AGAINST ALL HERESIES

by

Alfonso de Castro, O. F. M

Translated by
Rev. Paul M. Kimball

Dolorosa Press
Camillus, New York
www.dolorsapress.com

Copyright © 2021 Rev. Paul M. Kimball
All rights reserved.
ISBN: 978-1-7327175-8-9

To order additional copies, please contact us.

Dolorosa Press
www.dolorosapress.com
avemaria@dolorosapress.com

Contents

Topic	Page
Absolution	110
Adam and Eve	118
Adoration	101
Adultery	139
Almsgiving	386
Angels	140
Apostles	161
Baptism	172
Beasts and Brute Animals	253
Beatitude	222
Bishops	387
Blessings	253
Burial	988
Canonical Hours	578
Certitude	266
Character	261
Christ	274
Church	372
Church Buildings	1004
Circumcision	274
Colleges	996
Confession	316
Confidence	520
Confirmation	326
Contrition	332
Correction	336
Council	307
Counsels	332
Creatures	336
Cross	338
Devil	370
Earth	1008
Easter	824
Enemies	604
Eucharist	402
Eunuch	465
Evil and Wickedness	646
Excommunication	467
Exorcism	475
Faith	481
Fasting	583

Fate	478
Fear of God	1009
Flesh and the Human Body	264
Food	266
Foreknowledge	913
Fornication	527
Future Contingent	527
God	341
Gospel	396
Grace	531
Head	261
Hell	601
Heretic	576
Hope	993
Idolatry	581
Images	593
Indulgences	599
Injuries	605
Intercourse	312
John the Baptist	605
Judas	607
Judge	609
Judgment	608
Just Men	616
Killing	770
Kingdom of God	925
Language	644
Law	625
Liberty	631
Lies	659
Marriage	727
Martyrdom	654
Mass	669
Matrimony	656
Melchisedech	657
Mendicancy	663
Merit	666
Miracles	668
Monastic Life	719
Nudity	726
Oaths	610
Obedience	769
Penance	856
Pope	809
Poverty	826

Power	873
Prayer	798
Preaching	908
Precepts	875
Predestination	899
Priesthood	939
Prophets	914
Purgatory	916
Relics of the Saints	925
Restitution	931
Resurrection	933
Sacrament of Extreme Unction	1033
Sacrament of Holy Orders	803
Sacraments	972
Sacred Scripture	982
Saints	974
Satisfaction	981
Science	987
Shame	1016
Shoes	254
Silence	990
Simony	991
Sin	829
Singing	255
Soul	141
Strangers	854
Submission	999
Suffrages for the Deceased	1000
Temptation	1006
Tithes	338
Tyrants	1014
Usury	1066
Virginity	1019
Virgin Mary	650
Vows	1044
War	249
Water	168
Wine	1018
Women	722
Work	616
Works	771
World	723
Year	160

Biography of the Author

Rev. Friar Alfonso de Castro, O. F. M. (1495-1588)

Advisor of Charles V and Philip II

by

Rev. Friar Manuel Castro, O. F. M.

In this year of the Lord, 1958, we celebrate the fourth centenary of the death of two leading figures in the history of Spain: Emperor Charles V, and the Franciscan, Alfonso de Castro. Both belonged almost to the same generation: Charles was born in Ghent on February 25, 1500, and Castro was born in Zamora in 1495. They died in the same year of 1558: Castro, on February third, and Charles on September twenty-first.

Both were champions of the faith: the one defending it with the sword; the other with his polemic, which earned him the title of "staunch combatant of heretics," by the chronicler of the Order, Father Francisco Gonzaga. They had the same global vision regarding the mission of Spain. Being of one mind, they traveled all over Europe to defend the faith, and they succeeded: Charles V, in Mühlberg, helped by the Tercios[1] of the Duke of Alba; and Castro, in Trent, together with other Spanish theologians.

Charles V had a Titian[2] to capture his image for posterity; but for the humble Franciscan there was no brush to record his image, nor a Pedro Mexia to sing his exploits. And as one cannot comprehend the history of Charles without the unfailing collaboration of his dear friend and advisor, Alfonso de Castro, we wish that once again the names of both be united in this small monograph on the eminent figure of Alfonso de Castro, as a warm tribute and contribution to the fourth centenary that is being commemorated this year.

l. The First Years of his Life

The illustrious writer Friar Alfonso de Castro was born in the city of Zamora, which he calls his native soil.[3] The year of his birth we know only from the epitaph composed by Gaspar Tamayo from Salamanca, his disciple, to be placed on the tomb of his master in Brussels.[4] According to this epitaph, Castro died in 1558 at the age of sixty-three, which places his birth in the year 1495. Nor do we know who his relatives were, except for a brother named Bautista

---

[1] The Spanish Legion is grouped into four *tercios* (sing., *tercio*), a unit intermediate between a regiment and a brigade, each commanded by a colonel.

[2] Titian was a leading artist of the Italian Renaissance who painted works for Pope Paul III, King Philip II of Spain and Holy Roman Emperor, Charles V.

[3] Alfonsus a Castro, O. F. M. *Opera I*, Madrid (1773) p. VI. This edition shall be quoted thus hereafter, as long as it is not indicated otherwise.

[4] This epitaph is widely known; it can be seen in: Jacobo de Castro, O. F. M., *Arbol chronológico de la Providencia de Santiago*, I, Salamanca (1722) bk.3, c. 5, p. 111. Lucas Wadding, O. F, M, *Scriptores Ordinis Minorum*, Romae (1906) p. 12. Santiago Castillo Hernádez, *Alfonso de Castro y el problema de las leyes penales*, Salamanca (1941) p. 5.

Biography of the Author

de Castro, who was for some years royal judge in Avila and Logroño until he retired from office. After a number of years, he was returned to office by favor of the king, obtained through his brother, and of the Princess Governess of Spain to whom the king by letter expressed his will for Bautista de Castro's reinstalment.[1]

We also do not know where Alfonso de Castro began his first studies, whether in Zamora or Salamanca. There was in Zamora at that time a Franciscan monastery, whose foundation was prior to the year 1246,[2] and which had been made famous by several religious who lived in it, such as the famous Friar Enrique de Villalobos, Friar Alejo Hurtado and others. The Franciscans there maintained public schools for seculars, as in many other monasteries of the Province, so it may be presumed that the young Alfonso de Castro[3] learned his first letters there.

Amid such uncertainty, we do know that he was a Franciscan and that he took the habit in the monastery of Saint Francis of Salamanca.[4] Availing ourselves of the epitaph of Tamayo, we can deduce the year in which he took the habit, for it is said there that he lived under the Rule of Saint Francis for forty-eight years. Hence, he must have received the habit in the year 1510, when he was only fifteen years old, or at the latest, in January, 1511. The provisions of the *Constitutions of Barcelona*, which were then the regulations of the Observant Franciscans of Spain, concur well with this, which in chapter one, order that the aspirant had to be "at least sixteen years old."[5] Thereafter he always considered himself to be a true lover of his founder Saint Francis, and of his Order, which he cites in several places in his works. But the love he has for his Order is always wholesome, without letting himself be carried away by the presumption of some of the orators of his time, who dared to say in public that wearing the habit of their Order was an unequivocal sign of salvation, as if a simple cloth could confer more grace than the Sacrament of Baptism.

As Castro himself declares, and as we have already noted, he was enrolled to study within the Order, certainly first in Zamora and later in the monastery of Salamanca, to which he was subsequently incorporated, by virtue of his investiture of the habit which took place there. He studied in the recently founded University of Alcalá de Henares because his name is recorded in the history of the university.[6] A fellow disciple of his in the halls of the University of Al-

---

[1] The letter of Philip II to his sister, the Princess Governoress, is preserved in the General Archive of Simancas, *Secretary of State*, Leg. 809, fol. 135. It was published by Eloy Bullón, *Alfonso de Castro y la ciencia penal*. Madrid (1900) pp. 137-138. On this interesting work of Professor Bullón, see: Vicente Vignau, *Alfonso de Castro y la ciencia penal*, in: *Boletín Real Academia de Historia*, 36 (1900) p. 316.

[2] Lucas Wadding, *Annales Minorum*, 3.a ed. Quaracchi (1933) ad an. 1260, n. 59; ad an. 1430, p. 179. Atanasio López, O. F. M., *La Provincia de España de los Frailes Menores*, Santiago (1915) p. 155; Jacobo de Castro, O. F. M., *Arbol* I, p. 158.

[3] I would like to point out that our religious always signs with the name of *Friar Alonso*, and never with that of *Alfonso*, which surely was imposed by the translation into Spanish of the name *Alfonsus* or *Alphonsus* which invariably appears on the title page of his works, exception being of *De justa haereticorum punitione*. Lyon (1556) where he is called *Friar Alonsus a Castro*.

[4] *De potestate legis poenalis*, bk. 1, c. 8, *Opera II*, p. 285b. On the flyleaf of this vol. II, which exists in the Library of the Franciscan Fathers of Santiago, there is another note that says: "This volume with another by the same author, was used by Friar Marta, General Presidency of Jure, confessor of the nuns in Santa Clara de Astorga, and guardian for six continuous years in the monastery of Our Province of San Francisco de la Villa de Vivero, whose work with several others incorporated and put in the library of the said monastery for the use of its residents. In the year 1775."

[5] Antonio del Rincon, O. F. M., *Monumenta Ordinis Minorum*, 2. ed. Salmanticae (1511) p. 265v.

[6] Andrés Ocerín Jauregui, O. F. M., *Religiosos ilustres de la Seráfica Provincia de Santiago en la Universidad de Alcalá* in: *El Eco Franciscano* (= EF) 29 (1912) 817. Nicolás Aniceto Alcolea, O. F, M, *Seminario de nobles, taller de venerables y doctos, el Colegio Mayor de San Pedro y S. Pable fudado en la Universidad de Alcalá de Henares, para trece relgiosos de todas las provincias observantes de N. P.*

calá, Martín de Azpilcueta, more frequently known by the nickname [from his place of origin] of Dr. Navarro, wrote of him as "our fellow student in the University of Alcalá."[1] This means that Castro joined in the early years of the foundation of the University of Alcalá, since Dr. Navarro left for France around 1511.[2]

From the beginning, he did not propose in his studies any other end than to make known the Catholic faith and defend it from the attacks of the heretics who were then wreaking very noticeable havoc in the field of the Church of Jesus Christ. To this end he taught himself in all religious and secular subjects, thus becoming "one of the most learned men of his century and the most diligent in studying heresies."[3]

We have little information from which to follow Castro during these years of study. We do not know how long he was in Alcalá studying Sacred Theology, but once these years ended, he devoted himself to teaching the same subject at the monastery of Saint Francis of Salamanca for more than thirty years, since Friar de Medina, O. F. M.,[4] calls him his teacher.

The monastery of San Francisco of Salamanca was renown throughout the Franciscan Order, but especially in Spain. This ancient and royal monastery was founded outside the walls of the city, when King Alfonso X reigned in Castile and León, in the year of 1231. The main patron and founder was the Infante[5] Frederick of Castile, brother of Don Alfonso X the Wise, and his wife the Infanta Maria. In his will the Infante expressed his desire to be buried under the main altar of the church, and left it endowed with enough income that the Province would always have a place there for the study of sacred Theology. Further, the monastery would always be provided with religious who would study with a number of teachers and doctors, who with their letters, preaching and doctrines would serve the Church of God and the good of Spain.

At the death of Frederick in 1277, the houses of studies had already been extended notably by the Order, in which very learned men lived. This motivated the request for a dispensation from the Roman Pontiffs so that some of the monastery's income could be allotted to support the studies. And such was the prestige of the Franciscan *Studium* of Salamanca, that its founders "ensured that the most learned religious men who were formed therein would have such a name and opinion in this distinguished University [of Salamanca], and in all the other universities of the world, that they would consider themselves fortunate that they would merit to have a friar of Saint Francis, a son of the monastery of Salamanca, who would teach Sacred Scripture in those universities."[6] By this time the monastery was so adorned with very learned men, that there were more than forty Doctors and Masters who entered the schools

---

S Francisco de estos reynos, por el Card. D. Friar Francisco Cisneros, con su admirable vida. Madrid (1717) p. 152, where he cites the name of Alfonso de Castro among the illustrious men who studied at the said college.

[1] Martín de Azpilcueta, *Commentarium* in c. Int. verba XI, q. 3, prael. 2, n. 7. *Opera omnia I,* Lyon (1589) p. 3.

[2] M. Arigita, *Navarros ilustres. I. El Doctor Navarro, don Martín de Aspilcueta y sus obras. Estudio histórico crítico.* Pamplona (1895) p. 42.

[3] L. Alonso Getino, *Vida y procesos del Maestro Friar Luis de León,* Salamanca (1907) p. 395.

[4] Miguel De Medina, O. F. M., *Christianae paraenesis,* bk. 1, c. 4. Venice (1564) p. 5v. Riccardo Varesco, O. F. M., *I frati Minori al Concilio di Trento,* in: *Archivum Franciscanum Historicum* (This work will be cited as AFH from hereon) 41 (1948) pp. 146-147.

[5] An *Infante* or *Infanta* is a younger son of a Spanish or Portuguese monarch.

[6] *Chronica de la Provincia sancta de Santiago,* Manuscript, from the years 1612-1613, in the Archive of the Franciscan Fathers of Santiago, fols. 30v-31. About the same: Manuel R. Pazos, O. P. M., *Cronistas de la Provincia de Santiago,* in: *Archivo Ibero-Americano* (from henceforth referred to as AIA) 8 (1948) p. 158.

for the Major and Minor Acts;[1] and the more important and chief subjects were taught by the religious of this monastery.

Everything continued in this way until the reform of the Observants appeared in Spain around 1377. This reform was accomplished with the help of King Juan II and his wife, Doña Maria, but especially of Friar Sancho de Canales, an Observant religious and confessor to the queen,[2] who helped them in the reform. Juan de Santa Maria, Friar Pedro de Torquemada, Friar Antonio de Paz and Friar Alonso de Palenzuela, teachers in Theology and sons of the same monastery, entered this holy house in 1431.

Under the bull *Dum praeclara*,[3] promulgated by Eugene IV on February 9, 1446, in favor of the Observants, one of the consequences of the reform was that the religious did not hold the titles of Doctor and Master, which implied that they would have to give up the teaching of Sacred Scripture. The religious also ceased to be professors at the university. The monastery ceased to hold ownership of all property, so that from that time forward they ran the monastery with perfection and in conformity with the declarations of the Supreme Pontiffs and the Rule of the Friars Minor. In the Provincial chapter celebrated in Benavente in 1447, Juan de Santa Maria was elected the first Vicar Provincial of the Observants of Santiago.[4]

This is the reason why Castro never appears on the covers of his works with the titles of Doctor or Master, nor has he been able to teach or to be among the Doctors of the distinguished University of Salamanca. But he was no less famous than the most renowned Masters, his contemporaries in the city of Salamanca. "Both Friar Alonso de Castro, along with his brother in the Order, Luis de Carvajal,[5] contributed at the same time as Vitoria[6] to the rebirth of theology; although they did not have, like he, the most crowded classroom and the most brilliant students. Of course, the formation given in the classroom is much more intense than from the book, and no doubt that is why contemporaries, when speaking of theological restoration, mention only the head professor, Vitoria."[7]

There is no doubt that Castro, from the reduced ambit of the monastery of San Francisco de Salamanca, and with the scarce possibilities that the rigorous regulations of the Observance allowed him, gave a vigorous impulse to the restoration of Catholic theology. This was later continued by Soto, Suarez, Cano and the Salmanticenses, and made Spain the most fertile nation in first-class theologians. Hence, in 1553 Alfonso García Matamoros, alluding to this movement of theological restoration, could rightly say:[8]

---

[1] The "Major Acts" were public disputations, with precise ceremonies, between Doctors and teachers, that were more complete and required greater preparation, and to which were invited distinguished guests from outside of the university.

[2] Atanasio López, O. F. M., *Confesores de la Familia Real de Castilla*, in: AIA 31 (1929) pp. 62-63.

[3] *Annales Minorum*, ad an. (1447) n. 2.

[4] *Chronica* ms. fols. 65v-57. Castro, *Arbol I*, p. 78. Manuel Bandín Hermo, O. F. M., *Los orígenes de la Observancia en la Provincia de Santiago*, AIA 33 (1930) p. 362.

[5] Luis de Carvajal (born about 1500) was a Spanish Franciscan and theologian of the Council of Trent.

[6] Francisco de Vitoria O. P. (c. 1483–1546; also known as Francisco de Victoria) was a Spanish Roman Catholic philosopher, theologian, and jurist of Renaissance Spain. He is the founder of the tradition in philosophy known as the "School of Salamanca."

[7] Luis G. Alonso Getino, O. P., *El Maestro Friar Francisco de Vitoria*, in: *Ciencia Tomista*, 4 (1911-1912) p. 186. Para Carvajal: Pio Sagües, O. F. M., *Doctrina de Inmaculata B. V. Mariae Concepitone apud P. Ludovicum de Carvajal*, O. F. M. (+1552), in: *Antonianum*, 28 (1943) p. 152. AIA 4 (1915) p. 179; 3 (1943) p. 50; 5 (1945) p. 453; 15 (1955) pp. 248-249, 426.

[8] Alonso Garcia Matamoros, *Apologia pro adserendo, Hispanorum eruditione*. Edic. José López de Toro, CSI. Cientificas, Madrid (1943) n. 108 & 110.

Biography of the Author

It is beyond dispute that the Dominican Soto of Segovia, Alfonso de Castro of Zamora, Rodrigo,[1] Melchor Cano,[2] Bartolomé [Carranza] de Miranda,[3] to whom I might rightly add Luis de Carvajal, today attain nearly the peak of philosophy and theology.

And later, referring specifically to Castro, he adds:

A Franciscan monk, since when dealing with heretics he has refuted what is foreign [to the faith] just as very powerfully and eloquently as he ornately and copiously strengthens our [faith], I truly do not hesitate to compare him with many distinguished authors in points of doctrine.

And the same Carvajal, who shared the teaching chair with Castro for about thirty years in the monastery of San Francisco, answering an Erasmian epigram, in which the Rotterdamer rabidly attacks the Spanish monks; writes a list of the religious who having taught theology illustriously constitute the honor and prestige of their Orders, among whom he puts, in a very special place, Francisco de Vitoria, Francisco del Castillo y Velasco, and Alfonso de Castro.[4]

Such was the prestige that Castro achieved, after returning from Alcalá around 1512, that he took the chair of Theology in the Franciscan monastery of Salamanca. Let us not believe, notwithstanding the restrictions of the Observance, that the Franciscans lost all contact with the university. For, surely by the work of Castro himself and of other learned religious who lived with him, these contacts intensified daily. Thus, in 1518, the Provincial Friar Francisco de Zafra, who was a Doctor of Theology, donated, together with his Definitorium and the most serious Fathers of the Province, to Alfonso de Fonseca, Archbishop of Santiago, a part of the field called Saint Francis, belonging to the monastery of Salamanca, so that on it he could raise the building and college that he planned to found in the city. This the Archbishop did, in fact, only three years later, in 1521, being one of the most famous major colleges of that university, and which was called thereafter the College of the Archbishop. In the deed of donation there is this very interesting clause:

For which reason, I, the said Provincial Minister, with Reverend Father elect [in Provincial Minister, Friar Cristóbal Chacón], and the aforementioned Fathers of this Congregation, having seen and experienced... how just is what [Archbishop Fonseca] desires and requests, and the good and fruit that in general for all, and for us in particular, is to be derived from the establishment of the said College, in which His Grace places the clerics and also friars of our Collegiate Province, as His Grace said it to me, the said minister, and to Father Guardian, and the Fathers of the said Monastery....[5]

That is to say, that in 1518 the Provincial Chapter of Orense considered it a very special benefit for the Province, and expected to reap copious fruit from the foundation of the College, because it was going to give entrance to religious who were college students. Undoubtedly, in spite of the Observance, the desire for studies was in the heart of those religious, and university studies were not disregarded. For the Archbishop's College, which was already inaugurated in 1521, was a major college, and its college students were equal in everything to those of the university. The Franciscans Lope de Montenegro and Antonio de Robles studied here.[6]

---

[1] Rodrigo de Arriaga (1592–1667) was a Spanish philosopher, theologian and Jesuit.

[2] Melchor Cano (1509-1560) was a Spanish Dominican theologian and bishop.

[3] Bartolomé Carranza (1503–1576) (sometimes called de Miranda or de Carranza y Miranda) was a Navarrese priest of the Dominican Order, theologian and Archbishop of Toledo.

[4] Luis de Carvajal, O. F. M., *Apologia monástica relígionis*, Salamanca (1528) fols. 23r-24v.

[5] Castro, *Arbol* I, 146. This document was drawn up at the Provincial Chapter held in Orense on October 18, 1518, in which Father Cristóbal Chacón was elected Provincial Minister and Father Zafra resigned.

[6] Manuel R. Pazos, O. F. M., *Los estudios universitarios en la Provincia de Santiago*, in: *Liceo Fran-*

Did Castro teach at this school? We do not have documents that assure us apodictically, but neither do we have them to deny it; and the fact is that Father Castro, during his teaching in Salamanca, formed some distinguished disciples, who later felt obliged to remember him in their works. A vestige of his teaching may be considered, if we are not mistaken, in his *Copia lecturae in Esseiam ex Alveolo Friar Alfonsi de Castro*,[1] a commentary on Isaiah. They are the notes that one of his disciples took in class, surely at this time, for Castro still had little information about the Lutherans.

Castro was in Salamanca in 1524, where he was a professor. That same year, in the intermediate Chapter that the Province of Santiago celebrated in the monastery of San Francisco of Salamanca, he was named *custos custodum* to attend with vote to the next General Chapter. This is the first documented date that we have of the illustrious Franciscan lawyer, and also the first time that we find him holding a position in the Province. He did not occupy many, certainly, but his total dedication to his studies and his occupations at the side of Charles V and Philip II, as well as his multiple journeys, did not allow him to do so.

The office of *custos custodum* was a prestigious one, because it gave him the right to attend the next General Chapter in the company of the Provincial Minister, with the right to vote, representing all the *Custodes* [or "Guardians"] of the Province. Regarding Castro's particular case, the historian Wadding gives us precious information:[2]

On September first [1524] in the Chapter of the Province of Santiago, and in the monastery at Salamanca, Antonio de Guzman was commanded to continue in his office, and Alfonso de Castro was chosen as a Guardian [*custos*]. This is due to the singular virtue and merits of Castro, because he alone in the intermediate Chapter was elected as guardian. For in the other Chapters no one was appointed to this office of voting in the general elections, because before their indiction, the Chapter had to be celebrated in which the guardian was to be chosen. The first time of this happening belongs to this great man.

Castro was nearly thirty years old when he was appointed to this position, so he could perfectly comply with the provisions of the legislation of the Ultramontane Family of the Franciscans, in which it was ordained that "no one may henceforth have the office of superior unless he has completed thirty years of age."[3]

On Pentecost Sunday, 1526, which was celebrated on May twentieth, the General Chapter of the Order met in the monastery of Saint Francis of Assisi, at which Friar Castro attended as planned. He reminds us of his presence, when, regarding the fact that the sentence of the judge is not necessary for the offender to incur the penalty that by provision of the law *ipso jure* is predetermined, he adds, "such a law was established by the Order of the Friars Minor of the Regular Observance in the General Chapter celebrated in the year 1526, at which Chapter I attended as the *custos custodum* of the Province of Santiago."[4]

Not surprisingly, due to the fact that Castro, who in those years, although young, was adorned with so much prudence that he deserved to be elected to one of the main positions then existing in the Province, and endowed with so much wisdom and eloquence that he was already considered one of the most intelligent and cultured men of Salamanca, was appointed by the Emperor Charles V to advise him in difficult times and to remain in close contact with him, as we will see.

---

ciscano, Santiago, 4 (1951) pp. 65-82.
[1] Biblioteca Vaticana, *Vat. Lat.,* 12.807.
[2] *Annales Minorum*, ad an. (1524) n. 21. The Minister General, Father Francisco de Quiñones, presided over the Congregation.
[3] *Constitutiones barcinonenses*, c. 8. *Monumenta Ordinis*, fol. 273v.
[4] *De potestate legis poenalis*, bk. 2, c. 8. *Opera II*, 364a.

Biography of the Author

2. First Trip to the Netherlands, and his Relations with the Emperor

The chronicler Father Jacobo de Castro,[1] Nicolás Antonio,[2] and other authors agree in affirming that Father Castro accompanied the Emperor on several of his trips and that he was an acquaintance to him. Several historians, and among them Andrés Schott,[3] Alberto Mireo,[4] Wadding,[5] Hebrea,[6] and Friar Jacobo de Castro,[7] say, in addition, that he was confessor of the Emperor Charles V, but we do not know trustworthy testimonies that confirm this. According to Castro himself, he wrote, probably in 1530, and by order of the Emperor himself, a pamphlet defending the validity of the marriage contracted by Henry VIII of England with Catherine, daughter of the Catholic Monarchs. This matter, as is well known, aroused the attention of all Europe and brought sad consequences for England and for Catholicism. This pamphlet, contrary to what Castillo claimed,[8] was not printed, and this explains why it cannot be found, nor is there any trace of a copy. In this regard, Castro himself says:[9]

Concerning which matter [the marriage of Henry VIII] I was then a young man when that matter was discussed; I wrote a pamphlet, so that I might transmit by a published pamphlet my opinion, which was asked of me, as also of many other learned men,

He was then about thirty-five years old and was already beginning to be consulted by the Emperor on the serious problems of Christendom. This inclines us to suspect that by that time he was already in contact with Charles V, and that he even accompanied him in his retinue to Italy, in the spring of 1529, so that Pope Clement VII with his hands could impose the imperial crown on the Emperor. It is regrettable that the magnificent work of Foronda[10] does not give more details on the matter.

Let us add to this the fact that the many Spanish merchants residing in Bruges had invited Castro in those same days to go to this commercial emporium of Belgium to preach to them in their own language and to defend them from the Protestant attacks.

Castro's name, by this time, had gone beyond the borders of his homeland, as an excellent orator and eminent theologian.[11] This is what Juan Vaseo, a native of Bruges, affirms in a letter that is in the front of the *Homilias* on Psalm 50 by Alfonso, Salamanca edition of 1537.[12] Castro himself tells us that he traveled, and traveled much.[13] After the imperial coronation in Bologna, Father Castro must have gone to Bruges, since he reminds us several times in his works of his long stay in the Netherlands. He further refers to the polemics he held with the heretics, and even with the Catholics, on various religious questions. He also makes known some Flemish customs worthy of note, which he had the opportunity to observe:

---

[1] Castro, *Arbol I*, p. 110.
[2] Nicolas Antonio, *Bibliotheca hispana nova I*, Matriti (1783) p. 16.
[3] *Hispaniae bibliotheca, seu de Academiis ac bibliothecis II*, Frankfurt (1608) p. 249.
[4] *De scríptoribus ecclesiasticis saec.* XVI, Antuarpiae (1649) p. 52.
[5] *Scriptores Ordinis Minorum*, Roma (1906) p. 12. *Annales Minorum*, ad an. (1546) n. 9.
[6] José Antonio Hebrera, O. F. M., *Chrónica de la Sancta provincia de Aragón*. Parte II, Zaragoza (1705) Aparato, p. Xr.
[7] *Arbol I*, p. 102.
[8] Santiago Castillo Hernández, *Alfonso de Castro y el problema de las leyes, penales*, Salamanca (1941) p. 34.
[9] *De potestate legis poenalis*, bk. 1, c. 12; *Opera II*, p. 306b.
[10] Manuel De Foronda y Aguilera, *Estancias y viajes del Emperador Carlos V*, Madrid (1914) p. 420.
[11] Nicolas Antonio, *Bibliotheca hispaniae nova* I, 16.
[12] It can be seen in: Manuel de Castro, O. F. M., Friar Alfonso de Castro, O. F. M. (1495-1558). *Bibliographical notes*; in: *Collectanea Franciscana* 28 (1958) pp. 73-74.
[13] *De justa haereticorum punitione*, bk. 3, c. 2; *Opera II*, p. 200b.

Biography of the Author

Wherefore in different countries, heretics are killed by diverse kinds of death, because there is no type of death sanctioned by the civil and imperial law. In Flanders and in other parts of lower Germany, when I stayed there ten years ago [he wrote before 1547], I saw heretics punished by decapitation. Yet in Gelderland[1] heretics are bound hand and foot by order of Charles [II], then duke of Gelderland, and are cast alive into a river to drown. By the same type of death (as I heard from many who saw) a certain notorious Lutheran was punished in Antwerp by command of Margaret, aunt of Emperor Charles [V],[2] who at that time, on account of Charles' absence, governed that country. I also heard in Bruges, Flanders, from many trustworthy eyewitnesses that it was the custom in that city to cast heretics alive into boiling oil, so that they might be burned by it more quickly; but at the time when I was there, they were perishing only by beheading. In the other kingdoms or provinces of the Christian world, there is the new, constant and inviolable custom of burning heretics: thus I saw happen in France, especially in Paris. So also it was done in Spain, and I believe that it was always so done in Italy.[3]

This is a magnificent argument against the *black legend*, by which the Spaniards are falsely accused of being intransigent, as if in Paris and Italy as well, according to the illustrious Franciscan, heretics were not burned. Castro was in favor of the death penalty for heretics and this caused him some opponents abroad:[4]

For I saw many in Flanders, when I stayed there ten years ago, who, although they reckoned it to be just to punish heretics, still they thought ill of the punishments of the parent heretics to be extended to their children [i.e., their followers]. They were accusing the punishment of heretics, which is commanded by canon and civil law. Further, they were attacking Spain, because they had heard that all the rights, which were established by the supreme pontiffs or by the emperors, were consistently observed in Spain, and they were vehemently inveighing against me as a defender of the rights.

He was a great observer of the customs and laws of the Netherlands, and as he was there for a long time, he got to know them perfectly. He cites the law of the country, according to which, if an individual is robbed of something, the thief is sought, who, when found, is punished for stealing what was not his. However, the thing is not returned to its owner but remains before the judge, who in turn will punish the owner for not having kept it well; but the theologian wonders if such a law is just.[5] Also interesting are the customs on the penal laws existing in Bruges.[6]

He traveled through some German cities where he was able to learn more about Lutheran doctrines and observe their customs. The heretics began to say in Germany that the Church, in order to be pure, should not possess goods, and some even began to put it into practice.[7]

Luther assimilated these doctrines and instilled them in the princes so that, using them, he could take away the Church's property. Castro affirms, "Luther in our time defends the same error, persuading princes to loot the goods of the Church, which also we have heard has been done in many towns of Northern Germany."[8]

Protestants did not comply with the laws of the Church concerning fasting and abstinence:

---

[1] Gelderland is a province of The Netherlands with Arnhem as its capital.
[2] I.e. Margaret of Austria, regent of The Netherlands (1480-1530).
[3] *De justa haereticorum punitione*, bk. 2, c. 12; *Opera II*, p. 128a.
[4] *De justa*, bk. 2, c. 10; *Opera II*, p. 115b.
[5] *De potestate legis poenalis*, bk. 2, c. 5, *Opera II*, p. 340b.
[6] *De potestate*, bk. 1, c. 4; *Opera II*, p. 260b.
[7] Below, bk. 3, in the section on "Beatitude."
[8] Below, bk. 6, in the section on "The Church."

The Lutherans have embraced this same error in our time, who unrestrainedly eat meat on every Friday and Saturday, and on all days of Lent. I myself have heard from an upright man from Cologne, in this month in which I write these words, namely in the month of May in the year of the Lord 1533, that in the time of Lent when he went to the markets in Frankfurt, which city is in upper Germany, in nearly every town before Frankfurt no food was given by the hosts to him, his companions, or to any other visitors besides meat: which if anyone refused out of reverence for the season or the law of the Church, they were completely unwilling to sell him bread or wine. However, he told me that in Frankfurt the matter is treated more mildly on account of the markets which are held there during Lent, that more people would come to those markets.[1]

Not only the ecclesiastical goods were the object of the greed of the Protestants, but the monks were also the target of their anger:

In many German towns, monks were forced to abandon their own monasteries, because they were not permitted to live in them unless they took off their habits and married wives. I have decided to write nothing in this work against the error of all these men, lest perhaps it be said of me, because I myself am also a monk of the Franciscan Order, that I plead my cause and I seek the things that are my own and not those of Jesus Christ.[2]

During his stay in the Netherlands and in Bruges, Friar Castro prepared the first edition of the famous work, *Against All Heresies*,[3] as the author himself tells us when he recounts the dispute he had with a learned theologian who did not approve the writings of the Franciscan against the heretics, for fear that the latter would misuse them to defend their errors.[4] Castro was again accosted for writing this work against the heretics, and this time in Paris, where he was on September 28, 1534, the date on which the printing of the work was completed.[5] We do not know how long our theologian remained in Paris, but once the printing of *Against All Heresies* was finished, he returned to Spain, probably at the end of 1534, where he also had opponents, supported by the same reasons as the abovementioned theologian from Bruges.[6]

3. Teacher and Preacher

As we have already said, as a teacher the illustrious theologian did not occupy any chair within the University of Salamanca;[7] nevertheless, more than once he appears among the professors of the same.[8] This apparent contradiction is explained if one takes into account that during the sixteenth century and thereafter, the university was made up, in addition to the university cloister itself, of the monasteries and colleges incorporated into it. Included as

---

[1] Below, bk. 4, in the section on "Food."

[2] Below, bk. 10, in the section on "Monastic Life."

[3] For a description of Castro's works, see my article cited above: *Friar Alfonso de Castro, O. F. M. Obs. (1495-1558). Bibliographical notes*. In: *Collectanea Franciscana*. 28 (1958) pp. 59-88.

[4] *De justa haereticorum punitione*, bk. 1, c. 20; *Opera II*, pp. 71-72.

[5] *De justa*, bk. 2, c. 16; *Opera II*, p. 145b

[6] Castro's work later had more contradictors such as Abbé Fleury, *Histoire ecclésiastique XXI*. Nismes (1780) n. 47, pp. 189-190, where he accuses him of giving greater importance to polemics than to history, extensively refuting the new heresies, while barely tracing the history of the old ones. Card. Bellarmine also allowed himself to censure this work, branding several of its affirmations as erroneous, but from this accusation Castro has already been defended by Lucas Wadding, O. F. M. *Scriptores Ordinis Minorum*, Rome (1906) p. 12. *Annales Minorum*, ad an. (1546) n. 10.

[7] Enrique Esperabé y Arteaga, *Historia pragmática e interna de la Universidad de Salamanca II*. Salamanca (1917) p. 285.

[8] Alejandro Vidal y díaz, *Memoria histórica de la Universidad de Salamanca*, Salamanca (1869) p. 514; and Appendix, p. 10.

well were the guild of graduated teachers, Doctors and bachelors in the same, even if they held a chair in another place. Castro obtained the title of bachelor in Salamanca in the year of 1535, according to the list of graduates of that date,[1] having recently arrived from Paris. At that time our Franciscan was forty years old, but "at that time it was not unusual to see men of quite a few years sitting in the chapel of Saint Barbara to receive the investiture of Doctor, Master or Bachelor.[2] And Father Getino says that 'it would not be fair to omit..., that next to the professors of the university two Franciscan writers shone with the brightest light: Andrés Vega and Friar Alonso de Castro, both theologians of the Council of Trent.'"[3] Friar Beltrán de Heredia[4] "assures that Castro graduated in the aforementioned year of 1535." Castro recalls several times in his works the regulations of the University of Salamanca that he knew perfectly well.[5]

Although the *Statutes* of the University of Salamanca, made in 1538, do not expressly name the Franciscans or any other religious Order, there is no doubt that the following dispositions of that center had to do with them. In title XXIV it is ordered that "whoever passes from one department to another loses a course of those he has taken in that department from which he passed without being examined, except if he is a friar or a person who in another university has begun to study in this faculty."[6] Title XXXIV, also provides that "no course of friar or layman will be counted in theology unless it is done after having done all the courses in the arts that are necessary according to the constitutions of the university to be a bachelor; and with the friars of the monasteries of this city it is kept according to the constitution and how it has been kept until now for them."[7]

The students of the Salamanca monastery of Saint Francis took part, like those of other Religious Orders that had their schools incorporated to the university, in the Academic Acts of the latter. Title XXII of the Constitutions of 1538, says: "In theology there are every year ten major disputes given by the defender and challenger who are bachelors or graduates, or religious that have taken courses for bachelors or graduate students; and twelve minor disputes wherein they are auditors not graduated, although if it seems to the teachers convenient, they may admit bachelors in the minor disputes."[8]

These Minor Acts lasted at least three hours each. The topics were taken from the books of the *Sentences*, and the sessions were two, one in the morning and the other in the afternoon. The Constitutions add that, "in the major or minor dispute of theology, one religious of any of the four Mendicant Orders can argue, and no more."[9]

---

[1] Library of the University of Salamanca: *Catalógo de Catedráticos, Maestros, Doctores y Rectores que ha tenido esta Universidad*. Ms. 1221, s. f. Santiago Castillo Hernández, *Alfonso de Castro*, p. 22.

[2] J. Villalba, *Grados de Santa Bárbara*, Salamanca (1616) p. 84.

[3] Luis G. Alonso Getino, O. P., *El Maestro Friar Francisco de Vitoria*, in: *Ciencia Tomista* 4 (1911-1912) p. 190.

[4] Francisco de Vitoria, O. P., *Commentarios a la Secunda Secundae de Sto. Tomás*. Edition prepared by V. Beltrán de Heredia, O. P., Salamanca (1932) I, Introduction, XXXVI.

[5] On the appointment of Rector of the University, see: *De potestate legis poenalis*, bk. II, c. 6; *Opera II*, pp. 345-346. He cites the Constitutions of Martin V, Const. 25, on the renting of houses to students, and other details in: *De potestate*, bk. 1, c. 12; *Opera H*, p. 311b; bk. 2, c. 6; *Opera II*, p. 348; bk. 2, c. 8; *Opera II*, p. 366b; bk. II, c. 11; *Opera II*, p. 390a; p. 396a; bk. 2, c. 12; *Opera II*, p. 407a.

[6] E. Esperabé y Arteaga, *Historia pragmática e interna de la Universidad de Salamanca* I, Salamanca (1914) p. 163.

[7] E. Esperabé y Arteaga, *op. cit.*, I, p. 181.

[8] E. Esperabé, *op. cit.* I, p. 161.

[9] E. Esperabé, *op. cit.*, I, p. 162. Manuel Rodríguez Fazos, O. F. M., *Los estudios universitarios en la Provincia de Santiago*, in: *Liceo Franciscano* 4 (1951) pp. 73-4.

Biography of the Author

Castro defends the existence of the General Studies in the Order, and of the Universities, against the doctrines of John Wycliffe that maintained that they should be suppressed by the harm and vices to which they gave rise, such as envy, hateful comparisons of people and other evils.[1]

The epitaph of Tamayo says that Castro taught Sacred Theology in Salamanca for thirty years, and had very proficient disciples, such as Friar Miguel de Medina, Friar Francisco Orantes, Friar Antonio Rubio,[2] and Friar Andrés de Vega, although there is some doubt that the last named was a disciple of the eminent criminalist.[3]

Castro was an independent and eclectic genius. He revered Saint Thomas, Saint Bonaventure, Scotus and other Catholic doctors, but did not belong to any particular school. This he censured, in that it was intended to hinder understanding. He regretted that theologians were so subject to the authority of Saint Thomas or Scotus that they did not have the courage to abandon it, and to this end he wrote:[4]

I confess that I am not able to restrain my anger whenever I see some men to be so supportive of the writing of some men, that they assert that it is irreverent if someone deviates even in the least point from their opinion. For they want that the writings of men be received as oracles of a deity, and that honor to be shown to them which is owed to Sacred Writ alone. For we have not sworn on man's words, but on God's words. For I would call this miserable servitude, to be so devoted to human opinion that it would not be permitted to oppose it in any way. Those who subject themselves so much to the sayings of Blessed Thomas, or of Scotus, or of Ockham, suffer such [misery], so that from their opinions, to which they seem to have sworn, they choose names, some called Thomists, others Scotists, and other Ockhamists. Paul indeed commanded us to captivate our intellect, but in service to Christ, not in service to man. Hence it is that those who so lightly pronounce concerning heresy, not thinking about what they say, are often struck by their own arrows and fall into the pit which they prepared for others. For to reckon human writings among those of the Divine order, would not I have called this more truly heresy? Namely, what they do who assert that it is just as irreverent to dissent from human writings as from Divine writings? I have seen such persons to have descended to such madness, that they are unafraid to pour forth these words in a public sermon: "Whoever deviates from the opinion of Blessed Thomas, ought to be deemed suspect of heresy." O strong men of God's word, nay, I would have said more truly, O preachers of Thomas' words. Therefore will Blessed Bonaventure be considered suspect of heresy, because he deviates from Blessed Thomas in many things? Therefore will Blessed Anselm be called suspected of heresy, because contrary to the opinion of Blessed Thomas, he does not consider one a lover of the Virgin who refuses to celebrate the feast of her Conception? And yet I would not want these words said by me [to be taken] in such a way that someone think that I, by these words of mine, would want to hurt all the men of that [Dominican] institute or Order. For I have known many learned, wise, and truly pious men among them, who are very displeased when these things are done, or when they are said by the unlearned as generally happens. For it also greatly displeases me that our community [of Franciscans] also seems nearly to have sworn

---

[1] Below, bk. 13, in the section on "Colleges."

[2] On the disciples of Castro see the substantial article of Domingo Savall, O. F. M., *Friar Alfonso de Castro, ¿Sancto Padre?* in: EF 69 (1952) p. 299.

[3] V. Heynck, O. F. M., *Die Stellungdes Konzils theologen Andreas de Vega, O. F. M., zu Duns Skotus*, in: *Franz. Stud.* 27 (1940) p. 88, n. 4, where he gives a different interpretation to the words *magister meus*. Buenaventura Oromí, O. F. M., Friar Andreas Vega, O. F. M., *theologus concilii Tridentini*. AFH 36 (1943) pp. 3-31. For a bibliography on Vega, in: *Collectanea Franciscana. Bibliographia Franciscana* 7 (1940-1946) p. 143; 9 (1949-1950) pp. 285-289.

[4] Below, bk. 1, c. 7.

on the words of Scotus. I in fact venerate the holiness of Blessed Thomas, I concede much to his teaching, because it has enlightened the Church very much: yet I do not think that he should be so followed that it is necessary to agree with him in everything.

However, although Alfonso de Castro was not a Scotist, he frequently alleged the authority of the Subtle Doctor,[1] and rarely left the latter's opinion to adhere to that of Saint Thomas.[2] He combated Gabriel Biel and some Catholic theologians who at the Council of Trent pretended to defend that man could be certain of his righteousness, claiming that Scotus taught this doctrine. Castro demonstrated that the Subtle Doctor taught the opposite,[3] and in another place he stated it even more clearly.[4]

He also had great admiration for Aristotle, but he considered worthy of reprimand those authors who, without knowing theology, studied Aristotle with such faith that they had to reduce all questions to him.[5]

According to the epitaph of Tamayo, several times quoted, Father Alfonso de Castro carried out the office of preaching for forty-three years, so his first sermons to the public would have been around 1515. This seems to us to be too early, because although on the matter there was nothing established in the legislation of the ultramontane family of the Franciscans at that time, nevertheless, the general norm of the cismontane family was followed, which required that new preachers be twenty-five years old;[6] consequently, Friar Castro would have begun his preaching in about 1520.

He soon achieved fame as a preacher, since he was already famous when the very erudite Portuguese Andrés Resende, two years younger than our Franciscan, who was studying in Salamanca, attended his sermons, and stood nearby to be able to better observe and imitate his language and declamation. In a letter he wrote during these years to Quevedo, when he was Canon of the Church of Toledo, he expressly says, when speaking of Castro, that the people of the city liked him very much. He proposed him to himself as a model,[7] after the bishop of Laodicea, surely the one who had been chaplain of the Catholic Monarchs, García Bayón de Carvajal, O. P., famous preacher of his time who was named titular Bishop of Laodicea on March 20, 1493.[8]

Juan Vaseo, a native of Bruges, in the letter at the beginning of the *Homilias* on Psalm 50 of Friar Castro, Salamanca edition of 1537, writes how Castro was called with great honor to Bruges to preach in Spanish, by the Spaniards who in great numbers were then trading in that city, the most flourishing of all Belgium.[9]

---

[1] *De potestate legis poenalis*, bk. II, caps. 4 & 11; *Opera II*, pp. 333, 390.
[2] *Ibid.* bk. 2, c. 3, p. 325b.
[3] Below, bk. 7, in the section on "Grace."
[4] *Ibid.*, bk. 12, in the section on "Predestination."
[5] *De potestate legis poenalis*, bk. I, c. 8; *Opera II*, p. 285b.
[6] Bartolomé Belluco, O. F. M., *De sacra praedicatione in Ordine Fratrum Minorum*, Rome (1956) p. 58.
[7] Nicolas, Antonio, *Bibliotheca hispana nova*, I, Madrid (1783) p. 16; para Resende, *ibid*, p. 83. *La Epistola ad Bartholomeum Kebedium*, de Resende, in: Andreas Schorr, *Hispaniae illustratatae... scriptores varii II*, Frankfurt (1603) p. 1015.
[8] Conradus Eubel, O. F. M., Conv. *Hierarchia catholica medii aevi II*. Münster (1901) p. 190. *España Sagrada*, pp. 51, 160.
[9] The letter can be found in my article: *Fr. Alfonso de Castro. Bibliographical notes*; in: *Coll. Franc.* 28 (1958) p. 73. Egidio Caggiano, O. F. M., *Alfonso di Castro*. In: *Enciclopedia Cattolica*, I. Vaticano (1949) pp. 856-857. Ephren Longpré, O. F. M., *Alphonse de Castro*. In: *Catholicisme*, I, Paris (1948) p. 352.

Biography of the Author

As we have seen, our Franciscan was in Salamanca, after he returned from the Netherlands in 1535, judging by our calculations. Certainly he was there on July 12, 1537, since on this date, and in the Salamanca monastery, he signed the dedication of the *Homilias* on Psalm 50 to the King of Portugal, John III. The twenty-five homilies appeared published for the first time in Salamanca in 1537, and their author had preached them in the monastery of Saint Francis of the same city, which confirms us in our calculations that towards 1535 he was again in the city of the Tormes.

His fame as a preacher must have been great at the time he dedicated the *Homilias* on Psalm 50 to the King of Portugal. Master Gregorio Gallo, professor of that university, in his report to the bishop of Salamanca about the book *De potestate legis poenalis*, wrote that "the author of this work is a man of note and pleasing to the bishop himself, since he never abandoned the flock entrusted to him. On the contrary, for a long time his voice was heard throughout Salamanca."[1]

When considering the ravages of Protestantism, and seeing on the other hand the corruption of the clergy, which supplied powerful weapons to Luther's henchmen, Alfonso de Castro unleashed vehement invectives in which he exposed the heedless conduct of the unworthy priests and prelates, which were opposed to the doctrines they taught. In several places of his works, he indignantly censured the bad preachers, who, without knowing Latin or theology, preached without scruples of any kind, as parrots could do, previously learned sermons of someone else.

This lamentable decadence of sacred oratory was, in the opinion of our author, one of the causes that most contributed to foment the Protestant heresy. Its coryphaeus [or leader] knew how to take great advantage of the ineptitude and malice of many Catholic preachers, mainly those who, attentive to collect large sums of money, exaggerated the efficacy and merit of indulgences.[2] Castro describes pathetically the lamentable state in which was the oratory of his time, leaving us some very interesting data for the history of the same.[3]

Castro not only preached from the pulpit, but through his printed works, and developed a healthy apostolate of reviewing the Spanish life of his time, not sparing anyone who had something to be corrected.[4]

The evil was that the bishops, more enthusiastic in [conferring] the Sacrament of Holy Orders than in [conferring] the Sacrament of Confirmation, admitted to the priesthood all kinds of candidates. However, if someone was rigorous in this, there was no lack of another bishop to fulfill the wishes of the aspirant.[5]

His writing does not cease to be somewhat pessimistic when referring to the dereliction in which many Spanish bishops had left their dioceses, preferring to live in the Court or near

---

[1] My article: *Alfonso de Castro. Bibliographical notes.* In: *Coll. Franc.* 28 (1958) p. 79.

[2] Eloy Bullon, *Alfonso de Castro y la ciencia penal*, Madrid (1900) pp. 33-34. The hatred against the *buleros* [i.e., one charged with distributing crusading Bulls and charging for them] was then general, as is well revealed by the tasty criticism of them in *La vida de Lazarillo de Tormes*, treatise V. Edition by Julio Cejador y Prauca, "Clásicos Españoles", Madrid (1934) pp. 205-228; this work appeared for the first time in 1554, precisely when our friar was lashing out against the bad preachers.

[3] *De justa haereticorum punitione*, bk. 3, c. 3; *Opera II*, pp. 203a-204a, see also: *De potestate legis*, bk. I, c. 10; *Opera II*, p. 299ab. Castro also tells us of having seen some women who dared to preach of the highest things, if not in public then in their homes, to those who came to listen to them, a custom, he says, very widespread in many provinces and which was the cause of many errors: *De justa haereticorum punitione*, bk. 3, c. 3; *Opera II*, p. 206b.

[4] *De justa haereticorum punitione*, bk. 3, c. 4; *Opera II*, p. 217a. C. 4 & 5 of the same bk. 3, deal at length with the life of the clergy, *Opera II*, pp. 207-219.

[5] *Ibid*, bk. 3, c. 4; *Opera II*, pp. 210-211.

their relatives;[1] the imprudence of others in lavishing ecclesiastical censures without sufficient reason;[2] the superstitions that were discovered in the kingdoms of Catalonia,[3] Navarre and Galicia;[4] and other information of this sort, some of which is very interesting for the military history of Charles V.[5]

The seriousness of the anti-Christian distinction between new and old Christians demanded the intervention of the Cortes of Castile in 1532. Some Colleges, Orders and Confraternities excluded, by statute, those who were not old Christians. The request of the procurators was very moderate: that those who could prove that they come from Catholic parents, grandparents and great-grandparents be admitted, provided that said ancestors have not been condemned by the Inquisition, and provided that it cannot be proven by reliable deeds that they come from the lineage of Jews or Moors.[6]

Alfonso de Castro denies, against what Bernardo de Luxemburg affirms, that the Marranos[7] and Mozarabs[8] are heretics. He strongly protests against the custom of the Spanish people to call the descendants of the Jews "Marranos," since they are not to blame for the faults of their elders. In addition, the name is infamous and insulting, so that many of them, scorned, follow Jewish practices. For their part the Mozarabs are not heretics, but Catholics and very submissive to the Pope. They only differ from the other Catholics in the liturgy of the divine offices that they celebrate in some cities of Spain, especially in Toledo. With due authorization, they substitute the Gothic office abolished in time of Alfonso VIII to please the Queen, but to the displeasure of the people.[9] However, so that no one suspects him in the least, because of what could happen, he solemnly affirms:

I did not say all these things, I call up God and His Angels as my witnesses, so that I might defend my cause. Because I am foreign to all consanguinity of the Marranos, as could be evident to any who wants to thoroughly examine my genealogy, but I said this urged on by my conscience, so that I might avoid a common widespread error...[10]

To remedy many of these evils, the Inquisition was established.[11]

4. The Theologian of the Council of Trent

The first period: At Trent the Franciscan Observance had one of the most prestigious representations, in which the sons of the Province of Compostela excelled. Among these were Friar

---

[1] Below, bk. 6, in the section on "Bishops."
[2] *De justa*, bk. 1, c. 5; *Opera II*, p. 215.
[3] Below, bk. 10, in the section on "Works"; bk. 13, in the sections on "Relics of the Saints" and "Saints."
[4] *Ibid.*, bk. I, c. 13; *Opera I*, pp. 39-40; 49. The text to which this quotation alludes was published in my article: *Friar Alfonso de Castro, O. F. M. Bibliographical Notes*. In: *Coll. Franc.* 28 (1958) p. 60.
[5] *De justa haereticorum punitione*, bk. 2, c. 19; *Opera II*, p. 157.
[6] *Coleccion de Cortes de los antiguos reinos de España*. Edic. de la Real Academia de la Historia V (1903) p. 37.
[7] Moriscos were people with recent Muslim ancestors. They were Christian because either they were born Muslim and converted to Christianity during their life, or their parents or grandparents had converted. Even though Moriscos were officially Christian, there is evidence that many of them continued to practice Islam secretly.
[8] Mozarabs were Christians who lived under Muslim rule in Muslim Iberia (al-Andalus).
[9] *De justa*, bk. 1, c. 7; *Opera II*, pp. 31-33.
[10] *Ibid., Opera II*, p. 32a.
[11] *De justa*, bk. n, c. 17; *Opera II*, p. 150b; about the manner of proceeding of the Inquisitors: bk. 1, c. 22; *Opera* II, p. 76b; he speaks again of the rigor against heretics in Spain, which saved us from greater evils, in *Ibid.*, bk. II, c. 3; *Opera II*, p. 94a.

Biography of the Author

Andrés de Vega and Friar Alfonso de Castro, along with others of his Province, Friar Juan Ramírez, Friar Alfonso de Contreras, Friar Antonio de Ulloa and Friar Juan de Lobera.[1] Vega was already a professor at the University of Salamanca when he entered the Order, unlike the others, who could easily have held university chairs, although not by opposition, since this was forbidden by the *Statutes* of the Observance. There is no record that Fathers Ramirez, Contreras, Ulloa and Lobera, had done studies in a university. However, Friar Juan de San Antonio[2] affirms that among the Franciscan religious who came out of the of the University of Salamanca four theologians of the Tridentine must be counted, of which certainly two of them were Castro and Vega, and the others could be either Friar Luis de Carvajal and Fr Diego de Meneses or others from Compostela.

We cannot determine on what day Alfonso de Castro came to Trent, but since he attended as theologian of Cardinal Pedro Pacheco, Bishop of Jaén, it is not implausible to think that he arrived there with the prelate on July 24, 1545.[3] Certainly he attended the opening of the Council in company of Andrés de Vega, on December 13, 1545, judging by the writing that the Very Reverend Juan Maltei de Calvi, Minister General of the Franciscans, sent to Massarelli with the list of Franciscan theologians.[4]

During the first days of the Council, as the meetings and conciliar works were not abundant, Castro dedicated himself to the correction of his work, *Against All Heresies*, the second edition of which appeared in Venice in 1546,[5] with a dedicatory letter to Cardinal Pacheco signed in Trent on November 30, 1545. In Trent he was able to read and examine carefully the books of Luther and his followers. Diego de Mendoza, Imperial Ambassador at the Council at that time, provided him with a well-stocked library of Lutheran books, placed by him at the disposal of all those who wanted to refute them. This enabled Castro to correct the second edition of his work, as he tells us.[6]

---

[1] Buenaventura Oromí, O. F. M., *Los Franciscans españoles en el Concilio de Trento*. In: *Verdad y Vida* (cited as VV from hereon) 3 (1945) pp. 122-130. Ricardo Varesco, O. F. M., I, *frati Minori al Concilio di Trento*, AFH 41 (1948) pp. 88-160. AIA. 35 (1932) pp. 308-313; 2 (1942) pp. 506-7.

[2] *Biblioteca universal franciscana*, 3, Madrid (1733) p. 155.

[3] Constantino Gutiérrez, S. J., *Españoles en Trento*, Valladolid (1951) p. 977. *Concilium Tridentinum* (cited as CT from hereon), *Diariorum, Actorum, Epistolarum, Tractatuum*, nova Collectio, edit. Societas Goerresiana. Friburgi Brisg. (1901-1938). Alfonso Salmerón writes to Saint Ignatius from Trent on July 10, 1546 and tells him that Cardinal Pacheco "has in his company several persons learned in theology, such as Alonso de Castro y Vega..." Monumenta Historiae Societatis Jesu (cited as MHSJ from hereon): *Epistolae Salmerón* 1, Madrid (1906) p. 24.

[4] Massarelli says: "The [Minister] General told me that these theologians of the Order of Friars Minor were present for the opening of the sacred Council: The Very Reverend Father Minister General, the former minister general, Vicentius Lunel, Alfonso de Castro, Andrés de Vega, etc." Castro himself says in the dedicatory letter to Emperor Charles V, placed at the beginning of the 1547 Salamanca edition of his work, *De justa haereticorum punitione*, that he accompanied Friar Andrés de Vega. My article, Alfonso de Castro, O. F., M., *Notas bibliográficas*. In: *Coll. Franc.* 28 (1958) p. 76, where I put the text. Below, bk. 7, in the section on "Grace." The *Chronicle ms.* of the Province of Santiago says that the "Emperor, after being very well informed of the most learned men of Spain, which and what persons he could send to the said Council, had more particular knowledge of the letters, government, prudence and virtue of... Alonso de Castro, who had been Guardian of the said monastery [of Saint Francis of Salamanca], and in it the most famous preacher," fols. 75v-76.

[5] My article: *Alfonso de Castro...*, in: *Coll. Franc.* 28 (1958) p. 66.

[6] For the texts on this subject, see my article, pp. 61-62. C. Gutiérrez, *Españoles en Trento*, p. 41. Castro tells us in these words: "The illustrious man, Diego [Hurtado] de Mendoza, who was then the representative of the Emperor at the Council, prepared there a copious library filled with all the books of the Lutherans, so that whoever wished, could examine them in order to attack their teachings. Thus,

Biography of the Author

At the ninth session of the fifth Lateran Council held on May 5, 1514, under Pope Leo X, a law was promulgated governing book printers; this law was confirmed again on February 4, 1546, at the third session of the Council of Trent, which was attended by the professor of Salamanca.[1]

The Legates proposed to the Fathers of the Council to deal with the reception of the Scriptures and Traditions on February 11, 1546.[2] They wished to examine the reasons why some of our own and the adversaries do not accept certain books of Holy Scripture as canonical.[3] The principal Catholic author to whom the Legates referred was Cardinal Cajetan, who doubted that Saint Paul was the author of the Letter to the Hebrews, and deduced therefore that it was not to be counted among the canonical Scriptures.[4]

The task of refuting Cajetan was entrusted to Castro, who sent a memorial to the Council[5] wherein he argues harshly and impugns Erasmus and Luther for doubting the attribution of the Epistle to Saint Paul. This way of presenting the reasons for the admission of the Sacred Scriptures was rejected by many Fathers in the General Congregation of February twelfth.[6] It was decided in the General Congregation on the fifteenth that they would be simply accepted until time was given to the Fathers to weigh the reasons that exist on one side or the other.[7]

On February eighteenth, in the particular meetings, the Cardinal President proposed the same question, in which Castro intervened as envoy of the Cardinal of Jaen, sitting immediately after the Augustinian procurator, Claudius Jay.[8] Castro preferred to engage in the discussion the authority of the Church, because it is related to the Apostolic Traditions, for which some Fathers were inclined.[9] The next day the Legates established Congregations to hear the theologians in private meetings about what had been proposed to the Fathers. Having consulted the case with the Cardinals, the Cardinal of Jaen ordered that the three Franciscan theologians he had with him, Castro, Vega and Lunel, attend these Congregations.[10]

In the meetings of the twenty-third, Castro agreed with what was proposed by the Fathers regarding the Traditions, but regarding the decree he wished it to be written: "Besides these books, however, there are some things in God's Church which were not written, but are observed by the authority of the Church itself, to which Church they were handed down from the Apostles and came from hand to hand all the way to us."[11] Castro perhaps said this to prevent some of the Apostolic traditions from being forgotten, as happened to His Eminence Cardinal

---

I then penetrated Luther's mind, and came to know from what foundation he deduced this most wicked doctrine, and what flowed from it." Below, bk. 8, in the section on "Grace." In the library of Diego de Mendoza: CH. GRAUX, *Essai sur les origines du fonds grecs de l'Escurial*. Paris (1880) p. 40. The Legates used the library mentioned by Castro, CT, I, p. 570.

[1] *De potestate legis poenalis*, bk. I, c. 8; *Opera II*, p. 287b.
[2] CT, V, p. 3; X, p. 374.
[3] CT, I, p. 478.
[4] CT, X, p. 377; H1, p. 379; XII, p. 497, n. 4.
[5] *Epistolam ad Hoebreos S. Paulum esse auctorem défendit contra Caietanum et Lutherum*, CT, XII, p. 497.
[6] CT, V, p. 7; I, p. 478.
[7] CT, I, p. 480.
[8] CT, V, p. 10.
[9] CT, I, p. 484; V; 11. Oromí, *Los franciscanos...* VV 3 (1951) pp. 299-300.
[10] CT, I, pp. 466, 489.
[11] CT, V, p. 14; I, p. 491. Felix Asensio. S. J., *De Castro and the Tridentine Decrees on the Holy Scriptures. Scripture.* In: *Ecclesiastical Studies* 20 (1946) pp. 63-103.

Biography of the Author

of Jaen[1] in the meeting of February twenty-sixth, and he preferred that all the Traditions that existed in the Church at that time be accepted globally.

He did not attend the Congregation of the twenty-sixth because it was General, but his opinion was recalled by Cardinal de Santa Cruz,[2] and on the same day he was part of the Commission appointed for the drafting of the Decree on Traditions.[3] In fact, the Decree that Cardinal de Santa Cruz drafted and presented for approval to the Legates on March seventeenth, maintains the idea that we must accept the Traditions that are preserved in the Church, including those that, as from hand to hand, have come down to us, an idea that Castro had put forward.[4]

The Council considering the many abuses that had spread among the Christian people in the use of the sacred books, a Commission was formed on the fifth to correct them, of which Alfonso de Castro was a member.[5] On March ninth, our theologian spoke on the translation of Scripture in the vulgar language,[6] which he had already reproached in his work, *Against All Heresies*, as a source of heresy. Certainly, to his influence and writings we owe the position that Cardinal de Jaen took on this article in the following meetings.

On the fifteenth or the sixteenth, four commissioners presented the abuses with their respective remedies,[7] which were read at the meeting of March seventeenth, at which Cardinal de Jaen noted: "Ought a translation of the Bible into the mother tongue be granted?"[8] Hearing this, the Cardinal of Trent strongly opposed him, proving that such a version was in no way to be counted among the abuses. The Cardinal of Jaen replied that he did not affirm that such a translation was an abuse, but that it was necessary to consider whether it was, since he knew that in Spain there were laws, approved by Paul II, prohibiting such versions. This he said influenced by Castro, who writes in one of his works:

Wherefore the edict of the most illustrious Catholic Monarchs of Spain, namely Ferdinand and his wife Isabella, whereby under very grave penalties they forbade anyone to translate Holy Writ into the vernacular language, or to retain Bibles translated in whatever way.[9]

Notwithstanding, after a whole series of incidents, in which Castro's influence had to be great, on April third, "after many disputations, it is concluded that no mention ought to be made about this matter in the decree."[10] Castro at first felt a certain sympathy for Erasmus

---

[1] CT, V, p. 18.

[2] CT, I, p. 33.

[3] CT, II, p. 380

[4] CT, XII, p. 522.

[5] CT, V, p. 28; X, p. 411; I, p. 436. C, Gutiérrez, *Españoles en Trento*, p. 43.

[6] CT, I, p. 510. Francisco de Enzinas tells that when his translation of the New Testament was published in Antwerp in 1543, it was immediately banned, and before he was arrested, Friar Pedro de Soto put in his hands the treatise *Against All Heresies*, where the thesis that the generalized reading of the Sacred Scripture is an inexhaustible source of heresies was sustained; surely for this reason, the heretic from Burgos dared to brand the illustrious Zamoran as barbarous and ignorant. Marcelino Menéndez Pelayo, *Historia de los heterodoxos españoles III*, Madrid (1947) p. 289.

[7] CT, V, p. 514.

[8] *Ibid*, p. 30; I, pp. 37-8.

[9] Below, bk. 1, c. 13; *Opera omnia I*, Madrid (1773) p. 40b. *De justa haereticorum punitione*, bk. I, c. 20; *Opera II*, p. 75a. Alonso Getino, O. P., *La causa de Fr. Luis de León ante la critica y los nuevos documentos históricos*. In: *Rev. Archiv. Bibliotecas y Museos*, 9 (1903) pp. 268-279. Gaspar de Uzeda, lector of Saint Francis of Salamanca intervened in [that discussion] (p. 274). The author of this work cites the very respectable opinion of Alfonso de Castro on the reading of the Bible in the vernacular language (p. 271).

[10] CT, I, p. 437.

of Rotterdam, of whom he had no objection to issue a warm eulogy in the first edition of his work, *Against All Heresies*, when he says, writing about the versions of the Bible:

I cannot but refrain from passing on here, once more, the arguments presented in favor of this thesis by Erasmus of Rotterdam, a highly educated man, well-deserving for his learning, and, in my opinion, truly pious. If I render this testimony to his piety, it is because I see that certain persons do not hesitate to accuse him of impiety. Therefore, lest anyone think any such thing about me, due to the fact that I quote him here after Luther, as though I hold Erasmus to be a partisan of Luther, I have first of all borne witness to his piety and to his learning, so that all may be convinced that I am disagreeing with him, as with another Catholic man, which I do not think he will take badly.[1]

Similar praises are paid to Erasmus in the notice to the reader of the Cologne edition of 1539,[2] although they are surely not due to our Franciscan, but to the group of Erasmian theologians of Cologne. Castro must have known Erasmus personally when he was for the first time in the Netherlands, and we should not be surprised if he felt such sympathy for him, since, like him, he had a special love for classical culture.[3]

Things change after 1543, because from that date Erasmus appears censured in the treatise, *Against All Heresies*, in all the points in which his disagreement with Catholic doctrine is too scandalous: fasting, abstinence, monastic vows, etc.[4] With a very different criterion, then, with regard to his relations with Erasmus, Castro attended the fourth session of the Council of Trent on April 8, 1546, where the Canon of Sacred Scripture was determined.[5] He says, "While I was present in the fourth session, the Council of Trent, celebrated under Paul III and Emperor Charles V, embraced the same list of sacred books."

On April twelfth, outside of protocol, he was called to the meeting of those in charge, where they prepared the decree on lectors and preachers,[6] divided into nine chapters, which was read in the Congregation of the thirteenth day.[7] We do not know what part he took in the drafting of this decree, since the Fathers have not named him since April fifteenth. On May first, the Decree was already quite changed,[8] and on the seventh another was proposed that contained, no longer nine chapters, like the one Castro examined, but fifteen.[9] Finally, on June fifteenth, it was reformed in such a way that it had seventeen chapters.[10]

---

[1] *Adversus omnes haereses*, París (1534) bk. 1, c. 13, fol. 28.

[2] The eulogy in my article: *Alfonso de Castro. Bibliographical notes*. In: *Coll. Franc.* 28 (1958) p. 63. About Castro's Erasmism; Marcel Bataillon, *Erasmo y España, estudio sobre la historia cultural del siglo XVI*. Trad. Antonio Alatorre, Mexico (1950) II, pp. 90-92. This work is completed and summarized in: *Collectanea Franciscana* (Bibliographia) (1938-1939) pp. 126-127. Castro himself alludes to Erasmus on many occasions; we have some annotations taken from *Opera omnia I*. Madrid (1773) pp. 41, 226, 232, 277, 319, 353-354, 357, 361-362, 364-365, 392, 421, 436, 440, 464, 495.

[3] He quotes a passage from Plato's *Phaedo*: *De potestate legis*, bk. II, c. 3; *Opera II*, p. 328b, and publishes a list of classical authors less harmful to the Christian religion: *De justa haereticorwm punitione*, bk. 3, c. 9: *Opera II*, p. 234. He regrets not knowing Hebrew, for when speaking about the word *Sacerdos*, he expressly says: "What the Hebrew or Chaldaic word means, I frankly admit that I do not know, because I am completely ignorant of those languages..." (Below, bk. 10, in the section on "The Mass").

[4] In our article quoted several times, we have pointed out when Erasmus' texts are censured in some of the editions.

[5] Below, bk. 1, c. 2. *Ibid.*, bk. 12, in the section on "Penance."

[6] CT, II, p. 383; I, p. 535.

[7] CT, V, p. 108.

[8] *Ibid*, p. 122.

[9] *Ibid*, p. 125.

[10] *Ibid*, p. 241.

Biography of the Author

The Legates decided to propose for the fifth session the doctrine of original sin, for which the studies had already began on May fourth, in which Castro must have taken a good part, since on the sixteenth the Legates commissioned him and Friar Francisco de Palermo, O. F. M. Conv. "to pick out councils and decretals which prove original sin, which de Castro collected late into the night."[1]

If we were to examine his influence in these disputes, perhaps we would find it in the constancy with which the Cardinal of Jaen defends the Immaculate Conception of Mary during the whole time, and even in the same session. But it is rather to be believed that in this question the said Cardinal was helped by another Franciscan theologian, Friar Andrés de Vega, who later worked not a little in favor of the Blessed Virgin.

When the fifth the Decree was already finished, and on the sixth of June, before it was given to the Fathers it was shown to others, among them Castro.[2] However, we are inclined to believe that Alfonso de Castro did not work much in favor of the Immaculate Conception, for remembering that in the Council he was left free to give his opinion on this point, confirming the bull of Sixtus IV, *Grave nimis*, he writes:

I truly believe that Virgin who gave birth to God was conceived without sin. This is more befitting to the dignity of the Mother of God and not detracting from the dignity and excellence of her Son, the Redeemer of the whole human race. But still I do not hold this view with such a firm opinion that I consider it to be of Catholic faith, and hence for the defense of this opinion, I would not willingly lay down my neck to the sword."[3]

On June seventeenth, the fifth session was held, which Castro also attended, in which the opinion of the Lutherans which affirmed that the Sacrament of Baptism does not remove original sin, nor all sin, was condemned.[4]

The Legates had written to Rome on June eighteenth, to make known that they had decreed to propose to the Congregation the article of justification.[5] On the twenty-second the minor theologians met before the legates to discuss the articles, and the first to speak was Castro.[6] During the months of June to September his name hardly appears in the Acts, due, it seems, to his having been occupied in private work. The Minister General, Juan Maltei de Calvi, granted him permission on July twenty-seventh to publish his work, *De justa haereticorum punitione*, examined by his brother in the habit, Friar Andrés de Vega, which may explain why his intervention during these months appeared so little.

In the meantime, the new decree on justification was being actively prepared at the Council, mainly by Seripando and Cardinal de Santa Cruz, since the one drawn up by Vega, although praised for its doctrine, seemed to the Fathers to be obscure and diffuse. Massarelli showed the new decree to Castro on September first.[7] From this date he is no longer mentioned in the Acts or in the Journals, but what he writes in his work is so precise that it is necessary to admit that he was still in Trent during the months of October and November. In fact, on October

---

[1] *Ibid*, p. 170, n. 72.

[2] CT, X, p. 513. Buenaventura Oromí, O. F. M., *Los franciscanos españoles en el Concilio de Trento*, VV 3 (1945) p. 312.

[3] *De justa haereticorum punitione*, bk. 1, c. 8; *Opera II*, p. 34b; Below, bk. 6, in the section on "The Church"; bk. 12, in the section on "Sin." Domingo Savall, O. F. M., *Alfonso de Castro y la Inmaculada*. EP 72 (1955) pp. 20-21.

[4] Below, bk. 3 in, in the section on "Baptism."

[5] CT, X, p. 529.

[6] CT, V, p. 262.

[7] CT, I, 571. Alejandro de Villalmonte, O. F. M., Cap., *Andrés de Vega y el proceso de la justificación*. In: *Rev. Esp. de Teología* (1945) pp. 311-374.

fifteenth, the two articles on imputative justice and the certainty of grace,[1] about which Castro also gives information, were proposed for examination by the theologians.[2]

But although Castro remained in Trent at least until the end of November, it seems that he did not attend the sixth session which was held on January 13, 1547, because Massarelli does not put him in the list of theologians attending this session, nor does Castro express himself clearly on this point.[3]

When he tells us that he had to be absent due to illness, he is undoubtedly referring to the one that appeared in Trent in the spring of 1547, and because of which several Fathers of the Council asked for the suspension of the sessions or the transfer to another place,[4] to which Castro alludes.[5]

From his words it is clear that he did not go to Bologna, but came directly to Spain from Trent. In any case, on October 18, 1547, he was already in Salamanca where he signed the dedication to Charles V of his work, *De justa haereticorum punitione*. The work was written during his stay at the Council,[6] and he tells us the reasons that encouraged him to write it. Oromí affirms,[7] although we do not know on what grounds, that the following year, that is, in 1548, Castro was elected Provincial Definitor of the Province of Santiago;[8] Castillo agrees.[9] Nevertheless, I am inclined to believe that his charge was not Definitor, a position that, surely, he never carried out, but guardian of the monastery of Saint Francis of Salamanca. For which position he would have been elected on July 15, 1548, in the Provincial Chapter celebrated in Benavente. This seems confirmed by the fact that at the beginning of 1551, before the end of the mandate of this triennium, Castro was in charge of the guardianship of Salamanca. The Chapter in Benavente was presided over by the Very Reverend Andrés da Insua, in which Friar Gabriel de Toro was elected Provincial Minister for the second time.[10]

In Salamanca on September 17, 1550, Castro signed the dedicatory letter to Miguel Muñoz, Bishop of Cuenca, for the work *De potestate legis poenalis*, which appeared that year in that city, and for which he can be considered the founder of Penal Law. This work, which was

---

[1] CT, V, p. 523.
[2] Below, bk. 12, in the section on "Predestination."
[3] *Ibid.*, c. 7, in the section on "Faith."
[4] CT I, p. 137. Luis Pastor, *Historia de los Papas XII*. Barcelona (1911) p. 282.
[5] *De justa haereticorum punitione*, bk. II, c. 14; *Opera II*, p. 133a. where he alludes to the Protestants of the Schmalkaldic League who broke through the Danube in July 1546, and were defeated by Charles V on April 24, 1547 at the battle of Mühllberg; he had already written about this same war: *Ibid.*, bk. 1, c. 17; *Opera II*, p. 64b; Below, bk. 12, in the section on "Priesthood."
[6] My article: *Alfonso de Castro. Bibliographical notes*. In: *Coll. Franc.* 28 (1958) pp. 75-78. Castro himself alludes to this work on several occasions: "because of those things two years ago [he wrote in 1551] that I had set down in the work, *De justa haereticorum punitione*..." *De potestate legis poenalis*, bk. II, c. 9; *Opera II*, p. 373a: "In that work which I entitled, *De justa haereticorum punitione*, and which I published in 1547..." *Ibid.*, bk. II, c. 10; *Opera II*, pp. 376b, 377ab, 382a, 388b; c. 11, p. 390a. The work underwent some additions in successive editions: *De justa haereticorum punitione*, bk. 1, c. 7; *Opera II*, p. 29b.
[7] Buenaventura Oromí, O. F. M., *Los franciscanos españoles en el Concilio de Trento*. In: *Verdad y Vida* 3 (1945) p. 281.
[8] In the Franciscan Order, definitors are elected by the General and Provincial Chapters to assist the General or Provincial superiors in the government of the Order.
[9] Santiago Castillo Hernández, *Alfonso de Castro y el problema de las leyes penales*. Salamanca (1941). 7. This work is somewhat careless in form and substance; complete in the bibliography with: *Collectanea Franciscana* 15 (1945) pp. 242-244.
[10] Jacobo de Castro, O. F. M., *Arbol I*, p. 87.

Biography of the Author

written during the author's stay in Salamanca,[1] soon gave rise to lively discussions among the theologians of the time.[2] Nevertheless, it is his best thought-out work and with it he is the one who has most influenced the modern development of this important branch of law. And it was he who, long before Beccaria, wrote a complete scientific treatise on everything concerning the purpose and nature of punishment and its relationship to crime.[3] The reasons for the appearance of this work are expressly stated by Castro.[4]

The second period: 1551-1552. As in 1550 it was a question of reopening the Council, on December thirtieth of that same year Castro received a letter from the Emperor in which he was ordered to be in Trent, at the latest, for the following May first. Castro responded to this letter, sent from Augsburg, with one dated January 25, 1551,[5] in which he promised to be on his way as soon as he received license from the Reverend Andrés da Insua, Minister General, who was at the time making the canonical visitation in the Province of Andalusia.[6] The same day, and also from Salamanca, he wrote another letter to Her Highness Queen Ann of Bohemia, wife of King Ferdinand [I], in which he communicated to her that he had received a letter

---

[1] *De potestate*, bk. 2, c. 8; *Opera II*, p. 366b

[2] *Ibid.*, bk. 2, c. 8; *Opera II*, p. 360a; bk. IP, p. 7; *Opera II*, p. 109b. It underwent some corrections in the second Louvain edition of 1557; "After I had published this work, the general Council of Trent was again convoked by Pope Julius III, which had been suspended by Paul III, his predecessor. Thus, in the [fourteenth] session of this council held under Julius, many canons pertaining to errors were issued, the seventh of which pertained to the punishment of homicide... Therefore, when this decree was issued, my opinion, which I had just brought forth according to the thought of the old canons, now necessarily had to be rejected, and I reject it from now on, because the new decree of the Church enacted, one necessarily ought to obey." *De potestate*, bk. 2, c. 15; *Opera II*, p. 438b.

[3] The bibliographical production to which this work gave rise is abundant; taking into account what we have already indicated, we will add the following, without pretending to be complete: Hipólito Sancho, O. P., *Domingo Soto y Alfonso de Castro*, In: *Ciencia Tomista* 12 (1920) pp. 142-160. The article is a mixture of praises and insults to the memory of the illustrious Franciscan. Jaime Masaveu, *Contribución al studio de la escuela penal española. Alfonso de Castro and D. Manuel de Lardizábal*. Madrid (1922). C. Amor, *Alfonso de Castro, franciscano*, EF 43 (1926) pp. 608-610. Didimo Beaufort, O. F. M., *Alfonsus a Castro als Bron voor Hugo de Groots Mare liberum*, in: *Collec. Francisc. Neerlandica*, a (1926) p. 205. Domingo Savall, O. F. M., *Fr. Alfonso de Castro (1495-1558). La orientación voluntarista de su derecho penal*, AIA 38 (1935) pp. 240-255; Id., *La pena de muerte en el pensamiento español*, EF 49 (1932) pp. 470-473; Id., *Fr. Alfonso de Castro, O. F. M. en el cuarto centenario de su filosofia del derecho penal (1550)*, EP 67 (1950) pp. 271-272; Id., *Fray Alfonso de Castro y el Beato Escoto en la concepción de la ley*, EP 72 (1955) p. 286. Manuel Sanz López, *Juristas españoles de la Edad de Oro. Alfonso de Castro*, in: *Rev. Escuela Estudios Penitenciarios* (1946) n. 11, pp. 51-59; n. 13, pp. 34-40; n. 15, pp. 40-47; n. 21, pp. 21-28. (1947), n. 28, pp. 55-67; n. 29, pp. 29-37; n. 32, pp. 32-40. Antonio Alvarez de Linera, *El Padre Castro. Un friale penalista*, in: *Rev. Esc. Est. Penitenciarios* (1947) n. 26, pp. 22-27; n. 27, pp. 39-48. Teodoro Olarte, *Alfonso de Castro (1495-1558). Su vida, su tiempo y sus ideas filosófico-juridicas*. San José, Costa Rica, (1946). I could not get hold of this work; see: *Rev. Estudios Políticos* 16 (1946) pp. 427-435. Andrés E. De Mañarica Nuere, *La obligatoriedad de la ley penal en Alfonso de Castro*, in: *Rev. Esp. De Derecho Canónico* 4 (1949) pp. 35-54 Orolo Gómez Parente, O. F. M., *Hacia el IV centenario de Fr. Alfonso de Castro, fundador del derecho penal*, Madrid, (1957).

[4] *De potestate legis poenalis*, bk. 1, c. 10; *Opera II*, p. 301a.

[5] Spanish Historical Archive. *Colección de documentos indéditos para la historia de España y de sus Indias. I. El Concilio de Trento*. Selected documents by Manuel Ferrandis and Miguel Bordonau. Valladolid (1928) p. 243.

[6] Fernando Feux Lopes, O. F. M., *Friar Andre da Insua. Geral dos Observantes Franciscanos*. AIA 12 (1952) p. 24.

of the Emperor ordering him to go to the Council of Trent, and that he would obey as soon as the Minister General gave him authorization, which he trusted they would not deny him.[1]

He left Salamanca for Trent on February 26, 1551, as is evidenced by the payment orders that were allotted to him in the name of the king for his attendance at the Council.[2] The Governing Queen, who signed the royal decree in Valladolid on the indicated date, calls Castro the Guardian of the monastery of Saint Francis of Salamanca, a position to which he was appointed on July 15, 1548, in the Chapter celebrated in Benavente, wherefore he was at the end of his mandate.[3]

He was already in Trent in June of 1551, since Massarelli counts him among the assistants to all the sessions.[4] On July twentieth, Cardinal Cervini wrote to Massarelli to ask Castro where he saw and where he would find the work of Saint Isidore, *De viris illustribus*, which Castro had used in his book, *Against All Heresies*.[5] On November twenty-fifth, he was present at the fourth session held under the pontificate of Julius III.[6]

We do not know why he does not speak in the discussions of the theologians, except in the last one that deals with the Sacrifice of the Mass.[7] He examined, in the meeting of December ninth, the articles on the Sacrifice of the Mass and the Sacrament of Orders, proposed on the third of the same month. The Guardian of Salamanca later developed this doctrine, with the same order and the same arguments in the Council, as in the definitive edition of his work, *Against All Heresies*, book ten, in the section on the "Mass," published after the second period of the Council.

With this book he exerted great influence on the Fathers of the third period, who, when the discussion on the Sacrifice of the Mass began, proved, on his authority, that Christ immolated Himself at the Last Supper. This was proven in so strong a way that a dispute arose over his doctrine between the Bishop of Rieti and that of Modena, on December 17, 1562. Some other bishops, like that of Triestre, declared that they wanted to follow Castro's doctrine, although some did not like this author.[8]

On March 22, 1552, when it was treated about the safe-conduct for the Protestants, the treason of Maurice of Saxony against Charles V took place, forcing the sudden suspension of the Council on March 28, 1552. Castro resolutely opposed this suspension, and he made an address between March twenty-second and twenty-fourth of the same year,[9] which effect on the Spanish bishops was profound, moving them to resist the project of suspending the

---

[1] *Spanish Historical Archive. I. Councilio de Trento*, p. 24. It publishes it, as well as the one addressed to the Emperor, taken from the previous work: Ismael Rodriguez, O. F. M., *Felipe II envia al Concilio a su Consejero Alfonso de Castro*. In: *Truth and Life*, 3 (1945) pp. 230-231.

[2] The royal decree, granting to Alfonso de Castro a pension for the entire time he attended the Council of Trent, is preserved in the General Archive of Simancas: *Mercedes, privilegios, ventas y confirmaciones*, Legajo 50, fol. 35. Eloy Bullon published it, *Alfonso de Castro y la ciencia penal*, Madrid (1900) pp. 133-135.

[3] Castro, *Arbol I*, p. 87. The *Chrónica ms.* of the Province of Santiago, which is preserved in the archives of the Franciscan Fathers of Santiago, says that Friar Castro was Guardian of Salamanca, fols. 75v-76.

[4] A. Theiner, *Acta genuina S. oecumenici Concilii Tridentini I*, Agram (1874) p. 609.

[5] Oromi, *Los franciscanos españoles*, VV 3 (1945) p. 282.

[6] *De justa haereticorum punitione*, bk. 1, c. 10; *Opera II*, p. 57.

[7] A. Theiner, *op. cit.* I, p. 609. Isaac Vazquez, O.F.M., *Friar Alfonso de Castro, frente Protestant a las desviaciones protestantes sobre la misa*. In: *Verdad y Vida* 16 (1958) pp. 5-44.

[8] CT, II, p. 773. Oromí, *Los Franciscanos...*, pp. 322-323.

[9] *Spanish Historical Archive. I. El Concilio de Trento*, pp. 405-406. *Verdad y Vida* 3 (1945) p. 229.

Biography of the Author

Council. Our theologian continued in Trent until the end of November 1552, as evidenced by the previously mentioned payment orders that were allotted to him for going to the Council.

5. Preacher and Advisor to Philip II (1552-1558)

On his return to Spain, he rejoined his monastery of Saint Francis in Salamanca, where he resumed the erudite classes which he had abandoned during his absences. He devoted himself at the same time in the salutary ministry of the apostolate in the confessional. Given the reputation of wisdom that surrounded him, which he shared with his compatriot and neighbor Friar Francisco de Vitoria, O. P., many came to him in search of tranquility for their consciences.[1]

The year 1553 is full of events in the life of Father Alfonso de Castro. Being the Provincial of Santiago Pedro de Carvajal, who had begun his mandate in 1551, attended the General Chapter of the Order in the monastery of Saint Francis in Salamanca in the year 1553. The Very Reverend Clemente Dolerá de Moneglia was elected as Minister General, and Friar Antonio de Guzmán, who had been several times Provincial of the Province of Santiago, as General Definitor.[2] It is to be presumed that Father Castro took part in this Chapter, at least in the Theological Conclusions or in the celebrated sermons that were then held on the occasion of such elections.

This same year, Prince Philip subscribed, in the name of the Emperor, a certain *agreement* with Hernando de Ochoa, a merchant, the content of which can be summarized in the following fundamental clauses: 1. The Prince grants license to the abovementioned Hernando de Ochoa to introduce and sell in the Indies 23,000 black slaves, on condition that the fourth part of this number be women; 2. The merchant is obliged to pay his Highness 184,000 ducats; 3. The Prince grants the exclusivity of such slave trade and fixes the price at which each slave is to be sold as a monopoly, which is to expire in the year 1559; 4. The concessionaire also receives license to form a company with foreigners, notwithstanding the Castilian laws that state: "no foreigner can do business in the Indies."

Once the agreement was authorized, and in view of the protests made, principally by the Sevillian merchants, the Prince consulted several theologians and jurists, who, from different cities, sent their opinions in writing. In general terms, they felt the concession was inappropriate. Among those consulted were the Franciscans Friar Juan Belón, Guardian of the monastery of Zamora, Friar Pedro de Ibarra, who was the Guardian of the monastery of Valladolid, both of whom signed their opinions May 29, 1553.[3] Friar Alfonso does not shy away from

---

[1] Castro himself tells us of a complicated case of conscience that presented itself in the confessional, when a young man came to him to confess and he imposed on him the obligation to accuse his own father, who was a hidden heretic, to the inquisitors: *De justa haereticorum punitione*, bk. 2, c. 26; *Opera II*, p. 185a. On another occasion a gentleman, whose conscience was bothered by a grave calumny, went expressly from the Court to Salamanca to consult the case with Father Francisco de Vitoria, O. P., and being received harshly by the latter, went to Castro: Tomas de Mercado, O. P., *Tratos y contratos de mercaderes y tratantes decididos y determinados*. Salamanca (1569), pp. 168v-169. The same case, but told in a completely opposite way, since it says that the first consulted was Castro and the second Vitoria, is published by: Pablo Segneri, S. J., *El christiano instruido*, part. I, disc. 29, n. 35; I, Barcelona (1693) pp. 522-523.

[2] Castro, *Arbol I*, p. 87. *Chrónica ms.* fols. 145v-146v. *Annales Min.* ad an. (1553) n. 2.

[3] This opinion is preserved in the *Archivo General de Simancas: Diversos de Castilla* Católogo I. Legajo 6, fol. 52. J. Paz, *Archivo General de Simancas. Diversos de Castilla* Catalog I. Madrid (1904) n. 1189. It was published by Alfonso M. Guilarte, *Documentos y notas para la historia del Derecho. Alonso de Castro, consejero del Rey*. In: *Rev. de Estudios Penales* 3 (1945-46) pp. 83-86. P. Cereceda, S. J., also published it, together with the opinions of the other consulted theologians, *Un asiento de esclavos para América en el año 1553, y parecer de varios teólogos sobre su licitud*. In: *Missionalia Hispánica*

Biography of the Author

stating his opinion, saying that such a contract is unjust because it goes against the established law that "no foreigner may do business in the Indies." Further, since the law against passing slaves to the Indies was made for the good of the kingdom, it would be wrong for the Emperor and the Prince to authorize the sale of these 23,000 slaves for their own benefit, without hearing the opinion of the Spaniards residing in the Indies who might be harmed. This implies that by this time Father Castro was already admitted among the advisors of Prince Philip.

The royal preacher had dealt on several occasions with the subject of the recently discovered America,[1] so he was well informed of how things were going in those Spanish possessions. So he was consulted on some problems that affected these lands, and on November 13th, 1554 he sent to the Royal Council of Indies an opinion in favor of the Peruvian Indians.[2]

The difficulties of the treasury in the time of Charles V, due to the wars against the infidels, forced the emperor to ask the Pope for permission to sell jurisdictions with their vassals that the churches and their prelates held. Permission was granted by Julius III, and began to be used slowly, both because of the opposition of the Papal States, and because of the distrust that many had in buying such goods. King Philip II wanted to continue the same arbitration, and before doing so, he consulted with the most distinguished theologians of his kingdom. When His Highness was in the Court of Valladolid, Saturday, August 26, 1553, he had a meeting in his presence of seven theologians, among whom was Alfonso de Castro with the Franciscans Friar Bernardo de Fresneda, Friar Francisco Pacheco and Friar de Contreras. These theologians were unanimous in their opinion, that His Majesty could not in good conscience ask for this license, nor could His Holiness give it, and even if he could, the sale would not be safe in conscience, because His Holiness could not grant goods that were not his.[3]

Philip II, who always distinguished Castro with special predilection, wrote to Friar Toribio de Hevia, Provincial Minister of Santiago, the following letter:[4]

The Prince

Venerable Father Provincial Minister of the Province of Santiago in the Order of Saint Francis: because of the good relationship that we have of the person, writings, doctrine, life

---

3 (1946) pp. 580-597. He does not cite the work of Guilarte.

[1] In *Against All Heresies*, in the section on "Images," he speaks about the good news which the missionaries brought from the Indians, who had already learned to write Latin letters; in *On the Just Punishment of Heretics*, bk. 2, c. 14: *Opera II*, 134-5, he sets forth the reasons for showing when war which the king of Spain makes on the Indians is just.

[2] M. Morel-Fatio, *Catalogue des manuscrits de la Bibliotheque National [de Paris]*. Paris, 1892, 165; n. 550, fols. 347-8v; Fr. Alonso Getino, O. P. published it in: *Anuario de la Asociación Francisco de Vitoria* 4 (1931-32), 238-243. Juan de Solórzano Pereira, *De indorum gubernatione II*, Madrid, 1777, bk. II, chap. 1, 22; he seems to cite this when he says: "And the counsel of the Friar Alfonso de Castro's manuscript, which I have before me, which since it is dated January 13, 1558 (?), and as it appears that it was asked, whether our king can sell or grant in perpetuity these commenda of the Indians, he replies...".

[3] "Bernardo de Fresneda, Friar Alfonso de Castro, Friar Francisco Pacheco, Friar Melchor Cano, Bishop of the Canary Islands, Friar Bartolomé de Miranda, Friar Alonso de Contreras, and Master Gallo were asked if His Majesty could in good conscience ask His Holiness for permission to sell the vassals that the bishops and churches of these kingdoms have, to resist the Turkish Armada." Valladolid, August 26, 1553. It publishes it in full: Fermín Caballero, *Conquenses ilustres. II. Melchor Cano*. Madrid (1871) Appendix n. 16, pp. 478-481. La saca de la Biblioteca Nac. de Madrid, Ms. 1088 (Ant. E-170); see also pp. 89-90, 393-395. On this ms. see also: AIA 25 (1926) p. 204; 33 (1930) p. 457. *Inventario general de manuscritos de la Biblioteca Nacional III*, Madrid (1957) ms. 1088, p. 300. Pascual Gayangos, *Catalogue of the Manuscripts in the Spanish language in the British Museum*. II. London (1877) pp. 100, 299. VV 3 (1945) p. 297.

[4] Academy of History: *Collección Salazar*, A-52, fols. 279v-280. Baltasar Cuartero y Huerta, *Indice de la Colección de Don Luis de Salazar y Castro V*, Madrid (1951) n. 8631.

and example of Friar Alonso de Castro of the said Order, you have wished us to employ him and receive him as our Preacher. So that from now on he may reside in our Court and service, we beg you and charge you, taking into consideration what you have said, and the fruit that he can make with his sermons, to please give him license for it, and order him to come soon to serve us. In this you will do us pleasure and service.

The letter is not dated, but it is prior to October 18, 1553, the date on which the Prince signed in Valladolid the appointment of royal preacher in favor of our Franciscan. To him was assigned an annual salary of 60,000 maravedises, an allowance that Castro continued to receive until the day of his death, as can be seen in the letters of the payment orders.[1] By virtue of this appointment, he was to enjoy the titles enjoyed by the so-called "Fathers of the Province,"[2] but without the right to vote in the Chapters.[3] In addition to residing in the Court, he was to accompany the King in his travels.

When Edward VI of England died unexpectedly, Charles V proposed to open the way to important political connections by means of the marriage of his son with the new English queen, Mary Tudor, daughter of Henry VIII and Catherine [of Aragon], daughter of the Catholic Monarchs. Philip, although he had already fixed his eyes on the Portuguese Infanta Maria, daughter of Manuel the Fortunate and Philip's aunt Leonor, submitted to the will of his father. In Spain, such a marriage was not looked upon favorably because of the unequal age of the of the contracting parties, and because the King had to leave Spain without enjoying the supreme authority of the English. Theologians and jurists demanded that he have rulership as in a family, according to the right of the husband, with his wife necessarily obeying him.[4]

Prince Philip's trip to England was organized, and among the members of the entourage accompanying him was Alfonso de Castro.[5] His task was to make the purity of the faith clearly reappear and be restored in that kingdom. The royal preacher himself recalls it:[6]

For when having entered into the kingdom of England with Philip the Sovereign of the Spains, whom I served in public sermons, who came there to take as his wife Mary of England, Queen and Ruler of the kingdom, I heard that there are many in that kingdom, not only among the common people but also among the nobility, who had put away their own wives from their spouse on account of their adulteries, and had married others as wives. But afterwards when that kingdom, through the solicitude and persuasion of King Philip and Queen Mary, was brought back to the faith of Christ and union of the Church, divorce of this kind was never permitted.

---

[1] The appointment and the payment orders are preserved in the General Archivo of Simancas: *Quitaciones de la Casa Real*. Legajo 62, s. f. They are published by Eloy Bullon, *Alfonso de Castro y la ciencia penal*, Madrid (1900) pp. 129-131. *Chrónica ms.* fols. 76-78, where he refers us the fame of Castro as a preacher, and that of the monastery of S. Francisco de Salamanca, seedbed of very remarkable sacred orators.

[2] "Provincial Fathers" are religious who have held a position in their Order.

[3] Bartolomé Belluco, O. F. M., *De sacra praedicatione in Ordine Fratrum Minorum*, Roma, (1956) pp. 102-105.

[4] Luis de Cabrera, *Felipe II, rey de España*, Madrid (1619) p. 15.

[5] Andrés, Muñoz, *Viaje de Felipe II a Inglaterra*, Madrid (1877) *Sociedad Esp. de Bibliófilos Españoles*, XV, p. 29, gives the names of the theologians who accompanied the King: "The salaried theologians that His Highness takes for advice of conscience, are the following: the bishop of Lanchano; Friar Alonso de Castro, Franciscan; Friar Bartolomé de Miranda; Friar Juan (?) de Fresneda, Franciscan; Dr. Gurrionero, canon of Zamora; the Master of the Tower, clergyman, with each 600 ducats of apiece. They are those whom His Highness ordered to receive some of the goods of Castile...". *Chronica ms.* pgs. 147v-148.

[6] Below, bk. 11, in the section on "Marriage."

Biography of the Author

When in 1556 he published the second edition of his work, *De justa haereticorum punitione*, he was still very optimistic in his predictions about English Catholicism.[1]

Philip, when undertaking the trip to England, passed with his retinue by Santiago to kneel before the tomb of the Apostle [Saint James the Greater], Patron of Spain, and arrived at the Island [of England] on June 19, 1554. The royal wedding was celebrated with great solemnity on July twenty-fifth of the same year, the feast day of Saint James the Apostle.

Castro worked hard in England in the company of his friend Carranza. Dressed in the religious habit, they preached with great zeal, having recourse to every means to bring England back to the bosom of the Church.[2] Although at first they had to endure some scorn from the natives, gradually, with their knowledge and piety, they won the friendship and reverence even of the heretics. Cardinal Pole, elected Nuncio for the reconciliation of England, wrote to the royal confessor, Friar Bernardo de Fresneda from the monastery of Dilinghen on October 6, 1554, and said he expected much from the zeal of Friar Alfonso and Friar Carranza for the restoration of the Catholic faith in the Island.[3]

Castro gave himself with particular zeal to moderate the punishments inflicted on heretics. On February 9, 1555, the Bishop of London, Edmund Bonner, condemned six Protestants [to death]. But the next day our Franciscan gave before the King and Queen a speech in which he censured the actions of the government, and effectively achieved the suspension for a few days of the capital punishment launched against Ridley, Latimer and Cranmer.[4] He went to the prison to speak with Bradford in order to bring him back from his heresy, which he nearly succeeded in doing, as Bradford himself testifies.[5]

When Philip II married with the Queen of England, Mary Tudor, his father made him give away the kingdom of Naples, which by bordering to the States of the Church made good relations with the Holy See difficult. On May 23, 1555, John Peter Carafa was raised to the papal throne and took the name of Paul IV. Serious complications soon arose. The acts of hostility on the part of Paul IV towards the emperor reached such a point that the King of Spain wanted to expose the case to his best advisers to know their opinion and the conduct that he should follow in such circumstances. At first it was thought to form a meeting of the chosen personages, and they were summoned to the Court. Later it was thought preferable that, separately and in writing, they give their respective opinions, and so it was done. Among those consulted were several Franciscans: Friar Francisco de Córdoba, lector of the University of Salamanca; Friar Antonio de Córdoba, Guardian [of the Monastery] of San Juan de los Reyes; Father Pedro Ibarra, Guardian of Valladolid; and Father Alfonso de Castro, who on October 10, 1555, sent his opinion from London.[6]

---

[1] *De justa haereticorum punitione*, bk. 2, c. 5; *Opera II*, 100-101. In the *Epistola Nuncupatoria* to Philip II signed by the author in Antwerp on May 20, 1556, and which is in the front of his work, *Against All Heresies*; *Opera II*, he insists upon the matter.

[2] Luis Pastor, *Historia de los Papas XIII*, Barcelona (1927) p. 265.

[3] A. M. Quirini, *Collectio epistolarum Reginaldi Poli. IV*. Brixiae (1744) p. 168. R. Angel, *La réconciliation de l'Angleterre avec le S. Siege sous Marie-Tudor. Légation du Cardinal Polus en Angleterre (1553-4)*. In: *Rev. Histoire Ecclésiastique* 10 (1909) pp. 521, 744; José Maria Pou Y Martí, O. F. M., *Friar Bernardo de Fresneda, confesor de Felipe II, obispo de Cuenca y Córdoba, y arzobispo de Zaragoza*. AIA 33 (1930) pp. 582-603.

[4] Luis Pastor, *Historia de los Papas XIV*. Barcelona (1927) p. 314.

[5] Oromi, *Los Franciscanos*, p. 283: In: *Vie du Bienheureux martyr Jean Fisher*, in: *Analecta Bollandiana*, 12 (1893) p. 111, Castro is called "A Spanish Minorite, very famous."

[6] Fermín Caballero, *Conquenses ilustres. II. Melchor Cano*. Madrid (1871); Appendix, n. 40, p. 508 where he gives the list of those consulted; see also pp. 105-106, 280-281, 297-298. AIA 35 (1932) p. 213. I could not find this opinion of Castro at this time; Caballero and Friar Atanasio, in the places cited,

The talk between Maister Bradford and two Spanish Friers.

Meanwhile, the Pope negotiated an alliance with the King of France, Henry II, and consequently with the Sultan of Turkey, who was an ally of France. In Spain, however, opinion was divided, for while some were in favor of the king and his father, more than a few were repulsed by the fact that war was being waged against the pope. Among these were none other than Cardinal Siliceo and the members of the Royal Council. The Duke of Alba, from Italy, wrote to the regent of Spain, Princess Joanna [of Austria], warning her about the machinations of the Cardinal Archbishop of Toledo.[1]

Things changed completely when in February 1556 a five-year armistice was concluded in Vaucelles between the French, the emperor and King Philip, which made the anti-Spanish sentiment of Paul IV look very bad, and he sought the means to reach a peaceful settlement with Spain.[2] It must have been then, probably around February 20, 1556, when our Castro sent to Philip II, and I am inclined to believe that it was from England, a memorandum of the things that were to be asked of the Pope at this juncture.[3] I consider this the best of the *memoranda* that I know of Alfonso de Castro, where he demonstrates a serene criterion and a great love for Spain. According to his opinion, the Pope should give authentic confirmation of everything agreed upon in the Council of Trent. He advised the convocation of a national council presided over by a legate of the Pope, and that, if possible, he be a Spaniard. He further recommended asking that all holders of a benefice, [both] curate and simple, be patrimonial, as they already were in some bishoprics, for which Castro committed himself to present a plan. From this would be drawn many advantages for Spain, since the holders of the benefices would be more learned persons, which would redound to the good of souls. Further, they would not give so much money to Rome, since very many Spanish appointments would not have to go through the Roman Curia. It would be just to obtain a number of prebends[4] in each cathedral or collegiate church, which would be entrusted to doctors or graduates in theology and canons from a Spanish university, thereby raising the cultural level of the country.[5] Finally, it was necessary to ask the Pope that that no lawsuit be taken to Rome in the first instance, but only by way of appeal, after having been judged by the Ordinary.

We cannot specify the time that Alfonso de Castro lived in England, but on May twentieth, 1556, he was already in Antwerp, since in this city he signed the dedicatory letter to Philip II that goes into the front of the definitive edition of his work, *Against All Heresies*. He had corrected and increased this work during his trip to the Island [of England], as he affirms in the aforementioned dedicatory letter.[6]

On December 11, 1555, Pedro de Ribadeneira wrote to Saint Ignatius from Brussels[7] informing him that among the preachers at the Court was Alfonso de Castro, who would also

---

admit that this opinion was signed in England, in 1556, which is impossible, since at that time Castro was not on the Island, as we will see later.

[1] William Thomas Walsh, *Filipe II*, Madrid (1946) pp. 200-202. Ramón Lourido, O. F. M., *E; derecho de la Guerra en Fr. Alfonso de Castro, O. F. M.*, in: *Liceo Franciscano* 4 (1951) pp. 149-166.

[2] Luis Pastor, *Historia de los Papas XIV*, Barcelona (1927) p. 103.

[3] *General Archive of Simancas. Royal Board*, File 18-82. It can be read in its entirety in the Appendix, or, pp. 320-322.

[4] A prebend is the portion of the revenues of a cathedral or collegiate church formerly granted to a canon or member of the chapter as his stipend.

[5] In the session of April 13, 1546, the decree on lectors and preachers was read at the Council of Trent, and Castro approved the decree that deals with the creation of theological prebends in cathedrals. CT, V, p. 108.

[6] My article: *Fr. Alfonso de Castro, O. F. M., Notas Bibliográficas*. In: *Collectánea Franciscana* 28 (1958) pp. 67-68.

[7] MHSJ.: *P. Petri de Ribadeneira, S. J., confesiones, epistolae aliaque scripta inédita I*. Madrid (1920)

preach there during the next Lent together with Friar Bartolomé de Miranda. In 1556 he preached at the Court of the Archdukes with other famous preachers while the Jesuits, for their part, also wanted to be introduced.[1] That same year he strongly opposed, together with Friar Bernardo de Fresneda, the attempts made by the Society of Jesus to found a Jesuit College[2] in Jerusalem. We find him still there in 1557, when Bartolomé de Carranza, O.P., his collaborator in the Netherlands in the defense of the faith against the heretics, was promoted to the archbishopric of Toledo, who introduced Castro in his place.[3] And on January 3, 1558, Father Salmerón wrote from Brussels to Diego Laínez informing him that the king had many preachers there, among whom was Alfonso de Castro.[4]

Our Franciscan was still in Belgium when the Cardinal Archbishop of Santiago, Juan Alvarez de Toledo, died. Philip II, wanting to reward Castro's many merits and extraordinary services, named him to succeed the deceased in so high a position.[5] But Castro died in Brussels on February 3, 1558, before the arrival of the Papal Bulls.[6]

Some authors, even of special renown, such as the editors of the Tridentine Council of the Gorres publishing house,[7] erroneously state that he died on February eleventh. But we have proof of the third in the epitaph of Tamayo, where it is read: "He was called forth [from this life] on the third of February (*tertio nonarum Februarii*)." And Salmerón, in a letter of February 20, 1558, sent to Laínez from Brussels, says, "On the third day of this present month Our Lord took Father Alonso de Castro. May Our Lord grant him rest. Amen."[8] This is confirmed, moreover, from that date on which they stopped paying him the salary he received as royal preacher.[9]

This is the portrait of the humble Franciscan Friar Alfonso de Castro, an outstanding figure in the sixteenth century, so that after having read these poorly composed lines, we will perfectly understand the words of Cardinal Palavicini,[10] who said that Castro had been one of the best theologians who had attended the Council of Trent, and that he, together with Vega, were enough to make a century, and not only a religious house, famous.[11]

---

pp. 127, 156. MHSJ.: Polanco, *Vita Ignatii loiolae VI*, Madrid (1898) p. 441.

[1] MHSJ.: *Monumenta Ignatiana X*, Madrid (1910) p. 555.

[2] Polanco, *Vita VI*, pp. 457-458.

[3] Castro, *Arbol I*, p. 111. Carranza was appointed as the metropolitan of Toledo on December 10, 1557. Eubel, *Hierarchia* pp. 3, 334.

[4] MHSJ; *Epistolae P. Alphonsi Salmeronis I*, Madrid (1906) pp. 228-229

[5] Antonio Lopez Ferreiro, *Historia de la Santa M. I. de Santiago VII*, Santiago (1905) p. 18. The *Chrónica ms.* of the Province of Santiago, written in 1613, says: "The learned religious and great hound (*perseguidor*) of heretics, Fray Alonso de Castro, it is considered, certain died with a document from His Majesty King Philip II, by which he granted him the Archbishopric of Santiago." fols. 72v-73.

[6] L. Wadding, *Annales Min.* ad an. (1228) n. 90. He is quoted in the *Chronicon Werthense* of Enrique de Vroom, or Sedulio, published by David de Kok, O. F. M., in: *Collectanea Franciscana* 16 (1946) pp. 91-92. I asked Rome to search the Vatican Archives for the pontifical bulls mentioned in the text, but the result was negative.

[7] CT, XII, p. 497, n. 1; V, Index.

[8] MHSJ; Salmeron, *Epistolae I*, p. 236.

[9] General Archive of Simancas: *Quitaciones de la Casa Real*. File, 62, s. f. It is published by: Eloy Bullón, *Alfonso de Castro and penal science*, Madrid (1900) p. 131. F. Peri, *Chronographia sacra almae Provinciae Germaniae Inferioris, O. F. M.*, Bruxellis, p. 171; in *Collectánea Franciscana Neerlandica*, 1, (1926) p. 206, n. 1; p. 356, n. 3.

[10] Sforza Palavicini, *Istoria del Concilio di Trento III*, Mendrisio (1836) bk. 6, c. 5, n. 5, pp. 112-113.

[11] The Academy of Doctors of Madrid organized a commemorative act in honor and memory of Alfonso de Castro, on February 18, 1958, on the occasion of the fourth centenary of his death. See: *Rev. de la*

Biography of the Author

Appendix

Memorandum of Friar Alonso de Castro to Philip II on the things that had to be asked to the Pope when dealing with peace.[1]

S. C. R. M.[2]

Inasmuch as I have heard that the pope is trying to make some peace agreements, and if he does not do so now, things are at such a point that I believe he will be forced to ask for some agreements, I have thought of some things that it would be good to ask the pope then. These things seem to me to be very important for the service of Your Majesty and for the benefit of Christendom, especially of the kingdoms of Spain, which I put here as a memorandum so that Your Majesty may see them and command those of your Council who deal with them.

First of all, you must ask the pope to give authentic confirmation of everything determined in the Council of Trent. This is a very important thing, because things were ordered there, some of them very good, and some scandals have occurred between the prelates and the cathedral chapters (*cabildos*) over the keeping of some of them. All of which would have been eliminated if the pope had been willing to give confirmation of the said Council. And this confirmation the pope is obliged to give, since what was ordered there was with the authority and consent of the Apostolic Chair.

Likewise, seeing that the Council of Trent was not concluded, and as the world is now, it is not expected that a general council can be assembled again, it will be good that in Spain a national council of all Spain be assembled, as in the past many others were held in this nation, and for greater firmness of what is ordered there, it will be necessary that the pope be asked to appoint a legate, and if possible that he be a Spaniard, who with the pope's plenary authority will preside in the said council, and with this authority, when the pope wanted to undo something of what was ordered there, Your Majesty and your successors would have just title to resist him and not to consent to it.

Likewise, it should be requested that all the curated and simple beneficiaries who have the obligation of service, be patrimonial, as they are in the bishoprics of Burgos, Palencia and Calahorra. And because the way it is done in these three bishoprics is somewhat lacking and has some inconveniences, I offer myself for when it is to be treated that I will give a very good plan that has no inconveniences, but is very plain and well paid, that will eliminate all bribery and favoritism, and also all partiality and acceptance of persons. From this approbation there are very great benefits for the kingdom. The first and most important is the benefit of the souls, because all those holding benefices will be learned men and good examples, who will know how to govern their flock well and give them a salutary teaching. The second benefit is that, since the benefices are patrimonial, half of the Spaniards who now go to the Roman Curia will not go there. From this follows a third benefit, that not as much money will be taken from Spain to Rome as is now being taken.

In addition to the curated benefices and simple servants, it would be just that some number of prebends be requested in each cathedral or collegiate church, which would be deputed for doctors, or graduates in theology or canon law who have graduated from some university

---

Escuela de Estudios Pnitencios 14 (1958) 292-300.

[1] Amalia Prieto Cantero, *General Archive of Simancas. Catalog V. Patronato Real, I*, Valladolid (1946) n. 1609.

[2] SCRM comes from SCCRM, a phrase that Charles V of Spain started using when he became the Holy Roman Emperor (Crowned by the Pope in 1530). SCCRM stands for "*Sacra Cesárea Católica Real Majestade*" (Holy, Imperial, Catholic, Royal Majesty). Under Phillip II SCRM began to appear, which stands for "*Sacra, Católica, Real Majestad*" (Holy, Catholic, Royal Majesty).

in Spain, and not by rescripts from Rome. The Catholic Monarchs Ferdinand and Isabella obtained from Pope Sixtus IV two prebends in each cathedral church, one for a theologian and the other for a canonist; and it was seen by experience that by the hope of [gaining] these two prebends they were encouraged to study, which they had not done before. And with a certain number of residences for canons that Cardinal Fray Francisco Ximénez established in Alcalá for doctoral theologians, that university is preserved, and without them it would have been lost. Because, as Cicero says in the first Tusculan question: "Honors nourish the arts."[1] And we have seen by experience that as the Caesarean Majesty in the consultations that it had during the last twelve years, most of the bishoprics that fell vacant personally provided theologians. Then all the educated men who had children deputed for the Church sent them to study theology at Salamanca or Alcalá, and those who had begun to study canon law made them pass to theology. And if now some number of prebends were deputed in each cathedral or collegiate church, more than there are, many more would be encouraged to study, and there would be many more learned men. And it is not much that this be granted, since in the Council of Basel it was determined that at least a third part of the prebends of each church should be for theologians; which was not put into effect either, like the other things of that Council, because of the general hatred that the pope, who was then Eugene IV, had against him.

Likewise, it should be requested of the pope that no lawsuit may be brought to Rome in the first instance, except by way of appeal, after having been judged by the Ordinary. This is something of great importance because it would remove with it many annoyances and calumnies that are made by taking the lawsuits of the first instance to Rome; and it is not much that this would be now granted, since the Council of Basel orders that those who are distant from Rome for more than a hundred leagues, could not take the lawsuit to Rome, except for very serious causes. If all these things seem too many to be requested together, the two that concern the provision of benefices and other prebends can be left out. For, although they are the most important, they can be remedied by another way, which is by the national council, if it were to be held with the authority of the pope, wherein it could be put into effect by decree.

+Father Alonso de Castro
(Signed)

---

[1] Cicero, *Tusculan Disputations*, bk. 1, c. 2, n. 4.

The King's License

The King

Inasmuch as it has been related to us on your behalf, Juan Steelsio, bookseller, resident of our town of Antwerp, that our preacher, Friar Alonso de Castro of the Order of Saint Francis, has composed a new addition to the book he wrote entitled, *Adversus Omnes Haereses*: an addition so large as to be almost half again the size of the original work; and that you wished to publish it, which entails great expense; and that you besought and requested as a compensation that we would give you permission and authorization so that you, and no other person, may do this in our kingdom and dominion of Castile, for as long as we may be served, or as may be our favor: and we have approved of complying with your abovementioned request, since it is such a useful and beneficial book for the Christian state, and the income it provides for you thereby. Hence, by this decree we give permission and authorization to you, the aforesaid Juan Steelsio: and we command that you, or the person or persons who have your permission for this work, and no one else, may print and sell it; and that they do print and sell the aforesaid book in our aforementioned kingdom and dominion of Castile during the period of the next six years, which are reckoned from the date of this decree of ours and thereafter; under such penalty that whatever person or persons, without having your permission, publishes it, sells it or has it published or sold, shall lose all that they have printed, and the forms and apparatus for it, and moreover shall incur a fine of fifty thousand maravedis[1] for each time that they act contrary to this decree: one third of the aforesaid penalty will be for the person who makes the accusation, another third will be for the judge who passes sentence, and the other third, for our treasury and revenue; and each plate of the mold from the aforesaid publication shall be sold for a price appraised and controlled by our Council: and we command those of our Council, presidents and judges of our royal Audiences, mayors, sheriffs of our house, court, and chancellors, and all the chief magistrates, assistants, governors, wardens, judges, lords, provosts, and all other justices and judges of our aforesaid kingdom and dominions, who watch over and carry out this decree of ours, and supervise and execute what is contained in it, and let them not go against it, nor allow, nor consent to, nor permit, going against it, in any way: under penalty of our own and of ten thousand maravedis for our treasury, from each one who shall have done the contrary. Given in Brussels on the twenty-second day of the month of April, of the year one thousand five hundred fifty-six.

I, the King[2]
Promulgated by His Royal Majesty
Francisco de Erasso.

---

[1] I.e. old Spanish coins.

[2] I.e. Philip II, who assumed the throne on January 16, 1556, merely three months before authorizing this book to be published.

Letter to the King

Letter to the King

To the Most Serene and Catholic Philip King of Spain, England,[1] France[2] and Ireland, defender of the Church, Friar Alfonso de Castro, of the Order of Friars Minor, wishes all felicity.

So great, O Most Serene and Catholic King, is the desire of the heretics for harming, and so great is their fury for destroying souls, for whom Christ deigned to die, that Christ Himself, being also the Wisdom of God, willed to call them by the name of wolves, so that by this name He might urge His sheep to carefully avoid associating with them. "Beware of false prophets," He said, "who come to you in the clothing of sheep, but inwardly they are ravening wolves" (Mt. 7, 15). Our Savior indeed warned His sheep by these words, so that they would keep themselves away from heretics: who under the name of "Christian," as hiding under a kind of sheep's clothing, rage against the Lord's sheep, striving with obstinate determination to completely destroy them; so that they leave nothing untouched, until with the poison of their doctrine they do away with them, if they could.

They behead and maim the canon of Sacred Scripture, pulling out of it whatever contradicts their pestiferous doctrine, lest Catholics have evidence to refute them. Scripture itself, which they do not deny to be sacred, they distort into strange meanings. They despise the holy interpreters of Sacred Scripture, whom the Catholic Church has always venerated as almost prophets of God: and they do not merely make themselves equal to them, but dare with shameless temerity to prefer themselves to them, so that they might persuade insufficiently cautious people, by this simple reason that their doctrine is not merely human but is to be received as divine.

They contrive a thousand lies, so that they might draw the people and render them well disposed towards themselves. They seek with anxious solicitude the favor of kings and princes, so that with their help and power they may avail to force those who oppose them into silence. Now, in order that they might more easily chase after this favor, they flatter and applaud these same kings and princes, saying to them that whatever pleases them is lawful. Therefore, they leave no stone unmoved, so that their poisonous doctrine infects the Lord's sheep, that in this way they may be able to kill them.

Although heretics are so shrewd and eager, and so fierce in destroying souls—just as wolves do to sheep—so that they always lie in wait for them; nevertheless, God, Who is the best shepherd of souls and loves them with a certain intimate affection, does not wish to completely annihilate these wolves: so that He might in this way urge Christian men to greater caution and vigilance, and furnish them with an occasion for greater merit. For those who realize that they have enemies must live more carefully than those who are not maliciously begrudged. And cities which are near enemies should be guarded with greater diligence and be more fortified, lest perchance they become a booty of the enemy. According to Plutarch, of old, when the Carthaginians and the Greeks were destroyed, and a certain man in the Senate had said

---

[1] Passed by the English Parliament in 1554, the "Act for the Marriage of Queen Mary to Philip of Spain" granted Philip of Spain the privilege of using the titles of his wife, Queen Mary I of England.

[2] The kings and queens of England (and, later, of Great Britain) continued to claim the French throne for centuries, through the early modern period. The words "of France" was prominently included among their realms as listed in their titles and styles, and the French fleur-de-lys was included in the royal arms. This continued until 1801, by which time France had no monarch, having become a republic.

that the Roman Empire was now secure, Scipio Nasica[1] replied, "Nay, on the contrary, now we are in great danger, because we do not have anyone to fear." Therefore, lest the Christians, lacking enemies of the faith, become lethargic through leisure; and lest they become tepid in the same faith, the most benevolent God permits that in His Church after the Gospel has been preached and the faith has been accepted, scarcely ever is a heretic lacking who might agitate it. For from the Ascension of Christ our Savior into Heaven until this day, there has been no time in which have not arisen new heresies or old ones revived.

For in this time of ours—I will now omit other times—when everyone was thinking that some breath was given to the Church from the infestations of heretics; lest to this time of ours, full of vices, might be lacking heretics who had been in other happier times; behold suddenly Luther comes forth, dragging along nearly the whole heap of condemned heresies after him. For while other heretics proposed individual kinds of intricate and jeering questions to themselves, about which they conjectured and taught, this man indeed revived once again nearly all the teachings of the heretics, now rejected by the Church: so that dug out with various heresies from here and there, he became like a wide open trench through which the offscourings of all heresies flow and hide. For scarcely are there one or two sects of heretics, especially among those which err about morals, with whom Luther does not have something in common. For that old enemy of the human race harasses in such a way that heresies may never die from old age, and that there be no longstanding harmful doctrine, which either may be overthrown by time or be buried in oblivion.

And Luther did not come forth alone, so great is the misfortune of this age: as though he were to come forth surrounded by an escort, who seem to have expected him, so that afterwards they might fight under his banner. For Philip Melanchthon, [Wolfgang] Fabricius Capito, [Francis] Lambert, Konrad Pellikan, Andreas Osiander, and Martin Bucer enlisted under him, and many others with the passing of time inserted themselves en masse into his family. Others also came forth, who, even if they subscribe to Luther in many heresies, nevertheless disdained to fight under his banner, and thus other heresies were set up: between any of whom and Luther there is hardly agreement, so that anyone might in his own name establish his own battle line, of which he would be deemed to be the leader. For among the nearly infinite number of heretics, there always was, and is, a certain cupidity for popular glory, which wantonly drives them to contrive some new doctrine, that by the novelty of the doctrine they may draw others to the admiration of themselves. Oecolampadius parted from Luther, Zwingli separated himself from both. John Calvin separated from all these others in many things. Finally, the Anabaptists, of all the most pestilent, opposed them all.

Certainly so many and so great monsters were born in in our times that now it would be necessary for a new Hercules to be the tamer of them, who might dash them all down, and out of the Christian world. The greater part of Germany, however, chose to give ear to the serpentine hissing of all these heretics, rather than to the Divine voice of the Church. And would that this pestilence were contained solely within the confines of Germany, and were not fiercely and powerfully spreading in the other parts of the Christian world; so that now it is rare to find a province bearing the Christian name in which there are lacking those who publicly or secretly embrace Luther's and the others' errors, which are of the same dough.

Therefore, in order that I may partly heal, insofar as I can, this so widely spreading disease, twenty-two years ago, in the year 1534, I published a certain work divided into fourteen

---

[1] Publius Cornelius Scipio Nasica Corculum (died 141 BC) was a Roman statesman and member of the gens Cornelia. During the period 159-149 BC, Corculum was a political opponent of Marcus Porcius Cato and pleaded that Rome not destroy Carthage. According to Plutarch's conjecture and Appian's later definite assertion, that was because Corculum feared that the destruction of Rome's main rival would lead to the decline of Roman morals and discipline.

Letter to the King

books, in which I firstly took care to give a very accurate account of all the heresies that had arisen in the Church after Christ's Ascension: then I fought against them all one by one, so that in this way I might perhaps show that all these recent heretics have drawn their heresies from dregs already rejected long ago by the Church: and this was done in that hope that, knowing more clearly that these teachings were condemned as such by the Church, all might more easily escape their poisonous doctrines.

Which work, with God's help, and its just cause (I speak as a Christian) has pleased the eyes of all Catholics to such an extent that within those twenty-two years it has already been reprinted more than ten times in France, Germany and Italy. Which occurrence greatly motivated me to carefully revise this work again, so that if I might see anything lacking, I might take care to add it. I had indeed reviewed this work now more than once, and whatever I ascertained was then lacking I supplied: and what I thought to be less well arranged, I amended. Now, finally, so that I might put my hand to this work for the last time, I carefully revised it three times, and I learned by my literary venture that the last literary efforts are always the best. For I understood that several heresies were lacking, of which some I had prudently omitted, for the very reason that it was not fully established that they were heresies, and I did not wish in so serious a matter to determine anything. I found other heresies, however, doing a second revision, when I read with attentive eyes, [the works of] many authors regarding this matter. Lastly, other heresies after the publications of this work, came forth in public. Then, concerning those previous heresies, which I had described in other editions of this work, I have added many things which seemed to me necessary for more fully understanding, or for more easily overcoming, these heresies: [I have removed] other things, certainly of less importance, to put many and better things in their place. Therefore there are in it so many, and such important, things that are now added and changed after all the prior editions of this work, that it rightly ought now to be considered a new work, which also requires a new patron as well.

Even were I, wrapped in thought, to have searched after [likely patrons] with the greatest exertion, no one else besides you, O Most Serene and Christian king, could I have met, to whose patronage I could more suitably entrust this work. For since this work treats of the Catholic faith and fights against all heresies, it was reasonable to think that no one would give to it support, and help with more ardent desire and greater endeavor, than you, who—having derived succession by a hereditary right from your ancestors, the kings of Spain—wage a perpetual and irreconcilable war with the enemies of the Catholic faith. No one is more firmly bound with a greater obligation to protecting the Catholic faith than you, who by the title of King of England are called "defender of the Church."[1]

---

[1] "Defender of the Faith" is probably meant here. This title was granted on October 11, 1521, by Pope Leo X to King Henry VIII of England. The title was conferred in recognition of Henry's book *Assertio Septem Sacramentorum* (Defense of the Seven Sacraments), which defended the sacramental nature of marriage and the supremacy of the Pope. "About A. D. 1521, the Emperor Charles passing towards Spain landed at Dover, where the King met him and conducted him in great state to London, lodging him at Winsor; and in such bands of amity, the emperor and King Henry seemed to be linked, that in London this sentence was set up in the Guild-Hall over the door of the Council Chamber, *Carolus, Henricusque, Defensor uterque, Henricus fidei, Carolus Ecclesiae*. The reason of which titles, defender of the faith and Church was, for that Charles the Emperor had directed forth a solemn writ of outlawry against Doctor Martin Luther, who had then given a great blow to the triple crown [the papal tiara]; and King Henry had wrote a book against the said Luther, for the pope gave the title of 'Defender of the Church' to the emperor, and 'Defender of the Faith" to the king, and for the same cause he sent King Henry a consecrated rose." (William Howell, *Medulla historiae anglicanae: The ancient and present state of England* (London, Printed for T. Child [etc.], 1712), p. 174).

Letter to the King

Now you cannot be truly called "defender of the Church" unless you defend with all your strength the Catholic faith upon which God founded the Church itself. No one, even if he be more jealous than Zoilus,[1] would dare to deny that you have done enough, very completely and sincerely, in fulfilling the obligation of this title by those outstanding achievements, which were done long ago by you in the same kingdom of England. For after you married Mary, the Most Serene Queen of England, and for that reason you undertook the government of that kingdom, from that moment, lest you be seen to uselessly bear the name without the reality with pretentious and boastful vanity, with anxious care you saw to it that that kingdom, which for more than twenty years had deserted the Catholic faith, was led back to it.

Now the most benevolent God, Who hath searched the heart and reins,[2] and understood you to be a "man of desires" as another Daniel,[3] did not allow you be defrauded of your just desire, or to be left in suspense for a long time, but within a very short time He fulfilled your wish. For you applied yourself with so much diligence and prudence to this matter, that after only the period of four months from your nuptial celebrations, God having softened the hearts of the English, having assembled the principle men of the whole kingdom in the public place of assembly in London, in the name of themselves and the whole kingdom, they from afar offered to the Roman Pontiff the obedience, which they had withdrawn from him: and the Catholic faith, which they had previously rejected, they would henceforth embrace, and promised to remain steadfast in it for the future. Which promise nearly all have fulfilled so completely up until now, so that all of us who actually saw this event with our own eyes, might rightly hope that the whole kingdom is about to be brought back in a short time to that purity and sincerity of the Christian religion, which they had before their defection.

Therefore this work which I had published, and have enlarged while being in the kingdom of England, serving you in public sermons and matters of faith, and supported by your ample largess, I have taken care to dedicate to you, O Most Catholic King, and Deliverer and Protector of the Catholic faith, to whom many names were due: so that, since it is not enough to examine it, it may be protected by the shadow of your name. I humbly beseech Your Majesty and Highness that, by virtue of your royal benignity, you may deign to accept and support it, as a sort of soldier desirous of fighting under your standard. Farewell, O Most Christian King, and glory and ornament of the Christian religion. Signed in Antwerp, the twentieth day of May, in the year of the Lord, 1556.

---

[1] Zoilus (c. 400 – 320 BC) was a Greek grammarian, Cynic philosopher, and literary critic, especially notable for his role in the beginnings of Homeric scholarship. Cervantes calls Zoilus a "slanderer" in the preface to Don Quixote and there is also an old proverb, "Every poet has his Zoilus."

[2] Psalm 7, 10.

[3] Daniel 9, 23.

Preface

Among the many and various wicked deeds which enter into and devastate the whole of mankind, especially Christians, heresy is one that is worse than others, because it is the most pestilential: it spreads itself more widely, penetrates more deeply, adheres more tenaciously, and hence is more difficultly cured. For the harm is so great in that it assails the foundation of all piety, without which all other beneficial things are nothing. For "without faith," says Saint Paul, "it is impossible to please God" (Heb. 11, 6). Through faith the saints "conquered kingdoms, wrought justice, obtained promises, stopped the mouths of lions, quenched the violence of fire, escaped the edge of the sword, recovered strength from weakness, became valiant in battle, put to flight the armies of foreigners" (*ibid.* verses 33-34). This is the food for life's journey, as the Prophet says, "The just shall live in his faith" (Hab. 2, 4). This is, therefore, as I was just saying, the basis and foundation of the whole Christian structure, upon which, as upon, as it were, a most firm rock, God founded His Church. Upon which also Paul commanded us to be founded, as "grounded and settled, and immoveable from the hope of the gospel which you have heard" (Col. 1, 23).

Wherefore if from faith's goodness one can measure the malice of heresy, we will say by the opposite that heresy is the worst vice. For (according to the opinion of Augustine[1]) something evil is a worse evil to the degree that it deprives it of what is good. Hence, it is evident how undeserving of Christendom are those who fight against the faith, or those who will nod their head to heresy, or who protect those brought in: for the foundation being destroyed, it is necessary that whatever had been built upon it falls. Now heretics strive to destroy the foundation that was laid by Christ and shown to the world by His Apostles: for even if they oftentimes differ from each other in some things, nevertheless they all agree on one thing: that they raise up [military] plumes [on their heads] against the doctrine of Christ and of the Apostles. And those who did this are not few: which is especially to be lamented, and is a grave matter indeed, since they have gone out from us. And as many barbarous nations were of old stirred up against the sons of Israel, that many, nay more, have risen up against the Catholic faith and the Evangelical doctrine. And this attack has not yet ceased. Many camps of the enemy, in fact, are pitched around it, have walled it in on all sides, so that they might cast it down to the ground. From the East: Simon [Magus], Menander,[2] Valentinus,[3] and Mani.[4] From the

---

[1] "When, however, a thing is corrupted, its corruption is an evil, because it is, to that degree, a privation of the good. Where there is no privation of the good, there is no evil. Where there is evil, there is a corresponding diminution of the good" (*Enchiridion*, chap. 4, n. 12 (PL 40, 237)).

[2] "Of which heretics I will (to pass by a good deal) summarize some few particulars... Of these the first of all is Simon Magus, who in the Acts of the Apostles earned a condign and just sentence from the Apostle Peter. He had the hardihood to call himself the 'Supreme Virtue,' that is, the Supreme God; and moreover, (to assert) that the universe had been originated by his angels; that he had descended in quest of an erring daemon, which was Wisdom; that, in a phantasmal semblance of God, he had not suffered among the Jews, but was as if he had suffered. After him Menander, his disciple (likewise a magician), saying the same as Simon. Whatever Simon had affirmed himself to be, this did Menander equally affirm himself to be, asserting that none could possibly have salvation without being baptized in his name" (Pseudo-Tertullian, *Against All Heresies*, Chap. 1).

[3] Valentinus (c.100-c.160) the best known and most influential of the Gnostic heretics, was born, according to Epiphanius (*Haer.*, XXXI), on the coast of Egypt.

[4] Mani (216-274), the founder of the Manichaeism, is always called by Augustine, "*Manichaeus.*" His name is a title and term of respect rather than a personal name. He was born in what is now Iraq.

Preface

West: Priscillian,[1] Vigilantius,[2] and Peter Abelard.[3] From the South: Tertullian,[4] Novatian,[5] and Donatus.[6] From the North, from whence every evil is spread: Pelagius,[7] John Wycliffe,[8] John Hus,[9] and Martin Luther.[10]

Therefore [the faith] been having struck by four Angels, warlike engines on every side were moved against it.[11] O how many sophistical reasonings, how many distortions and mutilations of the Scriptures are laid down as true, so that what Christ laid down as the foundation, namely the faith, might tumble down? But after so many incursions of wars, after so many missiles hurled against it, the foundation remains fixed and immobile until the end of the world, be-

---

[1] Priscillian was the bishop of Avila, Spain, who followed Gnostic-Manichaean doctrines. He was executed by Emperor Maximus in 385 A.D., contrary to the wishes of Saint Martin of Tours, who expressing his disapproval of bringing an ecclesiastical case before a civil tribunal, temporarily obtained from the emperor a promise not to carry his condemnation to the extent of shedding blood.

[2] Vigilantius was born in about 370 A.D., at Calagurris in what is now southern France. He opposed the veneration of relics, the sending of alms to Jerusalem, the vow of poverty, and the high esteem of virginity. He was opposed in writing by Saint Jerome.

[3] Peter Abelard (1079-1142) was born in France and fell inadvertently into the errors of Arianism, Pelagianism, and Nestorianism. St. Bernard sums up the charges against Abelard, saying that when he "speaks of the Trinity savors of Arius; when of grace, of Pelagius; when of the person of Christ, of Nestorius" (PL 182, 358D-359A).

[4] Tertullian was an ecclesiastical writer in the second and third centuries, born probably about 160 A.D. at Carthage. In the year 206 he joined the Montanist sect, which held among other beliefs that certain sins committed after Baptism could not be forgiven, and which practiced a severe asceticism. He seems to have definitively separated from the Church several years later.

[5] "The errors of Novatus and Novatian were the following: they denied that the Church could use any indulgence with those who became idolaters through fear of persecution, or that she could grant pardon for any mortal sin committed after Baptism, and they denied the Sacrament of Confirmation. Like the Montanists, they condemned second marriages, and refused communion on the point of death to those who contracted them" (Saint Alphonsus Ligouri, *The History of Heresies, and Their Refutation* (Dublin, James Duffy, 1847), chap. 3, n. 7).

[6] Donatus, bishop of Casae Nigrae, in North Africa, followed the error of Donatism, an error that predated him but was later named after him, which held that the effectiveness of the Sacraments depends on the moral character of the minister. In other words, if a minister who was involved in a serious enough sin were to baptize a person, that Baptism would be considered invalid. Donatus died in 355.

[7] Pelagius (c. 390-419), probably born in Ireland, denied Original sin as well as the necessity of grace for performing works meritorious of salvation.

[8] John Wycliffe (1324-1384) was born in England and in 1415 was declared a heretic by the Council of Constance, which condemned forty-five of his errors, principally his denial of transubstantiation. He resembled the Protestant Reformers in his insistence on the Bible as the rule of faith, in the importance attributed to preaching, and in his sacramental doctrine.

[9] John Hus (1369-1415) was in southern Bohemia. He was tried by the Council of Constance, condemned, and burned at the stake on July 6, 1415. He publicly defended the condemned errors of Wycliffe, including the doctrine of impanation in the Eucharist.

[10] Martin Luther (1483-1546) was the leader of the great religious revolt of the sixteenth century in Germany.

[11] Cf. Apoc. 9, 15.

Preface -xlix-

cause the Lord promised that He would pray for the Church, that its faith would not fail.[1] But how could it fail, when He is praying for it, Who is always heard? Thus God gives her help by His countenance. He is in the midst thereof, so that it shall not be moved.[2] Hence it is that the battleline of heretics could never prevail against the Church, against which (God bearing witness) neither shall the gates of hell prevail.[3]

And nevertheless, heretics have not abstained from this infestation, nor will they ever abstain in coming generations. For they always attack, although they will never be able to conquer. For just as the Jebusite of old always remained among the sons of Israel, even in Jerusalem itself, and could never be annihilated, God so permitting or disposing for repelling the Jews' indolence,[4] namely so that they would know that they live among those whom it behooved them to fear, and to watch on account of them: so also now, no matter how much the Church is purged of heretics, the Jebusite will always be in its midst for our exercise. "There must be also heresies," Paul says, "that they also, who are approved, may be made manifest among you" (I Cor. 11, 19). Thus, because the Apostle foresaw that there would always be heretics, hence he admonishes with all the sedulity and solicitude he can, that we would avoid them, and abstain from associating with them: because he knew how much harm associating with them could cause. "Their speech spreadeth like a canker" (II Tim. 2, 17).

Motivated by this reason many Ecclesiastical writers have anxiously labored in examining heretics and their errors, so that they might describe them to us: so that consequently thereafter those whom, according to Paul's precept, one ought to avoid would be known to others in this way. Among whom the first of these who stands out, is Irenaeus, bishop of Lyon, very close to the times of the Apostles. This man composed an elegant work on the heresies divided into five books, in the first of which he enumerates all the heresies and their authors which had attacked the Church until his own time. But in the other books he disputes some of them. After this man, at nearly the same time, Tertullian came forth, who although he was afterwards a heretic, nevertheless previously when he was a Catholic, composed a book, *Prescription against Heretics*, the appendix of which is another small book on heresies.[5] In which brief compendium of all heretics who lived before him, he publishes the names and heresies; although he did not write down all their errors. Philastrius, the bishop of Brescia, whom Blessed Augustine testifies that he saw when in Milan with Blessed Ambrose, published a somewhat larger work, *De haeresibus*, and he does not omit those which were before Christ in ancient times among the Jews. At nearly the same time Epiphanius, bishop of [Salamis,] Cyprus, wrote a book in Greek on heresies,[6] divided into six books, moderately short, as Augustine bears witness.[7] In which book he enumerated only eighty heresies, having joined also to them those which of old had arisen among the Jews. Augustine, drawing from the books of these two bishops, impelled by requests of Quodvultdeus,[8] published a work about heresies for the same Quodvultdeus. In which book he describes only those which made an attack

---

[1] Cf. Lk. 22, 32.
[2] Cf. Common of many virgins in the Divine Office and Ps. 45, 6.
[3] Cf. Mt. 16, 18.
[4] Cf. Judges 2, 21-23.
[5] *Against All Heresies*, which is a spurious work formerly attributed to Tertullian.
[6] I.e., the *Panarion*, also called, *Against All Heresies*.
[7] "Epiphanius, bishop of Cyprus, who died not long ago, in treating eighty heresies also wrote six books, narrating everything in historical fashion without any refutation of error or defense of the truth. These books of Epiphanius are quite short" (*De Haeresibus ad Quodvultdeum* (PL 42, 23)).
[8] Quodvultdeus (Latin for "what God wills," died c. 450 AD) was a fifth-century Church Father and bishop of Carthage.

Preface

upon the Church after Christ's Ascension into heaven. Wherefore from the notorious Simon the Magician about whom mention is made in the Acts of the Apostles, he begins his history.

After all those outstanding men, Guy de Perpignan of the Carmelite Order, and afterwards bishop of Elna, composed a book about heresies,[1] in which he published those heresies which arose after Augustine, and not omitting those which in ancient times existed among the Jews. But he was not content to tell the bare history of the heretics, as Augustine and Philastrius did, but he tried to show the arguments in favor and against each heresy,[2] and, as it were, to challenge each one to battle. Which thing he does so unhappily, that frequently truth loses the competition, if a judgment must be given based on his fight. I omit that he fails also in the narration of the history itself. For as an insufficiently diligent investigator of history, he omits many heresies, even of those men who came forth around his time, such as the Albigenses, the Flagellants, Peter Abelard, Henry of Lausanne,[3] Amaury [of Bena], Durán de Baldach,[4] and many other heretics, whose errors Guy never mentions. Sometimes he mixes up heresies, attributing to this man what belongs to another. Sometimes also he attributes errors diametrically opposed to each other to the same sect, as, for instance, it is easy to find in his writings, when he speaks about the Armenians.

Finally, after all these men, a certain Brother Bernard of Luxemburg wrote down a *Catalogus* of all heretics, a certainly laborious work, although in it he often wanders in mind, including many men therein who ought to have been marked with a better stone,[5] such as Papias, and others of whom we will speak below. He also mixes in many other men there, who nowise seem to belong to the family of heretics, because they never put on Christ through Baptism, such as Avicenna and Averroes, since they never gave their names to Christ in Baptism, nowise can it happen that they be called heretics. For otherwise all the pagan philosophers would have to be written under the name of heretics.

Therefore, all who summarized the history of heretics, labored for this one thing, that they would write down the sects of the heretics, and in this way as by a list they might point out to others the enemies of the faith, from whose communion one needed to abstain. Which labor has benefited the Catholic Church not a little until the present time, and now daily benefits more: because the first step to gaining every virtue, as the Royal Prophet says, is to "decline from evil" (Ps. 36, 27): now this is the first [step] to doing good. For a ploughman firstly clears the field of thorns or whatsoever harmful plant, and in this way the land produces the crop from the seeds later planted. In this way a doctor prescribing rules for the sick person, whereby he can both attain and keep his health, firstly teaches him the food from which he ought to abstain. Also, in every teaching one ought not to labor less so that errors may be extirpated, than that the truth may be taught. For once the errors have been extirpated, the truth may be known more clearly, the thing known is loved more ardently, and lastly the thing loved is defended more vehemently and more carefully guarded. But if this is observed in any teaching, much more profitably will this happen in theology, that is, in the Evangelical teaching, in which (as written by Augustine[6]) nowhere else is error more dangerous, or the

---

[1] I.e., *Summa de haeresibus*.
[2] *Manus conferere*, which originally meant to fight hand to hand.
[3] Alias, Henricus Tolosanus in Latin. He was a disciple of Pierre De Bruys and was a French heresiarch of the first half of the 12th century. He fought against Masses for the dead, the invocation of the saints, celibacy, religious pilgrimages, the consecration of holy oils, feast days, and transubstantiation.
[4] Durán de Baldach (or Durandus de Valdach in Latin) was a French heretic and follower of the Beghards. He was condemned to death in 1323 in Gerona, Spain.
[5] People in ancient times often voted by casting stones. A white stone typically meant "yes" and a black stone "no."
[6] "In no other subject is error more dangerous, or inquiry more laborious, or the discovery of truth more

Preface -li-

discovery of truth more profitable. They therefore provided for our good, those who compiled the history of heretics, so that we might know therefrom those from whose society it behooved us to abstain.

But even though their labor was very useful, still they would have taken better care of our utility, in my opinion, if they had labored more to show the heresies and errors, from which one ought to have chiefly abstained, than the names of the heretics who were the authors of those heresies. For from the knowledge of the heresy anyone will very easily know that its pertinacious author or supporter is or was a heretic. But having proscribed the heretic, and, as it were, having defamed such a man, it is not in this way known what ought to be avoided in him. For most men know that Arius, Sabellius, and Nestorius were heretics, and as such cast out of the communion of the Church and condemned: yet they do not equally know the Arians, Sabellians, or Nestorians, namely because they do not know what was the reason why the Church branded Arius, or Sabellius, or Nestorius with such a mark.

I omit that in the *Catalogus* many heretics are listed by name, yet no heresy of theirs is cited on account of which it is established that they deservedly were so branded, such as Adelbert Gallus[1] and Clement Scotus,[2] Peter of Constantinople,[3] Petrus Olerius,[4] Waldemarius, Nicostratus, Evagrius Ponticus,[5] and very many others. How, I ask, does it help to know these men were heretics long ago, when the reason is unknown on account of which such a severe censure was declared regarding them, who should be avoided by the uneducated by this occasion, especially since the books of these men do not exist? Since therefore on account of the heresy which each teaches or maintains, the heretic ought to be avoided, and not vice versa on account of the heretic the heresy asserted by him [ought to be avoided]: those men, it seems to me, would have done better, if they would have labored more in putting in writing the heresies, than in listing the names of the heretics.

In which matter I see that no one up until now, among those whom I have read, has labored as is demanded: because even though Augustine, Philastrius, Tertullian, Guy, or the *Catalogus* have named the sects of all heretics, still none of them have enumerated all the errors of whichever heretic, nay any one of them omits many of them. Accordingly, Philastrius attributes some heresies to the Cataphrygians or the Gnostics, of which Augustine does not mention when speaking about the same heretics. Likewise, Augustine accuses the Manichaeans of some heresies, which Philastrius nowise mentions. Guy [the Carmelite], however, seems to follow Augustine, and it appears that he did not see another author besides Augustine about the old heretics to be enumerated, since about any heretic he discusses, he does not accuse

---

profitable" (*On the Trinity*, bk. 1, c. 3, n. 5 (PL 42, 822)).

[1] Aldebert, or Adalbert, was a preacher in 8th century Gaul. He claimed that an Angel had conferred miraculous powers on him at his birth and that another had brought him relics of great sanctity from all parts of the earth. He also claimed to be able to see the future and read people's thoughts, telling those who came to him that they had no need to confess, since he knew what they had done, and that their sins were forgiven.

[2] Clement Scotus I (fl. 745) was an Irish bishop and was condemned as a heretic, in part for urging his followers to follow Old Testament Law in such controversial matters as obliging a man to marry his widowed sister-in-law upon his brother's death.

[3] Peter (died in 666) was the Patriarch of Constantinople from 654 to 666. He was condemned as a heretic in the Third Council of Constantinople for the heresy of Monothelitism.

[4] Petrus Olerius was a Beghard in Spain, who was executed for heresy in 1336 for having held an opinion regarding Evangelical poverty peculiar to the Beguines. Cf. R.P. Natalis Alexandri, *Historia ecclesiastica* (Paris, Antonius Dezallier 1714), vol. 7, p. 101.

[5] Evagrius Ponticus was condemned at the II Council of Constantinople because his writings were associated with a theological strain of Origenism.

him of more errors than he reads in Augustine: although in the other authors, if he had read them, he could have found more. Hence it is very clearly proved that they only labored in this, so that they might show the heretics to us as by a list.

All which things having been closely examined by me, it seemed necessary to undertake the work, in which I will endeavor not only to enumerate all the heretics, insofar as I would write down all the heresies, which until our time I could find, the memory of which writing having been kept, supplying from one what another I shall have seen omitted. Which having been done, one collection will be made of all heresies, from which any Catholic ought to abstain. And in this way, anyone will easily know the poison which he ought to avoid, and the path which he ought to turn away from. Now so that from this labor of ours anyone may be able to profit more easily, the heresies themselves will be arranged not according to the time in which they arose, but according to the matter about which they deal. Wherefore the subjects themselves about which they treat, will be arranged by words, divided according to the order of the alphabet.[1] But under any word those heresies will be placed, which will seem to pertain to the subject matter signified by that word. This order having been observed, it will be very easy for anyone, after any topic has once been listed, to then know the heresies which have arisen about it, and which one ought to avoid.

And when I treat about each individual heresy, I will observe this order. Firstly, after having stated the heresy, I will state the archheretic, as the leader of that sect which later on fought under that leader: also, who thereafter recalled from hell the error then dead. Next, I will dispute against the error itself with some arguments, very brief ones at that, by which the heresy (certainly in my opinion) can be refuted. Other more learned teachers will carry this out more powerfully and efficaciously, I for my small measure will give what I can. I do not want to expand very extensively, although perhaps I could often do it very easily, in a very wide-open field, but I have heaped up everything within narrow limits, I have weighed out everything exactly, judging it to be better to impart few worthy words, than to overload the minds of many with my loquacity. Because if one had to dispute extensively about all the heresies, it would have been necessary, that our work would exceed the size of an even larger book: because not in three or four volumes, lest I say in one, could all the heresies be collected together. For that reason I have determined to be brief, and reduce everything into the form of a compendium. But those things will be left to other writers, whom if I know, I will give the reference, whence anyone can draw more plentifully. Last of all, if some council was celebrated, which has defined about that matter in any way, I will subjoin the definition and decree.

Now how much labor of ours was here, the upright and unenvious reader will easily judge, since for going over these heresies alone it was necessary to unroll and read many authors, to wander through many books; especially because frequently there is no agreement among recent authors, it was necessary to seek the truth from other older ones. Which labor having been finished, when I saw a greater number standing against me, namely [that I was] to fight against so many serpents, to vanquish so may monsters, I was deterred from the beginning, pressed by the weight of so many things: because I considered that I took up a matter hardly (according to Horace's precept[2]) suited to my abilities: and I would have turned back,[3] unless I had heard the Lord saying: "One of you shall chase a thousand" (Jos. 23, 10). For the Lord's hand is now neither weaker nor less powerful for strengthening me against the heretics, than of old He was for bestowing assistance and strength to Sampson against the Philistines, a

---

[1] Please note that the Latin order of the subjects will be kept in this translation, in order to keep the author's references to previous and subsequent subjects.

[2] "Ye who write, choose a subject suited to your abilities, and long ponder what your powers are equal to, and what they are unable to perform" (*The Art of Poetry: to the Pisos*, lns. 37-38).

[3] *Retraxissemque pedem.* Cf. Virgil, *Aeneid*, bk. 9, ln. 125.

thousand of whom he killed with the jawbone of an ass.[1] Wherefore even if the camp of all the heretics would stand against me, I will never fear, because I trust in the Lord that He will be "at my right hand, that I be not moved" (Ps. 15, 8). Therefore, fortified by this confidence, I go into the camp, to fight against each and every heresy. But before we go out to fight, it is firstly necessary to prepare the things needed for battle, namely it is necessary to show the creed of those enemies with whom one must fight, and the arms with which to battle, the judges under whom the contest is to be undertaken. For if there would be no judge, there will be no end to battling, especially against pertinacious men. But lest while I attack the deceptive errors of others, I fall into some error myself, by the devil's instigation and with God's permission, I firstly testify, and I always wish it to be testified, that I do never want to deviate even a hair's breadth from that faith which the Catholic Church holds. But if perhaps something of the sort is detected, I assert that it was said not deliberately, but through the negligence or ignorance of a man who could err, [who could have] slipped, and as already now I ask to be regarded as one who has recanted, I will say with Augustine, that "I could err, but I could never be a heretic."[2]

---

[1] Cf. Judges 15, 15.

[2] The idea is St. Augustine's; cf. *De Trinitate*, I, c. 3, n. 6 (PL 42, 822-23): "Neither can anyone, in any way, rightly ascribe the numerous and various errors of heretics to the holy testimonies themselves of the Divine books; although all of them endeavor to defend out of those same Scriptures their own false and erroneous opinions. The law of Christ, that is, charity, admonishes me clearly, and commands me with a sweet constraint, that when men think that I have held in my books something false which I have not held, and that same falsehood displeases one and pleases another, I should prefer to be blamed by him who reprehends the falsehood, rather than praised by him who praises it." See also *De Haeresibus* in the Preface (PL 42, 20 ff): "For not every error is a heresy, although every heresy which is grounded in vice cannot be a heresy except because of some error." The actual words, however, are St. Bonaventure's, who summarizes Augustine in *On the Trinity*, using the words quoted in the text. St. Bonaventure, *Commentaria in quatuor libros sententiarum*, Sent., 4, dist.13, dub.4 in *Doctoris seraphici S. Bonaventurae opera omnia* (near Florence, Ex typographia Colegii S. Bonaventurae, 1889), vol. 4, p. 313.

Introduction

Chapter I: What is heresy?

As I shall treat about heresies, I think that the subject ought to be considered beginning with the definition of heresy. For it is first necessary, according to Aristotle's precept, to establish the definition of heresy, in relation to which—as it is similar to the pin of a sundial—any assertion concerning heresy ought to be examined. Heresy, according to the true and full meaning of the term, means "choice," namely, because everyone chooses that school of thought which he considers to be best: and it comes from the Greek word αἵρεσις, which in Latin is *eligo*.[1] Hence, the sects or opinions of philosophers are called "heresies."

From which meaning of the word it might perhaps seem to someone that the Evangelical doctrine would be called heresy, since very many men, forsaking other errors, choose it for themselves, because they reckon it to be truer. But anyone immediately will reject this, if he were to consider the Evangelical doctrine has not come forth from men, or has not been invented by human reason, but is known solely by God's inspiration and revelation, and therefore it did not happen to come to anyone by his own choice, but only by God's will manifesting it. For no one relying only on his own prudence is able to attain to it. Hence, it is necessary that before anyone truly and firmly (as is fitting) embrace this doctrine, he firstly must be taught by God. For so says the Teacher of truth: "No man can come to me, except the Father, who hath sent me, draw him" (Jn. 6, 44). Wherefore according to the meaning of the word, in no matter how broad the sense, the Evangelical doctrine can hardly be called heresy.

Theophylactus favors this opinion, for when commenting on the passage, "Beware lest any man cheat you by philosophy, and vain deceit; according to the tradition of men" (Col. 2, 8), says: "You see how through some various human opinions and reasoning of men, deceptions of the same sort come forth. Hence, they are called heresies, because they are various opinions of men. But this faith of the Christians is in nowise established by any human understanding or judgment, and therefore neither is any name of this kind given, such that it is called heresy."[2] Therefore, the belief which everyone chooses according to his own judgment is called heresy.

Hence (this is my opinion) Catholic men, restricting the name of heresy, call an assertion deviating from the true faith heresy, as though it were not had from or revealed by God, but invented by the men's choice; nor conformed to Sacred Scripture, but opposed to the true faith. For every truth that pertains to the faith, and which we must believe by Divine law, has been revealed by God Himself and does not depend on the choice of men. If it depended on man's choice, anyone would be able to contradict it with impunity, which Paul clearly opposes. In his First Epistle to the Corinthians, chapter two, he speaks thus: "My speech and my preaching was not in the persuasive words of human wisdom, but in shewing of the Spirit and power, that your faith might not stand on the wisdom of men, but on the power of God" (v. 4). Therefore, if anything is invented by human reason, it is certainly not faith. Hence it is,

---

[1] I.e. "I choose."

[2] This quotation from Theophylactus's commentary on Colossians 2, 8 has an alternate translation of the Greek in *Migne's Patrology* which is translated from the Latin as follows, "Do you observe whence there is a deception? Namely, because human reasonings intervene. And accordingly they are called heresies, because they are human opinions. The faith of Christians, however, is not the doctrine of men: wherefore neither does it gain such a name" (PG 124, 1239A).

that if an assertion comes before us, which faith obliges us to oppose, then we may call this contrary assertion heresy.

Therefore it happens that this name of heresy—which for heathens applies to any opinion, be it true or false—to theologians, who use the word in a slightly stricter sense, is ignominious. For, in a matter of faith, in which it is necessary to submit the intellect in obedience to Christ, the opinion of one's own judgment is preferred to Sacred Scripture, or the definition of the Church, or the traditions of the Councils. Now he who contradicts Sacred Scripture or the definitions of the Church, contradicts the Holy Ghost, the Ruler of the former and the Author of the latter. "He that despiseth you, despiseth me; and he that despiseth me, despiseth him that sent me" (Lk. 10, 16). And elsewhere: "He that despiseth me, and receiveth not my words, hath one that judgeth him" (Jn. 12, 48). Therefore he who has scorned the Church or has disparaged Sacred Scripture, relying only on his own prudence, is so arrogant that it can be ascribed to him what [St.] Paul says, "Who is lifted up above all that is called God" (II Thess. 2, 4). Which pride the Doctor of the Gentiles also describes more clearly elsewhere: "If any man teach otherwise, and consent not to the sound words of our Lord Jesus Christ, and to that doctrine which is according to godliness, he is proud, knowing nothing, but sick about questions and strifes of words" (I Tim. 6, 3-4). "It is like the sin of witchcraft," as it is said in the First Book of Kings, "to refuse to obey" (v. 15, 23). Therefore, it is a very grave sin to adhere so tenaciously to one's own opinion, that because of it one condemns the Church, which is ruled by God.

Hence Gregory says: "For when the most wicked spirits involve the soul of any one in evil works, but cannot pollute the integrity of his faith, they pollute the inferior members, as it were, but as yet reach not to the head. But whoever is corrupted in the faith, is at once defiled even to the head. For a malignant spirit reaches, as it were, from the inferior even to the higher members, when, defiling the outward conduct, it corrupts with the disease of unbelief the pure loftiness of the faith."[1] You see here that as faith is the basis of all Christian virtue, so heresy is the fullness of all evil. For this reason, not without cause the word heresy is well known among Christians, but is unimportant among heathens: because for the latter it belongs to each person to think according to his own judgment. For us, on the other hand, no matter how much reason may urge, it will never be allowed to think other than how the Church does. Therefore, having shown the reason for the name, it remains for us to state its definition.

Heresy is a false doctrine opposed to the orthodox faith. Here we call a "false doctrine" every false declaration, whether someone dogmatizes it, or affirms it silently to himself: for both can be heresy. However, outside of a declaration of heresy, it cannot be discovered. For something merely carried out, without the judgment of the intellect prescribing, can be a sin but by no means heresy. For he who steals, even if he acts against Scripture forbidding it to occur, he is not a heretic, unless he believes that theft is not a sin. Sacred Scripture forbids fornication, but he who fornicates, unless he believes that this can be done with impunity, ought not to be deemed a heretic. Therefore, a mere deed with an error of the intellect is not heresy, no matter how much the deed is forbidden by Scripture. On account of which, it is necessary to warn that when you hear simony called heresy, you ought to understand that it is not the deed itself, by which simony is committed, which is heresy, but the error whereby one believes that spiritual things are sellable. For so is it called by Gregory Nazianzen in a certain passage cited by Gratian, question one, chapter one: *Qui studet*.[2]

---

[1] *Moralium Libri sive Expositio in Librum Beati Job*, XXV, c. 11, n. 28 (PL 76, 339C).

[2] *Decretum Gratiani* (2, C. 1, q. 1, c. 11 (PL 187, 482C-483B)). "It cannot be doubted that he who attempts to purchase a gift of God for a price, can remain in the Sacred Order by reason of another Order, or be recalled. Such a one ought to be cut off from communion in every way. That a gift of the Holy Ghost be compared a price, what else is this besides a capital crime and the simoniacal heresy? How

Introduction

But someone will object that if it is not heresy when an action is done while the intellect was nowise erring about it, why is someone who has been apprehended while performing a Jewish ceremony, such as observing the Sabbath, or eating the Passover lamb, or some Moslem rite, punished as a heretic? For if from a deed you say that a suspicion arises: in that how someone acts, so he believes he ought to act: why does not a thief or fornicator for the same reason give the same grounds for suspicion, so that we may suspect him to have acted thus because he believes he is permitted to do so?

To which objection it is replied, that there is a great difference between the former and the latter. For there are some sins towards which men are by nature inclined, as for example, seeking after the allurements of the flesh, the accursed greed for money, and the desire for honor. These things, therefore, are of such sort that we may be carried headlong into them, even seeking after them despite the resistance of our conscience. There are other sins, which are constituted otherwise, towards which the will is not drawn, for the very reason that they have nothing whereby they may entice the will. Wherefore when the will is indifferent or in doubt regarding them, it consults the intellect, so that it may know what ought to be done: and in regard to these sins, the will does not attempt to do something when the conscience is resisting. For the intellect serves the will by giving counsels. It often happens, however, that a king, not having consulted all his counsellors, or even after having the advice of all his counsellors, regarding that to which he is inclined, falls headlong, and does what he is inclined to do: even though he very often complies with his counsellors, and by their counsel commands all the things that are to be done: in those things therefore to which the will is not inclined, on no occasion does it do something after having scorned the judgment of the intellect.

Regarding the observance of these or those ceremonies, however, there is no inclination from nature in the will, unless perhaps that of carrying them out due to habit, which is a second nature. For this reason the suspicion is very strong that in this case the will is governed by the intellect, such that what it does, it likewise believes should be done. For so the Savior says: "By their fruits you shall know them" (Mt. 7, 16). For (as Aristotle says in *IV Ethics*) as every man is, so he speaks and acts.[1] For this reason alone, (in my opinion) the simoniacal man is called a heretic by Gregory in the *Register* [*of Letters*]:"Whoever is ordained through money is ordained to this end, namely, that he may become a heretic."[2] For by the fact that

---

horribly such is avenged in both Testaments is easily made evident by many examples. Giezi sold the gift of Naaman's health, the Syrian; he lost the same gift of health when Eliseus avenging, he was made a leper. Also Simon Magus, when he wished to buy the same grace of the Holy Ghost, heard his sentence of condemnation from Saint Peter: 'Keep thy money to thyself to perish with thee, because thou hast thought that the gift of God may be purchased with money.' Likewise, the Lord put out of the Temple those who by buying and selling this grace were sinning in regard to grace, rebuking one by one the sellers and buyers, and with scourging casting them out of the Temple; whereby it is clear that the sellers and buyers were devoid and empty of the grace of the Holy Ghost. "In the works of Blessed Gregory Nazianzen, many of which exist in Greek and Latin, no such passage is found. However similar words are found in the letter of Tarasius to [Pope] Hadrian [I]." (*Corpus Juris Canonici*, edited by Aemilius Friedberg (Graz, Akademische Druck- und Verlagsanstalt, 1959), p. 360).

[1] The author has given as a reference book 3 of the *Nicomachean Ethics*, whereas they are found according to more recent classifications in book 4, chapter 7, of the same book. Another similar passage is found in book 3, chapter 4: "According as a man is, such does the end seem to him."

[2] This text does not come from the *Register of Letters* of Saint Gregory the Great, but is an extract from *The Letter of Guido* of Arezzo called in Latin, *Epistola Widonis*. "The *Epistola Widonis* was considered an important historical document. Although Guido of Arezzo wrote this letter around 1031, during the reign of Archbishop Aribert of Milan (1018-1045), as a critique of the simoniacal practices in Milan, it was often attributed to a certain Paschasius or Paschalis. From the 1070's it appears in numerous canonical collections and polemical writings of the Investiture Contest, and, in a fragmentary form, also in

what is priceless is put up for sale, it is likely that he thinks badly of the Church's holiness, as though he believes that she wants spiritual things to be sold, yet he is bound to believe the Church is holy, immaculate, without spot and without stain.[1] Therefore the Church judges those things which appear outwardly, concerning which there is no doubt that they are evil. Now whether the intellect is an accomplice of the deed or not, God knows, Who beholds the heart.[2] Men, however, only know those things which appear outwardly: although the suspicion is very strong, that in these things there may be a great concurrence of the intellect to the deed. And for this reason, as a consequence of doing these things, one is punished as a heretic, who on account of other deeds, no matter how much they are forbidden by Sacred Scripture, will by no means be punished as a heretic. For it would not be allowed to suspect in the latter case that because one does the deed, one thus believes that it should be done.

Therefore, so that we may return to the proposed definition of heresy, let us conclude that nowhere can heresy be found without an error of the intellect, for every heresy is a false doctrine: but not every false doctrine is a heresy: since there are many errors in which (even if pertinacity is present) there is no sin. Nevertheless, it would have been a grave sin (as we said above) if it were heresy. Not every error, therefore, ought to be deemed heresy: because not every truth pertains to the Catholic faith. It is not required of a Christian that he know the number and the power of the elements; the motion, order and effects of the stars; the natures of the animals, fruits, springs, rocks, and countless other things. For in these things, even if a Christian were to be ignorant, or err about them by asserting what is false for what is true, there is no sin. Hence, Augustine says in his *Enchiridion*, chapter twenty-one: "In the case of these and other false impressions of the same kind, we are indeed deceived, but our faith in God remains secure. We go astray, but we do not leave the way that leads us to Him. Yet these errors, though they are not sinful, are to be reckoned among the evils of this life, which is to such an extent made subject to vanity that we receive what is false as if it were true, reject what is true as if it were false, and cling to what is uncertain as if it were certain. And although they are distinct from that faith whereby we reach true, certain, and eternal beatitude, yet they have much to do with that misery in which we are now living."[3] You now see how not every error ought to be called heresy, just as not every truth ought to be called faith. Hence, that error which is opposed to the Catholic faith is called heresy. Therefore, we have rightly defined heresy above, that it is a false doctrine opposed to the orthodox faith.

Wherefore it will reasonably be inquired, what are those things to which we are bound to assent with faith? Since opposite things are more easily known by comparing them, each to the other, in this way, once we have known the things which pertain to the Catholic faith, it clearly follows that we will with certainty know everything opposed to them which may be identified as heresy. Then it also will be shown what weapons are needed to overcome the heresy. Now the Catholic faith, which undoubtedly must be kept, is that which Sacred Scripture reveals: and not only this, but whatever (even without Sacred Scripture) holy Mother Church, by her universal Tradition, proposes to us for belief. Therefore, if we are bound by Divine law to believe anything, it is necessary that whatever is opposed to any of these things be deemed heresy. Thus, it is necessary that we discuss these individual things by chapters, and we shall firstly investigate which books of Scriptures must be held as canonical.

Gratian (C. 1, q. 3, c. 7) as the *Decretum* of Pope Paschasius or Pope Paschalis (Pope Pascal I, 817-825). [Footnote:] Forgeries were composed at the end of the eleventh century ascribed to Gregory I." (Detlev Jasper and Horst Fuhrmann, *Papal Letters in the Early Middle Ages* (History of Medieval Canon Law Series, Vol. 2, Washington D. C., The Catholic University of America Press, 2001), p. 102).

[1] Cf. Eph. 5, 27.

[2] "For men seeth those things that appear, but the Lord beholdeth the heart" (I Kings 16, 7).

[3] PL 40, 243.

Introduction

Chapter II: Concerning the Canonical Scriptures, with which heresies may be conquered.

When a fight against heretics has been assigned to us, it seems expedient to me that the arms would first be assigned with which it should be fought. For so we see in bodily warfare, that for the one provoking an individual combat and the one provoked there be similar arms. Wherefore it is that before meeting together, the arms ought to be presented with which the combative contest be undergone: in which affair it happens countless times that just before the fight there is an argument about selecting the spears, since they do not agree between themselves concerning this matter. The procedure for disputing is not much different from this practice. For there are principles in every science very well known in it, as weapons common to all, without which (as Aristotle would agree) no fighting would be possible, and there would be no spear by which you can stab the adversary.

Lest therefore it be debated many times afterwards concerning Scripture, it is necessary firstly to establish which books are canonical, which everyone is bound to believe. For just as in other sciences, no one who publicly acknowledges their first principles, denies them: so in the case of faith, it ought to be held as a sole and undoubted principle, by anyone who claims to be a Christian, that whatever is contained in the Sacred Books is true. For I think that it is rightly held not only by the Christian, but even by a heathen or by a moderately pious man, and in fact by one supposing only those things concerning God which can be known by natural reason, that God is so truthful that He cannot lie. Therefore, if God cannot lie, then Scripture likewise, having been composed by Him, cannot be false. Moreover, whatever God wished to make known to us through the mouths of others, will likewise be true, just as if it had come forth from His own mouth. For the Lord God has indeed spoken to Israel (as Zacharias said, quoted by Luke) "by the mouth of his holy prophets, who are from the beginning" (1, 70). And the Royal Prophet testifies that his "tongue is the pen of a scrivener that writeth swiftly" (Ps. 44, 2). By this epithet he is indicating the Holy Ghost, Whose grace (according to Ambrose's opinion) does not know sluggish efforts.[1] By this also, or by the testimony of the prophets themselves, it can plainly be seen, since it is usual for them to add these words: "Thus saith the Lord." St. Paul supports this opinion: "God, who, at sundry times and in divers manners, spoke in times past to the fathers by the prophets, last of all, in these days hath spoken to us by his Son" (Heb. 1, 1-2). Notice how by St. Paul's testimony it is evident that God has spoken by the mouth of the prophets. Blessed Peter teaches the same, saying: "For prophecy came not by the will of man at any time: but the holy men of God spoke, inspired by the Holy Ghost" (II Pet. 1, 21). And the Lord God Himself says to a certain prophet: "If thou wilt separate the precious from the vile, thou shalt be as my mouth" (Jer. 15, 19). Finally, the Lord in the Gospel, when He sends the disciples to preach, giving confidence to them as though they were inadequate to speak to fierce men, says: "For it is not you that speak, but the Spirit of your Father that speaketh in you" (Mt. 10, 20). From all these quotations it is clearly inferred that certain writings are inspired, namely, those which certain men inspired by God wrote: nay (so that I may speak more truly) those writings which God Himself wrote with the hands of men. To all these writings we ought to give full faith, and it is not permissible to oppose these writings any more than to oppose God, their Author.

Therefore, it is the quotations of these Scriptures—as first principles in this science and as common weapons which must be accepted by all—with which the heretic must defend himself, and with which we must fight against him. For Sacred Scripture is the tower of David fortified with bulwarks: "A thousand bucklers hang upon it, all the armor of valiant men"

---

[1] *"Enarrationes in XII psalmos Davidicos*, n. 52 (PL 14, 950C).

(Cant. 4, 4). This is also the brook from which David took up stones, with which he overthrew proud Goliath. (I Kings 17, 40). Saul's weapons, which weigh down more than they help, are reasoning emanating from human prudence. For (as Jerome says in his letter to Theophilus, Bishop of Alexandria) "pure faith and an open confession does not seek after trickeries or arguments of mere words."[1] Hence, it is clear that the Arian heretic, Felicianus,[2] had erred saying that in matters of faith, reasons rather than citations of Scriptures ought to be used. For the things about which our faith deals (as we will discuss elsewhere at greater length) are above all reason, and the little lamp of our intellect does not suffice to emit enough light for investigating them. Hence, Basil says the following in his exposition on Psalm 115: Therefore, in any study, which proceeds with order towards its object, it is impossible to seek proofs of the first principles. Rather, it is necessary for all arts which proceed by proofs, after having assumed the principles without investigation or reasoning, to show by use of reason the things which follow therefrom. So also the mysteries of Theology aim at a structure based on faith nowise proved by reason.[3] Therefore, to want to prove that Sacred Scripture is true by reason seems to me to be so much folly, as if someone would wish to support the first principles of a science with reasons. That Sacred Scripture is true is an axiom for anyone claiming to be a Christian, against whom alone we have taken up arms. For our discourse is not against the heathens and the Saracens, but against those who boast of being Christians, although they are nothing of the sort. All of whom are bound to believe as the first principle in this discipline that Sacred Scripture is true.

However, whether a particular writing is Divine or human, someone perhaps may doubt. For this reason, it must be seen which books ought to be held to be canonical: whose words, as a Divine oracle, it is not allowed to oppose, and by whose testimony heretics ought to be refuted. Therefore, in order that we may know the books which ought to be held as canonical, let us hear what the Synod of Laodicea defined in canon 59 of its decrees: "No psalms composed by common persons or any commonplace book, nor uncanonical books may be read in the church, but only the Canonical Books of the Old and New Testaments. Now those which ought to be read and accepted as authoritative are these: Genesis of the world; Exodus; Leviticus; Numbers; Deuteronomy; Josue, the son of Nun; Judges; Ruth; the four books of Kings; the two books of Paralipomenon; Esdras; the Book of Psalms numbering one hundred fifty; the Proverbs of Solomon; Ecclesiastes; the Canticle of Canticles; Job; Esther. The sixteen prophets, namely: Osee, Amos, Joel, Abdias, Jonas, Micheas, Nahum, Habacuc, Sophonias, Aggeus, Zacharias, Malachias, Isaias, Jeremias, Ezechiel, and Daniel.

"And the books of the New Testament, namely: the four books of the Gospels, Matthew, Mark, Luke and John. The Acts of the Apostles. The seven Catholic epistles: one of James; two of Peter, first and second; three of John, first, second and third; one of Jude; fourteen epistles of Paul, one to the Romans; two to the Corinthians, first and second; one to the Galatians; one to the Ephesians; one to the Philippians; one to the Colossians; two to the Thessalonians; two to Timothy, first and second; one to Titus; one to Philemon; and one to the Hebrews."[4]

---

[1] Letter 82, n. 5 (PL 22, 738).

[2] "Felicianus, the name of a person either real or imaginary, but of whom, if real, nothing is known, though he is called by Alcuin an Arian bishop. He is represented as one of the interlocutors in a dialogue carried on with St. Augustine on the nature of the Trinity. The treatise which contains this is entitled, *Contra Felicianum Arianum de Unitate Trinitatis*, and was formerly ascribed to Augustine." (William Smith and Henry Wace, *A Dictionary of Christian Biography, Literature, Sects and Doctrines* (Boston, Little Brown and Co., 1880), p. 476).

[3] The words of Saint Basil the Great, or Basil of Caesarea, are summarized here. Cf. PG 30, 103D-106A.

[4] PL 84, 135A-136B. The listing of the books is elsewhere given as Canon 60, and which canon is "of most questionable genuineness." ((Editorial comment on Canon 60, Nicene and Post-Nicene Fathers,

Introduction

Nevertheless, I already see how much the heretic rejoices by reason of the books enumerated in this list, since he sees a good many books omitted there, which are everywhere held to be canonical. For in fact heretics greatly desire that as many books as possible be eliminated from the canon, and that they would not be counted among those in the list of Sacred volumes. For they see that it is not permitted to oppose the authority of any book of Sacred Scripture: wherefore they try their utmost to reduce the Scriptures, lest we have weapons whereby we can wound them. For instance, a passage can be very efficacious, because if perchance a very clear quotation from a certain book of Sacred Scripture were cited against their assertion, such that it does not permit some adulterated exposition, it thus it cripples the heretics so that there is no crack left for them whereby they may escape. Wherefore they will immediately flee to this common refuge for them, namely, that they are not afraid to deny that the book is canonical, or pertains in any way to Sacred Scripture. Therefore some heretic will say, "Behold, the Synod of Laodicea, gathered in the Holy Ghost, defined concerning the canonical books, and yet it did not mention among them the book of Tobias, or Judith, or Wisdom, or Ecclesiasticus, or the books of Machabees, or the Apocalypse. Thus, these books should not be held as canonical." This reasoning is feeble to anyone even poorly instructed in logic. For even if the argument is sufficient for proving something, because this or that says the same thing, nevertheless it is not sufficient for denying something, because that thing is not said. Wherefore it is, that from the fact that the aforesaid books are omitted by the Synod of Laodicea in giving the list of sacred books, it does not follow that those books ought to be rejected from the Sacred register. For it could have been that the Synod Fathers were then in doubt concerning these books, and in a matter so important one would not want to decide rashly, but would wait until he were more fully informed. But the heretic insists: "If it was doubted by those gathered together in the Holy Ghost, how dare we assert as being certain, that about which they doubted?" What a strong argument! Why must something be perpetually doubted, because it was doubted at one time? Of old it was doubted concerning this matter, therefore now it is doubted: of old it was allowed to put into doubt, therefore now it is allowed to doubt. Let an even slightly educated logician reply, lest this reasoning seems sufficient.

The first argument is clearly shown to be deficient due to man's progress in gaining knowledge, in that he immediately makes progress by learning, hence it may be that he knows with certitude many things which of old either were doubtful to him, or completely unknown. Why is not the same thing said about the Church in her members? Will the Church always be in the same state, such that it may never make progress? Far be it. For it advances, for example, in virtues and goodness, as in knowledge and doctrine, God more fully enlightening her daily. On account of which, in the Canticle of Canticles the Church is compared to the dawn: "Who is she that cometh forth as the morning rising?" (6, 9). Now the dawn with the passing of time shines more, and it reddens more strongly. So would you also want the Church "to start from scratch" (as they say), with as little light as there was in the beginning of the nascent Church? Or do you wish to bring it back even to just Abel, or to Christ's death, when the new Church sprung forth from Heaven? For then to very few was that hidden mystery known,[1] to whom it was also given (I except the Apostles) to know it not so fully and perfectly then as afterwards. The dawn has certainly advanced, and the sun has arisen, spreading abroad more abundant rays of its light. Hence it is, that we now know many things which were either doubted or completely unknown to our first forefathers.

Second Series, Vol. 14, p. 159). The Canon of Scripture was defined in the Fourth Session of the Council of Trent in the year 1546 (Dz. 784).

[1] Here there is a subtle reference to the *mysterium absconditum* mentioned in Colossians 1, 26, "The mystery which hath been hidden from ages and generations, but now is manifested to his saints."

The second argument is shown to be deficient, nay void, due to the change of things, from which also arises the variety and change of decrees: hence it happened that of old what was permitted, may not now be permitted. For, since the matters that pertain to the faith are now stated and determined, and they do not depend on men's will, in this matter (as we shall say elsewhere) the newness of the decrees does not come forth from the newness of things, but from the new knowledge of those things: which things having been ascertained, the Church having been thoroughly instructed by the Holy Ghost, the Church defines. Which definition having been given, it will not be permitted to doubt concerning that which before was permitted to be doubted. (Blessed Cyprian in his letter to Donatus, among the many evils which he enumerates, this one is worthy of being mentioned: that [he doubted that] what he did could be done.)[1] Otherwise, if it were permitted to put into doubt everything which had been doubted of old, then it will be permitted to doubt whether we are obliged to observe matters decided by law, such as whether those baptized by heretics ought to be rebaptized. For these things were doubted of old by illustrious men of the Church, and nevertheless it is not now permitted to doubt upon these grounds, since the Church has forbidden rebaptizing to be done. Similarly it was doubted of old by some concerning the book of Wisdom, whether it were Solomon's. It was doubted by others concerning the book of Tobias, whether it were canonical. By others, it was doubted about the book of Judith, for the same reason. By some, it was doubted about the books of Machabees for a similar reason. By others it was doubted concerning the Epistle to the Hebrews, whether it were Paul's. By others it was doubted concerning the epistle published under the name of James, whether it were his. By others, lastly, it was doubted concerning the book of the Apocalypse. But now it is not permitted for anyone at this time to doubt about this, because the Church, after having been more fully enlightened, determined by verdict that the aforesaid books had to be enumerated better than before. This is evident from the Third Synod of Carthage, at which council Blessed Father Augustine was present.[2] The council in its decrees defined as follows: "It was also determined that besides the canonical Scriptures nothing be read in the Church under the title of divine Scriptures. The canonical Scriptures are these: the first is Genesis, the second Exodus, the third Leviticus, the fourth Numbers, the fifth Deuteronomy, the sixth Josue the son of Nun, the seventh Judges, the eighth Ruth, the ninth four books of Kings, two books of Paralipomenon, Job, the Davidic Psalter, five books of Solomon, the books of the twelve prophets, Isaias, Jeremias, Ezechiel, Daniel, Tobias Judith, Esther, two books of Esdras, two books of the Maccabees. Of the New Testament: four books of the Gospels, one book of the Acts of the Apostles, thirteen Epistles of the Apostle Paul, one epistle of the same to the Hebrews, two Epistles of the Apostle Peter, three of John, one of James, one of Jude, one book of the Apocalypse of John, which are twenty-seven."[3] You see here that no book was omitted of those which are widely published in the sacred volume, except the two books of Esdras: all the rest, however, are enumerated as Sacred Scriptures. [Saint] Pope Innocent, the first of this name, gave this same list of sacred books in his letter to [Saint] Exuperius, Bishop of Toulouse, towards the end of the letter; which letter is found in the Book of Councils under this title: "Decree of Pope Innocent." For

---

[1] "I used to regard it as a difficult matter, and especially as difficult in respect of my character at that time, that a man should be capable of being born again—a truth which the divine mercy had announced for my salvation,—and that a man quickened to a new life in the laver of saving water should be able to put off what he had previously been, and, although retaining all his bodily structure, should be himself changed in heart and soul. 'How,' said I, 'is such a conversion possible, that there should be a sudden and rapid divestment of all which, either innate in us has hardened in the corruption of our material nature, or acquired by us has become inveterate by long accustomed use?'" (n. 3 (PL 4, 199A-B)).

[2] Saint Augustine was ordained a priest in 391 and consecrated Bishop of Hippo in 396.

[3] Chapter 47 (PL 130, 338D).

Introduction

-9-

this holy and likewise learned pontiff said the following: "Which books are duly received in the canon, this brief appendix shows. These therefore are the matters concerning which you desired to be informed. Five books of Moses, that is, Genesis, Exodus, Leviticus, Numbers, and Deuteronomy; and Josue the son of Nun; and Judges; and the four books of Kings, together with Ruth; sixteen books of the Prophets; five books of Solomon; and the Psalms. Also of the historical books, one book of Job, one of Tobit, one of Esther, one of Judith, two of Maccabees, two of Esdras, two of Paralipomenon. And of the New Testament: of the Gospels, four; epistles of the Apostle Paul, fourteen; epistles of John, three; epistles of Peter, two; epistle of Jude; epistle of James; Acts of the Apostles; John's Apocalypse."[1] Behold the same books listed among the canonical books by the holy, and at the same time learned, sovereign pontiff, which the Third Synod of Carthage at nearly the same time judged to be sacred and canonical.

Blessed Augustine also gives the same list of books in chapter eight of his second book of *On Christian Doctrine*.[2] By which passage of Augustine this scruple is removed, which perhaps could beset someone resulting from the lists of sacred books cited above in the Synod of Carthage, and by Pope Innocent. In both passages five books are ascribed to Solomon, which could not be done unless Ecclesiasticus were assigned to Solomon; but it is evident this book cannot be Solomon's, but was written by Jesus, the son of Sirach. *This scruple is truly removed by what Augustine says in the eighth chapter of his second book of On Christian Doctrine.* For when listing the Sacred books, he says the following: "Three books of Solomon, namely, Proverbs, Canticle of Canticles, and Ecclesiastes. For two books, one titled Wisdom and the other Ecclesiasticus, are ascribed to Solomon from a certain resemblance of style, but the most likely opinion is that they were written by Jesus the son of Sirach. Still they are to be reckoned among the prophetical books."

But in fact, concerning that which he said, namely that the book which is called Wisdom was written by Jesus, the son of Sirach, he afterwards recants in chapter four of his second

---

[1] N. 7 (PL 130, 705B-C).

[2] "Five books of Moses, that is, Genesis, Exodus, Leviticus, Numbers, Deuteronomy; one book of Josue the son of Nun; one of Judges; one short book called Ruth, which seems rather to belong to the beginning of Kings; next, four books of Kings, and two of Paralipomenon—these last not following one another, but running parallel, so to speak, and going over the same ground. The books just mentioned are historical, which contain a connected narrative of the times, and follows the order of the events. There are other books which seem to follow no regular order, and are connected neither with the order of the preceding books nor with one another, such as Job, and Tobias, and Esther, and Judith, and the two books of Maccabees, and the two of Esdras, which last look more like a sequel to the continuous regular history which terminates with the books of Kings and Paralipomenon. Next are the Prophets, in which there is one book of the Psalms of David and three books of Solomon, namely, Proverbs, Canticle of Canticles, and Ecclesiastes. For two books, one titled Wisdom and the other Ecclesiasticus, are ascribed to Solomon from a certain resemblance of style, but the most likely opinion is that they were written by Jesus the son of Sirach. Still they are to be reckoned among the prophetical books, since they have attained recognition as being authoritative. The remainder are the books which are strictly called the Prophets: twelve separate books of the prophets which are connected with one another, and having never been disjoined, are reckoned as one book; the names of these prophets are as follows: Osee, Joel, Amos, Abdias, Jonas, Micheas, Nahum, Habacuc Sophonias, Aggeus, Zacharias, Malachias; then there are the four greater prophets, Isaias, Jeremias, Daniel, Ezechiel. The authority of the Old Testament is contained within the limits of these forty-four books. That of the New Testament, again, is contained within the following: Four books of the Gospel, according to Matthew, Mark, Luke, and John; fourteen epistles of the Apostle Paul—one to the Romans, two to the Corinthians, one to the Galatians, Ephesians, and Philippians; two to the Thessalonians, one to the Colossians, two to Timothy, one to Titus, Philemon and the Hebrews: two of Peter; three of John; one of Jude; and one of James; one book of the Acts of the Apostles; and one of the Apocalypse of John" (Chapter 8, n. 13 (PL 34, 41)).

book of *Retractions* saying as follows: "In the second book, however, with regard to the author of the book which many call the Wisdom of Solomon, I learned later that it is not certain that Jesus, the son of Sirach, wrote this book as well as Ecclesiasticus, as I have stated; and I found out that it is, indeed, more probable that he is not the author."[1] Who, even if he says that the book of Wisdom is not by Jesus son of Sirach, nevertheless neither does say that it is by Solomon, nor again does he retract that which he had said elsewhere, that both books, namely Wisdom and Ecclesiasticus, on account of a certain likeness with the books of Solomon, are said to be his. And so, whether or not Wisdom is by Solomon, we understand in what way it could happen that the books of Solomon are five, just as the Synod of Carthage attests: For even if Ecclesiasticus was produced by Jesus the son of Sirach, nevertheless on account of its likeness to the other books of Solomon, it is often said to belong to Solomon. Therefore, in my judgment it can deservedly be said to be Solomon's, since there are many things in that book borrowed from the books of Solomon. According to this manner, all those doctors ought to be kindly interpreted, who citing some passages from the book of Ecclesiasticus, cite them under the name of Solomon, as though he were the author of that book. For Pope Sixtus II, in his letter to Bishop Gratus, cites under the name of Solomon, those words which are found in Ecclesiasticus: "I came out of the mouth of the Most High, the firstborn before all creatures" (24, 5).[2] In like manner, Pope Marcellinus, in his letter to Bishop Solomon, cites under the name of Solomon these words: "I dwelt in the highest places, and my throne is in a pillar of a cloud," which words are evidently taken from chapter twenty-four.[3] But this opinion ought to be interpreted kindly, according to that manner by which we said that we interpreted Augustine, such that we may understand these words to have been said by Solomon, because they have a very great likeness with the words said by Solomon. Unless perhaps we would wish to say that those pontiffs, by citing the aforesaid passages of Sacred Scripture, had a lapse of memory, thinking that those words which are in Ecclesiasticus were contained in Solomon's Proverbs. For the fact that this happened to Pope John II is very clearly proven from his letter to Bishop Valerius, in which he cites these words under the name of Solomon: "He that made me, rested in my tabernacle," which words are contained in the aforesaid chapter twenty-four of Ecclesiasticus.[4] Now that in the quotation of those words was a lapse of memory is clearly shown by his words which he immediately added. For after the quotation of those words, he immediately adds these words: "And Ecclesiasticus, as it is from the beginning, so it is forever: neither was it increased in size, nor was it lessened in size."[5] From which difference of quotations it is clear that he had made a distinction between Ecclesiasticus and the books of Solomon, and that he had thought that the first passage quoted from it was not from Ecclesiasticus, but from the books of Solomon.

Then, after much time, the Council of Florence was celebrated, in which a special numbering of the canonical books of Sacred Scripture is found, and concerning them a special decree was made, with the tenor of the following words: "Seventhly, we pronounce that one and the same God is the Author of the Old and the New Testament—that is, the Law and the Prophets, and the Gospel—since the saints of both Testaments spoke under the inspiration of the same Spirit, of which the Church accepts and venerates their books, whose titles are as

---

[1] N. 2 (PL 32, 631).
[2] This letter is classified as doubtful in Migne's *Patrologia Latina*. This above mentioned passage is found in PL 5, 84C.
[3] Verse 7. "And so that the Son may be believed to dwell inseparably with the Father in the highest places, is proved by Solomon's testimony: 'I, wisdom, dwelt in the highest places, and my throne is in a pillar of a cloud'" (PL 7,1088B).
[4] Verse 12.
[5] PL 66, 28A.

Introduction

follows: Five books of Moses, namely, Genesis, Exodus, Leviticus, Numbers, Deuteronomy; Josue; Judges; Ruth; four books of Kings; two of Paralipomenon; Esdras; Nehemias; Tobias; Judith; Esther; Job; Psalms of David; Proverbs; Ecclesiastes; Canticle of Canticles; Wisdom; Ecclesiasticus; Isaias; Jeremias; Baruch; Ezechiel; Daniel; the twelve minor prophets, namely Osee, Joel, Amos, Abdias, Jonas, Micheas, Nahum, Habacuc, Sophonias, Aggeus, Zacharias, Malachias; two books of the Maccabees; the four gospels of Matthew, Mark, Luke and John; fourteen letters of Paul, namely, to the Romans; two to the Corinthians; to the Galatians; to the Ephesians; to the Philippians; two to the Thessalonians; to the Colossians; two to Timothy; to Titus; to Philemon; to the Hebrews; two letters of Peter; three of John; one of James; one of Jude; Acts of the Apostles; the Apocalypse of John."[1] In which words what especially ought to be noted is that none of those books which are published in common Bibles were omitted here, nay rather, the book of Baruch was added, which in no other Council was explicitly named. Yet I think that this book was omitted by the others because they deemed that it could be included under the name Jeremias, due to the fact that Baruch (as is evident from Sacred Scripture itself) was Jeremias' scribe.

Finally, so that we put an end to this matter, the Council of Trent held under Paul III, and Emperor Charles V, I being present, in the Fourth Session embraced the same list of sacred books, saying the following: "So that no doubt may arise in anyone's mind as to which are the books that are accepted by this Synod, it has decreed that a list of the Sacred books be added to this decree. They are written here below: Books of the Old Testament: The five books of Moses, namely, Genesis, Exodus, Leviticus, Numbers, Deuteronomy; Josue; Judges; Ruth; four books of Kings; two of Paralipomenon; the first book of Esdras, and the second which is called Nehemias; Tobias; Judith; Esther; Job; the Psalter of David consisting of 150 psalms; the Proverbs; Ecclesiastes; the canticle of Canticles; Wisdom; Ecclesiasticus; Isaias; Jeremias with Baruch; Ezechiel; Daniel; the twelve minor Prophets, that is, Osee, Joel, Amos, Abdias, Jonas, Micheas, Nahum, Habacuc, Sophonias, Aggeus, Zacharias, Malachias; two books of the Machabees, the first and the second. Books of the New Testament: the four Gospels, according to Matthew, Mark, Luke, and John; the Acts of the Apostles, written by Luke the Evangelist; fourteen epistles of Paul the Apostle, to the Romans; two to the Corinthians; to the Galatians; to the Ephesians; to the Philippians; to the Colossians; two to the Thessalonians; two to Timothy; to Titus; to Philemon; to the Hebrews; two of Peter the Apostle, three of John the Apostle, one of the Apostle James, one of the Apostle Jude, and the Apocalypse of John the Apostle. If anyone, however, should not accept the said books as sacred and canonical, entire with all their parts, as they were wont to be read in the Catholic Church, and as they are contained in the old Latin Vulgate edition, and if both knowingly and deliberately he should condemn the aforesaid traditions, let him be anathema."[2] By which words nothing can be more clearly said in confirmation of the list of sacred books.

After these Scriptures have now been enumerated, there is no other writing which may merit begin called canonical or divine Scripture. For although there may be many others that have great authority, nevertheless they are greatly unequal to the ones listed above. Since in fact the fifty *Apostolic Canons* by Blessed Clement (as it is said),[3] whether taken together as a whole or translated, hold the first place after Sacred Scriptures. For which reason Blessed [John]

---

[1] Session 11 (February 4, 1442).

[2] Dz. 783-784.

[3] The *Apostolic Canons* was a collection of eighty-five canons, mostly disciplinary and mostly taken from local Oriental councils of the fourth century. This collection was included in Book VIII of the *Apostolic Constitutions*, the whole being attributed to St. Clement. The Council in Trullo (692), while rejecting the *Constitutions*, retained and approved the Canons. The Canons, Saint John Damascene notwithstanding, were never generally considered to belong to the canon of Scripture.

Damascene in the fourth section of his book, *On the Orthodox Faith*, enumerated the list of canonical books, forthwith afterwards also adds, "the *Apostolic Canons* by Clement."[1] Blessed Isidore in that volume in which he had collected the decrees of all the Councils, placed the *Apostolic Canons* before the decrees of all the Councils: not because its authority is greater than the decrees of any assembled general council, as it is fitting, but, as I suspect, on account of the greater holiness and dignity of the Apostles than all the rest. Indeed the decrees of all the Councils properly assembled, as we shall show afterwards, have a most solid authority, which no one is permitted to oppose. And yet, this hinders not that the decrees of the Councils, and likewise the *Apostolic Canons*, should not be held as Divine writings, although it is not permitted for anyone to overturn the Divine precepts or alter the *Apostolic Canons* or the decrees of the Councils, when with the passing of time they have become obsolete in many instances. After the decrees of the Councils, the decretals[2] sent by the sovereign pontiffs hold the next place: yet their authority is much less, in those things which pertain to the Catholic faith, than the definitions of the Councils.

But because from this statement of mine someone will take the opportunity of suspicion that I in this place wish to teach that the pope is inferior to a council, I have decided to take away this suspicion: because since concerning this matter there are opinions of theologians not of the lowest sort, I do not wish at present to subscribe to one or the other. For it is not my intention to discuss the various opinions of men in this work, in which I have undertaken to treat the Catholic and pure faith alone. Therefore, whether the pope is superior to the rest of the council of Christians, or inferior, leaving to others and in another place to be disputed, I shall have constantly asserted this one thing, that those definitions of faith, which by a full and

---

[1] "There are two and twenty books of the Old Testament, one for each letter of the Hebrew tongue. For there are twenty-two letters of which five are double, and so they come to be twenty-seven. For the letters *Caph, Mem, Nun, Pe, Sade* are double. And thus the number of the books in this way is twenty-two, but is found to be twenty-seven because of the double character of five. For Ruth is joined on to Judges, and the Hebrews count them one book: the first and second books of Kings are counted one: and so are the third and fourth books of Kings: and also the first and second of Paralipomenon: and the first and second of Esdras. In this way, then, the books are collected together in four Pentateuchs and two others remain over, to form thus the canonical books. Five of them are of the Law, viz. Genesis, Exodus, Leviticus, Numbers, Deuteronomy. This which is the code of the Law, constitutes the first Pentateuch. Then comes another Pentateuch, the so-called *Grapheia*, or as they are called by some, the *Hagiographa*, which are the following: Jesus the Son of Nave, Judges along with Ruth, first and second Kings, which are one book, third and fourth Kings, which are one book, and the two books of the Paralipomenon which are one book. This is the second Pentateuch. The third Pentateuch is the books in verse, viz. Job, Psalms, Proverbs of Solomon, Ecclesiastes of Solomon and the Canticle of Canticles of Solomon. The fourth Pentateuch is the Prophetical books, viz. the twelve prophets constituting one book, Isaiah, Jeremiah, Ezekiel, Daniel. Then come the two books of Esdras made into one, and Esther. There are also the *Panaretus*, that is the Wisdom of Solomon, and the Wisdom of Jesus, which was published in Hebrew by the father of Sirach, and afterwards translated into Greek by his grandson, Jesus, the Son of Sirach. These are virtuous and noble, but are not counted nor were they placed in the ark. The New Testament contains four gospels, that according to Matthew, that according to Mark, that according to Luke, that according to John: the Acts of the Holy Apostles by Luke the Evangelist: seven catholic epistles, viz. one of James, two of Peter, three of John, one of Jude: fourteen letters of the Apostle Paul: the Revelation of John the Evangelist: the Canons of the Holy Apostles, by Clement." (bk. 4, chap. 17 (PG 94, 1179C)).

[2] Decretals (*epistolae decretales*) are letters of the pope that formulate decisions in ecclesiastical law of the Catholic Church. They are generally given in answer to consultations but are sometimes given due to the initiative of the pope himself. These furnish, with the canons of the councils, the chief source of the legislation of the Church, and formed the greater part of the *Corpus Iuris Canonici* before they were formally replaced by the *Codex Iuris Canonici* of 1917.

Introduction

entire council, and duly assembled (as it is fitting) were given, that is to say, to which things the pope and the rest of those assembled in the council subscribe, to be of greater strength and importance than those which merely the pope has defined. For it is most firmly believed by all true Christians until now that such a council which has been duly assembled with the authority and consent of the pope, cannot err in faith: and we elsewhere, with God as our guide, clearly prove [this] from Sacred Scripture. But the pope alone without the assembly of the council can err in those matters which pertain to the faith, many theologians, whose opinion has not been condemned, assert: on the contrary, it is evident that some supreme pontiffs erred in the faith.[1] Furthermore, if the authority of a pope alone were as great as the authority of an entire council fully and duly assembled, so much labor would be undertaken by the assembling of councils would be undertaken in vain. But since it shall always have been reckoned that the very great assemblies of the councils were times for removing disputes concerning matters of faith, which happen to arise from time to time: it is thence proved that there is a greater authority belonging to a whole council duly (as it is fitting) assembled, than the authority belonging to the pontiff alone.[2]

Hence Gratian's error is clearly detected, who in the volume of decrees in the beginning of the twentieth Distinction says the following: "Decretals, therefore, have the same legal force as conciliar canons."[3] Now by this, or from this, it is clearly shown to be false, because no right reason, which can deviate from correctness, can be allowed as a rule, and nowise may it be equated with the most correct, most certain and infallible rule. Because if perchance in discounting Gratian, someone will say that his statement only ought to be referred to the definitions of the matters under discussion, in deciding which matters, the pope's power is not less (always excepting matters of faith) than that of a whole council. Nevertheless, I do not know whether this interpretation, even if it have a true meaning, truly expresses the mind of the writer. For the same author in the nineteenth distinction of the book, in the chapter on

---

[1] "According to [the Dogmatic Constitution] *Pastor Aeternus*, the pope enjoys the infallible assistance of the Holy Ghost when he speaks *ex cathedra*, or "from the chair [of Peter]." An exegetical clause explains that the pope speaks *ex cathedra* when, 'in the exercise of his office as shepherd and teacher of all Christians, in virtue of his supreme apostolic authority, he defines a doctrine concerning faith or morals to be held by the whole church.' Therefore the pope does not exercise the charism of infallibility in all his statements. He may make a doctrinal error in his teaching as a private theologian or in his exercise of ordinary papal magisterium. He may err in his judgment on issues outside the scope of 'faith or morals,' such as political and scientific matters. He is still susceptible to sin. But when the pope issues a solemn judgment on an issue of faith or morals for the whole church, he enjoys 'the divine assistance promised to him in blessed Peter, that infallibility which the divine Redeemer willed his Church to enjoy in defining doctrine concerning faith or morals.' Since the pope has the charism of infallibility, his *ex cathedra* definitions are 'of themselves, and not by the consent of the Church, irreformable.'" (William Abraham, Jason E. Vickers, Natalie B. Van Kirk, *Canonical Theism: A Proposal for Theology and the Church* (Grand Rapids, William B. Eerdmans Publishing Company, 2008), p. 198.

[2] This opinion can no longer be upheld by Catholics. For Conciliarism was formally condemned by the First Vatican Council (1869-70), which defined papal primacy, declaring that the Pope had "full and supreme jurisdiction over the universal Church, not only in things which belong to faith and morals, but also in those which relate to the discipline and government of the Church spread throughout the world." He therefore possesses not merely the principal part but "all the fullness of this supreme power." (Dz. 1831).

[3] "Decretals, therefore, have the same legal force as conciliar canons. Now the question is about the interpreters of the sacred Scriptures; are their writings of the same rank [as the decretals] or are they subject to them? The more someone is grounded in reason, the greater authority his words seem to have. Many of the interpreters, being more eminent than others in the grace of the Holy Ghost and in ample learning, can be shown also to be better grounded in reason. Therefore, it seems, preference should be given to the sayings of Augustine, Jerome and other writers over the constitutions of some pontiffs."

the canonical Scriptures,[1] says that the decretals are counted among the divine Scriptures, and ought to be put into that category: Gratian having been motivated by a badly understood citation of Augustine. For Gratian cites it as follows: "In the matter of canonical Scriptures, the most skilled interpreter should follow the authority of the greater number of Catholic churches, among these, of course are those which the Apostolic See [possesses], and from it others deserved to receive letters."[2]

Which ordinance if Augustine were to read, he would strongly oppose: very much is lacking for it to be Augustine's. For from it arise very many detriments to the Catholic faith. Firstly, that ordinance has, 'it is necessary to count among the Sacred Scriptures not just the pontifical letters which they gave to others, but also those which they received from others.' Now these words are so clearly an absurdity that there is no need to oppose it. Now who does not see that from this ordinance this meaning may be found? For he says: "Certainly among which," namely the divine Scriptures, "are those which the Apostolic See [possesses], and from it others deserved to receive letters." Moreover those decretals letters by other later pontiffs, or by the same pontiffs from whom they were sent, can be revoked, as it is clear to have been done in many instances, for which reason it is a common proverb: "Equals do not have authority over one another."[3] By which phrase one intends to indicate that later pontiffs are not bound by the decrees of previous pontiffs, indeed it is a free matter for them, when they see fit, to revoke them. By which argument alone one clearly demonstrates that their decretals are not divine Scriptures, since it would not be allowed for the whole Church nor for the pontiff to make the latter void in any way. Once again, very many decretals of the pontiffs are abrogated by contrary custom, which can nowise apply to the canonical books of divine Scripture, since no custom, no matter how inveterate, can impede them. Comparing, which is great ignorance, even from afar, those letters which were published on account of certain temporal matters of little importance with divine Scriptures, there is so much lacking for them to be ascribed to the same category, adds to this argument. But if perhaps Gratian wanted to commend those decretals, through true and the most efficacious citations, which are not lacking, it should not have been done using false ones: for false and contrived citations rather detract from than enhance an assertion.

But now let us pass over the praises of the decretals, which are read in the nineteenth Distinction, [since] actually it suffices that they are approved by the consent of the universal Church. For among other condemned errors of John Wycliffe in the Council of Constance, eighth session, is one in which he says the following: "Decretals are apocryphal and seduce from the faith of Christ, and clergy who study them are foolish."[4] However, so that anyone may give fuller trust to our words, and may know that Augustine was not properly understood by Gratian, and was corruptly cited, it is worthwhile to bring forth the true writing of Augustine, and to publish the true meaning. For that blessed Father in chapter eight of the second book of his work, *On Christian Doctrine* (for from that book that fragment which Gratian cites is taken) says the following: "In reckoning the books of canonical Scriptures, let [the diligent searcher of the Scriptures] follow the authority of the greater number of Catholic churches."[5] Which words greatly differ from those which Gratian quotes. For in that passage our blessed father Augustine, while discussing the canonical books of Scripture, assigns this rule to us, that those books be held as canonical which are received by many Catholic churches. And

---

[1] I.e. Chapter 6.
[2] There is a corruption in this cited passage of Saint Augustine's *On Christian Doctrine*, bk. II, chap. 8, §12, as will be shown below.
[3] *Par in parem no habet imperium.*
[4] Error n. 38 (Dz. 618).
[5] Bk. 2, chap. 8, n. 12 (PL 34, 40).

Introduction

among which churches Augustine firmly believes those ought to be counted which had the seat of an Apostle: namely, you will understand [that he is speaking] concerning those which the Apostles ruled as their bishops. For Augustine believed that especially those churches, which merited to receive Apostolic epistles, that is to say, to which the Apostles sent letters, such as the Roman church, the churches of Corinth, Thessalonica, Colossia, Ephesus, Jerusalem, Antioch, or Alexandria, all of which the Apostles taught either by their words or writing [were principally to be regarded]. Wherefore Augustine reckoned that they ought to be more abundantly enlightened in the faith, because they had firmer and fuller Apostolic words. And it was not without reason that our blessed father believed this, because those provinces had not yet been captured and populated by the enemies of the Christian religion. Gratian, however, thought that the relative pronoun, namely, "which," where it is said, "among which, they truly, which were so blessed," etc., ought to be referred to the "Scriptures," to which it does not refer, but ought to be referred to the "churches." Because it is very clear from the words which follow, with which the previous words can no wise agree: for the Divine Scriptures did not have seats of the Apostles, nor could they receive Apostolic letters. But in order that the words could agree with his meaning, Gratian decided to change the words, and in place of the other relative pronoun put by Augustine in the nominative case, namely *quae*, he used the accusative case, and so he said *quas*. Where Augustine had said "the seat of an Apostle" in the accusative, he said "the seat of an Apostle" in the nominative case. But because by these changes in the text the meaning was hardly changed, he made sure to augment something and to diminish something; for from Augustine's text he took away this word, *to be*, and he added from his own head these three words, namely, "other [sees merited to receive] from it." And so, let us say finally, where Augustine's text has the following: "among which [churches], they truly, which were so blessed as to have Apostolic seats and to receive epistles from the Apostles, are specially and principally to be regarded," Gratian's text regarding the Divine Scriptures has the following: "among which [Scriptures] are those which the Apostolic See received, and the letters other sees merited to receive from it." Anyone will easily recognize the difference between those texts. From which passage any will easily surmise of how much importance it is whether you draw water from the purist sources, or from disturbed streams, or from putrid pools. For if Gratian had read that passage in Augustine, being an otherwise learned man (as I think), he would have clearly noticed the error, even though the text had been corrupted in the book which he was using. This is especially so if he had considered that Blessed Augustine, who acknowledged that he had composed his book, *On Christian Doctrine*, on account of his understanding of Sacred Letters would in no way have been speaking about the decretals of the sovereign pontiffs, nor would he have made mention of any of the words before or after those words. For "the meaning of words ought to be ascertained by considering the circumstances under which they were spoken" (as Blessed Hilary taught in his work, *On the Trinity*).[1] Therefore, since Blessed Augustine in the whole of that treatise, *On Christian Doctrine*, is always involved with the meaning of Divinely revealed doctrine, hence accordingly that passage in no way ought to be referred to the decretals. Gratian would also have been able to fully know this from Augustine's own words in the same chapter that follow the cited words. For just after giving the rules for recognizing the canonical Scriptures, he then listed them all by their names, saying: "Now the whole canon of Scripture on which we say this judgment is to be exercised, is contained in the following books:—Five books of Moses, that is, Genesis, Exodus, Leviticus, Numbers, Deuteronomy; one book of Joshua the son of Nun; etc." And listing in this way all the books which are found in the standard Bible, he does not include any decretals of the pontiffs, even though he had said that it was the complete canon of Scriptures, regarding which the careful consideration that he had mentioned

---

[1] Bk. 4, n. 14 (PL 10, 107C).

beforehand should have been taken. Nor ought anyone to be surprised that for proving this error of Gratian we have labored so much, because that discussion was about the head, and not about the shadow (as it is said) of the donkey. Indeed, it is not a matter of little importance whether such writings ought to be accepted as divine or as human writing. Therefore it was necessary to make this error evident to all, lest Gratian thenceforth give an occasion for erring to others, as hitherto he has given to many men with great names, who relying on Gratian's authority alone, cited those corrupted and lacerated words of Augustine in their writings, just as they had read in Gratian's *Decretum*. For [Cardinal] Juan de Torquemada[1] (in order that I may pass over many others) cites this passage of Augustine, just as Gratian had corrupted it, in the fourth book of his *Summa Ecclesiastica*, in part two chapter nine.[2] Cardinal Thomas de Vio Cajetan[3] in his book *On the Primacy of the Roman Church*, in chapter fourteen, gives these words of Augustine, as they are corruptly cited by Gratian, for proving the primacy of the Roman church. If however Cajetan, a man certainly highly educated and gifted with a keen intelligence, had read that passage in Augustine's own text, he would easily have recognized that Augustine had not said any word there which could in any way support the Roman primacy of the pontiffs.

Chapter III: That only the literal sense of the canonical books is effective for refuting heretics, and what ought to be called the literal sense.

Otherwise it is necessary to warn of the fact that Sacred Scripture often admits multiple meanings in the same passage. For therein is a history that tells the events which happened, which is called the literal sense, by its usual and widely used name. By allegory, wherein something is denoted by something else, it is shown what ought to be believed about the Divinity and humanity, Christ and the Church. By tropology, wherein by a type of figurative speech, it is discussed concerning the putting of morals in order. By analogy, whereby Scriptures treats of heavenly things, we are led to higher things. For example, if we wish to discuss Jerusalem, we say that according to history it is a city located in Judea. Allegorically, from the meaning of its name,[4] we say that it represents the Church on account of the very great peace existing in it, which the Angels announced when Christ was born; which Christ when dying strenuously commended to His disciples; which the disciples themselves kept, such that when the Spirit had not yet been received, while waiting in expectation for Him, they had one heart and one mind. What shall be said after having now received the Spirit, except that [would be realized] which Christ prayed for them, namely, that they would be one, as He and the Father are one? According to a tropology, Jerusalem means the soul of every just man, in whom the beasts of the vices are pacified, so that now nothing is in him [for which] his con-

---

[1] Cardinal Juan de Torquemada (1388–1468) was born at Valladolid. He was an uncle to the Inquisitor, Tomás de Torquemada.

[2] "Inter canonicas scripturas computandas point epistolas, quas apostolica sedes habere meruit, et alii meruerunt ab ea accipere."

[3] Thomas Cajetan (1469-1534) was an Italian philosopher, theologian, cardinal (from 1517 until his death) and the Master of the Order of Preachers 1508-18. He was a leading theologian of his day who is now best known as the spokesman for his opposition to the teachings of Martin Luther and the Protestant Reformation while he was the Pope's Legate in Wittenberg, and perhaps also for his extensive commentary on the *Summa Theologiae* of Thomas Aquinas.

[4] "Jerusalem is interpreted 'vision of peace'; and it signifies those who, from their desire for peace, come to Christ; 'Much peace have they that love thy law' (Ps. 118, 165)." (St. Thomas Aquinas, Commentary on the Gospel of Saint Matthew (Dolorosa Press, 2012), chap. 4, lect. 3).

Introduction -17-

science accuses him, but rather his "tabernacle is in peace," as Job says.[1] Finally, according to an analogy it represents that heavenly Jerusalem, "our mother, which (as Paul testifies) is free"[2]: whose peace is so great, that it exceeds all understanding: may which peace keep our hearts and bodies from the disturbances of men.

And there are so many others of the same kind in Sacred Scripture, that it would be laborious to enumerate them, nay, I speak more truly, it would be impossible for me. Therefore, since so many meanings can be accommodated to the same passage, it ought to be noted that none of the other meanings ought to be applied in addition, unless one truly and faithfully gives a literal narration, which (as I said) our theologians call the literal meaning. For since other meanings hide within the shell of the historical account, it is necessary that they be deduced by reasoning and discourse, and by certain comparisons of things. In which deductions there easily is an error, since this happens through human investigation. For in this manner Donatus, and Rogatus succeeding him, said that the Church was limited to them alone and their followers, and wishing to support their error by a passage of Sacred Scripture, they cited that passage from the Canticles: "Shew me, O thou whom my soul loveth, where thou liest in the midday (*meridie*)." By this passage they wished to reduce the Church to just the southern region (*Meridionalem plagam*) wherein they dwelt.[3] The argument is futile enough, and from the false interpretation, as it is evident: namely, from the mystical meaning being quite abstruse, and hardly apparent to the unbeliever. So also Luther, wishing to show that every man of every state of life or sex are priests, took up the passage, "But you are a chosen generation, a kingly priesthood" (I Pet. 2, 9) etc. But the literal meaning is more evident, since it may be drawn from the meaning of the words or from its closely related context: because it is only the literal sense that is capable of destroying or supporting a dogma. For thus Augustine says in his letter to the Donatist Vincentius: "For what else is it than superlative impudence for one to interpret in his own favor any allegorical statements, unless he has also evident citations, by the light of which the obscure meaning of the former may be made manifest."[4] Blessed Jerome, in book two of his commentary on the passages in Saint Matthew's Gospel concerning the leaven hidden in three measures of meal, after relating the exposition of certain men applying that parable to the Trinity of Persons and the unity of essence, adds these words: "This is a pious interpretation; but parables and doubtful solutions of enigmas,[5] can never bestow authority on dogmas."[6] Blessed Dionysius [the Pseudo-Areopagite] favors this opinion, who in a letter to [Titus] says that mystical theology does not prove, meaning that it does not give a sufficient argument to prove something.[7]

However, this rule is not always and everywhere kept, that the mystical sense of Sacred Scripture never ought to be admitted for proving a dogma. For if it can clearly be determined from some other citations of Scripture that the mystical interpretation of Scripture is according to its genuine and true meaning, then an argument for establishing some doctrine can be accepted from that mystical sense. For Augustine clearly indicates this in those words recently cited, where after he had said that it is "impudence for one to interpret in his own favor

---

[1] Job 5, 24.

[2] Gal. 4, 26.

[3] Donatus and his followers inhabited Northern Africa.

[4] Letter 93, chap. 8, n. 24 (PL 33, 334).

[5] "[The wise man] shall understand a parable, and the interpretation, the words of the wise, and their mysterious sayings (*aenigmata*)" (Prov. 1, 6).

[6] PL 26, 92A.

[7] The author incorrectly ascribes the addressee of this letter as Polycarp, when it is in fact Titus (Letter 9, chap. 1 (PG 3, 1103B-1107B)). "Dionysius says in his letter to Titus that symbolic theology is not conclusive" (Aquinas, *Comm. in I Sent.* dist. 11, art. 1, ad 1um).

any allegorical statements," he immediately excepts from this general view the particular and special case, saying the following: "unless he has also evident citations, by the light of which the obscure meaning of the former may be made manifest." In which words he very clearly teaches that an argument can rightly be taken from the mystical sense, when from elsewhere it can be determined that such a mystical meaning very well befits that passage, and is its true meaning.

This opinion of Augustine is clearly proved from Paul, who often used quotations from the Old Testament understood according to their mystical meaning for proving his doctrine. For when wishing to prove to the Galatians that the Mosaic Law was abrogated by the coming of the Evangelical Law, he cites the words which God said to Abraham: "Cast out the bondwoman and her son; for the son of the bondwoman shall not be heir with the son of the free woman" (Gal. 4, 30). Which words he so interprets, such that by the bondwoman he understands the Old Law which was a servant to many ceremonies, and by the son of this bondwoman, the Jewish people. By the free woman, however, he understands the Evangelical Law, free from all servitude, and by the son of this free woman, the Christian people. Which interpretation of the words (as it is sufficiently certain) is mystical, Paul himself stating this, saying that those words are said by way of allegory.

Furthermore, Paul likewise wishing to prove that the people are obliged by Divine Law to support those who teach them this gospel says: "Speak I these things according to man? Or doth not the law also say these things? For it is written in the law of Moses: 'Thou shalt not muzzle the mouth of the ox that treadeth out the corn.' Doth God take care for oxen? Or doth he say this indeed for our sakes? For these things are written for our sakes: that he that plougheth, should plough in hope; and he that thrasheth, in hope to receive fruit" (I Cor. 9, 8-10). But by interpreting oxen as the preachers of God's word, the sense is mystical (as is very clearly established), and not literal. From all which things it is proven that it is sometimes permitted to take an argument from the mystical sense for establishing some doctrine, if it can be clearly proved from elsewhere that the mystical sense very well befits that passage.

Nevertheless, the literal sense will always hold the first place in a disputation, and it will be stronger for confirming a doctrine. Therefore, since this sense is especially effective for refuting heresies, it will be worthwhile to inquire what the literal meaning is. The literal meaning can be found in multiple ways. Sometimes it can be found from the simple meaning of the words. Sometimes it is gathered not from the words themselves, but from the thing meant by the words. For it cannot happen that the sense of the text can be gathered from the primary meaning of the words: otherwise, many absurd things, and things which horrify pious ears, would be found in the sacred books, both in the New and in the Old Testaments. Such are all those things which seem to give to God bodily members, as when God is called a lamb, lion, rock, vine, worm, and many things of the same sort which Christ says by similitudes, and not according to their own meanings.

And in order that I may summarize very briefly, wherever a metaphor or translation or some figurative speech is found, the meaning therein of the text is not called the literal sense—the sense which the words express by their primary meaning—but that sense which is deduced from the likeness which the thing signified by the words has with another thing. There are many similar things in our everyday speech, as for example if you wish to call someone voracious, you call him a wolf: if you wish to call him greedy, you call him a mole,[1] not because these things are said literally, but rather because those thing are similitudes of whom they are said. Augustine says in book three of his *On Christian Doctrine*, "For he who follows the letter, takes figurative words as if they were proper, and does not carry out what is indicated

---

[1] Moles construct special underground "larders" which may contain over a thousand earthworms in them.

Introduction

-19-

by a proper word into its secondary signification; but, if he hears of 'the Sabbath,' for example, thinks of nothing but the one day out of seven which recurs in constant succession; and when he hears of a 'sacrifice,' does not carry his thoughts beyond the customary offerings of victims from the flock, and of the fruits of the earth. Now it is surely a miserable slavery of the soul to take the signs for the things, and to be unable to lift the eye of the mind above what is corporeal and created, that it may drink in eternal light."[1]

Furthermore, in the same book, chapter ten, he says: "But in addition to the foregoing rule, which guards us against taking a metaphorical form of speech as if it were literal, we must also pay heed to that which tells us not to take a literal form of speech as if it were figurative. In the first place, then, we must show the way to find out whether a phrase is literal or figurative. And the way certainly is as follows: Whatever there is in the word of God that cannot, when taken literally, be referred either to purity of life or soundness of doctrine, you may set down as figurative. Purity of life has reference to the love of God and one's neighbor; soundness of doctrine to the knowledge of God and one's neighbor."[2] When, therefore, it has already been established that something belongs to figurative speech, one ought to be wary lest it be supposed that it be determined in advance that once a thing be signified by some similitude, it is believed that this always and everywhere represents that thing. If one and the same thing has many characteristics, on account of which it has a likeness to many things, it thus also bears the signification of many things.

Hence it is that the same thing sometimes represents various things, and other times opposite things, according to the different characteristics found in it, whereby a likeness is found not only to different things, but even to opposite things. For a lion represents Christ on account of its constancy and fortitude, where it is said: "The lion of the tribe of Juda hath prevailed" (Apoc. 5, 5). And likewise, on account of it voracity it represents the devil, as it is said in the writings of Peter: "Your adversary the devil, as a roaring lion, goeth about seeking whom he may devour" (I Pet. 5, 8). I think that I have said enough about figurative speech according to the brevity which I resolved to have. Therefore, from what has been previously said, let this be the rule: It is the literal sense that the words or things expressed by words signify. Nevertheless, not every meaning is literal, but that meaning alone which the Holy Ghost intends. Which fact is indeed clearly inferred from the previous statement, if we recall that which we said shortly before, namely, that the Author of the sacred books is the Holy Ghost. For that is truly the genuine meaning of the text, which the writer intended. For in like manner we bear witness to our feelings and thoughts by our writings and words. Therefore since the Holy Ghost is the Author of Sacred Scripture, that ought to be held as the true meaning of the same Scripture, which is intended by the Holy Ghost. Every other meaning, however, is false and illegitimate. Hence Jerome commenting on the Epistle to the Galatians says: "Whoever understands Scripture in a manner other than that demanded by the meaning of the Holy Ghost in which it was written, even though he does not separate himself from the Church, can nevertheless be called a heretic."[3]

On the other hand, concerning the meaning of the parables, he who would want to limit the meaning to the literal sense, does not act rightly. If however he does not want to do this, I am not opposed. Still, regarding the same parables which are frequently used in the Gospels, I determined that it ought to be advised that (as Augustine says) they ought to be understood, not as they were in reality, but as they could be: as when (for example) it is said: "The kingdom of heaven is like to an householder, who went out early in the morning to hire labourers into his vineyard" (Mt. 20, 1). Which if it perhaps never actually happened, that the householder

---

[1] Chap. 5, n. 9 (PL 34, 69).
[2] N. 14 (PL 34, 71).
[3] *In Gal.* 5, 19-21 (PL 26, 417B).

went out and returned at those set times, and was always finding those whom he might send into his vineyard, nevertheless nothing prevents it from having happened: which suffices for a parable.

But it often happens that many literal meanings fit the same passage, apart from other meanings which are derived from the mystical meaning of things. In this case, one must beware lest any of them be rejected, as long as they have testimony from other passages of Sacred Scripture, that elsewhere those words have the meaning which is now given to them. And the meaning which comes from that signification of the words fits the passage if it is nowise opposed to the Catholic faith, and either of them will be deemed the genuine and true meaning of the text. For what hinders Sacred Scripture from being so fertile that it gives birth to two offspring? For so concerning the Doctors of the Church, who know how to draw out the literal meaning no matter how abstruse it is said mystically: "Thy teeth as flocks of sheep, that are shorn which come up from the washing, all with twins, and there is none barren among them" (Cant. 4, 2).

Now this is proved by the attestation of Blessed Augustine in book three of his On Christian Doctrine, chapter twenty-seven. For he says the following: "When, again, not one particular interpretation, but two or more interpretations are put upon the same words of Scripture, even though the meaning the writer intended remains undiscovered, there is no danger if it can be shown from other passages of Scripture that any of the interpretations put on the words is in harmony with the truth. And if a man in searching the Scriptures endeavors to get at the intention of the author through whom the Holy Ghost spoke, whether he succeeds in this endeavor, or whether he draws a different meaning from the words, but one that is not opposed to sound doctrine, he is free from blame so long as he is supported by the testimony of some other passage of Scripture. For the author perhaps saw that this very meaning lay in the words which we are trying to interpret; and assuredly the Holy Ghost, who through him spoke these words, foresaw that this interpretation would occur to the reader, nay, made provision that it should occur to him, seeing that it too is founded on truth. For what more liberal and more fruitful provision could God have made in regard to the Sacred Scriptures than that the same words might be understood in several senses, all of which are sanctioned by the concurring testimony of other passages equally Divine?"[1] And what has now been said suffices concerning this matter.

Chapter IV: That the interpretation of Sacred Scripture, which each and every faithful is held to embrace, pertains to the Church alone.

Although we have prescribed a rule for any designated meaning whereby one may know whether or not it actually be the true meaning, nevertheless many men abuse it: and they interpret Scripture freely and as they please, so that they drag it away as evidence of their error. For as Augustine says in his book, *Eighty-three Different Questions*, in question sixty-nine: "Their error, to be sure, could not spring up clothed with the name 'Christian' except from a failure to understand the Scriptures."[2] For also Blessed Peter testifies that the Pauline epistles have been wrongly understood by some, who were trying to twist them according to their error. For so he says: "As also our most dear brother Paul, according to the wisdom given him, hath written to you: as also in all his epistles, speaking in them of these things; in which are certain things hard to be understood, which the unlearned and unstable wrest, as they do also the other scriptures, to their own destruction" (II Pet. 3, 15-16).

---

[1] N. 38 (PL 34, 80).
[2] N. 1 (PL 40, 74).

Introduction

Arius took for proving his errors very many passages of Sacred Scripture, all nevertheless badly understood. The Novatians, Donatists, Pelagians, Nestorians, etc., with hardly any exceptions, have done the same. For to do this was a common thing for them all, so that they might defend their errors with Scripture wrongly understood and pestilently expounded. And we suffer this incursion today, alas, from the Lutherans, by whom the Gospels and the Pauline epistles [are cited] so frequently that they seem to breathe nothing else. Yet immense thanks ought to be given to God, who turns all these infestations of the Church to His glory and the glory of the Church, which struck by blows, is forced to advance to better things. For it happened that due to heretics of this kind, having put aside the trifles to which men have given themselves for the last three hundred years, they applied themselves to studying better things. Hence it is that the Church now possesses many more learned men than it had forty years ago. "For there must be also heresies," as Paul says, "that they also, who are approved, may be made manifest among you" (I Cor. 11, 19). Augustine expounding this passage in his book, *On Genesis Against the Manichaeans*, says: "Divine Providence permits many heretics with their differing errors so that at least, when they insult us and ask us what we do not know, we may shake off our sluggishness and long to know the Divine Scriptures. This is why the Apostle says, 'There must be also heresies that they also, who are approved, may be made manifest among you.' For those are approved before God who can teach well, but they can only become manifest to men when they teach. They are, however, willing to teach only those who seek to be taught. Yet many are slow to seek if they are not aroused as if from sleep by the troublesomeness and insults of the heretics... If these men are of solid faith, they do not give in to the heretics, but carefully seek what response they should make to them. God does not abandon them. When they ask, they receive, and when they seek, they find, and when they knock, the door will be opened for them (Mt. 7, 7)."[1]

If therefore there are heresies, and they arise from a wrong understanding of Sacred Scripture (as we will say below at greater length), it is necessary that there be someone who has the authority to interpret Sacred Scripture, to whose interpretation all the faithful are bound to assent. Otherwise there would be no way to refute a heretic, if it were permitted for anyone to interpret Scripture according to his own judgment. But because someone might doubt this, it is thus necessary to support it with reasons, as there may be some very shameless man who opposes. For which reason I address any individual heretic, and I ask whether he believes that anyone is, or ever has been, a heretic deviating from the true rule of faith. No one (I think) will have been so tainted that he would say that there never was anyone who deviated from the true rule of faith, unless perhaps he were from the sect of the Rhetorians: who (as Philastrius maintains)[2] thought that all heresies were true, and that heretics always opined well. Because the madness is so great, as Augustine says in his book, *On Heresies*, chapter seventy-two, it seems impossible that any man has become so senseless that he would assert this.[3]

I do not doubt that Arius reckoned Sabellius a heretic, and Sabellius vice versa Arius. Pelagius, if he were still alive, would judge Luther to have deviated from the true faith, Luther would bring this against Pelagius. For their assertions are so conflicting, that one can hardly agree with the other. If, therefore, (as is just) someone admits that the former man was a her-

---

[1] Book 1, chap. 1, n. 2 (PL 34, 173).

[2] Saint Philastrius (+397) was the Bishop of Brescia and composed a catalogue of heresies entitled *Diversarum Hereseon Liber*.

[3] "[Philastrius] calls the heresy that arose from a certain Rhetorius, an excess of astounding vanity, which affirms that all heretics were on a safe way and spoke truly: which is so absurd, that it seems unbelievable to me." (*De haeresibus ad Quodvultdeus* (PL 42, 44)). Cf. Philastrius, *Liber De Haeresibus*, n. 91 (PL 12, 1202B-1203A). This comment of Saint Augustine is quoted by Pope Leo XII in his encyclical, *Ubi Primum* (n. 13), in relation to Indifferentism.

etic, I will then ask [you] whether there is some way whereby a person he could be taught, such that, unless malice opposes, he could be awakened from his error?. And if he denies that there is a way, it necessarily ought to be acknowledged that no guilt should be imputed to the heretic for not giving up his error, seeing that this is because he labors under irremediable ignorance. For the Lord (as Augustine says in a certain sermon) "would not have condemned the slothful servant, if He commanded things which could by no means be done."[1] But if one admit that some way is open by which a person can be recalled from his error, and taught that he had understood Sacred Scripture wrongly, I ask by whom should he be taught? Not by another man, because it will be pleaded that he will be deceived by any man, and he would be unwilling to discuss on account of his own interpretation.

For every man is liable to err in the faith, even if he be the pope. For Platina[2] relates concerning Pope Liberius that that he had agreed with the Arians, and Anastasius II, the Pope bearing this name, favored the Nestorians, and he who reads history does not doubt this.[3] Pope Celestine also erred about Matrimony of the faithful, when one of spouses falls into heresy, the matter is manifest to all.[4] And this error of Celestine was not of the sort which ought to be attributed to negligence alone, such that we may say he erred as a private person and not as pope, who in defining any serious matter ought to consult learned men: because Celestine's definition was found in the old Decretals, beginning with the word, Laudabilem, entitled "On the Conversion of Infidels": which I myself saw and read.[5]

---

[1] *Sermon 54 on the New Testament* (Benedictine Edition), chap. 2, n. 2 (PL 38, 373).

[2] Bartolomeo Sacchi (+1481) is after his birthplace known as Platina, or in English, Bartolomeo Platina. In 1479 he wrote a work, most likely cited here, called *Lives of the Popes*.

[3] This is a false accusation about Pope Anastasius II. "During the medieval period, Anastasius II was often considered a traitor to the Catholic Church and an apostate. The writer of the *Liber Pontificalis*, supporting the opponents to Anastasius' efforts [to end the Acacian schism], argued that Anastasius II's death was Divine retribution and that he had broken with the Church. Similarly, the *Decretum Gratiani* writes of the pope that 'Anastasius, reproved by God, was smitten by divine command.' This Medieval view is described by modern commentators as a 'legend,' a 'misinterpretation,' a 'confused tradition,' and 'manifestly unjust.'" (Joseph Brusher, "Anastasius II," Catholic Culture, http://www.catholicculture.org. Retrieved October 20, 2014).

[4] "Pope Celestine III (1191-1198) is the only pope who apparently admitted the dissolution of the marital bond and subsequent remarriage. The case in point concerned a Christian husband, who during his married life denied Christ, left his wife, and took a pagan woman. It should be noted that the marriage was originally contracted by two Christians. The abandoned Christian woman also remarried another man with permission of the archdeacon. Celestine justified his unusual and rather inconsistent position by analogy with Pauline principle, that is, unbelief and subsequent refusal to cohabit peacefully are equal to contempt of the Creator and contempt of the Creator dissolves the law of marriage." (Juraj Kamas, *The Separation of the Spouses with the Bond Remaining: Historical and Canonical Study with Pastoral Applications* Gregorian Biblical Bookshop, 1997) p. 107), Cf. Ep. *Laudabilem*; in Mansi 22, 639-640.

[5] St. Robert Bellarine: "I respond: Neither Celestine nor Innocent stated anything certain on the matter; but each responded with what seemed more probable to them. That is manifestly gathered from the words of Innocent who, when he says his predecessor thought otherwise, shows in his opinion that the whole matter was still being thought out. On the other hand, Alphonsus [de Castro] says the epistle of Celestine was at one time among the epistles in the decretals. While certainly that is true, it cannot thence be gathered that a plainly Apostolic decree was made by Celestine, or even one *ex cathedra*; since it is certain that there are many epistles in the decretals which do not make any matter *de fide*, but only declare to us the opinions of the Pontiff on some affair" (*De Romano Pontifice*, bk. 4, c. 14 in *Disputationum Roberti Bellarmini..., S.J... de controversiis christianae* (Venice, Joannes Malachinus, 1721), vol. 1, controversy 3, pp. 415-416).

Introduction

If therefore we are obliged by law to believe no man regarding the interpretation of Sacred Writ, for the very reason that any man alone can err, the judgment of interpretation will necessarily belong to the whole Church, in whose power was the right of distinguishing Sacred Scriptures from human writings. For this Church cannot err, because it has been taught by the Holy Ghost. For no one can interpret some Scripture more correctly than the one who has the mind and the spirit of the writer. But it is certain that the Church has the Spirit of God. For so Christ promised: "I shall give you another Paraclete, who will bring to your mind all truth" (Jn. 14, 16).[1] And elsewhere He says concerning Himself, "I am with you all days, even to the consummation of the world" (Mt. 28, 20). Therefore if God always assists the Church, and His Spirit brings to its mind all truth, can she be able to be deceived, or not know how to interpret Scripture, who is daily taught by the Author of Scripture?

Add to this the fact that she is the spouse of Christ, in whom the heart of her Husband especially trusts, as it is said in the book of Proverbs.[2] But it would not have been well said that He trusts her, if He were to present her the Scriptures, whose keys He was keeping with Himself. This, however, would happen, if God were to not hand over the understanding of those Scriptures transmitted to the Church, but would keep it to Himself. Therefore if God did not want to hide from Abraham the things that He was about to do, how much less will He hide from the Church the understanding of Scripture?[3]

Moreover, the Church has this, that it can distinguish God's word from men's words: for otherwise we would not know that this is Matthew's Gospel, and that is certainly Mark's or Luke's, unless we had learned from the testimony of the Church asserting this. It is certain, however, that the Church does not have this power of distinguishing the Divine writings from human ones from another source, other than from God: and that for no other reason than lest the Church err in these matters, in which it was especially necessary not to err. Hence, it is clearly proven that if the power to distinguish God's words from men's words belongs to the Church, the power of discerning the Divine meaning from the human also belongs to the Church herself. For otherwise there would have been no benefit if the Church distinguishes by God teaching her the true Scripture from the false, if she were not to know in the true Scriptures how to distinguish the true meaning from the false. For the harm would have been no less if the Church were to accept the false meaning instead of the true, than if it were to have embraced human writings instead of Divine ones. Jerome says when commenting on the Epistle to the Galatians: "Let us not suppose that the essence of the Gospel is in the words, rather than in the actual meaning of Scripture: or on the surface, rather than in the inmost parts: or in the leaves of the words, and not in the root of the meaning."[4]

Hence it is, that by the law whereby we believe the Church saying that this writing is Divine, by the same law we may believe her saying that this or that is the meaning of the Divine writing. For it would not suffice if one were to say that the Church has the Scriptures, if it were deprived of their correct interpretation. For a dispute is not in words, but in things. It is fitting that the Greeks use Greek words, and the Latins use other words. One is the language of the Spanish, another of the French, another of the Germans, and another of the British. For there is not one language on the earth, even though the matters are the same about which men speak. It matters little whether you quote Christ's words in this or that language, provided that you relate the same meaning which He wished to be understood.

Likewise, it matters little to keep the same words, if they are expounded with opposite meanings by the different persons arguing with each other. For when we are adoring Christ

---

[1] This quotation is adapted also from Jn. 16, 13.
[2] "The heart of her husband trusteth in her" (Prov. 31, 11).
[3] "And the Lord said: Can I hide from Abraham what I am about to do" (Gen. 18, 17).
[4] Bk. 1, Chap. 1, verse 11-12 (PL 26, 322C).

and falling down before Him, we say, "Hail." The Jews mocking Him were saying, "Hail." The words are the same: who nevertheless does not know that there is a great difference due to the different meaning and the diverse intentions between our and their words? For the Jews spoke in mockery, but we show reverence by the same words. Since then it is so important that words should be grasped with this or that meaning, it was most necessary the authority for interpreting Scripture be in the possession of the Church, nowise distinct from the authority for distinguishing the Divine writings from the human.

Moreover, there would be no other way whereby heresy could be refuted. For since all heretics (as we said) support their errors with Scripture, which do not at all arise from Scripture, but from its adulterated meaning: how can that meaning be rejected if the heretic wishes to accept that meaning of the text as genuine? Or by whom will it be rejected, if no one possesses the authority for interpreting Sacred Scripture? You will perhaps say that the true meaning can be extracted by reasoning, arguments, and conjectures based on the context of the preceding and following words. I acknowledge that these help very much, and yet they do not completely solve the matter: because neither are the conjectures always cogent, nor are the arguments clearly conclusive, especially in matters of faith, where the strength of arguments is the weakest. In addition, there are many passages whose true meaning departs far from the words of the text, to such a degree that it is no help for conjecturing the meaning from it.

But lo, though we are girded for war, and we prepare weapons for battle, the signal has still in nowise been given for the fight, one of those whom we have determined to fight attacks us, namely Luther. We will tell who he is, when the heresies will be treated one by one. For in his book, *The Babylonian Captivity of the Church*, when he discusses the Sacrament of the Eucharist, he says the following: "No violence ought to be done to the words of God, neither by man, nor by Angel, but that, as far as possible, they ought to be kept to their simplest meaning, and not be taken out of their grammatical and proper signification, unless the circumstances manifestly compel us to do so, that we may not give our adversaries any opportunity of evading the teaching of the whole Scriptures."[1] O alleviation of very many heresies! Now I would like to interrogate Luther, whether words ought to always be taken according to their simplest meaning, and only according to their grammatical meaning, or whether it will sometimes be permitted to wander away from their grammatical boundaries? Because if he denies that it is permitted, then very many illustrious men have labored in vain in drawing out the very abstruse true meanings of Sacred Scripture: and it was unnecessary to expend so much labor on it, if only the grammatical meaning and the simplest meaning of the words would suffice.

Additionally, many things will then be found in Sacred Writ which a pious man would perhaps either laugh at a little or would abhor: such is the passage that one or another meaning may be adduced from among many: "And I dispose to you, as my Father hath disposed to me, a kingdom, that you may eat and drink at my table, in my kingdom" (Lk. 22, 29). To this a passage from Isaias seems to allude, when he is speaking about the retribution to be given to each man according to each man's works. For he says to those who pass this life in luxury and haughtiness: "My servants shall eat, and you shall be hungry: behold my servants shall drink, and you shall be thirsty," etc. (Is. 65, 13). Which passage, if it were taken according to the mere simplest meaning of the words (as Luther says), who does not see from this that it provides an occasion to Cerinthus[2] of fomenting his impious heresy, by which he says that in the awaited beatitude to come, there would be delights of the flesh? Perhaps the most well-known of all is that which Christ said: "The Father is greater than I" (Jn. 14, 28). If no

---

[1] Martin Luther, *First Principles of the Reformation or the Ninety-five Theses and the Three Primary Works* (London, William Clowes and Sons, Limited, 1883), p. 157.

[2] Cerinthus was a Gnostic-Ebionite heretic, contemporary with St. John; against whose errors on the divinity of Christ the Apostle is said to have written the Fourth Gospel.

interpretation is required there besides that which is drawn from the simplest meaning of the words, it is certain that therefrom weapons are freely given to the Arians, with which they may raise up their heresy, now buried for a long time. If no other exposition is applied to Sacred Writ besides that which can be drawn from the rules of grammar, thereupon the heretic Marcion[1] will exceedingly rejoice, and Mani,[2] his imitator, saying that the Old Law was bad: because Paul says: "The law entered in, that sin might abound" (Rom. 5, 20). Likewise, Mani thought that he had triumphed over the Catholics, when he said that all the Prophets had erred, because Christ said: "All others, as many as have come, are thieves and robbers" (Jn. 10, 8). These examples show in a clearer light that if Luther does not wish to agree with Cerinthus, or promote Arius, he should not only permit the interpretation of Holy Writ outside of the confines of the grammatical meaning, but even demand it.

Why does Luther, very often unmindful of his regulation, distort the Sacred Scripture, which is used as a defense by Catholics, with an exposition hardly according to the rules of grammar, and spin it into another meaning? For example, this is easy to see when he tears to pieces Christ's words whereby He turned bread into His own Body. For thus Luther explains "This," that is to say, this bread, "is My body." Indeed, in order that he may exercise his tyranny everywhere, he does not wish that the law that he had put forth to be permitted. For he wants (so that he may show that he truly has the leaven of the Pharisees) to impose unsupportable burdens, when nevertheless he does not wish to move them with his finger. For when previously he had established the law for inhibiting the interpretation of Scripture, he rejected that exposition which you saw, concerning which we will discuss in the section on the "Eucharist."

If therefore you, Luther, give to yourself the authority of expounding the Scripture which is used as a defense against you, why do you not permit so many wise men the faculty of expounding those passages which you use against us? Shall it be allowed for you to heedlessly distort Scriptures by your own judgment, and it will not be allowed for the Catholic Church to expound anything? For you wish these passages on which you rely not to be expounded, nor to be touched with the highest fingers, but to be taken according to the letter: and you say that it is not permitted to depart even slightly from the shell of the letter. Nevertheless, the passages which favor us, and the truth you touch with astounding liberty, you distort, making it into something else. Is this perhaps lest there be a different Scripture for you than for us, so that the former passages may not be expounded, but the latter are permitted to be torn to pieces? Or if perhaps Sacred Scripture is the same for you as it is for us, whence this audacity of you and of your accomplices, that the power of interpreting which you take away from us, you arrogate to yourselves? Has perhaps God's kingdom truly been taken away from us and given to you? If you assert that this is so, show yourself to be that people bearing fruit, to whom Christ promised that he would give this kingdom, and I will believe. Yet neither do we see, nor, as I expect, will we see that fruit, unless God by His most benign piety having had mercy on your errors, lead you back at some time from darkness into the light.

But if perchance vexation has now given Luther understanding that he permit us, just as himself, to interpret Sacred Scriptures: after this it will now happen that when there is no harmony between him and us concerning the correct understanding of the text, it ought to be in the power of some judge, who, removed from every contention, may show the true and Catholic meaning. Now it is necessary that he be such that he cannot be deceived. But every

---

[1] Marcion taught that the God of the Old Testament was not the true God but rather that the true and higher God had been revealed only with Jesus Christ. Marcion wrote the *Antitheses* to show the differences between the God of the Old Testament and the true God. Marcion was excommunicated in 144 A.D.

[2] The Persian founder of Manichaeism in the third century.

man can be deceived, as we showed shortly before. The Church, however, cannot be deceived, especially in those things which are very important. Therefore we have proved that in the Church's possession is the power both of distinguishing Divine from human writings, and of separating in the same Divine Scriptures the Divine meaning from the human meanings, to whose discretion and judgment every faithful is bound to obey in one just as also in the other.

Perhaps someone will object to us, in order that he may weaken this position of ours, and he will say the following: If it is the Church which alone cannot err, and we ought to receive [from Her] the true and undoubted meaning of Sacred Scripture with submission; never, or at least with great difficulty, would someone be able to obtain the true and certain meaning of Sacred Scripture, after he has once begun to doubt it. For the Church which has spread throughout the whole world cannot be assembled in some one place, so that it could teach one or another ignorant person. If you say that the whole Church can be represented by a general council, and the true meaning of Scripture can be sought from it, it would then be necessary for this reason to acknowledge that it is very difficult to acquire the true and certain meaning of Scripture because it would be very difficult to assemble a general council for every single doubtful meaning of Scripture.

I indeed admit that it would always be a difficult thing, and now alas, very difficult to assemble a general council, and thus I concede that it is not necessary to assemble such a council, so that by it we may know what the Church teaches concerning the true meaning of some passage of Sacred Scripture. For just as to know what writing the Church deems sacred, we not only need to give heed to the definitions of the general councils, but also (as Augustine teaches in book two of *On Christian Doctrine*, chapter eight) the opinion kept in many individual churches with unbroken succession. So also, in order to know what the Church holds regarding the true meaning of Scripture, we will have recourse to the venerable and holy doctors, who preceded us. What by unbroken succession and without any dispute has always been held as the true meaning of Scripture, that we believe without doubt to be the meaning which the Catholic Church teaches ought to be held.[1] For Saint Clement, martyr and Peter's disciple, teaches this in book ten of the *Recognitions,* saying the following: "It behooves you to learn the meaning of the Scriptures from him who keeps it according to the truth handed down to him from his fathers."[2]

Therefore, not from Luther, or Oecolampadius, or Melanchthon, or Bucer, or Zwingli, or any other man of similar ilk, one ought to learn the understanding of Sacred Scripture, because none of them hands down those things which were kept by our fathers, but what each one of them concocted as he pleased. Augustine agrees with Clement and in a certain letter to Paulinus says these words: "I prefer to understand in these words (he speaks about certain words of Sacred Scripture) what the entire, or almost the entire Church observes."[3] Furthermore, this is kept by perpetual use in the Church, that whenever a controversy happened to arise between Catholics and heretics about the correct understanding of Sacred Scripture, always in councils—which had been assembled for this reason—recourse was had to the opinion of the Fathers preceding from the time of the Apostles, and that which they under-

---

[1] "Now, in regard to the canonical Scriptures, he must follow the judgment of the greater number of catholic churches; and among these, of course, a high place must be given to such as have been thought worthy to be the seat of an apostle and to receive epistles. Accordingly, among the canonical Scriptures he will judge according to the following standard: to prefer those that are received by all the catholic churches to those which some do not receive." (N. 12 (PL 34, 40)).
[2] Chap. 42. This spurious quotation is taken from the *False Decretals of Pseudo-Isidore*. It is quoted in *Decretum Gratiani* (PL 187, 207A). Cf. *Epistola de Communi Vita et Reliquis Causis* (Letter V, PL 130, 59A).
[3] *Letter 147*, chap. 2, n. 16 (PL 33, 636).

Introduction

stood to have been handed down by them with uninterrupted succession, they deemed to be the teaching of the Catholic Church to be necessarily accepted. Yet this ought to be carefully noticed, that the inquiry was made only from the opinion of those Fathers, who before the controversy had arisen were considered more holy and learned, and who wrote about that matter not for the favor of some man, but only for God's honor. For so it is read in book nine, chapter nineteen of the *Historia Tripartita*.[1]

Chapter V: That there are some things to which from the definition of the universal Church whole-hearted faith must be applied, even if they cannot be proven by expressed testimonies of Sacred Scripture.

Now there are many doctrines of the heretics, which can by no means be disproved by the testimony of Scripture, but are rejected only by the tradition of the universal Church. Very many heretics scorn and deride this tradition of the Church. On the other hand, that which is derided by them is also examined by Job, saying "But now the younger in time scorn me" (30, 1): expounding which Gregory says, "All heretics when compared to the age of the Church Universal are fitly called 'younger' in time, because they went forth out of her, not she out of them. Whence it is rightly also said by John: 'They went out from us, but they were not of us: for if they had been of us, they would no doubt have continued with us' (I Jn. 2, 19). For 'they that are younger in time deride Holy Church,' when they that went out from her, set at naught the words of her instruction."[2] Hence, this very solid foundation has been laid, with which as a very strong garrison against heretics it will very often be necessary in the future to defend ourselves. The traditions or definitions of the universal Church in these matters which pertain to the faith, even if a clear passage of Scripture be lacking, are of no less authority than Sacred Scripture itself. Now it is necessary to support this assertion with many reasons so that it may not easily collapse.

The first reason is that the spoken word of someone teaching is no less effective for teaching faith and morals than writing: nay it is far more efficacious, and this is made sufficiently evident by citing the Scriptural editor Jerome in his letter to Paulinus concerning all the books of Sacred Scripture. For he writes as follows: "Spoken words possess an indefinable hidden power, and teaching that passed directly from the mouth of the speaker into the ears of the disciples is more impressive than any other"[3]

Therefore, say whether you can demonstrate the reliability of the Gospels by the fact that they were written by men, or because they were written by men inspired by God, Who was moving both their hearts and hands to write? I do not doubt that you are led to accept their reliability by the latter reason, namely that you believe those men were inspired in their writings by the Divine Spirit. What therefore prohibits the Divine Spirit from assisting the speaking Church, just as He does the Evangelist writing, since He says to the Apostles, "It is not you that speak, but the Spirit of your Father that speaketh in you" (Mt. 10, 20)? Has God already deprived His Church of His Spirit, such that He disdains to speak through her mouth? Far be it. For He says, "Behold I am with you all days, even to the consummation of the world" (Mt. 28, 20). If therefore you believe Divine Scripture, written by the hands of the Evangelists and Apostles, why do you not believe the Divine voice speaking through the mouth of the Church?

---

[1] PL 69, 1137A-B.
[2] *Moralia*, bk. 20, n. 15 (PL 76, 145C).
[3] Letter 53, n. 2 (PL 22, 541).

Introduction

But perhaps you say that you know that this writing is Divine, and so you give your ear to it: but you do not know whether that voice is also Divine, and hence you do not believe; but you would believe if on the other hand it were made known to you that that voice of the Church asserting this or that is Divine. Say, I beseech you, from whence do you know that this book was written by Matthew, that by Mark, that however by Luke, or that by John. Did you sit by the writers? Because if you say that you know this from the titles that were put on their writings, it will be for this reason that you may not more firmly cling to believing that the first of the four Gospels is Matthew's, than to believing that *The City of God* or *On the Trinity* are Augustine's, because if you agree to this, your faith certainly waivers, and has a very weak support. For who knows how very often the inscriptions of titles err, to such a degree you may discover that the same book has been inscribed with the different titles of two or three authors? That is why I seldom wish to try to defend such inscriptions. But lest I deny that the first Gospel is Matthew's, or that the Epistle to the Romans is Paul's, I will most willingly lay down my neck to the sword.

But perhaps you will say (as is befitting) that you believe that this Gospel is Matthew's, and that one is Luke's, because the Church so testifies. If therefore you believe the Church saying that this Gospel is Matthew's, and that one is Luke's, which is such an important matter, that upon it nearly every other depends: why do you not believe the same Church saying other things, even if she nowise confirms them with Scriptures? Was it necessary that Matthew would have testified concerning Luke that he wrote his Gospel, or that Luke testify this same thing concerning Matthew? If this be so, that any passage of Scripture always requires the testimony of another passage of Scripture for its approbation, who does not see that for this reason one must go on endlessly? Hence it will happen that one can never know with certainty about any passage of Scripture, whether or not it be human or divine.

But if this is not required, why do you believe the Church saying to you, without any testimony of Scripture, that this Gospel is Matthew's: while in other matters you do not wish to believe without the testimony of Divine Scripture? Is it not the same Church which asserts this and that? Is not the identification of Scriptures just as serious a matter as any other? Besides, in order that we may act more effectively and convince men more clearly, we freely concede this one point that you, without the testimony of Sacred Scripture and of the Church, but having been taught by the enlightenment of the Holy Ghost alone, know that the Gospel belongs to this or that Evangelist, and for that reason you say that you believe it: then tell me, why do you believe the Gospel and not the Church, of which the Evangelist himself was a member, since the Church excels the Evangelists to the same extent as the whole body surpasses its individual members? If you trust one member, why do you distrust them all together? If you give so much to a member, why do you give nothing to the whole body?

Besides, we do not read that Christ wrote anything, but merely taught by speech, of whose words the Evangelists have passed over many words, of which they make completely no mention. Hence John the Evangelist in the last chapter of his Gospel says, "There are also many other things which Jesus did; which, if they were written every one, the world itself, I think, would not be able to contain the books that should be written" (Jn. 21, 25). Therefore, it must be believed for equal reason that he did not write everything that Christ said: an example of which is the passage: "It is a more blessed thing to give, rather than to receive" (Acts 20, 35): which Paul testifies that Christ said, although nevertheless none of the Evangelists mention that saying. And Luke in the first chapter of the Acts of the Apostles relates concerning Christ Our Lord, that after His Resurrection He showed Himself to be alive to His disciples by many proofs, during forty days appearing to them, and speaking concerning the kingdom of God, of which words scarcely one or another will you find written. Yet it ought to be believed that the Apostles told others by word both deeds and sayings, and so by mouth

Introduction
-29-

on to us, and transferred from heart to heart until it came down to us without any testimony of any Scripture. Moreover, there were many teachings and precepts of the Apostles concerning the government of the Church, which were nowise commanded in writing. For it is said in chapter fifteen of the Acts of the Apostles that "Paul choosing Silas, departed, being delivered by the brethren to the grace of God. And he went through Syria and Cilicia, confirming the churches, commanding them to keep the precepts of the apostles and the ancients."[1] In like manner, in the following chapter it is said concerning Paul and his disciple, Timothy, in this manner: "And as they passed through the cities, they delivered unto them the decrees for to keep, that were decreed by the apostles and ancients who were at Jerusalem."[2] These things hardly serve our argument, since we find the *Apostolic Canons* which the Apostles themselves decreed for the then nascent Church. [Pseudo-] Isidore placed them, divided into forty-eight chapters, at the beginning of the Councils.[3] These canons having been translated (as it is said) by Clement, pope and martyr, the Supreme Pontiffs Zepherinus and Leo, and the sixth Synod, approved them.[4] Damascene gave them so much credit that in chapter eighteen of the fourth book of his book, *On the Orthodox Faith*, he seems to put them in the number of canonical books.[5] For when he treats of the canonical books, having enumerated their list, having made no distinction at all, he adds, "the *Apostolic Canons* by Clement."

However, putting these things aside, the words which Paul actually says in the Second Epistle to the Thessalonians especially confirm our assertion: "Therefore, brethren, stand fast; and hold the traditions which you have learned, whether by word, or by our epistle" (2, 14). Further, in the Second Epistle to Timothy he says: "Thou therefore, my son, be strong in the grace which is in Christ Jesus: and the things which thou hast heard of me by many witnesses, the same commend to faithful men, who shall be fit to teach others also" (2, 1-2). From these two citations it is clearly enough shown that Paul handed down some things by word only, which he had never put in writing. Then I ask whether the precepts have their force and strength from having been written, or from the intention of the one obliging? If they depend solely on the intention of the one commanding, since spoken words and writings equally bear witness to the intention, why is it that things transmitted by word from one to another do not have the force of obliging as do writings? Perhaps you will say that the same amount of trust ought not to be given to words as ought to be given to writings, for the very reason that they are more quickly and more easily entirely changed, diminished, augmented, and distorted than writings. Be that as it may, but then will words always be distrusted, and no one ever believed, unless they are confirmed by writing? Far be it. For then every human interaction in society would perish: I would not believe that I was born at a certain time, and I would not believe that such a person is my father and such a person is my mother. To believe no one, as well as to believe everyone, is madness.

---

[1] Verses 40 and 41.

[2] Acts 16, 4.

[3] *False Decretals of the Pseudo-Isidore* (PL 130, 15A-20B).

[4] "Wherefore not without cause did Gelasius in Holy Roman canon dist.15 put the *Apostolic Canons* among the apocrypha, which he seems to have done because some of the books were corrupted or added by heretics. Nor is it an obstacle that in canon 2 of the canons called those of the Sixth Synod, 85 of the *Apostolic Canons* are approved; for those canons are not from the true Sixth Synod but from some other Council celebrated later, which the Supreme Pontiff Sergius, who was then seated [on the Roman see], not only did not approve but even rejected, as is clear in Bede in his book, *On the Six Ages*, on Justinian." (St. Robert Bellarmine, *Disputations about Controversies of the Christian Faith* (Book 1, chap. 20).

[5] See footnote n. 29 in chapter 2 above.

Introduction

Are not witnesses very efficacious for proving a matter? "In the mouth of two or three [witnesses]," Christ says: "every word stands."[1] Now who can be a better witness than the Church, who is an eyewitness and having been breathed upon by the Spirit of Truth, cannot be a liar? For we prove that the Church is an eyewitness of those things which she relates, because the Church consists of all the faithful, not only the present ones but also the past ones and those who will come afterwards. Were it otherwise, it would be necessary to make as many churches as ages that have passed by. Nevertheless, the Spouse of the Church Himself clearly opposes this idea saying: "One is my dove, my perfect one is but one" (Cant. 6, 8). And the Apostles writes: "For I have espoused you to one husband that I may present you as a chaste virgin to Christ" (II Cor. 11, 2). He said "virgin" and not "virgins." If therefore she is one, it is necessary that it happen that this same Church which now is, has heard Christ preaching, saw Him dying, offered congratulations to Him rising, saw Him ascending into Heaven, was at the side of the Evangelists and Apostles writing, and assisted them teaching. If therefore the Church is an eyewitness of all these events, she ought to be believed during all ages, since it is certain that she neither wishes to lie nor assert what she does not know.

Furthermore, during the early ages of the nascent Church, when it was first beginning, after having received the Holy Ghost a space of time intervened until the first composition of the Gospel. At which time, no doubt one ought to have believed the Church about things commanded by Christ to be believed or done, even if at that time the Church lacked all protection of Scripture. Will it perhaps be said that the Church's authority is now less than it was then? Or will we reduce the Church into such narrow boundaries, that we may say that she now depends on the testimony of Scripture, who of old nowise so depended? Therefore one must hold fast without any hesitation to the universal traditions and definitions of the Church, even if these are not confirmed by any testimonies of Sacred Scripture, since regarding them the Holy Ghost equally moves the tongue now in speaking about those things upon which our salvation depends, just as of old He moved the hands of the writers to write the Sacred Scriptures.

However, lest I seem to have said these things only led by our reasoning, it is expedient that I will show that this same opinion belonged to any one of the most esteemed men who speak about this matter. Augustine, in his letter to Januarius, which is the fifty fourth in the collection of his letters, says: "As to those other things which we hold on the authority, not of Scripture, but of Tradition, and which are observed throughout the whole world, it may be understood that they are held as approved and instituted either by the Apostles themselves, or by plenary Councils, whose authority in the Church is most useful."[2] Hence, it is most insolent madness to say that these things ought to be disputed. Further, he says in his letter to the priest, Casulanus: "For in those things concerning which the divine Scriptures have laid down no definite rule, the custom of the people of God, or the practices instituted by their fathers, are to be held as law."[3] Therefore, just like transgressors of Divine laws, so despisers of ecclesiastical customs ought to be corrected.

There are very many other testimonies of the same most blessed Father conducive to this premise, perhaps of them all that one is outstanding which he says when writing to the grammarian Cresconius: "Furthermore, although there is no certain example of this thing which can be brought forth from the Scriptures, yet in this very thing do we hold the truth, when we do that which pleases the whole Church, which the authority of the Scriptures themselves commends, that seeing the Sacred Scripture cannot deceive, whosoever fears to be deceived

---

[1] "And in your law it is written, that the testimony of two men is true" (Jn. 8, 17). Cf. Deut. 19, 15 & Mt. 18, 16.

[2] Chapter 1 (PL 33, 200).

[3] Letter 36, chap. 1, n. 2 (PL 33, 136).

Introduction

in the obscurity of this question [whether heretics are to be again baptized], let him consult the same Church concerning it, which the Scripture indicates without any ambiguity."[1]

This is also confirmed by the testimony of John Damascene, who in chapter twelve of fourth book of his book, *On the Orthodox Faith*, when teaching how we ought to adore God towards the East, says: "But this tradition of the Apostles is unwritten. For much that has been handed down to us by Tradition is unwritten."[2] Likewise, also in chapter sixteen of the same book, he says: "But this is an unwritten tradition, just as is also the worshipping towards the East and the worship of the Cross, and very many other similar things."[3]

Origen also supports this view "with might and main" (as it is said). For he says the following in his fifth homily on the book of Numbers: "In the ecclesiastical observances there are some things of this sort, which everyone is obliged to do, and yet not everyone understands the reason for them. For the fact that we kneel to pray, for instance, and that of all the quarters of heavens, the East is the only direction towards which we pour out our prayers, the reasons for this, I think, are not easily discovered by anyone. Moreover, who would readily explain the reasons for the way we receive the Eucharist, or the rite by which it is celebrated, or the things that are done in Baptism, the words, actions, and their order, as well as the questions and answers? And yet, we carry all these things on our shoulders, though they are covered and veiled, when we fulfil them and follow them in such a way that we have received them as handed down and commended by the great High Priest and His sons."[4] You see here how Origen testifies that there are some things which are obligatory for us, even if no reason for them appears from Scripture, but solely from the practice of the Church. And likewise he teaches in the preface of his book, *De Principiis*.[5]

Irenaeus, Bishop and martyr of Leon, and disciple of a martyr,[6] also subscribes to this view, in chapter four of the third book of his *Adversus Haereses*, saying: "Since therefore we have such proofs, it is not necessary to seek the truth among others, which it is easy to obtain from the Church; since the Apostles, like a rich man [depositing his money] in a bank, lodged in her hands most copiously all things pertaining to the truth: so that every man, whosoever will, can draw from her the water of life. For she is the entrance to life; all others are thieves and robbers. On this account are we bound to avoid them, but to make choice of the thing pertaining to the Church with the utmost diligence, and to lay hold of the Tradition of the truth. For how stands the case? Suppose there arise a dispute relative to some important question among us, should we not have recourse to the most ancient churches with which the Apostles held constant intercourse, and learn from them what is certain and clear in regard to the present question? For how should it be if the Apostles themselves had not left us writings? Would it not be necessary [in that case] to follow the course of the Tradition which they handed down to those to whom they did commit the churches?"[7] The authority of this man is of no little importance. As it is well known, besides his holiness and doctrine by which he was influential, he was a disciple of the martyr, Polycarp, concerning whom many historical accounts testify

---

[1] Book I, chap. 33, n. 39 (PL 43, 466).

[2] PG 94, 1135B.

[3] PG 94, 1174A.

[4] N. 1 (PG 12, 603CD).

[5] I.e. *On First Principles*, which is one of the first philosophical expositions of Christian doctrine. "Seeing there are many who think they hold the opinions of Christ, and yet some of these think differently from their predecessors, yet as the teaching of the Church, transmitted in orderly succession from the Apostles, and remaining in the Churches to the present day, is still preserved, that alone is to be accepted as truth which differs in no respect from ecclesiastical and Apostolic tradition" (n. 2 (PG 11, 116B)).

[6] I.e. St. Polycarp.

[7] N. 1 (PG 7, 855BC).

that he was a disciple of John the Evangelist. Therefore let depart John Wycliffe, John Hus, Martin Luther and their accomplices, whom they want to scatter their follies and diminish the Church's authority as much as they wish. For the authority of these highly esteemed men throughout so many centuries would have sufficed for me, even if I had demonstrated no reason above.

Finally, for the complete confirmation, the Council of Trent celebrated under Paul III gave approval for this position, which Council in the fourth session in the first chapter of its decrees published, I being present, the suitable definition concerning this matter, saying the following: "The sacred and holy, ecumenical, and general Synod of Trent,—lawfully assembled in the Holy Ghost, the same three legates of the Apostolic See presiding therein,—keeping this always in view, that, errors being removed, the purity itself of the Gospel be preserved in the Church; which (Gospel), before promised through the Prophets in the holy Scriptures, our Lord Jesus Christ, the Son of God, first promulgated with His own mouth, and then commanded to be preached by His Apostles to every creature, as the fountain of all, both saving truth, and moral discipline; and seeing clearly that this truth and discipline are contained in the written books, and the unwritten traditions which, received by the Apostles from the mouth of Christ Himself, or from the Apostles themselves, the Holy Ghost dictating, have come down even unto us, transmitted as it were from hand to hand; (the Synod) following the examples of the orthodox Fathers, receives and venerates with an equal affection of piety, and reverence, all the books both of the Old and of the New Testament—seeing that one God is the author of both—as also the said traditions, as well those appertaining to faith as to morals, as having been dictated, either by Christ's own word of mouth, or by the Holy Ghost, and preserved in the Catholic Church by a continuous succession." And after these words, the Council lists the books of the whole Sacred Scriptures of both the Old and New Testaments, after having listed them all, immediately adds these words which follow: "But if any one receive not, as sacred and canonical, the said books entire with all their parts, as they have been accustomed to be read in the Catholic Church, and as they are contained in the Old Latin vulgate edition; and knowingly and deliberately contemn the traditions aforesaid; let him be anathema."[1]

Therefore let us affirm in that everything which is either to be believed or done, that one must be obedient to the Church, even if the authority of Scripture were lacking, although this cannot be lacking to her, since the Scriptures themselves give this authority to her. For otherwise how can we assert Mary's perpetual virginity, or say that her Son is consubstantial with the Father, since these things are scarcely found in Sacred Writ? Mary's perpetual virginity, in fact, is never clearly found in Sacred Writ, except perhaps in many figures and allegories, which (as we said in chapter three) hardly suffice for establishing a dogma. The Son's consubstantiality, even if it may be proved from the Gospel, nevertheless never is expressly found in the Gospel. Still we hold both by the Tradition of the universal Church, whose authority is most firm. There are also many other things of this sort which would be laborious to enumerate: even if they are not in Scripture, nevertheless the Church, having been breathed upon by the Holy Ghost deduced some things from the comparison of Scriptures, retained others through words alone passed down from one man to another through so many centuries: regarding which that passage of the Royal Prophet seems to allude: "Like the precious ointment on the head, that ran down upon the beard, the beard of Aaron, Which ran down to the skirt of his garment" (Ps. 132, 2). Just as the words transmitted by Christ the Head unto the Apostles, are again poured out from the Apostles onto His garment, unto the skirt of His garment, that is to say, unto the ends of the Church, which is the seamless coat which heretics attempt to tear apart. Besides which, if nothing ought to be affirmed except what can be proved from express words of Scripture, as Luther says, how can he himself testify that he believes that

---

[1] Dz. 783 & 784.

Introduction

Purgatory exists, since nevertheless he says elsewhere that Purgatory cannot be proved from Holy Writ? But it is not surprising, because Luther very often, just as "a thrush (as it is said in the Proverb), excretes his own trouble."[1]

Chapter VI: That general councils duly assembled sufficiently portray and represent the universal Church: that faith should be shown to the definitions and traditions of these councils which is due to the universal Church.

We have clearly enough shown (as I reckon) that one ought to comply without any hesitation with the traditions and definitions of the universal Church. But someone might perhaps wonder where in the world has the universal Church ever been gathered together to define something, or how can it ever be gathered together, since it is spread throughout the whole world? For there are certain heretics, namely the Wycliffites, the Hussites, and the Lutherans (whose histories we shall relate when we come to each of their heresies below) who, lest they be seen to attack the Church in open battle, deny whatever it has ever decreed, and hence fashion for us a certain invisible church: truly mathematical, abstracted from all perception. Which church, even if it were visible, could never define anything, because since it is spread so widely, by no means (as they say) could it ever be gathered together at the same time to define anything. Because this shield of theirs with which they are defended is very strong, the Church's authority will be consequently relied upon before all else as an objection to them for the reduction, nay I might more truly have said, for the destruction of their shield. For afterwards when we will fight against the heresies individually, the Church's authority will very frequently be for us like a most sharp spear with which we will pierce the heretics. Wherefore so that we may leave no shield for them in this matter with which they can protect themselves, this must be shown first, that the Church is visible and perceivable by men's senses, now often gathered together in some place, and of old often easily brought together.

But before all else it will be necessary to show, according to Aristotle's precept, what the Church is, lest from the matter having been misunderstood, there be a dispute. The Church, concerning which we now treat, which is called militant, is the gathering of all the faithful, which is one body, whose head is Christ: and every one of us are "members one of another" (Rom. 12, 5). For Paul bears witness in his Epistle to the Romans to the fact that we all are one body, whose head is Christ. "For as in one body we have many members, but all the members have not the same office: so we being many, are one body in Christ" (12, 4-5). Again, in his First Epistle to the Corinthians he likewise confirms this, saying: "For as the body is one, and hath many members; and all the members of the body, whereas they are many, yet are one body, so also is Christ. For in one Spirit were we all baptized into one body, whether Jews or Gentiles, whether bond or free" (12, 12-13). You already see how in Paul's opinion all the faithful who were once dedicated to Christ at Baptism, are made one body, whose head is Christ. Now that same body composed of all the faithful is the Church, as Paul likewise testifies in his Epistle to the Ephesians, where speaking of Christ our Redeemer, he says: "And he hath subjected all things under his feet, and hath made him head over all the church, which is his body, and the fulness of him" (1, 22-23). Again, to the Colossians he repeats nearly the

---

[1] In an ironic twist, some birdlime, an adhesive in olden times smeared on a branch (or any place a bird is wont to alight) with the distinct intention of entrapping birds, is created by the birds themselves. That is, by having birds ingest particular ingredients, allowing them to then mature within the stomach of the bird and be subsequently passed out through defecation, a bird can in fact create the very substance used to entrap it and its brethren. Such is the origin of the amusing Latin phrase *Turdus ipse sibi malum cacat*, or "The thrush defecates its own destruction."

same notion: "Fill up those things that are wanting of the sufferings of Christ, in my flesh, for his body, which is the church" (1, 24). Since the faithful individually are like the members of this body which is the Church, and they are visible, perceptible, and apparent to men's eyes, why is it that the Church, which is the whole body, is invisible? For it is not likely or consonant with reason that it be invisible, when all of the parts from which it coalesces are visible and conspicuous.

However, I see that those against whom we speak deny this, since the Head itself, which is Christ (as they themselves affirm), is invisible. But this cavil we will so repulse, such that no room is open for evasion. For whether you speak of Him before the glory of His resurrection, or afterwards, in either case you will find Him through the visible dispensation of assumed flesh. Does not the prophet Baruch say concerning him: "Afterwards he was seen upon earth, and conversed with men" (3, 38)? For if you speak concerning Him when He was liable of sorrows and death, what prohibits Him Who hungered, thirsted, was wearied, was saddened, was crucified, from also being seen? Does not what Isaias says concerning Him refer to that time: "We have seen him [as it were] a leper, and there was no sightlines" (53, 2 & 4). On the other hand, if you say it after He had received the stole of immortality, perhaps you will be convinced by that testimony alone of the Acts of the Apostles. "To whom also he shewed himself alive after his passion, by many proofs, for forty days appearing to them" (1, 3). Now how could He show Himself to the Apostles by many proofs that He had regained His life, unless the Apostles had seen Him? Moreover, did not the disciples going to the town which is called Emmaus (even if their eyes were held that they should not know Him) see Christ? Furthermore, to Thomas previously incredulous, afterwards however believing, the then glorified Head Himself says: "Because thou hast seen me, Thomas, thou hast believed" (Jn. 20, 29). The other fellow disciples say to the same Thomas: "We have seen the Lord" (*ibid.,* verse 25). And Paul in I Corinthians gives testimony concerning the many persons who saw Christ after His resurrection. For he says the following: "He was seen by Cephas; and after that by the eleven. Then he was seen by more than five hundred brethren at once: of whom many remain until this present, and some are fallen asleep. After that, he was seen by James, then by all the apostles" (15, 5-7).

Perhaps you will say, because He contained the rays of His brightness, therefore He was then visible, and He would have been invisible if He had poured out all the brightness of His glorified flesh. That this is false is proved by three witnesses, namely, Peter, James and John (Mt. 17, 1), so that "in the mouth of two or three witnesses every word may stand" (Mt. 18, 16). For these three having been led by Him into the high mountain, "And his face did shine as the sun" (Mt. 17, 2). The disciples thus truly saw Him transfigured. For if they did not see Him, how could they afterwards be witnesses of the event? And if Peter did not see, why therefore having been enticed does he say: "It is good for us to be here" (v. 4). Therefore if Peter and the other two saw Christ transfigured, why is it that we cannot now see Him clothed with the stole of glory, no matter how brightly He shines? For having been transfigured, He gave a certain representation of the future immortality; and in it there was the splendor in which He now sits again at the right hand of the Father. For so says the common Gloss, which is called "Ordinary," on Mark's ninth chapter. "He was in that clarity in which He will be after He shall have carried out the Judgment." And Bede says in the same place: "*Transfigured*: Our Savior then when transfigured did not lose the substance of real flesh, bit showed forth the glory of His own or of our future resurrection; for such as He then appeared to the Apostles, He will after the judgment appear to all His elect."[1] Therefore Christ is the visible Head of the Church at every time: and since concerning other members of the Church there is no one who would doubt they are visible, thence it is concluded that the whole body is visible.

---

[1] *Glossa Ordinaria* (PL 114, 212D); *Catena Aurea* (Mk. 9, 1).

Introduction

Additionally, the same Church is sometimes called a flock, according to that passage of Peter: "Feed the flock of God which is among you" (I Pet. 5, 2). Now the individual sheep of this flock are the individual faithful, whom the Lord entrusts to the same Peter to feed with word and teaching, saying: "Feed my sheep" (Jn. 21, 17). Or how will the shepherd feed the flock which he does not see, and which cannot in any way know him? For just as the shepherd must know the countenance of every one of his animals, so also the whole flock, in order to know how to distinguish his flock from another's flock. Therefore, it is necessary that the flock which ought to be fed by the shepherd be visible to him: and the individual visible members are its body, and its whole body itself must also be visible. For although the faith by which the body itself is united, the charity by which it is vivified, and the Holy Ghost by which it is ruled are all invisible, nevertheless nothing hinders the body from being visible: just as nothing prevents a man from being visible, although the soul, by which his body is animated, is invisible.

But because in matters of faith the testimonies of the sacred pages are more effective (as we said in the second chapter, and as we will discuss below at greater length in the section on "Faith") than all reasons no matter how impelling, therefore for the confirmation of this matter I will give some testimonies that are so clear that, unless malice has already blinded him, one may clearly see those things can be understood save only in respect to the visible Church. When sacred history describes the dedication of the Temple constructed by Solomon, among other things, it says: "The king turned his face, and blessed all the assembly of Israel: for all the assembly (*Ecclesiae*)[1] of Israel stood" (III Kings 8, 14). But if the Assembly [or Church] were invisible, how could Solomon turn his face towards it?

Furthermore, Christ teaching the steps by which fraternal correction ought to proceed, in the third place He orders that one must tell the Church. If, however, the Church is invisible, there is no possible way for someone to recognize the Church in order to denounce something to it.

What Paul admonished the ancients of the church of Ephesus gathered at Miletus agrees with this, as follows: "Take heed to yourselves, and to the whole flock, wherein the Holy Ghost hath placed you bishops, to rule the church of God, which he hath purchased with his own blood" (Acts 20, 28). Now how could a mortal man rule what he can nowise see? Again, Paul in his First Epistle to the Corinthians likewise says: "For I am the least of the apostles, who am not worthy to be called an apostle, because I persecuted the church of God" (15, 9). And once again to the Galatians he says: "For you have heard of my conversation in time past in the Jews' religion: how that, beyond measure, I persecuted the church of God, and wasted it" (1, 13). But it can hardly happen that a bodily persecution, such as that was, could be inflicted on what is invisible. Because if you contend that happened according to what Christ said to the same Paul: "I am Jesus whom thou persecutes" (Acts 9, 5): and yet Paul was not then seeing Jesus, inasmuch as He remains sitting at the right hand of the Father: who does not see that those words were said by Him for the same reason that He had said at another time: "Amen I say to you, as long as you did it to one of these my least brethren, you did it to me" (Mt. 25, 40). Therefore this persecution which Paul declares that he had inflicted upon the Church, Christ complains that He had suffered this same persecution, because it is natural for the head to suffer with the other members of the body.

We think that we have now said enough about this matter with howsoever few words: if perhaps any matters remain which ought to be discussed, they will be discussed in the section on the "Church."

Now let us undertake what remains, namely, let us prove that the Church which we have already shown to be visible, wherever it be gathered together in any place, can sometimes also be gathered together (no matter how widely it may be spread). Now this will be proved suffi-

---

[1] I.e. "Church."

ciently (as I reckon), if we show that a general council duly assembled sufficiently represents the universal Church. For by the same token it will be shown that so often does the universal Church assemble in one place, as often as a general synod of the Church shall have been duly assembled. Now, if the testimony of a council itself on this matter suffices, we will quickly prove our assertion, that a general council represents the universal Church. For indeed the Council of Constance, which without doubt was gathered in the Holy Ghost, decreed as a conclusion of the event, among other things which were defined during the fourth session, that: "First, that this synod, legitimately assembled in the holy Spirit, constituting a general council, representing the Catholic Church militant, has power immediately from Christ, and that everyone of whatever state or dignity, even papal, is bound to obey it in those matters which pertain to the faith and the eradication of the said schism."[1] Behold, you see how the Council of Constance bears witness that it represents the Catholic Church militant.

However, I know that there are not lacking those who object to this testimony, the same which the Pharisees objected to Christ: "Thou givest testimony of thyself: thy testimony is not true" (Jn. 8, 13). To whom the Council can rightly likewise reply that which Christ replied to the same Pharisees: "Although I give testimony of myself, my testimony is true: for I know whence I came, and whither I go: but you know not whence I come, or whither I go. You judge according to the flesh: I judge not any man. And if I do judge, my judgment is true: because I am not alone, but I and the Father that sent me" (*Ibid.*, verse 14-16). Now the Council could say: "I, and the Holy Ghost who teaches me, who brings to our mind all truth[2]... 'And in your law it is written, that the testimony of two men is true' (v. 17)." But even if these things do not convince the adversary, nevertheless they can well teach the disposition of our mind.

---

[1] This quotation here has been revised according to the chief collection of the Acts of the council and pertinent documents compiled by Hermann Von Der Hardt (*Magnum oecumenicum Constantiense concilium* (Frankfurt, Officina Christiani Genschius, 1697), Vol. iv, p. 88). "This council was summoned by John XXIII, the Pisan pope, with the support of Emperor Sigismund. It began on 5 November 1414 in the cathedral of Constance, with many bishops from all parts of Europe. Business in the council was transacted in a way that was largely new for an ecumenical council, namely, votes were cast not by individual persons but by nations. The council, from the very beginning, proposed the following three topics:
1. To bring unity back to the church and to make an end to the schism which had divided the church since 1378 and which the council held at Pisa in 1409 had not healed but rather aggravated when it elected Alexander V as a third pope. When the council of Constance opened, Christians owed obedience to three different popes: some owed obedience to Gregory XII of the Roman party, others to Benedict XIII of the Avignon party, and others to John XXIII, who had been elected after the death of Alexander V. John XXIII and Benedict XIII were deposed by the council, Gregory XII voluntarily resigned. Then Martin V was elected pope on 11 November 1417 and he was regarded as the legitimate pontiff by the church as a whole.
2. To eradicate heresies, especially those spread by John Wycliffe in Britain and by John Hus and Jerome of Prague in Bohemia.
3. To reform the corrupt morals of the church. This, however, was only partly accomplished in the final sessions of the council.
With regard to the ecumenical nature of the sessions, there is dispute about those before the election of Martin V and also about the significance and force of the approval which he gave to the matters transacted by the council. The decrees notably those of sessions 3-5 and the decree *Frequens* (session 39), appear to proceed from the Council's teaching. Objection has been made to them on the grounds of the primacy of the Roman pontiff. There is no doubt, however, that in enacting these decrees there was solicitude and care to choose the true and sure way ahead in order to heal the schism, and this could only be done by the authority of a council." (Tanner, *Decrees of the Ecumenical Councils* (Washington, D.C., Georgetown University Press, 1990), vol. 1, p. 1155).

[2] Cf. Jn. 14, 26.

Introduction

Therefore, we will reinforce our assertion otherwise. Firstly [we will do so] as follows, namely, that we discover that in the common and universal speech used by men, as often as all the leading men of some republic, to whom right of judging is entrusted by the people, gather in any place, we may say that the republic is gathered together, because all else depends on them. In this way when all the bishops, whom alone God has placed to rule His Church, assemble, it is then called the Christian republic, that is, the assembled Catholic Church. This is clearly shown in that passage from III Kings, which we applied above to a different matter. For after that sacred history described the magnificent construction of the Temple, it says the following: "Then all the ancients of Israel with the princes of the tribes, and the heads of the families of the children of Israel were assembled to king Solomon in Jerusalem: that they might carry the ark of the covenant of the Lord out of the city of David, that is, out of Sion" (8, 1). And after it had said that the ark was brought into the oracle of the Temple, it adds: "And the king turned his face, and blessed all the assembly (*omni ecclesiae*) of Israel: for all the assembly (*omnis ecclesia*) of Israel stood" (v. 14). From which passage it is clearly established that that assembly in which were gathered the ancients of Israel, the princes of the tribes, and the heads of the families is twice called the whole Church (*omnis ecclesia*).

Again, when the Council of Jerusalem was assembled to decide that important question, namely, whether prescriptions of the Law were to be observed along with the Gospel, after it said that the Apostles and the ancients had come together to consider this matter, and decided on the issue, it says: "Then it pleased the apostles and ancients, with the whole church (*omni ecclesia*), to choose men of their own company, and to send to Antioch" (Acts 15, 22). You again see here that assembly of the Apostles and ancients is being called the universal Church. Blessed Gregory likewise asserts this, who speaking concerning those four illustrious councils—and they have never been praised enough, namely, the First Council of Nicea, the First Council of Constantinople, the Council of Ephesus, and the Council of Chalcedon, also being the first—says the following: "But all persons whom the aforesaid venerable Councils repudiate I repudiate; those whom they venerate I embrace; since, they having been constituted by universal consent, he overthrows not them but himself, whosoever presumes either to loose those whom they bind, or to bind those whom they loose."[1]

Notice how Gregory asserts that the decrees in the councils are established with universal consent: which would hardly be true, unless the same most Blessed Father were to hold that a general council represents the universal Church: especially since the characteristic function of prelates is to teach, which hardly pertains to their subjects. For only to prelates is it said: "Feed the flock of God which is among you" (I Pet. 5, 2). And when Peter was chosen instead of the other Apostles, Christ said nothing other than "Feed my sheep" (Jn. 21, 17). Therefore it belongs to prelates to teach and command, but it belongs to subjects to learn and obey. A shepherd ought to feed the sheep, but it belongs to the sheep simply to be fed. For the prophet Malachias testifies this, who says: "For the lips of the priest shall keep knowledge, and they shall seek the law at his mouth: because he is the angel of the Lord of hosts" (Mal. 2, 7). If therefore priests are the ones from whom knowledge is sought, and the subjects are not: it will not be necessary that the subjects be summoned with the prelates to a council, which is for discussing some matter. Furthermore, if you say that all the subjects are members of this body, and thus ought to be summoned at the same time with the prelates, this is answered by what Paul says in his First Epistle to the Corinthians: "And if the ear should say, because I am not the eye, I am not of the body; is it therefore not of the body? If the whole body were the eye, where would be the hearing?" (12, 16-17). If indeed prelates, whose role is to teach and govern, fulfill the function of eyes, because they see for the other members, and they direct those things that the mind wanted; subjects, to whom it belongs to obey, exercise the function

---

[1] Book 1, letter 25 (*To John, Bishop of Constantinople, and the Other Patriarchs*). (PL 77, 478C).

of the ears, through which any doctrine and the faith are had. For "Faith cometh by hearing" (Rom. 10, 17). The subjects, because it is not allotted to them in the body, are not therefore excluded from the body, in that they are not admitted to that [teaching] office. Do we not say that a human body sees if its eyes see, even though the other members do not see? Will we then say that the body does not hear, because many members of the body do not hear, although the ears duly carry out the work committed it them? For then the whole body truly is said to execute it, when its member does what is incumbent upon it according to its function. Hence, we consequently may infer that the Church, which is one body, defines something when all those to whom it pertains are gathered together, and in agreement decree it. But when they are all summoned to a general council, it follows that we may say that the general council represents the universal Church in that matter to be defined, since they do what is recognized as pertaining to no one else.

But if perhaps you still contend that all the faithful ought to be summoned to that council, in which something concerning the faith is to be defined, we will challenge it will such clear testimonies of Scripture that no scruple will urge any longer. For the first council assembled by the Apostles is described in Acts 6. "And in those days, the number of the disciples increasing, there arose a murmuring of the Greeks against the Hebrews, for that their widows were neglected in the daily ministration. Then the twelve calling together the multitude of the disciples, said: It is not reason that we should leave the word of God, and serve tables. Wherefore, brethren, look ye out among you" etc. (v. 1-3). You see in this passage that the people or the common crowd, are nowise summoned, but simply the group of the disciples. Now what proves our assertion more effectively is what is written in chapter fifteen of the same book, in which a living image of the councils is described for us. For is it said as follows: "And some coming down from Judea, taught the brethren: That except you be circumcised after the manner of Moses, you cannot be saved. And when Paul and Barnabas had no small contest with them, they determined that Paul and Barnabas, and certain others of the other side, should go up to the apostles and priests to Jerusalem about this question" (v. 1-2). And a little further on it is said: "And the apostles and ancients assembled to consider of this matter" (v. 6). Finally, after they had looked into the matter, a decision was made by the Apostles and the ancients in this manner: "For it hath seemed good to the Holy Ghost and to us, to lay no further burden upon you than these necessary things: that you abstain from things sacrificed to idols, and from blood, and from things strangled, and from fornication; from which things keeping yourselves, you shall do well" (v. 28-29). Behold the clear model for celebrating a council: from which, in the passage of time, once the Church was freed from the persecution of tyrants, the other general councils took this manner and form for their celebration. Nevertheless, you nowise see in this passage the whole multitude of the Christian people called together, but only the Apostles and ancients came together, and having made a careful investigation from the comparison of the Scriptures, they made a judgment, which has been embraced by the Catholic Church until the present day. If, therefore, it was not necessary to summon a crowd of the common people for defining something about the faith, but only the ancients of the Church, because they are the ones who are concerned with defining the matter, and who represent the universal Church in treating the matter, it follows that a general council, to which the all leaders of the Church are summoned, also represents the universal Church. From which also it is surmised that the traditions of the general councils duly assembled, as emanating from the universal Church, ought to be accepted by all.

Furthermore, if general councils nowise represent the Church, and thus the power of deciding in matters of faith is arrogated by them, then absolutely everything in the Church will be ambiguous, and there will be no means whereby heresies can be extirpated. Nay, it would suggest inexhaustible material for attacking the faith, and it would allow anyone to stir up

Introduction

new heresies, or resurrect buried ones. For unless the public definition of the Nicene Council had assisted against Arius; and that of Constantinople against Eunomius and Macedonius; and that of Ephesus against Nestorius; and that of Chalcedon against Eutyches; their heresies would still be alive, and there would not have been lacking those who would serve as soldiers under their authors, since whatever would be objected to them from Scripture, they would distort by a depraved interpretation into another meaning. For it was done for this reason, so that at that time when the Church underwent the fury of tyrants, Christendom was divided into the splits of many heresies: namely, because the Catholic bishops had not been able to assemble together until the time of Constantine, from which time councils began to be assembled, due to the frequentation of which many heresies were countered. Again, we read this concerning the children of Israel, that when any matter of doubt arose among them, it was referred to Moses, so that he might decide on it. Then when Moses went up into the mountain to receive the Law, if perchance something would have arisen in the meantime, he provided a remedy. "If thou perceive that there be among you a hard and doubtful matter in judgment between blood and blood, cause and cause, leprosy and leprosy: and thou see that the words of the judges within thy gates do vary: arise, and go up to the place, which the Lord thy God shall choose. And thou shalt come to the priests of the Levitical race, and to the judge, that shall be at that time: and thou shalt ask of them, and they shall shew thee the truth of the judgment. And thou shalt do whatsoever they shall say, that preside in the place, which the Lord shall choose, and what they shall teach thee, according to his law; and thou shalt follow their sentence: neither shalt thou decline to the right hand nor to the left hand" (Deut. 17, 8-11). You see, therefore, that a doubtful question nowise ought to be brought before the people, or to kings or leaders, but to the priests of the race of Levi, whose decree he commands [them] to obey.

You also see how much God looks out for the synagogue, Who provides a remedy for it in every eventuality. For He well suggests this through the prophet Isaias, saying: "What is there that I ought to do more to my vineyard, that I have not done to it?" (Is. 5, 4). What then do you think that He has done for His Church? Should it be believed that He provided for the Church to the same extent as the synagogue: nay much more, since another prophet says concerning it: "Great shall be the glory of this last house more than of the first, saith the Lord of hosts: and in this place I will give peace" (Aggeus 2, 10). Therefore it ought to be said, just as it was explained concerning the old Fathers: "If anyone perceive that there be a hard and doubtful matter in judgment" (Deut. 17, 8) let him come to the chief men of the Church, who, after having assembled a council and thoroughly considered the matter, will teach it according to God's law, and their opinion shall be followed, not deviating to the right or to the left.

Hence, it is clear with how much vain labor was the Carmelite Guido wearied, who in his first book, *On the Heresies*,[1] betook himself to proving the things which were defined in those four first Councils: in which manner it behooved him also to prove all that was decreed in the rest of the Councils: which work would have been immense. Wherefore it would have been more advisable to prove the authority of the Councils and their certitude in defining: which when done, all the definitions of the Councils are strengthened in a short way.

Chapter VII: That the writings of however many holy men do not suffice for refuting heresy.

Up until this point we have discussed heresy and those things whereby heresy can be disproved: although in fact there are many men who have other, ever so deceptive gnomons, nowise reliable for carrying out that function. Nevertheless, they choose them for examining

---

[1] Guido Terreni wrote his *Summa de haeresibus*, between 1340 and 1342 when he was Bishop of Elne. He was a stanch defender of papal infallibility.

all assertions of heresy, and thus they very easily make pronouncements regarding heresy, having absolutely no reason with which to successfully prove it. For there are also many who so strive by means of the writings of certain men, that if perhaps they would see anyone who deviates even with a finger turned away from their opinion (I speak as an eyewitness) they immediately cry out heresy. Wherefore it is also necessary to show this, namely, that no writing of any man, no matter who learned and also no matter how holy, is effective for disproving heresy, unless it were established that it is derived from the testimony of Sacred Scripture or from the Church's definition.

Now anyone will easily examine this, if firstly he consider within himself, what kind of testimony is necessary to oblige us to believe something. For that alone will be effective for repulsing whatever one clearly identifies to be opposed to the faith. But because a testimony of this kind makes us liable to some credulity, it is necessary that it be had from a person of whom it be evident that he can neither deceive, nor wish to deceive. Because if he can be deceived or deceive, one will reject any testimony of his, without injury to the faith or stain of heresy: for it will immediately be supposed that he was deceived in that matter, or he wanted to deceive: because both of these could happen. For what prevents us from saying that which is false, just like him who can be deceived? But every man, due to the sin of our first parents, bears a weakened nature so that he can hardly fathom the true nature of things, hence it is that he is often deceived in judging. For among the inconveniences which we suffer in this life (as Augustine testifies) is our faulty judgment: And so the prophet said: "Every man is a liar" (Ps. 115, 11): and (as it is said in the proverb) "Sometimes even good Homer nods off."[1]

Hence, it is not right, or consonant with reason, that we be bound under threat of Hell to believe him who either is deceived or can be deceived, as is any ordinary man. For it would follow that it would very often happen that we would be held to accept something false as being true, and something true as being false: which is unlawful. Furthermore, since often there is no agreement between very learned and holy men concerning the same matter, it will be necessary to forsake one of them, and yet with no injury to the faith or mark of heresy, since it can nowise happen that someone assent to opposite assertions conflicting with each other. Jerome says that Paul only reprehended Peter in appearance and not really.[2] Augustine, how-

---

[1] This proverb is derived from the quote by Horace in *Ars Poetica* (line 359; c. 18 BC), *indignor quandoque bonus dormitat Homerus* ("I become annoyed when the great Homer is being drowsy").
[2] *Commentarioum in Epistolam ad Galatas*, bk. 1, chap. 2 (PL 26, 338C-342C) Cf. Letter 75 (to Augustine), chap. 2, n. 3-11 (PL 33, 252-257).

Introduction -41-

ever, says that Peter was truly and rightly reprehended by Paul.[1] Jerome[2] says that he who had two wives before baptism, after having received baptism can be promoted to the priesthood: which assertion Ambrose,[3] Augustine[4] and all others oppose. Augustine says that the fabric of the whole world was put together at one and the same moment of time as the varieties of natures,[5] and he allows absolutely so succession of time in that affair, but that series of days

---

[1] "I have been reading also some writings, ascribed to you, on the Epistles of the Apostle Paul. In reading your exposition of the Epistle to the Galatians, that passage came to my hand in which the Apostle Peter is called back from a course of dangerous dissimulation. To find there the defense of falsehood undertaken, whether by you, a man of such weight, or by any author (if it is the writing of another), causes me, I must confess, great sorrow, until at least those things which decide my opinion in the matter are refuted, if indeed they admit of refutation" etc. (Letter 28 (to Jerome), chap. 3, n. 3-5 (PL 33, 112-114)). "According to Jerome, Peter withdrew himself from the Gentiles by pretense, in order to avoid giving scandal to the Jews, of whom he was the Apostle. Hence he did not sin at all in acting thus. On the other hand, Paul in like manner made a pretense of blaming him, in order to avoid scandalizing the Gentiles, whose Apostle he was. But Augustine disapproves of this solution: because in the canonical Scripture (viz. Galatians 2:11), wherein we must not hold anything to be false, Paul says that Peter 'was to be blamed.' Consequently it is true that Peter was at fault: and Paul blamed him in very truth and not with pretense. Peter, however, did not sin, by observing the legal ceremonial for the time being; because this was lawful for him who was a converted Jew. But he did sin by excessive minuteness in the observance of the legal rites lest he should scandalize the Jews, the result being that he gave scandal to the Gentiles" (Aquinas, *Summa Theologiae*, I-II, q. 103, a. 4 ad 2um).

[2] Letter 69 (to Oceanus) (PL 22, 653-664). "Oceanus, a Roman nobleman zealous for the faith, had asked Jerome to back him in a protest against Carterius, a Spanish bishop who, contrary to the apostolic rule that a bishop is to be "the husband of one wife," had married a second time. Jerome refuses to take the line suggested on the ground that Carterius's first marriage having preceded his baptism cannot be taken into account. He therefore advises Oceanus to let the matter drop. The date of the letter is 397 A.D." (Introduction by Hon. William Henry Fremantle quoted in *A Select Library of the Nicene and Post-Nicene Fathers of the Christian Church*, second series, vol. 6). "St. Jerome further seems to speak of a custom generally observed when he declares that clerics, 'even though they may have wives, cease to be husbands.'" ("Celibacy of the Clergy," *Catholic Encyclopedia (1908 ed.), vol. 3, p. 484*).

[3] "And I have thought it well not to pass by this point, because many contend that having one wife is said of the time after Baptism; so that the fault whereby any obstacle would ensue would be washed away in Baptism. And indeed all faults and sins are washed away; so that if anyone have polluted his body with very many whom he has bound to himself by no law of marriage, all the sins are forgiven him, but if anyone have contracted a second marriage it is not done away; for sin, not law, is loosed by the laver, and as to baptism there is no sin, but law. That, then, which has to do with law is not remitted as though it were sin, but is retained. And the Apostle has established a law, saying: 'If any man be without reproach, the husband of one wife'(I Tim. 3:2). So then he who is without blame the husband of one wife comes within the rule for undertaking the priestly office; he, however, who has married again has no guilt of pollution, but is disqualified for the priestly prerogative." (Letter 63 (to the Church of Vercellæ), n. 63 (PL 13, 1206A)).

[4] "But since out of many souls there shall be hereafter one City of such as have one soul and one heart towards God; which perfection of our unity shall be hereafter, after this sojourn in a strange land, wherein the thoughts of all shall neither be hidden one from another, nor shall be in any matter opposed one to another; on this account the sacrament of Marriage of our time has been so reduced to one man and one wife, as that it is not lawful to ordain any as a steward of the Church, save the husband of one wife. And this they have understood more acutely who have been of opinion, that neither is he to be ordained, who as a catechumen or as a heathen had a second wife" (*Of the Good of Marriage*, chap. 18, n. 21 (PL 40, 387)).

[5] "On this question Augustine differs from other expositors. His opinion is that all the days that are called seven, are one day represented in a sevenfold aspect (*Gen. ad lit.* iv, 22; *De Civ. Dei* xi, 9; *Ad Orosium* xxvi); while others consider there were seven distinct days, not one only" (I, q. 74, a.2).

is interpreted as the alternations of angelic thoughts.[1] Which interpretation is contradicted so much, that I have never seen anyone of the sacred writers who agrees with him on this matter. There are also many other examples of this kind.

Therefore, who will be so mad that he would brand the mark of heresy on him who wants to embrace either side of these assertions, because it would oppose some sacred Doctor? Therefore calling something heresy because it opposes some sayings of the saints will never be anything short of temerity, provided that it does not oppose Sacred Scripture or a definition of the Church. Hence, Augustin in his letter to Jerome, which is the eighty-second in the list of his letters, says the following: "For I confess to your Charity that I have learned to yield this respect and honor only to the canonical books of Scripture: of these alone do I most firmly believe that the authors were completely free from error. And if in these writings I am perplexed by anything which appears to me opposed to truth, I do not hesitate to suppose that either the manuscript is faulty, or the translator has not caught the meaning of what was said, or I myself have failed to understand it. As to all other writings, in reading them, however great the superiority of the authors to myself in sanctity and learning, I do not accept their teaching as true on the mere ground of the opinion being held by them; but only because they have succeeded in convincing my judgment of its truth either by means of these canonical writings themselves, or by arguments addressed to my reason. I believe, my brother, that this is your own opinion as well as mine. I do not need to say that I do not suppose you to wish your books to be read like those of the Prophets or of the Apostles, concerning which it would be wrong to doubt that they are free from error. Far be such arrogance from that humble piety and just estimate of yourself which I know you to have." [2]

Hence, I confess that I am not able to restrain my anger whenever I see some men to be so supportive of the writing of some men, that they assert that it is irreverent if someone deviates even in the least point from their opinion. For they want that the writings of men be received as oracles of a deity, and that honor to be shown to them which is owed to Sacred Writ alone. For we have not sworn on man's words, but on God's words. For I would call this miserable servitude, to be so devoted to human opinion that it would not be permitted to oppose it in any way: those who subject themselves so much to the sayings of Blessed Thomas, or of Scotus, or of Ockham suffer such [misery], so that from their opinions, to which they seem to have sworn, they choose names, some called Thomists,[3] others Scotists, and other Ockhamists. Paul indeed commanded us to captivate our intellect, but in service to Christ, not in service to man. Hence, it is that those who so lightly pronounce concerning heresy, not thinking about what they say, are often struck by their own arrows and fall into the pit which they prepared for others.

For to reckon human writings among those of the Divine order, would I not have called this more truly heresy: namely, what they do who assert that it is just as irreverent to dissent from human writings as from Divine writings? I have seen such persons to have descended to such madness, that they are unafraid to pour forth these words in a public sermon: "Whoever deviates from the opinion of Blessed Thomas, ought to be deemed suspect of heresy." O strong men of God's word, nay, I would have said more truly, O preachers of Thomas's words.

---

[1] "Moreover, angelic knowledge is appropriately called 'day,' since light, the cause of day, is to be found in spiritual things, as Augustine observes (*Gen. ad lit.* iv, 28). In the opinion of the others, however, the days signify a succession both in time, and in the things produced" (*Ibid*).

[2] Chap. 1, n. 3 (PL 33, 277).

[3] "We admonish professors to bear well in mind that they cannot set aside St. Thomas, especially in metaphysical questions, without grave disadvantage" (Pope St. Pius X (1903-1914), *Pascendi Dominici Gregis*, September 8, 1907). The 1917 Code of Canon Law considered St. Thomas Aquinas to be the teacher for philosophy and theology in Catholic seminaries (CIC 589, 1366).

Introduction

Therefore will Blessed Bonaventure be considered suspect of heresy, because he deviates from Blessed Thomas in many things? Therefore will Blessed Anselm be called suspected of heresy, because contrary to the opinion of Blessed Thomas, he does not consider one a lover of the Virgin who refuses to celebrate the feast of her Conception?

And yet I would not want these words said by me [to be taken] in such a way that someone think that I, by these words of mine, would want to hurt all the men of that [Dominican] Institute or Order. For I have known many learned, wise, and truly pious men among them, with which things they are very displeased when these things are done, or when they are said by the unlearned as generally happens. For it also greatly displeases me, that also our community [of Franciscans] seems nearly to have sworn on the words of Scotus. I in fact venerate the holiness of Blessed Thomas, I concede much to his teaching, because it has enlightened the Church very much: yet I do not think that he should be so followed that it is necessary to agree with him in everything. And I would never have believed concerning Blessed Thomas' humility that he would want anyone to be so devoted to his words, since he himself was not so devoted to them, that he would not be ready to submit to one expressing better words.[1] For he often withdrew his own opinion. For in fact Blessed Augustine wishes the reader of his works not to be completely given up to his words. For so he says in chapter one of the third book of his *On the Trinity*: "Assuredly, as in all my writings I desire not only a pious reader, but also a free corrector, so I especially desire this in the present inquiry, which is so important that I would there were as many inquirers as there are objectors. But as I do not wish my reader to be bound down to me, so I do not wish my corrector to be bound down to himself. Let not the former love me more than the Catholic faith, let not the latter love himself more than the Catholic verity. As I say to the former, 'Do not be willing to yield to my writings as to the canonical Scriptures; but in these, when you have discovered even what you did not previously believe, believe it unhesitatingly; while in those, unless you have understood with certainty what you did not before hold as certain, be unwilling to hold it fast': so I say to the latter, 'Do not be willing to correct my writings from your own opinion or disputation, but from the Divine text, or from unanswerable reason.'"[2]

But what the glossator on the book of the *Decretals* says ought not to be passed over here, so that on this account we may at least take pity on his ineptness or laugh at his audacity. Whom, when accurately expounding on this cited quotation of Augustine, which is found in that book, distinction nine, in the chapter beginning with the word *Noli*, says the following: "This is said according to those times when the writings of Augustine and of other holy Fathers were not authentic, but today they are commanded to be kept to the least iota, as will be said below in distinction fifteen in the last chapter."[3] Who can now forebear that a man so clearly false be not pursued who in which book, in the last chapter of distinction fifteen, orders that the words of the holy Fathers ought to be upheld to the last iota? Or how can this be commanded, when the opinions of the holy Fathers often (as we showed above) oppose each other? God certainly cannot command contradictory things, so long as there is no command of the pope. Because if all the words of the holy Fathers to the last iota are commanded to be upheld, who does not see for this reason that contradictory things are commanded, since their opinions contradict each other. See what the glossators are like, in whom such trust is given. For now even by this argument alone it is clearly true what John Duns Scotus hurls against this glossator, saying: "They proclaim and disclaim, and yet nothing addresses the

---

[1] "Sacred doctrine makes use of these authorities as extrinsic and probable arguments; but properly uses the authority of the canonical Scriptures as an incontrovertible proof, and the authority of the doctors of the Church as one that may properly be used, yet merely as probable" (I q.1, a. 8 ad 2um).

[2] N. 2 (PL 42, 869).

[3] Juan de Torquemada (cardinal), *In Gratiani Decretum commentarii*.

point." But I know from whence the good man gets the springboard of his error. For in that last chapter of distinction fifteenth, Pope Galasius, whose decree that is, reviewing the books of Catholic men which can be read, mentions the Sovereign Pontiff Leo's letter to Flavian, in commendation of which he adds such words as follows: "If anyone disputes even one iota of whose text, and does not honorably receive it in all things, let him be anathema." The good glossator, hardly looking into the matter, thought that what it said in that letter alone ought to be applied to all the books listed.

Now how much he is deceived, one who actually knows grammar well will detect. We may conclude that the writings of the holy doctors of the Church are not to be so received that it is not free for us to think otherwise than they thought, especially since they do not agree among themselves, or on what other grounds their assertion may be established. But because in the same letter Pope Galasius approves the writings of very many holy men, it should thus be understood that we may infer for this reason that it is proved that they nowise oppose the Catholic faith, namely, that nothing may be found in their writings which deviates from the orthodox faith: nevertheless not as though all their words ought to be received as law. For there are many things which, even if they do not oppose the faith, nevertheless the Catholic faith does not oblige us to believe them. For example, that Heaven has matter very similar to this lower world is neither opposed to the Catholic faith, nor is the Catholic faith, but everyone is free to embrace the opinion that he wishes. So also those works of the holy men which are approved by Pope Gelasius, or any other work approved by any sovereign pontiff in the past, are approved as agreeing with the Catholic faith, namely, because they nowise deviate from it. Yet they are not passed on to us as being the Catholic faith, or commanded to be received by us as the faith, by that pontifical decree. Therefore one need not so tenaciously adhere to the writings of any man, possessing no matter how much holiness and learning, that when there is good reason, one would not be permitted to deviate.

Still, for this reason the words of illustrious men who have been approved for many centuries should not be rejected or deemed to be of no account. For this would pertain to great audacity and pride, which in our calamitous times the Lutherans show themselves to have, and in the past the Wycliffites have shown, and long ago Peter Abelard, as Blessed Bernard bears witness in his letter one hundred ninety.[1] For they were not ashamed, nor are they ashamed, to oppose the words of all the saints. For if objections are made to them from testimonies of any illustrious man, also no matter how holy, they immediately proclaim: "They are men like us." I admit that they are men, nevertheless is a man preeminent to another man in nothing? Does not an intelligent man differ from a foolish man in something? Is there not some order between a profane man and a saint? See what the prophet Ezechiel reprehends: "They have put no difference," he says: "between holy and profane: nor have distinguished" (22, 26). Certainly an account of the life as well as of the teaching ought to be considered, because (as Ecclesiasticus says) "The soul of a holy man discovereth sometimes true things, more than seven watchmen that sit in a high piece to watch." And Blessed John says in his Epistle: "His unction teacheth you of all things" (I Jn. 2, 27).

Also something ought to be taken into account regarding antiquity, not because I would want an estimation of things taken from years alone, because this is very foolish since it would be necessary by this law also to sanction vices which are found to be very old: but [antiquity ought to be taken into account] because when antiquity of life and doctrine are added, they produce a great weight. For he who despises a man praised for many centuries, by that very fact seems to despise all those by whom he was praised, and was held in esteem.

---

[1] "But you do not accept the Doctors since the Apostles, because you perceive yourself to be a man above all teachers. For example, you do not blush to say that all are against you, when they all agree together." (Chap. 5, n. 12 (PL 182, 1063D)).

Introduction

If therefore so much is bestowed upon a learned and at the same time holy man, and approved through many centuries, so that short of shamelessness it would not be permitted, unless prevailed upon by a reason, and this with reverence, to abandon him, how much weight should be given to all those agreeing on the same point? It certainly then would be temerarious to disagree with all, when there is agreement among them all about the same matter.

For even if they could err and stumble in some things, as they are men: still I will never believe that they unanimously erred in difficult matters pertaining to the faith: because this is greatly opposed to Christ's promise and the perpetual presence of the Spirit. For the words of Christ Himself are these: "I will ask the Father: and he shall give you another Paraclete, that he may abide with you for ever" (Jn. 14, 16). And afterwards: "But the Paraclete, the Holy Ghost, whom the Father will send in my name, he will teach you all things and bring all things to your mind, whatsoever I shall have said to you" (v. 26). If you say that these words ought to be referred to the Apostles alone, how will it be true what is said, "that he may abide with you for ever"? Or why does He promise these things to the Apostles? Is it for the Apostles' own sakes? Certainly not, but for the sake of the Church, which then was being enlightened by the Apostles. Since the Church now is the same which was then, and since she does not need the Spirit as her Enlightener any less now than then, these things were said for the sake of the Church, and those promises were made so that teachers may be given by God to the Church at all times. The Holy Ghost thoroughly teaches them all things necessary for salvation, and He brings to their minds the interpretation of those things which Christ said, so that by the interpretations of these teachers the Church may be enlightened: and in this way it will happen that the Spirit abides in her forever: which the Apostle clearly shows, saying: "And he gave some apostles, and some prophets, and other some evangelists, and other some pastors and doctors" (Eph. 4, 11). Notice how Paul testifies that besides Apostles the Lord gave doctors and prophets. Now Blessed Ambrose declares that prophets are interpreters of Sacred Writ.

But if Luther denies this, he cannot deny concerning the doctors that [the Apostle] said were given by God to the Church. Now for what purpose He gave them, the Apostle himself declares, adding: "That henceforth we be no more children tossed to and fro and carried about with every wind of doctrine, by the wickedness of men, by cunning craftiness by which they lie in wait to deceive. But doing the truth in charity, we may in all things grow up in him who is the head, even Christ" (v. 4, 14-15). If, therefore, they were given so that we may no more be carried about with every wind of doctrine by which they lie in wait to deceive, it is not possible that all who were sent so that we would not err, would have erred at the same time. Wherefore even if it be permitted to oppose one or another of the sacred doctors, nevertheless it will nowise be permitted to contradict them all when they are in agreement about the same matter. Hence it is that an agreement of the sacred doctors, both present and past, concerning the judgment of some matter is an equally effective argument for refuting heresy as a definition of the Church assembled in a council, because it is in no way believable that God would permit them all to err: nay, it is not believable that they would arrive at one and the same opinion unless they had been thoroughly taught by the Holy Ghost as the one Teacher of them all.

With this argument, Blessed Augustine in chapter forty-one of book eighteen of his *City of God*[1] proves the truthfulness of Sacred Scripture against the heathens: because in the numerous multitude of philosophers scarcely one or another teaching will be found (being clear exceptions) upon which they all agree. For even if the later ones have read the writings of their predecessors, nevertheless they disdain to agree with them. Hence it happened that the disciples of the prior philosophers fought among themselves, and having little esteemed the teaching of their masters, endeavored to teach their own doctrines, whereby each one could be seen to be wiser and more intelligent. Aristotle departed from Plato, Plato from Socrates, and

---

[1] N. 1-3 (PL 41, 600-602).

Socrates from Pythagoras. Now one should not reckon that the fact that the disciples opposed their teachers, and the disciples competed against each other, was due to any other reason besides the fact that they were led by their own haughty spirit.

Wherefore, except for that one Sacred Spirit, which everywhere and always has moved and taught the minds of the saints, it could nowise have happened that they would share the same opinion about anything, especially when many of those living at the same time were separated by great distances, and were divided by their languages, and so would hardly have read each other's books: but the Divine Spirit bringing [the correct meaning of revelation] to their minds, they subscribed to the same opinion. Therefore, when there is ardent unanimity of opinion among all the sacred doctors on any matter, which was never contradicted without punishment by the Church or by other Catholic men, this unanimity of opinion must be held as a true explanation of the Church, and ought to be most firmly believed as the Church's explanation: because the body of the Church is one, made up of the people and the Fathers.

I call the "Fathers" the bishops, pontiffs and all other prelates and teachers, or doctors, who teaching the faith well, beget us spiritually. It pertains to these Fathers to teach the people, among whom some, namely the prelates, are bound to do this by their office, while others are motivated by charity to do this, just like the other doctors and teachers. Now it does not pertain to the rest of the people to teach. For (as the Apostle says) "there are diversities of graces, but the same Spirit... Are all apostles? Are all prophets? Are all doctors?" (I Cor. 12, 29). Therefore if it be established that the men to whom it pertains to teach in the Church have taught some particular assertion without contradiction, such an assertion will doubtlessly be, as it were, Catholic, even if a citation from Scripture for its proof be lacking. For that which all agree to, even if they are far apart by place or time, must be deemed the faith of the whole Church. For the faith is not from the people, but from the Fathers. Therefore that must be judged to be Catholic faith which all the Fathers pass down, because the word "Catholic' in Greek means "universal" in Latin.

Now this was expressly inferred from the third council, which is one of the four to which Blessed Pope Gregory bears witness that they are received as the four Gospels. For that council, which is the First Council of Ephesus, in the letter from the whole council addressed to the heretic Nestorius (which was placed as a decree of the said council), says the following: "But it would not be sufficient for your reverence to confess with us only the symbol of the faith set out some time ago by the Holy Ghost at the great and holy council convened in Nicea: for you have not held and interpreted it rightly, but rather perversely; even though you confess with your voice the formula of words. But in addition, in writing and by oath, you must confess that you also anathematize those polluted and unholy dogmas of yours, and that you will hold and teach that which we all, bishops, teachers, and leaders of the people both East and West, hold."[1] In which words [the letter] makes no mention of anyone other than the bishops, teachers and prelates, whose faith the council affirms to be necessarily accepted.

Because if you say that those words should be referred to those who attended the assembled council: this response is so futile that one need not fight against it, except that we are dealing with men to whom even the clearest matter have to be proved. In fact, an assembly in one place is not required so that the Church may say something true, but the joining together of souls through the bonds of charity, which those men had concerning whom it is said: "There was one heart and one mind" (Acts 4, 32) is sufficient. For the Church does not depend on unity of place for it to be said to be one, but from the concord of souls in Christ. Now it is proved

---

[1] The Latin translation of the Greek text of this letter quoted here is that found in the *False Decretals of the Pseudo-Isidore* (PL 130, 294D-295A). But the original Greek text with an alternate Latin translation of this letter may be found in Migne's *Patrologiae cursus completus* among the letters of Saint Cyril of Alexandria (PG 77, 107D (*Epistola XVII*)).

sufficiently that this concord is among those who, even if they were separated by spaces of place or of time, nevertheless unanimously subscribe to the same opinion.

But if Wycliffe, or Luther, or any other imitator of them in this regard, be not moved by these reasons to believe that they are obliged to embrace the concord of all the sacred doctors concerning the faith, even if an explicit citation of Sacred Scripture nowise supports them, this at least they could hardly deny: that their sayings in support of this are strong, such that one may prove from them that what is found in the possession of those sacred authors, preserved through so many periods of time, is the Church's position. For if Cyprian erred in a difficult matter, he was afterwards corrected by Jerome, Augustine, and others following them. In what things Jerome also hallucinated it is noticed by those coming after him. Likewise, it also happened to Augustine, if he stumbled anywhere.

But although Jerome confirms the opinion of Cyprian, Ambrose subscribes to the same all the more after him, Augustine embraces the same, Blessed Gregory, Cassiodorus, Bede, and Bernard adhere to the same: hence it is proven sufficiently that this is the Church's opinion since the Church never contradicted the assertion of these men protracted though so many ages. For one sufficiently approves a matter (I speak of elevated matters, about which nothing is permitted to be overlooked through indulgence) if one does not contradict them when he can. It can never in fact be said more truly, that when a matter is so serious that to remain silent is pernicious, but to speak is useful and necessary, he who is silent seems to consent. If therefore the Church was silent regarding the common opinion of those men through so many centuries, by this fact it is certainly seen that she approved the opinion of all those men, and she thought likewise as they did. Therefore, one who contradicts the holy doctors when united concerning a lofty matter without ever any opposition is bound by nearly the same law as though he were to contradict the universal Tradition of the Church. Therefore will he rightfully be deemed most arrogant, who having belittled so many sacred doctors and having despised so many wise men, by whose teaching the Church shines as the sun and moon, clings to his own opinion.

For Ismael, the prototype of heretics represented such sort of man in figure, concerning whom it is said: "His hand will be against all men, and all men's hands against him" (Gen. 16, 12). For deservedly all men's hands are lifted up against him, whose hands rose up against them all. Hence, it is said by Solomon: "Lean not upon thy own prudence" (Prov. 3, 5); and Blessed Paul says: "Be not wise in your own conceits" (Rom. 12, 16). Theophylactus expounding which says: "That is to say, do not so trust in your own prudence or abilities that you think that you need no advisor, nor anyone pointing out what things are correct. For Moses, even if he was helped by speaking with God, still needed to consult his father-in-law."[1] To this end, it happens that Sacred Writ always sends us to others, so that we may learn from them. For in fact in Deuteronomy it is said: "Ask thy father, and he will declare to thee: thy elders and they will tell thee" (32, 7); and in the writings of Job: "For inquire of the former generation, and search diligently into the memory of the fathers" (8, 8). Further, in the Acts of the Apostles when Paul was then prepared to receive God's law and was asking the Lord, saying: "Lord, what wilt thou have me to do," the answer from the Lord is: "Arise, and go into the city, and there it shall be told thee what thou must do" (9, 7). The Lord indeed could have made known His will to Paul by Himself, and teach Him concerning His law: yet He did not want to do so, lest from this He would give anyone an occasion for taking pride, such that one would not want to be taught by another, asserting that he was already taught by the Lord. Thus for this reason He sends both Paul to Ananias and Cornelius to Peter.

Paul, in other respects a learned man and to whom the Lord designed to appear, is not ashamed to go to Ananias to be taught by him: and is Luther ashamed to go to Jerome, or

---

[1] Cf. Ex. 18, 17-23. PG 124, 510D.

Ambrose, or Augustine to learn something from them? Paul most willingly accepts the things said by Ananias, although nothing was said to him by the Lord about Ananias: and will Luther consider it very hard to receive the teaching of Cyprian, Chrysostom, Jerome, Augustine, Ambrose, and other illustrious men? Paul, fourteen years after having received the revelation, goes up to Jerusalem to discuss the Gospel that he was preaching to the Gentiles, expressly with those, "who seemed to be some thing" (Gal. 2, 2): and this was done in fact, lest perhaps he should run, or had run in vain: and do Luther or Wycliffe deign to discuss their Gospel with Jerome, Ambrose, Augustine, Cyprian, or Hilary? Unless perhaps Luther pleads that he is surer of his Gospel that he preaches than Paul was of his, and so it was necessary that Paul seek out someone with whom he may discuss his Gospel, but was it not necessary for Luther to do this? Add to this the fact that the sacred councils (whose authority is supreme[1] in the Church after Sacred Scripture concerning the faith) do not disdain to use the testimony of the holy Fathers to strengthen their explanations: and will Wycliffe or Luther also disdain to yield to all the highly renowned men agreeing who are at one with each other?

Accordingly the Fourth Synod of Toledo, in chapter [ten] of its canons, cites Cyprian and Hilary as a proof of its opinion[2]: and the [III] Council of Constantinople, which is called the Sixth [General] Council, in which Macarius, Bishop of Antioch, asserting that there is only one will in Christ and one operation, was condemned, uses the testimonies of very many holy men, namely, Athanasius, Ambrose, Cyril, Augustine, in whom full trust was given. And since explicit testimonies of Sacred Scripture were lacking, the unanimity of those holy men was considered to be sufficient to the whole council for refuting that heresy. What therefore will I say, I do not know, except that Luther ascribes more to himself than to all the councils, since he does not want to believe those whom the supreme councils gave its most complete trust on account of their holiness of life and eminence of doctrine. But if perhaps I do not persuade Luther or Wycliffe that this honor is due to the sacred authors—despite their having been praised through many centuries, such that it is not easily and at will permitted to deviate from their opinion—it suffices that those before whom the matter is treated are convinced.

---

[1] The dogma of Papal Primacy had not yet been defined at this time. This dogma was taught by both the Councils of Florence and Vatican I. "Therefore, relying on the clear testimonies of Sacred Scripture, and adhering to the eloquent and manifest decisions not only of Our predecessors, the Roman pontiffs, but also of the general Councils, We renew the definition of the Ecumenical Council of Florence, by which all the faithful of Christ must believe that the Apostolic See and the Roman pontiff hold primacy over the whole world, and that the Pontiff of Rome himself is the successor of the blessed Peter, the chief of the Apostles, and is the true vicar of Christ and head of the whole Church and faith, and teacher of all Christians; and that to him was handed down in blessed Peter, by our Lord Jesus Christ, full power to feed, rule, and guide the universal Church, just as is also contained in the records of the ecumenical Councils and in the sacred canons. Hence we teach and declare that by the appointment of our Lord the Roman Church possesses a sovereignty of ordinary power over all other Churches, and that this power of jurisdiction of the Roman pontiff, which is truly Episcopal, is immediate; to which all, of whatsoever rite and dignity, are bound, by their duty of hierarchical subordination and true obedience, to submit, not only in matters which belong to faith and morals, but also in those that appertain to the discipline and government of the Church throughout the world; so that the Church of Christ may be one flock under one supreme pastor, through the preservation of unity, both of communion and of profession of the same faith, with the Roman pontiff. This is the teaching of Catholic truth, from which no one can deviate without loss of faith and salvation." (I Vatican Council, Chapter III of *Pastor Aeternus* entitled "On the Power and Nature of the Primacy of the Roman pontiff" (Dz. 1826-1827).

[2] *Collectio Canonum Ecclesiae Hispanae: Ex Probatissimis Ac Pervetustis Codicibus* (Matriti: Ex typographia regia, 1808), p.

Introduction -49-

I will say nothing beyond these things except that which Valerius Maximus[1] recounts Marcus Aemilius Scaurus as having said, because it seems to me most useful on this point. For that man had a most renowned and proven probity of life,[2] when he was accused before the people by the insincere Varius of Sueca [Spain].[3] The accuser had harangued with a very long speech: the former used a very short summary, because he relied on his own conscience and that of the people, and so he disdained to contend by a speech: "Citizens of Rome,[4] the Spaniard[5] Varius affirms, [the Roman] Aemilius Scaurus denies: which think you should be believed more?" With which words, the people having applauded, the illustrious man evaded the futile accusation of that man. Which inquiry, it seems to me, befits no point of argument better than this one. For if Luther affirms, Cyprian denies: Luther affirms, Jerome rejects; Luther affirms, Augustine contradicts: Luther affirms, Ambrose stands against: Luther affirms, Gregory opposes: which side do you think should be believed more? I do not doubt that you will pass a silent verdict in favor of these highly renowned men, just as then was the verdict passed in favor of Marcus Aemilio. Yet Luther will have enough honor from this. For even if he was finally conquered, he will be said to have striven with so many illustrious men.

Chapter VIII: That it pertains solely to the Apostolic See or a general council to identify a heresy.

Although there are prescribed measuring rods, namely Sacred Scripture and the Church's definitions, according to which any assertion of heresy must be examined, nevertheless many men overlook them in numerous assertions. From which cause they do not know how to determine whether the assertions are heresies or not, because they do not recall Sacred Scripture or the Church's definitions in their entirety: or if they are remembered, they do not comprehend the meaning of Scripture, and they can nowise conclude anything, such that from it they may refute a heresy. For since men's capacities are different, they also interpret Scripture differently according to the quality of their understanding. Hence it is that often among learned and pious men there is no agreement even regarding a very serious matter: yet there would be an agreement if they could easily use the rules, and apply them to any proposition. Therefore, since contentions often occur, it is necessary that someone have the power to judge the matter and eliminate disputes. Otherwise an occasion would be given for stirring up new heresies at will, since there are not lacking writings, even if badly understood, on which they may rely, just as there is never a lack of heretics.

---

[1] *Valeri Maximi Factorvm et Dictorvm Memorabilium Libri Novem* (bk. 3, chap. 7, n.8).
[2] During the run-up to the Jugurthine War the historian Sallust wrote of the extensive bribery of Jugurtha in his attempts to persuade the Senate not to intervene on his brother's behalf. In describing the profligacy he commented on Scaurus' character: "A few, on the other hand, to whom right and justice were more precious than riches, recommended that aid be given to Adherbal and that the death of Hiempsal be severely punished. Conspicuous among these was Aemilius Scaurus, a noble full of energy, a partisan, greedy for power, fame, and riches, but clever in concealing his faults. As soon as this man saw the king's bribery, so notorious and so brazen, fearing the usual result in such cases, namely, that such gross corruption would arouse popular resentment, he curbed his habitual cupidity." (*Bellum Jugurthinum*, I. 15).
[3] Today the town is called Abalat which is in the province of Valencia.
[4] Lit. *Quirites*. Originally, the inhabitants of the Sabine town Cures were called the *Quirites*. After the Sabines and the Romans had united in one community, under Romulus, the name of *Quirites* was taken in addition to that of *Romani*, the Romans calling themselves, in a civil capacity, *Quirites*, while, in a political and military capacity, they retained the name of *Romani*.
[5] Varius *Sucronensi*, i.e., "of Sueca."

For Pelagius says that man by his power of free will alone can both avoid sins and merit glory. For if he cannot, he says, avoid sins, they are no longer sins for him, because no one sins in regard to what he cannot avoid. Again, he says: "He gave them power to be made the sons of God, to them that believe in his name" (Jn. 1, 12). If then it is in our power to become sons of God, one is not called a son except he have the right to an inheritance: thus he says that it is within our power to attain the eternal inheritance of glory. But Jerome, Augustine, and other Catholics object to Pelagius, and from among countless passages of Sacred Scripture, select that one of Paul: "For by grace you are saved through faith: and that not of yourselves, for it is the gift of God; Not of works, that no man may glory" (Eph. 2, 8-9). Thus see that the matter is addressed, and not in regard to the shadow of a donkey (as it is said),[1] but regarding the heart of the matter. Therefore a judge is required who may declare the judgment, with which it is necessary to comply.

Now such power of judging is not in any subordinate bishop, or in the chapter of the clergy which he oversees. Which perhaps will hereafter become clear, if firstly we show the quality and the manner of the faith that we are obliged to embrace. Now this is peculiar to the faith, that the faith in every existing land is one everywhere. For there is not a different faith belonging to the church of Salamanca, nor another allowed for the church of Zamora, or another of the church of Barcelona. For just as the universal Church is one, so the faith of all the churches is one, Paul bearing witness, who says: "One Lord, one faith, one baptism" (Eph. 4, 5). Hence, faith is called Catholic because in Latin it means "universal," because it is the one faith of the whole universal Church. Hence it is that the condition concerning the faith, which comes to the fore, is that the truth be such that pertains to the universal Church. Therefore, because it concerns all, it ought to be approved by all, or by him who rules in the place of all. Thus how can a subordinate bishop, or the whole chapter of clergy which he governs, pass judgment on a truth of faith, in such a way that the universal Church be subject to it? For this same reason the universality of some school, no matter how eminent a learning it possesses, cannot so decide concerning a heresy, that all would be bound to comply with its censures. Wherefore it is rightly accustomed to be said that "The Parisian decrees do not cross the mountains." Thus, a declaration of heresy need not be upheld by all, just because this or that school considered it to be heresy. For nothing prevents that whole assembly from possibly fumbling, since it is not that person for whom God prayed that his faith fail not.

By this principle we also prove that provincial councils do not have a full and complete power for deciding a matter of faith, since their opinions would not constrain other provincial councils: especially since such councils could also err regarding the faith, just as it is ascertained concerning other councils that they erred. For in fact the Synod of Carthage, in which eighty assembled bishops along with the holy martyr Cyprian unanimously decided that heretics, and those baptized by heretics, ought to be rebaptized when they recanted: there is no one who doubts that they erred. Yet if these provincial councils ever erred, they were corrected by general councils. Hence Augustine, in book two of his *Against the Donatists* says: "And the Councils themselves, which are held in the several districts and provinces, must yield, beyond all possibility of doubt, to the authority of plenary Councils which are formed for the whole Christian world."[2] Therefore since provincial councils are able to err, because they do not represent the universal Church, it is just and consonant with reason, that there not be in their possession the full power and established authority for deciding in so serious a matter, as the faith.

Many decrees of the pontiffs confirm this very thing. Pope Symmachus says: "Councils of the priests having decreed by annual ecclesiastical laws lose their force across the provinces

---

[1] I.e. a petty matter.
[2] Chap. 3, n. 4 (PL 43, 128-129).

because they do not have the presence of the pope."[1] And many other decretals, which are cited in distinction seventeen of the book of the *Decretum,* bear witness that councils assembled without the pope's authority are null and void. Add to this that all the rights both of the pontiffs and of the general councils, which permit or convoke the celebration of councils to the provinces, only extend that authority to those boundaries, namely, so that in that place dissentions may be cut off, grievances may be heard, morals corrected, yet not so that anything concerning the faith may be decided in that same place. Accordingly the Council of Nicea speaks thus concerning provincial councils: "The synods shall be held at the following times: one before Lent, so that, all disputes (if there are any) having been set aside, a solemn and unblemished fast may be offered to God."[2]

On the other hand, even if the bishop, or chapter of clergy, or the provincial council cannot decide concerning matters of faith regarding those points which may be doubted permissibly, nevertheless they can pronounce judgment in those matters which are already defined, or are grasped without any trickery from the clearest testimonies of Sacred Scripture. Further, they can punish the pertinacious defenders of the erroneous assertion. For without any doubt it does not belong to the council to pass sentence, but to execute the sentence already then given. For to this end that which is said in the chapter, *Ad Abolendam,*[3] goes further, namely that all heretics which the Roman Church, or bishops in their churches, shall have declared heretics, are excommunicated. For that ought to be understood concerning those caught in manifest heresy. When, however, the matter shall have been doubtful, the case should be devolved to the Apostolic See. A bishop or provincial council can also inhibit preaching, or any public assertion of a certain proposition on account of the conceived suspicion of heresy regarding such a proposition, or on account of the scandal which could arise from such preaching. But if perchance some were to be rebellious to a proposition of this kind, he could punish them (as it is fitting) according to the type of crime, not indeed as much as the heresy deserves, but according to the disobedience.

If therefore the power to judge a matter of faith belongs to anyone, and it does not belong to the individual bishops, nor to provincial councils, in that it is a matter common to all, whom neither the individual bishops nor the provincial councils govern, it follows that such power of deciding belongs to the whole Church. But since general councils (as we discussed

---

[1] Part 4, Dist. 17 (*Concilia*), chap. 242 (PL 161, 316D). The *Decretum* was compiled by Saint Ivo of Chartres, whose writings influenced nearly all the theologians and canonists of his day and for some time afterwards.

[2] Canon 5 (PL 84, 94C).

[3] *Ad abolendam* ("On abolition" or "Towards abolishing" from the first line, *Ad abolendam diversam haeresium pravitatem,* or 'To abolish diverse malignant heresies') was a decretal and bull of Pope Lucius III, written at Verona and issued on November 4, 1184. It instituted both the practice of episcopal inquisitions into heresy and the obligations of support for the process and penalty from the secular authorities, although the exact nature of the punishment was left unspecified. CLXXI (*Decretum contra haereticos*) (PL 201, 1297C)). "And though it sometimes happens that the severity of ecclesiastical discipline necessary to the coercion of sin is condemned by those who do not understand the virtue of it, we notwithstanding decree: that whosoever shall be notoriously convicted of these errors, if a cleric, or one that endeavors to conceal himself under any religious order, he shall be immediately deprived of all prerogative of the Church orders, and so being divested of all office and benefice, be delivered up to the secular power, to be punished according to demerit, unless, immediately upon his being detected, he voluntarily returns to the truth of the Catholic faith, and submits publicly to abjure his errors, at the discretion of the bishop of the diocese, and to make suitable satisfaction. And as for a layman who shall be found guilty, either publicly or privately, of any of the aforesaid crimes, unless by abjuring his heresy and making satisfaction he immediately returns to the orthodox faith; we decree him to be left to the sentence of the secular judge, to receive condign punishment, according to the quality of his offense."

above) represent the universal Church, it is inferred that they have the power for defining in these matters which pertain to the faith. The Apostolic See, however, because it represents the Church as its head, holds the first place after general councils for defining.[1] Therefore, these having been excepted, no one is permitted to have the right of deciding on those matters which pertain to the Catholic faith. Regarding general councils, I think that no one would doubt, who shall have perused the previous chapters.

Hence, there remains that we discuss regarding the Apostolic See. He who acknowledges this See to be the head of the entire Church will be easily persuaded. For that which governs all can judge all and decide concerning matters which bear upon all. There are very many testimonies of the holy Fathers about this matter. Innocent III says the following: "He distinguishes that the more important matters of the Church, especially those pertaining to the articles of the faith, ought to be referred to the See of Peter. For it was Peter, who, when the Lord asked whom the disciples said that He was, is observed to have replied: 'Thou art Christ, the Son of the living God'; and for him the Lord prayed that his faith fail not."[2] Furthermore, Pope Pelagius, writing to the bishops who had assembled at the [illicit] summons of John of Constantinople, says nearly the same words: "But the greater and more difficult questions (as the holy synod decreed, and the holy custom requires), are always referred to the Apostolic See."[3] Innocent I says: "Whenever a question of faith is in dispute, I think that all our brethren and fellow bishops ought to refer the matter to none other than Peter. That is, they ought to refer to the authority of his name and honor, just as your charity now refers to us, because it is able to benefit all the churches in the whole world."[4]

Blessed Cyprian, in his letter to Pope Cornelius, says: "For neither have heresies arisen, nor have schisms originated, from any other source than from this, namely that God's priest is not obeyed. Nor do they consider that at the present time there is one priest and judge in the Church taking the place of Christ;[5] whom, if, according to Divine teaching, all the faithful of the universal Church would obey, no one would stir up anything against the college of priests. No one, after the Divine judgment, after the suffrage of the people, after the consent of the co-bishops, would make himself a judge, not now of the bishop, but of God. No one would rend the Church by a division of the unity of Christ. No one, pleasing himself and swelling with arrogance, would found a new heresy."[6] Hence, it is made clearly established that Luther for this reason alone denies the primacy of the Roman bishop, that a way for introducing heresies might be more easily open to him.

Moreover, Blessed Jerome [wrote] to Pope Damasus: "This, most blessed Pope, is the faith that we have been taught in the Catholic Church. If anything therein has been incorrectly or carelessly expressed, we beg that it may be set aright by you who hold the faith and See of Peter. However, if this, our profession, be approved by the judgment of Your Apostleship, whoever may blame me will prove that he himself is ignorant, or malicious, or even not a Catholic but a heretic."[7] In support of this, let him see who wishes, there are also very many

---

[1] See the condemnation of Conciliarism quoted in footnote 31 above.
[2] Letter to Bishop of Arles, chapter *majores ecclesiae causas* (*Extra de baptismo et ejus effectu*). (Gregory IX, *Decretales*, bk. 2, tit. 42, c. 3 (Friedberg, II, 646)). Cited in II-II, q. 1, a. 10.
[3] *Decretum*, Dist. 17, chap. 5, n. 2 (PL 187, 95C).
[4] Pope Innocent I to the bishops of the Council of Milevum, letter 30 (PL 20, 590B) cited in *Decretum*, pars 2, causa xxiv, q. 1, chap. 12 (*Quoties*) (PL 187, 1269A). Also cited in *S.T.*, II-II, q. 11, a. 2 ad 3um.
[5] Namely, the Roman Pontiff.
[6] Letter 12, (PL 3, 802B-803A).
[7] *In Expositione Symboli*, (Among the supposititious works of St. Jerome). *Decretum Gratiani*, causa xxiv, q. 1 (PL 187, 1269B). Pelagius, *Letter and Confession of Faith to Pope Innocent I*, n. 14 (PL 45, 1718).

Introduction

testimonies of the holy Fathers asserting that the Apostolic See has never deviated from the right rule of faith, which are cited in the book of *Decretals, causa* twenty-four, question one.[1]

But here it ought to be observed that the name of the Apostolic See ought not to be taken for the supreme pontiff alone, since he can err in the faith, as we have shown above concerning Liberius, Anastasius,[2] and Celestine.[3] The Apostolic See which never erred includes both the curia by whose counsel the pontiff is helped, and the pontiff himself. Now concerning this See it is not correct that it erred at any time. Whether the whole College of Cardinals could err, however, I do not discuss: still I believe that the Lord will never permit that the whole College to be stained with heresy. For which reason it is just that in a matter of such great importance, such being the Catholic faith, it ought to consult the college of their brothers before it defines anything: having also been joined, if it were possible, by other men entirely eminent in holiness and learning. Nevertheless, Luther here, since he sees that a judge is necessary for eliminating strife that arose concerning the faith, says that Sacred Scripture is the true judge, to which every appeal ought to be made. But in the Old Law, the Law itself was not the judge, but only the priests of the Levitical race, to whose judgment one had to adhere.

Besides, if the dispute is about Scripture itself, how will Scripture itself be the judge? As for example, I ask whether you accept Paul's epistles. If you deny that they are Paul's, there is no testimony of Sacred Scripture whereby you can be refuted. Again, our Savior sent us to the Sacred Scriptures, so that we may get a testimony from them, but not judgment. "Search the scriptures," He said: "for they give testimony of me" (Jn. 5, 39). By which words He clearly taught that Sacred Scripture performs the role of a witness among us. From which it is clearly refuted that it cannot be the judge in the same case: because it is contrary to the order of justice, and contrary to natural equity, that in the same case treated in the external forum that the witness be the same as the judge. Moreover, all the Lutherans themselves, when disputing against the other heretics of this time, with whom they fight as it were diametrically, dispute about the meaning of Scripture. They very often use the Church's judgment, so that they may convict their enemies of error. For when they fight against the Anabaptists, and dispute about the meaning of Scripture, they flee to the Church's common opinion and to the teaching of the old Doctors.

Concerning which matter, Johann Gast renders sufficient witness. He being a Lutheran, in his book on the errors of the Anabaptists, he recalls a disputation he had with the Anabaptists of Basile. Replying to quotations of Scripture cited by the Anabaptists in confirmation of their errors, he flees to the common opinion of the Church, so that by it he may show that the true meaning of those quotations of Scripture is not that which the Anabaptists allege.[4] For they cite very many passages of Sacred Scripture, misunderstood by them, in favor of their most wretched errors. Against the baptism of infants, they cite that testimony of the Savior found in Mark: "Go ye into the whole world, and preach the gospel to every creature. He that believeth and is baptized, shall be saved: but he that believeth not shall be condemned" (Mk. 16, 15-16). From which words they surmise that baptism nowise benefits infants, due to the

---

[1] Pars 2 (PL 187, 1265ff).

[2] See footnote 61 above.

[3] "[I]f the pope speaks merely as a private individual, or as a private theologian, or as a temporal sovereign, or precisely as ordinary of the diocese of Rome, or precisely as metropolitan of the province of Rome, he should not be looked on as acting infallibly. ... What is required for an infallible declaration, therefore, is that the pope be acting precisely as pope; that is, as the supreme shepherd and teacher of all Christians so that his decision looks to the universal Church and is given for the sake of the universal Church" (Msgr. G. van Noort, *Dogmatic Theology* (Cork, Mercier Press, 1959), p. 292).

[4] *De anabaptismi exordio, erroribus, historijs abominandis, confutationibus adiectis, libri duo* (Basel, 1544), p. 134.

fact that they do not actually believe. In order that they may prove that it is not permitted for any reason to kill a man, they bring forward that precept of the Law: "Thou shalt not kill" (Deut. 5, 17). In order that they may prove that it is not permitted to swear for any reason, they bring forward that testimony of the Savior: "But I say to you not to swear at all, neither by heaven, nor by the earth" (Mt. 5, 34-35). Now to all these testimonies of Sacred Scripture the Lutherans responding said, and correctly, that those passages of Scripture ought not to be so understood as the Anabaptists think. But, because they reject the true meaning of those passages, the Lutherans, in order to persuade them of the true meaning of Scripture, found no other way besides the common opinion of the whole Church. This, for them, was seen to be more than enough to convince those Anabaptists of their errors, since the Church has been breathed upon by the Divine Spirit and it is certain that it cannot err. Hence, it is clearly proven that the Lutherans deal in a most iniquitous and Pharisaic manner, prescribing hard and intolerable laws for us, which they completely refuse to observe themselves. For when we dispute with them and invoke the Church's judgment, they immediately call upon Scripture, deferring all power of judgment to it. Contrariwise, when they fight against the Anabaptists or others like to them, whom they see that the testimonies of Scripture according to the apparent literal meaning favor, they immediately appeal to the Church's judgment, so that they may claim from it the true meaning of Scripture. If they once acknowledge it as the judge in the matter, it is necessary that they never reject it: because since it is, as Paul says, "the pillar and ground of the truth" (I Tim. 3, 15), and breathed upon by the Holy Ghost, it is certain that it cannot err. Now since no individual and private person may have this privilege of certitude, it follows that in a matter of the faith there is no such person who is the judge, whose judgment and opinions all Catholics are obliged to obey.[1]

Therefore, let inquisitors of heretical depravity take heed lest they easily pronounce concerning heresy. If the heresy has been condemned in the past, or is detected by the clearest passages of Scripture, and could not be precluded by human reasoning, then they are executers so that what the pontiffs' decrees command to be done concerning heretics should be carried out. However, if the matter is doubtful, whether it be heresy or not, it is not their function to pass sentence, nor can they judge concerning the heresy, since this belongs to the supreme pontiff alone. For in the case it is incumbent upon them by their office that they present their names, then the inquisitor must inquire concerning the aforesaid assertion, published in whatever way: How it was said by the asserter; with what words; how it was understood by him; for what reason was he motivated to assert it; and with what passages of Scripture it is supported. Which things having been done, if it can be nowise proved with the clearest testimonies, but the matter remains doubtful and stained with the blot of suspicion, the Apostolic See should be consulted. Further, it will not be permitted the inquisitors to decide anything when it has not been consulted (however much learned men be consulted). Now when they

---

[1] The pope may be so followed. Hence, this statement needs to be corrected by the more recent and solemn magisterium of the Church: "And so We, adhering faithfully to the tradition received from the beginning of the Christian faith, to the glory of God, our Savior, the elevation of the Catholic religion and the salvation of Christian peoples, with the approbation of the sacred Council, teach and explain that the dogma has been divinely revealed: that the Roman pontiff, when he speaks *ex cathedra*, that is, when carrying out the duty of the pastor and teacher of all Christians in accord with his supreme apostolic authority he explains a doctrine of faith or morals to be held by the universal Church, through the divine assistance promised him in blessed Peter, operates with that infallibility with which the divine Redeemer wished that His Church be instructed in defining doctrine on faith and morals; and so such definitions of the Roman pontiff from himself, but not from the consensus of the Church, are unalterable. But if anyone presumes to contradict this definition of Ours, which may God forbid: let him be anathema." (First Vatican Councils' definition of papal infallibility" (Dz. 1839-1840)).

receive the decision of the Apostolic See, it is incumbent upon them to execute that which was decided by the supreme pontiff.

Nevertheless, at this point he ought to admonish, because even though the Apostolic See or a general council could judge concerning the heresy, still it does not follow that an assertion will be heretical because the Church has decided, but because it opposed the Catholic faith. The Church does not make such an assertion to be heresy by its decision, since even if she had not decided, it would be heresy: but what the Church effects is that by her censure it is made clear to us that it is heresy, because previously it was unknown to us whether it could rightly be called such. For the whole Church (excluding its Chief Head), much less the supreme pontiff alone, cannot be the author of a new article of faith, yet it could establish that some proposition can be shown to be heretical.

Now it is proved by a clear reason that the Church cannot make a new article of faith. For every assertion indeed ought to be called Catholic provided it was revealed by God, either because it is contained in the book of Divine Scripture, or because the universal Church receives it. If there is none of these, at least it is concluded by clear deduction from either or both of them, or finally (so that nothing is lacking) because the supreme pontiff approves it. Certainly, there is no other way whereby something can be called Catholic. If therefore some truth is called Catholic, because it was revealed by God, since Divine revelation does not depend on the will of the pontiff or on the Church's approval, how is it that the pontiff's approval makes what is revealed by God to be Catholic? He indeed effects that we may believe that it is revealed by God, for Satan's angel may often be transformed into an Angel of light (II Cor. 11, 14), and plagues[1] occur by means of the bad Angels (Ps. 77, 49), and it could perhaps be doubted whether God reveals or the demon mocks. Therefore the Church discerns it to be God's revelation, yet it does not make the revelation to be true.

If, however, such a truth is called Catholic because it is contained in Sacred Writ, this does not depend on any human will, but on God alone, the Author of those Scriptures, and it is also evident for this reason, that the Church can do absolutely nothing so that that truth would pertain to the faith. For we have this from the Church, that we know what is Divine Scripture, according to those things which we treated above in chapter four. But since it was clear to us that Scripture is Divine, it is now established of itself that we are bound to believe it all. It is just as if witnesses were summoned for the proof of some book whereby Peter is bound to give John a hundred pieces of silver. Those witnesses do not make Peter obliged towards John; for even if Peter would deny, and the witnesses were lacking, Peter was truly a debtor. What they effect is that by the writing he can be proved as being subject to the debt. Therefore, if it be said that the truth is Catholic, because the universal Church now accepts it, then I ask in what way the Church has accepted it: because it was revealed by God to it, or because it is found in Sacred Scripture? Now, we have shown that neither of these depends on the will of the Church: either the Church accepts because it knows it through her experience or through natural reason, which ought not to be conceded to the Church in some way, because then our

---

[1] The word used here is *immissiones* which is translated in the cited Psalm as follows: "And he sent upon them the wrath of his indignation: indignation and wrath and trouble, *which he sent (immissiones)* by evil angels." St. Robert Bellarmine comments on this passage as follows: "*Which he sent by evil angels*, that is, which disturbance was effected through the interventions [*immissiones*] of evil angels. From which we understand that the plagues of Egypt, and especially the killing of the firstborn sons, were works done by the Angels, who do not harm, except insofar as God has permitted; since they are ministers of God, the Supreme Judge. The holy Angels, however, can also be called 'evil Angels,' who are called 'evil' from their effect, because they punish those whom God wishes to be punished. The impure Angels can also be called wicked Angels, who are truly evil, bearing an evil will. For God uses both" ("*Explanatio in Psalmos*," *Omnia Opera* (Naples, Joseph Guiliano Editor, 1860), vol. 5, p. 333).

faith would rest upon experience and natural reason alone. St. Paul clearly opposes this, saying: "My speech and my preaching was not in the persuasive words of human wisdom, but in shewing of the Spirit and power; that your faith might not stand on the wisdom of men, but on the power of God." (I Cor. 2, 4-5). However, if for another reason a truth be called Catholic, namely, because it is deduced by a clear inference from revealed truths or truths contained in Scripture: since the Church's definition does not make the inference firm—as is known to someone who has learned even a little logic—it follows that neither in this case does the Church make a truth to be Catholic.

Finally, it is left to be investigated whether an assertion may be said to be Catholic because it is decided by the pontiff, and then I will ask if the pontiff so defining relies on Divine Scripture, or Divine revelation. Is it evident that it is Catholic from Divine Scripture or from revelation, or does it rely on one's own prudence and will, in which case it is evident that it ought not for this reason to be accepted as a Catholic truth, since our faith depends neither upon the will nor the wisdom of men. Therefore, a truth is not deemed Catholic from the definition of the pontiff or the Church alone: but that which has always been Catholic, yet uncertain to us, is thereafter known by the Church's definition to be Catholic. Just as in a dispute about a debt, the judge rendering a just sentence does not make that person a debtor, since he was already a debtor from the thing borrowed, which he refuses [to return]. Rather, the judge make clear that the debt is owed, which before was, and the judge's sentence affects it such that by it he may be convicted as being pertinacious. For thus the judge justly said that this man is a debtor, because he truly is a debtor: and not thus such a man is a debtor, because the judge pronounced a just sentence. For if he was not a debtor, the sentence would have inflicted an injustice. So also, the Church defining that something ought to be held by faith, although it certainly defines, and cannot fail, yet it does not make by its definition that truth to be Catholic. Thus, the reason why she defined that truth to be Catholic is because that truth is Catholic: because if it were not Catholic, the Church defining it to be Catholic would have erred. Therefore, it was Catholic before the Church had judged. For in no way can it happen that the Church establishes a new article of the faith: but that which previously was the true faith, yet was unknown to us, the Church makes to be known to us by her censure.

Hence it is clear that the Lord Abbot erred, who when expounding the canon which begins, *Cum Christus*, which is found in the book of the *Decretals* under the title *De haereticis*, says that the pope can establish a new article of faith.[1] But that man, being ignorant and not carefully considering what he was saying, ought to be spared: I see that only this ought to be brought against him, namely that he "judged above the sandal."[2] For it is not the role of canonists to judge concerning heresy or the faith, but that of theologians, to whom the Divine right was entrusted. The duty of canonists is to discuss pontifical law. Therefore let them see lest, while they desire to "sit on two stools" (as it is said in the proverb), both be removed.[3]

---

[1] I.e. Nicolò Tudesco, Abbot of Maniacio (near Messina), and later Bishop of Panormo, whence his name, "Panormitanus," who wrote, "The pope can introduce a new article of faith" (*Lectura in Decretales* (on bk. 5, tit. 7, c. 7)).

[2] *Sutor, ne ultra crepidam* is a Latin expression meaning literally "Shoemaker, not above the sandal," and used to warn people to avoid passing judgment beyond their expertise. Its origin is set down in Pliny the Elder's *Naturalis Historia* (XXXV, 85) where he records that a shoemaker (*sutor*) had approached the painter Apelles of Kos to point out a defect in the artist's rendition of a sandal (*crepida* from Greek *krepis*), which Apelles duly corrected. Encouraged by this, the shoemaker then began to enlarge on other defects he considered present in the painting, at which point Apelles advised him that *ne supra crepidam sutor iudicaret* ("a shoemaker should not judge above the sandal"), which advice, Pliny observed, had become a proverbial saying.

[3] In 1517 Paschasius Berselius wrote in a letter to Erasmus, "I fear that while I try to sit on two stools,

Introduction

Because they conclude their opinion from the canon, *Cum Christus*, they do not act rightly. For Alexander III, whose proposition that is, did not establish an article of faith, because he did not make that proposition, namely, that "Christ is something besides man,"[1] to be true, nor consequently Catholic, since the truth depends on the thing itself, and is not derived from the pontiff's affirmation. Nothing changes in a thing because of our affirming or denying. The pope in defining [a truth] makes it not permissible to assert or suppose its opposite. Before the pontiff's decision, someone could have perhaps freely asserted [the opposite] without incurring the mark of heresy, because that truth had not been known. (Although I do not see how it could be unknown to someone unless he were completely untaught or badly disposed.) Thus in the past, if not being pertinacious someone were to assert the opposite, he would not be judged a heretic, and thus not deserving of excommunication.

For it very often happens that among pious and learned men that there is no agreement concerning the same matter, in which one of them necessarily errs, and yet that error is not immediately considered to be heresy. As for example, someone says that the Divine Persons are constituted in personal being (as they say) through relations of origin,[2] while others affirm that they are constituted by absolute properties.[3] Others say that they are not constituted by anything, but are [distinct] Persons in and of themselves [*seipsis*].[4] Who does not see that some of these err, in spite of which, any of them may adhere to his opinion with impunity, and without the mark of heresy. Yet it does not follow that such an error is not heresy, because it is not imputed to him. For if every error opposing the Catholic faith ought to be called heresy—according to that which we discussed above—it is certain that such an error is heresy, because it is opposed to the Catholic faith, although it is unknown to us. For the truth, to which that error opposes, is necessary, yet it is unknown to us whether it is truth, so we are nowise obliged to assert it, nor to disagree with the opposing error. Hence, it is a free matter for anyone to maintain his own opinion. Yet if the Church taught by the Holy Ghost decides concerning that

---

I fall between them," because he was trying to learn both Hebrew and Greek at the same time. (*The Correspondence of Erasmus: Letters 594-841, 1517 to* 1518 (Letter 674, n. 135, University of Toronto Press, 1974) p. 134) Oecolampadius adopted this phrase in 1528 when accusing the city of Basel of also trying to sit on two stools, because it had not outlawed Catholicism as he had wished, but instead it allowed a religious pluralism between Catholics and Protestants. (Carlos M. N. Eire, *War Against the Idols: The Reformation of Worship from Erasmus to Calvin* (Cambridge University Press, 2003), p. 115).

[1] This sentence was Abelard's; cf. *Opera sancti Bonaventurae* (ed. Quaracchi), vol. 3, p. 156 ff., Schol.

[2] This is the common opinion taught by St. Augustine (*De Trinitate*, V, c. 11, n. 12) and St. Thomas Aquinas, who wrote, "Now distinction in God is only by relation of origin" (I q. 29, a. 4).

[3] This is the position of St. Bonaventure (I Sent., dist. 25, a. 1, q. 1 in corp. (*Omnia Opera*, vol. 1, p. 437a) and Duns Scotus, who wrote, "The Divine Persons are constituted in their Personal being — and distinguished — through some absolute realities" (I *Ordinatio*, dist. 26, n. 59). Scotus held that there is a formal distinction — a distinction between the Divine essence and the property or properties proper to each Person — whereby the Divine Persons are distinct from each other. According to the *Liber Propugnatorius*, Scotus was oblige to publicly recant this position which was seen as coming close to the heresies of Arius or Sabellius.

[4] Praepositinus of Cremona first espoused this view, namely that that the distinction between the Divine Persons need not be explained by anything over and above the Divine essence. Saint Thomas Aquinas refutes this view as follows: "The Divine Persons are supposed to be distinguished in and of themselves (*seipsis*), insofar as the persons in reality are the relations themselves. But just as the person, as regards the manner of signifying, is not the same as the relation; so also they are not distinguished in and of themselves (*seipsis*), but by the relations; just as God of Himself is God, although the Deity is God, because He is His Deity." (*Super Sent.*, lib. 1, d. 26 q. 2 a. 1, ad 5um).

matter, doubtless the Church by her definition does not make a person to be this or that:[1] but teaches us that which, even though it was true from eternity, was nevertheless unknown to us. After the Church's definition, it will not be permitted to assert what was previously permitted. Therefore, it will necessarily be that just as the Church by her definition does not make a new truth of faith, so also she does not make the opposite belief to be a new heresy.[2]

However, because the Church sometimes defines some doctrine with clear and manifest words, which it draws out from some abstruse and hidden passages of Sacred Scripture, even if it is nowhere found clearly, for which reason it will sometimes happen that the Church may be said to establish an article of faith. This is not because she makes what not was the faith to be the faith, but because she expressed it with some precise words, by which it was never before expressed. For instance, we say that the Council of Nicea established a Creed of the faith, because it expressed the consubstantiality of the Son, which Sacred Writ had never expressed by this name. In this manner, it is also said that some heresy is new, not because the heresy did not exist before, but because no one asserted it before. For Pope Galasius speaks in this way: "Achatius was not made the inventor of a new error, but an imitator of an old one."[3] In fact, there are many errors which before they have promotors, were refuted by the holy Doctors, so that they might guard other men beforehand: because if someone at the time had begun to maintain them, they would have been called new errors for this reason. For thus it is related in the Acts of the Apostles concerning certain men saying about Paul that he was "a setter forth of new gods." (Acts 17, 18). They were in fact calling them "[new] gods," because they were newly preached by Paul. We discoursed at greater length in this chapter, because we saw that the matter needed a longer admonition, lest anyone believe that he is given the responsibility to make pronouncements concerning heresy.

Chapter IX: Who ought to be called a heretic?

Perhaps to someone who has only looked at the title of this chapter, what is herein going to be discussed will seem superfluous. For he will say to himself, since he is called a heretic who adheres to heresy; and what is a heretic has been shown above; why then is it necessary to repeat the topic of heretics? It is because it is not as it appears at first [glance]. For from time to time, it happens that he who asserts a heresy is nevertheless truly called a Catholic, as we shall say concerning Cyprian and others. Wherefore one ought to make a further investigation, so that we may find out who truly should be considered to be a heretic. Which matter, since it is not unimportant, requires a thorough investigation before anything may be settled.

Since the name of heretic is grievous and abhorrent to pious ears, it is unseemly to rashly fasten it upon anyone. For there is nothing more harsh or more bitter which you may inflict upon a Christian man as an insult than if you call him a heretic. Nevertheless, there are many men who have nothing else at hand besides the label of heresy, which they hurl at will, taking little account of the matter, or of what they say. From among those many men I cannot

---

[1] E. g. declared a heretic for having held the condemned proposition prior to the definition.
[2] "Accordingly we must conclude that, as regards the substance of the articles of faith, they have not received any increase as time went on: since whatever those who lived later have believed, was contained, albeit implicitly, in the faith of those Fathers who preceded them. But there was an increase in the number of articles believed explicitly, since to those who lived in later times some were known explicitly which were not known explicitly by those who lived before them" (II-II, q. 1, a. 7).
[3] *In commonitorio ad Faustum* quoted in the *Decretals* (Causa 24, q. 1, c, 1 ("Achatius") (PL 187, 1263B)). Pope Galasius I (492-496) wrote this letter of instructions to his Legate, Faustus, at Constantinople.

Introduction

hold back the stick from a well-known Brother Bernard of Luxemburg,[1] who in his list notes down many worthy men among the number of heretics, who may be reckoned with a better verdict. Such are [Saint] Papias, Bishop of Hierapolis, Praepositivus,[2] and Gilbert, surnamed Porretanus.[3] Now, I wonder why he struck out against the latter, such that he inserted him in the list of heretics, since he [Brother Bernard] himself admits that he had renounced his error. For whoever taught that someone ought to be called a heretic, who so held his error such that when admonished and proved wrong, was not ashamed to sing the palinode?[4] I keep silent about Berengarius,[5] whom, after putting him on his list of heretics, he [Brother Bernard] admits that he had so abandoned his error that he never returned to it (how true this is, we shall discuss elsewhere). And in in the same place he says that he was listed not because he was a heretic, but because he held an opinion that was at some time heretical.

However, since he named his book, *Catalogus haereticorum* [*omnium*],[6] what compels that they who at one time adhered to some heresy, by this name be channeled together into the same riverbed with others who most pertinaciously defended their errors? Did not Brother Matthaeus Grabow[7] follow heresy, which he renounced in the Council of Constance, Jean Gerson[8] being the witness? But he was a Dominican (just as others of the same institute who pertinaciously adhered to heresy), which perhaps knowing, he passed over, lest he seem to have insulted the Dominican institute to which he belonged. As if some of the glory of the Order of Preachers would have gone to ruin, because one or another of that sodality turned out

---

[1] Dominican theologian, controversialist, and Inquisitor of the Archdioceses of Cologne, Mainz, and Trier, who died in 1535 in Cologne. "As the author of the *Catalogus haereticorum*, he has been described as somewhat lacking in critical judgment; but he was otherwise a safe and indefatigable defender of the Faith against the heretics of his time" ("Bernard of Luxemburg," *Catholic Encyclopedia (1908 ed.), vol. 2, p. 503)*.

[2] I.e., Gilbert Prevostin, Chancellor of the See of Paris (1205-9), who "said that suffrages for the damned can be so multiplied that they are entirely freed from punishment, not absolutely as Origen maintained, but for a time, namely till the Judgment Day: for their souls will be reunited to their bodies, and will be cast back into the punishments of Hell without hope of pardon" (*Supp.* q. 71, a. 5).

[3] I.e., Gilbert de la Porrée (1076-1154). "The word 'God' can of itself be taken for the Divine essence. So, although to say of any of the *supposita* of the divine nature, 'God is the Trinity,' is untrue, nevertheless it is true of the Divine essence. This was denied by Porretanus because he did not take note of this distinction" (I, q. 39, a. 6 ad 1um).

[4] I.e., a recantation or to unsay what he had said. A palinode is an ode in which the writer retracts a view or sentiment expressed in an earlier poem.

[5] The heresy of Berengarius of Tours (999-1088), French theologian who denied transubstantiation while professing merely an intellectual or spiritual presence of Christ in the Eucharist. He was required to make a profession of faith in the Real Presence by the Council of Rome in 1079.

[6] I.e., "The Catalog of All Heretics."

[7] Matthaeus Grabow (c. 1421) was a Dominican friar and an inquisitor in Groningen and Wismar. Grabow dismissed all life spent outside the established monastic communities as without merit and not according to the Gospel. "In A. D. 1384, one Gerard Groot, of Deventer, a doctor of the University of Paris, and a canon of Utrecht, established a new order, called the *Brothers of Common Life*, consisting of persons of knowledge and piety, who lived in common, and employed themselves in the instruction of youth. Thomas à Kempis wrote the life of this Gerard, and greatly applauded his institution. During the sitting of the Council of Constance, one Grabow, a Dominican, wrote against it as unlawful, and contrary to the approved Orders; but Gerson answered Grabow, threatening him with the resentment of the Council, in the decisions of which his voice had the greatest weight; and in consequence of this, he was induced to retract what he had advanced." (*The Theological and Miscellaneous Works of Joseph Priestley* (Hackney, George Smallfield-Printer, 1831), vol. 9, p. 538).

[8] Jean de Charlier de Gerson (1363-1429).

to be a heretic. It certainly did not go to ruin any more that that holy community, concerning which it is said: "They went out from us, but they were not of us" (I Jn. 2, 19). For on no occasion is the Church beauty diminished, or her color darkened, because so many heretics withdrew from it.

On account of which I cannot but be annoyed with those who to praise their institute, are not afraid to boast and say before the people, that he who has once received the habit of that Order, cannot err or desert the faith. Is this not clear blasphemy, since by this more seems to be given to the habit with which one is clothed, than to the faith or God's grace? Is that cloth perhaps more powerful than God's grace or the faith? Far from us be such madness. But neither faith, nor the grace received in Baptism, does so protect man that he cannot fall into heresy. Why then is it that the habit may protect him: because if someone wishes to associate this to the [religious] profession, and not to the habit, so that the profession which he made in that institute may be said to have this power: who does not see that all men at Baptism profess to be Christians? Yet that profession which we then make does not make us immune from heresy. Still no one will be so imprudent that he would deny that that profession is much more important and efficacious than any other made afterwards. Therefore let them go away and leave the ditties that are to be sung to the poets, and preach better things to the people.

I attest before God that I lie not: for I was present when a certain man, preaching to the people at a public assembly on a day when the solemnity of the saint who had founded his Order—wishing to extol with praises his fraternity and society—said that he who had once put on the habit of his Order could not be a heretic. And I have heard from very many others that they have heard the same words from men of the same Order, when a sermon on the same subject to the people took place. I, in fact, when I was listening, detested the man's audacity and imprudence, and abhorred the prelate's patience, who when listening tolerated and nowise punished it. For which reason, not a small suspicion arose within me, such that I thought that the words spoken came from his mind. Lest I seem to assail the whole Order or society, I have deliberately kept silent the name of the order, so that I might seem rather to admonish as Christian charity requires, rather than to make public as envy suggests.

I willingly listen to the praises of holy men, but they do not become equal to God. I rejoice when someone praises the institute in which he is professed. For by this sign he shows that he has nowise fallen away from his original intention. Yet a limit ought to be applied to praises, lest one suppose that some particular assembly is more illustrious or beautiful than that assembly which is called the universal Church, which is spotless: yet when many heretics have gone away from it, it has lost none of its beauty. And so I attest before God that I will spare no one in this book whose heresy I find anywhere, even if he were to belong to the Franciscan institute, which I joined twenty-two years ago. For even if I have Blessed Francis as my Father, and his fraternity as my mother who fed and educated me, still I admit that I owe more to Christ, who died for me, and to the Catholic Church, which is indeed the mother of all men, in which we are born again through Baptism.

However, now it is necessary that the discourse return to our objective. Therefore, since it such a grievous matter to brand someone with the label of heretic, it ought to be diligently examined, and it is necessary to "check the stone with the plumb-line" (as it is said)[1] before we judge, and not to pronounce anything lightly. Thus, many things are required for someone to be rightly called a heretic. Firstly, it is required that he have accepted the Catholic faith

---

[1] This adage is taken from the practice of architects who do not believe their eyes, but check the straightness of a stone to a plumb-line. Hence its meaning is that one should proceed carefully and diligently when doing any operation. So it is used in a homily of Saint John Chrysostom: "Observe how again here he brings his stone to the plumb-line, everywhere seeking the edification of the Church" (St. John Chrysostom, *Homily 35 on I Corinthians* (14, 17) PG 61, 300).

Introduction

at baptism at some time. For he who was never set apart for Christ is an infidel, or pagan, or Jew, or Saracen, or will be classified by another name, but will not be called a heretic. Hence it is evident that Bernard of Luxemburg erred miserably, who when making a list of heretics, included some men therein who were never initiated into the Catholic faith, and so should not have been called heretics. Such were Avicenna and Averroes, who were listed in his *Catalogus haereticorum*, when nevertheless they can by no means be called heretics. For it is indeed evident that they had embraced the Mohammedan sect. Hence because if they should have been numbered among the heretics, since they were opposed to Christ's faith, why were Photinus,[1] Libanius,[2] Lucian,[3] Plutarch,[4] Apuleius,[5] and the other philosophers also included, who greatly opposed the Christian faith?

Next, after having received the faith, an error in the faith is required, more precisely, such that one embraces a heresy. On account of which a schismatic due to his schism alone is not properly considered a heretic, unless he be separated from the unity of the Church due to being guilty of heresy. But because (as Jerome testifies, commenting upon the Epistle to Titus) "there is no schism which does not trump up a heresy to justify its departure from the Church,"[6] hence it is that a schismatic is usually called a heretic: not because the schism itself is heresy, but because it is disposes to heresy. For as we discussed in the first chapter, an outward deed is never called heresy, unless credence in the mind be adjoined. Thus, schism cannot be called heresy unless an error of the intellect is added. Hence, in the same place Jerome says: "Between heresy and schism there is this difference, that heresy perverts dogma, while schism, by rebellion against the bishop, separates from the Church."[7]

Here it ought to be recalled that there is a twofold union. One which is through charity, whereby the members are joined together by joints, so that they adhere to their head, namely Christ, and whereby that body is constituted which is said to be spotless. And in this way the Church's unity consists in the unity of charity, by which the members love each other, and God. The other union of the Church is through faith, whereby all the faithful are a flock under one shepherd. For thus says Hugo of Saint Victor: "We obtain union by faith, vivification by charity."[8] This is that Church, which in the Gospel is sometimes compared to "a net cast into the sea, and gathering together of all kind of fishes" (Mt. 13, 47). Other times it is compared to ten virgins, of whom "five of them were foolish, and five wise" (Mt. 25, 2).

Schism (which in Latin means *scissura* or *divisio*)[9] is opposed to the first union, which is through charity. For it frequently happens that someone is called a schismatic, who still be-

---

[1] Photinus (died 376), was a Christian heresiarch and Bishop of Sirmium in Pannonia (today the town Sremska Mitrovica in Serbia). He was a dynamic Monarchian who, without denying the Virgin birth, regarded the Person of Christ as essentially human; and denied a hypostatic distinction of the Logos from the Father and a hypostasis of the Spirit. Hence it is surprising that he is here not considered a heretic since he was baptized in the Catholic Church.

[2] Libanius (314-394 A. D.) was a Greek-speaking teacher of rhetoric of the Sophist school.

[3] Lucian of Samosata (c. AD 125 - after AD 180) was a rhetorician and satirist who wrote in the Greek language.

[4] Plutarch (45-120 A. D.) was a Greek historian, biographer, and essayist.

[5] Apuleius (135-180 A. D.) was a Latin-language prose writer.

[6] *In Ep. ad Tit.*, iii, 10 (PL 26, 598A). As St. Jerome remarks, practically and historically, heresy and schism nearly always go hand in hand; schism leads almost invariably to denial of the papal primacy. This quotation was mistakenly attributed to Saint Augustine here in the text.

[7] *Ibid.* The text here cited Saint Jerome's commentary on Galatians, whereas it is found among his comments on the Epistle to Titus.

[8] *De sacramentis*, bk. 2, part 2, chap. 1 (PL 176, 416B).

[9] I.e. a split or division.

lieves that the Church is the mother of all men, and has the faith which the Catholic Church holds. He is separated for this reason alone: Namely, he denies that the pontiff was properly elected and is the true pontiff, and therefore does not want to be subject to him. Recent historical events call to mind such a schism which lasted nearly forty years in the Church, which then underwent having three men claiming to be the pope, which schism ended at the Council of Constance under the Holy Roman Emperor Sigismund. Who now still dares to brand the name of heretic upon any of those who said that they were the pope, or to those who were submitting to them, since the council itself never accused any of them of this, except perhaps Benedict,[1] who contradicting the council remained in schism? For although we are bound to believe by faith that the successor of Peter is the supreme pastor of the whole Church, we are not bound to believe with the same faith that Leo or Clement is the true successor of Peter: because we are not bound by the Catholic faith to believe anyone was duly and canonically elected. Hence it is that he who refuses obedience to Clement or Leo for this reason, namely because he says that he was not duly elected, even if he may be called a schismatic, yet he ought not to be deemed a heretic, since by doing this he does not oppose any Catholic truth. For those things do not pertain to the Catholic faith which now depend upon a fact (*ex facto*), but those things which are by law (*ex jure*). Otherwise, if those things were to pertain to the Catholic faith, it would be necessary to have happened that the Church was sometimes deceived in the faith, which no one in their right mind admits. Therefore, no one is considered to be a heretic unless he accepts an error in the faith. Wherefore the supporters and defenders of heretics—even if they are sometimes called heretics—if they defend only the persons and not the errors, are not deemed heretics, yet they will be subject to canonical penalties.

Thirdly, so that one may be truly called a heretic (according to the opinion of some) it is required that he not completely abandon the Catholic faith, but only one or several articles of it. For if one were to abandon the whole faith, they would not call him a heretic but rather an apostate. *Juan de* Torquemada, in his *Summa Ecclesiae*[2] upholds the same opinion. Likewise Sylvester Mazzolini[3] in his *Summa [Summarum]*, under the word: "Heretic."

And I at one time so thought, and thus I had so taught in the first edition of this work. For having followed in the footsteps of these doctors to the same opinion, I fell into the same pitfall into which they fell. Therefore now having considered the matter more deeply (as was necessary), I perceived most clearly that they and I had erred. For it is not consonant with reason that a heretic by increasing his heresy ceases to be a heretic. Who being of sound mind will say that a white man, by the addition of whiteness, ceases to be white? If whiteness makes a man white, it is necessary that the more whiteness that he have, the whiter he becomes: it is quite inconsistent that the white man could then cease to be white. If on account of only one thing stolen, someone is called a thief and a robber, then he who has snatched away by theft all the possessions of others is more deservingly deemed a thief. In the same way, concerning a heretic it seems to me necessary to say that if having abandoned one article of the faith makes its deserter a heretic, then having abandoned all the articles of the faith makes one not merely a heretic but a very great heretic. Therefore the apostate is not something so

---

[1] Antipope Benedict XIII (1328-1422).

[2] "A heretic is he who professing Christ's faith in general after having accepted the Christian religion, pertinaciously holds or follows one or more opinions in particular opposed to the Catholic truth…For as Saint Thomas says in II II, q. 11, art. 1, heresy pertains to those who profess Christ's faith, but corrupt its dogmas. Hence he thus departs from Christ's faith, who believes nothing of it, and completely departs from Christ's name and His truth, is not properly called a heretic but an apostate" (Bk. 4, part 2, chap. 13 (On who is properly called a heretic)).

[3] Sylvester Mazzolini, in Latin *Sylvester Prierias*, (1456/1457 – 1527) was a theologian born at Priero, Piedmont.

Introduction

distinct from the heretic that he cannot be a heretic at the same time as an apostate, as the aforesaid doctors seem to think, but the name "apostate" is like a kind of species of infidelity contained under the name "heretic." Thus, every apostate is a heretic, but not vice versa is every heretic an apostate. And Blessed Thomas teaches this opinion, who says that there are only three species of infidelity, namely Pagan, Jews and heretics, and under the name of heretics he says however many departed in any way from the Catholic faith which at one time they accepted.[1] And he teaches it more explicitly in the same part,[2] where he says that apostasy does not connote any species of infidelity, but a certain aggravating circumstance. William of Ockham writes the same opinion in the first part of his *Dialogus*.[3]

What makes someone fully a heretic is if you join pertinacity to the error. Augustine says against the Manichaeans: "In Christ's Church, those are heretics, who hold mischievous and erroneous opinions, and when rebuked that they may think soundly and rightly, offer a stubborn resistance, and, refusing to mend their pernicious and deadly doctrines, persist in defending them."[4] For it frequently happens that whenever the temerity of dogmatizing is begotten, pertinacity emboldens, nay increases. Wherefore it can be very well said to heretics that which the Lord said through the Prophet Ezechiel: "Their fathers, have transgressed my covenant even unto this day. And they to whom I send thee are children of a hard face, and of an obstinate heart" (2, 3-4). For such is the pertinacity of heretics, and it often does not hesitate to put their heads to the sword, so that they do not depart from their error: whom that passage of Paul well befits: "If I should deliver my body to be burned, and have not charity, it profiteth me nothing" (I Cor. 13, 3). Pertinacity put aside, however much someone errs, he ought not to be called a heretic. Hence Augustine says in his letter to Glorius and Eleusius: "Though the doctrine which men hold be false and perverse, if they do not maintain it with passionate obstinacy—especially when they have not devised it by the rashness of their own presumption but have accepted it from parents who had been misguided and had fallen into error—and if they are with anxiety seeking the truth and are prepared to be set right when they have found it, such men are not to be counted heretics."[5]

Hence, if someone is ignorant, who resolves within himself to always embrace that faith which holy Mother Church makes known to him, hears a preacher (by whom his simple mind is influenced), saying that the Holy Ghost proceeds from the Father but not from the Son, and he assents to it, ought not on that account be deemed a heretic. Whereas, even if he errs, still it is not due to malice, since he is prepared to obey the teaching Church. For he thus believes the preacher, because he supposes that the preacher says those things which are approved by the Catholic Church, and he would not believe if on the other hand if it were to become known that the preacher had departed from the true faith. Hence Augustine, in his book *On Baptism*,

---

[1] "Since the sin of unbelief consists in resisting the faith, this may happen in two ways: either the faith is resisted before it has been accepted, and such is the unbelief of pagans or heathens; or the Christian faith is resisted after it has been accepted, and this either in the figure, and such is the unbelief of the Jews, or in the very manifestation of truth, and such is the unbelief of heretics. Hence we may, in a general way, reckon these three as species of unbelief." (*II-II, q. 10 a. 5*).

[2] "The species of a quality or form are not diversified by the fact of its being the term 'wherefrom' or 'whereto' of movement: on the contrary, it is the movement that takes its species from the terms. Now apostasy regards unbelief as the term 'whereto' of the movement of withdrawal from the faith; wherefore apostasy does not imply a special kind of unbelief, but an aggravating circumstance thereof, according to II Peter 2, 21: 'It had been better for them not to know the truth [Vulgate: 'the way of justice'], than after they had known it, to turn back.'" (II-II, q. 12, a. 1 ad 3um).

[3] Bk. 4, chap. 12.

[4] *The City of God*, bk. 18, chap. 51, n. 1 (PL 41, 613).

[5] Letter 43, chap. 1, n. 1 (PL 33, 160).

Against the Donatists says: "Let us suppose that the one held the same opinions as Photinus about Christ, and was baptized in his heresy outside the communion of the Catholic Church; and that another held the same opinion but was baptized in the Catholic Church, believing that his view was really the Catholic faith. I consider him as not yet a heretic, unless, when the doctrine of the Catholic faith is made clear to him, he chooses to resist it, and prefers that which he already holds."[1] Moreover, he is not merely not a heretic, but also he does not sin in this, his ignorance excusing him, because just as he did not know, so neither was he not obliged to know. For not all are bound with the same obligation to believe. For untaught people it suffices for them to hold the articles of the faith which are set forth in the Apostles' Creed, being prepared to accept the rest which the Church has presented to him to be believed. But it is not the same for prelates and preachers, whom ignorance does not excuse, in that they are bound to know those things which pertain to their office, so that they preach nothing which they have not fully examined, and so they sin if they do not know. If nevertheless they are prepared to be corrected when the Church shall have taught something, although they sin in not knowing what they should have known, still they must not be considered to be heretics more than the unlearned common person, in that they are not pertinacious.

We say that someone is pertinacious who adheres so tenaciously to his own opinion that he is prepared to resist the Church no matter how much it admonishes him. Which pertinacity even in those things which are ambiguous, and where the Church has not yet defined anything, is so perverse that it alone suffices to make a man a heretic. For, if someone believes that the fire of Hell is like or unlike that that which we see here around us, he will not be considered a heretic, in that the matter has yet to be decided. However, if he embraces some opinion with such an intention that although the Church were to define the opposite he would be prepared to defend his opinion against the censure of the Church, he ought to be deemed a heretic. This is not because he defends this or that opinion (which perhaps is true), but on account of the pertinacity adjoined, by which he is ready to resist the Church teaching something; by that very fact he believes that the Church can err, which is heretical.

Otherwise, about those things which have been pronounced and put outside of all controversy, that is to say, which have been defined at some time by the Church, this rule should be held. He who opposes and contradicts these pronounced and previously decided matters, even if he were to say that he is prepared to be corrected by the Church or a Council, must be deemed a heretic: because by the very fact that he contradicts a known definition of the Church, he is pertinacious. For even if he may say that he is prepared to be corrected, still it is not so. For how is it that someone is prepared to be corrected by that which he now clearly opposes? And so the Church has not accustomed herself to put in question again what previously has been decided. Wherefore he who hears that which the Church has decided, ought to obey. Because if he opposes, he will rightly be considered pertinacious, and thus heretical. Hence Pope Galasius [I] said: "Our forefathers perceiving by Divine inspiration, necessarily took care that what a council had promulgated for the communion of faith and the Catholic and Apostolic truth against any heresy, was not permitted to be changed by new reconsiderations, lest an inappropriate occasion be given of repelling the things which were medicinally decreed. However, the author of any madness and likewise his error having been condemned, they judged it sufficient, that anyone who would come forth at any time as a sharer of this error, would be bound by the main judgment of its condemnation. Thus the council condemned Sebellius, and it was not necessary for his followers to be condemned afterwards, but according to the tenor of the old constitution, the universal Church ordered that those who showed themselves to be partakers of that depravity or that communion to be refuted. Thus Arius, so Eunomius, Macedonius, Nestorius, the council condemning their

---

[1] Bk. 4, chap. 16, n. 23 (PL 43, 169).

deeds at one time does not permit them to be brought before a new council in the future."[1] Further, Pope Felix [III] said: "Achatius was not the inventor of a new or his own error, such that a new ordinance would come forth concerning him, but he involved himself in another's crime by his communion. Therefore it is necessary that he fall under that judgment made with the correct scales of justice, which the author of the error had received with his successors with conciliar approval."[2] Finally, Pope Leo, writing to Martian Augustus about those things which were treated in the Council of Chalcedon, said the following: "Through our Lord Jesus Christ, who is the Author and Ruler of your kingdom, I entreat and beseech Your Clemency, that in the present Council you do not allow the faith, which handed down from the Apostles our blessed Fathers preached, to be retracted as though it were doubtful."[3] He wrote the same thing to Leo Augustus.[4]

Therefore, let Luther keep silence, and be ashamed to ask for a definition by a council in matters which were defined by many councils. For since it is evident that his errors came forth from the workshops of the Arians, Messalians,[5] Waldensians, Wycliffites, Hussites, whom many councils condemned, why does he ask for new definitions, when there are so many old ones? Still the subtle serpent[6] knows why he acts. For because he hopes it to be difficult in these times on account of the violent dissentions taking place to assemble a council, to summon to the council: which, if it were assembled, it would be scarcely attended. This was his cunning plan, and he afterwards openly declared success in the matter. For Emperor Charles V, seeing that Luther had appealed to a council, and hence hoping that Luther would depart as soon as the general council had assembled, with anxious solicitude pleaded before the Roman pontiff, that he celebrate a general council to put to rest the tumults of the heretics and restore peace to the Church. But Luther perceiving this, and fearing that he would be condemned by a general council, immediately afterwards began to disparage general councils, saying that it could err, and hence to protest that he would never submit to a definition of a council. With which words he clearly showed that his sole reason for appealing to a council was that he thought that it could nowise be assembled. Hence, so great was Luther's pertinacity in his opinion that he decided that he would never obey a definition of a whole general council.

And it is not surprising that he adheres so tenaciously to his error, because, as the Wise Man says: "Stolen waters are sweeter" (Prov. 9, 17). Are not "stolen waters" the opinions

---

[1] Letter XIII to Bishops of Dardania (PL 59, 62B-63A); *Decretum Gratiani*, p. 2, causa 24, q. 1, c. 2 (PL 187, 1263C).

[2] *Decretum Gratiani*, p. 2, causa 24, q. 1, c. 3 (PL 187, 1264C). Having summoned a council, Pope Felix III (483-92) condemned Achatius, Bishop of Constantinople (471-86), because he had revived the condemned heresy of Peter, Patriarch of Alexandria. More precisely, Pope Felix excommunicated Achatius for his apparent Monophysitism in the *Henotikon* of Zeno, issued in 472.

[3] Letter 90, chap. 2 (PL 54, 933B-934A). *The False Decretals of the Pseudo-Isidore*, letter 22 of Pope Leo (PL 130, 795D).

[4] "Therefore we must abhor and persistently avoid what heretical deceit is striving to obtain, nor must what has been well and fully defined be brought again under discussion, lest we ourselves should seem at the will of condemned men to have doubts concerning things which it is clear agree throughout with the authority of Prophets, Evangelists, and Apostles." Letter 162 (PL 54, 1144C); *The False Decretals of the Pseudo-Isidore*, letter 52 of Pope Leo (PL 130, 841A).

[5] The Messalians, or "praying folk," were an heretical sect which originated in Mesopotamia about 360 and survived in the East until the ninth century. They are also called Euchites from the Greek translation of their Oriental name (*euchetai* from *euchomai*, to pray); Adelphians from their first leader; Lampetians from Lampetius, their first priest (ordained about 458); Enthusiasts from their peculiar tenet of the indwelling of the Holy Ghost by Whom they thought themselves inspired or possessed (*enthous*).

[6] This is a reference to Genesis 3, 1: "The serpent was more subtle than any of the beasts of the earth."

and errors of the heretics? For elsewhere it is said: "Words from the mouth of a men are as deep water" (Prov. 18, 4). However, this water is stolen, since he uses the words of Sacred Scripture against the intention and will of the Holy Ghost, the Author of the same writing. But these waters, because they are stolen, taste sweeter to them, than if they had begged from others, and thus they adhere to them more tenaciously. Everyone enjoys himself more with his own contrivances than those of another. Therefore the Apostle James warned concerning this matter, saying: "If any of you want wisdom, let him ask of God, who giveth to all men abundantly" (1, 5). If he desires to have it from someone other than from God, he will have it by theft, because "All wisdom is from the Lord God, and hath been always with him, and is before all time" (Eccli. 1, 1).

Chapter X: Whether one who is in doubt concerning the faith ought to be called a heretic?

Concerning him who defends his error with a pertinacious mind, we discussed in the previous chapter. There remains that we discuss whether such a man deserves to be called a heretic, who adheres to no error, but only hesitates in the faith, such that he is wavering and doubtful as to which Father he may turn to. Which question is easily answered if firstly one takes into consideration what faith ought to be, such that it can truly be called faith.

For in order that something properly be called faith, it requires certitude and firmness in him who has it: otherwise, if certitude and firmness are lacking, some scruple will prompt one to think that it is not faith but it will be deemed an opinion or doubt. For by this reason alone faith is distinguished from opinion, because he who believes adheres tenaciously: no one can incline him to turn away to the opposite position. But he who has an opinion, so gives assent to his opinion, such that sometimes he hesitates and assents with a changeable understanding. Hence, it is that faith and opinion can hardly be united: therefore it will much more difficult for faith and doubt to unite, since these things instead fight against each other. Hence the Apostle James says: "But let him ask in faith, nothing wavering. For he that wavereth is like a wave of the sea, which is moved and carried about by the wind. Therefore let not that man think that he shall receive any thing of the Lord" (1, 6-7). It is therefore clearly implied that he who doubts in nowise believes. But in those things in which it is necessary to "bring into captivity every understanding unto the obedience of Christ" (II Cor. 10, 5), to not want to be brought into captivity in order to believe, is to openly fight against the faith. Now he who assaults the faith "by open force"[1] we showed in the last chapter to be heretical. Therefore, anyone who doubts those things which pertain to the faith ought to be called a heretic. Hence Pope Stephen says: "One who doubts the faith is an infidel."[2] This implies that everyone who doubts errs.

Since in the last chapter we showed that everyone who pertinaciously errs in the faith ought to be called a heretic, therefore it is clearly proved that everyone who doubts the faith may also be called a heretic. That one doubting the faith errs is proved by Augustine's testimony, who in chapter nineteen says the following: to err is "to receive what is false as if it were true, and to reject what is true as if it were false; or to hold what is uncertain as certain, and what is certain as uncertain."[3] He repeats nearly the same words in chapter twenty-one.[4] Those things which pertain to the faith are the most certain. Now since those things which are doubted are

---

[1] *Aperto Marte.*
[2] Gregory IX, *Decretales,* bk. 5, tit. 7, chap. 1. The Decretals cite merely "Pope Stephen to all the bishops" without specifying which Pope Stephen wrote these words.
[3] PL 40, 241-2.
[4] PL 40, 243.

held to be uncertain, it is concluded therefrom that he who doubts in matters of faith, errs: now everyone pertinaciously erring in the faith is a heretic: therefore, everyone who doubts the faith, in the same way will be considered a heretic.

This is also proved by many testimonies of Scripture. For after the Resurrection, when the Lord appeared to the disciples at the time when Thomas was not there, for which reason since Thomas likewise did not wish to believe unless he first put his hands into the prints of the nails, after eight days the Lord appeared to all eleven disciples and said to Thomas: "Put in thy finger hither, and see my hands; and bring hither thy hand, and put it into my side; and be not faithless, but believing" (Jn. 20, 27). Notice here that the Lord focuses upon Thomas' incredulity and infidelity on account of his doubt, which he had regarding His Resurrection. Now, because Thomas doubted, [Pope Saint] Gregory [I] in his homily on this lesson testifies saying: "Do you believe that this took place by chance; that this chosen disciple should be missing at this time, that coming in later he hears of these things, and that hearing he doubts them, and doubting he touches the Lord, and while touching Him he believed? Not by chance, but by Divine appointment, did this come to pass. For the Divine clemency acted in this so wondrous manner that the doubting disciple, when he touched the wounds in the Body of His Master, healed in us the wounds of our unbelief."[1] And [Saint] Cyril expounding in the twelfth chapter of his commentary the same passage says: "That the blessed disciple did not so much lack faith owing to infirmity of judgment, but rather was affected in this way by excess of joy, will not be wide of the mark. For we have heard the saying of the blessed Luke concerning all the others: 'But while they yet believed not, and wondered for joy' (24, 41). It was wonder, therefore, that made the disciples slow to be convinced. But as henceforward there was no excuse for unbelief, as they saw with their own eyes, the blessed Thomas accordingly unflinchingly confessed his faith in Him, saying: 'My Lord and my God' (Jn. 20, 28)"[2] You now see Thomas doubting, whom for this reason alone the Lord calls "faithless."

Furthermore, when Peter by Christ's command went to him on the water and he began to sink, and implored Divine assistance, it was said to him by the Lord: "O thou of little faith, why didst thou doubt?" (Mt. 14, 31). Theophylactus explaining which words says: "Now Peter did not completely doubt, but somewhat, that is to say, partly: for as to what he doubted, he was unbelieving, but as to that which he cried out: "Lord, save me" (v. 30), he cured his infidelity: thus he is said to be "of little faith," not "unbelieving."[3]

Moreover, Paul in his Epistle to the Romans commending Abraham's faith to them, says: "In the promise also of God he staggered not by distrust; but was strengthened in faith" (4, 20). From which words Paul very clearly showed that he who hesitates nowise has faith. Again Theophylactus expounding the passage in Romans: "For since those things which God has bestowed upon us by grace exceed human thoughts, deservedly faith is necessary for us. For if we begin to be curious scrutinizers of Divine things, we shall have lost everything."[4] Therefore, for such a clear matter, it suffices to have cited these testimonies.

Nevertheless, the latter things which we have said are things which ought to be referred only to him who doubts with a pertinacious mind, in the way we have said above concerning him who dissents pertinaciously. For if someone doubts, either from a certain weakness, such as arises in first movements[5] and in those things which men have from nature so that they are

---

[1] Homily 26 on the Gospels, n. 7 (PL 76, 1201C).
[2] *In Joannis Evangelium*, bk. 12 (PG 74, 734B).
[3] *In Mattheum ennaratio*, (PG 123, 302D).
[4] *Expositio in epistolam ad Romanos*, chap. 1 (PG 124, 351B).
[5] *In primis motibus*. "If some object of ardent natural desire were suddenly thrust upon us, leaving no time for deliberation, overwhelming us with the idea of its power to satisfy our appetite, it might be that no room was left for free choice, that we should be necessitated to action. There would be at least some

doubtful in any matter and are pressed upon by incessant scruples: or if one doubts due to ignorance, namely because he does not know that such a matter pertains to the Catholic faith: yet in either way is ready to assent without any hesitation when he shall be admonished or fully taught by the Church: such a man ought not to be called a heretic, and hence will not be subject either to excommunication or the other canonical penalties.

But if he doubts so pertinaciously that he does not wish to assent to the Church teaching, he is already a heretic for a twofold reason: both because he doubts about these things to which he is obliged to give his full and entire faith, and because he is someone who does not believe the Church admonishing. For from this the suspicion arises that he thinks that the Church can err in the faith, which is impious. But I reckon that this man ought to be admonished, because although it is not permitted for anyone to doubt matters which pertain to the faith, still it will be permitted to doubt concerning one's understanding of them. For it very often occurs that men, no matter how learned and pious, are perplexed about many passages of Scripture, namely, doubting about what lies hid beneath that covering of words, although nevertheless they firmly believe whatever God willed to make known to us by those words to be true. For most certainly, and without any hesitation, they believe that the meaning of that text is true: they rightly question, however, what is the true meaning of that text.

In this way even if the Virgin Mother of God believed when the Angel was announcing her future conception, yet she asks the manner whereby it could be done, and pondering concerning it asks: "How shall this be done, because I know not man?" (Lk. 1, 34). That question or doubt of the Virgin indeed lessened none of her most complete faith. Hence Blessed Ambrose expounding this passage says: "Therefore how can it happen that Zachary, who had not believed, was condemned to silence; but Mary, if she had not believed, would have been exalted by the infusion of the Holy Ghost? But neither did Mary not believe, nor ought one to assume so rashly that she did not believe the Angel and that she usurped Divine things. For neither was it easy to know the mystery hidden from ages in the Lord,[1] which not even the higher powers could not know: and yet she did not reject the faith, she did not shirk the responsibility, but conformed her will, by promising obedience. Even when she says, "How shall this be done," she did not doubt concerning the effect, but she sought the nature of that effect. How subdued her answer is, compared with the words of the Priest. She says [to the Angel], "How shall this be?" He [Zachary] answers, "Whereby shall I know this?" She treats of the affair: he in addition doubts concerning the decision. He refuses to believe that which he says he does not know, and seeks as it were still further authority for belief. She avows herself willing to do that which she doubts not will be done, but how it can be done, she is anxious to know."[2]

In this way also ought to be interpreted those commonplace questions of scholastic theologians, whereby they ask: whether God is one, whether the plurality of Persons can be reconciled with the unity of essence, and whether the Holy Ghost proceeds from the Father and the Son. It is not because they doubted these things to be so, but in order they may show how it could be so. I do not see why if someone ponders in this way he must needs incur the censure of heresy, provided that he believe the matter to be true, just as the Virgin Mother of God pondered about the manner by which she was to conceive God. They also seek those things, and stir up questions, so that they may be exercised as in a school of rhetoric, so that they may be

---

indeliberate motion towards the object, a movement of the will which divines call *motus primo-primus*. If in such a case the power of deliberation is not altogether smothered, but is exercised, though imperfectly, the movement of the will which follows is called *secundo-primus*" (Rev. Thomas Slater, SJ, *A Manual of Moral Theology* (London, Burns, Oates & Washbourne, 1925), p.3).

[1] Cf. Col. 1, 26.

[2] *Expositio Evangelii secundum Lucam*, Bk. 2, (PL 15, 1558B).

more ready to fight against heretics, more precisely, that they may be ready to give a reason of that faith which is in them.[1]

For in one way Arius asks whether the Son is equal to the Father in all things, and Thomas or Scotus, or other Catholics, ask in another way. For the former certainly asks because he does not believe that the Son is equal to the Father, and he asks so that he may pervert. But the latter asks so that they may convert; they ask so that they may find a way by which they can evade the wiles of the Arians: they strive to obtain the true knowledge of the faith. Now Blessed Cyril [of Alexandria] advises this to be done in this way, far from forbidding it. For he says the following: "For the truly wise hearer shuts up the more obvious teaching in the treasury of his understanding, not admitting any delay in respect of this. But as to the things the meaning whereof is hard, he goes about with his enquiries, and does not cease asking about them. And he seems to me profitably to press on to do much the same as they say that the fleetest dogs of the chase do, who having from nature great quickness of scent, keep running round the haunts of their game. And does not the wise and prophetic oracle call to some similar habit, 'If you seek, seek: return, come' (Is. 21, 12). For the seeker must seek, that is, must bring a most unflinching zeal thereto, and not go astray after empty speculations."[2] You see here how he advises men to seek, but to this end, namely so that they may possess the true faith, so that they be not seduced, and so that they not go astray from God after empty speculations. Heretics are seeking like Nicodemus saying: "How can these things be done?" (Jn. 3, 9), and like the Lord's Jewish disciples at Capharnaum saying: "How can this man give us his flesh to eat?" (Jn. 6, 53). They ask because they do not believe: which it is evident because they "went back" (Jn. 6, 67). Seeking Catholics ask like the glorious Virgin, who believing asks so that she may be taught.

Hence, I decided to publish these things, because I see certain men lash out against the scholastic doctors without cause, because they ask these things, about which it would be impious to doubt. As if as often as they propose a question with the word, "whether," it ought to be believed that they doubt the matter, and have a wavering faith. Far be it. They do not notice that although they believe the effect, they can rightly ponder concerning the nature of the effect, and concerning the means by which it takes place.

Therefore, one doubting those matters which pertain to the Catholic faith ought to be considered a heretic, provided that he doubts with a pertinacious mind, such that he does not cease to doubt even when the Church admonishes and teaches. Otherwise, if he does it without pertinacity, he will nowise be called a heretic: since even if he dissents in that way, he can by no means be truly called a heretic.

Chapter XI: Concerning certain causes from which heresies arise.

In order that one can more easily prevent heresies, lest (as the Apostle says) they spread imperceptibly like cancer, I have decided to show the causes and the roots from which they arise, so that once those things have been taken away, heresies may be quickly driven away. Since to recover health the first step is to know the cause from which arose the poor state of health, because as doctors say, it is more difficult to cure illnesses whose causes are hidden: those, however, whose causes are apparent, even if the sicknesses are very serious, one can more easily counteract.

The first root of all heresies is that which Augustine says is the sole root of all evils: namely, immoderate love of oneself. For this, as Augustine bears witness, built the city of the devil. And the Apostle clearly expressed this, saying: "Know also this, that in the last days shall

---

[1] Cf. I Pet. 3, 15.
[2] *In Joannis Evangelium*, bk. 4, on chap. 6, v. 53 (PG 73, 571C).

come dangerous times, and men shall be lovers of themselves, covetous, haughty, proud, blasphemers, disobedient to parents, ungrateful, wicked, without affection, without peace, slanderers, incontinent, unmerciful, without kindness, traitors, stubborn, puffed up, and lovers of pleasures more than of God: having an appearance indeed of godliness, but denying the power thereof" (II Tim. 3, 1-5). For when the Apostle in that passage wishes to enumerate the compendium of evils, he put love of oneself before all the evils, and perhaps by this indication he may be showing it to be the cause of the others. For thus Theophylactus, expounding that passage, namely "lovers of themselves," says: "He immediately relates what is the cause of all evils, he does not consider what is good for one's neighbor, but only what is good for oneself; for he is someone who only loves himself: from which it happens that in the end he does not in fact truly love himself."[1] Moreover, expounding the word, "lovers," he says: "When he indicates the root, he also individually mentions the branches sprung forth from it, of which covetousness is both the first and the greatest."[2] From this immoderate love of oneself arises that his own things are pleasing to himself, he delights in his own inventions, hence is born obstinacy and pertinacity, which are the very wide gates leading to heresy.

Besides this main root of all evils is another particular one, common nevertheless to all heresies, namely the desire for glory. For this is innate to all heretics, that they desire popular glory, and they desire to be considered as very learned men by all. But since those going by the royal road cannot attain this, they endeavor by some other way off the beaten track to arrive at their goal. Gregory says this, expounding a passage in Job, chapter six: "For neither do heretics try to attain truth by their investigations, but to appear to be the victors; and whereas they desire to appear as wise men outwardly, they through foolishness are inwardly bound with the chains of their own pride. Hence it comes to pass that they look out for contests of rivalry, and concerning God, Who is our Peace, they know not how to speak with peaceableness, and by what pertains to peace they become originators of strife. To whom it is well spoken by Paul: 'But if any man seem to be contentious, we have no such custom, nor the church of God (I Cor. 11, 16)'".[3]

From this cupidity for glory soon arises pertinacity, flexibility in nothing, and to such an extent that when he shall have fallen down in a contest, nevertheless he will not yield. For they prefer the overturning of any doctrine rather than admit that they have been defeated, namely on this occasion, or rather than that the least part of glory may go to ruin, which they strive to seize. Now so that they may not seem to the people to have fallen down, before whom and not before God they wish to have glory, they leave nothing untried, to such an extent that that even Sacred Scripture itself, which they know openly opposes their assertions, they pervert, twist, and cripple. Not only do they distort it into another meaning, but they cut out what permits no adulterated exposition on account of its most clear testimony. Eusebius of Caesarea expressly asserts that a certain Asclepiolotus, Theodotus, Apollonides, Hermophylus, and Artemonistas had done this. For he says the following: "But that those who use the arts of unbelievers for their heretical opinions and adulterate the simple faith of the Divine Scriptures by the craft of the godless, are far from the faith, what need is there to say? Therefore they have laid their hands boldly upon the Divine Scriptures, alleging that they have corrected them, etc."[4] Likewise, Theophylactus says concerning the Nestorians, when expounding this passage from the Epistle to the Hebrews: "That, through the grace of God he might taste death for all" (2, 9). For he says the following: "But the Nestorians, distorting this passage of Paul, do not say 'through the grace of God,' but 'without God,' that is, 'he might

---

[1] PG 125, 115D.
[2] PG 125, 118A.
[3] *Moralia*, bk. 8, chap. 3, n. 4 (PL 75, 803D-804A).
[4] *Church History*, bk. 5, chap. 28, n. 15 (PG 20, 515B-516A).

taste death for all' without the Divinity, because they suppose very wrongly. For they assert that when Christ was fastened to the Cross the Divinity was not present, because It was not in Him substantially, but was united to Him by a certain affection."[1]

Since therefore it came to be that the only refuge they have is to delete the Scriptures, with which they had been refuted; perhaps by this fact is proved that their own consciences fight against them, and that they know clearly that Sacred Scripture is opposed to them. For if they did not discover the clear opposition of the Scriptures, they would never have deleted the Scriptures, which they could somehow have distorted to fit their meaning. Therefore, why do they not profess the truth? Why do they not sing the palinode, since they discovered the Scripture that should oblige them to do this? Certainly nothing stops them from doing this except the desire for glory; for they say to themselves that passage of Paul: "For if I build up again the things which I have destroyed, I make myself a prevaricator" (Gal. 2, 18). If which words can apply to those who, coming back to their senses, preach the truth which they previously opposed, they would have first applied to Paul himself, regarding whom the churches of Christ then magnified God, hearing that he evangelized the faith which at one time he ravaged. For it is not possible that one pass from error to the truth, or from a grave sin to grace, without repentance. One who is ashamed to repent does this: namely, that whereas he is ashamed to correct his error, he is not ashamed to remain in his error, of which he ought to have been more ashamed.

About which it is very well said in the book of Ecclesiasticus: "There is a shame that bringeth sin, and there is a shame that bringeth glory and grace" (4, 25). Shame "bringeth sin" when someone is ashamed to change a depraved opinion, lest either he be considered inconstant, or he be held to have erred for a long time, himself being the judge. Shame, however, "bringeth grace" when being ashamed of one's own error, by repenting transfers oneself to the light of truth. Thus, the Apostle wishing to convince the Philippians of the true faith, firstly suggests to them that they flee all vainglory, because it could hinder very much the true faith. Thus he says the following: "Being of one accord, agreeing in sentiment, let nothing be done through contention, neither by vain glory" (2, 2-3). Hence Augustine in his book, *On the Profit of Believing*, says: "He is a heretic, who, for the sake of some temporal advantage, and chiefly for the sake of his own glory and pre-eminence, either gives birth to, or follows, false and new opinions."[2] By which words Augustine rather explains the cause rather than the definition of heresy.

For what will he who is desirous of glory not dare to do for acquiring this? He directs all his steps to that desired goal, to this end he speaks, for this end he writes, and from this cause he stirs up strife. Because if now another way does not appear for him to be seen, to be pointed out, to be called by men "Rabbi," it is necessary that he contrive a new doctrine, so that by the newness of the thing he may draw others into admiration. For which reason, heretics seem to me to be like the man who, because he was obscure and not powerful enough to leave behind, by things magnificently done, the remembrance of his power; hoped by a most wicked crime to become renown, and so decided to burn with fire the temple of Diana of Ephesus, built with marvelous workmanship and did so.[3] For very often, men have more strength for vice than for virtue. For so it happens with heretics, who when they were remaining in the true rule of faith were completely obscure, were not ashamed to invade God's Church and burn it with fire, so that thereupon they may become very well-known. For which reason it is just that they under-

---

[1] PG 125, 210D.

[2] Chap. 1, n. 1 (PL 42, 65).

[3] "A man was found to plan the burning of the temple of Ephesian Diana so that through the destruction of this most beautiful building his name might be spread through the whole world." (Valerius Maximus, *Factorum et Dictorum Memorabilium* (*Memorable Deeds and Sayings*), bk. 8, chap. 14, n. 5).

go the same punishments which history relates to have been decreed against that most renown criminal: namely, that the writer who would record that crime, would make no mention of that man, and his name be not recorded.[1] And so it happens that he would be punished in that which had suggested matter of sin to him. In this way also, the Church breathed upon by God's Spirit orders that the books of heretics be handed over to be burned with fire. For it is just that his vainglory, which is considered to be the mother and parent of such a great crime, perished when his books were burned; nor may anyone read those books, which having been disregarded there is left nothing from which he may receive the glory which he solely sought. Thus concerning them it can be said those words of Paul to the Romans: "They became vain in their thoughts" (1, 21).

However, someone will oppose this punishment, saying that it nowise ought to be inflicted for this reason: namely, that the punishment hinders the faithful who do not have the books of the heretics. For even if there may be some erroneous things in the books, there are nevertheless some other things said exceptionally well, which will hardly be found in other books which are according to the faith, and which to obstruct would be unjust.

To which we reply that it ought to be feared lest by love of those things which the heretics say well, the attracted readers may be drawn into subscribing to the other things said perversely. Wherefore the Church, thoroughly instructed by the Holy Ghost, deems it better to lack both, than to swallow both. So also we read in Saint Luke's Gospel, namely, that when the demons having been cast out from the bodies of men by Christ's power, cried out and said: "Thou art the Son of God," Christ "rebuking them suffered them not to speak" (4, 41). Were they not saying true things? Why then does He forbid them to speak? Certainly lest by this occasion the false things again spoken by them might be believed. For thus speaks Bede: "Now why the Lord forbids the devils to speak about the faith, the Psalmist makes clear, who says, 'Why dost thou declare my justices, and take my covenant in thy mouth?' (Ps. 49, 16) lest while someone listens to a preacher, he follow his error. For the devil is a wicked teacher, who often mixes together false things with the true, so that under the appearance of the truth he may cover up his testimony of deceit."[2]

Therefore, if the Lord on that occasion forbids the demons from crying out, what prevents the Church forbidding the offspring of devils from writing? Cannot writings harm as much as words? Nay, they do so much more. For even if words are more effective, nevertheless, once they have been uttered you cannot make them heard again: but writing lasts through many centuries, and so it can either harm or benefit many people. Therefore the Church rightly forbids the writings of these men, and tears them to pieces if they can be obtained, just as Christ forbade the words of those demons, even if what was being said by them were true. So also heretics, even if they say many true and fine things, nevertheless the false things mixed in with the other true things undermine the faith. Hence Gregory, expounding the passage of Job, "And indignation is come upon me" (3, 26), says the following: "Heretics have this especial peculiarity, that they mix good and evil, so that they may easily delude the mind of the hearer. For if they always said wrong, having been more quickly discovered in their depravity of thought, they would be the less able to win a way for that which they desire. Again, if they always thought aright, then surely they would never have been heretics. But with artfulness of deceiving they engage themselves with both, and by the evil they vitiate the good, and by the good they conceal the evil, to the end that it may be readily admitted: just as he that presents

---

[1] The above passage continues, "He revealed his mad scheme after he was put on the rack. The Ephesians made a wise decision and decreed that all evidence of this repulsive man's existence should be wiped out, but the very eloquent and talented Theopompus [of Chios, who lived from 378 to 320 B.C.] included the man's name in his historical work."

[2] *In Evangelium S. Lucae*, bk. 2 (PL 92, 381B).

Introduction

a cup of poison touches the brim of the cup with honeyed sweets, and while this that has a sweet flavor is tasted at the first sip, that which brings death is unhesitatingly swallowed. Thus heretics mix right with wrong, that by making a show of good things, they may draw hearers to themselves, and by setting forth evil they may corrupt them with a secret pestilence."[1] Therefore the Church, being fearful, prudently forbids the books of heretics, lest that happen which the Wise Man says: "He that toucheth pitch, shall be defiled with it" (Eccli. 13, 1).

Because even if there are some things found among them that are explained with precise investigation, it is much better to find out about them from other orthodox men than from heretics. Because if there still are such things, such that they are found in the writings of no orthodox man (which I hardly believe) those things nevertheless will always be suspect to me, because they were said by such a man, namely a heretic. For so Diogenes Laertius[2] relates in his book, *Lives and Opinions of Eminent Philosophers*, that when someone asked Aristotle: "What do people gain by telling lies?" he is said to have answered the same man: "Just this, that when they speak the truth," he said, "they are not believed."[3] Therefore, when a heretic is caught in heresy, why should he be trusted afterwards? It is thus not just that we accept the interpretation of a passage of Sacred Scripture from heretics, since we have discovered that their explanations have despised other passages. We dare not eat bodily food from the hand of the same man who once or twice has offered us poison; why would we want to accept the teaching of the faith from heretics, who many times have mixed in poisonous teachings?

Neither does one ever accept his master's food from his enemy, nor does a soldier undertake military service for enemies of the king, unless he be clearly a deserter or fugitive. The woman in Luke's Gospel looking for the groat (15, 8) looks within her house, not outside. So also, one ought to seek within the Church, if you desire to find what pertains to the true faith. The man who asks for bread in Luke's Gospel knocks at the door of his neighbor, not of a stranger. True doctrine ought to be sought from the true Christian. One's neighbors are all true Christians, living within one and the same city. From heretics, however, because they are strangers, nothing ought to be asked. If with these men (as Paul says) it is not permitted "so much as to eat" (I Cor. 5, 11), much less will it be permitted to ask for food from them.

Add to this that heretics do not have the right of interpreting Sacred Writ, nor does it belong to them in any way to give discourses about it. For since they are not sons to whom the inheritance has been bequeathed in a will, they have absolutely no right of examining the father's will, which is Sacred Scripture. If "the son of the bondwoman shall not be heir with the son of the free woman" (Gal. 4, 30), much less will a stranger be heir with the son of the free woman. If the bondwoman ought to be cast out with her son, namely the synagogue, all the more the "assembly of the malignant" (Ps. 25, 5) with its children shall have to be cast out, namely the heretics. Therefore, the heretics have been excluded from the father's will, and they also will not have the right of viewing the will, which is Sacred Scripture. If they do not have the right of viewing, how is it that they have the right of interpreting? Therefore in no way will it be permitted to accept the interpretation of Sacred Scripture from them, but rather shall it be obtained from elsewhere. Hence, Tertullian in his book, *Prescription against Heretics*, says: "Not being Christians, they have acquired no right to the Christian Scriptures; and it may be very fairly said to them, 'Who are you? When and whence did you come? As you are none of mine, what have you to do with that which is mine? Indeed, Marcion, by what right do you hew my wood? By whose permission, Valentinus, are you diverting the streams

---

[1] *Moralia*, bk. 5, chap. 11, n. 28 (PL 75, 694A-B).

[2] Diogenes Laertius (third century B. C.) was a biographer of the Greek philosophers. Nothing is known about his life, but his surviving *The Lives and Opinions of Eminent Philosophers* is a principal source for the history of Greek philosophy.

[3] Bk. 4, n. 17.

of my fountain? By what power, Apelles, are you removing my landmarks? This is my property. Why are you, the rest, sowing and feeding here at your own pleasure? This (I say) is my property. I have long possessed it; I possessed it before you. I hold sure title deeds from the original owners themselves, to whom the estate belonged. I am the heir of the Apostles. Just as they carefully prepared their will and testament, and committed it to a trust, and adjured (the trustees to be faithful to their charge), even so do I hold it. As for you, certain it is that they have always held you as disinherited, and rejected you as strangers and enemies.' But on what ground are heretics strangers and enemies to the Apostles, if it be not from the difference of their teaching, which each individual of his own mere will has either advanced or received in opposition to the Apostles? Where diversity of doctrine is found, there, then, must the corruption both of the Scriptures and its interpretations be found."[1]

Howbeit, because due to the occasion offered to us we have digressed a little, it is necessary that our discourse be redirected back to its initial objective. Therefore just as pertinacity arises from that most wicked root, namely the desire for glory, so also does deception of judgment, such that on account of their sins God permits them to be led into error. For so says Isaias: "He hath blinded their eyes, and hardened their heart, that they should not see with their eyes, nor understand with their heart."[2] The light of truth, as Gregory testifies, is hidden from proud minds,[3] and every sin is a certain blindness of the mind,[4] according to that which is written: "Their own malice blinded them" (Wis. 2, 21). Elsewhere it is said: "They shall walk like blind men, because they have sinned against the Lord" (Soph. 1, 17). Further, concerning the proud it is said by the Apostle to the Romans: "Their foolish heart was darkened, for professing themselves to be wise, they became fools" (Rom. 1, 21-22). [Hervé de Bourg-Dieu], expounding the words of Paul taken from his Epistle to the Ephesians, "That we be no more carried about with every wind of doctrine by the wickedness of men" (4, 14), says the following: "He said, 'By the wickedness of men,' because there is no heresy except in the soul subject to sins: because the sins committed are the causes for which God permits them to err into the abyss of heresy."[5]

Add to this that God does not permit man to be deceived solely on account of his own iniquity, but also on account of the sin of the one asking or learning: God permits a good man teaching someone to be deceived, so that he may deceive the iniquitous enquirer. For so we read in the book of the Prophet Ezechiel: "And the word of the Lord came to me, saying: Son of man, these men have placed their uncleannesses in their hearts, and have set up before their face the stumblingblock of their iniquity: and shall I answer when they inquire of me? Therefore speak to them, and say to them: Thus saith the Lord God: Man, man of the house of Israel that shall place his uncleannesses in his heart, and set up the stumblingblock of his iniquity before his face, and shall come to the prophet inquiring of me by him: I the Lord will answer him according to the multitude of his uncleannesses: That the house of Israel may be caught in their own heart, with which they have departed from me through all their idols.

---

[1] Chap. 37 & 38, (PL 2, 51A-C).

[2] The cited passage is worded as found in Jn. 12, 40. The original wording from Isaias is as follows: "Blind the heart of this people, and make their ears heavy, and shut their eyes: lest they see with their eyes, and hear with their ears, and understand with their heart" (Is. 6, 10).

[3] "The light of truth, which is concealed from proud and overbusied minds" (*Moralia*, bk. 27, chap. 14, n. 26 (PL 76, 414B)).

[4] "Day can be taken as our delight in sin and night as the blindness of the mind by which man lets himself stoop to commit sin" (*Ibid.*, bk. 4, chap. 13, n. 24 (PL 75, 650C)).

[5] This quotation is incorrectly attributed here to Saint Anselm of Canterbury, but instead belongs to Hervé de Bourg-Dieu (1080-1150), a French Benedictine exegete, in his *Commentaria in epistolas Pauli-In Epistolam ad Ephesios* (PL 181, 1248D).

Introduction

Therefore say to the house of Israel: Thus saith the Lord God: Be converted, and depart from your idols, and turn away your faces from all your abominations. For every man of the house of Israel, and every stranger among the proselytes in Israel, if he separate himself from me, and place his idols in his heart, and set the stumblingblock of his iniquity before his face, and come to the prophet to inquire of me by him: I the Lord will answer him by myself. And I will set my face against that man, and will make him an example, and a proverb, and will cut him off from the midst of my people: and you shall know that I am the Lord. And when the prophet shall err, and speak a word: I the Lord have deceived that prophet: and I will stretch forth my hand upon him, and will cut him off from the midst of my people Israel. And they shall bear their iniquity: according to the iniquity of him that inquireth, so shall the iniquity of the prophet be" (14, 2-10).

From which passage of Scripture it is clearly surmised that to a wicked people, on account of their sins heretical teachers are given by God: or, so that I may speak more truly, are permitted [by God]. Which perhaps in our time happened in parts of Germany, where Luther was made a false prophet and Pseudoapostle. For their works of the flesh are manifest, "Whose God is their belly; and whose glory is in their shame; who mind earthly things" (Phil. 3, 19). Wherefore what the Lord threatened through the prophet had to happen, namely, that according to the iniquity of the one asking, was the iniquity of the prophet. Because if they are to be recalled from error, there is no other way available than that which the Lord showed: namely, that they be converted from their evil way and repent of their evil actions, and that the change in their lives be for the better. Or at least if they shall have prayed to the Lord that He show them the way of truth, and fulfill His promise, Who said: "Ask, and you shall receive" (Jn. 16, 24), "Knock, and it shall be opened to you" (Mt. 7, 7). Because if only the sin of the one asking hinders the prophet, such that it be the cause of that deception, how much more do you think will the sin of the teacher himself hinder? Therefore, it will be without any doubt the most effective cause, such that He turns a blind eye, and he errs.

If therefore to the heretic Sacred Scripture be offered to one knowing letters, he ought to say: "I know no letters" (Is. 29, 12). But since he is led by the desire for glory, he will never admit his ignorance, nay rather, saying that he is a wise man he is caught in his foolishness. The Lord mocks such men as these though the Prophet Isaias saying: "For they seek me from day to day, and desire to know my ways, as a nation that hath done justice, and hath not forsaken the judgment of their God" (Is. 58, 2). By which words the Lord clearly suggests that he who has not done justice or has forsaken God's judgment can neither find Him nor know His ways. Christ says the same thing in Matthew's Gospel: "O generation of vipers, how can you speak good things, whereas you are evil? for out of the abundance of the heart the mouth speaketh" (Mt. 12, 34). Hence it is, that we in fact persuade by this evidence that holy men, "who by faith conquered kingdoms, wrought justice, obtained promises" (Heb. 11, 33), ought rather to be believed than other men whose lives are not approved by as many proofs, even if [the latter are] more learned. For as the book of Ecclesiasticus says: "The soul of a holy man discovereth sometimes true things, more than seven watchmen that sit in a high place to watch" (37, 18).

By this evidence it is also proved that the exposition of Sacred Scripture ought not to be accepted from heretics, except it shall have been established that his interpretation is true in another way. How do we know whether or not, having taken into account the heretics faults, God shall allow him to err in that same passage as in other ones? Therefore, so that we be not deceived, it is necessary that according to James' wise counsel, we "ask the Lord in faith, nothing wavering" (1, 6): hence let us consult those men who have been approved by the Church both for their lives and knowledge. Heretics however nowise ought to be consulted, because they ought to be held suspect on many accounts, firstly because they have been caught at some time in a lie, then because they are covered with sins, on account of which God permits them to err in Scripture, and to interpret it otherwise than it ought. Hence Gregory expounding the passage from Job, "who gnawed in the wilderness" etc., says the following: "That is wont to be 'gnawed,' which cannot be eaten. Now heretics because they apply themselves to make out Scripture by their own power, assuredly never can comprehend it, which same whilst they do not make out, they, as it were, do not eat. And because, not being aided by grace from on high, they are unable to eat it, they, as it were, 'gnaw' it with certain efforts. Since they handle it outwardly, when indeed they endeavor but do not attain to the interior parts of it. Which same because they are separated from the society of the Church Universal, are mentioned as gnawing not anywhere, but 'in solitude.'"[1]

After this desire for glory common to all heretics, then the particular cause of heresy follows. Now this will be the vice particular to any heretic: namely, that into which anyone is inclined, since there is in each man a certain inclination to some vice, even though in everyone it be not to the same one. Certain men have an inborn greed, others are prone to enticements of the flesh, others again desire honors, and they seek the first seats. Now, affection (as Aristotle maintains) draws the judgment of reason to itself, such that the intellect often chooses the same as the hands and feet, as it is said, towards which the will directs it, or to which direction it feels the will to be leaning. Hence those sects of philosophers arose placing human happiness into various vain and fallacious things. Everyone considers to be best what he desires more, the judgment yielding to the will. Because if perhaps the intellect does not approve that which it knows that the will desires, still it pretends to approve it, so that the vice may be more easily hidden, or at least the vice with which it is afflicted may be overshadowed. Wherefore if perhaps he shall be caught in this or that vice, he may be covered with this cloak, namely, that he acted in ignorance. Of which ignorance this indeed could have been the proof, namely, that he often bore witness that there was no crime in that affair, for surely he preferred to be branded with the mark of ignorance, than to not have that thing to which he claimed for himself.

For we know this by experience, and from the reputation which we have from our past deeds, that certainly no one ever approved a vice, which human society has opposed, or a virtue to which one was naturally inclined. There is perhaps someone who considers being subject to the will of another burdensome, and who thinks it hard to depend on the will of another. Hence, it happens that he shakes off the yoke of obedience, which he had at one time accepted, and from there he goes on to further things, so that he speaks ill of obedience itself, and treats monastic life with insults and scoffing. This in order that he may cover his error with this cloak, namely, that he shows to others that he left a place which he considered to be ignominious and irreligious.

There are so many very clear examples of this that they would be tedious to relate. As to this, if someone desires money immoderately, it would be due to his excessive and unbridled adherence to this thing that he would apply every effort to acquire it. He would move every stone (as it is said), and leave nothing untried which could perhaps assist this endeavor in the least: even to such an extent that, if it were necessary, he would plunder Sacred Writ. Diogenes Laertius relates that a certain philosopher, Menippus, hung himself with a rope on account of his money having been snatched away by a ruse.[2] See that as much as the love

---

[1] *Moralia*, bk. 20, chap. 9, n. 20 (PL 76, 149A-B).
[2] "Menippus was also a Cynic, and a Phoenician by descent, a slave by birth, as Achaicus tells us in his *Ethics*; and Diocles informs us that his master was a native of Pontus named Baton; but that subsequently, in consequence of his importunities and miserly habits, he became rich, and obtained the rights of citizenship at Corinth. He never wrote anything serious; but his writings are full of ridiculous matter; and in some respects similar to those of Meleager, who was his contemporary. And Hermippus tells us that he was a man who lent money at daily interest, and that he was called a usurer; for he used to lend

Introduction

of something had preceded, that much sorrow followed after the thing was lost. What did he not attempt, who did not hesitate to kill himself? What also did he not do, who did not shrink back from selling God? Was not the error rebuked by Christ also from this source, [namely the error] whereby the Pharisees were teaching the Jews that it was better to offer something in the Temple, than to distribute it to one's needy parents?[1] And it is not needful to dwell any longer on these things, since Paul in his First Epistle to Timothy explains it very clearly saying: "They that will become rich, fall into temptation, and into the snare of the devil, and into many unprofitable and hurtful desires, which drown men into destruction and perdition. For the desire of money is the root of all evils; which some coveting have erred from the faith, and have entangled themselves in many sorrows" (6, 9-10).

Moreover, Blessed Gregory, expounding this passage of Job, "The root of junipers was their food" (30, 4), says the following: "What then is there denoted by the 'root of the juniper' saving avarice, from which the thorns of all the sins are produced? Concerning which it is said by Paul, 'For the desire of money is the root of all evils' (I Tim. 6, 10). For that springs up covertly in the mind, and brings forth openly the prickles of all sin in the practice. Which same prickles arising from this root the great preacher immediately implies, when he subjoins, 'Which some coveting have erred from the faith, and have entangled themselves in many sorrows.' For he who spoke of 'many sorrows' made known as it were the prickles arising from this root. So by 'junipers' we understand sins, but by 'the root of junipers' what else do we understand, but avarice, i.e. the material of sins? So then, because heretics in their words generally go after external gains alone, yet are not ignorant that they make up what is wrong, but do not abandon the preachings of error whilst they wish to receive their emoluments as teachers, it is well said of them now by the voice of the holy man, 'and juniper roots for their meat.' Because whilst they think of avarice with all the faculties of their minds, they are as it were fed by that nourishment, wherefrom assuredly the prickles of sins ensuing are used to be produced. Which persons if ever in sacred Revelation they seemingly discover things with sagacity, which while they do not understand, they fancy make for their statements, they directly scatter these vociferating them to their wretched hearers, whom they covet not the souls of but the substance."[2]

Concerning the allurements of the flesh, that they are the roots of heresies, Paul testifies in his Epistle to the Romans: "Now I beseech you, brethren, to mark them who make dissensions and offences contrary to the doctrine which you have learned, and avoid them. For they that are such, serve not Christ our Lord, but their own belly" (16, 17-18). Theophylactus commenting on this passage says: "All heresies are born from the fact that their authors are exceedingly subservient to their inclinations and their stomach."[3] And again, writing to the Philippians, Paul gives the same opinion: "Be ye followers of me, brethren, and observe them who walk so as you have our model. For many walk, of whom I have told you often (and now tell you weeping), that they are enemies of the cross of Christ; whose end is destruction; whose God is their belly; and whose glory is in their shame; who mind earthly things" (3, 17-19).

That the allurements of the flesh impede the mind, such that the carnal man is unable to understand the hidden mysteries of the faith, Isaias clearly teaches saying the following: "Whom shall he make to understand the hearing?" To which question the Prophet himself answering

---

on nautical usury, and take security, so that he amassed a very great amount of riches. But at last he fell into a trap, and lost all his money, and in a fit of despair he hung himself, and so he died" (*The Lives and Opinions of Eminent Philosophers*, bk. 6, n. 99-100).

[1] Cf. Mt. 15, 4-6.
[2] *Moralia*, bk. 20, chap. 10, n. 21 (PL 76, 150B-C).
[3] *Expositio ad Epistolam ad Romanos* (PG 124, 555C).

says: "Them that are weaned from the milk, that are drawn away from the breasts" (Is. 28, 9), that is to say, those who are separated from carnal pleasures. If these alone God makes to understand the mysteries of faith which are said to them, then those who are not weaned from carnal pleasures, cannot understand the things that they have heard.

There are very many examples of this thing. From this source, Cerinthus went forth expecting the pleasures of the flesh as the beatitude that was promised. From this root Adamites[1] and the groups of the Fratricelli.[2] From the same root, the former heresy was indulging men in promiscuous and random sexual intercourse. For this reason the Arians heretics completely rejected fasting and asserted it to be of no value. From that source another heresy, namely of Jovinian, equated matrimony with virginity: and many other of this sort which will be described in their sections.

For the rest, concerning ambition, who does not know that it is the parent of many heresies? For just as when the world was born the beginning of all sins was pride, so when the same world was reborn through Christ, the beginning of every heresy was also pride. For what else motivated Simon Magus (for Eusebius of Caesarea relates that he was the first heretic[3]) to have offered money that in exchange he would own God's house, except pride? "And when Simon saw," Luke said in the Acts of the Apostles, "that by the imposition of the hands of the apostles, the Holy Ghost was given, he offered them money saying: Give me also this power, that on whomsoever I shall lay my hands, he may receive the Holy Ghost" (8, 18-19). For except that Simon was led by the desire for glory and honor, it would have sufficed for him to have asked for God's Spirit for himself. But because he considered it a small thing to possess, unless this were also known to others, thus he asked for the power of communicating [God's Spirit]. And this so that by this occasion many men would come to him to ask for God's gift, and many would venerate him as God, which is what he mostly wished for, as the outcome of the affair showed. For he pretended to the people that he was God, and accepted from the deceived people divine honors, as Blessed Justin Martyr relates in his discourse that he wrote in favor of our faith to the Emperor Antonius [Pius].[4] At approximately the same time there was a certain Thebuthis, concerning which Eusebius in his *Church History* relates: "because he was not made bishop, began to corrupt it [the faith]. He also was sprung from the seven sects among the people."[5] And concerning a certain Aerius, Augustine relates in his *Book of Heresies*,[6] that striving for a bishopric which he could not obtain, in order that he might seem no less than the bishops, asserted that priests are equal to bishops. From this root came forth afterwards the Wycliffites, the Hussites, and perhaps in our time the Lutherans: who in that

---

[1] The Adamites are an obscure sect, dating perhaps from the second century, which professed to have regained Adam's primeval innocence. Consequently they called their church "Paradise"; they condemned marriage as foreign to Eden, and they stripped themselves naked while engaged in common worship.

[2] The Fratricelli were various heretical sects which appeared in the fourteenth and fifteenth centuries, principally in Italy. A number of them separated from the Franciscan Order on account of the disputes concerning poverty. "The allegation that their religious services were defiled by immoral practices cannot be proved" ("Fraticelli," *Catholic Encyclopedia (1909 ed.), vol. 6, p. 249*).

[3] "We have understood that Simon was the author of all heresy" (*Church History*, bk, 2, chap. 13, n. 6).

[4] "There was a Samaritan, Simon, a native of the village called Gitto, who in the reign of Claudius Cæsar, and in your royal city of Rome, did mighty acts of magic, by virtue of the art of the devils operating in him. He was considered a god, and as a god was honored by you with a statue, which statue was erected on the river Tiber, between the two bridges, and bore this inscription, in the language of Rome:— 'Simoni Deo Sancto,' 'To Simon the holy God'" (N. 26 (PG 6, 367A-B)).

[5] Bk. 4, chap. 22, n.5.

[6] *De Haeresibus*, chap. 53 (PL 53, 39-40).

Introduction

they could not attain to the dignity of a bishop, lest in something they seem to be less than the bishops, they took care to make bishops equal to all priests.[1]

I think that these most manifest examples suffice for the proof of this matter, from which it is clearly shown that the heresies which deal with morals, have those men as founders, who have a proclivity by their nature to those vices. Wherefore, because they often fall into them, be it that the intellect yields to the will, they judge to be good that to which their will unrestrainedly adheres: and they also judge that to be bad which their wills forsake. For since the same virtue has two opposite vices, if anyone by nature is prone towards one, it will never happen that the one opposite to it is found to have been approved. There were, I say, those who condemned all sexual intercourse, and yet there were not lacking those who permitted and approved of all sexual intercourse. Yet if you demand historical accounts, you will never find him who has no share in associations with women, to have allowed all sexual intercourse to others: or he who was given to the allurements of the flesh, to have condemned all sexual intercourse. Hence, Augustine says: "When men are prone to estimate sins, not by reference to their inherent sinfulness, but rather by reference to their own customs, it frequently happens that a man will think nothing blamable except what the men of his own country and time are accustomed to condemn, and nothing worthy of praise or approval except what is sanctioned by the custom of his companions. And thus it comes to pass, that if Scripture either enjoins what is opposed to the customs of the hearers, or condemns what is not so opposed, and if at the same time the authority of the word has a hold upon their minds, they think that the expression is figurative."[2] In which words the most holy and learned Father most appropriately and "to life" (as it is said) depicted the heretics of the present time, to whom, if something were objected from Sacred Scripture which clearly was contrary to their sect, they immediately said that it is figurative speech.

Chapter XII: Concerning two other causes from which heresies also arise.

Besides those roots of heresy which we have mentioned, there is another root of heresy, which has absolutely no malice of itself, if there is moderation, but only from the vice of those using it badly. This is the constant reading of books of profane men, meaning of pagans. And this reading especially [is a root of heresy], if it were imbued in them from infancy without any discernment of things. For in fact Horace says: "The cask will long retain the odor of that with which it was once filled."[3] And through a certain prophet the Lord says: "If the Ethiopian can change his skin, or the leopard his spots: you may also do well, when you have learned evil" (Jer. 13, 23). For so efficacious is custom that it nearly passes into the nature, especially at a tender age, during which time things easily make a deep impression, and the impression adheres more tenaciously.

In pagan books you will find many things which oppose the Catholic faith as it were diametrically, many things which allure to vices, draw away from virtue, among the poets especially, among whom vices are prized and highly praised, since they do not disdain to ascribe them to their gods. There you will find irreconcilable discords of brothers, there very harsh punishments of children by their parents, there very pertinacious disobediences of children, there very indecent love affairs, adulteries, rapes, and the honors of kidnapped Ganymede.[4]

---

[1] Cf. Epiphanius, *Anacephal*, bk. 3, t. 1, n. 6 (PG 42, 872).

[2] *On Christian Doctrine*, bk. 3, chap. 10, n. 15 (PL 34, 71).

[3] *Epistles of Horace*, bk. 1, Ep. 2, v. 69.

[4] Ganymede was a handsome, young Trojan prince who was carried off to heaven by Zeus, or his eagle, to be the god's lover and cup-bearer of the gods.

Introduction

On account of which not undeservingly Plato banished the poets of this kind from his Republic, the kind of men most ready and able to harm.

But if you turn yourself to the philosophers and their wise men, you will find in their writings many things which are opposed to piety and the true religion. For what can oppose more the true faith than the multitude of gods which very many of them put forth? What is more injurious to God than to render violence to Him and to completely disjoin from Him His liberty in the production of things? Yet Aristotle and so many Peripatetic schools attributed this to Him. In his writings you will find an eternal world, lacking any beginning or end. This statement is theirs: "Nothing out of nothing, into nothing nothing can return." There are also many other things of this sort, for enumerating which it would be necessary to compose a list.

Wherefore the Apostle forewarned us to beware of philosophy, which he knew well, because he spent some time among the philosophers at Athens. "Beware lest any man cheat you by philosophy, and vain deceit" (Col. 2, 8). Hence Tertullian in his book, *The Prescription Against Heretics*, thinks likewise saying: "Indeed heresies are themselves instigated by philosophy. From this source came the Æons, and I know not what infinite forms, and the trinity of man in the system of Valentinus, who was of Plato's school. From the same source came Marcion's better god, with all his tranquility; he came from the Stoics. Then, again, the opinion that the soul dies is held by the Epicureans; while the denial of the restoration of the body is taken from the aggregate school of all the philosophers; also, when matter is made equal to God, then you have the teaching of Zeno; and when any doctrine is alleged touching a god of fire, then Heraclitus comes in. The same subject-matter is discussed over and over again by the heretics and the philosophers; the same arguments are used."[1] Add the fact that on account of them, those who were after Christ and His Apostles, do not merely fight with the Christian religion, but what is most pestilential of all things, they deride, mock and persecute it.

Hence, it often happens that the weak and feeble undergo scruples and suspicions therefrom concerning the Christian religion: which when once they have begun to vehemently vex the soul, they go away with difficulty and late. For from philosophers is born an astounding liberty of speech, to such a degree that they never yield to anything unless it be proved by clear arguments and evidence: hence it happens that those things which do not correspond to their opinion, they immediately reject. But faith does not rely on such evidence of arguments, but requires the captivity of the understanding unto the obedience of Christ.[2] Hence Paul rightly says: "The Jews require signs, and the Greeks seek after wisdom: but we preach Christ crucified, unto the Jews indeed a stumblingblock, and unto the Gentiles foolishness: but unto them that are called, both Jews and Greeks, Christ the power of God, and the wisdom of God: for the foolishness of God is wiser than men" (I Cor. 1, 22-25). Therefore, since such things are in the writings of the heathens, there is now no reason for anyone to doubt that the constant reading of them harms Christians very much, especially the incautious and weak. If books full of piety profit their readers, why cannot ungodly books impede the same readers? For so the Royal Prophet says: "With the holy, thou wilt be holy… and with the perverse thou wilt be perverted" (Ps. 17, 26-27).

If customs and social intercourse change men's morals, and allure men to follow them, it is beyond a doubt that the reading of books can do the same thing. Nay, often more effectively, because although words have move more strongly, draw more vehemently, and snatch away more quickly than writing, because the living word pierces more sharply. Nevertheless, things which are written, since they are produced by long reflection, ought to be better absorbed, ordered more accurately, than those in common speech, and for that reason it happens that writing is often more effective than the spoken word: because a premeditated speech has

---

[1] Chap. 7 (PL 2, 19B).
[2] Cf. II Cor. 10, 5.

Introduction

more force than one said *ex tempore*. Hence Basil, teaching his nephews how the books of the pagans, especially the poets, ought to be read, says: "But when they portray base conduct, you must flee from them and stop up your ears, as Odysseus is said to have fled past the song of the Sirens, for familiarity with evil writings paves the way for evil deeds."[1] There is in addition to this the fact that in whatever thing to be discussed they have great ornamentation, elegance, brilliance of speech: all of which things are influences most efficacious for alluring men's souls. Thus Paul says: "Now this I say, that no man may deceive you by loftiness of words" (Col. 2, 4). Theophylactus, expounding which words, says: "'I said this,' he said, because to Christ alone all things are more known and manifest, lest anyone deceive you with pandering and loftiness of words namely by a certain adornment, courteousness, and elegance of speech of theirs. For what if someone were to preach things which can greatly persuade, but he is ignorant of everything, that is to say, of the truth? It is indeed nothing other than to argue by subtleties and sophisms."[2] This also heretics have done, namely, that by the elegance of their speech they deceive the unwary, as Paul bears witness in his Epistle to the Romans where after warning them to beware of heretics, he adds: "By pleasing speeches and good words, seduce the hearts of the innocent" (16, 18).

Hence Origen, expounding the passage in Jeremias, "Babylon hath been a golden cup in the hand of the Lord, that made all the earth drunk" (51, 7), says the following: "Nabuchodonosor, wishing to deceive men through the deceitful 'cup of Babylon,' did not mix the potion he was preparing in a vessel of clay, nor in what was a little better, in an iron, copper or pewter vessel, or in what is superior to these, silver. Choosing rather a "golden" vessel in which he blended the drink so that whoever sees what is attractive about the gold, touched by the beauty of the radiant metal and entirely drawn with eyes to its splendor, does not consider what is inwardly hidden, and accepting the 'cup,' drinks, ignoring that it is the cup of Nabuchodonosor. You will understand what is called the 'golden cup' in the present text if you notice that the deadly words of the most evil teachings have a certain kind of arrangement of speaking, a kind of attractive eloquence, a kind of beauty of order. And you know how each of the poets, who are considered by you as the most well-spoken men, have blended the 'golden cup' and injected the venom of idolatry and the venom of obscenity, the venom of those teachings which slay the soul of man, the venom with the false name of knowledge. But my Jesus has done the opposite. For by knowing the 'golden cup' of Satan and taking care that no one coming to His faith would ever worry that what he left behind was the 'cup' of Christ and through a similarity of material would fear an error, He took care then that 'we have this treasure in earthen vessels' (II Cor. 4, 7). I have often seen a 'golden cup,' decorated with beauty of words, and when I consider the venom of its teaching, I have perceived that it is the 'cup of Babylon.'"[3] Nevertheless, I would not want anyone to think that I said these things because I think that elegance of speech conflicts with the Christian religion, or is in some way opposed to the Catholic faith. I indeed admit that those things can work together such that one may be at the same time truly Christian and eloquent, as were among the Greeks Basil, Gregory Nazianzen, and Chrysostom; and among the Latins Jerome, Cyprian, Ambrose and Hilary. And would that I were such, so that firstly on account of holiness and then on account of eloquence I might be deservedly numbered among their ranks. For elegance of speech and the cultivation of prayer are such things that are common to the good and wicked, Catholics

---

[1] Chap. 4 (PG 31, 570A).

[2] A variant rendition of the Greek is found in Migne's *Patrologia Graeca* as follows: "'I said this,' he said, because Christ alone has known all things, 'that no man may deceive you.' For what if someone were to speak persuasively? He has known nothing, and truly all this is a deception, and vain sophistry." PG 124, 1235D.

[3] PG 13, 538D-539C.

and heretics alike, which anyone can use both well and badly: for it is very good ornament to Catholic men, most useful for the persuasion to virtues and the censuring of vices. Because if this eloquence were to chance upon some heretic, it will render him more powerful for deceiving. For by charm of speech as though by some flatteries he draws the mind of the reader to his opinion. And so I said these things, namely, lest allured by mere brilliance of speech, as with a golden cup, he drink up poisoned teaching. Hence the Wise Man says: "Look not upon the wine when it is yellow, when the colour thereof shineth in the glass: it goeth in pleasantly, but in the end, it will bite like a snake, and will spread abroad poison like a basilisk" (Prov. 23, 31-32).

But when one shall have read it, he rather pays attention to what the writing relates, and not how it relates. For no one (as I believe) is so mindless, that he prefers poison in a golden vessel, rather than very good wine in a clay vessel. It indeed makes no difference for the health of the body whether you drink from the latter or the former, provided that it brings some utility when you pour it into the stomach: yet it helps for the pleasure of the eyes to use clean, ornate and also precious vessels. So also brilliance of speech and fineness of language delights in an amazing way: but they nowise reinvigorate unless under that coloring of words some solid food of true doctrine is concealed. For eloquence of speech seems to me to be like a condiment, so that food may be eaten more avidly. But to put out a condiment alone at a meal, is to stimulate hunger and not to prepare a meal. Because if the speech were plentiful and ornate in subject matter and words, it will certainly be a sumptuous meal, which no one attending could rightly disdain. Therefore for all these reasons it is now made sufficiently clear (as I think) how much the reading of the books of pagans can be prejudicial to true piety and the Catholic faith, in which there is much poison for killing, and very much honey for alluring.

But it is necessary here to advise that the books of pagans should not be completely abandoned on this account, because they can teach us many things, the knowledge of which is quite necessary for the understanding of Sacred Books. We have definitions and divisions from Logic and Metaphysics. Natural science shows the causes, origins, and properties of things, from the knowledge of which many hidden things in Scriptures are shown to us. About Moses it is said that he "was instructed in all the wisdom of the Egyptians" (Acts 7, 22). Augustine in fact asserts in chapter twenty-eight of book two of his book, *On Christian Doctrine*, that the pagan histories contribute very much for understanding of Sacred Scripture, and he shows that some men from their ignorance of them erred about the Scriptures.[1] And in chapter twenty-nine of book three of the treatise, he shows that the knowledge of tropes and figures, which is to be sought from grammarians and orators, are altogether necessary for understanding of Scriptures.[2] Finally, in chapter forty of book two he says the following concerning the teaching of all the philosophers: "Moreover, if those who are called philosophers, and espe-

---

[1] "Anything, then, that we learn from history about the chronology of past times assists us very much in understanding the Scriptures, even if it be learnt without the pale of the Church as a matter of childish instruction. For we frequently seek information about a variety of matters by use of the Olympiads, and the names of the consuls; and ignorance of the consulship in which our Lord was born, and that in which He suffered, has led some into the error of supposing that He was forty-six years of age when He suffered, that being the number of years He was told by the Jews the temple (which He took as a symbol of His body) was in building..." (N. 42 (PL 34, 55)).

[2] "Moreover, I would have learned men to know that the authors of our Scriptures use all those forms of expression which grammarians call by the Greek name tropes, and use them more freely and in greater variety than people who are unacquainted with the Scriptures, and have learnt these figures of speech from other writings, can imagine or believe. Nevertheless those who know these tropes recognize them in Scripture, and are very much assisted by their knowledge of them in understanding Scripture" (N. 40 (PL 34, 80).

Introduction

cially the Platonists, have said aught that is true and in harmony with our faith, we should not shrink from it, but rather claim it for our own use from those who have unlawful possession of it. For, the Egyptians had not only the idols and heavy burdens which the people of Israel hated and fled from, but also vessels and ornaments of gold and silver, and garments, which the same people, when going out of Egypt, appropriated to themselves, designing them for a better use. And they did this not on their own authority, but by the command of God, the Egyptians themselves, in their ignorance, providing them with things which they themselves were not making a good use of. In the same way, all branches of heathen learning have not only false and superstitious fancies and heavy burdens of unnecessary toil—which every one of us, when going out under the leadership of Christ from the fellowship of the heathen, ought to abhor and avoid—but they contain also liberal instruction which is better adapted to the use of the truth, and some most excellent precepts of morality. Moreover, some truths in regard even to the worship of the One God are found among them. Now these are, so to speak, their gold and silver, which they did not create themselves, but dug out of the mines of God's providence which are everywhere scattered abroad, and are perversely and unlawfully prostituting to the worship of devils. These, therefore, the Christian, when he separates himself in spirit from the miserable fellowship of these men, ought to take away from them, and to devote to their proper use in preaching the gospel. Their garments, also,—that is, human institutions such as are adapted to that intercourse with men which is indispensable in this life,—we must take and turn to a Christian use."[1]

Their teachings can also be beneficial for fighting against the pagans themselves: so that when we fight against them we may cut their throats with their own sword, just as David killed Goliath, according to sacred history.[2] For in fact by these weapons Justin Martyr fights in his *Apology* against the pagans, which he did concerning the same matter.[3] Hence Damascene says: "But if we are able to pluck anything profitable from outside sources, there is nothing to forbid that. Let us become tried money-dealers, heaping up the true and pure gold and discarding the spurious. Let us keep the fairest sayings but let us throw to the dogs absurd gods and strange myths: for we will prevail most mightily against them by those same things."[4] But here there is need of so much consideration, so that when we peruse pagan books, let us take care lest while we wish to read the flowers in their field, we be pricked by thorns. Wherefore it will be necessary that we act according to the manner of the bees, which in order to produce their honey, go out of their beehives, fly through the fields, wander here and there, settle down on the flowers, and yet not on them all. On the contrary, they know which are more suitable, and they do not try to take away all that adheres to them but taking as much as will be necessary to them for the work, they leave the rest. So also not every pagan book ought to be read: but only those, from which something useful can be gathered: and not everything from them ought to be taken, but only that which can aid piety and be of service to the Catholic faith.

---

[1] N. 60 (PL 34, 63).

[2] "[David] ran, and stood over the Philistine, and took his sword, and drew it out of the sheath, and slew him, and cut off his head" (I King 17, 51).

[3] E. g. "And the Sibyl and Hystaspes said that there should be a dissolution by God of things corruptible. And the philosophers called Stoics teach that even God Himself shall be resolved into fire, and they say that the world is to be formed anew by this revolution; but we understand that God, the Creator of all things, is superior to the things that are to be changed. If, therefore, on some points we teach the same things as the poets and philosophers whom you honor, and on other points are fuller and more divine in our teaching, and if we alone afford proof of what we assert, why are we unjustly hated more than all others?" (N. 20 (PG 6, 358C)).

[4] *De fide orthodoxa*, bk. 3, chap. 17 (PG 94, 1178B-C).

Introduction

Finally, there is another parent and origin of heresies, namely zeal, but not according to justice and discretion. And this cause is sterile in relation to other things, as can be seen. For although the other causes, concerning which we spoke, have so many offspring of heresies, this cause as of yet has produced very few that I know of. Yet there are some, such as the Novatians of old, concerning whom the *Historia Tripartita* relates that Novatian, their leader, withdrew himself from the communion of the Roman Church, because Pope Cornelius received into communion the faithful who sacrificed [to idols] during the time of the persecution made by Decius. Indeed, Novatian wanted everyone to be strong and constant, wherefore, it seemed to him, that the remission [of sins] ought not to be given to those who had deserted in their torments, even if they repented.[1] That he wanted them not to desert was a zeal to be praised: that he denied forgiveness to those repenting, was exceedingly harsh and a bitter point of view, and quite foreign to the Divine benignity.

Due to the same occasion (as Aeneas Sylvius[2] in his book, *De origine Bohemorum*) John Hus fell,[3] and perhaps in our era Martin Luther. For these men with zeal and hatred for the bad lives of clerics and of certain monks began to rave against the clergy, against the Roman pontiff, against ecclesiastical orders, and against all monks. And although they perhaps could have spoken ill of certain ignorant and corrupt men, they began to bark at all priests without any distinction, to overthrow all monastic life, to drive away all ceremonies from the Church, and they tried to jumble together all ecclesiastical orders. They indeed had matter for reprehension. For malice abounded and now (alas) it abounds to such an extent that we experience to have happened what the Prophet Osee says: "Cursing, and lying, and killing, and theft, and adultery have overflowed, and blood hath touched blood" (4, 2).

Yet he ought to have resisted this sickness in another manner. The clergy should have been admonished and corrected, but not done away with: one ought to have labored for the reform of the monks, not doing away with the monastic Orders. The people ought to have been thoroughly educated so that they would not put their hope in ceremonies, yet they ought not to have been entirely severed from all ceremonial worship. One indeed cures badly who cuts the throat of the sick person, even if one despairs of his health. Hence, regarding such men Paul says: "For I bear them witness, that they have a zeal of God, but not according to knowledge. For they, not knowing the justice of God, and seeking to establish their own, have not submitted themselves to the justice of God" (Rom. 10, 2-3). True Catholics certainly also have much more ardent zeal than Luther: yet it is "according to knowledge": because "knowing God's justice" they are by no means "seeking to establish their own," they are subject to God's justice, which does not permit a lesser evil to be taken away by another which is worse. Wherefore, even if they desired the reformation of the Church more fervently and sincerely, let them now patiently desire and yet tolerate, and pretend to be trained and expert doctors: who when they see that the sickness has gotten worse, and has invaded the marrows, dare not to try anything, but instead leave him to be cured by nature, fearing lest the remedial treatment strengthen the disease, which may kill the sick man in such a feeble state.

So also good and learned men, being zealous for the Lord of Hosts, seeing the Church undergoing so many very grave sicknesses in its members, commit it to be cured by God, Who is the true Doctor, and hence they pray without ceasing, they sigh, they beseech with boldness, having confidence in His words, Who said: "If you shall ask me anything in my name, that I will do" (Jn. 14, 14). Now what can be more truly asked in Christ's name than when we ask for the reform of the Church, which He acquired by His Blood? Because if they do not so quickly obtain their petition, they ought not to despair, nor ought others lose confidence:

---

[1] Bk. 8, chap. 9 (PL 69, 1116C).

[2] He was later to become Pope Pius II. He was born Enea Silvio Bartolomeo Piccolomini.

[3] Chapter 35.

because God often delays to give, so that he may make men more fervent in their petition. So we read that He did to the woman of Canaan, whom He seemed to have refused twice her petition, and when she acknowledged that she was a dog, He nowise refused her (Mt. 15, 22-28). Also, although He bore with Mary Magdalene weeping for a long time, at length showing Himself to her, He consoled her.

Therefore what hinders that we many not hope that He would now do likewise for His Church? Of old was not the synagogue likewise cast down? Were the priests then not likewise prevaricators of the Divine law, as now the popes? Were those priests unlike these now? Were Pharisees then unlike the monks now? Nay much more, as Sacred history bears witness, especially the Books of Kings and the Machabees.

Yet often when things were hopeless, God provided magnificently for His synagogue, restoring things to a better state. For one time He sets them free from the Babylonian Captivity, and another time he casts out Antiochus by the hands of Mathathias, recovers the city and purifies the Temple. What therefore do we think that He will do now? Is there now perhaps lacking a Jeremias, who deplores the squalid and nearly deserted Church? Or will there be lacking to the Church another Mathathias or Elias, the zealous man, who is zealous for the Lord? Hear what the Lord says to Elias, who thinks that he alone has withstood in Israel: "I have left me seven thousand men in Israel, whose knees have not been bowed before Baal" (III Kings 19, 18). What therefore shall we say? Was the Lord's hand shortened, so that He could not grant to the Church now what of old He granted to the synagogue? Or perhaps His goodness has lessened, so that what did for the synagogue, He disdains to do for the Church which He acquired by His Blood? Far be it, since He promised by a prophet greater glory to come of this last house than of the first.[1]

Hence, since holy men—which the Church by no means lacks—today know all these things, they sigh, praying to God that He remedy the current evils, to which they know themselves unequal, and hence do not care to apply a remedy. For they fear lest that happen which history relates to have happened of old to Rome, due to the new agrarian law promulgated by the Gracchi [brothers].[2] For these men dared to make a law concerning the lands to be divided which the nobility had wrongfully taken possession. But (as Blessed Augustine says): "To reform an abuse of so long standing was an enterprise full of peril, or rather of destruction, as the event proved."[3] For the goal not having been achieved, on this account a great multitude of both classes of Romans were killed, and also the Gracchi's themselves, who had been the cause of the upheaval, were killed in the upheaval itself. Likewise, it would be more than enough to endure the evils which the Church is undergoing, rather than to stir up an upheaval in taking them away. For this is a worse evil, since from it much worse evils would arise, as (alas) we now experience.

Therefore, observe that we have shown (as I think) all the intrinsic causes of heresies, among which some are completely evil, namely, the immoderate love of oneself, the desire for glory, the allurements of the flesh, greed, and ambition. Others are indifferent, because they are never evil except from fault of those using them badly, as is the reading of pagan books and zeal. For the latter, if ruled with discretion, greatly works in favor of God's honor: in that way, in fact if there is cautious examination of those books which are read, it can greatly avail [God's honor].

---

[1] "Great shall be the glory of this last house more than of the first" (Aggeus 2, 10).
[2] Tiberius Sempronius Gracchus was a Roman Popularis politician of the 2nd century BC, together with Gaius Gracchus, one of the Gracchi brothers. As a plebeian tribune, he caused political turmoil in the Republic with his reforms of agrarian legislation that sought to transfer wealth from the wealthy, patricians and otherwise, to the poor. Cf. *Life of Caius Gracchus* by Plutarch.
[3] *The City of God*, bk. 3, chap. 24 (PL 41, 105).

Therefore, he who wishes to get away from heresies should firstly pray to the God of all men to enlighten his understanding: then he should endeavor to root out those vices [above-mentioned]. Because if perchance he shall have fallen into some vice out of weakness, the will does not so adhere to it, such that it draws the intellect to itself. If he happens to wander through the fields of pagan books, let him take heed lest he be pricked by the thorns. Finally, if he has noticed the zeal for God or religion in himself, let him bridle it, lest he run unbridled, and overthrow himself and others.

Chapter XIII: Concerning three other causes, and they being external, whence heresies arise.

Besides all these causes and origins of heresies already enumerated, there still remain three others, somewhat dissimilar to the others mentioned above. Those concerning which we have spoken until now are in the heretic himself: wherefore they can be rightly called intrinsic causes, because they are causes such that the same person in whom they are either will stir up heresies or support ones already arisen. Those concerning which we now prepare to speak, are not adjoined to those persons themselves, but give cause and occasion to others for stirring up heresies: and hence we give to them the name of extrinsic causes, because they are outside the person who supports the heresy.

The first of these is the negligence of prelates, who are so sordid and slothful that they are nowise attentive to the flock committed to them, but are very far away from their duty with other things. It is indeed the office of prelates to watch over the flock committed to them, namely, lest something come up which could harm the flock. Hence, when Christ, the true and good Shepherd, was born, Luke says that "there were in the same country shepherds watching, and keeping the night watches over their flock" (2, 8). Expounding which passage Ambrose says: "Behold the beginning of the Church. Christ is born, and the shepherds watch; shepherds, to gather together the scattered sheep of the Gentiles, and to lead them into the fold of Christ, that they might no longer be a prey to the ravages of spiritual wolves in the night of this world's darkness. And that shepherd is wide awake, whom the Good Shepherd stirreth up. The flock then is the people, the night is the world, and the shepherds are the priests."[1] Paul, addressing priests and bishops, says: "Take heed to yourselves, and to the whole flock, wherein the Holy Ghost hath placed you bishops, to rule the church of God, which he hath purchased with his own blood" (Acts 20, 28).

For this is the office of the shepherd, namely, to look out for the flock committed to him, to take diligent care of it, which can easily be surmised from his title. For bishop in Greek[2] means *superintendens*[3] in Latin: from the Greek preposition ἐπί, which put into Latin means *super*:[4] σκοπός in Greek means *custos* or *speculator* in Latin.[5] Hence, one is called a "bishop" who watches for the protection of others. For this reason, according to Paul, we are bound to obey prelates, namely because they are held to watch over us. "Obey your prelates. For they watch as being to render an account of your souls" (Heb. 13, 17). How then can one be called a shepherd or bishop who has no concern for the sheep? Who never sees the flock committed to him, but wanders through the courts of princes? "I am the Good Shepherd," Christ says. But why is He the "good shepherd"? Because "I know mine," He says, "and mine know me" (Jn. 10, 14). By which words it is very clearly proved that he is a very bad shepherd, who

---

[1] *Expositio Evangelii secundum Lucam*, bk. 2, n. 50 (PL 15, 1571A-B).
[2] *Epískopos*.
[3] I.e. "overseer" in English.
[4] I.e. "over" in English.
[5] I.e. "guardian" or "watcher" in English.

Introduction

neither knows the sheep, nor is known by the sheep. Now the number of them is so many that the good shepherds in relation to them are like gems compared to a number of other common stones.

Hence, it happens that if perchance some heretic begins to spew his poison to the people, he will proceed the more boldly and freely the farther away he sees the shepherd to be: who, were he watching over the sheep, would try to oppose him and give an antidote to his poisons. For one knows that he [the absent shepherd] is not a pastor but a mercenary; wherefore also if he sees a wolf coming, he "flieth, because he hath no care for the sheep" (Jn. 10, 13): wherefore "the wolf catcheth, and scattereth the sheep" (v. 12). Who more truly scatters than a heretic, who separates from the single flock of the Church those whom he deceives? Wherefore we can rightly understand "heretic" by the word "wolf." Therefore if [the bad shepherd] flees when he sees the wolf coming, what do you think that he will do who never sees the sheep, neither knows whether a wolf ever enters the flock, nor what sickness they have caught? Concerning this [shepherd] I would not hesitate to call him a wolf rather than a mercenary:[1] because this is his sole concern and interest, that he tithe and fleece them, and that he suck their blood: but not that he feed them. These are those many shepherds who demolish the Lord's vineyard, that is, the Church. There is exceeding negligence of the shepherds in this case, so that not only is everyone free to think as he wishes, but also those things which he thought, he teaches with impunity.

For it is as in the parable of the sower in Matthew's Gospel, that "while men were asleep, the enemy came and oversowed cockle among the wheat" (Mt. 13, 25). The Truth Himself expounds what is the good seed, saying that it "is the word of God" (Lk. 8, 11), which was sown firstly by Christ Himself, Who gave us the true and sound doctrine. Now bishops and priests, to whom is entrusted God's word, are appointed to guard this seed and it is their responsibility to teach. But these men, namely the bishops and priests, sleep, seek after pleasure, and taken absolutely no care of their sheep. Wherefore the enemy, taking advantage of this opportunity, oversowes the cockle of false doctrine: he indeed oversows, and also in the middle of the wheat, because this is the practice of heretics, whereby they many harm more easily and securely, that they always mix together their heresy and erroneous doctrine with some other true and Catholic doctrines.

Now the reason for this perverse seed having been thrown on top is the sleep of prelates, which is so deep that they seem to snore. Concerning this matter so many examples could be given, but I will relate just one, which we now have as though before our eyes, although its origin is somewhat older. Aeneas Sylvius relates in his book, *De origine Bohemorum*, that the heresy of the Hussites (the author of which is a certain Bohemian, John Hus) began under King Wenceslaus, king of the Bohemians, about the year of the Lord 1400.[2] Before the aforesaid John Hus could rant and rave more, the bishop of Prague tried to prevent this true calamity. Who, since he was illustrious for his prudence and intelligence, ordered that the books of John Wycliffe, from which John Hus was drawing his poison, be brought to himself, and having consulted learned men, he ordered that all the books be publicly burned. Over two hundred volumes were handed over, beautifully written, and ornamented with precious covers. John Hus' preaching was interdicted, and threats were added moreover if he were ever heard to spread his prior errors among the people.

For which reason, John Hus left Prague, where there is a public school of the Bohemians, and was received in the small town of Husinetz, from where he originated, and from where he had taken his name. Nevertheless he did not put aside his madness there, because as much as the previous diligence of the bishop of Prague hindered him, to the same extent afterwards the

---

[1] Cf. Jer. 23, 1: "Woe to the pastors, that destroy and tear the sheep of my pasture, saith the Lord."
[2] Chapter 25. King Wenceslaus IV of Bohemia, "the Idle" (1361-1419).

later negligence of bishops and secular rulers, to whose dominions he had fled, increased the powers of his madness. For with the permission of the lord of that town of Huzinetz, to which John had come as it were to take refuge, he did not cease to assemble and teach the people, heaping many curses upon the Roman pontiff and many curses upon the other bishops of the Church. Now to win over more and more the minds of the people to himself, he was asserting that the tithes due to the priests were nothing but alms.

Now, when this evil was spreading every day, and was devastating nearly all of Bohemia, it was made known to King Wenceslaus, so that he might remedy this calamity: and although he could have very easily done away with it, he neglected through carelessness and sloth. Wherefore it happened that when he afterwards wanted to do the same, he was unable: because nearly the whole region was afflicted with this pestilence, and is even now (O the pain!) so afflicted. Because of the defense of this heresy, the whole kingdom withdrew obedience to the Roman Church until this day. Now how many wars were begun to wipe out this sort of heresy, it is not now necessary to say in detail, yet Aeneas Sylvius describes them long enough. Because if there had been as much diligence of the other bishops and King Wenceslaus in opposing the heresy when it was arising, as had been the diligence of the bishop of Prague, there never would have been so many and such bloody wars, and the whole kingdom would not have been infected with that poison so long.

The second cause of heresies is the lack of preaching of God's word, although this could also be traced back to the cause above. For because the people lack the preaching of God's word, the fault is of the prelates, to whom it pertains from their office to teach the people. For it is said to them: "Preach the gospel to every creature" (Mk. 16, 15), and to them it was commanded that they feed the sheep with the word of doctrine. Since it was indeed said to Peter: "Feed my lambs" (Jn. 21, 15). Likewise, Peter says to all the shepherds: "Feed the flock of God which is among you" (I Pet. 5, 2). Now what is the truer food of the soul than God's word, which not merely nourishes the soul, but also fattens it? And so not without reason Jeremias laments, saying: "The little ones have asked for bread, and there was none to break it unto them: (Lam. 4, 4). To prelates it also pertains to enlighten the people who lie in the darkness of ignorance. Now what other light can be used by them except the preaching of God's word? "Thy word is a lamp," says the Psalms, "to my feet, and a light to my paths" (Ps. 118, 105). And again: "The declaration of thy words giveth light: and giveth understanding to little ones" (v. 130). If therefore you withdraw the light by which one is guided, will not the one walking in the darkness very often stumble?

Therefore, it is not surprising if when the preaching of God's word has been taken away from the people that the people err: nay rather, it would be surprising if when the people have never heard God's word that they always judge rightly about the faith. For since those things which we believe exceed the weakness of the human intellect, no one can of himself rise up to perceive them. It is necessary to firstly believe and afterwards one may understand. "Unless you will have believed," says Isaias, "you will not understand" (7, 9).[1] It is not possible to believe, however, without a preacher, as Paul testifies: "How shall they believe him, of whom they have not heard? And how shall they hear, without a preacher?" (Rom. 10, 14). And a few words later he concludes: "Faith then cometh by hearing" (v. 17). Concerning this matter, it is not necessary to put forth many examples, since everywhere in the world, and in every na-

---

[1] The text here has: *Nisi enim credideritis, non intelligetis.* This wording is based on an Old Latin reading of the Hebrew text which predates the Latin Vulgate translation, namely, *Si non credideritis, non permanebitis* ("If you will not believe, you shall not continue"). This discrepancy is discussed by Saint Augustine in his book, *On Christian Doctrine* (Bk. 2, chap. 12, n. 17), where he says that both translations serve for edification, but the latter, which is in our Vulgate text, "sticks more closely with the words."

Introduction -89-

tion, it is known by experience that many errors are stirred up among rural and agrarian men, especially among those who live in uninhabited regions, who are very far away from human society. Because it is certain to happen, for no other reason than the fact that they do not hear God's word whence they could have been taught: which having been lacking, the malignant enemy stands nearby, always prepared to harm, and firstly he leads astray their feelings but afterwards their minds, and dislodges them into many errors.

Concerning this matter, our Spain can provide for us abundant testimonies. Less than ten years ago, in the region of Cantabria, which is now called Navarre, and the Basque country, among the men who live in the mountains, there were found various errors, many superstitions, and different forms of idolatry: to such an extent that the devil himself, depicted in the figure of a goat, is venerated. Because previously during many years it began to be done secretly among them: in which affair there were found more women than men. For that malignant enemy knew that from the beginning of mankind it is easier to seduce the woman than the man: and once she has embraced evil she will adhere to it more tenaciously.

We find that the same thing happened in other mountains of Spain, even if it is not as wicked, among the Asturians and the Gallicians, and some other similar peoples, to whom the word of God very rarely happened to be preached. For there are amongst them many superstitions and pagan rites, certainly for no other reason but on account of the lack of preachers. Which defect should to be partially attributed to their prelates and pastors. For even though those erring in this way sin, still their sin gives admittance to some excuse, in that no one assembled them and no one ever taught them. But however much preachers be lacking, if men themselves worship (as is fitting) God, and they pray to Him, God would never permit them to be deceived: because either He would teach them interiorly, or send someone to them, who would teach them exteriorly, just as He sent Peter to Cornelius.[1] Yet because they were immersed in other great crimes, their sins deserved that God permitted that no preacher would come forth to teach them.

Finally, the third parent and origin of heresies is the translation of Sacred Writ into the vernacular: hence it happens that they are read by men without any distinction of persons. Now so that we may prove this often was and is the cause of heresies, it is necessary to firstly establish the fact that heresies never arise from Sacred Writ, but from the misinterpretation of it. Hence, Hilary says: "There have risen many who have given to the plain words of Holy Writ some arbitrary interpretation of their own, instead of its true and only sense, and this in defiance of the clear meaning of words. Heresy lies in the understanding, not in the word written; the guilt is that of the expositor, not of the text."[2]

If therefore heresy arises from the misinterpretation of Scripture, who will more easily fall into heresy than a common man reading that which he can hardly understand?[3] It was certainly difficult to be believed that the unlearned common man would understand, that which the most learned men can scarcely grasp with lengthy study. Wherefore it was not permitted to the Jews (as Jerome testifies)[4] younger than thirty years old to read the book of Genesis and

---

[1] Acts 10.
[2] *On the Trinity*, bk. 2, n. 3 (PL 10, 51B-52A).
[3] "The solicitude of the Apostolic office naturally urges and even compels us…to desire that this grand source of Catholic revelation (the Bible) should be made safely and abundantly accessible to the flock of Jesus Christ" (Leo XIII, *Providentissimus Deus* (Nov. 18, 1893), n. 2.)"
[4] "I will come to the [exposition of] the prophet Ezechiel, whose difficulty the tradition of the Hebrews proves. For unless someone among them completed the age of priestly ministry, that is, his thirtieth year, it was not permitted to read the beginning of Genesis [i.e. the first three chapters], the Canticle of Canticles, or the beginning and end of the book [of Ezechiel], so that he approaches the full time of human nature for the perfect knowledge and mystical understandings" (*In Ezechielem*, bk. 1, chap. 1 (PL 25,

the Canticle of Canticles, because in them were many things difficult to understand. For there was danger in reading them, unless the books were approached by learned and distinguished men, lest from a misinterpretation they [the young Jews] might believe something distorted. In like manner, the Sibylline books were held in such esteem by the Romans that (as Fenestella[1] testifies, speaking in *De magistratibus et sacerdotiis Romanorum*)[2] it was permitted only to the Duumviri[3] to look at those books. However, afterwards, when the priesthood of the Duumviri was expanded to ten men, who were called the Decemviri,[4] the Sibylline Books were allowed to be read by those ten men alone.

Therefore all the more was it fitting for Christians to show that reverence to Sacred Writ, so that they would not be indiscriminately given to all men to be read, but to those only who were approved for their faith and considerable knowledge of other things. For concerning faith, it is said by Isaias: "Unless you will have believed, you will not understand" (7, 9). And concerning the knowledge of human affairs, that this is often necessary for the understanding of Sacred Scripture, we have already taught elsewhere. The Lord recommended both in one sentence saying: "Give not that which is holy to dogs; neither cast ye your pearls before swine, lest perhaps they trample them under their feet, and turning upon you, they tear you" (Mt. 7, 6). Expounding which words Theophylactus says: "The dogs are the infidels: the swine, however, are indeed the faithful, but those leading a filthy life. Thus, mysteries ought not to be shown to unbelievers, nor ought clear words concerning theology, similar to pearls, be communicated to the unclean. For swine trample, or despise the things that are said; the dogs, however, having turned around, tear us: which the philosophers did, when they heard that Christ was crucified. Now they tear us in pieces by their reasonings, jeering that it is impossible."[5]

Wherefore the worthy of praise edict of the most illustrious rulers of Spain, namely Ferdinand and his wife, Isabella, came to be whereby under most serious penalties they forbade anyone to translate Sacred Writ into the common language, or keep in any way Scriptures translated by someone else. For they in fact prudently feared that an occasion of erring would be given to the people whom they had been given to rule: and yet they did not fear for nothing and without reason: because it had been learned by long experience that many heresies had been stirred up of old by this occasion. Since indeed from this root the Waldensians came forth, who are called by another name the "Poor Men of Lyons." For Waldo, their head from whom they are called Waldensians, since he was an uneducated man, procured some books translated for himself, reading and not understanding which, he fell into many errors. From the same source burgeoned forth the Beghards, the Turelupini,[6] all unlearned men and entirely

---

17A)). "In the 119th Epistle [Jerome in his letter to Paulinus] confesses that there is much more in the Scripture of which he is ignorant than there is of what he knows. Origen and Saint Jerome, the former in his Prologue to his *On the Canticles*, the latter in his *On Ezechiel*, say that it was not permitted to the Jews before the age of thirty to read the three first chapters of Genesis, the commencement and the end of Ezechiel, or the Canticle of Canticles, on account of the depth of the difficulties therein, in which few persons can swim without being submerged. And now, everybody talks of them, everybody criticizes them, everybody knows all about them" (St. Francis de Sales, *The Catholic Controversy* (Benzinger Brothers, London, 1909), part 2, art. 1, chap. 10, pg. 131).

[1] The work was really published by A. D. Fiocchi, canon and papal secretary.
[2] Book 1, chap. 13.
[3] One of two persons jointly exercising the same office in Republican Rome.
[4] One of a body of ten magistrates in ancient Rome.
[5] PG 123, 211.
[6] This was a heretical sect which sprang up in the late fourteenth century in France, especially in the Dauphiné. It was condemned by the Inquisition in Paris in 1372 and by Pope Gregory XI in the follow-

ignorant of how to read and write. Yet here Luther objects saying that Sacred Scripture is very clear, especially the New Testament, and it is very easily understood, wherefore he says that Sacred Scripture ought to be put into such language so that it can be read and understood by all. But that in this matter Luther is irrational, and all the others who support him in this view, we shall prove by explicit testimonies of Scripture and efficacious arguments.

Firstly then, Blessed Peter speaking of the Pauline epistles says: "In which are certain things hard to be understood, which the unlearned and unstable wrest, as they do also the other scriptures, to their own destruction" (I Pet. 3, 16). And Paul, speaking of men of this kind, says that they "understand neither the things they say, nor whereof they affirm" (I Tim. 1, 7). And he says that his Gospel was "hid to them that are lost" (II Cor. 4, 3). Because if Peter says that in the Pauline epistles there are many things "hard to be understood," and Paul says that his Gospel is "hid to them that are lost," how will Luther persuade that Sacred Scripture can understood very easily, and is it very clear, to such an extent that it can be understood by all? Moreover, if Scriptures are so clear, how did Arius err? Macedonius? Nestorius?—especially since all these took an occasion of their error from Scripture misunderstood? Because if these men erred in understanding Scripture, and from thence stirred up heresies, will not he who is an unlearned common man also err? How will the common man understand the parables, of which there is frequent use in both Testaments? How will he apply the similitudes? How will he distinguish the figurative speech from the non-figurative speech? How will he consider the property of things, from the knowledge of which the literal sense often depends? In what way will he know to relate the preceding and the following words, and those common to both, so that from thence the people may conclude the true understanding of the text, who have not known how to put anything together, but are accustomed to think that there is completely no relation between things? But each of these things are very necessary for the understanding of anything, all the more I will say for the understanding of Divine Scripture.

Furthermore, there are many things in Sacred Writ which apparently seem to contradict diametrically: in which places is needed an interpreter so diligent and learned that he may reconcile those things and show them to be consistent: as for example, Christ in John's Gospel says: "The Father is greater than I" (14, 28). Likewise, in the same Gospel He says: "I and the Father are one" (10, 30). But where there is unity, no one can be greater or less. Likewise Paul's words, "The kingdom of God is not meat and drink" (Rom. 14, 17), seem to be opposed to Christ saying, "I dispose to you, as my Father hath disposed to me, a kingdom, that you may eat and drink at my table, in my kingdom" (Lk. 22, 29-30). The Royal Prophet also says: "Be angry, and sin not" (Ps. 4, 5), by which words he commands an anger, which he says is without sin. But Paul seems to contradict this, saying: "Let all anger and indignation be put away from you" (Eph. 4, 31). Now, when a common uneducated man reads these words, he will suppose that they are contradictory: hence, it will happen that he will doubt or waiver in his faith. Or else, temerariously reckoning, he may reject one part of Scripture. It could be, as is common to heretics if they perhaps discover that a passage is contrary to their error, that he may immediately reject it as non-canonical.

Again, Luther says that Jerome had hallucinated in his interpretation of Scripture, Augustine erred in the same, Ambrose, Cyprian, Hilary, Basil, and Chrysostom were often deceived. Yet the same Luther in his Latin treatise, *Assertion of All the Articles Wrongly Condemned in the Roman Bull*, acknowledges that they had exceptionally labored in the Lord's vineyard, and had used diligence in clarifying Scripture.[1] Therefore, if these most learned men, after

---

ing year. Its beliefs suggest a connection with the Beghards and the Brethren of the Free Spirit, both in an emphasis on poverty and in the notion that the 'perfect' cannot sin and are free to follow their inclinations.

[1] There is an incorrect reference in the text to Luther's book, *Prelude on the Babylonian Captivity of*

Introduction

long experience in Sacred Writ, after long meditation, after fervent and long prayer, have been deceived according to that witness, how will he say that the Scriptures are very clear, about which so many and such men after long and attentive study of them have been deceived? If they erred in one or another point, it is likely that the unlearned common man would err in a thousand points. Especially since he does not use so much diligence as they, nor does he meditate on those things as much as they, nor is his life such as theirs, as the affections enlighten the intellect, or rather, God's unction teaches them.

It is certainly possible that one man, however uneducated, exercised by long prayer, accustomed to fervent contemplation, whom God has introduced into His wine cellar, from thence may draw the interpretation of words and the true meaning of Sacred Scriptures, which another man, however accustomed to men's teachings, is unable to attain. But that scoundrels, drunkards, devourers of music, drinkers of wine, "whose God is their belly" (Phil. 3, 19), without any meditation, without any exercise of prayer, may penetrate the Scriptures which God has hidden from so many wise and holy men, is not credible to anyone. "I confess," Christ said, "to thee, O Father, Lord of heaven and earth, because thou hast hid these things from the wise and prudent, and hast revealed them to the little ones" (Mt. 11, 25). "To little ones," I say, not to proud men, trusting in themselves. "To little ones," I say, that is, to the humble, who in their own estimation crawl on the ground,[1] who do not walk among great and marvelous matters above themselves,[2] who count all earthly things as dung,[3] and thus despising those things they sigh after heavenly things. God certainly reveals His mysteries to these little ones, not to the ravenous, and not to drinking partners. For doubtlessly wine and bread fatten the body, nourish flesh and blood, but not the soul. Moreover, flesh and blood did not reveal to Peter that Christ is the Son of God, but God's Spirit Who is in heaven.[4]

Finally, so that we may wall in the man on all sides so that no exit may be open to him, have not the Lutherans divided amongst themselves? Carlstadt from Luther, Oecolampadius from both, have already separated. But for what reason are they divided? It is certainly for no other reason but that any one of them accuses another that he has closed his eyes to the meaning of Scripture. Therefore, if among those who want to be seen as leaders of the people there are disagreements, and anyone of them says that the other has nowise understood Scripture: why is it that the people may not err in many more things than any of them? Especially since the common man is not content with just reading [Scripture], but also may dispute concerning its meaning, to such an extent that scoundrels are also unafraid to challenge the most learned to a combat and dispute with them. And what is worse than all these things, not only are these things done by men, but also by women. Paul certainly does not permit a woman to teach, and yet in these times Luther especially favoring them, women are not ashamed to teach and

---

the Church. The correct reference is to Luther's *Assertion of All the Articles Wrongly Condemned in the Roman Bull*, written on November 29, 1520. The latter was the second and more complete response to the papal bull condemning Luther, *Exsurge Domine* written on June 15, 1520. It was written in Latin for his scholarly supporters. It ought not to be confused with a German version, later published on March 1, 1521 in simpler language for the common people. The reference then has been changed to the Latin version of Luther's response to *Exsurge Domine*: "Una est vinea, sed diversi diversarum horarum operarii, omnes tamen in ipsa vinea, non in sarculis aut cultris operariorum laborant. Satis est e patribus didicisse studium et diligentiam in scripturis laborandi: non omne opus eorum probari necesse est, siquidem et diligentia pluribus quandoque non dat, quod dat vel uni sola occasio et nescio quae spiritus incomprehensibilis impulsio" (*Assertio omnium articulorum M. Lutheri per bullam Leonis X, Novissimam damnatorum*, n. 35).

[1] *Humi*. This word means "ground" and is the etymological foundation for the word "humble."
[2] Cf. Ps. 130, 1.
[3] Cf. Phil. 3, 8.
[4] Cf. Mt. 16, 17.

Introduction

dispute about the faith: and so boldly, that you will more easily recall a hundred men from error than one woman.

From which things anyone will most clearly conclude that Luther for this reason alone translated Scripture into the vulgar tongue, because he perceived that this is an easy way for the fall of the people, whom having been deceived by error from the text badly interpreted, he can more easily bring into his darkness. I cannot contain myself, but I will also insert here the things which Erasmus of Rotterdam cites in favor of this matter. For concerning this matter among others, he was reproached and reprehended by the faculty of theology in Paris, since in many books authored by him has said that he desires that Sacred Writ be translated into every language so that they may be read by the farmer, the carpenter, the stonemason, and by the woman. To which censure Erasmus responded, and not recanting his opinion, he cited some things as proof of his opinion which hardly support his assertion. He firstly says that of old, Sacred Writ was translated into the common language, and Chrysostom recommends to the laity the study of the Divine books, and Jerome likewise praises [the study of the Divine books] by women: concerning whom he also relates that he translated the Sacred Books into the Dalmatian language. Because if it was then done with so much praise, it seems to Erasmus that it ought likewise to be done now.

Now this recapitulation is clearly proved to be bad, in that we have often seen it happen that something is legislated concerning some matter that men's actions might be guided, which—when experience has taught that it could be harmful, and has already done harm—is afterwards completely revoked. Long ago, during the evening vigils, men, women, girls, boys, monks, consecrated virgins, and every sort of men used to run to the martyrs' graves. When of old Vigilantius criticized this practice, Blessed Jerome wrote to him so sharply that Erasmus, in the argument written by him on that issue, was forced to wish for moderation in the part of Blessed Jerome. Now that which then Blessed Jerome so emphatically praised, the scandalous conduct which was permitted under the guise of piety, caused it to be completely abolished. And this was abrogated not solely through disuse, but by the definition of a council. The Synod of Elvira in fact, in chapter thirty-five of its decrees says that following: "Women are not to remain in a cemetery during the night. Some engage in wickedness rather than prayer."[1] Why does not Erasmus want to restore those vigils, since he may see that they were so popular in former times, and so praised from the heart by Jerome? Now, he does not do this, nay rather he reckons that they were deservedly abolished.

Also Christ's Body was formerly given in the hand, because everyone carried It home with them: so that when one wished, one could receive it at home. This is easily gathered from Eusebius' *Church History*.[2] But when many men were caught treating unworthily and abusing [the hosts] for magical arts, the custom was abrogated. There is now no truly Catholic and prudent man, as I think, who would wish to consider that the Eucharist be again given to the laity in the hand to be carried back to their homes, even though in former times it is evident that this was so done until the time of Pope Cornelius.

Therefore, we acknowledge that Sacred Writ was translated into the common language in former times, and yet it is not thus expedient that something similar be done now, because we have learned from experience that from this cause many uneducated men have fallen into

---

[1] PL 84, 305D-306A.

[2] "But I did not dare to do this; and said that his long communion was sufficient for this. For I should not dare to renew from the beginning one who had heard the giving of thanks and joined in repeating the Amen; who had stood by the table and had stretched forth his hands to receive the blessed food; and who had received it, and partaken for a long while of the body and blood of our Lord Jesus Christ." (Bk. 7, chap. 9, n. 4). The reference here in the text is to bk. 6, chap. 33, but this may be due to a previous division of the work.

detestable errors. For even if few uneducated men were authors of heresies, nevertheless there were, and now today are, many who support heresies. Even if Luther is certainly the author and prince of heresy, still he was one man who could have easily been restrained by the secular power: thus he strenuously strove to win over minds of the people to himself, so that he could more securely do his business. Now in order to attain this, he saw no easier way than if he were to translate Sacred Writ and his teachings into the common language: and just as he thought, so it happened: for this occasion among the others was not small, so that nearly all the people adhered to him.

Secondly, Erasmus adds as proof of his assertion saying that whatever heresy there is in the world, nearly all arose from philosophy, or from Sacred Writ itself misinterpreted. And as no one is kept away from the books of the philosophers, so then no one ought to be held back from Sacred Writ. Who does not see that there is a very great difference even in the matter about which we speak, between pagan books and Sacred Writ? For all the faithful read Sacred Writ as a Divine oracle: wherefore no one dares to contradict or doubt them, but holds whatever he reads there with a constant mind. Wherefore, if he shall have misunderstood something, he will believe it with no less constant mind than the rest, because according to the meaning which he adopts, he thinks that those words ought to be understood: and so he tenaciously defends his error, just as he believes it to be the Divine oracle. But no one initiated to Christ so reads the books of the philosophers as Divine oracles, unless perhaps someone be insane: but he reads them as books of men, who no matter how learned they were, they could still have erred, and so he does not fear to disagree with them, or doubt their opinion. But because it very frequently happens that on account of the arguments well laid out, which are read in them, or on account of the eloquent style of speech, they are drawn into the philosophers' errors, thus not without reason did we warn above that pagan books ought to be read with great caution. Therefore since greater harm is inflicted from Sacred Writ translated into the common language than from the reading of the pagan philosophers, it is rightly controlled and even if there otherwise be no prohibition. I think Erasmus should be pleased that we have disagreed with him on this matter. For he also teaches not just once that it is allowed for anyone to disagree with the opinion of any man, ever if he were holy, provided he do it with respect and motivated by some reason. He may take it well or badly, but I will never depart from my intention whereby I have decided to fight for the Catholic faith.

Chapter XIV: On recognizing heretics.

It is no small matter to distinguish heretics from true Catholics, on account of the utility of the matter and also on account of its difficulty. The utility is certainly very great, due to the reason that many men covered with the cloak of the name "Christian" scatter their heresies, and try to sell their poisonous teachings to the people: whom they deceive all the more easily, and draw into their errors, the more they are reputed to be faithful and true Catholics. Therefore Christ having very diligent care for us and foreseeing that many heretics would come under the guise of the Christian name, warns us saying: "Beware of false prophets, who come to you in the clothing of sheep, but inwardly they are ravening wolves" (Mt. 7, 15). And John in his first Catholic Epistle says: "Dearly beloved, believe not every spirit, but try the spirits if they be of God: because many false prophets are gone out into the world" (4, 1).

Now the difficulty is known from this, namely, that heretics do not keep the same manner [of acting], but each has his own way of acting, a thousand appearances, and a varied usage of things. For some of them are hidden so that they may appear more holy, so that they can deceive more easily the minds of ignorant men. Hence, concerning them Job says: "They dwelt in the desert places of torrents, and in caves of earth" (30, 6). Heretics dwell "in caves,"

Introduction

because daring not to preach their full error in public, lest they be resisted by wiser men, they take care to present themselves hiddenly and secretly to the unexperienced, so that they may draw them more securely into their error. Hence it is, that in the writings of Solomon, the woman, who is a type for heresy, says: "Stolen waters are sweeter, and hidden bread is more pleasant" (Prov. 9, 17). A thing is more dangerous the more hidden it is, because it is more difficult to heal that poison. Some do teach publicly, and truly impudently, persuading themselves that they can thus better defend their error. Some, in order to persuade others more easily of their error, try to appear more holy, and to perform many miracles, so that the more they are deemed to be better men, the more easily they may be believed. Others, on the contrary, despising the opinion of other men, and in no way caring about it, associate with the men having the worst lives, so that they may attain the vices they had desired, and may have happy and willing ministers of their errors. For he who recommends vices instead of virtues, or who rejects virtues as vices, will find no one more well-disposed to him than those who incline to those vices which he praises.

Since, therefore, there are so many different manners of heretics, and different inclinations, it would have been difficult to prescribe a rule whereby they can be recognized, had the Savior left it to us. For He, the Supreme and Best Shepherd and Teacher, when He had forewarned us to beware of false prophets, He adjoined whereby we may recognize them, saying: "By their fruits you shall know them. Do men gather grapes of thorns, or figs of thistles? Even so every good tree bringeth forth good fruit, and the evil tree bringeth forth evil fruit. A good tree cannot bring forth evil fruit, neither can an evil tree bring forth good fruit." (Mt. 7, 16-18). Yet since the fruits of heretics, as we have already said, are different, and are not the same for all, the same difficulty always remains. Nevertheless, although there are so many different manners of heretics, if there is perhaps some indication common to them all, as the genus of them all, they can be easily been recognized by it. After having diligently considered the matter (as was fitting), I have found in heretics three or four manners common to them all, whereby anyone may conclude whether or not any teacher deservedly incurs suspicion of heresy.

Firstly therefore, and I do not know whether it is the best proof, he wants to preach or teach new things, and which benefit little. For the fact that he is the friend of new things, and always wants to preach or teach them, is a sign that he wishes to please, that he seeks his honor among the people, and that he preaches himself and not Jesus Christ. From which it is proved that he speaks from himself, and not from God: because (as it is written in St. John's Gospel) "He that speaketh of himself, seeketh his own glory" (7, 18). Now he who seeks his own glory, hopes to obtain the same through the preaching of a new doctrine. Even if he contrives something erroneous, he will be pleased by its newness, and hoping that he will have glory therefrom, not only will he be fearless in preaching it, nay he will try to sell it as a precious gem to the people.

Moreover, the very newness of the teaching is easily detected, because Christ and His Apostles have given sufficient doctrine for attaining eternal life. After the Law given by Christ, there is no other law to be given again by God, because this testament is eternal. Therefore, if something new is now preached, not a vestige of which has been found in the Church from the Apostles until this day, it is suspect by the very newness of the thing. Because [if it were true] then it would be necessary to acknowledge that the Apostles did not perfectly or sufficiently preach the Gospel, and the Church which the Holy Ghost has undertaken to teach, was for so long a time in the darkness of ignorance. Blessed Augustine in his letter to Jerome, *On the Origin of the Human Soul*, when describing many opinions about the soul, concerning a particular one of them, which he believes to be erroneous, and yet not conceding that he could not overcome it, says: "It is formally refuted, by its very novelty."[1] Aeneas Sylvius speaking

---

[1] The reference here in the text for this quotation is to a book, *De ratione animae ad Optatum*, but the

about John Hus, the heresiarch of the Bohemians, in his book, *De origine Bohemorum*,[1] says that he always loved strange and new opinions. Again, Blessed Paul often condemns this novelty of doctrines, and he commands that it ought to be fled from as being condemned. Hence he says: "O Timothy, keep that which is committed to thy trust, avoiding the profane novelties of words, and oppositions of knowledge falsely so called, which some promising, have erred concerning the faith" (I Tim. 6, 20-21).

Then he who tries to introduce a new doctrine, ought to prove it with very effective and clear arguments: and what is more, if the doctrine is such that it be preached as being necessary for attaining eternal life, one ought to confirm it with the clearest working of miracles. For so we find that it was done as often as a new doctrine was commanded to the people by God. For firstly when Moses was sent to Pharao, he did not dare to go, in that he feared lest they on account of the novelty of the thing which he was to say to Pharao, Pharao and the rest of the Egyptians would not believe. Wherefore God bestowed upon him the power of performing miracles before Pharao and the Egyptians, so that having seen the clearest working of miracles, they may be persuaded to believe those things which Moses was to say to him.

Thereafter, when the Lord was preaching a new Law to the world, and unfolding a new and true interpretation of the Old Law, He confirms His doctrine with the clearest miracles. For after the long sermon that the Lord gave to his disciples and other men on the mount, in which sermon He taught them the precepts of the Decalogue according to their true meaning, immediately after the sermon was finished He worked a miracle. Namely, when the leper was asking and saying: "Lord, if thou wilt, thou canst make me clean" (Mt. 8, 2), He answered: "I will, be thou made clean. And forthwith his leprosy was cleansed" (v. 3). And lest you think that this was done by chance, namely, that when the Lord finished that sermon to the people who heard Him, that He healed the leper, Jerome assigns the reason for this deed, saying: "It is appropriate that after His preaching and teaching, an opportunity for a sign present itself. In this way the words He has just spoken are confirmed among His hearers by means of the power of a miracle."[2] Because if Christ had not performed such miracles, by which men were attracted to His teaching, no guilt would have been imputed to the Jews of that time who did not believe. For Christ Himself says: "If I had not done among them the works that no other man hath done, they would not have sin" (Jn. 15, 24). Hence, it is very clearly proved that the working of miracles is necessary for the confirmation of so excellent a doctrine as is the Gospel.

Moreover, after the Gospel was preached by Christ, and confirmed with many miracles by Him, when the Apostles after Christ's Ascension into Heaven preached the Gospel through various nations, they confirmed it by working various miracles. About which Mark says: "But they going forth preached everywhere: the Lord working withal, and confirming the word with signs that followed" (16, 20). [Ambrosiaster[3]] expounding the passage to the Romans: "By whom we have received grace" (1, 5) etc. says the following: "The witness of doctrine is power, so that because what it preached is unbelievable to the world, by deeds it may become believable."[4] And Bede, in his third book on Luke, ninth chapter, says: "Having firstly bestowed the power of miracles, He sent them to preach the kingdom of God, so that the great-

---

quote seems to rather be taken from the above cited letter of Saint Augustine to Saint Jerome (Letter 166, chap. 8, n. 23 (PL 33, 730-731)).

[1] Chap. 35.

[2] *Commentary on Matthew*, bk. 1, chap. 8, v. 1 (PL 26, 50D).

[3] "[Saint Ambrose] is not the author of the admirable commentary on the thirteen Epistles of St. Paul known as 'Ambrosiaster'" ("St. Ambrose," *The Catholic Encyclopedia* (New York, Robert Appleton Company, 1907), vol. 1, p. 387).

[4] *Commentaria in Epistolam ad Romanos*, chap. 1, v. 5 (PL 17, 50D).

Introduction
-97-

ness of the deeds would also bear witness to the greatness of the promises; the power shown would give belief to their words; and they might do new things who preached new things."[1]

Therefore, we have proved from all these arguments that a new doctrine of the faith ought to be confirmed with most evident miracles. Because if something new is preached without the confirmation of such miracles, it is suspect by its very novelty. And those who delight in such novelties, and eagerly seek after them, so that they may lay hold of vain glory therefrom, I conclude by this reason alone that he is a heretic, or is prone to heresy, and is one who may easily fall into it. Luther support us on this position to such an extent that he has fought against himself, perhaps not realizing what he was saying. For he wanted to assert that trust ought not be to given to any man, no matter how learned, no matter how holy, unless he has proved his teaching by very clear citations from Sacred Scripture. And in the introduction to his book, *Assertio omnium articulorum per Bullam Leonis X*, he says the following: "We read in the Acts of the Apostles that those who had heard 'with all eagerness, were daily searching the scriptures, whether these things were so' (Acts 17, 11). Therefore, if Paul's Gospel or the New Testament needed to be proved by the Old Testament whether the Apostle had authority given to him by God, so that its word would be believed, why do we ourselves not want the sayings of the Fathers, who had no authority to teach new things, but only the authority of preserving the things received through the Apostles to be subjected to the judgment of Scripture?"[2] There is no one (as I think) so out of his mind, who would deny that the sayings of any man are subject to the judgment of Scripture, because we have not sworn on the words of man, but on God's words: nor is it necessary to subject our intellect to the obedience of men, but to obedience of Christ. Therefore we allow the sayings of the saints to be subjected to the judgment of Scripture, but not as it [Scripture] is understood by Luther. Now the judgment of Scripture, that is, the interpretation of Sacred Scripture, as we have already taught elsewhere, does not belong to Luther, but to the whole Church.

What he says, however, that it is not permitted to anyone to teach new things, we agree with. But if it were not permitted to any of the saints to teach new things, but only to preserve what has been received from the Apostles, why will it be allowed to you, Luther, to invent so many novelties? Is it not a new doctrine that all Christians are priests? Is it not a new teaching whereby you assert that to receive the Eucharist it is not necessary first to cleanse the soul by contrition and the confession of sins? Is it not a new teaching that man's free will is a slave and not free? Is this not a new opinion, that no good works are necessary, but that faith alone suffices for attaining eternal life? Is it not a new doctrine that general councils duly assembled (as it is fitting) can err in the faith, and thus we are nowise obliged by their decrees? All these things certainly are new, unless perhaps you say that they are not new, because some heretics before you contrived them. For this is unique to you, that rarely being purged of wine, you very often draw from the excrements thrown away by the Church.

But even if this were so, still those things which are at one time antiquated, sometimes begin to be new, because then they are revived. So although you draw many errors from the Waldensians, Wycliffites and some other men of this sort; nevertheless because you have taken up again those which have been rejected and disapproved for a long time by the Church, it is as though you were to raise up from Hell those who have been buried; and hence your errors are said to be new. Therefore, if you still assert and pertinaciously defend these new things, which were never handed down from the Apostles nor preserved by their successors—although you have said that it is not permitted for anyone to preach new doctrines, but only to preserve things received from the Apostles—have you not fallen into the pit which you have

---

[1] *Homilia 105 Feria Quinta Pentacostes*, (PL 118, 571D).
[2] *An Assertion of All the Articles of Martin Luther Which Were Quite Recently Condemned by a Bull of Leo X*, n. 31.

made, and into the snare which you have prepared for other feet? Therefore, to you who introduce new doctrines, it is incumbent to prove the things which you assert, and confirm them by the clearest miracles, just as Christ did, and His Apostles did. Now to us who hold the old faith of the whole Catholic Church, it is not incumbent to prove. For the doctrine ought not to be called new, which has been preserved for so many centuries until this day, and confirmed by so many miracles: wherefore it is not necessary that we now prove the things which already have been proved and confirmed in the past.

A second characteristic, by which we can recognize a heretic, is the excessive liberty in making pronouncements, to which some are so inclined that they do not hesitate to assert anything which comes into their mouth. Now because temerity in defining went forth, pride afterwards defends, and very often pertinacity increases: because pride becomes compelling, such that what was once said temerariously, one does not wish to recant: wherefore pertinacity having been joined to error, it makes the heretic complete. Therefore, he who trusting himself makes pronouncements so very freely concerning matters that are serious and pertaining to the faith: who having been persuaded by very facile reasoning, without any further investigation, or advice of other learned men, immediately pronounces a decision, rightly incurs suspicion of heresy, so that he may be considered a heretic, or it may be reckoned that he is very close to falling into heresy.

Hence, Blessed James says: "And if any man think himself to be religious, not bridling his tongue but deceiving his own heart, this man's religion is vain" (1, 26). And again: "The tongue no man can tame, an unquiet evil, full of deadly poison" (3, 8). Hence, Blessed Gregory, expounding that passage of Job: "Answer, I beseech you, without contention: and speaking that which is just, judge ye" (6, 29), says the following: "He that fears to be reproved in respect of his words, ought first to examine what he says; that there may be a kind of just and discerning judge sitting between the heart and the tongue, weighing with exactness whether the heart presents right words, which the tongue receiving may usefully bring forward to the judgment of the hearers. Therefore, blessed Job, arguing against his friends, but also denouncing against our heretics, reproves their precipitation in speaking, gathers up their words to their mind, saying, 'And speaking that which is just, judge ye': as though he were to say clearly, 'If in that which you go out to us by a departure of speech, you do not wish to be reprehended, hold inwardly the scale of justice, so that as much as is said outwardly, may please from the weight of the truth, the more in proportion as the scales of discretion weigh it well within.'"[1]

Hence a third thing is permitted to indicate that someone is a heretic, which is characteristic of nearly all heretics: namely, that if one corrects him to recall him from his error, he on the spot shows impatience. In which matter, however much he is a hypocrite and strives to seem holy, his hypocrisy is thence uncovered, because as soon as he was admonished by anyone, immediately he hurls back a curse for the good deed, raging with protests and insults, impatient to have been taught by another. For if you remind him to come to his senses from his error, he does not become better but worse, and more pestilent. Concerning these men Paul says: "Evil men and seducers shall grow worse and worse: erring, and driving into error" (II Tim. 3, 13).

Of this thing Luther gave us a most clear example, who when he had babbled some few errors at the beginning and was admonished about them by many learned men, he was so far from wishing to recant that he added many more worse errors. Then, when he was corrected by the most Serene King of England by writing, and when he ought to have thanked him, or at least modestly reconsidered, he attacked him with protests and insults. Finally, when he was admonished by the Supreme Pontiff, Leo X, he did not want to obey, and lest the putrid

---

[1] *Moralia in Iob*, bk. 8 (PL 133, 175D-176B).

sheep infect the rest by contact, the good shepherd completely expelled him from the flock of the Church. Now Luther being impatient because of this censure, began to ridicule the Roman pontiff, and all the other ranks of the Church. Therefore, it is a clear sign of a heretic, to permit no medicine, and to allow no hand of one healing: hence it came to pass the he remained incurable. For how can he be cured who does not allow himself to be treated? Or how can he be treated, whom if you teach him something, he speaks nonsense? If you admonish anything, he is angered? If exhort anything, he resists? If you reconcile anything, he is incensed? Therefore impatience due to correction is the most effective indication that someone is a heretic, because it shows the pertinacity which makes the heretic complete.

Introduction

Preface to Book II

Thus far we have treated those things which were necessary for refuting heresies. For we have shown the weapons common to both, with which both we ought to fight against the heretics, and also the heretics ought to fight against us. We have pointed out the judges under whom the trial of combat will be undergone, to whom the authority has been conferred of judging concerning the victory: which was also especially necessary, since without them there would perhaps be no end of war. For since we are all influenced by the desire for victory, there will be no one who would want to throw away his sword during battle, or give fodder to his enemy: and thus for this reason war would be fought endlessly, unless the Church by being the judge one of the two is forced to cede the arena, especially when they, against whom we are dealing, are children with a stiff neck and indomitable heart. Therefore all things having been prepared for war (as is befitting), it is now necessary that we go down to the field, and begin to join battle among ourselves. Nevertheless have I not determined to fight against all the heresies at the same time, nor against the phalanx of all the heretics, but to contend with any heresy in a one on one combat.

Now the heresies themselves are not are ordered according to the times in which they arose (as we have stated in the preface to the whole work) but according to the subject matters, about which they pertain. Now so that the reader can more easily profit from this labor of ours, such order will be kept, that by the subject matters, about which heresies have arisen, arranged in alphabetical order, those heresies are put under each word, which shall be deemed to pertain to the subject indicated by that word. Therefore since the first letter of the alphabet is the letter "A," it will firstly be necessary to discuss those things whose names begin with the letter "A." Thus I have reckoned to be seen, in order that we may know first of all as it were concerning the first Commandment, what we ought to reverence or adore.

ADORATIO

Adoration

Among all the heresies which have hitherto arisen, I find only two among all authors I have read (which, God as my witness, are numerous enough), which ought to be placed in this section. The first is the heresy which affirms that the Lord's Cross ought nowise to be adored. The leader and teacher of this error was a certain Claudius, Bishop of Turin, as Thomas Netter[1] testifies in his book *De Sacramentalibus*,[2] having cited in favor of this the testimony from the Chronicles of Ivo of Chartres, which I admit that I have not seen. A certain John Wycliffe resurrected this same heresy, already buried, from Hell after some years, as the same Thomas Netter states in the place just cited. This John Wycliffe was an English priest and teacher in the arts, an ingenious, shrewd and eloquent man, and as much as the poverty of that time permitted (for he was born about the year of the Lord 1380), wrote many books, whereby he persecuted the Catholic Church. For in them he scattered many impious doctrines concerning the Divine law, human law, the Church, monks, ceremonies, tithes, obedience and many other things, which will be said in their places.

Now that time was opportune for committing any crime, when the Church was then torn apart in thirds by three men considering themselves as supreme pontiffs. But never is any crime more easily committed than in time of war, when everything is permitted, and everything happens without punishment. Finally, God having mercy, a General Council was convened in Constance for the uniting and reformation of the whole Church: during which, among other things done in the same place, forty-five articles extracted from John Wycliffe's books were condemned. And because he was already dead, a diligent examination having been previously made of his final impenitence and pertinacity, the council judged the aforesaid John to have been a heretic, and ordered "that his body and bones (if they can be identified among the corpses of the faithful) be exhumed and scattered far from a burial place of the church." All these things were done during the eighth session of the same Council.

Even if among the articles condemned during that Council this one concerning the adoration of the Cross is in fact nowise found, it ought not seem surprising to anyone. And, although it was not listed among them by the Council, it ought not be disbelieved that Wycliff was a heretic. For after the Council enumerated those forty-five articles it subjoined these words: "It was also found that his books contain many other articles of similar quality and incite insane doctrine hostile to the faith and morals in God's Church." Now after these words immediately follows the condemnation both of the aforesaid forty-five articles stated in the same place, and of others of the same sort which are said to be found in those books. For in fact Aeneas Sylvius relates in his book, *De origine Bohemorum*,[3] that he wrote two hundred books. Now we think that Thomas Netter, a learned man, and just as religious, reviewed his books to the last one, because he was also English as the other man, and so read them so that he could purge the country which he saw infested by the error of the Wycliffites (for he was a contemporary of John Wycliffe). Therefore let the history of this John Wycliffe be related here once and for all, because very often hereafter he will need to be called to judgment.

---

[1] Thomas Netter (1375–1430) was an English Scholastic theologian and controversialist. From his birthplace he is commonly called Thomas of Walden, or Thomas Waldensis.

[2] Title 2, c. 16.

[3] C. 35.

Thus having exposed to view the defenders of this heresy, it remains that we discuss the error itself. Firstly I am in doubt whether among these heretics there is a complete consensus concerning this matter. For even if it be established concerning the Wycliffites that they assert that the Cross itself, on which Christ truly hung, ought nowise to be adored, and much less ought others made in its likeness be adored: nevertheless it is not established concerning Claudius of Turin that he forbade either only these images of Christ's Cross or also the very Cross by which Christ worked our salvation to be adored: because I could find nothing else from him besides the fragment which is cited from Ivo of Chartres by Thomas Netter. Still whatever he may allege, it is certain that he ought to be smitten by the same sword by which John Wycliffe was struck down, since the latter forbade both.

Now therefore it is fitting to prove only the present proposition: that that Cross on which the Lord hung rightly ought to be adored. For that its images ought to be adored, pertains to another matter, when below in the section on "Images" we will discuss concerning all images at the same time, how they may be tolerated, and for what their use benefits in the Church. This adoration of the Cross, which we now investigate, the Prophet explains saying: "Adore his footstool, for it is holy" (Ps. 98, 5). Now what is more truly Christ's footstool than the Cross to which His feet were affixed? For even if there may be other things which deservedly can be called Christ's footstool, still nothing prevents that the Cross also may be called His footstool, which the Prophet commands to adore. Hence Jerome expounding that passage of the Psalm says the following: "There are many opinions concerning the footstool, but he properly called the Lord's Body this name, in which the majesty of the Divinity stood as upon a footstool. Now while He ascended the Apostles taught that It [His Body] ought to be adored, since [it is written]: 'They adoring went back into Jerusalem' (Lk. 24, 52). These things ought to be referred to the Lord's Cross, and to [every] holy soul."[1] You see here how according to Jerome's opinion the footstool is the Lord's Body, the footstool is the soul, and the footstool is also the Lord's Cross.

Now the Psalmist commands these things to be adored in one sentence, saying: "We will go into his tabernacle: we will adore in the place where his feet stood" (Ps. 131, 7). Cassiodorus treating this passage, after expounding it according to its allegorical sense, says: "Because if you wish to piously refer this to history, it perhaps signifies the Holy Cross, where He bodily stood, when He appeared fixed upon it. It is rightly said that He stood upon which [Cross], whereon His Body is shown to have been affixed. Therefore the Prophet rightly says that this place ought to be adored, which gave us the sign of faith and salvation."[2] Hence it is clear that Cassiodorus asserts that the Lord's Cross ought to be adored, and yet not merely from his own understanding, but having relied upon prophetic testimony. Now lest you object that a proof ought not to be taken from the mystical meaning, see what he said, namely that that exposition is according to history.

But lest you distrust Cassiodorus as the sole witness in this matter, I will put forth another witness of the same matter, so that "in the mouth of two or three every word may stand" (Mt. 18, 16). For in fact Damascene when discussing the wood of the Lord's Cross, says the following: "This same truly precious and august tree, on which Christ has offered Himself as a sacrifice for our sakes, is to be adored as sanctified by contact with His holy Body and Blood; likewise the nails, the spear, the clothes; His sacred tabernacles, which are the manger, the cave, Golgotha, which brings salvation, the tomb which gives life, Sion, the chief stronghold of the churches and the like, are to be worshipped. In the words of David, the ancestor of Christ, 'We will go into his tabernacle: we will adore in the place where his feet stood' (Ps. 131, 7). And that it is the Cross that is meant is made clear by what follows, 'Arise,

---

[1] PL 26, 1124A.
[2] PL 70, 950A.

O Lord, into thy resting place' (v. 8). For the Resurrection comes after the Cross. For if of those things which we love, house and couch and garment are to be longed after, how much the rather should we long after that which belonged to God, our Savior, by means of which we are in truth saved."[1] From which testimony among the many things you have one thing, namely the Cross ought to be adored, and this same testimony of the Prophet was supported by Cassiodorus.

But lest John Wycliffe escape to a certain spiritual cross which he contrives, to which he distorts the quotations, see what Damascene said: "On which Christ has offered Himself as a sacrifice for our sakes." But He did not offer Himself except upon material wood, and very heavy to carry. Furthermore the rite of the whole universal Church confirms this very adoration, and the custom which prescribes that on Good Friday after singing from John the Evangelist that noble triumph, which Christ gained on that day by means of the mount of the Cross, the cross is elevated by the priest so that it may be adored by the people: then the cross itself having been place in an honorable place, the priest adores it on bended knees, after which the other ministers serving the altar, after whom the others attending the ceremony similarly also adore. Now the tradition of the universal Church (as we discussed at greater length above) is of such weight, that he who opposes it is not deemed less of a heretic than if he were to expressly contradict Scripture, especially in serious matters, and in which to err would be a great peril. But where is it more important not to err than about giving worship? For God abhors nothing so much as idolatry, to such an extent that in Sacred Writ an idol is often designated by the word "abomination." It is not therefore very likely that through so many centuries the universal Church, for which the Lord prayed that its faith would not fail, would be stained by the blot of idolatry, as the impious and blasphemous Wycliffe accuses her.

The opinion of all the Saints concerning this matter adds to this. For besides Jerome, Damascene and Cassiodorus, whom we have already cited, there are many others who give testimony concerning this matter. Augustine says the following: "What does He reserve for His faithful one, when He has put such honor on the instrument of His own torture? Now the cross is no longer used among the Romans in the punishment of criminals, for whereon the Cross of the Lord came to be honored, it was thought that even a guilty man would be honored if he should be crucified."[2] Is it not the reason why Wycliffe mocks us, namely on account of the honor which we show to the Cross, although God gave it to him, as Augustine here says: "What does He reserve for His faithful One, when He has put such honor on the instrument of His own torture?"

Chrysostom says the following: "For this Cross saved and converted the world, drove away error, brought back truth, made earth Heaven, fashioned men into angels. Because of this, the devils are no longer terrible, but contemptible; neither is death, death, but a sleep; because of this, all that warreth against us is cast to the ground, and trodden under foot. If anyone therefore say to thee, 'Dost thou worship the crucified?' Say, with your voice all joy, and your countenance gladdened, 'I do both worship Him, and will never cease to worship.' And if he laugh, weep for him, because he is mad."[3] Therefore let us weep for the Wycliffites, and let us pity them, because according to Chrysostom's words they are mad: if they are mad, it were better to subdue them with chains than with arguments.

Therefore whom do you make yourself, Wycliffe, such that you despise Jerome, Augustine, Chrysostom, Damascene, Cassiodorus, and you rely solely on your own prudence? For when you are not ashamed to accuse the whole Church of so grave a crime as idolatry, why do you not cite even one witness in support of your accusation? You want to be believed without any

---

[1] *On the Orthodox Faith*, bk. 4, c. 11 (PG 94, 1130C-1131B).
[2] *Tractates (Lectures) on the Gospel of John*, tract 36, n. 4 (PL 35, 1665).
[3] *Homily 54 on Matthew*, n. 5 (PG 58, 538).

testimony of Scripture more than so many illustrious men? than even the whole universal tradition and customs of the Church?

Notwithstanding because you brand the Church with idolatry, let us discuss this, and let us see for what reason you say this. Is it perhaps because Christ's faithful genuflect before the Lord's Cross, and bow their uncovered heads? It is certainly a trifling reason for accusing the Church of so great a crime. For since outward adoration, like any outward act, is not deemed good or evil except in the degree that it proceeds from the interior, it ought to receive that character of goodness or wickedness, which the interior operation has from which it is derived. For this reason alone the genuflections of the mocking Jews and their adorations are blamed, because they proceed from a bad, namely mocking, root. On account of which it ought to be inquired, from which precise root does such exterior worship arise? If thus anyone genuflects before the Cross, or bows his head, because he believes it to be some deity, or some supreme good, rightly you will criminalize such a person, and we will not depart from you on these grounds. But if he genuflects because he recalls when seeing the Cross, that Christ hung on it or on another one like it for us, and gives thanks for such an immense benefit shown to us by genuflecting, why do you accuse of a crime in this case where there is no reason for accusing? Do you not believe that Christ was fixed to the Cross for us? Or if you believe, when you are reminded of it, do you not in return love the One loving? But if you deny either of these things, you are refuted by this argument alone. If, however, you agree to either of these, why do you accuse us because you agree to these things? For those prostrations, uncovering of the head, the elevating of the hands made before the Cross, signify nothing else but that by them we testify that we believe Christ hung on one similar for us: and on account of such a great benefit, the memory of which is revived by looking at the Cross, we profess our servitude and obedience by genuflecting. Since all these things are acknowledged by all, and even by Wycliffe himself, it is proved by this argument, that not only the Cross itself is rightly adored, on which the Lord hung, but also all the others which are its true images. For upon looking at them our mind is reminded of the Crucified, whom we truly adore by such genuflections.

In this all the others are surpassed by that one on which Christ hung, namely in that it was sanctified by contact with Christ's Body and Blood. And therefore by no means ought not the others to be adored. Hence Damascene in the place cited above says: "Moreover we worship even the image of the precious and life-giving Cross, although made of another material, not honoring the material (God forbid) but the image as a symbol of Christ. For He said to His disciples, admonishing them, 'Then shall appear the sign of the Son of Man in Heaven,' meaning the Cross. And so also the angel of the resurrection said to the woman, 'Ye seek Jesus of Nazareth which was crucified.' And the Apostle said, 'We preach Christ crucified.' For there are many Christs and many Jesus's, but one crucified. He does not say speared but crucified. It behooves us, then, to worship the sign of Christ. For wherever the sign may be, there also will He be. But it does not behoove us to worship the material of which the image of the Cross is composed, even though it be gold or precious stones, after it is destroyed, if that should happen. Everything, therefore, that is dedicated to God we worship, conferring the adoration on Him."[1]

Hence it now clearly appears how from that adoration which we show to the Cross, no suspicion of idolatry can trickle. For although we adore all things connected with God, in this we give reverence and worship of piety to God alone. Augustine also confirms this in his book, *On the Visitation of the Sick*,[2] saying: "The sacred mysteries of the Christians indeed have a

---

[1] *On the Orthodox Faith*, bk. 4, c. 11 (PG 94, 1131B).
[2] "Long unattributed, the main source of the *Visitation*, the PseudoAugustinian *De visitation infirmorum*, is now known to be the only religious prose written—written in two parts as letters to a gravely ill nephew—by the humanist poet Baudri de Bourgueil (1045-1130), abbot of the monastery of Saint-

certain venerable monument of that Cross of the Lord, which we also confess to be most worthy of all veneration, and we venerate for the remembrance of Our Crucified One. For there is found on the Cross an image of a man suffering scourges, by which the salutary Passion of Jesus Christ is renewed for us. This is to be humbly embraced, and simply venerated. Yet you will recall to yourselves these things:

The present figure which I presently see is neither God nor man,
But it is God and man, which the sacred figure represents:
True man and true God, yet both are one,
He suffers the reproach of the Cross, He undergoes death, and is buried:
He lives, and likewise triumphs over the enemy through these signs of the Cross,
The letter of this Cross makes it known to you,
Namely His Cross and the Crucified are known."[1]

From these words, he who is nowise blind, now will be able to perceive how this genuflection, and whatever other adoration before the Cross is made, and to Whom it is shown, for to God Himself, in whose memory we come through the sight of the Cross, and thus we show ourselves in some way grateful to the Cross, which makes us recall such a great benefit shown to us.

Nor is it surprising that the sight of the Cross renews the knowledge of Christ Himself, since Christ by His own voice called it, "the sign of the Son of Man in heaven." For speaking of His own Coming for the Judgement, He says, "And then shall appear the sign of the Son of man in heaven" (Mt. 24, 30). Expounding which, Theophylactus says: "The Cross will then appear in heaven shining brighter than the sun for rebuking the Jews. For Christ will come against the Jews having the Cross as the evidence and testimony of justifying, as if one struck by a stone were to show the stone. Now He calls the Cross a sign as being a trophy and insignia of kings."[2] You see here the Cross called a sign: because even if Theophylactus calls [It] a sign in that manner whereby it is a "trophy," or "banner," or "insignia," it nowise stands in the way. For these things also in some way bring to mind those things to which they pertain.

But Blessed Cyril explains this more clearly. For he in his sixth book against Julian when he replies to his mocking of the Christians because they adore the wood of the Cross, after having listed the benefits shown to us on the Cross, says: "The salutary wood stirs up the memory of all these things for us, and furthermore leads us to that thought (as the most wise Paul says) that One 'died for all, so that those who live, may not live to themselves, but unto him who died for them and rose again' (II Cor. 5, 15)."[3]

These things now suffice concerning this matter: since from them it is evident that the Lord's Cross, and others made in its likeness, deservedly ought to be adored. And yet on account of this the scruple of idolatry ought not to compel, since in that adoration we give nothing else to the Cross than that we believe Christ the Lord underwent death for us all on the Cross or figuratively on the crucifixes which represent it, and knowing such the great benefit, which we may recall by looking at the Cross, we profess our servitude by genuflecting and baring our head. Finally, even if the adoration itself be before the Cross, still our mind is carried to that alone, which the Cross itself represents, namely the Son of God hanging of old upon the Cross. Against this heresy wrote the very accurate Thomas Netter, in his book, *De Sacramentalibus.*[4] From him I certainly admit that I have taken some things, and also attribute

---

Pierre-de-Bourgueil in Brittany and, later, Archbishop of Dol." (Amy Appleford, *Learning to Die in London, 1380-1540* (Philadelphia, University of Pennsylvania Press, 2015), p.28.)

[1] C. 3 (PL 40, 1154).

[2] *Enarratio in Evangelium S.* Matthaei (PG 123, 415A).

[3] PG 76, 798D.

[4] Title 20 (*De adoratione sanctae crucis*).

many things [to him]. Of old a certain Jonas, Bishop of Orleans, had also written concerning this matter against Claudius, Bishop of Turin, the first parent of this heresy. Nevertheless I have not seen this work, but I have [it] merely from the relating of the history from the fragment of the Chronicles of Ivo of Chartres cited by Thomas Netter.

A **second heresy** has arisen concerning this subject, asserting that the Most Holy Eucharist ought not to be adored in any way, accusing the crime of idolatry to anyone adoring it. The author of this heresy is John Oecolampadius,[1] German by nationality, a man of three languages and highly educated in every kind of good learning. But at length, led by the spirit of pride, he wished "to be more wise than it behoveth to be wise" (Rom. 12, 3), and so it happened that by God's permission he was caught in his own foolishness. He firstly adhered to the Lutheran sect, and by Luther's example, when he was a monk of the Order of Saint Bridget, having rejected monastic life and having slighted the continency which he had vowed in religion, like a dog having returned to its vomit,[2] married a wife, such that by this evidence she in fact persuades us of his errors. Finally being impatient (as I suppose) to fight under Luther's banners, he thought up something more impious and blasphemous than the Lutheran sect, whereby he might appear more illustrious and could raise his own banner. For he says in fact that Christ is nowise contained in the Eucharist, and on account of this he calls those who venerate and adore the Most Holy Eucharist idolaters. Now when Luther could not be drawn into this blasphemy, Oecolampadius was divided from Luther for this reason. And it happened that those who followed Oecolampadius received a name from him, namely they are called Oecolampadians.

Now in order that we may refute this error, firstly it is necessary to show that Christ's true Body is truly and really contained under the accidents of the bygone bread. For by this reason alone (it seems to me) they forbid adoration of the Eucharist, but they would not forbid it if they believed that Christ's true Body is hidden under the covering of those accidents. Now this (God willing) we will show below in the section on the "Eucharist": wherefore the assault on this error will be deferred until that place. For I show there that Christ's true Body is contained under the accidents of bread: hence it will become clear that the Eucharist is rightly adored. But if perhaps someone is so ungrateful to Christ's humanity, which God by a dispensation assumed as an instrument for working our Redemption, that he also disdain to adore It, this alone will now be established, and that briefly, because I can hardly believe that a man who acknowledges that he has been redeemed by means of Christ's humanity would avoid adoring it. For although that nature of His is unworthy to be adored, nevertheless as it has been joined to the Divinity by such a union whereby it exceeds all human and angelic understanding, it certainly deserves all veneration.

On account of which I am unable not to be surprised, when I see Luther (now who he is we will state afterwards) actually asserting that Christ's true Body and His true Blood are in the Eucharist, but also denying that the Eucharist ought to be adored. And certainly the reason which motivates him to say that is very ridiculous. It is because (he says) the Lord did not command it. Oh insane argument that therefore the three very holy Wise Men did very badly, who came from the East, and entering the house genuflecting adored Him (Mt. 2, 11) Who was crying in the cradle. Luther will also say that Magdalene and the Canaanite woman, and the man born blind, and all the other who showed Divine honors to Christ acted badly, for the very reason that none of them did it because of God's command. What Luther says is of

---

[1] Berengarius of Tours was previously condemned by the Council of Vercelli in 1050 for denying the article of faith of the Real Presence, but retracted his heresy at the Council of Tours (1055), presided over by the papal legate Hildebrand. Perhaps because of his retraction, he is not accredited as being the first author of this heresy.

[2] Cf. II Pet. 2, 22.

course false, that there be no precept concerning this adoration. For the Divine precept is this: "The Lord thy God shalt thou adore, and him only shalt thou serve" (Mt. 4, 10).

Now if Luther were to say that this precept ought to be understood of the Divinity alone, the objection to him is that there is a very clear precept from the Royal Prophet, whereby God commands Christ to be adored existing in His two natures. "Adore him, all you his angels" (Ps. 96, 7). Which words Paul in his Epistle to the Hebrews teaches that they ought to be understood of the Person of Christ, not in fact concerning His Divinity alone, but concerning the whole Person existing in two natures. Otherwise Paul argued badly from that passage, wishing to prove from thence, that Christ is superior to the Angels, whom God the Father commanded to adore Christ, His own Son. For if the adoration ought only to be directed to the Divinity, it would not be permitted thence to conclude anything except that only Christ's Divinity was higher than that of the Angels, but not that Christ's Person contains two natures at the same time. I see here that Luther cannot reply anything except perhaps he may say that the command concerning Christ's adoration was given to the Angels, but not to men.

But this reply is so ridiculous that it would easily move a prudent and wise man to laughter. For according to this reason men would be of greater dignity and more excellent than Angels, since the Angels are obliged by precept to the adoration of Christ, but men are exempt from the obligation of this kind.

But putting aside these arguments, I will relate other very clear testimonies, by which not merely Christ's Divinity, but also His Body is commanded to be adored. Firstly there is the passage from the Psalms concerning the Cross which we mentioned above: "Adore his footstool, for it is holy" (Ps. 98, 5). For as it was shown there according to Jerome's authority, among the many things which can be understood by the word "footstool," the Lord's Body before all others can rightly be understood by the word, because on it the majesty of the Divinity stood as upon a footstool. Augustine agrees with Jerome's exposition, when expounding the same passage from the Psalms. For he says the following: "Explaining to us what His footstool is, Scripture says, 'The earth is My footstool.' I am in doubt; I fear to worship the earth, lest He who made the Heaven and the earth condemn me; again, I fear not to worship the footstool of my Lord, because the Psalm bids me, 'fall down before His footstool.' I ask, what is His footstool? And the Scripture tells me, 'The earth is My footstool.' In hesitation I turn unto Christ, since I am herein seeking Him: and I discover how the earth may be worshipped without impiety, how His footstool may be worshipped without impiety. For He took upon Him earth from earth; because Body is from earth, and He received His Body from the flesh of Mary. And because He walked here in very flesh, and gave that very Flesh to us to eat for our salvation; and no one eats that Body, unless he has first worshipped: we have found out in what sense such a footstool of our Lord may be worshipped, and not only that we sin not in worshipping it, but that we sin in not worshipping."[1]

We have many things here besides what Augustine intends: Firstly, that He gave His Body to be eaten. Now He nowhere else gave [His Body] than in the Eucharist. Therefore it is Augustine's understanding that Christ's Body is contained in the Eucharist. But concerning this [it will be discussed] elsewhere at greater length. Then he shows that the Body Itself ought to be adored, saying: "No one eats that Body, unless he has first worshipped." No one, Augustine? What will you say concerning Oecolampadius, who eating disdains to adore, fearing to fall into idolatry? My words (Augustine says) ought to be referred to Christians alone: among whom there is no one who eats without adoring. For if he refuses to adore, for this reason

---

[1] *Exposition on Psalm 98*, n. 9 (PL 37, 1264). This work is also known as the *Enarrationes in Psalmos*, a title attributed to Erasmus, which is best translated as "running explanations." (Michael Cameron, "Enarrationes in Psalmos," in *Augustine Through the Ages: An Encyclopedia*, ed. Allan Fitzgerald (Grand Rapids, Eerdmans, 1999), p. 291).

he will in fact nowise be called a Christian, but a heretic. For thus I said that we sin by not adoring.

Cassiodorus also agrees with Jerome and Augustine in his exposition of the same Psalm saying: "Now it ought to be said to us what his feet seem to signify in this verse, namely the stability of the Divinity, which always in the omnipotent glory of Its nature persists as the unfailing stability of the feet. Therefore the assumed Body of this Word, although glorious, although admirable, nevertheless on account of the humility of the humanity we suitably understand as the footstool of the feet. For when He says in Isaias: 'Heaven is my throne, and the earth my footstool' (66, 1): the earthly body which He took from the Virgin Mary, the footstool of His feet is well proved to be understood (as I think) by the same similitude."[1]

Now what he said, "As I think," he did not say this as though he was being distrustful, but as a man acknowledging the fragility of human understanding, which can easily be deceived. Wherefore in those things which are not expressed, holy men fear their own judgment and greatly fear, let perhaps they err, who wish to be very far from error. Not so the heretics, not so: because these hold onto their own opinions so firmly with their teeth that they can by no means be pulled away.

Again, the Royal Prophet likewise says speaking in the name of any true Christian that he, after he shall have entered God's house, which is the Church, would adore Christ's Body Itself: "I will come into thy house; I will worship towards thy holy temple" (Ps. 5, 8). Expounding which words, Cassiodorus says: "One must note that she[2] did not say in the temple but 'towards [thy holy] temple'; as has been previously said, even the syllables partake of the mysteries. The 'holy temple' is the Lord Savior's Body which the Church rightly worships because through It she has merited veneration; for He said of His Body, 'Destroy this temple, and in three days I will raise it up' (Jn. 2, 19)."[3]

Then the Royal Prophet likewise, what he said that he would do in the name of the Christian people, afterwards in another Psalm declares it to have been so done, saying the following: "All the fat ones of the earth have eaten and have adored" (Ps. 21, 30). Which words Blessed Augustine in his commentaries on the Psalms says: "The rich of the earth too have eaten the Body of their Lord's humiliation, and though they have not, as the poor, been filled even to imitation, yet they have worshipped."[4] These words Augustine wrote in his first exposition on the Psalms, since he made two expositions on this Psalm.[5]

The testimony of Alexander, the first pope of this name, who was the sixth pope counting from Blessed Peter, and was ultimately crowned with martyrdom, adds to all these testimonies. For he in his first letter which he wrote to all the faithful, discussing the sacrifice of the Mass, says the following: "For that reason also His Passion, by which we were redeemed, is commemorated in these words,[6] which are often recited, and these things[7] ought to be offered to the Lord: for by such offerings the Lord will be pleased and appeased, and He will forgive great sins. For nothing in sacrifices can be greater than Christ's Body and Blood, nor any

---

[1] *Expositio in Psalterium*, Ps. 98, v. 6 (PL 70, 694D-695A).
[2] I.e. the person of the Catholic Church speaking in this Psalm.
[3] *Explanation of the Psalms*, Ps. 5, verse 8 (PL 70, 56B-C).
[4] *Exposition on the Book of Psalms*, Ps. 21, 30 (PL 36, 170).
[5] Augustine never envisaged the Expositions of the Psalms as a single work. Later redactors collected Augustine's sermons and treatises on the Psalms to form the work as we now have it. The Expositions were either dictated essays or preached sermons. The dictated essays generally took three forms: exegetical notes, expositions or homilies. (*Johannes Quasten. Patrology, Vol. 4: The Golden Age of Latin Patristic Literature* (Allen, TX, Christian Classics, 1986), pp. 396-397.
[6] I.e. the words in Mt. 26, and I Cor. 11 which refer to the words of consecration used at Mass.
[7] I.e. Christ's Body and Blood.

oblation is more preferable, and it ought to be received with a pure heart, and venerated by all: and just as it is preferable to other [sacrifices], so it ought to be more honored and venerated."[1] From which words it is very clearly established that the Most Holy Eucharist ought to be adored with great reverence.

But concerning this matter it is necessary to caution that although we may say that Christ's humanity ought to be adored on account of its union with the Divinity, not on account of itself alone, but by reason of the Divinity to which it has been united, to which Divinity the adoration itself ought to be referred as to its ultimate cause. Because if perhaps it belongs to His humanity to be adored with the worship of *latria*, this will be by that singular adoration itself, by which Christ's Person is adored, in which the humanity subsists, by which all things subsisting in Him are adored with one adoration. Hence Damascene says: "Christ's Body, then, in Its own nature, if one were to make subtle mental distinctions between what is seen and what is thought, is not deserving of worship since it is created. But as It is united with God the Word, It is worshipped on account of Him and in Him. For just as the king deserves homage alike when un-robed and when robed, and just as the purple robe, considered simply as a purple robe, is trampled upon and tossed about, but after becoming the royal dress receives all honor and glory, and whoever dishonors it is generally condemned to death: and again, just as wood in itself is not of such a nature that it cannot be touched, but becomes so when fire is applied to it, and it becomes charcoal, and yet this is not because of its own nature, but because of the fire united to it, and the nature of the wood is not such as cannot be touched, but rather the charcoal or burning wood: so also the Body, in Its own nature, is not to be worshipped, but is worshipped in the Incarnate God, not because of Itself, but because of its union in subsistence with God the Word. And we do not say that we worship mere flesh, but God's Body, that is, God Incarnate."[2]

Wherefore Cassiodorus after having explained the figurative use of the word footstool, adds: "And notice that He did not say that He is holy; but 'for it is holy' (Ps. 98, 5), namely, so that you may not distinguish by your mind's consideration [the holiness of] His Body from the Deity, but rather so that you may relate [it] to the one Person, that is, to 'the Word which was made flesh, and dwelt amongst us' (Jn. 1, 14)."[3] Therefore just as Christ's Body does not subsist by itself, but in the Word, and It has the same hypostasis with the Word: so also It is neither adored by Itself, but in the Word; and with the same unique adoration by which we adore Christ, we venerate His Humanity which is in Its hypostasis.

And this ought not to seem surprising to anyone, because there are many things which on account of a connection which they have to other things much more noble than themselves, some things are obtained from them, which by themselves they could not attain, and yet by these things they do not give up any of their own nobility to the other: as for example, if you were to separate a body from the soul, it does not move, does not hear, does not see, does not taste, is not nourished, does not increase in size, and finally does not live, yet from its union with the soul it has all these things: for the body is said to live by the soul giving life to it, and yet for the same reason the soul does not receive any of the corruption of the body: so also it could happen that human flesh on account of its union with the Word receives this from it, namely that it be adored along with it.

But that is enough about these things. Assuredly these things so suffice, so that they may seem superfluous to someone: because if Christ's Flesh hides under the accidents of what was bread, as I have promised to demonstrate with God's help, it will also be for the same reason

---

[1] *Decretum*, part 2, c. 15 (PL 161, 164C). Previously cited in the *False Decretals of the Pseudo-Isidore* (PL 130, 94A).
[2] *On the Orthodox Faith*, bk. 4, c. 3 (PG 94, 1106A-B).
[3] *Expositio in Psalterium*, Ps. 98, v. 6 (PL 70, 965B).

by the unique existence of the Son of God therein, since in this particular case the human flesh which He at one time assumed, He never afterwards separated from Himself. But if Christ subsists there in His two natures, doubtlessly the Most Holy Eucharist rightly ought to be adored, whether or not His humanity ought to be adored. For we do not worship the accidents of bread, which we see, but that which is hidden under them, namely Christ, the Son of God, and through those things which we see, the soul rises to the worship of those things which it does not see. Hence Augustine says the following: "He, on the other hand, who either uses or honors a useful sign Divinely appointed, whose force and significance he understands, does not honor the sign which is seen and temporal, but that to which all such signs refer."[1]

Finally against this heresy there is a clear definition of the Catholic Church. For the Council of Trent celebrated under Julian III says the following: "Wherefore, there is no room left for doubt that all the faithful of Christ may, according to the custom ever received in the Catholic Church, render in veneration the worship of latria, which is due to the true God, to this most Holy Sacrament. For not therefore is it the less to be adored on this account, that it was instituted by Christ, the Lord, in order to be received; for we believe that same God to be present therein, of whom the Eternal Father, when introducing Him into the world, says: 'And let all the angels of God adore him' (Heb. 1,6); whom the Magi, 'falling down, adored' (Mt. 2, 11); who, in fine, as the Scripture testifies, was adored by the Apostles in Galilee. The holy Synod declares, moreover, that very piously and religiously was this custom introduced into the Church, that this sublime and venerable Sacrament be, with special veneration and solemnity, celebrated, every year, on a certain day, and that a festival; and that it be borne reverently and with honor in processions through the streets and public places. For it is most just that there be certain appointed holy days, whereon all Christians may, with a special and unusual demonstration, testify that their minds are grateful and thankful to their common Lord and Redeemer for so ineffable and truly divine a benefit, whereby the victory and triumph of his death are represented. And so indeed did it behoove victorious truth to celebrate a triumph over falsehood and heresy, that thus her adversaries, at the sight of so much splendor, and in the midst of so great joy of the universal Church, may either 'pine away' (Ps. 111, 10) weakened and broken; or, touched with shame and confounded, at length repent."[2]

There is another heresy, which in some way pertains to this matter, namely concerning completely removing images, but concerning this matter it will more properly be treated below under the heading, "Image." Moreover there are many other heresies, which could rightly be put here, namely all who worship idols: but we will give a more appropriate place to them, when we treat below concerning idolatry to be avoided, and so see them under the heading, "Idolatry."

ABSOLUTIO

Absolution

About absolution, which is bestowed in the Sacrament of Penance to sinners who have confessed, very few heresies have arisen, and they are recent ones. Therefore the **first heresy** is that which asserts that someone believing that he has been absolved, is absolved no matter how much he lacks contrition, and that absolution ought to be deemed efficacious, not because it is efficacious (ultimately one may or may not err by whom it may be done) but because it is believed to be efficacious. A certain Martin Luther became the

---

[1] *On Christian Doctrine*, bk. 3, c. 9, n. 13 (PL 34, 70).

[2] Sess. 13, c. 5 (Dz. 878).

leader and teacher of this error in our time. Who he is will be worthwhile to state once, since mention will often be made of him later on.

This Luther, a German by nationality, a native of Saxony (as I think), lived for a time under the Institute of the Hermetical Brothers of Blessed Augustine,[1] at length degenerating from his Father, namely [Saint] Augustine, who was a most bitter enemy of heretics, this degenerate son became a heretic, taking an occasion for his errors from Indulgences. For he had heard some ranting preachers of indulgences, who said so many and such things (as men of this sort are accustomed babble for the sake of greater gain), that he decided that he ought to resist them: with zeal, not animated by due discretion, he went forth into the public, not explaining the true meaning of indulgences, but completely distorting them, he said that they were of no importance. Who when he was contradicted by certain learned men, and he was encouraged to sing the palinode, he was so disinclined to do so, that he increased his madness, giving vent to worse things than before. Indeed it often happens that from a trifling accident on a small stone, one dashes his head against another greater stone and perishes. Afterwards he having been protected in the fortress of the duke of Saxony, became so strong that he corrupted nearly the whole of Germany.

Consequently the Supreme Pontiff Leo X, who then ruled the universal Church, perceiving that the man was obstinate in evil, and would not be healed either by reasons or warnings, and seeing the evil was increasing daily, completely drove off the putrid sheep from the flock of the Church, lest he infect the rest of the sheep by its contact. Luther, however, realizing the he had been cast out from the communion of the faithful, not only did not mourn, or lament his case, but as an impious man sunk into the depth of sins disdained the matter: and he was made a member of the devil, as he imitated his head, that is to say, the devil who is called a calumniator, for he also began to calumniate the Supreme Pontiff, and the whole Church. He overturned every ecclesiastical order, he wished that all monasticism be removed from the Church, by giving license to the monks to live as they pleased. Unless God in His goodness come quickly to the aid of this pestilence, it must be feared that it will spread further, and that it will infect the small remainder of Germany which is left. We have written Luther's rationalization beforehand, even though it may be well known at the present time, nevertheless it should not have been passed over, because we write not only for the present time, but also for the times to come afterwards. Therefore, he teaches this error, which we have related concerning absolution, among many others.

Now so that his insane mind may be more clearly known, I will cite his words: "If through an impossibility he who confessed was not contrite, or the priest did not absolve seriously, but in a jocose manner, if nevertheless he believes that he has been absolved, he is most truly absolved."[2] And after a few things which he interjected clarifying himself he adds: "Now I said, 'through an impossibility,' because it was sufficiently said above that faith without contrition cannot exist, since grace is not infused except with a great upheaval in the soul. For I wished to state and to recommend the power of faith, which alone accomplishes the remission of sins and the justification of peace."[3] From which words of Luther we can gather two things, of which one flows from the other, as a corrupt stream from a spoiled spring.

---

[1] Today it is called simply the "Order of Saint Augustine."
[2] Number twelve of the forty-one heretical sentences selected from Luther's writings listed in *Exsurge Domine,* the Bull of Pope Leo X condemning the errors of Martin Luther, issued June 15, 1520. This sentence was taken from Luther's *Assertio omnium articulorum Martini Lutheri per Bullam Leonis X novissimam damnatorum.*
[3] Martin Luther, *Varii argumenti ad Reformationis historiam imprimis pertinentia,* ed. by Hericus Schmidt (H. Zimmeri, 1868), vol. 5, p. 194.

Firstly he in fact asserts that only faith justifies, motivated by certain passages which nowise support his assertion even slightly: for even if there may be some passages of Sacred Scripture which say that faith justifies or purifies, still there is none which asserts that only faith justifies man: nay from them the opposite is proved, since all such passages ought to be understood as concerning faith informed by charity, which is the form of all the virtues. For unformed faith[1] does not justify. For Blessed James says: "The devils also believe and tremble" (2, 19). Now since they are not just, it is evident that unformed faith does not justify but rather formed faith does. But formed faith is never alone, but charity always exists with it at the same time: thus faith alone never justifies. Furthermore a priest absolves and remits sins by the power conferred upon him by God: therefore it is not true that a penitent is absolved by faith alone. Now that a priest remits and absolves is clear from that which Christ said to the Apostles: "Whose sins you shall forgive, they are forgiven them; and whose sins you shall retain, they are retained" (Jn. 20, 23).

Then I ask Luther whether Christ conferred some power by these words upon the Apostles or none? If he says that Christ conferred no power, he clearly makes Christ a hypocrite and deceiver, since He did something other than what He clearly stated with these words. If he gave some power, since it is none other than the power of remitting, as the words say, it will be necessary then to admit that the penitent is not absolved by faith alone, since the priest also absolves. Again, the priest says the words of absolution in the first person and in his own name: "I absolve thee": thus speaking in this manner he is either saying something true, or he is lying. No one will be so impious such that he would say that he administers the sacrament through lying words. But if he says true things, and the reality is as the priest says, it will be necessary to concede that the priest does something through the signification of those words. Hence it is clearly established that Luther erred miserably, when he says that only faith justifies and absolves the penitent: since from the aforesaid it is clear that the priest truly absolves.

Now in order to show that Luther is unable to oppose this Catholic belief without great impudence, it will be useful to show that this was the opinion of holy men, and that they all unanimously held that priests received the power of absolving penitents and remitting sin. Hence Blessed Ambrose against the Novatians denying that could it happen in any way that a priest may forgive sins, speaks thus: "Why do you baptize if sins cannot be remitted by man? If baptism is certainly the remission of all sins, what difference does it make whether priests claim that this power is given to them in Penance or at the font? In each the mystery is one. But you say that the grace of the mysteries works in the font. What works, then, in Penance? Does not the name of God do the work? What then? Do you, when you choose, claim for yourselves the grace of God, and when you choose reject it?"[2] In which words he teaches clearly enough that priests have the same power in the administration of the Sacrament of Penance as they have in the administration of the Sacrament of Baptism. Therefore since it is evident that the priest truly baptizes, there is no reason why Luther now denies that priests also truly absolve.

Chrysostom confirms the same opinion saying: "Yet one will not be wrong in asserting that they then also received some spiritual power and grace; not so as to raise the dead, or to work miracles, but so as to remit sins. For the gifts of the Spirit are of different kinds; wherefore He added, 'Whose sins you shall forgive, they are forgiven them,' showing what kind of power He was giving."[3] By which words he clearly expressed that the priest forgives sins.

Cyprian, a man most renowned for his martyrdom and doctrine, says the following: "I entreat you, beloved brethren, that each one should confess his own sin, while he who has

---

[1] I.e. faith without charity.

[2] *Concerning Repentance* (*De poenitentia*), bk. 1, c. 8, n. 36-37 (PL 16, 477C).

[3] *Homily 86 on the Gospel of John*, n. 3 (PG 59, 471).

sinned is still in this world, while his confession may be received, while the satisfaction and remission made by the priests are pleasing to the Lord."[1] You see now, O Luther, that Cyprian is saying that the remission of sins takes place through the priests.

But that [Luther] cites Jerome in favor of his opinion, he proceeds from a distorted understanding. Now so that it may be shown more clearly, it will be useful that we relate Jerome's words. For he, when expounding the passage from Matthew's Gospel, "And I will give to thee the keys of the kingdom of heaven" (Mt. 16, 19), says the following: "Not understanding this place of the bishop and the priest, they assume to themselves that it is some arrogance of the Pharisees, such that they perhaps condemn the innocent, or they decide to loose the guilty, when before God not the verdict of the priest, but the life of guilty men ought to be sought. We read in Leviticus (14, 2) about lepers, where they are ordered to show themselves to the priests, and if they have leprosy, then they are to be declared unclean by the priest. It is not that the priests make them lepers and unclean; rather, it is the priests who separate the leper from one who is not a leper, and they can distinguish the clean from the unclean. Just as in the Old Testament the priest makes the leper clean or unclean, so in the New Testament the bishop and priest binds or looses not those who are innocent or guilty, but by reason of their office, when they have heard various kinds of sins, they know who is to be bound and who loosed."[2]

It will be necessary to thoroughly discuss these words so that their meaning may appear more clearly. Firstly therefore it is necessary to bring to mind what Jerome said, namely that the priest by reason of his office has heard various kinds of sin, he knows who is to be bound and who loosed: but he did not say, "He knows who has been bound and who has been loosed": just as previously he had said concerning the priest of the Old Law that he distinguishes who is clean and who is unclean. From which words it is very clearly proved that Blessed Jerome was able to put some difference between the priest distinguishing concerning leprosy, and the evangelical priest absolving from sin, because the priest of the Old Law was not cleansing the leprosy, but was merely judging the one to be clean: the evangelical priest, however, the penitent who confesses his sins before him, by the key of knowledge and discernment judges whether such a one is worthy of absolution, or not: nevertheless he is not yet absolved before the priest says the words of absolution: just as the leper after having obtained cleanliness was truly clean before the priests judged him to be clean. Wherefore Blessed Jerome speaking about the priest of the New Law, did not say, "He knows who is bound": but he said, "he knows who is to be bound, and who loosed," because from the knowledge of the sins and disposition of the penitent himself he knows whether he ought to absolve or bind. For if he knew that the sinner is obstinate in evil, in such wise that he suspects that he has the intention of returning to his vomit, he would judge him unworthy to receive absolution. Therefore since Jerome said concerning the priest, that he knows who "is to be bound, or loosed," he intimates clearly enough that after the examination of the priest, that is to say, after the hearing of the sins, something still remains to be done, which ought to be done by the priest in regard to the penitent himself, namely to bind or to loose.

Now that which Jerome said, that "before God not the verdict of the priest, but the life of guilty men ought to be sought," it ought not to be understood that only the life of the guilty ought to be sought, but that it ought to be more principally sought as the foundation of the whole structure, upon which lies in a certain way whatever shall have been done afterwards by the priest. For if the sinner were in the resolve of sinning, however much the priest would say the words of absolution, the sinner will never be absolved. Thus the evangelical priest does something more in regard to the penitent than the priest back in the time of the Old Law did concerning leprosy. Then the Savior's words themselves very clearly express that, for

---

[1] *On the Lapsed*, n. 29 (PL 4, 489B).
[2] *Commentariorum in Evangelium Matthaei Libri Quattor*, bk. 3, c. 16 (PL 26, 118B).

He said the following: "Whose sins you shall forgive, they are forgiven them" (Jn. 20, 23). He did not say, "Whose sins you shall declare to have been forgiven, shall be forgiven": but He said: "Whose sins you shall forgive, they are forgiven them." By which words it is very clearly shown that He conferred upon the priests not merely the power of declaring sins to have been forgiven, but the power of truly forgiving sins. Thus since from the aforesaid it is evident that the priest truly absolves, and forgives sins, it is clearly proved that what Luther said is false, that faith alone justifies. According to what Luther said, it ought to be deduced from that corrupt principle, that one who believes that he has been absolved, even if he was not contrite, or the priest did not absolve seriously, but in a jocose manner: because by that faith by which he believes that he is absolved, as he says, "he is justified."

Now in order that it may appear more clearly with what darkness Luther is surrounded, it is necessary to inquire of him, what does he understand by "the one who has been absolved"? For either he understands him over whom the priest has said the words of absolution, or him who is already free from the punishment of Hell and has already been loosed from the bonds of his sins. If were to say that the one absolved is he over whom the priest has said the words of absolution, what he says is false, namely that he is absolved. For it is possible that someone who has the intention of sinning, upon whom the priest has said the words of absolution, may think that he has been absolved, because he believes the words of absolution said over him: yet who would say that this man has been justified? Likewise it is possible that a priest would err in the form of the absolution, namely so that he did not use any form, but merely said something else not pertaining to this matter, and yet the penitent who has confessed thinks that the priest said the correct words of absolution, for the very reason that he did not understand what the priest said, then that penitent thinks that he has been absolved, because he believes that the words of absolution have been said over him, and nevertheless he has not been truly absolved (according to the cited interpretation), because such words of absolution were not said over him.

If, however, Luther were to call him "absolved," who outside of the words of absolution which were said over him receives [absolution], [and so] is free from the bonds of his sins: then the meaning of such an assertion of his, namely that he would be absolved, that is to say, he is free from sin, who believes that he has been freed from sin. Which meaning is also proved to be false by that which Paul says: "For I am not conscious to myself of any thing, yet am I not hereby justified" (I Cor. 4, 4). For it does not follow from the fact that someone believes that he is without sin, that he would be without sin. Perhaps Luther will say that the meaning of his assertion, namely that he says that one is "absolved," that is to say, free from sin, who believes that he is absolved, that is to say, who believes that the true words of absolution were said over him.

Now we will clearly show that this assertion so understood is false: for even if we were to concede to Luther that faith alone justifies, it should have been understood of what is required of any of the faithful, without which it is impossible to please God, such that it is concerning those things which Christ taught. But about absolution it is not demanded of the penitent that he believe that the priest said the words of absolution, because that matter consists in the mere deed of the priest, who could have erred, but rather it is required of the penitent, that he believe that the words of absolution pronounced by the priest have such power from Christ, namely that they may loose the sinner from his sin.

Wherefore also if we were to concede to Luther the first proposition that he proposes, namely that faith alone justifies: it would only be allowed to infer therefrom that the penitent is absolved since he believes that a priest has such power, that by the words of absolution uttered by him absolve the penitent. But if it ought to be said that someone was thus absolved, meaning that he is free from sin, because he believes that he is absolved, meaning that the

ABSOLUTIO

words of absolution have said over him, it would follow therefrom that he who would have a sin in his desire, would be free from sin if the priest were to say that words of absolution over him. For such a man although he previously intended to sin in the future, yet rightly believes that he has been absolved (according to aforesaid interpretation) because he believes that the priest said the words of absolution.

Therefore, Luther's words, in order that they may have some semblance of truth, ought to be understood as follows. He is truly absolved, meaning free from sin, who believes that he has been absolved, meaning who believes that there is such power in the priest, such that by the words of absolution pronounced over the penitent by him the penitent may remain absolved, namely so that the penitent believes both, namely that the priest has said the words of absolution over him and also believes that by those words said by the priest upon the penitent, the penitent is absolved. And he says "from this faith," because it alone justifies.

Now in order that this may be shown to be clearly false, it is necessary to consider that the priest firstly says those words of absolution, by which the penitent believes that he is absolved. For if he believes that he is absolved by the words not yet completed, he would believe falsely, because he was not yet absolved. Unless perhaps Luther assumes so much credulity in the penitent that he would altogether nullify the words of absolution said by the priest. But if Luther were to say that the whole force of the absolution depends upon the mere credulity of the penitent, it is necessary that he would admit that he may be said to have been absolved, who believes that he has been absolved, even if no words were said over him, and thus those words were completely superfluous, and were said in vain. But if they are not said in vain, and do something in the penitent, then I ask what do they do? If [they work] justification, or absolution, it is then false that faith alone justifies, as Luther said: nay rather it would never be possible that faith justifies: because he who believes that he has been absolved, either believes rightly or wrongly. If he believes wrongly, then he has not been absolved, because it is not as he believed: he believed however that he has been absolved, therefore he has not been absolved. If however he believes rightly that he has been absolved, before the words of absolution were said: and the credulity of the penitent follows afterwards, I will ask of him when was this penitent absolved, when the words of absolution were completed before the credulity entered in, or after the penitent's faith was applied? If he was absolved then when the words were completed before faith was applied, it is clear that the penitent was not then justified by faith, but by the words of the absolution alone.

But if he was then absolved once the words of absolution have been said, the faith of the penitent entered in, by which faith he believes that he was absolved: then I ask Luther why does such a penitent believe, when he says that he was absolved due to his credulity? For either he merely believes that he was absolved, and this is nothing, and this credulity does not suffice so that anyone may be justified, we have already clearly shown. Or he believes that when the words of absolution were completed he was absolved from sin, and then he believes falsely, because (as he says) he was not yet absolved even when the words of absolution were completed, until faith entered in, thus when he believed that he had been absolved, [and so] he believes falsely. But no one is justified through a false faith.

If, however, he believes that he has been absolved through his own faith, it will be necessary to say that he was then absolved when he believes that he was absolved through his own faith: therefore so that someone may be said to believe that he was absolved, a certain reflexive faith is necessary, namely such that he believes that the priest said the words, and that he has the power conferred upon him by God: and then again that he believe through the prior faith which he had, that he was absolved. And it could never have been said before that he believed that he was absolved. For it is not possible, and moreover it is not intelligible, that by the same faith through which someone is absolved and justified, he believe by the same faith that he was already absolved. But if it is one faith by which he is absolved, and another by which he believes that he has been absolved, it is also necessary that what he said is false, namely so that he alone is absolved, who believes that he has been absolved: because if he is absolved by prior faith, even if the second faith does not enter in, still he will be absolved. Note well, I beseech you, O reader, and carefully take notice of all these things, and you will clearly see with how much darkness Luther is surrounded, and with what snares he is entwined, such that it is impossible for him to be explained.

Finally so that we may put an end to this business, among Luther's assertions condemned by Leo X, this is one about the matter we have treated up till now. Then the Council of Trent celebrated under Julius III in session four,[1] condemned the statement of Luther in the ninth canon, saying the following: "If any one saith, that the sacramental absolution of the priest is not a judicial act, but a bare ministry of pronouncing and declaring sins to be forgiven to him who confesses; provided only he believe himself to be absolved, or (even though) the priest absolve not in earnest, but in joke; or saith, that the confession of the penitent is not required, in order that the priest may be able to absolve him; let him be anathema."[2]

[Saint] John [Fisher], Bishop of Rochester, a learned and at the same time a pious man wrote against this error in that book which he composed against all the articles of Luther.[3] Jacques Masson[4] wrote at greater length on that defense, which he composed, of the condemnation made by the University of Louvain of Luther's articles.[5] I have not seen anyone else, however, who treated this matter, although I have read many authors who wrote against Luther.

There is a **second heresy** concerning this subject, which says that a child and a woman equally absolve as does the pope. The author of this heresy is Martin Luther, he about whom we shortly above gave an account. Now so that his insane mind might appear more clearly, I will cite his words and they are those which follow: "In the sacrament of penance and the remission of sin the pope or the bishop does no more than the lowest priest; indeed, where there is no priest, any Christian, even if a woman or child, may equally do as much."[6] By these words he mixes together two things. Firstly in fact he says that in the absolution of a penitent all priests are equal, namely such that all priests have equal power of absolving. Secondly he says that all Christians can absolve, even if one is a woman.

The first of these, if correctly understood, we concede to him, namely that all priests (insofar as the absolution of the guilt) have equal power. For since (according to Augustine) it is impious to hope for partial pardon from God, it never ought to be said that one is absolved from one sin and not from another. Wherefore it is necessary to acknowledge that a priest who absolves a penitent, absolves from all or no sins. And so when a simple priest absolves, he merely absolves from the guilt as does the pope. For it ought not to be imagined that the pope wipes out a greater part of the guilt by his absolution, and the lowest priest wipes out a lesser part, but both of them absolve from the whole guilt, or he does not absolve at all.

---

[1] Session XIV, which was the fourth session under Julius III.

[2] Dz. 919.

[3] *Assertionis Lutheranae confutatio* (Cologne, Maternus Cholinus, 1564), fol. 54v-55r.

[4] Jacques Masson (or Jacobus Latomus) (ca. 1475–1544) was a Flemish theologian, a distinguished member of the Faculty of Theology at the University of Louvain. He was a theological adviser to the Inquisition. The general focus of his academic work centered on opposing Martin Luther and the Protestant Reformation.

[5] *Articulorum doctrinae fratris M. Lutheri per theologos Lovanienses damnatorum ratio ex sacris literis et veteribus tractatoribus.*

[6] Dz. 753 (Proposition thirteen condemned in the Bull *Exsurge Domine*, June 15, 1520).

Now what is brought up concerning reserved cases, from which the lowest priest cannot absolve, nowise nullifies our assertion, because the fact that he may not absolve, is not from a lack of power, but from a lack of jurisdiction, namely because the penitent is not subject to him, which is especially required for this, namely that the judgment passed upon him be valid. A judgment in fact not passed by one's own judge is null. The pope therefore has wider power than the lowest priest, because he has more subjects than the lowest priest. Now the lowest priest in regard to his subject, if he is fully subject to him, has equal power of absolving with the pope, because he equally absolves from all guilt, as does the pope. But it is not the same concerning the punishment, because outside of absolution, regarding the punishment which remains to be paid, the pope can relax either part or all, as the circumstance present themselves. The lowest priest, however, outside of the absolution from guilt never by his own authority can absolve from the punishment in its entirety. Concerning the equality of priests, as to the absolution of guilt, it suffices to say these words.

Now it is necessary that we treat concerning the rest of what Luther says, that any Christian even if a woman or child, in the absence of a priest truly absolves equally as any priest. Now this assertion of his flows from the first heresy which we have discussed and opposed. For we have said above that Luther thinks that the whole power of wiping away guilt ought to be ascribed to the faith of the believer, and nowise to the minister. Wherefore on this basis he infers that even if a woman or child were to say these words, the sinner hearing and believing them is immediately absolved. Now in order that we may clearly prove this to be false and heretical, it is necessary to interrogate Luther, as to whether if the penitent were to hear from a parrot those words of absolution, would parrot have absolved and would the penitent have been absolved. If he would say that the parrot absolves, what can be said that is more absurd and more impious? But if he denies that the parrot absolves although he says the words of absolution, it is necessary that he acknowledge some power in the minister saying the words, which when lacking in the speaker of the words, absolution would be non-existent. For if there were no force or power in the minister, one who was the speaker of the words would effect nothing, even though he were to say the words entirely.

Now there is no one who does not see that these things are absurd. Because if power is necessarily required in the minister of the speech, and it is evident that this power was not conferred by Christ to women, it is hence proved that a woman may not absolve. But here I know that Luther denies that such power was nowise conferred upon women, rather he very constantly affirms that Christ gave that power to all Christians. Now it is evident that this is false, because such power was conferred by Christ by these words which after the Resurrection Christ said to His disciples: "Whose sins you shall forgive, they are forgiven them; and whose sins you shall retain, they are retained" (Jn. 20, 23). Now when Christ said those words, there was no woman present, to whom those words can pertain: but there were only the Apostles, to whom alone those words were addressed. But if Luther were to say that that power was conferred by God by those words found in Matthew's Gospel: "Whatsoever you shall bind upon earth, shall be bound also in heaven; and whatsoever you shall loose upon earth, shall be loosed also in heaven" (Mt. 18, 18): even if we were to concede this to Luther, the same reasoning fights for us, because then although those words were said, there was also no woman (as is evident from the account of the Evangelist) but there were only the Apostles and the other disciples, to whom those words were said. Hence it must be inferred that only Christ's disciples, and their successors, namely the priests, received that power from Christ.

But if Luther still contends that those words, which Christ said to His disciples alone, ought to be referred to all Christians, it is then necessary to grant that a woman could also consecrate Christ's Body: because when Christ said to His disciples: "Do this for a commemoration of me" (Lk. 22, 19), it would also be necessary to refer those words to all Christians. Likewise it would be necessary to concede that a woman could preach, because it was said to the Apostles: "Go, preach the gospel to every creature" (Mk. 16, 15). And yet Paul says that he does not allow a woman to preach.[1] Again, so that we may wall in the man on every side, it is necessary to discuss the fact that Luther said that a woman can absolve where there is no priest. Now these words greatly contradict another assertion of the same Luther. For Luther says (as we will discuss below at greater length) that all Christians are priests. If then according to Luther all Christians are priests, it is certainly not possible that there be a woman where there is not a priest. You see now reader, how with many snares Luther surrounds himself.

Finally this is one of Luther's many assertions condemned by Leo X, against which we have been disputing until now.[2] Then, the Council of Trent in fourth session celebrated under Julius III condemned this proposition of Luther by a public decree. For among the many propositions which it produced in that session, the tenth of them contains these words: "If any one saith, that priests, who are in mortal sin, have not the power of binding and of loosing; or, that not priests alone are the ministers of absolution, but that, to all and each of the faithful of Christ is it said: Whatsoever you shall bind upon earth shall be bound also in heaven; and whatsoever you shall loose upon earth, shall be loosed also in heaven; and, whose sins you shall forgive, they are forgiven them; and whose sins you shall retain, they are retained; by virtue of which words everyone is able to absolve from sins, to wit, from public sins by reproof only, provided he who is reproved yield thereto, and from secret sins by a voluntary confession; let him be anathema."[3] I do not wish to argue about this matter further, because below in the section on the "Priesthood," in the first heresy, it will be treated longer concerning it.

ADAM ET EVA

Adam and Eve

Concerning the first parents of the human race, namely Adam and Eve, various heresies have occurred. The **first heresy** is the one asserting that our first parents were cast into Hell with a perpetual damnation on account of their first sin of disobedience. The author of this error was a certain Tatian, a disciple of [Saint] Justin Martyr, who lived in the time of Emperor Antoninus [Pius] and Pope Pius I.[4] This Tatian never showed that he ever opined badly while his teacher, Justin, lived (as Eusebius of Caesarea testifies in his *Ecclesiastical History*).[5] But afterwards when [Saint] Justin finished his life by martyrdom,

---

[1] "But I suffer not a woman to teach, nor to use authority over the man: but to be in silence" (I Tim. 2, 12).

[2] "Sins are not forgiven to anyone, unless when the priest forgives them he believes they are forgiven; on the contrary the sin would remain unless he believed it was forgiven; for indeed the remission of sin and the granting of grace does not suffice, but it is necessary also to believe that there has been forgiveness." (Dz. 750 (Proposition thirteen condemned in the Bull *Exsurge Domine*, June 15, 1520)).

[3] Session 14 (Dz. 920)

[4] The text mistakenly has here Pope Julius I (337-352) but Pope Pius I (140-155) is more likely intended by the author.

[5] "Those who are called Encratites, and who sprung from Saturninus and Marcion, preached celibacy, setting aside the original arrangement of God and tacitly censuring him who made male and female for the propagation of the human race. They introduced also abstinence from the things called by them animate, thus showing ingratitude to the God who made all things. And they deny the salvation of the first man. But this has been only recently discovered by them, a certain Tatian being the first to introduce this blasphemy. He was a hearer of Justin, and expressed no such opinion while he was with him, but after

ADAM ET EVA

Tatian departed from the path of truth, and striving for the name of doctor, he chose rather to become a teacher of error than a disciple of truth. Now he followed the errors of previous heretics in many things, namely Valentinus, Marcion, and Saturninus[1]: he also invented many other heresies from his own mind. For Blessed Irenaeus,[2] Blessed Jerome in his commentary on Amos,[3] and Blessed Epiphanius[4] in his *Treatise Against Eighty Sects* testify that [Tatian] was the author and leader of the Encratites.[5] One of the other errors of this Tatian and the Encratites was that they assert that Adam and Eve were punished with eternal damnation on account of their sin.

But in order that we may prove that this opinion is heretical, although I think this opinion to be such, still (as I frankly admit) no clear passage of Sacred Scripture helps me, with which we may accomplish it: nor does anyone, among those who classify this assertion as heretical, and it is rejected by them as such, allege any clear passage of Sacred Scripture by which it may be disproved. Accordingly, Irenaeus when on account of this assertion brands Tatian with the note of heresy, nevertheless cites no passage of Scripture by which he may prove it.[6] Eusebius of Caesarea when pinning this error on Tatian, cites no testimony of Sacred Scripture in favor of this matter.[7] Philastrius of Brescia in that book which he published, *De haeresibus*, enumerating the Tatian's heresies, also assigns this one to him, and does not cite any testimony of Sacred Scripture in support of this.[8] Also Blessed Augustine says, "He denies the salvation of the first man,"[9] yet he puts forth no testimony of Scripture whereby he proves that this opinion is heretical.

I omit Guy the Carmelite,[10] because he, even though he intended to write against all heresies, still he examines many which he rejects with no testimony of Scripture, but merely by his own judgment, in which manner he mimicked a fable. For when discussing the errors of the Tatians and the Encratites, he asserts this error of theirs, not having given any citation of Sacred Scripture for this which refutes it, but he sends us to Anselm in his book, *Cur Deus Homo*,[11] and to Blessed Jerome in his letter to Evangelus,[12] in which [references] I found nothing of the sort of what he claims. On account of which I think that he did not read those

---

the martyrdom of the latter he left the Church, and becoming exalted with the thought of being a teacher, and puffed up with the idea that he was superior to others, he established a peculiar type of doctrine of his own, inventing certain invisible æons like the followers of Valentinus, while, like Marcion and Saturninus, he pronounced marriage to be corruption and fornication. His argument against the salvation of Adam, however, he devised for himself. Irenaeus at that time wrote thus" (Bk. 4, c. 29, n. 2-3).

[1] Saturninus of Antioch was an early Gnostic heretic mentioned by Saint Ireneus (*Adversus Haereses*, bk. 1, c. 24, n. 1 ff. (PG 7, 673B)).

[2] *Adversus Haereses*, bk. 1, c. 28, n. 1 (PG 7, 690).

[3] *Commentariorum In Amos Prophetam Libri Tres*, bk. 1, verse 12 (PL 25, 1010C).

[4] The *Panarion* ["Medicine Chest"] of Epiphanius of Salamis; bk. 2, heresy 27 (or 47 in the series), (PG 41, 850D).

[5] I.e. self-controlled.

[6] *Adversus Haereses*, bk. 1, c. 28, n. 1.

[7] *Ecclesiastical History*, bk. 4, c. 29, n. 3.

[8] *Diversarum haereseon liber*, sect. 2, n. 48 (PL 12, 1164A-1165A).

[9] *De haeresibus ad Quodvultdeus*, c. 25 (PL 42, 30).

[10] The Carmelite theologian, Guy de Perpignan (Guido Terreni), the *Doctor Breviloquus*, (c. 1260/70-1342) of Catalonia wrote his *Summa de haeresibus*, which was completed in 1342.

[11] "... we must not doubt that Adam and Eve obtained part in that forgiveness, though Divine authority makes no mention of this" (C. 16).

[12] The text here reads, "letter to Evagius," but in *Summa de haeresibus* (c. 24) it is written, "letter to Evangelus."

passages to which he sends us. For if he had read [them] he would also have found some useful for this purpose, and he would have most willingly (as is wont to happen) borrowed from them. For in refuting other heresies where there are very clear proofs against them, it is surprising how troubled the citer is, citing every testimony that he can from any place whatsoever. Yet here where some quotation from Scripture was necessary, lest it seem to be lacking to him, he sends us to other [places].

But even if the be no clear passage from Scripture for refuting this error, it ought not therefore to be thought that such is not a heretical statement: because the concordant opinion of all the sacred Doctors (as we have discussed at greater length above) is very effective testimony. For it is not possible, that they all err in unison, who in order that we may not go astray, were sent by God. For so says Paul in that epistle which is to the Ephesians: "And he gave some apostles, and some prophets, and other some evangelists, and other some pastors and doctors, for the perfecting of the saints, for the work of the ministry, for the edifying of the body of Christ until we all meet into the unity of faith" (4, 11-13). Now why he gave them, he adds saying: "That henceforth we be no more children tossed to and fro, and carried about with every wind of doctrine by the wickedness of men, by cunning craftiness, by which they lie in wait to deceive" (v. 14). You see how according to Paul's opinion doctors were given by God, so that we may not be "carried about with every wind of doctrine" for the avoidance of error. Wherefore it could not happen that all would err in unison, who, lest others err, were sent.

Now there is an agreement of all the sacred doctors that Adam was saved, and was one of the number of those whom when Christ descended into Hell (according to Zachary's prophesy) he led out the prisoners who were in the pit.[1] But lest we seem to have said this without foundation and as a guess, Blessed Irenaeus[2] inveighing again this error of Tatian, cites some other testimonies and fine arguments against him: which even if he does not argue from a clear passage of Scripture, still he infers very well from it. Therefore I do not disdain to insert these [arguments] into this work, yet [I do so] very briefly, since he having been endowed with a more copious style of speech expanded it at greater length. I will also add other things of my own, by which the truth itself may be better supported.

Therefore it is firstly necessary to state the fact that the human race was redeemed and saved by Christ, as Paul says: "As in Adam all die, so also in Christ all shall be made alive" (I Cor. 15, 22). Therefore if mankind is saved, it is necessary that the man who was first created be saved. For it is not just that he who was first captured by the enemy, would still remain a captive when his children were freed, whom he begot in captivity. For if someone having been captured by the enemy, begets children in captivity, whom someone else having pitied, assaults and attacks the enemy who took him and holds him captive; he who assaulted the enemy would act unjustly if he were to free the children from captivity while leaving the parents in captivity, on account of whom he had assaulted the enemy. Therefore since Adam was being held captive by the devil, on account of whom God clothed with flesh attacked the devil, it improbable that Adam's children would be freed while their parent would remain captive, on account of whom He assaulted the devil, so that He might avenge him.

Moreover, if he who was first made man by God so that he might live and fill up the angelic ruins from his children (according to the Prophet),[3] were to have remained in that very

---

[1] "Thou also by the blood of thy testament hast sent forth thy prisoners out of the pit, wherein is no water" (Zach. 9, 11).

[2] *Adversus Haereses*, bk. 3, c. 23, n. 8.

[3] "He shall judge among nations, he shall fill ruins: he shall crush the heads in the land of many." (Ps. 109, 6). "Neither can they die any more: for they are equal to the angels, and are the children of God, being the children of the resurrection" (Lk 20, 36).

"Thus it pleased God, Creator and Governor of the universe, that since the whole multitude of the angels

perpetual death on account of the serpent's injury, and in no way be returned to the life for which and on account of which He created him, it would then be necessary to say that God in some way was conquered by the serpent, since the affair succeeded according to the serpent's wickedness, and not according to God's will.

Furthermore, if Adam is punished with perpetual death on account of his sin, why does Paul insult death by saying: "O death, where is thy victory? O death, where is thy sting?" (I Cor. 15, 55). Because if Adam's sin still remains, and was never expiated, it is necessary that the sting of death would also remain: because (according to the same Paul) "the sting of death is sin" (v. 56). But no other sin was the sting[1] of death than Adam's sin: because by it death entered into this world. "By one man," says Paul, "death entered into this world" (Rom. 5, 12),[2] and this for no other reason than on account of his first sin. Thus the sin of Adam was the stimulus of death. If then Tatian says that Adam's sin remains [unforgiven], it may be stated that it is necessary that the sting of death be elsewhere. Therefore Paul wrongly insults death, declaring it to be conquered.

But these things will nowise move Tatian, because among his other insanities is this one, by which he detracts Paul the Apostle, asserting that he is also damned, for which reason he accepts no epistle of his. But concerning these matters we will discuss at greater length in book thirteen, under heading of Sacred Scripture. Furthermore it ought not to be doubted that God clothed with flesh for mankind fought with the devil, and conquered him: because besides the other testimonies of Scripture He showed it where the Lord speaking in a parable (as He was accustomed to do) says: "When a strong man armed keepeth his court, those things are in peace which he possesseth. But if a stronger than he come upon him, and overcome him; he will take away all his armour wherein he trusted, and will distribute his spoils" (Lk. 11, 21-22). By which parable He clearly shows His own triumph over the devil, which is clearly proved from the preceding words. For when the Jews object to Him that He had cast out by Beelzebub—the prince of devils—that devil which was mute: He took up this parable as a confirmation of this. Therefore Christ conquered the devil, and took away his armor and spoils. Now the devil's first spoil and his first possession was Adam, whom he held captive under his power. Therefore, so that the devil would acknowledge himself clearly conquered, these are the spoils which especially had to be taken away from him, on account of which such a difficult war was undergone. For the enemy would always behave insolently if those old spoils would have stayed with him.

---

had not perished in this desertion of Him, those who had perished would remain forever in perdition, but those who had remained loyal through the revolt should go on rejoicing in the certain knowledge of the bliss forever theirs. From the other part of the rational creation—that is, mankind—although it had perished as a whole through sins and punishments, both original and personal, God had determined that a portion of it would be restored and would fill up the loss which that diabolical disaster had caused in the Angelic society. For this is the promise to the Saints at the resurrection, that they shall be equal to the Angels of God. (Lk. 20, 36)
"Thus the heavenly Jerusalem, our mother and the commonwealth of God, shall not be defrauded of her full quota of citizens, but perhaps will rule over an even larger number. We know neither the number of holy men nor of the filthy demons, whose places are to be filled by the sons of the holy mother, who seemed barren in the earth, but whose sons will abide time without end in the peace the demons lost. But the number of those citizens, whether those who now belong or those who will in the future, is known to the mind of the Maker, 'who calleth into existence things which are not, as though they were,' (Rom. 4, 17) and 'ordereth all things in measure and number and weight' (Wis. 11, 21)" (St. Augustine, *Handbook on Faith, Hope, and Love*, c. 9, n. 29).

[1] *Stimulus mortis* can also mean the "stimulus of death," or here, the cause of death to mankind.
[2] The full quotation is, "by one man sin entered into this world, and by sin death."

Besides all these things, that punishment of Adam's sin would strengthen our argument, from which it can be clearly gathered what God would decide afterwards concerning him: for when punishing Adam God, did not so curse him, such that he would be called cursed, as those who were destined to eternal fire, but he cursed the land in his works, inflicting on him as a punishment weariness and earthly labor, and to eat bread in the sweat of his brow, and to be turned into the soil from which he was taken. Likewise also the woman was punish with weariness, labors, groans, griefs, and sorrows in giving birth: this however was done by God by dispensation, so that not cursed by God neither would completely perish, nor living without punishment would they treat God with contempt. Now every curse came upon the serpent who had seduced them: "Because thou hast done this thing, thou art cursed among all cattle, and beasts of the earth" (Gen. 3, 14). Likewise when Cain afterwards sinned by killing his brother, he received a curse from God, because he brought a curse upon himself, and did not return to God. For when asked by God where his brother was, he answered that he did not know, as though he could deceive God. And to increase that irreverence, as though with a certain indignation of mind he said: "Am I my brother's keeper?" (Gen. 4, 9).

No such thing happened in regard to Adam. He was seduced by someone else, namely by the woman: the woman, however, was seduced by the serpent. After Adam sinned, he immediately was struck with fear and trembling, and hid, but he did not think that he could deceive God: but instead was confounded in his mind, and due to shame and embarrassment for the evil committed, does not dare to come into His sight and to speak with God. Now "The fear of the Lord is the beginning of wisdom" (Ps. 110, 10). But the knowledge of sin especially motivates to penance, and God forgives the sins of the penitent. Therefore Adam's sin was forgiven, because from what he did he was driven to repent. He covered his body with fig leaves, which give no pleasure, but sting and prick, when nevertheless there were many other smoother leaves, which could have afflicted his body less. And so he carries no curse upon himself, because God foresaw that penance which he was going to do. Now that those things are indications of penitence, is proved thereafter, because by that, God immediately turned to mercy, clothing them with garments of skins to replace their fig leaves. And (as God is accustomed to prod the sinner to repentance, and once having been prodded to advance to what is better) seeing Adam had compunction of heart, after He had cast him out of Paradise, did not want him to live far away from Paradise. But He put him in the neighborhood of Paradise, so that the sight of it might be a continual remembrance of the place from whence on account of his sin he had been cast out, and thereby an occasion of continual sorrow might be suggested to him.

Concerning this matter I find no definition made in a Council of the Church, which occurred (as I think) for this reason, namely that then at that time in which that pest arose, while the persecution of the emperors was raging, Councils were unable to be assembled until the time of Constantine the Great, under whom peace was given to God's Church. Since, however, this error is found to have arisen from no one after Tatian, besides his disciple Severus, from whom the Severians are named, this, as I think, was the cause, that in the Councils which were celebrated long afterwards, nothing about this error was defined. After the first edition of this work, I found a clear testimony of Sacred Scripture for refuting this heresy, which it is now necessary to add. For the Wise Man speaking about Divine wisdom says the following: "She preserved him, that was first formed by God, the father of the world, when he was created alone, and she brought him out of his sin" (Wis. 10, 1-2). Which words clearly enough teach that Adam was saved.

A **second error** arose concerning this matter, asserting that Adam after his sin lost God's image. Ephiphanius, Bishop of Salamis, in a certain letter to John, Bishop of Jerusalem, attributed this error to Origen, which Blessed Jerome rendered from Greek into Latin, and which then is also found among the other letters of Blessed Jerome, in their second volume.[1] Now who this Origen was, it is not necessary to relate a long history, since the name of that man is so famous, such that he is known to nearly the whole world, wherefore I have deemed that nothing ought to be said concerning him. He who, however, desires to fully know his deeds may read Eusebius of Caesarea in his *Ecclesiastical History*, book six, which he treats nearly in their entirety in this account.

Now whether due to this and his other errors, concerning which it will be said in their proper places, whether or not he ought to be deemed a heretic, is a long question treated at length by others. Indeed Ruffinus[2] took up the cause of Origen of old against Jerome. But John, Bishop of Jerusalem, in opposition to Ephiphanius, Bishop of the city of Salamis in Cyprus, was defending Origen. There exists the *Apologia for Origen* by Pamphilus[3] Martyr (this is in fact his true title), which the priest Ruffinus translated into Latin. Finally John Picus, [Earl] of Mirandula, a man no less learned than eloquent, among the many conclusions which he accepted to dispute and defend at Rome in the time of Pope Innocent VIII, he took part in this one: "It is more pious to believe that Origen was saved than damned." Since others would want to reject this conclusion as heretical with twelve others: for the defense of it and the other twelve he composed a splendid apology. After so many illustrious men I will not dare to decide anything, because it would be temerarious, especially since the matter is very doubtful. Yet I will say that I think, namely concerning Origen and whomever else, as the Catholic Church thinks.

Thus, since it has already been related about his person, it remains that we discuss his error. Firstly it is doubtful to me whether Origen thought that man by sin lost something of his substance, or merely some qualities of the soul, or I will say in other words, whether he lost his image or only his likeness. For Victorinus Afer,[4] from whom Jerome relates that he had learned Rhetoric,[5] in the disputation which he wrote against Arius, expounding the passage in Genesis, "Let us make man to our image and likeness" (1, 26), says the following: "Therefore it is one thing to be 'according to the image,' which indeed is substance, but another thing to be 'according to the likeness' which is not a substance but the name of a quality manifest in the substance. But just as we understand God to be substance, so also the image, that is, Christ. But we understand perfection as signifying something qualified. And if 'like' signifies something qualified, necessarily, since we say that the soul is rational and perfectly rational, we say that the soul is perfect according to the likeness of the perfection of God. Therefore now and in this world it is 'according to the image,' but afterwards 'according to the likeness' by faith in God and in Jesus Christ, such as it would have been if Adam had not sinned. Therefore insofar as it is rational, it is 'according to the image' because of reason; insofar as it will be perfect, it is 'according to the likeness.'"[6] From which words it is evident (according to him) that an image differs greatly from a likeness, and Adam lost His likeness, not however His image.

[Pseudo-] Eucherius of Lyons, a man certainly no less renowned for his teaching than his sanctity, assigns this same difference between image and likeness, who expounding the same passage of Scripture, says the following: "There is this difference between 'likeness' and 'im-

---

[1] "For, among other wicked things, [Origen] has presumed to say this, too, that Adam lost the image of God, although Scripture nowhere declares that he did" (Letter 51, n. 6 (PL 22, 524)).

[2] Tyrannius Rufinus (340-410 A.D.) or Rufinus of Aquileia was a monk, historian, and theologian. He is most known as a translator of Greek patristic material into Latin, especially the work of Origen.

[3] I.e. Saint Pamphilus of Caesarea (died 309 A. D.).

[4] I.e. Gaius Marius Victorinus (fl. Fourth century).

[5] Jerome supplied his biographical information but was not his student.

[6] *Against Arius*, bk. 1, n. 20 (PL 8, 1054C-D).

age': God's image belongs to all, His likeness to a few. And in fact this image of God differs from the excellence of the Divine likeness, because God's image does not determine the soul not to be a sinner; but unless a soul were to be holy it would not attain to God's likeness: because that soul was created by nature, this soul will be given [the opportunity] to be consummated by grace: because God's image is nothing other than the power of reason naturally joined to the human soul, what else will be the likeness, except beatitude happily conferred? And so it is in fact a great thing, that man's power of reason was given to his nature made in God's image, which privilege the other animals lack: but it is more outstanding, that the likeness of His Creator would be given him in glory, so that there he may be similar to His Creator, where he will be equal to the holy Angels."[1]

If therefore Origen says that Adam lost God's image after sin, having accepted the word "image" according to that meaning which we have just said, namely that "image" consists in the nature, the error is clear, and Epiphanius justly accuses him for this reason: because regarding the demons, whose sin was far more serious, says Blessed Dionysius the [Pseudo-]Areopagite, their natural qualities remained intact in them: how much more ought that to be reckoned to have been done in man? Again, if sin were to take away something from the nature by sins becoming frequent, ultimately at some point those same sins would have consumed the whole nature of the soul, which is not permitted to say.

The passages of Scripture which Epiphanius cites in favor of this seem to me to hardly strengthen this position, although he boasts that, instead of the three citations which John of Jerusalem was requesting, he had produced seven:[2] because all the passages which he cites from Scripture, besides one or the other, merely prove that man was at first made or composed in God's image: that however after sin he remained in that image, this they never say, besides one from the Apostle Paul, and another from the Psalms, which also perhaps do not convince, although they greatly persuade. Now his passages are these:

In Genesis it is read: "And Adam lived a hundred and thirty years, and begot a son to his own image and likeness, and called his name Seth" (Gen. 5, 3). This passage adds nothing to the argument, and is very defenseless, so that it is unnecessary to refute it: for it is said there that Seth was begotten "to his own image and likeness," not however to God's image and likeness. Nor also could Adam have begotten a son according to God's likeness, while keeping the same meaning which we proposed above.

The second quotation is from the same book saying the following: "Saving that flesh with blood you shall not eat. For I will require the blood of your lives at the hand of every beast, and at the hand of man... for man was made to the image of God" (9, 4-6). From this quotation nothing is clearly proved, except that man was made according to God's image, not however that he persevered in it. The passage from Solomon's Wisdom also sounds completely the same: "God created man incorruptible, and to the image of his own likeness he made him" (2, 23).

And another passage from Blessed James' epistle also does not prove [the point], saying: "The tongue... an unquiet evil, full of deadly poison: by it we bless God and the Father: and by it we curse men, who are made after the likeness of God" (3, 8-9). Now because this passages said "men" and not "man," it seems to be concluded from it that not merely Adam but all men born after his sin were made according to God's likeness. To which it may be replied

---

[1] *Commenatarius in Genesim*, bk. 1; on chap. 1, v. 26 (PL 50, 900C). This text is found in an appendix in Migne's Patrology in which the work is considered doubtfully or wrongly attributed to Saint Eucherius.

[2] "Instead of the three proofs from Holy Scripture which you said would satisfy you if I could produce them, behold I have given you seven" (Letter LI. From Epiphanius, Bishop of Salamis, in Cyprus, to John, Bishop of Jerusalem (n. 7 (PL 22, 525)).

that other men then are said to be "made," because he was then formed, from whom all were to descend. Sacred writ does not abhor this manner of speaking. For in Genesis we read that after the perfect making of the world according to the diversity of species and forms: "These are the generations of the heaven and the earth, when they were created, in the day that the Lord God made the heaven and the earth" (2, 4). For Scripture asserts that all the generations were then made, although nevertheless afterwards it relates them to have been made through the alternation and succession of days, some on the first day, others on the second, and so forth until the seventh day. Still all creatures are said to have been made "in the day in which God created heaven and earth," because on that day the whole mass from which all corporeal substances were derived was made. In which way it can also be said although somewhat contracted that all men are said to have been made when Adam was made: for then just as Adam himself, so also all others were made according to God's image.

Now the passage from the Psalms: "Man passeth as an image: yea, and he is disquieted in vain" (Ps. 38, 7), and that from Paul's First Epistle to the Corinthians: "The man ought not to cover his head, because he is the image and glory of God" (11, 7): these two passages are more impelling, because they cannot be referred in some way to the first man alone, but it is certain that they are said of any man. Scripture does not always use the word "image" according to that specification which we gave above, such that an "image" is always attributed to the bare nature: but sometimes according to the qualities of the soul: as is evident in the Epistle to the Colossians: "Stripping yourselves," says Paul, "of the old man with his deeds and putting on the new, him who is renewed unto knowledge, according to the image of him that created him" (3, 9-10). From which citation it is clearly established that this distinction between the old and new man given by Paul, such that the old man who pertains to sin, does not have God's image, but the new man, who pertains to the grace recuperated by Christ, bears God's image. According to which it is necessary that therein the image not merely consists in the bare substance of the soul, but also in grace, by which man is Godlike. And [Ambrosiaster[1]] on Paul's Epistle [to the Colossians], expounding this passage from the Epistle to the Colossians recently cited, says the following: "This image ought to be understood as the leading of a good life, as he says in his First Epistle to the Corinthians: 'As we have borne the image of the earthly, let us bear also the image of the heavenly' (15, 49). He is therefore the Creator of man, Whose image he commands us to carry in holiness and good works, which descends from the knowledge of the Son of God."[2] From which words it is clearly gathered that the word "image" not only is meant in Sacred Writ according to what is found in the nature, which is also never lost: but sometimes also it is meant according to certain qualities of the soul.

But if perhaps Origen so meant the word "image," such that he made use of the word "image" for "likeness": who does not see that there is no suspicion of heresy there? Nevertheless, I have not said these things so that anyone would think that I wish to take Origen's side. For I say that I think concerning Origen and his doctrine that which Holy Mother Church thinks. On account of which I most firmly assert this, if the Church made a judgment this matter, it ought to be held. But I do not find anyone who accused Origen of this, besides Epiphanius alone. For Theophilus, Bishop of Alexandria, who in that book of his to which he gave the name Pascal [Letter], reviews Origen's errors, but makes no mention of this one.[3] Which I

---

[1] "[Saint Ambrose] is not the author of the admirable commentary on the thirteen Epistles of St. Paul known as 'Ambrosiaster'" ("St. Ambrose," *The Catholic Encyclopedia* (New York, Robert Appleton Company, 1907), vol. 1, p. 387).

[2] *Commentaria in Epistolam ad Colossenses* (PL 17, 435D-436A).

[3] Cf. Letter 96 of Saint Jerome who translated Theophilus's Paschal letter for the year 401 A.D. In it Theophilus refutes at length the heresies of Apollinaris and Origen (PL 22, 773-790).

think was perhaps thus done, because those words which Epiphanius attributed to Origen, even if they were found in Origen's books, are capable of a pious and Catholic meaning, namely which we related shortly before. Nevertheless there are some men with zeal, and not motivated according to prudence, who immediately proclaim everything which differs from their opinion to be heresy, and perhaps Epiphanius was such a man, as it is easy to know from that letter from this same man cited above, because there it is declared that he tore apart a cloth which he found in a shrine, merely on this pretext, that it had Christ's picture on it, or the picture of a saint. For he testifies that he did not recall of whom the image was, and he asserts that it is contrary to Sacred Scripture, to hang the picture of any man in the Church.[1] Yet whether this is correct, even one little educated can know, and we will discuss this further below in the section on "Images." Nevertheless, there are many who demand many things from others, which nevertheless they themselves do not do: and there are those who pardon many things through indulgence to their friends, and are willing to pardon themselves, who nevertheless harshly censure others. Therefore, since Epiphanius has some things for which indulgence is necessary, it was just that he also through indulgence pardon Origen some things, and not always show himself a Cato to him.[2]

A **third error** arose in this matter whereby it is taught that if Adam and Eve had remained in justice, they would never have had sexual intercourse, nor would the human race have been propagated by intercourse. This error was discovered in the Armenians, as Guy the Carmelite[3] testifies in his *Summa de haeresibus*.[4] For this is the eleventh error of the Armenians.

These Armenians live in Asia, in that region which is located between the Taurus and the Caucasus Mountains. Their country called Armenia stretches from Cappadocia to the Caspian Sea. These Armenians although they had been firstly taught the Catholic faith: at length after they left the true rule of faith they fell into many errors. They have their own primate, which they call *Catholicos*: they obey him as the supreme pontiff. They in fact despise the Roman Bishop, and say that he is not superior to the others. Now at what time, or for which reason they defected from the Church, it is still unknown to me. This is certain, namely that at the time of Philastrus, Bishop of Briscia, and at the time of Blessed Augustine, they were not yet separated from the Church, because neither of them, enumerating the authors of heresies, make any mention of the Armenians. Now since I can conjecture from many things, it is very likely that the Armenians were separated from the Church on account of the decrees of the Council of Chalcedon celebrated under Leo I and Emperor Marcian: because in that Council Eutyches, the Constantinopolitan abbot, and Dioscorus, the Alexandrian bishop, his imitator, were condemned. Now the Armenians favoring these heretics, disdained to receive the decrees of the Council of Chalcedon. Therefore among the other errors of the Armenians is this one, whereby they assert that Adam and Eve would never be joined in a carnal union, if they had remained in that state in which God had made them: asserting that the human species would be propagated otherwise.

The impious Amaury[5] afterwards revived this error, as Bernard of Luxemburg relates in his *Catalogus haereticorum*.[6] For although in the book of the *Decretal Letters*, in the title,

---

[1] Letters of St. Jerome, letter 51, n. 9 (PL 22, 526).
[2] Marcus Porcius Cato the Elder (234 B.C. – 149 B.C.) was distinguished as a rigid judge of morals; hence with the appellation, "the Censor."
[3] I.e., Guy de Perpignan (1270-1342).
[4] Guido Terrena de Perpiniano, *Summa de haeresibus et earum confutationibus* (Paris, Prelum Ascensianum, 1528), f. 32v-33r, c. 11.
[5] I.e., Amaury of Bena or of Chartres (1150-1206 A. D.).
[6] *Catalogus haereticorum omnium* (Paris, Jean Petit, 1524), bk. 2, fol. 21v.

"On the Holy Trinity and the Catholic faith,"[1] the aforesaid Amaury with his errors are condemned, nevertheless no error of his is related there, nor does the Gloss add anything. Thus Amaury, a teacher in Paris, who at the time of Innocent III was condemned by the same at the [IV] Lateran Council, agreed in this matter with the Armenians and increased their madness: because not only does he deny carnal union in that state, but also he asserts that no sexual difference would have come to be. Now this last proposition is such clear madness that it is not necessary to attack it. For at the beginning of Genesis it is read: "God created man to his own image: to the image of God he created him: male and female he created them" (1, 27). This is also more clearly expressed by Christ Our Redeemer, who in Matthew's Gospel says: "Have ye not read, that he who made man from the beginning, made them male and female?" (19, 4). But because He does not say that He made them male and female from the beginning, it is necessary to cite Mark also, which more clearly says these things saying: "But from the beginning of the creation, God made them male and female" (10, 6).

Now let us discuss another common error of these men. Firstly in fact their foundation is invalid. For thus the Armenians in that state deny future sexual intercourse, because they think that marriages are illicit, and they say that their use is a sin. How false this is we will show below, God willing. Therefore what they assert concerning the union of the flesh that it would nowise be in that state, is proved to be false from that which is said in Genesis. For after "God created Adam and Eve to His own image" and "male and female he created them," He immediately blessed them and said: "Increase and multiply, and fill the earth" (v. 1, 28).

But because they say that the human race was multiplied otherwise than by sexual intercourse: perhaps it will seem to someone that this passage does not hem them in very much: hence let us seek for weapons from elsewhere. In the same book, immediately after it is related that Eve was formed from Adam's side, these words of Adam himself are added, saying: "This now is bone of my bones, and flesh of my flesh; she shall be called woman, because she was taken out of man. Wherefore a man shall leave father and mother, and shall cleave to his wife: and they shall be two in one flesh" (2, 23-24). These words were said by Adam before He sinned, as is evident from the historical account. And a man and wife never become one flesh except through sexual intercourse, by which there is a mixture of seed for the generating of a man's body. But if they say that thus Adam and Eve were said to be one body, because Eve's body was taken from Adam's flesh: then for what reason is a man who is now with his wife said to be one flesh, since the wife's flesh was not derived from him?

Or perhaps those words of Adam were said only to Eve, such that they ought to be understood as to nowise refer to later spouses? Far be it: because God refuted the Pharisees using those words showing that it is not lawful to put away a wife, except it be for fornication (Mt. 19, 9): which He would not have done if those words of Adam were not to be referred to all spouses. Furthermore Adam had neither a father nor a mother, but was formed out of the earth by God. Therefore those words of Adam ought not to be referred to Adam himself but to others, since he says: "Wherefore a man shall leave father and mother," etc.

But if, as it is necessary, they admit that those words of Adam are to be applied to all men coming after him, and thus they say that any man is one flesh with his wife, because although the wife's flesh is not always taken from the flesh of her husband, still it suffices that of old that it was so done in the case of the first parents, because the rest were made according to their image: thus, for this reason it will also be that any man with any woman is one flesh, since any woman was made in the image of the first woman, who was taken from the side of her husband, which is absurd to accept. Also on the same principle it ought to be admitted that Adam and Eve before sexual intercourse were one flesh, which nevertheless from the words of the same [Adam] is evidently not so. For when Eve was formed from Adam's side, he

---

[1] Lib. 1, Tit. 1, Cap. 1

immediately uttered these words: "Wherefore a man shall leave father and mother, and shall cleave to his wife: and they shall be two in one flesh." He did not say, "they are two in one flesh," but "they shall be two in one flesh." Because if it was necessary for no other reason, that they would be made one flesh, it should have been said: "And they are two in one flesh." Since therefore he said, "they shall be two in one flesh," he signified that some other thing is necessary, namely sexual intercourse, so that husband and wife may be called "one flesh," even after the first joining of minds expressed by words, whereby alone they become spouses. For Adam speaks about spouses already joined by their minds, when he said: "they shall be two in one flesh": which is evident from the fact that he had said previously: "Wherefore a man shall leave father and mother, and shall cleave to his wife." And just after he said the name of his wife, he added: "And they shall be two in one flesh."

But if someone is so insane that for defending this he were to say that Adam said this without reflection: let him consider that those words were not just Adam's, but the words of God speaking through Adam's mouth: now that this is clear is evident from these words which Christ quoted in Matthew's Gospel. For when the Pharisees were asking whether it were lawful "for a man to put away his wife for every cause" (Mt. 19, 3), He answered: "Have ye not read, that he who made man from the beginning, made them male and female? And he said: For this cause shall a man leave father and mother, and shall cleave to his wife, and they two shall be in one flesh" (v. 4-5). You see from the Savior's words, how He who made then male and female from the beginning, that is, God, said this: "For this cause," etc. Hence Theophylactus commenting on Matthew's Gospel said: "But why is it written in Genesis (Gen. 2:24) that Adam said, 'Therefore shall a man leave his father and his mother,' while here Christ says that it was God Who said, 'For this cause shall a man leave father and mother.' We say, therefore, that what Adam spoke, he spoke from God, so that the speech of Adam is God's. Therefore, since they have become one flesh, joined together by means of marital relations and physical affection, just as it is accursed to cut one's own flesh, so is it accursed to separate husband and wife."[1] From which words the consonance of the words [of God and Adam] is evident: for that saying is attributed to Adam, as an instrument: to God, however, as to the motor cause of his tongue.

It is also evident from Theophylactus' words that a man and his wife are said to be one flesh namely when they are joined together through love and carnal intercourse: which we clearly also prove from the very words of Scripture. For in the First Epistle to the Corinthians Paul says: "Or know you not, that he who is joined to a harlot, is made one body? For they shall be, saith he, two in one flesh" (6, 16). From which words of Paul it is clearly proved that through sexual intercourse alone a man and woman become one flesh, not only in the intercourse of spouses, but also in fornication. On account of which the doctors rightly state that even from the intercourse of fornication arises a true affinity, such that it also ought to be deemed capable of impeding the contract of matrimony according to ecclesiastical ordinances. Therefore let the mad Armenians keep quiet and obey the Catholic Church.

The **fourth error** which is found in this matter was raised up by the monk Pelagius, who lived under [Emperors] Honorius and Theodosius the Younger. For he said (as Blessed Augustine says) that "Adam would have died even if he had not sinned, and that he died not by reason of his guilt, but from a condition of his nature."[2] This Pelagius was from Great Britain, and was a monk living in the East. Finally returning to his country, after he had scattered his errors elsewhere, he infected nearly his whole country with his errors. Now when the English sought the support and help in this matter from the French bishops, in that the teaching was

---

[1] PG 123, 350C-D.
[2] *De haeresibus ad Quodvultdeus*, c. 88 (PL 42, 48).

clearer to them, they received Germanus[1] and Lupus[2] bishops and brothers[3] (as Bede says in his book, *The Ecclesiastical History of England*[4]) as defenders of the Catholic faith, which bishops purged the island of the Pelagian heresy, confirming England in the faith both by the word of truth and by signs of miracles. There were two Councils celebrated against this Pelagius, one in Carthage[5] and the other in Milevum.[6] Among other errors of this Pelagius, therefore, this one is listed whereby he asserts that Adam did not die due to his guilt, but from the natural condition in which he was created, in which had he remained and had not withdrawn from God's command, he nonetheless would have died.

Now it might seem to someone that this error can be refuted from that which is said in Genesis: "In what day soever thou shalt eat of it, thou shalt die the death" (Gen. 2, 17). To which argumentation it will be replied that even if this conclusion is true and valid, the argument proves nothing, because that passage of Scripture ought to be understood as pertaining to spiritual death, which is sin, as [Psuedo-] Eucherius, Bishop of Lyons proves in the first book of his [*Commentarii*] *in Genesim* [*in tres libros distributi*]. For he says the following: "He says the death of the soul, not of the body: because they did not die at the time when they ate. Therefore we ought not to understand this with which God threatened man so much as the death whereby the flesh is separated from the soul, but that whereby it is alienated from God, Who is its life. For just as the body lives as a result of the soul, so the soul, so that it may live in beatitude, lives from God. Thus when the soul has turned away from God, according to justice it is said to be dead. From which death three deaths consequently follow, the first in the soul, the second in the flesh, and the third in damnation. But for these deaths to follow, the desertion of God came first."[7] Blessed Gregory interprets this passage in the same way in a letter to his companion Narses, which is his fourteenth letter of the sixth book [of the collection of his letters].[8] Hence having put aside this previous citation of Scripture, arms for us ought to be obtained from elsewhere.

---

[1] Saint Germanus (378-448 AD) was the Bishop of Auxerre.

[2] Saint Lupus (383-478), Bishop of Troyes.

[3] Saint Lupus' brother is not Saint Germanus as said in the text. Saint Lupus is, however, thought to be the brother of Saint Vincent of Lerin.

[4] The text here cites Saint Bede the Venerable's *Reckoning of Time*, but there one merely finds one sentence, "Pelagius the Briton impugned the grace of God" under the heading of the year of the world, 4376. But in *The Ecclesiastical History of England* (bk. 1, c. 17 (PL 95, 45A-47B)) the cited history, summarized here in the text, may be found. Hence the latter title has been inserted in the text in place of the former. "In the story of Germanus and Lupus he follows closely the *Life of Germanus* by Constantius of Lyons." (Introduction to *Bede's Ecclesiastical History of England* (London: George Bell and Sons, 1907) by A. M. Sellar).

[5] I.e. the Synod of Carthage in 416 A.D., although he was more solemnly condemned there again in 418 A.D. by bishops from all of Africa summoned by Pope Zosimus.

[6] I.e. the Synod of Milevum in 416 A.D.

[7] PL 50, 908B. This work is found among a long series of works in an appendix in Migne's *Patrologia Latina* attributed to Eucherius, "some of doubtful authenticity, others certainly apocryphal" ("St. Eucherius," *The Catholic Encyclopedia* (1909 ed.), vol. 5, pg. 595).

[8] "God had said, 'In the hour you eat thereof, in death you shall die' (Gen. 2, 17). When, therefore, Adam ate of the forbidden tree, we know that he did not die in the body, seeing that after this he begot children and lived many years. If, then, he did not die in the soul, the impious conclusion follows that He himself lied who foretold that in the day that he sinned he should die. But it is to be understood that death takes place in two ways; either from ceasing to live, or with respect to the mode of living. When, then, man's soul is said to have died in the eating of the forbidden thing, it is meant, not in the sense of ceasing to live, but with regard to the mode of living;— that he should live afterwards in pain who had been created to live happily in joy" (PL 77, 805B). The text here cites the "fifth book," but at least

Firstly therefore this error is most clearly refuted by that which the Apostle says in the Epistle to the Romans: "As by one man sin entered into this world, and by sin death; and so death passed upon all men, in whom all have sinned" (Rom. 5, 12). In the same Epistle he again says: "The body is dead, because of sin" (8, 10). This passage of Scripture clearly fights against Pelagius, such that he can be defended from it by no reasoning, because in it the Apostle clearly speaks about death, which is distinguished from sin, and he says that this [death] was introduced on account of sin.

Again, God, Who did not make death, "neither hath he pleasure in the destruction of the living" (as it said in the book of Wisdom),[1] "created man incorruptible, and to the image of his own likeness he made him" (Wis. 2, 23). If then He made man incorruptible, therefore He made him in such a condition of nature, in which, if he had persevered, he would not have died.

Finally the order itself of what occurred in regard to Adam shows that he incurred death in punishment for sin. Firstly, because He made him garments of skins, which could not be done except from a dead animal. Therefore this garment from the skin of a dead animal is given as to one already dead. Then when a curse of the earth is inflicted upon him as a punishment, when the Lord was saying: "In the sweat of thy face shalt thou eat bread till thou return to the earth, out of which thou wast taken: for dust thou art, and into dust thou shalt return" (Gen. 3, 19). Now it is evident that this was enjoined upon him on account of his sin. But a man never returns to the earth from which he was taken, except by way of death: it is therefore an indication that death was a punishment for sin. Afterwards when Adam is cast out of Paradise, God says: "Lest perhaps he put forth his hand, and take also of the tree of life, and eat, and live forever" (v. 22). From which it is seen that through eating of the tree of life he was being kept from death.

Against this error is the Synod of Milevum celebrated under Innocent I, and in the times of Emperors Arcadius and Honorius. For in chapter one of the acts of this Council it is said: "It hath pleased all the bishops, who were in the sacred synod to establish these things, which have decided in the present Council, that whoever says that Adam, the first man, was made mortal, so that, whether he sinned or whether he did not sin, he would die in body, that is he would go out of the body not because of the merit of sin but by reason of the necessity of nature, let him be anathema."[2] Therefore since the Church has already put an end to this dispute, there is nothing more that we may debate about this matter.

A **fifth heresy** arose about this matter, which asserts that our first parents, Adam and Eve, were blind before their sin, and then they firstly began to see themselves, when they ate from the food of the forbidden tree. Regarding what occasioned this to be asserted, Sacred Scripture relates that after their sin, their eyes were opened, and thus they considered their nudity. Now who the author of this heresy was, and at what time it arose, is not certain to me: because I see that only Philastrius mentioned this heresy, who since he says that such a heresy had arisen at some time, he nevertheless does not say at what time or place, or by what author it arose.

This heresy is easily refuted. For before they sinned, Sacred Scripture speaking about the woman says: "And the woman saw that the tree was good to eat, and fair to the eyes, and delightful to behold: and she took of the fruit thereof, and did eat" (Gen. 3, 5-6). If she were blind, she could not have seen the tree: she "saw," as Sacred Scripture relates, and thus she was not blind. Nor is it necessary in so clear a matter to exert oneself more. Now what they bring forth in favor of themselves, comes forth out of ignorance: because if they were to

---

according to the current classification of these letters it is found in the sixth book.

[1] Wis. 1, 13.
[2] PL 130, 369C; Cf. Dz. 101.

understand that passage rightly (as it ought), they would clearly acknowledge that it in nowise supports them. Thus let them hear Blessed Augustine, who interprets how it ought to be understood, saying the following: "Their eyes, therefore were open, but were not open to this, that is to say, were not observant so as to recognize what was conferred upon them by the garment of grace, for they had no consciousness of their members warring against their will. But when they were stripped of this grace, that their disobedience might be punished by fit retribution, there began in the movement of their bodily members a shameless novelty which made nakedness indecent: it at once made them observant and made them ashamed. And therefore, after they violated God's command by open transgression, it is written: 'And the eyes of them both were opened, and they knew that they were naked; and they sewed fig leaves together, and made themselves aprons' (Gen. 3, 7). 'The eyes of them both were opened,' not to see, for already they saw, but to discern between the good they had lost and the evil into which they had fallen."[1] In the same way Chrysostom[2] and [Psuedo-] Eucherius[3] interpret in their commentaries on Genesis, whose words I do not wish to cite at present, lest in so clear a matter a multitude of witnesses being so little necessary, the reader might grow weary.

There is a **sixth heresy**, which teaches that Eve, the mother of all nations, was not formed from Adam's rib according to the literal sense, as the history of the Book of Genesis relates. It asserts that Eve was formed by God of the slime of the earth, not from Adam's rib, at the same moment in which He formed Adam of the slime of the earth. The author and first inventor of this heresy was Thomas de Vio Cajetan. Although he is now known to the whole world, yet because we write not only for those in the present but also for those in the future, I have deemed it will be worthwhile to state fully who he was. This Thomas de Vio was a religious of the Order of Preachers,[4] having originated from Gaeta,[5] for which reason he is called Cajetan. He was so signally learned in Scholastic theology, he was second to none of those who lived at his time. On account of his eminence of writings and probity of morals, by the common consent of the brothers of his Order, he was elected master general of his Order, and hence was elevated to the dignity of cardinal priest by Leo X. Although he had lived twenty years in which position, he nevertheless acquired no ill repute from human vices in himself (as is usual for others). He wrote many and various works: but it happened what Solomon said to one writing many things: "In the multitude of words there shall not want sin" (Prov. 10, 19). For although he wrote many useful things, yet because he was relying much on his own intelligence, he fell into some errors, among which is this one, concerning which we now investigate, by which he asserts that Eve was not formed from Adam's rib.

---

[1] *City of God*, bk. 14, c. 17 (PL 41, 425).

[2] "... they did not know, after all, that they were naked, clad as they were in ineffable glory, which adorned them better than any clothing" (*Homily 16*, n. 1 (PG 53, 126)). "And eating from that tree did not open their eyes: for they also saw before eating; but because that eating was a proof of their disobedience, and transgression of the command given by God: wherefore they were afterwards stripped of the glory, which surrounded them, because they had made themselves unworthy of such an honor: furthermore Scripture observing its custom says that they ate 'and the eyes of them both were opened: and they perceived themselves to be naked'; having been stripped of the clothing of supernal grace, on account of the sin, they became aware of their sensible nudity, so that through the shame which came upon them, they would know with certainty into what great ruin the transgression of the Lord's command had brought them." (*ibid.*, n. 5 (PG 53, 131)).

[3] "For it follows that before sin [Adam] was unaware that he was naked, because his focus was upon higher things" (*Commentarii in Genesim in tres libros distributi*, bk. 1, on chap. 3, v. 10 (PL 50, 913B)).

[4] I.e. the Dominicans.

[5] Gaeta was then part of the Kingdom of Naples.

Now what Sacred Scripture says in the book of Genesis, he says ought not to be understood in a literal sense, but "by way of a mystery": not in fact by an allegory, but by a parable. For that sleep which the Lord cast upon Adam, as he says, bears a likeness to a defect of the manly power, whence a man is naturally produced: because a sleeping man is a partial man, and likewise the principle generating the woman is semi-manly; the removal of the rib from the man for forming the woman, insofar as the rib is a bone, as he says, is a similitude of the lessening of strength from the soul of the man on account of his wife: insofar as it is a rib, it is a similitude of the social life between a husband and wife, such that she is neither superior to her husband, nor a slave of her husband but was a companion to the man. Now insofar as the rib is one, he says that it is a similitude of the very little strength of the women both in body and soul, and hence the proportion of womanly powers to manly men, is somewhat the proportion of one rib to all the rest of the ribs. But he says that the restoring of the flesh for the rib is a similitude of representation which is in relation to the man, by giving him the carnal generation and propagation of children, in place of the lessened strength of soul on account of his marriage. These are the things which he teaches in his commentary on Genesis.[1] Now whether or not on account of this or his other errors he ought to be considered a heretic, let others be the judge. Since I discuss at present the teaching, not the person. He indeed could have erred (as we said in the first book of this work) and not be a heretic: especially if he did not adhere to his opinion with a pertinacious mind.

This related assertion is proved to be heretical, because it openly opposes Sacred Scripture and the consensus of the whole Church, and in it not one error is contained, but many. For (as Aristotle says) one false thing having been given admission, many false things thence follow. Firstly in fact (as I infer from his other statements) he thinks that Eve was formed by God at the same time with Adam. He is motivated to say that from what Scripture says elsewhere: "He created them male and female" (Gen. 5, 2). From which words he concludes that they were formed at the same time by God. But the Wise Man clearly opposes this opinion, who speaking about Divine wisdom says the following: "She preserved him, that was first formed by God the father of the world, when he was created alone, and she brought him out of his sin" (Wis. 10, 1-2). In which words it ought to be especially noted that he says: "when he was created alone." Therefore there was a time, according to the Wise Man, in which Adam after having been created was alone: hence it is that they were not both created at the same time. Furthermore, Paul, in his First Epistle to Timothy, says: "Adam was first formed; then Eve" (2, 13). And we certainly need not argue any more about this error, since Sacred Scripture so clearly contradicts it.

Let us proceed to the **second error** which asserts that Eve was not formed from Adam's rib, as the text of Sacred Scripture actually says. Paul teaches the opposite of this error, who when speaking to the Athenians in the midst of the Areopagus says the following: "God, who made the world, and all things therein; he, being Lord of heaven and earth, dwelleth not in temples made with hands; Neither is he served with men's hands, as though he needed any thing; seeing it is he who giveth to all life, and breath, and all things: and hath made of one, all mankind, to dwell upon the whole face of the earth" (Acts 17, 24-26). In which words what ought to be noticed is what he lastly said: "And He hath made of one, all mankind, to dwell upon the whole face of the earth." If Eve (as Cajetan claims) was not produced from Adam's rib, it follows that God did not make all mankind of one. And again in the First Epistle to the

---

[1] *Commentarii illustres planeque insignes in quinque Mosaicos libros Thomae de Vio Cajetani quondam cardinalis*, (Paris, 1539), fol. XXIV-XXV. According to Charles Boyer, Cajetan is here following the interpretation previously given by Origen (*Tractatus de Deo creante et elevante* (Gregorian Biblical Bookshop, Rome, 1957) pg. 196). Cajetan cites the ancient philosophers' opinion as the basis of his view that a woman is a "damaged man."

Corinthians Paul teaches the same thought, saying the following: "The woman is the glory of the man. For the man is not of the woman, but the woman of the man" (11, 7-8). Notice that you hear that the woman was made from the man: now it is nowhere else read that she was made of the man except when Eve was formed from Adam's rib. Therefore Paul maintains, according to that which the account of the book of Genesis relates, that Eve was formed from Adam's rib. And Ecclesiasticus clearly shows the same thing, who after he had said that man was created by God from the earth, afterwards speaking concerning the woman says: "He created of him a helpmate like to himself" (17, 5).

Furthermore according to that parabolic interpretation of the text which this heresy teaches, nothing is found concerning the formation of Eve: but only the manner by which other women are generated is stated, and the reason is expressed, when the woman rather than the man was generated. If in that passage, namely in the second chapter of the book of Genesis, Sacred Scripture says nothing about the formation of Eve, then when and where does it state Eve's formation, such that we can fully and clearly learn the matter from which she was formed? It is certainly surprising that it declared Adam's formation so clearly, saying that he was formed by God from the slime of the earth, and said absolutely nothing about Eve's formation: if indeed Scripture never said anything about Eve's formation in that second chapter of Genesis.

If you say, it then treated her formation when it said in the first chapter: "Male and female he created them," I admit that it then spoke about the creation of the woman and man. But by those words one cannot prove from what matter either of them were made, as it merely says that they were created by God, yet not from what they were produced by Him. For this reason Moses chose to teach more clearly and openly man's formation in chapter two: who obviously had known well that it could not be known by those things which he had treated in the first chapter. You might say that Moses then treated Eve's formation when he said: "And the Lord God formed man of the slime of the earth: and breathed into his face the breath of life, and man became a living soul" (Gen. 2, 7). For because this word, "man", belongs to the common genus which means both woman and man, perhaps from thence it could be suspected in that passage it refers to the formation of the woman as well as of the man. But this is not so, nor can this be proved from the word, because for this word, "man," the Hebrew text has in this passage, "Adam." Hence it is concluded that Moses then spoke only of the formation of the man.

Therefore where does Moses teach about Eve's formation, if he did not then teach [about it] when he said that she was formed from Adam's rib? Or how could Thomas de Vio know that Eve was equally formed from the slime of the earth as Adam, if Sacred Scripture never states this? For even if it says many times that Adam was formed from the slime of the earth, yet it never said this concerning Eve. For in the book of Genesis (as we just said) it speaks of Adam and not about Eve. And Tobias Junior praying to God said: "Thou madest Adam of the slime of the earth, and gavest him Eve for a helper" (Tob. 8, 8). Notice, you hear that Adam was made from the slime of the earth, but not Eve. And Solomon speaking about the first man, the father of the whole world, in the book of Wisdom says: "She brought him out of his sin ["out of the slime of the earth" in the text], and gave him power to govern all things" (10, 2).[1] Behold he says that Adam was formed out of the slime of the earth, but says no such

---

[1] The text here cites this verse in a variant wording, "And she brought him out of the slime of the earth." Many Latin manuscripts have this wording but according to François Lucas (1548?-1619), this substitution was made by an editor of the text who noticed that many letters are the same in *delicto* and *de limo,* and so thus "corrected" the text by substituting "sin" for "slime." (Lucas' Notations of the book of Wisdom found in *Commentarius in sacro-sancta quatuor Iesu Christi Euangelia, ut et reliqua, majorem ad S. Scripturae lucem, opuscula omnia, auctore eximio eruditissimoque viro Francisco Luca Brugensi, S. T. L. ecclesiae cathedralis audomaropolitanae theologo ac decano* (typis Christiani Ver-

thing of Eve. Therefore let this man, who denies Eve was formed from Adam's rib, show us the Sacred Scripture which clearly teaches us that she was made from something else, and we will believe him. Because he is unable to do this, it is necessary that he concede something to the Church teaching. Again if in that second chapter of Genesis where it is said that Eve was produced from Adam's rib, Sacred Scripture (as he says) does not treat of Eve's production, from whence could Solomon know that Adam was at some time alone? And from whence does Paul say that Adam was formed first and then Eve? For there is no other passage of Sacred Scripture whence Paul would have been able to say this, except this one.

Then, Adam's words themselves, which he said when he had seen the formed woman, show this very clearly. "She," he said, "shall be called woman, because she was taken out of man" (Gen. 2, 23). From which words it is evident that Adam according to what happened willed to give a name to the woman, so that just as the woman was produced from the man, so the woman's name was derived from the man's name. For "man" in Hebrew is "ish," but woman is "isha": if we wish to follow that analogy, from *vir* ["man"] we would say, *vira*. Which, because the Latin word not does not allow this word *vira*, Blessed Jerome expressed saying, *Virago* ["woman"], inasmuch as the law of Latin speech allowed. Therefore these things having been firstly noted, it is necessary to carefully observe what Adam said. "She," he said, "shall be called woman, because she was taken out of man." Imposing the woman's name by which words, he expressed its etymology and the reason for its derivation. For *Isha* is derived from *Ish*: he immediately gave in fact the reason why he gave such a name to the woman, saying: "because she was taken out of man."

Furthermore, the book of Genesis is historical, and hence the things which are said there historically ought to be understood literally. For even if in sacred histories the happenings which are related often contain other mysteries under the surface of the text, still historical truth ought to be firstly taken in them according to the grammatical meaning, and then the mystical sense ought to be sought. Unless perchance the writer expressly were to warn that it is a parable which he is relating in the historical text itself, for then the author himself obliges us to understand his words parabolically. Such is that which is said in the book of Judges concerning the trees seeking a king for themselves, which after Joatham had said, he immediately shows that it was said by him parabolically, when he explains the parable itself.[1] But since the book of Genesis is historical, and makes no suggestion of a parable in this passage, it is proved that all these things about Eve's formation ought not to be taken parabolically.

Add to this the concurring opinion of all the sacred Doctors, which (as we taught in the first book of this work, chapter seven) is of such importance that it ought to be held as a decision of the Church. Now since the time when Christ was born until the present day all the faithful have consistently thought that Eve, the mother of all nations, was formed from Adam's rib. And because all the faithful think that the matter is so very clear, I have decided not to cite their testimonies in favor of this position, lest I fill pages nowise needed about this matter, and I burden the reader with excessive wordiness. Now if someone wishes testimonies in favor of this fact, I will show him the places whence he could get them. See Augustine in his

---

mey, 1712), p. 113). Lucas was appointed to revise the Vulgate text in 1574 in relation to the "original sources" of the Hebrew, Greek, and Aramaic texts of the Old Testament, and the Greek and Syriac texts of the New Testament. The revised edition was entitled, *Biblia Vulgata Lovaniensis* and served as the basis for the successive papal Vulgate committees in Rome. (*Shaping the Bible in the Reformation: Books, Scholars and Their Readers in the Sixteenth Century* (Brill, 2012), p. 241).

[1] Judges 9, 8 ff.

Literal Meaning of Genesis[1] and *City of God*[2]; Chrysostom, homily 15 on Genesis[3]; Gregory in his *Morals on the Book of Job*[4]; Theophylactus in his *Commentary on Ephesians*[5] and *Commentary on First Corinthians*[6]; [Hervé, monk of Bourg-Dieu], on the same passages of Paul;[7] [Pseudo-] Eucherius, *On Genesis*[8]; Peter Lombard, *II Sentences*, distinction 18[9]; and all scholastic theologians who wrote after Peter Lombard.

And this teaching has not only been always accepted by the Christian faithful, but also by Jewish teachers. For Josephus, a certain Jewish man highly learned in Hebrew and Greek discoursing on the production of man in his *Antiquities* says the following: "But when he saw that Adam had no female companion, no society, for there was no such created, and that he wondered at the other animals which were male and female, he laid him asleep, and took away one of his ribs, and out of it formed the woman; whereupon Adam knew her when she was brought to him, and acknowledged that she was made out of himself."[10]

---

[1] "Finally, on waking up, full of prophecy so to say, when he saw his wife brought to him he immediately burst out with what the Apostle holds up to us as a great sacrament (Eph. 5, 32): 'And Adam said: This now is bone of my bones, and flesh of my flesh; she shall be called woman, because she was taken out of man. Wherefore a man shall leave father and mother, and shall cleave to his wife: and they shall be two in one flesh.' From this we may conclude that through the ecstasy which Adam had just experienced he could be treated by God as a prophet." (Bk. 9, c. 19, n. 36 (PL 34, 408)).

[2] "And therefore God created only one single man, not, certainly, that he might be a solitary, bereft of all society, but that by this means the unity of society and the bond of concord might be more effectually commended to him, men being bound together not only by similarity of nature, but by family affection. And indeed He did not even create the woman that was to be given him as his wife, as he created the man, but created her out of the man, that the whole human race might derive from one man" (Bk. 12, c. 21 (PL 42, 572)).

[3] "... after all the other beings He creates also woman. Notice how He teaches us precisely the process of creation, too." (n. 2 (PG 53, 119)).

[4] "Which silence of ours Adam also when sleeping rightly typified, out of whose side the woman presently came (Gen. 2, 21-22)" (Bk. 30, c. 16, n. 54 (PL 76, 554)).

[5] "'Because we are members of his body, of his flesh, and of his bones.' (Eph. 5, 30). For from our matter [Christ] was made, as Eve was from Adam... For He visibly communicated with us by flesh and blood: invisibly however He is the spiritual author of our reformation, as also Adam was the cause of Eve's creation" (PG 124, 1118).

[6] "'For the man is not of the woman, but the woman of the man. For the man was not created for the woman, but the woman for the man' (I Cor. 11, 8-9). He says the reasons why the man has charge over the woman: doubtlessly both because the woman is from the man's rib, and because the man exists not on account of her, but she on account of him." (PG 124, 698).

[7] "... Adam was made first, then Eve from his rib" (*Commenatarius in Epistolas Divi Pauli*, on I Tim. 2, 13 (PL 181, 1419A)). The text attributes this book to Saint Anselm of Canterbury, but it is the production of Hervé of Bourg-Dieu. The author here refers to Hervé's comments on I Corinthians where he merely says that Eve was made from Adam, but on I Timothy, as just cited, he explicitly says that she was taken from his rib.

[8] "'And the Lord God built the rib which he took from Adam into a woman' (Gen. 2, 22). How did God create the woman here, Who above rested from every work? He did not create her in her matter, but He produces her in her form: for she was made previously in Adam's side, whose rib afterwards was taken out from which the woman was made." (PL 50, 909).

[9] "In the same Paradise God formed the woman from man's substance: just as after he had made Paradise, and placed man in it, and after He had brought all the animals to him, and given them their names, Scripture subjoins, 'The Lord God cast a deep sleep upon Adam. And while he slept, He took one of his ribs, and formed it into the woman.'" (Bk. 2, dist. 18).

[10] Bk. 1, c. 2. (PL 192, 687).

Therefore I marvel at so great audacity of Thomas Cajetan, such that he is not afraid to teach contrary to the whole concordant opinion of Christians and Jews, as though he alone, all the others being blind, could understand the truth itself. Therefore miserable is the Church, which through so many centuries had remained in such great error, that she did not understand by what means Eve was formed. Of course Thomas de Vio had been expected, to whom alone the understanding of this matter was kept by God, so that by it the Church would be recalled from error, by which it had be heretofore infected. If he thought this to be so, it was necessary that he would confirm such a new teaching with a clear working of miracles, since he would make us submissive to him. And we would believe that this was revealed to him by God. But since he worked no such miracle in testimony of this new teaching, even if there were nothing else by which such a doctrine could be disproved, he was bound to displease learned men by its newness alone.

Add to this that this assertion was classified with the note of heresy by holy men many years before, and they were deemed heretics by them who adhered to such an opinion. Blessed Jerome interpreting the passage from book of Exodus: "They believed the Lord, and Moses his servant" (14, 31), says the following: "One and the same credulity is referred to Moses and to God: such that the people who believed in the Lord, equally believed regarding His servant. This is true, however, not merely in regard to Moses, but in regard to all His saints: so that whoever believed God, could not otherwise accept His faith, unless he also believe regarding His saints. For it is not perfect love and faith in God which would be dissolved by hate and infidelity towards His ministers. Now what I am saying is this: someone has believed in God the Creator: he could not believe unless he firstly believed that the things written concerning the saints are true: Adam was formed by God, Eve was made from his rib and side, Enoch was translated, Noe having been shipwrecked was alone saved in the world." And afterwards he relates many other similar works, and finally he subjoins: "These and the other things which were written concerning the saints, unless one believe the entirety, he will be unable to believe in the God of the saints."[1] In which words that ought to be noted which among the other things which he says necessarily ought to be believed, he intermingled the formation of Eve from Adam's rib, and if anyone would not believe this, he said that he cannot believe in God.

Finally, Pope Innocent III, decreeing that it is forbidden by Divine law that one have many wives at the same time, relies on this opinion as a most firm foundation, namely that at the beginning one rib was converted into one woman. Now this decree of Pope Innocent is found in the chapter, *Guademus,* under the title: *De divortiis.*[2]

But it is necessary that we discuss the reasons for which Thomas de Vio Cajetan was motivated to assert this heresy, and that we show them to be of no strength. Firstly in fact he objects that "an inevitable absurdity is incurred" (the words are his) "either that Adam was a monster before a rib was taken away from him, or that he was maimed after the rib was taken away from him both of which is clearly absurd: now it ought to be conceded by all that no absurdity should be claimed in the first production of things. And the consequence is evident

---

[1] *Commentaria in Epistolam ad Philemonem*, v. 5 (PL 26, 609A-C).

[2] "We have read that the Patriarchs and other just men before the Law and after the Law had many wives in common... But this seems incompatible and contrary to Christian Faith, where from the beginning one rib was turned into one woman, and it was testified in Divine Scripture that 'For this cause shall a man leave father and mother, and shall cleave to his wife, and they two shall be in one flesh' (Mt. 19, 5). It does not say, 'three' or 'to his wives,' but 'to his wife.' ... And so that the truth may prevail over falsehood, without any hesitation we state: that it was never in any way lawful for anyone to have several wives at once, unless it was conceded by Divine revelation..." (Decretals of Gregory IX, bk. 4, tit. xix, c. viii).

(he says) that if that rib was superfluous to man, then man was monstrous... but if that rib was necessary for man, it is evident that when it was removed man was maimed."[1]

Therefore let us discuss how much weight this reasoning has. If we were to concede that Adam before the rib was taken from him was a monstrous man, he refutes this opinion by this, namely that the common consensus of all teaches the contrary. For he says the following: "Now it ought to be conceded by all that no absurdity should be claimed in the first production of things." If this argumentation from the common consent of all is so valid that it alone was seen to be sufficient of itself for prevailing, we easily strike him down with his own sword. For it is the common opinion of all (as we have already shown) that Eve was formed from Adam's rib. Therefore it is necessary to admit that he erred, since contrary to the opinion of all he said that Eve was not formed from Adam's rib. For the same reason we refuse to admit that Adam was a monstrous man before his rib was taken from him, because we dare not hold an opinion contrary to the common teaching of all.

But then he assaults us, so that he may force us to admit that he was a monstrous man, because that rib was superfluous to man, since it was not necessary for the survival of the human nature, or if it was needed, it will be necessary to concede that Adam after the rib was removed from him was maim. Blessed Thomas unties this knot saying, "The rib belonged to the integral perfection of Adam, not as an individual, but as the principle of the human race,"[2] not in fact as man (because otherwise a man after he pours out seed, he would not be a man when the seed has been emptied out) but it belongs to the perfection of the begetter insofar as he is a begetter. So also that rib was in Adam after the manner of a seed, because it was the matter whence the woman was formed, and so it belonged to Adam's perfection, since he was the principle of the whole human race.

But he still presses the point, saying: "If Adam before the rib was taken from him was not a monstrous principle, because that rib was necessary for him to be the principle, it will at least be necessary to concede that he was a monstrous man because the rib was not necessary for him to be a man." But it is not necessary to concede this, just as a man having seed is not said to be monstrous, although that seed does not belong to man's perfection. For even if it be not necessary for the constituting of the individual, nevertheless it is necessary for the conservation of the species: and this suffices so that a man be not called monstrous. Because the individual not only retains that which is necessary for his own existence, but also that which is necessary for the conservation of the species.

Secondly he argues as follows: After Scripture had said that Adam named all the animals by their names, and "all the fowls of the air, and all the cattle of the field," it immediately adds: "But for Adam there was not found a helper like himself" (Gen. 2, 20). And from this text he argues as follows: "If this passage be understood according to the literal meaning, it signifies a ridiculous question. For in whose mind," he says, "could it be doubted whether a fitting helper for Adam could be found among the birds? Hence, this kind of Divine inquisition (introduced by Moses when he says, "there was not found a helper") is introduced for this purpose: so that we may understand the later formation of the woman from the man's rib was not to be understood according to the literal sense but as a similitude."[3]

O ridiculous argumentation, and deduced from a mere dream and a feigned text. Sacred Scripture does not actually say that God sought a helper for Adam among the birds or beasts, but only says, "Adam did not find a helper like himself." He will perhaps say that Scripture suggests it, namely that God sought a helper like Adam, because nothing is found except what was first sought. Granted that according to the true and legitimate meaning of the word, any-

---

[1] *Commentarii illustres*, fol. 14-15.
[2] I, q. 92, a. 3 ad 2um.
[3] *Commentarii illustres*, fol. 14-15.

thing found was firstly sought, still it does not thence follow that what is said to not have been found was also previously sought. For just as things which were not sought, are falsely said according to the rules of grammar to have been found, so that they are not truly said to have been found: because two contradictory things cannot be negated of the same thing. If Scripture had said that God had found a helper like Adam, perhaps it could thence be concluded that God had firstly sought such a helper. But since He said, "For Adam there was not found a helper like himself," I do not know on what pretext he relies for concluding that God sought a helper for Adam. Therefore what Scripture says after the beasts and birds had been named: "But for Adam there was not found a helper like himself" is the same as if it had said, "Adam did not have a helper like himself," although all the birds and beasts had females of their own species, with whom they could be helped with the generation of others.

And, so that his argumentation might further weakened, I will show that Sacred Scripture does not always use those words with such an exact meaning of the word: because in it many things are said to have been found by those who nowise sought them. And, so that I may cite one and another passage of Scripture from the many, David says: "Trouble and anguish have found me" (Ps. 118, 143). For it is certain that someone could not have sought tribulation and the rest of man's inconveniences which they nowise perceive. No one in fact seeks anything but that which he can perceive, or towards which he has a natural inclination. But that passage is much clearer which the Lord says through Isaias the Prophet concerning the Gentiles: "They have sought me that before asked not for me, they have found me that sought me not" (65, 1).

Thirdly Cajetan argues again so that he may persuade us of his error saying the following: "The same point is made by Moses' text about the sixth day in which it is clearly written that 'male and female He created them.' Truly in this way— in that Moses had written that the woman was created on the sixth day, and then subsequently describes her as formed from the man's rib after man had been transferred into Paradise— He opened the door to understanding this kind of formation from a rib not in the strict sense but as a similitude. If indeed the woman was brought forth on the sixth day, He did not suppose we should understand that she was brought forth a second time."[1]

I certainly cannot but marvel that a man otherwise so learned was so foolish that he knew not how to untie this knot. For out of ignorance of the custom of Scriptures this error crept up on him. The custom in fact of Sacred Scripture is often to relate some things with a brief summary, and afterwards to return to it, explaining the same thing at great length. For unless we acknowledge this to be the custom of Sacred Scripture, we would be forced to assert many things inconvenient and repugnant to the Catholic faith. It will indeed be necessary to assert, as Philastrius of Brescia asserted on account of the ignorance of this observation, that breath of life, which God breathed into Adam's face, is not Adam's soul: because it was said that Adam was created by God "to His image and likeness" (Gen. 1, 27), hence it follows that he already had a soul, because in consequence of it, and not in consequence of his body, he was God's image. Therefore since at that time Adam already had a soul, it will seem that it could not happen that that breath, which afterwards God is said to have breathed into him, would be his soul. Thus according to this argumentation of Cajetan it is necessary to understand that breath not literally but parabolically, lest the soul be said to have been produced twice. But that this is not so, we, God as our guide, will show below in the section on the "Soul," in book two of the heresies. It will also be necessary to concede that if that argumentation of Cajetan were valid, man's formation from the slime of the earth ought not to be taken literally, lest Adam be said to have been created twice. For just as Moses said in the first chapter of the book of Genesis that the woman was created, so also he said that man was created by God.

---

[1] *Commentarii illustres*, fol. 14-15.

"Male and female he created them" (v. 27). And in chapter two just as he discussed Eve's formation, saying that she was brought forth from Adam's rib, so also he treats about the production of Adam, teaching that he had been formed from the slime of the earth. Therefore lest Adam be said to have been made twice, it will be necessary, according to Cajetan's argumentation, to say that Adam's production ought to be understood parabolically.

Nevertheless we easily untie these and many other similar knots, attending to the custom of Sacred Scripture, which often returns to those things which it had already said one in summary form, so that it may relate those things more clearly and in greater length. Let us acknowledge that Eve was in fact created by God on the sixth day, as was Adam. But because Moses in that first chapter had not expressed the formation of both, that is of the man and woman, since they were different, he thus decided to again speak of the production of both sexes individually in chapter two. Hence Moses does not say that the woman was produced twice, although his words may be taken literally: but the things which were said by him more obscurely, he repeats those same things again, so that they may be related more clearly and fully.

Now I confirm the exposition of that text to be true and correct with the testimony of Blessed Augustine who says the following: "Thus, he had already been formed from mud, already put to sleep for the woman to be made from his side; but this had not been mentioned, and was mentioned at this point by way of recapitulation. For the male not was made on the sixth day, and later on after a lapse of time the woman made; but, 'male and female he created them and blessed them.' So how then, when man had already been placed in Paradise, was the woman made for him? Did Scripture readdress what had been left out? For Paradise was also made on that sixth day, and man was put there, and he was put to sleep so that Eve might be formed, and he awoke when she had been formed, and gave her a name. But these things could not have happened except through intervals of time. Therefore it did not so happen, as if all things were created at the same time."[1]

Therefore from all these things it is most clearly established how vain and futile are the arguments which motivated Cajetan such that thinking contrary to all the Catholic doctors, he fell into this pestilential error. And he certainly would have acted more prudently if he would have admitted his ignorance, saying that he does not know how to respond to such arguments, rather than on account of it to presume against the concordant opinion of all.

ADULTERIUM

Adultery

Concerning this matter I have found only one heresy, which teaches that matrimony legitimately contracted and perfectly consummated can be dissolved on account of the spouse's adultery, not merely as to a separation of bed, such that he who was free of guilt of the consummated and perpetrated adultery in the marriage, could completely put away the other adulterous spouse, and contract a true and legitimate marriage with another, and be joined to him without sin. But concerning this heresy I have decided to say nothing in this place, because there will be a more suitable and apt place below under the section on "Marriage," in which I decided to attack all the heresies which are opposed to this sacrament.

---

[1] *De Genesi ad litteram*, bk. 6, c. 2, n. 3 (PL 34, 341).

ANGELUS

Angels

About the subject of the Angels I find precisely one error among the authors which I have read, which assert that neither the good nor the bad Angels were created by God. The first author of this error among those who had professed Christ at one time at Baptism (for against only those have we taken up arms) was Herman Riswick, (as Bernard of Luxemburg relates in his *Catalogus haereticorum*),[1] who was a Batavian man, or (so that I many use the common word) he was a Hollander, who fell into many errors: finally when he was brought to repent, and sang the palinode, having obtained mercy with some justice, was condemned to life imprisonment in the year of the Lord, 1502. But when shortly afterwards he left prison, he relapsed into his prior madness, and he also babbled many things worse than before. On account of which he was arrested in the year of the Lord, 1512, was condemned by the inquisitors of heretical depravity, and handed over to the secular power, and was burned by its order.[2]

Therefore, among these errors into which this Herman fell into, this is one, whereby he asserts that the Angels, either good or bad, were not created by God, because (as he says) Scripture never affirms this.

This error is clear: because it is clearly said in the book of Job concerning the bad Angel: "Behold behemoth whom I made with thee" (40, 10). But by the name "behemoth" (as approved by Jerome and Gregory) nothing else is understood other than the devil. And in the same book it is said about the same [bad Angel]: "He is the beginning of the ways of God" (40, 14). Expounding which passage Blessed Gregory says: "For what do we understand by the 'ways' of God, but His doings? Concerning which He says by the Prophet: 'For My ways are not as your ways' (Is. 55, 8). And Behemoth is said to be the chief of the ways of God, because doubtless when He was performing all the work of creation, He created him first, whom He made more eminent than the other Angels."[3]

And in the writings of the prophet Ezechiel under the name of King Assur it is said of the same demon: "No tree in the paradise of God was like him in his beauty. For I made him beautiful and thick set with many branches" (31, 8-9), who is described to have been made "beautiful and thick set with many branches," because he was created superior to many legions of the celestial spirits.

Furthermore, it is said concerning all the Angels: "Who makest thy angels spirits" (Ps. 103, 4). For by these words of the Prophet [David], Blessed Paul in that epistle which is to the Hebrews shows Christ, the Son of God, to be superior to the Angels, namely because God made the Angels, but Christ was not made. For he says the following: "And to the angels indeed he

---

[1] *Catalogus haereticorum omnium*, bk. 2, fol. 44r.

[2] "This impious Riswick preludes the modern Deists of our age, and the whole crowd of unbelieving deniers of all revealed faith, who having been corrupted by this age find the sectarians so exceedingly easy of belief." (Schannat, *Concilia Germaniae* (Cologne, Joan. Krakamp, 1763), p. 996). "Herman Ruiswick, likewise a native of the Netherlands, asserted the eternity of matter, and denied the creation of the angels by God, the existence of Hell, and the immortality of the human soul. Christ was to him an impostor, the Christian religion a fraud, and the Bible a book of fables." (Birkhaeuser, J. A. (Jodocus Adolph), *History of the Church, from its first establishment to our own times: designed for the use of ecclesiastical seminaries and colleges* (New York, Fr. Pustet & Co., 1898), p. 480).

[3] *Moralia in Job*, bk. 32, c. 23, n. 47 (PL 76, 664D). *Books of the Morals of St. Gregory the Pope*, or *An Exposition on the Book of Blessed Job*, vol. 3, part 6.

saith: He that maketh his angels spirits, and his ministers a flame of fire. But to the Son: Thy throne, O God, is for ever and ever: a sceptre of justice is the sceptre of thy kingdom" (1, 7-8). Theophylactus expounding these words says the following: "The Angels in fact," he says, "are creatures and works: for of them it is said, 'He that maketh.' But the Son is not a creature, for not also of Him is it said, 'He that maketh': but rather King, Lord and God. For a throne is given to Him, which is an indication of a kingdom, and the throne is eternal."[1] What is said in John's Gospel adds to this: "All things were made by him: and without him was made nothing that was made" (1, 3). Thus either he concedes that the Angels were made by God or it is necessary that he profess that they are nothing. Therefore from manifest ignorance of Scripture he comes forth to say that it cannot be concluded that the Angels were made by God.

Finally against this heresy is an explicit decree of the Church. For the [IV] Lateran Council celebrated under Innocent III put forth such a decree. "One Beginning of all, Creator of all visible and invisible things, of the spiritual and of the corporal; Who by His own omnipotent power at once from the beginning of time created each creature from nothing, spiritual, and corporal, namely, Angelic and mundane."[2] These words are found in the book of the Decretals.[3]

ANIMA
Soul

Among those things which are unknown and more abstruse to us in this light under Heaven, is our soul, such that on account of it Blessed Bernard truly says: "Of myself I understand how incomprehensible God is; because I am unable to understand myself, whom He made."[4] To which saying of Bernard a passage of the Royal Prophet seems to, as it were, give his approval: "Thy knowledge is become wonderful to me" (Ps. 138, 6). The [Royal] Prophet indeed marvels at God's wisdom which is great of itself. For from the fact that man does not know himself, who nevertheless believes that he knows something, it is just that he marvel at the knowledge of Him Who knows all things, and nothing is hidden from His eyes. Therefore from this so obscure understanding of the soul regarding self-knowledge, it happens that many errors about its substance and qualities have arisen. I omit those which the pagan philosophers embraced: for we are not proceeding against them now, but against those who boast that they follow Christian philosophy and the Evangelical doctrine, which errors will not be delineated in the order of time whereby they arose, but as the subject matter itself requires according to the order of the teaching.

Therefore the **first error** is that which denies that rational soul is the form of the human body, not absolutely, but insofar as it is rational. It indeed acknowledges that the rational soul is the form of the body, yet not under this aspect whereby it is rational, because through this aspect it cannot inform the body. The advocate of this error is said to be a certain Pierre Jean

---

[1] PG 125, 198D-199A.

[2] Fourth Lateran Council, c. 1 (Dz. 428).

[3] *Decretals of Gregory IX*, bk. 1, t. 1, (*De summa Trinitate*), c. 1 (*Firmetur*).

[4] *Meditationes piissimae de cognitione humanae conditionis*, c. 1, n. 1 (PL 184, 485C). This quotation seems to be based on a similar and older saying of Saint Augustine: "For I understand by myself how wonderful and incomprehensible is Thy knowledge, by which Thou madest me, when I cannot even comprehend myself whom Thou hast made!" (Saint Augustine, *On the Trinity*, bk., 15, c. 7, n. 13 (PL 42, 1067)).

[Olivi],[1] who revived many errors of Abbot Joachim (about whom we shall speak later), in the time of Pope Clement V.

For attacking this error, because generally there is no theological discussion about it, lest we labor amidst ambiguity, it is firstly necessary to know what form is. Form is that which gives being to the thing, that is to say, which coming to the matter, gives being to the substance itself, and according to which there is a distinction of species, because matter is one and the same type in all corporeal substances. Therefore the variety of form causes a thing to differ from others, because especially from it a thing gets its being, and its perfection is examined according to it.

Therefore according to the above given notion of form the error is clear, which denies that the rational soul is the form of the human body insofar as it is rational. From that it assuredly follows that man himself is nowise rational, which is heretical. But that a man be rational, he has this either from the form or from the matter, for there is nowhere else from which it can come to him, since to be rational does not belong to him accidentally, but essentially. A thing has no other essential parts besides matter and form. It is certain that it does not arise from the matter that a man is rational, since following this reasoning it would be necessary that all substances, which have the same matter as man, be rational. Therefore it comes forth from his form that man is rational. For that is (according to the given definition) from which a thing has its own perfection.

But according to Pierre Jean's assertion the rational soul insofar as it is rational, is not the form of the body, hence from it man does not possess rationality, because in that respect (as he says) it is not the form. Thus it has rationality from no essential part of it, since neither from the matter nor from the form [does it have rationality]: thus it would not be reckoned simply, according to his assertion, that man is rational. Again, if the soul insofar as it is rational is not the form of the human body, thus neither is it an essential part of man: because since matter is not [the form], there is nothing else which it could be. Because if according to this notion the form is not part of man, anything pertaining to perfection that is normally attributed to it will necessarily, according to this explanation, be distinct from man, because it does not get its perfection from exterior things. For due to this cause man is said to be God's image, because that His image is impressed upon the soul, which is admitted by all for this reason alone, insofar as he is rational. Thus it would not be that man should be called God's image: he also ought not to be said to be free, because having taken away from man that he is called rational, it is also necessary to separate from him that which is free, because liberty cannot exist without reason. Because if you would take away liberty from man, there is no way by which he can merit or demerit: because that which is not free, is never imputed by God either to punishment or to glory. Therefore it will be necessarily conceded that the rational soul, even insofar as it is rational, is the form of the human body.

This error was condemned in the Council of Vienne under Clement V.[2] The definition is put in the book of the Clementine epistles under the title, *De summa Trinitate*, in the first chapter, with these words: "We reject as erroneous and contrary to the truth of the Catholic faith every doctrine or proposition rashly asserting that the substance of the rational or intellectual soul is not of itself and essentially the form of the human body, or casting doubt on this matter. In order that all may know the truth of the faith in its purity and all error may be excluded, we define that anyone who presumes henceforth to assert, defend, or hold stubbornly that the

---

[1] Pierre Jean Olivi was a Spiritual Franciscan and theological author. He was born at Sérignan, Diocese of Béziers in 1248-9 and died at Narbonne in 1298.

[2] The Council of Vienne was held in the years from 1311 to 1312.

rational or intellectual soul is not the form of the human body of itself and essentially, is to be considered a heretic."[1]

There is a **second error** (if it only deserves to be called an error), teaching that the breath that God breathed into Adam, is the soul itself. This assertion was reported by Philastrius among the heresies, yet no author of this assertion was named, nevertheless (with all due respect to His Excellency) I do not see why the note of heresy is stamped upon this assertion.

Firstly in fact I find this to be the teaching of many truly Catholic teachers asserting that that breath which He breathed into the man's face is man's soul, which He then created either by breathing, or by creating He poured [the soul] into the body. Hence Chrysostom says: "He intends also to teach us that the Lord's loving kindness intended that this creature shaped from the earth should have also a rational being by reason of a soul, by means of which this living thing emerged complete and perfect. 'He breathed into his face the breath of life,' the text says; the creature shaped from the earth, it means, was endowed with this breath as a vital force, and this became the origin of the soul's being. Hence it adds, 'and man became a living soul'"[2]

Eucherius also says this more expressly, who says the following: "Hence [the soul] is called the 'breath of life,' because both the very air and many other things are called *spiritus*; but nevertheless it is not called 'the spirit of life,' because it lacks life. But it is inquired whether God made the soul by breathing in [to the body]: or rather did He breathe into the body that [soul] which He had made? For I think that it is either, and have not a question about how He made the soul either by breathing in [the soul], or by creating He gave it, and not from some breathing of His, nor from Himself, but from nothing, [and] either He created by breathing into the body or He breathed into the body by creating: not because that breath was converted into the living soul, but instead He made the living soul."[3] Cardinal Hugh [of Saint-Cher][4] and Nicholas of Lyra[5] likewise say this in their expositions on Genesis: whose words I do not wish to insert here, because their words are commonly had. These men are all nevertheless Catholic men.

It is now necessary that we reply to the arguments that Philastrius cites in his favor. For firstly he says that the breathing in is a certain grace of the Divine Spirit, and hence he says the breath is the grace given to Adam's soul after his creation, just as (so he says) after the Resurrection [the Lord] breathing upon the Apostles said: "Receive ye," not the soul but "the Holy Ghost." (Jn. 20, 22).Then he cites Scripture, that by the word "spirit" God's grace is designated, as it is read concerning Saul that the Lord's Spirit departed from him, and an unclean spirit troubled him. (I Kings 16, 14). And he states that elsewhere it is read that the spirit of "wisdom will not enter into a malicious soul." (Wis. 1, 4).

---

[1] Decretal *Fidei catholicæ fundamento*; Dz. 481.

[2] *Homily 12 on Genesis*, n. 5 (*The Fathers of the Church* (Washington D.C., Catholic University of America Press, 1999), vol. 74, p. 166; PG 53, 103.

[3] *Commenatarius in Genesim*, bk. 1; on chap. 2, v. 7 (PL 50, 906C).

[4] "Concerning Adam's soul there is the question whether it was created with the Angels in heaven, and afterwards infused into the body: or was it created when it was being infused? But concerning other souls it is certain, that they are created when being infused, and they are infused when being created: and it is likewise sufficiently probable concerning it, that just as the creation of all the Angels is uniform, so also the creation of all souls." (*Postillae in universa Biblia juxta quadruplicem sensum, litteralem, allegoricum, moralem, anagogicum* (Lyons, 1703), Vol. 1, p. 4v, on Gen. 2, 7).

[5] "'And breathed into': to show that man's soul is from the outside [*ab extrinseco*] through Divine creation and infusion, because at the same time that it was created by the Lord it was also infused into the body." (*Postilla super totam Bibliam* (Venice, Bonetus Locatellus, 1488) on Gen. 2, 7).

All these things are certainly hardly convincing, and are equivocal. [The argument] comes forth due to ignorance in fact of the multiple meanings of this word, "spirit." For sometimes "air" in Scripture is called *spiritus*, as where it is written: "Storms of winds [*spiritus*] shall be the portion of their cup" (Ps. 10, 7). And elsewhere it is said: "He said the word, and there arose a great storm of wind [*spiritus*]" (Ps. 106, 25). And again: "A great and strong wind before the Lord overthrowing the mountains, and breaking the rocks in pieces: the Lord is not in the wind" (III Kings 19, 11). Sometimes also every soul, whether it be rational or irrational, is call a "spirit," as in Genesis it is read: "All things wherein there is the breath [*spiritus*] of life on the earth, died" (Gen. 7, 22). Other times only the rational soul is called a "spirit." For thus we read concerning Christ: "Bowing his head, he gave up the ghost." (Jn. 19, 30), that is, the soul which He gave up by His own power, as He had previously said: "I have power to lay it down: and I have power to take it up again." (Jn. 10, 18). Sometimes also "spirit" is taken for the Third Divine Person. Now this is very rarely found, that the name "spirit" is taken absolutely for God, unless with a certain contraction, consider for example, as when saying, "the Spirit of the Lord," or "Holy Ghost."

Thus the breath of life was given to Adam, meaning, his soul, which is clearly proved by that which is added, "And man became a living soul." For by this man became a living soul, namely that God "breathed into his face the breath of life." In the Apostles, however, when He breathes on them and says to them: "Receive ye the Holy Ghost." (Jn. 20, 22): Scripture does not add, "and they became living souls," as it had said concerning Adam. Thus that breathing ought not to be referred to the giving of natural life, as when He breathes upon Adam's face, but to the giving of spiritual life, that is, the giving of a certain grace. Therefore there is a great difference between that breathing whereby God breathes into Adam's face, from that whereby He breathed upon the Apostles: because the latter refers to a certain spiritual life, but the former ought to be referred to the natural life, which is by the soul, which it is allowed to infer from the words of Blessed Paul, who says: "The first man Adam was made into a living soul; the last Adam into a quickening spirit" (I Cor. 15, 45). For there Paul distinguishes between the first and second Adam, namely Christ. Because if that breath whereby the first man was made into a living soul, was a certain spiritual grace, it would also have been that the first man was made into a quickening spirit: and so there would not have been that difference better them which Paul distinguishes.

If however one were to still object from the fact that Scripture seems to say that man was completely formed before God breathed into his face, thus before that breath it is necessary that man have a soul, because man cannot exist without a soul. For Scripture says the following: "God formed man of the slime of the earth" and immediately it is added: "and breathed into his face the breath of life." From which it seems that the breath was one thing but the soul another. To which words we reply granting that man cannot exist without a soul: yet these things do not impede that it is accustomed to be said according to a certain law of speaking that such a man is in glory, when nevertheless only his soul now rests there, a man is buried in this or that place, although this can be referred to his body alone, and certainly Sacred Writ does not abhor this manner of speaking. For it often calls the soul the inner man, and the body the outer man, as if there were two men, though both are at the same time one man.

Thus from this business it is permitted to take for granted the argument that making a declaration of heresy is not easy, even if there be a statement of some learned man, no matter how learned. For Blessed Augustine in the Prologue of his book *De Haeresibus ad Quodvultdeum*, bears witness that this Philastrius classified many assertions as heresies, which nowise ought to be considered as heresies.[1] And as regards this assertion, he mocks those who believe that

---

[1] *Epistola* CCXXII, n. 2 (PL 42, 17-18). *De Haeresibus ad Quodvultdeum* "was Saint Augustine's response to a request from Quodvultdeus, a deacon (and future bishop) in Carthage, for a practical text

the breath, which God breathed into Adam's face is a certain grace conferred upon Adam's soul, and not rather the soul itself.[1]

There is a **third heresy** in regard to this matter, which teaches that man's soul was formed prior to the body. Blessed Jerome attributes this error to John, Bishop of Jerusalem, in a certain letter to Pammachius against the errors of the aforesaid John. Into the same error fell Philastrius of Brescia, who so firmly adhered to it, that in his small book on heresy, that he says it is heresy to assert that Adam's body was previously formed, and then the soul was created and inserted into it. And Philastrius tries to persuade [others of] this opinion of his by that which is written in chapter one of the book of Genesis it is said: "God created man to his own image" (v. 27). For because according to his soul man is God's image, and not according to the body, Philastrius thought that it was then only treated concerning the creation of the soul. But when in chapter two of the same book it is said: "And God formed man of the slime of the earth" (v. 7), he then believes that Moses is speaking about the formation of the body alone. And motivated by this reasoning he supposed it ought to be held by faith that the soul was created first and then the body was formed.

Thus this heresy, like others, arose from a distorted understanding of Scripture. For that good man did not understand that in both passages Scripture speaks of the formation of the whole man: and it is the custom of Sacred Scripture that it firstly says some things through anticipation in summary fashion, and afterwards returns to them to be discussed at greater length. For it had previously said that man was created by God in His image: but from what he had been made, or whether he had been made from nothing, it had not said. Hence in chapter two it repeats man's formation again, so that it may speak about it at greater length and more clearly. For that it is discussed in chapter one not of the body alone, but of the formation of the whole man, the very order of the words indicates this clearly enough. For it says the following: "God created man to his own image: to the image of God he created him: male and female he created them" (Gen. 1, 27). Notice you see the distinction of sexes, namely male and female. But this diversity of sexes is dependent upon the body, not upon the soul: wherefore it is that the body was then formed, since the distinction of the sexes is expressed.

Now that the body was firstly formed, and then the soul was created, the words which are written in the second chapter show clearly enough. For they relate these things: "And the Lord God formed man of the slime of the earth: and breathed into his face the breath of life, and man became a living soul" (Gen. 2, 7). When he said that man was "formed from the slime of the earth," he is indicating man's body: because the soul was not made from the slime of the earth, but the body. In saying, "breathed into his face the breath of life," he is indicating the soul: because this (as we taught in the aforesaid heresy) is the breath of life, which God breathed into Adam's face. Since therefore it is evident from the sequence of the text itself, that man was firstly formed from the slime of the earth, and afterwards God breathed into his face the breath of life, it is proven therefrom that the body was firstly made and then the soul was created by God.

Blessed Jerome confirms this opinion in his aforesaid letter to Pammachius, saying the following: "If the soul existed before Adam was made in Paradise (in any state and condition), and lived and acted (for we cannot think that what is incorporeal and eternal is dull and torpid

---

in Latin useful for instructing the clergy and laity about heresy... Augustine planned a two-part work, of which the first was a brief catalogue of all heresies after Christ, and the second was to be a theoretical discussion of what constituted heresy... The second part was never written, leaving *On Heresies* as a short reference guide. In it, Saint Augustine presents eighty eight heresies in chronological order, beginning with Simon Magus and ending with his contemporary Pelagians." (Christine Caldwell Ames, *Medieval Heresies* (Cambridge, Cambridge University Press, 2015), pp. 48-49).

[1] Cf. *The City of God*, bk. 13, c. 24.

like a dormouse), there must have been some precedent cause to account for the soul, which at first had no body, being afterwards invested with a body. And if it is natural to the soul to be without a body, it must be contrary to nature for it to be in a body. If it is contrary to nature to be in a body, it follows that the resurrection of the body is contrary to nature. But the resurrection will not be contrary to nature; therefore, according to you, the body, which is contrary to nature, when it rises again will be without a soul."[1] Jerome not merely asserts what we have said, but by many arguments he confirms our, that is, the Catholic position.

Finally Pope Leo I pronounced judgment concerning this matter. For in a certain letter to the Bishop of Astoria, which is the seventy-first letter [2] [of the *False Decretals of the Pseudo-Isidore*] in which he condemns the Priscillianists, afterwards he enumerates in the tenth place a certain error of theirs, in which they say that the souls of men were firstly in Heaven, and from thence on account of their sins were hurled down and inserted into human bodies, he subjoins these words: "This blasphemous fable they have woven for themselves out of many persons' errors: but all of them the Catholic Faith cuts off from union with its body, persistently and truthfully proclaiming that men's souls did not exist until they were breathed into their bodies, and that they were not there implanted by any other than God, who is the Creator both of the souls and of the bodies."[3] So saith Pope Leo, a truly holy as well as learned man. And about this matter in proportion to its worth I think I have said enough. Against this heresy I have found no other writer besides Blessed Jerome in that letter which we cited above: in which place he does not say many things against it, other than the few things which we just recently cited.

A **fourth error** adds that the soul is either God's substance or from God's substance. This monster was devised by certain heretics, who are called Gnostics, a word derived from the pretended knowledge which they flaunted. Different men relate that one of various persons was their leader. Philastrius in fact asserts that they derived their origin from the deacon Nicolas, of whom mention is made in the Acts of the Apostles.[4] Irenaeus, however, asserts that their author was Carpocrates, about whom we will say more later. I believe Irenaeus more, because he was more learned, diligent, and closer to those times.[5] Manichaeans resurrected this same error afterwards, of whom a certain Mani was the leader, insane according to his name, for μανία [*mania*] in Greek means to be insane. This is why his disciples in Greece (as Augustine says) avoiding the word for "madness,": "so to speak the more learned and therefore the more deceitful, called him *Mannich(a)eus*, doubling the letter 'n' as if he were one who pours out manna"[6] instead of *Manicheus*, that is, "the insane one."

Hence this Manes was a Persian, barbarous in his life and morals, having such a keen intellect that he seemed to be insane or filled with the devil: and, stirred up by an instinct of the devil, taught his detestable and execrable heresy to all. He pretended that he was Christ, and also was sometimes saying that he was the Paraclete. Therefore elated with this madness, and following the manner of Christ, choosing twelve disciples, sending them to preach, he sowed foolish, impious, borrowed teachings, which had been extinct for a long time before, and

---

[1] *To Pammachius Against John of Jerusalem*, n. 20 (PL 23, 371B).

[2] PL 130, 897D.

[3] Letter 15 (To Turibius), c. 10 (PL 54, 685A).

[4] Acts 6, 5. *De haeresibus*, c. 33 (PL 12, 1148A).

[5] *Adversus Haereses*, bk. 1, c. 25 (PG 7, 680A-685A).

[6] "The Manichaeans arose from a certain Persian called *Manis*; his disciples, however, when his mad doctrine began to be proclaimed in Greece, preferred to call him *Manichaeus* to avoid the word for 'madness'. This is why some of them, so to speak the more learned and therefore the more deceitful, called him *Mannich(a)eus*, doubling the letter N, as if he were one who pours out manna" (Augustine, *De Haeresibus*, n. 46 (PL 42, 34)).

poured out consummate poison upon the whole world. Thus from this Manes, the heresy of the Manichaeans arose, in the time of Emperor Probus and Pope Felix: which heresy greatly infected the Church, and lasting for a long time infected many regions. For from these men numerous dregs of heresies went forth. For many heretics fight under this heresy, though they are called by other names. To the Manichaeans are related the Audians, so named from Audaeus the Syrian, of whom his memory is treated in book seven, chapter eleven of the *Historia ecclesiastica tripartite*.[1] Apocaritae,[2] Brachitae,[3] Dicartitae, Tascodrugites,[4] Tesalitae, and Tetraditae,[5] of these all there is mention in the [Justinian] Code, [in the section] "Concerning Heretics and Manichaeans [and Samaritans],"[6] and also many other somewhat learned men, such as Faustus[7] and Felix,[8] against whom Blessed Augustine had various disputations, and wrote various tracts.

Therefore these Manichaeans agree on one point with the Gnostics, against the Lord and against the faith, which He through the Apostles and Prophets taught us: saying that man's soul is God's substance. Against this error is firstly that passage from the book of Genesis

---

[1] PL 69, 1077A-1078D. *Historiae Ecclesiasticae Tripartitae Epitome*, the abridged history (in twelve books) of the early Christian Church known as the *Tripartite History*, was the standard manual of Church history in Medieval Europe. The work was compiled, under the direction of Cassiodorus, in about 510 AD, by his assistant Epiphanius Scholasticus. Epiphanius was assigned the translation into Latin of the Greek Church histories of Socrates Scholasticus, Sozomen and Theodoret, written in the previous century.

[2] "The heresy of the Apocaritae arose from the Persian Manes, in the time of the Roman Emperor Tacitus and the Supreme Pontiff Eutychian, about the year 279. This heresy infected with its contagion and disturbed many and great regions. It was propagated with such great success that for two hundred years afterwards it could not be laid to rest" (Gabriel Du Préau, *De vitis, sectis, et dogmatibus omnium haereticorum, qui ab orbe condito, ad nostra vsque tempora & veterum & recentium authoru[m] monimentis prodotti sunt, elenchus alphabeticus... compactus* (Cologne, Geruuinum Calenium, & haeredes Ioannis Quentel, 1569), p. 48).

[3] The Brachitae were a branch of the Manichaeans, which seems to have belonged to the end of the third century A.D.

[4] Tascodrugites is the name given to a religious sect which arose in Galatia in the fourth century. The name is formed from the Greek words *taskos* "a wooden nail" and *drouggos* "a nose." According to Epiphanius (Bmr. xlviii.), the Tascodrugites were so called because while praying they placed the finger on the nose. They are said to have rejected the Creeds and Sacraments (so Theodoret).

[5] The Tetraditae were Manichaeans who admitted a quaternity instead of a Trinity in the Godhead, or four persons in lieu of three.

[6] In the *Codex Justinianus*, "Title V is label *De haereticis et Manichaeis et Samaritis* and contains twenty-two provisions from Constantine to Justinian. These designate the heresies along with the penalties, both penal and civil, which are meted out to their adherents" (Wilfried Hartmann and Kenneth Pennington, *The History of Byzantine and Eastern Canon Law to 1500* (Washington D.C., CUA Press, 2012), p. 126). "The Arians, Macedonians, Pneumatocahi, Appollinarians, Novatians or Sabbatians, the Eunomians, Tetraditae or Tessarescaedecatitae, the Valentinians, Montanists or Pricillianists, or Phrygians or Pepuzitae, the Marcianists, Borbarians, Messalians, Eutychians, or Enthusiasts, the Donatists, Audians, Hydroporatatae, Tascodrogist, Batrachists, Hermeiecians, Photinians, Paulians, Macellians, Ophites, Encratites, Apotactiles, Saccophori, and those who arrived at the deepest depth of crime, the Manichaeans, shall have no permission to meet and pray anywhere in the Roman Dominion" (Book 1, title 5, n. 5).

[7] *Contra Faustum Manichaeum libri XXXIII* (PL 42, 207-518).

[8] *De actis cum Felice Manichaeo libri II* is the record of the debate. In the *Corrections* 2, 34, Saint Augustine recalls that a certain Felix, a Manichaean preacher, came to Hippo "to sow this very error." The debate was held in the church at Hippo on two days, December 7th and 12th, in the year 404 A. D. The proceedings were taken down by shorthand stenographers (PL 42, 519-552).

which we discussed shortly before: "God formed man of the slime of the earth: and breathed into his face the breath of life," which breath we showed above is the soul itself, by that which is added: "and man became a living soul" (Gen. 2, 7). If the soul then is that breath which God breathed upon Adam's face, it follows that it is not from God's substance, just as the breath coming forth from a man's mouth is not from his substance, but from the surrounding air. Thus as we cannot make from our nature, whereby we are men, the breath when we breathe, but from the surrounding air, which by inhaling and exhaling we draw in and expel: so Almighty God, not from His nature, nor from the matter of His substance, but even out of nothing is able to make the breath, which putting into man's body, is very fittingly said breathe into or breathe upon. Because if perhaps from this they object that the soul is equal with God's wisdom, concerning which it is said: "I came out of the mouth of the most High, the firstborn before all creatures" (Eccli. 24, 5), to this objection we reply that it is not said that the wisdom was blown out of God's mouth: but it came out of His mouth. Then not everything which comes out of God's mouth is necessarily equal to God. For in the Apocalypse we read that the Lord saying to a certain man: "I would thou wert cold or hot. But because thou art lukewarm and neither cold nor hot, I will begin to vomit thee out of my mouth" (3, 15-16).

Besides if God had made the soul out of His substance, and the soul is of the same substance which is God's, it is necessary that it have the same properties which God has: just as a father and son, namely John and Peter, because they are of the same substance, they are in the same species, and they have the same properties, especially those which naturally belong to them, and nowise can be separated from them: as for example, if one is rational, the other is also: if one is risible, the other is also: if one is mortal, the other is also. But there are many properties which we necessarily attribute to God, which can in no way befit the soul. For God is omnipotent, our soul however not merely cannot do all things, but in fact there are very few things that it can do. God is immutable, according to the passage: "I am the Lord, and I change not" (Mal. 3, 6). And elsewhere it is said: "with whom there is no change nor shadow of alteration" (James 1, 17). In our soul, however, how many changes are there, O good God? Now happy, now sad, now angry, now meek: sometimes it wants, and other times it does not want the same thing: now it loves something, afterwards it pursues that very same thing with hatred: now it is given to vices, and at another moment it is striving after virtues. For it is not undeserved what Job said, that man "never continueth in the same state" (14, 2): which is no less true of the soul than it is of the body. If therefore these things belong to the soul, which are necessarily opposed to God, it follows that the soul is not of the same substance with God, nor does it come forth in some way from the Divine substance.

But after all these things let us hear what the Church has decided on this matter, because according to the things said above, one ought to obey a decision of the Church as a Divine oracle. The First Synod of Braga[1] in the fifth chapter of its decrees declared the following: "If anyone believes that human souls or Angels exist derived from God's substance, as the Manichaeans and Priscillianists said, let him be anathema."[2] Therefore lest someone be sub-

---

[1] The First Provincial Council of Braga was held in 563 A. D.
[2] This error was more recently condemned by the First Vatican Council "If anyone shall say that finite things, both corporeal and spiritual, or at least the spiritual, have emanated from the divine substance, or, that the divine essence by a manifestation or evolution of itself becomes all things, or, finally, that God is universal or indefinite being, because by determining Himself, He created all things distinct in genera, in species, and in individuals: let him be anathema." (Dz. 1804). The same teaching was also contained in Saint Leo IX's Symbol of Faith: "I also believe and declare that the soul is not a part of God but was created from nothing and was without baptism subject to original sin." (Dz. 348). Saint Augustine says, "The soul is not part of God; for if it were then it would be in every respect unchangeable and indestructible" (Letter 166, c. 2, n. 3 (PL 33, 721)).

ject to the anathema with the Manichaeans and Priscillianists, it is necessary that he obey the Church, saying that the souls created by God are not derived from God's substance, or from some underlying material, but instead from nothing. And Pope Leo I in the fifth chapter of his seventy-first letter [of the *False Decretals of the Pseudo-Isidore*] says the following: "Now in the fifth chapter it is related that they assert that man's soul is of Divine substance, and the nature of our being is no different from the nature of its Creator. Which impiety emanating from the opinion of certain philosophers and the Manichaeans, the Catholic faith condemns, knowing that nothing was made to be so sublime and outstanding that God Himself is its nature."[1] And he says many other things relating to this matter in that place, in which he treats the errors of the Priscillianists.

The **fifth error** is that which teaches that souls are not created by God. Now this error is still divided, as it is usual for heretics never to have unity. For some say that souls are made from the Angels, and made from fire and spirit. The authors of this error were Seleucus and Hermias of Galatia, as Philastrius says,[2] from whom the heresy of the Messalians[3] arose, as it is said in the *Tripartite History*.[4] Now others say that souls of children come to be from the soul of their father, just as the body is derived from his body. The author of this error is Tertullian, as Blessed Augustine says in his book, *De Haeresibus ad Quodvultdeum*.[5] Now who he was, and of what sort was his teaching, you can learn more fully from others, and especially from the book of illustrious men of Blessed Jerome. The opinion of this man was that man's soul is corporeal, although immortal and from the soul of the father as the body is generated from a body. Apollinaris, an Alexandrian, taught this error, of whom there is mention in the *Tripartite History*.[6] The Luciferians, so named their leader, a certain Lucifer, Bishop of Cagliari, of whom there is mention in book ten of the *Eccesiastical History* translated by Ruffinus,[7] hold this same error, and yet this error is not attributed to him. But Guy the Carmelite says that this error belongs to the Luciferians: still I do not know which authors ought to be followed in this matter: because Blessed Augustine in his *De Haeresibus ad Quodvultdeum*, discoursing about them,[8] is especially doubtful as to whether this is their assertion. Then also he doubts whether given that they renounced it, should they be considered heretics on account of it. And speaking about Tertullian in a passage near to the one cited,[9] and although he attributes this error to him, he nevertheless says that he ought not to be called a heretic on account of this assertion, but because joining the sect of the Cataphrygians,[10] he condemned second marriages as being adultery.

---

[1] Letter to Bishop of Astoria (PL 130, 896B).

[2] PL 12, 1169A.

[3] Also known as the Euchites.

[4] Bk. 7, c. 11 (PL 12, 1077D).

[5] "Tertullian therefore, as his writing show, indeed says that the soul is immortal, but he also maintains that it is the body; and not merely this, but that it is also God." (Bk. 1, n. 86 (PL 42, 46)). Cf. Augustine *De Genesi ad litteram*, bk. 10, c. 25-26 (PL 34, 427-428).

[6] Bk. 5, c. 44 (PL 69, 1023D-1023B).

[7] Bk. 1, c. 30 (PL 21, 501A). Rufinus translated Eusebius of Caesarea's *Church History* published in 325 and added a continuation of the history to the year 395. This "tenth book" is part of the added history authored by Rufinus and the passage here cited is classified in *Migne's Patrology* as part of Book One of the appended history by Rufinus.

[8] Chapter 81 (PL 42, 45).

[9] Chapter 86 (PL 42, 45-46).

[10] The Cataphrygians are more commonly known as the Montanists. "The province of Phrygia gave its name to the Cataphrygians (*Cataphrygius*), because they lived there. The founders were Montanus, Prisca, and Maximilla. They assert that the Holy Ghost was passed on, not to the Apostles, but to them."

For Blessed Father Augustine is likewise very often undecided and doubtful about what should be thought about the origin of the soul. For he believes (as he himself admits in his letter[1] on this matter sent to Jerome through the priest Orosius) that souls are created by God, and are not generated *ex traduce*[2]: but he doubts whether the Catholic faith obliges us to believe this: because (as he says) there is no clear passage of Sacred Scripture which proves this.

For if someone were to cite that passage: "Who formeth [*fingit*] the spirit of man in him" (Zach. 12, 1) and the passage of the Psalms: "He who hath made [*finxit*] the hearts of every one of them" (Ps. 32, 15). To these two citations we can reply that we say someone "makes" [*fingere*] something out of preexisting matter: just as we are accustomed to call potters [*figulos*] those who make vessels out clay, and so from any of these passages it can be very well proved that saying that souls are not created by God, but by Angels, as Seleucus and Hermias said, is heresy: still it is not proved that they were produced by God from nothing, because "to make" does not express that. In fact it is greater to create than to make, and yet "to create" in Sacred Writ does not always mean to produce from nothing: which for instance can be shown by that that passage of the Psalm where it is said: "Create a clean heart in me, O God" (50, 12). For the soul seeks to be created which already exists. And in another place it says: "Thou shalt send forth thy spirit, and they shall be created" (Ps. 103, 30). If then the already existing soul is created by a new reception of justice: what forbids that an already existing soul may be said to be made, because it acquired something new?

Now because in Ecclesiastes it is read: "And the dust return into its earth, from whence it was, and the spirit return to God, who gave it" (12, 7), this passage also most clearly proves that the soul was produced by God, but that the soul was produced by the same God from nothing, it does not show, rather (as Augustine says) it is easily replied to this objection, that the body returns into the earth from which the body of the first man was made, but the spirit to God, from which the first soul of man was made. For these men who defend this error will say, that just as our body although it was propagated from that first body, it nevertheless returns to that whence that same first body was made: so our soul although propagated from that first soul, returns not to nothing, because it is immortal, but to God, from Whom the first soul had been made.

Hence Augustine in the letter to Jerome, recalled above, speaking about this opinion, says the following: "Let it not be said to me that we ought to receive as supporting this opinion the words of Scripture in Zacharias: 'Who formeth the spirit of man in him' (12, 1), and in the book of Psalms: "He who hath made the hearts of every one of them" (32, 15). We must seek for the strongest and most indisputable proof, that we may not be compelled to believe that God is a judge who condemns any soul which has no fault. For to create signifies either as much or, probably, more than to form [*fingere*]; nevertheless it is written, 'Create a clean heart in me, O God' (Ps. 50, 12), and yet it cannot be supposed that a soul here expresses a desire to be made before it has begun to exist. Therefore, as it is a soul already existing which is created by being renewed in righteousness, so it is a soul already existing which is formed by the molding power of doctrine. Nor is your opinion, which I would willingly make my own, supported by that sentence in Ecclesiastes: 'Then shall the dust return to the earth as it was: and the spirit shall return to God who gave it'" (Eccle. 12, 7)."[3]

(Isidore of Seville, *Etymologies*, b. 8, c. 5, n. 27).

[1] Letter 166.

[2] I.e. having direct origin from the souls of the parents (literally, from a vine layer). The theory of Traducianism founded by Tertullian derives the rational soul *ex traduce*, i.e. by procreation from the soul of the parent.

[3] *On the origin of the soul* (Letter 166), c. 8, n. 26 (PL 33, 731).

And in his letter to Optatus concerning the origin of the soul, he says the following: "But when a matter, in its very nature difficult, surpasses our capacities, and Scripture assists us with nothing plain, it is only presumption if we attempt to define. Now according to the lives which they begin to have as their own, we say that they are born new men, whether regarding the soul or regarding the body. But actually according to original sin they are born old, and so they are renewed by Baptism. Thus nothing conclusive about the origin of the soul is yet found in Sacred Scriptures. For those who assert that new souls begin to exist without any progeny, among the references whereby they strive to establish this, they cite also those two which I previously mentioned: "Who formeth the spirit of man in him" (Zach. 12, 1) and "He who hath made the hearts of every one of them" (Ps. 32, 15), concerning which you see how one can reply to those opposing."[1] Thus although Augustine thinks that souls do not come into existence *ex traduce*, but are produced from nothing by God, still for this he says that there is no passage of Sacred Scripture obliging this to be believed.

And [Psuedo-] Blessed Eucherius, Bishop of Lyons, who lived at the same time as Augustine,[2] expounding the passage, "And the Lord God built the rib which he took from Adam into a woman" (Gen. 2, 22), says the following: "It is inquired whether the woman formed from the man's side received her soul from his soul? Whether new souls are always created by God out of nothing? Which question is difficult to decide: because there is nothing from holy men, or clearly stated by a passage of Scripture."

Furthermore Blessed Thomas treating this matter in his *Summa Contra Gentiles*, says that it is an error that souls are derived by progeny as bodies are derived.[3] After opposing this error he adds that this was the error of Apollinaris.[4] And yet neither he does depart from the preceding holy men to any extent, nor does he assert anything more certain about the soul. For although Blessed Thomas says that it is an error, still he does not say that it is a heresy. There is wide difference between heresy and error, because even if every heresy is an error, still vice versa it is not necessary that every error ought to be deemed a heresy, as we taught at the beginning of this work. And it is seen that this holy Doctor thinks the same thing since he called it an error, citing no passages of Scripture, because he was treating against the Gentiles in that book of his work, not against heretics.

Therefore for this reason we are able to conclude this one thing, that this assertion of Tertullian and Apollinaris, if it would be shown that there would be some passage of Sacred Scripture or a definition of the Church to which it opposes, it ought to be deemed heresy, but if no passage of Scripture or definition of the Church can be found for this position to which it opposes, even if it should not be called a heresy, it will still be called an error: since it is evident from natural reasoning that it deviates very far from the truth.

---

[1] Letter 190, c. 5, n. 16 (PL 33,862).

[2] The text incorrectly has here that Saint Eucherius "lived a hundred and some more years after Augustine."

[3] "Any principles whatever whose operations cannot be without the body cannot without the body begin to be at all; a thing's way of being and its way of operating are in mutual accord, since everything operates inasmuch as it is a being. Contrariwise, those principles whose operations are performed without the body are not generated through the generation of the body. Now, the nutritive and sensitive soul cannot operate independently of the body, as we have seen before. On the other hand, as we have likewise pointed out, the intellective soul does not operate through any bodily organ. Therefore, the nutritive and sensitive souls are brought into being through the body's engendering; but not the intellective soul." (Bk. 2, c. 86, n. 2).

[4] "Thus is excluded the error of Apollinaris and his followers, who said that 'souls are generated by souls, just as bodies are generated by bodies.'" (*Ibid.* n. 10).

To persuade someone of this, after those arguments which Blessed Thomas asserts in the place recently cited I will set forth in public one from my head, which does very much for proving the matter. If the soul is propagated from a soul, as the body from a body, it is necessary that some seed be emitted from the parents during sexual intercourse whence the soul is formed, as seed is emitted for the formation of the body: otherwise the soul will be said to be produced from nothing, and not from progeny, if nothing was emitted from the parents whence it may be formed. But since it often happens that women remains unchanged without any conceptions: it must then be asked what is made from the seed of the soul, whether it perishes or it remains? If you assert that it perishes, it will also be necessary that you say the soul is mortal: because it is impossible that if its cause and seed be mortal, that it is immortal. But if you deny that it perishes, and rather contend that it remains: why is the soul not generated, since its seed is emitted, whence it needed to be propagated? Will it not have to be said that as concerning the body, so the soul is not generated, because the required conditions disposing for its generation are lacking: so that as the woman from excessive coldness although having received the man's seed does not conceive, so also the soul, however much the man's seed has been received in the mother's womb, on account of the lack of the some similar required condition the soul is not produced? Which having been conceded, it will be necessary to say that the substance of the soul depends on some certain conditions, both in generation, as also in its conservation: such that those things having been applied to its seed the generation of the soul would follow: when those thing have been removed the soul can neither be generated nor subsist. But with those conditions some contrary things might be found (because otherwise nothing would impede, that when seed was emitted, to which souls are closely united, souls will come into existence from the seed itself, if nothing other opposed to their coming into existence) it would be necessary that those conditions be subject to corruption, and when they have been corrupted it is then necessary that the soul then be corrupted. And so it would be necessary to acknowledge that the soul is mortal. But even if this conclusion is very persuasive, and strongly urges, still it does not conclude from that argumentation that it is necessary to say that the assertion of these men is heretical: because in matters of faith authorities are more effective than any natural arguments, as Jerome says in a letter to Theophilus, Bishop of Alexandria: "It is not a pure faith and a frank confession which look for quibbles or circumlocutions."[1]

But what Tertullian says, if he indeed thinks that the soul is a body, such that it has parts, and it can be cut apart, one part in one place and another in another: this is clearly proved to be heresy, by the fact that Sacred Writ teaches that the soul is a spirit. But a thing which is a spirit is not a body, nor can it be. Since in fact the Lord after His Resurrection appearing to the His disciples, and they were thinking that He was a spirit, said: "See my hands and feet, that it is I myself; handle, and see: for a spirit hath not flesh and bones, as you see me to have" (Lk. 24, 39). Now that the soul is a spirit can be proved by many passages of Scripture. For Solomon in Ecclesiastes says: "Who knoweth if the spirit of the children of Adam ascend upward, and if the spirit of the beasts descend downward?" (3, 21). And the Lord commending His soul at death to His Father says: "Father, into thy hands I commend my spirit" (Lk. 23, 46). And showing that He had a free and prompt will in regards to undergoing His Passion, He says: "The spirit indeed is willing, but the flesh weak" (Mt. 26, 41), where by the word "spirit" He means the soul. And Paul describing the fight of the flesh and the soul says: "The flesh lusteth against the spirit: and the spirit against the flesh" (Gal. 5, 17). The soul therefore cannot be a body, since it is a spirit.

But it is now necessary that we set forth clear testimonies of Sacred Scripture against the Messalians, whereby we may prove that man's soul is not from the Angels (as they say) but

---

[1] Letter 82, n. 5 (PL 22, 738).

was created by God. Firstly it is clear that concerning man's creation Moses relates that the Lord said: "And he said: Let us make man to our image and likeness" (Gen. 1, 26). And a few words later Moses says: "And God created man to his own image" (v. 27). Perhaps the Messalians will say that by the words, "Let us make," God is speaking to the Angels whom He wanted to partake in the creation of souls. But this is easily proved to be false: because man was made in the image of those to whom He says, "Let us make." Man was not made, however, in the image of the Angels, but in God's image, and thus not to the Angels, but to the other Divine Persons God the Father says: "Let us make man to our image and likeness."

Furthermore, it is clearer that afterwards in the same book speaking about man's creation Moses says: "[God] breathed," he says, "into his face the breath of life" (Gen. 2, 7). But we have already shown above in the second heresy [or "error"] from the sacred Doctors that the "breath" was the soul, which God had infused into Adam's body. Then, there are many testimonies of Sacred Scripture which teach that God is the Creator of all things: and therefore also of souls. For Solomon says: "He created all things that they might be" (Wis. 1, 14). And Paul says to the Hebrews: "He that created all things, is God" (Heb. 3, 4). And the twenty-four elders in John's Apocalypse adoring God say: "Thou art worthy, O Lord our God, to receive glory, and honour, and power: because thou hast created all things; and for thy will they were, and have been created" (4, 11).

Finally against this heresy are many definitions of the Church. Pope Leo [the Great] in his letter to Turribius, Bishop of Asturias, says: "Men's souls did not exist until they were breathed into their bodies, and that they were not there implanted by any other than God, who is the Creator both of the souls and of the bodies."[1] The Creed of the Nicene Council says: "We believe in one God the Father almighty, Creator of all things visible and invisible."[2] The Council of Constantinople subscribed to the same statement.[3] The same statement was openly declared in the [IV] Lateran Council celebrated under Innocent III, the decree of which, because we have already cited it in the section on the "Angels," need not be repeated here.[4]

There is a **sixth heresy** which affirms that the souls of sinful men after death are changed into demons, and into whatever brute animals befitting their merits. Philastrius relates this heresy, yet no author of it is named. And Guy the Carmelite recalls it a long time afterwards in his book on heresies among the unnamed heresies, of which there is no certain author.[5] But I am very surprised concerning this Guy, namely that he gives this heresy without the name [of its author], especially since he read (as it is fair to believe) Augustine in his book, *De Haeresibus ad Quodvultdeum.*[6] For even if here he writes this error without the name of the author, following Philastrum in that regard: nevertheless afterwards reviewing those heresies which are not recalled neither by Philastrius nor Epiphanius, when discussing Tertullian, he says that Tertullian held that the souls of very bad men, after death were turned into demons.[7] And likewise Guy, when writing about the errors of Tertullian, attributes this error to him:[8] wherefore I am surprised that afterwards he placed it among the unnamed heresies. Tertullian therefore thought that men's souls, not all, as Guy indifferently attributes to him, but the souls of the worst men are changed into demons after death. Now whether he would say that those

---

[1] Letter 15, c. 10 (PL 54,685A).
[2] H. Denzinger, *Enchiridion symbolorum*, 54. Hereafter this source will be abbreviated as Dz.
[3] Dz. 86.
[4] Fourth Lateran Council, c. 1 (Dz. 428).
[5] Guido Terrena de Perpiniano, *Summa de haeresibus et earum confutationibus*, f. 72v, c. 76.
[6] C. 78 (PL 42, 45).
[7] C. 86 (PL 42, 47).
[8] *Summa de haeresibus et earum confutationibus*, f. 67v, c. 63.

souls are also changed into brute animals, Augustine does not say, and I am not sure. But if he denies this, this heresy in that part alone will be without a named patron.

Now what could motivate Tertullian that he would fall into this error, I certainly do not see: unless perhaps that which the Lord speaking to the very wicked Jews in Saint John's Gospel said: "You are of your father the devil" (8, 44). And concerning the transformation into brute animals, those who defend that error perhaps are motivated by that which John the Baptist said: "Ye brood of vipers, who hath shewed you to flee from the wrath to come?" (Mt. 3, 7).

But this ought to little motivate a man even moderately educated: especially if he were to consider that not all the words of Sacred Scripture ought to be taken merely according to the bare literal meaning. For Sacred Scripture is full of metaphors, and other figures of speech, in which on account of the agreement of things among themselves, the name of one thing is put for the name of another: as when Christ is called a lion and a lamb: it is not that He is both of these, rather He is neither of them, yet He is called both from a certain comparison, in that He has some likeness to them both. So also men are called beasts on account of their morals, which they have similar to the beasts. Thus the Jews are called "brood of vipers" by John the Baptist, because just as those vipers are born devouring their mothers, similarly after those men had killed their fathers, that is to say their teachers and prophets, then they are born spiritually doing penance. In this manner also ought to be taken that which is said: "You are of your father the devil": it ought not to be understood that according to their nature are they sons of the devil, but according to their morals whereby the sons imitate their parents. For whose works anyone does, of him he is also called a son. Which argument is clearly proved from that which Christ replies to the Jews saying that their father is Abraham: "If you be the children of Abraham, do the works of Abraham" (Jn. 8, 39).

Now for refuting this error perhaps that passage is sufficiently effective where Christ threatens to say on Judgment Day to the men too little merciful: "Depart from me, you cursed, into everlasting fire which was prepared for the devil and his angels" (Mt. 25, 41). From which words it is shown that there is a distinction between the souls of wicked men and demons. Likewise in the book of Wisdom it is said: "How could any thing endure, if thou wouldst not? or be preserved, if not called by thee. But thou sparest all: because they are thine, O Lord, who lovest souls" (11, 26-27). But how would He preserve souls, if they were turned into demons at some time? For it is necessary that what is turned into something else perish, so that it may be turned into something else. Wherefore from the same reason it would be necessary to say that the soul is mortal: which nevertheless Tertullian, Augustine bearing witness, denies. For that which is converted into something else, is then corrupted, when it turns into something else: as wine when it is turned into vinegar, or air when air is converted into water, ceases to be wine, and ceases to be air. Therefore if the soul is changed into a demon or into a brute beast, it is necessary that the soul ceases to exist in the change, and so it will be mortal: which is the error we wish to expose next.

There is a **seventh heresy**, which says that man's soul is corrupted at the same time with the body at man's death. And this error is further divided into two sects, by those saying that the souls perish at the same time as the bodies, but afterwards are raised up again with the bodies at the resurrection. This error (as Eusebius says)[1] arose in the regions of Arabia. But those heretics, because Eusebius names no author of them, Blessed Augustine says that we can call the Arabians,[2] by which name they are named by those in coming generations who wrote about their heresies. These heretics in a disputation with Origen being present, and speaking to them, Eusebius bearing witness,[3] quickly recanted.

---

[1] *Ecclesiastical History*, bk. 6, c. 37.

[2] *De Haeresibus ad Quodvultdeum*, c. 83 (PL 42, 46).

[3] *Ecclesiastical History*, bk. 6, c. 37.

Now others say that souls so perish with the body at man's death, that they never return afterwards, by which fact it seems that they also deny the resurrection. But concerning the latter error we shall discuss below at greater length, when we shall treat of the resurrection. This was the error of the Sadducees: which error I would have omitted, unless another had revived it afterwards: because I decided to treat only those heresies which arose after Christ's coming: not those which existed before Christ's coming, as Blessed Father Augustine also does in his book *De Haeresibus*. Thus the Hollander Herman Riswick whom we already mentioned above, after the Sadducees revived this error.

Hence even if these men are divided among themselves, still they agree on this, that they say that the soul through man's death perishes with his body at the same time. Wherefore they ought to be struck with the same sword. Firstly, therefore, before all things I decided that it ought to be noted that something is said to be immortal in two ways: in one way that one would merely deny the act of dying, such that something is said to be immortal because it will never die, though it would be able to die: in which way some say that Adam if he had persevered in justice, would have been immortal, such that he would not have died, although he would have had the potency (as they say) for death. In another way something is said to be immortal, in that one does not merely deny the act, but the potency of death, such that just as it will never die, so neither could die, in the same way that we say that God is immortal. In this last way to prove that the soul is immortal, it requires more work than our Enchiridion permits: wherefore we have now decided to omit, especially since for refuting these heretics it is enough to prove that man's soul however much the body dies, will never perish.

Now this is very clearly proved from the reward of good and wicked men, where it is said concerning both: "And these shall go into everlasting punishment: but the just, into life everlasting" (Mt. 25, 46). Now what will end at some time cannot be eternal. And concerning the just in particular it is said: "Their hope is full of immortality" (Wis. 3, 4). Furthermore, the various lives of men in this world, for which an unworthy reward befalls at the present time, seems to me to be such a strong argument that even if the testimony of Scripture were lacking, it would suffice to prove that man's soul remains after death: because we see in this present life sinners and the most wicked men prosper, and to pay off no punishments due to their deeds here: on the contrary the just are troubled with adversities, tortured with maladies, and suffer very many inconveniences. But if souls would not remain after men's death, the Ruler of the world, to Whom all things are subject, could be accused of being unjust, and reprehended of injustice, because He punished the just, and bestowed a reward upon wicked men. But God nowise ought to be accused of being unjust, because "The Lord is just, and hath loved justice" (Ps. 10, 8), hence it is proved that after man's death the soul has some life, in which everyone will receive a fitting reward for his deeds.

Still besides these things, there is a very clear testimony of Sacred Scripture. For in fact in the book of Wisdom it is read: "Their own malice blinded them. And they knew not the secrets of God, nor hoped for the wages of justice, nor esteemed the honour of holy souls. For God created man incorruptible, and to the image of his own likeness he made him" (2, 21-23). From which passage it is clearly proved that the soul is immortal and incorruptible: because, as it appears from the text, it speaks of man in regards to his soul, and not in regards to his body, according to which God's image is found in man. For it says the following: "Nor esteemed the honour of holy souls." And adding the reason it says: "For God created man incorruptible." And in the same book Solomon speaking about the souls of the just says: "The souls of the just are in the hand of God, and the torment of death shall not touch them. In the sight of the unwise they seemed to die: and their departure was taken for misery" (3, 1-2).

Also concerning the same just souls it is said in the book of the Apocalypse: "I saw under the altar the souls of them that were slain for the word of God, and for the testimony which they held. And they cried with a loud voice, saying: How long, O Lord (holy and true) dost thou not judge and revenge our blood on them that dwell on the earth? And white robes were given to every one of them one; and it was said to them, that they should rest for a little time, till their fellow servants, and their brethren, who are to be slain, even as they, should be filled up" (6, 9-11). And in the same book it is said elsewhere: "I saw a great multitude, which no man could number, of all nations, and tribes, and peoples, and tongues, standing before the throne, and in sight of the Lamb, clothed with white robes, and palms in their hands" (7, 9). Now who these are, concerning whom it speaks, one of the ancients explained saying: "These are they who are come out of great tribulation, and have washed their robes, and have made them white in the blood of the Lamb. Therefore they are before the throne of God, and they serve him day and night in his temple" (v. 14-15) etc.

Again in Luke's Gospel the soul of just Lazarus is brought by Angels, and placed in Abraham's bosom: and the soul of the rich feaster after his death was buried in Hell, where he is tormented, and from there he speaks with Abraham. Therefore the soul remains after man's death. Then the Lord in Matthew's Gospel says: "Fear ye not them that kill the body, and are not able to kill the soul: but rather fear him that can destroy both soul and body" (10, 28). Now if the soul were mortal, and it were to perish at the same time with the body, killing the body would also kill the soul at the same time, as in the brute animals, whose soul is killed by one killing the body. Add to this that the Lord in the same Gospel of Matthew says to the Sadducees denying the resurrection: "And concerning the resurrection of the dead, have you not read that which was spoken by God, saying to you: I am the God of Abraham, and the God of Isaac, and the God of Jacob? He is not the God of the dead, but of the living" (22, 31-32). Thus the soul lives however much the body has died, nor does it perish at the same time with the body.

Against this heresy exists an explicit definition of the Church given at the Lateran Council celebrated under Leo X, which is this: "Leo, bishop, servant of the servants of God, with the approval of the Sacred Council, for an everlasting record. The burden of Apostolic government ever drives us on so that, for the weaknesses of souls requiring to be healed, of which the Almighty Creator from on high has willed us to have the care, and for those ills in particular which are now seen to be pressing most urgently on the faithful, we may exercise, like the Samaritan in the Gospel, the task of healing with oil and wine, lest that rebuke of Jeremias may be cast at us: 'Is there no balm in Galaad? or is no physician there?' (8, 22) Consequently, since in our days (which we endure with sorrow) the sower of cockle, the ancient enemy of the human race, has dared to scatter and multiply in the Lord's field some extremely pernicious errors, which have always been rejected by the faithful, especially on the nature of the rational soul, with the claim that it is mortal, or only one among all human beings, and since some, playing the philosopher without due care, assert that this proposition is true at least according to philosophy, it is our desire to apply suitable remedies against this infection and, with the approval of the Sacred Council, we condemn and reject all those who insist that the intellectual soul is mortal, or that it is only one among all human beings, and those who suggest doubts on this topic. For the soul not only truly exists of itself and essentially as the form of the human body, as is said in the canon of our predecessor of happy memory, Pope Clement V, promulgated in the General Council of Vienne, but it is also immortal; and further, for the enormous number of bodies into which it is infused individually, it can and ought to be and is multiplied. This is clearly established from the Gospel when the Lord says, '[They] are not able to kill the soul' (Mt. 10, 28); and in another place, 'he that hateth his life in this world, keepeth it unto life eternal' (Jn. 12, 25) and when He promises eternal rewards and eternal punishments to those who will be judged according to the merits of their life; otherwise, the Incarnation and other mysteries of Christ would be of no benefit to us, nor would the resurrection be something to look forward to, and the Saints and the just would be (as the Apostle says) 'of all men most miserable'" (I Cor. 15, 19).

"And since truth cannot contradict truth, we define that every statement contrary to the enlightened truth of the faith is totally false and we strictly forbid teaching otherwise to be permitted. We decree that all those who cling to erroneous statements of this kind, thus sowing heresies which are wholly condemned, should be avoided in every way and punished as detestable and odious heretics and infidels who are undermining the Catholic faith. Moreover we strictly enjoin on each and every philosopher who teaches publicly in the universities or elsewhere, that when they explain or address to their audience the principles or conclusions of philosophers, where these are known to deviate from the true faith—as in the assertion of the soul's mortality or of there being only one soul or of the eternity of the world and other topics of this kind—they are obliged to devote their every effort to clarify for their listeners the truth of the Christian religion, to teach it by convincing arguments, so far as this is possible, and to apply themselves to the full extent of their energies to refuting and disposing of the philosophers' opposing arguments, since all the solutions are available.

"But it does not suffice occasionally to clip the roots of the brambles, if the ground is not dug deeply so as to check them beginning again to multiply, and if there are not removed their seeds and root causes from which they grow so easily. That is why, since the prolonged study of human philosophy—which God has made empty and foolish, as the Apostle says, when that study lacks the flavouring of divine wisdom and the light of revealed truth—sometimes leads to error rather than to the discovery of the truth, we ordain and rule by this salutary constitution, in order to suppress all occasions of falling into error with respect to the matters referred to above, that from this time onwards none of those in Sacred Orders, whether religious or seculars or others so committed, when they follow courses in universities or other public institutions, may devote themselves to the study of philosophy or poetry for longer than five years after the study of grammar and dialectic, without their giving some time to the study of Theology or Pontifical Law. Once these five years are past, if someone wishes to sweat over such studies, he may do so only if at the same time, or in some other way, he actively devotes himself to Theology or the Sacred Canons; so that the Lord's priests may find the means, in these holy and useful occupations, for cleansing and healing the infected sources of Philosophy and poetry. We command, in virtue of holy obedience, that these Canons are to be published each year, at the beginning of the course, by the local Ordinaries and rectors of universities where institutes of general studies flourish. Let nobody therefore..."[1]

There is an **eighth heresy**, which asserts that souls pass on from body to body: such that after the death of one man, his soul would pass on to enliven and supporting another body. Of old this was the opinion of the philosopher Pythagoras, to which the wicked Albanenses afterwards adhered.[2] The Albigenses heretics,[3] so called, because they arose from the group at Albi near Toulouse in the year of the Lord 1200 in the time of Pope Innocent III.

Which view, putting the faith aside for now but led by natural reason alone, anyone would easily abandon, if he were to consider that souls have remembered absolutely nothing of those things which were before. It was in fact necessary that they remembered the things that were done before. Nor is it likely, that this would be ascribed to the body, namely that the joining with the body would entirely extinguish the whole memory of those things which were done before. For as the body has now been put to sleep and to rest, whatever the soul alone sees by

---

[1] V Lateran (From the Bull *Apostolici Regiminis*, December 19, 1513), n. 1-14; Cf. Dz. 738.

[2] The Albanenses were Manichean heretics who lived in Albania, probably about the eighth century, but concerning whom little is known, except that they were one of the numerous sects through which the original Manicheism continued to flourish.

[3] Also called the Albigensians.

itself, many of those things are remembered, and often after a long time, when it has woken up declares what it saw in a dream: so also it would have remembered those things which it had done in another body before it came into this body.

But if someone perhaps would deny that there is any likeness to sleep, namely because when then body is asleep the soul still shares its operation with the body: such that it is not that which alone acts, but it is using the body as an instrument: for which reason I put forth another fitting comparison. Paul rapt up into the third Heaven saw the hidden things of God, which it is not permitted for a man to say: in which rapture, although he himself is doubtful whether his soul was in his body, or out of his body: still this is certain, that his soul nowise used the bodily senses, but it alone without any help of the body was in that contemplation of hidden things: because the bodily senses nowise avail for contemplating those things, and nevertheless afterwards he remembered those things which he saw. If therefore he remembers when he returned to his body what was outwardly seen for a very brief time: all the more the soul would remember those things among which it dwelt living for so long a time in another body.

But if someone perhaps were to say that he copies Plato: When he was transferred to another body, he drank from a certain cup of forgetfulness offered by I know not what devil, whereby it happens (as Plato says) that souls do not remember past things.[1] This certainly seems to be rather a creation of the poets, than of philosophers, and much less a teaching of theologians. For if the soul drinks of the cup of forgetfulness, which wipes out the memory of all things, then I will interrogate Plato, or him who follows him in this view, whence he knows that his soul was given to drink by the demon, since his soul is now in his body, and by this fact it would seem necessary that his soul drank of that cup of forgetfulness, such that he also lost the memory of that drink, and consequently he should not remember that he was given to drink? But if he forgets that cup, whence therefore does he now know that he drank the cup in the past? For if he remembers the demon, the cup, and the entrance into his body, why does he not also remember the other things? From which it is clearly proved that this doctrine is not merely foreign to the Catholic faith, but also to true philosophy.

And [Pseudo-] Blessed Athanasius in his book which is called *De beatitudine fidei* showing the rules of the faith says: "If anyone were to profess that men's souls return back again to the world, either to being men, brute animals or serpents, let him be anathema."[2] But lest anyone find fault with me that having forgotten my goal, I dispute with pagan philosophers: let him realize that I do not fight against this opinion because it belonged to Pythagoras or Plato, but

---

[1] "With reference to these objections, Plato, that ancient Athenian, who also was the first to introduce this opinion, when he could not set them aside, invented the [notion of] a cup of oblivion, imagining that in this way he would escape this son of difficulty. He attempted no kind of proof [of his supposition], but simply replied dogmatically [to the objection in question], that when souls enter into this life, they are caused to drink of oblivion by that demon who watches their entrance [into the world], before they effect an entrance into the bodies [assigned them]. It escaped him, that [by speaking thus] he fell into another greater perplexity. For if the cup of oblivion, after it has been drunk, can obliterate the memory of all the deeds that have been done, how, O Plato, dost thou obtain the knowledge of this fact (since thy soul is now in the body), that, before it entered into the body, it was made to drink by the demon a drug which caused oblivion? For if thou hast a remembrance of the demon, and the cup, and the entrance [into life], thou oughtest also to be acquainted with other things; but if, on the other hand, thou art ignorant of them, then there is no truth in the story of the demon, nor in the cup of oblivion prepared with art." (St. Irenaeus, *Adversus Haereses*, bk. 2, c. 33, 2). Plato, *Republic*, bk. 10).

[2] Bk. 6, PL 62, 281A The book was not written by Saint Athanasius, but possibly by Bishop Vigilius of Thapsus, who used "Athansasius" as his Pseudoname. He lived during the fifth century and was present at the Synod of Carthage in 484.

because the Albanenses and Albigenses, who gave their names to Christ at their Baptism, embraced the same view afterwards.

There is a **ninth** and last **heresy**, which I find on this subject, which asserts that the souls sinned before their infusion into the body, and as a punishment of their sin they were confined to their bodies as to a prison. The author of this error is Origen, as Epiphanius accuses him in his letter to John, Bishop of Jerusalem, which is found in the works of Jerome, because he translated it into the Latin language.[1] This same error Theophilus, Bishop of Alexander attributes to him in his Pascal letter,[2] which work Jerome also translated into Latin, and is found in that volume which is called *Antidotum haersum*.[3] The same heresy was afterwards defended by the Spaniard Priscillian, Bishop of Avila,[4] who drew the heresy from the dregs of all heresies, as Pope [Saint] Leo says in his letter to the Bishop of Asturias,[5] and Blessed Augustine in his book *De Haeresibus ad Quodvultdeum*.[6] But about the name of the city which this Priscillian ruled, Erasmus of Rotterdam, a man otherwise very well learned, was deceived. For in his leisure given to learning with which he embellished the book of Blessed Jerome concerning noteworthy men, when Blessed Jerome had said of him that he was the Bishop of Avila, when interpreting these words of Jerome, he says that Abila is a Phoenician city in Syria.[7] In which matter he greatly wandered in his mind: because although there is a city in Phoenicia called by this name, still Avila which Priscillian ruled, is a well-known city in a rather remote part of Spain, and is not one of its least cities. Now it is evident that Priscillian was Spanish from Augustine in his book *De Haersibus*, and Pope Leo in his letter to Turribius, Bishop of Asturias. And hence it happened that the Synod of Braga[8] was held against him.

Against this heresy those same argument militate, which we have adduced against the recently discussed heresy. Firstly therefore regarding Christ's soul it is evident that He never sinned, nor consequently ought it to be said that on account of sin it was cast into a body as into a prison. For as it is said in the First Epistle of Peter, "Who did no sin, neither was guile found in his mouth" (2, 22). For how could He deliver all from sin, if His soul was guilty of sin, was imprisoned as a punishment for sin? Furthermore since according to the Apostle, "This mortal must put on immortality" (I Cor. 15, 53), so that the body as well as the soul may receive the deserved reward for its merits: what madness is this to call the body the soul's prison, given to it as a punishment? For then the resurrection of a blessed soul would not be for a rest, but for a punishment, since by that resurrection it would be forced to return again to the prison, whence it had once been freed. And so the resurrection of bodies would be in

---

[1] "Can anyone, moreover, brook Origen's assertion that men's souls were once Angels in heaven, and that having sinned in the upper world, they have been cast down into this, and have been confined in bodies as in barrows or tombs, to pay the penalty for their former sins; and that the bodies of believers are not temples of Christ, but prisons of the condemned?" (Letter 51, n. 4 (PL 22, 520)).

[2] Letter 96, n. 18 (PL 22, 788).

[3] *Antidotum adversus haeresum venena* I.e. *The Antidote for [the Poison] Heresies*. It was written by Rev. Fr. Louis de Reyn against the errors of Luther and Calvin.

[4] He died c. 385.

[5] I.e. Turribius, Bishop of Asturias. "For there is no dirt which has not flowed into this dogma from the notions of all sorts of heretics: since they have scraped together the motley dregs from the mire of earthly opinions and made for themselves a mixture which they alone may swallow whole, though others have tasted little portions of it." (Letter 15).

[6] Chap. 70 (PL 42, 44).

[7] N. B. *Abila* is the Latin word for both the city in Spain called Avila and for the Phoenician city of Abila.

[8] I.e. the First Council of Braga in 563.

vain, if it were expedient for the souls to fly up more lightly to Heaven without the weight of their bodies.

Again, if the body were a prison and punishment for the soul, the soul would nowise love it, nor sorrow to be separated from it, nor in any way wish to return to it: all of which is proved false by one's experience: and Paul disproves the last of these things saying: "We would not be unclothed, but clothed upon" (II Cor. 5, 4), where Paul calls the body clothing, rather than a prison: and he teaches that there is a natural inclination of the soul to the body when he says: "We would not be unclothed, but clothed upon." That is, we flee and abhor the miserable condition of the body, not however the body itself: wherefore we do not want to be without the body, but without the miseries and calamities of the body: we would however want to be clothed with a new body, such as it will be in the resurrection.

Then if souls sinned before they entered their bodies, and not in their bodies, but in punishment for the sin which they did outside of the body they were enclosed into their bodies as into a prison, it was necessary that the Savior Himself who had come to free men, would not have assumed a body, since souls sinned without a body. It would also have been necessary that He would have freed the souls from their bodies at the time when He forgives sins at Baptism, and immediately free the one baptized from the prison of his body, since he says that the body was produced solely as a punishment for sin, and given to the soul. For it is unjust that the soul having been freed from sin, nonetheless still be bound in prison.

Add to this that Blessed Paul says regarding the twins in the womb of Rebecca: "For when the children were not yet born, nor had done any good or evil (that the purpose of God, according to election, might stand,), not of works, but of him that calleth, it was said to her: The elder shall serve the younger. As it is written: Jacob I have loved, but Esau I have hated" (Rom. 9, 11-13). From which saying of the Apostle it is evident that those brothers had done nothing good or evil before they were born.

But about these things one ought not to tarry longer, the Church some time ago made a definition. In fact the First Synod of Braga in the sixth chapter of its decrees says the following: "If anyone says that the souls of men sinned first in the heavenly abodes, and therefore were cast down into human bodies upon earth, as Priscillian said, let him be anathema."[1]

ANNUS

Year

Concerning this subject I only find an opinion which is numbered among the heresies by Philastrius (which in fact according to my judgment) nowise deserves the classification of heresy. For he, in his book, *De haeresibus*, says it is heresy to assert that the number of years from the origin of the world is uncertain. I am indeed surprised at this man, who pronounced so lightly about heresy, since it is such a serious matter to reckon about heresy that it is necessary that it be considered with long and careful examination before something be decided. For it is certain that there are different opinions about this matter: wherefore it is certain that none of them is certain, especially since the Church has not rejected any of them henceforth.

Eusebius in fact, whom Augustine imitated in his computation of times, numbers five thousand six hundred years from the creation of the world until the time in which Rome is captured by the Goths.[2] Bede in his book, *The Reckoning of Time*, numbers until the time of Theodosius

---

[1] PL 84, 563D.

[2] "They are deceived, too, by those highly mendacious documents which profess to give the history

the Younger, at which time he says that Rome was captured by the Goths, four thousand four hundred and two years.[1] Which diversity comes from the different translations of the Old Testament: for the seventy interpreters [of the Septuagint] in regard to the computation of the years, which are distributed through the various generations in the book of Genesis, differ greatly from the Hebrew text, which Blessed Jerome handed down to us. Concerning which discrepancy Blessed Augustine discusses for many chapters in book fifteen of His book, *City of God*. Eusebius and Augustine follow in their computation the seventy interpreters. Bede follows the Hebrew text. But Philastrius follows I know not which translation, since he follows neither of these. For in the computation of the years he departs from both. He puts in fact from the beginning of the world to the time in which he wrote that work, five thousand three hundred seventy years.

Now Philastrius lived a short time before Augustine, because Blessed Augustine in his prologue to the book *De Haeresibus ad Quodvultdeum*, states the he had seen him in Milan with Blessed Ambrose. Hence I do not know how he could make us accept his computation, since others exist which greatly differ from his, and they belong to men of no mean authority. Add to this that Philastrius himself is inconsistent with himself, using various computations. For in the chapter where he treats of this matter, from Adam to holy Heber,[2] in whose time the language of the whole world was confounded, he supposes there were two thousand eight hundred forty-two years, and yet treating about the variety of languages shortly before, he then numbers from Adam to Heber two thousand seven hundred years. Therefore it is not a heresy to assert (as Philastrius says) that the number of years from the beginning of the world is uncertain, since the Church has never defined concerning this matter, nor has it ever rejected any opinion of the preceding men.

APOSTOLI

Apostles

Concerning the life, state and condition of the Apostles, some heresies have arisen: one of which is that which asserts that the Apostles did not preach Christ's Gospel according to the spiritual meaning, but merely according to the literal sense. This is the error of Abbot Joachim [of Flora],[3] and Pierre Jean [Olivi], as Guy the Carmelite charges them.[4] This Joachim was raised in Calabria, was a monk of the Order of Saint Benedict, and was the abbot of the same Order in the monastery of Florence. He wrote many things, in which (in my opinion) he showed meagre ability: because in nearly all his books, in order to show that he was herald of future events, he was accustomed to mix in predictions, which is a sign of great levity and a desire for glory: especially when the event turned out differently afterwards than he had foretold. For, in order that I may be brief, he predicted, as he perhaps dreamed, that

---

of many thousand years, though, reckoning by the sacred writings, we find that not 6000 years have yet passed" (*City of God*, bk. 12, c. 10). Saint Augustine here follows the chronology of Eusebius, who reckons 5611 years from the Creation to the taking of Rome by the Goths; adopting the Septuagint version of the Patriarchal ages.

[1] PL 90, 560B.

[2] In Jewish tradition, Heber, the great-grandson of Sem, refused to help with the building of the Tower of Babel, so his language was not confused when it was abandoned. He and his family alone retained the original human language, Hebrew, a language named after Heber, also called *lingua humana* in Latin. This tradition is supported by Saint Augustine (*City of God*, bk. 16, c. 11).

[3] He was born c. 1132 and died in1202.

[4] *Summa de haeresibus et earum confutationibus*, f. 99r.

Emperor Frederick would be an enemy of the Church, of whom all historians relate that he remained in peace and tranquility with the Church until his death.[1] Abbot Joachim flourished under Pope Alexander III and Emperor Henry VI.

Now what pertains to the dogma at hand: I have not found in his writings—which I have read— that concerning what has just been mentioned, but I merely find him charged of this matter by Guy the Carmelite. Concerning which matter I am greatly surprised, because although in the [IV] Lateran Council celebrated under Innocent III, another particular error of this Abbot Joachim was condemned, about which we will say more afterwards, it is surprising that that Council made no mention of the other error: although nevertheless he had many other errors just as Guy charged him. But it was possible that those errors were so hidden that they did not reach the ears of the Council. Wherefore in this matter we trust Guy.

Thus among the other fables that this Joachim wanted to force upon the Christian people, this is one, whereby he says that there are three states of man. The first state is that in which men lived according to the state of the flesh: which state lasted from Adam until Christ. The second state, is that in which men led a middle life between the flesh and the spirit: and this state extended from Christ until Blessed Benedict. The third state is that in which one lives and will live according to the spirit: and this state extended from Blessed Benedict until the end of the world. Now into these three states he fits three orders, namely, of those married, of the clergy and of the monks. The order of the married began from Adam, (and as he said) began to fructify from Abraham. The sacerdotal order began from Ozias, who being from the tribe of Juda offered incense, but began to fructify from Christ, who is both king and priest. The order of monks began from Benedict, who was a holy man. Thus in the first state the carnal law was given. In the second state even if the spiritual law was given, namely the Gospel, still it was not preached by the Apostles except according to its literal sense. But in the third state which he proposes, he says it was to be preached according to its spiritual meaning, and this by those monks of Saint Benedict.

Pierre Jean [Olivi] assents to all of these things, except for the third state, which, since he belonged to the Order of [Friars] Minor, he says took its beginning from Blessed Francis, and that through the Brothers of his Order the spiritual life was due to be reformed, and the Gospel spiritually preached. And so it happened that each one tried to favor his institute under which he was fighting.

Therefore so that we may overturn everything in order, firstly let us show that the first state, namely, which they say was from Adam until Christ, was not life according to the flesh. For in fact Paul in the Epistle to the Romans says: "They who are in the flesh, cannot please God" (Rom. 8, 8). Now he says that those Apostles are in the flesh, who live according to the flesh. But how is it true what is added: "But you are not in the flesh, but in the spirit, if so be that the Spirit of God dwell in you" (v. 9)? Hence [Ambrosiaster] when expounding these words says: "Having been formed in the flesh, they are not said to be in the flesh, if assenting to the Apostle John, they do not love worldly things; for man's views form his nature, so that he may be named after what he thinks."[2] From which words it may be concluded that all the men of the first state were in the flesh, since, according to them, they lived according to the flesh. Those, however, who are in the flesh, according to Paul, do not please God. It is surmised from this that no man belonging to the first state pleased God. Furthermore in the same passage Paul says again more expressly: "For if you live according to the flesh, you shall die" (v. 13). Now this ought to be understood of the second death, as Theophylactus says. For otherwise those

---

[1] If this emperor was Frederick I (Barbarrosa) who lived at the time of Abbot Joachim, then his prediction was not entirely false, as the emperor challenged papal authority and was nearly excommunicated by the pope.

[2] *Commentaria in Epistolam ad Romanos*, c. 8 (PL 17, 120B).

words which follow cannot be reconciled. For thus it is subjoined: "But if by the Spirit you mortify the deeds of the flesh, you shall live." Now all those living in the spirit, will be dead in their bodies, but will live forever. If therefore it is necessary according to Paul that those who live according to the flesh die in Hell, it is necessary to acknowledge that all the men of the first state are dead in this way, such that no hope of eternal life remains for them.

Now to say that from Adam until Christ no man pleased God, and all were damned, is manifest heresy, which opposes many and very clear passages of Sacred Scripture. Concerning Abel, in fact, it is read that "the Lord had respect to Abel, and to his offerings" (Gen. 4, 4). And he did not have respect otherwise than by accepting, in the same way that "to Cain… he had no respect," because he did not please God (v. 5), but [Abel] pleased God. For Paul expounds this passage in this way in his Epistle to the Hebrews: "By faith Abel offered to God a sacrifice exceeding that of Cain, by which he obtained a testimony that he was just, God giving testimony to his gifts; and by it he being dead yet speaketh" (Heb. 11, 4). Therefore Abel was found to be just before God. For so it was proclaimed by the Divine Voice. "That upon you may come," Christ said, "all the just blood that hath been shed upon the earth, from the blood of Abel the just, even unto the blood of Zacharias" (Mt. 23, 35).

Furthermore Paul says in the same place concerning Enoch: "By faith Henoch was translated, that he should not see death; and he was not found, because God had translated him: for before his translation he had testimony that he pleased God" (Heb. 11, 5). Again it is proved sufficiently that David pleased God, by that which God said concerning the same David: "I have found…a man according to my own heart."[1] Now what more efficacious testimony can be cited which is concerning John the Baptist, who so merited to be exalted as the Divine herald that no one may be said to be greater then he among all those born of women?[2] To this man I would not dare, after the Virgin Mother of God, to prefer any of the Saints. How, I say, will we say that John the Baptist lived according to the flesh, who did not drink wine nor strong drink?[3] Who was fed on locusts? Who was not wearing soft garments, but clothing woven from camel's hair? For this is inimical to the flesh. Thus it is a very clear lie to say that all men from Adam until Christ lived according to the flesh.

Let us come then to the second state, in which they say that the spiritual law was given, namely the Gospel: but this they say was not preached spiritually and according to its true meaning, but merely according to the literal sense, and superficially. Thus it is necessary here to ask them (so that their temerity may appear more clearly), whether their reason why the Apostles did not preach according to the spiritual meaning was because they did not understand it in this way? Or if they understood [the spiritual meaning], why did they not wish to preach [it], keeping the true understanding to themselves, but announcing merely the literal sense?

No one would say that the Apostles were ignorant of the Gospel according to its spiritual meaning, since the Lord says: "To you it is given to know the mysteries of the kingdom of heaven" (Mt. 13, 11; Lk. 8, 10). Because if it is a mystery, then it is not merely literal. Hence who dares to say that Blessed John the Evangelist was ignorant of the spiritual meaning of the Gospel, to whom reclining upon the Lord's breast were revealed heavenly secrets?[4] And who will dare to say this concerning Paul, also, who, "caught up to the third heaven… heard secret words, which it is not granted to man to utter" (II Cor. 12, 2-4)? Who also did not receive the Gospel from men, but from God Himself (as he said)?[5]

---

[1] "I have found David my servant: with my holy oil I have anointed him" (Ps. 88, 21).

[2] Cf. Mt. 11, 11.

[3] Cf. Lk. 1, 15.

[4] Cf. Jn. 13, 23-25.

[5] Gal. 1, 12.

Furthermore if the Apostles were ignorant of the spiritual meaning of the Gospel, Paul wrongly rebuked the Jews because they were merely adhering to the outward part of the text, and did not hold the spirit of the text. Someone could object to him that quote of the poet: "Let the straight-limbed man deride the one with deformed foot, let the white man deride the black African."[1] The Apostle speaking concerning the Jews, however, says: "Even until this day... the veil is upon their heart. But when they shall be converted to the Lord, the veil shall be taken away. Now the Lord is a Spirit. And where the Spirit of the Lord is, there is liberty. But we all beholding the glory of the Lord with open face, are transformed into the same image from glory to glory, as by the Spirit of the Lord" (II Cor. 3, 15-18).

Someone could add to these words that Christ, soon before His death when about to depart from the Apostles, said to them: "But the Paraclete, the Holy Ghost, whom the Father will send in my name, he will teach you all things, and bring all things to your mind, whatsoever I shall have said to you" (Jn. 14, 26). Now what does it mean that He would bring to their mind, except that He will declare, He will express, the things more obscurely said by Christ which perhaps they had not understood on account of their dull mental capacity, so that when the Holy Ghost came all things were manifest to them?

If, however, the Apostles had a true and spiritual understanding of the Gospel: it is necessary to acknowledge that they preached [the Gospel] just as they understood [it]. Otherwise they would have been worse than if they had been ignorant: because knowing, and not willing to teach according to their knowledge, they would rightly be accused either of envy or of some other similar crime, having no ignorance excusing them.

Nor in this matter, in my opinion, must more time be spent, since the Apostle Paul said concerning it a clear statement. For he said the following: "Who also hath made us fit ministers of the new testament, not in the letter, but in the spirit. For the letter killeth, but the spirit quickeneth" (II Cor. 3, 6). Indeed nothing could be said more explicitly against these men. Therefore let them depart, and tell their fables near the fire to little old women, and not to learned men, who know how to distinguish wheat from cockle.

There is a **second heresy**, which asserts that the Apostles neither had nor received money, nor kept anything for the next day, and (what is worse) this heresy also teaches that none of these things was permitted to them. Wherefore it takes away the hope of salvation to everyone receiving money, or to anyone keeping something for the next day. The authors of this heresy were certain so-called the Apostolics, who lived about the time of Pope Boniface VIII. The leader of these men was a certain Gerard Segarelli from Parma, who was caught in his error, condemned and burned.[2] A certain [Fra] Dolcino of Novara,[3] who with his wife Margaret, accessory of the same crime, suffered death for his teaching. About these men can be said that passage of the Apocalypse: "Thou hast tried them, who say they are apostles, and are not, and hast found them liars" (2, 2). For these men boasted that they lived an Apostolic life, because just as the Apostles (as they said) so also they were not accepting money nor keeping anything for the next day. To asserting which they were motivated by that which Christ, the Redeemer and Teacher of all the Apostles, said: "Do not possess gold, nor silver, nor money in your purses" (Mt. 10, 9). And again: "Be not solicitous for tomorrow" (Mt. 6, 34). And other words of this kind which the Evangelists relate that the Lord said to His Apostles.

But this heresy arises from a distorted understanding of the text (as often happens). Hence against this heresy let us proceed in this order: firstly let us prove it to be heresy, then let us teach the true meaning of that Gospel Scripture.

---

[1] Juvenal, Satire 2, line 23.
[2] Gerard Segarelli (c. 1240 – 1300) was the founder of the Apostolic Brethren.
[3] Fra Dolcino (c. 1250 – 1307) was burned at the stake in Northern Italy in 1307.

Firstly, therefore, the Apostles had money, and that they carried it with them is sufficiently proved by that which is said in John's Gospel: When Jesus had come to a city of Samaria, which is called Sichar, He stayed near the well outside the city, while "His disciples were gone into the city to buy meats" (Jn. 4, 8). Again in the writings of John the Evangelist it is said, when the Lord said to Judas the traitor: "That which thou dost, do quickly" (13, 27), none of the Apostles understood this, "for they thought because Judas had the purse, that Jesus had said to him: Buy those things which we have need of for the festival day: or that he should give something to the poor" (v. 29). Discussing which words, Theophylactus says: "And how is it that He who admonishes others not to carry a scrip or money,[1] He Himself however was carrying a purse? He shows that it is necessary that one lacking possessions, and crucified to the world, have a great care for a portion of it, namely for the poor."[2] In which words it ought to be observed that Theophylactus thinks that Christ's words about not carrying money ought to be reckoned among the admonitions and counsels, and not among the precepts. Yet be this as it may, it is forever certain that Christ and His Apostles carried money with them, as the two passages which we very recently cited show most clearly. Wherefore one ought not to dispute this matter anymore, since this opinion about not carrying money is most effectively refuted by these quotations.

Therefore, we may now proceed to another element of this heresy. For what these Apostolics say about keeping for the next day is not literal, because (as they say) it was so forbidden to the Apostles to keep something for the next day: this is false as is the rest. It is in fact well proved that Christ and the Apostles kept [something] for the next day by that which is found in the writings of John. For when the Lord satisfied five thousand men with five loaves and two fishes, He afterwards said to the Apostles: "Gather up the fragments that remain, lest they be lost. They gathered up therefore, and filled twelve baskets" (Jn. 6, 12-13). You see that something was kept here. The Apostle also arranged that collections be made on the first day of the week, so that thereafter they might distribute to the needy:[3] nevertheless everything was not collected on one day, and then they were dividing, but rather as the need and want of the poor required. It was necessary therefore that something be kept the time thereafter. Likewise (as it is evident in the book of the Acts of the Apostles) many necessary things had been procured for the needs of the brethren on account of the pressing famine, which had been predicted by Agabus, and happened afterwards under [Emperor] Claudius.[4] Then Paul sailing, when he had appealed to Caesar, to whom he was sent, did he not take some food for the trip? Yet he did not provide for one day only, because a ship from Asia was not accustomed to arrive at Rome in one day: nay he was delayed many days on the trip.[5]

Although these passages are indeed very clear, still it is necessary that we reply to their objections. Therefore firstly they cite that passage of Matthew: "Do not possess gold, nor silver, nor money in your purses" (10, 9).

To this we reply in two ways. Firstly [we reply] that some things were forbidden to the Apostles at one time, which afterwards were permitted to them: hence it appears that such a prohibition was not absolute and everlasting, but temporary limited for a certain period of time. There were many suchlike things among those found in the tenth chapter of Matthew, when they were sent by the Lord to preach. For example, it is said there: "Go ye not into the way of the Gentiles, and into the city of the Samaritans enter ye not" (v. 5): which certainly

---

[1] Cf. Mk. 6, 8.

[2] MG 124, 163A.

[3] Cf. I Cor. 16, 2.

[4] Cf. Acts 11, 28. The famine occurred during the reign of Emperor Claudius, was in the fourth year of his office (45 A.D.), and was particularly centered in Judea.

[5] Cf. Acts 27, 9.

ought to be referred to that time in which they were sent to preach, so that they might not then go to the regions of the Gentiles: not, however, absolutely, namely so that they might never go to those places wherein the Gentiles dwelt. For in the same Gospel of [Saint] Matthew it is afterwards said that "Jesus retired into the coasts of Tyre and Sidon" (15, 21), which towns belonged to the Gentiles and in [Saint] John's Gospel it is found that He went to Samaria.[1] The Apostles also, after Christ's Ascension, having left Judea went to Samaria. Peter in fact was in Antioch and Rome, where he both died and was buried.

Also regarding this manner of not carrying money in purses, it was perhaps a command for the Apostles for that time alone during which they were sent. For Christ wanted to teach the Apostles how they ought to cast their care upon the Lord,[2] and that their hope ought to be placed in Him: which having been done He would feed them. Now in order that they might know this by their own experience, He sent them commanding them not to carry money, which having been cast away they might then experience how nothing would be lacking to them, because they to whom they preached were bound to feed them. "The workman," He said, "is worthy of his meat" (Mt. 10, 10). Wherefore when teaching at another time He also treated of this same matter. He said: "When I sent you without purse, and scrip, and shoes, did you want anything?" (Lk. 22, 35). Hence it seems that for this reason it was then forbidden them to carry money, so that they could then experience that the Lord takes care of them, and that nothing was lacking to them, even if they cast away their money, for which reason He might convince them that they ought not to fix their hope in money, whether gold or silver, but in God.

Interpreted otherwise, it can be said according to Blessed Augustine, who in many places says that it was not a precept but a counsel. For in the second book of his *Harmony of the Gospels* he says: "For when He said to the Apostles, 'Do not possess gold, nor silver, nor money in your purses,' etc., He immediately adds, 'For the workman is worthy of his meat' (Mt. 10, 9-10). And by this He makes it sufficiently obvious why it is that He would have them provide and carry none of these things. He shows that His reason was, not that these things are not necessary for the sustenance of this life, but because He was sending them in such a manner as to declare plainly that these things were due to them by those very persons who were to hear believingly the Gospel preached by them; just as wages are the soldier's due… This makes it apparent that by these instructions the Lord did not mean that the preachers of the Gospel should not seek their support in any other way than by depending on what was offered them by those to whom they preached the Gospel (otherwise Paul acted contrary to this precept when he acquired a livelihood for himself by the labors of his own hands, because he would not be chargeable to any of them), but that He gave them a power in the exercise of which they should know such things to be their due. Now, when any commandment is given by the Lord, there is the guilt of non-obedience if it is not observed; but when any power is given, anyone is at liberty to abstain from its use, and, as it were, to recede from his right… Accordingly, as our Lord ordained what the Apostle declares Him to have ordained— namely, that 'they who preach the gospel, should live by the gospel' (I Cor. 9, 14)— He gave these counsels to the Apostles in order that they might be without the care of providing or of carrying with them things necessary for this life."[3] And he repeats the same opinion in his book against the heretic Adimantus.[4] He straightforwardly speaks likewise in his book, *Against Lying.*[5]

---

[1] Cf. Jn. 4.

[2] Cf. Ps. 54, 23.

[3] Chap. 30, n. 73-74 (PL 34, 1113-1114).

[4] *Contra Adimantum Discipulum Manichaei*, bk. 1, chap. 20, n. 1 (PL 42, 165).

[5] "Moreover, it was said to the Apostles that they should take nothing with them for their journey, but

Now what they assert based on Matthew's Gospel, namely: "Be not solicitous for tomorrow" (Mt. 6, 34), wanting to prove from this that it is not permitted to keep anything for the next day, can nowise prove their opinion. Firstly in fact (as Blessed Jerome says commenting on Saint Matthew's Gospel) "tomorrow" in Sacred Writ not merely denotes the day soon to come after the present day, but all future and indefinite time: so the future is called "tomorrow," which will happen sometime, as in Genesis Jacob says: "And my justice shall answer for me tomorrow before thee when the time of the bargain shall come" (30, 33). Where it clearly appears that this adverb, "tomorrow," is used for a future time. "And in the apparition of Samuel, the woman with the pythonical spirit says to Saul: "Tomorrow thou and thy sons shall be with me (I Kings 28, 19)."[1] Yet on the next day Saul and his sons did not die, but when a number of days passed Saul died with his three sons. And so according to this interpretation it could be said that that text does not forbid keeping for tomorrow, that is to say the following day, but providing provisions for the whole future time.

We reply secondly, better and more clearly, saying that keeping for tomorrow is not forbidden, but rather solicitude for tomorrow: namely, lest we be so solicitous that the solicitude itself would separate us from God, Whom we are bound to serve. Now that the words themselves say the same thing, this is easily surmised from the preceding words. For He did not say, "Thou shalt keep nothing for tomorrow": but instead He said, "Be not solicitous for tomorrow." But someone can keep for tomorrow without solicitude, nay when one has kept for tomorrow, the solicitude itself is taken away, so that now there he has no care for tomorrow, but instead he may think about God. For in fact the Apostle says: "But having food, and wherewith to be covered, with these we are content" (I Tim 6, 8). Hence Theophylactus when expounding these words found that [Saint] Matthew's Gospel means: "For it suffices for you that you are weighed down with your daily troubles, but if you shall have been solicitous for tomorrow, when you will take time for God, always tormenting yourself about corporeal things?"[2] You see there that excessive solicitude is forbidden, and not the reservation or keeping of things for tomorrow alone. Therefore, the Apostolics err saying that it is not allowed to keep for tomorrow.

---

should live by the Gospel. And in a certain place too the Lord Himself signified why He said this, when He added, 'For the workman is worthy of his meat' (Mt. 10, 10) where He sufficiently shows that this is permitted, not ordered; lest haply he who should do this, namely, that in this work of preaching the word he should take anything for the uses of this life from them to whom he preached, should think he was doing anything unlawful. And yet that it may more laudably not be done is sufficiently proved in the Apostle Paul: who, while he said, 'And let him that is instructed in the word, communicate to him that instructeth him, in all good things,' (Gal. 6, 6) and showed in many places that this is wholesomely done by them to whom he preached the word, 'Nevertheless,' says he, 'we have not used this power' (I Cor. 9, 12). The Lord, therefore, when He spoke those words, gave power, not bound men by a command" (*De mendacio*, chap. 15, n. 30 (PL 40, 507-508)).

[1] "In the Scriptures 'tomorrow' refers to the time to come. Jacob says: 'My justice shall answer for me tomorrow' (Gen. 30, 33). And in the apparition of Samuel, the woman with the pythonical spirit (cf. Acts (16, 16)) says to Saul: 'Tomorrow thou shalt be with me.' (I Kings 28, 19)." (PL 26, 46B).

[2] PG 123, 210.

AQUA

Water

Concerning this matter I find only two heresies. The first is that which says that water was not created by God: but is coeternal with Him. Philastrius relates this heresy, with no named author: and also Blessed Augustine in his book, *De haeresibus*, in the seventy-sixth place among the heresies which he names, does not mention the author. Whoever was its author, I do not know what occasioned his error, unless perhaps that in the book of Genesis, in which Moses treats of the Creation, when he makes mention of the Creation of Heaven and earth, he nevertheless makes no mention of the Creation of water.

This heresy is easily refuted by that which is said in Psalm 88: "Thine are the heavens, and thine is the earth: the world and the fulness thereof thou hast founded" (v. 12). And in Psalm 134 it is said: "Whatsoever the Lord hath pleased he hath done, in heaven, in earth, in the sea, and in all the deeps" (v. 6). If therefore God created the sea, then it is also necessary that he created the waters: because "The gathering together of the waters, he called Seas" (Gen. 1, 10). And (as Ecclesiastes says) "All the rivers run into the sea" (1, 7).

Now what it objected by reason of their name, namely that no mention is made by Moses of the Creation of water in the book of Genesis, this is false, and proceeds from a false understanding of Scripture. For when He said: "In the beginning God created heaven, and earth" (Gen. 1, 1), in that passage by that word "earth" all corporeal things, which are under Heaven, are signified. For this word "earth" is taken in two ways in Sacred Writ, especially in the first chapter of the book of Genesis. For in fact sometimes "earth" is taken to mean that mass, from which all corporeal creatures were derived: concerning which it is said, that it was "void and empty" (v. 2), that is, unformed, as a certain unwrought and disorganized mass, from which various parts were taken for the undertaking of various forms. And these words are said concerning which [earth]: "In the beginning God created heaven, and earth," that is, that mass from which all corporeal things were derived, and consequently water. And the philosophers call this "earth" prime matter, because it is the first material, from which through the reception of various forms other corporeal substances were diversified.

Sometimes "earth" is taken, and that is more usual, to mean one of the four elements, and so it is meant in the same place when it is said: "Let the waters that are under the heaven, be gathered together into one place: and let the dry land appear. And it was so done. And God called the dry land, Earth; and the gathering together of the waters, he called Seas" (v. 9-10). Thus when the dry land is called "earth," the word "earth" is used in a more restricted sense, than when it is said: "In the beginning God created heaven, and earth": because in the latter case "earth" extends to the matter of all corporeal substances, and thus to the matter of water. Wherefore there is mention of water in the same place by the name of "earth."

But if in that same place there was no mention of water, it would nowise be permitted to conclude that water was not created: since this may be clearly proved from other writing no less canonical that is the book of Genesis. Against this heresy is the Creed of the Council of Nicea and the Creed of the Council of Constantinople, both of which state that God is the Creator of all things, visible and invisible. And likewise the Lateran Council celebrated under Innocent III, whose decree is found in the chapter *Firmiter*, [under Title one,] *De summa Trinitate et fide Catholica*.[1]

---

[1] Dz. 428.

The **second heresy** is that which says that blessed water has no more power or efficacy than non-blessed water. The first authors (that I know of) were certain men who were called the Flagellants. These men rose up in Italy about the time of [Blessed] Gregory X, and spread into Germany and France: who during forty years or so wandered through the world flagellating themselves. And so from their work they chose the name, so that they called themselves "Flagellants": because with knotted whips, in which thorns were inserted, they scourged themselves, saying that this flagellation was more effective for wiping away any sin, than any confession: nay they compared it or preferred it to martyrdom: because by it they (as they used to say) were shedding their own blood, but the martyrs were forced by others to suffer this. From this sect very bad errors were derived: among which is this one which we said.

After these men certain heretics, called the Lollards, succeeded them into the same error in England, drawing their origin from the sect of the Wycliffites, but did not adhere to this teacher of theirs, Wycliffe: and it is not surprising, because this is peculiar to heretics, that they do not know how to keep unity. To these Lollards, in the same error succeeded a certain German called John of Wessel,[1] in the time of Emporer Fredrick III: whose books at the same time on account of the many heresies found therein, were burned in Mainz by sentence of the Inquisitors for heretical depravity.

Thus all these men unanimously assert that blessed water is of no greater power than non-blessed water: because we cannot (as they say) make things better by our blessings than God made them by their nature. Wherefore the impious Lollards say that all blessing made upon wine, bread, oil, salt, wax, the walls or floor of the church, vestments, miters, chalices, and other similar things, are merely a work of necromancy rather than of true and Christian piety. For (as they say) by such exorcisms and blessings creatures are honored, by believing about those things that they are of greater power than they are in their own nature, since in the blessed creature no change is seen to have been made, but only by a false faith, which is the main thing in the diabolic art. But regarding exorcisms and blessings, we will show elsewhere that all those things are not futile and vain, and not separated from Christian piety. We now therefore are discussing only and specifically about water.

Firstly it is indeed evident that its blessing is not an invocation of demons, as the Lollards falsely assert, by that which is written in the book of Numbers about jealousy of the husband towards his wife. For so it is said: "If the spirit of jealousy stir up the husband against his wife, who either is defiled, or is charged with false suspicion, He shall bring her to the priest, and shall offer an oblation for her, the tenth part of a measure of barley meal: he shall not pour oil thereon, nor put frankincense upon it: because it is a sacrifice of jealousy, and an oblation searching out adultery. The priest therefore shall offer it, and set it before the Lord. And he shall take holy water in an earthen vessel, and he shall cast a little earth of the pavement of the tabernacle into it. And when the woman shall stand before the Lord, he shall uncover her head, and shall put on her hands the sacrifice of remembrance, and the oblation of jealousy: and he himself shall hold the most bitter waters, whereon he hath heaped curses with execration. And he shall adjure her, and shall say: If another man hath not slept with thee, and if thou be not defiled by forsaking thy husband's bed, these most bitter waters, on which I have heaped curses, shall not hurt thee. But if thou hast gone aside from thy husband, and art defiled, and hast lain with another man: these curses shall light upon thee: The Lord make thee a curse, and an example for all among his people: may he make thy thigh to rot, and may thy belly swell and burst asunder. Let the cursed waters enter into thy belly, and may thy womb swell and thy thigh rot. And the woman shall answer, Amen, amen. And the priest shall write

---

[1] His full name is John Ruchrath von Wesel (c.1400–81). The text mistakenly calls him John of Upper Westphalia, who was simply a printer.

these curses in a book, and shall wash them out with the most bitter waters, upon which he hath heaped the curses, And he shall give them her to drink" (5, 14-24).

What will the Lollards reply to this? Is that an exorcism of cursing and diabolic: or it is rather full of Divine piety, and uttered by the Divine voice? How then does that water have power and efficacy? Is it not through the devil's art? Far be it, but instead through the Divine power: and yet it seems that there was no change made in the water after the exorcism, as they seek. What therefore do they demand? If God did this at that time, why will He not also be ready to also do other similar things now through creatures upon the invocation of His name? Wherefore it was the very old custom of the Church, derived even from the very times of the Apostles unto our times, that water would be blessed and exorcized with salt: so that through the prayers, which are poured out to God in its blessing, God deigns to work similar things upon us through its sprinkling, such things which are previously besought by praying or blessing.

It is not that from the blessing itself that the water itself necessarily has that power: because the water of Baptism (according to the truer opinion) does not have this power: but because God assists and works through the words said upon the water: yet differently, because in Baptism God assists from a promise, and thus it never does not work: because "Heaven and earth shall pass, but [His] words shall not pass" (Mt. 24, 35). Wherefore unless the one washed by Baptism were to place the obstacle of sin, God always infuses grace in the one baptized.

But it is not so concerning blessed water, nor is He so obliged (just as I said), because He neither promised nor Himself instituted this sign: but one ought to rely upon Him, that he will give and effect that in us, that which is besought in the water when it was being blessed, for example when saying: "Pour down into this element the power of Thy blessing, prepared by many purifications. May this, Thy creation, become a vessel for Thy Divine grace to dispel demons and sicknesses, so that everything on which it is sprinkled, in the homes and buildings of the faithful, will be removed of all unclean and harmful things. Let no pestilent spirit, no corrupting atmosphere, remain in those places: may all the schemes of the hidden enemy be dispelled," etc.[1]

But if all these things are not always worked when the water is sprinkled, it is thence proved that it is not a Sacrament, namely because it is not an efficacious sign. Yet because through its sprinkling God has worked many wonders, we prove that even if it be not a Sacrament, nevertheless it has this, that it possesses much greater power than non-blessed water: because upon its sprinkling God works many things, which by the sprinkling of the other, not blessed, water are nowise worked. For, although I keep silent about other things, an account has been presented which in book nine of the *Tripartite History*[2] Theodoret,[3] one of the three authors from which the *Tripartite* receives the name, speaks as follows.

For he relates that when the most pious Emperor Theodosius commanded the temples of the idols to be destroyed, a certain prefect of the city of Apamea went to destroy the temple of Jupiter, which he doubted that he would be able to do, for the very reason that the building was so strong, the stones placed in it were so great, joined to each other so firmly, that he deemed it impossible for him to be able to break apart the joints of the stones. And when a certain man came there, he promised to do this. Boring through three surrounding columns on which the whole building was mainly supported, and under their bases supporting the very strong timber he lit a fire, and yet the fire was not kindled: because a hideous demon appeared, who prevented the flame to work according to its powers.

---

[1] *Rituale Romanum*, Titulus 8, cap. 2.
[2] Chapters 33-34 (PL 69, 1149B-1151A). Theodoretus, bk. 5, chap. 20.
[3] Theodoret of Cyrus (c. 393-458/466 A.D.) was an influential theologian of the School of Antioch, biblical commentator, and Christian Bishop of Cyrus (423–457).

And when they had frequently done this, and they could not accomplish the demolition, they sent word to Marcellus, the Bishop of that city; who going to the church ordered that a container of water be put under the altar: but he prayed to the Lord prostrated on the ground, that he might rout the tyranny of the demon: lest an occasion of greater exaltation to the infidels be produced from this. When he had said these things, having made the sign of the Cross on the water, he ordered Equitius, a deacon of his, who was fortified with faith and zeal, to take the water and run quickly, and to sprinkle the fire with faith, and apply the flame. Which when it was done, the demon fled, being unable to endure the power of the water. What will the impious Lollards say about this? Did not that water change its nature through the prayer of the holy bishop, so that it not merely extinguished the fire, but rather enkindled it?

[Saint] Epiphanius relates another example similar to this in his *Contra haereses*, of a certain Jew converted to Christianity, whose name was Joseph, where he says these words: Joseph received letters and power from Constantine, came into Tiberias, and he also had a draft on the imperial treasury. And so he began to build in Tiberias. But lime was needed, and the other building material. He therefore had many ovens set up outside the city. But the crafty Jews tried with certain incantations to bind and scatter the fire. Wherefore Joseph having been stirred up, and seized with zeal towards the demon, ran outside the city and ordered water to be fetched in a vessel and took this vessel of water in the sight of all —a crowd of Jews had gathered to watch, eager to see how it would turn out and what Joseph would try to do. Tracing the sign of the Cross on the vessel with his own finger, and invoking the name of Jesus, he cried out, "In the name of Jesus of Nazareth, may there be power in this water to set at naught all sorcery and enchantment these men have wrought, and to work a miracle on the fire that the Lord's house may be finished." And he took the water into his hand and sprinkled the water on each furnace. And the spells were broken, and in the presence of all, the fire blazed up.[1]

On account of these and other similar things, which were experienced by the faithful, the Church approves the blessing of water, and commands it to be done, and yet not from yesterday or the day before, but it was derived proceeding from the very times of the Apostles until our own times. Pope Alexander I in fact, who was the fifth Roman pontiff after Blessed Peter, in his decrees which are circulated widely in the book of the Councils, says the following: "We bless water mingled with salt for the people, that all of them who shall be sprinkled with it may be cleansed and sanctified; and we direct all priests to do this. For as of old the ashes of the sacrificed victims, sprinkled with blood, purified and sanctified the people, how much more will they be sanctified by water mingled with salt and blessed with prayer! And if the unfruitfulness of the water was so healed by prayer when the prophet Eliseus sprinkled salt over it, how much more likely is this water sanctified by prayer to remove the unfruitfulness of earthly things, to sanctify the unholy, to increase all good things, to turn away the assaults of the devil, and to protect men against treacherous deceits. For if we believe that the sick were healed by the mere touching of the Saviour's garment, how much more will the elements be sanctified by God through the power of His sacred words, whereby feeble man seeks health of body and soul! Now, since we have received these and other ancient teachings and practices, pay attention, ye priests of the Lord, to the wishes of each one, and be careful, by the power of the Holy Ghost and prayer, to fulfil, by virtue of your office, all these wishes. Bless the elements—those of which I have just spoken as well as others that are used in God's service and are necessary to human weakness."[2] From which words it is evident that the use

---

[1] *Panarion*, bk. 1, heresy 30, c. 12 (PG 41, 426A-427B).

[2] *Decretum Gratiani*, dist. 3 (*De consecratione*), p. 8, c. 20 (*Aquam*) (PL 187, 1787C-1788A). "The letter written under the name of Pope Alexander I, who lived in the second century, is apocryphal and of more recent times" (*The Catholic Encyclopedia* (New York: Robert Appleton Company, 1910), vol. 7., p. 432).

of blessed water is not new, which the Church now holds: its great power is not from the nature of water, but by power of the blessing, or of the prayer, made over it. Thus the sprinkling of blessed water is not an infernal club, as the most wicked Flagellants falsely assert: the blessings or prayers said over it are not curses of demons, or incantations of necromancy, as the impious Lollards murmur.

Now what the Lollards object, namely that we wish by our blessings to make things better than God made them by their nature, this is so clearly true, that even they themselves, however much they resist, are bound to concede. God in fact creates new souls every day, which even if they are good by nature, nevertheless He does not create them good in grace: otherwise there would be no original sin in any of them when firstly created it adheres to the body: nevertheless after the exercise of good works they advance in morals, in which they were not created by God. But if they can be no wise made better than God made them by nature, they are taught in vain, in vain is goodness persuaded to them, in vain is it preached to them. It adds to these things that they would not be blamed if they do not become better: because this would be impossible for them, and so the whole fault will be in God rejecting them, Who did not create them better.

All which things are absurd, and full of impiety. Therefore, the impious Lollards ought not to be surprised that we say that creatures are rendered better by men's blessings, than they were created by God by nature: this nevertheless does not happen by men themselves, but by God on account of the merits of the preceding blessings and prayers. Now the special tradition of this blessing (as Augustine says) remained in the synagogue, and is celebrated in the Church in the weddings: where God's creatures are joined under God's blessing, and they become better therein, yet not by the one blessing or praying, but by God, that they be multiplied upon the earth.

Concerning this matter, namely regarding blessed water, its power and efficacy, wrote Cardinal Juan de Torquemada of Saint Sixtus, of the Dominican Order, which I admit that I have not seen, nor was I able to find:[1] which I lament, because since I consider him a learned man, he would have given me (I think) great helps. Johannes Trithemius[2] in his book, *De Scriptoribus Eccesiasticis*, wrote that this Cardinal wrote a book on this subject.

BAPTISMUS

Baptism

There are many things which one ought to hold and firmly believe about Baptism, namely that Baptism is a sacrament, the matter of Baptism is water, the words whereby one may be baptized are: "In the name of the Father, and of the Son, and of the Holy Ghost" etc., the power and efficacy of Baptism itself such that by it original sin is remitted iand grace is poured in from God. Now to all these things contrary heresies have arisen, which we will put in order, so that we will speak firstly about those which are opposed to the substance of Baptism: then we will treat those which oppose its power and efficacy.

The **first heresy**, then, is that which pertains to the matter (as more recent theologians speak), namely they do not baptize with water but with fire. This is the error of Seleucus and Hermias of Galatia, of whom we spoke above. Augustine in chapter fifty-nine of his book,

---

[1] *De efficacia aque benedictae* (Nuremberg, 1515); *Tractatus de aqua benedicta* (Rome, Stefano Guillery, 1524).

[2] Johannes Trithemius (1462-1516) was a famous scholar and Benedictine abbot, born at Trittenheim on the Moselle.

BAPTISMUS

De Haeresibus [ad Quodvultdeum], speaking about Seleucus and Hermias says that they did not baptize with water, yet he does not state with what they baptized.[1] But when Philastrius discusses them, he states that they baptized with fire: taking the occasion from what John the Baptist says in Matthew's Gospel when speaking about Christ: "He shall baptize you in the Holy Ghost and fire" (3, 11). Although the word, "fire," is not found in the Greek copies (as the very learned Erasmus warns)[2]: nevertheless Jerome[3] and Hilary[4] so read, and Chrysostom,[5] who was Greek, so reads, and also Cyril, also Greek, in his book, *De recta fide ad reginas*,[6] so cites this passage.

Wherefore admitting that passage, as it is cited, we say that Christ was to baptize in the Holy Ghost and with fire, because the Holy Ghost is fire: or because in this life we are baptized in the Spirit and with water, in the future life however we are baptized with fire, according to that passage of the Apostle: "The fire shall try every man's work, of what sort it is" (I Cor. 3, 13). And Jerome expounds this passage with this twofold interpretation,[7] and Hilary[8] likewise: and Christian Druthmar[9] follows them. And that this correct exposition of the text concerning the baptism of fire in relation to the time to come is sufficiently evident from the passage which immediately follows: "Whose fan is in his hand, and he will thoroughly cleanse his floor and gather his wheat into the barn; but the chaff he will burn with unquenchable fire" (Mt. 3, 12). From which words it is clear that the passage had spoken about the fire of the Judgment to come. But Nicholas of Lyra thinks that it was said, "in the Holy Ghost and fire," because in the early Church the Holy Ghost descended in the form of fire.[10] To me (so that I may speak candidly) the prior exposition is more pleasing.

It remains that we overcome this heresy, in which business it is appropriate to spend but little time, since the matter is very clearly opposed to passages of Holy Writ: "Going therefore,

---

[1] PL 42, 42.

[2] "Quod in nostris additum est, *et igni*, in nonnullis Graecorum exemplaribus erasum est, fortassis odio quorundam haereticorum, qui pro lotione utebantur inustura [That which is additional in our texts, 'and fire,' has been deleted in many Greek versions, perhaps due to hatred of certain heretics, who used burning instead of washing]" (Anne Reeve (ed.), *Erasmus' Annotations on the New Testament. The Gospels: facsimile of the final Latin text (1535) with all earlier variants (1516, 1519, 1522 and 1527)* (Duckworth, London, 1986), p. 21).

[3] PL 29, 544B.

[4] PL 9, 518C.

[5] Homily 11, n. 4 (PG 57, 196).

[6] PG 76, 1259D.

[7] "'He shall baptize you in the Holy Ghost and fire' (3, 11)... because the Holy Ghost is fire, as the Acts of the Apostles teach, Whom when He descended, sat as a fire upon each one of the believers (Acts 2, 3); and the word of the Lord was fulfilled saying: 'I am come to cast fire on the earth; and what will I, but that it be kindled?' (Lk. 12, 49). Or it is because presently we are baptized with the Spirit, and in the future with fire. The Apostle is also in agreement with this meaning: 'The fire shall try every man's work, of what sort it is' (I Cor. 3, 13)" (*Commentary on Matthew*, chap. 3, v. 11 (PL 26, 30B).

[8] PL 9, 518C.

[9] *Expositio in Mattheum*, c. 5 (PL 106, 1293D-1294A). "Christian Druthmar was born in Aquitania in the first part of the ninth century. Before the middle of the century he became a monk of the Benedictine monastery of old Corbie. About 850 he was called thence to the abbey of Stavelot-Malmédy, in the diocese of Liège, to teach the Bible to the monks. It is not known whether he died there or returned to Corbie" (Schaff, Philip. *History of the Christian Church*. Volume IV: Mediaeval Christianity. A.D. 590-1073. (Christian Classics Ethereal Library, Grand Rapids, MI, 1884) p. 172).

[10] "*And fire*. Because upon the newly baptized in the early Church it frequently appeared, namely as a visible sign, just as it appeared upon the Apostles as fiery tongues." (*Biblia sacra cum glossis, interlineari & ordinaria, Nicolai Lyrani postilla et moralitatibus...* (Lyon, Gaspar Trechsel, 1545), p. 14v).

teach ye all nations; baptizing them in the name of the Father, and of the Son, and of the Holy Ghost" (Mt. 28, 19) etc. Now "to baptize" in Greek, is the same thing as "to immerge" in Latin: and "baptism" is likewise the same thing as "immersion" or "washing." No one, however, washes with fire, but burns with fire: but we are washed with water. Furthermore when the Apostle Paul mentions Baptism, he says that Christ washed us "by the laver of water" (Eph. 5, 26), not however with the burning of fire. For so he says: "Husbands, love your wives, as Christ also loved the church, and delivered himself up for it: that he might sanctify it, cleansing it by the laver of water in the word of life: that he might present it to himself a glorious church, not having spot or wrinkle" (v. 25-27). Notice that the Apostle says a Church cleansed "by the laver of water," not however burnt "with fire." Again, the Apostles themselves (as appears in many passages of the Acts of the Apostles) baptized with water, not however with fire. Add to this that Our Lord Jesus Christ Himself was baptized by John, and by the contact with His most pure Flesh He sanctified the waters, and they could be the instrument of the Divine goodness for expiating sins, and to give us an example, that we should be baptized with water. Lastly as often as the Old Testament speaks figuratively (as it is accustomed to do) about this Sacrament, it designates it by the name of water: as in the book of Zacharias the Prophet it is said: "In that day there shall be a fountain open to the house of David, and to the inhabitants of Jerusalem: for the washing of the sinner, and of the unclean woman" (13, 1). And in the book of Ezechiel it is said: "And I will pour upon you clean water, and you shall be cleansed from all your filthiness, and I will cleanse you from all your idols" (36, 25). Therefore, it is very clear from passages of Sacred Writ that Baptism is to be done with water, and not with fire.

Finally against this heresy is the definition of the Council of Florence celebrated under [Pope] Eugene IV, which when speaking about the Sacrament of Baptism says: "The matter of this sacrament is real and natural water; it makes no difference whether cold or warm."[1]

The **second heresy** is about the form of this Sacrament, that is, about the words whereby Baptism is confected: because the words which the Church uses and which Christ taught His Apostles are not used. But some men baptize thus: "In the name of the unknown father of the universe; and the truth, the mother of the universe; and in him who descended upon Jesus." These men are the Marcosians, the disciples of a certain Mark, an expert of magical art, who lived about the time of the Apostles, of whom Irenaeus[2] and Eusebius[3] make mention. For this Marcus, followed by Cerdo and Marcion in this matter, among the other errors that he taught, said that the God Who was preached in the Law and the Prophets is not the Father of Our Lord Jesus Christ: because the former in fact, as he said, was unknown: the latter, however, was known: concerning which error we shall discuss elsewhere. Wherefore based upon this error the disciples of this Marcus were confecting Baptism thus: "In the name of the unknown father of the universe" etc. But other followers of this same man terrifyingly say Hebrew words over those whom they initiate to frighten their hearers. Concerning the Paulianists[4] and the Cataphrygians[5] it is said that they nowise baptize in the name of the Trinity, as is found in [Gratian's *Concordia discordantium canonum*, Causa] I, q. [I,] c. [53] *Paulianistae*.[6] Wherefore it was decreed at the Council of Nicea that when some of them return to the Catholic

---

[1] Bull *Exultate Deo*, Nov. 22, 1439 (Dz. 696).
[2] *Adversus Haereses*, lib. 1, c. 13 (PG 7, 578-594). Note that the reference here incorrectly cited chapter eight, perhaps by a confused of the Roman numeral V for X.
[3] *Ecclesiastical History*, lib. 4, c. 11 (PG 20, 330B).
[4] The Paulianists were the followers of Paul of Samosata (200-275 A.D.).
[5] I.e. the Montanists.
[6] PL 187, 505B.

Church, they ought to be rebaptized, because they do not have the correct form of Baptism and consequently neither do they have true Baptism.[1]

Now it is never read what form for baptism were they using, neither in Philastrius,[2] nor in Augustine[3] nor in Guy [the Carmelite],[4] who all speak of this matter. Now who the Cataphrygians are and in what time they began will be stated in the following heresy. But concerning the Paulianists will be stated in the section on Christ, in the first heresy. We will fight against all these men with the same arms. Since after having shown the true form of Baptism, it will become clear that all the others are worthless.

The true form of Baptism, which Christ taught, is related in the Gospel of Matthew: "Going therefore, teach ye all nations; baptizing them in the name of the Father, and of the Son, and of the Holy Ghost" (Mt. 28, 19). From which words it is concluded that there are three necessary things for the form of Baptism, namely an express pronouncement of the Trinity, and a word expressing the act itself of Baptism, and a word expressing the person baptized: "Baptizing," He says, "them in the name of the Father, and of the Son, and of the Holy Ghost."

Concerning the first [requirement] it is said in the *Apostolic Canons*: "If any bishop or presbyter, contrary to the ordinance of the Lord, does not baptize into the Father, the Son, and the Holy Ghost, but into three Unoriginated Beings, or three Sons, or three Comforters, let him be deposed."[5] Now so that the act itself of baptizing be conformed to the words, it is also prescribed that in the Baptism itself there be a threefold naming, which we also find to have been decreed by the Apostles themselves. For fiftieth Canon of the Apostles says the following: "If any bishop or presbyter does not perform the one initiation with three immersions, but with giving one immersion only, into the death of the Lord, let him be deposed. For the Lord said not, 'Baptize into my death,' but, 'Go, teach ye all nations, baptizing them in the name of the Father, and of the Son, and of the Holy Ghost.'"[6] Note how great was the Apostles' concern regarding the naming of the Trinity at Baptism, such that they were not satisfied with an explanation of the words, unless it would be confirmed with the display of a triple immersion.

But what is said there concerning the triple immersion ought not to be understood such that without it, Baptism could not be valid: because whether one immerse once, twice, or thrice the Baptism will be valid, provided that the other things needed for Baptism be present. Now the minister is obliged to perform Baptism with one or three immersions according to the custom of the place in which he lives. For concerning this matter it has already been decreed at the [Fourth] Synod of Toledo that every church may keep its own custom.[7] Now Spain, to take away the occasions of heresy which were arising from the triple immersion, chose at that

---

[1] "Concerning the Paulianists who have flown for refuge to the Catholic Church, it has been decreed that they must by all means be rebaptized" (Canon 19 (Dz. 56)).
[2] *De haeresibus*, c. 49 (PL 12, 1165-66; c. 64 (PL 12, 1178)).
[3] *De Haeresibus ad Quodvultdeum*, c. 44 (PL 42, 34).
[4] *Summa de haeresibus et earum confutationibus*, fol. 49r, c. 42.
[5] Canon 49 (PG137, 135D). The *Apostolic Canons* are "a collection of ancient ecclesiastical decrees (eighty-five in the Eastern, fifty in the Western Church) concerning the government and discipline of the Christian Church, incorporated with the Apostolic Constitutions (VIII, 47)" ("Apostolic Canons," *The Catholic Encyclopedia* (1908 ed.), vol. 3, pg. 279).
[6] "In the so-called *Decretum* of Pope Gelasius (429-96) [the *Apostolic Canons*] are denounced as an apocryphal book, i.e. not recognized by the Church (Thiel, *epistolæ Rom. pontificum genuinæ*, 1867, I, 53-58, 454-71; Von Funk, op. cit., II, 40), though this note of censure was probably not in the original *Decretum*, but with others was added under Pope Hormisdas (514-23)" (*Ibid.*, pg. 280).
[7] Canon 6 (*Collectio Canonum Ecclesiae Hispanae: Ex Probatissimis Ac Pervetustis Codicibus*, p. 368. Note that the text mistakenly gives canon five of the Synod of Toledo as the reference which has been corrected here.

Council a single immersion, namely lest anyone might suppose that there is a triple substance of the Divine Persons, just as the immersions were triple. Nevertheless, whether one baptizes with a single or multiple immersions, still the words always ought to be the same, namely such that the three Persons are named with their own names.

But if anyone were to object that the action of the Apostles, who baptized merely in Christ's name, without naming the other Persons, as the Apostolic history narrates, for the Samaritans were converted at Philip's preaching and were baptized "in the name of Jesus [Christ]" (Acts 8, 12): to this objection it will firstly be replied that which Blessed Ambrose says, namely that by "in the name of Jesus Christ" the whole Trinity is designated.[1] For since *Christus* in Latin means the same thing as "anointed," by this name is denoted, by a certain connection of things, both He Who was anointed, namely the Son, and by Whom He was anointed, namely the Father, and the anointing itself whereby He was anointed, namely the Holy Ghost.[2] Wherefore since in the name of Jesus Christ the whole Trinity is designated, the Apostles could (as he says) baptize in the name of Jesus.

It is otherwise replied, and perhaps more exactly according to the common opinion of more recent theologians, [that this was done] on account of the exaltation of the Name of Jesus Christ, which was "a stumblingblock, and unto the Gentiles foolishness" (I Cor. 1, 23). Which occasion having been removed, namely since the Name of the Lord Jesus has been exalted, no one is permitted to baptize having invoked this Name alone. But if it be objected that one would be bound to baptize in Christ's Name alone, there are various opinions among the Doctors whether the Baptism was invalid and unfruitful. Concerning which matter I do not wish to now decide anything, because in this work, I have determined to treat not human opinions but only the Catholic faith.

Now concerning the second [necessary thing for the form of Baptism], namely that a word expressing the act of Baptism be required: and similarly concerning the third [necessary thing for the form of Baptism], namely [that a word expressing] the person baptized [be required], it is evident from the very words of Christ Himself: "Baptizing them in the name of the Father," etc. Wherein the participle "baptizing" is used to express the act itself, and the pronoun "them" is used to express the persons baptized. Now that the act of baptizing be expressed by the verb in the present or another tense, for example in the imperative, what is necessary is not determined, because it cannot be well determined, since Christ in His words expressed the act of Baptism by a participle and not by a verb: He said, "baptizing them" etc. Wherefore the Roman Church as to this permits and tolerates the Greeks, who baptize with another form than the Latins. For they say the following: "May Christ's servant be baptized in the name of the Father, and of the Son and of the Holy Ghost." For since in the beginning of the nascent

---

[1] "So they were baptized in the Name of Jesus Christ, and Baptism was not repeated in their case, but administered differently, for there is but one Baptism. But where there is not the complete Sacrament of Baptism, there is not considered to be a commencement nor any kind of Baptism. But baptism is complete if one confess the Father, the Son, and the Holy Spirit. If you deny one [Person] you overthrow the whole [Trinity]. And just as if you mention in words one [Person] only, either the Father, or the Son, or the Holy Ghost, and in your belief do not deny either the Father, the Son, or the Holy Ghost, the mystery of the faith is complete, so, too, although you name the Father, Son, and Holy Ghost, and lessen the power of either the Father, the Son, or the Holy Ghost, the whole mystery is made empty" (*On the Holy Ghost*, bk. 1, chap. 3, n. 42 (PL 16, 713B-714A)). "Nevertheless all modern theologians teach that baptism cannot be *today* conferred in the name of Jesus, but the express mention of the three Persons of the Most Holy Trinity is required" (Prümmer, *Manuale Theologiae Moralis* (Friburg, Herder & Co., 1928), vol. 3, n. 103, p. 85).

[2] "If you name Christ, you imply both God the Father by Whom the Son was anointed, and the Son Himself Who was anointed, and the Holy Ghost with Whom He was anointed" (*On the Holy Ghost*, bk. 1, chap. 3, *n.* 44 (PL 16, 715A)).

Church such a schism arose, that everyone would think that he belonged that the one who had baptized him, such that one would say, "I am of Cephas": another said, "I am of Paul": reprehending whom the Apostle says: "Was Paul then crucified for you? or were you baptized in the name of Paul?" (I Cor. 1, 13). In order to eliminate this schism it was ordered among the Greeks that no one would baptize saying: "I baptize thee in the name of the Father," etc. but one would say: "May Christ's servant be baptized in the name of the Father" etc. lest in any way one show oneself by some words to be the author of the Baptism, but only the minister [of the Baptism].

Now that the complete form is contained in those words is evident, because in that formula there is a clear expression of the Trinity; in those words is expressed the act of baptizing, although in the imperative tense, which does not matter; and the person baptized [is expressed], although in the third person: thus nothing is lacking. Therefore the Greeks are not to be judged as heretics on account of this, namely because they so baptize: but because baptizing in this manner they believe that the Latins by using a different form do not confect Baptism. On account of this [the Greeks] are judged to be heretics, since by saying: "I baptize thee in the name of the Father," etc. everything necessary is also stated for the due form and to be conformed to Christ's words. And because the Greeks taking this occasion were separated from the obedience to the Roman Church, as also did others, thus they are called schismatics. [This may be proved] otherwise, for Alexander the third pontiff of this name said: "If anyone dip a child thrice in the water saying, 'In the name of the Father, and of the Son, and of the Holy Ghost, Amen,' without saying, 'I baptize thee in the name of the Father, and of the Son, and of the Holy Ghost, Amen,' the child is not baptized."[1]

This is my opinion (unless someone knows better, and a definition of the Church being excluded, to which I always submit myself) namely that it must be understood that however much someone be triply immersed in water, he is not believed to be baptized, even if such immersion is made in the name of the Father, Son and Holy Ghost, unless with this the act itself of baptism be also expressed. Now whether the act of the baptism itself be expressed in the indicative or in the imperative tense, concerning this the Pontiff does not decide in that passage, because the question about that matter was not being discussed there: and one ought to especially take notice of this: because Blessed Hilary says that from the circumstances of writings their true meaning very often depends. But if those words are absolutely required and necessary, as they are given by the Pontiff in the same passage, it would also be necessary that the pronoun "I" must also be expressed: such that it would also be said, "I baptize thee in the name of the Father," etc. And nevertheless, the Gloss on this passage says that the omission of that pronoun nowise impedes Baptism from being truly conferred.

Likewise, this is inferred from a reply of Pope Zachary, which is included in the book of *Decretals*.[2] For to someone [Bishop Boniface] inquiring whether one ought to be rebaptized who was baptized with these words: "Baptizo te in nomine Patria, et Filia, et Spiritu Sancta,"[3] the pope replied that if the one so baptizing says words of this sort out of ignorance of the Latin language, and not so that he may introduce some error through those words, he baptized validly, nor ought the one so baptized by him be rebaptized. And yet in those words (as it is evident), the pronoun "I" is not used: hence it is clear that the pronoun is not necessary, and this all theologians acknowledge. Therefore we say that the Greeks using their form baptize validly, although so baptizing they sin, because they disdain to submit to the Roman Church. For the Council of Florence celebrated under Eugene IV defined this very clearly, saying the

---

[1] X, lib. 3, tit. 42 (*De baptismo et eius effectu*), c. 1-2; III, q. 66, a. 9 ad 4um; Dz. 757.

[2] Gratian, *Concordia discordantium canonum*, p. 3 (*De consecratione*), dist. 4, c. 86 (*Retulerunt*) (PL 187, 1828B).

[3] The feminine gender is incorrectly used here instead of the masculine.

following: "We do not deny that true Baptism is conferred by the following words: 'May this servant of Christ be baptized in the name of the Father and of the Son and of the Holy Ghost; or, 'This person is baptized by my hands in the name of the Father and of the Son and of the Holy Ghost.' Since the Holy Trinity is the principle cause from which Baptism has its power and the minister is the instrumental cause who exteriorly bestows the sacrament, the Sacrament is conferred if the action is performed by the minister with the invocation of the Holy Trinity"[1]

Therefore we have shown that the true and precise form of Baptism, which Christ taught, which also was evident from the Gospel and from the *Apostolic Canons*: in which [form] three things are necessary, namely words indicating the act of Baptism, words expressing the person baptized, and an expression of the whole Trinity by their proper names. But if even the least of these be lacking, then just as the form is invalid, so also the Baptism is invalid. From which arguments we have proved that Marcosians, Paulianists, and Cataphrygians have erred in performing baptisms. Wherefore the Council of Nicea rightly decreed that they, when they return to the faith of the Church, must be rebaptized.

The **third heresy** is that which pertains to the person baptized. For there are those who baptize the dead, and these are the Cataphrygians, as Philastrius says;[2] yet Blessed Augustine in his *Liber de haeresibus* [*ad Quodvultdeum*] does not charge them of any such thing.[3] These Cataphrygians are so called because they originated from the province of Phyrygia. Their originators were Montanus, who said that he was the Paraclete, and his two prophetesses, namely Prisca and Maximilla, whom he boasted that he, Montanus, made [prophetesses by his inspiration. He who wishes to know more about which may read Eusebius,[4] and yet in the entire discourse of his work he does not accuse them of this error: even though he states many other errors of theirs. Against these Cataphrygians (as Eusebius relates in that same place) wrote Apollonius [Claudius, bishop] of Hierpolis,[5] Miltiades,[6] and Apollonius [of Ephesus].[7]

A **second heresy** is similar to this, or perhaps is the same, because Philastrius when speaking about the Cataphrygians, saying that they baptize the dead, does not explain how they were doing this. Regarding the Marcionites, however, Theophylactus when expounding the passage, "Otherwise what shall they do that are baptized for the dead, if the dead rise not again?" (I Cor. 15, 29), says the following: "It is the custom of the Marcionite heretics when someone of them dies without Baptism, hiding a living person under the bed of the dead man, they approach the bed, asking the dead man whether he wishes to be baptized. And when he who was hiding responds that he wishes, they thus baptize him in place of the dead man. Then when they are accused about this, they defend themselves with this passage; affirming that the Apostle had said this, the stupid men produce this text."[8] Thus I have cited him, because I find none of those who wrote about the heresies, have mentioned this matter. For although

---

[1] Sess. 8, Nov. 22, 1439 (Decree of union with the Armenians).

[2] *De haeresibus* c. 49 (PL 12, 1166A).

[3] C. 26 (PL 42, 30).

[4] *Ecclesiastical History*, lib. 5, c. 16-19 (PG 20, 464-483).

[5] Saint Apollinaris Claudius was a Christian apologist and Bishop of Hierapolis in Phrygia in the second century.

[6] Miltiades was a rhetorician of Asia Minor who composed his *Apology for Christian Philosophy* during the years 161-180 A.D.

[7] Apollonius of Ephesus was an anti-Montanist Greek ecclesiastical writer, between 180 and 210, probably from Asia Minor.

[8] PG 124, 767C.

BAPTISMUS   -179-

Philastrius,[1] Augustine,[2] and Guy [the Carmelite][3] speak about Marcion and his errors, nevertheless they do not relate that he opined anything of the sort. And neither does Eusebius, who wrote about him in the fourth book of his *Ecclesiastical History*, ever accuse him of this error.[4] Likewise, nor does Tertullian, when enumerating the errors of Marcion in his book on heresies,[5] ever make mention of this. Finally, Irenaeus in the first book of his *Adversus Haereses* when discussing Marcion's errors, does not charge him with any such thing.[6]

Wherefore I do not cease to wonder from whence did Theophylactus, who succeeded these men after many centuries, determine that this error was Marcion's? But if we look more circumspectly, Theophylactus does not say that this was the error of Marcion, but of the Marcionites. Yet it is the custom of heretics, who follow in the footsteps of other heretics, that they are never content with the errors of their masters, but always strive to increase their madness, adding something of impiety. Hence it was possible that the followers of Marcion joined this heresy to their errors, and so those first writers did not mention it. Theophylactus, however, who lived later, could have said these things about the Marcionites, yet not about Marcion. Thus since we mentioned Marcion, it will now be worthwhile to discuss who he was.

Marcion (as Irenaeus and Tertullian wrote), by birth a Pontic, during the time of Antoninus Pius was firstly instructed especially in the teachings of the Stoic philosophers. Having then converted to the faith of Christ, followed the doctrine of Cerdo and attempted to insert many things from philosophical teaching into the Catholic faith: and coming to Rome he seduced many men there. When afterwards he found the martyr Polycarp there, saluting him, he said: "Do you know me?" To whom Polycarp said: "I know the firstborn of Satan."[7] He accepted no Gospel except Luke's Gospel, and it was shorted by him. Likewise he cut down the Epistles of the Apostle Paul, taking away from them whatever seemed opposed to his impiety. Many very weighty authors wrote against this man: Dionysius, Bishop of the Corinthians; Philip the Cretan;[8] Hippolytus [of Rome];[9] the Asian Rhodon;[10] Irenaeus, Bishop of Lyon; and Tertullian. Only [the writings of] the last two (as far as I know) still exist. Therefore, these things once said may serve for hereafter.

Now we have dealt with the error of both the Marcionites and the Cataphrygians, and between the two there is an agreement on this matter, namely that they think that Baptism benefits the dead. Which error is proved to be false from the fact that after death there is no longer time for doing well or badly. This life is granted to us by God, during which we may labor: which having ended, that which each has done in his life will be rewarded. For so the Wise Man says: "If the tree fall to the south, or to the north, in what place soever it shall fall, there shall it be" (Eccle. 11, 3). He designated man by the word "tree," which falls down when it dies. Now it falls to the south, which wind is hot and humid, when a man departs in grace. For

---

[1] *Liber de haeresibus*, c. 45 (PL 12, 1160-1162).
[2] C. 22 (PL 42, 29).
[3] *Summa de haeresibus*, f. 49v, c. 20.
[4] C. 11, n. 9 (PG 20, 331A).
[5] *De Praescriptione Haereticorum* (On the Prescription of Heretics), c. 30 (PL 2, 41-43).
[6] C. 29 and lib. 4, c. 57.
[7] *Ecclesiastical History*, bk. 4, c. 14, n. 7 (PG 20, 339A).
[8] I.e. Philip Bishop of Gortyna on Crete (died 180 A.D.).
[9] The text says that he was an African bishop, but this may be due to the fact that his life was not well known at that time. "Until the publication in 1851 of the recently discovered 'Philosophumena,' it was impossible to obtain any definite authentic facts concerning Hippolytus of Rome and his life" ("St. Hippolytus of Rome," *The Catholic Encyclopedia*, (New York, Robert Appleton Company, 1910), vol. 7, p. 360). But it was St. Hippolytus of Rome who wrote against Marcion in his *Refutation of All Heresies*.
[10] He wrote *Against Marcion*, a lost work mentioned in Eusebius' *Church History*.

when that wind is blowing, by which graces is designated, water rains down. Again, he is said to fall to the north, who dies in sin: which is rightly depicted by the north, because that wind is cold and drives away the rains. And he again says more expressly: "For the living know that they shall die, but the dead know nothing more, neither have they a reward any more: for the memory of them is forgotten. Their love also, and their hatred, and their envy are all perished, neither have they any part in this world, and in the work that is done under the sun" (Eccle. 9, 5-6). Therefore, if they do not have a reward hereafter, nor part in the work which is done under the sun: how can Baptism which is conferred upon a man brought down alive to the place of the dead, benefit a dead man? Furthermore, if from the dead man, as though he were someone who does not exist, praise perishes (as the other Wise Man says),[1] why will not Baptism also perish, which is the gate of the other Sacraments?

Again, when the Lord showed the necessity of Baptism, and He entrusted to the Apostles for it to be preached, He said: "Going therefore, teach ye all nations; baptizing them in the name of the Father, and of the Son, and of the Holy Ghost" (Mt. 28, 19). In which passage He did not say that one man may be baptized for another, but each one for himself. "Baptizing," He said, "them." And it is said more explicitly in Mark: "Go ye into the whole world, and preach the gospel to every creature. He that believeth and is baptized, shall be saved: but he that believeth not shall be condemned" (16, 15-16). Thus, he who dies without Baptism, no matter how much a substitute with his name takes his place, will never be said to have been baptized: hence it happens that he necessarily perished, because he was not baptized.

Then I will ask those men: Why do they think that he who died without Baptism attained glory? It is necessary that he go to Hell or to glory or be on the way to glory, meaning in Purgatory. It ought not to be said that he attained glory, nor that he is on the way to glory: otherwise, Baptism would not be necessary, since without it one could be saved. Therefore, he will be in Hell, because according to the Gospel, he who is not baptized will be condemned,[2] just as though he did not believe. If, therefore, he is in fact in Hell, "there is no redemption [in Hell]" (as the Church sings).[3] And the Wise Man says: "Whatsoever thy hand is able to do, do it earnestly: for neither work, nor reason, nor wisdom, nor knowledge shall be in hell, whither thou art hastening" (Eccle. 9, 10). And the Lord said in Saint John's Gospel: "The night cometh, when no man can work" (Jn. 9, 4): calling the time after death "night" (as Blessed Augustine says) in which it is not permitted for anyone to work.[4] Therefore, He said: "Work while it is day," that is to say, "while you are in this life: because after death you can do nothing."

Hence the insane Marcionites and Cataphrygians wickedly attempted to baptize the dead. Now the passage of Paul which they cite: "Otherwise what shall they do that are baptized for the dead, if the dead rise not again at all? why are they then baptized for them?" (I Cor. 15, 29) nowise supports their view: since in fact it is derived from a misunderstanding. Hence, Theophylactus when expounding this passage says: "All who are about to be baptized recite the Symbol of faith. For in that Symbol, among other things this is set forth, 'I believe in the resurrection of the dead.' Therefore, [Saint Paul] is saying: 'Those who have believed in the future resurrection of dead bodies, and were baptized with such hope, what will they do if they were deceived? Now why are men baptized precisely for the resurrection, that is to say in

---

[1] "Praise perisheth from the dead as nothing" (Eccli. 17, 26).

[2] Cf. Mk. 16, 16; Jn. 3, 5.

[3] Taken from the third nocturn of Matins of the Office of the Dead. *Peccantem me quotidie, et non poenitentem, timor mortis conturbat me. Quia in inferno nulla est redemptio, miserere mei, Deus, et salva me.* ("Sinning daily, and not repenting, the fear of death disturbs me. For there is no redemption in Hell, have mercy on me, o God, and save me.").

[4] *In Ioannis evangelium tractatus CXXIV*, 4-6 (PL 35, 1715).

expectation of the resurrection, if the dead are not raised up?'"[1] According to whom it matters so much that they are baptized for the dead, as though he were to say, they are baptized in expectation of the resurrection.[2]

But because this exposition is too forced, and departing from the literal meaning too much: thus it is replied with [Ambrosiaster], who in my opinion expounds much better and more literally. For He expounds as follows: "[Saint Paul] is so eager to defend the resurrection of the dead as signed, sealed and delivered that he cites the example of people who were so convinced of the coming resurrection that they had themselves baptized on behalf of the dead—if death had accidentally overtaken someone. It seems that people were baptized for the dead because they were afraid that someone who was not baptized would either not rise at all or else rise merely in order to be condemned. A living person would therefore be immersed on behalf of dead one, and Paul asks: 'Why are people baptized on their behalf?' In citing this example, Paul is not showing approval of their behavior, but merely illustrating what a firm faith in the resurrection had led to in their case. Remember that Jephte too was found faithful, even though it was in a matter which, according to the account which has come down to us, is unbearable—he sacrificed his daughter in order to keep the vow that he had foolishly sworn.[3] It is not the action, therefore, of which Paul approves, but the perseverance in faith to which it bears witness. Paul made a distinction between different types of people, making it clear that those who were baptized on behalf of the dead were not Catholics. What he said was, 'Why are they then baptized for the dead?' not 'Why are we being baptized on their behalf?'"[4] Thus from this excellent exposition of this passage it is evident that that custom, which Theophylactus ascribes to the Marcionites, that a living person would be baptized for one who is dead, already began by some at Paul's time, although it was not approved. Therefore, I again marvel that Theophylactus attributes it to the Marcionites, because Marcion, their leader, lived nearly a hundred years after the Blessed Apostle Paul: since he lived at the time of Antoninus Pius, but Paul died under Nero.

In order to avoid heresies of this kind, the Third Synod of Carthage made this decree: "It also seemed good that the Eucharist should not be given to the bodies of the dead. For it is written: 'Take, Eat,' but the bodies of the dead can neither 'take' nor 'eat.' Nor let the ignorance of the presbyters baptize those who are dead."[5]

A **fourth heresy** is about the efficacy and power of Baptism, which certain men try to diminish so much that they attribute no power to Baptism. Yet heretics tend to this end in various ways. For the Messalians, who are also the Euchites, that is, they are called "praying folk," but not the *Euchidiae* (as the *Catalogus haereticorum* corruptly names them),[6] give such power to prayer, that they say that is suffices for remitting all sins: wherefore they are called ευχεται, that is, "praying folk."[7] For this reason they belittle Baptism, saying that no

---

[1] *Expositio in Epist. I ad Corinthios* (PG 124, 767C).

[2] "By 'dead' the works of sin are understood. They are dead, because they lack the life of grace and lead to death: 'The blood of Christ shall cleanse our conscience from dead works' (Heb 9:14). And according to this the words are plain. 'What shall they do that are baptized for the dead?' i.e., for washing away their sins, if they are not to have the life of grace?" (Saint Thomas Aquinas, *Commentary on I Corinthians*, c. 15, v. 29).

[3] Judges 11, 30-40.

[4] *Commentaria in epistolam ad corinthios primam* (PL 17, 265D-266A). The text here cites Saint Ambrose but this text is commonly attributed to "Ambrosiaster," i.e. PseudoAmbrosius.

[5] *Codex canonum ecclesiasticorum*, Canon 18 (PL 67, 189D-190A).

[6] Fol. 37r.

[7] "They are also called Euchites from the Greek translation of their Oriental name (*euchetai* from *euchomai*, to pray)" ("Massalians," *The Catholic Encyclopedia* (1911 ed.), vol. 10).

benefit comes to those baptized from sacred Baptism, but only fervent prayer is useful for putting the devil to flight. These men are also called Messalians and Enthusiasts, that is, the inspired and prophetic.[1]

The *Catalogus Haereticorum*, however, in the section on "Messalians" calls them *Anthyatistas*, yet by way of a corruption of the word, not knowing what to say, since it was so written in the writings of some author whom he found.[2] Wherefore from a putrid lake it drew putrid water. It also errs in the section on "Elpulius,"[3] where it speaks of a certain old man of this pestilential faction, from whom Flavianus, an Antiochian ruler, by a marvelous trick and through flatteries wrested so that he would reveal the sect of those men to him. The *Catalogus* calls this man Elpulius, although in book seven, chapter two of the *Historia Tripartite*, where these things are told, he is called Adelphius, and not Elpulius.[4] And this change cannot be ascribed to the printer, because it lists the names of the heretics in alphabetical order: now it is placed among the names that begin with the letter "e." The leaders of this faction were (as the *Historia Tripartita* relates in the place just cited) Dadosius, Sabas, Alelphius, Hermas and Symeones.[5]

Otherwise regarding the present error, Blessed Augustine when treating of the Messalians in his *De Haeresibus*, does not mention this error.[6] Guy [the Carmelite], however, much later, makes absolutely no mention of the Messalians or Massalians, or under any other name. But we have taken these things from the *Historia Tripartita*. The Manichaeans, however, not due to the fact that they attributed much to prayer but because they wanted to detract Baptism, say that which is produced with water avails nothing for salvation to anyone. For Augustine relates this about them in his *De Haeresibus*.[7] After them others in their place are summoned forth, namely the Albigenses, who even say that Baptism has no efficacy. Now the Albigenses completely reject Baptism, whom we rightly insert here: for having proved against them its power and necessity, the Albigenses will be forced to receive the Sacrament of Baptism. Concerning these men as to who they are, however, we have already said above.[8] Finally Pierre Jean [Olivi], about whom we have already spoken elsewhere (as Guy the Carmelite accuses him) says that in Baptism grace and the virtues which are commonly call the theological virtues, are nowise infused.[9]

Now the Armenians remove the power of conferring grace from all the sacraments. To these men in this respect Martin Luther consents, who although he admitted very few sacraments, nevertheless he says about them in general that they do not confer any grace, for in his book, *The Babylonian Captivity of the Church*, he says the following: "It is a heretical opinion, but a common one, that the sacraments of the New Law give pardoning grace to those who do

---

[1] "They have also another designation which arose naturally from their mode of action. From their coming under the influence of a certain demon, which they supposed to be the advent of the Holy Ghost, they are called enthusiasts" (Theodoret, *Ecclesiastical History*, lib. 4, c. 10). An incorrect translation of *Enthysiastae* as "sacrificers," published by Cassiodorus has been deleted here.

[2] Fol. 57r.

[3] Fol. 37r.

[4] PL 69, 1078A.

[5] The spelling of these names has been modified following the spelling in the *Historia Tripartita* (PL 69, 1077D).

[6] PL 42, 40.

[7] Chapter 46 (PL, 42, 38).

[8] In the section on the "Soul" [*Anima*], in eighth heresy.

[9] *Summa de haeresibus et earum confutationibus*, fol. 103v, c. 1.

BAPTISMUS

not set up an obstacle."[1] Hence since he says this concerning all the sacraments, it ought to be referred to Baptism. Wherefore this assertion of his ought to have been adjoined to these.

It ought to be treated against all these heretics at the same time, since they all agree among themselves on this point. Firstly, therefore, this heresy is refuted by that which is said in Mark 16: "He that believeth and is baptized, shall be saved" (v. 16). But since no one may be saved without sanctifying grace, it ought to occur that Baptism itself confers grace, though which the one baptized is justified, and having been justified is saved. For "If the just man shall scarcely be saved, where shall the ungodly and the sinner appear?" (I Pet. 4, 18). To this Blessed Peter seems to somewhat allude saying: "They waited for the patience of God in the days of Noe, when the ark was a building: wherein a few, that is, eight souls, were saved by water" (I Pet. 3, 20): because Baptism also now saves us in a similar fashion. Blessed Peter explains the likeness between the figure and the thing figured, where he says: as those who lived in Noe's time were saved as to the bodily life through water: so now we may be saved as to the spiritual life of the soul through the water of Baptism, the cleaner of sins.

Therefore, Baptism has this efficacy and power that it may save men. Now this salvation cannot be without God's grace, as the Apostle says: "For by grace you are saved through faith, and that not of yourselves, for it is the gift of God" (Eph. 2, 8). Furthermore, the Lord says: "Unless a man be born again, he cannot see the kingdom of God" (Jn. 3, 3). Now such a rebirth from water and the Holy Ghost does not happen except through the water of Baptism, in which the grace of the Holy Ghost is conferred. In fact, the Holy Ghost never gives a spiritual rebirth without the infusion of His grace: because God's charity is poured out into men's hearts as often as the Holy Ghost is given to them. Again Blessed Peter speaking on the day of Pentecost to the Jews repentant by his preaching, says: "Do penance, and be baptized every one of you in the name of Jesus Christ, for the remission of your sins: and you shall receive the gift of the Holy Ghost" (Acts 2, 38). From which words two things are evident: Firstly that Baptism is beneficial for the remission of sins, because it is also evident from the Nicene Creed, where it is said: "I confess one baptism for the remission of sins." But without the conferral of grace there is no remission of sins.

The second point is that the gift of the Holy Ghost is received through Baptism: "You shall receive the gift of the Holy Ghost" (Acts 2, 38). Now the gift of the Holy Ghost is grace and faith, which are infused at Baptism: because "Without faith it is impossible to please God" (Heb. 11, 6), says Paul. Now if the one baptized would not please God, he would not be saved. But Baptism confers faith as well as grace: for both are the gift of God. Then this opinion is also proved by Paul's words, who says: "Know you not that all we, who are baptized in Christ Jesus, are baptized in his death? For we are buried together with him by baptism into death; that as Christ is risen from the dead by the glory of the Father, so we also may walk in newness of life. For if we have been planted together in the likeness of his death, we shall be also in the likeness of his resurrection. Knowing this, that our old man is crucified with him, that the body of sin may be destroyed, to the end that we may serve sin no longer" (Rom. 6, 3-6). From which words it is apparent that he attributes that renovation of life to Baptism.

Now such newness pertains to grace: because just as oldness refers to sin, so newness to grace. And he says: "As many of you as have been baptized in Christ, have put on Christ" (Gal. 3, 27). Now what is it to put on Christ, except to have His grace, by which we are covered as though by a garment? For so Jerome expounding these words says: "If anyone has received only the bodily Baptism of water that is visible to fleshly eyes, he has not clothed himself with the Lord Jesus Christ. For Simon [the magician] in the Acts of the Apostles had received the Baptism of water, yet he had not clothed himself with Christ because he did

---

[1] *Exsurge Domine*, §2, n. 1 (Dz. 741).

not have the Holy Ghost."[1] And Theophylactus when expounding the same words says: "He shows how we are sons of God by strengthening, namely through Baptism. Now He did not say, 'As many of you are baptized, you are made sons of God,' as though the conclusion was postulating; but what is much more tremendous, 'You have put on Christ.' For if we have put on Christ the Son of God, and we have been assimilated to Him: we are made one thought and one idea with Him, and by grace we are made what He is by nature."[2]

And Paul confirms the same opinion saying: "But when the goodness and kindness of God our Saviour appeared: not by the works of justice, which we have done, but according to his mercy, he saved us, by the laver of regeneration, and renovation of the Holy Ghost; Whom he hath poured forth upon us abundantly, through Jesus Christ our Saviour: that, being justified by his grace, we may be heirs, according to hope of life everlasting" (Titus 3, 4-7). Nothing could be said more expressly than these words: for he says that He saved us "by the laver of regeneration": moreover, He washed us, "that, being justified by his grace," "we may be made heirs of eternal life" (I Pet. 3, 22). Therefore, it is manifest that by these quite clear quotations of Scripture that Baptism has the efficacy and power of remitting sins and conferring grace.

Against this heresy is the decree of the Council of Florence, celebrated under Eugene IV: because speaking about the sacrament of Baptism he says the following: "The effect of this sacrament is the remission of every sin, original and actual, also of every punishment which is due to the sin itself. Therefore, no satisfaction must be enjoined for past sins upon those who immediately attain to the kingdom of Heaven and the vision of God."[3] By which words not only the Messalians, but also the error of Pierre Jean [Olivi] is refuted, because by Baptism sin is remitted, and the kingdom of Heaven bestowed, neither of which can happen without grace.

The **fifth heresy** asserts that Baptism does not benefit infants lacking the use of reason: because infants not having had the use of reason are unable to have faith, nor can they believe God's word which has been preached to them. This, however, they say is most necessary for everyone receiving Baptism: if anyone, however, without previous faith had received Baptism, they say that Baptism does not benefit him at all. The leader and originator of this heresy was a certain Peter of Bruis,[4] a Frenchman from the province of Narbonne: in which place he infected many men with this heresy and many others. Therefore he was burned in the town of Saint Gilles on account of his crimes, as Peter the Venerable, abbot of Cluny, relates in the small treatise which he wrote against his errors.[5]

From this Peter of Bruis the Petrobrusian heretics are named. After the death of this Peter of Bruis, a certain Henry received his standard, from whom also the Henricians are named, who not only accepted those heresies which Peter of Bruis had taught, but added many others in addition. Now at what time this Henry lived, and what sort of person he was is evident from a letter of Saint Bernard, which he wrote to Alphonsus,[6] a fellow citizen of Saint Gilles, where he says these things about this Henry who was living at that time: "An apostate who has cast off his religious habit (for he was a monk), and returned to the world and to the filthiness of the flesh like a dog to its vomit. Ashamed to live amongst kinsmen and those who know him, or rather not permitted to do so on account of his monstrous crimes, he has girded himself and taken to the road to where he is not known, becoming a vagabond and fugitive on the

---

[1] *Commentaria in Epistolam ad Galatas*, lib. 2 (PL 26, 369A-B).
[2] *Expositio in Epistolam ad Galatas* (PG 124, 995A).
[3] Decree for the Armenians (from the Bull *Exultate Deo*, Nov. 22, 1439), Dz. 696.
[4] He died about the year 1131.
[5] Blessed Peter of Montboissier, *Epistola sive tractatus adversus Petrobrusianos Haereticos* (PL 189, 719ff).
[6] Count of Saint Giles and Toulouse.

face of the earth. When he began to seek a living he sold the Gospel (he is an educated man), scattering the word of God for money and preaching so that he might live. If he is able to secure something over and above his keep from the simple people or some elderly women, he squanders it in gambling or more shameful ways. Frequently indeed after a day of popular adulation this distinguished preacher is to be found with prostitutes, sometimes even with married women."[1] Certain heretics commonly known as the Anabaptists recalled this heresy from Hell, buried for more than four hundred years until our time, who embraced all the heresies of the Petrobrusian and Henricians to the last one, and added others in addition.

Against this heresy there is a very clear and strong argument, namely that those not yet having the use of reason are capable of eternal salvation and the kingdom of Heaven, and hence it is very clearly concluded that they are capable of Baptism. Because without Baptism actually received, or at least willed when it cannot be actually received, someone is unable to attain eternal salvation or enter the kingdom of Heaven. "Unless a man be born again of water and the Holy Ghost, he cannot enter into the kingdom of God" (Jn. 3, 5). Therefore it is necessary to admit that infants are capable of Baptism: or if they try to deny this, they are then forced also to deny that children are capable of the kingdom of Heaven, because they cannot attain this without Baptism. But if these heretics wish to be so cruel to the infants, such that they are not ashamed to drive them away from the kingdom of Heaven, Christ our Lord immediately refutes these heretics themselves, saying: "Suffer the little children to come unto me, and forbid them not; for of such is the kingdom of God" (Mk. 10, 14). By which words the Savior doubly rebukes these Anabaptists, and indeed very clearly. Firstly in fact since He says: "Suffer the little children to come unto me, and forbid them not."

But let us see first who they are who come to Christ and how they come, and then we will more clearly know who they are who forbid [them] to come to Christ: who are here reprehended by Christ. Of those who come to Christ, not all depart from the same nor from an equally distant place, and thus do not come the same way. For there are many who remaining in the Catholic faith, fall into various mortal sins, and so withdraw from God. Concerning all these the Prophet Isaias said, and afterwards the Savior confirmed: "This people honoureth me with their lips: but their heart is far from me" (Is. 29, 13; Mt. 15, 8). And among these men the farther one goes away, so many the more and graver [sins] he commits. For so Blessed Gregory teaches, saying the following: "For the mind approaches by so many steps nearer to God, as it makes progress in so many holy emotions. And, again, it departs so many steps further from Him, as it becomes depraved by so many evil thoughts."[2] If all these men wish to come to God, they have only one way, namely repentance by which we may come to God.

Again there are others who completely lack the Catholic faith, and to these men the Catholic faith is necessary so that they can arrive at God. "He that cometh to God," Paul says, "must believe that he is, and is a rewarder to them that seek him" (Heb. 11, 6). For if he who lacks faith is moreover ensnared with mortal sin, the double way is necessary for this man so that he can reach God: because faith is not enough for him, unless he moreover adds repentance of his sins. But if he is not infected with any mortal sin, but merely lacks faith, for this man only faith with Baptism is necessary and sufficient so that he may be able to approach God. "He that believeth and is baptized," says the Savior, "shall be saved: but he that believeth not shall be condemned" (Mk. 16, 16).

Such are infants before Baptism, because even if they are not guilty of any mortal sin, because they can nowise commit it without the use of reason, still they lack the Catholic faith. On account of this defect and on account of original sin, in which they are born, they are so far away from God that they are called, and are, "children of wrath" (Eph. 2, 3). For without

---

[1] *Episotla* 241 (PL 182, 435B-C).
[2] *Moralium* p. 5, lib. 25, c. 5, n. 7 (PL 76, 323B).

it they cannot be reborn, nor be children of God. The Anabaptists, who drive away children from Baptism, are refuted by all these things. It is they who forbid the children lest they come to God, and whom Christ reprehends saying: "Suffer the little children to come unto me, and forbid them not; for of such is the kingdom of God" (Mk. 10, 14). And the latter phrase is the second phrase whereby the Anabaptists are reprehended by Christ's words. For Christ says that the kingdom of Heaven pertains to children. But the Anabaptists try to keep them away from the kingdom of Heaven, because without Baptism they cannot attain it.

Furthermore, the Savior likewise says: "Come to me, all you that labour, and are burdened, and I will refresh you" (Mt. 11, 28). This saying has exactly the same promise, although worded differently. For it is to say exactly the same thing to say, "I will refresh you" and to say, "for of such is the kingdom of God." And on the other hand, all who have the right to the kingdom of Heaven are also spiritually refreshed now by Christ dwelling in them through the grace of the Holy Ghost, and afterwards through eternal glory.

Thus since this and that promise are the same, it is necessary that we note who they are to whom He gives this promise, and what He requires from them so that they may enjoy this promise. "Come to me," He says, "all you that labour, and are burdened." He summons those who "labour, and are burdened," but who they are Theophylactus teaches us very well, saying the following: "He calls all mankind, not only the Jews, but also the Gentiles. By those "that labour" understand the Jews, who follow the strict observances of the Law and labor in the occupation of fulfilling the commandments of the Law. Those who are "burdened" are the Gentiles, who are oppressed by the burden of sins."[1] To all these He promises refreshment, and He commands them to come to Him. And saying: "Come to me," He excepts no one, He excludes no one, but He calls all to Himself, children as well as adults. For children are weighed down and burdened, although with not as great of a burden as an adult: because adults are weighed down with the weight of mortal sin, but children are burdened with just original sin (which is much smaller sin than mortal sin).

Perhaps at this point the Anabaptists will reply that those commands, which we have just recalled, were not given to children but only to adults: because children cannot come to God: because they can neither know Christ, nor consequently are they able to have that faith which is necessary for coming to Christ. This reply comes from an exceedingly crass ignorance. For they show that they are ignorant of how great is the difference between children and adults in their manner of coming to Christ. For the difference is the same in the manner of spiritually coming, which of old was in the manner of approaching to the very person of Christ corporeally. Since in fact adults, especially healthy adults who were healthy in body, who wished to approach Christ corporeally, approached with their own feet, and were going to Him: but the children were not coming to Christ with their own but others' feet (because they were unable to move themselves). In exactly the same way they are distinguished in their way of spiritually coming to Christ. For adults (in that they have the use of reason and free will) ought to come by their own faith if they wish to come spiritually to Christ. But children, because they do not have the use of reason or of free will, come by another's faith, that is to say, come to Christ by the faith of their parents, or at least by the faith of our mother, the Catholic Church, when they are carried by their parents or others to receive Baptism. Thus another's faith does this for receiving the fruit of Baptism for children, which one's own faith does for adults.

Blessed Bernard gives clear testimony concerning this matter in a letter to Master Hugo of Saint Victor saying the following: "Certainly infants who are unable to have this faith (their age prohibiting), meaning the conversion of the heart to God, consequently have not salvation if they die without having received Baptism. Not that they actually completely lack faith when they are baptized, without which 'it is impossible to please God' (Heb. 11, 6): but they

---

[1] PG 128, 258C.

are also themselves saved by faith, yet not their own but another's. It is doubtlessly fitting and it pertains to God's goodness that to those whose age does not permit them to have their own faith, He would graciously deign that another's faith would be beneficial for them."[1] Augustine supports the same view saying the following: "Men often inquire what benefit the sacrament of Christ's Baptism brings to children, since many die after having received it before they could know anything about it for themselves. In which matter it is piously enough and rightly believed that the faith of those by whom it is offered to be consecrated benefits the children. And the authority of the Church supports this, wherefore, anyone may perceive what benefit his own faith has for himself, when you can lend it to help others who do not yet have their own faith."[2] These words of Augustine are also cited by Gratian.[3]

Now if the Anabaptists contend that those words of Christ, "Come to me, all you that labour" refer only to adults, I will never argue with them about this, but I will rather use their opinion to confirm my view. For if they would say this, then this difference which we have shown to exist between children and adults about the way of coming to Christ, could be much better concluded from the variance of those two sayings of Christ, which we have cited recently above. For thus Christ said to the adults simply, or to the Anabaptists themselves: "Come all you to me," because adults could hear and understand the command, and fulfill it themselves. Inasmuch as those who come to Christ with their own feet and own movement, and use of their own reason and own will could believe in Christ and love Him. But He did not say to children, "Come," because they could not do this by their own will and own feet, but to their parents, or their guardians, whose help children need, Christ commands, "Suffer the little children to come unto me, and forbid them not." It is as though He were to say: "I want the children to come to me, but because they cannot do it by themselves and with their own feet, do not forbid them in any way, but help them instead."

And in order to say this more clearly, I wish to make this understood by another very similar example. By this precept: "Thou shalt not kill," it is not merely forbidden for any man to kill himself with a sword, with a rope, by starving, or by any other means: but it is also commanded the one avoid every, especially great danger of death. But because infant children are unable to avoid it of themselves, doubtlessly we understand that this was commanded to their parents or guardians, that they protect them and do not allow them to go headlong into a danger of death. If, however, due to exceeding negligence of the parents, their children fall into fire, or water or the sword and so die, the children themselves die by no fault of their own. Yet the parents themselves or their guardians will be judged before God regarding the matter of their death, due to the fact that they did not avoid the danger of death, when they were able to do so.

It happens in just the same way to children in the present case of Baptism: because although they ought to come to Baptism to gain the salvation of their souls, nevertheless it was not expressly said to them that they come, but it was commanded to us all that we allow them to come, such that we nowise prohibit them. But it was commanded to their parents or guardians not merely they would not prohibit them, but also that they carry them, or arrange for them to be carried to Baptism. And if perhaps on account of a great negligence of the parents or guardians it happens that a child dies without Baptism, no fault will be imputed to the child on account of the omission of Baptism, but only to his parents or guardians. From all these things it is clearly proved that the faith of another suffices for children, because they cannot have their own faith for the reception of Baptism, and by it they come very well to Christ.

---

[1] *De Baptismo allisque questionibus ab ipso propositis ad Hugonem de Santo-Victore*, c. 2, n. 9 (PL 182, 1037D).

[2] *De libero arbitrio*, lib. 3, c. 23, n. 67 (PL 32, 1304).

[3] *Concordia discordantium canonum*, p. 3 (*De Consecratione*), dist. 4, c. 7 (PL 187, 1794A-B).

For those children, concerning whom Christ said to His disciples, "Suffer the little children to come unto me," were not coming of themselves or with their own feet to Christ, but were being carried by others. "They brought," Luke says, "unto him also infants, that he might touch them. Which when the disciples saw, they rebuked them. But Jesus, calling them together, said: Suffer children to come to me, and forbid them not: for of such is the kingdom of God" (18, 15-16). It ought to be especially noted in which words that He said the children [ought to] come to Him, who nevertheless were carried by others.

Again from various figures of Baptism which preceded of old in the Old Testament it can be clearly proved that Baptism benefits children as well as adults. Nor is this a weak argument, since according to Paul's opinion all things happened to the Fathers in figures, and Paul himself often makes an argument from figures of this kind for proving those doctrines which now must necessarily be accepted by all in the time of the New Testament. Concerning which matter it can be somewhat seen above in book one, chapter three. Firstly, therefore, I present Noe's ark which no one can justly deny was a figure of Baptism, since Blessed Peter the Apostle teaches this very clearly, saying the following: "In the ark of Noe wherein a few, that is, eight souls, were saved by water. Whereunto baptism being of the like form, now saveth you also" (I Pet. 3, 20-21). In which words he clearly shows that the ark was a type of our Baptism. The ark constructed out of various pieces of wood signifies the Church composed of various peoples, namely the Jews and Greeks, gathered together: and the various rooms of the ark represent the various states in the Church. The ark was carried upon water to the port, and all the faithful are carried by Baptism to the port of salvation, that is, to eternal glory. The salvation of the body was through the ark, and the salvation of the soul occurs through Baptism. Few men, namely, only eight were saved by the ark, namely Noe, his three sons, Noe's wife and the three wives of his sons: so although many are called to Baptism, nevertheless few are chosen. They drowned in the flood and perished, nor only those who had sinned by their own will, and had provoked God's anger against themselves, but also countless children, who never sinned by their own free will, except that they had been born "children of wrath" (Eph. 2, 3). In like manner not only adults perish without baptism who sin by their own volition, but also children who have not yet sinned of their own volition, but are stained only with Adam's sin, and have been born in God's wrath.

Likewise in the ark not only men saved from the death of the body, who acknowledged their God: but also many beasts, which God had chosen for man's wellbeing on account of their service to men, which nevertheless nowise knew God Himself. In the same way through Baptism as many as are capable of it receive spiritual salvation, either acknowledge their Redeemer, or as beasts completely are ignorant of Him, and understand nothing of the salvation of their souls bestowed through Christ's merits, insofar as they are children, who although are capable of spiritual salvation, just as the adults, yet are like beasts and cannot know the salvation of their souls nor God Himself, the Author of that salvation. For children, although they outwardly have a human appearance and possess an immortal soul within themselves as much as adults, yet because they lack the use of reason, they are truly very similar to beasts, according to that which the Prophet says: "Man when he was in honour did not understand; he is compared to senseless beasts, and is become like to them" (Ps. 48, 13).

Another figure of Baptism is the Red Sea, through which the Israelites fleeing from Egypt, crossed and were saved, and delivered from Pharaoh's persecution. No one could without shame deny that that sea was a figure of Baptism: because Paul teaches this very clearly saying: "I would not have you ignorant, brethren, that our fathers were all under the cloud, and all passed through the sea. And all in Moses were baptized, in the cloud, and in the sea" (I Cor. 10, 1-2). Let us carefully consider this figure of Baptism, and afterwards we may clearly acknowledge that it greatly supports our and the Catholic view. Clouds and the sea jointed together at the same time make a true and complete figure of Baptism: because Baptism is accomplished by two things, namely water and the Spirit, as the Savior said, that the regeneration necessary for acquiring the kingdom of God is accomplished by water and the Holy Ghost.[1] The Red Sea signifies the water itself of Baptism, which is also red, not in fact by its natural color, but by the power and operation which it has from the merit of Christ's red and violet Blood, in virtue of the Holy Ghost working within. And for this reason he says that they are baptized in Moses, because as Moses was the leader of the nation that he saved, so now Christ being our leader and going before us to His Passion, we are saved by His merits through Baptism.

Clouds signify the Holy Ghost: because what protecting beneficent clouds confers upon those cooled by them, all that the Holy Ghost conveys to those baptized more abundantly, since He is the guide and protector of our actions, moderator and extinguisher of our concupiscences. The Israelites when crossing the Red Sea were freed only once from Pharaoh's tyranny, so Baptism received frees us only once from the devil's tyranny. Just as the all Israelites both children and adults crossed the sea, and all were saved, so also as man shall have been baptized whether young or old, all are freed from the devil's power. And Paul clearly taught this, since he said that all "were baptized, in the cloud, and in the sea." For by saying "all," he excepts no one, but he includes all, the children as well as the adults.

Finally the third figure of Baptism and the most important of them all is circumcision: which Paul also teaches was a figure of Baptism, when saying the following: "In whom also you are circumcised with circumcision not made by hand, in despoiling of the body of the flesh, but in the circumcision of Christ, buried with him in baptism" (Col. 2, 11-12). Theophylactus when interpreting which words in his Commentaries on Paul says: "He brought forth a benefit to be admired, namely that you were circumcised with Christ. For man's hand does not perform this circumcision, but the Spirit: and He does not circumcise part but the whole man. In the past a member was taken off by circumcision, the fleshly covering having been removed: but now our body takes off the sins which we accomplish through the flesh. Now with such circumcision not the Law but Christ circumcises in Baptism, taking away from the old life guilty with sins, and truly carnal."[2] From which words it is very clearly established that circumcision according to Paul's view was a figure of Baptism.

But circumcision not only benefited adults for the salvation of their souls, but it was also commanded for children, as it is evident from the book of Genesis, wherein God says these words: "This is my covenant which you shall observe, between me and you, and thy seed after thee: all the male kind of you shall be circumcised: and you shall circumcise the flesh of your foreskin, that it may be for a sign of the covenant between me and you. An infant of eight days old shall be circumcised among you" (17, 10-12). And further on it is written: "The male, whose flesh of his foreskin shall not be circumcised, that soul shall be destroyed out of his people: because he hath broken my covenant" (v. 14). Behold, you see that the precept of the circumcision of children was given by God. A child, who passed away from this world before circumcision perished without hope of eternal glory, as is evident from that which it says, "That soul shall be destroyed out of his people."

Now this is the same as if one were to say, "shall not be written." Sacred Scripture often says that those are "blotted out" who were never written. For in Psalm nine it is said: "Thou hast rebuked the Gentiles, and the wicked one hath perished: thou hast blotted out their name for ever and ever" (v. 6). Certainly, the Gentiles' name was not firstly written in the book of the living, of which there was mention there, unless perhaps according to the nature in Adam,

---

[1] "Amen, amen I say to thee, unless a man be born again of water and the Holy Ghost, he cannot enter into the kingdom of God" (Jn. 3, 5).

[2] *Expositio in Epistola ad Colossenses* (PG 124, 1242).

from which through his prevarication it was blotted out. And again, in another Psalm the Prophet says likewise: "They have persecuted him whom thou hast smitten; and they have added to the grief of my wounds. Add thou iniquity upon their iniquity: and let them not come into thy justice. Let them be blotted out of the book of the living; and with the just let them not be written" (Ps. 68, 27-29). The Prophet says these things concerning those who crucified Christ, and did not do penance afterwards, as Peter interpreted in the speech which he gave to his fellow disciples for the substitution of another Apostle in place of Judas after Christ's Ascension into Heaven.[1]

From these words of the Prophet it is evident that these three words are used by him for the same thing: "to blot out [*deleri*]," "not to write," and "not to enter into God's justice." Of these three the two latter express the first. Thus, "The male, whose flesh of his foreskin shall not be circumcised, that soul shall be destroyed [*deleri*] out of his people" is the same as "not to be written" and "to not enter into God's justice." And this happens likewise to a child, who now dies without Baptism. Circumcision, by virtue of the covenant performed upon a child, conferred upon him Divine grace and the salvation of his soul: because [God] says that it is a sign of the covenant between God and them, not only adults but also children. And hence it follows that Baptism performed now also confers to the one baptized grace for the salvation of his soul: unless perhaps someone wishes to be so foolish that he is not ashamed to say that Baptism has less efficacy than circumcision of old. Yet the Prophet teaches the contrary saying: "The Lord loveth the gates of Sion above all the tabernacles of Jacob" (Ps. 86, 2). By which words he teaches that the Sacraments of the New Law, which are the gates of the Catholic Church designated by "Sion," are reckoned by God to be of greater worth than all the sacraments and sacrifices of the Judaic Law. Therefore, it is necessary to believe that circumcision likewise conferred upon all males whether young or old what Baptism confers now. Yet this is important, namely that circumcision, in that the price of the Redemption was not yet paid, could not open the kingdom of Heaven to the dying, which Baptism now does, the reason being that Christ's Blood has now been poured out for us as the price of our redemption.[2]

The very ancient practice [of infant Baptism] perpetually kept in the Catholic Church adds to all these things in favor of the Baptism of children. For (as is apparent in the writings of various holy Fathers) from the very time of the Apostles until this day this was always preserved, that at least when obliged by necessity, children, even if lacking the use of reason, were baptized. For it is evident that it was so done at the time of the Apostles according to Dionysius the [Psuedo-] Areopagite.[3] And it is evident that afterwards [this practice] was kept two hundred years later, according to Cyprian.[4] That it was likewise kept at the time of Augustine is evident from his ninety-eighth epistle, which is about the Baptism of children.[5]

Finally, there are many decrees of the General Councils in favor of this practice, which all concordantly teach that Baptism benefits all men, children as well as adults, towards the

---

[1] Ps. 68, 26.

[2] Those who died before Christ paid the price of the redemption of the human race on the Cross were sent to Limbo until Christ's Ascension into heaven, when He brought these just souls with Him to heaven.

[3] *On the Ecclesiastical Hierarchy*, c.7, n.11 (PG 3, 583B).

[4] "But in respect of the case of the infants, which you say ought not to be baptized within the second or third day after their birth, and that the law of ancient circumcision should be regarded, so that you think that one who is just born should not be baptized and sanctified within the eighth day, we all thought very differently in our council" (Epistle 58, n. 2 (PL 3, 1015A)). The text here cites the "eighth epistle of the third book" which is an outdated reference according to a different numbering system.

[5] PL 33, 359 ff. Likewise the text here gives "Epistle 23" as the reference, which is also an outdated reference.

salvation of their souls. The [IV] Lateran Council celebrated under Innocent III says these words: "The sacrament of Baptism (which at the invocation of God and the indivisible Trinity, namely, of the Father and of the Son and of the Holy Ghost, is solemnized in water) rightly conferred by anyone in the form of the Church is useful unto salvation for little ones and for adults."[1] The Council of Vienne celebrated under Clement V among the other decrees gave this one regarding Baptism: "Besides, one baptism which regenerates all who are baptized in Christ must be faithfully confessed by all just as 'one God and one faith' (Eph. 4, 5), which celebrated in water in the name of the Father and of the Son and of the Holy Spirit we believe to be commonly the perfect remedy for salvation for adults as for children."[2] Finally the Council of Trent celebrated under Paul III determined the matter in this way: "If anyone shall say that infants, because they have not actual faith, after having received Baptism are not to be numbered among the faithful, and therefore, when they have reached the years of discretion, are to be rebaptized, or that it is better that their Baptism be omitted than that they, while not believing by their own act, be baptized in the faith of the Church alone: let him be anathema."[3]

This only do I now see remains, namely that I respond to the argument that the Anabaptists object to us, and by which they strive to firmly defend their most wicked heresy. Christ (they say) when teaching His Apostles about those things which after His Ascension into Heaven they were about to do said: "He that believeth and is baptized, shall be saved: but he that believeth not shall be condemned" (Mk. 16, 16). But infant children do not believe, because they do not have the use of reason. Thus it follows that if they would die then, they would be condemned, even if they were to receive Baptism; and hence they further deduce that Baptism does not benefit them for the salvation of their souls. And this argument they again confirm with Paul the Apostle's testimony saying: "Without faith it is impossible to please God" (Heb. 11, 6). Now children as long as they lack reason, do not have, nay nor can they have of themselves, faith, hence at that time (according to Paul's opinion) they could not please God, and consequently Baptism cannot benefit them at that time for the salvation of their souls. These are the strongest arguments, by which the Anabaptists oppose and think that they conquer us: but in reality they by no means do so and they are most crassly deceived by their ignorance.

For before those words Christ said: "Go ye into the whole world, and preach the gospel to every creature" (Mk. 16, 15) and after having said these words He immediately said those words which they object to us: "He that believeth and is baptized" etc. From which context of words it is very clearly proved that these last words ought to be understood of those only to whom He was commanding them to preach the Gospel. But the Gospel was not to be preached to children, but to adults: because children, even if the Gospel would be preached to them, could not understand: thus the Gospel was to be preached only to adults, who alone could understand the things which were said to them, and hence it is very clearly proved that the words are understood concerning only adults, when Christ says: "He that believeth and is baptized, shall be saved: but he that believeth not shall be condemned." Since in fact adults, when they come to be baptized, before they receive it, ought to orally confess the Catholic faith, and whenever they are taught concerning it. And so the Catholic Church from the time of the Apostles themselves until today has kept the practice uninterruptedly that adults would firstly be catechumens before they are baptized. For firstly they were catechizing, meaning instructing in the Catholic faith, adults. There exists concerning this matter the small book of Blessed Augustine, which is entitled, "On the Catechizing of the Uninstructed."[4]

---

[1] Chap. 1 (Dz. 430).
[2] Dz. 482.
[3] Sess. 7, "On Baptism," can. 13 (Dz. 869).
[4] *De Catechizandis Rudibus* (PL 40, 309-348).

Now that which they object from Paul's testimony proceeds from crass ignorance: because children even if they do not have the faith before they have received Baptism, still they have it after they are baptized, although they cannot use it. Concerning which matter Blessed Bernard brings forth testimony to us saying the following: "Let no man object to me that the infant has not faith. For his mother [the Church] communicates to him her own, wrapping it up for him [so to speak] in the sacrament [of regeneration], until he becomes capable of perceiving it unfurled and pure nor merely with his own mind but also with his assent. Do you think that [the faith of the Church] is like the [Prophet's] 'short covering which cannot cover two'?[1] Great is the faith of the Church. Is it less than the faith of the Canaanite woman, which was sufficient, as we know, to cover both herself and her daughter? Hence she deserved to hear, 'O woman, great is thy faith: be it done to thee as thou wilt' (Mt. 15, 28)." And shortly afterwards he adds: "This being so, no prejudice against the salvation of regenerated infants can be maintained from the fact that it is said, 'Without faith it is impossible to please God' (Heb. 11, 6). For those infants are not without faith, who in testimony of [the Church's] faith have received the grace of Baptism. Nor [can it be maintained] from that which is likewise said, 'But he that believeth not shall be condemned' (Mk. 16, 16). For what is it to believe except to have faith?"[2]

Augustine supports the same view saying the following: "Baptized children are reckoned among believers through the power of the sacrament and the pledges of the sponsors."[3] This passage is cited by Gratian.[4]

Therefore they have faith, but they cannot put it into operation until when attaining the use of reason and believing through hearing God's word, they may receive it. For as children, even if they have all the complete members of the body, and have life in them all and a living soul, still there is scarcely any member of theirs that performs its function correctly: because they neither walk with their feet, nor speak with their tongue, nor work with their hands: so also even though there is true faith in them, pleasing to God and charity vivifying, nevertheless it cannot go out into operation through some act of theirs, unless they firstly be taught: and by helped by some exterior teacher.

Blessed Bernard wrote against this heresy some few words in that sixty-sixth sermon on the Canticles [cited above], and in his seventy-seventh letter.[5] At the same time a certain Peter [the Venerable], abbot of Cluny, wrote somewhat longer.[6] Finally in this century of ours,

---

[1] "For the bed is straitened, so that one must fall out, and a short covering cannot cover both" (Is. 28, 20).

[2] *Sermons on the Canticle of Canticles*, Sermon 66 ("On the Heretical Doctrines concerning Marriage, Baptism of Infants, Purgatory, Prayers for the Deceased, and the Invocation of the Saints"), n.10 (PL 183, 1099B-C).

[3] "Where do we reckon the baptized children except among the faithful, just as the authority of the universal Church declares? Therefore we reckon them among those who have believed; for this is procured for them through the power of the Sacrament [of Baptism] and the pledges of the sponsors" (*De peccatorum meritis et remissione et de baptismo parvulorum*, lib. 1, c. 33, n. 62 (PL 44, 146)).

[4] *Concordia discordantium canonum*, p. 3 "De consecratione," c. 8 ("Filius Dei"), dist. 4 (PL 187, 1794B).

[5] *Ad Hugonem de Sancto Victore*, (PL 182, 1031 ff.) cited above.

[6] PL 189, 729ff cited above.

many have written: Johann Faber[1] Johann Eck,[2] Leopold [Dick],[3] but the lengthiest and most learned of all, Maerten Dunck: who published a whole volume divided into two books against the Anabaptists.[4]

The **sixth heresy** is about the unity of Baptism itself. For there are some who rebaptized those who have already received Baptism once. Now there are until the present time various sects of them. Accordingly, the Donatists (as Augustine relates in his book, *De haeresibus* [*ad Quodvultdeum*]) rebaptized those who came to them from the Catholic Church[5]: because (as they say) Baptism cannot be conferred outside the Church: they however were asserting that the Church was nearly only themselves. Wherefore they were rebaptizing those who falling away from the Church joined them, saying that they had not received true Baptism before. These Donatians or Donatists, firstly on account of Caecilian having been consecrated Bishop of Carthage against their will, made a schism, accusing him of crimes which they were unable to prove. But afterwards, having discovered the falsity of their accusation, they turned the schism into pertinacious defense of heresy: as though Christ's Church, on account of Caecilian's crimes—whether true or false—had perished throughout the entire world where it was promised to be, and while remaining in the African region of Donatus was annihilated in the other regions of the world by a certain contagion of communion [with Caecilian].

Now the Donatists are so called from a certain Donatus, who lived in the time of the Emperor Constantius and Pope Liberius: concerning whom we will say many things in the section on the Church, first heresy. The Armenians hold this same error (as Guy the Carmelite says),[6] who rebaptize those coming to them from the Roman Church, saying that in the Roman Church there is not the true Baptism, in that (as they say) the true and Catholic Church does not exist among them, but only among the Armenians themselves.

You clearly see here fulfilled what Christ foretold: "If any man shall say to you: lo here is Christ, or there, do not believe him. For there shall arise false Christs and false prophets, and shall shew great signs and wonders, insomuch as to deceive (if possible) even the elect. Behold I have told it to you, beforehand. If therefore they shall say to you: Behold he is in the desert, go ye not out: Behold he is in the closets, believe it not" (Mt. 24, 23-26). We certainly see these things now fulfilled; we have heard of many false Christs and false prophets. The Donatists say, "Behold Christ is among us and nowhere else": The Armenians say, "Behold Christ is with us." But according to Christ's warning it is necessary that we do not believe them, but instead remain in the Catholic Church, which is the only mother of all men. To this place also pertains the error of Cyprian and of all the African bishops who at the synod [of Carthage in 256] celebrated among them concerning this matter decreed that heretics ought

---

[1] Johannes Faber, (1478 – 1541) was a Catholic theologian known for his writings opposing the Protestant Reformation and the growing Anabaptist movement.

[2] Johann Maier von Eck (1486 – 1543) was a German Scholastic theologian and defender of Catholicism during the Protestant Reformation.

[3] Leopold Dick, a jurist in the Imperial Court of Chancery in Speyer, was the author of a booklet of 84 pages in Latin against the Anabaptists, *Adversus impios Anabaptistarum errores, longe omnium pestillentissimos* in 1530). In it he teaches Catholic doctrine of Baptism, that its administration to infants at a very early age is necessary for their salvation because of original sin, and its repetition is blasphemy. As proof he offers besides the Bible, from which he makes special reference to circumcision, quotations from the Church Fathers.

[4] Maerten Dunck (*Martinus Duncanus*) (ca. 1506-1593) of Wormer wrote his book, *Anabaptisticae haereseos conjutatio* in 1549 at Antwerp.

[5] PL 42, 43.

[6] *Summa de haeresibus et earum confutationibus*, fol. 34v, c. 15.

to be rebaptized when they returned to the Church, because (as they said) Baptism cannot be conferred among heretics.

Now in this matter they erred, motivated as I suspect with zeal and not according to discretion, and led by hate which they had conceived against the heretics. Nevertheless Cyprian and the others consenting to him ought not to be judged to be heretics on account of this error, because they nowise defended it with pertinacity: yea they stated their opinion being prepared to be corrected by others teaching better things. Which was evident by the very fact, that when they were thoroughly taught by the Supreme Pontiffs of the Church, namely Cornelius, Lucius, and Stephen, the Africans themselves decreed things contrary to their prior decrees. This error was not firstly in Africa, but it was in existence previously in many places such as Iconium (as Eusebius relates[1]).

Now in much more recent times a certain Baltasar [Hubmaier][2] arose, who teaches men to be rebaptized, saying that Baptism does not benefit children: wherefore when they shall have reached the age of reason, they ought to be rebaptized. This he is said to have done to many [children], and to have seduced many into his error, so that men of this faction are called Anabaptists, that is, "rebaptizers."[3] Against this Baltasar and his followers there is nothing more that we may do because since we have already shown that Baptism benefits children as it does adults, having overthrown their foundation, the structure of the whole error will fall down.

Now against all these others we will proceed in this order, namely that we firstly show that the malice of a minister nowise lessens the validity of Baptism, indeed it may be conferred by any minister, and as long as he keeps the other things that are necessary, the Baptism would be valid.

This is firstly proved by the passage which is found in John,[4] namely that Christ's disciples were baptizing, among whom was Judas, who although he was not [yet] a traitor, still he was a thief and a robber: and yet it is not read about those baptized by him that they were ever rebaptized. Furthermore, the words of John the Baptist confirm this fact more explicitly: "I saw the Spirit coming down, as a dove from heaven, and he remained upon him. And I knew him not; but he who sent me to baptize with water, said to me: He upon whom thou shalt see the Spirit descending, and remaining upon him, he it is that baptizeth with the Holy Ghost" (Jn. 1, 32-33). From which words it is evident that he who baptizes is Christ, the Son of God. For although the minister outwardly washes the body, yet it is Christ Who inwardly cleanses the soul. Thus it is He alone who baptizes with the Holy Ghost, but the others as ministers. "He it is," he says, "that baptizeth with the Holy Ghost," although He Himself was not then baptizing, but rather He was baptized by John: by which He wished to insinuate that it is Christ Himself who always baptizes, no matter how much the minister varies. If, therefore, it is He who baptizes, what could a wicked minister impede? For also Paul says: "Therefore, neither he that planteth is any thing, nor he that watereth; but God that giveth the increase" (I Cor. 3, 7). Hence it is proved that a wicked minister can hinder nothing, since the Lord Who baptizes is good.

Blessed Augustine confirms this also most elegantly, saying: "But he who is a proud minister is reckoned with the devil; but the gift of Christ is not contaminated, which flows through him pure... In a stony channel nothing grows, nevertheless it brings much fruit to the gar-

---

[1] *Ecclesiastical History*, lib. 7, c. 7, n. 5 (PG 20, 651A).
[2] Baltasar Hubmaier (c. 1480 – 1528) was an influential German/Moravian (Schwertler) Anabaptist leader.
[3] Greek *ana* means "again," and *baptizo* means "to baptize"; hence the name, Anabaptists, means "rebaptizers."
[4] "Jesus himself did not baptize, but his disciples" (Jn. 4, 2).

dens."[1] And in his *De baptismo contra Donatistas* he says the following: "Since baptism at the hands of a contemptible man is as valid as when given by an Apostle, it is known to be the baptism neither of this man nor of that, but of Christ... Accordingly we find the Apostles using the expressions, 'my glory,' (I Cor. 9, 15) though it was certainly in the Lord; and 'my ministry,' (Rom. 11, 13) and 'my knowledge,' (Eph. 3, 4) and 'my gospel,' (II Tim. 2, 8) although it was confessedly bestowed and given by the Lord; but no one of them ever once said, 'my baptism.' For neither is the glorying of all of them equal, nor do they all minister with equal powers, nor are they all endowed with equal knowledge, and in preaching the Gospel one works more forcibly than another, and so one may be said to be more learned than another in the doctrine of salvation itself; but one cannot be said to be more or less baptized than another, whether he be baptized by a greater or a less worthy minister."[2]

And Pope Zachary writing to Bishop Boniface says: "You mention also that some have been baptized by adulterous and unworthy priests without being questioned on their belief in the articles of the Creed. In such cases, you must hold fast to the ancient custom of the Church, because whoever is baptized in the name of Father, Son and Holy Ghost cannot be baptized again. For he has received this grace not in the name of the minister but in the name of the Trinity. Hold fast the teaching of the Apostles, 'One Lord, one faith, one baptism' (Eph. 4, 5)."[3] Therefore from these quite clear testimonies of Scripture and of the sacred Doctors it is clearly proved that the malice of the minister in no wise impedes Baptism, but rather through him Baptism can be validly conferred.

But someone may say that these citations suffice well enough for proving in regard to some crime, such as adultery, homicide, etc. that it does not impede in the minister from conferring valid Baptism: still in regard to a heretic they do not prove this. But if they would carefully examine, they equally prove this in regard to a heretic, just as in regard to one guilty of any other crime: because whether the minister is an adulterer, or a murderer, or a heretic, it is Christ Who baptizes with the Holy Ghost. Hence Augustine says: "Why therefore can [heretics] not baptize outside [the unity of the Church]? Is it because they are worse by the mere fact that they are outside? But however wicked the minister may be makes no difference, in respect of the validity of Baptism. For there is not as much difference between bad and worse as between good and bad; and yet, when the bad baptizes, he gives the selfsame [Sacrament] as the good. Therefore, also, when the worse baptizes, he gives the selfsame [Sacrament] as the less bad."[4] And likewise against Cresconium the grammarian, he says: "If among the good ministers, although one is better than another, the Baptism which is given by the better one is not better, and in no respect is the one given by a bad minister worse, since it is the same Baptism given. And so, through unequal ministers God's gift is equal, because it is not theirs, but His."[5]

Furthermore one baptized by a Jew or pagan rightly saying the words, and having the intention of doing what Christians do, is validly baptized, and does not need to be rebaptized: therefore one baptized by a heretic will also be validly baptized. The premise is proved by that which Pope Nicholas [I] replies to an emissary of the Bulgarians, and is recorded in the book of *Decretals*: "You say that many in your country have been baptized by someone, whether Christian or pagan you know not. If these were baptized in the name of the Trinity, or in the

---

[1] *In Evangelium Joannis Tractatus CXXIV* ("Lectures or Tractates on the Gospel According to Saint John"), tract. 5, n. 15 (PL 35, 1442).
[2] *On Baptism, Against the Donatists*, lib. 5, c. 13-14, n. 15-16 (PL 43, 184).
[3] *Epistola XIV. Gregorii Papae II ad Bonifacium Episcopum*, n.8 (PL 89, 525D).
[4] *On Baptism, Against the Donatists*, lib. 6, c. 24, n. 43 (PL 43, 212).
[5] *Contra Cresconium grammaticum et donatistam*, lib. 3, c. 6, n. 6 (PL 43, 499).

name of Christ only, as we read in the Acts of the Apostles[1] (for it is one and the same thing, as St. Ambrose has explained[2]) they must not be rebaptized."[3] Therefore, we have proved from these testimonies that the malice of the minister, even if he be a heretic, nowise impedes Baptism, but rather a heretic confers valid Baptism, if he does the things that are necessary for Baptism.

But here it is necessary to warn that the malice of the minister, even if it does not impede Baptism from being valid, still it does impede the one baptized, namely that he would not receive grace through such Baptism: because he places the obstacle of a fault, which he commits by so receiving Baptism from such a wicked minister. For he who with full knowledge receives Baptism from a wicked minister, especially a heretic, sins: both because he has communion with the heretic in these things in which it was especially unfitting to have communion: and also because an express prohibition of the Church about this was made. Hence in the *Apostolic Canons* it is said: "We ordain that a bishop, or presbyter, who has admitted the Baptism or sacrifice of heretics, be deposed. For 'what concord hath Christ with Belial? Or what part hath the faithful with the unbeliever?' (II Cor. 6, 15)"[4] Therefore one sins who knowingly and deliberately receives Baptism from a heretic: wherefore although he may receive valid Baptism, yet not the effect of Baptism.

Nevertheless, if being forced by necessity, he may do it, as for example when death is imminent and there is no one else from whom one may receive Baptism besides the heretic, one can receive Baptism from him: provided that he does not do it with the intention of assenting to his heresy, but as one wishing to receive the true Catholic faith. Hence Blessed Augustine says the following: "He that is separated may confer it, as he that is separated may have it; but as he has it to destruction, so he may confer it to destruction. But he on whom he confers it may receive it to his soul's health, if he, on his part, receive it not in separation; as it has happened to many that, in a Catholic spirit and with heart not alienated from the unity of peace, have received it under some pressure of impending death."[5]

Outside of an urgent necessity, anyone sins who is baptized by a wicked man, especially by a heretical minister. Nevertheless, he receives valid Baptism, but does not receive the effect of Baptism: because the Baptism is impeded by his fault, so that it would not have its effect for him. And from this, Augustine says in the place recently cited, Cyprian and the other African bishop took the origin of their error. "It appeared to some even eminent men who were bishops of Christ, among whom the Blessed Cyprian was specially conspicuous, that the Baptism of Christ could not exist among heretics or schismatics. This simply arose from their not distinguishing the Sacrament from the effect or use of the Sacrament; and because its effect and use were not found among heretics in freeing them from their sins and setting their hearts right, the Sacrament itself was also thought to be wanting among them."[6] If, therefore, as we have already fully shown, the malice of any minister does not impede that one baptized by him may receive valid Baptism from him, such that one baptized by him nowise ought to be rebaptized. And this is the second point that we promised to discuss.

---

[1] "Having heard these things, they were baptized in the name of the Lord Jesus" (Acts. 19, 5).

[2] Ambrose, *On the Holy Ghost*, lib. 1, c. 3 (PL 16, 712B-717B). N.B. "All modern theologians teach that today Baptism cannot be validly conferred in the name of Jesus, but the express mention of the three Persons of the Most Holy Trinity is required" (Prümmer, *Manuale Theologiae Moralis* (Friburg, Herder & Co., 1928), vol. 3, n. 103).

[3] *The Responses of Pope Nicholas I to the Questions of the Bulgars A.D. 866 (Letter 99)*, c. 104 (Dz. 335); *Decreta, De consecra*, p. 1, dist. 4, c. 148 (PL 161, 93D).

[4] Canon 46 (PG 137, 130C).

[5] *On Baptism, Against the Donatists*, lib. 6, c. 3, n. 5 (PL 43, 200).

[6] *On Baptism, Against the Donatists*, lib. 6, c. 1, n. 1 (PL 43, 197).

But because the Armenians (as we have said) rebaptized the Latins, still they are motivated by another reason than those African bishops and the Donatists, against whom we have already discussed: namely because they say that the Roman Church does not have the correct form of Baptism: and so this will be why the Latins are rebaptized by them. Now it was shown that the form of Baptism used by the Latins is valid, from the second error regarding Baptism disproved above. For the form which Christ taught, related in Matthew's Gospel, expresses three necessary things, which are: the verb expressing the act of Baptism, the noun designated the person baptized, and the explicit invocation of the Trinity. "Baptizing," He says, "them in the name of the Father, and of the Son, and of the Holy Ghost." "Baptizing," behold the first: "them," behold the second, namely the person baptized: "in the name of the Father" etc., there the third is shown. Now all these things are included in the form which the Roman Church has. For it is as follows: "I baptize thee in the name of the Father, and of the Son, and of the Holy Ghost." Since all the things that are necessarily required are in it, there is no reason why the Armenians deny that we have valid Baptism. Now against the wicked Anabaptists, who rebaptized at will not merely once and again, but three, four and five times: because they repeat Baptism, like Penance, as many times as they please: against them I say that it must be treated again.

Firstly, that which Paul says opposes their heresy: "One Lord, one faith, one baptism" (Eph. 4, 5). If, therefore, Paul bearing witness, Baptism is one, why do the wicked Anabaptists presume to confer baptisms to one and the same person three and four times? Besides this citation Paul confirms this more completely and explicitly in his Epistle to the Romans: "Know you not that all we, who are baptized in Christ Jesus, are baptized in his death? For we are buried together with him by baptism into death; that as Christ is risen from the dead by the glory of the Father, so we also may walk in newness of life" (6, 3-4). From which words and others from the same place it is evident that Baptism is a certain figure of Christ's death. For just as sin died by Christ's death, so also by Baptism our sin also vanishes, through nevertheless the merit of Christ's Passion. But Christ died once for our sins, but not two or three times: thus it is also necessary that we be baptized only once for our sins. Also, "Christ rising again from the dead, dieth now no more, death shall no more have dominion over him" (Rom. 6, 9): thus we also having been brought forth out of the water, ought not to return again to the bath of water. The Anabaptists, who presume to rebaptized, "crucify again to themselves the Son of God" (Heb. 6, 6). Paul was speaking explicitly about them, and not about others. For he who baptizes again, as much as is in him, also fixes Christ to the Cross a second time: because since Baptism is a figure of Christ's death, he who baptizes again, by this very fact shows that Christ had died a second time.

Again, the definitions of the sacred Councils confirm this fact. For in the Symbol produced by the Council of Nicea it is said: "I confess one baptism for the remission of sins." The First Synod of Carthage says the following: "Bishop Gratus presiding at the Synod said: Therefore if it pleases you, let us consider firstly the subject of rebaptism: hence I ask your holiness, whether it would be pleasing to you for one descending into the water, and asked about the Trinity according to the faith of the Gospel and the teaching of the Apostles, and having confessed a good conscience towards God concerning the Resurrection of Jesus Christ, if it would be allowed for him to be asked again in the same faith and dipped into water again? All the bishops said: Far be it, far be it. We decree rebaptisms to be unlawful, and is quite foreign to sound faith and Catholic discipline."[1] And the Council of Vienne celebrated under Clement V says: "One baptism which regenerates all who are baptized in Christ must be faithfully confessed by all just as 'one God and one faith' (Eph. 4, 5)."[2] These words are found in the

---

[1] C. 1 (PL 8, 775A-B).
[2] Dz. 482.

Clementine Decretals in the chapter *Fidei catholicae, de summa trinitate, et fide catholica*.[1] Also the Council of Florence, celebrated under Eugene IV teaches the same doctrine, saying the following: "Among these sacraments there are three: Baptism, Confirmation, and Orders, which imprint an indelible sign on the soul, that is, a certain character distinctive from the others. Hence they should not be repeated in the same person. The remaining four do not imprint a sign and admit of repetition."[2]

But if someone wishes to object to these definitions of the Councils the decree of the Synod of Carthage celebrated with Cyprian present, which says that valid Baptism cannot be conferred by heretics, and so those baptized by them ought to be baptized again, it can be replied to this, that the decrees of all the Councils are not equal. For the authority of the provincial councils is not so great that all are obliged to comply with its decrees: for provincial councils (as we taught at the beginning of the first book) can err. For God did not ask for that assembly that its faith would not err: nor does God promise to it that He would always be present. General councils, however, legitimately assembled can nowise err. Wherefore if something was decreed in a provincial council which seems to deviate from the true faith, it ought to be corrected by a general council (as Blessed Augustine teaches).[3] Which we find to have been done in the case. For in fact the African council of seventy-one bishops, in which it was decreed that heretics cannot confer valid baptism, was provincial, and not general: hence it could err, and is corrected by Cornelius the then Roman Pontiff, and afterwards was corrected by the First Synod of Carthage in the decree which was recently cited. The universal Church accepts this council, and so all its definitions together are held. Blessed Augustine wrote against this error in his book, *Concerning the One Baptism*, [*Against Petilian*], and again in his tract, *On Baptism, Against the Donatists*, divided into seven books. In our time Johann Faber wrote a large book against the Anabaptists.[4] Leopold [Dick], a German, [also wrote] against the same [heretics].[5]

The **seventh heresy** is about the sacramentals of Baptism itself, meaning, about those things which surround Baptism in its conferral from a certain rite of Mother Church. For the Armenians (as Guy [the Carmelite] says, whom we follow regarding the history of the Armenians, because we could find no other) says that Baptism cannot be conferred to anyone, unless the Sacrament of the Eucharist is conferred to the same person. Secondly they say that chrism is so necessary for confecting true Baptism, that unless the one baptized is anointed with oil, he would not be baptized.

Now both of these two assertions are erroneous and heretical. For that what they firstly say concerning the Eucharist [is erroneous and heretical], is clearly proved from the fact that when the Lord commanded His disciples to teach all nations and baptize them in the name of the Father, and of the Son, and of the Holy Ghost, He made no mention of receiving the Eucharist, yet He would have done so if it were required for the conferring of Baptism. Next, the Sacrament of the Eucharist was instituted long after Baptism: because on the day of the Lord's Supper, namely on Thursday the day before He suffered, He instituted the Sacrament of the Eucharist. Now Baptism was instituted long before. For in the fourth chapter of John's Gospel it is said that Christ's disciples were baptizing[6]: therefore, Baptism had already then been instituted, although not commanded under the threat of Hell, as after Christ's Resurrec-

---

[1] X, lib. 1, t. 1, c. 1.
[2] Decree for the Armenians (*Exultate Deo*, Nov. 22, 1439), Dz. 695.
[3] *On Baptism, Against the Donatists*, lib. 6, c. 1, n. 1 (PL 43, 197).
[4] *Sermones aliquot Salubres, Doctoris Ioannis Fabri, Adversvs nepharios, et impios Anabaptistas habiti, apud Moravos*.
[5] *Adversus impios Anabaptistarum errores, longe omnium pestillentissimos*.
[6] Verse 2.

tion. That some who were baptized by the Apostles were to be baptized again afterwards, we never read was done. Wherefore, from this it can be more rightly concluded that the Eucharist cannot be given except when Baptism has preceded, as it was instituted previously. Now that Baptism could not be given without the Sacrament of the Eucharist, it is supported by absolutely no reason: but it is merely said of one's own accord. Wherefore with the same facility by which it is said, it deserves to be contemned: although we are unable to do it now, for if we will contemn, we will do it induced by valid reason.

The second assertion is not less erroneous: for even if chrism is required in Baptism, yet Baptism does not require it: but the Church requires it of the minister performing Baptism: so that if chrism were not administered, excluding extreme necessity, the minister would sin, because he does not follow the precept of the Church: yet Baptism nonetheless would be so complete (if the other things are present) that it would not be necessary that he baptize again one so washed. For when Christ was instituting Baptism, He gave no precept about using chrism. For this same reason another error similar to this is rejected, of a certain Claudius, Bishop of Turin,[1] concerning whom we spoke above. For he said that is invalid if the sign of the Cross is not made upon the forehead of the one baptized. Now his error is clear: because if those things are performed which Christ commanded, it is evident that the Baptism is complete. Now it is evident that when Christ instituted Baptism, He never mentioned the sign of the Cross.

The **eighth heresy** is completely opposite to this. For the Waldensians say (as Aeneas Silvius says in his book, *De origine Bohemorum*[2]) that no mixing of holy oil with water is permitted for receiving Baptism. Now the Waldensians are so named because a certain [Peter] Waldo,[3] a citizen of Lyons, was their originator. They are also called the "Poor Men of Lyons," because that Waldo of Lyons, from whom they draw their origin, when he was very rich, having left his riches and given them to the poor, pretended that he would observe evangelical poverty: under which cloak he thought that he could cover his many errors. For since he was uneducated, he had some books produced for himself in his vulgar and maternal language, with some quotations of the Saints. Which books he could not understand as well as he ought. Nevertheless, puffed up by his own breath, he usurped the office of the Apostles by preaching. This sect of the Waldensians (as Guy says) began about the year of the Lord 1170, which (as he likewise says) was condemned in the General Council of Rome.[4] Hence among the other errors of the Waldensians is one whereby they assert that holy oil nowise ought to be mixed at Baptism. John Wycliffe followed this error afterwards, concerning whom we have already spoken.

Thus, for a clearer discussion of this error, it ought to be firstly observed that holy oil or chrism are given many times. For sometimes it is given after the Baptism itself has already been received, also with an interval of the space of a number of days or years: and this is a Sacrament distinct from Baptism or (so that I may speak more truly) it is the matter of that sacrament which is called Confirmation. And the present discussion is not about this. Sometimes also oil is given in the very conferring of Baptism. For there they are anointed with chrism on the chest and shoulders, and on the forehead. Now this is for designating the mercy which God shows to us by pardoning sins through the reception of Baptism. For oil very often signifies mercy in Sacred Writ. Hence Blessed Damascene says: "Olive oil is employed in Baptism because it signifies our anointing, and makes us "christs" [meaning "anointed

---

[1] He died in 827.

[2] Chapter 35.

[3] He lived from c. 1140 to c. 1205.

[4] *Summa de haeresibus et earum confutationibus*, fol. 79r. Pope Innocent III condemned them at Fourth Lateran Council in 1215.

ones"], and promises us God's mercy through the Holy Ghost: for it was also a dove that of old brought beyond all hope the branch of the olive to those who escaped the flood (Gen. 8, 11)."[1]

And there is also another not lesser reason: namely that by Baptism we descend into a kind of spiritual battle, and into a wrestling-match. For just as when one put into a combat, and going into a wrestling-match, is anointed, so that the can be held less by the opponent, and instead can more easily slip out of his hands: so also one going into this spiritual combat, is first anointed with oil: by which the one to be baptized is prepared for the combat, lest the devil catch him, that he might instead slip out of his power. Hence Blessed Ambrose says: "['We are the good odour of Christ unto God,'] as the holy Apostle said; and may there be in thee the full fragrance of faith and devotion. We came to the font, thou didst enter. Consider whom thou saw; consider what thou said, recall it carefully. A levite met thee, a presbyter met thee. Thou was anointed as Christ's athlete; as about to wrestle in the fight of this world, thou didst profess the objects of thy wrestling. He who wrestles, has something to hope for; where the contest is, there is the crown. Thou wrestled in the world, but thou art crowned by Christ, and thou art crowned for contests in the world; for, though the reward is in Heaven, yet the merit of the reward is placed here."[2]

From which it is evident that it is not a recent invention of the Church that holy oil be imparted at Baptism. But so that we may show that the thing is much older, it is necessary to cite Dionysius the [Pseudo-] Areopagite, the disciple of Paul the Apostle. For he says when discussing the rite of this sacrament: "For the Godlike bishop starts with the holy anointing, and the priests under him complete the Divine service of the chrism, summoning in type the man initiated to the holy contests, within which he is placed under Christ as Adjudicator: since, as God, He is Institutor of the awards of contest, and as the Wise One, He placed its laws."[3] A commentator or its expounder explaining which words says the following: "Athletes about to compete used to be anointed with fragrant and fortifying ointment, so that the slipperiness of those anointed would make them ungrippable, and unimpedible by the opponents: the smell sharpens the mind and consequently the senses, the absorption of it moistens the muscles and bones, it revives lifeless breathing, and thus strengthens the athlete."[4]

Therefore the Roman Church keeps until our time this not new but old rite, derived from the Apostles themselves (as we have shown). But if the oil were to be omitted, nonetheless if the other things were present, the Baptism would be valid: although the one so omitting it without an urgent need would sin. For the Apostles were baptizing with water alone without oil, as is evident from the Acts of the Apostles. Now, however, it would not be licit for it to be done, the Church having forbidden this. Why then do the wicked Waldensians murmur, since it is shown that the use of oil does no harm to Baptism? Wherefore the custom of the Church ought to be followed, which is ruled by the Holy Ghost, especially in the supervision and administering of the Sacraments.

There is a **ninth heresy** asserting that children do not need Baptism for the remission of original sin, namely because they deny that children before Baptism have any original sin. This is the error of Pelagius, as Blessed Augustine says in his book, *De Haeresibus* [*ad Quod-*

---

[1] *An Exposition of the Orthodox Faith*, lib. 4, c. 9 (PG 94, 1126B).
[2] *Concerning the Sacraments*, c. 1-2, n. 3-4 (PL 16, 437A-B).
[3] *De ecclesiastica hierarchia*, c. 2, p. 3, sect. 6 (PG 3, 402C-D).
[4] I.e. Thomas Netter (c. 1375 – 1430) who was an English Scholastic theologian and controversialist. From his birthplace he is commonly called Thomas of Walden, or Thomas Waldensis who in 1427 wrote his *Doctrinale antiquitatum fidei Catholicae Ecclesiae: ad vetera exemplaria recognitum & notis illustratum*. This quotation is taken from its third volume entitled *De sacramentalibus* (Venice, Typis Antonii Bassanesii, 1757), c. 50, p. 328.

vultdeum].[1] It is also the heresy of the Armenians, as Guy the Carmelite accuses them.[2] But for fighting against this error there will be a better place below, namely when we will treat about sin. For we will then show that children before Baptism are guilty of original sin, and due to it are liable to go to Hell. By which fact it becomes clear that they need Baptism for the remission of this original sin.

There are still others besides the Pelagians who defend this error, although not in the same way. For they say that children can be saved without Baptism and without martyrdom, not because they in fact lack original sin, as the Pelagians said: but because they believe that the faith of the parents, and their prayers, with the intention of baptizing them, when there would be the possibility, is sufficient for their spiritual salvation. The first of all those whom I know who taught this error was John Wycliffe, as Thomas Netter taught in his book, *De sacramentis*.[3] For in that place he says that Wycliffe asserted that children can be saved without the Baptism of water, yet he does not state the way whereby (according to Wycliffe's opinion) children can be saved without Baptism.

Jean Gerson, being excessively compassionate (as I suspect) towards infants, said that children can be saved without Baptism of water through the faith and prayers of their parents, when Baptism is not omitted due to the fact that their parents contemned it, but because they could not give it to their children. Cardinal Thomas de Vio, commonly called Cajetan, afterwards accepted this opinion. Now who he is I have stated above clearly enough when I discussed the formation of Eve from Adam's rib. But lest anyone excessively devoted to this Cajetan think that I have falsely attributed this to him, I will relate his own words, which he wrote in his commentary on part three, question sixty-eight, second article [of the *Summa Theologica*] of Saint Thomas: "In the case of necessity," he says, "Baptism in the desire of the parents seems to suffice for the salvation of children, especially with some exterior sign." And after some words he again adds: "A child from the baptism of desire can be saved by the accepted wish of the parents, if it were impossible that the infant to be baptized with water. The parent however ought in such a case to fortify the infant with the sign of the Cross with the invocation of the Trinity, and so to offer the dying infant to God, in the name of the Father, and of the Son, and of the Holy Ghost." And afterwards in his commentary on article eleven, he says these words: "In the eleventh article it suggests itself to be written and consequently ought to be said, yet subject to correction, that children being in danger in their mothers' wombs can be saved, as we said above concerning infants who cannot be baptized. Now I say that they can be saved not by actual sacrament of Baptism but by the sacrament of Baptism received in the desire of the parents, with some blessing of the child, or offering of him to God with an invocation of the Trinity."

Now I do not consider him to be a heretic due to this assertion, although it is heretical, because he does not assert it obstinately and pertinaciously, but saying it he submits himself to correction, as is evident from his words which we have cited. These words of the Savior clearly prove that this opinion is false and erroneous: "Unless a man be born again, he cannot see the kingdom of God" (Jn. 3, 3). Many things ought to be noted in these words. The first is that He says that it is necessary that one who is due to enter the kingdom of Heaven must be born again. But one who is not yet born, cannot be reborn. Therefore, children being not yet born in the wombs of their mothers, cannot according to the common law, be born again before such a birth, nor consequently enter into the kingdom of God. And Augustine states this, saying the following: Thus it is necessary to be born before one may be reborn.[4]

---

[1] C. 88 (PL 42, 48).

[2] *Summa de haeresibus et earum confutationibus*, fol. 30v, c. 3.

[3] *Doctrinale antiquitatum fidei Catholicae Ecclesiae*, v. 3 (*De Sacramentis*), c. 96.

[4] The reference here is for *De baptism parvulorum*, c. 13, but it does not seem to be correct. A similar

But lest the reader err here, I have decided to advise him that he understand that one is said to be born in this world who he comes forth into the light in some way, either his whole [body] or some member of his comes forth alive. For if the mother has died her womb may be cut, and the infant seems alive inside, it may be baptized, although it was not fully born. Something else deserves to be noted in these words of Christ, that the rebirth necessary for the entering of God's kingdom, ought to be by water and the Holy Ghost. And hence it follows that where water is lacking, there is not a perfect rebirth and one sufficient for entering God's kingdom.

The third thing finally that ought to be noted in these words of Christ is that those words are said in general and without any exception. For Christ speaks not merely about adults, but He spoke generally without the exception of children or of anyone else: "Unless a man be born again of water and the Holy Ghost, he cannot enter into the kingdom of God." Hence where the law does not make an exception, we also ought not to make an exception. And Augustine often teaches that those words of Christ ought to be understood both of children as well as of adults, especially in his book, *On [Merit and the Forgiveness of Sins, and] the Baptism of Infants*, saying the following: "[Children] belong, therefore, among those who have believed; for this is obtained for them by virtue of the Sacrament and the answer of their sponsors. And from this it follows that such as are not baptized are reckoned among those who have not believed, [based on the words of John's Gospel: 'Unless a man be born again of water and the Holy Ghost, he cannot enter into the kingdom of God.']"[1] Notice how Augustine concludes from these words of Christ that unbaptized children are not to be called believers, wishing thereby to show that they will be damned, according to the words of our Savior saying: "But he that believeth not shall be condemned" (Mk. 16, 16).

Moreover, from the words of Paul which he wrote to Titus, the opinion of Cajetan and of others is clearly refuted. "But when," says Paul, "the goodness and kindness of God our Saviour appeared, not by the works of justice, which we have done, but according to his mercy, he saved us, by the laver of regeneration, and renovation of the Holy Ghost; Whom he hath poured forth upon us abundantly, through Jesus Christ our Saviour" (Tit. 3, 4-6). By which words Paul clearly teaches that spiritual salvation is given to us by God, not due to our merits, but due to Christ's merits. And he does not say that this was given by a mere His word or command without any other means, but through "the laver of regeneration, and renovation of the Holy Ghost," meaning, through Baptism in which we are regenerated and renewed with the Holy Ghost helping in us. For Paul calls the sacrament of Baptism itself "the laver of regeneration, and renovation of the Holy Ghost": because by it we are washed from the stains of sins, and spiritually born after carnal birth, and having put off the old man[2] being renewed by the Holy Ghost, so that we may now receive again in Baptism the newness of innocence, which we had received in our first parent before he sinned.

And in the Epistle to the Ephesians Paul again teaches the same idea saying: "Christ also loved the church, and delivered himself up for it: that he might sanctify it, cleansing it by the laver of water in the word of life" (5, 25-26). In which words he called the Sacrament of Baptism the "laver of water and the word of life," without which things Baptism can nowise be conferred. Paul here calls the invocation of the Trinity "the word of life," which [invocation]

---

quotation, however, is found elsewhere in the same work as follows: "Nobody, however, is born again in Christ's body, unless he be previously born in the body of sin" (*On Merit and the Forgiveness of Sins, and the Baptism of Infants*, lib. 1, c. 29, n. 57).

[1] *On Merit and the Forgiveness of Sins, and the Baptism of Infants*, lib. 1, c. 33, n. 62 (PL 44, 146). The words in brackets are found only in the *Decretals* (Gratian, *Concordia discordantium canonum*, p. 3 (*De consecratione*), Dist. 4. c. 8 (*Filius Dei*) (PL 187, 1794B)).

[2] Cf. Eph. 4, 22.

the one baptizing does when he says: "I baptize thee in the name of the Father, and of the Son, and of the Holy Ghost." Thus by this "laver of water in the word of life," He cleansed the Church. And hence it follows that unbaptized children, because they have not been washed with this laver, are not clean, regenerated, or renewed: and consequently, if they were to die without Baptism, they would never arrive to that Church, which is "beautiful"[1] "not having spot or wrinkle,"[2] that is, to heavenly glory.

Again this view is proved to be erroneous by the testimony of John the Apostle, who in his First Epistle declares the way by which Christ comes for the salvation of our souls: "not by water only, but by water and blood." (5, 6). But it is necessary to inquire from whence He came. Did He come from Heaven into the womb of the Virgin to take up our flesh? Or [did He come] from thence for preaching the Gospel? Hardly: because He did none of those things through water and blood at the same time. Thus He so came to wash "the filth of the daughters of Sion... by the spirit of judgment, and by the spirit of burning," as Isaias the Prophet foretold.[3] Now such washing of filth was the remission of sins to be given to us through Christ's merits, Who having died for us poured out water and blood from His side. And this offering He also now makes daily in those who are baptized each day. For it is said concerning of Christ our Savior, that it is He Who baptizes "in the Holy Ghost and fire" (Mt. 3, 11): which is none other than that which was predicted by Isaias, as we just said, because He washed away "the filth of the daughters of Sion... by the spirit of judgment, and by the spirit of burning."

But let us proceed, and see the testimonies of this washing, which Blessed John relates in that passage: "And there are three that give testimony on earth: the spirit, and the water, and the blood: and these three are one" (I Jn. 5, 8). Bede, when interpreting which words in his commentaries on the Canonical epistles, says: "In us these things are one not by nature of the same substance, but by operation of the same mystery. For, as Blessed Ambrose says, 'The Spirit renews the mind, water is useful for washing, and blood refers to a price. For the Spirit made us children of God by adoption, the water of the sacred Font washed us, and the Lord's Blood redeemed us.'[4] Therefore one attains invisible testimony, the other a visible testimony by a spiritual sacrament."[5] From whose words it is evident that John refutes all those who say that children can be saved without Baptism: because John says that there are three witnesses, who ought to render testimony to the soul washed from the filth of sins. But there is lacking one witness for children who have died without Baptism, namely the water of Baptism, therefore they ought not to be reckoned cleansed. Then John says that Christ comes for the salvation of us all through water and blood at the same time, and not through only either one of them: and hence it follows that for children to whom the water of Baptism is lacking, Christ never spiritually comes.

Besides these quotations of Sacred Scripture, there are other very strong reasons which most clearly show that this opinion of Cajetan is erroneous. Firstly, therefore, I begin with this, that no one can, nor ever could attain grace, except by some prevenient good disposition of soul of one's own, or by another's, or by a Sacrament: except perhaps by some particular privilege God mercifully willed to bestow upon someone, as was John the Baptist, Jerome, and other similar men sanctified in the womb of their mother. Children in the wombs of their mothers or dead after birth before Baptism could have grace in none of these ways according to the common law given by God, and so without which they could not be saved: because without [grace] one cannot be saved, on account of that which Paul says: "The grace of God,

---

[1] Cant. 2, 13.
[2] Eph. 5, 27.
[3] Is. 4, 4.
[4] *De Spiritu Sancto*, bk. 3, c. 10, n. 68 (PL 16, 792A-B).
[5] *Super epistolas Catholicas: in primam epistolam s. Joannis*, c. 5 (PL 93, 114D-115A).

life everlasting" (Rom. 6, 23). They could not have grace through some other Sacrament, for since Baptism is the gateway of all the Sacraments, when Baptism is absent no other sacrament can be conferred upon children. Nor could one dispose and prepare himself for receiving grace though the own good movement of one's own will: for since they completely lack the use of reason, they could not have a good or bad movement of their own will.

It now only remains to ask whether through the merits of another, for example of parents or others, they could attain grace. But this could not happen, hence it is proved what the common opinion of all theologians teaches, that no pure man can merit the first grace for another, or first justification, without some movement of his own or affection of the one to be justified. For otherwise, an insane person being in mortal sin could be justified without any repentance of his own: the contrary of which Christ teaches: "Unless you shall do penance, you shall all likewise perish" (Lk. 13, 3). And Innocent III decrees the same thing in the chapter *Majores*.[1] And certainly if some could merit the first grace for a child, for the same reason he could merit its increase, nay he could do this much more easily, since then there would be no contrary disposition for the reception of grace in that child. And if perhaps someone would not be ashamed to accept this, by maintaining this opinion, he would then have to accept that an unbaptized child could have greater grace than a baptized child, as for example if many persons were to fervently pray for the former and no one would pray for the latter. Therefore, there is no means by which children dying without Baptism could attain grace, and consequently eternal life: because [he could attain grace] neither by a Sacrament, nor by his own or another's merit.

Furthermore, if by prayers and offerings, and other sacrifices etc. one could assist children in danger of death, for the same reason one could help those not in such danger by the same means: because danger of death does not make prayers and other suffrages to be a Sacrament, because otherwise [Baptism outside of danger of death] would be no Sacrament, nor can [danger of death] give a greater efficacy to those prayers for impetrating than they had before. And certainly it would seem to be a crime of sacrilege, if one wished to dispute the certitude of the salvation of such children, due to the prayers and offerings of the parents for these children. Because then anyone could easily prove that such prayers are a true Sacrament, according to the common and correct definition of a Sacrament. But, to dare to call another thing a true sacrament, besides those seven which the Catholic Church acknowledges, is a clear sacrilege: and if someone were to pertinaciously defend it, on these grounds alone he may be called a heretic, according to chapter *Ad abolendum*, "On heresies."[2] And hence it also clearly follows that neither Cajetan himself nor the parents of the children for whom they pray, can by their prayers be certain of the salvation of those children: for since those prayers or offerings are not a Sacrament, nothing certain can be established about their efficacious operation for the salvation of children.

Again, if children can be saved without Baptism, this grace would be common to all children, both the children of unbelievers and believers: because there is no reason which urges more for the latter or the former. For they are of the same condition and the sin of both is equal, nor have they merited more from God: nor do the latter or the former have less of an impediment to grace: and so the Sacraments can be equally given to the former and the latter, and the prayers of the just can be equally efficacious for both. And actually if children in the wombs of their mothers could be justified by the prayers of others according to the common law, there would then be absolutely no special privilege of John the Baptist and of the other

---

[1] X, lib. 3, tit. 42, c. 3.

[2] *Decretalium Gregorii papae* lib. 5, Tit.7, c. 9. *Ad abolendam* was a decretal and bull of Pope Lucius III, written at Verona and issued November 4, 1184. The bull was incorporated as Canon 3 of the Fourth Council of the Lateran of 1215 under Pope Innocent III.

BAPTISMUS

Saints who were sanctified in their mother's womb, because it could have happened to all others according to the law, if others prayed for them, as it was befitting.

Finally, if children could be saved without Baptism, then there would be salvation outside of the Church, which if one would perhaps not hesitate to accept, he would immediately be refuted by the authority of the [IV] Lateran Council celebrated under Innocent III, which defined in the first chapter of its decrees that outside of the Church there is no salvation[1]: which definition is found in the chapter, *Firmiter*, under the title, *De summa trinitate et fide catholica*,[2] Now what follows from that opinion of Cajetan is that salvation is outside the Church, hence one will easily understand, if he considers that the children whom he says are saved without Baptism are outside the Church: because they do not pertain to the Lord's flock, since they are not marked with His character. And since Baptism is the gateway through which one enters the Church, those who have not yet attained to be baptized, do not have the gate through which they could have entered it. Also, the Church is the congregation of all men believing in Christ, who are joined together to Christ by one faith, according to that which Hugo of Saint Victor says: "By faith we receive union; by charity we receive vivification."[3] But unbaptized children are unbelievers, because they do not actually believe as do adults: nor habitually as do baptized children. For Augustine in his book, [*De peccatorum meritis et remissione et*] *de baptismo parvulorum*, showing the difference between unbaptized children and those who have been washed with Baptism, says that the latter are believers, but not the former. And this view of Augustine is cited in [Gratian's *Concordia discordantium canonum*].[4]

The declared consent of the whole Church with very clear actions and words adds to all these things against the opinion of Cajetan. For until this day the Church has never prayed for children dying without Baptism, nor has it made any offerings for them, nor does she admit them to ecclesiastical burial, because doubtlessly she would have done those things, if she thought that they deserved those things. The consent of the Church is also evident from the testimonies of the holy Doctors, who even if at times were disunited, still were always in unison about this in this view that Baptism ought to be conferred upon children. Dionysius the [Psuedo-] Areopagite relates that at the time of the Apostles the Church received children for Baptism.[5] And likewise, that it was done afterwards by the Church is evident from Cyprian in his eighth letter of the third book, and from Augustine in his fifty-eighth epistle,[6] and from Augustine in his ninety-eighth epistle.[7] This is likewise evident from Bernard in his sixty-sixth sermon on the Canticles.[8] And likewise [that this practice] has been kept in the Church until this day is evident from the writings of those who lived afterwards, which I now prudently omit for the sake of avoiding tedium.

But the Church never would have given holy Baptism to infants if she would have thought that they could be saved without Baptism. For it would have then been better to defer Baptism for them until adolescence, in which having the use of reason they might do by their own free

---

[1] "One indeed is the universal Church of the faithful, outside which no one at all is saved" Dz. 430.

[2] *Decretalium Gregorii papae* lib. 1, tit.1, c. 1.

[3] *On the Sacraments of the Christian Faith*, lib. 2, p. 2, c. 1 (PL 176, 416B).

[4] P. 3 (*De consecr.*), dist. 4, c. 8 (*Filius Dei*); PL 187, 1794B. "In what class, then, do we place baptized infants but among believers... And from this it follows that such as are not baptized are reckoned among those who have not believed" (*On Merit and the Forgiveness of Sins, and the Baptism of Infants*, lib. 1, c. 32 & 33 (PL 44, 145D-146A)).

[5] *On the Ecclesiastical Hierarchy*, c.7, n.11 (PG 3, 583B).

[6] N. 2 (PL 3, 1015A).

[7] PL 33, 359 ff.

[8] N.10 (PL 183, 1099B-C).

will what now they do by another's [will]: and with their own mouth they would confess the faith, which they now confess by another's tongue. For (as Augustine teaches in his book, *On the Free Choice of the Will*, and by that fact it is sufficiently evident) an adult acquires greater grace in Baptism, who duly prepares himself for its reception, than a child, who receives it without any preparation of soul.[1] And certainly if this were a true and effective remedy, which Cajetan thought up for the spiritual welfare of children, I could rightly accuse the Church of ignorance, because for so many centuries it was ignorant about such a great and such a necessary matter. But if it was not hidden from her, she could be more correctly accused of negligence, due to the fact that she never cared to use such a remedy for children. Yet I with the heart, I [believe] unto justice; and with the mouth, I make confession unto salvation[2] that before Cajetan was born, the Church was not ignorant of something which is effective and necessary for the salvation of souls. For when the Holy Ghost descended upon the Apostles, He taught them every necessary truth. And hence I prove that such an opinion of Cajetan concerning the salvation of children dying without Baptism, which the Church was ignorant of until now, is not true.

It is also clearly established that the perpetual consent of the Church based on the testimonies of the holy Doctors, who all teach in unison not merely that Baptism ought to be given to children, but they say, moreover, that they cannot be saved without Baptism. From which testimonies I present a number of them. [Psuedo-] Augustine says the following: "We have also known children who did not have the use of reason, such that we could judge of their good or evil merits, carried in the arms of their parents for the grace of sacred Baptism, and several times, one of them died in the arms of its parents while the mystery of faith was being performed upon him by the hands of the priest, deprived of the Savior's grace. Who is the wise man understanding these things? Or who will be worthy to give a reason for these things? Let us say with David, 'The Lord is just in all his ways: and holy in all his works' (Ps. 144, 17). And 'How great are thy works, O Lord?' (Ps. 103, 24) 'O Lord, how great are thy works! thy thoughts are exceeding deep' (Ps. 91, 6). Let us also say with the Apostle Paul, 'O the depth of the riches of the wisdom and of the knowledge of God! How incomprehensible are his judgments, and how unsearchable his ways!'"[3] In which words besides saying that an unbaptized child, although carried for Baptism, was not granted God's grace, he answers the argument which the authors of this opinion make, who attempt to prove that salvation can be given to unbaptized children. For they say that this pertains to God's mercy, and it befits Him, that He would give some remedy to unbaptized children, as though God would have been called cruel if no remedy would have been left to them for their salvation. But Augustine humbly answers to these men, admitting his own ignorance and by leaving the decision of these hidden things to God's judgment, believing always that whatever God has done, it was done justly, and not account of this or whatever else ought God to be called cruel.

Gregory says these words: "It is not uncertain, because unless a man shall have been reborn by the grace of sacred Baptism, every soul is bound with the chains of original sin."[4] Isidore [of Seville] speaks thus: "Now to those of older age we believe that Baptism bestows a purgation of the original fault or for the ablution of actual sin: to children, however, it bestows that they are washed from original sin, which they contracted from Adam at the time of birth. Who if they pass away before being regenerated with water and the Holy Ghost, doubtlessly

---

[1] Lib. 3, c. 23, n. 67 (PL 32, 1304).

[2] "Now as my heart believes unto justice, so my mouth shall confess unto salvation" (St. Augustine or St. Anselm (uncertain), *Meditations,* c. 13 (PL 40, 910). Cf. Rom. 10, 10.

[3] *Hypognosticon contra Pelagianos,* lib. 6, c. 7, n. 11 (PL 45, 1663). The *Hypognosticon* is among the spurious works of Saint Augustine.

[4] *Epistolae,* lib. 9, *n.* 52: *Ad Secundinum* (PL 77, 983A).

are alienated from our Christ, the Lord bearing witness saying, 'Unless a man be born again of water and the Holy Ghost, he cannot enter into the kingdom of God.'"[1] Isidore deems that these words of the Savior were said equally in regard of children as to adults. Likewise, does Bede, who in the first book treating of the Canticles of Solomon says the following concerning the errors of Pelagius: "That which he says, namely that 'He Who is good would not condemn a man for what he could not avoid,'[2] contradicts the statement of the same good Redeemer and just Judge, in which he also speaks about children: 'Unless a man be born again of water and the Holy Ghost, he cannot enter into the kingdom of God.'"[3]

I could have brought forth testimonies of many holy men about this matter, but I did not wish to do it, lest I provoke the wearied reader unto nausea. For these things which I have already brought forth are enough to refute the opinion of Gerson and Cajetan, especially since all these holy Doctors have not spoken from their own ideas, but based upon the Savior's statement, which they assert to be understood of all men both children and adults. But so that nothing is lacking which might fully confirm this view, I decided to bring forth a clear decision of the Church on this matter, stated by a number of approved Councils.

The Synod of Milevum (as is evident to nearly everyone) declared that it is necessary to be baptized to obtain the remission of sins. And lest anyone dare to contradict this declaration, due to the fact that the council was provincial, I bring forth the statement which Pope Zosimus gave at that time to confirm that council, and which even if it is not found in the book of councils, nevertheless Augustine cites part of it, saying these words: "'For through Him we are born spiritually; through Him we are crucified to the world. By His death there is destroyed that sentence of death which was introduced and passed on to every soul and contracted by all of us through generation from Adam. Because of that sentence absolutely everyone who has been born is held guilty before being set free by Baptism.'"[4] These words are found in the writing of Augustine, who to show of what importance he deemed this declaration of the Roman Pontiff, immediately after those words of Zosimus, he added these words: "These words of the Apostolic See contain the Catholic faith that is so ancient and well-founded, so certain and clear, that is impious for a Christian to doubt it." Thus let them cease to assert that children can be saved without Baptism, or understand with certainty that they will nowise be reckoned as Christians by Augustine.

The Council of Florence celebrated under Eugene IV twice judged this matter. For in that instruction given to the Armenians, *De Sacramentis*, it declares by these words: "Since death entered into the universe through the first man, 'Unless a man be born again of water and the Holy Ghost, he cannot,' as the Truth says, 'enter into the kingdom of God' (Jn. 3, 5)."[5] And in the definition [from the decree for the Jacobites] it more clearly defined this doctrine, speaking as follows: "With regard to children, since the danger of death is often present and the only remedy available to them is the Sacrament of Baptism by which they are snatched away from the dominion of the devil and adopted as children of God, it admonishes that sacred Baptism is not to be deferred for forty or eighty days or any other period of time in accordance with the usage of some people, but it should be conferred as soon as it conveniently can; and

---

[1] *De ecclesiasticis officiis*, lib. 2, c. 25, n. 7 (PL 83, 822A).

[2] B. R. Rees, *The Letters of Pelagius and his Followers* (Woodbridge, The Boydell Press, 1991), pp. 53-54,

[3] *Allegorica expositio in Cantica canticorum*, lib. 1, (PL 91, 1076C-D).

[4] *Letter 190* (to Optatus), c. 6, n. 23 (PL 33, 865). The citation is from the now lost *Tractoria* of Pope Zosimus, which he wrote in the summer of 418.

[5] Dz. 696 (From the Bull, *Exultate Deo*, Nov. 22, 1439).

if there is imminent danger of death, the child should be baptized straightaway without any delay, even by a lay man."[1]

Finally the Council of Trent says these words: "In these words a description of the justification of a sinner is given as being a translation from that state in which man is born a child of the first Adam to the state of grace and of the 'adoption of the sons' (Rom. 8, 15) of God through the second Adam, Jesus Christ, our Savior; and this translation after the promulgation of the Gospel cannot be effected except through the laver of regeneration (can. 5 *de Bapt.*), or a desire for it, as it is written: 'Unless a man be born again of water and the Holy Ghost, he cannot enter into the kingdom of God' (Jn. 3, 5)."[2]

It remains that I reply to those things which Cajetan objects against us for the confirmation of his opinion. Firstly therefore Cajetan argues from the fact that Baptism succeeded circumcision, and it was figured by it. But circumcision was not so necessary in the Mosaic Law that if one were to die before the eighth day, he could not be saved without it: therefore if a child now dies without Baptism, because it could not be given to him, he could also be saved without it.

We indeed admit that Baptism took the place of circumcision: because Paul seems to teach it (Col. 2, 11),[3] and it is confirmed by testimonies of many Fathers, and finally it was certain decided in the chapter, *Majores*, concerning Baptism and its effects.[4] But we firmly deny that a Jewish child who died before the eighth day could be saved without circumcision, because it is opposed to Sacred Scripture saying: "The male, whose flesh of his foreskin shall not be circumcised, that soul shall be destroyed out of his people" (Gen. 17, 14). For on account of this reason alone (as the holy Doctors interpret[5]) Solomon says that he was the only begotten son of his mother,[6] although (as the book of Kings relates[7]) his mother, Bethsabee, gave birth to another son older than he, whom she conceived in adultery. But because he died before circumcision, he did not have a name any more than if he had not been begotten, nor could he be numbered among God's people. Which things being like this, Cajetan's argument can be easily flung back against him, much more strongly than he had hurled it against us. If, according to the Mosaic Law of old, an uncircumcised child could not be saved, then neither could a child dying without Baptism be saved according to the Evangelical Law, because the words of both Laws speak in the same manner, and have exactly the same force.

Concerning which matter there exists an explicit and clear definition of the Church in *Majores*, concerning Baptism and its effects,[8] where these words are found: "For just as the Mosaic Law was crying out without any distinction, 'The soul, whose flesh of his foreskin shall not be circumcised, that soul shall be destroyed out of his people' (Gen. 17, 14). So now the Evangelical voice without distinction resounds, 'Unless a man be born again of water and the Holy Ghost, he cannot enter into the kingdom of God' (Jn. 3, 5): and it is not excluding either

---

[1] Dz. 712 (From the Bull, *Cantata Domino*, February 4, 1442).

[2] Sess. 6, c. 4 (Dz. 796).

[3] "In whom also you are circumcised with circumcision not made by hand, in despoiling of the body of the flesh, but in the circumcision of Christ."

[4] X, lib. 3, tit. 42, c. 3.

[5] "On Proverbs 4, 3: 'I was...an only son in the sight of my mother,' a gloss says, that Bethsabee's other baby boy did not count because through dying before the eighth day it received no name; and consequently neither was it circumcised." (III, q. 70, a.3 ad 3um).

[6] "For I also was my father's son, tender and as an only son in the sight of my mother" (Prov. 4, 3).

[7] "Nevertheless, because thou hast given occasion to the enemies of the Lord to blaspheme, for this thing, the child that is born to thee, shall surely die" (II Kings 12, 14).

[8] X, lib. 3, tit. 42, c. 3.

sex or age from this generation."[1] In which words it is necessary to note many things against Cajetan. The first is that he says that no sex is excepted by these words of Christ, "Unless a man be born again," etc. Another thing is worthy of noting, is that he says that circumcision of old happened in the same way in the Mosaic Law: because it says concerning it, it was declared without any distinction, "The soul, whose flesh of his foreskin shall not be circumcised, that soul shall be destroyed out of his people." When I carefully examine these things, I do not cease to be amazed with what temerity Cajetan dare do say that the opinion which he states is probable, that a Jewish child having died before the eighth day without circumcision was saved by some blessing or offering. I certainly cannot understand how someone without temerity or some other worse note could say that some opinion is probable, which is contrary to those things defined by the Church.

Secondly, Cajetan objects to us that the martyrdom of children, which without any Baptism can benefit children for salvation. I indeed admit that martyrdom in place of Baptism avails for salvation, and takes the place of it, as Augustine says in his book, *De fide ad Petrum* [*sive de regula verae fidei*,[2] to which Isidore agrees in *De Ecclesiasticis officiis*[3] and Bernard in his *Epistle 77*,[4] and the whole Catholic Church teaches this. For Christ called martyrdom Baptism, when He said to the two brother, the sons of Zebedee: "Can you drink of the chalice that I drink of: or be baptized with the baptism wherewith I am baptized?" (Mk. 10, 38). He here called the shedding of blood unto death baptism. I admit also that children can obtain the palm and merit of martyrdom, as Blessed Thomas rightly asserts,[5] and to the whole Church consents. For the Church celebrates the solemn feast of the infants killed for Christ,[6] and Hilary calls their death martyrdom,[7] and Augustine in a sermon on the Epiphany.[8] And this is not a small privilege of the children, that the shedding of blood on account of Christ, although it is not by their will, takes the place of Baptism, and likewise completely works in them what the water of Baptism works if it had been conferred upon them. Thus adults acquire by their will the palm of martyrdom which the children obtained by God's grace and privilege. But it ought not to be hence concluded that just as martyrdom takes the place of Baptism, so also the prayers and offerings of parents have the power of Baptism, and can supply for it. For the one is so far from the other, that there is no comparison between the two.

Thirdly Cajetan objects that children are completely destitute of any remedy if when dying without Baptism they cannot be saved, which would be exceedingly cruel, and hardly befitting the Divine mercy. To this objection I could reply that which Augustine in his *Hypognosticon* replies to the complaints of a similar sort, saying the following: "But if after having given this reason you still wish to be contentious, and not acquiesce to the truth; yet cease to calumniate us that we reckon badly about the just and most merciful God: but rather reprove Lord Jesus Christ Himself, Whose Gospel we follow, if you dare: take up the quarrel to be

---

[1] Dz. 410.
[2] The authorship of this is uncertain. C. 3, n. 43 & c. 30, n. 73 (PL 40, 775).
[3] Bk. 2, c. 25, n. 2 (PL 83, 820C).
[4] *De Baptismo allisque questionibus ab ipso propositis ad Hugonem de Santo-Victore*, c. 2, n. 9 (PL 182, 1037D).
[5] II II, q. 124, a. 1 ad 1um.
[6] I.e. the feast of the Holy Innocents on December 28th.
[7] "They were appointed, through the glory of martyrdom, for the gain of eternity" (*Super Mattheum* c. 1, n.7 (PL 7, 923C).
[8] *Sermones ad populum*, serm. 373, c. 3 (PL 39, 1664-1665). "A man that does not believe that children are benefited by the baptism of Christ will doubt of your being crowned in suffering for Christ. You were not old enough to believe in Christ's future sufferings, but you had a body wherein you could endure suffering of Christ Who was to suffer." (*Summa theologiae* II-II q. 124, a. 1, ad. 1).

fought with Him; you calumniate Him of what is not the case, namely that He misunderstood His Father, when He said: 'Many are called, but few are chosen' (Mt. 22, 14). And, 'No man can come to me, except the Father, who hath sent me, draw him' (Jn. 6, 44). And, 'No man can come to me, unless it be given him by my Father'" (Jn. 6, 66).[1]

It can also be responded otherwise by denying that children are left without remedy, when they cannot attain Baptism: because martyrdom can (as I said) supply for Baptism. Hence, the parents' prayers, even if they do not suffice for the justification of their children, still could be useful such that by reason of those prayers God would keep their children unharmed until they can attain Baptism whom God would otherwise not preserve. And for this reason parents act prudently if after they come to know that the woman is certainly pregnant, they pray for the fetus, and make offering for him, so that God would keep him unharmed until Baptism.

Some time ago a certain Thomas Netter wrote a few things against this heresy in his book, *De sacramentis*.[2] From whom I have taken nothing in this disputation of mine, due to the fact that some quotations which he cites from Augustine alone hardly pertain to the matter, while the rest are erroneously cited, not through the fault of the author, whom I know was a learned man, but from the fault of the copyists and printers, who often copied very erroneously the things which he most correctly wrote.

There is a **tenth heresy** about this matter, which is nearly diametrically opposed to the preceding one: because it asserts the necessity of Baptism so much that it contends that an adult man, who not on account of contempt, but on account of impossibility passed away from this life without Baptism could not be saved, although at the time he wanted to be baptized, and was then converted to God with his whole heart. Who was the teacher or preacher of this heresy, I could not know to the present time: yet I know from Bernard[3] and Hugo [of Saint Victor][4] that this heresy had some advocate at their time, whose name they kept silent. Notwithstanding who the advocate of this assertion may be, nevertheless we will prove that it is heretical by many very clear arguments.

In the first place it is certainly clear that the Lord said through the Prophet Ezechiel: "The wickedness of the wicked shall not hurt him, in what day soever he shall turn from his wickedness" (33, 12). And again through the Prophet Zachary God says: "Turn ye to me... and I will turn to you" (1, 3). If conversion to God would not be enough, God would then not uphold His promise, whereby He promised to turn to us if we turned to Him.

Perhaps here the advocate of this heresy will reply saying that at that time the precept of Baptism was not given, and for this reason conversion alone without Baptism does not now suffice, which was sufficient at that time. But was not circumcision as necessary at that time as Baptism is now? For just as now it is said, "Unless a man be born again of water and the Holy Ghost, he cannot enter into the kingdom of God" (Jn. 3, 5): so it was said then, "The soul, whose flesh of his foreskin shall not be circumcised, that soul shall be destroyed out of his people" (Gen. 17, 14).

Therefore let us propose that there was some adolescent, uncircumcised dead Jew who repented perfectly for all of his sins, who not due to contempt, but merely on account of necessity omitted circumcision, and about this person I ask whether he was justified and saved or not? If you say that he was not saved, then God did not do according to His aforesaid promises, which He gave through the mouths of His prophets Ezechiel and Zacharias. Now if one were to say this, it would clearly be blasphemous. But if someone would say (as he ought

---

[1] *Hypognosticon contra Pelagianos*, lib. 6, c. 8, 12 (PL 45, 1663-1664).

[2] *Doctrinale antiquitatum fidei Catholicae Ecclesiae*, v. 3 (*De Sacramentis*), c. 96.

[3] Epistle 77: *De Baptismo allisque questionibus ab ipso propositis ad Hugonem de Santo-Victore*, c. 1, n. 1 (PL 182, 1031C).

[4] *On the Sacraments of the Christian Faith*, lib. 2, p. 6, c. 7 (PL 176, 452A ff.).

to say) that that Jew was then saved, he will be consequently forced to admit that he who now is fully converted to God, and while desiring Baptism dies without Baptism is saved: because God said, "The wickedness of the wicked shall not hurt him, in what day soever he shall turn [to Him]." He did not say, in this or that day, but "in what day soever."

And this argument is confirmed by the testimony of Paul saying in his Epistle to the Romans: "If, then, the uncircumcised keep the justices of the law, shall not this uncircumcision be counted for circumcision?" (2, 26) And shortly afterwards he adds: "For it is not he is a Jew, who is so outwardly; nor is that circumcision which is outwardly in the flesh: But he is a Jew, that is one inwardly; and the circumcision is that of the heart, in the spirit, not in the letter; whose praise is not of men, but of God" (v. 28-29). Haymo [of Auxerre][1] when interpreting these words says: "He who is only a Jew by race and name, and carnally practices circumcision, does not please God, nor deserves to be praised by Him, although he be praised by men. But he who is a Jew hiddenly and in his heart, that is, confessing Christ, and is circumcised in his heart from all infidelity, and from all bad will and thought, pleases God, and deserves to be praised by God, hearing from Him: 'Well done, good and faithful servant... enter thou into the joy of thy lord'" (Mt. 25, 21).[2] Now the things which Paul says about the hidden circumcision which is in the heart, the same entirely ought to be said of hidden Baptism received only in the heart: for Baptism replaced circumcision.

Again, Paul says in the same epistle: "With the heart, we believe unto justice; but, with the mouth, confession is made unto salvation" (Rom. 10, 10). Behold you hear Paul teaching that faith gives justice, which ought not to be understood of any [justice], but of that one alone which (as the same Paul says) "that worketh by charity" (Gal. 5, 6). Therefore, if someone perfectly believes in this way, he will be called "just," although he has not actually received Baptism: because one so believing has such a desire for Baptism that, if the possibility were present, he would receive it immediately. Now this desire when it cannot have the doing of the work, is so well accepted by God and esteemed by Him, as if the work itself were done. In testimony of which thing is that which Paul says when writing to the Corinthians, exhorting them, not to contribute more than they can for the support of the poor: but it is enough if they give what they can: because God requires nothing more from them. For he speaks thus: "For if the will be forward, it is accepted according to that which a man hath, not according to that which he hath not" (II Cor. 8, 12). It is as if he more clearly said: 'That willingness is pleasing to God, which is prepared to do what it is able: nor does God demand from someone that he do what he cannot.'"

That idea, it seems to me, seems to derive its origin from these words of Paul, which has now come to be a proverb: *Voluntas pro facto reputatur*.[3] Which idea is not only true when someone cannot do in deed what his will desire. For otherwise when he can do what he desires, and does not do it, then that will is not reputed before God as much as if he had done the work. For God, the Searcher of hearts[4] and "Weigher of spirits" (Prov. 16, 2), knows very well that the will which does not carry out when it can that which it desires, is tepid and remiss, and hence values it less. But that will, which does not perform the deed only because it is not able, He accepts and regards it as having value, as though it had performed the deed. And hence it clearly follows that God accepts the desire of Baptism in place of Baptism, in him who could not be baptized, if nevertheless he fully believes and has converted to God. Thus

---

[1] In Migne's *Patrologia Latina*, this passage is attributed to Haymo of Halberstadt, but as mentioned above (see the section, "Gospel," heresy 2), it has more recently been shown to have been written by Haymo of Auxerre.

[2] *Expositio in Divi Pauli epistolas: In epistolam ad* Romanos, c. 2 (PL 117, 384B).

[3] I.e. the will is to be taken for the deed.

[4] "For the Lord searcheth all hearts, and understandeth all the thoughts of minds" (I Par. 28, 9).

Bernard speaking about this matter elegantly says: "We read, 'Whosoever hateth his brother is a murderer' (I Jn. 3, 15). And likewise, 'He who shall look on a woman to lust after her, hath already committed adultery with her in his heart' (Mt. 5, 28). What is more clear than that the will is to be taken for the deed, where necessity excludes the deed? Unless perhaps it may be thought that the will is found to be more efficacious in evil than in the good before God, Who is charity, and the compassionate and merciful Lord is more inclined to take vengeance than to reward."[1]

Next, martyrdom undergone for Christ supplies for Baptism, thus complete faith with the desire of receiving Baptism, will also supply for Baptism. The whole Catholic Church confesses and teaches the assumed point of this argumentation: because even if Christ's martyrs are not explicitly exempted on account of their martyrdom from that general statement: "Unless a man be born again," etc. (Jn. 3, 5). Yet elsewhere this is specially granted by God when Christ said: "He that shall confess me before men, I will also confess him before my Father" (Mt. 10, 32). Now martyrdom does not have this privilege from anywhere but from faith alone: because martyrdom excluding faith is nothing more than a punishment, which in itself does not have much value before God. If faith is the only reason why martyrdom has this privilege, such that it can supply for Baptism, then that complete faith, "that worketh by charity" (Gal. 5, 6), also supplies for Baptism for the soul's salvation: because it was also specially said of it by Christ our Savior: "He that believeth in me, hath everlasting life" (Jn. 6, 47). And perhaps for this reason (as Bernard says[2]) our Savior afterwards had said: "He that believeth and is baptized, shall be saved", afterwards did not repeat, "but he that is not baptized": but He merely said, "but he that believeth not shall be condemned" (Mk. 16, 16). By which He wished to imply that sometimes faith alone suffices for salvation, and without it nothing suffices.

Add to all these things that the Church, always taught by the Holy Ghost, would immediately give Baptism to requesting catechumens, and to those perfectly disposed to receiving it, and never would delay until a set time, unless she most certainly believed that the will for receiving Baptism was sufficient for them for justification, and consequently for entering God's kingdom, if by force of necessity they were prevented by death, and died without Baptism. For otherwise, the Church would have done a great injury to those catechumens, by deferring their Baptism: because doing so it was placing them in the greatest danger, if per chance an accident would happen whereby having been seized by death, they would depart from this life without Baptism. For as many fatal accidents can happen unto sudden death, so many, nay many more, can prevent them from their long desired Baptism.

Besides all these reasons, there are also testimonies of many holy men in accord on this view, which until now none of the holy men has contradicted. Ambrose speaking about him in his funeral oration on the death of Valentianian [II] says these words: "I lost him whom I was to regenerate: but he did not lose the grace he prayed for."[3] Valentian died without the Baptism that he sought.

Augustine wholeheartedly supports the same opinion in many places, especially in his book, [*On Baptism,*] *Against the Donatists*, where he says these words: "That the place of Baptism is sometimes supplied by martyrdom is supported by an argument by no means trivial, which the Blessed Cyprian adduces from the thief, to whom, though he was not baptized, it was yet said, 'This day thou shalt be with me in paradise' (Lk. 23, 43). On considering which,

---

[1] *De Baptismo allisque questionibus ab ipso propositis ad Hugonem de Santo-Victore*, c. 2, n. 9 (PL 182, 1037B-C).

[2] *De Baptismo allisque questionibus ab ipso propositis ad Hugonem de Santo-Victore*, c. 2, n. 8 (PL 182, 1036C).

[3] *De obitu Valentiniani consolation*, n. 29 (PL 16, 1368B).

again and again, I find that not only martyrdom for the sake of Christ may supply what was wanting of Baptism, but also faith and conversion of heart, if recourse may not be had to the celebration of the mystery of Baptism for want of time."[1] Concerning which words I warn the reader about that example of the thief, whom He just said was not baptized, that he be not persuaded from this citation that he had died without Baptism. For the same Augustine afterwards in his book of *Retractions*, retracted this example which he had proposed of the thief as less suitable for proving the aforesaid opinion, due to fact that it is uncertain whether that thief was baptized or not.[2] Still that opinion concerning invisible baptism which would be sufficient for salvation, when visible Baptism cannot be received, he not only does not recant, but confirms it. And in fact in his *Questionibus super Leviticum*, after he set before some men, whom Scripture recalls as having been only invisibly sanctified without any exterior sign, at length subjoins these words: "Hence it is concluded that some have received the invisible sanctification without visible sacraments, and to their profit; but though it is possible to have the visible sanctification, consisting in a visible sacrament, without the invisible sanctification, it will be to no profit, which were changed for the different times, such that some were then and others now... Yet the visible sacrament ought not to be completely contemned, for its contemnor can nowise be invisibly sanctified."[3] In which words one ought to observe that he says one is deprived of the fruit of Baptism, who contemns, not however he who cannot receive the Sacrament.

Isidore [of Seville] subscribes to the same opinion saying the following: "Now there are three kinds of Baptism: the first of which is that by which the filth of sins are washed away through the laver of regeneration. The second is that whereby one is baptized in his own blood. The third, however, is the baptism of tears, by which one is more laboriously transfixed, as he who every night watered his couch with his tears,[4] who imitated the conversion of Manasses,[5] and the humility of the Ninivites,[6] by which they obtained mercy. Who imitated the prayer of the publican praying in the Temple, standing afar off, and striking his breast, and who dared not so much as lift up his eyes towards heaven."[7] By these words Isidore clearly asserts that true penitence is reputed to take the place of Baptism for the spiritual welfare of the penitent.

Bernard teaches the same opinion saying the following: "Just as someone who calls to mind—it may be at the point of death—that he is pledged to a creditor and lacks the wherewithal to discharge his debt, is believed nonetheless to win remission and be let off any judgment by simple dint of repentance and genuine sorrow, even so will faith alone and the conversion of the mind to God, without the shedding of blood and pouring of water, assuredly win salvation for whomsoever wishes to be baptized but, waylaid by death, is unable to put that wish into effect. And just as no repentance can remit the sin of the debtor who, when he can, does not restore what he has taken, even so no faith will avail the other who fails to re-

---

[1] Lib. 4, c. 22, n. 29 (PL 43, 173).
[2] Lib. 2, c. 55, n. 3 (PL 32, 653).
[3] *Quaestiones in Heptateuchum*, lib. 3 (*Quaestiones in Leviticum*), c. 84 (PL 34, 713).
[4] Cf. Ps. 6, 7.
[5] Cf. II Par. 33, 12-13.
[6] Cf. Jonas 3, 5-10.
[7] Lk. 18, 13. *De Ecclesiasticis officiis*, lib. 2, c. 24, n. 2 (PL 83, 820C).

ceive the sacrament when he is able."[1] Hugo teaches the same view in the place cited above,[2] and Peter Lombard.[3]

Besides all these so clear testimonies of holy men, there also exists a clear decision of the Church regarding this matter. For Pope Innocent III, having been asked by the Bishop of Cremona, replies with these words: "We reply to your question as follows: the priest whom you mentioned who ended his last day [on earth] without Baptism, because he persevered in the faith of holy Mother Church, and the confession of Christ's name, we unhesitatingly affirm that he has been absolved from original sin and has attained the joy of the heavenly kingdom."[4] Finally the Council of Trent celebrated under Paul III when giving the decree on justification says these words: "In these words a description of the justification of a sinner is given as being a translation from that state in which man is born a child of the first Adam to the state of grace and of the 'adoption of sons' (Rom. 8, 15) of God through the second Adam, Jesus Christ, our Savior; and this translation after the promulgation of the Gospel cannot be effected except through the laver of regeneration, or a desire for it, as it is written: 'Unless a man be born again of water and the Holy Ghost, he cannot enter into the kingdom of God' (Jn. 3, 5)."[5] In these words it ought to be especially observed that where he says that justification "cannot be effected except through the laver of regeneration, or a desire for it." For adding, "or a desire for it," he clearly enough declared that to actually receive Baptism is not necessary, but the desire for Baptism is sufficient for justification, when one omits Baptism not out of contempt, but from necessity alone.

But because although this opinion is pronounced in that Council, there were some, though few and less educated, to whom this decree was not pleasing, it is necessary to reply to their objections. Firstly they object to us that Augustine, in the book *Ecclesiasticis dogmatibus*, saying, "No catechumen, although having died with good works has eternal life, except by martyrdom, wherein the whole sacrament of Baptism is completed."[6] But to this objection we easily reply by denying that that work is Augustine's, as many others before me have denied this, saying that it is Gennadius'. And certainly since from many other passages, as also from this one, one may be persuaded that this book is not Augustine's: because it ought not to be believed that Augustine was so forgetful that in this book and in the others cited above, he would have written opinions so clearly contrary, especially since he did not recant in his last book, nor make mention of those others, which he had said in the past. If that book (as many think) has Gennadius as its author, then that testimony of his has little force, because he was not of such esteem, so that by the weight of his authority it would avail to impede us.

Secondly they object against the words which I cited from the Council of Trent, concerning Cornelius, they assert that the centurion, to whom, before he was taught about Christ's faith, the Angel had said: "Send men to Joppe, and call hither one Simon, who is surnamed Peter... who shall speak to thee words, whereby thou shalt be saved, and all thy house" (Acts 10, 5 & 11, 14). But if in these things which Peter was going to say to them Cornelius and his whole

---

[1] *De Baptismo allisque questionibus ab ipso propositis ad Hugonem de Santo-Victore*, c. 2, n. 8 (PL 182, 1037C-D).

[2] "You should, therefore, either confess that true faith and confession of the heart can fulfill the place of baptism in the moment of necessity or show how true faith and unfeigned charity can be possessed where here is no salvation." (*On the Sacraments of the Christian Faith*, lib. 2, p. 6, c. 7 (PL 176, 454B)).

[3] *Libri quattuor sententiarum*, lib. 4, dist. 4, n. 4 (PL 192, 847-848).

[4] X, lib. 3, tit. 43, c. 2 (PL 179, 624-625).

[5] Sess. 6, c. 4 (Dz. 796).

[6] C. 74 (PL 58, 997C). The PseudoAugustinian treatise, *De ecclesiasticis dogmatibus* is now universally attributed to Gennadius of Massilia.

house was to be saved, thus he was not yet just before he was instructed in the faith and baptized by Peter.

This objection is empty and lacking any strength. For Cornelius was truly just before he saw Peter, as Blessed Augustine teaches, saying the following: "For the centurion Cornelius, before Baptism, was better than Simon, who had been baptized. For Cornelius, even before his Baptism, was filled with the Holy Ghost (Acts 10, 44); Simon, even after Baptism, was puffed up with an unclean spirit (*Ibid.*, 8, 13 &18-19). Cornelius, however, would have been convicted of contempt for so holy a Sacrament, if, even after he had received the Holy Ghost, he had refused to be baptized."[1] But Augustine's testimony is not necessary, where there are so many and so clear testimonies of Sacred Scripture. For Scripture relates of him that he was a religious man and fearing God (10, 2): and that his alms were such that they "ascended for a memorial in the sight of God" (10, 4). All of which things could not be truly said except of a justified man.

But that quotation is clearer, namely "While Peter was speaking these words," to the crowd which had gathered in Cornelius' house, "the Holy Ghost fell on all them that heard the word" (Acts 10, 44), and they spoke in various tongues (v. 46), and afterwards Peter said: "Can any man forbid water, that these should not be baptized, who have received the Holy Ghost, as well as we? And he commanded them to be baptized in the name of the Lord Jesus Christ" (v. 47-48). Behold you see that not only Cornelius, but many others were filled with the Holy Ghost, before they had received Baptism. Now the words whereby they assert to prove that Cornelius was not just before the reception of Baptism are not from Sacred Scripture nor are they found in the holy Bibles which have gone around everywhere. For in the common Bibles which it has been allowed to see until now, there are not these words, "who shall speak to thee words, whereby thou shalt be saved, and all thy house." Now the words which Scripture relates that an Angel said to Cornelius, when he was speaking to him about Peter, are these: "He will tell thee what thou must do." Now from these words it can nowise be concluded that Cornelius was not then justified before having received Baptism: but only this can be gathered from those words, namely that although he was then already justified, he was still obliged to receive Baptism: because Peter ordered this to be done after he had instructed in the faith him and all the others who had gathered in his house. Now Baptism is necessary for salvation for every man no matter how much he is otherwise justified, we also confess, and that was clearly confirmed by the testimonies of Augustine and Bernard which were cited by me above.

An **eleventh heresy** has arisen about Baptism, which, although it concedes that by Baptism original sin is remitted, nevertheless it denies that through it every sin is removed. Because after Baptism has been received the concupiscence of the flesh or the rebellion of the flesh, remains, which (as the authors of this heresy teach) is truly a sin, although it is not imputed to God. Now that concupiscence is truly a sin, they try to prove on the grounds that (as they say) it is contrary to God's precept, "Thou shalt not covet."[2] The parent and first author of this heresy was Luther, whom afterwards Philip Melanchthon, the monk Martin Bucer, having apostatized from the Order of Saint Dominic, [Johannes] Brenz, and many other Germans of the same Lutheran faction followed.

In this heresy, as has just been related, two errors are mixed together, of which one arises from the other. The first is the error which asserts that Baptism does not remove every sin. The second teaches that concupiscence of the flesh is a sin against the precept, "Thou shalt not covet." Concerning this second error we will say nothing in this place: because below in the

---

[1] *On Baptism, Against the Donatists* lib. 4, c. 21, n. 28 (PL 43, 172-173).
[2] *Non concupisces*.

section on, "Precept," we will, with God as our Guide, contend against it, there will be a more suitable place for the disputation, and hence I send the reader to this place for this matter.

Therefore going forth to fight against that first error I now make as an objection that which the Prophet Micheas says: "He will put away our iniquities: and he will cast all our sins into the bottom of the sea" (Cant. 7, 19). In which words the prophet very clearly declared that the power and efficacy of Baptism is so great, that it swallows up all sins and allows none to remain. For that which the prophet says in the same place about Baptism, is clearly proved by that which Paul says: "Our fathers were all under the cloud, and all passed through the sea. And all in Moses were baptized, in the cloud, and in the sea" (I Cor. 10, 1-2). From which words it is clearly enough established that Baptism was represented by the sea, and compared to it. Thus the Prophet Micheas speaks concerning this sea when he says: "He will cast all our sins into the bottom of the sea." He did not say "some," but "all."

Perhaps Luther and his consorts will say that Baptism, according to Paul's view, is not represented by any sea, but only by the Red Sea through which our fathers passed, but Michaes did not speak about any particular sea, and hence they contend that the words of the prophet are distorted into a sense different from the literal sense (as they themselves are accustomed to do). But they cannot escape thus, as though we cannot refute them, because derived from their reply there is an ultimate argument against them. If the Red Sea through which our fathers passed was a figure of Baptism, it follows that the Egyptians, who followed after our fathers, represented the sins which pursue after us, and Pharao, the king of the Egyptians, was the figure of the devil, who (as it is written in the book of Job) is "king over all the children of pride" (Job 41, 25). But in that sea, in which the children of Israel were saved, all the Egyptians, who pursued them perished along with Pharao their king. "The waters returned," Sacred Scripture says, "and covered the chariots and the horsemen of all the army of Pharao, who had come into the sea after them, neither did there so much as one of them remain" (Ex. 14, 28). Thus in order that the figure truly corresponds to the thing figured, it is necessary that all sins perish in the water of Baptism, and not one of them remain.

Furthermore, the opinion is more clearly confirmed by that which God says through the Prophet Ezechiel: "I will pour upon you clean water, and you shall be cleansed from all your filthiness" (Ez. 36, 25). He did not say, "from some filthiness," but "from all," so that we may understand that there is none excepted, which is not washed away by the water. Now that these words of Ezechiel ought to be understood of the Sacrament of Baptism, all the holy Doctors unanimously teach: because there is no water that can wash away all filthiness except the water of Baptism alone. Again, when our Savior was proclaiming the necessity of Baptism, he called Baptism itself regeneration, saying the following: "Unless a man be born again of water and the Holy Ghost, he cannot enter into the kingdom of God" (Jn. 3, 5). And Paul, so that he might make Christ's words clearer, after he called Baptism "the laver of regeneration," immediately added, "and renovation" (Tit. 3, 5). By which words he declared what sort of regeneration it is which is obtained by Baptism, namely such which puts off the soul's oldness, and puts on newness.[1]

For on account of this reason Christ our Savior in Matthew's Gospel calls the resurrection of the body regeneration,[2] because by that resurrection the body is so completely renewed, putting off everything old, so that one may now seem to be born by a new birth. Now hunger has gone away, thirst has departed, sickness has fled, torture, sorrows, weaknesses, corruptions and finally everything old has passed away, and all things are made new. Only the substance of the body remaining the same, nearly all the characteristics of the body are changes. The same thing certainly happens to the soul by Baptism, because by it man who before was

---

[1] Cf. Eph. 4, 22 & 24.
[2] Mt. 19, 28.

the son of the devil by sin, afterwards is made a son of God by Baptism. Thus there is a renewal in the soul by Baptism, just as there is a renewal in the body by the resurrection. There would not have been a complete and perfect renovation, if something of the oldness of sin would remain.

Many things which Paul writing to the Romans relate to this opinion, and when discussing original sin and its remedy, which is Baptism, he says: "Where sin abounded, grace did more abound. That as sin hath reigned to death; so also grace might reign by justice unto life everlasting, through Jesus Christ our Lord" (Rom. 5, 20-21). If sin remains after the grace of Baptism has been conferred, then grace does not abound more, as Paul teaches, but rather sin. But so that we might more clearly refute Luther, it will be useful to examine the manner of the superabundance, which Paul declares: "So that as," he says, "sin hath reigned to death, so also grace might reign by justice." But since sin reigned in man, there was no grace of God in him: thus on the contrary when God's grace reigns in a baptized man, there will be no sin in him, otherwise it will not be said to reign in him, and hence it follows further that grace does not abound more, where sin had abounded, the contrary of which Paul teaches.

And although in this passage Paul clearly condemns Luther, still [Paul] does this much more clearly and strongly afterwards in the same epistle saying the following: "Know you not that all we, who are baptized in Christ Jesus, are baptized in his death? For we are buried together with him by baptism into death" (Rom. 6, 3-4). In which words Paul very clearly teaches that we become through Baptism members of the Mystical Body, whose Head is Christ: and then we undergo Christ's death in ourselves. For Christ having died upon the Cross for our sins, Who is our Head, then we who are His members die to sin with Him. For if you cut off the head of a man and kill him, necessarily all his members die together. After the same manner in which Christ died, so those who have been baptized die with Him, who then having received Baptism have been made His members. Still He dies in one way and we in another way through Baptism: because He died with His Body, but we die to sin. His Flesh died upon the Cross, and our sin died in Baptism.

Hence Blessed Chrysostom when explaining Paul's words quoted above says: "What does being 'baptized in His death' mean? [It means] that it is with a view to our dying as He did. For Baptism is the Cross. What the Cross then, and burial, is to Christ, that Baptism has been to us, even if not in the same respects. For He died Himself and was buried in the flesh, but we have done both to sin. Wherefore he does not say, planted together 'in His death,' but 'in the likeness of His Death.' For both the one and the other is a death, but not of the same subject; since the one is of the flesh, that of Christ; the other of sin, which is our own. As the former is real, so is the latter."[1] From which words it is established that it is Paul's doctrine, namely that in Baptism sin is fully dead, just as Christ on the Cross was so fully dead that nothing of human life remained in Him. But if after Baptism something would remain in the one baptized, which is truly a sin, then in Baptism sin would not die as fully as Christ died upon the Cross.

But Paul goes on further to teach the same opinion, by those words which he adds in the same place after the previous words, saying the following: "Knowing this, that our old man is crucified with him, that the body of sin may be destroyed" (Rom. 6, 6). He did not say that "sin may be destroyed," lest it might be thought that one or another sin is destroyed: but he said, "the body of sin may be destroyed": so that he might teach that nothing of sin remains. And if perhaps Luther tries to understand these words of Paul otherwise, let him hear, I beseech him, Blessed Chrysostom interpreting these words, who says the following: "Not giving that name to this body of ours, but to all iniquity. For as he calls the whole sum of wickedness the old man, thus again the wickedness which is made up of the different parts of iniquity he calls the body of that man. And that what I am saying is not mere guesswork,

---

[1] *Homily 10 on Romans*, n. 3 (PG 60, 480).

hearken to Paul's own interpretation of this very thing in what comes next. For after saying, 'that the body of sin might be destroyed,' he adds, 'to the end that we may serve sin no longer.' For the way in which I would have it dead is not so that you should be destroyed and die, but so that you sin not. And as he goes on he makes this still clearer. This he says of every man, that as he that is dead is henceforth justified from sin, lying as a dead body, so must he that has come up from Baptism, since he has died there once for all, remain ever dead to sin."[1]

Theophylactus interprets this passage in the same way saying the following: "For 'our old man,' that is to say, our malice, 'is crucified with him,' that is, just as Christ's Body was buried, in Baptism, 'that the body of sin may be destroyed,' that is, either vice composed from various parts and as coalescing into one body, or our body inclined to sin: hence he concludes, 'to the end that we may serve sin no longer.'"[2] In the same point of view [Hervé, monk of Bourg-Dieu], explaining the aforesaid words of Paul much more clearly, says the following: "'The body of sin,' that is, may sin be destroyed in all the members. For one vice is a member of sin: but the body is the totality of sins, of which the principle is original sin. Now Christ was not partly but entirely crucified, so that we might die to all sin and we may live to God. For God's grace does this through the Baptism of Christ, Who came in the likeness of sinful flesh, so that the body of sin may be destroyed."[3]

Paul teaches again the same opinion in the same epistle, saying the following: "There is now therefore no condemnation to them that are in Christ Jesus, who walk not according to the flesh. For the law of the spirit of life, in Christ Jesus, hath delivered me from the law of sin and of death" (Rom. 8, 1-2). Which words doubly slay Luther's opinion. If concupiscence of the flesh were a sin, as Luther says, then something of damnation would belong to those things which are in Christ Jesus: for every sin is of itself damnable. And since Paul says that nothing of damnation is in the baptized, the consequence is that there is no sin in them. Moreover, if concupiscence after having received Baptism is a sin, then the law of the Spirit of life did not completely free us from the law of sin, the contrary of which Paul teaches.

Then in another epistle Paul says: "For as many of you as have been baptized in Christ, have put on Christ" (Gal. 3, 27). But those who have put on Christ especially do not have a damnable sin: because "Wisdom will not enter into a malicious soul, nor dwell in a body subject to sins" (Wis. 1, 4). For "What fellowship hath light with darkness? And what concord hath Christ with Belial?" (II Cor. 6, 14-15). Nor is it enough for the evasion of all these arguments to say, as Philip Melanchthon says, that the concupiscence which is in the baptized, ought not to be imputed as regards punishment, although it is truly a sin: and Baptism does this, so that concupiscence may not be imputed, not however that it is not a sin. Because although it may not be imputed, if it is still truly a sin, it puts a stain on the soul, which cannot be in him who is fully cleansed by Baptism. For Paul says concerning those who are baptized: "You are washed, but you are sanctified, but you are justified" (I Cor. 6, 11).

Besides all these very clear testimonies of Sacred Scripture, there is also in favor of our and the Catholic view, the consensus of all the holy Doctors, which alone, even if express testimonies of Sacred Scripture were lacking, would be enough for condemning Luther's opinion. For besides Chrysostom, Theophylactus and Hervé, whom we have cited above, there is also Peter the Venerable[4] having the same opinion, who in his sermon on the washing of the feet says these words: "The Church was ornamented and honored as paradise, in the navel of its amplitude, containing the font of singular grace, creating rivers springing up unto eternal life,

---

[1] *Homily 11 on Romans*, n. 1 (PG 60, 487).

[2] *Expositio in Epistolam ad Romanos* (PG 124, 411).

[3] *Commenatarius in Epistolas Divi Pauli* (PL 181, 672C). The text attributes this book to Saint Anselm of Canterbury, but it is the production of Hervé, monk of Bourg-Dieu.

[4] The text here mistakenly has Cyprian, to whom this sermon was formerly ascribed.

having a living origin and perpetual running down. From this place four rivers of the Gospels going forth, through the whole world they carry with them the laver of regeneration, and fluid of this grace flows out from the hidden and most secret gift of the Holy Ghost, thus washing those whom the parental stain had spoiled, so that it does not leave any trace of actual or original stain after that washing."[1] By which words he clearly sufficiently condemns Luther's opinion, since he says, Baptism leaves no trace of sin.

Blessed Augustine subscribes to the same opinion in many places, especially in his book, *Contra Julianum pelagianum*, saying the following: "Grace perfectly renews man, since it brings him even to immortality of body and full happiness. It perfectly renews man now, also, as regards deliverance from all sins, but not as regards deliverance from all evils, nor from every ill of mortality, by which the body is now a load upon the soul."[2] And after many words he again says: "Although man's body is also sanctified in sacred Baptism, it is sanctified so that through the remission of sins he is not bound by any guilt for past sins, nor for the concupiscence of the flesh which exists in him. Every man at birth is necessarily answerable by the guilt of this concupiscence, and will be until death, if he is not reborn."[3] In which words he most clearly teaches that through Baptism every sin is remitted, and that concupiscence itself which before Baptism was a sin, yet afterwards when Baptism has been received, if it still remains, it is not a sin. And again after many words when teaching the same opinion more clearly, he says the following; "You are much mistaken in thinking: 'If concupiscence were an evil, he who is baptized would lose it.' Such a man loses every sin, but not every evil. More plainly, he loses all guilt for all evils, but not all evils. Does he lose bodily corruption? Is this not an evil weighing down the soul, so that he erred who said: 'The corruptible body is a load upon the soul' (Wis. 9, 15)?"[4] By which words nothing can be more clearly said against the whole opinion of Luther. For he says that concupiscence is not a sin, but is an evil, meaning, it is a punishment, which is called an evil by God Himself, through the Prophet Jeremias saying: "I will bring in evils" (Jer. 11, 11). Then he says that in Baptism "every sin is remitted," but "not every evil."

Which words having been carefully considered, I cannot but marvel how Philip Melanchthon in the Conference of public debate, which he had with [Johann Maier von] Eck[5] in Worms in the year of the Lord 1540 dared to say that Augustine always held this opinion, and never changed it, namely he said that the concupiscence, which is in the baptized, is truly and properly a sin. I certainly marvel, and with very good reason, at the brazen audacity of this man, such that in that Conference before such an illustrious gathering, he was not afraid to say such an open lie, and to accuse Augustine of such a false crime, that Augustine himself, if he were still alive, could not bear, and by no means would consent to. Philip Melanchthon indeed rightly said that Augustine always held the same opinion, yet not the one which Philip, consenting to Luther, teaches, but to that one which we defend, and the whole Catholic Church holds. For he teaches the same view in his *Enchiridion* to Lawrentius,[6] in his book, *Against Two Letters of the Pelagians*,[7] and in his book, *On Marriage [and Concupiscence]* to [Count] Valerius[8]: and the reader will find this last testimony in this work, in the section on, "Pre-

---

[1] *De cardinalibus operibus Christi usque ad Ascensum*, c. 7 (PL 189, 1650D).
[2] Lib. 6, c. 13, n. 40 (PL 44, 844).
[3] *Ibid.* c. 14, n. 44 (PL 44, 847).
[4] *Ibid.* c. 16, n. 49 (PL 44, 850-851).
[5] Johann Maier von Eck (1486–1543) was a German Scholastic theologian and defender of Catholicism during the Protestant Reformation.
[6] *De fide, spe et charitate*, c. 52 (PL 40, 257).
[7] Lib. 3, c. 7, n. 17 (PL 44, 600).
[8] Bk. 1, c. 23, n. 5 (PL 44, 428).

cepts," in the fourth heresy[1]: where it is proved that the concupiscence which remains in those who have been baptized, is not a sin. Therefore I send the reader to that place, because the things that we will say in that place help much for the expurgation of the present heresy. For when it shall have been proved that the concupiscence which remains in the baptized is not truly a sin, from that it will immediately be proved against Luther that no sin remains in one who has been baptized, since we dispute with the Lutherans about this concupiscence alone.

Cassiodorus teaches the same opinion as Augustine, in his commentary on the words, "Wash me yet more from my iniquity" (Ps. 50, 4), saying the following: "This laver, which so washes away the stains of sins, that it can cleanse what is soiled brighter than snow, is known to indicate the purity of salubrious Baptism, wherein all one's own crimes and original sin are cleansed, such that it restores us to that purity in which the first Adam is known to have been brought forth."[2]

Finally the Council of Trent celebrated under Paul III, at which I was present, pronounced this definition of faith concerning this matter: "If anyone denies that by the grace of our Lord Jesus Christ, which is conferred in Baptism, the guilt of original sin is remitted, or even asserts that the whole of that which has the true and proper nature of sin is not taken away, but says that it is only shaved off[3] or is not imputed, let him be anathema."[4]

But it is now necessary that we reply to those things which Luther objects to us, and after him Philip Melanchthon, all which things have but little strength. He objects to us that passage of Paul: "For I do not that good which I will; but the evil which I hate, that I do. Now if I do that which I will not, it is no more I that do it, but sin that dwelleth in me. (Rom. 7, 19-20). In which words Paul clearly calls concupiscence of the flesh "sin," which, since it remains in the baptized, evidently (as Luther says) shows that after Baptism has been received, always remains a sin. But this argumentation unsettles absolutely no one, except perhaps an uneducated and completely ignorant man: because it proceeds from ignorance of the metonymical[5] manner of speech, according to the use of which, we often attribute the name of the cause to the effect. For a language, owing to the fact that the tongue utters it, we call "a tongue," as it is said of the Apostles, that after the Coming of the Holy Ghost "they began to speak with divers tongues," even though each one of them had only one tongue by which he uttered his words. In the same manner we call a written work a "pen," due to the fact that it was written with a pen [in the expression, "The pen is mightier than the sword"].[6] According to the same manner of speech Paul says concupiscence is a sin: because it is caused by sin. For on account of the cause the Prophet said that he was conceived "in sins" (Ps. 50, 7), although there is only one original sin in every man, and not more. But because there are many punishments inflicted on account of original sin, calling them all "sins," he said that he was conceived in sins. Concupiscence can also be called sin, because it always tempts to sin, and often is its cause.

Then Philip Melanchthon objects to us again citing Paul: "I see another law in my members, fighting against the law of my mind, and captivating me in the law of sin, that is in my members" (Rom. 7, 23). In which words (as Melanchthon says) Paul calls concupiscence itself the law of his members, and he says that it is sin: and from this Melanchthon thinks that it is clearly concluded that sin remains in the baptized. But he errs by the whole breadth of the

---

[1] The text here has "first heresy," but the fourth heresy seems more correct, but this quotation of Saint Augustine does not seem to be present in this section titled, "Precept."
[2] *Expositio in Psalterium* (PL 70, 360C).
[3] Cf. St. Augustine, *Against Two Letters of the Pelagians*, bk. 1, c. 13, n. 26 (PL 44, 562).
[4] Sess. 5, n. 5 (Dz. 792).
[5] Here the author incorrectly used the word "synecdochical."
[6] "We call a writing or picture 'a hand'" found here in the text is based upon a Latin metonymy, not used in English, and so it has been replaced here with a common English metonymy.

heavens, because Paul, even if he calls concupiscence the "law of sin," still he does not say that it is truly and properly sin. Now he calls that concupiscence a "law," because carnal men and those given to concupiscence, obey the concupiscence of the flesh, just like the precept of some very powerful king. For we are accustomed to call the edicts and commands of a tyrant "laws," no matter how evil, just as the decrees of a good prince. And because that concupiscence always draws to sin, thus he called it the law of sin.

Haymo [of Auxerre] interprets this passage differently, not in fact of concupiscence of the flesh, which wages an irreconcilable and perpetual war with the spirit, but he associates it with the habit of sin, which leads us captive to sin.[1] But the previous interpretation pleases me more, which is according to the opinion of Chrysostom[2] and Theophylactus.[3] I wished to state it in this place so that Philip Melanchthon may know how much he erred from the true meaning of Paul, since all the sacred Doctors interpret all those words of Paul differently.

It is also similar to that which Philip cites from Paul: "The wisdom of the flesh is death" (Rom. 8, 6). For Paul calls "wisdom of the flesh" that which even if it is in the mind, is according to the inclination and appetite of the flesh. But Paul does not say that this wisdom is in all the reborn, and hence the argument is vain which Philip takes from this place to prove that sin always remains in the baptized. He cites other testimonies which because nowise support him not even superficially, hence they seem to me to be unworthy to waste time in responding to them. John Fisher, Bishop of Rochester, wrote against this heresy in the work which he published against Luther's errors.[4]

The **twelfth** and last **heresy** (that I know of) concerning this matter belongs to certain men who are called the Flagellants concerning whom we spoke above. These men said that Baptism of water already ceased, and was changed to baptism of blood. They prove that [heresy] from an inept allegory of Scripture. For they say that when Christ changed water into wine in Cana of Galilee at nearly the end of the marriage nuptials, He indicated that near the end of the world Baptism of water ought to be changed into baptism of blood. And just as the red wine pleased the guests and was valued more than all the wine previously served: so the new law of baptism of blood will be accepted by God more agreeably than all the laws previously given. Wherefore they said that after their coming into the world, no one could be saved and be a true Christian, unless he be baptized in his own blood shed from his body with a flagellum.

Which [heresy] ought to be called not only heresy, but also absurdity and madness. For what they firstly say, that Baptism has ceased, we will show to be false, when against them in the section on, "Gospel," we will prove that Gospel law will be eternal; there will be no other one afterwards. Now what they say, that Baptism was likewise changed into baptism of blood, without which no one can be saved, if they would show this from the literal sense of the Gospel, I might believe: but the allegorical sense of Scripture (as we taught above at the beginning of this book) nowise is efficacious to establishing a dogma. Furthermore, He Who said: "He that believeth and is baptized, shall be saved" (Mk 16, 16), did not say: "He who scourges himself, will be saved: but he who does not scourge himself, will be condemned."

If therefore the Lord did not say this, He Who kills and brings to life, and Who can send the body and soul into Hell: by what authority do they dare to condemn those who do not flagellate themselves? Again, even if the shedding of blood for Christ may supply (as Blessed Augustine says) in place of Baptism: nevertheless, it does not completely weaken its validity and power. For it is enough that it can take its place. Then it is necessary that the shedding

---

[1] *Expositio in Divi Pauli epistolas: In epistolam ad* Romanos (PL 117, 424D-425A).
[2] *In epistolam ad Romanos*, Hom. 13, n. 2 (PG 60, 509 ff.).
[3] *Expositio in Epistolam ad Romanos* (PG 124, 430B).
[4] *Assertionis Lutheranae confutatio* (Cologne, Maternus Cholinus, 1564), art. 2, fol. 63r-97v.

of blood, which deserves to take the place of Baptism, be inflicted by another, rather than the one patiently enduring it, so that it can take the place of Baptism. But since one who inflicts death upon himself, or such wounding of his body, from which the body would be in danger in regard to its life, as the wicked Flagellants say they have done, it does not merely not take the place of Baptism, but it deserves Hell.

BEATITUDO

Beatitude

Concerning this matter there is a heresy of the Armenians asserting that the Blessed do not see God's essence, but instead a certain brightness of his essence: in which vision they say beatitude consists. Afterwards a certain Peter Abelard[1] revived this error saying that God is not seen in His essence by the Blessed. This Peter was French, who, in the time of Pope Innocent II relying on his own ingenuity, began to despise all the opinions of the holy Doctors, and as another Ismael lifted up his hands against all men. Wherefore it was just that the hands of all men be lifted up against him. Therefore from this excessive confidence in himself it happened that he fell into many errors, which others having followed him tried to defend, especially an Italian named Arnold of Brescia, after whom (as I suppose) the Arnoldist heretics are named, who are excommunicated every year on Holy Thursday in Rome.[2] Against this Peter Abelard rose up Saint Bernard, who, in order to debate with him and recall him back to the true faith, came to the city of Rheims from his monastery located in Burgundy: yet Peter, afraid of being vanquished by Blessed Bernard, did not wish to meet with him. For so Blessed Bernard himself relates in a letter.[3] Among the other errors that Peter Abelard taught, one error was that he said God is not seen by the Blessed in His essence. After this Abelard rose up a certain Almalric of Bena, concerning whom we have already spoken above,[4] who defended this error, saying that God is nowise seen in Himself, but in His creatures. Among all these men therefore they agree in this, that they all assert that God is nowise seen, not even by the Blessed.

Now that this assertion is heretical, we will most clearly prove from explicit testimonies of Scripture. Paul in fact, in his first Epistle to the Corinthians when distinguishing between that knowledge which we have in this life about God and that which afterwards we will have in glory, says: "We see now through a glass in a dark manner; but then face to face" (13, 12). Notice that Paul clearly promises the facial vision of God in the time to come. But if God would only be seen through creatures, and not more, who does not see that that vision is through a glass? For in creatures a certain likeness of God appears: wherefore creatures themselves are a glass though which we see God. Hence it follows that the Blessed merely seeing God in creatures (as these heretics assert) still see God though a glass, and do not have a clearer knowledge than those who live in this world. Furthermore, Blessed John in the Apocalypse, speaking about the condition of the heavenly country, under the name and figure of the new Jerusalem, speaks thus: "And there shall be no curse any more; but the throne of God and of the Lamb shall be in it, and his servants shall serve him. And they shall see his face" (22, 3-4). Again the Lord Jesus Christ commending the little children who believe in Him says: "See that you despise not one of these little ones: for I say to you, that their angels in heaven always

---

[1] Peter Abelard lived from 1079 to 1142.
[2] X, lib. 5, tit. 7 (*De haereticis*), c. 15 (*Excommunicamus*); St. Gregory IX, edict *Excommunicamus*.
[3] Letter 190 (PL 182, 1055D ff).
[4] Actually, this is the first time he is mentioned in this work.

see the face of my Father who is in heaven" (Mt. 18, 10). Notice based upon our Savior's statement, that the Angels always see God's face. Thus, how do these heretics do not fear to say that God is never seen in Himself? It certainly appears that they have "assembled together against the Lord and his Christ" (Ps. 2, 2 & Apoc. 4, 26).

But if they would perhaps say that they spoke merely about men, and not about the Angels, so that they concede the vision of God to the Angels but they deny it to men: they ought to consider what is said by the same Savior: "For in the resurrection they shall neither marry nor be married; but shall be as the angels of God in heaven" (Mt. 22, 30). From which words it is apparent that Christ has equated men with the Angels in the other life. But this quotation (as I openly admit) only equates men to Angels in that they will have no use of matrimony, just as the Angels will not: it does not, however, make them equal as to the facial vision of God. Nevertheless even if He does not speak about men in that passage, they cannot deny that Paul and John in the quotations recently cited expressly speak about men. Wherefore if they restrict their assertion to men only, we object to them those two passages of Scripture. What the Royal Prophet petitions adds to these when saying: "Shew us thy face, and we shall be saved" (Ps. 79, 4). He does not ask for what is impossible to be given: otherwise, he would deserve to hear what the Lord said to the two brothers petitioning through their mother: "You know not what you ask" (Mt. 20, 22). Moses also asked for this, saying: "If I have found favour in thy sight, shew me thy face" (Ex. 33, 13). Notice the testimonies are very clear whereby we have shown that God is seen by the Blessed in His essence.

Now what motivated these heretics to so err, I do not find cited by anyone. For Guy [the Carmelite] also, who discusses this error of the Armenians,[1] does not cite any occasion for their error, just as he generally does not do for other errors. For he rejects the errors of other men in such a way that he never replies to their arguments: which nevertheless is as necessary as to reject their errors. For as Augustine says in his book, *On Christian Doctrine*, "It is, however, exceedingly desirable that whatever occurs to the mind as an objection that might be urged should be stated and refuted, lest it turn up at a time when no one will be present to answer it, or lest, if it should occur to a man who is present but says nothing about it, it might never be thoroughly removed."[2]

Therefore, regarding the present case they took (as I think) as an occasion of the error, that it is said in many places of Scripture that God is not seen by anyone. For example, in Exodus it is said, "Man shall not see me and live" (Ex. 33, 20). And Job speaking about the Divine wisdom says: "It is hid from the eyes of all living, and the fowls of the air know it not" (Job 28, 21). And Paul in his First Epistle to Timothy says: "Who... inhabiteth light inaccessible, whom no man hath seen, nor can see" (6, 16). And Blessed John in his First Epistle says: "No man hath seen God at any time" (4, 12). Therefore by these quotations of Scripture having been misunderstood it seemed to me that these heretics could have been led into the aforesaid error, which things it is necessary to put forward for discussion, and to respond to them, lest perhaps others reading, and not understanding, fall into the same error.

We indeed admit that God is seen by no one in this life: nay nor can He be seen (according to the law given) by a living man in this corruptible life: because He would either be seen by bodily sight, or by the intellect. Bodily sight (as it is evident) is not capable of the Divine vision. But the soul when it is in its mortal body, uses the ministry of the senses: because an artisan cannot do his work more nicely than the nature of his instrument allows, whereby he works intermediately. Therefore, since the soul uses the senses as an instrument for its operations, it will be unable to go beyond those things which pertain to the sensitive power. Now

---

[1] *Summa de haeresibus et earum confutationibus*, fol. 31r & v, c. 5.
[2] Lib. 4, c. 20, n. 39 (PL 34, 107).

the senses are unable to see God. Therefore, neither can the soul when it is within the mortal body see God using the ministry of the senses.

And the things that God says in Exodus, saying: "Man shall not see me and live" ought to be understood in this sense. And what John says, "No man hath seen God at any time" ought to be understood such that no one may see God while he lives in this mortal life. Now that which is said, namely that Paul when he was rapt up to the third Heaven saw God,[1] does not conflict with this view. For although Paul saw, this was done after his soul was previously withdrawn beyond the use and ministry of his senses. For even if the soul were within the body (which is unsure to Paul himself) nevertheless it had been separated from the ministry of the senses. Now this is so concluded because Paul says: "whether in the body, or out of the body, I know not: God knoweth" (II Cor. 12, 3). But if his soul then used the ministry of the senses, Paul certainly would have known that he was then in the body.

Now concerning other men whom Scripture relates to have seen God, it ought to be so understood, so that we may understand that they saw some Angels shining with great brightness somehow representing the Divinity Itself: wherefore, those who saw them, were saying that they had seen God. For thus Jacob said: "I have seen God face to face, and my soul has been saved" (Gen. 32, 30). This also is said of Moses: "And the Lord spoke to Moses face to face, as a man is wont to speak to his friend" (Ex. 33, 11). But if Moses had seen God clearly, he would have prayed to God in vain, saying: "If therefore I have found favour in thy sight, shew me thy face, that I may know thee" (Ex. 33, 13). Therefore all these men, and however many others, who have been found in Sacred Scripture to have seen God, saw God as an image: although some think regarding Moses that he clearly saw God, his soul nevertheless having then been withdrawn from the ministry of the senses.[2] For so is understood what was said by the Lord to the same Moses: "Man shall not see me and live."

And what Job says, that wisdom "is hid from the eyes of all living," namely those who live in this mortal life. But then that which Paul said now comes to the fore: "Who… inhabiteth light inaccessible, whom no man hath seen, nor can see." To which we reply that Paul called the Divine light "inaccessible," yet not simply as being inaccessible to all, but to man. Hence, to confirm this he immediately added, "whom no man hath seen." Therefore it is inaccessible, but to man. He is invisible, but to man, to human wisdom. Sacred Scripture in fact is accustomed to call all who live according to the flesh "men," and so brand the characteristics of humanity. Wherefore Paul says: "Whereas there is among you envying and contention, are you not carnal, and walk according to man?" (I Cor. 3, 3) And afterwards: "Are you not men?" (v. 4) Hence it is that when in the same epistle he cited the testimony of Isaias saying that "eye hath not seen, nor ear heard, neither hath it entered into the heart of man, what things God hath prepared for them that love him" (I Cor. 2, 9).[3] Afterwards Paul subjoins: "But to us God hath revealed them, by this Spirit" (v. 10). By which words he clearly separates himself from the name of man, in that he was not living according to the flesh. None, therefore, of those who on account of their life according to the flesh are called "men" see God, nay neither can they see God.

Concerning other men, however, that they will clearly see God in the next life, Paul could not testify more clearly, than saying: "We see now through a glass in a dark manner; but then face to face" (I Cor. 13, 12). Hence it is evident that men would at some time have the facial vision of God. Now concerning the Angels the Truth very clearly said: "Their angels

---

[1] II Cor. 12, 2.
[2] "Augustine (*Ep.* 147, 13; *ad Paulin., de videndo Deum*) concludes that 'possibly God's very substance was seen by some while yet in this life: for instance by Moses, and by Paul who in rapture heard unspeakable words, which it is not granted unto man to utter.'" (II II, q. 175, a. 3 s.c.).
[3] Cf. Is. 64, 4.

in heaven always see the face of my Father who is in heaven" (Mt. 18, 10). Nor does what Blessed Peter say oppose this saying of the Savior: "On whom the angels desire to look" (I Pet. 1, 12). For the Angels both see and desire to see, just as also other Blessed men seeing desire and desiring see. The Blessed in fact seeing God are satisfied, according to the passage of the Psalm: "I shall be satisfied when thy glory shall appear" (Ps. 16, 15). Certainly, a desire without its attaining what it desires has anxiety: and anxiety has pain. But the Blessed lack all pain of anxiety: because pain and beatitude can never be together. Wherefore from both, namely from satiety and desire, if we remove all that which seems to inflict pain, namely displeasure and anxiety, we will attribute to the Blessed satiety and desire, such that by removing anxiety from desire, we may say that they when desiring are satisfied, and by separating from the displeasure of satiety, we may say that they having been satisfied desire. Therefore Peter says well: "On whom the angels desire to look": because even if they see, still they desire to see: that is, they so enjoy the vision of God that although they are satisfied, still they have no displeasure therefrom. Therefore, for the refutation of this heresy I think that I have said enough, according to that brevity which I promised to have.

The **second heresy** is that which asserts that beatitude consists in the pleasures of the flesh. This error was of old found among certain Jews, who understand carnally all the things that were said by the Prophets concerning Christ.

From which error seems to have proceeded that petition of the mother of the sons of Zebedee asking from Christ: "Say that these my two sons may sit, the one on thy right hand, and the other on thy left, in thy kingdom" (Mt. 20, 21). Yet not on account those so erring regarding these things is this heresy placed here, since I stated at the beginning of this work that I would discuss only those heresies which arose after Christ's Ascension into Heaven, unless I find many of those who gave their names in Baptism to Christ to have fallen into this error.

Therefore, the first who revived this error was a certain Cerinthus, given over to very bad morals. Of which nation or race he was, it is not evident to me: I only know that he was a contemporary of Blessed John the Evangelist. For Blessed Irenaeus speaking about Blessed Polycarp says the following: "There are also those who heard from him that John, the disciple of the Lord, going to bathe at Ephesus, and perceiving Cerinthus within, rushed out of the bath-house without bathing, exclaiming, 'Let us fly, lest even the bath-house fall down, because Cerinthus, the enemy of the truth, is within.'"[1] Among the other errors of Cerinthus there is one whereby he asserts that after the resurrection the earth is going to be God's kingdom, and men will lead a life subject to concupiscences and lusts. Some accuse Papias, Bishop of Jerusalem, of this same error, who was a disciple of Blessed John the Evangelist.

Now those who accuse him are motivated by a certain statement of Blessed Jerome, who says the following: "He is said to have published a *Second coming of Our Lord* or *Millennium*.[2] Irenæus and Apollinaris and others who say that after the resurrection the Lord will reign in the flesh with the Saints, follow him."[3] But from these words of Jerome no such thing is established that Papias had thought the same thing as we now have related of Cerinthus. For the only thing that is established from Jerome's words is his view that Christ would reign again on earth according to the flesh: and that he thought that this is indeed true, as it is evident from many other authors. But Papias did not also teach that God's kingdom, which we call by another name beatitude or glory, would have perpetual pleasures of the flesh. For he did not think any such thing: Cerinthus, however, taught all these things. Wherefore it seems to me that the difference between Cerinthus and Papias is wide, although they agree in some

---

[1] *Against Heresies*, Bk. 3, ch. 3, n. 4 (PG 7, 853A-B).
[2] In Greek, δευτέρωσιν.
[3] *On Illustrious Men,* c. 18 (PL 23, 637B).

part of the error. For both of these men think that after the resurrection the Lord will reign on earth with His Saints for a thousand years.

Now Papias fell into this error motivated by that which Blessed John says in the Apocalypse, where when speaking about the just he says: "And I saw... the souls of them that were beheaded for the testimony of Jesus, and for the word of God, and who had not adored the beast nor his image, nor received his character on their foreheads, or in their hands; and they lived and reigned with Christ a thousand years. The rest of the dead lived not, till the thousand years were finished" (20, 4-5). On account of these words badly understood, he believed that Christ would reign on earth with the Saints for a thousand years: because he believed that those words of the Apocalypse ought to be understood superficially according to the literal and not according to the mystical sense. Hence Eusebius speaking about this Papias says the following: "The same writer gives also other accounts which he says came to him through unwritten tradition, certain strange parables and teachings of the Savior. To these belong his statement that there will be a period of a thousand years after the resurrection of the dead, and that the kingdom of Christ will be set up in material form on this very earth. I suppose he got these ideas through a misunderstanding of the Apostolic accounts, not perceiving that the things said by them were spoken mystically in figures. For he appears to have been of very limited understanding, as one can see from his discourses. But it was due to him that so many of the Church Fathers after him adopted a like opinion, urging in their own support the antiquity of the man; as for instance Irenæus and anyone else that may have proclaimed similar views."[1]

Although therefore Papias erred in this respect, still not on account of this did anyone of the ancients brand him with the censure of a heretic: perhaps because he was not pertinacious, such that he did not wish to submit to someone teaching better things. Pertinacity indeed is the main element that makes a heretic, as we have taught above. On account of which I am not able to refrain myself from being enraged with Brother Bernard of Luxemburg, who in his *Catalogus haereticorum* [*omnium*] did not hesitate to list this Papias with the other heretics,[2] especially since he perceived that it was not so done to him by any of the ancients. For Blessed Augustine in his book, *De Haeresibus ad Quodvultdeum*, when he enumerates all the heretics, he never mentions this Papias. Philastrius, Bishop of Brescia, in his book, *De haeresibus*, makes no mention of this Papias. Isidore [of Seville] also in the eighth book of his *Etymologies*, when he listed all the heretics which he could know, also makes not any mention of Papias. I omit Guy [the Carmelite], because he is too recent to be trusted in listing the old heretics. But if he ought to be trusted, he also never mentions this Papias.

Therefore, if none of these illustrious men numbered Papias among the heretics, for what reason has Brother Bernard of Luxemburg deemed him a heretic? For if due to the fact that Jerome said that Papias published a *Second coming of Our Lord* or *Millennium*, he ought to be immediately placed among the heretics, why also for the same reason did he not list Irenaeus, Apollinaris, Lactantius, Victorinus of Pettau,[3] since Jerome relates in the same place concerning all these men that they followed Papias in this matter? Therefore, either Papias ought not to be deemed a heretic, or the others who followed him in this matter for the same reason ought to be called heretics.

It is fitting to bring up all these things so that those may see who easily make pronouncements concerning heresy, how easily they also may err, and they may understand that one

---
[1] *Ecclesiastical History*, lib. 3, c. 39, n. 11 (PG 20, 299B).
[2] Papias is so mentioned under the heading of *Chiliastae*, *Catalogus Haereticorum* (Cologne, Johannes Parvus, 1524), fol. 33r.
[3] Saint Victorinus was the Bishop of Pettau in Pannonia was born in 207 A.D. and suffered martyrdom in 303 or 304 A.D under Diocletian.

ought not to be lightly judged of heresy, especially since there is no worse crime of which a Christian can be accused than if he be called a heretic. Therefore Papias and those who followed him thought that Christ would reign on earth for a thousand years with the just. And so thinking, they are called by the Greek word, Chiliasts.[1] From the Latin equivalent, we can call them Millenarians.[2]

Now Cerinthus asserts concerning Christ's kingdom, thinking there would be certain carnal pleasures during a thousand years on earth, that there would also be certain portentous vices of every lust. Besides this he also thinks that God's kingdom after a thousand years on earth, would be in Heaven, in the pleasures of the flesh, in gluttony and lust. In which matter he greatly deviates from Papias' meaning, and the meaning of others who followed Papias. Now that Cernithus asserted these two things, Eusebius shows in X his *Ecclesiastical History*. For speaking thus concerning Cerinthus he says: "The kingdom of Christ will be set up on earth after the resurrection, and the flesh dwelling in Jerusalem will again be subject to desires and pleasures. And being an enemy of the Scriptures of God, he asserts, with the purpose of deceiving men, that there is to be a period of a thousand years for marriage festivals. And Dionysius, who was Bishop of the parish of Alexandria in our day, in the second book of his work *On the Promises*, where he says some things concerning the Apocalypse of John which he draws from tradition, mentions this same man in the following words: 'But (they say that) Cerinthus, who founded the sect which was called, after him, the Cerinthian, desiring reputable authority for his fiction, prefixed the name. For the doctrine which he taught was this: that the kingdom of Christ will be an earthly one. And as he was himself devoted to the pleasures of the body and altogether sensual in his nature, he dreamed that that kingdom would consist in those things which he desired, namely, in the delights of the belly and of sexual passion, that is to say, in eating and drinking and marrying, and in festivals and sacrifices and the slaying of victims, under the guise of which he thought he could indulge his appetites with a better grace.'"[3]

From whose words and the others about Papias which we have cited above from the same Eusebius, it is evident that there is a vast difference between the errors of Papias and Cerinthus: for concerning Papias we have nothing else besides that he said that Christ would reign a thousand years on earth with the Saints after the resurrection. Now whether Papias thought that during that reign of a thousand years there would be carnal pleasures, or spiritual ones, is not evident to me. But if he said that they would be spiritual pleasures, the error was not grave. For Blessed Augustine when discussing this opinion in the twentieth book of *The City of God*, chapter seven, does not dare to label it an error, but an opinion. For so he says in the cited place: "And this opinion would not be objectionable, if it were believed that the joys of the saints in that Sabbath shall be spiritual, and consequent on the presence of God; for I myself, too, once held this opinion."[4] From which citation it again appears that Brother Bernard of Luxemburg judged badly when he reckoned Papias among the heretics: for Blessed Augustine says that that opinion of a thousand years is not objectionable, if in those years spiritual and not carnal pleasures are supposed. But Cerinthus (as we have just stated) says that there will be carnal pleasures not merely during that reign of a thousand years, but also afterwards, because he was saying that they would be in the kingdom of God, which one's own lust chooses: and supposed that the greatest happiness consists in them: and for this reason we have put the error of this Cerinthus in the section on of "Beatitude."

---

[1] Borrowing from Latin *chiliasta*, from Ancient Greek χίλιοι (*khílioi*, "thousand"), this word is synchronically analyzable as *chilia-* + *-ast*.

[2] I.e. *millenarii*.

[3] Bk. 3, c. 28, n. 2 (PG 20, 274D-275B).

[4] N. 1 (PL 41, 667).

Nor ought the reader be surprised that we have made a long discussion in relating the history of this heresy: for I see that many men have erred in this, namely that they confuse Cerinthus' error with Papias' error, thinking that they both had the same error: hence it was necessary to show the difference between the two. It remains now that we show that there will be no pleasures of the flesh in that kingdom of beatitude, as Cerinthus dreamt up.

First of all, Paul openly opposes this opinion, saying: "The kingdom of God is not meat and drink; but justice, and peace, and joy in the Holy Ghost" (Rom. 14, 17). Furthermore if God's kingdom, meaning beatitude, were to consist of the pleasures of the flesh, there would be no more direct way to that kingdom and to acquiring beatitude, than a life filled with the pleasures of the flesh: for no way is more direct to beatitude, than that which is most like to the end of the way, that is to say to beatitude itself. Hence true and faithful Catholics who place their beatitude in the knowledge and love of God, also teach that there is no shorter and more certain way to attaining beatitude, than the true knowledge of God and perfect love of Him. Thus if beatitude would be in the pleasures of the flesh: the pleasures of the flesh would most certainly be the way to acquiring beatitude. But nothing impedes the acquisition of beatitude more than carnal pleasures. For Paul the Apostle when listing those who are excluded from God's kingdom, enumerates among them those given over to pleasures of the flesh. For he says the following: "Neither fornicators, nor idolaters, nor adulterers, nor the effeminate, nor liers with mankind, nor thieves, nor covetous, nor drunkards, nor railers, nor extortioners, shall possess the kingdom of God" (I Cor. 6, 9-10). And again: "As we have borne the image of the earthly, let us bear also the image of the heavenly. Now this I say, brethren, that flesh and blood cannot possess the kingdom of God: neither shall corruption possess incorruption" (I Cor. 15, 49-50). By the words "flesh and blood" life according to the impulses of flesh and blood is designated: which is apparent from the fact that he thereby indicates the image of the earthly man. And elsewhere, namely in the Epistle to the Galatians, after he listed the works of the flesh, he adds: "They who do such things shall not obtain the kingdom of God" (5, 21). If therefore the works of the flesh are opposed to the attainment of God's kingdom itself: how is it that God's kingdom itself would consist in the same works of the flesh?

Again the Teacher of truth Himself condemns this error with His own voice: for when replying to the Sadducees disputing the resurrection He says: "In the resurrection they shall neither marry nor be married; but shall be as the angels of God in heaven" (Mt. 22, 30). If in the resurrection there are no marriages (according to the Savior's words) it ought necessarily to be admitted that there is no fornication there, or any other sexual intercourse. And because He says that men will be like the Angels of God, it is also necessary to concede that there will be no tasting of corporeal food for them. For one of those who stands before the Lord, namely Raphael, when speaking to Tobias, said: "When I was with you, I was there by the will of God: I seemed indeed to eat and to drink with you: but I use an invisible meat and drink, which cannot be seen by men" (Tob. 12, 18-19). Now this food which cannot be seen by man is God Himself: whom seeing and loving they taste. Hence the Royal Prophet says: "O taste, and see that the Lord is sweet" (Ps. 33, 9). For if God Himself were not the food of our souls, the Prophet would not have bid us to taste His sweetness. For He is not tasted except because he can be eaten and drank.

And concerning this spiritual food and drink those passages ought to be understood which in both Testaments of Sacred Scripture promise food and drink in the beatitude to come: namely in Isaias it is said: "My servants shall eat, and you shall be hungry: behold my servants shall drink, and you shall be thirsty" (Is. 65, 13). "I shall be satisfied," as the Royal Prophet says, "when thy glory shall appear" (Ps. 16, 15). So also ought to be understood what Our Savior says: "I dispose to you, as my Father hath disposed to me, a kingdom, that you may eat and drink at my table, in my kingdom" (Lk. 22, 29-30). For just as Christ the Son of

God is satisfied by the vision of His essence, which He receives from His Father through generation: so also we ought to be satisfied by the vision of the Divine essence: Christ obtained through the merits of His Passion that we might acquire that vision: and He then arranged a table for us when He merited that glory might be given to us, wherein seeing God, we may be satisfied with the vision of Him.

Cerinthus, since he was given over to the pleasures of the flesh, did not believe that there was one spiritual food for the soul, and another for the body: wherefore all the passages which speak about food and drink, of a banquet, of a supper, instead of that future beatitude, he conjectured that they ought to be understood carnally according to the literal sense. For if God's word (according to the statement of the Savior) is food nourishing the soul, how much more will God Himself nourish and refresh [the soul]? For in fact Moses was nourished without bodily food during forty days by merely speaking with God. The Savior describes these two foods namely corporeal and spiritual, and their difference, saying: "Labour not for the meat which perisheth, but for that which endureth unto life everlasting, which the Son of man will give you" (Jn. 6, 27).

The things which have been said against Cerinthus' error suffice: having omitted the other arguments, which are treated in the schools for proving that beatitude consists merely in the vision of God and the love of Him. For where the testimonies of Sacred Scripture are very clear, it is superfluous to add many arguments, as though one would wish to add light to the very bright rays of the sun. It has also been proved from the aforesaid arguments that Papias' error is different, concerning the reign of a thousand years, in which he said that Christ would reign after the resurrection according to the flesh. For the Savior said: "For in the resurrection they shall neither marry nor be married; but shall be as the angels of God" (Mt. 22, 30). From which words it is clearly proved that after the resurrection there will not be any sexual intercourse of man and woman, nor also the use of food and drink: and consequently, no life according to the flesh.

Now they nowise understood what they cite in confirmation of their opinion from the Apocalypse, and hence fell into error. For it is said in the Apocalypse as follows: "And I saw the souls of them that were beheaded for the testimony of Jesus, and for the word of God, and who had not adored the beast nor his image, nor received his character on their foreheads, or in their hands; and they lived and reigned with Christ a thousand years. The rest of the dead lived not, till the thousand years were finished. This is the first resurrection. Blessed and holy is he that hath part in the first resurrection" (Apoc. 20, 4-6). In these words the Apostle shows the difference between the good and wicked. For the good are they who have not adored the beast, meaning the devil, "and they lived," because even if their bodies are now dead, still their souls live by the grace and glory which they now possess. And this is called the first resurrection, which pertains to the grace and glory of souls. Wherefore Blessed John said: "Blessed is he that hath part in the first resurrection." The second resurrection is different, which will be when the bodies rising unto life will receive the stole of immortality.

And by opposition, death is also twofold. One is called "the first," and it is sin, which is the death of the soul: concerning which death the Savior says: "Let the dead bury their dead" (Lk. 9, 60): that is to say, let the dead in the soul bury the dead in the body. The second death is perpetual damnation. In which death they shall be cast who do not rise from the first, which is the death of sin. And thus rightly "Blessed is he that hath part in the first resurrection" (Apoc. 20, 6). Thus holy men who were beheaded "for the testimony of Jesus, and for the word of God, and who had not adored the beast," meaning the devil, "and they lived": because even if their dead bodies lie in sepulchers, still their souls have the life of grace and glory, and now reign with Christ a thousand years, meaning all the years which are to come until the Judgment. For until that time the Saints will have the life of their separated soul, and will rise first: but after that time they will have the second resurrection, meaning the life of the body and soul at the same time.

Now that the number thousand may be taken for universality, is clearly proved by that which is said in the Psalm: "He hath remembered his covenant for ever: the word which he commanded to a thousand generations" (Ps. 104, 8). And in Ecclesiasticus: "Better is one that feareth God, than a thousand ungodly children" (16, 3), meaning all the ungodly children. Furthermore, the number ten sometime is used for universality, as in Matthew it is said: "The kingdom of heaven," which is the Church Militant, "is like to ten virgins" (25, 1), by which number all men both good and bad are designated. But the number ten is the root of the number one thousand, which is cubed. For if the number ten is multiplied by itself, it makes a hundred. But if you again multiply ten by a hundred, it makes a thousand. Thus if the number ten it used for universality, a thousand which is derived from ten multiplied twice much more rightly is used for universality. Thus when Blessed John speaking about the Saints already dead said that they lived and reigned with Christ a thousand years, it ought to be so taken that it be understood that they lived and are to reign with Christ all the years to come until Judgment Day. In which years, even if they are dead as to their body, they nevertheless live by their souls, and reign with Christ.

John the Apostle when speaking about dead sinners says: "The rest of the dead lived not, till the thousand years were finished." For dead sinners, during the whole time until Judgment Day have no life: for their bodies lie dead, and their souls are dead through sin. Now when these thousand years have passed, that is during the whole time until Judgment Day, they will have some life, because even if their souls may be dead through sin, still they will recuperate their bodies, although miserable, through the resurrection. Or perhaps the number thousand is used there for the universality of the time to come after Judgment Day, such that the meaning of the Saints "lived and reigned with Christ a thousand years," meaning always, because after death of the body they will always live with Him in soul, even if they shall not always live in body. But the other dead, that is the sinners, will not live until the thousand years are completed, meaning they will never live: because they lost the true life of body and soul. Nor does the word "until" mean the end of a time. For so it is often used in Sacred Writ, such that it means no end of time: as it appears in the Psalm. "The Lord said to my Lord: Sit thou at my right hand: Until I make thy enemies thy footstool" (Ps. 109, 1). For there will never be a time when the Son will not sit at the right hand of the Father: and yet He said that He will sit until He makes His enemies the footstool of His feet. Hence it is proved that the adverb, "until," is without any limitation of time. In this way also is meant that which John the Evangelist said: "The rest of the dead lived not, till the thousand years were finished," meaning, until the universality of time be ended: that is, they will never live.

Let he who wishes read another exposition of these "thousand years" which Blessed Augustine gives.[1] I do not wish to get in the middle, because it does not please me. Now these things which we have related, are also stated by him: and it seems truer to me. Of old, Gennadius, a priest of Massilia, wrote against those Χιλιαστές, that is the Millenarians: as Johannes Trithemius testifies in his book, *De scriptoribus ecclesiasticis*,[2] which one may enjoy: it indeed (I think) provided great help to us.

The **third heresy** is that which asserts that there is neither perpetual beatitude nor misery. The author of this heresy is Origen. For he (if we believe Augustine and Theophilus of Alexandria) proposes certain alternations of beatitude and misery, so that having completed some number of courses of years, he says that the souls will return to their mortal bodies, and in them suffer vexations of the body, and from thence again be summoned to beatitude, and

---

[1] *City of God*, bk. 20, c. 7.

[2] *De scriptoribus ecclesiasticis* (Basil, J. Amerbach, 1494), fol. 32r.

from beatitude brought back to misery: in which manner there will be a perpetual rotation of beatitude and misery. And in the same way he also thinks concerning the wretched, namely that he says that they will at some time return to this world: and from there be again called to beatitude. Hence it happens that he says that the demons will be saved at some time.

This opinion is very clearly proved to be heretical, both by reason and by the testimonies of Sacred Scripture. Let us firstly go and question Origen whether the soul which has already attained beatitude knows that its beatitude will end at some time or whether is it is completely unaware of this? If it has no idea that its beatitude will end, it will then be necessary that Origen admit that we who live in this miserable world are more learned than the blessed are in that future beatitude: because we who live in this world know that beatitude will end at some time: but the blessed are unaware of the misery to come. We also who live in this world know (according to Origen's opinion) that the happiness of the blessed will cease at some time: which since they are unaware, it follows that we are more learned than they.

Now if the beatified soul knows that their happiness will end, for this reason alone it is proved to be miserable, because it will always be afraid of losing what it loves. But fear is a passion of the soul: and he who fears, suffers in some way, and undergoes some unhappiness. Furthermore that fear reduces the strength of love. For one love more lukewarmly what he knows that he will lose at some time. Wherefore it happens that the blessed, knowing that his beatitude will end at some time, loves it more remissly and tepidly. For by this single and very strong argument Christ wished to separate us from the love of riches, namely that they will end at some time. "Lay not up to yourselves treasures on earth: where the rust, and moth consume, and where thieves break through and steal" (Mt. 6, 19). Again, if the blessed knows that its happiness will end, the soul lives more happily and peacefully here in this world than there in that beatitude: and is so much the more happy the more certain is the hope of gaining the good than the fear of an imminent evil. The depraved living in this world in fact has hope of happiness to come: but the blessed suffer fear of the misery to come, to which (according to Origen) after the course of a number of years must summoned back.

Now having omitted some arguments, we treat the testimonies of Sacred Scriptures, because they are more convincing. Sacred Scripture in fact says not just once or twice that beatitude and the misery of the damned are unending. Hence Solomon says in the book of Wisdom: "The souls of the just are in the hand of God, and the torment of death shall not touch them" (3, 1). But if they ceaselessly go back and forth between beatitude with continual alternations, it is necessary that they undergo the torment of death. And again pointing out the different conditions of the blessed and the damned, after discussing the damned, he says concerning the blessed: "But the just shall live for evermore: and their reward is with the Lord" (Wis. 5, 16).

Accordingly in the book of Daniel it is said: "At that time shall Michael rise up, the great prince, who standeth for the children of thy people: and a time shall come such as never was from the time that nations began even until that time. And at that time shall thy people be saved, every one that shall be found written in the book. And many of those that sleep in the dust of the earth, shall awake: some unto life everlasting, and others unto reproach, to see it always. But they that are learned shall shine as the brightness of the firmament: and they that instruct many to justice, as stars for all eternity" (12, 1-3).

Again, the Angel Gabriel when speaking to the Virgin Mary about the Incarnation of the Son of God says: "He shall reign in the house of Jacob for ever and of his kingdom there shall be no end" (Lk. 1, 32-33). Now the "house of Jacob" which is elsewhere called the "house of Israel," that is to say heavenly glory, the greatness of which a prophet admires saying: "O Israel, how great is the house of God […It is great, and hath no end: it is high and immense]" (Bar. 3, 24-25). Jacob in fact is the same as Israel: thus the house of Jacob is the house of Israel. In this house the Angel says that Christ will reign forever. But how could He reign forever in that house if the house is not eternal? Thus it is necessary that that house of beatitude be eternal, so that Christ could reign in it forever.

Also the blessed are Christ's kingdom, who cry out in the Apocalypse: "Thou hast made us to our God a kingdom and priests, and we shall reign on the earth" (5, 10). For this is that kingdom which Christ declared before Pilate is not of this world.[1] And rightly so, because He speaking elsewhere concerning the just had said: "If you had been of the world, the world would love its own: but because you are not of the world, but I have chosen you out of the world, therefore the world hateth you" (Jn. 15, 19). If therefore the blessed are called God's kingdom, how will there not be an end of Christ's kingdom, if from beatitude the blessed will be at some time recalled from beatitude to misery? Thus it is necessary to acknowledge that beatitude is eternal, such that Christ's kingdom may be truly said to be without end.

The other point which is said about the damned is clearly proved by that in Matthew's Gospel which the Lord warns that He will say to sinners on Judgment Day: "Depart from me, you cursed, into everlasting fire which was prepared for the devil and his angels" (Mt. 25, 41). And in Luke's Gospel Father Abraham said to the rich feaster buried in Hell: "And besides all this, between us and you, there is fixed a great chaos: so that they who would pass from hence to you, cannot, nor from thence come hither" (Lk. 16, 26). Nothing clearer could be said than these words for disproving Origen's madness. Blessed Augustine writes against this error in his *City of God*,[2] in which place he only uses arguments, not citing any passage of Sacred Scripture. It is fitting to have been so done, because he was then arguing against heathen philosophers, whom the testimony of Sacred Scripture would hardly influence. Against the same error Blessed Gregory also argues in his *Morals on the Book of Job* when commenting on the passage, "He shall esteem the deep as growing old" (Job 41, 23).[3]

There is a **fourth heresy** concerning this matter which asserts that men in the present life can obtain final beatitude according to the degree of perfection which they will have in Heaven. Certain men in Germany stirred up this heresy, called the Beghards and certain women called the Beguines, who all proceed in a certain upright and religious manner. For today in lower Germany I myself have seen women so named Beguines, who respectably live in a certain community, yet without taking any expressed vow, with the retention of their own household furnishings: who when they wish, and when their manner of life displeases them, have the free choice of departing, and can leave the whole community. The Beghards are different, for they have a cloister and they render to the Lord three vows, as other monks. It is fitting to give this explanation here: because these names are completely unknown in other countries, such as Spain and Italy, and most of France. Thus these Beghards and Beguines, among the others who had errors, attempted to teach this error: namely that man in this life can attain the final beatitude which he will have in Heaven.

Now so that we may refute this error, it is firstly necessary to define beatitude, lest perhaps we fight about the word and not the reality. But because according to Aristotle's precept: an ambiguous word ought to be firstly divided into its different senses before being defined: hence it is firstly necessary to show the multiple meanings of beatitude. Beatitude in fact in Sacred Writ is sometimes and often used for the way to attaining beatitude. "Blessed is the man," says the Royal Prophet, "who hath not walked in the counsel of the ungodly, nor stood in the way of sinners, nor sat in the chair of pestilence. But his will is in the law of the Lord" (Ps. 1, 1-2). And elsewhere: "Blessed is the man that feareth the Lord: he shall delight exceedingly in his commandments" (Ps. 111, 1). And the Lord Himself assigns in the Gospel

---

[1] Jn. 18, 36.

[2] Bk. 12, c. 12 (PL 41, 269-372).

[3] Bk. 24, c. 19, n. 34 ff. (PL 76, 737C-739D).

of Matthew eight beatitudes, that is, eight ways whereby on arrives at beatitude. "Blessed are they that mourn: for they shall be comforted" (5, 5). Now in that blessed life, in which there is perfect happiness, there will be no mourning. For there "God shall wipe away all tears" (Apoc. 7, 17) from the eyes of the saints. Now mourning is called beatitude because mourning in this life and not to desire to be happy in this life is a sure way to the beatitude to come.

Faith is also called eternal life, in that it is a way to eternal life. For so Christ says, asking the Father for us: "Now this is eternal life: That they may know thee, the only true God, and Jesus Christ, whom thou hast sent" (Jn. 17, 3). Blessed Cyril discussing this passage says: "He defines faith as the mother of eternal life... And we affirm that to be true piety, which cannot be branded with the crime of strange and false worship."[1] Wherefore I am greatly surprised that certain scholastic theologians cite that passage of John to prove that the principal part of beatitude is the vision of God, while the lesser part is love: to prove which they cite no other passage of Scripture than that of John in which Christ says: "This is eternal life: that they may know thee, the only true God, and Jesus Christ, whom thou hast sent" (17, 3).

I omit how others interpret this passage, who defend the opposing view. For their interpretation is merely an arbitrary interpretation, and derived from their own imagination, not however from the words themselves. But if they were to ask for the meaning of that passage from the sacred Doctors, they would have wasted very much work in the matter. Yet I do not wish that because I have said these things, that one would think that I want to dispute that the greatest part of beatitude is vision: because neither for this side nor for the contrary side do I wish to dispute: since I do not wish to treat the different opinions of men, but only the Catholic faith. Yet I said these things so that those who teach that the principal part of beatitude is vision, may know upon how weak of a foundation they rest, since it is evident that this passage of John ought to be understood of the knowledge of the faith, which is the way to beatitude.

And this can be easily proved by having recourse to the text itself. For in that passage Christ does not ask the Father that He would glorify him through the clear vision of His essence, but through the knowledge of the faith. For then Christ is glorified, when it is clearly known by faith that He is the Son of God. Then He was glorified when men believed that He was the Son of God. Thus since Christ prays the Father that He glorify His Son, He asks this, namely that He give faith in His divinity to men, by which they may believe that He is the Son of God. And hence to show that He is not referring to Himself, but asks in regard to men, He adds: "Now this is eternal life: That they may know thee, the only true God, and Jesus Christ, whom thou hast sent." The meaning is that they will have eternal life if they shall believe in Thee and Me. Nor ought they be surprised that we call faith eternal life, since in John's Gospel the Lord also says: "He that believeth in the Son, hath life everlasting" (3, 36). He does not say "will have" but "hath": to clearly show that faith is called life everlasting: for it is a most straight way to acquiring eternal life.

Now Blessed Cyril teaches this exposition (as we have shown) in his commentary on John's Gospel. And in his book *Ad [religiosissimas] reginas de [recta] fide*, says the following: "If it is necessary that the knowledge of the only and true God be joined and associated with the knowledge of Jesus Christ, and this procures eternal life itself: to whom can it be unclear that Christ is true God?"[2] In which words it ought to be noticed that he said: "procures eternal life." Hence it clearly appears that Cyril thinks that this passage ought to be understood in regard to the knowledge of the faith: which thus he calls eternal life, because it procures eternal life.

Blessed Augustine also suggests this interpretation, yet not as expressly as Cyril, but in a sort of roundabout way: hence I omit his words, being content to have indicated this to the

---

[1] *Commentary on John*, bk. 11, c. 5 (PG 74,483D).
[2] PG 76, 1271B.

reader.[1] Blessed Hilary in his book, *On the Trinity*, when he had cited those same words of Christ to prove Christ's divinity, he immediately adds these words: "Learn, heretic, to confess, if you cannot believe, the faith which gives eternal life. Separate, if you can, Christ from God, the Son from the Father, God over all from the true God, the One from the Only: if, as you say, eternal life is to believe in one only true God without Jesus Christ. But if there is no eternal life in a confession of the only true God, which separates Christ from Him, how, pray, can Christ be separated from the true God for our faith, when He is not separable for our salvation?"[2] Therefore, since so many distinguished men teach that that passage of John ought to be understood of the knowledge of the faith, which is the way to eternal life: it is proved that they have relied upon a false foundation, who cite it to prove that the principle part of beatitude is vision. We have said this upon a favorable opportunity.

But now we return to the first point of our discussion, saying that the way to beatitude is sometimes called beatitude in Sacred Writ. Concerning this so-called beatitude, it is not our intention to speak now, since no one doubts concerning this matter that it is had in this life.

Sometimes the word beatitude is used for highest happiness, which we hope for in the next life. And thus concerning this is said in the Psalm: "Blessed are they that dwell in thy house, O Lord: they shall praise thee for ever and ever" (Ps. 83, 5). Severinus Boethius of blessed memory defines it as follows: "Beatitude is the state made perfect by the aggregation of all good things."[3] And it agrees with that which Augustine says: "Blessed is he who has what he wills, and wills nothing amiss."[4] That is to say, blessed is he who has every good which he can rightly want. From which it follows that he is blessed who perfectly possesses God: for then our will is satisfied: because when God is possessed every good is possessed. For so it is said concerning it: "Who satisfieth thy desire with good things: thy youth shall be renewed like the eagle's" (Ps. 102, 5). Then indeed our desire will be filled with good things when our youth will be renewed by the resurrection. Then our will shall be satisfied, according to what the Prophet says: "I shall be satisfied when thy glory shall appear" (Ps. 16, 15). Thus beatitude is not had unless the will has been satisfied and the desire fulfilled.

But no one can fill our desire for good things except God alone. Now no one has God unless he loves Him perfectly. "He that abideth in charity, abideth in God, and God in him" (I Jn. 4, 16). Now God cannot be perfectly loved in this life, because He cannot be perfectly known in it. For the things that we know less, it is necessary that they be loved less: because the things which cannot be known, cannot be loved. But God cannot be known by the common law in this life with clear and facial knowledge, according to that which is said in Exodus: "Man shall not see me and live" (33, 20). And Paul says: "We see now through a glass in a dark manner; but then face to face" (I Cor. 13, 12). If therefore no one can perfectly and clearly see God in this life, then neither can He be perfectly loved in this life: and consequently, nor possessed: from which it follows, our will cannot be satisfied in this world, nor our desires fulfilled. From which it is concluded that it cannot happen that a man in this world is happy with the beatitude of which we speak.

Furthermore, "The life of man upon earth," as Job says, "is a warfare" (7, 1): it necessarily follows that beatitude cannot be in this life: because beatitude has rest, calmness and security annexed, all of which things are very far from warfare. Indeed where there is labor, there is fear. Wherefore no one being a soldier claims to be happy [*beatus*], except after having achieved victory. Nor is anyone crowned during the fighting itself, but after the battle has ended. Thus since beatitude is a sort of crown of the blessed, it is proved that beatitude cannot

---

[1] *In Ioannis evangelium tractatus CXXIV*, tr. 111, n. 3 (PL 35, 1927-1928).

[2] Bk. 9, n. 32 (PL 10, 306A).

[3] *De consolatio philosophiae*, bk. 3, prosa 2 (PL 63, 724A).

[4] *On the Trinity*, bk. 13, c. 5, n. 8 (PL 42, 1019).

be had in this life, which is a sort of warfare. Again, the same Job when describing the life of man living in this world says: "Man born of a woman, living for a short time, is filled with many miseries" (14, 1). If man is filled with miseries, who is there who can be happy [*beatus*]? This life, I say, is filled with miseries and labors, filled with the need of food and drink, worn out by food and drink. Humors swell up, sorrows destroy, heats dry up, air infects, food swells, fasting wastes away, jokes dissipate, sadnesses consume, solicitude constrains, security dulls, old age bends over, sickness breaks, and death completely takes away this life. All which things fight as though completely opposed to beatitude: hence it is that man could not be happy in this life.

Finally besides all these so clear testimonies, there exists a decision of the Church regarding this matter. For the Council of Vienne celebrated under Clement V, among the eight errors of the Beguines and Beghards which it condemned, it decreed this in the fourth place[1]: its decree is found in the book of the Clementine Decretals in the title *De haereticis*, chapter *Ad nostrum*.[2] I know of no author who expressly wrote against this error of the Beguines: for which reason I am very surprised at Guy the Carmelite, who when he wrote his *Summa de haeresibus* [*et earum confutationibus*], never mentioned the blabbering of these Beguines nor of their errors, even though they lived a short time before him. And in the Council of Vienne (as we have said) they were condemned. Wherefore it ought not to have escaped his notice, especially since the Council of Vienne preceded Guy by no more than about forty years. Yet Guy examines other Beguines and Beghards at the end of his work: who (as it is established from Guy's words) were quite different from these, about whom we have just spoken. For the errors of the Beguines, about who Guy speaks, nowise agree with those which were condemned at the Council of Vienne.

There is a **fifth heresy** "that any intellectual nature in its own self is naturally beatified"[3]: and this heresy is also from the Beghards and Beguines, and is placed fifth among the eight propositions condemned at the Council of Vienne which we have recently related. For Paul says: "The grace of God, life everlasting" (Rom. 6, 23). And again: "Being justified freely by his grace" (Rom. 3, 24). Therefore if we are justified freely, all the more are we also beatified freely. And again: "It is not of him that willeth, nor of him that runneth, but of God that sheweth mercy" (Rom. 9, 16). Thus, not every intellectual creature in its own self is naturally beatified.

Furthermore, if (as Christ says) "None is good but God alone" (Lk. 18, 19), because He is good by nature, we however are not good by nature, but only by our own will: much more will it be necessary to say that no one is beatified due to his own nature, except God alone. Again if any intellectual nature in its own self is beatified, then no intellectual nature could be wretched: because the things which are naturally inherent can nowise be forsaken.

The things which we have said against the heresy just related also oppose this heresy: for if in this life no one can attain beatitude, it follows that man cannot be naturally beatified. Thus, let the Beguines be gone, and work the spindle and distaff, and nowise discuss the Divine Scriptures.

The **sixth heresy** teaches that no soul before Judgment Day is beatified: because (as it says) no soul before that day sees God. The authors of this heresy are the Armenians. The Greeks also maintain the same position. These men certainly (Guy bearing witness[4]) are much more deranged, because just as they deny that beatitude is given to the just before Judgment Day, so

---

[1] "That man can so attain final beatitude according to every degree of perfection in the present life, as he will obtain it in the blessed life." (Dz. 474).
[2] *Clementinae*, lib. 5, t. 3, c. 3.
[3] Dz. 475.
[4] *Summa de haeresibus*, fol. 22v, c. 7.

also they say that punishment is given to sinners before that day. After these men rose up Pope John XXII. But lest anyone distrust my words on this matter, I will cite the words of Pope Adrian [VI], who in his [*Questiones in*] q*uartum sententiarum*, near the end of a question on the Sacrament of Confirmation says the following: "It is very recently related concerning John XXII, that he publicly taught, declared, and commanded to be held by all that souls purified before the Final Judgment do not have the stole [of glory], which is the clear and facial vision of God: and it is said that he induced the University of Paris to this, that no one in it could obtain a degree in theology, unless he would firstly have sworn to defend this error, and adhere to it perpetually."[1]

Besides these men there are still other patrons of this error, illustrious men in fact, renowned for holiness as well as learning: namely the martyr for Christ, the most Blessed Irenaeus, Theophylactus, Bishop of Bulgaria, and Blessed Bernard. And no one ought to be surprised if such great men have fallen into so pestiferous an error: because (as Blessed James the Apostle says) "If any man offend not in word, the same is a perfect man" (James 3, 2). Yet here it is necessary to warn the reader, lest he think that this error detracts something from the holiness and doctrine of such great men: since at that time the Church had never defined anything about this matter, nor was that matter ever called into question, nor were there very explicit testimonies of Sacred Scripture for that doctrine, such that it could not be distorted into any other meaning whatsoever: they could at that time teach either view without heresy: especially since there are not lacking some testimonies of Scripture which somewhat seem to favor them.

Now so that I may leave my reliability in this matter suspect to no one: I now wish to cite their words, so that the fair reader may know that they so taught, just as we have testified about them. Irenaeus towards the end of his *Against the Heresies* wrote these words: "For as the Lord walked 'in the midst of the shadow of death' (Ps. 22, 4), where the souls of the dead were, yet afterwards arose in the body, and after the resurrection was taken up [into Heaven], it is manifest that the souls of His disciples also, upon whose account the Lord underwent these things, shall go away into the invisible place allotted to them by God, and there remain until the resurrection, awaiting that event; then receiving their bodies, and rising in their en-

---

[1] *Questiones in quartum sententiarum praesertim circa sacramenta* (Paris, in aedibus Josse Bade, 1518), fol. 23r. "In the last years of John's pontificate there arose a dogmatic conflict about the Beatific Vision, which was brought on by himself, and which his enemies made use of to discredit him. Before his elevation to the Holy See, he had written a work on this question, in which he stated that the souls of the blessed departed do not see God until after the Last Judgment. After becoming pope, he advanced the same teaching in his sermons. In this he met with strong opposition, many theologians, who adhered to the usual opinion that the blessed departed did see God before the Resurrection of the Body and the Last Judgment, even calling his view heretical. A great commotion was aroused in the University of Paris when the General of the Friars Minor and a Dominican tried to disseminate there the pope's view. Pope John wrote to King Philip IV on the matter (November, 1333), and emphasized the fact that, as long as the Holy See had not given a decision, the theologians enjoyed perfect freedom in this matter. In December, 1333, the theologians at Paris, after a consultation on the question, decided in favor of the doctrine that the souls of the blessed departed saw God immediately after death or after their complete purification; at the same time they pointed out that the pope had given no decision on this question but only advanced his personal opinion, and now petitioned the pope to confirm their decision. John appointed a commission at Avignon to study the writings of the Fathers, and to discuss further the disputed question. In a consistory held on January 3, 1334, the pope explicitly declared that he had never meant to teach aught contrary to Holy Scripture or the rule of faith and in fact had not intended to give any decision whatever. Before his death he withdrew his former opinion, and declared his belief that souls separated from their bodies enjoyed in heaven the Beatific Vision." ("Pope John XXII," *The Catholic Encyclopedia* (1910 ed.), vol. 8, pp. 432-433).

tirety, that is bodily, just as the Lord arose, they shall come thus into the presence of God."[1] In which words since he said: "they shall come thus into the presence of God," he clearly indicated that souls before the resurrection of their bodies are not received in heavenly glory.

Now Theophylactus, expounding the passage of the Apostle from the eleventh chapter of his Epistle to the Hebrews: "And all these being approved by the testimony of faith, received not the promise" (v. 39), says the following: "Why are you fearful, in that although you are in battle, you have not yet received a reward? All the aforesaid saints, even if they had testimony that they pleased God by faith, nevertheless they had not yet obtained the promises of heavenly goods. You certainly may thus conclude that some obtained temporal promises, such as David. Otherwise it was not that which was sought: but the things which are in Heaven, these are truly promises... Therefore is not God unjust to them, if they have preceded us with labors, they wait for us to be crowned? Not at all; for this is also pleasing to them, that they be perfected with their brethren... He gave to those who labored first, a certain foretaste, saying and commanding them that they ought to wait for their brethren for the complete banquet: who, since they are human, wait joyfully, so that they might rejoice together."[2] He says the same thing when discussing what our Savior said to the thief: "This day thou shalt be with me in paradise" (Lk. 23, 43).[3] I am surprised that printer warned the reader about some other opinions of his at the end of his exposition of the Gospels, yet he left this intact: perhaps he did not notice it.

Blessed Bernard in his third sermon for the Feast of All Saints wrote these words: "They will not enter that blessed dwelling without us, or without their bodies; that is, the Saints will not go without the people, nor the spirit without the flesh."[4] And in the sermon following next, which is the fourth on the same feast, speaking about the bosom of Abraham, he speaks thus: "Now the Savior, descending to this place, 'hath broken gates of brass, and burst the iron bars' (Ps. 106, 16) and led from their prison those who had been bound;[5] they were indeed seated, that is, at rest, but 'in the shadow of death' (Lk. 1, 79).[6] Then He set them beneath the altar of God,[7] hiding them in His tabernacle in the time of trouble and keeping them safe 'in the secret place of His tabernacle' (Ps. 26, 5) until the time should come when they should go forth, when the number of their brothers should be complete,[8] and they should see the kingdom prepared for them 'from the foundation of the world.' (Mt. 25, 34)"[9] In which words it ought to be noticed that he says that the Saints do not take possession of the kingdom which was prepared for them until the number of their brethren is completed.

But much more manifest are the words which he adds, for a few sentences later when expounding the passage from the Apocalypse, "I saw under the altar" of God, etc. (Apoc. 6, 9) he says the following: "Further, the altar we are going to talk about, I think, rightly be supposed to be nothing other than the very body of our Lord and Savior.[10] Moreover, I think

---

[1] Bk. 5, c. 31, n. 2 (PG 7, 1209B-C).

[2] PG 125, 366C-367A.

[3] PG 123, 1103B ff.

[4] N. 1 (PL 183, 469A).

[5] Is. 42, 7.

[6] See the antiphon *O Clavis David* for December 18.

[7] Cf. Apoc. 6, 9.

[8] Cf. Apoc. 6, 11.

[9] N. 1 (PL 183, 472A).

[10] Here a footnote in Migne's Latin Patrology reads: "These words of Bernard are not an absolute definition, but are his opinion, as is evident from the first paragraph of this sermon, where it is said that he wishes to be accepted reasonably, "allowing, of course, that it may have been revealed to others in another way." In the preface of the volume of Migne in which this sermon is found (PL 183, n. 20-21),

that this interpretation of mine agrees with His, particularly when I hear Him saying in the Gospel, 'Wheresoever the body shall be, thither will the eagles also be gathered together' (Lk. 17, 37). So in this interim time the Saints rest in joy under the human nature of Christ, a thing that the Angels themselves long to look upon,[1] until the time comes when they no longer lie beneath the altar but are raised above the altar. But what have I said? No one, neither human beings nor Angels, can attain—let alone surpass—the glory of Christ's human nature, right? How then can I say that those who are now at rest beneath the altar are to be raised above the altar? By vision and contemplation, not by authority! For the Son, as He promised, will show Himself,[2] not in the form of a servant but in the form of God.[3] He will also show us the Father and the Holy Ghost, and without that vision nothing will satisfy us, since this is life eternal, that we should know the Father,[4] the true God, and Jesus Christ Whom He sent,[5] and in Them, without doubt, the Spirit that is of both."[6] From which words it is more clearly established that he thought that the souls of the Saints before Judgment Day rested in the vision of Christ's humanity alone, and after that day they would be exalted up to the vision of His Divinity.

I beseech the reader here not to think that I have cited the words of these Saints in this place in order to lessen their glory and honor on this occasion even a little: for far be from me such a wicked intention: for even if I had wanted to do this, I am not so great that I could achieve this: wherefore they were free to so think without incurring the stain of heresy. But I have put the words of these Saints in this place, so that the reader may be warned, lest if he were to read them in their works, he might incautiously follow their opinion. If however he shall be convinced from another source that they had thought differently than I think, I beg the reader to deem me more unknowing and ignorant, who did not understand their words, than malevolent.

But now it is necessary that we show that the souls of the Saints, which departed from their bodies purified, or after the dissolution of their body were purified elsewhere, are already beatified and clearly seeing God. First of all I cite the testimony of the Psalms, where the Prophet speaking to Christ says: "Thou hast ascended on high, thou hast led captivity captive; thou hast received gifts in men" (Ps. 67, 19). Which words Blessed Paul repeating says: "Ascending on high, he led captivity captive" (Eph. 4, 8). What else was the detaining of the just in Abraham's bosom, than a sort of captivity? For here Paul having imitated the Prophet said "captivity," in that manner of speech whereby we are accustomed to call those who fight "an army." Thus God freed by His death these just, who were held by the devil on account to the sin of the first parent, and translated them to another sweet and desirable captivity, so that as before they were held captive by the devil, to whom they were at one time slaves, so afterwards they were held captive by God, so that they might serve His justice. For due to the same reason (as I think) he called the captivity itself "captive," because they are so detained in glory with a happy and desirable captivity just as before it was not permitted for them to leave Hell: so also now they are not free to depart from that blessed life even a little. Thus the Prophet speaking above this captive captivity says: "Thou hast led captivity captive."

---

it is shown that Saint Bernard spoke otherwise in some other works of his, but because we do not know the time when he gave these two sermons for the feast of All Saints, it cannot be immediately concluded that he later retracted his erroneous opinion stated here.

[1] Cf. I Pet. 1, 12.
[2] Cf. Jn. 14, 21.
[3] Cf. Phil. 2, 6-7.
[4] Cf. Jn. 14, 8-9.
[5] Cf. Jn. 17, 3.
[6] N. 2 (PL 183, 472C-473A).

But wither did He lead? Certainly He led into no other place than into that place into which He ascended: because when He ascended He brought them with Him. Now He ascended into Heaven: thus He led that captivity captive. "Ascending," he said, "into heaven, he led captivity captive." And they were not led into Heaven so that they would remain without the vision of God, for which they groaned for so many years. For otherwise what consolation would be theirs, or what better condition would they have through Christ's death, if they were to have merely a change of place? Thus since He led them into Heaven, wither He ascended, He assuredly translated them into the blessed life, just as they had desired. For so [Psuedo-] Jerome in his commentary on the Psalms expounding that verse says: "Ascending the heights of the heavens, He freed those who were held in the devil's captivity: and having led them away as captives after Himself, He restored them to eternal life."[1]

Furthermore, it is most evident that our Savior hanging upon the Cross said to the thief commending himself to Him: "This day thou shalt be with me in paradise" (Lk, 23, 43). If the purified souls do not see God before Judgment Day, what is that paradise in which the thief was promised that he would be on that day at the same time with Christ? Or perhaps we will say that he will be detained in the Elysian fields, or in the Fortunate Islands?[2] Far be this from the hearts of the faithful. For there is no analogy, as our Savior, Who had already given a spiritual law, and preached by His own mouth, and then confirmed it by His own death, would not revoke the earthly promises of the Old Law. He promised us spiritual things: the kingdom of Heaven in fact: and this same thing is what He now calls paradise, when He said to the thief: "This day thou shalt be with me in paradise."

Then in the Second Epistle to the Corinthians Paul, when exhorting them to enduring all hardships even unto death for Christ, says the following: "For we know, if our earthly house of this habitation be dissolved, that we have a building of God, a house not made with hands, eternal in heaven" (5, 1). [Hervé de Bourg-Dieu[3]] interpreting these words in his Commentary on the Epistles of Paul, says the following: "The Church's preachers after they departed from their bodies, were in no wise held back by periods of delays (as the ancient Fathers) from the perception of the attainment of the heavenly homeland: but as soon as they go out from the bonds of the flesh, they rest in a heavenly throne, as is shown in this passage. For it is not said: 'we will have an eternal house in heaven,' but 'we have': namely because that house is immediately had, as soon as this one is dissolved. However, before our Redeemer paid for the punishment of the human race by His death, the gates of Hell held even those who followed the path to the heavenly homeland, after having gone out of the flesh: not as though they suffered punishment as though they were sinners, but such that they were resting in remote places, because the intercession of the Mediator had not yet arrived, the guilt of the first sin prohibited the entrance to the kingdom. Now, however, anyone perfect is directly received into the kingdom."[4]

Again Blessed Paul writing to the Philippians says: "Having a desire to be dissolved and to be with Christ" (1, 23). But this desire would have been vain and useless, if when he died his soul could not yet get to Heaven, wherein it is evident Christ is. Thus he desires to be dissolved, because he believes without any hesitation that immediately after his dissolution

---

[1] *Brevarium in Psalmos* (PL 26, 1016).

[2] The "Fortunate Isles" or "Isles of the Blessed" were semi-legendary islands in the Atlantic Ocean, variously treated as a simple geographical location and as a winterless earthly paradise inhabited by the heroes of Greek mythology.

[3] This work was formerly ascribed to Saint Anselm and is so done here in the text. Hervé de Bourg-Dieu (1080-1150) was a French Benedictine exegete.

[4] *Commentaria in epistolas Pauli* (PL 181, 1041C-D).

he will attain the vision of God. Hence [Ambrosiaster][1] discussing these words of Paul in his commentary says: "He has a desire to die and go to be with Christ because he thinks it is much better to be in the presence of God and enjoy the things which have been chosen and promised to him."[2] From whose words it is established that the Saints, immediately after death enjoy the things hoped for and promised. But the vision of God is hoped for and promised, nay it is the greatest of all things which are promised to us.

And what is said in the Apocalypse is more explicit (if nevertheless it be taken according to the true meaning of the Saints) where Blessed John, speaking about the souls of those who were killed on account of the word of God and cry out from under the altar of God, says: "And white robes were given to every one of them one; and it was said to them, that they should rest for a little time, till their fellow servants, and their brethren, who are to be slain, even as they, should be filled up" (Apoc. 6, 11).

"Blessed Augustine"[3] discussing these words says: "He calls the Church the altar of God, under whose eyes they were made martyrs: and although the souls of the Saints are in Paradise, still because the blood of the Saints was poured out upon the earth, they are said to cry out from under the altar."[4]

And Ambrose Autpert[5] in his commentary on the Apocalypse when discussing these words says the following: "What therefore is designated in this passage by the white robes but the martyr's reward, the retribution of the wicked, and the joys of the heavenly homeland. Where also we understand, because the souls of the Saints, who now have received single robes and sometimes double ones, that is, double joys. Before the resurrection the elect indeed were granted to receive single robes: because they enjoy eternal beatitude in their still separated soul. They will receive double robes in the resurrection, when they are clothed with the perfect joy of their souls and incorruption of the body."[6]

[Pseudo-] Blessed Gregory[7] interprets this passage of the Apocalypse in the same way, who in his exposition of the seven Penitential Psalms when expounding the passage: "To my hearing thou shalt give joy and gladness" (Ps. 50, 10) wrote these words which follow: "For holy men trampling upon the glory of the world by their mind's contempt mortify all mortal pleasures in themselves, so that they may afterwards always live in God: For they who hardly avoid suffering the miseries of the world for God, acquire the recompense of eternal beatitude: which beatitude is certainly given both to their souls before the resurrection, and is conferred upon their bodies none the less after the Judgment: as John writes in the Apocalypse saying: 'I saw under the altar the souls of them that were slain for the word of God, and for the testimony which they held. And they cried with a loud voice, saying: How long, O Lord (holy and true) dost thou not judge and revenge our blood on them that dwell on the earth? And white robes were given to every one of them one; and it was said to them, that they should rest for a little time, till their fellow servants, and their brethren, who are to be slain, even as they, should be filled up' (Apoc. 6, 9-11). What in fact is it to give white stoles to each of them, except to confer upon them the immortality of eternal beatitude? But what is

---

[1] The text here falsely ascribes this commentary to Saint Ambrose.

[2] *Commentaria in epistolam ad Philippenses* (PL 17, 407A).

[3] This authorship of this work is uncertain.

[4] *Expositio in Apocalypsim Ioannis*, hom. 6 (PL 35, 2426).

[5] Ambrose Autpert (ca. 730 – 784) was a Frankish Benedictine monk. He was an official at the court of King Pepin the Short. He also played, in some way, the role of tutor to the future emperor Charlemagne.

[6] *In Sancti Iohannis Apostoli & euangelistæ Apocalypsim libri decem* (M. Godefridus Hitorpius, Cologne, 1536), bk. 4, pp. 138-139.

[7] According to the *Catholic Enclyclopedia* this work is "almost certainly spurious." ("Pope St. Gregory I ('the Great')", (1909 ed.), vol. 6, pg. 787).

the meaning of 'to rest until the number of the elect be filled up,' except to wait for the glory of the future resurrection? In which they each will indeed receive white robes again, because they will recover the immortal and incorruptible garments of their bodies."[1] Whose words so clearly express the Catholic faith that nothing more could be desired.

Bede relates the same view, who interpreting the aforesaid words in his *Explanation of the Apocalypse* says the following: "The souls of the Saints which rejoice in their blessed immortality, have now each one robe. But when their bodies arise, as Isaias says, "They shall receive double in their land (61, 7)."[2] Haymo [of Auxerre][3] and Richard of Saint Victor[4] in their commentaries which they published on the Apocalypse interpret in the same way. I have omitted their words lest I burden the reader with excessive prolixity.

Besides these very clear testimonies, the fact that it seems to be against justice to defer wagers to a laborer for so many centuries confirms this position of ours and of the whole Church: wherefore of old it was commanded in the Law: "The wages of him that hath been hired by thee shall not abide with thee" (Lev. 19, 13). Now all the just are a kind of laborers, laboring in the Lord's vineyard. The laborers, I say, are they who agreed with the lord of the vineyard, that is with God the Father, for a penny a day, namely the clear vision of God: and in hope of this pay the laborers willingly endure all their labors, however difficult. Therefore since all labors are so finished at death such that one may not then labor more to increase one's merits: it is necessary that the reward of their labors, namely eternal beatitude, be immediately given to those souls which are already purified: otherwise it would be an injustice to them, if the reward of their labors would not be immediately given to those faithfully laboring, when there is no cause existing in them which would impede that they be paid immediately. Further, God immediately gives grace to the sinner doing what he can: thus God will also immediately give glory to the just doing what he can even unto death. Add to these reasons that (according to the saying of the Wise Man) "Hope that is deferred afflicteth the soul" (Prov. 13, 12): hence it will happen that souls however holy when delayed in waiting for their future beatitude, are in continual affliction. But it is not just that he would undergo pain, who has already sufficiently paid for any sin which he may have committed.

Furthermore. the soul of a sinner immediately undergoes punishment after death: thus the soul of the just will also immediately after death have its reward: especially since God is more inclined to mercy than to punishment. Regarding the punishment for sins being immediately inflicted after death, Job testifies saying the following: "They spend their days in wealth, and in a moment they go down to hell" (21, 13). He said "in a moment" because they descend to Hell immediately after death without any rest, so that they may undergo due punishments for their sins. And what is said in Luke concerning the rich glutton it is very clear: "The rich man also died: and he was buried in hell" (16, 22). If God immediately inflicts due punishment upon sinners, it is unreasonable that He would not immediately render the due reward to the just.

Finally, among the Ecclesiastical dogmas which are listed in the book, *De Ecclesiasticis dogmatibus*, the seventy-eighth, pertaining to this matter, says the following: "After the Ascension of the Lord to Heaven, the souls of all the Saints are with Christ, and going out of the body go to Christ, waiting for the resurrection of their body, so that together with it both may be transformed to complete and perpetual beatitude: and just as the souls of sinners in Hell in

---

[1] *Expositio in psalmos poenitentiales*, exposition on the fourth penitential psalm, n. 10 (PL 79, 588C-D).

[2] Bk. 1, c. 7 (PL 93, 148B).

[3] *Expositio in Apocalypsin*, bk. 2, c. 7 (PL 117,1031A).

[4] Richard of Saint Victor was a Scottish theologian who died in 1173. *In Apocalysim libri* septem, bk. 2, c. 8 (PL 196,768A ff.).

a state of fear, wait for the resurrection of their bodies, so that with it both may be thrust into eternal punishment."[1]

Now there remains that we reply to the adversaries' objections. For they firstly object against us that Paul, who in his Epistle to the Hebrews, after listing many Saints who conquered kingdoms through faith, afterwards adds: "And all these being approved by the testimony of faith, received not the promise; God providing some better thing for us, that they should not be perfected without us" (Heb. 11, 39-40). From which words it is inferred that no soul before Judgment Day is beatified, until all the just are beatified at the same time: because he said that they "received not the promise." For we admit that they have not received the promise: because the resurrection of the bodies, which God promised to His saints, is still delayed, so that we may all rise together, seeing that in the common joy of all, the joy of each is greater. And so they wait until we all rise, God having so wisely ordained, so that they would not be perfected without us, that is, that they would not perceive the perfect beatitude of soul and body.

And for this reason He did not say that they would not be beatified without us, but that they will not be perfected without us: namely because souls may have obtained the beatitude of soul without us, yet they will not have attained perfect beatitude of body and soul without us. Hence, although the Saints are already beatified in their souls, they eagerly await us for their perfection and desire our liberation, both for their sakes and ours: and they pray for us, so that we may all be freed from the miseries of the present world. For they know clearly that they will not be perfected without us: because although they have poured out prayers and supplications to God for the resurrection of their own bodies, they have received the Divine reply, "That they should rest for a little time, till their fellow servants, and their brethren, who are to be slain, even as they, should be filled up" (Apoc. 6, 11). Therefore, the Saints have not yet received this promise, which was given concerning the immortality of the body, such that they have not possessed complete and perfect beatitude without us: yet the other promises, namely which were given regarding the glory of their souls, they have already received, because they already see God, and they are already filled with joy with God's countenance: they exult in Him and enjoy Him.

Otherwise Paul would not be consistent with himself, because when speaking concerning the Saints a little above, he had said: "By faith they conquered kingdoms, wrought justice, obtained promises" (Heb. 11, 33). Many and various are the dignities which souls have already received according to the variety of their merit: but besides all these promises there is still lacking the one concerning the incorruption of their bodies: and concerning this he say that "they received not the promise": and for this reason they do not have perfect and consummate joy until they also obtain the promise. Therefore God replies to the Saints desiring and asking from God the resurrection of their bodies in the manner whereby a father, who has many children, and to each one returning from the field and asking that food be given to him, replies: "Food is already prepared for all of you, but wait for your brothers, so that when you have been gathered in one place, you may all eat and feast rejoicing together."

They secondly object against us the passage from John's first epistle: "We are now the sons of God; and it hath not yet appeared what we shall be. We know, that, when he shall appear, we shall be like to him: because we shall see him as he is" (3, 2). But before Judgment Day it will not appear what we shall be: thus before that day we will not see Him as He is. To this objection we reply that although John says that we shall be like to God and see Him, when it shall appear what we shall be, yet he does not say that we will not see Him before it appears what we shall be: nevertheless this ought to have been said, so that the conclusion of the

---

[1] Gennadius of Massilia, c. 79 (PL 58, 998C).

argument would have been good: but since it was not said, we say that the conclusion of that syllogism is incorrect.

It can also be replied otherwise, such that we may say it has already appeared in the souls of the Saints what would be in them: because they already have the inheritance, for which they were adopted: they already see God, they already enjoy Him. "We are now," he says, "the sons of God." I say adopted sons, adopted for heavenly glory: but "it hath not yet appeared what we shall be," because it has not yet been shown to us to what we have been adopted: we do not know the inheritance kept for us: but we know that when this adoption shall have appeared, when the inheritance shall have been revealed, to which we were destined, then we shall see God as He is. For the vision itself is the inheritance for which we were adopted. Wherefore it cannot happen that what was destined for us would appear, except that we see God. Hence, just as we say the souls of the Saints see God before Judgment Day: so we say that it has already appeared in them what they were to be.

These are the testimonies of Scripture, which superficially seem to support the adversaries. Thus since these testimonies of Scripture are so hardly convincing, and the ones we have cited above are so clear, and confirmed with the authority of the Fathers: it is necessary that we most firmly believe, and nowise doubt that the souls of the Saints which departed from this world purified, or after the separation of their souls from their bodies were purified elsewhere, have already attained the facial vision of God and already reached eternal beatitude.

But to conclude this discussion, it is necessary that we cite the definition of the Church. Pope Innocent III, a man worthy of all veneration outside of his pontifical dignity, when replying to the Bishop of Cremona, asking about a certain unbaptized and already dead priest, whether he could be saved without Baptism, says the following: "We reply to your question as follows: the priest whom you mentioned who ended his last days [on earth] without Baptism, because he persevered in the faith of holy Mother Church, and the confession of Christ's name, we unhesitatingly affirm that he has been absolved from original sin and has attained the joy of the heavenly kingdom."[1] These words are found in the book of Decretal letters, with the title of *Presbytero non bapizato*, in the chapter which begins: *Apostolicam*.

After this decision, Pope Benedict XII, gave a much more extensive and explicit decision concerning this matter:

Benedict, the servant of the servants of God, for a perpetual remembrance of the matter: Blessed be God in all His gifts, and holy in all His works Who, guards the sacrosanct Roman Catholic and Apostolic Church which He planted with His right hand, and which as the chief head of all the churches as a conqueress, by the Lord saying to Peter: "Thou art Peter and upon this rock I will build My Church": by His compassion He has not abandoned, but guards through His Blessed Apostles, especially Peter and Paul, singular defenders of the same Church, with kind benignity and continual goodness, to the extent that having been governed by the same rulers, it may remain stable in itself having been founded upon a firm rock, and all the worshipers of the Christian faith may obey him, submit to him, live under his teaching, continue under his discipline and correction: not that he may recklessly propound a dogma, engraft incautiously, or impose something imprudent in the faith: and thus men may turn away from evil and do good, walk through straight ways, seek better things through holy desires, hope for the soon to come reward for the just of eternal life, fear the not remote calamities of Hell for the wicked: for it is written: "Behold, I come quickly; and my reward is with me, to render to every man according to his works" (Apoc. 22, 12). But if something were attempted by anyone otherwise, it would be completely rooted out immediately by his authority, after penalties have also been imposed, according as he sees to be useful. Our Savior Jesus Christ at the time of His Passion deigned to entreat the Father

---

[1] X, lib. 3, tit. 43, c. 2 (PL 179, 624-625).

for which [church] saying: "Simon, Simon, behold Satan hath desired to have you, that he may sift you as wheat: but I have prayed for thee, that thy faith fail not: and thou, being once converted, confirm thy brethren" (Lk. 22, 31-32), so that subsisting in itself it might instruct the other [churches].

The question recently arose, however, in the time of Our Predecessor of happy memory, John XXII, even among the many teachers of theology, about the [beatific] vision of the souls of just men after their death, in whom nothing was purgeable when they departed from this world, or if there was, it was already entirely purged, whether they see the Divine essence before they take up their bodies again at the General Judgment, and about many other things, some of whom expressed the negative opinion, others the affirmative opinion, while others were striving to express different things and in different ways according to their imaginations, about the vision of the Divine essence by such souls: as it is known to be evident from their sayings and writings: but about their rejected disputes, which we omit here for the sake of brevity, also because among themselves they fell away from Our conclusions. And since Our Predecessor, to whom the judgment of the aforesaid matters belonged, was preparing to end the disputes of this kind, in his public consistory and by more strictly enjoining, and by commanding both his brother Cardinals of the Holy Roman Church, of the number of whom we were then, and also the prelates and masters in theology, many of whom were present, that when requested by him, each one would say what he thought about the aforesaid subject of the [beatific] vision. Yet, having been prevented by death, as it was pleasing to the Lord, he was unable to do it.

Thus our aforesaid predecessor having died, we having assumed to the height of the highest Apostle with its lofty dignity, observing more diligently that due to their unsolved disputes, how many dangers hang over souls, and how many scandals could thence arise: in order that their variety of opinion may appear and the solidity of the truth may be made known, having first made a careful examination about the aforesaid matters, and careful consideration with our brother Cardinals of the aforesaid Roman Church, from the counsel of these brothers, by this Constitution which is to remain in force forever, we, with apostolic authority, define the following:

According to the general disposition of God, the souls of all the saints who departed from this world before the Passion of our Lord Jesus Christ and also of the holy Apostles, martyrs, confessors, virgins and other faithful who died after receiving the holy Baptism of Christ—provided they were not in need of any purification when they died, or will not be in need of any when they die in the future, or else, if they then needed or will need some purification, after they have been purified after death—and again the souls of children who have been reborn by the same Baptism of Christ or will be when Baptism is conferred on them, if they die before attaining the use of free will: all these souls, immediately (*mox*) after death and, in the case of those in need of purification, after the purification mentioned above, since the Ascension of our Lord and Saviour Jesus Christ into Heaven, already before they take up their bodies again and before the General Judgment, have been, are and will be with Christ in Heaven, in the heavenly kingdom and paradise, joined to the company of the holy Angels. Since the Passion and death of the Lord Jesus Christ, these souls have seen and see the Divine essence with an intuitive vision and even face to face, without the mediation of any creature by way of object of vision; rather the Divine essence immediately manifests Itself to them, plainly, clearly and openly, and in this vision they enjoy the Divine essence. Moreover, by this vision and enjoyment the souls of those who have already died are truly blessed and have eternal life and rest. Also the souls of those who will die in the future will see the same Divine essence and will enjoy it before the General Judgment.

Such a vision and enjoyment of the Divine essence do away with the acts of faith and hope in these souls, inasmuch as faith and hope are properly theological virtues. And after such intuitive and face-to-face vision and enjoyment has or will have begun for these souls, the same vision and enjoyment has continued and will continue without any interruption and without end until the Last Judgment and from then on forever.[1] We determine, moreover, that according to God's common ordination the souls of those dying in state of mortal sin, soon after their death their souls descend to Hell, where they are tortured with infernal flames: and because nonetheless all men will appear on Judgment Day before Christ's tribunal with their bodies to render an account of their own deeds, so that each one may receive what is due to their bodies, according as he has done good or evil. Having decreed our aforesaid definitions or determinations, each one ought to be held by all the faithful. Whosoever, however, henceforth knowingly and pertinaciously presumes to hold, oppose, preach, teach or defend by word or writing the contrary of our decrees or determinations, may it be proceeded in due manner against him as against a heretic. Thus it is permitted to no man to breach this writing of our decree etc. Given at Avignon on February fourth of the second year of our Pontificate.[2]

But for a greater confirmation of the same matter, I will cite concerning the same matter the definition of the universal Church. For the Council of Florence celebrated under Eugene IV, defined with these words: "It has likewise defined, that, if those truly penitent have departed in the love of God, before they have made satisfaction by the worthy fruits of penance for sins of commission and omission, the souls of these are cleansed after death by purgatorial punishments; and so that they may be released from punishments of this kind, the suffrages of the living faithful are of advantage to them, namely, the sacrifices of Masses, prayers, and almsgiving, and other works of piety, which are customarily performed by the faithful for other faithful according to the institutions of the Church. And that the souls of those, who after the reception of Baptism have incurred no stain of sin at all, and also those, who after the contraction of the stain of sin whether in their bodies, or when released from the same bodies, as we have said before, are purged, are immediately received into Heaven, and see clearly the one and triune God Himself just as He is, yet according to the diversity of merits, one more perfectly than another. Moreover, the souls of those who depart in actual mortal sin or in original sin only, descend immediately into Hell but to undergo punishments of different kinds."[3]

And I think that I have indeed said enough about this matter. Against this heresy wrote with sufficient length William of Ockham in his *Dialogus*[4]: and Blessed Thomas asserts a few things against this heresy in a small work which is entitled: *Reasons for the Faith Against Muslim Objections.*[5]

A **seventh heresy** asserts that all the blessed are equal in glory, nor is there any difference of rewards in Heaven: because there is no difference of merits in this life: but it asserts that all the just are equal in merits and rewards: and it says that all sinners are also equal in sins and punishments. The leader and teacher of this error was a certain Jovinian, a Roman, previously a monk, and afterwards having given up the monastic life returned to the world, which he had formerly left. He lived during the time of Popes Damasus and Siricius, Jovinian being a

---

[1] Dz. 530-531.

[2] *Magnum Bullarium Romanum* (Lyon, Sumptib. Philippi Borde, Laur. Arnaud, & Cl. Rigaud, 1655), v. 1, IV, pp. 240-241.

[3] Dz. 693.

[4] P. 2, c. 9. William of Ockham (1280-1349) was a philosopher and controversial writer, born at or near the village of Ockham in Surrey, England.

[5] *De rationibus fidei contra Saracenos, Graecos et Armenos ad Cantorem Antiochenum*, c. 9.

monk under Damasus, and giving up the monastic life under Siricius, he taught this among other heresies.

Now we will speak concerning the difference of merits and their different retributions: because it will be discussed below concerning the difference of sins, in the section on sin. What the Lord says in John's Gospel very clearly proves the diversity of merits and rewards: "In my Father's house there are many mansions" (14, 2). He called the heavenly kingdom the "Father's house," the greatness of which house a prophet having admired said: "How great is the house of God, and how vast is the place of his possession!" (Bar. 3, 24). This is that house of Jacob concerning which the Angel speaking to the Virgin said: "And He shall reign in the house of Jacob for ever" (Lk. 1, 32). For unless He were speaking about that heavenly house which would last forever, what He says could not be true: "And He shall reign in the house of Jacob for ever." For in that house which is not eternal, He could not reign forever. Therefore He now calls the house of Jacob His "Father's house," in which He will reign forever.

Now that He is speaking concerning this house in which He now reigns, and not concerning that house in which He fights through His members, that is this lower Church, the words which follow clearly declare. "If not, I would have told you: because I go to prepare a place for you. And if I shall go, and prepare a place for you, I will come again, and will take you to myself; that where I am, you also may be" (Jn. 14, 2-3). No one doubts Christ says to the Apostles that the place He says that He prepares is in Heaven, in the kingdom of Heaven: not this present place on earth in which He left the Apostles. Thus the place which He says that He will prepare for the Apostles, He likewise calls the "Father's house," concerning which He says: "In my Father's house there are many mansions." If therefore the house is the kingdom of Heaven, what will be the difference of mansions, unless a diversity of rewards is found in that kingdom according to the diversity of merits? Furthermore, in the First Epistle to the Corinthians Paul says: "As in Adam all die, so also in Christ all shall be made alive, but every one in his own order" (15, 22-23). If everyone will rise in his own order, then there will be diverse merits of those rising: otherwise if the merit of all those rising is the same, all will rise in the same order, and not "every one in his own order." And in same place Paul says: "One is the glory of the sun, another the glory of the moon, and another the glory of the stars. For star differeth from star in glory. So also is the resurrection of the dead" (v. 41-42).

But this passage, Jerome bearing witness, Jovinian so interprets so that he would say that star differs from star, because spiritual men differ from carnal men. Thus the stars will be, according to Jovinian's interpretation, carnal men, and they will be at the same time with spiritual heavenly men. Far be this opinion, nevertheless, from the hearts of the faithful. For by the word "stars" Paul does not include the whole human race, but only the just: because sinners themselves are darkness: to such an extent that they fail to give light to others. Thus it is evident that that those words were spoken about the just alone when he said: "One is the glory of the sun, another the glory of the moon": such that those greater in glory shine with brightness of the sun, and those who are in a lower degree shine with the brightness of the moon.

And again he says in another place: "He who soweth sparingly, shall also reap sparingly: and he who soweth in blessings, shall also reap blessings" (II Cor. 9, 6). You see here the diversity of reapers according to the diversity of sowers. Now all those doing good works are here called sowers, according to the passage of the Prophet: "They that sow in tears shall reap in joy. Going they went and wept, casting their seeds. But coming they shall come with joyfulness, carrying their sheaves" (Ps. 125, 5-7). And that which the praying Apostles say is clear: "Increase our faith" (Lk. 17, 5). If the measure of faith is one, how do the Apostles pray that their faith be increased? And Christ our Savior bearing testimony concerning John the Baptist says: "There hath not risen among them that are born of women a greater than John the Baptist: yet he that is the lesser in the kingdom of heaven is greater than he" (Mt. 11, 11). Likewise Christ speaking about the fulfillment and transgression of the precepts says: "He therefore that shall break one of these least commandments, and shall so teach men, shall be called the least in the kingdom of heaven. But he that shall do and teach, he shall be called great in the kingdom of heaven" (Mt. 5, 19). Now where there is greatest and least, it is necessary that not all have the same measure.

He also explains the same difference of greatest and least through the prophet Jeremias saying: "Behold the days shall come, saith the Lord, and I will make a new covenant with the house of Israel, and with the house of Juda: not according to the covenant which I made with their fathers" (31, 31-32). And after a few words he adds: "I will write it in their heart: and I will be their God, and they shall be my people. And they shall teach no more every man his neighbour, and every man his brother, saying: Know the Lord: for all shall know me from the least of them even to the greatest, saith the Lord" (v. 33-34). From the context of which words it is very clearly known that the prophet spoke concerning Christ's future kingdom in Heaven: nevertheless when He speaks of it He says: "All shall know me from the least of them even to the greatest." If all are to be equal, how will there be there greatest and least?

Again in the Second Epistle to the Corinthians Paul says: "We must all be manifested before the judgement seat of Christ, that every one may receive the proper things of the body, according as he hath done, whether it be good or evil" (5, 10). Then the Lord speaking through the Prophet Isaias concerning eunuchs says: "I will give to them in my house, and within my walls, a place, and a name better than sons and daughters: I will give them an everlasting name which shall never perish" (56, 5). Thus when He says, "I will give to them... a name better," he shows that a good place is given to the married in His house, but much lower: and "a name better," but less than the name given to the virgins. But lest a carnal person perhaps think from this promise something temporal ought to be hoped for, He immediately adds, "I will give them an everlasting name." But because the heretic could still escape saying that in this place "everlasting" ought to be taken for a long time, just as those things which are of very long duration, we are accustomed to call everlasting and eternal: hence so that every crack may be blocked to the heretic, he adds that it "shall never perish." Therefore what more does Jovinian seek? Why does he pour out the clouds of his perversity to block the serenity of the truth? This everlasting name which will not perish, whatever it is, certainly signifies a certain glory, which is promised to be proper to eunuchs, and will not be common with others who have procreated children. Thus, not everyone in that kingdom are measured to be equal.

He adds still that the angelic spirits are not all of the same condition, nor are all of the same merit. For among them some are called Angels, others Archangels, others Thrones, Dominations, Powers, Cherubim, and Seraphim. But in vain would be such a diversity of names, if there were no diversity of merits. If this diversity is in the Angels, why is not the same found in men especially since the Savior promised to just men that they "shall be as the angels of God" (Mt. 22, 30)? Furthermore, the Savior clearly showed the diversity of punishments according to the diversity of sins saying: "The servant who knew the will of his lord... and did not according to his will, shall be beaten with many stripes. But he that knew not, and did things worthy of stripes, shall be beaten with few stripes (Lk. 12, 47-48). You see here the clear distinction not in fact of the just and sinner, but of sinner and sinner. For both are sinners: wherefore both are beaten, although one more severely than the other: for one is beaten with few stripes, because he sinned less: the other, however, with many, in that he sinned more gravely. Since therefore one is punished more severely than the other according to the diversity of their sins: it is necessary that one also be given a greater reward than another according to the diversity of their merits.

But now it remains that we see what it is whereby Jovinian defends his heresy. To all those laboring in the Lord's vineyard, he says, an equal pay was given by the just householder: namely one penny. For some of them labored from the first hour of the day to the last, but others only worked one hour: now in the reception of their pay all were made equal: because all received just one penny. To this objection Blessed Augustine replies in his book, *On Holy Virginity*, with these words: "What is the meaning of that penny, which is given in payment to all alike when the work of the vineyard is ended? Whether it be to those who have labored from the first hour, or to those who have labored one hour? What assuredly does it signify, but something, which all shall have in common, such as is life eternal itself, the kingdom of Heaven itself, where shall be all, whom God has predestinated, called, justified, glorified? 'For this corruptible must put on incorruption; and this mortal must put on immortality' (I Cor. 15, 53). This is that penny, wages for all. Yet "star differeth from star in glory; so also is the resurrection of the dead" (*ibid.*, 41-42). These are the different merits of the Saints. For, if by that penny Heaven were signified, is it not common to all the stars to be in Heaven? And yet, 'One is the glory of the sun, another the glory of the moon, and another the glory of the stars' (v. 41). If that penny were taken for health of body, have not all the members, when we are well, health in common; and, should this health continue even unto death, is it not in all alike and equally? And yet, 'God hath set the members every one of them in the body as it hath pleased him' (12, 18); that neither the whole would be an eye, nor the whole hearing, nor the whole smelling[1]: and, whatever else there is, it has its own property, although it have health equally with all. Thus, because eternal life itself shall be alike to all, an equal penny was assigned to all; but, because in that eternal life itself the lights of merits shall shine with a distinction, there are many mansions in the house of the Father[2]: and, by this means, in the penny not unequal, one lives not longer than another; but in the many mansions, one is honored with greater brightness than another."[3]

In addition, Jovinian still objects many other things against us. But these things are so frivolous and so unimportant that it would be annoying to examine them, and we would disdain to answer them. Nevertheless, if anyone would like to know them, he may read the second book of Blessed Jerome's *Against Jovinian*, because in that place he ridicules all Jovinian's ditties, and answers them.

But now it is necessary that we hear the decision of the Church on the matter. The Synod of Telepte,[4] celebrated in Africa under the authority of Pope Siricius, says the following: "For it is a savage barking to show no reverence to virginity, observe no rule of chastity, to attempt to put everything on a same level, to abolish the different degrees of merit, and to introduce a certain meagerness in heavenly rewards, as if Christ had only one palm to bestow, and there were no copious diversity in His rewards."[5] The Council of Florence celebrated under Eugene IV teaches the same opinion. For in those words which we recently cited for the refutation of the preceding heresy, that is, the sixth heresy above, after it said that the souls of the Saints already see God clearly before Judgment Day, it immediately adds, "yet according to the diversity of merits, one more perfectly than another." And it says that those who go down to Hell "undergo punishments of different kinds."[6]

---

[1] Cf. v. 17.

[2] Jn. 14, 2.

[3] C. 26 (PL 40, 410).

[4] It was held in Telepte, a city in Byzacena in 418. Telepte was the metropolis of the Byzacene province.

[5] *False Decretals of the Pseudo-Isidore*, (PL 130 0689B); Saint Ambrose, Letter 42 (PL 16, 1123B); Appendix to the works of Leo the Great, c. 31 (PL 56, 566B).

[6] Dz. 693.

Blessed Jerome wrote *Against Jovinian* in two books: and in the second book he disputes against this heresy. Blessed Augustine disputes the same error in his book, *On Holy Virginity*. I have not seen others.

BELLUM

War

Concerning this matter there was one error of the Manichaeans saying that it is nowise licit to wage war: and for this reason (as Augustine bears witness[1]) they reprehend Moses that he waged wars. In our era John Oecolampadius raised up this error from Hell, as it were already buried, who differs from the Manichaeans in this, namely that he does not reprehend warring Moses: because at that time war was permitted either by God's command or permission. Now, however, (as he says) Christ having forbidden war, it is no longer permitted for Christians to wage war in any way.[2] [Heinrich] Cornelius Agrippa [of Nettesheim][3] teaches the same view in his book, *The Vanity of Arts and Sciences*.[4] For when discussing military science, after having assailed it with many insults, and afflicted it with jeers, he says the following: "Yet the Divine Plato praises this art, teaches it to his scholars, and commands them to enroll as soon as fit for service: and the famous Cyrus affirmed, 'That war was a necessary as agriculture': nay St. Augustine and St. Bernard, Catholic Doctors of the Church, have approved thereof, neither do the Pontifical Decretals at all impugn it, though Christ and His Apostles teach quite another doctrine. So that contrary to the doctrine of Christ, it has obtained no small honor in the Church."[5] In which words he openly teaches that Christ forbade war.

Against the opinion of the Manichaeans whereby they reprehend Moses waging war, it makes one ashamed to dispute: since from the testimony of Scripture it is evident that Moses waged war against barbarous and infidel nations due to the Lord's command. Thus let them either also reprehend God, or cease to calumniate Moses waging war. If you prefer a longer disputation of the matter, read Blessed Augustine's *Against Faustus*, book twenty-two, chapter seventy-four, and through the four following chapters.

Now concerning the remaining objection wherein Oecolampadius and Agrippa agree with the Manichaeans keeping men back from every type of war, it is necessary that we carefully investigate. Luke when recounting John preaching in the desert and baptizing says: "And the soldiers also asked him, saying: And what shall we do? And he said to them: Do violence to no man; neither calumniate any man; and be content with your pay" (3, 14). Now if war were

---

[1] *Contra Faustum Manichaeum libri XXXIII*, bk. 22, c. 74.

[2] "Alphonsus à Castro also attributes the same teaching to John Oecolampadius, in the section on 'War,' which seems strange to me, since Zwingli, his colleague, approved of war to such an extent that he perished on the field of battle, and in like manner Calvin, and Melanchthon, and other heretics of this time, by word and by deed teach that war should be carried on" (Saint Robert Bellarmine, *De Laicis*, c. 14).

[3] Heinrich Cornelius Agrippa was born in 1486, at Cologne; died at Grenoble or Lyons in 1534 or 1535. He was a nominal Catholic openly in sympathy with Luther.

[4] *De vanitate scientiarum* was published in 1527, has been translated into many European languages and is well described as a "compound of erudition and ignorance, gravity and vanity." It abounds in denunciations of Scholasticism, veneration of relics and the Saints, Canon Law and the hierarchy, and calls for a return to the Scriptures as the philosopher's stone (*Lydius lapis*) of Christian teaching.

[5] *The Vanity of Arts and Sciences* (London, Printed by J. C. for S. Speed, 1676), c. 79, p. 255.

completely unlawful, Blessed John ought to have replied: "Cast away your weapons, cease this warfare, strike no one, wound no one." Since, however, he said none of those things, but forbade calumny and told them to be content with their pay: by that very fact he is seen to approve war. Furthermore when the centurion said to Christ: "I also am a man subject to authority, having under me soldiers; and I say to this, Go, and he goeth, and to another, Come, and he cometh, and to my servant, Do this, and he doeth it" (Mt. 8, 9); Christ hearing these words, praised the centurion's faith: but He did not command the desertion of warfare: He would have commanded this, however, if war were nowise permitted. Again, Christ answered the Herodians asking whether it were lawful to give tribute to Caesar: "Render therefore to Caesar the things that are Caesar's; and to God, the things that are God's" (Mt. 22, 21). Now tribute is rendered so that wages may be paid to the army for the preservation of peace.

For so Paul says: when he discusses the obedience that ought to be given to a leader: "Wherefore be subject of necessity, not only for wrath, but also for conscience' sake. For therefore also you pay tribute. For they are the ministers of God, serving unto this purpose" (Rom. 13, 5-6). Hence, if it were nowise licet to wage war, it would follow that a wicked sinner would [not] act badly defending himself from the judge, so that he would not be captured for punishment, if the judge enters to arrest and punish. Now to assert this would be most absurd, and destructive of all human society, and very clearly contrary to Sacred Writ. For Blessed Paul says in his Epistle to the Romans: "Let every soul be subject to higher powers: for there is no power but from God... But if thou do that which is evil, fear: for he beareth not the sword in vain. For he is God's minister: an avenger to execute wrath upon him that doth evil" (13, 1 & 4).

Now the arguments that they put forth in their favor hardly support their position. They firstly in fact object that the Lord says: "But I say to you not to resist evil: but if one strike thee on thy right cheek, turn to him also the other" (Mt. 5, 39). To this objection Augustine replies that this saying is not a command of the deed, but a disposition of the mind, such that one would be prepared, if he would be struck again on the other, to also bear it patiently.[1] It can also be replied otherwise. For what impedes that the same objection be repelled in two ways? For it can also be said, not without reason, that this statement of the Savior does not belong to the number of precepts, but ought to be counted among the counsels. Now that this is so can be easily determined from the words which immediately follow, because the words which immediately follow nowise seem to belong to the number of precepts, but to the counsels: those words namely are: "And if a man will contend with thee in judgment, and take away thy coat, let go thy cloak also unto him. And whosoever will force thee one mile, go with him other two" (Mt. 5, 40-41). Which two sayings, no one contends to be precepts unless he be mentally deficient, but are merely counsels given to perfect men. If therefore that statement is a counsel, it is thence proved that that saying nowise supports the opinion of the Manichaeans.

They secondly object that a Christian man do battle by his prayers and supplications to God, so that God would have mercy upon them, and by those prayers repel the injury inflicted upon them, and recall the offenders from their wicked intention. Let us reply to this objection conceding the just warrior ought to do battle by his prayers made to God: for, as it is said in the First Book of Machabees, "The success of war is not in the multitude of the army, but strength cometh from heaven" (3, 19). Nevertheless not on that account ought one to abstain from war, and weapons ought to be cast away in general, because when Moses prayed on the mountain, Amalec was conquered by Josue's sword.[2]

---

[1] "For these precepts are to be taken as binding 'the mind to be prepared to fulfill them,' as Augustine says (*De Sermone Domini in Monte,* bk. 1, c. 19 (PL 34, 1239))." Cf. I-II, q. 108, a. 3 ad 2um.

[2] Cf. Ex. 17.

The **second heresy** is Martin Luther's: and I do not know whether it ought to be discussed a little more leniently or more severely and harshly. For he said that that it is not permitted for Christians to fight against the Turks, because (as he says) it would be to resist the will of God visiting and correcting our iniquities through them. Thus Luther does not restrict Christians from every war, but from waging war against the Turks, in which matter this opinion seems to me more severe than that of the Manichaeans. For if it be permitted for a Christian to fight against a Christian, why would it not be permitted against the Turks? For regarding war, so that it be just, the cause must be especially investigated, on which the justice of the war depends: but since the same cause is much more urgent in a war against the Turks than in a war waged against Christians, it follows that a war is more just which is begun against the Turk, than that which is waged against any Christian.

Now the reason on account of which a ruler can start a war, is that therefrom perfect peace may be obtained. Hence Augustine in his letter to the officer Boniface says: "We do not seek peace in order to be at war, but we go to war that we may have peace. Be peaceful, therefore, in warring, so that you may vanquish those whom you war against, and bring them to the prosperity of peace."[1] But nothing preserves and fosters peace more than justice, and nothing disturbs it more than injustice. "Justice," says the Prophet, "and peace have kissed" (Ps. 84, 11). Thus the cause on account of which one can justly wage war is the execution of justice and its conservation. Hence it is that if someone would wish to kill you or strike you unjustly, you could justly prevent him: and if someone by force and violence would want to rob you of your possessions, you could justly resist him. And if perhaps he stole either secretly, or in any other way, and there does not appear to be another way of regaining except by war, you could justly start a war so that you can regain your possessions: provided that you have the authority and power to draw up [an army for] war. For it does not pertain to just anyone to gather an army and to begin a war: but, as Augustine says in *Against Faustus*: this is the function of the head of state alone.[2]

Therefore when the cause of beginning a war is the same against the Turk, and when both the authority and power in the Emperor and other Christian kings are not lacking, it follows that it is equally just, nay and it could be more just to begin a war against them than against Christians, since the cause would be much more just in the former case than in the latter. For if a Christian attacks a Christian to slaughter and spoil, and on account of this the other justly resists, is it not so when the Turk attacks Christians to kill and spoil? Most certainly as he does much worse, namely he does this to force them to deny the faith, to renounce both Christ and the Gospel, so that, if he could, he may eliminate every Christian from the globe. Are not these things worse? If for the sake of regaining the patrimony from another Christian, it is allowed to go out against him in war: why will it not be allowed to fight against the Turk, who has seized from the Christians so many cities and towns, not to speak of kingdoms and an empire, with great dishonor, and very great harm inflicted? If then it is allowed to do battle with someone, as we have already shown above that it is allowed, it will be likewise permitted against no one as much as against the Turk. Machabeus fights against Antiochus, and other infidel kings for the sake of religion, the faith, and ceremonies, and he is praised for having done this. Why will the Christian fighting against the Turk for the faith and religion not also be praised?

Concerning this subject there are many decisions of the Church, not by the words which it taught, but by the deeds which it performed, whereby it more truly instructed us by example

---

[1] Letter 189, n. 6 (PL 33, 856).

[2] "A great deal depends on the causes for which men undertake wars, and on the authority they have for doing so; for the natural order which seeks the peace of mankind, ordains that the monarch should have the power of undertaking war if he thinks it advisable" (Bk. 22, n. 75 (PL 42, 447)).

than by word. In the Synod of Clermont celebrated under Urban II, in fact, it was decreed that there would be a war against the Turks, in which Urban was marvelously successful. After whose death a successor Pascal II (as [Bartolomeo] Platina bears witness) supported the war that had been begun.[1] Also Callistus II when he held the [First] Lateran Council of nine hundred Fathers[2] decreed with their consent that "with the first opportunity they might send recruits to the Christian army in Asia, then much weakened; the news whereof gave such courage to Baldwin, King of Jerusalem, that he set upon Gazis, a king of the Turks that inhabited Asia Minor, who was coming against him with a great army, vanquished him, and took him prisoner."[3] Also Lucius III having held the Synod of Verona exhorted all Christian princes to afford assistance to those oppressed for the faith in Asia.[4] Why then does Luther presume to teach against so many proofs of words and examples, that it is not allowed for Christians to wage war with the Turks? Certainly, so that I can infer from his life and works known to the world, that he has declared by this view he is an enemy of Christ, and a minister of the devil: because teaching these things, he seemed to want to completely wipe out the Christian name: because unless the Christians had resisted the Turks up until the present time, this would have already been done to Christendom. But thanks be to God, Who has better cared for His people than it seems Luther to have wanted to do.

Let us now see by what argument he established his view, namely that "to go to war against the Turks is to resist God Who punishes our iniquities through them."[5] O mighty arguer! Are you that Luther who mocks scholastic theologians, calling them sophists? Are you not now doing nothing but sophistry? I ask you, what kind of reasoning is this: God visits our iniquities by the war which is waged against us by the Turks, therefore it is not permitted for us to resist the Turks? Following this line of thinking it would not be permitted for us to make any provision against famine, to take medicine against sickness, or get any antidote against pestilence. For God visits our iniquities by all these things. Still even if He may visit [our iniquities through them], He does not bar us from preventing them by having applied some remedy. So likewise even if God would visit our iniquities by the Turks, still He does not bar defense. For God so visits His own, such that He does not abandon them. For the mercy that He always exercises towards us, exalts itself above His judgment.[6] "I will visit their iniquities with a rod: and their sins with stripes: But my mercy I will not take away from him" (Ps. 88, 33-34.

John [Fisher], Bishop of Rochester, wrote a whole article, namely number thirty-four, against this error in that work which he published against Luther's *Defense and Explanation*

---

[1] "He applied himself to the war in Asia, and to that end wrote letters and sent nuncios to all the Christian princes to exhort and animate them to it as much as possible" (*The Lives of the Popes* (London, Christopher Wilkonson, 1685), p. 224).
[2] I.e. three hundred bishops and more than six hundred abbots.
[3] *The Lives of the Popes*, p. 232.
[4] *Ibid.* p. 247.
[5] Leo X, Papal Bull *Exsurge* Domine, condemned proposition n. 34.
[6] Cf. James 2, 13.

of all the Articles.[1] Seventy years earlier Denis the Carthusian also wrote a book on waging war against Turks, in which he argues that war ought to be made against the them.[2]

BENEDICTIO
Blessings

The wicked Waldensians, due to their accustomed temerity and impiety, ridicule and mock all blessings that the Church gives or says upon wine, bread, water, oil, salt, wax, incense, olive and palm trees, vestments, chalices, any other thing necessary for use in Ecclesiastical functions, saying that all those things are of no importance. The Wycliffites imitate the Waldensians here (as everywhere else): who (in order to augment the insanity of their parents) say that such blessings are a true practice of necromancy rather than of sacred theology: to such an extent do they think that those blessings do not have any power. We have already said not a little about this error above when we discussed the power of holy water, in the section on of water, in the second heresy: and below in the section on of Exorcism, we will say many more things: wherefore we defer the discussion unto that place.

BESTIA ET BRUTUM
Beasts and Brute Animals

Concerning this matter I find just one heresy, and it is cited by Philastrius alone, which asserts that all beasts are capable of reasoning, and all brute animals, equally as man, not merely sense, but also understand. Philastrius attributes this heresy to the Gnostics and Manichaeans.[3] Augustine, however, in his *De Haeresibus ad Quodvultdeum*, when

---

[1] I.e. *Assertionis Lutheranae confutatio* (1523) reprinted in *Joannis Fisherii Opera Omnia* (Farnborough: Gregg Press, 1967) columns 660-716. "When some of his teachings were condemned by the papal Bull *Exsurge Domine* in June, 1520, Martin Luther (1483-1546) responded by publicly defending his views in a work entitled *Defense and Explanation of all the Articles* (1521). The most extensive episcopal response to Luther's defense of his forty-one condemned assertions was penned by John Fisher (1469-1535), the Bishop of Rochester England. Fisher later became a Catholic martyr of King Henry VIII and was eventually canonized together with Thomas More. Fisher's *Confutation of Luther's Assertion* (1523) comprehensively answered all forty-one of Luther's assertions in work that has never been translated into English and that has received little attention from Modern scholarship. In the sixteenth century, on the other hand, Fisher's literary activity was well known. The German Catholic theologian Johann Cochlaeus (1479-1552), who was Luther's first Catholic biographer, described Fisher as the greatest Catholic theologian in England at the time and the one who 'most seriously and thoroughly' refuted the two principle leaders among the heretics of this time, Luther and Oecolampadius." (Scheck, T. P. "Bishop John Fisher's Response to Martin Luther," (*Franciscan Studies*, vol. 71 no. 1, 2013, pp. 463, 464). The text here mistakenly states that this work was a refutation of the Luther's *Babylonian Captivity*. This has been corrected here.

[2] Denis the Carthusian (1402–1471), born in Ryckel, Belgium, was a theologian and mystic. To refute Mohammedanism he wrote the treatises, *Contra perfidiam Mahometi, et contra multa dicta Sarracenorum libri quatuor* in 1452 and *Dialogus disputationis inter Christianum et Sarracenum de lege Christi et contra perfidiam Mahometi*.

[3] *De haeresibus*, c. 88 (PL 12, 1200A-B).

he discusses the Gnostics[1] and Manichaeans,[2] never charges them with this error; nor does Irenaeus—who is much more ancient than Augustine and Philastrius—when enumerating the errors of the Gnostics, make mention of this error.[3] Now whether this opinion belongs to the Gnostics or the Manichaeans, I do not much care, since it is certain that such an assertion is erroneous, and very clearly contrary to Sacred Scriptures. "Do not become,' says the Prophet, "like the horse and the mule, who have no understanding" (Ps. 31, 9). Thus, it is false that all brute animals have the capacity of reasoning. And the Prophets says the same thing again: "Man when he was in honour did not understand; he is compared to senseless beasts, and is become like to them" (Ps. 48, 13). To what man has become like, he declared when he said that the man "did not understand." For by the fact that he did not understand, he was made like unto the beasts, because they do not understand. If brute beasts understand, in what, I ask, is he like unto the beasts, when he was in the honor in which God placed him, and he did not understand? Therefore, from these two very clear citations from Sacred Scripture, we have proved that beasts are incapable of reasoning.

CALCEAMENTUM

Shoes

Philastrius[4] and Augustine[5] cite a heresy concerning this matter, which teaches that it is not permitted for man to wear shoes. They do not assign any patron of this error: yet those holding it were name "Discalced" by the activity itself. But here it is necessary to warn that they are not condemned as heretics because they do not wear shoes, but because they believe that it is not permitted to wear them, they are hence condemned. For to lack shoes, and to walk unshod, is good and meritorious, such that one is far from being a heretic. In fact, one who walks barefoot afflicts his flesh and chastises his body, lest it resist the soul, and not obey it as it ought. And who doubts that the wearing away of the flesh is good? Thus it is good and useful to walk barefoot. Wherefore Blessed Francis, the Father of the Friars Minor, commanded those belonging to his institute, I am one of their number, a good one I hope, not to wear shoes except when required by necessity.

Yet to believe that it is nowise allowed to wear shoes, this is heretical. For the Lord, when appointing to the Jews the manner according to which they ought to eat the Pascal lamb, says: "You shall have shoes on your feet" (Ex. 12, 11). On account of which, so that the truth might be likened to the figure and the body to the shadow, priests solemnly celebrating the Holy Mass, in which the true Lamb, namely Blessed Christ, is eaten, have shoes on their feet, even those who would not otherwise wear them, such as the Friars Minor, who even if they otherwise walk barefoot, nevertheless when they celebrate Mass, have shoes on their feet. And the Lord says in Ezechiel: "Let thy shoes be on thy feet" (24, 17). And Christ our Redeemer when He sent His Apostles two by two before His face, sent them (as Mark says) "shod with sandals" (6, 9). Furthermore, what is never found to be refused, is understood to be granted. If, therefore, it was never forbidden to everyone to wear shoes, it is hence proved to be granted to us.

---

[1] *De haeresibus*, c. 6 (PL 42, 26).
[2] *Ibid.*, c. 46 (PL, 42, 38).
[3] *Contra Haereses*, bk. 1, c. 29 (PG 7, 691-694).
[4] *Liber de haeresibus,* c. 81 (PL 12, 1193B-1194A).
[5] *De Haeresibus ad Quodvultdeum*, c. 68 (PL 42, 29).

But perhaps here someone will object that the Lord forbade wearing shoes. For (as Matthew bears witness) when He sent the twelve Apostles to preach, among other things which He commanded, He also said this: "Nor scrip for your journey, nor two coats, nor shoes, nor a staff" (10, 10). Notice that shoes were forbidden in that passage."

We admit that shoe were forbidden there, but not to all. For He was speaking only to the Apostles, to whom alone those commands are discerned to pertain, as we have taught in other places. And also, those commands were not given in perpetuity and for always, but only for the time in which they were sent. In fact, it is said there: "Go ye not into the way of the Gentiles" (v. 5). And yet, it was commanded to them further on: "Preach the gospel to every creature" (Mk. 16, 15). In that passage he also forbade them to carry a purse: yet afterwards He says: "When I sent you without purse, and scrip, and shoes, did you want anything? But they said: Nothing. Then said he unto them: But now he that hath a purse, let him take it, and likewise a scrip; and he that hath not, let him sell his coat, and buy a sword" (Lk. 22, 35-36). From which words it is evident that those commands related in Matthew's Gospel were given to the Apostles for traveling on that trip, not however for the times to follow. Therefore, much less do those commands now pertain to us. Thus, since no prohibition was made about wearing shoes, it is very clearly proved that it is allowed to all to wear shoes, except perhaps to those who have obliged themselves to go without by a vow.

CANTUS

Singing

I have found just one heresy concerning this matter, which derides the singing which is done in church. The first author (in my opinion) of this error was a certain Hilary, concerning whom Blessed Augustine makes mention and presents his error.[1] And I do not know whether this Hilary was one of the Arians, who also removed the holy chants, because they heard praises of Christ in them, Whom they strongly desired to belittle. Hence Ambrose in his *Sermon against Auxentius on the Giving Up the Basilicas* says the following: "And so today, when Christ is praised, the madness of the Arians is scourged. The Gerasens could not bear the presence of Christ;[2] these, worse than the Gerasens, cannot endure the praises of Christ. They see children singing of the glory of Christ, for it is written: 'Out of the mouth of infants and of sucklings thou hast perfected praise' (Mt. 21, 16). They mock at their tender age, so full of faith, and say: 'Behold, why do they cry out?' But Christ answers them: 'If these shall hold their peace, the stones will cry out,' (Lk. 19, 40) that is, the stronger will cry out, both youths and the more mature will cry out, and old men will cry out."[3] From whose words it is evident that the Arians belittled the singing of Christ's praises in church. Nevertheless (as I think) they were belittling not because praises were being sung, but because Christ was being praised beyond their views, for they believed that Christ is a mere creature, wherefore they looked askance at the praises whereby Christ was extolled as the true God. Which praises annoyed them even if they were said in a low voice and without singing. I said that on account of Thomas Netter who seems to attribute this error to the Arians, motivated by this quotation of Ambrose, misconstrued (as I think). Whereas Hilary (as it appears from the Augustine's words) simply belittled chants. The Waldensians resurrected this error, who said that it was useless to waste time with Church singing. The English John Wycliffe followed them after-

---

[1] *Retractions*, bk. 2, c. 11 (PL 32, 634).
[2] Lk. 8, 37.
[3] N. 19 (PL 16, 1013B).

wards, who so belittled Church hymns that he called singers in church "priests of Baal," to whom when they were praying loudly Prophet Elias said: "Cry with a louder voice: for he is a God, and perhaps he is talking, or is in an inn, or on a journey, or perhaps he is asleep, and must be awaked" (III Kings 18, 27). Wherefore John Wycliffe says that they who sing in church are priests of Baal, because they so cry out as though God were sleeping and does not hear them, and so He would have been wakened by their voices.

Now in order that we might more clearly refute this error, it is firstly necessary to recall that there are two kinds of prayer to God. The first kind is private prayer, which is made by an individual person. The other is public prayer, which is made by a group of men gathered together. Silence is more conducive for the first prayer than praying aloud: since when one prays aloud he impedes others from being able to pray quietly in his presence, because by the sound of his words, he distracts the minds of others. Moreover, by so praying aloud in public, one makes one's prayers audible to the ears of the good and the wicked, which perhaps are not useful for others to know, and one may be mocked by those to whom he made his secrets known. And on account of this Anna, the mother of Samuel, is praised, concerning whom when praying to the Lord for a son it is said: "Now Anna spoke in her heart, and only her lips moved, but her voice was not heard at all" (I Kings 1, 13). And that which Paul says ought to be understood of this prayer: "If there be no interpreter, let him hold his peace in the church, and speak to himself and to God" (I Cor. 14, 28). Nevertheless if someone out of a certain impatience and fervent desire were to cry out while also praying privately, yet in a place where he does not disturb others and while so praying does not reveal the secrets of his heart, nor believes that God will not hear better when he cries out louder than when he prays in a low voice, when this man prays thus aloud he does not act badly, nay he acts well, if perhaps he intends that when another has heard his prayer he may be motivated to praise God. Hence the Prophet says: "In my trouble I cried to the Lord: and he heard me" (Ps. 119, 1).

Now lest heretics attempt to get around this by saying that those words ought to be understood of the cry of the heart, and not the cry of the mouth, let put forth Christ our Savior, Whose works no one can criticize except wickedly. For He (as John says) when about to resurrect Lazarus, "Lifting up his eyes said: Father, I give thee thanks that thou hast heard me. And I knew that thou hearest me always; but because of the people who stand about have I said it, that they may believe that thou hast sent me. When he had said these things, he cried with a loud voice: Lazarus, come forth" (11, 41-43). Notice here that you see Jesus crying with a loud voice, Who nevertheless could have been heard with a very low voice, nay Who had been able to resurrect without any sound. And so that our position might be strengthened, see what Matthew says: "And about the ninth hour Jesus cried with a loud voice, saying: Eli, Eli, lamma sabacthani? that is, My God, my God, why hast thou forsaken me?" (27, 46). Finally, so that we may prove with three witnesses, let us cite Paul, who when speaking about Christ, says the following: "Who in the days of his flesh, with a strong cry and tears, offering up prayers and supplications to him that was able to save him from death, was heard for his reverence" (Heb. 5, 7). What then do you say. impious Wycliffe, to these very clear quotations which are objected to you? But I certainly fear that you will also dare to incriminate Christ, you who have not hesitated to contemn and accuse the Church, His spouse.

The other kind of prayer is public prayer in which not merely the utility of the person himself praying is considered, but common benefits are taken into account. And in this prayer it helps to pray aloud, so that those praying hear each other, and while hearing each other compete from a certain holy emulation in praising God. For, in fact, two Seraphim cried one to another: "Holy, holy, holy, the Lord God of hosts, all the earth is full of his glory" (Is. 6, 3). In the likeness of whom there are two choirs in the church, who sing in alternation, and like two Seraphim cry one to another. It is also beneficial that prayer in common be done aloud so that others hearing it may be stirred up to praise God. Hence, the Lord in Matthew's Gospel says: "So let your light shine before men, that they may see your good works, and glorify your Father who is in heaven" (5, 16). And the Prophet says concerning that same prayer and praise: "I will bless the Lord at all times, his praise shall be always in my mouth. In the Lord shall my soul be praised: let the meek hear and rejoice. O magnify the Lord with me; and let us extol his name together" (Ps. 33, 2-4).

Hence, Rabanus says: "The Church frequently uses his psaltery with its melody of sweet songs, by which souls may be moved more easily to compunction. The primitive Church, however, so chanted the Psalms that it had the psalmist make his voice resonate with only a slight inflection, so that it was closer to speaking than to singing... A perfect voice is high, loud, and sweet: high, so that it can reach the high range; loud, so that it fills the ears; sweet, so that it soothes the spirits of the listeners. If a voice lacks any of these qualities, it is not perfect."[1] Blessed Isidore confirms the same opinion saying: "Therefore in singing hymns and Psalms, we have the example not only of the Prophets, but also of the Lord Himself and of the Apostles, and useful precepts concerning this matter to piously arousing the soul and inflaming the affection of Divine love."[2]

But if anyone is so pertinacious and wrongly indurate such that he would not be ashamed to deny that hymns themselves if rightly composed as they ought, can move the minds of those hearing to devotion of the spirit, the testimony of Augustine proves this view, who in book nine, chapters six and seven of his *Confessions* says these words: "How greatly did I weep in Thy hymns and canticles, deeply moved by the voices of Thy sweet-speaking Church! The voices flowed into mine ears, and the truth was poured forth into my heart, whence the agitation of my piety overflowed, and my tears ran over, and blessed was I therein. Not long had the Church of Milan begun to employ this kind of consolation and exhortation, the brethren singing together with great earnestness of voice and heart. For it was about a year, or not much more, since Justina, the mother of the boy-Emperor Valentinian, persecuted Thy servant Ambrose in the interest of her heresy, to which she had been seduced by the Arians. The pious people kept guard in the church, prepared to die with their bishop, Thy servant. There my mother, Thy handmaid, bearing a chief part of those cares and watchings, lived in prayer. We, still unmelted by the heat of Thy Spirit, were yet moved by the astonished and disturbed city. At this time it was instituted that, after the manner of the Eastern Church, hymns and Psalms should be sung, lest the people should pine away in the tediousness of sorrow; which custom, retained from then till now, is imitated by many, yea, by almost all of Thy congregations throughout the rest of the world."[3]

And in book ten, chapter thirty-three, he again says: "Now, in those airs which Thy words breathe soul into, when sung with a sweet and trained voice, do I somewhat repose; yet not so as to cling to them, but so as to free myself when I wish. But with the words which are their life do they, that they may gain admission into me, strive after a place of some honor in my heart; and I can hardly assign them a fitting one. Sometimes I appear to myself to give them more respect than is fitting, as I perceive that our minds are more devoutly and earnestly elevated into a flame of piety by the holy words themselves when they are thus sung, than when they are not; and that all affections of our spirit, by their own diversity, have their appropriate measures in the voice and singing, wherewith by I know not what secret relationship they are stimulated. But the gratification of my flesh, to which the mind ought never to be given over to be enervated, often beguiles me, while the sense does not so attend on reason as to follow

---

[1] *De clericorum institutione*, bk. 2, c. 48 (PL 107, 361D-362B).
[2] *De Ecclesiasticis Officiis*, bk. 1, c. 6 (PL 83, 743A).
[3] N. 14-15 (PL 32, 769-770).

her patiently; but having gained admission merely for her sake, it strives even to run on before her, and be her leader. Thus in these things do I sin unknowing, but afterwards do I know it.

"Sometimes, again, avoiding very earnestly this same deception, I err out of too great preciseness; and sometimes so much as to desire that every air of the pleasant songs to which David's Psalter is often used, be banished both from my ears and those of the Church itself; and that way seemed unto me safer which I remembered to have been often related to me of Athanasius, Bishop of Alexandria, who obliged the reader of the Psalm to give utterance to it with so slight an inflection of voice, that it was more like speaking than singing. Notwithstanding, when I call to mind the tears I shed at the hymns of Thy Church, at the outset of my recovered faith, and how even now I am moved not by the singing but by what is sung, when they are sung with a clear and skillfully modulated voice, I then acknowledge the great utility of this custom. Thus vacillate I between dangerous pleasure and tried soundness; being inclined rather (though I pronounce no irrevocable opinion upon the subject) to approve of the use of singing in the church, that so by the delights of the ear the weaker minds may be stimulated to a devotional frame."[1] From which words it is very clearly established how much the Church's singing can profit the minds of the hearers, if they be sung with sweet modulation, because Augustine himself testifies concerning himself, that he was moved to tears by the hymns of the Church.

Therefore, since the not small utility of singing now appears, it is necessary that we confirm it with the authority of the Scriptures. The Royal Prophet says: "Sing to him a new canticle, sing well unto him with a loud noise" (Ps. 32, 3). And lest Wycliffe be able by subterfuge to twist the passage to relating to mental prayer, he said, "sing well unto him with a loud noise." Furthermore, when Christ was born, "There was with the angel a multitude of the heavenly army, praising God, and saying: Glory to God in the highest; and on earth peace to men of good will" (Lk. 2, 13-14). Again, as Luke says, when Christ entered the city of Jerusalem, "They began with joy to praise God with a loud voice, for all the mighty works they had seen, saying: Blessed be the king who cometh in the name of the Lord, peace in heaven, and glory on high! And some of the Pharisees, from amongst the multitude, said to him: Master, rebuke thy disciples. To whom he said: I say to you, that if these shall hold their peace, the stones will cry out" (19, 37-40). From which words it is evident that the Wycliffites are similar to the Pharisees reprehending the disciples praising God aloud. Next, so that singing might be more approved, the Lord Himself deigned to sing with His disciples. For soon before His death, after the Last Supper "a hymn being said, they went out unto mount Olivet" (Mt. 26, 30).

Now so that it is may be more clearly perceived that this evidence supports us very much, it is necessary to state what a hymn is. The word "hymn" is Greek, in Greek ὕμνος, and in Latin it is equivalent to both "canticle" or "praise that is given to God." Hence Augustine in his exposition of the title of Psalm seventy-two says the following: "Hymns are praises of God accompanied with singing: hymns are songs containing the praise of God. If there be praise, and it be not of God, it is no hymn: if there be praise, and God's praise, and it be not sung, it is no hymn. It must needs then, if it be a hymn, have these three things, both praise, and that of God, and singing."[2] Isidore [of Seville] subscribes to the same opinion, who in his *Etymologies* says the following: "A hymn (*hymnus*) is the song of those giving praise (*laudare*), whence it is translated from the Greek as "praise" (*laus*) in Latin, being a song of joy and praise. Properly, then, hymns contain praise of God. Therefore if it is praise, but not of God, it is not a hymn; if it is both praise and praise of God, but it is not sung, it is not a hymn."[3] If then according to Matthew and Mark Christ said a hymn with His disciples, therefore He sung.

---

[1] N. 49-50 (PL 32, 799).

[2] *Expositions on the Psalms*, n. 1 (PL 36, 914).

[3] Bk. 6, c. 19 (PL 82, 253B-C).

And the action of Paul and Silas confirms this opinion, who when put in prison, were praising God aloud. For so it is said: "And at midnight, Paul and Silas praying, praised God. And they that were in prison, heard them. And suddenly there was a great earthquake, so that the foundations of the prison were shaken. And immediately all the doors were opened, and the bands of all were loosed" (Acts 16, 25-26). If, therefore, it is not permitted to pray loudly and aloud and with singing, why were so many miracles done upon the loud prayer of Paul and Silas?

Finally, the practice of the whole Church confirms this Catholic opinion, not a new one, but one kept from the very beginning of the Church until our times. And so that I may omit other testimonies, I will cite one, more efficacious than the others, which was uttered by a stranger and enemy of our religion. For Pliny the Younger, when speaking in a letter to Trajan concerning the then nascent Christians, says: "They asserted, however, that the sum and substance of their fault or error had been that they were accustomed to meet on a fixed day before dawn and sing responsively a hymn to Christ as to a god."[1] And so that we may further confirm the matter, we will cite another testimony also of a foreigner, but highly acclaimed. For the Jew Philo, who lived during the time of the Apostles and bordering upon the time of Christ, most clearly bears witness concerning the hymns of Christians. For Eusebius of Caesarea when relating how the Jew Philo described all the beginnings of the Ecclesiastical institution and the origin of the Apostolic tradition: says that he told this fact concerning the Christians, namely that when one of all them rose in their midst, he sang a Psalm regularly in time, and to the one intoning a verse the whole assembly responds.[2]

Next Socrates Scholasticus[3] relates whence originated the antiphons and responsories sung in the Church, saying the following: "Ignatius third Bishop of Antioch in Syria from the Apostle Peter, who also had communication with the Apostles themselves, saw a vision of Angels praising in alternate chants the Holy Trinity. Accordingly, he introduced the mode of singing he had observed in the vision into the Antiochian church; whence it was transmitted by tradition to all the other churches. Such is the account [we have received] in relation to these responsive hymns."[4]

After these very clear testimonies by which we have proved that the ungodly Wycliffe has erred, there exists a definition of the Church concerning this matter; For the Synod of Agde[5] defined the following: "And since it is suitable that the order of the Church be observed by all, it is decreed (as it is everywhere the practice) that after the antiphons, collects be said by the bishops or presbyters, and let the morning or evening hymns be sung every day; and at the conclusion of Matins or Vespers, after the hymns, let lesser sections from the Psalms be read; and in the evening let the congregation be dismissed with prayer and benediction by the bishop."[6] In which words it is clearly commanded that hymns be sung every day.

But let us now see by what argument they attempt to support their opinion, so that we may reply to it. For they say the following: Christ forbade praying aloud and singing, when He also forbade public prayer, by commanding that everyone pray in secret. For in Matthew's Gospel He says the following: "But thou when thou shalt pray, enter into thy chamber, and having shut the door, pray to thy Father in secret: and thy Father who seeth in secret will repay thee" (Mt. 6, 6). To which objection we reply that Christ does not forbid the action but

---

[1] Pliny the Younger, *Letters to the Emperor Trajan*, bk. 10, n. 96.

[2] *Ecclesiastical History*, bk. 2, c. 17, n. 22.

[3] Socrates Scholasticus was a historian of the early Church, born at Constantinople towards the end of the fourth century.

[4] *Ecclesiastical History*, bk. 6, c. 8 (PG 67, 691A).

[5] This synod was held in 506 at Agatha or Agde in Languedoc, under the presidency of St. Caesarius of Arles.

[6] Canon 30 (Mansi, vol. 8, col. 329E-330A).

the intention. For He does not forbid praying in public, but He forbids that one pray with this intention and this motive, that he be seen by others. Now this is inferred from the preceding words of Christ Himself. Indeed, the preceding and following words show the true literal meaning. Now the preceding words of Christ are these: "And when ye pray, you shall not be as the hypocrites, that love to stand and pray in the synagogues and corners of the streets, that they may be seen by men: Amen I say to you, they have received their reward" (v. 5). And He immediately adds: "But thou when thou shalt pray" etc. Now the preceding words forbid a bad intention, which is when one prays so that he be seen by men. Now in the words that follow He commands the good intention, namely that one pray with this intention alone, namely that one be seen by God. But if someone were to make public prayer with this intention, his intention is secret, that is to say, that it is done secretly, because he directs it to God alone, although the action is public. And in this he does well, nay it is often necessary that it be so done, because (as Blessed Augustine says[1]) if we did not have observers, we will also have no imitators. But if the one praying prefers to be seen by men, no matter how much he closes the door in the room in which he prays, still in Christ's estimation he prays in public: because Christ pays more attention to the intention than to the deed. And the deed itself is never deemed good or bad, unless because it proceeds from a good or bad intention.[2]

Secondly, they object using that which the Prophet Elias said to the prophets of Baal: "Cry with a louder voice: for he is a God, and perhaps he is talking, or is in an inn, or on a journey, or perhaps he is asleep, and must be awaked" (III Kings 18, 27). Wherefore John Wycliffe argues that it is not allowed to pray aloud, because (as he says) those praying in this manner are like the prophets of Baal who were reproached by Elias. We admit that the prophets of Baal were reprehended, or rather mocked by Elias, and yet not for this reason alone that they were shouting, but because when they were shouting they thought that God hears louder voices than quiet ones. Thus, those who so believed shouted when praying, so that God might hear their voices more easily. Therefore, Elias mocking their error says: "Cry with a louder voice" etc. Not because he reprehends shouting, but he reprehends the error whereby they believe that God needs louder voices so that He can hear. Now he who prays with shouting and singing, believing that God equally hears low voices as well as others, nay, what is more, He hears the cries of the heart, this man so believing even if when praying cries out from a certain fervent and impatient desire, does not err. For we have shown above that Christ prayed aloud, and He approved of the children crying out. In this way Christ reprehends prolixity of words in prayer, not simply and absolutely, but as the heathens do. For so He says: "And when you are praying, speak not much, as the heathens. For they think that in their much speaking they may be heard" (Mt. 6, 7). Augustine, when expounding these words, says: "And in reality, every kind of much speaking comes from the Gentiles, who make it their endeavor to exercise the tongue rather than to cleanse the heart. And this kind of useless exertion they endeavor to transfer even to the influencing of God by prayer, supposing that the Judge, just like man, is brought over by words to a certain way of thinking. 'Be not you therefore like to them,' says the only true Master."[3] Therefore, by those words Christ does not absolutely forbid much speaking and lengthy prayers: because He prayed long and longer. But He forbids much speaking in prayer as the heathens do, who think that in much speaking they may be heard,

---

[1] *On the Sermon on the Mount*, bk. 2, c. 2-3, n. 7-11 (PL 34, 1272-1274).

[2] Here the author speaks on the subjective level. For although an action may be objectively good or evil, still men will ultimately be judged according to their conscience regarding that deed.

[3] The author attributes these words to Rabanus Maurus, who indeed writes them in his *Commentarium in Matthaeum*, c. 6 (PL 107, 816D-817A), but he is merely quoting Saint Augustine in his *On the Sermon on the Mount*, Book 2, c. 3, n. 12 (PL 34, 1274). Hence Saint Augustine's name has been substituted here.

that is, He forbade that we believe that God will be more influenced by our speaking much rather than by greater fervor of soul.

Brother Thomas Netter wrote at sufficient length and abundantly against this error in his book, *De Sacramentalibus*,[1] from which I admit that I have taken some things, and also abridged many things.

CAPUT

Head

There is one error saying that there is not one head of the Church on earth, namely the pope. But concerning this we will speak longer in section entitled "Pope."

CHARACTER

Character

Among the many errors of Luther, that one is mentioned whereby he says that in no Sacrament is a character imprinted: and to assert this, he says is a mere fiction of theology. Now that this is quite false, we will prove with the testimonies of many sacred Doctors, whom Luther can neither call "recent" nor "sententiary theologians."[2] For by this name he very often designates others, the latchets of whose shoes he is not worthy to loose.[3]

But lest perhaps we argue about words, it is necessary to firstly show what is the character concerning which is this present discussion of ours. "Character" is a Greek word and means "sign" or "mark."[4] Thus the character, concerning which we prepare to speak, is a mark (now whether it is a quality or a relation is of little importance) which God imprints upon the soul as a seal by which He separates his flock from others. For sheep are distinguished from sheep and recognized by a mark imprinted upon them. Soldiers also are distinguished in war by an insignia. Sometimes a certain sign is accustomed to be borne as a symbol of a certain nobility, by which one can be distinguished from the people or from other men of an ordinary state, as in Spain some men wear on their chest a spatha[5] made of iron or of red cloth. Elsewhere some men wear a golden fleece hanging from a chain worn around the neck. In a similar manner a character is imprinted in three Sacraments, meaning a mark upon the soul whereby it may be distinguished from others not marked in this way.

By Baptism we receive grace, and are reckoned among the Lord's sheep, and we enter His sheepfold. Hence so that we may be distinguished from others who have not been baptized, who are like the sheep of the devil, we are signed by God with a character on the soul. And because, as Job says, "The life of man upon earth is a warfare," (7, 1) and the Church which is now on earth is called the Church Militant, for we fight in it against the devil, the flesh and the world: wherefore when grown up we receive the Sacrament of Confirmation, in which grace is given to us, whereby we may be strengthened in warfare, and be stronger in battle against our enemies. And thus Christ our Leader then marks us with the mark of his army, so that we

---

[1] Title 2.

[2] A sententiary is someone who read lectures, or commented, on the *Sentences* of Peter Lombard.

[3] Cf. Lk. 3, 16.

[4] I.e., *Signum* or *figura* in Latin.

[5] A spatha was a type of straight and long sword.

may be distinguished from the enemy, and from others of our group who have never attained to this army, so that at least we may be separated by this sign. But in the Sacrament of Orders, he who receives it is raised up to a higher state, and is advanced to the state of nobility from the plebian state: wherefore a quasi-sign of his state is then imprinted upon him by God. But lest Luther say that we waste time in allegories, it is necessary that we go through and prove with testimonies each one.

And firstly let us speak about Baptism. Blessed Jerome, when expounding the passage of Paul to the Ephesians: "Grieve not the holy Spirit of God: whereby you are sealed unto the day of redemption" (4, 30), says the following: "We are sealed with the Holy Spirit of God, that both our spirit and soul might have the impress of God's seal, and we might again receive that image and similitude, after which in the beginning we were created. This seal of the Holy Spirit is, according to the speech of our Saviour, put on by the impression of God."[1] From which words it is evident that our soul is sealed with God's seal, which seal we call a "character."

We do not argue about the name but the thing. But if he still argues about the name, let him hear Augustine, who uses the word "character" not just now and again. For he, when speaking against Cresconium the grammarian saying that one ought to be rebaptized who was baptized by heretics, says the following: "For neither on that account ought the royal character in a man be changed or disapproved, if he shall have asked from the king pardon for his error and his military rank, because a deserter imprints the same insignia [*character*] with which he assembles his followers to himself: nor for that reason ought the brandings [*signa*] be changed for the sheep, when they are associated with the master's flock, because a fugitive servant has branded [other sheep with] his master's branding."[2] By which words he twice calls "character" a "sign."

And when discussing the same matter in his *On Baptism, Against the Donatists* he says the following: "That such persons both have, and give, and receive the Sacrament of Baptism, was sufficiently manifest to the pastors of the Catholic Church dispersed over the whole world, through whom the original custom was afterwards confirmed by the authority of a plenary Council; so that even the sheep which was straying outside, and had received the mark [*characterem*] of the Lord from false plunderers outside, if it seek the salvation of Christian unity, is purified from error, is freed from captivity, is healed of its wound, and yet the mark of the Lord is recognized rather than rejected in it; since the mark itself is often impressed both by wolves and on wolves, who seem indeed to be within the fold, but yet are proved by the fruits of their conduct, in which they persevere even to the end, not to belong to that sheep which is one in many."[3] And in a sermon about his dealings with Emeritus, Bishop of the Donatists,[4] he repeatedly names the "character" of Baptism. Striving to be brief, I do not wish to cite [this passage], and he who wishes to read it may find it in the seventh volume of the works of Augustine.[5] You now see, Luther, how we have proved with the testimonies of Jerome and Augustine, that a character is imprinted in Baptism, and you cannot call these men "recent theologians" (as you are accustomed to say) nor "sententiary theologians," since both of them preceded the Master of Sentences, Peter Lombard, by more than six hundred years.

But now let us pass on to the Sacrament of Confirmation. Pope Innocent I, a learned man and renowned for sanctity, when writing to Decentius, Bishop of Gubbio, says the following:

---

[1] *Commentaria in Epistolam ad Ephesios*, bk 2, c. 4 (PL 26, 514B).

[2] *Contra Cresconium grammaticum et donatistam*, bk. 1, c. 30, n. 35 (PL 43, 464).

[3] Bk. 6, c. 1, n. 1 (PL 43, 197).

[4] Emeritus was a participant at the Synod of Carthage in 411; Augustine debated with him in Caesarea on September 20, 418.

[5] *Letter 87* (PL 32, 296-302).

"In regard to the signing of little children, it is evident that it may not be done by any other than a bishop. For the presbyters, although they are second priests, nevertheless do not possess the crown of the pontificate. That this power of a bishop, however, is due to the bishops alone, so that they either sign or give the Paraclete, the Spirit, not only ecclesiastical custom indicates, but also that reading in the Acts of the Apostles which declares that Peter and John were directed to give the Holy Spirit to those already baptized."[1] From which words we conclude two things. One is that Confirmation cannot be conferred except by a bishop. The other is that in this Sacrament those receiving it are signed. For so he called it, namely "signing."

But because he will perhaps distort this testimony into another meaning than he ought, let us conclude with one argument concerning all three Sacraments, namely Baptism, Confirmation and Orders. For in these Sacraments, the Holy Ghost teaching, the Church learned not to allow a repetition, simply because the sign of a character is conferred in those Sacraments, which can nowise be effaced. For although sinners repeatedly stain it, and from being bright they make it dark, and from being most pure they make it impure, yet those signed with that character indeed could never so uproot it, and they remain on Judgment Day marked as belonging to the Lord's flock, by whose sign they have been marked.

Now that these Sacraments cannot be repeated, Augustine testifies concerning Baptism and Orders, speaking in this manner: "They are both Sacraments, and given to man after certain consecration; the one at his Baptism, the other when he receives Holy Orders. Therefore it is not lawful in the Holy Catholic Church to repeat either of them."[2] Gregory ascribes to the same view who says the following: "But as to what you say about one who has been ordained being ordained again, it is exceedingly ridiculous, and outside the consideration of one disposed as you are, unless perchance some precedent is adduced which ought to be taken into account in judging him who is alleged to have done any such thing. But far be it from your Fraternity to entertain such a view. For, as one who has been once baptized ought not to be baptized again, so one who has been once consecrated cannot be consecrated again to the same order. But in case of any one's attainment of the priesthood having been accompanied by slight misdemeanor, he ought to be adjudged to penance for the misdemeanor, and yet return his orders."[3]

And so that we may conclude, it is useful to cite the decrees of the Councils. The Fourth Synod of Carthage[4] decreed: "No rebaptizings, nor reordinations should take place, and that bishops should not be translated."[5] And these words were put in the *VolumenDecretorum.*[6] Now concerning Confirmation, the Second Synod of Châlons says the following: "It has been said to us that some people have been confirmed twice, thrice or even more times by the same bishop. Hence it is clear to us the same Confirmation, as also Baptism, ought nowise to be repeated."[7] Gratian cites these words in his book, *Decretum,* [part three] *De consecratione,* distinction five, chapter [eight,] *Dictum est.*[8]

---

[1] Dz. 98. Cf. Acts 8, 14-17.

[2] *Contra epistolam Parmeniani,* bk. 2, n. 28 (PL 43, 70).

[3] *Register of the Epistles of St. Gregory the Great,* bk. 2, letter 46 (PL 77, 585A-B).

[4] Synod of Carthage (A.D. 419). The numbering of the African Councils differs very widely between the different writers.

[5] C. 48 of what is commonly called the *Code of Canons of the African Church.*

[6] *Concordia discordantium canonum,* dist. 4, c. 107 (*Non licet*). PL 187, 1833B.

[7] PL 187, 1858B.

[8] Gratian incorrectly cites these words as decreed by the Council of Terragona, but they are rather found among the canons of the II Council of Châlons held in 813, namely, Canon 27 (Jacques Sirmond, S. J., *Concilia Antiqua Galliae* (Paris, Cramoisy, 1629), p. 313). The author questions this reference in the text here, but since the correct reference is now known, his discussion of the point has been deleted.

From the aforementioned testimonies it is evident that those three Sacraments are unrepeatable. Now this comes about for no other reason but that a character is imprinted in them, which is indelible: since that character is not imprinted in the other sacraments, they may be received again. Finally, so that we may firmly establish our position, it will be useful to cite the definition of the Council of Florence on this matter, because it very clearly condemns the insane opinion of Luther. For it says the following: "Among these sacraments there are three, Baptism, Confirmation, and Orders, which imprint an indelible sign on the soul, that is, a certain character distinctive from the others. Hence they should not be repeated in the same person. The remaining four do not imprint a sign and admit of repetition."[1] Lastly, the Council of Trent celebrated under Paul III decreed these words: "If anyone shall say that in the three sacraments, namely, Baptism, Confirmation, and Orders, there is not imprinted on the soul a sign, that is, a certain spiritual and indelible mark, on account of which they cannot be repeated: let him be anathema."[2] And these things having been said suffice concerning this matter. None of those who have disputed with Luther against this error have written anything (that I know of), besides a king of England, who in that work, which he wrote for the defense of the Sacraments of the Church, mentions this error succinctly and thoroughly enough.[3]

CARO ET CORPUS
Flesh and the Human Body

This is one of the errors of the Manichaeans, saying that one's own body is evil by nature, and hence made by an evil principle. The Priscillianists defend this error, just as they do many other errors of the Manichaeans. This is also the error of the Patricians, so named from a certain Roman, Patricius (as Philastrius says[4]). These men say that the flesh was made by the devil, and thus ought to be assailed, and beaten to death. Which men hated their own flesh so much (as Philastrius as well as Augustine[5] testify) that they did not hesitate to voluntarily inflict death upon themselves, as though they could thereby be free from the flesh. Other men, called the Paternians, partly hold this same error, who by another name are called the Venustians (as Augustine says[6]). They say that the lower parts of the human body were made, not by God, but by the devil: wherefore giving license to all disgraceful actions of those parts, they lived in the greatest impurity. Concerning the remaining upper parts of the body they assert no such thing as the Patricians said. Yet for this reason I have chosen to put them together, because they ought to be cut asunder with one and the same sword. For I show that man's whole body was made by God, whence it will also be proved that the lowers parts of the body were made by God, since they also belong to the substance of the human body. Now at what time either the Patricians or the Paternians began, it is not established either from Augustine or from Philastrius.

---

[1] Dz. 695.

[2] Sess. 7, Canon 9 (Dz. 852).

[3] I.e., *The Defence of the Seven Sacraments* (in Latin, *Assertio Septem Sacramentorum*) written by King Henry VIII of England in 1521.

[4] "Still other heretics are the Patricians, named after a certain Patricius, who lived in the city of Rome. They claimed that human flesh was not made by God, but suppose that it was made by the devil" (*Liber de Haeresibus*, c. 62, (PL 12, 1177A)).

[5] *De Haeresibus ad Quodvultdeum,* c. 61 (PL 42, 42).

[6] *Ibid.*, c. 85 (PL 42, 46).

Therefore, we object firstly by citing what is said in Genesis: "And God created man to his own image: to the image of God he created him: male and female he created them" (1, 27). And this distinction of sex is not situated in the soul, but in the body, nor it is anywhere besides in the lower parts of the body. If therefore God made them male and female, it follows that He not only made the soul, since in relation to it there is no distinction of sex, but He also made the body: which is against the Patricians. And He not only made the upper parts of the body, but also the lower parts, in which especially there is a diversity of sex, and by this the Paternians are refuted. Furthermore, it is said afterwards in the same book: "Then the Lord God cast a deep sleep upon Adam: and when he was fast asleep, he took one of his ribs, and filled up flesh for it. And the Lord God built the rib which he took from Adam into a woman" (2, 21-22). Behold you see here that the Lord made flesh to replace the rib, and from the rib He again made the woman. Now He did not make her from the rib as to her soul, because it was created, and since it is spiritual it was made out of nothing, nor could it have been made out of a rib. It remains, therefore, that we ought to acknowledge that the woman as to her body was made by God from the rib. Again, the Royal Prophet says: "Thy hands have made me and formed me" (Ps. 118, 73).

Now the body is equally part of man's substance just as the soul, according to the saying of Athanasius: "The rational soul and body are one man."[1] Since, therefore, Scripture often testifies that God made man, no distinction having been made in this matter of body and soul, it is proved that He also made the body just as He made the soul. And in order that by no equivocation could this error be concealed, Job expressly speaks about the body, saying: "Thou milked me as milk, and curdled me like cheese" (10, 10). Now one is not curdled according to the soul, as it is clear, but according to the body. And Ecclesiasticus says: "God created man of the earth" (17, 1): which also ought to be referred to the body, since the soul was created out of nothing. Then when "God created man, and made them male and female, He blessed them, saying: Increase and multiply, and fill the earth" (Gen. 1, 27-28). By which words (as we have taught elsewhere) He commanded generation, which happens though the joining of bodies, and not though any parts of the body (as it is known to all) but through the lower parts, in which the distinction of sex especially consists. Therefore, those parts, by which generation is to be done, must be made by God, by Whom generation is commanded. And this is against the Paternians.

Paul more clearly confirms our position, saying: "Neither yield ye your members as instruments of iniquity unto sin; but present yourselves to God, as those that are alive from the dead, and your members as instruments of justice unto God" (Rom. 6, 13). Thus, since Paul calls the body and its members instruments of justice, it is thence proved that one's own nature is not evil, since it can be turned into instruments of justice.

Finally, when Christ assumed our nature, He was made true man, just as one of us. For He wanted (as Paul says) "in all things to be made like unto his brethren" (Heb. 2, 17). And John, when describing His Incarnation, said one phrase: "And the Word was made flesh" (1, 14). And Paul again says: "Who was made to him of the seed of David" (Rom. 1, 3). If, therefore, man's flesh or the human body was made by the devil, as the Patricians concoct, or the devil made only the lowers parts of the human body, as the Paternians pretend: it would then be necessary to say that Christ, the Son of God, retains something diabolic. Far be it, however, that we would fall into such a blasphemy. For "What fellowship hath light with darkness? Or what concord hath Christ with Belial?" (II Cor. 6, 14-15) And Christ Himself, the Son of God, says concerning the devil: "For the prince of this world cometh, and in me he hath not anything" (Jn. 14, 30).

---

[1] Athanasian Creed (Dz. 40).

But now let us hear the teaching of the Church. Pope Leo I in his fifteenth letter, in which he condemns the errors of the Priscillianists, says the following: "Their eighth point is that the formation of men's bodies is the device of the devil, and that the seed of conception is shaped by the aid of demons in the wombs of women: and that for this reason the resurrection of the flesh is not to be believed because the stuff of which the body is made is not consistent with the dignity of the soul. This falsehood is without doubt the devil's work, and such monstrous opinions are the devices of demons who do not mold men in women's bellies but concoct such errors in heretics' hearts. This unclean poison which flows especially from the fount of the Manichaean wickedness has been already arraigned and condemned by the Catholic Faith."[1] The First Synod of Braga decrees the following: "If anyone shall say that the creation of all flesh is not the work of God, but of the bad Angels, as Manichaeus or Priscillian said: let him be anathema."[2] Now the remaining error of the Patricians, whereby they believe that they ought to kill themselves, so that by this means they may be freed from the flesh, we will refute below, under the heading of "Killing." Likewise, concerning the other error of the Paternians, whereby they think that all disgraceful actions, which they can commit with the lower parts of the body are licit, we will discuss below under the heading of "Intercourse."

A **second heresy** teaches that the image of God, to which man is said to have been created by God, is located in man's flesh, and not in his soul. But we will discuss this error below, God willing, in the section on "Image."

CERTITUDO

Certitude

Concerning this matter, I have found only one heresy, which teaches that every just man knows with the certitude of the faith that he is in state of grace and is truly justified. And it adds, moreover, that every just man is obliged from the rules of faith to believe with certainty that he is in the state of grace. But if it should be unsure, on these grounds alone it says that he is not just. The first author and inventor of this heresy was Martin Luther, and Philip Melanchthon, Martin Bucer, John Calvin, and the all others who go by the name of Protestants, followed him in this matter. I do not wish to dispute against this heresy for the moment, because I have decided to put it in the section on "Grace," in the third place, and to dispute against it there.

CIBUS

Food

There is one error concerning this matter, saying that it is not allowed to eat meat. This is the error of Tatian and the Encratites, whom we have said above were followers of Tatian.[3] Concerning whom Irenaeus makes mention.[4] This error was afterwards revived by the Manichaeans. Aerius [of Sebaste] adhered to the same error, as Philastrius says:[5]

---

[1] C. 8 (PL 54, 684A-B).
[2] C. 13 (PL 84, 564B; Dz. 241).
[3] See the section on "Adam and Eve."
[4] *Against the Heresies*, bk. 1, c. 29 (PG 7, 690).
[5] "The Aerins are other heretics; they are named after a certain Aerius. They practice abstinence, and

Augustine, nevertheless, says that Epiphanius does not ascribe this error to him.[1] Now the Cathari increased this madness, saying that it is not allowed to eat eggs, cheese, milk, even if there were to be a necessity. Guy the Carmelite charges the Cathari with this error.[2] Now these Cathari who teach these things are not those who sometimes are called Novatians, but they are other men who lived after the Novatians, who belong to the family of the Manichaeans, whom Augustine does not call Cathari, but Catharists.[3] For in his book, *De Haeresibus* [*ad Quodvultdeum*], when distinguishing the Manichaeans, he says that they are divided into three groups. Some are called Manichaeans, keeping the name of the author: others are called Mattarii[4]: others are called Catharists, that is, "the Purified" or "the Purifiers," on account of certain horrifying and detestable purifications which they used to do.[5] The latter were extinct for a time, at length they revived in Germany after a number of centuries, under the Emperor Fredrick I, and were called Cathari, and would better have been called Catharists, as Augustine calls them: because they were not "the Pure," but "the Purified." The Priscillianists also avoid meats as unclean foods. The Greeks (as Guy [the Carmelite] charges[6]) condemn those who eat things suffocated, or other meats forbidden in the Old Law.

Scripture very often cries out against all these men. Firstly, the Lord says to Moses the words which he is to say to the children of Israel, in this manner: "On the tenth day of this month let every man take a lamb by their families and houses. But if the number be less than may suffice to eat the lamb, he shall take unto him his neighbour that joineth to his house, according to the number of souls which may be enough to eat the lamb." (Ex. 12, 3-4). Notice that you see how the Lord commands them to eat a lamb. But if meat were evil and unclean, God would nowise have commanded this. Furthermore, when God prescribes their laws, regarding what things the children of Israel could eat, speaking through Moses, He says: "These are the animals which you are to eat of all the living things of the earth: whatsoever hath the hoof divided, and cheweth the cud among the beasts, you shall eat." (Lev. 11, 3). He repeats the same judgment in the "repetition of the Law,"[7] that is, in Deuteronomy saying: "These are the beasts that you shall eat, the ox, and the sheep, and the goat, the hart and the roe, the

---

most of them live in the province of Pamphilia. They do not own anything and hate the foods which God gave to the human race with a blessing. They also condemn lawful marriages, saying that they were not instituted by God" (Philastrius, *Liber de Haeresibus*, c. 72 (PL 12, 1186).

[1] Augustine, *De Haeresibus ad Quodvultdeum*, c. 53 (PL 42, 40). "The Aerians. This Aerius was born in Pontus and still survives as a trial for this life. He was a priest of Bishop Eustathius who was accused of being an Arian. When this Aerius was not made a bishop, he taught many things against the Church. In terms of his faith, he was a complete Arian, but he taught other opinions. He says that one should not offer sacrifice for the dead; he forbids fasting on Wednesdays and Fridays, during Lent and Good Friday. He preaches renunciation but indulges in eating meat and every luxury. If one of his disciples wants to fast, he says that he should not do this on the appointed days, but whenever he wishes. 'For you are not under the law' (Rom. 6, 14). He claims that a bishop is no better than a priest" (Epiphanius, *Anacephal*, bk. 3, t. 1, n. 6 (PG 42, 872)).

[2] *Summa de haeresibus et earum confutationibus*, fol. 74v, c. 4.

[3] "(From the Greek *katharos*, pure), literally "puritans," a name specifically applied to, or used by, several sects at various periods. The Novatians of the third century were frequently known as Cathari, and the term was also used by the Manichaeans. In its more usual sense, Cathari was a general designation for the dualistic sects of the later Middle Ages" ("Cathari," *The Catholic Encyclopedia* (1908 edition), vol. 3, pg. 435). *De Haeresibus ad Quodvultdeum*, c. 46 (PL 42, 36).

[4] I.e., one who sleeps on a mat.

[5] C. 46 (PL 42, 34-48).

[6] *Summa de haeresibus et earum confutationibus*, fol. 28r, c. 26.

[7] In Latin the word *Deuteronomium* is derived from the Greek *Deuteronomion*, which means "a repetition of the Law," and this book of the Pentateuch gives a further explanation of the Law.

buffle, the chamois, the pygarg, the wild goat, the camelopardalus. Every beast that divideth the hoof in two parts, and cheweth the cud, you shall eat" (14, 4-6).

But because the impious Manichaeans reject the Old Testament, saying that it was made by an evil god, concerning which error we will dispute elsewhere, hence it is necessary that we strengthen our case with quotations from the New Testament. And firstly, the Apostolic trumpet of all men, namely Paul, cries out before us in the Epistle to the Romans, saying: "I know, and am confident in the Lord Jesus, that nothing is unclean of itself; but to him that esteemeth anything to be unclean, to him it is unclean" (14, 14). The Apostle here calls "unclean" (*commune*) food that is unclean and forbidden by Divine law: just as elsewhere Peter the Apostle said: "I never did eat anything that is common and unclean" (Acts 10, 14). And after the above cited words Paul adds in the same place: "All things indeed are clean: but it is evil for that man who eateth with offence" (Rom. 14, 20). Now Paul says this because in order to avoid scandal in one's neighbor, a man ought to abstain from meat, if he sees that another man would be scandalized by his eating meat, just as elsewhere he says: "If meat scandalize my brother, I will never eat flesh" (I Cor. 8, 13). And in the same previous place Paul, following the same view, adds: "But he that discerneth, if he eat, is condemned; because not of faith" (Rom. 14, 23).

Therefore Tatian, Mani, the Priscillianists, and the Cathari are condemned according to Paul, because when eating they discern the food, thinking that one ought not to eat some foods. Furthermore, in I Timothy he explains this more clearly saying: "Now the Spirit manifestly saith, that in the last times some shall depart from the faith, giving heed to spirits of error, and doctrines of devils, speaking lies in hypocrisy, and having their conscience seared, forbidding to marry, to abstain from meats, which God hath created to be received with thanksgiving by the faithful, and by them that have known the truth. For every creature of God is good, and nothing to be rejected that is received with thanksgiving: For it is sanctified by the word of God and prayer" (4, 1-5). Now I ask, what could have been said which would have been clearer than these words?

Again, Peter's vision confirms this view, concerning which it is said in the Acts of the Apostles as follows: "And being hungry, he was desirous to taste somewhat. And as they were preparing, there came upon him an ecstasy of mind. And he saw the heaven opened, and a certain vessel descending, as it were a great linen sheet let down by the four corners from heaven to the earth: wherein were all manner of four-footed beasts, and creeping things of the earth, and fowls of the air. And there came a voice to him: Arise, Peter; kill and eat. But Peter said: Far be it from me; for I never did eat anything that is common and unclean. And the voice spoke to him again the second time: That which God hath cleansed, do not thou call common. And this was done thrice; and presently the vessel was taken up into heaven" (Acts 10, 10-16). Next Christ Himself (as all the Evangelists bear witness) ate the Pascal lamb. Now if meat were itself unclean and illicit, Christ, the Model of every perfection and virtue, would never have eaten it.

A decree of the Church on this matter adds to all these testimonies. For the First Synod of Braga decreed the following: "If anyone considers the foods of the flesh unclean, which God has given for the use of men; and, not for the affliction of his body, but as if he thought it unclean, so abstains from these that he does not taste vegetables cooked with meats, just as Manichaeus and Priscillian have said, let him be anathema."[1] After such explicit testimonies of Sacred Scripture and the Church, there is no longer anything else to be discussed about the matter.

But there remains that we reply to a certain objection, which could be cited for supporting the error of the Greeks. For in the Council of Jerusalem celebrated by the Apostles, concern-

---

[1] Dz. 244.

ing which there is mention in the fifteenth chapter of the Acts of the Apostles, when there was a dispute about this matter, judgment was made as follows: "For it hath seemed good to the Holy Ghost and to us, to lay no further burden upon you than these necessary things: that you abstain from things sacrificed to idols, and from blood, and from things strangled, and from fornication; from which things keeping yourselves, you shall do well" (v. 28-29). Which words nowise oppose our view, because those things were forbidden by the Apostles for that time, and not because they are evil in themselves, or because they were prohibited by Divine law: but they were forbidden because of the Gentiles, who were recently converted to the faith. For the Jews especially very much abhorred things sacrificed to idols, or things belonging to the sacrifices of idols, something strangled. For the Apostles, fearing that the converted Jews, by occasion of the food which they abhorred, would be separated from the communion of the faithful, commanded the faithful to abstain from those foods, lest by occasion of the food their brothers might perish, whom perhaps they could convert to the Lord, by abstaining from such food.

Now we easily prove this to be so. For, so that I may not mention other things, among the food enumerated in that passage there are things offered to idols, concerning which the Apostle says that it is lawful to eat, provided one is not conscious of the idol: that is, as long as one does not do this on account of reverence for the idol, perhaps believing that there is something of divine power in the idol. For so he says in the First Epistle to the Corinthians: "But as for the meats that are sacrificed to idols, we know that an idol is nothing in the world, and that there is no God but one. For although there be that are called gods, either in heaven or on earth (for there be gods many, and lords many). Yet to us there is but one God, the Father, of whom are all things, and we unto him; and one Lord Jesus Christ, by whom are all things, and we by him. But there is not knowledge in everyone. For some until this present, with conscience of the idol: eat as a thing sacrificed to an idol, and their conscience, being weak, is defiled. But meat doth not commend us to God. For neither, if we eat, shall we have the more; nor, if we eat not, shall we have the less. But take heed lest perhaps this your liberty become a stumblingblock to the weak" (I Cor. 8, 4-9). From which words it clearly appears that it is licit to eat those things which were sacrificed to idols, provided that there was no "conscience of the idol." But even if this were licit, if one were to see another is scandalized by this, he ought to abstain from food otherwise licit, lest he destroy his brother by occasion of the food. Therefore, no food is forbidden by Divine law: but according to the permission given to us by the Savior, it will be lawful to eat all food which is set before us.[1]

There is a **second heresy** opposed to this last one, which asserts that any food whatsoever even on any day, is lawful without any distinction, no matter how much it were forbidden by Church law. This is the heresy of Jovinian, as it is clear from Augustine.[2] This Jovinian was a monk in Rome at the time of Jerome, against whom Jerome wrote. It is also the error of the Waldensians, who were eating meat, eggs and other forbidden things, saying that it is no sin to do this, nay they were saying that the Church could not command such abstinence of foods, and they were saying that there is no merit in such abstinence from meat. The Lutherans have embraced this same error in our time, who unrestrainedly eat meat on every Friday and Saturday, and on all days of Lent.[3]

---

[1] Cf. I Cor. 10, 27: "If any of them that believe not, invite you, and you will be willing to go; eat of any thing that is set before you, asking no question for conscience' sake."

[2] *De Haeresibus ad Quodvultdeum*, c. 82 (PL 42, 45-46).

[3] "Gregory VII (1073-85) speaks in no uncertain terms of the obligation to abstain on Saturdays, when he declares that all Christians are bound to abstain from flesh meat on Saturday as often as no major solemnity (e.g. Christmas) occurs on Saturday, or no infirmity serves to cancel the obligation (*cap. Quia dies, d. 5, de consecrat., ap. Joannes, Azor. Inst. Moral. I*, Bk. VII, c. xii)" ("Abstinence," *The Catholic*

I myself have heard in this month in which I write these words, namely in the month of May, in the year of the Lord 1533, from an upright man from Cologne, that when he went to the markets in Frankfurt, which city is in upper Germany, during the time of Lent in nearly every town before Frankfurt no food was given by the hosts to him, his companions, or to any other visitors besides meat: which if anyone refused out of reverence for the season or the law of the Church, they were completely unwilling to sell him bread or wine. In Frankfurt, however, he told me that the matter is treated more mildly on account of the markets which are held there during Lent, that anyone may more freely come to those markets. For he said that during the whole time of Lent both meat and fish are made available to all: by no means was food forced upon anyone, but there remained the free choice of eating what one wished.

Now Erasmus of Rotterdam gave to many not a small suspicion of heresy concerning this matter, a man truly both pious and learned: and I do not know whether he has fully and rightly purged himself from this suspicion: for in many of his writings he seems to teach this view very clearly: from which I will point out to the reader one or two, so that from them he may conclude what he wishes. In the preface to his *Paraphrase on the First Epistle to the Corinthians* he says the following: "It seems to me more like pure Christianity and more in keeping with the teaching of the Gospels and the Apostles to lay down for no man any specific form of food, but to instruct all men to eat in accordance with their habit of body, whatever is most conducive to each man's good health, with a view to moderation and not self-indulgence, with thanksgiving and a lively desire to think aright."[1] And in the paraphrase of chapter eight of First Corinthians he says the following: "I approve of what you say: 'meat doth not commend us to God' (I Cor. 8, 8). For since God created the universe for mankind to use and demands nothing from us except holy living, what difference does it make to Him whether we eat fish, or four-footed beasts, or birds. For none of these either adds to or detracts from holiness. Choosing among them may make someone superstitious, but it will by no means make him holy. Christ taught no distinction among them. Accordingly, it is foolhardy for some little human nobody to burden anyone with regulations of this sort. Let everyone eat whatever he wants according to the constitution of his body, as long as he does it soberly, sparingly and (above all) giving thanks to God."[2] I appeal to the upright reader through Christ's Passion and His supreme judgment, entirely apart from all passion, that he consider what he could conclude from these words of Erasmus. Does he not very openly and brighter than light teach here that there is no merit in the selection of food? in abstinence from meat and milk products? Nay he says that it is purer Christianity and more consonant with Evangelical and Apostolic teaching, not to abstain from any kind of food.

Concerning this matter he was branded by the theologians of Paris with their collective censure. But he so replied to their censure that it seems to me that he badly purged himself of suspicion of this heresy. For even if he admits that he does not wish to harm obedience to the rulers of the Church, nor does he wish that anyone by his own choice eat meat or other food against her laws at a time forbidden by the Church; yet he persists in that opinion, as he says

---

Encyclopedia (1907 edition), vol. 1, pg. 68).

[1] "[Noël] Béda and the Paris faculty criticized this sentence as encouraging disregard for Church rules about eating and fasting and agreeing with the Lutheran and other heretical beliefs. In response, Erasmus maintained that he had never scorned the practice of fasting and charged that Béda had purposely ignored the context of the sentence. He pointed as well to Paul's preference for the spiritual over the corporeal, but suggested that he would not criticize the contemporary Church for resorting out of necessity to "Judaistic vestiges" in order to help those of weak faith." (*Paraphrases on the Epistles to the Corinthians, Ephesians, Philippians* (University of Toronto Press, 2009), footnote 31).

[2] Erasmus defended these propositions in Divinationes ad notata Bedae (bk. 9, p. 474 b-e), *Elenchus in censuras Bedae* (bk. 9, p. 507d-e, and in *Supputatio* (bk. 9, pp. 680f-681c)).

that the distinction of food yields no benefit to piety: and it is more conformed to Christian doctrine, if such selecting of foods would be taken away by the law of the Church: because (as he says) Christ taught no such selection of foods. He also admits the abstinence of meat, but he prefers that this be free: such that one abstain from meat by his own choice, and not by being forced by the law. For in reply to the first censure of the Parisians concerning this matter, he says the following: "I think, however, that Christianity was purer in the times of the Apostles and martyrs than now, when the charity of men has grown so cold.[1] But in those times, when there was no regulation about the distinguishing of foods, many men were abstaining from meat more than they do now when forced by law." In which words he indicates plainly enough that is good to abstain from meat: but it is bad that some men are forced by law to do this. And if he so thinks, he falls into an error similar to the error of Aerius, who said that it is not good to force men to fast: but everyone is free to fast when He chooses.

But concerning this error of Aerius we will dispute below in the second heresy of the section entitled, "Fasting." Therefore, this error having been put aside, let us return to the previous heresy concerning the selection of food. The conquest of this heresy depends on something else which we will discuss below, namely whether the Church can establish a law from scratch: concerning which we will speak below under the heading of "The Church." But let us say something about it for the moment.

In the Old Testament we find abstinence from some foods and drinks praised, which also had not been forbidden by Divine law. For in the book of Numbers the law of the Nazarenes is so described: "When a man, or woman, shall make a vow to be sanctified, and will consecrate themselves to the Lord: they shall abstain from wine, and from every thing that may make a man drunk. They shall not drink vinegar of wine, or of any other drink, nor anything that is pressed out of the grape: nor shall they eat grapes either fresh or dried" (6, 2-3). But to this quotation or to others which we could cite from the Old Testament, they will perhaps reply that abstinence from such foods was licit, nay meritorious, because by it obedience was bestowed upon the Lord commanding it: in the Evangelical Law, however, such a distinction of foods is no longer permitted, since the Lord granted the eating of all foods.

But this can be very easily rejected, if one would consider that eating cows or sheep is no less licit in the Old Law than now in the Evangelical Law. For just as now all foods are permitted by God, so also then the cow, sheep, goat and other animals, which chew the cud and have a divided hoof, were permitted, as is evident from Leviticus and Deuteronomy.[2] But not withstanding this permission and allowance of those foods, at that time in the Old Law before the promulgation of the Evangelical Law, one licitly, nay meritoriously, abstained from those foods, and thus now one will licitly and meritoriously abstain from the same foods: since the reason for [abstaining from] those foods is the same for both [Laws] and the allowance of both foods is the same for both times.

Now what we have said for the time of the Old Law, namely that one abstained meritoriously from meat, is sufficiently proved by that which Matthew says concerning John the Baptist. "And the same John had his garment of camels' hair, and a leathern girdle about his loins: and his meat was locusts and wild honey" (Mt. 3, 4). Notice that you now see that John the Baptist abstained from meat: nor could they say that he had erred in this, who, as is evident, was sanctified from his mother's womb. But if he did not act meritoriously by doing this, why did the Evangelist praise him so much concerning this matter? Furthermore, after the Gospel was given and preached by Christ, in which Christ granted the eating of all foods, the Apostles having gathered together in Jerusalem, issued a decree in this fashion: "For it hath seemed good to the Holy Ghost and to us, to lay no further burden upon you than these

---

[1] Cf. Mt. 24, 12.

[2] Cf. Lev. 11, 3 and Deut. 14, 6.

necessary things: that you abstain from things sacrificed to idols, and from blood, and from things strangled, and from fornication; from which things keeping yourselves, you shall do well" (Acts 15, 28-29).

Next, I will now earnestly question the Waldensians and Luther whether the Apostles erred or decreed justly when so distinguishing [food]? Far be it that they say that the Apostles, after they had already received the Holy Ghost, all erred in unison on such a serious matter, especially when the Holy Ghost was assisting them: for so they say: "It hath seemed good to the Holy Ghost and to us." If, therefore, the Apostles then gathered together, motivated by a serious reason, could forbid the eating of things strangled and blood, why could not the Church today, or a general council representing it, forbid those same things, or other similar foods on account of some just reasons? Shall we now relegate the Church to more narrow limits than before, such that it cannot do those things which it could justly do before? But if they say this, let them show the letters sent from Heaven, whereby they revoke the authority and power, which He had bestowed upon His Church.

Again, among the *Ecclesiastical Dogmas* complied by Gennadius,[1] one is the following: "It is not Christian but Jovinian to set virginity on a level with matrimony, or to deny an increase of merit to those who, for the sake of mortifying the flesh, refrain from wine or flesh meat."[2] Add to this that from the very earliest ages of the Church it was the custom of apostolic men that they would abstain from meat. In fact, Philo, a very knowledgeable man, a contemporary of the Apostles, when speaking about the life of the Christians, says these words, as Eusebius cites him: "And how, on the days referred to they sleep on the ground on beds of straw, and to use his own words, 'taste no wine at all, nor any flesh, but water is their only drink, and the relish with their bread is salt and hyssop.'"[3]

Finally, let us now hear the decision of the Church. The Eighth Synod of Toledo decreed the following: "And also all those who during the days of Lent, which is reckoned a tenth part of the whole year, which are also consecrated in the offering of the fast to the Lord, whereby also the condition of the human race is most salutarily expiated, while man is brought to believe this religion from the four parts of the world, and is formed from the four elements, and on account of the transgression of the Decalogue, is fittingly afflicted four times ten days, temerariously condemn all these things, and does not restrain the gluttony of voracity, and what is worse, profanes the Pascal feasts with the consuming of illicit foods: to whom it is very strictly forbidden that anyone without unavoidable necessity, and clear weakness and sickness, or also by the impossibility of age, presumes to attempt the eating of meat during the days of Lent, not merely will be guilty of the Lord's Resurrection, but also will be excluded from Holy Communion on the same day: and this accrues to him as a punishment, that he abstain from the eating of meat during that whole year, because he has not observed the discipline on the holy days of abstinence."[4] Every Christian ought to rather obey the decree of this council rather than any "council of the malignant"[5] of the Waldensians or Lutherans.

But now let us see what they object against us. For firstly they object that which the Lord said to His disciples, when He sent them to preach: "In the same house," He said, "remain,

---

[1] The treatise entitled *De Ecclesiasticis Dogmatibus* ("On Church Doctrine") the author ascribes to "Blessed Augustine," but is now universally attributed to Gennadius of Massilia. Hence the text has been revised accordingly.

[2] *De dogmatibus ecclesiasticis*, c. 68 (PL 83, 1241B).

[3] *Ecclesiastical History*, lib. 2, c. 17, n. 22 (PG 20, 183B).

[4] Chapter 9 of the Eighth Provincial Council of Toledo held in 653 and cited in *Collectio Canonum Ecclesiae Hispanae ex probatissimis ac pervetustis Codicibus*, p. 437.

[5] Ps. 21, 17.

eating and drinking such things as they have" (Lk. 10, 7). And again: "And into what city soever you enter, and they receive you, eat such things as are set before you" (*ibid.* v. 8).

To which objection we reply that those words do not pertain to all Christians, but only to the Apostles: nor were they said for the whole time to come, but only for that time, in which they were sent on that journey. For it was then said to them: "Go ye not into the way of the Gentiles, and into the city of the Samaritans enter ye not" (Mt. 10, 5): afterwards it was said: "Go ye into the whole world, and preach the gospel to every creature" (Mk. 16, 15). Next, by those words (as Theophylactus warns) He teaches only the Apostles and the other preachers of the Gospel with the delegated power of the Apostles, that they be content with the food and drink which is offered to them, with whom they stayed, nor ought they to seek finer foods than those which are offered to them by those to whom they preach.[1] Add to this that even if these words were to pertain to all, nothing is concluded from them, except that any food was thenceforth permitted or allowed to us, even what had been forbidden in the Law: there was not a command there, but the free use was granted.

But if by the fact that these words are in the imperative mood, you contend that it is a command and not a permission, it will also be necessary that you likewise admit that what the Lord said in Leviticus is a command: "Whatsoever animal hath the hoof divided, and cheweth the cud among the beasts, you shall eat" (11, 3). But if you concede this, then you ought to also concede that John the Baptist sinned, because he did not act according to the precept, since he ate no such animal. It is certain, therefore, that that passage ought to be understood as a permission: such that the meaning is: "Whatsoever animal hath the hoof divided, and cheweth the cud among the beasts, you shall eat," meaning, you may eat. And in this way Blessed Augustine expounds the passage in his work, *De opere monachorum*.[2] In this way also ought to be taken those words of the Gospel: "And into what city soever you enter, and they receive you, eat such things as are set before you": that is, you are permitted to eat all that is put before you: so that you may clearly understand that there now is no food forbidden to you by Me, unless you yourselves shall have chosen to abstain at will, or afterwards it shall be forbidden to you by My successors.

Secondly, they object that which the Lord says in Matthew's Gospel: "Not that which goeth into the mouth defileth a man: but what cometh out of the mouth, this defileth a man" (15, 11). Thus, one who eats meat during Lent does not sin. We reply admitting that no food by its nature can tarnish the substance of the soul: but a depraved will, by which one eats meat contrary to Church law, is what defiles man. Now that depraved will soliciting disobedience, is internal to man, and it goes out from the heart, and from thence it reaches the mouth through the execution of the wicked deed. In this manner we also say (as Paul says) that "meat doth not commend us to God" (I Cor. 8, 8). For meat itself makes us neither better nor worse, but obedience, whereby we abstain obeying the Church's ordinance, commends us to God, and makes us better: disobedience, however, makes us worse.

But now it is necessary that we also discuss that which Erasmus cites in his own favor: Christ (he says) taught no distinction of food, therefore, it will be purer Christianity if no one makes a choice of foods. How much this argument is worth, even one poorly instructed, if he considers, will understand. For one ought to also argue in this manner that Christianity would be purer if all ceremonies would be completely removed from the Church, because Christ taught none or very few ceremonies. It will also be admitted for the same reason that it would belong to purer Christianity if the Lord's Body were to be given to those who have eaten, than if would be given to those fasting: because Christ our Savior neither by word or by example taught that it ought to be given those fasting, since He Himself gave His Body to the Apostles

---

[1] *Enarratio in evangelium Lucae* (PG 123, 835).

[2] C. 6 (PL 40, 553).

who had supped. For it does not follow that if Christ our Redeemer did not teach this or that, then it is far from pure and true Christianity. That is purer Christianity which draws closer to the life and imitation of Christ and His Apostles.

But Erasmus himself admits in his reply to the Parisians, that in the time of the Apostles, when there was no precept concern the choice of food, many more abstained from meat than now. Hence it belongs to purer Christianity to abstain from meat to control the rebellion of the flesh, than to eat meat, which supplies much power to the body so that it may exercise its tyranny. Besides, the stupidity of the Jews was perhaps the reason why Christ did not teach any distinction of foods. For the Jews thought that the foods which the Mosaic Law had forbidden were by nature evil and unclean, and hence forbidden: and if Christ our Savior were to still continue to forbid meat and other foods, they might have been confirmed in their error, and be led on to another, such that they might believe that meat is by nature evil, just like the Manichaeans wickedly supposing have thought. Hence, in order that Christ our Savior might recall the Jews from this error, He did not wish to teach any distinction of food.

But afterwards when the Church was assembled from the Gentiles—prompted by the Holy Ghost, that no food is by nature evil, but rather "For every creature of God is good, and nothing to be rejected that is received with thanksgiving" (I Tim. 4, 4)—Christ, Who is with us "even to the consummation of the world" (Mt. 28, 20), taught His Church to make laws, by which it would forbid some kinds of food at certain times: so that when excessive food nourishing the body has been taken away, it may be compelled to observe the commands of the soul. For horse trainers do not just use blows for training, but they withdraw food also or a kind of food, giving hay instead of barley, so that the excessive unbridled strength of the foals might be weakened by hunger. For there are certain foods, which not merely nourish the body for life, but inflame to lust. To abstain from these helps not a little for increasing true piety.

He who wishes to see more about this matter may read Josse Van Clichtove in his *Propugnaculum ecclesiae* [*adversus Lutheranos*],[1] which he published against the Lutherans, in which he treats this matter at great enough length.

CIRCUMCISIO

Circumcision

There is one error, asserting that still in the New Law infants ought to be circumcised. But we will speak about this error below in the section on "Law," where we will prove that all the legal prescriptions [of the Old Law] have now ceased: which having been done, it will also be resolved concerning circumcision.

CHRISTUS

Christ

Christ is the name of one Person having two natures, namely a Divine and human nature. For "this is the right faith," as Athanasius says and the Catholic Church proclaims, "that we believe and confess that our Lord Jesus Christ, the Son of God, is both God and man. As God, He was begotten of the substance of the Father before time; as

---

[1] Josse Van Clichtove (1472-1543) was a theologian, born at Nieuport (Flanders), who published this work in 1516.

man, He was born in time of the substance of His Mother."[1] Therefore, since many heresies have arisen about Christ's Person, we will treat them in this order: and firstly we will speak about those which deal with His Divine nature, then we will treat those which seem to touch upon His human nature alone. Afterwards we will discuss those things which regard the whole Person existing in two natures.

Therefore, the **first heresy** about this subject is that which denies that Christ was God, but instead had only a human nature. The first author of this heresy (that I know) was a certain Ebion,[2] a contemporary of the Apostles, because he lived in the eightieth year of the Lord under the Emperor Diocletian and Pope Cletus. Against this Ebion (as Blessed Jerome says in his book, *On Illustrious Men*), John "wrote the last of all the Gospels, at the request of the bishops of Asia... On this account he was compelled to maintain the Divine nativity."[3] After this Ebion, or so that I may speak more truly, at the same time in which Ebion lived, Cerinthus held the same error. Yet Philastrius attributes this error to a certain Carpocrates,[4] as its first patron, and after him to Cerinthus and then to Ebion, whom he says was a disciple of Cerinthus.[5]

After them (as the same Philastrius says) Theodotus,[6] a certain Byzantine, who in a persecution denied Christ the Savior. From which time he began to teach that Christ was a mere man and not God. Now he did this believing that he could cast off the opprobrium of his denial from himself. For he thought within himself that if someone were to accuse him of the crime of his denial, he would respond that he had denied a man and not God.[7]

After these men the same error was held by Paul of Samosata in Syria, who said that Christ was a just man, but not God. He lived under the Emperor Severus and Pope Victor I. To whom a certain Photinus succeeds as a student to his teacher, who so attempted to restore and strengthen the then declining error, that those defending the error are called "Photinians," and not "Paulians." Thus it was their common error that Christ was just a man, born from man and a woman, and He did not exist before Mary His mother. Now the Arians, even if they believe that Christ was not born of a father and a mother, nevertheless reckon that He was a mere creature, and they say that He was not the Son of God by nature but by adoption. But when it is objected to these men that it is proved from Sacred Writ that Christ is the Son of God, they admit this, yet they say that He is a creature, because they say that the Son of God Himself is a sort of creature of God, and the Holy Ghost is another creature produced by the Son. Hence

---

[1] Athanasian Creed (Dz. 40).

[2] It is an open question whether Ebion is the actual name of a person or a contrived generic name, as *ebion* in Greek means a "poor man."

[3] The Latin title of this work is *De Ecclesiasticis scriptoribus*. The pertinent passage is: "John, the Apostle whom Jesus most loved, the son of Zebedee and brother of James, the Apostle whom Herod, after our Lord's Passion, beheaded, most recently of all the Evangelists wrote a Gospel, at the request of the bishops of Asia, against Cerinthus and other heretics and especially against the then growing dogma of the Ebionites, who assert that Christ did not exist before Mary. On this account he was compelled to maintain His Divine nativity." (c. 9 (PL 23, 623A-B)).

[4] Carpocrates of Alexandria was the founder of an early Gnostic sect from the first half of the 2nd century.

[5] *Liber de haeresibus*, c. 35-37 (PL 12, 1151-1155).

[6] Theodotus of Byzantius, called "the Tanner," came to Rome about 190 A.D.

[7] Cf. Epiphanius, *Anacephalaeosis*, bk. 2, c. 1, n. 8 (PG 42, 865). The author here discusses whether Saint Augustine in *De Haeresibus ad Quodvultdeum*, (c. 33 (PL 42, 31)) has mistakenly written his name as Theodotion, but the Vatican codex of this work also has *a Theodoto,* where others have *a Theodotione*. Hence, since this point is no longer disputed, the section of the text which discusses this question has been omitted.

we do not now argue against these Arians, but we postpone this to another place, when we will discuss concerning God both the unity of His essence and the Trinity of Persons.

Therefore, since this is one of the main foundations of our faith, namely that Christ, the Son of God, is true God, it is necessary to show it to be a most firm foundation and supported by many quotations of Sacred Scripture. Hence, beginning from the first Gospel, namely Matthew's, let us go through the rest of the books of the New Testament. "And Jesus being baptized," Matthew says, "forthwith came out of the water: and lo, the heavens were opened to him: and he saw the Spirit of God descending as a dove, and coming upon him. And behold a voice from heaven, saying: This is my beloved Son, in whom I am well pleased" (3, 16-17). You see here not merely testimony from earth, but from Heaven, how Christ is the Son of God.

And again in the same Gospel: "And Jesus came into the quarters of Caesarea Philippi: and he asked his disciples, saying: Whom do men say that the Son of man is? But they said: Some John the Baptist, and other some Elias, and others Jeremias, or one of the prophets. Jesus saith to them: But whom do you say that I am? Simon Peter answered and said: Thou art Christ, the Son of the living God" (16, 13-16). And here He is called by Peter "the Son of the living God," and yet he was not reprimanded for saying this, nay he is praised instead. For after Peter finished his words, immediately Christ added: "Blessed art thou, Simon Bar-Jona: because flesh and blood hath not revealed it to thee, but my Father who is in heaven" (v. 17). Again, likewise Matthew, when relating that Christ was transfigured on the mountain, and Peter asked to stay there, says: "And as he (namely Peter) was yet speaking, behold a bright cloud overshadowed them. And lo, a voice out of the cloud, saying: This is my beloved Son, in whom I am well pleased: hear ye him" (17, 5). This is also related by Mark and Luke.[1]

Still besides this testimony, Mark has another more explicit testimony. In fact, when recording the interrogation which the high priest was making of Christ, he says: "Again the high priest asked him, and said to him: Art thou the Christ the Son of the blessed God? And Jesus said to him: I am" (14, 61-62). No more explicit testimony could be cited for confirming this truth of the faith. But Luke when recounting that the Angel Gabriel was sent to the Virgin, and relating the words of the same Angel to the Virgin, says the following: "He shall be great, and shall be called the Son of the most High; and the Lord God shall give unto him the throne of David his father; and he shall reign in the house of Jacob for ever. And of his kingdom there shall be no end" (1, 32-33). You see that He is called by the Angel "the Son of the most High." It continues: "And Mary said to the angel: How shall this be done, because I know not man? And the angel answering, said to her: The Holy Ghost shall come upon thee, and the power of the most High shall overshadow thee. And therefore also the Holy which shall be born of thee shall be called the Son of God" (v. 34-35). And when Elizabeth is visited by the Virgin Mary, already having Jesus in her womb, [Elizabeth] exclaims with a loud voice and says: "Blessed art thou among women, and blessed is the fruit of thy womb. And whence is this to me, that the mother of my Lord should come to me?" (v. 42-43). Jesus, small in body is still in the womb, and Elizabeth call Him her Lord. How, pray, can He be her Lord, if besides His human nature He does not have a Divine nature, according to which He is also the Lord of Elizabeth, nay of all creatures?

It is now necessary that we hear that sublime eagle, John the Evangelist, who reclined upon the Lord's breast, and to whom was revealed heavenly secrets: "In the beginning," he says, "was the Word, and the Word was with God, and the Word was God... All things were made by him: and without him was made nothing that was made" (1, 1 & 3). He continues: "And the Word was made flesh, and dwelt among us" (v. 14). He calls the Son of God "the Word," and he called him "God," saying: "and the Word was God." He declared that the Son of God

---

[1] Mk. 9, 6 and Lk. 9, 35.

was made man, saying: "And the Word was made flesh." Again, when Jesus had said to the Jews: "Abraham your father rejoiced that he might see my day: he saw it, and was glad. The Jews therefore said to him: Thou art not yet fifty years old, and hast thou seen Abraham? Jesus said to them: Amen, amen I say to you, before Abraham was made, I am" (8, 56-58). If Christ did not exist before the birth of His flesh, how is what He says true: "before Abraham was made, I am," since Abraham preceded Christ according to the birth of His flesh more than a thousand years? And elsewhere He is called "the son of Abraham."[1] Thus, it is not possible that a son be before his father, unless he have another nature, namely a Divine nature, according to which He is not the Son of Abraham, and is prior to him. Furthermore, likewise, Jesus Christ when He was about to raise Lazarus from the dead, when speaking to Martha, the sister of Lazarus, says: "I am the resurrection and the life: he that believeth in me, although he be dead, shall live: and every one that liveth, and believeth in me, shall not die for ever. Believest thou this? She saith to him: Yea, Lord, I have believed that thou art Christ the Son of the living God, who art come into this world" (11, 25-27).

Also Paul, the "vessel of election,"[2] who saw the secrets of God, gave testimony, not just once or twice but very frequently, regarding this matter. For in the Epistle to the Romans he first addresses them as follows: "Paul, a servant of Jesus Christ, called to be an apostle, separated unto the gospel of God. Which he had promised before, by his prophets, in the holy scriptures, concerning his Son, who was made to him of the seed of David, according to the flesh, who was predestinated the Son of God in power, according to the spirit of sanctification, by the resurrection of our Lord Jesus Christ from the dead; by whom we have received grace and apostleship" etc. (1, 1-5). Notice here that he firstly said that Christ's preaching is God's Gospel whereby it is clearly proved that Christ is God.

Then he adds that Christ is predestined or declared or shown to be the Son of God from His Resurrection from the dead. For by the fact that He raised Himself from the dead, He is declared to be God. For even if many men were raised from the dead, nevertheless, no one rose by his own power, but were raised by another, namely by God Himself, and by the ministry of some Saints, that is by their prayers to God, which God hearing, He raises the dead person for whom the Saint prays. Christ, however, rose Himself from the dead by His own power, by which He showed that He is the Son of God. And again Paul says: "According to thy hardness and impenitent heart, thou treasurest up to thyself wrath, against the day of wrath, and revelation of the just judgment of God, who will render to every man according to his works" (Rom. 2, 5-6). Behold you see here that Christ's judgment is called God's judgment. For Blessed Paul says, "we must all be manifested before the judgement seat of Christ, that every one may receive the proper things of the body, according as he hath done, whether it be good or evil" (II Cor. 5, 10). And since the Father "hath given all judgment to the Son" (Jn. 5, 22), and according to Blessed James, "there is one lawgiver, and judge, that is able to destroy and to deliver" (James 4, 12), it is hence proved that Christ is God, since there is no other judgment to come than that which Christ will do at the end of the world: now Paul calls this judgment Christ's judgment: therefore Christ is God.

And again in the same epistle he says: "For I wished myself to be an anathema from Christ, for my brethren, who are my kinsmen according to the flesh, who are Israelites, to whom belongeth the adoption as of children, and the glory, and the testament, and the giving of the law, and the service of God, and the promises: whose are the fathers, and of whom is Christ, according to the flesh, who is over all things, God blessed for ever. Amen" (Rom. 9, 3-5). Nothing could be said more explicitly to show Christ's Divinity.

---

[1] Mt. 1, 1; Lk. 19, 9.

[2] Acts 9, 15.

Again in his First Epistle to the Corinthians he says the following: "But as for the meats that are sacrificed to idols, we know that an idol is nothing in the world, and that there is no God but one. For although there be that are called gods, either in heaven or on earth (for there be gods many, and lords many). Yet to us there is but one God, the Father, of whom are all things, and we unto him; and one Lord Jesus Christ, by whom are all things, and we by him" (8, 4-6). If God is one, and there is no other besides Him, and the Lord Jesus Christ is assumed together into one nature of the Divinity, through which Paul says all things were made: therefore Christ is God.

And is his Second Epistle to the Corinthians he says: "You are our epistle, written in our hearts, which is known and read by all men: being manifested, that you are the epistle of Christ, ministered by us, and written not with ink, but with the Spirit of the living God; not in tables of stone, but in the fleshly tables of the heart" (3, 2-3). The Apostle of Christ calls the Corinthians his "epistle" because they were keeping Christ's commands and laws among themselves like monuments of his letters. Now Paul says that this epistle was ministered by himself: so that just as Moses was the minister of the Old Testament, so also he was the minister for spreading and preaching the Evangelical Law. And this epistle was "written not with ink, but with the Spirit of the living God." Therefore it was written by God in our hearts, as He had said through Jeremias the Prophet: "After those days, saith the Lord: I will give my law in their bowels, and I will write it in their heart" (31, 33). If, therefore, the Corinthians are Christ's epistle, and this was written by God, therefore Christ is God. For a letter is his by whom it is written, unless when perhaps someone is a minister of another, so that one writes while the other dictates: for then we say that the letter belongs to him who had dictated, even if he did not write it. Here, however, it is the same to dictate as to write, and the one dictating is the same as the one writing. For since the epistle was written by God, but God does not write with anyone dictating, thus the epistle is truly said to be Christ's: and so it is clearly proved that Christ is God.

And in the Epistle to the Philippians, he says that following: "Let this mind be in you, which was also in Christ Jesus: who being in the form of God, thought it not robbery to be equal with God" (2, 5-6). What can be expected to be clearer, than what Paul says here to confirm Christ's Divinity? And in the Epistle to Titus he exhorts saying the following: "Exhort servants to be obedient to their masters, in all things pleasing, not gainsaying: not defrauding, but in all things shewing good fidelity, that they may adorn the doctrine of God our Saviour in all things" (2, 9-10). These are the words of Paul, whereby he very clearly calls the Savior God.

From the all the rest of Paul's epistles I could cite similar testimonies: but lest I afflict the reader with tediousness, and so that I may not exceed the brevity which I determined to keep at the beginning of this work, by passing over all those, let us go to the epistle which he sent to the Hebrews, because in it Paul seems to discuss this matter as it were expressly and intentionally. For he says the following: "For to which of the angels hath he said at any time, Thou art my Son, today have I begotten thee? And again, I will be to him a Father, and he shall be to me a Son? And again, when he bringeth in the first begotten into the world, he saith: And let all the angels of God adore him. And to the angels indeed he saith: He that maketh his angels spirits, and his ministers a flame of fire. But to the Son: Thy throne, O God, is for ever and ever: a sceptre of justice is the sceptre of thy kingdom. Thou hast loved justice, and hated iniquity: therefore God, thy God, hath anointed thee with the oil of gladness above thy fellows" (1, 5-9). Paul says these and many other things there concerning Christ, whereby His Diving and human nature is proved.

But let us discuss the aforesaid words more fully. If then Christ is adored by the Angels, it is necessary that He be God, since only He ought to be adored. Next, if He is the Maker of the

Angels, and has a throne forever and ever, it is necessary that He be God, because no one else made the Angels, except God alone. Again, He who according to His human nature was made "a little lower than the angels" (Heb. 2, 7), how could He be the Creator of the Angels, if He were not to have another nature besides His human nature? Therefore, Christ is God. Now when it is said that He was anointed above His fellows, this ought to be understood according to His human nature: such that, namely, the anointing does not refer to the Divine nature but to the human. Thus, Christ is God and man: He is God by nature, but man by a certain dispensation, He was made similar to us, when He was made from a woman according to the flesh. As God He made the Angels, and as man He is anointed with the oil of gladness above His fellows. And these things are so clear that they could nowise evade, saying that Christ is the son of God by adoption: but it is necessary that they say that He is the Son of God by nature. For every just man is a son of God by adoption, who has been predestined by God unto the adoption of sons unto the inheritance of glory. But no mere man, however just, no matter how much adopted, made the Angels, nor is adored by the Angels, nor "sitteth on the right hand of the majesty on high" (Heb. 1, 3). Since all of these things befit Him alone Who is God by nature, it is proved that Christ is the true Son of God, and true God.

Also, Blessed Peter repeats his testimony of this matter. For in his First Epistle he says that Christ sits "on the right hand of God... being gone into heaven, the angels and powers and virtues being made subject to him" (3, 22). And in his Second Epistle he says the following: "For we have not by following artificial fables, made known to you the power, and presence of our Lord Jesus Christ; but we were eyewitnesses of his greatness. For he received from God the Father, honour and glory: this voice coming down to him from the excellent glory: This is my beloved Son, in whom I am well pleased... And this voice we heard brought from heaven, when we were with him in the holy mount" (1, 16-18). Blessed John the Apostle and Evangelist in his First Epistle gives very clear testimony concerning this matter, saying: "And we know that the Son of God is come: and he hath given us understanding that we may know the true God, and may be in his true Son. This is the true God and life eternal" (5, 20). How can the heretics prattle here, saying that Christ is the son of God not by nature but by adoption? See how many times that the Apostle rejects them with one verse. For he calls Jesus Christ the true Son of God. But he who is a mere son by adoption, is not truly a son, but is a son by addition, namely he is a son through adoption. And lest any there be any room for evasion, he added: "This is the true God and life eternal." No objection can be made to which words.

Furthermore, Christ Himself says: "The works that I do in the name of my Father, they give testimony of me" (Jn. 10, 25). Hence let us see His works and let us investigate whether we could prove from them that Christ is God. Firstly, for example, He forgives sins. For when some men presented a certain paralytic to Christ, so that health might be given by Him, "Whose faith when he saw, he said: Man, thy sins are forgiven thee" (Lk. 5, 20). Now to forgive sins belongs to God alone. For even if priests forgive sins, they do this by a certain ministry, and not authoritatively as the Savior did. In addition, He knows men's thoughts. We prove this by a double testimony. For when the Pharisees and Scribes heard Christ saying to the paralytic: "Thy sins are forgiven thee," "the scribes and Pharisees began to think, saying: Who is this who speaketh blasphemies? Who can forgive sins, but God alone? And when Jesus knew their thoughts, answering, he said to them: What is it you think in your hearts?" (v. 21-22) etc. And again when He had cast out a mute devil from a man, "the dumb spoke: and the multitudes were in admiration at it, some of them said: He casteth out devils by Beelzebub, the prince of devils. And others tempting, asked of him a sign from heaven. But he seeing their thoughts, said to them: Every kingdom divided against itself, shall be brought to desolation" (Lk. 11, 14-17) etc. You now see Christ reading men's hearts. But only God is

He who is able to read them. "For man," as it is said in the First Book of Kings, "seeth those things that appear, but the Lord beholdeth the heart" (16, 7).

Again, the splendor of the miracles which Christ worked affirm the faith of Christ's Divine nature. "From the beginning of the world it hath not been heard, that any man hath opened the eyes of one born blind" (Jn. 9, 32), as Christ opened his eyes, putting clay upon his eyes. Which man after having been healed in both eyes said: "Unless this man were of God, he could not do anything" (v. 33). This blind man had a more genuine faith in Christ than Cerinthus, Ebion, Paul of Samosata, or Photinus and others of the same ilk.

And so that we may omit other miracles, let us speak about those raised from the dead by the same Christ. He rose Lazarus by a mere word, saying: "Lazarus, come forth" (Jn. 11, 43). He raised the son of the widow by a mere word, saying: "Young man, I say to thee, arise" (Lk. 7, 14). And He raised the daughter of the ruler of the synagogue not merely by a word, but also with a touch of His hand. For so Matthew says: "And when the multitude was put forth, he went in, and took her by the hand. And the maid arose" (9, 25). Now how is He not Life according to His nature, to Whom the dead obey, He Who could drive away death not only by a word, but also by the touch of His hand, showing by this that His Body is vivifying: because it could not be so unless It was joined to Life, namely to the Divinity, in Which "we live, and move, and are" (Acts. 17, 28)?

Let us now see who it is who can by a mere command and word recall from death to life, but God alone? Because even if men also have raised the dead, still they did not do this by their own power, but in Christ's name. For it is one thing to ask, and another thing to command; it is one thing to merit, and another to give. For Elias raised the dead, but He did so praying, not commanding.[1] Eliseus also when he raised the son of the Sunamitess, He firstly prayed after having closed the door.[2] Now that he was configured to the dead person,[3] and raised him by the touch of His body, was done so that he would be a type and figure of the One to come, Who Himself, also being in human flesh died and was buried, could raise the dead.

Peter also when he raised Tabitha, first after kneeling down prayed, and afterwards "turning to the body, he said: Tabitha, arise" (Acts. 9, 40). And when he cured Eneas, the man ill of the palsy who had kept his bed for eight years, he spoke to him thus: "Eneas, the Lord Jesus Christ healeth thee: arise, and make thy bed. And immediately he arose" (*Ibid.* v. 34). You see in these passages explicit words of one beseeching, not of one commanding: and he was distrusting his own ability and power, trusting in the power of the Lord Jesus Christ. And when he strengthened the feet of the lame man asking alms at the entrance to the Temple, he said: "Silver and gold I have none; but what I have, I give thee: In the name of Jesus Christ of Nazareth, arise, and walk" (Acts. 3, 6). See how he does not act in his own name, but in Christ's name. Wherefore even if a word of command was used, he does this not as one presuming about his own power, or about the authority of his command, but as one trusting in Christ's merits and promises, Who said to them: "If you ask the Father anything in my name, he will give it you" (Jn. 16, 23).

What then can the heretics reply here? If Peter commands in Christ's name, is it not much better that Christ could likewise command in His own name? But they object saying that Christ likewise asks His Father, and He does this not just now and again, but He does this very often. We indeed admit what they object. Christ does in fact ask as man: but He commands as the Son of God. He also asks on account of the bystanders, namely when He is about to do something in front of them, lest they suspect something wicked about Him, just as it is evident that at other times the Pharisees said wicked things about Him. "He casteth not out the devils

---

[1] Cf. III Kings 17, 17-24.

[2] Cf. IV Kings 4, 32-35.

[3] I.e., by laying upon him.

but by Beelzebub the prince of the devils" (Mt. 12, 24). Thus lest they suspect some such thing about Him when He had worked something magnificent and remarkable before them, He asks His Father: so that they might believe those things were worked by God's power. Thus He asks the Father as man, Who was able to command as the Son of God.

Finally, so that we may now conclude, Christ Himself promised that He would give the Holy Ghost to the Apostles. Hence must not He Who sends the Holy Ghost, Who is God (as we will prove below, with God as our Guide), and gives Him to the Apostles, also be Himself God? Otherwise, God is both given and sent by a mere creature, which is impious to assert. Therefore, Christ, the true Son of God, not by adoption but by nature, has the true substance of the Divinity. For His works give testimony of Him.[1] Hence when rebuking the Jews He Himself says: "If I had not done among them the works that no other man hath done, they would not have sin" (Jn. 15, 24).

Besides all these clear testimonies of Sacred Scripture, there are also the decrees of many councils concerning this matter, by which the Catholic Church has shown what one ought to think about Christ according to the true faith. But we defer these decrees of the councils until the assault against the next heresy. For we shall show there the truth of the human nature in Christ against other heretics, and then we shall cite the decrees of the councils, professing the two natures in Christ, namely the Divine and the human in the unity of the Person.

Many men wrote against this heresy. Ambrose wrote a work, *Exposition of the Christian Faith*,[2] for Gratian divided into five books, in which he shows that Christ is true God equal to the Father. Blessed Cyril wrote a book, *De recta fide ad reginas*, in which he proves the same thing.[3]

There is a **second heresy** which denies that Christ had a human nature, and these heretics maintain that there is but one nature in Him, namely the Divine nature, and likewise one Divine Person. Now this heresy is broken up into still more factions. For it is usual for heretics that they do not know how to have unity. For some of them simply and absolutely deny that Christ had a human nature. The author of this error was Cerdo,[4] as Augustine says in *De Haeresibus ad Quodvultdeum*.[5] Nevertheless Irenaeus in his book, *Against the Heresies*, when speaking about this Cerdo, says that he lived at the time of Pope [Saint] Hyginus, who was the eighth pope after Blessed Peter, and when recounting the errors of this same Cerdo in the same place, never accuses him of this error. But Augustine relates that Cerdo so taught, as he said that Christ "was not born of a woman, and had no human nature, nor did He truly die or suffer at all, but simulated His Passion."[6]

The Proclinianites followed this error long afterwards, whom Philastrius says were Galatians. They, as Philastrius[7] and Augustine[8] testify, said that Christ did not come in the flesh. Now Apelles,[9] concerning whom Eusebius makes mention,[10] taught, as Augustine[11] and Philastrius[12] testify, that Christ did not take flesh from His mother, but obtained it from the

---

[1] Cf. Jn. 10, 25.
[2] *De fide ad Gratianum Augustinum libri quinque* (PL 16, 527 ff.).
[3] PG 76, 1202 ff.
[4] "Cerdo was a Syrian Gnostic who lived at Rome c. 140 A.D."
[5] C. 21 (PL 42, 29).
[6] *De Haeresibus ad Quodvultdeum*, c. 21 (PL 42, 29).
[7] *Liber de haeresibus*, c. 56 (PL 12, 1170A-1172A).
[8] *De Haeresibus ad Quodvultdeum*, c. 60 (PL 42, 42).
[9] Apelles was the founder of a Gnostic sect; he died at an advanced age late in the second century.
[10] *Ecclesiastical History*, bk. 5, c. 13 (PG 20, 459B-462A).
[11] *De Haeresibus ad Quodvultdeum*, c. 23 (PL 42, 29).
[12] *Liber de haeresibus*, c. 47 (PL 12, 1163A-11164A).

[four] elements, which when rising from the dead, He returned it to the world, and so ascended into Heaven (as he says) without His flesh.

The Manichaeans uphold a very similar error, saying that Christ was not a true man, but a certain imaginary man and an illusion, nor did He come forth from the womb of the Virgin. The Priscillianists embraced this error of the Manichaeans, who (as is established from a letter of Pope Leo I[1]) did not piously venerate either the day of the Lord's birth or the day of His Resurrection: because he did not believe that Christ was a true man.

Now others said that Christ was a true man, yet not of the same nature as us, because (as they say) when Christ was sent by the Father, He brought a heavenly body with Him, and took nothing from the Virgin, but instead He passed through her as through a crack or through a pipe without any flesh taken from her. The leader and teacher of this error was Valentinus, who lived at the same time as Cerdo, as Irenaeus says.[2] Apollinaris (as Augustine says[3]) also said that Christ did not assume flesh from the Virgin: and yet he does not on that account deny that Christ had flesh: because he said that in the very work of the Incarnation something of the Word was converted into flesh. He came from Laodicea in Syria,[4] and he lived under Constantine [II], son of Constantine the Great. He who wishes to know more about him may read the *Historia Tripartita*.[5]

Thus all these heretics whom we have listed "met together, against the Lord and against his Christ" (Ps. 2, 2): for they all, even if they take different paths, still tend to the this goal: that they may deny that Christ is a true and perfect man, of the same kind as we: wherefore they strive to separate from Him the human nature which is of the same species as ours. Thus, it will be fitting to fight against all these heretics at the same time. For when will shall show from Sacred Writ that Christ assumed true flesh from the Virgin Mother, and not from elsewhere, which flesh remaining in its own substance He united to His Divinity, keeping the properties of both natures: then all the aforesaid heretics will left vanquished. But before all these things it is necessary, lest perhaps we shall have labored in vain, that we lay this one foundation, the truth of the human nature consists in two substances, name a body and a rational soul, and man is nothing other than body and soul. Therefore, once this foundation has been laid, then we will go out against our enemies.

Christ was of the seed of Abraham. Now He is not the seed of Abraham according to His Divinity, as is very clearly established, and so it will be according to His humanity. But in His humanity there is nothing else but His body and soul. Hence, since the soul does not come to be from propagation, as we have proved above against Apollinaris, it remains that He is the seed of Abraham according to the flesh. If then His flesh is the seed of Abraham, we have proved that His flesh is not from Heaven, as Valentinus fables. For if He took His body with Him from Heaven, it could not happen that He was the seed of Abraham.

Now that Christ is the seed of Abraham, and was born according to the flesh from the seed of Abraham, that which we read in Genesis to have been said to Abraham by God through an Angel shows: "By my own self have I sworn, saith the Lord: because thou hast done this thing, and hast not spared thy only begotten son for my sake: I will bless thee, and I will multiply thy seed as the stars of heaven, and as the sand that is by the sea shore: thy seed shall possess the gates of their enemies. And in thy seed shall all the nations of the earth be blessed, because thou hast obeyed my voice" (Gen. 22, 16-18). Now so that we may not dispute about the meaning of these words, let us hear the Apostle Paul, who in his Epistle to the Galatians

---

[1] Letter 15, c. 4 (PL 54, 682A-B).

[2] *Against the Heresies*, bk. 3, c. 4, n. 3 (PG 7, 856).

[3] *De Haeresibus ad Quodvultdeum*, c. 55 (PL 42, 40).

[4] He was the bishop of Laodicea.

[5] Bk. 5, c. 44 (PL 69, 1023D-1024B).

elucidates these words in this way: "To Abraham were the promises made and to his seed. He saith not, And to his seeds, as of many: but as of one, And to thy seed, which is Christ" (Gal. 3, 16).

Furthermore in his Epistle to the Romans Paul calls Christ the "seed of David." For he says the following: "Paul, a servant of Jesus Christ, called to be an apostle, separated unto the gospel of God, which he had promised before, by his prophets, in the holy scriptures, concerning his Son, who was made to him of the seed of David, according to the flesh" (Rom. 1, 1-3). Here you see explicitly that Christ, according to the Apostle's view, was made from the seed of David. For if there were only a human nature in Christ, it would have sufficed to say, "who was made to him of the seed of David." But lest he would have given an occasion of supposing anything of the sort, he said: "who was made to him of the seed of David, according to the flesh," so that by this phrase he might give to be understood that there is another nature in Christ, according to which He was not of the seed of David. If then Christ is the seed of Abraham, and "was made to him of the seed of David, according to the flesh," Christ therefore had true flesh, against Cerdo and Manichaeus: and not from Heaven, as Valentinus said: or from the elements, as Apelles said: because if he brought his flesh from Heaven, or procured it from mere elements, then He is not of the seed of Abraham, or of David.

By the same argument Apollinaris is refuted, who was saying that something of the Divinity was converted into flesh. I omit for the moment that which never could have happened, as we will show. But if it could have happened, and it did happen, then Christ was not made according to the flesh of the seed of David, but from something of the Deity which was converted into flesh. For when one thing is changed into another, it is said to come to be from that which it was changed into something else: as for example, when wine is turned into vinegar, we say that vinegar was made from the preexisting wine. If then something of the Divinity was converted into Christ flesh, it will be necessary to say that Christ's flesh was made from the Divinity; not then from the seed of David. Again, Blessed Matthew the Evangelist when relating Christ's human generation at length, says the following: "The book of the generation of Jesus Christ, the son of David, the son of Abraham: Abraham begot Isaac" etc. (Mt. 1, 1-2). It continues further on: "And Jacob begot Joseph the husband of Mary, of whom was born Jesus, who is called Christ" (v. 16).

If Christ did not have true flesh, as Cerdo said: or if He had imaginary flesh, as Manichaeus lied: or brought His flesh from Heaven, as Valentinus dreamt: or procured it from the elements, as Apelles concocted: how will Christ be the Son of David and the Son of Abraham, if He did not have flesh derived from them? Furthermore, if Christ took nothing from the Virgin Mary, but passed through her as through a pipe (as Valentinus says), how will it be true what Matthew says, "of whom was born Jesus, who is called Christ"? and what the Angel said to the Virgin Mary according to Luke: "Behold thou shalt conceive in thy womb, and shalt bring forth a son; and thou shalt call his name Jesus"? For a Son receives the substance of his flesh from his mother, otherwise he is neither said to be born of her, nor rightly called her son. But if a mere passing through her would suffice so that he may be called her son, by the same reasoning we will call the menses and urine her son, and other things which a woman emits from herself. Now to assert this would be very clear folly. Therefore, Christ Who was both born of the glorious Virgin and is called her Son, has the substance of His flesh from her.

But the Apostle Paul rejects these heretics more clearly in his Epistle to the Galatians saying: "When the fulness of the time was come, God sent his Son, made of a woman" (4, 4). If He was "made of a woman," then He was not made of heavenly matter, nor did He receive a body from a union of the elements, but from the woman herself from who He was made. For if He received nothing from her, how could He come to exist from her? Therefore He received a body from the woman from whom He was made.

Add to this that we very often hear Christ's Blood named in the New Testament: which could not be truly said, unless Christ had the true substance of flesh. For Paul says in his Epistle to the Ephesians: "You, who some time were afar off, are made nigh by the blood of Christ" (2, 13). And in the Epistle to the Hebrews he says: "For if the blood of goats and of oxen, and the ashes of an heifer being sprinkled, sanctify such as are defiled, to the cleansing of the flesh: how much more shall the blood of Christ, who by the Holy Ghost offered himself unspotted unto God, cleanse our conscience from dead works, to serve the living God?" (9, 13-14). Blessed Peter also says: "You were not redeemed with corruptible things as gold or silver, from your vain conversation of the tradition of your fathers: but with the precious blood of Christ, as of a lamb unspotted and undefiled" (I Peter 1, 18-19). And Blessed John says: "The blood of Jesus Christ his Son cleanseth us from all sin" (I Jn. 1, 7). Thus it is necessary that He Who is said to have true blood, have the true substance of flesh.

Next, the actions of Christ Himself very clearly testify to the true substance of His flesh. To hunger, to thirst, to be tired, to sleep, to be sad, to feel pain, to suffer, to be crucified, to die, to resurrect is obviously human. Now that Christ was subject to all these things, is clearer than that someone would cite some testimony, which he would now be obliged to present. Furthermore, when His Passion drew near, He said out of His weariness and dread: "The spirit indeed is willing, but the flesh weak" (Mt. 26, 41). By which words He most clearly bore witness that He has flesh, whose weakness in the toleration of His Passion is declared.[1] Also after the Resurrection He remained on earth for forty days, and conversed with His disciples, speaking, walking, and eating with them, for no other reason than that He might show the true substance of His flesh, and that they might know that the same flesh which they has seen crucified and dead had risen. Hence Luke says: "To whom also he shewed himself alive after his passion, by many proofs, for forty days appearing to them, and speaking of the kingdom of God" (Acts 1, 3). For this reason He says to Thomas, incredulous concerning His Resurrection: "Put in thy finger hither, and see my hands; and bring hither thy hand, and put it into my side; and be not faithless, but believing" (Jn. 20, 27). He showed them the wound of His side, and all the signs of His very recent Passion of offered them to be touched, so that by this they might acknowledge the truth of the His flesh after the Resurrection, which they knew by His dying. Thus by very clear testimonies of Sacred Scripture it is shown that Christ had true flesh. Now Blessed John the Evangelist calls those who deny it in Christ Antichrists: "And every spirit that dissolveth Jesus, is not of God: and this is Antichrist" (I Jn. 4, 3).

Notwithstanding, whereas Apollinaris said that something of the Divinity was converted into flesh, it is necessary that we show that this could not possibly happen, although this heresy has been sufficiently refuted by the above arguments. For God is immutable, and is always remaining in one and the same state, He bearing witness Who says through a prophet: "For I am God, and I change not" (Mal. 3, 6). And Paul when speaking about Christ says: "And: Thou in the beginning, O Lord, didst found the earth: and the works of thy hands are the heavens. They shall perish, but thou shalt continue: and they shall all grow old as a garment. And as a vesture shalt thou change them, and they shall be changed: but thou art the selfsame, and thy years shall not fail" (Heb. 1, 10-12). Therefore, the whole nature is always simple and unchangeable in Its essence of Deity, neither receiving any loss or increase: such that it cannot be said to be greater by any addition, or less by the removal of any part. If, therefore, (as Apollinaris dreamt up) something of the Deity would have been converted into flesh, It would then be lessened by that conversion, because when that conversion was made, something of the Deity would have been lost, namely that which was converted into flesh.

---

[1] "In these words He shows that He took real flesh of the Virgin, and had a real soul, saying that His spirit is willing to suffer, but His flesh is weak in fearing the pain of the Passion." (Remigius, *Catena Aurea on Matthew*).

For what is turned into something else, does not keep its nature after such a change has been made: as when wine turns into vinegar, after such a conversion it does not keep being wine in its substance. Wherefore it would be necessary to say, according to Apollinaris, that in the Incarnation of the Word, the Divinity was diminished.

Now it proceeds from pure ignorance that Apollinaris cites that passage of John for the confirmation of his error: "And the Word was made flesh" (Jn. 1, 14), wishing by this to prove that the substance of the Word was converted into Flesh. For it is not necessary that as often as something changes any which way (if I may express it thus) by any manner of making or fashioning, one thing is changed into something else: especially when the thing that changes, does not change simply or absolutely, but rather gains some quality which it did not have before: for example, if some wood begins to be white, we then say that the wood became white, but not because the wood was turned into whiteness, but because while remaining wood in its substance, it receives whiteness onto itself, through the addition of which the wood is white. Similarly if the human body being cold at some time approaches the fire and gets warm, we say that the body became warm, and yet we do not therefore say that the substance of the human body was turned into heat, but that the substance itself of the human body staying the same, the body itself receives heat in itself, through in inhesion of which the body itself is said to be warm.

In this way (if some comparison of such an ineffable mystery can be made to fit) when we say, "The Word was made flesh," it ought to be so understood as when we say the body become warm, such that we do not understand that the Word was somehow changed into flesh, but that the substance of the Word remaining without any change to itself, receives the substance of our flesh to Itself, through the accession of which the Word was made flesh, meaning carnal, if I may so express myself. For otherwise, if by this which is said, "The Word was made flesh," ought to be have been understood such that the substance of the Word is changed into flesh, it will be necessary by the same rule to say that God's substance was changed into a curse: because Paul says: "Christ hath redeemed us from the curse of the law, being made a curse for us" (Gal. 3, 13).[1] But to assert this is impious and horrendous. Now Christ is said to have been made a curse for us, not through a conversion as such, but because He hung upon the Cross, upon which all who hung were said to be cursed.

But now it is necessary that we cite the definitions of the Church. The Council of Nicea of three hundred eighteen Fathers celebrated under Constantine says the following: "We believe in one God the Father Almighty, Creator of all things visible and invisible. And in our one Lord Jesus Christ the Son of God, the only begotten born of the Father, that is of the substance of the Father, God of God, light of light, true God of true God, born, not made, of one substance with the Father (which they call in Greek *homousion*), by whom all things were made, which are in Heaven and on earth, who for our salvation came down, and became incarnate and was made man, and suffered, and arose again on the third day, and ascended into Heaven, and will come to judge the living and the dead... But those who say: 'There was a time when he was not,' and, 'He was not before he was made,' and 'He was made out of nothing,' or 'He is of another substance' or 'essence,' or 'The Son of God is created,' or 'changeable,' or 'alterable,' these the Catholic Church anathematizes."[2] From the decree of which all the heretics named in the present and preceding error are struck down and fall.

The First Council of Ephesus of two hundred bishops celebrated under the Emperors Theodosius the Younger and Valentinian [III], at the beginning, that is to say in the letter which it sent to Nestorius, says the following: "Following in all points the confessions of the Holy Fathers which they made (the Holy Ghost speaking in them), and following the scope of their

---
[1] "He is accursed of God that hangeth on a tree" (Deut. 21, 23).
[2] Dz. 54.

opinions, and going, as it were, in the royal way, we confess that the Only begotten Word of God, begotten of the same substance of the Father, True God from True God, Light from Light, through Whom all things were made, the things in Heaven and the things in the earth, coming down for our salvation, deigned to lower Himself to being empty, was incarnate and made man; that is, taking flesh of the holy Virgin, and having made it His own from the womb, He subjected Himself to birth for us, and came forth man from a woman, without casting off that which He was; but although He assumed flesh and blood, He remained what He was, God in essence and in truth. Neither do we say that His flesh was changed into the nature of Divinity, nor that the ineffable nature of the Word of God has laid aside for the nature of flesh; for He is unchanged and absolutely unchangeable, being the same always, according to the Scriptures."[1]

The Council of Chalcedon under Emperor Marcian and Pope Leo I states the same opinion:[2] which in fact Leo in a letter to [Turribius], Bishop of Asturia, in which he condemns the errors of the Priscillianists, says the following: "The fourth head deals with the fact that the birthday of Christ, which the Catholic Church thinks highly of as the occasion of His taking on Him true man, because 'the Word became flesh and dwelt in us' (Jn. 1, 14), is not truly honored by these men, though they make a show of honoring it, for they fast on that day, as they do also on the Lord's day, which is the day of Christ's Resurrection. No doubt they do this, because they do not believe that Christ the Lord was born in true man's nature, but maintain that by a sort of illusion there was an appearance of what was not a reality, following the views of Cerdo and Marcion, and being in complete agreement with their kinsfolk, the Manichaeans. For as our examination has disclosed and brought home to them, they drag out in mournful fasting the Lord's day which for us is hallowed by the Resurrection of our Saviour: devoting this abstinence, as the explanation goes, to the worship of the sun: so that they are completely out of harmony with the unity of our faith, and the day which by us is spent in gladness is past in self-affliction by them. Whence it is fitting that these enemies of Christ's Cross and Resurrection should accept an opinion (like this) which tallies with the doctrine they have selected."[3] The Second Synod of Seville pronounces the same decision concerning this matter.[4] I now pass over the words of these two councils: because for the assault on the fourth heresy, which we shall put in writing concerning this matter, would have been repeated again by us. Wherefore he who wishes to apply those words to this matter may read the fourth error of this section, and its refutation, because it is very close to this place.

But it is necessary that we reply to the objections of the adversaries. For Valentinus says that Christ took flesh from Heaven because Paul says: "The first man was of the earth, earthly: the second man, from Heaven, heavenly" (I Cor. 15, 47). For in order that a man may truly be called heavenly, it suffices that the Divine nature in which he subsists be heavenly, just as on the contrary so that the Son of God may be said to have suffered and died, it suffices that the human nature, in which with the Divine nature He also subsists, shall have suffered and died. For on account of the union of those two natures in one supposit, whatever be predicated of either one of them alone is said likewise of the supposit, in which both subsist, although not in the same way of predication: because if something of the nature is said abstractly, it ought not to be so said of the supposit, but concretely: for example, Christ is not truly called humanity, but truly said to be a man. Wherefore Christ is said to be omnipotent, because it belongs to the Divine nature: He is said to be infinite for the same reason: He is also said to be weak and He is said to be limited, because these things are proper to the human nature. Hence, for

---

[1] The Second letter of Cyril to Nestorius with the Twelve Anathemas (PL 84, 153A-B).
[2] Dz. 148.
[3] Letter 15, c. 10 (PL 54, 682A-B).
[4] C. 13 (PL 84, 599B-608A).

this reason Christ is said to be a heavenly man, because according to the Divine nature He is heavenly: just as Adam is said to be earthly, although his soul, from which he is composed along with his body, is heavenly. Thus Paul gives a name to Christ from His principal nature, when he called Him "heavenly": but to Adam he gave a name from the less foremost nature, calling him "earthly."

Now Manichaeus objects as follows: Paul when speaking about Christ says: "Being made in the likeness of men, and in habit found as a man" (Phil. 2, 7). If Christ was made "in the likeness of men," then He is not a true man. Which argumentation is worthless and comes from an erroneous imagination, namely from the fact that he thinks that likeness in men does not include the likeness in their substance: which is quite false, and very foreign to Sacred Scripture's manner of speaking: because even if Aristotle says that likeness is based upon quality, and not in the substance, still Sacred Scripture is not bound to Aristotle's rules, which often calls things similar which are of the same species. For the Wise Man says: "Every beast loveth its like" (Eccli. 13, 19). And God says more explicitly concerning man: "Let us make him a help like unto himself" (Gen. 2, 18), when speaking about Eve, who is like Adam in that she is of the same species as he. For both are human. And in the same book shortly afterwards: "And Adam lived a hundred and thirty years, and begot a son to his own image and likeness, and called his name Seth" (Gen. 5, 3). Hence since Seth was made to Adam's likeness, it would be necessary, according to the Manichaeans' argumentation, that Seth would not have been a man, because he was similar to a man. Thus those things which are of the same species are said to be similar: which manner of speaking also is not completely foreign to the teaching of the philosophers. Hence in this way Christ, since He is a true man, is said to have been "made in the likeness of men," because He received a human nature, which is of the same species as ours.

Against this error Blessed Athanasius wrote a book, *On the Incarnation of the Word*,[1] in which He shows that Christ has two natures. Blessed Ambrose wrote another book, *The Sacrament of the Incarnation of Our Lord*,[2] in which he recalls and conquers nearly all the errors which we have enumerated here. Also Blessed Cyril, Bishop of Alexandria, made an elegant book which he entitled, *De recta fide ad Theodosium imperatorem*,[3] in which he reviews and refutes various errors of the heretics concerning the Lord's Incarnation.

There is a **third heresy** concerning the mystery of the Lord's Incarnation, which when putting two natures in Christ, also says that there are two persons, one of the Divinity and the other of the humanity: it does not think that there is one Christ in Deity and humanity, but teaches that there exists separately and apart one Son of God, and another Son of man, who is also called Christ: wherefore it does not call the Virgin Mary "the Mother of God," but merely "the mother of a man." Finally, it says that Christ is merely a man and not God, but one in whom God dwells by a certain special prerogative: and hence it says that Christ is called Emmanuel, which is interpreted, "God with us": not because He is God and man at the same time, but because the Divinity dwells in His humanity: wherefore it does not call Christ "God," but the "God-bearer." Everyone says that Nestorius, Bishop of Constantinople, was the author of this heresy, who (as Gennadius says[4] and it is evident from the *Historia Tripartita*[5]) lived at the time of Theodosius the Younger.

But Blessed Ambrose in his book, *The Sacrament of the Incarnation of Our Lord*, makes mention of this error, while keeping silence about the author of that error. But Blessed Am-

---

[1] PG 25, 96-198.
[2] PL 16, 817 ff.
[3] PG 76, 1134 ff.
[4] *De ecclesiasticis dogmatibus*, c. 5 (PL 58, 982B).
[5] Bk. 12, c. 4 (PL 69, 1205B).

brose preceded Nestorius by no small time, because Blessed Ambrose was the Archbishop of Milan during the time of Theodosius the Great: for he excommunicated Theodosius on account the cruelty done by him in Thessalonica, and forbade him entrance to the church. Now this Theodosius was the father of Emperor Arcadius. And Arcadius was the father of Theodosius the Younger, under whom Nestorius lived: wherefore I am surprised that everyone attributes this error to Nestorius as its first author. Yet it could have happened that although someone before him had asserted it, yet not as publicly as Nestorius, wherefore this heresy was spread more widely under Nestorius, and receiving from him its name for this reason, it was called the Nestorian heresy.

After Nestorius had died and was condemned at the Council of Ephesus, Peter the Fuller, Bishop of Antioch, who asserting two persons in Christ, dared to add a fourth phrase to the angelic hymn,[1] which is called by the Greeks the *Trisagion*, saying, "Holy God, Holy Mighty, Holy Immortal, Holy Who wast crucified for us."[2] He did this so that he might make the "Holy Mighty," by which name the Son of God is designated, other than He Who was crucified. Now this Peter the Fuller was condemned at the Fifth Synod of Constantinople.[3] This heresy has already been refuted from the refutation of the first heresy concerning this topic which we have set forth and rejected: because as it is sufficiently evident, the heresy of Nestorius coincides with the error of Paul of Samosata and Photinus, and of the others impiously thinking that Christ was a pure man, and His Virgin Mother was the mother of a mere man. Wherefore, since we have shown there from clear testimonies of Scripture that Christ was God, and in the attack on the second heresy we taught that Christ is a true man: hence Nestorius is sufficiently (I think) repelled. But because he tries to make us believe that there two persons, One Who is God and another who is man: and the things which are proper to God, he attributes to one Person existing in the Divine nature alone: and the things which are proper to man, he applies to a person existing in a mere human nature: hence it remains for us to prove that Christ is the same Person Who is God and who is man: such that one and the same Person is God and man.

Firstly, therefore, to the Virgin Mary asking the Angel about the manner whereby she was to conceive a son, the Angel replies: "The Holy Ghost shall come upon thee, and the power of the most High shall overshadow thee. And therefore also the Holy which shall be born of thee shall be called the Son of God" (Lk. 1, 35). By which words he very clearly expresses the human and Divine nature of the same Christ. For when he said, "shall be born of thee," he declared the possession of a human nature would be from the mother. Now when he said, "the Holy," he shows that He would be born without the contagion of carnal concupiscence. But when he says, "shall be called the Son of God," he very clearly shows the possession of a Divine nature. Since the Angel said all these things to the glorious Virgin concerning the Son Whom she was to conceive and give birth, it is evident that the Son of the Virgin is the same as the Son of God: it is also evident that that mother deservedly ought to be called the "Mother of God." For if the Son of the Virgin Mary, the Son of God, is also God, it could nowise happen that the Virgin not be the Mother of God. Furthermore, since the glorious Virgin when already pregnant visited her cousin Elizabeth, the same Elizabeth cried out, saying: "Whence is this to me, that the mother of my Lord should come to me?" (*Ibid.*, v. 43) For who else is

---

[1] The *Trisagion* is based upon the words of the Angels in Isaias 6, 3: "Holy, holy, holy."

[2] "[Peter the Fuller] gained the favor of the Monophysites by adding to the Trisagion the words *ho staurotheis di' hemas* (who wast crucified for us) in the monophysitic sense that the Father and the Holy Ghost were crucified with the Son" ("Peter Fullo", *Catholic Encyclopedia* (New York, Robert Appleton Company, 1911 ed.), vol. 11, p. 768).

[3] A synod at Constantinople (end of 476 or beginning of 477 A. D.) under Acacius condemned Peter the Fuller. He was also condemned in the Formula of Homisdas written in 519 A. D. (Dz. 171)

the Lord besides God? For He alone is the Lord, He alone is the Most High. Thus it is more necessary to believe Elizabeth filled with the Holy Ghost, who calls the Virgin the Mother of God, than Nestorius, troubled by a demonic spirit denies her to be the Mother of God.

Again Christ Himself says: "No man hath ascended into heaven, but he that descended from heaven, the Son of man who is in heaven" (Jn. 3, 13). By which words He expresses both natures in one Person, because when He calls Himself the Son of man, He nevertheless asserts that He had descended from Heaven: because according to His Divine nature taking His origin from His Father Who is in Heaven, He lowered Himself to accepting our humanity.

Next Paul teaches this clearly in many places. For in the Epistle to the Romans he says: "Paul, a servant of Jesus Christ, called to be an apostle, separated unto the gospel of God, which he had promised before, by his prophets, in the Holy Scriptures, concerning his Son, who was made to him of the seed of David, according to the flesh" (1, 1-3). From which words two things can be inferred which are worthy of notice, serving our purpose. Firstly, Paul said, "the gospel of God." And when he says elsewhere: "For we preach not ourselves, but Jesus Christ our Lord; and ourselves your servants through Jesus" (II Cor. 4, 5); and elsewhere: "For I judged not myself to know anything among you, but Jesus Christ, and him crucified" (I Cor. 2, 2), it is hence proved that Christ is God. Paul preaches "the gospel of God," and does not preach "but Jesus Christ crucified," therefore Jesus Christ is God.

But if some still contentiously resists the truth, who would say that there is Someone Who is God, and someone else who was crucified: let him see how Paul speaks concerning the Son of God: "Who was made," he says, "to him of the seed of David, according to the flesh." For that relative pronoun, "who," makes the words that follow [it] apply to the same person whom the pronoun represents. For if you were to say: "Aristotle taught that the world had no beginning, who also said that the world has no end: who is so insane that he understands by these words that there are two Aristotles, one who taught that the world has no beginning and another who said that the world has not end? For by these words it is indicated that it is the same Aristotle who taught [both] these things. For the relative pronoun is a kind of repetition of the same name. Thus, when Paul said concerning the Son of God: "Who was made to him of the seed of David, according to the flesh," it cannot be applied to anyone else besides the same Son of God. For it is as if he had said: 'And that Son of God was likewise made of the seed of David.' Thus, there is one and the same Person, Who is the Son of God according to His Divine nature, and Who was made of the seed of David according to the flesh.

What he says in the Epistle to the Philippians proves it by the same logic: "Let this mind be in you, which was also in Christ Jesus: who being in the form of God, thought it not robbery to be equal with God" (2, 5-6). It is certain that the pronoun, "who,"[1] refers to the one Person of Christ, not two. For if it referred to two, the pronoun would have been plural, and the verb would have been plural: since, however, it is connected to a singular verb,[2] it is evident that it refers to just one person and not two. If it refers to one person, I ask whether it is Divine or human? If human, then it follows that Christ's humanity is equal to the Divinity: because Paul says: "Who being in the form of God, thought it not robbery to be equal with God." But if you say that the pronoun refers to that Person Who exists in the Divine nature alone, how does it fit with the words which Paul adds in the same context saying: "But emptied himself, taking the form of a servant, being made in the likeness of men, and in habit found as a man. He humbled himself, becoming obedient unto death, even to the death of the cross"? (v. 7-8). For then it would be necessary that the Divine nature underwent the death of the Cross, which is blatant blasphemy.

---

[1] I.e., *qui* in Latin.

[2] I.e., *esset* in Latin.

Now so that we may avoid all these inconveniences, it is necessary to assert according to the true faith that there are two natures in Christ in the unity of a Person, which Person is equal to the Father as to His Divine nature, as He says: "I and the Father are one" (Jn. 10, 30). According to His human nature He is less than the Father, as He says: "The Father is greater than I" (Jn. 14, 28). According to His Divine nature He is immortal, as He says: "I am the resurrection and the life" (Jn. 11, 25). According to His human nature He was "obedient unto death, even to the death of the cross" (Phil. 2, 8): as He says: "Not as I will, but as thou wilt" (Mt. 26, 39). And in the Epistle to the Galatians he says: "When the fulness of the time was come, God sent his Son, made of a woman" (Gal. 4, 4). Thus, He is likewise the Son of God and the son of a woman, because it is said that He was made from her. And in the First Epistle to the Corinthians, he teaches this more explicitly saying: "If they had known it, they would never have crucified the Lord of glory" (2, 8). Nothing clearer against Nestorius could have been said: since he says that "the Lord of glory," meaning God, was crucified. Hence, there is one Person Who likewise was crucified and died, and Who is God and the "Lord of glory." I could cite many other testimonies of Scripture, which I omit striving to be brief. But I will now make only one argument against Nestorius.

And I enquire of him whether he believes that the Son of God was incarnated, or does he completely deny this? If he denies that the Son of God was incarnated, he contradicts John saying: "And the Word was made flesh" (Jn. 1, 14) and he contradicts the faith of the Nicene Council saying concerning the Son of God: "Who for us men, and for our salvation, came down and was incarnate and was made man."[1] But if (as is fitting) he concedes that the Son of God was incarnated, by the very word, "Incarnation," he clearly intimates two natures, one which was incarnated, and another by which He was incarnated. For the nature of the Deity was not Itself incarnated, but rather the nature of flesh had to have been incarnated. Therefore, so that the Son of God may be said to have been incarnated, it is necessary that the Son of God have flesh in Himself.

But if there were one person of flesh and another person of the Deity, He could nowise be said to have been incarnated. For something is never said to be such by the qualities existing in another person. Who would have been so insane that he would say that Peter is white on account of the whiteness adhering to John? In like manner it cannot happen that the Son of God be called incarnated on account of the flesh existing in another person, but on account of the flesh which He has in the unity of His supposit united to Himself. Also, the names of different natures are never said of each other either concretely or abstractly, unless those two natures exist in the same person: for example, unless whiteness and coldness exist in the same supposit, whiteness will never be said to be cold. For although whiteness may inhere to milk and coldness to steel, the white thing will never be said to be the cold thing. Yet if the whiteness and the coldness are found in snow, then we rightly say that the white thing is cold. But a man is called God, and those things which are proper to man are said of the Son of God: and those things which are proper to God, are said of the Son of man. Hence the Son of man and the Son of God are one Person.

For concerning Him it is said: "In the beginning was the Word, and the Word was with God, and the Word was God" (Jn. 1, 1): by which the Divine nature is shown. It is also said of the same Person: "And the Word was made flesh" (v. 14): and by this His human nature is indicated. Concerning Him it is said: "All things were made by him: and without him was made nothing that was made" (v. 3). It is said of the same Person that "He was made of a woman" (Gal. 4, 4), which is proper to man. The wise men adore Him (Mt. 2, 11), but this is due only to God: but they find Him lying in a manger, being fed by His mother, which pertains to a man (Mt. 2, 11). The infancy of the Child is show by the humility of the cradle (Lk, 2, 7), and

---

[1] Dz. 13.

the majesty of His Divinity is declared by the voices of the Angels (Lk, 2, 13-14). Diabolical cunning tempts (Mt. 4, 1 ff.) the same Man to Whom the Angels minister as God (Mt. 4, 11). He Who as man was wearied from a journey sits upon a well (Jn. 4, 6), and the same Man cries out and says: "Come to me, all you that labour, and are burdened, and I will refresh you" (Mt. 11, 28). He Who thirsts as a man, asks for a drink from the Samaritan woman (Jn. 4, 7), likewise says as God: "If thou didst know the gift of God, and who he is that saith to thee, Give me to drink; thou perhaps wouldst have asked of him, and he would have given thee living water" (v. 10) of which he who drinks will not thirst again. He Who hungered as a man (Mt. 4, 2), likewise as God satisfied five thousand men with five loaves and two fishes (Mt. 14, 19 & 21). He Who by the affection of compassion weeps for His dead friend (Jn. 11, 35), likewise as God when four days after burial the stone was taken away raises him brought back to life (v. 43-44). He Who as man was fixed to the Cross, likewise as God promise paradise to the thief (Lk. 23, 43), changes light into darkness (v. 44), and makes all the elements to tremble (Mt. 27, 51).

Yet although He be one man in two natures, there is one thing which is due to Him according the majesty of His Divinity, and another which He had by dispensation according to the humility of His humanity. In one He shines with miracles, according to the other He succumbs to injuries. And just as according to the Divinity He did not withdraw from the equality of His Father's glory, so according to the humanity He did not abandon the nature of our created form. And although sometimes He be named by the name of only one nature, not on that account ought one to think that the other is excluded from Him: as for example, if it would be said, "The Son of man shall be delivered to the Gentiles, scourged and spit upon": just because He is in this passage merely called the "Son of man," one ought not to believe on that account that the Son of God was not delivered [to the Gentiles], but the Person existing in a human nature alone. For both the Son of God also suffered and the Son of man also suffered: because He is likewise the Son of God and the Son of man.

However, when He is called the "Son of God" or the "Son of man," even if only one nature is expressed in some passage of Scripture, nevertheless two natures are given to be understood for two reasons. One reason is that the expressions "Son of man" or "Son of God" do not name the nature but the supposit: in which when there are two natures, both are given to be understood, because by naming the supposit it is given to be understood the whole supposit as it exists. And when the supposit exists in two natures, even if one nature is expressed, still it is not separated from the other by this. A second reason is that often by naming a part the whole is given to be understood, and by naming one nature the whole supposit is given to be understood as subsisting in two natures: as for example, man is a being composed of two things with quite different natures, namely body and soul, and yet by naming one of the them the whole man is often denoted: to which manner of speaking Sacred Writ is not adverse. For in Genesis, when all the men who entered Egypt with Jacob are numbered, we read the following: "All the souls that went with Jacob into Egypt, and that came out of his thigh, besides his sons' wives, sixty-six" (Gen. 46, 26). And again after a few words: "All the souls of the house of Jacob, that entered into Egypt, were seventy" (v. 27). Notice here you see that the whole man is designated by the word "soul. Notice also that he is named by the word "flesh." "My spirit shall not remain," God said, "in man for ever, because he is flesh" (Gen. 6, 3). But "flesh" is proper to just one of the two natures of which man is composed.

But if Nestorius had considered this well, he never would have fallen into such a wicked heresy, distinguishing two persons on account of the two natures he was considering: for from created things one can in some way attain to the knowledge of such a marvelous mystery. For even if man has two quite different natures, there is still only one person receiving different appellations on account of the diversity of natures; for he is called mortal, and this on account of the body alone which dies, although the soul is immortal. He is also called intelligent by reason of the soul, which alone in man understands. Let us say, thinking with the Catholic Church that Christ, that the Son of God has two natures, namely the Divine and human, unconfused in the unity of the supposit, united without any mixture of them, such that the Son of God is one and the same [Son] as the Son of man.

But he who thinks otherwise, such that he concocts two sons, one of man and the other of God, is the Antichrist, as John the Evangelist says: "And every spirit," he says, "that dissolveth Jesus, is not of God: and this is Antichrist" (I Jn. 4, 3): although in the Greek manuscripts it is not so found, but as follows: "Every spirit which does not confess that Jesus came in the flesh is not of God." But this variance of the text, such that there is a different text in the Latin manuscripts than what is now found in the Greek manuscripts, came about because (as the *Historia Tripartita* says[1]) heretics removed this meaning from the old copies, who wanted to separate the Divinity from the control of a man, and so erased that which as very clearly withstanding them, as it is evident they have very often done at other times.

But Erasmus of Rotterdam in his published *Annotations on the New Testament* suspects that this clause which is now found in the Latin manuscripts was added against the heretics, some of whom were so attributing the human nature to Christ that they eliminated His Divine nature: others were so giving to Christ the Divine nature, that they were eliminating His human nature. Now Erasmus confirmed this suspicion in some way, yet it does not hold firm, unless he gives to everyone the free choice of thinking as he wishes. Hence when speaking according to the liberty given by him, I say that it is more likely that that clause was not added. Firstly, because even though the Church has the custom to form new words on account of the new heresies that have arisen, still it will never be found that it added or subtracted anything in Sacred Writ.

But perhaps he will say that this was not added by the Church, but by some learned men, which afterwards with the passage of time was accepted by everyone. But it cannot be denied that those authors, from whose fragments joined together the *Historia Tripartita* receives its name, were Greek and wrote in Greek, which was translated from Greek into Latin by Epiphanius the Philologist, at the instigation of Cassiodorus. But that author, whence this was taken, says that in the old copies it is found as follows: "Every spirit that dissolveth Jesus, is not of God." Thus, it is not merely found among the Latins alone, but it is so found among the Greeks at that time. Hence, it could have happened that the old copies were lost, and only those that remain are those which were distorted by heretics, and which were reproduced from those copies. Furthermore, the same author of the history says that the old exegetes related this same thing, namely that some men have adulterated this epistle, wishing to dissolve the Man from God. But it is clear that that author, from which this is taken, is Socrates: because from the beginning of the eleventh until the end of the twelfth, in which this is told, no one else is given as the author besides Socrates, who, as it is evident from the last words of the history, lived during the time of Theodosius the Younger, at which time also lived Nestorius.

Again Blessed Pope Leo I in his letter to Flavian, Bishop of Constantinople, when acting against the heretic Eutyches cites those words: "Every spirit that dissolveth Jesus, is not of God."[2] Now this Leo lived very near to the time of Nestorius, nay (as best as I can reckon) a contemporary, although he may not have been the pope at the time of Nestorius: because Nestorius lived at the time of Pope Celestine [I], under whom was celebrated the Council of Ephesus, in which Nestorius was condemned. Now Celestine (as [Bartolomeo] Platina

---

[1] Bk. 12, c. 4 (PL 69, 1206C).

[2] PL 62, 506C.

testifies[1]) ruled the Church for ten years and ten months.[2] After Celestine Sixtus III ruled the same universal Church for eight years. Leo succeeded after him, concerning whom we now treat, who cites that clause as we now have it. But if it had been altered then, he would not have been so mindless that he would use a false or an altered quotation when fighting against a heretic. Hence I prefer that we would say that it is the correct literal text, which the Latin manuscripts retain, and the Greek manuscripts (as the *Historia Tripartita* relates) were distorted by heretics. And thus supported by this testimony of John we say that Nestorius had the spirit of the Antichrist, because "Every spirit that dissolveth Jesus, is not of God: and this is Antichrist." Now who is there who more truly dissolves Jesus than Nestorius, who separates the Divine nature from the human nature in Christ, proposing two persons, one of the Deity and another of the flesh, dissolving that marvelous union of both natures in the unity of the supposit?

Against this heresy is the decree of the Council of Ephesus, in which after many things which are decreed there against Nestorius based on testimonies of Sacred Scripture, decreed the following: "And since the holy Virgin brought forth corporally God made one with flesh according to nature, for this reason we also call her Mother of God, not as if the nature of the Word had the beginning of its existence from the flesh. For 'In the beginning was the Word, and the Word was God, and the Word was with God,' and He is the Maker of the ages, coeternal with the Father, and Creator of all; but, as we have already said, since He united to Himself hypostatically His human nature from her womb, also He subjected Himself to birth as man."[3] Blessed Cyril wrote against this heresy in his book, *De recta fide ad Theodosium imperatorem*[4]: in which book he disputes against many heretics, yet especially against this heresy of Nestorius. Pope Gelasius [I] published another small book on the same matter, but I have not seen the work of this pope.[5] John Cassian also wrote a small work, *De Incarnatione Domini contra Nestorium*,[6] which was recently printed in Germany.

The **fourth heresy** is completely opposite to the preceding one, and is somewhat similar to the second heresy. Now this fourth heresy says that there is one person in Christ, and on this point it correctly affirms [the truth] against Nestorius: but just as Nestorius on account of the two natures which he saw in Christ, also said that there were two persons, so also this heresy on account of the one person it held by faith to be Christ's, infers out of ignorance to propose only nature in Christ, namely the Divine nature. Yet because it saw clear testimonies of Sacred Scripture proving that Christ has true flesh, according to which He was born of the Virgin, and suffered and died for us, it says and admits that the Son of God is incarnated, but at the very moment of the Incarnation it was converted into the Divinity.

The author of this error is a certain Eutyches, abbot of a monastery in Constantinople at the time of Pope Leo I and Emperor Marcian. This Eutyches said that Christ had only one nature, namely the Divine, just as He was one Person: because even if he acknowledged the Incarnation of the Word, nevertheless after that union he was saying that the flesh was changed into the Deity, and so according to him He was made one substance of flesh and Deity: wherefore he was forced to concede that Christ suffered according to His Divine nature: because by the Incarnation the substance of flesh, as he used to say, was changed into the substance of the Divinity. When Flavian, Bishop of Constantinople, condemned this heresy along with Eu-

---

[1] *The Lives of the Popes* (London, Griffith, Farran, Okeden & Welsh, 1888), vol. 2, p. 103.
[2] The text here mistakenly reads, "eight years," but Platina wrote, "ten years."
[3] Second letter of Cyril to Nestorius (PL 84, 157B).
[4] PG 76, 1134 ff.
[5] PL 224, 763-87.
[6] PL 50, 9-272. John Cassian (ca. 360-435) was a monk and ascetic writer of Southern Gaul, and the first to introduce the rules of Eastern monasticism into the West.

tyches its author, a division arose on this account among the Eastern Christians, some defending Eutyches others condemning him. Hence, with the approval of Emperor Theodosius the Younger, the Council of Ephesus was convoked, in which Dioscorus, Bishop of Alexandria, presided, who was infected with the same error of Eutyches (as appeared afterwards), Eutyches was restored, and Flavian condemned. And this is called the Second Synod of Ephesus, which is rejected by all Catholics as to be execrated and cursed: for it was neither celebrated by the authority of the Supreme Pontiff nor was a universal assembly made to it from the Catholic Church: but such poisonous doctrine was decreed by only heretics gathered together.

A short time after this Eutyches and Dioscorus, his patron, other heretics arose called the Acephali,[1] so named because rising up together at the same time, no one was found who was their leader or teacher. These men denied the two natures in Christ, but affirming only one, namely the Divine, they said that the same was crucified. And because the opposite of this was defined in the Council of Chalcedon against Eutyches and Dioscorus, these men did not wish to acquiesce to the definitions of the same Council of Chalcedon. This heresy, if anyone considers well, remains refuted from the refutation of the three preceding heresies. Since it has been proved, as we have already proved, that there are two natures in Christ, namely the Divine and human, in the unity of the Person: it is necessary to next argue against those who assert that there is only one nature in Christ. But because they assert a mode and notion of only one nature, saying that the substance of the flesh was converted into the Divinity, and the Divinity suffered on the Cross: these two things ought to be driven away, with God showing the way, so that such a heinous blasphemy may not be heard.

If Christ has only one nature, either that nature is completely simple without any composition, or it is a composed nature. If that sole nature which they say is in Christ is simple without any without any composition, and that nature is Divine, Christ will thus only be God, and not man. For it cannot happen that one be called a man who does not have a human nature: just as something cannot be called white which does not have whiteness. Now we have rejected this in the refutation of the second heresy, where we proved that Christ was true man. And actually this heresy of Eutyches is very similar to the heresy of Valentinus, Apelles, or Manichaeus, because this Eutyches (as Flavian, Bishop of Constantinople, says in the letter which he sent to Pope Leo I, reporting the errors of Eutyches) said that "The Lord's flesh was not of the same substance with us, as if assumed from us and united to the Word of God hypostatically: but he said that the Virgin who bore him was indeed of the same substance with us according to the flesh, but the Lord Himself did not assume from her flesh of the same substance with us."[2] All which things we have already proved above to be impious and absurd.

However, if that nature which they put in Christ is not simple, but composed, such as a third nature merged from the two, then it would follow that the Father and the Holy Ghost are incarnated, and the Virgin Mother of Christ is God and man at the same time: all which things are heretical. Yet that it is necessary that they concede these things we have so proved, because Christ the Son of God (as the Catholic Church confesses according to the definition of the Nicene Council[3]) is consubstantial to the Father, meaning of the same substance and nature with Him. Thus, if the Son of God (as these heretics say) is said to be incarnate and is called a man, by the sole single nature which He has, then the Father, Who has the same nature as the Son, will also be said to be incarnate and called a man. It can be argued in the same way about the Holy Ghost, because the Holy Ghost (as the Church defined in the First Council of Constantinople[4]) is of the same substance with the Father and the Son: wherefore,

---

[1] The term *acephali* is taken from the ancient Greek word, ἀκέφαλοι, meaning "headless."
[2] Letter 22 of Pope Leo the Great (PL 54, 725A-727A).
[3] Dz. 54.
[4] No copy of the I Council of Constantinople's doctrinal decisions, entitled *tomos kai anathematismos*

for the same reason it will be said that the Holy Ghost is incarnate and is a man. None of the faithful will not see that all these things are erroneous. And because (as I can suspect from the words of Pope Gelasius [I] writing against Eutyches[1]) Eutyches proposed in this way one quasi composed nature in Christ, as a third nature resulting from the two, for Eutyches was saying that before the Incarnation there were two natures, but after the Incarnation only one nature remained, because then a sort of confusion or composition was made of the natures: and Pope Gelasius presents their example, by which they strive to establish their error.[2] Just as (they say) man is one nature composed from two others, by which composition and union having been made, a third results, which is neither of them: so it is, they say, in the Incarnation of the Word, such that before the Incarnation there were two natures, but after the Incarnation only one remained, the two joining together into one (as they say).

Hence, we argue against this composition a second time. So expounding, they never grant that Christ has two natures. For He did not have them before the union, because then according to everyone there was only one nature, namely the Divine. Nor [did He have them] after the Incarnation, because then according to them He is of only one composed nature. Furthermore, why is it that he says that before the Incarnation there were two natures, but after the Incarnation only one? For how could there be two natures before the Incarnation, since the Word was not yet incarnated? For either you say that the human nature which God united to Himself subsisted in itself before the union, and then you must say that the Son of God united a human person to Himself, and not a human nature: and then you must assert two persons with Nestorius: and so fleeing from Nestorius, you run for help to that same man. Or perhaps you say that even if the whole human nature did not precede the Incarnation, still His soul was previously in Heaven, or abode on earth, and then it was infused into the flesh at the time of the Incarnation. But if you assert this, you fall into the error of Origen concerning the souls firstly created in Heaven, and afterwards infused into the body. We have already vanquished, with God as our guide, that heresy above. Now I cannot think of another way whereby you could say that before the Incarnation there were two natures.

Again if there were two natures before the Incarnation, and afterwards there remained but one, then by the Incarnation either there is a loss of one of them, or there is a mixture and confusion of both: just as when water is mixed with wine, before the mixture there were two natures, and after the mixture there is only one. If by the Incarnation there is a loss of the flesh, there is now no Incarnation but rather (so to speak) it should have been called a "deincarnation." If there is a mixture or composition of both natures, so that a third nature will result from that composition, then it is necessary that He ought not to receive the name of either nature from which He is composed. For man (so that I may use their example) who is a certain third nature, consisting of two very different natures, namely body and soul, receives neither the name of the body or of the soul, because he is call neither body or soul, but he is only called man. So then it would be necessary that Christ would be called neither God nor man, after he has a certain nature composed of those two.

But if perhaps the example of water mixed with wine adduced by me pleases more, because after the mixture it retains the name of wine when the water was converted into wine: and so perhaps you may say, the name of water does not remain, but only the name of wine, because by the mixture the water was changed into wine: and so after the Incarnation it would be necessary to concede to you that Christ is not a man, because the humanity was converted into the

---

engraphos (record of the tome and anathemas), has survived. Indirect references from other sources, such as the synodical letter of the synod of Constantinople held in 382, do indicate, however, that the Council did define this point of the faith.

[1] *De duabus in Christo naturis contra Eutychen et Nestorium* (PL 224, Supplementum 3, pp. 763-87).
[2] C. 9.

Divinity. Then if there is only one nature in Christ, how according to it could he receive such opposite names? For it is impossible that one and the same nature would receive contrary substantial differences, because opposite things cannot be said of the same thing in the same respect. But if opposite things be said of the same thing, it would be necessary that it contain different things in itself, according to which it receives different names: for example man because he has a body and soul, can be called "corporeal" according to the body, "incorporeal" according to the soul: "mortal" according to the body, "immortal" according to the soul. But since Christ is called "mortal" and "immortal," "passible" and "impassible," "finite" and "infinite," it is necessary that he would have different natures, according to the difference of which He receives these different names. Thus there is not one composed nature in Christ, but two simple natures, either of which is specified by its properties.

Now this error of the Eutychians (as [Saint John] Damascene says in the third book, *An Exposition of the Orthodox Faith*[1]) and likewise of the Nestorians, it seems to me, arose from the fact that they did not know how to distinguish between nature and person. And hence Nestorius recognizing the two natures thought that there were two persons. Eutyches on the other hand, because he acknowledged and believed by faith that there is one Person of Christ, he consequently thought that there ought to also only be one nature. Yet both of them could have easily known and seen, if malice had not blinded them, that there are two natures in one supposit of man,[2] in which the plurality of natures does not imply a plurality of persons: nor the unity of the person shows a unity of nature. Thus, this example of man, in this respect only, is very appropriate, although it is very dissimilar in other respects: because in man there is a plurality of natures in the unity of a person by a natural composition of one from many: in Christ, however, there is a plurality of simple natures without any composition or mixture of them. And so in man there are three natures, of two kinds, namely of the body and soul, and a third resulting from them, namely man himself, who is neither of these. But in Christ there are only two natures, the Divine and the human, from which no other third nature is constituted.

But now it is necessary that we refute another common error and impious blasphemy of the Eutyches and the Acephali, whereby they say the Divinity suffered on the Cross. Who will tolerate this? Whose ears do not abhor to hear that the Divinity either felt pain or could suffer? For God Who is most perfect and is a sort of ocean of infinite perfection, cannot be subject to such miseries. "I am the Lord," He Himself says, "and I change not" (Mal. 3, 6). If He does not change, it necessarily follows that either He always feels pain and always suffers, which is the greatest misery: or He never feels pain, nay He can neither feel pain or suffer. For if at one time He is rejoicing and lacking all suffering, and afterwards He feels pain and suffers: it is necessary that He consequently changes.

Furthermore, Peter the Apostle says: "Christ therefore having suffered in the flesh, be you also armed with the same thought" (I Pet. 4, 1). He said that He suffered "in the flesh," not in the Deity. And Paul the Apostle says: "Do you seek a proof of Christ that speaketh in me, who towards you is not weak, but is mighty in you? For although he was crucified through weakness, yet he liveth" (II Cor. 13, 3-4) impassible and immortal, but by the power of His Divinity, which is so great that in Himself He could neither undergo death, nor withstand any suffering. Jesus Christ Himself also testifies that He suffered in the flesh. For when the Jews were speaking and requesting of Him: "What sign dost thou shew unto us, seeing thou dost these things? Jesus answered, and said to them: Destroy this temple, and in three days I will raise it up... But he spoke of the temple of his body," (Jn. 2, 18-19 & 21) which was destroyed at His death and raised up at His Resurrection. Wherefore, the Evangelist as though declaring this added: "When therefore he was risen again from the dead, his disciples remembered, that

---

[1] C. 3 (PG 94, 994B).

[2] I.e. body and soul, which are here called natures.

he had said this, and they believed the scripture, and the word that Jesus had said" (v. 22). You see here that suffering is related to the body, but not to the Divinity, because It could not suffer.

The Prophets also who preceded Christ's Passion spoke of His suffering in the flesh. Hence, in the Psalm it is said in the Person of Christ: "They have dug my hands and feet. They have numbered all my bones" (Ps. 21, 17-18). And Isaias, when showing that Christ's suffering was voluntary, in the Person of the same Christ says: "I have given my body to the strikers, and my cheeks to them that plucked them" (50, 6). And so that I may pass over many others, what else means those words of the Angels to Christ, with which they ask Him, saying: "Why then is thy apparel red" (63, 2). And again: "Who is this that cometh from Edom, with dyed garments from Bosra" (v. 1). It irks to cite many quotations. The relating of which should certainly have sufficed for the refutation, unless we were dealing with men of a hard neck and indomitable heart, of which sort are all heretics.

Against this heresy there are decrees of many councils. For the Council of Chalcedon says the following: "Following the holy fathers, we all teach that with one accord we confess one and the same Son, our Lord Jesus Christ, the same perfect in human nature, truly God and the same with a rational soul and a body truly man, consubstantial with the Father according to Divinity, and consubstantial with us according to human nature, "in all things like as we are, without sin";[1] indeed born of the Father before the ages according to Divine nature, but in the last days the same born of the Virgin Mary, Mother of God according to human nature; for us and for our deliverance, one and the same Christ only begotten Son, our Lord, acknowledged in two natures, without mingling, without change, indivisibly, undividedly, the distinction of the natures nowhere removed on account of the union but rather the peculiarity of each nature being kept, and uniting in one Person and substance, not divided or separated into two persons, but one and the same Son only begotten God Word, Lord Jesus Christ."[2] This decree of the Council of Chalcedon corrected not only the heresy of Nestorius, but also of Eutyches and the Acephali.

But because the wicked and cursed Acephali do not accept the Council of Chalcedon, we thus have recourse to the previous and following councils. For this heresy in fact existed before Eutyches and the Acephali. For Philastrius, who lived a long time before them, relates a certain heresy which said that the Divinity felt pain and suffered on the Cross.[3] Augustine,[4] also more ancient than the Acephali, also tells the same thing, although neither of them reveals the author of the heresy.

The Council of Ephesus, which is called the Third Ecumenical Council, near the end of its decrees, says the following: "In a similar way we say that He suffered and rose again, not that the Word of God suffered blows or piercing with nails or any other wounds in His own nature (for God, being without a body, is incapable of suffering), but because the body which became His own suffered these things, He is said to have suffered them for us. For God, Who cannot suffer, was in that body which suffered."[5] And the Second Synod of Seville says the following: "Thus as the immaculate faith and the holy Church of God teaches, we confess that Our Lord was eternally born God from the Father, born man in time from the womb of the glorious Virgin Mary, and for this reason having two natures existing in one Person: the

---

[1] Cf. Heb. 4, 15.
[2] Dz. 148.
[3] *Liber de haeresibus*, c. 92 (PL 12, 1203C).
[4] "There is another heresy which states that the Divinity in Christ suffered when His flesh was transfixed to the Cross" (*De Haeresibus ad Quodvultdeum*, c. 73 (PL 42, 44)).
[5] *Second letter of Cyril to Nestorius*, c. 13; this letter is cited in the *False Decretals of the Pseudo-Isidore* (PL 130, 301D-302A).

nature of the Divinity, whereby he was begotten before the world: and the nature of the humanity, in which he was brought forth in the last days: existing according to the form of God in the former, according to the form of a servant in the latter: remaining equal to the Father in the former, like unto our nature without sin in the latter: inviolable in the former, passible in the latter: in the former nature He could not die, He underwent death in the latter."[1] This council was expressly against the Acephali.

By which words all the aforesaid heresies that have arisen about the Person of Christ are smashed. Pope Gelasius [I] wrote against this heresy in the same book which he wrote against Nestorius.[2] Boethius also wrote a book, *De [persona et] duabus naturis*, against this same heresy.[3] And Blessed [John] Damascene disputes in the third book in a few chapters of his work *An Exposition of the Orthodox Faith*, against each of the aforesaid heresies.[4]

The **fifth heresy** is that which asserts that Christ only had a body and not a soul. The author of this heresy was Arius, as Augustine testifies about the Arians saying the following: "They are less known for maintaining this error: that Christ assumed flesh alone without a soul. I did not find this argued against them at any time by anyone. But Epiphanius testified to the truth of this, and I have certainly determined it from some of their writings and discourses."[5] But because it is not evident from these words whether Arius devised this poison, or his followers afterwards added it from their own brains: hence we keep silence about Arius for now. Apollinaris, concerning whom we have already spoken elsewhere, afterwards raised up this error, who is commonly called the author of that error. Philastrius reports this heresy, with no author of it named.[6]

This error is sufficiently refuted by those things which were said in the conquest of the second heresy. For if Christ had the true substance of a human nature, then He also had a soul, because without it He could not be a perfect man. But even if this very clearly refutes him, it will not cause displeasure to make particular arguments against him. Christ, when the time of His Passion was then at hand, said: "My soul is sorrowful even unto death" (Mt. 26, 38). And beforehand He said: "The good shepherd giveth his life [*anima* or "soul" in Latin[7]] for his sheep" (Jn. 10, 11). And again: "I have power to lay my life [*anima*] down: and I have power to take it up again" (v. 18). These words are clear enough, nor are redolent of any parable.

But Apollinaris replied to these passages from Scripture (as Augustine says[8]) saying that Christ did not have a rational soul, but only one which gave life to the body, and the Word Itself took the place of the rational soul. But by this he does not escape, without saying that Christ was not a whole and perfect man, with the same nature as us. But so that no way of escape be open to him, let us consider what Luke says about Him: "Jesus advanced in wisdom, and age, and grace with God and men" (Lk. 2, 52). Now the words which follow declare how He advanced in wisdom, because he adds: "in age, and grace with God and men." Thus according to the passage He advanced in wisdom just as he advanced in age. But since He only advanced in age according to His human nature alone, it follows that according to the same nature He advanced in wisdom, because according to the Divine nature, which is immutable

---

[1] C. 13 (PL 84, 601B-C).

[2] Tract 3: *De duabus naturis in Christo adversus Eutychem et Nestorium* which is printed in *Epistolae Romanorum pontificum genuinae et quae ad eos scriptae sunt a S. Hilario usque ad Pelagium* II, vol. 1 (Braniewo, Edward Peter, 1868), pp. 530-57 (PL 224, Supplementum 3, pp. 763-87).

[3] PL 64, 1337-1354D.

[4] C. 5-7 (PG 94, 999B-1011C).

[5] *De Haeresibus ad Quodvultdeum*, c. 49 (PL 42, 39).

[6] *Liber de Haeresibus*, c. 69 (PL 12, 1183-1184).

[7] The word used here in the Latin text is *anima*, which means both "life" or "soul."

[8] *De Haeresibus ad Quodvultdeum*, c. 55 (PL 42, 40).

and infinitely wise, He could nowise advance. Hence He advanced in wisdom according to His humanity.

But if the humanity which He received did not have a rational soul, then He could understand nothing according to His human nature, because He must understand by the rational soul, not according to the body, or by his truncated vegetative soul. Again, on account of this the Son of God took up our nature, so that by that nature received by Him He might aid our weaknesses, and He Who was without sin might remit our sins. Thus, it would have been of no benefit to us to take up only flesh without the soul, because our sins were in the soul, and not in the flesh, which cannot sin. But Christ redeemed the whole man, Who said: "I have healed the whole man on the sabbath day" (Jn. 7, 23).

Finally, this error was condemned by the decisions of many councils. The Synod of Rome under Pope Damasus says the following: "We anathematize those who say that instead of the rational and intellectual soul of man, the Word of God dwelt in a human body, although the Son Himself and Word of God was not in His own body instead of a rational and intellectual soul, but assumed our soul without sin (that is the rational and intellectual soul) and saved it."[1] The decrees of which Council are put in the book of the general councils, not among the councils themselves, but afterwards among the decrees of Pope Damasus. The Council of Ephesus says the following: "For we do not say that the nature of the Word was changed and became flesh, or that it was converted into a whole man consisting of soul and body; but rather that the Word having personally united to himself flesh animated by a rational soul, did in an ineffable and inconceivable manner become man."[2] The Council of Chalcedon says the following: "Following the holy Fathers, we all teach that with one accord we confess one and the same Son, our Lord Jesus Christ, the same perfect in human nature, truly God and the same with a rational soul and a body truly man" etc.[3]

I have not seen, nor until now have I known, anyone who wrote against this heresy besides Blessed Ambrose, who in his book, *On the Sacrament of the Incarnation of the Lord*, treats against it throughout the whole seventh chapter.[4]

There is a **sixth heresy** which asserts that there was only one will in Christ, namely the Divine. The author of this heresy was Macarius, Bishop of Antioch, who was condemned in the Sixth [General] Council, [the III Council] of Constantinople, celebrated under Pope Agatho. The promoters of this heresy are the Monothelites, not (as some incorrectly say) the Monoselites: and someone, and knowing his name I omit it, wishing to assign the derivation of the name, not less shamelessly as imprudently, said: "They are called Monoselites from Monosus, the author of the heresy. They are called Monothelites from the single will which they attribute to Christ: because μόνος in Greek in Latin means *tantum ac unus* ['one and only'], and likewise τέλειος which is *voluntas* ['will']."

We will accordingly proceed against this heresy, and firstly it must be sought from its defender, whether he acknowledges two natures in Christ. If he says that there is only one nature in Christ, just as one will, then he ought to be referred to one of the aforementioned heresies, which denied the two natures in Christ. But if he acknowledges two natures in Christ, then he ought to also acknowledge two wills in Christ: because just as one will belonging to one nature, so there are more wills belonging to more natures. For we say that there is one will of the Father, Son, and Holy Ghost, because there is one substance of Deity in those three Persons. So then in Christ, in Whom there are two different natures, namely of the Divinity and of the humanity, it is necessary that there are also two wills: one, which pertains to the Divinity: the

---

[1] Tome of Damasus, c. 7 (PL 13, 358C); Dz. 65.
[2] Second letter of Cyril of Alexandria to Nestorius (PG 77, 45B-C); Dz. 111a.
[3] *Symbolum 150 sanctorum patrum, qui in Constantinopolim congregati sunt* (PL 62, 514C); Dz. 148.
[4] PL 16, 833D-838B.

other, which regards the humanity. Furthermore, if there is only one will in Christ, then there will be only one nature in Christ: because just as one nature infers one will, so on the contrary one will shows one nature. For one will cannot belong to two natures.

Again, if there is only one will, either it will be Divine or human, or a third kind composed of them, as Eutyches had said above. If the will is only a Divine will, then Christ did not have a complete and perfect humanity of the same species as ours: because there can be no perfect humanity with a will. If, however, that one will is only a human will, then Christ will not be God, because He cannot be God without a Divine will. Now we have proved both of these positions to be heretical. But if one would say that the one will of Christ is of a third kind, composed of those two, then it follows that the will is neither Divine nor human: because a composed thing does not take its name from one of the parts out of which it is composed: and so according to these things it is necessary to say that Christ is not true God nor true man, because He has neither a Divine will (according to them) nor human will.

But putting aside these arguments, let us examine the Sacred Scriptures, because (as Christ said) they give testimony concerning Him.[1] Mark the Evangelist says: "He came into the coasts of Tyre and Sidon: and entering into a house, he would that no man should know it, and he could not be hid" (Mk. 7, 24). How could He not hide when He wished? Is not the Divine will omnipotent? Did not the Lord make all the things in Heaven and on earth that He wanted? Thus according to that which could not hide, according to it He wanted no one to know. But it is evident that He could not hide according to the humanity, because according to it He was not omnipotent, thus according to the same He wanted no one to know: and He did not so will according to the Divine will: hence the will of the Divinity is something else besides the will of the humanity.

Furthermore, when the time of Christ's Passion was near at hand, He said: "Father, if thou wilt, remove this chalice from me: but yet not my will, but thine be done" (Lk. 22, 42). Do you see here two wills of Christ explicitly mentioned, the one of the Divinity, and the other of the humanity? For if there were only one will of Christ, namely the Divine, how could it happen that Christ would pray to His Father saying: "Not my will, but thine be done"? For it is not possible that the Father's will be fulfilled, but not the Son's, since the Father's and Son's will is one. But because there are two wills in Christ, one of the Divinity, which is the same as the Father's will, according to which He asks nothing from the Father: the other of the humanity, according to which in some way He did not want the Passion: hence submitting His will, meaning the human, to the Divine, He says: "Not my will, but thine be done."

Again the Blessed Apostle Paul when speaking of Christ says: "He became obedient unto death, even to the death of the cross" (Phil. 2, 8). Now He was not obedient according to the Divine nature, because obedience denotes a certain subjection. But He was not subject to the Father according to the Divine nature, because according to it He "thought it not robbery to be equal with God" (Phil. 2, 6). Thus He "became obedient" according to the human nature. Now voluntary obedience is a certain subjection, and there can be no obedience without the will. For what happens by force and coercion does not happen through obedience. Therefore, since Christ "became obedient unto death" to the Father according to His human nature, He must necessarily have a will according to the same humanity, according to which He willed to suffer.

The [III] Council of Constantinople was celebrated against this heresy, which is called the Sixth [General] Council, under Pope Agatho. Thus after long discussions and disputations having been held about this matter, it was finally decreed as followed: "just as formerly the prophets taught us about Him, and our Lord Jesus Christ Himself has taught us, and the Creed

---

[1] Cf. Jn. 5, 39.

of the holy Fathers has handed down to us.[1] And so we proclaim two natural wills in Him, and two natural operations indivisibly, inconvertibly, inseparably, inconfusedly according to the doctrine of the holy Fathers, and two natural wills not contrary, God forbid, according as impious heretics have asserted, but the human will following and not resisting or hesitating, but rather even submitting to His Divine and omnipotent will. For, it is necessary that the will of the flesh act, but that it be subject to the Divine will according to the most wise Athanasius. For, as His flesh is called and is the flesh of the Word of God, so also the natural will of His flesh is called and is the proper will of the Word of God as He Himself says: "Because I came down from heaven, not to do my own will but the will of my Father who sent me," (John 6, 38), calling the will of the flesh His own. For the body became His own."[2]

I have found no writer against this heresy, besides [Saint John] Damascene, who disputes regarding this matter in the third book of *An Exposition of the Orthodox Faith*,[3] without naming the author of the error, as he is accustomed to do.[4] And Peter Lombard treats of this matter, although briefly and perfunctorily.[5] Now he who wishes to be more fully instructed about this matter may read the acts of the Sixth General Council, in which this topic is examined amply enough. Guy the Carmelite never mentions this heresy in his *Summa de haeresibus*, which greatly astonishes me, since it is known very well to learned men. Hence it is proved that he did not read the acts of the Sixth General Council. What we have said elsewhere is also evident, that he, when examining the old heresies, read nothing else besides the small work of Augustine, *De Haeresibus [ad Quodvultdeum]*, or the chapter of Isidore in his *Etymologies*, in which he relates the heresies which preceded his time. For since neither Augustine nor Isidore list this heresy, inasmuch as it was after them both, for that reason Guy does not mention it.

The **seventh heresy** is very ungrateful to Christ our Redeemer, because it does not acknowledge the benefit conferred upon us. For it denies that Christ was crucified, but instead asserts that Simon of Cyrene [was crucified], who was forced to bear the Cross. The author of this error was the impious Basilides at the time of the Apostles, concerning whom Eusebius speaks.[6] After this man a short time later Marcus, from whom the Marcosian heretics are so called, adhered to the same error, saying that Christ did not suffer in reality, but only in appearance.[7]

It irks to cite testimonies of Sacred Scripture against this error, since both Testaments are full of testimonies of Christ's Passion. And after having passed over the Old Testament, in which nearly everything is said in figures and enigmas, the history of the four Gospels relating Christ's Passion is very clear. None of them, however, say that the Cyrenian suffered, but merely carried the Cross, to which Christ was afterwards affixed. And Paul very often teaches this in his epistles. For in the First Epistle to the Corinthians he says: "But we preach Christ crucified" (1, 23). And again: "I judged not myself to know anything among you, but Jesus Christ, and him crucified" (2, 2). And so that I may omit all the others, Peter the Apostle on the day on which he received the Holy Ghost with the others, when preaching to the people

---

[1] Cf. Council of Chalcedon (Dz. 148).

[2] Dz. 290-291.

[3] C. 14 (PG 94, 1034B-1046C).

[4] Here the author makes a digression about whether Macarius was truly the first author of this heresy based upon the false claim of John Trithemius (*Liber de Scriptoribus Ecclesiasticis* (Basil, Johann Amerbach, 1494), p. 16v.) that Saint John Damascene lived about the year 450 A.D. and thus knew of this heresy long before Macarius of Antioch (+685) lived. But Saint John Damascene was actually born about 676 A.D. Thus, this discussion, for having no value, has been deleted.

[5] *Libri quattuor sententiarum*, lib. 3, dist. 17, n. 1-3 (PL 192, 790-792).

[6] *Ecclesiastical History*, bk. 4, c. 7, n. 3-8 (PG 20, 315B-318B).

[7] Cf. Augustine, *De Haeresibus ad Quodvultdeum*, c. 14 (PL 42, 28).

says: "Ye men of Israel, hear these words: Jesus of Nazareth, a man approved of God among you, by miracles, and wonders, and signs, which God did by him, in the midst of you, as you also know. This same being delivered up, by the determinate counsel and foreknowledge of God, you by the hands of wicked men have crucified" (Acts 2, 22-23). How therefore did He, who died through His suffering, not suffer in reality but only in appearance? But if He did not really suffer, Paul's preaching is false.

Against such madness it is not necessary to cite many things: because, as we stated from the beginning, we now treat against only those who gave their names to Christ by Baptism. But those who assert these things we show to be either heathens or Jews, because (as Paul says) to preach Jesus crucified is "unto the Jews a stumblingblock, and unto the Gentiles foolishness." (I Cor. 1, 23).

The **eighth heresy** is not less ungrateful to Christ Himself, not even acknowledging such an immense benefit, which He conferred upon us, namely our Redemption. The author of this heresy is a certain man named Colarbasus,[1] during the times of the Apostles, concerning whom I find mention made only by Philastrius.[2] This Colarbasus said that salvation ought not to be hoped for either in Christ's majesty or in his corporeal presence. A long time afterwards, Peter Abelard resurrected this error, who said the Son of God was not incarnated to free man. And so that his foolish mind may appear more clearly, I will cite his words here, which Blessed Bernard put in his letter 190. "'Therefore,' he says, 'as the doctors teach, the Son of God became incarnate under this necessity, that since man could not otherwise be freed, he might, by the death of an innocent man, be set free from the yoke of the devil. But as it seems to us,' he says, 'neither had the devil ever any power over man, except by the permission of God, as a jailer might, nor was it to free man that the Son of God assumed flesh.'"[3] Behold the new Goliath, who reproaches all the Catholic Doctors, saying that they all err. But this man, having been struck with the rock of the Catholic faith, with God as our guide, will fall down.

Firstly, therefore, what he says, namely that the devil has no authority or power over man, is clearly refuted by what the Lord says in John's Gospel: "For the prince of this world cometh, and in me he hath not anything" (14, 30). If he had no power over man, why is he called "the prince of this world"? And what follows shows this more clearly, namely: "and in me he hath not anything." But if he also had no authority or power over other men, why was it necessary to add: "and in me he hath not anything"? Now so that no interpretation or argumentation be needed, hear Blessed Paul saying this explicitly: "If peradventure God may give them repentance to know the truth, and they may recover themselves from the snares of the devil, by whom they are held captive at his will" (II Tim. 2, 25-26). Here you see the snares of the devil mentioned by Paul: and men "held captive at his will." Furthermore, if men were not held captive by the devil by sin, then Christ did nothing by His death: because if we were not captives, it would certainly not be necessary that we even be redeemed. For one is not redeemed unless he was held captive. But the ungrateful and blasphemous Peter Abelard assented to this, saying that the Son of God did not take flesh to redeem man.

But this error is condemned by many testimonies of Sacred Scripture. And, so that I may omit the Old Testament, I go on to the New. In Matthew's Gospel we read that an Angel said to Joseph concerning the Virgin Mary: "And she shall bring forth a son: and thou shalt call his name Jesus. For he shall save his people from their sins" (1, 21). And in John's Gospel likewise Christ says: "For God sent not his Son into the world, to judge the world, but that the

---

[1] The text here has "Bassus" but Saint Irenaeus in *Against the Heresies* (bk. 1, c. 14, n. 1) calls him "Colorbasus," and this is the earliest known reference to him. The author found him mentioned only by Philastrius, but that is probably due to variant forms of his name which are difficult to recognize.

[2] *Liber de haeresibus,* c. 43 (PL 12, 1159B-1160A).

[3] C. 5, n. 11 (PL 182, 1063A).

world may be saved by him" (3, 17). And at the Last Supper when giving His flesh as food to His disciples, He says: "Take ye, and eat: this is my body, which shall be delivered for you" (I Cor. 11, 24). And holding forth the chalice He says: "This is the chalice, the new testament in my blood, which shall be shed for you" (Lk. 22, 20).

And Blessed Paul says: "When the fulness of the time was come, God sent his Son, made of a woman, made under the law: that he might redeem them who were under the law: that we might receive the adoption of sons" (Gal. 4, 4-5). And elsewhere he says: "But God (who is rich in mercy) for his exceeding charity wherewith he loved us, even when we were dead in sins, hath quickened us together in Christ, (by whose grace you are saved)" (Eph. 2, 4-5). And in another place he says: "And you, when you were dead in your sins, and the uncircumcision of your flesh; he hath quickened together with him, forgiving you all offences: blotting out the handwriting of the decree that was against us, which was contrary to us. And he hath taken the same out of the way, fastening it to the cross: and despoiling the principalities and powers, he hath exposed them confidently in open shew, triumphing over them in himself" (Col. 2, 13-15).

And Blessed Peter the Apostle says: "Knowing that you were not redeemed with corruptible things as gold or silver, from your vain conversation of the tradition of your fathers: but with the precious blood of Christ, as of a lamb unspotted and undefiled" (I Pet. 1, 18-19). Finally, those four living creatures and the four and twenty ancients, which John saw falling down before the Lamb, were singing saying: "Thou art worthy, O Lord, to take the book, and to open the seals thereof; because thou wast slain, and hast redeemed us to God, in thy blood, out of every tribe, and tongue, and people, and nation" (Apocalypsc, 5, 9). Bchold those who were already enjoying the Redemption made by Christ acknowledge the Redemption. But Peter Abelard, because he was being kept back in diabolic captivity through sin, was not acknowledging the Redemption.

Against this heresy there are the decisions of many councils. In the Symbol of faith produced in the Council of Nicea it is said concerning Christ, the Son of God, as follows: "Who for us men, and for our salvation, came down and was incarnate and was made man; He suffered, and the third day He rose again, ascended into Heaven; from thence He shall come to judge the living and the dead."[1] And the same words were put into the Creed made in the Council of Constantinople, which is called the Second General Council.[2] The Council of Ephesus, which is called the Third General Council, says the following: "(For it is absurd and stupid to speak of the one who existed before every age and is coeternal with the Father, needing a second beginning so as to exist.) The Word is said to have been begotten according to the flesh, because for us and for our salvation He united what was human to Himself hypostatically and came forth from a woman."[3] And the Council of Chalcedon, which is called the Fourth General Council, says the same thing.[4] Behold all four Councils, which Blessed Gregory says are to be venerated like the four Gospels, are opposed to Peter Abelard. Therefore, let Peter Abelard become mute, and restrain his proud arrogance, whereby he was not afraid to think contrary to the common teaching of all the holy Doctors.

I have found no writer against this error besides Blessed Bernard, who in a letter to Pope Innocent,[5] which disputes about this matter, from which we have drawn some things. Guy [the Carmelite] also makes no mention of this heresy; nay he does not even make any mention of the impious Peter Lombard.

---

[1] Dz. 54.

[2] Dz. 86.

[3] Second letter of Cyril of Alexandria to Nestorius (PL 84, 159C).

[4] PL 84, 165B.

[5] Letter 190.

The **ninth heresy** denies that the spirit of the fear of the Lord was in Christ. And this poison was also invented by Peter Abelard, just as Blessed Bernard accuses him in that same letter,[1] although he does not argue against him. But the Prophet Isaias refuted and overcame this heresy, who when speaking of Christ says the following: "And there shall come forth a rod out of the root of Jesse, and a flower shall rise up out of his root. And the spirit of the Lord shall rest upon him: the spirit of wisdom, and of understanding, the spirit of counsel, and of fortitude, the spirit of knowledge, and of godliness. And he shall be filled with the spirit of the fear of the Lord" (Is. 11, 1-3). This rod, which rose up from the root of Jesse, is the Virgin Mary of the stock of David, who was the son of Jesse, as Matthew relates.[2] The flower, however, is Christ, Who says: "I am the flower of the field, and the lily of the valleys" (Cant. 2, 1). Upon this flower rested the sevenfold Spirit, which Isaias described, that is, the seven gifts of the same Holy Ghost, among which is listed the spirit of the fear of the Lord. Furthermore, why is he afraid to put the spirit of the fear of the Lord in Christ? Is it perhaps because fear belongs to imperfect things, according to which John says: "Perfect charity casteth out fear" (I Jn. 4, 18)? And so Peter Abelard fearing to deny the perfect charity in Christ, denied that there was the spirit of fear in Him.

But if it is so, then he certainly was afraid with fear, where there was no fear. For he did not know that fear of the Lord is multiple. For one fear of the Lord is servile, namely when someone on account of hatred of punishment, which he fears, flees sin: which is called servile fear, because slaves are accustomed to have such fear. It is also called initial fear, because it is a way and a beginning to the good. For one part of justice is to decline from evil, to which this servile fear introduces, and hence is called initial, concerning which it is said: "The fear of the Lord is the beginning of wisdom" (Ps. 110, 10). This fear belongs to those who are imperfect, because the perfect execution of any work ought to take its origin from charity. Now this fear does not arise from charity, but from the hatred of punishment. Perfect charity casts out this fear: because he who already so loves God that he does all things from love of Him, thereupon ceases to act on account of hatred of punishment. For he who acts out of hatred of punishment, acts as though forced by the punishment which he fears: which if he knew would never be inflicted, he would cease from the action. But if he acts out of love, he acts completely freely. Christ did not have this fear, because He had the most perfect charity that was permitted Him.

Another fear is filial fear of the Lord, namely when someone flees evil solely from love of his father, that is to say, lest he offend his father: hence it is called filial, because a good son ought fear his father with such fear. And charity not only does not expel this fear, nay charity produces it, and has its origin from it. And Christ had this fear, because He declined from many evils, nay from all evils, not from fear of any punishment, but from the love of God alone. Thus filial fear was in Him.

But if you still object saying that this filial fear has a certain intermixed pain, and due to this you say that it was not in Christ, Whose soul was beatified from the moment of His conception: this is no obstacle: because even if His soul was beatified, He was nonetheless sad during His Passion, which sadness was a much greater pain that that which was intermixed with filial fear. Thus, He Who could be sad when He was beatified, could also fear, especially with filial fear, and if there is some pain from it, it certainly is very little. Again the Blessed who are now free from every pain, fear the Lord, as the [Royal] Prophet says: "The fear of the Lord is holy, enduring for ever and ever" (Ps. 18, 10). Therefore, Christ's beatitude could nowise impede Him from fearing God. But they interpret this saying of the Prophet, in relation to another fear, which they call reverential, which is nothing other than a reverence for God

---

[1] *Ibid.*

[2] Mt. 1, 6.

Himself: and they say that the Blessed have this. But if this fear be different from filial fear, and they deny that filial fear exists in the Blessed, but only that which they call reverential, still Peter Abelard does not escape by this, as if there were not some spirit of fear of the Lord in Christ (as Isaias said): because since Christ revered God more that all others, to such an extent that Paul says that He was heard by God on account of that reverence:[1] it follows that He also feared God above all men with that fear which they call reverential. Therefore, there is no reason why Peter Abelard is afraid to attribute fear to Christ: because even if He did not have servile fear, which perfect charity casts out, nevertheless He had filial or reverential fear, which perfect charity produces.

The **tenth heresy** asserts that Christ underwent the wound of the lance while He was still alive. The author of this heresy was a certain Pierre Jean [Olivi], as Guy the Carmelite accuses him.[2] And I am certainly astonished that a man who knows even a little Latin and reads the Gospel of John, would fall into such a manifest error: unless perhaps by his proud malice blinding him: because when Blessed John is relating Christ's Passion, after he states the many torments undergone by Christ, he says the following concerning His death: "Jesus therefore, when he had taken the vinegar, said: It is consummated. And bowing his head, he gave up the ghost. Then the Jews, (because it was the Parasceve,) that the bodies might not remain on the cross on the sabbath day, (for that was a great sabbath day,) besought Pilate that their legs might be broken, and that they might be taken away. The soldiers therefore came; and they broke the legs of the first, and of the other that was crucified with him. But after they were come to Jesus, when they saw that he was already dead, they did not break his legs. But one of the soldiers with a spear opened his side, and immediately there came out blood and water. And he that saw it, hath given testimony, and his testimony is true. And he knoweth that he saith true; that you also may believe." (19, 30-35).

Now from the order of these words it very clearly appears that Christ was already dead when His side was struck with a lance. Thus, even if an Angel from Heaven were to announce another Gospel to us, he ought not to be believed.[3] Nor for the sake of devotion or of contemplation is it permitted to contrive a lie. Now this man in order to increase the sufferings of Christ's Passion, was saying that it could be licitly said and contemplated that Christ was struck with a lance while He was still alive. But God does not need our lies. Hence, this man was rightly condemned in the Council of Vienne under Pope Clement V. The decree of this council is found in the volume of the Clementine Decretals under the title, *De summa Trinitate et fide catholica*.[4] In this decree, after the Council cited that passage of John which we have recently related, it is defined as follows: "We, therefore, turning our attention to such remarkable testimony and to the common opinion of Apostolic reflection of the Holy Fathers and the Doctors in accord with which alone it is proper to declare these things, with the approval of the Sacred Council we declare that the above mentioned Apostle and Evangelist John had kept the right order of the deed accomplished in the aforesaid, when he said that Christ 'already dead… one of the soldiers with a spear opened his side.'"[5] Anyone ought to rather believe this definition of the Council of Vienne than the fantastic imaginations of heretics.

The **eleventh heresy** is that which denies that Christ resurrected. The teacher of this heresy is Cerinthus, concerning whom we have spoken elsewhere. This man (as Augustine testifies[6])

---

[1] Cf. Heb. 5, 7.
[2] *Summa de haeresibus et earum confutationibus*, fol. 107r, c. 3.
[3] Cf. Gal. 1, 8.
[4] Clement., bk. 1, tit. 1, c. 1.
[5] Dz. 480.
[6] *De Haeresibus ad Quodvultdeum*, c. 8 (PL 42, 27).

said that Christ did not resurrect, but would rise again at some time. This heresy is so easily refuted that he who wishes to defend it is forced to deny the four Gospels, which affirm with one voice that Christ rose again. For Matthew in the last chapter of his Gospel, as well as Mark and Luke in their last chapter, and John in the next to last chapter of his Gospel, all unanimously testify that Christ rose again. Furthermore, if Christ did not resurrect, then He is found to be a liar, Who had predicted to His Apostles that He would rise again from the dead after His Passion. The proofs also must be false and sophistical whereby (as Luke says) He wished to prove His Resurrection. For he says the following: "To whom also he shewed himself alive after his passion, by many proofs, for forty days appearing to them, and speaking of the kingdom of God" (Acts. 1, 3). Again, "If Christ be not risen again, your faith is vain" (I Cor. 15, 17). "Yea, and we are found false witnesses of God: because we have given testimony against God, that he hath raised up Christ; whom he hath not raised up, if the dead rise not again" (v. 15). Therefore, in so clear a matter it would be superfluous to compose a long disputation.

The **twelfth** and last **heresy** which I find concerning this matter, is that which asserts that Christ ascended into Heaven without His Body. Apelles taught this heresy, and with the same Apelles, as far as I know, it was buried. He (as Augustine says[1]) said that Christ rose without His Body, and ascended into Heaven without the same Body. What can be said more fanciful than this opinion? If fact it originates for no reason, it is supported by no argument, and it rests upon no foundation: but it appears as a mere dream or a pure fable. If Christ rose without flesh: Who was He Whom standing in the midst of the disciples Thomas touched on the octave day of the Resurrection? Whose were those wounds of the hands, and the wound of the side, which He showed to Thomas, and offered to be touched?[2] For the Divinity neither could be seen with bodily eyes nor touched with the hands, nor bear wounds.

Furthermore, Christ when appearing to the disciples after the Resurrection, and when they were troubled and frightened, because they thought that they saw a spirit, said: "Why are you troubled, and why do thoughts arise in your hearts? See my hands and feet, that it is I myself; handle, and see: for a spirit hath not flesh and bones, as you see me to have. And when he had said this, he shewed them his hands and feet. But while they yet believed not, and wondered for joy, he said: Have you anything to eat? And they offered him a piece of a broiled fish, and a honeycomb. And when he had eaten before them, taking the remains, he gave to them" (Lk. 24, 41-42). Therefore how did He resurrect without flesh, Who when rising, has hands and feet, and eats honeycomb? Again, if Christ ascended into Heaven without flesh, Who is He Whom Stephen saw when he was being persecuted, saying: "Behold, I see the heavens opened, and the Son of man standing on the right hand of God" (Acts 7, 55)? But the Son of God, if you exclude His flesh, will no more be called the Son of man. Add to these things that Christ when ascending into Heaven, the Angels said to the Apostles: "Ye men of Galilee, why stand you looking up to heaven? This Jesus who is taken up from you into heaven, shall so come, as you have seen him going into heaven" (Acts 1, 11). But since Jesus is to judge in human form, it is proved that He also ascended in human form. Against such an open lie, and such clear madness, it is not necessary to put forward many things. And certainly it would have embarrassed me to relate these things, if those heretics had been ashamed to assert them. But since their follies are already widely known, and told by many writers who mentioned them: it was necessary to insert them here, so that they might be condemned with the other heresies.

---

[1] *Ibid.*, c. 23 (PL 42, 29).

[2] Cf. Jn. 20.

CONCILIUM

Council

Concerning this subject I find only one error, common to nearly all heretics. For it always belongs to all heretics and until now proper to them, to take away the authority of councils, and to diminish it with all their strength: because they see that nothing is so effective to repressing their unbridled audacity, as the authority of a general council. Wherefore since all heretics obstinately defend their errors, it happens that if perhaps some error of theirs would have been condemned by a council, they take refuge in this common asylum for them, saying that the council erred in such a definition. Arius did this. For when he was condemned in the Council of Nicea, he and his followers not willing to acquiesce to the definition of the council, said that the council erred. In the same manner Nestorius found himself condemned in the Council of Ephesus, such that he and his followers preferred their own opinion to the decree of the Council of Ephesus. Eutyches and Dioscorus did no other thing when condemned in the Council of Chalcedon. The history of the Bohemian John Hus is also very well known, who when he had embraced the doctrine of John Wycliffe, and saw it condemned in the Council of Constance, nevertheless not on account of this did he desist to hold fast to his error, saying that the Council of Constance erred in the condemnation of John Wycliffe. Last of all Luther, although at the beginning of the preaching of his errors, he appealed to a council, fearing afterwards lest perhaps his poisonous doctrines might be condemned by an assembled council, he added this other poison, saying that a general council no matter how properly convoked (as is befitting), could err in faith and morals, and the Council of Constance erred in the condemnation of John Hus.

Therefore, against the dementia of all these heretics this must be proved, that a general council duly convoked cannot err in the faith. Now concerning local councils, which take place in particular provinces, it is not our intention to dispute, because it is evident that such councils can err, and some of them have erred. Certainly the Synod of Carthage with eighty bishops, which the martyr Blessed Cyprian attended, erred, defining that heretics and those baptized by heretics ought to be rebaptized. And the Donatists celebrated many other councils, in which they boasted that they had many centurias of bishops. And we have no doubt about them that they erred. But even if this or that provincial council erred, their error was not prejudicial to the whole Church, since an error of this kind would be corrected by the definition of a general council, just as Blessed Augustine teaches in his book, [*On Baptism,*] *Against the Donatists*, saying the following: "The Councils themselves, which are held in the several districts and provinces, must yield, beyond all possibility of doubt, to the authority of plenary Councils which are formed for the whole Christian world."[1] Therefore, we say concerning general councils duly convoked alone that they are not able to err.

Now in order that we may prove this clearly, it is necessary to question [the heretics] whether some certain way whereby someone who errs in the faith can be taught, so that recalled from his error, he may hold a certain rule of faith. If they say that there is no such certain way, two unfitting things follow. The first is that God did not rightly and sufficiently provide for His Church. The second is that no one, no matter how much he has erred in the faith, will sin by this: because he labors under irremediable ignorance. For it is wicked to say that God obliged someone to what is impossible for him. If no certain way appears whereby he could be recalled from error, it will then be impossible for him to hold a certain rule of faith:

---

[1] Bk. 2, c. 3, n. 4 (PL 43, 129).

wherefore since he lacked it, he will not sin. If, however, they say that there is some certain way by which he could be taught so that having abandoned his error he may return to the right faith, this will not be the teaching of any particular man, because any particular man can err in the faith, even if he is illustrious with the papal dignity. Therefore, a definition of a general council duly convoked will be the certain way. But if that same council could also err, neither is it a certain way: we would still be doubtful whether that council decided rightly or wrongly. That being the case, we would always be hesitant and like (as Blessed James says) "a wave of the sea, which is moved and carried about by the wind" (1, 6). But this Luther and his accomplices say that the study of Scriptures is the certain way, to which they say belongs every judgment for dispelling disputes about the faith: because Christ said: "Search the scriptures, because same are they that give testimony of me" (Jn. 5, 39).

To whom we object that in that passage it is merely maintained that Scriptures hold the place of the witnesses, not the place of the judge. But the office of witnesses is not to pronounce sentence, but merely to give testimony. But to the judge it belongs to hear and examine the words of the witnesses: which when they have been heard, he pronounces the sentence according to their testimony. Wherefore, we admit that the sentence ought to be given according to the testimony of Sacred Scripture: but there is need of a judge who seeks after, hears and examines the words of the witnesses: who when removed, the certitude also cannot be had from the testimony of Sacred Scripture, because each person will interpret the very same passage of Scripture as he pleases. Arius certainly cited many passages of Scripture for the confirmation of his error. Nestorius (as Gennadius says in his list of ecclesiastical writers[1]) attempted to confirm his heresy with sixty [-two] passages of Scripture.

And which heretic has not tried to prove his heresy with testimonies of Scripture? For if you ask any heretic teaching new things, whence do you prove that I ought leave the old faith of the Catholic Church: he will immediately cite a thousand testimonies, a thousand examples, a thousand assertions, from the Law, from the Psalms, from the Apostles, from the Prophets, with which he confirms his erroneous poisonous doctrine. Therefore, how will Scripture then be the judge, since the heretic and the Catholic use it at will? Arius and Athanasius dispute about the consubstantiality of the Son. Arius brings forth in his favor that saying of Christ: "The Father is greater than I" (Jn. 14, 28). Athanasius confirms his own and the Catholic faith by that which Christ said: "The Father and I are one" (Jn. 10, 30). Both of them say that they have searched the Scriptures, and that they bear witness to their teaching. Thus, it is not sufficient and a certain way of searching the Scriptures, because everyone interprets them as he pleases. Therefore a judge is needed, who may give judgment concerning the interpretation of those Scriptures, as to which meaning is correct. Now that judge, so that he may render us certain by his judgment, must be such a one who cannot be mistaken.

An individual man, however, whoever he may be, can err. Thus, a general council will necessarily be such a judge who cannot err, and make us certain about the true faith by his judgment. Either then there is no infallible judge whom we about bound to believe with certitude, or a general council will be such a judge who cannot err. But if you say that there is no such judge whom we are bound to believe with certitude, what kind of Church, O Good God, will we have then have? how inconstant, how fluctuating, how hesitant? certainly more changeable than Proteus himself.[2] How will all faith of Christians not vacillate, if it be not certain who we ought to believe? And certainly if everyone were to consider well that it is a very powerful foment of all heresies to say that a general council duly summoned could err: because if that were admitted, all heresies condemned by the authority of councils will rise again, and no way will be found whereby we may remove them from the Church. For if one

---

[1] C. 54 (*Liber De Scriptoribus Ecclesiasticis*, c. 53 (PL 58, 1088B-1089A)).

[2] Proteus is a sea-god of Greek mythology who was said to be as changeable as the sea.

argue against them with Sacred Scriptures, they will immediately either completely reject them, denying them to be canonical, or they will interpret them falsely, and distort their meaning, just as they have done, and experience now teaches us that they so do. And so the face of the Church would be completely confused, ugly and wretched.

Furthermore, in general councils duly convoked, the Holy Ghost, their director and guide, is present, Who instructs them in the faith. Hence just as neither the Spirit assisting them cannot err, so likewise nor the councils themselves directed by Him. But that God assists the general councils themselves duly convoked is proved by that which the Lord says: "If two of you shall consent upon earth, concerning anything whatsoever they shall ask, it shall be done to them by my Father who is in heaven. For where there are two or three gathered together in my name, there am I in the midst of them" (Mt. 18, 19-20). But if you see this promise to two or three gathered in the name of Christ, what do you think will happen when a whole general council shall have been assembled? This appears more clearly from the Council of Jerusalem celebrated by the Apostles, where the Apostles gathered together to decide about the cessation of the observances of the Law, pronounced judgment as follows: "It hath seemed good to the Holy Ghost and to us," etc. (Acts 15, 28).

Again, the Church has the Holy Ghost assisting it and governing it. For so Christ promised: "But the Paraclete, the Holy Ghost, whom the Father will send in my name, he will teach you all things, and bring all things to your mind, whatsoever I shall have said to you" (Jn. 14, 26). For neither ought these words to be referred to the Apostles alone: nor that mission of the Holy Ghost (as Bernard says[1]) was made on account of the Apostles alone. For why were the languages of all nations necessary for the Apostles, unless because they were to teach all nations? And the Truth Itself says: "I am with you even to the consummation of the world" (Mt. 28, 20). Which saying nowise ought to be referred to the Apostles alone, since they were not to remain in this miserable life until the end of the world. But it was said to the whole Church, to which God promised that He would present until the end of the world.

Now Solomon, saying this previously in Christ's name, had predicted: "My vineyard is before me" (Cant. 8, 12). Thus, Christ always stands by the Church as a bridegroom dwelling with His bride, as the head remaining attached to its members, so that it may enliven and rule them. But a general council (as we taught in the beginning of this work) represents the universal Church. Thus God Himself stands by a general council, in which the universal Church is represented, teaching it all things necessary for salvation. Then if a general council (as we have said) represents the universal Church, it follows that a general council cannot err in faith and morals, because the Church which is represented by a general council, cannot err in faith or morals. For the Truth Itself says: "The gates of hell shall not prevail against it" (Mt. 16, 18). The gates of Hell are each mortal sin, by which there is entrance to Hell. But if the universal Church could err in faith and morals, the gates of Hell would have prevailed against it. And in John's Gospel the same Truth again says: "I will ask the Father, and he shall give you another Paraclete, that he may abide with you for ever" (14, 16). Which words ought not to be referred to the Apostles alone, but to the universal Church, to which He promised the presence of the Holy Ghost until the end of the world.

And the Blessed Apostle Paul says: "Husbands, love your wives, as Christ also loved the church, and delivered himself up for it: that he might sanctify it, cleansing it by the laver of water in the word of life: that he might present it to himself a glorious church, not having spot or wrinkle, or any such thing; but that it should be holy, and without blemish" (Eph. 5, 25-27).

---

[1] This quotation seems to be rather taken from Oger, Abbot of Lucedia, who belonged to the Cistercian Order at the time of St. Bernard. At the time of this writing, this sermon was still attributed to Saint Bernard. It is now found among the *Sermones XV de Verbis Domini in ultima Coena*, serm. 9, n. 12 (PL 184, 920).

If, then, Christ presented the Church without spot and without wrinkle, how could the stain of heresy or the spot of sin stain it? Again, Paul in another epistle likewise calls the Church "the pillar and ground of the truth" (I Tim. 3, 15): from which words it is proved that it itself could not be involved with any error. For it is not possible that it, which is "the pillar and ground of the truth," would err. Therefore, from these and very many other citations which could be cited, we have proved that a general council rightly (as is befitting) assembled, is unable to err in faith and morals.

Now we say that a council is consequently general and rightly assembled, when it is convoked by the authority of the supreme pontiff and all those are summoned to whom it belongs to decide the matter. Hence, it is not surprising if the council of Ariminum erred: because it was assembled by the Arian heretics, favoring Emperor Constantius, and he himself having been infected with the Arian heresy, notwithstanding Pope Liberius contradicting. Wherefore, Pope Damasus entirely rescinded all the acts of this council in a council later convoked in Rome. For the same reason the synod of Constantinople[1] celebrated under [Emperor] Constantine [V] and [Pope] Stephen III[2] is void and pernicious, because it was assembled with [Pope] Stephen III kept away,[3] and contrary to his intention and of other Catholics, it was voted there that images ought to be completely removed from the churches: and thus this synod was later condemned at the Seventh Ecumenical Council which was [the II Council] of Nicea, under the Empress Irene.

Nor is it necessary in order that a council be called general, that all Christians be summoned, but only those to whom it belongs to teach and rule, such are the chief men of the Church, such as the bishops and the like. For it belongs to these men to teach and not to others. And this is very consonant with reason. For if all could teach, if all could define, it would belong to all to pass judgment concerning the faith, and then the whole body would be one member: yet Paul says: "For the body also is not one member, but many. If the foot should say, because I am not the hand, I am not of the body; is it therefore not of the body? And if the ear should say, because I am not the eye, I am not of the body; is it therefore not of the body? If the whole body were the eye, where would be the hearing? If the whole were hearing, where would be the smelling? But now God hath set the members every one of them in the body as it hath pleased him. And if they all were one member, where would be the body? But now there are many members indeed, yet one body." (I Cor. 12, 14-20). And after some interjected words he adds: "Are all apostles? Are all prophets? Are all doctors?" (v. 29). From which words of Paul we have proved that certain men are chosen by God to teach and define: it is the role of other men, however, to be taught and to receive the teachings of others. Thus, all those men to whom it belongs to teach, rule and define, ought to be summoned, but not the mixed multitude. For when there was a dispute in the very beginning of the Church about the ceremonies of the Old Law, some saying that they ought to be kept at the same time with the Evangelical Law, others however affirming the contrary, a council was assembled in Jerusalem for this reason: to which only "the apostles and ancients assembled to consider of this matter" (Acts 15, 6): and yet the things that were decided there concerned everyone.

There is something very similar to this matter which the Lord commanded in the Old Law: "If thou perceive that there be among you a hard and doubtful matter in judgment between blood and blood, cause and cause, leprosy and leprosy: and thou see that the words of the judges within thy gates do vary: arise, and go up to the place, which the Lord thy God shall choose. And thou shalt come to the priests of the Levitical race, and to the judge, that shall be

---

[1] Also known as the Council of Hieria (A.D. 754).

[2] The text here mistaken has Pope Gregory III as being the pope of that time. Pope Stephen III has been renamed Stephen II since 1961.

[3] Rather, it is not known if the pope was invited to attend.

at that time: and thou shalt ask of them, and they shall shew thee the truth of the judgment. And thou shalt do whatsoever they shall say, that preside in the place, which the Lord shall choose, and what they shall teach thee, according to his law; and thou shalt follow their sentence: neither shalt thou decline to the right hand nor to the left hand" (Deut. 17, 8-11). You see here how the Lord sends us for removing every wound of doubt, not to kings, not to princes, not to the common people, but to the priests of the Levitical tribe, and especially to the high priest of that time, to whom, more that to anyone else, it pertains (as we have said at the beginning of this work) to define concerning the faith. Thus, the chief men of the Church ought to be called to a council, and not the mixed multitude.

But if someone, no matter how lowly among the people, were to come, even though he were not called to the council, saying that he has somethings which pertain to the common utility of all, doubtlessly he ought not to be despised, but rather ought to be heard, and afterwards it will belong to the chief men to define. Hence, Paul says in his First Epistle to the Corinthians: "If there be no interpreter, let him hold his peace in the church, and speak to himself and to God. And let the prophets speak, two or three; and let the rest judge. But if anything be revealed to another sitting, let the first hold his peace" (14, 28-30). From which words of Paul it is established that those ought to be heard, and not despised, who would wish to teach what was revealed to themselves. Thus, when all those to whom it pertains have been summoned and assembled by the authority of the supreme pontiff, a general council will be said to have been duly assembled. But if all those so assembled unanimously and with one mind, or the majority of them consent with the supreme pontiff: that will be a certain decision and ought to be held as an infallible definition of a general council.

In support of this I could have cited testimonies of holy Doctors and the decrees of councils, but I have omitted to do so, because we are treating against those condemning councils, who will say to the council defining about itself: "Thou givest testimony of thyself: thy testimony is not true" (Jn. 8, 13). Nevertheless [Saint] John [Fisher], Bishop of Rochester wrote briefly enough in that work which he made against Luther's *Babylonian Captivity*,[1] namely chapters twenty-eight and twenty-nine. Also, the very learned Josse van Clichtove wrote in that work which he composed in support of the assertion of the truths defined at the Synod of Sens against Luther.[2] Sixty years previously, Denis the Carthusian of Ryckel [in Belgium] wrote *De auctoritate Concilii* in three books. I have not seen, however, the work of this author, but I have this by the testimony of Trithemius in his book, *De scriptoribus Ecclesiasticis*.[3] William of Ockham in his books of *Diologues* treats of this matter more profusely than he should have, and I do not know whether as well as the truth demands: because everything that he treats there, he leaves so unsettled, that you do not know which side he is on.[4] Jean Gerson also published many tracts, in which he discusses the power of the Church and the authority of Councils.[5] Juan de Torquemada, in his book, *De summa Ecclesiae*, Johann Eck, and many others treat this matter very plentifully.

---

[1] *Confutatio Assertionis Lutheranae*, written against Luther's *Defense and Explanation of all the Articles*, and not against Luther's *Babylonian Captivity*, as mentioned previously in a footnote.

[2] *Compendium veritatum ad fidem pertinentium contra erroneas Lutheranorum assertiones ex dictis et actis in concilio provinciali Senonensi apud Parisios celebrato* (Paris, in officina Henri Estienne Simon de Colines, 1529), c. 3.

[3] *De scriptoribus Ecclesiasticis* (Basil, J. Amerbach, 1494), fol. 118r.

[4] William of Ockham is a founder of Nominalism, a philosophical error which denies the existence of universals.

[5] *De potestate Ecclesiae, De Concilio Constantiensi, De Concilio unius obedientiae*, etc.

COITUS

Intercourse

Concerning this matter there was a bestial and disgraceful error. For the Simon the Magician, concerning whom there is mention in the Acts of the Apostles, taught that the promiscuous use of women was licit, such that anyone could make use of which without sin. A certain Saturninus[1] taught the same depravity about the same time in Syria. The Nicolaites were in the same error: wherefore it is said concerning them in the Apocalypse: "This thou hast, that thou hatest the deeds of the Nicolaites, which I also hate" (2, 6). These Nicolaites took an occasion of their error from Nicholas, who was one of the seven deacons who were assigned to the care of widows with [Saint] Stephen. For he when he was rebuked by the Apostles concerning his jealousy for the very beautiful wife, which he had, in order that that he might purge himself of jealously in front of the Apostles, he brought forth his wife in public saying that he who wished, could use her: by this he wished to show that he was not as jealous as they had accused him. From which deed, others taking occasion thought that it was permitted for anyone to use what women he wished: boasting that they had their origin from this Nicholas, they were called Nicolaites. Nevertheless, if anyone desires to know more about this, he may read Eusebius in the third book of his *Ecclesiastical History*, chapter twenty-nine.[2]

Philastrius also relates that there was such a custom among the Florinians, such that in the church after sunset, when the lamps were extinguished, promiscuously taking the women they wished they copulated with them.[3] But Augustine does not attribute this error to the Florinians, although he speak about them in *De Haeresibus ad Quodvultdeum*,[4] unless perhaps they are different from those about whom Philastrius speaks, because they are called Florians by Philastrius: but those whom Augustine mentions are called Florinians by him, so named from Florinus, a teacher of theirs. Now who was the leader of these Florinians, and at what time did he live, Philastrius does not say, nor could I find out in the writings of another author.

Certain men in Bohemia called the Adamites revived this same error of promiscuous intercourse, the chief and leader of who was a certain Picard from Belgic Gaul. For he (as Aeneas Sylvius says in his book, *De origine Bohemorum*[5]) entered Bohemia under the Holy Roman Emperor Sigismund, who by some deceptions drew to himself numerous people of men and women, whom ordering to walk naked, he called Adamites, but he called himself the son of God, commanded that he be called Adam. He permitted promiscuous intercourse for the Adamites: although without his consent it would be a crime to know a woman, but whenever anyone was enflamed with burning lust towards some woman, he took her by the hand, and approaching the chief, he said that he desired her. Having heard this, that Picard chief of theirs replied: "Go, increase and be multiplied." The Waldensians taught this same heresy, but with more obscene and unmentionable wickedness. For they (as Guy the Carmelite relates about them[6]) said with burning lust of the flesh, all carnal intercourse between both men and between women is licit.

---

[1] Saturninus was a native of Antioch and a disciple of Simon the magician.
[2] PG 20, 275C-278B.
[3] C. 57 (PL 12, 1173A).
[4] C. 66 (PL 42, 42).
[5] Chapter 41.
[6] *Summa de haeresibus et earum confutationibus*, fol. 87r, c. 18.

And I certainly am amazed at what could come into the mind of men, I do not say that I am amazed that they would do such a thing, but that they would believe that it could be licitly done. For I am certain that there were some liers with mankind, because Sacred Scriptures bear witness to this: but I can hardly believe that those do doing, would not believe that they are acting wickedly, or would not at least fear, their own consciences accusing them. For the Natural Law, which is implanted in the hearts of all men, is known with no one teaching, teaches that this unmentionable and most wicked crime must be avoided.

The Anabaptists, the most obscene and shameless of all heretics, teach in our time this heresy of the Adamites, adding in addition that the woman is obliged to having intercourse with any man choosing her, and vice versa with the same bond they bind every man to rendering as much to any woman asking them from him. All these heretics are convicted of a lie, if they will show from Sacred Writ that any intercourse is licit besides that which is had between a man and his own wife after marriage.

Now in order that this may appear more clearly, it ought to be firstly supposed that all possible intercourse that can be had is only of three kinds, namely either with an animal, or with a male or female human. Intercourse with an animal is condemned by the Natural Law, and God condemned it by the written Law saying: "Thou shalt not copulate with any beast, neither shalt thou be defiled with it. A woman shall not lie down to a beast, nor copulate with it: because it is a heinous crime" (Lev. 18, 23). And in the same book He again says: "He that shall copulate with any beast or cattle, dying let him die, the beast also ye shall kill. The woman that shall lie under any beast, shall be killed together with the same: their blood be upon them" (20, 15-16). The same Law also condemns intercourse with a male human. For He destroyed both cities Sodom and Gomorrha with fire, such that when Lot had left, all men, from the greatest to the least, were burned on account of this sin. And in Leviticus the Lord says: "Thou shalt not lie with mankind as with womankind, because it is an abomination" (18, 22). And again: "If any one lie with a man as with a woman, both have committed an abomination, let them be put to death: their blood be upon them" (20, 13). And the Apostle when speaking about the Gentiles says: "For this cause God delivered them up to shameful affections. For their women have changed the natural use into that use which is against nature. And, in like manner, the men also, leaving the natural use of the women, have burned in their lusts one towards another, men with men working that which is filthy" (Rom. 1, 26-27).

And I here call intercourse with a man, even if he copulate with a woman as with a man. For that intercourse is also against nature, and thus condemned. For all intercourse, which according to its kind or manner generation cannot be had, is reproved by the Natural Law. For the end to which Nature ordained intercourse is the generation and multiplication of the species: wherefore all such intercourse which takes place in such a manner that it would be impossible to have the generation of offspring from it, is condemned by the Natural Law. Therefore, this ought to suffice against the very obscene Waldensians.

Only the intercourse of a man with a woman remains. Now this intercourse may take place in three ways. For either someone copulates with her who is joined by marriage with him, or with her who is also joined by married to another, or he copulates with an unmarried woman, namely who is not married to another. If he copulates with the wife of another, such intercourse is called adultery, and is condemned by Divine law. For so the Divine law says: "If any man commit adultery with the wife of another, and defile his neighbour's wife, let them be put to death, both the adulterer and the adulteress" (Lev. 20, 10). And the Truth Itself lists adultery in the Gospel among the evils which defile a man. "From the heart come forth evil thoughts, murders, adulteries, fornications, thefts" etc. (Mt. 15, 19). But intercourse with an unmarried woman, who has been bound with no law of matrimony, is called fornication: and this intercourse is also condemned by Divine law, as appears from the Savior's saying just cited, where among the things which defile a man, after adulteries also lists fornications.

Yet the Greeks (as Guy [the Carmelite] accuses them[1]) say that simple fornication is not a sin. Martin le Maistre in his book, *De temperantis*, says that he admits that simple fornication is a mortal sin: yet he in addition says that to believe the opposite is not heretical, because (as he says), the testimonies of Scripture are not explicit, because even if fornication is forbidden in many passages, still those words cannot be interpreted such that the word "fornication" is universally taken for lust in general and because there are many species of that evil, hence he says that fornication understood by this name is condemned, because lust is evil *ex genere suo*.[2] But, to speak in his favor, I believe that Martin le Maistre, an otherwise learned man, erred in this regard, because, as we have said elsewhere, with Blessed Jerome supporting us,[3] the Gospel consists in the literal meaning, and not in the mere words [*nuda verba*].

Wherefore we have said that the interpretation of Scripture does not pertain to just anyone, but to the Church alone: or if such power resides in a particular person, it is in the supreme pontiff alone. Thus the Church which has the right and power of distinguishing Sacred Scriptures from profane writings, also has the power of distinguishing the true and legitimate meaning from the untrue meaning. Certainly it would have profited nothing to know certain writings are Divine Scripture, if afterwards we were to accept in the same Scripture a false meaning for the true. Hence, just as we believe the Church Teaching that this or that writing is Divine: so also it is necessary to believe the same Church Teaching that this or that is the meaning of the same Scripture. But the Catholic Church teaches that simple fornication is a sin, contrary to the Divine law, therefore it must be held that fornication is forbidden by the Divine law: and so it is necessary that someone is a heretic who pertinaciously shall say that simple fornication is not a sin. Furthermore, the common opinion of all the sacred Doctors about the same matter determines the faith, because even if many of them have erred in some matters, still it cannot happen that all would err in unison. For how is it possible that all would err, who (as Paul says[4]) who have been given to us by God lest we go astray? But the common opinion of all the holy Doctors is that simple fornication is a mortal sin, and no one ever asserted the opposite, among those who have been approved by the Church.

But now let us see whether the word "fornication" can always be taken in Sacred Write to mean lust in general. Firstly, it is certainly established that nowise can it be so understood in those words of the Savior, which we cited shortly above, unless we were to attribute inept speech to Christ. For He says the following: "From the heart come forth evil thoughts, murders, adulteries, fornications." Notice that He subjoined fornications after adultery. Now who,

---
[1] *Summa de haeresibus et earum confutationibus*, fol. 26v, c. 21.
[2] *De temperantia et luxuria Liber*, (Paris, 1511). Martin Le Maistre (1432-1482) was a professor of theology at the University of Paris as well as the chaplain and confessor to King Louis XI. He fell into this error through Probablism. Note here that some sins do not admit of slight matter, and these are mortal sins "from their whole nature" (*ex toto genere suo*), such as lust and blasphemy. In other sins the matter is not always grave, as in theft or injustice, and these are mortal "from their nature" (*ex genere suo*). Martin Le Maistre wrongly claimed here that the sin of fornication was merely a mortal sin *ex genere suo*.
[3] See the *Introduction* (chapter four) above: "Jerome says when commenting on the Epistle to the Galatians: 'Let us not suppose that the essence of the Gospel is in the words, rather than in the actual meaning of Scripture: or on the surface, rather than in the inmost parts: or in the leaves of the words, and not in the root of the meaning.'" (Bk. 1, Chap. 1, verse 11-12 (PL 26, 322C)).
[4] "And he gave some apostles, and some prophets, and other some evangelists, and other some pastors and doctors, for the perfecting of the saints, for the work of the ministry, for the edifying of the body of Christ: until we all meet into the unity of faith" (Eph. 4, 11-13).

except someone speaking ineptly, after having related the species would have afterwards added the genus of that species? The species, however, is fittingly added after the genus. For no one speaking rightly would say the following: "These many things were taken from the house, namely clothes, dishes, rams, and sheep. For by the very fact that rams are named, sheep are understood, because rams are sheep. Thus, when Christ subjoined fornications after adulteries: it is an indication that fornication cannot be understood as taking the place of the genus, such that it would signify all lust of the flesh: nor may it be taken to mean adultery, because it would be a useless repetition of the same thing.

Furthermore, Paul lists those vices of the flesh in this same order. For so it is said in the Epistle to the Galatians[1] according to the reading of [Ambrosiaster]: "The works of the flesh are manifest, which are adultery, fornication."[2] In which quotation fornication is again found after adultery, and hence it is necessary that it not be taken for adultery, nor for lust in general, but for a species distinct from adultery. Again, in the First Epistle to the Corinthians he says the following: "Do not err: neither fornicators, nor idolaters, nor adulterers, nor the effeminate, nor liers with mankind, nor thieves, nor covetous, nor drunkards, nor railers, nor extortioners, shall possess the kingdom of God" (6, 9-10). But no one having the use of reason is excluded from the kingdom of God except on account of mortal sin. Nor can it be said here that fornication is put for the genus of any type of carnal lust: because the rest of the species of lust would then be superfluously added, namely adulterers, the effeminate, liers with mankind: because by denying the genus, all the species of the genus are denied: just as if you were to say there is no animal in that house, by that same statement you have denied that there is a man, or horse or any brute animal there.

Moreover, if the word fornication is put for the genus, and not for the species, and every fornicator is forbidden to enter the kingdom of God: it follows that he who commits simple fornication (as they say), is prohibited from the kingdom of God, because simple fornication is a species of lust. Thus by denying the genus, the species is also denied. Hence, from these things is sufficiently evident that intercourse of an unmarried man with an unmarried woman, which it is called fornication, is forbidden by Divine law. Therefore, only intercourse which is of man with his own wife is lawful. Hence, promiscuous intercourse is explicitly forbidden by Divine law. For what intercourse can be more correctly called promiscuous than that which harlots undergo? Because they are prepared to copulate with anyone. And the intercourse of harlots is properly called fornication, from the brothels [*fornicibus*] in which harlots are accustomed to dwell.[3] Now such intercourse is forbidden by Divine law: "There shall be," the Lord says, "no whore among the daughters of Israel, nor whoremonger among the sons of Israel" (Deut. 23, 17). The passage afterwards continues, "because both these are an abomination to the Lord thy God" (v. 18). Add to this that if promiscuous intercourse were licit, and (as the disgraceful and obscene Florinians were doing) men would promiscuously copulate with women in the church with lamps extinguished, it would often happen that a son would have intercourse with his mother, a father with his daughter, which nature abhors, and Divine law condemns. Therefore, these things having been said suffice against all the aforesaid heretics.

There is a **second heresy** completely opposite to the preceding one, because it condemns all intercourse, saying that all intercourse is illicit. And many heretics concur with this opin-

---

[1] "Now the works of the flesh are manifest, which are fornication, uncleanness," etc. (Gal. 5, 19).

[2] *Commentaria in Epistolam ad Galatas*, c. 5 (PL 17, 368B).

[3] In Latin, the term *fornix* means arch or vault. In Ancient Rome, prostitutes waited for their customers out of the rain under vaulted ceilings, and *fornix* became a euphemism for brothels, and the Latin verb *fornicare* referred to a man visiting a brothel.

ion. But we will treat this matter below in the section on "Marriage," where we will prove, with God as our Guide, that marriages are licit and approved by God.

A **third heresy** teaches that carnal intercourse with burning lust of the flesh is not a sin, but an honorable kiss is a sin: because (as they say) nature does not incline to this, however, there is some natural instigation to this. And this is one of the heresies which the Beguines and the Beghards assert. Now this error involves two errors joined together. One is that by the flesh instigating carnal intercourse is not a sin, and these heretics and the Waldensians concur on this, whom we have already vanquished in the first heresy. The other error is that a kiss is a sin, even if they speak about any kiss which they call a true kiss, because a kiss by the fact that it is a solicitation for intercourse, is a sin, just as the intercourse itself is a sin. For every action is directed by its goal, and receives its classification, such that if the end is good, and the other things are present, the action is good. If the end is bad, then the action is bad. Thus, every kiss which is directed to soliciting the flesh is a sin.

But if they say about any kiss, that every kind is a sin, the error is clear, because a kiss which is given as a sign of peace and true love, such a kiss is not merely not a sin, but is rather an act of virtue, just as the peace itself of which it is a sign. For the disciples of Christ when kissing each other, were giving a sign of peace and true love. Wherefore Judas had given this sign to the Jews, saying: "Whomsoever I shall kiss, that is he, hold him fast" (Mt. 26, 48). For when Christ's disciples returned to Christ from somewhere, they used to give a kiss to His face as a sign of peace. Judas also did this, so that he might betray Christ with such a sign. Christ said to him: "Dost thou betray the Son of man with a kiss?" (Lk. 22, 48). Furthermore, not every kiss which is given for the sake of soliciting the flesh is a sin, especially if that intercourse is directed to whom it is licit, and happens with spouses. For if the wife demands from her husband that he have intercourse with her, and so that he may give this debt to his wife, the husband kisses his wife, namely so that the flesh may be excited by this to rendering the debt which he could not otherwise render, not only is it not a sin, but an act of virtue, just as the intercourse itself is also an act of justice, since by it the husband renders to his wife what is hers.

Finally, this opinion of the Beguines was condemned in the Council of Vienne celebrated under Clement V: the definition of which council is in the volume of the Clementine Decretals under the title *De haereticis*, chapter *Ad nostrum*, where eight errors of the Beguines are condemned, the error about which we treat, is listed in the seventh place by these words: "Seventh, that a woman's kiss, since nature does not incline to this, is a mortal sin; but the carnal act, since nature inclines to this, is not a sin, especially when the one exercising it is tempted."[1] Which error was condemned at the same time with the seven others listed there.

CONFESSIO

Confession

The confession of sins is a very difficult thing, whereby the sinner says all his sins to the priest, whispering into his ear, and nothing is found harder or more burdensome in the whole Evangelical law: hence, due to the difficulty of the work, many heretics not taking care of their own salvation or the salvation of others, have attempted to completely uproot it, yet they have tried to attack it in various ways.

---

[1] *Clementinarum*, bk. 5, tit. 3, c. 3. Dz. 477.

Thus, there is a **first error** about this matter, which denies that it was instituted by God, but rather established by merely human creation. A certain Peter [Martinez] de Osma,[1] a professor of theology at the University of Salamanca, taught this error in Spain. His Grace Alfonso Carrillo [de Acuña], Archbishop of Toledo and primate of the Spains,[2] after having taken council with many learned men, condemned this error, and declared it heretical by the authority specially delegated to him for this purpose by the Supreme Pontiff Sixtus IV. Sixtus afterwards likewise confirmed this definition: we will refer to his confirmation at the end of this heresy. This is also Luther's error: yea even before Luther some experts of Canon Law gave an occasion for this error. For the glossator of the decree at the beginning of the fifth distinction says concerning Penance that it is better to believe that the auricular confession of sins was instituted by a tradition of the universal Church, than by the authority of the New or Old Testament.

A **second error** is that which says that it is not necessary to confess to a priest, but it suffices to confess sins to God alone. This the error of certain Eastern heretics who are called the Jacobites,[3] and Luther follows them, saying that this secret confession which is whispered to the priest is not necessary, but it suffices that one would confess to God alone. He deduces this error from the first, as putrid water from a corrupt spring. For when the testimonies of Scripture commanding the confession of sins were cited, he interpreted them as pertaining to the confession which is to God, which he says is commanded by Divine law, and that it suffices. The third error says that Confession is superfluous and useless if contrition is present: and the author of this heresy is John Wycliffe. The fourth error says that it an examination of all sins is not necessary, nor ought all mortal sins be confessed, because (as Luther says) when we wish to clearly confess everything, we do nothing other than that we wish to leave nothing to be forgotten by God's mercy. The fifth error completely takes away Confession, and this is the error of the Waldensians, which coincides with the error of the Jacobites and Lutherans. There is a sixth error saying that in Confession grace, whereby a man is justified, is not conferred: and so it denies that Confession can be called a sacrament. And Luther teaches this error.

I have thus put together all these errors on purpose for the sake of avoiding prolixity, because the testimonies which we are about to cite refute at the same time sometimes two errors and other times three errors: hence lest we repeat the same quotation two or three times, we have joined these errors all together, so that when the testimony of some authority has been cited, we may point out in it all the things which fight against the errors. I omit the testimonies for this subject which could be cited from the Old Testament, because all the testimonies which could be cited on this subject from thence are so obscure that although they may support our position, still they cannot show it clearly. I also omit those which in the New Testament are said somewhat figuratively or as it were in a veiled manner. For example: Christ said to the ten lepers asking for their health from Him: "Go, shew yourselves to the priests" (Lk. 17, 14). And to the leper whom when descending down the mountain He purified with the touch of His hand He said: "See thou tell no man: but go, shew thyself to the priest, and offer your gift" (Mt. 8, 4). From which words even if it can be said that Confession is designated, because sin is symbolized by leprosy, wherefore by causing the leprosy to be

---

[1] Pedro Martínez de Osma (1427-1480) was a Spanish theologian and philosopher, known for his views on indulgences, which he retracted at the end of his life. He was born in Osma.

[2] It was until the union of the crowns of Castilla and Aragón that in both kingdoms the name *Las Españas* ("The Spains") started to be used to encompass the peninsular lands of both kingdoms. Only at the birth of Phillip II in 1527 was the name España used to encompass the confederated kingdom: for at his birth, he was proclaimed "Prince of Spain," the first of the combined monarchy proclaimed as such.

[3] The Jacobites are the Monophysites of Syria who derived their power of Orders from an ordained monk named James.

shown to the priest, it is shown that the confession of sins ought to be made to the priest: and that one cleansed from leprosy still ought to be shown to the priest, signifies that one cleansed from sin through contrition, still ought to show the remaining stains of the sins by making a confession to the priest: I say these things, even if they may be said piously, nevertheless are not effective for refuting a heretic: because no sense of Sacred Scripture (as we taught in the beginning of this work) is effective for strengthening the faith, and conquering heretics, unless it be the literal sense. For an effective argument against heretics can never be made from the mystical sense. But it is very clear that in that passage the sense is mystical. That which Christ said to the Apostles after Lazarus was raised is similar: "Loose him, and let him go" (Jn. 11, 44). From which it can also be inferred that although through the grace conferred by God in contrition the sinner is raised from the death of sin, nonetheless he is handed over bound to the priest to be loosed, so that he may be absolved from the bond by which he is held to a certain punishment for the satisfaction of sin. These things are certainly pious, and help much the faith of the Catholic Church: but because they are not so clear, it follows that they are not as effective as they need to be.

What can be cited more efficaciously and powerfully from the whole Holy Testament (at least in my opinion) are those words which Christ said to His disciples after His Resurrection: "Whose sins you shall forgive, they are forgiven them; and whose sins you shall retain, they are retained" (Jn. 20, 23). Which words need to be considerately discussed, because we can gather many supporting arguments for ourselves from these words. Firstly then it is said, "Whose sins you shall forgive, they are forgiven them." By which words according to the opinion of all the sacred Doctors He gave power to priests of absolving men from their sins. But priests cannot forgive sins, unless they firstly know them: because he who is going to pass judgment on some matter must first fully know that matter, as the Wise Man says: he who judges what he knows, is a judge of justice.[1] The sins of others, however, especially those which were committed secretly and within the hidden recesses of the heart, priests are unable to know, unless the sinners themselves reveal their sins to the priests. Thus, He Who gave the power of forgiving sins to priests, by those same words enjoined upon sinners the obligation of confessing their sins.

But someone will perhaps respond to this argument that from the Savior's words it can only be maintained that confession falls under His counsels as a good work, and most conducive for salvation: when that confession has been made priests have the power of absolving, which was conferred upon them by Christ by those words. But this response is easily rejected by that which is immediately added after those words: "whose sins you shall retain, they are retained." That priests retain sins is certainly nothing other than not to forgive. Hence the meaning of the verse is: "Whose sins you will not remit, they are not remitted." Thus, if in order that sins be remitted it is necessary that a priest remit them: then in order that sins be remitted, it is also necessary that the sinner manifest them to the priest.

Again, what if someone would perhaps say that from these words the necessity of secret confession cannot be maintained, which now is whispered to the priest: I do not dispute about this matter, provided that they concede that the necessity of Confession is maintained from these words, whether it be secret or public: because (as Jacques Masson contends far and wide against Luther[2]) the Sacrament of Penance can consist in both. For it is not so necessary for the Sacrament of Penance that the confession be done secretly, such that if it were done

---

[1] "He that speaketh that which he knoweth, sheweth forth justice" (Prov. 12, 17).

[2] He wrote that among the early Christians there were three kinds of Sacramental Penance: "secret, public and solemn." *Articulorum doctrinae fratris M. Lutheri per theologos Lovanienses damnatorum ratio ex sacris literis et veteribus tractatoribus.*

publicly it would not be a Sacrament: although one would act badly who were to confess publicly, unless there were to be some particular good reason urging.

Furthermore, from the words: "Whose sins you shall forgive, they are forgiven them" it is proved that grace is infused by God through the absolution of the priest. For when the priest is forgiving ministerially, God truly then forgives the sins. But since the remission of sins is never had without sanctifying grace: it follows that as often as the priest absolves the penitent, that many times God infused grace. But if grace is infused by God through it, it follows that it can rightly be called a Sacrament, because after the sensible words signifying the absolution of sins, if the sinner does not place an obstacle, the infusion of grace efficaciously follows. Thus, from these words we conclude many things, namely that confession is necessary, against the Waldensians: and it ought not to be made only to God, but also to the priest who is about to absolve the penitent from his sins, and this is against the Jacobites. We also have through confession grace infused, and hence it is a Sacrament, and this is against Luther.

Again, if confession was introduced by mere human invention, and by Divine precept, let them who say this show that it was a primitive fabrication of the Church: which since they do not know nor can show, it is necessary that they acknowledge that it is from God. For just as these men require of us clear testimony of Scripture, whereby we may prove that confession was instituted by God: so we require of them clear and true history, whereby they may teach that it was a primitive fabrication of the Church concerning making confession. We have brought forth the testimony from John's Gospel for our faith. In order that they, however, may teach that it was instituted by the Church, they will never show its first establishment by the Church.

But if someone were to say that it was instituted at the [IV] Lateran Council, in which was made that very famous Canon which begins: *Omnis utriusque sexus*.[1] I would easily believe this, if the objection was referring to annually making a confession, because before that Canon I do not know whether men were obliged to making a confession each year. But if it be simply said concerning confession that it began in the Church from the time of this council: it is evident that this is false, because Pope Innocent III, under whom this council was celebrated and the Canon was promulgated, attained the papacy (as [Bartolomeo] Platina says[2]) about the year of the Lord 1200, and before which lived Augustine, Jerome, and many others, who say that confession is necessary: and it is evident that it was practiced at the time of the Apostles. Accordingly, in the Acts of the Apostles it is said: "And many of them that believed, came confessing and declaring their deeds" (19, 18).

Next, the Catholic Church cannot err in those things which pertain to the faith and good morals. But the concordant opinion of all the sacred Doctors on some matter (as we taught in the beginning of this work) clearly shows it to be the mind and the explanation of the Church: because when there shall have been many Doctors equally distinguished in holiness as well as in knowledge living in different times and different places, who subscribe to the same opinion, whose opinion the Church has never condemned, but is silent regarding their assertion, which is never accustomed to keep silence about heresies that ought to be condemned, it is thence proved that that opinion to which all the Doctors subscribe, is the true mind of the Catholic Church and the true faith. When therefore there is a concordant opinion of the all the holy Doctors that the confession of all mortal sins which the sinner remembers must necessarily be made to a priest, and without which there can be no salvation, and that it was instituted

---

[1] Canon 21. This Canon commands every Christian who has reached the years of discretion to confess all his, or her, sins at least once a year to his, or her, own (i.e. parish) priest. It did no more than confirm earlier legislation and custom, and has been often but wrongly, quoted as commanding for the first time the use of sacramental confession. Dz. 437. Greg. IX *Decr.*, lib. 5, tit. 38, c. 12.

[2] *The Lives of the Popes*, vol. 2, p. 68-73.

by Christ: it is hence evident that this is the Catholic faith, namely that the confession of sins is of Divine precept and not introduced by human precept.

I omit in this matter Bernard, Hugo and Richard of Saint Victor, Bede, Rabanus, Isidore as well as Gregory, because the testimonies of these men is very well known. I pass on to the older authorities. Pope Leo I, in his letter to Theodore, Bishop of Forum Julii, says the following: "The manifold mercy of God so assists men when they fall, that not only by the grace of Baptism but also by the remedy of penitence is the hope of eternal life revived, in order that they who have violated the gifts of the second birth, condemning themselves by their own judgment, may attain to remission of their crimes, the provisions of the Divine Goodness having so ordained that God's indulgence cannot be obtained without the supplications of priests. For the Mediator between God and men, the Man Christ Jesus, has transmitted this power to those that are set over the Church that they should both grant a course of penitence to those who confess, and, when they are cleansed by wholesome correction admit them through the door of reconciliation to communion in the Sacraments. In which work assuredly the Saviour Himself unceasingly takes part and is never absent from those things, the carrying out of which He has committed to His ministers. saying: 'Behold I am with you all days, even to the consummation of the world' (Mt. 28, 20) so that whatever is accomplished through our service in due order and with satisfactory results we doubt not to have been vouchsafed through the Holy Ghost."[1] In which words many suitable things ought to be noticed which serve our purpose. For when He said, "the provisions of the Divine Goodness having so ordained," he intimates that it was not introduced by human arrangement, but was ordained by Divine law. But when he says, "God's indulgence cannot be obtained without the supplications of priests," he shows the necessity of confession. Now when he says that God always assists at the absolution and ministry of priests, he clearly enough stated the efficacy of the Sacrament.

Augustine says the following: "All you who have dishonored your wives with illicit intercourse, do the penance which is done in the Church, so that the Church may pray for you. Let no one say to himself, 'I repent before God, I will perform it secretly within my own heart; God will pardon me, as knowing my sincerity.' For at this rate, the keys would in vain be given to the Church; and the powers of binding and loosing would signify nothing. And shall we thus go about to defeat the Gospel, and to vacate the words of Christ our Savior? or shall we cheat you with a promise of granting you what He hath denied you?"[2] By which words he clearly says that the absolution of the priest is necessary, thus the confession of sins is necessary, because a priest cannot absolve sins which he has not known. And although he says the same thing in many other places, nevertheless he explains the same opinion more explicitly in his tractate forty-nine on John.[3] Let him see who wishes. For it is enough for me, who have promised to maintain brevity, as I have reminded the reader.

Jerome when expounding the passage, "If a serpent bite in silence" etc. says the following: "If the serpent, the devil, has secretly and without the knowledge of a third person, bitten anyone, and has infused into him the poison of sin; if unwilling to disclose his wound to his

---

[1] Letter 108, c. 2 (PL 54, 1011B-1012A).

[2] Sermon 392, c. 3 (PL 39,1711).

[3] "While you despise [Christ], you lie in the arms of death; and if your contempt reaches the lengths I have mentioned, you are buried as well: but when you make confession, you come forth. For what is this coming forth, but the open acknowledgment you make of your state, in quitting, as it were, the old refuges of darkness? But the confession you make is effected by God, when He cries with a loud voice, or in other words, calls you in abounding grace. Accordingly, when the dead man had come forth, still bound; confessing, yet guilty still; that his sins also might be taken away, the Lord said to His servants: Loose him, and let him go. What does He mean by such words? 'Whatsoever you shall loose on earth shall be loosed in heaven' (Mt. 16, 19)." (c. 24 (PL 35, 1757)).

brother or master, he is silent and will not do penance, his master, who has a tongue ready to cure him, can render him no service. For if the one who is ill is ashamed to make known his wound to the physician, the physician does not remedy what he does not know."[1] By which words he very clearly shows the necessity of confession, such that without it the wound of sin could not be cured.

Ambrose, when arguing against the Novatians denying that Penance can benefit sinners, says the following: "Why do you baptize if sins cannot be remitted by man? If Baptism is certainly the remission of all sins, what difference does it make whether priests claim that this power is given to them in penance or at the font? In each the mystery is one. But you say that the grace of the mysteries works in the font. What works, then, in Penance? Does not the name of God do the work? What then? Do you, when you choose, claim for yourselves the grace of God, and when you choose reject it?"[2] In which words Blessed Ambrose teaches very clearly that in Penance as well as in Baptism grace is conferred through the ministry of priests. Penance is never made complete through the ministry of priests except when the priest absolves the sinner confessing his sins. Therefore, through the Sacrament of Penance, that is through confession, a man receives grace: Luther says the opposite of this in the sixth error mentioned above. Ambrose likewise teaches the necessity of this Sacrament in book two of *Concerning Repentance*, chapter seven.[3] I skip these words to avoid prolixity, thinking it sufficient to refer the reader.

Blessed Cyprian when speaking of those who have sinned in their hearts says the following: "They who, although bound by no crime of sacrifice to idols or of certificate, yet, since they have even thought of such things, with grief and simplicity confess this very thing to God's priests, and make the conscientious avowal, put off from them the load of their minds, and seek out the salutary medicine even for slight and moderate wounds."[4] And he says shortly afterwards: "I entreat you, beloved brethren, that each one should confess his own sin, while he who has sinned is still in this world, while his confession may be received, while the satisfaction and remission made by the priests are pleasing to the Lord."[5] We conclude two things from these words of Cyprian. One thing, namely, is that confession ought to be made before God's priests, and not merely before God. The other is that it ought not to be done merely for public sins, but also for hidden sins which were committed within the recesses of the heart. Luther teaches the opposite of this. Concerning other hidden sins, however, which are so hidden that they are unknown to the sinner himself, or because he does not remember them, or because he firmly believes, through excusable ignorance, that they are not sins, about this, I say, we do not maintain that they need to be confessed. For no one was ever so senseless that he would think that the things which the penitent does not recall also need to be whispered to the priest.

But Luther cites this in his favor, saying that it is not necessary to confess everything, because (as he says) doing so leaves nothing to God's mercy to be forgiven: this is as if he were to say that it is also not necessary to so endeavor that all our good deeds may be done well, since so doing we would want much less to leave something to God's mercy: wherefore by that argument Luther would also persuade men not to want to do everything well. The same argument, whereby Luther now attempts to prove his impious assertion, Paul makes as an objection to himself, and condemns and rejects it as worthless and having no weight at all. For

---

[1] *Commentarius in Ecclesiasten* (PL 23, 1096B). The first lines are quoted in the Catechism of the Council of Trent (Qualities of Confession). The last line is cited by the Council of Trent (Dz. 899).

[2] *Concerning Repentance*, bk. 1, c. 8, n. 36-37 (PL 16, 477B-C).

[3] PL 16, 510B-512D.

[4] *On the Lapsed*, c. 28 (PL 4, 488B).

[5] *Ibid.* c. 29 (PL 4, 489A).

after Paul had said that God's Divine grace is much greater than our sins: such that "where sin abounded," he says, "grace did more abound" (Rom. 5, 20), he objects to himself saying the following: "What shall we say, then? shall we continue in sin, that grace may abound? God forbid." (6, 1-2).

It could perhaps come into the mind of some unlearned man that it is permitted for a man to sin, so that God might afterwards impart more abundant grace. Yet Paul does not admit this opinion, but deems it most absurd, saying: God forbid. It is never permitted, he says, to do evil so that there may come good.[1] Now so that Luther may understand that this is Paul's opinion, let him listen to Chrysostom interpreting these words of Paul, who says these words: "Since then he showed the greatness of the grace by the greatness of the sins it healed, and owing to this it seemed in the eyes of the unthinking to be an encouragement to sin (for if the reason, they would say, why greater grace was shown, was because we had done great sins, let us not give over sinning, that grace may be more displayed still), now that they might not say this or suspect it, see how he turns the objection back again. First he does it by his deprecation. 'God forbid.' And this he is in the habit of doing at things confessed on all hands to be absurd."[2] Add also to this that if sinners were to confess all sins, they still leave them all to God's mercy to be forgiven: because even if sinners were to confess all their sins, still God exercises immense mercy, remitting all the sins, since even if we were to perform all works howsoever meticulously, He shows us great mercy, since He accepts them for eternal life: because "the sufferings of this time are not worthy to be compared with the glory to come, that shall be revealed in us" (Rom. 8, 18).

But lest we seem to have taken testimonies from the Latin Doctors alone, it will be worthwhile to cite testimonies of some Greek Doctors. Origen[3] when expounding the passage: "If one shall have committed one of these sins, he will declare that he has sinned,"[4] says the following: "There is something marvelous in this mystery when it commands 'to confess sin.' And indeed, everything we do of any kind is to be proclaimed and brought out in public. If we do anything in secret, also if we commit anything secretly either in a single word or even an inward thought, it is necessary for everything to be revealed, for everything to be confessed. Indeed, it must be confessed either by us or by him, the accuser and inciter of sin."[5] You see here how he commands that everything be made known, and permits nothing to be concealed, if we wish to evade the devil's accusation.

[Pseudo-] Chrysostom, when speaking about those who were baptized by John, confessing their sins, says the following: "Confession of sins is the testimony of a conscience that fears God. Whoever fears the judgment of God is not ashamed to confess his sins, but whoever is ashamed to confess them does not fear God's judgment. Perfect fear removes all sense of shame. Confession is regarded as disgraceful where people do not believe in the punishment meted out by the future judgment. Do we not know that the confession of sins has a sense of shame and that to be embarrassed about this very thing is a grave punishment? But God orders us all the more to confess our sins so that we might experience discomfiture rather than punishment. For this itself is also part of the judgment."[6] In which words one ought to note that he says God ordered that we confess our sins, so that we may suffer shame as a punishment received for our sins. Which words nowise can be referred to the confession which is to

---

[1] Cf. Rom. 3, 8.

[2] Homily 10 on Romans, n. 4 (PG 60, 479).

[3] The text here mistakenly cites "Cyril, book three on Leviticus."

[4] The Vulgate here has "Let him do penance for his sin" (Lev. 5, 5), but the Hebrew has "and surely when he is guilty in one of these things, he shall confess that he hath sinned therein."

[5] *Homilies on Leviticus*, hom. 3 (PG 12, 429A).

[6] *Opus imperfectum*, hom. 3 (PG 56, 650).

God alone. I could certainly cite many testimonies of the holy Doctors about this matter, but I omit them lest I burden the reader with excessive prolixity.

But among so many testimonies one thing alone ought to be (in my opinion) very convincing, namely that by no human authority could a people ever be led to pour out their most secret crimes, the silent awareness of which makes them tremble, into others' ears, with as much shame as danger, without any hesitation. And there is certainly nothing of the like that could have happened, namely that so many priests hearing the confessions of the common masses would keep the secret, even those who at other times can keep nothing quiet, unless God Himself, Who instituted the Sacrament, would have defended such a salutary thing with special graces. The confession of sins, which is done to the priest, was instituted by God: in which all sins which the penitent recalls ought to be disclosed: which having been disclosed in confession, and after having been given absolution by the priest, God forgives the penitent his sins, and infuses grace: all which things have now been proved by various testimonies. But concerning the institution of confession, that this was done by God, the Supreme Pontiff Sixtus IV settled this matter by these words which are now appended.

Bishop Sixtus, servant of the servants of God, for the perpetual remembrance of the matter. Although those things, which are rightly done by our command obtain the full firmness of authority: nevertheless, we occasionally add the strength of our defense to them: so that by it they may remain more firmly unharmed, the more they shall have shared our protection. Recently in fact it was brought to our hearing, that recently in Western Spain and especially at the University of Salamanca, there were and still are not a few sons of iniquity, who publicly affirm to be true, pertinaciously maintain and defend certain false, contrary to the faith of holy Church, erroneous, scandalous and ill-sounding propositions, in very frequent gathering of men especially about the confession of sins, and ecclesiastical Sacraments in the study of the like: they challenge very clear passages of Sacred Scripture opposing their errors, by shamelessly violating their correct and clear meaning with their false interpretations: they also attempt sow their manifestly false teachings containing the blot of heretical depravity into the minds of others and ensnare simple souls: and so that they may reach the knowledge of many men, and they had presumed to such an extent, and were presuming so that the remembrance of them would be kept forever, they compose and publicly pass on books so that there would be an opportunity for all of reading them: We then, joined together with our venerable brother Alfonso [Carillo de Acuña], Archbishop of Toledo, by other letters, so that having taken up with him some teachers of theology, and other learned men (who had summoned those who had attempted and were trying for days to affirm that these propositions are true: and having heard the things which they said to support the truth of these propositions, and others were trying to assemble the Christians in order to explain the falsity of those propositions) he might declare and decide by our authority whether the things which were contained in the propositions of this sort were false, contrary to the faith, erroneous, and ill-sounding: and having made a declaration of this sort, he might find out whether those who are in the abovementioned errors are culpable would amend themselves according to the ordinances of the holy Fathers and canonical decrees, and after having completely put away the aforesaid errors from their hearts, having abjured the heretical stain of this kind, return to the unity of the Church, and according to their own declaration, acknowledge such propositions to be scandalous, false and heretical as well as ill-sounding, and moreover retract the published book of this sort, and if they were to refuse to actually reject [these propositions], wishing to pertinaciously follow those men and their errors, he may pronounce them heretics, and bound with the censures and punishments promulgated by law in such cases: moreover, having granted full authority to him, as is more fully contained in our letters thenceforth effected.

CONFESSIO

But afterwards, as We have heard, the aforesaid Archbishop, rightly proceeding to execute the said letters by having followed the rescript, ordered to be summoned to his town of Alcala in the diocese of Toledo our beloved sons Pedro [Ximénez] de Préxamo, [Saint] Pedro de Ocaña. Pedro de Coloca, and also Didacus de Betoño [O. P.], Martin and Alfonso de la Torre, Masters, Pedro Didacus de Constana and Juan [de la Cerda] de Quintanapalla, Licentiates in Theology: also Tello [de] Buendia of Toledo, Vasco [Ramírez] de Ribera of Talavera [de la Reina], archdeacons in the same church, Tomas de Cuenca, and Juan de Medina, Doctors of Canon Law: and Garcia Fernandez of Alcala, Licentiate in Canon Law, very many other Masters in Theology and Doctors and Licentiates in the same Canon Law: also very many other learned and educated men from various places of the aforesaid kingdoms: and likewise the beloved son Peter of Osma, author of the abovementioned propositions and his followers: and when the said Peter of Osma and his followers did not appear at all, after having waiting the due time, after having made mature deliberation upon all the aforesaid propositions, he declared those propositions with the unanimous advice and assent of the aforesaid professors and Doctors, by which Peter de Osma and his abovementioned followers were not fearing to pertinaciously affirm, that the confession of sins *in species* is to be found really in the statute of the universal Church, not in Divine law; that mortal sins with respect to blame and punishment of the other world are abolished without confession, by contrition of heart only; moreover, bad thoughts are forgiven by displeasure only; that it is not demanded of necessity that confession be secret; that those who confess should not be absolved, if penance has not been done; that the Roman Pontiff cannot remit the punishment of Purgatory; cannot dispense with respect to what the universal Church has established; also that the Sacrament of Penance, as far as concerns the accumulation of grace, is of nature, but not of the institution of the New or Old Testament:[1] and other propositions which on account of their enormity, so that they who have knowledge of them, may forget them, and those who do not have knowledge of them, may not be instructed in them from the present [Bull], we order them to be passed over in silence, he declared by power of the said letter and declared by power of the faculty granted to him by them: and he decreed about these propositions that they ought to be held and reputed as false, contrary to the holy Catholic faith, erroneous, and scandalous, and entirely at variance with the truth of the Gospels, also contrary to the decrees of the holy Fathers and other apostolic constitutions and to contain manifest heresy: as contained in certain authentic writings written above. And finally, (as shown by the abovementioned acts told to us in consistory) so that we might diligently be informed by our beloved sons, Stephen having the title of Santa Maria in Trastevere, and John having the title of Saint Praxedes, Cardinal priests, about the above acts by the archbishop himself: so that they may relate what things they find to us and our other brothers, the cardinals of the holy Roman Church: who both with such zeal of faith and so that they may comply with our commands, accepting the burden of this kind with a prompt will, they carefully examined all things: and they faithfully related what things they found to us and our other faithfully remembered brothers: the aforesaid propositions are erroneous by many authorities and reasons, besides those which they found in the proceedings of the archbishop, also showing zeal of renowned faith. We, therefore, to whom it pertains to extirpate errors of this kind (having the aforesaid account of the same Cardinals of Santa Maria in Trastevere and of Saint Praxedes) by our certain knowledge commending in the Lord the great skill and diligence of the archbishop himself in the abovementioned acts, and we, by our Apostolic authority, by the contents of the present letter, by the authority of the same [Cardinals] mentioned and of our other brothers, along with council and assistance, praise, confirm, and approve and also strengthen by the support of the present

---

[1] Dz. 724-732.

writing, the declaration of the archbishop, and decree of this kind, insofar as they concern these things, each and everything contained in the abovementioned executed writings of the archbishop supplying for each and every defect, if they have intervened in the same. And nevertheless, for the sake of greater caution, We declare each and all the above mentioned propositions to be false, contrary to the holy Catholic faith, erroneous, and scandalous, and entirely at variance with the truth of the Gospels, also contrary to the decrees of the holy Fathers and other apostolic constitutions and to contain manifest heresy.[1] We also entrust to and command the aforesaid archbishop that he not omit to proceed against the said followers of the said Peter of Osma as heretics, if they shall have refused to abjure the heresy of this sort in which they have fallen, abjuring their errors and amending themselves, and shall have refused to comply, as they have followed the same Peter as erring, or maliciously shall have delayed, according to the contents of our other letter. And so that things commendably and laudably done by him with the zeal of faith by our command and rightly approved by Us, more readily come to the knowledge of all the inhabitants of those regions: when this affair has been settled, so that they keep themselves more freely from sliding into the aforesaid errors, he ought not to omit making known this letter with the process done by it, and the abjuration of the said Peter to every bishop of that region: who after the same notice, should take care to publish those things for the clergy and the people of those cities and dioceses: and in general he should do everything which shall be necessary for the extirpation of the heresy of this kind, or the things that seem opportune to him in whatever way, notwithstanding the Apostolic constitutions and ordinances, and all those things, which we wished not to impede in the said letter, and by whatever other things to the contrary. Thus, it is nowise allowed for anyone, etc.[2]

But that confession is necessary, even if contrition were present, besides the testimonies cited, the definition of the Council of Constance bears witness. In which council, in session eight, forty-five articles of John Wycliffe were condemned: and among the others, this one is assigned to the seventh place, with these words: "If man is duly contrite, every exterior confession on his part is superfluous and useless."[3] Which opinion along with others was condemned in the same place.

Then the Council of Florence celebrated under Eugene IV in the definition of faith which it gave to the Armenians discussing the Sacrament of Penance says these things: "The fourth sacrament is penance, the matter of which is, as it were, the acts of the penitent, which are divided into three parts. The first of these is contrition of heart, to which pertains grief for a sin committed together with a resolution not to sin in the future. The second is oral confession, to which pertains that the sinner confess integrally to his priest all sins of which he has recollection."[4] From which words Luther denying that all sins must necessarily be confessed is refuted.

Finally, the Council of Trent celebrated under Julius III much more clearly and copiously defines those things which pertain to Sacramental Confession. For in the fourteenth session, in the third Canon it says these words: "If anyone says that those words of the Lord Savior: 'Receive ye the Holy Ghost; whose sins you shall forgive, they are forgiven them; and whose sins ye shall retain, they are retained' (John 20, 22 ff.), are not to be understood of the power of remitting and retaining sins in the Sacrament of Penance, as the Catholic Church has always understood from the beginning, but, contrary to the institution of this Sacrament,

---

[1] Dz. 733.

[2] Bull *Licet ea*, August 9, 1479 (Juan Tejada y Ramiro, *Coleccion de Canones* (Madrid, Don Pedro Montero, 1863), vol. 5, pp. 65-67).

[3] Dz. 587.

[4] Dz. 699.

distorts them to an authority for preaching the Gospel: let him be anathema."[1] And in the sixth Canon it again says: "If anyone denies that Sacramental Confession was either instituted by Divine law or is necessary for salvation; or says that the manner of secretly confessing to a priest alone, which the Catholic Church has always observed from the beginning and still observes, is alien to the institution and the mandate of Christ, and is a human invention: let him be anathema."[2] And again in the seventh Canon it says: "If anyone says that in the Sacrament of Penance it is not necessary by Divine law for the remission of sins to confess each and all mortal sins, of which one has remembrance after a due and diligent examination, even secret ones and those which are against the two last precepts of the Decalogue, and the circumstances which alter the nature of sin; but that this confession is useful only for the instruction and consolation of the penitent, and formerly was observed only for imposing a canonical satisfaction; or says, that they who desire to confess all their sins wish to leave nothing to be pardoned by divine mercy; or, finally, that it is not lawful to confess venial sins: let him be anathema."[3] In which words all the errors which we have listed above concerning Sacramental Confession are clearly condemned.

[Saint] John [Fisher], Bishop of Rochester, wrote about this matter against Luther, in that work which he published against [Luther's] *Confutatio Assertionis Lutheranae*.[4] Jacques Masson wrote at great enough length in that work which he composed against Luther in support of the declaration of the faculty of Louvain.[5] Caspar Schatzgeyer of the Order of Friars Minor also wrote [against Luther].[6] I have not seen the others which many men mention.

There is another error in some way regarding this matter, which says that all men of any state can hear confession and absolve penitents. This error belongs to Martin Luther saying that all men are priests. But we will dispute about this error below in the section on "Priests," where (with God as our Guide) we will prove that not all Christians are priests.

CONFIRMATIO

Confirmation

It is a heresy of the Greeks (as Guy [the Carmelite] says[7]) that Confirmation is not a Sacrament. Brother Bernard of Luxemburg, when speaking about the Greeks in his *Catalogus haereticorum*, says that they confer the Sacrament of Confirmation to children immediately after Baptism, and this is done by simple priests.[8] Thus, these two seem to attribute contrary things to the Greeks, and I do not know which of them should be believed. Now so that I may

---

[1] Dz. 913.
[2] Dz. 916.
[3] Dz. 917.
[4] The text here erroneously has Luther's *Babylonian Captivity*, but it was rather his *Confutatio Assertionis Lutheranae*, as mentioned previously in a footnote, and so has been corrected here.
[5] *Articulorum doctrinae fratris M. Lutheri per theologos Lovanienses damnatorum ratio ex sacris literis et veteribus tractatoribus* (Antwerp, 1521).
[6] Caspar Schatzgeyer (in Latin, Gaspar Sagerus) (c. 1464–1527) was a German Franciscan and a foremost opponent of the Protestant reformer Martin Luther in Germany. *Ecclesiasticorum Sacramentorum pia iuxta atque erudita assertio*, title 5 (*De poenitentia Evangelica...*).
[7] *Summa de haeresibus et earum confutationibus*, fol. 25r, c. 15.
[8] Fol. 42v. It is not expedient that those confirmed by Greek schismatic priests be reconfirmed unless they are to receive Holy Orders or they request to be conditionally reconfirmed (Holy Office, 14 January 1885, quoted in Prummer's *Manuale Theologiae Moralis* (Friburg, Herder, 1929), vol. 3, n. 159).

frankly say the truth, I do not trust either of them in this matter, because I see that neither has accurately investigated the matter, as one may infer from many other things. Hence, whether or not the Greeks hold the former or the latter view, it is certain that the Waldensians taught this error: although Guy when discussing their errors never attributes this error to them.[1] Yet Aeneas Sylvius, who afterwards was made supreme pontiff, and was called Pius II, in his book, *De origine Bohemorum*,[2] when recounting the errors of the Waldensians, he accuses them of this error among others. After them John Wycliffe, when restoring the sect of the Waldensians, said that Confirmation can be given by any priest: still he did not deny (as far as I know) that Confirmation is a Sacrament, because Thomas Netter who very diligently traced this man's error, merely assigns this error to Wycliffe, namely that he said that Confirmation can be conferred by any priest, and that only due to cupidity for temporal gain was it reserved to bishops.[3] Martin Luther drawing his teachings from putrid and infected pools (as he is accustomed to do), consents to the Waldensians saying that Confirmation is neither a Sacrament nor confers grace, but is a mere ceremony and a certain rite.

Now in order that we may prove that this is false, it is necessary to recall what we taught above at the beginning of this work: namely that many things ought to be held by faith, even if they cannot be explicitly proved by Sacred Scripture. Next, lest in the future we argue merely about the name, it is first necessary to warn that what is called Confirmation by more recent writers, is the same thing which in ancient and older times is called "consignation." Since indeed men in former times called it consignation from the rite and ceremony which is observed in the conferring of this Sacrament, because the bishop when conferring this Sacrament with chrism, that is, consecrated oil, anointed the forehead of the already baptized child, by having made the sign of the cross upon the forehead with the same chrism, whereby as with a most strong and impenetrable shield he may be fortified against the darts of the devil. But men in more recent times taking into consideration of the effect of this Sacrament call it Confirmation: because in this Sacrament grace is given whereby one is made stronger and more powerful for undergoing combat with the devil: and thus it is rightly called "Confirmation," because by it one is made more firm. Therefore, these things having been established, we will easily prove that Confirmation is a Sacrament conferring grace, which can be administered by bishops alone.

In the Acts of the Apostles we read that when the Apostles were in Jerusalem, "When the apostles, who were in Jerusalem, had heard that Samaria had received the word of God, they sent unto them Peter and John. Who, when they were come, prayed for them, that they might receive the Holy Ghost For he was not as yet come upon any of them; but they were only baptized in the name of the Lord Jesus. Then they laid their hands upon them, and they received the Holy Ghost." (8, 14-17). Notice that you see here that by the imposition of Apostolic hands the Holy Ghost descended upon those already baptized. Hence it is proved that the Sacrament of Confirmation confers grace to those receiving it, because the Apostles were conferring Confirmation in this way, by the imposition of hands joined to prayer, just as many holy and very ancient Doctors interpret: both holy and at the same time learned, as well as revered for their antiquity, supreme pontiffs so explain this passage: and the definition of a general council pronounces that this passage ought to be understood as concerning Confirmation. We will soon append all which things.

But (as we taught at the beginning of this work) that ought to be accepted as the true and indubitable meaning of Sacred Scripture which the Church gave to us as the true meaning. For just as it belongs to her to distinguish Sacred Scriptures from profane writings, so it be-

---

[1] *Ibid.* pp. 79r-89r.

[2] Chapter 35.

[3] *Doctrinale antiquitatum fidei ecclesiae catholicae* (Venice, 1571), vol. 1, bk. 2, c. 57. p. 317.

longs to her to separate the true from the false meaning. Thus, since the Church teaches us that this passage of Scripture ought to be understood of Confirmation or the consignation of the forehead, we ought not to doubt any more about it.

In that passage, however, it is very clearly said that by the imposition of hands the Holy Ghost is conferred. Now the fact that in this passage of the Acts of the Apostles there is no mention of the anointing with chrism, but of the imposition of hands alone, ought not to trouble us: because if this is there passed over in silence, still it is nonetheless certain that Christ so commanded that the one to be confirmed ought to be anointed with chrism, and that the Apostles did as Christ had commanded them. For [Pseudo-] Pope Fabian, martyr, in his letter to the Eastern bishops, when reprehending those bishops who were not confecting chrism each year on Holy Thursday, but were often using two or three years old chrism, says the following: "They are in error, however, who think so; and in making such statements they speak like madmen rather than men in their right senses. For on that day the Lord Jesus, after supping with His disciples, and washing their feet, according to the tradition which our Predecessors received from the holy Apostles and left to us, taught them to prepare the chrism. That washing of their feet signifies our Baptism, as it is completed and confirmed by the unction of the holy chrism."[1] And Luther cannot reject him as recent or tercentenary (as he is accustomed to do), because he was crowned with martyrdom under the Emperor Decius, nearly one thousand three hundred years ago.

Furthermore, in the same book of the Acts of the Apostles we again find something similar which was done by Blessed Paul. For he when he had met with some disciples baptized merely with John's baptism, he baptized them with the true Baptism in the name of Jesus, after which he imposed hands on them, and the Holy Ghost came upon them, and they were speaking in tongues and prophesizing. Notice again that you see that grace was given through the imposition of hands. But if grace is conferred in that same passage under some sensible sign appearing outwardly, nothing prevents it from being called a Sacrament. But take note of one thing here, that this imposition of hands was never done except by the Apostles alone, and it will never be found that it was done by the other disciples: hence the holy and ancient Doctors conclude that this Sacrament cannot be conferred by anyone besides a bishop, because the bishops succeed the Apostles, while the rest of the priests represent the disciples, and they succeed them.

It is necessary, however, to compare this testimony with the testimonies of the holy and ancient Doctors. [Pseudo-] Pope Damasus says the following: "The book of the Acts of the Apostles teaches, however, that it is belongs to the Apostles alone, and their successors, to impart the Holy Ghost, especially since it is not read that any of the seventy disciples imparted the Holy Ghost, whose place they take (he speaks about priests) in the Church, through the imposition of hands (as said before [concerning the bishops])."[2] This learned as well as holy, [Pseudo-] Pope Damasus died more than one thousand one hundred years ago.

Pope Innocent, a man cut from the same cloth as Damasus, because he was holy and learned, says the following: "But in regard to the signing of little children, it is evident that it may not be done by any other than a bishop. For the presbyters, although they are second priests, nevertheless do not possess the crown of the pontificate. That this power of a bishop, however, is due to the bishops alone, so that they either sign or give the Paraclete the Spirit, not only ecclesiastical custom indicates, but also that reading in the Acts of the Apostles which declares that Peter and John were directed to give the Holy Spirit to those already

---

[1] *False Decretals of the Pseudo-Isidore* (PL 130, 154D-155A). Pope Fabian was Bishop of Rome from 236 to 250 A.D. The letters ascribed to Pope Fabian are rejected by all as spurious.

[2] This is an apocryphal text. Letter 3 (PL 13, 436B).

baptized.[1] For to presbyters it is permitted to anoint the baptized with chrism whenever they baptize, whether without a bishop or in the presence of a bishop, but [with chrism] that has been consecrated by a bishop; nevertheless [it is] not [allowed] to sign the forehead with the same oil; that is due to the bishops alone when they bestow the Spirit, the Paraclete."[2] From these words it is evident that Confirmation, or consignation, confers grace to the one receiving it: and that such Confirmation cannot be conferred by anyone other than a bishop. And he says that it is not merely from ecclesiastical custom, but from Divine law, which is expressed in the Acts of the Apostles.

Pope Leo I says the same thing with nearly the same words as Pope Damasus in his letter to all the bishops of Germany and Gaul.[3] Let him see who wishes, because these letters of Leo were inserted into the book on the general councils.

Pope and martyr[4] [Saint] Melchiades in a letter to the bishops of Spain explains more explicitly the power of this Sacrament, saying the following: "The Holy Ghost, Who comes down on the waters of Baptism bearing salvation in His flight, bestows at the font the fullness of innocence; but in Confirmation He confers an increase of grace. And because while we live in this world we must pass amidst our invisible enemies in great danger, therefore in Baptism we are regenerated to life; after Baptism we are strengthened to fight. In Baptism we are born again unto life; after Baptism we are strengthened. Although the benefit of Regeneration suffices for those who are on the point of death, yet the graces of Confirmation are necessary for those who are to conquer. Confirmation arms and strengthens those to whom the struggles and combats of this world are reserved. And he who comes to die, having kept unsullied the innocence he acquired in Baptism, is confirmed by death; for after death he can sin no more."[5]

Next, [Pseudo-] Pope [Saint] Eusebius, who preceded Pope Melchiades in the papacy, and who underwent a glorious martyrdom under Diocletian for Christ's name, in his third letter, which is to the bishops of Tuscany and Campania, gives clearer testimony about this matter, saying the following: "Every single heretic converted by God's grace, has been baptized while believing in the Holy Trinity, holding the rule of the Roman Church, we command to be reconciled through the imposition of hands. The imposition of hands ought to be held in high esteem, because it cannot be performed by anyone except high priests. Nor is it read or known to ever have been carried out at the time of the Apostles by others besides the Apostles themselves. For if one shall have presumed otherwise, it will be held to be null and void, nor at any time reckoned to be ecclesiastical Sacraments."[6] In which words two things ought to be noted which serve our purpose. The first, in fact, is that he says that Confirmation is a Sacrament, which the Lutherans deny. Then he says that it cannot be conferred by anyone except the bishops, which John Wycliffe denied.

[Pseudo-] Pope and martyr [Saint] Urban [I] in a letter concerning the common life and offering of the faithful written to all bishops says the following: "All the faithful should, after Baptism, receive the Holy Ghost by the imposition of the bishop's hand, that they may

---

[1] Cf. Acts 8, 14-17.

[2] Letter of Pope Innocent I to Decentius, Bishop of Eugubium, c. 3. It is also found in the collection of papal constitutions of Dionysius Exiguus (*Collectio decretorum pontificum Romanorum* (PL 67, 239B)).

[3] Epist. 66, *False Decretals of the Pseudo-Isidore* (PL 130, 880D-882C). Epist. 88 (PL 55, 1325A-1327B).

[4] Pope Melchiades was counted as a martyr on many lists due to the sufferings he endured. His feast is traditionally kept on December 10th.

[5] *Epistola ad omnes hispaniae episcopos*, c. 2 (PL 7, 1119C-1120A).

[6] This letter, attributed to Saint Eusebius (d. 309 or 310), actually comes from the *False Decretals* (PL 130, 238A); there all the letters attributed to anti-Nicene popes are forgeries.

become perfect Christians: because when the Holy Ghost is infused, the faithful heart is widened regarding prudence and constancy."[1] [Pseudo-] Pope Urban clearly asserts that the Holy Ghost is infused by Confirmation or by "the imposition of hand." Also Pope and martyr [Saint] Clement, who was the fourth [pope starting] from Saint Peter, says the same thing in his fourth epistle near the end. The epistles of this [pope] are found in the book in which the decrees of all the councils have been collected together, in the beginning of that book.[2]

Now what Jerome says in his book, [*The Dialogue*] *Against the Luciferians*, namely that it is more on account of the honor of the priest than a decree from the necessity of the law, that only a bishop may confer the Holy Ghost through the imposition of hand,[3] does not disturb me, nor ought it disturb anyone: because it is better to rather believe Damasus and Innocent, and the other men who are just as holy as they are learned, whom we have cited, than Jerome alone, who elsewhere also maintained that there is no difference between a priest and a bishop from Divine law. And we do not belittle Jerome by saying this (far be it) nor does he lose any of his glory due to this: because Blessed Jerome himself thinking as a Catholic (as it fitting), wrote to the same Pope Damasus saying that he wishes to hold that faith alone which the Roman Pontiff and the true successor of Peter shall have taught him.[4] Nor also ought the action of Blessed Gregory disturb [anyone], who when writing to Bishop Januarius, permits that priests may confer the Sacrament of Confirmation to the baptized: because, as is evident from the same letter, he firstly had forbidden those priests to do this: yet because he knew that scandal would arise, he permits priests to confer it to avoid scandal and some greater evil. For thus from the same letter it is evident that this is a permission and not a concession. Now whether he acted wrongly or not by so permitting, I do not dispute, nor does it pertain to me, who do not now discuss particular cases. Still if I am forced to offer my opinion, I think that the holy and at the same time learned man neither wanted to err nor was he doing something which he did not understand.

But now it is necessary that we listen to the decisions of the councils about this matter. The Second Synod of Seville, which Blessed Isidore [of Seville] attended, when enumerating the things which are forbidden to priests and reserved to bishops alone, in the seventh Canon of its decrees among other things it lists Confirmation, saying: "Since it does not belong to them to bless a church, or to bless altars, nor to impart the [Paraclete] Spirit through the impositions of hand to the baptized faithful nor to those converted from heresy, nor to confect chrism, nor to sign with chrism the forehead of those baptized."[5]

Furthermore, among the forty-five articles of John Wycliffe condemned in the Council of Constance, this one is put in the twenty-eighth place, with these words: "The confirmation of youths, ordination of clerics, and consecration of places are reserved to the pope and bishops on account of their desire for temporal gain and honor."[6] Which article along with the others of the same John Wycliffe was condemned with one judgment upon them all.

---

[1] This passage is said to be apocryphal and a product of the *False Decretals* (PL 130, 140C).

[2] *Concilia generalia et provincialia, graeca et Latina* (Cologne, Severinus Binius, 1618), vol. 1, fol. 40b, A-B. This fourth epistle is also found in the *False Decretals of the Pseudo-Isidore* (PL 130, 56C).

[3] C. 9. Here Saint Jerome says that normally only bishops may confirm, but this power may also be delegated to priests.

[4] "I think it is my duty to consult the chair of Peter, and to turn to a church whose faith has been praised by Paul... My words are spoken to the successor of the Fisherman, to the disciple of the Cross. As I follow no leader save Christ, so I communicate with none but Your Blessedness, that is with the Chair of Peter. For this, I know, is the rock on which the Church is built!" (Letter 15, n. 1-2 (PL 22, 355)).

[5] PL 55, 1326C.

[6] Dz. 608.

Finally, the Council of Trent celebrated under Paul III in the seventh session, first Canon, "On Confirmation," condemns this heretical assertion saying the following: "If anyone shall say that the Confirmation of those baptized is an empty ceremony and not rather a true and proper Sacrament, or that in former times it was nothing more than a kind of catechism, by which those approaching adolescence gave an account of their faith before the Church: let him be anathema."[1] Again in the second Canon it says: "If anyone shall say that they who ascribe any power to the sacred chrism of Confirmation offer an outrage to the Holy Ghost: let him be anathema."[2] Again in the third Canon it says: "If anyone shall say that the ordinary minister of holy Confirmation is not the bishop alone, but any simple priest: let him be anathema."[3]

But because in these decrees nothing is said about the effect of this Baptism, it is necessary to add the Council of Florence celebrated under Eugene IV, which in the definition of faith given to the Armenians, when discussing the Sacrament of Confirmation, says these words: "The effect of this Sacrament, because in it the Holy Ghost is given for strength, was thus given to the Apostles on the day of Pentecost, so that the Christian might boldly confess the name of Christ. The one to be confirmed, therefore, must be anointed on the forehead, which is the seat of reverence, so that he may not be ashamed to confess the name of Christ and especially His Cross, which is indeed 'unto the Jews indeed a stumblingblock, and unto the Gentiles foolishness' (I Cor. 1, 23) according to the Apostle; for which reason one is signed with the sign of the Cross."[4]

There exist other councils which very much favor our case, namely, III Carthage and IV Carthage,[5] I Toledo,[6] and I Braga.[7] But it was not necessary to quote the words of these councils, because they are provincial, after we have already quoted the general councils.

I wish to point out one thing which deserves to be noted, namely that Eusebius of Caesarea in his book, *Ecclesiastical History*, when speaking about the heretic Novatian relates that the things which usually follow Baptism were not solemnly performed on him, nor was he signed with the seal of chrism, and on that account could never have been given the Holy Ghost.[8]

---

[1] Dz. 871.

[2] Dz. 872.

[3] Dz. 873.

[4] Dz. 697.

[5] "Let no presbyter make the chrism, nor prepare the unction, nor consecrate virgins, nor publicly reconcile anyone to communion" (Carthaginian Synod under Genethlius, A.D. 387 or 390, c. 3). "Neither the making of the chrism, nor the consecration of virgins, is to be done by presbyters, nor is it permitted to a presbyter to reconcile anyone in the public Mass (*in publica missa*), this is the pleasure of all of us" (Synod of Carthage (A.D. 419); *Codex canonum ecclesiasticorum*, Canon 6 (PL 67, 187C)). Note that the numbering of the African councils differs very widely between the different writers.

[6] "No one other than a bishop may confect chrism" (*Collectio Canonum Ecclesiae Hispanae ex probatissimis ac pervetustis Codicibus*, p. 326.

[7] "Also, it was decided, if a man be a priest, and after this interdict, shall have dared to bless the chrism, or the church, or to consecrate the altar, let him be deposed from their office, for the ancient canons also forbade this" (c. 19, *Collectio Canonum Ecclesiae Hispanae ex probatissimis ac pervetustis Codicibus*, p. 605).

[8] "And when he was healed of his sickness he did not receive the other things which it is necessary to have according to the Canon of the Church, even the being sealed by the bishop. And as he did not receive this, how could he receive the Holy Ghost?" (Bk. 6, c. 43, n. 15).

CONSILIUM

Counsels

Concerning this matter I find just one heresy, which has now recently arisen, invented by Luther as its first parent, which asserts that there is no difference between a counsel and a precept: for Luther says that everything which the Catholic Doctors call the Evangelical counsels, are Divine precepts, having no less force for obliging that the other Divine precepts. But I do not wish to dispute anything about this heresy at present, because I have chosen to discuss this matter below in the section on the "Precepts." Hence I send the reader to that place.

CONTRITIO

Contrition

Notice Luther comes up against us again, who is here to impede everyone wishing to behave well, and to deter every good deed. For he says, contrition and detestation of sin, which originates from the fear of Hell, is a sin: yet he is far from willing to prove it. But so that his inane mind may be apparent to all, I will cite his words. "Contrition," he says, "which is acquired through examination, remembrance, and detestation of sins, by which one reflects upon his years in the bitterness of his soul, by pondering over the gravity of sins, their number, their baseness, the loss of eternal beatitude, and the acquisition of eternal damnation, this contrition makes him a hypocrite, indeed more a sinner."[1] From which words two errors of Luther can be gathered: one is the error whereby he condemns contrition that arises from the consideration and hatred of Hell, and he says that such contrition is a sin. The other is the error whereby he says that it is not necessary for preparing true contrition to examine and remember all sins, by recalling their gravity, number, and hideousness.

He firstly clearly errs condemning contrition that arises from the consideration and hatred of Hell: because even if such detestation of sin, which arises from mere hatred of Hell is not perfect and meritorious, still it is not consequently evil. For if such detestation would be evil, either it has such evilness of itself or it contracts it from the motive from which it arises, namely the hatred of Hell. No one is so demented that he would say that such detestation of sin is evil of itself, because then the detestation of sin for any motive would be evil: such that even if such detestation were for God's sake, it would be evil. For an action that is evil by its nature, done for whatever motive, will be evil. For since wanting to steal is evil, when done for any reason, it will always be evil. Hence, since such detestation of sin is not evil of itself, it is necessary that it be evil due to the motive from which it arises, namely on account of the hatred of Hell.

But hatred of Hell is not evil. For one can licitly dislike Hell, because nature, even not corrupted, inclines to this very thing. This hatred of Hell inheres so tenaciously to nature that it can nowise love Hell. But if the detestation of sin is not evil in itself nor is hatred of Hell evil in itself, why is it that detestation of sin, which arises from the hatred of Hell, evil? Furthermore, if such detestation of sin were evil, it would then follow that servile fear of God is evil: because it is evident that such detestation of sin proceeds from servile fear. Luther actually

---

[1] Papal Bull of Pope Leo X, *Exsurge Domine*, n. 6 (Dz. 746).

agrees to this, hence it is necessary to vanquish this error: when this has been done, we will triumph over Luther as to both his errors.

Yet before we approach him, it is necessary to know well on what matter we wish to fight against him. To do this it is useful to point out that it could happen in two ways that someone would flee sin from fear on punishment. For it could happen that one would so flee sin by fear of punishment such that if he were to perceive that the punishment is very slightly reduced, he would never give up the sin. And such a person, although he flees the sinful deed, still he retains the will of sinning. Wherefore, we say that he who so detests sin by fear of punishment, acts badly, and in this man there is not even true servile fear of God: because he who truly fears God even with servile fear, avoids all sin. Hence, Blessed Ambrose says the following: "The flesh of the soul is carnal thoughts. Fear of the Lord and of His judgements pierces the flesh and bring it back to submission. But if the flesh rejects the nails of Divine fear, without a doubt it is said: 'My spirit shall not remain in men forever, because they are flesh' (Gen. 6, 3). Thus, unless the flesh be affixed to the Cross, and pierced with the fear of the Lord, God's Spirit will not remain in it."[1] Hence, we do not dispute against Luther about this fear and this kind of detestation of sin: in fact we agree on this point.

To detest sin from fear of punishment may occur in another way: namely such that both the deed of the sin and the will to sin are completely removed by the fear of punishment. For it happens that he who would consider Hell and its most grave punishment, which he greatly dislikes, and hence rises to the consideration of God, Who can inflict such punishment, and thus considering fears God as being able to inflict such punishment. And this fear is called servile, when God is feared on account of His power alone. The Lord Himself both persuades and motivates us to have this fear Who says: "Fear him that can destroy both soul and body in hell" (Mt. 10, 28). Then the sinner struck with this fear goes on to the consideration of his sin, which is the cause for such punishment to be inflicted upon the sinner: wherefore he considers how great is the gravity of the sin, how great its depravity, and also its enormity, which exacts such punishment. Finally, from the consideration of this gravity and depravity he comes to so completely and entirely flee sin such that there remains no will to sin in him, to such an extent that even if he would know for sure that punishment will never be inflicted, he would never want to sin: because he now fully realizes the enormity of sin, which (as is evident) arises from servile fear of God, for knowing which, nevertheless arose from the consideration and dislike of punishment. Thus such detestation of sin, which (as is evident) arises from servile fear, and proceeds from the consideration and dislike of Hell, is good.

Also, such servile fear of God is good, nay is a gift of the Holy Ghost: which is evident from that testimony of Ambrose which we just cited: "Unless the flesh be affixed to the Cross," he says, "and pierced with the fear of the Lord, God's Spirit will not remain in it." You see here that fear of the Lord pertains to God's Spirit. But the fact that he is speaking about servile fear is proved from what he says shortly afterwards in the same sermon: "For he," he says, "is worthy who has the fear of Christ, so that he would crucify carnal sin. Charity follows this fear."[2] From whose words it is evident that some fear of the Lord before charity is good, which nevertheless Luther denies: through which fear sin is expelled. And Ambrose does not reprehend him who abandons sin from that fear: in fact, he praises it.

Moreover, if that servile fear of God is evil, what is the fear which is "the beginning of wisdom" (Ps. 110, 10; Prov. 1, 7)? It certainly is not filial fear, because it is posterior to true wisdom itself, since it arises from charity, whereas charity does not arise from it. Why then is that which is the beginning of all good, and the first step towards acquiring virtue, evil? Again, David was awakened from the sleep of sin by this fear, and he was not rebuked for

---

[1] *Expositio in psalmum David CXVIII*, sermon 15, n. 37 (PL 15, 1423A-B).
[2] *Ibid.*, n. 40 (PL 15, 1424B).

this, but rather was praised. For his sin was forgiven through this detestation: far from making him a greater sinner, as Luther says. For when the prophet Nathan threatened David on God's behalf with afflictions and distress for the sin he had committed, David acknowledging his sin says: "I have sinned." And Nathan immediately replied: "The Lord also hath taken away thy sin" (II Kings 12, 13). Also, David himself testifies that he was motivated by that fear saying: "The sorrows of death surrounded me: and the torrents of iniquity troubled me. The sorrows of hell encompassed me: and the snares of death prevented me" (Ps. 17, 5-6).

Next, the prophet Isaias says: "Lord, they have sought after thee in distress, in the tribulation of murmuring thy instruction was with them. As a woman with child, when she draweth near the time of her delivery, is in pain, and crieth out in her pangs: so are we become in thy presence, O Lord. We have conceived, and been as it were in labour, and have brought forth wind" (26, 16-18). And where we have "in thy presence, O Lord," the Septuagint says "from Thy fear": and Jerome says that "in thy presence" and "from Thy fear" are the same.[1] The Royal Prophet also rouses sinners to penance, goading them with this fear: "Except you will be converted, he will brandish his sword: he hath bent his bow and made it ready" (Ps. 7, 13). John the Baptist also excited this fear in sinners saying: "Ye offspring of vipers, who hath shewed you to flee from the wrath to come? Bring forth therefore fruits worthy of penance" (Lk. 3, 7). And shortly afterwards: "For now the axe is laid to the root of the trees. Every tree therefore that bringeth not forth good fruit, shall be cut down and cast into the fire" (v. 9).

And so that we may conclude, how many times did Christ our Redeemer excite this fear in sinners? How often did He want to induce them to penance through this fear? "Unless you shall do penance," He says, "you shall all likewise perish" (Lk. 13, 3). He also encourages doing good through fear of the last and terrible Judgment. For when He had discussed the Judgment, and said that the day is uncertain, He added: "Watch ye therefore, because ye know not what hour your Lord will come" (Mt. 24, 42). You clearly see here how He stimulates with fear of the Judgment, so that He may induce to behaving well. But if it were evil (as Luther says) the Savior Himself would not have persuaded with this motive.

Also, the parable of the publican shows nothing else but that contrition, which is prepared by the consideration of sins and the consideration of their enormity, is good. For the Truth says about that publican that he "went down… justified" (Lk. 18, 14). But why was he justified? Namely because when praying the in Temple, standing afar off he was not daring to "so much as lift up his eyes towards heaven; but struck his breast, saying: O God, be merciful to me a sinner" (v. 13). Why was he not daring to lift up his eyes towards Heaven? He certainly knew the gravity and the multitude of his sins, and so judged himself unworthy, who could have gone closer, or lifted up his eyes towards Heaven: hence he was striking his breast, saying: "O God, be merciful to me a sinner." Notice that you see here the contrition of this publican which he prepared by examination, remembrance, and detestation of his sins. And he, who before was not just, was justified by that contrition: because Truth Itself says: "I say to you, this man went down [into his house] justified" (v. 14). But when he went up into the temple to pray, he was not just, but he went down just.

Finally, what else does the parable of the prodigal son teach us besides to be converted to God, and that such conversion is pleasing to God? For the son when he had wickedly used up all the substance which he had received from his father, was reduced to such poverty that he fed swine: and was oppressed with such hunger that he desired to be filled "with the husks the swine did eat; and no man gave unto him" (Lk. 15, 16). Behold you see the stimulus of grave punishment rousing from the sleep of sin. See how he is roused, because when he was perishing with hunger, "returning to himself, he said…" (v. 17): now what made him return to himself? Certainly the very great hunger which he was suffering made him, who went outside

---

[1] *Commentaria in Isaiam*, bk. 8, c. 26 (PL 24, 302C).

himself and away from his father into the far country of his vices, so that he might return to himself and his father, meaning, to the consideration of his depravity and of the paternal goodness. Fortunate necessity which compelled him to behaving well.[1] Thus "returning to himself, he said: How many hired servants in my father's house abound with bread, and I here perish with hunger? I will arise, and will go to my father, and say to him: Father, I have sinned against heaven, and before thee: I am not worthy to be called thy son," etc. (v. 17-19). Now that the contrition of this son was good is evident because he was received by his father, and the first robe was given to him, namely the first grace which had been taken off by sin, and there was rejoicing for him, and rightly so, because there is great "joy in heaven upon one sinner that doth penance" (v. 7). Thus, even if this son loved his father in the end, still the beginning of his conversion and the first step to that love was to know his own miserable condition and state in which he was in. Now the hunger that he was suffering incited and impelled to this knowledge. Therefore, what does Luther snarl, and does he wish to create a new Gospel for us? For this testimony is so clear that it pierces him through on all sides.

But now it will be worthwhile to cite the decision of the Church on this matter, so that we may enclose the enemy on all sides. The Council of Trent celebrated under Paul III says these words: "If anyone shall say that the fear of Hell, whereby by grieving for sins we flee to the mercy of God or refrain from sinning, is a sin or makes sinners worse: let him be anathema."[2] And likewise, the Council proceeding under Julius III says these words: "And as to that imperfect contrition which is called attrition, because it is commonly conceived either from the consideration of the turpitude of sin, or from the fear of Hell and of punishment, the Council declares that if with the hope of pardon, it excludes the wish to sin, it not only does not make man a hypocrite and a greater sinner, but that it is even a gift of God, and an impulse of the Holy Ghost, Who does not indeed as yet dwell in the penitent, but Who only moves him; whereby the penitent, being assisted, prepares a way for Himself unto justice, and although this attrition cannot of itself, without the Sacrament of Penance, conduct the sinner to justification, yet does it dispose him to receive the grace of God in the Sacrament of Penance. For smitten profitably with fear, the Ninivites at the preaching of Jonas did fearful penance and obtained mercy from the Lord. Wherefore falsely do some calumniate Catholic writers, as if they had maintained that the Sacrament of Penance confers grace without any good motion on the part of those who receive it: a thing which the Church of God never taught, or thought: and falsely also do they assert that contrition is extorted and forced, not free and voluntary."[3] In which words both of Luther's errors concerning which we discussed in this section are most clearly condemned.

Forty years earlier Brother Stephen Brulefer[4] wrote a distinguished tract on this subject, *De timore Domini servili*,[5] against a certain unnamed preacher, who when preaching to the people of that time, tried to teach the same things about servile fear, that Luther now teaches. [Saint] John [Fisher], Bishop of Rochester, also wrote in that work which he published

---

[1] Cf. Saint Augustine, epistle 127, n. 8: "Fortunate necessity, which compels to what is better" (PL 33, 487).

[2] Sess. 6, Canon 8 (Dz. 818).

[3] Sess. 3, chap. 4.

[4] Etienne Brulefer (or Brulifer) was a French ecclesiastic, a native of Bretagne, a Doctor of Paris, and a Franciscan, who taught theology at Metz and Mentz, and died in 1483.

[5] This tract may be found in his *Opuscula* (Paris, 1500, fol. 24 seq.) where he opposes certain theologians who had rejected servile fear as absolutely sinful; "Fear (which really excludes sin)," he says, "is a gift of the Holy Ghost, and theologians who teach otherwise are presumptuous, undiscerning, and foolish preachers, and they deserved to be punished as heretics." He was given the accolade, *Doctor Scotellus* ("little Scotus"), for his being a follower of Duns Scotus.

against Luther's *Defense and Explanation of all the Articles*:[1] to which matter he dedicates a whole article.[2] Jacques Masson, in a work which he wrote in support of the declaration of the faculty of Louvain against Luther, treats this matter more copiously than [the bishop] of Rochester.[3] But I have not seen any other.

CORRECTIO

Correction

There is one error about this matter saying that the common people can correct their wrong doing rulers as they wish, but we will dispute about this below in the section on "Subjects."

CREATURA

Creatures

The **first heresy** about this matter is saying that creatures were made by someone other than God. But this heresy is further divided in many sects. For some men said that this whole world was made by the Angels. The chief of this error was Simon the Magician, concerning whom there is mention in the Acts of the Apostles, whom his disciples, Menander and Saturninus, from whom the Saturninians[4] are named, followed. [It is the Saturninians] who say that only seven Angels made the world without the knowledge of God the Father.[5] And Cerinthus [also taught this].[6] Others said that creatures were made by an evil god. For they (as we will say below) posited two gods: one good, who did not create anything in this world and the other evil, from whom they say all creatures came forth. The authors of this heresy were those who were called the Gnostics. The wicked Manichaeus followed them. Nevertheless, Augustine when speaking about the Manichaeans says that they assert that the world was made by the good god, but it has in it a mixture of evil.[7] But Theophylactus says that the Manichaeans assert that creatures were made by an evil god. For when expounding the miracle which is in John's Gospel when from five loaves the Lord satiated with food five thousand men, says the following: "This passage confounds the Manichaeans, who say that bread and all such things were created by an evil god. The Son of the good God, Jesus Christ, multiplied the loaves. Therefore they could not have been naturally evil; a good God would

---

[1] The text here erroneously says that St. John Fisher wrote this against Luther's *Babylonian Captivity*.
[2] *Assertionis Lutheranae confutatio*, art. 6, pp. 176-194.
[3] *Articulorum doctrinae Fratris Martini Lutheri per theologos Lovanienses damnatorum ratio ex Sacris litteris et veteribus tractatoribus* (Antwerp 1521)
[4] Saturninians, Saturnians, or Saturnines an early sect of Syrian Gnostics, followers of Saturninus or Saturnilus. The theories of Saturninus are only known through the work of Irenaeus, *Against Heresies*.
[5] "The Saturninians were named from a certain Saturninus, who is said to have established the shameful doctrine of Simon in Syria; he also stated that seven Angels had made the world by themselves without the knowledge of God the Father." (Saint Augustine, *De Haeresibus ad Quodvultdeum*, c. 3 (PL 42, 26)).
[6] *Ibid.* c. 8 (PL 42, 27).
[7] *Ibid.* c. 46 (PL 42, 35).

never have multiplied what was evil."[1] And I Synod of Braga seems to attribute this same heresy to Manichaeus that Theophylactus attributed to him, as will be shown below. Afterwards Priscillian also taught the same error as Manichaeus.

This common heresy of all these men is refuted by that which is said at the beginning of Genesis: "In the beginning God created heaven, and earth" (1, 1). Thus, the Angels or the other hosts (*virtutes*) [did not create]. And Solomon says: "God created all things that they might be" (Wis. 1, 14). And Ecclesiasticus asserts this explicitly saying: "He that liveth for ever created all things together" (18, 1). But Manichaeus is not refuted by this testimony, because he says that the evil god is equally eternal as the good god: wherefore, he interpreted that passage of Ecclesiasticus of his evil god. But let him hear Malachias saying: "Hath not one God created us?" (2, 10). Behold, Manichaeus, the unity of God, and that one God is the Creator of us all. Therefore [creatures] were not created by the Angels, as Simon, Menander, or Valentinus said. Also [they were not created] by an evil god, as the wicked Manichaeus said, and Priscillian, his follower.

But because Manichaeus (as we will say elsewhere) rejects the Old Testament, let us have recourse to the New Testament. John, when speaking of the Son of God, says: "The Word was with God, and the Word was God… All things were made by him: and without him was made nothing that was made" (1, 1 & 3). And shortly afterwards he says: "He was in the world, and the world was made by him" (v. 10). And Paul the Apostle says: "He that created all things, is God." (Heb. 3, 4). And elsewhere speaking specifically about food, and reprehending those who teach to abstain from them, he says that they have a cauterized [i.e., hardened] conscience, who forbid "to marry, to abstain from meats, which God hath created to be received with thanksgiving" (I Tim. 4, 3). And the twenty-four elders falling down before the throne in the Apocalypse were saying: "Thou art worthy, O Lord our God, to receive glory, and honour, and power: because thou hast created all things; and for thy will they were, and have been created" (4, 11).

And the Council of Nicea, in order to reprimand this insane heresy of the Manichaeans added in its Creed that one must believe "in one God… the Creator of all things invisible and visible."[2] Finally, the IV Lateran Council celebrated under Innocent III, after it had said that all three Persons of the Trinity are one substance, adds these words: "One beginning of all, Creator of all visible and invisible things, of the spiritual and of the corporal; Who by His own omnipotent power at once from the beginning of time created each creature from nothing, spiritual, and corporal, namely, Angelic and mundane, and finally the human, constituted as it were, alike of the spirit and the body."[3] Which words are found in the book of the Decretals.[4] Then the [I] Synod of Braga decreed the following: "If anyone says that the creation of all flesh is not the work of God, but belongs to the wicked angels, just as Manichaeus and Priscillian have said, let him be anathema."[5]

Although Augustine wrote many times in various places against the Manichaeans, still he expressly wrote about this matter in his book, *On Genesis against the Manichaeans*.[6]

---

[1] This quotation of Theophylactus has been substituted from the *Catena Aurea* of Saint Thomas Aquinas (chap. 6, lecture 1, n. 72), because Maurice Hylaret (*In qvinqvaginta dvarvm dominicarvm totivs anni Evangelia* (Paris, Apud Claudivm Chappelet, via Iacobaea, sub signo Unicornis, 1604), etc., vol. 1, p. 351r) says that the Latin translation of Theophylactus' exposition on Saint John's Gospel from the Greek cited here was made by the heretic, Oecolampadius.

[2] Dz. 13.

[3] Dz. 428.

[4] *Decretalium Gregorii papae* lib. 1, tit.1, c. 1.

[5] Canon 13 (Dz. 243).

[6] PL 34, 173ff.

The **second heresy**, which Manichaeus deduced from the previous one, is that creatures are evil of themselves and from their creation, because (he says) they were created by an evil god. Priscillian afterwards subscribed to this view. Now this heresy is so clear that it would not be necessary to fight against it, if we were not disputing against men who are insolent and have a stiff neck. But let us pierce them through with their own spear.

Every creature is good of itself, because (as we have just proved) it is perceived that every creature has been made by one God, Who is supremely good. Furthermore, after the creation of all things was described by Moses, he immediately added: "God saw all the things that he had made, and they were very good" (Gen. 1, 31). Hence, why does Manichaeus rave, saying that all these things are evil? Again, the Wise Man says: "Thou lovest all things that are, and hatest none of the things which thou hast made" (Wis. 11, 25). But if creatures were evil of themselves, God would love that which is evil. But now we ought to have recourse to the New Testament because we are disputing against the Manichaeans. Paul says in his First Epistle to Timothy: "Every creature of God is good" (4, 4).

Finally, the First Synod of Braga defined the following in Canon seven of its decrees: "If anyone says that the devil was not first a good Angel made by God, and that his nature was not a work of God, but says that he came forth from darkness, and does not have any author of himself, but is himself the origin and substance of evil, as Manichaeus and Priscillian have said, let him be anathema."[1] And again in Canon eight it says: "If anyone believes that the devil made some creatures in the world and by his own authority the devil himself causes thunder and lightning, and storms and spells of dryness, just as Priscillian has asserted, let him be anathema."[2] And it is not necessary to cite many testimonies in a such a clear matter.

Blessed Augustine wrote against this heresy in many places, especially in the first book of *On the Free Choice of the Will*,[3] in which place he shows that nothing is evil except from our free will, and in the second book of *On the Catholic and the Manichaean Ways of Life*.[4]

CRUX

Cross

There is one error about this matter which nowise permits the Cross to be adored, but it calls him who either adores or in any way venerates the Cross an idolater. But we have already disputed about this matter above in the section on "Adoration," in the first error.

DECIMAE

Tithes

Some heretics taught that tithes ought not to be given to priests: although they were not all arguing from the same grounds. For there were some men called the Apostolics, whose leader and teacher was Gerard Segarelli of Parma about the year of the Lord 1260, who, when arrested and condemned by the judgment of the Church, was burned. Hence

---

[1] Dz. 237.

[2] Dz. 238.

[3] "A wanton will is the cause of all evils" (Bk. 3, c. 17, n. 48 (PL 32, 1294)).

[4] PL 32, 1345-1378.

these Apostolics (as Guy [the Carmelite] says[1]) said that tithes ought not to be given to the priests of the Roman Church, because they are not poor like the Apostles. After them John Wycliffe followed the same error, motivated by a different reason. For he said that tithes are pure alms and parishioners can withhold them as they wish due to the sins of their prelates.

But this opinion is proved to be heretical by the fact that no one is allowed to break a Divine precept. Now there is a Divine precept about giving tithes. "All tithes of the land," God says, "whether of corn, or of the fruits of trees, are the Lord's, and are sanctified to him" (Lev. 27, 30). Now these tithes are prescribed by God for several reasons. The first reason is so that there may be food in the house of the Lord. For so the Lord says through Malachias the prophet: "Bring all the tithes into the storehouse, that there may be meat in my house" (Mal. 3, 10), that is to say, for the sustenance of those who are in My house. This is according to that which had been said in the Law: "They shall not possess any other thing, but be content with the oblation or tithes, which I have separated for their uses and necessities" (Num. 18, 23-24). The second reason is that they may serve in the Temple and pray to God for the people. And this reason is assigned in the book of Numbers: "I have given to the sons of Levi," He says, "all the tithes of Israel for a possession for the ministry wherewith they serve me in the tabernacle of the covenant: that the children of Israel may not approach any more to the tabernacle... but only the sons of Levi may serve me in the tabernacle, and bear the sins of the people" *(ibid.* v. 21-23). To which is consonant that which the Apostle says: "They that serve the altar, partake with the altar" (I Cor. 9, 13). The third reason is so that they may attend to God's Law and teach the people. Which reason is described in the second book of Paralipomenon, where it is said: "He commanded also the people that dwelt in Jerusalem to give to the priests and the Levites their portion, that they might attend to the law of the Lord" (II Par. 31, 4). To which Paul is in accord, saying: "If we have sown unto you spiritual things, is it a great matter if we reap your carnal things?" (I Cor. 9, 11). The fourth reason is the indigence of the poor. For tithes are given to them not on account of the priests themselves alone, but also on account of the needs of the poor. Hence Augustine says: "It is a duty to pay tithes, and whoever refuses to pay them takes what belongs to another: and as many poor men shall have died in the places where he lives when he does not give tithes, he shall appear guilty of that many murders before the tribunal of the Eternal Judge, because the property which has been assigned by God to the poor, he kept back for his own use."[2] Notice that you see that God very wisely has repeated the command of giving tithes. Thus, they are not mere alms, since they are due by that right.

But what do the Apostolics and Wycliffe try to teach against God's precept? The Apostolics say: the priests are not poor: they have the means whereby they may live: hence tithes are not due to them, because there is already sufficient bread in the Lord's house. Be it so. But is this reason enough for tithes not to be given to them? But Wycliffe defends these things, saying that many of them neither serve in the temple nor pray to God for the sins of the people, but rather they are worse than the people, and do not teach the people entrusted to them: therefore, there is no reason why tithes ought to be given to them. We admit that many of the priests are like this, such that they are completely unworthy of the name of priest. But are tithes given to them on account of the priests alone? For we have shown that the indigence of the poor is a reason on account of which tithes ought to be given. And for this reason, the most expert theologians teach that even priests otherwise abounding in riches can receive tithes, as their dispensers, namely so that they may distribute them to the poor. And those who do not do this, retain them unjustly.

---

[1] *Summa de haeresibus et earum confutationibus*, c. 4, fol. 91r.

[2] *Serm. de Tempore* 277, n. 3 (PL 39, 2268); Gràtianus, *Decretum*, p. 2, causa 16, q. 1, cn. 66 (*Decimas*).

But be that the case, namely that a priest is neither as he ought to be, nor distributes tithes to the poor, ought he be denied what is due to him by Divine law? For by this principle it would happen that when anyone, including a layman, were to have the necessaries of food and clothing, if someone else, being unwilling to pay a debt beyond this, refuses money which by a contract of loan or by the sale of some goods he owed him, he would do this justly; because it is the common opinion of all holy men, that he who keeps something for himself beyond what he needs, is said to commit robbery. [Psuedo-] Ambrose says, "That which more than suffices for one's expenses has been violently obtained."[1] And [Psuedo-] Jerome says: "He is proved to have robbed another's goods, who is proved to retain for himself more than what things he needs for himself."[2] Augustine very wisely repeats the same view.[3] Thus, according to Wycliffe and the Apostolics this debtor could justly refuse a debt to a creditor having unnecessary possessions, because he unjustly has those unnecessary possessions.

But God forbid that we would concede this, because even if he acts badly by retaining, this man does not therefore act well by refusing [to pay] the debt, because it does not pertain to just anyone to punish one acting badly. So also although priests may not properly carry out the office committed to them, still the people do not act correctly by refusing [to give] tithes to them, because it does not pertain to the people to punish the sins of the priests, but to their superiors, such as bishops, archbishops, or the supreme pontiff, who ought to deprive priests living badly of their office and benefice, and substitute other good men in their place. But if they do not do this, they ought to be left to the Divine judgment to be punished. Nor is it necessary to spend more time on the matter, since there is an explicit decree on this matter. For among the forty-five articles of John Wycliffe condemned in the Council of Constance, this one is put in the eighteenth place, with these words: "The tithes are pure alms and parishioners can take these away at will because of the sins of their prelates."[4] Which article along with the others by one judgment upon them all is condemned by the Council of Constance.

But here I wish to warn the reader, that he should not reckon that I think that by Divine precept it is now enjoined upon everyone to give tithes to priests according to an actual and precise portioning of a tenth part. I say this because even if it is accepted by all that something ought to be offered to priests, and this is not merely by Divine law, but also by the Natural law, still whether that which is due, ought to be calculated according to an actual taxation of a tenth, about this there is a dispute among the Doctors: canonists say that the taxation of a tenth is still due to the priests by Divine law: theologians however say that such taxation of a tenth was a ceremony of the Old Law, and hence was abrogated by Christ's death, just as also the other ceremonies of the Old Law. Wherefore they say that something is due to the priests by Divine and Natural law: but that some such amount ought to be expropriated according to the taxation of an actual tenth, they say that in the Evangelical law this is now from human law alone. Concerning which matter at present it is not my intention to decide anything, because I have not accepted the burden of treating opinions, but the true faith against the heretics,

---

[1] *Concordia discordantium canonum*, dist. 47, c. 8 (*Sicut his*) (PL 187, 248A); Serm. 81 on Lk. 12, 18. On the attribution of this text to Rufinus, see Rudolf Weigand, *Die Naturrechtslehre der Legisten und Dekretisten von Irnerius bis Accursius und von Gratian bis Johannes Teutonicus* (Münchener Theologische Studien, Kanonistische Abteilung, 26; Munich: (1967) 308 n. 4.

[2] *Ibid.*, dist. 42, c. 1 (PL 187, 221C). This citation is to the *Regula Monachorum*, ("Rules for Monks"), a text once thought to be by Jerome but which was later shown to be apocryphal.

[3] The heretics are here claiming that one does not need to repay debts to anyone not in dire need of being repaid. But this is a distortion of the truth that anyone who is himself in dire poverty need not repay his debts until he obtains the sufficient means whereby he may do so without causing grave inconvenience to himself.

[4] Dz. 598.

against which I think it to be enough to have shown that tithes are due to priests from the Divine precept, which no one is allowed to transgress. But whether such a tithe actually be a tenth part of the whole or not, it hardly matters: because even if it were not imposed by Divine law, nevertheless it is commanded by papal law, to which all Christians are bound to submit.

DEUS

God

God is the most mysterious being and which being greatly escapes the understanding of all men: to such an extent that a certain prophet was obliged to say: "Thou art a hidden God" (Is. 45, 15). And this is not surprising, because (as Paul says) He "inhabiteth light inaccessible" and no eye can bear.[1] Hence when the Lord passed before the prophet Elias, "and a great and strong wind before the Lord overthrowing the mountains, and breaking the rocks in pieces," Elias "covered his face with his mantle" (III Kings 19, 11 & 13), namely because he knew that human eyes cannot bear so great splendor of the Divine majesty. For if "the children of Israel could not steadfastly behold the face of Moses" (II Cor. 3, 7), because he had a conversation with God in the mountain,[2] what do you think the human intellect would will do if it wanted to behold God's face, so that it might penetrate it with the shrewdness of its own intelligence? Certainly it must happen what the Wise Man says: "A searcher of majesty, shall be overwhelmed by glory" (Prov. 25, 27). Wherefore there is no being, in the perfect knowledge of which ought to more subdue our intellect unto the service of God, than God Himself, because for investigating that supreme mystery of the unity and Trinity no intellect destitute of faith suffices. Hence so many heresies concerning this matter have arisen (I omit the errors of the heathens and pagans) because relying on their own abilities, trusting in their own intelligence, they attributed more to human arguments than to the faith. And so it happened that wishing to scrutinize the Divine majesty, they were overwhelmed by glory, and fell into many heresies. Thus, because they put their mouths into heaven and touched that mountain which is above all mountains, it is needful that we block up their mouths with stones, according to the Lord's precept saying: "Every one that toucheth the mount... shall be stoned" (Ex. 19, 12-13). Thus, we shall go out to refute these errors in this order, such that firstly those will be treated which regard the Divinity Itself taken absolutely. Then we will discuss those which pertain to the individual Divine Persons.

Therefore, the **first heresy** is that which asserts many Gods. And this is divided into many factions. For this heresy is common, such that they never agree with themselves. For some said that there are two gods, one good, from whom are all good things: the other evil, from whom all evil things proceed. The first authors of this heresy were they who were called Gnostics: concerning whom we have already spoken elsewhere. After them a certain Apelles (concerning whom Eusebius [writes][3]) defended the same error of two gods, one good, the other evil, although he differs somewhat in this from the Gnostics. For Apelles did not say (as Augustine relates[4]) that those two gods are two principles of things, but says that there is only one principle, namely the good god, and from him was made the other god, who since he was malicious, made the world in his malignity.

---

[1] I Tim. 6, 16.
[2] Ex. 34, 29.
[3] *Ecclesiastical History*, lib. 5, c. 13, n. 5 (PG 20, 462A).
[4] *De Haeresibus ad Quodvultdeum*, c. 23 (PL 42, 29).

Some years later Manichaeus, having imitated these Gnostics, taught the same error, and it gained strength more under this man than under the Gnostics: to such an extent that it took its name from him, and now it is called [the error] of the Manichaeans. But this Manichaeus (as it is often the case when heretics revive heresies then buried, and so that they may appear more clearly, they manage to increase the madness, adding not a little from their own brain) said something worse than the Gnostics, namely that the two Testaments of Scripture came from those two gods. He says that the Old Testament was made by the evil god, but the New Testament by the good god, and he says that this creator of the New Testament is the Father of Our Lord Jesus Christ, but He did not make the Old Testament. The Albanenses called back this error from Hell after many centuries. For Guy [the Carmelite] accuses them of this:[1] and the *Catalogus haereticorum* attributes the same thing to the Albigensians.[2]

Other heretics, however, said that there are two gods, but they did not say that one is good and the other evil. The author of this error was a man by the name of Cerdo, although Philastrius says that Cerdo thought that there are two gods, one good and the other evil.[3] Blessed Augustine, nevertheless, says that Cerdo had proposed "two principles which are in mutual opposition, and that the god of the Law and the Prophets is not the Father of Christ, nor is he good, but just: another god, however, is the Father of Christ, and this god is good."[4] Notice that according to Augustine's opinion, Cerdo did not posit a god that is evil, because he says that he is just, although he is not good. Now in order that Blessed Augustine's opinion be confirmed, I will bring to the fore Irenaeus, more ancient than Augustine and Philastrius. For Irenaeus when speaking about this Cerdo says the following: "Cerdo was one who took his system from the followers of Simon, and came to live at Rome in the time of Hyginus, who held the ninth place in the episcopal succession from the Apostles downwards. He taught that the God proclaimed by the Law and the Prophets was not the Father of our Lord Jesus Christ. For the former was known, but the latter unknown; while the one also was righteous, but the other benevolent."[5] From whose words no such thing is found that Cerdo thought that there are two gods, one of whom is good, the other evil. Marcion of Pontus was a disciple of Cerdo and followed him.

At the same time in which the above-mentioned Cerdo lived (as Irenaeus says[6]) there was a certain heretic named Valentinus, who, although he was a Platonist (as Tertullian says[7]), taught many figments of his imagination, mixing the teachings of Plato with the Christian religion. For he said that there are two principles of all things, which he named depth and silence: and he said that depth is the father; from the marriage of depth and silence proceeded the mind and truth, and brought forth eight aeons in honor of the father, that is the eight ages.[8] Now from the mind and truth proceeded the Word and life, and brought forth ten aeons. From the Word and life proceeded man and the Church, and brought forth twelve aeons, which all together are thirty, that is, thirty ages. He says from the thirtieth age the devil was begotten, and from the devil other [devils] were born who made this world. Therefore he says all things proceeded from those two principles, namely depth and silence. All which things are mere figments of the imagination and mere fables, which can be supported by no reason, but are derived from the mind of a deranged and daydreaming man. Secundus followed these unlearned

---

[1] *Summa de haeresibus et earum confutationibus*, c. 1, fol. 76r.
[2] Fol 23v.
[3] *Liber de Haeresibus*, c. 44, (PL 12, 1160A)).
[4] *De Haeresibus ad Quodvultdeum*, c. 21 (PL 42, 29).
[5] *Contra Haereses*, bk. 1, c. 27, n. 1 (PG 7, 687B-688A).
[6] *Contra Haereses*, bk. 3, c. 4, n. 3 (PG 7, 856C-857A).
[7] *De Praescriptione Haereticorum*, c. 7 (PL 2, 19A).
[8] *Aeon* comes from the Greek *aiōn*, meaning "age."

fables, from whom are the Secundians: and a certain Ptolemy and Marcus, are followers of this Valentinus.

It is not hard to dispute against all these heretics since there are very clear testimonies of Sacred Scripture which teach that there is only one God: and He is the Supreme Good, from Whom all things proceed. In Deuteronomy it is said: "Hear, O Israel, the Lord our God is one Lord" (6, 4). And in the same book it is again said: "See ye that I alone am, and there is no other God besides me" (32, 39). The Royal Prophet, who also was himself an Israelite, says: "Who is God but the Lord? or who is God but our God?" (Ps. 17, 32). And again: "For thou art great and dost wonderful things: thou art God alone" (*Ibid.* 85, 10). The wise Solomon teaches the same faith: "For there is no other God," he says, "but thou, who hast care of all" (Wis. 12, 13). Isaias also commends the same faith, who portrays God as saying: "I am the Lord, and there is none else: there is no God, besides me" (45, 5). And in the same place: "I am the Lord, and there is none else" (v. 6). And again in the same place: "I am the Lord, and there is no other" (v. 18). And in the same place: "Am not I the Lord, and there is no God else besides me?" (v. 21). And he repeats the same assertion again in the same place, saying: "Be converted to me, and you shall be saved, all ye ends of the earth: for I am God, and there is no other" (v. 22).

But because both Cerdo and Manichaeus do not accept the Old Testament: so that no way may be open for them to escape, it is necessary to pierce them with testimonies of the New Testament. Paul in the First Epistle to the Corinthians says the following: "We know that there is no God but one. For although there be that are called gods, either in heaven or on earth (for there be gods many, and lords many). Yet to us there is but one God, the Father, of whom are all things, and we unto him" (8, 4-6). And in the Epistle to the Galatians he says: "A mediator is not of one: but God is one" (3, 20). And elsewhere he says: "One Lord, one faith, one baptism. One God and Father of all, who is above all, and through all, and in us all" (Eph. 4, 5-6).

Here I omit to cite philosophical reasons, because we do not dispute against pagans, but against those who gave their names to Christ in Baptism, and who pride themselves as being Christians, although they are by no means Christians. Aristotle very wisely strives to show that there is only one principle of all things.[1] But since the Scriptures are so clear, he is not necessary for our argumentations.

That which Cerdo says, namely that the God of the Law and Prophets is not the Father of our Lord Jesus Christ, to which Manichaeus subscribes, adding that the God of the New Testament is not He Who also gave the Old. This impiety is refuted by Paul's one saying: "God, who, at sundry times and in divers manners, spoke in times past to the fathers by the prophets, last of all, in these days hath spoken to us by his Son, whom he hath appointed heir of all things, by whom also he made the world" (Heb. 1, 1-2). But if you require yet another testimony, let the mute Zachary open his mouth and say: "Blessed be the Lord God of Israel; because he hath visited and wrought the redemption of his people" (Lk. 1, 68). It is evident that he is speaking about the Father of our Lord Jesus Christ, because He did not otherwise visit and work the Redemption of His people, except by sending His Son, so that the world might be saved through Him Thus, since He is speaking about this Father, He added: "As he spoke by the mouth of his holy prophets, who are from the beginning" (v. 70). Notice that it clearly appears that God, Who spoke through the Prophets, has also spoken in the New Testament in the Gospels, and worked our Redemption through His Son.

But if they still ask for a third witness, let us also ask for help from the Blessed Virgin Mary, so that she may give testimony in our favor concerning this matter: and she will not fail to

---

[1] "The first mover, then, of necessity exists; and in so far as it is necessary, it is good, and in this sense a first principle... On such a principle, then, depend the heavens and the world of nature" (*Metaphysics*, bk. 12, c. 7).

fulfill our request. She in fact when magnifying God because He regarded the humility of His handmaid, and He that is mighty did great things to her, and many other things which must necessarily to be referred to the Father of our Lord Jesus Christ: and finally she says: "He hath received Israel his servant, being mindful of his mercy: As he spoke to our fathers, to Abraham and to his seed for ever" (v. 54-55). Thus, the God Who showed mercy towards us: He, I say, spoke to our fathers, to Abraham and to his seed. Therefore there is not one God of the Old Testament, and another God of the New Testament: nor is there one Who spoke through the Prophets, and another who is the Father of our Lord Jesus Christ.

But Paul teaches this more explicitly, who in his Epistle to the Romans says: "It is one God, that justifieth circumcision by faith, and uncircumcision through faith" (3, 30). What then does Manichaeus rave? Is not the Old Testament designated by circumcision and the New by uncircumcision? But now let us see what else they say: namely that they propose that one of the two gods is evil. Is there any blasphemy that could be greater? What ears can tolerate this, or what mind could think this, such that he would charge God with wickedness? These things can nowise cohere, namely that He be God and evil: because if He be God, He is necessarily good: and if he be not good, he is certainly not God. That which Paul says when speaking to the Gentiles certainly befits these heretics: "When they knew God, they have not glorified him as God, or given thanks; but became vain in their thoughts, and their foolish heart was darkened" (Rom. 1, 21). For in saying that they are wise men, they were made foolish. Behold how these wicked and blasphemous heretics glorify God, who call Him evil. See what thanks they give to Him, they who accuse Him of supreme wickedness. Thus, since it is implanted by nature in the hearts of all men, that we acknowledge that God is good, it irks to cite testimonies of Scripture for something so clear: and if anyone desires them, they are most clear: thus, for example, the Gospel itself, which alone these heretics believe, says: "None is good but God alone" (Lk. 18, 19).

One ought not to assail against these heretics with arguments, but with stones, according to the Lord's precept saying: "The man that curseth his God, shall bear his sin: and he that blasphemeth the name of the Lord, dying let him die: all the multitude shall stone him, whether he be a native or a stranger. He that blasphemeth the name of the Lord, dying let him die" (Lev. 24, 15-16). Now who more truly curses God, than he who says that God is evil? Therefore this man deserves to be crushed by the whole multitude.

There is a **second heresy** which teaches that God is corporeal. The first author (as I think) of this heresy is Tertullian. Although Blessed Augustine excuses this Tertullian concerning this matter in his book, *De Haeresibus [ad Quodvultdeum]*,[1] saying that Tertullian ought not to be called a heretic on this account, because he could so think about God such that he said that He is a sort of body, not in fact such that He would have parts, some of which are larger and others smaller, which is also circumscribed in a place and contained within certain boundaries: but he could have called God a body, namely because he is not "nothingness," but is something, which is entire everywhere. But I do not really know whether such a thing which does not have parts, can fittingly and rightly be called a body.

But Blessed Augustine excused the use with a very light censure as much as he could. For he thought that no crime is more grievous and serious which could be hurled against a Christian than the crime of heresy: hence before we accuse anyone of this, it is necessary to first carefully examine the matter, and reduce the stone to a thread. Thus let them learn from Augustine—a person exceptionally zealous for the faith—those who so lightly make a pronouncement of heresy, lest if perhaps anyone would teach something, which deviates from their preference even by the breadth of a finger, they immediately cry out "heresy," allowing absolutely no excuse of the man even when he could easily be excused. Thus, since Bless-

---

[1] C. 86 (PL 42, 46-47).

ed Augustine excuses Tertullian in regard to this matter, I do not want to be a more severe judge against this same man. For I prefer (according to the opinion of [Pseudo-] Blessed Chrysostom) "to have to answer for mercy than for severity."[1] But although Tertullian was excused, nevertheless I will not on that account cease to fight against the heresy already related, because our combat is not against men, but against heresies, especially because there are not lacking followers of this heresy, who also defend it apart from Tertullian.

For there were certain heretics called the Audians, who said that God is corporeal, and has members as men have: they were motivated by the fact that very often in Sacred Writ, especially in the Old Testament, members are attributed to God, and Adam was said to have been made in God's image and likeness, hence they conclude that God has members just like Adam. These heretics having been allotted their name from their error, were called Anthropomorphites, because *anthropos* in Greek means "human."[2] Now this heresy arose in the regions of Egypt at the time of Pope Damasus and Theodore the Elder: Theophilus, Bishop of Alexandria, wrote against this heresy and refuted it (as it is said in the *Historia Tripartita*[3]).

[However,] Brother Bernard of Luxemburg in his *Catalogus haereticorum*[4] says that this heresy began under Pope Agapetus, and Emperor Berengar [II]. And it is certain that he is speaking of Agapetus II, because Agapetus I (as Platina relates[5]) was under the Emperor Justinian [I], to see whom he went from Rome all the way to Constantinople, where he also died. Thus it is necessary that this Agapetus of whom the *Catalogus* [*haereticorum*] speaks, be the second. Now from [Pope St.] Damasus, under whom this pestilence arose, until Agapetus [II] there intervened nearly six hundred years: wherefore I do not know in whose writings he read that this heresy began under Agapetus [II] and Berengar [II]. And what surprises me more, when speaking in the same place about the same Anthropomorphites, after he said that this heresy began under Agapetus [II] and Berengar [II], he added that Theophilus of Alexandria condemned the heresy of the Anthropomorphites: for the confirmation of which fact he cites a passage from Cassian's *Conferences of the Desert Fathers*.[6]

And these two things can hardly be reconciled, namely that the heresy began under Agapetus [II] and Theophilus of Alexandria condemned it, and so supposing he confused the calculation: because from Theophilus of Alexandria, of whom Cassian makes mention, until Pope Agapetus II there elapsed nearly six hundred years, and until Agapetus I nearly three hundred years, because this Theophilus (as is evident from the *Historia Tripartita*[7]) lived at the time of Pope Damasus. For [Theophilus] sent a certain legate, bishop Isidore, to [Damasus]. Hence it is allowable to infer that Brother Bernard of Luxemburg badly pieced together that work from many patches, having made no reasonable inference about these things. Perhaps he had read in one author that this heresy began under Agapetus [II], and then read nothing else about it. In Cassian he read something else, namely that Theophilus refuted it by disputation. And this man not considering whether those two things could be reconciled, joined them together.

Why should it have been easily detected by a man versed in learned authors, not to speak about the inconsistency of the things, that it is false that [this heresy] began under Agapetus [II]? It is because besides that which the *Historia Tripartita* relates, Augustine, who preceded both Agapetus' by a number of centuries, also mentions this heresy under the name of the

---

[1] *Opus imperfectum*, hom. 43 (PG 56, 878). *Catena Aurea*, in Mt., 23, lect. 1.
[2] *Morphe* means "form" in Greek.
[3] Bk. 10, c. 7 (PL 69, 1170-1171).
[4] Fol. 24r. He wrote that the heresy began in 949 A.D.
[5] *The Lives of the Popes* (London: Griffith, Farran, Okeden & Welsh, 1888), vol. 1 p. 125-126.
[6] Conference 10, c. 2 (PL 49, 820-823).
[7] Bk. 10, c. 10 (PL 69, 1172-1173).

Anthropomorphites.[1] I am forced to point out these things partly out of love for the truth, and partly enkindled by the heat of anger: when I see some men so unreliable and prolific in proclaiming and in writing, that whatever they shall have read, written even by just anyone, with no investigation into the matters, they immediately copy, and declare with confidence before the whole great multitude, thinking to themselves that it is sufficient that they read just any author.

Thus this opinion of the Anthropomorphites may be clearly refuted. If God is corporeal, and has a human shape, members and parts as a man, it is necessary that He be finite, and circumscribed by certain boundaries, because that which is infinite, can be of no shape, since it is necessarily required for a thing to have a shape that it be enclosed by a boundary or boundaries. But God Who is infinite, cannot be enclosed by any boundary, hence He has neither shape nor is enclosed in a place. "God is higher than heaven," as it is written in the book of Job, "and is elevated above the height of the stars" (22, 12). And the [Royal] Prophet says: "Great is the Lord, and greatly to be praised: and of his greatness there is no end" (Ps. 144, 3). But if there is no end of His greatness, there is also no shape of His.

Furthermore, if God were corporeal and would have members like a man, it would follow that He would not be entire everywhere, but part of Him in one place, and another part in another place, and so He will be divided by parts in places, which is greatly opposed to His supreme perfection. Again, it would also be necessary to grant that composition is in God, and to say that those things that are in God are not all of infinite perfection, because whatever things of which He is composed, are less than His entirety: and so are not equally perfect as the whole: wherefore it would be necessary finite, because what is infinite cannot be exceeded.

Many other similar arguments could be made from the imperfections which adjoin bodies: but avoiding prolixity I omit them, because without them we have very clear testimony from Sacred Scripture. For Truth Itself says in John's Gospel: "God is a spirit" (4, 24), hence He is not corporeal, and having human members, because the same Truth says in Luke's Gospel: "A spirit hath not flesh and bones, as you see me to have" (24, 39).

Now what the Anthropomorphites bring forth in their favor has little weight and proceeds from a warped understanding of Scripture. For although Sacred Scripture often mentions God's members, such as His head, eyes, tongue, ears, hands, arms and ones similar to these: still those words ought not to be taken in the literal sense, but according to a designated mystery hiding through those things. For there are very many things in the sacred books, especially in the Old Testament, because they were given to a carnal and still uneducated people, nowise ought to be taken according to the first signification of the letter, nor can they be taken, but what is signified by the letter according to its deeper meaning ought to be understood. For things themselves often also have a meaning, and affect the meanings, as well as the words. Because it is clear that it happens in all metaphorical speech, in which on account of the comparison found between things, one thing is called by the name of another. For example, if you call a voracious person a wolf, or an avaricious person a mole: it is not because they are such things, but because those things are similar to them. That it is necessary to interpret many things in Sacred Writ in the same way, and not according to the first meaning of the words, the Apostle bears witness, when saying that "the letter killeth, but the spirit quickeneth" (II Cor. 3, 6).

This is one and the chief among the many [explanations]. As often as some member or some shape is attributed to God, then you ought to understand by the said member that a power or strength is attributed to God by that word, which is more perfect than is found in that member: for instance when you hear mention of a head in God, understand the Divine

---

[1] *De Haeresibus* [*ad Quodvultdeum*], c. 50 (PL 42, 39).

essence, which is superior to all things. And when "head" is said in reference to the Mystical Body, which is the Church: understand His influx in the other members, which we are. When you hear "eyes," understand the power of so seeing that nothing can hide from Him. For the Apostle says: "Neither is there any creature invisible in his sight: but all things are naked and open to his eyes" (Heb. 4, 13). He is said to have ears, because there is such power in Him, that any word quietly uttered, cannot escape His notice, concerning Whom the Wise man says: "For the ear of jealousy heareth all things, and the tumult of murmuring shall not be hid" (Wis. 1, 10).[1]

But if the heretics are not persuaded by this explanation, but contend that everything ought to be understood according to the first meaning of the text, they will be forced to say that God is a monstrosity, nay some such thing which does not exist, since sometimes He is called a lion,[2] other times a worm,[3] and other times a locust.[4] Hence it is clearly proved that these things ought not to be taken according to the first meaning of the text, but according to that which the things themselves denoted by those words signify.

There is a book of [Psuedo-] Blessed Anselm about the mystical meaning of all these things entitled, *De [vestimentis et] membris [et actibus] Deo atttibutis*: in which he explains what each member attributed to God means.[5] There is also another treatise on the same subject ascribed to Jerome, which as a spurious treatise, and hardly redolent of Blessed Jerome, the very learned man, Erasmus of Rotterdam put into the fourth volume of his works, in which place he rejects all the works which hitherto had been falsely ascribed to Jerome. Theophilus of Alexandria, of whom we recently made mention, wrote against these Anthropomorphites.[6] Faustus, Bishop of Riez, and the monk, Ratherius, also wrote [against these Anthropomorphites] (as Johannes Trithemius testifies in his *De Ecclesiasticis scriptoribus*,[7]), but I have not seen any of these works.

There is a **third heresy**, which ought to rather be called blasphemy, asserting that God is a liar. This is the heresy of the Armenians, as Guy [the Carmelite] accuses them.[8] For they say that God said to Cain that he would be killed by no man, and yet (as they say) Cain killed himself, and thus proved that God said something false, since he was killed by a man. And certainly (as I frankly admit) I can hardly believe, even if Guy bears witness, that the Armenians fell into such a serious error, such that they would call God a liar, because this cannot come into a man's mind, that one would call Truth a lie, especially since the Armenians, even if they are heretics, still do not reject Sacred Scripture. For Guy never accuses them of this.

Therefore, if they accept Sacred Scripture, how can they say that God is a liar, since Scripture itself very often proclaims that God is most true? For "God is not a man," Scripture says,

---

[1] The text here has instead, "The ear of heaven," etc., which is taken from the Old Latin Bible.

[2] Osee, 11, 10; Apoc. 5, 5.

[3] Ps. 21, 7.

[4] Eccli. 43, 19.

[5] This treatise is rather an excerpt from Saint Augustine's *De essential unitatis*, bk. 1 (PL 42, 1200-1206). But it had been wrongly included in *Divi Anselmi archiepiscopi Cantuariensis Opera omnia quatuor tomis comprehensa*, (Cologne, Petrus Cholinus, 1612), vol. 3, pp. 185-187.

[6] "The Festal [Pascal] letter of Theophilus has not survived. But so far as we can tell from Gennadius' summary [*Lives of Illustrious Men*, chap. 34 (cap. 33 (PL 58, 1077B-1078B))], it demonstrated from Scripture that God was incorruptible and incorporeal, and moreover the only incorruptible and immutable nature, because all created natures, even intellectual ones, are corporeal, corruptible and mutable." (Normal Russell, *Theophilus of Alexandria* (London and New York, Routledge, 2007), p. 22).

[7] Faustus and Ratherius each wrote a treatise entitled *Contra Anthromophitas*. (*De scriptoribus Ecclesiasticis* (Basil, J. Amerbach, 1494), fol. 32v & 47r).

[8] *Summa de haeresibus et earum confutationibus*, c. 30, fol. 42r.

"that he should lie" (Num. 23, 19). And the prophet Jeremias says: "The Lord is the true God" (10, 10). And God Himself says: "I am the way, and the truth, and the life" (Jn. 14, 6). If God is truth, how could He have lied? Certainly not any more than coldness can heat, or blackness make white. Furthermore, how could God lie, Who abhors sin so much? Who very often deters men from lying, as from a most wicked vice? "Lying lips," says the Wise Man, "are an abomination to the Lord: but they that deal faithfully please him" (Prov. 12, 22). And elsewhere: "The mouth that belieth, killeth the soul" (Wis. 1, 11).

Again, if God is one time convicted of a lie, it follows that He should never be believed in the future. For this is the consequence of a man's lie, as Aristotle bears witness, that he is not believed when he says the truth.[1] But if God ought not to be believed, every law will perish, all social intercourse [will perish]: there will be no trust. And we certainly need not dispute more about this matter, since it is such clear madness, that anyone, even an infidel or pagan, acknowledges it. For there is no nation so barbaric that it does not abhor a lie.

The things which they assert about Cain are not found in Sacred Writ. For Sacred Scripture does not say that Cain killed himself, nay, neither does it make any mention of his death, although some Doctors are of the opinion that it was he whom Lamech killed, when thinking that [Cain] was a wild animal. Otherwise, even if Scripture said that Cain was killed by Lamech, or hurled himself down, God ought not on that account be accused of a lie, because God did not say that Cain was not going to be killed by any man, but rather He said: "Whosoever shall kill Cain, shall be punished sevenfold" (Gen. 4, 15). By which words He merely forbade the killing of Cain by any man: nevertheless He did not deny that it would happen.

The **fourth heresy** diminishes God's omnipotence. For Peter Abelard (as Blessed Thomas [Aquinas] accuses him[2]) says that God could not make things differently that He did, wherefore he said that all things happen by an absolute necessity. But we will dispute about this error below when we treat about the "Future Contingent."

There is a **fifth heresy** which denies the number of Persons in the Divinity. The author of this heresy was a certain Noetus, from whom the Noetians are so called.[3] Blessed Epiphanius [of Salamis] when discussing this Noetus, in his *Treatise Against Eighty Sects*,[4] says the following: "Another one, whose name was Noetus, an Asian from the city of Ephesus, arose in his turn after Bardesanes, not many years ago but about one hundred thirty years before our time. By the inspiration of a strange spirit he chose to say and teach things on his own authority which neither the prophets nor the Apostles [had proclaimed], and which the Church from the beginning had neither held nor conceived of. On his own authority he dared to say, with manic elation, that the Father suffered. And then, from further delirious conceit he called himself Moses, and his brother, Aaron. In the meantime, however, the blessed presbyters of the Church sent for Noetus because of the rumor about him, and questioned him about all these things, and whether he had put forth this blasphemy of the Father. At first he denied it when brought before the presbytery, since no one before him had belched out this frightful, deadly bitterness. But later, after, as it were, infecting certain others with his madness and winning about ten men over, inspired to greater pride and insolence [and] grown bold, he began to

---

[1] "Asked 'what those who tell lies gain by it,' he was said to have replied: 'They gain this,' said he, 'that when they speak truth, they are not believed'" (Diogenes Laërtius, *The Lives and Opinions of Eminent Philosophers* (London, Henry G. Bohn, 1853), p. 187).

[2] *De potential*, q. 1, a. 5.

[3] "Noetus of Smyrna, who was excommunicated in his own province about 239… held that God the Father of all is the only God and this one God became man, suffered and died." ("Sabellianism," *A Catholic Dictionary* (New York, Aeterna Press, 1887)).

[4] It is also called the *Panarion*, which in Greek mean "bread basket." In Latin it is entitled, *Adversus Haereses* ("Against Heresies"). Saint Epiphanius, Bishop of Salamis, died in 403 A.D.

teach his heresy openly. The same presbyters summoned him once more, and the men who unfortunately had become acquainted with him, and asked again about the same things. But now, with his followers in error, Noetus struck his forehead and openly opposed them. 'What wrong have I done,' he demanded, 'because I glorify one God? I know one God and none other besides him, and he has been born, has suffered, and has died!' Since he held to this they expelled him from the Church, with the men he had instructed in his own doctrine. He himself has died recently as has his brother, but not in glory like Moses; nor was his brother buried with honor like Aaron. They were cast out as transgressors, and none of the godly would lay them out for burial. Those whose minds he had corrupted confirmed this doctrine afterwards under the influence of the following texts, which had influenced their false teacher to begin with."[1]

Sabellius,[2] a disciple of this same Noetus (as Philastrius says[3]), from which Sabellius the Sabellians are so named, and this heresy is better known by this name than by the name of Noetus. This pestilence arose in Ptolemais of Egypt,[4] under the Emperor Gallienus and Pope Sixtus II. Thus, these men said that there is only one Person in the Divinity: nevertheless, that Person is named by different names. From that corrupt spring they also draw this vitiated river, namely that the Father suffered just as the Son also suffered: it was necessary that they assert this, since they said that the Father and the Son are the same Person. And so having been allotted their name from this teaching, they were called the Patripassians[5]: because they taught that the Father suffered. Afterwards Priscillian taught the same error (as Augustine says[6]).

The heresy of these men arose from the fact that (as Eusebius of Caesarea says[7]) they did not know how to distinguish between essence and person: or (to use the words of Eusebius) between substance and subsistence: even though there is a great difference between them. In fact, substance, essence, or nature, which vocabulary scholastic theologians use more, is something shared by many particular things whereby the single, individual things agree, and sets forth the whole perfection of any of those particular things. But a person is something singular and unique, endowed with a mind and reason, distinct from other individuals of the same nature by a singular property: as when you say "man" in general, you are referring to the human nature common to all men: I do not say common in reality, but merely as a manner of speech, but when you say Peter, John, Francis, you name persons, who agree in that human nature. They agree, I say, in a certain manner of speech (as I said), because any of them is called and is a true man. Or, if you prefer, they agree in the definition describing the perfection of the thing, which is found in any one of them. Hence in God His substance or essence is the very nature of the Deity, which expresses the whole perfection of the Deity.

But the Person is something singular in which the Deity exists, really separated from another individual, really, I say, not by nature, but by personal property: as when we say God,

---

[1] Heresy 57 (PG 41, 994D-995C).
[2] Sabellius (fl. ca. 215) was a third-century priest and theologian who most likely taught in Rome, but may have been a North African from Libya.
[3] *Liber de Haeresibus*, c. 54, (PL 12, 1168B).
[4] "He refers also in the same letter to the heretical teachings of Sabellius, which were in his time becoming prominent, and says: 'For concerning the doctrine now agitated in Ptolemais of Pentapolis...'" (Eusebius, *Church History*, bk. 7, c. 6).
[5] This name comes from the Latin *patri* "father" and *passio* "suffering."
[6] *De Haeresibus* [*ad Quodvultdeum*], c. 70 (PL 42, 44).
[7] The reference given here is to Eusebius' *Church History* (bk. 10, c. 29), but book ten and eleven of this work were added by Rufinus of Aquileia when he translated this work. Hence the citation more correctly refers to Rufinus' *Historia Ecclesiastica*, bk. 1, c. 29 (PL 21, 499D).

we express the substance of the Divine nature common to all the Persons. Common, I say, not (as we said concerning man) by a mere manner of speech, but truly and really common. But when we say Father, Son or Holy Ghost, we are speaking about a singular or unique Person in Whom the Deity subsists. Thus, since this mystery of the Trinity and unity is so deep that it surpasses the understanding of human and Angelic intelligence, it is necessary here to subject our understanding to the obedience of faith. Wherefore it is superfluous, nay ridiculous, to discuss this with reasons and arguments, but solely with testimonies of Scripture, from which we will clearly demonstrate, with God as our guide, the unity of the same God and Trinity of Persons.

In the book of Genesis, after having described the production of all the other creatures, when God decides about creating man, He says the following: "Let us make man to our image and likeness: and let him have dominion," etc., (1, 26). And a few words later He adds: "And God created man to his own image" (v. 27). By these words both the unity of the Divinity and the plurality of Persons is clearly shown. For He said the following: "And God saw that it was good. And he said: Let us make man" (v. 25-26). But since after the noun in the singular which is God, He added the verb in the plural [*faciamus*], namely "Let us make," He declared the plurality of Persons: because if there were only one Person, He would not have said in the plural, "let us make." Next that which follows also does not lack a mystery. For when saying, "let us make," He adds "image" and not "images": He said "to our likeness," not to our likenesses," intimating by this that even if the plurality of Persons is denoted when speaking in the plural, still one ought not think by this that there are many exemplars, but only one, in Whose image and likeness man was made. For if there were only one Person, as Sabellius falsely asserts, He would have said "My likeness," and not "our likeness."

Furthermore, in the same book, when the destruction of Sodom and Gomorrha is treated, it is so said: "And the Lord rained upon Sodom and Gomorrha brimstone and fire from the Lord out of heaven" (19, 24). If there is only one Person in the Divinity, Who is this "Lord" Who rained from the Lord? For when He said, "Lord… from the Lord," He shows the Son, through Whom (as John the Evangelist says[1]) all things were made: Who also is said to rain "from the Lord," because from the one whom one has existence, from him also one can act. Therefore when saying, "Lord… from the Lord," He shows the Father and the Son. For the Son is the Lord, and He is from the Lord, because He is begotten of the Father. Now the Father is the Lord, but not from the Lord, because He is unbegotten.

Again, the Royal Prophet, when speaking of Christ, relates the words of the Father said to Christ in this way: "Thou art my son, this day have I begotten thee" (Ps. 2, 7). "From the womb before the day star I begot thee" (Ps. 109, 3). Which words Paul the Apostle bears witness that they were said concerning Christ, the Son of God, who when speaking of Christ in this manner says: "For to which of the angels hath he said at any time, Thou art my Son, today have I begotten thee?" (Heb. 1, 5). Now it is not possible that the same person begets himself so that he may exist: nor can man's intellect conceive this, that the same thing be father of itself and son of itself. Thus there is One Who begets and another Who is begotten: One Who is the Father, and another the Son.

Next the Highest Truth Itself very often taught this truth. For to the Pharisees objecting that He gave testimony to Himself, and consequently His testimony was not true, He replies: "And if I do judge, my judgment is true: because I am not alone, but I and the Father that sent me. And in your law it is written, that the testimony of two men is true. I am one that give testimony of myself: and the Father that sent me giveth testimony of me" (Jn. 8, 16-18). Certainly nothing whatsoever could be said clearer against Sabellius. For if the Father and the Son are one Person (as Sabellius dreamt up) then the Son is said to be alone, even if He be

---

[1] Jn. 1, 3.

with the Father: just as if I were to say only Tullius wrote the *Tusculan Disputations*, even if Cicero wrote them, because Tullius and Cicero are one person, although the names are different. But what follows is still clearer. For wishing to prove that His testimony is true, He cited in favor of Himself the law saying that the testimony of two men is true. Notice with what argument He refutes the Pharisees. But if the Father and the Son are one Person, He would have argued badly, and would not have cited the Law in favor of Himself: because the Law approves the testimony of two men, not of one. Thus it is necessary that the Father and the Son are two Persons, if Christ's argument is of any value.

And again the Truth Itself says the same thing to the Jews: "I and the Father are one" (Jn. 10, 30). By saying "[we] are" in the plural, He clearly declared that He and the Father are two Persons: because otherwise He would have said "[I] am," and not "[we] are." But by saying "[we] are," He declared that the Deity of the same Persons is one. And again the Truth says when praying to the Father: "This is eternal life: that they may know thee, the only true God, and Jesus Christ, whom thou hast sent" (Jn. 17, 3). The meaning of those words is not, only God the Father is the true God, such that we would exclude Christ from the Deity, because we have already proved above against other heretics when speaking treating the Person of Christ that Christ is the true God. Thus the meaning is, that they may know that Thou, and Jesus Christ, whom thou hast sent, is the only true God. Hence when He enumerated the Father and Jesus Christ with a copulative conjunction, He called them the true God. From which words the plurality of Persons and the unity of the Divinity are clearly shown.

But even though these testimonies of Scripture are sufficient for proving the plurality of Persons along with the unity of the Deity, nevertheless they do not show the true Trinity, because from that which was said, "Let us make man to our image and likeness," it is proved that there are more than one person, yet it is not proved that there are three. Now in order to prove this, it is necessary that we cite other testimonies.

And firstly, that is the most efficacious of all, although hiding under a figure, which befell Abraham sitting by the oak of Mambre.[1] "When he had lifted up his eyes, there appeared to him three men standing near him: and as soon as he saw them he ran to meet them from the door of his tent, and adored down to the ground. And he said: Lord, if I have found favour in thy sight, pass not away from thy servant," etc., (Gen. 18, 2-3). You see here that three men firstly appeared and Abraham when speaking to these three men says as it were to one man: "Lord, if I have found favour in thy sight," etc.

David also, the prophet and king, to show the triune God says: "May God, our God bless us, may God bless us: and all the ends of the earth fear him" (Ps. 66, 7-8). For when he named God three times, lest perhaps from that someone might take occasion of surmising three gods, making the relation afterwards, he said in the singular, "all the ends of the earth fear him." For by naming God three times he declared the three Persons. But adding, "fear him," etc., he declared that all three are one God.

Isaias also when telling the words of the Seraphim praising God says: "Holy, holy, holy." But lest from that which he had said three times, the unity of the Divine substance be rent apart or that someone would suspect a division, he added, "the Lord God of hosts" (Is. 6, 3). Thus when he said "holy" three times, he showed the Trinity of Persons. But adding afterwards, "Lord God," in the singular, he declared the unity of the same Trinity.

The Truth Itself, namely Christ our Redeemer, when He had risen, now restored to life, being about to ascend into Heaven says: "Going therefore, teach ye all nations; baptizing them in the name of the Father, and of the Son, and of the Holy Ghost" (Mt. 28, 19). Notice here

---

[1] Gen. 18, 1. Here the Vulgate translates the Hebrew term *Eloney Mamreh* as *convalle*, which in the Douay translation is the "vale" of Mambre. But the text here follows the Old Latin reading which translated this Hebrew term as *illicem* or the "oak" of Mambre.

that you see all three Persons called by their own proper names. But although He names all three, He said "in the name," not "in the names," so that by this He might show that all three are one God, and have one substance of Divinity.

Blessed John in his Catholic epistle very clearly teaches this thing: "There are three," he says, "who give testimony in heaven, the Father, the Word, and the Holy Ghost. And these three are one" (I Jn. 5, 7). Now this testimony is so clear, that it cannot be concealed by any equivocation. For there you hear "three" and "one." "Three" against Sabellius, "one" against Arius": as we shall say below.

Paul also, to show the undivided operation of the Holy Trinity, says: "Of him, and by him, and in him, are all things: to him be glory for ever. Amen" (Rom. 11, 36). For when he presented Him three times, he showed the Trinity of Persons. But afterwards adding "to him," and not "to them," he showed that those three Persons are one. And elsewhere he says: "The grace of our Lord Jesus Christ, and the charity of God, and the communication of the Holy Ghost be with you all. Amen" (II Cor. 13, 13). See there that the three Persons are named, although their unity is not denoted. But this is sufficient for our present purpose, because we are now dealing against Sabellius denying that there are multiple Persons in the Divinity.

Finally, John in the Apocalypse, after he had described those magnificent animals, when still speaking about them says: "And they rested not day and night, saying: Holy, holy, holy, Lord God Almighty, who was, and who is, and who is to come" (4, 8). Which words are very similar to those which we recently cited from Isaias. Thus, since there are so many very clear testimonies about this matter, there is no reason for anyone to believe raving Sabellius: but everyone ought to subject his understanding in the obedience of the faith, believing that God is thee and one, three in Persons and one in essence. For if someone would wish to scrutinize this mystery with mere human reason, he would be overwhelmed by the glory of so great a mystery. For that passage of the Canticles seems to have been said to this end: "Turn away thy eyes from me, for they have made me flee away" (6, 4). For the more we try to investigate this mystery by reason alone, so much the less do we understand, and for this reason we make God Himself to flee away from us.

Pope Leo I condemns this heresy. For his fifteenth letter, which is to [Turribius,] Bishop of Asturia, in which he rejects the errors of the Priscillianists, says the following: "And so under the first head is shown what unholy views they hold about the Divine Trinity: they affirm that the Person of the Father, the Son, and the Holy Ghost is one and the same, as if the same God were named now Father, now Son, and now Holy Ghost: and as if He Who begot were not one, He who was begotten, another, and He who proceeded from both, yet another; but an undivided unity must be understood, spoken of under three names, indeed, but not consisting of three Persons. This species of blasphemy they borrowed from Sabellius, whose followers were rightly called Patripassians also: because if the Son is identical with the Father, the Son's Cross is the Father's passion (*patris-passio*): and the Father took on Himself all that the Son took in the form of a slave, and in obedience to the Father. Which without doubt is contrary to the Catholic faith, which acknowledges the Trinity of the Godhead to be of one essence (*homoousion*[1]) in such a way that it believes the Father, the Son, and the Holy Ghost indivisible without confusion, eternal without time, equal without difference."[2] These are the words of Pope Leo, a man, besides his pontifical dignity, was holy and at the same time learned.

Saint Hilary, Bishop of Poitiers, wrote *On the Trinity* about this matter in twelve books, in which he disputes against all heretics thinking incorrectly about the matter: although he especially argues against Arius. Blessed Augustine wrote *On the [Holy] Trinity* in fifteen books, in which he treats the same matter much more clearly and thoroughly than Hilary. [Psuedo-Au-

---

[1] I.e. ὁμοούσιον, meaning "one in being" or "of single essence."
[2] PL 54, 680C-681A.

gustine] also wrote again *De trinitate et unitate Dei,* in one book.[1] I have yet to see, however, a writer who specifically wrote against Sabellius alone concerning this matter.

There is a **sixth heresy** about the personal equality of the Divine Persons, because even if it acknowledges more than one Person subsisting in the Divine nature, still it says that they are unequal. Thus, let us firstly treat concerning the Person of the Son, then we will speak about the Holy Ghost.

Concerning the Person of the Son, therefore, there is one heresy, which says that the Son was less than the Father, and does not share the same essence with the Father, but is a mere creature. The author of this blasphemy (as far as I know) was Arius, an Alexandrian priest who lived at the time of Constantine the Great and Pope Silvester: he who would like to fully know the history of this matter may read the tenth book of *Historia Ecclesiastica* written by Rufinus,[2] and the first book of the *Historia Tripartita* from chapter twelve until the end.[3]

But there are some who charge Origen with this error, who preceded Arius by a hundred years: from which Origen they assert Arius drew [this error]. For [Pseudo-] Blessed Augustine when speaking about Origen says the following: "Origen himself further says that the Son of God compared to holy men is the truth: united to the Father, [He is a] lie: and the Apostles were as distant from Christ as the Son is from the Father. Hence the Son ought not to be prayed to with the Father, because He is not the author of granted petitions, but the supplicator."[4] [Pseudo-] Theophilus, Bishop of Alexandria, also charges Origen with this in his Pascal letter translated by Blessed Jerome from Greek into Latin, who in the [Pseudo-] second book of the same Pascal letter says that Origen taught that one ought not to pray to the Son, nor to the Father with the Son.[5] Epiphanius in a letter to John, Bishop of Jerusalem, which Jerome translated into Latin, says that Origen was the mentor of Arius, wanting to intimate that Arius' teaching was derived from Origen.[6]

The heresy of the Metangismonites closely approaches this same error. For they said (as Augustine says[7]) that the Son so dwells in the Father, like a small vase within a larger one, making the Son less than the Father. And from their doctrine they received their name, such that they are called Metangismonites. Ἀγγεῖον in Greek means vessel, and the compound expression, μεταγγισμός, means a pouring of one vessel into another. Hence Metangismonites, meaning (so to speak) "those pouring from one vessel into another" (Lat. *transvasantes*) or "those pouring into a vessel" (*invasantes*).

Augustine is silent, however, about who was their leader or chief. There exist so many favorers of this heresy after Arius that it would take a long time and be difficult to list them. For there never was any heresy that grew so strong and lasted for such a long time. In fact, from sunrise and noontime, meaning coming from Egypt, it passed through Greece into the north wind, and thence the Goths going out infected nearly the whole West with this poison, because they greatly favored the Arians. Now this pestilence lasted nearly three hundred years, or perhaps even longer. For we know that Spain suffered from this sickness at the time

---

[1] The authorship of this work is uncertain (PL 42, 1193-2000).

[2] PL 21, 467 ff. The text here erroneously has *Historia scholastica*, which work was not written by Rufinus of Aquileia, but by Peter Comestor.

[3] C. 12-20 (PL 69, 901C-920D).

[4] A note in Migne's Latin Patrology (PL 42, 34) states that this particular passage was removed from St. Augustine's writings based upon the authority of the old manuscripts.

[5] Another note in Migne's Patrology states that in the edition of Jean Martianay there erroneously is a second book of this Pascal letter. (PL 22, 773)

[6] "I have told you that you ought not to eulogize one who is the spiritual father of Arius, and the root and parent of some heresies." (Letter 51, n. 3 (PL 22, 520))

[7] *De Haeresibus ad Quodvultdeum,* c. 58 (PL 42, 41).

of Pope Gregory, from Gregory himself informing us: he relates that [Saint] Hermengild, the eldest son of Leovigild, king of the Spain, who had originated from the Visigoths and was an Arian, was converted to the true faith by Leander, Bishop of Seville.[1] Which Hermengild for this reason having been cast into chains and prison, when on Easter day he was unwilling to receive the Eucharist from an Arian bishop, he was killed by the command of his father, and was made a true martyr of God. After the father died, a second son named Reccared, succeeded him, who was also himself an Arian: but after his father died he was converted to the Catholic faith by Leander, just like his brother Hermengild. This Reccared little by little cast out all the Arians from Spain: and he never permitted anyone who was an Arian to fight under him. Now from Constantine, under whom Arius began to rave, until Reccared there were nearly three hundred years. I have recounted these things so that it may be seen for how much time this pestilence disturbed the Church.

I will list the favorers of this heresy, although not all of them at least the chief ones, namely those who were more famous. After Arius a certain Aëtius followed after in the same sect, after Aëtius another [heretic], Eunomius: after these men Acacius, at nearly the same time. These three men, namely Aëtius, Eunomius, and Acacius lived during the time of the Emperor Constantius, son of Constantine the Great. Now he who would like to know more about them may read the fifth book of the *Historia [ecclesiastica] tripartite*.[2] [There followed] a certain Varimundus, against whom the Spaniard, Hydatius [surnamed] "the brilliant" [is erroneously said to have] written and publicly disputed.[3] [There followed] Bishop Maximinus, against whom Augustine wrote and publicly disputed, which disputation is found in the sixth volume of the works of Augustine, in the Parisian edition.[4] [There followed] another heretic, Felicianus, with whom Father Augustine likewise publicly disputed, which disputation in found in the same volume of the works of Augustine.[5] [There followed] Pascentius, a certain count [of royal house[6]], with whom the same Father [Augustine] also disputed, and for which he sent several letters, which disputation is mentioned in Augustine's letters.[7] Peter Abelard also followed this error, because (as Blessed Bernard accuses him[8]) he put degrees in the Trinity, saying that the Persons are unequal: who even though he wanted to differ from Arius, nevertheless in reality he agrees with him. There were many more others who defended the Arian heresy, but these men were more famous.

---

[1] *Dialogues*, bk. 3, c. 31. The text here mistakenly calls Leander an archbishop.

[2] PL 69, 985 ff.

[3] A work, *De Trinitate adversus Varimadum*, was often falsely attributed to Hydatius, but rather belongs to Vigilius of Thapsus. For Saint Isidore of Seville makes no mention of any writings of Hydatius against Varimadus. But Saint Isidore wrote that Hydatius was surnamed *Clarus* (Latin for "brilliant") because of his knowledge and eloquence (*De viris illustribus*, c. 14 (PL 83, 1092A)).

[4] *Collatio cum Maximino* (PL 42, 709-742). *Opera omnia Diui Aurelii Augustini*, ed. by Desiderius Erasmus, (Paris, Carola Guillar, 1541), vol. 6, fol. 147, col. 1.

[5] *Contra Felicianum Arianum de unitate trinitatis liber unus, Vigilio (Tapsensi) restitutus* (PL 42, 1157 ff.). *Omnia Opera*, vol. 6, fol. 167, col. 3.

[6] Pascentius was a *comes domus regiae* (Possidius, *Life of St. Augustine*. c. 17). *Comes* in Latin means "companion." *Comes domesticorum* was the title used to designate both the military commanders of the various field armies and the special administrative representatives of the emperor. Possidius says that he collected taxes.

[7] Letters 238-241 (PL 33, 1038-1052).

[8] "In short, to describe this theologian in few words, he distinguishes with Arius degrees and inequalities in the Trinity; with Pelagius he prefers free will to grace; with Nestorius he divides Christ in excluding His humanity from union with the Trinity" (Letter 330 to Pope Innocent II (PL 182, 536A)).

This heresy can easily be refuted from those things which we have said elsewhere. In fact, when we treated about the Person of Christ, we showed from Scriptures that Christ, the Son of God, is true God. Thus, either Christ, the Son of God, is not God, or if He is God, it is necessary that He be one with God the Father, because God the Father Himself, when speaking through Isaias the prophet, says: "Before me there was no God formed, and after me there shall be none. I am, I am the Lord: and there is no saviour besides me" (Is. 43, 10-11). Hence if before God the Father there was no other God, nor will there be another (as He says) after Him: then the Son is not God. But if He is God, it is necessary that He be the same God as the Father: because neither before nor after Him is there another God.

Furthermore, if the Son is God, how can the Father precede the Son by some time (as Arius says) since God the Father says, after Me there will not be another God? If the Son is God, then He is coeternal with the Father. For if He is not coeternal with the Father, but posterior to the Father, then He is not God: because the Father says: after Me there will not be another God. You see by what perplexities Arius is pressed, saying that the Son is less than the Father, neither of the same substance with Him, nor coeternal with the Father, but posterior to the Father and created by Him. For saying these things, he is forced to deny that the Son of God is God, or if he admits that He is God, he is forced to posit two Gods, since He says that He is not the same God Who is the Father, but another God. If then the Father is one God, and the Son is another God, then there will be two Gods. But the Father contradicts this saying: "I am the Lord: and there is no other besides me." If the Son is God, and not of the substance of the Father (as Arius says) then God would be outside of the Father. And this argumentation seems so convincing to me, that it refutes any Arian. For it so encloses him that no crevice is open to him whereby he can escape.

Nonetheless, still, we will cite many testimonies against him. For in fact John the Evangelist when speaking about the Son of God says: "All things were made by him: and without him was made nothing that was made" (Jn. 1, 3). But if something exists, and was made, as Arius admits, then it was made by the Word of God, that is, by the Son of God: hence the Son of God was made by Himself and thus He existed before He was made. No mind can conceive all that of anything in reality, and even less so that it be truly said of the Son of God.

Again, if He is the Son of God, then He is equal to the Father, and of the same nature with Him, because it could not be otherwise possible that He be a son, if He is not of the substance of the Father. For it is not possible that one be the son of a man, who is not a man: hence much less will He be the Son of God, who is not God. If He is God, then either He is the same God as the Father, and that is what the Catholic faith teaches: or He is another God, and then there are many gods. As it is not possible that one be the son of a man, who is not of the same nature of the human race: so, consequently, it will not be possible that one be the Son of God, who is not begotten of the Divine substance. But if He was begotten of the same substance of the Father, and He is God just as the Father, then it is necessary that He be equal to the Father, otherwise He will be neither of the substance of the Father, nor will He be God. "Hereupon," John says, "therefore the Jews sought the more to kill him, because he did not only break the sabbath, but also said God was his Father, making himself equal to God" (Jn. 5, 18). The Arians are worse than the Jews, and duller in wit than they: because the Jews understood that Christ was preaching that He is equal to the Father by the mere fact that He said that He was the Son of God. For they saw that it could not otherwise happen that He was the Son of God, but that He also be God, and consequently equal to the Father, and of the same nature as He.

Furthermore, the Behemoth, which is a figure of the devil, is proclaimed to be "the beginning of the ways of God," (Job 40, 14): in that he is God's first creature. Thus, it is necessary for this reason to believe that the Son of God was not made, or to think that He was made after Behemoth: because otherwise it will not be possible that Behemoth is "the beginning of the ways of God."

Next, the Son of God Himself bears witness concerning this matter saying: "I and the Father are one" (Jn. 10, 30). Which passage (in my opinion) very clearly refutes Arius: although Erasmus of Rotterdam, a man well renowned for his good learning, thinks otherwise, saying that this passage is hardly persuasive against Arians: concerning which matter I now challenge, not because I think that he thinks like the Arians (far be which thing, both that he would so think and that I would believe this about him) but so that I may show that he has not considered that passage of John carefully enough: and this is not surprising, because sometimes (as the proverb says) good Homer nods. I certainly believe that he would think otherwise if he would reconsider and carefully study the passage. Now so that we may treat the matter more clearly, I will relate the words of the same Erasmus. For that most learned man in his annotations on the First Epistle of John when expounding the passage: "There are three who give testimony in heaven," etc., (5, 7), says the following: "In John [chapter] ten, the Lord says: 'The Father and I are one' (v. 30). How is an Arian going to be vanquished by this evidence, unless you tell him that the word 'one' in the Scriptures can only mean 'what is of the same substance'? Now, since the Scriptures provide innumerable passages which teach that it can be understood as referring to consent or mutual love, I fail to see how far this will help to confirm the opinions of the orthodox, or to repress the stubbornness of the heretic. However, that Christ is speaking there of the concord He has with the Father can be inferred with a high degree of likelihood, since He is not referring to His statement about being one with the Father, but to the fact that He called God His Father, and was thus in an extraordinary fashion calling Himself the Son of God."[1]

But with all due respect to this most erudite man, this passage very clearly refutes Arius. Now in order that we may show this, I see that it is required of us to prove that this passage in nowise can be understood of a concord of minds. For which matter it ought to be fully shown that which is more important than anything else, what is the subject matter of this passage about which the discourse was made: and what was Christ's intention in saying those words. For this is very necessary for understanding any passage of Scripture, namely to carefully examine the circumstances of the passage, and from the examination of these things the understanding of Scripture is easily extracted. For Christ in this passage when He was discoursing about His sheep said: "And no man shall pluck them out of my hand," meaning out of His power. For in Sacred Writ power is accustomed to be designated by the word, "hand." And so that I may omit many other passages, the passage is clear where it is said: "The word of the Lord came by the hand of Aggeus the prophet": "by the hand," that is to say, "in his power." So likewise here it ought to be understood when Christ says: "And no man shall pluck them out of my hand": unless perhaps we would wish to believe with the Anthropomorphites in a corporeal God, because even if it can be literally said of Christ that He has a hand according to His human nature, still this cannot be said of the Father, concerning Whom it is afterwards said: "No one can snatch them out of the hand of my Father" (v. 29). Christ, then, wishing to show that His sheep are safe says: "And no man shall pluck them out of my hand."

---

[1] *In Novum Testamentum Annotationes* (Basel, Froben, 1555), p. 803. Just before saying this quotation, Erasmus wrote: "So far we have dealt with what can be inferred from the verse. But here we are clearly dealing with the reliability of the witness, not about the substance of persons. For if this word 'one' in many other places means "agreement" rather than "the unity of an individual," what is so strange in our interpreting it here in a similar way? How often do we read in either Testament 'one heart,' 'one spirit and soul,' 'one voice,' 'one mind,' when this signifies agreement and mutual love? Since this trope is so familiar in the Scriptures, what is stopping us from assuming the same meaning here?"

Now to prove this, He added the following words, saying: "That which my Father hath given me, is greater than all" (v. 29).[1] For so Erasmus reads on the verse: "No one can snatch them out of the hand of my Father"[2] For in order that Christ might prove that no one can snatch His sheep out of His hand, He added that verse, namely that no one can snatch out of the hand of His Father. Hence, He infers that no one can also take out of His own hand. But if anyone would doubt about this inference, as to it being inferred incorrectly, He added: "I and the Father are one" (v. 30). By saying this He proved that this is rightly implied in His argumentation. For if He and His Father are one, one is not more able to snatch out of His hand than out of His Father's hand. And that this is the logical connection of the words, is apparent from the text itself, and both Augustine[3] and Theophylactus[4] explain it in this way. Hence, since Christ said those words for this purpose, it is very clear that they can nowise be understood of a unity of minds, as it is said elsewhere: "There was but one heart and one soul" (Acts 4, 32).

For if those words are interpreted concerning unity and consent of minds, Christ's argumentation will be of no value, as it is very clear. For He argues as follows: No one can snatch out of the hand of My Father, thus no one can pluck out of My hand. In case someone would deny that He had concluded correctly, He proves [His conclusion] saying: "I and the Father are one." One, I say, in power, concerning which there was then a question, and one, I say, in nature. It is certainly necessary that there be one hand of the Father and of the Son, so that the Son may correctly conclude that no one can pluck the sheep out of His hand, whereby no one can snatch out of the Father's hand. But if He were speaking about the unity of minds and mutual benevolence, what kind of argumentation was that? Who does not see that it is completely invalid? For in this way anyone in the state of grace could say and argue: No one can pluck this pen out of my hand, because no one can snatch it out of the hand of the eternal Father, Who is in Heaven. But is someone were to say that the argument is completely useless, he will add as proof of that argument what Christ said: "I and the Father are one."

We have now clearly enough shown, as I think, how effective is this quotation of Scripture against the Arians. But if Erasmus would have carefully considered, I know with certainty that he would have understood it more correctly. Truly he (apparently) did not look at the preceding words, but only at the words which follow, with which Christ answered the Jews. Indeed, for when the Jews heard those words, they understood them better than the Arians, concluding from them that Christ was calling Himself God, because He had said that He was one with the Father, which statement He in some way confirms by the words which follow.

---

[1] "The first sentence, "That which my Father hath given me, is greater than all," is rendered differently in the Greek manuscripts, namely in this manner: "The Father Who gave to me is greater than all" (Alfonso Salmeron, *Commentarii in Evangelicam Historiam, et Acta Apostolorum* (Madrid, Ludovicus Sanchez, 1500), tract 43, p. 438.

[2] *In Novum Testamentum Annotationes*, pg. 265.

[3] "And in this way it is better here, by the hand of the Father and Son, to understand the power of the Father and the Son; lest, in taking here the hand of the Father as spoken of the Son, some carnal thought also about the Son Himself should set us looking for the Son as somehow to be similarly regarded as the hand of Christ. Therefore, no one plucks them out of my Father's hand; that is, no one plucks them from Me. But that there may be no more room for hesitation, hear what follows: 'I and my Father are one'" (Tractate 48 on the Gospel of John, n. 7-8 (PL 35, 1744)).

[4] "'That which my Father hath given me, is greater than all: and no one can snatch them out of the hand of my Father,' and so neither out My hand: for my hand is also one of the Father's. For 'I and the Father are one,' namely according to power and strength. For He calls the 'hand' power and strength. 'I and the Father are one' according to substance, nature, power, and strength" (PG 124, 79D).

What Paul says when speaking about the same Son of God adds to this argument: "Who being in the form of God, thought it not robbery to be equal with God" (Phil. 2, 6). You see here God's equality. Why then, Arius, dare you say that God the Father is greater and the Son is less? Notice here also that Paul, when speaking about Christ according to His mentioned Divinity, said, "being in the form of God": he did not say, however, "having been made in the form of God," as elsewhere it was said of Him according to His humanity: "The Word was made flesh" (Jn. 1, 14). Thus he did not so speak, but rather thus, "being in the form of God," because to be is proper to God, according to that passage: "I am who am" (Ex. 3, 14). Also, from the same passage of Scripture Sabellius is refuted. For one who is alike and equal, needs to have another compared to him so that he may be recognized as equal. Thus from that equality the two Person are shown [to exist].

But now it is necessary that we show against the claim of Origen that one ought to pray to the Son of God. Now this does not entail much labor, since the testimonies of Scripture are very clear. For the [Royal] Prophet when speaking of the Son of God says the following: "Adore him, all you his angels" (Ps. 96, 7). Now Paul interprets these words to be said by the heavenly Father concerning His only begotten Son saying: "And again, when he bringeth in the first begotten into the world, he saith: And let all the angels of God adore him" (Heb. 1, 6). How is it then that one ought not to pray to Him Whom, as it is clear, ought to be adored? By which testimony Arius is no less overthrown than Origen. For if the Son of God is a creature (as Arius says), how is it that the Father commands [us] to adore Him, Who elsewhere so strictly forbade the adoration of every creature?[1] I omit the Wise Men's adoration shown to this Son even in the cradle. Furthermore, Stephen, when he was stoned by the Jews, prayed to Jesus Christ, the Son of God, saying: "Lord Jesus, receive my spirit. And falling on his knees, he cried with a loud voice, saying: Lord, lay not this sin to their charge" (Acts 7, 58-59). Peter also, so that he might deliver the paralytic Eneas from his malady, says: "Eneas, the Lord Jesus Christ healeth thee" (Acts 9, 34). Those words are certainly of one beseeching, not of one commanding, because one only commands those whom one believes are subject to himself. Finally, Paul says: "God hath given him a name which is above all names: that in the name of Jesus every knee should bow, of those that are in heaven, on earth, and under the earth" (Phil. 2, 9-10). Which the prophet Isaias had previously prophesied, who when speaking in the Lord's name said: "Every knee shall be bowed to me" (Is. 45, 24). Now such a genuflection is a sign of that adoration and of very humble deprecation.

Besides these so clear testimonies of Scripture there exists a definition of the Council of Nicea, which was celebrated under Constantine the Great, in which three hundred eighteen Fathers gathered together confessed the following creed for their and our salvation. "The Creed of the Council of Nicea. We believe in one God, the Father Almighty, the Creator of all things invisible and visible; and in one Lord Jesus Christ, the Son of God, the only begotten born of God the Father, that is of the substance of the Father, God of God, light of light, true God of true God, begotten not made, consubstantial to the Father (which the Greeks call ὁμοούσιον), by Whom all things were made, both those in heaven and those on earth," etc.[2] The Council of Constantinople, celebrated under Theodosius the Great, pronounced the same faith, and the Council of Ephesus under Theodosius the Younger, and the Council of Chalcedon under the Emperor Martian, and many other councils confessed this same thing, concerning which matter there exists a book of Blessed Hilary concerning the synods celebrated against the Arians,[3] in which book he gives an account of those councils which were celebrated against the Arians.

---

[1] "He that sacrificeth to gods, shall be put to death, save only to the Lord" (Ex. 22, 20). Cf. Deut. 5, 7-9.
[2] Dz. 13.
[3] *On the Councils* (*Liber de Synodis* seu *Fide orientalium*) (PL 10, 479-546).

But because the Arians cite many quotations of Scripture wrongly understood in support of their heresy, it suffices to warn the reader for discussing nearly all of them, that because in Christ there are two natures: one which is Divine, according to which He is equal to the Father, and the other which is human, according to which He is less than the Father: as often as Scripture attributes weakness to Christ, or inequality to the Father, or something else of this kind, it means that those things ought to be interpreted according to His human nature, according to which He was weak and feeble, and less than the Father. According to that nature He is called the Word made flesh, according to which He prays to His Father, and pours out prayers with a loud cry and tears. The other things ought to be understood of Him according to His Divinity.

Many men have written against this heresy. First and foremost [Pseudo-] Athanasius who, as it is related disputed with the same Arius, wrote *De unitate Trinitatis* in two books.[1] Blessed Cyril [of Alexandria] wrote a remarkable work, which he entitled, *Thesaurus [de sancta et consubstanitiali Trinitate]*, divided into fourteen books, in which he treats against many heretics, but especially against the Arians.[2] Among the Latin writers the first one who stands out (that I know) was Hilary, Bishop of Poitiers, who even though he disputes at length against Arius and other heretics in the [twelve] books of his *On the Trinity*, he published a special book about this matter against the Arians, *De patre et filii unitate*.[3] [Marius] Victorinus,[4] from whom Jerome is said to have learned Rhetoric, discusses this matter in the four books of his *Adversus Arium*, which work was printed in Basil five years ago among the other works which are bundled together in the *Antidotum [adversus] haeresum [venena]*.[5] Blessed Ambrose wrote his *Exposition of the Christian Faith* in one book.[6] Blessed Augustine very often disputed with the Arians (as we have already shown) and composed many books against them: *Against an Arian Sermon* in one book,[7] *Contra Maximinum haereticum Arrianorum episcopum* in two books,[8] and *Contra Felicianum Arianum De Unitate Trinitatis*.[9] [Psuedo-] Hydatius Clarus, the Spaniard, who (as I suspect) lived nearly at the same time as Augustine, wrote a notable work against a certain Arian, Varimadus [or Marivadus by way of a metathesis], which is also found in that book which is entitled the *Antidotum [adversus] haeresum [venena]*.[10] But I have not seen other books.

---

[1] "*De unita Deitate Trinitatis [ad Theophilum]* in seven books does not seem to me to belong to Athanasius; for it seems to have been written in Latin, not in Greek, as is apparent both from the style and because many times the author indicates how what he wrote in Latin is said by the Greeks." (Saint Robert Bellarmine, *De Scriptoribus Ecclesiasticis* (Cologne, Jost Kalckhoven, 1645), pp. 79-80).

[2] PG 75, 9-656. It is divided into thirty-five "Assertions."

[3] PL 10, 883D-888A.

[4] He was called Caius Marius as well as Marius Fabius; he is known as Afer from the region of his birth.

[5] A translation of the full title is as follows: *Antidote against the Poison of Heresies: Many Special Ways of Refuting Heterodox Adversaries to the Roman Church; in which the Conduct of Martin Luther and of John Calvin is Analyzed*.

[6] *De Fide Orthodoxa Contra Arianos* (PL 17, 549-568A).

[7] PL 42, 683-708.

[8] PL 42, 743-814.

[9] PL 42, 1155–1172. In Migne's Patrology it is written that this work was restored by Vigilius, Bishop of Thapsus. This work is, however, listed as dubious by the *Clavis Patrum Latinorum* under Vigilius (n. 808), and attributed to PseudoAugustine.

[10] *Contra Marivadum Arianum Diaconuum, sub nomine Idacii Clari Contra* in three books. This author of this work was rather Vigilius of Thapsus. (PL 62, 351-454.) "Vigilius, Bishop of Thapsus, assisted, February 1, 484, at a public disputation held at Carthage between Catholics and Arians. Under

There is a **seventh heresy** which denies that the Son of God is the Word. The authors of this heresy (as Augustine says[1]) are called the Alogians, as it were "without the Word." For *logos* in Greek is *verbum* [meaning "word" in English] in Latin. And because it is expressly stated that this [Word] is the Son of God, by this occasion they did not accept that Gospel, saying that it did not belong to John the Apostle.

Against this heresy there is no need to dispute, since there is such clear testimony of John the Apostle, which can nowise be denied. Having been put on that list, we have prescribed the weapons common to Catholics and the heretics with which it is needed for the heretic to defend himself and for the Catholic to fight. Thus since these heretics provoke Catholics to battle, they may not reject the weapons that they have now received as blameworthy. For the Wise Man says: "For while all things were in quiet silence, and the night was in the midst of her course, Thy almighty word leapt down from heaven from thy royal throne, as a fierce conqueror into the midst of the land of destruction" (Wis. 18, 14-15). Now it is evident that these words cannot be understood of speech uttered in the air,[2] because it [i.e. a word] is not omnipotent, but only God is omnipotent. And it is said more explicitly elsewhere: "The word of God on high is the fountain of wisdom" (Eccli. 1, 5). And the [Royal] Prophet speaking in the person of the Father says: "My heart hath uttered a good word" (Ps. 44, 2). Now it is evident that he speaks of the Son of God, because the words that follow belong to Him: "Thou art beautiful above the sons of men," etc., (v. 3). And Isaias clearly teaches this, who says: "The grass is withered, and the flower is fallen: but the word of our Lord endureth for ever" (40, 8). Now an uttered word passes away at the same time as the sound itself, and has a shorter duration than grass has: wherefore it cannot happen that Isaias' words refer to it, but to the Son of God Whose coming into this world is predicted in that chapter. Therefore that Word, which is eternal and omnipotent, and which is a fountain of wisdom, and which the heavenly Father uttered by begetting, and which went forth from the mouth of the Most High: that Word, I say, is the Son of God. Therefore, let the Alogi keep silence, and let them worship the things that they do not understand as a hidden mystery, and not want to measure Divine things by the capacity of their understanding.

There is an **eighth heresy** wrongly reckoning about the Person of the Son. For it says that the Son of God does not know the Last Day [i.e. Judgement Day]. The authors of this heresy (as Isidore [of Seville] says[3]) were called the Agnoites, because they affixed the charge of ignorance to God. Who was the first inventor of this heresy, or at what time did it begin, Isidore did not make known, nor could I find this in the writings of any other author. Now they were motivated to say this since Christ said in Matthew's Gospel: "Of that day and hour no one knoweth, not the angels of heaven, but the Father alone" (24, 36). And in Mark the Son is explicitly named, where it is said as follows: "of that day or hour no man knoweth, neither the angels in heaven, nor the Son, but the Father" (13, 32).

But before we reply to this objection, it is necessary that we firstly confirm our and the Catholic faith. The Royal Prophet says: "I have seen an end to all perfection [or literally: the end of every consummation]" (Ps. 118, 96). Hence since the last day is the end and consummation of time, it follows that He would have seen it. If perhaps you were to say that

---

his name have been printed nine treatises, of only two of which he is the undoubted author: a dialogue *Contra Arianos, Sabellianos et Photinianos*, and five books *Contra Eutychetem*. He himself, however, mentions two treatises which he wrote, but which have not been identified: a book *Against the Arian Marivadus* and *Against the Arian Palladius*" (Joseph Tixeront, *A Handbook of Patrology* (St. Louis, B. Herder, 1920), p. 346).

[1] *De Haeresibus ad Quodvultdeum*, c. 30 (PL 42, 29).

[2] Cf. I Cor. 14, 9.

[3] *Etymologies*, b. 8, c. 5, n. 68 (PL 82, 304B).

that saying of the Prophet ought not to be attributed to the Son of God, at least you cannot reject the saying of Isaias on this occasion: because when speaking of Christ, the Son of God, crucified for us, he says the follows under the name of the same Christ: "I have trodden the winepress alone, and of the Gentiles there is not a man with me: I have trampled on them in my indignation, and have trodden them down in my wrath, and their blood is sprinkled upon my garments, and I have stained all my apparel. For the day of vengeance is in my heart, the year of my redemption is come" (63, 3-4). Here you clearly see the Son of God asserting that He knows the Last Day, because he says: "the day of vengeance is in my heart." It is evident that these words were said in the Person of the Son of God, because it is He Who had said: "I have trodden the winepress alone," etc., and he continued the same sequence of words, saying: "the day of vengeance is in my heart."

Furthermore, Paul, when speaking about the Son of God, says: "In whom are hid all the treasures of wisdom and knowledge" (Col. 2, 3). If all the treasures of wisdom and knowledge [are in Him], then the knowledge of the Last Day also. Again, "All things were made by him." as John the Apostle says (1, 3), then time and all days were made by Him: hence the Last Day was already made by that mind Who knew all things which He would make before they were made. Next the Son of God Himself when speaking to the Father says: "All thy things are mine" (Jn. 17, 10). Thus, either the Son knows the Last Day just as the Father, or the Father does not know just as the Son, because otherwise it would be false that the Son says to the Father: "All thy things are mine." And in another place: "All things are delivered to me by my Father" (Lk. 10, 22). But if the Father kept the knowledge of that Last Day to Himself, it is necessary that the Father did not give all things to His Son. Add to this that if [the Son] does not know the Last Day, it is necessary that He would not know all the things that are before that day: because if He does not know the Last Day, He will also know that it is the only thing unknown to Himself: and if He knows everything preceding the Last Day, He will necessarily know that the day immediately following is the last, otherwise He would not be sure that He knows all the days preceding. But if He certainly knows all the days preceding the last, then He will know the day immediately following will be the Last Day, so He will know the Last Day. Thus, either He knows the Last Day, or if He does not know the last, it will be necessary that He does not know the days preceding it.

Consequently, after having shown that the Son of God knows the Last Day as well as the Father does, it remains that we state how [this passage] should be understood, since He says that He does not know that day. What will help us to do this is that which we read in the Acts of the Apostles, that the Apostles asked the Lord, saying: "Lord, wilt thou at this time restore again the kingdom to Israel?" (1, 6). To whom He responds: "It is not for you to know the times or moments, which the Father hath put in his own power" (v. 7). In this passage the Lord certainly does not deny that He knows, but merely says that knowledge of that day does not pertain to them. Hence it is surmised that that day is a secret, and should be revealed to no one. Because the prudent Lord Himself wanted to make us cautious and to make us watch, hence He said, "Of that day and hour no one knoweth." Now that He said this for this reason can be gathered from the context, for He immediately added: "Watch ye therefore, because ye know not what hour your Lord will come" (Mt. 24, 42). Now lest perhaps they might suppose that by labor, industry, or by some human reasoning they could know that day, He added, "not the angels of heaven," so that by having said this He might deter them from any scrutiny of this day.

But because the disciples might perhaps want to learn and ask about this from Christ Himself, their teacher (in order to remove them from this questioning) further added, "nor the Son, but the Father alone." As though by these words He were to say to them: "Do not be solicitous about the knowledge of that day, because no one has it: and do not ask Me, because neither do I know." Not that He simply does not know, but because even if He does know, still He ought not to reveal it to them: as when something was secretly entrusted to you, such that you may not reveal it to anyone else, and later someone were to ask you about that matter: you will reply, and rightly so, that you do not know, because even if you do know, still you do not know in such a way that you may reveal it. Now Sacred Scripture, since it was made for teaching men, uses the same manner of speaking by which men are accustomed to speak. Wherefore (as Augustine says[1]) it uses the same tropes, figures and metaphors which we use in our common speech. Thus the Son of God states that He does not know that day, because even though He does know it, yet not so as to reveal it. This opinion is clearly shown by His words: "It is not for you to know the times or moments, which the Father hath put in his own power." Now He did not want to openly say to them, "I know, but I do not want to reveal it to you": lest He sadden them by this reply, or He make them less fond of Him by this occasion. Blessed Hilary disputes at length about this matter.[2]

The **ninth heresy** also charges the Son with ignorance. For Origen (as Epiphanius [erroneously] ascribes to him in a letter to John, Bishop of Jerusalem) said that the Son cannot see the Father, nor can the Holy Ghost see the Son. And certainly Epiphanius is citing the words of Origen in the books of the *First Principles*,[3] where he cites the following: "For as it is unsuitable to say that the Son can see the Father, it is consequently unsuitable to suppose that the Spirit can see the Son."[4] To say the truth, I am surprised that such a learned man, such as Origen was, would have fallen into such a clear error, since there is such a clear passage of Scripture saying the following: "No one knoweth the Son, but the Father: neither doth any one know the Father, but the Son, and he to whom it shall please the Son to reveal him" (Mt. 11, 27).

And yet this is not so judged, because the things which are attributed to those Persons, which modern theologians call absolute and essential, are common to the three Persons, as also is the [Divine] essence itself. Wherefore even though an exclusive distinction is found in these words, by which at first glance some Persons are excluded: still none of them is excluded, but only those things are excluded by which the Divine essence does not so communicate itself. So that I may cite one of many examples, God the Father says through the prophet Isaias, saying: "I am the Lord, and there is none else forming the light, and creating darkness" (45, 6-7). Will we then say that the Son or the Holy Ghost does not form the light, because the Father said, "there is none else forming the light"? Far be it. For John says concerning the Son of God: "All things were made by him: and without him was made nothing that was made" (Jn. 1, 3). And when the water was created, the spirit of God moved over them (Gen. 1, 2). And concerning the same Holy Ghost David says: "By the word of the Lord the heavens were established; and all the power of them by the spirit of his mouth" (Ps. 32, 6).

In this manner ought to be interpreted that which is said, "No one knoweth the Son, but the Father: neither doth any one know the Father, but the Son." For knowledge is something said in respect to Itself, that is to say, something essential and common to all three Persons: wherefore even if the statement in that place is worded as exclusive, still it ought not be understood to exclude any Divine Person, in fact the Holy Ghost also knows the Father as the Son, and

---

[1] *On Christian Doctrine*, bk, 3, c. 29, n. 40 (PL 34, 80).

[2] *On the Trinity*, bk. 9, n. 62 ff. (PL 10, 330C ff).

[3] Origen here is merely excluding corporeal vision from the Divine Persons, which is certainly correct. For he explains his meaning slightly before the passage cited by Saint Epiphanius, "To see, then, and to be seen, is a property of bodies, which certainly will not be appropriately applied either to the Father, or to the Son, or to the Holy Spirit, in their mutual relations with one another" (Origen, *Peri archôn*, bk. 2, c. 4, n. 3 (PG 11, 202C)).

[4] Epiphanius, Letter 51, n. 4 (PL 22, 520).

also the Son as equally and perfectly as the Father. Now this which we say concerning the Holy Ghost, will appear clearer when in the assault on the following heresy, we prove from Sacred Writ that the Holy Ghost is consubstantial with the Father and the Son, meaning of the same substance with them: wherefore it will be necessary that all things that belong to the Father and Son, also belong to the Holy Ghost, such that of the Holy Ghost can be truly said what the Son said to the Father: "All my things are thine, and thine are mine" (Jn. 17, 10). Hence it is very clearly proved that the Holy Ghost knows the Father as well as the Son, and the Son as well as the Father.

The **tenth heresy** attacks the Holy Ghost, because it says that the Holy Ghost is less than the Father and the Son, and is not of the same substance with the Father, but instead is a true creature. The leader of this heresy is said to be a certain Macedonius, a Constantinopolitan bishop, in the time of the Emperor Constantius and Pope Liberius, from which Macedonius the heresy is called Macedonianism, although Arius had previously taught the same heresy, who just as he said that the Son is dissimilar to the Father, and is a creature, so also he taught concerning the Holy Ghost. But because his followers were divided, some affirming that the Son is in some way similar to the Father, although not of the same essence: a certain Eunomius, leprous in body and very skilled in debates, held that position: others, however, were affirming that the Son is completely similar to the Father, but that the Holy Ghost is entirely dissimilar to them and is a mere creature, and the leader of these men was Macedonius, hence it received the name from him, such that it was called the Macedonian heresy: for Arius disputed more about the Son than about the Holy Ghost. Those so thinking were called Pneumatomachi, meaning, "Combaters against the Spirit." πνεῦμα [*pneuma*] in Greek means the same thing as *spiritus* ["spirit"] in Latin. But if in Sacred Writ it is preceded by the article τό [meaning "the"] (as Didymus[1] points out in his book, *De Spiritu Sancto*[2]) it always signifies the Holy Ghost. μάχομαι in Greek has the same meaning as *pugno* in Latin [or "to fight" in English]. Hence the composed word, πνευματομάχοι, means "combators against the Spirit."

Here I cannot refrain from citing the charming etymology of that word that Bernard of Luxemburg relates in his *Catalogo haereticorum*, where he says the following: "They are so called from *pneuma*, meaning 'spirit,' and *tokos*, meaning 'mother,' because he was saying that the Holy Ghost proceeded from the mother herself and from the Son of God."[3] And it is certainly not surprising that he was mistaken, but I am very surprised that he is a person of such shameless arrogance that what he completely does not know, he does not hesitate to teach with such great self-assurance. But this can nowise be tolerated, namely because so that the etymology which he had fabricated out of his own head to agree with the matter at hand, he added that Macedonius thought that the Holy Ghost proceeded from the mother and from the Son of God, as though the Son of God having intercourse with the mother had given birth to the Holy Ghost. I am at a loss as to whether Brother Bernard dreamt up such a thing or found this written by someone writing about Macedonius. For Blessed Augustine, when speaking about Macedonius, does not accuse him of any such thing[4]: Philastrius, who does not call these heretics Macedonians but Semi-Arians, makes no mention of this fable.[5] The *Historia Ecclesiastica* when speaking of Macedonius attributed no such fabrication to

---

[1] Didymus the Blind, of Alexandria was born about 310 and died about 395, at the age of eighty-five. Didymus lost the use of his eyes when four years old, yet he became one of the most learned men of his period.

[2] *Liber Didymi Alexandrini de spiritu sancto, Sancto Hieronymo interprete*, n. 3 (PL 23, 106A).

[3] *Catalogus haereticorum omnium*, bk. 3 (Cologne, Godefridus Hittorpius, 1529).

[4] *De Haeresibus ad Quodvultdeum*, c. 52 (PL 42, 39).

[5] *Liber de Haeresibus*, c. 68, (PL 12, 1181A-1182A).

him.[1] The *Historia Tripartita* when discussing the heresies of Macedonius, did not propose any word of "mother" about the production of the Holy Ghost, but only says that Macedonius thought that the Holy Ghost is dissimilar to the Father and is His minister, and said things about the Holy Ghost which are said about the Angels.[2] Whether or not Angels are said in Scripture to have mothers, let Brother Bernard of Luxemburg see. Bede when mentioning Macedonius in his book, *The Reckoning of Time*, never relates that he thought anything such as Bernard of Luxemburg accuses him.[3]

Coming now to more recent authors, Platina, in the life of Pope Felix II, says the same thing concerning Macedonius, and in nearly the same words with which the *Historia Ecclesiastica* had discoursed concerning Macedonius.[4] Guy [the Carmelite], since he always follows Augustine and Isidore [of Seville], also here following his custom, merely relates the censure of Augustine and Isidore concerning Macedonius.[5] Thus where did Bernard of Luxemburg find that Macedonius gave a mother to the Holy Ghost, from whom and the Son of God he says that the Holy Ghost proceeded? Certainly I can conclude nothing else, unless perhaps he read something similar in a different author, without looking into the matter (as I have said elsewhere about him) he copied it into his work, or perhaps (which I think is more likely) he thought it up out of his own head, so that the etymology proposed by him would agree with the subject matter, and thus (as it is said in the Proverb) "He measured the plumb line by the wall."[6]

But it is now necessary that we go on to the refutation of the heresy. For which matter those things ought to be recalled which we brought forth against Sabellius. For there we showed that the Trinity of unity, namely that the Father, Son and Holy Ghost are one God. For the Truth Itself said to His Apostles: "Going therefore, teach ye all nations; baptizing them in the name of the Father, and of the Son, and of the Holy Ghost" (Mt. 28, 19). Since He said "in the name," and not "in the names," He showed clearly that one is the name and one is the substance of all three. Thus the Holy Ghost is God, and consubstantial with the Father. Furthermore, (as we have argued above about the Son) since there is only one God, and not many, it cannot be that the Holy Ghost would be God, unless He be one God with the Father and the Son, because otherwise there would be many gods, which the Catholic faith abhors. But, Paul the Apostle testifies that the Holy Ghost is God, who in the First Epistle to the Corinthians says: "Know you not, that your members are the temple of the Holy Ghost, who is in you, whom you have from God?" (I Cor. 6, 19). And lest anyone deny that the Holy Ghost is God Himself, he says immediately afterwards: "For you are bought with a great price. Glorify and bear God in your body" (v. 20). When he said, "bear God in your body," he is alluding to us that the Holy Ghost is God, Whose temple he had proclaimed that our bodies are. And he says in the same epistle: "And no man can say the Lord Jesus, but by the Holy Ghost. Now there are diversities of graces, but the same Spirit; and there are diversities of ministries, but the same Lord; and there are diversities of operations, but the same God, who worketh all in all" (12, 3-6). Notice that you see here that the Holy Ghost is called "Lord" and "God."

Furthermore, unless the Holy Ghost were God, how would it be possible that a sin against Him would be so serious that (as Christ says) "it shall not be forgiven, neither in this world, nor in the world to come" (Mt. 12, 32)? For it cannot happen that a sin against a creature

---

[1] Bk. 10, c. 25 (PL 21, 496C-497B).

[2] Bk. 5, c. 41 (PL 69, 1020C).

[3] C. 66 (PL 90, 558B).

[4] *The Lives of the Popes*, vol. 1 p. 84.

[5] *Summa de haeresibus et earum confutationibus*, c. 47, fol.62r & v.

[6] *Ad lapidem applicavit amussim*. Rather, the wall ought to be measured as being vertical by the plumb line.

would be more serious than one which is against God "in open assault" [*aperto Marte*].[1] But if the Holy Ghost were a creature (as Macedonius says) a sin against a creature would be more serious than a sin against God. Again, Peter said to Ananias, who had by fraud kept back from the Apostles part of the price of a piece of land: "Ananias, why hath Satan tempted thy heart, that thou shouldst lie to the Holy Ghost?" (Acts 5, 3). Now to explain that the Holy Ghost is God, he added: "Thou hast not lied to men, but to God" (v. 4). Thus, Him Whom he firstly had called the Holy Ghost, the same he afterwards called God.

Next the works of the Holy Ghost prove that He is God, because the ones which we know that He does are those which cannot be done except by God. He gives grace, as the Apostle says: "There are diversities of graces, but the same Spirit" (I Cor. 12, 4). Yet David says: "the Lord will give grace and glory" (Ps. 83, 12). Therefore, the Holy Ghost Who gives grace is both the Lord and God. He pours forth charity in our hearts. "The charity of God is poured forth in our hearts, by the Holy Ghost, who is given to us" (Rom. 5, 5). The Holy Ghost forgives sins, which is proper to God alone. For the Lord Jesus Christ having breathed upon the Apostles, said: "Receive ye the Holy Ghost. Whose sins you shall forgive, they are forgiven them" (Jn. 20, 22-23). The Holy Ghost was given to the Apostles, so that they could forgive sins. If therefore they forgive sins through the Holy Ghost, He forgives sins much better, in Whose power they do this. Thus, how is He not God, Who forgives sins on His own authority? The Holy Ghost spoke through the Prophets, just as the Father and the Son. For Zacharias said concerning God the Father: "He spoke by the mouth of his holy prophets, who are from the beginning" (Lk. 1, 70). And Peter said: "For prophecy came not by the will of man at any time: but the holy men of God spoke, inspired by the Holy Ghost" (II Pet. 1, 21). And Paul said: "All scripture, inspired of God" (II Tim. 3, 16). If the Holy Ghost speaks through the Prophets and Apostles, and all Scripture is Divinely inspired, then the Holy Ghost is God. The Holy Ghost is everywhere, which the [Royal] Prophet clearly shows saying: "Whither shall I go from thy spirit? or whither shall I flee from thy face? If I ascend into heaven, thou art there," etc., (Ps. 138, 7-8). The diligent reader can gather many other similar passages of Sacred Scripture.

But now let us hear the decision of the Church. The [First] Council of Constantinople, of a hundred and fifty bishops under Theodosius the Elder and Pope Damasus, after having condemned the Macedonian heresy, professed the following creed: "We believe in one God, Father omnipotent, maker of Heaven and earth," etc. It continues: "We believe in the Holy Ghost, the Lord, the Giver of life, Who proceeds from the Father, Who together with the Father and Son is worshipped and glorified, Who spoke through the prophets."[2] The Council of Ephesus teaches the same creed, the Council of Chalcedon embraced the same creed, and the [IV] Lateran Council celebrated under Pope Innocent III received the same creed, which decree is found in the book of the Decretals, in the title *de summa trinitate et fide catholica*.[3]

Didymus [the Blind], Bishop of Alexandria, wrote against this heresy in the one book of his *On the Holy Ghost*, which work Blessed Jerome translated into Latin.[4] Basil [of Caesarea] published *Against Eunomius* in five books.[5] Blessed Ambrose is more prolific on this subject,

---

[1] Cf. Seneca, *Oedipus* 275.

[2] Dz. 86.

[3] Gregory IX, *Decretales*, bk. 1, tit. 1, c. 1.

[4] PL 23, 109-162. The text here states that Didymus wrote "two books on the Holy Ghost," probably meaning that the book has two sections. But in Migne's *Patrologia Latina* (PL 23, 105) it is explained that this work is single book but could be subdivided into three chapters.

[5] PG 29, 497 ff. The text here states that Saint Basil the Great wrote this work in one book, but it is in fact five books.

who in the three books of his *On the Holy Ghost* which were published for the Emperor Gratian, strenuously fights for the Catholic faith.[1]

The **eleventh heresy** says that the Holy Ghost is the soul of the world. The instigator and teacher of this heresy was Peter Abelard. For Blessed Bernard accuses him of this in a letter to Pope Innocent [II].[2] The opinion is perceived to be heretical, if we recall a universal and well-known principle: every whole is greater than its part. Which is not only true of greater size (so to speak), or of surpassing by greater weight, but also of surpassing in regard to perfection, namely such that every whole is greater, meaning more perfect, than any of its parts taken from it. Having laid down this foundation, we will easily build up the doctrine of the true faith, namely that the Holy Ghost neither is nor can be the soul of the world, because from that it would follow that the Holy Ghost is less than the world, because He would be part of the world, since He is its soul. It also follows that the Holy Ghost is included, circumscribed and limited within the world's boundaries, yet to assert this is blatant blasphemy: because (as we have proved) the Holy Ghost is God. But God is not enclosed by any place's space. "Dost not thou think that God is higher than heaven, and is elevated above the height of the stars?" (Job 22, 12). "Heaven, and the heavens of heavens cannot contain him" (II Par. 2, 6). And how can the heavens contain Him "Who hath measured the waters in the hollow of his hand, and weighed the heavens with his palm?" (Is. 40, 12). Therefore, if the world cannot contain the Holy Ghost, it is not possible that the Holy Ghost would be the soul of the world, because every soul is contained by that body which it sustains and vivifies.

There is a **twelfth heresy** which denies that the Holy Ghost proceeds from the Father and the Son. The Greeks have taught and defended this heresy for many centuries, such that this heresy was one of the main reasons why they were separated from the Roman and Catholic Church. The Armenians teach the same error. For they say that the Holy Ghost proceeds from the Father, and not from the Son: to which error they were motivated from the fact that it is only found in the Gospel that He proceeded from the Father, and it is never found there (so they say) that He proceeded from the Son. And in the Nicene Creed and in the Symbol of Constantinople only the procession from the Father is stated, in which creeds there is no mention of the procession of the Holy Ghost from the Son. Wherefore they deny that the Holy Ghost proceeds from the Son.

But lest we labor in vain, disputing merely over words, let us investigate what is understood by "to proceed from another." And I cannot understand anything else but to be brought forth by another, and to be derived from another, just as a stream proceeds from a spring, because it takes its origin from it: heat proceeds from fire, from which it is brought forth: light proceeds from the sun, from which it is generated. So also the Son proceeds from the Father, from Whom He was begotten. The Holy Ghost proceeds from the Father and the Son, because He was brought forth by both. But if to proceed means anything else than to be brought forth from something, or to be derived by something, then we are fighting over the word, and we do not know what they are speaking about. But if they agree with us about the meaning of the word, we will clearly show from Sacred Writ that the Holy Ghost proceeds from the Son as well as the Father, because He is brought forth by the Son as well as by the Father.

Not that this is so, the Truth Itself teaches us, Who in John's Gospel says: "But when he, the Spirit of truth, is come, he will teach you all truth. For he shall not speak of himself; but what things soever he shall hear, he shall speak," etc., (16, 13). Didymus [the Blind], when expounding these words, says the following: "'For He will not speak of himself,' meaning

---

[1] PL 16, 703 ff.

[2] "...that the Holy Spirit is the *anima mundi*; that the world, as Plato says, is so much a more excellent animal, as it has a better soul in the Holy Ghost. Here while he exhausts his strength to make Plato a Christian, he proves himself a heathen." (Letter 190, c. 4, n. 10 (PL 182, 1062B)).

not without Me, and without My and the Father's decision, because He is inseparable from My and the Father's will, because He is not from Himself, but is from the Father and Me. For the fact that He subsists and speaks, belongs to Him from the Father and Me. 'I say the truth' (Jn. 8, 45), meaning, I inspire what He says. For He is 'the Spirit of Truth.'"[1] Him, because He was Greek, we have quoted more willingly, so that perhaps by this occasion his exposition may be more readily received by the Greeks.

The words which follow in John's Gospel confirm our faith still more: "He," Christ says concerning the Holy Ghost, "shall glorify me; because he shall receive of mine, and shall shew it to you" (16, 14). What is it to say, "He shall receive of mine"? It means that just as He has His essence from Me, through His being brought forth, so also all knowledge. For as the Son had said elsewhere that He had listened to His Father, so here He says the Holy Ghost listened to Him. Now He declares how He hears when saying, "He shall receive of mine," meaning, because He was brought forth, is brought forth and will be brought forth from my substance and from Me. Now do not be surprised that I said, "He shall receive of mine," because as He receives from the Father, so He receives from Me. For "all things which the Father hath are mine" (v. 15). Thus if He receives of the substance of the Father, it is necessary that He receive of mine. Hence if the Son is from the substance of the Father, it certainly cannot otherwise be but that He proceed from Him.

But so that I may render this interpretation of ours more firm and certain to the Greeks themselves, I present a witness from their family, worthy of belief, namely Cyril [of Alexandria], who when interpreting the aforesaid words of John, says these things: "And we must in no wise suppose that the Comforter, that is, the Spirit, is lacking in innate and inherent power in such a way that, if He did not receive assistance from without, His own power would not be self-sufficient to fully accomplish the Divine designs. Anyone who merely imagined any such idea to be true about the Spirit would with good reason undergo the charge of the worst blasphemy of all. But it is because He is consubstantial with the Son, and divinely proceeds through Him, exercising universally His entire activity and power, that Christ says, 'He shall receive of Mine.' For we believe that the Spirit has a self-supporting existence and is in truth that which He is, and with the qualities predicated of Him; though, being inherent in the substance of God, He proceeds and issues from it and has innate in Himself all that that nature implies. For the Divine substance is not His by participation or by relation, still less is it His as though He had a separate existence from it, since He is an attribute of it. For just as the fragrance of sweet-smelling flowers, proceeding in some sort from the essential and natural exercise of the functions or qualities of the flowers that emit it, conveys the perception thereof to the outer world by meeting those organs of smell in the body, and yet seems in some way, so far as its logical conception goes, to be separate from its natural cause, while (as having no independent existence) it is not separate in nature from the source from which it proceeds and in which it exists, even so you may conceive of the relation of God and the Holy Ghost, taking this by way of illustration. In this way then the statement that His Spirit receives something from the Only-begotten is wholly unimpeachable and cannot be caviled at. For proceeding naturally as His attribute through Him, and having all that He has in its entirety, He is said to receive that which He has."[2] Whom we have quoted at greater length as a witness against the Greeks, because he is Greek himself, and hence ought to be nowise suspected by them, nay rather highly esteemed and received by them with great respect on many accounts [*multis nominibus*[3]].

---

[1] PL 23, 133A-B.

[2] *On the Gospel according to John*, bk. 11, c. 1 (PG 74, 450A-C).

[3] This phrase is perhaps borrowed from Erasmus comment on Hebrews 13, 24 in his *Novum Intrumentum* where he raises doubts about the Pauline authorship of this epistle: "Caerte cuiuscumque est,

But I warn the reader, lest he err when reading Cyril's aforesaid words, thinking that this adverb, "naturally," when he said, "the Holy Ghost proceeding naturally through the Son," is taken from the accustomed usage of scholastic theologians, who always use it to mean what is opposed to "free." For if it were taken according to this meaning, it would be false that the Holy Ghost naturally proceeds from the Son, because He proceeds freely, since He comes forth from the Son through the will, through the free principle of production. Cyril, however, uses that adverb, "naturally, for "necessarily," such that he wishes to say that the Holy Ghost necessarily proceeds from the Son. Now that this is true, the whole school of theologians admits, and it does not follow from this that the Holy Ghost was not freely produced: because liberty is not opposed to necessity, but to force.

Furthermore, the Holy Ghost is likewise the Spirit of the Son, just as He is the Spirit of the Father, because it is not said that He proceeds only from the Son, just as it is not said that He proceeds only from the Father. For Paul in the Epistle to the Romans says: "Now if any man have not the Spirit of Christ, he is none of his" (8, 9). And elsewhere he says: "God hath sent the Spirit of his Son into your hearts" (Gal. 4, 6). From which it is proved that He proceeds from the Son just as He proceeds from the Father. Again, the Holy Ghost is sent by the Son, just as He is sent by the Father: thus, it is indicated that He proceeds from the Son just as He proceeds from the Father. For the Son says: "If I go not, the Paraclete will not come to you; but if I go, I will send him to you." (Jn. 16, 7). Thus, He Who is sent by the Son as by the Father necessarily proceeds from Son as from the Father. Add to this that Athanasius in his Creed says: "The Holy Ghost is from the Father and the Son, not made nor created nor begotten, but proceeding."[1] And he, too, is Greek.

But now, after all these proofs, let us hear the decision of the Church. The [IV] Lateran Council celebrated under Pope Innocent III professed its creed by these words: "Firmly we believe and we confess simply that the true God is one alone, eternal, immense, and unchangeable, incomprehensible, omnipotent and ineffable, Father and Son and Holy Spirit: indeed three Persons but one essence, substance, or nature entirely simple. The Father from no one, the Son from the Father only, and the Holy Spirit equally from both; without beginning, always, and without end; the Father generating, the Son being born, and the Holy Spirit proceeding; consubstantial and coequal and omnipotent and coeternal."[2] From the definition of which creed all the aforesaid heresies concerning God and His Persons which we have related to have arisen are overthrown. Now the creed of the council is found in the book of the Decretals under the title, *De summa trinitate et fide catholica*.[3]

And the [II] Council of Lyons celebrated under Gregory X, taught this creed more explicitly, saying the following: "In faithful and devout profession we declare that the Holy Ghost proceeds eternally from the Father and the Son, not as from two beginnings, but from one beginning, not from two breathings but from one breathing... But because some through ignorance of the irresistible aforesaid truth have slipped into various errors, we in our desire to close the way to errors of this kind, with the approval of the sacred Council, condemn and reject (those) who presume to deny that the Holy Ghost proceeds eternally from the Father and the Son; as well as (those) who with rash boldness presume to declare that the Holy Ghost

---

multis nominibus digna est, quae legatur a Christianis. Et ut a stilo Pauli, quod ad phrasim attinet, longe lateque discrepat, ita ad spiritum ac pectus Paulinum vehementer accedit. Verum ut non potest doceri certis argumentis cujus sit, quod nullius habeat inscriptionem, ita complutibus indiciis colligi potest, si non certis, certe probabilibus, ab alio quopiam quam a Paulo scriptam fuisse."

[1] Dz. 39.
[2] Dz. 428.
[3] Gregory IX, *Decretales*, bk. 1, tit. 1, c. 1.

proceeds from the Father and the Son as from two beginnings, and not as from one."[1] This decree is found in the sixth book, under the title, *De summa trinitate et fide catholica*, of the Decretals.[2]

But lest the Greeks reject these definitions of these councils using the pretext that they were celebrated by the Latins, it is necessary that we present to them the definition of a council celebrated with them present. The Council of Ephesus, which was celebrated under Theodosius the Younger, and is called the Third Ecumenical Council, in the letter sent by the whole council to Nestorius, near the end of the letter, says the following: "For although the Spirit is the same essence, yet we think of Him by Himself, as He is the Spirit and not the Son; but He is not different from Him; for He is called the Spirit of truth and Christ is the Truth, and He is sent by Him, just as, moreover, He is from God and the Father."[3] And they cannot calumniate saying that this is a letter of Cyril [of Alexandria] and not the definition of the council, because as is evident, the beginning of the letter has the following words: "To the most reverend and God-loving fellow-minister Nestorius, Cyril and the synod assembled in Ephesus."[4] In which inscription Cyril is put first, because the commission of Pope Celestine confided the council to him.

Now what the Greeks say, namely that the Gospel does not show the procession of the Holy Ghost from the Son, we have already shown to be false: because even if it is not stated there using the word "procession," still it is sufficiently declared with equivalent words. Also, even though the Councils of Nicea and Constantinople say that the Holy Ghost proceeds from the Father and are silent about the Son, nevertheless they merely say that He proceeds from the Father. How can those [councils] merely saying that He proceeds from the Father have testified that He proceeded from the Son? It is because (as Boethius says in his book, *De trinitate*[5]) opposite relations excepted, everything said of one Person, is also said of the others. Thus, since active spiration is not opposed to filiation, but only to passive spiration, which belongs to the Holy Ghost, it then follows that the Holy Ghost proceeds from the Father, wherefore it may be understood that He also proceeds from the Son.

The **thirteenth heresy** assails and afflicts with insults all the Divine Persons, because it says that power belongs only to the Father, and not merely appropriated to Him: wisdom to the Son, and goodness to the Holy Ghost. Saint Bernard also accuses Peter Abelard of this error in the letter which we have already often cited.[6]

This heresy is easily refuted if we firstly establish a thing is not truly proper to any one Person, which is discerned to befit multiple Persons. But since it is evident from Holy Writ that power, wisdom and goodness, just as all other things which are said of the Divinity, befit all three Persons, then it follows that none of those things are proper to any one single Person. He admits that the Father is powerful, but let him hear what is said concerning the Son: "All things were made by him: and without him was made nothing that was made" (Jn. 1, 3). And when He ascends into glory by the ministry of the Angels, to the Angels asking Who He is, the other Angels reply: "The Lord who is strong and mighty: the Lord mighty in battle" (Ps. 23, 8). And among the names which Isaias gave to the Son of God are these, namely, "God the Mighty, the Father of the world to come" (9, 6). But hear now the power of the Son and of

---

[1] Dz. 460.

[2] Boniface VIII ("*Liber sextus*"), *Decretales*, bk. 6, tit. 1, c. 1.

[3] Letter of Cyril to Nestorius with the Twelve Anathemas (PL 84, 156D-157A).

[4] The original letter speaks of those assembled "in Alexandria" (PG 77, 105) but this letter was "read and approved" at the Council of Ephesus. (Dz. 111a)

[5] C. 6 (PL 64, 1255). "Relation alone multiplies the Trinity of the divine persons" (quoted in the *Summa Theologica* I, q. 40, a. 2 *sed contra*).

[6] Letter 190, c. 3, n. 5-8 (PL 182, 1058D-1061B).

the Holy Ghost at the same time. "By the word of the Lord," says the Psalmist, "the heavens were established; and all the power of them by the spirit of his mouth" (Ps. 32, 6).

Peter Abelard concedes the Son's wisdom: hence let him hear Paul attributing wisdom to God the Father. For he at the end of the Epistle to the Romans says the following: "Known to God the only wise, through Jesus Christ, to whom be honour and glory for ever and ever. Amen." (Rom. 16, 26-27). Concerning the Holy Ghost, Wisdom Itself when speaking to His disciples says: "But when he, the Spirit of truth, is come, he will teach you all truth" (Jn. 16, 13). But how is He not Wisdom Who is capable of teaching all truth? And so that I may omit the remaining testimonies, among the other gifts of the Holy Ghost the Isaias lists wisdom, knowledge and understanding. (Is, 11, 2). Hence it cannot happen that He Who gives wisdom and knowledge to others, would not be wise Himself.

Now only remains to show that goodness is common to all three Persons. Since Peter Abelard attributes this to the Holy Ghost, it is only necessary that we show that it belongs to the Father and the Son. Concerning the Father, the Truth Itself testifies that He is good. For when in Luke's Gospel He commanded that we do good to those who hate us, he immediately added: "and you shall be the sons of the Highest; for he is kind to the unthankful, and to the evil" (6, 35). Now regarding the Son, Solomon testifies, who when speaking about Divine Wisdom, which is the Son of God, says the following: "For in her is the spirit of understanding: holy,... sweet, loving that which is good, quick, which nothing hindereth, beneficent" (Wis. 7, 22). If in Wisdom is a good spirit, how will He not be Goodness Itself? But Paul teaches us this more explicitly, who says the following in the Epistle to Titus: "But when the goodness and kindness of God our Saviour appeared," etc., (3, 4).

Now we concluded from all these testimonies that power does not belong only to the Father, nor wisdom to the Son, nor goodness to the Holy Ghost, but everything said of them is common to all the Persons. Yet they are said to be appropriated, because even though they are common to all the Persons, still they have some agreement and likeness to one Person: for example: power is common to all the Persons, yet it is said to belong to the Father because He is the source (as Augustine says[1]) of the whole deity, from which the other two Persons proceed. The Son likewise is called Wisdom, because even if the Father and the Holy Ghost are wise, nevertheless the Son was begotten by way of the Father's intellect, and He is a kind of knowledge produced by Him: and on account of this likeness wisdom is appropriated to Him, which is common to them all. In the same way we are accustomed to attribute goodness and love to the Holy Ghost, because the Holy Ghost was produced by the Father and the Son through their will, and He is the love produced by them both. On account of this agreement with Him, love is attributed to Him, although it is common to them all. Guy [the Carmelite] makes no mention of this heresy, just as he does not mention the other heresies which Peter Abelard taught.

DIABOLUS

Devil

Concerning this matter there is one error of the Manichaeans and the Priscillianists, whereby they teach that the devil is evil by his nature and cannot be good. Even though this heresy was already overthrown above when we disputed about "Creation" and all creatures, still nonetheless it will not be bothersome to cite some particular testimonies. For Christ when speaking about the devil said: "He stood not in the truth; because truth

---

[1] *De Trinitate*, bk. 4, c. 20, n. 29 (PL 42, 908).

is not in him" (Jn. 8, 44). From which saying it is evident that he was created in the truth, but by his malice he fell from it. For if he had never been in it, He would not have said, "He stood not in the truth," but rather He would have said, "He never was in the truth." Now He taught this more explicitly elsewhere saying: "I saw Satan like lightning falling from heaven" (Lk. 10, 18). Thus, he who fell from heaven necessarily was in heaven, where only the good are. Which is even more clearly shown by the fact that He said that the devil fell "like lightning": thus what was said is evident, because lightning has light at its commencement, which since it lasts but a short time and is quickly extinguished, it is turned into darkness with its fall. So likewise the devil, when he was created in the light of grace and of clear knowledge, remaining in it for a short time, fell from Heaven and was thrust into darkness. Hence He said: "I saw Satan like lightning falling from heaven."

Isaias likewise says concerning him under the name of the king of Babylon: "How art thou fallen from heaven, O Lucifer, who didst rise in the morning?" (14, 12). He said, "who didst rise in the morning," because he had light at the beginning of his formation or creation. The prophet Ezechiel likewise speaks about him under the name of the king of Tyre: "Thou wast the seal of resemblance, full of wisdom, and perfect in beauty. Thou wast in the pleasures of the paradise of God... Thou a cherub stretched out, and protecting, and I set thee in the holy mountain of God, thou hast walked in the midst of the stones of fire. Thou wast perfect in thy ways from the day of thy creation, until iniquity was found in thee" (28, 12-15). Notice with how many words he declares that the devil was good at one time. But if someone were to say that those words ought to be referred only to the king of Tyre, how could what He said befit him, "Thou wast in the pleasures of the paradise of God"? And again: "I set thee in the holy mountain of God"? Now here "the holy mountain of God" is Heaven, concerning which it is said by the [Royal] Prophet: "The mountain of God is a fat mountain..., a mountain in which God is well pleased to dwell" (Ps. 67, 16-17). And many other things are related in that same passage which can nowise befit the king of Tyre, as Blessed Jerome notes in his exposition of Ezechiel.[1]

Besides all these testimonies of Sacred Scripture, there is also the clear definition of the Church. For Pope Leo I in his letter to Torbius, Bishop of Asturia, in which he condemns the errors of the Priscillianists, says these words: "The sixth notice points out that they say the devil never was good, and that his nature is not God's handiwork, but he came forth out of chaos and darkness: because I suppose he has no instigator, but is himself the source and substance of all evil: whereas the true faith, which is the Catholic, acknowledges that the substance of all creatures spiritual or corporeal is good, and that evil has no positive existence; because God, who is the Maker of the universe, made nothing that was not good. Whence the devil also would be good, if he had remained as he was made. But because he made a bad use of his natural excellence, and 'stood not in the truth (Jn. 8, 44), he did not pass into the opposite substance, but revolted from the highest good to which he owed adherence: just as they themselves who make such assertions run headlong from truth into falsehood, and accuse nature of their own spontaneous delinquencies, and are condemned for their voluntary perversity: though of course this evil is in them, but is itself not a substance but a penalty inflicted on substance."[2] So wrote Pope Leo, a truly holy and hence learned man.

And the [IV] Lateran Council celebrated under Pope Innocent III says these things: "For the devil and other demons were created by God good in nature, but they themselves through

---

[1] *Commentariorum In Ezechielem Prophetam Libri Quatuordecim*, bk. 9 (PL 25, 269A-274C).
[2] Letter 15, c. 6 (PL 54, 683A-C). DS 286.

themselves have become wicked."[1] These words are found in the book of the Decretals, in the title *De summa trinitate et fide catholica*.[2]

Finally the First Synod of Braga defined regarding this matter, which is in chapter seven of its decrees, and says the following: "If anyone says that the devil was not first a good angel made by God, and that his nature was not a work of God, but says that he came forth from darkness, and does not have any author of himself, but is himself the origin and substance of evil, as Manichaeus and Priscillian have said, let him be anathema."[3]

Now the Manichaeans cite in support of themselves the saying of Christ regarding the devil: "He was a murderer from the beginning," which is hardly convincing: because it ought not to be understood to mean that the devil was a murderer from the beginning of his own creation, because then there was no man for him to kill such that he might be called a murderer: but he is called "a murderer" from the beginning of man's creation, when as soon as man was created by God, the devil resolved to kill him.

The **second heresy** is Origen's, saying that the devil would at some time be freed from Hell. For Augustine accuses him of this in his book, *De Haeresibus* [*ad Quodvultdeum*].[4] But we have already disputed about this matter above when we discussed concerning "Beatitude." For we showed there that both beatitude and the punishment of Hell are perpetual, and will never have an end. And besides those things which were said there concerning all the damned, what the Truth says in Matthew's Gospel especially refutes this heresy: that He will say to the wicked men at the Judgment: "Depart," He says, "from me, you cursed, into everlasting fire which was prepared for the devil and his angels" (Mt. 25, 41). From which words it is established clearly enough that the devil, just like the wicked men, will be punished with eternal punishment.

There is a **third heresy** which asserts that the devil's suggestions are made to us by contact with stones or herbs, just as their shrewd malice knew how to join each thing to each vice. But it is preferable to say nothing about this matter in this place, because we shall address it in a more suitable place below, namely, in the section on "Temptation." For in that place, by God's help, we will dispute about this matter.

ECCLESIA

Church

The word "Church" in Greek is ἐκκλησία, and means assembly or congregation, and is customarily used for the congregation of men itself: which meaning is found very often in Sacred Writ. Sometimes it also means the place in which the people are gathered, especially the place in which the people are gathered to praise God, which place by its proper name is called a temple. For so we find in the book of Judith: "And afterwards all the people were called together, and they prayed all the night long within the church, desiring help of the God of Israel" (6, 21). In which place (as it is clearly established) the word "church" is used for the place itself in which the people are gathered. But this meaning is rarer in Sacred Writ. Thus, leaving out this meaning (because we will discuss about the things related to it below in the section entitled, "Temple"), let us use the first meaning, concerning which we will find some heresies.

---

[1] Dz. 428.

[2] Gregory IX, *Decretales*, bk. 1, tit. 1, c. 1.

[3] PL 84, 563D-564A.

[4] C. 43 (PL 42, 34).

ECCLESIA

The **first heresy** is that which asserts that there are not good and bad men within the Church, but rather it asserts that only the good belong to it. The author of this heresy was a certain Donatus, from whom the Donatists are named. This Donatus (as Augustine relates[1]) coming from Numidia, which is part of Africa, infected nearly the whole of Africa with his error. Its origin and cause was that Caecilian was consecrated Bishop of Carthage against the will of Donatus. Alleging crimes to this Caecilian, which he could not prove, Donatus was judged to be a false accuser by judges who knew the matter very well. Wishing to fortify his falsity with pertinacious dissention, he changed the schism into heresy. For he separated himself from the Church, saying that the true Church was in the faction of Donatus: the Church was not in the other factions, however, which supported Caecilian, because although there were some good men there, nevertheless, they were sullied from their communion with bad men, and so the Church was perishing. Finally, for this reason Donatus, after bishops of the same faction had joined him, consecrated a certain Majorinus at Carthage, after who another Donatus succeeded him, of such doctrine and eloquence, that many think (as Augustine says[2]) that from him they were called Donatists.[3] And this second Donatus is he concerning whom Blessed Jerome mentions, although he says the Donatists are named after the former.[4] For Jerome relates that Donatus wrote a small work which is Arian in doctrine,[5] which Augustine attributes to the latter, and from whom he says on account of his eloquence many think the Donatists were so named. And in this matter I am more inclined to believe Augustine because he was an African like Donatus, wherefore he was better placed to know.

And I cannot omit here what things Bernard of Luxemburg says when speaking about the Donatists in his *Catalogus haereticorum*: for after saying that Donatus, namely the first (as is easily inferred from his text), lived at the time of the Emperor Constantius [II] and Pope Julius [I] (and he is indeed correct in saying this, as Platina supports him in the life of Pope Liberius[6]) afterwards adds, saying: "Cyprian of Carthage wrote various tracts and letters against this Donatus."[7] Now who can bear a man tripping so many times on the same stone? For "Cyprian lived in the time of Pope Cornelius, and was put to death under the Emperors Valerian and Gallienus on the same day that Cornelius was put to death at Rome, but not in the same year" (as Jerome says[8]). Now there were seventy or more years between the sufferings of

---

[1] *De Haeresibus ad Quodvultdeum*, c. 69 (PL 42, 43).

[2] *Ibid.*

[3] "For a long time it had been usual to distinguish these two, Donatus the Great and Donatus of Casae Nigrae. But in recent years doubt has been cast upon this distinction. We never hear of any Donatus residing at Casae Nigrae, but at Carthage. The Donatus who was called the Donatus of Casae Nigrae (which may have been his town of origin and not the seat of his bishopric) disappears after the Lateran Synod and the party is led thereafter by Donatus the Great at Carthage. The distinction between Donatus of Carthage and Donatus of Casae Nigrae is not found in the sources before the Synod of Carthage in 411. St. Augustine accepted the distinction with some hesitancy (*Retract*, c. 20, n. 3 (PL 32, 618)). But since his time the distinction became traditional. However, the fact that one Donatus disappeared as the other came upon the scene has led many moderns to doubt and to reject the distinction" (Rev. Liguori G. Müller, O.F.M., *The De Haeresibus of Saint Augustine* (*Patristic Studies*, (Washington, D.C., Catholic University of America, 1955), vol. 90 p. 196).

[4] *Lives of Illustrious Men*, chap. 93 (PL 23, 695).

[5] *De spiritu sancto.*

[6] *The Lives of the Popes* (London, Griffith, Farran, Okeden & Welsh, 1888), v. 1, p. 81.

[7] Fol. 35r.

[8] *Lives of Illustrious Men*, chap. 67 (PL 23, 677).

Cornelius[1] until Julius[2] under whom Donatus lived. Thus who can live, so that Cyprian could have written against Donatus, seventy years after himself?[3] And certainly (unless my memory fails me) there is no mention of any Donatus in all of Cyprian's works whose first letter[4] is to a certain Donatus, in which the word heresy was not used, nor any mention of heresy, but in that letter he merely tells Donatus how he converted from paganism to the faith of Christ: and he declares to him the snares of the world: so that on this occasion he would make him cautious. But this good man perhaps when reading just the title of the letter, thought that he was the arch-heretic Donatus, when nevertheless it is evident that he is another Donatus, more ancient than the heretic.

The Rogatists are related to these Donatists, being named after a certain Rogatus, of whom Augustine makes mention in letter ninety-three.[5] The Circumcellions also are related to them, concerning whom we will speak elsewhere. John Hus resurrected this error from Hell many centuries later: John of Rochezana succeeded him in the same error, who when attending the Council of Basil (as Aeneas Sylvius relates in his book, *De origine Bohemorum*[6]) being unwilling to submit to the Council departed. Luther, last of all, defended the same error.

Against this error is the quotation of the [Royal] Prophet: "And if he that hated me had spoken great things against me, I would perhaps have hidden myself from him. But thou a man of one mind, my guide, and my familiar, who didst take sweetmeats together with me: in the house of God we walked with consent" (Ps. 54, 13-15). Now the house of God is the Church, as Paul the Apostle testifies, saying: "These things I write to thee, hoping that I shall come to thee shortly. But if I tarry long, that thou mayest know how thou oughtest to behave thyself in the house of God, which is the church of the living God" (I Tim. 3, 14-15). Furthermore Paul the Apostle teaches that all the faithful belong to God's Church, who at the beginning of his [First] Epistle to the Corinthians says the following: "Paul, called to be an apostle of Jesus Christ by the will of God, and Sosthenes a brother, to the church of God that is at Corinth, to them that are sanctified in Christ Jesus, called to be saints, with all that invoke the name of our Lord Jesus Christ, in every place of theirs and ours," etc., (1, 1-2). From which words it ought to be noticed that he said, "the church of God," but he does not say, "of this or that man," as the heretics do, who restrict God's Church spread throughout the whole world, to a small number of them, yet they call it God's Church. He says, "sanctified in Christ Jesus," because they were regenerated in Christ by Baptism. And yet those very men whom he called "the church of God," and "sanctified in Christ Jesus" on account of the Baptism they received, he afterwards rebukes about many things. He states that there are contentions among them, by their saying, "I am of Paul; I am of Cephas" (I Cor. 1, 12). "I indeed am of Paul; and I am of Apollo; and I am of Cephas" (I Cor. 3, 4). And afterwards he reprehends some of them concerning fornication.[7] Thus he reprehends those men about many sins, whom he called "the church of God," because they were sanctified in Christ Jesus through Baptism. And when writing again to them in his Second Epistle to the Corinthians, he calls them "the

---

[1] Pope Saint Cornelius died in the year 253 A.D.

[2] Pope Saint Julius I died in the year 352 A.D.

[3] Saint Cyprian died in the year 258 A.D.

[4] The text refers to this letter as his second letter in his second book. Today this letter is classified as his first letter, and so the reference has been updated in this translation.

[5] C. 3, n. 11 (PL33, 326). According to an antiquated numbering convention this letter was referred to letter forty-eight in the text. The Rogatists were a sect that broke off from the Donatists.

[6] Pope Pius II, *De Bohemorum origine ac gestis historia* (Solingen, Johannes Soter, 1538), c. 52, p. 117.

[7] Cf. I Cor. 5, 1.

church of God" (1,1), even though he afterwards rebukes them, and threatens them unless they do penance.

Again, the Church is one body, according to Paul, the head of which body is Christ. Now the members of the body are all the faithful, those of whom who are just, are living and healthy members: those who are sinners, are dead and putrid members, ultimately to be cut off. Now this is evident from the words of Christ Himself, Who says: "I am the vine: you the branches" (Jn. 15, 5). And shortly before: "Every branch in me, that beareth not fruit, he will take away" (v. 2). Note that he did not say, "the branch that beareth not fruit is already taken away," but rather that it is to be taken away. From which is it proved that the faithful adhere to Christ through the true faith, who are tolerated by Him until death, when if they are found without fruit, they are completely separated as putrid members.

Next the Truth Itself taught by many parables that all the faithful are kept close in the bosom of the Church. "The kingdom of Heaven," He says, "is like to a net cast into the sea, and gathering together of all kind of fishes, which, when it was filled, they drew out, and sitting by the shore, they chose out the good into vessels, but the bad they cast forth. So shall it be at the end of the world. The angels shall go out, and shall separate the wicked from among the just, and shall cast them into the furnace of fire" (Mt. 13, 47-50). Observe here that the kingdom of Heaven is compared not to a multitude of good fish, but to a net, which contains the good and the bad. But the kingdom of Heaven of which He speaks, because it is evident that it is not Heaven, which is the Church triumphant, it follows that it is the Church militant, which is going to reign in Heaven. Also in the wedding feast, to which the kingdom of Heaven is compared, is there not someone not having a wedding garment?[1] It is evident that such a lack was a grave offense, because on account of it he is commanded to be bound hand and feet and cast into the exterior darkness, where there shall be weeping and gnashing of teeth.[2] Of the ten virgins to whom the kingdom of Heaven is compared, five were foolish, who when they took their lamps, did not take oil with them: and hence they were driven away as fools.[3]

Again, Blessed Paul in his Second Epistle to Timothy says: "But in a great house there are not only vessels of gold and silver, but also of wood and earth: and some indeed unto honour, but some unto dishonour" (2, 20). "Unto dishonour," namely those things which are of earth. Now the Apostle calls the Church "a great house," which is the house of God, in which the "vessels of gold and silver" are the just, while the "vessels of earth" are the sinners. Moreover, if it be so that the Church is composed (as John Hus says) solely of the predestined, and they, according to him, cannot be damned, nor be members of the devil, this church ought not to be called the Church militant, but the Church triumphant: because as they were predestined by God, so before God, to Whom all things are present, they are reputed triumphers. For he triumphs sufficiently, who was predestined.

Nor does that which the Lord, our Savior, commanded us to do with a brother sinning against us refute Luther any less: "If thy brother," He said, "shall offend against thee, go, and rebuke him between thee and him alone. If he shall hear thee, thou shalt gain thy brother. And if he will not hear thee, take with thee one or two more: that in the mouth of two or three witnesses every word may stand. And if he will not hear them: tell the church. And if he will not hear the church, let him be to thee as the heathen and publican" (Mt. 18, 15-17). Behold, you see that a brother sinning against us belongs to the Church, and is a member of it. For otherwise it would not have been commanded that his sin be denounced to the Church to be corrected by it: nor could the Church correct or punish him in any way. Because if he is not a member of the Church, and he not belong to it, the Church will have no power over

---

[1] Cf. Mt. 22, 11.

[2] V. 13.

[3] Cf. Mt. 25, 1-12.

him. For it will be said to him that which Paul says: "Who art thou that judgest another man's servant?" (Rom. 14, 4). Thus it would be necessary to admit, according to the opinion of the heretics, that anyone who has sinned mortally is by that very fact placed out of the power and jurisdiction of the Church. Now to concede this is so absurd, and foreign to the true faith, that no one is a learned man who would not see this clearly.

Furthermore, if it be so that the Catholic Church consists (as these heretics teach) of the just alone, it would be necessary to admit that the Church is invisible, that is to say, consisting of its spirit alone, which cannot be seen. For no one can know all those who are just, and who are sinners. For men often err in judging and determining these things, judging the just as unjust, and the unjust for the just. The reason for this deception is that men do not behold the heart, in which resides goodness or malice, but only see those things which appear outwardly. If they think that the Church is invisible, how will we denounce to the Church a brother sinning against us and unwilling to listen to us? How will we consult the Church, if we do not see it? How will we comply with the admonitions or commands of the Church, if we cannot know what is the Church? It is certainly necessary that the Church be visible, so that we can go to it, consult, revere and obey its commands. But we have disputed more than enough about this matter above in the first book. In which place we have shown by many quotations from Sacred Scripture and many very compelling reasons that the Church militant is visible and conspicuous to all men, hence it is not necessary to repeat anything from there now.

Finally, in Noe's ark—which is a type of this lower Church, because it crosses the sea of this world and although tossed by many waves, yet it will never be submerged—in it, I say, unclean animals are found along with clean ones. Thus in this lower Church, which militates here, all are found: only the unbelievers are found outside of it: all who firmly hold the orthodox faith, are enclosed within it. But if among them there are those who are sinners, the Church tolerates them until the shore of the sea, meaning until the end of the world. Then there will be a separation through the ministry of the Angels, who will put the good fish, that is to say, the good men, into their vessels, that is, into the places prepared for them by God: they shall cast the wicked, however, into the furnace of fire, where there shall be weeping and gnashing of teeth. When this separation has been made, Christ, her Spouse, will receive that glorious Church, not having spot or wrinkle, or any such thing; but holy, and without blemish. Also, before this separation has actually been carried out, separating mentally and by mere thought the wicked from the good, we now call the Church without blemish, a dove without gall,[1] such that we now consider it as it will be in the future: not that we separate the good from the wicked by this, because such separation is to be done by the shore of the sea, meaning at the end of the world. For that which the Apostle says, namely that the Church is without spot and without wrinkle,[2] Blessed Jerome says will be accomplished at the end of the world. For, when expounding the thirty-first chapter of Jeremias near the end of the chapter, he says the following: "See how many of these places the Church has! And see how the Apostolic saying, 'that she may be without spot or wrinkle,' is reserved for the future and the celestial realm. You hear of the corner [i.e. not in the straight line of truth, v. 38], you hear of the skin rash [Heb. *Gareb*, v. 39], you hear of destruction [or "dead bodies," v. 40] and the ashes (v. 40), and of the region of death (v. 40) and the darkness [Heb. Cedron, v. 40]—and do you still boast in your virtue and sinlessness?"[3]

---

[1] Doves have no gall bladders. Some medieval naturalists concluded they had no bile (gall), which in the theory of the four humors explained the allegedly sweet disposition of doves.

[2] Cf. Eph. 5, 27. St. Jerome had just referred the "building of the city" to "the Church" in this commentary.

[3] Bk. 6 (PL 24, 922A).

But what the Donatists and the Rogatists say, namely that the good are sullied from their communion with bad men, and for this reason they were saying that bad men do not belong to the Church, nor ought to be received into it lest the good be infected by their communion: this is very clearly refuted by the words which Christ said to His Apostles: "You are clean, but not all. For he knew who he was that would betray him; therefore he said: You are not all clean" (Jn. 13, 10-11). You see here Judas mixed in with the Apostles, and yet his malice did nothing to harm them, because Christ said that he was not clean, yet He said that the others were clean. We will prove below, with God as our guide, that Judas received the Sacrament of Communion, when we will treat about the Eucharist. Furthermore, the Lord says through the prophet Ezechiel: "They shall be in the mountains like doves of the valleys, all of them trembling, every one for his iniquity" (7, 16). He said, "his," not "another's" [iniquity]. And Paul when speaking about the retribution to be rendered to the good and the wicked says: "We must all be manifested before the judgement seat of Christ, that every one may receive the proper things of the body, according as he hath done, whether it be good or evil" (II Cor. 5, 10). He said, "proper,"[1] and not "another's." And he says elsewhere: "Let every one prove his own work" (Gal. 6, 4). He said, "his own." And again he says concerning those receiving the Lord's Body unworthily: "He that eateth and drinketh unworthily, eateth and drinketh judgment to himself" (I Cor. 11, 29). He said, "to himself," I say, not "to another." And John in the Apocalypse says: "The dead were judged by those things which were written in the books, according to their works" (Apoc. 20, 12). He said, "according to their works," not "according to the works of others."

Besides all these very clear testimonies of Scripture there is a universal pronouncement of the Church against the first part of this error. For among the articles of John Hus condemned at the Council of Constance during the fifteenth session, there are many pertaining to this matter. For the third article says the following: "The foreknown are not parts of the Church, since no part of it finally will fall away from it, because the charity of predestination which binds it will not fall away."[2] The fifth article says the following: "The foreknown, although at one time he is in grace according to the present justice, yet is never a part of the holy Church."[3] And the twenty-first article of the same man is this: "The grace of predestination is a chain by which the body of the Church and any member of it are joined insolubly to Christ the Head."[4] These articles along with the others of the same John Hus were condemned all together *lata sententia* at the Council of Constance.

Besides Augustine, I do not know of another writer against this error. For he published many treatises on this matter. There is a letter to the Donatist Vincentius,[5] another *Contra Fulgentium Donatistam*,[6] and in this [PseudoAugustine] disputes against the second part of the error whereby the Donatists teach that the good are sullied from their communion with bad men. There is another treatise of the same [Augustine] and this is especially against the letter of Petilian, in which he fights fiercely for the unity of the Church spread throughout the whole world.[7] Guy [the Carmelite] does not make any mention of these two errors, although

---

[1] *Propria*, which in Latin means "what belongs to oneself alone."
[2] Dz. 629.
[3] Dz. 631.
[4] Dz. 647.
[5] Letter 93 (PL 33, 321 ff.).
[6] PL 43, 763-774. The author of this work is "uncertain" (PL 43, 763) according to Migne, who strongly doubts that Augustine truly wrote it, though it is attributed to him in some manuscripts.
[7] *Answer to Petilian the Donatist* (*Contra litteras Petilliani donatistae Cirtensis episcopi* (PL 43, 245-388)).

he discusses the Donatists. And I am surprised, since Augustine, whom Guy always follows, attributes them to the Donatists.

There is **second error** which teaches that the Church can err. A certain [Pseudo-] John of Westphalia at the time of Emperor Fredrick III (as the *Catalogus haereticorum* says[1]) taught this error, who was condemned in Mainz on account of this and other errors, and his books burnt. Thus, this John taught this particular error among others, namely that the Church can err, and sometimes does err, and there is not such great certitude of the Church in defining that it could not err. If he is here speaking about an error in matters of faith and morals, it is evident that his teaching is heretical, which we have already refuted above, when we discussed the authority of councils.

If, however, he is speaking about errors which do not pertain either to faith or morals, his teaching is not heretical, because it is certain that the Church can err in such matters. For there is no danger, even if every single person were to think and pertinaciously assert that Emperor and King of the Spains Charles V never came to Italy, although we certainly know that he was in the towns of Italy many times, and in Bologna, which is an Italian city, received the crown of the empire by Pope Clement VII. Yet since this matter hardly pertains to salvation, there would be no injury to the faith even if the whole Church were to be mistaken about the matter. For all Catholic men admit that the Church can be mistaken especially in those things which do not regard the law [*jus*], but concern the deed [*res gesta*] alone: or (so that I may use more common words) the Church can err in those things which pertain to actions, just as it happens when someone contracts marriage with a woman with words in the future tense, whom afterwards he carnally knew without any marital affection: which having been done, he contracts marriage with another woman with words in the present tense, but (as is fitting) with a marital intention: in such an event the Church judges him to be bound to first woman, and decides that he is free and not bound to the second, because the Church piously believes that he had intercourse with the first woman with the intention of fulfilling and executing what he had previously promised: in which case she was his true wife, as the Church thinks. Yet in reality it was different, as we said before. The Church certainly knows that the woman whom he firstly had the intention of marrying is this man's true wife. However, that he had the intention to marry this or that woman, the Church cannot know with certitude, and consequently can be mistaken.

Now whether John of Westphalia taught about the former or latter [type of] error, when he said that the Church can err, it is not certain to me (as I frankly admit), because the good *Catalogus* did not say, nor have I found out from another author. Still I think that he thought what was said concerning the first error, and hence he was rightly condemned.

There is a **third heresy** which lessens the Church's authority. And the authors of this error were the Waldensians, or the "Poor Men of Lyons." Whom afterwards John Wycliffe followed, saying that the *Decretals* are apocryphal and of no importance, and he calls those who pay attention to them fools. The aforesaid John of Westphalia followed this man, who openly taught that neither the Apostles nor their successors, the prelates of the Church, have authority from Christ of making canons or laws. Luther teaches the same error in our time. Yet if someone were to say that what other teach, namely that obedience ought not to be rendered to

---

[1] Fol. 48v-49r. "Westphalus (John) an imaginary person, who [Louis] Moréri tells us was so named because he was born in Westphalia. He adds, that he was a Lutheran heretic, 'who about the year 1533, began to preach abominable errors; particularly that the Scripture doth not say that the Holy Ghost proceeds from the Son; that the Church hath erred, and several other impostures worth of Hell, from whence they proceeded.' He cites *Prateolous* v. Vest. *Gautier* in Chron. But we shall prove all this to be chimerical." (Pierre Bayle, Pierre Desmaizeaux, Anthelme, *The Dictionary Historical and Critical of Mr. Peter Bayle* (London, Printed for J. J. and P. Knapton; D. Midwinter, etc., 1738), vol. 5, p. 547).

the supreme pontiff, or to any other prelates of the Church, belong to this error, then this error will have many defenders. The Apostolics said that they do not submit to anyone except to Christ alone, just as (they say) the Apostles were subject to Christ alone. It was also a heresy of the Beghards and the Beguines, namely that a man existing in the state of perfection is not held to obey any man. Thus, the heresy of the latter heretics, namely of the Waldensians, the Apostolics, is more destructive than that of John Wycliffe and the others, because even if they deny that the Church can make laws and statutes to the observance of which all men are held, still they do not deny in general that subjects owe obedience to their prelates. Therefore, when we have proved that the Church can decree and establish something to which all are held to obey, and the transgression of which is deadly, we will be done with all these heretics.

Solomon gives testimony about this matter, saying: "My son, keep the commandments of thy father, and forsake not the law of thy mother. Bind them in thy heart continually, and put them about thy neck" (Prov. 6, 20-21). But if you were to say that these words ought to be referred to God's commandments alone, Who is our true and sole Father, I do not disagree. But tell me, who is that mother whose law he teaches ought not to be forsaken? For he joins two these things together, both the commandments of the father and the law of the mother. By which words he taught that the commandments of God the Father ought to be kept: and the precepts of the Church, our mother, in which we were reborn through the Baptism which we received in it, ought not to be despised. And again: "Pass not beyond the ancient bounds which thy fathers have set" (Prov. 22, 28). Notice here that he said "fathers," and not "father." Whence it is evident that those words cannot be understood of Divine commandments alone.

But if you say that those words should be understood of the Fathers of the Old Testament, to whom power was granted by God for deciding doubtful matters: why will not the same thing be said concerning the prelates of the Evangelical Law, especially since the holy Psalmist says: "Instead of thy fathers, sons are born to thee: thou shalt make them princes over all the earth" (Ps. 44, 17). And God Himself in Deuteronomy says: "But he that will be proud, and refuse to obey the commandment of the priest, who ministereth at that time to the Lord thy God, and the decree of the judge, that man shall die, and thou shalt take away the evil from Israel: And all the people hearing it shall fear, that no one afterwards swell with pride" (Deut. 17, 12-13). Because if such great authority and power of the priest of the Old Testament prevailed, such that no one would dare despise his power to command without danger of death, how much more will be the authority of the high priest in the New Law? It will certainly be much greater, since the priesthood of the latter is greater than the priesthood of the former.

But those replying to this argument, object to us from Paul saying: "If you are led by the spirit, you are not under the law" (Gal. 5, 18). And again: "You are bought with a price; be not made the bondslaves of men" (I Cor. 7, 23). By which words he wishes us to be freed by Christ from the Law of Moses, wherefore they say that it is no longer necessary for us to be subject to men. But this is not so, because even if Christ freed us from the slavery of sin, and from the servitude to the Mosaic Law, meaning from the yoke of its ceremonies and the ordinances, still He did not take away obedience to prelates, nay He commands it more strictly. Now by those words Paul does not turn away subjects from obedience to prelates, which we will show very clearly that He had commended elsewhere, but rather he turns away [subjects] from that servitude whereby everyone was claiming to belong to the person by whom he was baptized. One was saying, "I am of Paul": another, "I am of Apollo": and another, "I am of Cephas."[1] For Christ alone suffered for us, and hence we owe our whole selves to Him alone.

But putting aside the Old Testament, in which there are still many more examples that support us, let us go on to the New Testament, in which the Old Testament shines more clearly. For Christ commanded that a person secretly sinning, who after being corrected once does not

---

[1] Cf. I Cor. 1, 13 and 3, 4.

wish to listen, be delivered to the judgment of the Church: and if he will not hear the Church, He commands that he be considered as a heathen and a publican, meaning, that he be cut off from association with others, so that at least in this way, by being ashamed he may come back to his senses. Now an excommunication is only inflicted for a deadly and serious crime, and one to which pertinacity is attached. Thus it is evident that disobedience to the Church is a grave crime, which is punished with such a grave punishment.

But because some of these heretics (such a Luther) mock excommunications, for that reason let us present another testimony. Christ when speaking to His disciples, and in them to all prelates, their successors, says: "He that heareth you, heareth me; and he that despiseth you, despiseth me; and he that despiseth me, despiseth him that sent me" (Lk. 10, 16). From which words we conclude that the obedience which we proffer to men for God's sake, is not is human servitude, but is service to God: because He says: "He that heareth you, heareth me." It is also inferred that disobedience to the Church is considered by God Himself to be disobedience to God. And Paul in his First Epistle to the Thessalonians says: "For you know what precepts I have given to you by the Lord Jesus" (4, 2). And shortly afterwards he adds: "Therefore, he that despiseth these things, despiseth not man, but God, who also hath given his holy Spirit in us" (v. 8). Moses also taught this very clearly, when the people of Israel were murmuring against him and his brother Aaron, saying: "In the evening the Lord will give you flesh to eat, and in the morning bread to the full: for he hath heard your murmurings, with which you have murmured against him, for what are we? Your murmuring is not against us, but against the Lord" (Ex. 16, 8). From these two passages of Scripture just cited, it is clearly proved that the just precepts of rulers should not be called merely human, since they have their force and strength from the Divine command, especially since those despising them are reckoned before God as despisers of Divine commands.

Furthermore, the Truth Itself says again in Matthew's Gospel: "The scribes and the Pharisees have sitten on the chair of Moses. All things therefore whatsoever they shall say to you, observe and do" (23, 2-3). Now what is it that He says, "whatsoever"? Ought we to commit sins if they are commanded to us? Far be it. For by those words only obedience to those things which pertain to the chair is commanded to us, meaning those things which serve and open the way to more easily keeping God's Commandments. Concerning other commands, however, which turn men away from this observance of God's precepts, Truth Itself says elsewhere: "Why do you also transgress the commandment of God for your tradition?" (Mt. 15, 3). And afterwards He says: "This people honoureth me with their lips: but their heart is far from me. And in vain do they worship me, teaching doctrines and commandments of men" (v. 8-9). By which words Christ reprehends those traditions of men which are opposed to the Divine law, and not (as Luther imagines) all human laws.

Again, Paul in his Epistle to the Romans says: "For there is no power but from God: and those that are, are ordained of God. Therefore he that resisteth the power, resisteth the ordinance of God. And they that resist, purchase to themselves damnation" (13, 1-2). And when writing to Titus he says: "Admonish them to be subject to princes and powers, to obey at a word, to be ready to every good work" (3, 1). And he says in the Epistle to the Hebrews: "Obey your prelates, and be subject to them. For they watch as being to render an account of your souls" (13, 17). And what he says concerning ecclesiastical prelates is proved by that which he premised before in the same chapter: "Remember your prelates who have spoken the word of God to you" (v. 7). Moreover, Paul declares his authority over those disobeying when he says in the First Epistle to the Corinthians: "What will you? shall I come to you with a rod; or in charity, and in the spirit of meekness?" (4, 21). And again in the Second Epistle: "Therefore I write these things, being absent, that, being present, I may not deal more severely, according to the power which the Lord hath given me unto edification, and not unto destruction" (13, 10). And in the Second Epistle to the Thessalonians: "And if any man obey not our word by this epistle, note that man, and do not keep company with him, that he may be ashamed" (3, 14). Now there is no less power in the prelates of the Church now than there was then: hence prelates of the Church ought to be obeyed in those things which they know to conducive to the observance of the Divine law. Thus, why do the wicked Waldensians, Apostolics, Beghards, Waldensians, and Hussites bark, and despise obedience to the Church when it is confirmed by so many testimonies of Scripture?

But Luther, a more savage beast the more he is cautious on this point, admits obedience to the Church, but denies that it can be widened beyond the things which are explicitly stated in Holy Writ. But if it be necessary to follow this chimerical line of reasoning, all worship would perish and the whole religious government of Christendom would be destroyed, nay the whole Christian religion would fall to pieces, since faith, which is its foundation, by it alone would be overthrown. The festive solemnity of Sunday is not found enjoined in Sacred Writ, yet the Church prescribes that the Lord's day be observed. Nor was this invented after one hundred or three hundred years (as Luther and his followers are accustomed to object) but it came forth from the beginning of the early Church, and has been religiously observed by Christians ever since. Scripture never commands that images of the saints ought be venerated, yet the Seventh General Council which was assembled in Nicea [i.e. II Council of Nicea] decreed that they ought to be received by all Christians with worthy veneration.[1] Sacred Scriptures never commanded that we hear the Gospel standing and upright when it is read in public, or that we raise our hands when the Lord's Body is lifted up by the priest, or that we strike our breasts, or that we kneel before the altar when we pray. These and other pious ceremonies of this kind, I say, are not expressed in Sacred Writ, yet the Church established some of them, while others have been observed by perpetual custom until now. If all such things would be removed, because they are not written in the holy Bible, right away, within a few days, that which we call devotion, or (so that I may express myself better) the affection for sacred things will perish. For that worship which still flourishes in the hearts of Christians, however small it may be, is nevertheless fostered and nourished by these ceremonies. And unless Christians are required to do them, very quickly there is going to be either no or very cold worship of God.

But even though these things are so, still they are small compared to the things which we will now add. For Sacred Writ has never clearly stated Mary's perpetual virginity, hence someone might not now dare to call Mary, the Mother of Christ, a virgin, since Sacred Writ does not relate it. Sacred Writ never called the same most holy Virgin by the title, "Mother of God," but it merely calls her "Mother of Christ" or "Mother of Jesus": thus the Council of Ephesus wrongly decreed against Nestorius that she may be truly and rightly called *Theotokos*, meaning, the Mother of God. If all things were to be examined in relation to Luther's gnomon, which he prescribes for us, neither will we say that the Father is unbegotten nor will we assert that the Son is consubstantial to the Father, because none of these words are explicitly found in Sacred Writ, but are inferred from some reasoning by the infallible Church, declaring things which were obscure and drawing out things which were hidden.

But if it was permitted for the sake of the faith to establish this, why will it not also be permitted to establish those customs which are most conducive for the observance of God's Commandments? For otherwise we assert that the prelates of the Church cannot establish anything, whereas (as Paul says) power was given to the unto edification not for destruction.[2] Since God commanded us to worship Him, yet He did not specify when: the Church, however, using the power given to it by God, specified that we should worship God especially by

---

[1] Dz. 306.
[2] Cf. II Cor. 10, 8.

hearing Mass on Sunday. God also commanded fasting, and did not merely say this once or twice, but nearly countless times, yet He specified no day for fasting: wherefore lest it continually make no use of such fasting, since no particular day was designated, the Church specified the days on which one ought to fast. Thus, the precepts of the Church are specificative and declarative of God's Commandments, and they facilitate the observance of the Divine precepts. And so, the Church when establishing her precepts, does not decree something other than those things which God has decreed (as Luther accuses her), but it decrees the same things that God has decreed, since it decrees those things which tend to a better understanding and an easier observance of the God's Commandments.

For when Paul decreed not a few things which were not previously stated in Scripture, he immediately added: "If any seem to be a prophet, or spiritual, let him know the things that I write to you, that they are the commandments of the Lord" (I Cor. 14, 37). Furthermore, the Apostle similarly determined that a believing husband ought to remain with his unbelieving wife, and a believing wife with her unbelieving husband, if the unbelieving one of the spouses does not cause any injury to the faith of the other, and wishes to remain with the other believing spouse: and if [the unbelieving spouse] shall depart, being unwilling to remain with the believing spouse, he may depart, leaving the believing spouse free to marry someone else.[1] And yet when Paul decided or decreed this, he acknowledges that the Lord never said this. For he introduced this decree that he was able to give saying: "I speak, not the Lord" (I Cor. 7, 12). Again, the Apostle likewise commanded that women pray with their head covered, but men with their heads uncovered, which nevertheless is nowhere else stated in Scripture. Yet because he sees with a prophetic spirit some men in the future who would condemn the ordinances of prelates, afterwards giving this precept, he adds: "But if any man seem to be contentious, we have no such custom, nor the church of God" (11, 16).

Next, since a dispute had arisen about whether in the Evangelical Law men were obliged to the observance of the Legal precepts of the Old Law, the issue was referred to the Apostles and ancients who were in Jerusalem, who after mature deliberation was made (as was fitting) and the matter firstly carefully examined, pronounced this judgment: "It hath seemed good to the Holy Ghost and to us, to lay no further burden upon you than these necessary things: that you abstain from things sacrificed to idols, and from blood, and from things strangled, and from fornication; from which things keeping yourselves, you shall do well" (Acts 15, 28-29). It is certain that these four things, which the Apostles decreed to be necessary, are not enjoined upon us by God in the Evangelical Law, nay, nor are all these things now necessary. But the Apostles fearing that by this occasion communion of the Jews with the Gentiles might be impeded, and also by this occasion some of the Jews might be turned away from accepting the Evangelical Law, they forbade those four things for a time, so that the Church might merge together from the Gentiles and the Jews. Notice that the Apostles decreed things which are neither explicitly found in Scripture, nor did they ever hear them from God.

What then? Shall we thrust the Church down into such confines, or enclose it with such strict limits that we may say that it now has less authority for establishing something which is not expressed in Holy Writ, than there was then? If they say that the Church now does not have as much authority as then, let them show very clearly in Holy Writ (as they require of us) where it says that the Church's authority is now less, and that God has reduced the authority which He had once given to the Church: and once they have shown this, I will concede the point. Since, however, they cannot show it, why do they wish to enclose the prescriptions of the Church within the limits of Sacred Scripture, which of old was not hedged in by such limits? I could here cite many testimonies of holy men, but for the sake of avoiding prolixity,

---

[1] Cf. I Cor. 7, 12-15.

I omit them, both because those against whom we are now arguing, namely Wycliffe and Luther floccipend [i.e. regard as insignificant] the words of any holy man.

But besides all these very clear testimonies, this assertion of the heretics has already been condemned in many councils. For among the eight errors of the Beghards and the Beguines which were condemned in the Council of Vienne celebrated under Clement V, the third in the list is the error whereby they say that those who are in the state of perfection and in that spirit of liberty are not subject to human obedience.[1] Now the decree of this council is found in the volume of the *Constitutiones Clementinae* under the title, *De haereticis*, chapter *Ad nostrum*.[2] And the Council of Constance when condemning in the eighth session many articles of John Wycliffe, put this one among them, with these words: "The decretal letters are apocryphal and they seduce from the faith of Christ, and the clergy who study them are foolish."[3] Which article along with the others was condemned with one *latae sententiae* condemnation upon them all. And in the fifteenth session the same council again condemns many assertions of John Hus, among which this one is found, with these words: "Ecclesiastical obedience is obedience according to the invention of the priest of the Church, without the expressed authority of Scripture."[4] Therefore let us say that according to the Catholic faith, the Church's decrees ought not to be despised, but strictly observed. Now whether any particular transgression of them is a mortal sin, I do not discuss: because I see certain men, and not from the lowest rank among scholastic theologians, who assert that those transgressing the precepts of the Church, provided that they do not omit it out of contempt, but from a certain weakness, or perhaps negligence, do not sin mortally: I know others, however, who teach the opposite. Now since in this work I have intended to treat only the faith: I do not wish to dispute about the opinions of men thinking in diverse ways.

John Fisher, Bishop of Rochester, wrote against this heresy in the work which he published against Luther's [*Defense and Explanation of all the Articles*].[5] Josse van Clichtove also wrote at greater length in his *Antilutherus*, part one.[6]

There is a **fourth heresy** which teaches that the Church itself, meaning the clergy, cannot possess any riches, fields, or any possessions, because (as they say) the Apostles, whom the prelates of the Church succeeded, were poor, possessing absolutely nothing. The first inventors of this heresy (as Augustine relates[7]) were the Vadiani or Anthropomorphites: who by this occasion separated themselves from the Church, because they were saying that it is not allowed for bishops to possess riches, yet they seemed to be rich. After them, after a long lapse of time, arose the Waldensians, or the "Poor Men of Lyons," who said (as Aeneas Sylvius charges them) "Priests ought to be poor, and content with alms alone."[8] Yet Guy [the Carmelite] does not mention of this error when he recounts the heresies of the Waldensians. Marsilius of Padua,[9] a man in fact burning with hatred towards the whole Church and all ecclesiastics, taught this same error. This Marsilius lived under Pope John XXII and was con-

---

[1] Dz. 473.

[2] *Constitutiones Clementis V*, bk. 5, tit. 3, c. 3.

[3] Dz. 618.

[4] Dz. 641.

[5] *Assertionis Lutheranae confutatio*, a. 27, p. 431v ff. The text here erroneously has Luther's *Babylonian Captivity*, but it was rather his *Assertio omnium articulorum*, as mentioned previously in a footnote, and so has been corrected here.

[6] *Antilutherus* (Cologne, Ex officina Petri Quentell, 1525), bk. 1, c. 1-29, pp. 1r-62v.

[7] *De Haeresibus ad Quodvultdeum*, c. 50 (PL 42, 39).

[8] Pope Pius II, *De Bohemorum origine ac gestis historia* (Solingen, Johannes Soter, 1538), c. 35, p. 55.

[9] Marsilius of Padua was a physician born at Padua about 1270 and died about 1342, unreconciled to the Church.

demned by the same. He imitated the Waldensians on this point, just as John Wycliffe always did in other matters. Last of all Luther in our time defends the same error, persuading princes to loot the goods of the Church, which also we have heard has been done in many towns of Northern Germany.[1]

We have refuted the foundation of this heresy above, when we discussed the poverty of the Apostles.[2] For there we taught from Sacred Scripture that the Apostles possessed something. Likewise, above in the section on "Tithes," we showed that tithes are due to priests by Divine law: from which tithes the priest can take, and reserve for himself a first portion for things needed by himself, namely food and clothing.

But besides all these testimonies there are still other specific testimonies of Scripture. For priests of the Old Testament had possessions and fields. For after the people of Israel obtained the promised land, the Levitical tribe from which priests were taken, by the Lord's command received from the other tribes forty-eight cities with their suburbs. The Levites also received tithes from all the products of the land and of all the herds. Why will this not be also permitted for priests of the New Law, especially since this is not found to have been forbidden them by Christ, just as we taught above when we disputed about the poverty of the Apostles? Furthermore, Paul the Apostle when writing to Timothy about how a bishop should be, among other things he requires of him to be "given to hospitality" (I Tim. 3, 2). But hospitality cannot be exercised by him who has no possessions that he could administer to those whom he receives as guests. Paul also says in the same place that a bishop ought to rule his house well (v. 4), because (he says) "if a man know not how to rule his own house, how shall he take care of the church of God?" (v. 5). Now good management of a house includes providing for the wife and children one has as to food, clothing, and those things without which this miserable life cannot be conserved. Now no one can suitably accomplish this without possessions.

Again, the [Pseudo-] Pope and martyr Pius, in his letter written to the Italians, says the following: "It has been made known to the Apostolic See that there are contentions and jealousies among you, some men put to human uses properties given for religious purposes, and those given to the Lord God they take away from Him, to serve their own purposes. Wherefore the abuse of this usurpation must to be removed by all, lest the properties dedicated to the uses of the sacred mysteries be abused by certain plunderers: but if anyone would presume [to do the contrary], let him be held as sacrilegious and judged as sacrilegious."[3] So wrote Pope Pius, whom they cannot accuse of being wicked, since he ended his life as a martyr. Nor can they reject him for living after the first three centuries (as Luther is accustomed to do), because he was the tenth supreme pontiff from Peter. Thus, why does wicked Luther dare to persuade princes to loot and plunder the churches? Does he not see that those who do this are to be judged as sacrilegious by the very holy pope?

Another man cut from the same cloth agrees with this very holy pope, namely the [Pseudo-] Pope and martyr Urban, who published the following decree about this matter: "Thus the supreme pontiffs and other bishops, as well as the Levites and the rest of the faithful can benefit more if inheritances and lands, which they had previously sold, were delivered to the churches which the bishops presiding over, because from their both present and future revenues they can provide more and finer things to the faithful leading a common life, than from their price: they seized estates and lands to the churches which they were accustomed to sell, and to live from their revenues. But those things in the control of each parish priest, were,

---

[1] *Germania Superiora* is the expression used here which refers to the ancient Roman province with this name.

[2] See the second heresy of the section entitled "Apostles" above in book two.

[3] PL 102, 104C. A note explaining the historical dubiousness of this letter is found in PL 102, 1093C, where it is stated that it derives from the *False Decretals of the Pseudo-Isidore* (PL 130, 113B).

are still, and always ought to be for all time belonging to the bishops who hold the place of the Apostles. And from all these things, the bishops and faithful dispensers of them ought to supply all things needed to those wishing to live a common life, as best they can, so that none of them may be found to be in need."[1]

After Urban, [Pseudeo-] Pope and martyr Lucius confirmed the same opinion, which in his letter to the bishops of France and Spain condemned those ravaging the goods of the Church.[2] I could have cited many other testimonies of holy men on this matter, which I omit for the sake of brevity. Still if any curious reader desires to see them, he may read the *Decretum*, in which Gratian recorded many testimonies on this matter.[3] Add to this that many of the supreme pontiffs are numbered among the saints, even from the time when the Church possessed riches.

And there are decrees of many councils about not alienating the Church's goods and about the economy of the Church. And indeed, the Council of Chalcedon, which is one of those four which Blessed Gregory states are to be accepted like the four holy Gospels, strictly forbids clerics, following the death of their own bishop, to seize the things that belong to him.[4] Hence it is evident by the authority of the council that the ownership of things is allowed for bishops. Finally, among the many assertions of John Wycliffe condemned in the Council of Constance during the eighth session, there are some which pertain to this matter. For the tenth article says the following: "It is contrary to Sacred Scripture that ecclesiastical men have possessions."[5] The thirty-second says: "To enrich the clergy is contrary to the rule of Christ."[6] And in the following article it says: "Sylvester, the Pope, and Constantine, the Emperor, erred in enriching the Church."[7] And the thirty-sixth article is: "The pope with all his clergy who have possessions are heretics, because they have possessions; and all in agreement with these, namely all secular masters and other laity."[8] All these articles were simultaneously condemned in that eighth session of the Council of Constance. But here the ecclesiastical prelates ought to take notice that although it be permitted to them to possess riches, nevertheless it is not permitted to keep them greedily or to spend them inappropriately. Josse van Clichtove wrote about this subject in that work which he published support of the assertion of the truths defined at the Synod of Sens against Luther.[9]

---

[1] This letter is "deemed a fraud and forgery by learned men" (PG 10, 135B). It also derives from the *False Decretals of the Pseudo-Isidore* (PL 130, 137D-138B).

[2] *False Decretals of the Pseudo-Isidore* (PL 130, 168D-174C). This letter is "suspect" as are the other things found published by Psuedo-Isidore (PL 3, 975C).

[3] C. XII, q. 1-5.

[4] Canon 22.

[5] Dz. 590.

[6] Dz. 612.

[7] Dz. 613.

[8] Dz. 616.

[9] *Compendium veritatum ad fidem pertinentium contra erroneas Lutheranorum assertiones ex dictis et actis in concilio provinciali Senonensi apud Parisios celebrato* (Paris, 1529), c. 14.

ELEEMOSYNA

Almsgiving

There is one error about this subject, teaching that it is unlawful to give alms to mendicant brothers. The leader of this error was John Wycliffe, who asserted that everyone who collects alms for the brothers is *ipso facto* excommunicated. He is motivated to make this assertion by two reasons. One, because he condemns every order of monks, and he asserts that monks living a deprived life do not belong to the Christian religion. And the holy men who instituted the various orders of monks, sinned in doing this, and unless they repent of this, he contends that they are damned. The other reason which motivated him is that all begging is unlawful for brothers, because (as he says) brothers ought to gain their living by manual labor, and not by begging. Thus, this Wycliffe, in order to defend his error, asserts another more harmful or equal error; "the dish has a cover worthy of it."[1]

To defend being a monk, which he condemns in general, does not belong to the work at present: below, with God as our guide, we will make a longer disputation in its proper place. Now the fact that he requires monks to do manual labor for their living, I do not condemn in general, nor also do I generally approve. I, in fact, even though I am a monk, do not agree with the Euchites or Messalians, who were saying that all manual labor is unlawful for monks. For there are some monks who wish to labor with their hands, yet not all. But we will discuss this matter elsewhere under the heading or title, "Labor." We will prove, with God's help, in its proper place, when we will discuss it under that heading, that mendicancy is not merely licit, but also meritorious. Therefore, having removed the foundations by which this impious assertion of Wycliffe rests, it is necessary that it collapse. For if being a monk is licit, and it is licit for monks to beg, it will also be licit to give them alms. This assertion of Wycliffe is also one of the forty-five which were condemned in the eighth session of the Council of Constance. For the twentieth article condemned there says the following: "One bringing alms to the Brothers is *ipso facto* excommunicated."[2] Which assertion along with the other forty-four of the same Wycliffe were condemned in the same place. Thus, since the Church has put an end to this dispute, there is no reason why we ought to dispute the matter any further.

I have found no other error about this matter among any of those who wrote about heresies, or enumerated heresies. But Blessed Augustine says in *City of God*, book twenty-one, chapter twenty-two,[3] that he learned of certain men thinking that almsgiving is of such great excellence, that one who has done it, no matter how criminally and wickedly he lives, is not going to have eternal punishment: yea they were also saying that one who never gave alms or disdained to do so is destined to perpetual punishment. Since Augustine did not relate any author, I decided to omit it here: but because perhaps at a later time (as we experience daily in payment for our faults) someone may arise who tries to defend it, I changed my mind, and inserted it into this work, content with merely mentioning it. Accordingly, its very clear and effective refutation is the passage of Paul: "If I should distribute all my goods to feed the poor, and if I should deliver my body to be burned, and have not charity, it profiteth me nothing" (I Cor. 13, 3). If, however, someone would like to see more about this matter, he may read

---

[1] Cf. Erasmus, *Adagia chiliades*, I, X, 72.
[2] Dz. 600.
[3] PL 41, 736-737.

Blessed Augustine in the *City of God*, chapter twenty-seven, in which place he refutes this error, which he had related above in chapter twenty-two of the same book.[1]

EPISCOPUS
Bishops

Concerning this matter there is one error whereby it is taught that a bishop is not higher than a simple priest. The author of this error was Aerius [of Sebaste], although Philastrius when speaking about him, never attributes this to him. Yet Augustine when speaking about him says that while lamenting that that he could not be consecrated a bishop he fell into the Arian heresy, and added many other teachings, one of which was this, namely that there should be no difference between a bishop and a priest.[2] Marsilius of Padua afterwards subscribed to these things. John Wycliffe (as we have said elsewhere) always followed the Waldensians, and defended their errors: wherefore he, following his usual practice, taught this error: which error he derived from the same source, from that Aerius. Thomas Netter in his *Doctrinale [antiquitatum] fidei [Catholicae Ecclesiae]*,[3] says that John Wycliffe ambitioned the bishopric of Worcester, which nevertheless he did not obtain, and hence he began to despise what he had anxiously desired. For we have learned by experience that it very often happens that one who cannot obtain what he greatly longed for, takes refuge in the contempt and belittling of that thing, so that even by this remedy, he may heal his impotent desire, and persuade others that he hardly wanted what was not obtained. So likewise, because Aerius and Wycliffe could not procure a bishopric, they pretended to despise its dignity and degree of eminence. Luther agreed with John Wycliffe, who [i.e. Luther] in his pamphlet, *Against the Spiritual Estate of the Pope and the Bishops, Falsely So Called*, says these words: Bishops "are unlearned papal masks, unable to do anything but destroy truth, just like their creator [the pope]... hence episcopal government ought to be abolished and the bishoprics laid waste"[4] And again in *The Babylonian Captivity of the Church* he says: "All of us that have been baptized are equally priests,"[5] and any layman can consecrate churches, confirm children, etc.[6]

Yet before I go out to attack this heresy, I wish to warn the reader not to think that I contradict these heretics on this point such that I think the episcopacy is a different order from the priesthood. I have pointed this out because there are some who think that the episcopacy differs from the priesthood, just as the priesthood from the diaconate, such that a different character is imprinted in the consecration of a bishop than the one which had been imprinted when he was ordained a priest. Again, others teach that neither is a different character imprinted nor is the order of the bishop different from that of the priest, but they say they are

---

[1] PL 41, 746-752,

[2] *De Haeresibus ad Quodvultdeum*, c. 53 (PL 42, 39-40).

[3] Vol. 1, bk. 2, art. 3, c. 60.

[4] This pamphlet was originally published in 1522 in German under the title, *Wider den falsch genantten geystlichen stand des Babst und der bischoffen*. It was republished in Latin by Thomas Wolffe under the title, *Adversvs Falso Nomina tum ordinem Episcoporum libellus*.

[5] *On the Babylonian Captivity of the Church* (*Weimarer Ausgabe,* (abbrev. hereafter as WA), vol. 6, pg. 564, ln. 11).

[6] "Does the ordination of such babbling priests, the consecration of churches and bells, or the confirmation of children, constitute a bishop? Could not any deacon or layman do these things? It is the ministry of the word that makes a priest or a bishop" (WA 6, 566, lns. 7-9).

different degrees of the same order, such that within the same order there are two degrees, one superior to the other from its original institution. Concerning which matter it does not belong to me to decide at present: because (as I have often stated elsewhere) I do not treat here the opinions of men thinking differently, but the Catholic faith alone. Hence I leave this matter to be discussed by others. Thus, it belongs to my declared purpose merely to show that there is a difference between the episcopacy and the priesthood, which did not emanate from Caesar (as John Wycliffe murmurs), but that it proceeded from Christ and His Apostles, such that the bishop, by the Divine institution itself, merely has a different dignity, superior to the priest.

Now we prove this as follows. It is certainly necessary that a shadow be similar to the body, and a figure be similar to the truth. Now the things which preceded in the Old Testament were certain figures of those things which were to come in the New Law, Paul bearing witness, who says: "All these things happened to them in figure" (I Cor. 10, 11). But in the Old Law there was a distinction of priesthoods. For Aaron was the high priest; his sons, however, were lower priests. The high priest had different vestments than the lower ones. The high priest entered into the Holy of Holies, which was not permitted to other priests, as appears from the book of Leviticus, and the Epistle of Paul to the Hebrews. It belonged to the high priest alone to celebrate the feast of expiation, as appears from the same places. Thus, since there was such a vast distinction in the Old Law between priests, we infer therefrom that there was also a diversity of priesthoods in the New Law instituted by Christ. This argument of ours is also confirmed by the authority of [Pseudo-] Pope Leo [I], who in his letter sixty-six which is to all the bishops of the churches of Germany and Gaul, says the following: "For in Holy Writ by the Lord's command only Moses erected the altar in the tabernacle of God, only he anointed, who indeed was the high priest of God, as it is written of him: 'Moses and Aaron among his priests' (Ps. 98, 6). Therefore, that which was commanded only to the leaders of the priests to do, whose type Moses and Aaron were, it is indeed decreed that bishops or priests, who bear the figure of the sons of Aaron, may not presume to arrogate for themselves."[1]

Furthermore, Paul when writing to Titus says: "For this cause I left thee in Crete, that thou shouldest set in order the things that are wanting, and shouldest ordain priests in every city, as I also appointed thee" (1, 5). In this passage Paul by the word "priests" meant bishops, because (as Theophylactus[2] suggests and before him Chrysostom[3]) Paul did not want the whole island, namely Crete, to be entrusted to one bishop, especially since it is related that it was so large that it had a hundred walled towns. Hence, he wrote to Titus so that he would appoint a particular priest, meaning a bishop, for every city, thinking that in this way the people would be better cared for. Besides this testimony, also the context of the text proves this. For after he had commanded the ordination of priests, he then adds what qualities the one who has been ordained ought to have, using at the same time the word "bishop," by which evidence it is proved that he calls the same man a bishop, whom he had previously had called a priest. The latter word is now said for the former word firstly said.

Hence the bishop (so that we may return to our objective) ordains priests: on the other hand a simple priest cannot do this, as we will show, with God's favor, when we will treat about priests. Therefore, a bishop and a priest are not completely the same. Again, if by Divine in-

---

[1] Letter 88 (PL 2, 1325B-C). A discussion of the spurious nature of this letter is found in Migne's Patrology (PL 2, 760C ff).

[2] "[Paul] did not want the whole island to be committed to one man, but that each city would have its own pastor. For in this way both the labor would be lighter and the care more complete" (*Expositio in Epistolam ad Titum* (PG 125, 147)).

[3] "'For this cause left I you in Crete.' As though the whole world had been one house, they divided it among themselves, administering its affairs everywhere, each taking care of his several portion of it" (*In Epistolam ad Titum, homilia II* (PG 62, 671)).

stitution a priest and a bishop were completely the same, it would follow therefrom that just as a bishop ordains priests, so vice versa a priest would be able to consecrate bishops: which we read was never done: because even if Paul when writing to Timothy says: "Neglect not the grace that is in thee, which was given thee by prophesy, with imposition of the hands of the priesthood" (I Tim. 4, 14): nevertheless Chrysostom, Theophylactus[1] and the rest expound this of a bishop, Chrysostom adding that "priests were not enthroning [meaning consecrating] bishops."[2]

Next the bishops are the successors of the Apostles, and take their place, the other clerics, however, were put in the place of the seventy disciples. But no one doubts, which even Wycliffe himself concedes, as Thomas Netter testifies, that the Apostles by a certain singular prerogative were superior by merit and dignity to the other disciples. Now that the successors of the Apostles are bishops, but rest of the disciples are priests, this Wycliffe denies, but instead he says that all priests succeed the Apostles, and the deacons the rest of the disciples. Hence, he concludes from this that all priests are equal.[3] Thus so that we pierce him with his own dart, this must be sought with all our strength, that we show by the testimony of all that only bishops are the successors of the Apostles, but priests and the remaining clergy are the successors of the disciples. I added "the remaining clergy" because I see some men thinking that only priests were put in the place of the disciples. That this is not so is proved from the fact that the deacon Philip was of the number of disciples, as well as Stephen and the other deacons.

Therefore having omitted the more recent [testimonies], to which not as much confidence is due, Bede says the first of all the testimonies in our favor, who in his commentary on Luke says the following: "As no one doubts that the twelve Apostles also at the same time foreshadowed the order of Bishops, so also we must know that these seventy-two represented the presbyters, (that is, the second order of priests). Nevertheless, in the earliest times of the Church, as the Apostolic writings bear witness, both were called presbyters, both also called bishops, the former of these signifying 'ripeness of wisdom,' the latter, 'diligence in the pastoral care.'"[4] [Ivo of Chartes] puts forth the same view in a certain sermon in a synod that was held, saying the following: "Priests and their vicars are in fact the successors of the seventy disciples, who went before the Lord Jesus Christ into every city and place He was going to go. Thus priests, because they are helpers of the bishops, catechize the unlearned, incorporate those to be baptized into the unity of the Church, and administer all the Sacraments up until the imposition of hands. But the bishops are the successors of the Apostles."[5] And [Pseudo-] Blessed Damasus in a letter concerning chorepiscopi, whom he declares to be merely priests, after he had said that they are unable to administer the sacrament of Confirmation, says the following: "Now that it belongs only to the Apostles and their successors by the proper office to transmit the Holy Ghost, the book of the Acts of the Apostles teaches, especially since it is read that none of the seventy disciples, whose place in the Church these [chorepiscopi] take,

---

[1] "Priests were not consecrating bishops. Now see this horrendous thing, how much the imposition of sacerdotal hands can do" (*Expositio in Epistolam primam ad Timotheum* (PG 125, 59)).

[2] "He is not speaking here about priests, but about bishops: for priests were not enthroning [meaning consecrating] bishops" (*In Epistolam I ad Timotheum, homilia XIII* (PG 62, 565)).

[3] *Doctrinale antiquitatum fidei Catholicae Ecclesiae* (Venice, Antonius Bassanesi, 1757), vol. 1, bk. 2, a. 3, c. 60, n. 8, p. 564.

[4] *In Evangelium S. Lucae*, bk. 3, c.10

[5] Saint Ivo of Chartes, Sermon II: *De excellentia sacrorum ordinum, et de vita ordinandorum, in synodo habitus* (PL 162, 518C). The text here cites "Isidore" here, but this sermon is one of Saint Ivo of Chartes.

transmitted the gift of the Holy Ghost through the imposition of hands (as it was previously said)."[1]

You now see that three illustrious men gave testimony in our favor, who all assert that bishops are the successors of the Apostles, but priests hold the place of the disciples. But so that the case may be made stronger, let us summon still more witnesses in support of this case. [Pseudo-] Pope and martyr Urban in a letter on the common life and offerings of the faithful, when speaking about the goods of the Church to be distributed, by whom they ought to be distributed, says the following: "But these things in the control of the parishes were, still are and always ought to belong to the bishops, who hold the place of the Apostles."[2] By which words he clearly enough said that the bishops are the successors of the Apostles, no mention having been made of the priests.

[Pseudo-] Pope and martyr Anacletus, who ruled the Catholic Church [third[3]] from Blessed Peter the Apostle, in a letter concerning the patriarchs, the primates and the rest of the bishops, says the following: "My brethren, the order of priests is twofold, and as the Lord established it, it ought not to be disturbed by anyone. Now you know that the Apostles were chosen and appointed by the Lord, and afterwards were dispersed throughout various regions to preach. But when the harvest began to grow, seeing that the workers were few, He commanded that the seventy disciples be chosen to help them. Verily the bishops take the place of the Lord's Apostles: the priests likewise take the place of the seventy disciples."[4] In which words one especially ought to take note that he says that the Lord instituted the twofold order of priests. I would rather believe this Anacletus than a thousand Wycliffes, nay more than Jerome, Augustine or any other more recent [witness], no matter how holy or learned. For besides sanctity of life, which his martyrdom especially indicates, he saw the Apostles, and (as he testifies in the beginning of the letter which we have just cited) he was ordained a priest by Blessed Peter the Apostle. Hence it ought to be believed that he knew well the mind of the Apostles and had their spirit. And so that we may add something else, Blessed Augustine when enumerating the errors of Aerius, lists this one among them, namely that he made the priests equal to bishops.[5]

Besides all these many testimonies of illustrious men, that especially strengthens our argument, which we taught above when we were treating about Confirmation. For we showed there that the Sacrament cannot be conferred by just any priest, but by a bishop alone, and this is from Divine institution and not by the ordinance of the Church. If therefore the bishop administers Confirmation, and another priest cannot administer it, it is proved therefore that a priest and bishop are not the same.

But against all these things John Wycliffe objects against us that Blessed Jerome who when expounding the passage in the Epistle to Titus: "For this cause I left thee in Crete" etc., (1, 5) says the following: "Therefore a presbyter is the same as a bishop is, and before that by the instigation of the devil emulations in respect to religion arose, and people began to say: 'I am of Paul, and I of Apollos, and I of Cephas,' the churches were governed by the common

---

[1] The letter is found in Migne's *Patrologia Latina* among the apocryphal letters of Pope Saint Damasus (PL 13, 436B).

[2] This letter is found among the *False Decretals of the Pseudo-Isidore* (PL 130, 138B). It is found among Remigius' canons for his diocese (n. 47 (PL 102, 1110C)) which are described in Migne's *Patrologia Latina* as "spurious" and "very doubtful" (PL102, 1095B).

[3] The text here calls him the "fourth" pope of the Church. But he is now generally accepted as the second successor of St. Peter, though whether he was the same as Cletus, who is also called Anencletus as well as Anacletus, has been the subject of endless discussion. Cf. "Pope St. Clement I," *The Catholic Encyclopedia* (New York: Robert Appleton Company, 1908), vol. 4, p. 13.

[4] *False Decretals of the Pseudo-Isidore* (PL 130, 76B-C).

[5] *De Haeresibus ad Quodvultdeum*, c. 53 (PL 42, 40).

counsel of the presbyters. But, after that each one was accustomed to regard those whom he had baptized as his own disciples and not of Christ, it was decreed in the whole world that one chosen from among the presbyters should be placed over the others, and to whom all care of the Church should belong, that the seeds of schisms might be plucked up."[1] To which objection Thomas Netter replies in the place cited above,[2] that it is true that bishops are priests. For Jerome thinks this. But that there would be no distinction between the bishop and priest, this he did not say. But actually Thomas Netter is mistaken, in saying that in the whole discourse after the words just cited Jerome tries to do nothing else besides to show that by Divine institution there is no difference between the bishop and priest, but that such a distinction was afterward invented for eliminating a schism.[3] And the words of Jerome, about the elevation of bishops over other priests being invented by the Church, ought to be understood merely concerning precedence in a council, such that one bishop presides over the whole general council of priests in composing canons, which is not thought to have occurred so much by Divine institution as from human custom. And this saying of Jerome ought to be understood to mean that he is speaking about this precedence.

Now whether this exposition expresses the true meaning of Jerome and his true mind, I do not now wish to discuss, but I leave this to the reader, who when reading this passage of Jerome carefully will easily enough understand that this exposition is different from Jerome's reasoning. But so that it may appear more clearly what was Jerome's view on this matter, let us see what he says in his *Dialogue Against the Luciferians*. For there in about the middle of the dialogue, when discoursing in the person of Othrodoxus about the Sacrament of Confirmation, he says the following: "But if you now ask how it is that a person baptized in the Church does not receive the Holy Ghost, Whom we declare to be given in true Baptism, except by the hands of the bishop, let me tell you that our authority for the rule is the fact that after our Lord's Ascension the Holy Ghost descended upon the Apostles. And in many places we find it the practice, more by way of honoring the episcopate than from any compulsory law. Otherwise, if the Holy Ghost descends only at the bishop's prayer, they are greatly to be pitied who in isolated houses, or in forts, or retired places, after being baptized by the presbyters and deacons have fallen asleep before the bishop's visitation."[4] From which words it clearly appears that he thinks that it is not from the necessity of the law that only a bishop through the imposition of hands confers the Holy Ghost, but that this is from the institution of the Church for the honor of the priest. Therefore, it is necessary to reply otherwise to Jerome's testimony.

---

[1] *Commentaria in Epistolam ad Titum* (PL 26, 562C-D).

[2] *Doctrinale antiquitatum fidei Catholicae Ecclesiae*, vol. 1, bk. 2, a. 3, c. 60, n. 4, p. 562.

[3] Thomas Netter is here defended in a footnote added by a later editor of his work which says, "This proposition is so certain today among learned men, that he who would call it into doubt, would be considered by all as ignorant of ecclesiastical matters. Hence, I am surprised that the most illustrious Alfonso de Castro not merely asserts this to be doubtful, but completely false, and could rebuke Netter about it in book six of his *Adversus haereses*, in the section entitled *Episcopus* (Bishop). Certainly, in a clear matter to bring forth proofs is supervacaneous and tedious. But because it is fitting to satisfy such a great man, it will not be useless to bring forth in public some things to prove it. See the extended notes [which are found at the end of that volume]." In this extended note the editor also defends Saint Jerome who correctly wrote that bishops and priests shared the same name (*appelatio*) of presbyters but not the same power of Orders (*ordo*). The early Christians generally refrained from using the name "priest" which was at that time associated with the Jewish priesthood. Hence both bishops and priests were indiscriminately called presbyters. But with time, the ecclesiastical vocabulary became more precise. (*Ibid*. pp. 1007-1008)

[4] N. 9 (PL 23, 164C-165A).

But before I respond, it is useful to ask John Wycliffe why does he now fight against us with a testimony of Jerome, since elsewhere he rejects and treats as of little worth both Jerome and the other sacred Doctors? Thus, either he ought to accept him when he is cited in our favor, or nowise object his words to us. Then why does he object one man alone, Jerome, against so many men illustrious for holiness as well as eminent for learning? Does he prefer the saying of one Jerome to the opinion of so many brilliant men? Rather, does he perhaps prefer Jerome alone to the whole Catholic Church, or to a council representing it? In fact, the Second Synod of Seville (as we showed above when we treated about Confirmation) determines that Confirmation can be conferred by bishops alone,[1] and (as we will show afterwards[2]) the same council declared that a priest could nowise ordain someone to the priesthood or diaconate.[3] But if he shall have attempted to ordain, it judges his ordination to be invalid and that it must necessarily be repeated by a bishop, so that the one so ordained may exercise something [of his Orders]. But if by Divine institution a priest could administer it, although he would sin against the decree of the Church by so doing, his ordination would none the less have been valid, just as it is accustomed to be said about an excommunicated cleric confecting the Eucharist, who although he sins consecrating the Sacrament, nevertheless his consecration is none the less certain and valid.

Therefore, since there exists such an explicit declaration of a council, who will dare to oppose Jerome's opinion to it? Certainly, I highly extol the teaching of Blessed Jerome, I very much venerate his sanctity, yet such that I reckon that he was a man, who when he did things here on earth, was able to err: so also I prefer the decrees of many Catholic Doctors and pontiffs, such as were Damasus, Urban, and Anacletus to his opinion. And this ought not to be surprising to anyone. For besides the fact that those pontiffs were holy men like Jerome and some of them illustrious for martyrdom, and all eminent in doctrine, Jerome himself most willingly subjected his opinions to their decrees, as is evident from several of his letters to Pope Damasus. And no one ought to be surprised that Blessed Jerome, a man otherwise most learned, was so deceived, because sometimes "good Homer nods." Which could especially happen at that time, when that teaching had not yet been called into question, nor had the Church then defined anything about it: wherefore he could so think without any loss to the faith, especially since he had some testimonies of Scripture which seemed to support his view: which testimonies we should discuss individually.

Firstly therefore that which he says, in order to remove the schism whereby each person thought that they belong to the one who baptized him, and not to Christ, it was decreed that "one chosen from among the presbyters should be placed over the others, and to whom all care of the Church should belong"; how Jerome proves this, I do not know, nay the opposite can be inferred from the Acts of the Apostles, especially because that remedy which Blessed Jerome says was applied, was insufficient for removing the schism: because even if the schism which arose in one city was taken away by that means, nevertheless the schisms found in many cities were not taken away. Indeed, by that remedy it is not removed that all the men of one city were called Paulians, from Paul, the Bishop of that city: others Peterians, from Peter, the Bishop of another city. Which having been done, who does not see that the seeds of schism still remain, since it may still be said, "I am of Paul; I am of Cephas"? Effort was not made to prevent just this or that schism, but every schism. Hence it can be concluded from Apostolic history that another more effective remedy was used, namely that all Christians

---

[1] C. 7: "Since it does not belong to them to bless a church, or to bless altars, nor to impart the [Paraclete] Spirit through the impositions of hand to the baptized faithful nor to those converted from heresy, nor to confect chrism, nor to sign with chrism the forehead of those baptized" (PL 84, 596D).

[2] See below in book thirteen, in the section on "The Priesthood" (*Sacerdotium*).

[3] C. 5 (PL 84, 595C-D).

having been baptized in Christ, would be called by the word, "Christians," from Christ, Who is the Head of them all, Who also (as John the Baptist testifies) is truly the one who baptizes us.

For the confirmation of this matter, I will cite the testimony of [Vigilius, Bishop of Thapsus[1]]. For he when disputing against Arius rejecting this word, ὁμοούσιον,[2] on account of its novelty, and showing that the Church, on account of the novelties of arising heretics, was accustomed to formulate new words, says the following: "In the very beginning of the preaching of the Christian religion all who believed in Our Lord Jesus Christ were not called 'Christians,' but merely 'disciples.' And because there had existed many authors of new teachings opposing the Apostolic teaching, all their followers were called "disciples," nor was there any distinction between the true and false disciples, whether those of Dositheus,[3] or of Cephas, or of Theodas,[4] or of a certain Juda,[5] or even the followers of John, who claimed to believe in Christ, who were known by the one name of 'disciples.' Then when the Apostles came together in Antioch, as their Acts declare (Luke relating), all men call the disciples by a new name, that is, 'Christians,'[6] distinguishing them by the word from the false disciples; also in order that the word of the Divine prophecy through Isaias might be fulfilled, by whom [God] says: 'And the Lord God shall call his servants by another name' (65, 15)."[7] Rabanus when expounding this passage wherein is spoken about the imposition of the name, "Christians," says the following: "All sects were named after their authors, hence when the faith was founded, and becoming firmly established, firstly in Antioch, where the faith was flourishing more than in other places, the name 'Christian' was taken from Christ."[8] And certainly by this remedy schism is more truly avoided, than the custom (as Jerome says) "that one chosen from among the presbyters should be placed over the others, and to whom all care of the Church should belong."

But now let us see the testimonies which Blessed Jerome cites in favor of himself. "There are these words of the Apostle to the Philippians: 'Paul and Timothy, the servants of Jesus Christ; to all the saints in Christ Jesus, who are at Philippi, with the bishops and deacons. Grace be unto you, and peace' etc., (1, 1-2). Philippi is a city of Macedonia, and certainly there could not be several of those who in common parlance are bishops in one city. But because, at that time, they were accustomed to call the same persons bishops whom they also called presbyters, therefore he speaks of bishops without a distinction, as if he had spoken of presbyters... Then in the Acts of the Apostles it is written that when he had come to Miletus, he sent to Ephesus, and called the presbyters of that church, to whom among other things he afterwards said: 'Take heed to yourselves, and to the whole flock, wherein the Holy Ghost hath placed you bishops, to rule the church of God, which he hath purchased with his own blood' (Acts 20, 28). And observe this diligently," Jerome advises, "how calling together the

---

[1] The text here incorrectly attributes this quotation to Saint Athanasius.
[2] I.e. *homoousion*, meaning "one in being" or "of single essence."
[3] Dositheus was a Samaritan who formed a Gnostic-Judaistic sect, previous to Simon Magus.
[4] Cf. Acts 5, 36. He is mentioned by Josephus (*Jewish Antiquities* 20, 97-98).
[5] Cf. Acts 5, 27, where a Judas of Galilee is named. He is also mentioned by Josephus (*Jewish Antiquities* 20, 100).
[6] Cf. Acts 11, 26.
[7] *Dialogus contra Arianos*, bk. 1, c. 11 (PL 62, 162D-163A). -The quotation from Isaias in the text is worded according to the Greek Septuagint version: "*Servientibus vero mihi vocabitur nomen novum.*"
[8] This quotation is taken from a marginal note in the *Glossa Ordinaria* (Venice, Apud Juntas, 1601), vol. 6, p. 1115. The gloss is taken probably taken from Rabanus' *Tractatus super Actus* which is still unpublished.

presbyters of the one city of Ephesus, he afterwards calls the same [presbyters] bishops."[1] He cites other passages for his support which because they are weaker and less efficacious, I omit.

Thus it is not evident whether that first passage ought to be so understood as Jerome interprets, because by the word "bishops" [Ambrosiaster[2]] understands there Paul and Timothy. For he says the following: "'With the bishops and deacons,' meaning, with Paul and Timothy, who were certainly bishops: and at the same time he also mentioned the deacons who ministered to them. For he is writing to the people. For if he were writing to the bishops and deacons, he would have mentioned them by name. In particular, he would have written to the [one] bishop who was standing in for him, as he wrote to Titus and Timothy, and not to two or three of them."[3] From whose words it is sufficiently clear how differently he thinks from Jerome.

But because another testimony from the Acts of the Apostles is too clear to be eluded, wherefore it seems that it ought to be replied otherwise and more correctly that those words, namely presbyter and bishop, had at the time of their original institution a broader meaning than they have now. For the word "bishop" [*episcopus*] is derived from the Greek, and is composed from the Greek preposition, ἐπί, which means "over": but σκοπός means "watcher": and so "bishop" means "one who oversees," hence ἐπίσκοπος means "overseer." Thus the word "bishop" seems to be so derived, because he who rules others, ought to oversee their care. According to this basic interpretation no one will doubt that parish priests ought to be called bishops, for they also oversee the care of souls committed to them. "Presbyter" is also a Greek word, Πρεσβύτερος, which means "elder." Thus "presbyter" is a word pertaining to age, which should not be reckoned according to a number of years, but according to the maturity of understanding: just as the Wise Man says: "The understanding of a man is grey hairs, and a spotless life is old age" (Wis. 4, 8-9). Hence [Jerome] says the following: "For it was commanded also to Moses that he would choose presbyters, whom he knew to be presbyters (Num. 11, 16[4]) and hence it is said in the book of Proverbs: 'The dignity of old men, their grey hairs' (Prov. 20, 29). What is this grey hair? Doubtlessly it is wisdom, concerning which it is written: 'The understanding of a man is grey hairs' (Wis. 4, 8). And although we read that during the time from Adam until Abraham men lived more than nine hundred years (Gen. 5), no one else was previously called a presbyter, meaning an elder, except Abraham, who is shown to have lived many fewer years."[5] Therefore, men are called presbyters not on account of decrepit old age, but on account of wisdom.[6]

If then on account of wisdom, whereby he ought to be conspicuous, one is called a presbyter, it is evident from its institution that the word also meant more that it means now: for according to it all wise men ought to be called presbyters, when nevertheless there are many who are not now called presbyters. But if you argue that the word "presbyter" ought to be giv-

---

[1] PL 26, 563A-B.
[2] The text falsely attributes this to Saint Ambrose, as was commonly supposed at the time of its writing.
[3] *Commentaria in Epistolam ad Philippenses*, c. 1 (PL 17, 403D).
[4] "Moses, too, in choosing the seventy elders (*presbyteros*) is told to take those whom he knows to be elders (*presbyteros*) indeed, and to select them not for their years but for their discretion (Num 11, 16)." (Jerome, Letter 58, n. 1 (PL 22 0579)). "Gather unto me seventy men of the ancients (*presbyteros*) of Israel, whom thou knowest to be ancients (*presbyteros*) and masters of the people" (Num. 11, 16).
[5] The text here attributes the authorship of this quotation to "Pope Anacletus in a letter concerning the consecration of bishops," which is taken from the *False Decretals of the Pseudo-Isidore* (PL 130, 71C-D). But the text rather originates from Saint Jerome's *Commentaria in Isaiam*, bk. 2, c. 3 (PL 24, 59B). The full text of which has been substituted here.
[6] This last sentence is taken from the *False Decretals* just cited.

en to someone from the number of his years, it would be necessary to concede that all old men could rightly be called presbyters: still that it is not done so now. Hence the word "presbyter" taken from any derivation is common both to bishops and other priests. The word "bishop" also is common to all priests from its original institution, especially those to whom the care of souls has been committed. Thus the Church fearing lest on account of the unclear meaning of the words someone might suppose that the reality is also completely unclear, it restricted the meanings of the words in this way, such that he alone would be called a bishop who being superior to other priests, has the care of the whole city: he, however, is called a priest, who can confect or consecrate the Lord's Body. And so the Church when determining this, neither established a new order, nor a new degree of the same order, but deemed to name with specific names the old degrees of the priesthood, and those instituted by God, lest perhaps from the sharing or the identity of the names an occasion might arise of thinking that the realities designated by those names are completely the same. Now no one could doubt the Church regarding this for any good reason: because if the Church for new emerging reasons could impose new names for old things, what will forbid it from restricting old words to a stricter meaning for new emerging reasons?

But if someone having judged Jerome to be more correct, would still want to maintain Jerome's view, he will be fraught with great difficulties, as it would also be necessary that he say that deacons are bishops. For Paul when writing to Timothy, who was a bishop, calls him a deacon, saying: "Fulfill thy ministry" (II Tim. 4, 5). In which passage is found in the Greek, διακονίαν, meaning diaconate: where he clearly said "diaconate" for the office of a bishop. And not without reason, because the word "diaconate" (as we said concerning the other words) means according to his original meaning "ministry." Now a bishop since he is also a minister, as Christ said of Himself,[1] hence not without reason when writing to the bishop did he say: "Fulfill thy ministry." The Church restricted this word, "deacon," to that minister alone who ministers on a certain step at the altar.[2]

Now lest these things seem to have been fabricated out of our own head, I bring forth two witnesses of this matter. Theophylactus when explaining the first chapter of the Epistle to the Philippians says the following: "He calls bishops priests. For there were many bishops in one, city: since in fact there were not yet different names, but the bishops themselves were called priests and deacons."[3] In which words it is necessary to notice especially that he says, "since there were not yet different names": whereby he clearly shows that the distinction was made not of things but of words. Blessed Augustine intimates the same opinion in a letter to Blessed Jerome. For he says the following: "For although, so far as the titles of honor which prevail in the Church are concerned, a bishop's rank is above that of a presbyter, nevertheless in many things Augustine is inferior to Jerome."[4] It is especially necessary to observe in which words that he said, "so far as the titles of honor which prevail in the Church": he did not say, however, "so far as the degrees of honor which prevail in the Church." In these words he clearly implies that there was from the use of the Church a distinction of those words.

Therefore, after having thus settled these matters, we reply to Jerome, that it is true that at that time bishops were also called priests, because the distinction of words had not then been made: still it does not follow from this that that a bishop was completely the same thing as a priest. But someone will say, if the meanings of the words were then undistinguished, how will we be able from Holy Writ know the distinction of those things? To which question we reply that [we can know their distinction] by reasoning. For we know from Holy Writ that the

---

[1] "Even as the Son of man is not come to be ministered unto, but to minister" (Mt. 20, 28).
[2] A deacon typically stands one step lower than the priest celebrating a solemn high Mass at the altar.
[3] PG 124, 1142C.
[4] Letter 82, c. 4, n. 32 (PL 33, 290).

Apostles alone, whom the bishop succeeded, gave the Holy Ghost through the imposition of hands: because the other disciples, whose place the other lesser priests hold, never bestowed [this]. We know that the Apostles, and their successors, the bishops, ordained other men to be priests, but this is never read concerning the other disciples. Thence we prove that bishops had greater power than other priests. Now what I said about ordination, namely that only a bishop can ordain, Jerome himself acknowledges. For in his letter to Evangelus he says the following: "For what function, excepting ordination, belongs to a bishop that does not also belong to a presbyter?"[1] And at the end of the letter he says the following: "In fact as if to tell us that the traditions handed down by the Apostles were taken by them from the Old Testament, bishops, presbyters and deacons occupy in the Church the same positions as those which were occupied by Aaron, his sons, and the Levites in the Temple."[2] From which words it is evident that Blessed Jerome hardly agrees with himself on this matter: because if a bishop is in the Church what Aaron was in the Old Testament, a priest is what the sons of Aaron were, it is also proved therefrom that by Divine institution itself a bishop is greater than any priest: because (as we have recently taught) Aaron's priesthood from the institution of God Himself was greater than the priesthood of the sons of Aaron.

I have treated this matter at great enough length and beyond the determined brevity, because I have found no one else who wrote about this matter besides Thomas Netter, who even if he was able to help somewhat, still he nowise completed the work (as was befitting). Concerning Guy [the Carmelite] is it causes me shame to say that when enumerating the heresies of the Aerians, and imputing this one to them, although he cited testimonies against their other errors, he left this one alone untouched, citing no testimony of Scripture or of the holy Doctors, or any argument on account of which he would show that he has rightly censured that assertion as heretical.

There is also another error that has arisen about the persons of bishops, whereby it is taught that no sinner or unjust man can be a bishop. The authors of this error were the Waldensians saying that not the rank of the priests, but the worthiness of their lives made them more capable.[3] John Wycliffe imitated them. And if these men indeed said that he who is wicked and criminal should not have been consecrated a bishop, they would have rightly admonished, because Paul the Apostle often taught this. But because they teach that he who has once fallen into sin loses the rank and office of the episcopate, such that the two things could nowise be united in one person, namely that one be a bishop and wicked: they certainly thought wrongly. But because there are some who taught also this about any priest, others again thought the same thing also about any lay power, for that reason this matter is deferred to another place to be disputed, namely when we will treat about them all together under the title of "power."

EVANGELIUM

Gospel

Among the other heresies of the Flagellants there was one whereby they said that after the coming of their sect the Gospel ceased. Which error no one except foolish men, as were the Flagellants, could have taught: since there are such clear testimonies of Sacred Scripture testifying that the Gospel will last in perpetuity, meaning until the end of the

---

[1] Letter 146, n. 1 (PL 22, 194).

[2] N. 2 (PL 22, 1195).

[3] This synthesis of their error is taken from Aeneas Sylvius' *De Bohemorum origine ac gestis historia* (Solingen, Johannes Soter, 1538), c. 35, p. 59.

world. Accordingly, the Wise Man when speaking about the law given by God to men says: "He made an everlasting covenant with them, and he shewed them his justice and judgments" (Eccli. 17, 10). You see how the testament is called eternal, and it is evident that he is not speaking about the prior testament, because it was revoked, as Paul often proves, especially in the Epistle to the Hebrews. And the Lord when speaking through the prophet Baruch expressed this more clearly. "And I will make with them," he says, "another covenant that shall be everlasting, to be their God, and they shall be my people" (2, 35). And the Royal Prophet says: "He hath sent redemption to his people: he hath commanded his covenant for ever" (Ps. 110, 9). But another redemption was not given to us except in the coming of the Son of God, Who, when preaching by word and deed, left the Gospel to us as His testament which was in effect at His death: and then the previous one was revoked. Therefore, this Gospel which alone can be said to be the testament, because it alone is in effect; this testament, I say, He commanded us for eternity: thus it will never cease. And the Truth Itself confirmed this same testament, saying: "Amen, I say to you, this generation shall not pass away, till all things be fulfilled" (Lk, 21, 32).

Theophylactus when expounding Luke's Gospel says: "'This is the generation of them that seek him' (Ps. 23, 6). Now because He said that there would be disturbances, wars and changes both of the elements and of things: in order to prevent someone from suspecting that perhaps Christianity would be destroyed at some time, He said, 'This generation of Christians will not pass away.' Heaven and earth will indeed be changed, but My words and My Gospel will not perish, but remain. Even if all things may be moved, nevertheless faith in Me will not fail. Now it is evident in this passage that He prefers the Church to every creature: although the creature may be changed, nothing of the Church of the faithful, of His words and Gospel will be changed."[1]

Furthermore, in the words with which we daily transubstantiate the wine into Christ's Blood, it is said as follows: "For this is the chalice of My Blood of the new and eternal Testament, [the Mystery of Faith]; which shall be shed for you and for many" etc. Which words even if they are not explicitly found in the Gospel, still it certainly ought to be believed that the Church received them from Christ. But so that there may not be now any crack for escape, let them hear Paul saying this same thing: "And may the God of peace, who brought again from the dead the great pastor of the sheep, our Lord Jesus Christ, in the blood of the everlasting testament, fit you in all goodness" etc., (Heb. 13, 20-21).

Again, concerning those four animals which Ezechiel saw, and were shown to John in a vision, it is said that "they went and they turned not, when they went" (Ez. 1, 17). But that the four Gospels are signified by those four animals is too clear to be doubted or needing proof. What is it to say that they always went except that the Gospels will always remain? Time goes on and they also go on. But if the Gospel (as these Flagellants pretend) has already ceased: it would not be truly said of the animals that "they went and they turned not." The Old Testament, because it was indeed revoked, and now no longer obliges; it finished its course, and will not be said of it that "it went and turned not." Hence Blessed Gregory says: "The New Testament is also called eternal through the pages of the Old Testament, because its meaning never changes. Thus, it is well said that the wheels 'went… and they turned not when they went,' because the New Testament is not rescinded, while the Old Testament is now understood spiritually. They do not go backwards, because they remain immoveable until the end of the world. Thus they go, but do not go back, because they come spiritually to our hearts, and their precepts may no more be changed."[2]

---

[1] *Enarratio in Evangelium Sanctae Lucae* (PG 123, 1058).
[2] *Homiliae in Ezechielem*, hom. 6, n. 17 (PL 76, 836D-837A).

Additionally, those who think that the Gospel has ended, and another testament has been substituted in its place either deny that Christ has died or want Him to be crucified again. For if (as Paul says) a testament is in effect after the death of the testator, then the Gospel is now in effect or it will be that Christ has not died. But if Christ has died, and it is necessary that His testament be so firm that it can never be revoked, and if another testament after it will take its place, such that it also will be in effect, it will be necessary that the death of the testator occur: wherefore it would be necessary that Christ would die again, so that by His death that other testament would be in effect. Now who would dare to assert this? Certainly no one else other than he who crucifies the Son of God again to himself.[1] For Paul says: "Christ rising again from the dead, dieth now no more, death shall no more have dominion over him" (Rom. 6, 9). It would be irksome to cite more testimonies against this insane and wicked heresy.

There is a **second heresy** saying that the Gospel was not preached by the Apostles according to the spiritual meaning, but only according to the literal meaning. The author of this error (as Guy [the Carmelite] relates[2]) was Abbot Joachim [of Flora] who followed a certain other man, Pierre Jean [Olivi]. But we have disputed about this error above when we treated of those things pertaining to the Apostles.

A **third heresy** arose against the value and dignity of the Gospel, which denies that the Gospel is a law, according to the true and proper notion of law. Luther teaches this, whom Philip Melanchthon, [Johann] Brenz,[3] and all the rest of that sort follow. The reason why they teach this is so that they may claim to be free from the obligation of all good works. For they say that the Gospel is not a law because they assert that the Gospel commands absolutely nothing, but merely shows us the good news of Jesus Christ, the Son of God, that He alone is the expiator of our sins and the Redeemer of our souls by the merits of His Passion.

And (so that their opinion may be clear) I will cite their words. Luther in his [*Ad librum eximii Magistri nostri Ambrosii Catharini*[4]] says the following: "Whatever is compelled by law is a sin, hence in the New Testament there are not compelling precepts, but only exhortations and entreaties."[5] And again: "The Gospel is nothing else than preaching the resurrection of Christ... Here all works are abolished."[6] Philip Melanchthon in his *Loci Communes* says the following: "The New Testament is nothing other than a promise of all good things, without the Law, without any regard to our justices: because the good things are promised unconditionally, since nothing is required of us."[7] Then the teachers sent to the Council of Trent by the

---

[1] Cf. Heb. 6, 6.

[2] *Summa de haeresibus et earum confutationibus*, f. 99r.

[3] Johann Brenz (1499-1570) was a Swabian Protestant theologian of the sixteenth century.

[4] The reference here is wrongly ascribed to Luther's *Babylonian Captivity*. This work is Luther's response to Ambrosius Catharinus Politus (1484-1553), a Dominican controversialist. After beginning a career as a jurisprudent, he became a Dominican in 1517, taking the name Ambrosius Catharinus. In 1546 he was made Bishop of Minori and in 1552 Archbishop of Conza. Attacking Luther, in 1520 he wrote an *Apologia* and in 1521 an *Excusatio diputationis*, to which Luther responded with *Ad librum eximii Magistri nostri Ambrosii Catharini* in 1521.

[5] Martin Luther, *Omnia opera* (Jena, Thomas Rebarthus, 1581), vol. 2, p. 371v.

[6] Sermon on Mark 16, 14-20 delivered in 1522. *The precious and sacred writings of Martin Luther* (Minneapolis, Lutherans in all lands co., 1903), vol. 12, p. 201, n. 17. This sentence was included among the four hundred and four heretical theses listed by Johann Eck upon which he challenged the Protestant theologians to public debate. The challenge was not accepted; the only answer from the Protestant party was a torrent of abuse. Cf. Johann Eck, *Sub domini Jesu et Mariae patrocinio. Articulos 404, partim ad disputationes Lipsicam, Badensem et Bernensem attinentes* (Ingolstadt, 1530), n. 166.

[7] *Loci communes rerum theologicarum seu hypotyposes theologicae* (Erlangen, Leipzig Deichert, 1890), p. 212.

duke of Württemberg,[1] the chief of whom was [Johannes] Brenz, as a confession of their faith which they presented in writing, wrote these words: "The Gospel is nothing other than the good and joyful announcement of the Son of God, Our Lord Jesus Christ, because He alone is the expiator of our sins, the Redeemer and Our Saviour."[2]

From all the words of these heretics whom we have cited, it is especially necessary to point out two or three errors. The first is that which denies the necessity of good works, but we will discuss about this below, in the section on "Faith" and in the section on "Works." The second error is that whereby it is said that there is no precept in the Gospel Law, and concerning this we also will say nothing about this in this place, but we will dispute about it below, with God as our guide, in the section on "Precepts." There is a third error whereby they assert that Christ's Gospel ought not to be called a law, and the present disputation is about this, so that I may clearly prove this to be a manifest error.

The first in fact is that clear testimony against this assertion which God says through the prophet Isaias: "Behold my servant, I will uphold him: my elect, my soul delighteth in him: I have given my spirit upon him, he shall bring forth judgment to the Gentiles. He shall not cry, nor have respect to person, neither shall his voice be heard abroad. The bruised reed he shall not break, and smoking flax he shall not quench: he shall bring forth judgment unto truth. He shall not be sad, nor troublesome, till he set judgment in the earth: and the islands shall wait for his law" (42, 1-4). From these words it is very clearly established that the Gospel is called Christ's law. For Matthew very clearly declares that those words cited from Isaias ought to be understood of Christ our Savior, saying: all those things which were said concerning my chosen servant in those words of Isaias, were fulfilled in Christ our Savior.[3] Now concerning the servant chosen by God, which Matthew interprets to be Christ, God said through Isaias that "the islands would wait for his law," calling all souls "islands," which are surrounded by the turbulent sea of this world. But Christ our Savior gave no other law besides the Gospel. Therefore, the Gospel according to the prophecy of Isaias is a law.

Furthermore, the Lord through the prophet Jeremias says: "Behold the days shall come, saith the Lord, and I will make a new covenant with the house of Israel, and with the house of Juda: not according to the covenant which I made with their fathers, in the day that I took them by the hand to bring them out of the land of Egypt: the covenant which they made void, and I had dominion over them, saith the Lord. But this shall be the covenant that I will make with the house of Israel, after those days, saith the Lord: I will give my law in their bowels, and I will write it in their heart" (31, 31-33). Paul very clearly declared in the Epistle to the Hebrews that these words ought to be understood of the New Testament, which is the Gospel. For from those words of Jeremias, Paul wants to prove that by the coming of the Gospel and the New Testament, the Old Testament is abrogated. Because after those words of Jeremias he had fully cited, taking his proof from them, he says the following: "Now in saying a new, he hath made the former old. And that which decayeth and groweth old, is near its end" (8, 13). In which words Paul clearly notes the dissolution and death of the Old Testament.

Then from the same prophecy of Jeremias, Paul proves the eminence of the Gospel over the Old Testament. For after he had said that the Mosaic Law is imperfect, because its observance could not save, which the Gospel does in Christ's faith, in order to confirm the Evangelical grace, he cites the aforesaid words of Jeremias, saying the following: "And the

---

[1] I.e. Duke Christoph of Württemberg had the *Württemberg Confession* published in 1551 by the reformer Johannes Brenz on his behalf in response to the Council of Trent.

[2] *Monumentorum ad historiam Concilii Tridentini potissimum illustrandam spectantium amplissima collectio* (Leuven, *ex Typographia Academica*, 1784), vol. 4, 427.

[3] Cf. "That it might be fulfilled which was spoken by Isaias the prophet, saying: Behold my servant whom I have chosen" (Mt. 12, 17-18).

Holy Ghost also doth testify this to us. For after that he said: and this is the testament which I will make unto them after those days, saith the Lord. I will give my laws in their hearts, and on their minds will I write them" (Heb. 15, 15-16). In which words Paul indicates many things which the New Testament has over the Old. The first is that the New Testament is able through Christ's merits to so wipe out men's sins that they are completely forgotten, which the Old Testament had nowise been able to do. Next, the Old Law was given on stone tables, on account of their hard and stony hearts, because the Law was given to suchlike men: the New Testament, however, was given in men's hearts. For the prophet Jeremias spoke of that saying: "I will give my law in their bowels, and I will write it in their heart" (31, 33): and Paul interprets those words concerning the New Testament in the aforesaid place.

Haymo [of Auxerre][1] when interpreting the above-mentioned words of Paul which are found in Hebrews,[2] says these words: "There is a great difference between Law and Law, between Scripture and Scripture, between the teachers of the Law and the teachers of Gospel, between the letter and the grace of spiritual understanding. For the letter of the Law was written on stone tablets, but the grace of spiritual understanding was given to the faithful through the Holy Ghost, through Whom the charity of God was diffused in the hearts of the faithful. Now that which he says, 'I will give my laws into their mind, and in their heart will I write them,' specially pertains to the holy Apostles, who did not have the grace of the New Testament written on stone tablets, nor on parchments, but they had it Divinely furrowed in their mind and hearts... On the other hand, we have it partly in our hearts, but more fully written on the parchments left by them for us so that we may be exercised in meditating upon them."[3] And by which words it is very clearly established that the Gospel and the New Testament, according to the opinion of Jeremias and Paul, is a true law and more perfect law then the Mosaic Law. Again, Paul himself by his own judgment often calls the Gospel a law. For in the Epistle to the Romans when praising the Gospel he says the following: "For the law of the spirit of life, in Christ Jesus, hath delivered me from the law of sin and of death" (8, 2).

[Hervé de Bourg-Dieu[4]], when interpreting these words in his commentaries on Paul's Epistles, says the following: "The Law of Moses is spiritual but not a law of life: because it does not give life when sins have been forgiven. On the other hand, the law which the Holy Ghost ordains, is a law of life: because it gives life by forgiving sins. The Law of Moses is God's law, but it is a law of deeds; a law of works, a law which commands, but not a law which helps; a law which shows sin, not a law which takes away sin. The Law of the Spirit, is a law of faith, a law of grace, a law of mercy, a law which takes away sin, and frees from the law of the members,[5] which is not of God, but of sin and of death, because it makes one guilty

---

[1] In 1907, Edward Riggenbach in his study, demonstrated that the commentary from which this quotation was taken, attributed both here in the text and also in the *Patrologia Latina* (PL 117, 877C) to Haymo of Halberstadt, was actually the work of Haymo of Auxerre (fl. c. 840-860? perhaps as late as 875?). But Riggenbach judged it to have "virtually no independent value" since two-thirds of the exegesis was taken from the Latin translation of Saint John Chrysostom's homilies (Cf. *Die ältesten lateinischen Kommentare zum Hebräerbrief*, published in *Historische Studien zum Hebräerbrief*, Leipzig, vol. 1, pp. 19, 24).

[2] "I will give my laws into their mind, and in their heart will I write them" (Heb. 8, 10).

[3] PL 117, 877C-878A.

[4] The text ascribes this citation to Saint Anselm of Canterbury, but it is the work of Hervé, monk of Bourg-Dieu (Cf. PL 181, 13).

[5] This is a reference to the law that Saint Paul said was in his members. "But I see another law in my members, fighting against the law of my mind, and captivating me in the law of sin, that is in my members" (Rom. 7, 23).

and works death."[1] In which words he very frequently calls the Gospel a law, and he does this not based on his own imagination, as Luther does, but based on the judgment of Paul. And in the Epistle to the Galatians Paul again calls the Gospel itself a law, speaking thus: "For I, through the law, am dead to the law" (2, 19). By which words he teaches what is the whole purpose of the epistle, that through the coming of the Gospel the Mosaic Law is dead. Thus, the Gospel in Paul's opinion is a law through which we have died to the Mosaic Law, that is, we have been freed from it. For to live [according] to the Law is to be, according to the Paul's own expression which he uses in the Epistle to the Romans, "under the Law."[2]

And, on the contrary, to die to the Law is to be free from the Law, because when a debtor has died, he is now free from the exaction of the creditor. And all the holy interpreters, who have published commentaries on Paul's epistles, teach that this is the mind of Paul. Haymo [of Auxerre] when interpreting the aforesaid words says: "'For I through the law,' supply the words, 'of the Gospel,' 'am dead to the law' of Moses, meaning, I owe nothing to it because I am not subject to it."[3] Chrysostom gives a twofold meaning to those words of Paul, and one which we have just cited from Haymo, he put in the first place, saying the following: "This may be viewed in two ways; it is either the law of grace which he speaks of, for he is wont to call this a law, as in the words, 'For the law of the spirit of life hath delivered me' (Rom. 8, 2)."[4] Chrysostom imitates Theophylactus in this opinion, as he nearly always does elsewhere.[5] [Hervé de Bourg-Dieu[6]] completely subscribes to the same opinion,[7] and any Catholic so reckons. Nor have I seen any orthodox interpreter of Paul, among the many whom I have managed to see, who have departed from this meaning.

Next, from the very notion and definition of law it is clearly proved that the Gospel is a law. For by the word "law" Sacred Scripture calls whatever compels us to do something. For on account of this reason (as Chrysostom[8] and Theophylactus[9] teach) Paul calls the concupiscence of the flesh a law.[10] Because even if it does not force, still it vehemently incites us to do act wickedly: and men yield to that which is pleasurable just as to a commanding law. But with the Gospel there are some precepts (as the Württembergers themselves acknowledge in their confession of faith[11]) which not merely motivate, but compel us to do something: thus the Gospel is a law. But they say that although there are precepts in the Gospel, still they are not new but old, namely those which were in the Mosaic Law taken from the Natural law. And they say that these are declared in the Gospel, and they contend that no other new precepts

---

[1] *Commentaria in epistolas Pauli, Expositio in Epistolam ad Romanos*, c. 7 (PL 181, 697C).
[2] Rom. 6, 14 & 15.
[3] *Expositio in D. Pauli epistolas, In Epistolam ad Galatas*, c. 2 (PL 117, 678C).
[4] *Commentarius in Epistolam ad Galatas*, c. 2, n. 7 (PG 61, 644).
[5] Theophylactus (PG 124, 979).
[6] The text ascribes this citation to Saint Anselm of Canterbury, but it is the work of Hervé, monk of Bourg-Dieu (Cf. PL 181, 13).
[7] "The Law of the Spirit, is a law of faith, a law of grace, a law of mercy, a law which takes away sin, and frees from the law of the members" (*Commentaria in epistolas Pauli, Expositio in Epistolam ad Romanos*, c. 8 (PL 181, 697C)).
[8] "... so here he calls sin a law, owing to those who are so obsequious to it, and are afraid to leave it."
[9] "The Spirit calls the law of the Spirit something holy, just He calls the law of sin, sin itself." (PG 124, 434).
[10] Cf. Rom. 7, 23.
[11] "Even if in the writings of the Evangelists and of the Apostles many precepts of the Divine law are contained, and Christ Himself teaches [precepts]" etc. (*Monumentorum ad historiam Concilii Tridentini potissimum illustrandam spectantium amplissima collectio* (Leuven, *ex Typographia Academica*, 1784), vol. 4, 427).

are given in it. Now we will clearly show below that this is false and heretical in the section on "Precepts."

Furthermore, that definition and description of the Gospel given by them, is completely insufficient and nowise including all the things which pertain to the Gospel. For according to that definition it would be necessary to say that the Old Law is the Gospel, nay the Gospel was before that law: because right from the time of the fall of man an announcement of the remedy to be had through the coming of Christ, the future Mediator, was given, without faith in Whom (as Peter taught[1]) there is no salvation. Thus, all just men before the Incarnation of the Word knew that good news, and consequently, according to their definition, they knew the Gospel. For due to this reason Christ is called in the Apocalypse "the Lamb, which was slain from the beginning of the world" (13, 8), because from the beginning His Passion was promised to men as the remedy for their sins, and His Passion had been accepted by God the Father. Thus, that announcement of our Lord Jesus Christ, the Son of God, was common to all men, although what has been shown to us was merely promised to men of former times. But this is not an obstacle, because the promise given to them was also a joyful announcement for them, because they were rejoicing by hope alone, according to that which Paul says: "Rejoicing in hope" (Rom. 12, 12). Add to all these testimonies what Paul when writing to the Galatians calls "another Gospel" (Gal. 1, 6), namely the teaching asserting that the ceremonial precepts of the Old Law are necessary for eternal life: thus, by opposition, the teaching which asserts that those things are not necessary will be called, according to Paul, the true Gospel. And from this it further follows that the Gospel is not merely that joyful announcement, but also faith in those things that ought to be believed.

Against this heresy I saw no one who wrote expressly about it. Herman van Lethmate alone wrote a few things here and there in that work *De instauranda religione*.[2]

Finally, this heresy was condemned in the Council of Trent celebrated under Paul III, for it drew up canons in the Sixth Session, one of which is the twentieth and another the twenty-first on the list, which consist of these words: "If anyone shall say that a man who is justified and ever so perfect is not bound to observe the commandments of God and the Church, but only to believe, as if indeed the Gospel were a mere absolute promise of eternal life, without the condition of observation of the commandments: let him be anathema. If anyone shall say that Christ Jesus has been given by God to men as a Redeemer in whom they should trust, and not also as a legislator, whom they should obey: let him be anathema."[3]

EUCHARISTIA

Eucharist

Concerning this marvelous Sacrament and most excellent of all the Sacraments many heresies have arisen, the authors of them all have fared badly, God being zealous for His glory and punishing ingratitude towards such great benevolence shown to us. For all the originators or supporters of these heresies came to an unhappy end in this life: nay having in store an unhappier, in fact the unhappiest end in the other world. But in discussing the heresies of this kind let us proceed in this order, so that firstly we may treat of those heresies

---

[1] "Neither is there salvation in any other. For there is no other name under heaven given to men, whereby we must be saved" (Acts 4, 12).

[2] Hermas Letmatius, bk. 8, c. 9: *De authoritate scripturarum* (Basel, Johannes Oporin, 1544), pp. 178-182.

[3] Dz. 830-831.

which pertain to the substance of the Sacrament. But afterwards we will treat those heresies which attempt to lessen the efficacy of this same Sacrament. Finally, we will speak about those heresies which eliminate the correct preparation for the reception of this Sacrament.

There is a **first error** about this matter saying that Christ's Body can nowise be confected from bread, in that they say that bread is a creature of the devil. Guy the Carmelite assigns this error to the Cathari,[1] which error the Cathari are very far from having: unless perhaps he found other Catharists besides the Novatians. But I see upon what occasion this man shot this target. For Blessed Augustine when discussing the Manichaeans was saying that they used to call all food unclean on account of the admixture of the evil principle, and they were purifying it by having adhibited certain execrable purgations.[2] For into the flour, from which the bread for the Eucharist was going to be made, they mixed human seed, saying that the flour is purified when mixed with seed, and with that flour (as they were saying) when purified by the mixture of seed, they were confecting the detestable sacrament.

On account of these things, namely the detestable purifications of foods, Blessed Augustine does not call them Cathari, which means "the pure," but Catharists, meaning "the purifiers." By understanding this passage incorrectly this man (as I think) was deceived, such that he attributed this error to the sect of the Cathari. For Augustine here called the Manichaeans Catharists, on account of that purification of foods, not because the Manichaeans belonged to the sect of those heretics, who were commonly called Cathari. For there is no unanimity between the Manichaeans and the Cathari. For the Novatians were called Cathari (as we shall say elsewhere) on account of the cleanliness of soul about which they boasted, due to which they left the Church, because she was embracing repentant sinners as a kind mother. Yet is it evident that good Guy thought that these Cathari are they who are called Novatians. Because when discussing these Cathari, he says that he already spoke about elsewhere, namely since he had discussed the Novatians.

This error was rejected sufficiently (in my opinion) from those things which we taught when disputing above against the Manichaeans; more specifically we taught that every creature is good, and all things came forth from one source, namely God. But if bread is good by its nature, it does not need that horrendous purification so that from it the Eucharist could be confected. Wherefore there is no reason to fight any more against this error.

There is a **second heresy** about the matter of this Sacrament which asserts that the Sacrament cannot be confected with unleavened bread, but only with leavened bread. This is the error of the Greeks, who among other wrong teachings, due to which they left the Roman Church, they defend this one: scoffing at the Roman and Catholic Church, because it confects [the Sacrament] with unleavened bread. They call all Latins "Azymites" [i.e., unleavenders] on this issue, they anathematize them (as Blessed Anselm testifies in a letter De [*Tribus Waleranni Quaestionibus, ac praesertim*] *Azymo ac Fermentato*[3] and Guy the Carmelite bearing witness,[4] they do not permit Latin priests to confect the Sacred Mystery on their altars. But if without their knowing or against their will it happens that [Latin priests] celebrate, they wash the altars, because they believe that they are polluted by reason of the false (as they claim) sacrifice confected by a Latin priest with unleavened bread. The Armenians also embrace this heresy, and the Ruthenians hold the same heresy.[5]

---

[1] *Summa de haeresibus et earum confutationibus*, c. 12, f. 74v.
[2] *De Haeresibus ad Quodvultdeum*, c. 46 (PL 42, 36).
[3] PL 158, 541-8.
[4] *Summa de haeresibus et earum confutationibus*, f. 26v, c. 20.
[5] The Ruthenians rejoined the Catholic Church with the Union of Brest in 1595-96. They were permitted to continue to offer Mass with leavened bread.

Now lest they appear to have said this groundlessly, they confirm their opinion with this argument. This Sacrament ought to be confected by us with that bread with which Christ Himself confected when He instituted It: for He gave an example by that very action so that just as He did, so also we would do. Now John's Gospel testifies that Christ confected [this Sacrament] with leavened bread, saying that He supped with His disciples before the feast day of the Pasch, in which supper this Sacrament was instituted, and He gave us the power of confecting. But before the Pasch the Jews were eating leavened, not unleavened bread, just as during the seven days of the Pasch they were eating (according to the Law) unleavened bread, and it was not permitted to eat leavened bread.

But this argument is completely futile, since it neither starts with a true premise, nor does it deduce well. For if their deduction were solid, we would very quickly stab them with their own sword. In fact, it would be fitting for that reason to necessarily confect with unleavened bread, because it is very clearly established that Christ confected with unleavened bread (provided that it be not denied that He celebrated the Pasch with the Jewish rite) from three Gospels, to which we will show that John nowise opposes.

Now so that everything may be shown more clearly, the text of those Gospels will be cited. Matthew has the following [account]: "And on the first day of the Azymes, the disciples came to Jesus, saying: Where wilt thou that we prepare for thee to eat the pasch? But Jesus said: Go ye into the city to a certain man, and say to him: the master saith, My time is near at hand, with thee I make the pasch with my disciples. And the disciples did as Jesus appointed to them, and they prepared the pasch. But when it was evening, he sat down with his twelve disciples... And whilst they were at supper, Jesus took bread, and blessed, and broke: and gave to his disciples, and said: Take ye, and eat. This is my body" (26, 17-20 & 26). From which passage it is clearly proved that Christ at the time when it was then not permitted to eat leavened bread instituted this Sacrament, and gave to His disciples to eat. But since Christ at that time did not destroy the Law, nay He showed that He wished to observe it, it is concluded that He did not eat leavened bread nor did He give leavened bread to His disciples to eat. Thus, He confected with unleavened bread.

Now Mark's account is very similar to this. For it has the following words: "Now on the first day of the unleavened bread, when they sacrificed the pasch, the disciples say to him: Whither wilt thou that we go, and prepare for thee to eat the pasch? And he sendeth two of his disciples, and saith to them: Go ye into the city; and there shall meet you a man carrying a pitcher of water... And when evening was come, he cometh with the twelve... And whilst they were eating, Jesus took bread; and blessing, broke, and gave to them, and said: Take ye. This is my body" (14, 12-13, 17 & 22). Mark also shows that He confected on that day and at that time when it was already not permitted for the Jews to be fed with leavened bread.

Finally, Luke relates the same things: "And the day of the unleavened bread came," he says, "on which it was necessary that the pasch should be killed. And he sent Peter and John, saying: Go, and prepare for us the pasch, that we may eat... And they going, found as he had said to them, and made ready the pasch. And when the hour was come, he sat down, and the twelve apostles with him... And taking bread, he gave thanks, and brake; and gave to them, saying: This is my body, which is given for you. Do this for a commemoration of me" (22, 7-8, 13-14, & 19). Notice that Luke is agreeing in everything with the others.

Now that John says that these things were done "before the festival day of the pasch" (13, 1), Scripture itself teaching declares. For the feasts of the Jews were reckoned from evening to evening. And Scripture specifically says concerning the feast of the Pascal lamb: "And you shall keep it until the fourteenth day of this month: and the whole multitude of the children of Israel shall sacrifice it in the evening" (Ex. 12, 6). And again in Leviticus it is said: "The first month, the fourteenth day of the month at evening, is the phase of the Lord: and the fifteenth day of the same month is the solemnity of the unleavened bread of the Lord. Seven days shall you eat unleavened bread. The first day shall be most solemn unto you" (23, 5-7). Hence it is clear that the solemnity of the unleavened bread begins on the fourteenth day of the month, and that day which is the fifteenth is the most solemn of the whole Pascal solemnity. Which day for this reason is called "the Pasch," as is found in John's Gospel when it is said: "The Jews went not into the hall, that they might not be defiled, but that they might eat the pasch" (18, 28).

Not in fact the Pasch, meaning the Paschal lamb, because the Jews also already ate it on the previous evening when Christ supped with His disciples, which is proved by Mark saying: "Now on the first day of the unleavened bread, when they sacrificed the pasch, the disciples say to him: Whither wilt thou that we go, and prepare for thee to eat the pasch?" From which words it is evident that the Jews ate the Paschal lamb on the same day as Christ. Thus, when John says that the Jews on the Friday when Christ suffered "went not into the hall, that they might not be defiled, but that they might eat the pasch," by the word "Pasch" he named there the unleavened breads which they were bound to eat for seven continuous days, the first and most solemn of which was the day on which Christ suffered. But it was not permitted for unclean men to eat them and so they kept out of the house of a Gentile man, lest having been defiled by this occasion they would have been prevented from eating them.

Hence, if the fifteenth day of the month, first day of the Azymes, and the most solemn day, which ought to be computed from the evening of the preceding day according to the Law, and the lamb ought to be eaten in the evening of the already waning fourteenth day, it is clearly inferred that that evening of the fourteenth day on which the lamb is eaten, is the beginning of the first day of the Asymes, which is celebrated on the fifteenth day. Wherefore it is that at that time they would join together the first day of the Azymes and the Pasch, or the day of the Pascal lamb. And so it is evident that it was already not permitted for the Jews to eat unleavened bread in the supper of the Pascal lamb, because already from that time the first day of the Azymes was computed. Therefore, that day which Mark called "the first day of the unleavened bread," namely the fourteenth day of the month, because on its eve those breads were firstly eaten," John was calling the Pasch, the first day of the Pascal solemnity, which was to be celebrated on the fifteenth day of the month, [when] he said "before the festival day of the pasch."

Thus, since we have now shown the agreement between John and the other Evangelists on this matter: there is no reason why the impious and blasphemous Greeks would calumniate saying that the other Evangelists erred on this point (as they maintain), and for this reason were corrected by John who wrote later. For if even a very small lie in Holy Writ be admitted once (to use the words to Augustine[1]), nothing else will remain certain in them, whereby an adversary may be refuted. Furthermore, the author of the Gospels and all the other books of Sacred Scripture is the Holy Ghost: the Evangelist himself, however, was the pen by which means the Holy Ghost composed Sacred Scripture. But who will be so insane that he would impute a lie to a pen, which cannot move itself, and not rather to the one moving the pen of the writer? Wherefore it is that he who asserts that a lie, however small, is found in Sacred Scripture, charges that crime to God, its author, and not to the writer. But to brand God with the mark of a lie is blasphemy.

Therefore, let the blasphemous Greeks keep quiet, and put their hands on their mouths, and cease to blaspheme God, saying that Matthew, Mark, and Luke erred when recounting the Lord's Supper, and they were corrected by John. For neither did they err, nor do they differ from John in any way. And if they differ (which we adamantly deny) there would be no reason why John ought to be believed more than the other three in agreement, since "in the mouth

---

[1] Letter 28, c. 3, n. 3 (PL 33, 113-114).

of two or three witnesses every word may stand" (Mt. 18, 16). Thus, let he who wishes to be reckoned a Catholic acknowledge that Christ consecrated with unleavened bread.

Hence if the argument of the Greeks were valid, we would rather conclude that one is unable to celebrate with leavened, than with unleavened bread. For if this Sacrament must be confected with that bread with which Christ confected: now it is evident that Christ confected with unleavened bread: it will be necessary that we also confect with unleavened bread. This nevertheless this is not so. For one can confect with leavened bread just as with unleavened, because when sanctifying unleavened and leavened bread, one sanctifies true bread. And when we read that the Lord confected His Body with bread, we read that He "took bread," and although it is certain that it was unleavened, nevertheless the Evangelists were silent about it. And since elsewhere He also called His flesh bread,[1] and neither said "unleavened" or "leavened" bread: perhaps He intentionally omitted it, so that even by this fact it might be shown that it remains free for us to choose with which bread to confect. For unleavened and leavened bread do not differ substantially: just as neither the new man before sin, and man made old with the leaven of sin do not differ.

But you will say, if the Greeks when confecting with leavened bread confect validly, why do we accuse them of heresy in this matter? To which objection we reply that they are not deemed heretics because they confect with leavened bread: but because confecting in this way they think that one cannot confect with unleavened bread: which we have shown to be false, since we have shown that the Lord confected with it. Furthermore, when He celebrated He said: "Do this for a commemoration of me." Now if He had wanted that we, whom He commanded this through the Apostles, would not confect with unleavened bread, He would have forewarned us, through them, and said: "Do not do this with unleavened bread." Thus when saying "Do this," He did not except unleavened bread, even though He Himself consecrated with it. Who will dare to except what He Himself did not except, and forbid what He not only did not forbid, but even confirmed by His action? However, we so confecting with unleavened bread, believe that the Greeks validly confect with leavened bread, although confecting in this way they sin on account of the division of the Church which they make and have separated themselves from its obedience.

For the Church, even if it knows that one can confect legitimately with both, still for certain just reasons, has restricted all the faithful to one particular matter, namely, to unleavened bread. Firstly, it is because Christ confected with it, doing which He not merely did not forbid that we confect with unleavened bread, but rather He suggested it, saying, "Do this for a commemoration of me," supply, "what I do." Next it is because by unleavened bread sincerity is denoted, while by leavened bread malice is denoted, according to the Apostle saying: "Therefore let us feast, not with the old leaven, nor with the leaven of malice and wickedness; but with the unleavened bread of sincerity and truth" (I Cor. 5, 8). And the Lord in the Gospel says: "Beware ye of the leaven of the Pharisees, which is hypocrisy" (Lk. 12, 1). Wherefore in the Law it was commanded: "Every oblation that is offered to the Lord shall be made without leaven, neither shall any leaven or honey be burnt in the sacrifice to the Lord" (Lev. 2, 11). Doubtlessly He is signifying by this trope that in every good work all vain glory ought to be completely avoided. Thus, since leaven denotes malice, which by no means can be found in Christ's humanity, the Church rightly decreed that [this Sacrament] be celebrated with unleavened bread, so that the exterior sign, namely the appearance of the bread, would be more conformed to the thing signified. The Greeks opposing this precept, even if they validly confect, still sin by confecting in this way, because they despise Christ in the prelates of the Church, as He Himself says: "He that despiseth you, despiseth me" (Lk. 10, 16).

---

[1] Cf. Jn. 6, 52.

EUCHARISTIA

Which matter was settled in the Council of Florence, which was celebrated for the union of the Greeks under Eugene IV. For that council defines that "the body of Christ is truly effected in unleavened or leavened wheaten bread; and that priests ought to effect the Body of Our Lord in either one of these, and each one namely according to the custom of his Church whether that of the West or of the East."[1] Blessed Anselm made a very brief yet compendious tract [on this matter] which is titled, *De fermentato ac azymo*.

There is a **third heresy** about the words with which this Sacrament must be confected. For the Waldensians (as Guy the Carmelite says in *De haeresibus Waldensium*[2]) consecrate without the usual form of the Church, with which Christ consecrating, handed down the manner of consecrating to us: but by saying the Our Father seven times and blessing the bread and the wine, they were saying that they consecrate. But Aeneas Sylvius, who is also Pope Pius II, a man in my opinion certainly more careful regarding historical research than Guy, when recounting all the errors of the Waldensians until the present time in his book, *De Bohemorum origine*, does not concoct any such thing.[3] Also [Saint] Antoninus [Pierozzi], Archbishop of Florence, in the fourth part of his *Summa*,[4] when listing the errors of the Poor Men of Lyons, who are also called Waldensians, makes no mention of this matter. Bernard of Luxemburg in his *Catalogus* [*haereticorum*], neither in the title "The Poor Men of Lyon," nor in the title "Waldensians" (for he lists them twice among the heretics by their two names) does not attribute anything of the like to them, nay in the title, "Waldensians," having followed the history of Aeneas Sylvius in his book, *De Bohemorum origine*, he mentions something contradicting this assertion. For when Aeneas Sylvius lists the assertions of these men, whom Bernard of Luxemburg also follows, he says the following: "A priest in any place, at any time can consecrate the Body of Christ, and administer it to those who desire it; it is sufficient, if he repeat only the sacramental words."[5] From which words we infer that they rather keep a true form for confecting, than omit it. Furthermore, that assertion is so insane that I can hardly be persuaded that a man initiated to Christ, and nourished among Christians, taught it, since there is no passage of Sacred Scripture whence a suspicion of this matter can be had, unless perhaps they took occasion for this error from that phrase which is included in the Lord's Prayer, namely, "give us this day our daily bread." But since these men attribute so much to the Lord's Prayer, such that they admit no other besides it (as we shall show in the section on "Prayer") it is possible that they would deem it effective for the consecration of Christ's Body, especially since the sect of the Waldensians (as we have said elsewhere) was established by a man completely ignorant of letters.

We disdain to fight against a heresy which is so mindless and foolish, since the testimonies of Scripture found in Matthew, Mark and Luke, saying that Christ consecrated bread which was taken up saying: "This is my body." One of whom, namely Luke, adds that Christ said after the consecration was done, "Do this for a commemoration of me." By which short saying, He ordered to do this and with the same words with which He did this. And Paul in the First Epistle to the Corinthians recalls the same words, which words I omit since they are as clear as day.

---

[1] Dz. 692.

[2] *Summa de haeresibus et earum confutationibus*, c. 9, p. 80r.

[3] *De Bohemorum origine ac gestis historia*, c. 35, pp. 57-63. In Bohemia the Waldensians merged with the Hussites in the fourteenth century. Hence the errors of the Bohemians given in this chapter apply to both.

[4] *Summa historialis*, also called, *Chronicon partibus tribus distincta ab initio mundi ad MCCCLX* (Lyon, *Ex officina Iuntarum*, 1587), part 3, tit. 21, c. 5, sec. 1. The reference in the text is to the *Summa*, title 2, chapter 7. Perhaps this reference is taken from a different edition.

[5] *De Bohemorum origine ac gestis historia*, p. 60.

EUCHARISTIA

The **fourth heresy** is that which denies that the true Body of Christ is really contained in the Sacrament under the appearances of bread, and the Blood under the appearances of wine: in which error many concur, but among themselves they are (as is the custom of heretics) very diverse. For certain men said that the flesh of some man is therein, whether he was just or a sinner, one ought not to care, into which flesh the preexisting bread therein is converted, which flesh (as they were asserting) was profiting unto the remission of sins. Others again were saying that the bread is converted into the flesh of man, yet not of any man without distinction, but into the flesh of a just and sanctified man, who was God's temple, who possessed the Divinity dwelling in him. And Nestorius seems to have held this error according to the First Council of Ephesus. For Nestorius (as we have shown above) said that there are two persons in Christ: one which was man, and the other which was God, dwelling in that man as in a temple. Hence, he was saying that true flesh is contained in the Eucharist, but it is the flesh of a mere man, and not of God. Thus, there is agreement between those errors about this, namely that the flesh of the Son of man is contained therein, but not the flesh of God. But they differ from each other in that the first men assert that it is the flesh of any man, whether of a just man or a sinner. Now those who are the authors of this error, I did not find in any book, except that the Council of Ephesus condemned it.[1] Others say that the flesh of some mere man is contained therein, yet a just man. Thus both deny that the flesh of the Son of God is there.

There are still others who completely deny that flesh is contained therein. Now these claim that absolutely no flesh is really contained therein: yet they say that the flesh of the Son of God is not truly and really there, but only symbolically and figuratively, just it was contained in other things which represented Christ in the Old Testament, as were the Pascal lamb,[2] the cow sacrificed outside the gate of the city for the sins of the people,[3] and the rock which struck with the rod supplied water to the thirsty people,[4] by all which things Christ was contained, not really, but symbolically, because they were certain signs representing Christ Himself. Wherefore, those words with which Christ then converted into His Body, and we also now do by His command in remembrance of Him, by saying: "This is my body," they distort to this meaning, such that they say that those words ought to be understood in the same way as when Paul said: "And the rock was Christ" (I Cor. 10, 4). But the rock is Christ, not because Paul said that it was a true rock, but because that rock represented Christ, and so it is called Christ from Him: as though He had said more explicitly, what that rock signified is Christ. In this way they say ought to be understood what Christ says: "This is my body," because the true Body of Christ is not there, but merely a certain sign representing Christ.

The originators of this error (as it seems correct to Guy [the Carmelite]) were the Armenians. Yet I do not know which authors Guy followed in this, so that he would pin this heresy upon the Armenians, which no one else whom I found attributed to them. For all those whom I have found who have mentioned this perverse teaching, assert that this was the innovation of Berengarius. This Berengarius, French by nationality, was an [arch-] deacon of the Church of Saint Maurice in Angers, a man poorly educated (as Guitmund bears witness[5]) but completely

---

[1] Can. 11 (Dz. 123).

[2] Cf. Ex. 12.

[3] Cf. Num. 19.

[4] Cf. Num. 20, 11.

[5] Guitmund, *De veritate corporis et sanguinis Christi in Eucharistia adversus Berengarius* (PL 149, 1427C-1428A). Guitmund was a Benedictine monk who later was appointed Bishop of Aversa, Italy. He became a stanch defender of the Catholic doctrine of transubstantiation against the heretical Berengarius of Tours. Sometime between 1073-77 he wrote, at the instance of one of his fellow-monks by the name of Roger, this famous treatise in defense of the Holy Eucharist. It is written in the form of a dialogue between himself and Roger and contains an exposition as well as a refutation of the doctrines

given to certain dialectical sophisms, through which he was hoping to capture the fallacious glory of this world that he greatly desired. From which motive it happened that he broke out into this madness which we have just related. Disturbed by this occasion Leo IX, the then supreme pontiff of the Church, a man according to the testimony of all historians renowned for holiness of life, assembled the Synod of Vercelli, to which Berengarius was summoned, and being nowise willing to come (as Lanfranc says[1]), with his accomplices, unless they very speedily retracted, he was condemned with perpetual anathema. Nevertheless, Leo died shortly afterwards and Berengarius persisting in his obstinacy, spread the poison of his heresy through all parts of France. For which matter Victor II, who succeeded Leo IX, celebrated the Synod of Tours through Hildebrand, then cardinal of the Roman Church and presiding in his place over the council: in which council Berengarius was refuted by certain very learned men, and especially by Lanfranc, Archbishop of Canterbury, but nowise amended. For going out from it like a dog he returned to his vomit.[2] For which reason Nicholas II, who succeeded Victor in the administration of the Church, assembled a council in Rome with one hundred thirteen bishops, at which Berengarius attending, either amended, or pretending to have amended from fear of punishment, sang the palinode, which is recorded in the book of the *Decretals*.[3]

A certain impious Amaury [of Bène or of Chartres[4]] succeeded Berengarius after a hundred or more years, of whom we have already mentioned above.[5] He was saying that Christ is not otherwise in the Eucharist than in any other bread, or any other thing. So Bernard of Luxemburg relates of him in his *Catalogus [haereticorum]*,[6] citing a certain monk, Caesarius [of Heisterbach],[7] However, I have found no one else who attributes this to Amaury. For Antoninus of Florence in his *Summa [Theologica]*, when enumerating the errors of Amaury, does not mention any such thing.[8] And Platina, when relating the life of Innocent III, under whom in the [IV] Lateran Council the teachings of Amaury were condemned, when he lists his other errors, yet makes no mention of this one.[9] Caesarius, whom the *Catalogus* cites, I have not seen. Thus, having followed that *Catalogus*, I have decided to include this Amaury here, because the teaching of this man is not very different from Berengarius: wherefore he also ought to be struck with the same sword as he. A hundred or more years after these men, John Wycliffe embraced the same error, as is evident from the Council of Constance.[10]

Finally, in our time, John Oecolampadius, whose life we have already briefly described above,[11] brought back from Hell this heresy buried for so many years, and he fortified it as much as he could with passages both from the Bible and from the sayings of the Saints, some badly quoted, others detruncated, yet all badly understood. For he so expounds those words

---

of Berengarius concerning the Holy Eucharist. He died between 1090-95.

[1] "After that, the synod of Vercelli was called and convened the following September with the same pope presiding. To that synod you were summoned and did not attend" (*Liber de corpore et sanguine Domini*, c. 4 (PL 150, 413C)).

[2] Cf. Prov. 26, 11 and II Pet. 2, 22.

[3] *Decretum Gratiani*, p. 3 (*De consecratione*), dist. 2, c. 42 (*Ego Berengarius*) (PL 187, 1750A-1751A).

[4] In Latin he is called, Arnoldus Amalricus. He died in 1225.

[5] Cf. book two, "Adam and Eve," third heresy.

[6] Fol. 21v-22r.

[7] *Dialogus miraculorum* (Cologne, *Sumptibus J. M. Heberle*, 1851), dist. 5, c. 22, p. 304.

[8] *Summa Theologica in quatuor partes distributa* (Verona, *Typographia seminari apud Carattonium Augustinum*, 1740), part 4, tit. 11, c. 7, p. 593D-E.

[9] Baptista Platina, *De vitis ac gestis summorum pontificum, ad sua usque tempora, liber unus* (Cologne, *apud JasperumGennepaeum*, 1551), p. 185.

[10] Sess. 8, c. 1-3 (Dz. 581-583).

[11] Cf. book two, "Adoration," second heresy.

of Christ with which we daily confect the Sacrament, namely, "This is my body," to mean, "this signifies my body," or "this is a figure of my body." Now so that this may be made clearer, I will cite his words. Oecolampadius: "It is time that we go on to the chief point of the discourse: namely that we prove that the words of the Lord's Supper were said with the same figure, whereby the Apostles said: 'Now the rock was Christ': that is to say, the rock signified Christ, or was a figure of Christ. For the whole disagreement is about this. For if we would expound 'is' ὑπαρκτικῶς [i.e. 'really'][1] and substantively without trope: we would be asserting that Christ's Body is present on the altar not so much "sacramentally" (as they say) but just as He truly is in Heaven. But if our exposition fits, there would be no suspicion of transubstantiation, or of consubstantiation (one may use the words of one's adversaries). In this way from small words emerge great questions. And I would not dispute about this, if by 'body' one would understand the figure of the body, which renders the same meaning, whether you would interpret 'is' as 'it signifies,' or 'body' as the figure and sacrament of the body. We seek the meaning not the words."[2]

O illustrious expositor of Scripture! As though it were permitted to expound Scripture in this manner, or I should rather say, to mutate or deprave Scripture: inexhaustible matter would be suggested for raising up heresies. Also, every sword would be taken away by which the heretic could be run through. In fact, there will be no part of Scripture which could not be corrupted with equal facility. Indeed, the Cerdonians[3] and Manichaeans[4] of old would exult very much about this new trope, and anyone who denied that Christ had a true body, and was a true man. The Arians, Eunomians, Aerians, and all others who denied Christ is God. For everything that was seen to oppose them may be easily conciliated to them by expounding the word "is" to mean "signifies": as if one were to say, "God was the Word" means that He was the Word by a certain figure of the Deity. And the passage, "And the Word was made flesh," would be expounded to mean: "the Word was made a certain figure of flesh," or as follows: "the Word signifies the flesh by a certain figure." But what orthodox man can endure such things so repugnant, so distorted, and so foreign to the literal meaning?

Otherwise, I do not deny the fact that he cites many passages of Sacred Scripture in which tropes of this kind are perceived. For Sacred Scripture often uses figures and tropes (as Augustine shows in the second book of his *On Christian Doctrine*[5]), and yet from the fact that it often uses figures, it ought not to be concluded that all the language of Scripture is figurative. Wherefore, from the fact that Sacred Scripture elsewhere may have used some trope, Oecolampadius does not rightly conclude that it also now uses figurative speech. For even if he shows two thousand passages to which figurative speech appertains, still all these will never cause that some figurative speech is present in these words, as he pretends. No one will ever say that this is a correct conclusion. Paul used a trope when he said: "And the rock was Christ": and did Christ thus similarly use a figure when He said: "For this is my body"? And so, it still remains to be proved by Oecolampadius that in these words, namely: "For this is

---

[1] I.e. "spiritual" as used in I Cor. 10, 4: "the *spiritual* rock that followed them, and the rock was Christ."

[2] *De genuina verborum Domini, hoc est corpus meum, iuxta vetustissimos authores expositione liber* (Basel, 1525).

[3] Theses followers of the Gnostic Cerdo, mentioned above, rejected the Old Testament and the New, except part of Saint Luke's Gospel and of Saint Paul's epistles.

[4] Mani, the founder of the Manichaeans, rejected the whole of the Old Testament, but admitted as much of the New as suited him; in particular he rejected the Acts of the Apostles, because it told of the descent of the Holy Ghost in the past. The Gospels were corrupted in many places, but where a text seemed to favor him the Manichaeans knew how to parade it. One has to read St. Augustine's anti-Manichean disputes to realize the extreme ingenuity with which Scripture texts were collected and interpreted.

[5] C. 6, n. 7-8 (PL 34, 38-39).

my body," some trope is underlying, which he will never do. Furthermore, even if we were to admit some figurative speech in Scripture, still not the kind which Oecolampadius concocts, that by the word "is" we may understand "signifies."

For the passage which he cites from Paul, namely: "And the rock was Christ," by no means helps his case. For Paul did not say that Christ is a corporeal rock, but a spiritual rock: which is clearly proved from preceding words. For he says the following: "And they drank of the spiritual rock that followed them, and the rock was Christ" (I Cor. 10, 4). You now see what rock Christ is, namely a spiritual rock, from which they were drinking, which being a companion of that people, helped them by many miracles. But if you still contend that it ought to be referred to the corporeal rock, pray tell where may that sensible rock be found from which water came forth, and followed the people wherever they went? Moses did not actually mention such a great miracle, although he related other lesser miracles. But Paul attributes this to that rock which he said was Christ. "They drank," he says, "of the spiritual rock that followed them." For [Ambrosiaster] expounds this passage as follows: "The rock which followed them is said to be Christ, because at times when human help was lacking, Christ was present with them. He followed them precisely in order to be able to come to them in such circumstances. Nor was it a rock which gave water, but Christ himself."[1]

But we learn these things much more clearly from Chrysostom, who, when explaining this passage of Paul, says: "When he had said that they drank spiritual drink, he added: ...'That rock was Christ.' For not the nature of that stone flowed out water, then then it would have flowed out before that time, but another certain spiritual stone wrought all these things, that is, Christ being present everywhere did all the miracles, and therefore he said, 'that followed.'"[2] Finally, Theophylactus interprets this passage in the same way, saying: "What concerns the food needs no confirmation. For it was completely extraordinary. But concerning the drink, that the rock was extraordinary by reason of its abundance requires proof. Hence he says that it was giving drink in abundance not from the nature of the rock (for otherwise it would have also flowed before), but some other spiritual rock provided everything, namely Christ. Now he said, "followed" to show that Christ was with them everywhere, and performed all the miracles."[3] From these very clear proofs it is now very clear that Paul did not say that Christ was a corporeal rock, from which water flowed: but Christ is that spiritual rock figured by something else that was corporeal. And so it will not be necessary to expound "is" by "signify": since Christ truly and really is that rock about which Paul speaks, namely the spiritual rock.

In this way also when Christ praised John the Baptist, He did not say absolutely: "This is Elias": but He says: "And if you will receive it, he is Elias that is to come" (Mt. 11, 14). Which Chrysostom also comments, saying: "Wherefore did He did not simply say, 'This is Elias,' but, 'If you will receive it, he is Elias,' that is, if with an upright mind you attend to his deeds. And He did not stop even at this, but to the words, 'He is Elias that is to come,' He added, to show that understanding is needed, 'He that hath ears to hear, let him hear.' (Mt. 11, 15)."[4] And Theophylactus, who the same Oecolampadius translated into Latin for us, when expounding this passage of Matthew says: "'If you will,' He says, 'receive it,' that is, if you judge the matter with a rational, and not an envious mind, he is the one whom the prophet Malachias called Elias who was to come.[5] For both the precursor and Elias have the same ministry. The one was the precursor of the first coming, while Elias will be the precursor of

---

[1] *Commentaria in Epistolam ad Corinthios primam*, c. 10 (PL 17, 234A-B).
[2] Homily 23 on I Corinthians, n. 2 (PG 61, 191).
[3] *Commentarius in Epistolam I ad Corinthios* (PG 124, 679).
[4] *In Matthaeum*, homily 37, n. 3 (PG 57, 422).
[5] Cf. Mal. 4, 5: "Behold I will send you Elias the prophet, before the coming of the great and dreadful day of the Lord."

the second coming."[1] Notice here also that it is clearly established that it is not necessary to expound "is" for "signifies," since John was not truly and really Elias absolutely, but [he signified] that Elias who was to come. I indeed admit that Elias signified John, and so John was not truly and really Elias, but he who signified Elias.

I have discussed these two passages because they are the chief ones cited by Oecolampadius, with which he attempts to prove that this word "is" can be expounded by the word "signifies" in which passages by an unnatural and spurious exposition, as we have proved (I think) clearly enough. But if we would wish to freely give in to Oecolampadius, that in the recently cited passages from Matthew and Paul, and in many other passages that it would be necessary to expound this word "is" for "signifies," will it not be a necessary consequence to expound "is" in all the words of Christ to mean "signifies"? Certainly, even a slightly educated logician sees that this conclusion is weak. In Paul's words when he says: "The rock was Christ," the word "is" ought to be expounded by "signifies": thus in Christ's words when he says: "This is my body," the word "is" also ought to be expounded by "signifies."

For in order that this reasoning to be valid, it would be necessary to support it by adding a universal assertion such as this: "In all the sayings of Christ and Paul, the word "is" ought to be expounded for the word "signifies." Without such a universal assertion you would never conclude that these words of Christ ought to be expounded by the word "signifies," from the fact that those words of Paul are so expounded: nay from any other passage of Paul it will nowise be concluded that the verb "is" found in that passage ought to be expounded by "signifies," on account of the fact that elsewhere it should be so expounded, unless perhaps you would universally premise that it should be done so everywhere. But I do not think that Oecolampadius has gone so insane that he would admit this universal assertion.

Also, I do not think that it ought to be disregarded that Oecolampadius and his followers have compiled Sacred Writ to be passed on to the common people in their native language, so that it may be read by anyone without distinction. For from this matter their temerity is proved: especially if we were to repeat certain words of Oecolampadius recently cited. For he said the following: "From small words emerge great questions." If from small words great questions emerge, how can you claim on the contrary that Sacred Scripture is so clear, that it can be understood by the people? Would a man with little education and not enlightened by the Spirit of God (for not all men are given this Spirit of God) be able to solve these questions, which learned men can hardly explain? Or perhaps the common man, entangled with the cares of this world, could detect a trope or figurative speech in these words of Christ, "This is my body," which none of the so enormous multitude of men, highly renown for holiness and learning, who have lived from the time of Christ's Passion until now, was able to find beside one man, Berengarius, and the other, Oecolampadius? But if Sacred Scripture is so clear, that it may be handed over to people without distinction to be read and understood by them, since so many holy men renown for sanctity as well as for learning never detected this trope in these words, it is certain that none is there.

Up until now the only thing that we have done was to show that the arguments of Oecolampadius are futile and void, and nowise capable of establishing their pernicious teaching. Hence it remains that we confirm our position: which, by God the Creator, Who always stands with the truth, we will easily (as I hope) accomplish: because the many testimonies support us in this matter, and they are so explicit, that they cannot be concealed by any equivocation. I will cite a few of them: but he who wishes to have the rest, I will show him abundant sources whence he may draw *ad nauseam*.

Firstly, then, those words of Christ are brought forth by which He says: "This is my body." Certainly nothing could be said more explicitly: nor in a matter of such great importance,

---

[1] *Ennaratio in Evangelium Matthaei* (PG 123, 251C).

such as this, ought it to be believed that Christ would have used some trope or figurative speech, lest He give us an opportunity for erring by this occasion. But since we have spoken sufficiently about this matter, it is necessary that we show from other testimonies that there is no trope there, and Christ's Body is there, which was born of the Virgin, and hung on the Cross for us, was laid in the sepulcher, and from thence rose again, and ascended into the Heaven.

Now the whole sixth chapter of John's Gospel confirms this, in which He repeats this truth very often, such that no doubt remains to us. "I am," Christ said, "the living bread which came down from heaven... If any man eat of this bread, he shall live for ever; and the bread that I will give, is my flesh, (which I will give) for the life of the world" (Jn. 6, 41 & 52). Notice here that the words, "I will give," are used twice,[1] the first time so that you call to mind the gift in the form of food, and the second time to call to mind the Passion, in which He gave Himself up to death for the life of us all: as though He had said slightly more explicitly: "The bread which I am about to give you to eat is My Flesh, that Flesh, I say, which I will give for the life of all of you."

But, as perhaps you already began to do, you also here interpret the verb "is" for "signify," such that you say that it ought to be understood thus: "The bread which I will give, signifies My Flesh, or is a kind of figure of My Body." But if you corrupt this passage in this way, you clearly reckon yourself among the Jews of Capharnaum, who when they heard this saying of Christ which they could not grasp, they were disputing among themselves, saying: "How can this man give us his flesh to eat?" (Jn. 6, 53). Wherefore it will be necessary that we put to you the words which Christ answered to this objection: "Amen, amen I say unto you: Except you eat the flesh of the Son of man, and drink his blood, you shall not have life in you" (v. 54).

Notice that Christ now repeats the same truth, showing that His Flesh is truly food, and because He foresaw that one man, Berengarius, and another, Oecolampadius, would expound this verb "is," for "signifies," lest they could rightly suspect such a thing, He now repeats this verb "is," but He says: "Except you eat the flesh of the Son of man, and drink his blood, you shall not have life in you." From which words no such thing can now be concocted such that "eat" can be taken to mean "signify": unless perhaps one again takes refuge by expounding "flesh" as a figure of flesh, saying that it ought to be understood as follows: "Except you eat the flesh," meaning the figure of the flesh, "of the Son of man," etc. Who does not see that this exposition is so foreign to literal meaning that it can nowise fit with it?

But that some such thing cannot now be concocted, the words which Christ subjoins clearly show, saying: "He that eateth my flesh, and drinketh my blood, hath everlasting life: and I will raise him up in the last day. For my flesh is meat indeed: and my blood is drink indeed" (v. 55-56). Notice that He does not now merely say, "My flesh is meat," but lest "is" could be expounded in some way for "signify," He added "indeed," saying, "My flesh is meat indeed." But if Christ's flesh in the Eucharist is only significative, and by a certain likeness, it is then not truly food, but is food significatively and by likeness. Which passage you the reader will note well, for this passage before all others especially runs the adversary through and confirms our position. "My flesh," He says, "is meat indeed [*vere*, which in Latin also means 'truly']," as though He were to say, "not significatively or figuratively, but is truly food." For if it were food just figuratively, it nowise is "truly meat."

For likenesses or figures are never said to be truly those things of which they are likenesses. For who would say that God's image [*imaginem* in Latin also means both "image" and "likeness"] is truly God? I do not think that Oecolampadius would say this. For if he were

---

[1] "The Greek has, "But the bread which I will give is My Flesh, which I will give for the life of the world." And so read the Syriac, S. Cyril, Theophylact and Theodoret." (Cornelius à Lapide, *Commentaria in Joannem. Cap. VI* (Würzburg, Sumptibus Martini Veith, 1747), p. 343).

to say this, besides other inconveniences against the faith of all men, this would be against Oecolampadius in particular, namely that images ought to be tolerated, since God's image is truly God. Yet Oecolampadius (as it will be said elsewhere) does not tolerate images. Thus, if an image or figure is not said to be truly that thing whose image it is, but just significatively: how could Christ's flesh, which is nowise eaten (as Oecolampadius says), be said to be truly food? If, however, you say that it can be called food in the way whereby God's word is said to be food, as it is said: "Not in bread alone doth man live" (Mt. 4, 4): it is certain that in that passage God's word is not said to be truly food, but by a certain metaphor, or similitude: so that just as bodily food put into the stomach, when digested with sufficient heat nourishes the body, and confers life to it: so when God's word has been heard, and well consigned to the memory, when so digested with charity that one fulfills in deed what he heard by word, it nourishes his soul, and confers spiritual life to it. "If any man," He says, "keep my word, he shall not see death for ever" (Jn. 8, 51). Thus, from these words of Christ it is very clearly proved that Christ's true Body is contained in the Eucharist under the appearances of bread, and His Blood under the appearances of wine.

But because Oecolampadius tries to escape by a kind of crack, saying that this sixth chapter of John nowise relates to the Eucharist, but to a spiritual eating of flesh, by which, as he says, we have eternal life: it is necessary that we show that a whole multitude of men renown for holiness and learning understood and thus expounded this sixth chapter in relation to the Eucharist. For in the beginning of this book we showed that the meaning of Sacred Scripture ought to be sought from the Church. For by its authority we accept these Scriptures as Divine, so likewise it is necessary that by the same authority we obtain the meaning of these Scriptures. It yields little benefit to have the words, but to completely ignore the meaning. And the difficulty is not about the words alone, whose meaning a grammarian can know, but about the meaning. And Oecolampadius himself said in the words cited above: "We seek the meaning not the words." If then the meaning ought to be sought more than the words, since from the decision of the Church we hold that this or that book is Divine Scripture: it will be necessary from its decision also to hold the meaning of Scripture which it has given to us. Our faith certainly depends on the meaning of Scripture, not on the bare words. Therefore, it is necessary to hear the Church concerning this matter, and let us see what it settles for us.

And let us firstly show one by one that it was the common opinion of various Fathers on this matter, that this chapter of John ought to be understood of the Eucharist. And first of all, I put Theophylactus at the head of the army, translated into Latin by Oecolampadius himself. For when expounding the passage of John: "The bread that I will give, is my flesh, (which I will give) for the life of the world" (Jn. 6, 52), he says the following: "Manifestly does Christ speak unto us of the mystical Communion of His Body. For he says, 'The bread that I will give, is my flesh, for the life of the world.' And showing His power, that He should be crucified not as a servant, and less than the Father, but willingly, He says: 'I will give My Flesh for the life of the world.' For although He is said to have been given by the Father (cf. Jn. 3, 16), Christ also gave Himself. From the former statement, 'I am the living bread which came down from heaven,' we learn that the Son is of one mind with the Father. He then says, 'I will give... My Flesh,' so that we would not be ignorant of Son's free will. Note well, however, that the bread which we eat in the Sacrament of Communion is not merely a figure of the Lord's Flesh but is rather the very Flesh of the Lord. For He did not say, 'The bread which I will give is a figure of My Flesh,' but 'It is My Flesh.' For that bread by the mystic blessing and coming of the Holy Ghost, with the secret words is transformed into the Flesh of the Lord. And lest it should trouble any man, that the bread is to be believed Flesh: when our Lord walked in the flesh, and took food of bread, that bread that was eaten was changed into His Body, and was made like unto His holy Flesh and it went unto augmentation and sustenance after the condition of the nature of man. Therefore, now also the bread is changed into the Flesh of Our Lord. Why, then, someone will say, do we not see flesh, but bread? Because, if flesh were seen, it would revolt us to such a degree, that we should be unable to partake of it. And therefore in condescension to our infirmity, the Mystical Food is given to us under an appearance suitable to our minds."[1] I have quoted Theophylactus at greater length, because it especially supports our case, and solves all Oecolampadius' sophisms by these words alone.

Blessed Cyril [of Alexandria] expounds those words which are said by Christ in the sixth chapter of John of this marvelous Sacrament, as anyone can see there. However, so that you the reader may see this without your labor, I decided to insert those words here, which he eloquently says in his *Commentary on John*, as follows: "Again He contrast the Mystic Blessing[2] with the provision of the manna, and the partaking of the cup from the waters flowing forth from the clefts of the rocks. And what He said before in other words, this He again says here, weaving the same discourse in many ways. For He does not advise them to marvel overmuch at the manna, but rather to receive Him, as the Bread from Heaven, and the Giver of eternal life. For 'Your fathers,' He says, 'did eat manna in the desert, and are dead. This is the bread which cometh down from heaven; that if any man eat of it, he may not die.' (Jn. 6, 49-50) For after the food of manna had relieved the needs of the body, and the danger of starvation had been removed, the body again became feeble, since it was not infusing eternal life to those eating it. Thus, it was certainly not true food and bread from heaven. But the holy Body of Christ is the true food, nourishing unto immortality and life everlasting. But they also drank water from the rock. And what resulted from this, He says, and what was the benefit for those who drank? for they died. Therefore, it was true drink; but the true drink, so that we may speak correctly, is found to be the drink of the Precious Blood of Christ, which uproots from the foundation all corruption, and dislodges death which dwelt in the flesh of man. For it is indeed not the Blood of any common man, but is by its very nature Life Itself. Wherefore, we are called both the Body and members of Christ, as being those who through the Blessed Eucharist [*eulogia*] receive the Son Himself in ourselves."[3] From which quotation it is clearly established that those words which are repeated concerning the Mystical Bread in the sixth chapter of John ought to be interpreted of the Sacrament of the Eucharist. In which quotation I would like to alert the pious reader that whenever he finds Cyril saying "mystic blessing" of bread, he ought to take it to mean this admirable Sacrament. For he very often uses this expression, both here and also elsewhere.

Chrysostom also expounds these words of the most excellent Sacrament in his forty-fifth homily on John, where he shows which words befit this Sacrament, and which words do not. For when explaining these words: "I am the bread of life" (Jn. 6, 35), he says the following: "Now He proceeds to commit unto them mysteries. And firstly He discourses about His Godhead, saying, 'I am the bread of life.' For this is not said of His Body, concerning that He says towards the end, 'And the bread which I shall give is My flesh' (v. 52): but at present it refers to His Godhead. For That, through God the Word, is Bread, as this bread also, through the Spirit descending on it, is made Heavenly Bread."[4] Chrysostom clearly distinguishes between those words of Christ which are seen to pertain to His Divinity, and those which pertain to His Body, as veiled under the mysteries. And he teaches that the words about these Mysteries, meaning, about this Sacrament (for He calls this Sacrament Mysteries) begins from this verse:

---

[1] *Enarratio in Evangelium S. Joannis* (PG 123, 1307).

[2] Saint Cyril here refers to the Holy Eucharist as the "mystic blessing. The Greek word, *eulogia*, means "blessing." Cf. "Eulogia," *The Catholic Encyclopedia* (New York: Robert Appleton Company, 1908), vol. 5, p. 603.

[3] *In Joannis Evangelium*, bk. 4, c. 2 (PG 73, 582-583).

[4] *Homiliae LXXXVIII in Joannem*, n. 2 (PG 59. 253).

"And the bread which I shall give is My flesh." Which you the reader will note well, because this will help you very much to avoid the wiles of this sort of heretics.

Blessed Augustine very clearly refers all those things which are said about Christ's Flesh in the sixth chapter of John to this Sacrament of the Eucharist. So that you the reader may know this very clearly, I will cite this one of the many things which he says. For when expounding that passage, namely: "He that eateth my flesh, and drinketh my blood, hath everlasting life" (Jn. 6, 55), he says the following: "This epithet, eternal, which He used, answers to both. It is not so in the case of that food which we take for the purpose of sustaining this temporal life. For he who will not take it shall not live, nor yet shall he who will take it live. For very many, even who have taken it, die; it may be by old age, or by disease, or by some other casualty. But in this food and drink, that is, in the Body and Blood of the Lord, it is not so. For both he that does not take it has no life, and he that does take it has life, and that indeed eternal life."[1] Wherein he is explaining the said words of Christ concerning the Eucharist he very clearly asserts there that It is the true Body and the true Blood of Christ. For so he said: "But in this food and drink, that is, in the Body and Blood of the Lord." Nothing can be said more explicitly than this.

There are also very many other holy Doctors, who even if they do not expound John's Gospel in its entirety, still among those things which they wrote in other places, they expounded parts of this chapter, because they seemed to be useful for subject about which they were discussing. It will not be irksome to list which things, and all the more because they cannot be found very easily: which quotations we noted down when doing other things so as to be used later for this matter. For Cassiodorus when mainly expounding Psalm [109]: "Thou art a priest forever," says the following: "For with whom can these words be truly and clearly associated except the Lord Saviour, who in saving fashion consecrated His Body and Blood in the distribution of bread and wine? As Christ Himself says in the Gospel: 'Except you eat the flesh of the Son of man, and drink his blood, you shall not have life in you' (Jn. 6, 54). But the human mind must not imagine that there is anything bloody or corruptible in this Flesh and Blood—as Paul says: 'He that eateth and drinketh unworthily, eateth and drinketh judgment to himself' (I Cor. 11, 29)—but rather the substance that gives life and salvation and has become peculiar to the Word itself. Through it are granted remission of sins and the gift of eternal life."[2] Cassiodorus clearly states that in the Eucharist [Christ's] Body and Blood are contained, and he proves this by the quotation cited from the sixth chapter of John, which seems most suited to his purpose. Blessed Gregory when expounding the passage in Job: "Will the wild ass bray when he hath grass?" says: "Then 'the ox' had not an empty manger, when to the Jewish people, looking for His Flesh, the Law showed Him forth, Whom it prophesied to them whilst long kept in expectation of Him. Whence too the Lord, when He was born, is placed in a manger, that it might be signified, that the holy animals, which under the Law had long been found hungry, are filled with 'the fodder' of His Incarnation. For at His birth He filled a manger, Who gave Himself for food to the souls of mortal beings, saying, 'He that eateth my flesh, and drinketh my blood, abideth in me, and I in him' (John 6, 57)."[3] Gregory, when asserting that God gave Himself as food, cites a testimony for this matter from the sixth chapter of John.

Ambrose in his book, *On the Sacraments*, says: "As our Lord Jesus Christ is the true Son of God, not after the manner of men, through grace, but as a Son of the essence of His Father, so He is 'meat indeed,' as He Himself said,[4] which we receive, and His true Blood is our drink.

---

[1] *Tractate 26 on the Gospel of John*, n. 15 (PL 35, 1613-1614).

[2] *Expositio in Psalterium* (PL 70, 797B).

[3] *Morals on the Book of Job*, bk. 7, c. 7, n. 54 (PL 75, 770D-771A).

[4] Jn. 6, 56.

EUCHARISTIA

But perchance you may say—what the disciples of Christ also then said when they heard him saying: 'Unless a man eat my flesh and drink my blood, he shall not abide in me, nor shall he have eternal life'[1]—perchance you may say: 'How are these things real? I who see the likeness, do not see the reality of blood.' First of all, I told thee[2] of the word of Christ, which acts so that it can change and alter the appointed forms of nature. Then when the disciples of Christ endured not His saying, but hearing that He gave His Flesh to eat and gave His Blood to drink, they turned back; but Peter alone said: 'Thou hast the words of eternal life, and how shall I withdraw from thee?' (v. 69). Accordingly, lest others should say this, feeling a shrinking from actual blood, and that yet the grace of Redemption might remain, therefore you receive the Sacrament in a similitude, but truly obtain the grace and virtue of the nature. 'I am,' says He, 'the living bread which came down from heaven' (v. 41). But flesh did not come down from Heaven, that is to say, He took flesh of the Virgin on earth. How then did bread come down from Heaven, and that, too, living bread? Because our Lord Jesus Christ is alike a sharer both in Divinity and body. And you who receive His Flesh partake of His Divine essence in that food."[3] Wherein the reader should note how clearly he asserts that we eat Christ's Flesh, and how he expounds the words which are found in the sixth chapter of John of the true Flesh of Christ, which he says we eat under the appearance of bread.

Hilary says the following: "The words in which we speak of the things of God must be used in no mere human and worldly sense, nor must the perverseness of an alien and impious interpretation be extorted from the soundness of heavenly words by any violent and headstrong preaching. Let us read what is written, let us understand what we read, and then fulfil the demands of a perfect faith. For as to what we say concerning the reality of Christ's nature within us, unless we have been taught by Him, our words are foolish and impious. For He says Himself, 'For my flesh is meat indeed: and my blood is drink indeed. He that eateth my flesh, and drinketh my blood, abideth in me, and I in him' (Jn. 6, 56-57). As to the verity of the Flesh and Blood there is no room left for doubt. For now both from the declaration of the Lord Himself and our own faith, it is verily flesh and verily blood. And these when eaten and drunk, bring it to pass that both we are in Christ and Christ in us."[4] In which words he very clearly shows that we eat Christ's true Flesh: and drink His true Blood, having cited the testimony for this matter which he thought suitable from the sixth chapter of John.

Cyprian says the following: "And we ask that this bread should be given to us daily, that we who are in Christ, and daily receive the Eucharist for the food of salvation, may not, by the interposition of some heinous sin, by being prevented, as withheld and not communicating, from partaking of the Heavenly Bread, be separated from Christ's body, as He Himself predicts, and warns, 'I am the bread of life which came down from heaven. If any man eat of my bread, he shall live forever: and the bread which I will give is my flesh, for the life of the world' (Jn. 6, 51-52). When, therefore, He says, that whoever shall eat of His bread shall live forever; as it is manifest that those who partake of His Body and receive the Eucharist by the right of communion are living, so, on the other hand, we must fear and pray lest anyone who, being withheld from communion, is separate from Christ's Body should remain at a distance from salvation; as He Himself threatens, and says, 'Except you eat the flesh of the Son of man, and drink his blood, you shall not have life in you' (Jn. 6, 54). And therefore we ask that our Bread—that is, Christ—may be given to us daily, that we who abide and live in Christ may not depart from His sanctification and Body."[5] You the reader see how Cyprian

---

[1] The quotation is a conflation of Jn. 6, 54-55, & 57.
[2] *On the Sacraments*, bk. 4, c. 4, n. 13-20 (PL 16, 439-443).
[3] Bk. 6, c. 1, n. 1-4 (PL 16, 453C-455B).
[4] *On the Trinity*, bk. 8, n. 14 (PL 10, 247A-B).
[5] *On the Lord's Prayer*, c. 18 (PL 4, 531A-532A).

asserts that he who is separated from the communion of the Eucharist, is also separated from Christ's Body, and hence from salvation. To which he applies the passage from John, chapter six: "Except you eat the flesh of the Son of man," etc. And in the first book of *Against the Jews* [PseudoCyprian] confirms the same view by a quotation cited from that passage.[1]

Finally, Origen says the following: "And the things that were formerly signified in a riddle now are fulfilled plainly and in truth. And so the one who was explaining the forms of the figures and riddles as says: 'For I would not have you ignorant, brethren, that our fathers were all under the cloud, and all passed through the sea. And all in Moses were baptized, in the cloud, and in the sea: And did all eat the same spiritual food, and all drank the same spiritual drink; (and they drank of the spiritual rock that followed them, and the rock was Christ)' (I Cor. 10, 1-4). You see the manner in which Paul solves the riddle of the Law and teaches the forms of the riddles and says that 'the rock' was a riddle to Moses, before he was married to this Ethiopian woman of ours.[2] Now, in outward reality, 'the rock is Christ,' for now God 'speaks mouth to mouth' through the Law. Previously, Baptism was 'in a riddle, in the cloud and in the sea,' but now, plainly, it is a 'laver of regeneration, and renovation of the Holy Ghost.'[3] At that time the manna was food 'in a riddle,' but now, 'plainly,' the Flesh of the Word of God is 'meat indeed,' just as He Himself says: 'My flesh is meat indeed: and my blood is drink indeed' (Jn. 6, 56)."[4] From which passage many things support us. For when he discusses those things which were had figuratively and now are had really, he puts forth three examples, one of which is the manna, which was the food of the Israelites, but figuratively: for it was prefiguring the Eucharist, in which we are fed with Christ's Flesh really and not figuratively, as Oecolampadius says: for the confirmation of which matter, as you the reader see, Origen cited a passage from the sixth chapter of John, which he perceives to suit very well his statement. Therefore, it is evident from the testimonies of so many very renown men, that those things which are said concerning the bread, and Christ's Body and Blood, ought to be referred to the Sacrament of the Eucharist.

But so that we may bury the man with the testimonies of authors, and so that we may show him to be a heretic, separated from the unity of the Church: I will bring forth in addition other testimonies of illustrious men, which clearly prove that Christ's Body and Blood are contained under the appearances of bread and wine in this most excellent Sacrament.

[Pope] Leo I, renown for holiness as well as for doctrine, writes the following in a letter to the people of the city of Constantinople: "In God's Church it is so constantly in men's mouths, that even the tongues of infants do not keep silence upon the truth of Christ's Body and Blood at the rite of Holy Communion. For in that mystic distribution of spiritual nourishment, that which is given and taken is of such a kind that receiving the virtue of the celestial food we pass into the Flesh of Him, Who became our flesh."[5]

Also the priest Juvencus, more ancient than Jerome, when describing the Gospel history by a poem, in [dactylic] hexameters, says:
When He had spoken thus He broke the bread with His hands,
And divided it up, solemnly blessed it and handed it out,
Telling His disciples that they were thereby eating His own Body.
Then the Lord took the cup and filled it with wine,

---

[1] *Against the Jews*, bk. 1, c. 22 (PL 4, 694). "*Adversus Judaeos* is perhaps by a Novatianist and Harnack ascribes it to Novatian himself" ("St. Cyprian of Carthage," *The Catholic Encyclopedia* (New York: Robert Appleton Company, 1908), vol. 4, p. 588).

[2] I.e. the Ethiopian wife of Moses. Cf. Num. 12, 1.

[3] Cf. Tit. 3, 5; Jn. 3, 5.

[4] *In Numeros*, hom. 7, n. 2 (PG 12, 613B-C).

[5] Letter 59, c. 2 (PL 54, 868B).

EUCHARISTIA

Consecrated it with words of thanksgiving and handed it around to drink,
Telling them that He had distributed His own Blood.
He said, "This Blood will remit the sins of the people.
Drink this—it is Mine. For you must believe the truth of My words."[1]

Arnobius [the Younger][2] says the following: "'Praise' of the Trinity 'and magnificence' of the Deity, 'His work': His justice continues immutable 'forever,' in which justice He that hath made a memory of His marvelous works, saying, as often as ye shall do these things, you shall do them in remembrance of Me. When said our merciful and gracious Lord this? Then without doubt when He gave the food of His Body to them that fear Him, and this covenant the Lord will remember forever, by which He hath declared unto His people the virtue of His works."[3] You the reader see how Arnobius asserts that the Lord gave us the food of His Body.

Irenaeus also confesses this faith saying: "When, therefore, the mingled cup and the [man-]made bread receives the Word of God, and the Eucharist of the Blood and the Body of Christ is made, from which things the substance of our flesh is increased and supported, how can they affirm that the flesh is incapable of receiving the gift of God, which is life eternal, which [flesh] is nourished from the Body and Blood of the Lord, and is a member of Him?—even as Blessed Paul declares in his Epistle to the Ephesians, that 'we are members of his body, of his flesh, and of his bones.' (Eph. 5, 30). He does not speak these words of some spiritual and invisible man, for 'a spirit hath not flesh and bones' (Lk. 24, 39); but [he refers to] that dispensation [by which the Lord became] an actual man, consisting of flesh, and nerves, and bones—that [flesh] which is nourished by the cup which is His Blood, and receives increase from the bread which is His Body."[4] [Abbot Johannes] Trithemius in his book, *De scriptoribus ecclesiasticis* teaches that Irenaeus was a martyr,[5] and Jerome testifies that he was a disciple of the martyr Polycarp,[6] and who also asserts that the same martyr Polycarp was a disciple of John the Evangelist[7]: from which it is evident that this Irenaeus was taught by Christ's Apostle by means of Polycarp. I said these things so that his testimony many be more convincing.

Finally, Ignatius, whom I believe was a disciple of Christ, or at least a contemporary of the Apostles, in a letter to the Romans says the following: "I desire the bread of God, the heavenly bread, the bread of life, which is the Flesh of Jesus Christ, the Son of God, who became

---

[1] *Historia evangelica*, bk. 4, n. 448-454 (PL 19, 316A-317A). Juventus was a native of Spain and has left us the Life of Christ in hexameter verse. He flourished about the year 329, under Constantine the Great.
Haec ubi dicta dedit, palmis sibi frangere panem.
Divisumque dehinc tradit sancteque precatus
Discipulos docuit, proprium sic edere corpus.
Hinc calicem sumit Dominus vinoque repletum
Gratis sanctificat verbis potumque ministrat,
Edocuitque, suum se divisisse cruorem,
Atque ait: "Hic sanguis populi delicta redemit;
Hoc potate meum. Nam veris credite dictis."

[2] Arnobius was a Christian apologist who flourished during the reign of Diocletian (284-305 A.D.).

[3] *Commentarii in Psalmos* (PL 53, 497C).

[4] *Against the Heresies*, bk. 5, c. 2, n. 3 (PG 7, 1125-1127).

[5] Folio 7v.

[6] *Liber de viris illustribus*, c. 35 (PL 23, 649B).

[7] *Ibid.* c. 17 (PL 23, 635B).

afterwards of the seed of David and Abraham; and I desire the drink of God, namely His Blood, which is incorruptible love and eternal life."[1]

I have prudently omitted very many other authors, and they are illustrious ones, whose testimonies could also support us, lest I burden the reader, and I would seem to have forgotten the brevity (which I promised at the beginning of this work). We shall still cite them afterwards against other errors about the Eucharist: when you read them, I ask you, the reader, to notice that many things in them serve this argument. These testimonies of such men certainly ought to suffice, even if there were no citations of Scripture, to confirm any point of faith, even though it be contrary to the mind of Oecolampadius. But since so many illustrious men are contrary to Oecolampadius, how is it that he does not fear being against to so many renown men, nay to stretch forth his neck against the whole Church? That certainly applies to him which Cyril says concerning the disputing Jews who were also saying: "How can this man give us his flesh to eat?" (Jn. 6, 53). For Cyril [of Alexandria] says the following: "They were perplexed: they senselessly repeat 'How' to God, as though they knew not that it is a word replete with all blasphemy. For the power of accomplishing all things without toil belongs to God, but they, being 'sensual' men, as Blessed Paul says, 'perceived not the things that are of the Spirit of God,' but the so dread Mystery seems 'foolishness' (I Cor. 2, 14) to them."[2] Thus in this way such a magnificent mystery seems a kind of foolishness to Oecolampadius (as is evident), and he neither understands what is concealed within nor considers that nothing is impossible with God. Now why he does not understand is clear: because, as Paul bears witness, "The sensual man perceiveth not these things that are of God" (I Cor. 2, 14).

But who is more sensual than Oecolampadius, whose works of the flesh are manifest? For when he was a monk of the Order of Saint Bridget, having rejected continency which he vowed in monasticism, he married a wife: yet although he was of the age,[3] as it were to remain unmarried in the world, he ought to have abstained from having a wife, by having imitating Sara, who said: "I am grown old," and "shall I give myself to pleasure?" (Gen. 18, 12). But perhaps he was one of those old men who burned with concupiscence towards Susanna.

Otherwise, in order to entirely complete the matter, it remains that we cite the councils which were celebrated in confirmation of this matter. Firstly, the third of those four councils which Blessed Gregory states should be venerated "like the four Gospels," which is, namely, the First Council of Ephesus with two hundred bishops, in which Cyril, Bishop of Alexandria, presided representing the Supreme Pontiff, in a letter sent by the whole council to the heretic Nestorius, Bishop of Constantinople, concerning whose teaching it was discussing, who was saying that there are two persons in Christ, one of God and the other of a man, as we have already discussed concerning this elsewhere, it is said thus: "So we proceed to the mystical thanksgivings and are sanctified having partaken of the holy Flesh [*corpus*] and Precious Blood of Christ, the Savior of us all. This we receive not as ordinary flesh, Heaven forbid, nor as that of a man who has been made holy and joined to the Word by union of honor, or who had a Divine indwelling, but as truly the life-giving and real Flesh of the Word [*ut vere vivificatricem et ipsius Verbi propriam factam.*]. For being Life by nature as God, when He became one with His own Flesh, He made it also to be life-giving, as also He said to us: 'Amen, amen I say unto you: Except you eat the flesh of the Son of man, and drink his blood.' For we must not think that it is the flesh of a man like us (for how can the flesh of man be life-giving by its own nature?), but as being made the true Flesh [*vere proprium eius factam*] of the One Who for our sake became the Son of man and was called so."[4] By which decree all

---

[1] C. 7 (PG 5, 694B).
[2] *Commentarium in Evangelium Joannis*, bk. 4 (PG 73, 574A-B).
[3] Oecolampadius married a twenty-four year old widow when he was forty-five years old.
[4] *Third letter of Cyril to Nestorius*.

the heretics who deny that Christ's real Flesh and real Blood are contained in the Eucharist, howsoever they deny it, are here clearly rejected.

But when Oecolampadius saw this, when considering what great arrogance it is to directly oppose a whole council, he took refuge in this, namely he says that this decree is not from the acts in the council, but is in a letter from Cyril sent to Nestorius. Now the falsity of this is clearly proved from the title of the same letter. For the inscription of the letter is the following: "To the most reverend and God-loving fellow-minister Nestorius, Cyril and the synod assembled in Alexandria" [Ephesus is found in the text here in place of Alexandria].[1] From this inscription of the letter it is clearly gathered that the letter was sent to Nestorius from the whole council: which is why is it included in that council, to be accepted as part of its acts.

Several centuries later Leo IX, as we said, celebrated the Synod of Vercelli, in which the impious teaching of Berengarius was condemned. Next under Victor II another council was celebrated in Tours with Hildebrand, cardinal deacon of the Roman Church, presiding: in which council the teaching of Berengarius was rejected as by the whole council, as also by Berengarius himself.[2] Finally a Roman council under Nicholas II with one hundred thirteen bishops was convened for this reason, namely it was ascertained that Berengarius had returned to his vomit, in which again Berengarius accepting the decision of the council, renounced his teaching. We do not have the acts of these councils due to the negligence of the writers. For in that book of councils which was published in Paris, from the Fifth Council of Constantinople until the Council of Constance no other council is put in between: during which interval of time it is evident that there were many councils celebrated, and they were not of little importance. Thus, after the councils of Vercelli, Tours and Rome, I find nothing else besides the abjuration which was presented by the Roman Council to Berengarius, so that he would read it before the whole assembly, and acknowledge it in this way. Which abjuration is in fact found in the book of the *Decretals*.[3] Finally, after all these councils, the Council of Constance when listing the errors of John Wycliffe, it puts this one in third place with these words: "In the same sacrament Christ is not identically and really with His own bodily presence."[4]

Next the Council of Trent celebrated under Julius III says these words: "First of all the holy Synod teaches and openly and simply professes that in the nourishing Sacrament of the Holy Eucharist after the consecration of the bread and wine our Lord Jesus Christ, true God and man, is truly, really, and substantially contained under the species of those sensible things. For these things are not mutually contradictory, that Our Savior Himself is always seated at the right hand of the Father in Heaven according to the natural mode of existing, and yet that in many other places sacramentally He is present to us in His own substance by that manner of existence which, although we can scarcely express it in words, yet we can, however, by our understanding illuminated by faith, conceive to be possible to God, and which we ought most steadfastly to believe. For thus all our forefathers, as many as were in the true Church of Christ, who have discussed this most holy Sacrament, have most openly professed that Our Redeemer instituted this so wonderful a Sacrament at the Last Supper, when after the blessing of the bread and wine He testified in clear and definite words that He gave them His own

---

[1] *Epistola* 17 (PG 77, 106-122). The 12 anathemas and the preceding explanatory letter, which had been produced by Cyril and the synod of Alexandria in 430 and sent to Nestorius, were read at Ephesus and included in the proceedings.

[2] Berengarius signed a profession of faith at the Council of Tours wherein he confessed that after consecration the bread and wine are truly the Body and Blood of Christ.

[3] P. 2 (De consecratione), dist. 2, c. 42 (*Ego Berengarius*) (PL 187, 1750A-1751A).

[4] Dz. 583.

Body and His own Blood; and those words which are recorded by the holy Evangelists,[1] and afterwards repeated by St. Paul[2] since they contain within themselves that proper and very clear meaning in which they were understood by the Fathers, it is a most disgraceful thing for some contentious and wicked men to distort into fictitious and imaginary figures of speech, by which the real nature of the Flesh and Blood of Christ is denied, contrary to the universal sense of the Church, which, recognizing with an ever grateful and recollecting mind this most excellent benefit of Christ, as the pillar and ground of truth,[3] has detested these falsehoods, devised by impious men, as satanical."[4] But lest any exceedingly audacious person think that he can contradict this teaching with impunity, the Council pronounced a canon *latae sententiae* against the contradictors of this sort, the words of which are those which follow: "If anyone denies that in the sacrament of the most holy Eucharist there are truly, really, and substantially contained the body and blood together with the soul and divinity of our Lord Jesus Christ, and therefore the whole Christ, but shall say that He is in it as by a sign or figure, or force, let him be anathema."[5]

The first one of old to write against this impious heresy was Lanfranc, Archbishop of Canterbury, when Berengarius was defending it.[6] After him Guitmund, a monk and afterwards Bishop of Aversa, [also wrote against this heresy].[7] At the same time the scholar Alger [of Liège], a monk from the monastery of Cluny [also wrote against this heresy].[8] A certain Adelmann, well educated in Liège and afterwards Bishop of Brescia, also wrote against him, Johannes Trithemius bearing witness,[9] who had been a fellow student of the same Berengarius.[10] A certain Hildebert [von Lavardin], Bishop of Le Mans and afterwards Archbishop of Tours also wrote against him,[11] as Trithemius likewise bears witness in the book, *De scriptoribus ecclesiasticis*.[12] I confess that I have not seen the last two works, but I have read the works of the other authors. After all these men in our time Bishop John [Fisher] of Rochester, a man no less renowned for his life than for his teaching, who rightly can be compared with those more ancient writers, wrote at much greater length and more intelligently against Oecolampadius.[13] But if many bishops would maintain the churches under their governance as he does, we would not so weep over the churches falling into error as we now (alas) lament. I hope, with God's help, if one were to happen be doubtful, you may be strengthened, and you may forsake all scruples being grounded on the firmest rock of faith. Josse van Clichtove also wrote

---

[1] Mt. 26, 26 ff.; Mk. 14, 22; Lk. 22, 19 ff.

[2] I Cor. 11, 23 ff.

[3] I Tim. 3, 15.

[4] Sess. 13, c. 1 (Dz. 874).

[5] Canon 1 (Dz. 883).

[6] *On the Body and Blood of the Lord* (*The Fathers of the Church: Mediaeval Continuation* (Washington D.C., Catholic University of America Press, 2009), vol. 10, pp. 29-90). PL 150, 407-442.

[7] *On the Truth of the Body and Blood of Christ in the Eucharist* (*Ibid.*), pp. 91-218 (PL 149, 1427-1494).

[8] *De sacramento corporis et sanguinis Domini*, (PL 180, 739-854). The author here mistakenly says that Alger of Cluny was a monk from Corbi in Saxony. This error is corrected by Jean François in *Bibliotheque Generale Des Ecrivains De L'Ordre De Saint Benoit* (*La Societe Typographique*, 1777), vol. 1, p. 37.

[9] *De scriptoribus ecclesiasticis* (Bertholdo Rembolt, 1512), fol. 74r.

[10] *Ad Berengarium epistola* (PL 143, 1289-1296).

[11] *Carmina miscellanea*, XL. Epitaphium Berengarii (PL 171, 1396-1397).

[12] Fol. 79r.

[13] *De Veritate Corporis et Sanguinis Christi in Eucharistia* (Cologne, Petrus Quentell, 1527).

EUCHARISTIA

against the same Oecolampadius,[1] others I have not seen, although I hear that many others have written [against him].

A **fifth heresy** arose about this matter, which asserts that in the Eucharist after the consecration has been done the same bread remains which was there before the consecration. But this heresy is divided into two factions. For some said that the bread exists at the same time with the Eucharist, and they do not rave any further.[2] The leader of such men was John Wycliffe, of whom we have already often made mention. But others increasing the madness so assert that the bread is there, because they assert that the bread is Christ's Body.[3] Now this heresy has been recently invented, namely coming forth from Martin Luther, who says that these statements are true: the bread is Christ's Body and the wine is Christ's Blood. Between these two men, namely Wycliffe and Luther, they agree on this, that both admit that after the consecration the bread remains in existence: they were instigated by this reasoning, namely that this Sacrament is often called bread in the New Testament, such as in the Acts of the Apostles it is said: "And on the first day of the week, when we were assembled to break bread, Paul discoursed with them, being to depart on the morrow" (20, 7). And in the First Epistle to the Corinthians it is said: "The bread, which we break, is it not the partaking of the body of the Lord? For we, being many, are one bread, one body, all that partake of one bread" (10, 16-17). And again in the same epistle it is said: "For as often as you shall eat this bread, and drink the chalice, you shall shew the death of the Lord, until he come" (11, 26).

There is a dispute between them, however, about this matter, because Wycliffe does not accept that the bread which existed before the consecration can be called Christ's Body, Luther, on the other hand, assents to this, asserting that these things are true, namely, the bread is Christ's Body and the wine is Christ's Blood: motivated by the following reasoning, which is so convincing to him that no one could object to it.[4] "Scripture," he says, "... is not to be taken otherwise then in its proper and grammatical sense; lest occasion should be given to the adversaries to undervalue the whole Scriptures. But," says he, "the Divine words are forced, if that which Christ called bread, be taken for the accidents of bread; and what He called wine, for the form of wine. Therefore, by all means, the true bread," says he, "and true wine remain upon the altar, lest violence be done to Christ's words, if the species be taken for the substance." The Evangelists (he says) never mentioned "transubstantiation." But (he says) this word is something recently invented, in the last three hundred years and not before. Therefore, Luther says that the words of consecration ought to be understood as follows: "This," meaning this bread, "is My Body." "This," meaning this wine, "is My Blood." Notice on what trickeries Luther relies to seduce as many knowledgeable men as there are in the Church. Perhaps he thinks that we are all still babes in cribs, such that he can delude us with similar ditties.

One ought to fight against all these men with one and same sword. For once we shall have shown that when the consecration has been made no bread remains, at the same time it will also be apparent that this statement, namely that the bread is Christ's Body, is nowise true. Firstly, then, let us show that this interpretation of Luther is very far removed from the literal meaning: which can even be clearly proved from the fact that since the article, or demonstrative pronoun, *hoc*, is neuter [in Latin], it can nowise refer to bread [*panis*], which is masculine. Perhaps you will say that it is used substantively there, as a neuter adjective, according to the grammatical rule that a neuter adjective can substitute substantively: and so you will say that this is the meaning: "This," meaning this thing (pointing to the bread), "is My Body."

---

[1] *De Sacramento Eucharistiae contra Oecolampadium* (Paris, Quentel, 1526).
[2] This heretical doctrine is called consubstantiation.
[3] This heresy is properly called impanation.
[4] *The Babylonian Captivity of the Church*, Prelude.

Let us now come to the words of the chalice, in which words you will not be able to find any such subterfuge. For it is said there: "This [*hic*] is My Blood." You see how the article or demonstrative pronoun used there is masculine, but since the word wine [*vinum*] is neuter, how can it be that the pronoun *hic* would refer to wine, which is neuter? For if He had said, *Hoc est sanguis meum*, He would have given the occasion of thinking that the wine remains there. But since He says, "This [*Hic*] is My Blood," who does not see that the masculine article can nowise be referred to the wine, which is neuter? Is this the grammar, O Luther, according to which you say that God's words ought to be interpreted according to the bare words? For this interpretation is so bare that it completely strips the literal sense of its true meaning, and leaves nothing of the true meaning in the literal sense.

But if you call us back to the Greek language, or the source of the New Testament, thinking that perhaps this argumentation can nowise stand, you are deceived. For the demonstrative pronouns used in the Greek are both neuter. For the words by which the Body is consecrated are: τοῦτό ἐστιν τὸ σῶμά μου. And the words whereby the Blood is consecrated are: τοῦτο γάρ ἐστιν τὸ αἷμά μου. You see that both pronouns are neuter, namely τοῦτο. The Greek noun meaning body is τὸ σῶμά, and the noun meaning blood is τὸ αἷμά. From which it is evident that in both cases that the demonstrative pronoun must agree with the following noun, but nowise ought to be referred to the preceding noun: for since the noun used there for bread is ἄρτος, which is evidently masculine, it is proved that the neuter pronoun can nowise be referred to the bread. And wine in Greek is οἶνος, which is also evidently masculine. We thus conclude that Christ's words nowise support Luther, nay they rather are completely opposed to him. In fact, He could not have said more explicitly that nothing remains therein of the bread than when He said: "This is My Body." For He did not say, "Here [*hic*]," meaning in this place, "is My Body": or "With this which you see, is My Body," as though He were at the same time with the bread or in the bread, but He said, "This is My Body," indicating most clearly (so that He would stop the mouths of the heretics) that this whole thing which He was holding up in His hand is His Body.

Otherwise so that the matter may be clearer, and no room may be left for equivocating, let us cite the words of the Evangelists. For Matthew says the following: "And whilst they were at supper, Jesus took bread, and blessed, and broke: and gave to his disciples, and said: Take ye, and eat. This is my body. And taking the chalice, he gave thanks, and gave to them, saying: Drink ye all of this. For this is my blood of the new testament, which shall be shed for many unto remission of sins" (26, 26-28). But Mark recounts as follows: "And whilst they were eating, Jesus took bread; and blessing, broke, and gave to them, and said: Take ye. This is my body. And having taken the chalice, giving thanks, he gave it to them. And they all drank of it. And he said to them: This is my blood of the new testament, which shall be shed for many" (14, 22-24). These, however, are the words of Luke: "And taking bread, he gave thanks, and brake; and gave to them, saying: This is my body, which is given for you. Do this for a commemoration of me. In like manner the chalice also, after he had supped, saying: This is the chalice, the new testament in my blood, which shall be shed for you" (22, 19-20). From all these words of the Evangelists it is evident that there is no verse in which after the consecration has been made the Sacrament is called bread or wine, but only Body or Blood. For if Christ had not made any change in the bread He took up, and had given it to the disciples as He had taken it up, nowise transformed, it would rightly be said that He gave mere bread to the disciples. But since before He gave it to the disciples, He converted it into Flesh: it can nowise be said that the bread that He took up into His hands, He gave to the disciples, but He instead gave His Body into which He had converted the bread.

But Luther objects saying the following: "The Evangelists relate that Christ took up bread into His hands. And we likewise acknowledge this same thing."[1] But when the Apostles receive, you no longer hear It called bread, but His Body: nor wine, but Blood. Now what Luther and his imitators say, namely that this marvelous Sacrament can be called bread, and hence they conclude that either bread is there, or bread itself is Christ's Body, they do not conclude correctly. For Sacred Scripture typically calls what can be eaten in any way "bread": wherefore as Ecclesiasticus says: "The chief thing for man's life is water and bread" (29, 27). In this way the manna was called bread, as the Prophet wrote: "He had given them the bread of heaven" (Ps. 77, 24), "having in it all that is delicious" (Wis. 16, 20). Notice that Scripture calls bread what it elsewhere said is "like coriander seed."[2] In this way also the Son of God according to the substance of His Divinity was called bread, because when spiritually eaten it inwardly refreshes. For so He says: "I am the living bread which came down from heaven" (Jn. 6, 41). Which words (as we pointed out above[3]) nowise ought to be referred to His Body, but to the substance of His Divinity, because this Divinity descended from Heaven, but not His Body. Similarly, we acknowledge that Christ's Body is called bread in a general sense, namely because being covered with the appearance of bread it is eaten by us unto the spiritual refreshment of the inward man.

We can also give another reason why it is so-called, and the reason is not completely unsuited, but rather in conformity to the common manner of speech, and also to Sacred Scripture itself. In fact, it is a very common way of speaking, such that we call something by the name whereby a thing is named by what produced it. For if you gave wine to someone, which he afterwards either artificially or naturally turned into vinegar, which he again gives to you to be eaten as some other thing, he might say to you, and not incorrectly, "Here is your wine which you gave me": in fact by this expression he is indicating that the vinegar originated from wine that was given, or the wine that has turned into vinegar. Wherefore it happened that the vinegar now also enjoys the name of wine, because it was produced from its matter: even though the vinegar cannot truly and according to the proper meaning of the word be called wine, because the things are different in species and substance.

And Sacred Writ does not despise this manner of speaking. See what is said in Exodus: "And Aaron took the rod before Pharao, and his servants, and it was turned into a serpent. And Pharao called the wise men and the magicians: and they also by Egyptian enchantments and certain secrets did in like manner. And they everyone cast down their rods, and they were turned into serpents: but Aaron's rod devoured their rods" (7, 10-12). Now here you see that Aaron's rod turned into a serpent, and after that transformation it is again called a rod, although it is far from being a rod. For it also devoured two other rods, which nowise befits a rod. Yet it is called a rod after that transformation, because that serpent was made by God from that matter. In this way also in the Most Holy Eucharist, when the bread is turned into Christ's Body, since it is that from which it turned into that Body, [the Body] may be called by same name by which the bread transformed into the Body was called, not because It is bread, but because It took that place of the bread, and thus keeps the name of the bygone bread.

But about this so many arguments were not necessary, since the Church has already put an end to this dispute. But we have done this, so that we may reply to the scoffing of the heretics and may show the reason of that faith which is in us.[4] The Council of Constance when listing

---

[1] "Since the Evangelists write clearly that Christ took bread and blessed it, and since the book of Acts and the Apostle Paul also call it bread, real bread and real wine must be understood" (*The Babylonian Captivity of the Church*, Prelude).

[2] Ex. 16, 31 and Num. 11, 7.

[3] Cf. the previous heresy in the quotation of Saint Ambrose's book, *On the Sacraments*.

[4] Cf. I Pet. 3, 15.

the forty-five errors of John Wycliffe, put this one in the first place, in these words: "In the sacrament of the altar the material substance of bread and likewise the material substance of wine remain."[1] Which error, along with the forty-four other, the council condemns all together *lata sententia*.

But even if this sufficiently shows that the bread does not remain, still it does not show that the bread is transubstantiated into Christ's Body, which Luther denies and ridicules saying that this transubstantiation is recently invented, and is no older than three hundred years. If the dispute is about the word alone, the matter is completely undeserving that we fight like gladiators for it, and there is simply unanimity between us about this matter. The reality is, however, that the bread does not remain after the consecration, and it is converted into Christ's Body. But whether one were to call that conversion transubstantiation, or transmutation, or conversion, I do not much care, provided one acknowledges that the bread does not remain after the consecration and it is turned into Christ's Body. The first of these we have already shown both from other proofs and from the definition of the Council of Constance. It remains to show the other, namely that the bread is turned into Christ's Body, and that it is not a recent innovation of scholastic theologians, namely within the last three hundred years, as Luther says. For which matter I will cite many testimonies of the holy Fathers: all which testimonies, if you the reader considers well, also clearly fight against the aforesaid heresy of Berengarius and Oecolampadius.

First of them all I bring forth [Hervé de Bourg-Dieu[2]], a man truly renown for holiness as well as for learning, whom Luther cannot say, as he is accustomed to do, that he is within the last three hundred years: and from this man I will gradually proceed by going back to other older men, until those who lived close to the times of the Apostles. Therefore this [Hervé de Bourg-Dieu] when expounding the passage from the First Epistle to the Corinthians, "This chalice is the new testament in my blood" (11, 25), says these words: "We have obtained a new testament in Christ's Blood, by which we may arrive at a new inheritance, because the Blood is a witness of the Divine benefit. Hence we receive His Sacraments for the protection of our bodies and souls, because His Flesh was offered for the salvation of our bodies: but His Blood was shed for our souls, so that both substances of our may receive the inheritance of eternal life."[3]

Haymo [of Auxerre], a man also illustrious among theologians, born seven hundred years ago, when expounding the passage from the First Epistle to the Corinthians, "For we, being many, are one bread, one body" (10, 17), says these words: "The Body which the Word of God the Father assumed in the virginal womb in the unity of His Person, and the bread which is consecrated in the Church, are one Body of Christ. For the fulness of the Divinity which was in Him, also fills this Bread, and the Word's Divinity Itself, which fills Heaven and earth and all things that are in them, the same [Divinity] fills Christ's Body, which is consecrated by many priests throughout the whole world, and makes Christ's Body to be one: and just as that Bread and Blood are changed into Christ's Body, so all men who worthily eat It in the Church, are one Body of Christ, as He Himself says: 'He that eateth my flesh, and drinketh my blood, abideth in me, and I in him'" (Jn. 6, 57).

Theophylactus when expounding the passage of John, "The bread which I shall give is My flesh" (6, 52), says the following: "Note well, however, that the bread which we eat in the Mysteries is not merely a figure of the Lord's Flesh but is rather the very Flesh of the Lord. For He did not say, 'The bread which I will give is a figure of My Flesh,' but 'It is My Flesh.'

---

[1] Sess. 8 (Dz. 581).

[2] The text ascribes this citation to Saint Anselm of Canterbury, but it is the work of Hervé, monk of Bourg-Dieu (c. 1080–1150 A.D.).

[3] *Commentaria in epistolas divi Pauli* (PL 181, 934D).

EUCHARISTIA

For that bread by the mystic blessing and coming of the Holy Ghost, with the secret words is transformed into the Flesh of the Lord. And lest it should trouble any man, that the bread is to be believed Flesh: when our Lord walked in the flesh, and took food of bread, that bread that was eaten was changed into His Body, and was made like unto His holy Flesh and it went unto the increasing and sustentation after the condition of the nature of man. Therefore, now also the bread is changed into the Flesh of Our Lord."[1] Nothing could be said more clearly than those words. For he said that the bread is "transformed into the Flesh," and again he says "changed into flesh": obviously calling what recent theologians have named "transubstantiation," "transformation."

Isidore [of Seville] supports the same belief, saying the following: "For 'the bread that we break' (I Cor. 10, 16) is the Body of Christ Who says: 'I am the living bread' (Jn. 6, 51) etc.; and the wine is His Blood, and this is what is written: 'I am the true vine' (Jn. 15, 1). The bread, because it nourishes and strengthens our bodies, is therefore called the Body of Christ; and the wine, because it makes blood in our flesh, is called the Blood of Christ. Now these two things are visible, but, being sanctified by the Holy Ghost, they become the Sacrament of God's Body."[2] Isidore teaches clearly enough transubstantiation, when he says that the bread and wine become Christ's Body. Now that which he said, namely that one ought to believe that the Bread is Flesh, he said in the same way as we expounded above, namely that the bread is turned into Flesh, that is to say, the name of the previous thing has been kept for the reality of the latter thing.

Damascus also said this same belief, although with different words, for he says the following: "The Body which is born of the Holy Virgin is in truth Body united with Divinity, not that the Body which was received up into the heavens descends, but that the bread itself and the wine are changed into God's Body and Blood. But if you enquire how this happens, it is enough for you to learn that it was through the Holy Ghost, just as the Lord took on Himself Flesh that subsisted in Him and was born of the Holy Mother of God through the Spirit. And we know nothing further save that God's word is true and powerful and is omnipotent, but the manner of this cannot be searched out. But one can put it well thus, that just as in nature the bread by the eating and the wine and the water by the drinking are changed into the body and blood of the eater and drinker, and do not become a different body from the former one, so the bread of the table and the wine and water are supernaturally changed by the invocation and presence of the Holy Ghost into the Body and Blood of Christ, and are not two but one and the same."[3] You see here that the transformation of bread into the Body and of wine into the Blood is mentioned three times. Now that you cannot refer to the bread and the Body, what he said at the end: "are not two but one and the same," because they are not two things, but one and the same, the above words show, in order that you may not understand any such thing. For in fact he had said above that the body which is nourished by food, and the food is changed into it, is not another body different from that the one which existed before eating the food. So likewise, the bread in the Eucharist is not converted into another body of Christ, different from that which He had before the consecration, namely so that there are not two bodies, one which was before the consecration, and another into which the bread was transformed after the consecration was done. Now Luther cannot call this Damascene recent, unless perhaps Luther considers him to be such, such that those thousand years are like a yesterday which pasted: because he lived during the time of Emperor [Leo the Isaurian] from whom to our present time [eight hundred] or more years have elapsed.[4]

---

[1] *Enarratio in Evangelium S. Joannis* (PG 123, 1307C).

[2] *De Ecclesiasticis officiis*, Bk. 1, c. 18, n. 3 (PL 83, 755A-B).

[3] *Exposition of the Orthodox Faith*, bk. 4, c. 13 (PG 94, 1143A-1146B).

[4] Trithemius is cited here but he erroneously said that Saint John Damascene lived at the time of

Augustine supports this belief saying the following: "In the appearances of bread and wine, which we see, we honor invisible things, that is, his flesh and blood. We do not regard these two species the same as we did before the consecration, since with faith we acknowledge that before the consecration they were bread and wine which nature formed, but after consecration they are really the flesh and blood of Christ which the blessing has consecrated."[1]

In which words he clearly indicates that the bread does not remain earthly after the consecration has been done. For two times, he distinguishes things that are mutually opposed to each other, in which he shows there are different conditions of the things, one before the consecration, and the other after the consecration. In the first time there is only bread without Christ's Body, in the second, he says that there is only Christ's Body, and not the bread.

Ambrose clearly teaches this belief, saying the following: "[You may say, perhaps,] 'My bread is ordinary bread.' But that bread is bread before the words of the Sacraments; when consecration has been added, from bread it becomes the Flesh of Christ. Let us therefore prove this. How can that which is bread be the Body of Christ? By consecration. But in what words and in whose speech is the consecration? Those of the Lord Jesus. For all the other things which are said in the earlier parts of the service are said by the priest—praises are offered to God, prayer is asked for the people, for kings, and others; when it comes to the consecration of the venerable Sacrament, the priest no longer uses his own language, but he uses the speech of Christ. Therefore, the word of Christ consecrates this Sacrament. What is the word of Christ? That, to be sure, whereby all things are made. The Lord commanded, and the heavens were made; the Lord commanded, and the earth was made; the Lord commanded, and the seas were made; the Lord commanded, and every creature was produced. Do you see, then, how effective is the word of Christ? If, therefore, there is such power in the word of the Lord Jesus, that the things which were not, began to be, how much more is it effective, that the things which were, should be changed into something else?"[2] And shortly afterwards in the same book He again says: "Before it is consecrated, it is bread, but when the words of Christ have been added, it is the Body of Christ. Therefore, hear Him saying: 'Take ye, and eat. This is my body' (Mt. 26, 26). And before the words of Christ it is a chalice full of wine and water. When the words of Christ have operated then and there it is made to be the Blood of Christ which redeemed the people. Therefore, see in how many ways the word of Christ is mighty to change all things."[3] Nothing clearer can be desired than these words. For he said that Christ's Flesh came to be out of the bread, and the bread was changed and converted into Christ's Body. Now how often when one thing becomes something else, the first thing does not remain in existence from which the latter thing was made. As for example, when from wood fire is made, the wood does not remain from which the fire was made. And it happens likewise in everything from which something else comes to be.

"Theodosius" the Great (*De scriptoribus ecclesiasticis*, fol. 23v.), but the author assumes that he is "Theodosius the Elder." The text has been here corrected accordingly.

[1] Cf. Lanfranc, *De corpore et sanguine Domini*, c. 13 (PL 150, 423C); Gratian, *Concordia discordantium canonum*, dist. 2, c. 41 (PL 187, 1749C). The *Decretals* here cite Prosper of Aquitane's *Liber sententiarum*, but "in 1926, M. Lepin traced the process by which Lanfranc's *De Corpore et Sanguine Domini* (PL 150,421-425), was chopped up, rearranged, abridged and entered eucharistic controversy for 500 years primarily, but not exclusively, as Augustine's *Sentences* of Prosper" (Wayne J. Hankey, "*Magis...Pro Nostra Sentencia*"..., *Augustiniana*, 45, fasc. 3-4 (1995), p. 7).

[2] *On the Sacraments*, bk. 4, c. 4, n. 14-15 (PL 16, 439B-441A). The Roman edition omits the words, *ut sint quae erant et in aliud commutentur* which have thus been omitted in this translation, and the same reading was known to Lanfranc (Ambrose, *On the Mysteries and the Treatise on the Sacraments by an Unknown Author*, trans. T. Thompson, (New York: Macmillan, 1919), p. 111).

[3] *Ibid.*, c. 5, n. 23 (PL 16, 444A).

Basil the Great supports the same belief saying the following: "We beseech Thee, O Lord, that Thy Holy Ghost may come upon us and upon these offered gifts, and bless and sanctify them and make this same bread the precious Body and the wine the precious Blood of our Lord Savior Jesus Christ, which was shed for the life of the world."[1] In which words it is necessary to comment that which we commented on the words of Ambrose.

Gregory of Nyssa, the brother of this Basil, when expounding upon the subject of the food of manna given to the Fathers in the desert, under which figure he discusses the Eucharist, saying the following: "Thus He is this marvelous bread, which without sowing and reaping is also the Word. He changes His power in diverse ways to suit those who eat. For He knows not only to be bread, but also to become milk and Flesh, and greens and finally whatever is suitable and beneficial for the one receiving (as the Apostles says[2]), He Who prepared this table for us, is changed into that."[3] By which words He says once and again that the bread is changed into Flesh.

[Faustus, Bishop of Riez],[4] in a sermon on the Last Supper, beginning with the words, *Magnitudo coelestium*, says these words: "The heavenly Authority justly confirms [this Real Presence], for 'My flesh is meat indeed: and my blood is drink indeed' (Jn. 6, 56). Therefore, let every doubt of unbelief depart, seeing that the Giver of the Gift, is also the witness of its truth. For the invisible priest converts visible creatures into the substance of His Body and Blood by His word through a hidden power, saying: 'Take ye, and eat. This is my body' (Mt. 26, 26). Therefore, just as at the command of the directing Lord suddenly from nothing there existed the heights of the heavens, the depths of the waters, the vastness of the earth, so by equal power of the spiritual Sacraments, when the power of the Word commands, the effect follows."[5] It is very clearly established that nothing could be said more clearly than those words.

[Arnold, abbot of Bonneval[6]], says these words: "That bread which Our Lord offered to the disciples, changed not in outward appearance, but in nature, was made Flesh by the omnipotence of the Word; and as in the Person of Christ the humanity was plain while Godhead was latent; so the Divine essence infused itself in the visible Sacrament, that loving worship might in our religion attach itself to the Sacrament, and a purer access might lie open to the verity of Him Whose Body and Blood the Sacraments are, reaching even to a participation of Spirit; so that this union should attain not consubstantiality with Christ but the truest and most intimate union."[7] Nothing clearer could than these words could be said, since he says that the bread is "changed not in outward appearance, but in nature, was made Flesh by the omnipotence of the Word." For this change of the nature of bread whereby it is made Flesh we call a conversion or transubstantiation.

[Arnold of Bonneval] likewise teaches the same belief still more clearly saying the following: "Therefore the Lord gave at the table, in the which he made his last banquet with the Apostles, bread and wine with His own hands; but on the Cross He gave His Body to be wounded by the hands of the soldiers, that the pure truth and the true pureness, having been

---

[1] *Liturgiae, sive Missae sanctorum Patrum* (Antwerp, Sainctes, 1562), p. 44.

[2] Cf. Heb. 5, 12-14.

[3] *Mystica interpretatio vitae Moysis* (PG 44, 367C-D).

[4] The text wrongly attributes these words to Eusebius of Emesa. Cf. the note in Migne's Patrology (PL 30, 280C).

[5] Letter 38 or *Homilia de corpore et sanguine Christi*. (PL 30, 280D-281A).

[6] The text incorrectly attributes these words to the martyr, Saint Cyprian, as was commonly supposed at his time.

[7] *De cardinalibus operibus Christi usque ad Ascensum*, c. 6 (*De coena Domini, et prima institutione consummantis omnia sacramenta*) (PL 189, 1643D-1641A).

privately impressed in the Apostles, might set forth to the Gentiles, how wine and bread are His Flesh and Blood, and in what ways the causes agree with the effects, and diverse names or species are brought to one essence, and things signifying and things signified should be called by the same names."[1] In which words he not merely agrees with us concerning the conversion of bread into Christ's Body, and of wine into His Blood, but he also answers those objections which our adversaries usually raise against us on this subject. For he says that there is only one substance or essence which are called by two names, namely bread and flesh, and the name of the prior substance, which he calls the cause, is assigned to the latter substance, namely Christ's Body, which he calls the effect: and for this reason he says that Christ's Body is called "bread." If Arnold says that there is only one essence there, and there are two names for it such that according to him bread is not there, but only Christ's Body, because otherwise there would not be just one essence called by two names.

[Pseudo-] Pontian, pope and martyr, (also supports this belief), who lived during the time of the Emperor Alexander. For he says the following: "Now we have heard you concerning the priests of the Lord who help and assist against the snares of depraved men, know that in doing this they please God very much Who has received them unto Himself to serve Him, and He willed them to be so closely joined to Himself, that He would also accept the offerings of others through them, and He would forgive sins of others, and reconcile them to Himself. Also, they confect the Body of the Lord by their own mouths, and distribute it to the people."[2] In which words one ought to especially notice that he says that the priests confect Christ's Body. Now they cannot confect the Lord's Body unless by their words through God's secret power assisting therein, they change the bread into the Body and the wine into the Blood of Christ.

Irenaeus, who lived close to the time of the Apostles, says the following: "When, therefore, the mingled cup and the man-made bread receives the Word of God, and the Eucharist of the Blood and the Body of Christ is made, from which things the substance of our flesh is increased and supported, how can they affirm that the flesh is incapable of receiving the gift of God, which is life eternal, which [flesh] is nourished from the Body and Blood of the Lord, and is a member of Him?"[3]

[Psuedo-] Telesphorus, pope and martyr, in his decretal letter which he wrote to all the faithful of Christ when speaking about the celebration of Masses says these words: "Masses are nowise to be celebrated before the third hour of the day [i.e., nine to twelve o'clock in the morning], because it is read that at that hour Christ had ascended the Cross and the Holy Ghost had descended on the Apostles. And likewise, the Angelic hymn [the *Gloria*] is to be solemnly recited by the bishops when the Mass is solemnly celebrated according to the time and place. For they, who with their own proper mouth confect the Body of the Lord, must be heard, obeyed, and feared of all."[4] These are the words of Pope Telesphorus, who was slightly more ancient than Irenaeus: for the latter lived under Emperors Severus and Pertinax, but Telesphorus, as [Pseudo-] Damascus relates in his [*Liber*] *pontificalis*, lived under the Emperor Antoninus Pius.[5] And it is necessary to likewise comment on the words of this Telesphorus what we commented above on the words of Pontian. For if by the priest's words the bread is not changed into Christ's Body, there is no other way by which the priest can confect that

---

[1] *Ibid.*, c. 8 (*De unctione chrismatis et aliis sacramentis*) (PL 189, 1656A).

[2] *False Decretals of the Pseudo-Isidore* (PL 130, 141B).

[3] *Against the Heresies*, bk. 5, c. 2, n. 3 (PG 7, 1125-1126).

[4] *False Decretals of the Pseudo-Isidore* (PL 130, 105D).

[5] *The Book of the Popes* (New York, Columbia University Press, 1916), vol. 1, p. 12. In the Middle Ages it was supposed that Saint Jerome wrote this book at the request of Pope Damasus based on two letters of correspondence between the two which were later discovered to be forgeries. Cf. "Liber Pontificalis," *The Catholic Encyclopedia* (New York: Robert Appleton Company, 1908), vol. 9, p. 224.

Body. Because he does not beget it or produce it in any way, and does not have any efficient power on the substance of that Body. Nor would it be sufficient for this if he were to make that Body to descend from Heaven to earth by his words: because he moves something from one place to another, not on this account is it rightly said that he truly confects it.

Thus, these testimonies so numerous and of such great men ought to suffice to show to Luther that transubstantiation is not new, nor three hundred years old, as he asserts, but much older, namely having come forth from very beginnings of the Church. But if he contends that the word is new, we do not care about words, but about things: because to investigate the characteristics of words is the work of grammarians, not of theologians. For if the newness of a word for a thing is evident, this should not offend an orthodox believer, as [Vigilius, Bishop of Thapsus[1]] says in that disputation which he had against Arius.[2] For when new heresies arose the Church knew to formulate new words to express that reality more clearly and to avoid heresies. For since at the very beginning of the Church one would take the name from him, by whom he was baptized or by whom he was taught, such that they were saying: "I am of Paul; and I am of Apollo; and I am of Cephas" (I Cor. 3, 4), for this reason it happened to obviate this pestilence, that all men initiated to Christ were called by the general word, "Christians," which name history relates that it firstly originated in Antioch on this occasion.[3] Also the Church after seeing that heretics arose who were saying that the bread remains at the same time with the Body, to indicate that the bread nowise exists after the consecration, but is changed into the Body, coined the name of transubstantiation, with which she would label the reality, so that it would appear so clearly that no heresy would leave a trace behind it. Now whether she explains fittingly, ornately or refinedly, I do not care, provided she teaches faithfully and Catholically. And I do not see any reason why the Church would not have this authority of coining words, just as any government is reckoned to have, from their suitability and concordant formulation, the words receive their force of meaning.

But now it is necessary for us to show Church deciding this matter. The [IV] Lateran Council celebrated under Innocent III defines as follows: "One indeed is the universal Church of the faithful, outside which no one at all is saved,[4] in which the priest himself is the sacrifice, Jesus Christ, Whose Body and Blood are truly contained in the Sacrament of the altar under the species of bread and wine; the bread (changed) into His Body by the Divine power of transubstantiation, and the wine into the Blood, so that to accomplish the mystery of unity we ourselves receive from His (nature) what He Himself received from ours."[5] And these words are written in the book of the *Decretals* under the title, *De summa trinitate et fide catholica*, in the chapter, *Firmiter credimus*.[6]

Finally, the Council of Trent celebrated under Julian III teaches what must necessarily be thought about this matter, saying the following: "But since Christ, our Redeemer, has said that that is truly His own Body which He offered under the species of bread,[7] it has always been a matter of conviction in the Church of God, and now this holy Synod declares it again, that by the consecration of the bread and wine a conversion takes place of the whole substance of bread into the substance of the Body of Christ our Lord, and of the whole substance of the wine into the substance of His Blood. This conversion is appropriately and properly

---

[1] The text here incorrectly attributes this quotation to Saint Athanasius.
[2] *Dialogus contra Arianos*, bk. 1, c. 11 (PL 62, 162D-163A).
[3] Cf. Acts 11, 26.
[4] St. Cyprian: "There is no salvation outside the Church," (Ep. 73 to Jubaianus, n. 21 (PL 3, 1123B).
[5] Dz. 430.
[6] *Decretalium Gregorii papae* lib. 1, tit.1, c. 1.
[7] Cf. Mt. 26, 26 ff.; Mk. 14:22 ff.; Lk. 22, 19 ff.; I Cor. 11, 23 ff.

called transubstantiation by the Catholic Church."[1] And after having given the teaching by the Council, lest anyone teach or presume to think against it, it issued canons *latae sententiae* against presumptuous persons of this sort, the words of which are these: "If anyone says that in the sacred and holy Sacrament of the Eucharist there remains the substance of bread and wine together with the Body and Blood of our Lord Jesus Christ, and denies that wonderful and singular conversion of the whole substance of the bread into the Body, and of the entire substance of the wine into the Blood, the species of the bread and wine only remaining, a change which the Catholic Church most fittingly calls transubstantiation: let him be anathema."[2] In which words everything which seemed necessary for this matter are defined.

The **sixth heresy** is that which asserts that for the consecration of the chalice wine need not be used, but only water. This is the error of certain men who were called from the effect, Aquarians. For so Blessed Augustine calls them[3]: still he does not say why they do this. But from the Church definition just cited it is evident that they love sobriety to such an extent that for the sake of keeping it they also think that wine should be avoided for the consecration of the chalice. Who the author was of this heresy, and at what time did it begin, I could not find written by any author. Three Evangelists oppose this error, namely Matthew, Mark and Luke. For when relating how the Last Supper took place, they say that Christ gave the chalice the disciples, and so that they might show what liquid Christ gave the disciples to be drank in the chalice, they added the words of Christ saying: "I will not drink from henceforth of this fruit of the vine, until that day when I shall drink it with you new in the kingdom of my Father" (Mt. 26, 29). From which words it is shown clearly enough that the liquid which Christ gave to the disciples in the chalice to be drunk was the "fruit of the vine," that is to say, wine.

But if any pertinacious person perhaps contends that those words ought to be understood of some other fruit of the vine, this is rejected by the definitions of many councils, which assert that wine in the chalice is necessary for the consecration of the Blood, just as bread is necessary for the consecration of the Body. For the Lateran Council celebrated under Innocent III, among other things, defines: "One indeed is the universal Church of the faithful, outside which no one at all is saved, in which the priest himself is the sacrifice, Jesus Christ, Whose Body and blood are truly contained in the Sacrament of the altar under the species of bread and wine."[4] From which it is evident that the Blood is hidden under the appearances of wine, and not under the appearances of water. There are other councils moreover which state this, because they are to be again cited against the heresy next to be discussed, I omit them until then. Furthermore, signs ought to be somewhat similar to the things signified. But between water and blood there is no similarity, especially if we believe the scientists saying that pure water gives no nourishment. Thus, it was not suitable that water be instituted as a sign of blood.

There is a **seventh heresy** which is nearly diametrically opposed to the last one related. For this heresy puts wine into the chalice in such a way that it is not mixed with any water, and it asserts that none should be mixed in. This is an error of the Greeks, listed as the eleventh error by Guy the Carmelite among the errors of the Greeks.[5] This is also an error of the Armenians, which Guy lists as their twenty-fourth.[6]

For the refutation of this error one foundation must firstly be laid, namely that when a little water is mixed with wine, it is converted into the substance of wine, or remaining in its own

---

[1] Dz. 877.

[2] Canon 2 (Dz. 884).

[3] *De Haeresibus ad Quodvultdeum*, c. 64 (PL 42, 42).

[4] Dz. 430.

[5] *Summa de haeresibus et earum confutationibus*, f. 23 r&v.

[6] *Ibid.* f. 40r.

substance without conversion, since it is a small amount and less potent than wine, it does not change the wine from its nature. Now whether either one be truer, I am not so demented that I would dare to decide what the supreme pontiff, Innocent III, besides being a very learned man, dared not to decide, as appears in the book of the *Decretales*.[1] Thus, having laid the foundation, we will easily build on top our, that is to say, the Catholic, teaching. For this Sacrament is in memory of the Lord's death, Paul bearing witness, who says: "As often as you shall eat this bread, and drink the chalice, you shall shew the death of the Lord, until he come" (I Cor. 11, 26). But when Christ died (as it is written in John's Gospel) "One of the soldiers with a spear opened his side, and immediately there came out blood and water" (19, 34). Hence so that the Sacrament of the chalice would represent it as a perfect sign, it is necessary that water be mixed with wine in the chalice, which represents the water coming out from Christ's side at the same time with the Blood. Which even if it were not from Christ's institution, nevertheless the Church could have established this, since the water does not destroy (as we said) the wine with which it is mixed.

Now that this ought to be so done, and was so done from the very beginnings of the Church, we will teach thoroughly with many testimonies. Cyprian [of Carthage] says these words: "But when the water is mingled in the cup with wine, the people is made one with Christ, and the assembly of believers is associated and conjoined with Him in whom it believes; which association and conjunction of water and wine is so mingled in the Lord's cup, that that mixture cannot anymore be separated. Whence, moreover, nothing can separate the Church—that is, the people established in the Church, faithfully and firmly persevering in that which they have believed—from Christ, in such a way as to prevent their undivided love from always abiding and adhering. Thus, therefore, in consecrating the cup of the Lord, water alone cannot be offered, even as wine alone cannot be offered. For if any one offer wine only, the blood of Christ is dissociated from us; but if the water be alone, the people are dissociated from Christ; but when both are mingled, and are joined with one another by a close union, there is completed a spiritual and heavenly sacrament."[2]

[Pseudo-] Alexander I, who lived near to the time of the Apostles (for he ruled the Church under Emperor Aelius Hadrian[3]) says the following in his decretal letters, which is included in the first volume of the *Conciliorum [Oecumenicorum] Generalium[que Decreta]:* "In the offerings of the Sacraments which are offered to the Lord within the solemnities of Masses, let only bread and wine mixed with water be offered as a sacrifice. For either wine alone or water alone must not be offered (as we have received from the Fathers) in the chalice of the Lord, but both mixed, because it is read that both, that is, Blood and water, flowed from the side of Christ."[4] You see here a holy as well as learned pope, and one living near to the time of the Apostles, testifies that he so received from the Fathers, namely from the Apostles and their disciples.

And among the Eucharistic teachings found in the book, *De ecclesiasticis dogmatibus*, of [Gennadius of Massilia[5]] is the following: "In the Eucharist pure water ought not to be of-

---

[1] "You have asked (also) whether the water with the wine is changed into the blood. Regarding this, however, opinions among the scholastics vary... But among the opinions mentioned that is judged the more probable which asserts that the water with the wine is changed into blood." (*Decretalium Gregorii papae*, bk. 3, tit.41 (*De celebratione missarum*), c. 6 (*Cum Marthae*)).

[2] Letter 63, c. 13 (PL 4, 384A).

[3] "His pontificate is variously dated by critics, e.g. 106-115 (Duchesne) or 109-116 (Lightfoot)" ("Pope St. Alexander I," *The Catholic Encyclopedia* (New York: Robert Appleton Company, 1908), vol. 1, p. 285.

[4] *False Decretals of the Pseudo-Isidore* (PL 130, 93C). Cf. Dz 698.

[5] The author attributes this work rather to Saint Augustine, but was aware that others living at his time

fered, as some erroneously maintain under the pretext of sobriety, but wine mixed with water, both because wine was in the mystery of our Redemption, since [the Lord] said: 'I will not drink from henceforth of this fruit of the vine' (Mt. 26, 29): and water mixed [with wine ought to be offered], not [merely] because it was served after the [Last] Supper, but because water with Blood came forth from His side pieced by a lance, He showed wine extracted from the true vine of His Flesh mixed with water."[1]

Furthermore, in the collection which Blessed Martin, Bishop of Braga, made of the Eastern councils it is stated as follows: "It is not necessary that anything else be offered in the sanctuary besides bread, wine and water, which are blessed as a figure of Christ, because when He hung upon the Cross, water and Blood flowed from His Body. These three things are one in Christ Jesus, this Victim and Offering of God as an odor of sweetness."[2] Again the Third Synod of Carthage has the following in its decrees: "Nothing else may be offered in the Sacraments of the Body and Blood of the Lord, except what the Lord Himself handed down, that is, bread and wine mixed with water."[3] But even if there is no explicit text of Scripture, still it is certainly proved to me that I should think that Christ mixed water with the wine for the sake of sobriety. Solomon's words seem to allude to it: "Wisdom hath built herself a house, she hath hewn her out seven pillars. She hath slain her victims, mingled her wine, and set forth her table. She hath sent her maids to invite to the tower, and to the walls of the city: whosoever is a little one, let him come to me. And to the unwise she said: Come, eat my bread, and drink the wine which I have mingled for you" (Prov. 9, 1-5).

After the [III] Synod of Carthage [in 257 A.D.], the [Pseudo-] Sixth General Council [Council of Trullo[4]] specifically defined against the Armenians themselves in canon thirty-two by the following words: "Since it has come to our knowledge that in the region of Armenia they offer wine only on the Holy Table, those who celebrate, the unbloody sacrifice not mixing water with it, adducing, as authority thereof, John Chrysostom, a Doctor of the Church, who says in his interpretation of the Gospel according to St. Matthew… Now, lest on the point from this time forward they be held in ignorance, we make known the orthodox opinion of the Father. For since there was an ancient and wicked heresy of the *Hydroparastatae* [i.e., 'those who offer water'], who instead of wine used water in their sacrifice, this divine, confuting the detestable teaching of such a heresy, and showing that it is directly opposed to Apostolic tradition, asserted that which has just been quoted. For to his own church, where the pastoral administration had been given him, he ordered that water mixed with wine should be used at the unbloody sacrifice, so as to shew forth the mingling of the Blood and water which for the life of the whole world and for the Redemption of its sins, was poured forth from the precious side of Christ our Redeemer; and moreover in every church where spiritual light has shined this divinely given order is observed. For also James, the brother, according to the flesh, of Christ our God, to whom the throne of the church of Jerusalem first was entrusted, and Basil, the Archbishop of the church of Caesarea, whose glory has spread through all the world, when they delivered to us directions for the mystical sacrifice in writing, declared that the holy chalice is consecrated in the Divine liturgy with water and wine. And the holy Fathers who assembled at Carthage provided in these express terms: 'That in the holy Mysteries nothing besides the Body and Blood of the Lord be offered, as the Lord himself laid down, that is bread and wine mixed with water.' Therefore, if any bishop or presbyter shall not perform the

---

thought that Gennadius was its author, which is now certain.

[1] C. 75 (PL 58, 997D-998A).

[2] *Concilia Hispaniae*, c. 55 (PL 84, 582B).

[3] *Concila Africae*, c. 24 (PL 84, 192B).

[4] The Council in Trullo, also known as "The Quinisext Council," which was intended to be a continuation of the VI Council of Constantinople, but did not received the necessary papal approval.

holy action according to what has been handed down by the Apostles, and shall not offer the sacrifice with wine mixed with water, let him be deposed, as imperfectly shewing forth the mystery and innovating on the things which have been handed down."[1]

Finally, the Council of Florence celebrated under Eugene IV in the definition of the faith given to the Armenians, when speaking of the most holy Sacrament of the Eucharist, says these words: "The third is the Sacrament of the Eucharist, its matter is wheat bread and wine of grape, with which before consecration a very slight amount of water should be mixed. Now it is mixed with water because according to the testimonies of the holy Fathers and Doctors of the Church in a disputation made public long ago, it is the opinion that the Lord Himself instituted this Sacrament in wine mixed with water; and, moreover, this befits the representation of the Lord's Passion."[2] Therefore from all these [testimonies] it is evident, against the Greeks and Armenians, that water ought to be mixed with wine in the confection of the chalice.

There is an **eighth heresy** not opposing the substance of the Sacrament, but its power and efficacy: which asserts that this most holy food neither benefits nor harms anyone. The teachers and authors of this heresy were the Messalians, who are also called εὐχίται, that is "praying folk," or ἐνθουσιασταί, that is, "inspired" or "possessed," the history of whom we have related above.[3] The Armenians defend this same heresy, as Guy the Carmelite charges them, listing this as their twenty-third error.[4] But these latter are divided from the Messalians in that the Messalians assert that [the Sacrament] neither benefits nor harms. But the Armenians say that it only benefits the health of the body. Yet all these men with a concordant opinion assert that it brings no benefit to the soul. To whom it may be justly said that which the Lord says through the Prophet Malachias: "To you, O priests, that despise my name, and have said: Wherein have we despised thy name? You offer polluted bread upon my altar, and you say: Wherein have we polluted thee? In that you say: The table of the Lord is contemptible" (Mal. 1, 7). Does not one make the table of the Lord contemptable who say that it benefits no one? Now this assertion is proved to be clear heresy by what was said by Christ in approval and praise of this Sacrament, in which words the power of this most excellent Sacrament is shown more than once. "He that eateth my flesh," He says, "and drinketh my blood, hath everlasting life" (Jn. 6, 55).

But if you refer this to the future, namely such that it may be understood that the one who shall eat It, will afterwards have life everlasting, but at the time when it is firstly eaten, it confers no benefit: but even by saying this you admit that there is some benefit for the receiver. For even though the mere hope of future things does not make man happy, still one ought not to doubt that he who hopes (even if he has nothing) is much happier than he who despairs. For he who hopes has a kind of beginning of possession: hence it is that hope is nourished in the very privation of the thing. For so Blessed John says: "We know, that, when he shall appear, we shall be like to him: because we shall see him as he is. And every one that hath this hope in him, sanctifieth himself, as he also is holy" (I Jn. 3, 2-3). Thus you acknowledge a great benefit of the Eucharist when you admit that from the eating of it we acquires a certain right to possessing eternal life after death. Furthermore, such a right of possessing beatitude hereafter, no one who is without grace can have. For although beatitude is God's gift, as the Apostle says, "the grace of God, life everlasting" (Rom. 6, 23), as another translation says, "Life everlasting is God's gift": nevertheless, we never receive this grace from Christ's fullness[5] except for another grace with which it is necessary that we are firstly justified in this world, so that

---

[1] Canon 32 (PG 137, 615B-618B).

[2] Dz. 698.

[3] See the section on "Baptism" above, fourth heresy.

[4] *Summa de haeresibus et earum confutationibus*, f. 39v.

[5] Cf. Jn. 1, 16.

we may come to that pardon whereby it is said: "The just shall go into life everlasting" (Mt. 25, 46). Therefore, it is necessary that he who worthily receives this Sacrament, if he is to have glory for this reason, that he also receive grace in the present life.

But in order that the matter may be clearer, let us cite other words of Christ which follow: "He that eateth my flesh," He says, "and drinketh my blood, abideth in me, and I in him" (John 6, 57). And as Blessed John says in an epistle: "Whosoever abideth in him, sinneth not" (I Jn. 3, 6): hence it is clearly proved that having eaten this Body of Christ, all guilt of sin is completely removed from us, which is no small gain. Also, one never abides in God, or God in him, in that special existence except by charity. "He that abideth in charity," John says, "abideth in God, and God in him" (I Jn. 4, 16). Thus, if he who eats Christ's Flesh, and drinks His Blood abides in Him, he consequently abides in charity and love. For if he would not love, he would not abide in Him, because as Blessed John says: "He that loveth not, abideth in death" (I Jn, 3, 14). For which reason Christ elsewhere was instructing us to abide in His love, so that we could bear some fruit, wherefore it is that he who receives this Sacrament, also receives charity whereby he abides in God.

Now so that Christ might confirm this design more, He repeats the same statement three times, saying: "As the living Father hath sent me, and I live by the Father; so he that eateth me, the same also shall live by me" (Jn. 6, 58). The living Father sent His Son, because He became incarnate by the will of the Father; He lives by the Father as God, not because He does not have life in Himself, but because proceeding the Father, not from Himself, He had life by proceeding, having been begotten by Whom He has the Divinity. He also lives on account of the Father insofar as He is a man, because having been made man by the Father's will, He gave life to the body which He assumed. Hence He says: "As the living Father hath sent me, and I live by the Father; so he that eateth me, the same also shall live by me," meaning, just as I was made man by the Father's will, and having been made man, I live and I fill My Body with life: so He who eats My Flesh, will live on account of Me: because he has My Flesh, which is vivifying on account of the Divinity dwelling in It. Notice, therefore, Christ's clear words, by which He often testifies the great utility that will come to those eating this Sacrament, namely eternal life.

Again, He indicates the very word of the thing. For It is called the Eucharist, which means "good grace" [*bona gratia* in Latin], the name having been taken from the effect, because It confers great grace to those receiving. Next, since in this Sacrament not only is Christ's Body or humanity received, but the Divinity Itself which is joined to His humanity: who would think that God dwells in someone, to whom He does not confer great gifts? Wherefore [Hugh of Saint Victor[1]] preferring this Sacrament to the others, says: "In this Sacrament not merely grace, but He from Whom there is all grace, is received." By which words he states that it is better to receive the very Source of all grace, since He is not corporeally in the other Sacraments in the manner mentioned, than to receive the grace which all the Sacraments confer. Therefore, the Sacrament of the Eucharist confers great grace, for which in the future It gives eternal life. From which words many other things come to light, as the Saints bear witness, of which I will only cite one or another.

Cyril [of Alexandria] says the following: "Therefore, you should devoutly resolve to live correctly and virtuously, and thus be partakers of the Eucharist [*eulogia*[2]], believing that it drives away not only spiritual death but also our vices. When Christ is within us, He puts to

---

[1] The text incorrectly attributes this sermon to Saint Bernard.

[2] The term *eulogia* (ευλογία), Greek for "a blessing," has been applied in ecclesiastical usage to "a blessed object." It was occasionally used in early times to signify the Holy Eucharist, and in this sense is especially frequent in the writings of St. Cyril of Alexandria. The origin of this use is doubtless to be found in the words of St. Paul (I Cor. 10, 16): "The chalice of benediction (*eulogias*), which we bless."

sleep the raging law in the members of our flesh. He stirs up piety towards God and deadens our passions, not imputing to us the sins we are in but rather healing us as people who are ill. He binds together what has been broken apart, He raises what has fallen, and He does this as the Good Shepherd Who gives His life for the sheep."[1] What he said, "not imputing to us the sins we are in," He said about venial sins, concerning which it is said: "A just man shall fall seven times a day" (Prov. 24, 16).[2] And [He also said this] on account of the sins which are hidden from us, about which it is also said elsewhere: "from my secret ones cleanse me, O Lord" (Ps. 18, 13). Now this can be established from the preceding things which he relates in the same chapter of the same book.

Blessed [John] Chrysostom speaks thus concerning the Blood conferred to us in the Sacrament: "This Blood poured forth washed clean all the world; many wise sayings did the Blessed Paul utter concerning It in the Epistle to the Hebrews. This Blood cleansed the innermost chamber, the Holy of Holies. And if the type of it had such great power in the Temple of the Hebrews, and in the midst of Egypt, when smeared on the door-posts, much more the reality. This Blood sanctified the golden altar; without it the high priest dared not enter into the innermost chamber. This Blood consecrated priests, this Blood in types cleansed sins. But if it had such power in the types, if death so shuddered at the shadow, tell me how would it not have dreaded the very reality? This Blood is the salvation of our souls, by this the soul is washed, by this is beautiful, by this is inflamed, this causes our understanding to be brighter than fire, and our soul more beaming than gold; this Blood was poured forth, and made Heaven accessible. Truly awe inspiring are the [Eucharistic] Mysteries of the Church, awesome in truth is the altar. A fountain went up out of paradise sending forth material rivers, from this table springs up a fountain which sends forth spiritual rivers. By the side of this fountain are planted not fruitless willows, but trees reaching even to Heaven, always bearing seasonable fruit timely, which never decay. If anyone be scorched with heat, let him come to the side of this fountain and cool his burning. For it quenches drought, and comforts all things that are not burnt up by the heat of the sun, but are consumed by fiery darts. For it has its beginning from above, and its source is there, whence also its water flows. Many are the streams of that fountain which the Paraclete sends forth, and the Son is the Mediator, not holding mattock to clear the way, but opening our minds. This fountain is a fountain of light, spouting forth rays of truth. By it stand the celestial virtues looking upon the beauty of its streams, because they more clearly perceive the power and the unapproachable rays of the Sacrament [*res*] put forth."[3] I have cited Chrysostom at length so that these heretics may see, or those who will afterwards follow them, how much this saint attributed to this most excellent Sacrament, who although he very elegantly said many things, still he did not finish, because What he was praising is in reality greater than all praise.

After the testimonies of these holy men, so that we may make our opinion more certain and firmer, it will be worthwhile to bring forth the decision of the Church. The Council of Florence, celebrated under Eugene IV, in the definition of the declaration of faith given to the Armenians, when discussing the Sacrament of the Eucharist, says these words: "The effect of this Sacrament which He operates in the soul of him who takes it worthily is the union of man with Christ. And since through grace man is incorporated with Christ and is united with His members, it follows that through this sacrament grace is increased among those who receive it worthily; and every effect that material food and drink accomplish as they carry on corporal life, by sustaining, increasing, restoring, and delighting, this the Sacrament does as it carries on spiritual life, in which, as Pope Urban says, we renew the happy memory of our Savior,

---

[1] *In Joannis Evangelium*, bk. 4, c. 2 (PG 73, 586A).
[2] "A day" is found in some manuscripts but is not in the Vulgate.
[3] *On the Gospel of John*, Homily 46, n. 3-4 (PG 59, 261-262).

are withdrawn from evil, are greatly strengthened in good, and proceed to an increase of the virtues and the graces."[1]

The Council of Trent, celebrated under Julius III, subscribes to the same belief, saying the following: "Our Savior, therefore, when about to depart from this world to the Father, instituted this Sacrament in which He poured forth, as it were, the riches of His Divine love for men, 'making a remembrance of his wonderful works' (Ps. 110, 4), and He commanded us in the consuming of it to cherish His 'memory' (I Cor. 11, 24), and 'to shew the death of the Lord, until he come' to judge the world (I Cor. 11, 26). But He wished that this Sacrament be received as the spiritual food of souls, by which they may be nourished and strengthened, living by the life of Him who said: 'He that eateth me, the same also shall live by me' (Jn. 6, 58), and as an antidote, whereby we may be freed from daily faults and be preserved from mortal sins. He wished, furthermore, that this be a pledge of our future glory and of everlasting happiness, and thus be a symbol of that one 'body' of which He Himself is the 'head' (I Cor. 11, 3; Eph. 5, 23), and to which He wished us to be united, as members, by the closest bond of faith, hope, and charity, that we might 'all speak the same thing and there might be no schisms among us' (cf. I Cor. 1, 10)."[2] And after giving this definition, lest anyone dare to think contrary to it, it issued a fifth canon containing a *lata sententia* [censure] against the pertinacious, the words of which are these: "If anyone says that the special fruit of the most Holy Eucharist is the remission of sins, or that from it no other fruits are produced: let him be anathema."[3]

There is a **ninth heresy** which also opposes the efficacious power of this Sacrament. For it asserts that this excellent Sacrament confected on the day of the Lord's Supper, that is to say, on the Thursday of Holy Week, is more efficacious than when consecrated on any other day. The leaders of this error were the Greeks, as Guy the Carmelite testifies[4]: who when discussing this error also says that based on this pretext they confect this Sacrament on no other day of the year besides the day of the [Lord's] Supper, and having confected it they keep the Sacrament throughout the whole year from that day, and therefrom It is administered to the sick. The Waldensians followed the Greeks. For so Guy also charges them, who says that this is their ninth error,[5] yet I do not know which authors he followed, because in no one else's writing have I found this mentioned as being one of their errors. Aeneas Sylvius when discussing the Waldensians' errors does not relate that they said any such thing, although he relates many other which Guy never mentions.[6] Wherefore, as elsewhere so also here, I am astonished at this good man, nor could I ever know who the source is from which he is copying.

This error is clear madness: because when we say the words of Christ upon genuine bread, we truly confect Christ's Body, on whatever day this happens. For the Sacrament does not depend upon time, but upon the matter and form, namely the bread and Christ's words said with the correct intention. For Christ, when saying to the Apostles: "Do this for a commemoration of me" (Lk. 22, 19), did not say that they should through the course of the years confect the Sacrament on only the day when it happened. He said no such thing, He prescribed no law of time for them, but He simply said: "Do this for a commemoration of me." And Blessed Paul when instructing the Corinthians, says that He is handing down to them what He had received from the Lord.[7] Now so are His words in the passage, among others, which He adds: "as often as you shall eat this bread, and drink the chalice, you shall shew the death of the Lord, until he

---

[1] Dz. 698.

[2] Sess. 13, c. 2 (Dz. 875).

[3] Dz. 887.

[4] *Summa de haeresibus et earum confutationibus*, c. 18, f. 26r.

[5] *Ibid.*, f. 80r.

[6] *De Bohemorum origine ac gestis historia*, c. 35, p. 57ff.

[7] Cf. I Cor. 11, 23.

EUCHARISTIA

come" (I Cor. 11, 26). He did not say, "on the anniversary day of the Lord's Supper," but He says: "as often as." If on any day at any hour Christ's words are said with the correct intention over bread, Christ's Body is truly confected, why then is it that when confected on the day of the Lord's Supper, this Sacrament has greater efficacy than on any other day? If the same Body which is under the appearance of bread is confected on any day, then insofar as pertains to the Sacrament, the operation will be the same. For this happens in natural operations, namely that when a cause remains unchanged, and the thing acted upon remains the same, the consequent effect is always the same.

In free actions, however, such as this one, a variation of the action arises only from a change of the will. But when God stated the power and efficacy of this Sacrament, He said simply: "He that eateth my flesh, and drinketh my blood, abideth in me, and I in him" (John 6, 57). He did not say, "He that eateth me on this or that day, abideth in me": but after simply saying, "He that eateth my flesh, and drinketh my blood," immediately added, "abideth in me, and I in him." But if He had wanted to establish a distinction of days, He certainly would have added: "He that eateth my flesh, and drinketh my blood on this day will have more of me," or "he will receive more grace than on any other day." But since He did not suggest any such thing, why do the insane Greeks make up a story? But it is not surprising, because this is the fondness of the Greeks, that they never cease to speak nonsense, they always waste their time in concocting old-womanish tales. For Blessed Cyril in the sixth book of his *Against Julian the Apostate* relates that Solon[1] was moved by this reproof by a certain Egyptian: "You Greeks, when will you leave your childhood or infancy?" Still at his time he considered them to be children and vain.[2]

There is a **tenth error** about the preparation of the soul for the reception of this Sacrament, asserting that this preparation is not necessary to be done by an examination of one's sins and the confession of them: nor is any repentance required, but only faith, meaning a faith whereby men believe and trust they then will receive grace. Martin Luther became the author of this pestilential heresy, having no one as his leader in this matter: which rarely happens with him. For there is no other assertion of these poisons of his spread by him throughout Germany which did not have [as its source] another author rejected by the Church (as Luther now is), besides this one which we have just stated, or perhaps another which Luther finds with his damnation. And although this heresy also existed long ago according to the quotation of Cyprian that will appear cited below, still not with the impunity as Luther teaches it now. Now in order that the senseless mind of Luther may appear more clearly, I will add his words, which are the following: "Great is the error of those who approach the Sacrament of the Eucharist relying on this, that they have confessed, that they are not conscious of any mortal sin, that they have sent their prayers on ahead and made preparations; all these eat and drink judgment to themselves. But if they believe and trust that they will attain grace, then this faith alone makes them pure and worthy."[3]

Cardinal Thomas de Vio, commonly called Cajetan, somewhat taught this same error. For he teaches that it is not necessary by Divine law that someone who is aware of being in mortal sin prepare himself by sacramental Confession for receiving the Eucharist: but he says that

---

[1] Solon (640 B.C.-558 B.C.) was an Athenian statesman, lawmaker and poet.

[2] "Moreover, Plato himself, the son of Ariston, says in the *Timaeus* that Solon of Athens arrived in Egypt and there heard one of the false prophets, or priests, saying: 'Solon, Solon, you Greeks are always children and an aged Greek there is none, for are all young in your minds. You have no ancient opinions among you, nor learning hoary with age. Of this you have no knowledge because many generations have died without leaving a written record." (N. 19 (PG 76, 523D)). Cf. Plato, *The Cratylus, Phaedo, Parmenides, and Timaeus* (London, B. & J. White, 1793), p. 446.

[3] *Exsurge Domine*, n. 15. (Dz. 755).

this only necessary once a year by the determination of the Church, namely when it is necessary to receive the Eucharist during Eastertime, but at other times he says that contrition of heart suffices. Now so that full trust may be given to my words, I will cite his words, which he presents in his *Summa de peccatis*, in the title, *De confessione*, saying the following: "Now I know of no other necessary time for making an actual confession than the time of danger of death by Divine law, and once a year by the determination of the Church. But for administering the Sacraments without a new mortal sin, and receiving the same, and other things of the same kind, which require a clean- conscience: it is evident that contrition suffices."[1] Cajetan not only teaches those things which we said, but affirms them indubitably and clearly.

Now so that we may show that this assertion is heretical, it is necessary to firstly consider the genus and species of this Sacrament. Is it not food? I am quite sure that Luther will not refuse to acknowledge this, who does not rave to the extent that he would deny with Oecolampadius the reality of Christ's Body and Blood. Nevertheless he wished to rave in this way, and he anxiously sought a way to do it, as he himself testifies in a letter sent to the people of Strasburg concerning this matter, which I confess that I have not read, besides a fragment which the Lord Bishop [John Fisher] of Rochester cites in the second to last chapter of the whole work, *De veritate corporis et sanguinis adversus Oecolampadius*.[2] Now I can greatly trust [the bishop] of Rochester since on account of his luster of life that he would not put such words into Luther's mouth: the words of Luther which he cites, I have decided to insert here. "Neither can I nor will I deny," says Luther, "the fact that if Carlstadt, or any other could have convinced me five years ago that there was nothing in the Sacrament but mere bread and wine, he would have done me a great service. For I sweated much in investigating this matter being disturbed with much anxiety, and I tried with all my strength to extricate and free myself, since I rightly saw that thereby I could best greatly inconvenience the papacy."[3] Notice, I beseech the reader, by what spirit Luther is led, with what intention he examines the Sacraments, namely to that he might inconvenience the papacy. He who desires to do harm to another certainly does not have the Spirit of God. But he who lacks the Spirit of God, with what spirit will he enter the innermost chamber of the Sacraments and of the Divine Mysteries? By his own mind? By no means: because they immediately cease to be mysteries, if our spirit were able to investigate and thoroughly examine them.

But now let us return to the work that has been begun. Thus, Luther acknowledges that Christ's real Body and real Blood are in the Eucharist, and he admits that this most holy Sacrament is food, yet not merely for the body, but rather for the soul, because it nourishes and fattens it. For due to this Paul reprehends the Corinthians, not without displeasure, that they made no distinction of this food from others which are consumed as sustenance of the

---

[1] *Summula de peccatis* (Lyon, apud Jacobum Giuncti, 1539), f. 39r. Cf. *Concilium Tridentinum*, tome 7, pt. 4, vol. 1, pg. 126, footnote n. 4. In the same work Cajetan also wrote: "The person receiving Holy Communion without having repented of his mortal sin or sins does, indeed, sin mortally... On the other hand, one who [in the state of mortal sin] received Holy Communion without going to sacramental confession beforehand, if he has a reasonable motive for so doing, is excused since the precept of confessing oneself before receiving Holy Communion is not of divine right" (*Summa de peccatis*...fol.24). "Doctors are wondering whether the commandment of going to confession before receiving Holy Communion is of human or of divine origin. The most commonly held judgment and, in my view, the most certainly true and trustworthy one, is to consider this command as being of divine right" (F.M. Cappello, SJ. *Tractatus canonica-moralis, De Sacramentis*, (Rome, Marietti, 1945), vol.2, p.402).

[2] Bk. 5, c. 39, f. 169r.

[3] *Epistola ad Argentinenses* (*Letter to the Christians at Strasburg in Opposition to the Fanatic Spirit*), December 17, 1524; *Luther's Works*, vol. 40, pg. 68. The passage continues: "...But I am a captive and cannot free myself. The text is too powerfully present, and will not allow itself to be torn from its meaning by mere verbiage."

body alone. But since nothing is nourished except it be alive, it is necessary that whoever would receive this Sacrament, firstly have life, so that it can nourish him: now "whosoever sinneth... abideth in death" (I Jn. 3, 6&14). Hence it is necessary that anyone who is going to receive the Mystery must take care that he be free from sin. But he who has been stained with sins, not having made any expiation through repentance, faith alone (as we have shown above, and we will discuss at still greater length below) nowise cleanses him. Therefore, it is necessary that he who has sinned, because he has died to God, firstly recover his life through repentance before he would receive this Sacrament, if he wants to be nourished and fattened by it, because this is the food of the living, and not of the dead.

Furthermore, when Paul reprehends the Corinthians for not having made any distinction of this food from other food, he teaches them how it is necessary that they should prepare for the reception of this Sacrament, saying: "But let a man prove himself: and so let him eat of that bread, and drink of the chalice. For he that eateth and drinketh unworthily, eateth and drinketh judgment to himself, not discerning the body of the Lord" (I Cor. 11, 28-29). What, I ask, is it to prove oneself, except to examine one's life, to investigate the nature of one's works: are they upright or do they need expiation? And it is just as He said elsewhere: "But let everyone prove his own work, and so he shall have glory in himself only, and not in another" (Gal. 6, 4). And elsewhere: "But prove all things; hold fast that which is good" (I Thess. 5, 21). Thus, for Paul to "prove" is to test, investigate, to carefully examine. Therefore, Paul commands that a man prove himself, meaning, that he would carefully examine what he has within himself, of what sort are his works, what is his intention for the future.

Now this examination or proving is not commanded to be done for no reason: certainly so that if by the previous examination his conscience troubles him about some matter, he ought to abstain until he cleanses his sins though repentance. But if with sufficient and favorable examination no anxiety weighs down upon him, he may then eat of that Bread. But if that examination be not for this purpose, in vain does Paul command it, if when it has been neglected one would nonetheless receive this Sacrament worthily. That this is far from being Paul's opinion, his following words declare. For when he had said: "Let a man prove himself: and so let him eat of that bread," he added: "For he that eateth and drinketh unworthily, eateth and drinketh judgment to himself." By which words he showed that one eats unworthily who has not firstly proved or examined himself. Now it is evident that this interpretation is faithful to the text from the words of Paul himself: nay it is so faithful that the interpretation cannot be thought differently, since it is nothing other than Paul's own words.

Otherwise, so that the matter may appear more clearly, I will cite Theophylactus, the excellent interpreter of Paul, who when expounding this passage of Paul says the following: "It is customary for Paul that if during the middle of his discourse, something else comes up that needs to be discussed, he discusses that also: so here also, during his discussion about the meals, he takes advantage of the opportunity to speak about the Mysteries, and shows them to be the best of all good things, that one should approach them with a pure conscience, and says: 'I do not appoint another person to be your judge, but you must judge yourself.' Therefore, judge and explore your conscience, and in this way approach [the Mysteries], not [only] when there shall be [feast] days, but when you find yourself pure and worthy."[1]

Next it greatly confirms this same thing if we would consider the order of things which Christ observed when He gave His disciples His Body to be eaten. For before He presented His Body to the Apostles, He firstly fulfilled the Law concerning the eating of the Pascal lamb, and afterwards He washed the feet of the disciples. And it ought not to be supposed that He did it without mystery, Who at other times allowed the disciples, as the Gospel testifies,[2]

---

[1] *Expositio in Epistolam I ad Corinthios* (PG 124, 707).

[2] Cf. Mt. 15, 2 & 20.

to eat with unwashed hands. For by that fact He indicated that the affections of the soul, which are signified by the feet, ought to be firstly purified before anyone would presume to approach this so sublime Sacrament. A figure of which thing preceded in the book of Exodus, where it is said: "And water being put into it, Aaron and his sons shall wash their hands and feet in it: when they are going into the tabernacle of the testimony, and when they are to come to the altar, to offer on it incense to the Lord, lest perhaps they die" (30, 18-21). So also, when Christ the true priest, yet according to the order of Melchisedech, was about to lead the Apostles to the true altar, namely the Lord's table, on which His Body, more precious than all incense, was to be offered, firstly washed their feet, and purified their affections. Wherefore He said: "You are clean, but not all" (Jn. 13, 10), so that one might understand that that washing of feet ought to be referred to the affections of the soul, whereby Judas was no wise washed, even though Christ washed his outward feet as of all the other Apostles.

Then, after doing these things, when giving the Apostles His Body and Blood, He instructed them that as they would do these things, they should remember such an immense benefit shown to them. Certainly He was motivating them to a reciprocated charity towards Him by saying this, namely so that when doing these things we would love Him in return, Who has shown His extraordinary love by such a great benefit having been bestowed upon us. After these things the Evangelists recall that Judas, who received this Sacrament with not enough pious affection, exchanged his life with a bad death, certainly so that we would take heed not to receive unworthily, lest something similar happen to us, just as Paul related to have happened to many others afterwards. For after he warned that one who has eaten or drank unworthily, "eateth and drinketh judgment to himself," he added: "Therefore are there many infirm and weak among you, and many sleep" (I Cor. 11, 30), as though he had said: "Because many have received unworthily, even in this life, they are punished with sickness and a sudden death. Hence, what do you expect in the next life, except that they will be punished much more severely?"

Besides these proofs, the Lord commands in Leviticus saying: "I am the Lord. Say to them and to their posterity: Every man of your race, that approacheth to those things that are consecrated, and which the children of Israel have offered to the Lord, in whom there is uncleanness, shall perish before the Lord" (22, 2-3). But if for either offering or touching the figure of things to come God required so much cleanliness, how much greater cleanliness ought one to believe that He will require for the offering or reception of His Body and Blood? Again (so that I may use the words of [Pseudo-] Blessed Jerome[1]) "Wherefore that just Joseph buried the Lord's Body wrapped in a clean linen cloth in the sepulcher, prefiguring that those who would receive the Lord's Body, ought to have both a clean and new soul."[2]

But if besides these testimonies of Scripture, one would desire others of the holy Fathers because those testimonies would explain the matter more clearly than Luther could evade, we will now append them. [Pseudo-] Augustine in a letter to his comrade, Julian,[3] says the following: "From these [sins] may the pity of the Lord Jesus Christ deliver us, and may He give Himself to be eaten, Who said: 'I am the living bread which came down from heaven... He that eateth my flesh, and drinketh my blood, hath everlasting life' (Jn. 6, 41 & 55). But everyone before he receives the Body and Blood of Our Lord Jesus Christ, 'Let a man prove him-

---

[1] Alexander Souter in his study, *The Earliest Latin Commentaries on the Epistles of St. Paul* (Oxford, Clarendon Press, 1927) attributes the commentary from which this quotation was taken to the heretic, Pelagius. The quotation is found in his second book, *Pelagius's Expositions of Thirteen Epistles of St. Paul. II: Text and Apparatus Criticus* (Eugene, Wipf and Stock Publishers, 2004), p. 193.

[2] The spurious text attributed to Saint Jerome is found in *Expositio in Epistolam I ad Corinthios* (PL 30, 784B, or 752D in another edition).

[3] Very few manuscripts have Julian as the addressee of this letter (PL 40, 1045).

self,' according to the Apostles' command, 'and so let him eat of that bread, and drink of the chalice. For he that eateth and drinketh unworthily, eateth and drinketh judgment to himself, not discerning the body of the Lord' (I Cor. 11, 28-29). For when we ought to receive Him, and if we are aware of punishable sins in us, let us make haste to wash [them] through Confession and true repentance, lest we perish with Judas the traitor, concealing the devil within us."[1] Nothing could be said more clearly than these words for refuting Luther's temerity.

Also Hesychius [of Jerusalem], a disciple of Gregory Nazianzen (according to Johannes Trithemius[2]), when expounding the passage: "Keep my sabbaths, and reverence my sanctuary" (Lev. 26, 2), says the following: "Wherefore let us fear His holy place, that we neither defile our own body, nor rashly come to the Body of Christ, in which is all sanctification ('for in him dwelleth all the fulness of the Godhead' (Col. 2, 9)) without diligent examination of ourselves. But let us try ourselves remembering Him that said: 'Whosoever shall eat this bread, or drink the chalice of the Lord unworthily, shall be guilty of the body and of the blood of the Lord. But let a man prove himself: and so let him eat of that bread, and drink of the chalice' (I Cor. 11, 27-28). Of what kind of proving does he speak? The proving is that he would intend to do penance for the sins he has committed in the past, so that he may partake of the holy [Mysteries] with a clean heart and conscience for the remission of his sins."[3] These are the words of Hesychius who very clearly confirms our belief, meaning the Catholic belief.

Gregory of Nyssa, brother of Basil the Great subscribes to this belief saying the following: "It ought not to be overlooked that after they crossed the sea, after the bitterness of the waters was changed into sweetness by the power of the wood for the thirsty, and after refreshing rest by the springs and palms, and finally after they drank from the rock, the supplies from Egypt ran completely out. And thus, when they had no more of the foreign food which they had laid by in Egypt, there flowed down from above food which was at the same time varied and uniform. In appearance the food was plain and single. How was it varied? It changed itself according to each person's desire. What then do we say here? We say that we ought to make our souls clean and pure, more precisely, through faith, Baptism, effort, every virtue, and the whole Evangelical doctrine, so that we would completely separate ourselves from foreign behavior and the Egyptian life, more precisely, from the crowd of all vices, and finally the purified and purged soul ought to receive the heavenly food, which no sowing by the skill of agriculture produced for us, but it is bread without seed, prepared for us without ploughing, without any human labor."[4]

Blessed Jerome when indicating the virtues of a bishop, writes thus: "But if laymen are asked to abstain from relations with their wives for the sake of prayer, what should one then think of the bishop, of him who must be able to present spotless offerings to God every day, for his own sins and for those of the people? Let us reread the books of Kings, and we will find the priest Abimelech did not at first want to give David and his young men the loaves of proposition, until he had asked him whether they were clean from women, just not from other women, but from their wives. And until he heard that they "from yesterday and the day before" (I Kings 21, 5) had ceased from the marital act, by no means would he have granted the loaves which he had previously refused. Now the difference that there is between the loaves of proposition and Christ's Body is as great as between a shadow and substances, between a picture and the reality, between models of future things and the things themselves which were prefigured by the models. This is why, together with meekness, patience, sobriety, temperance, unselfishness, hospitality, and good will, the priest especially—in a more pronounced

---

[1] *De salutaribus documentis*, c. 33 (PL 40, 1059).
[2] *De scriptoribus ecclesiasticis*, fol. 21r. Hesychius calls him Esytius.
[3] *In Leviticum*, bk. 7 (PG 93, 1139B-C).
[4] *Mystica interpretatio vitae Moysis* (PG 44, 367A-B).

way than lay people—must practice the chastity proper to his state, and, so to speak, priestly purity, so that not only will he abstain from impure acts, but his mind, meant to consecrate the Body of Christ, will be freed from glances of the eye and straying of thought."[1] There are the words of Jerome, who even though he does not mention anything about faith [in the Holy Eucharist], but presupposing it, commands not just any, but a wholly complete abstinence from vices.

Likewise the most blessed martyr Cyprian, whose teaching he certifies with his sanctity, vigorously opposes this insane assertion of Luther saying: "Moreover, beloved brethren, a new kind of devastation has emerged; and, as if the storm of persecution had raged too little, there has been added to the heap, under the title of mercy, a deceiving mischief and a fair-seeming calamity. Contrary to the vigor of the Gospel, contrary to the Law of the Lord and God, by the temerity of some, Communion is extended to heedless persons—a vain and false peace, dangerous to those who grant it, and likely to avail nothing to those who receive it. They do not seek for the penitence necessary to health nor the true medicine derived from atonement. Penitence is driven forth from their breasts, and the memory of their very grave and extreme sin is taken away. The wounds of the dying are covered over, and the deadly blow that is planted in the deep and secret entrails is concealed by a dissimulated sorrow. Returning from the altars of the devil, they draw near to the holy place of the Lord, with hands filthy and reeking with smell, nearly still belching from the deadly idol-meats; and even with jaws still exhaling their crime, and reeking with the fatal contact, they intrude on the Body of the Lord, although the Sacred Scripture stands in their way, and cries, saying, 'If any one that is defiled shall eat of the flesh of the sacrifice of peace offerings, which is offered to the Lord, he shall be cut off from his people' (Lev. 7, 20). Also, the Apostle testifies, and says, 'You cannot drink the chalice of the Lord, and the chalice of devils: you cannot be partakers of the table of the Lord, and of the table of devils' (I Cor. 10, 21). He threatens and denounces, moreover, the contumacious and obstinate, saying, 'Whosoever shall eat this bread, or drink the chalice of the Lord unworthily, shall be guilty of the body and of the blood of the Lord' (I Cor. 11, 27). All these warnings being scorned and contemned—before their sin is expiated, before confession has been made of their crime, before their conscience has been purged by sacrifice and by the hand of the priest, before the offense of an angry and threatening Lord has been appeased, violence is done to His Body and Blood; and they sin now against their Lord more with their hand and mouth than when they denied their Lord. They think that that is peace which some try to sell with deceiving words: that is not peace, but war; and he is not joined to the Church who is separated from the Gospel. Why do they call an injury a kindness? Why do they call impiety by the name of piety? Why do they hinder those who ought to weep continually and to entreat their Lord, from the sorrowing of repentance, and pretend to receive them to communion? This is the same kind of thing to the lapsed as hail to the harvests; as the stormy season to the trees; as the destruction of pestilence to the herds; as the raging tempest to ships. They take away the consolation of eternal hope; they overturn the tree from the roots; they creep on to a deadly contagion with their pestilent words; they dash the ship on the rocks, so that it may not reach to the harbor. Such a facility does not grant peace, but takes it away; nor does it give communion, but it hinders from salvation."[2] From which citation the reader now perceives that at another time lived those who upheld this madness of Luther, those whom Blessed Cyprian sharply censures, and he would do no less now against Luther if he were still alive.

---

[1] *Commentaria in Epistolam ad Titum* (PL 26, 568D).

[2] *On the Lapsed*, n. 15-16 (PL 4, 478A-479C).

EUCHARISTIA

Finally, so that we may now conclude the matter, ecclesiastical decrees also oppose Luther on this point. For among the ecclesiastical decrees collected by Gennadius[1] in one volume, this decree is cited in the fifty-third place: "I neither praise nor condemn the daily reception of the Eucharist. Nevertheless, I urge and encourage the faithful to receive Communion of the Eucharist on all Sundays, if, however, they be free from affection to sin. For those still having the intention of sinning are rendered guiltier by receiving the Eucharist, instead of being made more holy. And even though one has been bitten by sin, he should not have intention of sinning again, and before communicating he ought to make satisfaction with tears and prayers, and trusting in the Lord's compassion, Who is accustomed to forgive sins for pious confession, he may approach to the Eucharist fearless and secure. But I say this concerning him who are not burdened with grievous and mortal crimes. For one whom mortal sins committed after Baptism burdens, I exhort to firstly make satisfaction by public penitence, and so having been reconciled by the judgment of the priest to be joined to communion, if he wishes not to receive the Eucharist to his own judgment and condemnation. But we do not deny that criminal sins are also forgiven by secret satisfaction, but first having changed one's secular clothing, and by religious profession through correction of life, nay and perpetual lamentation to the compassioning God, in such a way that he does things contrary to those for which he repents, and he may receive the Eucharist on all Sundays being suppliant and submissive unto death."[2] Since Luther opposes this decree, he is proved to opposed the whole Church, to which he is reckoned to belong, and thus he is rightly deemed a heretic, and ought to be avoided as such.

Therefore, having rejected Luther's poisonous teaching, assenting to the salutary traditions of the Church, let us acknowledge that for one who does not want to receive this Sacrament unworthily, contrition and Confession are necessary. Yet those who approach [to receive the Holy Eucharist] after having received the Sacrament of Confession, knowing how great He is Whom they are about to receive, they ought to say what is written in Luke's Gospel: "We are unprofitable servants; we have done that which we ought to do" (Lk. 17, 10). After all these things it is necessary to pray to God, from Whom are holy desires, right counsels, and just works, so that He may prepare a worthy dwelling for Himself in our soul, without which we are unable to do anything well.

But because out of trust for Cajetan and respect for him, many wished to support him, and by deed they were acting according to his teaching daring to receive the Eucharist without previous Sacramental Confession, wherefore the Church wishing to attack this so very pernicious disease, in the Council of Trent under Julius III it declared the following decree: "If it is not becoming for anyone to approach any of the sacred functions except solemnly, certainly, the more the holiness and the Divinity of this heavenly Sacrament is understood by a Christian, the more diligently ought he to take heed lest he approach to receive it without great reverence and holiness, especially when we read in the Apostle those words full of terror: 'He that eateth and drinketh unworthily, eateth and drinketh judgment to himself, not discerning the body of the Lord' (I Cor. 11, 29). Therefore, the precept, 'Let a man prove himself' (I Cor. 11, 28), must be recalled to mind by him who wishes to communicate. Now ecclesiastical usage declares that this examination is necessary, that no one conscious of mortal sin, however contrite he may seem to himself, should approach the Holy Eucharist without a previous Sacramental Confession. This, the holy Synod has decreed, is always to be observed by all Christians, even by those priests on whom by their office it may be incumbent to celebrate, provided the recourses of a confessor be not lacking to them. But if in an urgent necessity

---

[1] The text here is "collected by Blessed Augustine or by Gennadius" but St. Thomas Aquinas wrote: "[*De dogmaticis ecclesiasticis*] is not the book of Augustine but of Gennadius" (Quodlibet XII, q. 7, a. 2).

[2] *De ecclesiasticis dogmatibus*, c. 53 (PL 58, 994A-C).

a priest should celebrate without previous confession, let him confess as soon as possible."[1] After this teaching given by the Council of Trent, lest anyone temerariously dare to think or teach against it, against temerarious audacious men it issued a *latae sententiae* canon which contains these words: "If anyone says that faith alone is sufficient preparation for receiving the sacrament of the most Holy Eucharist: let him be anathema. And that so great a Sacrament may not be unworthily received, and therefore unto death and condemnation, this holy Council ordains and declares that Sacramental Confession must necessarily be made beforehand by those whose conscience is burdened by mortal sin, however contrite they may consider themselves. If anyone moreover teaches the contrary or preaches or obstinately asserts, or even publicly by disputation shall presume to defend the contrary, by that fact itself he is excommunicated."[2] From which words it is evident that the error stated above, namely of both Luther and Cajetan, is clearly condemned. But against the opinion of Cajetan one ought to especially notice that in the words of the council it did not say that it is establishing a new precept, but only is only stating what was of itself necessary.

[John Fisher,] Bishop of Rochester, writes against this heresy in that work which he published against all of Luther's errors.[3] To which matter he dedicates the fifteenth article of his work. From whom I have borrowed nothing, besides that quotation of Cyprian which I recently cited; the other quotations of holy men, however, whereby we have further embellished the matter, we have collected by our own labor. The reason why I mentioned this to you, the reader, was so that even if you have read this summary of ours, you should not then think that you need not read [the work of Bishop John Fisher], because you will find there many things which can instruct you.

There is an **eleventh heresy** about this Sacrament asserting that they who were burdened with some sins, even if they approach to the Lord's table, and receive consecrated bread from the priest, do not receive the Lord's Body. I could never find any author of this heresy, although I find that this heresy did not lack a patron. For Peter Lombard, who is commonly called the Master of the Sentences, in the fourth book of his *Sentences*, in the ninth distinction, after he quoted the testimonies of some holy men which seem to specifically support this error, he added these words: "Certain men when reading these words and others of this kind with a dull mind, where it is treated concerning spiritual eating, have been surrounded with the darkness of error, to such an extent that they said that Christ's Body and Blood are received only by the good, and not by the wicked."[4] From which words it is evident that of old there were some who maintained this error. Still none of all those who published commentaries on the Master of Sentences mentions any author of this error, which nevertheless was required of them since they accepted the burden of commenting.

Nevertheless, whoever is the author of this error, if it be so that it has been asserted at one time, it is necessary for us to refute it: which duty we discharge with a few quotations having God as their author. For when the Apostle says: "He that eateth and drinketh unworthily, eateth and drinketh judgment to himself" (I Cor. 11,29), he is clearly saying that no matter how unworthy, one can eat Christ's Body, although such eating is very detrimental for him, indeed which brings in a judgment of damnation upon him. Likewise, it is evident from the Gospel concerning Judas the traitor that he received the Lord's Body at the Last Supper with the other Apostles, and yet unworthily, since "the devil having now put into the heart of Judas to betray him" (Jn. 13, 2).

---

[1] Sess. 13, c. 7 (Dz. 880).

[2] Canon 11 (Dz. 893).

[3] *Assertionis Lutheranae confutatio*, a. 15, p. 251r-270r.

[4] N. 2 (PL 192, 858).

EUCHARISTIA

But because I hear that some men vehemently deny it, in order that we may consider this matter more clearly, it is necessary to cite the words of the Evangelists. For when Matthew recounts the Last Supper, he says the following: "But when it was evening, he sat down with his twelve disciples. And whilst they were eating, he said: Amen I say to you, that one of you is about to betray me... And whilst they were at supper, Jesus took bread, and blessed, and broke: and gave to his disciples, and said: Take ye, and eat. This is my body. And taking the chalice, he gave thanks, and gave to them, saying: Drink ye all of this" (26, 20-21 & 26-27). Now Mark and Luke relate those things which pertain to the Supper in this way with almost exactly the same words. You see here that at first all twelve were present, and afterwards absolutely no mention was made of the departure of Judas to the leading men and priests: "And whilst they were at supper, Jesus took bread... and gave to his disciples." In which passage since no one is excepted, it ought to be understood that He gave to all the attending disciples, and thus He also gave to Judas. Now this is proved more explicitly from the distribution of the chalice, where it is said: "Drink ye all of this": therefore Judas also drank, since it is evident that he was present. But if he drinks from the chalice, why did he not also eat the bread since Christ's substance is also entire in the chalice (as we will soon show) as in the bread?

But if you still contend that Judas was nowise present, and you say that the Supper was made when there were eleven, at which he immediately left before the consecration to go to the leading men and priests so that he might meet with them, and when he made an agreement with them about the manner of the betrayal, and so he received neither the Body nor the Blood which the others received: this is easily refuted from John's Gospel. And so that the matter may be clearer, it is necessary to consider here how Christ (as John testifies) sat twice at the supper, such that they firstly made the supper according to the Judaic rite by eating the Pascal lamb: no one can doubt that Judas was present at this supper, since Matthew, Mark and Luke testify that he was present. After this supper was finished, rising from the supper, He washed the feet of the disciples, about which matter only John makes mention. Since the other Evangelists omit that, one could scarcely be informed from them how Christ sat twice at the Supper, since they discuss the Supper with a continuous narration, none of them making any distinction of one supper from the other. Therefore, after washing the feet of the disciples, Christ returned again to the table. John stated this clearly enough saying: "Then after he had washed their feet, and taken his garments, being set down again, he said to them: Know you what I have done to you?" (13, 12). And further on, after these words, he mentions the morsel given to Judas, when they were still at table. From which words it is clearly concluded that Christ reclined twice to eat at the table: once before He had washed the feet of the disciples, and again after He washed their feet.

And in this second reclining at table Christ gave His Body to the disciples. It is concerning the first supper that Matthew, Mark and Luke say: "But when it was evening, he sat down with his twelve disciples" (Mt. 26, 20). To the second supper, done after the washing of the feet, pertains what they say: "And whilst they were at supper, Jesus took bread, and blessed, and broke: and gave to his disciples, and said: Take ye, and eat. This is my body" (*ibid.*, v. 26). Now during the latter supper it happened what the Evangelists relate, that Christ said: "One of you is about to betray me" (v. 21), and afterwards to indicate to John that it would be Judas, they say that He gave the dipped bread to Judas.[1] Now that these things were done in the second supper, in which He consecrated His Body, John and Luke[2] clearly bear witness.

---

[1] "And it is to be observed that the part put into the chalice ought not to be given to the people to supplement the Communion, because Christ gave dipped bread only to Judas the betrayer." (III q. 83, a. 5 ad 9um).

[2] Cf. Lk. 20, 20-21.

That the other Evangelists recall the consecration of Christ's Body after Christ had said: "One of you is about to betray me," is certainly due to the common manner of speaking which Sacred Writ uses, such that after they related some things about the washing of the feet, they return again to the previous things which remained to be discussed more clearly. In this way, likewise, Matthew, Mark and Luke, when discussing this supper using the word "supper" in the singular, as though it were one, notwithstanding that the washing of the feet intervened, with an uninterrupted narration they add those things which Christ said, namely: "One of you is about to betray me," and the things which follow. But after recounting these things, returning to the history of the supper, about which some things had been passed over, they add: "And whilst they were at supper, Jesus took bread, and blessed, and broke," etc. (Mt. 26, 26), so that you may know a certain going back was done from that point in the story, instead of a continuation: which one could suspect from the use of the conjunction, "and" [*autem*]. For if that were a continuation of the story, he would have said: "Whilst they were at supper, Jesus took bread." But since he said, "And whilst they were at supper," it ought to be supposed that they are returning to previous things which remained to be told.

Now I have dwelt upon these things so that it might consequently be apparent that Judas remained with other eleven until the end of the Supper. Wherefore if Judas was present, he also ate the Lord's Body and drank His Blood, especially since Christ said: "Drink ye all of this." And Mark testifies that they all did as the Lord had commanded saying: "And they all drank of it" (Mk. 14, 23). And Luke very clearly supports this opinion, who after he related the words of consecration immediately adds: "But yet behold, the hand of him that betrayeth me is with me on the table" (22, 21). From which words it is sufficiently evident that Judas was present when Christ consecrated the chalice and gave it to the disciples. And since Mark says, "They all drank of it," it is also proved that Judas drank of it.

Now lest it may seem that these things were said coming from my own head, I will bring forth the holy authors whom I have followed in this opinion. Theophylactus [when commenting upon]: "And whilst they were at supper, Jesus took bread…" (Mt. 26, 26), says the following: "Matthew added the words 'whilst they were at supper,' to reveal the cruelty of Judas. For worse than a beast, Judas did not become more meek when he partook of the common meal. Not even when reproved did he listen, but he went so far as to taste of the Lord's Body, and still did not repent."[1] And Chrysostom in a homily on Judas' betrayal subscribes to the same opinion saying: "At one time the Jewish Passover existed, but now it has been abolished; it was succeeded by the spiritual Passover, which Christ delivered unto us. It is said that as they were eating and drinking, Jesus took bread, broke it and said: 'This is my body, which shall be delivered for you' (I Cor. 11, 24). Those who have been initiated know these words. In turn He took the chalice and said: 'This is My Blood … which shall be shed for many unto remission of sins' (Mt. 26, 28). And Judas was present when Christ said these things. This is the Body which you, O Judas, sold for thirty pieces of silver; this is the Blood over which, a little while ago, you made shameless agreements with the ungrateful Pharisees. Oh, what love of Christ for mankind! Oh, what madness of Judas! What folly! Judas sold Him for thirty pieces of money, but even after that, Christ would not have failed to offer the Blood that had been sold for the forgiveness of the sins of him who had sold it, if the latter had in fact wished it."[2] Here Chrysostom explicitly affirms that Judas was present at the Lord's table, and Christ gave him His Blood.

Now Augustine repeats this opinion in many places, such that I do not know which of them to prefer to the others. For the sake of the brevity that I have decided to maintain, they cannot all be cited. He says the following: "Such was this man Judas, and yet he went in and

---

[1] *Enarratio in Evangelium Matthaei* (PG 123, 443).
[2] *De proditione Judae*, hom. 1 (PG 49, 379-380).

out with the eleven holy disciples. With them he came even to the table of the Lord: he was permitted to have intercourse with them, but he could not contaminate them. Of one bread did both Peter and Judas partake, and yet what communion had the believer with the infidel? Peter's partaking was unto life, but that of Judas unto death. For that good bread was just like the sweet savor. For as the sweet savor, so also does the good bread give life to the good, and bring death to the wicked. 'For he that eateth and drinketh unworthily, eateth and drinketh judgment to himself' (I Cor. 11, 29)."[1] Nothing could be said more explicitly to support our opinion than these words.

Therefore, from these holy Doctors as well as the text of the Gospel, it is evident that Judas received the Lord's Body and Blood. But when he received it, "the devil having now put into the heart" (Jn. 13, 2) to sell his Lord and Master. Hence it is clearly inferred that he who unworthily approaches the Lord's table, receives the true Body of Christ, even though it nowise benefits him, nay it harms him very much, not from the nature of the Bread itself, but from the receiver's own fault. And this is what more recent theologians have said using different words, namely that such an unworthy man, although he eats sacramentally, yet he does not eat spiritually, because however good the eaten Body is, it harms him from the malice of the one receiving. For we often find things which are very good harm some people due to their malice. For if the goodness of the thing were to suffice for the receiver, the Lord would have commanded in vain when He said: "Thou shalt follow justly after that which is just" (Deut. 16, 20). Therefore, it would be superfluous to add anything else for the confirmation of the matter, since our argument is sufficiently proved from the things which have been said.

There is a **twelfth heresy** which asserts that Christ's true Body is not in the Eucharist, but only when it is used, meaning, when one uses it by receiving and eating it. But otherwise, it teaches that outside of Communion, Christ's Body is not in it. From this error they deduce another similar error, like the putrid water from a corrupt source. For they say that the Eucharist never ought to be kept on the altar, or in any other place after the celebration of Mass on account of any likely necessity in the future. The inventors of this pestiferous error are the Lutherans, but whether Luther himself, their leader and teacher, taught this very error, is not evident to me, nor have I found anything similar in his works which I have been able to see up until the present time. But I read this only in a certain book published by Martin Bucer, the title of which is, *Liber Reformationis*, and afterwards it was revised with some modifications, published under the title, *Consultoria diliberationis*. And I now hear that this error is now publicly taught by all the Lutherans. They try to prove this heresy of theirs with the argument that Christ instituted the Eucharist, as they suppose, only for Communion. It can easily be proved that this is false from those things which we have said in the refutation of the aforesaid heresies, and it can be much more easily established from those things which we will say below in the section entitled, "The Mass."

I prove that this opinion of theirs is heretical by their own argument. For as often as they argue against some doctrine of ours, they always demand of us God's word and Sacred Scripture, that clearly states what we affirm and teach, and since such clear Scripture is lacking to us, they immediately proclaim it to be a tradition of men and a Satanic teaching. Wherefore it is necessary that "with the same measure" (Lk. 6, 38), according to the Lord's precept, we "mete" the Lutherans, whereby they wish to measure us. For as the Wise Man says, "Diverse weights and diverse measures, both are abominable before God" (Prov. 20, 10). And in the Law of Moses it was forbidden for anyone to "have divers weights in his bag, a greater and a less" (Deut. 25, 13). Hence let us demand from these Lutherans that they bring forth to us God's word and Sacred Scripture which clearly states this assertion of theirs. Now it is very well known that they could not show this teaching [to be in Scripture]. And so it necessarily

---

[1] *Tractate 50 on the Gospel of John*, n. 10 (PL 35, 1762).

follows, according to their rules, that we may call this teaching of theirs a human tradition and Satanic invention.

For Christ when making a covenant with us concerning His Bodily presence in the Eucharist after the words of consecration have been pronounced by the priest, He did not add any condition about Communion needing to be given: and when He gave the power of consecrating and confecting this most Blessed Sacrament to the priests, He did not place a condition about Communion needing to be given. But He merely said, "Do this for a commemoration of me" (Lk. 22, 19). In which words there is no mention of Communion, but only of consecration. Thus, the Lutherans from their own temerity, want to add the necessity of Communion for the validity of the consecration, which Christ Himself did not establish. Furthermore, if the willing of someone to receive Christ's Body were necessary for the true and real presence of Christ's Body, it would follow from this that the validity of the words of consecration and the priest's power to consecrate depends on the will of the one receiving, such that when one wants to be a partaker of Holy Communion, then Christ is present there, and if there is no one having such a wish, Christ is nowise present in that place.

Now it would be wicked and temerarious to think this, since it is opposed to the decision of the whole Church. For the Council of Florence, celebrated under Eugene IV, in the definition of the faith given to the Armenians, when discussing the Sacrament of the Eucharist says these words: "The words of the Savior, by which He instituted this sacrament, are the form of this sacrament; for the priest speaking in the person of Christ effects this sacrament. For by the power of the very words the substance of the bread is changed into the body of Christ, and the substance of the wine into the blood."[1] In which words it is very clearly declared that the whole power of confecting Christ's Body is in the priesthood, and in the words of consecration without any willing of the communicant, such that as often as a priest shall pronounce the words of consecration upon bread with the correct intention, Christ's Body is truly present there. And this is true even if there would be no one present who wishes to communicate.

Again, if the power of the priest for consecration were to depend on the will of the communicant, no priest could ever be sure that he has validly confected the Sacrament of the Eucharist, because he could never be certain of the will of another, whether he wishes to communicate or not. Next let us suppose someone present who immediately after the consecration of the priest decides to receive the Eucharist from his hand, then according to their view, Christ's Body will be immediately really present there after the consecration: because nothing was then lacking that is required by them for the real and corporeal presence of this kind. But after this consecration has been completely done it could happen that he who had been prepared for communion changes his mind and does not wish to communicate. Consequently, there is no doubt that Christ's Body is truly and really in the Eucharist even though there would be no subsequent communion of that Eucharist. Besides these convincing reasons there are very many testimonies of holy men, which teach that the Most Holy Eucharist ought to be kept for many necessities which are accustomed to occur, especially for the Communion of the sick.

To begin with I cite Cyril [of Alexandria] who, in a letter to Calosirius, Bishop of Arsinoë, when speaking about certain other men of a similar grain,[2] says these words: "I hear that some are so foolish as to say that the mystic blessing [i.e. the real presence] departs from the Sacrament, if any of its fragments remain until the next day: for Christ's consecrated body is not changed, and the power of the blessing, and the life-giving grace is perpetually in it."[3] From which words it is evident that there were some other men who maintained this error of the

---

[1] Dz. 698.

[2] I.e. the Audians of Mesopotamia who were Anthropomorphites.

[3] PG 76, 1075A. Cf. III q. 76, a. 6 ad 2um.

EUCHARISTIA -451-

Lutherans at the time of Cyril, and Blessed Cyril says that they had gone insane. Therefore, the Lutherans are also insane teaching such a foolish error.

Blessed Ambrose in his funeral oration upon the death of his brother, Satyrus, when praising his singular piety and devotion towards God, relates of him that he was going to enter the sea and foreseeing the death which then is often accustomed to occur, "fearing not death but lest he should depart this life without the Mystery, asked of those whom he knew to be initiated the Divine Sacrament of the faithful; not that he might gaze on secret things with curious eyes, but to obtain aid for his faith. For he caused it to be bound in a napkin, and the napkin round his neck, and so cast himself into the sea, not seeking a plank loosened from the framework of the ship, by floating on which he might be rescued, for he sought the means of faith alone. And so believing that he was sufficiently protected and defended by this, he sought no other aid... nor did his hope fail nor his expectation deceive him. And then, when preserved from the waves, he was brought safe to land in the port."[1]

Blessed Jerome relates in a letter to the monk Rusticus that Exuperius, Bishop of Toulouse, carried the Lord's Body enclosed in a wicker basket.[2] [Pseudo-] Augustine teaches that it is good and useful to bring this Sacrament to the sick as a most salutary viaticum.[3] Eusebius [of Caesarea] quotes a part of a letter sent by Irenaeus, Bishop of Lyons, to Pope Victor, from which it is most clearly proved that the Roman pontiffs were accustomed to send the Eucharist as a sign of a friendly visitation to the Catholic bishops who had come to Rome from elsewhere.[4] And in the *Historia Tripartita* it is related that a certain priest, when due to bodily illness could not go to a sick man, sent a small portion of the Eucharist to the house of the sick man.[5] Lastly, [Pseudo-] Clement, a disciple of Peter and successor in his chair, among the many things which he relates that he received from Blessed Peter, there is one which greatly commends our teaching, saying the following: "The Sacraments of the Divine Secrets are committed to three degrees, that is to the priest, deacon, and minister, who, with fear and trembling of the clergy, ought to reserve the remains of the fragments of the Lord's Body, that there be no corruption found in the tabernacle; lest great injury should be done to a portion of Our Lord's Body by their negligent behavior."[6] These are the words of [Psuedo-] Clement, pope and martyr, who teaches clearly enough that the Eucharist is kept in the tabernacle for its time, and that the Eucharist so kept in it is the true Body of Christ.

From all these testimonies it is evident that it is a very ancient custom of the Church to fittingly and reverently keep the consecrated Eucharist after the celebration of the Mass for future necessities (especially for the Communion of the sick). It is not necessary for this matter to use many testimonies of holy men, since there is the very clear decision of the Church about it, not given once, but often repeated: for the decree of the Synod of Worms, which Gratian cites,[7] contains these words: "Let the priest always have the Eucharist ready, so that,

---

[1] *On the Death of Satyrus*, bk. 1, n. 43-44 (PL 16, 1304B-1305A).

[2] "In fact he has bestowed his whole substance to meet the needs of Christ's poor. Yet none is richer than he, for he carries the Body of the Lord in a wicker basket, and the Precious Blood in a glass cup" (Letter 125, n. 20 (PL 22, 1085)).

[3] *De visitation infirmorum*, bk. 2, c. 4 (PL 40, 1154). The author of this work is uncertain.

[4] "But none were ever cast out on account of this form; but the presbyters before you who did not observe it, sent the Eucharist to those of other parishes who observed it." (*Church History*, bk. 5, c. 24, n. 15 (PG 20, 506B-507A)).

[5] Bk. 6, c. 44 (PG 20, 634A).

[6] PG 1, 485C. This letter is "falsely attributed to Pope St. Clement I" ("Pope St. Clement I," *The Catholic Encyclopedia* (New York: Robert Appleton Company, 1908), vol. 4, p. 14).

[7] *Concordia discordantium canonum*, dist. 2, c. 93 (PL 187, 1780B). The Council of Worms was held in 868 A.D.

when anyone fall sick, he may take Communion to him at once, lest he die without it."[1] And in the following chapter [of Gratian] is put the another decree, of the [Fourth] Synod of Arles, in which is a penalty is imposed upon him who does not keep well the Eucharist.[2]

But lest anyone perhaps disparage the aforesaid decrees since the councils by which they were produced were not general councils, but provincial, wherefore it is necessary that I cite decisions of general councils. The [IV] Lateran Council, celebrated under Innocent III, at which both the Greeks and Latins assembled, says these words: "We decree that in all churches the chrism and the Eucharist be kept in properly protected places provided with locks and keys, that they may not be reached by rash and indiscreet persons and used for impious and blasphemous purposes."[3] After this Innocent, under whom was celebrated the aforesaid council, Honorius III succeeded in the [Roman] pontificate: who gave a decree at much greater length concerning this matter, saying the following: "Lest the wrath of God blaze up in the future against the irreverent because of the carelessness of priests, We strictly enjoin by precept that the Eucharist be reserved always devotedly and faithfully in a place of honor that is clean and designated for It alone... At the same time, the priest should carry It in becoming apparel covered with a clean veil and should bring It back before his breast and with respect. The priest should be preceded by a torch, since the Eucharist is the radiance of Eternal Light, so that the faith and devotion of everyone be increased."[4]

Last of all the Council of Trent, celebrated under Julius III, decreed these words: "The custom of reserving the Holy Eucharist in a holy place is so ancient that even the age of the Nicene Council recognized it. Moreover, the injunction that the sacred Eucharist be carried to the sick, and be carefully reserved for this purpose in the churches, besides being in conformity with the greatest equity and reason, is also found in many councils, and has been observed according to a very ancient custom of the Catholic Church. Therefore this holy Synod decrees that this salutary and necessary custom be by all means retained."[5] After having given this decree, lest anyone dare to contradict it, it added a *latae sententiae* canon against the temerarious of such kind, saying the following: "If anyone says that it is not lawful that the Holy Eucharist be reserved in a sacred place, but must necessarily be distributed immediately after the consecration among those present; or that it is not permitted to bring it to the sick with honor: let him be anathema."[6] From all these words it is very clearly established that the heretical assertion of the Lutherans saying that Christ's Body is not really and truly in the Eucharist, except only during that time in which someone wishes to be a partaker of that Communion.

The **last heresy** (that I know) concerning this matter is that which asserts that one must necessarily communicate under both species, namely the bread and wine, such that he who communicates only under one species, even if he be a layman, sins, because (as they say) he acts contrary to Christ's precept, who prescribes that one communicate under both species. Now the authors of this heresy were the Greeks, whom afterwards the Bohemians followed, remaining as yet in their condemnation, and by this occasion are until now separated from the obedience to the Roman Church. Yet John Hus, their prophet, revived this error, not as

---

[1] *Liber decretorum*, bk. 5, c. 10 (PL 140, 754C). Cf. III, q. 83, a. 5 ad 11 um.

[2] "They who do not keep proper custody over the Sacrament, if a mouse or other animal consume it, must do forty days' penance: he who loses it in a church, or if a part fall and be not found, shall do thirty days' penance." (dist. 2, c. 94 (PL 187, 1780B)). Cf. III, q. 83, a. 6 ad 7um.

[3] Canon 20 (H. J. Schroeder, *Disciplinary Decrees of the General Councils: Text, Translation and Commentary*, (St. Louis, B. Herder, 1937). p. 259),

[4] *Sane cum olim* or *Expectavius hactenus*, November 22, 1219, *Bullarium Romanum*, Honorius III, n. 40, vol. 3, p. 366a-366b. Cf. Gregory IX, *Decretales*, bk. 3, tit. 41, chap. 10.

[5] Session 13, c. 6 (Dz. 879).

[6] Canon 7 (Dz. 889).

one of the Bohemians. For after the madness of this John had begun and had spread a little (as Aeneas Sylvius testifies in his book, *De Bohemorum origine*[1]) the German, Peter of Dresden, brought this new pestilence to Bohemia, after having been driven out of his country, he being known by his people that he had been infected with the Waldensian leprosy, and fleeing from there, headed to Prague, a city of Bohemia, as an asylum for heretics. Then in that city a certain Jacob of Mies,[2] eminent for the excellence of his moral and learning, was in charge of instructing the people by his preaching. When Peter met this man, he said that he was surprised that a learned as well as holy man, who had received the burden of instructing the people, had not noticed the error of Eucharistic Communion, which had taken hold for a long time in the Church, wherein the Lord's Body is administered to the people under only one species, although in John's Gospel it is commanded to be received under both species of bread and wine, when the Lord says: "Except you eat the flesh of the Son of man, and drink his blood, you shall not have life in you" (6, 54). The above-mentioned Jacob having been disturbed by these words, after the old books of saints had been carefully searched, when he had found that Communion of the chalice was sometimes used and fully praised, he instructed the people not to henceforth neglect Communion of the chalice, without which no one could be saved. Other heretics who already lived in Bohemia agreed with this man, and were not a little joyful because they had found an opinion based on "the Holy," as they used to call the Gospel, whereby they could rebuke the Roman See either of ignorance or wickedness.

Luther followed this pestilential teaching a hundred or more years later, infected nearly the whole of Germany with this error; wherein even the laity, like the priests, communicate under both species, lest not doing so (as they say), they would incur damnation. Now so that it may appear to all how tenaciously Luther holds this teaching, I will cite his words. For since he had preached sound doctrine in times past, after greatly repenting his behavior, he bursts out with these words: "I recanted this article in the book, *On the Babylonian Captivity*, and I recant it again in this writing, and I say that the Bohemians and Greeks on this point are neither heretics nor schismatics, but most Christian and evangelical, and whom by these words I ask and implore in the Lord, that they remain firm in this opinion, since they have an explicit text of the Gospel and the long Catholic practice of the Church of God kept until this day among the Greeks as their support. And may they not be moved by the destructive and wicked decrees of that Roman tyrant and Antichrist, whereby the other part of the Sacrament is forcibly taken away from them to whom Christ has given it."[3]

For the refutation of this error it is necessary to firstly establish that the whole Christ is entirely contained under either species of this Sacrament, because nearly the whole strength of this argumentation depends on this. Now this is especially proved from what the Apostle says: "Christ... dieth now no more, death shall no more have dominion over him" (Rom. 6, 9). But if under the appearance of bread Christ would exist bloodlessly, it would be necessary the He would also be lifeless, and a corpse, because a soul can nowise bloodlessly animate the body. For if that were to happen then as often as the bread would be consecrated, so often Christ would be present as He laid dead in the sepulcher, and so often His Body would become a new corpse. Now so that this would not occur, it will be necessary that it be conceded that Christ's Body is animated under the appearance of bread, and hence animated with the Blood.

Now the Body once it was assumed by the Divinity was never afterwards removed from it. And since it was never separated from the Divinity, it will also be necessary to admit that the whole Christ is there in both natures. Wherefore it ought to be likewise said concerning the

---

[1] Chapter 35.

[2] Jacob of Mies was called *Jacobellus* (i.e. Jacob the Short), from his small stature.

[3] *Assertio omnium articulorum Martini Lutheri per Bullam Leonis X. novissimam damnatorum* (*An Assertion of Martin Luther of All the Articles Condemned by the Bull of Leo X*), a. 16.

Blood. For since it was once shed for us upon the altar of the Cross, Christ resumed it at His Resurrection, never to be shed again. Whence it is also proved that all His true Blood is also never anywhere without His true Body. But if under the appearance of wine only the Blood would remain, it would be necessary that the Blood be shed each time the wine is consecrated, because having been made present by the power of the consecration, it would then be separated from the Body. Now so that we may evade this, it should be acknowledged without any hesitation that in the Sacrament of the Eucharist under both species, namely of the bread and wine, the whole Christ is also integrally contained.

But lest anyone dare to doubt about this matter, I cite the definition of the Council of Florence, celebrated under Eugene IV, which in its declaration of faith[1] concerning the Sacraments of the Church, when it discusses the Sacrament of the Eucharist, contains these words: "For the priest speaking in the person of Christ effects this Sacrament. For by the power of the very words the substance of the bread is changed into the Body of Christ, and the substance of the wine into the Blood; yet in such a way that Christ is contained entire under the species of bread, and entire under the species of wine. Under any part also of the consecrated host and consecrated wine, although a separation has taken place, Christ is entire."[2]

And although this is true concerning the things contained, still it is not equally true concerning the signification. For even though under those appearances of bread the whole Christ hides, still those appearances do not signify the whole Christ, but only that Body which was offered up for us on the altar of the Cross, more precisely at the time when it was bloodless, the Blood having been separated from the Body in its entirety. In like manner, the appearance of wine, even though they contain the whole Christ, still they do not signify anything other than that Blood shed when it was separated from the Body. And yet they do not signify that it is separated [from the Body], because the sign would be false, but they signify it alone, how it was alone when it was separated from the Body, such that the signification does not refer to the separation, but to the Blood.

A second foundation must be laid for our argument, meaning for confirming the Catholic doctrine, namely that grace is conferred in the Sacrament, not being so much conferred by the power of the sign, as by the power of the thing signified. For those appearances of bread and wine, which appear outwardly, are not such that they are the things which vivify the soul of themselves, which are able to restore a man unto the number of the elect, or which make us to be in God and God in us: but all these things happen by the power of the Flesh, which on account of the life dwelling in it, namely the Divinity, is deemed to be vivifying.

From these two [foundations] a third now clearly arises, namely that no more grace is conferred by the power of the Sacrament to one who receives both species, namely the bread and the wine, than to one who receives only one. For since besides the appearance, which can nowise confer grace, one receives only one thing, namely the whole Christ integrally, who receives one species, just as he who receives both. There is no reason why one receives more grace by the power of the Sacrament than the other, especially since it is one Sacrament, and not two, even though the appearances are two, or are two signs. Thus, since these things are so, it is evident that the laity are not deprived of any grace on account of withholding the other species, meaning, the wine.

After all these foundations a fourth ought to be added to the argument, so that a square structure may arise, namely that there is no command given by Christ about eating the Eucharist under both species. For the passage from the sixth chapter of John which they principally cite: "Except you eat the flesh of the Son of man, and drink his blood, you shall not have life in you" (v. 54): we certainly admit, and embrace with open arms (as they say) that those

---

[1] I.e. the Decree for the Armenians.
[2] Dz. 698.

words ought to be understood of the corporeal and visible eating of the Eucharist. And it does not please me that Caspar Schatzgeyer,[1] a man otherwise learned and Catholic, strenuously combating for the faith against Luther, says that these words are to be understood of a spiritual eating, which is through faith and charity, motivated by those words which Christ added afterwards in the same chapter: "It is the spirit that quickeneth: the flesh profiteth nothing. The words that I have spoken to you, are spirit and life." (v. 64). From which words he concludes that the former words ought to be understood of spiritual eating.[2] But these words are not so construed, as is evident to one reading Theophylactus, Cyril, Chrysostom, and Augustine, who in their expositions of John's Gospel all acknowledge that those words are to be referred to corporeal and visible eating. And we have reviewed the words of all these men above in the fourth heresy.

Now that which is subjoined: "It is the spirit that quickeneth: the flesh profiteth nothing," Theophylactus[3] and Cyril[4] expound as follows: This Flesh which I called lifegiving when someone receives it, will not be able to effect this by its own nature, yet it will effect this due to the indwelling Spirit of the Son of God in it. For this Spirit is the One Which truly vivifies, while flesh alone could not profit anything, but because it is joined together with the Word, it has been raised to a higher dignity, so that it can be lifegiving. For it is just as if you were to pour in and mix in some honey to a liquid, it makes the whole liquid sweet, and gives it a characteristic which it would not otherwise have: so the Divine Word united to flesh, because the Word is life, It also made the flesh itself lifegiving: and hence flesh of itself "profiteth nothing," but it has from the Spirit that it can vivify. But the reason why He said: "The words that I have spoken to you, are spirit and life," was because He saw the Jews murmuring, supposing that Christ had commanded them, after the manner of wild beasts, to eat human flesh, and drink blood: and so reproaching them for that carnal understanding of His words, He instructs them that there is a hidden mystery, and His words ought to be so understood, not such that they would think that His Body is to be ground with the teeth, but eaten as a Sacrament.

Thus, we say and acknowledge that those words, namely: "Except you eat the flesh of the Son of man," etc., ought to be understood of bodily eating, and yet we do not admit that Christ commanded us by those words to receive the Eucharist under both species. For there is no mention in those words of the appearances of bread and wine, but only of the things signified, namely the Body and Blood, which are contained under those signs. For He did not say: "Except you eat the flesh of the Son of man under the appearance of bread, and drink his blood under the appearance of wine, you will not have life in you." He did not so speak, but as follows: "Except you eat the flesh of the Son of man, and drink his blood, you shall not have life in you." But since we said that the Body is contained under the appearance of bread at the same time along with the Blood, it follows that he who receives the Eucharist under the appearance of bread eats the Flesh and drinks the Blood, since the consuming of the Blood may be truly called drinking, just as the receiving of the Flesh is called eating. Still it will not be enough for a confecting priest to receive one without the other on these grounds: because the confecting and consecrating priest represents Jesus Christ, the High Priest Himself, Who

---

[1] Caspar Schatzgeyer, OFM (c. 1464-1527) was a German Franciscan and a foremost opponent of the Protestant reformer Martin Luther in Germany.

[2] "In the heat of the Reformation controversy, theologians, such as that remarkable man Kaspar Schatzgeyer (1463-1527), were saying that Christ is not present in the Sacrament in His natural form, but in a spiritual way, *in mysterio*. He dared to use this terminology even in the Reformation situation, though he had no thought of weakening the reality of the Presence. (Cf. Erwin Iserloh, *Der Kampf um die Messe*, Münster, 1952, 39-46, 57, 58.)

[3] *Ennaratio in Evangelium Joannis* (PG 123, 1314D ff).

[4] *In Joannis Evangelium*, bk. 4 (PG 73, 603B ff).

offered for us His Body and Blood on the altar of the Cross, as Christ Himself stated, saying: "Do this for a commemoration of me." What does "do this" mean but "confect this," "consecrate this"?

Nevertheless, I know that there are some of these heretics who very skillfully deny this, nay they mock such an interpretation, as when we say that "do this" (Lk. 22, 19) means the same as though He had said, "consecrate this." For a certain Johannes Rivius of Atthendorn[1] in a letter about Communion under both species,[2] mocks this interpretation, saying the following: "For since τοῦτο ποιεῖτε [literally, 'this do'] is read in the writings of the Evangelist, 'do this' cannot be interpreted to mean 'sacrifice this.' For the Greek word clearly spits out this interpretation." It was not necessary so that we would acknowledge the correct interpretation of the text to cite the Greek text, which nowise differs in this phrase from the Latin, nor does it "spit out" our interpretation (as Johannes Rivius says) any more than the Latin text. For we are not so uneducated or ignorant of the Latin or Greek language that we would think that this word "to do" [*facere*], or this Greek word corresponding to it, ποιέω, means by its own definition the same thing as "to consecrate" or "to sacrifice."

But even if this were so, still because it is usual, and often done by very learned men, that a general noun or verb be accommodated to its particular aspects, hence it happens that often its meaning is changed, according to subject matter being discussed. Now this verb, "to do," or the Greek word corresponding to it, namely ποιέω, is a general verb for expressing all kinds of causality. For one who reads, writes, paints, sings, drinks or jumps, is said "to do" something. Hence if someone were to jump across a torrent with one leap, and afterwards says to others, "You do it," no one will deny that he commands it to others by these words, or that they leap across the torrent in like manner. Similarly, if an expert painter when painting in front of his disciples, were to say afterwards to his disciples: "Do this," everyone hearing would understand that the master commands his disciples to paint something similar. And yet this verb "to do" neither means to paint or to jump by its own and suitable definition, even though it means all those things by a general signification.

Christ's words should be understood in exactly the same way when He says: "Do this for a commemoration of me." For by those words He commanded the Apostles that they would themselves afterwards do what they had seen Him do. But Christ had taken bread into His hands, blessed, consecrated and distributed the consecrated bread to these same Apostles. Thus, when saying to the Apostles: "Do this," He commanded them to take bread, bless and consecrate it. Therefore, it is not absurd (as Johannes Rivius says) but the correct interpretation of the text when we explain those words of Christ: "Do this," by these words, "consecrate" and "sacrifice." For they were then ordained priests by Christ enjoining upon them that they do this for a commemoration of His Passion. This is what Paul explicitly said: "This chalice is the new testament in my blood: this do ye, as often as you shall drink, for the commemoration of me" (I Cor. 11, 25). If "to do" is here used for "to consecrate," which pertains to priests alone (as we shall discuss elsewhere): it is evident that it was said to priests alone, that as often as they will drink, they will make a commemoration of Him.

Now that it was a future commemoration of that thing, the subsequent words show. "For as often as you shall eat this bread," He said, "and drink the chalice, you shall shew the death of the Lord, until he come" (v. 26). Thus, the priest commemorates upon the altar the Lord's death, but not the one who receives [Communion] from the priest: wherefore the priest is bound by this law, that as often as he celebrates, he would neither consecrate bread without wine, nor receive one species without the other: because even if the whole complete Christ

---

[1] Johannes Rivius of Atthendorn (1500-1553) was a German humanist and Protestant theologian.

[2] *Assertio communionis sub utraque specie, contenta quatuor epistolis, ad Joannem Fabianum* published in *De Conscientia libri III* (Leipzig, Nicolaus Wolrab, 1541), Ep. 3, p. 4v.

hides under either species, still not any species signifies or represents the whole Christ, but the species of bread signifies only the Flesh, the species of wine represents only the Blood, and commemorates it alone. Hence if he were to consecrate the bread alone, or receive the consecrated bread alone, he would commemorate only the oblation whereby Christ offered His Body, but there would then be no commemoration of His Blood shed and offered for us by Christ, because the species of bread, even though it contains the Blood, still does not represent the Blood or commemorate it. In this same way, if only wine were to be consecrated, or it having been consecrated were alone received, there would be a commemoration of the offered and shed Blood alone, but not of the Body.

But since consecrating priests are bound to consecrate in memory of the Lord's death which He underwent for us, it is thence inferred that they are obliged to do it under both species, since neither one without the other represents Christ's complete oblation. Christ intimated this when He said after the consecration of the bread and wine: "Do this for a commemoration of me." "What is that that they are going to do for a commemoration of Thee?" "All," I say, "that I have just done in your presence." But since nothing is prescribed for the one receiving from the hand of the one consecrating, such that he is to receive for a commemoration of the Lord's offering, he who receives from the hand of another, whether he be layman or priest, is never bound to receive in like manner for the same commemoration such that he may not receive one without the other. For they do not do something at the same time regarding the Sacrament, and so it was not said to them: "Do this for a commemoration of me." Nor is it said to them: "Drink ye all of this," but only to those to whom it was given, namely to the Apostles, who were taking the place of all future priests, whom through the Apostles were commanded to confect this Sacrament for a commemoration of Christ. Thus, it is said to them alone: "Drink ye all of this." Unless perhaps it be said that those words ought to be referred to all Christians, and all Christians (as Luther says) are priests. But we will dispute about these things elsewhere at greater length.

But what they infer from this, namely that the Eucharist ought to be received under both kinds because He gave it to His disciples under both kinds, they certainly ineptly infer. For if the argument were to be taken from all Christ's actions in regard to this Sacrament (I omit His other deeds) for necessarily doing likewise, then the Greeks when confecting with leaven bread, would not licitly confect, since as we have shown above in this section, Christ confected with unleavened bread: yet we have said that they can confect licitly in this way. Again, if everything that Christ did at His Supper, when He gave His Apostles His Body and Blood under the appearances of bread and wine, necessarily had to be done by priests when they administer the Eucharist to others, it would also be necessary to wash the feet of others before this distribution of the Eucharist. For Christ Himself, as it is evident from the Gospel, washed the disciples' feet before He gave His Body and Blood to the disciples. And He not merely washed, but gave them an explicit command for them to do in like manner afterwards, saying the following: "If then I being your Lord and Master, have washed your feet; you also ought to wash one another's feet. For I have given you an example, that as I have done to you, so you do also" (Jn. 13, 14-15). Now this command of Christ, according to the literal meaning of the text, obliges no less than these words of the Lord: "Drink ye all of this." But the Catholic Church does not use this washing of the feet, although it used to do it long ago, as is evident from the ancient Doctors, especially Cyprian and Augustine.

Now, Augustine explains why this custom was at first adopted saying the following: "As to the feet-washing, since the Lord recommended this because of its being an example of that humility which He came to teach, as He Himself afterwards explained, the question has arisen at what time it is best, by literal performance of this work, to give public instruction in the important duty which it illustrates, and this time [of Lent] was suggested in order that the lesson taught by it might make a deeper and more serious impression. Many, however, have not accepted this as a custom, lest it should be thought to belong to the ordinance of Baptism; and some have not hesitated to deny it any place among our ceremonies."[1] Augustine clearly teaches that such washing of the feet was rejected lest it be supposed that it is a rebaptism. For the Church thought that it is much better to omit that external ceremony than to give an occasion of a so very harmful error by its pertinacious retention. Furthermore, if everything must necessarily be done in this Sacrament in imitation of Christ, it would not be permitted to receive the Eucharist fasting, since Christ gave His Body to His disciples not fasting but after having supped. Now this, which Christ did then, although was kept for some time thereafter, as is evident from the First Epistle of Paul to the Corinthians,[2] nevertheless was afterwards rejected, not only by custom, but by precept of the [Council in Trullo].[3]

Blessed Augustine praises this same ordinance of the Church, and strongly reprehends those who reprove this ordinance of the Church saying the following: "As to the question whether upon that day it is right to partake of food before either offering or partaking of the Eucharist, these words in the Gospel might go far to decide our minds, 'And whilst they were at supper, Jesus took bread, and blessed, and broke' (Mt. 26, 26); taken in connection with the words in the preceding context, 'But when it was evening, he sat down with his twelve disciples. And whilst they were eating, he said: Amen I say to you, that one of you is about to betray me' (v. 20-21). For it was after that that He instituted the Sacrament; and it is clear that when the disciples first received the Body and Blood of the Lord, they had not been fasting. Must we therefore censure the universal Church because the Sacrament is everywhere partaken of by persons fasting? Nay, verily, for from that time it pleased the Holy Ghost to appoint, for the honor of so great a Sacrament, that the Body of the Lord should take the precedence of all other food entering the mouth of a Christian; and it is for this reason that the custom referred to is universally observed. For the fact that the Lord instituted the Sacrament after other food had been partaken of, does not prove that brethren should come together to partake of that Sacrament after having dined or supped, or imitate those whom the Apostle reproved and corrected for not distinguishing between the Lord's Supper and an ordinary meal. The Savior, indeed, in order to commend the depth of that mystery more affectingly to His disciples, was pleased to impress it on their hearts and memories by making its institution His last act before going from them to His Passion. And therefore, He did not prescribe the order in which it was to be observed, reserving this to be done by the Apostles, through whom He intended to arrange all things pertaining to the churches. Had He appointed that the Sacrament should be always partaken of after other food, I believe that no one would have departed from that practice. But when the Apostle, speaking of this Sacrament, says, 'Wherefore, my brethren, when you come together to eat, wait for one another. If any man be hungry, let him eat at home; that you come not together unto judgment.' He immediately adds, 'And the rest I will set in order, when I come' (I Cor. 11, 33-34). Whence we are given to understand that, since it was too much for him to prescribe completely in an epistle the method observed by the universal Church throughout the world, it was one of the things set in order by him in person, for we find its observance uniform amid all the variety of other customs."[4] In which

---

[1] Letter 55 (to Januarius), c. 18, n. 33 (PL 33, 220).

[2] I Cor. 11, 20-22.

[3] "It is not permitted to hold what are called *Agapæ*, that is love-feasts, in the Lord's houses or churches, nor to eat within the house, nor to spread couches. If any dare to do so let him cease therefrom or be cut off" (Council in Trullo, canon 74 (PG 137, 766B)). The text here incorrectly labels this particular council held in Constantinople in 692 A.D. "the Sixth General Council" and the canon number has also been corrected.

[4] Letter 54 (to Januarius), c. 6, n. 7-8 (PL 33, 203).

words the foremost thing to notice, among other things, is how much importance Augustine gave to the decrees of the Church, which he most firmly believed to be always governed by the Holy Ghost.

Next, it would not be permitted to mix water with the wine in the chalice, because even though it was thought that Christ did this for the sake of His sobriety, still the Evangelists make no mention of it. But these men, against whom we are now disputing, are unwilling to accept anything not stated in Holy Writ: wherefore they [assume that they] must not mix water with the wine, because none of the Evangelists stated that Christ mixed water with the wine in the holy chalice. You now see well enough (as I think) how worthless is the argument whence they conclude that we are obliged to give the Eucharist to the laity under both species: because Christ so gave to the Apostles.

I omit the reply of certain men [to our assertion that there was] a separation of those appointed, because the Apostles were ordained priests by Christ by those words: "Do this for a commemoration of me." For from these words it is not evident that when the consecration was done whether Christ immediately said those words before He gave the Eucharist under both species to the Apostles or afterwards. Because if He said this before He gave the Eucharist, it is evident that He gave it to priests. But if Christ said those words after the Eucharist was given to them, it is then clear that He did not give it to priests. Which matter seems to me to be proved more by the context. Still, the argument is not sufficient (as we have said) to make us obliged to accept it.

But if that argument proves anything, it certainly proves that it is not contrary to the Gospel account of the institution to give the Eucharist to the laity under both species, which we most firmly admit. For long ago, for many centuries to do so was customary among all Catholics, as we learn from the writings of many holy men. [The Second Council of Châlons in the year 813 A. D. decreed[1]] the following: "Upon Maundy Thursday, the receiving of the Eucharist is by some neglected, whereas the use of the Church demonstrates that it is to be received on that day by all the faithful (except those to whom for great crimes it is inhibited), seeing even penitents are on that day reconciled to receive the Sacraments of the Lord's Body and Blood."[2] The martyr Cyprian [in 251 A. D.] gives testimony of the same thing in his sermon, "On the Lapsed," when speaking of a certain girl obsessed by the devil, who had been brought to the same Cyprian celebrating the Divine Mysteries [i.e. the Mass], he says these words: "When, however, the solemnities were finished, and the deacon began to offer the cup to those present, and when, as the rest received it, its turn approached, the little child, by the instinct of the Divine Majesty, turned away its face, compressed its mouth with resisting lips, and refused the cup. Still the deacon persisted, and, although against her efforts, forced on her some of the Sacrament of the cup. Then there followed a sobbing and vomiting. In a profane body and mouth the Eucharist could not remain; the draught sanctified in the Blood of the Lord burst forth from the polluted stomach. So great is the Lord's power, so great is His majesty."[3]

[Lanfranc of Canterbury in the first quarter of the twelfth century] gives testimony to this ecclesiastical usage saying the following: "When the host is broken, and the Blood from the chalice is poured into the mouths of the faithful, what other thing is designated than the immolation of the Lord's Body upon the Cross, and the effusion of His Blood from His side?"[4]

---

[1] This quotation was falsely attributed in the text to Pope Soter, the twelfth pope of the Catholic Church, in the text, based upon Gratian's *Concordia discordantium canonum, p. 3* (*De consecratione*), dist. 2, cap. 17 (*In coena Domini*) (PL 187, 1738C)) but has been corrected here.

[2] Canon 47. Mansi, *Sacrorum Conciliorum Nova Amplissima Collectio* (Venice, Antonius Zata, 1769), vol. 14, col. 103.

[3] C. 25 (PL 4, 485B-486A).

[4] *On the Body and Blood of the Lord*, c. 13 (PL 150, 423A). This quotation is falsely attributed to Saint

That this custom was still in the Church in the time of Blessed Pope Gregory is evident from the things which he relates in a Pascal homily. For when speaking to the people he says the following: "What the Blood of the Lamb is, you have already learnt, not by listening to explanations, but by drinking it. A person proceeds to put the Blood on both doorposts, when he swallows it not only with the mouth of the body, but also with the mouth of the heart."[1]

And the *Historia Tripartita* mentions that this was done at one time in the Catholic Church. For in this history, one of those three authors from whose combined extracts it receives the name "Tripartite," namely Theodoret, when recounting the words of Blessed Ambrose with which he excommunicated Theodosius on account of his immense cruelty which he had exercised in Thessalonica, and how he forbade him from entering the church, says the following: "With what eyes, then, will you gaze upon the temple of the Universal Lord? With what feet will you tread its holy pavement? How will you stretch forth the hands from which even now unjust blood is dripping? How will you receive the sacred Body of the Lord into such hands? With what presumption will you feel the cup of the Precious Blood at your mouth when so much blood has been unjustly shed by the fury of its speech? Withdraw, then: withdraw, lest to your former wickedness you hasten to add a second sin."[2] From which words two things ought to be noted. The first is that long ago the Eucharist was given in the hand: which is gathered from other histories and from this passage. For he said the following: "How will you receive the sacred Body of the Lord into such hands?" The second thing is that the laity then received the Eucharist under appearances of wine. For after he had spoken about the reception of the Body, he added: "With what presumption will you feel the cup of the Precious Blood at your mouth."

Yet someone may perhaps say that Theodoret, the author of this historical account, was Greek and for this reason he recounted according to his custom, because it is the custom of the Greeks (as we have said) to receive the Eucharist under both kinds. But it is shown from those words that this was done at one time, which nevertheless the Church after having carefully considered the matter abolished, and not without reason, since it lacked neither authority nor reason for doing this.

Now there were many reasons for abolishing it. The first was the numerous multitude of the faithful was growing daily, there was a danger of spilling when distributing it, which in former times was not feared so much on account the small number of people. The second reason is close to this, which is the transferal of the wine to more distant places for giving Communion to the sick, in which case it was to be greatly feared that by an accidental fall of the carrier the Blood would be spilt. For due to a similar cause, it is read in the life of Saint Donatus, bishop and martyr that long ago, when Communion was given to the laity under both kinds, the Lord's Blood was spilt by the deacon, wherein these words are found: "And one day after he had celebrated Mass for the people, and was being reverentially refreshed by Christ's Body, the deacon administering the Sacred Blood to the people fell, and spilt the holy chalice."[3] Next [the third reason is] lest the wine kept for the sick turn into vinegar, which often happens. The fourth reason is that there is a scarcity of wine in the countries of many peoples, due to which it would be very difficult, and sometimes impossible, that all the people would communicate under the species of wine: for there would not be enough wine to suffice for such a great multitude.

Augustine in the text based upon Gratian's *Concordia discordantium canonum*, dist. 2, c. 37 (PL 187, 1748A).

[1] Hom. 22, n. 7 (PL 76, 1178B). Cf. *Concordia discordantium canonum*, dist. 2, c. 73 (PL 187, 1770A).

[2] Bk. 9, c. 30 (PL 69, 1145B-C).

[3] Ado of Vienne, *Martyrologium*, August 7 (PL 123, 321A).

EUCHARISTIA

And what was more pressing than all these things was to prevent men by this occasion from being led into the error of believing that the whole Christ is not equally contained under both species of the Eucharist, as it is said of certain men, namely the Nestorians, that they fell into this error. Hence it might happen that when faced with serious difficulties the species of wine was withheld due to some urgent reasons, one might suspect that he had not fully communicated. Therefore, there are sufficient reasons, and they ought not to be despised: and authority is not lacking.

For if due to the fact that Christ one time gave Communion to the disciples under both kinds, we acknowledge that it could be done licitly, if the Church does not forbid it: hence, if we would show that Christ at some time gave Holy Communion to the disciples under only one species, it will also be necessary to acknowledge that this is also licit, namely to distribute Holy Communion to the people under only one species, especially since it is evident concerning the Apostles were wont to do this sometimes after Christ. Concerning Christ, it is evident. For Luke, when relating the history of the disciples going to the town which is called Emmaus, whom the risen Christ met on the way, says: "And it came to pass, whilst he was at table with them, he took bread, and blessed, and brake, and gave to them. And their eyes were opened, and they knew him: and he vanished out of their sight" (24, 30-31). Now it can be proved that this bread was the Eucharist from the fact that he says, "He blessed and brake." For that consecration is never called anything else in the Gospel and in the Epistles of Paul except "blessing." "And they knew him in the breaking of the bread" (v. 35), namely because they saw Him observing the same manner that he had at the Last Supper when He gave His Body to the Apostles.

But lest these things which have been said so far be attributed a deceptive opinion of ours, I will cite very weighty authorities thinking the same way. Hence Theophylactus when expounding this passage in Luke says: "And when He permits, then their eyes are opened and they know Him. But He also implies another thing, that the eyes of those who receive the sacred bread are opened that they should know Christ. For the Lord's flesh has in it a great and ineffable power."[1] Augustine also testifies to this saying the following: "Not unsuitably may we suppose that this impediment in their eyes came from Satan, with the view of precluding their recognition of Jesus. But, nevertheless, permission that it should be so was given by Christ unto the point at which the mystery of the Bread was taken up. And thus the lesson might be, that it is when we become participants in the unity of His Body, that we are to understand the impediment of the adversary to be removed, and liberty to be given us to know Christ."[2] [Pseudo-] Chrysostom[3] is of this opinion and likewise Bede[4] asserts the same thing. I disdain to bring forth their words in order to avoid prolixity.

---

[1] *Enarratio in Evangelium Sanctae Lucae* (PG 123, 1119A).

[2] *The Harmony of the Gospels*, bk. 3, c. 75, n. 72 (PL 34, 1206).

[3] "The Lord not only blessed bread on the road but from his own hand gave it to Cleophas and his fellow traveler. And as Paul was sailing, he not only blessed bread but offered it with his own hand to Luke and the other disciples. But whatever has been offered by the hand of a priest should not be given to animals or offered to the unbelieving, because it is not only sanctified but also a means of sanctification. (*Opus Imperfectum in Matthaeum*, hom. 17 (PG 56, 729)). This work had been falsely ascribed to Saint John Chrysostom.

[4] "It was done for the sake of a mystery, that another shape in Him would be shown to them, lest anyone suppose that they recognize Christ if he be not a partaker of His Body, that is, the Church, whose unity the Apostle commends in the Sacrament of Bread, saying: "We... are one bread, one body" (I Cor. 10, 17): so that when He gave them Blessed Bread, their eyes would be opened, they would recognize Him. They were indeed opened to the knowledge of Him, namely when the obstacle was removed, whereby they were held lest they recognize Him. Now we do not incongruously interpret that this obstacle was in

Thus, when Christ then gave the Sacrament, Luke only mentions that He gave bread, making no mention of wine. Suppose that Christ then did not give His Body, because I do not wish to settle anything about this matter: yet the Apostles likewise make use of this same [manner of expression]. For in the Acts of the Apostles it is said concerning those who were converted through Peter's preaching, that "they were persevering in the doctrine of the apostles, and in the communication of the breaking of bread, and in prayers" (2, 42). You see here that no mention was made of wine. And elsewhere in the same book it is said: "And on the first day of the week, when we were assembled to break bread, Paul discoursed with them, being to depart on the morrow" (20, 7). Nor is there here any mention made of wine.

And not only at the time of the Apostles, but also long afterwards we can prove the rite of Communion was under only one kind from various testimonies. For Cyprian in a letter to Antonianus relates that priests who abandoned the faith and later repented, were not accustomed to receive priestly Communion, but only lay Communion, which could not be anything else but that which is given under only one kind, because there can be no other distinction between lay and priestly Communion except that a layman communicates under only one kind, but a priest under both.[1] And Blessed Ambrose also gives a clear testimony about this matter, who when discussing Communion of the laity, makes absolutely no mention of wine but only mentions the bread. And hence in the funeral oration of his brother Satyrus, he declares (as we have just cited in the preceding heresy) that he carried the Sacrament of the Eucharist in his handkerchief,[2] and by It was saved in a shipwreck. From which testimony it is clearly gathered that one species of the Sacrament separated from the other was then given. There is still another example which we also just related in the previous heresy for a different purpose, and because it greatly supports this argument for a different reason, it is necessary to repeat it here. In the *Historia Tripartita* it is related that when [an old man[3]] named Serapion who was near to death asked for the Eucharist from a priest, the priest gave it to a boy so that he might bring It to the sick man, because he could not come to the sick man on account of the

---

their eyes from Satan, lest Jesus be recognized, and yet permission was given by Christ until the Sacrament of Bread was partaken, so that having partaken in the unity of His Body, it may be understood that the impediment of the enemy was removed, so that Christ could be known." (*In Evangelium S. Lucae*, bk. 6, c. 24 (PL 92, 628B-C)).

[1] "Trophimus was received, for whom the return of the brethren and salvation restored to many made atonement. Yet Trophimus was admitted in such a manner as only to communicate as a layman, not, according to the information given to you by the letters of the malignants, in such a way as to assume the place of a priest." (Ep. 52, n. 11 (PL 3, 778A; PL 4, 345B)).

[2] The author here writes that Satyrus put the host in his prayer book (*in libello precum suarum*), since Saint Ambrose wrote that it was put in an *orarium*. But although in the Middle Ages this word then could mean a Latin book of private prayer, especially that issued in England under Henry VIII. in 1546, or the one published under Elizabeth in 1560. But Rev. Alban Butler states that Satyrus rather used a handkerchief, saying: "Satyrus, attempting to go to Africa to recover some money due to his brother, was shipwrecked; and, not being baptized, desired some that were there to give him the Holy Mysteries, that is, the Blessed Eucharist, to carry with him; for the faithful carried it in long voyages, that they might not die deprived of it. As none but those who were baptized were allowed even to have a sight of it, Satyrus begged them to wrap it in an *orarium*, which was a kind of long handkerchief, at that time worn by the Romans about their necks. This he wrapped about him, and threw himself into the sea, without seeking a plank to support him; yet, by swimming, he was the first who came to land. It seems to have been in the isle of Sardinia" (*The Lives of the Fathers, Martyrs and Other Principal Saints* (Dublin, R. Coyne, 1833), vol. 7, p. 998).

[3] The text mistakenly calls him a "boy," but in *Historiae Ecclesiasticae* it is written, "Serapion, a certain old man" (PG 20, 630B).

inclemency of the night and his sickness. And that history relates that in these circumstances only the species of the Bread was given to the boy, making no mention of the wine.[1]

Next, Leo I in a certain decree[2] and in his fourth sermon on Lent[3] commands that there would not be Communion under one species only, on account of the heresy of the Manichaeans and of others who were preaching that Christ assumed an imaginary body without blood, and for this reason they contended that the Eucharist ought to be received without the Blood. From which decree of Leo it is clearly inferred that before Pope Leo it was the custom for the laity to communicate under one kind only, and that custom was removed by the decree of Leo, and from that time for due cause the custom began of communicating under both kinds, which afterwards lasted for a certain period of time, but finally for many other reasons the custom was abolished. Thus, if Christ once communicated His disciples in only one kind: if the Apostles often communicated others also in only one kind, if that custom was afterwards kept in the Church for a long time, it is proved that all Christians are nowise obliged from Christ's command. to receive under both species.

Additionally, in the sixth chapter of John's Gospel in which there is mention of this Sacrament, reference is often made to bread, but never to wine. For even if there would be mention of the Blood, still there is no mentioning that it must be received. Next, one of the petitions in the Lord's prayer which are recorded in Matthew's Gospel is about this Sacrament having these words: "Give us this day our supersubstantial bread" (Mt. 6, 11): in which petition there is no mention of the species of wine. I pass over the figures of this Sacrament, which since they are many, nevertheless very rarely prefigured by the species of wine, but nearly all prefigured by the species of food, such as the manna, the Pascal lamb, and the loaves of proposition. Now what is said in Genesis: Melchisedech offered "bread and wine," was indeed a figure of this Sacrament under both kinds, yet not in relation to a common man, but to a true priest of God: because it ought to be understood that he did not offer those things to Abraham. For if these would have been given to Abraham, he was not Christ's priest. But it ought to be understood that he offered those things to God, rendering thanks to Him for the victory which Abraham had over the enemies.

Thus, since it is proved by so many testimonies that there was no Divine precept about this matter, namely that all Christians receive the Eucharist under the twofold species: what prevents the Church from decreeing that the laity are restricted to only one species, especially since so many impelling reasons support decreeing this, and no inconvenience ensues as a result? Therefore, it ought to be most steadfastly maintained that the practice of the Church

---

[1] "He gave the boy a small portion of the Eucharist, telling him that after having soaked it in water, to let the drops fall into the old man's mouth" (Bk. 6, c. 44 (PG 20, 631A)).

[2] Either this decree of Pope Leo is contained in his fourth sermon of Lent, or more likely, the author here is referring to the decree attributed by Gratian to Pope Gelasius: "We find that some taking only a portion of the Body, abstain from the cup of the Holy Blood, which persons (because they seem to adhere to I know not what superstition) let them either take the Sacrament entirely, or else be wholly kept from them, because the division of one and the same Mystery cannot be without great sacrilege." (*De Consec.*, dist. 2, c. 12 (PL 187, 1736C)).

[3] "For they reject the mystery of man's salvation and refuse to believe that Christ our Lord in the true flesh of our nature was truly born, truly suffered, was truly buried and was truly raised. And in consequence, condemn the day of our rejoicing by the gloom of their fasting. And since to conceal their infidelity they dare to be present at our meetings, at the Communion of the Mysteries they bring themselves sometimes, in order to ensure their concealment, to receive Christ's Body with unworthy lips, though they altogether refuse to drink the Blood of our Redemption. And this we make known to you, holy brethren, that men of this sort may be detected by you by these signs, and that they whose impious pretenses have been discovered may be driven from the society of the saints by priestly authority" (Sermon 42, c. 5 (PL 54, 279B-280A)).

observed until the present time of giving Communion only under one kind to the laity is nowise inconsistent with Holy Writ, but rather is justified and truly Catholic. Wherefore, the Greeks, Bohemians and Lutherans asserting the opposite, ought to be reckoned as heretics, and as such avoided.

But it is unfitting to detain the reader any longer on these matters, since this matter has already been decided by many councils. For the Council of Constance defines by these words: "Since in some parts of the world certain ones have rashly presumed to assert that Christian people should receive the sacrament of the Eucharist under both species of bread and wine, and since they give communion to the laity indiscriminately, not only under the species of bread, but also under the species of wine, after dinner or otherwise when not fasting, and since they pertinaciously assert that communion should be enjoyed contrary to the praiseworthy custom of the Church reasonably approved which they try damnably to disprove as a sacrilege, it is for this reason that this present Council... declares, decides, and defines, that, although Christ instituted that venerable sacrament after supper and administered it to His disciples under both species of bread and wine; yet, notwithstanding this, the laudable authority of the sacred canons and the approved custom of the Church have maintained and still maintain that a sacrament of this kind should not be consecrated after supper, nor be received by the faithful who are not fasting, except in case of sickness or of another necessity granted or admitted by law or Church; and although such a sacrament was received by the faithful under both species in the early Church, yet since then it is received by those who consecrate under both species and by the laity only under the species of bread [another reading: And similarly, although this sacrament was received by the faithful in the early Church under both species, nevertheless this custom has been reasonably introduced to avoid certain dangers and scandals, namely, that it be received by those who consecrate it under both species, and by the laity only under the species of bread], since it must be believed most firmly and not at all doubted that the whole body of Christ and the blood are truly contained under the species of bread as well as under the species of wine. Therefore, to say that to observe this custom or law is a sacrilege or illicit must be considered erroneous, and those pertinaciously asserting the opposite of the above mentioned must be avoided as heretics and should be severely punished, either by the local diocesan officials or by the inquisitors of heretical depravity."[1] And the Council of Basel, in which this matter was disputed at greater length with the Bohemians, confirms this same opinion of the aforesaid council in the thirtieth session.[2]

---

[1] Sess. 13 (Dz. 626).

[2] "That the faithful laity, or clergy communicating but not consecrating, are not bound by the Lord's precept, to receive under each kind, that is of bread and wine, the Holy Sacrament of the Eucharist. But the Church, which is governed by the Spirit of truth remaining with her forever, and Christ remains with her, as the divine Scripture saith, even to the end of the world, hath to order how it may be ministered by those who do not consecrate, as shall seem expedient, both for the reverence of the Sacrament and the salvation of the faithful. Whether, therefore, anyone do communicate under one kind, or under both, according to the ordinance or observance of the Church, it is profitable to salvation unto those who communicate worthily. Nor is it in any wise doubtful, that not the Flesh only under the species of bread, nor the Blood only under the species of wine, but the whole Christs under either species is entire. The laudable custom also of communicating the lay-people under one kind, reasonably introduced by the Church and holy Fathers, and hitherto long observed even by the Doctors of the Divine law, having much knowledge of the Holy Scriptures and canons, and now of a long time commended, is to be accounted as law; nor is it lawful for anyone to reject it, or without the authority of the Church to change it. Given at Basel, in our solemn and public session, the tenth before the kalends of January (December 23), in the year from the Lord's nativity, 1437." *Monumenta conciliorum generalium seculi decimi quinti. Concilium Basiliense*, (Vienna, Typis C.R. officinae typographicae aulae et status, 1873), vol. 2, p. 1112.

If someone were to ask me, when did Communion under both kinds cease among the laity, I (so that I may speak candidly) do not know. For even though I have made much effort to investigate this matter, I still could not find the beginning of this practice in any writer, nor have I found any definition of the Church on this matter before the Council of Constance. Hence it is fair to believe that it is from the common silent consent of the faithful and of the orthodox prelates that Communion under only one kind was accepted. But it is not evident to me when it first began.

A certain Carthusian, Johannes [Bremer von] Hagen, wrote against this heresy some time ago (as Johannes Trithemius testifies[1]). Afterwards, in our time, many betook themselves to write [against this heresy], of whom I have seen Caspar Schatzgeyer in his *Scrutinium divinae Scripturae*,[2] and Bishop [John Fisher] of Rochester, who in that work which he published against all of Luther's errors, he made one whole article on this subject[3]: and Josse van Clichtove in that compendium of the truths defined in the Synod of Sens which he made.[4] Albert Pighius in his book of controversies held in Ratisbon [also wrote against this heresy].[5]

EUNUCHUS

Eunuch

There was a no less cruel and temerarious than erroneous opinion of certain men saying that it is necessary for serving God well that one be castrated and a eunuch. The authors of this heresy (as Augustine says[6]) were certain men named the Valesians, who castrated not only themselves, but also those whom they received as guests, supposing that they ought to serve God in this way.

This error is clearly enough refuted by that which is one of the Commandments of the Law, namely that we do not kill anyone. By which Commandment not merely killing is forbidden (as the Truth Himself explained), but everything which tends to it in whatever way. For just as in the affirmative Commandments not only the things expressed there are commanded, but those things are also commanded without which the Commandments could not be kept: so likewise in the negative Commandments, that is to say in the prohibitions, not only are the things stated there forbidden, but also all other things are interdicted which strongly impel and open a wide way to them.

And it is certain that he who is castrated is put into such danger that his life is greatly imperiled. For I myself have seen a man castrated by a surgeon, as he would otherwise suffer from

---

[1] *De scriptoribus ecclesiasticis*, fol. 179r. He is otherwise called Johannes de Indagine (c. 1415–1475) and wrote a tract entitled, *De communion sub utraque specie*. In total, he wrote about three hundred tracts on various subjects, but only fifty of which are still extant.

[2] *Scrutinium divinae Scripturae pro conciliatione dissidentium dogmatum circa subsciptas materias* (Cologne, Johannes Soter, 1523), conatus VIII (*De communione sub utraque specie*).

[3] Article 16, *Assertionis Lutheranae confutatio*, p. 270 ff.

[4] *Compendium veritatum ad fidem pertinentium contra erroneas Lutheranorum assertiones ex dictis et actis in concilio provinciali Senonensi apud Parisios celebrato* (Paris, 1529), c. 11 (*De communione laicorum sub una specie*), p. 53 ff.

[5] *Controversiarum præcipuarum in Comitiis Ratisponensibus tractatarum... explicatio* (Paris, Joannes Ruellius, 1549), controversia 7 (*De communione de utroque aut altera specie*), fol. 124r ff. Albert Pighius (c. 1490-1542) was a Dutch theologian, archdeacon at Utrecht and opponent of Luther. At Ratisbon in 1541 he took part in the efforts at reunion with the Protestants.

[6] *De Haeresibus ad Quodvultdeum*, c. 37 (PL 42, 32).

a truly incurable sickness, who nevertheless died from this operation alone. Hence since to castrate someone is so dangerous that that it is likely to cause the death of the one to be castrated, it is proved from this that castration is forbidden by the same Commandment whereby the killing of a man is forbidden. And it will never be permitted except for the sake of gaining health, which cannot be obtained by another easier way. Moreover, if it were necessary that everyone be castrated, marriages would vanish, which God has approved, commanding that no one put away his wife, "except it be for fornication" (Mt. 19, 9). And Paul commands the husband to render the debt to his wife, namely so that they would not defraud each other.[1] But how could a castrated man render the debt to his wife, since such rendering cannot be done in another way than by carnal intercourse?

Again, if it were necessary to castrate all men, the human race would very quickly end, not by God's command and will, but on account of a lack of propagation. But the command of the Lord precludes this opinion, for He says: "Increase and multiply" (Gen. 1, 22). Which precept obliged all men at the beginning of the world for the sake of the multiplication of the human race, but now since it has already been sufficiently propagated, and widely diffused, does not oblige except if there would be an urgent necessity, for example if it would happen that the human race were reduced to such a small number from some calamities, that it would be necessary for its preservation that that men would have carnal intercourse with women. For in such an urgent case, that precept of the multiplication of the human race would perhaps then resume its force of law, and oblige as it did at the beginning of human society. For due to this reason alone the daughters of Lot who had intercourse with their father are excused from the sin of incest, namely that they thought that all men had perished after the burning of Sodom and Gomorrha, and that that there was no other man in existence besides their father.

For holy men thought that this precept has such force of law that they deemed that it extended to the intercourse of a father with his daughter in order to avoid the extermination of the human race. For Blessed Irenaeus when speaking of Lot says the following: "Thus, according to their simplicity and innocence, did these daughters [of Lot] so speak, imagining that all mankind had perished, even as the Sodomites had done, and that the anger of God had come down upon the whole earth. Wherefore also they are to be held excusable, since they supposed that they only, along with their father, were left for the preservation of the human race; and for this reason it was that they deceived their father."[2]

Origen agrees with him, who says in a homily on Genesis: "Although their crime appeared great in lying with their father by stealth, nevertheless their impiety would have appeared more serious if, in preserving their chastity, they had, as they supposed, abolished the hope of human posterity. For this reason, therefore, they enter upon a plan with the lesser fault, in my opinion, but with the greater hope and intrinsic worth: they soothe and relax their father's grief and severity with wine. Having gone in individually on individual nights, they conceive from an unknowing man; they do not repeat the deed later nor do they seek to do so. Where is the fault of pleasure proven here; where the crime of incest? How will one be given to a vice which is not repeated in deed?"[3]

Nevertheless, Augustine attributes some fault to those women saying: "It would have been better for them never to have been mothers, than to have become mothers by their own father."[4] But although Augustine reckons that these women sinned, still he excuses them very much, namely because they were not motivated by an ardor of lust, but they acted only for the sake of the conservation of the human race, supposing that the human race would then perish

---

[1] Cf. I Cor. 7, 3 & 5.

[2] *Against the Heresies*, bk. 4, c. 31, n. 2 (PG 7, 1069B).

[3] *Homiliae in Genesim*, Homily 5, n. 4 (PG 12, 191C-192A).

[4] *Against Faustus*, bk. 22, c. 43 (PL 42, 426).

if they would not use their father. And this, in fact, is sufficient for our testimony: because if the intention of conserving the human race through intercourse would not be good of itself, it could nowise have freed them from as much malice as such incest could have enkindled in them. [Psuedo-] Eucherius of Lyons supports Origen's opinion, with the same words of Origen, and not changing a single word.[1]

One may add to these testimonies that in the Gospel the Lord did not commend men born eunuchs from their mother's womb, nor eunuchs who were made eunuchs by men, but He commended those eunuchs who castrated themselves for the kingdom of Heaven. Now this castration ought not to be so understood that they cut off their male sexual organs: because if Christ would have praised such eunuchs, for the same reason He would have also praised those who had been born eunuchs from their mother's womb, or those who were made eunuchs by men, which He did not do. Besides, even if in that way venereal act is completely removed, still the evil willing of that act is not taken away, which especially should have been avoided: since from that willing the goodness or wickedness of the act depends. I knew a man from whom the male organ had been removed due to a pressing infirmity, who nevertheless (as he himself stated afterwards) was suffering from vehement desires of the flesh, and often lamented that he could not carry out what the flesh was coveting. Hence, what had he gained from having been castrated? Certainly, he gained little for the salvation of his soul, since the ardor of lust burned his flesh, and a depraved will was still lurking within the hidden depths of his soul. Therefore, let the Valesians depart, and castrate their souls from a depraved will, and leave their bodies intact.

EXCOMMUNICATIO

Excommunication

Once someone has declared himself to be someone's enemy, he looks for a way to harm him in any way that he can, and tries to lessen, take away and, if possible, completely remove his power. This is easy to recognize in the Wycliffites, the Hussites, and Lutherans: because all these men, as broods of vipers, never cease to gnaw the heart of their mother, the Church: and although they were born in it through Baptism, leaving it through heresy, they wish to kill it, and take away all power from it. Hence among the other things that they strive to sever from the Church is the power of excommunicating. For Wycliffe says, "The excommunication of the pope or of any prelate whatsoever is not to be feared, because it is the censure of the Antichrist."[2] And John Hus asserts that the clergy procure the laity [for themselves, for their own exultation] by excommunications and other censures.[3] Luther,

---

[1] *Commenatarius in Genesim*, bk. 2; on chap. 15, v. 31 (PL 50, 964D). The author of this commentary is uncertain as was stated above in the section on "Adam and Eve," second heresy.

[2] Council of Constance, sess. 8, thirtieth error of John Wycliffe (Dz. 610).

[3] "By ecclesiastical censures of excommunication, suspension, and interdict, the clergy for its own exaltation supplies for itself the lay populace, it multiplies avarice, protects wickedness, and prepares the way for the Antichrist. Moreover, the sign is evident that from the Antichrist such censures proceed, which in their processes they call fulminations, by which the clergy principally proceed against those who uncover the wickedness of the Antichrist, who will make use of the clergy especially for himself." (Council of Constance, see. 15, nineteenth error of John Hus (Dz. 645)). "Verily, even so I do now say again, that every excommunication, by which a man is unjustly excommunicated, is unto him a blessing before God; according to the saying of the prophet, I will curse where you bless: and contrariwise, They shall curse, but thou, O Lord! shalt bless." (John Foxe, *The Acts and Monuments of John Foxe* (R.B. Seeley and W. Burnside, 1837), vol. 3, p. 466).

however, attempting to rebuild the walls of Jericho once destroyed, says that "an excommunication is not merely not to be feared, but received and procured with joy."[1] Hence, so that we may stop up the mouths of these men, let us show from Holy Writ that the Church has the power of excommunicating: then we shall relate the troubles from the excommunication alone which happen to one who has been excommunicated, so that in this way Luther may perhaps acknowledge how much it ought to be feared.

Christ gave the Church the power of excommunicating when in Matthew's Gospel He said: "If thy brother shall offend against thee, go, and rebuke him between thee and him alone. If he shall hear thee, thou shalt gain thy brother. And if he will not hear thee, take with thee one or two more: that in the mouth of two or three witnesses every word may stand. And if he will not hear them: tell the church. And if he will not hear the church, let him be to thee as the heathen and publican" (18, 15-17). Now what is it to say, "Let him be to thee as the heathen and publican"? Certainly, it is the same as if He were to have said, "Have completely no association with him," because Christians are forbidden to associate with unbelievers. Hence Paul says: "Or what part hath the faithful with the unbeliever?" (II Cor. 6, 15). And Blessed John says in his second epistle: "If any man come to you and bring not this doctrine, receive him not into the house nor say to him: God speed you. For he that saith unto him: God speed you, communicateth with his wicked works. (Behold I have told you beforehand, so that in the day of the Lord you may not be confounded[2])" (1, 10-11). Thus, what the Canaanite was to the people of Israel, that is what an unbelieving man is to the Christian man. Hence when He said, "Let him be to thee as the heathen": it is the same as if he would have said that one ought not to have any association with him.

Now so that no one would doubt that the sentence of the Church excommunicating someone is ratified and firm, He adds: "Amen I say to you, whatever you shall bind upon earth, shall be bound also in heaven; and whatsoever you shall loose upon earth, shall also be loosed in heaven" (Mt. 18, 18). Blessed Jerome expounding which words in his commentary on Matthew says: "Because He had said, 'If he will not hear the church, let him be to thee as the heathen and publican,' and there could be this hidden response or tacit thought of this brother who despises [the Church]: 'If you despise me, I also despise you: if you condemn me, you will also be condemned by my judgment': He gave authority to the Apostles, so that they who are condemned by such distinguished men may know that the human verdict is corroborated by a Divine verdict: 'And whatsoever you shall bind upon earth, shall also be bound in heaven.'"[3] You see here Jerome attributing the power of excommunication to the Church, and he does not do this based upon his own reasoning (as heretics do) but upon the words of the Gospel, which he reckons ought to be understood concerning this power.

---

[1] Gabriel DuPréau (Prateolus), *Elenchus Haereticorum omnium* (Cologne, Arnoldus Quentelius, 1605), bk. 10, p.268, Lutheran heresy n. 17. Luther's actual words are: "Be it known to you [i.e. Pope Leo X], that I and all other Christians shall consider your See as the seat of Antichrist, possessed by Satan himself; which not only will we not obey, nor own ourselves subject to, or incorporated with, but shall detest and execrate, as the chief enemy of Christ; being prepared in this our decision, not only to bear with joy your stupid censures, but even to request that you never absolve us, or number us among your followers, as we would rather fulfill your cruel tyranny by offering up to you our lives" (*Adversus execrabilem Antichrisit bullam M. Lutherus* in *D. Martini Lutheri Opera...*, ed. by Henricus Schmidt (Frankfurt, C. Heyderi et H. Zimmeri, 1868), vol. 5, p. 143). Additionally, Luther begins this key paragraph of his response to his condemnation with the words, *Te igitur, Leo X*, as a sacrilegious mockery of the first words of the Canon of the Mass.

[2] This insertion is found in some manuscripts but was expurgated in the Vulgate since "the Fathers passed it over it as superfluous" ("*Romanae Correctiones*," *Biblia sacra vulgatæ editionis Sixti V. & Clementis VIII* (Venice, Remondinus, 1774), p. 604).

[3] *Commentaria in Evangelium Sancti Matthaei* (PL 26, 131D).

Chrysostom agrees with Jerome, who, when expounding those words of Matthew, says: "Do you see how He binds by a twofold constraint, both by a present penalty (namely, the casting out by the Church: 'Let him be to thee as the heathen and publican') and by a future punishment (which is to be 'bound in heaven')?"[1] Christian Druthmar says the same thing, and with nearly the same words with which Jerome [expounds this passage], hence it was not necessary to repeat them, but it suffices to have indicated this to the reader.[2] [Psuedo-] Pope and Martyr Urban also teaches the same opinion in his letter concerning common life and the offerings of the faithful. For in that letter, after he inhibits the Church's possessions to be taken and converted to other uses, and having threatened an excommunication upon anyone usurping them, lest anyone belittle such an excommunication, he says: "As to the fact that in the churches of the bishops there are found elevated seats set up and prepared like a throne, they show by these that the power of overseeing and of judging, and the authority to loose and bind, are given to them by the Lord. Whence the Savior Himself says in the Gospel: 'Whatever you shall bind upon earth, shall be bound also in heaven; and whatsoever you shall loose upon earth, shall also be loosed in heaven.' And elsewhere : 'Receive ye the Holy Ghost: whose sins you shall forgive, they are forgiven them: and whose sins you shall retain, they are retained.' (Jn. 20, 22-23). These things, then, we have set before you, most dearly beloved, in order that you may understand the power of your bishops, and give reverence to God in them, and love them as your own souls; and in order that you may have no communication with those with whom they have none, and that you may not receive those whom they have cast out."[3] This letter of [Pseudo-] Pope and Martyr Urban is found in that book in which are kept the decrees of all the councils.[4]

Now I have cited the Doctors so that Luther may see how the holy Doctors have interpreted that passage of the Gospel, concluding from it that the Church has the power of excommunicating. And if ecclesiastical prelates indeed have such power, still they ought not to inflict it haphazardly and for very small faults: because since it is a very bitter punishment, no one ought to be punished with that penalty except for a lethal crime, and not just any such fault, but (as it is evident from the context of the Gospel passage) only for that crime alone to which pertinacity is involved. Hence Pope Leo I in his letter to the bishops stationed throughout the province of Vienne, says the following: "No Christian should lightly be denied communion, nor should that be done at the will of an angry priest which the judge's mind ought to a certain extent unwillingly and regretfully to carry out for the punishment of a great crime. For we have ascertained that some have been cut off from the grace of communion for trivial deeds and words, and that the soul for which Christ's Blood was shed has been exposed to the devil's attacks and wounded, disarmed, so to say, and stripped of all defense by the infliction of so savage a punishment as to fall an easy prey to him. Of course, if ever a case has arisen of such a kind as it is in due proportion to the nature of the crime committed to deprive a man of communion, he only who is involved in the accusation must be subjected to punishment: and he who is not shown to be a partner in its commission ought not to share in the penalty."[5] From whose words there are many things which will be noted hereafter. What serves our purpose now is that an excommunication ought not to be inflicted upon anyone except for guilt, and that which is serious.

---

[1] *Commentaria in Matthaeum*, hom. 40, n. 2 (PG 58, 586).
[2] *Expositio in Mattheum*, c. 41 (PL 106, 1410C).
[3] *False Decretals of the Pseudo-Isidore* (PL 130, 139C).
[4] Bartholomé Carranza de Miranda, *Summa Conciliorum et Pontificum a Petro usque Paulum III* (Madrid, Petrus Marin, 1781), p. 25-26.
[5] Ep. 10, C. 8 (PL 54, 635B).

For before someone may be excommunicated, the quality of the crime ought to be examined. Because if a crime shall be found in him, he ought to be corrected, and by all means induced to repentance. And if despising admonitions he shall refuse to repent and return to the straight path, then deservedly he ought to be excommunicated so that perhaps having been shaken and ashamed he may come to his senses. For herein is one reason for which someone ought to be excommunicated, namely for the benefit of the one excommunicated. Hence Blessed Paul, when speaking about that Corinthian who was having intercourse with his stepmother, says the following: "I have judged... To deliver such a one to Satan for the destruction of the flesh, that the spirit may be saved in the day of our Lord Jesus Christ" (I Cor. 5, 3 & 5). You see how he is delivered to Satan so that his spirit may be saved. And in the First Epistle to Timothy when saying that some have suffered shipwreck of the faith, he adds: "Of whom is Hymeneus and Alexander, whom I have delivered up to Satan, that they may learn not to blaspheme" (1, 20). And in the Second Epistle to the Thessalonians, he says: "And if any man obey not our word by this epistle, note that man and do not keep company with him, that he may be ashamed" (3, 14). Thus, firstly by excommunication one provides for the benefit of the one excommunicated himself, namely so that when he sees himself cast out of the communion of the faithful, having been put to shame in this way he may perhaps repent of acting wrongly.

For very often it has been found that after one has been corrected by an excommunication, he amends those things which he had previously done wrong. Very many examples could be cited of this thing, the one that is the greatest of them all is that which is told in *Historia Tripartita*[1] concerning Emperor Theodosius, who on account of the cruel slaughter of many men in Thessalonica done by his command, was excommunicated by Ambrose, Bishop of Milan, and forbidden from entering the church. The emperor was patiently bearing this excommunication, because he knew that it was justly inflicted upon him: he refrained from entering the church for eight consecutive months, and remaining at home, he was doing penance with tears and groans, and was asking pardon from the Lord. Ambrose knowing this well, after those eight months gave him communion in the Church. Now it never happened that the emperor was indignant towards Ambrose on account of this, even with other provoking matters: nay he praised Ambrose concerning this matter in Constantinople. That excommunication benefitted Theodosius very much, which brought him to the knowledge of his sin, and obliged him to do penance for it. For "Happy is the necessity which leads us to do better things."[2] And for this reason it is called a medicinal excommunication, because its purpose is to heal the sinner suffering from the sickness of sin. For the excommunication will be medicinal if one does not despise it, but rather considering his own shamefulness, amends those things which he had previously done wrong.

But if despising the excommunication, one neglects to repent, then the excommunication is not medicinal for him, but lethal. But even though it be lethal, still the excommunication ought not to be revoked due to this, because the one excommunicating not only takes into consideration the utility of the one excommunicated himself, but also the safety of the rest of the whole community. For since one sick sheep infects all the sheep: hence the infected sheep is isolated, lest it infect the rest of the sheep by its contact. And the shepherd is not judged to be cruel on account of this, but conscientious: rather he would have been deemed cruel, apathetic, and lazy, if he did not do this. Hence Ambrose says the following: "Since a part of the body which has putrefied is amputated with sorrow, it is also treated for a long time, in case it can be cured with medicine: but if it cannot be cured, then it is cut off by a good doctor. In

---

[1] Bk. 9, c. 30 (PL 69, 1144C ff.).

[2] "Happy is the necessity that compels us to do the better things" (Augustine, ep.127, n. 8 (PL 33, 487)). Cf. II-II, q. 88, a. 4 ad 1um.

this way the bishop's desire is good, in that he chooses to cure the sick, to singe some spreading wounds, not to amputate, but afterwards to cut off with sorrow what cannot be healed."[1] Hence, Mother Church ought not to be deemed cruel (as Luther objects) in that she punishes her son with such fierce punishment, because she does so for the son's benefit, although if the son despises the punishment, she takes into consideration the safety of the other children, namely because she prefers, and rightly so, to lose one rather than to lose all. Therefore, from all these proofs it is sufficiently evident that the Church has the power of excommunicating, and upon whom and for what purpose such excommunication ought to be exercised.

Besides all these proofs for confirming the same matter, the ancient custom of the universal Church has not little, but rather the greatest weight, which is known through the writings and decrees of the supreme pontiffs and also of holy and very learned men. Next, the decrees of many councils exist today in which it is said: "If anyone were to do such and such, let him be excommunicated," or "let him be condemned [*anathema sit*]": which is the same thing. Lastly, in the eighth session of the Council of Constance forty-five assertions of John Wycliffe are condemned, one of which is this: "No prelate should excommunicate anyone, unless he first knows that he has been excommunicated by God; and he who so excommunicates becomes, as a result of this, a heretic or excommunicated."[2] And another assertion of his is this: "The excommunication of the pope or of any prelate whatsoever is not to be feared, because it is the censure of the Antichrist."[3] Which propositions with the others of the same man are all condemned *latae sententiae*.

Therefore, now it is necessary that we show what are the effects of an excommunication, so that Luther may acknowledge that they ought not to be desired (as he says), but ought to be especially avoided. Firstly, then, one who has been excommunicated is handed over to Satan, so that he may be tortured more easily and freely by him. For even though one on account of sin is already in the power of the devil before the excommunication, because he is made the slave of the devil through sin: still by the excommunication the devil has greater power over him, such that he can torture him more easily as he wishes. For before the excommunication even though he had lost charity through sin, wherefore he is not livingly joined to Christ, still he is not completely separated from Christ: because he has some union: although he is a withered member lacking life, because he is joined to the body by sinews and skin, and he is kept somewhat warm by the heat of the body. And on account of this faith and union he is a partaker of the common prayers which are made by the Church. And hence the devil does not have so much power over him such that he may trouble him as he wishes, because the power of the rest of the members to whom he is joined by faith puts up resistance.

But after the excommunication he is deprived of this help, and is separated more from the body [of Christ], and so the devil can torture him more than before. For it is certain that he that is filthy (as it is said in Apocalypse 22, 11) can be filthier still: just as he who is just, can be justified still. So, he who is in the devil's power can still be put under his power more. In fact, John relates that a devil entered into Judas after having received the morsel of bread,[4] and yet the devil was already in him before the morsel was received, because John previously said that the devil had put into the heart of Judas to betray Christ.[5] Notice that the devil who had already possessed Judas enters into him again, receiving more power over him. So also in the one excommunicated, who through sin before the excommunication was already possessed by the devil, having been made his slave: but after the excommunication the devil

---

[1] *On the Duties of the Clergy*, bk. 2, c. 27, n. 135 (PL 16, 139A-B).
[2] N. 11 (Dz. 591).
[3] N. 30 (Dz. 610).
[4] Cf. Jn. 13, 27.
[5] Cf. Jn. 13, 2.

receives greater power over him. For he is no longer warmed by the body as before, because he is now neither a partaker of the goods of the Church nor it is it permitted to pour out public and solemn prayers for him.

A clear proof of this is that on Good Friday the Church prays for all men, even for the pagans, yet only for the excommunicated, who were publicly denounced, does she not pray. But if an excommunicated person is deprived of such helps, it is probable that the devil has a greater power over him than before the excommunication, even if he had been in sin. Now this is proved by the testimony of Paul. For it is certain that the Corinthian who had taken his father's wife was then possessed by the devil, yet Paul judged to deliver him to Satan. And concerning Alexander and Hymeneus who had erred from the true faith, he testifies that he delivered them to Satan. Hence it is quite evident that Paul delivered to Satan those who had already been possessed by the devil. But if they were possessed by him, how did he deliver them to the devil, and why? Certainly, they who were possessed were not completely under his sway, and hence he delivers them so that they may be more subject to him, and he may torture them more freely.

Now so that this truth may appear more clearly— that this is the meaning of Paul's words—I will cite testimonies of some holy men. What we have cited above from the letter of Pope Leo especially makes [the matter clearer]. His last words are these: "For we have ascertained that some have been cut off from the grace of communion for trivial deeds and words, and that the soul for which Christ's Blood was shed has been exposed to the devil's attacks and wounded, disarmed, so to say, and stripped of all defense by the infliction of so savage a punishment as to fall an easy prey to him."[1] Even though he reprehends those who haphazardly inflict an excommunication he still clearly enough shows this effect of excommunication which we have stated.

[Pseudo-] Blessed Augustine in a book on the Apostle's words teaches the same opinion, saying the following: "Every Christian, dearly beloved, who is excommunicated by the priests, is delivered to Satan. Why? It is namely because the devil is outside the Church, just as Christ is in the Church: and one who is removed from ecclesiastical communion is delivered thereby, as it were, to the devil. Hence those whom the Apostle preaches to be then delivered to Satan he shows to have been excommunicated by himself."[2]

And [Ambrosiaster], when expounding what the Apostle says concerning Alexander and Hymeneus, namely: "whom I have delivered up to Satan, that they may learn not to blaspheme," says the following: "This handing over means that the Apostle was moved by their blasphemies to pronounce sentence against them. The devil, who is ready to take those who have turned away from God into his power, seized them when he heard their sentence, so that they would understand that they were being subjected to punishment because they blasphemed."[3]

Origen teaches the same opinion, who in his second homily on the book of Judges, says the following: "Not only through His Apostles has God 'delivered' sinners into the hands of their enemies, but also through those who preside over the Church and have the power not only to loose but also to bind. Sinners are handed over 'for the destruction of the flesh' (I Cor. 5, 5) when on account of their transgressions they are separated from the body of Christ."[4] Which words are in the book of the *Decretals*, in the eleventh cause, third question, in the chapter *Audi*, erroneously cited under the name of Jerome, because besides the fact that Jerome did

---

[1] Ep. 10, C. 8 (PL 54, 635B).

[2] This chapter is quoted by Gratian in *Concordia discordantium canonum*, causa 11, quest. 3, c. 33 (PL 187, 853A-B). The authorship is "uncertain."

[3] *Commentaria in Epistolam ad Timotheum Primam*, c. 1 (PL 17, 465C).

[4] *Homiliae in librum Judicum*, hom. 2, n. 5 (PG 12, 961).

not write a commentary on the book of Judges, those words as cited under the name of Jerome are found word for word in the second homily of Origen on the book of Judges.[1] But let us return to our task.

[Jerome[2]] also teaches this same opinion, who in his [letter to Heliodorus] says the following: "Under the Old Law he who disobeyed the priests was put outside the camp and stoned by the people, or else he was beheaded and expiated his contempt with his blood.[3] But now the disobedient person is cut down with the spiritual sword, or he is expelled from the Church and torn to pieces by ravening demons."[4] Whose martyrdom [referring to Pseudo-Pope and Martyr Saint Anterus] received for Christ greatly commends his doctrine. Yet Luther for the confirmation of his error (which he reckons to be the truth), was most reluctant to undergo martyrdom, because he so kept himself within the corridors of Saxony that he dared not leave from there, thinking that he would not be safe elsewhere.[5]

[Pseudo-] Blessed Pope and Martyr Urban [I][6] concurs with these things in the letter cited above which is about the common life [and offerings] of the faithful. For this holy pontiff, when forbidding that the goods of the Church be changed for other uses, says the following: "These things, brethren, are carefully to be guarded against, and greatly to be feared. For the property of the Church, not being like personal, but like common property, and property offered to the Lord, is to be dispensed with the deepest fear, in the spirit of faithfulness, and for no other objects than the above-named, lest those should incur the guilt of sacrilege who divert it from the hands to which it was consigned, and lest they should come under the punishment and death of Ananias and Sapphira, and lest (which is yet worse) they should become anathema maranatha, and lest, though their body may not fall dead like that of Ananias and Sapphira, their soul, which is nobler than the body, should fall dead, and be cut off from the company of the faithful, and sink into the depths of the pit."[7] By which words he is saying that an excommunication is worse than death.

Why, then, does Luther dare to say that an excommunication ought not to be feared? Do not all men have from nature that they dread and are afraid of death? Much more then should an excommunication be dreaded and feared, which is worse than death. Also from these words it is proved to be false what Luther says, that an excommunication is merely an external punishment, because when the one excommunicated (as we have already proved sufficiently) is delivered to Satan, to be harassed by him; and left without any defenses, is given over to the assaults of the devil; and his soul may be more possessed by the devil than before the excommunication: from this it is deduced that an excommunication is also an internal punishment.

---

[1] This error was corrected in later editions. Cf. C. 21 (PL 187, 838B).

[2] The author erroneously attributes this citation to Pope and Martyr Saint Anterus in a letter to the bishops of Baetica and Toledo, based on the *False Decretals of the Pseudo-Isidore* (PL 130, 149B).

[3] Deut. 17, 5 & 12.

[4] Letter 14, n. 8 (PL 22, 352).

[5] When Luther was excommunicated in 1521 and consequently put under the ban of the Holy Roman Empire, Frederick the Wise, the Elector of Saxony, harbored Luther for ten months in his castle of Wartburg.

[6] "This letter is held to be fictitious and spurious by all learned men" (PG 10, 135B).

[7] PG 10, 138A. Note that this decree and others similar ones "which date from before the eighth century ought to be understood of ecclesiastical goods before their distribution and the erection of benefices, when clerics were still living in common; at which time we admit that neither a bishop nor any individual cleric were their owners, but only administrators, the ownership still remaining in the custody of the Church itself or the community, as it still is now in monasteries" (Billuart, *Summa sancti Thomae hodiernis academiarum accommodate* (Paris, Victor Palmé, 1900), dissert. 3, art. 5 ad 1um, vol. 4, p. 33).

EXCOMMUNICATIO

The second effect of an excommunication is to be separated from the social interaction and companionship with others, such that we may not speak with them, nor receive them as guests. For Paul, in the First Epistle to the Corinthians, says: "If any man that is named a brother, be a fornicator, or covetous, or a server of idols, or a railer, or a drunkard, or an extortioner: with such a one, not so much as to eat" (5, 11). And in the Second Epistle to the Thessalonians: "And if any man obey not our word by this epistle, note that man, and do not keep company with him, that he may be ashamed" (3, 14). And Blessed John, in his Second Catholic Epistle, says the following: "If any man come to you, and bring not this doctrine, receive him not into the house nor say to him, God speed you. For he that saith unto him, God speed you, communicateth with his wicked works. (Behold I have told you beforehand, so that in the day of the Lord you may not be confounded[1])" (1, 10-11). From these words of John, it is clearly established that the excommunicated person is deprived of benefit of hospitality and familiar conversation with other men.

And [Pseudo-] Blessed Pope and Martyr Callistus in his letter to all the bishops of Gaul, includes all these penalties of excommunication that are external in one sentence saying: "Also no one may receive those who have been excommunicated by the priests before a sufficient examination of both parties, nor may he communicate with them in prayer, or food, or drink, or kiss, nor say: God speed you to them: because whosoever shall knowingly communicate with excommunicated persons in these or in other forbidden things will himself be likewise subject to excommunication according to the institution of the Apostles."[2] His letter is among the pontifical letters which [Pseudo-] Blessed Isidore prefixed to the book of general councils.[3] And the Fourth Synod of Carthage[4] and the First Synod of Braga[5] forbids under penalty of excommunication that someone would communicate with an excommunicated person.

How does it seem to you, Luther? Are all these things so good that they rightly (as you teach) ought to be desired? If they ought to be desired and sought after, Paul would not have decreed that those things ought to be inflicted for their embarrassment. For no one is ashamed when he enjoys those things which he greatly desired. The Apostles certainly were not confounded by the reproaches they bore for Christ, because they greatly desired them. Hence when they were afflicted, "They went from the presence of the council, rejoicing that they were accounted worthy to suffer reproach for the name of Jesus" (Acts 5, 41). So if an excommunication were good, and one ought to desire it, when it is imposed, no one ought to be ashamed. And yet Paul wanted a sinner to be excommunicated so that the one excommunicated would be ashamed, so that perhaps in this way he might repent. If a bishop excommunicates someone (as it was evident from the opinion of Blessed Ambrose above) he ought to be sorrowful, because he excommunicates another: all the more it is necessary that the one who is excommunicated be sorrowful, because the bishop does not lament for his own sake, but on account of the severe punishment which he inflicts upon another.

But here it is necessary to instruct the reader, so that he does not suppose that communion with excommunicated persons is so forbidden to the extent that it would not be allowed to associate with them in any way. For if someone were to speak with the excommunicated person so that he might teach him the right way, and turn him away from the very bad way, and

---

[1] See the note above at the beginning of this section about this addition to the passage.
[2] *False Decretals of the Pseudo-Isidore* (PL 130, 132C).
[3] I.e. the *Collectio Hispana* attributed to Saint Isidore of Seville.
[4] "He who shall communicate or pray with an excommunicated person, whether clerical or lay, let him be excommunicated" c. 73 (PL 84, 205).
[5] "No one may presume to communicate with those who are excommunicated for heresy or for some other crime, just as the ancient canons also decreed; which if anyone voluntarily despises he will deliver himself to another condemnation." (C. 15 (PL 84, 567B)). The text here refers, however, to canon 33.

lead him back to the flock of the Church, from which he was expelled as was demanded due to his faults, he then acts most correctly: and if he persuades the excommunicated person to repent and to subject himself to the Church, he will receive a great reward from God, to such an extent is he who does this far from sinning. Hence Blessed Augustine, when expounding Psalm fifty-four, says the following: "Let us love our enemies, and correct them, punish them, excommunicate them, even cast them out from our society, with love let us even separate ourselves from them. See what the Apostle says: 'And if any man obey not our word by this epistle, note that man, and do not keep company with him.' (II Thess. 3, 14). But lest anger creep in to you, and inflame your eye, 'Do not,' he says, 'esteem him as an enemy, but admonish him as a brother' (v. 15). The Apostle prescribes separation from such a person, but does not cut off love from him."[1] Therefore, since excommunication does not forbid love of one's neighbor: it likewise follows that conversation which proceeds from charity and is ordered to charity, is also not forbidden.

EXORCISMUS
Exorcism

The Waldensians seem to have been born for this reason only, to overthrow the Church if they could. They move every stone (as it is said), to attack it. They tried to take away all exorcisms from the Church, saying, all blessings of water, candles, palms, vestments, chalices and patens, altars, and cemeteries should be ridiculed, and have absolutely no importance. Now the Wycliffites, since they seem to swear by the words of the Waldensians more than the words of Christ or the Church, here (as everywhere and always) defend the sect of the Waldensians. For they say that such blessings are rather derived from true necromancy than from sacred theology, because if we believe that through such exorcisms and blessings we improve nature (as they say) it is false.

Now so that we may repel the calumnies of these men, we will firstly say what exorcism is. Exorcism is a Greek word and means the same thing as adjuration. And more precisely, an exorcism is that invocation of the Divine name which is upon the possessed, that is, those having an unclean spirit, by adjuring him by the Divine power to go out from them. Hence Augustine says: "To exorcise is to drive out an unclean spirit by adjuring through holy things."[2] Whence every blessing of anything which is used against the demons or against other similar poisons are also called an exorcism, such as the blessing of water, salt, candles, palms, etc. For upon all these things we invoke the Lord's name, beseeching that those things may be, with His favor, Who alone can do this, a help and protection for us against the devil. But I do not know how this invocation can be rightly accused, since it is so clear in Sacred Writ. I pass over here what Bede relates on chapter nineteen of the Acts of Apostles quoting Josephus,[3] that King Solomon "taught to his people methods of exorcism (that is, of adjuration) by which unclean spirits which were driven out of a person would not dare to return anymore."[4]

Let us proceed to the Gospel. The disciples when returning from the preaching which Christ the Master of all had commanded, say to Him: "Lord, the devils also are subject to us

---

[1] *Expositions on the Psalms*, n. 9 (PL 36, 635).
[2] *De beata vita*, c. 3, n. 18 (PL 32, 968).
[3] "[Solomon] left behind him the manner of using exorcisms; by which they drive away demons; so that they never return: and this method of cure is of great force unto this day." (Josephus, *Antiquities of the Jews*, bk. 8, c. 2, n. 5).
[4] *Commentary on the Acts of the Apostles*, c. 19, v. 13 (PL 92, 983A).

in thy name." (Lk, 10, 17). What is it to say, "in thy name," but at the invocation of Thy name? And the Lord Himself when ascending into Heaven promises that He will never be wanting towards their invocation, saying: "In my name they shall cast out devils" (Mk. 16, 17). Now the fact that it does not always happen that when the name of Jesus has been invoked the devil departs, is due to the little faith in the one invoking. For if he had fully believed, he would have done this and greater things. And only to those, namely those with perfect faith, God's promise seems to pertain, because He had said just before those words: "And these signs shall follow them that believe" (v. 17). And in Luke the Lord says: "If you had faith like to a grain of mustard seed, you might say to this mulberry tree, Be thou rooted up, and be thou transplanted into the sea: and it would obey you" (17, 6). But a mulberry tree does not have understanding, and fulfills the commands of the believing person commanding.

Thus, it is not surprising that the demons obey the faithful, not in fact due to the natural power of the faithful themselves, but on account of the faith that they have. What then? Will Christ's disciples and His Apostles be called necromancers and magicians, because when the name of Jesus has been invoked, demons are cast out from the bodies of obsessed men? And what exalts this invocation of His name still more is that demons are sometimes cast out through reprobate men upon the invocation of the name of Jesus, and this is for the condemnation of the ones invoking themselves or for the benefit of those seeing and hearing. In confirmation of both things is that which we read in the Acts of the Apostles, namely that when the Apostles cast out devils, "Some also of the Jewish exorcists who went about, attempted to invoke over them that had evil spirits, the name of the Lord Jesus, saying: I conjure you by Jesus, whom Paul preacheth. And there were certain men, seven sons of Sceva, a Jew, a chief priest, that did this. But the wicked spirit, answering, said to them: Jesus I know, and Paul I know; but who are you? And the man in whom the wicked spirit was, leaping upon them, and mastering them both, prevailed against them, so that they fled out of that house naked and wounded. And this became known to all the Jews and the Gentiles that dwelt at Ephesus; and fear fell on them all, and the name of the Lord Jesus was magnified" (19, 13-17). From which words it is evident that there were exorcists among the Jews, concerning whom Christ says in Luke: "If I cast out devils by Beelzebub; by whom do your children cast them out?" (Lk. 11, 19). It is also evident how powerful the invocation of the name of Jesus is, and that by its power an abjuration, even when done by the reprobate, does such great things.

Therefore, those things ought not to be attributed to magic (as the wicked and blasphemous Wycliffites teach) but to God alone, Who is present near to everyone invoking Him with faith and humility. Hence Augustine says the following: "It is by true piety that men of God cast out the hostile power of the air which opposes godliness; it is by exorcising it, not by propitiating it; and they overcome all the temptations of the adversary by praying, not to him, but to their own God against him. For the devil cannot conquer or subdue any but those who are in league with sin; and therefore, he is conquered in the name of Him Who assumed humanity, and that without sin, that Himself being both Priest and Sacrifice, He might bring about the remission of sins."[1] These things suffice concerning exorcisms which are done for casting out demons.

Now let us go on to the blessings of other things. The blessings of altars originated from the Old Law. For Moses Himself erected and anointed the altar in the tabernacle by the Lord's command. From which evidence [Pseudo-] Pope Leo I deduces that to bishops alone, whom the high priest prefigured, is it permitted to consecrate and bless altars.[2] [Pseudo-] Blessed Pope Damasus teaches this same thing in his letter concerning the chorepiscopi.[3] Likewise

---

[1] *City of God*, bk. 10, c. 22 (PL 41, 299-300).

[2] *False Decretals of the Pseudo-Isidore*, ep. 66 (PL 130, 881A-B).

[3] *False Decretals of the Pseudo-Isidore* (PL 130, 670B).

EXORCISMUS

the Second Synod of Seville decrees the same thing.[1] Finally the Synod of Agde decrees as follows: "It has seemed good for the altars to be consecrated not merely with the anointing of chrism, but likewise with the priestly blessing."[2] We have already disputed sufficiently above concerning the blessing of water, which the reader ought not to disdain to see, because he will draw from it many things applicable to this topic.

The blessings of bread and of other foodstuffs are not new and invented by men (as the Wycliffites accuse the Church), but have proceeded from God Himself, Who by deed and word taught us to do so. For when God created the fish, "He blessed them" (Gen. 1, 22). And in Exodus it is read: "Thou shalt not adore their gods, nor serve them. Thou shalt not do their works, but shalt destroy them, and break their statues. And you shall serve the Lord your God, that I may bless your bread and your waters" (23, 24-25). And in Leviticus the Lord commands the people of Israel, saying: "When you shall have entered into the land which I will give you, and shall reap your corn, you shall bring sheaves of ears, the firstfruits of your harvest to the priest: Who shall lift up the sheaf before the Lord, the next day after the sabbath, that it may be acceptable for you, and shall sanctify it" (23, 10-11). And in Deuteronomy the Lord commands that all firstfruits be offered to the Lord and given to the priest, so that he may invoke the Lord's name upon them.[3] And in Ezechiel He says explicitly: "You shall give the firstfruits of your meats to the priest, that he may return a blessing upon thy house" (44, 30). Jerome when expounding this says: "Our firstfruits are offered to priests, so that we do not taste the new fruits before the priest has tasted them. Now we do this so that the priest may return our blessing and offering in his house, or so that the Lord may bless our homes upon his prayer. For great is the dignity of priests, but also, when they sin, great is their ruin."[4] What will you say wicked Wycliffites? Did God teach the people of Israel necromancy, or the expertise of magical arts? Far be such impiety from all hearts. For God very strictly forbade and most hatefully abhors idolatry, and yet upon which idolatry magic is based.

Let us go on to the New Testament. When Christ was about to give bread to the Apostles, He blessed it and likewise when about to give the chalice He gave thanks: and when He had supped, He said a hymn, teaching us that when we eat, we ought to do likewise. But if someone were to reply that those words were said of mystic bread alone and of the mystic blessing: let him hear the Apostle Paul, who says the following in the First Epistle to Timothy: "Every creature of God is good, and nothing to be rejected that is received with thanksgiving: for it is sanctified by the word of God and prayer" (4, 4-5). Theophylactus when expounding those which words says: "Then will it be unclean unless it be sanctified? By no means: but he states this as a concession. For firstly after insisting that he calls nothing unclean, then we admit (he says) that it may become unclean: still you have something that you can apply as a remedy: make the sign of the Cross, give thanks, glorify God, in this way all uncleanliness and filthiness will vanish. For thanksgiving cleanses all things."[5] Concerning sacred vestments, altar cloths, and vessels as to their importance and reverence with which they ought to be treated, [Pseudo-] Pope and Martyr Clement teaches in a letter to James, the Lord's brother, which is entitled *De sacratis vestibus et vasis*.[6] Let him read it who wishes to be taught about this matter.

Concerning the blessing of candles, I will only cite the decree of the IV Synod of Toledo. For that council when pronouncing a decision concerning the blessing of the Pascal candle

---

[1] C. 7 (PL 84, 596C).
[2] C. 14 (PL 84, 265D). Mansi, vol. 8, col. 327B.
[3] Cf. Deut. 26, 2-3.
[4] *Commentaria in Ezechielem*, bk. 13 (PL 25, 443D).
[5] *Expositio in Epistolam I ad Timotheum* (PG 125, 54D-55A).
[6] *False Decretals of the Pseudo-Isidore* (PL 130, 38C ff.).

says the following: "The lamp and candle are not blessed in some churches during the [Easter] vigil and they inquire why they are blessed by us. We solemnly bless these things, in fact, on account of the glorious mystery of this night, so that we may commemorate the mystery of Christ's sacred Resurrection, which has come at the time of this votive death, by the blessing of the sanctified light. And because this observance is approved in the churches in many places and in the provinces of Spain, it is fitting that for the sake of peace that it be observed in the Gallic churches. No one, however, will be without punishment who despises this, but on the contrary, he will be subject to the regulations of the Fathers."[1] About which citation it will only be necessary to point out that although it is not contrary to the faith to omit the blessing of such a candle, still it will be against the faith, nay it is deadly, to despise as worthless and without importance the things which the Church assembled together has decreed. Therefore, let the wicked Wycliffites go away and be afraid to call so many holy men magicians and necromancers, by whose doctrine and sanctity the Church shines as the sun and the moon. For they themselves ought rather to be called necromancers and spellcasters, who with diabolic shrewdness delude and bewitch ignorant and simple men, turning them away from the truth of the faith, and turning them towards wicked teachings.

But it is necessary that we reply to their objections. For the Wycliffites object to us that we ourselves wish by our blessings to make creatures better then God made them by their natures. Now such advancement of creatures, that they be made better, is not known (as they say) by any experience. Thus, it is ridiculous to bless them. What a persuasive argument! Tell me, is it not established from the Gospel that he who shall have faith like the grain of a mustard seed, has such power, that if he would say to a mulberry tree, be transplanted, it will immediately be transplanted?[2] But since before he received the faith he could not do this, it is proved that through the coming of the faith he becomes better. What then forbids us from saying the same thing of other things which receive a blessing such that they may become better than they were by nature? It is not because man makes things better, but God, upon the prayers of the one blessing. But we have already made a longer disputation about this matter in the section above entitled, "Water": wherefore we send the reader to that place.

FATUM

Fate

Although there were various opinions of philosophers about this matter, I will not discuss any of them here, but instead, keeping to my original plan, I will only relate what those who profess and brag to be Christians thought, even if they are not by any means. Thus, there was a certain error asserting that men's behaviors ought to be imputed to fate. The author of this error was (as Augustine says[3]) a Syrian named Bardesanes, a learned man: whom Augustine says that he was firstly a Catholic, and afterwards fell into the errors of Valentinus, and from him learned this error. But Eusebius of Caesarea when speaking about Bardesanes, thinks differently from Augustine about him. For he says that he was brought up in the school of Valentinus, but afterwards when he had come to know his teacher's errors, he returned to the correct rule of faith, although he asserts that he did not relinquish all his errors.[4] For he also says that he wrote against Marcion and other heretics, and to Emperor

---

[1] C. 9 (*Collectio Canonum Ecclesiae Hispanae ex probatissimis ac pervetustis Codicibus*, p. 369-370).

[2] Cf. Lk. 17, 6.

[3] *De Haeresibus ad Quodvultdeum*, c. 35 (PL 42, 31-32).

[4] *Church History*, bk. 4, c. 30 (PG 20, 402B-403A).

Antoninus a dialogue, *On Fate*, which dialogue Eusebius does not censure for any error, but rather calls that dialogue very convincing. Now whether he so thought as Augustine accused him, I cannot settle.

Bishop Epiphanius when discoursing on this Bardesanes, thinks otherwise than Eusebius and Augustine about him. For he says the following: "Their successor was a person named Bardesanes. This Bardesanes, the founder of the Bardesianist sect, was a Mesopotamian and a native of the city of Edessa. He was the finest sort of man at first, and while his mind was sound composed no few treatises. For originally he belonged to God's holy Church, and he was learned in two languages, Greek and Syriac. At first he became friends with the ruler of Edessa, Abgar, a very holy and learned man, and assisted him while taking a hand in his education. He survived after Abgar's death until the time of Antoninus Caesar—not Antoninus Pius, but Antoninus Verus. He argued at length against fate in reply to the astrologer Abidas, and there are other works of his which are in accord with the godly faith. He defied Antoninus' companion Apollonius besides, by refusing to say that he denied that he called himself a Christian. He nearly became a martyr, and in a courageous defense of godliness replied that the wise do not fear death, which would necessarily come, he said, even if he did not oppose the emperor. And thus the man was loaded with every honor until he came to grief over the error of his own sect and became like the finest ship, which was filled with a priceless cargo and then wrecked beside the cliffs of its harbor, losing all its freight and occasioning the deaths of its other passengers as well. For he unfortunately fell in with the Valentinians, drew this poison and cockle from their unsound doctrine, and taught this heresy by introducing many other principles and publications, as well as elaborations denying the resurrection of the dead."[1]

Even though Saint Epiphanius says that he fell into the errors of Valentinus, still he clearly says that he wrote against the heresy dealing about fate. But even if this Bardesanes did not uphold this heresy, there were not lacking those who strongly supported it. For Priscillian taught this error, who said that men are bound to the destining stars, and our body itself is composed according to the twelve constellations of the heavens, Aries constituting the head, Taurus in the neck, Geminis in the shoulders, Cancer in the breast, etc., in this way he distributed the other constellations through the other parts of the body down to the feet, which he attributed to Pisces: because the astrologers teach that this is the last constellation. And Guy makes no mention of this error when he speaks about the Priscillianists: which surprises me very much: since Augustine whom Guy always imitates clearly related it.

Now this teaching is easily proved to be a heresy, because it clearly takes away man's free will, such that he has absolutely none in choosing: for if man is free in choosing, such that he could do things otherwise than he does, it follows that man is not bound to the destining stars. But if whatever man is going to do depends upon the power of the stars, and not upon his own choice: then free will does not belong to man. But that man is free in his choices, we will show below, God willing, from Holy Writ. Furthermore, if all things in man are governed by fate, there will be nothing we may praise or reprehend in man. For in those things which are inherent by nature, we neither praise nor reprehend. Again, if men are led by fate, no seeking of advice will be necessary, because in those things which cannot happen otherwise, all advice is superfluous. For no one will be so mindless that he would ask advice about tomorrow's or yesterday's rising of the sun, because no matter what advice has been given, it is not within our power to stop the sun from rising today or tomorrow.

Likewise, it will not be necessary to fight against vices: since the matter is (as they say) subject to fate. In vain, therefore, is the love and attainment of good encouraged, and vice discouraged. In vain did the Prophet say: "Decline from evil and do good" (Ps. 36, 27). In vain also did Paul say: "Fly fornication" (I Cor. 6, 18). Who then would persuade someone [to

---

[1] *Panarion*, heresy 56, n. 1-2 (PG 41, 990B-991B).

do] those things which are not within his power? No one except a madman would persuade someone that he overturn the order of the heavens. Next, if men are subject to fate, laws will be unnecessary. Why is peace commanded to me, if the fate impels me to war? Theft is unjustly forbidden to me, if fate forces me to steal. Justice will also perish for this reason, which wishes that a reward be appointed for the good, and punishment for the troublesome. A thief or adulterer is unjustly punished, if both are so forced by fate, that neither the latter could in any way avoid adultery, nor the former theft. Certainly, there will be no reason due to which a reward is given to someone doing good rather than an evildoer: why this man is punished, but not that man, since both act by necessity and not freely. But if good or evil comes to be imputed to someone, it will be imputed to fate, which impels to good or evil. But since such fate is according to these men a certain arrangement of the stars in causing or influencing, which certain arrangement is proved to be ordained given to the stars by God so that men's evils may be referred to God, Who so disposed fate such that man would be forced to do evil. Now this is so impious that the ears are horrified to hear that God is the main author of our vices.

Add to these things that which we have known from experience and the testimony of others. For it often happens that twins having different characters are born from the same womb, such as is clearly evident of Jacob and Esau, how great was the dissimilarity of whom, the book of Genesis very clearly shows. But if perhaps you may say concerning those twins that one was born before the other, and so by the interval of that time which was between the birth of the one and the birth of the other, there was one or another star seen, and so one or another fate: then I will ask them, since they were in one and the same womb, from what fate was it ordained that one was born before the other, although it often happens that both twins are conceived simultaneously from the same woman and from one copulation? Thus, since they were conceived from the same seed and from the same copulation, it is proved that at least within one and the same womb there is the same fate of both. But if it was the same, how could it happen that one went out before the other, led or impelled by the same fate?

All these things are so clear that it is unnecessary in a matter so clear to ponder many things: but let us merely listen to the definition of the Church about this matter. The First Synod of Braga says the following in the ninth canon: "If anyone believes that human souls are bound by a fatal sign, just as the pagans and Priscillian have affirmed, let him be anathema."[1] And again in the tenth canon it says: "If anyone believes that the twelve signs or stars, which the astrologers are accustomed to observe, have been scattered through single members of the soul or body, and say that they have been attributed to the names of the Patriarchs, just as Priscillian has asserted, let him be anathema."[2] Pope Leo I also condemns this heresy. For in a certain letter to the Bishop of Asturia in which he condemns the errors of the Priscillianists, he says the following: "Their eleventh blasphemy is that in which they suppose that both the souls and bodies of men are under the influence of fatal stars: this folly compels them to become entangled in all the errors of the heathen, and to strive to attract stars that are, as they think, favorable to them, and to soften those that are against them. But for those who follow such pursuits there is no place in the Catholic Church; a man who gives himself up to such convictions separates himself from the body of Christ altogether."[3] These are the words of a man who was truly as holy as he was learned.

[Pseudo-] Thomas Aquinas wrote a small work, *On Fate*, about this matter, which is the twenty-eighth of his small works.[4] But in the treatise he argues little or nearly nothing against

---

[1] Dz. 239.

[2] Dz. 240.

[3] Letter 15 (To Turribius of Asturia), c. 11 (PL 54, 685C-686A).

[4] This small work may have been authored by St. Albert the Great. St. Thomas addressed the subject of fate in the *Summa Theologiae* (I q. 116).

this error, digressing to other matters. Blessed Gregory of Nyssa wrote a small, but elegant book about fate.[1] Now the one who discussed this matter more copiously and more exactly (in my judgment) is Blessed Augustine.[2] In which place I beseech the reader that you also read the Commentaries of the very learned man, [Juan] Luis Vives,[3] because he will help you very much for understanding the various sects of philosophers concerning fate.

FIDES

Faith

Of all the heretics Peter Abelard alone produced the strongest pretext for his heresies. For it is certain that the greatest part of heresies, nay so that I may speak more truly, the whole confluence of heresies whence they have arisen, namely that heretics want to restrict the faith within the limits of our intellect, so that they suppose that those things ought not to be believed which our intellect cannot comprehend by reason. Now although this disease was common to all heretics, nevertheless only Peter Abelard laid bare the sickness. For he said (as Blessed Bernard accuses him[4]) that nothing ought to be believed, which exceeds the power of our intellect. To support this he cites the passage of the Wise Man: "He that is hasty to give credit, is light of heart."[5] "He says that a hasty faith is one that believes before reason."[6] Now Paul clearly rejects this error, saying: "Faith is the substance of things to be hoped for, the evidence of things that appear not" (Heb. 11, 1). Whether these words of Paul pertain to the definition of faith, or (as it seems right Erasmus in his *Annotations*[7]) they are an encomium of faith, and were not said as a definition, what is certain is that Paul declared that the faith is true. What then is it to say "the evidence of things that appear not," except what Chrysostom expounds, "the proof of those things which are not seen"?[8] It is as though faith forces us to believe those things which we do not see, and we are unable to investigate by reason.

But here Erasmus suggests that Paul is not speaking about that faith whereby we believe those things which are to be believed, but of the faith whereby we trust someone, meaning confidence.[9] But I beg his pardon: because the same words of Paul prove otherwise. For after

---

[1] *Contra fatum, disputatio cum ethnic philosopho* (PG 45, 145-174).

[2] *City of God*, bk. 5, c. 1-11 (PL 41, 141-154).

[3] Juan Luis Vives (1493–1540) was a Spanish humanist and educational theorist who strongly opposed scholasticism and made his mark as one of the most influential advocates of humanistic learning in the early sixteenth century. His works are not limited to education but deal with a wide range of subjects including philosophy, psychology, politics, social reform and religion.

[4] "What is the use of speaking of doctrine unless what we wish to teach can be explained so as to be intelligible?" Letter 190 (to Pope Innocent II), c. 1, n. 2 (PL 182, 1055C).

[5] Eccli. 19, 4.

[6] Letter 190, c. 1, n. 1 (PL 182, 1055B).

[7] "Here some argue about this definition, as they call it, although it is an encomium of faith rather than a dialectic definition. Jerome and Theophylactus, however, call it a definition, because it has some semblance of a definition, whereby the dialecticians explain the nature of a thing. Since this short introduction indeed commences his praising of the faith, shortly afterwards he likewise shows how much power faith has, demonstrating this by examples." (*In Novum Testamentum Annotationes* (Basel, Inclyta Rauracorum, 1527), p.656).

[8] *Homiliae XXXIV in Epistolam ad Hebraeos*, hom. 21, n. 2 (PG 63, 151).

[9] "I will add to that, in this passage 'faith' ought not to be taken in its proper sense, whereby we believe the things that ought to be believed, but whereby we hope, that is, it is the same as 'confidence.'"

that either encomium or definition of faith he adds many things which nowise can be referred to confidence: for instance, "By faith we understand that the world was framed by the word of God" (v. 3). But confidence does not properly pertain to past things, just as to future things. Then when speaking about Enoch he says: "For before his translation he had testimony that he pleased God. But without faith it is impossible to please God" (v. 5-6). Now in order that he might indicate more clearly about what faith he was speaking, he added: "For he that cometh to God, must believe that he is, and is a rewarder to them that seek him" (v. 6). But I do not see how believing that God exists can be referred to confidence. [Pseudo-] Basil the Great interprets this passage of Paul as regarding true faith, whereby we believe, and not as regarding confidence.[1] Blessed Augustine expounds this passage of Paul as concerning faith and not as concerning confidence.[2] Blessed Bernard in the letter recently cited also expounds this passage of Paul of faith, citing it against Peter Abelard.[3] And Theophylactus also expounds it of faith.[4] Wherefore I hope that Erasmus will not take it badly if we differ here from him, since he himself differs from Augustine, Basil, and others.

But now let our discourse return to the subject of this discussion. Paul the Apostle, in that epistle which is to the Romans, when speaking about Abraham, says: "Who against hope believed in hope; that he might be made the father of many nations" (4, 18). But how is hope against hope? Namely because there was no natural hope that he could then beget, in that he was worn out by much age, because he was nearly a hundred years old, and his wife, Sara, from whom offspring was promised him, was affected by a twofold affliction, namely old age and sterility. Hence naturally speaking there was no hope, nor likelihood, that Sara, being both old and sterile, would conceive of an old man. But even if reason was not suggesting this, still he had hope, believing that those things which God had promised him are possible. But if those things ought not be believed which are above reason, Paul undeservedly praised Abraham, because he believed against hope in hope. Undeservedly also was Zachary, the father if John the Baptist, punished, because did not believe the birth of his wife, whom he knew was old and sterile. For he, according to Peter Abelard, ought to have been rewarded rather than punished, because (as he cited in support of himself), because "He that is hasty to give credit, is light of heart" (Eccli. 19, 4). In the First Epistle to the Corinthians Paul says: "My speech and my preaching was not in the persuasive words of human wisdom, but in shewing of the Spirit and power; that your faith might not stand on the wisdom of men, but on the power of God" (2, 4-5).

(*Annotationes*, p. 656).

[1] *Homilia in Psalmum CXV* (PG 30, 106B). There is evidence that this homily preexisted before the time of St. Basil (PG 29, 250).

[2] "So then: Faith, as it is defined elsewhere, 'the substance of things to be hoped for, the evidence of things that appear not' (Heb. 11, 1). If they are not seen, how can you be convinced that they exist? Well, where do these things that you see come from, if not from One you cannot see? Yes, of course, you see something, in order to believe something, and from what you can see to believe what you cannot see. Please don't be ungrateful to the One Who made you able to see, which is why you are able to believe what you are not yet able to see." (Serm. 126, c. 2, n. 3 (PL 38, 699)). The reference in the text, *Quinquaginta homiliae*, hom. 32, is according to an antiquated ordering of St. Augustine's works no longer followed.

[3] "I am satisfied, I confess, with his definition of faith, even though this man stealthily accuses it. Faith is the substance of things to be hoped for, the evidence of things that appear not (Heb. 11, 1)... For faith is not an opinion, but a certitude." (Letter 190, c. 4, n. 9 (PL 182, 1063A-B)).

[4] "'Evidence,' that is, a demonstration and manifestation of things which are not visible. For he asserts that we may perceive these things with our mind, nowise differently than if they were present." (*Expositio in Epistolam ad Hebraeos* (PG 125, 342)).

What will Peter Abelard reply here? If things ought not to be believed (as he says) unless those things which can be comprehended by reason: then our faith will depend upon human reason. Yet Paul says that our faith is not based upon men's wisdom, but upon God's power. And Blessed Gregory says: "Faith for which human reason gives proof has no merit."[1] And Blessed Augustine expresses the same teaching saying: "Believers firstly seek the mysteries and secrets of the kingdom of God, that they may understand. For faith is understanding's step; and understanding faith's attainment. This the Prophet expressly says to all who prematurely and in undue order look for understanding, and neglect faith. For he says, 'Unless ye believe, ye shall not understand' (Is. 7, 9).[2] Faith itself then also hath a certain light of its own in the Scriptures, in prophecy, in the Gospel, in the Apostolic readings.... You see then, brethren, how exceedingly unregulated and disordered in their haste are they who like immature conceptions seek an untimely birth before the birth; who say to us, 'Why do you ask me believe what I do not see? Let me see something that I may believe. You ask me to believe while I still do not see; I wish to see, and by seeing to believe, not by hearing.' Let the Prophet speak. 'Unless ye believe, ye shall not understand.' You wish to ascend, but you forget the steps. Surely, out of all order. O man, if I could show you already what you might see, I should not exhort you to believe."[3] By which words Augustine assails Peter Lombard clearly enough and seems to direct his words to someone who perhaps thought similarly to this Abelard.

Blessed Basil, when expounding Psalm 115, at the beginning of the Psalm says the following: "Faith draws the soul to assent more than some way of proceeding relying upon reasoning. It brings forth the works of the Spirit, not by the necessary conclusions of geometry. 'In the name of Jesus Christ of Nazareth, arise, and walk.' (Acts 3, 6). What followed this command was the work of the Spirit, and those who witnessed this miracle were compelled to admit the Divinity of the Only-begotten. Tell me, what is more compelling for assent, a complicated set of syllogistic premises entailing the logical conclusion, or a clearly seen miracle so great that it surpasses all that is humanly possible?... Finally in every study, which proceeds with method and order to an end, proofs cannot be sought of the first premises; but it is necessary that he who admits the principles of the practical sciences based upon reason would consequently accept what is a consequence of the principles already laid down, in those things which he sees then follow. Certainly then, in this way too, the mystery of theology requires assent based on faith devoid of proof."[4]

But someone will say to me, "Why do you spend so much time citing testimonies of men?" It is because Peter Abelard holds in contempt the opinions of all men, no matter how holy or learned, and rejects them at will. I acknowledge that I called him unto judgment on this account in the first book of this work: but even if those testimonies do not have any impact on him, they will nevertheless influence the upright reader. And if he does not accept other teachers, still he will accept Paul, from whom we have proved that faith is above all human understanding. The passage which Peter Abelard cited from Ecclesiasticus in support of himself, namely, "He that is hasty to give credit, is light of heart," ought not to be understood as pertaining to faith in God, but rather as pertaining to the mutual credulity among men them-

---

[1] *Homiliae in Evangelia*, hom. 26 (PL 76, 1197C).

[2] St. Augustine uses the Old Latin translation, which is closer to the Septuagint version—μὴ πιστεύσητε, οὐδὲ μὴ συνιῆτε. In the Vulgate this verse is translated as: *nisi credideritis, non permanebitis* ("If you will not believe, you shall not continue"). Cf. *On Christian Doctrine*, bk. 2, c. 12, n. 17 for St. Augustine's reconciliation of these two different translations.

[3] Sermon 126, c. 1, n. 1-2 (PL 38, 698).

[4] *Homilia in Psalmum CXV*, n. 1 (PG 30, 103B-106A). This homily was formerly considered doubtful (PG 30, 10) but is now considered authentic (Cf. Mark DelCogliano, "Basil of Caesarea's Homily on Psalm 115." Sacris Eruditi, vol. 56 (January 2017), pg. 7.

selves. For otherwise the Most Glorious Virgin would be accused of overcredulousness, in that she believed the Angel saying that God would be conceived of her flesh, with no proof sought or shown about this, whereby it could be proved to be possible. Therefore, let us ourselves bring into captivity our understanding unto the obedience of Christ,[1] so that we may believe Christ and His true disciples, and so believing, we will more easily understand those things which could not be previously be understood by us.

There is a **second heresy** which so exalts faith that it detracts from good works. A certain Arian, Eunomius, first taught this error (as Augustine relates[2]), who said that all men who held the faith that he was teaching would be saved, even if they were to commit sins, no matter how grave, and persevered in them. Luther, by a pythonic spirit, or rather by a diabolical instinct, raised up from Hell this error long ago buried, saying that faith alone justifies: wherefore he says that works are not necessary for attaining eternal life, because if they are done, he asserts that they nowise justify. But about this, we defer to another place. Thus we will now dispute only about the first point, proving that faith alone does not suffice, but good works are also required of us: for otherwise it would be necessary to admit that neither murder, nor perjury, nor adultery, nor theft will be imputed to man, provided he believe that he is to be saved through the power of the promise made at Baptism. For Luther teaches that this faith suffices. For he says the following: "See, how rich therefore is a Christian, the one who is baptized! Even if he wants to, he cannot lose his salvation, however much he sin, unless he will not believe. For no sin can condemn him save unbelief alone."[3] O impious speech, fomentation of all wickedness! O poisonous offspring of the serpent! Of course the most crafty serpent knew that God will render to each man according to the quality of the good or evil works he did while alive: hence he devised how he could make men heedless of works so that he might trick them out of their reward.

I beg you to pay attention, and you will see how many poisonous rivulets spring forth from this corrupted source. If faith alone justifies, then man will never be justified through the reception of any Sacrament. Notice that you now see all power of the Sacraments have been lost. The confession of sins does not help at all, but only faith. Alms, fasting, prayer and things of this kind are of no importance, because only faith (according to Luther) justifies. No crime, no matter how deadly, is harmful, provided one believes that faith alone suffices for salvation. Who can put up with these things? A Christian man certainly could not: nay an upright pagan philosopher could not tolerate it even slightly. For which pagan does not abominate theft? Who does not abhor murder of whatsoever kind? Who does not execrate parricide? Who does not hate adultery? What perjurer was ever not blamed? Whoever praised the violation of a just agreement? Nevertheless, all these things, and if there be other worse things, Luther permits to one having faith. Hence excommunication is contemned by him, because he thinks that faith alone suffices: wherefore if one believes, however much and howsoever he be excommunicated, he thinks that the excommunication does not hinder him at all.

For it often happens to a man wandering about, and leaving the right way to enter a dense forest, thinking that he is on the correct and straight path: going forth a short distance, the dense branches of trees impede him: he, however, lest he go back, tries to break them. But if further on some other obstacle opposes him more strongly, whatever it may be, he just tries to break or tear it away, or tries to remove it in whatever way, lest he abandon the path once begun. It seems to me that Luther has acted in this manner. For when this man, who we said, began to defend his error, the efficacious power of the Sacraments stood in his way, he threw out all the Sacraments: contrition blocked him, he threw out contrition; satisfaction for sins

---

[1] Cf. II Cor. 10, 5.

[2] *De Haeresibus ad Quodvultdeum*, c. 54 (PL 42, 40).

[3] *On the Babylonian Captivity of the Church* (WA 6, 529, lns. 11-13).

impeded him, he completely removed satisfaction. Now he did all these things, lest he abandon that first error: and so it happened that what his temerity in dogmatizing brought forth, his pertinacity in defending afterwards kept and increased. "You more speedily shatter than straighten," said Quintilian, "things which have solidified out of shape."[1]

But let us get back on track, and having omitted arguments from reason, let us return to the judgment of Scripture. But before we begin to dispute, it is necessary to firstly point out two things so that we may understand what we intend to prove and we may not dispute in vain, not knowing for what we are fighting. Firstly, it is necessary to point out beforehand in this section that we are speaking only about that justification whereby someone becomes just from being a sinner, which is called the first grace by scholastic theologians. For there is another justification, whereby the just man becomes more just, as John says in the Apocalypse: "He that is holy, let him be sanctified still" (22, 11). But we do not speak about this justification at present, because we will give a more suitable place to this discussion, in the section on "Works" [*Opera*]. The other thing which is necessary to point out is that there are different meanings of the word "faith," not only in the writings of secular authors but also in Sacred Writ.

For sometimes faith has the same meaning as fidelity, which is opposed to deceitfulness. And according to this meaning we say that someone does something faithfully when he does it without deceit and without negligence. Cicero defined this faith saying the following: "Faith is truth and fidelity to promises and agreements. From which meaning (although this will perhaps seem inaccurate, still so that we may attempt to imitate the Stoics, who diligently investigate the etymology of words) we think, because what was promised 'happens' [*fiat*], it is called 'faith' [*fides*]."[2] And Terence[3] says: "There is a grave sternness in his features, and truthfulness [*fides*] in his words."[4] In which citations the word "faith" is used to mean truth without deceit and without a lie. From this word "faith," he who is truthful is said to be faithful. So Paul very often uses the word, especially in his First Epistle to Timothy where he says: "A faithful saying, and worthy of all acceptation, that Christ Jesus came into this world to save sinners" (1, 15). He said, "A faithful saying," as meaning "truthful." And he used this word "faith" according to the same meaning in the same epistle, saying: "A faithful saying: if a man desire the office of a bishop, he desireth a good work" (3, 1). John also uses the same word with the same meaning in the Apocalypse when he said that Jesus Christ is "the faithful witness" (1, 5). The [Royal] Prophet used this meaning of faith when he invites us to praise God, giving the reason he says: "For the word of the Lord is right, and all his works are done with faithfulness" (Ps. 32, 4), meaning that all of God's works are true and not counterfeit, or pretended.

The word "faith" is used in another way, for a promise or swearing whereby we oblige ourselves to do something. Virgil used the word in this way when he said, "Receive, and give me, the pledge of honor [*fidem*],"[5] according to this meaning we are accustomed to say in Latin, *liberare fidem*, for meaning, "do what has been promised." According to this meaning among those who know well the Latin language, *fides publica*[6] is said, meaning that which we commonly call, safe passage [*salvum conductum*], or public promise of security. Blessed Paul

---

[1] *De Institutione Oratoria*, I, 3, 3.

[2] "*De Officiis*, bk. 1, n. 8.

[3] I.e. Publius Terentius Afer who was born in Carthage about 185 or c.195 BC, and died about 159 BC. He was a Roman writer of comedies.

[4] "*Tristis severitas inest in vultu, atque in verbis fides*" (*Andria*, Act 5, scene 2).

[5] "*Accipe daque fidem*" (*Aeneid*, bk. 8).

[6] I.e. "public trust" of the Roman people, whereby one is given a passport for safe conduct or passage through some territory.

used this meaning in his First Epistle to Timothy where he says these words: "But the younger widows avoid. For when they have grown wanton in Christ, they will marry: having damnation, because they have made void their first faith" (5, 11-12). He said "faith" for the vow or the promise of keeping chastity which they had made in their widowhood, and because they had not fulfilled this promise, but instead violated it by marrying, he thus says that they had made void their first faith. And what Paul likewise says in his Epistle to the Romans can also be taken in this sense: "Shall their unbelief make the faith of God without effect?" He said "faith" for "promise," according to which God does not fail, such that He would not bestow what He promised. For if He did not bestow it was not by His fault, but rather the disbelief of the Jews which made them unworthy of receiving God's promises. For God had not promised the reward to everyone, but only to believers. And that this is Paul's true meaning is clearly proved by those words which he immediately adds: "But God is true," Paul says, "and every man a liar, as it is written, That thou mayest be justified in thy words, and mayest overcome when thou art judged" (v. 3-4).

Faith is accustomed to being used in a third way for trust. Terence uses it in this way saying: "That you should put so little confidence [*fidem*] in me,"[1] meaning, "you have little trust in me." Cicero also uses this meaning in his oration, *Pro Quinto Ligario*, when he said: "And observe, I entreat you, with what good faith I am defending his cause"[2]: in which words Cicero wanted to show how much confidence he had of proving the contention of Quintus Ligarius, which he had accepted to defend. In Sacred Scriptures the use of this meaning is frequent and clear. And firstly, that is the clearest passage where Blessed James says: "But if any of you want wisdom, let him ask of God, who giveth to all men abundantly, and upbraideth not; and it shall be given him. But let him ask in faith, nothing wavering" (1, 5-6). He said to ask in faith, which is to say, to ask with trust and confidence in the Divine goodness, because He will give what has been asked. Our Savior, Christ Himself, used the word according to this meaning when He said: "All things, whatsoever you ask when ye pray, believe that you shall receive; and they shall come unto you" (Mk 11, 24). In which words, He said "believe" [*credite*] for "have confidence" [*confidite*]. And according to this manner of speech that which He said to Peter, reprimanding him, ought to be understood: "O thou of little faith, why didst thou doubt?" (Mt. 14, 31). It is also evident what John, when speaking about Christ, our Savior, said: "Now when he was at Jerusalem, at the pasch, upon the festival day, many believed in his name, seeing his signs which he did. But Jesus did not trust himself unto them, for that he knew all men" (Jn. 2, 23-24). He said that He did not trust Himself unto them, meaning that He did not have confidence [*fidere*] in them.

The word "faith" is used in a fourth way for what we commonly call "conscience." Cicero takes the word in this way in his oration, *For Marcus Caelius*, where he says these words: "But nevertheless it belongs to your wisdom, judges, if the cause is just to oppose Marcus Caelius, not on that account to think that you also have a reasonable ground for consulting the indignation of others rather than your own good faith."[3] In which words, he said to consult faith, for what is commonly accustomed to be said, to act according to conscience. Paul used this meaning when in his Epistle to the Romans he said, "For all that is not of faith is sin" (14, 23). By which words Paul wanted to signify that all that is done with a protesting conscience is a sin. For so Theophylactus interprets this passage, who on this passage says these words: "For when one was not sure, nor thought that the food was clean, but tasted it with a bad conscience, he has certainly sinned."[4] And according to this meaning, it is said by lawyers and

---

[1] "Ita ne parvam mihi fidem esse apud te?" (*Phormio*, act 5, scene 3).

[2] *Pro Quinto Ligario*, sect. 6.

[3] Sect 9, n. 21.

[4] *Expositio in Epistolam ad Romanos* (PG 124, 531).

by theologians that someone is a "possessor in good faith." For they call him a "possessor in good faith," who possesses something with a right conscience, and judges it to be his own. But he is said to be a possessor in bad faith who, knowing a thing to be another's, possesses it.

Faith is taken in a fifth way for the object of faith, that is, for the things to be believed themselves: so likewise Paul uses the word 'hope,' when he says, "Looking for the blessed hope" (Tit. 2, 13). In this meaning Paul likewise uses the word "faith," where he says: "One faith, one baptism" (Eph. 4, 5). For all are obliged to believe the same faith, and it is not permitted to divide into various sects, just as faith is divided by heresies. Athanasius takes "faith" in this way saying in his Creed: "This is the Catholic Faith, which except a man believe faithfully, he cannot be saved."[1]

In a sixth way the whole evangelical state and religion is called faith by Paul, which contains all the good things granted to us through Christ in this life. "Wherefore the law," says Paul, "was our pedagogue in Christ, that we might be justified by faith. But after the faith is come, we are no longer under a pedagogue" (Gal. 3, 24-25). He said that the faith came, because the Evangelical law has now been established. And this state, which we have received after having received the Gospel, we are accustomed to call the state of faith and of grace, distinguishing by this name from the state of the Mosaic Law. According to none of these meanings which we have thus far enumerated, have we taken this word "faith," when we argue that faith alone does not justify.

There is a seventh sense of this word, much more frequent in Holy Writ, and it is a certain belief or persuasion, or firm and certain assent, but obscure concerning all that has been revealed to us by God through His prophets, and through Himself, and through His Apostles. And not only very learned and eloquent ecclesiastical authors, such as Cyprian, Lactantius, Jerome, Ambrose, and Augustine, but also secular authors, who are deemed leaders of the Latin language in the judgment of all men, have used the word with this meaning. Cicero says that faith ought not to be put in the dreams of those who are sleeping.[2] And Pliny says: "The flooding of the Nile gives credibility [*fidem*] to all these things by a wonder exceeding all others."[3] He said "gives credibility" for meaning "makes someone believe." Livy says: "These were the principal events at home and in the field that marked the reign of Romulus. Throughout ... we find nothing incompatible with the belief [*fidei*] in his divine origin and his admission to divine immortality after death."[4] Virgil says: "I believe it well – nor is my belief [*fides*] vain – that he is sprung from gods."[5]

From all these quotations we have proved that the Lutherans unjustly reproach us, because we use this word, faith, in this sense. For they say that it is not Latin, nor conformed to Holy Writ, and hence they tell their followers not to use it in this sense. But whether they wish it or not, we use it just as the most eloquent sacred Doctors have used it when they speak about faith, which is a theological virtue, or about its act. For both of these, namely the act and the habit tending to the acts, whether it be infused or acquired, is called "faith": because it is customary that the acts, and the habit which inclines to those acts, be given the same name. But in this section we are disputing about the act of faith, not about the habit: because we do not merit by habits, but by acts. Thus having premised all these things, we now need to go forth

---

[1] Dz. 40.

[2] "If one cannot have faith in the visions of the insane, because they are false, I do not understand why we believe the visions people have when they are asleep, which are much more confused" (*On Divination*, bk 2, sect. 122).

[3] *The Natural History*, bk. 9, sect. 84 (58).

[4] *The History of Rome*, bk. 1, sect. 15.

[5] *Aeneid*, bk. 4, line 12.

to the fight against the Lutherans, and let us prove that faith alone does not always justify the sinner, but works are also necessary for justification.

When the [Royal] Prophet had asked the Lord who would dwell in His tabernacle, He immediately replied, saying: "He that walketh without blemish, and worketh justice" (Ps. 14, 2). He said, "worketh." And shortly afterwards when He had listed some works of the virtues, ending the Psalm He adds: "He that walketh without blemish, and worketh justice" (Ps. 14, 2). He did not say, "He who believes these things," but, "He who does these things," in order that He might show the power and necessity of works. Furthermore, the Lord, through the prophet Isaias, commends good works to us by these words: "Cease to do perversely, learn to do well: seek judgment, relieve the oppressed, judge for the fatherless, defend the widow" (1, 16-17). But why is it necessary to cite so many quotations, since all the books of the prophets are full of admonitions, with which they exhort, entice, and impel us to do good works?

But if you appeal to the New Testament, perhaps rejecting the Old on this matter, I would like you to come with me to the New Testament, and hear Christ saying in Matthew's Gospel: "Not everyone that saith to me, Lord, Lord, shall enter into the kingdom of heaven: but he that doth the will of my Father who is in heaven, he shall enter into the kingdom of heaven. Many will say to me in that day: Lord, Lord, have not we prophesied in thy name, and cast out devils in thy name, and done many miracles in thy name? And then will I profess unto them, I never knew you: depart from me, you that work iniquity" (7, 21-23). Now who is he who says to Christ: "Lord, Lord," except he who has faith, whereby he believes him to be the true Lord? And yet not every such person enters the kingdom of Heaven. Therefore, faith alone does not justify man.

Now that these words of Christ ought to be understood of a believer not having works of charity, all the interpreters of this sacred passage bear witness, some of whom I will cite, so that at least we may make our opinion more sure from thence, showing that it was the teaching of holy men. Theophylactus, when expounding this passage in Matthew, says the following: "Here Jesus shows that He is Lord by saying, 'Not everyone that saith unto Me, Lord, Lord.' Jesus in fact is saying that He is God. He teaches us that we derive no benefit from our faith if it is without works. 'He that doeth the will of My Father.' He did not mean, 'that did the will of My Father on one occasion' but 'that doeth the will of My Father continually until his death.'"[1] And Christian Druthmar[2] when expounding these same words says: "Someone may not rely on the fact that he is a Christian, because if he does not do the works of Christianity, he will not enter into eternal life: for he who says that he knows God and does not keep His Commandments, is a liar."[3]

Blessed Jerome treats those words in this way: "Just as He had said above,[4] that those who were not wearing the garment of a good life must not be received on account of the wickedness of their dogmas, so now He asserts the converse, in order to prevent the faith from being accommodated to those who, though they may be strong with the soundness of faith, live basely and by their evil works destroy the soundness of their doctrine."[5]

Blessed Basil instructs those seeking to be monks in this manner: "How can anyone, without charity, acquire so great a faith as to remove mountains, or distribute his goods to the poor, and deliver his body to be burned?" Now to this question of the monks Basil answers with these words: "If we remember the Lord Who said: 'All their works they do for to be seen

---

[1] *Ennaratio in in Evangelium Matthaei* (PG 123, 215A).

[2] He is also known as Christian of Stavelot, as he was a teacher at the Benedictine abbey of Stavelot-Malmedy.

[3] *Expositio in Evangelium Matthaei*, c. 14 (PL 106, 1322C-D). Cf. I Jn. 2, 4.

[4] Cf. Mt. 7, 15.

[5] *Commentaria in Matthaeum*, bk. 1 (PL 26, 49A).

of men' (Mt. 23, 5), and His answer to those who said: 'Lord, Lord, have not we prophesied in thy name, and cast out devils in thy name, and done many miracles in thy name?' when He said to them: 'I do not know you, or where you come from' (Cf. Mt. 7, 22-23). It is not because they had lied, but because they had misused the grace of God according to their own will, which assuredly is alien to God's charity."[1] These quotations of holy men suffice, by which we have proved that the exposition which we put forth above is the true and authentic exposition of the text. It is also evident from the concordant testimony of all these men that faith alone without works does not suffice.

But let us run through the rest of the quotations from the New Testament. In John's Gospel Our Lord Jesus Christ says: "Every branch in me, that beareth not fruit, [My Father] will take away" (Jn. 15, 2). Now to "take [a man] away," as He Himself says below (v. 6), is to cast him into the fire so that he may burn. Now since he is condemned for no other reason than that he had not borne fruit, it is thence proved that works are necessary. Again, when the Lord was discoursing about the Last Judgment, He promises everlasting life to those who have performed works of piety towards the poor and needy, and decrees eternal fire for those who have despised to do works of the same sort. Thus, let Luther come, and lifting himself up above all that is called God,[2] revoke God's sentence, and promise glory to wicked men, if they believe. Certainly, promises of this kind are promises of the old serpent, who, promising knowledge to our first parents, took away their knowledge, and substituted ignorance in its place. It seems to me that Luther acts in this way, who, while he promises eternal glory to one merely believing, prepares eternal fire for himself and for him.

Next, to the young man asking the Lord, by doing what may he possess eternal life, Christ, the true Teacher, replies: "If thou wilt enter into life, keep the commandments" (Mt. 19, 17). Notice that you see here that the Commandments are required as necessary for obtaining eternal life. For if they were not necessary, they then ought not to be called precepts, but counsels. For I consider this to be the difference between a precept and a counsel, namely that the latter is urged as something good, yet not required as necessary: but the former is so required that an account is to be rendered for it. But if they are not necessary, they ought not to be called precepts. For things are not commanded, unless they ought to be done. Now the Lord again repeats this concerning keeping the Commandments, when being about to ascend into Heaven He says to His disciples: "Going therefore, teach ye all nations; baptizing them in the name of the Father, and of the Son, and of the Holy Ghost. Teaching them to observe all things whatsoever I have commanded you" (Mt. 28, 19-20). He did not say, "Teaching them to believe only," but "to observe all things." Therefore, faith alone does not suffice. And in Mark's Gospel upon the same occasion He says: "He that believeth and is baptized, shall be saved" (16, 16). From which it is also evident that besides faith, Baptism is required. Thus, faith alone does not suffice for salvation: or if it alone did suffice, Baptism is not necessary. But although He said, "But he that believeth not shall be condemned": He taught that Baptism without faith does no good, just as faith without Baptism.

Paul also in the Epistle to the Romans says: "Not the hearers of the law are just before God, but the doers of the law shall be justified" (2, 13). Here He calls "hearers" those who believed by hearing: for "faith cometh by hearing" (Rom. 10, 17). And in the First Epistle to the Corinthians he says: "If I should have all faith, so that I could remove mountains, and have not charity, I am nothing" (13, 2). By which words He very clearly shows that faith alone does not suffice, but charity is also necessary. And again, when exhorting the same Corinthians, He says: "Stand fast in the faith, do manfully, and be strengthened" (16, 13). By which words

---

[1] *Regula S. Basilii*, interrogatio 187 (PL 103, 548D-549A); *Regulae Brevius Tractae*, inter. 179 (PG 31, 1202B-C).
[2] Cf. II Thess. 2, 4.

after the exhortation of faith he added the works of charity, implying that faith without them does not suffice for salvation. And in the Second Epistle to the same Corinthians he says: "We must all be manifested before the judgment seat of Christ, that every one may receive the proper things of the body, according as he hath done, whether it be good or evil" (5, 10). Notice that it is evident that rewards are distributed to each one according to the quality of their works.

But why do we tarry on a matter so clear? For Blessed James in his Catholic epistle says: "But he that hath looked into the perfect law of liberty, and hath continued therein, not becoming a forgetful hearer, but a doer of the work; this man shall be blessed in his deed." (1, 25). And in a different chapter of the same epistle: "But wilt thou know, O vain man, that faith without works is dead?" (2, 20). And again, in the same place: "Do you see that by works a man is justified; and not by faith only?" (v. 24). And again: "For even as the body without the spirit is dead; so also faith without works is dead" (v. 26). Do you see how clearly Blessed James teaches this teaching without any obscurity?

Certainly these quotations are so clearly in our favor, that is, in favor of the Catholic teaching, that Luther perceiving their clarity and strength, not knowing where to turn, fled to the common refuge for all heretics, saying that this letter does not belong to James the Apostle, and is unworthy of his Apostolic spirit. Also, for the same reason he denies the book of the Apocalypse: without a doubt it is because by its testimony Luther's teaching was convicted of being temerarious. For in that book the following is said: "Blessed are the dead, who die in the Lord. From henceforth now, saith the Spirit, that they may rest from their labours; for their works follow them" (14, 13). And again: "And another book was opened, which is the book of life; and the dead were judged by those things which were written in the books, according to their works" (20, 12). And once again: "Behold, I come quickly; and my reward is with me, to render to every man according to his works" (22, 12). Thus, on account of so clear testimonies of these books, which war against Luther, Luther decided not to rely upon these books, saying that they are not to be counted among the sacred books.[1]

But we have discussed this matter in chapter two of the first book of this work. For before we went out to fight, lest perhaps something similar to the present case were to happen in the future, we discussed about the weapons common to both sides, so that we firstly agreed among ourselves about the weapons to be used to fight with. Thus, we showed there that these books are canonical: wherefore it is not necessary that we discuss the matter further. Additionally, if faith alone would justify (as Luther says), everything would be fulfilled in one commandment, namely in faith. Yet Paul says that all things are fulfilled in the one commandment, namely in charity, not however in faith. But when naming charity, he includes faith, which is its foundation.

But if perhaps Luther on account of these testimonies would say that he understands faith as being formed faith, which is living through charity animating it, then we are in agreement, because we also say that such faith justifies, although we do not accept concerning faith that it alone justifies. For if faith needs charity in order to justify, it is much truer to call charity the justifier, from whence faith has the ability to justify, than faith itself, which justifies through charity. For from the form, which bestows the completion of the thing, the thing comes to be a substance, and likewise to have a specific nature and name.

Now Paul says that the end of the law is charity and not faith. Furthermore, how can faith be alone without works, if it is animated by charity? For charity is not idle, because (as Paul says): "In Christ Jesus neither circumcision availeth anything, nor uncircumcision: but faith

---

[1] "St. James' epistle is really an epistle of straw, compared to the others, for it has nothing of the nature of the Gospel about it." (*Luther's Works: Word and Sacrament I*, vol. 35, ed. E. T. Beckmann (Philadelphia, Fortress, 1960), pg. 362).

that worketh by charity" (Gal. 5, 6). And the Lord says in John's Gospel: "If you love me, keep my commandments" (14, 15). Thus, if charity is present, it works. But if it does not work, then there is no sign that charity is present. Hence Blessed John in his First Catholic Epistle says the following: "He that hath the substance of this world, and shall see his brother in need, and shall shut up his bowels from him: how doth the charity of God abide in him?" (3, 17). Hence, "The proof of love (as Blessed Gregory says) is to show it in deeds."[1] Therefore, let us say then that faith alone does not justify, but also works are necessary.

But someone being content with faith alone, who considers it sufficient for himself to be without works, seems to me to be like that man, concerning whom it is said in the Gospel, that he "began to build, and was not able to finish" (Lk. 14, 30). For faith is the foundation, upon which, as upon a most firm rock, God founded His Church: upon which Paul commands that we all be grounded, so that we may be "settled and immoveable from the hope of the gospel" (Col. 1, 23) which we have heard. Wherefore Blessed Augustine in his book, *On Faith and Works*, when interpreting that passage of Paul from First Corinthians,[2] where he says that Christ is the foundation, says these words: "But if Christ [is the foundation, then] doubtlessly faith in Christ [is the foundation], since it is 'by faith,' as the same Apostle says,[3] that Christ dwells 'in our hearts.'"[4] Thus if faith is the foundation, something will be built thereon, because he who lays a foundation, thinks about the rest of the building. But that which has been built thereon, in order that the building may become worthy of praise, is good works. Hence Paul in First Corinthians says: "Now if any man build upon this foundation, gold, silver, precious stones, wood, hay, stubble: every man's work shall be manifest" (3, 12-13). From which words of Paul it is evident that those things which are to be built upon God's foundation are works. Therefore, he who being content with faith alone, despises works, rightly began to build and could not finish.

Due to these very convincing reasons, which most clearly prove that works are necessary for attaining beatitude, Lutheran descendants, wishing to correct the opinion of their leader, openly admit the necessity of works: because without them, as they say, true faith cannot exist: yet they say that those works avail absolutely nothing for man's salvation. For a certain Johann Rivius of Attendom from the faction of the Lutherans' sect in a letter to an unnamed friend which is entitled, *De sola fide*, afterwards had joined works of faith, objects and replies to himself, saying the following: "Thus someone will say that works are required. I agree, but not so that we may attain justice through them, and become heirs of eternal goods, because we are immediately that from being born again: but rather so that we may prove our faith through them, and so that we may make our faith clear, known and testified to all. For that faith is then indeed sound and complete which is effective through charity, as the Apostle says. For just as a tree is known to be of a certain kind from its fruits: so whether faith is true or not is perceived from the works and deeds... For err you not, not just any simple credulity is full and perfect faith in God, but the firm persuasion is joined with hope and confidence towards God: such that there be no less hope than credulity in faith. For that simple persuasion about God, is only a certain approach and as it were a gate to that solid and perfect faith."[5]

A certain [Johann] Spangenberg in his *Margarita theologica*, in the section on [good] works, where he says the following: "Faith cannot exist with a bad conscience, because it is the trust that God is merciful unto us; a bad conscience judges the contrary. Likewise those

---

[1] *Homiliae in Evangelia*, hom. 30, n. 1 (PL 76, 1220C).

[2] "For other foundation no man can lay, but that which is laid; which is Christ Jesus" (I Cor. 3, 11).

[3] Eph. 3, 17.

[4] C. 16, n. 27 (PL 40, 215).

[5] *Ad amicum quondam epistola, de sola fide*, published in *De Conscientia*, bk. 3 (Leipzig, Nicolaus Wolrab, 1541), Ep. 5, pg. 5r-6v.

who do not repent, but indulge their wicked desires, do not keep their faith."[1] And in the same book, in the section on "Faith," he again says: "Faith is not only a knowledge of the history of Christ, but it is true trust of the heart, which consents to the promise of the Gospel, but especially it signifies trust in the mercy promised for Christ's sake."[2]

Philip Melanchthon, more learned than them all, and, as I think, the leader and teacher of them all, in his book, [*Hypotyposes theologicæ seu*] *loci communes* in the section on grace and justification,[3] says the following: "Those who do not repent, but indulge their wicked desires, do not keep their faith."[4] And earlier in this section, he says the following: "Faith doubtlessly here means, in this passage of Paul's writings, trust in the promised mercy on account of Christ. And if, however, certain sycophants ravingly contradict loudly, and deny that by faith, confidence in mercy is meant, still I have no doubt that it will not disturb all good and learned men."[5] And shortly afterwards he adds: "Faith, therefore, is correlatively related to mercy as to its object. For which reason when it is said, 'We are justified by faith,' this expression can be rightly understood in this way when it is transformed into a correlative. We are justified through the promised mercy on account of Christ. But this mercy is laid hold of by faith. For Paul treats this [in Rom. 3] so that men may be reconciled through confidence in another's help, not on account of one's own dignity, or quality of works."[6] And after some words detracting scholastic theologians, he again says: "When Scholastics say that man is justified by grace, they then say nothing about confidence in mercy, but instead they dream that man is pronounced just on account of his own dignity and that newness, or their own cleanliness, without confidence in mercy."[7]

In which words there are many things worthy of reproach, and ought to be pointed out individually so that his malice may become clear. Firstly, he makes a clear calumny against scholastic theologians saying that they dream up that man is just on account of his own dignity without confidence in the Divine mercy. May I perish if any scholastic theologian among those who are deemed by the Church to be Catholics, ever asserted this. For all men acknowledge that no one can be saved or justified without Divine mercy. All scholastics acknowledge with Paul that we become saved, not from works of justice which we ourselves do, but according to God's mercy, "by the laver of regeneration, and renovation of the Holy Ghost" (Tit. 3, 5).

Next because he denies that man is justified by grace, mocking the scholastic theologians asserting this, he contradicts Paul in his Epistle to Titus saying: "Being justified by his grace, we may be heirs, according to hope of life everlasting" (Tit. 3, 7). And certainly if Philip Melanchthon were to observe well the power of grace and the condition of his own nature, he would clearly understand that we attribute more to the Divine mercy and goodness when we say that man is justified by grace, than if we would say that he is justified by trust in the promised mercy. For that trust in the promised mercy is our work, although the mercy itself in which he trusts is Divine. And hence it necessarily follows that he who says that man is justified through trust in the promised mercy, also says that man is justified by his own work, which seems to greatly derogate Christ's merit, especially according to their view. Or when

---

[1] *Margarita theologica* (Leipzig, Nicolaus Wolrab, 1541), q. 5, pg. 49.

[2] *Ibid.*, pg. 66.

[3] The text here refers to the section as being *de bonis operibus*, which title was added in a later edition of the work.

[4] *Corpus reformatorum* (abbrev. hereafter as CR) (Braunschweig, C.A. Schwetschke, 1854), vol. 21, col. 432.

[5] *Ibid.*, pg. 422.

[6] *Ibid.*, pg. 423.

[7] *Ibid.*

we say that man is justified by [*per*] grace, we concede all of Christ's glory, arrogating absolutely nothing of that justification to ourselves, because grace has nothing from us, but it all is produced by God, according to that which the [Royal] Prophet says: "The Lord will give grace and glory" (Ps. 83, 12).

Philip Melanchthon also clearly shows his ignorance in the aforesaid words, and he very clearly shows that his error proceeds from it. He indeed ignores, or at least he shows himself to ignore, that this preposition, "by [*per*]," has various meanings, and denotes various types of causes, according to the varieties of words to which it is joined. For sometimes it means an efficient cause, other times the instrument by which something happens, other times the formal cause, other times the means or disposition for acquiring something. As (for example) if Peter the painter paints a table with a paint brush, and he makes it white, we can say that the table is white by the whiteness, as by the formal cause: by the paint brush, as by an instrument: by Peter, as by the efficient cause. Examples of these things agree with the writings of the Latin authors. For Columella says: "Pour into their jaws a *sextarius* of wine at a time by means of a horn."[1] Terence said in his third comedy: "who by [*per*] another person, discloses to me his own sentiments."[2] In which words, the preposition, "by," denotes means, [i.e., "by means of"]. Cicero said, "He had been cheated by [*per*] his imprudence,"[3] where it is evident that the preposition indicates the efficient cause, such that one may say that the imprudence was the cause of the deception. Terence says, "I deliver to you my female servants; permission is [given] by me for you to examine them with any tortures you please."[4] In this quotation "given" is inferred, and "by me" means "by me the authority and the one permitting." And the quotation of Persius ought to be understood in the same way: "All things are to be painted white by me henceforth."[5]

After having examined all these things beforehand, our view will be easily understood and received by all with open arms, as they say, unless perhaps by him who is determined to be obstinate or is insane. We say that man is justified by Christ, insofar as He is God, as by the cause which effects our justification in us. Moreover, we are justified by Christ, insofar as He is man, as by the meritorious cause of our justification. We are also justified by Christ's Blood as by means of or by the instrument whereby Christ has merited our justification. We are also justified by grace, which is true justice, as by the form inhering in us, just as by whiteness a body is said to be white, and by blackness, black. We also say that man is justified by faith, as by the means whereby we tend to justification. For faith is a means, and a necessary disposition preparing the soul for justification to be received from God. Therefore we take away nothing from Divine mercy or faith: nor do we take away confidence in His mercy, due to the fact that we have said that man is justified by grace, because each one of these things which we have said, has its own and unique causality in man's justification.

There is another error in these words of Philip Melanchthon and of the others, whereby they assert that faith is lost by any mortal sin. But I do not wish to dispute about his error at the moment, because it does not belong to the first theme of our disputation, and we shall specifically discuss it in the in the next heresy once we have finished taking this one by assault.

There still remains one other error contained in these cited words of Philip Melanchthon and the others. For they say that the faith whereby we are justified is "trust [*fiducia*] in the promised mercy on account of Christ," and when Philip Melanchthon said these words, I would have wished for modesty and politeness in his words. For he calls us unlearned, sy-

---

[1] *On Agriculture* (*Res Rustica*), bk. 6, c. 2, n. 7.
[2] *The Self-Tormenter* (*Heautontimorumenos*), act 2, scene 1, n. 7.
[3] *For Quintus Roscius the actor*, c. 7, n. 21.
[4] *The Mother-in-Law* (Hecyra), act 5, scene 2, n. 7.
[5] Satire 1, n. 110.

cophants and raving men, because we contradict their opinion, and he says that we deny that faith means trust in mercy. I truly do not wish to retaliate the injury, although I could easily do so, especially if I would wish to reply not on behalf of myself but for others, yet I strive to do but one thing, namely to show before the learned and good men, whom he has provoked, that those who contradict the aforesaid assertion of those men are not unlearned or sycophants.

But it is necessary before all else, that all understand that he maliciously and mendaciously makes a calumny against us, when he says that we deny that faith means trust [*fiducia*]. For we have clearly acknowledged and clearly approved at the beginning of this disputation that it is often taken in Holy Writ, and in the writings of the "most Latin" [*Latinissimos*] authors. Still we deny that the faith Sacred Scripture ascribes whereby we are justified, is confidence, and it is necessary to prove this very thing now, partly by reasons, partly by the testimonies of Sacred Scripture, partly also by the testimonies of holy and learned men.

And firstly I object to them Paul, concerning whom they glory in vain, and by whose testimony they falsely assert their teaching is defended. For he, in the Epistle to the Ephesians, very clearly gives testimony in our favor, when he, speaking about Christ, says these words: "In whom we have boldness [*fiducia*] and access with confidence by the faith of him." (3, 12). Notice that he said that "boldness [*fiducia*]" arises from faith, because he says that we have it "by the faith." You said that you make an appeal in this matter to all learned and good men. Do you recuse Paul, saying that he is not good, and not learned? But perhaps you say that Paul ought not to be interpreted in this way, as we suppose. But lest a way of escape be open to you by this route, I offer the testimony of Theophylactus who, when interpreting the aforesaid passage of Paul, says these words: "But we are not led as captives, nor as sinners, but instead we have freedom: and not that alone, but with confidence and trust. But whence are these things good for us? By faith, he says: for when freeing from these sins, it established freedom and confidence in us."[1] From which words it is very clearly evident that Paul thought that trust [*fiducia*] is caused in us by faith, and furthermore it follows that faith whereby we are justified, is not the trust but the cause of trust. And our Savior very clearly shows this same thing when He said to the woman who was suffering from an issue of blood: "Be of good heart [*confide*], daughter, thy faith hath made thee whole" (Mt. 9, 22). From which words it is clearly proved that faith is the cause of trust. For He commands her to be of good heart, because she already has such faith that she obtained the health of her body.[2] Moreover, that faith, which Paul praises so much in the Epistle to the Hebrews, is the faith whereby we are justified. For speaking of it he says: "Abel... by which he obtained a testimony that he was just" (11, 4) and he says without which "it is impossible to please God" (v. 6).

But that faith of which Paul speaks in that same passage is not trust, although Erasmus of Rotterdam in his *Annotations* on that passage of Paul to the Hebrews says that faith in that passage of Paul is to be taken for trust.[3] And noticing this now, I clearly understand the hidden poison in the words of Erasmus, and from these words, as also from his other words, I perceive that the proverb is true, which was commonly said by German Catholics: "Erasmus laid the eggs, but Luther hatched the chicks."[4] For I believe that the Lutherans took occasion

---

[1] *Commentarius in Epistolam ad Ephesios* (PG 124, 1074B).

[2] The text here has "health of the soul (*salus animae*)," but "health of the body" seems more in accord with the Gospel account.

[3] "I add that in this passage 'faith' is not properly used for that faith whereby we believe the things that are to be believed, but whereby we hope, meaning, confidence itself." (*Omnia Opera* (Leiden (Netherlands), Pieter van der Aa, 1705), vol. 6, pg. 1012 on Heb. 11, 1.

[4] "Erasmus wittily dismissed the charge, claiming that Luther had hatched a different bird entirely." (Terrence M. Reynolds, *Was Erasmus Responsible for Luther? A Study of the Relationship of the Two Reformers and Their Clash Over the Question of the Will*, Concordia Theological Journal, vol. 41

from this sentence of Erasmus, so that they would say the faith whereby we are justified is trust in the promised mercy on account of Christ. But passing over these things, let us get back on track, so that we may prove that "faith" in this passage of the Epistle to the Hebrews does not mean trust.

For Paul, when speaking about the faith, says: "He that cometh to God, must believe that he is, and is a rewarder to them that seek him" (Heb. 11, 6). And again, "By faith we understand that the world was framed" (v. 3). But to believe and to understand are operations of the intellect, and hence it follows that they do not pertain to the will, because this is an act, or passion, of the will, or rather it is evident from that fact that it is closely related to hope and follows after it.

But if Philip tries to deny this, I will refute him by the judgment of a learned and good man, certainly one of those to whom he said he has appealed. Seneca says these words: "Nevertheless I shall tell you what I think,—that at present I have hopes for you, but not yet perfect trust."[1] From which words it is clearly evident that, according to his judgment, trust is something greater than hope, and follows after it, and hence it is proved that trust pertains to the will, just as hope, which precedes it. Next there are many things, taken simply as they are, about which faith is concerned: that God is triune and one, that the Son of God is incarnate, He was born of the Virgin Mary, He was crucified, died and was buried, rose and ascended into Heaven, sits at the right hand of the Father, about all which things in no way can there be trust, nor when taken in a certain respect, because trust is always in regard to future things, and never in regard to present things, nor to past things. But all those things, which we have just listed as pertaining to faith, are past things, except one which is always present, namely the unity of God and the Trinity of Persons.

Furthermore, Paul when writing to the Corinthians separates faith from hope, and consequently from trust. "And now," says Paul, "there remain faith, hope, and charity, these three: but the greatest of these is charity" (I Cor. 13, 13). If faith (as the Lutherans say) includes hope in itself, there are not three things, but two. If there are three things (as Paul says) one must necessarily separate faith from the other two.

After these so very clear testimonies of Scripture it is necessary that we seek the testimony of holy and very learned men, because Philip Melanchthon, as is evident from his words which we have cited above, appealed to men of this kind. Augustine, when discoursing on the faith by which we are justified, says these words: "We now speak of that faith which we employ when we believe anything, not that which we give when we make a promise; for this too is called faith. We use the word in one sense when we say, 'He had no faith in me,' and in another sense when we say, 'He did not keep faith with me.' The one phrase means, 'He did not believe what I said'; the other, 'He did not do what he promised.' According to the faith by which we believe, we are faithful to God; but according to that whereby a thing is brought to pass which is promised, God Himself also is faithful to us; for the Apostle declares, 'God is faithful, who will not suffer you to be tempted above that which you are able.' (I Cor. 10, 13)."[2] From which words it very clearly appears that the faith by which we are justified is not trust, but an operation of the intellect, whereby we believe God revealing or saying something. And when Augustine says these words, he never thought of trust or confidence.

Basil, when defining faith, says the following: "Faith is an unhesitating assent."[3] Chrysostom says the following: "See from this also [the Wise Men's] faith, how they were not... saying, 'And yet, if this Child be great, and has any might, what need of flight, and of a clandestine re-

---

(1977), n. 4, pg. 18.

[1] *Moral letters to Lucilius*, letter 16, n. 2.

[2] *On the Spirit and the Letter*, c. 31, n. 54 (PL 44, 235).

[3] *De fide* (PG 31, 678D).

treat?'... For this most especially belongs to faith, not to seek an account of what is enjoined, but merely to obey the commandments laid upon us."[1] And in his explanation of the Creed [PseudoChrysostom] again says: "The faith of the Catholic religion is the light of the soul, the gate of life, and the foundation of eternal salvation."[2] "Faith is a lamp; and as a lamp gives light to a house, so also faith gives light to the soul."[3] From which words it is evident to all that that faith is not trust, for since it is not an operation of the intellect, it is evident that the mind cannot be illuminated by it.

But let us put these things aside for now, and in order that we may refute Philip and his accomplices more, let us grant them, for the sake of argument, that faith is trust in the promised mercy for the sake of Christ: even so, they will never establish from this that man will be justified by such faith. For I ask them, about what trust do they speak, since they say that man is justified by trust in the promised mercy for the sake of Christ. If they mean confidence in the mercy already received, man can nowise be justified by it: because it precedes, at least by its nature, justification itself, as the object about which the trust itself tends. For it is absurd to say that man is justified by something later than justification itself. But if they mean trust in mercy not yet received but to be received, this alone cannot be enough for accomplishing man's justification. Because this confidence, if it does not have hope and charity with it, and the works of God's Commandments, on which it relies, will be vain confidence, and unworthy to attain what it hopes for.

There is very clear testimony of this matter because there were and are many having this trust, who nevertheless were deceived by it and did not obtain what they hoped for. For Solomon in Proverbs says: "The way of a fool is right in his own eyes" (12, 15). And again, in the same book he says: "There is a way which seemeth just to a man: but the ends thereof lead to death" (14, 12). And again, Ecclesiastes says: "There are wicked men, who are as secure, as though they had the deeds of the just" (8, 14). And Ecclesiasticus says: "Justify not thyself before God, for he knoweth the heart" (7, 5). But much more powerful and clear than all these testimonies is that which the Angel said in John's Apocalypse concerning the Bishop of Laodicea: "Because thou art lukewarm, and neither cold, nor hot, I will begin to vomit thee out of my mouth. Because thou sayest: I am rich, and made wealthy, and have need of nothing: and knowest not, that thou art wretched, and miserable, and poor, and blind, and naked" (3, 16-17). Nothing clearer can be said against the temerarious trust of many men, and their vain security. That Gospel Pharisee also, praying in the Temple, gives us great evidence for refuting this vain trust. For he doubtlessly considered himself just when, relying upon his justification, he was giving thanks to God that he was not like other men, and yet not he, but the publican who was not thinking any such thing about himself, was standing afar off and was striking his breast saying: "O God, be merciful to me a sinner" (Lk. 18, 13), went down justified.

Next, if this opinion of theirs were true, there would be many more just and saved Christians than damned sinners: because there is hardly any Christian who does not have this confidence. For Solomon also bears witness to this same thing in Proverbs saying: "Every way of a man seemeth right to himself: but the Lord weigheth the hearts" (21, 2). In which words Solomon teaches that men are often deceived in the estimation which they have of themselves, because they are not such before God as they seem to themselves. Chrysostom also testifies concerning this vain trust in his homily on the first chapter of Matthew, where

---

[1] *On Matthew*, hom. 8, n. 1 (PG 57, 83).

[2] Eusebius of Emesa, *De Symbolo*, hom. 2 (*D. Eusebii Emiseni episcopi Homeliae ad populum* (Paris, Nicolaus Dives, 1547) pg. 28v.

[3] *Opus imperfectum in Matthaeum*, hom. 52 on chap. 25 (PG 56, 930). This second quotation is presented in the text as a continuation of the previous sentence, but it is in fact drawn from another source.

he says: Every one of us "may set his hopes on nothing else, after God's mercy, but on his own virtue."[1] [Pseudo-] Augustine says: "Hope is deceptive, which leads one to expect to be saved amidst the foments of sin."[2] And again: "It is [more] advantageous to fear well than to be too confident."[3] But let us hear Bernard who clearly condemns this vain confidence, in his third sermon on the Annunciation, after where he cited the words of the Savior to the adulterous woman, "Neither will I condemn thee. Go, and now sin no more" (Jn. 8, 11), says these words: "O voice of mercy, O saving utterance of joy! 'Cause me to hear thy mercy in the morning; for in thee have I hoped' (Ps. 142, 8). Only hope of compassion finds a place with Thee; not even the oil of mercy, unless Thou put it in the vessel of trust. But it is, at any rate, a faithless trust deserving only malediction, when we openly sin in hope. It should not, though, be called trust, but a kind of insensibility and dangerous pretense. For what trust is there for one who gives no heed to danger; what remedy for fear, where neither fear is felt nor the cause of fear perceived? Trust is a consolation, but he needs no consolation 'who is glad when he has done evil, and rejoices in most wicked things' (Prov. 2, 14)."[4] These are the words of Bernard who could not have said anything clearer against this vain trust of these Lutherans.

But now, lest we pass over something deserving of reprehension in the words of Philip Melanchthon cited above, it is necessary that we warn the reader about the ridiculous exposition which he gave to this proposition, "We are justified by faith." For he says, "Faith is correlatively related to mercy as to its object. For which reason when it is said, 'We are justified by faith,' this expression can be rightly understood in this way when it is transformed into a correlative, by saying the following: 'We are justified through the promised mercy on account of Christ.'" Who will not laugh when hearing these things? Or who ever thought that faith is correlative to mercy rather than to any truth to be believed? Also, whoever thought of substituting the one correlative for the other? The Patripassian heretics of old would certainly have greatly rejoiced, if this new kind of interpreting Sacred Scripture were followed. For as often as we read in Holy Writ, the Son of God suffered, they interpret it of the Divine Father, saying that the Son is correlative to the Father, and just as it is permitted to interpret one correlative for another, so it is permitted to substitute the Father in place of the Son. But who does not laugh at these things? Who does not abominate these things? Luther, the leader of all these men, when discoursing on the Sacrament of the Eucharist in his book, *The Babylonian Captivity* [*of the Church*], certainly teaches that Sacred Scripture ought to be interpreted in the simplest meaning of the words, and never outside of the proper meaning of the grammar, lest an occasion for deceiving be given to his adversaries. Thus, I beseech the honorable reader to note carefully and at length give judgment whether the simplest and proper meaning would be to interpret something relative by another relative thing, its correlative.

Finally, so that we may wall in Philip on all sides, although we were to concede to him that the correct and true interpretation is that interpretation which he gives to the proposition, "We are justified by faith," according to that interpretation he attributes nothing more to faith than to works, even if he takes faith to mean trust. For I ask of this Philip and his followers, whether one may say that man is justified by the trust in the promised mercy alone, or by the mercy of God alone. If he says that man is justified by the promised mercy alone, then trust in mercy does not work justification any more than penitence, or other suchlike works of piety and religion. If he says that man is justified by trust, since that is our work, it follows that they should also say that we are justified by some work of ours, which nevertheless they abhor to

---

[1] Hom. 5, n. 4 (PG 57, 59).
[2] *De Singularitate Clericorum* (PL 4, 837C).
[3] *Ibid.* (PL 4, 838A).
[4] N. 2 (PL 183, 394A-B).

hear, so far from it being the case that they would grant that. Against this heresy also militates all the things which we will bring forth for the storming of the upcoming heresies.

There remains that we reply to Luther's objections. Firstly, he objects by citing that passage of the Apostle to the Romans: "Being justified therefore by faith, let us have peace with God" (5, 1); and the passage to the Ephesians: "By grace you are saved through faith, and that not of yourselves" (2, 8); and in the Epistle to the Hebrews: "Without faith it is impossible to please God" (11, 6); and in the Acts of the Apostles Blessed Peter, when speaking about the Gentiles having converted to Christ, says: "And God, who knoweth the hearts, gave testimony, giving unto them the Holy Ghost, as well as to us; and put no difference between us and them, purifying their hearts by faith" (15, 8-9); and by the prophet Habacuc it is said: "The just shall live in his faith" (2, 4). In all which passages of Scripture and very many others justification and purification are attributed to faith, without any mention of works. It is a sign, Luther says, that faith alone justifies man.

Now we reply to this objection that what is said in those passages of Scripture is true, namely because faith justifies man, and without it no one is just: yet it is not said that faith justifies such that something else which was a share in its production is excluded: as for example, if someone were to say that Peter is begotten of John, by this it is not excluded that he is born of a mother, even though the mother is not mentioned: or if one were to say that he was made from a father and mother, it is not then inferred from this that he means to say: "Peter was not produced by God." Thus Scripture, even though it says that justification depends on faith, still it does not say that it depends only on faith.

But they say, when speaking about justification, [God] expressly says faith, but no mention is made of works. We acknowledge that He was then silent about works, still He did not exclude them from justification. For if by the fact that they are not mentioned, they ought to be considered as being excluded, it would also be necessary to say that Baptism is not necessary, as though without it anyone could be saved, because in none of those passages of Scripture which we have just cited is there any mention of Baptism: thus will faith without Baptism save? Far be it. But if Luther were to say that the necessity of Baptism is expressed elsewhere, even though it is not mentioned in these passages, and he asserts that this suffices: and we also will reply this same thing to him, that although in these cited passages of Scripture, or in any others in which works are omitted when there is a discussion about justification, they are not understood to be excluded by this, because it is enough for the assertion of them, that the power and efficacy of works was expressed elsewhere, just as in the testimonies firstly cited by us.

Furthermore, if by this fact that works are omitted, it is allowed to exclude them, or to infer their exclusion, for the same reason it will be allowed to also exclude faith from justification, because often justification is attributed to works, with not mention made of faith. And so that I may put forth other testimonies of this thing, for example, that is clear which is said in commendation of alms: "Alms deliver from all sin, and from death." (Tob. 4, 11). See what he said, "from all sin." And again, concerning the same matter: "Water quencheth a flaming fire, and alms resisteth sins" (Eccli. 3, 33). And again, Truth Itself says: "Give alms; and behold, all things are clean unto you" (Lk. 11, 41). Notice what He said, "all." Therefore, someone could so argue in the same way as Luther: "Behold the Savior commends almsgiving to us, and making completely no mention about faith, he says all things are clean to us. Therefore, faith is not necessary, but almsgiving alone suffices, especially because on Judgment Day (as the Lord Himself says in Matthew's Gospel[1]) He will ask an account of this, and He also then does not make any mention of faith." Far be it, however, that someone would say that almsgiving alone suffices for eternal life, since Paul says: "If I should distribute all my goods to

---

[1] Mt. 25, 35-45.

feed the poor, and if I should deliver my body to be burned, and have not charity, it profiteth me nothing" (I Cor. 13, 3).

Thus, however often faith, or any other virtue is praised, or something honorable is attributed to it, it always ought to be understood conditionally, if it rightly fulfills its function. Its function is then said to have been rightly fulfilled, if it does not omit other things elsewhere commanded. For just as almsgiving ought to be called good, whenever proceeding from faith, it be done with a care for God alone: so also faith will then be sufficient, when necessary works are conjoined to it. For not by the fact that one or another virtue is praised that immediately one ought to look askance at the others, because virtues do not envy each other, as men are accustomed to do, who consider the praises of other men to be affronts to themselves, and deem the praise of anyone else to be a detriment to their own glory. But the virtues are not like this: but rather all being content with their own condition, and each one acknowledging its own position, neither despises a lower one, nor envies a higher one. Therefore, by these things which we have said, it can be easily replied (as I think) to any objection, admitting that faith justifies, that faith is required, that faith purifies, but not alone, but all those things with it, which are found to have been commanded elsewhere. For otherwise they would be commanded in vain.

But there still remains one doubt left for us to remove, since Paul says in that epistle which is to the Romans: "For we account a man to be justified by faith, without the works of the law" (3, 28); and in the Epistle to the Galatians: "But knowing that man is not justified by the works of the law, but by the faith of Jesus Christ; we also believe in Christ Jesus, that we may be justified by the faith of Christ, and not by the works of the law: because by the works of the law no flesh shall be justified" (2, 16). Lutherans especially glory in these two passages of Scripture, because (as they say) in them man's justification is so attributed to faith itself, that works are excluded.

To which things we reply that Paul in those two passages speaks about the works of the Old Law, for instance the ceremonies and other rituals, which were all abolished by Christ's death, and having absolutely no power, they consequently could not justify anyone. He was not, however, speaking about the works of the other precepts of the Decalogue. Now the very subject matter which is treated in these epistles clearly proves it to be so, because (as Blessed [Augustine] says) "The Scriptural context usually sets the meaning of Scripture in a clear light."[1] Now it is certain that Paul occupies himself with this in these two epistles to show that the Mosaic Law, which was given to the Jews alone, then ceased, and Christ's New Law is for all men. Thus, after those words, which were cited from the third chapter of the Epistle to the Romans, he immediately added: "Is he the God of the Jews only? Is he not also of the Gentiles? Yes, of the Gentiles also. For it is one God, that justifieth circumcision by faith, and uncircumcision through faith" (v. 29-30).

And regarding the Epistle to the Galatians, it is evident that he wishes to teach the Galatians in this epistle that they should believe that the precepts of the Law should no longer be followed. For he testifies that it was for this reason that he reprehended Peter, namely because he was forcing the Gentiles to Judaize by simulation. In either epistle, namely to the Romans or Galatians, there is no mention of any other works besides the works of the Old Law. Thus, those passages of Scripture do nothing against us: because we also admit that those works of the Old Law are now worthless.

---

[1] The text here cites St. Hilary, but these words seem rather to have been said by St. Augustine as follows: "The Scriptural context usually sets the meaning in a clear light when the surrounding verses which bear on the question at hand are treated to careful examination" (*Eighty-three Different Questions*, q. 69, n. 2 (PL 40, 75)).

One can reply still another way to the argument, that we may say that in those passages Paul is speaking about works done before faith has been received, which all agree merit nothing before God, and concerning them we ourselves also admit that they do completely nothing for man's justification. For even though they are sometimes necessary for justification, such as penitence in the sinner, still justification is never imputed because of them. Now the works about which we now dispute as to their being necessary for justification are the works done after the reception of faith, and these are the ones about which the Apostle James says these words: "Faith without works is dead" (2, 26). Bede interprets this passage in this sense, who in his commentary on James' epistle says these words: "Since the Apostle Paul, preaching that man is justified by faith without works,[1] was not well understood by those who took this saying to mean that when they had once believed in Christ, even though they should commit evils and live wickedly and basely, they could be saved by faith, [James] explains how the passage of the Apostle Paul ought to be understood to have the same meaning as this epistle. And all the more therefore he uses the example of Abraham about faith being useless if it does not issue in good works, because the Apostle Paul also used the example of Abraham[2] to demonstrate the man can be justified without works. For, when [James] recalls those good works of Abraham which accompanied his faith, he shows well enough that the Apostle Paul did not so teach, by the example of Abraham, that a man is justified by faith without works to the extent that if someone were to believe, he would have no obligation to perform good works, but rather that no one should think he has come to the gift of justification which is in faith by the merits of his former good deeds. In this matter the Jews wished to set themselves above the Gentiles who believed in Christ, because, they said, they had come to Evangelical grace by the merits of the good works which are in the Law. And so many of those who believed were scandalized that the grace of Christ was being given to uncircumcised Gentiles. Hence the Apostle Paul says that a man can be justified by faith without works, that is to say, previous works. For how can one who has been justified by faith act otherwise than justly?"[3]

Now what he says, that one who has been justified by faith cannot act otherwise than justly, ought not to be so understood such that he who been once justified cannot fall away from his justification, or that he would be forced to act well, but he spoke thus because when one has acted unjustly, by that very fact he will lose his justification. Thus, he thinks that these two things cannot be united: man justified by faith and him to act unjustly. I know that these passages of Paul are expounded otherwise by others, and to the objection of the aforesaid passages is otherwise answered by them, yet these two meanings please me more, because they are more faithful to the literal meaning. Theophylactus[4] expounds these passages according to the first way whereby we have expounded them. [Ambrosiaster[5]] interprets them in the same way. And [Pseudo-] Blessed Jerome teaches that passage from the Epistle to the Galatians ought to be interpreted in the same way.[6]

Philip Melanchthon thirdly objects to us that passage of Paul to the Romans: "Abraham believed God, and it was reputed to him unto justice" (Rom. 4, 3). From which words Philip Melanchthon thinks that it is clearly inferred that Abraham was justified by faith alone. But Philip is mistaken about this, not understanding what "reputed unto justice" means. For it is

---

[1] Rom. 3, 28.

[2] Rom. 4, 1-25.

[3] *Commentary on James* (PL 93, 22C-D).

[4] *Commentarius in Epistolam ad Romanos* (PG 124, 390A-C); *Commentarius in Epistolam ad Galatas* (PG 124, 978C-D).

[5] *Commentaria in Epistolam ad Romanos* (PL 17, 80D); *Commentaria in Epistolam ad Galatas* (PL 17, 355C-D).

[6] *Commentarii in epistolas Pauli* (PL 30, 810C-D).

not, as Philip supposes, to acquire the first justification, but it is reckoned among the works of justice. And Paul so teaches in these words that the faith whereby "Abraham believed God" was a work of justice, and Paul correctly so teaches. Because it is just that everyone would believe God (Who is most truthful) saying something.

Now that "to be reputed to justice" means what we have said, I show clearly from another passage of Scripture. For the Royal Prophet when praising the action of Phinees, the priest killing the Jew fornicating with the Madianite woman, says: "Then Phinees stood up, and pacified him: and the slaughter ceased. And it was reputed to him unto justice, to generation and generation for evermore" (Ps. 105, 30-31). Notice the killing of a man was reputed to Phinees unto justice, as Chrysostom says,[1] whose words are cited by Gratian.[2] Now it is certain that in these words of the Prophet, the killing "was reputed to him unto justice," do not mean that Phinees was justified by such killing, but it only means that he by killing those fornicators in this way, performed a work of justice, and such killing was accepted by God as a work of justice. Thus Paul ought to be interpreted in the same way when he said that Abraham's faith "was reputed to him unto justice," not because he was justified by this alone, but because by so believing he did a just work.

Perhaps Philip and his followers thought that they would sway us by that which Paul immediately adds saying: "Now to him that worketh, the reward is not reckoned according to grace, but according to debt. But to him that worketh not, yet believeth in him that justifieth the ungodly, his faith is reputed to justice" (v. 4-5). From which words Philip perhaps concludes that faith without works justifies. But those words of Paul ought to be understood quite differently from what he supposes. For Paul in that passage, after he had said that Abraham's faith "was reputed to him unto justice," immediately treats about works performed after faith and grace have been received. Thus Paul in that passages distinguishes two men already justified. For there are some who after having received faith and grace did good works, and a reward (that is, eternal glory which is the true reward) is due to them not according to grace, that is, not gratis and from pure liberality, but according to debt: because eternal glory is due to good works, not by nature or by their natural worth, but from the Divine promise. There are others who after having received faith and grace have performed no good work, perhaps because no time was given to them in which they could have acted virtuously, as happens to those who died immediately after having received Baptism, and to these faith alone is reputed to justice, not merely so that they may be just in this life, but also unto eternal glory, which Chrysostom when expounding this passage calls full and complete justice.[3] And this is given to them not according to debt, primarily, but according to grace and God's pure liberality, and this is what Paul says, "according to the purpose of the grace of God" (v. 5).

Now that a reward is not given to the latter, as something due, as to the first group, hence it happens that the first group have some work of their own, in which they served God, and hence a reward is in some way due to them: but the second group had only faith, which, as Paul says, is "the gift of God" (Eph. 2, 8), and hence cannot properly be said to be our work, because no one can acquire it by his own powers according to that which the Savior says: "No man can come to me, except the Father... draw him" (Jn. 6, 44). Blessed Augustine,[4] and

---

[1] "But Phinehas became a manslayer, and it was reputed to him, he says, unto justice" (*Homilies on Matthew*, hom. 17, n. 5 (PG 57, 262-263)).

[2] *Concordia discordantium canonum*, c. 14 (*Occidit*), C. XXIII, q. 8 (187, 1250A).

[3] "Justice is a recompense which most fully comprehends several rewards" (*Homilies on Romans*, hom. 8, n. 2 (PG 60, 456)).

[4] "'Now to him that worketh, the reward is not reckoned according to grace, but according to debt' (Rom. 4, 4). Paul here spoke of the way men give rewards to men. For God gave by grace, since He gave to sinners, so that by faith they might live justly, that is, do good works. Therefore the good works we

the Gloss,[1] which is commonly called the *Glossa Ordinaria,* and Blessed Thomas[2] expound these words of Paul according to this manner. These three authors give another interpretation to these same words which we have just cited. But the interpretation which I have just related is much more pleasing, because it seems to me to be more truly the literal meaning.

They fourthly object to us the passage of Paul: "Other foundation no man can lay, but that which is laid; which is Christ Jesus. Now if any man build upon this foundation, gold, silver, precious stones, wood, hay, stubble: every man's work shall be manifest; for the day of the Lord shall declare it, because it shall be revealed in fire; and the fire shall try every man's work, of what sort it is. If any man's work abide, which he hath built thereupon, he shall receive a reward. If any man's work burn, he shall suffer loss; but he himself shall be saved, yet so as by fire" (I Cor. 3, 11-15). From these words of Paul, the Lutherans suppose that they prove that faith alone suffices for salvation. For Paul, as they think, teaches by these words that all will be saved who have Christ as the foundation of their spiritual edifice, whatsoever they build afterwards. For they say that Paul designated only two groups of those building upon Christ, and both will be saved, namely those who build thereupon wood, hay and stubble are saved by fire, but those who build thereupon gold silver and precious stones are saved without fire. Therefore since all those have Christian faith, they hold fast Christ, because as Paul says, He dwells by faith in our hearts.[3] And for the same reason Paul himself glories that he had laid the foundation in the case of the Corinthians, because he delivered the faith of Christ to them, hence Lutherans suppose that he clearly implies that all who believe in Christ will at length be saved, either through the fire of tribulation consuming the bad deeds done, or without fire of this kind, those who did nothing bad but only good works.

But this argumentation of theirs comes from a wrong and distorted understanding of Paul's words. And certainly, if these words of Paul were rightly examined as they ought, it will be very clearly known that they support us rather than them. For from those words, as we shall prove below at greater length in the section on "Purgatory," it is gathered that Purgatory is fire after this life, and there is a difference between mortal and venial sins, and the punishment of venial sins is only for a time. But having passed over these things which we leave to be disputed in another place, it is necessary for reaching our goal, that we prove that no such thing is contained in Paul's works, such as the heretics think.

Firstly, in fact, they are deceived thinking that those who have perpetrated evil deeds, and keep their affection for them, dwell in Christ, and have Him for a foundation. For Blessed John says in his First Epistle: "If we say that we have fellowship with him, and walk in darkness, we lie, and do not the truth" (1, 6). And again, in the same epistle: "He that saith he abideth in him, ought himself also to walk, even as he walked" (2, 6). But he who commits sin, does not walk like Christ, "Who did no sin, neither was guile found in his mouth" (I Peter 2, 22), therefore he, according to John's judgment, does not abide in Christ. And in

---

do once we have received grace are not due to ourselves, but to Him Who justifies us by grace. For if He had wanted to render a just reward, He would have rendered the punishment due to sinners" (*Expositio propositionum ex Epistola ad Romanos,* n. 21 (PL 35, 2066)).

[1] "'According to the purpose' (Rom. 4, 5). It is as though he were to say: 'the wicked man is justified without preceding works,' and this 'according to the purpose [*propositum*] of the grace of God,' meaning, according to God's grace offered to all believers, but according to what God offered long before" (PL 114, 482B).

[2] "The nature of grace is repugnant to reward of works, according to Rm. 4:4: "Now to him that worketh, the reward is not reckoned according to grace but according to debt." Now a man merits what is reckoned to him according to debt, as the reward of his works. Hence a man may not merit the first grace" (I-II, q. 114, a. 5, s.c.).

[3] Cf. Eph. 3, 17.

the same place: "He that hateth his brother, is in darkness, and walketh in darkness" (I Jn. 2, 11). From which words of John, it is very clearly proved that he who hates his brother, does not abide in Christ, Who is the truest light, because as Paul says, "What fellowship hath light with darkness?" (II Cor. 6, 14). And once again John likewise says: "Whosoever abideth in him, sinneth not" (I Jn. 3, 6). And again: "He that loveth not, abideth in death: whosoever hateth his brother is a murderer. And you know that no murderer hath eternal life abiding in himself" (v. 14-15). If one does not have life, then he does not have Christ, Who is the true life. Finally, Solomon when discussing Divine Wisdom, which is Christ, says: "Wisdom will not enter into a malicious soul, nor dwell in a body subject to sins" (Wis. 1, 4). Therefore, since from all these passages it is clearly evident that Christ does not dwell in the hearts of sinners, it is consequently also proved that they do not dwell in Christ, because Christ is in all who are in Him. And so, it further follows that that they who have sins do not have Christ for the foundation of their spiritual edifice.

And the fact that Paul is not speaking about such men as these in the aforesaid words, but only about the just in whom God dwell by grace is easily established by that which Paul likewise adds immediately after those words: "Know you not, that you are the temple of God, and that the Spirit of God dwelleth in you? But if any man violate the temple of God, him shall God destroy" (I Cor. 3, 16-17). Please notice what he says. He says, "shall destroy" and not "shall save." From which words it is clearly proved that he who, even if he have faith, yet joins mortal sins to the faith, does not build upon the foundation which is Christ.

And I confirm that this is Paul's true meaning by the testimony of Augustine in his book, *On Faith and Works*, where when explaining the aforesaid words of Paul, after he said that faith is also the foundation, as is Christ, says these words: "For not the faith of devils, whereas they themselves both believe and tremble, and confess that Jesus is the Son of God, can be taken as a foundation. For what reason, save because that is not faith which worketh through love, but which is wrung out through fear? Thus the faith in Christ, the faith which is of Christian grace, that is, that faith which worketh through love, being laid as a foundation, suffereth no one to perish."[1]

There is still something else to be carefully considered in the words of Paul, which clearly shows that the Lutherans were mistaken in their understanding of his words. For Paul, when distinguishing those building upon the foundation of the spiritual edifice, does not mention any other edifice built thereon except "gold, silver, precious stones, wood, hay, stubble." But mortal sins are neither gold nor silver nor precious stones, because all these things are precious, but mortal sins are so very worthless that they have no price or value, except perhaps among those "who are glad when they have done evil, and rejoice in most wicked things" (Prov. 2, 14). But neither are wood nor hay nor stubble compared to mortal sins in Sacred Scripture, because these material things are easily consumed by fire, whereas mortal sins have "everlasting fire which was prepared for the devil and his angels" (Mt. 25, 41). And for this reason, those sins are compared in Sacred Scripture to lead, iron, and heavy stones, which press down by their weight, and draw from the heights of Heaven down to Hell.

Venial sins, however, in that they are light and can be purged by the fire of tribulation are compared to very light things which can be easily consumed by fire, namely wood, hay and stubble. Thus, Paul mentions two groups of those building upon Christ. But both are just men. The first are those who build thereon gold, silver or precious stones, who have nothing to be purged, these men receive the reward of eternal glory immediately after death. But others, who build thereon wood, hay or stubble are those who have committed only venial sins, or if they have committed mortal sins, they have repented of them, but have not made full satisfaction, and it is necessary that they be purged before they may receive the reward of glory, and

---

[1] C. 16, n. 27 (PL 40, 215).

this either through the fire of tribulation in this present life, or by the fire of purgatory in the future life. And this is what Paul said, that they "shall be saved, yet so as by fire."

Fifthly they object to us some testimonies of Sacred Scripture, in which every believer without distinction, and without any requirement of good works, is promised justice and life everlasting. For Christ, Our Savior, in John's Gospel, says: "And as Moses lifted up the serpent in the desert, so must the Son of man be lifted up: that whosoever believeth in him, may not perish; but may have life everlasting. For God so loved the world, as to give his only begotten Son; that whosoever believeth in him, may not perish, but may have life everlasting" (3, 14-16). And Paul when writing to the Romans says: "Even the justice of God, by faith of Jesus Christ, unto all and upon all them that believe in him" (3, 22). And hence the Lutherans suppose that they rightly conclude that faith alone without works is enough for attaining justice.

To this objection I know others reply differently, passing over those responses which seem to deviate far from the literal meaning, I will relate others which are more in accordance with the literal meaning. Therefore I firstly reply that all those quotations of Sacred Scripture ought to be understood of living faith which truly works by love,[1] and on this matter Blessed Augustine supports us in the book, *On Faith and Works*, where after he said the good morals and faith are interrelated to each other, just as love of God and love of neighbor, of which one cannot exist without the other, he says these words which follow: "And so at times we find that Scripture makes mention of the one without the other, either this or that, in place of the full doctrine, so that even in this way we may understand that the one cannot exist without the other: because both he who believes in God ought to do what God commands; and he who therefore does it because God commands it, must of necessity believe in God."[2] Which words are very noteworthy, and ought to be retained as an outstanding rule, because it helps very much for understanding many other passages of Sacred Scripture, and is also effective for confirming those things which we said in the solution of the first argument.

And he supports this solution of our still more clearly in the same work saying the following: "Paul hath laid down, that not any faith whatsoever whereby God is believed in, but that whose works proceed from love, is saving, and truly according to the Gospel; 'but faith,' he says, 'that worketh by charity' (Gal. 5, 6). Whence that faith which seems to some to be sufficient unto salvation, he so asserts to be of no avail, as that he says, 'If I should have all faith, so that I could remove mountains, and have not charity, I am nothing' (I Cor. 13, 2). But where faithful love worketh, there without a doubt is a good life, for 'Love is the fulfilling of the law' (Rom. 13, 10)."[3]

It can be replied in another way to the aforesaid objection, by an outstanding and very noteworthy rule for the understanding of Sacred Scripture, which Ralph of Flaix,[4] a highly learned man, notes down in his commentary on Leviticus. For he says, regarding general statements which are found in Sacred Scripture, one ought to examine before all else, whether a particular statement is found in the same passage or elsewhere which contradicts the general statement. And if such be found, he says that the general statement ought to be understood with the exception of that particular statement which has been found to contradict it. Because unless the passage be interpreted in this way, it would be necessary to grant that many contradictions are found in Sacred Scripture, which would be absurd and a grave sin to concede.

---

[1] Cf. Gal. 5, 6.

[2] C. 13, n. 20 (PL 40, 210-211).

[3] C. 14, n. 21 (PL 40, 211).

[4] Radulphus (Ralph), a Benedictine Friar, surnamed Flaviacensis because he belonged to the Convent of St. Germer de Flaix, in the diocese of Beauvais, flourished in 1157. *In mysticum illum Moysi Leviticum libri 20* (Cologne, Eucharius Cervicornus, 1536).

Now so that I may make this rule well understood, I will give some examples in which a manifest contradiction will be found unless they be reconciled according to this rule. First of all is that very well-known saying which, as Sacred Scripture bears witness, [King] Assuerus said to Esther his queen: "This law is not made for thee, but for all others" (Esth. 15, 13). Since he said, "for all others," one must necessarily exclude Esther herself, such that the meaning would be, "for all others, except you." Furthermore the passage is also very clear which is read in the book of Job: "None is free from sin, not even the infant which has lived but a day upon the earth" (14, 4-5 LXX).[1] In this general saying, it must necessarily be understood that the exception of Christ, our Savior, and of the Virgin Mary, His mother, and of other Saints, whom were sanctified in their mother's womb is encompassed, as Sacred Scripture testifies. For if this aforesaid exception encompassed in the general statement would not be understood, it would be necessary to acknowledge that the general statement is false.

Paul used this rule when interpreting the passage of the [Royal] Prophet: "Thou hast subjected all things under his feet" (Ps. 8, 8). For since based upon it, someone perhaps misunderstanding it might have been tempted to infer that the Heavenly Father Himself was also put under Christ's feet; to eliminate this incorrect inference, in the First Epistle to the Corinthians he says: "For he must reign, until he hath put all his enemies under his feet. And the enemy death shall be destroyed last: For he hath put all things under his feet. And whereas he saith, all things are put under him; undoubtedly, he is excepted, who put all things under him." (15, 25-27). Behold, you see that the Prophet had spoken generally without any exception. Yet Paul teaches that in a general statement it is necessarily understood that what has been established elsewhere to contradict the general statement is excepted.

Along the same line, I say that all those general statements whereby it is asserted that every believer is just, ought to be understood with this exception: except those who have not fulfilled the works of the Divine precepts, because concerning all such men clear and numerous testimonies of Sacred Scripture say that they are not just nor worthy of eternal life. For Paul, when writing to the Ephesians, says: "For know you this and understand, that no fornicator, or unclean, or covetous person (which is a serving of idols), hath inheritance in the kingdom of Christ and of God. Let no man deceive you with vain words. For because of these things cometh the anger of God upon the children of unbelief" (Eph. 5, 5-6). These last words would seem to have been said on account of the Lutherans, and other teachers of the same grain. For they seduce men with vain words teaching them that works are not necessary, but by faith alone one can be justified and attain eternal life. Again, concerning these men in the Epistle to Titus he says: "They profess that they know God: but in their works they deny him; being abominable, and incredulous, and to every good work reprobate" (1, 16). And John in his First Epistle says: "He who saith that he knoweth him, and keepeth not his commandments, is a liar, and the truth is not in him" (2, 4). Lastly, Our Savior replies to the man asking Him by what deeds can one possess eternal life: "If thou wilt enter into life, keep the commandments" (Mt. 19, 17). From which words it is evident that they who do not keep God's Commandments, do not enter into eternal life, and consequently are not just. Therefore, that all these men, whom have been evidentially excluded from eternal life by Christ's and the Apostles' testimony, ought to be understood to be excepted in those general statements whereby eternal life, or justification, is promised to every believer.

A third response to the aforesaid objection can moreover be given, and it certainly ought not to be despised, since it is very much in accord with the literal meaning. Therefore, I say to them that the general statements ought to be so interpreted that they be not referred to each and every individual, but to each class of those individuals. And this is what recent logicians say with other words, that the application is not to every individual of each class, but to every

---

[1] This passage is quoted according to the Septuagint version.

class of individuals. And there is no one who dares to deny that this manner of speech is frequently used in Holy Writ, except perhaps those who are not versed in it, or do not understand it. For instance, that which the Royal Prophet says is clear: "All kings of the earth shall adore him: all nations shall serve him" (Ps. 71, 11). Certainly, there are many kings today who do not adore Christ, and many nations which do not serve him. Nevertheless, out of every people and out of every nation some kings have adored or at some time they will adore Christ, and some people out of every nation will serve Him. In the same manner ought to be interpreted that which the [Royal] Prophet likewise says in another Psalm: "All the nations thou hast made shall come and adore before thee, O Lord" (Ps. 85, 9).

And lest this diction of speech be said to be found only in the Old Testament, I cite an example from the New Testament. In the parable of the king who made a marriage for his son, the king says to his servant: "As many as you shall find, call to the marriage" (Mt. 22, 9). But it is certain that not all men come to Christ's faith, which is signified by the name of marriage in that passage, but some men from every race and from every nation have come to Christ's faith or at least will come. According to this this manner of speech, we say that Paul ought to be interpreted when he said: "Even the justice of God, by faith of Jesus Christ, unto all and upon all them that believe in him" (Rom. 3, 22), such that we understand not every single believer is just, but that from every people and every nation some believers will be justified, such that not only believing Jews but also believing Gentiles can be justified. And Paul's words themselves clearly prove that this is the true and actual meaning of the text. For after those words Paul immediately adds: "For there is no distinction: for all have sinned, and do need the glory of God... Is he the God of the Jews only? Is he not also of the Gentiles? Yes, of the Gentiles also" (v. 22-23 & 29). The Jews certainly thought that they alone are just before God, and the Gentiles are incapable of [receiving] Divine grace, and hence to check this arrogance of theirs, he said that God's justice is "unto all and upon all," meaning not merely unto the Jews, but also unto the Gentiles.

Sixthly, they object to us testimonies of some holy men who seem to say that faith alone without works justifies: among whom is Bernard,[1] Theophylactus,[2] Pope Leo,[3] Hilary,[4] and perhaps some others which do not presently come to my mind. But none of these nor anyone else approved by the Church has ever said that faith alone without works always justifies. Some have said, as I frankly admit, that faith alone justifies, but not faith alone without works, because there is a great difference between these two. For when they say that faith alone justifies, by that exclusive expression the word "alone" does not set aside works, but all other sects, which do not agree with Christ's faith, in which sects there is not salvation, nor justification. Thus, when it is said, "faith alone justifies," it means the same thing as if he were to say, "In no sect is there justice except in the sole faith of Christ." For long ago there was a certain heretic saying that every man living well in his own law can be saved, whether he be a Jew, Saracen, or pagan,[5] concerning which heresy we will dispute below in the section on "Law."

---

[1] "Wherefore, whosoever feels compunction for his sins, and hungers and thirsts for justice, let him believe in Thee Who justifies the impious, and thus, justified by faith alone, he shall have peace with God." (*Sermons on the Canticle of Canticles*, sermon 22 (PL 183, 881D)).

[2] "The Gentiles having justice by faith were truly justified" (*Commentarius in Epistolam ad Romanos*, c. 9 (PG 124, 474A)).

[3] "...faith that justifies the godless" (Serm. 35 (On the Epiphany), c. 2 (PL 54, 251A)).

[4] "The sins of his soul that the Law could not remit are remitted him; for faith alone justifies" (*Commentarius in Evangelium Matthaei*, c. 8, n. 6 (PL 9, 961A)). The reference here is to chapter nine, but this does not seem correct.

[5] Philastrius of Brescia relates that certain men, whom he calls "Rhetorians," from a certain Rhetorius,

But the Saints, in order to refute this error, were accustomed to say that faith alone justifies, which is the same as though it were said, "Outside the Catholic faith there is no true justice." And in order to confirm this interpretation I cite an example from the Bull of Pope Martin V, whereby the errors of John Wycliffe and John Hus are condemned, in which after the condemnation of these heretics these words are found: "When in fact to the rest of those infected in any way by this kind condemnable sect, who after suitable warning, and one has used frequent exhortation, which one kindly makes to them in hope of their correction, emendation, and conversion to a better life, and they do not wish to renounce their sect and the aforesaid errors and fully acknowledge and confess the flock, and unity of Holy Mother the Church and the Catholic faith, which alone can save, without which to no one obtains assistance for true salvation, the severity of justice, insofar as the quality of the deed demands, ought to be tempered with the sweetness of mercy."[1] In which, as its content clearly shows, [Pope Martin says] that faith alone saves, just as Paul said elsewhere, "Without faith it is impossible to please God" (Heb. 11, 6). Thus by that exclusive expression only other sects and not works are excluded, except only those which were done before faith, because these works nowise justify, nor is justice attributed to them in any way, although something of them, namely repentance, is necessary for salvation. And in confirmation of this is that which Augustine says in his book, *On the Spirit and the Letter*: "But the statement that 'the doers of the law shall be justified' (Rom. 2, 13) must be so understood," he says, "as that we may know that they are not otherwise doers of the Law, unless they be justified, so that justification does not subsequently accrue to them as doers of the Law, but justification precedes them as doers of the Law."[2]

Those words, "faith alone justifies," can have still another and truly Catholic meaning, such that that exclusive expression excludes works, not indeed all, but those which precede faith, and this is universally true, because even though those works, as we said, are sometimes necessary, still justification is never imputed to them. It can also be understood such that it excludes works following faith, but then that exclusive expression is not taken universally, such that faith alone is always understood to always justify, but it ought to be understood particularly, that faith alone without an external work following it sometimes justifies man, namely when after having received the faith there is no time in which man can do some exterior work which he ought to do.

And it is evident that this is the true understanding of those words from [Pseudo-] Blessed Chrysostom in his homily, *On Faith and the Law of Nature*, wherein when interpreting the passage of the [Royal] Prophet, "I, as a fruitful olive tree in the house of God" (Ps. 51, 10), says these words: "Thus it is necessary both that faith shine before works and be what follows on foot after faith: and lest someone vituperate faith on account of sterility and works on account on incredulity, you ought to be a 'fruitful olive tree,' but 'in the house of God.' The 'fruitful olive tree' is understood of works; but the words, 'in the house of God,' show faith... Yet faith ought to be put on before works. You cannot prove that he who performs works of justice without faith was alive: but I can show that the believer without works both was alive

---

taught in Egypt that any man could be saved in his church, or in his own religion, provided that he live rightly in it, whether he be a Jew, Pagan or Saracen: for they approved of all heresies, praised all heretics, and claimed that none of them erred in Christ's faith. (*Liber de Haeresibus*, c. 91, (PL 1202B-1203B)). St. Augustine wrote concerning this heresy, "This is so absurd that it seems unbelievable to me." (*De Haeresibus ad Quodvultdeum*, c. 72 (PL 42, 44)). And yet this all-encompassing heresy, propagated by Freemasonry, is widely accepted today.

[1] Bull *Inter cunctas* of February 22, 1418 (Mansi, *Sacrorum Conciliorum Nova Amplissima Collectio*, vol. 27, col. 1205-1206).

[2] C. 26, n. 45 (PL 44, 228).

and has attained the kingdom of Heaven. No one has life without faith. The thief, however, merely believed and was justified.[1] And do not say to me here that there was no time for him in which he could live justly, and perform virtuous deeds. For I did not dispute this, but I have asserted something else, namely that faith alone of itself saved him. For if he had lived longer, and was negligent of works, he would have been cut off from salvation. This is what is being investigated and treated now, that faith of itself saved him: works, however, of themselves have never justified anyone doing good works."[2]

From which words it is clearly enough established in what sense ought to be understood what he says: "faith alone justifies," namely because it can sometimes so happen, as for example when there was not the time needed to do something, as is clear in the example of the thief which was crucified at the same time with Christ. It is also evident that the exclusive expression, "alone," does not exclude all works, but only external works. For otherwise it would be false that faith alone without charity or love of God could make one saved. It would also be false that the thief who was given as an example would have faith alone, since it is evident from the words which he said that he had true hope in Christ, love of Him, and repentance for his sins.

I do not see what is left for me to do against this heresy so that I may pluck it out by its roots, except to cite the definition of the Catholic Church which clearly condemns it. The Council of Trent celebrated under Paul III very carefully (as was fitting) examined this matter (I being present there), and finally after long discussion and study, in the sixth session, published the teaching which ought to be embraced about this matter, which extending from the third chapter of the decrees of that session until the end of the eighth chapter contains the following words:

But although "Christ died for all" (II Cor. 5, 15), yet not all receive the benefit of His death, but those only to whom the merit of His Passion is communicated. For, as indeed men would not be born unjust, if they were not born through propagation of the seed of Adam, since by that propagation they contract through him, in conception, injustice as their own, so unless they were born again in Christ, they never would be justified, since in that new birth through the merit of His Passion, the grace, whereby they are made just, is bestowed upon them. For this benefit the Apostle exhorts us always to "give thanks to the Father who has made us worthy to be partakers of the lot of the saints in light" (Col. 1, 12), and "has delivered us from the power of darkness, and has translated us into the kingdom of the Son of his love, in whom we have redemption and remission of sins" (Col. 1, 13-14).

In these words a description of the justification of a sinner is given as being a translation from that state in which man is born a child of the first Adam to the state of grace and of the "adoption of sons" (Rom. 8, 15) of God through the second Adam, Jesus Christ, our Savior; and this translation after the promulgation of the Gospel cannot be effected except through the laver of regeneration, or a desire for it, as it is written: "Unless a man be born again of water and the Holy Ghost, he cannot enter into the kingdom of God" (John 3, 5).

It [the Synod] furthermore declares that in adults the beginning of that justification must be derived from the predisposing grace of God through Jesus Christ, that is, from his vocation, whereby without any existing merits on their part they are called, so that they who by sin were turned away from God, through His stimulating and assisting grace are disposed to convert themselves to their own justification, by freely assenting to and cooperating with the same grace, in such wise that, while God touches the heart of man through the illumination of the Holy Ghost, man himself receiving that inspiration does not do nothing at all inasmuch as he can indeed reject it, nor on the other hand can he of his own free will without the grace of

---

[1] Cf. Lk. 23, 40-43.
[2] N. 1 (PG 48, 1081-1082).

God move himself to justice before Him. Hence, when it is said in the Sacred Writings: "Turn ye to me, and I will turn to you" (Zach. 1, 3), we are reminded of our liberty; when we reply: "Convert us, O Lord, to thee, and we shall be converted" (Lam. 5, 21), we confess that we are anticipated by the grace of God.

Now they are disposed to that justice when, aroused and assisted by Divine grace, receiving faith "by hearing" (Rom. 10, 17), they are freely moved toward God, believing that to be true which has been divinely revealed and promised, and this especially, that the sinner is justified by God through His grace, "through the redemption that is in Christ Jesus" (Rom. 3, 24), and when knowing that they are sinners, turning themselves away from the fear of Divine justice, by which they are profitably aroused, to a consideration of the mercy of God, they are raised to hope, trusting that God will be merciful to them for the sake of Christ, and they begin to love Him as the source of all justice and are therefore moved against sins by a certain hatred and detestation, that is, by that repentance, which must be performed before Baptism;[1] and finally when they resolve to receive Baptism, to begin a new life and to keep the Commandments of God. Concerning this disposition it is written: "He that cometh to God must believe, that he is and is a rewarder to them that seek him" (Heb. 11, 6), and, "Be of good faith, son, thy sins are forgiven thee" (Mt. 9, 2), and, "The fear of the Lord driveth out sin" (Eccli. 1, 27), and, "Do penance, and be baptized every one of you in the name of Jesus Christ for the remission of your sins, and you shall receive the gift of the Holy Ghost" (Acts 2, 38), and, "Going therefore teach all nations, baptizing them in the name of the Father and of the Son and of the Holy Ghost, teaching them to observe all things whatsoever I have commanded you" (Mt. 28, 19), and finally, "Prepare your hearts unto the Lord" (I Kings 7, 3). Justification itself follows this disposition or preparation, which is not merely remission of sins, but also the sanctification and renewal of the interior man through the voluntary reception of the grace and gifts, whereby an unjust man becomes a just man, and from being an enemy becomes a friend, that he may be "an heir according to hope of life everlasting" (Tit. 3, 7). The causes of this justification are: the final cause indeed is the glory of God and of Christ and life eternal; the efficient cause is truly a merciful God who gratuitously "washes and sanctifies" (I Cor. 6, 11), "signing and anointing with the Holy Ghost of promise, who is the pledge of our inheritance" (Eph. 1, 13-14); but the meritorious cause is His most beloved only-begotten Son, Our Lord Jesus Christ, Who "when we were enemies" (Rom. 5, 10), "for the exceeding charity wherewith he loved us" (Eph. 2, 4), merited justification for us by His most holy Passion on the wood of the Cross, and made satisfaction for us to God the Father; the instrumental cause is the Sacrament of Baptism, which is the "sacrament of faith,"[2] without which no one is ever justified. Finally the unique formal cause is the justice of God, not that by which He Himself is just, but by which He makes us just, that, namely, by which, when we are endowed with it by him, we are renewed in the spirit of our mind, and not only are we reputed, but we are truly called and are just, receiving justice within us, each one according to his own measure, which the "Holy Ghost distributes to everyone as he wills" (I Cor. 12, 11), and according to each one's own disposition and cooperation. For although no one can be just but he to whom the merits of the Passion of our Lord Jesus Christ are communicated, yet this does take place in this justification of the ungodly when by the merit of that same most holy Passion "the charity of God is poured forth by the Holy Ghost in the hearts" (Rom. 5, 5) of those who are justified, and inheres in them. Hence man through Jesus Christ, into Whom he is ingrafted, receives in the said justification together with the remission of sins all these [gifts] infused at the same time: faith, hope, and charity. For faith, unless hope and charity be added to it, neither unites one perfectly with Christ, nor makes him a living member of his body. For this reason it is most

---

[1] Cf. Acts 2, 38.
[2] Cf. Mk. 16, 16.

truly said that "faith without works is dead" (James 2, 17), and is of no profit, and "in Christ Jesus neither circumcision availeth anything, nor uncircumcision, but faith, which worketh by charity" (Gal. 5, 6). This faith, in accordance with Apostolic tradition, catechumens beg of the Church before the Sacrament of Baptism, when they ask for "faith which bestows life eternal," which without hope and charity, faith cannot bestow. Thence also they hear immediately the word of Christ: "If thou wilt enter into life, keep the commandments" (Mt. 19, 17). Therefore, when receiving true and Christian justice, they are commanded immediately on being reborn, to preserve it pure and spotless as the "first robe" (Lk. 15, 22) given to them through Christ Jesus in place of that which Adam by his disobedience lost for himself and for us, so that they may bear it before the tribunal of our Lord Jesus Christ and have life eternal. But when the Apostle says that man is justified "by faith" and "freely" (Rom. 3, 24), these words must be understood in that sense in which the uninterrupted consent of the Catholic Church has held and expressed, namely, that we are therefore said to be justified by faith, because "faith is the beginning of human salvation,"[1] the foundation and root of all justification, "without which it is impossible to please God" (Heb. 11, 6) and to come to the fellowship of His sons; and are, therefore, said to be justified gratuitously, because none of those things which precede justification, whether faith, or works merit the grace itself of justification; for, "if it is a grace, it is not now by reason of works; otherwise (as the same Apostle says) grace is no more grace" (Rom. 11, 6).[2]

And after giving this doctrine about justification, lest anyone dare to teach or speak against it, it adds some Canons. This is the ninth canon: "If anyone shall say that by faith alone the sinner is justified, so as to understand that nothing else is required to cooperate in the attainment of the grace of justification, and that it is in no way necessary that he be prepared and disposed by the action of his own will: let him be anathema."[3] And again in the twelfth canon it says: "If anyone shall say that justifying faith is nothing else than confidence in the divine mercy which remits sins for Christ's sake, or that it is this confidence alone by which we are justified: let him be anathema."[4]

But Calvin laughs at this definition of the Council, and raves like the Bacchantes at it, because it declared that Paul said that man is justified by faith, because faith is the beginning of justification.[5] For Calvin laments that the Council attributed so little to faith,[6] in that it said that it is the beginning and not the complement, but it is not correct that he raves like the Bacchantes at the holy Synod, as though on account of a new and unheard of teaching. For Ambrose when interpreting the verse, "The beginning of thy words is truth" (Ps. 118, 160), says: "Faith is the beginning of the Christian, but justice is the completion of the Christian."[7] Augustine says these words: "Therefore it remains, that we ascribe not faith itself (from whence all justice takes its beginning, for which it is said unto the Church in the Canticle of Canticles: 'Thou shalt come and pass through from the beginning of faith,'[8]) unto man's free

---

[1] *Rituale Romanum*, Ordo Bapt. n.1.

[2] Dz. 795-801.

[3] Dz. 819.

[4] Dz. 822.

[5] Chap. 8 (Dz. 801).

[6] "There is no room for the vulgar quibble that Paul is speaking of the beginning of Justification" (*Selected Works of John Calvin: Tracts and Letters*, vol. 3, *Acts of the Council of Trent with the Antidote*, ed. Henry Beveridge and Jules Bonnet (Grand Rapids, Baker, 1983, pp. 114-115); CR 35, 447.

[7] *Expositio in psalmum CXVIII*, serm. 20, n. 57 (PL 15, 1502B).

[8] This wording of Cant. 4, 8 is a mistranslation of the *Septuagint* version incorporated into the *Vetus Latina* translation. (Cf. Elizabeth A. Livingstone, *Papers Presented at the Eleventh International Conference on Patristic Studies Held in Oxford, 1991* (Louvain, Peeters Publishers, 1993, pg. 323).

will, whereof they are proud; nor to any merits going before, for all good merits whatsoever they are begun from thence; but that we confess it to be the freely given gift of God, if we think of true grace, which is without merits."[1] Herein Augustine also says that faith is the beginning of justification, and not full justification. Let Calvin read these words and grieve over his own temerity, because he spoke evil of the holy Synod. Afterwards, the Council did not only say that [faith] is the beginning of justification, but also its root and foundation. But the root produces the fruit of the tree, and the foundation helps to complete a house up to the roof.

Long ago Blessed Augustine wrote a book against this heresy entitled, *On Faith and Works*. Many other authors in our time wrote against the Lutherans, namely Thomas Cardinal Cajetan,[2] Jacob van Hoogstraaten,[3] Josse van Clichtove,[4] Ambrosius Catharinus,[5] and at greater length than all these authors, Albert Pighius in his book of controversies.[6]

There is a **third heresy** which teaches that faith is lost by any mortal sin. The inventor of this heresy is also Luther, because this heresy necessarily follows from the one which just preceded. For if faith alone, as Luther says, justifies, then every believer is just, and hence it also necessarily follows moreover that no one who is not just is a believer. For Luther thought that charity was necessarily born from faith, and so great is the connection between faith and charity that one cannot exist without the other. For Luther's words are these: "Faith is perceived in no better way than in works of charity, as the Lord says, 'By this shall all men know that you are my disciples, if you have love one for another' (Jn. 13, 35)."[7] And in the book, *On Christian Liberty*, he again says: "God the Father has made everything to depend on faith, so that whosoever has it has all things."[8]

Everyone who call himself a Lutheran shares this opinion with Luther. For Philip Melanchthon in his *Loci Commune*, in the section on good works, says these words: "Those who do repent, but indulge their wicked desires, do not keep their faith. For faith seeks the remission of sins; it does not delight in sins."[9] A certain Johann Spangenberg in his *Margarita theologica*, when treating of the first cause of good works, says these words: "Faith cannot exist with an bad conscience, because it is the trust that God is merciful unto us; a bad conscience judges the contrary. Likewise those who do repent, but indulge their wicked desires, do not keep their faith."[10] Calvin derides the distinction of faith which is accustomed to be made by scholastic

---

[1] Ep. 194, c. 3, n. 9 (PL 33, 877).

[2] *Faith and Works—Against the Lutherans* (1532).

[3] Or Jacobus Hochstratus (c.1460–1527). He was a Flemish Dominican theologian and inquisitor. *Epitome de fide et operibus, aduersus chimaericam illam atque monstrosam Martini Lutheri libertatem, quam ipse falso ac perdite Christianam appellat* (Cologne, Peter Quentel, 1525).

[4] *Compendium veritatum ad fidem pertinentium contra erroneas Lutheranorum assertiones ex dictis et actis in concilio provinciali Senonensi apud Parisios celebrato* (Paris, 1529).

[5] Or Lancelotto Politus. *De perfecta justifactione a fide et operibus* (Lyons, *apud* Antonium Vincentium, 1541).

[6] *Controversiarum præcipuarum in Comitiis Ratisponensibus tractatarum... explicatio* (Cologne, Melchior von Neuss, 1545), *controversia* 2 (*De Fide, Operibus, et Justificatione Hominis*).

[7] "Thus everyone should beware lest he has in his heart a dream and fancy instead of faith, and thus deceives himself. This he will not learn anywhere as well as in doing the works of charity. As Christ also gives the same sign and says: 'By this shall all men know that ye are my disciples, if ye have love one to another' (Jn. 13, 35)." ("Sermon on the Ten Lepers" (WA 8, 362, lns. 17-21). This sermon was published in German in a pamphlet in 1521. The reference given here incorrectly cites "the book of the ten precepts."

[8] WA vol. 7, p. 53, lns. 9-10.

[9] CR 21, 432.

[10] *Margarita theologica* (Leipzig, Nicolaus Wolrab, 1541), question 5, pg. 49.

theologians between formed and unformed faith, and he says that it is "nugatory," "putrid,"[1] and "absurd," because he thinks there is no faith which is not formed by charity.[2] And when writing against the decree of the Council of Trent on the justification of the ungodly which we have just cited in the preceding heresy, he says that "faith devoid of charity" is a dream and "vain figment," and "they can no more separate faith from charity than Christ from his Spirit."[3]

This opinion of all Lutherans is proved to be heretical by very strong reasons and by very clear testimonies of Sacred Scripture. Firstly, in fact, it is established by natural reason that nothing necessarily depends upon what comes after it, because otherwise it must happen that the same thing exists and does not exist at the same time, which natural reason abhors. For it is evident that what depends upon another cannot exist without it, otherwise it would not depend upon it. But if that on which it depends comes after it, it could not exist before the existence of that later thing: if it cannot exist before the existence of that thing, then it does not exist prior to that thing. Thus, it is clearly proved that it could not be brought about that that what is prior would require for its existence something else which is later in time. Therefore, natural reason teaches this, namely that which is prior can exist without some other thing which is later, but not the contrary, namely that which is later in time could exist without something prior, upon which it depends.

Now, so that I may make this clearer, I wish to demonstrate this by a very clear example. The essential parts of which a whole man is composed, and from which man himself depends for his own existence, namely body and soul, are prior to the man himself, and hence it happens that because man is comes after these things, he cannot exist without a body and soul, but the body and soul, because they are prior, can exist without the man himself, as happens after the man's death, when those parts remain separate, and then man does not exist at that time. Among the operations of the soul, all philosophers and theologians always unanimously have taught up until now that this order is necessary, namely that understanding is prior to willingness or unwillingness, and hence it happens that willingness or unwillingness could not exist without preceding knowledge, according to the well-known phase of Augustine, "The will is not borne towards the unknown."[4] Now knowledge, because it is prior, can exist without subsequent willingness or unwillingness.

And this is not merely true about apprehensive knowledge, but also concerning judicative knowledge, by which we judge something is to be done or avoided, as happens in those who know rightly and act wrongly. From all these things it is clearly proved that faith can be without charity, because faith pertains to the intellect, and the proper act of faith is an operation of the intellect, and on the other hand, charity pertains to the will: and the act of charity, which is love, is an operation of the will.

Perhaps the Lutherans will deny that faith is a work of the intellect, due to the fact that they say that faith is confidence, but we proved that this is false in the preceding heresy by the words of Paul: "He that cometh to God, must believe that he is" (Heb. 11, 6): and by the words of the same Paul: "By faith we understand that the world was framed by the word of God" (v. 3). But to believe that God exists, and to understand that "the world was framed," does not pertain to confidence, but is an operation not of the will, but of the intellect. Thus, that faith, about which Paul discusses in that passage, can be without charity and love of God, just as an

---

[1] This word he uses in the *Acta Synodi Tridentinae: Cvm Antidoto* (Geneva, Girard, 1547), Sess. 6, pg. 181.
[2] *The Institutes of Christian Religion*, bk. 3, c. 2, n. 8.
[3] *Acta Synodi Tridentinae: Cum Antidoto*, pg. 181.
[4] The Latin axiom, *Voluntas non fertur in incognitum*, is adapted from St. Augustine's words, "No inquisitive person, loves things he does not know" (*De Trinitate*, bk. 10, c. 2, n. 4).

act of the intellect without an act of the will. Furthermore, it is clear that this faculty of our will could do something contrary to the judgment of conscience, because otherwise it would not be free, if the intellect could force it by its judgment. Since then faith is only ready belief and an assent of the intellect whereby it persuades oneself that all the things which ought to be believed are true, it is proved that with this judgment persisting, the will can, even with the conscience protesting, do something which supposing that it happens, as we see to happen daily, then it is clear that what we are discussing can actually happen, namely that faith can exist without charity and consequently remain at the same time with mortal sin.

But Luther responds to this argumentation denying that it could happen, such that he who has once accepted that faith, could do something with the conscience protesting. For in the [*Judgement of Martin Luther on Monastic Vows*] he delivers these words: "He who retains the faith, cannot sin against his conscience."[1] Notice what kind of men and how bold faced these heretics are, that they are not ashamed to deny the most evident things, when they do not agree with their own opinion. Perhaps Luther already at that time had such a blinded, broken, and inconsiderate conscience that whatever he might do, he always thought that it was allowed for him, and hence he considered himself to be the conscience of all others, and said that no one could act against his conscience.

But let him say what he likes, nevertheless Scripture shows that he is false in this matter. Firstly, therefore, what is said in Job clearly proves it: "He hath struck them, as being wicked, in open sight. Who as it were on purpose have revolted from him, and would not understand all his ways" (Job 34, 26-27). What, I ask, O Luther, is "on purpose have revolted from God" except to do something which is bad and displeasing to God with the conscience protesting? But if you are not ashamed to reject this interpretation, which is so manifest and so correct according to the clear literal meaning, I bring forth Blessed Gregory in testimony of this interpretation, which in his *Morals on the Book of Job*, when interpreting the aforesaid passage, says these words: "Those persons sinned intentionally, of whom the Master Himself said, 'If I had not come, and spoken unto them, they would not have sin, but now they have no excuse for their sin' (Jn 15, 22). And a little after, 'They have both seen and hated both Me and My Father' (v. 24). For not to do good is one thing, to hate a teacher of goodness another: as it is one thing to sin from precipitancy, and another thing to sin deliberately. For a sin is often committed from precipitation, which yet is condemned on thought and deliberation. For it frequently happens that a man through infirmity loves what is right, and cannot perform it. But to sin deliberately is neither to love nor to do what is good."[2] From the words of this [citation] it is evident that to sin intentionally is to sin with knowledge and awareness of the sin. What our Savior says in Luke is also clear: "The servant who knew the will of his lord, and prepared not himself, and did not according to his will, shall be beaten with many stripes" (12, 47). And James the Apostle says: "To him therefore who knoweth to do good, and doth it not, to him it is sin" (4, 17). Notice that Christ our Savior and His Apostle James bear witness that there are some men possessing faith, who nevertheless act against their conscience.

But perhaps Luther and his followers, as they are bold faced and pertinacious, will deny those words of Christ and His Apostle ought to be understood of knowing good through the true faith, but instead they say that they only ought to be understood of those things which they come to know to be good through natural reason with faith. Bede clearly contradicts this

---

[1] "Behold! This is the faith which Scripture teaches. If a man has this faith, he cannot act against his conscience because he can no longer have any doubt that he is pleasing to God because of Christ Who was given for him. If a man does not have this faith, he cannot but act against his conscience all the time because he doubts that he is pleasing God." *De votis monasticis Martini Lutheri judicum* (WA 8, 594, lns. 9-11). The text here cites a sermon of Luther concerning the Anabaptists.

[2] Bk. 25, c. 11, n. 28 (PL 76, 338).

opinion, who when interpreting the aforesaid words of James, teaches that they ought to be understood of the faithful, when speaking thus: "Throughout the whole text of this epistle Blessed James has shown that they to whom he wrote had the knowledge to do good things and at the same time they had so learned a right faith that they presumed to be able to become teachers even for others; but still they had not yet attained perfection of works or humility of mind or restraint of speech. Hence it terrifies them now to no small degree that he says amidst other words of rebuke and encouragement that someone who knows how to do good and does not do what he knows has a greater sin than the one who fails through ignorance, although neither the one, who has sinned unwittingly, can be entirely free from guilt, for the ignorance of good is itself no small evil. Truly the Lord says, then, 'The servant who knew the will of his lord, and prepared not himself, and did not according to his will, shall be beaten with many stripes' (Lk 12, 47- 48)."[1] Which citation clearly indicates that those words of the Apostle ought not to be only understood of him who knows the good things to be done by natural reason alone without the faith, but also of him who knew the good through true faith.

It is not necessary, however, to dwell at great length on this matter since it is clear that by that opinion the whole power of our free will is taken away, because if he who knew the good, also by faith, cannot act against his conscience, then it would evidently follow that the will is forced by the judgment of the intellect. Again, if faith were to be lost by every mortal sin, it would follow that everyone who has been stained with mortal sin, especially if he had pertinaciously persevered in it, is a heretic, but this would be quite absurd to assert. For then it would further follow that every such person who sins mortally would err about absolutely every article of the faith, because there does not appear to be any reason why he errs in one article rather than in another, and so it is necessary to grant that he has either erred in every article of the faith or in none. But concerning this I do not wish to dispute further because we will say something specifically against this error below in the third heresy in the section "Heretics."

Besides all these pressing reasons, whereby it is clearly proved that faith is not lost by each and every mortal sin, there are many testimonies of Sacred Scripture, which prove it much more strongly. And the first of them all, which the Lord says in Matthew, is clear: "Not everyone that saith to me, Lord, Lord, shall enter into the kingdom of heaven: but he that doth the will of my Father who is in heaven, he shall enter into the kingdom of heaven. Many will say to me in that day: Lord, Lord, have not we prophesied in thy name, and cast out devils in thy name, and done many miracles in thy name? And then will I profess unto them, I never knew you: depart from me, you that work iniquity" (Mt. 7, 21-23). Behold, you see these men to whom Christ was speaking were in mortal sin, because they are driven away from the kingdom of God, from which no one is ever driven away without mortal sin. But these men so driven away by God had the faith, because they were confessing Christ to be the Lord, in whose name they were prophesying, casting out devils, and performing many miracles. And we will prove that this is the correct meaning of Christ's words in the next heresy with the testimonies of Theophylactus, Jerome, and Basil.

The parable of the ten virgins put forth by Our Savior in Matthew also provides us with proof about this matter. For that cry of the five foolish virgins, "Lord, Lord, open to us" (25, 11), clearly shows that they had the faith. That they lacked charity, however, is evident from the fact that the door was shut to them: and also by the fact the spouse said to them, "I know you not" (v. 12). And certainly [Pseudo-] Chrysostom gathers from this parable that faith is not lost by any mortal sin, and that those virgins were deceived in that they thought faith alone without works was sufficient for justification.[2] Furthermore, Our Savior in John when

---

[1] PL 93, 35C-D.

[2] "But the five foolish virgins are those who keep the faith of Christ whole but have no works of justice" (*Opus Imperfectum in Matthaeum*, hom. 52 (PG 56, 930)).

commending the faithful concerning their faith said: "He gave them power to be made the sons of God, to them that believe in his name" (1, 12). By which words He taught that faith is the beginning of the adoption as sons, not however that there is a completed adoption by faith.

Again, the parable of the king making a marriage for his son most clearly shows this same thing. For in that marriage feast, there was a man not clothed with a wedding garment, whom the king himself reprehends, due to the fact that he came into the marriage feast without a wedding garment, and the king commanded his ministers that having bound his hands and feet to cast him out into the exterior darkness where there shall be weeping and gnashing of teeth.[1] Theophylactus when interpreting this parable says: "The entry into the wedding takes place without distinction of persons, for by grace alone we have all been called, good and bad alike; but the life thereafter of those who enter shall not be without examination, for indeed the king makes an exceedingly careful examination of those found to be sullied after entering into the faith. Let us tremble, then, when we understand that if one does not lead a pure life, faith alone benefits him not at all. For not only is he cast out of the wedding feast, but he is sent away into the fire."[2]

Blessed Gregory subscribes to the same opinion in a homily on that part of Matthew's Gospel where this parable to narrated. "What symbolism," Gregory says, "shall we attribute, dear brothers, to this nuptial dress? Shall we say that it represents Baptism, or faith? But who could have entered the wedding hall without Baptism or faith? For he who has not yet believed is by that very fact outside [of the Church]. What must we understand by the nuptial dress, if not charity? He indeed enters for the wedding, but he enters without the nuptial robe, the one who is in the holy Church and has faith, but lacks charity."[3] And shortly afterwards he again says, "It is quite astonishing, dear brothers, that while calling this man his friend, he condemns him. It is as if he were telling him more clearly: 'You are my friend, and you are not my friend: you are my friend by faith, but you are not my friend by works,'" or charity.[4] Jerome supports the same interpretation, saying these words: "The marriage garment is the Commandments of the Lord, and the works which are done under the Law and the Gospel, and form the clothing of the new man."[5]

Notice that I have brought forth the concordant testimony of three very holy as well as learned men, who all teach that faith can remain without charity and without good works. For they say that the entrance to the marriage happens by faith, and the nuptial garment is charity, without which, as it is evident in the Gospel, some enter the marriage. Furthermore, this opinion is confirmed by the testimony of John the Evangelist saying: "Many of the chief men also believed in him; but because of the Pharisees they did not confess him, that they might not be cast out of the synagogue. For they loved the glory of men more than the glory of God" (12, 42-43). From these words it is evident that those men, of whom the Gospel speaks, had faith but not charity, because although they believed correctly, having been thoroughly frightened by the Pharisees they dared not confess it with their mouths. And lest anyone dare to reject this interpretation of ours as foreign to the text, I cite as evidence Bede, who when in-

---

[1] Cf. Mt. 22, 1-13.

[2] *Enarratio in Evangelium S. Matthaei* (PG 123, 386-386).

[3] Homily 38, n. 9 (PL 76, 1287C).

[4] *Ibid.*, n. 12 (PL 76, 1289C).

[5] *Commentaria in Matthaeum*, bk. 3 (PL 26, 161A). This quotation continues in the text as follows: "On the other hand, everyone clothed with the old and tattered garments, which they have as it were inherited from the old Adam, to them the Lord says what is also in this Gospel: 'Friend, how camest thou in hither not having a wedding garment?' (Mt. 22, 12)" Though these latter words are not found in Migne's *Patrologia Latina*, they are quoted by Johann Eck in his *Homiliae adversus haereticos* (Paris, Petrus Regnault, 1541), vol. 2, pg. 298.

terpreting the aforesaid words, says these words: "Whilst our Lord Jesus Christ was speaking among the Jews, and giving so many miraculous signs, some believed who were foreordained to eternal life, and whom He also called His sheep; but some did not believe, and could not believe, because that, by the mysterious yet not unrighteous judgment of God, they had been blinded... But others were not confessing their faith, whom the Evangelist has branded with the words, that 'they loved the praise of men more than the praise of God' (Jn. 12, 43)... The praise of God is to publicly confess Christ, as the holy martyrs did, of whom the Lord Himself says in another place: 'He that shall confess me before men, I will also confess him before my Father' (Mt. 10, 32)."[1]

Again, Paul in his First Epistle to the Corinthians favors this same opinion, saying these words: "If I should have all faith, so that I could remove mountains, and have not charity, I am nothing" (13, 2). In which words Paul very clearly teaches that faith can remain without charity. Yet the Lutherans seeing them pressed by the weight of these words, distort those words into a different meaning, saying that Paul did not say what could happen, but he argued from the supposition of something impossible. Thus wishing to exaggerate the matter more than it actually is so that he might show that charity is also necessary for justification, he granted point but did not concede it, as the Dialecticians are accustomed to say when arguing,[2] regarding what has been granted but not admitted, that faith could be without charity, and so without it man would not be justified.

But this interpretation of theirs contradicts the teaching of all holy men, because all the holy Doctors when interpreting Paul say that he was not speaking in hyperbole based upon the presupposition of something impossible, but he said what could happen, and does happen daily. For Haymo [of Auxerre[3]] when interpreting the aforesaid words, says these words: "'If I should have all faith,' that is, perfect and complete [faith], which is compared by the Lord to a grain of mustard seed, not account of its meagerness but on account of its hotness: because when crushed, it shows what potency it has, so also faith, when crushed by adversities, shows its strength, such that I may remove mountains from place to place, or I may cast out demons from those suffering. 'If I have not charity,' that is love of God and neighbor, 'I am nothing,' this will make me good for nothing. Some of the Corinthians were doing this through the invocation of God's name, and hence considered themselves to be nearly perfect. But he exhorts to that which is the most important, that is to say, for charity."[4] From whose words it is evident that Paul was not speaking about what was impossible, but of what he saw happening among the Corinthians. [Hervé de Bourg-Dieu[5]] when interpreting the aforesaid words of Paul supports the same view, saying the following: "The Savior had said that faith which was 'as a grain mustard seed' could move mountains (Mt. 17, 19), and now the Apostle says, there is 'all faith' which removes mountains. Hence it is understood that faith is perfect which is compared to a grain of mustard seed, and this is said not because of its smallness, but on account of its completeness. But faith without charity is able to do nothing towards salvation, because even the demons have this sort of faith."[6] [Hervé de Bourg-Dieu] teaches clearly

---

[1] *In Evangelium S. Ioannis*, c. 12 (PL 92, 797C-D). Ven. Bede is here partly quoting St. Augustine from his work, *In Joannis Evangelium tractatus CXXIV*, tract 54, n. 1 (PL 35, 1780).

[2] In Latin, *Datum, sed non admissum/concessum*, meaning that the point is granted merely for the sake of the argument, but not truly conceded.

[3] In Migne's *Patrologia Latina*, this passage is attributed to Haymo of Halberstadt, but as mentioned above (see the section, "Gospel," heresy 2), it has more recently been shown to have been written by Haymo of Auxerre.

[4] *Expositio in Divi Pauli epistolas*: *In epistolam I ad Corinthios* (PL 117, 528A-B).

[5] This citation was incorrectly ascribed to St. Anselm of Canterbury.

[6] *Commentaria in epistolas Pauli: In epistolam I ad Corinthios*, c. 13 (PL 181, 953C).

enough from the passage of Paul that not just any faith but perfect faith, meaning complete faith, can remain without charity.

Next, James the Apostle teaches this view of ours with many very clear words: "What shall it profit, my brethren," James says, "if a man say he hath faith, but hath not works? Shall faith be able to save him?... [faith], if it have not works, is dead in itself" (2, 14 & 17). Luther, who as we said, was the first author of this heresy, seeing that the aforesaid words of James completely destroyed his own opinion, being in this situation took refuge is the common asylum of heretics, such that he denied that that epistle was the epistle of Blessed James, and said it was unworthy that someone would use his testimony for proving some Catholic dogma. But it is not necessary that we fight against this opinion, because we have shown, above in the second chapter of the first book of this work, the list of books of Sacred Scripture which necessarily should be received by all Catholics. Subsequent Lutherans, such as Melanchthon and others, seeing the madness and temerity is great to want to cast out a book from the canon of Sacred Scripture, admit that the epistle was written by Blessed James, but say that the words of James the Apostle do not oppose their opinion, because James says that the faith which consists without works is dead, and hence they deduce that it is not true faith, just as a dead man is not a true man.

But they do not escape our hands in this way, because James the Apostle does not compare faith itself to a living man, but only to the body, which receives life from the soul, and thus faith takes its life from charity and its works. "For even as the body without the spirit is dead," James says, "so also faith without works is dead" (v. 26). And hence it necessarily follows that just as a body without a soul, although it is dead, is still a true body, so faith without charity and its works is true faith. I say true faith, but not living faith; for it is one thing to be living and another to be true; because true faith is opposed to feigned or false faith: living faith, however, is opposed to dead faith. Hence, just as dead faith and feigned faith are not necessarily the same, so neither on the contrary are living and true faith necessarily the same, because faith can be true, although it is not living.

And many very learned and very holy men teach that this is the true interpretation of James' words. For [Hervé de Bourg-Dieu[1]] when interpreting the words of Paul to the Galatians, "faith that worketh by charity" (5, 6), says these words: "'For even as the body without the spirit is dead,' James says, 'so also faith without works is dead' (James 2, 26): and not the faith of the Old Testament, serving out of fear, but the Evangelical faith, doing good works out of charity, not expecting a temporal reward, but in order to perpetually see the face of the Creator. This is the faith of the elect, which leads to salvation. For the demons also believe and tremble, yet they neither love nor do good works. And so, faith which does not have charity and good works is the faith of demons, not of Christians. Therefore, only that faith alone which burns with charity and sweats with good works avails in Christ Jesus."[2] From which words it clearly established that James the Apostle compared faith to the body alone, not to the whole complete man; charity and works, on the other hand, he compared to the spirit, whereby the body is vivified.

Blessed Jerome supports the same opinion saying the following: "In vain do we make our boast in him whose Commandments we keep not. 'To him that knows what is good, and does it not, it is sin.' (James 4, 17). As the body apart from the spirit is dead, even so faith apart from works is dead. And we must not think it a great matter to know the only God, when even devils believe and tremble."[3] Bernard teaches this opinion, saying these words: "The death of faith is the departure of love. Do you believe in Christ? Do the works of Christ so that your

---

[1] This citation was incorrectly ascribed to St. Anselm of Canterbury.
[2] *Ibid.*, c. 5 (PL 181, 1183A).
[3] *Against Jovinian*, bk. 2, n. 2 (PL 23, 283D-284A).

faith will live; love will animate your faith, deeds will reveal it."[1] Bernard teaches clearly enough that the life of faith is charity, without which faith is dead. As a body without the soul, which is its life, is a true body, although it is dead: so faith without charity, which is its true life, is true faith, although it is dead.

And certainly, if we consider the rest of the words of James the Apostle, it will be clearly established that he thinks that faith without works, although it is dead, is true faith. For he says that the faith without works is idle. But how can it be truly said to be idle, which does not exist? Thus, faith which is indeed idle, is true faith. Next, the Apostle proves by a clear example that faith can exist without charity in a man being in mortal sin. "Thou believest that there is one God. Thou dost well: the devils also believe and tremble" (2, 19). In which words the Apostle compared the faith of those who lack charity and works to the faith of demons. From which passage of James, some holy Doctors conclude that faith alone cannot justify man. For Cyril says these words: "'Thou believest that there is one God... the devils also believe and tremble.' Shall one then say to those who think that a faith bare and alone will be sufficient to enable them to get possession of the fellowship that is from above,—will even the band of demons return to the fellowship with God, since they believe that He is one?"[2] [Hervé de Bourg-Dieu] agreeing with this opinion, says these words: "But faith without charity is able to do nothing towards salvation, because even the demons have this sort of faith."[3]

Finally, there is a clear definition of the Catholic Church against this heresy, which the Council of Trent celebrated under Paul III pronounced, of which these are the words: "Against the crafty genius of certain men also, who 'by pleasing speeches and good words seduce the hearts of the innocent' (Rom. 16, 18), it must be maintained that the grace of justification, although received, is lost not only by infidelity, whereby even faith itself is lost, but also by any other mortal sin, although faith be not lost, thereby defending the doctrine of the Divine law which excludes from the kingdom of God not only the unbelievers, but also the faithful who are 'fornicators, adulterers, effeminate, liers with mankind, thieves, covetous, drunkards, railers, extortioners' (I Cor. 6, 9-10), and all others who commit deadly sins, from which with the assistance of Divine grace they can refrain and for which they are separated from the grace of God."[4] After giving this teaching, lest anyone dare to speak against it, it pronounced the *latae sententiae* canon, which is listed as the twenty-eighth, the words of which are these: "If anyone shall say that together with the loss of grace by sin faith also is always lost, or that the faith that remains is not a true faith, though it be not a living one, or that he, who has faith without charity, is not a Christian: let him be anathema."[5]

But Calvin ridicules this definition of the Council, because the Council said that faith without charity is held to be true faith, and he does not consider it to be permitted that the Council would call it true faith, yet deny that it is living faith.[6] For it does not necessarily follow that

---

[1] *Sermons on the Canticles of Canticles*, serm. 24, n. 8 (PL 183, 898B).

[2] *Commentary on John*, bk. 10 on Jn. 15, 7 (PG 74, 366-367).

[3] *Commentaria in epistolas Pauli: In epistolam I ad Corinthios*, c. 13 (PL 181, 953C).

[4] Sess. 6, c. 15 (Dz. 808).

[5] Dz. 838.

[6] "I deny not that, even during the most grievous lapses, some seed of faith remains, though in a smothered state. However small it is, I admit that it partakes of the nature of true faith: I add, living faith, since otherwise no fruit could come from it. But since it does not appear for a time, nor exhibit itself by the usual signs, it is, in respect of our sense, as if it were dead. But nothing of this kind entered the minds of the Fathers [of the Council of Trent] or their dictatorial monks. All they wished was to establish their absurd dogma of an informal and a formal faith. Hence they maintain that faith is true which is manifestly dead; as if faith could be the life of the soul, (as Augustine, in accordance with the uniform doctrine of Scripture, elegantly terms it), and yet not be itself alive. To the same purpose they contend that men

what is true be living. Because as we have already said a dead body is a true body, although it lacks life. But perhaps Calvin will press us with the testimony of some holy and very learned men, who deny that faith without works is true faith. Gregory says: "True faith demands that one does not contradict in one's conduct what one affirms by his words... Indeed, we are truly believers only if we fulfill in our works what we promise in our words."[1] Theophylactus commenting upon the passage, "He that doth not believe, is already judged" (Jn. 3, 18), says that those who lead an unclean life, are not truly believers.[2] But all these Doctors, and however many others who use this kind of speech, take the word "true" for "perfect and complete," such that for them "true faith" is that which is perfect and complete, and is that kind which (as Paul says) "worketh by charity" (Gal. 5, 6). And all men use this type of speech in common and ordinary conversation. For if someone were to say that when he was sleeping he heard others conversing, one is wont to respond to him, that there was no true sleep of his, because if he was slumbering or sleeping, his sleep was not full and perfect. Likewise, if someone who had been scourged says that he did not suffer from the beating of the lashes, it will be replied to him that it was not a true lashing. By which words he does not deny that he underwent the lash, but it is denied that it was a perfect and vigorous lashing. According to this manner of speaking holy men sometimes say that dead faith is not true faith, not because they deny that it is faith, but they deny that it is full and perfect.

It can also still be objected against the aforesaid definition of the Council that many saints say that faith cannot exist without charity. Bede in his *Commentaries on the Epistle of James* when interpreting the passage of the same Apostle, "Faith if it have not works, is dead" (2, 17), says these words: "Nor is that contrary to this statement which the Lord uttered, 'He that believeth and is baptized, shall be saved' (Mk. 16, 16), for it must be understood there that only he truly believes who carries out in deed what he believes. And because faith and charity cannot be separated from one another—as Paul bears witness by saying, 'and faith which works through love' (Gal. 5, 6)—appropriately the Apostle John brings forward a statement about charity akin to James' about faith, saying, 'He that hath the substance of this world, and shall see his brother in need, and shall shut up his bowels from him: how doth the charity of God abide in him?' (I Jn. 3, 17)."[3] Cyprian says: "But how can a man say that he believes in Christ, who does not do what Christ commanded him to do? Or whence shall he attain to the reward of faith, who will not keep the faith of the commandment? He must of necessity waver and wander, and, caught away by a spirit of error, like dust which is shaken by the wind, be blown about; and he will make no advance in his walk towards salvation, because he does not keep the truth of the way of [salvation[4]]... He who does not hold this unity does not hold God's law, does not hold the faith of the Father and the Son, does not hold life and salvation."[5] From which words it is evident that both clearly teach that faith cannot exist without charity.

But we reply firstly concerning Bede, that he does not absolutely deny that faith without charity cannot exist, but only in the order to justification, concerning which James, whom he was interpreting in this quotation, was clearly speaking. Thus faith, although it can be of itself separated from charity, still when he considers justification, it cannot be separated from

---

are Christians though they have no charity, and anathematize those who think otherwise; in other words, according to them, we anathematize the Holy Ghost if we deride a false profession of Christianity, and set it at naught." (*Acts of the Council of Trent with the Antidote*, on sess. 6, can. 28 (CR 35, 482-483)).

[1] *Homilies on the Gospels*, hom. 29 (PL 76, 1214D-1215A).

[2] "If someone has led an unclean life, is he not judged? Very much so, indeed. Men of this kind are not truly believers." (*Enarratio in Evangelium Joannis* (PG 123, 1214B)).

[3] *Commentary on the Seven Catholic Epistles: on the Epistle of Saint James*, c. 2 (PL 93, 21C-D).

[4] The text mistakenly here has "unity" instead of "salvation."

[5] *The Unity of the Church* (PL 4, 496B-497A & 504A).

it, because if it exists without it, it is unable to justify. Cyprian, however, does not deny that faith exists without charity, but by those words he merely shows that a faith which is without works is languid, feeble, and inadequate for salvation, and hence it is reckoned by him as though it did not exist, because that faith could not be proved by the testimony of good works. Now "what cannot be proved (as Bernard adroitly says in his book, *On Precept and Dispensation*[1]) to me was not done." And it is evident that this is the true mind of Cyprian from the words which he himself says at the end of the cited book, where he teaches that one does not completely depart from the faith, but it is made languid and grows weak through mortal sin.

FIDUCIA

Confidence

There is one heresy that has arisen concerning this matter, which asserts that it is nowise allowed to put confidence of attaining grace or glory in our works. The author of this heresy is Luther, Philip Melanchthon, Martin Bucer, and everyone who call himself a Lutheran. These men deduce this heresy from their previous errors, just as putrid water comes from a corrupt source. For they say that all our works are sins, and by them men cannot merit eternal life, and hence they deduce that no confidence ought to be put in our works for the attainment of eternal life, but they say that all our confidence ought to be placed in Christ's merits alone, because we were redeemed and saved by Him alone. We will dispute concerning those errors which pertain to the goodness of good works and their merits below in their places, in the section on "Merit" and in the section on "Works" [*Opera*]. It is necessary to dispute now, however, about the confidence that ought to be placed in works. But before discussing anything, lest we labor in vain, it will be worthwhile to inquire what is confidence, and then afterwards it will become clearer in what one ought to place it. Confidence is either hope, or the firmness or strength of that hope. Now which of these it is, I myself to not wish to decide at present, because whether it be the former or the latter matters little for the clarification of the present subject. Blessed Thomas says, "Confidence is hope strengthened by a strong opinion."[2] Thus confidence is a certain hope, and not any hope, but only that hope which has vigor and strength from a strong opinion.

But because I know well that Luther and his followers wish to despise Blessed Thomas, just because he is named a scholastic theologian, I will cite pagan authors, whom they greatly revere, to prove this opinion of his. Cicero, when defining confidence, says: "Confidence is the sure hope of the soul of bringing to the end the thing begun."[3] And Seneca in his sixteenth letter to Lucilius says: "Nevertheless I shall tell you what I think,—that at present I have hopes for you, but not yet perfect confidence."[4] From which words it is evident that confidence is hope, yet not every hope, but only vehement hope. And because Seneca has little or faint hope for Lucilius, hence he said that he did not yet have confidence. Confidence adds something to plain hope. What confidence adds to plain hope, Thomas said, is a certain strength, by which

---

[1] *Quod probari non potest, mihi infectum est.* (C. 17, n. 56 (PL 182, 891B)).
[2] II-II, q. 129, a. 6 ad 3um.
[3] This quotation literally seems to have been taken from a Medieval compendium of Cicero, the *Moralium dogma philosophorum* (Section 1, subsection C) in which are synthesized two quotations of Cicero: "Confidence is that feeling by which the mind embarks in great and honorable courses with a sure hope and trust in itself" (*On Invention*, bk 2, n. 54) and "Confidence, that is, firm assurance of mind..." (*Tusculan Disputations*, bk. 4, n. 80) into the quotation cited in the text.
[4] *Moral letters to Lucilius*, letter 16, n. 2.

the hope itself is made strong. Cicero however said that it is sureness, such that there is no fluctuation, hesitation, timidity, diffidence of soul in hoping. For all these things conflict with confidence and are opposed to it.

Nevertheless, I warn the reader here in regards to the words of Cicero saying, "Confidence is a sure hope," that they ought to be understood of the certitude which comes not from the object, meaning from the thing hoped for, but from that which is on the part of the one hoping himself. For it can often happen that someone hesitating and fearing hopes for what is certainly going to happen: and on the contrary, that someone without any hesitation hopes for what will never happen, as it happened to the rich man in the Gospel, who having collected many riches, said that he would be well off in his life, and yet on the following evening the demons took his soul. He certainly had confidence of living, because without any hesitation he was hoping that he would have a long, perfect, quiet life, but he wrongly placed that confidence in riches, which cannot give life. Confidence arises from the firm opinion, which is had about something. For if someone believes that Peter is truthful, capable of doing something, he immediately has confidence in his promises and the more he was persuaded of Peter's truthfulness, capability, and goodness, the more he hopes to have what he promised and more firmly trusts in him.

And hence it is clearly deduced that we are all obliged to have greater confidence in God's promises than in the promises of any man, no matter how truthful, powerful and good. Because I am obliged to believe that God is more truthful and good, and also powerful than any mere man. Thus the Royal Prophet said: "Put not your trust in princes: in the children of men, in whom there is no salvation" (Ps. 145, 2-3). For they are not completely truthful, and they are not so powerful that they can do everything they wish to do. Next, confidence which is put in a man comes from the opinion had of the man, which is always mixed with fear. On the other hand, confidence which is had in God, arises from faith, whereby we believe that God is truthful, good, and omnipotent. But the persuasion of God's truthfulness, goodness and power, which is had by faith, because it is without any doubting and without any fear, is much firmer than an opinion, which always (as we said) has fear mixed with it. Hence Paul said that faith is the foundation upon which hope relies. "Faith is the substance of things to be hoped for" (Heb. 11, 1). The translator said "substance" for the Greek word ὑπόστασις, as though he were to say, it is that which supports something else, so that it holds it up, just as the foundation supports the whole building. For we hope in the resurrection because we believe that God is truthful, Who said that it would happen, and we believe that God is so powerful that He can call back the dead to life.

Therefore, all these things having been presupposed, we say that confidence of having grace and glory ought to be placed in Christ insofar as He is God, because for that reason alone is He able to give grace and glory, according to that which the [Royal] Prophet says: "The Lord will give grace and glory" (Ps. 83, 12). Now this confidence arises from what Christ said: "Do penance, for the kingdom of heaven is at hand" (Mt. 4, 17). We believe, however, that God is true Who cannot lie, and able to do what He has promised. But in Christ insofar as He is man, we have confidence of obtaining grace and glory, as in Him through Whose merits these things are to be bestowed upon us. For it is He Who heals all our diseases, Who redeems our life from destruction: Who crowns us with mercy and compassion.[1] "For there is no other name under heaven given to men," as Peter says, "whereby we must be saved" (Acts 4, 12). "By whom also we have access" (Rom. 5, 2), says Paul, to the Father. He is the true shepherd,[2] Who put the hundredth wandering sheep upon His shoulders, and bought it back

---

[1] Cf. Ps. 102, 4.
[2] Cf. Jn. 10, 11.

in this way to the sheepfold.[1] He is the true vine, without which the branches cannot produce fruit.[2] "In whom," as Paul says, "we have redemption through his blood, the remission of sins, according to the riches of his grace" (Eph. 1, 7). And so, "In whom," as Paul again likewise says, "we have boldness and access with confidence by the faith of him" (*Ibid.* 3, 12). And on account of all these things we say with Paul that "Another foundation no man can lay, but that which is laid; which is Christ Jesus" (I Cor. 3, 11). And this is and always was the opinion of all scholastic theologians, and I do not know of any scholastic theologian till now, whom it is permitted to read, who taught the contrary view.

For which reason I cannot restrain myself at this point, from berating Philip Melanchthon for the manifest calumny which he makes against scholastic theologians, saying that they think that man can be just without confidence in the Divine mercy. But lest anyone detract from the credibility of my words, saying that I am falsely accusing Philip Melanchthon, I will cite his words which he says, and they are these: "When the Scholastics say that man is justified by grace: they say nothing on that occasion about confidence of mercy, but they dream that man on account of his own dignity, and that newness or his own sinlessness, is pronounced just without confidence of mercy."[3] From which words it is clearly established how many lies the heretics concoct, so that by certain trickeries such as these they may delude men, so that they may turn them away from the true faith and men would recoil in terror from its teachers. If scholastic theologians so think, as Philipp accuses them, why did he not name someone? Why did he not cite the words of someone, so that from them he might establish what he attributes to scholastic theologians? But because there is no one who teaches as he says, he censured no one in particular. For we all admit and publicly declare and teach the people about this matter, that all confidence of attaining grace and glory ought to be put in Christ Jesus, as in our true and sole mediator, and in Him is to be placed (as it is said) "the prow and the stern."[4]

Yet our assertion does not in fact take away even the least part of confidence, to place it in our works. For it is not opposed (as the Lutherans think) to put confidence in two things at the same time. For they make confidence placed in God so jealous and intolerant of co-partnership that they suppose that no other confidence is admitted with it. For it is not beyond the notion of confidence that someone confides in two things, so that in both equally, or in a certain order, such that it is firstly and primarily in one and afterwards less principally in another. For when a man is sick and has some hope of health, he puts his first confidence of health in God, and then in many other things, namely in medicine, in [*Compendium*] *aromatorium*,[5] the bloodletting, in the location where he resides, in his physical constitution, his regimen. For since all these things (as is very clearly evident) help for recuperating health, no one is so senseless that he would deny that a sick man can put confidence of his health in all these things.

Next, if we wish to say with the comparison of the foundation used by Paul, the same thing will be clearly established. For in building a house, upon the first stone, which is placed is like the foundation of the building, is placed another stone, which is the second, upon which is erected a third, upon which third stone is set a fourth, and so forth until the completion of the peak. For just as we do not deny that the first stone is the foundation of the whole work, because it supports all the upper stones, and upon it all the stones rest, so one ought not to

---

[1] Cf. Lk. 15, 4-5.

[2] Cf. Jn. 15, 5.

[3] *Loci Communes*, c. 8 (*De gratia et justificatione*) in CR 21, 423.

[4] I.e. *puppim et proram*.

[5] I.e. an important work on pharmacy influenced by the Arabic treatises written by Saladin of Ascolo which was first published in 1488.

deny that the peak of the house rests upon the fourth stone, and the third, and the second, because when they have been removed, even while the first stone remains, the peak of the house would fall, because without them it cannot be supported.

In the same way it is necessary to say concerning confidence of obtaining glory, that this confidence ought to be put firstly and especially in Christ's merits, as on the first foundation of the whole spiritual structure, and without which all the rest will be able to do completely nothing. After these merits of Christ come man's good works, without which, even with Christ's merits remaining, no one can gain eternal life, because Christ said: "If thou wilt enter into life, keep the commandments" (Mt. 19, 17). Thus, since a reward has been set for good works (as we will say later elsewhere, in the section on "Merit"), which cannot be obtained without them, it is then proved that confidence of obtaining eternal glory can be rightly placed after Christ in good works. Nevertheless, we do not say that this confidence is so placed in our good works as though the reward of eternal life is due to them by their nature. And trusting in our good works in this way, we detract nothing from the Divine honor, as the Lutherans object to us, but rather we increase the Divine honor in this, because that confidence which we place in our works we refer back to God's goodness and mercy, because we acknowledge that by it happens to us that we can perform good works, and that by it we are able to merit something before God. Thus, all our confidence is referred unto Christ: because we know and acknowledge that we accomplish nothing without Him. For "Such confidence we have," as Paul says, "through Christ, towards God. Not that we are sufficient to think anything of ourselves, as of ourselves: but our sufficiency is from God… Having therefore such hope, we use much confidence" (II Cor. 3, 4-5 & 12).

Now when Paul elsewhere commands that we ought not to be confident in ourselves, he does not command to abstain from all confidence, but only from that whereby someone so trusts in himself or his works so that he puts absolutely no confidence in God, and we also condemn this confidence, because (as we said) never ought we to place any confidence in our own deeds unless we firstly and principally have placed confidence in God. And that this is Paul's true meaning, the words which he added clearly show. For after he had said, "that we should not trust in ourselves," he immediately added, "but in God who raiseth the dead" (II Cor. 1, 9).

Now it can be proved from the testimonies of Sacred Scripture and of the Holy Doctors that such confidence can be rightfully placed in our works, as we have thus far declared. Firstly, that testimony is clear which Tobias says: "Alms shall be a great confidence before the most high God, to all them that give it" (4, 12). In which words Tobias clearly teaches that confidence before God can rightfully be placed in having given alms. Furthermore, "The life of man upon earth is… like the days of a hireling. As… the hireling," Job says, "looketh for the end of his work, so I also have had empty months, and have numbered to myself wearisome nights" (7, 1-3). Now the hireling hoping for a reward of his labor, not only has confidence in the truthfulness and goodness of the employer by whom he was hired to labor, but he also trusts in his own labor. Because he understands well that he will not receive a reward from the employer, even they he is good and truthful, except on account of his own labor.

Again, when that woman who was suffering from an issue of blood, and was desiring to be healed by Christ, "came from behind and touched the hem of His garment," saying within herself: "If I shall touch only his garment, I shall be healed," Jesus said to her: "Be of good heart, daughter, thy faith hath made thee whole" (Mt. 9, 20-22). In which words He clearly taught that she could rightly have confidence of health, because she had faith. Thus, he commanded that she trust in Him, and in the faith which she had conceived about Him. Next, John the Apostle very clearly teaches this saying the following: "If our heart do not reprehend us, we have confidence towards God: and whatsoever we shall ask, we shall receive of him: because we keep his commandments" (I Jn. 3, 21-22). Notice, Lutherans, I beseech you, and do not harden your hearts, because John teaches us that from the fulfilment of God's Commandments we can conceive confidence of obtaining whatever we ask from God when praying.

Paul also testifies that he had confidence in his own good works of obtaining a crown of glory: "I have fought a good fight, I have finished my course, I have kept the faith. As to the rest, there is laid up for me a crown of justice, which the Lord the just judge will render to me in that day" (II Tim. 4, 7-8). See how much confidence Paul says he has of attaining a crown of glory on account of the excellent works which he recalls that he did unto God's glory. And, so that we may press the adversaries more from this testimony of Paul, it is necessary to note these words of the Apostle that he said that a crown of justice is laid up for him, not a crown of mercy: and that the Lord by bestowing it would be a just judge, and he did not say a merciful judge. For by these words he very clearly teaches that a crown will be given to him by God, not only out of the liberality of Divine mercy alone, but also from a debt of justice. For that which has been once promised, nature teaches, is reckoned to be a debt in justice. Now God promised eternal life to everyone keeping His Commandments well: hence God is a debtor of bestowing eternal life to anyone fully keeping His Commandments. Still God's very great mercy is in this, because He has deigned to promise men such a great reward on account of deeds that are lowly and unworthy of so great a reward. Therefore, after having given this promise a man does not act proudly who trusts in God, that He will give eternal life on account of his own good works.

Hence Augustine says: "A reward is due to good works, if they are performed; but grace, which is not due, precedes, that they may be done."[1] From which words it is plainly established that God out of pure liberality gives man the first grace of justification, but out of a debt of justice He renders eternal glory for good works. Thus, one ought not to be reprehended who places confidence, especially a moderate confidence, in those works to which God out of His goodness promises to render the reward of eternal life. Many holy and most learned men commend this confidence put after Christ in our works, and give testimony in favor of it.

Thomas Aquinas when interpreting the passage from the Epistle to the Hebrews: "Do not therefore lose your confidence" (10, 35), says these words: "He shows what remains for them to do, i.e., to retain the confidence obtained from their good works... Inasmuch as you have done so many good things in the first days of your conversion, it should cause you to have much confidence in God; do not, therefore, throw away your confidence, which you will lose, if you stop doing good."[2]

Before Thomas, [Hervé de Bourg-Dieu[3]] supports the same opinion, who when interpreting the aforesaid words of Paul says these things: "There is a logical inference from that which he said, that they had borne so much, and hence they expected eternal life, meaning, 'a lasting substance' (v. 34). It is as though he said, 'Because in the beginning of the faith you suffered so many adversities, you will confidently hope for an eternal reward,' and 'Do not therefore lose your confidence,' meaning, by forsaking your firm hope based upon the patience of faith, because by the loss of patience you will also lose you hope of eternal life. And lest the loss of hope seem to be a small loss he adds: 'which hath a great reward.' Therefore, hope with certitude for the ineffable remuneration, 'That eye hath not seen, nor ear heard' (I Cor. 2, 9), as though you already had it. Or you have it in Divine predestination. Truly you ought not to lose though impatience confidence of an everlasting reward."[4] And before [Hervé de Bourg-

---

[1] *Opus Imperfectum, contra Julianum*, c. 133 (PL 45, 1133). Cf. Dz. 191. The author here cites a spurious work attributed to St. Augustine, *De vera innocentia*.

[2] *Commentary on the Epistle to the Hebrews*, c. 10, lect. 4, n. 541-542.

[3] This citation was incorrectly ascribed to St. Anselm of Canterbury.

[4] *Commentaria in epistolas Pauli: In epistolam ad Hebraeos*, c. 10 (PL 181, 1641B-C).

Dieu], Theophylactus teaches the same opinion who when interpreting the aforesaid words of the same Paul, says these words: "When he says, 'Do not lose,' he shows that they had not yet fallen away, for they had need of strengthening and fortifying. Now he said, 'confidence,' because those who patiently undergo such things for God's sake, have great confidence."[1]

Before all these men Chrysostom teaches this opinion more clearly, who in his *Commentaries on the Psalms* when interpreting the verse, "Open ye to me the gates of justice," says these words: "He who submits to discipline can confidently say, 'Open ye to me the gates of justice.' The statement is to be taken anagogically, in fact, and is understood as the gates of Heaven, which are closed to the wicked, on which you have to knock with virtue, with alms-giving, with righteousness."[2] And again in another Psalm when interpreting the verse, "The Lord is gracious and merciful" etc. (144, 8), says these words: "Do you see the inspired author dwelling on these more gracious attributes, and more effusive in his language? He is well aware, in fact, that God's riches consist of these qualities most of all: it would not be possible to be saved were His clemency not enormous, it would not be possible for us to continue in existence did we not enjoy great goodness. Hence, He Himself also said, 'I am he that blot out thy iniquities for my own sake, and I will not remember thy sins' (Is. 43, 25). See how He shows His ineffable clemency: to sinners. He is not only merciful, but He also gives evidence of a further form of clemency of no little significance, His leniency and patience, so that they may come to repentance, and with His clemency be saved by their own effort and diligence, and have confidence on the basis of their good deeds. Now, he did not say simply 'merciful' but 'plenteous in mercy,' showing that this richness cannot be measured but surpasses all calculation."[3] I beg you Lutherans to take note and see how clearly Chrysostom teaches our opinion. For he said that God from His goodness and clemency conceded this to us, so that we may place some confidence in our works. Thus, if we place some confidence in our works, it is not because we may reckon our works of their own nature so worthy that by them we may be able to attain eternal life.

Jerome in his commentary on the Epistle to the Ephesians when interpreting the passage from the same epistle, "In whom we have boldness and access with confidence by the faith of him" (3, 12), says these words: "Faith in Christ is the beginning and source of confidence and access."[4] In which words there are two things that ought to be especially noted. The first is that according to Jerome's opinion it is allowed not merely to trust in Christ, but also in the faith of Christ, which is at the same time our work and God's gift. The other thing is that Jerome did not say that all confidence is in Christ alone or in His faith, but he said that faith alone is the beginning and source of confidence. If faith is the sole beginning and source of confidence, it is thence clearly proved that there is something beyond faith in which we can place confidence, because it would not be the beginning of confidence, but the whole confidence.

Finally, this opinion of the heretics was condemned in the Council of Trent celebrated under Paul III, in the sixth session of which this teaching was promulgated. "To men, therefore, who have been justified in this respect, whether they have preserved uninterruptedly the grace received, or have recovered it when lost, the words of the Apostle are to be submitted: 'Abound in every good work, knowing that your labor is not in vain in the Lord' (I Cor. 15, 58); 'for God is not unjust, that he should forget your work and the love which you have shown in his name' (Heb. 6, 10), and: 'Do not lose your confidence, which has a great reward' (Heb. 10, 35). And therefore to those who work well 'unto the end' (Mt. 10, 22), and who trust in God,

---

[1] *Expositio in Epistolam ad Hebraeos* (PG 125, 338-339).
[2] *Expositio in Psalmos*, Ps. 117, n. 5 (PG 55, 335).
[3] *Ibid.*, Ps. 144, n. 3 (PG 55, 468).
[4] *Commentaria in Epistolam ad Ephesios*, bk. 2, c. 3 (PL 26, 485A).

life eternal is to be proposed, both as a grace mercifully promised to the sons of God through Christ Jesus, 'and as a recompense'[1] which is according to the promise of God Himself to be faithfully given to their good works and merits."[2] After having given this teaching, lest anyone temerariously dare to contradict it, it decreed two *latae sententiae* canons against those who oppose this teaching, whose words are these: "If anyone shall say that the just ought not to expect and hope for an eternal recompense from God and the merit of Jesus Christ for the good works which have been performed in God, if by doing well and in keeping the Divine commandments they persevere even to the end: let him be anathema."[3] "If anyone shall say that the good works of the man justified are in such a way the gifts of God that they are not also the good merits of him who is justified, or that the one justified by the good works, which are done by him through the grace of God and the merit of Jesus Christ (whose living member he is), does not truly merit increase of grace, eternal life, and the attainment of that eternal life (if he should die in grace), and also an increase of glory: let him be anathema."[4]

But it is necessary that we reply to the Lutherans' objections. They object to us the Royal Prophet reprehending those who trust in their works: "They that trust in their own strength, and glory in the multitude of their riches" (Ps. 48, 7). And Solomon in Proverbs says: "He that trusteth in his own devices doth wickedly" (Prov. 12, 2). But to all these testimonies, and if there are others which are similar, it can be easily responded by that which we have said while arguing, namely that the confidence that is reprehended in all those passages, is that which is placed in our works alone, not however that which is placed firstly and principally in Christ, and then secondly and less principally in our works. They also object to us the Pharisee praying in the Temple, whom they say was reprehended by God in that he was recalling his own good works and was trusting in them. But they are mistaken, because he was not reprehended for this reason, but on account of the Pharisee's pride and contempt. For after the Savior had said that the Publican had went down from the Temple more just than the Pharisee, He stated the reason, saying: "Every one that exalteth himself, shall be humbled: and he that humbleth himself, shall be exalted" (Lk. 18, 14). And certainly, if the words which Luke cites in that passage are carefully considered, so far from him being able to use this passage for supporting his teaching, from them Luther's error is clearly proved. "And to some who trusted in themselves as just," Luke says, "and despised others, he spoke also this parable" (v. 9). Thus, he reprehends those who although they were not just, were trusting in themselves as though they were just. By which words He clearly stated that those who are just can trust in themselves in some way.

I have not seen anyone who wrote against this heresy except for just one author, Josse van Clichtove, who in his *Antilutherus*,[5] occasionally wrote a few things.

---

[1] Cf. St. Augustine, *On Grace and Free Will*, c. 8, n. 20 (PL 44, 893).
[2] Dz. 809.
[3] C. 26 (Dz. 836).
[4] C. 32 (Dz. 842).
[5] Bk. 3, c. 13, pp. 160r-162r.

FORNICATIO

Fornication

Among the other errors of the Greeks which Guy enumerates, there is one pertaining to this topic. For they say (as he says[1]) that simple fornication, meaning intercourse of an unmarried man with an unmarried woman, is not a mortal sin. But we have already disputed against this error above in first heresy of the section on intercourse, to which place therefore we send the reader.

FUTURUM CONTINGENS

Future Contingent

There is one error about this matter, whereby it is taught that nothing contingent happens in things, but all things which are, happen by an absolute necessity. The author of this error was Peter Abelard: after whom John Wycliffe followed, saying that God's power and the actual creation are of the same measure, such that He could not create more things than He creates, nor make things differently than He did. Luther now upholds the same error, saying that everything that happens occurs with such absolute necessity so that it is impossible that they would happen differently than they do. Hence, we have proved what we have said elsewhere to be true, namely that the greatest cause of heresies is that they measure according to the power of the mind, such that they think that only those things ought to be believed which their minds can understand. For because Peter Abelard's and John Wycliffe's very lowly minds, or rather blinded minds, cannot know other things that those which were made, they thence conclude that God could only make those things which were made. Thus, they wish to enclose the Divine omnipotence and surround it with limits of their minds, which is a very great blasphemy.

For Paul says that God's ways are "unsearchable."[2] Origen when treating this passage says: "His judgments are said to be inscrutable and His ways unsearchable only because there is no creature which is able to either search into or to scrutinize them. For it is only the Son Who has known the Father, and it is the Holy Ghost alone who 'searcheth all things, yea, the deep things of God' (I Cor. 2, 10): and hence these deep things of God, which he calls inscrutable and unsearchable, he says are inscrutable to every creature."[3] Why then do the very proud heretics attempt to scrutinize what is inscrutable? And to search into what is unsearchable? For they want to act like those Babylonians who tried to build a tower to go up into Heaven: but God cast them down while they strove to raise themselves up above the height of Heaven, and they "became vain in their thoughts, and their foolish heart was darkened: For professing themselves to be wise, they became fools" (Rom. 1, 21-22). Augustine certainly acts better, who bringing into captivity his understanding unto the obedience of the Divine omnipotence, says the following: "Let us grant that God can do something which we must admit to be beyond our comprehension. In such wonders the whole explanation of the work is the power of Him by whom it is wrought."[4]

---

[1] *Summa de haeresibus et earum confutationibus*, fol. 26v, c. 21.
[2] Cf. Rom. 11, 33.
[3] *Commenataria in Epistolam B. Pauli ad Romanos*, bk. 8 (PG 14, 1201A-B)
[4] Letter 137 (to Volusianus), c. 2, n. 8 (PL 33, 518).

For the rest, because Peter Abelard and John Wycliffe agree on this one thing, so that to themselves alone, against the precept of the Wise Man, they may be prudent, and having disregarded the opinions of all holy men, they may glory in their own understanding alone, we consequently proceed against them, bringing forth testimonies from Sacred Scripture alone. And firstly the Wise Man pronounces testimony in our favor, who when speaking about the journey of the Israelites through the desert, says the following: "Because some being deceived worshipped dumb serpents and worthless beasts, thou didst send upon them a multitude of dumb beasts for vengeance; that they might know that by what things a man sinneth, by the same also he is tormented. For thy almighty hand, which made the world of matter without form, was not unable to send upon them a multitude of bears, or fierce lions, or unknown beasts of a new kind, full of rage: either breathing out a fiery vapour, or sending forth a stinking smoke, or shooting horrible sparks out of their eyes: whereof not only the hurt might be able to destroy them, but also the very sight might kill them through fear. Yea and without these, they might have been slain with one blast, persecuted by their own deeds, and scattered by the breath of thy power: but thou hast ordered all things in measure, and number, and weight" (Wis. 11, 16-21). You see how many things that Wise Man enumerates which he says God could have made, even though they were never made. Therefore, He can make other things, and make things differently than He made them. And after those words the Wise Man again says: "Thou hast mercy upon all, because thou canst do all things, and overlookest the sins of men for the sake of repentance" (v. 24). Notice that he praises God's compassion, which he thereafter proves, because although He could immediately take a sinning man out of the world, He grants life to him, whereby he may repent and deserve pardon. The Wise Man also repeats the same opinion in the same book, although in a different chapter.[1]

And Wycliffe cannot escape by that direction in which he tries to go, saying that if God could have done many things which He did not do, then, if He so wished, He could have done wicked things. But we ourselves will say that He could do things, even if He not did want to do those things: for if He wanted, He would have done them: hence it is proved that He did not want to do things, because He did not do them.

Furthermore, Christ our Redeemer on the day before He suffered, and when He was about to be arrested, said to Peter, who had cut off with a sword the ear of the high priest's servant: "Thinkest thou that I cannot ask my Father, and he will give me presently more than twelve legions of angels? How then shall the scriptures be fulfilled, that so it must be done?" (Mt. 26, 53-54). Peter wanted to defend the Master with force and arms, to prevent, if he could, Him from being arrested. But the Master Himself, wanting to show that it is in His hands if He wished not to suffer, says that He could ask His Father to give Him twelve legions of Angels, who could accomplish this more easily. But although He said that He could, still it is evident that He did not do as He could have done. And in John's Gospel when showing that He was going to suffer by His own will, and not by an absolute necessity as the heretics say, He says: "Therefore doth the Father love me: because I lay down my life, that I may take it again. No man taketh it away from me: but I lay it down of myself, and I have power to lay it down: and I have power to take it up again" (10, 17-18). He clearly indicates by which words that He has the power of impeding the power of the men machinating His death: hence He said, "No man taketh it away from me": as though He were to say to the Jews more openly: "You thirst for My blood and anxiously desire my death: know this, however, that none of you would prevail if it were against my will and I were unwilling."

Again Blessed Paul, in that epistle which is to the Hebrews, when speaking of Christ speaks thus: "Who in the days of his flesh, with a strong cry and tears, offering up prayers and supplications to him that was able to save him from death, was heard for his reverence" (5, 7). What

---

[1] Cf. Wis. 12.

clearer testimony can be desired than this? Paul says that God could have freed Christ from death, meaning, He would not have suffered such a death. Yet since He did not do this, it is proved that God could do something else and otherwise than He did. And in the First Epistle to the Corinthians he says: "God is faithful, who will not suffer you to be tempted above that which you are able" (10, 13). Now we suffer, or allow (for to suffer here means to tolerate or to permit) only those things we do not wish to prevent from happening, which would otherwise happen: those things which we do not impede, but allow to remain as they are, we are then said to suffer, permit or tolerate. For no one correctly, and speaking as he ought, would say: "I suffer fire to be hot," because no one of us can make fire to be cold, or prevent it from being hot. Thus, when Paul says about God, that He does not suffer us to be tempted above that which we are able, it is an indication that it could happen otherwise, namely that we be tempted above our power. Now even though this could happen, still God does not permit it to happen in that way, and hence Paul says that He will not suffer us to be tempted above that which we are able. From which passage, if it be rightly considered, it is also clearly shown that God can do things otherwise than He does.

Next, the very change of operations which happen in creatures by God's command very clearly show that God can do things otherwise than He does. For it often happens that things are and act differently than it was permitted to them by nature: which change proves, that when it was done differently, we may believe that it so happened, not by necessity, but by God's mere will. For that a woman sterile in youth, such as Sacred history relates concerning Sara, afterwards gave birth when she became old, happened outside the order of nature.[1] Balaam's ass speaks—it exceeds the limits of its condition.[2] The sun when relinquishing its own motion, stood in favor of the sons of Israel—this was beyond natural laws.[3] The almond branch placed [in the Temple] with Aaron's name, flowered without root against the natural order, and although it was dry, produced fruit.[4] The three young men enclosed in the fiery furnace were not incinerated;[5] out of a dry rock, which contained no character of wetness, flows water in great abundance, to such a degree that it satisfied six hundred thousand souls.[6] Since all these things occur beyond the natural order, we are taught that when there is something according to the order of nature, we may believe that then also God could do otherwise.

Add to these things that if nothing happens contingently, but all things happen by an absolute necessity, prayers will be entirely useless. Why do we pray to God if what has been once decreed necessarily happens? For we pray in vain if that which we request will also happen to those who do not petition: or if it was not to be, it is impossible that it would happen. Do we therefore pray in vain? Far be it. For the Lord taught us to pray.[7] And when King David with fasting and tears, hoped that he could obtain from God that his son would not die, although Nathan the prophet had said to him: "The child that is born to thee, shall surely die" (II Kings 12, 14). And afterwards when he saw his son dead, David said to his servants, who had reproached him on account of his fasting and weeping: "While the child was yet alive, I fasted and wept for him: for I said: Who knoweth whether the Lord may not give him to me, and the child may live? But now that he is dead, why should I fast?" (v. 22-23). Notice that David believes that God could have done regarding his son differently than he did: and Peter Abelard does not believe this. Wherefore he seems to me to be like another Goliath, who provokes all

---

[1] Cf. Gen. 21, 2.
[2] Cf. Num. 22, 28 ff.
[3] Cf. Jos. 10, 13.
[4] Cf. Num. 17, 8.
[5] Cf. Dan. 3, 24.
[6] Cf. Num. 20, 11 & Num. 11, 21.
[7] Mt. 6, 9 ff.

the children of Israel, meaning all the holy Doctors, to war: but see that he has already now been struck and killed by David.

Furthermore, Christ when praying to His Father, says: "Father, if it be possible, let this chalice pass from me" (Mt. 26, 39). But Christ Who was foreseeing the future knew that He would drink the chalice: hence according to this opinion of theirs, it was impossible that He would not drink. Does He then pray in vain? Far be it that we would burst out with such a great blasphemy, such that we would say that Christ asked the Father for what was impossible to be given to Him. Now that which He said: "if it be possible," another Evangelist, when relating the same prayer, said: "Father, if thou wilt" (Lk. 22, 42). From the combination of those two passages it is shown that Christ's words ought to be understood thus: "Father, if it be possible," meaning, "if it can happen without it being against Thy will." For Christ was not wanting to contradict this will, but wanted to fulfill it, and hence He adds: "Nevertheless not as I will, but as thou wilt" (v. 39). Jerome,[1] however, and Christian Druthmar,[2] who imitates him, expound this passage otherwise: although their exposition does not contradict what we firstly set forth. Notwithstanding, Mark's words prove that those words were not words of someone doubting God's power. For after that prayer Mark relates that Christ said the following: "Abba, Father, all things are possible to thee" (14, 36): by which words he very clearly signifies that God could remove the chalice from Him, namely that He would not drink it. Since however it was not so done, we have proved that God could do things differently than He does. Those things which we will say below in favor of the assertion of free will militate against this error. Thus, the reader may get many things from that place, if he desires them: because having shown free will, it is proved that not all things happen necessarily.

Finally, from the forty-five articles of John Wycliffe condemned in the eighth session of the Council of Constance, the twenty-seventh says: "All things happen from absolute necessity."[3] Which article, along with the others, was condemned *latae sententiae*. Thomas [Netter] of Walden wrote against this error.[4] But he was somewhat lukewarm in that place, because he very rarely cited quotations of Sacred Scripture, but more frequently cited some holy Doctors: which ought not to have been done, especially because there exist explicit quotations of Sacred Scripture, and because he was waging war against men who, as is evident, do not accept the testimonies of men.

---

[1] "He prays a second time that if Ninive [or the Gentile world] cannot be saved unless the gourd [i.e. the Jews] be withered, His Father's will may be done, which is not contrary to the Son's will, Who Himself speaks by the Prophet, 'That I should do thy will: O my God, I have desired it' (Ps. 39, 9)." *Commentaria in Evangelium Matthaei*, bk. 4, c. 26 (PL 26, 199B).

[2] "He says for the benefit of the Jews: 'If it is possible for the Gentiles to be saved without the dereliction of the Jews, such that they do not bring about my death, let it be done. Nevertheless, let not what I say with human affection, but rather what I have disposed with Thee in the Divinity be done.' And here we ought to follow His example of praying, such that whenever we supplicate God for our own temporal good, we ought to always ask at the end for His good pleasure, so that if we are asking against our salvation, He Who is our Savior, may govern and hear us according to His plan." (*Expositio in Evangelium Matthaei*, c. 56 (PL 106, 1478D-1479A)).

[3] Dz.4 607.

[4] *Doctrinale antiquitatum fidei Ecclesiae Catholicae* (Venice, Jordanus Zilettus, 1571), bk. 1, art. 1 from chapter 10 to chapter 14 (pp. 36-43).

GRATIA

Grace

It is the most novel error of Pelagius, who attributed so much to free will, that he would say that man can fulfill all of God's precepts without Christ's grace, and attain eternal life by his own merits. And when he was reproved by others about this matter, he submitted to the admonition to the extent that he would say that grace ought not to be discarded as completely useless, but it ought to be embraced, because eternal glory can be had more easily when it comes, by which words he was implying that beatitude can be acquired without grace, although more difficultly than with grace. Caelestius, a [lay-] monk (as I suppose), taught this error after him; I do not know of which nationality he was because when Gennadius [of Massilia] discusses about him in his *Lives of Illustrious Men*,[1] he omits his country of origin. From his description, however, it is evident that he was a contemporary of Pelagius, at the time of Pope Innocent I. Augustine, however, says that the supporters of this error were also called Caelestians from this Caelestius. Julianus, bishop [of Eclanum],[2] "a man of vigorous character, learned in the Divine Scriptures," as Gennadius says,[3] wrote a number of books against Blessed Augustine, his opponent.[4]

It is necessary to go forth against this error with such due balance, so that we may defend the necessity of grace in such wise, that we do not take away from free will: again, that we affirm free will such that we prove that it needs grace. Now in order that we may do this better, it is necessary that we point out that there are three kinds of liberty. There is a liberty from guilt, concerning which the Apostle says: "For when you were the servants of sin, you were free men to justice" (Rom. 6, 20). And elsewhere he says: "Where the Spirit of the Lord is, there is liberty" (II Cor. 3, 17). This is not the liberty whereby we say that man's every choice is free. There is another liberty which is opposed to the servitude of wretchedness, about which the Apostle also says: "The creature also itself shall be delivered from the servitude of corruption, into the liberty of the glory of the children of God" (Rom. 8, 21). Nor is this liberty useful for our argument, because man's choice is not said to be free from it. There is a third liberty, which is opposed to necessity, or rather to force, because there is some necessity, as for example the procession of the Holy Ghost, the mutual love of the Divine Persons, which happen freely, although necessarily, yet not as a result of force or violence, because they do not go against something opposite. From this liberty we call man's choice free. Man has this liberty from his own nature, and it is so ingrafted in him, that it cannot be separated from him. Now it is not now necessary that we prove this liberty of choice, because we are arguing against Pelagius, who favors human free will more than is correct. Now if there are some who oppose this liberty, they ought not to be cited now, because we will dispute elsewhere against them.

---

[1] "Caelestius, before he joined Pelagius, while yet a very young man, wrote to his parents three epistles *On monastic life*, written as short books, and containing moral maxims suited to everyone who is seeking God, containing no trace of the fault which afterwards appeared but wholly devoted to the encouragement of virtue." (C. 44 (PL 58, 1083B-1084A)).

[2] The text erroneously here reads, "of Capua."

[3] *Lives of Illustrious Men*, c. 45 (PL 58, 1084A).

[4] I.e., *Ad Turbantium* (419) composed of four books, and *Ad Florum contra Augustine librum secundum de nuptiis* composed of eight books.

Otherwise, so that we may show the necessity of free will and of grace at the same time, it ought to be further noted that the operations of our will are threefold. For one of which is good, such as to wish to give alms to the needy for God's sake. Another is evil, such as to want to steal. Another is in the middle, which is reckoned as neither good nor bad, such as to want to rub one's beard, or to walk, for no deliberate purpose to which these actions are directed: for these actions are directed to some end, they can receive from it goodness or badness.

Thus, having laid these foundations, I add five Catholic assertions. The first is: Free will of itself and by its nature can chose any wicked choice. The second Catholic assertion is: Free will by the very condition of its nature (I do not exclude here or in the first assertion the general concurrence of God) can choose any indifferent work, namely which is neither good nor bad. The third Catholic assertion is: Man's free will from its own power alone, even having added God's general and common concurrence, cannot do something good without some special help of God, because some admonition, attraction, inspiration, or some aforesaid gift to nature, which help God Himself gives completely freely to those whom He is pleased to choose. The fourth Catholic assertion is: After God has motivated our will to good, this power is in man's will itself to consent or dissent to God advising and inspiring. The fifth Catholic assertion is: After our will begins to do some good with God's help, it cannot without special help of God Himself complete the good begun and persevere in it. Thus, from these five assertions it very clearly appears how much power is in our free will, how great also is the need for Divine grace in our free will. We and Pelagius agree on the first, second and fourth assertions: wherefore there is no need for us to take pains to support them now. Therefore, it remains for me to prove only two, namely the third and fifth assertions.

The Lord shows clearly enough our inability by the prophet Isaias saying: "Shall the axe boast itself against him that cutteth with it? or shall the saw exalt itself against him by whom it is drawn? as if a rod should lift itself up against him that lifteth it up, and a staff exalt itself, which is but wood" (10, 15). Notice that you see how God compares Himself to a craftsman, but us to an axe or saw, or some other instrument by means of which the craftsman works. Neither an axe nor a saw cuts wood unless it be moved by some man to do this: so also our free will is never able to do something good, unless it be moved by God to do it. Therefore, as if a saw would be exalted against him who cuts with it, so also does everyone who glories about a good work, and does not glory in the Lord. There is something very similar to this that the holy Psalmist says: "My tongue is the pen of a scrivener that writeth swiftly" (Ps. 44, 2). Isaias show our weakness for works, by the cited example of a saw in support of this truth. David teaches the same inability about forming words, comparing his tongue to a pen. For just as a pen never writes unless the hand of the writer moves it: so also no one can say something good, unless his tongue is moved by God. "For it is not you that speak," Christ says to His disciples, "but the Spirit of your Father that speaketh in you" (Mt. 10, 20). And Paul says: "No man can say the Lord Jesus, but by the Holy Ghost" (I Cor. 12, 3). Moreover, the prophet Jeremias says: "I know, O Lord, that the way of a man is not his: neither is it in a man to walk, and to direct his steps" (10, 23). See what he says. He does not deny that man has the power to walk, for man can do this with God's general concurrence: but he denies that the power to walk rightly is in man's power, namely so that he would direct his steps to the end which we all seek, namely eternal glory.

David, however, teaches this more explicitly: "With the Lord shall the steps of a man be directed" (Ps. 36, 23). Hence acknowledging his own weakness, he asks for help from the Lord saying, "Perfect thou my goings in thy paths: that my footsteps be not moved" (Ps. 16, 5). And again: "Direct my steps according to thy word: and let no iniquity have dominion over me" (Ps. 118, 133). Let Pelagius be ashamed saying that everyone is governed by his own will. And Jeremias prays to the Lord saying: "Heal me, O Lord, and I shall be healed:

save me, and I shall be saved, for thou art my praise" (17, 14). If Jeremias could have healed himself, why does he ask it of God? Again, God teaches by the prophet Osee the same belief, saying: "Destruction is thy own, O Israel: thy help is only in me" (13, 9). Let these testimonies from the Old Testament suffice.

Let us now go on to the New Testament, in which the truth shines more brightly. "Without me you can do nothing" (Jn. 15, 5). If we can do nothing, how could we attain eternal life without Him? And again, the same Truth says: "No man can come to me, except the Father, who hath sent me, draw him" (Jn. 6, 44). Furthermore, it is said in the prayer which the true Teacher teaches us: "Thy kingdom come" (Mt. 6, 10). By which words we ask God for heavenly glory, which is God's eternal kingdom. And again, in another petition it is said: "And lead us not into temptation. But deliver us from evil. Amen" (v. 13). The one and true Teacher taught us to ask for all these things from His Father. From which it is easily proved that no one can obtain eternal life, or avoid every sin without God's special help.

But here Pelagius will say that such petitions are vain, because even if our free will can do all these things, still they are difficult for it. Thus, the reason why we ask, he says, is so that we can attain more easily with His help things which we could attain only with difficulty without His help. But this is rebutted by Paul's testimony, who in his Epistle to the Romans says: "Whom he justified, them he also glorified" (8, 30). He did not say, "whom He found to be just": but instead he said, "whom He justified": so that by these words he might teach us that all our justification is from God, and not from us. Hence he says again: "It is not of him that willeth, nor of him that runneth, but of God that sheweth mercy" (Rom. 9, 16). By which words he very clearly teaches that we can do nothing without God's special help. For what, pray tell, is it that he says, "nor of him that runneth"? For by those words he teaches that not only the remiss and tepid will, but also the will which burns with very great desire, and which howsoever vehement an effort it makes, it cannot attain eternal life of itself, but this depends on God's mercy alone. For this is to say, "it is not of him that willeth, nor of him that runneth": because he who runs, seeks after movement, and drives on his members with a stronger impulse than if he were to walk at a slower pace. And he says in another epistle: "Not that we are sufficient to think anything of ourselves, as of ourselves: but our sufficiency is from God" (II Cor. 3, 5). What will Pelagius reply here? If we are not sufficient to think, and are less sufficient to will, because the things which we do not know, we cannot will. And if we cannot will something good, nor will we be able to do something good. "Our sufficiency," he says, "is from God."

And what does Pelagius say? "Our sufficiency," Pelagius says, "is from ourselves, but the facility is from God." Thus, Pelagius very clearly opposes Paul's teaching, that is, the Catholic faith. And in another epistle, he repeats the same opinion, saying: "And God is able to make all grace abound in you; that ye always, having all sufficiency in all things, may abound to every good work" (II Cor. 9, 8). Behold you see what grace bestows upon us, certainly not merely the facility for good works, as Pelagius says, but it confers upon us all sufficiency. Hence we are not sufficient without God's grace. Moreover, when Paul likewise asked the Lord three times to take away from him the sting of the flesh, it was responded to him by the Lord: "My grace is sufficient for thee" (II Cor. 12, 9). For He did not say to Paul: "You yourself suffice," but He said, "My grace is sufficient for thee." But if Paul had been able to do what he asked for, although it were difficult to do, the Lord would have rightly answered that which it is related that Blessed Agatha replied to Blessed Lucy praying to the same Agatha for her mother's health: "Maiden Lucy, why seekest thou of me," she said, "that which thou thyself canst presently give thy mother?"[1] But because Paul could not resist such a strong

---

[1] First responsory at Matins of the feast of St. Lucy.

temptation of Satan even with great difficulty, wherefore the Lord says to him: "My grace is sufficient for thee."

Again, the Apostle likewise says in the Epistle to the Ephesians: "For by grace you are saved through faith, and that not of yourselves, for it is the gift of God; not of works, that no man may glory" (2, 8-9). Pelagius seems to completely eliminate the Divine help when he says that faith is God's gift, and without it we cannot be saved, and hence he says that we owe to God that He gave us knowledge whereby we can truly know Him and know what things ought to be done: once that knowledge is had, he says that we do not need the further gift of grace of charity, because he does not want to admit that charity is God's gift, nor does he say that it is necessary, but faith alone suffices with our power of choice: and in this way he interprets this quotation of Paul which we have just cited: "by grace you are saved through faith."

But Pelagius ought to notice that Paul does not say that we are saved by faith alone, but by grace, and this through faith. For Paul likewise testifies that faith alone or knowledge does not suffice, saying: "If I should have all faith, so that I could remove mountains, and have not charity, I am nothing" (I Cor. 13, 2). Next, in the Epistle to the Philippians he says: "For it is God who worketh in you, both to will and to accomplish, according to his good will" (2, 13). If it is God Who works, then knowledge does not suffice. Now when he said, "to will and to accomplish," he taught that we should believe that God's grace is necessary not only for beginning something good, but also so that we can persevere in the good begun. For this it to "accomplish," because he who "began to build, and was not able to finish" (Lk. 14, 30), he is not a perfect man: "but he that shall persevere unto the end, he shall be saved" (Mt. 10, 22). This salvation is not had except by God's grace. For Paul in his Epistle to Titus says: "The goodness and kindness of God our Saviour appeared: who not by the works of justice, which we have done, but according to his mercy, saved us, by the laver of regeneration, and renovation of the Holy Ghost; whom he hath poured forth upon us abundantly, through Jesus Christ our Saviour: that, being justified by his grace, we may be heirs, according to hope of life everlasting" (3, 4-7). I could have brought forth here very many testimonies of holy men, but since Sacred Scripture bears witness so clearly, it would be superfluous to cite testimonies of men.

Therefore, we conclude that the beginning of any good, and the perseverance of the same, depends on Divine grace, and not on man's free will alone. A sign of which thing is that which the Lord commands, saying: "And you shall offer in that place your holocausts and victims, the tithes and firstfruits of your hands" (Deut. 12, 6). What are the firstfruits of our hands according to the moral sense, except the beginning of our good works? And what can be more suitably understood by tithes than perseverance, and the completion of every good work? The whole Law is contained in the Ten Commandments, by which we can attain eternal life. We are bound to offer the firstfruits and tithes, because the beginning of good works and their completion ought to be attributed to the Lord, Who works them in us and by us.

But it is necessary that we respond to the Pelagians' objections. Firstly, they object to us as follows: no one sins in what he cannot avoid. Therefore, if man is not free to fulfil all the precepts, and to avoid all sins, when he does not avoid them, he does not sin, because he could not avoid this very thing. To which we respond that it is within the power of man's free will that he may consent to God admonishing and cooperate with God collaborating. Now God never denies Himself to us, nay He is always ready to motivate and help us. For Paul says: "God is faithful, who will not suffer you to be tempted above that which you are able" (I Cor. 10, 13). Hence it follows that man is rendered guilty, not because he does not act alone, since this would be impossible for him, but because he does not listen to God admonishing him, he is not roused by His voice, and he does not answer the One calling him. For the Lord complains about sinners regarding this matter saying: "I called, and you refused: I stretched out my hand, and there was none that regarded. You have despised all my counsel, and have neglected my reprehensions. I also will laugh in your destruction, and will mock when that shall come to you which you feared" (Prov. 1, 24-26). Note that you now see about what matter the Lord calls sinners to account, namely because He called and they did not want to answer Him; they did not want to act according to His counsel. And they could not plead their own inability or weakness, because He extends His hand to help them, yet they neglected His help. "I stretched out my hand," He said, "and there was none that regarded." If anyone were to accidentally fall into a pit, out of which he was unable to arise and get out, and someone else were to extend his hand to him to assist him and thus he would get out, would he not rightly be blamed if refusing the help, he were to choose to stay in the pit? But if afterwards he were to be reproached for staying in the pit and not getting out, could he rightly plead that he was unable to get out? Certainly not: because even though he could not do so alone, still he could have done so with the help of another, which help he did not wish to utilize. So also although a man cannot fulfill all God's precepts by himself alone, and avoid all sins, still he can do all these things with God's help: wherefore the sinner is guilty, because he does not listen to God admonishing, and he disregards God helping, Whose help he does not want.

Secondly, they object as follows: If God performs every good deed that we do, then there will be no merit of ours and no reward of ours. To which therefore I respond by objecting in like manner: If our free will can perform by itself alone all good works, there is no reason why we render glory to God from the good deeds done by us, but we could claim glory by right for ourselves, who have performed them. Yet far be it that anyone would think this within himself. For the holy Psalmist says: "Not to us, O Lord, not to us; but to thy name give glory" (113, 9). And again: "All they that love thy name shall glory in thee" (5, 12). And Paul says: "He that glorieth, may glory in the Lord" (I Cor. 1, 31). Thus Pelagius, who glories in himself and not in the Lord, does not love the Lord's name, because all who love the Lord's name, glory in it: attribute to it the glory of all their works, and imputing to themselves their evil deeds. "Why dost thou glory in malice," Pelagius, "thou that art mighty in iniquity?" (Ps. 51, 3). Since you are not as powerful for good as much as for evil, what is this is malice of yours, namely that you glory about good, who are powerful in iniquity? See what God Himself says: "I will not give my glory to another" (Is. 42, 8). But what dost Thou give us, O Lord? "Peace I leave with you," He says, "my peace I give unto you" (Jn. 14, 27). Peace is ours, glory is His. The Angels sang about this distribution of things when the Lord was born: "Glory to God in the highest," they say, "and on earth peace to men" (Lk. 2, 14). The Angels give glory to God, peace to men. Speak, Pelagius; do you wish to snatch away the glory from God, which all the choirs of Angels render unto Him, and which He kept for Himself? But if you are forced to render glory to God, how do you give glory to Him if you say that you perform all things?

But lest we seem to evade the objection with an objection, we will respond more clearly, thus rendering glory to God, such that we do not empty out our merits: again, so asserting our merit, such that we detract nothing from the Divine glory. For our free will (as we have already taught above) but for God's admonition, anticipation, and cooperation, could not undertake something truly good. Still, since it was advised and anticipated by God, it can obey God advising, and cooperate with God operating. Notice two things, namely God's advice and our obedience: God's operation, and our cooperation: which two things Paul mentions simultaneously saying: "The Spirit helpeth our infirmity" (Rom. 8, 26). And elsewhere he expresses this same thing more clearly saying: "For we are God's coadjutors" (I Cor. 3, 9). From which words we clearly enough conclude that both God and we act simultaneously in the same work. And again after he had said that many good works were performed by himself, and that he had labored more than all, lest perhaps someone think that he had arrogated the glory of the good works to himself, he added: "Yet not I, but the grace of God with me" (I Cor. 15, 10). He did not say, "by me": lest perhaps someone infer therefrom that he was like an instrument in acting: but he said, "the grace of God with me," to show thereby that he was God's cooperator. Thus, God anticipates by advising, by motivating: we, however, follow Him, provided that we obey Him advising by consent: and when we act according to his advice, He helps our weakness.

Two other things correspond to these two things, namely glory and merit, such that we ourselves render glory to God, but He bestows [glory] to us according to our merit. For since he anticipates us in the action, motivating us to do it, and He helps us in the act itself, without Whose help we could do nothing: hence we owe Him the glory as the first source of that work. On the other hand, from the fact that we consent to His advice, we who could dissent, a recompense and reward are due to us, and hence our merit [exists]. [A reward] is due to us, I say, not from the nature of the work, because (as Paul says) "The sufferings of this time are not worthy to be compared with the glory to come, that shall be revealed in us" (Rom. 8, 18): but it is due by the right of a promise. For nature taught us this law, namely that what someone promises, he would think that he owes. Hence the work which can be called merit, could not be accomplished without two things, namely without God's anticipating and assistance, and without our consent and cooperation. In the first is God's glory; in the second is our merit. The Prophet taught us all which things in one phase, saying: "Thou hast wrought all our works for us" (Is. 26, 12). For when he said, "our works," he shows our action in regard to it: because if we would do nothing in regard to it, they would not be called "our works." On the other hand, when He said to God, "Thou hast wrought," he likewise shows that our work is God's work, because God helps our weakness in that same work, working with us. Saying, "for us," however, he intimates our merit: because although He works with us, still His cooperation is for our benefit, not for His own, because He does not stand in need of our good works.

They thirdly object to us, saying: If our free will can fall from good to evil, when could it not also rise from evil to good? To which things we reply that someone cannot as easily get out of pit as he can easily fall into it. So also, although someone may fall by his will alone into the pit of sin, nevertheless he cannot get out of it by his will alone without God's grace helping him. But you will say: "Why is this? Do we lose free will by sin?" Far be it. But we lose Divine grace by sin, by the help of which our free will can do good, which when it has been taken away we cannot do the good which leads to eternal life.

But it is now necessary that we bring forth the definition of the Church. The [Second] Synod of Milevum in canon four defines concerning this matter by these words: "In like manner, whoever says that the same grace of God through Jesus Christ, our Lord, helps us not to sin only for this reason, that through it the understanding of the commands is revealed and opened to us, that we may know what we ought to strive after, what we ought to avoid, but that through this [the power] is not also given to us to love and to be able to do that which we know ought to be done, let him be anathema."[1] And again in canon five it says: "It has likewise been decided that whoever says that the grace of justification is given to us for this reason: that what we are ordered to do through free will, we may be able to accomplish more easily through grace, just as if, even if grace were not given, we could nevertheless fulfill the Divine commands without it, though not indeed easily, let him he anathema. For when the Lord was speaking about the fruits of His commands, He did not say: 'Without me you can accomplish with greater difficulty,' but rather He said: 'Without me you can do nothing' (Jn 15, 5)."[2]

Likewise, the Council of Trent celebrated under Paul III in the sixth session teaches: "If anyone shall say that man can be justified before God by his own works which are done either by his own natural powers, or through the teaching of the Law, and without Divine grace

---

[1] Dz. 104.

[2] Dz. 105.

through Christ Jesus: let him be anathema."[1] "If anyone shall say that Divine grace through Christ Jesus is given only so that man may more easily be able to live justly and merit eternal life, as if by free will without grace he were able to do both, though with difficulty and hardship: let him be anathema."[2] "If anyone shall say that without the anticipatory inspiration of the Holy Ghost and without His assistance man can believe, hope, and love or be repentant, as he ought, such that the grace of justification may be conferred upon him: let him be anathema."[3]

Jerome wrote three books of *Dialogues against the Pelagians*.[4] Blessed Augustine published many tracts against the same men, namely: *On Merit and the Forgiveness of Sins, [and the Baptism of Infants]*[5] written to Marcellinus in three books; *On Nature and Grace*[6] against Pelagius in one book, *On the Grace of Christ [and Original Sin]*,[7] against Pelagius and Caelestius in two books; *Against Two Letters of the Pelagians*[8] written to Boniface in four books; *Against Julian*[9], the Pelagian, in six books; *On Grace and Free Will*[10] written to Valentinus in one book; *Hypomnesticon contra Pelagianos [et Caelestianos]* in six books,[11] in the third book of which he discusses this matter, although Erasmus thinks that the latter work is not Augustine's. Blessed Bernard wrote another small work, *On Grace and Free Will*.[12] Johannes Trithemius,[13] in a list of ecclesiastical writers, relates that Gennadius [of Massilia] also wrote *Adversus Pelagium*,[14] but I admit that I have not seen this work.

The **second heresy** teaches that grace once received in Baptism cannot afterwards be lost. The author of this heresy was Jovinian, a Roman monk, who having cast off the monastic state returned to his vomit like a dog.[15] This man taught among other errors this one, saying that those who were reborn with full faith by Baptism cannot afterwards sin again. Pelagius also taught this error (as Augustine relates[16]) saying "that the life of the just in this world is absolutely without sin," as if he who is just at one time, already can sin no more. Luther resurrected this error then long buried for more than a thousand years, whose words, as Eck cites them in his list of errors, are these: "We have no doubt whatever that we are saved when we are baptized... since the promise there made is not mutable with respect to any sins... Hence one baptized, even though he so will, cannot lose salvation, because no sin but unbelief can condemn him. All others are swallowed up by faith in a moment."[17]

---

[1] Can. 1 (Dz. 811).
[2] Can. 2 (Dz. 812).
[3] Can. 3 (Dz. 813).
[4] PL 23, 491-590A.
[5] PL 44, 109-200.
[6] PL 44, 247-290.
[7] PL 44, 359-410.
[8] PL 44, 549-638.
[9] PL 44, 641-874.
[10] PL 44, 881-912.
[11] PL 45, 1611-1664. This spurious text formerly attributed to St. Augustine is commonly called the *Hypognosticon*.
[12] PL 182, 1001-1030.
[13] *De scriptoribus Ecclesiasticis* (Bertholdo Rembolt, 1512), fol. 47r.
[14] This work has been lost.
[15] Cf. II Pet. 2, 22.
[16] *De Haeresibus ad Quodvultdeum*, c. 88 (PL 42, 44).
[17] Luther, *De captivitate Babylonica* (WA vol. 6, p. 527, lns. 37 ff.; p. 528, lns. 25 ff.; p. 529, lns. 11-15). Excerpted by Johann Eck, *Four hundred and four Articles; some pertaining to the disputations at Leipzig, Baden, and Bern*, n. 193.

Nevertheless, heavenly along with earthly things oppose this erroneous doctrine. For we have already shown above in the section on the "Devil" that the devils were created by God in grace. These Angels, however, were not steadfast in grace, nor in the truth, nay iniquity was found in them. "I saw Satan," He says, "like lightning falling from heaven" (Lk. 10, 18). What therefore do you think will happen to us? "And in his angels he found wickedness" (Job 4, 18), "how much more shall they that dwell in houses of clay, who have an earthly foundation, be consumed as with the moth" (Job 4, 19)? If falls are in Heaven, how much more on earth? If that Lucifer, "who didst rise in the morning" (Is. 14, 12), and who "was in the pleasures of the paradise of God" (Ez. 28, 13), and is described as adorned with "every precious stone" (Ez. 28, 13), fell, who will presume about his own constancy? Are men stronger than Angels? Far be it that someone would presume of himself.

But now let us descend to man. God created man upright, and yet afterwards having despised God's command, to please his wife, he ate of the fruit of the forbidden tree.[1] Lot in Sodom is found just, wherefore when the whole city perished with fire, he is saved, and after a short time he becomes drunk by his own fault, and has intercourse with his daughters.[2] David, from following the ewes great with young" (Ps. 77, 70), is chosen as king, and anointed by Samuel according to God's command, and yet afterwards commits adultery and murder. Solomon, the son of this man, having been firstly loved by the Lord, and endowed by Him with wisdom above all men: yet who doubts that he was afterwards infatuated with women and an idolater? I could bring forth very many examples from the Old Testament, but I omit them for the sake of brevity.

Let us come to the New Testament. The day before the Lord Jesus Christ suffered, when He was having supper with His Apostles, He said to Peter, when He wished to wash him: "He that is washed, needeth not but to wash his feet, but is clean wholly. And you are clean, but not all" (Jn. 13, 10). He denotes by these words that the Apostles are in the state of grace. But it is evident that what He says, "but not all," was said on account of Judas who then wanted to betray Christ. But those who "are clean," afterwards having abandoned the Master all fled, and were scandalized, and Peter denied the Master thrice. What could Jovinian reply to these things; what also could Pelagius reply? But if you would like still another example, listen. Nicolaus, the Antiochian deacon is chosen by the Apostles as a man of good testimony, and full of the Holy Ghost, such that he ministered with Stephen and the other five deacons to the widows, nevertheless afterwards had a bad character, on account of which the Lord says in the Apocalypse that He "hatest the deeds of the Nicolaites" (2, 6).

Which men fell from the height of virtue into many vices on account of these and other similar things, by the devil greatly instigating and impelling. God, when speaking about the devil's great power and cunningness under the name of Behemoth, says to Job: "He shall strew gold under him like mire" (Job 41, 21). Which words (as is evident) cannot be taken literally, just as all the other things which He treats concerning Behemoth and the Leviathan: for otherwise if you attempt to take these words literally, God does not point out the Leviathan's power very much by the fact that "he shall strew gold under him like mire," since any weak and feeble man can tread upon gold as upon mire. Hence since a mystical sense of this passage is required, let us listen to Blessed Gregory, who wonderfully interprets (as is his custom) the text, saying the following: "In this place therefore 'gold' is taken for the brightness of sanctity; but nothing hinders our understanding by 'clay,' either covetousness in earthly things, or the infection of wicked doctrines, or the filth of carnal pleasures. For because this Leviathan subjects at that time to himself many, who seemed within Holy Church to be resplendent with the brightness of justice, either by the desire of earthly things, or by the infection of erroneous

---

[1] Cf. Gen. 3.

[2] Cf. Gen. 19.

doctrine, or by carnal pleasures, he doubtless 'strew gold under him like mire.' For to 'strew gold like mire,' is to trample down in some persons purity of life by unlawful desires; so that even they may follow his filthy footsteps, who used before to flash forth against him with the splendor of their virtues. The ancient enemy then deceives some at that time under a show of sanctity, but intercepts others by the foul sins of a carnal life. But he will then openly attack in these ways, but now he rules secretly in the hearts of many, as the Apostle Paul says, 'That he may be revealed in his time; for the mystery of iniquity already worketh.' (II Thess. 2, 6-7). He therefore even now 'strews gold under him like mire,' as often as he overthrows the chastity of the faithful through the sins of the flesh. He tramples on gold as clay, as often as he distracts the understanding of the continent by unclean desires."[1]

Furthermore, in the prayer which the Lord taught us, we say: "Forgive us our debts, as we also forgive our debtors" (Mt. 6, 12). And again: "And lead us not into temptation" (v. 13). But if (as Jovinian says) a man who has been baptized with full faith, cannot be subverted by the devil, this prayer does not befit a baptized man, and hence neither befits the whole Church. Yet the Church sings it daily. Again, that vessel of election chastises his body, and brings it into subjection, lest perhaps when he has preached to others, he should become a castaway.[2] And when writing to the Corinthians he says: "I fear lest, as the serpent seduced Eve by his subtilty, so your minds should be corrupted, and fall from the simplicity that is in Christ" (II Cor. 11, 3). But if there is such security after Baptism, why does Paul tremble with fear where there is no fear?[3] Also why does he warn elsewhere, saying: "He that thinketh himself to stand, let him take heed lest he fall" (I Cor. 10, 12)? And he reprehends the Galatians because they departed from the right way. For he says: "You did run well, who hath hindered you, that you should not obey the truth?" (5, 7). Lastly, the Lord in the Apocalypse says through John the Apostle to the Angel of the Church of Ephesus: "I know thy works, and thy labour, and thy patience... [because] thou hast endured for my name, and hast not fainted. But I have somewhat against thee, because thou hast left thy first charity" (2, 2-4). Thus, upon what basis do Jovinian and Pelagius promise security to those who have been at one time justified at Baptism? Hence these heretics seem to me to be those of whom the Lord complains through the prophet Jeremias saying: "They healed the breach of the daughter of my people disgracefully, saying: Peace, peace: and there was no peace" (6, 14).

But now let us see upon what foundation they rely, and let us show that it is so weak that we can overturn it with one finger. For they cite in their favor the passage of John in his First Epistle: "Whosoever is born of God, committeth not sin" (3, 9). But this immediately collapses, because the words which follow clearly show that it ought not to be understood as they suppose. For he immediately added, giving the reason for saying what he had said: "For," he says, "his seed abideth in him" (*ibid.*). He called grace or charity, through which we are made sons of God, "his seed." For it is impossible that someone would be in the state of grace and would sin. For those two things ought to be referred to the same time such that they could not be united at the same time, namely to be in the state of grace and in the state of sin. For if you would refer to different times, such that he who at one time had been in the state of grace, could not afterwards sin, then you would make John to disagree with himself. For he had said in the same epistle: "If we say that we have no sin, we deceive ourselves, and the truth is not in us" (1, 8). And again: "My little children, these things I write to you, that you may not sin" (2, 1). If everyone who has been born of God, cannot sin afterwards, in vain does he warn us not to sin. Blessed Bernard expounds this passage otherwise, who in his book, *Concerning Grace and Free Will*, says that the passage ought to be understood of the predestined, whose

---

[1] *Morals on the Book of Job*, bk. 34, c. 15, n. 28 (PL 76, 733D-734B).
[2] Cf. I Cor. 9, 27.
[3] Cf. Ps. 13, 5 & 52, 6.

sins, if they exist, are not imputed to punishment, because they are purified in this world, and hence they do not sin, with a sin, I say, unto death.[1]

In addition, in confirmation of their error they cite that which the Savior says in Matthew: "A good tree cannot bring forth evil fruit" (Mt. 7, 18). But this citation makes as little impact as the previous one, because it also arises from a faulty understanding, such that Jovinian supposes that it favors himself. Now Jerome explains in his book, *Against Jovinian*, how this passage ought to be understood when saying the following: "The truth is that a good tree does not bear evil fruit, nor an evil tree good fruit, so long as they continue in their goodness, or badness."[2]

But if they cite in their favor that passage of Paul: "Charity never falleth away" (I Cor. 13, 8), it does not disturb us at all, because there Paul does not deny that charity had at one time can be lost in this world, but teaches that the charity which shall have been had in this world, does not fall away in the world to come: it is just as he teaches concerning faith, which in the other life, when replaced with clear vision, we do lose. Hence in that passage he compares charity to faith and prophecy, and the rest of the virtues, which when he says that they do not exist in the other life, yet he says that charity alone remain there.

There exists a definition of the Synod of Milevum concerning this matter which says the following: "It has likewise been decided that what St. John the Apostle says: 'If we say that we have not sin, we deceive ourselves, and the truth is not in us' (I Jn. 1, 8), whoever thinks that this ought to be interpreted thus: that he asserts that this ought to be said on account of humility, namely, that we have sin, and not because it is truly so, let him be anathema."[3] And again: "It has likewise been decided that whoever wishes that the words themselves of the Lord's Prayer, where we say: 'Forgive us our debts' (Mt. 6, 12) be said by the saints so as to be spoken humbly, not truthfully, let him be anathema. For who would tolerate one praying and lying, not to men, but to the Lord Himself, who says with his lips that he wishes to be forgiven, and in his heart holds that he does not have debts to be forgiven?"[4]

But the Council of Trent celebrated under Paul III condemned this heresy much more clearly. For in the sixth session it published a canon concerning this matter, namely the twenty-third, the words of which are these: "If anyone shall say that a man once justified can sin no more, nor lose grace, and that therefore he who falls and sins was never truly justified; or, on the contrary, that throughout his whole life he can avoid all sins even venial sins, except by a special privilege of God as the Church holds in regard to the Blessed Virgin: let him be anathema."[5]

Blessed Jerome wrote *Against Jovinian* in two books, and in the second he disputes against this heresy. I have not seen another work which he wrote expressly against it.

The **third heresy** teaches that every just man knows that he is in the state of grace, and is certain of his own justice. The first inventor of this pestiferous heresy is Martin Luther, who seems to have been impelled by the devil that by him he would make all, or at least many, Christians listless, call them away from the practice of all good works.

When I first commissioned this work, *Against All Heresies*, to be published, namely in the year 1534, I had not seen Luther's work in which he had written this teaching therein, nor did I know of anyone who had written against it at that time, although I had read many authors

---

[1] "But this is said of them that are predestined unto life, not meaning that they do not sin at all, but that sin is not imputed to them, being either punished by befitting penance, or in love put utterly away." (C. 9, n. 29 (PL 182, 1017A)). The author mistakenly cites the name of this work as "On Nature and Grace."

[2] Bk. 2, n. 25 (PL 23, 322C).

[3] Can. 6 (Dz. 106).

[4] Can. 8 (Dz. 108).

[5] Dz. 833.

who had published very many volumes of books against Luther's other errors, but I had only seen the censure of the faculty of theology in Paris, which condemned this along with other assertions of Luther. And hence it happened that I had at that time written very little in this work against this heretical teaching of Luther, because I had not fully understood at that time upon what foundation Luther had relied, and from which principles he had deduced this assertion of his, nor had I considered for what purpose he was teaching it, nor what evils could arise from it. But after the first and second edition of this work, namely in the year 1545, Paul III, supreme pontiff of the whole Church, with Emperor Charles V as procurator, assembled the Council of Trent to extirpate all the recent heresies, which I attended by the command of Philip [II], king of all Spains. Hence my being there allowed me to read the books of Luther and of all his followers, and to investigate whatever escaped notice, because the illustrious man, Diego [Hurtado] de Mendoza,[1] who was then the representative of the Emperor at the Council, prepared there a copious library filled with all the books of the Lutherans, so that whoever wished, could examine them in order to attack their teachings. Thus, I then penetrated Luther's mind, and came to know from what foundation he deduced this most wicked doctrine, and what flowed from it.

It is now apparent, and known to nearly the whole world, that Luther's doctrine is that man is justified by faith alone, and that man's justice nowise depends on works, but on faith alone. For about this matter it has already been written and refuted by us above in the section on "Faith." And from this very false principle Luther and his followers endeavored to conclude that every just man knows that he is in the state of grace and is certain of his own justification, because faith, whereby man is justified, can be certain to anyone, nay is always most certain, according to that which [Pseudo-] Augustine says: "Nothing is more certain than his faith."[2] Hence, although someone may commit many sins, as well as many disgraceful acts and wicked deeds, Luther says that none of them are imputed to a believer, that is, according to his interpretation, to one having confidence in Christ, that by God's mercy and Christ's merits, his sins have been remitted. And because this faith is known to anyone having it, he infers from this that whatsoever be a man's works, as long as his faith be firm and fixed, he will always be certain of his salvation. Martin Bucer, a native of Strasburg (I think), an apostate monk of the Order of Preachers, and a follower of Luther in his book, *De concordantia certitudinis gratiae*, complains of us that we falsely ascribe to them this doctrine of the certitude of grace, as for instance they teach that no matter how impurely and wickedly men live, they still ought to firmly believe that through Christ they are pleasing to God.[3]

Wherefore lest someone suppose that this crime is falsely ascribed to them, nay rather so that he may realize that Bucer complains about us regarding this for no good reason, I will cite their own words, referencing also the exact places where they wrote them. [In his response to Lancelotto Politi] Luther says these words: "There is no sin except unbelief; there is no justice except faith."[4] In his book, *The Babylonian Captivity* [*of the Church*], he says:

---

[1] A compendium containing selections of the Reformers' writings, *De sacris concionibus recte formandis deque ratione theologiae dicendae*, was compiled by Father Alfonso Zorilla, secretary to Diego Hurtado de Mendoza, and published in 1543.

[2] Augustine did, however, write something similar: "Everyone sees his own faith in himself." (*On the Trinity*, bk. 13, c. 2, n. 5 (PL 42, 1017)).

[3] *De vera ecclesiarum in doctrina, ceremoniis, et disciplina reconciliatione et compositione* (Strasbourg, Wendelin Rihel, 1569), pg. 190v. The work, *De concordantia certitudinis gratiae*, could not be found.

[4] The work cited here is a sermon of Luther against Carlstadt. But this quotation was instead taken from Luther's response to Ambrosius Catharinus' *Apologia pro veritate catholicæ et apostolicæ fidei ac doctrinæ, adversus impia ac pestifera Martini Lutheri dogmata* ("Defense of the True Catholic and Ap-

"Even if he would, a man cannot lose his salvation by any sins however great, unless he refuses to believe; for no sins whatever can condemn him, but unbelief alone."[1] "Nor should someone having faith doubt about his own salvation, because the promise made there is not changeable by any sins, but only by unbelief."[2] And in his book, *De votis monasticis*, he again says: "There are no works so wicked of a believer in Christ that they could indict and condemn him."[3] Bucer in his commentary on the Epistle to the Romans says: "Since all our works are uncertain, nay of themselves are nothing, no reckoning ought to be had of them."[4] From which words it is evident that these heretics thus assert that man's justification nowise depends on our works, so that they can make their own justification certain to themselves. For they themselves well understood that if they were to admit that man's justification in some way depends on his works, they could never establish this certitude of the state of grace. And Bucer likewise, in his booklet, *De concordantia certitudinis gratiae*, again says: "Since no one in this world can always exclude all doubt about his salvation and the paternal care for him which God exercises, and this doubt is a fault and a sin, every Christian must certainly strive to his utmost, with trustful consideration of God's promises, and then adjoined prayer for an increase of faith, to strengthen his confidence."[5] From which words it is evident that he teaches that even in the state of sin a believer is certain about his state of grace by faith alone, and that the sin of doubting, which no man can avoid, does not harm man on account of faith alone.

Take note, I beseech you upright reader, and consider in what great confusion Bucer get himself into. How can these two things coexist, that someone having a serious doubt about his state of grace as to whether he has fallen into the state of sin, is certain about his state of grace? For if he is certain about his state of grace, it necessarily follows from this that he does not have a doubt about it which is a sin. Again, if he has the sin of doubting, it follows that he is not certain. Now so that the Lutherans may increase their madness and demonstrate their ignorance more, they wished to go further and said that not every man is certain about his state of grace, but every such man is obliged to believe that he is in the state of grace. And he who does not believe, is not (so they teach) just, nor a believer. For the Lutherans call it "Catholic faith," whereby anyone in particular most surely believes that his sins are remitted by Christ. Philip Melanchthon teaches this most clearly, speaking thus: "The mind extremely frightened by the perception of sins, ought to hold the opinion that his sins are freely forgiven on account of Christ, by His mercy, not on account of the worthiness of his contrition, love or other works. When the mind raises itself up, the remission of its sins and reconciliation are bestowed. For if it had judged that we would not have the remission of sins, not until there was sufficient contrition or love, the soul would be driven to despair. Wherefore so that he may have certain and firm consolation, the matter depends not upon the condition of our

---

ostolic Faith and Doctrine against the Disease-spreading Dogma of Martin Luther") entitled, *Ad librum eximii Magistri Nostri Magistri Ambrosii Catharini, defensoris Silvestri Prieratis acerrimi responsio* (WA 7, 764, l. 37).

[1] *On the Babylonian Captivity of the Church* (WA 6, 529, lns. 12-13).

[2] Domingo de Soto, *De natura et gratia* (Antwerp, Joannes Steelsius, 1550), bk, 2, c. 5, pg. 102. He is rephrasing the sentence following the one just cited literally from Luther's *Babylonian Captivity*: "All other sins—so long as the faith in God's promise made in Baptism returns or remains—all other sins, I say, are immediately blotted out through that same faith, or rather through the truth of God, because He cannot deny Himself."

[3] WA 8, 608, lns. 19-20.

[4] *Metaphrasis et enarratio in epistolam Divi Pauli Apostoli ad Romanos* (Basel, Pietro Perna, 1562), c. 2, pg. 101A.

[5] *De vera ecclesiarum in doctrina*..., pg. 193r.

worthiness, but upon the promised mercy alone on account of Christ."[1] And Johann Spangenberg in his *Margarita theologica*, in the chapter on penitence, firstly says that there are only two parts of penitence, namely contrition and faith, and then asking, "What is the faith part of penitence?," he answers with these words: "It is confidence whereby each one believes that his sins are forgiven freely on account of Christ. This faith ought to hold the opinion that your sins in particular are forgiven."[2] From whose words it is evident that no sinner can, according to his view, be justified, unless he believe that he is justified, because he lacks that faith, which, as he supposes, is part of penitence. And all Lutherans openly assert this view in their *Augsburg Confession*, in the fifth article of which these words are found: "They are condemned ...who wish their consciences to doubt whether they have obtained the remission of sins, and add to this that this doubt is not a sin."[3] If it is a sin to doubt, then just as everyone is bound to avoid sin, so also everyone is bound not to doubt. Philip Melanchthon in his *Defense of the Augsburg Confession* says these words: "The adversaries give men bad advice when they bid them doubt whether they obtain remission of sins."[4] Calvin teaches likewise, and at greater length in his book, *Institutes of the Christian Religion*.[5]

After all these men, among others a Catholic man, Claude Guilliaud of Beaujolais,[6] fell into this error. And lest someone think that I falsely accuse him of this, I will cite his words, which he wrote in his commentaries on the last chapter of II Timothy, in the second conciliation.[7] "Now as to what pertains to the certitude of our salvation," he says, "let us discuss it in a few words. You are certain that whatever God promises you, 'he is able also to perform' (Rom. 4, 21). Hence if you believe in Him, you are certain and not doubtful (since faith excludes doubt and fear) that you are loved by Him: since He promised to those believing in Him to be saved, and called sons of God. Wherefore Paul having conceived the persuasion regarding God's infallible promises, says: 'There is laid up for me a crown of justice, which the Lord the just judge will render to me in that day: and not only to me, but to them also that love his coming' (II Tim. 4, 8)... And so that we may get to the point, certainly no one of himself and by his own nature 'knoweth not whether he be worthy of love, or hatred' (Eccle. 9, 1), but he knows by faith from God's word and promises. Nor is there anyone, if he has knowledge of Christianity and is truly a Christian, who is not certain by faith that he holds his salvation to be sure, infallible, and laid up in God's hands. For everyone who 'hears the voice of the Son of God' (Jn. 5, 25), as it is said in John, 'and believeth in him, has life everlasting' (Jn. 6, 40)."[8]

From which words it is very clearly established the he thinks entirely the same as the Lutherans concerning the certitude of justification, and uses the same argument whereby they prove this certitude of theirs. And it confirms this censure of ours that he teaches about man's justification entirely the same thing and with the same words that the Lutherans teach. For in those same commentaries on Paul, when interpreting the passage, "The just man liveth by faith" (Rom. 1, 17), he says these words: "The sacred writer[9] when teaching about the over-

---

[1] *Loci Communes*, c. 8 (*De gratia et justificatione*) in CR 21, 421.
[2] *Margarita theologica*, pg. 56
[3] CR 26, 354.
[4] CR 27, 447.
[5] "Wherefore, as often as we fall, we must recall the remembrance of our baptism, and thus fortify our minds, so as to feel certain and secure of the remission of sins. For though, when once administered, it seems to have passed, it is not abolished by subsequent sins" (Bk. 4, c. 15, n. 3 (ed. 1559, CR 30, 963)).
[6] Claude Guilliaud (1493-1551) was a canon of the Autun cathedral and doctor of theology of Paris.
[7] The author reconciles apparently conflicting passages of Scripture in certain sections of his commentary called conciliations.
[8] *Collatio in omnes divi Pauli apostoli Epistolas* (Lyon, Sebastian Gryphius, 1543), pg. 331v-332r.
[9] The word "prophet" is used here instead of "sacred writer," but afterwards in the cited text (p. 10v)

throw of the proud, adds: 'the life of the just consists in faith, not in knowledge of the Law': that is, when with confidence of mercy we propose to ourselves that God is propitious to hear us, He wants to deliver us, and we expect salvation, we are justified, and are vivified, knowing with the remission of sins and with the reconciliation the gift of the Holy Ghost is conjoined."[1] From which words it is very clearly established that he thinks that man's justification consists in faith alone, and that faith is confidence in the Divine mercy: all which things are from the particular teaching of the Lutherans. Now I have not said these things so that I may brand this Claude Guilliaud, whom otherwise I reckon to be a Catholic man, as a heretic, but so I may warn readers of that work, lest they be deceived when reading these passages, due to the fact that he is reckoned among Catholics, to suppose that this opinion about the certitude of the state of grace is also Catholic, which he very clearly teaches.

Likewise in every respect, it is necessary to warn about that book which is entitled, *Enchiridion Christianae institutionis*. For in the section on justification when treating about the certitude of justification, it teaches the same opinion and with the same words as the Lutherans, saying the following: "Hence justification is from faith, such that the promise is firm according to grace. But if someone troubles himself about the passages: who knows 'whether he be worthy of love, or hatred' (Eccle. 9, 1); likewise, 'Who hath known the mind of the Lord? Or who hath been his counsellor?' (Rom. 11, 34). It surely will not be necessary hereupon to look back upon our works. For these works will forthwith make us doubt, but it is plainly necessary that faith come to our aid, and to this end it will be necessary here that the truth come to one's mind, namely what lies hidden about us in the Father's heart, the same thing is revealed to us by His Spirt, and His Spirit testifying to our spirit, persuades that we are sons of God, but it persuades by calling and justifying freely by faith."[2] This book contains these and many other similar words.

Hence, I think that this book was not published by that Synod of Cologne,[3] and it itself clearly indicates this. For in a letter at the beginning of that book, Hermann [of Wied], Archbishop of Cologne, in whose name it is published, says that the book was promised by him in that council, and he now presents it. But that Hermann shortly afterwards showed himself to be a heretic, for which reason he was deprived by the Apostolic See of his archbishopric in Cologne. This assertion of these men, as just quoted, contains two manifest heresies in it. The first is that which asserts that every just man is certain of his justification, with the certitude of the Catholic faith. The other heresy is that which asserts that every just man is obliged to certainly and firmly believe that he has obtained grace by God's merit. I wish now to attack these two heresies with all my strength, because I know clearly that they are the parents and the proximate causes of many, nay of all vices. For this false and most pestilential certitude, which the Lutherans preach, calls away their hearers from the performance of all good deeds, and loosens the reins of concupiscence, such that it grazes withersoever. They permit [their hearers] to stray because they reckon that they are justified by faith alone, and by that [faith] they believe that they are certain of their salvation. This certitude of theirs is also injurious to God, and a blasphemy against Him. For nothing can be more injurious to God that to say that He receives into His friendship thieves, assassins, parricides, and any other kind of shameful and most villainous men, moreover dwells above with them, and grants many spiritual gifts to

---

the word "prophet" is defined as "all sacred writers."

[1] *Ibid.*, pg. 7r.

[2] Johannes Cardinal Gropper, *Enchiridion christianae institutionis in concilio prouinciali Coloniensi aeditum* (Lyon, Antonius Vincentius, 1544), pp. 288-289. This book was criticized by St. Robert Bellarmine "which paved the way to its being put on the *Index librorum prohibitorum*, in 1596" (Brian Lugioyo, *Martin Bucer's Doctrine of Justification* (Oxford, Oxford University Press, 2010), pg. 107.

[3] The Synod of Cologne was a provincial council held in 1536.

them as long as there is firm and fixed faith in them. Therefore, it is necessary to fight against these denounced things with full force, so that they may completely perish, or rather depart from the whole world.

But before all else, it is necessary to state what certitude is, and how many kinds of certitude there are, and afterwards to show of which certitude is this assertion, lest we labor in ambiguity, and thus afterwards we may seem to dispute in vain. For when this subject was discussed in the Council of Trent, by learned and Catholic men, who attended in large number, and was very carefully examined, and many as well and long disputations took place about it, I saw some men who because they did not know about what certitude we were arguing, they were deviating far from the main point of this matter, and from the goal of this disputation. Thus it is necessary to firstly establish what is and how many kinds of certitude there are, so that by that by having stated its multiplicity it can be known to all with what certitude a just man can be certain of his justice, and with what certitude he will necessarily always be uncertain, unless a Divine revelation renders him certain. And what we will now say about certitude will also be useful for assailing the other heresy which teaches that man can certainly believe that he is predestined without God's special revelation. We will dispute about that heresy afterwards in the section on "Predestination."

The word certitude in its proper sense denotes firmness of the intellect in the judgment which it makes about something. Doubt or wavering of the mind is opposed to this certitude, because one who is certain in his judgment, rests in such great firmness in it that although he be strongly assailed, he is not ready to depart even a little from it. Now although certitude properly belongs to the intellect, still by a certain likeness it is accustomed to be attributed to the will and to natural virtue. For the will is often doubtful and indifferent to the love or hate of something, and not inclined more to one side or the other: but when it firmly chooses one side, then it is said to be certain, and with what greater firmness it chooses it, the more certain it is said to be. Virgil used this meaning when he said: "It is certain that in the woods, amid wild beasts' dens, it is better to suffer."[1] And again elsewhere: "Aeneas, on the lofty stern, now certain to go, was enjoying sleep, [all] things now duly ready."[2] He is said to be certain, for having decided or determined.

I think that what Paul says to the Romans ought to be understand in this manner: "For I am certain that neither death, nor life, nor angels, nor principalities, nor powers, nor things present, nor things to come, nor might, nor height, nor depth, nor any other creature, shall be able to separate us from the love of God, which is in Christ Jesus our Lord" (Rom. 8, 38-39). When saying that he is certain, he expresses the most firm deliberation of his will in God's love. For he asserts that he loves God with such great fervor and such great firmness that no creature seems capable of tearing him away from God's love. And Ambrose supports this interpretation of ours, who in place of what we have in the Vulgate, "I am certain," he reads, "I am confident."[3] And Jerome, when citing this passage of Paul, put "I am confidant"[4] for "I am certain," but it is evident that trust or confidence pertain to the will and not to the intellect. Chrysostom, however, supports our opinion much more clearly when interpreting the aforesaid words of Paul he says these words: "This Paul says not as if the Angels attempted it, or the other Powers, far from it, but as wishing to show quite to the utmost the charm he had toward Christ. For Christ he loved not for the things of Christ, but for His sake the things that were His, and to Him alone he looked."[5] From all which testimonies it is evident that

---

[1] *Eclogues*, X, n. 53-54.

[2] *Aeneid*, bk. 4, n. 554-555.

[3] *On the Duties of the Clergy*, bk. 3, c. 1, n. 7 (PL 16, 147B).

[4] *Epistola CXXI. ad Algasiam*, c. 9 (PL 22, 1028).

[5] *Homily 15 on Romans* (PG 60, 546).

Paul said that he is certain, not actually because it could not happen otherwise, but because he had so firmly decided that he would do so, taking certitude to mean a determination of his will. For this same reason (as we said concerning the appetitive potency) [this determination of the will] is given the name of certitude by a likeness of nature, because it has a determinate object about which it operates.

In this manner philosophers say that nature always operates with certainty: which ought not to be so understood such that nothing ever happens outside of or against nature, but that nature always operates about something determined, and not about a vague or indifferent object, although in its very operation it may often fail in attaining that which it intends, on account of obstacles which impede it. For this reason, Aristotle says that virtue is more certain than art,[1] because the artisan is not determined by his art to one certain material nor to one mode of operation, but can work in one way or another. Virtue, however, has a determined object to which it is directed, and a determined manner of operation, according to which it acts, although it often fails (as we said concerning nature) in its operation, on account of the malice of him who acts against its inclination. All these things having been stated, perhaps more extensively than was necessary, it is necessary that we establish in the first place that we are presently discussing about that certitude alone which pertains to the intellect, and not about some other certitude which improperly and only by metaphor may be called certitude.

All those who rightly speak about this certitude, however, reckon that it is not just one, but threefold. For there is the certitude of evidence. A second is the certitude of the Catholic faith. Finally, there is a third certitude of human faith, which is otherwise called moral or probable certitude by some men. The certitude of evidence is the firmness of the cognitive faculty in its judgment, caused by the evidence of the same judgment and assent. For because man knows from evidence that something is true it follows that he judges it to be so with firmness and without any doubt. Thus, because this certitude is caused by and depends upon evidence, then it is necessary that that same certitude be as multiple as the evidence itself is multiple from which the certitude arose, and also there are as many degrees in the certitude itself as there are in the evidence which produces that certitude. For there is some evidence of necessary things which cannot happen otherwise. There is also evidence of contingent things. Necessary things are of two kinds, for some of them are first principles very well known to all which are immediately known from the mere knowledge of the subject and the predicate. Among all evidences these obtain the first place, and so also they have the first degree of certitude among them all. There are other necessary things of which the evidence does not depend upon the mere knowledge of their terms, but is produced and caused by other things more evident than they. Such are all the conclusions which are deduced from those first principles because the evidence of these things depends upon the evidence of the antecedent and the evidence of the syllogism [*collectio*] or inference [*consequentia*]. If either of these two is lacking, the conclusion deduced from them could not be evidence, because it is not possible that the effect be more perfect than its cause.

Now the assent whereby someone consents to the conclusion, is in fact the effect caused by the assent to the premises and to the syllogism. And hence it is clearly proved that the conclusion could not be evident, when one of the premises or the syllogism is not evident. Likewise, it ought to be said in general concerning certitude, that the conclusion is not certain when one of the premises by which it is proved or the syllogism is not certain, but doubtful. Evidence

---

[1] "Virtue, like nature, is more certain and better than art." (*Nicomachean Ethics*, bk. 2, c. 6, n. 116b). "The same method is not used in all products made by art; but each workman works with the material in a way suited to that material, in one way with the soil, in another with clay, in still another with metal. Now the matter of moral study is of such a nature that perfect certitude is not suitable to it" (Thomas Aquinas, *Commentary on the Ethics of Aristotle*, bk. 1, lect. 3, n. 1).

can also be had of contingent things, but differently than concerning necessary things, because necessary things are known universally from evidence, and through abstractive knowledge of them. But contingent things are not known except through directly apprehended knowledge, which is had in the presence of some particular thing, and is caused by that thing. Thus future contingent things, because firsthand and direct knowledge cannot be had of them, thus cannot be known from evidence: and hence it follows that certitude of evidence cannot be had of them, because when the evidence which is the cause of this certitude is lacking, it is necessary that the certitude which arises from it also be lacking.

The second certitude is of the Catholic faith, and this is the firmness of the intellect about its object which is everything revealed by God. Everyone who is a true believer has this firmness and certitude about those things which require the faith, otherwise if he doubts and vacillates he by that alone loses the faith. Thus Athanasius, after he expressed a complete account of the faith, immediately added: "This is the Catholic Faith, which except a man believe faithfully and firmly, he cannot be saved."[1] Of this certitude of faith ought to be understood that which Paul said before King Agrippa. According to the most sure sect of our religion he lived a Pharisee.[2] He called the sect of the Pharisees "the most sure [*certissima*] sect" on account of the faith they had concerning the future resurrection of the dead, which the Sadducees denied. Now this faith about the resurrection of the dead is most certain, by no other certitude than by the certitude of the Catholic faith, which teaches the future resurrection of all men.

This certitude has in common with the certitude of evidence that no one who has either of those certitudes can err or be deceived in his judgment. Still there is this difference between the two that the certitude of evidence arises from the manner of proceeding in the object, that is to say, from the knowledge of the terms in the first principles, or if it is a conclusion deduced from those principles, it arises from the demonstration whereby it becomes evident and certain. On the other hand, the certitude of the Catholic faith arises rather from the object itself, which is most certain in itself and cannot deceive.

And by this difference the scholastic theologians can be easily reconciled (as I think) who when comparing the certitude of science with the certitude of the Catholic faith, and enquiring which of them is greater, fight against each other. For some say that science is more certain than faith, while others assert on the contrary that the certitude of faith is greater than the certitude of science. But this controversy is easily removed (as I said), if we wish to have the different considerations of certitude. For there is a certitude in regard to us, which is called by some certitude of the subject: and there is another certitude of the thing in itself, which is called by some certitude of the object. It is necessary that both of these certitudes be in a thing, so that certitude may be truly said to belong to the thing. But we would be able to be sure of many false things if the firmness of the one judging alone were to suffice, because many defend their errors as firmly without any doubt and tenaciously as other truths are firmly embraced. But no one with a sound mind will say that those who think false things are equally certain as those who think true things. Again, if on the contrary only the certitude of the object without the firmness of the one judging would suffice, such that someone may be called truly certain, it would necessarily follow that someone could be certain and doubtful at the same time. For those who doubt the Catholic faith in this way would be said to be certain, because although he doubts the matter, still it is something most certain. Therefore, lest we concede such absurd things, it is necessary that we say that these two things are necessary, so that someone be said to be truly certain, namely the certitude of that thing in itself and firmness of judgment without vacillation of him who judges concerning that matter.

---

[1] "The Athanasian Creed," *The Catholic Encyclopedia* (1909 ed.), vol. 2, pg. 34.
[2] Cf. Acts 26, 5.

And it is necessary that we understand this present disputation with respect to this twofold certitude, because if it be understood in regard to the certitude of the subject alone, we would not fight with the Lutherans about this matter. For (as we said) many men are certain of their errors with this certitude alone. Due to the lack of certitude regarding the object, we say that no one of himself can be certain about some future contingent thing, because it has no certitude in itself but only from elsewhere, for example that something would come to him by decree of the Divine will. If we wish to consider the certitude of someone's assent from the certitude of the thing from which the judgment is obtained, then we will truly say that the certitude of the faith is greater than the certitude of science. For it is much more certain that all things revealed by God (from which things alone is the Catholic faith) are true, than every other created thing. For just as God is the source of all goodness and is alone perfectly good: so He is the source of all truth and is alone perfectly true.

Now we only believe all things which we are obliged to believe from the Catholic faith, from whomsoever they may be said, because they were firstly said by God, or firstly revealed by God Himself, and afterwards by His command were proclaimed by man. Wherefore it is that the word of the Catholic faith preached by man, may not so much be called man's word as God's word, as Paul teaches to the Thessalonians, writing: Now there is nothing as certain as God's word, which is so true that it cannot deceive.[1] Therefore the Catholic faith on the part of its object, which is God's word, is more certain than science. And according to this notion of certitude which is on the part of its object, it is necessary to acknowledge that the knowledge of God which the Blessed have is not more certain than the faith of wayfarers: because the object of both is equally certain, namely God Himself.

But if we consider certitude not by reason of the object, but by reason of the mode of tending to the object, then we say that science is more certain than faith: because science tends by evidence of observation to conclusions, but faith either by pious affection, or by probable reason, or it tends by both at the same time to the things that are to be believed. Now this manner of proving is never as certain as the observation itself. Furthermore, science permits no doubt with it, whereas faith admits some doubt: because unless the doubt is so great that it draws man to the opposite side, it is unable to destroy faith. For what is said in the first chapter concerning heretics, "One who doubts the faith is an infidel,"[2] ought not to be understood of every doubt, but of that only which can turn the soul to the opposite position, such that it fluctuates between both sides and does not rest in either of them. For it can be that someone remaining firm in some opinion, doubts slightly from weakness alone, as happens in a surreptitious doubt which happens in the first movement, and in those who have this by nature, that they are of two minds in any matter, and oppressed by constant scruples of doubts. For these persons even if they doubt, they nevertheless doubt slightly, because they conquer the doubt, remaining firm in the faith. Faith, therefore, because it admits with itself some or light doubt, is less certain from the manner of tending to the object than science which permits absolutely no doubt with it. Again, that habit or act is more certain from the manner of tending to the object, which renders the one having it firmer in the object and less separable from it.

Now it is evident that it is more difficult for a man to depart from what he knows through science, than from that which he understands by faith. For from that which is known by faith, men frequently withdraw, as the experience itself regarding heretics teaches. On the other hand, from what was known through science, if it was truly known, a man never withdraws, because the science itself forces the intellect and in this way holds fast the intellect so that it cannot depart from that judgment even when commanded by the will. And hence it is very

---

[1] Cf. I Thess. 2, 13.

[2] Gregory IX, *Decretales,* bk. 5, tit. 7, chap. 1. The Decretals cite merely "Pope Stephen to all the bishops" without specifying which Pope Stephen wrote these words.

clearly evident that science from its manner of tending to the object is more certain than faith, because science makes the one knowing firmer in his judgment than faith makes the believer.

Finally, there is the third certitude of human faith, which some call moral or probable certitude, and it is the firmness of the cognitive power about its object, caused by an upright affection of the will or a probable reason. This certitude differs from the first two by the fact that falsity cannot be present with either of those two, nor can someone who has something of them err or be deceived by it. Now this moral certitude is often about false things, and those having it often err and are deceived in it. For this certitude does not depend in any way upon the certitude of the object, as we said above concerning the other two certitudes, but it depends only upon the manner of tending to the object, which, because it has no or very light doubt mixed with it, is then said to be certain, although the matter itself with which it is concerned is not certain. Besides these three which we have said, there is no other mode of certitude. For that certitude which some call conjecture, is not properly certitude, because it does not have such firmness that it excludes all doubt and all fear. Hence it is that if something was not certain in one of these three ways, it ought to be reckoned truly uncertain.

All these things having been presupposed, it is necessary that we go on now to assailing the two aforesaid heresies, so that we may prove firstly that no one according to the common law without a special revelation of God can be certain of his being in the state of grace, with as much certitude as he has concerning the articles of the Catholic faith. And firstly, those things cast down and overthrow this heresy which we adduced above in the second heresy of the section of faith against that heresy which teaches that faith alone justifies man. For when that heresy of justification from faith alone is the foundation upon which this heresy of the certitude of grace rests, it is necessary that the former having been overthrown, this one also would fall down with it. For Luther and his followers (as we have recently shown from their words) say that faith alone is sufficient for man's justification, such that in this way men can be certain of their state of grace, because if works were necessary, the Lutherans themselves admit, no one could be certain of his justification.

Yet Blessed Peter teaches us otherwise, who advises us to labor that by good works we may make sure our calling and election.[1] Assuredly the matter itself can be certain in itself, although we ourselves may be doubtful and uncertain about it. Thus, we make certain by good works not only our present justification, but also our future glory, because Christ said: "If thou wilt enter into life, keep the commandments" (Mt. 19, 17). But although these things may be certain in themselves, still they are not certain in regard to us, meaning, we are not certain about them, because we do not know whether our works are good and pleasing to God. Therefore, a very strong argument is taken from the words of Peter the Apostle against the Lutherans. For if without good works there cannot be in oneself a certain vocation and election, then no one who is not certain that he has done good works and no bad works could be certain of his vocation and election: because (as we have said above in the presuppositions to this disputation) a twofold certitude, namely of the subject and the object, is necessary so that someone may be said to be truly certain about something, and we have established that this contention of ours ought to be understood about this twofold certitude. Hence, since no one (as the Lutherans themselves admit) can be certain about his works that they are good, it is proved that no one also can be certain that he is just.

And this argument shackles Philip Melanchthon and the other later Lutherans more strongly and the authors of that *Enchiridion Christianae institutionis*, which has in its title, although falsely, to have been published at the Synod of Cologne. For these men seeing the very clear testimonies of Sacred Scripture, by which it is most evidently proved, that man without good works, or with some bad works, cannot be just, have acknowledged that good works are nec-

---

[1] Cf. II Pet. 1, 10.

essary for man's justification, but they deny that any justification is imputed to good works, although they were done after the justification itself, but they say that the whole justification is to be attributed to faith alone. The words of Philip Melanchthon in the section on good works in his *Loci communes* are these: "Those who do not repent, but indulge their wicked desires, do not keep their faith. For faith seeks the remission of sins; it does not delight in sins. And the Holy Ghost does not remain in those who do not restrain wicked desires, according to that saying of John: 'He that committeth sin is of the devil' (I Jn. 3, 8). These numerous motives of necessity join together, which rightly ought to sharpen in us attentiveness to acting correctly."[1] Johann Spangenberg in his *Margarita theologica* says the same thing in nearly the same words, in question five, where he treats of the first cause of good works.[2] And in the booklet which in the name of the Lutherans was shown to Charles [V], when he was is in Regensburg, in article five these words are found: "Because this renewal is imperfect and enormous weakness remains in them, it should nevertheless be taught that those who truly repent may always hold with the most certain faith that they are pleasing to God on account of Christ the Mediator."[3] And in his elaboration of this article Bucer states that the famous article admonishes only those repenting, and truly repenting and having living faith to be convinced by most firm faith that they have attained to be in the state of grace.[4] And those men from Cologne, whoever they may be, who published that small book connected with the Synod of Cologne, which is called the, *Enchiridion Christianae institutionis*, after they said the words which we have cited above concerning the certitude of the state of grace, when discussing about the things which are needed so that faith can justify, say these words: "This faith also requires many aids, with which not only does it not exist, but also it cannot be understood. For in the first-place repentance is required." And after listing many other works, namely sorrow, groans, tears, and other things of this sort, at the end it says these words: "Even though these things neither merit nor obtain justification, unless faith enters in, still without a doubt that justifying faith requires, nay includes, those things as prerequisites and necessary aids. For when that faith is conjoined with affection and desire for the remission of sin, it cannot delight in sins, whose remission it seeks."[5] These words are very similar to the words of Philip Melanchthon which we cited. From all which words it is evident that in their opinion works are necessary for justification.

But Luther himself, although he often said elsewhere that works are not necessary, nevertheless openly admits their necessity, in his assertion in the twelfth article of the articles condemned by Leo X, saying these words: "If through an impossibility he who confessed was not contrite, or the priest did not absolve seriously, but in a jocose manner, if nevertheless he believes that he has been absolved, he is most truly absolved."[6] And shortly afterwards he adds: "I spoke by an impossible supposition [*per impossibile*], because it was said sufficiently above that faith cannot be without contrition, since grace is not infused except with a great disturbance in the soul."[7] Thus the Lutherans teach that great contrition or (as Bucer

---

[1] CR 21, 432.

[2] Pg. 49.

[3] *Interim of Ratisbon* (CR 4, 200).

[4] "And living faith is what we call the movement of the Holy Ghost, by which those who truly repent of their old life are lifted up to God and truly apprehend the mercy promised in Christ, so that they now truly perceive that they have received the remission of sins and reconciliation on account of the merits of Christ, through the free goodness of God." (*Ibid*. pg. 199).

[5] Pg. 297.

[6] Dz. 752.

[7] *Assertio omnium articulorum per Bullam Leonis X. novissimam damnatorum* (WA vol. 7, p. 120, lns. 27-29).

says) true repentance is necessary for justification, although they say that neither contrition nor repentance do anything towards justification. But I do not wish to dispute about this last point at present, because I will discuss this matter below in the section on "Works" [*Opera*].

But if great contrition and true repentance are necessary for the sinner to obtain the state of grace, it is thence proved that no one according to the common law can be as certain about his own state of grace as he is certain about other articles of the faith: because no one according to the common law can have this great certitude that his repentance is true, or that his contrition is as great as was necessary. Therefore, although justification is attributed to faith alone, still it will never be able to make men certain of their own state of grace if they admit that works are necessary for impetrating justification, or for its conservation: because no one can be sure of the value and worth of those works before God. For someone can have vincible ignorance about the evilness of some work, as often happens to merchants, who suppose that many agreements are licit, which they would clearly understand to be usurious if they chose to consult (as they ought) learned and good men.

Furthermore, so that we may refute the Lutherans more, let us grant them, although we do not concede, that good works are not in any way necessary for justification, yet it is necessary to abstain from sin, so that one may obtain the grace of justification, because Luther himself teaches that "the best repentance is a new life."[1] Now man cannot be certain that he abstains from sin, therefore he cannot be certain about his justification. What was assumed is clearly proved because, as is very clearly evident, a man can be culpably unaware that he has omitted something, which he was bound to do under threat of Hell, and can also do something which he is unaware is a sin. Now whether some such thing happens to oneself, no one can be certain of himself. Hence it follows that it is proved that no one without a special revelation of God can be certain of his own justification. For due to this reason the [Royal] Prophet said: "Who can understand sins? from my secret ones cleanse me, O Lord" (Ps. 18, 13). He calls those sins which a man does not know "secret ones," and hence he asks to be cleansed from them, because of those which he does not know to be sins, he cannot repent. For the same reason Paul said: "I am not conscious to myself of anything, yet am I not hereby justified" (I Cor. 4, 4).

He said this because he knew very well that some sins could be in him which were completely hidden from him, and hence he reckoned that it is not enough to be not conscious to himself of anything so that by this fact he would believe that he was just. Wherefore [Hervé de Bourg-Dieu[2]] when interpreting the aforesaid words of Paul says: "He was truly not conscious of any sin. But because he had read, 'Who can understand sins?', he tempered his opinion, lest perhaps he sin through ignorance, and so added: 'yet am I not hereby justified.' For seeing that his own judgment would also not suffice for his perfection of holiness, he says, 'I am not hereby justified.' But why he did believe not himself about himself, he gives the reason when he added, 'but he that judgeth me, is the Lord.' And it is as though he were to say clearly: 'And I do not believe about myself by thinking by my own judgment, because He judges me, Whose judgment I do not comprehend. For I know that I am accurately examined by Him Who judges me.' That is to say, I recall to mind that I have done rightly, but I do not presume of my merits, because our life is brought to His examination, under which our virtues also tremble."[3] [Hervé de Bourg-Dieu] gives testimony clearly enough from Paul's opinion against the certitude of the state of grace.

[Ambrosiaster] supports the same position in his commentaries on Paul, where, when interpreting the aforesaid words of Paul, says: "It is clear that he, having a pure conscience, was

---

[1] *Exsurge Domine*, condemned proposition. n. 7 (Dz. 747)
[2] This commentary is here erroneously ascribed to St. Anselm.
[3] *Commentaria in epistolas Pauli* (PL 181, 850B-C).

not concerned about himself. 'Yet am I not hereby justified.' He now humbles himself, and the man speaks who could incur guilt unaware."[1] From whose words it is established to be true what we assumed at the beginning of this argument, namely that man can have culpable ignorance of his own sin, which having been granted he will easily be deceived if due to the fact that he is unaware of his sin, he deems himself justified.

Perhaps Luther foreknew this argument, and hence in order to escape its power and strength, said (as is very clearly established from his words which we cited at the beginning) that no sin no matter how serious can impede man's justification, if he has fixed and firm faith, but he says that all those sins are covered and abolished by faith alone. Notice how his temerity in defining advances. For whenever someone defends what has been temerariously uttered at one time by himself, he is not ashamed to give himself headlong to whatsoever most absurd and pestilential errors. For Luther, seeing that the necessity of good works cannot be reconciled with the certitude of grace, excludes the necessity of good works. Also understanding that the certitude of grace cannot stand if one must necessarily abstain from sins, he said that it was not necessary, but faith alone suffices for justification, so that anyone can make certain his own justification. But neither by this does he establish this certitude nor could he escape the force of our argument. Because he and his followers teach otherwise, (as we have shown in the third heresy in the section on "Faith") faith is lost by any mortal sin, from which assertion it is very clearly exposed to be false what they afterwards assert, that faith covers all mortal sins, and abolishes them all, and that there is no mortal sin except unbelief alone.

[Quintilian] certainly very well said that every liar needs a good memory.[2] For these two things are diametrically opposed to each other: "Faith is lost by any mortal sin" and "faith covers all mortal sins except unbelief." If faith is lost by any mortal sin, then it cannot cover and abolish it. And again, if faith covers all mortal sins, then it is not lost by any of them. Behold now in these Lutherans we experience it to be true what the prophet Jeremias said about other similar men: "They have taught their tongue to speak lies: they have laboured to commit iniquity" (9, 5). For it is necessary that a liar labor much so that they may not be caught in their lie.

But putting these things aside, let us proceed to another argument. If every just man is certain about his state of grace which he now has, then every just man is also certain that he will have eternal glory. This conclusion is clear according to Luther's teaching: because (as we showed in the preceding heresy) he asserts with Jovinian and Pelagius, that he who has been justified cannot become unjust anymore. If he who has acquired grace at one time cannot lose it anymore, then it is certain that every such man is going to have eternal glory, because Christ promised He would give it to all just men dying in the state of grace. "The just shall go into life everlasting" (Mt. 25, 46). If perhaps Luther, which is his temerity, would dare admit all these things, I will not dispute against him to overcome such a temerarious assertion, because I have decided to fight specifically against it in the section on "Predestination."

Again, the Lutherans defend this certitude of justification only because they suppose that justification depends solely upon that faith, whereby they believe that their sins are forgiven through Christ. But they cannot be sure that this faith alone is enough, nay is necessary, for justification unless they are completely blind to the fact that it is uncertain for them. Because they themselves admit that not any faith justifies, but only that faith which is true and perfect. But faith is not perfect, if by it someone does not believe all the articles of faith, and so it follows that although someone may think that his sins are forgiven unto him through Christ, yet if he errs in another article of faith he does not have perfect faith, and consequently cannot

---

[1] *Commentaria in Epistolam ad Corinthios Primam*, c. 4 (PL 17, 203A).

[2] "*Mendacem memorem esse oportet.*" (*Institutio oratoria*, bk. 4, c. 2, l. 91). Aristotle is incorrectly cited here as the author of this quotation.

be justified by it alone. For Athanasius clearly teaches that this alone is not perfect faith, nor suffices for justification, who after stating one by one everything that is necessary to believe concerning Christ's Divinity and humanity, immediately adds these words: "This is the Catholic Faith, which except a man believe faithfully, he cannot be saved."[1]

Although the Lutherans also are sure that they have faith whereby they suppose that their sins are freely forgiven through Christ, this is not enough so that they can immediately be certain of their own justification: because it would also be necessary that they be sure that such faith suffices for justification. But they cannot be sure that they have this certitude that faith alone suffices. If, however, they say that they are sure about this assertion, they ought to show very clear testimonies of Sacred Scripture, of such a sort as they are accustomed to demand of us in other occasions, whereby they may prove that assertion. Or if they lack testimonies of Scripture, they ought to at least show testimonies of the holy Fathers, who were always highly esteemed by the universal Church, in favor of that matter. And because they cannot cite any such testimony, it is thence proved that they cannot be sure of that assertion, since it is a figment of their own imagination not confirmed by any certain testimonies. For there were some men before Luther, as for example Eunomius and his heretical followers, who said that faith alone is enough for a man to be saved, but no one before Luther said that man is justified by that faith alone, whereby he believes his sins are freely forgiven through Christ.

Next, this assertion of general certitude of the state of grace is refuted by the fact that as a great and special favor it is related concerning some persons in particular that the remission of all their sins was told to them. For Christ said concerning Mary Magdalene in her presence: "Many sins are forgiven her, because she hath loved much" (Lk. 7, 47). And He said to a certain sick of the palsy lying in a bed: "Be of good heart, son, thy sins are forgiven thee" (Mt. 9, 2). And to another paralytic He said: "Behold thou art made whole: sin no more, lest some worse thing happen to thee" (Jn. 5, 14). And to Zacheus He said: "This day is salvation come to this house, because he also is a son of Abraham" (Lk. 19, 9). And to a woman who was troubled with an issue of blood twelve years, came behind him, and touched the hem of his garment, Christ said to her: "Be of good heart, daughter, thy faith hath made thee whole" (Mt. 9, 22). And concerning Blessed Francis, the father of all the other Friars Minor, Blessed Bonaventure relates in the history of his life as a great favor granted to him by God, that God revealed to him that all his sins to the least were forgiven him by God.[2] But if this remission of sins was certain to every believer from the faith, it was not necessary that God make these particular revelations, because without them all those men were certain from the faith, according to the opinion of the Lutherans, that their sins were forgiven them. Thus the Lutherans make no small injury to God by their assertion of the universal certitude of the state of grace, because they are forced to own that God makes superfluous and completely worthless revelations, and yet Aristotle says that "God and nature do nothing in vain."[3]

Additionally, it was not expedient that this certitude of grace be given to all the just due to the many evils which could arise from it. For this certitude of one's own justice would give no small occasion to self-exaltation, as Blessed Gregory teaches when interpreting the passage of Job, "Although I should be simple, even this my soul shall be ignorant of" (9, 21), where he says these words: "Most commonly if we know the good things that we do, we are led to entertain pride; if we are ignorant of them, we cannot keep them. For who would not, in however slight degree, be rendered proud by the consciousness of his virtue? Or who, again,

---

[1] Dz. 40.

[2] "Now on a day, while in a certain lonely place he was bewailing the remembrance of past years, the joy of the Holy Spirit came upon him, and he was assured of the remission of all his offenses." (Saint Bonaventure, *The Life of Saint Francis* (London, J.M. Dent, 1904), c. 3, n. 6, pp. 26-27.

[3] *De caelo* (Oxford, Clarendon Press, 1922), bk. 1, c. 4, pg. 271, -ll. 34-35.

would keep safe within him that good, of which he does not know? What then remains as a provision against either of these evils, saving that all the good things that we do, in knowing we should not know; so that we both look upon them as right things, and as a mere nothing, that thus the knowledge of their rightness may quicken the soul to a good guard, and the estimation of their littleness may never exalt it in pride."[1] Gregory here teaches clearly enough that there is hardly anyone who if he were aware of his justice would not take pride in it. Now what he said, "All the good things that we do, in knowing we should not know," is as if he were to have said, "We believe those things to be good, yet with fear and doubt, such that we neither know for sure that they are good, nor are we totally ignorant of the same."

And from this consideration of one's own justice the Pharisee praying in the Temple took occasion of despising the Publican praying in the same Temple. And perhaps (so I may say something more important) from the same root arose that horrendous pride of Lucifer, whereby he wanted to put his seat in the highest places, and be equal to God in all things.[2] For he, (just as the poets fable about Narcissus[3]) perceiving his own extraordinary beauty in which God created him, infusing grace into him, to the extent the he was desperately in love with himself, such that, elated with pride, he thence fell, and strove to be equal to God. This certitude of one's own justification would also be an occasion of sloth, sluggishness, and idleness, especially in an imperfect man, which (as the Wise Man says) is apt to teach much evil.[4] For all the sacred Doctors unanimously teach that God made the hour of death uncertain to us, lest men take occasion therefrom of living disgracefully and wickedly until that time, with hope of doing penance at the time of death. Likewise, if men would be sure of their justification it would certainly happen that thinking themselves to be already just, they would no longer care about acquiring justice, and hence they would easily come to lose the justice acquired at one time.

But I now deem it necessary that having finished the arguments which proceed rather from natural reason, we now go on to the testimonies of Sacred Scripture, so that with them we may fight against the Lutherans, lest they, as they are accustomed to do, call us sophists. For as often as Catholics fight against their heretical assertions with such effective and evidential arguments, such that they can answer nothing face to face with the truth, they immediate cry out that it is a sophism, and they call us all sophists for that reason, when actually they themselves are nothing other than real sophists. Therefore lest they take occasion in this most serious matter of crying out the same thing against us, I judge it worthwhile for me to stop using arguments proceeding from human reason alone, although the faith was presupposed, and fight against them with most clear testimonies of Sacred Scripture, upon which they rely too much.

But before I do this, it is necessary to point out to the reader that in the Council of Trent, where this matter was carefully examined for a long time, there were some Catholic men, although few and not very learned, who were maintaining that certitude of justification, without God's special revelation, is possible. But they differed much from the Lutherans in the defense of this assertion, because they were denying that every believer is obliged to rely upon their sins having been freely forgiven on account of Christ. They were also denying that every just man is certain of his justification. They were merely teaching that through the Sacrament of Baptism or Penance, without any special revelation of God, a man can be certain with the certitude of the Catholic faith that he is in the state of grace. And one of them said, and afterwards publicly asserted by a book published on this subject, that not only those who

---

[1] *Morals on the Book of Job*, bk. 9, c. 25, n. 37 (PL 75, 878C-D).
[2] Cf. Is. 14, 12 ff.
[3] In Greek mythology, Narcissus was a hunter from Thespiae in Boeotia who was known for his beauty.
[4] Cf. Eccli. 33, 29.

receive the Sacrament of Baptism or Penance are by that fact certain, but also those who long after having received the Sacraments burn with the fervor of ardent charity, then have the certitude of the Catholic faith about God's grace being in them. And because some testimonies of Sacred Scripture, among those which I will cite shortly, fight in the same way against these men as against the Lutherans, I decided to state the assertion of these men at the beginning, so that when I cite one of those testimonies, I will then show that they fight against them all together at the same time.

When I first published this work of mine, *Against All Heresies*, among the few testimonies which I then brought forth against this heresy, the first was that of Solomon in Ecclesiastes, because it then seemed to me very clear on this matter: "Yet man knoweth not whether he be worthy of love, or hatred, but all things are kept uncertain for the time to come" (Eccle. 9, 1-2). Afterwards, when considering these words more carefully I clearly understood (as I openly admit) that they give doubtful evidence for supporting us in this dispute. For many learned and holy men, such as Bernard,[1] Gerson,[2] and Denis the Carthusian,[3] interpret those words of Solomon not regarding God's love or hatred according to present justice, but according to final perseverance. Which meaning seems to be derived from those words which Solomon immediately added, saying the following: "But all things are kept uncertain for the time to come."

For otherwise, if those words were to be understood of the present life, it would be false (as is very clearly evident) that no one knows whether he is worthy of hatred. Because even if no one can know that he is loved by God, many nevertheless, namely thieves, adulterers, murderers, and all others involved with similar crimes, know that they are at that time hated by God, because they know, unless they become completely insane, that God hates the wicked. Hence, they think that Solomon is speaking about that love alone and of that hatred whereby God so loves some that he chooses them for eternal glory, and hates others such that he ordains them unto eternal punishment. And concerning this love and this hatred (as Paul interprets[4]) is understood that which God says through the prophet Malachias: "I have loved Jacob, but have hated Esau" (Mal. 1, 2-3). Therefore the opinion of Solomon, according to their interpretation, is that no one can know of himself whether he has been chosen by God or not, but all these things are kept uncertain unto the future, until the Judgment Day, in which He "will bring to light the hidden things of darkness, and will make manifest the counsels of the hearts" (I Cor. 4, 5).

No one can know anything about these things from the consideration of external things, either favorable or adverse, because all these things can happen to a just man in the same way as to a sinner. And so, Solomon after the aforesaid words concerning the ignorance of love

---

[1] "For 'No man knoweth not whether he be worthy of love, or hatred, but all things are kept uncertain for the time to come' (Eccle. 9, 1). Therefore, let the renown of these saints be in the heart of God, for 'The Lord knoweth who are his' (II Tim. 2, 19), and He Himself knows whom He has chosen from the beginning" (*Sermo 5: In festo omnium sanctorum* (PL 183, 476C)).

[2] "Furthermore, what sort of consolation can there be for one who has constantly before his eyes the lake of burning fire and sulfur? In the sight of it he must be in dread lest at any moment he fall into it. Nor is he ever free from this fear while he lives, for no human being knows his end, viz. 'not whether he be worthy of love, or hatred' (Eccle. 9, 1)." (*The consolation of theology*) *De consolatione theologiae* (New York, Abaris Books, 1998), p. 61).

[3] "Notwithstanding, many know for certain, or could know for certain, that they are in the state of mortal sin, and due to this are hateful to God according to the present justice; but what will finally happen to them, they do not know" (*Enarratio in librum Ecclesiastae*, art. 9, n. 1 in *Omnia opera* (Montreuil, Cartusiae S.M. de Pratis, 1896), vol. 7, p. 264.

[4] Cf. Rom. 9.

and hatred, under which he said that we all labor, he immediately added: "All things equally happen to the just and to the wicked" (Eccle. 9, 2). Olympiodorus [the Deacon of Alexandria][1] interprets according to this meaning in his commentaries on Ecclesiastes.[2] Therefore having rejected that testimony, because it is doubtful, and there is not unanimity among all about its meaning, it is necessary the we take testimonies from elsewhere, and thankfully many such testimonies present themselves to us.

The well-known very holy Job, "a simple and upright man, and fearing God" (Job. 1, 8), offers so many and such manifest testimonies for the incertitude of grace that I do not know which ones I will cite first. "If he come to me," he says, "I shall not see him: if he depart I shall not understand" (9, 11). Which words, as is very clearly evident, cannot be understood of local motion, for since there is no place where God is not present, it is proved that he cannot come to any place, nor leave any place. Thus those words ought to be understood of God's coming to man's soul through the infusion of grace, concerning which coming Our Savior spoke when He said: "If any one love me, he will keep my word, and my Father will love him, and we will come to him, and will make our abode with him" (Jn. 14, 23). Hence Job when speaking of this coming says: "If he come to me, I shall not see him: if he depart I shall not understand." By which words Job acknowledges that he does not know when God has infused his grace into him, or if when it has been given at one time, He has removed it afterwards on account of a sin committed by him. Blessed Gregory supports this interpretation of ours, who when interpreting the aforesaid words in his *Morals on the Book of Job*, says these words: "Therefore the coming and going of God are not at all discoverable by our faculties, so long as the issue of alternating states is hidden from our eyes; in that there is no certainty concerning the trial, whether it be a test of virtue or an instrument of our destruction; and concerning gifts we never find out whether they are the reward here of such as are given up, or whether they are a support on the road to bring men to their native country."[3] If Job, a most holy man, to whom, God giving testimony in his favor, there was no one similar upon earth at that time, asserts that he does not know the grace conferred upon him by God, for this reason all Lutherans as well ought to be afraid to boast that they are certain about God's grace dwelling in them.

Now that Job says that he does not understand God's departure, meaning, His withdrawal of Divine grace, ought not to be attributed to all sinners, such that they are unaware that they lack Divine grace, but rather these words ought to be referred to Job himself alone and others like him, who although they have performed many good deeds, still they do not know whether some sin hides in them, on account of which God deservedly withdrew from them. Job goes further to show this incertitude of his state of grace and says: "If I should have any just thing, would not answer, but would make supplication to my judge" (v. 15). See, I beseech you, the modesty of this holy man, who although he was actually just, did not dare to say that he has anything just, but spoke conditionally, speaking thus: "If I should have any just thing, would not answer, but would make supplication to my judge." And so that he might more openly declare his incertitude, he immediately adds: "And if he should hear me when I call, I should not believe that he had heard my voice" (v. 16). What could he say more clearly to show the incertitude of his justification?

But not content with this, he adds yet more shortly afterwards: "If I would justify myself, my own mouth shall condemn me: if I would shew myself innocent, he shall prove me wick-

---

[1] Olympiodorus, a Greek monk said also to have been a deacon of a church in Alexandria, is believed to have lived in the first part of the 6th century A.D.

[2] *Commentarius in Ecclesiastes* (PG 93, 586A-B).

[3] Bk. 9, c. 13, n. 20 (PL 75, 870D).

ed. Although I should be simple, even this my soul shall be ignorant of" (v. 20-21). Blessed Gregory when interpreting these words says:

But there are some things which are not easy to be ascertained by us, even when they are done by us. For often we are inflamed with a right earnestness against the sins of transgressors, and when we are transported by passion beyond the bounds of justice, we account this zeal for just severity. We often take upon ourselves the office of preaching, that we may in this way minister to the service of our brethren; but unless we be acceptable to the person, whom we address, nothing that we preach is received with welcome. And when the mind aims to please on useful grounds, it lets itself out after the love of its own praise in a shameful way, and the soul which was busied in rescuing others from captivity to bad habits, being itself made captive, begins to be enslaved to its own popularity. For the appetite for the applause of our fellow creatures is like a kind of robber, who, as people are going along the straight road, joins them from the side, that the wayfarer's life may be barbarously taken by the dagger secretly drawn. And when the intention of purposed usefulness is drawn off to our own interests, in a way to make one shudder, sin accomplishes that identical work, which goodness began...

Often while we sift ourselves more than is meet, by our very aim at discernment we are the more undiscerningly led wrong, and the eye of our mind is dimmed, in proportion as it strives to perceive more; for he too, who determinately looks at the sun's rays, turns dark-sighted, and is necessitated to see nothing from the very thing in which he strives to see too much. Therefore whereas, if we are negligent in our examination, we know nothing at all of ourselves, or, if we search ourselves with an exact scrutiny, we are very often dim-sighted to distinguish between virtue and vice, it is rightly said here: "Although I should be simple, even this my soul shall be ignorant of."[1]

And shortly afterwards when expounding the passage of the same Job, "And I shall be weary of my life" (v. 21), he says the following: "The just man is weary to live, in that both by doing works he does not cease to seek after life, and yet cannot discover the merits of that same life."[2] But Job, in order to confirm his testimonies, wishes to now give the reason for his opinion which he had expressed concerning the incertitude of his own justification, showing that no one is certain of the goodness of his works, and says: "I feared all my works, knowing that thou didst not spare the offender" (v. 28). Blessed Gregory, after he enumerated the splendid and numerous works of Job, when interpreting which words, says these words: "How then is it, that while doing works to be admired, he even fears for these same, being in alarm, when he says, 'I feared all my works,' save that we gather from the deeds and the words of the holy man, that if we really desire to please God, after we overcome our bad habits, we must fear the very things themselves that are done well in us?... Therefore, because our very good actions themselves cannot escape the sword of ambushed sin, unless they be guarded every day by anxious fear, it is rightly said in this place by the holy man, 'I feared all my works.' As if he said with humble confession, 'What I have done publicly, I know, but what I may have been secretly subject to therein, I cannot tell.' For often some good works of ours are spoilt by deceit robbing us, in that earthly desires unite themselves to our right actions; oftentimes they come to naught from sloth intervening, in that, love waxing cold, they are starved of the fervor with which they began. And so because the stealth of sin is scarcely got the better of even in the very act of virtue, what safeguard remains for our security, but that even in our virtue, we ever tread with fear and caution?"[3] Such great firmness was in Blessed Job about the uncertainty of his good works, which are necessary for justification, that not content with his previous words he wished to go further speaking thus: "If I be washed as it were with snow

---

[1] *Morals on the Book of Job*, bk. 9, c. 25, n. 37-39 (PL 75, 878D-880A).

[2] *Ibid.*, n. 39 (PL 75, 880B).

[3] *Ibid.*, n. 52-53 (PL 75, 888C-889B).

waters, and my hands shall shine ever so clean: yet thou shalt plunge me in filth" (v. 30-31), meaning, as Blessed Gregory interprets: You will declare me filthy and you will clearly show me to be filthy.[1] Hence Job said this because he knew that no matter how much his works were examined and he wished to cleanse his conscience, hidden sins could still be in them which were hidden from him, due to which his justification was deservedly impeded.

And in another place Job again says: "Whether his children come to honor or dishonor, he shall not understand" (14, 21). In the interpretation of which words Gregory says these words: "With no unfitness by the word 'children' are works denoted, as Paul saith of woman, 'Yet she shall be saved through childbearing' (I Tim. 2, 15). For it is not that a woman, who being devoted to continency and never bearing children, shall not be saved, but she is said to be 'saved through childbearing,' because by the performance of good works she is united to everlasting salvation. Thus the children in honor are good deeds, and the children in dishonor are bad deeds. And often man strives to do things with a good intention, yet by reason of the many occasions that creep upon him, how his actions are accounted of in the sight of Almighty God is a thing uncertain. And so 'Whether his children come to honor or dishonor, he shall not understand,' in that his works being sifted with a searching scrutiny, whether they be approved or condemned he cannot tell."[2] I have cited Gregory at such great length because the asserters of certitude try to claim him as being in their favor of them. Hence so that it may be evident to all that they falsely boast that Gregory gave his opinion in their favor, I wished to cite so many testimonies from Gregory whereby our opinion about the incertitude of the state of grace may be most clearly confirmed.

All these which we have brought forth from Blessed Job, not only militate against the Lutherans, but also against the Catholics whom we have said above favor in one way or another the certitude of the state of grace. For if the renowned very holy Job, to whom there was no similar man on earth, did not know God's coming into his soul, or departure from it: if he was unaware of his own innocence, who will be so perfect that he, outside of every revelation of God, could glory that he knows with certainty God's coming into his soul, and that He abides in it? If Job feared his own good works, who will be so perfect that he may know his own works are perfectly good and pleasing to God? If someone is sure about his state of grace, there is no reason why he would be afraid of his works. For he who is in God's grace, and knows this with certitude, necessarily also knows with certitude, without any doubt, that he has some good works that are also pleasing to God, especially when he exercises himself in some works of God's Commandments.

I know that there are some men who will respond in general to all these testimonies from the book of Job, that Job said all those things not because they were true, but on account of his humility, so that he might completely remove vainglory from himself. But certainly it can be rightly said of this response that saying of the poet: "He falls into Scylla in endeavoring to escape Charybdis."[3] For that response includes another assertion no less pestilential than that of the [certitude[4]] of the state of grace, for defending which they wish to fall into this. For they say in this response of theirs that it is licit for a man for the sake of humility to lie, which is manifestly erroneous, as we will prove below, with God as our guide, in the section on "Lies," because evil things ought not to be done so that good things may consequently happen.

---

[1] "For God 'to plunge us in filth' means His shewing us to be stained with filth." (*Ibid.*, n. 57 (PL 75, 891B)).

[2] Bk. 12, c. 21, n. 26 (PL 75, 999C-D).

[3] "*Incidit in Scyllam, cupiens vitare Charybdim*" (Philip Gualtier de Châtillon (ca. 1135-1201) was a poet from Lille, France and wrote this celebrated verse in his poem, *Alexandriad*, bk. 5, v. 301).

[4] The text mistakenly has here "incertitude."

Again, I wish to confirm this our and the Catholic assertion of the incertitude of the state of grace with the testimonies of the prophet David, and the first one is that whereby when admonishing kings he says: "Serve ye the Lord with fear: and rejoice unto him with trembling" (Ps. 2, 11). Now so that this testimony of the prophet may be understood more clearly, let us hear Cassiodorus interpreting the aforesaid words, who says these words: "A short but full warning, through which we serve the Lord God with amiable fear, for just as careless complacency incurs faults, so desireable fear always keeps sins at bay. Then, so that God's service might not be thought exceedingly hard or grim, the prophet added: 'And rejoice unto him with trembling,' for fear of the Lord leads not to misery but to joy, for it creates blessed men and produces saints. But on the other hand, to ensure that this rejoicing does not become negligent, the prophet added 'with trembling.' Thus both emotions combined could suitably express celestial reverence."[1] There is another testimony of the same prophet in another Psalm, where he says these words: "Who can understand sins?" (Ps. 18, 13). Which manner of speaking by way of a question suggests that there is no one or but a few who can understand all his sins. For the fact that man can understand some sins, he himself taught elsewhere, speaking thus: "For I know my iniquity, and my sin is always before me" (Ps. 50, 5). And again elsewhere: "I have acknowledged my sin to thee" (Ps. 31, 5). Therefore, man can know some sins, but not all, because there are many which we often commit unaware, or commit by omission; there are also others which after they have been committed, remain unknown to us. From which words it is proved that no one can be certain about his own justification.

Nor is the response of certain men valid saying that the prophet in that place spoke not about mortal sins, but only of venial sins. For the prophet spoke indiscriminately about sins in general, without any distinction. Therefore, it is unreasonable that what the prophet said unrestrictedly, someone would want to restrict to venial sins only, because where the law does not distinguish, neither ought we to distinguish, especially because it is clearly evident from the text itself that those words ought rather to be understood of mortal sins rather than of venial sins, because after those words he immediately added: "From my secret ones cleanse me, O Lord" (Ps. 18, 13). Hence, he speaks of the former sins, which make man unclean and dirty. Moreover, mortal sins render man much more unclean and dirty, and therefore they also are sins which many men often do not perceive. And those words of the prophet certainly ought to be interpreted of mortal sins of this kind. For both [Hervé de Bourg-Dieu][2] and Bernard[3] interpret [the passage] of those sins which can impede man's justification.

Furthermore, what the Lord says through Jeremias the prophet very clearly proves this position of ours concerning the incertitude of justification: "The heart is perverse above all things, and unsearchable, who can know it? I am the Lord who search the heart and prove the reins" (17, 9-10). If man cannot search out his heart, then he cannot know with certitude that he is in the state of grace: because many things could be hidden in our heart, which suffice for impeding grace. This quotation not only opposes the Lutherans, but also the Catholics who defend the certitude of the state of grace. But so that it may be known to all, how much efficacy this quotation has against all those men, one ought to hear Blessed Bernard who argues from those words of Jeremias that the just are uncertain of their justice. For he says the following: "The heart is perverse above all things, and unsearchable, such that no one may know 'the things of a man, but the spirit of a man that is in him' (I Cor. 2, 11), and not even he himself entirely. For when the Apostle says: 'To me it is a very small thing to be judged by you, or by man's day,' he adds, 'but neither do I judge my own self' (I Cor. 4, 3). Why?

---

[1] *Explanation of the Psalms* (PL 70, 41C).
[2] *Commentaria in epistolas Pauli, In Epistolam I ad Corinthios*, c. 4 (PL 181, 850B-C).
[3] *De moribus et officio episcoporum*, c. 6, n. 24 (PL 182, 824D). The text cites this treatise as "Letter forty-two, which is to the Archbishop of Sens."

It is because even I myself am not able, he says, to pronounce a judged sentence on myself. 'For I am not conscious to myself of any thing, yet am I not hereby justified' (v. 4). I do not entirely believe my own conscience: of course, since it is unable in fact to comprehend me wholly. Nor can it judge of the whole as it does not hear the whole. 'But he that judgeth me, is the Lord' (*ibid.*) The Lord, he says, Whose knowledge he assuredly does not escape, does not avoid judgment even upon what is hidden from his own judgment. God hears in the heart of the one thinking, which he himself who thinks does not hear... Notwithstanding, 'Who can understand sins?' (Ps. 18, 13). For if I could say with Paul which it is certainly far from me, 'I am not conscious to myself of anything' (I Cor. 4, 4), it would still be unbefitting for me to boast that I am justified. 'For not he who commendeth himself, is approved, but he, whom God commendeth' (II Cor. 10, 18). If man's day would applaud me, I deem it a very small thing, because He shines so much upon my face. 'for man seeth those things that appear, but the Lord beholdeth the heart' (I Kings 16, 7). Wherefore Jeremias not content with popular opinions, as though he were moved by some rays of man's day, but confidently spoke to God: 'I have not desired the day of man' (17, 16). Thou knowest, if my day has smiled upon me, 'neither do I judge,' he says, 'my own self,' because neither do I myself know myself enough. Rightly only He 'was appointed by God, to be judge of the living and of the dead' (Acts 10, 42). I pay attention to the Judge alone, Whom I know also judges alone. The Father 'hath given him power to do judgment, because he is the Son of man' (Jn. 5, 27). I, a servant, do not usurp unto myself, or upon myself, the power of the Son: nor do I number myself among those of whom He is wont to complain thus: 'Men took judgment away from me.[1] ...Willy, nilly, I shall have to stand before Him and give Him an account of my actions in the flesh, to Him Whom no word eludes nor thought escapes.' In the presence of so exact a surveyor of merits, so profound a prober of secrets, who would boast of being chaste of heart? Surely, what will find grace in the eyes of loving-kindness is only that virtue which does not make a habit of boasting, has not learned how to quarrel, is not used to disputing: and that is humility. 'God resisteth the proud, and giveth grace to the humble' (James 4, 6). A genuinely humble person does not argue with the judge or justify himself, but pleads: 'Enter not into judgment with thy servant' (Ps. 142, 2). He declines judgment and asks for mercy, more confident of obtaining grace than of establishing his own justice."[2]

And in his third sermon of Advent, after he had said that those who care for souls incur danger, he says the following: "One truly approaches to the height of care, and burden of fear, since it is necessary to guard my and my neighbor's conscience, neither of which is known to me. Both are an inscrutable abyss. Both are night to me, and nonetheless the guardianship of both is required of me. 'Watchman, what of the night? watchman, what of the night?' (Is. 21, 11)."[3] Bernard could say nothing clearer in favor of the incertitude of justification. And I wished to cite him as such great length so that I might prove with his own words, that those who attempt pull Bernard to the opposite opinion labor in vain, saying that he gave his opinion in favor of the certitude of the state of grace. For one ought not to think that such a learned and holy man said things opposed to himself. For in these words which we have just now cited from him, he very clearly teaches the incertitude of the state of grace.

On the other hand, what some men cite from Bernard in favor of the certitude of the state of grace, is wrongly understood by them, because he does nothing to support this contention. For in his sermon on the four types of prayer,[4] upon which the authors of the *Enchiridion Chris-*

---

[1] Cf. Jn. 5, 22: "For neither doth the Father judge any man, but hath given all judgment to the Son."
[2] *De moribus et officio episcoporum*, c. 6, 22-24 (PL 182, 823C-823D; 824D-825B; 825B-825C).
[3] *De adventu Domini*, serm. 3, n. 6 (PL 183, 46C-D).
[4] *Sermo 25. De verbis Apostoli, Volo primum fieri obsecrationes,...* (PL 183, 605A ff.).

tianae institutionis chiefly rely,[1] Bernard does speak not about the certitude of faith, under which something false cannot come, but about the certitude of human faith, which excludes doubt, and under it something false can come. And from the words which he says there it is very clearly evident that this is Bernard's opinion in that citation. Because those proofs from which he wants to prove that certitude, are only some conjectures which human faith produces, and can deceive, and are not necessarily inferred from the Catholic faith. And he explains well enough that he is speaking about certitude of confidence, which one can have in one's petitions, who has the indications which he lists.

Our adversaries cite another testimony of Bernard from sermon seventy-four on the Canticle of Canticles, but neither is that sermon about the point at hand, because there Bernard does not speak about the coming of God through the infusion of grace, but of His coming to the soul previously justified, when He comes through the bestowal of spiritual sweetness and of other spiritual consolations. For otherwise if he had spoken about God's coming into the soul through the infusion of the first grace, it would follow that the renown Bernard said there that he was certain that he had often sinned mortally: because he says that he certainly knew that God had withdrawn from him and he also says this same thing in the [thirty-seventh[2]] sermon on the Canticles, when expounding the passage, "Return... my beloved" etc. (2, 17). Concerning which coming, which happens through the bestowal of spiritual consolations, man can be completely certain, because he can experience them in himself. But from them it cannot be inferred with the certitude of the Catholic faith about God's indwelling grace in man, because all these consolations, with God's permission, can be given by the devil, who often "transformeth himself into an angel of light" (II Cor. 11, 14).

There are other testimonies of Bernard which our enemies cite for the certitude of the state of grace, which they preach, and yet they say nothing in favor of it, because he only says that the just know their good works, and he says this in his third sermon on Advent.[3] Now we ourselves also acknowledge this, because (as Gregory says above) unless one were to know that he does well, he would immediately cease from good works: and hence he very well says that it is necessary that "knowing we should not know."[4] Now what he said in the [thirty-seventh] sermon, hardly bearing upon the testimony of justification, ought not to be understood of the justification of a particular man, but of the justification which is in the body of the Church, which is His body. But no one knows whether he is a member in which God so dwells by grace.

Next, many other prophets besides Jeremias confirm this incertitude of the state of grace by their testimonies. For Daniel says to King Nabuchodonosor: "Redeem thou thy sins with alms, and thy iniquities with works of mercy to the poor: perhaps he will forgive thy offences" (Dan. 4, 24). In which words the word, "perhaps," ought to be especially noticed, which

---

[1] *Enchiridion christianae institutionis*, pp. 287-288.
[2] In the section on justification in the *Enchiridion christianae institutionis* the reference to St. Bernard's sermons on the Canticle of Canticles is to sermon 37 (n. 3 (PL 183, 972B)), and not sermon 17, as cited here in the text. The reference in the *Enchiridion* is: "Blessed Bernard very clearly said, 'This joy in engendered in the heart of him who sows for himself unto justice, by the assurance of his pardon (meaning justification) [note here that these two added words give a heretical interpretation]; provided, however, that such assurance is confirmed by the efficacy of the grace received in enabling him to live thereafter more holily. Everyone of you, my brethren, who is conscious of these operations in his interior, knows what the Spirit says, for His words and works are ever in harmony.'" (p. 282).
[3] "Wherefore the wise man fears all his works; he examines, investigates, judges all these works. Of course, he respects the truth, who also both truly knows and humbly acknowledges himself and all his works in that state." *De adventu Domini*, serm. 3, n. 7 (PL 183, 47B).
[4] *Morals on the Book of Job*, bk. 9, c. 25, n. 37 (PL 76, 878D).

all agree is an indication of doubt. Now this doubt does not arise from God's hardness and austerity, Who is certainly most merciful, but from the imperfection of our works, about which we ought to doubt, whether they are such that they can obtain mercy. If Daniel was doubting whether God would pardon, then neither he nor Nabuchodonosor could be certain of the remission of sins. Hence Jerome in his *Commentary on Daniel* when interpreting the aforesaid words says: "In view of the fact that the blessed Daniel, foreknowing the future as he did, had doubts concerning God's decision, it is very rash on the part of those who boldly promise pardon to sinners."[1]

Next the prophet Joel when exhorting God's people to convert themselves with their whole heart to the Lord, because He is gracious and patient, says: "Who knoweth but he will return, and forgive, and leave a blessing behind him" (2, 14). Jerome, when interpreting these words in his *Commentary on Joel*, says: "Do not despair of His mercy, no matter how great your sins, for great mercy will take away great sins, ... and if we do penance for our sins, He regrets his own threat and does not carry out against us the evils He had threatened. So by the changing of our attitude, He Himself is changed... lest the magnitude of His clemency make us lax and negligent, he adds this word through His prophet: "Who knoweth but he will return, and forgive, and leave a blessing behind him, sacrifice and libation to the Lord your God?" (Joel 2:14). In other words, he says: 'I exhort you to repentance, because it is my duty, and I know that God is inexhaustibly merciful, as David says: "Have mercy on me, O God, according to thy great mercy ..." (Ps. 50, 3). But since we cannot know the depth of the riches and of the wisdom and knowledge of God, I will temper my statement, expressing a wish rather than taking anything for granted, and I will say: "Who knoweth but he will return, and forgive?"' (Joel 2, 14). Since he says, 'who,' it must be understood that it is impossible or difficult to know for sure."[2]

The testimony is also clear, which the Ninivites, upon the preaching of Jonas having decided to do penance for their sins and to make some satisfaction for them to God, said: "Who can tell if God will turn, and forgive: and will turn away from his fierce anger, and we shall not perish?" (Jonas 3, 9). Upon which words Jerome says: "Also, when it is said: 'Who can tell if God will turn, and forgive,' doubt and uncertainty are set out, for when people are doubtful about their salvation they repent more heartily and call out to God for mercy all the more."[3] By Jerome's elucidating the mind of the prophet, he very clearly showed his own opinion about the uncertainty. The words which the Apostle Peter said to Simon Magus have the same meaning: "Do penance therefore for this thy wickedness; and pray to God, that perhaps this thought of thy heart may be forgiven thee" (Acts 8, 22). These testimonies of the prophets which we have just cited from Daniel, Joel, and Jonas no less oppose the Catholic advocates of the certitude of the state of grace then they do the Lutherans.

Paul also gives very clear testimony against all these men in favor of the incertitude of the state of grace, saying the following: "But to me it is a very small thing to be judged by you, or by man's day; but neither do I judge my own self. For I am not conscious to myself of anything, yet am I not hereby justified; but he that judgeth me, is the Lord. Therefore judge not before the time; until the Lord come, who both will bring to light the hidden things of darkness, and will make manifest the counsels of the hearts; and then shall every man have praise from God" (I Cor. 4, 3-5). I have cited this passage of Paul at length because many things seem to me to be contained in it, which very clearly prove the incertitude of the state of grace. But before we evaluate the strength and value of those words, it is firstly necessary to advise the reader so that he may understand that Paul does not show his uncertainty about

---

[1] PL 25, 517A.

[2] PL 25, 967C-968A.

[3] *Jerome's Commentary on Jonas* (PL 25, 1144A).

his own state of grace in these words, because he was not really speaking about himself, who by Divine revelation was sure not merely about his present justification, but also about the crown of justice which he most certainly believed and most firmly hoped that he would very certainly have from the just Judge. Paul (as he is accustomed to often do elsewhere) wishing to instruct others about what they ought to do, spoke using his own name, so that his teaching might be more readily accepted, and they might more patiently bear his reprehension of their confidence about their own conscience.

And Theophylactus noted this before me, who upon the words, "to me it is a very small thing...," says: "Certainly he is not really speaking about himself (for they were not judging him at all), but lest they judge others, he corrects in his own person, what he wants [to correct in others]."[1] And afterwards upon the words: "Judge not before the time," he again says: "For Blessed Paul is always accustomed to transfer in this way the things which are another's to his own person, and to teach in himself the things which he is going to teach others."[2] And before Theophylactus, Chrysostom teaches this very same thing upon the same words of Paul saying the following: "Howbeit, let no one condemn Paul of arrogance; though he says that no man is worthy to pass sentence concerning him. For first, he says these things not for his own sake, but wishing to rescue others from the odium which they had incurred from the Corinthians."[3]

Therefore, based upon this foundation, the first thing to be noticed in Paul's words is that the testimony of one's own conscience, whereby it testifies that one does not have knowledge of any sin, does not suffice for a man to believe with certainty that he is just. "For I am not conscious to myself of anything," he says, "yet am I not hereby [*in hoc*] justified," meaning, "Not on account of this can I declare myself just." For Paul is accustomed to use this preposition, 'in,' for the preposition, "on account of" [*propter*], or for the preposition, "through" [*per*]. He so used it when speaking to the Ephesians, when he said, "...sit together in the heavenly places, through [*in*] Christ Jesus" (2, 6), meaning "through [*per*]" or "on account of [*propter*]." And again: "But now in Christ Jesus, you, who some time were afar off, are made nigh by [*in*] the blood of Christ" (2, 13), meaning, "through the blood of Christ." The second thing to be noticed in Paul's words is that no one can fully search out all the secrets of his heart, but only God is He "that searcheth the reins and hearts" (Apoc. 2, 23). And hence he said, "but neither do I judge my own self; but he that judgeth me, is the Lord." The third thing to be noticed Paul derives from the second thing said, namely that no one can make a true judgment about himself, because one can only truly judge what he perfectly knows. And hence he warned that we should not want to judge "before the time; until the Lord come, who both will bring to light the hidden things of darkness, and will make manifest the counsels of the hearts." What is understood about the judgment of one's own heart, ought to be understood as well as about the judgment of someone else.

And all the holy Doctors clearly teach that this is Paul's true meaning, wherever they have interpreted those words of Paul. Jerome, when treating the aforesaid words, says: "He who was saying this, was truly not conscious of any sin in himself, but because he had read, 'Who can understand sins?' (Ps. 18, 13); 'There is a way which seemeth just to a man: but the ends thereof lead to death'; and again: 'Every man seemeth just to himself, but God directeth men's hearts' (*LXX*: Prov. 21, 2),[4] for that reason he moderates his opinion, lest perhaps he had sinned through ignorance, especially since Scripture testifies: 'A just man perisheth in his

---

[1] *Commentariius in epistolam I ad Corintheos* (PG 124, 610D).
[2] *Ibid.* (PG 124, 611A).
[3] *Homily 11 on First Corinthians*, hom. 11 (PG 61, 88).
[4] St. Jerome here quotes the Septuagint version for this verse, which in the Vulgate is: "Every way of a man seemeth right to himself: but the Lord weigheth the hearts."

justice' (Eccle. 7, 16), and elsewhere: 'Thou shalt follow justly after that which is just" (Deut. 16, 20), lest we turn away by our opinion of the truth from justice."[1]

Augustine when expounding the verse from Psalm 41: "Deep calleth on deep" (v. 8), in passing interprets those words of Paul, saying the following: "The holy preachers of God's word call on the 'deep': are they not themselves a 'deep' also? That you may know that they also are a 'deep,' the Apostle says, 'It is a very small thing to be judged by you, or by man's day.' Nay, how profound a deep he is, hear ye farther. 'But neither do I judge my own self.' Do not you believe that there is in man a 'deep' so profound as not to be seen through by him in whom it is? How profound a depth of infirmity lay concealed in Peter, when he knew not what was passing in himself, and rashly promised to die either with or for his Lord![2] How profound was the abyss: yet was that abyss bare to the eyes of God! For that which he knew not of within himself, Christ forewarned him of. Every man then, though holy, though just, though advancing in many things, is still a 'deep.'"[3]

And Chrysostom when expounding the passage, "Judge not before the time," says: "For if in what things I myself have sinned, says he, I am conscious of nothing clearly, how can I be worthy to pass sentence on other men? And how shall I, who know not my own case with accuracy, be able to judge the state of others? Because if these things were hidden to Paul, much more are they hidden to us. For he was speaking in this way, not to call himself blameless, but to show that even should there be among them some such person, free from transgression, not even he would be worthy to judge the lives of others: and that if he, though conscious to himself of nothing, declare himself guilty, much more they who are conscious of many more sins in themselves."[4]

And Haymo [of Auxerre[5]], when expounding upon the aforesaid words of Paul, says: "'If I find myself irreprehensible, who knew myself better than you, how can you judge my conscience; I do whatever I do, especially since no man knows the things which are in man, "but the spirit of a man that is in him" (I Cor. 2, 11).' Happy conscience, which dares to speak so securely. And lest it seem that the Apostle asserts such things presumptuously and proudly, he added: 'Yet am I not hereby justified.' Supply the words 'before myself' or 'before God': it is as though he were to say with other words: 'Although I find in myself nothing evil and nothing worthy of reproach, as some men unjustly accuse me, others applaud themselves, yet I am not then justified in my own eyes nor do I believe by this that I am justified before God, because I do not know whether the things that I do please Him, or how he accepts them, Who knows better what happens in me than I do, because even if I have not sinned by very great sinful deeds, I have at least sinned in thought, and so have sinned. I indeed know myself better than you who judge and detract me, and God better than I.'"[6] And again after a some few words he says: "For however much men can judge another, a man can judge himself more: but God can judge man more, than a man can judge himself. For there is such great depth in man, that many things in him lie concealed from man himself. What depth of weakness in Peter, when he inwardly knew not what he was doing, and he temerariously promised that he would die with the Lord and for the Lord. For Christ foretold this to him when he himself did

---

[1] *Dialogus contra Pelagianos*, bk, 2, n. 3 (PL 23, 537B).

[2] Cf. Jn. 13, 37.

[3] *Exposition on Psalm 41*, n. 13 (PL 36, 472).

[4] *Homily 11 on First Corinthians*, n. 2 (PG 61, 90).

[5] In Migne's *Patrologia Latina*, this passage is attributed to Haymo of Halberstadt, but as mentioned above (see the section, "Gospel," heresy 2), it has more recently been shown to have been written by Haymo of Auxerre.

[6] *In epistolam I ad Corinthios* (PL 117, 530D-531A).

not know what was in himself."[1] Haymo's words are nearly the same as those which we have just now cited from Augustine. [Ambrosiaster] on Paul's epistles,[2] [Hervé de Bourg-Dieu] on the same,[3] and Bernard,[4] whose words were cited above for a different purpose in this disputation, interpret those words of Paul in the same way, and so it is unnecessary to repeat them now.

Furthermore, that testimony is also clear against the Lutherans, which in the Second Epistle to the Corinthians, Paul says: "For not he who commendeth himself, is approved, but he, whom God commendeth" (10, 18). From which words what Luther says is clearly proved to be false: "Believe yourself to have been absolved, and you will truly be absolved."[5] And that saying of Philip Melanchthon [is also proved to be false]: "If you firmly believe that your sins are forgiven through God's mercy and through Christ's Blood, you are justified."[6] "For not he who commendeth himself, is approved, but he, whom God commendeth." And in the same epistle he again says: "Try your own selves if you be in the faith; prove ye yourselves" (13, 5). If men were certain of their justification, it would not be necessary to admonish them to try themselves. And again, he says elsewhere: "If any man think himself to be something, whereas he is nothing, he deceiveth himself" (Gal. 6, 3). From which words it is very easily gathered that everyone who, without God's special revelation, firmly believes that he is just, has deceived himself, because every such person not only thinks himself to be something, but to be something great. For he who is just, is great before God.

Although the testimonies of Sacred Scripture, which we have cited up until now in favor of the incertitude of the state of grace are very convincing, still for a great confirmation of this position I wish to show that this is and always was the position of the whole Catholic Church, by the fact that all Catholic Doctors have always taught it. And assuredly the quotations of those holy men which we have presented above for showing the correct meaning of those passages of Sacred Scripture which we have cited to prove the incertitude of the state of grace could suffice for this matter. But because the curious or doubtful reader will perhaps desire more testimonies, I wish to present them to him now, among which I will cite some fully and entirely, but others, lest by excessive prolixity I would weary other readers fully convinced of our and the Catholic position, I will give the reference to the places where they can be found.

Cyprian, in his sermon on almsgiving, says these words: "Let us then acknowledge, beloved brethren, the wholesome gift of the Divine forbearance; and let us, who cannot be without some wound of conscience, heal our wounds by the spiritual remedies for the cleansing and purging of our sins. Nor let anyone so flatter himself about his pure and immaculate heart, lest relying upon his own innocence, he would think that medicine need not be applied to his wounds; since it is written, 'Who shall boast that he has a clean heart, or who shall boast that he is pure from sins?' (LXX Prov. 20, 9).[7] And again, since in his epistle, John takes for granted, and says, 'If we say that we have no sin, we deceive ourselves, and the truth is not in us. (If we confess our sins, he is faithful and just, to forgive us our sins)[8] (I Jn. 1, 8). But if no one can be without sin, and whoever should say that he is without fault is either proud

---

[1] *Ibid.* (PL 117, 531B).
[2] *Commentaria in Epistolam ad Corinthios Primam*, c. 4 (PL 17, 203A).
[3] *Commentaria in epistolas Pauli* (PL 181, 850B-C).
[4] *De moribus et officio episcoporum*, c. 6, n. 24 (PL 182, 824D). The text refers to this treatise as Letter 42 (to the Archbishop of Sens).
[5] *Exsurge Domine*, condemned proposition n. 11 (Dz. 751).
[6] "Scripture also teaches that we are justified before God through faith in Christ, when we believe that our sins are forgiven for Christ's sake" (*Augsburg Confession* (1530), art. 24).
[7] "Who can say: My heart is clean, I am pure from sin?" is found in the Vulgate.
[8] The author here has extended the quotation cited by St. Jerome to include the second verse.

or foolish, how needful, how kind is the Divine clemency, which, knowing that there are still found some wounds in those that have been healed, even after their healing, has given wholesome remedies for the curing and healing of their wounds anew!"[1]

Jerome, besides the quotations cited above, teaches still the same opinion in his commentaries on Jeremias,[2] and on Micheas, chapter six.[3] Augustine on the passage of the Psalm, "The uncertain and hidden things of thy wisdom thou hast made manifest to me" (50, 8), says these words: "What hidden things? What uncertain things? Because God pardons even such. Nothing is so hidden, nothing so uncertain. For this uncertainty the Ninevites repented, for they said, though after the threats of the prophet, though after that cry, 'Yet forty days, and Ninive shall be destroyed' (Jonas 3, 4): they said to themselves, 'Mercy must be implored'; they said in this sort, reasoning among themselves, 'Who can tell if God will turn, and forgive?' (v. 9) It was uncertain, when it is said, 'Who can tell?' on an uncertainty they did repent, certain mercy they earned: they prostrated themselves in tears, in fastings, in sackcloth and ashes. They prostrated themselves, groaned, wept, and God spared. Did Ninive stand, or was Ninive destroyed? One way indeed it seems to men, and another way it seemed to God."[4] And he teaches likewise in his book, *Eighty-three Questions*,[5] his *Sermons on the New Testament*,[6] and in his book, *On the Predestination of the Saints*.[7] Gregory, besides the so very many testimonies which we have cited from his *Morals on the Book of Job*, still more openly teaches the same thing in a letter to Gregoria, lady of the bedchamber (*cubicularia*) to the Empress.[8]

---

[1] *On Works and Alms*, n. 3 (PL 4, 604B-C).

[2] The references here are to the third and thirteenth chapters of Jeremias, but nothing pertinent to the subject can be found there. Instead there is a suitable comment on Jer. 17, 9: "The heart is perverse above all things, and unsearchable, who can know it?" as follows: "And so, lest we think that human judgment is trustworthy, he adds that the hearts of almost all people are corrupt, as the Psalmist says: 'Who can understand sins? from my secret ones cleanse me, O Lord' (Ps. 18, 13)" (bk. 3 (PL 24, 789B)).

[3] "For just as He commands us 'to do judgment, and to love mercy' (Micheas 6, 8): so it is commanded that we be prepared to 'walk' with the Lord our God; we ought at no hour to sleep, at no time to be secure, but always to wait for the coming Householder, and to fear the day of judgment" (*Commentary on Micheas*, bk. 2 (PL 25, 1211C)).

[4] Cf. Jonas 3, 4-10; *Exposition on Psalm 50*, n. 11 (PL 36, 592).

[5] "Wherefore since every person either can nowise or scarcely render a true judgment about himself, how can he judge another, because no one knows what is done in man, 'but the spirit of a man' (I Cor. 2, 11)?" (*De diversis quaestionibus*, q. 59, n. 3 (PL 40, 46)). The text cites question 58, but nothing there relates to the matter being discussed.

[6] The reference here is to sermon sixteen of *On the Words of the Apostle* (*De verbis Apostoli*), but as this was part of the popular medieval collection, *Sermones de verbis domini et apostoli*, it seems likely that the following text, found elsewhere therein, is what the author had in mind: "But as says the Apostle, 'But to me it is a very small thing to be judged by you...' My conscience is not therefore good, because you praise it. For how do you praise what you do not see? Let Him praise, who sees; yea let Him correct, if He sees ought there which offends His eyes. For I too do not say that I am perfectly whole; but I beat my breast, and say to God, 'Be merciful, that I sin not.'" (*Sermones de Scripturis*, serm. 138, c. 11, n. 14 (PL 38, 762)).

[7] "But do you say, God's will concerning myself is to me uncertain? What then? Is your own will concerning yourself certain to you? And do you not fear—'He that thinketh himself to stand, let him take heed lest he fall?' (I Cor. 10, 12)." (c. 10, n. 21 (PL 44, 976)). The reference here is to chapter 20, which contains nothing relevant to this topic.

[8] "Thou oughtest, ever suspicious and ever fearful, to be afraid of faults, and wash them with daily tears. Assuredly the Apostle Paul had already ascended into the third Heaven, had also been caught up into Paradise, and heard secret words which it was not lawful for a man to speak (II Cor. 12, 2, ff.), and

Isidore [of Seville] in his *Sententiae* writes: "There are those who quickly promise security to penitents, of whom it is well said by the prophet: 'And they healed the breach of the daughter of my people disgracefully, saying: Peace, peace: and there was no peace' (Jer. 6, 14). Therefore, he heals the breach disgracefully who promises security to someone sinning and not rightly repenting... Although atonement for sins is through repentance, still a man ought not to be without fear: because the satisfaction of repentance depends upon Divine, not human judgment. Hence because God's pity is hidden, it is necessary to weep without intermission. Indeed, the one repenting never ought to have security about his sins. For security begets negligence, and negligence often makes one reckless regarding faults committed."[1] Isidore very clearly teaches our and the Catholic teaching.

Jean Gerson in a tract, *De signis bonis et malis*, which is in the fourth part of his work, says these words: "It is a bad sign to judge oneself to be in the state of grace with certitude, unless it be had through a clear revelation, since a probable conjecture suffices for the present life. For 'Man knoweth not whether he be worthy of love, or hatred' (Eccle. 9, 1), both because he does not know whether his works are accepted before God; and because he does not know with what severity they will be judged, or with what end of life they will be completed; and because the mind's eye sees poorly, sometimes thinking concerning grace, that grace freely given or acquired [*gratia gratis data*, i.e. a gratuitous grace or charism] is sanctifying grace [*gratia gratis faciens*]; and finally because 'Satan himself transformeth himself into an angel of light' (II Cor. 11, 14) extinguishing through some hidden pride the flame of charity, conserving nonetheless some light of acquired or habitual virtue."[2] He teaches this same teaching in his tract, *De praeparatione ad missam*, which is in the second part of his works.[3]

After all these illustrious men comes a whole crowd of scholastic theologians, among whom many were renowned for holiness as well as for doctrine, who all unanimously teach this our and the Catholic assertion about the incertitude of indwelling grace. I will not cite the words of these men, but it will be enough to indicate the references to the reader. Alexander of Hales in his *Summa Universae Theologiae*,[4] Saint Bonaventure in his *Commentaria in*

---

yet, still fearful, he said, 'But I chastise my body, and bring it into subjection: lest perhaps, when I have preached to others, I myself should become a castaway' (I Cor. 9, 27). One who is caught up into Heaven still fears; and shall one whose conversation is still on earth desire already not to fear? Consider, most sweet daughter, that security is wont to be the mother of carelessness. Thou oughtest not, then, in this life to have security, whereby thou mayest be rendered careless. For it is written, 'Blessed is the man that is always fearful' (Prov. 28, 14). And again it is written, 'Serve ye the Lord with fear: and rejoice unto him with trembling' (Ps. 2, 11). In short, then, it must needs be that in the time of this life trembling possess your soul, to the end that it may hereafter rejoice without end through the joy of security." (Bk. 7, letter 25 (PL 77, 878B-879A)).

[1] *Sententiae*, bk. 2, c. 13, n. 16 & 18 (PL 83, 616B-617A).

[2] *Joannis Gersonii Opera omnia* (Antwerp, Sumptibus societatis, 1706), vol. 3, p.160A.

[3] "No one has clear certitude without a special revelation of God that he is sufficiently disposed and worthy to celebrate the Mysteries of the Mass. It is evident that then someone would clearly know the he is in the state of sanctifying grace, and that he has sufficiently done whatever is required for this, such that God has infused this grace into him, and that moreover he places no obstacle in any way for the reception of this kind of grace... Furthermore, who does not know that it could happen that a man is given unto a reprobate sense due to past faults such that he does not see his own sins, and thus is unaware of anything, and yet he is not hereby justified, as the Apostle fearfully testifies. (I Cor. 4, 4). Perhaps such a man is like proud Aman himself, who comes to the banquet, supposing this to be a special honor for himself, which was for his hanging..." *Ibid.*, p. 324.

[4] P. 3, q. 61, mem. 6, a. 3, §1 (Whether someone can know scientifically and with certitude that he has grace?). An incorrect reference to p. 3, q. 27 was found here and corrected.

Librum Primum Sententiarum,[1] Saint Thomas in his *Summa Theologica*,[2] Richard of Middletown in his *Super sententias Petri Lombardi*,[3] Durandus of Saint-Pourçain in his *In quatuor libros sententiarum quaestionum resolutions*,[4] and Gabriel Biel in his *Super quatuor Libros Sententiarum*.[5] In the latter work Gabriel Biel undeservedly reprehends the *Doctor Subtilis*, John [Duns] Scotus, saying that it is surmised from his works that he thinks that man can be certain about his own justification. And many of the Catholics, who were willing to defend the certitude of grace in the Council of Trent were trying to draw Scotus in favor of their opinion, motivated by the authority of Gabriel, who attributes it to Scotus.

But actually Gabriel, and however many others who attribute it to Scotus, are mistaken: because they nowise comprehend his mind. For he teaches in many places very clearly that no one without a special revelation of God can be certain of his justification. For he teaches this very clearly in his commentary on the first book of the *Sentences*, where he says that no one "with certitude [knows] that he exists in charity."[6] He speaks likewise when commenting on the third book.[7] Commenting on the fourth book when wishing to prove the goodness of the minister is not necessary for the reception of Baptism, he says these words: "For since nearly no one can be sure of his own goodness, all the more can one not be sure of the goodness of another: thus if Baptism depends upon the goodness of the minister, one could never be certain that he has truly received Baptism, which is unsuitable."[8] And when discussing the necessary preparation for receiving the Eucharist worthily, he says that it is not necessary that a man would know that he is in the state of grace, because otherwise no one could receive worthily: because no one can know with certitude that he is in the state of grace.[9] Therefore since the *Doctor Subtilis* very clearly said in so many places that no one can be certain about his justification, rightly ought they to be reprehended who dared to falsely attribute to him the opposite assertion.

But it is necessary that we respond to the argument whereby Gabriel and his followers try to persuade that Scotus thought man can by the common law be certain of his justification. For they say that it is Scotus' opinion that for the reception of grace through some Sacrament, it suffices not to place an obstacle, meaning, not to then be in mortal sin. Now anyone can know that he has not placed an obstacle, meaning that he is not in mortal sin when he receives the Sacrament: thus anyone receiving the Sacrament in this way will be certain that he is in the

---

[1] Dist. 17, p. 1, a. 1, q. 3 (Whether anyone can know with certitude, that he is in charity?).

[2] I-II, q. 112, a. 5 (Whether man can know that he has grace?)

[3] Bk. 1, dist. 17, a. 1, q. 5 (Whether someone in this mortal life can know that he has charity with certain knowledge?) An incorrect reference to dist. 1, a. 2, q. 5 was found here and corrected.

[4] Bk. 1, dist. 17, q. 4 (Whether he who is in charity can know with certainty that he is in charity?)

[5] Bk. 2, dist. 27, dubium 5 (Whether wayfarers can know that they have grace?)

[6] "As to the first article one can say that from no act which we experience, whether from the substance of the act, or from the intensity of the act, or from the pleasure or ease in doing it, or from the goodness or the moral rectitude of the act, can we conclude that some such supernatural habit is present; because from none of them can anyone possessed of charity know with certitude that he exists in charity, namely from the fact that an act with such and such intensity is experienced to exist within him, or to be in him with pleasure and ease, or to be consonant with right reason." (*Lectura* 1, dist. 17, q. 3, n. 21).

[7] "A theological persuasion is added, that if no one can have the perfect act of virtue of loving God above all things from his purely natural powers, then he who would find himself inclined to such an act, could know that he is in charity, because without charity there is no such inclination. The conclusion is false; ergo." (*Lectura 3*, dist. 27, q. 1, n. 14).

[8] *Lectura* 4, dist. 5, q. 1, n. 5.

[9] "If it were necessary that the communicant know that he is in charity, anyone by communicating would expose himself to danger, not knowing whether he sins by that act." (*Lectura* 4, dist. 9, q. 1, n. 2).

state of grace. But in this argument Gabriel errs twice, and those who are on his side. Firstly, because according to Scotus' teaching, not only he who is in mortal sin places an obstacle, but also he who when approaching the Sacrament has no contrition or attrition for his sins. Thus not to place an obstacle, as Scotus teaches, ought not to be considered merely negatively, but rather it is to have some attrition for sin, which even in the best circumstances, would not be a sufficient disposition for acquiring grace. Scotus very clearly teaches this commenting on the fourth book of the *Sentences*.[1] And he also says there that someone sins who recalls that he has sinned and does not lament.[2] Secondly Gabriel errs in his argument, because he reasons incorrectly, even if we would grant to him that not to place an obstacle is the same thing as not to sin mortally. For in order that the one receiving the Sacrament be certain with a certitude of the faith that he has received grace, it is necessary that he be certain with the same certitude that he has received the Sacrament. But no one can be certain about this with certitude of the faith, because no one can be so certain about the intention of the minister, without which, as it was defined in the Council of Florence, he cannot confect the Sacrament. Thus Scotus remains in favor of our and the Catholic position concerning the incertitude of the state of grace, and not in favor of the contrary opinion into which some men were attempting to draw him unwilling and resisting.

From all these things which we have brought forth in favor of the incertitude of the state of grace, the second part of the Lutheran assertion is easily refuted, which says: "Every believer is obliged to believe with certitude that his sins are freely forgiven on account of God's mercy and the merit of Christ's Passion." If no one can be certain about his justification, it necessarily follows that no one is bound to have this certitude: because otherwise man would be obliged to the impossible, which is absurd and injurious to God. Furthermore, if all believers and just men are obliged (as the Lutherans say) to believe with certitude that they are just, it is necessary that the Lutherans themselves show a clear and manifest Divine precept, which they are accustomed to demand from us in other matters, which clearly obliges all believers to this certitude, which they preach. But since such a precept cannot be found in Holy Writ, it is then demonstrated that no such precept exists. And this argument more than the others refutes the Lutherans, because they say that nothing ought to be accepted which in not found in Holy Writ. Again, if all believers are bound to believe with certitude that they are just, then he who does not believe it ought to have been considered as a heretic. Yet until now the Church has never declared someone a heretic on account of this, nay on the contrary, she has called those who fear there being guilt where it is no guilt, pious souls.

After all these arguments, so that we may complete this whole disputation about certitude, it will be worthwhile to bring to the fore the Church's definition. In the last chapter of [a section of the Decretals entitled] *Purgatio canonica*, Innocent III declares it to be "confused, temerarious and senseless"[3] for someone to swear that he is devoid of sins, even though he has done penance for them. And he proves this by the words of Job: "Although I should be simple, even this my soul shall be ignorant of" (9, 21).

---

[1] "I say then the God does not justify one who is unwilling, according to the saying of Augustine: 'He Who created thee without thee, will not justify thee without thee' (Serm. 169, *de verbis Apostoli* (Phil. 3, 3-16), c. 11, n. 13 (PL 38, 922)). This man, who actually has an obstacle against grace, for example unbelief, or some sin which he then commits by an act of the will, or which he previously committed, and nowise displeases him, in no way receives grace" (*Lectura* 4, dist. 4, q. 5, n. 2). *Lectura* 4, dist. 14, q. 2, art. 3, n. 90 ff.; "That absolution is not useful unless some contrition or attrition precedes" (*Lectura* 4, dist. 16, q. 1, n. 7).

[2] "Similarly, a person who thinks about sin, without any displeasure, sins." *Lectura* 4, dist. 49, q. *ex latere*, n. 76.

[3] *Liber Extra* bk. 5, tit. 34, c. 16 (*Accepimus*).

Finally, the Council of Trent celebrated under Paul III, after long and very careful examination made upon this matter, made known its most Christian decision with these words: "Although it is necessary to believe that sins are neither forgiven, nor ever have been forgiven, except gratuitously by Divine mercy for Christ's sake, yet it must not be said that sins are forgiven or have been forgiven to anyone who boasts of his confidence and certainty of the forgiveness of his sins and rests on that alone, since among heretics and schismatics this vain confidence, remote from all piety, may exist, indeed in our own troubled times does exist, and is preached against the Catholic Church with vigorous opposition. But neither is this to be asserted, that they who are truly justified without any doubt whatever should decide for themselves that they are justified, and that no one is absolved from sins and is justified, except him who believes with certainty that he is absolved and justified, and that by this faith alone are absolution and justification effected, as if he who does not believe this is doubtful of the promises of God and of the efficacy of the death and resurrection of Christ. For, just as no pious person should doubt the mercy of God, the merit of Christ, and the virtue and efficacy of the Sacraments, so everyone, when he considers himself and his own weakness and indisposition, may entertain fear and apprehension as to his own grace, since no one can know with the certainty of faith, which cannot be subject to error, that he has obtained the grace of God."[1] And after having given this definition of the faith, lest anyone dare to heedlessly say anything against it, it added two *latae sententiae* canons, the words of which are those that follow: "If anyone shall say that it is necessary for every man in order to obtain the remission of sins to believe for certain and without any hesitation due to his own weakness and indisposition that his sins are forgiven him: let him be anathema."[2] "If anyone shall say that man is absolved from his sins and justified, because he believes for certain that he is absolved and justified, or that no one is truly justified but he who believes himself justified, and that by this faith alone absolution and justification are perfected: let him be anathema."[3]

But lest by these words having been misunderstood, some reader were to fall into an error, I wish to admonish the reader so that he may perceive well and rightly understand those words of the council. Since no one is able to know with the certitude of the faith, which cannot be subject to error, that he has attained to be pleasing to God. For they do not say by those words that no one can believe that he is in the state of grace, such that there cannot be any error to that faith: but they say that no one can know with the certitude of the faith, which cannot be subject to error. For it can be that some just man by some conjectures given by the Holy Ghost, meaning which the Holy Ghost suggests to him, may believe with human faith alone, that is, based upon human reasoning, that he is just and that faith cannot be subject to error: because since the Holy Ghost suggests that he so believe, that faith cannot be subject to error. But someone so believing will not be certain of his justification with the certitude of the faith, which cannot be subject to error. Because even if the Holy Ghost were to suggest to him those conjectures, still he does not know that they were given by the Holy Ghost, which would have been necessary so that he would be certain with the certitude of the faith, which is not subject to error. For otherwise, even if the matter is certain in itself, still he will not be certain, because he could often rightly doubt. Thus, the words of the council ought to be understood of both certitudes, namely of the thing in itself and in relation to us, such that no one can have both certitudes about his state of grace without God's special revelation.

If, however, he were to know that that suggestion is certainly from the Holy Ghost, then it can be said to be a special revelation. Because it is not given to all the just that they know which suggestions are from the Holy Ghost, and which from the evil spirit. For if all were to

---

[1] Sess. 6, chap. 9 (Dz. 802).

[2] Can. 13 (Dz. 823).

[3] Can. 14 (Dz. 824).

know this, John would not have said: "Believe not every spirit, but try the spirits if they be of God" (I Jn. 4, 1). But because "Satan himself transformeth himself into an angel of light" (II Cor. 11, 14), it is thus necessary to "try the spirits if they be of God." And hence it necessarily follows that he who certainly knows that some spirit is from God, he knows this by a special revelation. Now he who knows it, can be rightly certain about his justification with the certitude of the faith, which is not subject to error: because he who from such a revelation certainly believes that he is just, relies upon Divine revelation, which evidently cannot be subject to error. And just as that revelation is a special revelation for him, so the faith whereby he believes with certitude, as he is then bound to believe that he is just, is a special and not Catholic faith for him, because it does not oblige others to whom that special revelation was not made. Therefore, since the Council said that no one can certainly know with the certitude of the faith, which is not subject to error, this is the same as if it had said, with the certitude by a way, whereby one cannot be deceived. And he has such a way, who relies upon Divine revelation. On the other hand, he who through conjectures given by the Holy Ghost, but not knowing for sure that they are from the Holy Ghost, believes with certitude that he is in the state of grace, is not certain with the certitude of the faith, which is not subject to error. Because even if the matter is certain in itself, still the way whereby he believes it is not infallible, because it is only a human probable reason, which is subject to error. And this moral certitude, which is had by a fallible way, which we call "human faith," the council does not deny, nor do we deny that it can happen by the general law to many just.

And hence it is very clearly established how little the passage of Paul achieves in support of the certitude of the state of grace: "The Spirit himself giveth testimony to our spirit, that we are the sons of God" (Rom. 8, 16). Those who were trying to defend the certitude of the state of grace at the Council of Trent were making much of this saying of Paul. But from these things which we have now said it is clearly evident that it does not support them at all. We indeed admit that the Holy Ghost gives testimony to the just through the good works which they do, or through other conjectures, that they are the sons of God, but it is not certain to them all that it is the Holy Ghost's testimony. For this, as we said, is most necessary so that a man can be truly certain of his justification. Furthermore, not every testimony which the Holy Ghost gives to man about his justification is a testimony of certitude. For a witness does not always testify from sight, but sometimes from hearing, sometimes from credulity, and from probability. So also the Holy Ghost, and if He gives testimony to the just that they are the sons of God, still it is not equal to all, but the more fully it has been stamped upon our mind, and the more fully it is brought to light by our works, the more certain it is that He "giveth testimony to our spirit that we are the sons of God." He does not give this testimony to all, but only to those to whom He reveals His justification.

I see that this alone now remains for me, namely to answer some arguments, with which the assertors of certitude fight against us and the Catholic truth. Firstly, in fact they argue against us, and say that those who deny that the certitude of salvation can be had, torment and torture consciences, and they lead them to despair, if they always make those consciences to doubt. I answer that we do not wish them to doubt. For one who is uncertain does not doubt because there is an intermediary between certitude and despair, namely a probable faith or opinion about his justification. But these men wish to pass from one extreme to the other without intermediary, because from the denial of the certitude of the state of grace they wish to infer despair of salvation, as they act according to that which someone said: "While fools in avoiding a vice, they run into its opposite."[1] To these arguments we can respond with that which Horace said to other similar men in his first satire or conversation (*sermo*), saying the following: "I certainly, when I bid you not be a miser, am not bidding you turn fool and spend-

---

[1] Horace, *Satires*, bk. 1, Sat. 2, l. 24.

thrift. There is a mean between a Tanais and Viselius' father-in-law.[1] There is a measure in everything. There are fixed limits beyond which and short of which right cannot find a resting place."[2] I reply in this manner because by denying certitude, I do not wish to concede despair, but I merely wish to give an intermediary in between, namely a probable opinion about one's own justification.

Now this probable opinion can be conceived from many testimonies. For there are two principal and more certain signs of this justice and interior grace, which can render more security to those who know with certitude that they keep to the Catholic faith. The first is sorrow for all sins committed against God. The second is the intention of avoiding every offense to Him and of keeping all the Divine Commandments in all respects. And those who certainly know that they are of this mind, such that they lament beyond measure for all the offenses, which they perpetrated against God, and they desire to avoid them henceforth with the greatest care and diligence that they can, notwithstanding any inconveniences or dangers whatsoever, reasonably have a very probable conjecture of their justification, and can rejoice within themselves with their whole heart and soul for so great and such an excellent favor. Contempt of the world and of all earthly things, the desire of the heavenly homeland, to willingly hear God's word, to delight in Divine things, a prompt will for the execution of God's Commandments, to have no remorse of conscience for mortal sin, and fear of offending God are also signs of the state of grace. But all these things are not so certain signs of justification that the one having them could not be deceived in judging that he is just: because some hidden mortal sin could be present with them all. Yet they are very strong signs for giving (as I said) a probable opinion, or moral certitude, about one's justification.

And this moral certitude is one which can console a man not a little. This is that testimony of conscience in which, according to Paul's opinion, they cannot glory in and rejoice in vain. Hence Chrysostom says: "Our conscience not having whereof to condemn us, as when for evil doings we are persecuted. For though we suffer countless horrors, though from every quarter we be shot at and in peril, it is enough for our comfort, yea rather not only for comfort, but even for our crowning, that our conscience is pure and testifies unto us that for no evil-doing, but for that which is well-pleasing to God, we thus suffer; for virtue's sake, for heavenly wisdom's sake, for the salvation of the many."[3] In these words one ought to notice that he merely said the we have comfort and consolation from the testimony of our conscience, and not full certitude and security.

But lest from this consolation and testimony of conscience someone would take pride, and would desire to take greater glory than is fitting, let him hear what Blessed Bernard says. "I wish," he says, "thee to glory in the testimony of thy conscience,[4] but I also desire that the same should humble thee. It is rare to find a man who can say with the Apostle, 'I am not conscious to myself of anything' (I Cor. 4, 4). The knowledge of the evil that is in thee shall make thee more careful of the good. Wherefore, as I have said, know thyself, not only that amidst the reverses and disappointments which shall not be wanting, thou mayest have the testimony of a good conscience for thy consolation; but also and more especially that thou

---

[1] The poet offers the example of two men, as much unlike as the miser is to the prodigal. "On this line the scholiasts comment that Tanais was a eunuch (*spado*) and Visellius' father-in-law herniated (*herniosus*). Clearly the two men represent opposite extremes of the sexual scale: Tanais, as a spado, was impotent, whereas Visellius' father-in-law had suffered a rupture from over-liberal gratification of his sexual urges." (Lindsay C. Watson, "Of Hernias and Wine-Jugs: 'Catalepton' 12," *Mnemosyne* (Fourth Series, Vol. 61, Fasc. 2 (2008)), p. 252.

[2] *Ibid.*, Sat. 1, ll. 103-107.

[3] *Homily 3 on Second Corinthians* (PG 61, 405).

[4] Cf. II Cor. 1, 12: "For our glory is this, the testimony of our conscience."

mayest understand what is yet wanting to thee.[1] For where is the man to whom something is not always wanting? Indeed, he who considers that he is wanting in nothing proves himself thereby to be wanting in everything."[2]

Secondly, they argue against us using that which is contained in the Apostles' Creed, "the remission of sins." From which words they want to infer that whoever has been absolved by a priest is obliged to believe that his sins have been forgiven. But this does not disturb us at all, because we acknowledge the forgiveness of sins is given through the absolution of the priest, and all are obliged to believe that such forgiveness is given if everything else is present which is needed for obtaining such forgiveness. Yet no one can know with certitude that all those things are present, because no one can know with certitude that he has prepared himself well by fully examining his conscience such that he perfectly repents of all his sins, nor also can he establish with certitude the intention of the priest, which is always necessary for the administration of any Sacrament. And for this reason, an adult who comes to be baptized, although he knows with certitude that he repents of his sins, still cannot know with certitude that he is in the state of grace, because he cannot establish with certitude the intention of the one baptizing.

Thirdly, they object to us that saying of the Apostle: "Now we have received not the spirit of this world, but the Spirit that is of God; that we may know the things that are given us from God" (I Cor. 2, 12). From which words our enemies attempt to infer that the Apostles through the infusion of the Holy Ghost alone, and not by a special revelation, knew that God's gifts were conferred upon them, and hence they conclude that it was granted to all the just to know God's gifts, among which grace is included. And they confirm this by saying that unless it were granted to them, they could not give thanks to God as they ought for the befits which they received from God. But these arguers are mistaken about many things when arguing in this way. Firstly, because the Apostle there, as is evident from the context, is not speaking about the special gifts which God specially grants to some men, but about the common favors which God has granted to the whole human race, such as the Redemption, the teaching of the faith, and the Sacraments by which we can be justified. Now all the just, nay even all the faithful, by the gift of faith know with certitude that they have received all these things from God. And the words which follow clearly demonstrate that Paul is speaking in the passage about gifts of this kind. For after those words cited above, he immediately adds these words: "Which things also we speak, not in the learned words of human wisdom; but in the doctrine of the Spirit" (v. 13). But Paul and the other Apostles, his comrades, were not preaching the justification of a particular man, or some other particular gifts of a man, but those common gifts which we have enumerated above. Next, they are deceived about the quality of knowledge, which they suppose to be necessary. For they object that man cannot give thanks to God as he ought for benefits received if he does not know them: they indeed say the truth and we acknowledge it, but to give thanks it suffices to know those gifts by a probable opinion had about them, and certitude of the faith is not needed for this. And what the Apostle likewise says in the same place ought to be understood about this knowledge: "What man knoweth the things of a man, but the spirit of a man that is in him?" (v. 11). For even though we may know with certitude and plainly our interior acts, nevertheless we do not so know our interior habits, but rather we only know them through conjectures and by a probable opinion.

Fourthly, they object to us the saying of John: "If our heart do not reprehend us, we have confidence towards God: and whatsoever we shall ask, we shall receive of him: because we keep his commandments, and do those things which are pleasing in his sight" (I Jn. 3, 21-22). From these words our enemies suppose that they prove the certitude of the state of grace, and

---

[1] Cf. Ps. 38, 5: "... that I may know what is wanting to me."
[2] *Treatise on consideration*, bk. 2, c. 7, n. 15 (PL 182, 750D).

to lack remorse of conscience is sufficient testimony for that certitude, and the keeping of God's Commandments arises from that peace of conscience. But John says nothing of the sort in that passage: because John did not say in those words that we have certitude if our heart does not reprehend us: but instead he said, "we have confidence." But confidence is very far apart from certitude, because certitude, as we said in the beginning, pertains to the intellect, but confidence pertains to the will. Now for having this confidence of obtaining from God the things which we ask for, a probable persuasion that we are pleasing to God and the things which we do are pleasing to Him suffices. Which persuasion is born from the fact that we keep His Commandments, and our conscience does not accuse of any sin.

Fifthly, they object to us John's words taken from the same place: "We know that we have passed from death to life, because we love the brethren" (v. 14). Now passing from death to life is through justification, because sin is the soul's death and grace is the soul's life, and hence it follows that passing from death to life is the passing from sin to grace. Thus, when John says that we know this passing, it seems to infer from that that we also know when we are in the state of grace. But this argument is defective in many things. For firstly it proceeds from the mystical sense, which is incapable of proving a dogma. For to understand sin by the word "death" and grace by the word "life," the meaning is mystical, which hardly agrees with this passage and is nowise understood from this text. For John was speaking in the passage about true bodily death and of eternal life unto which the just are transferred when they leave this world.

Next there is a mistake in the argument, in thinking that by the verb, "we know" [*scimus*], which is used in John's text, evident and certain knowledge is signified, which is the knowledge which is had through a demonstrative syllogism, or by beholding something present. For often we say that we know those things about which we have only Divine faith, or human faith, or a probable opinion. For Peter when speaking to the Jewish people said: "Let all the house of Israel know most certainly, that God hath made both Lord and Christ, this same Jesus, whom you have crucified" (Acts 2, 36). In which words it is evident that "know" is used from "believe." And John, in the same epistle and in the same chapter in which the first words were taken, often uses this verb, "know," for "believe": "We know, that, when he shall appear, we shall be like to him: because we shall see him as he is" (I Jn. 3, 2). And again: "And you know that no murderer hath eternal life abiding in himself" (v. 15). In these two passages it is evident that knowledge is taken for Divine faith, whereby we believe everything revealed by God to be true. And according to this meaning that verb ought to be understood in the passage previously cited, where John said: "We know that we have passed from death to life, because we love the brethren." For the just believe that they are to pass from the death of this body to eternal life, as long as they truly believe God. For the word, "because," in that passage means the same things as if he had said, "as long as" or "if." And because they most firmly believe and hope for it, he used on account of the certitude the past tense for the future tense, "we have passed," for "we shall pass." For this very frequently happens in Sacred Scripture as is evident from many passages of it. "Their sound hath gone forth," David said, "into all the earth" (Ps. 18, 5). And again in another Psalm: "Thou hast delivered my soul out of the lower hell" (Ps. 85, 13). And again: "I am become as a man without help, free among the dead" (Ps. 87, 5-6). In all these passages and in many others, the past is put for the future on account of the certitude of an event to come, which is held to be as certain as if it had already happened. And John likewise does this in the aforesaid passage.

Sixthly, the Lutherans object to us the passage of Paul from his Epistle to the Romans: "Therefore is it of faith, that according to grace the promise might be firm to all the seed; not to that only which is of the law, but to that also which is of the faith of Abraham, who is the father of us all" (4, 16). From this passage Philip Melanchthon supposes that he triumphs over us, because he says that Paul in those words taught us that justice is consequently from faith alone, such that we can be certain of the remission of our sins which God promised us.[1] But certainly Philip distorts Paul's words exceedingly into another meaning. For Paul in that passage does not speak about the promise of the remission of sins, but of the promise of the Incarnation of the Son of God, Who was going to assume flesh of the seed of Abraham and for this purpose He gave another promise about the son whom Sara would give birth unto him. Concerning this second promise Paul says in the same epistle: "For this is the word of promise: According to this time will I come; and Sara shall have a son" (Rom. 9, 9). On account of these two promises Paul says in another epistle: "To Abraham were the promises made" (Gal. 3, 16). This promise of the Incarnation of the Son of God was given to Abraham before the Law, and hence Paul said that the promise given to Abraham or to his seed was not through the Law, because if it were given through the Law it would be understood that Christ was promised only to the Jews of the seed of Abraham according to the flesh. Therefore, Paul says that that promise was given on account of Abraham's faith, so that it could benefit every believer in Christ, whether Jew or Gentile, because they all are true sons of Abraham and his true seed according to the spirit.

Now this promise was made firm and certain not on account of our works, but by God's grace alone. And it is certain that this is Paul's true meaning from the commentaries of all the sacred Doctors and especially from [Hervé de Bourg-Dieu[2]] who better interprets, in my opinion, that passage, saying the following: "For it would not be firm, but rather weak and void, unless He were to fulfil it by His grace. Thus, it is not from the power of our will, but instead He promised from His predestination. For He promised what He was going to do, not what men were going to do. Because even if men do good works which pertain to worshipping God, He Himself enables them to do the things which He commands, and they do not do things so that He may accomplish what He promised. Otherwise, it would not be in God's power, but in man's, that God's promises are fulfilled: and what was promised by the Lord, would be rendered to Abraham by them. But it could not so happen: thus by God's grace, granted to us by a free gift, His promises are fulfilled when by the gift of His grace He enables us to believe and act well, and thus we are made heirs. The promise is 'firm to all the seed' of Abraham: meaning, not to part of the seed, but to the whole seed. For the Jews wanted it to be firm in regard to themselves: but in regard to the Gentiles, void. But God did not so promise, when He said, 'In thy seed shall all the nations of the earth be blessed' (Gen. 22, 18). It is 'firm to all the seed,' that is, to all the people of believers, the imitators of Abraham."[3] From whose words it is very clearly established that the Lutherans incorrectly interpret Paul's words and distort them into a different meaning.

Seventhly, they object to us the passage of John in the Apocalypse: "To him that overcometh, I will give the hidden manna, and will give him a white counter, and in the counter, a new name written, which no man knoweth, but he that receiveth it." (2, 17). From this passage some of the Catholics, who in the Council of Trent were arguing in favor of the possible certitude of grace, were trying to prove that certitude, and they thought that they triumphed in this matter. But their excessive fondness for their own opinion was deceiving them. For since those words of John are very obscure, and which words are not easily understood by

---

[1] "Paul joins the promise and the faith as correlatives, teaching that it is necessary that the promise be accepted by faith. Therefore faith signifies confidence, which relies upon the Divine promise. This testimony is so perspicuous that it cannot be shaken by any calumnies. Thus 'Therefore is it of faith, that according to grace the promise might be firm,' meaning, I require faith, whereby the promise of reconciliation is accepted." (*Commenarius in epistolam Pauli ad Romanos* in CR 15, 516).

[2] This commentary is here erroneously ascribed to St. Anselm.

[3] *Commentaria in epistolas Pauli* (PL 181, 650C-D).

all, they ought not to be used to prove a dogma, especially since the understanding of those words is not agreed upon by all the sacred Doctors. And what astonishes me more about these argumentators is that none of the sacred Doctors who interpret that passage support their opinion, such that one would say that by "manna," grace or justification is meant, and the Doctor is rare who would say by the word "new" the appellation of the true Christian or true adoptive son of God is meant. For nearly all interpret the passage of the reward of Heaven to be received in the future life. [Berengaudus[1]] in his commentary on the Apocalypse,[2] which the diligence and labors of Cuthbert Tunstall, Bishop of Durham, brought to light, gave two expositions to these words of John, and in neither of them does he say that the word "new" ought to be understood as an appellation of the true Christian: for in the first exposition he says that by the word "new" Christ's name is understood.[3] And [Bede in his *Explanatio Apocalypsis*[4]] says that the phase, "which no man knoweth, but he that receiveth it" ought to be understood according to the passage of the same John in another place: "He who saith that he knoweth him, and keepeth not his commandments, is a liar" (I Jn. 2, 4). In the second exposition [Berengaudus] says that the happiness of Heaven is signified by the word "new," and no one knows this word except those who receive it. "Because," as he says, "no one succeeds in knowing how great that heavenly beatitude is but those who merit to reach it, as Isaias the prophet says: 'The eye hath not seen, O God, besides thee, what things thou hast prepared for them that wait for thee' (64, 4)."[5] And Gregory embraces this latter interpretation.[6]

After the Council of Trent's definition against this heresy was given, two learned men of Spain, the first of whom is named Dominic Soto, of the Dominican Order, who composed a work, *De natura et gratia* divided into three books, in the third of which he disputes against this heresy. The other is Andreas de Vega, of the Franciscan Order, who wrote a large work for the defense and explanation of the Tridentine decree on the justification of man,[7] and in the ninth book of this work he discusses this subject fully and copiously enough.

HERETICUS

Heretic

There were some men so out of their senses that said that all heretics reasoned well: which opinion (as Philastrius says[8]) some men, called Rhetorians, asserted. But this opinion is so repugnant to reason, Augustine says,[9] that it seems impossible that anyone who is mentally competent could think this. For although there are many heresies dia-

---

[1] This commentary is here erroneously ascribed to St. Ambrose, as it was commonly supposed at the time of this writing.

[2] *Expositio super septem visiones libri Apocalypsis.*

[3] PL 17, 861D.

[4] The author attributes this application of I Jn. 2, 4 both to Berengaudus and to Bede, whereas only Bede so applies it in bk. 1, c. 2 (PL 93, 139B). Berengaudus understands the white counter similarly, however, as being given to those who accept the teaching of the Gospel (PL 17, 862A).

[5] PL 17, 862D-863A.

[6] "To have 'a new name written on a white stone' is in an eternal recompense to have the knowledge of God strange to the faculties of men, which no man can know saving he that receiveth it." (*Morals on the Book of Job*, bk. 19, c. 2, n. 4 (PL 76, 98A)).

[7] *Tridentini decreti de justificatione exposition et defensio lib. XV distincta.*

[8] *De haeresibus*, c. 91 (PL 12, 1202A-B).

[9] *De Haeresibus ad Quodvultdeum*, c. 72 (PL 42, 44).

metrically opposed to each other, it is impossible that both of them be believed to be true, any more than to believe that two contradictory things are true. Wherefore, it is not against this madness that we will fight. We think that it has been conquered merely by its narration, because it conquers itself.

There is a **second heresy** which teaches that heretics ought not to be punished with any corporal punishment, but left to the Divine judgment. But we will say nothing about this matter at present, because we are preparing a special treatise about his matter which will be entitled, *De justa haereticorum punitione*.

There is a **third heresy** which teaches that everyone who sins mortally in any way ought to be deemed a heretic. Nicholas Eymerich[1] states in his *Directorium Inquisitorum* that this heresy was propagated during the time of Pope Gregory XI, yet [he does] not [state] who the author was who propagated it: but he only says that Gregory XI first having held a council of learned men condemned this assertion as heretical, and deviant from the true rule of Catholic faith.[2]

Perhaps what some of the Lutherans assert, when disputing about faith and works, pertains to this error. For some of them attempting to teach that faith alone justifies man, and seeing many testimonies of Sacred Scripture which very clearly teach the necessity of good works, say that faith does not exist when there are not the necessary works. Thus, it becomes necessary, according to their view, that every time someone commits a deadly crime, he loses the faith: because (as they say) faith cannot remain without works. So teaches a certain Johannes Rivius of Atthendorn in a letter which is entitled, *De sola fide*, to an unnamed friend, where he puts in these words which follow: "For it cannot happen," he says, "that where there is true and sincere faith, one would then act wickedly against God."[3] And shortly before these quoted words he teaches this same thing more explicitly, saying the following: "As long as we are truly sons of God, we are also heirs. Now we are clearly sons all the while we retain faith in Christ. When it has been lost, the heavenly Father does not recognize [us] as His sons. Now it is lost if you live wickedly and do not repent of your wickedness." If faith is lost by any mortal sin, then everyone who sins mortally is an unbeliever. If one is an unbeliever, it necessarily must be that one is either a Jew, Saracen, pagan or heretic. Because no other kind of unbelief has been until now assigned by learned men. Therefore, since an otherwise truly Christian man, on account of the crime of adultery or theft alone having been committed by him, is not deemed a Jew, Saracen, or pagan, it will be necessary, according to Johann Rivius' opinion, to confess that he is a heretic.

And certainly, unless the difficulty of the question solely depends upon the meaning of the word, it is very clear that not every sinner, even if his crime is deadly, is a heretic. For since there are two kinds of sins, one when some things happen which ought not to be done, and the other when some things are omitted which we are obliged to do: if someone sins in the second way, how will you call him a heretic, who has clearly has not done or taught anything? Furthermore, it can happen that someone commits a grave fault, and he knows that he has done wrongly: for otherwise what our Savior said would not be true: the son who knew the will of his father, and did not do according to his will, shall be beaten with many stripes.[4] But Christ our Savior Who is Truth Itself could not lie. Thus, it can happen that someone may act wrongly although he believes that he acts wrongly. For our will is not so compliant that it

---

[1] Nicolas Eymeric (1320-1399) was a Spanish Dominican theologian and inquisitor.
[2] "The tenth heresy is: that everyone sinning mortally is most properly a heretic." (*Directorium Inquisitorum* (Venice, Simeon Vasalini, 1595), Pt. 2, q. 10, p. 263C.
[3] Published in *De Conscientia libri III*, p. 5v.
[4] Cf. Lk. 12, 47.

always yields to the intellect advising it, nay very often its advice is disdained, and when its advice has been rejected one does whatever he wills.

Accordingly, it is certain that not every sin is from pure ignorance, but many sins are from pure malice, which can be very clearly established from that which is read in the book of Job: "He hath struck them, as being wicked, in open sight. Who as it were on purpose have revolted from him, and would not understand all his ways: so that they caused the cry of the needy to come to him, and he heard the voice of the poor" (34, 26-28). From which words it is clearly proved that someone can act badly, although he certainly knows that he acts against God's precepts.

Therefore, he who acts in this manner against God's precepts, sins, yet will not be deemed a heretic by any educated and Catholic man. For how could it happen that someone who does not adhere to any heresy be a heretic? But where there is no error in the faith, there cannot be a heresy: because heresy is opposed to the faith. Hence, he who acts badly and knows that he acts badly, ought not to be called a heretic. Wherefore it is that not every sinner should be called a heretic. Furthermore, if every sinner would be deemed a heretic, it would be necessary that to avoid every sinner after the first and second admonition: because the Apostle Paul says: "A man that is a heretic, after the first and second admonition, avoid" (Tit. 3, 10). Yet Christ taught us to do otherwise, Who did not say that someone sinning a second time ought to be avoided, but ought to be denounced to the Church.[1] And there is no need for us to dispute longer against this condemned heresy, especially because in the first book[2] we showed from the teaching of holy men who really ought to be called a heretic: from which men it is very clearly established that not every sinner ought to be branded of heresy.

HORAE CANONICAE

Canonical Hours

Among the other errors which Aeneas Sylvius accuses the Waldensians in his book, *De origine Bohemorum*, there is one whereby they teach "Time is spent uselessly in singing and reciting the Canonical Hours."[3] Nevertheless, good Guy does not mention this error when he enumerates the errors of the Waldensians.[4] Afterwards John Wycliffe revived this error, saying that although it is good to pray, still it is unjust that a man be forced to pray at a certain and determined time, because (as he says[5]) this is opposed to Christian liberty, but he says that everyone ought to be free to pray when he wishes. It is as though Christian liberty were to consist in one's not being obligated by any human law. As we showed above, the Church has the power from God of making laws, to which all Christians are obliged. Hence Christian liberty consists in this, firstly that one is free by Baptism from the servitude of sin, which is the greatest servitude. Next, we are free from the yoke of servi-

---

[1] Cf. Mt. 18, 17.
[2] Chap. 9.
[3] *De Bohemorum origine ac gestis historia*, c. 35, p. 60.
[4] *Summa de haeresibus et earum confutationibus*, fol. 79r ff.
[5] "But Wycliffe will say that these things [i.e. prayers] ought to be done, such that Christ's liberty be kept: so that when praying one neither be forced regarding their use, nor regarding their time" (Thomas Netter, De *sacramentalibus in quo doctrinae antiquitatum fidei Ecclesiae catholicae, co[n] tra Witcleuistas [et] eorum asseclas Lutheranos aliosq[ue] haereticos continentur* (Salamanca, Juan Maria de Terranova, 1556), tit. 3, c. 23, p. 55v.

tude to the Mosaic Law: true Christian liberty is established in these two things. And this is the liberty "wherewith," as Paul says, "Christ has made us free" (Gal. 4, 31).

He did not so free us, however, such that we are free to despise all human laws whatsoever, because we are bound to submit to them when they are just. Hence it is just that we pray to God and render thanks to God for the benefits we have received from Him (for God commanded this, although he did not specify the time when this ought to be done). The Church when fixing the time for praying, does nothing other than to prescribe the time in which that Divine precept ought to be fulfilled, just as in the precept of the sanctification of the Sabbath she declares that it is fulfilled by hearing Mass on Sunday. Thus, all those to whom a certain time for praying has been prescribed, are obliged to pray at that time, and when so doing they do not act in vain, because they obey the Church commanding. And those who hear the Church, hear Christ, her Spouse. Now who will be so senseless that he would say that we obey God to no purpose? Certainly "Obedience is better than sacrifices: and to hearken rather than to offer the fat of rams" (I Kings 15, 22).

Besides, the Church, when instituting set times for praying, so that on any day at set hours appointed for this He would be entreated by some men, does rightly, because as the Wise Man says: "All things have their season, and in their times all things pass under heaven" (Eccle. 3, 1). Hence if there is "A time to weep, and a time to laugh. A time to mourn, and a time to dance… A time to keep silence, and a time to speak" (v. 4 & 7), why is there not also a time to pray? The Blessed Apostle Paul writes to the Corinthians so that "all things be done decently, and according to order" (I Cor. 14, 40). If "all things," then prayer also ought to be done according to order. But what kind of order will it be, if there will be no set time appointed for prayer, in which one is to assemble at the Church, but instead everyone prays or comes to the Church when he chooses? Surely all things then will be in disorder.

Again, we know from the teaching of Sacred Scripture that it is not a human contrivance that hours for praying ought to be fixed. Daniel "went into his house: and opening the windows in his upper chamber towards Jerusalem, he knelt down three times a day, and adored, and gave thanks before his God, as he had been accustomed to do before" (Dan. 6, 10). Behold, you see Daniel praying three times, and this not just on one day or another, lest perhaps you might think that he did this by chance, but he was always accustomed to do so. And in the Acts of the Apostles it is said that "Peter and John went up into the temple at the ninth hour of prayer" (3, 1). And in the same book it is again said that "Peter went up to the higher parts of the house to pray, about the sixth hour" (10, 9). From which passages of Scripture it is proved that of old among the Jews there were certain set hours, and they were appointed for prayer, which the Apostles observed, and from whom these times for praying have come down unto us.

And not without cause were the Jews of old and now the Christians praying at these three times, namely at the third, sixth and ninth hours, because (as Blessed Cyprian says[1]) in these three spaces of hours the threefold mystery of the Trinity is denoted. "For both the first hour in its progress to the third shows forth the consummated number of the Trinity, and also the fourth proceeding to the sixth declares another Trinity; and when from the seventh the ninth is completed, the perfect Trinity is numbered every three hours"[2] Thus long ago God's adorers were keeping these spiritually determined spaces of hours at set and legally appointed times for prayer. Besides these three times for praying there was also among the Jews of old the silence of the middle of the night allotted to prayer by holy men. Following their example,

---

[1] "And in discharging the duties of prayer, we find that the three children with Daniel, being strong in faith and victorious in captivity, observed the third, sixth, and ninth hour, as it were, for a sacrament of the Trinity, which in the last times had to be manifested" (*On the Lord's Prayer*, n. 34 (PL 4, 541B)).

[2] *Ibid.* (PL 4, 541B-C).

religious men in the New Law rise in the middle of the night to recite praises to God. For the divine Psalmist says: "I rose at midnight to give praise to thee" (Ps. 118, 62).

And lest the impious Wycliffe escape, saying that the argument ought not to be taken from one action of David, so that we may do this on any night we choose: let him hear that the same prophet was not doing this just on one or another night, but each night. "Every night I will wash my bed: I will water my couch with my tears" (Ps. 6, 7). Blessed Hilary teaches that this passage of nightly prayer ought to be so understood when expounding the passage of the Psalm: "In the night I have remembered thy name, O Lord" (Ps. 118, 55). For he speaks thus: "He knows that the Divine name ought to be especially remembered by us at nighttime. He knows that the guarding of God's law ought to be especially kept at the time when impure desires creep up upon the soul: when the stings of the vices through the recent taking of food vexes the body. At that time God's name ought to be remembered: then His law obliging chastity, continence, and fear of the Lord. He knew that especially at this time was the Lord to be besought, implored, and conciliated, saying in another place: 'Every night I will wash my bed: I will water my couch with my tears' (Ps. 6, 7). The soul is not slackened by the quiet of the night vigils, but it is occupied in prayers, petitions, and confessions of sins: so that when the opportunity is especially given to bodily vices, particularly then the same vices are broken by the remembrance of the Divine law."[1]

From whose words it is established that the prophet David praised God not only one or another night, but he did this each night. And elsewhere he exhorts us also to do the same saying: "In the nights lift up your hands to the holy places, and bless ye the Lord" (Ps. 133, 2). And in the Acts of the Apostles it is said that "At midnight, Paul and Silas praying, praised God. And they that were in prison, heard them. And suddenly there was a great earthquake, so that the foundations of the prison were shaken. And immediately all the doors were opened, and the bands of all were loosed" (Acts 16, 25-26). What will the Waldensians say here, supposing it to be vain to rise at midnight for prayer, when God worked such clear miracles upon Paul's and Silas' night prayer? Thus, it is not vain (as they suppose) "to rise before light" (Ps. 126, 2). And God does not promise a crown to those snoring deeply, but those watching. "Blessed is that servant, whom the Lord when he cometh, shall find watching."[2]

Notice that you now see that of old the hours were observed by the Jews so that they might pray to God in them, namely midnight, the third, sixth and ninth hours. But the Church, so that the Christians' justice might abound more than that of the Pharisees and Scribes, chose those other hours in addition, namely the first hour of the morning, vespers and compline, namely when the first watch of the night begins. Hence Blessed Cyprian in his exposition of the Lord's Prayer, after he listed the hours appointed by the Jews for prayer, says the following: "But for us, beloved brethren, besides the hours of prayer observed of old, both the times and the mysteries have now increased in number. For we must also pray in the morning, that the Lord's Resurrection may be celebrated by morning prayer. And this formerly the Holy Ghost pointed out in the Psalms, saying, 'O My King, and my God, for to thee will I pray: O Lord, in the morning thou shalt hear my voice; In the morning I will stand before thee, and will see [thee]' (Ps. 5, 3-5). And again, the Lord speaks by the mouth of the prophet: 'They will rise early to me [saying:[3]] Come, and let us return to the Lord'. (Osee 6, 1). Also, at the sunsetting and at the decline of day, of necessity we must pray again. For since Christ is the true sun and the true day, as the worldly sun and worldly day depart, when we pray and ask that light may return to us again, we pray for the coming of Christ, which shall give us the

---

[1] *Tractatus super psalmos, littera VII* (Zain), n. 6 (PL 9, 550C-551B).

[2] Cf. Lk. 12, 43.

[3] This word is found in the Old Latin translation.

grace of everlasting light."[1] I omit many testimonies of holy men concerning this matter, because the Scriptures are clear. If anyone wishes to see them, he may read Thomas Netter in his book, *De sacramentalibus*, where he copiously discusses this matter.[2]

The universal custom of the Church adds to these things, which has observed these fixed hours for praying for many centuries in the larger churches and monasteries. And lest perhaps they calumniate this custom saying that it was derived merely from the Church's tolerance, let them hear the Church's decision commanding to do this. For the Synod of Agde teaches the manner whereby one ought to pray at certain hours. For it says the following: "And since it is fitting that the order of the Church be maintained equally by all, it is to be encouraged that, as is done everywhere, bishops and priests say the collects in order after the antiphons, and every day hymns for Matins and Vespers be sung on all days, and after the hymns, at the conclusion of Masses, Matins and Vespers, versicles of the Psalms be said, and at Vespers, after having prayed a collect, the people be dismissed with a blessing."[3] In which words it not merely designates certain hours to be prayed, but the manner whereby one then prayed.

Therefore, let the heretics cease to reprehend all ecclesiastics, nay the whole Church praising God at set hours. For God consecrated the same hours with mysteries. For He is born at midnight from the Virgin Mother. He rose reanimated from the tomb at the first hour of the morning. At the third hour the Holy Ghost came down upon the Apostles and the other disciples. He was crucified at the sixth hour. He died at the ninth hour. He supped with the disciples in the evening (*vespere*), and refreshed them with His Most Sacred Body. At the close of the day (*tempore completorii*), which is the first watch of the night, He went up the mountain to pray alone, to prepare for the ordeal which he was to undergo. "Seven times a day," according to the [Royal] Prophet, let us give praise to God,[4] so that by the trumpets of the Divine praises, the engines of the devil and the world fall down, just as of old the walls of Jericho fell by the priests sounding seven trumpets.

IDOLOLATRIA

Idolatry

I could not but be astonished when I discovered that there were some worshippers of idols among those who gave their names to Christ, because all who have even barely tasted (*summis labiis*[5]) Christ's doctrine, can very easily comprehend that there is nothing more injurious to God than if something besides God Himself be worshipped as the highest being. Yet even though God's law abominates idolatry, nevertheless there were not lacking among those who boasted of being Christians, who worshiped something besides God, and taught that it ought to be worshiped. For there were some (as Augustine says[6]) who worshiped the serpent and venerated it as God. For they said that the serpent which deceived Adam and Eve was Christ. And for this reason they used to feed and venerate a living serpent, which was going out of its den upon the incantation of the priest, and went up onto the altar which was over the den, and licked the oblations which they were offering, and after this was finished it returned to its den. Now Augustine relates the opinion of others, that the worship of the

---

[1] *On the Lord's Prayer*, n. 35 (PL 4, 541D-542A).
[2] Tit. 3.
[3] *Concilia Galliae*, c. 30 (PL 84, 267D). Mansi, vol. 8, col. 329E-330A.
[4] Cf. Ps. 118, 164.
[5] I.e. "with the ends of their lips."
[6] *De Haeresibus ad Quodvultdeum*, c. 17 (PL 42, 28).

serpent arose from the Nicolaites or Gnostics. These worshippers of the serpent were called Ophites from a Greek word, because ὄφις means snake, hence they were called Ὀφιανοί, which is the same as though they were called "the Serpentines": who were rightly so called from the serpent which they worshipped.

Others were the Cainites, who venerated Cain, saying that he had been made by one power, namely the devil's, and Abel by another, and that greater power which was in Cain himself prevailed such that he killed his brother. These things are taken from Philastrius,[1] because Augustine in his book on heresies[2] does not report this error of theirs as clearly. Augustine accuses these men of other errors in that place of which Philastrius makes no mention. But we will discuss them elsewhere. There were others called the Sethiani, in that they were venerating Seth, the son of Adam, with a falsity full of fables, saying that "he was born of a celestial mother, whom they claim united with a celestial father to produce another divine race, the sons of God, as it were."[3] [Epiphanius] says that some of them thought that Seth himself was Christ.[4] But Augustine does not accuse them of any such thing when speaking about them.[5] [Pseuedo-[6]] Tertullian, however, in his small book on heresies, calls these heretics *Sethoitas*,[7] not Sethiani as Philastrius and Augustine: and when he speaks about them, he does not accuse them of any such thing, namely that they believed that Seth was Christ. There were others who adored Angels, and hence they were called Angelici. Augustine lists them among the heretics in the thirty-ninth place.[8] All these sects are so antiquated, and have been effaced from men's memories, that it no longer known who were their inventors and at what time they began.

I find in Augustine no other error which pertains to idolatry. Philastrius, however, enumerates many other forms of idolatries. For he says that some adore the sun, whom he calls Heliognostics[9]: others again adored mice, and these he calls Musorites[10]: and he lists many other idolatries, which I omit, because he so relates them such that he says that they existed long ago among the Jews before the coming of Christ. I, however, determined to relate only those which arose among Christians after Christ's Passion. Wherefore I am surprised why Augustine included those three aforesaid heresies, namely the Ophites, the Cainites, and the Sethiani, in his work, since he stated that he would recount only those heresies which have arisen after Christ's Ascension into Heaven. Yet Philastrius enumerates those same aforesaid three heresies which were before Christ's coming. For when firstly discussing the heresies of the Jews, he inaugurates his book from the Ophites.

---

[1] *De haeresibus*, c. 2 (PL 12, 1116A).

[2] *De Haeresibus ad Quodvultdeum*, c. 18 (PL 42, 29).

[3] *Ibid.*, c. 19 (PL 42, 29).

[4] Philastrius is cited here, but he merely states that the Sethiani hold that Christ descended from Seth, which is certainly correct. He seems to have misinterpreted Epiphanius, the source of his knowledge of the Sethiani, who rather accused them of claiming that Christ was Seth reincarnated. (See notes of Fabricius and Galeardus in Migne (PL 12, 1117B)).

[5] *De Haeresibus ad Quodvultdeum*, c. 19 (PL 42, 29).

[6] In Migne's *Patrologia Latina* edition, the text contains not just forty-four chapters, but a further eight containing a list of heresies. These additional chapters are found separately in the Cluny-collection MSS as the spurious work *Adversus Omnes Haereses*, and appears as an appendix to *De praescriptione haereticorum* only in the Gagny/Mesnart edition of this work, where a marginal note indicates the join is the work of the editor.

[7] *De praescriptionibus adversus haereticos*, c. 47 (PL 2, 65B).

[8] *De Haeresibus ad Quodvultdeum*, c. 39 (PL 42, 32).

[9] *De haeresibus*, c. 10 (PL 12, 1123A-1124A).

[10] *Ibid.*, c. 12 (PL 12, 1124B-1125A).

It is not difficult to dispute against these heresies, especially since the authors boast that they are Christians, wherefore it will be necessary that they accept Sacred Scriptures, in which there are very clear quotations referring to idolatry. For that quotation is plain which the Lord cited against the devil, the father of heretics: "The Lord thy God shalt thou adore, and him only shalt thou serve" (Mt. 4, 10).[1] And in Deuteronomy: "When there shall be found among you within any of thy gates, which the Lord thy God shall give thee, man or woman that do evil in the sight of the Lord thy God, and transgress his covenant, so as to go and serve strange gods, and adore them, the sun and the moon, and all the host of heaven, which I have not commanded: and this is told thee, and hearing it thou hast inquired diligently, and found it to be true, and that the abomination is committed in Israel: thou shalt bring forth the man or the woman, who have committed that most wicked thing, to the gates of thy city, and they shall be stoned" (Deut. 17, 2-5). And the prophet Isaias, when enumerating many reasons due to which the people of Israel were abandoned by God, says that the chief reason was idolatry. For he says the following: "For thou hast cast off thy people, the house of Jacob: because they are filled as in times past, and have had soothsayers as the Philistines… And their land is filled with horses: and their chariots are innumerable. Their land also is full of idols: they have adored the work of their own hands, which their own fingers have made. And man hath bowed himself down, and man hath been debased: therefore forgive them not" (Is. 2, 6-9). And many other things follow thereafter for warding off idolatry. Furthermore, many thousand men of the children of Israel were punished because they adored the golden calf.[2] The three boys, because they were unwilling to adore the statue, were rewarded by God. For they, having been cast into the furnace by the king's command, were protected by God's Angel, lest the flame harm them.[3] John also when he fell before the feet of the Angel who showed the vision to him, and wanted to adore him, the Angel forbade him to do this saying: "See thou do it not: for I am thy fellow servant, and of thy brethren the prophets, and of them that keep the words of the prophecy of this book. Adore God" (Apoc. 22, 9). It is irksome to cite more quotations in such a clear matter, because if anyone would like them, Sacred Scripture is full of them.

JEJUNIUM

Fasting

The **first heresy** is that which says that fasting has no merit before God. For Jovinian and those who revived his error, the Waldensians, the Wycliffites, and the Lutherans, do not merely condemn the choosing of foods, but add still more saying that there is no merit in fasting, citing as proof of their error a passage of Paul wrongly understood by them: "Bodily exercise is profitable to little" (I Tim. 4, 8).

And I am truly astonished that a man who boasts that he is a Christian and accepts the Sacred Scriptures would say that there is no merit in fasting, since only the lovers of pleasure could teach this, who teach the things which their inordinate desires dictate. For if virtues ought to be loved, and the true lovers of them have merit, fasting will necessarily have some merit, since it is [an act of] virtue and part of temperance. For since gluttony is a fault which is committed in excessive eating or drinking, it cannot be that fasting, whereby we are sparing with food and drink, would not be [an act of] virtue. And if fasting is a zealous act done for God's sake, why is it that He would not render some reward, just as He does for any good

---

[1] Cf. Deut. 6, 13.
[2] "There were slain that day about three and twenty thousand men" (Ex. 32, 28).
[3] Dan. 3, 20-49.

work? Furthermore, fasting is not only [an act of] virtue, but it helps many other virtues, and prepares a very open way to them, wherefore it is fitting that a reward correspond to it, just as to the other virtues to which it agrees. For when Paul says that they who consent to those who act wrongly are deserving of punishment, why will they also not be worthy of a reward who consent to those acting rightly? Will God be more profuse in punishing than in rewarding? Far be it. Therefore, it is necessary that fasting be given a reward, just as the virtue to which it opens the way.

For fasting prepares the way to chastity, which is certainly a virtue. For if gluttony fosters lust, it is necessary that fasting aids chastity, because contrary effects have contrary causes. What made Sodom to sin except the "fulness of bread" (Ez. 16, 49)? "When the belly is heated with drink it soon boils over with lust."[1] Thus if you withdraw bread and wine, you block the way to sin, because (as someone said[2]) "Without Ceres and Liber, Venus freezes." Fasting also helps prayer, a sign of which is that the Lord, when He wished to teach the way whereby we ought to pray to the Heavenly Father, firstly expounded upon fasting and almsgiving, and forthwith teaches His prayer. He joins together fasting and almsgiving in one discourse so that He might suggest by this that fasting and almsgiving are two wings by the help of which prayer lifts itself on high.

For when the people had eaten and drank, they did not rise up to pray but to play; not to adore God, but to adore the golden calf.[3] Moses received the Law with a fast of forty days, but the satiated people made the calf which they adored, after which Moses broke the tablets on which the Law was written: and fittingly, because a full stomach is not apt to receiving the Divine Commandments, nor to understanding them. The three young men are cast into the furnace, the heat was so great that the flame rose up more than forty cubits: yet those who entered fasting[4] went out of the furnace unharmed. Daniel, a "man of desires," when he fasted for three weeks, made the lions fast, into whose lair he was cast, because although they were fasting, so that they would devour him more avidly, they nevertheless did him no harm. Next, after fasting for three weeks the same Daniel saw a vision in which it was said to him by an Angel: "From the first day that thou didst set thy heart to understand, to afflict thyself in the sight of thy God, thy words have been heard: and I am come for thy words" (Dan. 10, 12). How then does fasting have no merit, because it merits being heard? Elias prays fasting, and at his prayer rain does not fall upon the earth for three years and six months.[5] He again prays fasting and he obtains rain from God.[6] He comes to the mountain of God fasting, in which the Divine presence resides, although he does not see God, because reputing himself as being unworthy he covered his face with his mantle when the Lord passed by. Therefore, fasting receives the Law, voracity lost the Law. Fasting frees from burning, the fires of lust grow with the nourishments of foods. Fasting prepares the mind for prayer, excessive drinking darkens the mind.

Let us proceed to the New Testament, whence we can have even much clearer testimonies. The prophetess Anna, the daughter of Phanuel is praised in Luke's Gospel because she "departed not from the temple, by fastings and prayers serving night and day" (2, 37). But if fasting were of no importance (as the heretics teach) why is she praised for it? Besides, when the Lord cast out the unclean spirit from the body of a certain child, His disciples asked him: "Why could not we cast him out?" (Mt. 17, 18). To whom the He replied: "This kind is not

---

[1] St. Jerome, Letter 69 (To Oceanus), n. 9 (PL 22, 663).
[2] Terence, *Eunuchus*, scene 5, act 4, l. 732.
[3] Cf. Ex. 32, 6.
[4] They ate pulse and drank water for ten days (Dan. 1, 12).
[5] Cf. III Kings 17, 1.
[6] Cf. III Kings 18, 42 & 45; Mk. 9, 27-28; Mt. 17, 18-20.

cast out but by prayer and fasting" (v. 20). Why is it then that it is a thing of no importance, which is so powerful that it can cast out devils? Again, the Teacher of truth Himself when teaching the manner according to which we ought to fast says: "But thou, when thou fastest anoint thy head, and wash thy face; that thou appear not to men to fast, but to thy Father who is in secret: and thy Father who seeth in secret, will repay thee" (Mt. 6, 17-18). Notice that you now see the very clear merit of fasting. For the Father repays us for fasting. Now He never renders a reward except for merit. Therefore, if the Father repays for fasting, it is necessary to admit that some cause of merit exists in fasting. These testimonies are very clear: wherefore there is no need to cite more.

Nevertheless, it remains that we reply to the objections of the heretics. Firstly, they object to us that passage of Paul in his First Epistle to Timothy: "Bodily exercise is profitable to little: but godliness is profitable to all things, having promise of the life that now is, and of that which is to come" (4, 8). To which objection we reply that this passage of Paul is nowise opposed to our position for two reasons. One reason is that fasting is not properly called a bodily exercise, and Paul is not speaking about it there. Hence Theophylactus when expounding that passage of Paul says the following: "Some men call fasting a bodily exercise, but it is not: for this is a spiritual exercise. Actually, he means bodily exercise which having many labors, benefits the body a small amount and for a very short time."[1] Notice it is clear how fasting is not an exercise of the body, but a spiritual exercise, because it applies to the spirit. But be it that fasting is a bodily exercise, there will still be another reason why this passage will not oppose our position. For in that passage Paul does not deny absolutely that bodily exercise is useful, but rather he says that it is of small benefit if it does not have piety conjoined to it. And that this is the meaning of those words is proved from the preceding words. For he had firstly said to Timothy that he should "exercise himself unto godliness," and he immediately added, "bodily exercise is profitable to little: but godliness is profitable to all things." It is as though he said, "Do not rely so upon the maceration of the flesh, such that you would think that this alone without godliness [*pietas*] suffices, because without godliness it is useful for little, wherefore exercise yourself unto godliness, which is much more preferable than the maceration of the flesh." And [Ambrosiaster] interprets in this manner saying: "Now he says, 'bodily exercise is profitable to little.' For to fast and to abstain from food by the admonishing command of the Creator does not profit much, unless piety be added to this, the works of which are helped by the prayers of many to be worthy to the Lord... Now exercise of the body is nothing other than the bridling of the flesh. Thus, if anyone, because this thing is a great mercy, nevertheless suffers a slipping of the flesh, what will happen to such a person? Doubtlessly he will be flogged, because it should have been done, and this nowise ought to be omitted."[2]

Secondly they object to us those words of the Lord said by Isaias the prophet to the Israelite people: "Is this such a fast as I have chosen: for a man to afflict his soul for a day?... Is not this rather the fast that I have chosen? loose the bands of wickedness, undo the bundles that oppress, let them that are broken go free, and break asunder every burden. Deal thy bread to the hungry, and bring the needy and the harbourless into thy house: when thou shalt see one naked, cover him, and despise not thy own flesh. Then shall thy light break forth as the morning, and thy health shall speedily arise" (58, 5-8). By which words God very clearly approves of fasting and abstinence from sins, to which is adjoined the doing of good works, especially works of piety towards the poor and needy.

Now we repel this objection in the same way whereby we repelled the preceding one. We certainly admit that fasting alone, if other things are lacking, is of no consequence. For

---

[1] *Expositio in Epistolam I ad Timotheum* (PG 125, 55).
[2] *Commentaria in Epistolam ad Timotheum Primam* (PL 17, 473D-474A). Cf. Lk. 11, 42.

fasting without piety and the rest of the good works avails little or not at all. But it does not thence follow that fasting with piety and the rest of the good works is of no consequence, nay when the other works are present, it has much value. "Prayer is good with fasting and alms" (Tob. 12, 8). Therefore, the Lord by these words of the prophet condemns only fasting that is defective, and to which many other sins are adjoined. Now this becomes clear from what he previously said. "Behold," he said, "in the day of your fast your own will is found, and you exact of all your debtors. Behold you fast for debates and strife, and strike with the fist wickedly. Do not fast as you have done until this day, to make your cry to be heard on high" (Is. 58, 3-4). He did not only say, "Do not fast," but he added, "as you have done until this day." What does it mean, "as you have done until this day"? It means that they should not "strike with the fist," they should not "fast for debates and strife," and they should not carry out their own wills as before.

Now there is another fasting which is motivated by charity, so that the flesh may be subject to the spirit, and nonetheless the poor are not abandoned. Such fasting, I say, is praised by God, and He says that a reward is prescribed for it by the Father. Otherwise, if by the fact that fasting done wrongly is reprehended you wish to infer that even if it were done correctly it would avail nothing: in the same way it will be necessary to say that the celebration of the sabbath in the Old Law was of no important, because those who were honoring the sabbath not as God wished, the Lord reprehended through the same prophet, saying: "My soul hateth your new moons, and your solemnities: they are become troublesome to me" (Is. 1, 14). And concerning those sacrificing and offering incense in sin He says: "Offer sacrifice no more in vain: incense is an abomination to me" (v. 13). And about all these men He says: "I am weary of bearing them. And when you stretch forth your hands, I will turn away my eyes from you: and when you multiply prayer, I will not hear: for your hands are full of blood. Wash yourselves, be clean, take away the evil of your devices from my eyes" (v. 14-16). Therefore, let them begone, and let them also condemn based upon these words the keeping holy of the sabbath, the offering of incense, and every sacrifice: and let them say that it merely suffices that we take away the evil of our thoughts. Far be it, however, that someone be so foolish that he would dare to condemn these things. For the Lord in that passage is condemning those who were either not sacrificing as they ought or honoring the sabbath with a certain profane joy, and they were doing all these things in the state of mortal sin, thinking to themselves that it suffices that they had done those exterior things. Now the Lord commanded the sanctification of the sabbath: that is very far from condemning it. He afterwards spoke in this way about fasting, such that He condemned fasting which is without piety and with mortal sin, but the rest He left intact.

Finally, the opinion of these heretics was clearly condemned by the definitions of many Councils. The Synod of Gangra[1] says the following: "If any of the ascetics, without bodily necessity, shall behave with insolence and disregard the fasts commonly prescribed and observed by the Church, because of his perfect understanding in the matter, let him be anathema."[2] The anathema, therefore, applies to Jovinian, Luther and any other supporters of this heresy: because they all condemn all fasting, since they say that it has no merit before God. The Synod of [Milan] in which not only these, but the other heresies of Jovinian were condemned, after it defined concerning chastity, finally when speaking about fasting says these words: "And fitting it is that these men should despise widowhood, which is wont to keep fasts, for they regret that they should have been mortified by these for any time, and avenge

---

[1] The Synod of Gangra was held during the fourth century in what once was the capital of Paphlagonia, now part of modern-day Turkey. It issued twenty canons which were declared ecumenical by the Council of Chalcedon in 451.

[2] Canon 19 (PL 67, 58-60).

the wrong they inflicted on themselves, and by daily banquets and habits of luxury seek to ward off the pain of abstinence. They do nothing more rightly than in thus condemning themselves out of their own mouth."[1] And after some quotations of Paul cited in the same place, the Council thereafter adds, "If what the Apostle has said is not enough, let them hear the [Royal] Prophet saying, 'And I covered my soul in fasting' (Ps. 68, 11). He therefore who fasts not is uncovered and naked and exposed to wounds."[2]

Blessed Jerome wrote against this error in the second book of his *Against Jovinian*, in which place he intertwines many praises of fasting. Blessed Ambrose made an elegant book which is entitled, *De Elia et jejunio*, in which he extols fasting in a marvelous manner.[3] Josse van Clichtove in our time wrote at great length about this subject in the work which is entitled, *Propugnaculum ecclesiae adversus Lutheranos*.[4]

A **second heresy** teaches that fasting ought not to be fixed to a certain and set time, but that anyone may fast when he wishes. Aerius first taught this heresy (as far as I know): unless perhaps this is a heresy of a certain Eustathius,[5] who is condemned by the Synod of Gangra, because he condemned ecclesiastical fasting. This heresy is not the same as the one which Jovinian taught, because Augustine when discussing Aerius does not say that he despised fasting in general, but he ascribes to him only that he said that the legally fixed fasts ought not to be observed, but one ought to fast whenever he wished, lest one seem to be subject to the law.[6] Thus Aerius did not criticize fasting, but only criticized the laws of fasting, nowise admitting that the Church can oblige to fast: because even if fasting is salutary and beneficial for the soul, still he does not want that someone be forced to do it, but rather he wanted it to be free for anyone to fast when he wishes. I said these things because I see some men disputing about fasting, who place Aerius in the same error with Jovinian, although there is a great difference between the two.

Erasmus of Rotterdam also gave occasion to many for suspecting him of this error, from which suspicion he never (as far as I know) cleared himself entirely. For in his *Paraphrases* he says these words: "Fastings are sad which the law prescribes: and wherefore displeasing to God, Who loves the cheerful giver."[7] Which words of Erasmus in fact were condemned by the theologians in Paris with a common censure of them all. Erasmus nevertheless replied to their censure, giving an explanation of the aforesaid words. But his explanation was such that it allowed the suspicion of heresy to remain. I will cite his words, so that his mind may be more clearly understood. For in reply to the Parisians he uses these words: "Further, he who fasts by fear, will not fast unless the law compels; in this respect the fasting of this man is certainly sad and displeasing to God, because it lacks alacrity of spirit, with which God is especially pleased. Therefore, I call back no one from obedience to superiors, but I show what is more pleasing to God. For the weak are not consequently free from their constitutions,

---

[1] Letter 42, n. 9 of St. Ambrose to Pope Siricius (PL 16, 1126C) which was approved by the Synod of Milan in 389 A.D.

[2] *Ibid.*, n. 11 (PL 16, 1127C-1128A).

[3] PL 14, 697-728. For an English translation of this text, see *De Helia et Ieiunio: A commentary, with an Introduction and Translation* (*Patristic Studies*, trans. by Sr. Mary Joseph Aloysius Buck, Washington, D.C., CUA, 1929), vol. 19.

[4] *Propugnaculum ecclesiae adversus Lutheranos* (Paris, Ex officina Simonis Colinaei, 1526), bk. 3, pp. 406 ff.

[5] Eustathius (300- ca. 377 A. D.) was the Bishop of Sebaste in Armenia

[6] *De Haeresibus ad Quodvultdeum*, c. 53 (PL 42, 39-40).

[7] *Paraphrases in Novum Testamentum* (Berlin, Haude and Spener, 1778), p. 347.

because God prefers those fasting with alacrity and spontaneity to those who fast by force of law rather than from their heart."[1]

In which words he teaches clearly enough that fasting is better by one's own choice than when forced by law. For which reason he wishes that the Church would remove fasting of this kind. This is not because he thinks that the Church cannot make such laws, or having been so made that they ought to be temerariously violated: but because he reckons that fasting done spontaneously is of a better sort before God than that which one is forced to do. And he thinks that there would be many more men who spontaneously fast and abstain from meat than now do so being forced by the law. For in his reply to the first censure of the Parisians concerning fasting and the enjoyment of food, he says these words: "Now I think that Christianity was purer at the times of the Apostles and martyrs than it is now, when the charity of men has grown cold as you see. But at those times when there was no prescript about distinguishing food, many more were abstaining from meat than they do now when forced by law."[2]

In his pamphlet, [*On Eating Meat*,[3]] he says these words: "If anyone is sufficiently steadfast to moderate himself with temperance at all times, there is no absolute need for prescribed fasts, except when God's anger must be placated in some circumstances with this sort of sacrifice. 'But,' you will say, 'it is for the ignorant and dull witted that fixed days are prescribed.' Let us accept that this is quite tolerable. It is laid down that there must be only one light meal, and the type of food is laid down, too. But this is not enough; eternal damnation is threatened for anyone who violates this human custom."[4] From which words it is more clearly established that Erasmus maintains that some days of fasting are wrongly prescribed: but he reckons that this is a tolerable evil: yet he reckons it to be an intolerable evil that fastings are prescribed under threat of Hell: and he deems it harsher that in fastings of this kind some specific kinds of food are forbidden.

Therefore Erasmus (as it is plainly evident from the things which we have said) seems to think the same thing as Aerius. Still, their error (as we recently said) is different from the error of Jovinian. But even though the latter error is different from the former, it is not necessary to think up new stratagems against it: because (as we have shown above, when we treated the power of the Church) the Church can establish laws, especially those which seem to be conducive to the observance of the Divine Commandments, which laws all Christians are obliged to observe. But since we have just now shown against Jovinian and his followers that fasting is useful, and Aerius himself (as I think) would not deny this, we have thence proved that the Church can prescribe fasts, and those things which have been prescribed by her ought to be observed by all Christians, such that no one may disregard them with impunity. And certainly this error attacks the Church's authority more than the efficacy of fasting.

Wherefore since it belongs to the Church's authority to prescribe what shall seem useful, the case is closed concerning this error, especially since there are some fasts instituted by the Apostles, or perhaps by Christ, according to the common teaching of all. For it is said concerning Lent by many men, not of the meanest sort but by those of the greatest authority, and

---

[1] "Declarationes ad Censuras Lutetiase, vulgatas sub nomine Facultatis Theologiae Parisiensis," *Desiderii Erasmi Roterodami Opera omnia emendatiora et auctiora* (Leiden, Pieter van der Aa, 1706), vol. 9, p. 833C.

[2] *Ibid.*, p. 827E.

[3] This quotation is taken from Erasmus' work, *On Eating Meat* (De *interdicto esu carnalium*). Our author, however, cites here, *Notes on the Letter about Abstinence* (De *ciborum delectu* [*scholia*]), scholium 23, which is Erasmus' subsequent commentary on the cited passage. For the English translation of these works see *Collected Works of Erasmus* (Toronto, University of Toronto Press, 2015), vol. 73 ("Controversies").

[4] *Ibid.*, p. 1202A.

not recent, but the oldest authors, that the Lenten fast was instituted by Christ, such that the obligation to it depends not merely upon human but Divine law. Hence Maximus bishop [of Turin] says: "We have brought forth the examples of Sacred Writ, by which we might prove that this number, forty [days of fasting in Lent], was not constituted of men, but consecrated of God: not invented by human cogitation, but commanded by the heavenly Majesty... These things are not so much the precepts of priests, as of God; and so he that despises them, despises not the priesthood, but Christ, Who speaks in His priests."[1] Theophilus of Alexandria says that we observe a forty days fast as ordered and appointed by the Apostles.[2] And the martyr [Pseudo-] Ignatius in a letter to the Philippians, which is the fourth of the series, says the following: "Despise not the period of forty days, for it comprises an imitation of the conduct of the Lord. After the week of the Passion, do not neglect to fast on the fourth and sixth days."[3]

From which testimonies, even if it is perhaps not sufficiently established that that [fast of forty days] was instituted by Christ by precept, still it is evident that following Christ's example it was observed by the Apostles, and enjoined by precept upon the Christians, and after the death of the Apostles, the Church has decreed in many councils that it ought to be strictly observed. For the First Synod of Braga defined as follows: "If anyone on the Thursday before Easter, at the *Coena Domini*, does not, at the appointed time, after None, keep Mass [*missas non tenet*] fasting in the church, but, after the manner of the Priscillianist sect, keeps the festival of that day, after Terce, with their fast discontinued by a Mass for the dead, let him be anathema."[4] And in the collection of [mostly] Greek synods by Martin, [Arch] bishop of Braga, it is said as follows: "The fast must not be broken on the fifth day of the last week in Lent [i.e., on Maundy Thursday], and the whole of Lent be dishonored; but it is necessary to fast during all the Lenten season."[5] And the [VIII] Synod of Toledo commands this more clearly and strictly, namely so that one fast and abstain from meat during the whole Lent.[6] Pope and martyr [Pseudo-] Telesphorus, who was the seventh to hold the papacy after Blessed Peter the Apostle, also published a decree about abstinence from meat in Lent.[7] Even though prior to him one would fast for forty days, as is evident from the quotation of the martyr Ignatius just now cited, still it is not evident to me whether before Telesphorus such fasting was done with abstinence from meat, or only by a reduction of the amount of food, namely so that one would fast with eating meat once a day and less than other days: since I am not sure about the matter, I state nothing. Nevertheless it is certain from the testimony of Philo

---

[1] *Homilia* 37 (PL 57, 307C-308C). St. Maximus of Turin was born about 380 A.D. and died shortly after 465 A.D.

[2] "Having to celebrate Easter, let us begin our Lent from the eighth day of the month, which with the Egyptians is called Pharmenoth; and God giving us strength let us fast more carefully on the Great week, howbeit so, that according to the Evangelical Traditions, we end the fasts late at night, on the eighteenth day of Pharmuth" (Letter 98, n. 25 (PL 22, 811)).

[3] C. 13 (PG 5, 938A).

[4] Can. 17. *Collectio Canonum Ecclesiae Hispanae ex probatissimis ac pervetustis Codicibus* (Madrid, Typogr. Regia, 1808), p. 601.

[5] Synod of Laodicea, c. 50 (*Collectio orientalium canonum ad Concilium Lucense missa*); *Concilia Hispaniae* (PL 84, 581D).

[6] Can. 9: "Whoever without necessity, and manifest languor produced by weakness, or the inability arising from the time of life, shall dare to use flesh during the days of Lent, let him be an alien from the Communion of the sacred day of the Lord's Resurrection" (*Collectio Canonum Ecclesiae Hispanae ex probatissimis ac pervetustis Codicibus*, p. 437). The reference in the text was to canon eight, but has been corrected here.

[7] "The fast of Lent was instituted by Telesphorus." This fictitious decree supposedly mentioned in the *Chronicle of Eusebius* is spurious. See PL 27, 1067B.

cited by Eusebius that there was abstinence from meat at the time of the Apostles.[1] Finally, the Synod of Gangra decreed concerning all the fasts prescribed by the Church as follows: "If any of the ascetics, without bodily necessity, shall behave with insolence and disregard the fasts commonly prescribed and observed by the Church, because of his perfect understanding in the matter, let him be anathema."[2] I could have cited the decrees of many other councils on this point, but these should suffice.

For the rest, what Erasmus says, that it is better to fast spontaneously than by order of the law, is proved to be false by that which is said in the First Book of Kings: "Obedience is better than sacrifices" (15, 22). Thus, it is better than fasting. And obedience is rightly preferred to fasting, because fasting pertains to temperance: but obedience pertains to justice, which renders to each one what is his due. Accordingly, by obedience we give what we owe to a superior. He who spontaneously fasts, has only the merit of fasting: but he who fasts by the incentive of the law, and hence fasts to obey the law, he has besides the value of fasting, the merit of obedience. Therefore, the condition of him who fasts obeying the precept is better than of him who spontaneously fasts by his own choice: because the latter has only one merit, namely of fasting: but the former has double, the merit of fasting and of obedience. The things which we will say below in the section on "Vows" also deal with this matter. For in that place (with God's guidance) we will prove that those things which are done from the obligation of a vow are better than those things done spontaneously. From which things it is also proved that works which are done from the obligation of a precept are better than those done by one's own choice.

Next, he clearly errs and he speaks ineptly when he says the one fasts out of fear who otherwise would not fast if the law had not commanded. For he who does something that he was not going to do unless the law prescribed, acts out of obedience, and fear of punishment does not necessarily follow from that, about which (as is evident) Erasmus was then speaking, namely that he is one who always has sadness and not filial fear in himself. Now that not everyone, who does what he was not going to do unless commanded, acts out of servile fear, is proved on the grounds that otherwise it would be necessary to admit that every such person sins and is a transgressor of the same law. For (as Augustine says[3]) "He who carries out a command out of fear acts otherwise than he should, and therefore is deemed here to have done nothing [meritorious]."

Now to say that everyone sins, who does what he was not going to do unless the law commanded, is a manifest error. Because if every such person sins, it will be necessary by the same principle to acknowledge that every legislator sins when he commands something besides the Divine law, because by his law he forces all men to do what they were not otherwise going to do. Therefore, according to Erasmus' teaching, it would never be allowed to prescribe anything except those things which all men were going to do, the law being excluded, lest the legislator by his law oblige someone to sin, namely by obliging him to do something which that law being excluded, he was not going to do. Yet far be it that a Christian would accept this. For it necessarily follows, as Erasmus supposes, that anyone who does by the precept of the law what he was not otherwise going to do, acts sorrowfully and sadly. For he who has acquired the virtue of obedience, and from its inclination and impulse does what has been prescribed by law, even though was not going to do it the law being excluded, does

---

[1] The early Christians during their vigils "taste no wine at all, nor any flesh, but water is their only drink, and the relish with their bread is salt and hyssop." (*Church History*, bk. 2, c. 17, n. 22 (PG 20, 183B)).

[2] Can. 19 (PL 84, 114C).

[3] Cf. Gregory IX, *Decretales,* bk. 5, tit. 41, chap. 8. A footnote in the *Decretals* states that this passage is of uncertain origin.

it not with less, nay often with greater alacrity of soul, than if the law being excluded he had acted merely by his own choice. For a habit (as Aristotle teaches[1]) not merely gives facility to the one acting, but also pleasure.

Furthermore, even if we were to freely grant to Erasmus that everyone is gloomy and sad who by the motivation of the law does what he was not otherwise going to do, still it does not necessarily follow that that work done out of obedience to the law is always displeasing to God. Because God does not require so much cheerfulness in the giver that he have absolutely no sadness, but that alacrity of soul suffices unto God which overcomes and conquers sadness, restraining in opposition. For the sadness which Christ had during the Passion did not prevent even slightly the Passion from being most pleasing to God the Father. Thus it is false what Erasmus said by these words: "Further, he who fasts by fear, will not fast unless the law compels; in this respect the fasting of this man is certainly sad and displeasing to God, because it lacks alacrity of spirit, with which God is especially pleased." From which words it is clearly established that Erasmus wrongly thought that sadness could not exist with alacrity of spirit, whereby God is enjoyed.

But let us see what Erasmus puts forth in his favor. "God," he said in his response to the Parisians, "condemns Pharisaical fasts in Isaias, and Christ also detests them, which nowise ought to be equated with spontaneous fasts, which the Apostles would fast without the need of any precept after having imbibed the Heavenly Spirit."[2]

I certainly admit that God condemned the Pharisaical fasts through Isaias, but not due to the fact that they were fasting on the prescribed days, or according to the precept of the law: but because they were relying upon their fast alone, such that having neglected all other virtues and good works, they believed that by fasting alone they would satisfy God. Now in order to make these things clearer, it is necessary to cite Isaias' words: "Behold in the day of your fast your own will is found, and you exact of all your debtors. Behold you fast for debates and strife. and strike with the fist wickedly. Do not fast as you have done until this day, to make your cry to be heard on high" (58, 3-4). In which words it is evident that there is no mention made of the precept of fasting: nor was the fasting of Pharisees reproached on this account, namely that they fasting being obliged by law and not by their own choice.

Next it is necessary to notice that He did not absolutely forbid fasting to them, but He merely forbade the kind of fasting which they were doing. For He did not say absolutely: "Do not fast," but He added, "as you have done until this day, to make your cry to be heard on high." He condemned their fasting on account of the boasting and the other sins which they were perpetrating on days of fasting, not however because they were fasting because being prescribed by law. Therefore, fasting ought not to be reckoned as if it were Pharisaical, which is done on account of the precept of the law.

The **third heresy** is of the Beghards and Beguines saying that man is not obliged to the ecclesiastical fasts, since they have reached the state of perfection. And this error differs somewhat from Aerius' error, because the Beghards and Beguines do not exempt all Christians from the obligation of fasting, as Aerius taught, but only those who have reached the state of perfection. But they deduce this error from another error of theirs whereby they teach that those who are in the state of perfection are not subject to human laws, and hence they say that they are also not bound to ecclesiastical fasts. It will not be necessary to furnish new arguments against this error, because we have already proved above that all Christians, of whatever state they may be, are bound to the observance of laws instituted by the Church. But if they say that they are not bound to fasting, namely because he who has acquired the state

---

[1] *Nichomedian Ethics*, bk 2, c. 1 & 3.

[2] *Omnia Opera...* (Basel, Froben, 1540), vol. 9, *Propositionum Erasmicarum censurae facultatis Parisiensis*, declaratio 7, p. 670.

of perfection does not need fasting for the salvation of his soul, then it is necessary to draw up other arguments.

And firstly, that testimony of Paul militates against them: "the flesh lusteth against the spirit: and the spirit against the flesh; for these are contrary one to another: so that you do not the things that you would" (Gal. 5, 17). Because if the flesh is so rebellious, it is necessary to restrain its rebellion with the bridle of fasting. But perhaps the Beghards will say that he who has reached the state of perfection, does not suffer in himself from this struggle of the flesh and the spirit, but has his tabernacle in peace.[1] This is such clear madness that it is unnecessary to attack it, because to the Virgin Mother of God alone is this privilege given that she would have such peace in her. Hence Richard of Saint Victor says the following: " In other saints it is held to be a great thing that they cannot be overcome by vices, in this woman it is seen that she could not even in the least be attacked by vices. In other saints in general it is publicly declared that sin does not reign in their bodies, only to this woman is it singularly given that sin does not reside in her mortal body."[2]

Furthermore, the vessel of election, Paul the Apostle, who was caught up to the third Heaven and saw the hidden things of God which it is not granted to man to utter: he, I say, chastises his body, and brings it into subjection: and he does not do this in vain, because he fears lest when he has preached to others, he himself should become a castaway.[3] The great John the Baptist, than whom among them that are born of women there has not risen a greater, who was also filled with the Holy Ghost from his mother's womb, also chastises his body, abstaining from wine and strong drink,[4] not eating meat, but "his meat was locusts and wild honey" (Mt. 3, 4). What therefore do the wicked Beghards and the libidinous Beguines presume? Do they not arrogate a greater perfection of virtue to themselves than to Paul and John the Baptist? But let us say something more astounding and more sacred, He Himself Who knew no sin,[5] neither was guile found in his mouth,[6] fasted for forty days and nights, not because He had need of fasting, but so that He might give an example to us, that however perfect one may be, he might recognize that fasting is necessary for him. For as long as we are here below, we have enemies in our house, who lie in wait like thieves for us. Within the gates of Jerusalem the Jebusite was always in the midst, and could never could be eliminated[7]: so likewise within our flesh, no matter how perfect anyone may be, some stimulus to evil always remains. Wherefore it is necessary to fast, so that by fasting the malice of the flesh may be held in check.

Finally, among the eight errors of the Beghards and Beguines condemned at the Council of Vienne under Clement V, this is the second.[8] Now the decree of the Council is found in the book of the *Clementine Decretals*, under the title *de hereticis*, chapter [III] whose beginning is *Ad nostrum*...[9] He who wishes may see it there.

---

[1] Cf. Job 5, 24.
[2] *De Emmanuele*, bk. 2, c. 31 (PL 196, 664B-C).
[3] Cf. I Cor. 9, 27.
[4] Cf. Lk. 1, 15.
[5] Cf. II Cor. 5, 21.
[6] Cf. I Pet. 2, 22.
[7] Cf. Judges 1, 21.
[8] "That it is not necessary for man to fast or to pray, after he has attained a degree of such perfection; because then his sensuality is so perfectly subject to the spirit and to reason that man can freely grant to the body whatever it pleases" (Dz. 472).
[9] *Constitutiones Clementis V*, bk. 5, tit. 3, c. 3.

IMAGO

Images

Long ago there was an error, which has been renewed in our times, teaching that images ought to be removed from the Church, saying that to have images in churches is idolatry, whether they be of Christ or of any holy man. I can scarcely find the first author of this heresy. Platina in the life of Pope Adrian I says that the Felician heresy of removing images was abrogated at the Synod of Frankfurt held under this pontificate.[1] Now although he called it "Felician," still he did not make clear from which Felix it originated. Yet he had previously said in the life of Pope Constantine that a certain Felix, Archbishop of Ravenna, was transferred by the Emperor Justinian to Pontus, who after abandoning his former heresy returned to his own country under Emperor Theodosius.[2] But in this place he also does not say what was the heresy of this Felix. But if from those two places some would want to conclude that this heresy was named after this Felix, I do not object: although I know that before this heresy there was not lacking someone who taught this heresy.

For it is evident that Blessed Pope Gregory I lived more than a hundred years before Pope Constantine, at the time of whom this Felix lived. But Blessed Gregory rebuked by letter a certain Serenus, Bishop of Marseilles, that with inconsiderate zeal he had broken the images of the Saints, fearing that they would be adored by the people.[3] And Epiphanius [Bishop of the city of Salamis in] Cyprus preceded Blessed Gregory by more than a hundred and fifty years. Now he in a letter to John, Bishop of Jerusalem, near the end of the letter says that he tore a curtain which he saw hanging on the doors of a certain church. He tore it, however, because it had the image of Christ or of some saint (for when he wrote these things he did not recall whose image it was) and said it was "contrary to the teaching of the Scriptures that an image of a man should be hung up in Christ's church."[4] Notice to what times we trace back this error. But even though the two bishops so thought, still they are not known for this heresy. The reason is that the matter was not so clear, nor had yet the Church defined the matter before that time: wherefore it was then free for them to so think without it being heresy. Additionally, those thinking this way were not adhering to their opinion with a pertinacious mind, such that they were not prepared to submit to the Church teaching.

Many Greek emperors were supporters of this error. For Leo III, emperor of Constantinople, was deprived of his rule [over the Exarchate of Ravenna] and communion with the faithful on account of this error by Pope Gregory III (as Platina bears witness[5]). Emperor Constantine V, who died stricken with the sickness of elephantiasis, adhered to this heresy. Emperor Leo IV, son of this Constantine, supported this heresy. Yet the wife of this Leo, named Irene, when Leo was dead, being the regent of the empire in the name of her son, namely Constantine VI, assembled the Second Council of Nicea, in which it was defined by three hundred and fifty bishops gathered in the said place, that "those who were to say that

---

[1] *The Lives of the Popes: From the Time of Our Saviour Jesus Christ, to the Reign of Sixtus IV* (London, Printed for Christopher Wilkinson, 1685), p. 148. Bishop Felix of Urgel was condemned by the Synod of Frankfurt in 794 A. D.

[2] *Ibid.*, pp. 128-130.

[3] "For indeed it had been reported to us that, inflamed with inconsiderate zeal, you had broken images of Saints, as though under the plea that they ought not to be adored." (Bk. 11, letter 13 (PL 77, 1027C)).

[4] Letters of St. Jerome, letter 51, n. 9 (PL 22, 526).

[5] *The Lives of the Popes*, p. 134.

holy images ought to be destroyed are to be marked with a perpetual anathema."[1] When Constantine VI became old, having been deceived by the persuasion of evil men, he did not want to accept this definition of the Church. And this matter was one of the main reasons why the Latins separated themselves from the Greeks. Much later the Waldensians revived this error, with whom (as they always do) the Wycliffites agreed. A certain Carlstadt and another man, Balthasar Hubmaier, Lutherans, although they deviated from Luther, their teacher, on this matter, because he approved of images of the saints, recalled this long-buried error from Hell in our times in some parts of Germany.

This error is easily refuted if we consider how by the Lord's command there were images among the Jews, yet He had strictly forbidden them to have graven images. For when He commanded Moses to make the propitiatory out of the purist gold, he immediately added, saying: "Thou shalt make also two cherubims of beaten gold, on the two sides of the oracle. Let one cherub be on the one side, and the other on the other" (Ex. 25, 18-19). Behold you see the images of Cherubim, and not in a common place, but on the propitiatory, which was the covering of the ark of the testimony. Furthermore, when the people of Israel, on account of the murmurings which they had said against God and Moses, suffered from the bites of serpents, Moses prayed to the Lord, to whom the Lord says: "Make a brazen serpent, and set it up for a sign: whosoever being struck shall look on it, shall live. Moses therefore made a brazen serpent, and set it up for a sign: which when they that were bitten looked upon, they were healed" (Num. 21, 8-9). Notice again another image made by the Lord's command, the use of which was not completely useless, since upon looking at it those struck by the serpents were healed.

Nevertheless, King Ezechias afterwards broke the brazen serpent, not because it was wrong to keep the image, but because he saw that the people bestowed Divine honors to it, as though there were something of the Divinity in it. The history in the books of Kings itself clearly enough declares that this was the reason why the king broke it, saying: "He destroyed the high places, and broke the statues in pieces, and cut down the groves, and broke the brazen serpent, which Moses had made: for till that time the children of Israel burnt incense to it: and he called its name Nohestan" (IV Kings 18, 4). You see the reason why the serpent was broken, namely because the children of Israel were burning incense to it. For the Wise Man had reckoned that the people were prone to idolatry, inasmuch as they worshipped idols not merely once or twice, but very often: thinking that the people could not be otherwise recalled from that error unless he broke the serpent, he thus rightly broke it. And lest they would have from the breaking of the serpent an occasion of sadness, believing that they had lost something Divine, he imposed a name upon the serpent which when heard they would know and understand that it was not as they thought. Hence the old author, the monk Angelomus [of Luxeuil], in his commentaries on the books of Kings when expounding this passage, says the following: "'And he called its name Nohestan…' indeed since Nohestan means 'their brass': so that they might know by his words that what they worshipped as something Divine is not God since it is metal."[2]

Thus, if the Christian people were now equally prone to idolatry as the people of Israel were then, and could not otherwise be recalled from error than by having the images broken, I would think that they rightly ought to be broken. For those things which are not necessary, no matter how good they may be, still often ought to be removed, or completely abrogated on account of the evils which are known to arise therefrom. So then, even if the use of images is good and useful to the Church, nevertheless if idolatry were to arise therefrom, which could not be otherwise avoided according to the judgment of the superiors than by breaking the images, then it would be just that they be removed or broken by the command of the superiors,

---

[1] *Ibid.*, p. 148.
[2] *Enarrationes in libros Regum* (PL 115 524B).

and not by the free choice of just anyone. But the Christian people are not prone to idolatry, as the Jewish people were, because they have never been initiated to Beelphegor,[1] nor have adored Astaroth, the goddess of the Sidonians,[2] nor worshipped Baal, nor constructed temples to idols: hence there is not now an urgent reason on account of which images ought to be broken, as there then was that the serpent would be broken, because even if one or another would err by a certain simplicity, he ought to be taught, and not for his sake ought images to be entirely removed. For laws and statutes have a view, not to a minority but to the majority of the people. We have discussed these things at such great length, because from rightly praising this deed of King Ezechias, heretics wish to prove their detested error. Now that we have very clearly exposed the matter, it will now clearly appear how unfounded their opinion is.

But now let us return to reinforcing our position. Solomon made Cherubim, palms, and pomegranates, and under the sea of brass he put twelve oxen, and on the bases of the sides, lions with oxen. And Solomon was not reprehended for the painting or sculpting of these things, rather he was exceedingly praised. Thus, if it was then allowed to sculpt twelve oxen, when one had more fear about idolatry, why will it not be allowed to paint the twelve Apostles, of whom those twelve oxen bore the figures? If it was allowed to raise the serpent before the people prone to idolatry, so that by looking at it the children of Israel might be freed from the serpents' bites, why will it not be allowed now to depict Christ raised up upon the Cross, so that we may recall by looking at His image the immense benefits which He procured for the human race when dying upon the Cross? If it was allowed to paint obscure images, why will it not be allowed to paint bodies?

Again, the use of images is useful, because images are the written language of the unlettered, seeing which they read them like books, and by seeing them they impress upon their memories that which otherwise would not be remembered. For seeing the story depicted wherein a naked man bound to a column, wounded with many stripes, and others on his right and left, taking turns to whip him, when we see these things, I say, we recall that God was made man for us having suffered similar things in the flesh, which when it comes to our minds, fosters love and compassion in us, in that He suffered such things for us. We venerate images for no other reason than that they may remind us by the representations and hence they can move our affections. This is not because such veneration stops at the image itself, but because it passes on to that whose image it is. For (as Blessed Basil says) "the honor given to the image passes over to the prototype."[3] Wherefore let us not fear regarding idolatry, if the simple and uneducated are taught that their minds ought not to stop at the image when we come before it, but rather that images help to stir up our minds to know and love the things of which they are images. Thus, if writings are permitted to readers, since Sacred Writ is also held in highest veneration, why may not images also be permitted, even if they be considered valuable, provide this be not beyond justice? For "picture," in Greek ($\zeta\omega\gamma\rho\alpha\varphi\iota\dot{\alpha}$) means a "living writing,"[4] because an image is, as it were, another kind of writing.

The clearest proof of this is that in that part of the world which the Spanish sailors by vast and long navigation to the west sailing beyond the columns of Hercules, under Charles I as King of the Spains, and [who was also titled] Charles V as Emperor, discovered, no writing was found among the men of that land, but they used images in place of writing. Accordingly, they painted images in such a way that they could clearly illustrate what things they wished. And this was not just in one or another place, but although they had gone more than six hundred leagues as by land, they never found any vestiges of writing, but merely the use of im-

---

[1] Cf. Num. 25, 3.

[2] Cf. Judges 10, 6.

[3] *De Spiritu Sancto*, c. 18, n. 45 (PG 32, 150C).

[4] I.e. "Picture" ($\zeta\omega\gamma\rho\alpha\varphi\iota\dot{\alpha}$/zografiá) = "living" ($\zeta\omega\dot{\eta}$/zoí)) + "writing" ($\gamma\rho\alpha\varphi\iota\alpha$/graphía).

ages. And this ought not to be ascribed to their rusticity, since the nation is of otherwise very vivacious intelligence, and one which works very finely in some mechanical arts, and has cities with a very large population. For they who have seen Tenochtitlan [now Mexico City] say about it that it is a city having more than two hundred thousand houses. And although there are all these houses, still they lacked writing, being content with just images. But now they have been taught writing by the Spanish who made a colony there, especially by the Friars Minor, who labor magnificently among them, such that the people of that land were writing with the Latin alphabet. It was fitting to bring this up because it seemed to me to be a powerful argument to show that an image takes the place of writing and consequently it can likewise be used as writing. Thus, if the use of images is useful, and it was never forbidden by Divine law, nay it was approved, as we have shown, it is thence very clearly proved that it is wrong to remove images from the Church.

Next, if there were no other proof for the confirmation of this matter than the use of the universal Church, even this alone would suffice, especially since the use of images is not something new in the Church, but very old, and continually maintained from the Apostles themselves until the present time. Eusebius of Caesarea bears witness about this matter, who when speaking about the city of Caesarea Philippi, says the following: "Since I have mentioned this city, I do not think it proper to omit an account which is worthy of record for posterity. For they say that the woman with an issue of blood, who, as we learn from the sacred Gospel, received from our Savior deliverance from her affliction, came from this place, and that her house is shown in the city, and that remarkable memorials of the kindness of the Savior to her remain there. For there stands upon an elevated stone, by the gates of her house, a brazen image of a woman kneeling, with her hands stretched out, as if she were praying. Opposite this is another upright image of a man, made of the same material, clothed decently in a double cloak, and extending his hand toward the woman. At his feet, beside the statue itself, is a certain strange plant, which climbs up to the hem of the brazen cloak, and is a remedy for all kinds of diseases. They say that this statue is an image of Jesus. It has remained to our day, so that we ourselves also saw it when we were staying in the city. Nor is it strange that those of the Gentiles who, of old, were benefited by our Savior, should have done such things, since we have learned also that the likenesses of his Apostles Paul and Peter, and of Christ himself, are preserved in paintings."[1] The *Tripartite History* under the name of Socrates when speaking of the Emperor Julian, relates, however, that this statue was destroyed by Julian the Apostate out of envy towards Christ, which in book six, chapter forty-one, says the following: "Having heard that at Caesarea Philippi, otherwise called Panease Paneades, a city of Phoenicia, there was a celebrated statue of Christ, which had been erected by a woman whom the Lord had cured of a flow of blood. Julian commanded it to be taken down, and a statue of himself erected in its place; but a violent fire from the heaven fell upon it, and broke off the parts contiguous to the breast; the head and neck were thrown prostrate, and it was transfixed to the ground with the face downwards at the point where the fracture of the bust was; and it has stood in that fashion from that day until now, still showing evidence of the lightning. The statue of Christ was dragged around the city and mutilated by the pagans; but the Christians recovered the fragments, and deposited the statue in the church in which it is still preserved."[2] Therefore why do heretics dare to remove images from the Church, the use of which God has confirmed by many miracles, and the Catholic Church from the very times of the Apostles (Eusebius bearing witness) has preserved until present times?

Finally this heresy of removing images has been condemned in many councils, namely in the II Council of Nicea, celebrated under the Empress Irene and Emperor Constantine [VI],

---

[1] *Church History*, bk. 7, c. 18, n. 1-4 (PG 20, 679B-C).
[2] PL 69, 1057D- 1058A.

her son, and called the "Seventh Synod": and in the Synod of Frankfurt under Pope Hadrian I, at which Bishops Theophylactus and Stephen presided, representing the supreme pontiff.

But it is necessary that we respond to the objections of the adversaries. Firstly they object to us that God in Exodus and Deuteronomy strictly forbids all images, saying: "Thou shalt not make to thyself a graven thing, nor the likeness of anything that is in heaven above, or in the earth beneath, nor of those things that are in the waters under the earth" (Ex. 20, 4). To which we reply, that that prohibition was made by God to avoid idolatry, such that to this end all images were understood to have been forbidden, not that they may not be possessed such that they may not be made absolutely, but rather that they may not be made in order to worship them. Now that this is the correct meaning of the passage is easily proved from the preceding and subsequent words. For before He makes a such like prohibition in Exodus, he premises these words: "Thou shalt not have strange gods before me" (v. 3), after which words the prohibition of idols immediately follows, which prohibition having been made, He immediately adds when speaking about those images: "Thou shalt not adore them, nor serve them" (v. 5). Hence from the preceding and subsequent words we conclude that the images are forbidden unto this end, namely that they may not be held to be gods. But when we worship images, we do not venerate them as gods, because we refer (as we have said) our adoration not to them, but to their exemplars.

Secondly they object those words of Christ in John's Gospel: "The true adorers shall adore the Father in spirit and in truth. For the Father also seeketh such to adore him... in spirit" (4, 23-24). Whence the heretics strive to conclude that images are not necessary, because when we worship them, we do not adore in spirit, but with the body. We certainly admit that the true and principal adoration is in spirit, namely since by faith, hope and charity (as Augustine says[1]) "we tend towards God": but because our mind sometimes sleeps, it is forgetful of God and tepid in affections, not loving God as one ought. It is then necessary to stir up our mind by some external things, so that by looking at and considering them the mind may be led back to the remembrance of God and the affections be inflamed.

Long ago Pope Gregory III,[2] Pope Adrian I,[3] and John [Chyrsoras],[4] a monk [of St. Benedict], during the time of Pope Gregory III wrote against this heresy. I have not seen these works, but I have knowledge of them only by the testimony of John Trithemius, who in his list of ecclesiastical writers[5] refers to the aforesaid men as having written against this heresy. Blessed [John] Damascene discourses not a little about this matter.[6] Thomas Netter in his book, *De Sacramentalibus*, disputes more copiously against this heresy.[7] We also have said many things above in the section on "Adoration," first heresy, which can be fittingly adapted to this place, to which place the reader may go, from whence he can derive many things if he wishes.

The **second heresy** asserts that God's image in which man was made by God, is impressed upon the body, and not the soul. Philastrius, Bishop of Brescia, in his work *De haeresibus*,[8] relates this heresy among the others, and yet he does not reveal who is its author. Blessed

---

[1] "We tend towards Him by love" (*City of God*, bk. 10, c. 3, n. 2 (PL 41, 281)).
[2] *Commonitorium, Ad eosdem, & Contra eosdem.*
[3] *De veneratione imaginum.*
[4] *Adversus Leonem imperatorem* in two books. It was written against Emperor Leo III, the Isaurian.
[5] Cf. *De scriptoribus ecclesiasticis* (Basel, Bertholdo Rembolt, 1512), fol. 60v & 61v.
[6] *An Exposition of the Orthodox Faith*, bk. 4, c. 16.
[7] Tit. 13. This book is the third part of the book, *Doctrinale antiquitatum fidei ecclesiae catholicae*.
[8] C. 97 (PL 12, 1209B-1210B).

Augustine in his small book, *De Haeresibus ad Quodvultdeum*,[1] mentions this heresy after Philastrius: but he does not indicate the author.

Now it is not evident to me what motivated the author of this heresy to think as he did, because neither Augustine or Philastrius, among those whom I have read, said anything about this. Still I think that this error derived from another, whereby it is taught that God is corporeal and has all the members of a body, just as a man has: and those who thought this way (as I reckon) argue from this that God's image is in man's body, and not in the soul. John Cassian clearly favors this suspicion of ours, who in his *Conferences*[2] when discussing the heresy of the Anthropormorphites says that the patrons of this heresy assert that God is corporeal because Scripture says the man is made to God's image. But that error we, with God helping us, have already destroyed above, in the section on "God," in the second heresy. From the assault of which heresy these things, which we have now in hand, may easily, in my opinion, be dashed to the ground. For if God is not corporeal, nor has members as man does, it cannot happen that man according to his body may be called God's image. Furthermore, anything ought to be called the image of something because it represents its principal parts: because if it relates only to its least part, it would undeservedly be called its image. For no one would say that Peter is the image of John because Peter has a mole on his chin, or a wart on his forehead, just as John has. If, however, he has similar eyes, and similar lips, similar color of cheeks, he contracts his forehead in a similar way, has a similar face, and also similar the rest of the bodily features, it will rightly be said that Peter is John's image, especially if he acted like him: because he expresses and represents his principal parts.

But in God intelligence, memory and will are His principal parts (if among the infinitely perfect things one thing is more principal than another). For upon these things nearly all the other Divine perfections are founded as it were upon certain bases. For the Divine omnipotence is founded upon His will. Furthermore, God is certainly called and is omnipotence because He can do everything that He wishes: nor can anything happen except what He wills or permits. If God would lack an intellect and will, He could neither be wise, prudent, just, merciful, the Creator, Governor, nor Ruler. For it could not happen that one who does not understand or will, would govern fully and well. Thus, the intellect and will are, as it were, certain bases and foundations of all the Divine perfections. Now man has an intellect, memory and will not according to the body, but according to the soul. The soul remembers, not the body. The soul wills, not the body. For the body without the soul cannot do any of these things, nor other acts of life. For it cannot see, hear, speak, eat, walk, or do other things of this sort. From which things we conclude that when the body does all these things, it gets its powers from the soul. Hence, since the soul alone has an intellect, memory and will, it follows that likewise according to the soul alone man carries God's image.

Again, if God's image is in man's body, and not in the soul, it would be necessary that some brute animals which have a similar form of their body have a likeness to man (some such things are said to be in the sea) carry God's likeness, and are made to God's image, just as man. Yet Sacred Scripture very clearly contradicts this opinion. For after "God created the great whales, and every living and moving creature, which the waters brought forth, according to their kinds, and every winged fowl according to its kind" (Gen. 1, 21): also after He made "beasts of the earth, according to their kinds" (v. 24), and "everything that creepeth on the earth after its kind," and arriving at man's creation, God said: "Let us make man to our image and likeness: and let him have dominion over the fishes of the sea, and the fowls of the air, and the beasts, and the whole earth, and every creeping creature that moveth upon the earth" (v. 26). Now of no other animal was it said that it was made to God's image, except

---

[1] C. 76 (PL 42, 45).

[2] Conf. 10, c. 1-3 (PL 49, 817-824).

of man alone. On the other hand, if God's image were impressed in man's body, some brute beasts that are like man according to his body would also have that image of God. I could have heaped together many testimonies of the Saints, but I do not want to burden the reader with excessive prolixity in such a very clear matter.

INDULGENTIA
Indulgences

Many heretics despise and mock the indulgences which the Pontiffs grant sinners, namely by remitting the punishment which the sinner is obliged to bear even after the guilt has been forgiven. For instance, the Waldensians assert that the pope has completely no power for granting indulgences: which if he grants, they say that they are without effect. John Wycliffe also taught this error, who never abandons the Waldensians: the latter teach another more despicable error whereby they support their error. For they say that there is no fire of Purgatory, and hence they deduce that there are no indulgences. After these men Luther succeeded as heir of those men in the same error, although he deduces his error from another source no less vitiated. Accordingly, Luther admits Purgatory, yet he denies that there will be any satisfaction for sins. For he says that one who has been absolved from guilt is not obliged to the satisfaction of any punishment, but rather he says that as soon as one is absolved from guilt, he is also free from all punishment.[1]

I will fight against this error with a few words, because among all the matters about which we dispute in this work, there is none which Holy Writ shows less clearly, and about which the ancient writers said less. Nevertheless, indulgences ought not to be despised by this occasion, because their use in the Church seems to have been received at a late hour, for there are many things known to later writers about which those ancient writers were completely ignorant. For mention about the transubstantiation of bread is rare in the ancient writers: about the procession of the Holy Ghost from the Son is much rarer: there is nearly none about Purgatory, especially among the Greek writers. For which reason Purgatory is not believed in by the Greeks until this day. Still who, except a heretic, will dare to deny these things, because among the ancient authors these things were not spoken of by such names? For the Church makes progress in her members, by God enlightening it more each day. Wherefore the Church is compared to the dawn. "Who is she," He says, "that cometh forth as the morning rising?" (Cant. 6, 9). But the dawn in its rising has faint light, which increases with the progress of time: so also the Church. Hence, I do not doubt that there may be many things that will appear more clearly and plainly which are now completely unknown to us. Why then is it surprising if it has happened in this way concerning indulgences, that among the ancients there is no mention of them? Especially because the charity of Christians was then more fervent, such that there was little need of indulgences. Many were longing for martyrdom. There were few wicked deeds of men, and what ones there were, were emended by the very weighty punishments of the canons. They wished to make satisfaction in the present life, they wanted to leave nothing to be punished in the future, wherefore there is no mention of indulgences. On the other hand, the charity of many has grown cold in present times, and hence many sins are committed, and for the sins committed Christians want to make less satisfaction, hence it was necessary to flee to indulgences as to a refuge, so that some help may be given to sinners.

---

[1] "Nay, when God remits sin, he remits the guilt and the punishment at the same time" (Martin Luther, *Asterisci Lutheri adversus Obeliscos Eckii* (i.e., *The Asterisks of Luther against the Obelisks of Eck*), WA 1, 284, lns. 15-16).

INDULGENTIA

Additionally, the use of indulgences is not so recent as the heretics charge. For among the Romans their very ancient use is related, as can somewhat be inferred from the very frequent use of the stations[1] in Rome. And it is related of Blessed Pope Gregory I that he granted some [indulgences] during his time.[2] But even though a clear testimony of Sacred Scripture for the approbation of indulgences is lacking, still they ought not be despised, because their usage, retained for many centuries by the Catholic Church, is of such great authority, such that he who despises it is rightly deemed a heretic, especially since such usage did not creep into the Church by chance, but it was introduced by the decision of the Church. For the [IV] Lateran Council celebrated under Innocent III in order to reprimand the temerity of some abbots, declared that abbots are nowise able to grant indulgences, but it says that this function has been granted by God to bishops alone: but lest they be regarded as worthless from their easy concession, or lest sinners relying upon them would be more tepid regarding works of satisfaction, laws are prescribed to the bishops themselves, that they may not grant indulgences beyond a certain number. Now the decree of this council can be found in the *Decretals*[3] The Council of Constance, in the eighth session, condemned forty-five articles of John Wycliffe, one of which pertains to this matter. For its forty-second article says the following: "It is foolish to believe in the indulgences of the pope and bishops."[4] Which article along with the others is condemned with one *latae sententiae* [excommunication] upon them all.

[Bishop John Fisher] of Rochester wrote about this matter in the work he published against Luther's [*Defense and Explanation of all the Articles*];[5] and Jacques Masson in a work which he made for the assertion of the conclusion of the faculty of Louvain against Luther.[6] A certain Tuberinus [i.e., Johannes Mathias Beuschel][7] wrote more copiously about this matter against Luther, but in my judgment less ornately, and much less exactly than the Bishop of Rochester settled the matter. John Eck in his *Enchiridion locorum communium adversus Lutheranos*,[8] as much as a summary format permits, disputes about this matter. But if he discussed this matter at greater length, it is not apparent to me. Nevertheless, I hear that he wrote many things against Luther.

---

[1] I.e. stational churches.

[2] This claim is disputed; Cf. Eusebius Amort C.R.L., *De origine, progressu, valore ac fructu indulgentiarum, necnon de dispositionibus ad eas lucrandas requisitis notitia* (Venice, apud Joannem Baptistam Recurti, 1738), pp. 38-40.

[3] *Decretales Gregorii IX*, bk. 5, tit. 38 *De poenitentiis et remissionibus*, c. 14 *Cum ex eo*.

[4] Dz. 622.

[5] *Assertionis Lutheranae confutatio* (Venice, Gregorius de Gregoriis, 1526, pp. 92v-107v (assertions 17-22)). The text here mistakenly states that this work was a refutation of the Luther's *Babylonian Captivity*. This has been corrected.

[6] *Articulorum doctrinae fratris Martini Lutheri per theologos Lovanienses damnatorum ratio ex sacris literis, & veteribus tractatoribus* (Antwerp, Michael Hillenius, 1521).

[7] Alias, Johannes Mathias Tuberinus. *Contra falsas Luteris positions* (Tübingen, Morhart, 1524).

[8] *Enchiridion locorum communium Joannis Eckii, adversus Lutheranos* (Venice, Patavinus, 1535), c. 24, pp. 112v-116r.

INFERNUS
Hell

Among the other errors which Brother Bernard of Luxemburg accuses Amaury [of Bène] in his *Catalogus haereticorum*, one is that Amaury said that Hell does not exist, but he who has committed a mortal sin, is said to have Hell in himself."[1] Guy [the Carmelite] relates that the Albigensians think that there are no other pains in Hell than those which we experience in this world.[2] The *Catalogus* says of Herman Riswick that he said that there is no Hell at all.[3]

And certainly, regarding Amaury's opinion, in order to say the truth, one of the greatest punishments of Hell is the accusation of one's own conscience, which always assails the sinner, it always pricks him, and never ceases. And this accusation of the conscience many think is meant by the word "worm." Hence Blessed Jerome, when expounding the passage in Isaias, "Their worm shall not die" (66, 24), says the following: "But the worm that will not die and the fire that will not be quenched are understood by many to be the conscience of sinners, which tortures those who are held in punishment. Therefore, due to their vices and sins, they are deprived of the good of the elect, in accordance with which it is said, 'I am turned in my anguish, whilst the thorn is fastened,' (Ps 31, 4) and in the Proverbs, 'As a moth doth by a garment, and a worm by the wood: so the sadness of a man consumeth the heart' (25, 20)."[4] And the heathens dreaded this accusation of conscience as a very great punishment. For [Juvenal[5]] says: "Whatever is committed with bad example, displeases even the author of it. This is the first revenge, that himself being judge, no guilty person is absolved... But why should you think these to have escaped, whose mind, conscious of dire fact, keeps them astonished, and smites with a dumb stripe, their conscious the tormentor shaking a secret whip? But it is a vehement punishment, and much crueler, than those which either severe Caeditius invented, or Rhadamanthus, night and day to carry their own witness in their breast."[6] But even though this is a great punishment, and one of the worst which is in Hell, still in this world it does not torment the mind as much as it will torment after this life, because as everyone will come to know their sins more openly and clearly, so this consciousness of sin will prick more sharply: wherefore even though a sinful man may be tortured in this world by the consciousness of his sins, still it ought not to be thence said that he suffers Hell.

Next, even if this consciousness of sin were the harshest punishment, nevertheless there are others equally serious which are not experienced in this world by sinners: wherefore it

---

[1] I.e., "like a rotten tooth in his mouth" (*Catalogus haereticorum omnium* (Paris, Joannes Parvus, 1524)), fol. 21v-22r.

[2] *Summa de haeresibus* (Paris, Prelum Ascensianum, 1528), c. 7, fol. 78r, l. 24-26.

[3] *Catalogus haereticorum*, fol. 44r. "He was condemned to perpetual imprisonment in 1499 and having made his escape out of it, and continuing to vomit forth his blasphemies, he was burnt alive at the Hague in 1512." (Louis Ellies Du Pin, *A New History of Ecclesiastical Writers* (Abel Swalle and Tim. Childe, 1699), vol. 13, p138).

[4] *Tinea ossium cor intelligens* is the Massoretic text wording of this verse as cited here by St. Jerome for this passage, but some verses of the book of Proverbs were later made to conform with the Septuagint by means of the *Vetus Itala* version. The wording used here is according to the Vulgate and Douay-Rheims translation. Cf. "Proverbs," *The Catholic Encyclopedia* (New York: Robert Appleton Company, 1911), vol. 12, p. 506. *Commentaria in Isaiam*, bk. 18, c. 65 (PL24, 676C-D).

[5] The text here mistakenly cites Seneca *ad Lucilium*, letter 16.

[6] *Satire* 13, l. 1-3 & 192-198.

cannot be said that a sinner in this world has Hell, since many other punishments remain to be endured, such as fire, worms, sulfurous smoke and darkness. Isaias says: "Their worm shall not die, and their fire shall not be quenched" (66, 24). But if you say that these words of Isaias ought to be understood of that worm of conscience which continually gnaws upon the mind with remorse, I will cite the words of the Wise Man who expresses the matter more clearly saying: "The vengeance on the flesh of the ungodly is fire and worms" (Eccli. 7, 19). These words nowise can be understood of the worm of conscience, because he did not say, "The vengeance on the mind of the ungodly," but he said: "The vengeance on the flesh of the ungodly is fire and worms." And it is said in the book of Judith: "For he will give fire, and worms into their flesh, that they may burn, and may feel forever" (16, 21). Job bears witness to the darkness of the damned, when saying in their name: "I waited for light, and darkness broke out" (30, 26). And again, he says more clearly: "From the wicked their light shall be taken away" (38, 15). Now David testifies to the sulfurous smoke, saying: "He shall rain snares upon sinners: fire and brimstone [*sulfur*] and storms of winds shall be the portion of their cup" (Ps. 10, 7). And the voice of the third Angel in the Apocalypse says: "If any man shall adore the beast and his image, and receive his character in his forehead, or in his hand; he also shall drink of the wine of the wrath of God, which is mingled with pure wine in the cup of his wrath, and shall be tormented with fire and brimstone in the sight of the holy angels, and in the sight of the Lamb. And the smoke of their torments shall ascend up for ever and ever" (14, 9-11). And Hell itself is called in the same book a pool of fire and of brimstone. For when speaking of the wicked it says: "These two were cast alive into the pool of fire, burning with brimstone" (19, 20).

Why therefore do impious Amaury and the blasphemous Albanenses dare to teach that Hell is nowhere else than in this life? I believe that they now think otherwise. For since they now experience the pains of Hell, I think that they now know that there is another Hell, and other pains of Hell which were not experienced by them in this world.

A **second heresy** teaches that the pains of Hell are not everlasting. All who wrote about this heresy testify that the author of this heresy was Origen. Philastrius states that there was a heresy saying that Christ in His descent into Hell forgave those there, so that those confessing [the faith] in that place may be saved. Yet he does not indicate any author of this heresy. The Armenians (as Guy [the Carmelite] relates) assert that when Christ descended into Hell, he led out all the souls from there.[1] Augustine mentions this heresy among the others, yet without the name of the author.[2] Now we combine these men's opinion with Origen's error, because it is somewhat close to his, and it is overthrown with the same testimonies. For when we have shown that the punishment of Hell is everlasting, both errors are dealt with.

But Sacred Writ very clearly teaches that the punishment of Hell is everlasting. For nearly all the quotations which we cited against the recently mentioned heresy contradict this heresy. For the quotation of Isaias is very clear, and the other from the book of Judith, and yet another from the Apocalypse need not be repeated, lest we fill up pages for no reason. Besides these quotations there are other from the Gospels. The Teacher of truth Himself, when speaking in Mark's Gospel, says: "If thy hand scandalize thee, cut it off: it is better for thee to enter into life, maimed, than having two hands to go into Hell, into unquenchable fire: where their worm dieth not, and the fire is not extinguished. And if thy foot scandalize thee, cut it off. It is better for thee to enter lame into life everlasting, than having two feet, to be cast into the Hell of unquenchable fire: where their worm dieth not, and the fire is not extinguished. And if thy eye scandalize thee, pluck it out. It is better for thee with one eye to enter into the kingdom of God, than having two eyes to be cast into the Hell of fire: where their worm dieth not, and

---

[1] *Summa de haeresibus*, c. 13, fol. 33v-34v.

[2] *De Haeresibus ad Quodvultdeum*, c. 79 (PL 42, 45).

the fire is not extinguished" (9, 42-47). Behold you see Christ teaching three times in one discourse that the pains of Hell are everlasting. Furthermore, that saying is very clear which He threatens that he will say to sinners on Judgment Day: "Depart, you cursed, into everlasting fire which was prepared for the devil and his angels" (Mt. 25, 41). It is unnecessary to cite more testimonies since these are very clear. He who desire more about this matter, may see those things which we said above in the section on "Beatitude," third heresy, because in that place we discussed this error of Origen more freely.

The **third heresy** is that which denies that Christ descended into Hell. Neither Augustine nor Philastrius mention this heresy. Yet Isidore [of Seville] enumerates it among the heresies, although he does not disclose any author of this error.[1]

This heresy is refuted by that which the Wise Man under the name of Wisdom, meaning the Son of God, says: "I will penetrate to all the lower parts of the earth, and will behold all that sleep, and will enlighten all that hope in the Lord" (Eccli. 24, 45). But if someone playing with allegories distorts this quotation into something else, and says that wisdom penetrated and penetrates all the lower parts of the earth by its knowledge, which is so great that nothing can harm it, but everything, no matter how hidden from us, nevertheless is bare and open to its eyes: at least that quotation of Paul is clear enough, namely when discussing Christ's Ascension he says: "Now that he ascended, what is it, but because he also descended first into the lower parts of the earth?" (Eph. 4, 9). And the Apostle Peter on the day of Pentecost having already received the Holy Ghost, when preaching about Christ before the people, says the following: "Whom God hath raised up, having loosed the sorrows of Hell, as it was impossible that he should be holden by it. For David saith concerning him: I foresaw the Lord before my face: because he is at my right hand, that I may not be moved. For this my heart hath been glad, and my tongue hath rejoiced: moreover my flesh also shall rest in hope. Because thou wilt not leave my soul in Hell, nor suffer thy Holy One to see corruption" (Acts 2, 24-27). Furthermore, in the Apostles' Creed it is said: "He descended into Hell."[2] And the [IV] Lateran Council celebrated under Innocent III defined this same thing. For when speaking about Christ our Redeemer, it says the following: "Who also, for the salvation of the human race, having suffered on the wood of the Cross and died, descended into Hell, arose from the dead and ascended into Heaven."[3] Which words are found in the *Decretals*, in the chapter *Firmiter*, [Title one], *de summa Trinitate et fide Catholica.*[4]

And this is certainly one place in which we can refute Luther, who wants the clearest testimonies of Sacred Scripture without any reasonings or argumentations, but the things which very clearly teach an opinion. Next, he says that nothing ought to be defined which is not expressed in Holy Writ. He also admits no judge in a dispute about things pertaining to the faith, except Sacred Scripture alone. And certainly, if these gnomons are all examined, it will not be necessary to say that Christ descended into Hell, because Sacred Writ does not teach this with such explicit words which he elsewhere asks from Catholics. For these words are

---

[1] St. Isidore did not actually write that the heresy denied Christ's descent into Hell, but rather extended its effect to the liberation of all men from Hell. For he wrote, "Other heresies are without founder and without names... Some believe the liberation of all men from Hell took place with the descent of Christ." (*Etymologies*, bk. 8, c. 5, n. 69 (PL 82, 304C)). St. Augustine likewise wrote: "Another heresy believes that upon Christ's descent into Hell the unbelievers believed and all were liberated from Hell" (*De Haeresibus ad Quodvultdeum*, c.79 (PL 42, 45)). This is a heresy promulgated by Origen. But Johann Parsimonius (d. 1589), who was a pupil of Luther and Melanchthon, denied Christ's descent into Hell.

[2] Dz. 6.

[3] Dz. 429.

[4] *Decretals of Gregory IX*, bk. 1, tit. 1, c. 1.

never found in Sacred Writ in the form, "Christ descended into Hell." But even though these words are not found in that form: still other words are found which mean the same thing, and from which words they are deduced by the very clear argumentation which is sufficient for a Catholic man, who is bound to bring into captivity his understanding[1] to the definitions and interpretations of Scripture which the Church has handed down, and not to his own innate prudence alone.

INIMICUS

Enemies

There is an error of the Greeks whereby they assert that it is licit to deceive an enemy, and it is not a sin if someone does harm to his enemy, even if he be helped by perjuries or whatever lie to do this. Guy [the Carmelite] accuses them of all these things, when recounting their twenty-fifth error.[2]

And certainly, I can hardly believe that they are so demented that they would think these things, because those things are clearly contrary to the Natural law, such that any pagan philosopher would condemn that error of theirs, not to speak of a Christian. Whoever has not abhorred lies? Who does not detest perjury? And these things ought not to be done not only to friends, but also to enemies: because if it is permitted in war to use artifices for enemies, it is still not permitted to deceive with lies. Accordingly, in Leviticus the Lord says: "You shall not lie, neither shall any man deceive his neighbor" (19, 11). But no matter how much someone may be an enemy to another, he is still his neighbor: which is even proved from the fact that the Samaritan showing mercy to the wounded man, was judged to be a neighbor by Christ's words, however much the Samaritans underwent from the Jews.

Moreover, from the Evangelical law no one is permitted to have enemies, because even if another person is inimical to me, nevertheless I am bound not to be so to him. "Not rendering evil for evil," says Peter, "nor railing for railing, but contrariwise, blessing: for unto this are you called, that you may inherit a blessing" (I Pet. 3, 9). And Blessed Paul in his Epistle to the Romans says: "To no man rendering evil for evil... Revenge not yourselves, my dearly beloved; but give place unto wrath, for it is written: Revenge is mine, I will repay, saith the Lord. But if thy enemy be hungry, give him to eat; if he thirst, give him to drink. For, doing this, thou shalt heap coals of fire upon his head. Be not overcome by evil, but overcome evil by good" (12, 17 & 19-21). And in his First Epistle to the Thessalonians he says: "See that none render evil for evil to any man; but ever follow that which is good towards each other, and towards all men" (5, 15). Finally, the Teacher of truth Himself, when rebuking the Jews, says: "You have heard that it hath been said, Thou shalt love thy neighbour, and hate thy enemy. But I say to you, Love your enemies: do good to them that hate you: and pray for them that persecute and calumniate you: that you may be the children of your Father who is in heaven, who maketh his sun to rise upon the good and the bad, and raineth upon the just and the unjust" (Mt. 5, 43-45). Therefore, if God views His children in this way, the Greeks are proved not to be God's children, because they do not do good to their enemies.

---

[1] Cf. II Cor. 10, 5.
[2] *Summa de haeresibus*, fol. 27v.

INJURIA

Injuries

It is Luther's opinion that it is not lawful for Christians to seek reparation of an injury before a judge. Wherefore Luther seems to me to have not a little of the leaven of the Pharisees, because he binds heavy and insupportable burdens, and lays them on men's shoulders; but with a finger of his own he will not move them.[1] For does not the one who says that it is not lawful to seek reparation of an injury before a judge, if some injury is inflicted upon him by someone, repulse it shamelessly, not to say atrociously? He certainly repels one injury with a hundred harsher ones, and what is worse, also when he receives none, he attacks with a thousand insults him who has touched him with just the tip of his finger. See that the wound is such that it cannot even be touched. "He that hateth to be reproved," Ecclesiasticus says, "walketh in the trace of a sinner" (21, 7). Hence Luther is a sinner, because he cannot stand being corrected, nor admonished by anyone.

The proof of this matter is very clear, because whoever has either corrected or admonished him in writing, whether he be noble or common, whether king or emperor, bishop or pope, he has been attacked by a thousand injuries by Luther. For upon the most serene King of England, who gently enough, as befitted his royal dignity wrote against him, with no respect had to his royal dignity, he [Luther] hurled a thousand abusive words, he derided him with a thousand scoffs. Concerning the things which he babbled against the sovereign pontiff, it is better to pass over in silence, and I would be ashamed to relate them, because one ought not to write that shameful thing. Thus, what will you say to these things, O Luther? If you are permitted to repel an injury, why will it not be permitted for others to seek reparation of an injury before a judge? Certainly, it is just that no one be a judge in his own case. Wherefore if it is permitted to repel an injury with one's own hands, much more will it be permitted to repulse an injury through the hands of a judge, or to seek reparation for an injury already inflicted.

There seems to me to be no need for other arguments to disprove this error, but those which we have put forth above against the same Luther, in the section on "War," suffice. For we proved there that war is permitted for Christians, provided that the other things be present which are required for a just war. Now for a just war it is required that what can be corrected without war may not be done by means of war. Therefore, it is more just that someone seek correction from a judge, than that he wish to have it by war, if it is permitted to have it. But when it is permitted to seek it from war (as we demonstrated above), it will thus also be licit to seek it from a judge.

JOANNES BAPTISTA

John the Baptist

Bernard of Luxemburg, in his *Catalogus haereticorum*,[2] when speaking about the Manichaeans, says that they had so lost their senses that they said that John the Baptist, the precursor of Christ our Savior, was damned, because he did not believe in Christ. For

---

[1] Cf. Mt. 23, 4.

[2] *Catalogus haereticorum omnium* (Paris, Joannes Parvus, 1524), fol. 54v. Bernard of Luxemburg gives reference to Tomasinus de Lambertis de Ferraria, O.P. (fl. 1390-1447) when making this accusation.

when John was in prison, he sent two of his disciples to Christ to ask him: "Art thou he that art to come, or look we for another?" (Mt. 11, 3). The Manichaeans (as Bernard of Luxemburg accuses them) think that John the Baptist did and said this out of disbelief. But I can scarcely believe that the Manichaeans were so insane, though it is evident that they said many other things of greater madness. For Philastrius of Brescia in his book, *De haeresibus*, when he discusses the heresies of the Manichaeans makes no mention of this error.[1] Blessed Augustine his book, *De Haeresibus ad Quodvultdeum*, recounts the errors of the Manichaeans, and yet does not include this among them.[2] Hence I conclude that they were far from having this error: because Blessed Augustine who knew their errors very well, since he had adhered to their sect at one time, by no means would have said nothing about this error.

Still be it that they so thought just as Bernard of Luxemburg relates, it is not necessary that we spend much time refuting this error since Christ our Savior's testimony concerning John himself is so clear. For He praised John for his fortitude and constancy of mind, when He said the he was not like a reed shaken by the wind, which is moved by every blowing of the wind. He commended him moreover for his temperance, when saying the he was not clothed in soft garments. He shows that he is far from adulation, when He said that he is not in the houses of kings, because those who are stricken with this sort of malady, tend to dwell with kings. And when multiplying reasons for praise, He said that he is a prophet, and more than a prophet: He said that he is an angel, because he led an angelic life: since although he was in the flesh, he nevertheless lived contrary to the flesh. Lastly, to conclude, as it were, by a flourish of the pen, He says: "[There has not risen] among them that are born of women a greater than John the Baptist" (Mt. 11, 11). And all these things were said by Christ our Savior about John the Baptist at the very same time in which the Manichaeans claim that John sinned. For after Christ responds to the question made by John's disciples, just as soon as they left, He immediately said these acclamations of praise about John the Baptist. From which we prove incontestably that John nowise sinned (as the Manichaeans say) by that question.

Now they are mistaken that John the Baptist asked motivated by disbelief. For he does not ask in his own name and for himself, but for the sake of his disciples whom he saw were wavering in their faith in Christ. And for this reason, he sends them to Christ, so that by having seen miracles performed by Him, they would be strengthened in their belief in Him. Since Christ knew this very well, He gave no reply to them: but He tells them to return to John so that they might relate what they had seen, namely the many miracles He had performed in their presence. Certainly, for no other reason but that therefrom John might instruct his disciples, whom he knew were not firmly enough grounded in faith, more clearly about faith in Christ, and strengthen them through this instruction. For Blessed John Chrysostom so interprets that question of John, imitating Theophylactus here as he always does elsewhere.[3] Because the latter's words are much briefer, I will cite them here. "John did not ask as if he himself did not know Christ. How could this be when he had borne witness to Him, saying, 'Behold the Lamb of God'? But because his disciples were jealous of Christ, John sent them

---

[1] *De haeresibus*, c. 61 (PL 12, 1175A-1176A).

[2] C. 46 (PL 42, 34-38).

[3] "Although [John's disciples] could not suspect anything of the kind of their own master, the common people might from the inquiry of John's disciples form many strange suspicions, not knowing the mind with which he sent his disciples. And it was natural for them to reason with themselves, and say, 'He that bore such abundant witness, has he now changed his persuasion, and does he doubt whether this or another be He that should come? Can it be, that in dissension with Jesus he says this? That the prison has made him more timid? That his former words were spoken vainly, and at random?' It being then natural for them to suspect many such things, see how He corrects their weakness, and removes these their suspicions." (*Homilies on Matthew*, hom. 37, n. 1 (PG 57, 419).

to acquire more evidence, so that by seeing the miracles they might believe that Christ is greater than John. This is why he himself pretends to ask, 'Art Thou He that cometh?' that is, He Whose coming in the flesh is awaited in the Scriptures."[1] And this is enough about this matter.

JUDAS

Judas

No matter how wicked and disgraceful someone may be, there will never be lacking one by whom he is praised, and his wicked deed commended: because (as the old saying goes) "Cicada loves cicada, ant is dear to ant."[2] A sufficient testimony of this matter is for instance, that there are not lacking those who commended the very wicked crime of Judas: seeing that Augustine relates that the Cainites suppose Judas to have been of Divine nature and they consider his crime was beneficial.[3] For they say, as Augustine relates, that Judas foreknew how much Christ's Passion was going to benefit the human race, and for that reason had handed Him over to the Jews, so that by His death the human race would profit. Philastrius, nevertheless, when speaking about these Cainites in his book, *De haeresibus*, does not accuse them of any such thing, but he merely explains this heresy without mentioning any advocate of it.[4] Yet [Pseudo-] Tertullian in his small book on heresies, accuses this of those whom he calls Chaldeans, and they are the same men (as I suspect) who are called Cainites by Augustine, because the same errors which are attributed by Augustine to the Cainites are those of which [Pseudo-] Tertullian accuses the Chaldeans.[5]

For the refutation of this error sufficient proof is, for instance, when the Lord wishing to wash His disciples' feet said: "You are clean, but not all. For he knew," says the Evangelist, "who he was that would betray him; therefore he said: You are not all clean." (Jn. 13, 10-11). Hence Judas was not clean, of whose uncleanness no other reason the Evangelist indicated other than the fact that he wanted to betray Christ. And in the Acts of the Apostles Peter says: "Men, brethren, the scripture must needs be fulfilled, which the Holy Ghost spoke before by the mouth of David concerning Judas, who was the leader of them that apprehended Jesus: who was numbered with us, and had obtained part of this ministry. And he indeed hath possessed a field of the reward of iniquity, and being hanged, burst asunder in the midst: and all his bowels gushed out" (1, 16-18). If the betrayal whereby Judas betrayed Christ was good, how could it happen that the reward given to him for the betrayal is "the reward of iniquity"? If the thirty pieces of silver are the reward of iniquity, then the betrayal, for which those silver pieces were given, is iniquitous. But what Christ our Redeemer says about him in Luke's Gospel is clearer: "And the Son of man indeed goeth, according to that which is determined: but yet, woe to that man by whom he shall be betrayed" (22, 22). And it is unnecessary to cite more proofs against such a blatant blasphemy, especially since this heresy is not found to have been revived afterwards by anyone: and the proofs adduced overthrow it sufficiently.

---

[1] *On Matthew*, c. 11, v. 2-4 (PG 123, 247).
[2] Theocritus, *Idylls*, Idyll 9, ll. 31-32.
[3] *De Haeresibus ad Quodvultdeum*, c.18 (PL 42, 29).
[4] C. 2 (PL 12, 1115A-1116A).
[5] Perhaps our author depended upon a faulty text here because PseudoTertullian also called them "Cainites." *Adversus Omnes Haereses* (an appendix to the work *De praescriptionem haereticorum*), c. 2. Cf. *De praescriptionem haereticorum*, c. 47 (PL 2, 65A-B).

JUDICIUM

Judgment

So great is the devil's craftiness in deceiving men, that he suggested to some men that there is not going to be a judgment, so that perhaps by this occasion he might draw them the more easily into any vice, the less they believe that punishment is to be inflicted on account of it. Philastrius attributes this error to the Borborians,[1] and they are those who are called Gnostics by Augustine.[2] He also accuses this of the Florinians,[3] the Manichaeans,[4] and the Proclinianites,[5] whom he calls Prodianites, unless perhaps the spelling in Philastrius is incorrect, because those who in Augustine are called Proclinianites, in Philastrius are called Prodianites, and an error between the two spellings is easily made.[6] For if the letters c and l are joined together, you make the letter d. But if you separate the same letter, such that you separate from long complete ascender and put the rest by itself, you will consequently find two letters, namely c and l. From which I surmise by this occasion somewhere the mistake was made by the fault of the writers. Now whether the error is in Philastrius, or rather in Augustine, is not certain to me because I do not find any mention of these [heretics] in the writings of the older authors. However it may be, it is of small importance: still one thing is sure, that Augustine does not accuse any of these heretics of this error, neither of the Borborians, nor the Gnostics, nor the Florinians, nor the Manichaeans, nor the Proclinianites. Which surprises me very much, since Augustine saw Philastrius' work. Perhaps it could have happened because he did not find it in the writings of anyone else, and hence omitted it, having little trust of Philastrius about this, or perhaps he discovered that it was not as Philastrius related.

Nevertheless, whoever's error this may be, it can be easily refuted. For in Matthew's Gospel when the Lord was reproaching the cities in which He had performed many miracles, because they had not done penance, He says: "But I say unto you, it shall be more tolerable for Tyre and Sidon in the day of judgment, than for you" (11, 22). And again, when speaking to the Capharnaites He says: "I say unto you, that it shall be more tolerable for the land of Sodom in the day of judgment, than for thee" (v. 24). And again, in the same Gospel, He says: "The men of Ninive shall rise in judgment with this generation, and shall condemn it… The queen of the south shall rise in judgment with this generation, and shall condemn it" (12, 41-42). And in John's Gospel, He says: "He hath given him power to do judgment, because he is the Son of man. Wonder not at this; for the hour cometh, wherein all that are in the graves shall hear the voice of the Son of God. And they that have done good things, shall come forth unto the resurrection of life; but they that have done evil, unto the resurrection of judgment." (5, 27-29). And Paul in his Epistle to the Romans says: "For we shall all stand before the judgment seat of Christ. For it is written: As I live, saith the Lord, every knee shall bow to me, and every tongue shall confess to God. Therefore every one of us shall render account to God for himself" (14, 10-12). And again, he says in his Second Epistle to the Corinthians: "We must all be manifested before the judgment seat of Christ, that every one may receive the proper

---

[1] Or Barbeliotes. *De haeresibus*, c.73 (PL 12, 1186).

[2] *De Haeresibus ad Quodvultdeum*, c.6 (PL 42, 25).

[3] *De haeresibus*, c.57 (PL 12, 1172A-1173A).

[4] *Ibid.*, c. 61 (PL 12, 1176A).

[5] *Ibid.*, c. 56 (PL 12, 1171A-1172A).

[6] The spelling, "Prodianites," which was used in earlier editions is incorrect. See PL 12, 1170D in footnote l.

things of the body, according as he hath done, whether it be good or evil" (5, 10). And in the Creed published at the Council of Nicea it is said as follows: "He will come to judge the living and the dead."[1] And in the Creed made at the Council of Constantinople it is said: "He sits at the right hand of the Father, and is coming again with glory to judge the living and the dead."[2]

The **second heresy** is that of the Albanenses, saying that the Universal Judgment has already taken place, and there will not be another in the future. For Guy [the Carmelite] attributes this to them, who when recounting their errors puts this in the seventh place.[3]

This error is clearly refuted from the fact that the resurrection of all men is due to precede the Universal Judgment, as is evident from the same testimonies which we have just cited against the previous heresy, and in the twenty-fourth chapter of Matthew more explicitly, where the coming of the Antichrist is firstly described, then the general resurrection, and afterwards the Judgment, and finally the end of the world: and then (according to Blessed Peter) the elements of the world are purified by fire. But it is evident that none of these things has occurred, because neither the general resurrection, nor the end of the world has taken place, nor have the elements been purified by fire.

JUDEX

Judge

It is the error of the Waldensians whereby they teach that no judge can condemn a man to some punishment. Guy [the Carmelite] accuses them of this error,[4] although Aeneas Sylvius does not mention this error when enumerating the errors of the Waldensians in his book, *De origine Bohemorum*.[5] But it ought not to be surprising if the Waldensians so thought, because this is typical of wicked men, to desire impunity for their wicked deeds, whereby they could do more freely and securely the wicked deeds they wish to perpetrate. The Waldensian act in this manner, who in order that they can suggest their errors to men, attempt to teach before all else that no judge can condemn another man to some punishment. In support of they cite the passage: "Judge not, that you may not be judged" (Mt. 7, 1).

Against this error is that saying which the Lord says: "Appoint of them [rulers]... Who may judge the people at all times" (Ex. 18, 21-22). And again, elsewhere He says: "Thou shalt appoint judges and magistrates in all thy gates, which the Lord thy God shall give thee, in all thy tribes: that they may judge the people with just judgment" (Deut. 16, 18). But if someone distorts these passages to other judgments, and not to the infliction of punishments, let him consider that there are many laws in the Old Testament specifying such and such punishment is to be inflicted upon him who has committed such and such crime. And in the New Law these things are clearly found. Peter punished Ananias and Saphira with death, because they by fraud kept back the price of the sold land. And likewise, he says elsewhere: "Be ye subject therefore to every human creature for God's sake: whether it be to the king as excelling; or to governors as sent by him for the punishment of evildoers, and for the praise of the good" (I Pet. 2, 13-14). Notice that you see the punishment of the wicked. And shortly afterwards he says: "For what glory is it, if committing sin, and being buffeted for it, you endure?" (v.

---

[1] Dz. 54.
[2] Dz. 86.
[3] *Summa de haeresibus* (Paris, Prelum Ascensianum, 1528), c. 7, fol. 78r, lns. 23-24.
[4] *Summa de haeresibus*, c. 3, fol. 81v-82v.
[5] Pope Pius II, *De Bohemorum origine ac gestis historia* (Solingen, Johannes Soter, 1538), c. 35, pp. 59-63.

20). From which words we can conclude that it rightly happens that someone is beaten on account of sin by the command of the judge. And Blessed Paul says regarding higher authority: "If thou do that which is evil, fear: for he beareth not the sword in vain. For he is God's minister: an avenger to execute wrath upon him that doth evil" (Rom. 13, 4). Why then do the Waldensians, being no less ignorant than wicked, dare to teach? If a judge is God's minister to execute wrath upon him who does evil, why do they dare to accuse a judge for punishing evildoers? Do they not rather also accuse God on this account, Whose minister the judge is? Thus, begone Waldensians, and since they are the most ignorant of all heretics, let them be ashamed to teach others.

Now what they cited to support themselves, does not support them in the least: because when the Savior said: "Judge not, that you may not be judged": He did not forbid every judgment, especially that of a judge having authority, but He forbids the rash judgment of many men, who when the matter is hardly known, concluding from very paltry suspicions, immediately settle the matter to themselves, reckoning that such a person is evil or wanted to do something evil. This judgment, I say, the Lord forbids: but not that which when the matter has previously been well known (as it ought), is settled by one having authority. Now we prove that this is so by that which the Savior likewise said in John's Gospel: "Judge not according to the appearance, but judge just judgment" (Jn. 7, 24). By which words, although He forbids one judgment, namely a rash one: He clearly allows another, namely a just judgment, which, when the matter has been previously thoroughly examined, is made according to justice.

JURAMENTUM

Oaths

Among the other errors which Guy the Carmelite accuses the Waldensians, there is one whereby they assert that oaths are forbidden for Christians, such that one is never allowed to swear.[1] He attributes the same error to the Cathari,[2] which surprises me very much: because the Cathari are the same as those who are the Novatians. But no one ever accuses the Novatians of anything similar, but the *Catalogus haereticorum* when discussing the Albanenses says that there are some other Cathari, whom it asserts are divided into three groups.[3] It says that the Albanenses[4] belong to the first sect of the Cathari, the Concorrezenses[5] belong to the second, and the Bagnolenses[6] to the third. And if these are called Cathari, they are certainly different from the Novatians, who are called the first Cathari, on account of the cleanliness about which they boasted. For there is no agreement of the Novatians with these Cathari. Wherefore it is evident that Guy the Carmelite erred miserably, who when he begins to discuss the errors of these Cathari, says that he had already said other things about them: by which words he clearly implies that he thinks that those Cathari and Novatians are the same, yet since those Cathari were very different from the other Cathari who are called Novatians. Those about whom we now speak ought not to be called the Cathari (as Guy and

---

[1] *Summa de haeresibus*, c. 2, fol. 80r-81v.

[2] *Ibid.*, c. 37, fol. 56r, l. 6.

[3] Fol. 123r-v.

[4] I.e., from Desenzano, between Brescia and Verona, or from Alba in Piedmont, Albano, or perhaps from the provinces of Albania.

[5] I.e., probably from Concorrezo in Lombardy.

[6] I.e., from Bagnolo in Italy.

the *Catalogus* calls them), but Catharists. For so Blessed Augustine calls them,[1] as we showed above in the section on "Food" [*Cibus*], in the first heresy. The Apostolics also taught this error.[2]

To refute this error those words which the Lord says in Deuteronomy suffice: "Thou shalt fear the Lord thy God, and shalt serve him only, and thou shalt swear by his name" (6, 13). And again, He says: "Thou shalt fear the Lord thy God, and serve him only: to him thou shalt adhere, and shalt swear by his name" (10, 20). But here those who defend this error respond that this was permitted to the Jews in the Old Law, namely that they swear by God: this is not allowed to Christians who have the perfect law. They say that this is not licit because Christ in Matthew's Gospel forbade one to swear in general.[3] And they confirm this view by the testimony of Jerome[4] and Theophylactus,[5] who when expounding the fifth chapter of Matthew, say that oaths were permitted to the Jews, but it was completely forbidden to the Christians. And Hilary[6] and [Pseudo-] Chrysostom[7] seem to think the same thing when expounding the same passage, although the latter does not speak as explicitly as the former.

But this is countered by the fact that we find that God has often sworn. Whereas if an oath were evil in itself, such that the Jews could swear solely by permission, God, Who cannot do evil, would not have sworn at all. And to this objection they respond that an oath befits God alone, because He alone is true, and cannot lie: but every man is a liar. And they support this view by the testimony of Ambrose.[8] But neither by this way could they escape, as though we could not demonstrate to them that an oath is permitted to men. For they cannot deny that Paul the Apostle swore many times: since in the Epistle to the Romans he speaks thus: "God is my witness, whom I serve in my spirit in the gospel of his Son, that without ceasing I make a commemoration of you always in my prayers" (1, 9-10). And again, he says elsewhere: "But I call God to witness upon my soul, that to spare you, I came not any more to Corinth" (II Cor. 1, 23). And again: "God is my witness, how I long after you all in the bowels of Jesus

---

[1] *De Haeresibus ad Quodvultdeum*, c. 46 (PL 42, 36).

[2] *Summa de haeresibus*, c. 9, fol. 92r-v.

[3] Cf. Mt. 5, 34.

[4] "Finally, consider that the Savior here has not prohibited swearing by God, but by heaven and earth and Jerusalem and by your own head. This had been conceded by the Law, as it were to children, so that in what manner they were offering victims to God so as to avoid offering them to idols, thus also they were permitted to swear to God. It is not that they were right in doing this, but that it was better to exhibit it to God than to devils. But the Gospel truth does not admit swearing, since entirely faithful words have replaced swearing on oath." (*Commentary on Matthew*, bk. 1, on c. 5, v. 34ff. (PL 26, 40A-B)).

[5] "The Lord says that swearing, which is more than "Yea" and "Nay," is of the devil. But, you will ask, is the law of Moses, which bids us to swear, also evil? Learn, then, that at that time it was not evil to swear. But after Christ, it is evil. And so it is with circumcision and, in short, with all the Judaic practices." (*Enarratio in Evangelium Sancti Matthaei*, on c. 5, v. 37 (PG 123, 199B)).

[6] "For those who come in the simplicity of faith, there is no need for the observation of an oath" (*Commentarius in Matthaeum*, c. 4, n. 23 (PL 940B)).

[7] "... it is a sin even to swear honestly..." (*Opus imperfectum*, hom. 12 (PG 56, 698)). Elsewhere he wrote: "Again he who swears, says he, even if he fulfil his oath, does the works of the wicked one" (*Three Homilies on the Devil*, hom. 1, n. 7 (PG 49, 256)).

[8] "The Lord, when he came to teach little ones, to initiate beginners, to confirm the perfect, said in the Gospel: 'not to swear at all,' because he was speaking to weak souls. He was not speaking to the Apostles only but to the crowds. He did not want you to swear for fear that you might perjure yourself. And he added not to swear at all, either by heaven, or by the earth, or by Jerusalem, or by your own head, because of course not one of these things is within your power. 'The Lord hath sworn, and he will not repent.' Therefore He who could not repent of His oath may swear" (*In Psalmum CXVIII Expositio*, c. 14, n. 14 (PL 14, 307)).

Christ" (Phil. 1, 8). Notice that Paul is invoking God each time as witness of his words. But he who swears by God, does nothing other than invoke God as witness of the things which he says: from which we may clearly conclude that Paul swore. Thus an oath is not completely forbidden to the Christian: because otherwise Paul would have sinned when swearing.

Furthermore, an oath is not evil in itself, but rather something good, provided those things which are required are present: since by an oath we show reverence to God, and we show what estimation we have of God, because so swearing by God, we bear witness that we believe that God sees all things: for one who does not know a matter thoroughly, cannot be a good witness. Hence a comical poet wisely said: "Of more value is one eye-witness than ten hearsays."[1] We also show that we believe that God is true, Who cannot lie. Therefore, because we believe that God is such a Being Who has known all things, and Who cannot lie, hence in confirmation of those things which we say, we swear by God, invoking Him as a witness. From which it is evident that by an oath we reverence God, if the other things are present which are required for a just oath. A clear indication of which is that in Deuteronomy, as often as there is mention of an oath, it is always subjoined after the precept of adoration: "Thou shalt adore [literally, fear[2]] the Lord thy God, and shalt serve him only, and thou shalt swear by his name" (Deut. 6, 13). And again: "Thou shalt fear the Lord thy God, and serve him only: to him thou shalt adhere, and shalt swear by his name" (Deut. 10, 20). Notice that an oath is twice joined to adoration and the serving of God. Thus, if it is good to adore God, and to serve Him, it will also be good to swear by His name, as long as it be done rightly and as it ought.

Again, that an oath is licit for a Christian is confirmed by many definitions of the Church. The Council of Ephesus writes to Nestorius, so that he may recant of his heresies, and because the Council did not trust Nestorius' words, it required an oath from him in these words: "But in addition, in writing and by oath, you must confess that you also anathematize those polluted and unholy dogmas of yours, and that you will hold and teach that which we all, bishops, teachers, and leaders of the people both East and West, hold."[3] And the Council of Constance in the eighth session condemned forty-five assertions of John Wycliffe, among which this one is put in the forty-third place concerning oaths, wherein it says: "Oaths are illicit which are made to corroborate human contracts and civil commerce."[4] Which opinion was condemned along with the others of the same man with the said censure. And the same Council of Constance, in the twenty[-second] session decreed that for the confirmation of the agreement made between the Roman emperor and the king of Aragon for eliminating the schism, an oath was sought from all, and afterwards all those attending the Council, from the greatest to the least swore.[5]

But there remains that we reply to the objection of the adversaries. For they object thus: the Lord forbids oaths in the Gospel of Matthew, saying: "But I say to you not to swear at all, neither by heaven, for it is the throne of God: nor by the earth, for it is his footstool: nor by Jerusalem, for it is the city of the great king: neither shalt thou swear by thy head, because thou canst not make one hair white or black. But let your speech be yea, yea: no, no: and that which is over and above these, is of evil" (Mt. 5, 34-37). And Blessed James says: "But above all things, my brethren, swear not, neither by heaven, nor by the earth, nor by any other oath. But let your speech be, yea, yea: no, no: that you fall not under judgment" (5, 12). To

---

[1] Plautus, *Truculentus: The Churl*, act 2, scene 6, 1. 489.
[2] This quotation has been modified based upon Mt. 4, 10.
[3] *Epistola synodica*, Letter of Cyril Bishop of Alexandria to Nestorius, Bishop of Constantinople (PL 67, 13A).
[4] Dz. 623.
[5] This Treaty of Narbonne was signed on December 13, 1415 (*Histoire des conciles œcuméniques* (Paris, Éditions de l'Orante, 1965), vol, 9, p. 376).

this objection we reply in many ways. Firstly, in those words the Savior did not forbid one to swear by God, and Jerome noted this when commenting on that passage. Now he says that "not to swear at all" is not a prohibition of all oaths,[1] because those words refer to the words which follow, such that one ought not to swear at all by Heaven or earth, namely so that when one must swear, he nevertheless never swears by Heaven and earth. Now the reason for this prohibition was lest men when swearing by those elements, should venerate those elements as some kind of deities: because that by which one swears, either he loves or venerates exceedingly. Thus, lest those things be venerated or loved more than is due, He forbids one to ever swear by them. And Jerome and Theophylactus also acknowledge this when commenting on that passage, by whose authority those who teach the opposite view defend themselves. And since they acknowledge this, I am surprised that afterwards it made them think that oaths are completely forbidden. For so Theophylactus says: "Therefore, in prohibiting them from swearing by these things, the Lord does not say, 'Do not swear by them because Heaven is good and great, and earth is useful.' Instead He says, 'Do not swear by them because the one is the throne of God and the other is His footstool,' so that idolatry would not occur. For they might make gods out of those elements by which they swore, which indeed had happened before."[2] And Jerome teaches the same view.

But someone will object to these things those final words of Christ: "But let your speech be yea, yea: no, no: and that which is over and above these, is of evil" (v. 37). We certainly admit that oaths come from evil, but are not evil. And Christ did not say that they are evil, but are "of evil": from the evil, I say, of him who swears and on account of which he swears. For the malice of him for whom he swears, is the reason why the other swears. For if the one hearing had trusted the words of the one speaking, it would not have been necessary for the speaker to confirm his words with an oath. Thus, it comes from the evil of the one for whom one swears that something more is said then "yes, yes" and "no, no." And Augustine give this exposition on that passage of the Gospel in his book, *On Lying*.[3]

It can be otherwise responded that Christ by those words does not absolutely forbid oaths, but the over-readiness to swear, lest from the readiness come the custom, and from the custom one come to commit perjury. Hence Ecclesiasticus says: "Let not thy mouth be accustomed to swearing" (23, 9). And again: "For as a slave daily put to the question, is never without a blue mark: so everyone that sweareth, and nameth, shall not be wholly pure from sin" (v. 11). Augustine also gives this exposition in the place just cited.[4] Blessed Bishop Chromatius[5] gives this and a more excellent exposition to this passage in a distinguished booklet which he made upon the fifth and sixth chapters of Matthew. Here are his words: "For, first, He wanted to remove from us the use of oaths and the habit of human error, lest each of us through swearing by these elements accord a creature the honor of Divine veneration, or believe one

---

[1] "Finally, consider that the Savior here has not prohibited swearing by God..." (as cited above).
[2] *Enarratio in Evangelium Sancti Matthaei*, on c. 5, v. 34-35 (PG 123, 198D-199A).
[3] "But I say unto you, 'Swear not at all.' For here also all swearing is cut off; but from the mouth of the heart, that it should never be done with approbation of the will, but through necessity of the weakness of another; that is, from the evil of another, when it shows that he cannot otherwise be got to believe what is said, unless faith be wrought by an oath; or, from that evil of our own, that while as yet involved in the skins of this mortality we are not able to show our heart: which thing were we able to do, of swearing there were no need" (C. 18, n. 37 (PL 40, 512)).
[4] "'I say unto you, Swear not at all': that is, lest by swearing one come to a facility in swearing, from facility to a custom, and so from a custom there be a downfall into perjury. And therefore he is not found to have sworn except in writing, where there is more wary forethought, and no precipitate tongue withal" (C. 15, n. 28 (PL 40, 507)).
[5] St. Chromatius was Bishop of Aquileia and died about 406-407.

has impunity in swearing falsely if one swears by the elements of the world. For it is written, 'Nor has he sworn deceitfully to his neighbor' (Ps. 23, 4)." And shortly afterwards when expounding the rest of the verse, he says that by the words: "That which is over and above these, is of evil," lies ought to be understood, and that which is over and above "yea, yea, no, no," is over and above the truth, and he says that it "is of evil," meaning from the devil, who is a liar and the father of lies.[1] From which words it is clear according to Chromatius, that Christ by those words only forbade perjury, and the use of swearing. It can also be said that that prohibition of Christ ought not to be numbered among the precepts, but among the counsels, and that it pertains to the perfect alone. It can be inferred that in that passage Christ is depicting Christian perfection, because He treats many things in that same place which no sane person doubts are counsels, and not precepts, such as that which He immediately adds: "But I say to you not to resist evil" (Mt. 5, 39). And more modern theologians, whom they call the scholastics, interpret this passage of the Gospel in this way.

But they are not the only ones, as some think. For Blessed Bernard when inveighing against some heretics who were saying that that oaths are not licit, yet it is licit for them to perjure, lest the secrets of their sect become known to others, says the following: "But it is manifest that whilst you superstitiously abstain from taking lawful oaths you have no scruple at all about the heinous crime of perjury. O unspeakable perversity! What was intended simply as a caution, viz., 'I say to you not to swear at all,' these heretics observe pertinaciously and consider a command; and at the same time, according to their whim, and as if it were something quite indifferent, they dispense themselves in that which has the sanction of immutable law, namely the prohibition against perjury."[2] They cannot call this man a scholastic. Christian Druthmar holds the same view. For he says the following: "Lest the Jews swear by the names of idols, the Lord permitted them to swear by His name. And He likewise did not restrain us, but taught us the perfection: that trust ought to be had among Christians such that it should be not necessary to bring in the Lord's name as a witness. Perjury was forbidden both to them and to us."[3] They cannot call Christian Druthmar a scholastic, since he is not by any means: nor is he tricentenary (as Luther and his followers are accustomed to accuse) because he lived more than seven hundred years ago, if we wish to believe Johannes Trithemius.[4]

And Bede when expounding the words of James: "But above all things, my brethren, swear not" etc. (5, 12) says in the same place that the custom of swearing is forbidden, lest from it one come to commit perjury. For he says the following: "'Hence, I restrain you from the fault of swearing,' James says, 'for the reason that in swearing often to the truth you may also sometimes fall into perjury, and also that you may be further from the vice of perjury the more you do not wish to swear solemnly to the truth except under pressing necessity.'"[5] And Rupert of Deutz, a man renown for his learning and holiness, makes a distinction regarding that passage of Matthew concerning oaths in this way, saying that not to swear at all is a counsel: not to swear, on the other hand, by Heaven and earth etc. is a precept, such that if one must swear due to some necessity then he ought to swear by God, and not by any other thing.[6] See

---

[1] His actual words are: "'That which is over and above these, is of evil.' He is teaching that all speech that comes forth from us ought to contain nothing but the truth, since all falsehood, that is, 'that which is over and above these,' traces back to the devil as its author, who is ever a liar from the beginning, just as he is also its father (Jn. 8, 44)" (*Tractatus in evangelium S. Matthaei*, tract 10, c. 3 (PL 20, 352D-353B)).

[2] *Sermons on the Canticle of Canticles*, serm. 65, n. 2 (PL 183, 1090A).

[3] *Expositio in Mattheum*, c. 9 (PL 106, 1310D).

[4] *De scriptoribus ecclesiasticis* (Paris, Bertholdo Rembolt, 1512), fol. 67r.

[5] *Commentary on James* (PL 93, 39A).

[6] *Commentarius in Matthaeum*, bk. 5 (PL 168, 1416B). Abbot Rupert of Deutz (+1129) was a Benedictine theologian and exegete.

JURAMENTUM

then that the Gospel passage has been sufficiently discussed, which we have shown nowise contradicts our position.

But if they perhaps object to us Jerome and Theophylactus, who seem to think that it is not allowed for a Christian to swear, we in return object against them Augustine, Chromatius, Christian Druthmar, Bernard, Bede, and Rupert. I have said but little; rather I should mention the definition of the Church, the authority of which is so great that it outweighs a thousand men like Jerome and Theophylactus, even though they were illustrious men, renown for holiness as well as learning.

There is **second heresy** which is completely opposite with the previous one. For this one permits oaths so much, that it even says that perjury is allowed. Blessed August attributed this error to Priscillian. For the Priscillianists (as Augustine relates[1]) were teaching their disciples that when questioned and required by oath to reveal their doctrine, they used to say that perjury is allowed to hide their doctrine: wherefore they often used to say, "Swear, perjure yourself, but do not betray the secret." Some heretics at the time of Blessed Bernard held this same error, about whom he makes mention in his *Sermons on the Canticle of Canticles*,[2] and he says that they are called Apostolics, namely because they boasted that they were the successors of the Apostles.[3] The wicked Flagellants (as the *Catalogus haereticorum* asserts[4]) defend the same error.

This error is clearly refuted by that which the Lord in Leviticus says: "Thou shalt not swear falsely by my name, nor profane the name of thy God" (19, 12). For he who swears falsely profanes God's name, because he summons God as a witness of the lie. Now what can be more profane or vile than to encourage lying? Furthermore, the Wise Man when enumerating men's sins, especially those of the pagans, also includes perjury, saying: "All things are mingled together, blood, murder, theft and dissimulation, corruption and unfaithfulness, tumults and perjury" (Wis. 14, 25). And Blessed Paul when saying that "The law is not made for the just man, but for the unjust and disobedient, for the ungodly, and for sinners, for the wicked" (I Tim. 1, 9), he immediately adds, "for liars, for perjured persons" (v. 10). From which it is very clearly concluded that perjury is forbidden by Divine law.

Next, the very reason on account of which they say that perjury is licit, is very bad. For they say that it is licit to swear falsely, namely so that their doctrine may not be revealed to others. Then it is necessary to question them whether their doctrine is in conformity to the Gospel or opposed to it? If it is opposed to it, then they are not true Christians who teach that doctrine. If it is in conformity to the Gospel, why then do they hide it? Why do they conceal it among themselves? For Christ says: "That which I tell you in the dark, speak ye in the light: and that which you hear in the ear, preach ye upon the housetops" (Mt. 10, 27). And when He commands the preaching of the Gospel to His disciples, He says: "Go ye into the whole world, and preach the gospel to every creature" (Mk. 16, 15). He did not say to the Priscillianists only, or to the Apostolics only, or to the Flagellants among themselves only, but to every creature. For He does not want His law to be revealed to the Jews only, so that it would be known in Judea only: but He wants it to be known to the whole world. Hence, He wants His Gospel to be manifest to all, because He wants all men "to come to the knowledge of truth" (I Tim. 2, 4). Hence the Apostle says: "If our gospel be also hid, it is hid to them that are lost" (II Cor. 4, 3). Thus, the Priscillianists and Apostolics are lost, who want to hide the Gospel. And elsewhere the Apostle likewise says: "With the heart, we believe unto justice; but, with the mouth, confession is made unto salvation" (Rom. 10, 10). Now so that anyone may acquire salvation, it

---

[1] *De Haeresibus ad Quodvultdeum*, c. 70 (PL 42, 44).
[2] Serm. 65 & 66.
[3] Serm. 65, n. 8 (PL 183, 1098A).
[4] *Catalogus haereticorum omnium* (Cologne, Iohannes Kempensis, 1537), error 43.

JUSTUS

is necessary that he so confess with the mouth, as he believes with the heart. Against such a clear heresy it is not necessary to cite more things.

JUSTUS

Just Men

Blessed Augustine asserts that Jovinian thought that he who has once been justified through the laver of regeneration cannot sin anymore.[1] And Blessed Jerome likewise accuses him.[2] Augustine testifies that Pelagius taught the same error.[3] We have already disputed against this error above in the section on "Grace," in the second heresy, wherefore it is not necessary to discuss it any further.

A **second heresy** is that of Luther, saying that a just man sins in every good work. But we will discuss this error below in the section on "Works" [*Opera*], and at greater length in the section on "Sin" [*Peccatum*]. Thus, we refer our reader to those places.

There is a **third heresy** belonging to this place, which asserts that every just man is sure of his justification, and is obliged by the Catholic faith to have this certitude, such that if he doubts about it, he cannot be called a Catholic believer. The first inventor of this heresy is Luther, but nothing needs to be said against this heresy, because we have disputed enough against it in the section on "Grace," in the third heresy.

LABOR

Work

There were long ago in Syria monks saying that no manual work is permitted to monks, even for the sake of sustaining life. For they made their profession to be monks so that being free from all manual work, they might always attend to prayer. The authors of this heresy are called in the Syrian language, Psallians: for so Augustine names them.[4] But the *Historia Tripartita*,[5] when discussing these heretics, calls them Massalians, and says that they are called in Greek ευχεται, that is, "praying folk," in that they were saying that one must always pray. They are also called in the same place, Ἐνθουσιασαί, that is, "[Enthusiasts]."[6]

---

[1] *De Haeresibus ad Quodvultdeum*, c. 82 (PL 42, 45).

[2] *Against Jovinian*, bk. 2, n. 1-3 (23, 281D-286A).

[3] *De Haeresibus ad Quodvultdeum*, c. 88 (PL 42, 48).

[4] *De Haeresibus ad Quodvultdeum*, c. 57 (PL 42, 40-41). The text here has Psallians, but Massalians is in most manuscripts and in accord with the Greek. (PL 42, 40, footnote 4).

[5] "In that tempest of the Massalians, whom they call 'Praying folk,' a heresy arose. Now they are called by another name, *Enthysiastae*, that is, 'sacrificers.' For these men wait for the action of a certain demon and they consider this to be the presence of the Holy Ghost. But those who partake of its full malady, are opposed to working with their hands as though it were something wicked, and indulge themselves with dreams of iniquities which they call prophetic imaginings." (*Historia ecclesiastica tripartite*, lib. 7, c. 11 (PL 69, 1077C)).

[6] The meaning of this Greek word, Ἐνθουσιασαί, given here in the text is "sacrificers" or "priests," but it actually means "Enthusiasts." The incorrect translation, which has been corrected here, comes from Cassiodorus who "had the *Jewish Antiquities* of Flavius Josephus translated and also the ecclesiastical histories of Theodoret, Sozomen, and Socrates. He himself made extracts from the translations of these three historians and combined them in the *Historia Tripartita*, a hasty composition, teeming with errors

Other monks in Africa shortly afterwards defended the same error, especially at Carthage, as is evident from Augustine in his book, *On the Work of Monks*. For at the beginning of this work he states that he is writing this book at the request of Aurelius, the Bishop of Carthage at that time, for the refutation of this error, which had then arisen in Carthage.[1] The Waldensians resurrected this error long since buried in Hell, saying that a perfect man ought not to work with his hands. For so Guy [the Carmelite] accuses the Waldensians in his *Summa de haeresibus*.[2] But Aeneas Sylvius when enumerating the errors of the Waldensians does not mention this error.[3]

This error is easily refuted from the fact that Paul the Apostle, who rightly ought to be reckoned among the perfect, worked with his own hands. For although he was able not to work, and live from the Gospel without labor, because those to whom he preached were obliged to feed him: yet to not burden those to whom he preached the Gospel, he chose to work with his own hands, so that he would earn his living from his own labor. For so he says in the First Epistle to the Corinthians: "Know you not, that they who work in the holy place, eat the things that are of the holy place; and they that serve the altar, partake with the altar? So also the Lord ordained that they who preach the gospel, should live by the gospel. But I have used none of these things" (9, 13-15). If Paul, who could have lived from the Gospel, works with his hands, how much more are monks obliged to work with their hands, who do not preach?

Paul clearly reprehends those same idle monks in the Second Epistle to the Thessalonians, saying: "For yourselves know how you ought to imitate us: for we were not disorderly among you; neither did we eat any man's bread for nothing, but in labour and in toil we worked night and day, lest we should be chargeable to any of you. Not as if we had not power: but that we might give ourselves a pattern unto you, to imitate us. For also when we were with you, this we declared to you: that, if any man will not work, neither let him eat. For we have heard there are some among you who walk disorderly, working not at all, but curiously meddling. Now we charge them that are such, and beseech them by the Lord Jesus Christ, that, working with silence, they would eat their own bread" (3, 7-12). And in the Epistle to the Ephesians he again says: "He that stole, let him now steal no more; but rather let him labour, working with his hands the thing which is good, that he may have something to give to him that suffereth need" (4, 28). And in the Acts of the Apostles when from sending Miletus to Ephesus, he called the ancients of the church, he says to them: "I have not coveted any man's silver, gold, or apparel, as you yourselves know: for such things as were needful for me and them that are with me, these hands have furnished. I have shewed you all things, how that so labouring you ought to support the weak, and to remember the word of the Lord Jesus, how he said: It is a more blessed thing to give, rather than to receive" (20, 33-35). Behold the Apostle Paul working with his own hands, who very often exhorted others that they also would work with their hands.

Furthermore, all the holy men who instituted a manner of living in a monastery, commanded their monks that working with their hands they would avoid idleness, the enemy of the soul. For Blessed Jerome, when speaking about the monks of Egypt in a letter to the monk Rusticus, says the following: "In Egypt the monasteries make it a rule to receive none who are not willing to work; for they regard labor as necessary not only for the support of the body

---

and contradictions, but nevertheless much used throughout the Middle Ages as a manual of history" ("Cassiodorus," *Catholic Encyclopedia* (New York: Robert Appleton Company, 1908), vol. 3, p. 406).

[1] From *The Retractations*, bk. 2, c. 21 (PL 32, 639).
[2] *Summa de haeresibus* (Paris, Prelum Ascensianum, 1528), c. 19, fol. 87r, lns. 36-45.
[3] Pope Pius II, *De Bohemorum origine ac gestis historia* (Solingen, Johannes Soter, 1538), c. 35, pp. 59-63.

but also for the salvation of the soul. Do not let your mind stray into harmful thoughts, or, like Jerusalem prostituting herself to everyone who passed by."[1]

Blessed Basil teaches his monks the same thing, who in his monastic rule presents monks raising the following question to him, speaking thus: "Therefore, if we ought not to be anxious about the necessities of life[2] and there is the other precept of the Lord that says: 'Labour not for the meat which perisheth' (Jn. 6, 27), is it superfluous to work with our hands?" Responding to which question Basil says: "The Lord himself explained his own precept in another place. For there He said that we must not seek anything for this life when he says: 'Seek not you what you shall eat, or what you shall drink… for all these things do the nations of the world seek' (Lk. 12, 29-30), and added: 'Seek rather the kingdom of God and his justice' (Mt. 6, 33). He also indicated how we ought to seek, for in the same place, having said: 'Labour not for the meat which perisheth,' he added, 'but for that which endureth unto life everlasting' (Jn. 6, 27). And what this was He showed in another place, saying: 'My meat is to do the will of him that sent me' (Jn. 4, 34). Now the Father's will is that we give food to the hungry and drink to the thirsty, clothe the naked and the rest like this. Then it is necessary that we also imitate the Apostle who says: 'I have shewed you all things, how that so labouring you ought to support the weak' (Acts 20, 35), and again when he teaches: 'Let him labour, working with his hands the thing which is good, that he may have something to give to him that suffereth need' (Eph. 4, 28). When therefore the Lord in the Gospel or the Apostle delivers these things to us, it is clear that we ought not be anxious or labor for ourselves, but we ought to be anxious and to work diligently on account of the Lord's commandment and on account of our neighbors' necessities, and that above all because the things that we do for His servants the Lord receives to Himself and promises in return for these services the kingdom of Heaven."[3] From which words it is evident that he enjoins upon his monks to labor, not so much on account of the need of their own livelihood, as in order that they could fulfil God's Commandments by working, and from their work relieve the needs of their neighbors.

Blessed Benedict in his *Rule* says: "Idleness is the enemy of the soul. Therefore the brethren should be occupied at certain times in manual labor, and again at fixed hours in sacred reading. To that end we think that the times for each may be prescribed as follows. From Easter until the Calends of October, when they come out from Prime in the morning let them labor at whatever is necessary until about the fourth hour, and from the fourth hour until about the sixth let them apply themselves to reading. After the sixth hour, having left the table, let them rest on their beds in perfect silence; or if anyone may perhaps want to read, let him read to himself in such a way as not to disturb anyone else. Let None be said rather early, at the middle of the eighth hour, and let them again do what work has to be done until Vespers. And if the circumstances of the place or their poverty should require that they themselves do the work of gathering the harvest, let them not be discontented; for then are they truly monks when they live by the labor of their hands, as did our Fathers and the Apostles. Let all things be done with moderation, however, for the sake of the faint-hearted."[4] Blessed Benedict prescribed these things to his monks in the Rule.

Likewise the seraphic holy father, the founder of the Friars Minor, also [prescribes these things] in his rule: "Let those friars, to whom the Lord has given the grace to work, work faithfully and devoutly, in such a way that, having excluded idleness, the enemy of the soul, they do not extinguish the spirit of holy prayer and devotion, which all other temporal things must serve zealously. Indeed concerning the wages of labor, let them receive on their (own)

---

[1] Letter 125, n. 11 (PL 22, 1079). Cf. Ez. 16, 25.

[2] Cf. Mt. 6, 31.

[3] *The Rule of St. Basil*, interrogation 127 (PL 103, 533D-534B).

[4] C. 48 (PL 66, 703A-704B).

behalf and that of their brothers the things necessary for the body, excepting coins or money, and this humbly, as befits the servants of God and the followers of most holy poverty."[1] And in his *Testament*: "And I used to work with my hands, and I want to work; and all the other brothers I firmly want, that they work at their job, because this pertains to honorableness. Those who do not know how, let them learn, not for the sake of the cupidity to receive a price for work, but for the sake of the example (it gives) and to repel idleness."[2]

Finally, the Fourth Synod of Carthage perceiving how harmful is the idleness of the body to all the clergy, commands that they work with their hands, saying: "Let a cleric, in so far as he can do so without injury to his office, maintain himself either by handicraft or by husbandry."[3] And again in the following chapter it says: "All ecclesiastics, whose health will permit it, must study and must acquire some handicraft."[4] It is profitable to believe the decisions of this council more than the idle Massalians, or the uneducated Waldensians.

But now it is necessary that we see with what arguments the Massalians defend their heresy. For firstly they cite in their favor the words which our Savior said in John's Gospel: "Labour not for the meat which perisheth, but for that which endureth unto life everlasting" (6, 27). Secondly, they object that the Lord reprehended Martha for her labor, saying: "Martha, thou art careful, and art troubled about many things" (Lk. 10, 41). And in Matthew's Gospel He restrains the same solicitude when He says to all men: "Be not solicitous therefore, saying, What shall we eat: or what shall we drink, or wherewith shall we be clothed?" (6, 31). And again, He says: "Be not therefore solicitous for tomorrow; for the morrow will be solicitous for itself. Sufficient for the day is the evil thereof" (v. 34).

And certainly these passages of Sacred Scripture ought not to understood in the way that the Massalians suppose, thinking that Christ by those words forbade labor. Blessed Basil, however, teaches how those words ought to be interpreted in his words which we have cited above. But against the Massalians Theophylactus shows more clearly their meaning, who in his exposition of the Gospel of John when expounding those words which we have just now cited from John, says the following: "For because there are many who wish to live without working; notably, the Massalians, who defend their way of life of idleness by referring to this passage, it will be worthwhile to explain these words. The intent of Our Lord Jesus Christ was not to forbid bodily labor and encourage sloth. 'For idleness hath taught much evil' (Eccli. 33, 29), and, if truth be told, 'the meat which perisheth' is in fact the desire to live without working. He who wants to follow Christ must work in order to have the means to share with others. For this has the reward and the promise of the kingdom to come." And shortly afterwards he responds to the other two quotations which we have cited from Matthew and Luke in favor of the Massalians, saying: "The Lord's words to Martha are not about the relative merits of working or not working at a daily occupation. Rather, He is instructing her to recognize the right time for each, and not to fret over preparing food for the stomach when an opportunity to profit from spiritual teaching is at hand. When the Lord says, 'Be not solicitous,' He is forbidding anxious thought, not daily labor. It is possible to work without worrying. The Lord is teaching us not to be obsessed by worldly cares, and not to be preoccupied with how we will refresh ourselves tomorrow. He desires that we labor each day, saying, 'Be not therefore solicitous for tomorrow.' It is as though He were to say, 'Be not solicitous how by working today you may rest tomorrow, but in earning your living by daily labor, you should not worry about the future.'"[5] From these words of Theophylactus it is evident that the Massalians are

---

[1] *The Regula Bullata*, c. 5.
[2] C. 2.
[3] C. 52 (PL 84, 204B).
[4] C. 53 (PL 84, 204C).
[5] PG 123, 1295B-1298A.

slain by their own sword. For from the same passage of Matthew which they cited to support themselves, their idleness is rebuked.

Blessed Augustine wrote a book which is entitled, *On the Work of Monks*,[1] against this heresy. And John Cassian in his *On the Institutes of the Coenobia* in twelve books,[2] from the seventh until the last book does nothing other than show that it is necessary for the monk to work with his hands, so that the vices which idleness begets may be lopped off through labor.

The **second heresy** is one which is as it were diametrically opposed to the one just recounted, asserting that all monks without any distinction are bound to perform manual labor, so that they may earn a living for themselves: and they cannot earn a living for themselves in any other way then by manual labor. The first author of this heresy was a certain William of Saint-Amour, a very bitter enemy of mendicant monks. He said that all monks who did not have community property from which they may live, ought to labor with their hands, so that they may earn a living for themselves therefrom.[3] He taught this and other heresies under Pope Alexander IV, by whom he was also condemned by the Bull which begins, *Romanus Pontifex*.[4] John Wycliffe succeeded after him, who desired to rebuild more strongly the destroyed Jericho. For this man not only spoke about mendicant monks, but about all monks without distinction, saying that all monks ought to make a living and their own clothes for themselves by the labor of their hands. Luther, however, and all his accomplices teach this error more mildly, namely that they do not want to force those who are occupied with preaching God's word to work with their hands: on the other hand, they force all others to earn their living by some craft: and one is nowise allowed to live among the Lutherans by begging.

And certainly if they were to speak with due distinctions about enjoining working with one's hands upon monks, we would not have called them into dispute here: but rather there would be an agreement among ourselves about this matter, because as we have taught in the heresy just related, some laborious work is highly necessary for monks. But since they say that all without distinction ought to work, then we rightly now brand them of heresy: because we will prove from the teaching of Christ and the Apostles that there are many ways of life among monks which do not require this labor: but such monks can be well off even if they have not eaten from the labor of their own hands.

Who will be so cruel towards his neighbor, that he would want to force him who is sick and is afflicted with illness to work? Certainly no one, unless he be such a man who is unwilling to do to others what he would want others to do to him. "Sufficient for the day," the Savior says, "is the evil thereof" (Mt. 6, 34). For the illness itself suffices, and it is not right to lay upon him, on top of the illness, another burden, which since he cannot bear it, it is necessary that either he refuse it, or accepting it he be crushed. And yet we do not here speak only about those sick men, who were at the time afflicted with sickness, but also those who even though they may be well at times, still often relapse after a short time, whom doctors call valetudinarians.

For Timothy belonged to this category of men, who suffered from a stomach infirmity and other frequent infirmities. For Paul when writing to him says the following: "Do not still drink water, but use a little wine for thy stomach's sake, and thy frequent infirmities" (I Tim. 5, 23). He said "frequent," and not "continual." For if he had been afflicted with continual infirmity, Paul, who was burning with such great charity, such that had he been afflicted with any other

---

[1] PL 40, 547 ff.

[2] PL 49, 53A ff.

[3] "Such men, or rather all Christians who have no other means by which to live but are nevertheless able in body, ought without exception to live by physical labor even if they are suited for better spiritual works" (*De periculis novissimorum temporum* in *Magistri Guillielmi De Sancto Amore... Opera omnia* (Coutances (France), Apud Alitophilos, 1632), c. 12, p. 48).

[4] The bull, *Romanus Pontifex de summi*, was issued on October 5, 1256 (Dz. 840-844).

infirmity, would not have enjoined upon him the work of preaching, the care of souls, the ministry of widows, all which things require at least a man's mediocre health. Thus Timothy, because he was infirm in this way, could not work with his hands: he exhorts, admonishes and consoles him as follows. "Labour," he says, "as a good soldier of Christ Jesus" (II Tim. 2, 3).

And lest he think that he could earn his living through business as merchants do, he added: "No man, being a soldier to God, entangleth himself with secular businesses; that he may please him to whom he hath engaged himself. For he also that striveth for the mastery, is not crowned, except he strive lawfully" (v. 4-5). But because Timothy could have objected that he was unfit due to his infirmity, Paul immediately added: "The husbandman, that laboureth, must first partake of the fruits" (v. 6). By which words he does not advise him to work with his hands, as he is accustomed to advise others to do: but he shows him the way whereby he can live from the Gospel without manual labor. And when he was in Miletus, he taught all the priests whom he had summoned from Ephesus to that place, that the weak ought to be supported from the labors of other men. "I have shewed you all things, how that so labouring you ought to support the weak" (Acts. 20, 35). Notice that Paul is teaching that by the labor of those who are well, the weak should be supported. Hence [Julianus Pomerius[1]] says the following: "Even the poor, if they can help themselves by their crafts and labors, should not usurp what the weak and the sick ought to receive, lest the Church in her capacity of furnishing the necessities of life to those destitute of every comfort be embarrassed by the fact that even such as are in no need at all are recipients of her aid and be unable to assist those she should."[2] It is clear that it is unjust that the weak be forced to labor which they are unable to bear.

Blessed Augustine thinks something similar of the rich who having been brought up softly and delicately in the world, having despised all things entered the monastery, distributing those things which they owned to Christ's poor. For Augustine thinks that those men, because they cannot bear labor, having been reared more softly and nowise accustomed to labors, should not be forced to do labor. For he says the following: "Wherefore even those who having relinquished or distributed their former possessions, whether ample or in any sort opulent, means, have chosen with pious and wholesome humility to be numbered among the poor of Christ; if they be so strong in body and free from ecclesiastical occupations, (albeit, bringing as they do so great a proof of their purpose, and conferring from their former possessions, either very much, or not a little, upon the indigence of the same society, the common fund itself and brotherly charity owes them in return a sustenance of their life), yet if they also work with their hands, that they may take away all excuse from lazy brethren who come from a more humble condition in life, and therefore one more used to toil; therein they act far more mercifully than when they divided all their goods to the needy. If indeed they be unwilling to do this, who can venture to compel them? Yet then there ought to be found for them works in the monastery, which if more free from bodily exercise, require to be looked unto with vigilant administration, that not even they may eat their bread for nought, because it is now become the common property. Nor is it to be regarded in what monasteries, or in what place, any man may have bestowed that which he had upon his indigent brethren. For all Christians make one commonwealth."[3] From whose words it is clear that those men ought not to be forced to do labor in the monastery, who when they entered the monastery, had possessions in this world, which they distributed to the poor.

And he previously had confirmed the same position from Paul's opinion saying the following: "Setting apart, then, this power, which the preachers of the word have over them to whom

---

[1] This work was here ascribed to Prosper of Aquitaine, as was formerly supposed.
[2] *On the Contemplative Life*, bk. 2, c. 10 (PL 59, 454B-C).
[3] *On the Work of Monks*, c. 25, n. 33 (PL 40, 573).

they preach, he often testifies; speaking, moreover, of the saints who had sold all that they had and distributed the same, and were dwelling at Jerusalem in an holy communion of life, not saying that anything was their own, to whom all things were in common, and their soul and heart one in the Lord[1]: that these by the Churches of the Gentiles should have what they needed bestowed upon them, he charges and exhorts. Thence is also that to the Romans: 'But now I shall go to Jerusalem,' he says, 'to minister unto the saints' (15, 25)."[2]

There are also other men who not by lesser, nay perhaps greater or at least more noble justice, can spend their lives without working with their hands. Now these are the preachers of God's word, and all teachers, who by words or writing teach others God's law. For it does not matter by which way someone teaches, namely by word or writing, provided that he teaches about God's law. It is proved that all these men can eat without manual labor from the fact that they have from the Lord the right of receiving those things which are necessary for life from those whom they teach. For when Christ sent His Apostles to preach, He said to them: "Do not possess gold, nor silver, nor money in your purses: nor scrip for your journey, nor two coats, nor shoes, nor a staff; for the workman is worthy of his meat" (Mt. 10, 9-10). For He moreover held these things back from them so that when they needed them, they would receive them from those to whom they preached God's word.

But lest someone suppose that this right was granted to the Apostles alone, let him hear what the Evangelist Luke says about other preachers. "And after these things the Lord appointed also other seventy-two: and he sent them two and two before his face into every city and place whither he himself was to come. And he said to them: The harvest indeed is great, but the labourers are few. Pray ye therefore the Lord of the harvest, that he send labourers into his harvest. Go: Behold I send you as lambs among wolves. Carry neither purse, nor scrip, nor shoes; and salute no man by the way. Into whatsoever house you enter, first say: Peace be to this house. And if the son of peace be there, your peace shall rest upon him; but if not, it shall return to you. And in the same house, remain, eating and drinking such things as they have: for the labourer is worthy of his hire" (Lk. 10, 1-7). Notice that you now see that what had been previously granted to the twelve Apostles was likewise granted to the seventy-two disciples.

But if someone were to say that this power was given to pastors alone, and not to others to whom the duty of preaching was not enjoined, but they obtrude themselves to preaching, anyone will easily reject this who considers well that this power of living from the Gospel is not founded upon the office of pastor, but solely upon the preaching of God's word, nor does it depend upon anything other than the office of preaching. Hence if a monk labors only in the preaching itself, not having the office of pastor, as opposed to a secular pastor or curate, why will he not also have his meat or his hire as others do? "For the labourer is worthy," Christ says, "of his meat" (Mt. 10, 10). And again: "The labourer is worthy of his hire" (Lk. 10, 1-7). Notice that he said "labourer" both times, he did not however say "prelate," or "pastor," or "curate," or "superior": but in order to intimate that hire is due to the work, and not to the preferment, He said, "labourer." But since a monk preaches, he is also a "labourer," just like anyone else: thus hire is also due to him. For if those who freely volunteer do not work as much as the others, it is just that they also have an unequal hire. But if their work is in preaching is greater, why will they not have at least an equal reward? Moses certainly acted more justly than these heretics wish to do, who gave hire not only to Beseleel and Ooliab, skilled men and chosen by the Lord to do the work of the sanctuary, but also to other expert men who volunteered to do the same work, and distributed the offerings of the children of Israel

---

[1] Cf. Acts 2, 44, and 4, 32.

[2] *On the Works of Monks*, c. 16, n. 17 (PL 40, 562).

LABOR

to them as to the others.[1] But these heretics wish to oppress monks with Egyptian and Pharaonic slavery, namely such that straw be not given, and the same amount of work be required. They want that the necessaries of life not be given to preachers, and the work of preaching be required of them.

Paul the Apostle says in his Epistle to the Romans: "For if the Gentiles have been made partakers of their spiritual things, they ought also in carnal things to minister to them" (15, 27). And again, in the First Epistle to the Corinthians he says: "Who serveth as a soldier at any time, at his own charges? Who planteth a vineyard, and eateth not of the fruit thereof? Who feedeth the flock, and eateth not of the milk of the flock? Speak I these things according to man? Or doth not the law also say these things? For it is written in the law of Moses: Thou shalt not muzzle the mouth of the ox that treadeth out the corn. Doth God take care for oxen? Or doth he say this indeed for our sakes? For these things are written for our sakes: that he that plougheth, should plough in hope; and he that thrasheth, in hope to receive fruit. If we have sown unto you spiritual things, is it a great matter if we reap your carnal things?" (9, 7-11). Let these enemies of monks now fear to muzzle the mouths of those treading.

Or perhaps a preaching monk does not plant a vineyard when he preaches? Was not Paul saying on account of his preaching, "I have planted" (I Cor. 3, 6)? Does not a preaching monk also feed? Does he not also thrash? If he plants, they should allow him to eat the fruit of the vineyard. If he feeds the flock, they should permit him to eat its milk. If he thrashes, they ought not to muzzle his mouth contrary to God's precept. And when writing to Timothy he again says: "The husbandman, that laboureth, must first partake of the fruits" (II Tim. 2, 6). Behold you now see that the preachers of God's word by Divine decree are free from the obligation of corporal labor. Now these are all they who are dedicated to the Divine ministry. For in the First Epistle to the Corinthians Paul says: "Know you not, that they who work in the holy place, eat the things that are of the holy place; and they that serve the altar, partake with the altar? So also the Lord ordained that they who preach the gospel, should live by the gospel" (9, 13-14). Observe that in one sentence Paul asserts that not only the Evangelists, but all those serving the altar have this power, so that they may be well off, even if they would not eat of the labor of their hands. For so Blessed Augustine, who when speaking about the Massalian monks, says: "But these brethren of ours rashly arrogate unto themselves, so far as I can judge, that they have this kind of power. For if they be Evangelists, I confess, they have it: if ministers of the altar, dispensers of Sacraments, of course it is no arrogating to themselves, but a plain vindicating of a right."[2]

Why then do these heretics bark like dogs at monks? Why do they forbid with such a general sentence bread to all monks, which the Lord grants with such benevolence to Evangelists and those serving the altar? Besides these men, however, whom we have shown to be exempt by Divine law from working and manual labor, anyone else who were to be a monk is obliged to labor. And if they would not work, certainly I do not think that it is permitted for them to eat. For the monastic life was not instituted so that one may have a life of idleness in it, which perhaps he did not have in the world. Hence Blessed Augustine says the following: "But, as for them who before they entered this holy society got their living by labor of the body, of which sort are the greater part of them which come into monasteries, because of mankind also the greater part are such; if they will not work, neither let them eat. For not to that end are the rich, in this Christian warfare, brought low unto piety, that the poor may be lifted up unto pride. As indeed it is by no means seemly that in that mode of life where senators become men of toil, there common workmen should become men of leisure; and whereunto there come,

---

[1] Cf. Ex. 36, 3.
[2] *On the Work of Monks*, c. 21, n. 24 (PL 40, 567).

relinquishing their dainties, men who had been masters of houses and lands, there common peasants should be dainty."[1]

This pestilential assertion of these heretics has been condemned by the decision of the whole Catholic Church. For the twenty-fourth of the forty-five articles of John Wycliff condemned during the eighth session of the Council of Constance says the following: "Brothers are bound to acquire their food by the labor of hands and not by begging. Regarding this article, the reasons for the condemnation are included in the acts as follows: The first part is scandalous and presumptuous inasmuch as it speaks in general terms and without distinctions; the second part is erroneous inasmuch as it asserts that begging is not permitted to friars."[2]

But now it is necessary that we respond to the objections of these heretics. For firstly they object that Paul worked: thus since monks are imitators of the Apostles, they themselves are also bound to work. Now to this objection we reply admitting that Paul worked with his hands, we do not admit however that he did this by reason of necessity or obligation, but for the sake of perfection or supererogation. For even if he had not worked with his hands, but instead had chosen to live from the Gospel, he would not have sinned, since it is evident that Peter and the other Apostles supported themselves from the Gospel alone, without manual labor.

The Apostle himself also bears witness to this, who in the First Epistle to the Corinthians says the following: "My defence with them that do examine me is this. Have not we power to eat and to drink? Have we not power to carry about a woman, a sister, as well as the rest of the apostles, and the brethren of the Lord, and Cephas? Or I only and Barnabas, have not we power to do this? Who serveth as a soldier at any time, at his own charges?" (9, 3-7). And after having interjected some arguments with which he proves that he had the power of living from the Gospel just like the other Apostles, he adds: "But I have used none of these things" (v. 15). And in the Second Epistle to the Thessalonians he says: "For yourselves know how you ought to imitate us: for we were not disorderly among you; neither did we eat any man's bread for nothing, but in labour and in toil we worked night and day, lest we should be chargeable to any of you. Not as if we had not power: but that we might give ourselves a pattern unto you, to imitate us" (3, 7-9). From which words it is clearly proved that although monks are imitators of the Apostles, still it is not necessary that all work without distinction: because not all the Apostles did this, but rather Paul, who not out of necessity, but for the sake of perfection, testifies that he did this.

Secondly, they object to us those words which Paul, when writing to the Thessalonians, says: "For when we were with you, this we declared to you: that, if any man will not work, neither let him eat" (v. 10). But this objection has absolutely no strength if the subsequent words are adjoined to those which were related, because from those which the Apostle subjoined, it is clearly enough shown that he does not inhibit food by a universal ruling for anyone not working, but only for the idle who have absolutely no occupation by which they may deserve to eat bread. For he speaks as follows: "For we have heard there are some among you who walk disorderly, working not at all, but curiously meddling. Now we charge them that are such, and beseech them by the Lord Jesus Christ, that, working with silence, they would eat their own bread" (v. 11-12). Notice to whom Paul speaks, namely to those walking disorderly, working not at all, but curiously meddling. To these men, I say, he commands that working with silence, they would eat their own bread, and if someone is unwilling to work, neither let him eat. But monks preaching God's word, serving the altar, are not doing nothing: hence they can eat. But if those words of Paul were to oblige all monks, by the same rule they would oblige all Christians because the Apostle when writing to the Thessalonians wrote not only

---

[1] *Ibid.* c. 25, n. 33 (PL 40, 573).

[2] Dz. 604. Mansi, *Sacrorum Conciliorum* (Venice, Zatta, 1784), vol. 27, p. 633.

to monks, nor did he make any mentions there of monks, but rather he wrote to all without distinction: and yet those words are not directed to all men, but only to those who lead an idle life, whom we also acknowledge to be unworthy to eat bread.

Brother Thomas [Netter of] Walden wrote against this error in *Doctrinale antiquitatum fidei Ecclesiae Catholicae*.[1]

LEX

Law

A certain heresy about this matter arose long ago in the very beginnings of the early Church, asserting that the Old Law ought to observed as to all its precepts along with the New Law. It is not apparent to me who was the first author of this heresy. Yet I do know, based upon the testimonies of Philastrius[2] and Augustine[3] that Cerinthus, Ebion, and the Nazarenes taught this heresy.

But I do not know which of them was the most ancient, because the beginning of the Nazarenes is not clear, since no one has stated who was their leader. I am speaking about the heretical Nazarenes, not however about those [i.e. the Nazarites] whom the book of Numbers mentions.[4] Regarding Cerinthus and Ebion, it is evident that they were contemporaries of John the Evangelist. For Blessed Jerome says that Blessed John "wrote a Gospel at the request of the bishops of Asia, against [Cerinthus and other heretics and especially against the then growing dogma of] the Ebionites, who assert that Christ did not exist before Mary," wherefore he was compelled to treat both natures of Christ, namely the Divine and human.[5] But Irenaeus says, "John the disciple of the Lord, going to bathe at Ephesus, and perceiving Cerinthus within, rushed out of the bath-house without bathing, exclaiming, 'Let us fly, lest even the bath-house fall down, because Cerinthus, the enemy of the truth, is within.'"[6] Therefore since both of these men were contemporaries of John, although I suspect that Cerinthus was somewhat older then Ebion, due to the fact that Irenaeus when enumerating the heretics who molested the Church until his time, speaks about Cerinthus before Ebion.[7] For he speaks about Ebion in [the second part of] chapter twenty-six and he accuses him of this heresy which we will forthwith discuss. But on the other hand, he treats about Cerinthus in [the first part of the same chapter] and yet he does not attribute this heresy to him. But [Pseudo-]Tertullian also does not mention this error when discussing the same Cerinthus in his booklet about heresies, even when enumerating his other errors.[8] Philastrius, however, ascribes all those things to Cerinthus which Irenaeus ascribes to Ebion: and the same Philastrius says that Ebion was a disciple of Cerinthus. But in assigning these heresies, such that to each heretic be attributed what is his, I will much more willingly believe Irenaeus than Philastrius, because he was much more learned and he lived much earlier than Philastrius.

The Sampsaeans and the Elcesaites, who universally embraced the teaching of the Ebionites, also defended this heresy. Wherefore Epiphanius when enumerating heresies (as Au-

---

[1] Vol. 1, bk. 4, art. 1, c. 12, p. 506 ff.
[2] *De haeresibus*, c. 8, 36-37 (PL 12, 1122A; 1152A-1155A).
[3] *De Haeresibus ad Quodvultdeum*, c. 8-10 (PL 42, 27).
[4] Cf. Num. 6, 1-21.
[5] *De viris illustribus*, c. 9 (PL 23, 623A-B).
[6] *Against the Heresies*, bk. 3, c. 3, n. 4 (PG 7, 853).
[7] *Against the Heresies*, bk. 1, c. 26 (PG 7, 685-686).
[8] *De praescriptionibus adversus haereticos*, c. 47 (PL 2, 66B-67B).

gustine bears witness[1]) combines the Sampsaeans and the Elcesaites with the Ebionites, as though their heresy were the one and the same. Now no one, whom I know, taught this heresy after these men, until the present time, in which I hear that certain Germans among those bordering on the Rhine, tolerated circumcision after having received Baptism, saying that circumcision is necessary for attaining eternal life.

Nevertheless, Paul confutes all these men when writing to the Galatians, who had been infected with the same error, saying: "But before the faith came, we were kept under the law shut up, unto that faith which was to be revealed. Wherefore the law was our pedagogue in Christ, that we might be justified by faith. But after the faith is come, we are no longer under a pedagogue" (3, 23-25). And again, when speaking about the two testaments under the figure of the two sons of Abraham, he says: "But as then he, that was born according to the flesh, persecuted him that was after the spirit; so also it is now. But what saith the scripture? Cast out the bondwoman and her son; for the son of the bondwoman shall not be heir with the son of the free woman. So then, brethren, we are not the children of the bondwoman, but of the free: by the freedom wherewith Christ has made us free" (4, 29-31). Observe that Paul clearly testifies that the Old Law ought to be cast away, which was as it were the bondwoman of the Evangelical Law. And again, in the same Epistle he says: "Behold, I Paul tell you, that if you be circumcised, Christ shall profit you nothing. And I testify again to every man circumcising himself, that he is a debtor to the whole law. You are made void of Christ, you who are justified in the law: you are fallen from grace. For we in spirit, by faith, wait for the hope of justice. For in Christ Jesus neither circumcision availeth anything, nor uncircumcision: but faith that worketh by charity" (5, 2-6).

And in the Epistle to the Hebrews when disputing about the same thing, he says: "If then perfection was by the Levitical priesthood, (for under it the people received the law), what further need was there that another priest should rise according to the order of Melchisedech, and not be called according to the order of Aaron? For the priesthood being translated, it is necessary that a translation also be made of the law" (7, 11-12). And again, he says: "There is indeed a setting aside of the former commandment, because of the weakness and unprofitableness thereof: (For the law brought nothing to perfection), but a bringing in of a better hope, by which we draw nigh to God" (v. 18-19). Finally, a judgment was given about this matter by all the Apostles gathered together in the very famous Council of Jerusalem: because (as the Apostolic history relates) "Some coming down from Judea, taught the brethren: that except you be circumcised after the manner of Moses, you cannot be saved... For there arose some of the sect of the Pharisees that believed, saying: They must be circumcised, and be commanded to observe the law of Moses" (Acts 15, 1 & 5). On account of which teaching, no small contest was made by Paul and Barnabas resisting this assertion. For which cause the Apostles and ancients assembled to make a judgment about this matter. And after having made a thorough examination of the matter, as ought to have been done, they pronounced their judgment which they sent by letter to those who were in Antioch, in this manner: "For it hath seemed good to the Holy Ghost and to us, to lay no further burden upon you than these necessary things: that you abstain from things sacrificed to idols, and from blood, and from things strangled, and from fornication; from which things keeping yourselves, you shall do well" (v. 28-29). Who will there be, therefore, who would dare to oppose the judgment of such an illustrious council?

And certainly if after the Evangelical Law was given, it would still be necessary to observe the Old Law, God would have seemed to have acted contrary to the same Law, Who made the following law in Leviticus: "Thou shalt not take thy wife's sister for a harlot, to rival her, neither shalt thou discover her nakedness, while she is yet living" (18, 18). Which things were

---

[1] *De Haeresibus ad Quodvultdeum*, c. 32 (PL 42, 31).

certainly rightly commanded, lest if perhaps someone were to be married to a wife and her sister at the same time, jealousy would be stirred up between the sisters dwelling together, whence strife and quarrelling would have been engendered. God had indeed espoused the synagogue to Himself: the Church is its sister which God also chose to join to Himself. But lest there be any occasion of contention between them, He did not want to replace the second while the first was still alive. Hence it was necessary that the synagogue be buried at the time when God espoused to Himself the Church, His new spouse, lest there would have been jealousy between the sisters dwelling together, just as long ago Lia was jealous of Rachel. For when Rachel asked Lia to give her some of the mandrakes which her son had brought from the field, she answered: "Dost thou think it a small matter, that thou hast taken my husband from me, unless thou take also my son's mandrakes?" (Gen. 30, 15). Which words very clearly indicate a burning inward jealousy. For this reason (as the Apostle Paul bears witness) the bondwoman Agar and her son were cast out, namely because her son, Ismael, persecuted Isaac, the son of Sara the wife, for which reason Sara was complaining that she was being despised by the bondwoman.

But the heretic could perhaps object to us in defense of his heresy that which is found in Exodus, where after the description of the priestly vestments with which Aaron had to be vested, the Lord added through Moses saying: "It shall be a law for ever to Aaron, and to his seed after him" (Ex. 28, 43). And in Leviticus when commanding the manner of the sacrifice which ought to be offered for sin, He says: "And this shall be an ordinance forever, that you pray for the children of Israel, and for all their sins once in a year" (Lev. 16, 34). From these two passages the heretic may perhaps want to conclude that the Law of Moses ought to be observed forever. But this is not so: because it is not said, "an ordinance forever," because it would last forever, but because it was somewhat disposing to eternal life. Or it is otherwise, and in my opinion better, "forever" is said because it was a figure of the eternal testament. And so "forever" is said not in itself, but in relation to that of which it is a figure. And the interlinear Gloss on Exodus so expounds that word, "forever," "because (it says) it signifies eternal things."[1]

There is a **second heresy** completely opposite to the first, asserting that the Old Law is evil. Many writers attribute this heresy to Manichaeus as its first patron: they are most certainly mistaken in this matter, because even though Manichaeus defended it, still he did not teach it first. For the Pontic Marcion lived more than a hundred years before him, from whom the Marcionite heretics are named. And he taught that the Old Law was evil, and proceeded from an evil principle, just as the Manichaeus taught afterwards. Now this Marcion was a disciple of another heretic named Cerdo, whom Marcion in his madness imitated. Thus the first author and originator of this error was this Cerdo, who, as Irenaeus attests, came to Rome under Pope and martyr Hyginus.[2] Augustine also says that the Cainites taught this heresy as well.[3] Yet Irenaeus treats the Cainites under the Marcionites, because when discussing the errors of Marcion in that place he says that he honored Cain[4]: and all the other errors that he attributes to Marcion, Augustine attributes to the Cainites. Whence I begin to suspect that the Cainite heretics proceeded from Marcion. But since Marcion, as we said, was taught by Cerdo, it is necessary that we attribute the beginning and teaching of the present heresy to this Cerdo.

Now the falsity of this pestiferous assertion is refuted by the testimony of Paul in the Epistle to the Romans saying: "What shall we say, then? Is the law sin? God forbid. But I do

---

[1] *Biblia sacra* cum *glossis, interlineari & ordinaria, Nicolai Lyrani postilla et moralitatibus*… (Venice, apud Juntas, 1603), vol. 1, p. 799.

[2] *Against the Heresies*, bk. 1, c. 27, n. 1 (PG 7, 687B).

[3] *De Haeresibus ad Quodvultdeum*, c. 18 (PL 42, 29).

[4] *Against the Heresies*, bk. 1, c. 27, n. 3 (PG 7, 689A).

not know sin, but by the law" (7, 7). Since Paul discussed many things about the Law, due to which someone perhaps could suspect that he blamed the Law: he objects to himself what he sees another would object to him. For he had firstly said that the passions of sins are by the Law. He also had said that "we are loosed from the law of death, wherein we were detained" (v. 6). He also had said that "the law entered in, that sin might abound" (Rom. 5, 20). Which words of Paul were giving a handle of suspicion to the weak, that Paul was of that opinion, such that he wanted to condemn the Law. Hence to remove this suspicion Paul objects to himself what the weak could object to him, saying: "What shall we say, then? Is the law sin? God forbid. But I do not know sin, but by the law; for I had not known concupiscence, if the law did not say: Thou shalt not covet.[1] But sin taking occasion by the commandment, wrought in me all manner of concupiscence" (7, 7-8). By which words Paul teaches that the Law is not evil, but good, although it was not sufficient for salvation without grace. Wherefore he says that the Law was not given so that sin might be effaced in man, but so that it might show and reveal to men that which was unknown to them: whether something was a sin or not. For there were many things which even though they were sins, men nevertheless did not know that they were sins, or they did not know that they were so serious and would be punished so severely, except that the Law taught this. Hence the Law did do this, meaning it taught man what is sin.

The Apostle puts forth one example from among many of these things. "For I had not known concupiscence," he says, "if the law did not say: Thou shalt not covet": that is to say, "I had not known that concupiscence was something evil, until I heard that it was forbidden by the Law." But lest you suspect that the Law was the cause of this evil, he did not say: "I had not concupiscence, except by the Law": but he says: "I had not known concupiscence." Nor did he say: "I did not commit sin except by the Law": but "I do not know sin, but by the law." So that you may understand more clearly, the Law did not foster sin, but the knowledge of sin. Yet there is something in the Law which, when it has been given, we immediately are inflamed and incited by the desire for those things which are forbidden by the Law. And this is what the Apostle afterwards adds, saying: "But sin taking occasion by the commandment, wrought in me all manner of concupiscence." For the Law was given so that man who, abusing his liberty, was falling down headlong by each vice, might be refrained by the bridle of the Law, to not fall down so unforeseeingly into precipices. And because such is our carnal nature, that it desires forbidden things more ardently than if they were not forbidden: hence Paul says that the occasion of sin was taken from the prohibition of the Law. For (as a certain man said[2]) "We are ever striving after what is forbidden, and coveting what is denied us."

Similarly also, the devil seeing that the Law is given to man as a help, so that by it men may be refrained from sins as by a bridle, he then incites man more to sin and tempts more vehemently, so that they may turn the Law into harm, which was given to be a benefit. Hence it is evident how by occasion taken through the commandment, he made all manner of concupiscence in us. For concupiscence was less when we were sinning unconcerned before the Law. It was less when it moved only our sensuality. There is all manner of concupiscence when the Law having been known, we neither fear nor are ashamed to transgress it. But this evil is not from the Law, but it comes forth from our malice, which converts medicine into poison. For the Law does not force us to sin, but we take occasion of sinning from it, although the Law itself does not give such occasion. Hence the Apostle did not say: "But [sin] giving occasion." Instead he said: "But sin taking occasion by the commandment, wrought in me all manner of concupiscence."

So that you may clearly understand that it comes forth from our malice, and not from the Law, when after the Law has been given we desire to act against the same Law; Paul therefore

---

[1] Cf. Ex. 20, 17; Deut. 5, 21.

[2] Ovid, *Amores*, bk. 3, elegy 4, l. 17.

taught these and other things about the Law, whereby he shows that the Law is not evil, he afterwards adds praises of the Law, saying: "Wherefore the law indeed is holy, and the commandment holy, and just, and good" (v. 12). In the previous words the Apostle defends the Law against crime, but in these words he extols it with due praises. Crime was objected by these words: "What shall we say, then? Is the law sin?" The defense of the crime was in these words: "God forbid." Hence now the Apostle is not content to defend it from crime, unless he also praises it, wherefore he adds: "Wherefore the law indeed is holy, and the commandment holy, and just, and good." By "law" he means prohibitions, but by "commandment" he means precepts: and he teaches that both are holy. Furthermore, in the First Epistle to Timothy he again says: "But we know that the law is good, if a man use it lawfully: knowing this, that the law is not made for the just man, but for the unjust and disobedient" (1, 8-9).

He says that the Law was not made for the just, which is the same as he said elsewhere, namely that the Law "was set because of transgressions" (Gal. 3, 19). Now this ought to be so understood, because (as we said) the Law was given as a kind of bridle to refrain men from sin. Thus, when someone naturally does those things which are of the Law, and is a law unto himself, keeping himself from sin, he has not need of the Law, but is like a horse well trained and obedient to the rider, needs no bridle to be well controlled. The Law "was set because of transgressions" so that by it men may be kept away from transgression. He, however, who without the Law is ready to do the things which the Law would command has no need of the Law.

But even if the just man does not need it, the Law is still holy. For by the Law evil men are refrained from sins, and urged to the amendment of sins committed. And this is what the Apostle says: "The Law is good, if a man use it lawfully." The meaning is, if one does as the Law itself intends, that is to say, if by it one attains justifying grace. For one uses the Law lawfully who understanding why the Law was given, through its threats takes refuge in liberating grace: and hence the Law is good, because it also very much benefits a bad man, as long as it brings him by its threats to grace. If, however, someone who has known the Law acts against it, he uses the Law badly: even though the Law is good in itself, yet to this man it is not good: because sin through the good [Law], works death to such a man. For he sins more gravely by the commandment, who knows by that same commandment how grave an evil it is which he commits.

And this is what he had said in the Epistle to the Romans: "Was that then which is good, made death unto me? God forbid. But sin, that it may appear sin, by that which is good, wrought death in me; that sin, by the commandment, might become sinful above measure" (Rom. 7, 13). And it is as though he were to say: "The commandment is not a cause of death to me, but I brought death upon myself, who by sinning committed things which are worthy of death." Again, in the Epistle to the Galatians the Apostle says: "Wherefore the law was our pedagogue in Christ, that we might be justified by faith" (3, 24). Thus, the Law is our tutor. For pedagogue is the same word in Greek, which means a tutor [lit. "guide"] of children. Hence if the Law was our pedagogue, let us see wither it guides us: and it is evident from Paul's words that the Law led us to Christ's faith, so that by it we may be justified. For he says the following: "Wherefore the law was our pedagogue in Christ, that we might be justified by faith." If then Christ's faith is good, it is impossible that the Old Law, which led to it, would not have been good. One cannot be a bad pedagogue who instructs children well. Nor can one be a bad guide who leads to the selected and predetermined goal.

Finally, the Teacher of truth Himself and our Savior commends the Law by word and deed. For having been circumcised, offered in the Temple, eating the Pascal lamb with His disciples, He kept its precepts. He also commanded others to observe them. For He commanded the cleansed leper to show himself to the priest according to the Law of Moses.[1] And when preaching He very often cited passages of the Law and of the prophets. But if the Law were bad, Christ would not have given such great honor to it, such that He would use its passages in preaching.

There is a **third heresy** which says that every man who lives uprightly according to his own law can be saved, whether he be a Jew, or Saracen, or pagan. I have not found any patron of this heresy, but I know from being told by others that a defender was not lacking. For Juan de Torquemada in his book, *De summa Ecclesiae*,[2] says that there were heretics saying that everyone can be saved in his own law, if he has kept it well, yet he did not disclose who was the first author of this heresy, or who at any time was its patron.[3]

This heresy is clearly refuted by that which Paul says in his Epistle to the Hebrews: "Without faith," he says, "it is impossible to please God" (11, 6). Now unless someone pleases God, he cannot attain eternal life: therefore, without faith no one can be saved. And hence it is clearly concluded that in no other law can someone be saved, except in the Evangelical Law alone. Furthermore, in the same epistle, when Paul is proclaiming the praises of the faith, he says: "Faith is the substance of things to be hoped for, the evidence of things that appear not" (v. 1). What does "the substance of things to be hoped for" mean except the foundation and basis upon which the hope for those things which are rightly expected rests? Now the thing which is truly worthy to be desired and sought after is eternal life. Thus, the foundation of this is the Catholic faith, because upon it and from it arises hope of the future beatitude. Hence the Apostle likewise says in the First Epistle to the Corinthians: "Other foundation no man can lay, but that which is laid; which is Christ Jesus" (3, 11). The Gloss, which is called the Ordinary, when interpreting this passage says: "That is, Christ's faith, which works through love, whereby Jesus dwells in hearts. There is no other foundation."[4] If faith is the first and only foundation, upon which hope of future beatitude is firstly founded, it necessarily follows that when faith has been removed, hope of eternal life collapses: because where a foundation is lacking, nothing can be built on top.

Again, Blessed Paul the Apostle reprehends and condemns those who observe the ceremonies of the Mosaic Law, while placing hope in them. "If you be circumcised," he says, "Christ shall profit you nothing" (Gal. 5, 2). But without Christ no one can attain eternal life: because it is He alone Who "by his own blood, entered once into the holies, having obtained eternal redemption" (Heb. 9, 12). Therefore, it is false that a Jew also, if he keeps the Mosaic Law very well, can be saved without Christ's faith. For Paul when speaking about Christ our Savior, says: "He became, to all that obey him, the cause of eternal salvation" (Heb. 5, 9). He did not say, "that obey Moses"; but he said, "that obey Christ Himself."

Finally, the [IV] Lateran General Council celebrated under Innocent III, decreed about this matter, saying the following: "One indeed is the [universal] Church of the faithful, outside

---

[1] Cf. Mt. 8, 4.

[2] *De summa Ecclesiae* (Venice, apud Michaelem Tramezinum, 1561), bk. 1, c. 21, pp. 23v-25r.

[3] Philastrius of Brescia relates that certain men, whom he calls "Rhetorians," from a certain Rhetorius, taught in Egypt that any man could be saved in his church, or in his own religion, provided that he live rightly in it, whether he be a Jew, Pagan or Saracen: for they approved of all heresies, praised all heretics, and claimed that none of them erred in Christ's faith. (*Liber de Haeresibus*, c. 91, (PL 1202B-1203B)). St. Augustine wrote concerning this heresy, "This is so absurd that it seems unbelievable to me." (*De Haeresibus ad Quodvultdeum*, c. 72 (PL 42, 44)). And yet this all-encompassing heresy, propagated by Freemasonry, is widely accepted today.

[4] *Biblia sacra* cum *glossis, interlineari & ordinaria*, vol. 6, p. 218.

which no one at all is saved."[1] These words are found in [the book of the *Decretals* under the title,] *De summa trinitate et fide catholica*, in the chapter, *Firmiter credimus*.[2]

I certainly could have and ought to have brought forth many proofs of this matter, if I had taken up this disputation against the pagans, Jews, or Saracens: but because we now dispute only against heretics, who boast that they are Christians, I do not wish to cite many proofs against them, because these things seem to me to be sufficient against them.

LIBERTAS
Liberty

Since there is nothing of which we have a more certain experience than the liberty of our free will, which we experience in ourselves each day, it is certainly astounding that some men were so brazen that they were not afraid to deny that there is any liberty inherent in our human will. And these men who think such things are divided among themselves: for even though they tend to the same end, they still proceed by different ways, as very often happens with heretics, who tend not to be unified. For Bardesanes (as we said above in the section on "Fate") said that all the behavior of men ought to be ascribed to fate, and not to man's free will, because, as he used to say, it is subject to the stars. After this man rose up Manichaeus, claiming that sins can nowise be avoided, but he was saying that they proceeded from the evil mind. For he was saying that in man there are two minds: one which he said is evil, and from an evil principle, namely that which we call concupiscence of the flesh. But he said that there is another good [mind], which we call the rational soul. Sins which occur in man proceed from the bad soul, and he taught that they cannot be impeded by free will. Priscillian imitated Manichaeus in this regard, who accepted nearly all of Manichaeus' teaching. Peter Abelard said that everything comes from the absolute necessity of things, and God, not to speak of man, cannot do things otherwise than He does. John Wycliffe imitated this man, agreeing with him entirely about this. Guy the Carmelite asserts that Albanenses thought that man has no free choice.[3] Many of the recent heretics defend this heresy long since buried. The leader and chief of whom is Martin Luther, saying that man's will is not free, nor does it have any active power in its actions, because he maintains that it is not active, but rather passive.[4] Many followed this man, namely John Oecolampadius, who has already left this life, and Philip Melanchthon, and many others unknown to me, who have infected a large part of Germany with this error. All those things which we have presented above in the section on "Fate" oppose this heresy.

But it is necessary that we present still more specific arguments, and assault with might and main such a pestiferous heresy, because it is the kindling-wood of all wickedness. But because the word "liberty" is equivocal in Holy Writ, lest such equivocation give some occasion of erring to us, it is necessary that we show its various meanings. For sometimes liberty means grace, whereby we are free from the servitude of sin, to which it is opposed. According

---

[1] Dz. 430.

[2] *Decretalium Gregorii papae* lib. 1, tit.1, c. 1.

[3] *Summa de haeresibus*, c. 17, fol. 78v, lns. 74-76.

[4] "A sword contributes nothing whatever towards its motion but is entirely passive; however, in inflicting the wound it has through its motion, cooperated with him who wielded it. Therefore, just as a sword does not cooperate toward setting itself in motion, so the will does not cooperate towards its willing. This willing is a motion which the Divine Word produces. It is merely something that is done to the will" (WA 5, 177, lns. 21-27).

to this meaning the Apostle says: "Where the Spirit of the Lord is, there is liberty" (II Cor. 3, 17). And elsewhere he says: "For when you were the servants of sin, you were free men to justice" (Rom. 6, 20). And we are not speaking about this liberty, because not in this sense do we say that man's every choice is free.

There is another liberty, which is only had in glory, or it is the glory itself. And of this liberty the Apostle also writes: "The creature also itself shall be delivered from the servitude of corruption, into the liberty of the glory of the children of God" (Rom. 8, 21). Neither from this liberty is it said, "man's free will." There is still another liberty which is opposed to necessity, or, so that I may speak more correctly, to coercion. Hence when we say, "Man's will is free," we understand these words as pertaining to this liberty: such that with that meaning we may say that someone is free, namely because when he works, he is able not to work: and when he does no work, he could work. Now we will very clearly demonstrate, with God's guidance, this liberty from Holy Writ: because there is hardly any book of Sacred Scripture in which is not found some clear proof of free will.

In the book of Genesis we read that God said to Cain: "If thou do well, shalt thou not receive? but if ill, shall not sin forthwith be present at the door? but the lust thereof shall be under thee, and thou shalt have dominion over it" (4, 7). If man has dominion over his appetite, it is false that man cannot avoid sins which arise from the appetites, as Manichaeus said. Luther is confounded, making man's will a slave, which God testifies that He made a master. And in Exodus it is written as follows: "All both men and women with devout mind offered gifts, that the works might be done which the Lord had commanded by the hand of Moses. All the children of Israel dedicated voluntary offerings to the Lord" (35, 29). He said "voluntary offerings," not "necessary ones." In Leviticus it is stated as follows: "The man that offereth a victim of peace offerings to the Lord, either paying his vows, or offering of his own accord, whether of calves or of sheep, shall offer it without blemish, that it may be acceptable" (22, 21). And shortly after he adds: "An ox or a sheep, that hath the ear and the tail cut off, thou mayst offer voluntarily: but a vow may not be paid with them" (v. 23). Notice how clearly He shows that liberty is distinct from necessity, since He says, "either paying his vows, or offering of his own accord." In the book of Numbers[1] the Lord enacts a law that a woman vowing is not bound by the vow except with her husband's consent: such that if the husband consents to his wife's vow, she is obliged to fulfil it. If, however, her husband has gainsaid it, she is free from the obligation. Thus, since the option is given to the husband, it is proved that he has a choice, whereby he can choose either option: because if he is necessarily directed towards one option, whichever it may be, the choice is given to him for no reason.

Also [man has free will] because the Lord gave the precepts of the Law, and He did not give things that were impossible to observe. In Deuteronomy He says the following: "I call heaven and earth to witness this day, that I have set before you life and death, blessing and cursing. Choose therefore life, that both thou and thy seed may live" (30, 19). But there is no choice except of those things which are within our power. For no one is properly said to choose what, must happen, whether he wills it or not. For it does not depend upon our choice to be tall or short, to be a man or a beast, because those things are not subject to our choice that they would happen otherwise. Therefore, if a choice is given to man, and he can choose, it follows that he also has free will. And elsewhere the choice was given to the Jews, whether they would follow God or not.[2] The option of choosing one of three afflictions was given to King David, for the Lord had hitherto decreed that He would exclude some of those afflictions. If there is an option, then there is free will, because beasts have neither an option nor a choice. And to Solomon, the son of this man, it is said: "Ask what thou wilt that I should give

---

[1] Cf. Num. 30, 4-16.
[2] Cf. Jos. 24, 15.

thee" (III Kings 3, 5). There are also many other similar proofs in Sacred Scripture which give to man an option and choice. Now an option (as we have just said) cannot fit with those things which are brought by inevitable necessity to act.

Furthermore, King David, when exhorting the people of Israel to make offering to the Lord for the construction of the Temple, says: "If any man is willing to offer, let him fill his hand today, and offer what he pleaseth to the Lord" (I Par. 29, 5). Again, how great is the number of proofs in the Psalms for free will! "I will freely sacrifice to thee, and will give praise, O God, to thy name: because it is good" (53, 8). And again: "The free offerings of my mouth make acceptable, O Lord: and teach me thy judgments" (118, 108). And again: "My soul is continually in my hands" (v. 109). What does it mean the one's soul in in his hands? It means that it is in one's own power, so that it turns towards that which one wills. And in another Psalm he says: "My heart is ready, O God, my heart is ready: I will sing, and will give praise, with my glory" (107, 2). And again: "Be thou my helper, forsake me not; do not thou despise me" (26, 9). When one asks God for help, one shows that he is the doer: because if our will does nothing, but only receives (as Luther says), God ought not to be called our helper, but the entire and sole doer. And in the book of Wisdom, Solomon says: "For thy sustenance shewed thy sweetness to thy children, and serving every man's will, it was turned to what every man liked" (16, 21). Observe the clear power of free will, that it can change something to what one likes. But also what is found in Ecclesiasticus is much clearer: "God made man from the beginning, and left him in the hand of his own counsel. He added his commandments and precepts. If thou wilt keep the commandments and perform acceptable fidelity forever, they shall preserve thee. He hath set water and fire before thee: stretch forth thy hand to which thou wilt. Before man is life and death, good and evil, that which he shall choose shall be given him" (15, 14-18). What could be said more clearly to show the liberty of our free will? Certainly (in my opinion) the liberty of our free will is taught so clearly in that place, that by its excessive brightness, it makes the heretics to tightly close their eyes.

But there was not lacking a refuge for the heretics to which they are accustomed to flee. For the Lutherans deny that the book of Wisdom and the book of Ecclesiasticus are canonical, and hence they are insufficient for confirming a teaching, which pertains to the Catholic faith. But it is unnecessary to refute this cavil here, because in the first book of this work, chapter two, we showed the canon of the sacred books from many councils, among which these two books are also found. All the prophets also very clearly stated this. For in Isaias the Lord when speaking about the people of Israel under the appellation of the vineyard, says: "And he looked that it should bring forth grapes, and it brought forth wild grapes" (5, 2). If everything happens by absolute necessity, and man's choice is forced to act by God's foreknowledge, as the Lutherans say, why was He looking for grapes from the vineyard, since He knew that it would produce wild grapes? And through the same prophet He again says: "If you be willing, and will hearken to me, you shall eat the good things of the land. But if you will not, and will provoke me to wrath: the sword shall devour you" (1, 19-20). And in Jeremias something similar is had: "If that nation against which I have spoken, shall repent of their evil, I also will repent of the evil that I have thought to do to them. And I will suddenly speak of a nation and of a kingdom, to build up and plant it. If it shall do evil in my sight, that it obey not my voice: I will repent of the good that I have spoken to do unto it" (18, 8-10). This double type of choice between two opposite sides in both of these quotations very clearly indicates that the free power of acting rightly well or badly is present in man, which can be turned to that which he wishes according to his choice. For if such power of choosing either did not exist within man, God would have proposed the two in vain to man.

And through the prophet Ezechiel the Lord says: "If the wicked do penance for all his sins which he hath committed, and keep all my commandments, and do judgment, and justice, living he shall live, and shall not die... But if the just man turn himself away from his justice, and do iniquity according to all the abominations which the wicked man useth to work, shall he live? all his justices which he hath done, shall not be remembered" (18, 21 & 24). In which words that type of choice is again doubled, just as was done in Isaias and Jeremias: wherefore we can argue by a similar reasoning here as we did there.

Also the deliberation and choice of Susanna when put in difficult straights very clearly shows man's free will, whereby she, after having considered about which of the two choices ought to be chosen, chooses what seems better to her, after having rejected the other. For when Susanna was solicited to do shameful things by the two wicked old men, with a sigh she says: "I am straitened on every side: for if I do this thing, it is death to me: and if I do it not, I shall not escape your hands" (Dan. 13, 22). Thus far pertains to her consideration. Hear now her determination and choice: "But it is better for me to fall into your hands without doing it, than to sin in the sight of the Lord" (v. 23). Now by this choice she chose one option, after having rejected the other, which she could have embraced. From which act it is proved clearly enough that man's free will exists: because if she were not free to choose the option then she would have deliberated in vain. For no one is so foolish that he would deliberate about whether or not tomorrow will come after today: whether or not fire will consume the material next to it. For these things are not within our power to happen or not, nor are they the kinds of things about which one rightly ought to deliberate. It would be quite laborious, and too lengthy to cite all the other prophets, and cite quotations from all the books of the Old Testament: because even if I had wanted to take up this labor, it would have exceeded the bounds of the promised brevity.

Hence let us proceed to the New Testament. Christ our Savior in Matthew says: "Jerusalem, Jerusalem, thou that killest the prophets, and stonest them that are sent unto thee, how often would I have gathered together thy children, as the hen doth gather her chickens under her wings, and thou wouldest not?" (23, 37). Behold, when God is willing, men are unwilling. Thus man's will is so free that it is not forced by God's will, and consequently much less is it forced by His foreknowledge. And in Luke the Savior similarly says: "If any man will come after me, let him deny himself, and take up his cross daily, and follow me" (9, 23). When He says, "If any man will," He intimates our liberty, it being shown by these words that to be able and unwilling lies within our grasp. For if there were no liberty, there was no need to speak conditionally. For no one is so foolish that he would speak thus about fire: "If a fire is hot, it will not cease to be hot." For since it is necessary that all fire is hot, the applied condition is superfluous, because that kind of condition implies that the matter could not occur otherwise.

And John the Evangelist utters a clear enough proof regarding this matter saying: "He gave them power to be made the sons of God" (1, 12). Now this power was not given only to the just: because these men since they are just, are already included in the number of the just: hence a new power was not needed for them whereby they could become sons of God, since they already were such. Thus, this was conferred upon sinners, because if they prepare themselves according to their ability to receive grace, God will not withdraw Himself from them, but rather He will give them grace whereby they may be received unto the adoption of sons. For so Augustine expounds these words of Blessed John. "Let us listen also to the Evangelist, when he says, 'He gave them power to be made the sons of God'; that we may not imagine it as altogether beyond our own power that we believe: but in both let us acknowledge His beneficent acting. For, on the one side, we have to give Him thanks that the power is bestowed; and on the other, to pray that our own little strength may not utterly fail."[1] And Hilary taking occasion from this same quotation from John, says, "To be sons of God, it is a work of the

---

[1] *Tractates on the Gospel of John*, tract. 53, n. 8 (PL 35, 1778).

will, not of necessity: because God's gift having been presented to all men, (filiation) is not produced by the nature of those begetting, but the will attains the reward."[1]

Next those words, which the Apostolic history relates, that Peter the Apostle said to Ananias, who by fraud kept back part of the price of the sold field, very clearly show man's liberty. For Peter says to Ananias as follows: "Ananias, why hath Satan tempted thy heart, that thou shouldst lie to the Holy Ghost, and by fraud keep part of the price of the land? Whilst it remained, did it not remain to thee? and after it was sold, was it not in thy power?" (5, 3-4). What is it to say, "after it was sold, was it not in thy power?" The meaning is, "After you sold [the land], you had power of not bringing the price, and of putting it before the feet of the Apostles, which power if Ananias had used, Peter would not have either punished or reprimanded him: but because having this power, he pretended that he did not want to use it, but feigned that he wanted to offer the whole price of the field to the Apostles for the common life, having been reprehended by the Apostle, he was at length punished by death. Hence from this it is proved that not everything happens necessarily, and man's will is free, because Ananias when subtracting from the price of the field, had the power of doing otherwise.

But now let us go on to Paul, from whom we can take many proofs. For in the First Epistle to the Corinthians he says the following: "He that hath determined being steadfast in his heart, having no necessity, but having power of his own will; and hath judged this in his heart, to keep his virgin, doth well" (7, 37). Notice that he says, "having power of his own will." Paul clearly attributes power to our will, and are the shameless heretics not embarrassed to take it away? And in the same epistle he again says: "I have laboured more abundantly than all they: yet not I, but the grace of God with me" (15, 10). And again: "Every man shall receive his own reward, according to his own labour. For we are God's coadjutors" (3, 8-9). From which it is proved that our will does something, otherwise the labor would not be said to be ours. And lest someone suppose, as Pelagius did, that all ought to be ascribed to our will, he added: "For we are God's coadjutors." Therefore, by this quotation Pelagius and Luther are overthrown.

And in the Second Epistle to the Corinthians, when exhorting to giving alms, he says: "Everyone as he hath determined in his heart, not with sadness, or of necessity: for God loveth a cheerful giver" (9, 7). If there is no liberty of free will, it would necessarily follow that whatever it does, it does out of necessity. And when writing to Philemon, he says: "But without thy counsel I would do nothing: that thy good deed might not be as it were of necessity, but voluntary" (1, 14). Observe how clearly Paul distinguished voluntary from necessary, one opposing the other. Thus the Wycliffites, Hussites and Lutherans, and other heretics ought to be ashamed, saying that everything comes to pass by an absolute necessity, and there is no liberty of free choice.

And Blessed Peter when instructing the priests how they ought to take care of the people committed to them, says: "Feed the flock of God which is among you, taking care of it, not by constraint, but willingly, according to God: not for filthy lucre's sake, but voluntarily: Neither as lording it over the clergy, but being made a pattern of the flock" (I Pet. 5, 2-3). See how Peter also distinguishes and separates what is spontaneous and voluntary from constraint. And in John's Apocalypse God says about Jezabel, who seduces God's servants, and teaches them to fornicate: "And I gave her a time that she might do penance, and she will not repent of her fornication" (2, 21). If everything happens by absolute necessity, and there is no liberty of free will, God gave in vain Jezabel time for repentance, if she were unable to repent. For since afterwards He says that she did not want to repent of fornication, according to the opinion of the heretic, it is proved that she could not repent. And if she could not, it is surprising that God gave her time to do what was impossible to do.

---

[1] *On the Trinity*, bk. 1, n. 11 (PL 10, 33A).

After all these proofs from Sacred Scripture, so that the matter may be clearer, it will be beneficial to show that this was the opinion of all holy men. But lest I burden the reader with excessive lengthiness, or I go beyond the limits of the promised brevity, I will cite very few testimonies, namely those which are more abstruse, and whose authors are not easily available to all. The other citations, however, I will give as a list of references, whence he who wishes to have them can find them. Blessed Irenaeus very often teaches the liberty of the human will, but he makes a special disputation about this matter in his book, *Against the Heresies*, wherein these words are found: "Now the passage which says, 'How often would I have gathered together thy children, as the hen doth gather her chickens under her wings, and thou wouldest not?' (Mt. 23, 37), showed the ancient law of man's liberty, because God made him free from the beginning, possessing his own power, even as he does his own soul, to obey God's behests voluntarily, and not by God's compulsion. For force from God does not occur, but a good way of thinking is always found in Him. And so He gives good guidance to all. And in man, as well as in Angels, He has placed the power of choice."[1] And shortly afterwards he discusses many things about free will.[2]

And Tertullian in the second book of his *Against Marcion* subscribes to the same opinion, saying: "But the reward neither of good nor of evil could be paid to the man who should be found to have been either good or evil through necessity and not choice. In this really lay the law which did not exclude, but rather prove, human liberty by a spontaneous rendering of obedience, or a spontaneous commission of iniquity; so patent was the liberty of man's will for either issue."[3] Blessed Cyprian in a letter to Pope Cornelius, says the following: "Nor let any one wonder that the servant placed over them should be forsaken by some, when His own disciples forsook the Lord Himself, Who performed such great and wonderful works, and illustrated the attributes of God the Father by the testimony of His doings. And yet He did not rebuke them when they went away, nor even severely threaten them; but rather, turning to His Apostles, He said, 'Will you also go away?' (Jn. 6, 68) manifestly observing the law whereby a man left to his own liberty, and established in his own choice, himself desires for himself either death or salvation."[4]

Blessed Jerome in a letter to Hedibia, teaches the same opinion, saying: "But God made all men in the same condition: He gave them free will, so that each one may do what he chooses, whether good or evil. Notwithstanding that He gave such great power to all, however, the wicked voice disputes against his Creator, and scrutinizes the motives of His will."[5] And in another letter to Pope Damasus, [PseudoJerome] says the following: "Free will we do so own, such that we may say that we always stand in need of God's help; and that they who say with Manichaeus that a man cannot avoid sin, err as much as they who affirm with Jovinian that a man cannot sin; for both of these take away the freedom of the will. But we say that a man is always able either to sin or to not sin, so as to always avow that we possess free will."[6]

And Blessed Basil in a small work, in which he proves that God is not the author of evils, says the following: "Now from this question deservedly springs forth another thought and question about the devil. Where does the devil come from, if evil things do not come from God? What then do we say? the same reason which we already gave about the depravity of men, suffices to us for this question also. For whence is man evil? from his own will. Whence

---

[1] C. 37, n. 1 (PG 7, 1099B-C).

[2] Bk. 4, c. 39, n. 1-3 (PG 7, 1109C-1111B).

[3] C.6 (PL 2, 292B).

[4] Letter 12, n. 7 (PL 3, 806A).

[5] Letter 120, c. 10, n. 2 (PL 22, 999).

[6] Pelagius, *Letter and Confession of Faith to Innocent I*, n. 25 (PL 48, 491B-C). This text had been incorrectly attributed to St. Jerome by Peter Lombard (*Sententiae*, bk. 2, dist. 28, n. 8 (PL 192, 718-719)).

is the devil evil? from the same cause; since he also has a free life, and is under his own control either to adhere perseveringly to God or to depart from good."[1] These are the words of Basil, who in one fell swoop, when discussing the will of men and Angels, says that both are free. And his brother [Pseudo-] Gregory [of Nyssa] argues in a whole chapter in favor of free will, which is also entitled, *On Free Will*.[2]

And Blessed Cyril in the third book of his *Contra Julianum apostatam*, at the beginning supports the same opinion, saying: "It was fitting [for God] to clothe the creature endowed with reason with choice in acting, and to show [His] skill in [man's] good deeds, the fruit of [his] free will."[3] And in the sixth book of the same work near the end of the book he again says: "Now what he says, that He could not change the plans of His friends, is childish. For it seems to me that he has forgotten, though he has heard very often, that man is free and spontaneously goes to whatever seems good to him. And so it pleased the Creator of all things that both those who choose to act rightly, would obtain praise, and those who take a different route, are rightly vituperated by all."[4]

Hesychius [of Jerusalem] in his commentary on Leviticus thinks likewise. For when expounding the passage in Leviticus: "But the crop of the throat, and the feathers he shall cast" (1, 16), he says the following: "The subtility of the words of the Law is admirable, because it describes not merely various practices, but moreover some practices according to the Law, others however, over and above the Law. For according to the Law there are oblations of oxen and sheep, even though they are called voluntary. Why according to the Law? It is because even though one very rightly gave a gift in the power of the offerer (God certainly made man to have free will) nevertheless such is not freely offered, unless perhaps bad things be offered."[5]

And John Damascene teaches the same assertion, speaking thus: "We are left then with this fact, that the man acting and making himself the author of his own works, is also a creature endowed with free-will. Further, if man is the author of no action, the faculty of deliberation is quite superfluous: for to what purpose could deliberation be put if man is the master of none of his actions? For all deliberation is for the sake of action. But to prove that the fairest and most precious of man's endowments is quite superfluous would be the height of absurdity. If then man deliberates, he deliberates with a view to action. For all deliberation is with a view to and on account of action."[6]

Blessed [John] Chrysostom, teaches this opinion elegantly, as usual, saying: "For if they be not bad willed, you do not punish your servant nor reprove your wife for what errors she may commit, neither beat your son, nor blame your friend, nor are you insulted by your offending enemy: for all these deserve to be pitied, not punished, unless they offend on purpose. 'But I cannot philosophize in this way,' one may say. And yet, when you perceive that they are not responsible, but some other cause, you can philosophize. When at least a servant being taken with sickness does not the things enjoined him, so far from blaming thou dost rather excuse him. Thus you are a witness, that the one thing is of one's self, the other not of one's self... And in another way too it is easy to stop the mouths of such men, for great is the abounding power of the truth. For wherefore do you never find fault with your servant, because he is not of a beautiful countenance, that he is not of fine stature in his body, that he is not able to fly? Because these things are natural. So then from blame against his nature he is acquitted, and

---

[1] Homilia: *Quod Deus non est auctor malorum*, n. 8 (PG 31, 346C-D).
[2] Nemesius of Emesa, *On the Nature of Man*, c. 39 (PG 40, 762A-766B).
[3] PG 76, 619D.
[4] PG 76, 830C-D.
[5] *Commentarius in Leviticum*, bk 1 (PG 93, 801B-C).
[6] *An Exposition of the Orthodox Faith*, bk 2, c. 25 (PG 94, 958C-D).

no man gainsays it. When therefore you blame, you show that the fault is not of nature but of his choice. For if in those things, which we do not blame, we bear witness that the whole is of nature, it is evident that where we reprove, we declare that the offense is of the choice. Do not then bring forward, I beseech you, perverse reasonings, neither sophistries and webs slighter than the spider's."[1] Chrysostom teaches in such a way that he would even convince his adversary. Thus, these cited testimonies ought to suffice.

But if the curious reader desires more testimonies, then we will show him the authors from whom he can get them. [Prosper of Aquitaine bears witness in his book], *The Call of All Nations*.[2] Ambrose [does also] in book one of *Jacob and the Happy Life*.[3] Augustine teaches this opinion so many times, and everywhere so clearly, that I do not know which of them to cite. [The following are some of these passages:] in the book, *On the True Religion*.[4] And in the third book of [PseudoAugustine's] *Hypognosticon*, nearly through the whole book.[5] And in the [*Acts or Disputation*] *Against Fortunatus*, in the second disputation near the beginning.[6] And in *Against Cresconius the Grammarian*.[7] Finally, he wrote an elegant work, *On Free Will*, divided into three books.[8] Lactantius in the second book of the *Divine Institutes*.[9] John Cassian in his book, *Conferences of the Desert Fathers*.[10] Pope Leo, in his sixteenth sermon on the Passion.[11] Prosper Aquitaine published his book, *De gratia Dei et libero arbitrio contra collatorem*, in which he asserts that we need God's grace, notwithstanding he asserts our free will.[12] Theophylactus very often teaches this, but especially in Luke when expounding the parable of the man having two sons, the prodigal one of whom asked of his father the

---

[1] *Homilies on Matthew*, hom. 59, n. 2 (PG 58, 575-576).

[2] "Every human soul, as far as we can know it by experience, is endowed with a will manifesting itself in some manner or other. It desires what is pleasing and turns away from what is displeasing." (Bk. 1, c. 2 (PL 51, 650A-B)). The author mistakenly ascribes this work to St. Ambrose, as was commonly supposed in his time.

[3] "For man is not bound to obedience out of servile necessity, but by free will we either incline to virtue or lean toward vice." (Bk. 1 (PL 14, 598A-599A)).

[4] "Therefore, it is by the will that sin is committed. And since there is no doubt that sins are committed, I cannot see that it can be doubted that souls have free choice in willing." (C. 14, n. 27 (PL 34, 134)).

[5] PL 45, 1621-1640. It is more properly called the *Hypomnesticon*.

[6] "Wherefore, if it is manifest that there is no sin where there is not free exercise of will, I wish to hear what evil the soul which you call either part, or power, or word, or something else, of God, has done, that it should be punished by God, or repent of sin, or merit forgiveness, since it has in no way sinned?" (n. 20 (PL 42, 121)).

[7] "And indeed it does not make sense to complain, 'But you should respect my freedom!' Indeed, why do you not proclaim that you should allow free will to have its way in questions of murder and debauchery and other evil deeds and crimes? God did indeed give humans free will, but He neither wished that the good should go unrewarded nor that the wicked should go unpunished." (Bk. 3, c. 51, n. 57 (PL 43, 527)).

[8] PL 32, 1221-1310.

[9] C. 9 (PL 6, 293A-306B).

[10] Conf. 3, c. 12 & conf. 7, c. 8 (PL 49, 575A-576A & 677B-678B).

[11] "'Father, if it be possible, let this chalice pass from me... Thy will be done' (Mt. 26, 39 & 42). As therefore He had conquered the tremblings of the flesh, and had now accepted the Father's will, and trampling all dread of death under foot, was then carrying out the work of His design, why at the very time of His triumph over such a victory does He seek the cause and reason of His being forsaken, that is, not heard, save to show that the feeling which He entertained in excuse of His human fears is quite different from the deliberate choice which, in accordance with the Father's eternal decree, He had made for the reconciliation of the world?" (Serm. 67, c. 7 (PL 54, 372B)).

[12] PL 51, 213-276A.

portion of his substance.[1] Blessed Bernard [does the same] often, but especially in the book, *Concerning Grace and Free Will*.[2] [Pseudo-] Blessed Anselm in his book, *Super epistolas Pauli*, when expounding the passage from the Second Epistle to Timothy, "The Lord knoweth who are his" etc. (2, 19).[3] He also wrote a special tract, *De libero arbitrio*,[4] and another, *De concordia gratiae et liberi arbitrii*.[5]

Now I ask the reader, who do you think should be believed more, so many respected men, illustrious for holiness as well as sanctity, or a single man, Luther or John Wycliffe, or Peter Abelard, their father? I attribute more to any of those illustrious men than to a thousand Wycliffes or Luthers.

And certainly even if there were no proofs from Sacred Scripture, and none of the holy Doctors had taught us about this matter, nature itself teaches us that the human will is free: because when that liberty has been removed, all foresight perishes, all consultation perishes, laws become useless, a reward is reckoned undeserved to the good, and punishment for the wicked. Man's nature would certainly be worse than that of any beast, nay than of a stone or any piece of wood. For to these things no one imputes any sin or blame, because whatever they do, they do by nature. But man, who according to the opinion of these heretics, when he sins, sins necessarily, is requited for his sin not only with blame or temporal punishment, but eternal damnation, if the sin were not forgiven him.

Furthermore, if this assertion of the heretics were true, God ought not then to be called good and merciful, but a cruel tyrant. Is not one rightly called a wicked and cruel tyrant who would contrive that his weak and infirm subjects do battle with an enemy much stronger than they, and to be conquered, and afterwards would rebuke those fettered on account of this, and have them tortured? Now who is so wicked that he would dare accuse God of these things? For I will sing with the [Royal] Prophet: "Thou art just, O Lord: and thy judgment is right" (Ps. 118, 137). Thus, these wicked heretics lie, finding fault with human nature, hurling it down to the level of brute beasts and other animals, and blaspheming the Divine goodness, who ascribe our sins not to our will, but to Divine predestination.

Finally, this heresy has been condemned by the clear definitive judgment of the Church. For the [II] Synod of Orange says: "Freedom of will weakened in the first man cannot be repaired except through the grace of Baptism; once it has been lost, it cannot be restored except by Him by whom it could be given. Thus Truth Itself says: 'If therefore the son shall make you

---

[1] "'Father, give me the portion of the property that falleth to me.' The essential property of man is his rational mind, his reason, always accompanied by his free will (*autexousia*), for all that is rational is inherently self-governing. The Lord gives us reason for us to use, according to our free will, as our own essential property. He gives to all alike, so that all alike are rational, and all alike are self-governing. But some of us use this generous gift rationally, in accordance with reason, while others of us squander the Divine gift. Moreover, everything which the Lord has given us might be called our property, that is, the sky, the earth, the whole creation, the Law and the prophets. But the later sinful generation, the younger son, saw the sky and made it a god, and saw the earth and worshipped it, and did not want to walk in the way of God's law, and did evil to the prophets. On the other hand, the elder son, the righteous, used all these things for the glory of God. Therefore, having given all an equal share of reason and self-determination, God permits us to make our way according to our own will and compels no one to serve Him who is unwilling. If He had wanted to compel us, He would not have created us with reason and free will" (*Ennaratio in Evangelio Lucae* (PG 123, 950D-151A)).

[2] "Where, therefore, there is consent, there is an act of the will. Moreover, where there is an act of will, there is freedom. In this sense it is that I understand the term free will" (C. 1 (PL 181, 1003A)).

[3] This work is spurious. ("St. Anselm," *The Catholic Encyclopedia* (New York, Robert Appleton Company, 1907), vol. 1, p. 549).

[4] PL 158, 489B-506C.

[5] *De concordia praescientiae et praedestinationis cum libero arbitrio*, q. 3 (PL 158, 521B-542A).

free, you shall be free indeed' (Jn. 8, 36)."[1] In these words one ought to especially notice that the council did not say that freedom of will was not completely removed by sin: but it only said that it was weakened, and afterwards repaired through the grace of Baptism. But what is weakened has some, but not full, power. Now after having been repaired through the grace of Baptism it has full power for doing good, according to that which Paul says: "I can do all these things in him who strengtheneth me" (Phil. 4, 13).

But the Council of Trent celebrated under Paul III defined much more copiously and clearly about this matter, which in the sixth session published three canons for this matter, namely the fourth, fifth and sixth, the words of which are those which follow: "If anyone shall say that man's free will moved and aroused by God does not cooperate by assenting to God Who rouses and calls, whereby it disposes and prepares itself to obtain the grace of justification, and that it cannot dissent, if it wishes, but that like something inanimate it does nothing at all and is merely in a passive state: let him be anathema."[2] "If anyone shall say that after the sin of Adam man's free will was lost and destroyed, or that it is a thing in name only, indeed a title without a reality, a fiction, moreover, brought into the Church by Satan: let him be anathema."[3] "If anyone shall say that it is not in the power of man to make his ways evil, but that God produces the evil as well as the good works, not only by permission, but also properly and of Himself, so that the betrayal of Judas is no less His own proper work than the vocation of Paul: let him be anathema."[4]

But it is necessary that we reply to the objections of the adversaries. Firstly, they object to us that which Christ says in John's Gospel: "Without me you can do nothing" (Jn. 15, 5). "What is this 'nothing,'" Luther says, "which free will does without Christ? It prepares itself for grace, they say, by morally good works. [But in this way Christ here does nothing; therefore one prepares oneself by nothing.] A marvelous preparation, that happens by [doing] nothing?"[5] I answer that Luther makes his case with a very futile sophistry, who so many times sneers at sophistries: because according to this manner of arguing it would also be permitted to conclude that no natural cause can produce anything, since it is evident that such a cause without God cannot produce anything. Next, I will ask, what is that "nothing," which no one can do without God? Thus even though no creature can do something without God, still it is not permitted to conclude from this that one cannot do anything even with God's help: as for example, a man cannot beget without a woman; it does not follow from this that even with the help of a woman he cannot beget. We admit therefore that God assists free will, and all other causes, such that without His assistance and concurrence they can do nothing, which nevertheless they with His help can do their own movements. Nevertheless, so that free will acts well, it needs Divine help, without which even if it can act, still it cannot act well. And the meaning of that "nothing" is that without God, that is, without His grace, our will can do nothing.

For it is customary in Holy Write that those things which are not suggestive of eternal life, are called "nothing." For so Paul in the First Epistle to the Corinthians says: "Circumcision is nothing, and uncircumcision is nothing: but the observance of the commandments of God" (7, 19). And again: "And if I should have prophecy and should know all mysteries, and all knowledge, and if I should have all faith, so that I could remove mountains, and have not

---

[1] Can. 13 (Dz. 186).
[2] Can. 4 (Dz. 814).
[3] Can. 5 (Dz. 815).
[4] Can. 6 (Dz. 816).
[5] *An Assertion of All the Articles of Martin Luther Which Were Quite Recently Condemned by a Bull of Leo X*, assertion n. 36 (WA 7, 142, lns. 31-35). The author's modified citation of Luther has been changed here to Luther's original wording.

charity, I am nothing" (13, 2). Therefore, we can do nothing without God, because without His concurrence no creature can do anything: because even though "there are diversities of operations, nevertheless the same God, who worketh all in all" (12, 6). Also when this general assistance and concurrence of God is had, [we can do] nothing, that is to say, free will can do no meritorious work without God's special help, that is, without God's grace, whereby one has grace so that he can merit eternal life: according to that which Paul says: "The grace of God, life everlasting" (Rom. 6, 23). Thus when this grace has been excluded, even though our free will can do many things with God's general help, still it cannot merit, and in this way it cannot produce of itself the fruit of eternal life. And this is what the Savior said: "He that abideth in me, and I in him, the same beareth much fruit: for without me you can do nothing" (Jn. 15, 5). Who is it who abides in God, except he who has His grace? "He that abideth in charity, abideth in God" (I Jn. 4, 16). Thus this man abiding in God, namely he who has God's grace, bears much fruit: because eternal life, which is "much" to such an extent that all other things which can be desired cannot be compared with it.

Now he who does not have grace, does not abide in God, and hence cannot produce the fruit of eternal life of himself without the root of grace: wherefore as a fruitless branch he will be cut down in death, and thrown into the fire of Hell.[1] And in this way also ought to be understood many other passages in Holy Writ. "I know, O Lord," says Jeremias, "that the way of a man is not his: neither is it in a man to walk, and to direct his steps" (Jer. 10, 23).[2] And John the Baptist was saying: "A man cannot receive anything, unless it be given him from heaven" (Jn. 3, 27). And Paul the Apostle says: "Not that we are sufficient to think anything of ourselves, as of ourselves: but our sufficiency is from God" (II Cor. 3, 5). And Blessed James in his Catholic epistle says: "Every best gift, and every perfect gift, is from above, coming down from the Father of lights" (1, 17). All these passages and other similar ones, which are very many, do not take away the liberty of the will, but they show the insufficiency of our will, which without God's help cannot do something. Wherefore Paul spoke very circumspectly when he said: "Not that we are sufficient... but our sufficiency is from God": so that he might clearly show that he does not take away liberty, but the sufficiency of liberty.

Secondly, they object to us the words of the Savior in John's Gospel: "No man can come to me, except the Father, who hath sent me, draw him" (6, 44). By these words (the Lutherans say) all liberty of the will is taken away, because free will is drawn by God, and without this drawing it cannot go to him. Now "drawing" speaks of a certain violence: therefore, there is no free will. I reply that what they affirm is false, namely that this Divine drawing is a violence, because it is nothing other than an inward calling, exhortation and admonition, whereby He moves our will to act well. Now man, being disobedient, often resists this calling and admonition, from which it is proved that such a calling is not violent. For the Lord also accuses this man, saying: "I called, and you refused: I stretched out my hand, and there was none that regarded. You have despised all my counsel, and have neglected my reprehensions" (Prov. 1, 24-25). Therefore, we acknowledge the drawing of the Father through prevenient grace, excluding which our will cannot be moved to doing good. But when God so draws us forth, He sends us forth in our liberty, so that we may acquiesce to Him calling and admonishing, or harden our hearts when we shall have heard His voice.[3] And our liberty to do good consists in this, namely that after God has advised us to do good, we are then free to turn towards that which is more pleasing to us, whether good or evil. Yet before the admonition power for doing evil exists in us, but not for doing the good. We have taught all these things at greater length and more clearly above in the section on "Grace," in the first heresy. Hence

---

[1] Cf. Mt. 3, 10.

[2] Cf. Prov. 3, 6.

[3] Cf. Heb. 3, 15.

we send the reader to that place: because we showed there the concordance of grace and free will, how both so come together with each other, that one does not detract from the other.

Thirdly, they object the words of Paul in his Epistle to the Romans: "It is not of him that willeth, nor of him that runneth, but of God that sheweth mercy" (9, 16). And again: "Therefore he hath mercy on whom he will; and whom he will, he hardeneth" (v. 18). I reply that those words of Paul ought to be taken in relation to the will of predestination and of Divine reprobation, because in the whole context of that chapter he discusses nothing else but predestination and Divine reprobation. For Paul says that that Divine predestination, whereby [God] preordained some from eternity to eternal life, does not depend upon our merits, but only upon Divine mercy, which chose us without our merits for such a great good. And he likewise gives his understanding of reprobation, namely that it is not a positive act of His will, but a mere privation of predestination, whereby He does not ordain someone to eternal life. This reprobation, I say, is also without our demerits, but by the will of the Divine majesty alone, whereby He does not destine this man to glory. He cannot argue about this matter, because since God is indebted to no one, He also injures no one, since He does not give what He does not owe.

But if perhaps someone would murmur against God about this, and seek after why he was not predestined, the Lord will reply to him: "Friend, I do thee no wrong... Take what is thine, and go thy way" (Mt. 20, 13-14). Now another reprobation, which occurs by a positive act of the will, whereby God sentences someone to eternal punishment, never happens without demerits: because (as Augustine says[1]) God is never an avenger but that firstly someone is a sinner.

But even though God predestines some men to life without any merits or demerits of theirs, and others He chooses not to predestine, still such predestination and reprobation carries no necessity to our works, nor takes away the power and liberty of choice. For after such predestination and reprobation both the elect and the reprobate act freely. And the fact that such predestination is infallible does not force our will to act according to it, because He Who foresees the end of the predestined, namely eternal glory, also foresees the means whereby such an end is acquired: namely good works, which they will do with God's help. Hence Blessed Peter admonishes us to do good works, that is to say, lest Divine predestination makes us unconcerned about them, but rather, we should work, in order that we may merit to attain the end of that same predestination. For so he says: "Wherefore, brethren, labour the more, that by good works you may make sure your calling and election" (II Pet.1, 10). And Paul, who certainly knew that he was predestined, was a most diligent executor of good works. For he who knew that a crown of justice was laid up for him by God the just Judge,[2] was chastising his body, and was bringing it into subjection, lest perhaps when he had preached to others, he himself should become a castaway.[3] From which argument it is proved clearly enough that Divine predestination neither carries with it completely any necessity for our good works, nor lessens the liberty of our will in any way. I omit other arguments because they are weaker.

After those old authors whom we enumerated above, Johann Cochlaeus wrote *De libero arbitrio hominis, adversus locos communes Philippi Melanchthonis*, in two books. And Johann Eck wrote amply enough, as he is accustomed to do, against Luther on the same subject.[4] Bishop John [Fisher] of Rochester disputes about this matter in the work which he published

---

[1] "Was [God] an avenger before [the devil] was sinner? Far be it." (*De Genesi ad litteram*, bk. 11, c. 17, n. 22 (PL 34, 438)).

[2] Cf. II Tim. 4, 8.

[3] Cf. I Cor. 9, 27.

[4] *Enchiridion of Commonplaces Against Luther and Other Enemies of the Church* (Grand Rapids, Baker Book House, 1979), chap. 31 ("On Free Will"), p. 31 ff.

against Luther, in one whole article.[1] Also those things which we said above in the section on "Fate," on the future contingent, and on grace can certainly be of use for this topic.

There is a **second heresy** which teaches that man after having lost Divine grace, cannot do anything other than sin. The author of this heresy is also Luther, saying that man's will, destitute of God's grace, the more it tries [to dispose itself for grace], the more it sins gravely.

This heresy is overthrown by those things which we have just now taught: because if man's will of itself and by its nature is free, he cannot lose his liberty by any accruing sin, and consequently even when in the state of sin, just as he can sin, so he also can avoid sin, and perform good deeds, although they are not meritorious. Some quotations among those which we cited above specifically prove this, such as this one: "He gave them power to be made the sons of God" (Jn. 1, 12). For this power, as we said, seems to have been granted more to sinners than to the just: because the just, by the grace which they have, are already sons of God, and they do not need to again become sons of God. And the quotation from the Apocalypse [also proves this] wherein God says concerning Jezabel: "And I gave her a time that she might do penance" (2, 21). Time is given to no purpose if she cannot repent. Furthermore, admonitions are very frequent in Sacred Scripture, whereby sinners are exhorted to penance for past sins. "Be converted," say the Lord, "and do penance for all your iniquities: and iniquity shall not be your ruin" (Ez. 18, 30). And through another prophet He again says: "Be converted to me with all your heart" (Joel 2, 12). And the Savior Himself says: "The kingdom of God is at hand: repent" (Mk. 1, 15). Now sinners are admonished to repentance without cause if they can do nothing else but sin.

This heresy was condemned in the Council of Trent celebrated under Paul III, because among the many canons which he promulgated during the sixth session, he confirmed the seventh one against this heresy in the form of these words: "If anyone shall say that all works that are done before justification, in whatever manner they have been done, are truly sins or deserving of the hatred of God, or that the more earnestly anyone strives to dispose himself for grace, so much the more grievously does he sin: let him be anathema."[2]

The **third heresy** teaches that free will after the grace of Baptism has been received cannot sin anymore. Jovinian the monk was the first to teach this heresy. Augustine also accuses Pelagius of this.[3] But we have already disputed about this heresy above in the section on "Grace," in the second heresy: and from those things which we have just said against the first heresy of this section, it is proved clearly enough, because just as sin does not take away the liberty of free will, so neither does grace, for liberty is naturally implanted in the human will, such that by no subsequent event can it be taken away. Wherefore it is that just as someone in the state of sin could avoid other sins on account of the power of his liberty, so also someone in the state of grace can commit sins in the time to come on account of the same liberty of the will. And we proved above with very weighty proofs that he is so endowed [with free will] in the section on "Grace," in the second heresy.

---

[1] *Assertionis Lutheranae confutatio* (Cologne, Maternus Cholinus, 1564), art. 36, p. 357 ff.
[2] Dz. 817.
[3] *De Haeresibus ad Quodvultdeum*, c. 88 (PL 42, 48).

LINGUA

Language

Philastrius in his book, *De haeresibus*, reckons that it is a heresy to say that before the building of Babel there was only one language: because (as he says[1]) it ought to be firmly believed that there were many languages before that time, nevertheless by a sort of inspiration given by God they were understanding all these languages up until that time. But as to the fact that Scripture says that "the earth was of one tongue" (Gen. 11, 1), he thinks that this was said because even if there were many kinds of language, all men still understood each other: because (as he says) all the languages were known to them all.

I, however, differ so much from this opinion of Philastrius that I think that what he teaches is heresy. For Sacred Scripture very clearly says that there was one language, such that nothing could be said more plainly. "The earth was," it says, "of one tongue." If there were varieties of languages, it would not be truly said that the earth was of one tongue, although some man might know all the languages. For even though an Italian understands a Spaniard, and a Spaniard vice versa understands an Italian, still no one with a right mind will deny that their language is meaningless. Likewise, no one will say that that there is one language of both, since each one has his own language. Certainly the understanding of languages cannot bring about that two or three languages may be called one. Hence it is that although all would understand each other, it cannot be said that the earth was of one tongue, if there was a variety of languages. Furthermore, that variety of languages was superfluous, if all men were understanding the languages of all. For language was invented for this alone, that by it we may make public our ideas: because (as Blessed Augustine says) "The word that sounds outwardly is the sign of the word that [gives light] inwardly."[2] If, then, one language was sufficient for each one to make his mental concepts and affections known to others, what need was there to add in addition so many languages? On the other hand, however, after the sin of pride which was shown in the building of Babel, this multitude of languages cannot be called inane and superfluous: because it was introduced by God to check their pride, and kept until our day to also reprimand our pride.

Next Sacred Scripture says that at the time when Babel began to be built, the tongue of the whole earth was confounded. What is it to say that the tongue was then firstly confounded, except that it was then firstly divided, and made multiple and diverse? For where there is unity, there can be no confounding: but where there is a multitude, there also is confounding. But before the building of Babel the tongue of the whole earth was not confounded: thus, before that time it was not diverse and multiple, but it was simply the sole tongue.

Again all the holy Doctors who wrote about this matter teach this opinion of ours: and there is not one of them who supports the opinion of Philastrius. [Pseudo-] Blessed Augustine in his book, *De mirabilibus sacrae scripturae*, says the following: "Since until that time all the people of the world who had come to that work spoke one language, He gave each one his own language, namely so that by His most correct judgment of decision, he who had no fear of divisions with a deep rooted swelling of pride, might certainly feel pain in the manner of his very fragile stability of language. And this which came about happened not only to the ancestors themselves: but such a condition passed on through all the generations of their chil-

---

[1] C. 104 (PL 12, 1217B-1219A).
[2] *On the Trinity*, bk. 15, n. 20 (PL 42, 1071). The author here quotes St. Augustine using the word *latet* ("hides") for *lucet* ("gives light").

dren: so that those who sought an eternal fame for themselves unto their posterity, would find a reproach of their presumption remaining through all the time of the ages to come in their offspring."[1] In these words it ought to be especially noted that he said that in the beginning He gave each his own language, and not (as Philastrius says) knowledge of different preexisting languages. [Pseudo-] Eucherius, Bishop of Lyon, says the following: "Now at the time when a variety of languages was made, the language which previously existed, remained in the family of Heber alone."[2] From which words it is clearly enough established that he thinks that only one language existed at that time, namely the Hebrew language.

And it is not necessary to cite many testimonies for this matter, but I will bring forth only one, which is of very great weight, namely the Sibylline testimony. For Josephus relates in his book, *The Antiquities [of the Jews]*, that the Sibyl said these words which follow: "When all men were of one language, some of them built a high tower, as if they would thereby ascend up to Heaven. But the Gods sent storms of wind, and overthrew the tower, and gave everyone his peculiar language. And for this reason it was that the city was called Babylon."[3] In which words one ought to note that he said that "everyone was given his peculiar language": he did not say that everyone was given his own knowledge of the ancient languages. Thus, one must firmly believe that there was only one language before the building of Babel.

Philastrius, however, was deceived by a distorted understanding of Scripture. For before Scripture began to speak about the building of this tower, when it enumerates the seven sons of Japheth in order, it said these words: "By these were divided the islands of the Gentiles in their lands, every one according to his tongue and their families in their nations" (Gen. 10, 5). Philastrius, not understanding that these words were said in anticipation, thought that at the time before Babel was built there were already many languages. Yet he should have recalled that the custom of Sacred Scripture is to relate some things by anticipation: meaning that they are related, as by a rough sketch, before they occurred, since whatever event took place is afterwards described at great length in its proper order. For this is one and not the least of Ticonius' rules for understanding Sacred Scripture, which Blessed Augustine highly praises in his book, *On Christian Doctrine*.[4] For Sacred Scripture had previously said by anticipation that every people had its own language, and yet it had not said how, but instead it went on to describe the offspring of the other sons of Noe: but then returning to that which it had omitted, it relates how or for what reason the division or confounding of many languages was made, and it says: "the earth was of one tongue" etc. And Blessed Augustine teaches that this is the correct meaning of the text, when saying the following: "But though these nations are said to have been dispersed according to their languages, yet the narrator recurs to that time when all had but one language, and explains how it came to pass that a diversity of languages was introduced. 'The whole earth,' he says, 'was of one tongue, and of the same speech.'"[5]

And I surely think that I have said enough about this matter, being content with this alone, if I shall have once admonished the reader that he notice how dangerous it is to lightly pronounce about heresy. For Philastrius, an otherwise learned man, and fighting for the Catholic

---

[1] Bk. 1, c. 9 (PL 35, 2160). The true author of this book was an Irish pseudonymous writer of the mid-seventh century, Augustinus Hibernicus. St. Thomas recognized already in his time that St. Augustine of Hippo was not its true author (III, q. 45, a. 3 ad 2um).

[2] *Commentarii in Genesim*, bk. 2 (PL 50, 941C).

[3] Bk. 1, c. 4, n. 3.

[4] "The sixth rule Tichonius calls the recapitulation, which, with sufficient watchfulness, is discovered in difficult parts of Scripture. For certain occurrences are so related, that the narrative appears to be following the order of time, or the continuity of events, when it really goes back without mentioning it to previous occurrences, which had been passed over in their proper place" (bk. 3, c. 36, n. 52 (PL 34, 86)).

[5] *City of God*, bk. 16, c. 4 (PL 41, 482).

faith, although he brands others for heresy, he falls into error, condemning the truly Catholic assertion. And I am not surprised: because (as it is said in the proverb) "sometimes [even] good Homer nods off."[1] But Philastrius himself (as Blessed Augustine mentions about him[2]) was not completely learned: wherefore he could easily err in his censures.

MALUM ET MALITIA
Evil and Wickedness

According to Aristotle's rule, every equivocation ought to be firstly divided into its different meanings, and afterwards one ought to speak about each one separately.[3] Hence, since this word "evil," or this word "wickedness," means many different things in Holy Writ, it is necessary that before we speak about its meaning, we would show its many meanings. For there are many evils, and they are all extrinsic or accidental. For nothing is evil by nature, as we have already shown above, with God's help, against the wicked Manichaeus, in the section on "Creatures," in the second heresy. Thus, the evil which happens to a thing is twofold. For one is the evil of guilt: the other is the evil of punishment, which in my opinion can be more correctly called a loss [*damnum*]. Therefore, according to this division of evil, the heresies which deal with evil have also been divided.

The **first heresy**, then, says that evil is from God and God made evil things. The author of this heresy was a certain Florinus, from whom the Florinians are named. This Florinus lived during the time of Emperor Commodus, and Pope Eleutherius. Florinus imitated a certain other man named Blastus in the same error. And Blessed Irenaeus (as Eusebius of Caesarea testifies[4]) wrote against these two heretics: a letter to Blastus, *On Schism*, and another letter to Florinus, *On Monarchy*, or *That God is not the Author of Evil*. The Seleucians and Hermians, so named from their founders, Seleucus and Hermias, afterwards revived this same error. These men were saying that evil is sometimes from God, other times from matter.

The Teacher of truth Himself very clearly condemns this error, saying: "A good tree cannot bring forth evil fruit, neither can an evil tree bring forth good fruit" (Mt. 7, 18). Thus, either God is not good, or He cannot produce evil things. But God is good, nay He alone is good: because He is good of Himself [*a se*] and from Himself [*ex se*]: therefore, He cannot bring forth evil things. Furthermore, Paul the Apostle in the epistle which is to the Romans, says: "If the root be holy, so are the branches" (11, 16). But no one can be called holy except God, Who alone is holy, just as He alone is the Lord. For about these two things the Seraphim cried one to another: "Holy, holy, holy, the Lord God of hosts" (Is. 6, 3). If then God is holy, how can it be that the branches which spring forth from Him are not holy? For the Apostle is not mistaken, saying: "If the root be holy, so are the branches." Again, if God is the cause of evils, either He is the cause of evils which are evil by nature, or of other evils which are contrary to justice and uprightness, which by other name are called vices and sins. We have shown above in the section on "Creatures" against Manichaeus that there are no evils by their own nature. But if nothing is evil by nature, and God (as Florinus says) is the author of evils, it is necessary that He be the author of our vices and sins, and consequently of our destruction. But He Himself contradicts this view, Who says through the prophet Osee: "Destruction is thy own,

---

[1] Cf. Horace, *Ars Poetica* (line 359).

[2] "... we found Epiphanius much more learned than Philastrius" (Letter 222, n. 2 (PL 33, 999)).

[3] "One commonplace rule, then, in regard to obscurity is, 'See if the meaning intended by the definition involves an ambiguity with any other'" etc. (Aristotle, *Topics*, bk. 6, c. 2).

[4] *Church History*, bk. 5, c. 20, n. 1 (PG 20, 483).

O Israel: thy help is only in me" (13, 9). And certainly, if God were the cause of our evils, He would be exceedingly unjust, if He would punish us on account of the evils which He Himself did. But since God, Who is just and can do nothing unjustly, punishes sinners, and does this most justly, it is thence proved very clearly that He is not the cause of our evils.

But here someone might object those words of the Apostle: "O man, who art thou that repliest against God? Shall the thing formed say to him that formed it: Why hast thou made me thus? Or hath not the potter power over the clay, of the same lump, to make one vessel unto honour, and another unto dishonour?" (Rom. 9, 20-21). From which words it will perhaps seem to someone that Paul asserts that evils are from God, when he says that God made some things unto dishonor. But this is not the case.

To understand this more clearly it is necessary to firstly recall that it is the custom Holy Writ to call God's permission His action, such that those things which God permits, it says that He does. "I," God says, "shall harden the heart of Pharao" (Ex. 4, 21). For God then hardens the hearts of sinners, when He tolerates them due to the greatness of His goodness, not punishing them immediately, but waiting for their repentance, on account of Whose goodness and patience, which sinners abuse, they are daily made worse just as a master having a bad servant, whom by treating humanely and kindly, he makes worse: not in fact because the master imbues the servant with wickedness, but because the servant has abused the master's kindness to augment his own wickedness. Thus, God is said to harden Pharao, because He permitted him to be hardened. For so it ought to be understood that which the Lord says through the prophet Ezechiel, when responding to the sinner inquiring in his wickedness: "I the Lord have deceived that prophet" (14, 9). He in fact "deceived," not because He gave deceptive knowledge, but because He permitted him to be deceived, and this is on account of the wickedness of the one asking. Hence the Lord Himself continues, saying: "According to the iniquity of him that inquireth, so shall the iniquity of the prophet be" (v. 10).

In the same way ought to be understood those words of the Apostle Paul recently cited, in which he says that God makes some vessels unto honor, others unto dishonor. For God makes all things in regard to their substance, but He treats them in different ways according to their goodness or wickedness. For God makes their goodness with their free will, which works at the same time with God. But He does not do their wickedness, but only gives them free will. Thus, God is said to make vessels unto dishonor, not because He made them dishonorable, but because after God made the vessels, meaning, men as regards their substance, they with God's permission fell into disgrace. In this way, therefore, it ought to be understood, when it is said that God makes vessels unto dishonor, such that "makes" is understood to mean "permits, just as we also find to be done in many other passages of Scripture. And these things which have been said suffice for this heresy.

A **second heresy** teaches that there are some creatures evil in themselves, and it says that they were not produced by God, the supreme good, but by some other principle of all evil things, which it says is the supreme evil. This heresy is attributed to Manichaeus as its first author, and this is perhaps because it is better known from him, or perhaps because it succeeded more under him to deceive more men. For some incorrectly attribute this heresy to Manichaeus as its parent, although its origin is much older. Cerdo in fact (as Augustine testifies[1]) put forth two principles of things, one good from which he said good things proceed, and another evil from which all evil things proceed. Before Cerdo those heretics who are call the Gnostics also taught this error. For Augustine attributes this error to them.[2] Thus Manichaeus said that there are two principles, one good, from which good things were produced, namely invisible and incorporeal things, according as they are super-celestial and Angelic substances,

---

[1] *De Haeresibus ad Quodvultdeum*, c. 21 (PL 42, 29).
[2] *Ibid.*, c. 6 (PL 42, 27).

and rational souls; the other evil, from whom (as he says) were produced all evil things, and he says that these things are all corporal and visible things.

We have already disputed against this heresy in many places. For in the section on "Creatures," in the first heresy, we showed that all creatures have been produced by one God. And in the second heresy of the same section we proved from Holy Writ against the same Manichaeus that all creatures are good. And in the section on "God," in the first heresy, we very clearly proved from Sacred Writ that God is one, who established the Old and the New Testament. Thus, the reader may have recourse to those places, because from them this heresy is clearly enough overthrown. And if the curious reader desires to know more things about this matter, he may seek after them from Augustine, who very often disputes against this heresy. In his book, *On Free Will*,[1] he shows that nothing is evil by its nature, nor from God, but from our free will. He likewise proves this very extensively and effectively in the second book of his work, *On the Catholic and the Manichaean Ways of Life*.[2] In the disputation which he had with Fortunatus the Manichaean, the same subject is treated.[3] In the book, *On the Two Souls*, [*Against the Manichaeans*], he treats the same matter.[4]

The **third heresy** denies that God made any evil, whatsoever it may have been. The author of this heresy (as Philastrius and Augustine testify) was a certain Colluthus the Egyptian, from whom are named the Colluthiani. And although Augustine when writing about these Colluthiani omits their author,[5] Philastrius nevertheless states this.[6] Yet neither of them reveal at what time he lived: nor was I able to find this in any other author.

This opinion is classified as a heresy because afflictions and tribulations are called evils in Holy Writ, not because they are evil in themselves, but because they are or seem to be evils to those enduring them. On one hand, some afflictions do harm and are a torment to those upon whom they are inflicted: yet on the other hand, they are useful, since through the suffering of them the wicked are corrected, and the good become better. Thus, because Colluthus by a universal judgment was asserting that God was not the doer of any evil, he was condemned as a heretic, and rightly so, because it is evident from Holy Writ that afflictions are inflicted by God, and they are called evils. For the Lord says through the prophet Isaias: "I am the Lord, and there is none else: I form the light, and create darkness, I make peace, and create evil" (45, 6-7). Here He called war an evil, not because it is evil in itself, but because it is an evil to those who undergo it: it is indeed an evil, because it is harmful. Now that by the word "evil" there one may understand war, is proved from the context, in which there is an opposition of contraries. For just as darkness is opposite to light, so also war is to peace. Hence, since "evil" is put opposite to "peace," it is proved that war is the "evil."

Furthermore, God shows this same thing more explicitly through the prophet Jeremias, when speaking thus to the Jewish people: "Behold I will bring in evils upon them, which they shall not be able to escape" (11, 11). And the words which follow prove that He had called afflictions evils in that passage: "They shall cry to me, and I will not hearken to them. And the cities of Juda, and the inhabitants of Jerusalem shall go, and cry to the gods to whom they offer sacrifice, and they shall not save them in the time of their affliction" (v. 11-12). Notice that afflictions are very clearly called some sort of evils, which the Lord threatens that He will bring upon the cities of Juda, from which those cities cannot be saved through the help of the gods which they worshipped. Again, the prophet Jonas when describing how the Ninivites re-

---

[1] PL 32, 1221-1310.

[2] PL 32, 1345-1378.

[3] *Acts or Disputation Against Fortunatus* (PL 42, 111-130).

[4] PL 42, 93-112.

[5] *De Haeresibus ad Quodvultdeum*, c. 65 (PL 42, 42).

[6] *De haeresibus*, c. 79 (PL 12, 1189A).

pented upon his preaching, says: "And God saw their works, that they were turned from their evil way: and God had mercy with regard to the evil which he had said that he would do to them, and he did it not" (3, 10). Next, the Teacher of truth Himself when forbidding solicitude for tomorrow, says: "For the morrow will be solicitous for itself. Sufficient for the day is the evil thereof" (Mt. 6, 34). That is to say, it suffices for each day that one endure the troubles and difficulties required for the needs of that day. Finally, in the book of the prophet Amos it is said: "There is no evil in a city, which the Lord hath not done" (3, 6). By which words He wished to imply that there is no tribulation or distress which does not come from the Lord, either by Him doing or permitting it.

There is **fourth heresy** which Philastrius lists among the others, which (as he says) taught that evil kings or false prophets did not come by their own will, but it says that they come forth by God's command.[1] But he did not indicate any author of this heresy. Still, whoever may be the author of this opinion, it is evident that it is foreign to the Catholic faith. For Jeremias when speaking to Sedecias, the king of Juda, and to his people, says: "Bend down your necks under the yoke of the king of Babylon, and serve him, and his people, and you shall live. Why will you die, thou and thy people by the sword, and by famine, and by the pestilence, as the Lord hath spoken against the nation that will not serve the king of Babylon? Hearken not to the words of the prophets that say to you: You shall not serve the king of Babylon: for they tell you a lie. For I have not sent them, saith the Lord: and they prophesy in my name falsely: to drive you out, and that you may perish, both you, and the prophets that prophesy to you" (27, 12-15). These words of Jeremias are clear for the assaulting of this heresy, so that they do not need an interpretation: because when speaking about the false prophets, the Lord says that He did not send them. And the Lord when speaking through the prophet Osee about bad kings says: "They have reigned, but not by me: they have been princes, and I knew not" (8, 4). By which words God rebukes the ten tribes because Jeroboam and the kings succeeding him set up kings apart from God's will, and they ruled not according to God's plan. Therefore, bad kings are not sent by God to be bad, but they become bad by their own wills.

But here the author of this heresy will object to us that in the books of Kings it is read concerning the prophet Ahias the Silonite, that he tore apart his garment into twelve pieces: and in fact gave ten to Jeroboam, and foretold to him that he would be king of ten tribes: and afterwards when dissuading King Roboam from the war which he was preparing to make against the Israelites to put them back under his control, God said: "For this thing is from me" (III Kings 12, 24), by which words God testified that He gave the kingdom of ten tribes to Jeroboam. Thus, He reigned due to God. To which objection we reply that there are many things in Holy Writ which are said to have been done by God because He permitted those things to happen, not that we should actually think that they occurred by God's preceding plan and will, but by His permission, namely such that He did not want to impede the wicked wills of men, but rather He permitted them to act according to their own wills.

For so it ought to be understood what Paul says concerning the pagans: "God gave them up," he says, "to the desires of their heart, unto uncleanness, to dishonour their own bodies among themselves" (Rom. 1, 24). Now when we are abandoned by Him, we fall into any of the greatest sins. For so He testifies by the [Royal] Prophet saying: "I let them go according to the desires of their heart: they shall walk in their own inventions" (Ps. 80, 13). For so ought to be understood what the Lord says through the prophet Ezechiel concerning the bad prophet, who was given to the nation on account of its iniquity: "And when the prophet shall err, and speak a word: I the Lord have deceived that prophet" (14, 9). For there is no likelihood at all that God Who has so strictly forbidden deceptions and deceits to men, would Himself wish to deceive. Wherefore, that which he says, "I have deceived that prophet," ought to be taken to

---

[1] *De haeresibus*, c. 101 (PL 12, 1215A-1216A).

mean that He permitted him to be deceived, and not that He wanted him to teach deception. So likewise, when He said: "This thing is from me," namely, that Jeroboam would rule ten tribes, understand this to be a Divine permission. But when He said, "They have reigned, but not by me: they have been princes, and I knew not," you ought to take it to mean that it happened not by God's plan or command.

But so that these things might be clearer, I decided to bring to mind that one ought to consider two things in any bad prophet and in any bad king. One thing is the person's own wickedness; another thing is that a wicked person would prophesize or rule others. The first thing, namely the guilt of the king or prophet, is never from God. And if this opinion, which teaches that bad kings or prophets are from God, understands as to this, such that it thinks that their sin is from God: it is not merely a heresy, but an open blasphemy towards God. The second thing is that although the king or prophet is already bad of himself, meaning by his own free will, God sends him to prophesy or rule a wicked nation on account of their sins. The person, however, having been so sent, is not sent by God in order that he may deceive by prophesying, or may exercise tyranny by ruling; but after having become wicked by his own free will, God sends him for some good reason, namely He allows him to act according to His wickedness, so that he may punish the nation in some way. And this is quite true. For (as Job says) God "maketh a man that is a hypocrite to reign for the sins of the people" (34, 30). God does not make him to be a hypocrite: but since he is already a hypocrite and wicked, God makes him reign on account of the nation's sins. And the Lord says through the prophet Isaias: "Woe to the Assyrian, he is the rod and the staff of my anger, and my indignation is in their hands. I will send him to a deceitful nation, and I will give him a charge against the people of my wrath, to take away the spoils, and to lay hold on the prey, and to tread them down like the mire of the streets. But he shall not take it so, and his heart shall not think so" (10, 5-7). See here how God sent the Assyrian, although he did not understand that he was sent by God. And Paul the Apostle says: "Because they receive not the love of the truth, that they might be saved. Therefore God shall send them the operation of error, to believe lying that all may be judged who have not believed the truth" (II Thess. 2, 10-11). And according to this meaning it is not heresy to say that bad kings come by God's will, just as we will say elsewhere in the section on "Power."

MARIA VIRGO

Virgin Mary

It is not surprising that heretics attempt to lessen the honor of the Mother of God, since they are even unafraid to dishonor the name of God Himself. Thus Helvidius, one of those who have been caught in such folly, asserted that the Blessed Mother of God was known carnally by Joseph, her husband, after Christ's birth. He was prompted to teach this error from that which is said in Matthew's Gospel: "Before they came together, she was found with child" (1, 18). And again: "Joseph knew her not till she brought forth her firstborn son" (v. 25). From which passages Helvidius concluded that the Mother of God was carnally known by Joseph after she bore Christ, and she gave birth to other children whom (as he says) the Gospel calls Christ's brethren. For in Matthew's Gospel the Jews say to Christ: "Behold thy mother and thy brethren stand without, seeking thee" (12, 47). But Helvidius having understood wrongly from the text fell into error. Now from which country or nation he was, it is not evident to me. I gleaned from Gennadius that he was a disciple of Auxentius[1] and

---

[1] Auxentius was an Arian bishop, the predecessor of St. Ambrose.

a contemporary of Jerome.[1] The supporters of this heresy were called Antidicomarianites.[2] Augustine also accuses Jovinian of this error.[3] Yet Jerome, who fights against this error in his work, *Against Jovinian*, in two books, never makes mention of it.

Firstly, therefore, let us show Mary's perpetual virginity: then we will reply to Helvidius' objections. For showing Mary's perpetual virginity, even though a clear quotation from Scripture is lacking, still there are not lacking other proofs equally or almost as powerful. For the authority of the Church is of no less weight than Sacred Scripture, because just as Sacred Scripture, because it was produced by the Holy Ghost, cannot err, so the Church, in that it is governed and taught by the Holy Ghost, can neither deceive or be deceived. Now the Church declares that the Mother of God was perpetually a virgin, because it so preaches this everywhere in the world, so that it calls her by the name of inviolate and undefiled ever Virgin. Furthermore, the concordant opinion of all the holy Doctors (as we taught in the first book) ought to held to be the true faith, because it would impossible that all would think concordantly, except that they were all taught by the Holy Ghost, the one Teacher and Guide of them all, especially since many of them were separated from each other by place and time, such that they could not know one another, nor see each other's works: wherefore it could not happen that all would think concordantly, if the Holy Ghost, the common Teacher of them all, had not enlightened their minds to think in this way.

Now, that the holy Doctors think that the Blessed Mother of God was always a virgin, the matter is so clear that it is not necessary to cite their testimony here, because you will hardly find any book of sermons to the people in which there are not very many testimonies of the holy Doctors in favor of this matter. And not only the Latin writers think this, but the Greek writers also proclaim the same thing. For Theophylactus, the most recent of the Greek writers thinks this; [John] Damascene also often proclaims the same thing, Chrysostom teaches the same thing, [Pseudo-] Basil thinks the same thing, especially in his homily, *De humana Christi generatione*.[4] It is unnecessary to speak about Origen, since in many places he proclaims her a perpetual virgin. Blessed Irenaeus, Bishop of Lyon, who lived very close to the time of the Apostles, who was a disciple of the martyr Polycarp: he, I say, never calls the Mother of God (as far as we know) by any name save "the Virgin." And so that I may show one of the many citations, in the third book of *Against the Heresies*, in chapter twenty-two and often in the following chapters, he calls her "the Virgin."[5] Blessed Ignatius [of Antioch], a fragment of whose [Pseudo-] letter to the Virgin Mother of God is extant, very often bears witness that she was a virgin. Next, not only the Doctors think this, but the whole Christian people, impelled by the Holy Ghost, are persuaded of this opinion. Why then do the wicked heretics attempt to teach against the consent of all the holy Doctors and of the whole Christian people?

It is necessary therefore that (just as it is said of Ismael, the type of heretics) the hands of all Catholics be raised up against Helvidius, because he tried to raise up his hands against all Catholics. I omit here the figures and enigmas in which Sacred Scripture puts forth Mary's perpetual virginity, because these things (as we taught in the first book) avail little to convince heretics. Again, if the Blessed Mother of God was known by her husband after she bore Christ (as Helvidius says), and begot children, why did Christ, when He was dying, not entrust her to some one of these other children? For it would seem that He did an injury to the other children, by entrusting His mother to someone other than her child, because by this it would seem

---

[1] *De scriptoribus ecclesiasticis*, c. 32 (PL 58, 1077B).

[2] This name comes from the Greek word, ἀντιδικομαριανῖται, which literally means "opponents of Mary."

[3] *De Haeresibus ad Quodvultdeum*, c. 82 (PL 42, 45-46).

[4] Also entitled, *In sanctam Christi generationem* (PG 31, 1458-1476).

[5] PG 7, 955C ff.

that He had little confidence that they would provide due care for His mother. But since those whom Helvidius asserts were children of the Virgin would have been holy children, it ought to have been believed that they would have given diligent care for the Mother of God if she were their mother. For (so that I pass over the others) it is evident that James, who is called the brother of the Lord, was a very holy man. If then he was a son of the Mother of God, it was not necessary to entrust her to John, nor would Christ ever have entrusted her to John, because this would seem to be done out of ill-will for the other children. Furthermore, just as before Christ, no one was put in Christ's tomb, so after Christ. If then such honor was shown to Christ's dead body, that no one else was put into His tomb out of reverence for Him, it is necessary that much more honor would have been shown to the Virgin's womb, so that neither before nor after Christ, any man would have entered her womb, especially because in it was not merely Christ's dead body, as in the tomb, in which laid merely the body without the soul, although joined to the Divinity, but the whole entire Christ was enclosed.

Add to these things also that passage of Matthew which Helvidius objects to us. For it is necessary to pierce the same Helvidius with his own sword, as another Goliath. For Matthew says the following: "He knew her not till she brought forth her firstborn son" (1, 25). Then it is necessary to inquire of Helvidius, why Joseph abstains from touching his wife until the day of the birth? It is certain that he abstained for no other reason beside his reverence for Him Whom was carried in the womb of the Virgin. For Joseph had heard the voice of the Angel saying to him in his sleep: "That which is conceived in her, is of the Holy Ghost" (v. 20). Thus, will not he who abstains on account of the voice of the Angel made to him in his sleep, abstain much more when he sees with his own eyes the countless miracles which were very clearly demonstrating to Joseph himself the majesty and Divinity of the Child born, and the dignity of His mother? For Joseph sees her giving birth without pain, without a midwife, contrary to the common law of other women; he hears the multitude of Angels singing and saying: "Glory to God in the highest" (Lk. 2, 14). He sees the shepherds declaring, the Wise men adoring. Hence since he saw these things and very many other things after the birth, it ought to be believed that he then reverenced the Virgin Mother of God, and abstained from her more than before the birth. For if all are forbidden to touch the mountain upon which Moses went up to receive the Law, due to the fact that the Lord appeared there, how much more will Joseph be forbidden to touch the glorious Virgin, who is that mountain whence was cut without hands, Christ our God?

But now it is necessary that we reply to Helvidius' objections. For thus he argues: Matthew says that "before they came together, she was found with child": it then follows that they came together afterwards: for otherwise she would not be found before they came together, because that word, "before," seems to indicate a reference to what follows. To this we reply that it was not so, namely that the word, "before," indicates a reference and relation to future things that will occur; but rather, by the common way of speaking it is often said in relation to the things which would come about, if their occurrence would not have been hindered in some other way: as for example, if someone wanted to ask for something from someone else, and that person spontaneously gave it without even being asked, and if he had not so given, the other was indeed going to ask, but did not ask, because the one spontaneously giving prevented the request of the other: then if he be asked whether he asked for what he had decided to ask for, he will reply that he did not. If he be asked why he did not ask, he will answer saying: "Before I could ask, another gave it." And yet, after the one gave, the other did not ask. Nevertheless, it is said that it was given before asking, because even if he did not ask, he was still going to ask had not the other by giving prevented his asking.

And Holy Writ does not look askance at this manner of speaking. For in the book of the prophet Isaias, God says: "Before they call, I will hear" (65, 24). For since God grants many things to us not asking, He is said to hear us before we call. And yet the word there, "before," does not indicate reference to the things that will occur, because no one calls after he has been heard. For no one is so mindless that he would ask for that which has already been given to him. In this manner it is said in Matthew that "before they came together, she was found with child," because even though she was afterwards found with child, they never came together, yet perhaps Joseph would have wanted to have intercourse with her except that he was previously informed by the Angel about the marvelous impregnation of the Virgin.

Secondly Helvidius objects those words of Matthew which he says about Joseph: "He knew her not till she brought forth her firstborn son." If he did not know her (Helvidius says) till she brought forth, then after she brought forth, he knew her: for otherwise he would not have placed an end point saying, "till she brought forth, but he would have said absolutely, he did not know her." To this objection we likewise reply that it is false that the adverb which he says, namely "till [*donec*]," means an end point and an end of the act designated by the verb which it modifies, such that immediately after that end, there was no such act or operation designated by the verb which it modifies. But we say that such adverbs, such as "unto" [*usque*], "until" [*donec*], and if there be any other similar ones, only signify a continuation of the act designated by the verb which it modifies, with no reference had to future acts, whether that same act follows afterwards, or not. For if it be asked about Peter, who is in Spain until he returns from Flanders, where he went? Someone can correctly reply that he went to Paris, to Bordeaux, or to Bayonne, even though he went past these cities.

And this manner of speech is frequent in Holy Writ. For in Isaias the Lord says the following: "Even to [*usque*] your old age…I will carry you" (46, 4). And yet, after we grow old, He will not carry us less. And in the Psalm Seventy He says: "Unto [*usque*] old age and grey hairs: O God, forsake me not, until [*donec*] I shew forth thy arm to all the generation that is to come" (v. 18). Notice that you see both adverbs used there, namely "unto" and "until," and yet David did not ask to be forsaken after that time. And in Matthew's Gospel, Christ says: "I am with you all days, even to the consummation of the world" (28, 20). From which words, according to Helvidius' interpretation, one ought to conclude that once the world has been consummated, Christ will not be with us. Yet far be it that anyone would fall into such an error. Concerning the raven which Noe sent from the ark, it is said that "It did not return, till the waters were dried up" (Gen. 8, 7), yet it never returned afterwards, even when the waters were dried up. And it is said in the Psalm: "Our eyes unto the Lord our God, until he have mercy on us" (122, 2). After God has mercy on us, will we no longer lift up our eyes to God? Far be it; because he who said this, says elsewhere: "The meditation of my heart always in thy sight" (Ps. 18, 15). And again: "O how have I loved thy law, O Lord! it is my meditation all the day" (Ps. 118, 97). And Blessed Paul when speaking about Christ says: "He must reign, until he hath put all his enemies under his feet" (I Cor. 15, 25). What does Helvidius say to these things? After Christ has put His enemies under His feet, will He not reign any longer? Far be it. For "Of his kingdom," the Angel said, "there shall be no end" (Lk. 1, 33).

But now Helvidius tries to escape by another route. "If Christ is the firstborn son of the Virgin," he says, "then she had other sons thereafter, in relation to whom Christ is called 'the firstborn.'" And in regard to this Helvidius also is dreaming, because the word "first" or "firstborn" is not always said in relation to a subsequent second or third, but also that which is alone is sometimes called in Holy Writ "the first [*primum*]," and other times "firstborn [*primogenitus*]." Which two words are found together in one sentence in the book of Numbers. For there the Lord says to the priests: "Whatsoever is firstborn [*primum*] of all flesh, which they offer to the Lord, whether it be of men, or of beasts, shall belong to thee: only for the firstborn [*primogenitus*] of man thou shalt take a price" etc. (18, 15). Notice that you have here in one sentence even that which is alone called "the first" and "firstborn." For otherwise he who has only one son, would not be held to offer him to God and redeem him until he had another son who in relation to whom [the first son] might be called the first. Now this is proved to be false, because the Blessed Mother of God when she offered her Son to the Lord in the hands of Simeon, did so according to the Law, as Luke testifies. But the Gospel of Matthew testifies, and Helvidius admits, that at that time the Blessed Mother of God did not have any other son besides Christ.

Now the fact that it is said in the Gospel that Christ had "brethren [*fratres*, or 'brothers']" has little effect, because it is usual in Holy Writ that those who are joined by any consanguinity are called "brethren," even though they are not born of the same parents. For example, Lot is called Abraham's brother,[1] whom nevertheless the same book of Scripture states was the son of Abraham's brother. Therefore, since those things to which Helvidius objects are of no importance, and the authority of the Church is so great that we are bound to believe its definitions, it is necessary to confess that the Blessed Mother of God was perpetually a virgin, because the Church so teaches.

Blessed Jerome wrote a single tract against Helvidius.[2] Blessed Ildephonsus, Archbishop of Toledo, two hundred years or more after Jerome wrote about the same matter against certain heretics who attempted to revive this heresy of Helvidius in Spain.[3] Hugh of Saint Victor published a small book about the perpetual virginity of Mary.[4]

There is a **second heresy** asserting that the Blessed Virgin Mary ought not to be called the Mother of God, but only the mother of a just man. For this heresy says that there are two persons in Christ, just as there are two natures, and it says that one person is God alone, and the other man alone: and it says that the Blessed Virgin is the mother of the person which it says is man alone. And so it denies that the Blessed Virgin is the Mother of God. The author of this heresy was Nestorius. But it was already discussed sufficiently above about this error in the section on "Christ," in the third heresy. Hence the reader may refer to that place, because there will be found the conquering of this error.

MARTYRIUM

Martyrdom

There was an error which Basilides taught saying that it is not a crime to deny Christ in time of persecution. Wherefore he was saying that it is madness to suffer death for this reason, since Christ can be denied without crime. By which opinion he was discouraging men from martyrdom. Certain heretics called the Elcesaites taught this same error, although differently and for another reason than Basilides. For Basilides (as Philastrius says about him[5]) was not directly discouraging men from martyrdom, but was merely saying that death ought not to be endured for the confession of Christ's death and crucifixion. Now he was saying this because (as we said above) Basilides denied that Christ was crucified, but he said that Simon the Cyrenian, who was forced to carry the Cross, was crucified in Christ's place. Hence for this reason he laughed at those who suffered death lest they deny Christ Who was crucified for us, because he was saying that they suffered for a lie. We have already overturned the foundation of this error above in the section on "Christ," in the seventh heresy.

---

[1] "We are brethren" (Gen. 13, 8).
[2] *The Perpetual Virginity of Blessed Mary* (PL 23, 183-206).
[3] *De virginitate perpetuâ sanctae Mariae adversus tres infideles* (PL 96, 53-110).
[4] *De virginitate Beatae Mariae* (PL 176, 857-876).
[5] *De haeresibus*, c. 32 (PL 12, 1147A-1148A).

Hence there is no need for us to dispute more against this heresy. But the Elcesaites think differently. For they say that it is not a sin to deny Christ in time of persecution, because he who is fixed in his heart, even if he shall have denied Christ with his mouth out of necessity, yet with his heart he remains in the faith. Wherefore they say that such a person so denying with his mouth does not sin, since God looks more at the heart than the tongue. Eusebius relates these things about the Elcesaites.[1]

This heresy is refuted by very clear testimonies of Scripture. For the Wise Mas says: "The mouth that belieth, killeth the soul" (Wis. 1, 11). But he who denies with his mouth, but confesses with his heart, lies: thus he kills his soul, even if he confesses with his heart. He rather ought then to suffer the death of his body by confessing Christ, lest when he has denied Him with his mouth, he kill his soul, which is much better than his body. For Christ our Redeemer says in Matthew's Gospel: "Fear ye not them that kill the body, and are not able to kill the soul: but rather fear him that can destroy both soul and body in hell" (10, 28). And shortly afterwards the Savior likewise concludes, saying the following: "Everyone therefore that shall confess me before men, I will also confess him before my Father who is in heaven. But he that shall deny me before men, I will also deny him before my Father who is in heaven" (v. 32-33). Furthermore, the Teacher of truth itself says: "Blessed are they that suffer persecution for justice' sake: for theirs is the kingdom of heaven" (5, 10). Again, Blessed Paul says that the confession of the mouth is as necessary as the faith of the heart. For he says as follows: "If thou confess with thy mouth the Lord Jesus, and believe in thy heart that God hath raised him up from the dead, thou shalt be saved. For, with the heart, we believe unto justice; but, with the mouth, confession is made unto salvation" (Rom. 10, 9-10). Next, the Teacher of truth Himself, when speaking to His disciples, says: "You shall be witnesses unto me in Jerusalem, and in all Judea, and Samaria, and even to the uttermost part of the earth" (Acts 1, 8). Hence, if the disciples when placed in persecution would have denied Christ with their mouths, even if they would have confessed in their hearts, they would have been witnesses of a lie and false witnesses. Now "A lying witness," the Wise Man says, "shall perish" (Prov. 21, 28). Therefore, in no way it is permitted that on account of any persecution one deny the faith with his mouth, no matter how much it he upholds it in his heart: but instead, it is better to endure death, rather than to deny the truth, so that he be a good martyr, that is to say, a true and faithful witness. For the word "martyr" in Greek means "witness."

There is a **second heresy** which teaches that those who kill themselves for their sins, ought to be called martyrs, due to the fact that they punish in themselves what they lament that they have committed. The author of this heresy was Petilian, a certain Donatist, against whom there exist a number of tracts of Augustine.[2] This error is refuted by the action of Judas, who lamenting the sin which he had committed, hung himself. Now the fact that he did this lamenting his sin, Matthew bears witness, who says: "Then Judas, who betrayed him, seeing that he was condemned, repenting himself, brought back the thirty pieces of silver to the chief priests and ancients, saying: I have sinned in betraying innocent blood" (27, 3-4). No Catholic, however, doubts that Judas was damned, since the testimony of Scripture is so clear. For the [Royal] Prophet, when speaking of Judas, says: "When he is judged, may he go out condemned; and may his prayer be turned to sin. May his days be few: and his bishopric let another take" (Ps. 108, 7-8). And Blessed Peter testifies that these words ought to be understood of Judas in the discourse which he made to the other disciples after Christ's Ascension into Heaven, when speaking of the substitution of another man into Judas' place.

---

[1] *Church History*, bk, 6, chap. 38, n. 6
[2] *Answer to Petilian the Donatist* (*Contra litteras Petilliani donatistae Cirtensis episcopi* (PL 43, 245-388)).

The **third heresy** is still more pestilent, not to say more atrocious, because it asserts that all who voluntarily suffer death, ought to be called martyrs, no matter whether they suffer such a death at the hands of others, or if they inflict it upon themselves. Augustine calls the authors of this heresy, "Circumcellions," saying that "They are a rude country people, notorious in their insolence, who not only perpetrate savage crimes against others, but do not spare the members of their own sect in their mad fury. It is their practice to commit suicide in various ways, particularly by leaping off cliffs, by drowning, or by fire, and they seduce others whom they can... to follow the same madness."[1] But if others disdain to do this, they threaten them with death, saying that in this way they will become martyrs. Philastrius calls these heretics *Circuitores*, because they roved about through regions to perpetrate these crimes.[2] Neither Augustine nor Philastrius related who was the author of this insane heresy, or at what time it began. Augustine says that they are associated with the Donatists and they fight under them.

Their error is very clearly refuted by what is said in the Law of the Lord: "Thou shalt not kill" (Ex. 20, 13). By which words the killing of any man is forbidden, except for that killing which is by order of a judge as a punishment for evil doers. Thus, if it is not allowed to kill another, much less it is allowed to kill oneself. Furthermore, he who kills himself, acts against the natural inclination of all men, not only against the bad inclinations which are in our corrupted nature, but against the inclination of perfect human nature. But since such an inclination is always correct, he who acts against it, is clearly shown to act badly. Now it is evident that the inclination to life is natural to man even before sin, because Christ, in Whom there was no sin, recoiled from death, which would not have happened unless there was a natural inclination to life in Him. Again, the keeper of the prison in which Paul and Silas were kept, "Seeing the doors of the prison open, drawing his sword, would have killed himself, supposing that the prisoners had been fled. But Paul cried with a loud voice, saying: Do thyself no harm, for we all are here" (Acts 16, 27-28). If one killing himself would be deemed a martyr, Paul would never have prevented the keeper from killing himself. But since Paul with a loud voice called him off from killing himself, saying: "Do thyself no harm [*malum*, or "evil"]," it is proved that killing oneself, far from deserving to be called martyrdom, is something evil. The same argumentation which we made against the heresy just related opposes this heresy. And since the matter is so clear, it is not necessary to present more evidence.

MATRIMONIUM

Matrimony

Although there were not lacking and now are not lacking heresies which attack matrimony, still nothing will be said about them now, but below in the section on "Marriage" [*Nuptiae*] it will be treated about the heresies of this kind. For I had decided to defer the matter to that place, because the word "marriage" is more frequently used by the older authors than the word "matrimony," and the matters dealing with matrimony are discussed by them using the word "marriage." The word "matrimony" is certainly rarely used by them, and in Holy Writ the word "marriage" is more frequently used than "matrimony," although this word is also often found in Holy Writ.

---

[1] *De Haeresibus ad Quodvultdeum*, c. 69 (PL 42, 43).
[2] *De haeresibus*, c. 85 (PL 12, 1198A).

Melchisedech

Certain men, deceived by error, hardly understanding Sacred Scripture as it ought, said that the priest Melchisedech who blessed Abraham returning from the victory of the five kings, was not a mere man, but was Christ, or some other power of God. Augustine calls the supporters of this error Melchisedechians, and puts them in the thirty-fourth place among the heresies when enumerates in his book, *De Haeresibus* [*ad Quodvultdeum*].[1] From which book it is gathered that the book which is entitled, *Questions of the New and Old Testament*, is not Augustine's, although it is circulated under his name.[2] For besides other arguments which Erasmus of Rotterdam brings forth to prove this, this is the most powerful, that in Question one hundred nine [the book's author] tries to prove by very inept arguments that Melchisedech was not a mere man, but a certain power of God, namely the Holy Ghost. But [Augustine] never retracted this in his book of *Retractions*, nay he never mentions that book throughout the whole text of his *Retractions*. Therefore, when in his book, *De Haeresibus* [*ad Quodvultdeum*], he states that this assertion is heretical, Augustine was not so foolish that he would teach opposite assertions contradicting each other. I point out these things lest perhaps if someone would come upon this Question, he be pressured by Augustine's authority to deviate from steadfast rectitude. Who was the leader of this heresy, or at what time did it begin, however, Augustine does not state, nor could I find this in any other author. Yet Epiphanius [of Salamis] says in his book, the *Panarion*, in heresy fifty-five,[3] that Hieracas, a remarkably learned man, taught this heresy, but he does not say that he is the first one found by him. And he repeats the same thing in heresy sixty-seven, where he speaks longer about this Hieracas.[4]

Now so that we may show this opinion to be erroneous, it is necessary to cite the same Sacred Scripture which speaks about him, when relating Abraham's victory, and how Melchisedech went out to meet him. For it says the following: "But Melchisedech the king of Salem, bringing forth bread and wine, for he was the priest of the most high God, blessed him, and said: Blessed be Abram by the most high God, who created Heaven and earth. And blessed be the most high God, by whose protection the enemies are in thy hands. And he gave him the tithes of all" (Gen. 14, 18-20). Hence let us now discuss this text. If Melchisedech is the Holy Ghost, how is it said there that he was the king of Salem? Now Salem is a city in the land of Chanaan near Sichem. For in the same book of Genesis, when the Scripture is recounting how Jacob returned from Mesopotamia, it says the following: "And he passed over to Salem, a city of the Sichemites, which is in the land of Chanaan, after he returned from Mesopotamia of Syria" (33, 18). Therefore, if Salem is an earthly city, how is the Holy Ghost said to be the king of Salem, since He governs from sea to sea, from the river to the ends of the world? Especially because in the same passage Scripture recounts other kings who went out to Abraham, namely the king of Sodom and the king of Gomorrha: and having named these kings, and stated the lands in which they reigned, Melchisedech is immediately described,

---

[1] PL 42, 31.

[2] PL 35, 2213-2386. For many years, the *Questions on the Old and New Testaments* were thought to have been written by Augustine of Hippo and were placed among his works. Scholars have long since determined that it was not written by Augustine.

[3] PG 41, 979D. Epiphanius dates Hieracas in the time of Diocletian (PG 42, 183C).

[4] PG 42, 171C-183B.

and Scripture did not give him another kingdom. Has the Holy Ghost separated the kingdom of the land of Chanaan, so that He is the king of Salem alone, and the others are the kings of Sodom and Gomorrha? Far be it. For the heavens are His, and the earth is His, and the world and the fullness thereof He has founded.[1]

Now what the good author of that question one hundred nine, just cited, puts forth as evidence is that Salem by interpretation is "peace," and so the king of Salem by interpretation is, according to the Apostle, "king of peace"[2]: now the king of peace is none other than God, therefore Melchisedech is God. This is an inept conclusion, because in the first book of this work, chapter three we taught that no other sense of Sacred Scripture is effective for confirming an assertion besides the literal sense, and not the mystical sense. But when we taught that there is a town in the land of Chanaan which is called Salem, that will be the literal sense whereby it will be said that Melchisedech is the king of that town. For according to this other manner [of argumentation] it would also be said that Isaac is God, because Isaac is interpreted to mean "joy": and Jeremias for the same reason, because Jeremias is interpreted to mean "God's loftiness." But no one can truly be called joy essentially except God alone, Who is our joy, who is also our future reward.

Now when the Apostle had said that action of Melchisedech prefigured Christ's action, to show that Melchisedech deservedly was a figure of Christ, he presents the interpretation of his name, which fits Christ very well. Furthermore, in the same passage he says that he was "the priest of the most high God" (Gen. 14, 18). But God is not a priest belonging to God, thus Melchisedech is not God. "For every high priest," Paul says, "taken from among men, is ordained for men" (Heb. 5, 1). Hence either the Holy Ghost was not a priest taken from among men, or He was taken from among men, so that He was then truly a priest, as Christ was. But the good author of the previously oft-quoted question, claims that the Holy Ghost then appeared in human form, in the same way as the Son of God did afterwards. See with how many snares, whoever he is, he entangles himself so that he may persuade us of this error. Let him come forth, who now contends that this work is Augustine's, and let him say whether Augustine thinks that the Holy Ghost became incarnate. Again, if the Holy Ghost were a priest, and is ordained for men, as Paul says of every priest, and appeared in human form, as this author allows, then the Holy Ghost was a mediator between God and men, because He was God with God, and a man with men, just as Christ. And if they acknowledge this, they will certainly oppose Paul saying: "One mediator of God and men, the man Christ Jesus" (I Tim. 2, 5). If the Holy Ghost were a priest, then there are two mediators, not one, as Paul says.

Next, the very manner of blessing whereby he blessed Abraham proves that Melchisedech was not God. For he says the following: "Blessed be Abram by the most high God, who created heaven and earth. And blessed be the most high God, by whose protection the enemies are in thy hands" (Gen. 14, 19-20). If Melchisedech were God, why did he give thanks to God for Abraham's victory? Did Christ as God in this way render thanks for the miracles He performed? For when He wanted to raise Lazarus, He said the following: "Father, I give thee thanks that thou hast heard me. And I knew that thou hearest me always; but because of the people who stand about have I said it, that they may believe that thou hast sent me" (Jn. 11, 41-42). Christ gives thanks because of the people who stand around, but certainly it was not necessary that God would give thanks to God. But how were the people meant to understand that act of thanksgiving? It was namely so that they would believe that Christ was sent by the Father. But since Abraham was so faithful, that when he was instructed by God he believed without any hesitation, and so there was no need to give such thanks or praises to God to strengthen him in the faith. Regarding these things, when Paul was speaking about this

---

[1] Cf. Ps. 88, 12.
[2] Cf. Heb. 7, 2.

Melchisedech, he says that he was "likened unto the Son of God" (Heb. 7, 3). But everything that is likened to another, does not share the exact same nature with it. The Holy Ghost has the same nature as the Son of God, hence Melchisedech is not the Holy Ghost. For you will never find that the Son of God is said to be similar to the Father, although He is correctly called the image of the Father, because an image, as we said above in the section on "Adam and Eve," in the second heresy, properly pertains to the nature, but likeness pertains to a quality, such that those things are called similar which have different natures, yet have some things which are of the same species. Hence what is the same in nature, cannot be properly called similar. Now Paul says about Melchisedech that he was likened in every respect to the Son of God; namely in regard to all those things which Paul mentioned: that he is without father and without mother. But the Holy Ghost in not likened unto the Holy Ghost in this, because the Son of God according to His Divinity is not without the Father. But Melchisedech is said to be without father and without mother, not because he did not have parents, but because Scripture never mentioned either his father or his mother, nor did it make known any genealogy of his: so also, Christ according to His lower and human lineage lacks a father. For He was born of the Virgin, and of her alone, according to the flesh. And according to the Divinity He lacks a mother, because according to It He was begotten from the Father alone before all ages. And furthermore, Christ is without genealogy, because His genealogy is unutterable, as the prophet Isaias says: "Who shall declare his generation?" (53, 8).

But they still object to us another comparison which Paul makes, which nowise can befit Melchisedech if he is a mere man, because he says concerning him: "Having neither beginning of days nor end of life" (Heb. 7, 3). Now if Melchisedech was a man, he was both born and died like other men. But this is refuted as in the preceding objection. For the reason why it is said that Melchisedech did not have a beginning of days or an end of life is because although he was born and died, nevertheless to us he did not have a beginning or end because Scripture did not express his birth or death.

Blessed Jerome wrote a letter to Evangelus about this matter, which is in the third volume of his works according to the division which is found in the second publication made in Basel.[1]

MENDACIUM

Lies

I have found only one heresy about this subject, which teaches that it is licit to lie to save a man's life, or to gain a great benefit for man. [Lying is permitted] not only for these reasons, but also for the sake of humility, namely so that one may conceal his virtues by a lie. John Cassian under the name of Abbot Joseph teaches this error. For in conference seventeen, from chapter fifteen to chapter twenty he treats the first part of this error, and tries to persuade one of this error of the intellect by some quotations of Sacred Scripture.[2] But from chapter twenty-one to chapter twenty-five of the same conference he pertinaciously defends the second part of this error.[3]

Sacred Scripture clearly condemns this error. For the Royal Prophet says: "Thou wilt destroy all that speak a lie" (Ps. 5, 7). He who said "all" did not wish to exclude him who lies officiously. And again in another Psalm when asking who shall dwell in God's tabernacle, or who shall rest in His holy hill, that is to say, in heavenly glory, he answers saying: "He that

---

[1] Letter 73 (PL 22, 676-681).

[2] PL 49, 1060C-1075A.

[3] PL 49, 1075A-1081C.

speaketh truth in his heart, who hath not used deceit in his tongue" (Ps. 14, 3). By which words he clearly excludes him who uses deceit in his tongue. But everyone who lies officiously uses deceit. Hence every such person is excluded from God's hill: not actually that one falling into that sin cannot attain glory: far be it: but because it is necessary before he may be placed there, he must be purged by worthy satisfaction: such that when he shall have passed over thither, he may then not have any sin. And in the book of Wisdom it is said: "The mouth that belieth, killeth the soul" (1, 11). But this quotation has little force: because it seems to speak only about pernicious lies. On the other hand, the words which Ecclesiasticus says are very clear: "Be not willing to make any manner of lie" (Eccli. 7, 14). He who has forbidden every kind of lie, does not permit any lie. Therefore, it is not permitted to say a lie for any reason.

All the holy Doctors wholeheartedly[1] agree with this opinion. Augustine says: "Lest any should imagine that the perfect and spiritual man ought to lie for this temporal life, in the death of which no soul is slain, neither his own, nor another's. But since it is one thing to lie, another to conceal the truth (if indeed it be one thing to say what is false, another not to say what is true), if haply one does not wish to give a man up even to this visible death, he should be prepared to conceal what is true, not to say what is false; so that he may neither give him up, nor yet lie, lest he slay his own soul for another's body."[2] His words are able to remove all doubt. For due to ignorance of this distinction which Augustine now makes, comes the error of Cassian or Abbot Joseph. For they did not know how to distinguish between lying and hiding the truth: to say what is false, and to be silent about what is true. The first of these is never allowed, but the second can be done without sin: just as it happened when Abraham was saying about Sara his wife: "She is my sister" (Gen. 20, 2). But he in fact said the truth, and hid the truth. He indeed said the truth that she is his sister: because he was joined to her by blood. And all who are of the same kindred (as Blessed Jerome teaches against Helvidius[3]) are called brethren in Sacred Scripture. Thus, Sara is truthfully called Abraham's sister: yet Abraham did not deny that she was his wife: and hence he did not lie. And Augustine again confirms this opinion elsewhere saying: "Suppose a man should seek shelter with you who by your lie may be saved from death?... 'The mouth that lies slays the soul' (Wis. 1, 11)... How can a man be said to love as himself that man, for whom that he may secure a temporal life, himself loses life eternal?"[4]

Blessed Gregory when expounding that passage from Job: "My lips shall not speak iniquity" (27, 4), says the following: "All lying is very seriously to be guarded against, though sometimes there is a certain sort of lying which is of lighter complexion, if a man lie in rendering good. But seeing that it is written, 'The mouth that lies slays the soul' (Wis. 1, 11), and, 'Thou wilt destroy all that speak a lie' (Ps. 5, 7), this kind of lying also those that are perfect avoid with the greatest care, so that not even the life of any man should by deceit of theirs be defended, lest they hurt their own souls, whilst they busy themselves to give life to another's flesh; though the same particular kind of sin we believe to be very easily remitted."[5] From which words it is evident that an officious lie is a sin, although a slight sin. But Cassian, the Abbot in whose name he speaks, not only thought that a lie is no sin, but he considers it a sin not to lie when there is an urgent necessity.

---

[1] Lit., *manibus ac pedibus eunt* ("they go by their hands and feet").

[2] *Expositions on the Psalms*, Ps. 5, n. 7 (PL 36, 85).

[3] "Moreover they are called brethren by kindred who are of one family, that is πατρία, which corresponds to the Latin *paternitas*, because from a single root a numerous progeny proceeds" (n. 14 (PL 23, 197B)).

[4] *Concordia discordantium canonum*, causa 22, q. 2, 17 (PL 187, 1136A-B). *On Lying*, c. 7 (PL 40, 494-495).

[5] *Moralia*, bk. 18, chap. 3, n. 5 (PL 75, 40C-D).

MENDACIUM

Isidore [of Seville] says the following: "Flee in particular every kind of lie, lest you say what is false accidentally or deliberately: you ought not want to lie, even to assist others: nor ought you defend the life of others by any deceit. Beware of lies in all circumstances."[1] Next Blessed Augustine condemns lies which are said for the sake of humility to conceal one's virtues, saying the following: "When you lie for humility's sake, if you were not a sinner before you lied, by lying you are made what you had avoided. The truth is not in you, unless you in such wise say you are a sinner, as you know yourself to be. Now this is truth, that what you are, you say. For how is there humility, where falseness reigns?"[2]

But besides all these proofs of Sacred Scripture and of holy men, reason itself urges us to believe that we ought not to act in this way. For something evil in itself, cannot be good no matter how good the intention or on account of any other good circumstance: because (as [Pseudo-] Blessed Dionysius [the Areopagite] says) good results from a complete cause, while evil results from any single defect.[3] But the matter is so clear, that a lie is something evil in itself, that it does not need any proof: because it is opposed to the truth, which is something good in itself. And this was known not only to Christians, but also to the pagans. For Aristotle says: Lying is in itself evil and to be shunned, while truthfulness is good and worthy of praise.[4] If a lie is in itself evil, then it will also be evil when said for saving the life of a man. Otherwise for the same reason theft would be good which happens under the pretext of coming to the aid of the poor: yet none of the saints ever conceded this. Also, for the same reason it would be said that they who killed Christ's Apostles did not sin, because in so doing (as the Savior says[5]) they thought that they were doing a service to God. Now it is much better to do a service to God, than to take a man away by the death of his body. Hence it is that if saving a man's life could free a lie from guilt, the service which one thinks that he does to God, could deliver the slayer of the Apostles from sin.

Lastly, in order that we may put an end to this dispute, there is a clear declaration of the Church about this matter. For Pope Innocent III, when writing to the Archbishop of Palermo, says the following: "Since the crime of usury is detested in the pages of both Testaments, we do not see that any dispensation for this can be made: because since Sacred Scripture forbids one to lie for the sake of another's life, much more should it be forbidden that anyone be involved with the crime of usury even for the sake of redeeming the life of a captive."[6]

But it remains that we refute the objections of Cassian or of Abbot Joseph. For to prove that it is licit to lie for the sake of an urgent necessity, he cites some examples of the patriarchs of the Old Testament, who appear to have lied for some similar reason. We reply to all those objections at the same time, that they were not lies, because even though they concealed the truth, still they did not say something false, as we taught above concerning Abraham, when he said that Sara is his sister. Next, even if some patriarchs said something false, or acted by dissimulating, Sacred Scripture does not praise such falsity. For not all their actions which are related there are praised, simply because they were written there: otherwise it would happen that some of their sins, which they committed as men, would also be praised. In this way Scripture relates the lie which Judith said to Holofernes, yet it does not praise her lie,

---

[1] *Concordia discordantium canonum*, causa 22, q. 2, c. 16 (PL 187, 1136A). *Synonyma de lamentatione animae peccatricis*, bk. 2, n. 53 (PL 83, 857C).

[2] *Sermons on the New Testament*, sermon 181, c. 5, n. 5 (PL 38, 981).

[3] *The Divine Names*, c. 4, sect. 30 (PG 3, 730C).

[4] "For the man who loves truth, and is truthful where nothing is at stake, will still more be truthful where something is at stake; he will avoid falsehood as something base, seeing that he avoided it even for its own sake; and such a man is worthy of praise" (*Ethics*, bk. 4, c. 7).

[5] Jn. 16, 2.

[6] Gregory IX, *Decretales*, bk. 5, tit. 19 (*De usuris*), c. 4.

but her virile courage whereby she was not afraid to pass through the middle of the enemy's camp, kill the general of the army lying on his bed, and bring away the general's head with her into the city. It praises this courage, this daring, more than the womanly misdeed; it does not praise the lie whereby she deceived both the general and his soldiers. It may also be that some of the things done or said by those patriarchs, which on the surface appear to be lies, and are praised, ought (as Blessed Augustine teaches[1]) to be taken according to a hidden mystery, not according to the outwards appearances: just as Jacob said that he was Esau, the firstborn of Isaac; which according the outward appearance of the text was not true, yet by the spirit of prophecy which he used, he said the truth. For by that deed he prefigured and prophesied that the younger people, namely the Gentiles, would one day take the place of the firstborn, namely the Jewish people. For Pope Innocent III testifies that Jacob is excused of lying.[2]

To confirm the second part, wherein he teaches that one ought to lie for the sake of humility, such that when one is asked about the abstemiousness that he has, he may say that he does not have it, in chapter twenty-one of the aforementioned conference, he cites the following passages, in which Christ speaks thus: "Do not appear to men to fast, but to thy Father who is in secret" (Mt. 6, 18). And again He says: "Let not thy left hand know what thy right hand doth" (v. 3); and again concerning those who do their works in public, He says: "Amen I say to you, they have received their reward" (v. 2). To these we cannot reply other that what Blessed Augustine says in a certain homily: By these words, God did not forbid the deed but the intention. He forbade in fact the desire for vain glory, such that even if our works are done in public they ought not be done for the intention of being seen.[3] Still He did not forbid the manifestation itself of the good works: otherwise He would have contradicted Himself, Who elsewhere had said: "So let your light shine before men, that they may see your good works, and glorify your Father who is in heaven" (Mt. 5, 16). Hence he who has some virtue, when asked, admits that he has it, and gives thanks to God for this, gives his glory to God from Whom he receives: he does not act contrary to God's precept, "Let not thy left hand know what thy right hand doth" (Mt. 6, 3). And this is enough about this matter.

I do not know of anyone who specifically wrote against this error, besides Blessed Augustine alone, who wrote a work in which he disputes against every lie.[4]

Nevertheless I advise the reader not to count Cassian among the heretics by reason of this error: because as we taught in the first book of this work, it can happen that someone teaches a heresy, and not be reckoned as a heretic: because he would not defend it so pertinaciously that he would not be prepared to obey the Church teaching otherwise. Perhaps for this or some

---

[1] "And to this rule they apply all the instances of lying which are produced from the Old Books, and are found not reprehended, or cannot be reprehended: either they are approved on the score of a progress towards improvement and hope of better things, or in virtue of some hidden signification they are not altogether lies" (*On Lying*, c. 5, n. 7 (PL 40, 492)).

[2] Gregory IX, *Decretales*, bk. 4, tit. 19 (*De divortiis*), c. 8 (*Gaudemus*).

[3] "'That they may glorify your Father which is in Heaven'; that when a man who does good works is seen by men, he may have only the intention of the good work in his own conscience, but may have no intention of being known, save for the praise of God, for their advantage to whom he is thus made known." (*Sermons on the New Testament*, serm. 54, n. 3 (PL 38, 373)). "And hereby it is evident that He has said this, not to prevent us from acting rightly before men, but lest perchance we should act rightly before men for the purpose of being seen by them, i.e. should fix our eye on this, and make it the end of what we have set before us." (*On the Sermon on the Mount*, bk. 2, c. 1, n. 2 (PL 34, 1271)).

[4] *On Lying* (PL 40 517-548).

MENDICITAS

Mendicancy

There were not lacking those who calumniated mendicancy with long lasting outcries as the chief evil of the human race. For those who call people happy who have riches, also call miserable and unhappy those who so lack them, such that they are forced to beg on account of their want of necessaries. Accordingly, John Wycliffe, with the horde of his disciples, teaches that begging is not lawful: on which account he abhors mendicant monks, saying that they ought to live by manual labor, and not by begging. Luther revived this same error in our times, saying that begging is forbidden by law. Wherefore, since he himself was a monk of the Order of Hermits of Saint Augustine, and for this reason he begged (for that Order of monks is one of the four mendicant Orders), yet afterwards blinded by the devil, to whom he adheres, he rejected the monastic life, and condemned mendicancy, and so like a dog he returned to his vomit.[3]

Now since we are heedful, with God's assistance, of Franciscan mendicancy, which we vowed in our youth, we take pains to vindicate mendicancy. And because we fight for religion, we place our confidence in God that we will triumph over our enemies: because we will show from Holy Writ that such mendicancy is not forbidden, nay is praised and meritorious, to which the Apostles by Christ's institution needed to have recourse for their daily living. And although it is not so read or believed of Christ Himself that He sometimes begged, because some upright women who were listening to and accepting His teaching were ministering to Him from their own means without Him needing to beg, yet it does not follow from this that mendicancy it not licit for sustentation of life. For there are many things which it is certain that Christ did not do, which nevertheless are licit to men, so that they may provide the necessities for their lives therefrom. For did Christ sew shoes, or make baskets from withes, or smooth wood, or polish stones? By no means! Let it be assumed that Christ never begged, yet it does not follow from this that it is not allowed for others to beg for sustentation of life.

But now let us show mendicancy from the Gospels. When Christ was sending His disciples to preach, He commanded an absence and want of all things necessary for life, so that casting away all things, and casting their care upon the Lord alone,[4] they would believe that they would be taken care of by Him. "Do not possess," He says, "gold, nor silver, nor money in your purses" (Mt. 10, 9). Notice that money is interdicted. Yet because money has been excluded, they could bring something with them for the journey; lest they do this, He immediately added, saying: "Nor scrip for your journey, nor two coats, nor shoes, nor a staff; for the workman is worthy of his meat" (v. 10). Now lest someone suppose that the Apostles were then given over to chance, He shows them whence they would have food, saying: "The labourer is worthy of his hire" (Lk. 10, 7). Or as another Evangelist says: "The workman is worthy of his meat" (Mt. 10, 10). By which words He pointed out to them that those to whom the Apostles preached were obliged to give them food. Paul in the First Epistle to the

---

[1] I.e. "... it contains some erroneous doctrines" ("John Cassian," *Catholic Encyclopedia* (1908 ed.), vol. 3, p. 404).
[2] *Concordia discordantium canonum*, dist. 15 (PL 187, 78A).
[3] Cf. Prov. 26:11; II Pet. 2, 22.
[4] Cf. Ps. 54, 23 (as worded in the *Vetus Italica*).

Corinthians teaches this more explicitly, saying the following: "Who serveth as a soldier at any time, at his own charges? Who planteth a vineyard, and eateth not of the fruit thereof? Who feedeth the flock, and eateth not of the milk of the flock?... If we have sown unto you spiritual things, is it a great matter if we reap your carnal things?" (9, 7 & 11). Notice that the Apostles were stripped of all possessions, who from the labor of their preaching were due to earn their living.

But let us suppose that the hearers were so ungrateful and merciless that none of them would have given food to the Apostles, and none of them would have invited the Apostles to their home, for this possibility could happen, since it is evident that Christ on Palm Sunday, even after He had preached to the inhabitants of Jerusalem, was not invited by anyone of that city, but returned to Bethania, so that He might eat there; hence all the more it could happen to the Apostles. What then were the Apostles to do? Were they obliged to suffer death? By no means, since they could avoid it by making known to others their poverty. Thus, if they could reveal to others their poverty, then they could beg, because I call this beggary [or mendicancy]. For so Augustine defines mendicancy. "But what is it to beg, save living on the mercy of men, as they (i.e. the Jews) live beneath the kings of those nations into which they have been carried away?"[1] Augustine says these words when expounding the verse of the Psalms: "Let his children be carried about vagabonds, and beg" (108, 10).

But if the heretics say that that request of the Apostles at that time ought not to be called mendicancy since at that time the Apostles were asking for what was due to them by right, Ambrose contradicts them, who in his small book, *De vinea Naboth*, says the following: "We have heard the voice of the rich man asking for another's property; let us hear the voice of the poor man begging for his own. 'May God not permit,' he says, 'that I give thee the inheritance of my fathers.'"[2] By which words he expressly says that Naboth begged for his own property. Hence if this is the case, it would be necessary that he who has been placed in extreme necessity and asks for alms, ought not to be said to beg, since he asks for that which is due to him by right. Thus, it was necessary for the Apostles to beg, since all money had been forbidden to them at that time by Christ. Hence, Theophylactus when expounding the passage of Luke: "In the same house, remain, eating and drinking such things as they have" (10, 7), says the following: "See then how He taught His disciples to beg, and wished them to receive their nourishment as a reward." These words of Theophylactus are according to the old translation, which Thomas [Aquinas] uses in the *Catena Aurea*.[3] For the translation which Oecolampadius recently published expresses this differently. And I suspect that Oecolampadius deliberately changed the words, because he also was infected with this same error, as he also denied that it is lawful to beg.[4]

Furthermore, so that one may truly be said to beg, it matters little whether he asks himself or through someone else, because however he asks, he will be said to beg, whether or not he asks himself or through someone else, or also for himself or for another. And if this is to beg, then it is clearly established that Paul the Apostle begged. For, as is evident from the First Epistle to the Corinthians, in the churches of Galatia collections were made each Sunday for the saints who were in Jerusalem. And in the Second Epistle to the Corinthians the Apostle likewise states that he made plans to make collections for the saints in the church of Macedonia, and testifies that he did the same in the churches of Corinth.

---

[1] *Expositions on the Book of Psalms*, Ps. 108, n. 18 (PL 37, 1439).

[2] *De Nabuthe Jezraelita*, c. 3, n. 13.

[3] *Catena Aurea*, in Lk. 10, lect. 3.

[4] The wording found in Migne's *Patrologia Graeca*, however, is: "See how He provides for the disciples against poverty, although they possess nothing" (PG 123, 835D).

Again, the Council of Vienne, which was celebrated under Clement V, decreed that the way of life of the Friars Minor by mendicancy was not merely lawful, but also meritorious.[1] Finally among the forty-five articles of John Wycliffe condemned at the Council of Constance in the eighth session, the twenty-fourth says the following: "Brothers are bound to acquire their food by the labor of hands and not by begging."[2] Regarding which article the council passes sentence by these words: "The first part," it says, "is scandalous and presumptuous inasmuch as it speaks in general terms and without distinctions; the second part is erroneous inasmuch as it asserts that begging is not permitted to friars."[3]

But it is necessary that we reply to the objections of the adversaries. For firstly they object to us that which is written in Deuteronomy: "There shall be no poor nor beggar among you" (15, 4). From which passage they conclude that it is not allowed for anyone to beg, since this (as they say) was forbidden by God. To this objection we reply that those words are not prohibitory, but promissory. For God there promises this to those keeping His Law, so that if, namely the Jews, had kept the Law which God gave to them through Moses, none among them would be poor or a beggar. And because the Jews transgressed the Law, for that reason God did not deal with them according to His promise. Since God promised the Jews, as carnal men, only temporal goods as a reward for keeping the Law, as it was said: "If you will hearken to me, you shall eat the good things of the land" (Is. 1, 19). So likewise, it is a promise when He says: "There shall be no poor nor beggar among you." For if those words were prohibitory, then Elias begging from the widow,[4] and Lazarus full of wounds, sinned, whose mendicancy was praised in the Gospel.[5]

Thomas Netter replies to the aforesaid objection in this way.[6] Yet it can be replied otherwise, and, in my opinion, much better and in greater conformity to Holy Writ. I acknowledge that those words of Deuteronomy express a prohibition: yet that prohibition was not given to the poor, and God was not then speaking with the poor: but rather God was speaking to the rich about assisting the poor (as it can be easily inferred from the context of the passage), commanding them that they would have such care of the poor, that they would not allow them to beg on account of poverty. Now the words which follow clearly indicate this. "There will not be wanting," He says, "poor in the land of thy habitation: therefore I command thee to open thy hand to thy needy and poor brother, that liveth in the land" (Deut. 15, 11).

Secondly, they object the passage from the Psalms saying: "I have not seen the just forsaken, nor his seed seeking bread" (36, 25). From which passage they wish to conclude that those men are not just who seek bread through begging. To which objection we reply according to the teaching of Augustine,[7] that those words ought not to be understood of corporal bread which it is evident was sought by many just men, because (so that I may pass over others) Da-

---

[1] "Moreover since the rule itself expressly contains that the friars may appropriate nothing to themselves neither house nor place nor any thing, and [thus] has it been declared by the same predecessor, Pope Gregory IX, and by not a few others, that this ought to be observed not only individually but also in common, which so strict an abdication insensate cleverness has distorted with livid detractions, lest the clarity of the perfection of the same friars wound with unskillful sermons of such ones, We say that the abdication of this kind of property over all things not only individually but also in common is in the sight of God meritorious and holy." (Confirmation of the Rule of the Friars Minor in 1279 by Pope Nicholas III, *Exiit qui seminat*, n. 7).

[2] Dz. 604

[3] Mansi, *Sacrorum Conciliorum* (Venice, Zatta, 1784), vol. 27, p. 633.

[4] Cf. III Kings 17, 10.

[5] Cf. Lk. 16, 23 & 25.

[6] *Doctrinale antiquitatum fidei Ecclesiae Catholicae*, vol. 1, bk. 4, c. 7.

[7] *Enarrationes in Psalmos*, sermo 2, *Habitus Die Dominico*, n. 14-15 (PL 36, 315-317).

vid sought the loaves of proposition from the priest. But those words ought to be understood of the spiritual bread of God's word, which bread God never denied to the just, nor did He so forsake any just man that he would suffer a famine of God's word. Yet as to corporeal bread, or also other corporeal things, God very often forsakes the just, so that through suchlike afflictions they may be more able to attain God's kingdom.

Thomas Netter wrote against this heresy in the first volume of his *Doctrinale antiquitatum fidei*, in the fourth book.

MERITUM

Merit

Among the other errors of Luther there is this one whereby he says that there is no merit of man for attaining glory. For he attributes so much to grace, that he leaves no place for free will. Hence since (as he says[1]) all depends on God's grace and free will can nowise cooperate, he says that a work of man cannot be called merit, especially since our works in relation to eternal glory are found to be insignificant. If Luther understands merit to mean that for such a work which of its nature and of itself is equal to the reward, certainly his opinion would not be branded as an error, because there is no such work of ours which of itself can be equated to eternal glory. For the Apostles says: "The sufferings of this time are not worthy to be compared with the glory to come, that shall be revealed in us" (Rom. 8, 18). But merit is not always so understood that it signifies such equality and natural obligation, but some equality which does not arise from the nature of things, but from a sort of agreement: which agreement having been entered upon, the work will be equal which previously would not have been said to be equal: and it will be called a debt, which otherwise would not be so called. Take for example, if in a tournament which perhaps lasts for no longer than the space of an hour, the king promises to anyone swinging his spear the most when two men meet, a gem or some precious jewel worth six thousand gold coins; then if Peter or John has done this better than then others, it will be said without a doubt that he has merited the gem, and that the king owes it to him. Now this debt is not from the nature of the deed, that the gem is due to him, but it proceeds from the agreement of the king, and his free promise, who by promising to give, obliged himself.

So also, even if our works may be of themselves unworthy of glory, and we could have no right by them to eternal glory, and glory was never owed to us; still because the merciful God promised to one keeping His Commandments that he would give him eternal life, after that promise God is indebted to give glory to the one keeping His Commandments. Which debt does not arise in God from our works, but from His beneficent will, Who by promising us, willed to oblige Himself. And according to this way of understanding the meaning of merit, it is evident that we take away nothing from the Divine majesty, when we say that our works are meritorious of eternal life, because in this way we do not say that God is obliged, or He is a debtor to our works, but we say that He is obliged from His promise, and is a debtor to His promise.

Now that He has promised, ought to be simply and absolutely attributed to grace. It is a heresy to deny merit in this way, because Holy Writ very often shows this meaning of merit.

---

[1] "Furthermore, we are certain and secure that we please God, not by reason of the merit of our works, but by reason of His mercy promised to us; so that, if we have done too little, or badly, He does not impute it to us, but paternally pardons and free us from our faults. This is the glorying of all the saints in their God." (*De servo arbitrio*, WA 18, 783, lns. 36-39).

For the wise Ecclesiasticus says: "All mercy shall make a place for every man according to the merit of his works" (16, 15). Notice that you see there the word "merit" adequately described. Why then is Luther abhorring the word "merit" so much which Ecclesiasticus is not afraid to mention? Furthermore, Christ's parable of the householder sending the laborers into his vineyard denotes nothing else, when he made an agreement of a penny a day, but when the labor was finished, the householder said to his overseer: "Call the labourers and pay them their hire" (Mt. 20, 8), namely that which the householder had promised the laborers when he sent them to the work. Which the householder expressed more clearly when he said to the one murmuring in that he was not given a greater reward than a penny: "Didst thou not agree with me for a penny? Take what is thine, and go thy way" (v. 13-14). He said, "thine," by which word he shows that such a penny was owed to him. But whence was it owed? Certainly from the agreement. Again in Mark's Gospel Christ speaks to His disciples in this manner: "Whosoever shall give you to drink a cup of water in my name, because you belong to Christ: amen I say to you, he shall not lose his reward" (9, 40). And Paul the Apostle in the First Epistle to the Corinthians says the following: "And every man shall receive his own reward, according to his own labour" (3, 8). If there were no merit, a reward would not be distributed according to the amount of labor, but according to the will of the one giving. And in the Epistle to the Hebrews he expresses the word "merit" more clearly, saying: "And do not forget to do good, and to impart; for by such sacrifices God's favour is obtained [*promeretur*]" (13, 16). And the Wise Man when speaking about the just says: "God hath tried them, and found them worthy of himself" (Wis. 3, 5). And Paul when writing to the Thessalonians about the tribulations which they were undergoing, says: "Which you endure, for an example of the just judgment of God, that you may be counted worthy of the kingdom of God, for which also you suffer" (II Thess. 1, 4-5).

But if you say that Paul does not assert that we are worthy of ourselves, but that God made us worthy; I also think this same thing, because we are not sufficient of ourselves to deserve glory, but that we may merit it is by God's grace which both precedes us and accompanies us as we go. Hence God, by the grace which He gives us, makes us worthy of Him. Thus, Luther was unable to deny this, that the just man is really worthy of God, although He becomes worthy by God Himself. But if He is worthy, then he has some sort of merit.

I omit here the testimonies of the holy Doctors, who all attribute merit to man by the help of God's grace. For he who is destitute of God's grace certainly cannot merit anything which pertains to eternal life. We will say still many more things about this heresy in the section on "Works," in the fourth heresy.

There is a **second heresy** completely opposite to the this one just related, because it says that man without the help of God's grace can merit eternal life by his own strength. The author of this heresy was Pelagius. But it is not necessary to dispute about this heresy at present, because we discussed it sufficiently (as I think) above in the section on "Grace," in the first heresy.

MIRACULUM

Miracles

Guy the Carmelite, when discussing the errors of the Waldensians, says that they think that "no true miracles occur in the Church."[1] But Aeneas Sylvius when enumerating the errors of the Waldensians never mentions this error.[2] And if they so thought, as Guy accuses them, one will be allowed to very clearly conclude how great was their madness and their ignorance of Holy Writ, since there are so many testimonies of Sacred Scripture for the confirmation of miracles. But the Waldensians were uneducated and completely ignorant: wherefore it is likely that they did not know what a miracle is. Hence it is firstly necessary to define a miracle, before we dispute about it.

A miracle is an unusual occurrence effected above the power of nature. Hence two things must be involved so that something can be called a miracle, namely that it be above the power of nature, such that it is not a common occurrence. And if either of these are lacking, it will nowise be called a miracle. Hence for this reason the creation of a human soul ought not to be reckoned a miracle, because even though its creation exceeds the power of nature, still it is not an unusual occurrence, since God daily creates new souls. For the same reason if one man were to be born with seven fingers on either hand, it will not be called a miracle, because even though it is unusual, still it does not exceed the power of nature, because this can proceed from natural causes. Yet if something is unusual and exceeding natural powers, it rightly will be called a miracle. Now it is irksome to enumerate how many true miracles of this kind there were, because both Testaments are full of miracles.

From the Old Testament it is sufficient to recall to mind the miracles which God worked in Egypt when He led out the children of Israel from thence. And perhaps the Waldensians were among those about whom the [Royal] Prophet said: "And they forgot his benefits, and his wonders that he had shewn them. Wonderful things did he do in the sight of their fathers, in the land of Egypt, in the field of Tanis" (Ps. 77, 11-12). But if you contend by asserting that they were marvelous events, but not miracles, although from the definition of a miracle given you may be refuted, still I want Scripture itself to refute this. When Moses said to the people of Israel by God's command, how on the following night every firstborn both of animals and of men were going to die, he immediately added these words: "But with all the children of Israel there shall not a dog make the least noise, from man even to beast: that you may know how wonderful a difference the Lord maketh between the Egyptians and Israel" (Ex. 11, 7). And in the book of Numbers when Scripture says that the earth swallowed up Core, many others dying, when the fire burned two hundred and fifty men, says the following: "And there was a great miracle wrought, that when Core perished, his sons did not perish" (Num. 26, 10-11).

If they want us to cite from the New Testament, there also sentence will be passed in our favor. For there you will find the blind restored to sight, the lame walking, paralytics healed, among whom there was one who had been infirm for thirty-eight years,[3] many lepers cleansed, the dead raised up, and innumerable other miracles, which nowise could happen by the power of nature. Who then will be so temerarious that he would dare deny that those things truly happened and that they were true miracles? But if the Waldensians restrict their assertion to

---

[1] *Summa de haeresibus et earum confutationibus*, f. 86r-v, c. 15.
[2] *De origine Bohemorum*, c. 35.
[3] Cf. Jn. 5, 5.

miracles which are said to have been done by the saints, their assertion will still deserve to be called heresy. For the Apostolic history says of Peter, that at the voice of Peter the feet of a lame man asking for alms before the gate of the Temple were strengthened[1]: and another man, Eneas, was healed, who was a paralytic keeping to his bed for eight years.[2] And the Apostolic history relates very many other miracles, which they could not deny were miracles.

But there are not lacking other hidden (as I suppose) Waldensians, who deride the miracles performed by the saints, saying that they are done by God alone, because (as the [Royal] Prophet says) "Who alone doth great wonders" (Ps. 135, 4). Wherefore they grieve when they hear others saying that such a holy man, or holy woman, performed a miracle, because they say that those things are done by God, and ought to be nowise attributed to men. I certainly admit that all those miracles are done by God, but the merits of the saints are the reason why God did them: for the exaltation of whom God wishes to work miracles. And because God does this on account of the merits of the saints, they are said to have been done by the saints. And this manner of speech is not foreign to Holy Writ. For the Teacher of truth Himself says in John's Gospel: "Amen, amen I say to you, he that believeth in me, the works that I do, he also shall do; and greater than these shall he do" (14, 12). Notice that He did not say, "I will do greater than these on account of his merits," but He said, "He also shall do, and greater than these." And in Mark's Gospel He again says: "These signs shall follow them that believe: In my name they shall cast out devils" etc. (16, 17). Therefore let the mockers of miracles go away, and let them not want to make melodramas[3] against those who say that miracles happen by the saints, since the Lord says about anyone believing in Him, that he will do those things which He did, and still greater things.

MISSA

Mass

Among the many proofs of God's benevolence towards us which He left in the world, the chief is the most excellent of all the Sacraments, which on account of the abundant and overflowing grace which is conferred in It, is called the Eucharist. And just as It is the most excellent, so it was necessary for confecting It that a more eminent rite of religion would be instituted, so that from the exterior rite the hearts of all those present might be drawn to show greater reverence towards that Sacrament. For when men see the preparation of the priest, the ceremonies which precede and follow the consecration of this Sacrament, they are greatly moved to revere it more. Hence, we call the consecration of this ineffable Sacrament, with the ceremonies pertaining to it, the Mass. Therefore, it is not surprising if those who despise this same Sacrament, disparage the consecration of this Sacrament, saying that the Mass was not instituted by Christ, but it was introduced by the human inventions of the Church. The first teacher of this pestiferous assertion was John Wycliffe, who said that it was not based upon the Gospel that Christ composed the Mass. If John Wycliffe here takes the word "Mass" such that the entire order of the ceremonies which precede and follow the consecration of the Eucharist, for instance that the Introit is said first, then the *Kyrie eleison* is said three times, and the *Christe eleison* three times etc., by taking the word Mass in this way, I do not think that his assertion ought to be considered heresy: because it is certain that Christ did not institute all those things; the Apostles instituted part of them, the other parts the

---

[1] Cf. Acts 3, 6-7.
[2] Cf. Acts 9, 33-34.
[3] This was a favorite phrase of Erasmus.

Church instituted with the passage of time. For the Angelic hymn, namely the *Gloria in excelsis Deo*, [Pseudo-] Pope and martyr Telesphorus ordered that it be sung in the Mass before the offering of the sacrifice.[1] And Pope Gregory I instituted that at the beginning of the Mass the antiphon, which is commonly called the Introit, be sung.[2] He also instituted that after the Introit the *Kyrie eleison*, *Christe eleison* be sung. And in this way the other [prayers] were added by other [popes] through the course of time.

But if the word "Mass" is understood as it ought, namely so that it signifies only those things which are the essential elements, namely the consecration of the Eucharist under both species, its offering to God in Christ's memory, and the receiving of the same offering: by understanding the Mass in this way, it is certain that Christ instituted the Mass, and consequently, it is certain that the assertion of John Wycliffe is rightly branded as heresy. For Christ at the Last Supper, after He had given His Body to His disciples to be eaten under the appearances of bread, said: "Do this for a commemoration of me" (Lk. 22, 19). By which words He commanded the disciples that what He Himself did, they would do for a commemoration of Him. Christ "blessed," that is, He consecrated, because by that blessing Christ consecrated: and so the consecration of the Eucharist is called by the ancient Doctors of the Church, especially by the Greeks, "the mystical blessing." For so Gregory Nazianzen calls it.[3] It is very often called by the same name by Cyril [of Alexandria].[4] It is also so called in the letter which the Council of Ephesus sent to the heretic Nestorius.[5] From this source originates that the priest before he says the words of consecration, blesses the bread, so that he may imitate Christ, Who before He gave it to the disciples, He blessed it.

But even though it is not read in the Gospel that any other ceremony was instituted by Christ for this Sacrament, still those ceremonies which the Catholic Church uses ought not to be despised, especially since we read that a good part of them were instituted by the Apostles. For Hugh of Saint Victor in his book, *Sacraments of the Christian Faith*,[6] and Isidore [of Seville] in his *De ecclesiasticis officiis*,[7] and Remigius [of Auxerre] in his book, *De officio missae*,[8] testify that the order of prayers, whereby the sacrifices offered to God are consecrated,

---

[1] The *Liber Pontificalis* says that Telesphorus "ordered that... on the Birth of the Lord Masses should be said at night... and that the Angelic hymn, that is, the *Gloria in excelsis Deo*, be said before the sacrifice." (Ed. Duchesne, vol. 1, p. 129). "None of the statements in the *Liber pontificalis* and other authorities of a later date as to liturgical and other decisions of this pope are genuine" ("Pope St. Telesphorus," *Catholic Encyclopedia*, vol. 14, p. 477).

[2] "Thus [Pope] Caelestine [I (422-432)] instituted that Psalms be sung at the Introit of the Mass. From which Pope Gregory [I] afterwards composed by setting to music the antiphons for the Introit" (Honorius of Autun, *Gemma animae*, bk. 1, c. 87 (PL 172, 572C)).

[3] This phrase, "mystical blessing," was not found among St. Gregory Nazianzen's works in Migne's Greek Patrology. He does, however, refer to essential notion of consecration when he said, "... the mystical (or Sacramental) table to which you have approached, the Bread of Which you have partaken, the Cup in Which you have communicated, being consecrated by the Sufferings of Christ" (*Oratio* 40, c. 31 (PG 36, 403A)).

[4] "Except ye eat the Flesh of the Son of Man and drink His Blood, ye have no life in you. For wholly destitute of all share and taste of that life which is in sanctification and bliss, do they abide who do not through the mystical blessing [*mysticam eulogiam*] receive Jesus." (*Commentary on John*, bk. 4, c. 2 (PG 73, 578B)).

[5] "... we celebrate the unbloody sacrifice in the churches, and we thus approach the mystical blessings and are made holy, becoming partakers of the holy Flesh and of the precious Blood of Christ, the Saviour of us all." (Letter 17 of Cyril of Alexandria (PG 77, 114C)).

[6] PL. 176, 472A. It was written in 1133 A.D.

[7] Bk. 1, c. 15 n. 1 (PL 83, 752). It was written in 610 A.D.

[8] C. 40, *De celebratione missae et eius significatione*, of the tract of PseudoAlcuin's *Liber de divinis*

was instituted by Saint Peter, whom they relate celebrated the first Mass in Antioch, in which only three prayers are recited from the first beginning of the faith, and at that time the priest began from the place where it is said: *Hanc igitur oblationem* etc.[1] But the other prayers were added with the passage of time. All the holy Doctors who made mention of the Mass testify that the Mass, both portrayed and shown in the Gospel, was instituted by Christ according to the meaning of this word. I will cite some more ancient ones, so that it may be evident therefrom that the Catholic Church always believed and taught this.

Rabanus when speaking about the institution of the Mass says these words: "Our Lord Jesus Christ instituted this manner of sacrifice when He entrusted His Body and Blood to the Apostles before He was betrayed, as it is read in the Gospel. 'He took,' it says, 'broke, and gave to them, and said: Take ye. This is my body. And having taken the chalice, giving thanks, he gave it to them. And they all drank of it' (Mk. 14, 22-23). For with blessing and thanksgiving the Lord firstly dedicated the Sacraments of His Body and Blood, and gave them to the Apostles: which the Apostles thenceforth did in imitation, and which they taught their successors to do, and [which practice] now the all the Church throughout the whole world universally maintains."[2] Isidore [of Seville], slightly more ancient than this man, when discussing the Mass, says: "Now the order of Mass, and of the prayers, whereby the sacrifice offered to God is consecrated, was firstly instituted by Saint Peter, the celebration of which the whole world uses, in one and the same manner."[3] In which words the only thing that ought to be noticed it that he says that the order of prayers which are said at the consecration and in the offering of the Eucharist were instituted by Blessed Peter. For he says that the consecration itself of Christ's Body and Blood, which is the real Mass, were instituted by Christ, as he himself testifies elsewhere in the work which we will cite for the assailing of the next heresy.

Ambrose in the [Ambrosian rite of] Mass for Holy Thursday in the *Communicantes* of the Mass, says these words: "And what can we not hope for from Thy mercy, who have received so great an office that we are entitled to offer such a Victim to Thee, namely the Body and Blood of Our Lord Jesus Christ, Who delivered Himself to that benevolent and venerable Passion for the redemption of the world: Who when instituting the form of the perpetual sacrifice of salvation, firstly offered Himself as the Victim, and firstly taught that it should be offered?"[4] In which words there are many things that ought to be noted. The first is that the Body and Blood of our Lord Jesus Christ is contained in the Eucharist: and this is against Berengarius, Oecolampadius, Carlstadt, Zwingli, and the rest of those denying that Christ's true Flesh and true Blood is contained in the Eucharist. The second thing to be noticed is that we offer the Victim, namely Christ's Body and Blood: and this testimony helps for conquering the upcoming heresy which denies that the Mass is a sacrifice. Thirdly, it ought to be noted that he says that Christ instituted the form of the perpetual sacrifice, and taught that it should be offered: and this is opposed to this heresy, about which we now are disputing, which denies that the Mass was instituted by Christ. For we call this oblation and this sacrifice the Mass.

[Pseudo-] Eusebius of Emesa when speaking about the Lord's Supper and the Passion, says these words: "And because He was going to remove His Body, which He had assumed, out of sight, and to convey it into Heaven, it was necessary that on the day of the Supper the Sacrament of His Body and Blood should be consecrated for us; that what was once offered as a ransom might be perpetually celebrated in a mystery; that, because our Redemption flows

---

officiis (PL 101, 1246C). But Dom Jean Mabillon, O.S.B. and others attribute this section of the tract to Remigius of Auxerre (*Acta sanctorum ordinis S. Benedicti*, vol. 5, p. 325).

[1] "[We] therefore [beseech Thee, O Lord, to graciously accept] this oblation…"

[2] *De clericorum institutione*, c. 32 (PL 107, 322A-B).

[3] Bk. 1, c. 15 n. 1 (PL 83, 752).

[4] Jacques de Pamèle, *Liturgica latinorum* (Cologne, G. Calenius, 1571), vol. 1, p. 340.

with a daily unwearied stream for the salvation of all, the Oblation of that redemption might be perpetuated; and that this lasting Sacrifice might always live in the memorial, and might ever be present by grace, that true, perfect and only Sacrifice, to be estimated by faith, not by appearance; to be valued not by the outward sense, but by inward affection."[1] In which words one ought to note all those things which we noted in Ambrose's words.

Chrysostom, in the Greek rite instituted by him, orders that the priest, when the Cherubic Hymn[2] is sung, say the following prayer: "No one bound by fleshly desires and pleasures is worthy to approach, or draw nigh, or to minister to Thee, O King of Glory, for to serve Thee is a great and fearful thing, even to the heavenly powers themselves. Nevertheless, through Thine unspeakable and infinite love to man, Thou hast in reality and in truth become man, and hast ordained Thyself our High Priest, and hast delivered to us the celebration of this sacramental and unbloody Sacrifice, as Lord of all."[3] In which words he says both that the Mass is an unbloody sacrifice and that the Lord delivered its consecration, which we call the Mass.

Cyprian, when teaching that the chalice ought not to be offered with wine alone, nor with water alone, says these words: "For if Jesus Christ, our Lord and God, is Himself the chief priest of God the Father, and has first offered Himself a sacrifice to the Father, and has commanded this to be done in commemoration of Himself, certainly that priest truly discharges the office of Christ, who imitates that which Christ did; and he then offers a true and full Sacrifice in the Church to God the Father, when he proceeds to offer it according to what he sees Christ Himself to have offered. But the discipline of all religion and truth is overturned, unless what is spiritually prescribed be faithfully observed... It behooved Christ to offer about the evening of the day, that the very hour of sacrifice might show the setting and the evening of the world; as it is written in Exodus, 'The whole multitude of the children of Israel shall sacrifice it in the evening' (Ex. 12, 6). And again, in the Psalms, 'The lifting up of my hands, as evening sacrifice' (140, 2). But we celebrate the Resurrection of the Lord in the morning. And because we make mention of His Passion in all Sacrifices (for the Lord's Passion is the sacrifice which we offer), we ought to do nothing else than what He did."[4] These are the words of the very holy and very learned martyr Cyprian. In which words he says, "the Lord's Passion is the sacrifice which we offer": and he often says that God commanded that we offer this sacrifice to Him. And because this very sacrifice is called the Mass, it is thence proved that this Mass was instituted by God's precept.

[Pseudo-] Pope Alexander I, who is counted from Blessed Peter as the sixth supreme pontiff says these words: "In the sacramental oblations which in Mass are offered to the Lord, only bread, and wine mixed with water, are to be offered in sacrifice. For they ought not (as we have received from the Fathers and reason itself teaches) to offer either only wine or only water in the Lord's chalice, but both mixed together: because it is read that both flowed from His side during the Passion. Truth Itself certainly instructs that the chalice and the bread be offered, when He says: 'Jesus took bread, and blessed, and broke: and gave to His disciples,' and said: 'Take ye, and eat. This is My Body, which shall be delivered for you. In like manner, after he had supped, He takes the chalice and gave it to His disciples, saying: Take and drink from it all of you: because this is the chalice of my Blood, which shall be shed for you unto remission of sins.'"[5] These are the words of [Pseudo-] Pope Alexander, a true martyr of

---

[1] Fifth homily on Easter. *Maxima Bibliotheca veterum Patrum*, vol. 6, p. 636. This sermon is also attributed to St. Caesarius of Arles (PL 67, 1052C).

[2] Also called the *Cherubikon* or Cherubim chant.

[3] PG 63, 912.

[4] Epistle 63 (to Caecilius), c. 14-17 (PL 4, 385B-386C).

[5] *The False Decretals of the Pseudo-Isidore*, epistle 1 of Pope Alexander I (PL 130, 93C-D). This epistle is "suspect" (PG 5, 1058, footnote 7). Cf. Mt. 26, 26-28; I Cor. 11, 24-25.

Christ. In which words one ought to note among other things that he says that in the Mass sacrifice is offered, and this is done not from a human or popish statute, as the modern heretics say, but by Divine institution.

[Pseudo-] Martial, one of the seventy[-two] disciples of the Lord, the inseparable companion of Peter the Apostle,[1] in a letter to the inhabitants of Bordeaux, in the third chapter, says these words: "That which the Jews through envy did sacrifice, thinking thereby to blot out His name upon earth: that same do we for our salvation offer upon a sanctified altar, knowing well that by this only remedy life is given unto us, and death is put to flight."[2] These are the words of [Pseudo-] holy Martial. In which words one ought to specially notice that he says that we offer by the Lord's precept the same Body which the Jews killed through envy. Thus, the Mass is not from a human tradition, as the heretics lie, but from the Divine precept as all these men testify.

There are still other testimonies of holy and very ancient men, who even though they do not say that the Mass was instituted by Christ, still when mentioning the Mass, they call it by the name of "Mass," and they say that in it the Sacrifice of the Lord's Body and Blood is offered to God, which nowise could a priest do without God's command and authority. [Pseudo-] Pope and martyr Telesphorus, in the letter which he wrote to all the faithful of Christ, when speaking about the celebration of Mass, says these words: "Mass nowise ought to be celebrated before the third hour of the day: because also at that same hour the Lord was crucified and, it is read, the Holy Ghost descended upon the Apostles. Now the Angelic hymn [the *Gloria in excelsis Deo*] ought to be sung at Mass in [its proper] time and place and solemnly recited. For these bishops who confect the Lord's Body with their mouth, ought to be heard, obeyed and respected by all."[3] Notice that you hear the word "Mass" written more than a thousand four hundred years ago, which these heretics say ought to be abolished as being of recent origin.

But so that I may more clearly convict these heretics of their shameless lie, I wish to cite other more ancient witnesses. [Pseudo-] Pope Clement I, and disciple of Peter the Apostle, in his third letter commands priests and other clerics not to do anything without the permission of their own bishop, and not to celebrate Mass without his authorization. And shortly afterwards he adds, "It is not permitted to offer and celebrate Mass in other places without the permission of the bishop of those places."[4] [Pseudo-] Abdias of Babylon, consecrated a bishop by the Apostles, who testifies that he saw Christ in the flesh, in his Apostolic history, wherein when recounting the deeds of Matthew the Apostle and Evangelist, after he had said that Matthew prayed publicly to God, for Iphigenia, daughter of Aeglippus, king of the Ethiopians, whom Hirtacus the successor of the kingdom wished to marry, even though she had vowed her virginity to God, he relates these words which follow. "When they had answered, 'Amen,' and the Mysteries of the Lord had been celebrated, and the whole Christian assembly

---

[1] St. Martial was the Bishop of Limoges in the third century. "A *Life of St. Martial* attributed to Bishop Aurelian, his successor, in reality the work of an eleventh-century forger, is now regarded as spurious; but from the account it gives has arisen the popular belief that St. Martial was sent to Gaul by St. Peter himself, that he had been one of the seventy-two disciples chosen as missionaries by Our Lord etc." ("St. Martial," *Catholic Encyclopedia* (New York: Robert Appleton Company, 1910), vol. 9, pp. 721-722).

[2] *Sacrae Bibliothecae Veterum Patrum seu Scriptorum Ecclesiasticorum* (Paris, Compagnie du la Grand Navire, 1610), vol. 3, epistle 1, c. 4, p. 47B. "Two Epistles inserted in the *Bibliotheca Patrum* are attributed to St. Martial, but they are apocryphal" ("St. Martial," *Catholic Encyclopedia* (1910 ed.), vol. 9, p. 722).

[3] *False Decretals of the Pseudo-Isidore* (PL 130, 105D-106A).

[4] *The False Decretals of the Pseudo-Isidore*, letter 3 (130, 50C). This letter is "the work of Pseudo-Isidore" ("Pope St. Clement I," *Catholic Encyclopedia* (1908 ed.), vol. 4, p. 14).

had heard Mass, [Matthew] remained, so that next to the altar where he had confected the Sacrament of Christ's Body, there he would exult in Apostolic martyrdom. Therefore, not long afterward, the executioner sent by Hirtacus, stabbing from behind with one blow of the sword, made the Apostle, praying with his arms extended, Christ's martyr."[1] Notice that we find the word, "Mass," which is abhorred by today's heretics, held in veneration by Christ's disciples and Apostles. And hence it is also proved that the Mass is not something "papist," as heretics unjustly call it, but something instituted by Christ Himself.

Rightly, therefore, this kind of assertion of John Wycliffe was condemned as heretical. For among the forty-five articles of John Wycliffe condemned in the Council of Constance, the fifth article says the following: "It is not established in the Gospel that Christ arranged the Mass."[2] Which assertion, along with all the others, was condemned *lata sententia*. Thomas Netter copiously disputes against this heresy in his book, *De sacramentalibus*.[3]

The **second heresy** is much more pestilential: because it not only denies that the Mass was instituted by Christ, but it moreover denies that the Mass is a sacrifice, nay what is much worse, it denies that the Mass is a good work. The first author and public defender of this heresy is Martin Luther, and no one else among those who acknowledge that Christ's true Body and true Blood are contained in the Eucharist has ever dared until now to openly disparage the Mass, and openly deny that it is a sacrifice. Albeit Erasmus of Rotterdam, who wrote before Luther, to speak frankly, gave me no little suspicion that he held this most pestilential opinion. For in his *Annotations* on the thirteenth chapter of the Acts of the Apostles, where in the Vulgate translation is found, "And as they were ministering to the Lord" etc. (v. 2), he annotates that ["ministering"] ought to be changed to "sacrificing": because in the Greek is found, λειτουργούντων, which he says "is characteristic of those working with holy things": and afterwards he adds these words, "Now no sacrifice is more pleasing to God than to communicate the Evangelical teaching."[4] From which words it is proved that he either denies that the Mass is a sacrifice, or he says that it is not as pleasing to God as to communicate Evangelical teaching. But putting Erasmus aside, because he has not of yet clearly stated his opinion on this matter, we say that the first author of this wicked heresy was Martin Luther, who hounded the Mass with so much hatred that he was not ashamed to write a book against it, which he entitled, *De abroganda missa [privata]*.[5] These are Luther's words in this book, *De abroganda missa*: "The Mass, which they call a sacrifice, is the highest idolatry and wickedness... nay, the custom of calling the Mass a sacrifice and of using the title of priest is to deny Christ."[6] And in his book, *The Babylonian Captivity of the Church*, he says: "It is a most wicked abuse, established in the Church, that the Mass is a good work and a sacrifice."[7] And again in the same book: "The Mass is the very height of perversity."[8] These words of Luther are so blasphemous and so horrendous that I would not dare write them here, except that the very nature of the disputation compels me to faithfully cite the adversary's own words, so that the reader may thence know that I do not mendaciously attribute to Luther anything fabricated by me, but I merely cite what he himself stated in his own words. Yet on the other hand, he and all his other followers are accustomed to do this, who when they cite the opinions of

---

[1] *De historia certaminis Apostolici* (Cologne, Maternus Cholinus, 1569), bk. 7, p. 249.

[2] Dz. 585.

[3] *Doctrinale antiquitatum fidei ecclesiae catholicae* (Paris, Reginaldus, 1523), vol. 3, tit. 4, c. 28, fol. 69v-72r.

[4] *In Novum Testamentum annotationes* (Basel, Officina Probeniana, 1540), P. 302.

[5] WA 8, 411-476.

[6] WA 8, 417-418.

[7] WA 6, 512, lns. 7-9.

[8] WA 6, 564, lns. 4-5.

Catholics, they always mix in a thousand lies, and often attribute to Catholics things which never came into their minds.

All the heretics of the present time agree with this most wicked assertion, or at least those whom I have known by name, one of whom, held in greater esteem by them, I wish to cite. John Calvin, in his book, *The Institutes of Christian Religion*, wherein after he had said that the scholastic theologians teach that the Mass is a sacrifice, says these things which they say: "Let them begone with their thorny subtleties, which, however they may be defended by using sophisms, are to be repudiated by all good men, because, all they do is to enclose the brightness of the Supper in great darkness. Therefore, having commanded them to begone, let my readers understand that I am here combating that opinion with which the Roman Antichrist (Calvin and Luther, and all the heretics of this time call the pope by this name) and his prophets have imbued the whole world—viz. that the Mass is a work by which the priest who offers Christ, and the others who participate in the oblation, gain merit with God. And this is not merely the general opinion of the common people, but the very act has been so arranged so that as a kind of propitiation, it makes reparation to God by atonement for the living and the dead."[1]

The Wittenbergers assert completely the same thing in the book which they published for the confession of their faith, wherein when discussing the Sacrament of the Eucharist, and citing the Catholic view, say these things among others. "Another error is this, that the Eucharist is such a sacrifice, as ought to be offered daily in the Church, for the purging of the sins of the living and the dead, and for the obtaining of other benefits, both corporal and spiritual. This error is clearly opposed to the Gospel of Christ, which testifies that 'by one oblation Christ hath perfected forever them that are sanctified' (Heb. 10, 14). And because Christ, by His Passion and death, has purchased remission of sins for us, (which also is declared unto us by the Gospel in the New Testament), therefore it is not lawful to sacrifice any more for sin."[2] In which words they bring forth two heresies at the same time. One, whereby they deny that the Mass is a sacrifice: the other, whereby they deny that it can be offered for the sins of the living and the dead, or for other things, whether corporal or spiritual. About this second heresy we will say nothing in this chapter, but in the one immediately following.

On account of these and many other horrible and detestable things which Luther and his followers have dared to utter in contempt of the Mass, it seems to me that we can rightly say to Christ that which the Royal Prophet says: "They that hate thee have made their boasts, in the midst of thy solemnity" (Ps. 73, 4). For of all Christ's solemnities, which are celebrated on earth, the greatest is the celebration of the Mass, through which at the voice of the priest Christ's true Body descends from Heaven to earth hidden under the appearances of bread, and His Blood under the appearances of wine. But the Lutherans have hated Christ in the middle of this solemnity, they who despise so great a gift and take little account of so great a solemnity, and despising in this way, boast as though they have done something great. Hence it seems to me that Luther in this regard is very similar to Antioch Epiphanes, the king of Syria. For this Antioch, as the history of the Machabees relates, when he wished to completely take away the Law of the Jews, and to force them to use the rites of the Gentiles, among other things which he did unto this end, he forbade the sacrifices to be offered in the Temple according to the regulations of the Mosaic Law. Luther, however, in order to abrogate the whole of Christ's law, and to hand down the laws of the Pagans or Saracens, forbade the most excellent sacrifice of the Evangelical Law, when he abrogated the Mass, and denied that

---

[1] Bk. 4, c. 18, n. 1.

[2] The Wittenberg Confession, art. 19 (*Monumentorum ad historiam Concilii Tridentini*, vol. 4, p. 437-438).

it is a true sacrifice. It is necessary to fight in various ways against this heresy, so wicked and displeasing to God, so that we may clearly subdue it and force it to depart from the arena.

Firstly then, one ought to ask Luther whether for the era of the Evangelical Law some sacrifice was established by that same law, and distinctive to it. One ought not to say that there is no sacrifice distinctive to the Evangelical Law: because for the same reason it will be necessary to say that there is not distinctive priesthood of the same Law, and hence it will follow further that there is also no Evangelical Law. For there is such a close connection between the law and the priesthood, that one cannot be separated from the other. If Paul infers the translation of the law from the translation of the priesthood, in the same way it will be permitted to likewise infer the abolition of the law from the abolition of the priesthood and the sacrifice. Furthermore, in every law, whatsoever it was, there were always some sacrifices distinctive to that law. For in the law of nature, which was the same in all men, there were some sacrifices, as it evident from the life and actions of Job, who lived in the law of nature alone. For he, as his history relates, offered holocausts each day, lest perhaps his children should sin.[1] It is not necessary to dispute about the Mosaic Law, since it is clear that the whole of it abounds with sacrifices and oblations. It is also evident regarding the Gentiles, that they had different sacrifices according to the diversity of their idols, such that there never was a nation so barbaric which did not have some kind of sacrifice which it offered to God, that is to say, to him whom they thought was God. And this came about for no other reason but that it was put into all men by nature that everyone ought to worship God. Thus, much more in the Evangelical Law, in which we have a clearer knowledge of God, is it necessary that there be in it some distinctive sacrifice much more excellent than all the sacrifices of the other laws. Now we find no such sacrifice can be found unless the Mass be a sacrifice, in which Christ's true Body and His true Blood be offered to God. Therefore, the Mass is a sacrifice.

But let us leave off these and other similar arguments, although they are very strong, and lest the heretics call us sophists, as they are accustomed to do when they do not know how to respond to our arguments, we will fight against these heretics with testimonies of both Scripture and holy men, and also with definitions of the Councils. But lest we dispute in vain about the meaning of the word, as heretics are often accustomed to do, it is necessary to firstly establish the meaning of true sacrifice, so that according to it we may prove that the Mass is a true sacrifice. For the Wittenbergers seeing, as I think, some testimonies of holy men which clearly bear witness to the Mass being a sacrifice, they have recourse to saying that the Mass is a sacrifice in a wide and very broad meaning of this word. Their words, when they speak about the Sacrament of the Eucharist are these: "Moreover, seeing that the word, 'sacrifice,' is very large, and does generally signify a holy worship; we do willingly grant, that the true and lawful use of the Eucharist may in this sense be called a sacrifice."[2] And after these words they deny that the Mass is a true sacrifice, as is evident from those words which we have already cited above.

But because we say that the Mass is a true and proper sacrifice, which excels all other sacrifices, I think that it is necessary to firstly show the meaning of true sacrifice, so that our adversaries may understand the thing, in behalf of which we dispute against them, and so that they may not take refuge in the broad meaning of sacrifice. Augustine states what things are necessary so that something be a true sacrifice, speaking thus: "Four things are to be considered in every sacrifice: to whom it is offered, by whom it is offered, what is offered, for whom it is offered."[3] Among these four things, only the first is beyond all controversy, but the three last ones are controverted. For if someone would establish who is offering, what is

---

[1] Cf. Job 1, 5.

[2] The Wittenberg Confession, *Monumentorum ad historiam Concilii Tridentini*, vol. 4, p. 436.

[3] *On the Trinity*, bk. 4, c. 14, n. 19 (PL 42, 901).

offered, and for whom it is offered: it would be very clear that it is God alone to Whom the gift is offered. Of these three controverted things, only one will now be discussed, namely what is offered, since we will discuss for whom it is offered in the next heresy. Now who it is who offers, we will show in the section on the "Priesthood," in the first heresy: where we will prove by many testimonies that only a priest ordained by a bishop has the power of confecting and offering the Eucharist. Thus, it only remains that we examine about that which is offered.

What and what kind of thing ought to be offered, so that it can be called a true sacrifice, the same Augustine teaches, saying these words: "A true sacrifice is every work which is done so that we may be united to God in holy fellowship, and which has a reference to that Supreme Good and End in which alone we can be truly blessed. And therefore, even the mercy we show to men, if it is not shown for God's sake, is not a sacrifice. For, though made or offered by man, sacrifice is a Divine thing, as those who called it 'sacrifice' meant to indicate. Thus, man himself, consecrated in the name of God, and vowed to God, is a sacrifice in so far as he dies to the world that he may live to God."[1] From which words it is clearly gathered that every good work which is offered to God, is a true sacrifice. And Calvin himself accepts this definition of sacrifice, who in his *Institutes of Christian Religion* says these words: "Some, on what rational ground I see not, extend the term sacrifice to all sacred ceremonies and religious acts. We know that by the uniform use of Scripture, the name of 'sacrifice' is given to what the Greeks called at one time θυσια (*sacrifice*), at another προσφοπὰ (*offering*), at another τελετὴ (*ceremony*). This, in its general acceptation, includes everything whatever that is offered to God."[2] From whose words it is established that we and he agree on the definition of true sacrifice. And since Christ's sacred Body and His precious Blood are the best things, it is evidently gathered that the offering of those things is a true sacrifice, and whoever offers those things to God the Father, is said to have truly sacrificed. Thus, in order that we may clearly prove that the Mass is a true sacrifice, one needs to do nothing else except to prove that the priest celebrating Mass offers in it Christ's true Body and His true Blood to God.

Now I hope to do this easily, with God's help, by clear testimonies of Sacred Scripture, taken from both the Old and the New Testaments. The testimonies of the Old Testament are taken partly from figures of the Sacrament of the Eucharist, many of which preceded it, and partly from prophecies. From so many figures of the Eucharist, lest I give displeasure to the reader by excessive prolixity, I wish to cite and discuss only two, because these clearly prove that the offering of the Eucharist by the priest in the Church is done now. Which since it does not happen elsewhere than in the Mass, we may prove that the Mass is a sacrifice.

But perhaps the heretics wishing to break the force of the argument, which is to be made from figures, will say that one cannot take an argument from the mystical sense to prove some teaching, because Augustine clearly teaches this in his letter to the Donatist Vincentius. I certainly admit that a demonstrating argument cannot always be taken from the mystical sense to prove a teaching. Still if it can clearly establish from other passages of Scripture that mystical interpretation of Sacred Scripture is its true and genuine meaning, then an argument for proving some teaching can rightly be taken from the mystical sense. For to this end Augustine teaches the same thing in that same letter to the Donatist Vincentius, which is cited against us, wherein he says these words: "For what else is it than superlative impudence for one to interpret in his own favor any allegorical statements, unless he has also evident citations, by the light of which the obscure meaning of the former may be made manifest."[3] From which words it is sufficiently established that an argument can be taken from the mystical sense, when it can be established from elsewhere that such a mystical meaning very well befits that

---

[1] *The City of God*, bk. 10, c. 6 (PL 41, 283).
[2] Bk. 4, c. 18, n. 13.
[3] Letter 93, chap. 8, n. 24 (PL 33, 334).

passage, and is its true meaning. Which opinion of Augustine is very clearly proved from Paul's example, who in chapter four of the Epistle to the Galatians,[1] and in chapter nine of the First Epistle to the Corinthians,[2] used the passages of the Old Testament understood according to the mystical sense to prove a teaching.

Hence having once laid this most firm foundation, I wish to show, according to that which I had firstly proposed, that some very clear figures of the Most Holy Eucharist in the Old Testament preceded, from which it is evidently proved that the Mass, in which the Eucharist is consecrated and offered to God, is a most true sacrifice. That Melchisedech, the king of Salem, was a figure of Christ, the true and high Priest, and the priesthood of Melchisedech was a figure of the Evangelical Law, Paul clearly teaches in the Epistle to the Hebrews wherein among other things he says, those words of the Royal Prophet ought to be understood of Christ: "Thou art a priest forever, according to the order of Melchisedech" (7, 17).[3] Hence it is necessary that between the figure itself and the thing figured there be a true similitude, and that the shadow very well fit the body.

Let us see then what was in Melchisedech, and in his priesthood, that we are compelled to have similar things in Christ, and in His priesthood which He instituted for the Evangelical Law. Paul very well shows in the aforesaid epistle that the things which pertain to the person of Melchisedech, fit Christ. Hence it is necessary that we compare Melchisedech to Christ according to the order of the priesthood, so that we may see how according to this rank he was similar to Christ. Because unless in the rite itself of Melchisedech's priesthood something be found which was a figure of Christ's priesthood, it could not be truly said that Christ is a priest "according to the order of Melchisedech." Now concerning Melchisedech's priesthood and its rite, Scripture states nothing except that he offered bread and wine to God for the victory which Abraham had against the five kings. Thus, so that the body may correspond to the shadow, it is necessary that in the priesthood of the Evangelical Law some similar sacrificial offering be had, which agrees with bread and wine. But since no such corporal and visible sacrificial offering, which is offered to God, is had in the Evangelical Law, except the Most Holy Eucharist, in which under the appearances of bread hides Christ's Body, and under the appearances of wine His Blood, it is thence clearly proved that the Mass in which such a sacrificial offering is offered to God is a true sacrifice.

The heretics acknowledging the strength of this argumentation, and seeing that they are strongly pressed, sought some small cracks, though which they could escape its force. In fact, they firstly deny that Melchisedech was a figure of the priesthood of the Evangelical Law. They indeed acknowledge that he was a figure of Christ, because Paul teaches that so clearly that it could not be denied without impudence: nevertheless, they deny that Melchisedech was a figure of the Evangelical priesthood, because nothing (as they say) preceded in Melchisedech which could only fit the Evangelical priesthood. But this response of theirs is easily refuted by the testimony of Paul, who, wanting to prove that the priesthood of the Evangelical Law is much more noble and excellent than the priesthood of the Mosaic Law, proves this from the deed of Melchisedech regarding Abraham: because Melchisedech blessed Abraham in whose loins at that time was Levi, of whose tribe was the Aaronic priesthood. For "That which is less," Paul says, "is blessed by the better" (Heb. 7, 7). But if by Melchisedech only Christ is figured, and not the Evangelical priesthood, which after Christ's death perpetually remains in the Church, Paul's argumentation would have no strength: because by that is it only proved that Christ is better than Aaron. It is evident, however, that Paul in that passage is

---

[1] "For it is written that Abraham had two sons: the one by a bondwoman, and the other by a free woman" etc. (v. 22).

[2] "Thou shalt not muzzle the mouth of the ox that treadeth out the corn" etc. (v. 9).

[3] Cf. Ps. 109, 4.

not disputing about this point, but only about the nobility of the Evangelical priesthood, from which he strives to prove that the Levitical priesthood has ceased. Because the better priesthood having come, it was necessary that the less good priesthood would give way. And hence he concludes that the Mosaic Law had already ceased: because he considers it necessary that the priesthood having been translated, the translation of the Law would occur. Furthermore, many ancient holy and very learned Doctors bear witness that the priest Melchisedech was not merely a figure of Christ the priest, but also of the Evangelical priesthood.

[Pseudo-] Eucherius, Bishop of Lyons, who lived more than a thousand years ago, in his *Commenatarius in Genesim,* when explaining the deeds of the priest Melchisedech, says these words among others: "Now the fact that the great patriarch gave tithes to the priest Melchisedech after the blessing, spiritually shows that the priesthood amongst the Gentiles would be better than the Levitical priesthood in Israel which would be born of it, and the future priesthood of the Church being uncircumcised would bless in circumcised Abraham the priesthood of the synagogue."[1]

And before him, Augustine, after he said that Melchisedech blessed Abraham after the five kings were conquered by him, says these words which follow: "For then first appeared the sacrifice which is now offered to God by Christians in the whole wide world, and that is fulfilled which long after the event was said by the prophet to Christ, who was yet to come in the flesh, 'Thou art a priest forever, according to the order of Melchisedech,'—that is to say, not after the order of Aaron, for that order was to be taken away when the things shone forth which were intimated beforehand by these shadows."[2] Augustine not merely says that Melchisedech was a figure of the Evangelical priesthood, but he says that in him there was a figure of the sacrifice which is offered in the whole wide world. And lest a heretic could distort his words into another meaning, by saying that he spoke of some other sacrifice, he said that the sacrifice which is offered in the whole wide world is that sacrifice by which the prophecy is fulfilled which said, "Thou art a priest forever, according to the order of Melchisedech." Thus, Augustine says that the same sacrifice now offered in the whole wide world, is that which Christ the true Priest offered. But Christ, as Paul says, offered Himself: therefore, the Evangelical priests now offer the same Christ in the whole wide world.

Chrysostom, when interpreting the words of Paul: "The priesthood being translated, it is necessary that a translation also be made of the law" (Heb. 7, 12), says these words: "But if there must be another priest, or rather another priesthood, there must needs be also another law. This is for those who say, 'What need was there of a new Testament?' For he could indeed have alleged a testimony from prophecy also, namely: 'This is the covenant which I made with your fathers' etc. (Heb. 8, 9).[3] But for the present he contends on the ground of the priesthood. And observe, how he says this from the first. He said, 'According to the order of Melchisedech.' By this he excluded the order of Aaron. For he would not have said, 'According to the order of Melchisedech,' if that priesthood [of Aaron] had been better."[4]

Theodoret [of Cyrus] in his commentaries on Genesis says these words: "What was Melchisedech's ancestry? Since the Divinely inspired Paul says, 'Without father, without mother, without genealogy' (Heb. 7, 3), who could know the truth of this matter? He probably belonged to those nations that inhabited Palestine; for he was both their king and priest. Now he was a priest of the God of the universe. For [Paul] says, he was a 'priest of the most high God' (v. 1). Hence, the Patriarch Abraham offered him tithes of the spoils and, being a just man, and a friend of God, he received a blessing from him. For, [Melchisedech] was a figure

---

[1] Bk. 1; on chap. 14, v. 18 ff. (PL 50, 952B).
[2] *The City of God*, bk. 16, c. 22 (PL 41, 500).
[3] Cf. Jer. 31, 32.
[4] Hom. 13 (PG 63, 321).

of the Lord's priesthood."[1] These are the words of that Theodoret, Bishop of Cyrus. From all these testimonies it is sufficiently established that King Melchisedech was not merely a figure of Christ the true priest, but also of the Evangelical priesthood, which after Christ died, remains in the Church.

Thus, the Evangelical priest ought to offer something which is in some way similar to the bread and wine which Melchisedech offered. They respond differently to this argumentation of ours, as I hear; certain ones of these recent heretics, denying that Melchisedech was a priest, as we now use the word "priest': because they say that the word found in the Hebrew or Chaldaic language, not only means "priest," but also "ruler": and they say it ought to be understood according to the meaning of "ruler" in that passage of the book of Genesis, where Scripture treats of Melchisedech. But those who say this, want to cover one lie with another. What the Hebrew or Chaldaic word means, I frankly admit that I do not know, because I am completely ignorant of those languages: and I do not wish to speak a foreign language. I clearly understand, however, from the context that the Hebrew word was not used in that passage to mean "ruler," since he says, "For [Melchisedech] was [king of Salem,] priest of the most high God." For since he had just called him "king," he would have repeated the same thought for no reason when saying: "He was a priest of the most high God," that is to say, according to their interpretation, "ruler of the most high God": which words are completely superfluous, especially since they are so close to the other words, by which he had said that he was a king. Next, the very same Scripture relates that Melchisedech blessed Abraham, and Abraham offered him tithes. But to bless and to receive tithes, are not functions of rulers, but of priests. Therefore, Melchisedech was a true priest of God.

There are again other heretics who respond in another way to the argument which we put forth from the figure of Melchisedech the priest. For they deny that Melchisedech, according to the order of his priesthood, offered bread and wine to God: because this, as they say, Scripture does not relate: but they say that the only thing that it relates is that Melchisedech brought forth bread and wine to Abraham returning from his victory over the five kings. So teaches Zwingli, who revived the heresy of Berengarius among the Swiss with Oecolampadius, denying that Christ's true Body and His true Blood is contained in the Eucharist. Andreas Osiander, the prophet of Nuremberg, responds in the same way. Yet this assertion of theirs was not invented by them: because the Jews who preceded them by many centuries, wishing to disfigure and mutilate the Scriptures, which spoke figuratively of Christ, distorted this history of Melchisedech, as Nicholas of Lyra relates on that passage,[2] in the same way into a perverse meaning, just as we said these heretics think.

But that what they say is false, is very clearly proved from the context itself of the passage. For those four kings for whom Abraham fought, had carried with them the things which were needed for food, which Abraham and his servants made use of, as Abraham himself bears witness when saying to the king of Sodom, who offered him all the spoils besides the persons: "I will not take of any things that are thine... except such things as the young men have eaten" (Gen. 14, 23-24). Nor was it necessary that Melchisedech would offer food and drink to the fighters, who were returning from battle with such abundant spoils, bringing with them

---

[1] *Questiones in Genesim*, q. 64 (PG 80, 171A).
[2] "Afterwards here is put the blessing of Abraham himself. About which it ought to be known that the Jews, the adversaries of the Christian faith, try to disfigure the Scriptures which speak about Christ, among which is Psalm 109 in which there is mention of the priesthood of Melchisedech. And by occasion of that Psalm, which speaks about Christ, they strive to perversely expound this passage, saying that this Melchisedech brought forth bread and wine, not in sacrifice, but rather for refreshing Abraham and his people who were coming from battle." (*Biblia sacra cum glossis, interlineari & ordinaria, Nicolai Lyrani postilla et moralitatibus...* (Lyon, Gaspar Trechsel, 1545), p. 64r B).

all the captured goods. Furthermore, for no reason would Scripture have mentioned that he was a priest, if he were bringing forth bread and wine not in sacrifice: because bringing those things which pertain to nourishment, is not the function of priests, but of laymen. And by no means was it befitting a lay king to bring forth foodstuffs with his own hands to the victors, because it was befitting to his royal dignity if he would have sent foodstuffs by his ministers. But when he blessed Abraham, he did so not with another's hand but with his own: thus when he brought forth bread and wine, he gave not with another's hand, but with his own: because Scripture relates that he did all these things in the same way.

Next, if Melchisedech did not offer bread and wine to God, as these heretics say, they would [not] give him the rite and order which Melchisedech had in his priesthood. For it is foolish to say that Scripture did not state any order of his priesthood, while nevertheless Sacred Scripture says elsewhere that Christ is a priest "according to the order of Melchisedech."[1] And certainly if the words of Scripture are carefully considered, one will understand that it is clearly proved from them that Melchisedech offered bread and wine, not to Abraham, but to God. For after he said that Melchisedech offered bread and wine, wishing to show the reason for this, he immediately added, "For he was the priest of the most high God" (Gen. 14, 18). For someone could be surprised that a king would have offered, wherefore he immediately added, "For he was the priest of the most high God." If he had used a copulative conjunctive, saying: "And he was the priest of the most high God," it could deservedly be doubted, to whom he had offered bread and wine: but since he used a causal conjunctive, saying: "For he was the priest of the most high God," it is seen that those words were used to give the reason why he offered bread and wine, namely because he was a priest. But the office of a priest is not to offer to the victors, but to God. Hence Melchisedech offered to God, and not to Abraham.

Add to these proofs all the testimonies of many illustrious men, renown for holiness as well as for learning, who all unanimously teach that Melchisedech was a priest, and offered bread and wine to God, and thus was a figure of Christ the priest. I omit the more recent theologians, who even though they are very learned men, still they are not held in such high esteem by all. I wish to begin from Haymo [of Auxerre[2]], the most recent of all of these, who says these words: "But why it is said that he is a priest 'according to the order of Melchisedech,' and not 'according to the order of Aaron,' there are several reasons. The first in fact is because Melchisedech was not a priest according to the Legal commandments, but according to the dignity of a singular priesthood, offering bread and wine to God, not the blood of brute animals. In the order of whose priesthood, Christ was made a priest, not a temporal but an eternal priest: not offering Legal victims, but like him, bread and wine, to wit, His Flesh and Blood: concerning which things He spoke saying, 'My flesh is meat indeed: and my blood is drink indeed' (Jn. 6, 56). Also, these two gifts, namely bread and wine, He entrusted to His Church to be offered in memory of Him. Hence it is evident that the sacrifice of cattle died out, because it was of the order of Aaron: and rather, that [sacrifice] remains which was of the order of Melchisedech, both because Christ confirmed it, and because He left it to the Church to be kept."[3] In which words he clearly teaches that Melchisedech offered bread and wine, and in this he was a figure of Christ, and Christ left His Body and Blood to the Church, so that it could offer them to God in His memory.

Cassiodorus when interpreting the verse, "Thou art a priest forever, according to the order of Melchisedech" (Ps. 109, 4), says these words: "For with whom can these words be truly

---

[1] Cf. Heb. 6, 20.
[2] In Migne's *Patrologia Latina*, this passage is attributed to Haymo of Halberstadt, but as mentioned above (see the section, "Gospel," heresy 2), it has more recently been shown to have been written by Haymo of Auxerre.
[3] *In epistolam ad hebraeos*, c. 5 (PL 117, 855B-C).

and clearly associated except the Lord Savior, Who in saving fashion consecrated His Body and Blood in the distribution of bread and wine? As Christ Himself says in the Gospel: 'Except you eat the flesh of the Son of man, and drink his blood, you shall not have life in you' (Jn. 6, 54). But the human mind must not imagine that there is anything bloody or corruptible in this Flesh and Blood—as Paul says: 'For he that eateth and drinketh unworthily, eateth and drinketh judgment to himself' (I Cor. 11, 29)—but rather the substance that gives life and salvation and has become peculiar to the Word Itself. Through it are granted the remission of sins and the gift of eternal life. It was Melchisedech, that most just king, who by a mystical parallel established this dispensation, when he offered fruits of bread and wine to the Lord. It is certain that sacrifices of cattle died out, and that the order of Melchisedech remained, which is celebrated throughout the whole world in the distribution of the Sacraments."[1] Thus far the words of Cassiodorus, who clearly teaches that Melchisedech offered bread and wine to God, and in this offering figured Christ our Savior.

Isidore [of Seville] likewise says these words: "Christ our Lord and Teacher first instituted the Sacrifice, which is offered by Christians to God, when He entrusted His Body and Blood to the Apostles before He was handed over, as it read in the Gospel: 'Jesus took bread,' and the chalice, 'and blessing... gave to them' (Mk. 14, 22-23). Indeed, Melchisedech, the king of Salem, first offered this Sacrament figuratively in a type of the Body and Blood of Christ. He first expressed the mystery of this great Sacrifice, as an image, presenting beforehand the likeness of Our Lord and Savior Jesus Christ the eternal Priest, to whom it is said: 'Thou art a priest forever, according to the order of Melchisedech' (Ps. 109, 4)."[2] Thus far the words of Isidore, who also very clearly teaches everything needed for the overthrow of this heresy. For he says that Melchisedech offered in a type of Christ's Body and Blood, and that He was a figure of Christ the Eternal Priest, and that Christians now offer this same sacrifice, which He Himself offered, by Christ's institution.

But because the heretics will perhaps not be afraid to reject these three men, although the most recent of them was born seven hundred years ago, and Isidore nine hundred years ago, as being recent theologians, I wish to bring forth older and more illustrious witnesses. Jerome in his letter to Evangelus when discoursing about Melchisedech, and saying who he was, relates the opinions of very ancient illustrious men, saying the following: "I consulted Hippolytus, Irenaeus, Eusebius of Caesarea, Eusebius of Emesa, Apollinaris [of Laodicea] also, and our Eustathius, who was the first of all the bishops to sound the very clear signal for war against Arius, and I observed that after several detours and different reasonings, they all agree to say the man Melchisedech was a Canaanite king of the city of Jerusalem, which firstly was called 'Salem,' then 'Jebus,' and finally 'Jerusalem.' It is not surprising if the 'priest of the most high God' is described without circumcision or other ceremonies of the Law, or as being of the family of Aaron: since we see that Abel, Enoch and Noah pleased God and offered victims; and that we read in the book of Job that he also offered gifts, was a priest, and daily immolated sacrificial offerings for his children.[3] They also say that Job was not of the family of Levi, but of the race of Esau; although the Hebrews think otherwise. Now just as Noah was inebriated in his house, uncovered, and mocked by his middle son, gave a type of the Savior, and Cham gave a type of the Jewish nation; Samson also, the lover of the harlot and pauper Dalila, who, to signify the Passion of Jesus Christ, killed more enemies by dying than he had during his life; nearly all the holy men, the Patriarchs and the prophets, have portrayed a figure of the Savior in something, so also Melchisedech, because he was a Canaanite and not of the Jewish race, figured as a type the priesthood of the Son of God, of whom he it is said in Psalm one

---

[1] *Explanation of the Psalms* (PL 70, 797B).

[2] *De ecclesiasticis officiis*, bk. 1, c. 18, n. 1 (PL 83, 754C).

[3] Cf. Job 1, 5.

hundred nine: 'Thou art a priest forever, according to the order of Melchisedech.' (v. 4) Now his 'order' is interpreted in many ways: that he alone was both king and priest together; that he exercised the functions of the priesthood before the establishment of circumcision, which shows that the Gentiles did not receive the priesthood from the Jews, but the Jews from the Gentiles; that he was not anointed with priestly oil, as the precepts of Moses appointed,[1] but with an oil of joy and by the anointing of pure faith; that he did not immolate victims of flesh and blood, nor did he take up the entrails of brute animals; but with bread and wine, as a simple and pure sacrifice, he dedicated Christ's Sacrament."[2] In which words he related not his own opinion, but that of many other illustrious men, whereby they unanimously assert that Melchisedech made a sacrifice of bread and wine, and by it pointed out Christ's Sacrament, that is, the Most Holy Eucharist.

But it is necessary that we also hear Jerome's opinion, which he clearly expresses saying these words: "Now the Blessed Apostle, writing to the Hebrews, makes mention of Melchisedech as 'without father or mother', and relates him to Christ and, through Christ, to the Church of the Gentiles. For all the glory of the head is assigned to the members; because, while he was uncircumcised, he blessed Abraham who had been circumcised; and in Abraham he blessed Levi; and through Levi he blessed Aaron from whom the priesthood afterwards descended. For this reason, he maintains one should infer that the priesthood of the Church which is uncircumcised blessed the priesthood of the synagogue which is circumcised. And as to the Scripture which says: 'Thou art a priest forever, according to the order of Melchisedech' (Ps. 109, 4), our mystery is foreshown in the word 'order': not at all, indeed, in the sacrifice of non-rational victims through Aaron's agency, but when bread and wine, that is, the Body and Blood of the Lord Jesus, were offered in sacrifice."[3] In which words he has very clearly said everything that could support us in the present disputation. For he said that Melchisedech figured Christ, but also the priesthood of the Church assembled from the Gentiles. He also said that Melchisedech himself sacrificed bread and wine, and figured our sacrifice of Christ's Body and Blood. But more clearly still, he passes down to us the same teaching in [PseudoJerome's[4]] commentary on the Psalms, wherein when interpreting the verse from Psalm one hundred nine, "Thou art a priest forever, according to the order of Melchisedech," (v. 4) he says these words: "Let us only say this, why he said, 'according to the order.' Thou will nowise be a priest 'according to the order' according to the Judaic victims: but Thou will be a priest according to the order of Melchisedech. For just as Melchisedech, king of Salem, offered bread and wine: so also Thou wilt offer Thine Body and Blood, the true bread and wine. This Melchisedech, these mysteries which we have, He gave us. It is He Who said, 'He that eateth my flesh, and drinketh my blood' (Jn. 6, 55). According to the order of Melchisedech He delivered to us His Sacrament."[5] Jerome clearly supports our and the Catholic opinion, so that nothing clearer could be reasonably desired.

[Pseudo-] Eusebius of Emesa, praised by the same Jerome, and on the previous passage cited by him, when speaking about the Eucharist, says these words: "We find, therefore, the form of this Sacrament expressed in the pages of the Jews. For we read about Melchisedech in Genesis. 'And Melchisedech the king of Salem, brought forth bread and wine... and blessed Abraham. Now Melchisedech was the priest of the most high God' (Gen. 14, 18-19). Thus this Melchisedech, whose genealogy or origin escaped notice of that time, by this offering of

---

[1] Cf. Lev. 8, 12.
[2] Letter 73, n. 3 (PL 22, 677).
[3] *Hebrew questions on Genesis*, on Gen. 14, 18 (PL 23, 961B-C).
[4] This work is now accepted as an amalgam of Jerome's *Commentarioli in psalmos* and his *Tractatus sive homiliae in psalmos*, as well as drawing on other authors.
[5] *Brevarium in Psalmos*, Ps. 109 (PL 26, 1165D-1166A).

bread and wine prefigured Christ's sacrifice, about which the [Royal] Prophet foretells: 'Thou art a priest forever, according to the order of Melchisedech' (Ps. 109, 4)."[1] Even though Eusebius of Emesa reads that Melchisedech brough forth bread and wine, still he does not fear on that account to assert that he by the offering of bread and wine figured the sacrifice of Our Lord Jesus Christ the High Priest.

Eusebius of Caesarea supports this opinion, saying the following: "[The Psalmist] rightly exempts [Christ] from Aaron's ministry, which was figurative, and declares [Him to be] a priest Who would come according to the order of Melchisedech. And the fulfilment of the prophecy is truly wondrous, to one who contemplates how Our Saviour Jesus, Who is the Christ of God Himself, performs by the rite of Melchisedech those things which pertain to the priesthood to be transacted among men, through His ministers. For just as he, who was priest of the Gentiles, is not seen as offering corporal sacrifices, but rather bread and wine, as he blesses Abraham himself, certainly so likewise our Lord and Saviour Himself first, and then all the priests, in all nations, who go forth from Him, performing the spiritual office of the priesthood according to ecclesiastical ordinances, represent with wine and bread the mysteries of His Body and salutary Blood, which Melchisedech certainly had known beforehand by the Divine Spirit, and so had used images of things to come, as the Scripture of Moses testifies, where it says: 'And Melchisedech the king of Salem, brought forth bread and wine. For he was the priest of the most high God, and he blessed Abraham.'"[2] Eusebius asserts clearly enough that Melchisedech had used bread and wine as specific sacrifices.

Finally, Cyprian, the most ancient of all these men, in his letter to Caecilius, wherein he teaches that neither wine without water, nor water without wine can be consecrated in the Lord's chalice and offered to the Lord, says these words: "Also in the priest Melchisedech we see prefigured the Sacrament of the Sacrifice of the Lord, according to what Divine Scripture testifies, and says, 'But Melchisedech the king of Salem, bringing forth bread and wine, for he was the priest of the most high God,' (Gen. 14, 18). And he blessed Abraham. Now that Melchisedech bore a type of Christ, the Holy Ghost declares in the Psalms, saying in the Person of the Father to the Son: 'Before the day star I begot thee; the Lord hath sworn, and he will not repent: Thou art a priest forever according to the order of Melchisedech' (Ps. 109, 3-4); which order is assuredly this coming from that sacrifice and thence descending; because Melchisedech was a priest of the Most High God; because he offered wine and bread; because he blessed Abraham. For who is more a priest of the Most High God than Our Lord Jesus Christ, Who offered a sacrifice to God the Father, and offered that very same thing which Melchisedech had offered, that is, bread and wine, to wit, His Body and Blood?"[3] In which words he teaches clearly enough everything which was needed for us to refute the heretics, such that nothing further can be desired.

Besides this figure of Melchisedech's priesthood, there is another of the Paschal Lamb, whereby, inasmuch as it is necessary that a shadow be similar to the body, very clearly proves that the Mass is a sacrifice, in which Christ's true Body hidden under the appearances of bread, and His true Blood under the appearances of wine, is offered. For John the Baptist bears witness that this lamb was a figure of Christ, when pointing to Christ with his finger he said: "Behold the Lamb of God, behold him who taketh away the sin of the world" (Jn. 1, 29). But John the Evangelist gave much clearer testimony about this matter, when relating why the soldiers did not break Christ's legs, when they broke the legs of the others, the thieves who were crucified with Him. "For these things were done, that the scripture might be fulfilled:

---

[1] Fifth homily on Easter. *Maxima Bibliotheca veterum Patrum*, vol. 6, p. 636. This sermon is also attributed to St. Caesarius of Arles (PL 67, 1054C-D).

[2] *Proof of the Gospel*, bk. 5, c. 3 (PG 22, 367A-B).

[3] Epistle 63, c. 4 (PL 4, 375B-376A).

You shall not break a bone of him." (Jn. 19, 36). Which words so cited by John, are found in Exodus, where it is treated about the rite according to which the Pascal Lamb was to be eaten.[1] Hence since it is evident that Christ was figured in the Pascal Lamb, it is necessary that what was done of old with that typical lamb in figure, the same is now done in reality with the true Lamb, Who takes away the sins of the world. Certainly, Christ is called a lamb on account of His patience and meekness: because just He was "dumb as a lamb before his shearer" (Is. 53, 7), and "when he was reviled, did not revile: when he suffered, he threatened not" (I Pet. 2, 23). Just as by the blood of the Paschal Lamb every firstborn of Egypt perished,[2] so by Christ's Blood every sin perished, which is the firstborn of the devil. The Israelites were freed by the blood of that lamb from the destroyer, so by Christ's Blood we are freed from the devil, and from eternal death, which he tries to inflict upon us. The eating of that lamb figured the eating of Christ's Body, which today in the Evangelical Law, Christ's faithful receiving the Sacrament of the Eucharist, eat. Now those things the Law commanded to be done in the eating of the Pascal Lamb, are a figure of those things which the Christian faithful are bound to do, when they receive the Most Blessed Sacrament of the Eucharist.

Gregory amply enough explains these things, and Abbot Rupert [of Deutz] interprets those things no less accurately. "We have learned what is the blood of the lamb," Gregory says, "not now by hearing, but by drinking. This blood is put on the two door posts when it is drunk not merely by the mouth of the body, but also by that of the heart. The blood of the lamb is put on both door posts, when the Sacrament of the Passion of the Lord is received with the mouth in view of the Redemption, and one also wholeheartedly intends to imitate it. For whoever receives the Blood of his Redeemer without necessarily imitating His Passion puts this Blood on only one post, which also was to be put on the transom of the houses... We indeed eat the Lamb at night, since we now receive the Body of the Lord in the Sacrament, since all of us still do not see our own consciences. Nevertheless, its flesh must be roasted in the fire: in a cooking with water, the flesh disintegrates under the action of the fire, whereas it is made firm if it is cooked with fire without water. The flesh of our Lamb is thus hardened, because it is the vehemence of His Passion that gave Him more power in His Resurrection and strengthened Him unto incorruption. For when He was strengthened by death, His Flesh was made firm by fire. Hence, He also says through the Psalmist, 'My strength is dried up like a potsherd' (Ps. 21, 16). For what is a potsherd before going into the fire, except soft clay? But it is heated by the fire, in order to be hardened. Thus, the strength of the Lord's human nature was dried up like a potsherd, since by the fire of the Passion, He increased as to the power of incorruption. But merely receiving the Sacraments of our Redeemer does not suffice for the feast of the spirit, if good works are not joined to them also. For what does it profit to receive the Body and the Blood of the Lord with our mouth, if we go against him by bad morals? Hence rightly it is further added that one is to eat 'unleavened bread with wild lettuce' (Ex. 12, 8). A person eats unleavened bread who does virtuous deeds without corrupting them with vain glory; who fulfils the precepts of mercy without admixture of sin; who shows that he does not recklessly smash, as it were, what he has properly put in order. In reproof of some who had mingled the leaven of sin with their good deeds, the Lord spoke by the voice of the prophet, 'Come ye to Bethel [meaning, "the house of God"], and do wickedly.' And shortly after, 'And offer a sacrifice of praise with leaven' (Amos 4, 4-5). He 'offers a sacrifice of praise with leaven,' who intends to offer a sacrifice to God with stolen goods. Now 'wild lettuce' is very bitter. The flesh of the lamb then ought to be eaten with wild lettuce, so that when we receive the

---

[1] Cf. Ex. 12, 46.
[2] Cf. Ex. 12, 12.

Redeemer's Body, we afflict ourselves with weeping for our sins, since the very bitterness of repentance purges the humor of a wicked life from the soul's stomach."[1]

There are still some things in this figure of the Paschal Lamb to be explained, which although Gregory passes over them, Rupert of Deutz explains very well, saying the following: "Firstly, the full moon itself when a lamb is immolated, is mystically that fulness of time about which the Apostle says: 'But when the fulness of the time was come, God sent his Son, made of a woman, made under the law: that he might redeem them who were under the law: that we might receive the adoption of sons' (Gal. 4, 4-5). For in the fulness of time, when the number of the elect was already filled up by many of those awaiting their redemption in the region of Lower Egypt,[2] then came the Son of God, then came the Lamb of God to take away the sins of the world. Why is it that it is immolated not before but after the spring equinox? Assuredly starting from the spring equinox, the daytime begins to surpass nighttime: for before that time we have longer darkness and shorter daytime. Thus, it is the same in this mystery, namely because from the immolation of the pure Lamb and immaculate Christ, the light of justice began to surpass the darkness of sins. For previously there was the long and deep night of sins; short and cloudy, however, was the light of Legal justice. But does not the very month of Nisan, that is, the spring temperateness of April, when the earth blooms again, and the whole world becomes young again as though after old age, teach the intelligent man, inasmuch as he be renewed in the spirit of his mind,[3] verdant by faith, joyful by hope, flowering by charity, that he ought to attend the spiritual banquets of the Pascal Lamb?"[4]

Even though Rupert wanted to carefully explain nearly all the circumstances of the time, still he omitted one which ought not to be disregarded, which is concerning the evening of the day on which the lamb was immolated and eaten; but Cyprian explained this very well in his letter to Caecilius, saying the following: "It behooved Christ to offer around the time of the evening of the day, that the very hour of sacrifice might show the setting and the evening of the world; as it is written in Exodus, 'And the whole multitude of the children of Israel shall sacrifice it in the evening.' (12, 6). And again, in the Psalms, 'The lifting up of my hands, as evening sacrifice' (140, 2)."[5] There is still one more very important thing to be explained in the rite itself of the Paschal Lamb, which greatly supports our and the Catholic opinion about the sacrifice of the Mass. For the Law commands that Pascal Lamb to be immolated before it be eaten. The words of the Law are these: "The whole multitude of the children of Israel shall sacrifice it in the evening. And they shall take of the blood thereof, and put it upon both the side posts, and on the upper door posts of the houses, wherein they shall eat it. And they shall eat the flesh that night roasted at the fire, and unleavened bread with wild lettuce" (Ex. 12, 6-8). And shortly afterwards it adds: "When your children shall say to you: What is the meaning of this service? You shall say to them: It is the victim of the passage of the Lord" (v. 26-27).

Although this immolation of the Paschal Lamb was a figure of the immolation whereby Christ on the altar of the Cross immolated Himself to God the Father for us: still the figure of immolation which is in the Mass is much more expressive, when the priest after the consecration of the Eucharist, offers it to God in his own name and in the name of the Church, speaking thus: "We offer unto Thy glorious Majesty of Thine own gifts and benefits, a pure [Victim], a holy [Victim], an unspotted Victim, the Bread of eternal life, and the Chalice of everlasting

---

[1] *Homilies on the Gospels*, hom. 22 (PL 76, 1178B-1179B).

[2] I.e. Limbo (As this quotation of Rupert to be cited below indicates his meaning here: "He descended to those who were detained in lower Egypt, that is, in infernal darkness" (PL 167, 613D)).

[3] Cf. Eph. 4, 23.

[4] *De Trinitate et operibus eius, In Exodum commentariorum*, bk. 2, c. 5 (PL 167, 612D-613B).

[5] Letter 63, n. 16 (PL 4, 386C).

salvation."[1] For the immolation on the Cross was not made before the eating of the Paschal Lamb, but after it. But on the contrary that offering which is performed by the priest in Mass, always precedes the consuming of Christ's Body and the drinking of His Blood, because the priest firstly consecrates and offers Christ's Body and Blood to God, and always afterwards he consumes and drinks, and sometimes he gives others to eat. But if before this oblation the priest either were to eat or give to others to eat, without any doubt he would sin: because he would take away the true notion of sacrifice, and thus would make that the reality would not perfectly correspond to the figure. For the same reason he would also sin who would offer the Eucharist and not eat or drink it: just as long ago a Jew would have sinned, who after the Paschal Lamb was immolated, would not want to eat it.

Hence the Twelfth Synod of Toledo rightly pronounced the following decision on this matter: "It has been related to us that certain priests do not received the gift of Holy Communion every time that they offer Mass, but if in one day they themselves offer many sacrifices to God, they put off receiving Holy Communion in all the oblations, and they receive the grace of Holy Communion solely in the last oblation of the sacrifice alone, as though a priest would not be guilty of that real and singular sacrifice, as often as he omits partaking of the Body and Blood of Our Lord Jesus Christ. For behold the Apostle says, 'Are not they who eat the victims partakers of the altar?'[2] Therefore, if those who eat victims are partakers of the altar, it is certain that they who when sacrificing do not eat are guilty of the Lord's Sacrament. Therefore, whosoever of the priests henceforth shall approach the Divine altar to offer sacrifice, and abstains from Communion, from which same Communion he unfittingly has deprived himself, let him know that he will be refused the grace of Communion for one year."[3]

But a slight doubt about the priest could arise here, who before eating, either would delay the oblation, or impetrate grace by the consecration alone. I do not know of anyone who has raised this question as of yet, nor do I raise it now so that afterwards I may give about it an exact, definitive treatment, but rather so that I may offer an occasion for discussion to others. For I prefer to listen to the opinion of other Catholics on this subject, than to put mine in writing. Still I will not leave the matter untouched. I will say what I think, yet I am prepared to yield to a contradictor if he shows me a strong reason which may deservedly force me to abandon my view. The Eucharist can be considered in two ways, namely as a sacrifice and as a Sacrament: because according to the Catholic faith, it is both a Sacrament and a sacrifice. If the Eucharist be considered as sacrifice, it seems to be that the priest would not obtain any grace on this account *ex opere operato*, as it is usually said: because the priest has neither eaten the Eucharist nor offered it. But the consecration alone without the offering and eating, ought not to be called a sacrifice. But if we were to consider the Eucharist as a Sacrament, neither in this respect, as it seems to me now, has the priest obtained grace *ex opere operato*, because although he has confected the Eucharist, still he has not received it. But it is common to all the Sacraments that a Sacrament only confers grace to the one receiving it. For Christ did not say: "He that believeth and baptizes shall be saved": but he only said: "He that believeth and is baptized, shall be saved" (Mk 16, 16). For although the Sacrament of the Eucharist has this, that its substance can exist without its reception, because it is not like any other Sacrament: yet this is not unique to it, that to someone not receiving, it cannot confer any grace. I have said these things in passing, outside of the plan I intended: for in this work I had decided to address only the Catholic faith, and not men's opinions.

---

[1] Taken from the prayer, *Unde et memores*, recited in the Canon of the Tridentine Mass.

[2] Cf. I Cor. 9, 13.

[3] The author here cited from *The False Decretals of the Pseudo-Isidore* (PL 130, 556D-557A), but this citation has been replaced with more accurate wording taken from *Collectio Canonum Ecclesiae Hispanae ex probatissimis ac pervetustis Codicibus*, p. 496.

After having completed the argumentation from the two chief figures of the Old Testament, now I will argue against the aforesaid heresy from two other prophecies of the same Testament. In the prophet Daniel, where it is treated about the Antichrist, these words are found: "But at that time shall Michael rise up, the great prince, who standeth for the children of thy people: and a time shall come such as never was from the time that nations began even until that time. And at that time shall thy people be saved, every one that shall be found written in the book. And many of those that sleep in the dust of the earth, shall awake: some unto life everlasting, and others unto reproach, to see it always" (Dan. 12, 1-2). When Daniel had heard these words from the Angel Gabriel who appeared to him, he said, asking the same Gabriel: "How long shall it be to the end of these wonders?" (v. 6) To which Gabriel answers and swearing by Him Who lives forever; he said that that tribulation would last "for a time, and times, and half a time" (v. 7), that is, for three and a half years. And afterwards when stating from what time ought these three and a half years be reckoned, he says: "And from the time when the continual sacrifice shall be taken away, and the abomination unto desolation shall be set up, there shall be a thousand two hundred ninety days" (v. 11). Here is the whole account which needed to be cited in its entirety, because from its words, the strength of our argumentation will appear more clearly.

It is necessary to especially note from these words that in the end it is said: "From the time when the continual sacrifice shall be taken away, and the abomination unto desolation shall be set up, there shall be a thousand two hundred ninety days." In which words the celebration of the Mass, as we will with God's help show just now, is clearly called a sacrifice. For by those words the Angel Gabriel taught the prophet Daniel that the celebration of the Mass would cease at the time of the Antichrist. Because bad priests, terrified with the fear of Antichrist's persecution, will not dare to publicly celebrate Masses. But the good priests, even though not terrified by fear, will nevertheless forego [celebrating Mass] for three and a half years, lest so lofty a Sacrament be held in contempt, and treated unworthily and irreverently. And then "the abomination unto desolation shall be set up": because the Antichrist himself will sit in the temple of God, so that he may be adored by men.[1] Now so that our argumentation may have greater force, it will be necessary to show that there is no other sacrifice, about which the words of the prophecy just cited can be understood, except the Mass. Once this has been proved, it will then be proved that the Mass is a sacrifice.

Now to do this more clearly, it is necessary to firstly lay this foundation, that that prophecy does not speak about the perpetual sacrifice of the Mosaic Law, which was due to cease at the time of the Mass: because he had already spoken of the former in chapter nine. Now the words which are said about that cessation of the sacrifice, are opposed to these words which have just now been cited from chapter twelve of the same Daniel. For the words which are said there are these: "And he shall confirm the covenant with many, in one week: and in the half of the week the victim and the sacrifice shall fail: and there shall be in the temple the abomination of desolation: and the desolation shall continue even to the consummation, and to the end" (9, 27). In which words he clearly teaches that the cessation of the Jewish sacrifice would be perpetual. But from these words which we are now examining, as the prophecy itself relates, it will not be perpetual: but it will last for a thousand two hundred ninety days, that is for three and a half years.

And this prophecy ought not to be understood, as the demented Porphyry said, of the persecution made by Antioch Epiphanes, the king of Syria, during which time the Mosaic sacrifice ceased in Judea. For on account of this interpretation Jerome bitterly reprehends Porphyry in

---

[1] Cf. II Thess. 2, 4.

his *Commentary on Daniel*,[1] and after Jerome, Nicholas of Lyra [does the same].[2] And Porphyry is rightly reprehended on this matter: because that cessation of sacrifice, which was under Antiochus, in whatever way it may be computed, as Lyra proves well, [lasted "only three years"[3]]. But this cessation, about which we now dispute, Gabriel predicted would not last more than three and a half years: thus this prophesy has not been fulfilled in the persecution made under Antiochus. Furthermore, the Angel predicted about the time, namely that "a time shall come such as never was from the time that nations began even until that time" (Dan. 12, 1). But the tribulation under Antioch was not greater than all the preceding ones: because the one which Nabuchodonosor inflicted was much greater. For he destroyed the Temple and the walls of the city, and he led the king and all the chief men of the nation captive, and he did not leave some of the common people, except a few poor men, who would cultivate the fields. Antiochus did none of these things. Hence it remains that this prophecy is understood as owing to be fulfilled at the time of the Antichrist, as all the Catholic Doctors have reckoned that it ought to be understood.

For Jerome most constantly affirms the it cannot be understood of another time.[4] Rupert of Deutz thinks the same thing.[5] Nicholas of Lyra interprets it in the same way.[6] The gloss, which they call interlinear, agrees with all these men, which when explaining these words, "A time shall come such as never was from the time that nations began even until that time" (Dan. 12, 1), upon these last words, "that time," says: "of the Antichrist."[7] And certainly, as I think, it is not necessary to quote the Doctors, since Christ, the Teacher of truth Himself,

---

[1] "And because Porphyry saw that all these things had been fulfilled and could not deny that they had taken place, he overcame this evidence of historical accuracy by taking refuge in this evasion, contending that whatever is foretold concerning Antichrist at the end of the world was actually fulfilled in the reign of Antiochus Epiphanes, because of certain similarities to things which took place at his time. But this very attack testifies to Daniel's accuracy. For so striking was the reliability of what the prophet foretold, that he could not appear to unbelievers as a predicter of the future, but rather a narrator of things already past. And so wherever occasion arises in the course of explaining this volume, I shall attempt briefly to answer his malicious charge, and to controvert by simple explanation the philosophical skill, or rather the worldly malice, by which he strives to subvert the truth and by specious sleight of hand to remove that which is so apparent to our eyes." (PL 25, 491B-492A).

[2] "Porphyry explains this passage in the following way, such that the forty-five days beyond the one thousand two hundred ninety [Dan. 12, 11-12], signify the interval of victory over the generals of Antiochus, when Judas Machabeus fought with bravery and cleansed the Temple and broke the idol to pieces, offering victims in the Temple. But the book of Machabees says that the Temple was polluted for only three years [cf. I Mach. 1, 57 & II Mach. 5, 52]." (*Biblia sacra cum Glossis, interlineari et ordinaria, Nicolai Lyrani Postilla* (Lyon, Anthoine Vincent, 1545), on Dan. 12, 12, vol. 4, p. 328r A). Nicholas of Lyra is here quoting St. Jerome's *Commentary on Daniel* (on Dan. 12, 12 (PL 25, 579A-B)).

[3] The text here reads, "exceeded four years," but Nicholas de Lyra's own words which are "for only three years," as cited in the footnote above, have been substituted instead as a correction.

[4] *Commentary on Daniel* (on Dan. 12, 12 (PL 25, 579A-B)).

[5] "Why then did he say, 'two and forty months' (Apoc. 11, 2), which months are not longer than three and a half years? Namely because for making known the greatness of Antichrist's persecution, which will be so great, that it alone can scarcely be known or foreknown, and it alone is computed for all persecutions, as though the other persecutions compared to it are not or were not persecutions... We understand 'a time, and times, and half a time' (Dan. 7, 25) to be three and a half years... which he more clearly states afterwards by saying the number of days as follows: 'And from the time when the continual sacrifice shall be taken away, and the abomination unto desolation shall be set up, there shall be a thousand two hundred ninety days' (12, 11)." (*Commentaria in Apocalypsim*, bk. 6, c. 11 (PL 169, 1018D-1019A)).

[6] *Biblia sacra cum Glossis*, on Dan. 12, 12, vol. 4, p. 328r A.

[7] *Ibid.*, p. 327r.

very clearly teaches it in Matthew's Gospel, where he cites this passage of Daniel, saying: "When you shall see the abomination of desolation, which was spoken of by Daniel the prophet, standing in the holy place: he that readeth let him understand" (Mt. 24, 15). Now that Christ is speaking about these words which were written in the twelfth chapter of Daniel, and not about the other words which are written in the nineth chapter of Daniel[1], as some badly observing teach, is clearly proved from the other words which Christ our Savior said there, which completely agree with those words which were said in the twelfth chapter of Daniel. For in that chapter, Daniel says these words: "A time shall come such as never was from the time that nations began even until that time" (v. 1). And Christ when speaking about the time of Antichrist in Matthew says: "For there shall be then great tribulation, such as hath not been from the beginning of the world until now, neither shall be" (24, 21). Which words, as is manifestly evident, cannot be understood of any other time but of the time of Antichrist. "Then those days of great tribulation shall be shortened for the sake of the elect" (v. 21-22), and these words correspond to the words of Daniel in the aforesaid vision, which he says that the tribulation will last "a thousand two hundred ninety days" (12, 11). It is thus established from all these words that that prophecy of Daniel, which we cited from his twelfth chapter, will be fulfilled at the time of Antichrist.

It therefore remains to investigate what is that "continual sacrifice," which is going to cease for three years and a half. It is certainly not a corporal sacrifice like those which long ago existed in the Mosaic Law: because no such sacrifice is a continual sacrifice in the Evangelical Law. Prayer and Divine praise are not that sacrifice, about which the Royal Prophet says: "Offer to God the sacrifice of praise" (Ps. 49, 14). Neither is that sacrifice the affliction of the flesh by fastings, flagellations, pilgrimages, vigils, and other similar toils of the body, about which Paul says: "I beseech you therefore, brethren, by the mercy of God, that you present your bodies a living sacrifice, holy, pleasing unto God' (Rom. 12, 1). Nor is that sacrifice contrition for sins, or any tears shed in some other way for God's sake, about which the [Royal] Prophet says: "A sacrifice to God is an afflicted spirit" (Ps. 50, 19). Of none of these sacrifices, nor of any other similar one can be understood that which the Angel Gabriel said to Daniel, namely that the continual sacrifice will cease at the time of the Antichrist. Because although at that time "iniquity shall abound and the charity of many shall grow cold" (Mt. 24, 12): nevertheless, not the charity of all men [shall grow cold].

Although many will follow the Antichrist, still not all, nay many will courageously resist him, having been set aflame with Christ's love, and for this reason they will be killed by him, as the Angel Gabriel foretold in the words which he spoke to Daniel, saying the following: "Many shall be chosen, and made white, and shall be tried as fire" (12, 10). Upon which words the interlinear gloss says, "As gold in the furnace" (Wis. 3, 6). For otherwise it would be necessary to say that the whole Church, which is Christ's spouse, will vanish at that time, if there would not then be some just men, who would withstand it. For no matter how much iniquity shall abound, and sins be increased in number, God always keeps, and leaves for Himself, some thousands of men, "that have not bowed their knees to Baal" (Rom. 11, 4). Thus, those just men, who will then be alive at the time of Antichrist, seeing Antichrist's persecution will pray more fervently to God for help: and with greater devotion will praise God for having kept them from falling into so great wickedness of worshipping Antichrist.

Having remembered at that time their past deeds, whereby they had perchance formerly offended God, they will groan more bitterly over them: and fearing lest perhaps that having exasperated God by their sins He brought in such tribulations to afflict their bodies, so that even in this way they could placate God, as of old the men of Ninive did.[2] And the Angel Gabriel

---

[1] Verse 27.
[2] Cf. Jonas 3, 9-10.

also stated this, when speaking thus to Daniel: "And the wicked shall deal wickedly, and none of the wicked shall understand" (Dan. 12, 10). Whereupon the interlinear gloss says: "They shall not understand that all these things happen for a trial of the saints." And afterwards the Angel adds, "But the learned shall understand." Upon which words the interlinear gloss says: "The just and the elect, those taught by God's discipline, understand these things, and will willingly endure [these things]."[1] From which words it is very clearly proved that spiritual sacrifices of this kind, which we listed above, although they will be given up by many at the time of the Antichrist, yet they will not completely cease.

When the very wicked King Achab reigned, when there was such an abundance of wickedness, and so great a multitude of wicked men, such that Elias thought that he was the only one who worshipped God, God said to the same Elias that He had left "seven thousand men in Israel, whose knees have not been bowed before Baal" (III Kings 19, 18). Thus, since the glory of the Church is greater than that of the synagogue, and God now has greater concern for the Church, than of old for the synagogue, we are forced to believe that God at the time of the Antichrist, will not abandon His Church to such an extent, that He would not keep for Himself in it more than seven thousand men, who have not bent their knees before the Antichrist. And if of none of these sacrifices can be understood those words which the Angel Gabriel said to Daniel, namely that the continual sacrifice will cease at the time of Antichrist, it is thence proved that they must necessarily be understood of the Mass, which, because it is celebrated every day, and in it Christ's true Body and His true Blood are daily offered to God, is called the "continual sacrifice." And this will cease at the time of the Antichrist: because although many Masses at that time, as it is right to be believed, will be celebrated, still they will not be celebrated as frequently or as publicly as before: and this not so much on account of fear of the Antichrist, as lest so excellent a sacrifice come into greater contempt and mockery. Certainly, they will act according to the precept of the Savior saying: "Give not that which is holy to dogs; neither cast ye your pearls before swine" (Mt. 7, 6). Therefore, this sacrifice whereby God is greatly worshipped, the Antichrist will attempt to completely eliminate, so that he may be worshipped and adored in place of God. For in order to eliminate all true worship of God, the Antichrist would find no better means than to take away the sacrifice of the Mass. Because as [Pseudo-] Rupert says in his book, *De glorificatione filii hominis*,[2] when the sacrifice of the Mass has been taken away, devotion will immediately perish. And hence it is proved that Luther and all those who imitate him in this regard are precursors of the Antichrist, and his ministers: because they strive to take away the sacrifice of the Mass from the Church, just as the Antichrist, their teacher, will do afterwards.

There is another prophecy, of the prophet Malachias, which also clearly proves that the Mass is a sacrifice. For when Malachias was recounting how God was going to abrogate the sacrifices of the Old Law, and in its place, He would substituted another, says these words: "I have no pleasure in you, saith the Lord of hosts: and I will not receive a gift of your hand. For from the rising of the sun even to the going down, my name is great among the Gentiles, and in every place there is sacrifice, and there is offered to my name a clean oblation: for my name is great among the Gentiles" (1, 10-11). Notice that you see that the sacrifices of the Old Law are repudiated, when he says: "I will not receive a gift of your hand." And lest it might seem that the people are left completely without sacrifice, he immediately discloses that a much better sacrifice will be substituted in its place, when he said: "in every place there is sacrifice, and there is offered to my name a clean oblation." But there is no other oblation which can be simply and absolutely called "clean," except the Eucharist which is offered in

---

[1] *Biblia sacra cum Glossis*, on Dan. 12, 12, vol. 4, p. 327v.
[2] These words possibly originate from a lost work having this same title, but was written by Gerhoh of Reichersberg, whose theology was strongly influenced by Rupert of Deutz.

the Mass: because as a certain prophet says, "All our justices" are such before God, "as the rag of a menstruous woman" (Is. 64, 6).

And if there is some oblation which may be called clean, it is not clean of itself before God, but from the cleanliness and goodness from the one offering. "The Lord had respect (the Scripture says) to Abel, and to his offerings" (Gen. 4, 4). To Abel first, then to his offering, and hence He had respect to the offering, because He had respect to the person. Now that oblation of which the prophet Malachias speaks is absolutely called "clean," without having indicated the person from which it takes its cleanliness. From which it is inferred that it is clean of itself, and thus it is the Eucharist. But if you were to say that it ought to be understood of that oblation whereby Christ offered Himself on the Cross once for us all to His Father, that which the Lord says stands in the way, saying that this oblation is offered "in every place." Therefore, the prophet does not speak about that oblation. Nor also is this clean oblation about which the prophet speaks prayer, alms, fasting or any such similar thing. For if we were to speak about oblations of this kind, they are not offered in only one place and by all, but the prayers are different, the alms are distinct according to the diversity of persons offering them. And oblations of this kind were also offered in the Old Testament to God. This one, however, about which the Lord speaks through the prophet, was not in the Old Law, because he says that it would be substituted in place of the other sacrifices which would be rejected. Thus the oblation which is clean of itself without any respect to the person offering, and which is one and the same to be offered by all in every place, cannot be found except in the Eucharist, which is offered to God daily in the Mass by the whole Church spread out through the whole world. Thus, the Mass in which such an oblation is offered, is the sacrifice.

But because the Lutherans distort the words of Malachias, as they are always accustomed to do elsewhere, into another meaning, saying that those words ought not to be understood of the oblation of the Eucharist, but of other spiritual sacrifices, besides the reasons whereby I proved this that this ought not to be understood as they say, I wish to cite as evidence of our above mentioned interpretation, several ancient Doctors who concordantly interpret those words of Malachias of the oblation of the Eucharist, which is done in the sacrifice of the Mass. Haymo [of Auxerre], the most recent of these Doctors, but died nearly seven hundred years ago, when interpreting the aforesaid words in his commentary on Malachias, says: "The prophecy is very clear, and does not require a deeper exposition, however, it properly speaks to the priests who were offering unlawful victims, and hence the good-will of God, Whom they were exasperating, was not towards them: it also teaches at the same time that spiritual sacrifices would replace their carnal sacrifices, and not only in one region of the Jews, but in every place a clean oblation would be offered to God, that is, the sacrifice which the Church now repeats."[1] Although Haymo does not explicitly name the Eucharist, still his words clearly indicate that he spoke about it. For he says that that oblation, of which Malachias spoke, is "the sacrifice which the Church now repeats." But the sacrifice repeated by the Church is none other than the sacrifice of the Mass, which is daily celebrated in the Church.

But [John] Damascene interprets Malachias' words about the sacrifice of the Mass much more clearly, who when speaking about the Most Holy Eucharist, and showing that it was figured in many passages of the Old Testament and foretold by the prophets, says these words: "(With bread and wine) Melchisedech, the priest of the most high God, received Abraham on his return from the slaughter of the Gentiles.[2] That table prefigured this mystical table, just as that priest was a type and image of Christ, the true High Priest. For he says, 'Thou art a priest forever, according to the order of Melchisedech' (Ps. 109, 4). The loaves of proposition figured this bread. This surely is that pure and bloodless sacrifice which the Lord through the

---

[1] *Enarratio in duodecim prophetas minores, In Malachiam prophetam*, c.1 (PL 117, 282B).

[2] Cf. Gen. 14, 18.

prophet said is offered to Him 'from the rising of the sun even to the going down' (Mal. 1, 11). The Body and Blood of Christ changes into an enlivening both of our soul and of our body, which are neither consumed nor corrupted, nor go into the sewer (God forbid!), but go unto our standing firm and preservation, a protection against all kinds of harm, a cleansing from all filthiness, just as if one were to receive adulterated gold, one purifies it by smelting; lest in the future we be condemned with this world."[1] These are the words of Damascene, who clearly enough supports our and the Catholic opinion.

Eusebius of Caesarea, when teaching that the sacrifices of the Old Testament have ceased, and that other ones have been substituted in their place in the Evangelical Law, says these words among others: "And so all these things, which were Divinely foretold from the beginning, are being celebrated by all nations at this present time through our Savior's Evangelical teaching, the Truth bears witness by Whose voice God, having rejected the Mosaic sacrifices, Divinely announces that our practice of these things would come, saying: 'For from the rising of the sun even to the going down, my name is great among the Gentiles, and in every place there is sacrifice, and there is offered to my name a clean oblation: for my name is great among the Gentiles' (Mal. 1, 11). We sacrifice, therefore, to the Most High God the sacrifice of praise, the complete sacrifice, and bringing forth dread, and a sacrosanct sacrifice, and we sacrifice in a new manner, according to the New Testament, the clean sacrifice. But a contrite heart is called a sacrifice to God: therefore 'a humble and a contrite heart God wilt not despise.'[2] And we offer again and again that prophetic incense in every place, and we rightly offer to Him the fragrant fruit of the Eucharist [*theologia*] abounding in every virtue, making this same [sacrifice], having directed our prayers to Him. This same thing another prophet certainly also teaches, who says: 'Let my prayer be made as incense in thy sight.'[3] Therefore, we sacrifice and offer incense, at one time indeed renewing the memory of that great sacrifice, according to those things which have been handed down from Him, celebrating the Mysteries, and giving thanks to God for our salvation, and offering to Him religious hymns and holy prayers: at other times consecrating our entire selves to Him, and to the High Priest, truly devoting our words, body and mind to Him."[4] Even though Eusebius of Caesarea says that many oblations ought to be understood of that "clean oblation," which Malachias foretold, still among them he includes that oblation which is done in memory of that great sacrifice, namely which Christ offered for us upon the Cross. And it ought to be especially noted in Eusebius' words that he said the celebration of this oblation is according to the Mysteries handed down from Christ. From which words it is established that the celebration of Mass is not "papist," as Luther unjustly calls it: but rather, was instituted by Christ Himself.

Before all these men lived the philosopher, Justin [Martyr], renowned for his martyrdom and teaching, who, when disputing with the Jews in his *Dialogue with Trypho*, interprets the same words of Malachias about the sacrifice of the Eucharist, saying the following: "God Himself bears witness, saying that in every place among the Gentiles sacrifices are presented to Him, well-pleasing and pure. Now God receives sacrifices from no one, except through His priests. Accordingly, God, anticipating all the sacrifices which we offer through His name, and which Jesus the Christ enjoined us to offer, i.e., in the Eucharist of the bread and the chalice, and which are presented by Christians in all places throughout the world, bears witness that they are well-pleasing to Him. But He utterly rejects those presented by you and by those priests of yours, saying, 'And I will not receive a gift of your hand; for from the rising of the sun even to the going down, my name is great among the Gentiles,' He says, 'and you have

---

[1] PG 94, 1150C-1151A.
[2] Cf. Ps. 50, 19.
[3] Cf. Ps. 140, 2.
[4] *Proof of the Gospel*, bk. 1, c. 10 (PG 22, 91D-94A).

profaned it' (Mal. 1, 11-12)."[1] In which words by the testimony of the prophet Malachias he asserted that the Eucharist of the bread and wine is the sacrifice pleasing to God, and it was handed down from Christ.

But let us hear Irenaeus, a contemporary of the Apostles, who when speaking of the cessation of the old sacrifices, says these words: "From all these it is evident that God did not seek sacrifices and holocausts from them, but faith, and obedience, and justice, because of their salvation. As God, when teaching them His will in Osee the prophet, said, 'I desire mercy, and not sacrifice: and the knowledge of God more than holocausts' (Osee 6, 6). But Our Lord also exhorted them the same thing, saying, 'For if you knew what this meaneth: I will have mercy, and not sacrifice: you would never have condemned the innocent' (Mt. 12, 7). Thus does He bear witness to the prophets, that they preached the truth; but accuses these men (His hearers) of being foolish through their own fault. But when giving instruction to His disciples, to offer to God the first-fruits of His creatures—not as if He stood in need of them, but that they might be themselves neither unfruitful nor ungrateful—He took that which is one of His creatures, bread, and gave thanks, and said, 'This is My body' (Mt. 26, 26). And the chalice likewise, which is a creature like us, He confessed to be His Blood, and taught the new oblation of the New Testament; which the Church receiving from the Apostles, offers to God throughout all the world, to Him Who gives us as the means of subsistence the first-fruits of His own gifts in the New Testament, concerning which Malachias, among the twelve prophets, thus spoke beforehand: 'I have no pleasure in you, saith the Lord of hosts: and I will not receive a gift of your hand. For from the rising of the sun even to the going down, my name is great among the Gentiles, and in every place there is sacrifice, and there is offered to my name a clean oblation: for my name is great among the Gentiles, saith the Lord of hosts" (Mal. 1, 10-11)—indicating in the plainest manner, by these words, that the former people [the Jews] shall indeed cease to make offerings to God; but that in every place sacrifice shall be offered to Him, and that a clean one; and His name is glorified among the Gentiles."[2] So speaks the martyr Irenaeus, a disciple of Polycarp.

Let the Lutherans listen, and carefully consider the testimonies of these men, and they will understand that it is not a new or recent teaching, whereby it is taught that the Mass is a true sacrifice, but a teaching received in the Catholic Church from the very times of the Apostles. And these holy men handed down this teaching, not from their own judgment alone, as the heretics do: but they drew it from Sacred Scripture itself, the right and genuine interpretation of which ought to be received from them, rather than from heretics. And I have cited their testimonies for this very important reason, so that it may be established from them, what is the true and genuine meaning of Sacred Scripture, and finally so that I might clearly prove from Scripture itself that the Mass is a sacrifice. Therefore, let the very shameless and very mendacious heretics keep silent, who do not fear to reproach us, that we confirm our Catholic teaching only by the opinions of recent theologians, and not by God's word, about which they most mendaciously and arrogantly boast.

I could cite still more quotations from the Old Testament about this matter, but they do not show so clearly this Catholic opinion, due to the fact that their meaning is not so apparent, nor can it be so easily gathered from the opinions of the holy Fathers, as in other testimonies of the same Testament which I have cited until now: and hence I have decided to omit them, lest perhaps those who seek occasions on every side could expose Catholic men to be derided by the people.

Let us go on to the New Testament, in which there is much greater clarity of all things than in the Old Testament. If the deeds and words, which Christ our High Priest according

---

[1] C. 116-117 (PG 6, 746A-B).

[2] *Against the Heresies*, bk. 4, c. 17, n. 4-5 (PG 7, 1023B-1024A).

to the order of Melchisedech in that most holy Supper did and said be diligently pondered, it will be very clearly proved therefrom that the Mass is a sacrifice. Now so that I may do all these things more clearly, it is necessary to cite the words of Luke's Gospel, with which he describes the Lord's Supper, saying the following: "And taking bread, he gave thanks, and brake; and gave to them, saying: This is my body, which is given for you. Do this for a commemoration of me" (22, 19). In these words, Luke manifestly declares what Christ did, and what He said. In these words which He said, He commanded the Apostles and all future priests, that they do for a commemoration of Him, that which He did.

And because I do not know of any controversy about this, wherefore I do not want to tarry in proving this point, especially since Blessed Cyprian, in the letter to Caecilius cited above, teaches this clearly, and leaves the matter beyond doubt. If, then, I will have proved that Christ our Redeemer not only on the Cross, but also at the most holy Supper offered His Body to God the Father for us all: it will be fully proved that the Gospel priests, who consecrate the Eucharist at Mass, are obliged to offer the same Body of Christ to God which they consecrated: because Christ commands them to do what He did for a commemoration of Him. By this very strong argument Blessed Cyprian in the above mentioned letter proves that in the Sacred Mysteries it is necessary that water be mixed with wine: because the Lord did so, and afterwards He commands the priests to do what He did, saying: "Do this for a commemoration of me."

Now that Christ our High Priest offered His Body for us to God the Father in that most blessed Supper, is clearly established from Holy Writ and the testimonies of many holy men. Firstly, in fact, what Christ our Savior says in Luke's Gospel is clear: "This is my body, which is given for you." In which words one ought to especially notice that He did not speak in the future tense, "will be given," but rather He spoke in the present tense, "is given"; so that by this very clear speech He might show that not merely afterwards on the Cross, but then also He offers His Body under the appearances of bread for us to God the Father. And He spoke in the same manner of the chalice as follows, according to the original Greek wording, saying: "This is the chalice, the new testament in my blood, which is 'poured out' [*funditur*] for you" (Lk. 22, 20). For even though in the Vulgate and the Old Latin versions of the New Testament it is found in the future tense, *fundetur*: nevertheless, in the Greek version it is in the present and not in the future tense. For the Greek word corresponding to that word is ἐκχυννόμενον, which is a participle in the present tense, not in the future. And this same participle is used in Matthew and Mark, where both speak of the administration of the chalice.

Wherefore I cannot but be surprised that the interpreter of the old translation, in all three Evangelists, translated the word in the future tense, *effundetur*, since in all three Evangelists, in Greek is found the abovementioned participle, which is manifestly in the present tense. Perhaps that man translated it in the present tense, and afterwards uneducated writers not understanding the matter thought that they would correct the text, and they corrupted it by changing the present tense into the future. Erasmus of Rotterdam, a man very learned in Greek, in his translation of the New Testament, in all three Gospels put the word in the present tense, *effunditur*. And in the First Epistle to the Corinthians, where it is found in the Old [Vulgate] translation: "This is my body, which shall be delivered for you" (11, 24), Erasmus translated not by the word in the future tense, but by the word in the present, saying as follows: "This is my body which is broken for you." For in that passage of Paul, in Greek is found, ἔκλασεν, which also is a present participle, and hence was necessarily ought to be translated by the word in the present tense, and not by the word in the future.[1]

---

[1] "It is firmly to be believed that the form of consecrating the chalice is comprehended in these words: 'This is the chalice of My Blood of the new and eternal testament: the mystery of faith: which shall be shed for you, and for many to the remission of sins." These words are for the most part taken from

Therefore, from the words of the three Evangelists, and of Paul, according to the Greek original, it is clearly proved that Christ in that most blessed Supper offered to God for us His Body and Blood: because He then says that He delivers His Body and sheds His Blood: which cannot be said according to the truth unless He then offered His Body to afterwards undergo the Passion, and His Blood afterwards for making a shedding. And on account of this oblation which Christ then made of His Body and Blood, as often as we eat this most holy Bread and drink the Lord's chalice, as Paul says, we show the Lord's death until He comes for judgment.[1] For when we do these things, we do them in commemoration of Him, as Christ Himself commands. Now there would not be a commemoration of Christ's death unless He at His most blessed Supper had offered in some way His Body and Blood to God the Father. Thus, He offered in His blessed Supper His Most Sacred Body and Blood, yet otherwise than on the Cross. For on the Cross He offered His visible and palpable Body to God: but in the Supper He offered His Body in a form nowise visible to men, but rather hidden under the appearances of bread and wine. On the Cross He offered His palpable and passible Body: at His Supper, on the other hand, He offered it under a form in which He could not suffer or be touched.

Furthermore, from the very rite and order of the priesthood according to which Christ our Savior was a priest, it is proved that at the Supper He offered His Body and Blood to God the Father. But the rite and order of Melchisedech, as we have already proved above by very clear testimonies, was the offering of bread and wine: hence, so that Christ may according to truth be called a priest according to the order of Melchisedech, it is necessary that He would have made a similar offering, namely His Body under the appearances of bread, and His Blood under the appearances of wine. On the Cross, however, He did not offer His Body hidden under the appearance of this kind: but naked and visible to all, scourged, sprinkled with His own Blood, hurt with many wounds. If Christ was not a priest on the Cross according to the rite and order of Melchisedech, because there was not any likeness to a sacrificial victim there, one ought to necessarily acknowledge that He exercised such a priesthood according to the order of Melchisedech at the most sacred Supper. For there Christ had a similar victim,

---

Scripture. Some of them, however, have been preserved in the Church by Apostolic tradition… Of the legitimacy of this form we cannot entertain a shadow of doubt." (*Catechism of the Council of Trent*, On the Sacrament of the Holy Eucharist). "Cyprian adds [the words of the institution] for the wine: 'He took the chalice the day before He suffered, blessed it and gave it to His disciples saying: 'Drink you all of this, for this is the Blood of the New Testament which shall be shed for you (notice the future [tense], as at Rome) for the forgiveness of sins…' He insists on the necessity of doing just as Our Lord did at the Last Supper: 'Since it is commanded by the Lord, and the same thing is confirmed and handed down by His Apostle, that as often as we drink we should do in memory of the Lord what the Lord did, we see that we should not obey what is commanded unless we also did the same things that the Lord did' (Letter 63, n. 10)." (Adrian Fortescue, *The Mass: A Study of the Roman Liturgy* (Albany, PCP Publications, 1997), p. 46). "When the Vulgate translates the Greek participles by the future (*effundetur, fundetur*), it is not at variance with facts, considering that the mystical shedding of blood in the chalice, if it were not brought into intimate relation with the physical shedding of blood on the Cross, would be impossible and meaningless; for the one is the essential presupposition and foundation of the other. Still, from the standpoint of philology, *effunditur* (*funditur*) ought to be translated into the strictly present, as is really done in many ancient codices. The accuracy of this exegesis is finally attested in a striking way by the Greek wording in St. Luke: *to poterion… ekchynnomenon*. Here the shedding of blood appears as taking place directly in the chalice, and therefore in the present. Overzealous critics, it is true, have assumed that there is here a grammatical mistake, in that St. Luke erroneously connects the 'shedding' with the chalice (*poterion*), instead of with 'blood' (*to aimati*) which is in the dative. Rather than correct this highly cultivated Greek, as though he were a school boy, we prefer to assume that he intended to use synecdoche, a figure of speech known to everybody, and therefore put the vessel to indicate its contents." ("Sacrifice of the Mass," *Catholic Encyclopedia* (1911 ed.), vol. 10, p. 10)."

[1] Cf. I Cor. 11, 26.

namely His Body under the appearances of bread, and His Blood under the appearances of wine. If, then, Christ truly acted as a priest, and truly sacrificed and offered a victim: then the Evangelical priests, who are priests according to the order instituted by Christ and begun by the same Christ, sacrifice in the same way, and offer to God the same Victim which Christ offered: especially since by Christ's command, and power given to them for this by the same Christ, they do the same thing which Christ Himself did.

Additionally, the concordant testimony of many holy men who were illustrious for teaching as well as holiness, whereby they all bear witness in one accord that Christ at the Last Supper offered His Body for us to God. And I firstly cite Rupert Deutz, the most recent of all the ancient witnesses, who, when explaining the rite and ceremonies of the Paschal Lamb, how it figured those things which are associated with Christ's Body, at length when coming to the immolation of the lamb, about which we spoke above, says these words: "Finally in the evening of the fourteenth day, when He ate the lamb of the old Pasch with His disciples, then He, the Lamb of the new sacrifice, was to be taken immediately, and to be led away to be immolated, already agonizing in the distress of the Passion, firstly immolated Himself with His own hands to God the Father, taking bread and wine, and changing these things with marvelous and unspeakable power of sanctification into the Sacrament of His Body and Blood. For since thereafter the same Lamb was crucified and died by the hands of sinners, immediately He was the salvation of all past and present men, and He descended to those who were detained in lower Egypt, that is, in infernal darkness, who had been brought together in that same place for five days, through the five previous ages of the world. Hence it is also evident that for five days, namely from the tenth to the fourteenth of the month, the lamb was kept: because from which [time] as a type of the same Son of God, Abel firstly offered a lamb, five ages of the world flowed, at the end of which this true Lamb of God would be immolated... But because by His own hands, as was said above, the High Priest Himself offered His Body and Blood under the appearances of bread [and wine], and He said, 'Do this for a commemoration of me' (Lk. 22, 19), He is the salvation of those who are detained in this world, for whom this world is Egypt, for whom captivity under the devil, the ruler of this world, is ignorance of God."[1] Even though Rupert is the most recent of those whom we are going to cite, nevertheless he lived more than four hundred and fifty years ago: and he says so clearly that Christ at the Last Supper offered His Body to God, that nothing clearer could be desired.

Several centuries before this man was Bede, who, when interpreting the words: "And whilst they were eating, Jesus took bread" (Mk. 14, 22), says these words: "When the rites of the Passover were finished, He passed to the new, which He wanted the Church to repeat in memory of His Redemption: that is, to substitute the Sacrament of His own Body and Blood, for the flesh and blood of the lamb, in order to shew that He, Himself, is that Person to whom the Lord swore, 'Thou art a priest forever, according to the order of Melchisedech' (Ps 109, 4).'"[2] In Bede's words one ought to notice that he said that at the Last Supper Christ exercised His priesthood according to the order of Melchisedech, which He did not do except for when He offered His Body and Blood.

[Pseudo-] Jerome teaches this much more clearly, who when interpreting the passage, "Thou art a priest forever, according to the order of Melchisedech," says these words: "For as Melchisedech, the king of Salem, offered bread and wine: so also Thou wilt offer Thy Body and Blood, true bread, and true wine. This Melchisedech gave to us these Mysteries which we have. It is He who said: 'He that eateth my flesh, and drinketh my blood' etc. (Jn. 6, 55).

---

[1] *De Trinitate et operibus eius, In Exodum commentariorum*, bk. 2, c. 6 (PL 167, 613C-614A).
[2] Homily 53 (PL 94, 393C-D).

According to the order of Melchisedech He delivered His Sacrament to us."[1] Jerome could not say anything clearer to support our opinion.

Ambrose in the [Ambrosian rite of] Mass for Holy Thursday in the *Communicantes* of the Mass, says these words: "And what can we not hope for from Thy mercy, who have received so great an office that we are entitled to offer such a Victim to Thee, namely the Body and Blood of Our Lord Jesus Christ, Who delivered Himself to that benevolent and venerable Passion for the redemption of the world: Who when instituting the form of the perpetual sacrifice of salvation, firstly offered Himself as the Victim, and firstly taught that it should be offered?"[2] In which words he asserts two things at the same time, by which things this whole disputation is resolved. For he says that Christ in that most sacred Supper offered Himself as a victim, and taught us that we should offer ourselves the same Victim.

Before Ambrose lived Eusebius, Bishop of Caesarea, who, when proving how the sacrifices of the Old Law ceased, and in their place another sacrifice in the Evangelical Law was substituted, says these words: "After all this, Christ offering up in due manner such a wonderful sacrifice and most excellent Victim to His Father, for the salvation of us all, He instituted the memorial [of it] that we should continually offer it to God for a sacrifice."[3] In which words, although they are few, still they encompass many things which support our and the Catholic teaching. For firstly he says that he offered Himself to God the Father. Secondly, he says that we offer the same thing in commemoration of Him. Thirdly, he says that this sacrifice which we ourselves offer is by Christ's institution, and not from human judgment or by papist invention, as the heretics are accustomed to say by a very mendacious blasphemy. Of these three things which I said Eusebius asserted, the last two he says so clearly that no one can rightly doubt about them.

About the first, someone will perhaps argue, and will say that Eusebius there spoke about the sacrifice made on the Cross when He offered Himself to God. Now so that it may be clearly shown that He spoke about the sacrifice made at the Supper, and not on the Cross, it is necessary to examine the words which he immediately adds without any intermediary words, saying the following: "Also, David, the chief of the prophets, who had foreseen what was to come by the Divine Spirit, prophesied, where he says: 'With expectation I have waited for the Lord, and he was attentive to me. And he heard my prayers, and brought me out of the pit of misery and the mire of dregs. And he set my feet upon a rock, and directed my steps. And he put a new canticle into my mouth, a song to our God' (Ps. 39, 2-4). He then states afterwards what this new canticle is, where he says: 'Burnt offering and sin offering thou didst not require: then said I, Behold I come. In the head of the book it is written of me that I should do thy will: O my God, I have desired it,' and he adds, 'I have declared thy justice in a great church' (v. 7-10). He plainly teaches that in the place of ancient sacrifices and holocausts, Christ is to come through the assumption of a human body, and His perfect Body is to be offered to God; and this was announced with joy to His Church as a great mystery, which by the prophetic voice was declared and expressed in the head of the book. Thus since we have received a commemoration of this sacrifice which is to be made with certain signs of His Body and His salutary Blood, on the table, according to the traditions of the New Testament: we are again instructed by the prophet David to say: 'Thou hast prepared a table before me against them that afflict me. Thou hast anointed my head with oil; and my chalice which inebriateth me, how goodly is it!' (Ps. 22, 5) Clearly therefore in these words he indicates the sacrifices of Christ's table carrying forth mystical anointing and fragrance, when performing the sacred rites with those things which we have been taught to offer to the most high God through our

---

[1] *Breviarium in Psalmos*, Ps. 109 (PL 1165D-1166A).

[2] Jacques de Pamèle, *Liturgica latinorum* (Cologne, G. Calenius, 1571), vol. 1, p. 340.

[3] *Demonstratio evangelica*, bk. 1, c. 10 (PG 22, 90D).

whole lives, unbloody and reasonable victims sweet to Him."[1] Thus far the words Eusebius of Caesarea written more than a thousand two hundred years ago. From which words it is clearly established that he spoke about the sacrifice made in the Lord's Supper, and we offer to God an unbloody Victim in commemoration of that Supper: and he says that we do this by reason of the teaching of the Supreme Pontiff of all men, namely Jesus Christ our Savior.

Cyprian, Bishop of Carthage and martyr, preceded Eusebius of Caesarea by [nearly[2]] a century, when explaining the verse, "Thou art a priest forever, according to the order of Melchisedech" (Ps. 109, 4), says these words: "Which order is assuredly this coming from that sacrifice and thence descending; that Melchisedech was a priest of the most high God; that he offered wine and bread; that he blessed Abraham. For who is more a priest of the most high God than our Lord Jesus Christ, who offered a sacrifice to God the Father, and offered that very same thing which Melchisedech had offered, that is, bread and wine, to wit, His Body and Blood?"[3] The martyr Cyprian wrote these words more than a thousand three hundred years ago.

Behold seven illustrious men renown for holiness as well as doctrine, who all assert with one accord that Christ at the Last Supper offered to God the Father His Body and Blood under the appearances of bread and wine. And they assert this, not from their own judgment alone, as is the custom of heretics, but having been persuaded by the testimony of Sacred Scripture. If Christ in that most sacred Supper offered His Body and Blood to God the Father, then the Evangelical priests offer the same Body and the same Blood to God the Father: because He said to them: "Do this for a commemoration of me." For by these words, as all the sacred Doctors interpret them, He commands the priests to do the same thing which He had done. Now Christ, as we proved, offered Himself in the Last Supper: thus, priests are obliged to offer Him in the Mass, which is a commemoration of that Supper. Therefore, the Mass is a sacrifice.

Finally, this our and the Catholic opinion is proved by the definitions of many councils, in all of which the Mass is said to be a sacrifice. For the First Synod of Toledo calls the Mass a" sacrifice."[4] The Twelfth Synod of Toledo does likewise.[5] But perhaps someone will say that those were provincial councils, and hence were able to err. I acknowledge that they were provincial councils, but their judgment ought not to be contemned on that account: because it was confirmed by other general councils. For the [IV] Lateran Council celebrated under Innocent III says these words: "One indeed is the universal Church of the faithful, outside which no one at all is saved, in which the Priest Himself is the sacrifice, Jesus Christ, whose Body and Blood are truly contained in the Sacrament of the altar under the species of bread and wine; the bread (changed) into His Body by the Divine power of transubstantiation, and the wine into His Blood, so that to accomplish the mystery of unity we ourselves receive from His (nature) what He Himself received from ours."[6] Before this council, preceded by many centuries, the [Council in Trullo[7]], which when declaring that the wine mixed with water necessarily is to be offered in Mass, say these words: "Since it has come to our knowledge that in the region of Armenia they offer wine only on the Holy Table, those who celebrate the unbloody Sacrifice not mixing water with it, adducing, as authority thereof, John Chrysostom, a Doctor of the Church, who says in his interpretation of the Gospel according to St. Matthew... Now

---

[1] *Ibid.* (PL 22, 90D-91B).

[2] The text here incorrectly says, "by more than a whole century."

[3] Letter 63, n. 4 (PL 4, 376A).

[4] Canon 5 (*Collectio Canonum Ecclesiae Hispanae ex probatissimis ac pervetustis Codicibus*, p. 323).

[5] Chapter 5 (*Ibid.*), p. 496.

[6] Chap. 1 (Dz. 430).

[7] The Council of Trullo is here called the "Sixth General Synod."

so that they may now be freed from ignorance, we make known the orthodox opinion of the Fathers. For since there was an ancient and wicked heresy of the *Hydroparastatae* [i.e., 'those who offer water'], who instead of wine used water in their sacrifice, this divine [Doctor], confuting the detestable teaching of such a heresy, and showing that it is directly opposed to Apostolic tradition, asserted that which has just been quoted. For to his own church, where the pastoral administration had been given him, he ordered that water mixed with wine should be used at the unbloody Sacrifice, so as to show forth the mingling of the Blood and water which was for the life of the whole world and for the Redemption of its sins"[1] In which words it often says that that Mass is a sacrifice: and not any kind, but such kind in which Christ's true Blood is offered. Also, the Council of Ephesus, which was celebrated many centuries before the [Council in Trullo], in a letter sent to Nestorius, says these words: "Proclaiming the death according to the flesh of the only begotten Son of God… we offer the unbloody service of Sacrifice in the churches."[2] In which words it very clearly asserts that the Mass is a sacrifice: because from the words which it immediately adds afterwards, it is evident that it speaks about the celebration of Mass.

I do not see anything that remains for me for fully showing and proving the Catholic truth about the sacrifice of the Mass, except only to reply to the objections of the heretics, whereby they attempt to prove that the Mass is not a sacrifice. Firstly, in fact, Luther objects to us Christ's example, which he says necessarily ought to be imitated, saying the following: "The Mass is a commemoration of the Lord's Supper, in which Christ supped with His Apostles shortly before His death. But Christ did not sacrifice when having the Supper, nor did He then offer His Body and Blood, but only afterwards when dying on the Cross. Therefore, the priest does not sacrifice in the Mass, nor offers Christ's Body and Blood." Luther tries to prove this inference or consequence from the fact that we ought, as he says, to imitate in this mystery Christ's works and His mystery. For He said at the Supper: "I have given you an example, that as I have done to you, so you do also" (Jn. 13, 15).[3]

This argumentation of Luther has completely no force, because it assumes what is false, and reasons badly. Firstly, it is false in fact that the Mass is a commemoration of the Lord's Supper alone. For even though it is true that the Mass is a certain representation of the Lord's Supper, still not of the Supper alone, but also of Christ's death and Passion, Paul attesting to the this, who in the First Epistle to the Corinthians says: "As often as you shall eat this bread, and drink the chalice, you shall shew the death of the Lord, until he come" (11, 26). Thus, since Christ when dying sacrificed Himself, and offered Himself to God the Father on the Cross, priests have the right in the Mass, which is a certain representation of Christ's Passion, to sacrifice Christ's Body, and offer it to God the Father. It is also false that Christ in the most holy Supper did not offer His Body and Blood to God the Father. For above we proved from Christ's own words and from the testimonies of many holy men, that Christ at that Last Sup-

---

[1] Canon 32 (PG 137, 615B-618B).

[2] PL 67, 15B.

[3] "They all [i.e., the papist priests] imagine that they are offering Christ Himself to God the Father as an all-sufficient victim; and that they are doing a good work on behalf of all men, who, as they allege, will profit by it… To all these [arguments whereby the Mass is preached by the papists to be a sacrifice], which beset us so pertinaciously, we must oppose with the utmost constancy the words and example of Christ. [His words express merely a testament, not a sacrifice.] Again, we have the example of Christ on our side. For Christ did not in the Last Supper, when He instituted this sacrament [i.e., a sacred sign or mystery] and established this testament, offer Himself to God the Father, or accomplish any work on behalf of others, but, as He sat at the table, He declared the same testament to each individual present and bestowed on each the sign of it" (Luther, *On the Babylonian Captivity of the Church*, preface (WA 6, 522-523)).

per offered an unbloody Victim to God the Father, namely His Body and Blood. For unless we say that He offered these things, it could never be found when Christ exercised His office as a priest according to the order of Melchisedech. For He did not exercise this office on the Cross, because then, as we said above, He offered His Body openly perceivable to all, and hidden not under the appearances of bread and wine. But "Christ [the Lord]," as the Church sings of Him, "a priest forever according to the order of Melchisedech offered bread and wine."[1] Now since it is evident that Christ never did this except when at the Supper, is proved that Christ at the Last Supper offered His Body and Blood to God the Father. Thus, He twice offered His Body and Blood for us to God the Father: firstly, when He supped, and secondly, when He was fixed to the Cross.

The consequence [or logical inference] of the Lutherans is also wrong: because even if we were to freely grant to Luther that Christ at the Last Supper did not offer His Body and Blood to God the Father, it would not necessarily follow therefrom that the Evangelical priests no-wise offer Christ's Body and Blood in the Mass. For it is not necessary that whatever Christ then did at the Supper, priests now do in the Mass: and the things which He did not do then, priests also do not now dare to do. For according to this rule, it would not be permitted for priests to celebrate clothed in sacred vestments and in silver and gold vessels, because Christ in that most holy Supper of His, had none of these things. It also would be necessary that priests celebrate feasting, and only give the Lord's Body to those who have already feasted: because Gospels teach that Christ did so. Yet the Catholic Church, spread throughout the whole world and taught by the Holy Ghost, teaches and commands to do the opposite of all these things. For many things, as Jerome rightly says, befit a master, which do not befit a young slave, and hence are not permitted.[2] If everything in the Mass were to be done in imitation of Christ, why does he permit Mass to be celebrated among themselves in the presence of more or less than twelve men, since Christ consecrated the mystical Supper with only twelve? Why, when one Mass has finished, does he permit another to be said on another day, since Christ celebrated that most sacred Supper only once? Why when Luther is celebrating Mass, does he not get ready and prepare himself, so that when the Mass has been completed, he pray apart from his followers, and from there proceed to the death of the Cross, just as Christ did? But where it was necessary to imitate Christ, on that point Luther is far from doing so: and where it is not necessary, nor it is permitted to imitate Christ, on that point he contends that all should imitate Him.

What Luther cites to prove his opinion, "I have given you an example, that as I have done to you, so you do also" (Jn. 13, 15), does not support him at all. Because Christ did not say those words when sitting at the Supper when He gave His Body and Blood under the appearances of bread and wine to his disciples: but when, as it is clearly evident from John's Gospel, He washed the feet of His disciples. For He then commanded them that from what they had seen Him do, they would take the example of humility to wash the feet of each other. Thus, what Christ had said about the washing of feet alone, Luther tries to extend to all of Christ's actions. Behold what sort of arguments are Luther's, in which he brings forth nothing true, nay not even what has a semblance of truth, but mere nonsense, and distortions of Sacred Scripture, whereby he has deceived uneducated and completely illiterate people, and drew them to his own wicked teachings.

The Lutherans, secondly, argue that those saying that the Mass is a sacrifice rob Christ of the great honor of the eternal priest. Now so that the strength of this argument will be more apparent to all, I will faithfully cite the words of John Calvin, who treats this argument at

---

[1] First antiphon of the first Vespers of the feast of Corpus Christ.
[2] "Observe carefully how He decrees the precepts according to the persons" (*Commentaria in Epistolam ad Titum*, c. 2, v. 9 (PL 26, 560B ff.)).

greater length and more energetically. "Christ was not appointed priest and pontiff by the Father for a time merely, as priests were appointed under the Old Testament. Since their life was mortal, their priesthood could not be immortal, and hence there was need of successors, who might ever and anon be substituted in the room of the dead. But Christ being immortal, had not the least occasion to have a vicar substituted for him. Wherefore he was appointed by his Father a priest forever, after the order of Melchisedech, that He might eternally exercise a permanent priesthood... But nowadays they sacrifice daily; it is necessary that they appoint priests over the oblations, whom they substitute as successors and vicars of Christ. By this substitution they not only rob Christ of his honor, and take from Him the prerogative of an eternal priesthood, but attempt to remove Him from the right hand of His Father, where He cannot sit immortal without being an eternal priest. Nor let them allege that their priestlings are not substituted for Christ, as if He were dead, but are only substitutes in that eternal priesthood, which therefore ceases not to exist. The words of the Apostle are too stringent to leave them any means of evasion—viz. many other men were made priests: because they were impeded by death to continue. Thus Christ, who was not impeded by death, is one, and does not need partners."[1]

In the words of this argument Calvin clearly, as other heretics, his consorts, are accustomed to do, represents our stance as weak and defenseless, so that he may be able more easily to persuade uneducated people that he triumphs over us. For he contrives to give us an inept and exceedingly absurd response to his argument, which in fact we did not think of, even in our dreams. For we admit that Christ is a true priest according to the order of Melchisedech, as the heavenly Father had declared He would be by an oath. We do not say, however, that the Evangelical priests are His successors, as of someone deceased, as the priests of the Old Law were; when one of whom died, another was substituted in his place. And we do not say that the Evangelical priests, as Calvin falsely accuses us, are Christ's 'vicars' or His 'partners': but rather they are His ministers by whom He exercises His priesthood forever. For He alone is the true and perfect Priest Who really consecrates, offers and truly performs all the rest of the proper functions of a priest: we however are merely His ministers, through whom He acts. For in the Sacrament of Baptism, as often as some priest administers this Sacrament, it is Christ Who truly and effectively baptizes, as John the Baptist bore witness, saying the following: "He who sent me to baptize with water, said to me: He upon whom thou shalt see the Spirit descending, and remaining upon him, he it is that baptizeth with the Holy Ghost" (Jn. 1, 33). From these words of John, Blessed Augustine proves that the wickedness of a priest, even if he be a heretic, does not prevent him from conferring valid Baptism: because it is Christ who baptizes,[2] the priest however does not baptize the soul: but only says the words, and washes the body exteriorly. Entirely the same thing ought to be said about the Sacrament of the Eucharist, in the confection of which, although the priest takes bread, blesses, and pronounces the words of consecration upon it, still he does not actually convert the bread into Christ's Body: but Christ Himself is the one makes that change of substance: because just as it is He Who invisibly baptizes, so it is He Who invisibly consecrates the bread, and converts it into His Body.

As proof of this, I cite [Pseudo-] Eusebius of Emesa who says these words: "For the invisible Priest by secret power converts the visible creatures with His word into the substance of

---

[1] Cf. Heb. 7, 23-24. *Institutes of the Christian Religion* (ed. 1559), bk. 4, c. 18, n. 2 (CR 30, 1052).

[2] "You are then not better than John: but the Baptism given through you is better than that of John; for the one is Christ's, but the other is that of John. And that which was given by Paul, and that which was given by Peter, is Christ's; and if Baptism was given by Judas it was Christ's." (*Tractates on the Gospel of John*, Tract. 5, n. 18 (PL 35, 1423)).

His own Body and Blood."[1] Eusebius of Emesa said these words more than a thousand two hundred years ago. In which words he calls Christ by the name of the invisible Priest, due to the fact that He now is not seen by people, although He does those things which pertain to the real function of a priest. Not merely does Christ our God consecrate bread and convert it into His Body, but He also offers His Body to God the Father by an unbloody oblation, as often as the Evangelical priests validly celebrate Mass. Priests truly offer Christ's Body in the name of the whole Church to God the Father, as Christ's ministers. Christ, however, is the one Who at that time, principally through the priests and through the Church, offers Himself to God the Father. Hence Haymo [of Auxerre] when interpreting the words from the Epistle to the Hebrews: "Every high priest is appointed to offer gifts" (8, 3), says these words: "For because sacrifice is due to no one, except to God alone, our Pontiff offered a clean oblation for us to God the Father, being at the same time the priest and sacrifice. He also offers the sacrifice acceptable to God the Father through His Church. For while we offer the Sacraments of His Body, He Himself offers [the same]."[2]

And because Christ daily offers through the priests of the Church, hence He daily exercises His priesthood according to the order of Melchisedech. He also daily exercises the sacerdotal office, whilst He prays as our advocate, because the office of the priest is to pray. Nevertheless, when he so prays, He does not show himself in this to be a priest according to the order of Melchisedech, rather than according to the order of Aaron: because the latter order is not distinguished from the former by prayers and supplications, but by victims and sacrifices, and by the manner of offering them. Thus, Christ is a priest according to the order of Melchisedech, whilst He daily offers Himself through the priests of the Church to God the Father under the accidents of bread. If Calvin had understood well this our and the Catholic doctrine, he would not have accused us, saying that we rob Christ of the honor of the eternal priest. For when we say that the Evangelical priests offer to God Christ's Body and Blood, we do not exclude from this offering Christ Himself, nor do we make other priests His assistants or partners: but we only say that they are ministers of Christ, the true Priest, through whom He, the true and invisible Priest, acts daily. From all these things it is very clearly established that we much better attribute the glory and honor of the eternal Priest to Christ than does Calvin, who when he denies that the Mass is a sacrifice, denies that it is an oblation to be offered by the Evangelical priests, through which also Christ is a priest forever according to the order of Melchisedech.

Thirdly, the heretics object to us, especially John Calvin, that we diminish the power of Christ's Passion and death, when we say that the Mass is a sacrifice: because by this very fact, as he says, we are forced to confess that the sacrifice of Christ's death is not sufficient for the remission of sins, since it is necessary that it be repeated so many times in the Mass. These are Calvin's words: "For if, on the Cross, He offered Himself in sacrifice that He might sanctify us forever, and purchase eternal redemption for us, undoubtedly the power and efficacy of His sacrifice continues without end. Otherwise, we should not think more honorably of Christ than of the oxen and calves which were sacrificed under the Law, the offering of which is proved to have been weak and inefficacious because it was often repeated. Wherefore, it must be admitted, either that the sacrifice which Christ offered on the Cross lacked the power of eternal cleansing, or that He performed this once forever by His one sacrifice. Accordingly, the Apostle says, 'But now once at the end of ages, he hath appeared for the destruction of sin, by the sacrifice of himself' (Heb. 9, 26). Again: 'In the which will, we are sanctified by the oblation of the body of Jesus Christ once' (Heb. 10, 10). Again: 'For by one oblation he hath perfected forever them that are sanctified' (v. 14). To this he subjoins the celebrated passage:

---

[1] This sermon is also attributed to St. Caesarius of Arles (PL 67, 1053A).
[2] *Expositio in D. Pauli epistolas, In epistolam ad hebraeos*, c. 7 (PL 117, 874C).

'Now where there is a remission of these, there is no more an oblation for sin' (v. 18). The same thing Christ intimated by His last words, when, on giving up the ghost, He exclaimed, 'It is consummated' (Jn. 19, 30). We are accustomed to observe the last words of the dying as oracular. Christ, when dying, declares, that by His one sacrifice is perfected and fulfilled whatever was necessary to our salvation. To such a sacrifice, whose perfection He so clearly declared, shall we, as if it were imperfect, presume daily to append innumerable sacrifices? Since the sacred word of God not only affirms, but proclaims and protests, that this sacrifice was once accomplished, and remains eternally in force, do not those who demand another, charge it with imperfection and weakness?"[1]

In which words he plainly displays his ignorance. For he clearly shows that he does not know what is apparently true by the authority of Sacred Scripture, and which we proved by the testimonies of the holy Fathers, that Christ made two very different oblations, one unbloody in the Supper: the other bloody on the Cross. There was one and the same sacrificial Victim in both oblations, namely His Body which He offered to God in both oblations, but because He offered His same Body twice and in different ways to God the Father, whence I say that He made two and different oblations of His Body. For on the Cross He offered His wounded Body, sprinkled with His own Blood, and that sacrificial Victim was bloody, and that sacrifice was bloody. In the Supper, on the other hand, He offered His Body, not wounded, nor reddened with His own Blood, but whole and sound, and not bathed with any blood, hidden under the accidents of bread. And hence the holy Doctors, whom we cited above, call Christ's Body offered in this manner, a sacrificial Victim and unbloody oblation, and the Council of Ephesus named it an "unbloody service of sacrifice." And the Council in Trullo, in the words cited above, said "the unbloody sacrifice," so that by this epithet the oblation of the Last Supper and the sacrifice made in it might be distinguished from the oblation and sacrifice made on the Cross.

Therefore, since these two oblations are so different, it follows that different conditions and different merits be allotted. By the oblation which was made in the Supper, the human race was not redeemed: because "Without shedding of blood," as Paul says, "there is no remission" (Heb. 9, 22). By the oblation made on the Cross, however, we were redeemed from the slavery to the devil by which we were held captive at his will. For "By the blood of thy testament," as the prophet Zacharias foretold, "he hast sent forth the prisoners out of the pit" (Zach. 9, 11). This oblation made on the Cross is not done a second time, nor ever repeated: because "Christ rising again from the dead," as Paul says, "dieth now no more. Death shall no more have dominion over him" (Rom. 6, 9). Paul spoke about this oblation made on the Cross in the Epistle to the Hebrews, when speaking of Christ, he says: "Who needeth not daily (as the other priests) to offer sacrifices first for his own sins, and then for the people's: for this he did once, in offering himself" (7, 27). And in the same epistle he again says: "Christ was offered once to exhaust the sins of many" (9, 28). And again, in the same place he says: "For by one oblation he hath perfected forever them that are sanctified" (10, 14). In all these passages, and in other similar ones, Paul, as it is very clearly evident, speaks about that oblation which Christ made on the Cross, and not about the one which He made in the Last Supper. For by that one alone which was made on the Cross, did He "exhaust the sins of many," and "perfect forever them that are sanctified." It was not necessary to repeat the oblation made on the Cross: because having been made once, it was sufficient for exhausting the sins of many. Priests do not need to do a second time or repeat this oblation made by Christ on the Cross when they sacrifice and offer to God. Because even though they celebrate Mass in commemoration of the Lord's Passion, still there is not such an oblation of Christ's Body in the Mass,

---

[1] *Institutes of the Christian Religion* (ed. 1559), bk. 4, c. 18, n. 3 (CR 30, 1053-1054).

such as He made on the Cross: but such as He made at the Last Supper, namely an unbloody one, and without any shedding of blood, and without the death of the victim offered.

From all these things it is very clearly established that the sacrifice of the Mass does not at all derogate from the power of Christ's Passion, nor does it lessen the power and efficacy of the oblation which Christ made on the Cross. For we do not sacrifice and offer the Body and Blood of Our Lord Jesus Christ in the Mass, so that by such an oblation we may supply for a defect of the oblation made by Christ on the Cross. Far be it! For that oblation had no defect, nay on the contrary, it had all superabundance. Just as He has "trodden the winepress alone" (Is. 63, 3), so also, He alone without the assistance of anyone "exhausted the sins of many," and satisfied for them all. We celebrate Mass, so that by the Eucharist, as by the other Sacraments, the power and merit of Christ's Passion may be applied to the priest celebrating, and to those for whom he celebrates. Christ's Body and Blood is offered in Mass to God the Father by an unbloody oblation in satisfaction for our sins: and hence it is necessary that such an oblation take place in the Mass, which can be repeated: so that by it we can daily expiate the sins which we daily commit, and repeat daily.[1] And this doctrine is not new, nor it is fabricated from our imagination, as the doctrine of all heretics: but it is very old, accepted by the holy and ancient Doctors of the Church. [Pseudo-] Eusebius of Emesa says these words: "And because He was going to remove His Body, which He had assumed, out of sight, and to convey it into Heaven, it was necessary that on the day of the Supper the Sacrament of His Body and Blood should be consecrated for us; that what was once offered as a ransom might be perpetually celebrated in a mystery; that, because our Redemption flows with a daily unwearied stream for the salvation of all, the oblation of that redemption might be perpetuated; and that this lasting Sacrifice might always live in the memorial, and might ever be present by grace, that true, perfect and only Sacrifice, to be estimated by faith, not by appearance; to be valued not by the outward sense, but by inward affection."[2] Eusebius of Emesa said these words, who lived more than one thousand two hundred years ago. In which words it is necessary to note that when he said that Christ "was once offered as a ransom," he afterwards said, "the oblation of that redemption might be perpetuated." The one and bloody oblation made on the altar of the Cross was as a ransom: the perpetual oblation of the redemption, however, is unbloody, and is that which is made daily in the Mass: because to put this into effect, Christ instituted the Sacrament of His Body and Blood.

John Chrysostom, a contemporary of Eusebius or shortly after him, teaches the same opinion, saying the following: "And because that sacrifice was offered once, it was offered in the holy of holies. This sacrifice is the exemplar of that. For we always offer the same, not one sheep now and tomorrow another, but always the same thing: so that the sacrifice is one."[3] In which words what ought to be especially noticed is that he says that our sacrifice is the same as Christ's sacrifice: because we offer the same sacrifice which Christ offered, although we do not offer in the same manner.

---

[1] "Nevertheless, because that His priesthood was not to be extinguished by His death, in the Last Supper, on the night in which He was betrayed, to the end that He might leave to His own beloved spouse the Church, a visible sacrifice, such as the nature of men requires, whereby that bloody [sacrifice], once to be accomplished on the Cross, might be represented, and the memory thereof remain even unto the end of the world, and its salutary virtue be applied unto the remission of those sins which we daily commit, declaring Himself constituted 'a priest forever, according to the order of Melchisedech'" (Council of Trent, Sess. 22, chap. 1).

[2] Fifth homily on Easter. *Maxima Bibliotheca veterum Patrum*, vol. 6, p. 636. This sermon is also attributed to St. Caesarius of Arles (PL 67, 1052C).

[3] *Homiiae in Epistolam ad Hebraeos*, Hom. 17 (PG 63, 549).

After these two most illustrious men Haymo [of Auxerre[1]] teaches this same opinion more clearly and more copiously, who, when interpreting the verse from the Epistle to the Hebrews, "For then they would have ceased to be offered: because the worshippers once cleansed should have no conscience of sin any longer" (Heb. 10, 2), says these words: "'For then,' that is, if they had been freed from all sins, those sacrifices would have ceased to be offered, because 'they should have no conscience of sin,' that is, memory and remembrance of sins: from which His worshippers were once cleansed. But because this could not happen, and greater sins and crimes could never be cleansed: 'there is made a commemoration of sins every year' by those sacrifices. For example, if someone had offered sacrifices in the present year for the sin of adultery, or sacrilege, or parricide, it was necessary that he do it every year, because he could not be perfectly expiated by that sin-offering. Hence an accusation of sins was what was being done, not a release from them: an accusation of weakness, not an exhibition of strength. For by the fact that they were always being offered, was a reproof of sins: by the fact that they were always necessary, however, is a reproof of the weakness of the sacrifices themselves. Wherefore, he says, He commanded that [the sacrifices] be always offered on account of weakness, because one could not be perfectly cleansed, and so that a remembrance and reproof of sins might be made. What then ought to be said? Do not our priests do the same thing while they continually offer? They indeed offer, but they are doing so for the remembrance of His death. And because we sin daily, we need to be cleansed daily. And because He cannot die anymore, He gave to us this Sacrament of His Body and Blood, so that just as His Passion was the redemption and cleansing of the world, so also this oblation is the redemption and cleansing to all those offering in good faith, and having a good intention. For in this, our sacrifice, which is similarly repeated, differs from the old sacrifice frequently repeated: because the former is the reality, and the latter is a figure: the former makes man perfect, the latter nowise does this: and the former is not repeated due to its weakness, because it would be unable to confer perfect salvation, but rather in commemoration of Christ's Passion: just as He said, 'Do this in commemoration of me': and this sacrificial Victim is one, not many, as they were. How is it one and not many, since it is offered by many, in different places, and at different times? Thus one ought to pay very close attention, because the Divinity of God's Word Which is one, and fills all places, and is whole everywhere, this same Divinity makes that there are not many sacrifices: but one sacrifice, albeit it is offered by many, so that there is one Body of Christ with that sacrifice: because it received in the virginal womb not many bodies. And indeed, we do not offer one thing great, another thing less great, one thing today, another thing tomorrow: but something always having the same equal greatness. Hence there is this one sacrifice of Christ, not different ones: as there were of the former sacrifices. For if it were otherwise, because they are offered in many places, there would have been many Christs; thus there is one Christ everywhere: and the full Christ is existing in this place, and the full Christ is existing elsewhere having one Body. And just as that which is offered everywhere is one Body and not many bodies: so likewise there is also one Sacrifice."[2] Haymo lived more than seven hundred years ago. In which words he made the same argument against himself whereby all the Lutherans now attack us, and he obviates it very well. From all which words Calvin's pride is exposed, who acknowledging and confessing that the doctrine of the sacrifice of the Mass has deep roots in the Church, boasted that he by these arguments of his could cut asunder and overthrow all those things as by a very strong sword. For we have

---

[1] In Migne's *Patrologia Latina*, this passage is attributed to Haymo of Halberstadt, but as mentioned above (see the section, "Gospel," heresy 2), it has more recently been shown to have been written by Haymo of Auxerre.

[2] *Expositio in D. Pauli epistolas: In epistolam ad Hebraeos*, c. 10 (PL 117, 888D-889C).

clearly shown, by God's help, the weakness and lameness of their arguments is so great, that they seem like a sword made of butter.

Fourthly, Luther argues that he can prove that the Mass is not a sacrifice, saying the following: the Eucharist is Christ's testament, thus it is not an oblation made by priests. He proves what has been assumed by the testimony of Luke, who relates that Christ in the Last Supper called the Eucharist a testament. "And taking bread," Luke says, "he gave thanks, and brake; and gave to them, saying: This is my body, which is given for you. Do this for a commemoration of me. In like manner the chalice also, after he had supped, saying: This is the chalice, the new testament in my blood, which shall be shed for you" (22, 19-20). Paul wrote similar words to the Corinthians.[1] Luther proves the conclusion of his argument by the fact that, as he says, these two things, a testament and a sacrifice, or oblation, oppose each other. Because a testament, as Luther says, is a promise of the testator: but a sacrifice is offered on an altar. Now to promise and to offer, as he says, oppose each other.[2] See the principal foundation upon which Luther tries to build his pestiferous doctrine: and hence he takes the utmost pains to show how the Eucharist is a testament: and firstly he assigns the definition of a testament, not taken from Ulpian[3] or from some other approved expert in juridical science, but contrived from his own head.

"A testament," Luther says, is a [promise[4]] made by a man about to die, by which he assigns his inheritance and appoints heirs. Thus the idea of a testament implies, first, the death of the testator, and secondly, the promise of the inheritance, and the appointment of an heir… Christ testifies of His own death," Luther says, "when He says: 'This is my body, which is given for you' (Lk. 22, 19). And again: 'This is my blood, which is shed for you.'[5] Christ announced the inheritance when He said, 'unto remission of sins.'" For the remission of sins, says Luther, is the inheritance promised in the testament of the Eucharist. "And He appoints heirs when He said, 'For you and for many,' that is, for those who believe the promise; for it is faith," Luther says, "which makes us heirs." Therefore, he says, "that the Mass is a promise of the remission of sins made to us by Christ, and confirmed by His death. For a promise and a testament only differ in this, that a testament implies the death of the promiser; a promise, however, does not."[6] And from this he consequently concludes that if the Mass is Christ's testament and promise, it could not be a sacrifice.

Behold Luther's whole scheme, and engine for hurling missiles, whereby he attempts to shake to its foundation and overthrow the teaching of the Catholic Church that the Mass is a sacrifice. He very prolixly discusses this matter with many words, but I decided to summarize with fewer words, lest I burden the reader with excessive wordiness. However, so that I would be faithful in the recitation of his argument, I wished to omit nothing which is pertinent to the matter and could help it in any way. But if the readers wish to attend well, and have a good disposition, this scheme could not terrify them in the least: because they will easily understand that this whole scheme from itself hurls absolutely nothing but empty and completely

---

[1] Cf. I Cor. 11, 24-25.

[2] "For unless we hold fast to the truth, the Mass is a promise or testament of Christ, as the words clearly say, we shall lose the whole Gospel and all our comfort…Therefore, as distributing a testament, or accepting a promise, differs diametrically from offering a sacrifice, so it is a contradiction of terms to say the Mass a sacrifice; for the former is something that we receive, while the latter is something that we offer" (Luther, *On the Babylonian Captivity of the Church*, preface (WA 6, 523-524)).

[3] Note: Ulpian was a celebrated Roman jurist under the emperor Septimius Severus.

[4] The author here uses the word "arrangement" (*dispositio*), but "promise" was the word Luther actually used, which the author later uses when again citing Luther's definition of a testament.

[5] Cf. Mt. 26, 28.

[6] Luther, *On the Babylonian Captivity of the Church*, preface (WA 6, 513).

useless thunder. For by that argumentation of his, which has been summarized, he assumes what is false, and reasons very badly.

For it is false that the Mass is a testament, according to the correct and proper definition of a testament, which experts in juridical science are accustomed to give, from whom in preference to all others one ought to take: and not according to the one which Luther himself gives, saying that a testament is a promise [made by a man about to die[1]], by which he assigns his inheritance to certain heirs. For the Eucharist is not a promise, but it is a gift which Christ gave when near to death. But what a testator gives before his death, is neither a testament, nor likewise an inheritance proceeding from a testament. Also, what is given is not comprehended under the word "promise": because when the giving has taken place, the right of the promise passes away.

But the heretics wishing to escape this argument say that the Eucharist is called a promise because a remission of sins is promised in it, and they contend that it was given only so that by it we may have the remission of sins, which they say is the promised inheritance. But actually, they err by the whole extent of the heavens [*toto coelo*]. Because Christ did not promise at the Supper a remission of sins to his heirs, as Osiander and Bucer teach in defense of their master Luther: but He merely foretold that which afterwards would be done, namely the shedding of blood unto the remission of sins. But although we may grant [for the sake of argument] to Luther that Christ by those words not merely predicted, but also promised the remission of sins, still it could never be inferred therefrom that the Eucharist was given unto the remission of sins. Because Christ by those words did not promise the remission of sins to those receiving the Eucharist: but He promised that He would shed His Blood unto the remission of sins, making absolutely no mention of those receiving the Eucharist. "This chalice," Christ says, "is the new testament in my blood, which shall be shed for you and for many unto the remission of sins."[2] In which words what especially ought to be noted is that He did not say that the Blood is to be "received," but to be "shed" unto the remission of sins.

Furthermore, if Luther speaks of a testament, as it is fit to be supposed, according to the usage of theologians and not of the experts of human law, I will admit that a testament is a promise and a pact and a covenant, as Innocent III teaches, occasioned by the testimony of Paul saying: "Therefore he is the mediator of the new testament... so that they who are called may receive the promise of eternal inheritance" (Heb. 9, 15).[3] But although a promise is called a testament according to theological usage, still it is not necessary that such a promise be of someone near to death: because then the Old Law given by Moses could not be called a testament. For that promise was not made by one near to death: because as long as that Law lasted and that Law was in force, God, Who had established that testament, did not undergo death. And that testament was not [made by a man about to die], nay rather on the contrary, it was revoked by Christ's death, and the New Testament was substituted and confirmed in its place. And for this reason, the Evangelical Law is called the "Eternal Testament"[4]: because Christ will never die again, such that by His death He could confirm another testament.

But if Luther uses the word testament according to the usage of experts in juridical science, he defines "testament" very badly: because no expert in juridical science ever said that a testament is a promise. For Ulpian when defining a testament says these words: "A testament is

---

[1] Instead of "made by a man about to die," the author here has "confirmed by death," but for consistency with the previous citation of Luther's definition it has be changed to Luther's original wording.

[2] Cf. Lk. 22, 20 & Mt. 26, 28.

[3] "Furthermore, not only Sacred Scripture, but also a promise is called a testament, according to what the Apostle himself writes: 'Therefore he is the mediator...'" (Letter *Cum Marthae circa* to John, Archbishop of Lyons (PL 214, 1120B)).

[4] Cf. the words of consecration of the Precious Blood at Mass.

the just determination of what one wishes to be done after one's death."[1] His glossator, Accursius, says that "with an appointment of an heir"[2] needs to be added to this definition: because without an appointment of an heir, as he says, it would not be a valid testament [or will]. And all experts in juridical science embrace this definition. According to this definition the Old Law in certain ways can be called a testament: because it was God's just determination, and just choice about what He wished to be done. But it was not confirmed by death: it thus could not properly and perfectly be called a testament, but merely metaphorically and figuratively: because it was, in a certain way, confirmed by the death and blood of the calf, which prefigured Christ's death. For Paul says that it was not "dedicated without blood" (Heb. 9, 18). The Evangelical Law is more properly called a testament, not merely according to the theological usage, but also the juridical usage, as Paul teaches when writing to the Hebrews.[3] For it was confirmed by Christ's death, and it was the just determination of Christ's will, about what He wished to be done after His death, and in it He left to us the Sacraments for the present life, and eternal beatitude for the future life.

Nevertheless, the Mass or Eucharist for no reason ought to be called a testament: because nearly nothing which pertains to the notion of a testament can accord with it. Firstly, in fact, the Mass or the Eucharist is not a determination of Christ's will, or a judgment of His will, whereby He would have declared what was to be done regarding His goods after His death. Furthermore, there is a lacking a testator in this sort of testament: because Christ could not be called its testator. For as Paul says, "Where there is a testament, the death of the testator must of necessity come in" (9, 16). Thus, if the Mass were a testament, it would be necessary that Christ would die as many times as the Mass is celebrated, otherwise it will not be a strong testament. Again, if the Mass or Eucharist is a testament, it would be necessary that it would have been declared before witnesses, so that it may be firm and valid. Tell therefore, O Luther, who are the witnesses before whom it was made. If you say that it was the Apostles, because they alone were present when Christ consecrated bread and wine, and celebrated the first Mass, it is proved that they could not be witnesses of such a testament: because according to your teaching they were then appointed heirs in the same testament. For according to the best law it is forbidden, as "He who is appointed heir in a will cannot be a witness to the same will," as it is said in *Corpus Juris Civilis*.[4] I bid you to take note of what kind of testament Luther wants to propose, of which no testator can be given, and in which the heir himself is the witness.

Next, there is no inheritance appointed for the heirs in this testament, which they say is the Mass. For that which Luther says, that the remission of sins is the promised inheritance in that testament, is completely false. Because such a remission of sins cannot be called an inheritance, because Paul says that the just are "heirs of God, and joint heirs with Christ" (Rom. 8, 17), that is, partakers of the same inheritance, of which Christ is also a partaker. But Christ was not called to the remission of sins: He Who had no sin which could be remitted Him. Therefore, the remission of sins is not the inheritance: because Paul says that the just are heirs not of any other inheritance, but of that which Christ is heir. I certainly admit that the remission of sins is a sure way to acquiring the true inheritance: because by such a remission we are made adoptive sons of God, and hence we are constituted "heirs of God, and coheirs of Christ." But that such a remission is an inheritance, was never put forth in Holy Writ. And

---

[1] Modestinus (a disciple of Ulpian), *Digest of Justinian*, bk. 28, tit. 1, section 1. His definition is derived from Ulpian's definition: "A will is our intention duly attested and solemnly declared, to take effect after our death" (Ulpian Fragment, tit. 20).

[2] *Codex Juris Civilis Justinianei* (Lyon, Prost, 1627), vol. 2, p. 375.

[3] Cf. Heb. 9.

[4] Ulpian, Justinian's *Digesta*, bk. 28, tit. 1, section 20, § *Qui testamento*.

hence I cannot but be astounded how Luther dares to call it an inheritance, since he elsewhere often contends that nothing about the dogmas of the faith ought to be asserted, which is not found in Holy Writ. I find eternal life called an inheritance by Blessed Peter, who says these words about Christ our Savior: "Swallowing down death, that we might be made heirs of life everlasting" (I Pet. 3, 22). The remission of sins is never found to have been called an inheritance either in Holy Writ or in the writings of the holy Doctors. Moreover, even if we were to grant Luther that the remission of sins is the inheritance, still it is not the whole and entire inheritance, because there is something much greater, namely eternal life: Christ made no mention of which in the words of consecration of the bread and wine, whence it is proved that the Mass cannot be a testament: because in it the will of distributing the whole inheritance was not declared. For "No one can die partly testate, and partly intestate."[1]

Although I have clearly proved that the Mass or Eucharist cannot be called a testament, it is still necessary that I reply to Luther, who objects to us Christ's words in Luke, saying: "This is the chalice, the new testament in my blood" (22, 20). To this objection some of us respond, saying that those words were only said of Christ's Blood, not of His Body, and hence they say that nothing is proved by those words: because in the Mass not only is the consecration of Christ's Blood contained, but also of His Body. I, however, think that one ought to reply otherwise and much better. For I say that those words in Luke ought to be understood in the same way as the words in Matthew and Mark, who related that Christ said: "This is my blood of the new testament" (Mt. 26, 28; Mk. 14, 24). For the Evangelists are not opposed to each other, but they have the same meaning, although expressed in dissimilar words. The words of Matthew and Mark show how those words which Luke relates in this place ought to be understood. Now it is said, "the chalice of the New Testament in Christ's Blood," because the New Testament was confirmed by Christ's Blood. Bede interprets these words in this way saying the following: "Now that which He says, 'This is the chalice, the new testament in my blood,' regards a distinguishing from the Old Testament, which was dedicated with the Blood of calves and goats, the Legislator saying when sprinkling: 'This is the blood of the testament, which God hath enjoined unto you' (Heb. 9, 20)."[2] Bede, who clearly teaches that the chalice of Blood is called a testament, because by it the New Testament was confirmed, just as the Old Testament was by the blood of calves.

Haymo [of Auxerre[3]] agrees with this in his commentaries on Paul when interpreting those words from the Epistle to the Hebrews: "This is the blood of the testament, which God hath enjoined unto you," says these words: "It is as though He were to say: 'This is the confirmation of this testament, which God commanded you. This blood figured that Blood, which flowed from Christ's side on the Cross. Christ sprinkled us with this Blood, and confirmed His testament, as He Himself said: 'This is the Blood of the New Testament unto the remission of sins.'"[4] Pope Innocent III interprets these words in the same way, saying: "'This is My Blood of the new and eternal testament,' that is, the confirmation of the new and eternal promise, as the Lord guarantees saying, 'He that eateth my flesh, and drinketh my blood, hath everlasting life' (Jn. 6, 55)."[5] So says Innocent, a man very learned in addition to his pontifical dignity.

---

[1] Justinian's *Institutes*, bk. 2, tit. 14 (*De Heredibus Instituendis*), sect. 5, § *non autem*; *Digesta*, bk. 50, tit. 17, sect. 7, § *Jus nostrum*.

[2] Cf. Ex. 24, 8. *In Evangelium S. Lucae*, bk. 6, c. 22 (PL 92, 597C).

[3] In Migne's *Patrologia Latina*, this passage is attributed to Haymo of Halberstadt, but as mentioned above (see the section, "Gospel," heresy 2), it has more recently been shown to have been written by Haymo of Auxerre.

[4] *Expositio in D. Pauli epistolas*: *In epistolam ad Hebraeos*, c. 9 (117, 885D).

[5] Letter *Cum Marthae circa* to John, Archbishop of Lyons (PL 214, 1120B-C). *Gregory IX, Decretales*, bk. 3, tit. 41 (*De celebratione missarum*), c. 6.

And no one ought to be surprised that we say that these words of Christ ought to be so understood, because from other places it is evident that Sacred Scripture uses this kind of speech. For we read in Exodus that Moses took up the blood of a calf and sprinkled it upon the people, and said: "This is the blood of the covenant which the Lord hath made with you concerning all these words" (24, 8). He said, "the blood of the covenant," with that blood the Lord confirmed the covenant which He had made with the children of Israel. Now lest someone could doubt that this is the meaning of those words, Paul the Apostle, in the Epistle to the Hebrews, deigned to interpret those words, speaking thus: "For where there is a testament, the death of the testator must of necessity come in. For a testament is of force after men are dead: otherwise it is as yet of no strength, whilst the testator liveth. Whereupon neither was the first indeed dedicated without blood. For when every commandment of the law had been read by Moses to all the people, he took the blood of calves and goats, with water, and scarlet wool and hyssop, and sprinkled both the book itself and all the people, saying: This is the blood of the testament, which God hath enjoined unto you" (9, 16-20).

From all these words of Paul it is evident that he so interprets the "blood of calves" to have been called by Moses "the blood of the testament," because by that blood that testament was confirmed. For to this end He cited those words of Exodus, so that by them he might prove that the first testament was confirmed with blood. It is evident that those words which Moses said are very similar to those which Christ said, and hence it follows that both are to be understood in the same way. Hence [Hervé de Bourg-Dieu[1]] when interpreting those words from the Epistle to the Hebrews, says these words: "And Christ being about to sprinkle in like manner the New Law and the whole world with His Blood, said at the Supper to His disciples: 'This is My Blood of the New Testament, Which shall be shed for many.' Notice how harmoniously both testaments are of one accord with each other. Notice how accurately Moses predicts the words which the Savior will use at the Supper."[2] It is now established how Christ's words in Luke ought to be understood; and from all the aforesaid words it is also established that the Mass or the Eucharist is not a testament, according to the correct meaning.

Still if we wish to use this word, "testament," by a certain figure of speech we can say by a trope, the Most Sacred Eucharist is a testament: because it is the gift which Christ left us as a pledge of His love for us in His testament. For in this way we are accustomed to call peace His testament: because when Christ was near to death, He commended it to us as a testament. Mathathias used this figure of speech when speaking to his sons, saying: "Phinees our father, by being fervent in the zeal of God, received the covenant of an everlasting priesthood" (I Mach. 2, 54). In which words he calls the priesthood a testament: because it was committed to the charge of Phinees himself on account of the zeal which he had for observing the Divine law. It seems to me that this manner of speech has that figure, which Christ used when saying: "My chalice you shall drink" (Mt. 20, 23). In which words, He used the word, "chalice," to signify that which is contained in the chalice. By using the same figure, we can say that the Mass or Eucharist is a testament: because it is one of the greatest things contained in Christ's testament. In this sense Nichola of Lyra ought to be understood, who [in his commentary] on Psalm One Hundred Ten, calls the Mass a "testament."[3] But by this figured appellation of "testament," it is not allowed to infer that the Mass is not a sacrifice. Because although this conclusion would be good using the word "testament" according to its proper and true mean-

---

[1] The text attributes this book to Saint Anselm of Canterbury, but it is the production of Hervé, monk of Bourg-Dieu.

[2] *Commenatarius in Epistolas Divi Pauli* (PL 181, 1621D).

[3] "'He hath commanded his covenant [*testamentum*] forever' (v.9), because He then instituted the Sacrament of the Eucharist, which is called a 'testament.'" (*Biblia Sacra cum glossis, interlineari & Ordinaria, Nicolai Lyrani Postilla...* (Lyon, Gaspar Trechsel, 1545), vol. 3, p. 253v).

ing, nevertheless it is not good by using that word according to its figurative meaning. For the same thing cannot be inferred from the figurative or metaphorical metonymy, which can be inferred from the true and proper appellation of the thing.

For example, from the fact that something is truly and really a vine, it is very well inferred that it cannot understand, not see, not hear, not feel pain, and lastly not sense: because none of these things can befit an inanimate wood.[1] But from the fact that a thing is called a vine by comparison it is not permitted to infer any of those things: because Christ understands and senses, even though He is called a vine by comparison and properly. Completely the same thing ought to be said of a testament and a sacrifice. If you use the word testament according to its true and proper meaning, it will be permitted to infer that something is not a sacrifice, from the fact that it is a testament: and according to this meaning I deny that the Mass is a testament. Yet if when speaking figuratively and by a synecdoche we say that the Mass is a testament, from this appellation of a testament it is not permitted to infer that the Mass is not a true sacrifice: because it is both of those things, both a testament and a sacrifice, yet in different respects and considerations. It is called a testament, because it is contained in Christ's testament, and entrusted to us in it. It is called a sacrifice, because in it are offered to God the Body and Blood of Christ His Son. I wanted to treat this argument at such great length, because Luther boasts that he triumphs over Catholics and sounds the trumpet before the victory. Therefore, it was necessary to try all the strengths of this argument, so that I might make it clear to all that it is weak, and completely lacking any strength.

Fifthly, Luther argues from the notion of a gift, saying the following: The Eucharist is God's gift, because Christ said, "Take ye all, and eat of it": therefore it cannot be our sacrifice. For a gift and an offering, as he says, are opposed to each other: because one cannot rightly offer to another what one receives from him.[2]

I reply to this argument conceding that the Eucharist is God's gift, and certainly a great one: because by it He gave His Body and Blood to us under the appearances of bread and wine: nevertheless, it does not follow from this that we cannot offer that gift to God. For by this same reason it would be necessary to say that we can offer nothing to God, because we have nothing which was not given to us by Him. The sacrifices of the Old Testament which they were offering to God of beasts and birds, were apparently true sacrifices, yet those birds and beasts which were offered to God, were God's gifts, God Himself bearing witness to it, Who says through the prophet: "All the beasts of the woods are mine: the cattle on the hills, and the oxen" (Ps. 49, 10). Spiritual sacrifices also, such as the praise of God, a humble and contrite heart, all of which Luther himself acknowledges are true sacrifices, all are God's gifts. "What hast thou that thou hast not received?" (I Cor. 4, 7).

Augustine supports this opinion of ours, who says these words: "Our heart when it rises to Him is His altar; the priest who intercedes for us is His Only-begotten; we sacrifice to Him bleeding victims when we contend for His truth even unto blood; to Him we offer the sweetest incense when we come before Him burning with holy and pious love; to Him we devote and surrender ourselves and His gifts in us."[3] In which words what especially ought to be noted is that he said we offer God's gifts in us to God Himself. Thus, there is no opposition, according to Augustine's view, between a gift and an offering.

King David had understood this assuredly better than Luther, who when seeing the very spontaneous offerings of the people, and the repeated gifts which the people were offering

---

[1] Cf. Ez. 15, 2: "wood of the vine."

[2] "[The priests] communicate and make an offering out of the sacrament and testament of God, whereas they ought to have received it as a good gift" (Luther, *On the Babylonian Captivity of the Church*, Concerning the Lord's Supper (WA 6, 521)).

[3] *City of God*, bk. 10, c. 3, n. 2 (PL 41, 280).

for the future construction of the Temple, giving thanks to God for such a great multitude of offerings, among other things said this: "All things are thine: and we have given thee what we received of thy hand" (I Par. 29, 14).

The Catholic Church acts in the same way when sacrificing and offering the Most Holy Eucharist to God, and says: "Mindful, therefore, O Lord, not only of the blessed Passion of the same Christ, Thy Son, our Lord, but also of His Resurrection from the dead, and finally His glorious Ascension into Heaven, we, Thy ministers, as also Thy holy people, offer unto Thy supreme majesty, of Thy gifts bestowed upon us, the pure Victim, the holy Victim, the all-perfect Victim: the holy Bread of life everlasting and the Chalice of unending salvation."[1] In which words the Church clearly enough and humbly acknowledges that the Victim which it offers to God is God's gift given by Himself. And hence it is clearly proved that Luther wrongly calumniates the Church, and accuses it of a false crime, when he says that it supposes that it offers something of its own: as if the Church would think that the offering is properly our work, and our merit, whereby we merit for ourselves and for others, and that we offer it as though we were giving God something absolutely our own. It is very clearly evident that the Church thinks none of these things, based on the words of the Canon of the Mass which we have just cited, in which she clearly acknowledges that she offers the said Victim not from herself, but from God's gifts.

Therefore, it is evident from all these things that it is not contrary to natural reason that a thing be both a gift and an offering. Assuredly a gift firstly, and afterwards an offering. Through giving, a thing becomes ours which previously was not ours. Afterwards once it has been given, if he who has received it would wish to offer it, he would then offer not from another's, but from that which was made his own. "The Son (of God)," says Isaias, "is given to us" (9, 6): and so He can rightly be called ours. And the Father not only gave the Son to us, but also all the things which belong to the Son, namely His Body, Blood, hunger, thirst, tears, labors, and lastly His death. "He that spared not his own Son," Paul says, "but delivered him up for us all, how hath he not also, with him, given us all things?" (Rom. 8, 32). Thus, since the Son of God and all His merits have been given to us, we can rightly offer Him and all His goods to God, as if they were now ours. For he was offering Christ's Passion and death to God, in satisfaction for his sins, who was saying: "What shall I render to the Lord, for all the things he hath rendered unto me? I will take the chalice of salvation; and I will call upon the name of the Lord" (Ps. 115, 12-13). He was acknowledging that he had received many good things, and wishing to render something to God, he found nothing of his own that he could give to God: and hence the chalice of salvation, that is, Christ's Passion which is our salvation, he determined to take, so that he may offer it to God in compensation for so many sins.

Sixthly, Luther argues saying the following: the same thing cannot be received and offered at the same time, nor can it be given and received by the same person: thus a priest cannot be said to offer the Eucharist, which he entirely receives.[2] For it is the nature of a sacrifice that it be all be offered to God, and nothing be left for men. Why then do priests eat the whole bread and drink all the wine, leaving nothing for God? For this is rather to take away from God, and to give to ourselves, than to offer to God. Thus, there is a contradiction between the Mass and a sacrifice, because a sacrifice is offered, the Mass is received. This is Luther's argumentation related with nearly the same words it was written out by him. I cannot be but be surprised that Luther would support himself with such a worthless and manifest sophism, when he not just

---

[1] *Unde et memores* (Prayer in the Canon of the Tridentine Mass).

[2] "It is a contradiction in terms that the Mass should be a sacrifice; since we receive the Mass, but give a sacrifice. Now the same thing cannot be received and offered at the same time, nor can it be at once given and accepted by the same person." (Luther, *On the Babylonian Captivity of the Church*, Concerning the Lord's Supper (WA 6, 523-524)).

once or twice drives away all argumentations and dialectic reasonings from sacred matters, and accuses recent theologians that they mix them with sacred theology. Wherefore I can now very fairly say that saying of the poet: "Let the straight-limbed man deride the one with deformed foot, let the white man deride the black African."[1]

But let us pass these matters by [*Sed haec missa faciamus*[2]], and let us return to the reply to the argument, and let us show the intolerable impudence of Luther who does not fear very blatant lies, and to assume things plainly opposed to Sacred Scripture in his argument for the proving of his pestiferous heresy. For what he says is false, namely that it is the nature of a sacrifice that all be offered to God, and nothing left for men. For very many sacrifices of the Mosaic Law were eaten by the priests who were offering them. Was God eating everything that was being offered to Him? Listen to God Himself reprehending the future madness of Luther. "I will not take calves out of thy house: nor he goats out of thy flocks. For all the beasts of the woods are mine: the cattle on the hills, and the oxen. I know all the fowls of the air: and with me is the beauty of the field. If I should be hungry, I would not tell thee: for the world is mine, and the fulness thereof. Shall I eat the flesh of bullocks? or shall I drink the blood of goats?" (Ps. 49, 9-13) If God was not eating the flesh which was offered to Him, was it perishing? Certainly not; but much remained by the Lord's command in the disposal of the priests. I admit that there was a sacrifice which was called the holocaust, because the whole was consumed with fire; and hence none of it remained which could be eaten by the priests. Still this was not from the nature of a sacrifice, but from the special way of offering it. Because otherwise, it would be necessary that all the sacrifices were of the same sort, if this happened in the holocaust from the very nature of a sacrifice, so that nothing would remain from it in the disposal of those offering. Now it is evident that there were many sacrifices in that Law, of which at least some part the priests were bound by the precept of the Law to eat, as it is manifestly evident from the second, fifth and seventh chapters of Leviticus.

There are the strongest arguments whereby the heretics attempt to prove that the Mass is not a sacrifice. Luther makes still others, John Calvin also makes others: but because they are very weak, for the sake of avoiding prolixity, I have passed over them. In fact, they seemed to me unworthy that I would fill up sheets of paper, or that I would spend the least time answering them.

Many have written against this heresy, namely Josse van Clichtove in his *Antilutherus*,[3] Caspar Schatzgeyer of the Order of Friars Minor,[4] and Albert Pighius in his book of controversies held in Ratisbon.[5] John Eck composed a whole book on the sacrifice of the Mass, in which he studies this matter at sufficiently great length.[6] After all these men Johann Hoffmeister, an Augustinian, who also defends the canon of the Mass, which Luther was not afraid to calumniate, and to attack with a thousand insults.[7]

---

[1] Juvenal, Satire 2, line 23.

[2] I.e. "Pass those matters by". This phrase is taken from Terence, *The Eunuch*, act 1, scene 2, line 10.

[3] Bk. 3, c. 10, pp. 83r-85r.

[4] *Tractatvs de missa tribus distinctus sectionibus* (Tübingen, Hulderichus Morhardus, 1527), part 2, assertions 15-16.

[5] *Controversiarum prœcipuarum in Comitiis Ratisponensibus tractatarum... explicatio* (Paris, apud Vivantium Gaulterot, 1549), controversia 5 (*De Missae Sacrificio, atque ejus valore*), fol.108r-122v.

[6] *De sacrificio missae contra Lutheranos : libri duo* (Augsburg, Simprecht Ruff, 1526). N.B. there are actually three books contained in this work, and so the title should be "*libri tres*," as found in the later editions.

[7] *Dialogorum libri duo, quibus aliquot ecclesiae catholicae dogmata Lutheranorum et verbis et sententiis roborantur*, (Ingolstadt, Weissenhorn, 1546), bk. 2, fol. 34r-43r.

The **third heresy** is that which says that the Mass cannot be offered for sins, nor can it benefit the living and the dead, but only the priest himself. The author of this error is also Luther, saying that it is impious if the Mass is celebrated for the dead.[1] Notice by which steps the devil proceeds to lead men to Hell [*Tartara*[2]]. Firstly, he allures and incites to sin, next he calls away from the remedy, lest one be healed of the wounds of sins. But let us close our ears to his voice or the hissing of the venomous serpent, and let us listen to Paul saying: "For every high priest taken from among men, is ordained for men in the things that appertain to God, that he may offer up gifts and sacrifices for sins" (Heb. 5, 1). But since the Evangelical priesthood (as we showed in the preceding heresy) has no other sacrifice than the Eucharist, it is thence proved that a priest can offer it for sins, not only his own, but also for the sins of the people. For after the words just quoted, Paul, when making a discourse about the same priests, adds: "Who can have compassion on them that are ignorant and that err: because he himself also is compassed with infirmity. And therefore he ought, as for the people, so also for himself, to offer for sins" (v. 2-3). Notice how according to Paul's testimony every priest offers sacrifices not only for his own sins, but also for those of the people. And since the Evangelical priesthood has no other sacrifice that it can offer, it follows that a priest can offer it for the sins of the people and his own. Furthermore, the long-standing practice of the Church confirms this same thing, which is not [merely] tolerated by the Church's permission, but kept until the present time by the precept and ordinance of the same Church. For according to that rite of celebrating which the Catholic Church hands down to be observed, the priest, before the consecration of the Eucharist, prays silently for the living, that the oblation of the sacred Mysteries may profit them for the health of soul and body. But after the consecration the supplicant priest prays to God for the deceased, that by the power of the most sacred oblation God would deign to "grant a place of comfort, light and peace."[3] And this practice, which the Church maintains today, is not recent, such that by this occasion Luther would dare to contemn it. for [Pseudo-]Blessed Chrysostom bears witness that this practice emanates from the Apostles. For he speak thus: "It was not without good reason ordained by the Apostles that, in the dreadful Mysteries (to wit, of the Mass), there should commemoration be made of those that were departed, for they knew well the great benefit and utility they were to receive thereby."[4]

---

[1] "It is a manifest and impious error, to offer or apply the Mass for sins, for satisfactions, for the dead, or for any necessities of our own or of others" (Luther, *On the Babylonian Captivity of the Church*, preface (WA 6, 521)).

[2] I.e. Hell. In Greek mythology Hell was divided into two mansions, the one called Elysium, on the right hand, pleasant and delightful, appointed for the souls of good men; the other called Tartara (or Tartarus), on the left, a region of misery and torment, appointed for the wicked.

[3] This phrase is taken from the Canon of the Tridentine Mass, in the *Memento* for the dead.

[4] Homily 69 of *Homilias LXXX ad populum Antiochenum*, translated by Luca Bernardo (*Bernardus Brixianus*), *Omnia Opera Divi Ioannis Chrysostomi, Archiepiscopi Constantinopolitani* (Basel, Cratander, 1525), vol. 4, fol. 128r; not located in PG. Note, however, that he writes something similar in his Homily 41 on First Corinthians, n. 4: "But grant that he departed with sin upon him, even on this account one ought to rejoice, that he was stopped short in his sins and added not to his iniquity; and help him as far as possible, not by tears, but by prayers and supplications and alms and offerings (*oblationes*). For not unmeaningly have these things been devised, nor do we in vain make mention of the departed in the course of the Divine Mysteries, and approach God in their behalf, beseeching the Lamb Who is before us, Who takes away the sin of the world—not in vain, but that some refreshment may thereby ensue to them. Not in vain does he that stands by the altar cry out when the tremendous Mysteries are celebrated for all that have fallen asleep in Christ, and for those who perform commemorations in their behalf. For if there were no commemorations for them, these things would not have been spoken: since our service is not a mere stage show, God forbid! Yea, it is by the ordinance of the Spirit that these things are done." (PG 61, 360).

But Chrysostom writes the same thing much more plainly in the rite of Mass which was published by him, which Gentian Hervet recently translated into Latin. For close to the beginning of the same rite, he says these words: "It ought to be known that if there are many priests, who perform the sacred ministry, the priest who made the oblation, also begins the sacred ministry. He also says the exclamation. The deacon in a high voice: 'In peace let us pray of the Lord.' *The choir:* 'Kyrie eleison.' *The deacon:* 'For the peace from above, and the salvation of our souls, let us pray of the Lord.' *The choir:* 'Kyrie eleison.' *The deacon:* 'For the peace of the whole world, the welfare of the Holy churches of God, and the union of them all, let us pray of the Lord.' *The choir:* 'Kyrie eleison.' *The deacon:* 'For this holy house, and them that with faith, reverence, and fear of God, enter into it, let us pray of the Lord.' *The choir:* 'Kyrie eleison.' *The deacon:* 'For our Archbishop (name), the honorable Presbytery, the Diaconate in Christ, all the clergy and the people, let us pray of the Lord.' *The choir:* 'Kyrie eleison.' *The deacon:* 'For our most religious kings, in the keeping of God, all their court and their army, let us pray of the Lord.' *The choir:* 'Kyrie eleison.' *The deacon:* 'That He would fight with them, and put down every enemy and foe under their feet, let us pray of the Lord.' *The choir:* 'Kyrie eleison.' *The deacon:* 'For this holy abode (name), every city, county, and the faithful dwelling in them, let us pray of the Lord.' *The choir:* 'Kyrie eleison.' *The deacon:* 'For favorable weather, plenty of the fruits of the earth, and peaceful times, let us pray of the Lord.' *The choir:* 'Kyrie eleison.' *The deacon:* 'For them that travel by land or by water, sick persons, laborers, and prisoners, and their salvation, let us pray of the Lord.' *The choir:* 'Kyrie eleison.' *The deacon:* 'That He would deliver us from all trouble, wrath, peril, and want, let us pray of the Lord.' *The choir:* 'Kyrie eleison.'"[1] Behold Chrysostom teaching that the sacrifice of the Mass is offered not only for the priest, but also for all others, even the laity, present and absent: and not only for spiritual things, but also corporal things.

Now that it can be offered for the dead, and help them, Chrysostom likewise shows in the beginning of the same tract where he teaches for whom the priest ought to offer, saying the following: "For the remembrance and remission of sins, of those who built this holy edifice. *Then he remembers the bishop who ordained him, and of others who have died, whom he wishes, by name. And afterwards he adds the following*: 'And of all who have slept in the hope of the resurrection and of eternal life, the orthodox fathers, our brothers, O good and merciful Lord.' *Then he elevates a particle. The deacon, however, having himself received the oblation, and the holy lance, remembers those whom he wishes of the living and of the dead, and afterwards says the following:* 'Remember also, O Lord, my unworthiness, and forgive me my willful sins. *Then, he also remembers those whom he wishes, from among the living and the dead:* [2] *and likewise in another oblation of those who have died."* Chrysostom says all these words in that rite of Mass of his.

But perhaps the heretics will say that Chrysostom in all these places teaches that one ought to pray for the living and the dead; Christ's Body, however, ought not to be sacrificed and offered for them. Yet lest they could escape this way without being condemned by the same Chrysostom, let them hear this same Chrysostom in the same tract, what he commands the priest to secretly say in the prayer of the faithful, after he unfolds the corporal. For these are the words of the prayer which he determined ought to be said by the priest. "We thank Thee, O Lord God of hosts, that Thou hast vouchsafed to us even now to appear before Thy holy altar, and to have recourse to Thy tender mercies for our own sins, and the ignorances of Thy people. Receive, O God, our prayer, make us worthy to offer unto Thee our prayers, supplications, and the unbloody sacrifice for all Thy people; and render us fit, whom Thou hast

---

[1] PG 63, 907. Marguerin de La Bigne, *Magna bibliotheca veterum patrum et antiquorum scriptorum ecclesiasticorum* (Paris, Aegidius Morellus, 1644), vol. 12, p. 305.

[2] PG 63, 905. *Magna bibliotheca veterum patrum...* ,v. 12, pp. 302-303.

ordained for this Thy ministry, by the power of Thy Holy Spirit, unblameably and without condemnation to call upon Thee with the witness of a pure conscience at all times and in all places: so that Thou wilt hear us, and be merciful unto us in the multitude of Thy goodness." In which words he very clearly shows that the priest in the Mass not merely offers prayers and supplications, but also the unbloody sacrifice of Christ's Body and Blood for the living and the dead, for peace, for war, and for many other things of the same sort, both temporal and eternal goods.

And Blessed Ambrose in a letter of condolences to Faustinus for the death of his sister, adduces clear testimony about this matter, when he says: "Wherefore I deem that you ought not so much to deplore her, as to offer for her your prayers; make her not sorrowful by your tears, rather commend her soul to God by oblations."[1] Blessed Augustine in the nineth book of his *Confessions*,[2] commends his Catholic and holy mother, that when the day of her death approached, she was not concerned about the honor of her burial-place, but only about one thing, that she would be regularly remembered in the sacrifice of the altar, in which she knew that holy Victim is offered, whereby the handwriting of sin was blotted out.[3]

Cyprian the martyr, much more ancient than all these men, when writing a letter about a certain Victor, who against the decree of the bishops had appointed a certain priest as the executor of his will: when providing the tenor of that decree he says that the bishops his predecessors had religiously ordained that no brother departing from this world should name a cleric for executor or guardian. Because if anyone would do this, no offering should be made for him, nor any sacrifice be celebrated for his repose. These are the words of the decree of the bishops before Cyprian, from the words of which it is very clearly proved that at that time the sacrifice of the altar was offered for the deceased. But let us hear what Cyprian resolves ought to be done according to the aforesaid decree of the bishops: "And therefore," Cyprian says, "since Victor, contrary to the rule lately made in council by the priests, has dared to appoint Geminius Faustinus, a presbyter, his executor, it is not allowed that any offering be made by you for his repose, nor any prayer be made in the church in his name, that so the decree of the priests, religiously and needfully made, may be kept by us; and, at the same time, an example be given to the rest of the brethren, that no one should call away the priests of God to secular disturbances."[4]

But Tertullian also, nearly a whole century more ancient than Cyprian, mentions this custom being kept in the Church, who in the book, *On the military garland*, among the other old customs of the Church which he attributes to the authority of the Apostles, although they were passed down to us without writing, he also reckons among them this oblation of sacrifice.[5] [Pseudo-] Pope Alexander I preceded Tertullian by seventy or eighty years, who in a letter which he sent to all the faithful, when discussing the oblations of the Lord's Body and Blood, which are offered to God in the Mass, says these words: "For by these things of sacrifice having been offered to the Lord, crimes and sins are blotted out. On that account His Passion, by which we were redeemed, ought to be commemorated in these things, and more

---

[1] Letter 39, n. 4 (PL 16, 1099D).
[2] C. 11, n. 27-28 (PL 32, 775-776).
[3] Cf. Col. 2, 14.
[4] N. 66 (PL 4, 399A-B).
[5] "Even when pleading tradition, written authority, you say, must be demanded. Let us inquire, therefore, whether tradition, unless it be written, should not be admitted. Certainly we shall say that it ought not to be admitted, if no cases of other practices which, without any written instrument, we maintain on the ground of tradition alone, and the countenance thereafter of custom, affords us any precedent... As often as the anniversary comes round, we make offerings for the dead on the anniversary of their birth into Heaven" (*De corona militis*, c. 3 (PL 2, 79A-B)).

often recited, and these things offered to God. For by such sacrifices the Lord will be pleased and placated, and He will forgive enormous things. For nothing can be greater in sacrifices than Christ's Body and Blood, and no other offering is more preferable than this, but this one excels them all: which ought to be offered with a pure conscience to the Lord, and received with a pure mind, and venerated by all, and it is preferable to all, and so it ought to be honored and venerated more."[1] Pope and martyr Alexander said these things, who held the episcopacy of the Roman See as the sixth starting from Blessed Peter.

In which words one ought to note many things. The first is that he says, the oblation of Christ's Body and Blood is made in Mass: and afterwards he adds, such oblations avail for the remission of crimes and sins. Thirdly, he says that this oblation is the most excellent of them all, and most pleasing to God. From which opinion a very strong argument is taken up for proving that the sacrifice of the Mass can profit not only the priest, but also others. For the sacrifices of the Natural Law benefited not only those offering, but also those for whom they were offered, as is clearly established by Job's testimony, who was offering each day for his children lest perhaps they would have sinned.[2] Likewise the sacrifices of the Mosaic Law benefited not merely the sacrificing priest, but also those for whom they were offered, as is evident from the many oblations which the Law commanded to be made for sins, some of which were for the sins of the priest, others for the sin of the prince, others for the sins of the people.[3] Therefore, since the sacrifice of the Mass, as Pope and martyr Alexander related, is more excellent that all other sacrifices, it is thence proved that it can also be offered for others and benefit others, just as the sacrifices of the Natural Law and the Mosaic Law. Therefore, what does Luther dare to say against such an ancient custom of the Church, approved by so many testimonies of holy men? Thus, it is better that we imitate the fully certain custom of the Church, rather than Luther's presumptuous novelty.

Finally, the decree of the Synod of Chalon-sur-Saône determines about this matter thus: "The holy Church keeps this custom from antiquity that both in rite of Mass and in other prayers the souls of the deceased are commended [to God's mercy], as Augustine says: 'There should be no omitting of the supplications that should be made for all the [departed[4]] in Christian and Catholic communion.'"[5] But I would admit as true that the decrees of this kind of council are not found in one book, in which there are the decrees of all the councils brought together: but I have the fragment from Gratian, who in the book of *Decretals*[6] cites that decree of the synod.

But it is necessary to reply to Luther's objections. For he argues thus: The Communion of one lay person cannot benefit another lay person: therefore, the Mass of the priest cannot benefit the people.[7] Luther is miserably blind in this place, not seeing here that there is

---

[1] PG 5, 1064B-1065A.

[2] Cf. Job 1.

[3] Cf. Lev. 4.

[4] This quotation is from Gratian's *Decretals*, which incorrectly cites St. Augustine's *On the Care of the Dead* (c. 4, n. 6 (PL 40, 596)), and has *laudamus* in place of *defunctis*, and hence has been amended here. Perhaps *laudamus* is a gloss which surreptitiously became incorporated into the text as suggested in the footnote in *Corpus juris canonici* ((Leipzig, Bernhard Tauchnitz, 1839), vol. 1, col. 1147): "*Ceterum glossa fecit, ne mutaretur.*" The Synod's canon lacks the word *laudamus*. Cf. *Concilia Generalia, Et Provincialia, Graeca...*, vol. 3, issue 1, part 2, p. 195.

[5] Can. 39. The provincial council of Tertia Lugdunensis (Tours) was held at Chalon-sur-Saône in the year 813 A.D.

[6] *Concordia discordantium canonum*, p. 3 (*De consecratione*), dist. 1, c. 72 (*Visum est*) (PL 187, 1730C).

[7] "When the priest is performing Mass publicly, let him understand that he is only receiving and giving

a difference between the priest and the laity, which existed long ago between the Apostles receiving the Eucharist from Christ's hand, and Christ Himself extending His hand to the Apostles. For just as a lay person now receives from the hand of the priest, so also then the Apostles received from Christ's hand. Now a priest does what Christ then did: because he confects the same Body from bread, which Christ then did. He offers the same Body to God, which Christ afterwards offered on the altar of the Cross. Now who does not see that the argument is very foolish whereby one would want to prove that Christ's consecration nowise benefits us, because the Apostles when receiving benefitted nothing for us? If this is an invalid argument, there is no one who would not see why also, by a very similar argument, it will be clear folly, when he argues that one priest cannot offer for other men, because one layman cannot communicate for another? Because (as we said) the priest takes Christ's place, but a communicating layman represents the person of the Apostles.

Secondly, as though stumbling upon the same stone, Luther objects as follows: One man cannot be baptized for another, nor can he marry a wife for another, thus nor could he offer for another.[1] To this objection we reply that not all the Sacraments ought to be measured by the same measuring stick [*gnomon*], since there is not equal strength and power of them all. Thus, since this Sacrament of the Eucharist surpasses by far all the other Sacraments, it does not come to be measured by the same measure as the rest. And if we freely grant this to Luther, that this Sacrament is equal to the rest, still it is not thence inferred that such an exact comparison to the others would be allowed. For by the same argument it would also be proved that a priest could not receive the Eucharist consecrated by himself, but it would be necessary that he would receive it from the hands of another priest, because even though a priest has the keys by which he can absolve another penitent, still he cannot on that grounds absolve himself. Therefore, in the same way it would be necessary to assert that although one can confect, and give Communion to another, nevertheless he cannot give Communion to himself. But this is not the case, because it is not necessary that the Sacraments be so similar to each other, that there would be no difference among them. More will be said about this matter when we will dispute about the suffrages of the deceased.

MONACHATUS

Monastic Life

The old enemy of the human race, even to this day, can try to harm man and impede him from the attainment of eternal beatitude for which he was created by God. Thus since the devil sees many men have escaped his snares through entering into monastic life, and have attained eternal glory; lest others likewise escape his snares by their example, he strives to do one thing: to detract the monastic life, so that at least in this way he may deter men from entering into it. And in order to do this, there were not lacking those ministers,

---

to others the Communion in the Mass; and let him beware of offering up at the same moment his prayers for himself and others, lest he should seem to be presuming to offer the Mass. The priest also who is saying a private Mass must consider himself as administering the Communion to himself. A private Mass is not at all different from, nor more efficient than, the simple reception of the Communion by any layman from the hand of the priest, except for the prayers, and that the priest consecrates and administers it to himself. In the matter itself of the Mass and the Sacrament, we are all equal, priests and laymen" (Luther, *On the Babylonian Captivity of the Church*, preface (WA 6, 525)).

[1] "If then in one sacrament and testament there is no good work communicable to others, neither can there be any in the Mass, which is itself nothing but a testament and a Sacrament…" (*On the Babylonian Captivity of the Church*, preface (WA 6, 521)).

whom he deceived by his serpentine craftiness, so that they would afterwards induce others into the same damnation. Therefore, the first ministers of the devil were the Waldensians, who broke out into such madness that they would say that "the religions of mendicants were the invention of wicked demons." For Aeneas Sylvius charges them with this.[1] Guy [the Carmelite], however, makes no mention of this error even when he lists the errors of the Waldensians. At nearly the same time of the Waldensians, or shortly afterwards, a certain William of Saint-Amour wrote a book in which he tried to persuade men that they could not be saved in the mendicant Orders.[2] But Pope Alexander IV condemned this book as heretical, and commanded under pain of excommunication that it be burned by anyone who had a copy of it. After these men John Wycliffe revived this same error, who fiercely inveighed against not merely the mendicant monks, but against all monastic life. For he said that no one can be saved in "private religion,"[3] nay he says that everyone who is in "private religion" is unfit and unsuited for the observance of the laws of God.[4] Wherefore he added that those who instituted private religious communities, namely the Benedictines, Franciscans, Dominicans etc. were damned, because they instituted them, unless perhaps they repented of this.[5]

This insane and wicked error of John Wycliffe, hitherto buried, Martin Luther raised up from Hell in this century of ours, saying that it is not permitted that a man be obliged to do something beyond that which Our Lord commanded, but rather one ought to live freely, and not under human law. Wherefore he gave monks the free power of leaving their monasteries, and of marrying a wife if they wished. What is more, in many German towns, monks were forced to abandon their own monasteries, because they were not permitted to live in them, unless they took off their habits and married wives. I have decided to write nothing in this work against the error of all these men, lest perhaps it be said of me, because I myself am also a monk of the Franciscan Order, that I plead my case, and I seek the things that are my own, and not those of are Jesus Christ's.[6] And it seems to me that it would result in greater glory for the monastic life, if the case were treated by men other than myself. And since there were not lacking those who have strenuously fought for us on our side, there is no reason why we should take up arms.

John [Fisher], Bishop of Rochester, in the work which he published against Luther's [*Defense and Explanation of all the Articles*[7]], triumphs over Luther in favor of the monks.[8] Josse Van Clichtove, a man no less pious than learned, published a book in favor of monastic life, and elsewhere he often defends the cause of monastic vows, especially in the work which is called *Antilutherus*, in the third book of which he fights for this cause alone,[9] and in another which he made in support of the assertion of the truths defined at the Synod of Sens against Luther.[10] Long ago Blessed [John] Chrysostom wrote *Against the Opponents of the Monastic*

---

[1] *De origine Bohemorum*, c. 35, p. 59.
[2] In 1256 he published his attack on the mendicants, entitled *De periculis novissimorum temporum*.
[3] He calls "private religion" that which adds to the precepts the counsels of perfection.
[4] Cf. Wycliff's *De religione privata* (*John Wicliff's Polemical works in Latin* (London, Trubner & Co., 1883), vol. 2, pp. 524-536).
[5] Cf. Dz. 624.
[6] Cf. Phil. 2, 21.
[7] The text here mistakenly states that this work was a refutation of the Luther's *Babylonian Captivity*. This has been corrected here.
[8] *Assertionis Lutheranae confutatio* (Cologne, Maternus Cholinus, 1564), fol. 432v-435v.
[9] *Antilutherus* (Cologne, Ex officina Petri Quentell, 1525), c. 1-29, fol. 1r-62v.
[10] *Compendium veritatum ad fidem pertinentium contra erroneas Lutheranorum assertiones ex dictis et actis in concilio provinciali Senonensi apud Parisios celebrato* (Paris, in officina Henri Estienne Simon de Colines, 1529), c. 10, fol. 48r-53r.

Life[1] in three books. And if someone does not disdain our [monks], Blessed Thomas [Aquinas] wrote one book against the above-mentioned William of Saint-Amour.[2] Albert the Great composed *Defensorium mendicantium*.[3] Thomas Netter the Carmelite in *Doctrinale antiquitatum fidei* near the end makes a long tract about this, which in my opinion very clearly shows that all the calumnies of the adversaries have no force.[4]

But lest anyone accuse me that I put this opinion of these heretics among the heresies, without having put forth the reason on account of which it is deemed to have been deservedly condemned, I will bring forth the definition of the Catholic Church, which alone is of greater weight than a thousand reasonings or syllogistic arguments. Among the forty-five articles of John Wycliffe condemned in the eighth session of the Council of Constance, there are many pertaining to this matter. For the twenty-first says the following: "If anyone enters any private religious community (*religionem privatam*) of any kind, of those having possessions or of the mendicants, he is rendered unfit and unsuited for the observance of the laws of God."[5] The twenty-second article says the following: "Saints, instituting private religious communities, have sinned by instituting them."[6] The twenty-third article says the following: "Religious living in private religious communities are not of the Christian religion."[7] Articles thirty-four, thirty-five, and forty-five pertain to the same matter.[8] Now all these articles were condemned in the eighth session of the Council of Constance. Therefore, since there is such an explicit judgment of the Church, it is not necessary for monks to fight for themselves, or recall the case again for battle. And if someone were to invite us for a debate, it would be better not to debate, but to show that judgment of the case has already been pronounced in our favor.

For the rest, I would like to inform the reader here about just one thing: that he notice who they are who criticize monastic life; because no one has ever criticized monastic life except hedonistic men, given over to sinful allurements, such as I have often known. And so they are like dogs in the manger, as it is said in the proverb[9]: because they themselves do not wish to enter upon the way of virtue, and to those entering upon it, if there be those, they impede with barking and bites. For one who has led a perverse life, will incite others to live wretchedly, because he supposes that he will conceal his shameful deeds if he has other imitators of his misdeeds, and he thinks that he will be noticed so much the less, the more he has many partakers in his crime. And on the other hand, the more he fears to be confounded by shame, the more there will be many practicers of virtue. For vice appears vile from comparison to virtue. Some other things which pertain to the monastic life are already discussed above when mendicancy was treated, and we will say more below when we dispute about vows.

---

[1] PG 47, 319-386.

[2] *Contra Impugnantes Dei Cultum et Religionem*.

[3] This work of St. Albert the Great seems to never have been typeset. (Cf. Johannes Franciscus Bernardus Maria de Rossi, *De gestis et scriptis ac doctrina Sancti Thomae Aquinatis dissertationes criticae et apologeticae* (Venice, Pasqualis, 1750)), p. 216a.

[4] *Doctrinale antiquitatum fidei Catholicae Ecclesiae: ad vetera exemplaria recognitum & notis Illustratum* (Venice, Typis, Antonii Bassanesii, 1757), vol.1, bk 4, art. 3, c. 33-39, pp. 932-957.

[5] Dz. 601.

[6] Dz. 602.

[7] Dz. 603.

[8] Dz. 614, 615 & 625.

[9] This proverb alludes to the fable of the dog that lay in a manger to prevent the ox and horse from eating the hay. It seems that it has been derived from Lucian's *Timon*.

MULIER

MULIER

Women

There is a heresy asserting that women can rightly be promoted to the priesthood. The authors of this heresy are the Pepuzians, so called (as Augustine says[1]) from a certain town which was called Pepuza,[2] from which place the heretic Montanus originated. This error, buried a thousand three hundred years ago, Luther tried to revive, who seems to have been born for nothing else than for recalling and bringing back to the Church pestilential errors long ago driven out and expelled from the same Church.[3]

This heresy is easily refuted if we would consider what is the duty of priests, or what is their function and work. There are three duties of the priest, according to which a priest is distinguished from someone who is not a priest. For it belongs to the priest alone to confect Christ's Body from bread. It is the proper duty of the same priest to hear sins in Confession, and having heard them to absolve the sinner from them. It also pertains to the priest to teach by virtue of his office. And since none of these can befit a woman, it is proved that a woman cannot in any way be promoted to the priesthood. For that a woman would not have the power of consecrating the Eucharist, is inferred from the fact that such power was conferred by Christ upon men to serve as priests at the Last Supper, when He said to the Apostles: "Do this for a commemoration of me" (Lk. 22, 19). But when Christ said these words, there was no woman there to whom those words could be referred. Therefore, such power was not then conferred upon a woman.

But if they cannot consecrate, neither then can they absolve penitents, because this power which is exercised in regard to Christ's mystical body, rests upon another power, which is in regard to Christ's true Body, as a shadow is cast from a body, because Christ conferred the first power upon the priests at the Last Supper before death: but the second only after He had risen from the dead, namely when being in the midst of the Apostles He said to them: "Whose sins you shall forgive, they are forgiven them" etc. (Jn. 20, 23). Thus, if you take away the first power from a woman, it necessarily happens that you would also take away the second. Moreover, when He gave this power of absolving to the Apostles, no woman was present, but only men, namely the ten Apostles, as John the Evangelist relates, thus (as we concluded regarding consecration) such power of absolving was not conferred by God upon women. Again, if there was not any testimony of Scripture for proving that women cannot hear the confessions of sinners, this alone would suffice, that women hear badly with respect to keeping silent, and this is not said undeservedly, since this is inborn and innate, that they keep very little quiet if they hear something more secret. For they are garrulous by nature. Wherefore it is that the more you have obliged her to a secret, the more ready she is afterwards to spread

---

[1] *De Haeresibus ad Quodvultdeum*, c. 27 (PL 42, 30-31).

[2] Pepuza is located in modern day Turkey.

[3] "Should no distinction be made among the people, and should women, too, be priests?" This Luther answered as follows: "As Paul says in Gal. 3, 28, you must pay no attention to distinctions when you want to look at Christians. You must not say: 'This is a man or a woman; this is a servant or a master; this person is old or young.' They are all alike and only a spiritual people. Therefore they are all priests. All may proclaim God's word, except that, as St. Paul teaches in I Cor. 14, 34, women should not speak in the congregation. They should let the men preach, because God commands them to be obedient to their husbands... If, however, only women were present and no men, as in nunneries, then one of the women might be authorized to preach." (*Sermons on the First Epistle of St. Peter* (1523), c. 2, v. 5, WA 12, 308-309).

it abroad. Therefore, we think that God acted more knowingly than Luther teaches. For it is nowise advantageous that we would pour out everything into the ear of her who has a thoroughfare and wide-open road from ears to tongue.

The third duty which befits a priest by virtue of his office is teaching. For it is incumbent upon them to teach others, according to that which the Lord says through Malachias the prophet: "The lips of the priest shall keep knowledge, and they shall seek the law at his mouth: because he is the angel of the Lord of hosts" (2, 7). Now that this duty cannot be permitted on any terms to women, the Apostle Paul bears witness, who most clearly forbids women that they would not presume to teach, saying: "Let the woman learn in silence, with all subjection. But I suffer not a woman to teach, nor to use authority over the man: but to be in silence" (I Tim. 2, 11-12). Therefore, if a woman cannot teach, nor confect the Eucharist, nor absolve, it is proved that she also cannot be a priest.

Add to these things the constant practice of the Catholic Church which never permits a woman to execute the office of the priest. And certainly, if anyone considers how great the dignity of the priesthood is, and how much it exceeds all other dignities, he will know right away that such a dignity was rightly denied to women. For it behooves women to be subject to men, because (as Paul says) "The husband is the head of the wife" (Eph. 5, 23). Women suffer from a lack of prudence, and hence are easily deceived. For the first woman was seduced into transgression. Women are by nature inconstant and fickle. As the Wise Man says: "One man among a thousand I have found, a woman among them all I have not found" (Eccle. 7, 29).[1] And again elsewhere: "Who shall find a valiant woman? far and from the uttermost coasts is the price of her" (Prov. 31, 10). Women are frail by nature, and hence Blessed Peter calls the woman "the weaker vessel" (I Pet. 3, 7). Theophylactus when interpreting the words of Paul: "The woman being seduced, was in the transgression" (I Tim. 2, 14), says the following: "A woman taught once, and the whole world was also overthrown: for this reason, this sex may not teach. For it is inconstant, [it easily submits,] and can easily be seduced. For notice that he did not say, 'Eve being seduced,' but 'the woman,' that is to say, as though he were discussing the feminine gender itself. For in the same manner that the whole race perished in Adam, so through Eve inconstancy spread unto all woman; by that inconstancy to be sure that same transgression took place firstly in Eve."[2] Therefore, since women suffer so many natural defects, it ought not to be believed that such an office was committed to them; for the due execution of which, it is especially required that he who ought to execute it, would lack all those defects.

MUNDUS

World

Here we very clearly find to be true what we taught in the first book of this work, that a good part of the heresies have arisen from the reading of pagan books. For since many heresies arose about the nature of the world and its qualities, nearly all came forth from the workshops of the philosophers. For there is a certain heresy teaching that "the matter of the elements, from which the world was made, was not made by God, but is coeternal with God." The authors of this error were Seleucus, from whom the Seleucians are

---

[1] Though not used in the text, a side reference here cites Proverbs, chapter six, possibly referring to: "The woman catcheth the precious soul of a man" (v. 24), suggesting that a female priest would be a distraction, if not a danger, for men.

[2] *Expositio in Epistolam ad Timotheum* (PG 125, 39A-B).

named, and Hermias, from whom the Hermians are named. For so Blessed Augustine relates of them.[1] The Albanenses a long time later taught the same error. A certain Hollander, Herman Riswick, about whom there has already been mention above, adhered to the same error. Now these men and the Albanenses absolutely said that the world was from eternity. Who does not see that this error came forth from the school of Aristotle? If we had to fight against Aristotle, it certainly would be hard and laborious, because the testimonies of Sacred Scripture would do little against him. But since the fight designated for us is against those who gave their names to Christ in Baptism, we will triumph very easily over them. And John the Evangelist, when speaking of the Son of God, says: "All things were made by him: and without him was made nothing that was made" (1, 3). And again, in the same place: "He was in the world, and the world was made by him" (v. 10). Therefore, no one may dare to say that the world was from eternity, since Blessed John says so clearly that the world was made by God.

The **second heresy** teaches that the world must not end. This error was also taught by Aristotle. After Aristotle, however, among those who boasted that they are Christians, the Albanenses defended the same error, saying that the world must never end, but will always remain in this same state. But if they take the world for only the substance of the elements and the heavens, their opinion certainly ought not to be reckoned to be heresy, because even when the General Judgment has taken place the heavens will remain, and the elements will remain according to their substance, in fact, purer than they are now. But if they take the world for the inhabitants of the world, as John takes it when he says, "The world knew him not" (v. 10); and again, "God so loved the world, as to give his only begotten Son"; according to this signification of the world, it is a clear error to say that the world is not going to end, such that it would never lack generations of men dwelling in it; because (as we proved above against the same Albanenses) there will be a General Judgment, in which all men will be present so that each one may receive his reward, either good or bad, according as he conducted himself in his body. But if the world will not end, the General Judgment could not happen, because what is infinite could never be united together. Therefore, since it is evident that there will be a General Judgment, it is necessary that the world would end at some time.

The **third heresy** teaches that the world was not created by God, but by the Angels. This error also seems to have come forth from the Aristotelian workshop. For although Aristotle denied that the world was created, still he said that all things which were made in these lower regions, were made by intelligent beings, because the things which are immediately done by God, Aristotle said happen necessarily, wherefore he was saying that contingent things are made by intelligent beings. Heretics seem to have drawn from that error, saying that the world was made by the Angels. The first author of this heresy was Simon the Magician, whom many others followed, namely Menander, a disciple of the same Simon, and Saturninus, from whom the Saturnians are named, the Nicolaites, the Carpocratians, Cerinthus, and the Archontics, who were so called from the princes[2] to whom they attributed the creation of the world. The common error of all these men was thrown to the ground in the section on "Creatures," in the first heresy. For in that place we proved from Holy Writ that the world was made by God, and by no one else.

The **fourth heresy** was of certain men saying that the world was made by God; but these men allege many gods, of whom they attribute to one the making of this world; a second, however, they say produced nothing. And this error also seems to be derived from myth-filled paganism. For nearly all pagans believed in a multitude of gods. We have already discussed about this error above in the section on "God," in the first heresy. For there we showed from

---

[1] *De Haeresibus ad Quodvultdeum*, c. 59 (PL 42, 41-42).

[2] In Greek ἄρχοντες *(archontes)* means "princes."

MUNDUS

Holy Writ that there is only one God, and He is the Creator of Heaven and earth. Therefore, he who desires to know the authors of this error, may learn from that place.

There is a **fifth heresy** about this matter, which asserts that this world, even after the resurrection of the dead, will remain in the same state as it is now; and it will not be changed such that there will be a new heaven and a new earth. Philastrius of Brescia enumerates this heresy among the others, yet he does not disclose any author.[1] After Philastrius, Augustine also mentions this heresy and also does not indicate any proponent of it.[2]

Clear testimonies of Sacred Scripture condemn this heresy. For in Psalm One Hundred One the [Royal] Prophet says: "They shall perish but thou remainest: and all of them shall grow old like a garment: And as a vesture thou shalt change them, and they shall be changed" (v. 27). See how many times he indicates the change of the heavens. For he says that they shall perish, and are to be changed as a vesture, which doubtlessly is the same thing. For the heavens will not completely perish, but will be changed for the better. For Blessed Jerome in his commentary on Isaias, chapter sixty-five, after he cited these words which we just now brought forth from David, adds these words: "In which it is clearly shown that the perishing and destruction is not an annihilation into nothing, but a compete change into something better. For neither does that which is written in another place: 'The light of the moon shall be as the light of the sun, and the light of the sun shall be sevenfold' (Is. 30, 26), signify a destruction of the former things, but a complete change into better. So that one may be able to understand this, let us set forth examples of our circumstances. When an infant has grown into a boy, and a boy into a young man, and a young man into a man, and a man into an old man, he nowise perishes through each age. For he is the same thing which he was before; but he is slowly changed, and is said to have perished to his previous age. Understanding this, Paul was also saying: 'for the fashion of this world passeth away' (I Cor. 7, 31). Let us consider what he said, 'the fashion passeth away,' not the substance."[3] In whose words there is a clear enough understanding of the truth.

Moreover, Our Savior, in Matthew, says: "Heaven and earth shall pass" (24, 35). Which words of Our Savior (as [Pseudo-] Blessed Jerome in his commentary on the Psalms teaches[4]) teach the same thing that the prophet David teaches in Psalm One Hundred One. Next Blessed Peter very clearly teaches this opinion, saying the following: "But the day of the Lord shall come as a thief, in which the heavens shall pass away with great violence, and the elements shall be melted with heat, and the earth and the works which are in it, shall be burnt up. Seeing then that all these things are to be dissolved, what manner of people ought you to be in holy conversation and godliness? Looking for and hasting unto the coming of the day of the Lord, by which the heavens being on fire shall be dissolved, and the elements shall melt with the burning heat? But we look for new heavens and a new earth according to his promises" (II Pet. 3, 10-13). These words of Peter the Apostle so clearly fight against this heresy that there is no need for refuting it with many testimonies.

But these words require some interpretation, especially in the passage where he says: "the heavens being on fire shall be dissolved." These words ought not to be understood of those heavens in which the sun, moon and the stars are located, which are very distant from us, but ought to be taken for the lower heaven, which is called the atmosphere (*aëris regio*). For regarding the higher heavens, whether they are to be dissolved by heat, Augustine doubts, who when commenting on Psalm One Hundred One, having thoroughly surveyed these words of

---

[1] *De haeresibus*, c. 80 (PL 12, 1191B-1193B).
[2] *De Haeresibus ad Quodvultdeum*, c. 67 (PL 42, 42).
[3] *Commentaria in Isaiam*, bk. 18, c. 65 (PL 24, 64C-D).
[4] "'They shall perish but thou remainest' (Ps. 101, 27). According to the words: 'Heaven and earth shall pass, but my words shall not pass' (Mt. 24, 35)" (*Breviarium in Psalmos*, Ps. 101 (PL 26, 1129A)).

Blessed Peter, speaks thus: "He has said then that the heavens have already perished by the flood: and we know that the heavens perished as far as the extent of this atmosphere of ours. For the water increased, and filled the whole of that space in which birds fly; thus perished the heavens that are near the earth; those heavens which are meant when we speak of the birds of heaven. But there are the heavens of heavens higher than these in the firmament: but whether these also shall perish by fire, or those only which perished also by the flood, is a much harder question among the learned, nor can it easily, especially in a limited space of time, be explained. Let us therefore dismiss or put it off; nevertheless, let us know that these things perish, and that God endures."[1] According to Augustine's opinion it is established that the heavens are taken in that place for the atmosphere in that place in which Blessed Peter said: "the heavens being on fire shall be dissolved."

Still when Peter adds afterwards: "But we look for new heavens and a new earth according to his promises": there we can understand the heavens to be those which are also above very distant from us, because they also will be changed for better according to the prophecy of Isaias. "And the light of the moon shall be as the light of the sun, and the light of the sun shall be sevenfold, as the light of seven days: in the day when the Lord shall bind up the wound of his people, and shall heal the stroke of their wound" (30, 26). And according to this meaning of the heavens Blessed Jerome interprets another prophecy of Isaias in which he says: "For behold I create new heavens, and a new earth" (Is. 65, 17).[2] He calls everything new, not because they are other things, but because all things shall be changed for the better: just as we taught above from Jerome's opinion. And I think that I have spoken more than enough about this matter. For it is not necessary in a matter so very clear to burden the reader with a multitude of testimonies, especially since we know of no advocate of this heresy whom one would need to overcome.

NUDITAS

Nudity

There was a heresy of certain men saying that nudity is good and decent. Certain men held this error, called the Adamites, so called because the nudity which Adam had in Paradise before sin they wished to imitate, and so the males and females always went around naked. They heard readings naked, they prayed naked, they celebrated the sacraments naked: and on account of this they called their church, that is their congregation, paradise. Now who was the first author of this heresy, and in what time it began, I could not find in any author.

These brazen and shameless heretics, even though they imitate Adam's nudity in Paradise, nevertheless do not preserve innocence, nay they augment their sin, because although before sin Adam and Eve were naked, still after sin, as Scripture says, they "made themselves aprons" (Gen. 3, 7), and God made for them "garments of skins" (v. 21). And a long time afterwards He prescribed for the people of Israel a certain type of clothing, by which they might be distinguished from other nations.[3] And the priest by God's precept wore a special vestment when he was obliged to offer and to enter the Holy of Holies.[4] Finally, the Teacher

---

[1] *Exposition on the Psalms*, Ps. 101, serm. 2 (second part of the Psalm), n. 13 (PL 37, 1313).

[2] PL 24, 644A-645B.

[3] "Thou shalt make strings in the hem at the four corners of thy cloak, wherewith thou shalt be covered" (Deut. 22, 12).

[4] "And he made, of violet and purple, scarlet and fine linen, the vestments for Aaron to wear when he

of truth Himself, Who taught by word and example the way of God in truth, had clothing, one of which was a "coat without seam, woven from the top throughout" (Jn. 19, 23).

NUPTIAE
Marriage

The **first heresy** which arose about this matter teaches that marriage is unlawful, and they say that all those who join themselves together by the marriage contract sin. The first author of this heresy was Tatian, from whom, as we said above, the take their origin. But if the things which the *Catalogus haereticorum*[1] relates about the Heracleonites are true, Heracleon, their leader, was the first inventor of this error: because Heracleon who was a disciple of the heretic Valentinus, was more ancient than Tatian, who was (as we said elsewhere) a disciple of Justin Martyr. But as I frankly admit, I have little confidence in this matter as to those things which the *Catalogus* relates, because Augustine in his book, *De haeresibus ad Quodvultdeus*, when speaking about Heracleon, does not accuse him of any such thing, namely that he condemned marriage.[2] And Philastrius in his book, *De haeresibus*, when enumerating the errors of this Heracleon, never mentions this error.[3] Wherefore unless something stands in the way, I would think that Tatian was the first author of this error and so this error is commonly called the error of the Encratites, whose leader was Tatian. But Blessed Jerome testifies that this was the error of Marcion, saying the following: "For ourselves, we do not follow the views of Marcion and Manichaeus and disparage marriage."[4] And hence in Jerome's opinion it is necessary that we attribute the beginning of this error to Marcion, since he was more ancient that Tatian. The Adamites upheld the same error, saying that if Adam had not sinned there would have been no marriages: wherefore they, wishing to imitate Adam in Paradise, shun marriage. Concerning the foundation on which the Adamites rely, it is not necessary now to dispute, because we have overthrown this foundation from the bottom above in the section on "Adam and Eve," in the third heresy. The Aerians were in the same error, who (as Augustine relates in his report about them) "admit to communion with them only the continent."[5] Augustine relates concerning the Priscillianists that "they separate spouses whom they have succeeded in convincing of this evil, husbands from wives who refuse to accept this, wives from husbands who likewise refuse to accept it."[6] Now why they did this, either because they condemned marriage, or perhaps they thought that the marriage contract once entered upon could be rescinded by the choice of either spouse, Augustine does not state.

Foreseeing these heresies by the prophetic spirit, Blessed Paul, in his First Epistle to the Timothy, says the following about them: "Now the Spirit manifestly saith, that in the last times some shall depart from the faith, giving heed to spirits of error, and doctrines of devils, speaking lies in hypocrisy, and having their conscience seared, forbidding to marry" (4, 1-3). Therefore, the Encratites and those others forbidding to marry, according to Paul's censure

---

ministered in the holy places, as the Lord commanded Moses" (Ex. 39, 1).

[1] Bernard of Luxemburg, *Catalogus haereticorum*, fol. 44r. Heracleon was a Gnostic who flourished about 175 AD, probably in the south of Italy.
[2] C. 16 (PL 42, 28).
[3] *Diversarum haereseon liber*, n. 41 (PL 12, 1158A-1159A).
[4] *Against Jovinian*, bk. 1, n. 3 (PL 23, 213A).
[5] *De Haeresibus ad Quodvultdeum*, c. 53 (PL 42, 40).
[6] *Ibid.*, c. 70 (PL 42, 44).

ought to be called liars, giving heed to the spirits of error and the doctrines of devils. Furthermore, if marriages were not lawful, Christ would not have honored them with His presence. But since Christ attended a wedding, and at it performed the first of all His miracles, it is proved that marriage is not unlawful.[1] Again, if marriage is evil, it would be necessary to grant that God is the author of evils, because God Himself is the institutor of marriage, Who when He created the first man said: "Increase and multiply, and fill the earth" (Gen. 1, 28). And lest someone could refer this only to that state of innocence, Christ approves of the same institution of marriage, Who replies to the Pharisees asking whether it is lawful for a man to put away his wife for every cause saying: "Have ye not read, that he who made man from the beginning, made them male and female? And he said: For this cause shall a man leave father and mother, and shall cleave to his wife, and they two shall be in one flesh. wherefore now they are not two, but one flesh. What therefore God hath joined together, let no man put asunder" (Mt. 19, 4-6). Why then do the heretics attempt to separate what God has joined?

And Paul in the First Epistle to the Corinthians says: "But to them that are married, not I but the Lord commandeth, that the wife depart not from her husband" (7, 10). And again: "Art thou loosed from a wife? seek not a wife. But if thou take a wife, thou hast not sinned. And if a virgin marry, she hath not sinned" (v. 27-28). And again, in the Epistle to the Hebrew he says: "Marriage honourable in all, and the bed undefiled" (13, 4). And Blessed Peter commands women to be subject to their husbands and he commands husbands to give honor to their wives as to the co-heirs of the grace of life.[2] Now if marriage were unlawful, Blessed Peter would not teach spouses the manner according to which they ought to live.

Furthermore, those who support this heresy, condemn themselves by it. For they owe their existence to marriage, and were begotten from a woman, and from the seed of man: hence it is that they necessarily either condemn themselves, or approve of marriage. For if they think that they are in good state, it is necessary that they say that marriage, whence they came into being, is good. But if they say that marriage is abominable, it is necessary that whatever has come forth from it is also abominable.

Blessed Augustine writes about this subject numerous times.[3] Against this heresy there are some decrees of the councils. For the Synod of Gangra[4] says the following: "If any woman shall forsake her husband, and resolve to depart from him because she abhors marriage, let her be anathema."[5] The First Synod of Braga decrees the same thing.[6]

The **second heresy** is that which allows first marriages, yet condemns second ones. The authors of this heresy are the Cataphrygians, whose leader was Montanus. Afterwards Tertullian taught the same error, who although he previously had fought against the Cataphrygians about this matter, nevertheless later turned around to join them, defending their error. There exists still to today the book which he had made for the defense of this error, which is entitled *De monogamia*.[7] After these men followed Novatus, a certain Roman priest at the time of Pope and Martyr Cornelius, from which Novatus the Novatians are named, who by another name are called the Cathari, that is "the Purfied," so called on account of the purity which they

---

[1] Cf. Jn. 2.
[2] Cf. I Peter 3, 1 & 7,
[3] E.g. *Of the Good of Marriage* (PL 40, 373-396).
[4] The Synod of Gangra was held in 340. Although merely a local synod, its decisions were later ratified by the Council of Chalcedon.
[5] C. 14. This canon is found in the *Corpus Juris Canonici,* Gratian's *Decretum,* part 1, dist. 30, c. 3 (PL 187, 165A).
[6] C. 11 (PL 84, 564B).
[7] PL 2, 930C-954A.

very proudly and very loathsomely boasted.[1] Guy the Carmelite in his *Summa de haeresibus* [*et earum confutationibus*] says that this is one of the errors of the Greeks.[2]

This error is easily refuted by that which is found in Deuteronomy: "When brethren dwell together, and one of them dieth without children, the wife of the deceased shall not marry to another: but his brother shall take her, and raise up seed for his brother: and the first son he shall have of her he shall call by his name" (Deut. 25, 5-6). Notice here that you see that a second marriage is not merely permitted but commanded by precept. But if you would say that this was then permitted to them in the time of the Old Law, not however now in the time of the Law of Grace, there stands in the way that which Paul says in that epistle which is to the Romans: "A woman if her husband be dead, she is delivered from the law of her husband; so that she is not an adulteress, if she be with another man" (7, 3). And in the First Epistle to the Corinthians he confirms this opinion more explicitly saying: "A woman is bound by the law as long as her husband liveth; but if her husband die, she is at liberty: let her marry to whom she will; only in the Lord" (7, 39). Nothing more explicit could be said for taking this error by assault. But the wicked and blasphemous Cataphrygians, seeing that the testimony of Scripture is so clear that no way of escape is left open to them, do not accept Paul, saying that he had not fully received the Holy Ghost, but merely partially prophesied, and hence they assert one ought not to believe him, but rather to believe Montanus, their leader and teacher, in whom they say the Holy Ghost fully descended. Their error ought not to be refuted with reasons but curbed with avenging punishments.

Furthermore, many holy men, whose names are written in the Book of Life, contracted second marriages. Thus, if second marriages are condemned, it is necessary to condemn those who ended their lives in them. Abraham, after the death of Sara, his first wife, married a certain Cetura as his second wife.[3] Ruth, a holy woman by the testimony of Scripture, when her first husband, the son of Noemi, died, married a second husband, who was called Booz.[4] Sara, the wife of Tobias Junior, also a woman commended by the testimony of Scripture, after seven husbands whom she had, and the devil killed,[5] married Tobias Junior, in which marriage she remained serving the Lord,[6] "so that they were acceptable both to God, and to men, and to all that dwelt in the land."[7] The Samaritan woman who had five husbands, was not reprehended by the Lord on account of this, but because he who she then had was not her husband.[8] For from the fact that He called those five men her husbands, it seems that he approved of the marriage of them. For if there had not been a true marriage with the second, third, fourth or fifth, none of them would have been her husband, but it is through marriage that a husband has power over the wife's body, and the wife has power over the husband's body. Thus, if she had five husbands, then she contracted five valid marriages: for which matter since she was not reprehended by Christ, it is proved that the second, third and all the following possible marriages were not unlawful.

Finally, against this heresy there exists a definition of the Council of Nicea. For there the Council commands that any of the Novatians who wishes to return to the Catholic Church may not be received unless he firstly profess in writing that he "will communicate with per-

---

[1] Cf. Augustine, *De haeresibus ad Quodvultdeus*, c. 38 (PL 42, 32).
[2] Fol. 22v-23r, c. 8.
[3] Cf. Gen. 25, 1.
[4] Cf. Ruth 4, 13.
[5] Cf. Tobias 6, 14.
[6] Cf. Tobias 8.
[7] Tobias 14, 17.
[8] Cf. Jn. 4, 18.

sons who have been twice married."[1] And the Council of Florence, which was celebrated under Pope Eugene IV for the union of the [Jacobites[2]], defines about this matter by the following words: "It is asserted that some people reject fourth marriages as condemned. Lest sin is attributed where it does not exist, since the Apostle says that a wife on her husband's death is free from his law and free in the Lord to marry whom she wishes, and since no distinction is made between the deaths of the first, second and third husbands, we declare that not only second and third marriages but also fourth and further ones may lawfully be contracted, provided there is no canonical impediment. We say, however, that they would be more commendable if thereafter they abstain from marriage and persevere in chastity."[3]

The **third heresy** denies that there is a Sacrament in marriage, saying that the indissoluble bond of man and woman is not a Sacrament, nor is any grace conferred by it. The first authors of this heresy are the Armenians, who say about all the Sacraments that they do not confer any grace. After these men the first teacher of this error among those who approve of marriage is Luther, who although he so treats the other Sacraments such that he denies that some of them were instituted as a sign, in others he denies that there is a grace promised; but in Matrimony he denies both. But although Luther denies these things, we with God as our Helper will show both from Holy Writ.

Paul the Apostle very clearly teaches in the Epistle to the Ephesians that Matrimony is a Sacrament instituted as a sign, saying: "Let women be subject to their husbands, as to the Lord: because the husband is the head of the wife, as Christ is the head of the church. He is the saviour of his body. Therefore, as the church is subject to Christ, so also let the wives be to their husbands in all things. Husbands, love your wives, as Christ also loved the church, and delivered himself up for it: that he might sanctify it, cleansing it by the laver of water in the word of life: that he might present it to himself a glorious church, not having spot or wrinkle, or any such thing; but that it should be holy, and without blemish. So also ought men to love their wives as their own bodies. He that loveth his wife, loveth himself. For no man ever hated his own flesh; but nourisheth and cherisheth it, as also Christ doth the church: because we are members of his body, of his flesh, and of his bones. For this cause shall a man leave his father and mother, and shall cleave to his wife, and they shall be two in one flesh. This is a great sacrament; but I speak in Christ and in the church" (5, 22-32).

See here that Paul very clearly teaches that the marriage of a man and wife is a Sacrament because it represents the union of Christ with the Church: and so he compares the man to Christ and the wife to the Church. He says that the man is the head of the body which he makes one with the woman: but he says that Christ is the head of His body which He makes one with the Church. He proposes no other reason why a man ought to love his wife other than that he may not be an unlike sign to Christ, Whom he represents,[4] Who loved His spouse the Church so much, that He deigned to undergo death for it. He teaches the woman, however, the she ought to fear and respect her husband: in order to more correctly and easily persuade her of this, he draws her by the example of the Church whose image she bears, which obeys Christ its Spouse in all things. Thus the Apostle discusses nothing else in that place than to admonish spouses to mutual charity between themselves by the example of Christ and the

---

[1] Can. 8 (Dz. 55).

[2] The text here has "the Greeks," but this Bull, *Cantate Domino* issued in 1443, was in behalf of the Jacobites of Egypt, more commonly known today as the Copts.

[3] Luigi Tomassetti et alii, *Bullarium Romanum* (Tomi XXIV), *Bullarum diplomatum et privilegiorum sanctorum romanorum pontificum Taurinensis editio* (Turin, Seb. Franco et Henrico Dalmazzo editoribus, 1860), vol. 5, p. 64, §26.

[4] This exposition is taken in part from *The Defense of the Seven Sacraments* (New York, Benziger Brothers, 1908), p. 370.

Church whom they represent, that is to say, lest they be fallacious signs, but rather they ought to truly resemble those things whose image they bear.

Furthermore, the Church, which (as we have often shown above) cannot err, reckons there to be seven Sacraments: because among the many articles of John Hus which the Council of Constance in the fifteenth session condemned, one of which says the following: "Priests living criminally in any manner whatsoever, defile the power of the priesthood, and as unfaithful sons they think unfaithfully regarding the seven Sacraments of the Church."[1] Now this assertion of John Hus since it is condemned there, whence we conclude that the Church thinks that there are seven Sacraments. Therefore, Matrimony is a Sacrament.

Again, that Matrimony is a Sacrament, not only teach those whom through contempt Luther calls "Sententiaries,"[2] but also the ancient Doctors of the Church. [Ambrosiaster] when expounding the passage of Paul which we recently cited, says: "Paul indicates that in the union of man and woman there is a great sacrament of mystery. He does not contradict this but brings out another instance which tallies with the above-mentioned mystery and which he knows contributes to the advancement of the human race. This is the mystery of the Savior and the Church. Just as a man must leave his father and mother and cleave to his wife, so the Church must leave every error and cleave and submit to its Head, Who is Christ."[3]

Augustine supports the same opinion in the book, *Of the Good of Marriage*, where he says these words: "To such a degree is that marriage compact entered upon a matter of a certain Sacrament, that it is not made void even by separation itself, since so long as her husband lives, even by whom she has been left, she commits adultery in case she be married to another: and he who left her is the cause of this evil. Hence neither can she, while the adulterer is alive, marry another: nor can he, while the adulteress is alive, marry another woman, as the Apostle teaches."[4] Hence "it is not in a man's power to put away a wife that is barren... And yet it is not allowed; and now indeed in our times, and after the usage of Rome, neither to marry in addition, so as to have more than one wife living..." which is "not lawful, as the Divine Rule seems to prescribe, who is there but it must make him attentive to learn what is the meaning of this so great strength of the marriage bond? Which I by no means think could have been of so great avail, were it not that there were taken a certain sacrament of some greater matter from this weakened mortal state of men, so that, men deserting it, and seeking to dissolve it, it should remain unshaken for their punishment. Seeing that the contract of Marriage is not done away by divorce intervening; so that they continue wedded persons one to another, even after separation."[5] And he speaks likewise elsewhere in the same book.

From these testimonies of [Ambrosiaster] and Augustine which we have just now cited, the lie of John Calvin is refuted which he contrived in favor of the Lutheran heresy. For he, in that work of his, *Institutes of the Christian Religion*, says these words: "The last of all is marriage, which, while all admit it to be an institution of God, no man ever saw to be a Sacrament, until the time of Gregory."[6] That this which Calvin says is false, is very clearly proved by that which is undisputed, namely that Ambrose and Augustine preceded Gregory by a whole century or more. But these two men called Matrimony a Sacrament, therefore before the times of Gregory some men knew that Matrimony is a Sacrament. [As Augustine wrote:] "It is certainly not fecundity only, the fruit of which consists of offspring, nor chastity only, whose bond is fidelity, but also a certain Sacramental bond in Marriage which is recommend-

---

[1] Art. 8 (Dz. 634).
[2] I.e., one who read lectures, or commented, on the *Sentences* of Peter Lombard.
[3] *Commentaria in Epistolam ad Ephesios*, c. 5 (PL 17, 399B).
[4] Cf. I Cor. 7, 10-11.
[5] C. 7 (PL 40, 378-379).
[6] Bk. 4, c. 19, n. 34.

ed to believers in wedlock. Accordingly, it is enjoined by the Apostle: 'Husbands, love your wives, as Christ also loved the Church' (Eph. 5, 25)."[1]

But here Luther objects to us that in the cited passage of Paul the word "sacrament" is not found, but "mystery": therefore, it ought not to be called a "Sacrament" but a "mystery." O indissoluble knot![2] If the reality is clear, why tarry to make a fight about a word? If the conjugal union of a husband and wife represents the union of Christ with the Church, then it is a sign of the other thing, he may now concede the point, although we call such a thing a Sacrament; if he want to call it a "mystery," it matters little, because all the Sacraments are certain mysteries. As a very powerful proof of which thing is that which is found in the words of consecration, which the whole Catholic Church uses for confecting Christ's Blood from the wine. For in those words, the Sacrament of the Eucharist Itself is called the "mystery of faith." Because it is said for no other reason except that the Church believes that a "Sacrament' and a "mystery" are the same thing. Thus, Luther wrongly concludes that Matrimony is not a Sacrament, by the fact that Paul when speaking about it called a mystery: because as we have shown, a "Sacrament" and a "mystery" are the same thing.

Secondly, Luther argues against us, saying the following: "Furthermore, since marriage existed from the beginning of the world and is still found among unbelievers, it cannot possibly be called a Sacrament of the New Law and the exclusive possession of the Church. The marriages of the Patriarchs were no less sacred than are ours, nor are those of unbelievers less true marriages than those of believers, and yet they are not regarded, as Sacraments."[3] In which words he manifestly assumes two false things, and hence it is not surprising if he concludes incorrectly. Firstly, in fact it is false that the marriages of the holy Patriarchs were not, in our opinion, Sacraments.[4] For all Catholic theologians teach with concordant opinion that the marriages of those holy men, who lived in the Law of Nature or of Moses, were true Sacraments, for since they had by God revealing to them belief in Christ's future Incarnation, their Matrimony was a sign of that union whereby Christ was to be joined with His Church. Secondly, it is false that marriages of infidels are equal to the marriages of Christians, since there were such marriages among the pagans, such that hardly any of them were valid and proper marriages, but rather it was a brothel and prostitute.

For Aristotle says that of old it was the practice among the Greeks "of buying each other's wives."[5] And Caesar when speaking about the customs of the Britons says: "Ten and even twelve have wives common to them, and particularly brothers among brothers, and parents among their children; but if there be any issue by these wives, they are reputed to be the chil-

---

[1] *On Marriage and Concupiscence*, bk. 1, c. 10, n. 11 (PL 44, 420).

[2] The author here is most likely referring to the Gordian knot, an intricate knot tied by Gordius, the king of Phrygia, and cut by the sword of Alexander the Great after he heard that whoever undid it would become ruler of Asia.

[3] *On the Babylonian Captivity of the Church* (WA 6, 550, lns. 33-37).

[4] This opinion of the author can hardly be upheld without straying from the faith, since Pope Pius IX writes: "It is a dogma of the faith that Matrimony was elevated to the dignity of a Sacrament by Our Lord Jesus Christ" (Letter to the King Victor Emmanuel II of Sardinia, September 19, 1852 (*Pii IX Pontificis Maximi*, p. 1, vol. 2 (Rome, *Ex typographia bonarum artium habita facultate*, 1855), p. 295)). Rather the more common opinion is that Christ elevated the contract of Matrimony to the dignity of a Sacrament when He honored the marriage celebrated in Cana of Galilee. Sts. Cyril of Alexandria, *In Joannis Evangelium*, bk. 2, c. 2, v. 1-4 (PG 73, 223), Epiphanius, *Adversus Haereses*, Haer. 67, c. 6 (PG 42, 179), and Augustine, *Tractates on the Gospel of John.*, tr. 9, n. 2 (PL 35, 1459) all favor this opinion. Moreover, as the author himself says below, "Baptism is the gateway to all the Sacraments such that before it no one can receive any Sacrament validly."

[5] *Politics*, bk. 2, c. 8.

dren of those by whom respectively each was first espoused when a virgin."[1] And Pomponius Mela relates that a certain tribe in Africa, called the Augilae, whose women "on their wedding night, have a religious obligation to be available for sexual intercourse with every man that comes bearing a gift. On that occasion, it is a very great honor to sleep with many men, but the rest of the time chastity is manifested."[2] Plutarch relates that the Lacedaemonians share their wives with their friends. He also says that among them "a worthy man who admired some woman for the fine children that she bore her husband and the modesty of her behavior as a wife, might enjoy her favors, if her husband would consent, thus planting, as it were, in a soil of bountiful fruitage, and begetting for himself noble sons, who would have the blood of noble men in their veins."[3] Solinus says something worse about the Garamantic Ethiopians, whose words are these: "The Garamantic Ethiopians do not have private marriage, but permit everyone to have sexual relations in common. Thence it is that only mothers recognize their sons; there is no deference for the paternal name. For who could truly know his father in this extravagance of uncleanliness run riot? The Garamantic Ethiopians are thus counted as degenerate among all peoples. This is not undeserved, seeing that they have overthrown chastity and have destroyed knowledge of descent through their wicked custom"[4]

Now concerning the Scots when they were unbelievers, Jerome says these words: "The Scots have no wives of their own; as though they read Plato's *Republic* and took Cato for their leader, no man among them has his own wife, but like beasts they indulge their lust to their hearts' content."[5] And because he mentioned Cato, it will be worthwhile to hear what Augustine says about him. "'In the city of our God, in his holy mountain' (Ps. 47, 2), namely the Church, which regards Matrimony not only as a contract but also a Sacrament. Consequently, she does not allow a man to give his wife to another, as Cato is said to have done in the day of the Roman Republic, and for this he was not in the least censured but was even praised."[6] But concerning Plato's *Republic* which Jerome mentions above, Lactantius relates that in that *Republic* all things even wives were common, "so that many men may flock together like dogs to the same woman, and he who shall be superior in strength may succeed in obtaining her."[7] Wives were also repudiated among unbelievers so frequently that in the Roman Empire which was much more upright than other governments, one was free to repudiate his wives for a light reason, and marry other ones. Now who will dare to say that all these shameful things, nay rather adulteries and lewdness, were true marriages?

But let it be granted that their many wedlocks were valid and legitimate marriages, it is not follow from this that any of them will have been a true Sacrament and hence the Matrimony of Christians. Because although the marriages of unbelievers may have an indissoluble bond, still it does not truly represent the union of Christ and the Church, because such marriages are without faith in the Incarnate Word and are made outside God's Church, and for this reason cannot be considered true Sacraments just as the marriage of Christians. For all the scholastic theologians confess with one voice that Baptism is the gateway to all the Sacraments such that before it no one can receive any Sacrament validly. Although Innocent III says that the Sacrament of Matrimony exists among unbelievers,[8] and Blessed Augustine also says that the

---

[1] *Commentarii de Bello Gallico*, bk. 5, c. 14.

[2] *De situ orbis*, bk. 1, c. 46.

[3] *Life of Lycurgus*, c. 15.

[4] *De mirabilibus mundi*, c. 30, n. 2.

[5] *Against Jovinianus*, bk. 2, n. 7 (PL 23, 296A).

[6] *On Faith and Works*, c. 7, n. 10 (PL 40, 203).

[7] *The Divine Institutes*, bk. 3, c. 21 (PL 6, 418A).

[8] "…since the Sacrament of Marriage exists among the faithful and unbelievers…" (*Decretals of Gregory IX*, bk. 4, tit. 19 (*De divortiis*), c. 8 (*Gaudemus*)).

Sacrament of marriage is common to all unbelievers, but the holiness of the Sacrament only exists in the city of our God.[1] But these words are only said on account of the indissoluble bond of marriage, which exists just as much among unbelievers as among the faithful, and this bond of marriage Augustine calls the "sacrament" of marriage: but not because it is a true sign really representing the union of Christ and the Church. And in the same way ought Innocent III to be interpreted in the passage just cited, because there as it is evident from the context, he was not treating about the true notion of the Sacrament, but only about its indissoluble bond.

Besides these arguments of Luther, Calvin objects to us another argument much inepter and more calumnious. For in that book of his, *Institutes of the Christian Religion*, he says these words: "Marriage... which Christ our Lord sanctified by his presence, and which he deigned to honor with his first miracle, they presume to stigmatize as pollution, so extravagant are the terms in which they eulogize every kind of celibacy."[2] And again he says: "There is also another absurdity in these dogmas. They affirm that in a Sacrament the grace of the Holy Ghost is conferred; this [carnal] intercourse they hold to be a Sacrament, and yet they deny that in intercourse the Holy Ghost is ever present."[3] But in all things there are many lies, and many calumnies against Scholastic theologians. For no theologian said that Matrimony is carnal "pollution." Because even though conjugal intercourse is the business of Matrimony, or a certain consummation of Matrimony; nevertheless they do not say that it is the true Sacrament of Matrimony, because when it is excluded, provided the other necessary things are present, it is a true Sacrament. Let it be granted that it is the Sacrament, or an integral part of the Sacrament, still no one has truly dared to call that intercourse of Matrimony "pollution" or "uncleanliness" of the soul. Such intercourse, although it may take place without sin, can indeed be rightly called pollution of the body, because by it the body is polluted, although the soul is clean. For on account of this reason the effusion of human seed which is accustomed to occur in sleep is called in Holy Writ nocturnal pollution,[4] although it occurs without sin. Also for this reason [Pseudo-] Abdias [of Babylon], Christ's disciple, in book seven of the book which he wrote about the lives of the Apostles, which is about the life of Saint Matthew, calls Matrimony "pollution," because by its intercourse the body is polluted.[5]

But all our theologians deny that Matrimony is the pollution of the soul, and rightly so, because Paul said: "Marriage honourable in all, and the bed undefiled" (Heb. 13, 4). If the bed is undefiled, it follows that intercourse is unpolluted and without stain. It is also false that we deny that in intercourse the Holy Ghost is ever present. For if in intercourse the Holy Ghost had never been present, marriage would not have been honorable, because without the Holy Ghost, nothing is truly honorable. For we acknowledge that he who has intercourse with his wife, that he renders the debt to his wife asking, not for the sake of satisfying lust, but only on account of God, so that he may beget offspring for the service of God, has the Holy Ghost

---

[1] "And so complete is the observance of this bond (*sacramenti*)in the city of our God, in His holy mountain — that is to say, in the Church of Christ— by all married believers..." (*On Marriage and Concupiscence*, bk. 1, c. 10, n. 11 (PL 44, 420).

[2] Bk. 4, c. 13, n. 3.

[3] Bk. 4, c. 19, n. 36. Shortly before this Calvin wrote: "Marriage being thus recommended by the title of a sacrament, can it be anything but vertiginous levity afterwards to call it uncleanness, and pollution, and carnal defilement? How absurd is it to debar priests from a Sacrament [i.e. of Marriage]! If they say that they debar not from a Sacrament but from carnal intercourse, they will not thus escape me..."

[4] Cf. Deut. 23, 10.

[5] "Therefore, marriage has the pollution of intercourse; it does not have the crime of lewdness." (*Historia Certaminis Apostolici* found in Fabricius, *Codex Apocryphus Novi Testimenti* (Hamburg, Schiller & Kisne, 1719), vol. 2, pp. 656).

unless something extraneous enters in which would impede the presence of the Holy Ghost. For he who so acts performs justice, and hence merits an increase of grace; because "to them that love God, all things work together unto good" (Rom. 8, 28). Wherefore [Ambrosiaster] when discussing that passage of Paul, calls Matrimony by both names, namely by the name of "mystery," and by the name of "sacrament," as was evident from his words recently cited.

We have proved that Matrimony is a Sacrament. It remains that we clearly show that grace is infused when contracting marriage, because Luther also denies this. Now in order that we may show this more clearly, let us turn our eyes and look at the beginning of this Sacrament, namely whence it took its origin, and how. For when God, the institutor of this Sacrament, joined our first parents in marriage, He sanctified marriage with His blessing. For Scripture says the following: "Increase and multiply" (Gen. 1, 28). Now it is unlikely that when God gave the blessing to man, He would have had in mind only the body, as in the other animals, but the soul capable of reason He left destitute of His blessing. But if He grants that blessing extending unto the soul, it is necessary that He also grant that grace then be bestowed upon the soul, because in no other way are our souls blessed by Him, than through the infusion of His grace. For so are they blessed by Him who are called to partake in the glory of the eternal kingdom.[1] Also the [Royal] Prophet was asking for this blessing, saying: "May God, our God bless us, may God bless us" (Ps. 66, 7-8). But if Luther concedes that from that Divine blessing grace was imparted to the first parents, yet he denies that it happens in others, this is easily refuted; because He who joined the first parents, is likewise He Who joins the rest of men in Matrimony. And there is not anyone who has been bound by marriage, who was not bound by God. Those whom "God hath joined together," Christ says, "let no man put asunder" (Mt. 19, 6). If He joins all, it ought to be believed that he also blesses all. For it is not likely that He would always join, and only bless once, but rather that He renews the grace of His blessing as often as He resumes the function of joining.

Furthermore, the Apostle Paul in the Epistle to the Hebrews, when speaking about marriage, speaks thus: "Marriage honourable in all, and the bed undefiled" (Heb. 13, 4). A bed cannot be without stain if marriage lacked grace. For marriage would not have an undefiled bed, if the grace which is infused in marriage did not turn it into something good, because otherwise it would be a sin. A miraculous occurrence performed at a marriage teaches us this. For why was it that water was turned into wine at a marriage, except that the tasteless carnal concupiscence of water was turned by God's hidden grace into wine of the best flavor? Again, after the sin of the first parents, marriage was given as a remedy for carnal concupiscence, which was first instituted for a reason: namely so that he who is not continent may contract marriage, by means of which he can exercise without sin what otherwise could not be done without sin. The Apostle so teaches us this, who advises one who is restraining himself badly to marry lest he sin, saying: "It is better to marry than to be burnt" (I Cor. 7, 9). Therefore, if marriage was given as a remedy, how can it be a remedy for carnal concupiscence if grace is not given in it whereby that burning of carnal concupiscence is lessened? Certainly, by the exercise and use of marriage that flame of lust burns more than is extinguished, because even if for a time it the ardor is lulled from the weakness of bodily strength, still when the body regains its strength, then more intense ardor appears, as coals which hide within ashes. Thus it is necessary to acknowledge that by virtue of this Sacrament grace is conferred to those who with an upright intention enter into the contract of marriage, so that by the grace conferred in this Sacrament they may better contain themselves, who otherwise could not contain themselves. For then it would not serve as a remedy, but rather as an enkindling of carnal concupiscence. Add to this the practice of the Church, whereby those who are about

---

[1] "Come, ye blessed of my Father, possess you the kingdom prepared for you from the foundation of the world" (Mt. 25, 34).

to receive this Sacrament are commanded that they clean their souls through the confession of sins, so that having been so cleansed they may be prepared to receive the grace which is infused in this Sacrament. For otherwise, if no grace were infused therein, there was not any need to make a confession of sins.

I think that I have spoken enough about this matter for the brevity which we promised, and for what the book itself requires. He who desires to know more things may read the *Defense of the Seven Sacraments* which is published under the authorship of the king of England, and the defense of the same tract which John [Fisher], Bishop of Rochester, made.[1]

The **fourth heresy** teaches that it is licit for any man to have two wives united to himself by Matrimony at the same time. The first authors of this heresy in our age are the wicked Anabaptists, unless perhaps someone wishes to trace back this heresy to the error of the Adamites who, as we taught above in the section on "Intercourse," said that promiscuous marriage is licit. But certainly, from those things of this kind which Aeneas Silvius relates in the book, *De origine Bohemorum*, about the Adamites, it cannot be concluded that they thought that such promiscuous marriage are true marriages. If they thought this, it is clearly proved therefrom that they thought that it is not only licit for anyone to have two wives, but as many as they wanted. But if they permitted promiscuous marriages not for this intention, such that they considered them to be true marriages, I do not know for what reason this heresy of plurality of wives could be attributed to them. And because this is not evident to me about them, wherefore I said that the Anabaptists are the first authors of this heresy, although they also permit promiscuous marriages just as the Adamites, yet the Adamites do not say that such marriages are true marriages, but only permissions on account of the burning ardor of lust.

Cardinal Thomas de Vio, commonly called Cajetan, although he does not accept that the plurality of wives is lawful, nevertheless says that the law of oneness of a wife is not written in Holy Writ, and adds that this is the opinion of theologians. Lest someone however suppose that I falsely accuse Cajetan of this, I will cite his words, which he wrote in his commentaries on the tenth chapter of Mark. For in that place after he had said that the bond of Matrimony is dissolved by the adultery of a wife, about which we will dispute below in the heresy immediately following, he adds these words which follow. "Here the plain meaning of the text appears, which I have explained precisely so that what the theologians say may be understood to be true, namely that a law concerning one wife is nowhere written in the canonical books."[2] I see some learned men who gather from these words of Cajetan that he thinks that the law concerning one wife is not Divine, but merely human, because he said that it is nowhere written in the sacred books, and hence they were trying to deduce that he thought that the pope is able to dispense from the law concerning one wife.

---

[1] I.e. the *Confutation of Luther's Assertion*.

[2] On Mk. 10, 11, *Omnia Opera Quotquot Sacrae Scripturae* (Lyons, sumptibus Iacobi, & Petri Prost, 1639), vol. 4, p. 155., Jacques-Paul Migne, *Scripturae Sacrae cursus completus: ex commentariis...et a magna parte episcoporum necnon theologorum Europae Catholicae... conflatus* (Paris, Migne, 1840), vol. 22, p. 135. "If these words [of Cajetan] be understood in the sense that it is not explicit in Sacred Scripture, they state the truth: because it is not found anywhere explicitly that it is not allowed to have two wives. But if they be understood to say that this is so neither explicitly nor implicitly, such that it may not be deduced from the testimony of Sacred Scripture, it is an error" (Andreas a Matre Dei, O.C.D., *Collegii Salmanticensis FF. Discalceatorum B. Mariae de Monte* ... (Venice, Pezzana, 1764), vol. 2, tract 9, c. 5, point 1, n. 11, p. 80. John Eck listed this error about polygamy as one of the errors of Cardinal Cajetan (*Enchiridion locorum communium adversus Lutheranos* (London, apud Theobaldum Paganum, 1561), p. 446).

From this quotation I nevertheless cannot conclude that Cajetan was of the opinion, that he would say that the law of one wife is merely human and not Divine.[1] For from the fact that a law is not written in the canonical books, it does not follow that it is not a Divine law. For there are many Divine laws, as we proved in the fifth chapter of the first book, which are not written in the sacred codices, but are kept only by word through the traditions in the Church. There are also many laws of the Natural law, although not of its first principles which also are rightly called Divine laws, and yet are not clearly written in Holy Writ. It is not a light suspicion, however, that it is believed that Cajetan thought in this way. For Blessed Thomas, upon whose words he seems to have sworn, teaches this same view. For in his commentary on the *Sentences*, where he asks whether it was sometime licit to have many wives, he replies by these words: "The law prescribing the one wife was framed not by man but by God, nor was it ever given by word or in writing, but was imprinted on the heart."[2] Which words are nearly the same as those which Cajetan said, and my suspicion is that he took them from there. I wanted to say these things in his favor, so that I might free him if I can from the suspicion of error which some try to brand him.

But I find other words of the same Cajetan upon the nineteenth chapter of Matthew's Gospel which draw me to the other opinion, so that I greatly suspect that he thought that the law concerning one wife is not Divine. Now so that the reader may understand that my suspicion in this matter is not light, I will cite the words of the same Cajetan below. If Cajetan thinks this, as his words indicate, he errs twice in this regard: firstly, when he says that this law is not found in the canonical books of Scripture; secondly, when he says that this is the opinion of theologians. Thus, although Cajetan differs from the Anabaptists by the fact that he does not say that it is licit to have a plurality of wives, as they say, yet there is this in common between him and the Anabaptists, that both deny that the law about one wife is written in the canonical books, and hence on this point it is necessary to strike them at the same time with the same sword. But I will firstly prove against the wicked Anabaptists that a plurality of wives is not licit, and then against Cajetan. And I will show by very clear testimonies that the law about one wife is written in the canonical books.

That no man is allowed to marry another wife while his wife is still alive is very clearly proved by the fact that the man contracting with the second woman, hands over nothing to her: whence it follows that neither does the woman hand over to him anything, and consequently that no contract is made in this matter between them, and no marriage. For in every marriage some contract intervenes whereby they exchange their bodies in relation to the act of generation, when both give the power of their body to the other. For the woman when she marries a man, does not hand over to him the power over her body gratis, but on account of equal compensation: namely because he also hands over the power over his body to the woman. And for this reason, this contract of marriage is accustomed to be called by jurists and theologians, *do ut des*, or I give if you give. Because no one gives freely the power over his own body to another, but only on condition of retribution. Paul clearly teaches about this contract of mutual giving of bodies entered upon between the spouses in the First Epistle to the Corinthians, saying the following: "The wife hath not power of her own body, but the

---

[1] In his commentaries on Genesis and Leviticus, Cajetan says without any qualification that "having a plurality of wives is not against the Law of Nature" (*In Genesis*, c. 16, v. 1; *In Levitici*, c. 18, v. 18; *Omnia Opera Quotquot Sacrae Scripturae*, vol 1, pp. 71 & 313). St. Thomas, on the contrary, wrote: "To have several wives is contrary to the Natural law by which even unbelievers are bound" (Supp. 59, a. 3, ad 4um). "If anyone says that it is lawful for Christians to have several wives at the same time, and that it is not forbidden by any Divine law (Mt. 19, 4 ff.): let him be anathema" (Council of Trent, Sess. 24, c. 2 (Dz. 972)).

[2] Super Sent., bk. 4, dist. 33, art. 1, q. 2 and *Summa Theologica*, Supp. q. 65, a. 2.

husband. And in like manner the husband also hath not power of his own body, but the wife" (7, 4). Now the husband only has this power over the body of the wife from the giving of the wife, and the wife only has power over the body of the husband from the giving of the husband. Thus, there is a mutual giving of their bodies between the spouses, and consequently a manifest contract. From all these things it is clearly proved that the man who contracts with a second woman while his first wife is still alive, gives no power over his body to her; because when he contracted with the first wife, he retained no power over his body for himself. Hence, he could not give to the second what he does not have, because he no longer possesses it; because no one can give what he does not have. If he cannot give over the power over his body to another woman while his first wife is still alive, then neither can he receive from the other woman power over her body, but only by exchanging it for the power over the body of the man. If those two cannot exchange the power over their bodies, then neither can they contract marriage between themselves.

Perhaps someone will respond, conceding that the man handed over the power over his body to the first wife, yet not the full and complete power, but kept some for himself which afterwards he could hand over to the second. But this response is very easily refuted by that which Paul says: "The husband also hath not power of his own body, but the wife." Paul was not content to say, "The wife has power over the body of the husband," but he chose to say, "The husband does not have power over his own body," to plainly show that he has kept nothing in this matter for himself, which he could hand over to another woman. Furthermore, if the husband contracting with the first wife retained some power over his own body for himself, so that he could give it to another, this will clearly establish that he contracts marriage neither with the first nor with the second woman: because with neither of them does he make an equal exchange of his body, since he does not give as much power over his own body to the woman as he receives from her. For the woman, since she could not have, as the Anabaptists themselves admit, two husbands at the same time, always gives the entire power over her body to the man she marries. Therefore, the man with whom she contracts, is bound to also render her the entire power over his body. And certainly, if the man does not give as much power over his body as he receives from the woman, such a contract is unjust and forbidden by Divine law.

For Paul, when writing to the Thessalonians, says: "No man should overreach, nor circumvent his brother in business: because the Lord is the avenger of all these things, as we have told you before, and have testified" (I Thess. 4, 6). To "overreach" in this passage, as [Hervé de Bourg-Dieu[1]] teaches in this place, is to receive something of greater value in business than what one pays. To "circumvent," however, is to deceive another in some business by trickery or fraud.[2] Paul clearly enough teaches that both of these are sins by that which he immediately adds: "because the Lord is the avenger of all these things." Now the Lord never takes vengeance except on account of sin. From this, therefore, it is very clearly proved that a husband who contracts marriage with a second woman while his first wife is alive, overreaches the second woman in the business of the matrimonial contract, because he does not give in return to her as much as he tries to take from her. But if he contracted with the first having this intention, namely, that he did not wish to give in return the entire power over his body, but kept some power for himself which he could hand over to another, then he has not merely overreached the first woman, but also circumvents her, because he neither gave to the woman

---

[1] This quotation is here incorrectly attributed to St. Anselm.
[2] "For it is overreaching whenever that which is of greater value is lured forth in exchange for what is of lesser value; circumvention, however, is whenever a brother is deceived by trickery in the buying or selling itself" (*Commentaria in epistolas Pauli, In Epistolam I ad Thessalonicenses*, c. 4 (PL 181, 1371C).

as much power over his body as she gave to him over her body, nor did he give as much as she hoped and as much as she could justly think that would be given back by her husband to herself. And hence it is proved that he did not contract a valid marriage with either one of them.

Again, if the husband while the first wife is alive could still marry a second, with equal reason he could marry a third wife in addition to the two living women, and a fourth, and a fifth, and thereafter as many as he would be able to feed. If the Anabaptists are not ashamed to concede this, by this very fact they show that they are Mohammedans rather than Christians, and they will concede that a man can hand over very little power over his body to any woman, when, nevertheless, any of them hands over to him the entire power over her body to him.

Next, let us propose that all those wives ask for the conjugal debt at the same time from that man; I ask the Anabaptists to state to which of them is the man obliged to render the debt. Either he is obliged to render to all, or to none of them, because he is not obliged to one more then another. He is not obliged to all at the same time, however, because he cannot render to all at the same time; thus he is then obliged to none, and hence it follows that none of them then have power over his body, and consequently none of them is his true wife. Add to all these things that that plurality of wives is a very great inducement of discord, because it will give a perpetual occasion for much strife and contention. For any of them, so that she may make the man more favorable towards her and a more ardent lover of herself, will always endeavor to make him more hostile and inimical towards the other wives. And the wives of Jacob, Lia and Rachel, furnish very clear proof of this for us, who even though they were sisters, and hence ought to love each other more, yet by the vice of zelotypia[1] were quarrelling with each other. But since God has commended nothing more to us than peace, and for the sake of its better observance, he removed all occasions of war and discord, it follows that He also forbade the plurality of wives itself, because it can easily furnish a perpetual occasion of discord.

Putting aside all these arguments which very clearly prove against the Anabaptists that the plurality of wives is unlawful, it is necessary that I now prove that the law of one wife is written in the canonical books. The law of one wife is very clear in those words which, when Eve was formed, God said through Adam's mouth: "For this cause a man shall leave his father and mother; and shall cleave to his wife. And they two shall be in one flesh" (Mk. 10, 7-8; Gen. 2, 24). In which words it is necessary to notice that he did not say, "shall cleave to his wives," but "shall cleave to his wife"; nor does he say: "They shall be three, or four or more in one flesh," but He said: "They two shall be in one flesh." By which words God clearly shows it is sanctioned by Him that one man have one and not many wives at the same time. Now that these are God's words and not Adam's, our Savior Himself clearly teaches in Matthew, where to the Pharisees asking if it is lawful for a man to put away his wife for every cause, He replies: "Have ye not read, that he who made man from the beginning, made them male and female? And he said: For this cause shall a man leave father and mother, and shall cleave to his wife, and they two shall be in one flesh." (19, 4-5). These words said by God and through Adam's mouth, as proclaimed through the mouth of a Divine herald, very clearly declare the law of one wife. And our Savior cited those words against the Pharisees in this meaning, wishing to prove by them, as it is evident from the context, that it is not permitted for a man, while his first wife is alive, to marry, nor to put away the first.

But because Cajetan tries to make an assault upon the above-mentioned words, so that he might distort them into a different meaning, and very far away from the literal meaning, I wish to prove by the testimonies of the holy Fathers, that their true meaning is that which we just gave. Jerome, in his commentaries on Matthew, when interpreting the aforesaid words of our Savior, says: "This is written in the beginning of Genesis. This teaches that second

---

[1] I.e. jealousy.

marriages are to be avoided, for He said not male and females, which was what was sought by the putting away of the first, but, male and female, implying only one tie of wedlock. In a similar way, He says: 'He will cleave to his wife,' not wives. The reward of marriage is the making of one flesh out of two. Chastity, when united with the Spirit, makes one flesh."[1] And he teaches the same opinion again in *Against Jovinian*, speaking thus: "At the beginning one rib was turned into one wife. 'And they shall be,' he says, 'two in one flesh': not three, or four; otherwise, how can they be any longer two, if they are several. Lamech, a man of blood and a murderer, was the first who divided one flesh between two wives.[2] Fratricide and bigamy were abolished by the same punishment—that of the deluge."[3]

Chrysostom renders these words the same meaning, who says these words: "But mark Him arguing strongly not from the creation only, but also from His command. For He said not, that He made one man and one woman only, but that He also gave this command, that the one man should be joined to the one woman. But if it had been His will that he should put this one away, and bring in another, when He had made one man, He would have formed many women. Now both by the manner of the creation, and by the manner of lawgiving, He showed that one man must dwell with one woman continually, and never break off from her. And see how He says, 'He who made man from the beginning, made them male and female,' that is, from one root they sprung, and into one body came they together, for 'they shall be two in one flesh.'"[4] In which words one ought to especially note that he says that God by these words commanded that "the one man should be joined to the one woman." And hence it is established that he thinks by those words the law of one wife was delivered.

Theophylactus is in accord with Chrysostom, who in his commentaries on Matthew, when explaining the above-mentioned words of Christ, says these words: "He shows that monogamy is the work and law of Him Who created us at the beginning. For at the beginning, He says, God joined together one man and one woman. So it is not right that one man should be joined to many women, or one woman to many men. But as they were joined together at the beginning, so they should remain, not sundering the marital union without good cause. Jesus did not say, 'It is I Who made them male and female,' not wanting to vex the Pharisees; but He phrased it more indefinitely, 'He Who made them.' The goodness of wedded union is of such importance to God that He even permitted women to leave their parents and to cleave to their husbands. But why is it written in Genesis that Adam said, 'Wherefore a man shall leave father and mother' (2, 24), while here Christ says that it was God Who said, 'For this cause shall a man leave father and mother.' We say, therefore, that what Adam spoke, he spoke from God, so that the speech of Adam is of God."[5] In which words one ought to also note that which he said in the beginning, namely that Christ showed by His words that God Who created us at the beginning gave the law of monogamy.

And Pope Innocent III when asked by the Bishop of Tiberias whether pagans after having been converted to Christ's faith can retain all the wives which they had in paganism, replies by these words: "But this seems incompatible and contrary to Christian Faith, where from the beginning one rib was turned into one woman, and it was testified in Divine Scripture that 'For this cause shall a man leave father and mother, and shall cleave to his wife, and they shall be two in one flesh' (Mt. 19, 5). It does not say, 'three' or 'to his wives,' but 'to his wife.'" And after some words he proves the same opinion with another testimony, speaking thus: "Certainly this opinion is proved true also by the testimony of Truth Himself, bearing

---

[1] *Commentary on Matthew*, bk. 3 (PL 26, 134A-134B).

[2] Cf. Gen. 4, 18-19.

[3] Bk. 1, n. 14 (PL 23, 223C).

[4] *Homily 62 on Matthew*, n. 1 (PG 58, 597).

[5] *Ennaratio in Evangelium Sancti Matthaei* (PG 123, 350B-C).

witness in the Gospel: 'Whosoever shall put away his wife, except it be for fornication, and shall marry another, committeth adultery' (Mt. 19, 9). If, therefore, when the wife has been put away, another cannot be married according to law, and all the more when the same wife is retained." From this it clearly appears that plurality [regarding marriage] in either sex, since they are not judged unequally, must be condemned." Now this decree of Pope Innocent is found in the chapter, *Guademus*, under the title, *De divortiis*.[1]

But this last argument which Innocent formulated from Christ's testimony, Cajetan himself considers to be of little weight, because he, as we will say in the heresy immediately following, teaches that a man who has put away his adulterous wife can marry another wife. Thus Cajetan denies the antecedent[2] of the argument which Innocent formulated, saying: "If, therefore, when the wife has been put away, another cannot be married according to law, and all the more when the same wife is retained." And lest someone suspect that I have falsely accuse Cajetan, that he esteems Innocent's argument as nothing, I will cite the words of the same Cajetan, which he says in his commentaries on Matthew, chapter nineteen, and they are the words which follow. "Notice that hereupon Innocent III in the *Decretals of Gregory IX*, under the title *De divortiis*, in the chapter *Gaudemus*, accepts that it is not permitted to have many wives. For if it were permitted to have many wives, he who having put away an adulteress marries another would not commit adultery, but would be married to the second; in the text however it is said that he commits adultery. But if Mark had not added 'against her" (10, 11), Innocent's argument would lack difficulty."[3] In which words he clearly teaches that Innocent's argument is invalid. And in these words, it seems to me, that Cajetan very clearly shows that he thinks that it is not prohibited by Divine law to have two wives at the same time.

There are still other testimonies of Sacred Scripture for refuting the plurality of wives, besides those which Innocent III cites in the chapter, *Gaudemus*. For that testimony is clear which Paul, in the First Epistle to the Corinthians, says: "Let every man have his own wife, and let every woman have her own husband" (7, 2). In which word two things ought to be noted. The first is that he allows only one wife to each man, and not more. For he said, "his wife," not "his wives." The other thing is that he says, "his own" wife, and "her proper [*proprium*]" or "her own" husband. Now nothing can truly be truly proper to someone, unless it is singular and not common to another in those things which he has as a possession, because if many possess it, it will be proper to neither one or another. And hence it is very clearly proved that if a man would have many wives, none of them would have their own husband. Yet Paul says that every woman should have her own husband.

Furthermore, Christ has only one spouse, namely the Church, therefore it is not allowed for anyone to have two wives at the same time. It is evident that this conclusion therefrom is correct, because Matrimony is a Sacrament, signifying the union of Christ with the Church, and so it will be necessary that one man have only one wife, as Christ has one spouse, namely the Church. After having considered all these things well, I cannot but be surprised that Cajetan dared to say that the law of one wife is not written in the canonical books, since Christ our Savior (as Jerome, Chrysostom, Theophylactus and Innocent interpret His words) clearly taught that that law was given by God at the beginning of the human nature, and was written in the book of Genesis. Next, I am much more surprised that he says that this is the opinion of all theologians. Did he perhaps not consider Jerome, Chrysostom, Theophylactus and Innocent to have been theologians? If he strives to relegate all these men outside the school of theologians, I do not know who could more truly be called theologians. Yet I suspect that he

---

[1] *Decretals of Gregory IX*, bk. 4, tit. 19, c. 8.

[2] An antecedent is the first half of a hypothetical proposition, whenever the if-clause precedes the then-clause.

[3] *Commentaria in S. Evangelia et Actus Apostolorum* (Lyon, Prost, 1639), on Mt. 19, 9 in p. 86.

understood by the word theologians, only the scholastic theologians. But albeit he spoke only about them, what he said will be false, namely that they assert that the law of one wife was not written in the canonical books.

For so that I be begin from their first leader, Peter Lombard, who gained the name, "Master of the *Sentences*," in the fourth book of the *Sentences* very clearly teaches that the plurality of wives is prohibited by Divine law, for to support this opinion he cites those words of Genesis: "A man shall cleave to his wife, and they two shall be in one flesh" (2, 24).[1] Saint Bonaventure on the Fourth book of the *Sentences,* when inquiring whether it is against the Natural law that one man have many wives, answers by these words: "If what is in the Law and written in the Gospel be called the Natural law, in this way the Natural law is that there be one woman belonging to one man. And both in the Old and in the New Testaments it says, 'And they two shall be in one flesh.'"[2] Richard of Middleton on the fourth book of the *Sentences* asserts completely the same thing.[3] I would have been able to cite more scholastic theologians in support of this opinion, but being prudent I omit them for the sake of avoiding prolixity, because these are enough for proving that what Cajetan says is not true, namely that theologians say that the law of one wife is not written in the canonical books. Now I think that Blessed Thomas said, "although the law prescribing the one wife was framed by God, nevertheless it was it never given by word or in writing, but was imprinted on the heart,"[4] because this law is not in a clear and plain formulation of words, as befits a law, placed in Holy Writ: which I think is likely. For these particular words, "No man can have many wives," or others as clear as these, are never found in Holy Writ. But this idea is gathered from other words of Sacred Scripture. Now so that something be truly called a law, it is necessary that it be clearly stated and not under veils.

It remains now that we reply to the arguments which the Anabaptists object to us, for proving that the plurality of wives is permitted. For they object to us the examples of the holy Patriarchs, some of whom, namely Abraham and Jacob, had many wives. We indeed acknowledge that those men had more than one wife at the same time, but Blessed Augustine answers this objection very well, and I decided not to make any other reply, but only that which he replies in chapter thirteen of the book, *Of the Good of Marriage*, saying the following: "In the times when the mystery of our salvation was still hidden under the veil of prophetic symbols, even those who were like that before marriage entered into marriage because of the duty to continue the race. They did not do this under the domination of lust, but in response to their sense of duty. If they had been offered the same alternative as is offered now with the revelation of the New Testament, when the Lord says,, 'He that can take, let him take it' (Mt. 19, 12), they would have accepted it even with joy. No one will doubt this who reads with care and attention how they treated their wives. Even when one man was allowed to have several wives, they behaved toward them with greater chastity than is shown now toward one wife by any of those others, when we see what the Apostle allows them as something excusable.[5] They had those wives because of their task of having children,. 'not in the disease of desire, as the nations which know not God' (I Thess. 4, 5)."[6] And again in chapter fifteen he replies more clearly about those Patriarchs, saying the following: "Now there is not the same need for offspring as there was then. At that time, in order to have a larger number of descendants, even when one's wife was able to have children, one was allowed to marry others as well, but

---

[1] Dist. 33, n. 4 (PL 192, 926).

[2] On dist. 33, a. 1, q. 2 (*Opera Omnia* (Venice, Orlandini, 1754)), vol. 4, p. 793.

[3] On dist. 33, q. 1.

[4] Super Sent., bk. 4, dist. 33, art. 1, q. 2 and *Summa Theologica*, Supp. q. 65, a. 2.

[5] "But I speak this by indulgence, not by commandment" (I Cor. 7, 6).

[6] N. 15 (PL 40, 384).

this is certainly not allowed now. Making a clear distinction between the different circumstances of the times has such an effect on whether it is right or wrong to do something that, unless celibacy is impossible, it is now better not to have even one wife, whereas then even those who would much more readily have stayed celibate, had not piety demanded otherwise at that time, were blameless in having several wives."[1] Augustine, who clearly teaches that one very different notion of marriage exists in this time under the New Testament, and another very different notion in times past when the Old Testament had full power and efficacy. For just as for the diversity of times human regulations vary, so God for the diversity of times made different laws, and also different dispensations of the same laws. For from the beginning of the world (as our Savior says) God made them male and female, and established marriage between only two, so they would be only two, and not more, in one flesh.[2] And if the first parents had persevered in justice, marriage would always have been celebrated during the whole succession of time between only two, as it was established at the beginning. But since afterwards men's malice so increased that nearly all men served idols and worshipped false gods, with very few remaining in the worship of God, God decreed that the men who were His servants would be joined to many women through marriage, so that the true worshippers of God would be multiplied, and in this way the downfalls of the Angels might be more quickly repaired. Therefore, God in His good will towards the human race dealt kindly in this dispensation, so that in this way He might quickly repair the walls of the heavenly Jerusalem with men as with living stones, which were broken when the Angels sinned. Innocent III in that chapter, *Gaudemus*, in the title, *De divortiis*, says that those holy Patriarchs took many wives on account of the Divine revelation made to them about this.[3]

Secondly, Anabaptists object to us, and Cajetan could also object in favor of himself, that which Augustine says in the book, *On the Good of Marriage*: "And, the case being thus, enough and more than enough answer has been made to the heretics, whether they be Manichaeans, or whosoever other that bring false charges against the Fathers of the Old Testament, on the subject of their having several wives, thinking this a proof whereby to convict them of incontinence: provided, that is, that they perceive that that is no sin, which is committed neither against nature, in that they used those women not for wantonness, but for the begetting of children: nor against custom, forasmuch as such things were usually done at those times: nor against command, forasmuch as they were forbidden by no law."[4] From which words there are two things which seem to militate against us. The first is that at that time there was a custom of having many wives. The second it that that custom was not prohibited by any law. But I reply to these two things, as Saint Bonaventure replies in the passage recently cited, that that custom was then not merely the custom of men, but was also approved by God's decision and dispensation. Now that Augustine says that that custom was not prohibited by law, Saint Bonaventure interprets concerning the written law. And he rightly indeed so interprets, because it is clear that at that time that the Divine law was not written.

It can thirdly be objected against our and the Catholic position about having one wife, that in the Mosaic Law there was permission not merely for some individual persons, but for all to have two wives at the same time. For Moses said in Deuteronomy: "If a man have two

---

[1] N. 17 (PL 40, 385).

[2] Cf. Mt. 19, 4-5.

[3] "Never is it permitted to anyone to have several wives at one time except to whom it was granted by divine revelation." (*Decretals of Gregory IX*, bk. 4, tit. 19, c. 8).

[4] C. 25, n. 33 (PL 40 0395). The author probably took this quotation from Hugh of St. Victor's *De sacramentis* (bk. 2, part 11, c. 10 (PL 176, 497A)) which gives a modified version of this quotation and also attributes it to St. Augustine's *De virginibus*, as cited in the text. But the original wording of St. Augustine has been substituted here.

wives, one beloved, and the other hated, and they have had children by him, and the son of the hated be the firstborn, and he meaneth to divide his substance among his sons: he may not make the son of the beloved the firstborn, and prefer him before the son of the hated. But he shall acknowledge the son of the hated for the firstborn, and shall give him a double portion of all he hath" (21, 15-17). In which words the Law clearly presupposes that a man can have two wives at the same time: because if this were not permitted for a man, the Law would not have appointed anything about the children of two wives; because then one of them would not be a true wife. I reply to this argument that if these aforesaid words of the Law are carefully considered it will be clearly known that they say absolutely nothing against us. For that law is not in the present tense, speaking thus: "If a man has [*habet*] two wives"; but it uses the past tense, saying the following: "If a man have [*habuerit*] two wives." From which tenor of the words it is merely gathered that a man can have two wives successively, yet not both at the same time. The Law indeed allowed a man that he could give a bill of divorce to his wife, whom he hated, and marry another. Now lest a man a man extend the hatred which he had conceived towards the first wife also to her son, so that he would deprive him of his rights as the firstborn son, the above-mentioned law decreed that the rights of the firstborn son would always be firm towards the son of the first wife who had been put away. Therefore, the Law speaks about two wives which a man had successively, not however about two wives retained at the same time; because the Law never permitted this.

There is a **fifth heresy** which teaches that the contract and bond of marriage can be dissolved by the choice of the spouses. The author of this heresy was Montanus, from whom the Cataphrygians arose, although Augustine, when speaking about the Cataphrygians, in the place wherein he discusses about the this Montanus, does not accuse him of any such thing;[1] nor does Philastrius attribute this error to Montanus,[2] but Eusebius [of Caesarea] relates that Montanus so thought.[3] The Greeks and the Armenians maintained this same error, if we believe Guy the Carmelite, who in his book, [*Summa*] *de haeresibus*, enumerates this among their errors.[4] Priscillian seems to have taught the same error, because the things which Blessed Augustine relates of him closely approach to this view.[5] The Apostolics taught that men can leave their wives, and wives can leave their husbands, to go over to their sect or order, saying that marriages can be dissolved by joining and supporting their sect. For so writes Nicholas Eymerich about the Apostolics;[6] nevertheless, Guy does not mention this error even when he listed the errors of the Apostolics.[7]

After all these men in our times certain men relying upon their own prudence, and wanting "to be more wise than it behoveth to be wise" (Rom. 12, 3), who even though they do not concede that marriage can be dissolved at the choice of the spouses, nevertheless say that on account of adultery the bond of marriage is thus dissolved, such that by Divine law the innocent man is free to entirely leave that wife, and marry another wife. Erasmus of Rotterdam teaches this opinion in his *Annotations on the New Testament* on the seventh chapter of the First Epistle to the Corinthians, where exceeding the measure and limits of the annotation, he makes a lengthy disputation about this matter, and says it is merely by human law, and not by Divine law, that an innocent man, whose wife has committed adultery, is forbidden

---

[1] *De haeresibus ad Quodvultdeus*, c. 26 (PL 42, 30).

[2] *Diversarum haereseon liber*, n. 49 (PL 12, 1165A-1166A).

[3] "[Montanus] is he who taught the dissolution of marriage" (*Ecclesiastical History*, bk. 5, c. 18 (PG 20, 475B)).

[4] Fol. 24r, c. 10.

[5] *De Haeresibus ad Quodvultdeum*, c. 70 (PL 42, 44).

[6] *Directorium Inquisitorum*, pt. 2, q. 11, p. 269B.

[7] *Summa de haeresibus*, fol. 89r-94r.

to marry another wife, although he can drive her away from his bed and his domicile. For he says that the Evangelical law grants to such a man free power of marrying another wife, as well as of driving away the adulteress. Then he says that the human law is exceedingly hard and unjust, which took away this right of marrying another wife from innocent men, and tries to persuade that such a law ought to be completely abrogated.[1] Luther instructed, as I suspect, by Erasmus' *Annotations*, taught this same opinion after Erasmus. And in consequence of his teaching, as I have heard, many men in Germany drive away their wives from themselves on account of adultery and marry other wives.

Cardinal Thomas de Vio, commonly called Cajetan, embraces the opinion of Erasmus in many passages of his works, especially in his commentaries on Matthew 19, Mark 10, and I Corinthians 7. And as far as I can surmise everything which Cajetan asserts in support of this opinion, he takes from Erasmus' *Annotations*, as he has followed him in many other things which he said concerning the New Testament: in which matters he would have acted much more prudently if had kept far away from him. Still he used some prudence in this opinion. For on chapter nineteen of Matthew he says these words: "Therefore I understand from this law of our Lord Jesus Christ that it is licit for a Christian to put away his wife on account of the carnal fornication of his wife, and can marry another wife, always without violation of the decision of the Church, which until now is not clear. For the pontifical decretals on this matter are not of definitive faith, but are made as juridical. Now the Roman pontiffs themselves publicly declare that they sometimes have erred in these definitions about marriage."[2] In which words he acted prudently submitting himself to the definition of the Church: but when saying that no definition about this matter has been given by the Church until now, he was deceived. For a definition was very clearly given about this matter in the Council of Florence, which we will later cite, and the definition of the faith will be established from that very definition, and not a judicial definition of fact, like the others which are in the book of the *Decretals*.

---

[1] "So, just as good men have always sought to revise opinions for the better, and just as it is appropriate to adapt laws and remedies to suit the nature of the ailments that confront us, let us consider whether a similar course would be desirable in this case; if we conclude that it would, let us consider whether it is permissible to dissolve certain marriages, not rashly, but where proper grounds exist; not on the authority of ordinary men, but on that of those set in authority over the Church or duly appointed judges; and for such marriages to be dissolved in such a way that either party is free to remarry with whomsoever he or she wishes, at least insofar as he or she did not give cause for the divorce… We see, however, so many thousands of people tied to one another by unfortunate marriages that benefit neither party, when they could probably be saved by separation. But if it could happen that without infringing any Divine commandment, this should in my view be welcomed by all pious people, but if not, nevertheless I deem it a pious wish, and indeed, especially since charity often hopes for things which cannot happen… If because the Jews are so hard-hearted, a Jew is permitted to repudiate his wife on any grounds, lest anything worse should happen and if we see that among Christians there is not only constant dispute between the spouses, but also more serious iniquity, such as murder, poisoning and incantations, why then do we—thus confronted by the same ailment that afflicted the Jews—not employ the same cure?" (*In novum Testamentum... annotationes* (Basel, apud Inclytam Rauracorum, 1527), p. 418-419 & 426.

[2] "…although indeed our predecessor seems to have thought otherwise…" (*Decretals of Gregory IX*, bk. 4, tit. 19 (*De divortiis*), c. 7 (*Quanto*)) & Dz. 405; "…although some think otherwise and also judgment has been rendered in another way by certain of our predecessors" (bk. 4, tit. 4 (*De sponsa duorum*), c. 3 (*Licet*)) & Dz. 397. Cajetan, *Opera omnia quotquot in Sacrae Scripturae expositionem reperiuntur* (Lyon, Prost, 1639), vol. 4, p. 86.

NUPTIAE

Ambrosius Catharinus of Siena,[1] of the Order of Saint Dominic, who had branded many opinions of the aforesaid Cajetan with the character of infamy (*nigro carbone*[2]), calling some of them heretical, others however erroneous, yet this opinion about complete divorce granted on account of adultery, he left intact, although he could have much more justly left out some others which he undeservedly branded with a very severe censure. About which matter, although many were surprised that in the second edition of that work which he wrote against Cajetan, he gave the reason for this omission or silence, saying the following: "Concerning the putting away of a wife due to adultery, I hear that not a few are surprised that in the first edition of my *Annotationes*, that I did not touch upon this article in the least, although it was for this that Cajetan himself was censured, because he thought that marriage could be dissolved due to adultery, not merely as to the bed, but also as to the bond. Therefore, so that I may take away the astonishment of all, I will frankly make known the reason for my silence. I did not sharpen my pen towards men, but towards teachings, where they seemed deserving of an annotation. For I could not prudently reprehend, what I also did not know how to suitably confute. Not that I would approve the bold venture of the man, but because he seemed to have some occasion for this venture, so that I dared not to reprehend him in this place. Now it is not hidden from me that the common opinion of recent theologians, indeed from Augustine to the most recent in our time, that in the case presented just now, marriage is not completely dissolved, that is to say, in regard to the bond. Which opinion from the time of Augustine himself, who has always deservedly been a man of great authority, seemed to have put down more firm roots."[3] And after these words he immediately adds arguments whereby he seems to confirm Cajetan's opinion, and he says that those arguments seems to him to be so strong, that he does not know how one could respond well to them.

Now Erasmus had put forth all these argument before Catharinus himself, in his *Annotations* on the seventh chapter of the First Epistle to the Corinthians. And hence I conjecture that all those who in our time teach this opinion have taken the occasion for their error form Erasmus' *Annotations*. But although Catharinus was inclined towards this opinion, and we may prove that the opinion itself is heretical, still not on this account does he come to the point that he ought to be branded with the crime of heresy, because he fully subjects himself in this matter to the judgment of the Church, saying the following: "I know that now schools universally teach otherwise. And I think with them, if I am forced by faith, and I render my intellect captive."[4] It is necessary to fight fiercely against this teaching so that we may clearly prove it to be heretical, lest others deceived by it fall down headlong into sin. For when having entered into the kingdom of England with Philip the Sovereign of the Spains, whom I served in public sermons, who came there to take as his wife Mary of England, Queen and Ruler of the kingdom, I heard that there are many in that kingdom not only among the common people but also among the nobility, who had put away their own wives from their spouse on account of their adulteries, and had married others as wives. But afterwards that kingdom through the solicitude and persuasion of King Philip and Queen Mary was brought back to the faith of Christ and union of the Church, divorce of this kind was never permitted.

---

[1] Lancelotto Politi (name in religion Ambrosius Catharinus) (1483–1553) was an Italian Dominican canon lawyer.

[2] Literally, with a black coal. The Romans marked in their calendars auspicious days with white chalk, the inauspicious days with black coal. Accordingly, Horace wrote, "Are such outrageous individuals to be marked with chalk as sane, of sound mind, or with charcoal as insane? (*Creta, an carbone notandi?*)" (*Satires*, bk. 2, Satire 3, line 246).

[3] *Annotationes in commentaria Cajetani super sacram Scripturam* (Lyon, Mathias Bonhomme, 1542), pp. 500-501.

[4] Cf. II Cor. 10, 5. *Annotationes in commentaria Cajetani*, p. 508.

Now for refuting this opinion which says that divorce is permitted as to the bond on account of adultery, the words which our Savior says in Mark and Luke seem to me to suffice. For in Mark He says these words: "Whosoever shall put away his wife and marry another, committeth adultery against her. And if the wife shall put away her husband, and be married to another, she committeth adultery" (10, 11-12). But in Luke these are Christ's words: "Everyone that putteth away his wife, and marrieth another, committeth adultery: and he that marrieth her that is put away from her husband, committeth adultery" (16, 18). In which words one ought to especially notice that those words were said universally and without any exception for the case of fornication. From which words it is very clearly gathered that even when the adultery of the wife exists, the husband is not allowed to so depart that he marry another wife, because then, as Mark says, he commits adultery in respect to her. And Augustine certainly holds that it is very well proved from these words of Mark and Luke that a husband while his first wife is alive, cannot marry another after he has repudiated the first on account of her adultery.[1]

But perhaps our adversaries will say that those words which are in Mark and Luke ought to be interpreted with the exception of the case of fornication, because Matthew put that exception. For it is often necessary to interpret the words of one Evangelist by the words of another, so that the dissonance, which seems to arise from their words, may be brought back into consonance. I indeed acknowledge that often one Evangelist ought to be interpreted by another, when it seems that one is opposed to the other. But here there is not even a superficial discrepancy between Matthew and the other two, Mark and Luke. And if there were some apparent discrepancy between them, there is not an evident reason which proves that Mark and Luke agreeing between themselves ought rather to be interpreted by the words of Matthew, then on the contrary, Matthew ought to be interpreted by the words of Mark and Luke.

But passing over these things I wish to show that there is no discrepancy, even an apparent one, among these three Evangelists. Now so that I may do this very clearly, there are two things which ought to be especially considered. The first is that Mark and Luke bring up two things at the same time, namely putting away a wife and marrying another, which if someone were to do, they say that according to the Lord's reckoning he is an adulterer.[2] Now Matthew, although he twice discusses this matter, namely in chapter five and afterwards in chapter nineteen, only in chapter nineteen joined those two things together, and in the same place he speaks about him who has put away his wife, and has married another after the first has been driven away. Thus when speaking about this, and pronouncing a universal sentence about men of this kind, he added an exception, after he had stated only one of the those things, namely the putting away of the wife, and he had not afterwards stated those two, which are the putting away of the first wife and the introduction of the second. For Matthew speaks thus: Whosoever shall put away his wife, excepting for the cause of fornication, and shall marry an-

---

[1] "'Why then,' you say, 'did the Lord make special reference to the case of adultery, and not say instead quite generally, "Anyone who divorces his wife and takes another wife commits adultery," if the one who takes another wife after divorcing a wife who commits adultery is also guilty of adultery?' I think it is because the Lord wanted to talk about the more serious case. No one would deny that if someone takes another wife after divorcing a wife who has not committed adultery, this adultery is worse than remarrying after divorcing a wife who commits adultery. It is not that there is not adultery in the other case, when the remarriage is after divorce from a wife who commits adultery, but it is less serious. The Apostle James says something similar, when he says: 'To him therefore who knoweth to do good, and doth it not, to him it is sin' (James 4, 17). Does it follow from this that someone who does not know the right thing to do, and therefore does not do it, does not also commit a sin? This person does, of course, commit a sin, but the sin is worse if the person knows and still does not do it. Being a less serious sin does not make it no sin at all" (*Adulterous Marriages*, bk. 1, c. 9, n. 9 (PL 40, 456)).

[2] In Latin, *adulter* or *moechus*.

other, commits adultery. From which words it is evident that Matthew makes no exception for him who after he has put away his first wife, shall have married another, about which alone Mark and Luke spoke: but he makes an exception for him who merely puts away his wife. Thus Matthew even though he pronounces a universal sentence, nevertheless he partly limits it and restricts it to him who not on account of fornication puts away his wife, and concerning him who so puts away and marries another, Matthew says that he is an adulterer. Mark and Luke, however, spoke universally about every man, who in whatever way puts away his wife and afterwards marries another; and they say that every such man is an adulterer.

Therefore it is not necessary to insert the exception of the case of fornication in the words of Mark and Luke, which Matthew made, and if someone contends that it ought to be inserted, he ought to place it in that same place in which Matthew placed it, so that he only excepts from the first part and not from the second. And then having inserted that exception, there will be a limited sentence in Mark and Luke, just as in Matthew. But it is better to say that in Mark and Luke there is universal sentence, but a limited one in Matthew. For so teaches Augustine, saying the following: "Although the adultery committed by the man who marries someone else after divorcing his wife for some reason other than her adultery is worse, and this is the kind of adultery Matthew referred to, nevertheless he is not the only one who commits adultery. As we find in Mark, 'Whosoever shall put away his wife and marry another, committeth adultery against her. And if the wife shall put away her husband, and be married to another, she committeth adultery' (Mk. 10, 11-12); and in Luke, 'Everyone that putteth away his wife, and marrieth another, committeth adultery: and he that marrieth her that is put away from her husband, committeth adultery' (Lk. 16, 18). I have already discussed the testimony of these witnesses sufficiently in the previous book."[1] In which words one ought to note that those words of Matthew, "except it be for fornication," Augustine does not say is an exception, but a certain limitation or restriction, which hence is as if he had said, "not in the case of fornication," or "without the reason of fornication," or "not on account of fornication." And according to this interpretation, which Augustine had stated more completely before these words, it does not follow from Matthew's words that the one putting away on account of fornication, and marrying another, does not commit adultery.

Yet Catharinus in his *Annotationes* against Cajetan, is not pleased with the interpretation of Augustine, because he says that those words in Matthew, "not on account of fornication," are then superfluous, if he who puts away his wife on account of fornication, also commits adultery. But if everything is carefully considered which is in Matthew's words in chapter nineteen, Catharinus' argument is completely of no avail against Augustine's interpretation, because although it is true that he who on account of his wife's fornication puts her away, and marries another, commits adultery; nevertheless, it does not thence follow that those words, "not on account of fornication," are superfluously added in Matthew's words: "Whosoever shall put away his wife, not on account of fornication, and shall marry another, committeth adultery." For Matthew added those words, so that by them he would show that a wife's fornication is sufficient for putting away the wife as to the bed. Yet I said these things, in favor of Augustine, so that I would defend him from Catharinus, who seemed to me to attack him without cause.

But besides this explanation of Augustine, which can be very well defended, I reckon that those words of Matthew can be understood otherwise and perhaps better, unless the love for my arguments deceives me. Now so that I may be able to make this clearer, there is something that ought to be considered in Matthew alone, and carefully noted, which certainly in my opinion, greatly helps for the correct understanding of this matter, although I do not know that it has been noted up until now by anyone. Matthew indeed twice discusses about the divorce

---

[1] *Adulterous Marriages*, bk. 2, c. 9, n. 8 (PL 40, 476).

of a husband and wife, namely in chapter five and chapter nineteen. But the things which he said in chapter five are very different from those which he afterwards said in chapter nineteen. The words found in chapter five are these: "Whosoever shall put away his wife, excepting for the cause of fornication, maketh her to commit adultery: and he that shall marry her that is put away, committeth adultery" (v. 32). The words which are found in chapter nineteen are these: "Whosoever shall put away his wife, except it be for fornication, and shall marry another, committeth adultery: and he that shall marry her that is put away, committeth adultery" (v. 9).

Within these words there is actually great difference in the two passages. Firstly, in fact, in the latter words which are found in chapter nineteen these words are included: "and shall marry another," and Mark and Luke relate them also, which nevertheless are not said in Matthew chapter five. Next, in chapter nineteen Matthew says that he commits adultery who "shall put away his wife, except it be for fornication, and shall marry another." And in chapter five he does not say that he commits adultery, who "shall put away his wife, excepting for the cause of fornication," but merely says that he makes his wife to commit adultery. Now it is evident that it is not the same thing, that someone commit adultery, and that someone makes his wife to commit adultery, although he himself does not commit adultery. Someone can also, on the contrary, commit adultery, although he does not make his wife to commit adultery. For if someone being far away and for a long time from his wife, whom he knew ardently desires the husband's intercourse, keeps chastity, which the wife on account of the mere absence of her husband violates, he is not truly said to commit adultery, and yet it would said correctly that he made his wife to commit adultery. For to make his wife to commit adultery, is nothing other thanto give the occasion to the wife for committing adultery. Also, if someone having a chaste and continent wife, and living with her voluptuously has relations with another woman without the wife knowing, he truly would commit adultery, and yet he does not make his wife to commit adultery. Therefore, since there is such a great difference between committing adultery and making one's wife to commit adultery, it is necessary that also be a difference of the circumstances of the persons and their different actions, on account of which such a different sentence against them is pronounced.

And from this difference of things and persons it is clearly proved that Matthew spoke both times about the putting away of the wife merely as to the bed, but not as to the bond, which our adversaries deny, and hence take the occasion of their error. For he who makes his wife to commit adultery, but is not reckoned to commit adultery, about whom Matthew speaks in chapter five, is he who has put away his wife, but has not yet married another. And hence it is very clearly proved that Matthew in chapter five spoke about the putting away of a wife, as to the bed alone and not as to the bond, because no one in the Evangelical law, even according to the opinion of the adversaries, can show that he completely puts away his living wife as to the bond, except when he marries another wife. For after he separated her from the bed, and cast her away from his company and cohabitation, he can still repent of doing so, and call her back to himself, and be reconciled to her, as Paul clearly teaches.[1] Now if the husband wishes to reconcile her to himself, it is not necessary to contract a new marriage between them, and to repeat the words again, by which they had formerly contracted marriage. From which things it is most evidently proved that the bond of the previous marriage was not dissolved through fornication; because otherwise it would have been necessary that they would contract a new marriage between themselves, when they were reconciled to each other. And in the same manner it is proved that Matthew in chapter nineteen ought to be interpreted of the mere putting away as to the bed, who if he had spoken about the putting away as to the bond, would have superfluously added those words: "and shall marry another"; because those words are

---

[1] "And if she depart, that she remain unmarried, or be reconciled to her husband" (I Cor. 7, 11).

included in the word signifying putting away, since no one perfectly shows that he puts away his living wife as to the bond, as we have said just now, except when he marries another.

And from this we can easily hurl back the argument against Catharinus, which he hurled against Augustine. For as we said above, Catharinus, in order to condemn Augustine's exposition, objects to him the superfluity of words, which would have been in Matthew's words, according to Augustine's exposition; but there would certainly have been greater superfluity in Matthew, if he were to be interpreted according to Catharinus' opinion about the putting away as to the bed, and as to the bond. And in truth this greatly obliges us to believe that Matthew in that passage spoke only about the putting away as to the bed, and not as to the bond. Next, he who puts away his wife and marries another, about whom Matthew spoke in chapter nineteen, is not deemed to have made his wife to commit adultery, but only that he commits adultery. From which sentence it is clearly proved, in my judgment, that Matthew in that chapter spoke about him alone, who on account of the cause of the wife's fornication put her away, and married another. For if he had spoken about him who without the fornication of the wife put her away and married another, as the words of that passage in the literal sense seem to indicate, then he would not only have said about him that he commits adultery, but also that he makes his wife to commit adultery, as he had said in chapter five about him who without the wife's fornication had put her away, although when so putting her away, he had not married another in addition. Thus, since in chapter nineteen he says that he commits adultery and does not say that he makes the wife to commit adultery, it is thence proved that Matthew in that passage spoke only about him who on account of the wife's fornication put her away, and married another, since there is no one else who, because he puts away his wife and marries another, rightly ought to be reckoned that he commits adultery, and not because he makes his wife to commit adultery.

But because the text of Matthew in that chapter nineteen seems according to the surface to say something else, and to except from that sentence him who put away his wife for the reason of fornication, it is thus necessary to acknowledge that the text suffers a certain eclipse, that is a certain defect of those words, which necessarily ought to be supplied, so that the true meaning of the text is disclosed, saying the following: "Whosoever shall put away his wife for no other reason except on account of fornication, and shall marry another, commits adultery." And one ought not to be surprised that I say that this text suffers a certain eclipse; because such eclipses are frequent in Holy Writ, not only in the Old, but also in the New Testament. For which thing although there are many examples, I now wish to present only a few, so that I may leave this opinion proved by two testimonies.

And I firstly cite that which the Royal Prophet says: "Lift not up your horn on high: speak not iniquity against God. For neither from the east, nor from the west, nor from the desert hills" (Ps. 74, 6-7). In which passage it is necessary to supply these words, "is flight accessible," or other similar words, because otherwise the sentence would be lame and without any meaning. Now that those words or other similar words ought to be supplied, is evident from those words which the Prophet immediately adds, saying the following: "For God is the judge" (v. 8). The prophet indeed wanted to signify that the sinner cannot be safe anywhere, because the judge who is going to judge him is God, Who is in every place, and beholds all things. I cite a second example from Paul in the Epistle to the Galatians, where he says these words: "Be ye as I, because I also am as you" (4, 12). In which text it is necessary to supply these two words, "am" and "was," so that the meaning of the text may be clear and disclosed in this way: "Be as I am, because long ago I was as you, zealous about the ceremonies of the Jews." I wish to bring forth yet a third example from the same Matthew, about whose text we are now disputing: so that when I shall have shown that he had a clear absence of words elsewhere, I may convince that it is not surprising if we say that something similar happened to him in the nineteenth chapter, about which we now dispute. For when Matthew is recounting that the Scribes and the Pharisees accused in Christ's presence His disciples, because they were not washing their hands when they ate bread, he says that Christ responded to them: "Why do you also transgress the commandment of God for your tradition? For God said: Honour thy father and mother: And: He that shall curse father or mother, let him die the death. But you say: Whosoever shall say to father or mother, The gift whatsoever proceedeth from me, shall profit thee. And he shall not honour his father or his mother" (15, 2-6). Which text, as all the holy Doctors when interpreting it acknowledge, is very defective, and hence it is necessary to add many words so that its meaning may be clear and understandable. And Erasmus openly admits this, against whom we now dispute, in his *Annotations* on this passage of Matthew.[1] And hence in the New Testament which he translated from Greek into Latin, he added many words in that passage of Matthew in his translation, which are not in the Vulgate, nor in the Greek.[2] Thus one ought not to be surprised if I shall have said that the same Matthew in chapter nineteen has a similar defect of words, which one necessarily ought to supply by an addition of words.

[Alonso Tostado] of Avila[3] in his very copious commentaries, which he published on Matthew, in question seventy-six on the nineteenth chapter of Matthew says that in this text very many more words ought to be added than those which I added a little above. For he, to make clearer that text which seemed to him to be maimed and obscure, modified it as follows: Whosoever shall have put away his wife, except it be for fornication, even if he does not marry another, commits adultery; and he who when putting her away, puts her away in whatever way, if he marries another in addition, commits adultery.[4] But in actual fact this wording does not please me, because so many words have been added in it, that it completely alienates the text itself. Next, that wording is not completely correct, because it is evident that what was put in its first part is false, where the following is said: Whosoever shall have put away his wife, except it be for fornication, even if he does not marry another, commits adultery. For he who without the cause of fornication puts away his wife, yet does not marry another wife, although he makes his wife to commit adultery, still he himself does not commit adultery.

Therefore, I say that in those words of Matthew, from the nineteenth chapter, only these very few words ought to be added: "for no other reason"; by adding these words alone the meaning of the text will be very clear and quite correct, and will agree with those words which Mark and Luke say on the same matter. Thus it will be necessary to modify the text of Matthew in this way so that he says the following: "Whosoever puts away his wife, for no other reason except on account of fornication, and shall marry another, commits adultery." In which sentence only these words are added: "for no other reason," and once these words

---

[1] "The obscurity of the passage was the reason why the interpreters divined various meanings... Further, in ὃ ἐὰν ἐξ ἐμοῦ ["whatever if by me" (Mt. 15, 5)], clearly something has to be supplied, in order to express the full sense of the Greek clause; and it is permissible to supply that which best fits the meaning, 'is' or 'will be,' or something similar" (*In novum Testamentum... annotationes*, p. 64).

[2] The Vulgate version of Mt. 5, 5 is: "Vos autem dicitis : Quicumque dixerit patri, vel matri: Munus, quodcumque est ex me, tibi proderit" ("But you say: Whosoever shall say to father or mother, The gift whatsoever proceedeth from me, shall profit thee"). Erasmus's translation of the same verse is: "Vos autem dicitis : Quicumque dixerit patri, vel matri: quicquid doni a me profecturum erat, id in tuum vertitur commodum" ("But you say: Whosoever shall say to father or mother, Whatever gift proceedeth from me, it is turned into your profit"). *(Novum Testamentum omne, multo quàm antehac diligentius ab Erasmo Roterodamo recognitu, emedatum ac translatum* (Basel, Johann Froben, 1519), p. 33.

[3] Alonso Tostado (ca. 1410–1455), known in Spanish as *El Abulense,* was a Spanish theologian, councilor of John II of Castile and briefly Bishop of Ávila.

[4] *Commentaria in quintam partem Matthaei* (Venice, [s.n.], 1615), p. 199b.

have been added, the meaning becomes very clear. And from that particular case, which is expressed in these words about a man putting away his wife on account of her adultery, the universal ruling is very clearly inferred about all who put away their wives, and marry other wives, just as Mark and Luke stated it without any limitation or exception. For, as the dialecticians teach, "If what seems to belong less belongs, then what seems to belong more will belong."[1]

Now the reason will appear less, namely that he who on account of the wife's fornication put her away, and married another, was deemed to commit adultery. And thus from that alone, about which some doubt could arise, Matthew spoke in chapter nineteen, so that therefrom all would understand that much more justly the same thing ought to be said about all the rest of men, who without the cause of fornication put away their wives, and marry other wives. For in chapter five, Matthew had said about him who on account of the wife's fornication puts her away, but does not marry another wife, that he does not make her to commit adultery; because even if she afterwards would commit adultery, it is evident that she does not do this because her husband gave her the occasion of committing adultery by putting her away; since when staying with the husband she also committed adultery. And because, from this sentence of Matthew stated in chapter five a doubt could have arisen about him who on account of his wife's fornication had put her away, whether just as he is free from blame in the putting away, he is consequently also free to marry another wife, hence in chapter nineteen, he spoke only about the man of this kind putting away his wife in this way, so that he would eliminate all doubt about the matter, and he spoke according to the understood truth: "Whosoever puts away his wife, for no other reason except on account of fornication, and shall marry another, commits adultery." From all these things it is evident that Matthew, Mark and Luke are of one accord on this point, and all together are diametrically opposed to Erasmus, Cajetan, and Catharinus. And Innocent III supports this interpretation of mine, who cites those words of the Savior: "Whosoever shall put away his wife, except it be for fornication, and shall marry another, committeth adultery." From the citation of which words it is evident that Innocent, by those words, "except it be for fornication," understood merely the cause of fornication, and that he spoke about it alone in that passage.[2]

Again, this opinion, which teaches that marriage is dissolved as to the bond on account of the wife's fornication, is clearly proved to be false from Christ's words in Matthew, wherein after he had said no one can put away his wife except it be for fornication, immediately added these words: "And he that shall marry her that is put away, committeth adultery" (19, 9). And in another place when he speaks about the question of the Pharisees, he again says: "And he that shall marry her that is put away, committeth adultery" (5, 32). And in Luke it is said: "He that marrieth her that is put away from her husband, committeth adultery" (16, 18). From which words it is evidently inferred that the adulterous wife put away by her husband cannot marry any other man. If the wife who has been put away cannot marry another man, then neither can the man putting her away marry another woman; because if the bond of marriage was dissolved through adultery, it would be necessary that it be dissolved for both parties. For there are no just grounds for permitting that a contract entered into by two persons be binding for one party but not for the other. For it is necessary that both be bound or both be freed, because both are equally held to the contract. Thus, it is necessary that if a man is freed from bond of marriage, so also is the wife, and if the wife is not freed from that bond, neither is the husband.

Erasmus and his followers, Cajetan and Catharinus, foresaw this argument; and hence Erasmus to escape from this argument said that this was given as a punishment for the adultery

---

[1] Boethius, *De differentiis topicis*, bk. 2, c. 4 (PL 64, 933A).

[2] See *Decretals of Gregory IX*, bk. 4, tit. 19, c. 8 cited above.

to the adulterous wife, that she cannot marry after having been put away by the husband. Therefore, he says that bond on marriage is dissolved for both parties, but by the bond having been dissolved only the husband can proceed to a second marriage, and not the wife, as a punishment for the adultery perpetrated. But this response does not take away the force of the argument, whereby his slyness is detected, by Christ's words which He says: "He that marrieth her that is put away, committeth adultery." Now he would not commit adultery who marries her if she were not the wife of another man, especially if he who marries her were not otherwise freed from the bond of marriage. For no one can be truly said to commit adultery even if he has intercourse with a woman who is not his own, unless she be the wife of another man, or that he be the husband of another woman. Thus, I ask Erasmus and his followers, Cajetan and Catharinus, whether that woman put away by the husband on account of adultery, and married to another man, is the wife of the other man or of no one. If she is the wife of no one, then he who marries her, if he is not bound by the bond of marriage to another wife, does not commit adultery, which is the opposite of what Christ declares. And therefore, she is the wife of someone; but who's? Certainly not his who marries her, because if she were his, he would not be said to commit adultery by marrying her who is his. It necessarily follows then that that woman is the wife of him by whom she was put away; because otherwise it could not happen that he who marries her, if he is free from another marriage, by marrying her commits adultery. This argument is so convincing to me that I will frankly admit that I do not know how he could answer it.

Next, so that we may hem in the adversaries by an argument taken from the text of Matthew, let us freely grant to them that to the adulterous wife was given as a punishment for her adultery that having been put away by the husband she could not marry another. But what will he say about an innocent wife who on account of the husband's adultery departs from him? Is the same punishment not given to her, that she cannot marry again? Far be it, because, as Augustine say, God is never an avenger but that firstly someone is a sinner.[1] An innocent woman, however, who departed from the husband on account of his guilt, Paul bears witness that the Lord commanded, "that she remain unmarried, or be reconciled to her husband" (I Cor. 7, 11). If an innocent wife who has put away the adulterous husband cannot, while he is alive, marry another, then neither could a chaste man, who has put away the adulterous wife, marry another wife; because in the things which pertain to marriage, they are always reckoned to be equal.

And certainly, this testimony of Paul, as I think, clearly refutes the adversaries, although Catharinus would say that this passage of Paul can be very easily answered. For he says the meaning of this passage is that a woman may not depart from the husband, namely without the cause of fornication, because if she shall depart, namely without the cause of fornication, she ought to remain unmarried. But this interpretation of Catharinus greatly distorts Paul's words, so that he alienates it from its true meaning. For when Paul said: if she shall depart, the Lord commanded her to remain unmarried, he was speaking about that departure whereby it was permitted for her to depart from the husband, which is on account of the cause of fornication. Because if he was speaking about the other departure, which is for another cause besides fornication, he would not have been content to say that she ought to remain unmarried, but he would have said that she makes the husband to commit adultery, as the Lord said about the man who without the cause of fornication puts away the wife, that he makes her to commit adultery.

Erasmus interprets this passage of Paul otherwise, saying: Paul in that passage makes a distinction in this case between a man, such that in the case of the divorce of husband and wife they are not equal. For he says that the husband after he has put away the wife on ac-

---

[1] *De Genesi ad litteram*, bk. 11, c. 17, n. 22 (PL 34, 438).

NUPTIAE

count of adultery, can by the Savior's permission marry another;[1] but the wife cannot do this on account of the Lord's precept, which he says Paul stated in this passage.[2] And in support of this exposition he cites [Ambrosiaster] in his commentaries on Paul's Epistles, where the aforesaid words of Paul are interpreted, in which place this opinion of Erasmus, Cajetan and Catharinus is very clearly taught.[3] Gratian gives a synopsis of this interpretation of [Ambrosiaster].[4] But seeing that this opinion is very bad and contrary to the faith, he says that those words are not Ambrose's, but were inserted into Ambrose by some forgers.[5] Peter Lombard thinks the same thing.[6]

But Erasmus mocks this censure of Gratian and Peter Lombard, and Catharinus much more, saying the following: "But certain men say that this was patched on in Ambrose's books by heretics. Which heretics? Was this question ever perhaps bandied about among the heretics? I truly have not read of it. Finally, just as this is easily said, and not proved, so also it can be easily and truly disregarded."[7] I admit that this question was not bandied about at that time among the heretics, because the Church had not then defined about the matter; and hence, neither Peter Lombard nor Gratian said that those words were added by heretics in Ambrose, but by forgers, who then teaching that opinion, which Erasmus now taught, perhaps wanted to be supported by the authority of Ambrose; and hence decided to add those words to Ambrose. Now it is evident that there were at that time those who constantly asserted this opinion. For the well-known Pollentius, for whom Augustine wrote that work of his, *Adulterous Marriages*, was of that opinion, as Augustine relates there.[8]

But whether is was so done, it is not evident, but I have many reasonable inferences which urge me very much to believe that it was so done. The first is that Augustine, who was very devoted to Ambrose and a most diligent observer of his deeds and writings, when treating about this question, in the whole work of *Adulterous Marriages* never relates that Ambrose wrote that opinion, which I have no doubt that he would have done if he had read it in Ambrose, especially since I see Augustine in that same work cite Cyprian regarding another question about marriage related closely enough to this one. A second reasonable inference is that I see in those words which are attributed to Ambrose, one intolerable error, which neither Erasmus, nor Cajetan, nor Catharinus, as I think, would take up to defend.

Now so that I may show this more clearly, it is necessary to cite all those words which are said to be Ambrose's in the place, and they are those which follow: "It is not permitted for the wife to marry if she puts away her own husband because of adultery, or apostasy, or if he seeks to use her illicitly under the impulse of lasciviousness, since the woman, as the inferior

---

[1] "And I say to you, that whosoever shall put away his wife, except it be for fornication, and shall marry another, committeth adultery" (Mt. 19, 9).

[2] "But to them that are married, not I but the Lord commandeth, that the wife depart not from her husband" (I Cor. 7, 10).

[3] Erasmus here cited "Ambrose's" *Commentaria in Epistolam ad Corinthios Primam* on I Cor. 7, 11, but this commentary was written by an unknown author. The essential part of his citation is: "... a man is not bound by the law in the same way as his wife, since a woman's head is her husband" (PL 17, 218C).

[4] "Hence [the law] burdens the wife, does not apply to the husband, because the husband is permitted to marry another wife" (*Decretum Gratiani*, p. 2, c. 32, q. 7, c. 17 (*Uxor*) (PL 187, 1501A)).

[5] Actually, in a footnote Gratian cites Peter Lombard, who says that these words contradict other words of St. Ambrose etc.

[6] "But this is believed to have been put into Ambrose's book by forgers" (*IV Sentences*, dist. 35, n. 3 (PL 192, 929)).

[7] *Annotationes in commentaria Cajetani*, p. 507.

[8] "Therefore, [in Pollentius' opinion] it is permitted both of [husband and wife] to remarry after the adultery, just as though after death." (Bk. 2, c. 2, n. 2 (PL 40, 471-472)).

party, does not enjoy the same rights as the man, who is the superior. But if her husband commits apostasy or desires to enjoy his wife in a perverted manner, the wife can neither marry another man nor return to her husband. 'And let not the husband put away his wife.' Supply, however, 'except it be for fornication.' The reason why Paul does not add, as he does in the case of the woman, 'If he depart, that he remain unmarried,' is because it is licit for a husband to remarry if he dismisses a sinful wife, because he is not bound by this law as is his wife, because a husband is the head of his wife."[1] I suspect that these words attributed to Ambrose were added there by someone else.

In which words one ought to especially notice that he says, "If the husband commits apostasy… the wife can neither marry another man nor return to her husband." This is so clearly false that no one who professes to be a Catholic would wish to endorse it: because Paul in the same seventh chapter of the First Epistle to the Corinthians clearly condemns these words, saying the following: "If any woman hath a husband that believeth not, and he consent to dwell with her, let her not put away her husband. For the unbelieving husband is sanctified by the believing wife" (v. 13-14). And Paul says these words about the woman whose husband was unbelieving when she contracted marriage with him, which could be more easily dissolved than if after the marriage was contracted, he had withdrawn from the faith. Thus it is false that the woman who on account of her husband's apostasy had left him, could not return to him, especially if he remaining in his apostasy does not wish to impede the wife from remaining in the true faith.

If perhaps you say that those words which are found in [Ambrosiaster] ought to be understood of the case when the apostate man tries to turn his wife away from the true faith. I certainly admit that then she ought not to remain with the husband; but neither then ought the husband to remain with the wife. Because Paul says the same thing about both in this case; and he makes them equals, saying the following: "But if the unbeliever depart, let him depart. For a brother or sister is not under servitude in such cases" (v. 15). Also it ought to be noticed in these words [of Abrosiaster], and carefully considered, the reason why the author of these words, whoever he is, is motivated to make the husband and wife unequal in the case of divorce, such that after the marriage is dissolved the husband can marry another wife, but the wife cannot marry another husband, even if she is completely innocent. "Because a husband is the head (he says) of his wife." And it is certainly undeserved that such a very bad reason could be attributed to such a great man as Ambrose was. For Paul did not say that the husband is the head of the wife, because the husband has greater power for taking carnal pleasures than the wife, but rather that the man ought to rule and govern the woman, just as the head does for the whole rest of the body. And certainly if a woman's nature is considered well, that same reason will teach that more is conceded in this regard to the wife than to the husband; because, as Blessed Peter says, the woman is a "weaker vessel" (I Pet. 3, 7) than the man, and hence it was more correct to assist this weakness, than to assist the man, who ought to be much stronger.

A third reasonable inference which seems to urge me very much to think that those words are added by someone else in Ambrose is that in the commentaries of the same Ambrose on Luke I find the opposite opinion to that which is found in his commentaries on Paul. For when interpreting those words of Christ in Luke: "Everyone that putteth away his wife, and marrieth another, committeth adultery" (16, 18), he says many things to persuade a man not to put away his wife, and among them he says these words: "Listen to the law of the Lord, Whom they also serve, who make the laws: 'What therefore God hath joined together, let no man put asunder' (Mt. 19, 6). Not merely a heavenly precept, but also a certain work of God is dissolved here. Will you allow, I pray you, while you are still alive, that your children be

---

[1] Ambrosiaster, *Commentaria in Epistolam ad Corinthios Primam* on I Cor. 7, 11, (PL 17, 230A–B).

under the care of a stepfather; or the mother still being alive, to live under a stepmother? Suppose the woman you have repudiated marries. Her necessity is your crime; what you consider to be marriage, is adultery."[1] In which words there are many things which Ambrose clearly testifies in the case of divorce to make the spouses equal, such that neither of them after the fact of the divorce can join to themselves someone else through marriage. For when saying, "Will you allow, I pray you, while you are still alive, that your children be under the care of a stepfather?" he clearly shows that that the wife cannot marry someone else. Because her children could not otherwise be under a stepfather, unless the wife, who is their mother, were perhaps to marry another man. Also, when saying afterwards, "or the mother still being alive, to live under a stepmother?" he also clearly stated that the matter is unlawful and intolerable, if a man after a divorce were to marry another wife. For children cannot, while the mother is living, live under a stepmother, unless their father, while the mother is alive, marries another wife, which he says ought not to be tolerated. Then he says that the marriage of the wife is adultery, if she marries another man. Now it would not be adultery if she, at the time after the divorce, were not the wife of the first husband.

See the three reasonable inferences, truly not light, but weighty enough, by which I am motivated to think that those words cited above, upon which the adversaries rely, are not Ambrose's, but inserted by someone else into his commentaries. For even though Blessed Ambrose is a man of great estimation and authority on account of the excellence of his teaching joined with sanctity, still one ought not to defer to someone of such great honor and authority such that one ought to believe him alone more than all others renowned for holiness and doctrine, and of one accord in the same opinion. Now all the holy Doctors whom it is permitted to examine when speaking about this matter, teach in unison that a man and wife are equal in all things which pertain to the substance of marriage, such that when one can marry, the other also can do the same, and when one cannot, neither can the other.

Now so that I may leave this matter sufficiently proved, it will be worthwhile in the present circumstances to cite a number of testimonies of holy men. [Hervé de Bourg-Dieu[2]] in his commentaries on Paul, when interpreting the passage from the First Epistle to the Corinthians, "And let not the husband put away his wife" (7, 11), says these words: "What was firstly said about the wife, ought to be understood likewise concerning the husband, that if the husband shall put way the wife on account of her fornication, that he remain unmarried, or if he cannot contain herself, he ought to be reconciled to his wife."[3] Long before this man [Pseudo-] Primasius, Bishop of Hadrumetum,[4] who in his commentaries on Paul, when interpreting the above-mentioned words of Paul, says: "Men know that it is not permitted to them to know another wife besides their own, because by an equal lot they are under obligation and debtors to each other."[5] Augustine teaches this opinion in so many places that I do not know which I ought to rather cite from among them as a testimony; but at length it seems suitable to choose from his book, *On the Sermon on the Mount*, wherein when interpreting those words of Paul, "And let not the husband put away his wife," he says these words: "Wherefore did he not add, 'except it be for fornication,' which the Lord permits, unless because he wishes a similar rule to be understood, that if he shall put away his wife (which he is permitted to do for the cause of fornication), he is to remain without a wife, or be reconciled to his wife? For it would not be a bad thing for a husband to be reconciled to such a woman as that to whom,

---

[1] *Exposition of the Holy Gospel According to Saint Luke* (PL 15, 1767A).
[2] This quotation is here incorrectly attributed to St. Anselm.
[3] *Commentaria in epistolas Pauli* (181, 877C).
[4] Primasius (died around 560) was bishop of Hadrumetum and Primate of Byzacena, in Africa.
[5] *Commentaria in epistolas S. Pauli* (PL 68, 521A).

NUPTIAE

when nobody had dared to stone her, the Lord said, 'Go, and sin no more' (Jn. 8, 11)."[1] Jerome is clearly favorable to this view, who in a certain letter to [Amandus[2]] says these words: "The Apostle thus cut away every plea and has clearly declared that, if a woman marries again while her husband is living, she is an adulteress. You must not speak to me of the violence of a ravisher, a mother's pleading, a father's bidding, the influence of relatives, the insolence and the intrigues of servants, household losses. A husband may be an adulterer or a sodomite, he may be stained with every crime and may have been left by his wife because of his sins; yet he is still her husband and, so long as he lives, she may not marry another. The Apostle does not promulgate this decree on his own authority but on that of Christ who speaks in him. For he has followed the words of Christ Who says in the Gospel: "Whosoever shall put away his wife, excepting for the cause of fornication, maketh her to commit adultery: and he that shall marry her that is put away, committeth adultery' (Mt. 5, 32)."[3] Chrysostom teaches the same opinion saying the following: "Elsewhere I grant He gives to the man abundant precedence [over the woman]… But in this place we hear no more of greater and less, but it is one and the same right… There is great equality, and no prerogative."[4]

Now then, it is necessary to ask Erasmus, Cajetan and Catharinus whether it is more rightful to believe Ambrose alone, rather than so many holy and learned men agreeing together on this opinion? What am I saying? Nay, rather than Paul. For if they wish to correctly attend to Paul's words, they will clearly know that he made the husband and wife equal in this matter. Because before Paul prescribed that law for the wife, that if she would want to depart from her husband, she must remain unmarried, he said that he commands it not on his own authority, but on God's. "But to them that are married," Paul says, "not I but the Lord commandeth, that the wife depart not from her husband. And if she depart, that she remain unmarried, or be reconciled to her husband. And let not the husband put away his wife" (I Cor. 7, 10-11). Now this precept which pertains to the woman, the Lord gave nowhere, as it is very clearly established from Jerome's words which we have just cited, except where He said: "Whosoever shall put away his wife, excepting for the cause of fornication, maketh her to commit adultery: and he that marry her that is put away, committeth adultery" (Mt. 5, 32). In which words alone is there express mention of the man putting way the wife, and there is completely no mention of the wife putting away the husband. Nevertheless, the Apostle says that the Lord gave this precept to the wife, which he could not say in any way except because he held it to be a most certain and undoubted fact that a husband and wife are equal in the case of divorce, and hence all those things which Christ said about a husband putting away the wife, Paul derived the necessary consequences for the wife putting away her husband. And for this reason he said that these things were commanded by the Lord, although they were not expressed by the same words by him. And for the same reason Paul, in the same place when speaking about the husband, did not care to clearly explain all those things which he had said about the wife, because he had seen that Christ had spoken clearly enough about them, from Whose words he had gathered the precept about the woman. And this argument refutes and hems in the adversaries to such an extent that there is no small crack left open whereby they could slip away.

These things are enough for proving that a husband and wife in the case of divorce are equal; now it remains that we resume our disputation in regard to the first goal of this dispute. And so to continue where we had left off, this opinion which teaches that a man when putting away his wife on account of her adultery can marry another wife, is manifestly proved to be

---

[1] Bk. 1, c. 16, n. 43 (PL 34, 1251).

[2] The author incorrectly wrote that this letter was written to Pope Damasus, when in fact it was written to Amandus, a priest, and afterwards bishop, of Burdigala (Bordeaux).

[3] Letter 55, n. 3 (PL 22, 562-563).

[4] *Homilies on First Corinthians*, hom. 19 (PG 61, 152).

false by that which Paul says in the Epistle to the Romans: "The woman that hath an husband, whilst her husband liveth is bound to the law. But if her husband be dead, she is loosed from the law of her husband. Therefore, whilst her husband liveth, she shall be called an adulteress, if she be with another man" (7, 2-3). And in the First Epistle to the Corinthians he repeats the same opinion, saying the following: "A woman is bound by the law as long as her husband liveth; but if her husband die, she is at liberty" (7, 39). If the woman is bound to the law for as long as her husband lives, then after she has committed adultery she is still bound to the husband, because her husband does not cease to live on account of the wife's adultery. If she was still bound to the husband as his wife, also after the adultery has been committed [she remains bound]. Therefore, that husband cannot, while the wife is alive, marry another wife, because then he would commit clear adultery, since no one, according to the Divine law, can have two wives at the same time.

Perhaps someone will respond to this argumentation, and will say that that husband then ceases to be the husband of that wife, who was an adulteress, such that although he lives bodily, yet he does not live as her husband. But this response does absolutely nothing except beat the air, and utters words in vain; because it is immediately caught in its craftiness, by those words which Paul himself immediately adds, speaking thus: "But if her husband be dead, she is loosed from the law of her husband" (Rom. 7, 2). And after a few words he repeats the same thing, speaking thus: "But if her husband be dead, she is delivered from the law of her husband; so that she is not an adulteress, if she be with another man" (v. 3). From which words it is very clearly established that Paul says that only the husband's death is what frees the woman from the law of the husband, and which makes her free from the bond of marriage, so that she is not an adulteress if she would be with another man. And hence it is very clearly established that although she had committed adultery, nevertheless if her husband is not dead, she is bound to the husband. Now it is evident that the husband is not dead at that time when his wife commits adultery, nor when the husband repudiates her; thus, the wife is at that time bound to him.

Blessed Augustine is well aware of all these things, and when discussing the aforesaid words of Paul says: "It follows that the rational doctrine is this: 'A woman is bound by the law as long as her husband liveth' (I Cor 7, 39), that is, as long as he has not departed from the body. A woman subject to a husband is bound by the law while he is alive, that is, while he is still in the body. 'But if her husband be dead, she is loosed from the law of her husband. Therefore, whilst her husband liveth, she shall be called an adulteress, if she be with another man: but if her husband be dead, she is delivered from the law of her husband; so that she is not an adulteress, if she be with another man' (Rom 7, 2-3). These words of the Apostle, so often repeated, so often insisted on, are true. They are alive. They are sound. They are clear. A woman does not begin to be the wife of any second husband, unless she has ceased to be the wife of the first. She ceases to be the wife of the first, however, if her husband dies, not if he commits adultery. It is not wrong, therefore, for a wife to be divorced for adultery; but her obligation of chastity remains, and this makes anyone who marries a divorced woman guilty of adultery, even in this case of divorce because of adultery."[1]

Next, besides all the testimonies of Sacred Scripture quoted above one of the *Apostolic Canons*, which Blessed John Damascene lists among the canonical writings, proves this our and the Catholic opinion. Now of those canons, which is the forty-eighth, contains these words: "If any layman put away his wife and marry another, or one who has been divorced by another man, let him be excommunicated."[2] Add to all these things the concordant opinion of

---

[1] *Adulterous Marriages*, bk. 2, c. 4, n. 4 (PL 40, 473).
[2] PG 137, 134D. The *Apostolic Canons*, Saint John Damascene notwithstanding, were never generally considered to belong to the canon of Scripture.

all the holy Doctors about this matter, which, as I proved in the first book of this work in chapter seven is of such great weight that it is not at all permitted to oppose it; because it would be just as if one were to contradict the opinion of the whole Church. Now all the holy Doctors, who have discussed this matter, whom I was able to see, teach in unison that by adultery marriage can be dissolved as to bed and habitation, but not as to the bond. Among all those men, whom I knew have discussed this matter, I decided to cite some testimonies, so that I may make known to all their concord in this regard. I omit here all the scholastic theologians, who originated with their leader and teacher, Peter Lombard, although all these men are of one accord in this our and the Catholic opinion, because all of them, even though they also have a great esteem and authority among Catholic and upright men, nevertheless for Erasmus, the modern leader in battle of this error, they have little credibility, and their writings are spread far and wide; and it is known that they approved of these things.

Wherefore I wish to select testimonies from only those who lived before Peter Lombard, and I cite Anselm [of Laon[1]] as the first witness, who in his commentaries on the fifth chapter of Matthew says these words: "Here He commands that one may not put away his wife but only 'excepting for the cause of fornication' (v. 32). For if she shall have broken the law of marriage, the husband can separate himself from her, so that he may take away the sexual intercourse from himself, which she violated; but nevertheless the Sacrament of Matrimony remains, so that he may not marry another wife."[2] And on the nineteenth chapter of the same Matthew again he says these words: "Fornication alone is a reason for separation. For after the woman who is married to her husband, and was one in carnal intercourse, shall have deserted that unity unto other flesh, and divided it by fornication, she assuredly does not break the bond of marriage: but deserves not to have carnal intercourse with her husband any longer: because she sinned against the marital bond."[3]

Theophylactus teaches the same opinion in much fewer words when interpreting the passage, "[A man] shall cleave to his wife" (Eph. 5, 31), where he says these words: "Notice another strengthening of the [marriage] state, namely, a man having left his parents is joined to his wife. And he did not say, 'shall live with,' but 'shall cleave to,' signifying an indivisible union."[4]

Bede supports the same opinion in his commentaries on the tenth chapter of Mark, saying the following: "In Matthew it is more fully expressed, 'Whosoever shall put away his wife, except it be for fornication' (Mt. 19, 9). The only carnal cause then is fornication; the only spiritual cause is the fear of God, that a man should put away his wife to enter into religion, as we read that many have done. But there is no cause allowed by the law of God for marrying another, during the lifetime of her who is quitted."[5]

Before all these men Blessed Isidore taught this same opinion saying these words: "Thus it was called a Sacrament between the spouses, because the Church cannot be separated from Christ, so neither the wife from the husband. Therefore, that which is in Christ and the Church, is this Sacrament of union in every single husband and wife that cannot be separated. Hence the Apostle also says: 'Not I but the Lord commandeth, that the wife depart not from her husband' (I Cor. 7, 10). For he forbids them to be sent away for whatever reason, in order that they not be married to others according to the custom of the Jews, which the Lord

---

[1] Anselm of Laon (1050-1117), known as *Doctor Scholasticus*, was educated under St. Anselm of Canterbury, who made him acquainted with the new scholastic theology. Anselm's chief work is his *Glossa interlinearis*, a commentary on the whole Vulgate.
[2] *Ennarrationes in Matthaeum* (PL 162, 1298D).
[3] *Ibid.* (PL 162, 1412B-C).
[4] *Commentarius in Epistolam ad Ephesios* (PG 124, 1118C).
[5] *In Evangelium Sancti Marci*, bk. 3, c. 10 (PL 92, 230C).

forbade, saying: 'Whosoever shall put away his wife, excepting for the cause of fornication, maketh her to commit adultery' (Mt. 5, 32)."[1] In which words there are two things which one ought to especially notice. The first is that he says that between husband and wife there is a Sacrament of union that cannot be separated. The other is that he says that the Apostle forbids that the wife be put away for any reason, lest she be joined to another.

It is not necessary to now cite Augustine for this opinion of ours because his three testimonies which were cited by us above in this disputation adequately suffice. Catharinus when acknowledging that there are so many and such great men united in this opinion, says that they all followed Augustine, and from him this opinion began to have strength. What defect does it have because it began from Augustine? Ought it then be rejected? By no means; nay it ought to be embraced with open arms, because all men after him accept it. But Catharinus is mistaken saying that this opinion began to have strength from Augustine; because it is evident that it had great strength during so many centuries before Augustine that a Christian would be considered foolish and insane who would dare to fight against it. Did not the Apostles precede Augustine by many centuries? And there were the legislators of the canon which we cited above. And besides these men there were still others older than Augustine, who taught the same opinion. For Jerome, although he was a contemporary of Augustine, was nevertheless more ancient than he was, and wrote before him; and he in his commentaries on the nineteenth chapter of Matthew says these words: "And since it could have happened that someone brought a false charge against an innocent person, and on account of the second marriage-union hurled a charge at the first wife, it is commanded to put away the first wife in such a way that he have no second wife while the first one is living."[2]

And Chrysostom was slightly more ancient than Jerome, because by the same Jerome he was enumerated among the Ecclesiastical writers. And this man clearly teaches the same opinion as Augustine, saying the following: "That is, the former, though he take not another wife, by that act alone has made himself liable to blame, having made the first an adulteress; the latter again has become an adulterer by taking her who is another's. For tell me not this, 'The other has cast her out'; nay, for when cast out she continues to be the wife of him that expelled her."[3] And he again says: "For He said not, that He made one man and one woman only, but that He also gave this command that the one man should be joined to the one woman. But if it had been His will that he should put this one away, and bring in another, when He had made one man, He would have formed many women. But now both by the manner of the creation, and by the manner of lawgiving, He showed that one man must dwell with one woman continually, and never break off from her… For not merely did He bring the woman to the man, but also commanded that father and mother ought to be left. And neither did He make it a law for him merely to come to the woman, but also 'to cleave to her,' intimating by the meaning of this phrase that they nowise ought to be severed."[4]

Origen lived nearly two centuries before Chrysostom, who, when interpreting the words of the Savior from the nineteenth chapter of Matthew about the putting away of the wife on account of the cause of fornication, says these words: "Even some prelates of the Church have permitted a woman to marry, even when her husband was living, doing contrary to what was written, where it is said, 'A woman is bound by the law as long as her husband liveth' (I Cor.7, 39), and 'Therefore, whilst her husband liveth, she shall be called an adulteress, if she be with another man' (Rom. 7, 3), not indeed altogether without reason, for it is probable this concession was permitted in comparison with worse things, contrary to what was from the beginning

---

[1] *De ecclesiasticis officiis*, c. 20, n. 11 (PL 83, 812C-813A).
[2] *Commentary on Matthew*, bk. 8, on Mt. 19, 9 (PL 26, 135A).
[3] *Homilies on Mattthew*, hom. 17, n. 4 (PG 57, 259).
[4] *Ibid.*, hom. 62, n. 1 (PG 57, 597).

ordained by the Law, and written. But perhaps among those who dare to oppose the teaching of our Savior, some Jewish man will say that when Jesus said, 'whosoever shall put away his wife, excepting for the cause of fornication, maketh her to commit adultery: and he that shall marry her that is put away, committeth adultery' (Mt. 5, 32), He also gave permission to put away a wife like as well as Moses did, who was said by Him to have given this law for the hardness of heart of the people, and will hold that the saying, 'she find not favour in his eyes, for some uncleanness' (Deut. 24, 1), is to be reckoned as the same as fornication on account of which with good cause a wife could be cast away from her husband. But to him it must be said that, if she who committed adultery was according to the Law to be stoned, clearly it is not in this sense that the unseemly thing is to be understood. For it is not necessary for adultery or any such great indecency to write a bill of divorce... But as a woman is an adulteress, even though she seem to be married to a man, while the former husband is still living, so also the man who seems to marry her who has been put away, does not so much marry her as commit adultery with her, according to the declaration of our Savior."[1] Origen has said many noteworthy things here against our adversaries. And these words of Origen are according to Erasmus' translation. For which reason I am very surprised that Erasmus was so brazen in this place, that in that lengthy annotation of his on the seventh chapter of the First Epistle to the Corinthians he was not afraid to say that Origen does not reprehend those bishops who permitted men to marry other wives, while their first wives were still alive, when on the contrary Origen clearly says that the acted against Scripture.

Clement of Alexandria, the teacher of Origen, says: "Now that the Scripture counsels marriage, and allows no release from the union, is expressly contained in the law, 'You shall not put away your wife, except for the cause of fornication'; and it regards as fornication, the marriage of those separated while the other is alive."[2] And he who wishes to see these words will find them on page eighty-three of the Florentine edition.

[Pseudo-] Pope Evaristus preceded this Clement by more than a whole century; because he, as it is clear from the [*Liber*] *pontificalis* of Damasus,[3] lived during the times of Domitian, Nerva, and Trajan. Now he in his second letter clearly supports this opinion of ours, saying the following: "Just as a husband ought not to commit adultery against his wife, so neither ought a bishop against his church, that is to leave that church for which he was consecrated without an unavoidable necessity, or by Apostolic or canonical change, and not join himself to another church due to ambition. And just as a wife is not permitted to put away her husband so that she might marry another man while he is alive, or commit adultery against him, even if her husband has committed fornication; but according to the Apostle she either ought to be reconciled to her husband or remain unmarried. So it is not permitted to put away a church, or to separate its bishop from it, while he is alive, so that he may accept another; but he either ought to keep it or remain unmarried, that is, it may not receive another bishop while he is alive, lest it incur the crime of fornication or adultery."[4]

For Catharinus says (as we have already related above) that these words ought to be interpreted in this way. I command the wife not to depart from the husband, except for the cause of fornication, because if she shall depart, namely without the cause of fornication, she ought

---

[1] *Commentary on the Gospel of Matthew*, bk. 14, c. 23-24 (PG 13, 1246A-1250B).
[2] *Miscellanies* (or *The Stromata*), bk. 2, c.23 (PG 9, 1095B).
[3] *The Book of the Popes* (New York, Columbia University Press, 1916), vol. 1, p. 10. In the Middle Ages it was supposed that Saint Jerome wrote this book at the request of Pope Damasus based on two letters of correspondence between the two which were later discovered to be forgeries. Cf. "*Liber Pontificalis*," *The Catholic Encyclopedia* (New York: Robert Appleton Company, 1908), vol. 9, p. 224.
[4] *False Decretals of the Pseudo-Isidore* (PL 130, 84C-D).

to remain unmarried or be reconciled to her husband.[1] And according to this interpretation of his, he says that Paul doe not command the wife who departed from her husband on account of his fornication to remain unmarried or to be reconciled to her husband. But this opinion of Catharinus is proved to be very clearly false by the words of Evaristus saying that the Apostle commanded that the wife who departed from her husband, even if he had committed fornication, ought to remain unmarried while he is living, or be reconciled to her husband. For when the Apostle said, "And if she depart" (I Cor. 7, 11), he does not allow that which was forbidden to the woman, about which it was not necessary to dispute any more about what she could do in that state in which she was able to rightly be; but he allows that which it was lawful for the woman to do, which is, to depart from the husband on account of his fornication. And then he goes further stating what she could then do, and says that she could not marry another, but instead must necessarily remain unmarried or reconciled to her husband. From all these testimonies cited so far, it is already clear established as false what Catharinus says, that this opinion of ours took strength from Augustine; because many illustrious men more ancient than Augustine taught it, and no man of any fame dared to reject it. For those bishops whom Origen relates did the contrary, he himself said that they acted outside of Scripture and against Scripture.

Besides the words Evaristus mentioned above, spoken in passing about this subject, there are still other proclamations of the popes specifically given about this matter. For Pope Innocent III when wishing to prove that the plurality of wives is forbidden by the Divine law, says these words: "Certainly this opinion is proved true also by the testimony of Truth Himself, bearing witness in the Gospel: 'Whosoever shall put away his wife, except it be for fornication, and shall marry another, committeth adultery' (Mt. 19, 9). If, therefore, when the wife has been put away, another cannot be married according to law, all the more when the same wife is retained."[2] Innocent when saying these words established nothing new, but merely argues from that which he certainly believed to be of Divine law.

Alexander III, who preceded this Innocent [III], decreed by these words: "Because no one is permitted to put away his wife except for the clear cause of fornication, and in this case he ought to reconcile her to himself, or as long as she lives to be continent; we command, regarding the same man who has put away the abovementioned woman, that he, preceded by a warning, be forced by ecclesiastical censure to return to his wife and treat her with marital affection."[3] This Alexander III decreed nothing new in this matter, but commanded that one act according to existing law.

Before these two supreme pontiffs, Innocent I preceded them by many centuries, who in a letter to Exuperius, Bishop of Toulouse, by whom he was asked about this matter, in the sixth chapter replies by these words: "You have inquired also about those who, after obtaining a divorce, have married again. It is clearly evident that both parties are adulterers. Those men who, while the wife is still living, hasten to another union, though their marriage seem to have been dissolved, evidently cannot be other than adulterers. This is so true that those women to whom the men in question have united themselves have also committed adultery according to that which we read in the Gospels: 'Whosoever shall put away his wife… and shall marry another, committeth adultery: and he that shall marry her that is put away, committeth adultery' (Mt. 19, 9)."[4] Innocent I was certainly a man very famous for holiness and doctrine. In whose words what especially ought to be noted is that he did not issue any new decree, but merely answers the question proposed to himself through the testimonies of Sacred Scripture.

---

[1] Cf. *Annotationes in Commentaria Cajetani*, pp. 502-504.

[2] *Decretals of Gregory IX*, bk. 4, tit. 19 (*De divortiis*), c. 8 (*Gaudemus*). Dz. 408.

[3] *Decretals of Gregory IX*, bk. 4, tit. 1 (*De sponsalibus et matrimoniis*), c. 9 (*Ex parte*).

[4] C. 6, 12 (PL 20, 500B-501A).

And it is necessary to observe this on account of Erasmus who says that it is merely forbidden by the decrees of the popes, and not by a Divine commandment, for a man who left his wife on account of adultery to marry another wife. Catharinus also in those *Annotationes* of his against Cajetan says these words: "It is enough that I pay reverence to the decrees of the pontiffs, so that I also teach and interpret favorably according to them."[1] And certainly, so that I may speak frankly, I am much more surprised that Catharinus erred on this point rather than Erasmus, because Catharinus was at the beginning of his studies a professional lawyer, and in that capacity he gained a name before he made his profession in the Order of Saint Dominic. Hence he could have adverted to, if he wanted, that no pontiff has decreed anything about this matter on his own authority, as though he issued his own law: but when he spoke about this matter, he merely stated what the Lord had declared in the Gospel. And for this reason after I cited those words of those three pontiffs, I noted this in them all, so that I might thence show that they all taught that this opinion of ours is from the Divine law, and not from their own creation.

I see that nothing now remains for me, so that I may leave fully proved this our and the Catholic opinion, except that I bring forth the clear definition of the Catholic Church about this matter. The Synod of Milevum decrees regarding this contention by these words: "It seemed good that according to Evangelical and Apostolic discipline a man who had been put away from his wife, and a woman put away from her husband should not be married to another, but so should remain, or else be reconciled the one to the other; but if they spurn this law, they shall be forced to do penance, covering which case we must petition that an imperial law be promulgated."[2] Although we admit that this council was provincial, still we know, Augustine bearing witness, that it was confirmed by Innocent I. Now these words for their greater confirmation were afterwards repeated in the African Council[3] word for word.

But lest someone still contend that both these councils were provincial, I bring forth the Council of Florence, because beyond any doubt it was a general council, at which the Greeks and the Latins came together. Now this council in the formula of the faith given to the Armenians, when speaking about the Sacrament of Matrimony, issued the decree in these words: "Moreover, there is allotted a threefold good on the part of Matrimony. First, the progeny is to be accepted and brought up for the worship of God. Second, there is faith which one of the spouses ought to keep for the other. Third, there is the indivisibility of Marriage, because it signifies the indivisible union of Christ and the Church. Although, moreover, there may be a separation of the marriage couch by reason of fornication, nevertheless, it is not permitted to contract another marriage, since the bond of a marriage legitimately contracted is perpetual."[4]

Nevertheless, if any contentious person wishing to defend Cajetan shall say that this formula of the faith for the Armenians was not given by the whole council, but was published by Pope Eugene alone after the closing of the council, it could nowise help him in this way; because Cajetan himself teaches elsewhere that the pope cannot err in definitions of the faith. Next, Cajetan clearly bears witness in the tract of his, *On the Comparison of the Authority of Pope and Council*, that this teaching about the Sacraments given to the Armenians was published by the whole council.[5] And he published this tract long before he had undertaken

---

[1] *Annotationes in Commentaria Cajetani*, pp. 508.

[2] II Synod of Milevum, can. 17 (Mansi, *Sacrorum Conciliorum nova et amplissima collectio*) vol. 4, p. 331; *False Decretals of the Pseudo-Isidore* (PL 130, 372B).

[3] XI Synod of Carthage (407 AD), Can. 102 (Mansi, *Sacrorum Conciliorum nova et amplissima collectio*) vol. 3, p. 806.

[4] Dz. 702.

[5] "These words also are found in the ecumenical Council of Florence under Eugene IV, where the union of the Greeks and Armenians with the Roman Church was accomplished, 'We define...'" (James

commenting on Sacred Scripture, in the commentaries of which he brought forth this opinion about divorce. Wherefore I do not see how on this point he can be excused, since it is evident that he knew the definition of the general council very well, against which he was not afraid to think and publicly oppose. Yet I do not say these things because I wish to accuse his person on this account. For in this work, as I have often said elsewhere, I determined not to speak out against persons, but against false and heretical doctrines. It is also possible that although he had read that formula of the faith given by the Council of Florence to the Armenians when he wrote that tract, nevertheless since a long time had afterwards elapsed when he wrote those commentaries on the Gospels, he did not remember that Council of Florence which he had previously read. For we do not always keep in memory everything we have read. And hence I do not wish to condemn his person on account of this error, especially since in regard to this opinion, as I already said in the beginning, he submitted himself to the decision of the Church.

But now it is necessary that I respond to the arguments of the adversaries, which they say motivated them to defend the aforesaid teaching. Firstly in fact Erasmus and Catharinus argue that it is hard that he who without any fault of his own, but solely due to the wife' fornication puts her away, is forced to keep continence, especially if such a man is inclined by nature towards carnal intercourse. Catharinus greatly amplifies this reasoning, and expends many words about it. But the well-known Pollentius had put forth this reasoning many centuries before, for whom Augustine wrote that tract of his, *Adulterous Marriages*. Thus, I could not respond to Erasmus and Catharinus better than Augustine responds to Pollentius in the second book of *Adulterous Marriages*, in the tenth chapter saying the following: "In reply to this you say to me: 'The celibate life is only for the few. Therefore, those who divorce partners who commit adultery, because there is no possibility of reconciliation, see themselves put so much at risk that they proclaim that Christ's law is not human but a law of death.' My brother, as far as concerns those who are not continent, they may well have their numerous complaints about Christ's law being a law of death and not human. Just the same, we must not change or pervert Christ's Gospel because of them. You yourself would be inclined to respond only to the complaints of those who divorce their wives on the grounds of adultery, if they are not allowed to remarry. Celibacy, you would say, is only for the few, and they ought to be encouraged to undertake it by praising it, not forced to it by law. You think, therefore, that if there is no remarrying after a wife has been divorced, the complaint about human celibacy is legitimate. Pay attention, though, to how often we shall have to allow adultery to be committed, once we choose to accede to the complaints of the unchaste. What if a spouse is afflicted by a lasting and incurable disease, and this prevents the partners from having intercourse? What if imprisonment or some other external force keeps them apart, so that the husband knows that his wife is still alive, but he is denied access to her? Do you think the mumbling of the unchaste should be acknowledged and adultery be permitted in that case? What about the very case the Lord was asked about, when he answered that it ought not be done, and said that because of the hardness of their hearts Moses had allowed them to give a bill of divorce and put aside their partner for any reason at all? Is not Christ's law distasteful to men who are unable to be celibate, but whose wives are quarrelsome, hurtful, bossy, fussy, and reluctant to comply with their marital obligation, and they would like to get rid of them by divorcing them and marrying someone else?"[1]

Innocent III replies in the same way.[2] But as to the example of the man separated from his wife which Innocent presents there, some bring up as an objection a certain statement

---

Henderson Burns, *Conciliarism and Papalism* (New York, Cambridge University Press,1997)), c. 1, p. 4; c. 7, pp. 29-30.

[1] Bk. 2, c. 10, n. 9 (PL 40, 476-477).

[2] "And notwithstanding that perhaps it is objected by some that the faithful man having been aban-

of Gregory the Younger [i.e. Pope Gregory II], which is cited by Gratian.[1] Yet Gratian also replies well to this that that Gregory erred deciding the matter in this way,[2] although a gloss in that place endeavors to excuse Gregory.

Secondly, the adversaries argue from the fact that a man is not bound to his wife, nor the wife to the husband, except for rendering the carnal debt, and for cohabitation, and mutual support. Now by divorce the innocent spouse, in favor of whom the divorce is granted, is freed from all these things. Therefore, at all events he could go on to a second marriage. It is easily responded to this argument by denying its first assumption. Now so that I may show its falsity more clearly, I advise the reader to notice that after any marriage has been contracted and ratified a double mutual obligation arises. One is affirmative, whereby they are bound to render the carnal debt and mutual support to each other: and these things are taken away by divorce. The other is negative, whereby either of them is bound not to render carnal intercourse to anyone except to that person alone to whom the spouse is bound by marriage, and this is not taken away except through the death of the other spouse. And concerning this bond alone is understood the saying of Paul: "A woman is bound as long as her husband liveth" (I Cor. 7, 39). And from the understanding of this obligation a clearer response to the preceding argument is also inferred, so that Erasmus and Catharinus may understand that it is not hard and severe to force the man to continence who left his wife on account of her adultery, and who does not want to reconcile himself to her. For when he contracted marriage with her, he obliged himself to this hardness and severity, whereby it is that what he promised from the beginning, he is obliged afterward to keep. And in this there is no injury to him, because knowing that such a bond exists in marriage, he voluntarily bound himself to such a bond. Now "An injury is not done," as the rule says, "to one who knows and wills it."[3]

Thirdly, the adversaries argue that what the Lord said according to the tenor of ancient law, "Whosoever shall put away his wife, let him give her a bill of divorce" (Mt. 5, 31), ought to be understood of the complete dismissal, which is not merely as to the bed, but also as so the bond, which one cannot deny, because of old the law was understood in this way. Therefore, what the Lord said about Evangelical dismissal, which is on account of fornication, ought to be understood in the same way of complete dismissal, not merely as to the bed, but also as to the bond. Catharinus makes so much of this argument, that he says that he does "not see what [more] could be said, which would satisfy a learned mind."[4] And he certainly was not the first inventor of this argument, because before him Erasmus had written in his *Annotations*, on the seventh chapter of the First Epistle to the Corinthians, saying the following: "The Church

---

doned ought not to be deprived of his right [to marital life] without his fault, although this may happen in many cases, as though the other spouse is cut off. By this response, however, the malice of certain men is prevented, who out of hatred of their spouses, and when they are displeased with each other, if in this case they could put them away, they might simulate heresy, so that once they have married other spouses they will rebound from that heresy." (*Decretals of Gregory IX*, bk. 4, tit. 19 (*De divortiis*), c. 7 (*Quanto*).

[1] "As regards your question what a husband is to do, if his wife has been attacked by illness, so that she is incapable of conjugal intercourse, it were best if he could continue as he is and practice self-restraint. But since this demands exceptional virtue, the man who cannot live in continence had better marry. But let him not fail to furnish her with support, since she is kept from married life by sickness, not debarred from it by some abominable offence" (*Concordia discordantium canonum*, C. 32, q. 7, c. 18 (PL 187, 1501B)).

[2] "That citation of Gregory is found to be completely opposed to the sacred canons, nay to the Evangelical and Apostolic teaching" (*Ibid.*). Cf. Gregory II's letter 14 (*Desiderabilem mihi*) (PL 89, 525A-B).

[3] *Digest* of Emperor Justinian, bk. 47, tit. 10, sect. 1, § 5, quoting Ulpian, *On the Edict*, Bk. 56. It is literally translated as, "No injury is committed against one who consents."

[4] *Annotationes in commentaria Cajetani*, p. 502.

allows divorce and separation of man and wife to be made, so far that after the separation, neither party marries again. I pray thee tell me, is Christ speaking about this kind of divorce? The question was put to Him from the Jews, and He made the answer again unto the Jews. But the Jews knew no other kind of divorce, but that which did bar them from taking that woman again, whom they had put away, and gave them liberty to marry another."[1]

But this argument which they make so much of, I make little of: because I carefully and attentively consider certain other words which Christ our Savior said shortly before those words about which we now dispute. "Unless your justice abound more than that of the scribes and Pharisees, you shall not enter into the kingdom of heaven" (Matt. 5, 20). Which words having been premised, He proceeded to reform those errors with which the Pharisees and Scribes were infected, and were infecting the people. Thus, He corrected in all those errors, those things which they were previously accustomed to teach incorrectly. And one of them was the repudiation of wives, by which repudiation they thought that they were freed from the bond of the wife, whom they were repudiating. In which matter they erred greatly: because although it was permitted for them that after one wife having been repudiated, they could marry another, nevertheless in doing so they were sinning: because they were acting contrary to the Natural law, from which no one can dispense, except He Who is above Nature. Thus, the permission was serving them for this, namely that they were not punished for this, when putting away their wives in this manner: they were not, however, free from sin. For because they were sinning in this way, wherefore Christ afterwards did not say, "God permitted," but "Moses permitted." And Jerome pointed this out in his commentaries on Matthew when interpreting those words of the Savior, "Moses by reason of the hardness of your heart…" (19, 8), whereupon he says these words: "What He means to say is this: Is God able to contradict Himself? Does he first command one thing and then break his own judgment by a new command? One must not understand things in this way. Rather, when Moses saw that, on account of the desire for second marriages to women who were richer, younger, or prettier, the first wives were either killed or were leading an evil life, he preferred to grant the discord than to allow hatred and murder to continue. At the same time, consider what He did not say: 'By reason of the hardness of your heart, God permitted you.' Rather He says, 'Moses.' This is in agreement with the Apostle, [who says[2]] that it is a counsel of man, not a command of God."[3]

There is still something else that ought to be considered: that Christ did not say that Moses "commanded," but "permitted." And hence it is inferred that the bill of divorce was something bad, because bad things are those which are permitted to happen; but good things are either commanded, or counsels are given concerning them. And [Pseudo-] Chrysostom noted this in his *Imperfect Work on Matthew*, whoever is the author of that work, saying these words: "He well said that Moses permitted this, not that he commanded it. It is one thing to order something and another thing to permit it. For what we order always pleases us, but what we permit, we order even though we do not want to because we cannot fully prevent the evil will of people."[4] Now in permitting this way Moses did not act badly, but well; because to avoid a greater evil, such as murder, he permitted a lesser evil.

Still it is necessary, so that everything may be understood correctly, to consider three things in the matter. The first of which Moses forbade, the second thing he permitted, and the third thing he commanded. He indeed forbade putting away one's wife without cause. He permitted one to put away his wife for the cause of disgraceful behavior, if she was disgraceful. He

---

[1] *Desiderii Erasmi Roterodami Opera omnia: emendatiora et auctiora* (Leiden, Pieter van der Aa, 1705), vol. 6, p. 698E.

[2] "But I speak this by indulgence, not by commandment" (I Cor. 7, 6).

[3] *Commentary on Matthew*, bk. 3, on Mt. 19, 8 (PL 26, 134C-D).

[4] Hom. 32 (PG 56, 801-802).

commanded that one give a bill of divorce, if one were to put away that woman, so that by the giving of this bill he might deter those men from putting away the wives of this kind. For after having given the bill of divorce one could no longer return to that wife, as it is stated in Deuteronomy,[1] and could not afterwards be reconciled to her. And in this, as in certain other things, that bill of divorce of the Old Law differs from the divorce of the Evangelical Law, in the Evangelical Law spouses can be reconciled after the divorce was made. In the giving of the bill of divorce, which was commanded, there was no sin. In the putting away of the wife, however, which was permitted, sin was committed, because the bond of marriage was dissolved, which was indissolvable from the Natural law.

Thus Christ, when speaking to the Jews, although He wants to discard the bill of divorce which was commanded in the Old Law, used the expression of "putting away," according to the meaning in which the Jews were accustomed to understand. When, however, after having abrogated the bill of the Old Law, He established divorce according to the Evangelical Law, He does not use those words to signify putting away as to the bond, but only as to the bed. Because just as He was establishing, or in order that I may speak more correctly, He was restoring, a law stricter than the Old Law, so also He then used a stricter meaning of the words, wishing that our justice would "abound more than that of the scribes and Pharisees" (Mt. 5, 20). And that He uses this meaning, Christ Himself very clearly shows, by the words which He immediately adds, saying: "He that shall marry her that is put away, committeth adultery" (v. 32). For by those words He clearly indicated that she who was put away by her husband is the wife of him by whom she was put away: because as we have already said above, he would not have committed adultery who married her unless she were the wife of him by whom she was put away. Hence Christ says that she is "put away" by the husband, who was only put away as to the bed.

But Erasmus mocks the use of these words in so strict a meaning, saying that these words, "to put way," are never found among approved authors to be taken to mean merely the putting away as to the bed.[2] Does Erasmus wish to oblige Christ to follow the rules of philology? Or does he want to accuse Christ Himself of having incorrectly used the meaning of that word? Does not Erasmus himself often admit elsewhere that there are many things in Holy Writ which ought not to be depicted according to the exact philology? But putting these things aside, I wish to show to Erasmus an approved author who used this word to signify the separation from the bed alone. For Chrysostom in the above-mentioned homily in the *Imperfect Work* used this word according to that meaning, speaking thus: "He who divorces his wife and does not take another wife is still married... Therefore, when he accepts another wife then he fully divorces the first wife."[3] In which words it is evident that he distinguishes two ways of putting away, one whereby someone so puts away his wife that he marries another; and this he calls full divorce. The other is whereby someone puts away his wife in such a way that he nevertheless does not marry another wife; and he who puts away the wife in this way is still the husband of her whom he put away.

After now having sufficiently replied to the adversaries arguments to the extent that I would be able to satisfy any wise man, I can easily turn back their very argument against themselves, as I mentioned in passing earlier above. If Christ spoke about the putting way as to the bond,

---

[1] Cf. Deut. 24, 4.

[2] "But I do call that to be a true divorce, that which was then known [in the time of the Jews], and none other, when a man might lawfully take another wife after he was separated from his wife. For, was there ever any of the old theologians and jurists who did so define such that divorce is when husband and wife no longer live together, though the bond of marriage nevertheless still remains?" (*In novum Testamentum... annotationes*, on I Cor. 7, 11, p. 425).

[3] Hom. 32 (PG 56, 802).

then He superfluously added those words, "and shall marry another" (Mt. 19, 9), because only then does a man put away his wife as to the bond, when he marries another; because before he marries another, he can still reconcile to himself the wife that was put away. But Christ does not say any superfluous words; because as the Royal Prophet said of Him, "His leaf shall not fall off" (Ps. 1, 3). Therefore, Christ did not speak about the putting away as to the bond, but only as to the bed.

Fourthly, the adversaries argue thus. If Christ had spoken about putting away as to the bed alone, the reason of fornication was not alone excepted: because the separation from the bed could also be permitted for other reasons, such as if with the consent of both they enter into religion, or on account of uxorcide. I certainly admit that there are other reasons on account of which a separation as to the bed could be permitted, nevertheless those dismissals have greater reason than fornication does for separation as to the bed, because the fornication of the spouse is in itself opposed to the fidelity of the marriage; and hence it is just that henceforth the other spouse be not obliged to that spouse who did not keep fidelity. But uxorcide is more opposed to marriage, by which life is taken away and the wife's own existence, than adultery by which the fidelity is taken away without the taking away of life. Uxorcide is against the union of souls; adultery is against the union of bodies. Now "It is not intercourse," as [Pseudo-] Chrysostom says, "but the will that creates marriage."[1] Next, there is a greater obligation of the wife to conserve her own life than for rendering the debt of the wife. And hence all theologians reckon that no spouse is bound to render the conjugal debt to the other, when such rendering of the debt turns into manifest harm of one's own health: because one is more bound to the conservation of one's own individual being than to the conservation of the species, to which such rendering of the conjugal debt tends.

Concerning the other inconveniences, however, which men are accustomed to give to wives, I think none of them is sufficient for making even the separation from the bed. But those who enter religion with mutual consent, are not deemed to put each other away, but that anyone may renounce his right which he has upon another. For putting away does not mean merely the separation of the spouses, but denotes besides this a crime in the one who is put away. For on account of this only the innocent spouse is said to put away the other who committed adultery, and on the contrary, it is not called adultery to put away the innocent spouse.

Fifthly, Cajetan argues as follows. If one infidel spouse converts to the faith, the marriage contracted between them can be dissolved on account of the spiritual fornication of the other; therefore, it can also be dissolved on account of the carnal fornication of the other. Catharinus in his *Annotationes contra Cajetanum* replies to this argument and says that there is a great difference between those two marriages. Because the marriage of infidels is not ratified,[2] and hence can be dissolved. Innocent III makes this distinction in the chapter, *Quanto*, in the title, *De divortiis*.[3] It can be still replied otherwise to the argument, and I say that spiritual fornication, which is through unbelief, is much greater than carnal fornication; and hence the former can be very correctly be inferred from the latter, such that if the if the latter dissolves, then the former also, by arguing affirmatively from the lesser to the greater. It is not allowed,

---

[1] *Imperfect* Work, hom. 32 (PG 56, 802).

[2] 'A ratified marriage is a valid marriage contracted between two Christians which has not yet been completed by conjugal intercourse" (Prümmer, *Handbook of Moral Theology* (New York, P. J. Kennedy & Sons, 1957), p. 399).

[3] "For even though true marriage indeed exists between infidels, still it is not ratified. Between the faithful, however, it is in fact true and ratified, because the Sacrament of faith, which having been once received, is never lost; but it makes the Sacrament of Marriage ratified, so that same Sacrament perdures in the spouses during that marriage" (*Decretals of Gregory IX*, bk. 4, tit. 19 (*De divortiis*), c. 7 (*Quanto*)).

however, to infer the latter from the former by arguing thus: If the former dissolves, then the latter dissolves. Because by so arguing, one argues affirmatively from the greater to the lesser, which is a very inept argument. For it is not necessary that that which is the lesser, could do that which the greater does. A certain Johannes Dietenberger wrote against this error, when Erasmus firstly began to teach it.[1] After this man, Robert Céneau from the Academy of Paris shortly afterwards wrote against the same error of Erasmus.[2]

A **sixth heresy** arose against marriage or matrimony, which extols marriage to such an extent that it does not fear to equate it with virginity. But concerning this heresy we will discuss below in the section on "Virginity." I decided to fight for virginity itself in that place, and may I be able to conquer its carnal enemies as easily as I hope, with God as my Helper, to easily triumph over its spiritual enemies.

OBEDIENTIA
Obedience

All criminal and villainous men, so that they may commit more easily and freely the crimes they wish to commit, wish for liberty, or so that I may speak more truthfully, unimpeded slavery, because according to that liberty which they desire they deliver themselves to slavery, as Our Savior says, "Whosoever committeth sin, is the servant of sin" (Jn. 8, 34). Some heretics fearing that they would be punished on account of their crimes and poisonous teaching by the prelates of the Church according to the power given to them by God, fled to this refuge, so that many of them denied that obedience ought to be given to the prelates of the Church. The first authors of this error were the Waldensians, wicked and very wretched men, who after the manner of vipers, endeavored to gnaw the womb of Mother Church, from which they were given birth through Baptism.[3] For these men wanted to remove all the Church's authority and Orders, saying that one need not obey the Roman pontiff, or the other prelates of the Church. The Apostolics, Wycliffites, and Hussites taught the same error: and now the Lutherans say that one need not obey the Church's prelates, except in those things which are very clearly expressed in Sacred Scripture. The Beghards and Beguines said that those who have reached the state of perfection are not subject to any human power. Concerning all these heretics, and the error common to them all we have already spoken sufficiently (as I opine) in the section on the "Church," in the third heresy: in which place we showed that the Church can make laws and statutes which were not expressed in Holy Writ: whose regulations all without exception are bound to obey. Therefore, there is no need to repeat those things again.

---

[1] Johannes Dietenberger O. P. (c. 1475-1537) was a renowned professor of theology, and an inquisitor of heretical depravity, whose work cited here is *Phimostomus scripturariorum* (Cologne, Petrus Quentell, 1532), c. 16 (*De divortio tract.*).

[2] *De divortio matrimonii mosaici per legem evangelicam refutato* (Paris, Thomas Richard, 1549). Robert Cenalis (1483-1560) was a French bishop, historian, and controversialist.

[3] "On the third day [the viper] hatches its young in the uterus, and then excludes them, one every day, and generally twenty in number; the last ones become so impatient of their confinement, that they force a passage through the sides of their parent, and so kill her" (Pliny the Elder, *Natural History*, bk. 10, c. 82).

OCCIDERE

Killing

Among the other errors of the Waldensians which Guy [the Carmelite] lists, there is one whereby they teach that no man can be justly killed, even if it were to happen by the command of a judge. A certain Nicolaus Galecus[1] originating from Bohemia, who was one of the legates sent from Bohemia to the Council of Basel, afterwards taught this same error.

This error is clearly refuted, because by it human social intercourse is taken away, and all upright administration of government is overthrown: because by this doctrine there will be no peace: because when peace has been taken away, no government can remain undisturbed, nor can men live quietly in it. Therefore, since peace is so necessary to us that Christ commended it to us with the greatest affection, and shortly before death bequeathed it to us, as it were, by a testament, it is proved that this doctrine is erroneous by which the peace of the whole country is disturbed. Now peace is disturbed unless criminals and evildoers are killed. Therefore, it is a heresy to assert that they cannot killed. For every country is like a human body, whose head is its chief of state and ruler: now other men are members in relation to each other. Paul the Apostle calls the Christian commonwealth, that is the Church, one body, whose head is Christ: individual men, however, its members one towards another. Now if in the human body a particular member suffers from some sickness, the man whose member is sick, takes care to restore it in every way that he can to its former health, takes medicine, applies the bandages which he can. But if in no way he can cure that member, he willingly allows its amputation, because it is better to lose one member than to lose the whole body. It is the same in a country, since every citizen is like a particular member in the body which is the country. If some man shall commit a serious crime, one ought to strive for his correction. But if there is no hope of his correction, it is necessary to do away with him even by death, and to amputate him from the whole body, lest he infect the rest of the members. For one cow infects every cow.

But if death were never inflicted, the land would be full of thieves, the sea with pirates, and no possessions would be safe. Thus, so that there may be due quiet and tranquility among the people, it is expedient that the wretched man be killed, lest the entire race perish. Furthermore, when we treated about war above, we showed that war can be justly waged by a man having authority, if those things are present which are required for a just war. But since men cannot be gathered together in war without the killing of men often happening in it to many men, it is thence proved that if it be licit to wage war, then it is also licit to kill. Again Blessed Peter the Apostle punished Ananias and Saphira with death, because after having sold a piece of land they kept back part of the price, not bringing the whole price before the Apostles, but keeping back some of the price for themselves.[2] And this example alone suffices for throwing to the ground the heresy of these heretics, because this was done in the time of the New Law, during which time they say that on account of the benignity of the Law it is not permitted for any reason to kill a man. Yet Peter knowing this benignity, did not hesitate to punish Ananias

---

[1] Nicholas of Pelhřimov (ca. 1385-1460) was the first Bishop of the Czech Thaborites, a militant group of Bohemian Hussite reformers. In 1444 his teachings were condemned at the Prague Chamber. From 1452 he was imprisoned, died in the prison of Poděbrady. He is the founder of the *Nicolinistae* sect. He wrote a special treatise against the death penalty entitled, *De homicidio*, which along with his other writings was put on the *Index of Forbidden Books*.

[2] Cf. Acts 5, 1-10.

and Saphira with death; because he knew that true mercy also has justice in its retinue with it, which does not allow malefactors to live upon the earth.

But in this place the heretics object to us the Divine precept which forbids killing, saying: "Thou shalt not kill" (Mt. 5, 21). Now we reply to this objection by saying that those words did not forbid all killing, but that which was done by a private person, not however that which is determined to be inflicted by a judge for a just cause. Now that this is so is proved by the fact that in the Old Law there was that same precept, and in the same words, namely, "Thou shalt not kill" (Ex. 20, 13); and yet there were many other laws whereby the killing of a man was commanded on account of some sins, as it is clear concerning the punishment of blasphemy, and concerning the punishment of nocturnal theft.[1] But if by those words, namely, "Thou shalt not kill," any killing of a man was forbidden, it would then be necessary to grant that God commanded contradictory things, which nowise could happen. Far be it, however, that we would say that God commanded something impossible. Hence so that there be no contradiction in God's commandments, it is necessary to acknowledge in that precept, "Thou shalt not kill," all killing was not forbidden, because in the Evangelical Law the Savior Himself is seen to confirm the Law of killing a man who killed a man, when He said: "All that take the sword shall perish with the sword" (Mt. 26, 52). For so Christian Druthmar interprets this passage.[2] And Blessed Jerome says: "To punish murderers, impious men and poisoners is not shedding blood but administering the law."[3]

There is **second heresy** which is nearly diametrically opposed to the one just related, teaching men to kill themselves so that they may deserve to attain the palm of martyrdom. For the Circumcellions said that those who kill themselves ought to be reckoned martyrs, because they voluntarily underwent death. But we have already discussed this heresy above in the section on "Martyrdom."

There is a **third heresy**, which asserts that it is licit for any man to kill a tyrant, even by underhanded deceptions, notwithstanding any pledge made between them, even if it had been confirmed by oath. But we will dispute about this error below in the section on "Tyranny."

OPERA

Works

Luther thought that he had not done enough—in that he rejected human works, saying that they are not necessary—unless he would also condemn them, asserting that the works of each and every man, no matter how well they were done, are sins. "The just man," he says, "sins in every good work."[4] Now he deduces this error from another not less pernicious error. For Luther thinks that by the first and greatest Commandment, which is con-

---

[1] "He that blasphemeth the name of the Lord, dying let him die" (Lev. 24, 16). "If a thief be found breaking open a house or undermining it, and be wounded so as to die: he that slew him shall not be guilty of blood." (Ex. 22, 2).

[2] "Jesus says to them, 'For all that take the sword' (supply the words, "for evil doing") shall perish with the sword.' [They will perish] if not with a material sword, then with an invisible sword, meaning with the sword of God's word. But we also frequently see that he who unjustly kills someone, unless he does penance, he also frequently dies in the present life. That judgment seems to be the judgment which He said to Noe, saying: 'Whosoever shall shed man's blood, his blood shall be shed' (Gen. 9, 6)." (*Expositio in Mattheum*, c. 56 (PL 106, 1480D)).

[3] *Commentary on Jeremias*, bk. 4, on Jer. 22, 1 ff. (PL 24, 811D).

[4] Bull *Exsurge Domine*, condemned proposition 31 (Dz. 771). Cf. WA 1, 356, lns. 23-24.

cerning the love of God, men are obliged to the consummate perfection of charity. Because no one in this life is able to reach this, since that charity is expected to be as a reward, wherefore Luther says that as many times as something done out of charity lacks the highest perfection of charity, so many times does a man sin.[1] Luther also thought that the precept, "Thou shalt not covet," prohibited the desire of the flesh, which no man of himself is able to eliminate, although he is able to repress it: "For the flesh lusteth against the spirit: and the spirit against the flesh; for these are contrary one to another: so that you do not the things that you would" (Gal. 5, 17), wherefore he says that the just man sins in every good work, and all our works, however good, are to be deemed sins, namely, because in every such work the flesh resists and fights against the spirit: wherefore he says that such a work is a sin, because it is a work done with concupiscence and so is opposed to that precept, "Thou shalt not covet" (Rom. 13, 9). Behold Luther's foundation, upon which he tries to build the structure of the present error.[2] We will overturn this foundation, with God's guidance, when we will treat of the precepts. For there we shall show, from Sacred Scripture and from the teaching of the holy Doctors, that those two precepts are not to be understood as Luther understands them. Therefore, deferring this subject until that place, we ought to discuss the error that we first presented, so that we may teach against Luther that neither all our works are sins nor does the just man sin in every work.

Firstly, therefore, we put forth as our evidence that magnificent work of Abraham, who when obeying God's command, wanted to immolate his only begotten son, Isaac, whom he loved. In remuneration of which God promised him that He would take flesh from his offspring. For so He says, "In thy seed shall all the nations of the earth be blessed" (Gen. 22, 18). Which words, according to Paul, are to be understood of Christ: "He saith not, And to his seeds, as of many: but as of one, And to thy seed, which is Christ" (Gal. 3, 16). If Abraham's obedience was a sin, he would not have been promised so great and such an honorable reward. Likewise, after Job had suffered so many tribulations and had spoken words which bore witness to his very great patience, Scripture immediately praises him, saying, "In all these things Job sinned not by his lips, nor spoke he any foolish thing against God" (Job 1, 22). If Job did not sin in all these trials, not each and every work of man, therefore, is a sin. Again, Blessed Paul, speaking about those who are joined in Matrimony, said, "Art thou loosed from a wife? seek not a wife. And if a virgin marry, she hath not sinned" (I Cor. 7, 27-28). Paul says that one who marries does not sin, and Luther is not ashamed to say that every work of ours is a sin. If therefore the act of marrying, according to Paul, is not a sin: what do you think about the other works about which Paul is about to speak, which he deems to be better than marrying? And Blessed Peter after enumerating a number of virtues necessary for attaining glory, immediately adds, "For doing these things, you shall not sin at any time" (II Pet. 1, 10). And Blessed John in his first canonical epistle says, "Whosoever abideth in him, sinneth not" (3, 6). Lest we dispute while inquiring who is it who abideth in God, he, in the same epistle declares this saying, "God is charity: and he that abideth in charity, abideth in God, and God in him" (4, 16). Pay attention therefore, Luther, and see how clearly John condemns your

---

[1] "Whoever does less than he ought, sins. But every righteous person in doing good does less than he ought. Well, then, I shall prove the minor premise in the following way: Whoever does not do good out of complete and perfect love of God does less than he ought. But every righteous man is that kind of a person. I shall prove the major premise through the commandment: 'Thou shalt love the Lord thy God with thy whole heart, and with thy whole soul, and with thy whole strength' etc. (Deut. 6, 5), of which the Lord says in Matt. 5 [v. 18], 'One jot, or one tittle shall not pass of the law, till all be fulfilled.' Therefore, we must love God with all our might, or we sin" (Heidelberg Disputation held in 1518 (WA 1, 368, lns. 9-20)).

[2] *Assertio omnium articulorum*, art. 31 & 32 (WA 7, 103-108 & WA 7, 137-138).

opinion. Everyone who abides in charity, abides in God. Everyone who abides in God, does not sin. Everyone who abides in charity, does not sin. Therefore, either you ought to deny that just men are in charity, or you are forced to confess that a just man does not sin doing a good work: for everyone who abideth in charity, does not sin.

Observe, O reader, I beseech you, and consider by what confines Luther is enclosed, so that no flight is possible for him. For if he perhaps tries to escape like a snake, saying that the work is with perfect charity such that we may abide in God and God in us: such charity, however, (as Luther says) may not be had in this life: therefore, according to this reply, it would be said that God dwells in no man due to the state of this misery, because no man has that perfect charity which Luther requires. But lest some way of exit be open to Luther, Blessed John blocks this small crack, when in the same epistle he declares what perfect charity is. For he speaks as follows, "He that keepeth his word, in him in very deed the charity of God is perfected" (2, 5). What therefore will Luther say? Will he not go further such that he denies that anyone has kept God's words, that is, God's Commandments? If he is not ashamed to deny this, let him hear the divine Psalmist saying, "My soul hath kept thy testimonies: and hath loved them exceedingly" (Ps. 118, 167). And if Luther does not accept the words of the prophet, because the prophet bears witness to himself, let him hear God bearing witness to the prophet. For speaking to Jeroboam He says, "Thou hast not been as my servant David, who kept my commandments, and followed me with all his heart, doing that which was well pleasing in my sight" (III Kings 14, 8).

Next, there are many perfections in Sacred Scripture which we are admonished to have lest we sin. But if the just man sins in every work however good, we are admonished in vain about that which it is not possible for us to avoid. "Be angry," says the prophet, "and sin not" (Ps. 4, 5). It is possible, therefore, for man to be angry and not to sin. Hence it is concluded that not every work is a sin; because not all anger is a sin. And the Lord said to him, whom after thirty eight years in his infirmity He restored to his pristine health, "Behold thou art made whole: sin no more, lest some worse thing happen to thee" (Jn. 5, 14). If all our works are sins, then it would be the same thing to say, "do not sin," and to say, "do no work": because it would not be possible to do a work without sin. But since God, Who has forbidden sin, has commanded many works, it is concluded from this that those works which God commanded or counseled are not to be reckoned as sins. For otherwise it would be necessary to admit that God had commanded contrary things, things opposed to themselves, since He commanded works and forbade sin. Far be it, however, that we impugn God, such that we would say that He had commanded us such things which in no wise could be done. Wherefore let us say with all the Catholic Doctors that there are many good works, done from grace and charity, which merit eternal life, according to the Divine law now promulgated: which works in nowise ought to be called sins.

Besides all these things which clearly vanquish Luther's heresy, the consideration of the many fruits which Sacred Scripture testifies are produced by good works can in addition clearly refute it, which fruits could by no means be produced by good works if they were truly sins. Firstly, for example, good works are called "light" by Solomon, saying, "the path of the just, as a shining light, goeth forwards, and increaseth even to perfect day" (Prov. 4, 18). For if the good works were done in public, they are said to shine and to enlighten those before whom they are done, just as our Savior taught, speaking thus, "So let your light shine before men, that they may see your good works, and glorify your Father who is in heaven" (Mt. 5, 16). In which words our Savior calls good works "light," and then He said that they give light, when they are done in a place wherein they can be seen by men. If, however, they who see the good works of the just, and from their example are motivated to do other similar good works, then they glorify our Father Who is in Heaven. But none of these things are in harmony with sin: because sin is not called "light" in Sacred Writ, but "darkness." For the Wise Man, describing the difference that God put between the Egyptians and the sons of Israel, said, "For the whole world was enlightened with a clear light, and none were hindered in their labours. But over them only was spread a heavy night, an image of that darkness which was to come upon them. But they were to themselves more grievous than the darkness" (Wis. 17, 19-20). In which words not only Hell, whereunto they were to go afterwards, but also sinners themselves are called "darkness." But Paul teaches this more clearly in that epistle which is to the Romans, speaking thus: "Let us therefore cast off the works of darkness, and put on the armour of light" (13, 12). In which words, as is shown clearly enough, he calls good works "the armour of light" and he said that sins are "the works of darkness." Now, he who does these works of darkness does not glorify the Father Who is in Heaven, but instead dishonors Him: as elsewhere the Savior Himself said to the Jews, "You have dishonoured me" (Jn. 8, 49). For, as Solomon said, "To do mercy and judgment, pleaseth the Lord more than victims" (Prov. 21, 3). And Paul calls afflictions of the body well received "a living sacrifice, holy, pleasing unto God" (Rom. 12, 1).

Not only do works themselves please God, but works themselves are often causes for their authors to also please God. For as Paul testifies concerning hospitality, certain men by it pleased God, and "have entertained angels" (Heb. 13, 2). Now sin never pleases God, nor does the sinner during the time in which he remains in sin. "But to God," as Solomon says, "The wicked and his wickedness are hateful alike" (Wis. 14, 9). For the proud have never pleased God: but the prayer of the humble and the meek hath always pleased God (Judith 9, 16). For, on account of this, God turned away His face from Cain and did not wish to look upon him, nor upon his gifts: because neither he nor they pleased Him (Gen. 4, 5). But on the other hand, the sinner converting himself to God, by his conversion placates God angered against him, as Isaias clearly taught, saying as follows, "They shall return to the Lord, and he shall be pacified towards them, and heal them" (Is. 19, 22). Concerning the killing whereby Phinees killed the Israelite going into a harlot,[1] the Royal Prophet testifies that by doing this he had pleased God: "Phinees stood up, and pacified him: and the slaughter ceased" (Ps. 105, 30). The Lord was angered against the Ninivites to such an extent that through the prophet Jonas He threatened them that their city was to be overthrown within the space of forty days: but by fasting and other corporal afflictions they pleased God. For "God saw," as Jonas says, "their works, that they were turned from their evil way: and God had mercy with regard to the evil which he had said that he would do to them, and he did it not" (Jonas 3, 10).

Now God is never pacified by sin, nay He is instead angered. "Cast them out: for they have provoked thee, O Lord" (Ps. 5, 11). And again, "The wicked hath provoked God? for he hath said in his heart: He will not require it" (Ps. 9, 34). And once again, "The sinner hath provoked the Lord" (Ps. 9, 25). If God is provoked by sin, how can it be that the just man sins in his good work, by which God Himself is pacified? For it cannot happen, nay, neither can it be understood, that God, on account of the same work, is at the same time pacified and angered. Furthermore, by good works a reward is due, owing to the Divine promise, but punishment is due to sins, as Sacred Writ often teaches.[2] For Christ says that He will come in the glory of His Father with His Angels, and then will render to each one according to His works. What He will render to the just, and what to the sinner, He declared afterwards by the same Evangelist, saying, "These shall go into everlasting punishment: but the just, into life everlasting" (Mt. 25, 46). Therefore, it will happen, according to Luther's opinion, that the just man on account

---

[1] Num. 25, 7.

[2] "For to everyone that hath shall be given, and he shall abound: but from him that hath not, that also which he seemeth to have shall be taken away" (Mt. 25, 29).

of the same work is deserving of punishment and an eternal reward, and nothing more absurd or inept than this opinion can be said.

This last insane heresy was condemned in the Council of Trent, which was celebrated under Paul III. In the sixth session, against this error, among many others, it published in the twenty-fifth place the *latae sententia*[1] canon: "If any one saith that in every good work the just sins venially at least, or (which is more intolerable still) mortally, and consequently deserves eternal punishments; and that for this cause only he is not damned: that God does not impute those works unto damnation; let him be anathema."[2] These are the words of the Council of Trent.

It still remains for us to reply to Luther's objections. He firstly makes an objection to us from a passage of the Wise Man: "For there is no just man upon earth, that doth good, and sinneth not" (Eccle. 7, 21). We indeed acknowledge that no man is just without God's grace, nor can a just man avoid all sin without God's help. For just as grace is required at the beginning of a good work, so also it is required for its execution. Wherefore every man, however just, if not helped by God, subsequently sins. And to show that these words of Ecclesiastes have this meaning, it is only necessary to read the preceding words, which are as follows: "Wisdom hath strengthened the wise more than ten princes of the city," which is to say, God's grace strengthens man more than all human aid. To give the reason for this, he immediately adds, "There is no just man upon earth that doth good and sinneth not." It is as though he were to say, "Hence it is proved that God's grace strengthens man more than all the princes in the world, because helped by God's grace he will be able overcome all sin; but he who lacks God's grace, even if he has the help of the world's princes, will not be able to avoid all sin." From which interpretation it is clear that the passage in Ecclesiastes in no way is opposed to our position.

Secondly, Luther objects to us from the passage of Saint John in his first epistle: "If we say that we have not sinned, we make him a liar, and his word is not in us" (I Jn. 1, 10). To this objection we reply that there are many venial sins from which no one, however just, may be free; and in fact he falls into many: for, as Saint James says, "In many things we all offend" (James 3, 2). He did not say we offend in all things, but "in many things"; likewise, it does not follow therefrom that every work is a sin. See here that Luther, who was accustomed to call scholastic theologians "sophists," now thinks that he has deceived the sophists with a very naughty sophism. Who does not see the fallacy of this reasoning: "Every just man has some sin, therefore every deed is a sin"? So Luther, according to his logic, learned to infer from the particulars to the universal.

In like manner the passage of the Psalmist ought to be understood, "And enter not into judgment with thy servant: for in thy sight no man living shall be justified" (Ps. 142, 2). It is certainly true that no man, if examined according to the rigor of Divine justice, would be found to be just, because (as we have just said, citing the Apostle James) "in many things we all offend." No one, therefore, would be found just if God wished to judge very strictly. But what kind of reasoning is this: "No man examined strictly will be found just, therefore no work of man is good"? For although a man may have some work for which he ought not to be called just, nevertheless one ought not to infer from this that every work of the man is a sin. In this way also ought to be understood what Augustine says in his *Confessions*, "Woe (he

---

[1] *Latae sententiae* is a Latin phrase, meaning "sentence (already) passed," used in the Canon Law. A *latae sententiae* penalty is one that follows *ipso facto* or automatically, by force of the law itself, when a law is contravened. It is opposed to a penalty that binds a guilty party only after it has been imposed on the person, which is known as a *ferendae sententiae* (meaning "sentence to be passed") penalty. (Cf. Can. 1314 of the 1983 Code of Canon Law.)

[2] Sess. VI, Canon 25.

says) to the life of men, no matter how commendable, if they be judged without mercy."[1] He said, "Woe to the life of men," and he did not say, "woe to all men's works"; because even if no man's life be so perfect that it not have many venial sins mixed into it, nevertheless there are many works which Augustine does not doubt to be without sin; for in the same passage, Augustine says, speaking of his mother, that she did many good works, on account of which he gives thanks to God. He also acknowledges other good works that are in need of the Divine mercy, for which he says God should be besought.[2]

Luther thirdly objects to us from the passage of Isaias that says: "And we are all become as one unclean, and all our justices as the rag of a menstruous woman" (64, 6). By this testimony he thinks that he has triumphed, because the prophet seems to condemn all our works, since he compares all our justices to a menstruous rag, which is splattered with many stains. But even though that testimony of Isaias apparently seems to favor Luther, nevertheless, if the words are examined well and as they ought to be, it is very clearly known that it says nothing in favor of Luther. For in that passage, the prophet is not speaking in his own name, but in the name of the people; nor even in the name of the whole people, but only in the name of the Israelite people. Nor in that name does he speak in a manner such that his words refer to every time, but only to that time in which the prophet was saying those things; in which time sin was abounding in the Israelite people on account of which God was about to permit that they be led into captivity. Therefore the prophet, foreseeing this, prays to God for the people, and speaking concerning that time he says, "We are all become as one unclean, and all our justices as the rag of a menstruous woman." He utters these words in the name of his people. But if those words are referred to all men, how are the words which follow true? "And we have all fallen," he says, "as a leaf, and our iniquities, like the wind, have taken us away. There is none that calleth upon thy name: that riseth up, and taketh hold of thee" (v. 7). Did Isaias never call upon God's name? Let not anyone dare to say this. If, therefore, these words cannot be referred to Isaias or to other men who worshipped God and called upon His name, nor likewise can the other words, which Luther cites in his objection, be referred to them, since all those words of prayer are said in the same discourse concerning the same persons. And that those words may be referred only to that time of the captivity can be easily concluded from the words which the prophet adds shortly afterwards, saying, "Be not very angry, O Lord, and remember no longer our iniquity: behold, see we are all thy people. The city of thy sanctuary is become a desert, Sion is made a desert, Jerusalem is desolate. The house of our holiness and of our glory, where our fathers praised thee, is burnt with fire and all our lovely things are turned into ruins" (v. 9-11). Now these words are very clearly said about the Israelite people, to which time the rest of the words of that chapter refer. But from the fact that at that time all justices were as menstruous rags, it may not be concluded that it was the same at every time. Add to this the fact that Jerome refers those words to be interpreted of the works before Christ's Incarnation,[3] namely, at the time of the Mosaic Law, and not of the works done under the Evangelical Law; so that if someone now living under the Evangelical Law would wish to keep the ceremonies of the Old Law, all his justices would be as menstruous rags. We have proved from all these arguments that the passage from Isaias in no way favors Luther.

Fourthly, Luther objects to us that Blessed Gregory, who in his *Morals on the Book of Job*, says these words, "Because he sees that all the worth of our goodness is evil if it be strictly

---

[1] Bk. 9, c. 13, n. 34 (PL 32, 778).

[2] "I therefore, O my Praise and my Life, God of my heart, laying aside for a while her good deeds, for which I give thanks to Thee with joy, do now beseech Thee for the sins of my mother" (*Confessions*, bk. 9, c. 13, n. 35 (PL 32, 778)).

[3] "All our works in the Law are reputed as the rag of a menstruous woman" (*Against the Pelagians*, bk. 2, n. 25 (PL 23, 564A)).

accounted of by the Judge of the interior, the holy man lightly subjoins: 'If he will contend with him, he cannot answer him one for a thousand' (Job 9, 3)."[1] In which words, so that I may faithfully relate the argument of the adversaries, two things are to be noted. The first is that this utterance of Gregory is universal as regards every good work. The second is that he says those words are said by Blessed Job, not indeed merely because of his humility, on account of which just men are accustomed to say things against themselves: but he says that they are said because they are true. For he said that the holy man saw that all the merits of our virtues are defective. We only "see," however, that which is real. The Lutherans think that by this quotation of St. Gregory they triumph over us.

But in reality I am very surprised that they are not afraid to cite this testimony against us, since they reject by their own choice the testimonies of all holy men, saying they were men as we are, who hence could have been deceived, just like us. Then, in that testimony of Gregory is something which testifies that another doctrine of theirs is false. For they deny that there is any merit in our good works, which nevertheless Gregory clearly affirms in the words cited above. If a citation of Gregory has some strength, then it is necessary that they acknowledge that there is some merit in our virtues, because Gregory testifies that this is the case. If they reject Gregory in this part, why do they not fear to cite the other part to us? It is indeed just, that in a duel the weapons ought to be equal. It is also just that by what measure one would want to measure another, with the same measure he ought to measure himself: because it is forbidden by Divine and Natural law that one would have diverse weights or diverse measures in his bag.

But lest I may seem to flee from the main point of the argument by of this kind reasoning, I wish to reply to the citation of Gregory, and will show that nothing in it supports them. For Gregory did not state absolutely and without any limitation that all merit of our virtue is a vice, but immediately adds a conditional limitation by saying, "if it be strictly accounted." And we also acknowledge that if this condition be added, every good work of man is defective, if God were to make a strict account, on the basis of debts by which we are by our nature debtors to Him: and not on the basis of His mercy, whereby He willed to temper that rigor of his justice. For God could, if He willed, demand many more and greater things of us than He now requires: because He confers so many and such great things upon us that if we would give Him all that we could do, and do it for Him alone, we would still not pay back half of our debt. Therefore Chrysostom says, "For if we were to die a thousand deaths, and to practice every virtue, we could not make a suitable return to God for the things which we have received from Him."[2] And again, in a certain homily [PseudoChrysostom] says, "Should our whole lifetime be spent in obedience, in singing praises and giving thanks; yet could we never repay what we most justly owe."[3] And this is what Job said: "Indeed I know it is so, and that man cannot be justified compared with God. If he will contend with him, he cannot answer him one for a thousand" (9, 2-3). It is as though he were to say, "If anyone would wish to make an account of what has been given and received, for as many thousand as you wish of things received from God, he would be unable to ascribe [to himself] one that he gave." And hence he says that he truly knows that man compared with God will not be justified, meaning man considered in comparison with God. If God would wish to judge according to this rigor of justice, many and countless things would be lacking for the payment of so many debts: many things in our works would also be deficient, no matter how rightly they were done, on account of which they can rightly be condemned.

---

[1] Bk. 9, c. 2, n. 2 (PL 75, 859D, n. 288).
[2] *On Compunction of Heart*, bk. 2, n. 5 (PG 47, 418).
[3] *Homily 60: Dominica in Septuagesima* (PL 95, 1207B).

Therefore Blessed Gregory, considering God's supreme goodness and the excellent benefits conferred upon us by Him, observed that we are not merely indebted to God, but that if God wanted to exact our debt from us according to the reckoning of the debt, we would never be able to pay it. Thus, for this reason he said that all the merit of our virtue is a vice, and all our justice is injustice, if man were strictly judged by God. Because no matter how much we may try, we can never serve God both from the heart and as purely and fervently as He could require of us if He wanted. But on account of His mercy, considering that we are flesh and fragile clay, and that our strength is not the strength of stones, nor is our flesh bronze, He did not want to exact of us so many and such great things, but merely the observance possible to us of the Ten Commandments. Therefore, by this very great mercy shown to us by God, many works are truly not sins, which otherwise, if God wished to judge according to the rigor of His justice, would rightly be reckoned as sins.

Against this error of Luther, [Saint] John [Fisher] of Rochester wrote splendidly in two articles of his *Assertionis Lutheranae Confutatio*.[1] The learned Josse Van Clichtove in his *Antilutherus* also wrote on this subject,[2] as also the Franciscan Caspar Schatzgeyer in his *Scrutinio divinae Scripturae*, third edition.[3] And we also will yet say something else below in the sections on Sin and the Precepts.

The **second heresy** teaches that no work is good, no matter from what motive it is done, even the hope of one's eternal reward, unless it comes from a pure and sincere heart. The first author of this error was Bugarius of Montefalcone, who, when teaching this in parts of Catalonia, was condemned along with his error by Archbishop Sancium of Tarragona. These facts are stated by Brother Bernard of Luxemburg in his *Catalogus haereticorum [omnium]*.[4] This error was condemned by the words of the prophet saying, "I have inclined my heart to do thy justifications for ever, for the reward" (Ps. 118, 112). And the Lord counseling alms says, "Make unto you friends of the mammon of iniquity; that when you shall fail, they may receive you into everlasting dwellings" (Lk. 16, 9). By which words He teaches us to give alms on account of eternal life. And elsewhere, often after he had commanded something, He immediately adjoins the promise of eternal life to anyone doing it, so that through the hope of the reward He might entice man to do the work commanded. "Do penance," He says, "for the kingdom of heaven is at hand" (Mt. 4, 17). But if a work done from the hope of eternal life were evil, Christ would not encourage us to do it through hope of a reward.

Furthermore, the Apostle Paul says, "That he that plougheth, should plough in hope; and he that thrasheth, in hope to receive fruit" (I Cor. 9, 10). And likewise, Paul often exhorts to doing works of virtue also through hope of a reward. "Know you not that they that run in the race, all run indeed, but one receiveth the prize? So run that you may obtain" (v. 24). By which words, through a metaphor taken from those who in their competition run to obtain a crown set before them, he admonishes to running quickly on the way of God's Commandments, on account of acquiring the reward of eternal life at the end of the race. He also admonishes Timothy, his disciple, to doing good works through hope of a reward, speaking thus: "For bodily exercise is profitable to little: but godliness is profitable to all things, having promise of the life that now is, and of that which is to come" (I Tim. 4, 8). Peter, the Prince of the Apostles, did the same thing in his second canonical epistle, saying these words: "Labour the more, that by good works you may make sure your calling and election" (1, 10).

---

[1] Art. 31 & 32, pp. 310r-332v.

[2] Bk. 1, c. 27, pp. 57r-59r.

[3] Kaspar Schatzgeyer, O. F. M., *Scrutinium Divinae Scripturae pro conciliatione dissidentium dogmatum* (Cologne, Johann Soter, 1522), conatus 3 (*De bono opere*).

[4] Bk. 2.

Again, Blessed Paul praises some on account of their good works, which nevertheless he himself testifies were done for hope of a reward. "Grace be to you and peace from God our Father, and from the Lord Jesus Christ. We give thanks to God, and the Father of our Lord Jesus Christ, praying always for you, hearing your faith in Christ Jesus, and the love which you have towards all the saints, for the hope that is laid up for you in heaven, which you have heard in the word of the truth of the gospel" (Col. 1, 3-5). And in his Epistle to the Hebrews he praises Abraham for his faith and obedience, which he had on account of the hope of eternal life, speaking thus: "By faith he that is called Abraham, obeyed to go out into a place which he was to receive for an inheritance; and he went out, not knowing whither he went. By faith he abode in the land, dwelling in cottages, with Isaac and Jacob, the co-heirs of the same promise. For he looked for a city that hath foundations; whose builder and maker is God" (Heb. 11, 8-10). When saying "a city that hath foundations," he signifies heavenly glory: because this city has such a firm foundation, that it could never collapse. For the foundation upon which it rests is the Divine promise which says: "These shall go into ... life everlasting" (Mt. 25, 46). In hope of this city having such a firm foundation, Abraham wished to dwell in the Promised Land as in a foreign land, dwelling in cottages. Since therefore Paul praises that work of Abraham done on account of the hope of a reward, it is thereby clearly proved that every work done from the hope of an eternal reward is not evil.

Next, in the same epistle he praises Moses for his faith by which he despised all the things of this world, giving the reason for this contempt to be none other than hope of an eternal reward. For he speaks thus: "By faith Moses, when he was grown up, denied himself to be the son of Pharao's daughter; rather choosing to be afflicted with the people of God, than to have the pleasure of sin for a time, esteeming the reproach of Christ greater riches than the treasure of the Egyptians. For he looked unto the reward" (Heb. 11, 24-26). When he denied that he was the son of the daughter of Pharao, he despised the royal dignity, and hence he showed that he deemed the honors of this world to be nothing. "Rather choosing to be afflicted with the people of God," who were serving in mud and bricks, "than to have the pleasure of sin for a time," he openly declared how little he valued the pleasures of this world. But when he says "the reproach of Christ," that is, injuries patiently born either for Christ or in the likeness of Christ, which he deems to be of greater value than the treasures of the Egyptians, he clearly shows what he thinks of the riches of this world. Paul expresses the reason for all this contempt of temporal things saying, "For he looked unto the reward." Moses truly believed that other, much better, good things would remain afterwards, which God was going to give to the humble and to the despisers of this world, and on account of this remuneration which he believed would come, he wanted to despise the riches, honors and pleasures of this world, so that in another life he would have never failing riches and pleasures.

Therefore a work which is done from hope of an eternal reward is not evil, although I will not consider such a work to be meritorious unless it proceeds from charity: for charity is the root from which all power of merit arises. And in fact, if such a work is done exclusively out of hope of a reward, it is not meritorious; nevertheless it is not therefore evil: for just as not every good work is meritorious, so neither is every work evil which lacks grounds for merit. A work can also arise from charity, and that the one doing it is motivated to do it out of hope of a reward, yet such that if he were prevented from being rewarded, he would not cease doing the work, because he acts out of charity although he is motivated by the hope of a reward. Hence, such a work done in this manner will be good and meritorious, and done with hope of an eternal reward. And he who does a work in this way ought not to be considered as the kind of mercenary Our Savior depicts when He distinguishes the good and bad shepherd. For that man does not act out of charity, according to which he would have an affection for the sheep, but he feeds the sheep only out of hope of a reward. "And the hireling flieth," the Savior says, "because he is a hireling: and he hath no care for the sheep" (Jn. 10, 13). The one, however, who has care for the sheep is he who truly has an affection for them and truly tends them as though they were his own. And he, although he may hope for some reward for his labor, is not considered a mercenary: because even if he had no hope for such a reward, nevertheless he would take care to feed them, and although he were to see a wolf coming towards the sheep, he would not flee. And therefore just as the latter shepherd who hopes in this way for the reward of his labor is not deemed before God to be a bad mercenary, so also he is accepted by Him for the labor of this kind unto eternal life.

Finally, this opinion of Luther was condemned in the Council of Trent, which was celebrated under Paul III, which in the sixth session declared a canon concerning this matter, whose words are these: "If anyone shall say that the one justified sins, when he performs good works with a view to an eternal reward: let him be anathema."[1] These are the words of the Council of Trent. I do not know of anyone who has written *ex professo* against this heresy, although I have seen many who have written against the errors of Luther and of his followers.

The **third heresy** teaches that it belongs to an imperfect man to exercise himself in virtuous deeds: wherefore it says that a man, come to the final state of perfection, ought not to do good works. The authors of this demented error were Beghards and Beguines. Nevertheless Luther, a more savage beast, increased their error, saying that not merely for a perfect man but for no man are works necessary for obtaining eternal life: for, he says, faith alone without works suffices. We have in fact already fought against this error in the section above on Faith, where we showed to the heretics from Sacred Scripture that it is said that works are necessary for every man so that he may attain eternal life.

Against the Beghards and Beguines, who concede that works are necessary for imperfect men but not for perfect men, there is the testimony that Christ gave concerning John the Baptist, saying: "There hath not risen among them that are born of women a greater than John the Baptist" (Mt. 11, 11). By which words He clearly taught that John the Baptist had reached that degree of virtue, beyond which no other man among those born of women attained. But concerning the same John the Baptist, the Evangelist relates that he exercised himself in works of abstinence, and Christ praised him before the Jews for his admirable temperance and fortitude, such that he was not cast down by adversities nor elated by good fortune. Therefore, it is not limited to imperfect men to exercise themselves with laborious works. Furthermore, Paul the Apostle says, "And they that are Christ's have crucified their flesh, with the vices and concupiscences" (Gal. 5, 24). Therefore, a man, no matter how perfect, ought to crucify his flesh with its vices, otherwise he will not belong to Christ. But if one wished to make an attack based upon the verb in the past tense, such that Paul says that they are Christ's who have already crucified their flesh, not however they who crucify it—because at the time when one works there is the disposition for perfection, which afterwards is had when the works have been done, not when they are being done—this is rejected by the testimony of the same Paul, who says of himself, "But I chastise my body and bring it into subjection: lest perhaps, when I have preached to others, I myself should become a castaway" (I Cor. 9, 27). And the man who says this was caught up to the third heaven, and saw the secret things of God, which it is not granted to man to utter.[2] He was a man, I say, chosen by God, so that he would be the vessel into which God would pour His grace. This man chastised his body, and the impious Beghards are not ashamed to assert that it belongs to an imperfect man to exercise himself in laborious works. Again, Christ Himself, the font and origin of all perfection, fasted and performed other acts of virtue: nevertheless, no one short of impiety will be so demented as to taint Christ with some imperfection.

---

[1] C. 31 (Dz. 841).

[2] II Cor. 12, 2-4.

Finally, this error was condemned by the Council of Vienna, celebrated under Clement V, wherein eight errors of the Beghards and Beguines were condemned, one of which is that concerning which we have just spoken.[1] Now the definition of this council is found in the book of the Clementine Decretals.[2]

The **fourth heresy** teaches that no work of men, however good, is meritorious of eternal life, nor necessary for attaining eternal life. The inventor of this heresy and first author is Luther, who always disparaged human works. Now in order that it might seem that he had not said this without reason, he covered this heresy under the appearance of piety, saying those who give to human works the merit of glory derogate from Christ's merits, by which alone we are saved. But if our good works would merit eternal life, we may be saved, as Luther says, not solely by Christ's merits. This heresy necessarily follows from another of Luther's, about which we discussed in the first heresy of this section on Works. Now in that place we said that he asserted that all works of man, no matter how well they were done, are sins[3] and he says that "the just man sins in every good work."[4] For if every work of men is a sin, it necessarily follows that by no work would man be able to merit eternal life. For it would be absurd and contrary to all reason if it were to be said that man merits eternal life through sins: because punishment and not reward is due to sin. No one is so senseless that he would say that man merits before God a reward through his offense, whereby he provoked and exasperated Him.

Therefore, by having well considered this error, I cannot but be surprised how many others from Luther's faction are able to agree with each other. For Philip Melanchthon, John Calvin, Martin Bucer, Johann Spangeberg, and in short, all Protestants in the Augsburg Confession, acknowledge the merit of our works: for they saw the testimonies of Sacred Scripture and of the holy Doctors are so clear that they were forced to acknowledge that there is some merit in our works. Philip Melanchthon in *Loci Communes*,[5] in the section on "Good Works," near the end of the chapter, writes: "Thirdly it ought to be known that rewards are offered for good works, or in other words, good works merit corporal and spiritual rewards. ... Now here it ought to be known that we are speaking about the good works of the just. For firstly the remission of sins, reconciliation, and acceptation to eternal life, must be received with faith, and this is given through mercy on account of Christ, so that it may be certain." And at the end of the chapter he finally says, "And as I have now often said, a reward is given to works so that the remission of sins may not be uncertain. Likewise, lest Christ's benefit be transferred into the dignity of our works, a person is freely justified before God by faith, which relies only upon mercy, and afterwards good works please God and merit a reward."[6] These are the words of Philip Melanchthon. In which words, even if he admits that good works merit corporal and spiritual rewards, nevertheless he never openly asserts that we merit eternal life though good works.

And Johann Spangenberg, who in his theological work, *Margarita* [*theologica*], in the section on "Good Works," asking whether good works merit eternal life, declares this opinion of Philip Melanchthon much more openly, saying these words, "By no means should it be

---

[1] "That it is characteristic of the imperfect man to exercise himself in acts of virtue, and the perfect soul gives off virtues by itself." (Errors of the Beghards and the Beguines Concerning the State of Perfection, n. 6 (Dz. 476)).

[2] *Clementinarum* [*Clementis V Constitutiones*], bk. 5, tit. 3 (*De haereticis*), c. 3 (*Ad nostrum*). *Ad nostrum* was a papal bull of Pope Clement V issued in 1311.

[3] Bull *Exsurge Domine*, condemned proposition 32: "A good work done very well is a venial sin" (Dz. 772).

[4] Dz. 771.

[5] Otherwise titled, *Hypotyposes theologicae Philippi Malanchthonis, recogniti ab Autore* (1523).

[6] CR 21, 433-434.

thought that on account of the dignity and purity of good works is eternal life given. But it is a gratuitous benefit, and is given through mercy on account of Christ. And the reason is that our obedience is still always unclean, and is not pleasing in itself, but is pleasing on account of Christ. ... And we may not allow ourselves to be deluded by sophistry, which feigns a synecdoche, namely, even if good works are not completely meritorious, nevertheless there is a partial and less primary merit: because in this way faith relies upon it partially, which is impossible. For it is a contradiction to state that we may receive eternal life through mercy on account of Christ, and to imagine that our obedience merits eternal life. ... Therefore, it ought to be understood in this way, that if our obedience is not meritorious of eternal life, neither are we saved on account of it, but freely on account of Christ: nevertheless it is a duty which necessarily ought to follow, and merits corporal and spiritual rewards, which are given partly in this life and partly after this life."[1] In which words he asserts the necessity of works for acquiring eternal life: because he says obedience "is a duty which necessarily ought to follow, and merits corporal and spiritual rewards," yet he clearly denies that they merit eternal life.

Likewise, John Calvin speaks absolutely in that tract of his which he published against the decrees given by the Council of Trent in the sixth session, chapter sixteen and canon thirty-two.[2] All these men assert that in our works there is something meritorious, to which corresponds corporal and spiritual rewards, although not eternal life. And all these men equally say, "The just man sins in every good deed." Which two assertions very clearly contradict each other. For, as I have already said, it is not possible that by sin someone merit before God something spiritual, since Sacred Scripture clearly testifies, "To God the wicked and his wickedness are hateful alike" (Wis. 14, 9). But Calvin, understanding very well this contradiction of statements, in order to reconcile them, said, "Our works, although of themselves are sins, nevertheless on this account are acceptable to God: because He with paternal indulgence overlooks whatever is defective in them."[3] It truly seems to me that in this conciliation of his, Calvin has failed to achieve his goal and wasted his time: for he by no means does what he is trying to do. For God overlooks what is culpable in our works either when they are done or after they are done. If He overlooks this when they are done, Calvin is obliged to acknowledge that some works of men are not sins. If, however, God overlooks this after they are done, it is necessary that he acknowledge that those works are not meritorious when they were being done, or that they are at the same time meritorious and sins. Therefore, Luther is more consistent in this regard than all his followers: for Luther, as I said at the beginning, affirming that all works of man are sins, consequently asserted no work of men merits eternal life. All these men, even if they oppose each other somewhat, nevertheless unitedly assert that in no human work, however good, is there merit of eternal life.

Now in order that we may clearly refute this heretical assertion, it is necessary before all else that we establish what merit is, lest perhaps we labor equivocally, or we fight about various meanings of the word. And because every equivocal word, as Aristotle teaches, ought firstly to be divided before being defined, it is thus necessary to distinguish the different meanings of merit, and afterwards we will define merit according to the meaning that we should use in the present disputation. Among the Latin writers and approved authors, merit is attributed not only to good, but also to bad works of men, such that they can say that by bad

---

[1] *Margarita theologica* (Leipzig, Nicolaus Wolrab, 1541), q. 5, pp. 52-53.

[2] *Acts of the Council of Trent with the Antidote* (*CR*,35, 468-469 & 485-486).

[3] Calvin's actual words are these: "It is, indeed, a gross and impious delusion, not to acknowledge that every work which proceeds from us has only one way of obtaining acceptance, viz., when all that was vicious in it is pardoned by paternal indulgence. Another delusion almost similar to this is their not reflecting, that even if we should have merited anything by any one work, the whole of the merit, be it what it may, is lost by contrary transgression" (*Ibid.*, *CR* 35, 472).

works men may be said to merit a punishment, just as by good works they merit a reward. Ovid said, "The punishment which he alone deserved (*meruit*), he brought down upon us all."[1] And likewise in the fifth letter [of Heroines] he said the same thing, "What is deservedly (*ex merito*) suffered must be borne with calmness."[2] Vatinius, in a certain letter to Cicero, said, "You know my good fortune, and I do not know how I found detractors so easily, not through my merit (*merito*), by Hercules."[3] In which words, as it is clearly established, merit is used for guilt.

And the word "merit" is not found to be used only among profane authors to denote evil works. For Jehu, the Lord's prophet, as sacred history relates, said to Josephat, King of Juda, "Thou helpest the ungodly, and thou art joined in friendship with them that hate the Lord, and therefore thou didst deserve (*merebaris*) indeed the wrath of the Lord: but good works are found in thee" (II Par. 19, 2-3). And in that epistle which he wrote to all the provinces subject to himself concerning Aman after he had been hung, Assuerus said, "Not we, but God repaying him as he deserved (*meruit*)" (Esth. 16, 18). And Sophar the Naamathite, speaking to Job, said, "I wish that God would speak with thee, and would open his lips to thee, that he might shew thee the secrets of wisdom, and that his law is manifold, and thou mightest understand that he exacteth much less of thee than thy iniquity deserveth (*meretur*)" (Job 11, 5-6). Finally Paul, writing to the Hebrews, said, "A man making void the law of Moses, dieth without any mercy under two or three witnesses. How much more do you think he deserveth (*mereri*) worse punishments, who hath trodden underfoot the Son of God, and hath esteemed the blood of the testament unclean, by which he was sanctified, and hath offered an affront to the Spirit of grace?" (Heb. 10, 28-29). In all these passages it is clearly said that iniquity merits punishment.

Concerning this merit there is no mention in the *status questionis*[4] of the present disputation: but only concerning that merit of good works, to which corresponds a good reward. This merit, however, the scholastic Doctors say is twofold, calling one type of merit "condign"[5] and the other kind of merit "congruous."[6] Nevertheless, not all the scholastic Doctors approve of this division of merit: for some of them entirely reject this division of merit, as though the latter never deserves to be called merit: for which reason it neither from its dignity nor from the law deserves a reward, but only by a fittingness is it freely accepted towards obtaining a reward.[7] About which matter I do not wish to dispute: because those who are disputing about accepting or rejecting congruous merit seem to me to be disputing more about the name than the thing itself. And so, if I were to say that congruous merit is to be accepted, that would be very far away from the subject of the present disputation: for we are speaking only about condign merit when we say, "The just man merits eternal life through good works."

There are still other scholastic theologians who, trembling with fear where there was no reason for being afraid, sought a third type of merit, which they call "worthy merit." For seeing Paul saying, "The sufferings of this time are not worthy (*condignae*) to be compared with the glory to come, that shall be revealed in us" (Rom. 8, 18); and on the other hand, seeing the

---

[1] *Quam meruit poenam solus, digessit in omnes* (Metamorphoses, book 14, n. 469).

[2] *Leniter ex merito quidquid patiare ferendum est* (*Heriodes*, Letter 5, n. 7).

[3] *Scis meam fortunam, nescio quomodo facile obtrectatores invenerim, non meo hercle merito* (*Epistulae ad Familiares*, book 5, n. 9).

[4] I.e. the subject proposed for debate.

[5] I.e. *de condigno*, or merit in the strict sense of the word.

[6] I.e. *de congruo*, or merit in a broad sense.

[7] God does not reward our good works by strict justice, since they do not deserve the reward that they will be given, but still, there is a fittingness that for using ten talents well that one be given charge over ten cities, and for five talents, five cities, as Our Lord said.

Divine promises, by which God promised those keeping His Commandments that they would be given eternal life; they were forced to acknowledge that the merit of eternal life is in the observing of God's Commandments, which they call "worthy merit." These theologians in fact did not notice that among the Latin and approved authors, "worthy" and "condign" are completely the same, and neither of them is more excellent than the other: but both signify a certain equivalence or equality between the merit and the reward. And the fact that Erasmus of Rotterdam, in his translation of the New Testament, when translating that passage of Paul, due to which these theologians undeservedly took occasion to tremble, did not translate the Greek word ἄξια with "condign" or "worthy," but with "equal" (*pares*), thus saying, "For I reckon that the sufferings of this time are not equal with the glory that shall be revealed in us," bears witness to this truth. From which words it is established that Paul merely denied the equality between our works and the glory which is to be given to us. But since this equality is as well expressed by the word "worthy" (*dignus*) as by the word "condign" (*condignus*), in vain do they attempt by the former word to contrive a third type of merit, which is not called "congruous" or "condign" but "worthy": especially since in reality those works which give "worthy" merit to good works in relation to glory in no way differ from those which give condign merit. Therefore, since the subject of the present controversy is only about condign merit, it is fitting at present to define only that type of merit.

Condign merit is a free work for which a reward is due from its natural and own dignity, or from the law. When I say merit is a "work," by "work" I understand not only the doing of some deed, but also an omission, as all scholastic theologians teach that this ought to be understood in that well-known definition whereby Augustine defines sin, speaking thus, "Sin is a word, deed, or desire contrary to God's law."[1] In which definition, in order that it may be complete, by "word" also ought to be understood an omission of a word: and by "deed," an omission of a deed. Therefore let the reader understand that I have brought this to his attention, since I know that there are some scholastic theologians who assert that man, not only by a deed, but also by an omission of a deed, is able to merit. Concerning which matter I do not wish to fight, because in this work I have resolved to debate not to please men but solely for the Catholic faith. And therefore in order that I may put every view of men into the definition of merit, I have brought this to the reader's attention that by "deed" one may understand, if he wishes and it agrees with his opinion, also the omission of a deed.

Now the work itself, in order that it could be called merit, ought to be free: for what lacks liberty of will, cannot have the notion of merit. For nothing human is able to please God, which does not proceed from man's will. And thus, in every oblation which is offered to God, the first thing that God asks from man is the offering of his own will. "My son," Divine Wisdom says, "give me thy heart" (Prov. 23, 26). And rightly it is now said as a common proverb, "a forced service does not please God," on account of that which Paul says, "Every one as he hath determined in his heart, not with sadness, or of necessity: for God loveth a cheerful giver" (II Cor. 9, 7). Also no one, as Augustine teaches, sins in what he cannot avoid[2]: and hence it follows that no one may merit in what he does necessarily and not freely. For merit does not require less freedom of will than sin: because in the things which are inherent from nature, as Aristotle says, we are neither praised nor blamed.[3] And Tertullian says, "But the

---

[1] "Sin, then, is every deed, word, or desire contrary to the eternal law" (*Contra Faustum*, bk. xxii, n. 19), quoted by Peter Lombard as, "Sin, as Augustine says, is every word, deed, or desire which is done against God's law" (*Sent.* II, dist. 35), and by St. Thomas Aquinas as, "Sin is a word, deed, or desire, contrary to the eternal law" (*Summa* I II, q. 71, a. 6, ad 1um).

[2] *Of Two Souls*, c. 10-11, n. 13-15 (PL 42, 103-105); *On the Free Choice of the Will*, bk. 3, c. 18, n. 50-52 (PL 32, 1295-1296). Cf. *Summa Theologica* I II q. 109, a. 8, obj. 1.

[3] *Nicomachean Ethics*, bk. 2, c. 5; Cf. St. Thomas Aquinas (*De veritate*, q. 17, a. 1, s. c. 7).

reward neither of good nor of evil could be paid to the man who should be found to have been either good or evil through necessity and not choice."[1] We also said that for the notion of perfect condign merit it is necessarily required that the reward, in respect to which it is called merit, be due to a good and free work, either from the very nature of the work or from law. For it is not always necessary that the reward be due from the very nature of the work: but it is sufficient that it be due from the law. For the law can make equal, things which were of their nature unequal.

The Natural law teaches that every promise is a debt, and hence it happens that when a promise has been given, things become equal which, apart from that promise, were not equal. Now in order that I may make myself clear, I put forward as an example that promise which King Saul gave when that giant Goliath, who was much stronger than all the sons of Israel whom he was provoking to an individual combat, was instilling fear and terror. "The man that shall slay him," he said, "the king will enrich with great riches, and will give him his daughter, and will make his father's house free from tribute in Israel" (I Kings 17, 25). After having given this promise, David struck Goliath and killed him, and was made worthy to have the king's daughter for his wife. Apart from this promise of the king, although David on account of that victory would have been worthy of some great reward, yet not so great that the king would give his daughter for his wife. For David, who fed sheep and was the youngest of his brothers, was still unequal to the king's daughter: and hence he was unworthy to take her for his wife. For, as a certain man said very well, "Oxen of unequal size are badly matched for the plough."[2]

Given this definition of merit, it is necessary that we ask Luther's sycophants, or followers, whether this definition of merit pleases them, and according to it one may say that human works are not meritorious for eternal life; or on the other hand, whether they would like to add to or remove something from that definition. Perhaps they will say that this definition is not pleasing to them, for the very reason that perhaps they think it is necessary for the true notion of merit, that a work by its own nature be worthy of such a reward, and that reward be due from the natural dignity of the work: and that what is due to it from law is not enough. If they say that they reason in this manner, it will be established on this ground alone, that they dispute with us merely about the word, and merely about the meaning of the word. For according to this meaning of the word, we all admit that no human work, however good, is meritorious of eternal life: because it is not equal to it from its nature, because earthly things are not equal to heavenly things, nor temporal things to eternal things. Obviously, according to this natural condignity, or equality, we understand Paul saying, "The sufferings of this time are not worthy to be compared with the glory to come, that shall be revealed in us" (Rom. 8, 18). And concerning this same dignity and equality we understand all the holy Doctors, whenever they say that our works are not meritorious or worthy of eternal life. For then they are considering in relation to it only the natural value of good works, and they prudently said that it is very distant by its value and the just estimation of eternal life. In fact, Chrysostom truly and piously said in his book, *On Compunction of Heart*, "For if we were to die a thousand deaths, and to practice every virtue, we could not make a suitable return to God for the things which we have received from Him."[3] And in his homily for Septuagesima [PseudoChrysostom] again says, "Whatever you have accomplished, it is little: whatever you might do, it is less. For all merit is small in comparison with the gifts: number the benefits if you can, and then consider

---

[1] *Against Marcion*, bk. 2, c. 6 (PL 2, 283A).
[2] Ovid, *Letters of Heroines*, letter 9 (Deïanira to Hercules), ln. 29.
[3] "*Etiamsi enim sexcenties moriamur, etiamsi omnem exhibeamus virtutem, nihil dignum reddimus honoribus, quibus ad Deo affecti sumus*" (*De Cordis Compunctione*, lib. 2, n. 5 (PG 47, 418)).

what you deserve."[1] And shortly [before[2]] he says, "Should our whole lifetime be spent in obedience, in singing praises and giving thanks; yet could we never repay what we most justly owe... Let the merit of men be excellent, let him observe the rights of nature, let him be obedient to the commandments of the laws; let him fulfill his faith, keep justice, exercise virtues, condemn vice, repel sins, show himself an example for others to imitate: if he have performed anything, it is little."[3]

We willingly acknowledge all these things, and with open arms as they say: for we are neither so unlearned nor arrogant that we would wish to equate the natural value of our works (which in fact are very small) to the most excellent dignity and immense value of heavenly glory. And in light of this, we show clearly that Luther and all his sycophants falsely calumniate us and accuse us of arrogance, as though we would wish to equate our works with the inestimable value of eternal life. Therefore, supposing the word "merit" to mean an equality of measure between it and its reward, we do not dispute concerning this very thing with Luther, but there is agreement between us and him on this point, because human works, however good, are not truly meritorious of eternal life. Nevertheless, one who would be desirous of contention (which I vehemently abhor) could contend, not without reason, about the meaning of the word with Luther and his followers. For if it is necessarily required for the true and perfect notion of merit, that merit itself, according to its natural value, be equated with the reward, and from a natural right the reward itself be due to that merit, there will scarcely be any merit, not only before God, but also among men. Therefore, it would be necessary to completely remove the word "merit" from the Latin language, for the very reason that it would be the name of nothing.

But let us pass over these things, because it is not right nor does it befit a Christian man, especially a theologian, to argue except where the matter itself obliges. Since Luther and his imitators gave that definition to merit, they accept, and according to it say, that no works of men, however good, are meritorious of eternal life: and so necessity itself obliges us to argue with them. For this opinion is clearly opposed to Sacred Scripture and the consensus of the whole Church. Sacred Scripture often testifies that God has promised eternal life for good works. "Do penance," our Savior said, "for the kingdom of heaven is at hand" (Mt. 4, 17). In which words not only the remission of sin, but also the kingdom of Heaven, which is eternal life, is promised. And in St. John's Gospel He said, "Amen, amen I say unto you, that he who heareth my word, and believeth him that sent me, hath life everlasting; and cometh not into judgment, but is passed from death to life" (5, 24). And after a few words He adds, "For the hour cometh, wherein all that are in the graves shall hear the voice of the Son of God. And they that have done good things, shall come forth unto the resurrection of life" (v. 28-29). And to everyone keeping His Commandments He promises eternal life, saying as follows, "If thou wilt enter into life, keep the commandments" (Mt. 19, 17). And shortly afterwards He again adds these words, "And everyone that hath left house, or brethren, or sisters, or father, or mother, or wife, or children, or lands for my name's sake, shall receive an hundredfold, and shall possess life everlasting" (v. 29). In which words eternal life is clearly promised, not in fact *gratis*, but on account of the works enumerated in the same passage. Paul also bears testimony of the Divine promise, when he says, "Godliness is profitable to all things, having promise of the life that now is, and of that which is to come" (I Tim. 4, 8). And perhaps Paul said this on account of those words which Christ foretold that He would say on Judgment Day to the merciful, "I was hungry, and you gave me to eat; I was thirsty, and you gave me to drink; I was a stranger, and you took me in" (Mt. 25, 35). And just before He said, "Come,

---

[1] *Homily 60: Dominica in Septuagesima* (PL 95, 1207D).
[2] The text has "after" but in the homily cited it is before, hence "before" has been substituted here.
[3] *Ibid.* (PL 95, 1207B-C).

ye blessed of my Father, possess you the kingdom prepared for you from the foundation of the world" (v. 34). In which words the Savior clearly promises the kingdom of Heaven to the merciful, on account of the works of mercy done by them. The Apostle James also bears witness that God promised eternal glory on account of the afflictions of this life borne patiently. "Blessed be the man that endureth temptation," he says, "for when he hath been proved, he shall receive a crown of life, which God hath promised to them that love him" (James 1, 12).

Not only for these works, but also to those receiving the Sacraments, Christ promises eternal life. For to those receiving Baptism He said, "He that believeth and is baptized, shall be saved: but he that believeth not shall be condemned" (Mk. 16, 16). And to the one receiving the Sacrament of the Eucharist He said, "He that eateth my flesh, and drinketh my blood, hath everlasting life: and I will raise him up in the last day" (Jn. 6, 55). And to all these promises conforms that parable of Christ our Savior, concerning the householder "who went out early in the morning to hire labourers into his vineyard. And having agreed with the labourers for a penny a day, he sent them into his vineyard" (Mt. 20, 1-2). In which parable, that "penny" promised for a day's labor, as all the Latin and Greek sacred Doctors consistently interpret, signifies the heavenly glory promised by God to all who labor in the Lord's vineyard. Therefore, given this promise, and having made an agreement with us, the good works of men with the help of God's grace become worthy of eternal life, and are equal to it, which apart from that promise of God, would have been completely unworthy of eternal life. And this was that supreme mercy of God, upon which depends all our merit: namely, that the reward of eternal life, entirely inestimable and of its nature above all our merit, He willed to value by the price of our works done in sanctifying grace, and to promise it in remuneration for our works. For which reason He made us much more to be debtors to Him, so that having acknowledged so great a benefit we may strive to serve Him more ardently, as the greatest remunerator of our labors.

But lest from so liberal and magnificent a promise we might take occasion of being proud, for we might suppose that by our works alone we could attain eternal life, God did not wish to promise it for works howsoever good, except they have His grace joined to them: "Without me you can do nothing" (Jn. 15, 5). If [we can do] "nothing," therefore [we cannot do anything], neither to attain eternal life, nor to do that which is needed to attain that life. Helped by God's grace we can merit eternal life, according to that which Paul says, "I can do all things in him who strengtheneth me" (Phil. 4, 13). By this grace, which makes us capable of meriting glory, we are pleasing to God and accepted for eternal life, and then our works are pleasing to God, and by Him accepted for eternal life. Indeed, God firstly looked upon Abel and afterwards upon his works (Gen. 4, 4). Therefore, this order of things well considered, it is easily understood that we refer all the glory of our merit to God alone, from Whose grace alone it proceeds, so that we might be pleasing to Him, and by it work well, and we might be able to merit eternal life. Nevertheless, from the Divine promise alone, the utility of merit appears to us, to whom on account of good works done with God's grace, is due eternal life. And this same fact is proved from this same parable, in which the householder said to him who bore the burden of the day and the heat, "Take what is thine, and go thy way" (Mt. 20, 14). For the only reason why He said that the day's penny was his, was that it due to him by agreement on account of his labor. And this does not take away even slightly from God's glory and dignity, nay rather it confers upon Him greater glory and honor. As, for instance, it exalts God's immense goodness, because although He was rich, He willed to become poor for our sakes, so that by His neediness we might be rich[1]: thus He shows His most abundant generosity and very magnificent benevolence towards us, because although He owes nothing

---

[1] Cf. II Cor. 8, 9: "Being rich he became poor, for your sakes; that through his poverty you might be rich."

to men, He, by His own goodness, willed to make Himself a debtor, so that He might truly make us rich. He made Himself a debtor, as Blessed Bonaventure teaches, not indeed to men, to whom He could owe nothing, but to Himself, that He might be faithful to His promise, such that Heaven and earth would pass away rather than some promise of His might become void.

Because if Philip Melanchthon and John Calvin shudder at giving this name "debtor" to God, as they are in this regard supercilious, or to be more precise, superstitious, let them hear what Augustine says, who was a most ardent defender of God's grace: "For the things which we already have," Augustine says, "let us praise God the giver: for the things which we do not yet have, we have God as a debtor. For He is become our debtor, not by receiving anything from us, but by His promising what it pleased Him."[1] And again he says in his sermon on the days of Easter, "Therefore let us praise the Lord, because we hold fast to His faithful promises; we have not yet received [their fulfillment]. Do you consider it a trifling matter to hold Him as One Who has made a promise so that we may prove that He is our Debtor? God, the Promiser, has become our Debtor; He has become our Debtor because of His goodness, not because of any just claim on our part."[2]

If these enemies of ours do not wish to believe Augustine's testimony, let them hear the declaration of the Second Synod of Orange,[3] which in canon eighteen is contained these words, "A reward is due to good works if they are performed: but grace, to which we have no claim, precedes them, to enable them to be done."[4] Take note, I beseech all ye Lutherans, and see how clearly Augustine and the Synod of Orange assert that God is not only a debtor to Himself, as Bonaventure said, but also to us, such that we can demand the debt from Him. If eternal glory is the debt, as Augustine says, which is due to the just man on account of his good works done with the help of God's grace, nothing actually prevents it from being said that he merits eternal life through such good works. From the testimonies of Scripture already cited it is proven that the fiction of Philip Melanchthon and John Calvin is vain and ridiculous, who acknowledging the force of the arguments proving good works to be meritorious, flee to this asylum, namely that they would say that those good works merit temporal goods and some spiritual goods, but not eternal life. Nevertheless in these testimonies of Sacred Scripture—which we have now just cited—eternal life, expressed by its own name or by "the kingdom of heaven," which is nothing other than eternal life, is promised; and hence it is evidently shown that good works, on account of which eternal life is promised, are meritorious of the same life.

Furthermore, Sacred Scripture very often says that eternal life is the reward of our merits, and thus it is necessarily concluded that the works themselves are the merit of that reward. For merit and reward are correlative terms: just as a father is necessarily the father of a child. Therefore, when one is taken away, the rest is necessarily taken away: and when one is stated the other necessarily follows: for they are joined one to the other. Therefore, it becomes necessary that if you deny that good works are meritorious of eternal life, you would be forced to also deny that eternal life is the reward of good works: or if you concede that eternal life is the reward of good works, it would also be necessary to acknowledge that the good works themselves are the merit of that life. But it is very clear to those versed in Sacred Letters that eternal life is the reward of good works.

---

[1] *Sermo* 158, c. 2, n. 2. (PL 38, 863).

[2] *Sermo* 254, c. 5, n. 6 (PL 38, 1184).

[3] The Second Synod of Orange was a local council held in 529 in France, which condemned Semi-Pelagianism.

[4] Dz. 191. Cf. Augustine, *Opus imperfectum contra secundam responsionem Iuliani*, bk. 1, c. 133 (PL 45, 1133).

Nevertheless, Calvin, in that tract against the Acts of the Council of Trent at the end of Session Six, openly denies this, saying the following, "First, I differ from them in this, that they make eternal life the reward; for if God rewards works in eternal life, they will immediately make out that eternal life itself is the reward which is recompensed for them."[1]

But Calvin badly depicts our case to the reader: because we are not moved by so feeble an argument, namely, that we appoint eternal life to be the reward of good works, but on the contrary this assertion is based on the clear testimonies of Sacred Scripture and of the holy Doctors. For it is evident that God said to Abraham, "I am thy protector, and thy reward exceeding great" (Gen. 15, 1). And that contrivance of theirs does not here serve John Calvin or Philip Melanchthon, namely, that one may say that not beatitude itself, but some other spiritual good on earth or in Heaven is the reward of our works. For God Himself says that He is our "protector," and "reward exceeding great." The Wise Man says that this same reward is to be rendered to the just, saying as follows, "But the just shall live for evermore: and their reward is with the Lord" (Wis. 5, 16). To the holy Patriarchs who were waiting for a more open and accessible heavenly gate, and beatitude to be given through Christ's merits, and were kept in suspense with exceedingly long and anxious expectation, the prophet Isaias said these words for their consolation, "Behold the Lord God shall come with strength, and his arm shall rule: Behold his reward is with him and his work is before him" (40, 10). Now in order that God shows that He is the one whom Isaias had then foretold, in the Apocalypse of John He says, "Behold, I come quickly; and my reward is with me, to render to every man according to his works" (22, 12). And these things also are to be understood of the eternal vision of God, or rather one can easily prove that the just were then waiting for it, and for it alone we now all hope, saying with David, "For what have I in heaven? and besides thee what do I desire upon earth?" (Ps. 72, 25).

It is also evident because our Savior said in that sermon which He gave on the Mount: "Blessed are ye when they shall revile you, and persecute you, and speak all that is evil against you, untruly, for my sake: be glad and rejoice, for your reward is very great in heaven" (Mt. 5, 11-12). Now Chromatius shows in his commentary on the Lord's Sermon on the Mount, that this reward "very great in heaven" is beatitude itself and heavenly glory, and interpreting the aforesaid words, says: "How glorious is the endurance of this persecution, the reward for which the Lord says is laid up in Heaven! And so, taking into consideration the reward of the proposed glory, we should be ready with devout faith for every endurance of suffering, so that we may merit to be made sharers in the glory of the Prophets and Apostles, through Christ our Lord, Who is blessed forever."[2] In which words one ought not only to note that he declares that the "very great" reward in Heaven is heavenly glory, but he says that we merit it through endurance of the persecutions together with Christ's merits. The word "retribution," by which heavenly glory is itself designated, also pertains to this passage: because through it the Lord repays (*retribuit*) every just man according to the merits of his works. When speaking about keeping the Commandments, the Prophet says, "In keeping them there is a great reward (*retributio multa*)" (Ps. 18, 12). In which words the Prophet agrees with Christ saying that the "reward is very great in heaven." Hence Cassiodorus, interpreting that Psalm, says, "For the gifts of Divine clemency were so great that they cannot be comprehended. For so the Apostle speaks of them: 'That eye hath not seen, nor ear heard, neither hath it entered into the heart of man, what things God hath prepared for them that love him' (I Cor. 2, 9). Therefore, many things are rightly said: because all these things cannot be comprehended."[3]

---

[1] *Acts of the Council of Trent with the Antidote* (*CR*, 35, 471).
[2] *Tractatus in evangelium S. Matthaei*, tract 3, c. 9 (PL 20, 337C).
[3] *Expositio in Psalterium*, on Ps. 18 (PL 70, 142B).

And certainly whoever will have carefully examined the style of Sacred Scripture will find that it never uses the word "retribution" or "merit," but only "free gift," as often as it speaks of the call to grace, or of first justification, or of predestination to glory. By this manner of speech it is clearly shown that all those things are given freely and without merit. For the Holy Ghost, as Christ says, "breatheth where he will" (Jn. 3, 8). And He says again, "You have not chosen me: but I have chosen you" (Jn. 15, 16). And Paul says, "It is not of him that willeth, nor of him that runneth, but of God that sheweth mercy" (Rom. 9, 16). And again, "He hath mercy on whom he will; and whom he will, he hardeneth" (v. 18). Now when it speaks of the conferring of heavenly glory, then it uses the word "retribution" or "reward," so that it may show that it is not freely given, but often given on account of some merits of one's own, namely for all adults. For even if God freely and without any merit of ours predestines to eternal glory, nevertheless He does not freely render it to a man who is already an adult and has the use of reason. The Royal Prophet uses this manner of speaking in one and the same Psalm, and in the same context of words, saying the following, "He saved me, because he was well pleased with me. And the Lord will reward me according to my justice; and will repay me according to the cleanness of my hands" (Ps. 17, 20-21). In the first part where he treats of predestination, and of the vocation to grace, he used an expression of a free gift, saying, "because he was well pleased with me (*quoniam voluit me*)."[1]

In the second verse where he does not now treat of the call to service, but of the rendering of the reward, he does not use an expression signifying a free gift, but an expression of retribution, saying the following, "And the Lord will reward me according to my justice" (Ps. 17, 25). And Cassiodorus, when commenting on the Psalms, observed this before me, where interpreting the first part of the verse, he says that these words, "Because he was well pleased with me" (Ps. 17, 20), mean "Because He chose me, Who calls all men freely, and did not firstly receive any service before He deigned to give, as He says in the Gospel, 'You have not chosen me: but I have chosen you.' (Jn. 15, 16)"[2] Jerome favors this interpretation, who on the same passage says these words, "He called me by His own will and not due to my merit, as the Apostle says: 'By grace you are saved through faith, and that not of yourselves' (Eph. 2, 8)."[3] Cassiodorus, however, expounding the second verse, says these words, "[The Church] did well to maintain both points. Earlier she said, before she was assumed, 'because he was well pleased with me': and now she says, 'He will reward me according to my justice.'"[4]

Again, Sacred Scripture itself, not merely once or twice but many times, says that the saints are worthy of eternal life: which would not be said unless they merited it by their good works. For the Wise Man, speaking about the just men who for God's sake endured evils, says, "Afflicted in few things, in many they shall be well rewarded: because God hath tried them, and found them worthy of himself" (Wis. 3, 5). He did not say that He found them worthy of some other good, but "worthy of himself," so that we might clearly refute with this reason the contrivance of John Calvin and Philip Melanchthon. And God did not say that He had made them worthy, but had "found them worthy." "Afflicted in few things, in many they shall be well rewarded." Affliction, therefore, in few things endured for God, along with God's grace, makes just men to be worthy of God Himself. And Paul, writing to the Thessalonians, favors the same views, speaking thus, "The charity of every one of you towards each other, aboundeth: so that we ourselves also glory in you in the churches of God, for your patience and faith, and in all your persecutions and tribulations, which you endure, for an example of the just judgment of God, that you may be counted worthy of the kingdom of God, for which

---

[1] Literally, "because He chose me."

[2] *Expositio in Psalterium*, on Ps. 17 (PL 70, 129D).

[3] *Breviarium in Psalmos* (PL 26, 867C).

[4] *Expositio in Psalterium*, on Ps. 17 (PL 70, 129D-130A).

also you suffer" (II Thess. 1, 3-5). And concerning certain Sardiceans, who did not defile their garments, God says, "They shall walk with me in white, because they are worthy" (Apoc. 3, 4). If they are worthy to walk with God in white, then they merited this very thing: for to merit some reward is nothing other than to be worthy of it.

Then from another consideration of good works it can easily be further proved that they merit eternal life. For good works are said to cause and yield eternal life in the man who does them. Now they cannot be called the cause of beatitude, except by that reason whereby they are the merit of it, nor can they have any production regarding it, except that production which merit has regarding the reward. For this reason alone Paul says that Christ "became, to all that obey him, the cause of eternal salvation" (Heb. 5, 9). He said "the cause of eternal salvation" because He merited eternal salvation for all who obey Him. In this way ought to be interpreted that which Christ our Savior Himself said to a certain blind man along the road sitting and begging sight from Him. "Receive thy sight: thy faith hath made thee whole" (Lk. 18, 42). For faith, which is something spiritual, could not produce corporeal vision, but Christ said that faith made him see, because it is through such faith that the blind man merited that God would restore his sight. Now, that good works may be said to cause or produce beatitude in man is clearly proved from the words of Jerome and Augustine, who clearly teach this. For Jerome, in his commentaries on Matthew, interpreting those words of the Savior, "Blessed are ye when they shall revile you" (Mt. 5, 11), says, "That curse is to be despised, which creates beatitude, because it is uttered by the erroneous mouth of the one cursing."[1] In which words one ought to note that he says that the one enduring the curse creates his beatitude. Augustine says, "What will make [the soul] blessed, unless its own merit, and its Lord's reward? But [the soul's] merit, too, is His grace, whose reward will be its beatitude."[2] Augustine plainly says that man's merit makes him blessed.

And although these two illustrious men clearly and openly say this, nevertheless we can much better prove this from the words of St. Paul, saying, "For that which is at present momentary and light of our tribulation, worketh for us above measure exceedingly an eternal weight of glory" (II Cor. 4, 17). He said "worketh" so that by this word he might show that the merit of beatitude exists. For Augustine concludes from these words of Paul that our good works are the price by which heavenly glory is purchased, saying these words: "What is, 'worketh for us an eternal weight of glory,' [to us] for whom it works? 'While we look not at the things which are seen, but at the things which are not seen. For the things which are seen, are temporal; but the things which are not seen, are eternal' (II Cor. 4, 17-18). Be not slothful laboring for a short time, and you will rejoice incessantly. ... This is everlasting rest. This rest will be without end, without end there will be this joy, without end there will be this rejoicing, without end there will be incorruption; you will have eternal life, rest which will not have an end. How much labor is rest which does not have an end worth? If you wish to truly compare and truly judge, eternal rest is rightly bought with eternal labor. Truly this is so: but do not fear; God is merciful. For if you would have eternal labor, you would never attain eternal rest. ... Therefore, so that you may at some time attain that which you purchase, one must not labor eternally: not because it is not worth so much, but so that what is bought may be possessed. It is indeed worthy to be bought with perpetual labor; but it is necessary that it be bought with temporal labor. What are ten hundred thousand years of labor worth? Ten hundred thousand years have an end: 'What I will give you,' God says, 'will not have an end.' What kind of mercy is God's? Neither does He say, 'Labor for ten hundred thousand years,' nor does He say, 'labor for a thousand years'; He does not say, 'labor for five hundred years': labor while you live, during a few years: immediately thereafter there will be rest, and it will not have an end.

---

[1] *Commentariorum in Evangelium Matthaei Libri Quattuor*, lib. 1, cap. 5 (PL 26, 35).

[2] *De Trinitate*, lib. 14, cap. 15, n. 21 (PL 42, 1051-1052).

... Therefore, it is true what the Apostle said, 'For that which is at present momentary and light of our tribulation, worketh for us above measure exceedingly an eternal weight of glory.' Behold how much of a price we give: in a way, one husk for receiving everlasting treasures: a husk of labor for unbelievable rest."[1] Thus speaks Augustine, who even if he acknowledges that all our labors are very unequal to everlasting glory, nevertheless he says that they are the price by which eternal glory is purchased. The price in fact is not from its nature, but from the Divine mercy, which willed to put it up for sale with such a small price so that we could acquire it, which, had it been sold for a just price, it could never be obtained.

Even now I beseech Calvin to tell us why he reproaches monks so rashly, and mocks and ridicules them for the very reason that they say that by good works man merits eternal life, as though only monks had said this, and not all the sacred Doctors before them. Now, so that the reader may know Calvin's temerity, shamelessness, and abusive language, I have decided to cite his words. In his tract Against the Acts of the Council of Trent near the end of the sixth session, where he treats of the merit of good works, after he denied that eternal life is the reward of good works, he says these words which follow: "It is not strange, however, that addle-pated monks who, having never experienced any struggle of conscience, and who, moreover, being intoxicated with ambition or excessive drinking, only desire to raise themselves in the esteem of their idol (he always calls the pope by this name), should thus prate of the perfection of the Law. With the same confidence do they talk of a heaven for hire, while they themselves meanwhile continue engrossed with the present hire, after which they are always gaping."[2] From which words, just as "[you know] the lion by its claws," as it is said in the proverb,[3] the intelligent reader will easily be able to appraise Calvin: for as Solomon says, "The learning of a man is known by patience" (Prov. 19, 11). I could indeed very easily retaliate, if I wished, but I prefer to keep silent and patiently endure such abusive language for Christ's name: because the Savior said, "Blessed are ye when they shall revile you, and persecute you, and speak all that is evil against you, untruly" (Mt. 5, 11). But let us see the reason why he heaped such abusive language upon monks: because, as he says, we "talk of a heaven for hire." If this were the reason why he sets us on fire, for this same reason he ought to be angered more vehemently, and to inveigh against Augustine, because he before us, as it was shown from his words previously cited, taught this clearly: and we relying on his authority dare to say it. But I think that Calvin did not read those words: otherwise he would not have spared him less than the monks.

Finally, this impious assertion of theirs was condemned by the definition of the whole Church. For the [Fourth] Lateran Council, celebrated under Innocent III, in the first chapter of its decrees says these words: "Moreover, not only virgins and the continent but also married persons pleasing to God through right faith and good work merit to arrive at a blessed eternity."[4] These are the words of the Lateran Council and are found in the chapter, *Firmiter*, [in the book of the *Decretals* under title one,] *De summa Trinitate et fide Catholica*. And the Council of Trent, celebrated under Paul III, in the sixth session, in the thirty-second canon of its decrees, says: "If any one saith that the good works of one that is justified are in such manner the gifts of God, as that they are not also the good merits of him that is justified; or, that the said justified, by the good works which he performs through the grace of God and the

---

[1] *Enarratio in Psalmum XCIII*, n. 24 (PL 37, 1211).

[2] *Acts of the Council of Trent with the Antidote* (CR 35, 471-472).

[3] *Leonem ex unguibus [aestimes]* was a popular cliché of the sixteenth century used by Erasmus (*Adagia*, I, ix, 34). It was originally a classical Greek adage (Ἐκ τῶν ὀνύχων τὸν λέοντα) found in the writings of Plutarch and Lucian, alluding to the sculptor Phidias' famed ability to judge the size of a lion given only its severed paw.

[4] Dz. 430.

merit of Jesus Christ, whose living member he is, does not truly merit increase of grace, eternal life, and the attainment of that eternal life (if he should die in grace), and also an increase of glory: let him be anathema."[1] All these facts are more than enough to refute the assertion of these heretics, whereby they say that men are unable through good works to merit eternal life.

Nevertheless, it is necessary to reply to their objections, so that the truth of our and the Catholic position may be more clearly seen. Firstly, for example, they object to us that we are very ungrateful to Christ our Redeemer, for the very reason that we arrogate the merit of beatitude to ourselves and our works, as though Christ does not merit it for us, or His merit were not sufficient for obtaining it for us, but instead it is necessary for it to be helped by our works. Now to assert such things is an impiety, such that there is no Christian man who does not abhor to hear them. This argument is either a mere calumny, or it proceeds from crass ignorance: because all who make this objection to us, by that very fact, show that they do not understand our position, and why we say that good works merit eternal life.

For, as we now have often said, we do not have this of ourselves that we can merit eternal life by good works: nor are our works of themselves of such value and or so great dignity that heavenly glory is due to them: but men and their works are exalted to this dignity and to this value only by the Divine clemency whereby God wished to promise eternal life to those submitting to Him. Apart from this promise, by no good works of ours, however good, could men acquire it: because all our good works, no matter how good, are unequal to so great a reward, and consequently are undeserving of it. Now men and their good works are pleasing to God, having been accepted for eternal life through Christ's merit, Who offered His Passion and death for them to God His Father, and Who prayed for all those whom He knew to be predestined to glory. "When he cometh into the world, He said: 'Sacrifice and oblation thou wouldest not: but a body thou hast fitted to me: holocausts for sin did not please thee. Then said I: Behold I come: in the head of the book it is written of me: that I should do thy will, O God.' ... In the which will, we are sanctified by the oblation of the body of Jesus Christ once" (Heb. 10, 5-7 & 10).

Next, precisely when He wished to go out of the world, after He prayed to God the Father for His disciples soon before His Passion, He immediately added, "And not for them only do I pray, but for them also who through their word shall believe in me, that they all may be one" (Jn. 17, 20-21). Now this prayer, as all His others, as Paul says, God the Father heard, for that reverence that He showed to Him (Heb. 5, 7). Therefore, it follows that just as all grace and all glory originate from His first merit: so also all Divine acceptation depends upon His first merit, whereby He accepts men and their works towards eternal life. "Being justified freely," says St. Paul, "by his grace, through the redemption that is in Christ Jesus, Whom God hath proposed to be a propitiation, through faith in his blood" (Rom. 3, 24-25). And again he says, "Being justified therefore by faith, let us have peace with God, through our Lord Jesus Christ" (Rom. 5, 1). And once again, "As by the offence of one, unto all men to condemnation; so also by the justice of one, unto all men to justification of life" (v. 18). And in another epistle, not only concerning men, but also concerning good works accepted through Christ by God, he says, "He gave himself for us, that he might redeem us from all iniquity, and might cleanse to himself a people acceptable, a pursuer of good works" (Titus 2, 14). And Peter, exhorting us to lay aside all malice, guile, and dissimulation, and teaching the way how we may do this correctly, says, "Offering up spiritual sacrifices, acceptable to God by Jesus Christ" (I Pet. 2, 5). Since, therefore, we acknowledge all these things with our whole heart and full mouth, we take away none of Christ's glory: but rather we exalt His glory, and we attribute to Him whatever in us has some notion of merit. For we do not merely say that He has merited eternal

---

[1] Dz. 842.

life for us, but also that we are able to merit this by our good works supported by His merits: which is of much more glory.

And nevertheless, Christ did not give in this way the honor of merit to our good works, as though His without ours were insufficient for meriting eternal life. Far be it. For Christ's merit was and is, without our works, most sufficient: but He did not want to apply all the sufficiency of His merit to adults without some good work of theirs, although He easily could have done this if He wished: just as He confers upon infants. Nor by saying this do we share the glory of merit between ourselves and Christ. For we give all glory to Christ, and none to ourselves in this regard, lest we presume to snatch away the glory which God willed to be kept for Himself. For even if we give some notion of merit to our works, nevertheless we ascribe it to Christ Himself; from Whose merit it was given to us that we may merit something by our good works. And therefore, Blessed Bernard, considering this, said, "My merit, therefore, is nothing but the mercy of the Lord. Hence, I cannot be poor in merit so long as He is rich in compassion. And if 'the mercies of the Lord are many' (Ps. 118, 156), many too must my merits be. ... And if 'the mercies of the Lord are from eternity and unto eternity' (Ps. 102, 17), 'the mercies of the Lord I will sing forever' (Ps. 88, 2) also. But shall I sing my own justice? 'O Lord, I will be mindful of Thy justice alone' (Ps. 70, 16). For Thy justice is also my justice, because Thou art made unto me 'justice of God' (I Cor. 1, 30)."[1] These are the words of Bernard, who acknowledging merit, gave it all to God's glory: because he understood that such merit comes about from God's mercy.

Secondly, they object to us that our works, whereby we say that we merit, are God's gifts: because unless they were God's gifts, those good works would not exist on account of what the Apostle James says, "Every best gift, and every perfect gift, is from above, coming down from the Father of lights" (1, 17). If our works are God's gifts, it follows that, as the heretics say, men are unable to merit eternal life through them: for it is not consonant with reason that by what someone gave to us, we may merit something in relation to him.

If this argument were valid, it would also prove that man through good works is unable to merit before God not merely eternal life, but neither does he merit other spiritual goods, nay, nor temporal goods: because if our good works were compared to those other goods, God's gifts will not be less [unmerited], than if [our good works] were compared to eternal life. But Philip Melanchthon, John Calvin and the Wittenbergers admit that our works merit temporal and spiritual rewards before God. Therefore, we say that our good works are God's gifts, and at the same time are meritorious of eternal life. And we do not say this from our imagination, as the heretics do, but relying upon the testimonies of the holy Fathers: who said this many centuries before us, of whom I chose to cite some in the present circumstances—especially those same Fathers whom the heretics cite in their favor—so that henceforth it may be evident to all how badly do they boast of their approbation.

Bernard says these words, "Regarding merit it suffices to know that one's own merits do not suffice. But just as it is sufficient for merit not to presume on one's own merits, so to lack merit is sufficient for judgment. On the other hand, no regenerated infant is without merits, for they have the merits of Christ. Yet one renders himself unworthy of a participation in the merits of Christ by not joining thereto merits of his own, if this is due not to incapacity but to negligence; which, however, is a danger more for adults than for infants. Study therefore, my brethren, to acquire merits, which you should know were given. You should hope for God's mercy as the fruit of your merit. And in this way you shall avoid all danger of poverty, of ingratitude, and of presumption. The worst kind of poverty is lack of merit, whilst presumption of spirit is but deceitful riches. Hence the Wise Man prays to the Lord, 'Give me neither beggary nor riches' (Prov. 30, 8). Happy the Church to which are wanting neither merits without

---

[1] *Sermones in Cantica Canticorum*, Sermo LXI, n. 5 (PL 183, 1073).

presumption, nor presumption without merits! She has indeed grounds whereon to presume, but these grounds are not her own merits. She has merits for meriting, but not for presuming. Not to presume it, is not this to merit it?"[1] In which words it ought to be especially observed that he said that our merits are bestowed gifts, and the reward corresponding to our merits is from God's mercy, and hence one ought not to presume concerning merits.

Augustine, disputing with the Pelagians, who falsely supposed that man's merit precedes God's grace, said, "For, just as in the beginning we obtained the mercy of faith, not because we were faithful but that we might become so, in like manner He will crown us at the end with eternal life, as it says, 'with mercy and compassion' (Ps. 102, 4). Not in vain, therefore, do we sing to God: 'His mercy shall prevent me' (Ps. 58, 11),[2] and 'His mercy shall follow me' (Ps. 22, 6). Consequently, eternal life itself, which will certainly be possessed at the end without end, is in a sense awarded to prior merits, yet, because the same merits for which it is awarded are not effected by us through our sufficiency, but are effected in us by grace, even this very grace is so-called for no other reason than that it is given freely; not, indeed, that it is not given for merit, but because the merits themselves are given to whom [grace] is given."[3] Behold these two [Fathers], namely Augustine and Bernard, concerning whom the heretics boast that they approve of their position even though they actually deviate very far from it, as their words, which we have now just cited, very clearly establish.

[Pseudo-] Chrysostom also agrees with these Fathers, who in his first homily on Adam and Eve, after many arguments by which he strives to prove that every good work of ours originates from God, and that we are unable to do a truly good work without God's help, says the following words: "Therefore by these ecclesiastical regulations, and having cited examples by Divine authority, the Lord thus helping we are confirmed that of all good affections and works, and of all efforts and of all virtues, by which from the beginning of faith one tends towards God, let us acknowledge God as the author, and let us not doubt that from His grace all of man's merits come forth; through Whom likewise it happens that we are able to will and do something good. Indeed, by which help and gift of God, free will is not taken away, but freed, so that it becomes light from darkness, straight from crooked, healthy from weak, grave from imprudent. For so great is God's goodness towards all men that he wills that merits be ours, which are His gifts."[4] These are the words of Chrysostom who could not have spoken more clearly in support of our position.

Finally, Pope Celestine I says, "So great is God's goodness towards all men that he wills that merits be ours which are His gifts: and for those which He has given, He is to give an eternal reward."[5]

From these testimonies of illustrious men it is already evident enough how little the objection of the heretics is valid, by which they endeavor to obstruct by this objection that men's merits are God's gifts. And by these testimonies it is also evident why Paul called grace "life eternal" itself saying, "But the grace of God, life everlasting" (Rom. 6, 23). And Zacharias says, "He shall give equal grace to grace" (4, 7). For grace is said to be eternal life itself, because although it is given on account of merit, nevertheless the merits themselves are God's

---

[1] *Sermones in Cantica Canticorum*, Sermo LXVIII, n. 6 (PL 183, 1111).

[2] Literally translated this verse would be "His mercy shall come before me."

[3] *Epistola ad Sixtum presbyterum*, letter 194, c. 5, n. 19 (PL 33, 880).

[4] *Homilia de Adam et Eva*. According to St. Robert Bellarmine, this homily was not written by St. John Chrysostom but by a later author. (See *De Scriptoribus Ecclesiasticis* (Brussels, 1719), lib. 1, p. 128). It is included in the writings of Prosper of Aquitaine in Migne's Patrology. (*De gratia Dei et libero voluntatis arbitrio*, c. 8 (PL 51, 210)).

[5] Letter 21 (to the bishops of Gaul), c. 10, n. 14 (PL 50, 535B-C). Pseudo-Isidore, *Collectio decretalium*, c. 12 (PL 130, 754B).

free gifts, and merits would not exist without grace. Therefore, considering the first origin of merit, we say that the glory which we render by merits is a grace, because the works themselves, so that they may be merits, have [merit] from God's grace.

Thirdly they object to us from that the passage of the Savior in St. Luke's Gospel: "When you shall have done all these things that are commanded you, say: We are unprofitable servants; we have done that which we ought to do" (Lk. 17, 10). [They say that] if we are unprofitable, then by the fulfilment of the Commandments we do not merit life everlasting: because if by such fulfilment of the Commandments we merit eternal life, we are not only profitable in that regard, but we shall be judged by a very profitable merit. For eternal life in itself is the highest and most profitable good which can happen to us. Hence, if we did what we should have done, it follows that by acting in this manner we merit nothing. For he who renders what he owes has enough, because by this he is freed from debt and from the punishment which from him would be rightly required, if he had not rendered the debt.

I admit that all of us, even after we have carried out God's Commandments, ought to consider ourselves to be unprofitable from our nature, and from the very nature of those things which we do: because neither the fulfilment of the Commandments themselves is by its nature of such value that it be worthy of the reward of eternal life, nor do we ourselves have so many and so great powers that by ourselves alone, without God's special help, are we able to carry out all His Commandments. For concerning the execution of God's Commandments, as it was defined in the [Second] Synod of Milevum[1] in chapter five of its decrees, "The Lord was speaking [of the fruits of His commands] when He said, 'Without me you can do nothing' (Jn. 15, 5).[2] Therefore from the Divine mercy alone, as we have now often said, both things occur: namely, the Divine help for executing God's Commandments, and the liberality of God Himself, which promises that He will give eternal life to us, if we shall have kept His Commandments.

And because all these things are not from us, but proceed from God's mercy, wherefore Christ our true Teacher teaches us that we may not take pride in the works that we do: but let us call ourselves "unprofitable servants," deeming ourselves to have been able to do none of them without God's special aid. And although we may do this, nevertheless not due to this would we be worthy, such that on account of the works themselves would He render a reward to us: just as neither is a fervent man worthy of a reward on the grounds that he served his Lord, to whom he is bound to obey due to his servitude. And so, Christ also teaches that acknowledging this we may say, "That we have done that which we ought to do." And this is the other not less mercy of God, that when He could have required this of us had He so wished, just as a master demands the execution of his commands from his servants without any expectation of a reward, He nevertheless—as perhaps might motivate us to a more prompt observance of His Commandments by this hope—willed to promise so great a reward to us from His mercy.

And this is the true and genuine sense of Christ's words, as the words which precede evidently prove. For before those words Christ said these words which follow, "But which of

---

[1] The Second Synod of Milevum (or Mileum) was held in 416 and appealed to Pope Innocent I for the repression of the Pelagian heresy. The city was formerly situated in the Roman province of Numidia. The city is now called "Mila" and is located in Algeria.

[2] "Can. 5. It has likewise been decided that whoever says that the grace of justification is given to us for this reason: that what we are ordered to do through free will, we may be able to accomplish more easily through grace, just as if, even if grace were not given, we could nevertheless fulfill the Divine commands without it, though not indeed easily, let him be anathema. For concerning the fruits of His commands the Lord spoke not when He said: 'Without me you can accomplish with greater difficulty,' but when He said: 'Without me you can do nothing' (John 15, 5)" (Dz. 105).

you, having a servant ploughing or feeding cattle, will say to him, when he is come from the field: Immediately go. Sit down to meat. And will not rather say to him: Make ready my supper and gird thyself and serve me, whilst I eat and drink; and afterwards thou shalt eat and drink? Doth he thank that servant for doing the things which he commanded him? I think not" (Lk. 17, 7-10). Having said this parable Christ immediately adds these words about which we are now discussing. "So you also, when you shall have done all these things that are commanded you, say: We are unprofitable servants; we have done that which we ought to do" (v. 10). From the context of the words it is clearly evident that we therefore are called unprofitable servants, because from the execution of God's Commandments we are worthy of no reward: just as a servant is also unworthy of a reward from the fact that he served his master.

And Theophylact[1] favors this interpretation, who interpreting the aforesaid parable of Christ says, "For it is shown by this parable that one ought not be exalted for any good work, not even in the fulfilment of all the Commandments. For necessity is incumbent upon a servant that he do the Lord's Commandments, as one ought to ascribe a good work to Him. Of course, if he will not work, he is more worthy of blows: when, however, he shall have worked, he may be content that he shall have escaped blows. Hence, he ought not seek from this a price or honor. For it belongs to the Lord's liberality to give, nay, to give generously. And so also, he who serves God, even if he carries out all the Commandments, ought not to be elated, for he has done nothing great. But woe will be to him unless he will have done it: as the Apostle says, 'Woe is unto me if I preach not the gospel' (I Cor. 9, 16). Hence if one shall have procured gifts, he ought not to take pride in them and boast about them. For they are benefits conferred upon him through God's mercy, not because the Lord owes something to him; nay, the servant owes to his Lord that he does all His commands."[2]

I know that others interpret Christ's words differently, saying therefore, "we are unprofitable servants," because we give no benefit to God from our merits. And Bede in his commentary on Luke favors this interpretation, where interpreting the aforesaid words of Christ he gives both expositions of these words, saying the following, "If a man demands from a man who is his servant, not a single but multiple services, and nevertheless he does not gain his favor: how much more you, who without Me can do nothing, ought not to reckon the merits by the length of time of the labors, but to always increase [your merit] by new efforts with love and spontaneous service. Therefore say, 'We are unprofitable servants.' You are truly servants, because you were purchased with a price. But 'unprofitable,' because the Lord does not need you. Now if one is unprofitable who does all the things [commanded], what ought to be said of him who either is unable through weakness, or, what is worse, despises through pride, to carry out what was commanded? Or it is interpreted otherwise. We are unprofitable servants because 'The sufferings of this time are not worthy to be compared with the glory to come that shall be revealed in us' (Rom. 8, 18)."[3]

These are the words of Bede, who gave two expositions to these words of Christ, of which the second pleases me much more: because it belongs to the literal sense to be truer: the first, however, as I think, goes far away from the literal meaning: for that reason it does not fit with the parable, according to which example He admonished us to say that we are unprofitable servants. For a servant who serves a man, is profitable to his master, although not to himself: therefore the Lord was not thinking of the profit which comes to the Lord, but of the profit coming to the servants themselves, when He admonished us that we say that we are unprofitable servants. Therefore we are unprofitable to ourselves, because we merit nothing from the nature of our works, however good they be: just as a servant does not merit from his service

---

[1] Theophylact of Ohrid (1055-1107) was Archbishop of Bulgaria.
[2] *Enarratio in Evangelium S. Lucae* (PG 123, 987A-B).
[3] *In Lucae Evangelium Expositio*, lib. 5, c. 17, n. 27-29 (PL 92, 541D).

which he renders to his master: because he does what he is obliged to do by reason of his servitude.

Fourthly, they object to us, saying that if men merit eternal life though good works, by that very fact it would be allowed for them to put trust in their good works, and from them to hope for eternal life: he who accepts this would seem to be foolish, according to Solomon's judgment, saying, "He that trusteth in the Lord, shall be healed. He that trusteth in his own heart, is a fool" (Prov. 28, 25-26). And he is not merely foolish, but Jeremias also deems him to be subject of a curse, saying, "Lord: Cursed be the man that trusteth in man" (17, 5). And therefore David, fearing this mishap, said, "For I will not trust in my bow: neither shall my sword save me" (Ps. 43, 7). If it be not allowed to hope for eternal life from our works, but only from God's mercy, it is hence proved that we do not merit eternal life by our good works. For anyone would be able to hope for a reward from his merits.

To this objection we have already replied sufficiently above, in the section on "Confidence." For in that place we clearly showed from Holy Writ and from the testimonies of holy men that it is permitted to trust in one's works and from them to hope for eternal life: as long as one does not put all one's hope in them, but principally and mostly one may put confidence in Christ's merits and the Divine mercy. Therefore, to this place I send the reader: for from there he shall be able to take up many arms by which he may be able to fight strongly against the present heresy.

ORATIO

Prayer

Certain men attribute so much to prayer that they say that is alone suffices for possessing eternal life, even though they lack everything else, even Baptism. The author of this pestiferous heresy was a certain Adelphius of the Psallians, or Messalians, who is the same. This Adelphius (as *Historia Tripartita* relates[1]) was saying that no benefit comes from holy Baptism to those baptized, but only assiduous prayer drives out the in-dwelling devil... but when he has been driven out by assiduous prayer, the Holy Ghost was coming, giving both visible and sensible signs of His presence: and he said that then the body is freed from every impulse of the passions, and the soul is freed from bad will, such that for the future one nowise needs either to macerate the body by fasting or to bridle it by doctrine. He also was saying that he who impetrated these things by prayer, is not only freed from the passions of the body, but also foresees things to come, and perceives [the Holy Trinity[2]] with his eyes.

Now whether this error was common to all the Messalians, I am not certain, but I suspect it to be so. For in the *Historia Tripartita*, when discussing the heresy of the Messalians, it merely says that Flavian, Bishop of Antioch, when investigating this heresy went to a certain old man named Adelphius, whom he believed was infected with the heresy of the Messalians, so that he might have knowledge of the content of their doctrine. Now from this Adelphius the aforesaid bishop through flattery and certain pretenses extorted those things which we have just now related. Hence, I suppose that this was the opinion of all the Messalians.

There is no need to dispute against this heresy, because even though prayer is good and meritorious if made properly, still it is evident from Holy Writ that it alone does not suffice,

---

[1] Bk. 7, c. 11 (PL 69, 1078B-C). Cf. Theodoret, *Ecclesiastical History*, bk. 4, c. 10 (PG 82, 1143D-1146A).

[2] The author repeats "future things" here, but the *Ecclesiastical History*, which is his source, has instead, "the Holy Trinity."

since the Lord commanded many other things in the law besides prayer as being necessary. And above in the section on "Baptism" we proved against these Messalians, or Psallians, that Baptism is necessary. And in the section on "Fasting" we showed the strengths of fasting, and its necessity. From which things it is clearly proved that prayer alone is insufficient for attaining eternal life.

The **second heresy** teaches that one ought to never cease praying. It is evident that this heresy belongs to the Messalians, or Psallians. For Augustine says, "They pray so much that it seems incredible to those who hear this about them."[1] [He further says,] "In Greek, however, they are called Εὐχίται[2] because of their praying."[3] Guy does not mention this heresy in his *Summa de haeresibus*, nay, neither does he make any mention of the Messalians in that whole work.

Now to refute this heresy it is not necessary to sweat very much, because it is very clear that it is impossible for a man to pray always. For it is necessary to sleep, at which time no one can pray, because then there is no use of the mind, which is especially required in prayer. For there is no one, except Christ our Savior, who can truly say that which is found in the *Canticles*: "I sleep, and my heart watcheth" (5, 2). It is also necessary to eat and drink, and to employ some moderate labor to acquire these things, without being solicitous. It is also necessary to take care of one's family, because Blessed Paul, when speaking about widows, says: "If any widow have children, or grandchildren, let her learn first to govern her own house, and to make a return of duty to her parents: for this is acceptable before God... But if any man have not care of his own, and especially of those of his house, he hath denied the faith, and is worse than an infidel" (I Tim. 5, 4 & 8). And this is not only necessary for the laity, but also for ecclesiastics. For among the other things which the Apostle enumerates as necessary for someone to properly fulfill the office of a bishop, he adds this also, namely that he rule well his own house. "But if a man know not how to rule his own house," he says, "how shall he take care of the church of God?" (I Tim. 3, 5). But who does not see how much the care of a household impedes from prayer?

I do not speak about food and drink, because when these things are taken, there is no room left for prayer, especially vocal prayer, about which these Messalians (as I conjecture) speak. For other prayer which is formed in the depths of the heart, anyone can pray even when eating and drinking. For Moses prayed in this way, to whom when silent the Lord said: "Why criest thou to me?" (Ex. 14, 15). For he cried in his heart, although his mouth was silent. Thus, when someone eating or drinking, or doing anything else, thinks about God, for the love of Whom he does those things, then he truly prays. Wherefore Blessed Paul was admonishing the Corinthians, saying: "Therefore, whether you eat or drink, or whatsoever else you do, do all to the glory of God" (I Cor. 10, 31). And when writing to the Colossians he again says: "All whatsoever you do in word or in work, do all in the name of the Lord Jesus Christ, giving thanks to God and the Father by him" (3, 17). And in this way ought to be understood that which Paul says elsewhere: "Pray without ceasing" (I Thess. 5, 17). So that he is said to pray without ceasing who does everything that he does for God's glory. For otherwise, it is impossible to pray without ceasing. "Can we genuflect without ceasing, bow the body, lift the hands, form words, so that he do what Paul said, 'Pray without ceasing?'"[4]

But the Messalians object to us another passage, whereby they think to beset us. For our Savior in Luke says: "We ought always to pray, and not to faint" (18, 1). And from this passage the Massalians infer that one never ought to cease praying. Yet these words of Christ

---

[1] *De Haeresibus ad Quodvultdeum*, c. 57 (PL 42, 40).

[2] I.e. "praying folk."

[3] *Ibid.*

[4] Hervé de Bourg-Dieu, *Commentaria in Epistolas divi Pauli*, on I Thess. 5, 17.

support them not at all, because they ought not to be interpreted as they suppose. Augustine says that these words ought to be interpreted to mean, "that set times for prayer should not be missed on any day."[1] So that to Augustine it is the same thing to "pray always," and "pray without ceasing," as to pray every day. [Hervé de Bourg-Dieu[2]] in his *Commentaria in Epistolas divi Pauli* interprets Christ's words, and similarly those of Paul from the First Epistle to the Thessalonians, in the same way.[3] Yet Bede gives double exposition to these words, speaking thus: "Now who is able thus to pray always, and to be instant in prayers without failing and without intermission, so that one has time neither for eating or sleeping? Either then it ought to be said that he prays always, and without failing or intermission, who does not cease to beseech and praise the Lord by canonical hours according to the rite of ecclesiastical tradition by psalmodies and continual prayers. And this is what the Psalmist was saying, 'I will bless the Lord at all times, his praise shall be always in my mouth' (33, 2). Or certainly everything that the just man does and says according to God ought to be reckoned as prayer."[4]

But even though the expositions of these illustrious men please me, still those words can be understood otherwise and perhaps (certainly in my opinion) are comprehended better, namely that Christ and His Apostles used in those words a certain hyperbole for exaggerating the matter, and as also elsewhere in Holy Writ that manner of speech is often found: because (as Blessed Augustine says[5]) Sacred Scripture, which was written in the form of common speech, uses the same tropes and figures which the common manner of speaking uses. And so that the matter may be clearer, I will cite one or two examples from Holy Writ, in which this hyperbole is found. In the Acts of the Apostles, when that history is recounting the coming of the Holy Ghost, and wishing to signify the multitude of races and peoples which were then in Jerusalem, says: "Now there were dwelling at Jerusalem, Jews, devout men, out of every nation under heaven" (2, 5). Because unless a hyperbole be admitted here, it will be necessary to admit that at that time in Jerusalem there were Spaniards, Frenchmen, Englishmen, Scotts, Ethiopians, Sicilians, Balearicans, Sarmatians, and the other countless peoples, which Ninive, which was "a great city of three days' journey" (Jonas, 3, 3) could scarcely have contained, not to speak of Jerusalem, which was a small or middling city.

Similarly, when Christ was wanting to persuade us that alms ought to be given as secretly as possible and without any boasting, He said: "But when thou dost alms, let not thy left hand know what thy right hand doth" (Mt. 6, 3). But since the mind is the same in both hands, it cannot happen that the left hand would not know what the right hand does. But there is therein a certain hyperbole, or a certain exaggeration for commending the matter more. In this way likewise Christ, to commend to us frequency of prayer, said: "We ought always to pray" (Lk. 18, 1), making use of "always" as a kind of hyperbole. Paul used the same hyperbole, when saying: "Pray without ceasing" (I Thess. 5, 17). For otherwise it could not happen that we pray always and without ceasing, for whom it is necessary to eat, drink, sleep, to take care of a household, and to do many other things without which in this miserable life we could not

---

[1] *De Haeresibus ad Quodvultdeum*, c. 57 (PL 42, 40).

[2] The text attributes this book to Saint Anselm of Canterbury, but it is the production of Hervé of Bourg-Dieu.

[3] "But he who now wishes to cease to pray, does not desire to cease." (PL 181, 1383B). See also the words of Hervé, monk of Bourg-Dieu, in the text quoted shortly before.

[4] *In Evangelium S. Lucae*, bk. 5, c. 18 (PL 92, 550C).

[5] "Moreover, I would have learned men to know that the authors of our Scriptures use all those forms of expression which grammarians call by the Greek name tropes, and use them more freely and in greater variety than people who are unacquainted with the Scriptures, and have learned these figures of speech from other writings, can imagine or believe... for the speech of the vulgar makes use of them all" (*On Christian Doctrine*, bk. 3, c. 29, n. 40-41 (PL 34, 80-81)).

exist; some of which things lessen attention in prayer, others take it away completely. And there is nothing more we will dispute against this heresy.

There is a **third heresy**, which is diametrically opposed to these two preceding ones: because it teaches that prayer is completely useless, and of no efficacy. This heresy has many promoters, who although they do not proceed the same way, yet they all tend to the same end, that they belittle the efficacy of prayer, and completely enervate it. For Pelagius, Augustine bearing witness,[1] said that the prayers which the Church makes for unbelievers and other sinners that they be converted, or for the faithful that they persevere, are made in vain, because he said that the power of our free will suffices for all these things, and so it is not necessary to ask from God those things which we ourselves can attain. But the foundation of this heresy we have already completely overthrown above in the section on "Grace," in the first heresy. Hence, it is not necessary that we summon Pelagius to this contention. I decided merely to say this about the Pelagians, that these men are like the ancient giants, who (as Ecclesiasticus says) "did not obtain pardon for their sins"; hence they "were destroyed trusting to their own strength" (16, 8). There are others who lay a foundation no less pernicious, upon which they attempt to build this pestilential workshop. For Peter Abelard, John Wycliffe, John Hus, and Martin Luther say that everything happens by an absolute necessity, and all things cannot happen otherwise than they do. From this putrid spring here gushes forth a no less foul rivulet, namely prayers which are sent to God are superfluous and useless; because if everything happens by an absolute necessity, one prays to God in vain for something, which, if it is going to happen even if one does not pray, it will happen; and if it is not going to happen, even if one does pray, it will never happen. Thus, for this reason many of the Lutherans in their camps completely rejected prayer as entirely useless. Yet Luther approves of prayer, in which matter he is nowise consistent with himself, since elsewhere he says that everything happens by an absolute necessity.[2]

Against this heresy there are so many testimonies of Sacred Scripture, and so clear, that it is astounding that a man even moderately versed in Holy Writ, would have fallen into it, unless such a man is one who wishes to detract from Holy Writ. What is very clear before all else, is that the Teacher of truth Himself taught us to pray. For when He said that much-speaking is not necessary in prayer, He afterwards added the way in which we ought to pray, saying: "Thus therefore shall you pray: Our Father who art in heaven, hallowed be thy name. Thy kingdom come…" (Mt. 6, 9-10). If prayer is something useless, then Christ would have taught us the way by which we ought to pray for no reason. Not merely did He teach us by His words to pray, but also by His actions; because He Himself prayed repeatedly, nay so that I may speak more truly, His whole life was a certain perpetual prayer. For having taken up Peter, James and his brother John, He went up into the mountain to pray, and it happened that while He prayed His countenance was changed. And when His death drew near, dreading its bitterness, "He fell upon his face, praying, and saying: My Father, if it be possible, let this chalice pass from me" (Mt. 26, 39). And those who were waiting for the coming of the Holy Ghost, "were persevering with one mind in prayer" (Acts. 1, 14). How then will prayer be reckoned useless, which prepares the way for the Holy Ghost, so that He might deign to come to us? When Christ our Savior cast out a devil from the body of a certain man, which His disciples previously could not cast out, He said to His disciples: "This kind is not cast out but by

---

[1] *De Haeresibus ad Quodvultdeum*, c. 88 (PL 42, 48).
[2] "Because for no one is it at hand to think the least thing of good or evil, but everything… happens by an absolute necessity." (*Assertio omnium articulorum* (WA 7, 146, lns. 6–8)). When Luther translated the *Assertio* into German as *Grund und Ursach aller Artikel* [*Defense and Explanation of All the Articles*] in March 1521, his rejection of free will did not contain any reference to the idea of absolute necessity. Cf. WA 7, 446-451.

prayer and fasting" (Mt. 17, 20). Certainly, the power is great which avails to cast out devils. Furthermore, when Paul and Silas, praying earnestly in prison, praised God, "Suddenly there was a great earthquake, so that the foundations of the prison were shaken" (Acts 16, 26).

Again, Blessed James in his canonical epistle enumerates many strengths of prayer. "Is any of you sad? Let him pray. Is he cheerful in mind? Let him sing" (5, 13). Notice that it is for dispelling sadness of the mind. Afterwards he adds: "Is any man sick among you? Let him bring in the priests of the church, and let them pray over him, anointing him with oil in the name of the Lord. And the prayer of faith shall save the sick man" (v. 14-15). Notice how prayer helps for gaining well-being of the body. But hear now what he says about the well-being of the soul: "Confess therefore your sins one to another," he says, "and pray one for another, that you may be saved. For the continual prayer of a just man availeth much." (v. 16). Let the impudent heretics now be ashamed to detract prayer, saying that is avails nothing, which James the Apostle asserts avails much. And so that he may reinforce his statement, he confirms it with the testimony and example of Elias the Prophet, saying: "Elias was a man passible like unto us: and with prayer he prayed that it might not rain upon the earth, and it rained not for three years and six months. And he prayed again: and the heaven gave rain, and the earth brought forth her fruit" (v. 17-18). You now see how great is the power of prayer, which holds back the rains within the sky, and avails to bring them down from thence. Finally, so that we may summarize the power of prayer in a few words, Christ our Savior says: "Whatsoever you shall ask in prayer, believing, you shall receive" (Mt. 21, 22). Christ makes so much of prayer that if it shall be accompanied by faith, He says that it suffices for impetrating everything that we ask: and heretics are not afraid to say that it is of no importance.

After these very clear testimonies there is a definition of the Church about this matter. For the Fourth Synod of Toledo, in the ninth chapter of its decrees, when discussing the Lord's Prayer, after it commanded that it be said each day by every priest, when explaining the power of that prayer, says: "Thus 'this prayer certainly takes away the very small sins of daily life. It takes away also those which at one time made the life of the believer very wicked, but which, now that he is changed for the better by repentance, he has given up.'[1] Therefore as Christ commanded, so the Apostle has instructed. And just as the ecclesiastical Doctors instituted, because we daily sin either by thought or by word, so we ought to daily pour out this prayer in God's sight. Therefore, whosoever of the priests or lower clergy daily omits this Lord's Prayer, either in public or in private, having been judged for his pride is deprived of the honor of his order."[2] And the [Second] Synod of Milevum in the eighth canon of its decrees against Pelagius, says the following: "It has likewise been decided that whoever wishes that the words themselves of the Lord's prayer, where we say: 'Forgive us our debts' (Mt. 6, 12) be said by the saints so as to be spoken humbly, not truthfully, let him be anathema. For who would tolerate one praying and lying, not to men, but to the Lord Himself, who says with his lips that he wishes to be forgiven, and in his heart holds that he does not have debts to be forgiven?"[3] From definition of which council we conclude two things. One is that all men, as long as we are in this life, are subject to sins. The other is that in regard to this, so that they may be forgiven, the Lord's prayer is useful, in which it is said: "Forgive us our debts."

The **fourth heresy** asserts that prayers which are specially applied to one person, do not benefit him more than if they were made generally for all. The author of this heresy is John Wycliffe, saying that one ought not to pray for a particular person, because (as he says) prayer for one person alone does not benefit him more than others. God Himself condemns

---

[1] St. Augustine, *Enchiridion*, c. 71 (PL 40, 265-266).

[2] *False Decretals of the Pseudo-Isidore* (PL 130, 467D-468A). *Concilia Hispaniae*, c. 10 (PL 84, 370A).

[3] Dz. 108.

this heresy with His own mouth, Who commanded Eliphaz the Themanite to ask Job that he pray to God for him, and for his other two friends, who had offended God in that they had reprehended Job so bitterly. And "The Lord," as Scripture testifies, "was turned at the penance of Job, when he prayed for his friends" (42, 10). Furthermore, when Peter the Apostle was in prison, "Prayer was made without ceasing by the church unto God for him" (Acts 12, 5), and at length the prayer of the Church benefitted Peter, because "the Lord hath sent his angel, and hath delivered me out of the hand of Herod, and from all the expectation of the people of the Jews" (v. 11). And nevertheless, that prayer did not benefit everyone else who had been put into prison. Thus, special prayer gives more benefit to the one for whom it is made, than for others. Again, Blessed Paul when writing to the Thessalonians says that he made prayer for them. "We give thanks," he says, "to God always for you all; making a remembrance of you in our prayers without ceasing" (I Thess. 1, 2). If prayers equally benefit all, for what purpose did Paul mention that he made a remembrance of the Thessalonians in his prayers? Next, Paul himself often exhorts, asks for, commands that special prayers be made both for himself, and for others. "I beseech you therefore, brethren, through our Lord Jesus Christ, and by the charity of the Holy Ghost, that you help me in your prayers for me to God" (Rom. 15, 30). And elsewhere: "That he will yet also deliver us, you helping withal in prayer for us" (II Cor. 1, 10-11). And again: "Be instant in prayer; watching in it with thanksgiving: praying withal for us also, that God may open unto us a door of speech to speak the mystery of Christ" (Col. 4, 2-3). And in another place: "Pray for us, that the word of God may run, and may be glorified" (II Thess. 3, 1). From these last two testimonies that custom originated in the whole Catholic Church of invoking the Virgin Mother of God at the beginning of any kind of preaching of God's word, so that she would deign to ask God to open to the preacher the door for speaking, and to the others for hearing the mystery of Christ. For no reason Paul asks so many times for prayers for himself, if the prayers of all men could equally benefit him.

And he also admonishes that special prayers be made for others, saying: "I desire therefore, first of all, that supplications, prayers, intercessions, and thanksgivings be made for all men: for kings, and for all that are in high station: that we may lead a quiet and a peaceable life in all piety" (I Tim. 2, 1-2). Hence preachers of God's word, imitating Paul in this regard, exhort the people in their preaching to offer special prayers to God for the king and other rulers and ecclesiastical prelates, so that the small boat, which is thrown about by the waves in this vast and spacious sea, may convey them to the chosen port.

Finally, among the forty-five articles of John Wycliffe condemned at the Council of Constance in the eighth session here is the nineteenth, which says the following: "Special prayers applied to one person by prelates or religious are not of more benefit to that person than general (prayers), all other things being equal."[1] Which article along with the others of the same Wycliffe was condemned with one *latae sententiae* [excommunication] upon them all.

ORDO SACRAMENTUM

Sacrament of Holy Orders

There is scarcely one or two Sacraments which Luther did not detract. Some of them he denies are Sacraments; others he says do not confer grace; others, moreover, he holds in slight esteem. Now he so treats Orders that he tries to completely remove it from the Church. For he says that Orders neither is a Sacrament, nor is there any inequality in it, so that one Order is greater than another both in dignity and power; but all Christians, he says, have

---

[1] Dz. 599.

the same rank. It is necessary to successively overcome three things. Firstly, then, Luther says that Christ's Church has no knowledge of the Sacrament of Orders. For according to him the Sacrament of Orders is nothing other than a certain rite of choosing a preacher in the Church; wherefore he [secondly] asserts the he who does not preach, is not a priest, except equivocally; as for instance, a picture of a man is a man. Finally, he says the Orders themselves are a figment of the imagination, nothing to those who understand about ecclesiastical realities or the Sacraments.

Firstly then, I wish to show that in the transmission of Orders grace is conferred; then I will show from Holy Writ that there is a sensible sign of this thing. From which two things it is concluded that Orders is a Sacrament. That grace is conferred to the one receiving Holy Orders is shown by that which Paul writes to Timothy, saying: "Neglect not," he says, "the grace that is in thee, which was given thee by prophesy, with imposition of the hands of the priesthood" (I Tim. 4, 14). By which words Paul clearly enough shows that Timothy received grace when he was promoted to the rank of the priesthood. And in the Second Epistle which he wrote to the same Timothy, he gives testimony in favor of this case in this way: "I admonish thee, that thou stir up the grace of God which is in thee, by the imposition of my hands" (1, 6). Moreover, from the very ancient rite of the Church coming forth from the Apostles it has always been observed that both the one ordaining and the one ordained, especially in Holy Orders, comes to Orders fasting. And Scripture itself testifies to this, which relates that the Apostles were fasting and praying when they imposed hands upon Paul and Barnabas, whom they sent to preach the Gospel by the command of the Holy Ghost.[1] If in the transmission of Orders no grace would be infused, there was no need for such preparation. But because the Apostles certainly believed that the grace of the Holy Ghost is conferred to those who were promoted to Sacred Orders, hence they fasted and prayed, so that in this way they would be prepared to receive the grace of the Holy Ghost; just as formerly when they were waiting for the coming of the Holy Ghost, "they were persevering with one mind in prayer" (Acts 1, 14).

And Pope Leo I assigns this reason for fasting, whose words I will cite below, because they also are of service for another point. And [Pseudo-] Blessed Augustine in his book, *Questions on the Old and New Testaments*, in question ninety-three (provided this book is Augustine's),[2] also teaches this very clearly. But because above in the section on "Melchisedech" we clearly proved that that word is not Augustine's, hence I do not consider it to be worthwhile to cite those words. Yet if someone is convinced that this book is Augustine's, I have indicated the place to him in which he may find that opinion.

See, therefore, that we have shown that grace is conferred in the bestowal of Orders; now it is necessary that we show in such bestowal there is an exterior sensible sign. Now those words of Paul from his epistles to Timothy, which we have just now cited, show this very clearly, because from them it is evident that he who was ordaining someone, imposed hands upon him, by which imposition of hands he was conferring the Order to the other man, which is also gathered from many other passages of Scripture. For Paul when admonishing Timothy not to lightly promote anyone to the priesthood, unless he diligently examine the merit of the person, says the following: "Impose not hands lightly upon any man" (I Tim. 5, 22). And when the Apostles, after having chosen seven men from the multitude of disciples, made deacons, "praying," as the Apostolic history says, "they imposed hands upon them" (Acts 6, 6). Notice again when the Apostles promote to the deaconate, they do so praying, just as when they impose hands upon Paul and Barnabas, namely because grace was conferred in that pro-

---

[1] Cf. Acts 13, 2-3.
[2] PL 35, 2213-2386. For many years, the *Questions on the Old and New Testaments* were thought to have been written by Augustine of Hippo and were placed among his works. Scholars have long since determined that it was not written by Augustine.

ORDO SACRAMENTUM

motion. The Fourth Synod of Carthage decreed that the bishop, priest and deacon ought to be ordained by the imposition of hands.[1] And from this sign, which the Apostles used, one can also be persuaded that grace is conferred in the reception of Orders: because it is not likely that hands were imposed by the Apostles on those ordained so that they might touch the body with a useless contact, and the souls would not have benefited by a spiritual grace. For it was no particular benefit to impose hands on the body, if from this imposition of hands the soul should benefit nothing. If therefore grace is conferred in the reception of Orders, and under some sensible sign, it is thence proved that Orders is a Sacrament.

And so that we may show that this is not a recent invention of scholastic theologians, I will cite the testimonies of a number of ancient Doctors. Pope Leo I, a man illustrious for holiness as well as doctrine, in the nineth epistle which is to Dioscorus, the Bishop of Alexandria, when saying that Orders ought to be conferred and received by those fasting, says the following: "For besides the weight of custom which we know rests upon the Apostles' teaching, Holy Writ also makes this clear, because when the Apostles sent Paul and Barnabas at the bidding of the Holy Ghost to preach the Gospel to the nations, they laid hands on them fasting and praying: that we may know with what devoutness both giver and receiver must be on their guard lest so blessed a Sacrament should seem to be carelessly performed."[2] From which words we gather two things, namely that Orders is a Sacrament, and that in its bestowal grace is conferred, because the reason why he says that fasting and prayer preceded, is so that the blessing which in this Sacrament is conferred may be worthily received.

Augustine, when speaking about the same Baptism and Orders, says the following: "For each of them is a Sacrament, and both are given to a man by some consecration; the one, when he is baptized; the other when he is ordained. And so it is not lawful to repeat either of them in the Catholic Church... Injury must not be done to either Sacrament."[3] And he added about the Sacrament of Orders: "Just as he who does not have it rightly, if he withdraws from unity, but yet has it, and therefore when he returns into unity it is not given to him again, so also he does not give it rightly if he withdraws from unity and yet he gives it."[4] And again, returning to both, he adds: "Therefore they do not cease to be Sacraments of Christ and the Church, merely because they are unlawfully used, not only by heretics, but by all kinds of wicked and impious persons. These, indeed, ought to be corrected and punished, but the Sacraments should be acknowledged and revered."[5] In which words not [merely] once does he confess that Orders is a Sacrament. I now think that anyone sees with what brazen audacity Luther reveled that Christ's Church has no knowledge of the Sacrament of Orders, and that it is its new invention, when from Augustine and Pope Leo it is clearly evident that it is a Sacrament. For he cannot drive away Augustine or Leo from Christ's Church, whom the same Church reckoned to be venerated as holy men: nor will he say that they are recent theologians, as he is accustomed to do, unless he considers himself to be such a one that for him "a thousand years are as yesterday, which is past" (Ps. 89, 4).

Therefore, this only remains for us to prove, namely that we show that not all Orders are equal among themselves, but there are different grades within this Sacrament, such that one Order is greater than another in dignity and power. And certainly whoever shall consider with due attention those things which were ordained in the Old Mosaic Law, concerning the tabernacle, the altar, the priests, and other ministers serving the altar: will easily from thence know,

---

[1] Canons 1-4 (PL 84, 199-200).

[2] C. 1 (PL 54, 625B-626A).

[3] *Answer to the Letter of Parmenian*, bk. 2, n. 28 & 30 (PL 43, 70 & 72).

[4] *On Baptism, Against the Donatists*, bk. 1, c. 1, n. 2 (PL 43, 107). *Answer to the Letter of Parmenian*, bk. 2, n. 30 (PL 43, 72).

[5] *On Baptism, Against the Donatists*, bk. 3, c. 10, n. 13 (PL 43, 144).

as it were, the body from its shadow, that various orders ought to be given in the Church, which perform different offices in the ministry of the altar. "For the law," as Paul says, "had a shadow of the good things to come" (Heb. 10, 1). Thus, from the shadow to its body, from the figure to the truth of the reality corresponding to it, will be a very good and most efficacious argument. For Paul used this sort of argumentation, when wishing to prove that it is licit for those who preach the Gospel, to live from the Gospel: because he who worked in that old tabernacle, was living from the tabernacle, and he who served the altar, partook of the altar.[1] Therefore, Paul argues there from shadow and figure to the body and truth.

Since then this kind of argumentation is so efficacious, according to Paul, we manifestly will prove by it that there are many orders in the Catholic Church, and various grades of those who minister at the altar. Because for the ministry of that old tabernacle various orders and diverse grades were instituted by God, such that one was the pontiff or high priest, others were lesser priests, others Levites, who even though they were not priests, still ministered to the altar. The things which pertain to the high priest, and those which relate to the lower priests, are described in Exodus where some offices and some vestments are specified for the high priest, and others for the lower priests.[2] Upon the head of Aaron, and of any other high priest, the oil of holy unction was poured out. The sons of Aaron, the lesser priests and their successors, were not anointed with holy oil on the head, but only on their hands. Their tunics were linen, but the vestments of the high priest were made of gold, hyacinth, purple and precious gems. Regarding the rite of consecration of the Levitical order, it is found in the book of [Numbers[3]], in which although one rite of consecration for all the Levites is described, still different offices were distributed among them.[4] For they are distributed among the three classes under their heads and leaders, and a place is assigned to each one in the watches and ministry, according to the command of the priests.

If this order was so great, and so distinct in that old figure, it is necessary that we concede that there is a diverse order clearly distinct, of those who ought to minister at the altar where they now consecrate the Eucharist. Unless perhaps we wish to make the Catholic Church a very confused Babylon in which there is no order, even though it is very clearly evident that the old synagogue, which is a type of it, was like a very noble city, very orderly arranged. But if someone is so impious and brazen that he does not fear to admit it, he certainly is forced to diminish either the Divine wisdom, Divine power, or ultimately, the Divine goodness: namely because he is force to confess that God either did not know, or could not, or ultimately did not want to form the Church just as He previously foreshadows and delineates it in that ancient people. Certainly since the sacrifice which is now offered by the priests of the Church is much more excellent than all the sacrifices of the Old Law, it is necessary that greater honor be given to it, and also a greater order in its ministry be kept, and more orders of ministers for its administration be deputed.

I omit here the minor Orders, because even though not little mention is made of them in the ancient authors, nevertheless many theologians do not admit the minor orders within the number of the Sacraments; wherefore nor also are they called sacred Orders; nay concerning the subdiaconate, Hugh of St. Victor reckons that it is not a Sacrament, although others place it within the Sacraments, within the distinctions of a Sacrament.[5] We spoke about this matter

---

[1] Cf. I Cor. 9, 13.

[2] Cf. Ex. 28.

[3] The text here cites the book of Leviticus, but the ordination rite described in Lev. 8 pertains to priestly ordinations.

[4] Cf. Num. 8, 5-22.

[5] "The sacred canons define that no one is to be elected as bishop except one who has first lived religiously in the sacred orders. Now they decree that only the diaconate and the presbyterate are to be

in some measure about in the section on "Bishops": in which place we showed that a bishop from Christ's institution is greater in dignity and power than a simple priest.

The Apostolic history relates that deacons were ordained by the Apostles.[1] What is more, concerning the other orders, it is evident that their offices and names existed at the time of the Apostles. For Blessed Ignatius, a disciple of John the Evangelist, in his epistle to the Trallians extols the dignity of bishops, priests and deacons.[2] And in the [Pseudo-] epistle to the Antiochians he conveys these words: "I salute the holy presbytery. I salute the sacred deacons, and that person most dear to me, whom may I behold, through the Holy Ghost, occupying my place when I shall attain to Christ. My soul be in place of his. I salute the subdeacons, the readers, the singers, the doorkeepers, the laborers, the exorcists, the confessors."[3] The *Canons of the Apostles* seem also to suggest a distinction between the bishop and priest, the deacon, subdeacon, lector and cantor. This appears in canons forty-two and forty-three.[4] But the *Apostolic Canons* promulgated by Clement, are of such great authority, that Blessed Damascene inserted them into the list of canonical books of Sacred Scripture.[5]

Therefore, so that we may now put an end to this matter, it will be necessary to bring forth the testimony of the Fourth Synod of Carthage,[6] which delineates all the grade of Orders, and pronounces the manner whereby their ordination ought to be done. For in the first and second chapters of its decrees it assigns the manner whereby the bishop ought to be ordained,[7] in the third chapter it treats about the ordination of the priest;[8] in chapter four, about the ordination

---

called sacred Orders, because the primitive Church is described as having only these three, and only of these have we the precepts of the Apostle." (*On the Sacraments of the Christian Faith*, bk. 2, part 3, c. 13 (PL 176, 430A)).

[1] Cf. Acts 6, 3-6.

[2] "In like manner, let all reverence the deacons as an appointment of Jesus Christ, and the bishop as Jesus Christ, who is the Son of the Father, and the presbyters as the Sanhedrin of God, and assembly of the Apostles." (C. 3 (PG 5, 677C)).

[3] C. 12 (PG 5, 907A).

[4] "Canon 42: If a bishop or presbyter, or deacon, is addicted to dice or drinking, let him either give it over, or be deposed"; "Canon 43: If a subdeacon, reader, or singer, commits the same things, let him either give over, or be excommunicated. So also laymen" (PG 137, 126C).

[5] A collection eighty-five canons was included in Book VIII of the *Apostolic Constitutions*, the whole being attributed to St. Clement. The Council in Trullo (692), while rejecting the *Constitutions*, retained and approved the Canons. The *Apostolic Canons*, Saint John Damascene notwithstanding, were never generally considered to belong to the canon of Scripture.

[6] The IV Synod of Carthage was held on Nov. 8, 398, under Aurelius of Carthage, at the head of two hundred and fourteen or two hundred and fifteen bishops, including St. Augustine. One hundred and four canons were published, chiefly relating to the life and conduct of the clergy. These canons later became known as the *Statuta ecclesiae antiqua*, which were apparently composed in Gaul in the late fifth century and then circulated as the product not of a Gallic council, but of an African one. (Cf. "The 'Second Synod of Arles' and the Spirit of Compilation and Codification in Late Roman Gaul," *Journal of Early Christian Studies*, vol. 5, n. 4 (1997), p. 548.

[7] "Canon 1: He who is to be ordained a bishop, must previously be examined in order to ascertain whether he is prudent by nature, docile, temperate in his manner, sober, chaste, affable to the humble, merciful, learned, instructed in the law of the Lord, cautious in the interpretation of Scriptures" etc. (PL 84, 199B-200B). "Canon 2: When a bishop is ordained, let two bishops place and hold the Gospels book on his neck, and while the blessing is pronounced over him, let the other bishops present touch his head with their hands" (*Ancient Statutes of the Church* in Dz. 150).

[8] "When a priest is ordained, while the bishop is blessing [him] and holding his hands over his head, let all the priests also, who are present, hold their hands close to the hands of the bishop above his head" (Dz. 151).

of the deacon;[1] in chapter five, about the ordination of the subdeacon;[2] in chapter six, about the ordination of the acolyte;[3] in chapter seven, about the ordination of the exorcist;[4] in the eighth chapter, about the ordination of the lector;[5] in the nineth chapter, about the ordination of the porter;[6] I have omitted to cite the words of all those decrees for the sake of avoiding prolixity, thinking it to be enough to point out the place to the reader. He who desires to know more about this matter, let him read Hugh of Saint Victor, that renowned Doctor who having an authority not to be scorned treats of each order, explaining the power and ordination of them all.[7]

From these things which we have said, the error of the Greeks and Waldensians is left refuted. For the Waldensians (as Guy [the Carmelite] accuses them[8]) said that there are three orders in the Church, namely the diaconate, the priesthood, and the episcopate. But Aeneas Sylvius in the book, *De origine Bohemorum*, when enumerating the errors of the Waldensians, never mentions this error, nay he attributes another to them, which seems to be somewhat diametrically opposite to this. For he says that they think that a bishop is not either by dignity or power superior to any priest.[9] Concerning which matter we have disputed in the section on "Bishops." The Greeks, according to the same Guy, besides the sacred Orders admit none of the minor Orders beside lector: the others, however, namely porter, exorcist, and acolyte, they say ought not to be numbered among the Orders.[10] Nevertheless, we have already shown that their names and offices existed in the Church from the time of the Apostles, and the manner of ordination was stated in the [IV] Council [of Carthage]: wherefore there is nothing more to dispute about this matter. All those things which we will say below in the section on the "Priesthood," in the first heresy militate combat against this heresy.

---

[1] "When a deacon is ordained, the bishop only, who pronounces the benediction over him, shall lay his hand upon his head; because he is not consecrated to the office of the priesthood, but to the ministry, or inferior services of the Church" (Dz. 152).

[2] "When a subdeacon is ordained, because he does not receive an imposition of hands, he receives from the hand of the bishop an empty paten and chalice, but from the archdeacon, a cruet with water, a basin and hand-towel" (Dz. 153.).

[3] "When an acolyte is ordained the bishop shall inform him how he is to behave himself in his office: and he shall receive a candlestick with a taper in it, from the archdeacon, that he may understand that he is appointed to light the candles of the church. He shall also receive an empty cruet to furnish wine for the Eucharist of the Blood of Christ" (Dz. 154).

[4] "When an exorcist is ordained, he shall receive at the hands of the bishop a book, wherein the forms of exorcising are written, the bishop saying, Receive thou these and commit them to memory, and have thou power to lay hands upon the energumens, whether they be baptized or only catechumens" (Dz. 155).

[5] "When a lector is ordained, let the bishop speak a word concerning him to the people, pointing out his faith, his life, and his ability. After this, while the people look on, let him hand him the book, from which he is about to read, saying to him: Take this book, and be thou a reader of the word of God, which office if thou fulfill faithfully and profitably, thou shalt have part with those that minister in the word of God" (Dz. 156).

[6] "When a porter is ordained, after he has been instructed by the archdeacon as to how he ought to live in the house of God, at the suggestion of the archdeacon let the bishop hand him the keys of the church from the altar, saying: So act as about to render an account of those things which are kept under these keys" (Dz. 157).

[7] *On the Sacraments of the Christian Faith*, bk. 2, part 3 (PL 176, 421B ff.).

[8] *Summa de haeresibus*, fol. 85r-86r, c. 14.

[9] C. 35.

[10] *Summa de haeresibus*, fol. 26r, c. 19.

PAPA

Pope

Luther, who has been so many times thrown to the ground by us, having heard just the name of the pope recovers his strength, so that he can fight with us once more about this matter. For he has imbibed so much hatred for the pope, that even if he were to be reduced to ashes, he would come back to life to harass the pope. For there is one goal of all his writings, namely to hurl down the pope from his throne, deprive him of that power which he received from God on earth: and to accomplish this, he leaves nothing untried; there is no stone he does not move. For the sake of this end alone he undertakes to overthrow the whole house of the Church. Now anyone will surmise that he acted out of hatred of the pope, and not out of zeal, if he shall fully know the series of things done by him. For when this Luther had tried to teach some things foreign to the true faith, he was admonished about this matter by Leo X, who then presided over the universal Church. When the same Luther disdained to obey that admonition, Leo X, as a good shepherd, excommunicated this Luther, and as a corrupt sheep he was cast out of the flock of the Church, lest he infect the rest of the sheep coming into contact with him. As a consequence of this affair, Luther, who had previously approved of the primacy of Peter and his successors, and had taught this in published books, after this excommunication inflicted upon him, detracted the papacy to such an extent that he was not content to diminish its power, but he also inflicted upon it very bitter reproaches, and spoke ill of it with atrocious insults. For he says that the "Supremacy of the Pope [*pontificium*] is but a vain name, and is effectually nothing but the kingdom of Babylon, and the power of Nemrod the mighty hunter"[1]: because he says that by mere tyranny it happened that the pope was exalted over the other bishops.[2] Thus it is permitted to infer from this by what spirit Luther is led, who is ruled more by emotion than by reason in treating the Catholic faith.

Nevertheless, the first author of this error was not Luther. For the infamous old serpent firstly persuaded the Greeks of this error, who were separated from the unity of the Church on account of the errors of Nestorius, Dioscorus, and Eutyches: because Nestorius was condemned at the Council of Ephesus, while Dioscorus and Eutyches at the Council of Chalcedon. For

---

[1] Henry VIII, *The Defense of the Seven Sacraments*, p. 198. "We need pay no attention to the masks of these masqueraders when they distinguish between the power of the keys and the use of the keys, a distinction they feign by their own temerity. Next, according to the custom they do very wrongly when begging the question. For when it is incumbent to them to prove that their power is different from that of the common power of the whole Church, they rush on as if this were already demonstrated, and then add this fictitious distinction that the power of the keys belongs to the Church, their use however, to the bishops [*pontificum*]. These things are worthless, and fall down by themselves. Christ here gives the power and the use of the keys to each Christian, when he says, 'Let him be to thee as the heathen' (Mt. 18, 17). For who is that 'thee' to whom Christ refers when he says, 'let him be to thee'? The pope? Indeed, he refers to each and every Christian." (Luther, *Concerning the Ministry* (*De Instituendis*), WA, vol. 12, p. 183-184). "The kingdom of Babylon, and the power of Nemrod the mighty hunter" *Babylonian Captivity of the Church*, prelude (*Babylonian Captivity* (WA, vol. 6, p. 498, lns. 5-6)).

[2] "For first, he denied the pope's supremacy to be of Divine right: but now, (contrary to himself) he affirms it to be of neither of them; but that the papacy, by mere force has assumed, and usurped tyranny. Formerly he was of the opinion, that power was given to the Roman pontiff over the universal Church by human consent, and for the public good: and so much was he of that opinion, that he detested the schism of the Bohemians, who denied any obedience to the See of Rome; saying, 'That they sinned damnably who did not obey the Pope': having written these things so little time before, he now embraces what then he detested" (Henry VIII, *The Defense of the Seven Sacraments*, p. 200).

the same reason the Armenians withdrew themselves from the unity of the Church, namely because they disdained to accept the decrees of the Council of Chalcedon, and from this time began to deny obedience to the Roman pontiff until the time of Eugene IV, at which time the Council of Florence was celebrated, at which the Greeks and Armenians attended, after a long disputation which was held with the Latins about this matter, finally fully acknowledging the truth, they submitted themselves to the Roman Church.

After the Greeks came the wicked and foolish Waldensians, no less enemies of all the bishops than the Greeks and Armenians had been to the Roman pontiff. For these Waldensians teach that all priests are equal, and one is not superior in authority over another. A certain Marsilius of Padua consented in this regard to the Waldensians. Concerning John Wycliffe and John Hus there is no need to speak, because the former seem to have sworn to the words of the Waldensians, and the latter to the words of Wycliffe. Therefore, the common error of all these men now long buried, Luther called back from Hell in this age of ours, so that he could teach in an easier way the heresies which he had concocted. For there is no other way more open to introducing heresies than if you shall have withdrawn the primacy of Peter from the Church. Wherefore it is necessary to apply all our strength to this work, so that we may clearly make known the primacy of the supreme pontiff, lest a way may be open to the heretics for introducing their heresies.

There is a clear testimony for supporting this point, that which the Lord says to Peter: "That thou art Peter; and upon this rock I will build my church, and the gates of Hell shall not prevail against it. And I will give to thee the keys of the kingdom of heaven. And whatsoever thou shalt bind upon earth, it shall be bound also in heaven: and whatsoever thou shalt loose upon earth, it shall be loosed also in heaven" (Mt. 16, 18-19). In which words there are many things which are seen to manifestly teach Peter's primacy.

Firstly, the fact that Simon's name having been changed, He called him by the name of Peter, which thing could not happen without a great mystery. For God never bestowed a new name to anyone to whom He had not given great favors. For so in the Old Testament a new name was given by God to Abraham and Sara, whom he would make into a "great nation" (Gen. 17, 20), and from whom Christ was to be generated according to the flesh. In this way also Jacob, because he had been "strong against God" (Gen. 32, 28), having changed the name of Jacob, was called Israel. And so that we may go on to the New Testament: Christ called James of Zebedee and his brother John "Boanerges," that is, "the sons of thunder" (Mk. 3, 17). Now the Gospel account itself teaches that these two brothers were raised up higher than the other Apostles, after Peter. For He took up those two along with Peter as witnesses of His glorious transfiguration.[1] He permitted them alone to enter the house of Jairus, the ruler of the synagogue, when He wished to raise up his daughter.[2] And when, His Passion being at hand, He prayed, He also took up these men with Him[3]: so that perhaps from thence we could infer that it was not without cause that He had given them new names. Therefore, since a new name was imposed by God upon Peter, a great future mystery is designated in it: especially if anyone averts well to what sort of name was given to him. For the name Peter (*Petrus*) seems to have been derived from rock (*petra*). But since Christ, according to Paul, will be called a rock,[4] it is thence proved that such a name was given to Peter which would be very similar to Christ's name, and took its derivation from the name of Christ: so that perhaps by this reasoning we might be instructed that Peter would dwell on earth in Christ's place, Whose name we know that he then received.

---

[1] Cf. Mt. 17, 1.

[2] Cf. Lk. 8, 51.

[3] Cf. Mt. 26, 37.

[4] Cf. I Cor. 10, 4.

Secondly, in that passage of Matthew cited above, it is necessary to notice what follows. For He afterwards called the same Peter the rock upon which the Church would be founded. "That thou art Peter," He says, "and upon this rock I will build my church." Consider then what sort of person Peter is going to be, upon whom the Church is promised to be built. For so Theophylactus says when expounding those words of Christ: "The Lord gives Peter a great reward, that the Church will be built on him."[1] By which words he shows clearly enough that Peter is the rock upon which God had decided to found His Church. Jerome also expounds in the same way.[2] Hilary interprets in the same way.[3] Although Erasmus, having attempted to distort the words of this man, added these words in the margin, "Faith is the foundation of the Church."[4] By which words he wished Hilary to be interpreted, as though Hilary thought that faith is the foundation and the rock, but not Peter. Hilary, nevertheless, very clearly speaks of Peter, as it is easy to see. Chrysostom thinks likewise.[5] Augustine often expounds this passage in a similar manner, especially in the book, *Contra epistolam Donati*,[6] and [Pseudo] Augustine likewise in the twenty-sixth sermon on the Saints.[7] In the same way Leo [I] expounds that passage in the sermon delivered on the anniversary of his elevation to the pontificate.[8] Blessed Gregory [the Great] subscribes to all these things.[9] I omit to cite the words of all these holy men for the sake of avoiding prolixity. Tertullian also thinks the same thing in his book, *Prescription against Heretics*, whose words we will subjoin below.

The third thing that deserves consideration in those words of Christ said to Peter is that to Peter by name alone did Christ promise the keys of the kingdom of the heavens (*coelorum*):

---

[1] *Explanation of the Gospel of Matthew* (PG 123, 319A).

[2] "'Upon this rock' the Lord founded the Church; from this rock, also, the Apostle was allotted his name" (*Commentary on Matthew*, bk. 1, on Mt. 7, 26 (PL 26, 50A)).

[3] "O in this bestowing of a new name is a happy foundation of the Church, and a rock worthy of that building, which should break up the laws of Hell, burst the gates of Tartarus, and all the shackles of death" (PL 9, 1010A).

[4] *Éditions anciennes d›Érasme* (Mons (Belgium), Centre universitaire de l'État, 1967), p. 42. The side note of Erasmus' annotation on Matthew 16, 18 (*Quia tu es*) has 'The Church is not founded on Peter' (*In novum Testamentum... annotationes*, p. 68). The Spanish Inquisitors ordered this to be expunged from Erasmus. "[St. Robert] Bellarmine saw and justly reprehended this error of Erasmus" (PL 9, 1009C). Cf. *De Romano Pontifice*, bk. 1, c. 10 (*Disputationes Roberti Bellarmino... de controversiis Christianae* (Ingolstadt, Sartorius, 1588), vol. 1, p. 643).

[5] "And I say unto you, 'Thou art Peter, and upon this rock will I build my Church'; that is, on the faith of his confession. Herein shewing that many should believe what Peter had confessed, and raising his understanding, and making him His shepherd" (*Homilies on Matthew*, hom. 54, n. 2 (PG 58, 534)).

[6] This work has been lost, but reference is made to it in his *Retractions* as follows: "I have said in a certain place of the Apostle Peter, that it was on him, as on a rock, that the Church was built" (*Retractions*, bk. 1, c. 21, n. 1 (PL 32, 618)).

[7] This sermon is spurious. Cf. Serm. 201 (PL 39, 2119-2120). Formerly this sermon was titled "*de sanctis* 126."

[8] "The dispensation of Truth therefore abides, and Blessed Peter persevering in the strength of a rock, which he has received, has not abandoned the helm of the Church, which he undertook. For he was ordained before the rest in such a way that from his being called the rock..." (Serm. 3, c. 3 (PL 54, 146B)).

[9] "For the more you fear the Creator of all, the more fully may you love the Church of him to whom it was said, 'Thou art Peter, and upon this rock I will build my Church, and the gates of hell shall not prevail against it'; and to whom it is said, 'I will give to thee the keys of the kingdom of heaven. And whatsoever thou shalt bind upon earth, it shall be bound also in heaven: and whatsoever thou shalt loose upon earth, it shall be loosed also in heaven.' Whence it is not doubtful to us with what strong love you will bind yourself to him through whom you earnestly desire to be loosed from all sins" (Bk. 13, letter 39 (PL 77, 1289B)).

because even though the keys were given to the other Apostles, still not [the keys] of all the heavens, but of heaven (*coeli*). For to Peter it is said: "Whatsoever thou shalt loose (*solveris*[1]) upon earth, it shall be loosed also in [the] heaven[s] (*coelis*[2])" (Mt. 16, 19). But when the keys are given to all the Apostles at the same time, it is said thus: "Amen I say to you, whatsoever you shall bind upon earth, shall be bound also in heaven; and whatsoever you shall loose (*solveritis*[3]) upon earth, shall be loosed also in heaven (*coelo*[4])" (Mt. 18, 18). Behold you see that here is it said, "in heaven" in the singular: and yet when the keys are promised to Peter, the keys of the "heavens" are promised: and what he shall bind is said to be bound "in the heavens," not in one heaven: namely so that from this diverse manner of speech you may understand that stronger and more powerful keys were given to Peter than to the other Apostles.

And Origen noted this same thing in his exposition of Matthew,[5] and before Origen, Tertullian seems to have noted this same thing. For he, in the book, *Prescription against Heretics*, when disputing against those who were saying that the Apostles did not know everything necessary in regard to the faith, says the following: "What man, then, of sound mind can possibly suppose that they were ignorant of anything, whom the Lord ordained to be masters [or teachers], keeping them, as He did, inseparable [from Himself] in their attendance, in their discipleship, in their society, to whom, when they were alone, He used to expound all things which were obscure,[6] telling them that to them it was given to know those mysteries,[7] which it was not permitted the people to understand? Was anything withheld from the knowledge of Peter, who is called the rock on which the Church should be built, who also obtained the keys of the kingdom of Heaven, with the power of loosing and binding in Heaven and on earth? Was anything, again, concealed from John, the Lord's most beloved disciple, who used to lean on His breast,[8] to whom alone the Lord pointed out Judas as the traitor,[9] whom He commended to Mary as a son in His own stead?[10] Of what could He have wanted those to be ignorant, to whom He even exhibited His own glory with Moses and Elias, and moreover the Father's voice from Heaven?[11] Not as if He thus disapproved of all the rest, but because by three witnesses must every word be established."[12]

By which words after He had given to all the Apostles to know the mysteries which it was not permitted to the people to know: when afterwards naming the things which were individually allotted to each of the Apostles, he points out that it was given to John to recline upon

---

[1] *Solveris* in Latin means "you (singular) shall loose." Note that the Vulgate is followed here instead of the Douay-Rheims translation, which is smoother and not literal here.

[2] *Coelis* in Latin means "heaven" in the plural.

[3] *Solveritis* in Latin means "you (plural) shall loose."

[4] *Coelo* in Latin means "heaven" in the singular.

[5] "Are the keys of the kingdom of heaven given by the Lord to Peter only, and will no other of the blessed receive them? But if this promise, 'I will give to thee the keys of the kingdom of heaven' (Mt. 16, 19), be common to the others, how shall not all the things previously spoken of, and the things which are subjoined as having been addressed to Peter, be common to them? For in this place these words seem to be addressed as to Peter only, 'Whatsoever thou shalt bind upon earth, it shall be bound also in heaven (*caelis*)' etc. (*ibid.*)" (*Commentary on the Gospel of Matthew*, bk. 12, n. 11 (PG 13, 1602A)).

[6] "And without parable he did not speak unto them; but apart, he explained all things to his disciples" (Mk. 4, 34).

[7] "To you it is given to know the mysteries of the kingdom of heaven" (Mt. 13, 11).

[8] Cf. Jn. 21, 20.

[9] Cf. Jn. 13, 25-26.

[10] Cf. Jn. 19, 26.

[11] Cf. Mt. 17, 1-8.

[12] C. 22 (PL 2, 34A-B).

the Lord's breast; and that to the same John, James and Peter it was given to have seen the Lord in the transfigured majesty of His glory. He says that to Peter, however, it was given to be the rock of the Church, and having obtained the keys of the kingdom of Heaven, the power of binding [and loosing] in Heaven and on earth. All which things inasmuch as they were said to Peter alone, from them it is clearly proved that Peter was set above the other Apostles. For he alone among the Apostles was set in place as the rock upon which the Church is founded: to him alone are promised the keys of the kingdom of Heaven: he alone receives the power of binding and loosing in Heaven and on earth.

Wherefore I cannot pass over in silence the things which Beatus Rhenanus[1] when speaking about this matter says. For he in an argument which he prefaced to the book of Tertullian, *Prescription against Heretics*, insinuates that he thinks that the Roman pontiff was not established by God as the superior of the other bishops, and he says that this is Tertullian's opinion in that book and elsewhere.[2] Now so that he may show that Tertullian thought this, he reasons as follows. Tertullian when naming the Roman church, names it among the Apostolic churches, and yet he does not put it before the others: he lists it among the eminent churches, yet he never says that it is the highest. But if he had believed it to be the highest church, he would have at some point called it the highest church. [Tertullian] never called it the highest, therefore he did not believe that it is the highest. O strong arguer! O another Aristotle! Is this classic dialectic, to conclude something negatively by an argument from authority? Who does not know that this inference is invalid? Such or such a Doctor does not say this, therefore it is not so, or he believed it is not so? For if it were allowed to always reason in this manner, many incongruous things would follow therefrom. It would follow that the Father is not unbegotten; Mary would not have been a perpetual virgin: because Holy Writ did not express either of these, even though it made mention of these things. Let Rhenanus, not Happy (*Beatus*)[3] but Miserable, go away: and if he should wish to confirm his opinion, let him do so with true testimonies, and not with mere calumnies and impostures, as we have now proved that he has done. For although he accuses Tertullian of thinking that the Roman Church is not the highest, we showed that Tertullian thought that Peter was placed over the other Apostles, and we showed that he clearly taught this in the same book in which Rhenanus had prefaced such an argument.

Furthermore, when Christ was teaching the Apostles who among them would be the greater, He said to Peter: "Simon, Simon, behold Satan hath desired to have you, that he may sift you (*vos*[4]) as wheat. But I have prayed for thee (*te*), that thy faith fail not: and thou, being once converted, confirm thy brethren" (Lk. 22, 31-32). By which words Christ clearly taught that Peter would be greater than the other Apostles by the fact that He enjoined upon him, whom the devil had desired to sift as wheat, the duty of confirming the other Apostles. Now so that Peter could better exercise the office committed to him, Christ promises to him that He would ask the Father that He would not permit his faith to be lost. Theophylactus when expounding which words says the following: "'And thou, being once converted, confirm thy brethren.' The sense is plain: because I will make you the chief of the disciples, when you have wept and come to repentance after having denied me, confirm the others. For this befits you, who after Me are the rock and foundation of the Church."[5] Peter therefore was declared by Christ

---

[1] Beatus Rhenanus (1485–1547), born as Beatus Bild, was a German humanist, religious reformer, classical scholar, and book collector.
[2] *Tertulliani Opera* (Basel, Frobenius et Episcopius, 1539), p. 118.
[3] Beatus was his first name.
[4] *Vos* in Latin means "you" in the plural.
[5] *The Explanation of the Holy Gospel According to Luke* (PG 123, 1074C-D).

to be greater than the other Apostles, because to him it was enjoined the duty of strengthening the other Apostles.

Again, Christ commits to Peter the care of all the sheep, when He twice said to him: "Feed my lambs" (Jn. 21, 15-16). And He said again a third time: "Feed my sheep" (v. 17). By which words Christ very clearly declared that the whole flock both of the lambs and the sheep, that is the universal Church, was committed to Peter. For (as the [Royal] Prophet says), "We are the people of his pasture and the sheep of his hand" (Ps. 94, 7). God committed to Peter the care of these sheep. But Luther in fact and his followers, because they are not among these sheep, but among the number of those goats which the Lord will set on His left hand,[1] consequently do not want to be under the care of this shepherd, namely the Roman pontiff.

Next, things which Peter did very clearly show that he was set over the other Apostles. For Peter paid the drachma for himself and for Christ. For when the tax collectors of the drachmas questioned Peter whether his Master paid the drachma, Christ said to Peter: "Go to the sea, and cast in a hook: and that fish which shall first come up, take: and when thou hast opened its mouth, thou shalt find a stater: take that, and give it to them for me and thee" (Mt. 17, 26). Now so that from this passage we may more clearly make our point, it is necessary to firstly know what sort of collection was this collection of the drachma. To understand this better let us listen to what Blessed Jerome says about this matter. For, when discussing this passage, he says the following: "From the time of Augustus Caesar, Judaea was made tributary and all the inhabitants were taxed per head [of the family]. Hence also Joseph, along with his wife Mary, was registered in Bethlehem. Again, because the Lord was brought up at Nazareth, which is a town of Galilee subject to Capernaum, it is there that according to the custom they ask Him for the tribute; but due to the greatness of His miracles, those who collected it did not dare to ask Him Himself, but address His disciple."[2] If the tribute (as Jerome says) was paid by the head [of the family], why is it that Peter is commanded to pay a stater, that is two drachmas, for himself and for Christ, except that Christ was then intending to leave Peter as the head of the Church after Himself?

But if it be denied that the tribute was paid for this reason, why is the drachma paid for Peter rather than for the other Apostles, since such a tax was paid not otherwise than by the head [of the family]? No other reason for this can be found, except that Peter was to be put before the others; [hence] one ought to acknowledge that Peter, who was ordered to pay the tribute which was only required of the head [of the family], was for this reason declared the head of the family. Now the fact that he was joined with Christ in the payment of the drachma, such that one coin, namely he paid one stater for himself and for Christ, shows that Peter would be the head of the same family, namely the Church, whose head is Christ. Still, it does not thence follow that the Church's body is a two-headed monster (as Luther objects to us[3]), because we do not say that Peter is the head equal to Christ, but the head under Christ. For we say that Christ is the first and supreme head of the Church; but we do not say that Peter is the first head of the whole body which is the Church, but the vicarious head, that is, the head substituted in Christ's place, and the second head after Christ, meaning, the head of the all the others apart from Christ. Wherefore Peter ought not to be called the superior of all simply, but superior in comparison to the others, apart from Christ. But Christ is absolutely and simply the head of the whole Church, Who is the founder. And in this way it is evident that there are not two heads of the same whole body, because only Christ is the head of that whole body, and of this

---

[1] Cf. Mt. 25, 33.

[2] *Commentary on Matthew*, bk. 3 (PL 26, 127A).

[3] "If the pope were the head of the Christian church, then the church were a monster with two heads, seeing that St. Paul says that Christ is her head. The pope may well be, and is, the head of the false church" (*Table Talk*, n. 1266 (WA TR (*Tischreden*) vol. 2, p. 17)).

body Peter is one member, yet superior to the others. But Peter is the head of the mystical body, which forms from other men by Christ: and in this way he is not the head of the whole entire body: because he is not the head of Christ Who belongs to this Church.

Very similar to this is that which we see in other things. For a governor is the head of that province which he administers, although the consul is superior to him, and the first head of all the provinces. The viceroy is the head of the country of which he has charge: yet the king is superior to him, and the first head of all his countries. For the viceroy or the governor is the head of part of the body, namely of some country, or some province: the ruler however is the first head of the whole entire body. So Peter and Christ [are related]. In this way one also ought to understand that which we said above, namely that Peter is the rock and foundation of the Church. I do not say the first foundation, namely on which the structure of the whole Church rests, because such a foundation is Christ alone, of Whom Paul says: "Other foundation no man can lay, but that which is laid; which is Christ Jesus" (I Cor. 3, 11). And, in comparison to this foundation, Peter is as one of the other stones which rest on the foundation. But after the first stone has been laid as the foundation, there are other stones in the same structure, namely those which are supported by the first, yet they support all the rest which have been placed upon them in the building. And any of these can be called a foundation, not simply and absolutely in respect to all the stones, but in respect to those stones which it supports.

And according to this manner of speech there are many foundations of the Church. For Blessed John says of all the Apostles that they are foundations of the Church. For when speaking in the Apocalypse about the new city descending from Heaven, which is the Church, he says the following: "And the wall of the city had twelve foundations, and in them, the twelve names of the twelve apostles" (Apoc. 21, 14). Notice that you hear all the Apostles called the foundations of the city, because by their teaching the Church is supported until now. Why then is Luther surprised if we say that Peter is the foundation of the Church? But although they all are and may be called foundations, still Peter stands out before the others: because even though he is not the first stone laid in the foundation, still he is the first after Christ: and in this way he will be the foundation, not indeed of all the stones which are in the spiritual edifice, because he is not the foundation of Christ, Who belongs to this building, but he is the foundation of all the other spiritual stones, and so he is the second foundation after Christ, because he is the first rock after Christ the Rock. And so the whole structure of the Church is founded upon this Rock, which is Christ: but upon another rock, which is Peter, the rest of the Church is founded by Christ, that is, the whole Church except Christ the Head.

Now Theophylactus signified these things in one saying among the words of his commentaries on that passage of Luke which we just cited above. For when so expounding Christ's words, he says: "Because I have you as prince of the disciples, when, having denied me, you have wept and come to repentance, confirm the rest. For this befits you, who after me are the rock and foundation of the Church." From Theophylactus' words it is evident that Peter is called the foundation of the Church, not indeed absolutely and in respect to all, but the foundation after Christ, that is, the foundation of all the other apart from Christ. And so there are not two first stones: because only Christ is the primary stone: Peter is not properly the first, but the first after Christ. We have discussed this matter at length and beyond the set limits of brevity, because this is a very strong arrow which Luther shoots at us, and by which he attempts to defend himself: since more than enough has already been said about which matter, it is necessary that we briefly go through Peter's other actions.

When an Angel was appearing to Mary Magdalene and her other companions visiting Christ's tomb, he says to them: "You seek Jesus of Nazareth, who was crucified: he is risen, he is not here, behold the place where they laid him. But go, tell his disciples and Peter that he goeth before you into Galilee" (Mk. 16, 6-7). Why is it that only Peter's name is stated, while the names of all the others is passed over in silence, except that Peter surpasses all the others? For if Peter were not more superior to the others, it would have been enough to have said: "Go, tell His disciples." But since He added, "and Peter," he suggests that there is something singular in Peter on account of which he ought to have been designated by his own name, as being the prince of the others. Next when Peter and John came to the sepulcher, although John runs faster than Peter, and arrived first at the sepulcher, nevertheless he did not dare to enter before Peter, showing honor to Peter by this, as to his superior.[1] John, who had reclined upon the Lord's breast, indeed could have entered the sepulcher. For he who was worthy to recline upon the living body, was much more worthy to enter the sepulcher in which the dead body laid. But even though he was worthy of this, he still refused to enter, wishing to defer the honor to Peter, such that because Peter was superior in dignity, so also he should enter the sepulcher first. And when Christ had already ascended into Heaven, Peter makes a discourse to the other disciples, persuading them that another be substituted in Judas' place[2] Unless Peter had been chosen by God to be the superior of the others, he would not have been so arrogant, and desirous of glory, that not having been asked by the others he would rise up in their midst, and give a discourse to all.

But if you were to claim that this was done before the Spirit was received, let us see what he did after the coming of the Holy Ghost. For on the day on which the Holy Ghost descended in fiery tongues, when the Apostles were speaking in all languages, and the whole multitude marveled at the newness of the thing, and attributed it to drunkenness, Peter taking up the cause of all of those same fellow disciples of his, made a speech to the people, teaching them that the disciples are not drunk, as they thought; having heard which speech, about three thousand of those hearers were converted.[3] Why does Peter alone reply for them all, unless because he alone is set over them all? For it is the office of the shepherd to defend his sheep from the wolves' disturbances. Hence Peter, as a good shepherd wishing to defend his sheep, made a speech in their favor to the people. After these things when Peter and John went up to the Temple at the ninth hour of prayer, to a certain lame man asking for alms at the gates of the of the Temple, Peter says: "Silver and gold I have none; but what I have, I give thee: In the name of Jesus Christ of Nazareth, arise, and walk" (Acts 3, 6). And forthwith his feet received strength. Now this was the first miracle which we read to have been done by any Apostle, namely so that he who was superior to the others in dignity and power, would also first show the power of his God by working miracles. And it is not lacking in mystery that when John is in Peter's company, John is silent, and Peter alone heals the lame man. For he who afterwards raised the dead woman, Drusiana,[4] could well have strengthened the feet of the lame man. But because John acknowledged Peter as his superior, he did not want put to a test anything in his presence, lest he seem to lessen his honor. The Lord also after His Ascension into Heaven, when wishing to teach His Church that the distinction of foods, which had been commanded in the Law of Moses, ought not to be made now, made a revelation about this to Peter alone. For Peter being in an ecstasy of mind is shown a great linen sheet let down from Heaven to the earth, wherein were all manner of four-footed beasts, and creeping things of the earth, and fowls of the air, and afterwards a voice was made to him: "Arise, Peter; kill and eat" (Acts 10, 13). Which matter, although it touched upon them all, still only to Peter is it revealed: because Peter was a public person (*persona communis*) having the care of all. Also, when the question arose about the cessation of the Legal observances, some saying that they

---

[1] Cf. Jn. 20, 3-6.

[2] Cf. Acts 1, 15-26.

[3] Cf. Acts 2, 1-41.

[4] Drusiana was said to have been raised from the dead by St. John the Apostle in the Apocryphal book, *Acts of John*.

are necessary, others however saying the contrary, and for the deciding of this question the Council of Jerusalem was assembled: Peter rising up in their midst speaks first, and all consent to his decision. Peter speaks first, even though he was in the diocese in which there was another bishop, namely James. Therefore, from all these things which Peter did, we conclude that he had been put in charge of the other Apostles.

Furthermore, whenever a list of Apostles is made in the Gospel, Peter is always listed in the first place: which would not have been done if Peter were not superior to the others: especially since in the listing of the others, the same order is not kept by all the Evangelists. For Andrew, whom Matthew put in the second place,[1] Mark puts in the fourth.[2] Matthew puts Thomas seventh,[3] whom Mark and Luke name eighth.[4] And Luke himself does not keep the same order: because in the Gospel he put Andrew second, whom in the Acts of the Apostles he puts fourth.[5] In the Gospel he puts Bartholomew sixth;[6] but in the Acts of the Apostles he wrote the same Bartholomew seventh.[7] But Peter, the order never having varied, all the Evangelists everywhere write first. And it cannot be said that it was done that he is always written first because he was called first, because it is evident that Andrew was called before him, and Peter was brought by Andrew to Christ.[8] Thus, Peter, who having been called afterwards, is written everywhere before all, for this reason is declared to be superior to all the others. And certainly, unless it had been so instituted by God, that there would be one high priest in the Church, it would have necessarily have come to pass what is said in the book of Judges: "In those days there was no king in Israel: but everyone did that which seemed right to himself" (21, 24).

And for this reason alone (as I think) the heretics attempt to diminish the primacy of Peter and of his successors, namely so that they might be able to teach more easily what heresies they will. For Cyprian thinks that from this root heresies arise in the Church, who in the first book of his letters, in the [twelfth] letter, which is to Pope Cornelius, says the following: "For neither have heresies arisen, nor have schisms originated, from any other source than from this, that God's priest is not obeyed; nor do they consider that there is one person for the time priest in the Church, and for the time judge in the stead of Christ; whom, if, according to Divine teaching, the whole fraternity should obey, no one would stir up anything against the college of priests; no one, after the Divine judgment, after the suffrage of the people, after the consent of the co-bishops, would make himself a judge, not now of the bishop, but of God. No one would rend the Church by a division of the unity of Christ. No one, pleasing himself, and swelling with arrogance, would found a new heresy."[9] Wherefore if there be any room for conjectures about this matter, we could justly conjecture that heretics for this reason alone have been motivated to overthrow Peter's primacy, so that they could spew out more easily the heresies which they have conceived.

After these very clear testimonies of Sacred Scripture, there also exists the concordant opinion of all the holy Doctors about this matter: whose words I will omit to cite, lest I transgress the promised brevity. But if the curious reader desires to see them, I will indicate the places in which the holy Doctors affirmed this. And so (so that I may omit more

---

[1] Cf. Mt. 10, 2.
[2] Cf. Mk. 3, 18.
[3] Cf. Mt. 10, 3.
[4] Cf. Mk. 3, 18 & Lk. 6, 15.
[5] Cf. Acts 1, 13.
[6] Cf. Lk. 6, 14.
[7] Cf. Acts 1, 13.
[8] Cf. Jn. 1, 37-42.
[9] C. 5 (PL 3, 802B-803A).

PAPA

recent authors) [the following Doctors have asserted this:] Blessed Gregory;[1] Theophylactus on Matthew chapter sixteen[2] and Luke twenty-two;[3] Leo I in his letter to Dioscorus, Bishop of Alexandria,[4] and again in his sermon delivered on the anniversary of his elevation to the pontificate;[5] Augustine very often, especially in the fifty-sixth tract on John,[6] in the second book of [*On Baptism,*] *Against the Donatists,*[7] in the one hundred twenty-fourth sermon of the time,[8] in sermon twenty-six on the saints,[9] and letter one hundred fifty-seven;[10] Jerome

---

[1] "'But go, tell his disciples and Peter that he goeth before you into Galilee' (Mk. 16, 7). We must ask ourselves why, after having mentioned the disciples, the Angel still designates Peter by name. But if the Angel had not mentioned the name of the one who had denied his Master, he would not have dared to come among the disciples. He was therefore called by name, lest he should despair because of his denial. We must consider here why Almighty God allowed the one whom he had decided to put at the head of the whole Church to tremble at the voice of a servant and deny his God. We know that it was by a disposition of the great goodness of God, that the one who should be the Shepherd of the Church learn by his own fault how he should have pity on others. God revealed Peter to himself before putting him at the head of others, so that the experience of his own weakness would make him know with what mercy he should bear the weaknesses of others" (*Homilies on the Gospels*, bk. 2, hom. 21, c. 4 (PL 76, 1171D-1172A)).

[2] "'And I say also unto thee, that thou art Peter, and upon this rock I will build My Church'; and the gates of Hades shall not prevail against it. The Lord gives Peter a great reward, that the Church will be built on him" (PG 123, 319A).

[3] "'And thou, being once converted, confirm thy brethren.' The sense is plain: because I have you as prince of the disciples, when, having denied me, you have wept and come to repentance, confirm the rest. For this befits you, who after me are the rock and foundation of the Church. And this must be understood not only of the Apostles that they would be strengthened by Peter, but of all the faithful who were about to be, even to the end of the world. For you, Peter, being once converted, you will be a good example of repentance to all, so that none of the believers might despair: you who since you were an Apostle and you denied, yet once more you received the first of all places, and the rulership of the world through repentance" (*The Explanation of the Holy Gospel According to Luke* (PG 123, 1074C-D).

[4] "For since the Most Blessed Peter received the headship of the Apostles from the Lord, and the church of Rome still abides by his institutions..." (Letter 9, PL 54, 625A).

[5] "The dispensation of Truth therefore abides, and Blessed Peter persevering in the strength of a rock, which he has received, has not abandoned the helm of the Church, which he undertook. For he was ordained before the rest in such a way that from his being called the rock..." (Serm. 3, c. 3 (PL 54, 146B)).

[6] "For who can fail to know that the Most Blessed Peter was the first of the Apostles?" (C. 1 (PL 35, 1787)).

[7] "But is it in any way greater than that of the Apostle and martyr Peter, of whom the said Cyprian speaks as follows in his epistle to Quintus? 'For neither did Peter, whom the Lord chose first, and on whom He built His Church...' Here is a passage in which Cyprian records what we also learn in holy Scripture, that the Apostle Peter, in whom the primacy of the Apostles shines with such exceeding grace" (C. 1, n. 2 (PL 43, 126-127)).

[8] This sermon is spurious. Cf. Serm. 79 (PL 39, 1899-1900). Formerly this sermon was titled "*de tempore* 124."

[9] This sermon is spurious. Cf. Serm. 201 (PL 39, 2119-2120). Formerly this sermon was titled "*de sanctis* 126."

[10] Letter 190 (formerly this letter was titled "Letter 157"). "Its authors, or at least its fiercest and most notorious advocates, are Pelagius and Caelestius, and by the vigilance of the councils of bishops along with the help of the Savior Who watches over His Church, as well as two venerable bishops of the Apostolic See, Pope Innocent and Pope Zosimus, they have been condemned throughout the whole world, unless they amend and do penance." (C. 6, n. 22 (PL 33, 865)). "These words of the Apostolic See contain the Catholic faith that is so ancient and well-founded, so certain and clear, that it is impious for a Christian to doubt it" (C. 6, n. 23 (PL 33, 865-866)).

also very often and very clearly, but especially in many letters to Pope Damasus;[1] [Ambrosiaster[2]] when expounding on the first chapter of Paul's Epistle to the Galatians,[3] and [Ambrose] in a certain sermon, "On the repentance of Peter";[4] Chrysostom in homily fifty-six on Matthew;[5] [Pseudo-] Athanasius in a letter to Pope Liberius;[6] Eusebius of Caesarea;[7] Hilary in his commentary on Matthew,[8] and in *On the Trinity*;[9] Cyprian in many letters, especially the third letter in book one of his letters,[10] and in the eighth letter of book four, in which place

---

[1] "I think it my duty to consult the chair of Peter, and to turn to a church whose faith has been praised by Paul. I appeal for spiritual food to the church whence I have received the garb of Christ. The wide space of sea and land that lies between us cannot deter me from searching for the pearl of great price. 'Wheresoever the body shall be, there shall the eagles also be gathered together' (Mt. 24, 28). Evil children have squandered their patrimony; you alone keep your heritage intact. The fruitful soil of Rome, when it receives the pure seed of the Lord, bears fruit a hundredfold… My words are spoken to the successor of the fisherman, to the disciple of the Cross. As I follow no leader save Christ, so I communicate with none but your blessedness, that is with the chair of Peter. For this, I know, is the rock on which the Church is built!" (Letter 15, n. 1-2 (PL 22, 355)).

[2] "[Saint Ambrose] is not the author of the admirable commentary on the thirteen Epistles of St. Paul known as 'Ambrosiaster'" ("St. Ambrose," *The Catholic Encyclopedia* (New York, Robert Appleton Company, 1907), vol. 1, p. 387).

[3] PL 17, 344C.

[4] This incorrect title was mistakenly taken from St. Maximus of Turin's homily 53 (PL 57, 349C-352B), the content of which is at least in part derived from St. Ambrose's *Commentary on Luke* (bk. 10, c. 22) where we find these words: "Peter therefore cuts off the ear. Why Peter? Because it is he who has received the keys of the kingdom of Heaven. He condemns, as he absolves, because he has received the power to bind as that of loosening. He cut off the ear of those who listen badly; by the spiritual sword he cuts off the interior ear of one who understands wrongly" (N. 67 (PL 15, 1821A)).

[5] "And I say unto you, 'Thou art Peter, and upon this rock will I build my Church'; that is, on the faith of his confession. Herein shewing that many should believe what Peter had confessed, and raising his understanding, and making him His shepherd" (*Homilies on Matthew*, hom. 54, n. 2 (PG 58, 534)). Note that this homily was formerly homily 55, though the reference here is mistakenly to homily 56.

[6] Letter 1 (PL 8, 1403D). Cf. *Monitum in Epistolas Amoebeas Liberii et Athanasii* (PL 8, 1395-1396).

[7] "During the reign of Claudius, the all-good and gracious Providence, which watches over all things, led Peter, that strongest and greatest of the Apostles, and the one who on account of his virtue was the speaker for all the others, to Rome against this great corrupter of life. Clad in divine armor like a noble commander of God, He carried the costly merchandise of the light of the understanding from the East to those who dwelt in the West" (*Church History*, bk. 2, c. 14 (PG 20, 171A)).

[8] "And plainly the confession of Peter received a worthy reward, because he had seen the Son of God in a man. Blessed is this man, who is praised to have seen and have contemplated [this truth] beyond human eyes: beholding not what was of flesh and blood, but seeing the revelation of the Son of God from the heavenly Father; and worthy and just, was he such that in Christ of God he was the first to recognize [the Divinity]. Oh! By appellation of a new name the fruitful foundation of the Church, her rock is of a worthy build, [the rock] which destroys the hellish laws, the gates of Hell, and all the barriers of death. O blessed door-keeper of Heaven, to whose will have the keys of the eternal gates been delivered, to whose earthly judgment the authority was decreed beforehand in Heaven: so that what was bound or loosed on earth, obtains the condition of the same status in Heaven" (*Commentary on Matthew*, c. 16, n. 7 (1009C–1010A)).

[9] "This faith [of Peter] is the foundation of the Church. Through this faith the gates of hell cannot prevail against her. This is the faith which has the keys of the kingdom of Heaven. Whatever this faith shall have loosed or bound on earth shall be loosed or bound in Heaven" (Bk. 6, n. 37 (PL 10, 187A-B)).

[10] Letter 54 (to Pope Cornelius; Erasmus: lib. 1, ep. 3), n. 5 (PL 3, 802B-803A). Full citation is given above.

he clearly confesses the Roman church to be the mother of all churches;[1] Origen in homily six on Matthew;[2] Irenaeus;[3] and [Pseudo-] Pope and martyr Anacletus, who ruled the Catholic Church [third[4]] from Blessed Peter the Apostle, in a letter concerning the patriarchs, the primates and the rest of the bishops.[5]

Thus, let the reader attend to and consider well whether it is reasonable to believe Luther alone rather than so many holy Doctors illustrious for holiness as well as doctrine, some of whom were crowned with martyrdom. The concordant opinion of these men suffices for captivating our understanding,[6] even if the testimony of Sacred Scripture were lacking (which I do not think could happen) I surely know that such an error would not be imputed as to guilt, if out of humility he preferred to trust the judgment of others than to uphold his own opinion. But after so many, very clear testimonies, even this one could suffice, that after the world was made peaceful, Christians were obedient to the Roman pontiff. All the bishops revered him as their superior. All the councils which have force, were confirmed by his authority. In the Council of Nicea Bishop Hosius of Cordova presided as the delegate of Pope Julius. In the Council of Ephesus the delegate of the Apostolic See was [Bishop] Cyril of Alexandria, who presided in the name of the pope in that council. In the Council of Chalcedon the delegates of Pope Leo I, were Paschasinus, Bishop of Lilybaeum [Marsala, in Sicily], Bishop Lucentius of Ascoli, Bishop Julian of Cos, and Boniface, a Roman priest. In the fifth synod, [the Synod of Constantinople held in 536 A. D.], the delegates of Pope Agapetus were five bishops, as is clearly evident from the second session of the same council.[7] In the sixth synod [III Constan-

---

[1] "We have exhorted them to acknowledge and hold the root and mother of the Catholic Church. But since our province is wide-spread, and has Numidia and Mauritania attached to it; lest a schism made in the city should confuse the minds of the absent with uncertain opinions, we decided—having obtained by means of the bishops the truth of the matter, and having got a greater authority for the proof of your ordination, and so at length every scruple being got rid of from the breast of every one—that letters should be sent you by all who were placed anywhere in the province; as in fact is done, that so the whole of our colleagues might decidedly approve of and maintain both you and your communion, that is as well to the unity of the Catholic Church as to its charity" (Letter 44 (to Pope Cornelius; Erasmus: lib. 4, ep.8), n. 3 (PL 3, 710B-711A)).

[2] "Jesus… sends Peter to drag up the fish into the net, in the mouth of which He said that a stater would be found which was to be given for Himself and Peter. It seems to me, then, that thinking that this was a very great honor which had been bestowed on Peter by Jesus" (Bk. 13, n. 14 (PG 13, 1130A)). Book 13 is the sixth book of this commentary, which may be the reason why the author cites it as the sixth "homily."

[3] "Since, however, it would be very tedious, in such a volume as this, to reckon up the successions of all the Churches, we do put to confusion all those who, in whatever manner, whether by an evil self-pleasing, by vainglory, or by blindness and perverse opinion, assemble in unauthorized meetings; [we do this, I say], by indicating that tradition derived from the Apostles, of the very great, the very ancient, and universally known church founded and organized at Rome by the two most glorious Apostles, Peter and Paul; as also [by pointing out] the faith preached to men, which comes down to our time by means of the successions of the bishops. For it is a matter of necessity that every church should agree with this church, on account of its preeminent authority (*potiorem principalitatem*), that is, the faithful everywhere, in which, always, that which is the tradition from the Apostles has been preserved by those who are from all parts" (N. 2 (PG 7,848)).

[4] The text here calls him the "fourth" pope of the Church. But he is now generally accepted as the second successor of St. Peter, though whether he was the same as Cletus, who is also called Anencletus as well as Anacletus, has been the subject of endless discussion. Cf. "Pope St. Clement I," *The Catholic Encyclopedia*, vol. 4, p. 13.

[5] *False Decretals of the Pseudo-Isidore* (PL 130, 76B-C).

[6] Cf. II Cor. 10, 5.

[7] I.e. Sabinus of Canusium, Epiphanius of Aeclanum, Asterius of Salernum, Rusticus of Faesulae, and

tinople] the delegates of Pope Agatho presided, namely, Theodore and George, priests, and John, a deacon. Finally, there has been no general council up until now, in which if the pope was not present, his delegates did not preside.

The [II] Council of Milevum, in which Pelagius was condemned, was confirmed by Pope Innocent [I], because all at the council asked the pope to approve and ratify its decrees: which the pope also did, as it is evident from the letters [176[1] and 182[2]] of Augustine. The III and IV Synods of Carthage were confirmed by Pope Zosimus.[3] The Synod of Thelepte which also was an African synod, in which Jovinian was condemned, sought confirmation of its judgment from Pope Siricius, who confirmed the decrees of the synod, as appears from the decrees of the same Pope Siricius, which are found in the book of the general councils.[4] The rest of the African synods were confirmed by the authority of Boniface, who sent to them a certain Bishop Faustus as his legate.[5] The First Synod of Braga was celebrated after having first sought authorization from the Roman pontiff, as is evident from the acts of the same council.[6]

Now not only provincial councils showed this honor to the supreme pontiff, but also the general councils, because all those councils sought confirmation of their decrees from the Bishop of Rome. For the Council of Nicea requested Silvester, then the Roman pontiff, that he deign to confirm the things which were enacted in the council: which he did, as it evident from the acts of the same council.[7] The Council of Chalcedon did the same thing with Leo, as is evident from the third session of the same council at the end.[8] Pope Leo [II] gave the confirmation of the sixth synod [III Constantinople], at the request of Emperor Constantine [IV], which is found at the end of the same synod.[9]

And the Roman pontiff not only exercised the primacy in councils, but also in settling disputes: because to him as to the supreme judge cases have always devolved from the whole

---

Leo of Nola (Mansi, *Sacrorum conciliorum nova et amplissima collectio*, vol. 8, p. 925E).

[1] "Because by a special gift of His grace the Lord has placed you in the Apostolic See... We ask that you be so good as to apply your pastoral care to the great dangers of the weaker members of Christ. A new and very dangerous heresy [of the Pelagians] on the part of the enemies of the grace of Christ is attempting to rise up... But we think that with the help of the mercy of the Lord our God, Who deigns to guide you when you consult Him and to hear you when you pray to Him, those who hold such perverse and destructive ideas will more easily yield to the authority of Your Holiness, which is derived from the authority of the holy Scriptures, so that we may rejoice over their correction rather than be saddened by their destruction" (*The Council of Milevum to Pope Innocent I warning him of the grave dangers posed by the heresy of Pelagius written in 416 A. D.*; n. 1, 2, & 5 (PL 33, 763-764)). Formerly, this was letter 92, though it is cited as letter 90 in the text.

[2] "In the midst of other cares of the Roman church and the tasks of the Apostolic See whereby, on the basis of faith and with an aim to heal, we respond to questions coming from various sources, our brother and fellow bishop Julius unexpectedly brought me the letter of Your Charity, which you sent from the Council of Milevum out of a more ardent concern for the faith, to which you added the writings of the Synod of Carthage on a similar question" (*Pope Innocent to Silvanus, the primate of Numidia, and to the participants in the Council of Milevum in response to Letter 176, which they had sent him*; n. 1 (PL 33, 784)). Formerly, this was letter 93, though it is cited as letter 91 in the text.

[3] These two synods were held in Carthage is 418 A. D. and Pope Zosimus sent letters for both. Cf. Mansi, vol. 4, pp. 373-376.

[4] Mansi, vol. 4, pp. 379-380. Letter 5 (PL 13, 1155C-1162A).

[5] Mansi, vol. 4, pp. 451-452; Letter 2 (PL 20, 791B).

[6] Mansi, vol. 9, p. 776E; PL 85, 656B-C.

[7] Mansi, vol. 2, p. 719B-720E.

[8] Mansi, vol. 7, p. 499B; D. Severin Binius, *Concilia Generalia, Et Provincialia, Quotquot Reperiri Potuerunt* (Cologne, Gymnicus et Hierat, 1606), vol. 2, p. 86.

[9] Mansi, vol. 11, p. 715.

world. For when in the first beginnings of the steadily springing forth Church a question arose between the easterners and westerners about the celebration of Easter, Polycarp, Bishop of Smyrna, a disciple of John the Evangelist, came to Rome about the matter, so that Anicetus, the Roman pontiff of that time, might consider the matter.[1] Afterwards since the easterners wanted to always celebrate Easter on the fourteenth day of the new moon according to the Jewish custom, and were unwilling to obey Pope Victor [I] commanding the opposite, Pope Victor wanted to excommunicate them: but Irenaeus who had [written[2]] from Lyons to Victor about this matter, feared that the Church would be disturbed because of this, and perpetual discord would remain between the easterners and the westerners, advised Victor not to do this: by whose advice Victor gave way. When Athanasius was expelled by the Arians from his Alexandrian See, he was likewise restored by Pope Julian I.[3] When Chrysostom was expelled from his Constantinopolitan See as brought about by Theophilus,[4] Bishop of Alexandria, [an attempt was made] by Pope Innocent [I to restore him to his See[5]]: I keep silent about Spain and France, because the bishops of these regions always obeyed the Roman pontiff, and never withdrew from him, except perhaps one or another heretic. For this is easily known from the letters of the supreme pontiffs to the bishops of these nations, especially from the letters of Innocent I, Leo I and Gregory I.

Therefore, if the Roman pontiff acquired such great and so widely spread power, not by God's command, but by his force (as Luther says[6]), I beseech Luther to show when such extensive power was first acquired, by what votes, by what army he usurped this tyranny. For it is not likely that the beginning of such immense power is hidden. Let him trace from history the beginning of the thing. Certainly anyone is forced to give no trust to this fable if he takes notice of the fact that it could nowise happen that an unarmed priest, alone, not accompanied by any army (such would have been necessary before he could have acquired this tyranny), propped up by no right, supported by no title, among so many fellow bishops, in such varied and distant nations, obtains so great power, such that not only bishops, but kings and emperors, who live outside his diocese obey him. Also, who is so senseless that he could believe that all peoples, kingdoms, provinces were so prodigal of their own rights and liberty, that to a foreign priest, to whom they were not under obligation by any reason for subjection, would have given such power to him, as much as he perhaps would have dared to choose, or at least

---

[1] Cf. Eusebius of Caesarea, *Church History*, bk. 5, c. 24, n. 16 (PG 20, 507A).

[2] St. Irenaeus did not come in person to Rome, as stated here in the text, but instead wrote to Pope Victor, as mentioned by Eusebius in these words: "Among them was Irenæus, who, sending letters in the name of the brethren in Gaul over whom he presided, maintained that the mystery of the Resurrection of the Lord should be observed only on the Lord's Day. He fittingly admonishes Victor that he should not cut off whole churches of God which observed the tradition of an ancient custom" (bk. 5, c. 24, n. 11 (PG 20, 499A)).

[3] "Can you be ignorant, that this is the custom, that we should be written to first, so that from here what is just may be defined" (Letter of Pope Julius to the Antiochians, c. 22 (PL 8, 905B-C)).

[4] Cf. Photius, *Bibliotheca*, c. 59, (PG 103, 105-113).

[5] Pope Innocent I was unable to restore St. John Chrysostom to his See, as incorrectly stated here in the original text. "When the circumstances of his deposition were known in the West, the pope and the Italian bishops declared themselves in [St. John Chrysostom's] favor. Emperor Honorius and Pope Innocent I endeavored to summon a new synod [to reinstate Chrysostom], but their legates were imprisoned and then sent home" ("St. John Chrysostom," *Catholic Encyclopedia* (New York, Robert Appleton Company, 1910), vol. 8, p. 455).

[6] "That wretched man, the Roman bishop, neither rules nor feeds his own church, but neither can he. Then he arrogates to himself his Curia, the swamp of all crimes [which] he also nourishes and fosters, for ruling the churches of the whole world, nay he could not even rule his own person now for many centuries" (*Assertio omnium articulorum M. Lutheri per bullam Leonis X*, (WA 7, 128, lns. 12-15)).

request? Therefore, let the heretics be gone, and we, holding the faith of the Catholic Church, acknowledge that there is one high priest in it, so that just as it is one flock, so there is one shepherd of it.

There exists a definition of the Council of Constance about this matter. For the aforesaid council in the eighth session condemned forty-five articles of John Wycliff, of which this is the thirty-[seventh]: "The Roman Church is a synagogue of Satan, and the pope is not the next and immediate vicar of Christ and His Apostles."[1] Which assertion along with the others of the same man is condemned there. And in fifteenth session of the same council many assertions of John Hus are condemned, some of which are pertinent to the matter.[2] And the Council of Florence, celebrated under Eugene IV for the reunification of the Greeks, issued a more explicit definition about this matter. For it speaks thus: "We likewise define that the holy Apostolic See, and the Roman pontiff, hold the primacy throughout the entire world; and that the Roman pontiff himself is the successor of Blessed Peter, the chief of the Apostles, and the true vicar of Christ, and that he is the head of the entire Church, and the father and teacher of all Christians; and that full power was given to him in Blessed Peter by our Lord Jesus Christ, to feed, rule, and govern the universal Church; just as is contained in the acts of the ecumenical Councils and in the sacred canons."[3] The Greeks who were present subscribed to this council.

I have not cited Luther's objections here because they are all frivolous, and we have already replied to their main points when we disputed against him.

Johann Eck wrote an excellent and large book against this heresy, which is entitled, *De primatu Petri*;[4] Johann Faber also wrote in a large work which he made against Luther.[5] [Bishop] John [Fisher] of Rochester treats the same matter very well in the twenty-fifth article of the assertion which he made for Luther's condemnation.[6] Jacques Masson also wrote a short booklet on Peter's primacy.[7]

There is a **second heresy**, which even though it does not take away the pope's power, still it asserts that it depends on his holiness, such that if the pope were not good, he would have absolutely no power. The authors of this pestiferous sect were the so called Apostolics, who taught that the pope cannot absolve anyone unless he possessed that sanctity which Blessed Peter was rich in. Wherefore these men asserted that all the power which Christ granted to the Roman pontiff and Peter's successor, is now rendered void, and was completely lost on account of the wickedness of the Roman pontiffs.[8] John Wycliff agrees with these Apostolics in

---

[1] Dz. 617.

[2] "Peter is not nor ever was the head of the Holy Catholic Church"; "The papal dignity has sprung up from Caesar, and the perfection and institution of the pope have emanated from the power of Caesar"; "No one without revelation would have asserted reasonably regarding himself or anyone else that he was the head of a particular church nor is the Roman Pontiff the head of a particular Roman Church" (n. 7, 9, & 10 (Dz. 633, 635 & 636).

[3] Dz. 694.

[4] *De Primatu Petri adversus Lutherum libri tres* (Paris, Petrus Vidoveus, 1521).

[5] *Malleus Haereticorum, sex libris ad Hadrianum VI summum Pontificem* (Cologne, Johann Soter, 1524; Rome, 1569).

[6] *Assertionis Lutheranae confutatio* (Paris, Apud Petrum Drouart, 1545), fol. 197v-235v.

[7] Jacques Masson (or Jacobus Latomus), *De primatus pontificis adversus Lutherum* (Antwerp, Michael Hillenius, 1526).

[8] Guy the Carmelite, *Summa de haeresibus et earum confutationibus*, c. 1-3, fol. 89r-91r.

this matter[1]: John Hus however always copied this [error][2]: who universally says about both secular and ecclesiastical power that it is lost by mortal sin.[3] Wherefore we defer the expurgation of this error to that place where we will speak about power in general. For in that place, with God as our Helper, we will prove that no power is lost on account of mortal sin alone.

There are other errors which pertain to this subject, about which we have already examined in other places according to our power. For the fact that the pope can make regulations, and by them can oblige all Christians, we proved in the section on the "Church," in the third heresy, against the Waldensians, Beghards, Wycliffites, etc. We have spoken somewhat about the power of granting indulgences above in the section on "Indulgences."

PASCHA

Easter

There was in former times among the Asiatic bishops an error of such a kind, that they would invariably celebrate Easter Sunday on fourteenth day of the new moon, and they taught that one must necessarily do so. About which matter there was a dispute between the eastern and western bishops; the former were saying that Easter must necessarily be celebrated on the fourteenth day of the new moon, on whatsoever day of the week it fell: because on that day according to the Old Law was the Pasch celebrated. The latter, however, namely the western bishops, were asserting on the contrary that it ought to be celebrated on Sunday in memory of the Lord's Resurrection. And this question arose in the Church in the time of Pope Anicetus and lasted until the time of Pope Victor I, who tried to excommunicate the easterners unwilling to obey the Roman custom and its decrees on this matter, and he would have done so except that Irenaeus reproved him about this. After Victor this question was raised again at some time, but finally it was completely resolved in the Council of Nicea. For in that council it was decreed that Easter would be celebrated by everyone on Sunday in memory of the Lord's Resurrection which occurred on that day, because the majority of the Church always observed this practice that Easter would always be observed on Sunday. The said decree is not found among the decrees of the Council of Nicea which now exist, but it is found in the *Historia Tripartita*.[4] Otherwise, it is necessary to point out to the reader here that he ought not to think that the upholders of this error ought to be called heretics, because

---

[1] Errors of John Wycliffe: "If the pope is foreknown and evil, and consequently a member of the devil, he does not have power over the faithful given to him by anyone, unless perchance by Caesar" (n. 8 (Dz. 588)).

[2] Errors of John Hus: "The pope is not the true and manifest successor of Peter, the first of the other apostles, if he lives in a manner contrary to Peter; and if he be avaricious, then he is the vicar of Judas Iscariot. And with like evidence the cardinals are not the true and manifest successors of the college of the other Apostles of Christ, unless they live in the manner of the Apostles, keeping the Commandments and counsels of our Lord Jesus Christ"; "If the pope is wicked and especially if he is foreknown, then as Judas, the Apostle, he is of the devil, a thief, and a son of perdition, and he is not the head of the holy militant Church, since he is not a member of it"; (n. 13, 20, & 30 (Dz. 641 & 646)).

[3] "No one is a civil master, no one is a prelate, no one is a bishop while he is in mortal sin" (Dz. 595 & 656).

[4] "The great and holy Council of Nicea having been convened by the grace of God... We also give you the good news that, according to your prayers, the celebration of the most holy Paschal feast was unanimously rectified, so that our brethren of the East, who did not previously keep the festival at the same time as those of Rome, and as yourselves, and, indeed, all have done from the beginning, will henceforth celebrate it with you" (Bk. 2, c. 12 (PL 69, 931C-932C)).

they celebrate Easter on the fourteenth day of the new moon, but rather because they thought that it is necessary to do so. For Easter itself could have been celebrated on the fourteenth day of the new moon with impunity, if the Church had chosen this, and then they would not be doing wrong if they then celebrate it in this way. But the Church, in remembrance of the Lord's Resurrection which it is believed took place on a Sunday, decreed that Easter would always be celebrated on Sunday.

Now he who celebrates Easter on the fourteenth day of the new moon, no matter what day it occurs, although he does wrongly, still he ought not to be deemed a heretic, unless he shall believe that it necessarily ought to be so done. For if he thinks that Easter must necessarily be celebrated on the fourteenth day of the new moon, no matter what day it occurs, then he is truly a heretic. And those doing so are called Tessarescaedecatitae,[1] that is, Quartodecimans, so called from the fourteenth day of the new moon, on which they think that Easter necessarily ought to be celebrated. Augustine does not declare the author and first inventor of this heresy in his book, *De haeresibus*; although he lists it as the twenty-ninth among the others, but he only says that they care called Tessarescaedecatitae.[2] Yet [Pseudo-] Tertullian in his book on heresies names a certain Blastus whom he says was the author of this heresy.[3] The Anthropomorphites (Augustine bearing witness) adhered to this error.[4]

Thus, the opinion of these men is hence proved to be heresy, because above in the section on "Law," we showed it to be heresy to assert that the ceremonies and judgments of the Old Law oblige in the time of the Evangelical Law. But at what time Easter ought to be celebrated pertains to ceremonies, hence it is necessary that such a precept about the celebration of Easter on the fourteen day of the new moon is also made void by Christ's death. For Paul, when reprehending the Galatians in that they thought that the ceremonies of the Law ought to be observed, says among other things: "You observe days, and months, and times, and years" (4, 10). By which words he clearly taught that the observation of days, which were prescribed in the Law, is now wrong: all the more so that one would believe that it obliges under precept.

He who desires to know more fully the events which took place may read Eusebius in his *Church History*[5]: because there he relates in what way this question was sorted out. The *Historia Tripartita* also relates something further.[6]

---

[1] "Tessarescaedecatitae, because they contend that Passover to be observed with the Jews on the fourteenth day of the new moon. For the word *tessares* (τέσσαρες) signifies four, and *deka* (δέκα) ten." (St. Isidore of Seville *Etymologies*, bk. 8, c. 5, n. 61 (PL 82, 303C)).

[2] St. Augustine, *De haeresibus ad Quodvultdeus*, c. 29 (PL 42, 31).

[3] "In addition to all these, there is likewise Blastus, who would latently introduce Judaism. For he says the Passover is not to be kept otherwise than according to the law of Moses, on the fourteenth of the month. But who would fail to see that Evangelical grace is escheated if he recalls Christ to the Law?" (*The Prescription Against Heretics*, c. 53 (PL 2, 72B). In Migne's *Patrologia Latina* edition, the text contains not just forty-four chapters, but a further eight containing a list of heresies. These additional chapters are found separately in the Cluny-collection MSS as the spurious work *Adversus Omnes Haereses*, and appears as an appendix to *De praescriptione haereticorum* only in the Gagny/Mesnart edition of this work, where a marginal note indicates the join is the work of the editor.

[4] *De Haeresibus ad Quodvultdeum*, c. 50 (PL 42, 39).

[5] Bk. 5, c. 24 (PG 20, 494B-507B).

[6] Bk. 9, c. 37-38 (PL 69, 1152C-1156C).

PAUPERTAS

Poverty

There is one error concerning this matter whereby it is taught that no one can arrive at eternal life unless he were so poor that he has nothing of his own: because (as its upholders say) such was the life of the Apostles. The authors of this error, Augustine bearing witness,[1] are called the Apostolics, who with great arrogance gave themselves such a name, saying that they follow the life of the Apostles. This opinion is very clearly proved to be heretical, because there is nothing opposed to eternal life, except what has been interdicted by an express prohibition. For what has never been forbidden, is understood to be conceded, and consequently it cannot, when it shall have been done, impede someone from entering into glory. But to own property was never forbidden to all without distinction by God: hence it will be lawful.

But if someone were to say that Christ interdicted to all the ownership of things by that which is found in Luke: "Every one of you that doth not renounce all that he possesseth, cannot be my disciple" (14, 33): it is false: because by those words Christ merely forbade the affection for temporal things, not however ownership. For a man is seen by Christ to have renounced all things, who, although he may have riches, is prepared to lose all things before he would offend God on account of them. And if someone were to contend that those words ought to be understood of the renunciation as to the deed and not of the renunciation in the affection, let him then say in what way should it be understood that which in the same Luke is found: "Amen, I say to you, there is no man that hath left house, or parents, or brethren, or wife, or children, for the kingdom of God's sake, who shall not receive much more in this present time, and in the world to come life everlasting" (18, 29-30). Notice how He commands to leave one's house: because in the same way He commands it to be left, in that way He commands parents, brethren, wife, and children to be left. But all these things He does not wish to be so left by us, such that we lack them, but lest we so fix our heart upon them, that the love of those things separate us from the love of God. For he who has parents cannot leave them such that he would lack them, unless the parents die, because no matter wherever he may turn, as long as he lives, they will be his parents. Now to kill one's parents is wicked. Thus it is not so commanded to leave one's parents that the parents cease to be his own: and consequently it is also not so commanded to leave one's house or other possessions, so that they cease to be one's own, but it is thus commanded that he would leave such like things, namely lest the affection for those things in whatever way make us either completely cold or tepid. Hence one ought to possess them so that it may happen according to the counsel of the [Royal] Prophet saying: "If riches abound, set not your heart upon them" (Ps. 61, 11).

And if someone were to object that which Christ said to the His disciples when He sent them to preach: "Do not possess gold, nor silver, nor money in your purses" (Mt. 10, 9): to which we respond, that those words do not pertain to all Christians, but to the Apostles alone: and not to them at all times, but only for that time in which they were being sent to preach. But we have disputed at greater length concerning this matter above in the section on the "Apostles," in the second heresy. Moreover, when a certain young man inquired of Christ what good things he ought to do, so that he could have eternal life, Christ answers him saying: "If thou wilt enter into life, keep the commandments" (Mt. 19, 17). But when explaining what these Commandments were, He did not state any about abdicating the ownership of things: hence

---

[1] *De haeresibus ad Quodvultdeus*, c. 40 (PL 42, 32).

it is not necessary to actually abdicate things, although it belongs to greater perfection: which the context itself of Christ's words very clearly shows. For after He said that the observance of the Commandments is sufficient for attaining eternal life, wishing to explain the state of greater perfection, He then said: "If thou wilt be perfect, go sell what thou hast, and give to the poor, and thou shalt have treasure in heaven: and come follow me" (v. 21). This, I say, is the work of greater perfection, not of necessity. Again: If it be unlawful to own any property, why does Blessed Paul command to render to all men their dues? "Tribute, to whom tribute is due: custom, to whom custom" (Rom. 13, 7)? For if it is not lawful to own property, there will be no tribute or custom due to the ruler. But tributes are due to rulers, therefore it is lawful to own property. Let the haughty Apostolics be gone then, and let them renounce their property if they wish: and they will do well if they do not preclude the way of salvation to others who retain some property for themselves.

There is a **second heresy** which extols poverty to such an extent that it says that all sins are consumed by poverty alone.[1] The author of this heresy was a certain William [Cornelius] of Antwerp, as is testified in the *Catalogus haereticorum* [*omnium*].[2] But I could not learn at what time this William lived, since the *Catalogus* was silent about this, nor I could not learn this from another source.[3] Nevertheless it says that William was a man given over to the pleasures of the flesh, and afterwards he renounced his possessions saying that by poverty all sins are effaced, and better is a poor common prostitute than any chaste person owning something. And, certainly, if he were speaking about poverty of spirit, we would not have taken up arms against him, because this poverty of spirit, which is the contempt of all earthly things, when it has charity with it, as though annexed to it, does not allow mortal sin to be with it, just as neither does charity. Hence Christ says: "Blessed are the poor in spirit: for theirs is the kingdom of heaven" (Mt. 5, 3). But it is evident that this heretic is not speaking about this poverty, but about that poverty which by another name is called want, which is a certain defect, and the mere privation of riches.

Against this heresy is that which the Lord says: "Thou shalt not favour [*misereberis*, meaning "feel pity for"] a poor man in judgment" (Ex. 23, 3). If the Lord commands a poor man to be condemned in judgment, then it is a sign that it can happen that a man is poor and guilty. Furthermore, among the three things which the Wise Man hates, one is a proud poor man. "Three sorts my soul hateth," he says, "and I am greatly grieved at their life: a poor man that is proud: a rich man that is a liar: an old man that is a fool, and doting" (Eccle. 25, 3-4). Notice that you see a proud poor man. If he is proud, then he is a sinner: and consequently, it is necessary that poverty does not consume all sins, since it allows pride to be with it. Again, the Teacher of truth Himself says: "If thou wilt be perfect, go sell what thou hast, and give to the poor, and thou shalt have treasure in heaven: and come follow me" (Mt. 19, 21). If poverty would suffice to consume all sins, after Christ had commanded the young man to sell all that he had, and to give to the poor, it was not necessary to add, "and follow me." But because it was possible to sell all things, and to distribute as alms for the poor, and to sin with these things: hence Christ afterwards added those words, "and follow me." Which thing Paul wishing to express more clearly, said: "If I should distribute all my goods to feed the poor, and if I should deliver my body to be burned, and have not charity, it profiteth me nothing" (I Cor.

---

[1] The official charges against William Cornelius of Antwerp summarized his doctrine this way: "As rust is consumed by fire, all sin is consumed by poverty and annulled in the eyes of God. Simple fornication is not a sin for those who live in poverty" (Paul Fredericq, *Corpus documentorum Inquisitionis hereticae pravitatis Neerlandicae*, Ghent, 1889–1900 (Vuylsteke, 1903), vol. 1, pp. 119-120).

[2] Bk. 2.

[3] He died around 1253. Cf. Raoul Vaneigem, *The Resistance to Christianity: A Chronological Encyclopedia of the Heresies from the Beginning to the Eighteenth Century*, p. 349.

13, 3). Behold that poverty, not alone, but joined to almsdeeds, does not avail to consume sin, because it, Paul says, can be had without charity, and profited nothing.

The **third heresy** is nearly diametrically opposed to the second one, which was just related. For it says that poverty is not merely useless, but even harmful. The author of this heresy was a certain Desiderius [Sigerius] of Lombardy[1] in the time of Pope Alexander IV, saying that it is illicit to leave all things for Christ, unless one enters such a religious order that has possessions, or unless he is such a person who can live from the labor of his hands. At the same time there was another man, William of Saint-Amour, who wrote a tract against the mendicant monks, especially against the Franciscans and Dominicans, in which book he tried to argue that habitual poverty is licit, not however actual poverty, that is, the readiness of the soul to leave all things when forced by necessity is licit: yet outside of this necessity he says that the poverty whereby someone renounces everything he owns, in order to be at liberty to serve God more freely, is illicit.[2] And although there are different words of these two men, nevertheless there is agreement between the two on this same matter because both condemn poverty according to which someone leaves all things for Christ. But they seem to fight for different things, because Desiderius intimates that he approves of that poverty which is had in the religious congregations having possessions: yet he condemns the poverty to which was annexed mendicancy. But William of Saint-Amour condemns all actual poverty.

We have shown above clearly enough (as I think) that mendicancy is licit and meritorious in the section on "Mendicancy." But to extol poverty, that suffices which the Teacher of truth said to the young man asking what good things he ought to do in order to possess eternal life. For after He had said to him the keeping of the Commandments is effective enough for gaining it, wishing to show him the life of greater perfection, He added: "If thou wilt be perfect, go sell what thou hast, and give to the poor, and thou shalt have treasure in heaven: and come follow me" (Mt. 19, 21). But if perhaps someone were to say that this ought to be understood of the affection, namely that one would despise all things, not however that one would leave all things in deed: this is clearly refuted by that which is said in the same passage, "give to the poor." For one ought to sell the things with the intention that one would give to the poor. But he who gives to the poor, not merely relinquishes by his affection, but also by his deed.

But perhaps you will say that that act of giving to the poor was also commanded to that young man insofar as to the affection alone. In this way anyone could interpret that all the commands ought to be understood of the mere affection, and so there will be no actual deeds fulfilling the precept. Furthermore, if only the affection were commanded, and not the actual deed, why did the young man when he had heard Christ's counsel go away sad? For there would not have been sadness in his affections, if nothing had been said to him about the renouncing of his goods, and the assistance of the poor that ought to be exercised. "And when

---

[1] He is a French theologian mentioned by St. Thomas Aquinas in his *Liber contra impugnantes Dei cultum et religionem* (*An Apology for the Religious Orders*), part 2, c. 5: "The error of Vigilantius has been handed down by a succession of heretical teachers to our days. It is still perpetuated by the sect of the Cathari, and is expounded in a treatise written by a certain heresiarch of Lombardy named Desiderius, who, amongst other heretical propositions, condemns the conduct of those who sell all that they may live in poverty with Christ." Pope Clement IV approved of this small work of St. Thomas and condemned the writings of those attacking the religious congregations, and removed them from their posts and degrees as teachers, and banished them from Paris during the reign of King Louis IX of France. Cf. Alonso Chacon & Denis François Camusat, *Bibliotheca libros et scrptores* (Paris, apud viduam Georgii Jouvenel, 1731), pp. 669-670. Cf. Bernard of Luxemburg, *Catalogus haereticorum omnium*.

[2] "Such men ought to live by the labor of the body: nay, even all Christians, who do not have the means wherefrom they may live; yet as long as they have a strong body, not withstanding, even if they do not labor for the sake of spiritual works" (*De Periculis Novissimorum Temporum* in *Opera omnia Magistri Guillielmi de Sancto Amore* (Constance, apud Alithophilos, 1632), p. 48).

the young man had heard this word," the Evangelist says, "he went away sad: for he had great possessions" (v. 22). Notice the reason why he went away sad, namely because he had great possessions which the Lord commanded him to distribute to the poor. For so Theophylactus says: "For the Lord promised him treasure in Heaven, but the avaricious young man did not give heed, because he was a slave of his money. Therefore, when he heard what the Lord had asked of him, he was sorrowful. For the Lord had counseled him to deprive himself of his wealth."[1] In which place he says many other things in praise of poverty, clearly explaining those words of Christ of a renunciation in actual deed, for acquiring that perfection which God was counselling the young man. But all these things I omit for the sake of brevity. Again, the Apostles left all things for Christ: for having left all things they followed Him. And Peter in the name of them all says to Christ, the teacher of them all: "Behold we have left all things, and have followed thee: what therefore shall we have?" (Mt.19, 27). Then the Church whose judgment in matters of faith is infallible, recognized the poverty of mendicant monks not only to be licit, but also meritorious. Therefore, one ought to believe more the Church praising poverty than the heretics vituperating it.

Alexander IV published two decrees against this heresy.[2] Blessed Bonaventure wrote twice against it. For he wrote *Apologia pauperum*,[3] and another tract, *De paupertate Christi*,[4] against the aforesaid William; which two tracts are had among the opuscula of Blessed Bonaventure which are widely circulated. Blessed Thomas wrote one tract against this heresy, the title of which is, *Liber contra impugnantes [Dei cultum et] religionem*, which is found in the book of his opuscula.[5]

There is a **fourth heresy** which deals with the poverty of ecclesiastics, asserting that ecclesiastics ought to be poor men, content with alms alone. But we have disputed about this heresy above in the section on the "Church," in the fourth heresy. For in that place showed that it is licit for ecclesiastical men to have possessions and income.

PECCATUM

Sin

Heretics up until the present time have been greatly mistaken about those things which the Catholic faith proposes to us to be believed about sin. Firstly, in fact, some have erred saying that there is no Original sin: for which reason they say that infants do not have Original sin. The teacher of this error was the monk Pelagius, saying that infants are not baptized because they have sin which ought to be remitted through Baptism, but because they have not received the grace of adoption as sons of God, which he says they receive through Baptism, so that they may be admitted to the kingdom of Heaven. For those infants who die without Baptism, he says, have a certain blessed and eternal life, yet outside of God's king-

---

[1] *Ennaratio in Evangelium Sancti Lucae*, on Lk. 18, 23 (PG 123, 1011B).

[2] In the Bull *Quasi lignum vitae*, dated April 14, 1255, the pope settled the dispute between the University of Paris and the mendicant friars; and in the Bull *Romanus Pontifex*, dated October 5, 1256, he condemned William of Saint-Amour's treatise, *De Periculis novissimorum temporum*. Cf. "Mendicant Friars," *Catholic Encyclopedia* (New York, Robert Appleton Company, 1911), vol. 10, p. 184.

[3] *Sancti Bonaventurae Opera* (Rome, ex typographia Vaticana, 1596), vol. 10, pp. 411-466. *Defense of the Mendicants* (Bonaventure Texts in Translation Series, ed. by Robert J. Karris, O.F.M., St. Bonaventure, NY, Franciscan Institute Publications, Saint Bonaventure University, 2010, vol. 15.

[4] *Ibid.*, pp. 387-409.

[5] *An Apology for the Religious Orders* (London, Sands & Co., 1902).

dom. Pelagius opens the door to all these unsuitable things, because he denies Original sin, which he cannot understand. The Armenians maintain the same error, although in a different way, because even though they say that there is no Original sin, still they admit that Baptism is necessary for attaining eternal life. But they deny infants who die without Baptism have eternal life, but they say that they go to an earthly paradise if they are children of believers: because if they were children of unbelievers, they say that they descend to Hell with their parents. Thus, overlooking the errors which nowise agree with this stance, it is evident that this is a common error, which the Armenians share with Pelagius in that they deny Original sin. The Albanenses promote the same error.

Erasmus of Rotterdam gave no light suspicion that he thinks wrongly about Original sin, for in his *Annotations on the New Testament*, when explaining the words of Paul from the Epistle to the Romans: "in whom all have sinned" (5, 12), says that Paul said that all have sinned in Adam because all men imitate him by sinning.[1] Thus, he says that Adam's Original sin is transferred by imitation, not by propagation: because having been born of Adam they receive only the imitation of sinning, and not some sin. By which words he very clearly does away with the correct meaning of Original sin: because since newborn infants do not at that time imitate Adam in actual sin, then, according to Erasmus' teaching, they will have no sin.

Against this heresy is that which is found in the Third Book of Kings: "There is no man who sinneth not" (8, 46). But since infants are men just as adults are, it is thence proved that they also have some sin. They do not have, however, actual sin, since they do yet have the use of reason, which is especially required so that sin could be imputed to someone: therefore, it is necessary that infants have Original sin, since there is no other sin with which they could be stained, except Original and actual sin. For otherwise it would not be true that every man is at some time guilty of sin, which according to the Divine Writ is true of every man, because even if a small child has been baptized, he then lacks all sin, yet at some time he was under sin, namely before Baptism. Nevertheless, if there is no Original sin, there will be many men, namely infants, who never sinned.

Furthermore, the Royal Prophet, acknowledging his misery more correctly than Pelagius, says: "For behold I was conceived in iniquities; and in sins did my mother conceive me" (Ps. 50, 7). For when asking for God's mercy, so that he may more readily obtain it, he brings up his misery, and proneness to sin, which he had contracted from his parents. It is as though he were to say: "Thou ought to be have compassion upon me, because not from my malice, but from my weakness I have sinned: now I suffered this weakness when conceived in the very womb of my mother." If there is no Original sin, let Pelagius and his imitators show what this iniquity is, and what that sin is, which an infant has in the womb of its mother. Thus, since there cannot be another sin besides Original sin, it is thence proved that Original sin is.

Again, the Wise Man in Ecclesiasticus says: "A heavy yoke is upon the children of Adam, from the day of their coming out of their mother's womb, until the day of their burial into the mother of all" (40, 1). What other yoke upon all the children of Adam is there besides Original sin, which coming down from Adam passes on to all men? Now Original sin is called a yoke, because a yoke arises from the joining of two things, and bears down upon the one on which it is imposed. So likewise, every man who is conceived from the joining of a man and woman contracts Original sin. Wherefore Christ our Redeemer, even though He was a true man and a son of Adam according to his bodily substance, still never received the yoke of Original sin, because by the working power of the Most High He was incarnated from the Holy Ghost, and not from the joining of two, namely of a man and woman. Now Ecclesiasticus said that this yoke is upon all the children of Adam until the day of their burial because even if Original sin

---

[1] "Death reigned not only in Adam, but also in all who sinned according to his example" (*In Novum Testamentum Annotationes* (Basel, Inclyta Rauracorum, 1527), p. 347.

is effaced through Baptism, nevertheless many misfortunes and miseries remain for the whole time of this present life, which have arisen from Original sin as their source.

Next Blessed Paul, in that epistle which is to the Romans, says: "All have sinned, and do need the glory of God" (3, 23). If all have sinned, then infants have sinned. Now they have not sinned by actual sin, who have not yet attained the use of reason: therefore, they have sinned by Original sin. And in the same epistle he again says: "As by one man sin entered into this world, and by sin death; and so death passed upon all men, in whom all have sinned" (5, 12). If death entered upon all men, then infants die unjustly because before they have reached the age of discretion, they have no sin according to the teaching of these heretics. Likewise, these heretics can be asked why infants undergo pain, suffer from hunger and thirst, are very often bothered by demons, if they have no sin, from which all these things have proceeded? Hence since infants suffer all these things, it is evident that they have some sin due to which they are punished in this way: otherwise, God would be unjust, Who punishes someone before he is a sinner. But it is a wicked crime of injustice to accuse God of the crime of injustice: thus, it is wicked to assert that there is no Original sin.

But if Original sin is something real, it ought to be taken away through Baptism: because if a small child dies after having been baptized, he is saved, according to that saying of the Savior: "He that believeth and is baptized, shall be saved" (Mk. 16, 16). But if after having received Baptism the sin remains, one would not be saved: because into that holy city, the supernal Jerusalem, nothing defiled shall enter[1]: wherefore it is necessary that he who wishes to enter into glory would efface the stain of Original sin by the laver of Baptism. For so the Savior says: "Unless a man be born again, he cannot see the kingdom of God" (Jn. 3, 3).

Concerning this matter there exists a definition of the Council of Milevum, which in the second chapter of its decrees defines about this matter against Pelagius in these words: "Likewise it has been decided that whoever says that infants fresh from their mothers' wombs ought not to be baptized, or says that they are indeed baptized unto the remission of sins, but that they draw nothing of the Original sin from Adam, which is expiated in the bath of regeneration, whence it follows that in regard to them the form of Baptism 'unto the remission of sins' is understood as not true, but as false, let him be anathema."[2] Finally, the Council of Trent celebrated upon Paul III condemned this same heresy, in the fifth session, saying the following: "If anyone asserts that the transgression of Adam has harmed him alone and not his posterity, and that the sanctity and justice, received from God, which he lost, he has lost for himself alone and not for us also; or that he having been defiled by the sin of disobedience has transfused only death and the punishments of the body into the whole human race, but not sin also, which is the death of the soul, let him be anathema, since he contradicts the Apostle who says: 'By one man sin entered into the world, and by sin death, and so death passed upon all men, in whom all have sinned' (Rom. 5, 12)."[3] "If anyone asserts that this sin of Adam, which is one in origin and transmitted to all is in each one as his own by propagation, not by imitation, is taken away either by the forces of human nature, or by any remedy other than the merit of the one Mediator, our Lord Jesus Christ, Who has reconciled us to God in His own Blood, 'made unto us justice, sanctification, and redemption' (I Cor. 1, 30); or if he denies that that merit of Jesus Christ is applied to adults as well as to infants by the Sacrament of Baptism, rightly administered in the form of the Church: let him be anathema. 'For there is no other name under heaven given to men, whereby we must be saved...' (Acts 4, 12). Whence that word: 'Behold the lamb of God, behold Him who taketh away the sins of the world' (Jn. 1, 29). And that other: 'As many of you as have been baptized, have put on Christ' (Gal. 3,

---

[1] Cf. Apoc. 21, 27.

[2] Dz. 102.

[3] C. 2 (Dz. 789).

27)." In which words not only the error of the Pelagius and the Armenians, but also of Erasmus is condemned.

[Pseudo-] Augustine writes against this heresy in the book which is called *Hypognosticon* [*contra Pelagianos*], in the fifth book.[1] He also made another tract which is titled, *On [Merit and the Forgiveness of Sins, and] the Baptism of Infants*, which is found in the book of his letters, in his letter [to Marcellinus].[2]

Otherwise, that the Armenians say that the infants of unbelievers, dying without Baptism, descend into Hell with their parents, this will be shown to be false in the heresy immediately following, because there we will show that no one is damned except for their own sins.

The **second heresy** teaches that all men before Christ's Passion were damned on account of the sin of the first parents. Guy [the Carmelite] asserts that the authors of this heresy are the Armenians. For he says that the Armenians think that the sin of the first parents was so harmful that it harmed their whole posterity until Christ's Passion, and drew it into Hell, not actually because of Original sin, which those being born derived from the first parents, because they say (as appeared in the heresy immediately preceding) that sin does not exist, but they say that all men were damned on account of first parents' personal sin, even if they would have had no sin in themselves.[3] This heresy is so insane and foolish that its narration alone would suffice to exterminate it. But because we are proceeding against brazen and stiff-necked men, hence it is necessary that we hurl some dart against them, whereby we may pierce them.

Firstly then, it is evident that it is false, namely that all men up until Christ's Passion were damned. For Abraham, Isaac, and Jacob lived many centuries before Christ's Passion, and yet Scripture itself clearly teaches that they were saved. "Many," Christ says, "shall come from the east and the west, and shall sit down with Abraham, and Isaac, and Jacob in the kingdom of heaven" (Mt. 8, 11). See that Christ clearly teaches that those three Patriarchs belong to the kingdom of Heaven: thus they were never damned in Hell: because otherwise they would have never gone out of there, since "There is no redemption in Hell."[4] Furthermore, Christ, when showing what a broad distance there is between the rich man and the poor man, said that the gluttonous rich man after death was buried in Hell, while on the contrary Lazarus the beggar was carried by the Angels into Abraham's bosom.[5] If both were damned, what is this differentiation between these men? One is carried by the Angels, but the other is buried by the demons. If Lazarus was damned, why does the rich man ask for his help from Abraham? If Lazarus had been damned, how could he, touching the tongue of the rich man with his finger, temper its burning? Again, if they were just men, it is impossible that they, dying in justice, would be damned: because God is not unjust, that He would damn the just with the wicked.

But Scripture testifies concerning many men that they were just, such as Abel, Enoch, Abraham, Moses, and David: hence, none of these men were damned. But let it be that all men were damned (as the Armenians assert), it is impossible that those men were damned on account of the sin of the first parents alone, unless they themselves also had some personal sin. For God would be unjust if He damned someone without their own guilt: because even though God sometimes inflicts a temporary and transitory punishment upon someone on account of the sin of another, still He never eternally damns someone on account of the sin of another. For when God punishes someone with temporal punishment on account of the sin of

---

[1] PL 45, 1647-1658. The *Hypognosticon* is among the spurious works of Saint Augustine.

[2] PL 44, 109-199.

[3] *Summa de haeresibus et earum confutationibus*, c. 11, fol. 32v-33r.

[4] The phrase comes from a responsory of the Office of the Dead, in the third Nocturn of Matins: "Sinning daily, and not repenting, the fear of death disturbs me. Because there is no redemption in Hell, have mercy on me, O God, and save me.'

[5] Cf. Lk. 16, 22.

another, for example when a son is punished on account of the father's sin, and in the contrary case; or a ruler on account of his subjects, and vice versa: then He punishes the same one who sins in what belongs to him, namely the father in his son's death. But He does not properly punish the son who did nothing wrong, since for [the son's] greater good God inflicts such a penalty on him. And so that penalty is a punishment in relation to the father: but to the one suffering himself, namely the son, that that penalty ought not to be called a punishment, because God never inflicts it except so that He may allow it for the benefit of the one suffering. But he who has been eternally damned [is said to be punished by God], from the fact that no greater good could be attained: wherefore God never inflicts such damnation to anyone, unless their own demerits demand it.

For God when wishing to punish David on account of his adultery committed with Bethsabee, made the son born from that adultery to die, by which death He punished David, taking away from him what was his own, and what he greatly loved, namely his son. Now his son cannot be said to have been punished, since he had no guilt, because even though he died, still this death conferred a greater good to him, because "He was taken away lest wickedness should alter his understanding" (Wis. 4, 11), and he should commit things like unto his father. But if the son had perished unto eternity, what, I ask, benefit could have come to him from that damnation? Therefore, God never condemns anyone to eternal death, except on account of misdeeds. For He Himself promised through the prophet Ezechiel that he would act in this way, saying: "Behold all souls are mine: as the soul of the father, so also the soul of the son is mine: the soul that sinneth, the same shall die" (Ez. 18, 4). And shortly afterwards when speaking about the good son having a father who is a sinner, He adds these words: "This man shall not die for the iniquity of his father, but living he shall live. As for his father, because he oppressed and offered violence to his brother, and wrought evil in the midst of his people, behold he is dead in his own iniquity. And you say: Why hath not the son borne the iniquity of his father? Verily, because the son hath wrought judgment and justice, hath kept all my commandments, and done them, living, he shall live. The soul that sinneth, the same shall die: the son shall not bear the iniquity of the father, and the father shall not bear the iniquity of the son" (v. 17-20). Therefore, let the impious Armenians be afraid to say anything against the plain testimony of Scripture, especially since by their opinion one would ascribe a very great injustice to God, namely that He would condemn a just man, on account of another man's guilt.

Against this error also militates those things which we brought forward against the error of the Donatists in the section on the "Church," in the first heresy: in which place we showed that the wickedness of one person nowise hinders another in regard to eternal life.

The **third heresy** asserts that sin is not from free will, but from the devil. The author of this heresy was Valentinus, to whom afterwards the impious Manichaeus adhered. The Armenians raised up the same heresy, saying (as Guy [the Carmelite] accuses them[1]) that there would have been no sin if there were no devils, who impelled men to sin by their temptation: wherefore they say that sin is simply from the devil, and nowise from free will. The Albanenses consent to the Armenians in this regard.

This heresy is refuted by that which the Wise Man says in Ecclesiasticus: "God made man from the beginning, and left him in the hand of his own counsel. He added his commandments and precepts. If thou wilt keep the commandments and perform acceptable fidelity forever, they shall preserve thee. He hath set water and fire before thee: stretch forth thy hand to which thou wilt. Before man is life and death, good and evil, that which he shall choose shall be given him" (15, 14-18). From whose words it is evident that sin is also from free will, just as a good work, because man can stretch forth his hand to water and fire, to life and death, to good

---

[1] *Summa de haeresibus et earum confutationibus*, c. 16, fol. 35v.

and to evil. Furthermore, if man's will be free, then he can turn and turn back to either side, because otherwise he would not be free. Therefore, when he turns himself according to this liberty to evil, then the evil will be from himself, and not from the devil, since the devil does not choose, but man's will itself. Again, if you say that sin is from the devil, or consequently from the devil forcing our will to sin, and then our will shall not be free, since it could be forced. But we showed above in the section on "Liberty" that the will is free.

Or you say that sin is from the devil's persuasion, because he merely persuades without force: and then it is necessary that sin be from free will, which the devil persuades to choose evil. Then because the Armenians say that there would have been no sin if there would not have been devils who tempted men: this is proved to be false: because even if man's first sin proceeded from the devil's temptation, still man could have then sinned even if the devil did not tempt him; man had been created free by God, wherefore he could act well or badly. Add to this that the sin of the bad Angels proceeded from no other devil, but from their own free will. If then the first sin of the devil was committed without any temptation of another devil, then man also could have sinned if no temptation of the devil had preceded: because the Angels' strength is much greater than men's. Thus, if "in his angels he found wickedness: How much more shall they that dwell in houses of clay?" (Job 4, 18-19). Moreover, "Every man is tempted," James the Apostle says, "by his own concupiscence, being drawn away and allured" (1, 14). Hence there is no need of the devil's temptation so that he can commit sin. Finally, if sin were from the devil, and not from free will, it would be useless to persuade men not to sin. But if this were possible, one ought to persuade the devil, from whom is sin. Nevertheless, Christ said to a certain man whom he had healed from his infirmity: "Behold thou art made whole: sin no more" (Jn. 5, 14). And Paul in the First Epistle to the Corinthians says: "Awake, ye just, and sin not" (15, 34). If sin is from the devil, and not from free will, in vain does he advise us to beware of sin. Against such a clear error these very few words suffice.

I do not know of anyone who wrote specifically against this error: although Augustine often disputed against it, especially in his books, *On Free Will*,[1] and in the second book of his *On the Morals of the Catholic Church*.[2]

The **fourth heresy** teaches that every work no matter how well done, is a sin. The author of this error is Luther, saying that the just man sins in every good work.[3] From which putrid source he deduces another error, saying that no one is certain that he does not sin mortally.[4] But we have already disputed above about this error, in the section on "Works." For we showed there from Scriptures, there are many good works which have entirely no mixed evilness, and in them it is certain that many men did not sin mortally when they did them. But if someone desires to see something in addition to those things which we said in the section on "Works," he may read John [Fisher], Bishop of Rochester, in his work which he made for the confutation of Luther's *Assertio* [*omnium articulorum per Bullam Leonis, X. novissimam damnatorum*].[5]

Aëtius teaches a **fifth heresy**, saying that no sin, no matter how grave, is imputed to a man having faith. Luther raised up in our age this same error buried for a long time, saying that faith alone without any other work is enough for attaining eternal life. But we have already refuted this error above from Sacred Scripture. For in the section on "Faith," in the second heresy, we very clearly showed by testimonies of Sacred Scripture that faith alone nowise suffices for reaching eternal glory, but other works are also necessary, namely those which

---

[1] PL 32, 1221-1310. This work is divided into three books.
[2] PL 32, 1345-1378.
[3] Proposition 31 condemned in the papal Bull *Exsurge Domine* (Dz. 771).
[4] *Ibid.*, proposition 35 (Dz. 775).
[5] *Assertionis Lutheranae confutatio* (Cologne, Maternus Cholinus, 1564), art. 35, fol. 352r-357v.

have been enjoined to us by explicit precepts. But if works are also required, and faith alone does not suffice, it is very clearly concluded that it can happen that a sin may be imputed to someone having faith.

The Armenians invented the **sixth heresy**, saying that some sins are completely irremissible, which cannot ever be remitted by any priest. Against this is that which Christ said to Peter: "Whatsoever thou shalt bind upon earth, it shall be bound also in heaven: and whatsoever thou shalt loose upon earth, it shall be loosed also in heaven" (Mt. 16, 19). He who says all things, excludes nothing. But Christ did not say: "If you loose this or that, it will be loosed in heaven": but "Whatsoever," He said, "thou shalt loose upon earth, it shall be loosed also in heaven." Therefore, there is not any sin which cannot be remitted by Peter. Furthermore, it is said to all the Apostles: "Whatsoever you shall loose upon earth, shall be loosed also in heaven" (Mt. 18, 18). And again: "Whose sins you shall forgive, they are forgiven them" (Jn. 20, 23). Behold, you see the power of loosing not this or that sin, but every sin, was not only given to Peter, but to all the Apostles. "Whatsoever," He said, "thou shalt loose upon earth, it shall be loosed also in heaven."

But the Armenians can object to us those words of the Savior saying: "Every sin and blasphemy shall be forgiven men, but the blasphemy of the Spirit shall not be forgiven. And whosoever shall speak a word against the Son of man, it shall be forgiven him: but he that shall speak against the Holy Ghost, it shall not be forgiven him, neither in this world, nor in the world to come" (Mt. 12, 31-32). From which passage they seem to infer that a sin against the Holy Ghost cannot be forgiven by any priest. But this is not the case, because Christ did not speak universally of every sin against the Holy Ghost, but of some. For He did not say no sin against the Holy Ghost would be forgiven, but said that the blasphemy of the Spirit would not be forgiven. And "He that shall speak against the Holy Ghost," He says, "it shall not be forgiven him, neither in this world, nor in the world to come." And we admit that there is some sin which is never remitted, not will be remitted. Now this is the hardness of heart, whereby a man refuses until the end of his life to accept the remission of sin through repentance. Such sin, I say, will never be remitted, not because it was unremittable, but because the sinner never repented of it, hence it will never be remitted in this life: but after death, even if he were to repent, it will not be remitted: because "Confession perishes from the dead, as from one that is not" (Eccli. 17, 26). As long as the sinner lives, as the Apostle says, God's patience waits for us to repent.[1] And if he shall do penance, and does not disdain to receive absolution from the priest, his sin, no matter how grave, without a doubt will be remitted in this world. But if he perseveres in iniquity, as the Apostle added in that same place, "According to his hardness and impenitent heart, he treasurest up to himself wrath, against the day of wrath, and revelation of the just judgment" (v. 5). Augustine interprets that passage of Matthew in this way in a letter to his companion Boniface.[2]

Yet Richard of Saint Victor interprets this passage otherwise, who says that these words of Christ ought to be understood not of the remission of guilt, but of punishment. For he says

---

[1] Cf. Rom. 2, 4: "The benignity of God leadeth thee to penance."

[2] "Whosoever therefore has resisted or fought against this gift of the grace of God, or has been estranged from it in any way whatever to the end of this mortal life, shall not receive the remission of that sin, either in this world, or in the world to come, seeing that it is so great a sin that in it is included every sin; but it cannot be proved to have been committed by any one, till he has passed away from life. But so long as he lives here, 'the benignity of God,' as the Apostle says, 'is leading him to penance;' but if he deliberately, with the utmost perseverance in iniquity, as the Apostle adds in the succeeding verse, 'according to thy hardness and impenitent heart, thou treasurest up to thyself wrath, against the day of wrath, and revelation of the just judgment' (Rom. 2, 4-5) he shall not receive forgiveness, neither in this world, neither in that which is to come" (Letter 185, c. 11, n. 49 (PL 33, 814-815)).

that he who has sinned against the Son will be treated more leniently than he who has sinned against the Holy Ghost: because he who sinned against the Son, has an excuse, in that he acted through ignorance, and so is deserving of pardon, namely whereby some of the punishment due to the sin would be forgiven him. He, however, who sinned against the Holy Ghost, has no excuse, in that he acted out of pure malice, and so is not deserving of pardon, namely whereby some of the punishment due to the sin may be forgiven him. Hence, he says that this is the difference between he who sins against the Father or the Son, and he who sins against the Holy Ghost, namely that he who sins against the Father or the Son sins out of weakness, or out of ignorance: and wherefore is worthy that some of the punishment due to the sin be forgiven him, whether he repents or does not repent. But he who sins against the Holy Ghost, sins out of pure malice: wherefore completely nothing will be forgiven him of the punishment due to the sin, in that he has no excuse, since he sinned out of pure malice: because even if his sin may be remitted through repentance, still he will pay all the punishment due to the sin: and so if he shall do penance, he will be freed from the guilt, but nowise from the punishment. Richard of Saint Victor discusses all these things in a small tract of his which is entitled, *De spiritu blasphemiae*.[1]

Theophylactus interprets [this passage] in nearly the same way, although he seems to think that who has sinned out of weakness or ignorance, either against the Father or against the Son, which is the same thing, is deserving of pardon: so that even if he would not repent, it would be forgiven him, because weakness or ignorance excuses him not only from part of the punishment, but also from the guilt.[2] Richard, however, does not want to excuse him from guilt, but from part of the punishment: and he says that this ought to be understood through forgiveness, such that it ought to be referred to the punishment alone. Otherwise, they agree with each other about the sin of the Holy Ghost, since both think that it is not forgiven because it has no excuse, on account of which some of the punishment due to him may be forgiven, such that although repentance having been made, the guilt is forgiven, still it is necessary that he pay the whole punishment due to the sin. And this is for them [how it is that] this sin is not forgiven. Read them, and perhaps it will seem to you that their exposition is more faithful to the text than Augustine's, although the interpretation of the latter is not to be despised.

The **seventh heresy** asserts that no capital sin ought to be tolerated, even if it be permitted for the sake of avoiding any greater evil. The authors of this heresy are the Waldensians, although Guy the Carmelite, when enumerating the errors of the Waldensians in his *Summa de*

---

[1] PL 196, 1189B-1191B.

[2] "He is saying here that every other sin, such as fornication or theft, has some defense, however slight. For we take refuge in human weakness and we may be forgiven. But when one sees miracles performed by the Spirit and slanders them as being the work of a demon, what defense will he have? For it is clear that such a slanderer knows that these things are of the Holy Ghost, yet he speaks evil of his own will. How then can such a man be forgiven? When the Jews saw the Lord eating and drinking, associating with publicans and harlots, and doing all the other things He did as the Son of Man, then they slandered Him as a glutton and drunkard; yet for this they deserve forgiveness, and not even repentance will be required. For they were understandably scandalized. But when they saw Him working miracles and were slandering and blaspheming the Holy Ghost, saying that it was something demonic, how will this sin be forgiven them, unless they repent? So, then, know that he who blasphemes the Son of Man, seeing Him living as a man, and says that He is a friend of harlots, a glutton, and a drunkard because of those things which Christ does, such a man will not have to give an answer for this, even if he does not repent. For he is forgiven, as he did not realize that this was God concealed. But he who blasphemes the Holy Ghost, that is, the spiritual deeds of Christ, and calls them demonic, unless he repents, he will not be forgiven. For he does not have a reasonable excuse to slander, as does the man who sees Christ with harlots and publicans and then slanders" (*Enarratio in Evangelium S. Matthaei* (PG 123, 270A-271A)).

haeresibus, never mentions this error. But Aeneas Sylvius, who afterwards was called Pope Pius II, in his book, *De origine Bohemorum*, lists this among the errors of the Waldensians.[1]

Against this heresy is that in Matthew which Christ our Redeemer, when speaking to the Jews, says: "Moses by reason of the hardness of your heart permitted you to put away your wives: but from the beginning it was not so" (19, 8). Notice that the divorce of a man and woman was permitted by Moses. But such divorce Christ shows to be bad, saying: "What therefore God hath joined together, let no man put asunder" (v. 6). And in these words (as Jerome testifies in the same place[2]) He did not give a new precept, but he renewed the old one, and restored it. And Christ Himself states this clearly enough, saying: "But from the beginning it was not so" (v. 8). By which words He taught that marriage from its institution was indissoluble. But Moses seeing his nation prone to allurements, and fearing that when some wife would not be pleasing to her husband, she would be killed by the husband, so that he might be able to have a more beautiful wife, he permitted them to be able to repudiate their wives when they wished, so that they would avoid uxoricide. "Moses permitted you," Christ says, "by reason of the hardness of your heart to put away your wives." If he permitted, then He never approved such a misdeed: because (as [Pseudo-] Chrysostom points out in the same place[3]) we permit those things which we do not approve.

Moreover, a lesser evil compared to a greater evil has some aspect of goodness, namely the lack of that degree of evilness, by which the greater evil exceeds the lesser. Now all avoidance of evil is good. And according to this reckoning of good it can be in a certain way accepted by the will. Again, those things which are done through fear are very often excused, which apart from that fear ought not to be excused. Now they are not excused except by reason of a pressing greater evil near at hand, thus anyone can licitly choose the lesser evil as a means whereby one can avoid the greater evil which is imminent. For it is evil if someone were to cast merchandise into the sea, which could be kept without harm, so that it could be put to good use. But if a storm impels, one rightly sinks it, when fearing that if he would choose to keep it, he himself would be sunk.

And if this is allowed for a particular and private person: why will it not also be allowed for a public person? If men's chastity is firmly trusted, it is evil to permit harlots among the people. But if the latter having been expelled from the people, the fidelity of marriage would be violated, such that, as a certain prophet says: "Everyone neighed after his neighbour's wife" (Jer. 5, 8), and "would change the natural use into that use which is against nature...," as the Apostle says, "men with men working that which is filthy" (Rom. 1, 26-27), and if these consequences are truly feared, it is expedient to tolerate harlots rather than to expel them. Add to these things the command of the goodman of the house, who commands his servants wishing to remove the cockle from the field in which wheat was sown, that they suffer those things until the harvest, lest perhaps gathering the cockle, the wheat be rooted up also at the same time.[4]

---

[1] *De origine Bohemorum ac gestis historia*, c. 35, p. 59.

[2] "'They say to him: Why then did Moses command to give a bill of divorce, and to put away?' They betray the calumny that they had been preparing. And surely the Lord had not brought forth His own opinion, but He had recalled the ancient history and the commands of God. 'He saith to them: Because Moses by reason of the hardness of your heart permitted you to put away your wives: but from the beginning it was not so.' What He meant to say is this: 'Is God able to contradict Himself? Does He first command one thing and then break His own judgment by a new command? One must not understand things in this way'" (*Commentary on Matthew*, bk. 3 (PL 26, 134B-D)).

[3] "What we permit, we order though we do not want to because we cannot fully prevent the evil will of the people" (*Opus imperfectum*, hom. 32 (PG 56, 801-802)).

[4] Cf. Matt. 13, 29.

Next, this opinion is confirmed by the testimony of Blessed Gregory, who when interpreting those words of Job: "The sinews of his testicles are wrapped together" (40, 12), says these words: "The sinews of (leviathan's[1]) testicles are wrapped together, because the arguments of his suggestions are bound together by complicated devices; so as to make many sin in such a way, that, if they wish perchance to escape a sin, they cannot escape it without being entangled in another sin; and that they commit a fault in avoiding it, and that they are unable to release themselves from one, unless they consent to be bound by another… There is, however, a plan which may be usefully adopted to overthrow (behemoth's) craft, namely, that when the mind is straightened between lesser and greater sins, if no outlet for escape is open without sin, the lesser evils should always be preferred: because even he who is shut in by a circuit of walls on every side lest he escape, hurries himself to where the wall is found lowest."[2]

The Eighth Council of Toledo supports the same opinion, saying these words: "Although one must carefully guard against being forced to choose between two evils, if an inescapable danger compels us one to perpetrate one of two evils, we must choose the one that makes us less guilty. We should investigate which of the two is less and which is more serious by the acuity of pure reason. For when we are compelled to lie, we offend the Creator, but we stain only ourselves. When we perform a crime because of a promise, we hold God's command in contempt through pride, harm our neighbors with faithless cruelty, and cut ourselves down with a still crueler sword. In the former case we perish by a twofold lance of guilt, in the latter we are slain in three ways."[3] From which words it is very clearly proved that a king, or any other public authority, can licitly and without any guilt permit the people subject to him some lesser sin, so that by allowing it he may turn away the same people from some other graver sin, into which he justly fears that they will fall. For it is much less to permit than to choose: because permission can be without approval, nay it can be with great disapproval of the thing permitted; choice, however, is never without some approval of the thing chosen. Now all these things which we have said, we want to be understood of only that permission which merely excludes the punishment of guilt, and not the guilt itself. A king, or any other public authority, can permit, that is, not punish some sin, so that in this way the people may abstain from some greater sin. Nevertheless, he cannot permit, that is, so indulge the pardon of guilt, such that by doing what has been permitted, if it is against the Divine law, one would not sin: because no one can dispense in this way from the Divine law.

The **eighth heresy** asserts that all sins are equal, just as the *Paradoxa Stoicorum*[4] maintains. Augustine attributes this heresy to the monk Jovinian.[5] Yet Blessed Jerome who disputed against the errors of the Jovinian in two books,[6] never mentions this error, nor does he accuse this Jovinian of this error: still from which it is not allowed to conclude that Jovinian did not think in this way. For it could have happened that that this error did not come to the

---

[1] I.e. the Devil's.

[2] *Moralia*, bk. 32, c. 20, n. 36 & 39 (PL 76, 657B-6591A). Cf. Gratian, *Concordia discordantium canonum*, dist. 13, p. 1, c. 2 (PL 187, 67C-70A).

[3] C. 2 (PL 84, 419C-D). Cf. Gratian, *Concordia discordantium canonum*, dist. 13, p. 1, c. 1 (PL 187, 67B).

[4] The *Paradoxa Stoicorum* (English: *Stoic Paradoxes*) is a work by the Academic Skeptic philosopher Cicero in which he attempts to explain six famous Stoic sayings that appear to go against common understanding. The third of which is: "All the vices and all virtues are equal." His facetious logic is as follows: If you are not virtuous and wise, you are totally bad and foolish. The wise are totally happy, the foolish totally unhappy. Whatever strides you may have made towards virtue, you are no happier till you get there.

[5] *De haeresibus ad Quodvultdeus*, c. 82 (PL 42, 45).

[6] *Against Jovinianus* (PL 23, 211-338).

notice of Jerome, and hence he did not write against it, although he had meant to write against all of Jovinian's errors. But let it be assumed that this was not asserted by Jovinian: since now it is known about this error, it is necessary that we bring forth some things against it.

For Christ our Redeemer very clearly teaches that there is an inequality among sins. For in Matthew, He speaks thus: "I say to you, that whosoever is angry with his brother, shall be in danger of the judgment. And whosoever shall say to his brother, Raca, shall be in danger of the council. And whosoever shall say, Thou Fool, shall be in danger of hell fire" (5, 22). By these words a difference of sins is clearly shown, from the difference of punishments. For it is worse to be in danger of hell fire, than to be in danger of the judgment, or to be in danger of the council: thus it is worse to say, "Thou fool," than to say, "Raca." Furthermore, when Christ was speaking to His disciples about those who had not received them with hospitality, He says: "Amen I say to you, it shall be more tolerable for the land of Sodom and Gomorrha in the day of judgment, than for that city" (Mt. 10, 15). If it will be more tolerable, then their sin will be reputed less, because according to the measure of the sin will be the extent of the misfortune. Again, a sin against the Holy Ghost is more serious than a sin against the Father or the Son: which is proved from the fact that the former is not be forgiven, neither in this world, nor in the world to come,[1] but the latter is forgiven. Next, the same Teacher of truth. when speaking to Pilate. said: "He that hath delivered me to thee, hath the greater sin" (Jn. 19, 11). Notice the very clear testimony whereby the inequality of sins is proved. Wherefore it is not necessary that we dispute longer about this matter. And it is not necessary to bring to the fore arguments from the workshop of the philosophers, because we do not dispute here against the Stoics, but against Jovinian, or any other patron of this error, who boasts that he is a Christian.

The **nineth heresy** teaches that a man who has been once justified by grace, cannot sin anymore. Blessed Jerome pins this heresy on Jovinian in his work against the same man, in the second book.[2] Augustine, in his book on heresies, attributes it to Pelagius, as well as to Jovinian.[3] After a long time the Beghards and Beguines revived this same heresy, although not such that they would affirm their assertion universally about every just man, as Jovinian and Pelagius do, but speaking more narrowly, they said that a man could acquire such great perfection of virtue in this miserable life, that he is rendered completely unable to sin. And certainly, if the Beghards and Beguines were to say that this can happen from a certain privilege, and by the very special help of God granted to someone, no one would have branded them on account of this as heretics. For God can by a certain exceptional privilege so assist the will of some man, that He would not permit it to fall into sin.

For many and illustrious theologians confess this was granted to the Virgin Mother of God after she conceived the only-begotten Son of God in her womb[4]: I will cite one of them, Rich-

---

[1] Cf. Mt. 12, 32.

[2] "The second proposition of Jovinianus is that the baptized cannot be tempted by the devil. And to escape the imputation of folly in saying this, he adds: But if any are tempted, it only shows that they were baptized with water, not with the Spirit, as we read was the case with Simon Magus. Hence it is that John says, 'Whosoever is begotten of God does no sin' (I Jn. 3, 9-10)" (N. 1 (PL 23, 281D)).

[3] *De haeresibus ad Quodvultdeus*, c. 82 & 88 (PL 42, 45 & 48).

[4] St. Thomas wrote that some "say that in her first sanctification, the *fomes* [*peccati*, or inclination to evil] remained essentially, but was fettered; and that, when she conceived the Son of God, it was entirely taken away… but by reason of the abundant grace bestowed on her in her sanctification [at conception], and still more perfectly by Divine Providence preserving her sensitive soul, in a singular manner, from any inordinate movement. Afterwards, however, at the conception of Christ's flesh, in which for the first time immunity from sin was to be conspicuous, it is to be believed that entire freedom from the *fomes* redounded from the Child to the Mother." (III q. 27, a. 3).

ard of Saint Victor who speaks thus: "It is believed the banishment of sin that happened in the Blessed Virgin Mary will, it is hoped, take place in all the saints. It will take place, I say, not yet in their mortal body, but in their body at the time when it has been made immortal. First it is indeed necessary that 'This corruptible must put on incorruption; and this mortal must put on immortality' (I Cor. 15, 53). But this was in the Blessed Virgin marvelous above measure, and singular among all the other saints, that so much corruptibility could be together at the same time in her with so much incorruptibility. Corruptibility in those things which pertain to her suffering, incorruptibility in those things which pertain to guilt."[1] From Richard's words it is evident that such a privilege was granted to the Virgin Mother of God, so that she would be completely impeccable: which privilege he asserts was granted to no one else among men. But he says that we hope to have this in the other life, because the Blessed Virgin had it in this life.

But the impious Beghards and Beguines teach that any man could acquire this in this life, if through advancement in virtue one reaches the degree of perfection which they assign. And on account of this they were deservedly condemned, because it is said to every man existing in this life: "He that thinketh himself to stand, let him take heed lest he fall" (I Cor. 10, 12). And the Lord, when teaching us to pray, commands that we say: "Forgive us our debts" (Mt. 6, 12). Which prayer all men can truthfully say until the end of their lives. And Blessed John in his first canonical epistles says: "If we say that we have no sin, we deceive ourselves, and the truth is not in us" (1, 8). Therefore, the truth is not in these heretics saying that there is such a man in this life, who could not sin.

But against the Beghards and Beguines there is a definition of a general council,[2] in which eight errors of these men were condemned, among which this one, about which we now treat, is the first. The decree of this council is had in the book, *Constitutiones Clementinae*, in the title, *De haereticis*, in the chapter whose beginning is *Ad nostrum*.[3]

There is a **tenth heresy** which asserts that there is no mortal sin, except incredulity. The first author and inventor of this heresy is Martin Luther; and Philip Melanchthon, John Calvin, Martin Bucer, and as many others classified by the Lutheran name have followed him on this point. Luther deduces this error from another very pestilential error of his, which is a copious source from which innumerable errors gush forth. For he says that faith alone justifies, and that alone is sufficient for attaining eternal life: but works are not necessary for justification, nor for attaining eternal life. From this opinion it is evidently inferred that only incredulity is a mortal sin, which truly takes away justification and grace. For if [something] besides infidelity would be a mortal sin, it would very clearly follow therefrom that something else besides faith is necessary for justification, and consequently for attaining eternal life. Because if something other than infidelity is truly called a sin, it is an omission of some work: thus, that omitted work was necessary for justification: otherwise the one who had omitted it would not have sinned. If that sin was the perpetration of some evil deed, then it was necessary for justification to abstain from it for keeping justification: otherwise, the one who committed that wicked deed would not have sinned. Thus, it is evident that no sin ought to be called a mortal sin except infidelity alone, if one concedes that faith alone justifies. Therefore, since this heresy is very clearly inferred from the other heresy, it will not be necessary to dispute at the present time, because the other heresy upon which it rests and from which it depends,

---

[1] *De Emmanuele*, bk 2, c. 31 (PL 196, 664C).

[2] I.e., the Council of Vienne.

[3] "That man in the present life can acquire so great and such a degree of perfection that he will be rendered inwardly sinless, and that he will not be able to advance farther in grace; for, as they say, if anyone could always advance, he could become more perfect than Christ" (Dz. 471). *Clementinae*, lib. 5, t. 3, c. 3.

we have already conquered in the section on "Faith," in the second heresy. I merely add here that the decree of the Council of Trent, which was celebrated under Paul III, in the sixth session, pronounced many canons of the faith, among which the twenty-seventh contains these words: "If anyone shall say that there is no mortal sin except that of infidelity, or that grace once received is not lost by any other sin however grievous and enormous, except the sin of infidelity: let him be anathema."[1]

There is an **eleventh heresy** which teaches that there is no difference between mortal and venial sin because, as it says, there is no venial sin, but every sin is a moral sin. John Calvin teaches this heresy in his work, *Institutes of the Christian Religion*.[2] In which view he departs somewhat from his leader, Martin Luther: because the latter says, concerning unbelievers, that all their sins are mortal sins, but he says that the sins of believers are venial, besides incredulity, which alone he says is a mortal sin. It is not necessary to dispute now against Luther: because that which he says, that all the sins of unbelievers are mortal sins, although I believe that it is false, still it is not evident that it is heretical, nor has the Church defined anything yet (as far as I know) about it, but it is still controverted among scholastic theologians. The Council of Trent indeed condemned the opinion saying: All works done before justification are truly sins[3]: but it did not on that account condemn the opinion saying: All the works of unbelievers are truly sins. But the rest of what he says, namely that there is no mortal sin besides infidelity alone, pertains to the heresy immediately preceding.

Therefore, we now take up arms against John Calvin alone: because it is he alone who utterly mocks that distinction of sins which all theologians teach, saying: Some sins are mortal, and others are venial. For he says that every sin is mortal, and none are venial. Calvin's words in that tract which he wrote against the definitions of the Council of Trent are these: "Every sin, inasmuch as it is condemned by the law of God, is mortal."[4] He says these words against canon twenty-seven of the sixth session of the aforesaid council. And against the teaching given by the same council in the eleventh chapter of the same session, he says these words: "If they consider what they call lighter lapses as nothing, the dreadful sentence of the Supreme Judge thunders forth, 'He who shall *despise* [sic] one of these least commandments shall be called the least in the kingdom of heaven' (Mt. 5, 19). Although I should like to know what sins they call light, for so they speak by way of extenuation."[5] When disputing against him, we will point out some things in passing against Luther.

Firstly, I am certainly very surprised that Calvin fell into such great madness, that he would not only want to contradict all others, but even himself. He assuredly ought to have remembered another lie, lest afterwards he be convicted of having lied on both sides: for Calvin asserts that he followed Luther in another teaching, that a just man sins in every good work. If a just man sins in every good work, and every sin, as he says, is mortal, then a just man sins mortally in every good work, and consequently every good work will be a mortal sin. What, I ask, more absurd and foolish thing can be said? How can it happen, or how can it be understood, that a good work be reckoned a mortal sin? Furthermore, if some man is deemed just, it is necessary that he then lack mortal sin. Now if he sins mortally, he cannot be truly be called just: because mortal sin takes away true justice. These two things therefore are, so

---

[1] Dz. 837.

[2] "Here they take refuge in a foolish distinction, that some sins are venial, and some mortal; that a great satisfaction is due for mortal sins; but that those which are venial are purged away by easier remedies... But though they are incessantly talking of venial and mortal sins, yet they have never been able to discriminate one from the other." (Bk. 3, c. 4, n. 28 (ed. 1559, CR 30, 479)).

[3] Cf. Dz. 817.

[4] *Acts of the Council of Trent with the Antidote* (CR 35, 482).

[5] *Ibid.* (CR 35, 462).

to speak, diametrically opposed: a just man sins in every good work and every sin is mortal. But putting aside the other teachings of this Calvin, I will now clearly prove that this teaching about which we now dispute is false and heretical, by the testimonies of Sacred Scripture and of the holy Fathers, and by the clear definitive judgment of the whole Catholic Church.

Nevertheless, before we enter upon the disputation, it is necessary to state what in this regard do we understand by mortal sin and what by venial sin, lest perhaps it happen that we fight in regards to a misunderstanding, and dispute only from the meaning of the words. A mortal sin is that sin through which is taken away the spiritual life of the soul, which is by grace, which when taken away God immediately leaves the soul in which He was dwelling, and hence death immediately follows. Hence Augustine says: "The life of your flesh is your soul: the life of your soul is your God. As the flesh dies in losing the soul, which is its life, so the soul dies in losing God, who is its life."[1] This is that death about which God threatened the first parent, when after having forbidden eating of the tree of the knowledge of good and evil, He said to him: "In what day soever thou shalt eat of it, thou shalt die the death" (Gen. 2, 17). For Adam did not die a bodily death immediately on that day on which he ate the forbidden fruit: but he immediately died a spiritual death of the soul, because he immediately lost justice, and consequently God.[2] Hence only mortal sin is that wickedness about which Solomon says: "For a man killeth (his own soul) through malice" (Wis. 16, 14).[3] And Jeremias also says: "Everyone shall die for his own iniquity" (31, 30). And Lord says through Ezechiel: "The soul that sinneth, the same shall die" (18, 4). Likewise ought to be understood, concerning the same sin, what Paul says: "Know you not, that to whom you yield yourselves servants to obey, his servants you are whom you obey, whether it be of sin unto death, or of obedience unto (life)?" (Rom. 6, 16).[4] Sin is also something mortal [or deadly] on account of the other death, which devours the soul and body, and this is everlasting Hell, about which the Royal Prophet says: "They are laid in hell like sheep: death shall feed upon them" (Ps. 48, 15). And John, in the Apocalypse, says: "And hell and death were cast into the pool of fire. This is the second death" (20, 14). Therefore, it is called mortal sin because the sinner who commits it, unless he repents, will be punished with eternal death. "The lovers of evil things deserve (death)" (Wis. 15, 6).[5]

Now sin is accustomed to be called venial in many ways, and hence it is necessary to show its various meanings, so that afterwards I may say according to which meaning we use it in this place, when we distinguish it from mortal sin. A sin is sometimes called venial on account of the cause from which it arises, which usually diminishes the guilt itself, and so also gives some reason for pardon. Such are the sins proceeding from ignorance or from weakness, which are not as grave as are those which proceed from pure malice, and hence they deserve some pardon (*veniam*), so that the former are not punished as severely as the latter. Other times a sin is called venial from the outcome which happens to it: namely that pardon was given to it. And according to this meaning, no sin is so grave that it may not be called venial, if worthy penance is done for it. For so Ambrose ought to be understood when he said that all

---

[1] *Tractates on the Gospel of John*, tractate 47, n. 8 (PL 35, 1736).

[2] A side reference to "Luke 15" without any corresponding text is found here, perhaps because a deletion in the text was made. Most likely it made reference to the spiritual death of the prodigal son, about whom it was said that he "was dead, and is come to life again" (v. 24).

[3] This wording is taken from the *Vetus Latina*. The *Vulgate* here reads: "A man indeed killeth through malice."

[4] The author here again uses the *Vetus Latina*, whereas the *Vulgate* reads: "... unto justice."

[5] The *Vulgate* here reads: "The lovers of evil things deserve to have no better things to trust in." Cf. François Luc de Bruges, *Romanæ Correctionis in Latinis Bibliis editionis vulgatæ* (Antwerp, Ex officina Plantiniana, 1603).

mortal sins become venial through repentance.[1] [Pseudo-] Augustine ought to be understood, who in his book, *De vera et falsa poenitentia*, says: "For there are some sins which are mortal, and through repentance become venial."[2] He said, "through repentance become pardonable," instead of saying, "through penance become venial." According to neither of these two meanings do we use the words "venial sin" in the present disputation, in which we strive to prove that venial sin differs by nature from mortal sin.

In a third way a sin is called venial from its own nature and considered strictly, and it is that sin which of itself and by its nature is so light and so small, that it is not able to strip someone of Divine grace, or make him an enemy of God, or render him deserving of eternal death. Now this lightness of sin sometimes is inherent to it by its nature, and from its genus, because the matter itself, or the thing itself about which it deals, is light by its nature, such as immoderate laughter is, or an idle word whereby no one is harmed. Sometimes the very lightness of sin does not come from the matter itself, but from the imperfection of the work, which can happen, even where the matter itself is very grave. Now such imperfection of the work can arise from the parvity of the matter, as happens in the theft of a very small thing, or in the small detraction by which the neighbor's reputation is injured in a very small matter. Such imperfection of the work can also arise from the lack of deliberation which happens in sudden movements, on account of which defect the work itself cannot be called fully voluntary, and hence does not have the full essence of mortal sin: and hence it comes about that it is venial, because otherwise it would have been mortal. Which distinction of sins is thence made, namely that mortal sin causes the death of the soul, which is the privation of grace, and the eternal death of Hell: venial sin, however, does not cause either one of these deaths, but only makes, of itself, one deserving of temporal punishment.

Having explained all these things, we reply to Calvin saying that he would like to know what we would call light sins. We indeed say that we call all venial sins light sins on account of the light matters about which they deal, or on account of the light punishment, that is, the temporal punishment, to which they deserve, because they did not have the full completion of sin. This distinction of sins so explained, as it was always received by all Catholics up until now, we by God's help will prove with manifest arguments and testimonies of Sacred Scripture, so that we may show that Calvin unjustly and foolishly mocks and ridicules it. Firstly, in fact, I offer the testimony of the [Royal] Prophet saying, "I said I will confess against myself my injustice to the Lord: and thou hast forgiven the wickedness of my sin. For this shall every one that is holy pray" (Ps. 31, 5-6). When he says, "for this," one ought to understand implicitly, as Jerome points out, the impiety of sin, or the [iniquity[3]] of sin, which [both] give the same meaning. From which words of the Prophet, it is proved that there are some sins, which are not mortal, but venial [i.e. pardonable]. For if one is "holy," one does not pray for the impiety of mortal sin, or for [iniquity]: because if one is holy, he does not have the impiety of mortal sin, for which he would pray that it be forgiven him. If, however, he formerly had some impiety of mortal sin, it is necessary that it would have been forgiven at that time, when he is holy. And again, if someone has the impiety of mortal sin, for which he prays that he be forgiven, it cannot happen that he is holy: because mortal sin, about which we are now disputing, takes away all holiness and grace. From which words it is very clearly proved that that impiety of sin, for which every holy man prays to God, is only venial and not mortal.

---

[1] "That fault is pardonable which is followed by an admission of guilt" (*On Paradise*, c. 14, n. 71 (PL 14, 310B)).

[2] C. 18, n. 34 (PL 40, 1128). This latter work has often been incorrectly ascribed to St. Augustine and is of unknown authorship.

[3] Here the text has "remission." St. Jerome, whom he is quoting, instead uses the word, "iniquity."

The same argument can be made from the words of Solomon saying: "A just man shall fall seven times and shall rise again: but the wicked shall fall down into evil" (Prov. 24, 16). If a man is just, he does not fall: if he falls, he is not just. Thus, it is necessary that there is some falling into sin, which does not take away justice. And Bede supports this interpretation, who when explaining the aforesaid words of Solomon in his commentary on the third chapter of the Epistle of James, says these words: "For although the just man may offend perhaps through the frailty of the flesh or through ignorance, nevertheless he does not cease to be just, because even as there is daily an unavoidable offense of this kind, so also there is the daily remedy of prayers and good works that quickly raise up the upright offender, so that he may not tumble to the ground and befoul with the dust of vices the marriage garment of charity and the clothing of faith."[1] In which words he clearly teaches that there is a type of offense which does not befoul the clothing of charity.

Furthermore, this distinction of sin between mortal and venial is very clearly gathered from the words of our Savior, saying: "Whosoever is angry with his brother, shall be in danger of the judgment. And whosoever shall say to his brother, Raca, shall be in danger of the council. And whosoever shall say, Thou Fool, shall be in danger of hell fire" (Mt. 5, 22). In which words three sins are delineated, the first two of which are light, but the third is more serious than the other two. Now the difference is clearly gathered from the very diversity of punishments, by which it is said that those sins ought to be punished. For "According to the measure of the sin," as the Divine law says, "shall the measure also of the stripes be" (Deut. 25, 2). Thus, since among these sins only the third and last is said ought to be punished with hell fire, that is, everlasting death: and neither of the first two are condemned to such a punishment, but to some much lighter punishment, it is thence very clearly proved that only the third of those sins is a mortal sin, but the remaining two are venial.

And that this is the true meaning of these words, Chrysostom clearly teaches when interpreting the aforesaid words, saying these words: "'Raca,' is not an expression of a great insolence, but rather of some contempt and slight on the part of the speaker. For as we, giving orders either to our servants, or to any very inferior person, say, 'Away with you; you here, tell such a one': so they who make use of the Syrians' language say, 'Raca,' putting that word instead of 'you.' But God, the lover of man, roots up even the least faults, commanding us to behave to one another in seemly manner, and with due respect; and this with a view of destroying hereby also the greater." After these words Chrysostom enumerates the many and very grave evils which are accustomed to arise from wranglings, and after having enumerated them he immediately says these words which follow: "All which kind of evils Christ checking beforehand, had condemned first him that is angry without a cause to the judgment, (this being the very reason why He said, 'He that is angry shall be in danger of the judgment'); then him that says 'Raca,' to the council. But as yet these are no great things; for the punishments are here. Therefore for him who calls 'fool' He has added the fire of Hell, now for the first time mentioning the name of Hell. For having before discoursed much of the kingdom, not until then did He mention this; implying, that the former comes of His own love and indulgence towards man, this latter of our negligence. And see how He proceeds little by little in His punishments, all but excusing Himself unto you, and signifying that His desire indeed is to threaten nothing of the kind, but that we drag Him on to such denunciations. For observe: 'I bade you,' says He, 'not be angry for naught, because you are in danger of the judgment. You have despised the former commandment: see what anger has produced; it has led you on straightway to insult, for you have called your brother "Raca." Again, I set another punishment, "the council." If you overlook even this, and proceed to that which is more grievous, I visit you no longer with these finite punishments, but with the undying penalty of Hell, lest

---

[1] *Super epistolas Catholicas* (PL 93, 25D).

after this you should break forth even to murder.'"[1] Chrysostom clearly enough notes our Catholic teaching in Christ's words, saying that some sins are greater, for example, which are deserving of eternal death, but others are very small and light, namely those which do not deserve such great punishment.

Gregory interprets these words of Christ in the same way in his *Morals on the Book of Job* where he says these words: "Now the Lord so 'considers the ways' of each one, and so 'numbers all his steps,'[2] that by His judgment not even the minutest thoughts or the very slightest words, which have become insignificant in our eyes from use, remain unexamined. Hence He says, 'Whosoever is angry with his brother, shall be in danger of the judgment. And whosoever shall say to his brother, Raca, shall be in danger of the council. And whosoever shall say, Thou Fool, shall be in danger of hell fire' (Mt. 5, 22). 'Raca' in the Hebrew speech is a word of interjection, which indeed shews the temper of one who is angry, but does not give forth a full word of anger. Thus anger without utterance is first blamed, then anger with utterance, but not yet shaped by a complete word, and at last also when it is said, 'Thou fool,' anger is reproved, which, along with excess of the voice, is fulfilled by the perfecting of speech as well. And it is to be noted that He tells that by anger he is 'in danger of the judgment;' by a voice of anger, which is 'Raca,' 'in danger of the council;' and by a word of the voice, which is 'Thou fool,' in danger of Hell fire. For by the steps of offence, the order of the sentence increased, because in 'the judgment' the case is still under examination, but in the council the sentence of the case is now determining, while 'in the fire of Hell' the sentence, which proceeds from the council, is fulfilled. And therefore because of human actions 'the Lord numbers the steps' with exact scrutiny, anger without the voice is made over 'to the judgment,' but anger in the voice 'to the council,' and anger in speech and voice to 'hell fire.'"[3] From these words of Christ Luther's error is also refuted, who says that every sin in those who have been reborn is venial. For "Whosoever shall say, Thou Fool, shall be in danger of hell fire."

Again, the distinction of mortal and venial sin is clearly gathered from other words of our Savior that He says: "Whosoever shall speak a word against the Son of man, it shall be forgiven him: but he that shall speak against the Holy Ghost, it shall not be forgiven him, neither in this world, nor in the world to come" (Mt. 12, 32). From which words it is evident that there are some sins which can be forgiven in this world: others which can be forgiven in the next. But mortal sins are not forgiven in the world to come, because they lead man to eternal death. And the tree which falls to the south, as Solomon says, will remain there.[4] Hence the sins which are forgiven in the other world necessarily are venial: because these alone are those which are consumed in the fires of Purgatory. And certainly Blessed Gregory thinks that he proves from these words of Christ in the fourth book of the *Dialogues* that the place of Purgatory exists, in which the souls which died in the state of grace are purified from lighter sins after this life.[5] Bernard does likewise.[6]

---

[1] *Homilies on Matthew*, hom. 16, n. 7-8 (PG 57, 248-249).
[2] Cf. Job 31, 4.
[3] Bk. 21, c. 5, n. 9 (PL 76, 194B-D).
[4] Cf. Eccles. 11, 3.
[5] "But yet we must believe that before the Day of Judgment there is a purgatorial fire for certain small sins: because our Savior saith, that he which speaketh blasphemy against the Holy Ghost, that 'it shall not be forgiven him, neither in this world, nor in the world to come.' Out of which sentence we learn, that some sins are forgiven in this world, and some other may be pardoned in the next" (Bk. 4, c. 39 (PL 77, 396A-B)).
[6] "These heretics further maintain that there is no purgatorial fire to be feared after death, but that every soul, as soon as it has been separated from the body, immediately either ascends to Heaven or descends into Hell. Let them, therefore, demand of Him Who has declared that there is a certain sin, which 'shall

Next, this distinction of sins is gathered from many passages of Paul. For he manifests mortal sins in many places, when he says concerning many sins that they exclude men from God's kingdom, from which no one is cast out, as we said in the beginning, except on account of mortal sin.[1] All these testimonies of Paul evidently also refute Luther saying that every sin in those who have been reborn are venial, besides unbelief, which he says is mortal. Calvin, however, is refuted by another testimony of Paul from the First Epistle to the Corinthians, where he teaches clearly enough that there are some venial sins, saying the following: "For other foundation no man can lay, but that which is laid; which is Christ Jesus. Now if any man build upon this foundation, gold, silver, precious stones, wood, hay, stubble: Every man's work shall be manifest; for the day of the Lord shall declare it, because it shall be revealed in fire; and the fire shall try every man's work, of what sort it is. If any man's work abide, which he hath built thereupon, he shall receive a reward. If any man's work burn, he shall suffer loss; but he himself shall be saved, yet so as by fire" (3, 11-15). In which words by gold, silver, and precious stones, he signified good works done from grace and charity: because only they who do works of this kind receive an eternal reward from God. By wood, however, hay, and stubble, which burn when placed in fire and are consumed, venial sins are signified, and not mortal sins: because they who build those things upon the foundation which is Christ, Paul says that they "shall be saved, yet so as by fire." And that this is Paul's true meaning, we have already proved above in the section on "Faith," in the second heresy against the heretics who strive to distort those words of Paul into another meaning: and below in the section on "Purgatory," in the first heresy, we will prove this same thing with the testimonies of the holy Fathers.

There is still another testimony of Paul in favor of venial sin in the Epistle to the Hebrews, where, when treating the office of the priest, he says these words: "Every high priest taken from among men, is ordained for men in the things that appertain to God, that he may offer up gifts and sacrifices for sins: who can have compassion on them that are ignorant and that err: because he himself also is compassed with infirmity. And therefore he ought, as for the people, so also for himself, to offer for sins." (5, 1-3). From which words Jerome concludes that there are some sins which remain at the same time with justice: because their wickedness is not so great, nor so opposed to justice, that when they occur justice would immediately be lost. For he says the following: "If he were not himself just, he would never be commanded to offer for others. Nor, again, would he offer for himself if he were free from sins of ignorance."[2] From whose words it is very clearly established that he thinks that a just priest being in venial sin, and praying for his own sin, and offering a victim impetrates from God pardon of his own sin. For if he were to pray in mortal sin, he would not only not impetrate forgiveness for his own sin, but rather would augment his sin, and incite God to anger.

The Apostle James is in accord with Paul, who teaches once and again that there some sins which are not mortal. "But every man is tempted by his own concupiscence," he says, "being drawn away and allured. Then when concupiscence hath conceived, it bringeth forth sin. But sin, when it is completed, begetteth death" (1, 14-15). In which words he shows two kinds of sins: one which is not consummated, and about this sin he does not say that it begets death. The other is consummated, and he says that this begets death. The first sin is the disordered affection begotten from concupiscence of the flesh, in which the will hesitates slightly without true deliberation of reason, and this is a venial sin. It is not, however, called a consummated

---

not be forgiven neither in this world or in the world to come,' let them ask Him, I say, why He spoke thus, since, as they believe, there can be no remission or purgation of sin in the next life" (*Sermons on the Canticle of Canticles*, serm. 66, n.11 (PL 183, 1100A).

[1] "They who do such things, are worthy of death" (Rom. 1, 32).

[2] *Against the Pelagians*, bk. 1, n. 32 (PL 23, 526C).

sin, because it was done without that advertence and deliberation which is necessary for the consummation of sin. When, on the other hand, the mind duly adverts, and with will did not wish to restrain those movements proceeding from concupiscence, and did not want to "dash thy little ones against the rock" (Ps. 136, 9), but consents after deliberation, then it is now a consummated sin, and then it begets death, and it is called for this reason a mortal sin.

And that this is the correct and true meaning of those words of James, one can easily establish from those words which Bede says in the commentaries which he made on the Epistle of James, where, when interpreting the aforesaid words, he says these words: "'Temptation acts in three ways: by suggestion, by delectation and by consent,'[1] by the suggestion of the enemy, or by the delectation, or also by the consent of our frailty. But if at the enemy's suggestion we are unwilling to take delectation in or to consent to the sin, the temptation itself carries us on to the victory by which we deserve to receive the crown of life. If in fact at the enemy's suggestion we begin gradually to be drawn from the right intention and lured into vice, we offend by taking pleasure but we do not yet incur the falling of death. But if bringing forth evil action also follows the delectation in wickedness conceived in the heart, then the enemy departs victorious from us, now deserving of death."[2] In which words he clearly teaches, based upon James' words, that there are some offenses to God whereby we do not incur the fall of death, and again there are others which make us condemned to death.

But it is necessary to warn the less cautious and not well instructed reader that by those words of Bede, "bringing forth evil action," he ought not to understand only the deed outwardly perpetrated, but also the willing whereby one wills to do the evil action: because the willing is what is more correctly called the action rather than the external deed, and which truly is the mortal sin without the external deed. And by this testimony of James, along with Bede' commentary, not only Calvin is refuted, but also Luther, saying that every sin of a baptized man is a venial sin, besides unbelief. For James spoke about every sin which arises from concupiscence. "Sin, when it is completed, begetteth death." From which testimony it is most evidently concluded that not only unbelief is a mortal sin.

There is yet another testimony of James, whereby it is clearly proved that not every sin is mortal, but some sins are venial. "In many things," he says, "we all offend" (3, 2). Which words can nowise be understood of mortal sin, because it would be false that all, even if we were to be speaking only about adults, offend God by many mortal sins. For the whole Church up until now has always taught that there were some saints who never sinned mortally, as for instance, the most Blessed Virgin Mother of God, John the Baptist and Jeremias; the latter two were sanctified in their mother's wombs. Now Bede testifies that James spoke about venial sins of this kind in his commentary on the same epistle, wherein when explaining the aforesaid words, he says these words: "He appended, 'in many things,' and added '[we] all,' that all might more carefully acknowledge themselves imperfect in acting or speaking the more they know most definitely that not even the perfectly good and those who proceed under the guidance of the grace of the Holy Ghost are able to pass along the way of this life without committing some offense, according to what has been written elsewhere, 'The heavens are not pure in his sight' (Job 15, 15), and as Solomon says, that 'There is no just man upon

---

[1] "For although these words may be understood of the fire of tribulation, which men suffer in this world: yet if any will interpret them of the fire of Purgatory, which shall be in the next life: then must he carefully consider, that the Apostle said not that he may be saved by fire, that buildeth upon this foundation iron, brass, or lead, that is, the greater sort of sins, and therefore more hard, and consequently not remissible in that place: but wood, hay, stubble, that is, little and very light sins, which the fire doth easily consume."

[2] *Super epistolas Catholicas* (PL 93, 14C-D).

earth, that doth good, and sinneth not' (Eccle. 7, 21)."[1] Behold you see, Calvin, that perfectly good men are in sin, and not in mortal sin: because such sin does not admit the perfection of goodness, thus there is some sin which is not mortal sin.

Besides all these very manifest testimonies of Sacred Scripture, one argument occurs to me, which seems to me to be enough for refuting Luther and Calvin at the same time. For although these two men are placed at opposite extremes, and both are, as it were, diametrically opposed, yet both have blasphemed God, and inflict a manifest injury upon Him. For Calvin, when saying that every sin is mortal and deserving of eternal death, pronounces God to be exceedingly harsh, severe, not to say, cruel. The severity and harshness would not be small, if on account of any very light offense God were to adjudicate a man to perpetual death. Christ's yoke certainly could not be called sweet and His burden light: but rather His burden would be so heavy that neither we nor our fathers, nay nor any other man, would be able to bear it.[2] For scarcely any man could be just, if God were to hold any very small offense to be a mortal sin: because there is nearly no one who does not often sin. God would also be a fickle and inconstant friend, if on account of any very small offense he would at once rescind the contracted friendship. For nature itself teaches us that many things ought to be condoned to friends. Therefore, considering all these things I cannot but have compassion on Calvin, and feel sorry for him: because I fear lest, according to that which James says: God will do judgment without mercy to him, due to the fact that he reckoned him to be not merciful enough.[3] I fear lest according to that [severity] which he supposes that God gave as law to all, He would want to examine and judge him, punishing every sin of his just as though it were truly a mortal sin. Because if God were to decide to do so, I wonder whether anyone will suffer a bitterer and more intolerable Gehenna in Hell.

Luther does no less of an injury to God, when he says that every sin after having received Baptism is venial, besides unbelief, which alone he says is a mortal sin: for when saying these things, he considers God to be exceedingly remiss, and insufficiently just, due to the fact that He would easily be indulgent to the most evil and wicked men, who harm their neighbors in many and very serious matters. Now this very great ease in pardoning, as is evident from the matter itself, would give men a clear incentive for committing offenses. But if Luther is not ashamed to attribute this to God, he says a manifest blasphemy against God: because it is evident that God was so anxious and careful about averting men from sins, that He was not content to forbid sins to us, but also all occasions of all sins. It is not enough to believe that God is merciful, unless we also believe that He is just: because, as the Wise Man says, "Mercy and truth preserve the king" (Prov. 20, 28). And the Royal Prophet says: "The king's honour loveth judgment" (Ps. 98, 4).

Add to these things the concordant opinion of all the holy Doctors: because all Catholics beyond all controversy always up until now have taught that some sins are mortal and others are venial. Although some older Doctors used some other names, saying that some sins are grave, others are light. Those which they previously called grave, they afterwards call mortal: and those which they called light, they afterwards call venial. I do not wish to cite scholastic theologians at present, because Luther and Calvin reject them all for this reason alone, yet undeservedly, because they are scholastics. Richard of Saint Victor is outside of the school [of Scholasticism], and he published a tract with this title and inscribed with this name, *On the Difference between Mortal and Venial Sin*.[4] [Hervé, monk of Bourg-Dieu[5]] on the passage

---

[1] *Super epistolas Catholicas* (PL 93, 25C).

[2] Cf. Acts 15, 10.

[3] Cf. James 2, 13.

[4] PL 196, 1191D-1194D.

[5] The text attributes this commentary to Saint Anselm of Canterbury, but it was in fact written by Hervé

from the Apostle's First Epistle to the Corinthians: "If any man's work burn, he shall suffer loss" etc. (3, 15) clearly teaches that there are some light sins which are consumed in relation to the just by the purgatorial fire in the world to come.[1]

Haymo [of Auxerre[2]] when explaining the same words of Paul in his commentaries on Paul's Epistles teaches completely the same view, but much better than [Hervé]: and hence I decided to cite the words of this man here, after having forgone to cite [Hervé's] words. "By gold," Haymo says, "and silver, and precious stones, we can understand good works and excellent virtues: but by hay, wood, and stubble, light sins, such as an idle word, unseemly laughter, and other such things. But by lead, iron and tin,[3] which the holy Doctors add,[4] are grave and very enormous sins which exclude from the kingdom of Heaven. Hence just as gold, silver and precious stones are tried by fire,[5] and yet they are not consumed: so in the Day of Judgment those who shall have good works and good commendation, although they may pass through fire, still they will undergo no punishment or affliction: but those who shall have light sins, will expiate by passing through fire: because [the sins] will be consumed there as hay or stubble, or will be burned by the fire as wood, yet they will not remain in the fire, but after having been cleansed and tried they will ascend to the Lord. But, those who shall have serious sins, which exclude from the kingdom of Heaven, just as iron, lead or tin, they liquify, but do not vanish through the fire: so they, being weighed down by the weight of sins, will remain in the fire, and will undergo punishments that do not vanish."[6]

Therefore, let Calvin cease to be astounded, and cease to rebuke the Fathers of the Council of Trent, due to the fact that they said in their definitions that some light sins exist, as though they were the first to have said that some sins are light. Certainly [Hervé of Bourg-Dieu] lived more than five hundred years ago and Haymo [of Auxerre] more than seven hundred years ago: and both teach that some light sins exist, and they are so-called, because they do not deserve to be punished with eternal death. It is not necessary to cite testimonies from Bede, Gregory, Jerome, and Chrysostom, because those which I have already cited in this disputation suffice.

Augustine very often calls venial sins by this name, and says that they are light, and very different from mortal sins. In his book, *On the Good of Marriage*, he says these words: "For intercourse of marriage for the sake of begetting has not fault; but for the satisfying of lust, but yet with husband or wife, by reason of the faith of the bed, it has venial fault: but adultery or fornication has deadly fault."[7] And in the same book he again says: "Truly we must consider, that God gives us some goods, which are to be sought for their own sake, such as wisdom, health, friendship: but others, which are necessary for the sake of something else, such as learning, meat, drink, sleep, marriage, sexual intercourse. For some of these are nec-

---

of Bourg-Dieu.

[1] "For concerning some light sins, it ought to be believed that there is a purgatorial fire before the resurrection of the bodies" (*Commenatarius in Epistolas Divi Pauli* (PL 181, 844D)).

[2] In Migne's *Patrologia Latina*, this passage is attributed to Haymo of Halberstadt, but as mentioned above (see the section, "Gospel," heresy 2), it has more recently been shown to have been written by Haymo of Auxerre.

[3] Cf. Num. 31, 22-23: "Gold, and silver, and brass, and iron, and lead, and tin, and all that may pass through the fire, shall be purified by fire."

[4] "The Apostle said not that he may be saved by fire, that buildeth upon this foundation iron, brass, or lead, that is, the greater sort of sins, and therefore more hard, and consequently not remissible in that place" (St. Gregory the Great, *Dialogues*, Bk. 4, c. 39 (PL 77, 396C)).

[5] Cf. Prov. 17, 3: "As silver is tried by fire, and gold in the furnace: so the Lord trieth the hearts."

[6] *Expositio in Divi Pauli epistolas: In Epistolam I ad Corinthios*, c. 3 (PL 117, 526A-B).

[7] C. 6, n. 6 (PL 40, 378).

essary for the sake of wisdom, as learning: some for the sake of health, as meat and drink and sleep: some for the sake of friendship, as marriage or sexual intercourse: for hence subsists the propagation of the human kind, wherein friendly fellowship is a great good. These goods, therefore, which are necessary for the sake of something else, whoever uses not for this purpose, wherefore they were instituted, sins; in some cases venially, in other cases damnably."[1] In which words he very clearly distinguishes venial sin from mortal sin. And he uses the name "light sins" in his book, *On the Spirit and the Letter*, saying the following: "It will be sin in the man who lives by faith ever to consent to an unlawful delight — by committing not only frightful deeds and crimes, but even trifling faults; sinful, if he lend an ear to a word that ought not to be listened to, or a tongue to a phrase which should not be uttered."[2] And in the first book on the Creed when speaking to catechumens he says: "I do not tell you that you will live here without sin; but they are venial, without which this life is not. For the sake of all sins was Baptism provided; for the sake of light sins, without which we cannot be, was prayer provided."[3] Accuse Augustine, O Calvin, on account of the fact that he said that some sins are light: mock and ridicule him on account of the same reason you ridiculed the Fathers of the Council of Trent. But they do not wish to retaliate your ridiculing, but rather emulating Christ our teacher, with those who hated peace they wish to be peacemakers, because they follow goodness. Nevertheless, they fear that it may happen to you that which Solomon when speaking about God says: "He shall scorn the scorners" (Prov. 3, 34).

But now it is necessary that we respond to the argument whereby Calvin supposes that he crushes us. "If they consider what they call lighter lapses as nothing, the dreadful sentence of the Supreme Judge thunders forth, 'He who shall *despise* [sic] one of these least commandments shall be called the least in the kingdom of heaven' (Mt. 5, 19)."[4] In this argument of Calvin he cuts apart the very text of the Gospel, so that he can use that passage for proving his error, just as heretics often do elsewhere, removing from Holy Writ those things which conflict with their assertions. For Calvin did not present in their entirety in those words of Christ which he now cited for supporting himself, but he removed from them those words upon which the whole force of that passage depended. For he removed these words: "and shall so teach men." For Christ spoke thus: "He therefore that shall break one of these least commandments, and shall so teach men, shall be called the least in the kingdom of heaven." From which words it is evident that not for this reason alone will someone be called by Christ the least in the kingdom of Heaven, namely because he broke one of the least commandments: but because in breaking them, he teaches others that one ought to do so. Thus, although by breaking the least commandments one would sin venially, still by teaching others that they should act in this way, one sins mortally, because he lies perniciously, and puts a stumbling block (*scandalum*) of iniquity in front of his neighbor, by saying that it ought to be so done by all, as he does.

Next, even if he does not teach others to do what he does, but teaches whatever else: still because a greater perfection of justice is required in the teacher than in the disciple, hence what in others is a small and light sin, in him it is deemed great and serious. And Jerome supports this opinion of ours, who in his commentaries on Matthew, when interpreting these words, says: "This passage is rooted in the preceding verse in which He had said: 'One jot, or one tittle shall not pass of the law, till all be fulfilled.' Therefore, He is taunting the Pharisees who despised God's commands and were establishing their own traditions. He means that their teaching among the people is of no benefit to them, if they destroy even a little bit from

---

[1] C. 9, n. 9 (PL 40, 380).

[2] C. 26, n. 65 (PL 44, 245).

[3] *A Sermon to Catechumens on the Creed* (*Sermo I de symbolo*), c. 7, n. 15 (PL 40, 635).

[4] *Acts of the Council of Trent with the Antidote* (CR 35, 462).

what was commanded in the Law. We can also understand it in another way, that the learning of a teacher, even if he is guilty of a small sin, demotes him from the greatest position. Nor is it advantageous to teach a justice that the smallest fault destroys. Perfect blessedness is to fulfill in deed what you teach in word."[1]

Calvin errs still again about the interpretation of those words of Christ which he cites to support himself, for Christ does not call in that passage the least commandments those things whereby only venial sins are forbidden, as is the commandment of avoiding idle words, or immoderate laughter, or of other commandments of that sort: because He was not discoursing about them: but He called those precepts "the least," not on account of the matter concerning which they treat, because these things are actually great matters: but on account of Himself, Who was then giving them, or at least interpreting them, He tempered His words out of humility, having spoken modestly He said "the least commandments": because they were His own. And that this is the correct meaning of those words of Christ, Chrysostom testifies in his sixteenth homily on Matthew, where, when interpreting the aforesaid words, he says these things: "For what cause then does He call these commandments least, though they were so great and high? Because He Himself was about to introduce the enactment of them; for as He humbled Himself, and speaks of Himself frequently with measure, so likewise of His own enactments, hereby again teaching us to be modest in everything."[2]

Finally, this opinion of Calvin was often condemned by decree of the Council of Trent. For in the sixth session which was celebrated under Paul III, in the eleventh chapter when teaching the faithful those things which are necessary for salvation, among others it says these words: "For although in this mortal life men however holy and just fall at times into at least light and daily sins, which are also called venial, they do not for that reason cease to be just. For that word of the just, 'Forgive us our trespasses' (Mt. 6, 12), is both humble and true."[3] And afterwards in chapter fifteen, it says these words: "Against the crafty genius of certain men also, who 'by pleasing speeches and good words seduce the hearts of the innocent' (Rom. 16,18), it must be maintained that the grace of justification, although received, is lost not only by infidelity, whereby even faith itself is lost, but also by any other mortal sin, although faith be not lost, thereby defending the doctrine of the Divine law which excludes from the kingdom of God not only the unbelievers, but also the faithful who are 'fornicators, adulterers, effeminate, liers with mankind, thieves, covetous, drunkards, railers, extortioners' (I Cor. 6, 9), and all others who commit deadly sins, from which with the assistance of Divine grace they can refrain and for which they are separated from the grace of God."[4] From which two definitions it is established that Luther's and Calvin's assertions were condemned at the same time.

Next, afterwards during the same council under Julius III, in the fourteenth session, which was celebrated under him, it was decreed that the confession of all mortal sins is necessary from Divine law for recovering the grace lost by sin: the confession of venial sins, however, is not necessary, but voluntary.[5] From which decree it is proved that mortal sin from its nature, and from its own kind is distinguished from venial sin. Now I do not wish to cite the words of this definition or decree, because below in the section on "Penance," in the first heresy, they ought to be cited by me for another proposition: and I do not wish to sing the same song twice. If anyone were to say that Calvin does not accept the decrees of the Council of Trent, because he wrote against it, I indeed admit it to be so, and yet that council will not lose its authority,

---

[1] Bk. 1 (PL 26, 36C).

[2] N. 4 (PG 57, 243).

[3] Dz. 804.

[4] Dz. 808.

[5] Dz. 899.

because Calvin disapproved of it: just as the [First] Council of Nicea did not lose its authority due to the fact that Arius and his supporters contemned its decrees.

The **twelfth heresy**, even though it admits that there is some distinction between mortal and venial sin, still not that distinction which has been received by all Catholics; but what cannot be acknowledged by any man, and has been condemned by the definition of the whole Church. For John Wycliffe, the first inventor and author of this heresy, says: Every sin of a predestined man is venial: because no such sin is punished by eternal death: and every sin of a reprobate man is mortal, because every such sin, as he says, ought to be punished with eternal death.[1]

This assertion is clearly proved to be heretical by the testimony of the sin of Adam, the first parent. For that his sin was manifestly mortal is proved by those words which God said to him after having forbidden eating of the tree of the knowledge of good and evil: "In what day soever thou shalt eat of it, thou shalt die the death" (Gen. 2, 17). Which words ought to be understood rather of the spiritual death of the soul than of the body, as [Pseudo-] Blessed Eucherius, Bishop of Lyons, proves very well when saying these words: "He is speaking about the death of the soul, not of the body, because they did not die at the time when they ate. Thus, this death which God now threatened man, we ought not to take so much as that death whereby the flesh is separated from the soul, but that death whereby the latter is alienated from God, Who is its life; for just as the body lives from the soul, so that soul, so that it may live happily, lives from God. Therefore, the soul having been deserted by God, is rightly said to be dead: from which three deaths afterwards followed: the first in the soul, the second in the flesh, and the third in damnation. But so that these deaths would follow, the desertion of God preceded as their beginning."[2] Blessed Gregory interprets those words of God in the same way as [Pseudo-] Eucherius.[3]

If Adam's soul immediately died after sin, then that sin, which was the cause of this death, was truly mortal: because that is truly deadly, which inflicts death upon someone. Now it is evident that Adam was predestined to eternal life from the fact that he attained that life, concerning which Solomon gave testimony, when, relating the strength and power of Divine wisdom, he says: "She preserved him, that was first formed by God the father of the world, when he was created alone, and she brought him out of his sin" (Wis. 10, 1-2). And it is unnecessary to bring forth many arguments for Adam's salvation: because above in the section on "Adam and Eve," in the first heresy, we proved against Tatian that Adam was saved. If Adam was saved, and his sin, as we proved, was mortal: then not every sin of a predestined man is venial.

---

[1] "A sin can be called mortal which according to the judgment of our God is worthy of being punished by the second death [i.e., eternal damnation]. And so only the sin of final impenitence (which is a sin against the Holy Ghost) is properly mortal; but any other sin, since it is deserving of pardon, can reasonably be called venial... Every sin of the reprobate [*praesciti*, i.e., foreknown to be damned] ought to be punished at the same time with one eternal punishment... Nevertheless, it does not seem to me that any sin called mortal, in a man ultimately fruitfully penitent, is worthy of eternal punishment... Nevertheless, it ought to be admitted that there are many reprobate in a present state of grace, while many predestined [to glory] sin gravely in their present state of sin. Yet the reprobate are never in a state of final persevering grace, just as the predestined are never finally obstinate.... For by this it is known that the reprobate sin infinitely more gravely than the predestined, and they are not equal in grace or sin" (*Trialogus cum supplemento trialogi* (Oxford, Clarendon Press, 1869), pp. 145, 149, & 150).

[2] *Commenatarius in Genesim*, bk. 1; on chap. 2, v. 17 (PL 50, 908B). This text is found in an appendix in Migne's Patrology wherein the work is considered doubtfully or wrongly attributed to Saint Eucherius.

[3] "For when this is written, that when Adam sinned his soul died, the writer shows afterwards how it is said to have died, namely that it lost the blessedness of its condition. Whosoever denies this is not Catholic" (Bk. 5, letter 14 (to the Count Narses) (PL 77, 806A)).

Furthermore, David was predestined to eternal life, which cannot be denied, unless perhaps by him who is not ashamed to reject Sacred Scripture. For besides other testimonies of his predestination, one is especially clear, namely that Paul in the Epistle to the Hebrews lists him among the saints.[1] The sin of adultery, however, that David committed with the wife of Urias is proved to have been mortal by that which the prophet Nathan said to David himself, that he is a "child of death," that is, deserving of the punishment of death.[2] Which death, as all theologians teach in unison, is never inflicted by the Divine law, to anyone except on account of mortal sin. For because the death of the body, as is evident from the words of [Pseudo-] Eucherius cited above, firstly arose from the spiritual death of the soul, hence after the example of that first death, as often as someone had to be punished with bodily death from Divine law, it was necessary that a mortal sin would have preceded, which would have rightly required such a death. And now in the Evangelical Law, no one is ever justly killed except on account of a preceding mortal sin.

Again, the prodigal son who consumed his whole substance by living luxuriously, returning to his father from whom he had been far removed, was received with joy by him. Yet the father said concerning that son, when he received him, that this son "was dead, and is come to life again" (15, 24). By which words he clearly showed that the sin of that prodigal son was mortal: because when he committed it, he was then dead: and he came to life again, when he repented of his past life.

Next, from this assertion of Wycliffe many absurd and incongruous things follow. Firstly, in fact, it follows that the sins which God forgave Mary Magdalene, because she loved much, would all have been venial sins. Yet the Evangelist suggests the contrary, when he said antonomastically that there was a sinful woman in the city.[3] For she would not have been called par excellence a sinful woman in the city on account of venial sins alone. It also follows that no predestined person could rejoice for this reason, nay nor give thanks to God, because some mortal sin was ever forgiven him. It thirdly follows that the Sacrament of Penance was not instituted for the predestined, because venial sins need not be said in an auricular confession, but only mortal sins, which the predestined can never, as Wycliffe says, commit: therefore, the Sacrament of Penance will never be necessary for the predestined. But the Sacrament of Penance never benefits the reprobate either: because a mortal sin will never be remitted by that Sacrament. For if it were remitted, then surely, according to Wycliffe's opinion, it will not be mortal: because only that sin, says Wycliffe, is a mortal sin, which leads to eternal death. In vain, therefore, was the Sacrament of Penance instituted, if it benefits neither the reprobate nor the predestined. And hence it further follows that the form of absolution is false, as often as the priest when absolving some reprobate person says: "I absolve you from all your sins." Nor will only the Sacrament of Penance be useless, but also penitence itself, which is called a virtue, will be useless: because no mortal sin is forgiven the reprobate by it. Yet God promised the contrary through the prophet Ezechiel, saying: "But if the wicked do penance for all his sins which he hath committed, and keep all my commandments, and do judgment, and justice, living he shall live, and shall not die" (18, 21). Which words, since they are said absolutely and without any limitation, necessarily ought to be understood of all men, both the reprobate and the predestined. Add to this that no one, no matter how learned, would be able to know about any sin whether it is mortal or venial: because no one, except by a special revelation from God, could know about himself, nor about another, whether he is predestined or reprobate.

---

[1] Cf. Heb. 11, 32.

[2] Cf. II Kings 12, 5-7.

[3] Cf. Lk. 7, 37.

Finally, this opinion was condemned in the Council of Trent, which, in the sixth session celebrated under Paul III, declared among the many other canons this seventeenth one: "If anyone shall say that the grace of justification is attained by those only who are predestined unto life, but that all others, who are called, are called indeed, but do not receive grace, as if they are by Divine power predestined to evil: let him be anathema."[1] By which words it clearly declared that the reprobate are sometimes in the state of grace just as the predestined. From which words it is further deduced that mortal sin is sometimes forgiven the reprobate, and not every sin of his is mortal: because when he is just, he can fall into some sin, by which he does not lose justice, as was proved in the preceding heresy.

All those things which we will say below in the section on "Predestination" will oppose this heresy. Thomas Netter wrote against this error of Wycliffe in his book, *De Sacramentis*.[2]

There is another heresy, which agrees with this proposition, and pertains somewhat to the present matter. But we will dispute about it in the section on "Power," because it is more suitably and fittingly put there.

PEREGRINUS

Strangers

About this matter I have found only one heresy, and actually very cruel and completely foreign to all human reason, which teaches that hospitality ought not to be extended to strangers. The pestiferous author of this error (as Bernard of Luxemburg in his *Catalogus haereticorum* says[3]) was a certain Diotrephes, a contemporary of the Apostles, about whom Blessed John the Apostle and Evangelist in his third Catholic epistle says the following: "I had written perhaps to the church: but Diotrephes, who loveth to have the pre-eminence among them, doth not receive us. For this cause, if I come, I will advertise his works which he doth, with malicious words prating against us. And as if these things were not enough for him, neither doth he himself receive the brethren, and them that do receive them he forbiddeth, and casteth out of the church" (v. 9-10). Venerable Bede, when expounding these words in his commentaries on the Catholic epistles, speaks thus: "Diotrephes (as it seems) was an archheretic of his time, proud and insolent, preferring to usurp the pre-eminence of knowledge by teaching new things, rather than to humbly hear the ancient commandments of holy Church which John was preaching. Hence 'Diotrephes' is understood as 'a fair fool,' or 'a raving beauty,'' so that he signifies a treacherous heart even by his name."[4]

But neither from the words of Blessed John the Evangelist, nor of Bede his expounder, is it evident that Diotrephes thought such a thing such as Bernard of Luxemburg accuses him in his *Catalogus*. It is indeed evident that he was a heretic, yet his heresy is not indicated. For on account of this that Blessed John says of him: "Neither doth he himself receive the brethren, and them that do receive them he forbiddeth" (v. 10), it is not permitted to suspect that he thought that all strangers ought not be received, but only the Catholic faithful, because Blessed John call them "brethren" in that place. And it assuredly always was the custom of heretics that they were hostile to the true faithful. For this happen among the Lutherans now, who do

---

[1] Dz. 827.

[2] *Doctrinale antiquitatum fidei Catholicae Ecclesiae* (Venice, apud Iordanum Zilettum, 1571), v. 2 (*De Sacramentis*), c. 155, fol. 254r-256r.

[3] Bk. 4.

[4] *Super epistolas Catholicas* (PL 93, 124A). This meaning come from interpretation of his name from Hebrew (cf. St. Jerome, *De nominibus Hebraicis* (PL 23, 852)).

not wish to receive the faithful among themselves, and if perhaps they permit them, they treat them badly, yet they do not teach that hospitality ought not to be extended to strangers. The same thing could happen in Diotrephes, such that when they were separated from the Church for some other reason, he did not wish to receive the "brethren," that is the true faithful, and forbade others to do it.

Nevertheless, let it be assumed that he so thought, as Bernard of Luxemburg accuses him: it is not difficult to dispute against this heresy, in that there are very clear testimonies of Sacred Scripture which oppose it. For God Himself seems to have taken care of strangers when He forbade any bothering to them, saying the following: "Thou shalt not molest a stranger" (Ex. 23, 9). He not only forbade bothering, but elsewhere He commanded works of mercy, saying: "And when you reap the corn of your land, you shall not cut it to the very ground: neither shall you gather the ears that remain; but you shall leave them for the poor and for the strangers" (Lev. 23, 22). And again, in another place: "Give it to the stranger, that is within thy gates, to eat" (Deut. 14, 21). Furthermore, if it were not a sin to deny hospitality, Job would not have excused that from himself, saying: "The stranger did not stay without, my door was open to the traveller" (Job 31, 32). Next, the Savior himself shows how serious this sin is when he says in Matthew that He will reproach some men with this sin on Judgment Day. "I was a stranger," He says, "and you took me not in" (25, 43). And afterwards He adds, saying to them who committed the sin of this kind: "Depart from me, you cursed, into everlasting fire which was prepared for the devil and his angels" (v. 41). It is therefore evident that it is not a small sin for which its perpetrator is condemned to eternal punishment: on the contrary, however, to those who brought strangers and foreigners into their homes, He will say: "I was a stranger, and you took me in" (v. 35) And in consequence of this: "Come, ye blessed of my Father, possess you the kingdom prepared for you from the foundation of the world" (v. 34). It is not a small virtue which merits to receive the kingdom of Heaven.

Again (as Origen noted), Lot was delivered from the burning of Sodom and Gomorrha on account of hospitality alone. For the sacred history does not relate any outstanding deed of his, besides hospitality which he extended to strangers, on account of which he merited to be delivered from the fire.[1] Finally, so that this heresy may be overthrown on all sides, I will show that it has been hated not only by the Christians, but even by the pagans, and condemned by them. For Aristotle, when speaking about the eagle, says: "In old age the upper beak of the eagle grows gradually longer and more crooked, and the bird dies eventually of starvation; there is a folklore story that the eagle is thus punished because it once was a man and refused hospitality to a stranger."[2] See, even to pagans, how much a violation of hospitality was abominable, so that on account of this alone, a man is fabled to have been changed into an eagle. And I have perhaps said more than what was needed about a very clear matter.

---

[1] "When the Angels who were sent to destroy Sodom desired to expedite the task with which they were charged, they first had concern for their host, Lot, in consideration of his hospitality, they might deliver him from the destruction of the imminent fire... We do not read of other good deeds of his. The hospitality alone occurring at that time is mentioned. He escapes the flames, he escapes the conflagration, for this reason alone: because he opened his house to strangers. Angels entered the hospitable house; fire entered the houses closed to strangers" (*Homilies on Genesis*, hom. 5, n. 1 (PG 12, 188C-189A)).

[2] *The History of Animals*, bk. 9, c. 32.

POENITENTIA

Penance

There is one error of Luther concerning this matter, whereby he teaches that there are not three parts of penance, but instead he says that the best penance is a new life. Which error he fabricated out of his own head, and did not draw it forth from the workshop of another heretic, which we know has rarely happened with Luther. For although he put forth more than a hundred errors up until now, scarcely three or four are found which he did not draw out of the putrid reservoirs of the heretics now cast out of the Church for a long time: but on this point he did not have (as far as I know) a teacher of this error. And although he, in a certain book which he published, *Assertion of the Articles condemned by Pope Leo X*, seems to reject this assertion as not being his own, saying that he does not deny all three parts of penance, but only satisfaction, because contrition and confession he says are found and proved [to exist from Holy Writ]: but he denies that satisfaction is supported from Holy Writ: wherefore he says that no satisfaction ought to be done for sins: but that when guilt is forgiven, all punishment due to sin is also remitted at the same time.[1] Yet even though Luther says that he admits contrition and confession, still he denies them by his deeds. For he ridicules contrition which comes to be through the examination of sins, and the detestation of those same sins, saying that it is mere hypocrisy. He denies that auricular confession is necessary. He does away with satisfaction universally. From which things it is sufficiently evident that Luther does not admit the three parts of penance, as is admitted by Catholic men. We have disputed against Luther about contrition and confession in these sections. Wherefore there alone remains that we show from Holy Writ that satisfaction is necessary.

Now in order that we may prove it more clearly, it is firstly necessary to show that after guilt is forgiven through contrition, there remains some punishment to be paid according to the measure both of the punishment and time decreed by God. Now this is sufficiently gathered from that which God replied to Moses praying for the people of Israel. For when Moses prayed to the Lord, saying: "Forgive, I beseech thee, the sins of this people" (Num. 14, 19): the Lord responds, "I have forgiven... But yet all the men that... have tempted me... shall not see the land for which I swore to their fathers" (v. 20-23). Notice that after the guilt has been forgiven, the punishment is still retained. Furthermore, it ought not to be doubted that Moses and Aaron immediately lamented and came to their senses about the sin of incredulity and diffidence which they had committed at the waters of contradiction: yet the punishment determined by the Lord to them was not relaxed on account of this, because they never entered the promised land, as the Lord had threatened them.

Again, King David, knowing the enormity and gravity of the guilt which in the adultery and homicide he had incurred, was immediately forgiven the guilt, because it was so declared to him by the prophet Nathan: "The Lord also hath taken away thy sin" (II Kings 12, 13). And yet after the said remission of guilt the prophet likewise predicted to him many calamities and punishments that he would suffer on account of the sin committed, all of which he afterwards suffered, as it is testified in the Second Book of Kings.[2] Notice here that David's sin was forgiven, yet for which he afterwards underwent many punishments. Likewise, David, when

---

[1] On article 5; "They have maliciously compiled this article, for I have not denied contrition and confession, as the article nevertheless cries out, and they wish to make it appear that I taught such things, but I have denied satisfaction, such as they teach" (WA 7, 112, lns. 7-10).

[2] Cf. II Kings 12, 18; 15, 14.

seeing the Angel of the Lord killing his people with a very pestilential plague on account of the sin which he had previously committed in numbering the same people, acknowledges his sin, saying: "It is I; I am he that have sinned, I have done wickedly: these that are the sheep, what have they done? let thy hand, I beseech thee, be turned against me, and against my father's house" (24, 17). After that humble confession it ought not to be doubted that his sin was immediately forgiven, just as we have related was done at other times. And yet the guilt already having been forgiven, he is commanded by Gad the prophet to build an altar to the Lord in the in the threshing floor of Areuna the Jebusite, and to offer on it a holocaust to placate God's anger. But this oblation would not have been enjoined upon him, unless after the sin was forgiven some punishment was to be paid, in satisfaction of which such an oblation needed to be made. And these things seem to me to suffice for showing that after the guilt of sin has been forgiven there remains some temporal punishment to be paid.

But if some punishment remains to be paid after the guilt has been forgiven, then in compensation of that punishment a man can further undergo some punishment, and this voluntary and free acceptance of punishment is satisfaction for the other due punishment. Now we will show by explicit testimonies of Sacred Scripture that this is true. The prophet Daniel exhorted the king of Babylon to make satisfaction of this kind for his sins, saying the following: "Redeem thou thy sins with alms, and thy iniquities with works of mercy to the poor" (Dan. 4, 24). But sins as to the guilt of the fault are not redeemed with alms, because someone can give alms and be in sin. Therefore, it is the punishment due to sin, which is redeemed by the giving of alms. And this releasing from sin not only the recent, but also the very ancient Doctors, call satisfaction for sin. I have said this because Luther abhors the word, "satisfaction." Now where the reality is clear, it is of no use to fight about mere words. But insofar as I suspect, Luther rather hates satisfaction itself than the word, "satisfaction." For it is permitted (as it is said in the proverb) to appraise a lion from its claws.[1]

Furthermore, that alms satisfies for sins, the Teacher of truth Himself bears witness, Who after He had reprehended the Pharisees for "rapine and iniquity" (Lk. 11, 39), said to them: "That which remaineth, give alms; and behold, all things are clean unto you" (v. 41). And it is evident that He is speaking about satisfaction for punishment, and not for the guilt of the fault: for to someone in the state of sin, alms alone will not make that all things would be clean. Again, regarding prayer, that it satisfies for sin, the Wise Man testifies when he says: "My son, hast thou sinned? do so no more: but for thy former sins also pray that they may be forgiven thee" (Eccli. 21, 1). Let Luther give heed and see that renewal of life is not enough for true penance. For after the Wise Man had commanded amendment of life saying, "do so no more," as though this were not sufficient, he added, "for thy former sins also pray that they may be forgiven thee."

Next, for showing all satisfaction in general, that which John the Baptist says when preaching is very efficacious: "Bring forth fruit worthy of penance" (Mt. 3, 8). Chrysostom when treating that passage says: "But how shall we bring them forth? If we do the opposite things: as for instance, have you seized by violence the goods of others? Henceforth give away even your own. Have you been guilty of fornication for a long time? abstain even from your wife for certain appointed days; exercise continence. Have you insulted and stricken such as were passing by? Henceforth bless them that insult you, and do good to them that smite you."[2] From which words it is evident what things ought to be done as compensation for sin. Blessed Gregory interprets that passage in the same way.[3] Blessed Paul, in that epistle which is to the

---

[1] "Painting the lion from a single claw" (Plutarch, *Moralia, De Defectu Oraculorum*, n. 3, wherein Alcaeus is cited (*Bergk, Poet. Lyr. Graec.* III, p. 184, Alcaeus, no. 113)).
[2] *Homilies on Matthew*, hom. 10, n. 6 (PG 57, 190).
[3] "These words: 'Bring forth fruit worthy of penance' therefore take the conscience of each one into

Romans, gives testimony in favor of this cause, saying: "As you have yielded your members to serve uncleanness and iniquity, unto iniquity; so now yield your members to serve justice, unto sanctification" (Rom. 6, 19). Theophylactus, when expounding these words, says: "For after some sin has been committed by you, you do not stop here, but having increased the amount of your iniquity, this same amount is for you a motivation. Therefore, with equal measure yield your members to serve justice, that is, every virtue, so that you may lead a life in temperance and sanctification for your previous uncleanliness."[1] From which words it is evident that this passage of Paul ought to be understood of making compensation or satisfaction for sins as the measure of offense requires, such that according to the measure of the offense is the amount of the affliction, not only in the other life, but also in this.

Add to these things that all the holy Doctors hold in unison that some satisfaction ought to be made for sins, even after the sins were forgiven through contrition. I will bring forwards the sayings of some of them, so that the matter may appear more clearly. For Hesychius [of Jerusalem] says the following: "The cleansing of leprosy is penance. Now it has necessary works, which by virtues and the exertion of action avails to eliminate sins. On account of which John the Baptist, as Matthew testifies, was saying to the people of Jerusalem: 'Bring forth fruit worthy of penance.' For he considered, as a clever lawmaker, them who could not present everything which pertains to the strict reckoning of penance. For penance has need of attentive prayer, alms, vigils, holy fasting, and last of all also those things which David says: 'My tears have been my bread day and night' (Ps. 41, 4), and 'Every night I will wash my bed: I will water my couch with my tears' (Ps. 6, 7). But also 'I did eat ashes like bread, and mingled my drink with weeping' (Ps. 101, 10)."[2] In which words it especially ought to be noted that penance has need of perfect prayer, alms, vigils, holy fasting, tears, and other labors of the present life.

Now when he says that all these things are necessary for penance, he is speaking about Sacramental Penance, and all its integral parts: which include at the same time contrition, confession, and satisfaction as its three integral parts. For they are not all three essential parts of penance, such that without any of them there could be no Sacramental Penance: because the integral confession of sins with any small displeasure of them is true penance, which avails to eliminating all guilt: but it is not integral and complete penance, because it lacks one part, namely satisfaction, which of itself is not ordered to the elimination of sin, but only to the elimination of punishment. Now when I say that confession is part of Sacramental Penance, I understand by the name of confession not only that making known of one's sins which the sinner makes in the presence of the priest, but also the absolution of that priest: because otherwise there would be more than three integral parts of Sacramental Penance, and it would be necessary to add a fourth, namely the absolution of the priest. The Council of Florence, however, named but three, and hence it is necessary that we understand by the word, "confession," also absolution.[3] Hence Hesychius, when saying that those laborious works are necessary for penance, stated clearly enough that satisfaction is part of penance, and avails for removing the punishments due to sin after the guilt has been forgiven. For those works, as is evident, are not necessary for contrition, nor for confession, nor for the elimination of guilt: hence that which is necessary, besides confession and contrition for the elimination of guilt,

---

consideration, and invite him to constitute by penance a treasure of good works, all the richer because his faults have earned him heavier punishments" (*Homilies on the Gospels*, hom. 20, n. 8 (PL 76, 1164A)).

[1] *Commentarius in epistolam ad Romanos* (PG 124, 418A-B).
[2] *Commentarius in Leviticum*, bk. 4 (PG 93, 958A-B).
[3] Dz. 699.

we call satisfaction, which is not for the removal of guilt, but avails as some recompense for the punishment due to sin.

Blessed Fulgentius[1] says the following: "Converted, let us never despair of the forgiveness of sins, holding on to the faithful promise of the Lord, Who says, 'If you return and be quiet, you shall be saved' (Is. 30, 15). Let us put up with the pressures and trials of the present time with longanimity and let us never depart from the fear of the Lord. For the Apostle command us to be 'patient in tribulation' (Rom. 12, 12), who also bears witness that the correction of the present time is of great avail to us for the avoiding of the punishment of the future Judgment, saying, 'Whilst we are judged, we are chastised by the Lord, that we be not condemned with this world' (I Cor. 11, 32)."[2] By which words he clearly teaches that through the punishments of this life, punishments of the other life are avoided: and he taught these things not out of his own head (as Luther does), but by the testimony of Paul saying the same thing.

[Pseudo-] Eucherius, Bishop of Lyons says the following: "If the Lord took away David's very detestable sin, why is it that he afterwards underwent all the things which were said by the Lord through the prophet to him? But undoubtably the Lord took that sin away, but did not leave it without taking vengeance. For either the same penitent man punishes this sin in himself, or God strikes this sin taking vengeance upon the man. Thus, He nowise spares the sin, because He nowise forgives without avenging. For so David deserved to hear after his conversion: 'The Lord hath taken away thy sin' (II Kings 12, 13). And yet he was afterwards stricken with many afflictions and when fleeing, he paid for the guilt of the fault which he had committed. In the same way the water of salvation washed us from the guilt of the first parents: but nevertheless, when washing away the guilt of the same fault, after we have been cleansed, we still also physically die, because He cuts off our sins either through us, or through us when He loosens. For He strives to rub off from His elect by corporeal afflictions the stains of iniquities, which He does not wish to forever avenge in them."[3] Nothing clearer could have been said in support of that satisfaction of sins which we try to assert.

Christian Druthmar subscribes to the same opinion, who in his *Expositio in Mattheum*, speaks thus: "To 'bring forth fruit worthy of penance' is to punish past evil deeds with tears, and on the contrary to do good deeds, so that just as we yielded our members to serve injustice, so we ought to yield the same to serve justice unto sanctification, or 'fruits worthy of penance' is to do good deeds, and redeem the misdeeds with alms."[4] I certainly could cite more testimonies of holy men for the defense of this truth: but for the sake of avoiding prolixity I omit them: and if someone desires to see them, he will find them cited by Bishop John [Fisher] of Rochester in the fifth article of that great work which he made against Luther,[5] and in Jacques Masson in the work which he made in support of the declaration of the faculty of Louvain against Luther.[6] For both of these men collected together many testimonies of holy men in support of this matter. I preferred, however, to bring forth these few from my labor, because none of these men has requested their testimony. Hence, I cited the testimonies of these men so that we might show more firmly the matter fully confirmed by those men.

---

[1] St. Fulgentius (468-533 A.D.) was the Bishop of Ruspe in the province of Byzacene in Africa.

[2] Letter 7 (to Venantia, on correct penance), c. 15 (PL 65, 360A-B).

[3] *Commenatarii in libros Regum*, c. 7; on II Kings 11 (PL 50, 1092B-C). This text is found in an appendix in *Migne's Patrology* in which the work is considered doubtfully or wrongly attributed to Saint Eucherius.

[4] C. 4 (PL 106, 1292C).

[5] *Assertionis Lutheranae confutatio*, fol. 104r-117v.

[6] Jacobus Latomus, *Articulorum doctrinae fratris M. Lutheri per theologos Lovanienses damnatorum ratio ex sacris literis et veteribus tractatoribus*.

Finally, this assertion of Luther is proved to be heresy by the decrees of some general councils. For the Council of Florence, celebrated under Eugene IV, in the definition of faith which it gave to the Armenians, when discussing the Sacrament of Penance, says these words: "The fourth Sacrament is Penance, the matter of which is, as it were, the acts of the penitent, which are divided into three parts. The first of these is contrition of heart, to which pertains grief for a sin committed together with a resolution not to sin in the future. The second is oral confession, to which pertains that the sinner confess integrally to his priest all sins of which he has recollection. The third is satisfaction for sins according to the decision of the priest, which is accomplished chiefly by prayer, fasting, and alms."[1]

The Council of Trent condemned this assertion at much greater length and copiously. For in the sixth session celebrated under Paul III, in the fourteenth chapter, when declaring the manner whereby those who have fallen can be renewed through penance, says these words: "For on behalf of those who after Baptism fall into sin, Christ Jesus instituted the Sacrament of Penance, when He said: 'Receive ye the Holy Ghost; whose sins you shall forgive, they are forgiven them, and whose sins you shall retain, they are retained' (Jn. 20, 22-23). Hence it must be taught that the repentance of a Christian after his fall is very different from that at his Baptism, and that it includes not only a cessation from sins, and a detestation of them, or 'a contrite and humble heart' (Ps. 50, 19), but also the Sacramental Confession of the same, at least in desire and to be made in its season, and sacerdotal absolution, as well as satisfaction by fasting, almsgiving, prayers, and other devout exercises of the spiritual life, not indeed for the eternal punishment, which is remitted together with the guilt either by the Sacrament or the desire of the Sacrament, but for the temporal punishment, which (as Sacred Writ teaches) is not always wholly remitted, as is done in Baptism, to those who ungrateful to the grace of God which they have received, have grieved the Holy Ghost,[2] and have not feared to 'violate the temple of God' (I Cor. 3,17). Of this repentance it is written: 'Be mindful, whence thou art fallen, do penance, and do the first works' (Apoc. 2, 5), and again: 'The sorrow which is according to God, worketh penance steadfast unto salvation' (II Cor. 7, 10), and again: 'Do penance' (Mt. 3, 2; 4, 17), and, 'Bring forth fruits worthy of penance' (Mt. 3, 8)."[3] And after having given this teaching, lest anyone dare to teach or assert in any way against it, the same council published a canon of anathema against temerarious men of this kind, which having been put in the thirtieth place contains these words: "If anyone shall say that after the reception of the grace of justification, to every penitent sinner the guilt is so remitted and the penalty of eternal punishment so blotted out that no penalty of temporal punishment remains to be discharged either in this world or in the world to come in purgatory before the entrance to the kingdom of Heaven can be opened: let him be anathema."[4]

But afterwards the same council proceeding under Julius III, in the fourteenth session celebrated under the same Julius, declared much more clearly everything which necessarily ought to be believed concerning the Sacrament of Penance: which new teaching it divided by chapters, and in the third of these, it states the integral parts, speaking thus: "The matter, as it were, of this Sacrament, on the other hand, consists in the acts of the penitent himself, namely contrition, confession, and satisfaction. These, inasmuch as by the institution of God they are required in the penitent for the integrity of the Sacrament for the full and perfect remission of sins, are for this reason called the parts of Penance."[5]

---

[1] Dz. 699.
[2] Cf. Eph. 4, 30.
[3] Dz. 807.
[4] Dz. 840.
[5] Dz. 896.

And afterwards in the other chapters it discusses the above-mentioned parts of penance one by one, and because its definitions pertaining to contrition and confession, were already cited above in their sections, it is unnecessary to repeat them now. Those, however, which relate to satisfaction, are contained in the eighth and ninth chapters of the definition given in that above-mentioned session, and are those which follow: "Finally with regard to satisfaction, which of all the parts of Penance has been recommended by our Fathers to the Christian people in all ages, and which is especially assailed in our day under the pretext of piety by those who 'have an appearance of piety, but who have denied the power thereof' (II Tim. 3, 5), the holy Synod declares that it is absolutely false and contrary to the word of God that the guilt is never forgiven by the Lord without the entire punishment also being remitted. For clear and illustrious examples are found in the Sacred Writings,[1] besides which Divine tradition refutes this error with all possible clarity. Indeed the nature of Divine justice seems to demand that those who have sinned through ignorance before Baptism may be received into grace in one manner, and in another those who at one time freed from the servitude of sin and the devil, and on receiving the gift of the Holy Ghost, did not fear to violate the temple of God knowingly,[2] and to grieve the Holy Ghost.[3] And it befits Divine clemency that sins be not thus pardoned us without any satisfaction, lest, seizing the occasion,[4] and considering sins trivial, we, offering injury and affront to the Holy Ghost,[5] fall into graver ones, 'treasuring up to ourselves wrath against the day of wrath' (Rom. 2, 5; James 5, 3). For, without doubt, these satisfactions greatly restrain from sin, and as by a kind of rein act as a check, and make penitents more cautious and vigilant in the future; they also remove the remnants of sin, and destroy vicious habits acquired by living evilly through acts contrary to virtue. Neither was there ever in the Church of God any way considered more secure for warding off impending punishment by the Lord than that men perform these works of penance with true sorrow of soul.[6] Add to this that, while we suffer by making satisfaction for our sins, we are made conformable to Christ Jesus, who made satisfaction for our sins,[7] from whom is all our sufficiency,[8] having also a most certain pledge from Him that if we suffer with Him, we shall also be glorified.[9] Neither is this satisfaction which we discharge for our sins so much our own as it is through Jesus Christ; for we who can do nothing of ourselves, as if of ourselves, with the cooperation of Him who comforts us, we can do all things.[10] Thus man has not wherein to glory; but all our glorying is in Christ,[11] in whom we live, in whom we move,[12] in whom we make satisfaction, bringing forth fruits worthy of penance[13] which have their efficacy from Him, by Him are offered to the Father, and through Him are accepted by the Father. The priests of the Lord ought, therefore, so far as the Spirit and prudence suggest, to enjoin salutary and suitable satisfactions, in keeping with the nature of the crimes and the ability of the penitents, lest, if they should connive at sins and deal too leniently with penitents, by the

---

[1] Cf. Gen. 3,16 ff.; Num. 12, 14 ff.; 20, 11 ff.; II Kings 12, 13 ff., etc.
[2] Cf. I Cor. 3, 17.
[3] Cf. Eph. 4, 30.
[4] Cf. Rom. 7, 8.
[5] Cf. Heb. 10, 29.
[6] Cf. Mt. 3, 2; 4, 17; 11, 21 etc.
[7] Cf. Rom. 5,10; I Jn. 2, 1 ff.
[8] Cf. II Cor. 3, 5.
[9] Cf. Rom. 8, 17.
[10] Cf. Phil. 4, 13.
[11] Cf. I Cor. 1, 31; II Cor. 10, 17; Gal. 6:14.
[12] Cf. Acts 17, 28.
[13] Cf. Lk. 3, 8.

imposition of certain very light works for grave offenses, they might become participators in the crimes of others.[1] Moreover, let them keep before their eyes that the satisfaction which they impose be not only for the safeguarding of a new life and a remedy against infirmity, but also for the atonement and chastisement of past sins; for the ancient Fathers both believe and teach that the keys of the priests were bestowed not only to loose, but also to bind.[2] Nor did they therefore think that the Sacrament of Penance is a tribunal of wrath or of punishments; as no Catholic ever understood that from our satisfactions of this kind the nature of the merit and satisfaction of our Lord Jesus Christ is either obscured or in any way diminished; when the Innovators wish to observe this, they teach that the best penance is a new life, in order to take away all force and practice of satisfaction. It teaches furthermore that so great is the liberality of the Divine munificence that not only by punishments voluntarily undertaken by us in atonement for sin can we make satisfaction to God the Father through Jesus Christ, or by punishments imposed by the judgment of the priest according to the measure of our offense, but also, (and this is the greatest proof of love) by the temporal afflictions imposed by God and patiently borne by us."[3]

This is the teaching given by the Council of Trent, but lest anyone recklessly teach against this doctrine, or dare to think in any way otherwise, it pronounced many *latae sententiae* canons against the temerarious contradictors of this kind, the fourth of which contains these words: "If anyone denies that for the full and perfect remission of sins there are three acts required on the part of the penitent, as it were, the matter of the Sacrament of Penance, namely contrition, confession, and satisfaction, which are called the three parts of Penance; or says, that there are only two parts of Penance, namely the terrors of a troubled conscience because of the consciousness of sin, and the faith received from the Gospel or from absolution, by which one believes that his sins have been forgiven him through Christ: let him be anathema."[4] The twelfth canon has these words: "If anyone says that the whole punishment, together with the guilt, is always pardoned by God, and that the satisfaction of penitents is nothing other than faith, by which they perceive that Christ has made satisfaction for them: let him be anathema."[5] The thirteenth canon has the following words: "If anyone says that for sins, as far as temporal punishment is concerned, there is very little satisfaction made to God through the merits of Christ by the punishments inflicted by Him and patiently borne, or by those enjoined by the priest, but voluntarily undertaken, as by fasts, prayers, almsgiving, or also by other works of piety, and that therefore the best penance is only a new life: let him be anathema."[6] The fourteenth canon is drawn up by the following words: "If anyone says that the satisfactions by which penitents atone for their sins through Jesus Christ are not a worship of God, but the traditions of men, obscuring the doctrine of grace, the true worship of God, and the very beneficence of the death of Christ: let him be anathema."[7] The fifteenth and last canon concerning Penance has the words which follow: "If anyone says that the keys have been given to the Church only to loose, and not also to bind, and that therefore priests, by imposing penalties on those who confess, act contrary to the institution of Christ; and that it is fiction that, after eternal punishment has been remitted by virtue of the keys, there usually remains a temporal punishment to be discharged: let him be anathema."[8]

---

[1] Cf. I Tim. 5, 22.
[2] Cf. Mt. 16, 19; Jn 20, 23.
[3] Dz. 904-906.
[4] Dz. 914.
[5] Dz. 922.
[6] Dz. 923.
[7] Dz. 924.
[8] Dz. 925.

There now remains that we reply to those things which Luther and the other followers of his object to us. Firstly, in fact, they object to us that which the Lord promised through Ezechiel the prophet, that He would not remember any longer all the iniquities of the wicked if he did penance from all his sins. If, the wicked having done penance, God does not remember his iniquities, then after the guilt has been forgiven, God requires no punishment for sin: because if God were to require some punishment after the forgiveness of guilt, He now remembers the iniquities of the wicked after his penance.[1] This argument is very easily solved if God's very words in Ezechiel the prophet are read with attention. For God does not promise that He will not remember the iniquities of the wicked if he were merely contrite of heart for his sins, but rather He promised this with this condition, if the wicked did penance. But full penance, as we said, also includes satisfaction, just as it requires contrition and confession: and hence it is that he does not make full and perfect penance, who does not satisfy God for his sin: and so it is not surprising if God remembers his sin, such that He punishes it with some temporal punishment.

But if we wanted to freely grant to Luther that the word "penance" in the aforesaid words of God mean contrition of heart alone, still Luther could gather nothing from those words against us. Because in those words God not only asks for penance from the wicked so that He would not remember his iniquity, but in addition He requires from Him that He "do judgment and justice." Unless perhaps the contrition of heart is very great, which rightly would compensate for the lack of exterior penance. Because He does not wish to inflict punishments according to the measure of the sin. We can still reply otherwise that by those words God does not promise so much indulgence as Luther thinks. For when saying that He will not remember the iniquities of the wicked, He only promises that He will no longer hold his as an enemy, but this does not hinder that after the friendship is contracted He would punish him amicably, especially because according to Paul's teaching: "He scourgeth every son whom he receiveth" (Heb. 12, 6).

Secondly, Luther objects to us that Christ satisfied for all of us, and hence it seems to Luther that the sinner does an injury to Christ who tries to satisfy God for his sins: because by that very fact he seems to lessen the glory of Christ's Passion, as though it were not sufficient for satisfying for our sins. The Lutherans extol this argument very much, and by it they think that they triumph over us: but in reality this argument does not have even a little force, which could move learned men a tiny bit, but it merely has a certain appearance of a counterfeit religion and a false piety which can deceive unlearned men. For if this argument proves anything, by it would also be proved that penance is not necessary. But if a sinner was made by sin a slave of the devil, and held captive by him, it can be argued that to ransom him it is not necessary that he be sorry for the sin, or that he confess it, or do anything else: because Christ "gave himself a redemption for all" (I Tim. 2, 6). If the sinner incites God's anger, and is made His enemy through sin, it can also be argued that it is not necessary that we by our contrition, or by our sorrow, try to appease our God, and make Him propitious to us: because He was made, as John says, "the propitiation for our sins: and not for ours only, but also for those of the whole world" (I Jn. 2, 2). Therefore, let us not weep, because Christ wept for us: let us not be sad, because He was sad for us.

Behold what Luther's argument is capable of doing, namely that it is capable of hurling us into many horrendous ruinations, if that argument were capable of doing anything. Certainly, Christ did not hang upon the Cross to degenerate us and make us lazy and permit us to have a splendid life. "Christ also suffered for us," says Peter, "leaving you an example that you should follow his steps" (I Pet. 2, 21). Certainly, Christ did not suffer for us so that we would

---

[1] "But if the wicked do penance for all his sins which he hath committed, and keep all my commandments, and do judgment, and justice, living he shall live, and shall not die" (Ez. 18, 21).

eat sumptuously or occupy ourselves with the other delights of the body, but so that by His example we would bear our Cross for His sake. Hence, we acknowledge that Christ satisfied for us, in a way whereby He was made a redemption, propitiation, and a reconciliation for us. Thus, just as notwithstanding the prior Redemption made through Christ, those who sin after Baptism are obliged to do penance so that they may be freed from the slavery of sin, and be bought back from the captivity of the devil: so also notwithstanding the prior satisfaction made through Christ, those who sin after Baptism are obliged to satisfy for themselves, and to join their satisfaction, which otherwise would not be effective, with Christ's satisfaction, so that by that satisfaction it may do that which by itself it could not do. For the Royal Prophet when asking what he could render to God in satisfaction for his sins, said: "I will take the chalice of salvation; and I will call upon the name of the Lord" (Ps. 115, 13).

Now so that we may make these things clearer, it will be worthwhile to explain how all these propositions ought to be understood, which are contained in various passages of Sacred Scripture. "Christ redeemed all men." "Christ gave Himself as a redemption for all" (I Tim. 2, 6). "In Christ all shall be made alive" (I Cor. 15, 22). "God will have all men to be saved" (I Tim. 2, 4). For this proposition about which we now dispute, Christ satisfied for the sins of all men, ought to be interpreted in the same way. All these propositions have a certain universality, which is called by recent dialecticians "befitting distribution,"[1] such that the word denoting universality does not extend to everything signified by the word closely joined to it, but only to those things which are specified by the adjective which follows it, or by the predicate. Thus, all those propositions ought to be interpreted in this way. "Christ redeemed all men," that is, Christ redeemed all the redeemed or all who are going to be redeemed; or, no man is redeemed except by Christ. "In Christ all will be made alive," that is, all who going to be made alive, will be made alive in Christ; or, no one who is made alive, has life except through Christ. "God wills all men to be saved," that is, God wills all men who are going to be saved, to be saved; or, no one is saved except by God willing it. And certainly, unless all these propositions be understood according to this manner, their truth could hardly be established. For there are many men in the devil's perpetual captivity and held by him in slavery: many also have been condemned in perpetual death, and buried in Hell, who were not redeemed in any way, nor made alive in Christ, and consequently were not saved.

Yet this does not happen because the redemption offered through Christ was insufficient for them as well as for the others who were redeemed. Nor is it because Christ was not able to give them life, or save them, just as the others: but because they did not want to use the redemption given through Christ, and they did not want to accept the condition of the redemption, reconciliation, and perpetual life and salvation. For He did not offer redemption, reconciliation and perpetual salvation to all: but to them only who shall keep God's Commandments. "You are my friends," Christ says, "if you do the things that I command you" (Jn. 15, 14). And again: "If you love me, keep my commandments" (Jn. 14, 15). And once again: "If thou wilt enter into life, keep the commandments" (Mt. 19, 17). Notice that He promises His friendship and afterwards life, yet on this condition, that they keep His Commandments. And so, it is that he who does not keep God's Commandment, is not His friend, nor will attain eternal life, and consequently was not redeemed from the devil's captivity. Thus, in order that we

---

[1] *Distributio accomoda.* "Again, it is customary to posit a certain 'distribution of aptitude,' as 'Every man fears the sea,' that is, man is born apt to fear the sea. Or again, it is customary to posit 'befitting distribution,' as 'Heaven touches all things apart from itself' and 'God created all things apart from Himself.' But these two kinds of distribution are not as proper as the other." (Peter of Spain, later Pope John XXI, *Summulae logicales cum versorii Parisiensis clarissima expositione* (*Little Summaries of Logic*) (Venice, apud F. Sansovinum, 1572), tract 6 (On Suppositions), fol. 246D).

may truly say with Paul that Christ redeemed all men, and in Christ all men were made alive, it is necessary to interpret all those words according to the meaning which we have just said.

But lest anyone suppose that I concocted this interpretation of Paul's words out of my own head, and hence thinks that it rightly ought to be rejected, I bring forth for a confirmation of this interpretation the testimony of Blessed Augustine who says these words: "Just as what is said, 'In Christ all will be made alive,' since so many are punished by eternal death, it was so said, that all, whosoever receive eternal life, do not receive it unless in Christ; so too, what is said, 'all men to be saved,' is so said, that all men who are saved… are not saved unless as Christ wills."[1] And in the book, *On the Soul and its Origin* [which he sent] to Jerome when interpreting the words of Paul: "As in Adam all die, so also in Christ all shall be made alive" (I Cor. 15, 22), he says these words: "For, according to this Apostolic, Divine, and perspicuous declaration, it is sufficiently plain that no one goes to death otherwise than through Adam, and that no one goes to life eternal otherwise than through Christ. For this is the force of all in the two parts of the sentence; as all men, by their first, that is, their natural birth, belong to Adam, even so all men, whoever they be, who come to Christ come to the second, that is, the spiritual birth."[2] Thus from the interpretation of the above-mentioned words of Paul, it is gathered that this proposition ought to be understood in the same way, Christ satisfied for all, that is, Christ satisfied for all who satisfy for their own sins. Or otherwise and better, no one except through Christ satisfies for their own sins. For even if one were to fast, pray, give alms, or do any other penal work, by that he will never satisfy for his sins except by means of the merits of Christ's Passion, on account of which we have this most plentiful gift from God, that through our works we can satisfy God for our sins: by which works we would never satisfy God, unless Christ by His Passion had impetrated this for us.

And hence it is easily established that we do not detract anything from God's glory, when we say that our satisfaction is necessary for us, for obtaining the perfect remission of sins. For when saying this we rather increase God's glory, and extol the merit of Christ's Passion: because we say that Christ by the Passion not only satisfied for us, but also merited that our works would be satisfactory, which apart from Christ's Passion could not have such great worth. Next, we admit that Christ satisfied for all sinners, but this satisfaction is not applied to any sinner except by means of some Sacrament or good work of the sinner himself. And so it is that he who does more or greater good works on account of God for the remission of sins, Christ gives more to him of the merit of His Passion for satisfying for his sins. Hence Paul says: "A faithful saying: for if we be dead with him, we shall live also with him. If we suffer, we shall also reign with him" (II Tim. 2, 11-12). Now when by means of a Sacrament the satisfaction of Christ's Passion is communicated to the penitent, the more excellent and more efficacious the Sacrament will have been for the remission of sin, so much the more by it is communicated to man the merit of the Passion for the redemption of sin, and satisfaction for him. Now the Sacrament of Baptism, as we will say below, is more excellent than the Sacrament of Penance, and hence although by both Sacraments the guilt is forgiven, still the punishment is not so remitted by the latter.

Thirdly, Luther objects to us that the word, "satisfaction," which he says was falsely contrived by scholastic theologians, because it is never found in Holy Writ, nor was it ever used, as he says, by the holy Fathers. Now so that Luther's thinking, nay rather his madness, may be known to all, I have decided to cite here his words, which he says in that attack upon the Bull of Leo X, in the fifth article, and are those which follow: "Wherefore I have said the truth, that this arbitrary satisfaction is not found in Scriptures or the Fathers; the irremissible punishment imposed by God is however found… Now I have greatly hated, and I would wish

---

[1] Letter 217 (to Vitalis), c. 6, n. 19 (PL 33, 985-986).
[2] Letter 166, c. 7, n. 21 (PL 33, 729).

that this word, 'satisfaction,' be taken away, which not only is not found in Scriptures, but also has a dangerous meaning, as though anyone could make satisfaction to God for any sin, although He freely forgives all sins."[1] Even though Luther says that he hates the word, "satisfaction," still he execrates much more bitterly, as I said, the thing itself than the word. For he abominates fasting, flagellation, chastity, vigils, pilgrimages, and all the rest of labors of the body: and he loves the allurements of the flesh. And hence it is evident that he has detested satisfaction itself, because it consists of hard and austere works.

But let us see what he objects about the word. He firstly says that it is not found in Sacred Scriptures. Since he contends about the word, and not about the thing itself, I reply about the word itself that what he says is false. For the word, "satisfaction," is found in Lev. 10, 20; Acts 17, 9 & 24, 10; and I Pet. 3, 15, although in none of these passages is the word used for that satisfaction which is made to God for sins. But so be it that this word is not found in Holy Writ, still it does not thence follow that it is not permitted for Catholic men to use the word. For Holy Writ prescribes to us laws about works, which we ought to do, and about things we are obliged to believe: yet it does not prescribe the words which necessarily ought to be used. Because when it is evident about the reality, it matters little whether we use this or that word. Certainly, the word, "consubstantiality," is nowise found in Holy Writ, and yet the Church does not hesitate to use it, when saying that the Son is consubstantial to the Father: although Arius was objecting to the newness of the word. So also, now the Catholic Church uses, and will use, the word, "satisfaction," although Luther and his followers say that they are offended by this word.

Next, Luther says that this word was not used by the holy Fathers, not is it found in their writings. But when saying this, either he lies, or he shows clearly that he, when he wrote this, was insufficiently versed in the reading of the holy Doctors, because there are many of them who use this word. I omit the more recent ones, and from the ancient ones I firstly bring forth Gregory who in the thirty-fourth homily on the Gospels, which is on the parable of the erring sheep, says the following: "We must reflect seriously that one who remembers having committed unlawful actions must strive to refrain even from some that are lawful, since he makes satisfaction to his Creator in this way. A person who has committed things that are prohibited should cut off from himself even what is allowed."[2] In this homily he uses the same word in that meaning whereby it shows us to satisfy God for sins by our works. Gregory also uses this same word in homily [fourteen], which is on the parable of the [good shepherd] in that meaning whereby he shows us that we by our works satisfy God for our sins.[3]

Pope Leo I says these words: "The Mediator between God and men, the Man Christ Jesus, has transmitted this power to those that are set over the Church that they would both give a satisfaction of penitence to those who confess, and, when they have been cleansed by the same salutary satisfaction, admit them through the door of reconciliation to communion in the Sacraments."[4] These are the words of Pope Leo, a man renowned for his holiness as well as his learning.

---

[1] *Assertion of All the Articles Wrongly Condemned in the Roman Bull* (WA 7, 112 lns. 21-21 & 113, lns. 16-19).

[2] N. 16 (PL 76, 1256C).

[3] "The Good Shepherd has laid down His life for His sheep in order to change His Body and Blood into a Sacrament for us, and to satisfy (*satiaret*) the sheep He had redeemed with His Blood as food. The way of contempt for death which we are to follow has been shown to us, the mold which is to form us is there. The first thing we are to do is to devote our external goods to His sheep in mercy" (N. 1 (PL 76, 1127C-D)). The text incorrectly refers to "homily twenty-five, which is on the erring sheep." It has been amended here.

[4] Letter 108 (to Bishop Theodore of Forum Julii), c. 2 (PL 54, 1011B-1012A).

Jerome commenting on [Joel[1]] says: "He who is a sinner and whose own conscience gnaws at him, let him be girded with the sackcloth of penance and let him mourn either his own sins or those of the people, and let him go into the church from which he had departed [on account of his sins], and let him lie down, or 'sleep' in sackcloth, to compensate for past pleasures, through which he had offended God, by austerity of life."[2] Jerome here uses the word "compensation" for "satisfaction, because both words have the same meaning, and it is customary among approved authors to very often put one for the other.

Ambrose in the book, *De lapsu virginis consecratae*, says these words: "Therefore a sinner if he did not spare himself, is spared by God. And if he shall have compensated for the future everlasting pains of Hell in this short period of life, he frees himself from eternal judgment. For a great destruction a deep reaching and prolonged remedy is needed. A great crime has need of much satisfaction."[3] Ambrose used both words, "compensation" and "satisfaction."

Cyprian, when reprehending the error of certain men, who having been led astray by a semblance of mercy were reconciling to the Church without hesitation those who had fallen into idolatry, says these words: "They interfere such that Christ is not besought with prayers and satisfactions, Who professes that he who denies Him He will deny... Efforts are used that the sins may not be atoned for with just satisfactions and lamentations, that the wounds may not be washed away with tears. True peace is done away by the falsehood of a false peace."[4] And in his sermon, *On the Lapsed*, when inveighing against those who deny that the lapsed need to make satisfaction for their sins, he says that they are much more pernicious and much crueler than tyrants persecuting the Christians, and at the end says these words: "God, in proportion as with the affection of a Father, is always indulgent and good, in the same proportion is to be dreaded with the majesty of a judge. Even as we have sinned greatly, so let us greatly lament. To a deep wound let there not be wanting a long and careful treatment; let not the repentance be less than the sin. Think you that the Lord can be quickly appeased, Whom with perfidious words you have denied, to Whom you have rather preferred your patrimony, Whose Church you have violated with a sacrilegious participation? Think you that He will easily have mercy upon you whom you have declared not to be your God? You must pray and entreat more vehemently; you must pass the day in grief; wear out nights in watchings and weepings; occupy all your time in wailful lamentations; lying stretched on the ground, you must keep using ashes, be clothed with sackcloth and mourning garments; after having lost the raiment of Christ, you must be willing now to have no clothing; after the devil's meat, you must prefer fasting; be earnest in righteous works, whereby sins may be cleansed; frequently apply yourself to almsgiving, whereby souls are freed from death... He who has thus made satisfaction to God; he who has done penance for his deed, who by shame for his sin, has conceived more both of virtue and of faith from the very grief of his fall, heard and aided by the Lord, shall make the Church which he had lately saddened glad, and shall now deserve of the Lord not only pardon, but a crown."[5] Cyprian does not merely explain the very matter of satisfaction, but when explaining this, often uses the word, "satisfaction."

---

[1] The text incorrectly has "Malachias" here.

[2] On Joel 1, 13-14 (PL 25, 958D).

[3] C. 8, n. 36 (PL 16, 378B). "The genuineness of the touching little work 'On the Fall of a Consecrated Virgin' (*De lapsu virginis consecratæ*) has been called in question, but without sufficient reason. Dom Germain Morin maintains that it is a real homily of Ambrose, but like so many more of his so-called 'books,' owes its actual form to some one of his auditors" ("St. Ambrose," *Catholic Encyclopedia* (New York: Robert Appleton Company, 1907), vol. 1, p. 387).

[4] Letter 12 (to Pope Cornelius), n. 12-13 (PL 3, 812B-C).

[5] N. 35-36 (PL 4, 492B-C & 494B).

Tertullian in his book, *On Repentance*, also uses this word, when saying these words: "For confession is counselled by [a desire to make] satisfaction... by confession satisfaction is settled... by repentance God is appeased."[1]

From all these testimonies of most illustrious men it is very clearly proved to be false what Luther asserted with great temerity, that the word of "satisfaction" is not found in the holy Fathers. After having considered all these things well I cannot but be astonished at the madness of Luther and his followers: because while they want to make God excessively merciful, they strive to make Him unjust. For it would be unjust to forgive whatever very grave crimes without punishment. Next, they all confess that Original sin, which we contract by another's will, is forgiven us through Baptism in such a way that afterwards its punishment remains, namely concupiscence of the flesh, which also through Christ's satisfaction, as they say, cannot be effaced without it being a sin. From which opinion it is proved that they think that Original sin is much more serious than a mortal actual sin, because when a mortal sin has been forgiven no punishment remains: when Original sin has been forgiven, however, punishment inflicted on account of it remains, which is so serious, according to their view, that it is always a sin for man, and it is never an occasion of merit. It is also proved incontestably for the same reason that they make Penance of more value than Baptism: because when actual sin has been forgiven through Penance, as they say, all punishment is forgiven which is due to it: when Original sin has been forgiven through Baptism, however, all punishment is not taken away. Now to claim this is a great impiety: because the holy Fathers have always taught that the Sacrament of Baptism is much more excellent than Penance, and the Fathers in the Council of Trent defined this in the fourteenth session celebrated under Julius III, where in the second chapter of their teaching, published these words while I was present there:

"Moreover, it is clear that this Sacrament differs in many respects from Baptism. For aside from the fact that in the matter and form, by which the essence of a Sacrament is effected, it differs very widely, it is certainly clear that the minister of Baptism need not be a judge, since the Church exercises judgment on no one who has not first entered it through the gateway of Baptism. 'For what have I to do,' says St. Paul, 'to judge them that are without?' (I Cor. 5, 12). It is otherwise with those of the household of the faith, whom Christ the Lord by the laver of Baptism has once made members of his own body.[2] For these, if they should afterwards have defiled themselves by some crime, He did not now wish to have cleansed by the repetition of Baptism, since that is in no way permitted in the Catholic Church, but to be placed, as it were, as culprits before the tribunal, so that by the sentence of the priests they may be freed not only once, but as often as they, repentant for the sins committed, have had recourse to Him. Furthermore, the fruit of Baptism is one thing; that of Penance is another thing. For by putting on Christ by Baptism,[3] we are made an entirely new creature in Him, obtaining a full and complete remission of all sins, to which newness and integrity, however, we can in no way arrive by the Sacrament of Penance without many tears and labors on our part, for Divine justice demands this, so that Penance has justly been called by the holy Fathers, 'a laborious kind of Baptism.' This Sacrament of Penance, moreover, is necessary for the salvation of those who have fallen after Baptism, as Baptism itself is for those as yet not regenerated."[4]

From which words it is evident how much the Sacrament of Baptism excels the Sacrament of Penance: since by the former all punishment is remitted, but not by the latter. For even though after Baptism concupiscence remains, it is not left as a punishment, but for caution, so that we might be more vigilant and cautious by this occasion, just as one who has a domestic

---

[1] C. 8-9 (PL 1, 1243A-B).
[2] Cf. I Cor. 12, 13.
[3] Cf. Gal. 3, 27.
[4] Dz. 895.

enemy. For God decreed for this reason that when the Promised Land was subdued by the children of Israel, the Jebusite would always remain among them, and never be extirpated, lest they would be torpid through idleness.[1] In this way also, so that necessity would force us to labor and caution, God left an enemy to our spirit, namely, concupiscence of the flesh, whose perpetual snare it would be necessary to always fear. Hence God left to us after Baptism the impulses of the flesh opposing the spirit rather for our caution and benefit than for a punishment: because although they occasion no little trouble, still we will obtain great profit, if we overcome them. In Baptism, therefore, not only the guilt is forgiven, but also all punishment, which ought to have been paid on account of actual sin. "We, who are baptized in Christ Jesus," as Paul says, "are baptized in his death. For we are buried together with him by baptism into death; that as Christ is risen from the dead by the glory of the Father, so we also may walk in newness of life" (Rom. 6, 3-4). Thus, just as no vestige of corporeal life remained in Christ after He died and was buried, so no vestige of sin remains in the one baptized, because he was buried together with Christ through Baptism.

By Penance, on the other hand, sin has not so died, neither by it is the penitent buried together with Christ: nor by it is he called a new creature, as by Baptism. Because even though by the Sacrament of Penance the guilt is remitted, still the whole punishment is not always remitted. And this is what Paul says to the Hebrews. "For if we sin wilfully after having the knowledge of the truth, there is now left no sacrifice for sins" (10, 26). He says this because Christ's Passion ought not to be offered for us again for the death of sin, as it is offered in Baptism. For Christ, as Paul says elsewhere, died once for us.[2] If for the sins committed after death Christ's Passion would always suffice for impetrating the full remission of sin through the Sacrament of Penance, as through Baptism, it would thence follow that Christ would die for us many times, and not once, and that there would be other victims for sins after having received the knowledge of truth. For Paul proves elsewhere by this argument that Baptism ought not to be repeated: because he who repeats it, crucifies to himself the Son of God.[3]

And that this is the correct meaning of Paul, [Hervé, monk of Bourg-Dieu], who in his commentaries on Paul, when interpreting those aforesaid words from the Epistle to the Hebrews, says these words: "For Christ ought not to be immolated again for sins, which was done once, and a second time is not necessary, but rather it would be necessary that we remain in faith and good works. Penance ought not to be excluded, but a second Baptism. For I say, there is no further penance or remission, but a victim, that is, the second cross: because one suffices, and we should no longer wait for this, but we should do penance, because we cannot be rebaptized in Christ's death. For he who repeats Baptism, repeats again Christ's death, so that from this having been repeated the remission may be repeated. But this is impossible. No such victim is left to us, if after Baptism we shall have inquinated."[4] Haymo interprets these words in the same way in his commentaries on Paul's epistles.[5] Against this most pestilential error it is not necessary to dispute more, because by those things which we have said, it is proved clearly enough about its falsity.

There is a **second heresy** which says that penance which arises from the fear of Hell, is not merely useless, but even harmful. The author of this heresy was also Luther, who to this end seemed to direct his teaching, so that he might turn away sinners from penance, and incite them to sin. For he says that penance is pestiferous which has arisen from fear of Hell.

---

[1] Cf. Jud. 2, 21-22.

[2] Cf. Heb. 9, 28.

[3] Cf. Heb. 6, 6.

[4] PL 181, 1636D. The text attributes this commentary to Saint Anselm of Canterbury, but it was in fact written by Hervé of Bourg-Dieu.

[5] PL 117, 895A-B.

Wherefore he says that it is wrong to scare sinners with this fear, so that therefrom they would bring themselves to penance. But we have already discussed this error above in the section on "Contrition": hence there is no need to repeat those things here.

The **third heresy** takes away all power of penance, saying that they who have fallen one time, never afterwards obtain forgiveness, no matter how much they repent afterwards. The author of this heresy was Novatian, a certain priest of the Roman church, from whom the Novatians are named. They are called by another name, Cathari, that is, "the Pure," on account of the purity which they very proudly proclaimed about themselves. And this name they very arrogantly gave to themselves. He who desires to fully know the history of this affair, may read Eusebius of Caesarea in the sixth book of his *Ecclesiastical History*, in the forty-third chapter.[1] But although everyone who wrote about heresies attributes this error to this Novatian as its first inventor, nevertheless Blessed Jerome says that this error was also the error of Montanus,[2] who is evidently more ancient than Novatian, because the former lived under Emperor Commodus and Pope Soter: but the latter under Decius and under Pope Cornelius. Thus, whoever was the first inventor of this heresy, he certainly invented a harsh opinion, and quite incongruous with the Divine mercy.

Wherefore I think that those who taught this heresy did not attain mercy: because (as James the Apostle says) "Judgment without mercy to him that hath not done mercy" (2, 13), especially since nothing else is put forth as many times and as clearly in the holy codices as the mercy which God exercises towards sinners, especially the repentant, granting them pardon of their sins. If penance does not merit pardon of sins, in vain did he do penance in sackcloth and ashes, and beseech God for his sins, saying: "Thou indeed hast numbered my steps, but spare my sins" (Job 14, 16). In vain he asks, who is sure that he cannot obtain what he asks. But holy Job thinking better of the Divine mercy than Novatian, asks for that which he believes he can obtain. And David, when repenting of the adultery which he has committed, entreats the Lord, saying: "Have mercy on me, O God, according to thy great mercy. And according to the multitude of thy tender mercies blot out my iniquity" (Ps. 50, 3). David recognizes that the Divine mercy is great, and he knows the multitude of His mercies: hence he asks for mercy from God with confidence, just as from one who could give it. For the goodness of omnipotence and the omnipotence of goodness is so great in God, that there is no sin that He does not want to forgive or that He could not forgive the repentant sinner. For if there were some sin which He could not forgive, He would not be omnipotent: or if although He could forgive, He does not want to forgive, then He is not fully merciful, since it is required for full mercy that He would want to forgive all that He could, if the bad will of the one asking does not impede. The king in the Gospel, by whom the Lord represented Himself by the parable, forgave the whole debt to his servant, because he asked him: and because that servant had not exercised the same mercy to another fellow-servant, he was fastened in chains and thrown into prison.[3]

Furthermore, Solomon in the book of Wisdom says: "No evil can overcome wisdom" (7, 30). But if there were some sin which goodness could not or would not forgive, wisdom would have been overcome by evil: or its power would have been conquered, if it could not

---

[1] "After this, Novatus, a presbyter of the church at Rome, being lifted up with arrogance against these persons, as if there was no longer for them a hope of salvation, not even if they should do all things pertaining to a genuine and pure conversion, became leader of the heresy of those who, in the pride of their imagination, call themselves Cathari" (PG 20, 615B).

[2] "Montanus and Novatus would smile at this, for they contend that it is impossible to renew again through repentance those who have crucified to themselves the Son of God, and put Him to an open shame" (*Against Jovinian*, bk. 2, n. 4 (PL 23, 286B)).

[3] Cf. Mt. 18, 23-34.

forgive: or mercy would have been conquered, if it did not want to forgive. In the same book it is again said: "God overlooks the sins of men for the sake of repentance" (11, 24). What is to overlook, except not to punish when one could? Now He does not punish, because God's [goodness[1]] (as the Apostle says) leads the sinner to penance.[2] But if penance were of no use to the sinner, in vain would God wait for him, since from such waiting the sinner can have no benefit. But because through such penance the sinner attains the remission of his sins, and afterwards everlasting life, then God does not immediately punish the sinner after having committed sin, but He waits so that he may do penance, saying: "I desire not the death of the wicked, but that the wicked turn from his way, and live" (Ez. 33, 11). Thus, He Who prefers the conversion of the sinner, prefers [this] on account of the benefit of the sinner himself, and not on account of His own benefit, because God has no need of our goods.[3] Ecclesiasticus also teaches this same opinion saying: "My son, hast thou sinned? do so no more: but for thy former sins also pray that they may be forgiven thee" (21, 1). If sin were not forgiven through penance, in vain would Ecclesiasticus advise the sinner that he ask God for the forgiveness of his sins.

Again, the prophet Isaias promises the sinner pardon of his sins if he would repent, saying: "Let the wicked forsake his way, and the unjust man his thoughts, and let him return to the Lord, and he will have mercy on him, and to our God: for he is bountiful to forgive" (55, 7). And the Lord says through the prophet Jeremias: "If that nation against which I have spoken, shall repent of their evil, I also will repent of the evil that I have thought to do to them" (18, 8). The Lord promises this same thing through the prophet Ezechiel saying: "If the wicked do penance for all his sins which he hath committed, and keep all my commandments, and do judgment, and justice, living he shall live, and shall not die. I will not remember all his iniquities that he hath done: in his justice which he hath wrought, he shall live" (18, 21-22). Why then do the very cruel Novatians presume to teach contrary to so many and such clear testimonies? God promises to the penitent sinner that he will forgive and pardon sins, and these men are not afraid, contrary to the Divine promises, to deny forgiveness to the penitent.

But see how they explain their teaching, supposing that it can be defended without difficulty. For they claim that sins committed before Baptism can be effaced through Baptism, those however which were perpetrated after Baptism, they deny can be forgiven through Penance. But then it will be necessary to ask them whether Baptism lessens God's power or mercy, or perhaps it helps the wickedness of sin, so that the victory against God's mercy may be able to appear? Far be it that someone would fall into such great blasphemy, that he would say that our wickedness could ever conquer the Divine mercy and wisdom. But wisdom would need to admit that it was conquered if it could not or would not forgive sins committed after Baptism. For it not only ought to be believed that wickedness sometimes does not conquer wisdom, but that it never does.

Furthermore, the Lord Himself says: "They that are in health need not a physician, but they that are ill. Go then and learn what this meaneth, I will have mercy and not sacrifice. For I am not come to call the just, but sinners [to penance]" (Mt. 9, 12, 13). It is surprising that God would have come from Heaven to call sinners for what is completely useless, namely for penance, which according to the opinion of these heretics is something completely useless for a baptized sinner. Again, in those very same words the Savior says that He came as a physician for the sick. If therefore He is a skilled doctor, He can cure all infirmities. For one's medical skill is not perfect, which cannot cure some infirmity. But if he can cure all infirmities, but does not want to cure, then the doctor is cruel, and ought not to be call merciful, who does not

---

[1] The *Vetus Latina* text cited here, had God's "patience" instead of "goodness," as in the Vulgate.
[2] Cf. Rom. 2, 4.
[3] Cf. Ps. 15, 2.

have compassion on the sick, because he does not help him when he can. But God is merciful, of whose mercy there is no number[1]: and so He wants all men to be saved, if they themselves do not oppose their own salvation. Wherefore it is necessary that we praise Him with the Royal Prophet on account of this immense mercy of His, saying: "Bless the Lord, O my soul: and let all that is within me bless his holy name. Bless the Lord, O my soul, and never forget all he hath done for thee. Who forgiveth all thy iniquities: who healeth all thy diseases. Who redeemeth thy life from destruction: who crowneth thee with mercy and compassion" (Ps. 102, 1-4). What sin in us could be unforgivable, if the Lord forgives all our iniquities? Or how will it be said that some wound of sin is incurable, if the Lord heals all our weaknesses? Or how does one not obtain the benefit of full remission, who is crowned with mercy and compassion. Thus, God, Who heals all our infirmities, ought also to forgive the repentant sinner the sins committed after Baptism.

Next, there are many parables in the Gospel whereby Christ taught us to believe that the forgiveness of sin would be given to the repentant sinner. For the prodigal son, who having received the substance which was due to him by hereditary right, going away into a far region, had wasted his substance by living riotously. After having returned to himself, he repented of acting badly and returned to his father, and was received by him, and yet not roughly and harshly, but rather kindly and with great joy, because the son who had perished was found. Neither is there any other prodigal son than the sinner: nor another father of his than God, Who from His exceedingly great goodness receives the sinner converted to Himself, and does this with joy: because "There shall be joy in heaven upon one sinner that doth penance, more than upon ninety-nine just who need not penance" (Lk 15, 7).

The man wounded by robbers, going down from Jerusalem to Jericho, the Samaritan brought to an inn, poured wine and oil into his wounds, gave two pence to the host to be spent for medicine for the wounded man, and promised that he would afterwards pay whatever the host had spent in addition on the infirm man. This wounded man represents the sinner. The Samaritan having such solicitous care of him is Christ our Redeemer. Now if the health of the infirm man were already despaired of, the Samaritan would not have been so solicitous for his health. But because he hoped that the infirm man could be restored to pristine health, if the due medicine were applied to him: hence he applies every care that he could so that he might recover his health.

Finally, the Synod of Rome was celebrated against this heresy by Pope Cornelius, [sixty] bishops, and many more priests and deacons, in which this pestiferous heresy was condemned. And although the decrees of this council do not exist, nevertheless Eusebius of Caesarea bears witness about this matter.[2] But if some obstinate person does not believe Eusebius, let him hear the Council of Nicea, which forbade any of the Novatians to be received into the communion of the Church, unless they firstly abjured this heresy. For the aforesaid council says the following: "Concerning those who call themselves Cathari [Novatians] that is, clean, if at any time they come to the Catholic Church, it has been decided by the holy and great Council,

---

[1] Cf. Ps. 146, 5.

[2] "After this, Novatian, a presbyter of the church at Rome, being lifted up with arrogance against these persons, as if there was no longer for them a hope of salvation, not even if they should do all things pertaining to a genuine and pure conversion, became leader of the heresy of those who, in the pride of their imagination, call themselves Cathari. There upon a very large synod assembled at Rome, of bishops in number sixty, and a great many more presbyters and deacons; while the pastors of the remaining provinces deliberated in their places privately concerning what ought to be done. A decree was confirmed by all, that Novatian and those who joined with him, and those who adopted his brother-hating and inhuman opinion, should be considered by the Church as strangers" (*Church History*, bk. 6, c. 43 (PG 20, 615B-C).

that, provided they receive the imposition of hands, they may remain among the clergy. However, because they are accepting and following the doctrines of the Catholic and Apostolic Church, it is fitting that they acknowledge this in writing before all; that is, both that they communicate with the twice married and with those who have lapsed during a persecution."[1]

And the Council of Trent celebrated under Paul III condemns this heresy in the sixth session. For in the teaching on the justification of a sinner, which was given in the fourteenth chapter of that session, these words are contained: "Those who by sin have fallen away from the received grace of justification, will again be able to be justified when, roused by God through the Sacrament of Penance, they, by the merit of Christ, shall have attended to the recovery of the grace lost. For this manner of justification is the reparation of one fallen, which the holy Fathers have aptly called a second plank after the shipwreck of lost grace."[2] But lest anyone temerariously think contrary to this teaching, it put forth the twenty-ninth *latae sententiae* canon, the words of which are these: "If anyone shall say that he who has fallen after Baptism cannot by the grace of God rise again; or that he can indeed recover lost justice, but by faith alone without the Sacrament of Penance, contrary to what the holy Roman and universal Church, taught by Christ the Lord and His Apostles, has hitherto professed, observed, and taught: let him be anathema."[3]

Blessed Cyprian wrote against this heresy a treatise in the form of a sermon, which is entitled, *On the Lapsed*.[4] Blessed Ambrose wrote a work on penance divided into two books, the first of which fights against Novatian.[5] Blessed Chrysostom made another book which is entitled, *De reparatio lapsi*.[6]

POTESTAS

Power

There is one heresy about this subject which asserts that all power, both secular and ecclesiastical, is lost through mortal sin. The authors of this heresy were the Waldensians, saying that one need not submit to a person who is guilty of a mortal sin, because such a person, they say, cannot hold an ecclesiastical or secular office. Blessed Bernard, who is more ancient than the Waldensians, attributes this error to certain heretics of his time, whose names he does not state, but he merely says that they boast that they are the successors of the Apostles, and live an Apostolic life.[7] Which thing gives an occasion of suspicion to me, that those men about whom Bernard speaks, are those whom we call the Apostolics: because both this error and the others which Bernard enumerates there, are defended by the Apostolics. But to this suspicion can be objected that Gerard Segarelli and Dolcino of Novara,[8] who are

---

[1] C. 8 (Dz. 55).
[2] Dz. 807.
[3] Dz. 839.
[4] PL 4, 463D-494B.
[5] PL 16, 465A-496C.
[6] This book is the first letter of the *Two Exhortations to Theodore after his Fall* (PG 277-308).
[7] "For they proudly proclaim themselves to be the successors of the Apostles and call themselves the Apostolics, although they are unable to show any proof of their apostolate... 'The successors of the Apostles,' they say, archbishops, bishops, and priests, are all sinners, and are thus incapable of validly either administering or receiving the Sacraments.' They hold indeed that to be a real prelate and to be a sinner are two things absolutely incompatible. But this is evidently false" (PL 183, 1098A & 1100A).
[8] Fra Dolcino (c. 1250 – 1307) succeeded Gerard Segarelli as the leader of the Apostolics and was

called leaders of the Apostolics, lived much later than Bernard. And certainly, whoever they were, they upheld completely the same errors as did the Waldensians. John Wycliffe revived this heresy of the Waldensians, just as he did many others, after a number of years. John Hus imitated John Wycliffe in this regard. These two men say that he who is guilty of a serious fault, is not king, nor count, nor duke, nor pope, nor bishop, nor any such [office]. And if some [office] is said to belong to these men, or they are named to be such, they claim that they are named by an equivocal denomination, just as a painted man is said to be a man, although he has nothing truly human.

Now they support themselves for asserting this by this argument: All power is from the Lord God: now God does not give His gifts to sinful and wicked men. Therefore, a man guilty of sin has no power. But this argument is completely worthless, and has no force, in that it assumes something false when it says that God does not grant His gifts to sinners. Now it is proved that this is false, for instance, from what the Lord, when speaking through the prophet Jeremias to some pagan nations, says: "And now I have given all these lands into the hand of Nabuchodonosor king of Babylon, my servant: moreover also the beasts of the field I have given him to serve him. And all nations shall serve him, and his son, and his son's son: till the time come for his land and himself: and many nations and great kings shall serve him" (27, 6-7). See wicked Nabuchodonosor, and he is called "king": and Wycliffe cannot say that he is called a king equivocally, because as it is said, he is a king. For God to Whom it belongs to give kingdoms, gave him the kingdom. "I," God says, "have given all these lands into the hand of Nabuchodonosor the king." Therefore, God also gives kingdoms to sinners, just as to the just: because He (as it is written in Job) "maketh a man that is a hypocrite to reign for the sins of the people" (34, 30). See that a hypocrite reigns not merely by God permitting, but by God making him to reign. But who can doubt that a hypocrite is a bad man?

Furthermore, Christ, when speaking about rendering obedience to superiors, says: "The scribes and the Pharisees have sitten on the chair of Moses. All things therefore whatsoever they shall say to you, observe and do: but according to their works do ye not; for they say, and do not" (Mt. 23, 2-3). From which words it is very clearly proved that it can happen that those who ought not to be imitated, who say and do not do, sit upon a throne: who "bind heavy and insupportable burdens, and lay them on men's shoulders; but with a finger of their own they will not move them" (v. 4). Again, Blessed Peter says: "Servants, be subject to your masters with all fear, not only to the good and gentle, but also to the froward" (I Pet. 2, 18). Notice that Blessed Peter calls the froward "masters," and the heretics are not afraid to deny that this is possible, namely that a man be a sinner, and have some power and rulership. And lest they escape to the equivocation of the word, saying that because they were called "masters" equivocally, just as a painted man is called a man, he commands that they be subject to such froward men. From which it is clearly established that they not in name only are called "masters," but in reality, since obedience and fear is due to them.

Next, there were some sinners about whom the Gospel testifies that they then had some official dignity of power. Judas was an Apostle, and was then a sinner: and if John Wycliffe is not ashamed to deny this, the Truth Itself by His own mouth refutes and confounds him. For He speaks thus: "Have not I chosen you twelve; and one of you is a devil?" (Jn. 6, 71). Behold, Judas is a sinner, and yet he is an Apostle, because he was chosen by the Lord. Unless perhaps him whom God chose, Wycliffe wants blocked from the choice. Caiphas also when he was the priest of that year prophesied. He was a priest, and he sentenced Christ to death.[1] Thus it is possible that someone be a sinner and be pope, or bishop, or king, or anything of

---

burned at the stake in Northern Italy in 1307. Gerard Segarelli was executed in 1300.

[1] Cf. Jn. 11, 51.

this kind. For He "who maketh his sun to rise upon the good, and bad" (Mt. 5, 45), also gives kingdoms to the just and to sinners.

Deservedly, therefore, this opinion was condemned in the Council of Constance. For the fourth of the forty-five articles of John Wycliffe condemned in that council in the eighth session, says the following: "If a bishop or priest is living in mortal sin, he does not ordain, nor consecrate, nor perform, nor baptize."[1] And the fifteenth article of his is this: "No one is a civil master, no one a prelate, no one a bishop, as long as he is in mortal sin."[2] Which two articles along with the others were condemned with one *latae sententiae* [excommunication]. And in the same council in the fifteenth session some articles of John Hus were condemned, the last of which has the same sentence [of excommunication], and was promulgated with the same words as the fifteenth of John Wycliffe.[3] And the Council of Trent celebrated under Paul III and Julius III condemned this same heresy to the extent that it speaks about priests. For in the seventh session celebrated under Paul III, among the many canons which it composed, it composed the twelfth with these words: "If anyone shall say that a minister who is in mortal sin, although he observes all the essentials which pertain to the performance or conferring of the sacrament, neither performs nor confers the sacrament: let him be anathema."[4] And afterwards in the seventh session celebrated under Julius III it published many canons, the tenth of which contains these words: "If anyone says that priests who are in mortal sin do not have the power of binding and loosing…"[5]

Thomas Netter wrote against this error of John Wycliffe in his first volume of his *Doctrinale antiquitatum fidei Catholicae Ecclesiae* in three chapters of the same book, namely chapters eighty-one, eighty-two and eighty-three.[6]

PRAECEPTUM

Precepts

The **first heresy** is that which teaches that there is no precept in the whole Evangelical Law. The inventor of this heresy is Luther, who seems to direct his whole doctrine to this end alone, namely that he might turn men away from the way of truth, and lead them astray to any vice whatsoever. Philip Melanchthon followed Luther on this point in his *Loci Communes*.[7] Luther's words in his *Preface to the New Testament* are these: There is not anything which was commanded in the Gospel by God.[8] In his sermon on Moses he says these words: "This text makes it clear that even the Ten Commandments do not pertain to us. For

---

[1] Dz. 584.
[2] Dz. 595.
[3] Dz. 656.
[4] Dz. 855.
[5] Dz. 920.
[6] Bk. 2, art. 3, pp. 399-407.
[7] CR 21, 303 ff.
[8] "We see, also, that He does not command us but invites us as a friend, saying, 'Blessed are the poor in spirit…'; and the Apostles use the same language, they exhort, they entreat, they pray, so that you may from hence readily perceive that the Gospel is not a law book, but properly a declaration of benefits conferred by Christ upon us, and of their efficacy through the condition of belief. But Moses in his Law urges, insists, and threatens; his punishments are severe, for they are those of a task-master as well as of a legislator. Hence it comes that no law is given by which he who believes is justified before God" (*The Prefaces to the Early Editions of Martin Luther's Bible* (London, Hatchard, 1863), p. 78).

God never led us out of Egypt, but only the Jews."[1] Luther in his tract, *On Christian Liberty*, so extols faith, that he says by it one fulfills the whole law, and the faithful are freed from the other precepts of the law.[2]

When I firstly read all these words of Luther I could not help being astonished, that a man who professes himself to be a Christian would be so bold faced that he would not hesitate to assert an opinion so temerarious and contrary to the Gospel, and attempt to sell it to the people through public writings. But because Luther did not seek God's glory in his teaching, but only the applause and favor of the people, he always cared to teach those things which he knew would be more pleasing to the people. And certainly this was the greatest reason why in a short period of time such a great multitude of men defected to Luther's teaching. For the majority of people always praises those things more which are amicable to the flesh: and these things Luther took care to teach. For it happens to Luther what long ago happened to Epicurus, who, as Lactantius relates, had more followers than the other philosophers, because he taught the delights of the flesh, which the other philosophers were avoiding.

Nearly the whole Gospel opposes this most pestilential heresy. "I am not come to destroy the law," Christ our Savior says, "but to fulfill" (Mt. 5, 17). Now he fulfilled the Old Law, when He added precepts to it, which were not in it, so that by those having been added the law would become complete and perfect. Now Jerome teaches that He fulfilled in this way, who in his commentaries on Matthew when interpreting the aforesaid words of Christ, says these words: "This means either that He fulfilled what was prophesied about Himself through others, or that by His own preaching He has fulfilled the things that previously had been rough or imperfect, owing to the weakness of the hearers, removing wrath and the law of retaliation, excluding even the lust hidden in one's heart."[3]

Chrysostom interprets those words in the same way, saying these words: "Why, who suspected this? Or who accused Him, that He should make a defense against this charge? Since surely from what had gone before no such suspicion was generated. For to command men to be meek, and gentle, and merciful, and pure in heart, and to strive for righteousness, indicated no such design, but rather altogether the contrary. Wherefore then can He have said this? Not at random, nor vainly: but inasmuch as He was proceeding to ordain commandments greater than those of old, saying, 'It was said to them of old: Thou shalt not kill'; but I say unto you, Be not even angry; and to mark out a way for a kind of Divine and heavenly conversation."[4] After Chrysostom says many other things in the same homily, when interpreting those words of Christ, "He therefore that shall break one of these least commandments…," says these words: "For what cause then does He call these commandments least, though they were so great and high? Because He Himself was about to introduce the enactment of them; for as He humbled Himself, and speaks of Himself frequently with measure, so likewise of His own

---

[1] WA 16, 373, lns. 16-18.

[2] "From all this you will again understand, why so much importance is attributed to faith, so that it alone can fulfil the law, and justify without any works. For you see that the First Commandment, which says, 'Thou shalt worship one God only,' is fulfilled by faith alone. If you were nothing but good works from the soles of your feet to the crown of your head, you would not be worshipping God, nor fulfilling the First Commandment, since it is impossible to worship God without ascribing to God the glory of truth and of universal goodness, as it ought in truth to be ascribed. Now this is not done by works, but only by faith of heart. It is not by working, but by believing, that we glorify God, and confess Him to be true. On this ground faith alone is the righteousness of a Christian man, and the fulfilling of all the Commandments" (WA 7, 55-56).

[3] *Commentary on Matthew*, bk. 1 (PL 26, 36A).

[4] *Homilies on Matthew*, Hom. 16, n. 1 (PG 57, 238-239).

enactments, hereby again teaching us to be modest in everything."[1] From which words it is clearly proved that Christ gave precepts in the Gospel, and established a New Law, so that He deserves to be called not only the Redeemer, but also the Lawgiver.

Tertullian agrees with Chrysostom and Jerome in his explanation of the above-mentioned words of Christ, who in the fourth book of *Against Marcion* says these words: "Did Christ rescind the previous Commandments, of not killing, of not committing adultery, of not stealing, of not bearing false witness, of loving one's father and mother? Or did He both keep them, and then add what was wanting to them?... Therefore, this saying in the Gospel is upheld: 'I am not come to destroy the law, or the prophets... but to fulfill.'"[2]

Furthermore, Christ, when speaking to the Apostles, said: "If you keep my commandments, you shall abide in my love; as I also have kept my Father's commandments, and do abide in his love" (Jn. 15, 10). From which words it is evident that Christ gave some precepts to the Apostles; it is also evident that not only sinners, but also the just, are subject to the Divine precepts. For the Apostles, when Christ said these words, were just, and approved by Christ's testimony, Who said to them: "Now you are clean by reason of the word, which I have spoken to you" (v. 3). That which Christ said elsewhere to His Apostles is also manifest for refuting Luther's error: "Going therefore, teach ye all nations; baptizing them in the name of the Father, and of the Son, and of the Holy Ghost. Teaching them to observe all things whatsoever I have commanded you" (Mt. 28, 19-20). From which words it is very clearly proved that Christ gave precepts, Who commands the Apostles that they teach all nations to keep them. When saying, "all nations," He excludes no one, whether or not he be just, or a sinner: so that He might show that for this reason no one is free from obeying God's Commandments.

Now so that Luther may understand that from those words of Christ it is evidently inferred that Christ gave precepts, let him listen to what Jerome says, when interpreting the aforesaid words: "Observe the order of these injunctions. He bids the Apostles first to teach all nations, then to wash them with the Sacrament of faith, and after faith and Baptism then to teach them what things they ought to observe. And lest we suppose the things commanded to be insignificant or few, He adds, 'all things whatsoever I have commanded you,' so that whoever has believed, who has been baptized in the Trinity, should do everything that has been commanded."[3] Behold, Luther. See how from the Savior's judgment we are bound to keeping some precepts after the faith of the Gospel has been received.

But let us descend to particular precepts of the Gospel, because from those particular precepts the truth will shine more brightly then from universal or indefinite elocutions. It is clearly evident that Christ's faith was prescribed in the Gospel from these words of Christ: "He that believeth and is baptized, shall be saved: but he that believeth not shall be condemned" (Mk. 16, 16). If he who does not believe is damned, it manifestly follows that it was commanded to all men to believe under pain of mortal sin: because no one is damned except for mortal sin. Luther himself confesses that faith is so necessary that he says nothing is a sin except unbelief. And hence I cannot understand how he can be consistent with himself when saying that there is no precept in the Gospel: because if faith is necessary, it follows that it is precepted.

In the same way it is proved that the precept of Baptism was given, because Christ expressed its necessity for salvation when saying: "Unless a man be born again, he cannot see the kingdom of God" (Jn. 3, 3). That necessity for salvation clearly indicates a precept: because no one is excluded from the kingdom of God, except on account of a transgression of some precept. For Christ has promised eternal life to those keeping all the precepts. And

---

[1] N. 4 (PG 57, 243).
[2] C. 36 (PL 2, 450A).
[3] *Commentary on Matthew*, bk. 4 (PL 26, 218C).

hence it is evidently inferred that Baptism is under precept, because otherwise, a man could be saved without it, if he had kept the other precepts. For Christ said: "If thou wilt enter into life, keep the commandments" (Mt. 19, 17). Therefore, an adult man justified before Baptism, could be saved without Baptism and without the desire for it, if Baptism were not under precept. Therefore, Baptism is under precept for those to whom it has been duly preached, such that those who have sufficient preaching and do not want to be baptized when they could, are not only damned due to other sins, but also on account of the neglect of Baptism.

It is proved that penance is under precept not only from those words, "Do penance, for the kingdom of heaven is at hand" (Mt. 4, 17): but much more clearly from those words of the same Savior: "Unless you shall do penance, you shall all likewise perish" (Lk. 13, 3). For that threat of Hell is a clear indication of a Divine precept obliging unto death. Nor could the force of the precept be more clearly stated by other words than by the threat of such punishment. That grave and frequent reproach of God also clearly indicates the precept of penance whereby He strikes sinners not only because of other sins, but also on account of impenitence. For when rebuking the children of Israel through Jeremias the prophet, He shows that He is more offended and exasperated on account of impenitence and obstinacy, than on account of their other most serious wicked deeds. "Thou hadst a harlot's forehead, thou wouldst not blush... as a woman that despiseth her lover, so hath the house of Israel despised me" (Jer. 3, 3 & 20). By which words God clearly calls this same impenitence contempt. And the same prophet reproaches this obstinacy of theirs, saying: "Thou hast struck them, and they have not grieved: thou hast bruised them, and they have refused to receive correction: they have made their faces harder than the rock, and they have refused to return" (5, 3). The prophet Ezechiel reproaches them in the same way in chapter three.[1]

And the Divine Wisdom being indignant about the impenitence of sins, says to them: "You have despised all my counsel, and have neglected my reprehensions. I also will laugh in your destruction, and will mock when that shall come to you which you feared" (Prov. 1, 25-26). The Divine Wisdom would never speak so harshly unless It were exasperated on account of the impenitence of sinners. But by all these things He indicates much more clearly the precept of penance, because procrastinated penance increases the punishment very much beyond that which would have been required on account of other sins. And Paul indicated this same thing, when addressing the sinner, he said: "But according to thy hardness and impenitent heart, thou treasurest up to thyself wrath, against the day of wrath, and revelation of the just judgment of God" (Rom. 2, 5). He said, "treasurest," as meaning, to add punishments to punishments. But if you ask in which precept of the Decalogue that precept is contained, it can be replied, that in the precept of the love of God: because it belongs to true friendship not to offend one's friend, and after the offense has been committed, to grieve on account of it. And according to this opinion it will also be necessary to say that every sin is opposed to the precept of the love of God, just as on the contrary, every precept, as Paul teaches, is contained in the precept of the love of God.[2]

It can be replied otherwise, and perhaps better, by saying that the precept of penance is not one but multiple: because penance for whatever sin is contained in that same precept, against which the sin was committed. For just as by any precept sin is forbidden, so also perseverance in it, and hence the precept of penance is inferred: because one cannot forsake it without penance. But all these things which we have said about penance, only prove about the penance which is a virtue, that it is under precept. Concerning the Sacramental Penance,

---

[1] "The house of Israel will not hearken to thee: because they will not hearken to me: for all the house of Israel are of a hard forehead and an obstinate heart" (v. 7).

[2] "Now the end of the commandment is charity" (I Tim. 1, 5).

however, it has already been proved above, in the section on "Confession," and in the section on "Penance," that it is commanded by God.

Again, Luther, denying that there is some precept in the Gospel, we can easily slay with his own sword. For he accuses all Catholics obedient to the Roman pontiff, whom he calls "Papists," for this reason, namely that the laity do not receive the Eucharist under both species, nor do priests give them the Eucharist under both species. For he says, as we related more fully in the section on the "Eucharist," that Christ commanded us to receive the Eucharist under both species. If Christ commanded this, how it is true what he says now, that there is no precept given by Christ in the Gospel? Next, if there is no precept in the Gospel, then there is no sin in those who live under the Gospel [Law]. For Paul teaches that there is there is no transgression, where there is no law.[1] If there is no prevarication, then is there no sin? Because the Royal Prophet declares that all sins are transgressions.[2] Therefore, this is the Evangelical liberty which Luther preaches, that men are allowed to do whatever they like, without [committing] sin.

Besides these particular precepts of the Gospel, it is necessary to prove that those precepts of the Decalogue pertain to Christians, just as to the Jews: which certainly will not be difficult for us to do. For those precepts are from the Natural Law, and all, besides the three precepts of the first tablet, are deduced from those first two principles of natural reason. "All things therefore whatsoever you would that men should do to you, do you also to them" (Mt. 7, 12). What you do not wish others to do to you, do not do to others. But since Christ in the Gospel confirmed these two principles of the Natural Law, it is also established therefrom that He confirmed all the precepts of the Decalogue, which is necessarily derived from those two principles. He confirmed some precepts of the Decalogue, however, more clearly, in that excellent sermon which He gave on the mount, when discoursing about murder, adultery, and perjury wherein he ordered that they be observed more strictly than they were of old by the Jews, which is so much different from that He would want men living under the Evangelical Law to be free from their observance. Furthermore, to the young man asking what he should do to gain eternal life, Christ responds to him: "If thou wilt enter into life, keep the commandments" (Mt. 19, 17). And when the young man had further asked that those Commandments were, He again responds to him: "Thou shalt do no murder, Thou shalt not commit adultery, Thou shalt not steal, Thou shalt not bear false witness. Honour thy father and thy mother" (v. 18-19). Now all these Commandments, as it is very well known, since they pertain to the Decalogue, I do not know with what impudence and temerity Luther dared to say that the Ten Commandments do not pertain to Christians, but to the Jews.

Again, if it ought to be believed that those ten precepts of the Law only pertain to the Jews, because God brought them alone ought of Egypt, for the same reason one ought to say that they now do not pertain to any men, because He brought neither the Saracens nor the pagans out of Egypt. They do not, however, oblige the Jews more than the Christians: because the Mosaic Law having been completely revoked after Christ's death as to the ceremonies and the judicial precepts. But the moral precepts, as are all the precepts which belong to the Decalogue, were not given to them alone, nor only after the departure from Egypt, but were written at the same time as the very creation of man, as Paul teaches, in men's hearts.[3] For if they would have been given only after the departure from Egypt, it would then follow that before that time men would not have sinned when transgressing them. It also would follow that no men besides the Jews ever sinned on account of the transgression of any precept of the

---

[1] Cf. Rom. 4, 15.

[2] "I have accounted all the sinners of the earth prevaricators" (Ps. 118, 119).

[3] Cf. Rom. 2, 14-15.

Decalogue, because the Law which had been given by Moses, and not before, obliged only the Jews.

Finally, this most pestilential assertion of Luther was condemned in the Council of Trent in the sixth session celebrated under Paul III, For in the teaching about the justification of the sinner, which was in that session, in the eleventh chapter these words are had: "But no one, however much justified, should consider himself exempt from the observance of the Commandments."[1] And after having given the whole teaching about justification, many canons were added containing a *latae sententiae* [excommunication] against the temerarious detractors, the nineteenth of which contains these words: "If anyone shall say that nothing except faith is commanded in the Gospel, that other things are indifferent, neither commanded nor prohibited, but free, or that the Ten Commandments in no way pertain to Christians: let him be anathema."[2] The canon next after it is written out with the following words: "If anyone shall say that a man who is justified and ever so perfect is not bound to observe the Commandments of God and the Church, but only to believe, as if indeed the Gospel were a mere absolute promise of eternal life, without the condition of observation of the Commandments: let him be anathema."[3]

But it is necessary that we reply to Luther's arguments, or rather, to his petty tricks. For he objects to us Paul saying: "Christ hath redeemed us from the curse of the law, being made a curse for us" (Gal. 3, 13). And again: "You, brethren, have been called unto liberty" (*ibid.* 5, 13). But all these quotations, and many others similar to them, speak about that liberty alone whereby Christ freed us from the servitude of the Mosaic Law, so that now after Christ's death we are not obliged to keep the ceremonies and judicial precepts of the Mosaic Law. And that this is the true and faithful meaning of those words, is clearly proved from the main question of that epistle to the Galatians, from which the above-mentioned testimonies were taken. For in that whole epistle Paul is trying to do this, namely, to teach the Galatians that the ceremonies and judicial precepts of the Old Law ceased after Christ's death, and now have no force of law: the Galatians were supposing the contrary of which, having been seduced by some false apostles, who had taught them that the Law of Moses ought to be kept at the same time with the Gospel. Thus, that same Law, insofar as it contained judicial precepts and ceremonies, he called a "yoke of bondage" (Gal. 5, 1) and a "curse" (*Ibid.* 3, 13): just as elsewhere the Apostles gathered together called it a heavy burden, "which neither our fathers nor we have been able to bear" (Acts 15, 10).

But lest anyone misunderstand this liberty, just as Luther thinks, that by it one is free from obeying the rest of the Commandments, which pertains to good men alone, Paul said in the same place, "For you, brethren, have been called unto liberty: only make not liberty an occasion to the flesh, but by charity of the spirit serve one another" (Gal. 5, 13). Jerome, when interpreting these words in his commentaries on the Epistle to the Galatians, says these words: "Someone may say: If I have ceased, O Paul, to be under the Law and have been called from slavery to liberty, then I must live in a way that befits this liberty and not be bound by any precepts. But whatever pleases and whatever desire suggests to me, that I must do, that I must fulfill, that I must chase after. To which the Apostle replies that we are indeed called to liberty of the Spirit, provided that same liberty does not serve the flesh. We should not think that everything is expedient just because everything is permissible. Rather, because we have ceased to be slaves to the Law and have been made free, let us serve one another more through charity, so that the manifold precepts of the Law may be collected under the one heading of love."[4]

---

[1] Dz. 804.

[2] Dz. 829.

[3] Can. 20 (Dz. 830).

[4] Bk. 3 (PL 26, 408B-C).

In the same way ought to be understood also that quotation from the Second Epistle to the Corinthians: "Where the Spirit of the Lord is, there is liberty" (3, 17). For before these words the Apostle had said: "The letter killeth, but the spirit quickeneth" (v. 6). By which words he taught that the literal meaning of the Old Law in Scripture ought not now to be taken in the observance of the Law, but the spiritual meaning. Which meaning the Jews do not arrive at, because they have a veil put over their eyes, and they lack the Spirit of the Lord. For "Where the Spirit of the Lord is, there is liberty." Because where the Spirit of God is, there will not then be a veil over the eyes of the mind, but the veil having been removed, it understands that through Christ's merits it is now freed from the servitude of the Mosaic Law. It can also be understood otherwise, that there is liberty from the servitude of sin, where there is the Spirit of the Lord. Concerning which liberty and servitude Christ said the opposite to it: "Whosoever committeth sin, is the servant of sin. Now the servant abideth not in the house for ever; but the son abideth forever. If therefore the son shall make you free, you shall be free indeed" (Jn. 8, 34-36).

Those words of Paul can be understood still in another way, as [Hervé of Bourg-Dieu] says, of liberty in the execution of God's Commandments, such that he who has the Spirit of the Lord spontaneously performs justice not forced by fear of punishment, but led by the love of God.[1] And [Hervé of Bourg-Dieu] says that what Paul says elsewhere: "The law is not made for the just man" (I Tim. 1, 9), ought to be likewise understood according to this meaning. For he interprets him in that place as follows: "Concerning the hardness of the Old Testament the Apostle says, 'The law is not made for the just man, but for the unjust.' For he who spontaneously does those things which the law morally commands or more, why is the necessity of the law imposed upon him? For he does what he does by liberty, not by necessity."[2] Theophylactus supports the same interpretation in his commentaries on Paul, where when interpreting the aforementioned words, says: "Understand here a just man who practices virtue: who not from fear of the law, but on account of his uprightness both hates wickedness and embraces virtue, and performs more than the law asks, not resenting to have it as his teacher, who would bring lashings to himself: but being full of manly strength, he transcends childish things, even as a doctor is on hand for the wounded or sick, not for someone in good health: and a bridle is necessary for a horse acting disorderly and disobediently, not for one that is submissive and tame."[3]

Notice how little these quotations of Paul help Luther, even though he vainly boasts that he triumphs over us by their strength. And there is no likelihood that Paul would ever have given support for this very horrendous and pestilent teaching of Luther, who elsewhere often excludes adulterers, murderers, perjurers, fornicators, thieves, and all other transgressors of the Commandments of the Decalogue, and judges them worthy of death. There is no need to dispute more against this heresy, because it is so temerarious, that it is hardly credible that a man who reads Holy Writ, would have fallen into such great insanity. But when I consider how much pride and the pleasures of the flesh are able to blind man's mind, I am not surprised that Luther, in whom these two vices reign, will have fallen into so many and such horrendous errors.

There is a **second heresy** which asserts that there entirely is no difference between a precept and a counsel, and that there is not any counsel in the Gospel, but all the things which are recommended to us are precepts. All Lutherans teach this error in unison, yet I do not know

---

[1] "But also in action there is always this liberty, wherever this Spirit dwells, because it makes one to do good not from fear of punishment, but from love of justice." (*Commentaria in epistolas Pauli*, on c. 3 (PL 181, 1030D)

[2] PL 181, 1408C.

[3] *Expositio in Epistolam I ad Timotheum* (PG 125, 18B-C).

whether they received it from Luther, their forerunner: because I did not find it in the works of Luther that I was able to read, nor did I discover it noted by anyone about this matter. The first in whose writing I read this error is Philip Melanchthon, who in his book, *Loci Communes Rerum Theologicarum*, in the section on the distinction between precepts and counsels, he says these words: "Certain men have contrived that in the Gospel there are counsels of not taking revenge, of poverty, and of virginity. And some men think that in the Gospel it is taught to this end, that these works merit reconciliation or salvation more than other works. Then they contrive that these works are perfection. But these things are full of errors and superstitions. There is one law of God, which contains nothing except precepts."[1] From which words, and from those which we said in the preceding heresy that he taught, the reader will clearly gather that he contradicts himself. For it was noted in the preceding heresy that he said that there was no precept in the Gospel. But now he says that there is no counsel in the Gospel, but they are all precepts. Yet that prior assertion, whereby he denied that men after the Gospel has been given are bound to any precept, he said in his book, *Loci Communes*, when burning with a youthful age he began to deviate from the straight path: but afterwards understanding his error, he corrected it in the same book, and in the *Apology of the Augsburg Confession*, and he fell into this error about which we now are disputing, whereby he says that there is no counsel in the Gospel, but they are all precepts. Therefore, this Philip acted according to that saying of Horace, "When fools try to avoid errors, they run into the opposite errors."[2]

After this Philip, a certain Johann Spangeberg of the family of Lutherans teaches this same heresy, who in his *Margarita theologica*,[3] in the section on counsels, wrote nearly the same words which we have cited above from Philip Melanchthon, and in all of the *Margarita* of his he wrote nearly nothing else but what he stole from Philip Melanchthon's *Loci Communes*. After these men I cite John Calvin in that work of his, *Institutes of the Christian Religion*, in which, when reprehending monks due to the fact that they say that they have vowed the Evangelical counsels, he says these words which follow: "But let them say I calumniated them when I declared that they were not contented with the rule prescribed by God. Still, though I were silent, they more than sufficiently accuse themselves; for they plainly declare that they undertake a greater burden than Christ has imposed on his followers, since they promise that they will keep Evangelical counsels regarding the love of enemies, the suppression of vindictive feelings, and abstinence from swearing, etc., counsels to which Christians are not commonly astricted. In this will they show antiquity to us? None of the ancients ever thought of such a thing: all with one voice proclaim that not one syllable proceeded from Christ which it is not necessary to obey. And the very things which these worthy expounders pretend that Christ only counselled, they uniformly declare, without any doubt, that he expressly commanded."[4]

In which words he introduces and heaps up so many lies, that I scarcely find one truth. For among other things which he says it is especially false and a pure calumny, that monks deem it to be a counsel and not a precept given by God about loving enemies, and about not desiring revenge. For no monk up until now, as far as I know, has written that the love of enemies was only given as a counsel: but all whom I have read, confess that it is was given as a precept. All of us condemn the desire for revenge, and we say that it was forbidden by Divine precept, although reparation of an injury or of damage, which sometimes is accustomed to be called revenge, one is not forbidden to seek before a judge, but only he gave the counsel that it be not sought.

---

[1] CR 21, 407.

[2] *Satire* bk. 1, satire 2, ln. 24.

[3] Pg. 100.

[4] Bk. 4, c. 13, n. 12 (CR 30, 933).

And Calvin was not content to inflict this calumny upon all monks, but he undertook to also detract all scholastic theologians by the same calumny. For in the chapter wherein he discusses the Divine law he says these words: "Wherefore, nothing could be more pestilential than the ignorance or wickedness of the scholastics in converting the precepts respecting revenge and the love of enemies (precepts which had formerly been delivered to all the Jews, and were then delivered universally to all Christians) into counsels which it was free to obey or disobey, confining the necessary observance of them to the monks, who were made more righteous than ordinary Christians, by the simple circumstance of voluntarily binding themselves to obey counsels."[1] I have not hitherto seen any scholastic theologian, even though I have read many on this point, who deny that love of enemies was commanded to us by Christ as a precept, but rather all confess with one mouth that God often gave a precept about it. Therefore, Calvin should have named one scholastic theologian who taught about love of enemies and about not desiring revenge such as he asserts.

Calvin also lies saying that the obeying of these two things was relegated to monks alone. Because even though in every monastery vows concerning certain things are made, for instance of poverty and of chastity, still there is no monastic institute, as far as I know, in which a vow is made to God of loving enemies, and of not desiring revenge. Wherefore I cannot but be astonished at such shamelessness of the man, that he does not fear to pour out so many and such plain lies in such harmful things, which I think does not come forth from elsewhere than from envy of the monastic life. But he lies still more clearly when he says that all the ancients with one voice proclaim that not one syllable proceeded from Christ which it is not necessary to obey. Why, O Calvin, did you not cite one or another of the ancients who gives testimony in favor of this to confirm this opinion of yours? But there was none of those ancients approved by the Church, who wished to support your lie, lest he be similar to you. But I, with God's favor, will cite below their testimonies, so that by their testimonies which you very mendaciously boasted supported you, I will clearly convict you of the lie. Nevertheless, it will firstly be necessary to assail against these heretics with testimonies of Sacred Scripture.

But before we enter the disputation, lest we fight only about the meaning of the word, it is necessary to establish what we understand by the word "precept," or by the word "counsel." A precept is sometimes taken to mean, even in the writings of good authors, "a teaching": and it comes down from this word, "precept," that it is often use for "to teach": and from it is derived the name "preceptor," which means "an instructor," or "a teacher." But we do not use this word in this meaning in this disputation, in which to fight to differentiate precepts and counsels. For if according to this meaning we use the word precept, we also admit that counsels are precepts: because Christ also taught us counsels, as well as precepts. Whatever has been recommended to someone in any way is sometimes also called a commandment, even if one is not forced to do it. And according to this meaning counsels are also called "commandments": because Christ when exhorting also recommended counsels to us, but not obliging us to them, and hence we will not use at the present time the word "commandment" according to this meaning. Thus, a precept or commandment, about which we now dispute, is a law or rule which obliges those to whom it is given, to do or omit something; he who will not obey which law or precept will hear the sentence of eternal damnation from the just judge. A counsel, however, is a certain exhortation to good, obedience to which is praiseworthy, but its transgression is blameless. And I have collected these proper and true meanings of the words from Jerome, who, although he sometimes uses the words "precept" and "commandment" according to the first and strange meaning of these words, still in the first book of *Against Jovinian*, where he specifically treats the matter, he clearly distinguishes a precept and a counsel, when saying the following: "For what is enjoined is commanded,

---

[1] Bk. 2, c. 8, n. 56 (CR 30, 306).

what is commanded must be done, and that which must be done implies punishment if it be not done. For it is useless to order a thing to be done and yet leave the individual free to do it or not do it... If counsel be given, a man is free to proffer obedience; if there be a command, he is a servant bound to compliance."[1]

Using the words with these meanings, let us investigate whether there are counsels of this kind distinct from precepts in the Gospels. Christ our Teacher taught the difference of counsels from precepts by all those things which He replied to a certain young man asking Him questions. For when he asks, by doing what may he possess eternal life, Christ our Savior responds to him: "If thou wilt enter into life, keep the commandments" (Mt. 19, 17). Now when the youth had said that he had kept all these things from his youth, Christ our Savior said to him: "If thou wilt be perfect, go sell what thou hast, and give to the poor, and thou shalt have treasure in heaven: and come follow me" (v. 21). In which words one ought to note that He said that one thing is needed for reaching eternal life, and something else for obtaining perfection. For not all men who enter eternal life, as Jovinian said, are equal in glory. For just as one is the brightness of the sun, another the moon, another the stars: so also the splendor of glory is various in the souls of the Blessed. For certain men were only beginning to enter the way of virtue: others who had advanced a little further: others who succeeded so much in virtue, that they never offended God in any serious matter, and rarely in smaller ones. "He who offends not in word, the same is a perfect man" (James 3, 2). Now since no one is perpetually excluded from eternal life on account of an offense of one idle word alone, it is proved that some men are worthy of eternal life, who nevertheless when they lived here, were not perfect. For reaching eternal life He only said that it is necessary to keep the Commandments, among which the abdication of one's own possessions was not numbered. But for acquiring the state of perfection alone, He said that one ought to sell the things which one has, and follow Him. But no one is obliged to obtain perfection, so that by it he can enter eternal life: therefore, no one is obliged to sell his own goods and give to the poor, for reaching eternal life. And hence it is proved that the abdication of such goods is not preceptive, but only given as a counsel, because it is not shown by Christ as being necessary for [eternal] life, but as a step to perfection.

Chrysostom clearly favors this opinion in his *Homilies on Matthew*, wherein, when interpreting the above-mentioned words of the Savior with which He exhorts the young man to perfection, says these words: "Do you see how many prizes, how many crowns, He appoints for this race? If he had been tempting, He would not have told him these things. But now He both says it, and in order to draw him on, He also shows him the reward to be great, and leaves it all to his own will, by all means throwing into the shade that which seemed to be grievous in His advice. Wherefore even before mentioning the conflicts and the toil, He shows him the prize, saying, 'If thou wilt be perfect,' and then says, 'Sell that thou hast, and give to the poor,' and straightway He says the rewards, 'Thou shalt have treasure in heaven; and come follow me.' For indeed to follow Him is a great recompense. 'And thou shalt have treasure in heaven.' For since his discourse was of money, He advised him to strip himself even of all things, showing that he loses not what he has, but adds to his possessions. He gave him more than He ordered him to give up; and not only more, but also as much greater as Heaven is greater than earth, and yet more so. But He called it a treasure, showing the plenteousness of the recompense."[2] In which words he teaches clearly enough that those words of Christ are a counsel and recommendation.

Jerome also favors this same opinion, who in his *Commentary on Matthew*, when interpreting the same words, says these words: "It is in our power whether we want to be perfect. Yet

---

[1] N. 12 (PL 23, 227B-C).

[2] Hom. 63, n. 2 (PG 58, 604-605).

whoever wants to be perfect ought to sell what he has and sell not merely a part of it, as Ananias and Sapphira did,[1] but sell everything. And when he has sold it, he must give everything to the poor. In this way he prepares himself a treasure in the kingdom of Heaven."[2] From Jerome's words it is established that that perfection, for the attainment of which Christ requires the abdication of one's own possessions, is not commanded, but placed in our power, and left to our choice. And certainly Peter taught this same thing, when reprehending Ananias due to the fact that he had retained part of the price of his sold possessions, he said to him: "Whilst it remained, did it not remain to thee? and after it was sold, was it not in thy power?" (Acts 5, 4) He said that it was in his power: because they were not compelled by any precept to sell, but it was within his liberty to sell, and after having sold the field, it was a free matter for him to give or not give away the price of the sold land. From which words of Peter that interpretation which John Wycliffe and after him all Lutherans give to those aforesaid words of Christ is proved false, and completely inconsistent with the text. For they say that Christ spoke there about that renunciation of goods alone, which, when persecution rages, is necessary for the confession of the true faith: and they say that this is under precept. But this interpretation is clearly opposed to Christ's words: because this abdication of goods when the confession of faith is pressing, is not only necessary for perfection, but also for entering into eternal life.

Now Christ did not speak, as the context of the text itself shows, about the abdication of goods as being necessary for entering eternal life, but about the abdication whereby one goes to perfection, which, as Jerome said, is left to our free choice. Next, those who were selling all their goods, and were bringing the price of them to the feet of the Apostles, were acting according to this teaching of Christ: and yet a persecution of some tyrant was not forcing them to do this: nor was Ananias punished with death by Blessed Peter, because when a persecution was raging they did not want to abdicate from themselves the ownership of all their belongings: but because when choosing the persecution which Christ had taught in the Gospel, he had not acted according to that perfection which he had chosen: but instead kept something for himself from the price of the sold land.

There is another small testimony of Christ our Redeemer for the confirmation of the counsels. For when the disciples had heard that it is unlawful for a man to put away his wife except on account of fornication, they said to him: "If the case of a man with his wife be so, it is not expedient to marry" (Mt. 19, 10). To whom Christ responds: "All men take not this word, but they to whom it is given. For there are eunuchs, who were born so from their mother's womb: and there are eunuchs, who were made so by men: and there are eunuchs, who have made themselves eunuchs for the kingdom of heaven. He that can take, let him take it" (v. 11-12). In which words Christ delineates three kinds of eunuchs: the first two of which were forced into chastity of the body: because even if they would have wished, they could not do otherwise. They are of the third kind who castrated themselves on account of the kingdom of Heaven. And these men of their own free will keep chastity, and the reward of the kingdom of Heaven is promised to them.[3] But because this thing was very difficult, He did not want to make a precept about it: but instead he merely exhorted, saying: "He that can take, let him take it": and this admonition, as it is very clear, does not have the force of a precept, but only indicates a counsel.

Hence Jerome in his *Commentary on Matthew* when explaining these words of the Savior says: "It is as though the voice of the Lord were exhorting and encouraging on His soldiers to the reward of chastity, that he who can fight might fight and conquer and triumph."[4] When

---

[1] Cf. Acts 5, 1-10.
[2] Bk. 3 (PL 26, 137B).
[3] Note that "in no case is it allowable to maim oneself" (II-II, q. 65, a. 1 ad 3um).
[4] Bk. 3, (PL 26, 136B).

Jerome says that it is the voice as of one exhorting, he clearly teaches that it is a counsel, not a precept. But Chrysostom teaches this opinion much more clearly in his *Homilies on Matthew*, wherein when interpreting the above-mentioned words of Christ, says these words: "At once making them more earnest by showing that the good work is exceeding in greatness, and not suffering the thing to be encompassed in the compulsion of a law, because of His unspeakable gentleness. And this He said, when He showed it to be most possible, in order that the emulation of the free choice might be greater. And if it is of free choice, one may say, how does He say, at the beginning, 'All men take not this word, but they to whom it is given'? That you might learn that the conflict is great, not that you should suspect any compulsory allotments. For it is given to those who will it. But He spoke thus to show that much help from above is needed: which is indeed prepared for all, if we wish to go forth higher in this combat."[1] When Chrysostom says that Christ did not wish to encompass this in the compulsion of a law, he stated clearly enough that it was not given as a precept, but as a counsel.

But why do I tarry seeking interpreters of Christ's words, since Paul explains them very clearly, saying that it is a counsel, and not a precept? "Now concerning virgins," he says, "I have no commandment of the Lord; but I give counsel" (I Cor. 7, 25). Jerome, when interpreting these words, says: "The reason is plain why the Apostle said, 'Concerning virgins I have no commandment of the Lord.' Surely because the Lord had previously said, 'All men take not this word, but they to whom it is given' (Mt. 19, 11) and 'He that can take, let him take it' (v. 12). The Master of the Christian race [*Agonothetes*[2]] offers the reward, invites candidates to the course, holds in His hand the prize of virginity, points to the fountain of purity, and cries aloud: 'If any man thirst, let him come to me, and drink' (Jn. 7, 37). He does not say, you must drink, you must run, willing or unwilling: but whoever is willing and able to run and to drink, he shall conquer, he shall be satisfied. And therefore, Christ loves virgins more than others, because they willingly give what was not commanded them. And it belongs to greater favor to offer what you are not bound to give, than to render what is exacted of you."[3]

[Ambrosiaster] gives the same interpretation of the above-mentioned words of God, saying the following: "He says that he has not received any precept about virgins, because the Author of marriage could not order anything which goes against marriage without bringing down recrimination on His ancient decree. Paul says that he is giving a counsel, not because it would displease or be tinged with flattery, but because he has received the grace to be capable of giving salutary counsels."[4]

But he teaches much more clearly everything which pertains to the main point of the present disputation in his book, *Concerning Widows*, where, when interpreting the aforesaid words of Paul, he says these words: "Marriage, then, is honorable, but chastity is more honorable, for 'he that giveth his virgin in marriage, doth well; but he that giveth her not in marriage doth better' (I Cor. 7, 38). That, then, which is good need not be avoided, but that which is better should be chosen. And so it is not laid upon any, but set before him. And, therefore, the Apostle said well: 'Concerning virgins, I have no commandment of the Lord; but I give counsel' (I Cor. 7, 25). For a command is issued to subordinates, a counsel is given to friends. Where there is a commandment, there is a law; where counsel, there is grace... You will see the difference between precept and counsel, if you remember the case of him in the Gospel, to whom it is first commanded to do no murder, not to commit adultery, not to bear false witness; for that is a commandment which has a penalty for its transgression. But when he said that he had fulfilled all the commandments of the Law, there is given to him a counsel that he should

---

[1] Hom. 62, n. 3-4 (PG 58, 600).
[2] *Agonothetes* is Greek for a person who presided over the ancient Olympic Games.
[3] *Against Jovinian*, bk. 1, n. 12 (PL 228A-B).
[4] *Commentaria in Epistolam ad Corinthios Primam* (PL 17, 221C).

sell all that he had and follow the Lord,[1] for these things are not imposed as commands, but are offered as counsels. For there are two ways of commanding things, one by way of precept, the other by way of counsel. And so, the Lord in one way says: 'Thou shall not kill,' where He gives a commandment; in the other He says: 'If thou wilt be perfect, go sell what thou hast.' He is, then, not bound by a commandment to whom the choice is left. And so, they who have fulfilled the commandments are able to say: 'We are unprofitable servants; we have done that which we ought to do' (Lk 17, 10). The virgin does not say this, nor he who sold all his goods, but they rather await the stored-up rewards like the holy Apostle who says: 'Behold we have left all things, and have followed thee: what therefore shall we have?' (Mt. 19, 27). He says not, like the unprofitable servant, that he has done that which was his duty to do, but as being profitable to his Master, because he has multiplied the talents entrusted to him by the increase he has gained, having a good conscience, and without anxiety as to his merits he expects the reward of his faith and virtue. And so it is said to him and the others: 'You, who have followed me, in the regeneration, when the Son of man shall sit on the seat of his majesty, you also shall sit on twelve seats judging the twelve tribes of Israel' (Mt. 19, 28). And to those who had faithfully preserved their talents He promises rewards indeed, though smaller saying: 'Because thou hast been faithful over a few things, I will place thee over many things' (Mt. 25, 21). Good faith, then, is due, but mercy is in the rewards. He who has kept good faith has deserved that good faith should be kept with him; he who has made good profit, because he has not sought his own benefit, has gained a claim to a heavenly reward. So, then, a commandment to this effect is not given, but a counsel is [given]. Chastity is commanded, entire continence counselled. All men take not this word, but they to whom it is given. 'For there are eunuchs, who were born so from their mother's womb' (Mt. 19, 11-12) in whom exists a natural necessity, not the virtue of chastity. And there are eunuchs which were made eunuchs of men. And there are eunuchs who have made themselves eunuchs, of their own will, that is, not of necessity. And, therefore, great is the grace of continence in them, because it is the will, not incapacity, which makes a man continent."[2] I have cited Ambrose at length, because he clearly makes apparent the difference between a precept and a counsel, and he shows clearly that poverty and chastity, which the Lutherans have especially hated, are Evangelical counsels.

Now Augustine gives so many testimonies in favor of the distinction between a precept and a counsel, that I do not know which to cite, yet it is necessary to cite some, so that we may make a square foundation of testimonies for making the truth stable and firm. When interpreting the words of Paul, "Concerning virgins, I have no commandment of the Lord; but I give counsel" (I Cor. 7, 25), he says these words: "This is not to have us think that this counsel is different from what the Lord would give, since he immediately goes on to say, 'as having obtained mercy of the Lord, to be faithful' (*ibid.*). The counsel he gives, therefore, is faithful according to the will of God in that Spirit about Whom he says, 'I think that I also have the spirit of God' (I Cor. 7, 40). Notwithstanding, an order given by God commanding is one thing, but a faithful counsel, in accordance with the mercy of charity, which was inspired and given to him by the Lord, is something else. In the former case it is not permitted to do something; in the latter case it is permitted, certainly such that the thing permitted is indeed partly expedient, but partly not expedient. It is expedient in the instance when not only it is permitted through justice, which is before the Lord, but also when no impediment to salvation from it is occasioned to men: just as when the Apostle gives to virgins the counsel of not marrying: hence he testifies that he does not have a precept from the Lord: it is permitted to do something, that is to say, to marry, and yet to enter the married state is less good than continence. And the same licit thing is also expedient: because it so rescues the tottering weakness

---

[1] Cf. Mt. 19, 18-21.

[2] C. 12-13, n. 72-75 (PL 16, 256B-258A).

of the flesh by the honorableness of marrying, such that it impedes no one regarding salvation; although it would be more expedient, and it would be more honorable, if the virgin were to take the counsel, whereby a precept does not compel her. On the other hand, that which is permitted is not expedient in the instance when it is indeed permitted, but the use of the option occasions an impediment of salvation to others."[1]

From these testimonies of four very holy men it is evidently established that Calvin lied more shamelessly, when he temerariously asserted that all the ancients with one voice proclaim that there is not one syllable proceeded from Christ which it is not necessary to obey. For Augustine, Jerome, Ambrose, and Chrysostom are deservedly reckoned among the ancient Doctors of the Church: because any one of them passed away more than one thousand one hundred years before this century. But perhaps they are not reckoned to be ancient by Calvin, because perhaps he considers himself such a man as could say: "Before all these men lived, I am."

Next, I would like to ask Calvin and Philip Melanchthon, and all the other Lutherans, where is that Evangelical liberty which they daily sell to the people? How could it truthfully be called liberty, if there is no counsel in the Gospel, but everything is a commandment? For Christ said that we ought not to resist anyone offending us: if someone strikes us on one cheek, we ought to offer him the other also. If someone wants to contend with us in judgment and take away our coat, we ought to let go our cloak also to him, and He stated several other things of this kind found in the Sermon on the Mount, and elsewhere.[2] If we were obligated to do all these things under precept, the Lord's yoke would not be sweet and his burden light,[3] but it would be no less unsupportable, nay more unsupportable, than the Mosaic Law. And hence Augustine in his exposition on the Sermon on the Mount, says that many of these things are counsels and not precepts.[4]

It is unnecessary to dispute more against this heresy, because those things which we have objected against it very clearly refute it. And I do not respond to the arguments of those who assert it, because they do not give any arguments for supporting themselves, but they put forth this bare heresy, and completely unsupported by any reason. But because counsels as well as precepts were said by Christ by a verb in the imperative mood, perhaps from this they thought that they were all precepts. And certainly many Catholics, misled for this reason alone, hallucinated about some counsels, thinking that they are precepts. Hence so that I might do something about this occasion of deception, I decided to show to the reader some rules whereby he can distinguish counsels from precepts. The first rule ought to be taken from the consideration of the two precepts of charity, which are the love of God and love of neighbor: from which two, as Christ taught us, the whole Law and the prophets depend.[5] Whatever, therefore, is necessary for keeping the love of God or of neighbor, every such thing ought to reckoned a precept for us: because 'Love is,' as Paul says, 'the fulfilling of the law' (Rom. 13, 10). However, that which is suitable for increasing the love of God or of neighbor, and is not necessary for its conservation, is held to be only a counsel.

The second rule is taken from the reward which is promised to one obeying, from the punishment that ought to be inflicted upon the transgressor. For if the transgressor is condemned to temporal or eternal death, it is thence very clearly proved that it is a precept obliging under

---

[1] *Adulterous Marriages*, c. 18, n. 21-22 (PL 40, 463).

[2] Cf. Mt. 5, 39 ff.

[3] Cf. Mt. 11, 30.

[4] "And if a man will contend with thee in judgment, and take away thy coat, let go thy cloak also unto him,' is rightly understood as a precept having reference to the preparation of heart, not to a vain show of outward deed" (Bk. 1, n. 59 (PL 34, 1260)).

[5] Cf. Mt. 22, 40.

pain of mortal sin. And in this way, we judge that everything contained in the Decalogue is a precept because the Savior said that all those things are necessary for entering into eternal life. In this way also we likewise judge to be mortal sins those works of the flesh about which Paul says, "that they who do such things shall not obtain the kingdom of God" (Gal. 5, 21), because no one is excluded from the kingdom of God except on account of mortal sin. And hence it is evidently inferred that abstaining from all those things is under precept. If, however, a reward is promised to the one obeying, but no punishment is designated to the transgressor, we can justly believe that it is a counsel and not a precept. In this way we know that virginity is a counsel: because the kingdom of Heaven is promised by Christ for it, saying: "There are eunuchs, who have made themselves eunuchs for the kingdom of heaven" (Mt. 19, 12). But if after having possessed virginity one chooses marriage, no punishment is inflicted upon him by God on account of it, Paul bearing witness who says: "If a virgin marry, she hath not sinned" (I Cor. 7, 28). In the same way we know that Evangelical poverty is given only as a counsel, and not as a precept: because to the possessor of riches no punishment is assigned because of this: and to one renouncing them a reward is promised by God. By this same rule we know that fasting was never given in the Gospel by Christ as a precept, but only as a counsel, because Christ never threatened death, or any similar punishment, to one not fasting, and promises a reward to one fasting on account of God alone, when He said: "Thy Father who seeth in secret will repay thee" (Mt. 6, 18).

The third rule can be applied not to this matter alone, but to all matters which pertain to faith and morals, and it is the consent of the whole Church, such that we may hold those things to be precepts which were always held by the Catholic Church as precepts, and we may reckon those things as counsels, which the concordant consent of all the holy Doctors always judged to be counsels, and not precepts. For since the Church is, as Paul says, "the pillar and ground of the truth" (I Tim. 3, 15), and Christ is with it "even to the consummation of the world" (Mt. 28, 20), it follows that in those things which are necessary for salvation, it is unable to err.

The **third heresy** asserts that nothing is good and pleasing to God except that which has been commanded and ordered by Him. The authors and first inventors of this heresy are also the Lutherans, and yet I was unable to find it in any of the works of Luther that I have seen. Johann Spangenberg of the family of Lutherans, in his *Margarita theologica*, in the section on counsels, when speaking about poverty, proposes the question to himself, and replies to it saying these words: "How many kinds of forsaking of riches are there? Two. The one is by our election without the commandment and calling of God. This forsaking of riches is not the worshipping of God. 'In vain do they worship me, teaching doctrines and commandments of men' (Mt. 15, 9). The other is that which has the commandment and the calling of God, and when tyrants compel us either to lose our goods or to forsake the Gospel. This Christ praises. He who has left land, house, etc. on account of the Gospel, that is on account of the confession of the Gospel, will receive a hundredfold."[1] Martin Bucer, one of the chief leaders of the Lutherans, in his *Apology of the Augsburg Confession* firmly asserts that no work of ours is pleasing to God, unless it were firstly commanded by God, and says that Erasmus of Rotterdam taught this same opinion. Yet I, so that I may confess the truth, have not read it in Erasmus, nor have I seen the *Apologia* of Bucer, and so I cannot cite his words in that place: but I read the *Apologia adversus Martini Buceri* [*calumnias*] of Albert Pighius, wherein he relates that Bucer asserted this,[2] and for this reason and many others, he fights the same Bucer in that *Apologia*.

---

[1] Cf. Mk. 10, 29-30. P. 103.

[2] "If Erasmus taught what Bucer affirms about him, that 'works cannot be pleasing to God except those which according to His precept pertain and avail unto Him, so that they may more closely provide for

This heresy is deduced from the one immediately preceding, which says that there are no counsels in the Divine law, but they are all precepts. If there are no counsels, as they say, then every good action is commanded: because there is no good action pleasing to God which He did not show to us either in a precept or counsel. It follows, therefore, that having rejected counsels, all good actions accepted by God are contained under precept. I wished to state this here so that the reader may understand that those things which we objected against the preceding heresy also completely oppose this heresy, for having destroyed the foundation upon which it rests, the structure of this heresy will necessarily fall. If it is evident that there are some counsels in the Gospel, which are not precepts, it will also be consistent that many human actions are good and pleasing to God, which nevertheless God has not commanded: because those things which God counsels necessarily ought to be admitted to be good. But even though those things that we said in the preceding heresy suffice for the conquest of the present heresy, still it is necessary to now add some things which fight against it more properly and specifically, and by them also refute it.

Firstly then, the just Abel is placed first in the battleline, whose offering, Sacred Scripture testifies, pleased God, yet God's word does not say that this offering was commanded him.[1] The just man Noe, when the flood was then over and the land had dried somewhat, went out of the ark, built an altar to the Lord, and taking of all the clean animals and birds offered holocausts upon the altar. Concerning which matter no precept had been given by God to him, and yet that that offering was pleasing to God, Sacred Scripture testifies saying these words: "And the Lord smelled a sweet savour" (Gen. 8, 21). In which words He did not say that it was merely pleasing, but what is more, that it was sweet. Phinees, the son of Eleazar, the son of Aaron the priest, without any command of God, killed an Israelite man having intercourse with an Madianite woman. Yet, the words which God said to Moses in favor of Phinees, and as to his reward, on account of this deed, clearly show that this killing of them pleased God very much: "Phinees the son of Eleazar the son of Aaron the priest," God said, "hath turned away my wrath from the children of Israel: because he was moved with my zeal against them, that I myself might not destroy the children of Israel in my zeal. Therefore say to him: Behold I give him the peace of my covenant, and the covenant of the priesthood forever shall be both to him and his seed, because he hath been zealous for his God, and hath made atonement for the wickedness of the children of Israel" (Num. 25, 11-13).

It is also clear that the conscientiousness of the Rechabites, who without God's precept were not drinking wine, and were in many other ways living an austere life which Jonadab their father enjoined upon them by precept. Yet in their obedience they were nowise holding fast by Divine precept, as Sacred Scripture clearly testifies.[2] The prophet Daniel received

---

living well and piously,' as he also taught in many other places" (Albert Pighius, *Aduersus Martini Buceri calumnias* (Paris, Joannes Foucherius, 1543), fol. 7v).

"But when the Lord having pitied His Church, willed that He would come to the aid of its so great and calamitous oppression, He firstly brought to the fore Erasmus of Rotterdam, who with great shrewdness, and lively arguments, with that eloquence and dexterity he possesses in abundance, he began to forcefully bring to mind that our salvation cannot either be repaired or conserved with ceremonies: but with true confidence in Christ: and works cannot be pleasing to God except those which according to His precept pertain and avail unto Him, so that they may more closely provide for living well and piously. And so that this salutary teaching could be restored solidly and completely, he was the studious author of sacred things, he influenced by his very effective persuasion unto this, so that having sent away the Scholastic commentaries, which they obtained in that more corrupt age, he read and discoursed on the writings of the holy Fathers, and especially Holy Writ, with the greatest diligence" (Bucer, *De vera ecclesiarum in doctrina reconciliatione et compositione* (Strasburg, Rihel, 1542), fol. 8r).

[1] Cf. Gen. 4, 4.

[2] Cf. Jer. 35, 18-19.

absolutely no precept of fasting from God, and yet by that fasting he so pleased God that from the very day on which he began to afflict himself, God heard his prayer.[1] God was angered against the Ninivites, but they humbling themselves with ashes and fasting pleased Him, which they could not done by those works, according to Bucer's teaching: because their works were not commanded them by God, yet Scripture says, "God saw their works, that they were turned from their evil way: and God had mercy with regard to the evil which he had said that he would do to them" (Jonas 3, 10).

What shall I say about John the Baptist? Was he not praised by Christ due to the fact that he was clothed with rough garments?[2] Yet this roughness of clothing was never commanded him by God. Paul praises many holy men due to the fact that "they wandered about in sheepskins, in goatskins, being in want, distressed, afflicted: of whom the world was not worthy; wandering in deserts, in mountains, and in dens, and in caves of the earth" (Heb. 11, 37-38). And he says that all these men would receive the fulfillment of the promise on account of those works, which were not commanded by God.

But let us skip over all these things, and let us come to poverty about which that good Spangeberg said is not pleasing to God, when it is by our choice without God's commandment. Peter the Apostle and the rest of his fellow disciples were poor by their own choice without God's commandment. For even though God said, "Unless a man renounce all that he possesseth, he cannot be my disciple" (Lk. 14, 33): yet when they firstly came to be followers of Christ, no such thing was said to them: but without any command of Christ "leaving all things, they followed him" (Lk. 5, 11). Now as to this forsaking of property being pleasing to God, He Himself declared when He replies to Peter asking what reward he and his fellow disciples would have due to the fact that they had left all things: "Amen, I say to you, that you, who have followed me in the regeneration, when the Son of man shall sit on the seat of his majesty, you also shall sit on twelve seats judging the twelve tribes of Israel. And everyone that hath left house, or brethren, or sisters, or father, or mother, or wife, or children, or lands for my name's sake, shall receive an hundredfold, and shall possess life everlasting" (Mt. 19, 28-29). Next, after Christ's Ascension into Heaven, as the Apostolic history relates, "All they that believed, were together, and had all things common. Their possessions and goods they sold, and divided them to all, according as everyone had need" (Acts 2, 44-45). God did not command this forsaking of their property, nor did any tyrant force them to undertake it: yet that it was pleasing to God, Scripture itself testifies, which praises them on account of that forsaking, which would not have been done unless it had been pleasing to God. Add to all these things that Christ our Redeemer was poor insofar as He was a man: and this poverty He undertook by His own choice, and not being forced by a command of the Father or by any tyrant. Now it is absurd and very wicked if anyone would dare to say that that poverty of Christ was not pleasing to God, due to the fact that it was not commanded Him by God the Father: because by it He merited even to the extent that we would be rich. "For you know the grace of our Lord Jesus Christ, that being rich he became poor, for your sakes; that through his poverty you might be rich" (II Cor. 8, 9).

I have not seen anyone who expressly wrote against this heresy except only Albert Pighius, who in the above-mentioned *Apologia* said a' few words.[3] But before him Blessed Augustine, as I think, breathed upon by the Spirit, and foreseeing this heresy, wrote some things of not small importance against it saying these words: "There are many things that we should do freely from charity and not because they are commanded by the law; and among our duties those we undertake by choice, when it would not be wrong not to undertake them, are the

---

[1] Dan. 10, 12.

[2] Cf. Mt. 11, 7-11.

[3] *Aduersus Martini Buceri calumnias*, fol. 7v-9r.

more pleasing ones. That is why the Lord Himself paid the tax, although He had firstly shown that He was not obliged to pay it, in order not to scandalize those whose eternal salvation was His concern in becoming man.[1] Now the Apostle extols this way of acting, as his words bear witness, when he says: 'For whereas I was free as to all, I made myself the servant of all, that I might gain the more' (I Cor. 9, 19). Just before this he had said, 'Have not we power to eat and to drink? Have we not power to carry about a woman, a sister, as well as the rest of the apostles, and the brethren of the Lord, and Cephas? Or I only and Barnabas, have not we power to do this? Who serveth as a soldier at any time, at his own charges? Who planteth a vineyard, and eateth not of the fruit thereof? Who feedeth the flock, and eateth not of the milk of the flock?' (v. 4-7). And a little further on he says, 'If others be partakers of this power over you, why not we rather? Nevertheless, we have not used this power: but we bear all things, lest we should give any hindrance to the gospel of Christ' (v. 12). Then a few words afterwards he says, 'What is my reward then? That preaching the gospel, I may deliver the gospel without charge, that I abuse not my power in the gospel' (v. 18). Immediately he adds the words I cited a little earlier: 'For whereas I was free as to all, I made myself the servant of all, that I might gain the more' (v. 19). Likewise, in another passage about certain questions relating to food, he says: 'All things are lawful to me, but all things are not expedient. All things are lawful to me, but I will not be brought under the power of any. Meat for the belly, and the belly for the meats; but God shall destroy both it and them' (I Cor 6, 12-13). Likewise, he elsewhere says concerning the same point: 'All things are lawful for me, but all things are not expedient. All things are lawful for me, but all things do not edify. Let no man seek his own, but that which is another's' (I Cor. 10, 22-24). And to show the reason why he speaks, he says, 'Whatsoever is sold in the shambles, eat; asking no question for conscience' sake' (v. 25), although he also said in another place, 'I will never eat flesh, lest I should scandalize my brother' (I Cor. 8, 13). In another place, too: 'All things indeed are clean: but it is evil for that man who eateth with offence' (Rom. 14, 20). In this way he shows that those things that are allowed (that is to say, not forbidden by any precept of the Lord) should be treated in the way that is more expedient, following the counsel of charity rather than the prescription of the law. These are the things which are generously spent upon the wounded man, who was brought by the compassion of that Samaritan to the inn to be cared for.[2] And hence they are not said to be commanded by the Lord, although they are encouraged to be offered by the Lord; so that they may be understood to be so much more pleasing, the more they are shown to be not obligatory."[3] I have cited Augustine at such great length because he says so many things and speaks so clearly against this heresy, that it seems that he expressly disputes against it. For he does not merely say that works done without God's command can be good and pleasing to God, but rather are sometimes better, and more acceptable to God than others which are done because of His command.

And Jerome and Ambrose also said the same thing in the other testimonies of theirs which we cited in the preceding heresy.

The **fourth heresy** pertaining to this subject of precepts was also invented by Luther. For he says that God commanded us things which are impossible to be kept by us: and he gives the example of the two precepts of the Decalogue, namely of the precept of the love of God, and of the precept, "Thou shalt not covet." For these two things, he says, cannot be kept in this life: and he gives the reason for this impossibility in the precept of love, because it is necessary that living in this life we would love some things other than God: because when we do, we then do not love God (as he says) with the whole heart. Wherefore he concludes that

---

[1] Cf. Mt. 17, 23-26.

[2] Cf. Lk. 10, 33-35.

[3] *Adulterous Marriages*, bk. 1, c. 14, n. 15 (PL 40, 459-460).

it is impossible to love God in this life from the whole heart: which nevertheless (as he says) is commanded to us in the first precept.[1] But concerning the impossibility of observing the other precept, namely: "Thou shalt not covet," he assigns the following cause, namely he says that concupiscence which is left in the one baptized is a sin, properly so-called, and a transgression of this precept: "Thou shalt not covet." And because the flesh has been infected with such concupiscence it concurs for every good work of free will, hence it is that every human work becomes a sin.[2] But we have shown this last point to be false in the section on "Works [*Opera*]." For in that place, we taught from Sacred Scripture against this same Luther, that not every human work is a sin. Therefore, now it remains that we show that the observance of all God's precepts is possible for us with the help of God Himself, which nevertheless He is always prepared to grant us, if we want to use it.

After the Lord had given precepts to the children of Israel, He wanted to show that everything which He had commanded them is possible, lest perhaps when they had neglected them afterwards, they might allege that they were impossible. For so it is said in Deuteronomy: "This commandment, that I command thee this day is not above thee, nor far off from thee: nor is it in heaven, that thou shouldst say: Which of us can go up to heaven to bring it unto us, and we may hear and fulfill it in work? Nor is it beyond the sea: that thou mayst excuse thyself, and say: Which of us can cross the sea, and bring it unto us: that we may hear, and do that which is commanded?" (30, 11-14). Nothing could be said more explicitly than these words to show that the observance of God's Commandments is possible, especially because in the immediately preceding words He had spoken about the precept of the love of God from the whole heart, and in the words following He again repeats the same precept: from which it is clearly gathered that that precept is possible for us, with God's help, which He is prepared to grant us: it is that precept about which He specifically says: "The commandment, that I command thee this day is not above thee." Furthermore, the Lord says in Matthew: "My yoke is sweet and my burden light" (Mt. 11, 30). The Lord calls His precepts a yoke and burden, and He says that these things are light: therefore they are not impossible, as Luther says. For if it were impossible to keep them, then they ought not to be called light, but very heavy. Again, Blessed John says concerning God's commandments in his first canonical epistle: "His commandments are not heavy" (5, 3). Notice that John says that God's commandments are not heavy, and Luther is not afraid to say that they are impossible. For nothing can be heavier to someone, than that which he can nowise keep. Thus, if God's commandments are not heavy, it is necessary that they are not impossible.

Next, it is very great insanity to say that God commanded impossible things, because then God would act unjustly. For by the Natural Law we are taught that no one is obliged to what is impossible. There is a very strong saying of Augustine: No man sins in what he cannot avoid.[3] And in a certain sermon he says: "(The Lord) would not condemn the slothful servant, if he commanded those things which could by no means be done."[4] And Blessed Ambrose says in his book, *Jacob and the Happy Life*: "No one is held to guilt unless he has gone astray by his own will."[5] Blessed Basil in his *Rule* for monks, when speaking about the love of enemies, says: "For He who is just and merciful would never have commanded this, unless He also granted to us the capacity to do so."[6] And [Pseudo-] Jerome says to Damasus: "We also detest

---

[1] Heidelberg Disputation held in 1518 (WA 1, 368, lns. 9-20).
[2] *Assertio omnium articulorum*, art. 31 & 32 (WA 7, 103-108 & WA 7, 137-138).
[3] "For who, then, sins through something he, by no means, can avoid?" (*On Free Choice of the Will*, bk. 3, c. 18, n. 50 (PL 32, 1295)).
[4] Serm. 54, c. 2, n. 2 (PL 38, 373).
[5] C. 1, c. 3, n. 10 (PL 14, 602D).
[6] Question 156 (PG 31, 1199C).

the blasphemy of those who say that something impossible was commanded to man, and the Commandments cannot be kept by a single man."[1] Chrysostom testifies this same thing, saying: "It is possible, if only we have the will, to overcome every weakness of nature by strength of will, and none of the commandments of Christ are impossible to man."[2]

It ought not to be omitted here that Luther is inconsistent with himself, because he very often labors under this vice. For when he speaks about the confession of sins, he says that it is not necessary to confess venial sins, but neither also all mortal sins: because it is impossible to know all the mortal sins: no one is obliged, he says there, to what is impossible.[3] Also when wishing to prove that Peter the Apostle was not placed by God above all the other Apostles, he argues as follows: "And everything which God commands are fulfilled at least by some men... This primacy was never in fact fulfilled even for one hour. Now it was impossible for it not to have been fulfilled, if it had been either commanded or promised."[4] All of these words are, as it were, diametrically opposed with his present teaching.

But now it is necessary that we examine whether those two precepts of the Decalogue, which were put forth by him as his own examples of his assertion, are correctly understood by him. Concerning the precept of the love of God it is evident that Luther thinks wrongly, because it is not commanded us that we love God with the whole heart such that we love nothing but God, or that we apply all the strength of our will to such love: but we are so commanded to love God, that we love nothing opposing God's precepts. Wherefore he ought to be said to love God with the whole heart, who, when loving God, keeps all the rest of His Commandments. Now the Lord expressly taught us this same thing, Who, when encouraging love of Him to us, seems to oblige nothing else from us than the observance of His Commandments. For He says the following: "If any one love me, he will keep my word" (Jn. 14, 23). When expounding these words Blessed Gregory speaks thus: "For we truly love God only if we restrain ourselves from our pleasures to follow His commandments."[5] Notice how according to Gregory's testimony perfect love of God is acquired by keeping God's Commandments, such that he is said to fulfill the precept of the love of God, who has kept the rest of the Commandments.

Furthermore, Blessed John in his first canonical epistle says: "This is the charity of God, that we keep his commandments" (5, 3). Thus, charity is kept by the fact that we keep His Commandments. Again, Blessed Paul says that the whole law is fulfilled in one commandment, namely in this: "Thou shalt love thy neighbour as thyself" (Rom. 13, 9). Therefore, he has fulfilled the whole law, who loves his neighbor truly and as he ought. But since the Lord has commanded us to love our neighbor, He sent us to work, intimating by this that the precept of the love of neighbor ought to be fulfilled not so much by affection as by deeds. For when He had commanded us to love our neighbors, He immediately added, saying: "Do good to them that hate you" (Mt. 5, 44). Hence, we fulfill the precept of love of neighbor when loving our neighbors as ourselves, we keep that precept of the Natural Law: "Whatsoever you would that men should do to you, do you also to them" (7, 12).

---

[1] N. 10 (PL 45, 1718). This quotation is taken from a tract of the heretic Pelagius entitled, *Libellus fidei Pelagii*, which was formerly attributed by some to St. Jerome, but by other to St. Augustine. Cf. Peter Johannes van Egmond, *Haec Fides Est: Observations on the Textual Tradition of Pelagius's "Libellus Fidei"*, Augustiniana, vol. 57, no. 3/4 (2007), pp. 345-385.

[2] *In praise of Saint Paul* (*De laudibus sancti Pauli Aposotoli*), hom. 6 (PG 50, 503).

[3] "By no means may you presume to confess venial sins, nor even all mortal sins, because it is impossible that you know all mortal sins. Hence in the primitive Church only manifest mortal sins were confessed" (Luther's eighth article condemned in the papal bull, *Exsurge Domine* (Dz. 748)).

[4] *Assertio omnium articulorum*, art. 25 (WA 7, 127-128).

[5] *Homilies on the Gospels*, hom. 30, n. 1 (PL 76, 1220C).

Yet all these things ought not to be so understood that someone would think that he fulfills the precept of charity through the performance of deeds without any actual love. For the latter is also especially required, because among the many evils of men which the Apostle enumerates in his Second Epistle to Timothy, he also adds this one: "Without affection" (3, 3). Thus it is necessary to have affection for God: and if with this latter anyone would have kept all the rest of His Commandments, he ought to be said to love God with his whole heart in that manner according to which the love of God is commanded us in this life. For the love of God, for producing which the soul applies all its strength and makes every effort, such I say cannot be had in this life: nor is it commanded us in this life, but it is that which is expected as the reward. Blessed Paul, when speaking about the knowledge of God, says: "Now I know in part; but then I shall know even as I am known" (I Cor. 13, 12). Thus, just as he says about knowledge, one ought to think about the love which follows knowledge, namely that here we love in part, and afterwards we hope to love in its totality.

Now this interpretation of the love of God is proved by the testimony of Blessed Bernard, who speaks thus: "Charity, my brethren, must be exercised in two ways, in action and in affection. And in fact, concerning the former, which pertains to actions, I think that a law was given to men, and a definite law. For who could so be in his affections as it is commanded? Therefore, the former is commanded for merit, the latter is given in reward. The beginning and advancement of which we do not deny can indeed be experienced by Divine grace in the present life, but I by all means defend that its consummation is for the happiness to come."[1] And Blessed Augustine teaches the same opinion, when saying the following: "That wisdom also and the knowledge of God, is then perfected in us, and that in the Lord there is such rejoicing that it is a full and a true security, who will deny, unless he is so averse from the truth that on this very account he cannot attain unto it? But these things will not be in precepts, but in reward of those precepts which should here be observed... Here, then, it is prescribed that we sin not; there, the reward is that we cannot sin. Here, the precept is that we obey not the desires of sin; there, the reward that we have no desires of sin. Here, the precept is, 'Understand, ye senseless among the people: and, you fools, be wise at last' (Ps. 93, 8); there, the reward is full wisdom and perfect knowledge. For 'We see now through a glass in a dark manner,' Says the Apostle, 'but then face to face. Now I know in part; but then I shall know even as I am known' (I Cor. 13, 12). Here, the precept is, 'Rejoice to God our helper' (Ps. 80, 2), and, 'Rejoice in the Lord, O ye just' (Ps. 32, 1); there, the reward is to rejoice with a perfect and unspeakable joy."[2] Augustine says many things in this place whereby he teaches that in this miserable life the perfection of justice is not commanded, but to expect it as a reward. From which words it is clearly enough gathered that Luther wrongly understood the precept of the love of God.

Next, if that precept should be understood as Luther teaches, no one would be found, nay no could be found, who shall have kept it in this life. But there are many about whom Sacred Scripture testifies that they either loved God, or sought Him, or served Him with their whole heart. For God, when speaking to Jeroboam about David, says: "Thou hast not been as my servant David, who kept my commandments, and followed me with all his heart" (III Kings 14, 8). Notice that David followed God with his whole heart and kept God's commandments, and yet David had tinder [*fomes*] of the flesh, which, as happens in all other men, was held in check by the will. Thus, it is proved from this passage that neither is concupiscence of the flesh a sin against God's precept, nor also does it impede whereby one loves God with the whole heart, as He was commanded to be loved by us in this life. And likewise, David did not fear to say to God: "With my whole heart have I sought after thee" (Ps. 118, 10). And again:

---

[1] *Sermons on the Canticle of Canticles*, serm. 50, n. 2 (PL 183, 1020C-1021A).
[2] *Against Two Letters of the Pelagians*, bk. 3, c. 7, n. 17 (PL 44, 600-601).

"I entreated thy face with all my heart" (v. 58). And again: "I will seek thy commandments with my whole heart" (v. 69). And once again: "I was directed to all thy commandments: I have hated all wicked ways" (v. 128). If David is directed to all the commandments, then he is directed to the commandment of the love of God. And it is certainly necessary to admit that he is directed to another of these commandments: "Thou shalt not covet," or else to say that they are not commandments as Luther interprets them: or to say that David was not directed to all the commandments. But David testifies that he was directed to all God's commandments: therefore, those commandments of God ought not to be understood as Luther interprets them.

King Ezechias testifies that he had done this same thing when he prayed to the Lord God, saying: "I beseech thee, O Lord, remember how I have walked before thee in truth, and with a perfect heart, and have done that which is pleasing before thee" (IV Kings 20, 3). Perhaps this man did not have resisting tinder? He certainly had. Hence how could he walk before the Lord with a perfect heart, if such love of God which Luther teaches, is required of us in this life, or if concupiscence of the flesh is a sin against God's precept? Furthermore, in Deuteronomy it is said: "Thou shalt find God: yet so, if thou seek him with all thy heart, and all the affliction of thy soul" (Deut. 4, 29). Let us inquire of Luther whether anyone ever found God? If he denies, that passage stands in the way which the spouse says in the Canticles: "I found him whom my soul loveth" (3, 4). And concerning those who lived in the kingdom of Juda at the time of King Asa, it is said: "For with all their heart they swore, and with all their will they sought him, and they found him" (II Par. 15, 15). Now if it is acknowledged, as it ought, that every just man finds God, it is also necessary to acknowledge that every such man sought God with his whole heart: otherwise he would not have found God: because in order that one is able to accomplish this, such diligence is required of him, namely, such that he would seek God with his whole heart. Wherefore, from all these things it is very clearly proved that the precept of the love of God ought not to be understood as Luther interprets it. Now this is very clearly gathered from the Fourth Book of Kings, in which place it is so said about King Jehu: "But Jehu took no heed to walk in the law of the Lord the God of Israel with all his heart." And adding the reason for this thing, he says: "For he departed not from the sins of Jeroboam, who had made Israel to sin" (10, 31). For because he transgressed one or another commandment, it was said that he did not walk with his whole heart. Hence it is proved that he walks with the whole heart, who fulfills all the commandments.

Concerning the other precept, namely: "Thou shalt not covet," it is also evident that Luther erred. For from the aforesaid things, it is sufficiently evident that by that precept concupiscence of the flesh is not prohibited, because although such concupiscence shall have been found in all men, besides Christ and perhaps His Virgin Mother, there would be no one who would have kept such a precept. But David kept all the Lord's commandments, and hence this commandment also. He would not have kept it, however, if concupiscence of the flesh had been forbidden by it. Thus, we proved that by that precept concupiscence of the flesh is not prohibited, but rather the interior affection of the will. In order to show that more clearly, I will bring forth some testimonies of holy men.

But before I present them, I would like to point out one thing, namely, that this word, "sin," is equivocal in Holy Writ. For sometimes it is taken for the victim which is offered for sin. So it is taken by Paul the Apostle in the Second Epistle to the Corinthians, when he says: "Him, who knew no sin, he hath made sin for us" (5, 21), as though he were to say: "Christ, Who even as Man, had not become guilty of any guilt, the Heavenly Father made Him to undergo death for us: by having undertaken which death for our sins, Christ Himself was made sin, that is, a victim for sin." But from this meaning of sin someone is never called "a sinner." And so, Paul when speaking about Christ, did not say that the Father made Him "a sinner," but that He made Him "sin." Sometimes also the cause drawing to or impelling to sin, or the punishment of sin is called "sin": and Paul used the word "sin" in this way when he said: "If then I do that which I will not, I consent to the law, that it is good. Now then it is no more I that do it, but sin that dwelleth in me" (Rom. 7, 16-17). In this passage Paul calls concupiscence of the flesh "sin," because it always impels to evil, or because it was given as a punishment for the first sin. Now this is apparent from the words which follow. For after he had said that the sin which dwells in him does the evil, he immediately added: "For I know that there dwelleth not in me, that is to say, in my flesh, that which is good" (v. 18). And from this meaning of sin no one is ever called a "sinner." Hence Blessed Augustine in his commentaries on the Epistle to the Galatians, says: "It is one thing not to sin and another not to have sin."[1]

This word is taken in another sense for guilt, and an offense against God, which our will by transgressing God's precept commits, and on account of which the will, sinning in this way, is made to be condemned to some punishment to be inflicted. And this is its most common meaning which Holy Writ also uses more frequently. And only from this meaning of sin is someone called a sinner. Thus, when speaking of this meaning in regard to sin, we say that concupiscence or the tinder of the flesh is not a sin, and consequently, it is not prohibited by that precept: "Thou shalt not covet." Richard of St. Victor when showing the excellence of the Blessed Virgin Mary over all other saints says: "To the saints in general it is commanded that sin may not reign in their mortal bodies: to this woman alone it is singularly given that sin would not inhabit her mortal body. 'Let not sin,' the Apostle says, 'reign in your mortal body' (Rom. 6, 12). Take note that he commands that it would not reign, but does he command that it would not inhabit? Notice what he says elsewhere: 'For if the evil that I will not, that I do… it is no more I that do it, but sin that dwelleth in me' (Rom. 7, 19-20)."[2] In which words it ought to be observed that he says that it was commanded to us that sin would not reign in our mortal body: it was not commanded that it would not dwell in our mortal body. From which it is evident that concupiscence of the flesh was not interdicted, because this concupiscence is that "sin" which dwells in our body.

Blessed Augustine very often teaches this same opinion, namely in the first book of the *City of God*,[3] but more explicitly and at greater length when writing to Boniface in his *Against Two Letters of the Pelagians*. For in that place he says: "They also say that Baptism does not give complete remission of sins, nor take away crimes, but that it shaves them off, so that the roots of all sins are retained in the evil flesh. Who but an unbeliever can affirm this against the Pelagians? I say, therefore, that Baptism gives remission of all sins, and takes away guilt, and does not shave them off; and that the roots of all sins are not retained in the evil flesh, as if of shaved hair on the head, whence the sins may grow to be cut down again. For it was I that found out that similitude, too, for them to use for the purposes of their calumny, as if I thought and said this. But concerning that concupiscence of the flesh of which they speak, I believe

---

[1] N. 48 (PL 35, 2140).

[2] *On Emmanuel*, bk. 2, c. 31 (PL 196, 664C).

[3] "And if that lustful disobedience, which still dwells in our mortal members, follows its own law irrespective of our will, surely its motions in the body of one who rebels against them are as blameless as its motions in the body of one who sleeps" (Bk. 1, c. 25 (PL 41, 38)). "For when the carnal part which the Apostle calls sin, in that place where he says, 'It is not I who do it, but sin that dwelleth in me' (Rom. 7, 17), that part which the philosophers also call vicious, and which ought not to lead the mind, but which the mind ought to rule and restrain by reason from illicit motions—when, then, this part has been moved to perpetrate any wickedness, if it be curbed and if it obey the word of the Apostle, 'Neither yield ye your members as instruments of iniquity unto sin' (Rom. 6, 13), it is turned towards the mind and subdued and conquered by it, so that reason rules over it as a subject" (Bk. 15, c. 7, n. 2 (PL 41, 445)). The second reference here in the text is to Bk. 14, c. 10, but this seems incorrect and has been replaced here by the second quotation which cites and expounds Rom. 7, 17, which speaks of the indwelling of "sin."

that they are deceived, or that they deceive; for with this even he that is baptized must struggle with a pious mind, however carefully he presses forward, and is led by the Spirit of God. But although this is called sin, it is certainly so called not because it is sin, but because it is made by sin, as a writing is said to be some one's hand because the hand has written it. But they are sins which are unlawfully done, spoken, thought, according to the lust of the flesh, or to ignorance—things which, once done, keep their doers guilty if they are not forgiven. And this very concupiscence of the flesh is in such wise put away in Baptism, that although it is inherited by all that are born, it in no respect hurts those that are born anew."[1] And in the first book of *On Marriage And Concupiscence* to Valarius, he teaches the same opinion through many chapters.[2] I commit to the curious reader all which things to be read, he thinking that I have done enough since I showed that place where he would be able to find the things he wishes.

Besides all these testimonies of holy men, there also is a clear definition of the Church against this wicked and blasphemous opinion of Luther. For the Council of Trent, celebrated under Paul III, in the fifth session condemned this particular opinion of Luther about concupiscence, speaking thus: "This concupiscence, which at times the Apostle calls sin (Rom. 6, 12 ff.) the holy Synod declares that the Catholic Church has never understood to be called sin, as truly and properly sin in those born again, but because it is from sin and inclines to sin. But if anyone is of the contrary opinion, let him be anathema."[3] Then the same council in the sixth session condemned the teaching asserting that God's precepts are impossible, saying these words: "No one should make use of that rash statement forbidden under an anathema by the Fathers, that the Commandments of God are impossible to observe for a man who is justified. 'For God does not command impossibilities, but by commanding admonishes you both to do what you can do, and to pray for what you cannot do, and assists you that you may be able';[4] 'whose commandments are not heavy' (I Jn. 5, 3), 'whose yoke is sweet and whose burden is light' (Mt. 11, 30). For they who are the sons of God, love Christ: 'but they who love him, (as He Himself testifies) keep his words' (Jn. 14, 23), which indeed with the Divine help they can do."[5] And after having given this teaching, lest anyone rashly dare to say something against it, it adds a *latae sententiae* canon [of excommunication], which among the many others published in that session, having been put in the eighteenth place, contains these words: "If anyone shall say that the commandments of God are even for a man who is justified and confirmed in grace impossible to observe: let him be anathema."[6]

Jacques Masson, in that work which he made for the defense of the judgment of the Louvain against Luther, wrote abundantly against this heresy in regard to both of its parts.[7] Bishop John [Fisher] of Rochester wrote most eloquently, as he is accustomed to do, against the second part of this heresy, namely the part which is about concupiscence, in the second article of that work which he made against the forty-one articles of Luther previously condemned by Leo X.[8]

---

[1] Bk. 1, c. 13, n. 26-27 (PL 44, 562-563).

[2] PL 44, 413-474.

[3] C. 5 (Dz. 792).

[4] St. Augustine, *On Nature and Grace*, c. 43, n. 50 (PL 44, 271).

[5] C. 11 (Dz. 804).

[6] Dz. 828.

[7] *Articulorum doctrinae fratris M. Lutheri per theologos Lovanienses damnatorum ratio ex sacris literis et veteribus tractatoribus* (Antwerp, 1521).

[8] *Assertionis Lutheranae confutatio* (Cologne, Maternus Cholinus, 1564), fol. 89r-92r.

PRAEDESTINATIO

Predestination

The monk Sigebert [of Gembloux][1] relates in his *Chronicon* that, under the Emperor Honorius and Pope [Innocent I[2]], a certain heresy arose which taught that the labor of "good works did not benefit those living piously, if they had been ordained to death by God: and any evil deeds or heinous crimes committed by them did not harm wicked sinners, if God had predestined them to eternal life."[3] The promoters of this heresy, Sigebert says, are called "the Predestined," receiving their name from their teaching. Now Sigebert passes over in silence, nor could I find in any other author, who was the originator of this heresy, because none of those who wrote about the heresies, mention this heresy, besides Bernard of Luxemburg in his *Catalogus haereticorum*, who says nothing else but what he found in the *Chronicon*.[4] The Bohemian John Hus raised up this error from Hell, after it had then been buried for nearly a thousand years, saying that he who was predestined by God to life, even if he does evil deeds, can never be a member of the devil: and he who was ordained by God to death, no matter how well he may live, can never be a member of God. Some common and uneducated men embraced this most pestilential heresy in the year 1534 in Holland and Phrygia, saying that a good deed does not benefit nor does an evil deed harm any man, but everything depends on predestination and the Divine foreknowledge alone.

This teaching withdraws just men from the exercise of good works, and incites sinners to perpetrating any evil deed whatsoever. Thus, let us show by very clear testimonies of Sacred Scripture the falsity of this teaching, lest from this doctrine sinners make take an occasion of behaving badly. No one doubts that Cain was damned, who despaired of the Divine mercy, saying: "My iniquity is greater than that I may deserve pardon" (Gen. 4, 13). But when the Lord did not have respect to Cain's offerings, on this account Cain was angry, and his face fell, and the Lord said to him: "Why art thou angry? and why is thy countenance fallen? If thou do well, shalt thou not receive?" (v. 6-7). Notice that God promises to the foreknown man the reward of good deeds, if he wished to do them: and heretics do not fear to take away the power of acting uprightly from those whom were ordained by God to death. For God neither so forces by necessity those predestined to good by His predestination, that they cannot act badly and perish: nor does He so force those ordained to Hell, that they cannot act well and merit life. For (so that I may use the words of [Pseudo-] Augustine) God would know how to change the sentence, if man would begin to change his life.[5] Hence God Himself speaks through Jeremias the prophet saying: "If that nation against which I have spoken, shall repent of their evil, I also will repent of the evil that I have thought to do to them" (18, 8).

Furthermore, it is certain that King David was predestined to eternal life, and yet, when on account of the adultery committed by him, the prophet Nathan came to him proposing to the king a parable about a rich man taking a little lamb from a poor man, which the same

---

[1] Sigebert of Gembloux (c. 1030-1112 A.D.) was a Benedictine monk and chronicler known for his *Chronicon ab anno 381 ad 1113*, a universal history widely used as a source by later medieval historians.

[2] The text mistakenly has Pope Zosimus, as also incorrectly stated in Bernard of Luxemburg's *Catalogus haereticorum*.

[3] *Chronicon ab anno 381 ad 1113* (Paris, Henricus Stephanus, 1513), fol. 7v.

[4] Fol. 44v.

[5] "O that the sinner would quickly have recourse to penance as quickly as God wants to change the sentence… Who upon our conversion desires to change the sentence" (Serm. 29, n. 2 (PL 39, 1802)).

poor man lived upon: King David said that a rich man such as this was a son of death. Which having been said, the prophet Nathan said to David: "Thou art the man" (II Kings 12, 7). By which words the prophet very clearly stated that King David on account of that evil deed was a son of death, and one who deserved to be punished with eternal death, unless God having pity on him, gave him life whereby he could repent of his wrongdoings.

Again, Blessed Peter the Apostle was predestined by God to eternal life, which he also now enjoys: yet when he rebuked Christ because He said that He was going to die and was prepared to die, He heard from the same Christ: "Go behind me, Satan" (Mt. 16, 23). Behold predestined Peter, who nevertheless was at one time a Satan. But if he was a Satan, it is necessary that he belong more to the devil than to Christ. For Theophylactus when expounding that passage of Matthew, speaks thus: "'Satan' means 'the adversary.' 'Get thee behind me,' that is, do not oppose Me, but follow My will. He calls Peter this because Satan, too, did not wish Christ to suffer."[1] But because it is not very clear that Peter then sinned mortally, although he was called Satan (for he was so called, because he was opposing the Divine will. For Satan means the same thing as an adversary), wherefore we bring forth another very grave sin of his, namely the triple denial, whereby swearing he denied his Teacher and the Teacher of all men.[2]

Next, Paul, the vessel of election, who bears witness that a crown of justice was laid up for him by God,[3] acknowledges that previously he was a blasphemer.[4] If he was at that time a blasphemer, then at that time he was a sinner and wicked, and consequently at that time deserving of death. Unless perhaps these heretics reckon that a blasphemer is deserving of an eternal reward. And if he was a sinner at that time, it is necessary that he was at that time a member of the devil. Hence Blessed Gregory, in a homily for the first Sunday of Lent, says the following: "The devil is undoubtedly the leader of all the wicked, and all the wicked are the members of this leader."[5]

Finally, among all the assertions of John Hus which the Council of Constance condemned in the fifteenth session, the second in the list is the one which follows: "Paul never was a member of the devil, although he did certain acts similar to the acts of those who malign the Church."[6] And the fifth assertion of the same John Hus is put there in these words: "The foreknown, although at one time he is in grace according to the present justice, yet is never a part of the holy Church; and the predestined always remains a member of the Church, although at times he may fall away from additional grace, but not from the grace of predestination."[7] Now these two assertions, along with the many others of the same John Hus, were condemned in the Council of Constance.

There is a **second heresy** about predestination which asserts that a man without a special revelation can know that he is predestined by God to eternal life. This heresy firstly appeared in public in this pitiful century of ours, very apt to reviving any heresy, in which time whatever one is pleased to spread abroad about dogmas, he is permitted to do so. But it is well that until now those who think this way have not so progressed that they published their error in writing, which is apt to harm more widely than words: but they have manifested their rash and very presumptuous judgment by word only.

---

[1] *Explanation of the Gospel of Matthew* (PG 123, 322C).
[2] Cf. Mt. 26, 70-74.
[3] Cf. II Tim. 4, 8.
[4] Cf. I Tim. 1, 13.
[5] Hom. 16 (PL 76, 1135C).
[6] Dz. 628.
[7] Dz. 631.

For in the Council of Trent, at which I was present, when among the many learned men who were present there, by command of the synod, the question of the certitude of human justification was treated, and the matter was controverted among them, behold one or another sprang forth, who with a presumptuous temerity before such a great multitude of learned men were not ashamed to say that man without a special revelation of God can certainly know not merely that he is just, but that he has been predestined. Now one of them, to make his own rashness and proud presumption complete, proposed himself as an example, saying: For I in fact certainly know that I am predestined. Hearing which I was astounded, surprised that a man even somewhat educated and in his right mind, had fallen into such an insane error, and was not ashamed to spread it abroad in the presence of such and so great gathering. But afterwards when going over the matter within myself, and reflecting upon it with careful consideration in my mind, I greatly suspected that these assertors of so presumptuous a heresy, cherished Luther in their hearts, and swore allegiance to his words, although they sold themselves to us as Catholics, and desired to be thought by us as being such.

For even though Luther never, as far as I know, openly taught this heresy, still it is evidently gathered from other assertions of his. For Luther asserts that every believer certainly ought to believe that he is justified freely through God's mercy. He moreover says that a believer, even if he wants, cannot lose that salvation which was given to him in Baptism, unless he does not want to believe. From which two assertions this third is manifestly deduced. Because if man is sure that he is just, and is sure that he cannot lose his justice, the consequence is that he is also sure that he will attain eternal life, which without God's predestination to it, cannot be attained. I have already disputed against those two first heresies of Luther above in the section on "Grace," and everything which I said against those two heresies in that place also strongly fights against that heresy about which we now treat. For if man cannot be sure of his own justification, much less can he be sure about his predestination. But I still wish to specifically fight against this heresy, and to refute it with clear testimonies of Scripture, and with evident arguments, so that at last having been refuted and confuted, it may depart from the whole Christian world.

Now so that we may make the matter clearer, let us imagine a man who without any special revelation of God certainly knows that he has been predestined, and let us call him Peter. And in this way I prove that Peter, without God's revelation, could never know it, because apart from God's revelation no way is open whereby it could have been certain for Peter. Firstly, in fact, Peter could not be certain with a certitude of evidence about his predestination: because it could not be evident to him in any way that he is predestined. For from the knowledge of the terms alone it could not be evident, because only the first principles known by themselves are evident in this way. But since it is not a first principle known by itself that Peter is predestined, it follows that it could not be evident in this way. And certainly, if it could be evident to Peter in this way, that he is predestined, it would be evident to any other man that Peter is predestined: because anyone else could know the words and language of this sentence, "Peter is predestined," and so it is necessary that any other man could evidently know that Peter is predestined.

To claim this, however, would be very great insanity. It can also not be evident to Peter through demonstration that he is predestined: because that Peter is predestined is not something necessary, but merely contingent, which obviously depends on God's free will alone. Paul very clearly reminds us about this point in the Epistle to the Romans: "It is not of him that willeth, nor of him that runneth, but of God that sheweth mercy. For the scripture saith to Pharao: To this purpose have I raised thee, that I may shew my power in thee, and that my name may be declared throughout all the earth. Therefore, he hath mercy on whom he will; and whom he will, he hardeneth" (9, 16-18). Therefore, it is established that predestination, which depends on God's free will alone, is something contingent and not necessary. Now contingent things cannot be proved through demonstration: because (as Aristotle teaches[1]) certain knowledge cannot be had of contingent things.

Nor can it be evident to Peter through experience that he is predestined: because it is necessary that what is evident in this way be known immediately and by direct perception. But no one, unless by God willing and showing, is able to directly perceive that predestination whereby Peter is predestined, which is an act of the Divine will, and what is more marvelous, even if someone were to see God Himself, still it would not then be necessary that he directly behold that Divine volition, whereby He decides to give eternal life to Peter. For (as Blessed [Bonaventure] excellently teaches[2]) God is a kind of voluntary mirror; making known and showing what things He wishes, and hiding what things He wishes. Thus, it is not possible that to Peter, who is unable to directly perceive the decree of the Divine will, it would be evident through experience that he is predestined.

Add to this that God's judgments are so hidden and unknown to men that not only are they unable to directly perceive them, but also they cannot know them in any other way. Hence the Royal Prophet, when wishing to show to us how much the Divine judgments are hidden from us, said: "God's judgments are a great deep" (Ps. 35, 7). And the son of this man, King Solomon, says: "Who among men is he that can know the counsel of God? or who can think what the will of God is? For the thoughts of mortal men are fearful, and our counsels uncertain. For the corruptible body is a load upon the soul, and the earthly habitation presseth down the mind that museth upon many things. And hardly do we guess aright at things that are upon earth: and with labour do we find the things that are before us. But the things that are in heaven, who shall search out? And who shall know thy thought, except thou give wisdom, and send thy Holy Spirit from above" (Wis. 9, 13-17).

And Paul in the Epistle to the Romans says: "O the depth of the riches of the wisdom and of the knowledge of God! How incomprehensible are his judgments, and how unsearchable his ways! For who hath known the mind of the Lord? Or who hath been his counsellor?" (Rom. 11, 33-34). Wherefore the Lord speaks through the prophet Jeremias about the heart of man, that it is unsearchable, saying: "The heart is perverse above all things, and unsearchable, who can know it? I am the Lord who search the heart and prove the reins" (17, 9-10). If no one can know the things which are in man's heart, much less could one know the things which God decides in His heart, unless He will reveal them. Therefore, it is great temerity that someone would say that without God's special revelation he certainly and clearly knows that he is predestined to eternal life, even though Solomon said that no one can know the Lord's thought, except He give wisdom, and send His Holy Spirit from above. Wherefore it ought to be asked of him, who says that he certainly knows that he is predestined, in accord with Paul's

---

[1] "In the case of that which is or which has taken place, propositions, whether positive or negative, must be true or false... When the subject, however, is individual, and that which is predicated of it relates to the future, the case is not similar." *On Interpretation* (*Peri Hermeneias*), c. 9.

[2] "There are two kinds mirrors, a natural mirror and a voluntary mirror. Just as a natural mirror naturally receives, so it also naturally gives, and in this way it hides nothing: hence the mirror opposite to it reflects not only itself, but also everything which shines in it. A voluntary mirror, however, is not in the act of showing those things which are contained in it, unless when the will does this, and such is a spiritual mirror." (*In Librum Secundum Sententiarum,* Dist. 8, part 2, art. 1, q. 6, ad 6um in *Sancti Bonaventurae Opera* (Venice, Joan. Baptista Albritius, 1753), vol. 2 p. 229). The author here cites St. Augustine, but the analogy was used by St. Bonaventure who cites St. Augustine who wrote these related words: "For [the Angels] have the power, I believe, of hiding their thoughts by spiritual means, just as we can hide our bodies from the eyes of others by setting up some obstacle to obstruct their view" (*Literal Meaning of Genesis*, bk. 12, c. 22, 48 (PL 34, 473)).

teaching: How have you known the mind of the Lord? Have you been his counsellor? And in the First Epistle to the Corinthians he again teaches that the Divine judgments are hidden to us, which nevertheless we are able to know very well once God has revealed them. "The things also that are of God no man knoweth, but the Spirit of God. Now we have received not the spirit of this world, but the Spirit that is of God; that we may know the things that are given us from God" (2, 11-12). From all these things it is very clearly concluded that no one without a clear vision of God can certainly know with a certitude of evidence that he has been predestined to eternal life.

It remains that we also show that no one without a special revelation of God can know that he is predestined with the correctness of the Catholic faith. Now anyone will easily understand that this is true, if he observes that nothing is certain with the certitude of this kind, except that alone which we are held to believe from the Catholic faith. Otherwise, it will be necessary to confess that from a probable reason alone, and a pious affection towards the one speaking, we certainly know that it is as certain to us as those things which we believe by the Catholic faith. But if someone concedes this, he will act wickedly. Because we can be deceived about those things which we believe from a probable reason and pious affection: but about those things which we believe from the Catholic faith, we cannot be deceived. If, however, it were to happen that those things which are believed by a probable reason and pious affection are the kind of things about which one believing them in this way could not be deceived, which would happen if someone moved by this reason alone would believe some demonstrable geometric proposition, or some particular article of the Catholic faith, yet the one believing in this way would not be certain with so great certitude, as he who believes the same things from the Catholic faith inclining him to believe in this way. Because even though both are equally sure about the fact that neither of them believing in this way could be deceived, because the objects of both are of themselves equally certain: yet from that way of grasping the object, they are very disparate. For one of them is moved by human truth alone and probable reason, but the other relies upon Divine truth and is moved by it to believing: because he believes that God is most true: hence he very firmly believes that everything revealed by God is true. Now there is no one who does not see the great difference between the latter and the former motive, and how much more certain the latter motive is than the former. From which it becomes very clear that nothing which is believed by human faith alone, is equally certain as that which is believed from the Catholic faith inclining and moving the soul to believing in this way.

And hence it necessarily follows that no one without a special revelation from God can be certain with this certitude of the Catholic faith that he is predestined to eternal life. Because whoever shall say that he is certain of his predestination with such certitude, is forced to confess that it is an article of faith that he is predestined, or through an evident and clear conclusion deduced from some article of faith. For otherwise (as we just said) one cannot be sure about his predestination with such certitude. Nevertheless, both of these are very clearly false. For it is so manifest that it is not an article of the Catholic faith that Peter or John are predestined to eternal life that it does not need proving. If someone, however, is so brazen that he does not fear to deny it, it ought to be asked of him where does he show it in the Apostles' Creed, or in one of the books of Sacred Scripture, but because these things are too clear for us to spend time on them, hence I pass on to something else.

Peter also cannot deduce from the articles of faith as an evident conclusion that he is predestined. For if that could be done, not only Peter, but whoever would know to make such a deduction would certainly know regarding himself and regarding any other predestined person that they are predestined to eternal life. Not only would he know with the certitude of the Catholic faith, but he would be so held to believe under threat of Hell. Because all are held to believe under threat of Hell those things which are deduced from the articles of faith as evident conclusions. Besides if this could be deduced from some article, it would certainly not be deduced from another than that in which God promises that He will give eternal life to one acting well and obeying his Commandments. "If thou wilt enter into life," our Savior says, "keep the commandments" (Mt. 19, 17). But from this promise alone one cannot be sure about his predestination because it is not a bare and absolute promise, but conditional, namely under this condition that one would keep the Commandments.

But no one without a special revelation of God can be sure that he has that fulfillment of God's Commandments, which is enough, according to God's promise, to certainly attain eternal life. For that obedience whereby someone now at this moment in time performs the Divine Commandments, even if he certainly knew that he then perfectly obeys the Divine Commandments, does not enable a man to rendered sure of attaining eternal life: because not according to any obedience, but only according to that obedience which will be unto final perseverance God promises that He will give eternal life. "He that shall persevere unto the end," the Savior says, "he shall be saved" (Mt. 10, 22). And Paul says: "He is not crowned, except he strive lawfully" (II Tim. 2, 5). Now one does not strive lawfully who, although he carried out many and outstanding deeds in war, at length spontaneously, and not being forced, wants to surrender to the enemy. Finally, Solomon says: "If the tree fall to the south, or to the north, in what place soever it shall fall, there shall it be" (Eccle. 11, 3).

Jerome in his *Commentary on Ecclesiastes* speaks thus: "A tree, if in this life it falls and is cut in its state of mortality, either must sin before while it stands and is then placed in the north afterwards, or if the south winds takes away all its worthy fruit, it will lie wounded in the south."[1] The saintly Bishop Salonius[2] states this opinion much more clearly in the questions on Ecclesiastes which he made in the form of a dialogue, speaking thus: "This verse ought to be understood spiritually. For by the tree man is designated: because everyone is like a tree of the forest of the human race. By the south, which is a warm wind, the rest of paradise is designated: by the north, which is cold, the punishment of Hell is designated. And the meaning is this. Every man shall have prepared a place of living for himself, when he shall have fallen to the south, that is, when he shall be dead, he will remain forever in the rest of paradise and the glory of the heavenly kingdom. But if by living badly he shall have prepared a place for himself to the north, he will undergo the punishments of Hell forever."[3] These are the words of Salonius [said] to his brother Veranus. From all which things it is clearly gathered that the end of predestination, which is eternal life, is not given by God on account of any justice except in that which is found at the last gasp of life. And hence, it is clearly proved, from the mere thought of the present justice, even if someone certainly knows that he has it, he cannot be sure about his predestination with the certitude of Catholic faith. Because even if we would admit (which is false according to Paul's teaching) that Divine predestination proceeds from men's foreseen merits, such that the cause of Divine predestination is the foreknowledge of merits, nevertheless this would be understood of those merits alone which

---

[1] On Eccle. 11, 3 (PL 23, 1102C).
[2] Saint Salonius was a confessor and bishop of the 5th century. He was born about 400, a son of St. Eucherius of Lyon. He was educated at Lérins Abbey, first by St. Hilary of Arles, then by Salvianus and St. Vincent of Lérins. In 440, he was elected Bishop of Geneva and, as such, took part in the Synod of Orange (441), the Synod of Vaison (442), and the Synod of Arles (451). He has also been listed as the Bishop of Genoa, but it is not clear if this was a later appointment or if the word Geneva was miswritten as Genova. He was an accomplished Latin ecclesiastical writer. The author had titled him here as "Bishop of Vienne," and although he was a bishop in France, it is unknown of what city. (Cf. Louis Ellies Du Pin, *A New History of Ecclesiastical Writers* (London, Edward Jones, 1693), vol. 4, p. 149).
[3] *Expositio mystica in Ecclesiasten* (PL 53, 1009A).

God foreknew would be had at the moment of death, so that according to Solomon's opinion, he perpetually remains in that state in which he fell through death.

But perhaps someone striving to pertinaciously maintain the aforesaid error will fall into the heresy of Jovinian and Pelagius, saying that he who has once received the grace of Baptism can no longer lose it, and consequently also cannot sin, but will be sure of his perseverance and hence of eternal life. And from this he perhaps will deduce that he who is sure that he has attained the grace of Baptism, is thence sure of his predestination to eternal life, because he certainly believes that he is unable to fall away from that grace. But he who would flee to this refuge, would support a worse error than the previous one. For it is evident from Holy Writ that King David was good and just when by God's command the prophet Samuel anointed him as king. Yet afterwards when taking leisure at home he desired the wife of Urias, and at length firstly committed adultery with her and then committed murder. But perhaps because Jovinian and Pelagius will reject this example, due to the fact that David did not have the grace of Baptism, which had not been instituted at that time, let us for this reason go on to those who received the grace of Baptism.

It is evident that the Apostles were baptized before Christ's death, even from that passage of John wherein our Savior when speaking to them said: "He that is washed, needeth not but to wash his feet, but is clean wholly. And you are clean, but not all" (Jn. 13, 10). For those words are understood by holy men of the washing by the Sacrament of Baptism, such that when saying that they are "clean," He shows that they are in the state of grace. It is evident, however, that He adds "but not all," on account of Judas, who was then planning the death of Christ our Savior. Yet shortly after these words, namely on that same night, all the Apostles were scandalized when having left their master they all fled. And Peter who was boasting that he was stronger and more constant than the others, sinned worse than all when cursing and swearing, he denied his master three times. And it is unnecessary to dispute more against his heresy of Jovinian, because I remember that I said enough against it above in the section on "Grace," in the second heresy. And from all those things it is clearly proved that any man no matter how just, unless confirmed by God in grace, can sin mortally and consequently lose the grace of Baptism. And from this it is evidently concluded that no one from the mere knowledge of his present justice, even if he were to know it more certainly, can certainly know with the certitude of the Catholic faith that he is predestined to eternal life.

Perhaps he who contends that he is sure about his predestination, having been conquered by the above-mentioned reasons, will say that he has certainly persuaded himself with the certitude of the Catholic faith that he is predestined to eternal life, not from the thought of his present justice alone, but also from the thought of his final perseverance. But he who says this adds error to error: because no one without a special revelation from God can certainly know his own final perseverance. For concerning this alone ought to be understood that which Solomon says: "Man knoweth not whether he be worthy of love, or hatred: but all things are kept uncertain for the time to come" (Eccle. 9, 1-2). Even though Jerome has translated these words differently from the Hebrew into Latin than we have cited them, according to the Vulgate edition, nevertheless the meaning of his words do not differ from ours. Jerome's translation is as follows: "Man indeed knows not love or hatred, nor anything from its appearances." Now so that it can be established for all that the meaning of these words does not differ from our Vulgate edition, it is necessary that we hear Jerome himself interpreting his own translation, who speaks thus: "Man knows neither friendships nor enmities; but everything is uncertain regarding them, because similar things happen to all men, the just and the unjust. Hence the meaning is this: 'I also applied my heart to this matter, and wanted to know whom it is that God loves, and whom it is that He hates. And I found that the works of the just are truly in the hands of God: and yet, whether they are loved by God or not, they cannot now know; and they fluctuate undecidedly, whether they are undergoing the things that they undergo unto approbation or unto punishment.'"[1] Which words explicate the meaning which the Vulgate edition teaches.

Furthermore, Solomon teaches the same thing elsewhere. "Boast not for tomorrow, for thou knowest not what the day to come may bring forth" (Prov. 27, 1). By "the day to come" the Wise Man means the time to come, or it is the following day, or if you prefer, any other day after that. Our Savior used this meaning of the word when, wishing to withdraw us from the care and solicitude of providing the things needed for the body in the future, He said: "Be not solicitous for tomorrow" (Mt. 6, 34). For He did not only forbid us to be solicitous regarding the next day, but still more so regarding other days further away in time. Thus, Solomon forbids that we glory in time to come, because we do not know what we will do at that time. But if a just man would be sure of his perseverance in justice, he could indeed, and rightly, glory about his present goodness and justice: because he would know what the following day could procure for him. For if, as Paul teaches, a man could glory about the goodness in the Lord,[2] nothing prohibits that one could glory in tomorrow, if he is sure that he will not lose tomorrow what he has today. But because Solomon, enlightened by the Divine Spirit, knew very well that men of themselves do not know what they will do in the future, he thus forbids them to glory in the time to come. Hence Blessed Augustine, in his book concerning the shepherds, reckons as rash judgments those whereby men judge about themselves or others, what sort of things they will do, since they cannot know this. "Everything is full of rash judgments. One we despaired of is suddenly converted and becomes one of the best. One about whom we greatly trusted falls away and becomes one of the worst. Neither is our fear certain, nor is our love certain. What any man is today, the man himself scarcely knows: yet only what he is today. But what he will be tomorrow, not even he himself knows."[3] Again, all those things, whereby Sacred Scripture admonishes us to be cautious regarding the future and to watch over ourselves, fight against the certitude of perseverance. "He that thinketh himself to stand, let him take heed lest he fall" (I Cor. 10, 12). And Solomon says: "Blessed is the man that is always fearful" (Prov. 28, 14). If once a man has been justified he would be sure of his perseverance, it would be unnecessary to admonish him to about caution and fear.

Next, all the sacred Doctors testify in unison that perseverance in good, or one's own predestination, is not known to any man without a special revelation of God, some of whom I have decided to cite as witnesses. Bernard, when discussing the heavenly begetting of the elect, says these words: "But who shall speak of this begetting? Who can say, 'I am one of the elect, one of those predestined to life, I am numbered among the children?' Who can say that, when Scripture says in no uncertain terms, 'Man knoweth not whether he be worthy of love, or hatred' (Eccle. 9, 1). We have not certainty, but confident hope consoles us; otherwise we could be utterly crucified by anxiety and doubt."[4] Bernard, not relying upon his own judgment, but upon the testimony of Sacred Scripture, clearly teaches that no one knows that he will persevere in good, or that he is predestined by God to eternal life.

Blessed Gregory, when interpreting that saying of the Savior, "The Spirit breatheth where he will; and thou hearest his voice, but thou knowest not whence he cometh, and whither he goeth" (Jn. 3, 8), says these words: "The Spirit indeed comes and goes, because he abandons the reprobate, and adopts the elect. And because the judgment of Almighty God is inscrutable, man does not know whence He comes and wither He goes: because it cannot be known whether someone is destined to persevere forever in the grace which he receives. Thus, the

---

[1] *Commentary on Ecclesiastes* (PL 23, 1080B).

[2] Cf. I Cor. 1, 31: "He that glorieth, may glory in the Lord."

[3] *Sermones de Scripturis*, serm. 46 (*De Pastoribus*) on Ez. 34, 1-16, c. 12, n. 27 (PL 38, 285).

[4] Sermons for Septuagesima, serm. 1, n. 1 (PL 183, 163A-B).

Spirit is said to come from him who falls away and to go to him who is going to persevere: because some He abandons in time, yet others He adopts and does not abandon."[1]

Blessed Bishop Salonius, more ancient than Gregory, favors the same opinion, who in his commentary which he made in the form of a dialogue on Ecclesiastes, when interpreting that saying of Solomon: "Who knoweth if the spirit of the children of Adam ascend upward, and if the spirit of the beasts descend downward?" (3, 21), says these words: "The children of Adam signify the saints and the elect, who rightly are called men, because they live reasonably, holily, and spiritually. But by the beasts, carnal men are signified due to the fact that they live bestially and carnally like animals and beasts. For, as a consequence, the holy prophet David says: 'Men and beasts thou wilt preserve, O Lord' (Ps. 35, 7). For it commonly happens that they who seem to be just men, sin, and are turned around from their justice, and work iniquity. On the contrary, those who are bad and wicked, are turned around from their iniquity, and work justice and equity. Hence Solomon says: 'Who knoweth if the spirit of the children of Adam ascend upward, and if the spirit of the beasts descend downward?' Yet the state of this life is uncertain, so that both the sinner who is called a beast, having been converted through penance may rise and ascend into Heaven, and the just man may fall from his justice into sin, and may plunge into Hell."[2]

But Blessed Augustine teaches this opinion much more clearly in many places. For in his letter to Proba, when treating that saying of Paul, "Judge not before the time" (I Cor. 4, 5), says these words: "No one is known to another so intimately as he is known to himself, and yet no one is so well known even to himself that he can be sure as to his own conduct on the morrow."[3] And in *The City of God*, when speaking about just men, he says these words: "These, though they are certain that they shall be rewarded if they persevere, are not certain that they will persevere."[4] And in the book, *On the Gift of Perseverance*, he says these words: "I assert, therefore, that the perseverance by which we persevere in Christ even to the end is the gift of God; and I call the end, that by which this life is finished, and so long as one is in which life, there is peril of falling. Therefore, it is uncertain whether any one has received this gift so long as he is still alive."[5]

Finally, the Council of Trent celebrated under Paul III, in the sixth session, declared by a manifest definition what necessarily ought to be believed about this matter, speaking thus: "No one moreover, so long as he lives in this mortal state, ought so far to presume concerning the secret mystery of Divine predestination, as to decide for certain that he is assuredly in the number of the predestined, as if it were true that he who is justified either cannot sin any more, or if he shall have sinned, that he ought to promise himself an assured reformation. For except by special revelation, it cannot be known whom God has chosen for Himself. So also as regards the gift of perseverance of which it is written: He that 'shall persevere to the end, he shall be saved' (Mt. 10, 22; 24, 13) (which gift cannot be obtained from anyone except from Him, 'who is able to make him, who stands, stand' (Rom. 14, 4), that he may stand perseveringly, and to raise him, who falls), let no one promise himself anything as certain with absolute certitude, although all ought to place and repose a very firm hope in God's help. For God, unless men be wanting in His grace, as He has begun a good work, so will He perfect it, 'working to will and to accomplish' (Phil. 2, 13). Nevertheless, let those 'who that thinketh themselves to stand, let them take heed lest they fall' (I Cor. 10, 12), and 'with fear and trembling work out their salvation' (Phil. 2, 12) in labors, in watchings, in almsdeeds, in prayers

---

[1] *Commentarii in librum I Regum*, bk. 6, c. 3, n. 21 (PL 79, 460A-B).
[2] *Expositio mystica in Ecclesiasten* (PL 53, 1001D-1002A).
[3] Letter 130, c. 2, n. 4 (PL 33, 495).
[4] Bk. 11, c. 12 (PL 41, 328).
[5] C. 1, n. 1 (PL 45, 993-994).

and oblations, in fastings and chastity.[1] For they ought to fear, knowing that they are born again unto the hope of glory,[2] and not as yet unto glory in the combat that yet remains with the flesh, with the world, with the devil, in which they cannot be victors, unless with God's grace they obey the Apostle saying: 'We are debtors, not to the flesh, to live according to the flesh. For if you live according to the flesh, you shall die. But if by the spirit you mortify the deeds of the flesh, you shall live' (Rom. 8, 12 ff.)."[3] And after having given this teaching about predestination and the gift of perseverance, lest anyone henceforth dare to assert something by a rash attempt against it, it decreed a *latae sententiae* canon, and it is expressed in the following words: "If anyone shall say that he will for certain with an absolute and infallible certainty have that great gift of perseverance up to the end, unless he shall have learned this by a special revelation: let him be anathema."[4]

But even if no one without a special revelation of God can know certainly and infallibly that he is predestined, or will persevere in goodness and justice until the end of life, still nothing impedes that by some signs and conjectures one can conjecture that he is among the number of the predestined. For the holy Doctors show us many signs about this matter, strengthened by the testimonies of Sacred Scripture, and they are those which follow: Patience in tribulations, mercy towards the poor and afflicted, humility, contempt of worldly things, abundance of tears especially for the desire of our heavenly home, willing and eager hearing of God's word, and perhaps many other things of the same sort. But although someone may recognize all these things in himself by certain experience, he ought not on that account to be sure and certain about his predestination: because it is possible that those things which he has in himself are not such as he thinks. It can also happen that many of those things are present with mortal sin, as happened to some pagan philosophers, who having been endowed with many virtues of this kind were idolaters.

PRAEDICATIO

Preaching

Among the many errors of which Aeneas Sylvius accuses the Waldensians in chapter thirty-five of his book, *De origine Bohemorum*,[5] there is one whereby they teach that preaching of God's word is permitted to any Christian, such that however much it has been forbidden by a superior, they assert that he can still preach God's word. But Guy the Carmelite, when enumerating the errors of the Waldensians in his *Summa de haeresibus*, never mentions this error. Afterwards John Wycliffe taught the same error. And John Hus followed this man as a disciple following his master. And because later heretics, so they can lay hold of the vainglory which they especially seek, strive to increase the madness of preceding heretics, hence this John Hus, when teaching this assertion of free preaching of God's word, says that he who ceases to preach God's word on account of the superior's prohibition, is by that very fact excommunicated from God.

Blessed Paul condemns this opinion in the Epistle to the Romans, saying: "How shall they preach unless they be sent?" (10, 15). For Paul thinks that no one can justly exercise the office of preaching unless it has been committed to him, and he has been sent to do it. And in the

---

[1] Cf. II Cor. 6, 3 ff.
[2] Cf. I. Pet. 1, 3.
[3] C. 12-13 (Dz. 1540-1541).
[4] Can. 16 (Dz. 826).
[5] P. 59.

Epistle to the Hebrews, he again says: "Neither doth any man take the honour to himself, but he that is called by God, as Aaron was" (5, 4). And although Paul speaks in this passage about priests, still because it is the office of the priest to teach, as is evident from many passages of Paul: wherefore it is not unsuitably said about preaching, that no one of them may take the honor to himself, but he who is called by God as Aaron. Furthermore, the first preachers of the Gospel, whom God chose to go for this, so that their sound might go forth into the whole world,[1] were called by Christ "Apostles," that is to say, "sent,"[2] so that from the meaning of the word anyone might know that no one ought to preach unless he were sent for this. Now one is sent when he is granted faculties for preaching from the superior having the authority.

And the great John the Baptist, than whom "There hath not risen among them that are born of women a greater" (Mt. 11, 11), never dared to preach until the time when he was commanded by God. For Luke speaks thus: "Now in the fifteenth year of the reign of Tiberius Caesar, Pontius Pilate being governor of Judea... the word of the Lord was made unto John, the son of Zachary, in the desert. And he came into all the country about the Jordan, preaching the baptism of penance for the remission of sins" (Lk, 3, 1-3). Theophylactus when interpreting these words says: "Now the word of the Lord was made unto John, so that you may learn that he did not rashly, nor beyond his calling, jump into testifying about Christ, but was moved by the Divine Spirit. By 'word' understand the Holy Ghost, or God's command."[3] And John the Evangelist relates more expressly about the Baptist: "There was a man sent from God," he says, "whose name was John. This man came for a witness, to give testimony of the light, that all men might believe through him" (Jn. 1, 6-7). Behold John the Baptist, who does not dare to give testimony of the light, unless he had firstly been sent from God: and the proud heretics are not afraid to preach contrary to the order of the superior.

Add to these things the example of the Old Law in which this was consistently upheld that none of the holy prophets, such as Elias, Jeremias, Ezechiel, and the like, ever preached to the people, save only after they had been sent by God to do this. Not even Moses himself, who was the leader and lawgiver to the Israeli people, ever dared to explain the Divine commandments to the people, save only God firstly commanded it to him. And for this reason, the pseudoprophets, who by their own will, without God's command, intruded themselves to prophesying, the Lord reprehends through the prophet Jeremias, saying: "I sent them not, neither have I commanded them, nor have I spoken to them: they prophesy unto you a lying vision, and divination and deceit, and the seduction of their own heart" (14, 14). And He says again by the same prophet in another chapter: "I did not send prophets, yet they ran: I have not spoken to them, yet they prophesied" (23, 21). And these are they of whom Christ our Savior spoke when He said: "All others, as many as have come, are thieves and robbers: and the sheep heard them not" (Jn. 10, 8).

Theophylactus when interpreting these words says: "Consider these words carefully. 'As many as have come,' He says, not 'as many as have been sent.' For the prophets indeed came having been sent: the pseudoprophets, however, and those seditious men were so-called, came not having been sent by anyone, and as the Lord said: 'I did not send them, yet they ran.'"[4]

And Bede agrees with this interpretation speaking thus: "They came of themselves, because they were not sent by Him, as the Apostle says: 'How shall they preach unless they be sent?' (Rom. 10, 15). And because they came of themselves, and were not sent by Him, they are thieves and robbers. For before Christ's coming there were false prophets in God's people,

---

[1] Cf. Ps. 18, 5: Rom. 10, 18.
[2] "The word 'Apostle' comes for the Greek ἀποστέλλω (*apostello*) meaning 'to send forth'" ("Apostles," *Catholic Encyclopedia* (New York, Robert Appleton Company, 1907), vol. 1, p. 627).
[3] *Enarratio in Evangelium Sancti Lucae* (PG 123, 735C).
[4] *Enarratio in Evangelium Sancti Joannis* (PG 124, 70A).

just as after His coming there were just as many false teachers under the Christian name: not teachers, but seducers."[1] Thus they who were not sent to preach, but came of themselves, as our Savior says, are thieves and robbers. Thieves, I say, because they took the truth away from the hearers, and afterwards killed their souls, drawing them to their errors and vices by their seductions. No one, therefore, is an apostle, save those who have been sent: no one also is a true preacher, unless the office of preaching has been committed to him.

Hence Blessed Jerome says the following: "Paul wanted to make a clear distinction between himself, as one sent by Christ, and those sent by men, and so he began his epistle, 'Paul, an apostle, not of men, neither by man' (Gal. 1, 1). The word 'apostle,'[2] which means 'one who has been sent'... Hence we can understand why John the Baptist should be called both a prophet and an apostle, given that Scripture says, 'There was a man sent from God, whose name was John' (Jn. 1, 6)... There are four kinds of apostles. The first is the one who is sent 'not of men, neither by man, but by Jesus Christ, and God the Father.' The second is sent by God but through human agency. The third is sent by man but not by God. The fourth kind is sent not by God, nor through human agency, nor by man; he sends himself on his own initiative. To the first category belong Isaias, the rest of the prophets, and the Apostle Paul himself, who are sent not by men nor through human agency but by God the Father and Christ. An example of the second kind of apostle is Josue the son of Nun, who was made an apostle by God but through the man Moses.[3] The third kind is when someone is ordained because of the favor and efforts of men. Today we see a great many appointed to the episcopacy not because God has deemed them worthy but because they have garnered the favor of the common people. The fourth category is comprised of false prophets and false apostles, concerning whom the Apostle says, 'Such false apostles are deceitful workmen, transforming themselves into the apostles of Christ' (II Cor. 11, 13). They claim that the Lord says certain things, but the Lord has not sent them."[4] From whose words it is apparent that one is not called an apostle, but a false apostle, who has neither been chosen by God nor by men, but who intrudes himself, and usurps the office of preaching.

Now if a heretic were to say that he has been sent by God to preach, just as Paul who was made an Apostle neither by man nor through man, but from God: then it is necessary that the heretic show by miracles and signs that he has been sent by God. For Moses in the presence of Pharaoh proved by the splendor of his miracles that he had been sent by God. And when Christ sent the Apostles to preach, he first gave them power over unclean spirits, so that they might cast them out and cure every disease and every sickness. Again, as it is evident from Holy Writ, the preaching of God's word was forbidden even to those knowing it, when some reason compelled for some time and place. Thus, as often as such a reason is present, one will rightfully be impeded from preaching God's word. For the Teacher of truth Himself, when he sent the Apostles to preach, forbade them to go into the way of the Gentiles.[5] Jerome when commenting on Matthew assigns the reason for this prohibition, saying: "It behooved Christ's coming to be announced to the Jews first, lest they should have a valid excuse, and say that they had rejected our Lord because He had sent His Apostles to the Gentiles and Samaritans."[6] Here is one just reason on account of which someone can be justly forbidden not to preach in some place, namely so that by such preaching in that place, one cease to preach to others to whom one is more obliged. For if some pastor of souls having left his own sheep

---

[1] *Expositio In Evangelium S. Ioannis* (PL 92, 764C-D).

[2] In Greek, ἀπόστολος (*apostello*).

[3] Cf. Deut. 34, 9.

[4] *Commentary on Galatians*, bk. 1 (PL 26, 311D-312C).

[5] Cf. Mt. 10, 5.

[6] *Commentary on Matthew*, bk. 1, on Mt. 10, 5 (PL 26, 62B).

to whom he is bound by his office to preach, goes to preach in another place, he can be justly forbidden in that same place so that perhaps having been prohibited in this way hasten back to his own flock.

There can also be another reason for a just prohibition, namely lest God's word preached in some place or at some time be contemned by the hearers. For holy Paul and Timothy were forbidden by the Holy Ghost to speak God's word in Asia: and when they wanted to preach in Bithynia, the Spirit of Jesus suffered them not.[1] And Bede when commenting on the Acts of the Apostles gives the reason for his prohibition, says: "God, Who knows hearts, on account of His kindness, withdrew [His] teacher from Asia lest, if what is holy were given to dogs,[2] the error of their wicked heart might be judged more reprehensible on account of their contempt of his preaching."[3] Thus as often as it is apparent that God's word would be despised by the hearers, then the preaching of God's word can be justly prohibited by the superior. Now it can happen in many ways that God's word is despised. For sometimes it is despised simply on account of the wickedness and hardheartedness of the hearers. Other times also the wickedness of the preacher himself is the reason why God's word is despised. For as Blessed Gregory says, "He whose life is despised, it remains that his preaching be also despised."[4] Wherefore when the wicked life of the preacher is public, then the superior can justly forbid him to preach: nay he does unjustly if he does not forbid him, lest by the occasion of the bad life of the preacher, God's word be held up to scorn. For God said to the sinner: "Why dost thou declare my justices?" (Ps. 49, 16). Sometimes also contempt is procured without the wickedness of the one preaching or the one hearing, but on account of the age of the very one teaching. For young men, in that they are less experienced, are not suited to teaching, but better suited to being taught. Thus, if a boy or young man were to teach, his teaching would be despised by the common people, because the uneducated people would not consider so much what is said, as by whom it is said. Wherefore Christ, Who was born a small child with the greatest wisdom, did not wish to preach before He was thirty years old, as Luke bears witness[5]: and His precursor, John the Baptist, began to preach at the same age: because that is the perfect age in which all the powers of man flourish the most. And for this reason, as far as I know, it happened that the Church decreed that bishops, to whom belongs the duty to preach, are not consecrated before thirty years of age. Thus, those on account of whose young age God's word will probably be contemned, the superior can justly restrict from preaching, lest God's word be exposed to contempt. Hence Blessed Gregory excludes young and immature men from the office of preaching, saying: "They are to be admonished to consider that, if women bring forth their conceived offspring before it is fully formed, they by no means fill houses, but tombs. For hence it is that the Truth Himself, Who could all at once have strengthened whom He would, in order to give an example to His followers that they should not presume to preach while imperfect, after He had fully instructed His disciples concerning the power of preaching, immediately added, 'But stay you in the city till you be endued with power from on high' (Lk. 24, 49)."[6]

A third reason can still be assigned, and the greatest of them all, on account of which the preaching of God's word can, nay ought, to be interdicted to someone by the superior, namely if such a man by his preaching scandalizes the Church and disturbs it. Concerning these men

---

[1] Cf. Acts 16, 6-7.

[2] Cf. Mt. 7, 6.

[3] *Commentary on the Acts of the Apostles*, c. 16 (PL 92, 977D). Cf. St. Gregory the Great, *Homiliae in Evangelia*, hom. 4, n. 1 (PL 76, 1089D).

[4] *Homilies on the Gospels*, Hom. 12, n. 1 (PL 76, 1119A).

[5] Cf. Lk. 3, 23.

[6] *Pastoral Rule*, bk. 3, c. 25 (PL 77, 98B).

Paul the Apostle, when writing to the Galatians, says: "There are some that trouble you, and would pervert the gospel of Christ" (1, 7). And afterwards towards the end of the epistle when giving judgment about such men, he says: "I would they were even cut off, who trouble you" (5, 12). And the Wise Man in the book of Proverbs says: "Cast out the scoffer, and contention shall go out with him" (22, 10). Bede, when interpreting these words in his commentary on Proverbs, says: "Cast out from the Church," he says, "the heretic whom you cannot correct, and when you have taken away from him permission to preach, you give aid to Catholic peace."[1] See that there are many reasons on account of which the preaching of God's word can justly be forbidden to someone. And generally speaking (as we have already shown) we say that no one can rightfully preach unless he has been sent by God or by some man having authority for this, so that no man "take the honour to himself, but he that is called by God, as Aaron was" (Heb. 5, 4). Therefore, Blessed Francis [of Assisi], the founder of the Franciscans, thinking much better than these heretics about the preaching of God's word, commands the following things to his monks in his rule: "Let the friars not preach in the diocese of any bishop, when he has spoken against them. And let no friar at all dare preach to the people, unless he will have been examined by the minister general of this fraternity and approved, and there be conceded to him by the same the office of preaching."[2] Yet heretics since they stand a long way off from the humility of Blessed Francis, are also very far from this ruling of his.

Finally, in the Council of Constance this assertion was condemned. For among the forty-five articles of John Wycliffe, which the Council of Constance condemned in the eighth session, the thirteenth says the following: "Those who cease to preach or to hear the word of God because of the excommunication of men, are themselves excommunicated, and in the judgment of God they will be considered traitors of Christ."[3] And the fourteenth article speaks thus: "It is permissible for any deacon or priest to preach the word of God without the authority of the Apostolic See or a Catholic bishop."[4] Which two articles along with the others of the same John Wycliffe were condemned in the same place with *latae sententiae* [excommunication] upon them all. And in the same council, in the fifteenth session, many articles of John Hus were condemned, among which there are three which support this condemned teaching.[5] Thomas Netter wrote against this heresy in the first volume of his *Doctrinale antiquitatum fidei Catholicae Ecclesiae*.[6] And we also will say more things against it below in the section on the "Priesthood" [*Sacerdotium*], in the first heresy.

---

[1] *Allegorica expositio in Parabolas Salomonis*, bk. 2, c. 22 (PL 91, 1003C).

[2] The *Regula Bullata*, c. 9.

[3] Dz. 593.

[4] Dz. 594.

[5] "17: Priests of Christ, living according to His law and having a knowledge of Scripture and a desire to instruct the people, ought to preach without the impediment of a pretended excommunication. But if the pope or some other prelate orders a priest so disposed not to preach, the subject is not obliged to obey. 18: Anyone who approaches the priesthood receives the duty of a preacher by command, and that command he must execute, without the impediment of a pretended excommunication" (Dz. 643-644). "Likewise, whether he believes that it be freely permitted to individual priests to preach the word of God, wheresoever, and whenever, and to whomsoever it may be pleasing, even though they are not sent" (Questions to be proposed to the Wycliffites and Hussites, n. 38 (Dz. 688)). The text here gives the wrong numbers of these propositions, which has been corrected here.

[6] Bk. 2, a. 3, c. 70-73, pp. 361-376.

PRAESCIENTIA

Foreknowledge

Among the many errors of which Guy the Carmelite accuses the Albanenses, there is one pertaining to this matter. For they say that "God does not foreknow of Himself any evil thing, but through His adversary, namely the devil."[1] About what evil they mean, however, Guy did not indicate. For Sacred Scripture teaches that evil is twofold. For there is the evil which is called sin or guilt: and this is the most well-known evil. There is also the evil which is called punishment, about which God, speaking through Isaias the prophet, says: "I am the Lord, and there is none else: I form the light, and create darkness, I make peace, and create evil" (45, 6-7). He here calls war evil, not because it is evil in itself, but because it is a misfortune to them who undergo war. Jonas the prophet speaks of both, who when describing how the Ninivites did penance upon his preaching, says: "And God saw their works, that they were turned from their evil way: and God had mercy with regard to the evil which he had said that he would do to them, and he did it not" (3, 10). In which place it is evident that a twofold wickedness is designated. For when he said, "they were turned from their evil way," he indicated the evil of guilt. But when saying, "God had mercy with regard to the evil which he had said that he would do to them," he clearly meant the evil of punishment.

Now concerning which evil the Albanenses think that God does not know, Guy did not indicate. Yet about whatever evil they speak, it is evident that their opinion is heretical, and blasphemous towards God. Concerning both evils there is a very clear testimony which God Himself said to Moses when He sent him to Pharaoh. "But I know," He says, "that the king of Egypt will not let you go, but by a mighty hand: and I will stretch forth my hand and will strike Egypt with all my wonders which I will do in the midst of them" (Ex. 3, 19-20). In which words He foretold the sin of the king, and the plagues with which he and his people were going to be struck. Thus, God foreknew both evils. Concerning the evil of guilt that which John says is very clear: "For Jesus knew from the beginning, who they were that did not believe, and who he was, that would betray him" (Jn. 6, 65). You see here that from the beginning Christ foreknew Judas' betrayal, which was not a light sin.

Concerning the evil of punishment there are so many predictions of the prophets, whereby they foretold evils to the people, that it is unnecessary to relate them, but that suffices for refuting this heresy which Luke the Evangelist, when speaking about Christ our Savior, says: "If thou also hadst known, and that in this thy day, the things that are to thy peace; but now they are hidden from thy eyes. For the days shall come upon thee, and thy enemies shall cast a trench about thee, and compass thee round, and straiten thee on every side, and beat thee flat to the ground, and thy children who are in thee: and they shall not leave in thee a stone upon a stone: because thou hast not known the time of thy visitation" (19, 42-44). Notice how many afflictions, which are evils, Christ foretold, Who described events which afterwards happened.

Now that which the Albanenses say, that God foreknew evils through His adversary, namely the devil, is such a clear blasphemy that we disdain to dispute against it. For "What concord hath Christ with Belial?" (II Cor. 6, 15). "Who hath been his counsellor? Or who hath first given to him, and recompense shall be made him?" (Rom. 11, 34-35). And it is written in Job: "Shall anyone teach God knowledge, who judgeth those that are high?" (21, 22). These men are worse than the Pharisees who reproached Christ that "He casteth out devils by Beelzebub,

---

[1] C. 8, fol. 78v, lns. 79-80.

the prince of devils" (Lk. 11, 15). But Christ did not put up with this, much less then would He have tolerated the Albanenses if they had said that by the devil teaching God would foreknow something. It is unnecessary that we spend time in overthrowing so plain a blasphemy, because I do not think that there is any baptized person into whom this idea could insinuate itself. For although Guy accuses the Albanenses of this, still I do not know whether I trust him on this point.

PROPHETA

Prophets

There is a rather wicked heresy about this matter, which when it detracts the prophets, it blasphemes God. For Apelles said that the prophets were inspired by an opposing spirit, and hence they said contradictory things. Wherefore he was saying that prophecies are false, and that there is no truth in them, in that they refute (as he says) themselves and are self-contradictory. Thus, because Apelles was finding in the prophecies some things which on the surface seemed to contradict, which he did not know how to reconcile, he was not afraid to accuse the prophets of lying. And since he taught that the prophecies are self-contradicting, and that contradictory things could not be from the same principle, so that he could support this error more easily, he fell into another, worse error, saying that there are two principles of things, from which two principles, diverse or divided between themselves, he said the prophecies were inspired, so that they said contradictory things. These things are taken from Eusebius [of Caesarea] in his *Church History*.[1]

Although this heresy involves two errors at the same time, only one ought to be discussed now. For that there is only one principle, we already proved in the section on "God," in the first heresy. For in that place we showed God's unity from Holy Writ against Apelles and other heretics. There remains that we repel the other error of this heresy, whereby it is taught that the prophets taught false things, and contradicted each other among themselves. For who doubts that it is a supreme blasphemy to accuse God of lying? But he who says that the prophets taught false things, pass that falsity on to God, Who inspired the prophets to speak as they did. For God spoke (as Zachary says in Luke) "by the mouth of his holy prophets, who are from the beginning" (1, 70). And the Royal Prophet bears witness that his "tongue is the pen of a scrivener that writeth swiftly" (Ps. 44, 2), by this epithet designating the Holy Ghost, Whose grace (as Ambrose says) "knows no tardy efforts."[2] Now no one is so insane that he would accuse the falsity of a writing to the pen, and not rather to the writer who moved the pen. If then God is the writer, and the prophet the pen, those things which He taught the prophet should rather be attributed to God than to the prophet: whereby it will happen that if a prophet taught false things, as Apelles says, God ought to be accused of falsity, and not the prophet. Far be it that someone would fall into such a great blasphemy, that he would presume to call God a liar. Furthermore, Blessed Paul, in the Epistle to the Hebrews, says: "God, who, at sundry times and in divers manners, spoke in times past to the fathers by the prophets, last of all..." (1, 1). Here you see Paul asserting that God spoke by the mouth of the prophets. And Blessed Peter says: "For prophecy came not by the will of man at any time: but the holy men of God spoke, inspired by the Holy Ghost" (II Pet. 1, 21). And it is unnecessary that we dispute more against such a clear blasphemy.

---

[1] Bk. 5, c. 13 (PG 459B-462B).

[2] *Expositio Evangelii secundum Lucam*, bk. 2 on Lk. 1, 39 (PL 15, 1560A).

PROPHETA

The **second heresy** teaches that the prophets were delirious, not understanding those things about which they were speaking. The author of this heresy was Montanus, whom afterwards Priscillian followed on this point. For Bernard of Luxemburg in his *Catalogus haereticorum* accuses him of this.[1] For not in the writings of any other author who wrote about heresies do I find that Priscillian was branded concerning this matter. Not does Bernard of Luxemburg himself say by whose testimony he relies for attributing this to Priscillian.

This heresy is very clearly refuted by that which is contained in the First Book of Kings: "For he that is now called a prophet, in time past was called a seer" (9, 9). If a prophet is a seer, how can it happen that he is not also understanding? For so great is the knowledge which the prophets have about those things which they prophesize, that it is close to that knowledge which by common usage they call "intuitive": and for this reason the prophets are called "seers," and their prophecies are called "visions." Accordingly, Isaias calls his prophecy by this name, saying: "The vision of Isaias the son of Amos" (1, 1). And the prophet Ezechiel speaks the same way, saying: "I saw the visions of God" (1, 1). And the prophecy of Nahum the prophet has such a beginning: "The book of the vision of Nahum" (1, 1). And concerning this vision of the prophets it is said in Daniel: "There is need of understanding in a vision" (10, 1). Wherefore it is that he who does not understand the things which he says ought not to be called a prophet, even though he were to say some prophecy. For "after death Eliseus' body prophesied" (Eccli. 48, 14), as Ecclesiasticus relates about it[2]: yet no one having a sound mind will say that that dead body was a prophet. Furthermore, if the prophets were delirious, not understanding what they were saying, it ought to be confessed that their prophecies were not from God, because (as it is written in Job) "The inspiration of the Almighty giveth understanding" (32, 8). From which words it is clearly proved that if the prophets were not understanding, they were also not inspired by God. but if they were inspired by God, it is necessary that they were also understanding, because "The inspiration of the Almighty giveth understanding." Next, Blessed Paul in the First Epistle to the Corinthians very clearly teaches that the prophets were understanding. For him alone, Blessed Paul reckons, ought to be called a prophet, who those things which he speaks he know how to interpret and explain for the benefit and edification of the hearers. For he speaks thus: "He that prophesieth, speaketh to men unto edification, and exhortation, and comfort. He that speaketh in a tongue, edifieth himself: but he that prophesieth, edifieth the church. And I would have you all to speak with tongues, but rather to prophesy. For greater is he that prophesieth, than he that speaketh with tongues: unless perhaps he interpret, that the church may receive edification" (14, 3-5). Notice that you see that a man is called by Paul a prophet, who is able to interpret the things which he says, for the edification of the Church. But it cannot happen that he who is the interpreter is not understanding. Add to these things that Sacred Scripture very clearly testifies concerning some prophets that they understood those things which they prophesied. Hence about Daniel the prophet it is said that God gave to him the understanding of all visions and dreams.[3] And the prophet Ezechiel, when describing the vision whereby he saw Cherubim moving together with wheels, says, "I understood that they were cherubims" (Ez. 10, 20). The prophet bears witness that he understood, and Montanus and Priscillian do not hesitate to say they did not understand. Therefore, it is more reasonable that we believe that those heretics were delirious, and stirred up by the devil: the prophets, however, whom God inspired, understood very well those things which they prophesied: to such an extent that on account of the excellent knowledge, almost a direct perception, which they had, they are called "seers."

---

[1] Bk. 2, fol. 66r.

[2] Cf. IV Kings 13, 21.

[3] Cf. Dan. 1, 17.

PURGATORIUM

Purgatory

One of the most well-known errors of the Greeks and Armenians is that whereby they teach that Purgatory is not a place in which souls that have passed away from this world are purified from the stains which they contracted when alive, before they deserve to be received in the eternal tabernacle. The Waldensians imitated the Greeks and Armenians on this point. John Wycliffe, however, even though elsewhere he always accepts and upholds the errors of the Waldensians, on this matter, nevertheless, is not blamed by anyone except Brother Bernard of Luxemburg, who, in a certain small work on Purgatory which he added at the end of the *Catalogus haereticorum*, accuses John Wycliffe and John Hus of this error. Yet the Council of Constance in which both were condemned, did not brand either one of them with this error. And Thomas Netter who very diligently investigated all the errors of John Wycliffe, never mentions this error in order to accuse him. Nevertheless, I would easily believe that John Hus so thought, that he would have taught that there is no Purgatory fire, because the Bohemians who were seduced by this John Hus, pertinaciously have maintained this error (as it is said) until now. Finally, Luther in this century of ours, although he acknowledges Purgatory, still he denies that is can be shown [to exist] from Holy Writ. Regarding which matter I am astounded how he has forgotten his own opinion whereby he teaches that nothing ought to be believed which cannot be clearly gathered from Holy Writ. If Holy Writ does not teach [the existence of] Purgatory, why, Luther, do you believe it? Or what reason do you give to someone asking you a reason of that faith which is in you? For Peter the Apostle commanded that we be ready always to satisfy everyone that asks the reason of that faith which is in us.[1] For if you believe something which cannot be confirmed by any quotation of Sacred Scripture, you will deservedly be judged inconsistent according to your opinion, especially since according to your teaching the Church can only force someone to believe those things which are expressed in Sacred Scripture. Thus, lest we be judged inconsistent as Luther, when believing that Purgatory is after this life, we ought to give a reason of that faith which is in us.

Firstly, therefore, this ought to be very clear, that in the beatitude to come there is no spot, and also there is no filth. For Isaias the prophet clearly bears witness to this, saying: "It shall be called the holy way: the unclean shall not pass over it" (35, 8). John in the Apocalypse agrees with him: "There shall not enter," he says, "into it anything defiled" (21, 27). For that holy city is the spouse, whom, according to Paul, Christ her Spouse sanctified, "cleansing it by the laver of water in the word of life: that he might present it to himself a glorious church, not having spot or wrinkle, or any such thing" (Eph. 5, 26-27). For then alone will it be fulfilled that the Church has no spot or wrinkle when she shall be blessed, not however in this life, in which we ought to say daily when praying: "Forgive us our debts" (Mt. 6, 12). For Augustine bears witness about that sole spouse, that she is without spot, in his book, *The City of God*,[2] and in his book, *De haeresibus ad Quodvultdeus*.[3] And Blessed Jerome in his

---

[1] Cf. I Pet. 3, 15.
[2] "[The Church] shall then be purged by the last judgment, as a threshing-floor by a winnowing wind, and those of her members who need it being cleansed by fire" (Bk. 20, c. 25 (PL 41, 700)).
[3] "[The Pelagians] go to such lengths as to say that the life of the just in this world is absolutely without sin, and that through them the Church of Christ is brought to perfection in this mortality so that she is absolutely without spot or wrinkle" (C. 88 (PL 42, 48)).

PURGATORIUM

Commentary on Jeremias teaches the same thing.[1] From these testimonies therefore we prove that it will be necessary that no soul, which has some spot or wrinkle, may enter into celestial glory before it has been cleansed from such a spot.

Or there are many souls who when departing from this world have many wrinkles of venial sins, which they never cleansed while they lived here. Now such souls do not go down to Hell, because no one dying with charity is perpetually damned on account of venial sins alone. Nor do they ascend to glory, because they have not yet been cleansed from the wrinkles of venial sins. Therefore, it is necessary to grant that there is a third place in which those souls are taken until they have been cleansed like gold in a furnace, so that having been purified in this way they can enter into the holy city of Jerusalem, into which nothing defiled enters.[2]

Furthermore, we taught above in the section on "Penance," that after sin has been forgiven there remains some punishment to be endured as a punishment for sin, so that in some way the sinner may satisfy God for the debt for which the sinner is held accountable. Thus, if someone dies after sins have been forgiven for which he has not yet satisfied, one ought to ask these heretics wither does such a soul go when it is be first separated from the body? It is certainly unfair and unbefitting to the Divine mercy that it would go down to Hell on account of sins which have already been forgiven him. And it is unjust that it would enter celestial glory, since it has not yet satisfied for its sins, nor paid off the just punishments for them. For just as no good deed goes unrewarded, so there is no evil deed which ought not to be punished: now an evil deed would have been without punishment if someone after his sins have been forgiven, for which he was not punished in this life, would immediately after death enter into glory.

And certainly (unless I am mistaken) even if there were no testimony of Sacred Scripture for proving Purgatory: from these two argumentations which we have now brought forth, it can be very clearly proved. But so that the truth of the faith may appear clearer to all, it is necessary that we bring forth some testimonies of Scripture. In Isaias we read that "The Lord shall wash away the filth of the daughters of Sion, and shall wash away the blood of Jerusalem out of the midst thereof, by the spirit of judgment, and by the spirit of burning" (4, 4).

And Malachias the prophet says: "Behold he cometh, saith the Lord of hosts. And who shall be able to think of the day of his coming? and who shall stand to see him? for he is like a refining fire, and like the fuller's herb: and he shall sit refining and cleansing the silver, and he shall purify the sons of Levi, and shall refine them as gold, and as silver, and they shall offer sacrifices to the Lord in justice" (3, 1-3). From which words it is clearly enough gathered that there are some Purgatorial pains in which souls are purged. But if someone perhaps would say that those words of Malachias ought to be understood of that purgation which happens on Judgment Day, in which the good will be purged by the fact that they will be separated from the wicked: the words Malachias himself show that this is not so, whereby he says: "He shall refine them as gold, and as silver, and they shall offer sacrifices to the Lord in justice. And the sacrifice of Juda and of Jerusalem shall please the Lord" (v. 3-4). By which words the prophet teaches that those who will be cleansed, shall offer sacrifices of justice to the Lord, that is to say, themselves now justified. For then they will be victims most pleasing to God. And lest someone be surprised that we have interpreted these words of the fire of Purgatory, let him read Blessed Augustine in the twentieth book of *The City of God*, chapter twenty-five.[3] For in that place it is clear that he likewise thinks that the Purgatorial punishments after this life can be proved by these two testimonies.

---

[1] "And see how the Apostolic saying, 'that she might be without spot or wrinkle' (Eph. 5, 27), is reserved for the future and celestial realm" (Bk. 6, c. 31 (PL 24, 922A)).

[2] Cf. Apoc. 21, 27.

[3] "From these words it more evidently appears that some shall in the Last Judgment suffer some kind of Purgatorial punishments..." (PL 41, 700).

Again, the Teacher of truth Himself, in Matthew, says: "Whosoever shall speak a word against the Son of man, it shall be forgiven him: but he that shall speak against the Holy Ghost, it shall not be forgiven him, neither in this world, nor in the world to come" (12, 32). By which words He clearly insinuates that there are some faults which are forgiven in the other world. For if no faults are forgiven in the other world, why was it necessary to add, "nor in the world to come"? For it was enough to say that it shall not be forgiven him in this world. But since no word was said by Christ idly or in vain, it is thence proved that that clause was added due to the fact that some faults in this world are completely forgiven: others, namely venial sins, are forgiven in the other world, when one did not satisfy for them in this world. Blessed Gregory uses this testimony for proving Purgatory in the fourth book of the *Dialogues*, chapter thirty-nine.[1] Blessed Bernard uses the same quotation against certain heretics who were calling themselves the Apostolics, denying Purgatory.[2]

Finally, after Paul had said that Christ is the foundation, He immediately adds: "Now if any man build upon this foundation, gold, silver, precious stones, wood, hay, stubble: every man's work shall be manifest; for the day of the Lord shall declare it, because it shall be revealed in fire; and the fire shall try every man's work, of what sort it is. If any man's work abide, which he hath built thereupon, he shall receive a reward. If any man's work burn, he shall suffer loss; but he himself shall be saved, yet so as by fire" (I Cor. 3, 12-15). From which word the Purgatorial fire is inferred clearly enough. For what he says, "If any man's work burn, he shall suffer loss," cannot be understood of mortal sin not yet forgiven in this life, because he immediately subjoins, "but he himself shall be saved." But those who are in Hell, will never be saved. Thus, there is another place in which the souls suffer loss, and are afterwards saved. That place we call the Purgatorial fire. But if someone granting the place of Purgatory, denies that there is fire in it, but saying that the loss which the souls suffer is only the privation of the Divine vision, let him direct his attention to what Paul says: "If any man's work burn,' he says, 'he shall suffer loss; but he himself shall be saved, yet so as by fire." Notice that you now hear in what he who is to be saved suffers loss.

But lest someone accuse us that we have misinterpreted this passage, distorting it in a way other than is befitting, I will cite two or three very renown interpreters of Sacred Scripture, whom I have followed on this point. And firstly I bring to the fore Origen, who, when treating this passage of Paul, after he had said that by wood, hay and stubble ought to be understood threefold way of evil, says the following: "He who is saved, therefore, is saved through fire so that if he has, by chance, any lead mixed in himself, the fire may melt it away and separate it, that all may be made good gold because 'the gold of that land,' which the saints are to have, is said 'to be good.'[3] And just as a furnace tests gold, so temptation tests just men.[4] All, therefore, must come to the fire; all must come to the melting furnace, for the Lord sits and melts

---

[1] "But yet we must believe that before Judgment Day there is a Purgatorial fire for certain small sins: because our Savior saith, that he who shall speak blasphemy against the Holy Ghost, it shall not be forgiven him, neither in this world, nor in the world to come (cf. Mt. 12, 31-32). Out of which sentence we learn, that some sins are forgiven in this world, and some others may be pardoned in the next: for that which is denied concerning one sin, is consequently understood to be granted touching some others." (PL 77, 396A-B).

[2] "Let them, therefore, demand of Him Who has declared that there is a certain sin, which 'shall not be forgiven him, neither in this world, nor in the world to come,' let them ask Him, I say, why He spoke thus, since, as they believe, there can be no remission or purgation of sin in the next life" (*Sermons on the Canticle of Canticles*, serm. 66, n. 11 (PL 183, 1100A)).

[3] Cf. Gen. 2, 12.

[4] Cf. Prov. 27, 21; I Cor. 3, 12-13.

down and purifies the sons of Levi.[1] But when one comes to that place, if he brings many good works and very little iniquity, that little is separated by fire like lead and is purified and the whole is left pure gold. And if someone brings more lead to that place, more is burned away, so that he is diminished to a greater extent, so that even if there is very little gold, it may be left purified nevertheless. But if someone should come to that place totally lead, this which has been written will happen to him: He will sink in the depth like lead in very deep water."[2]

Blessed Augustine, in his *Enchiridion*[3] addressed to Laurentius, after he had expounded this passage of Paul as referring to the fire of tribulation in this life, speaks thus: "It is a matter that may be inquired into, and either ascertained or left doubtful, whether some believers shall pass through a kind of purgatorial fire, and in proportion as they have loved with more or less devotion the goods that perish, be less or more quickly delivered from it. This cannot, however, be the case of any of those of whom it is said, that they 'shall not possess the kingdom of God' (I Cor. 6, 10), unless after suitable repentance their sins be forgiven them."[4] And [Pseudo-Augustine] treats this passage of Paul at much greater length and interprets it of the fire of Purgatory [in his one hundred and fourth sermon].[5]

Blessed Jerome near the end of the eighteenth book of his *Commentary on Isaias*, says the following: "As we believe the torments of the devil, and of all that deny the faith, and of those wicked men who have said in their heart, 'There is no God,'[6] to be eternal: so for those who are sinners and wicked, but yet Christians, whose works are to be tried and purged in the fire, we believe that the sentence of the Judge shall be moderate, and mixed with clemency."[7] Blessed Gregory in the fourth book of the *Dialogues*, also cites this passage of Paul for proving the Purgatorial fire.[8]

Add to all these things this custom of the universal Church derived from the Apostles, and preserved until these times, whereby the priest in the celebration of Mass prays to God for the dead, and offers sacrifice to God for them. Now he does not pray for those who already peacefully enjoy God, because they do not need our prayers, nor can they also be helped by them in any way. And also he does not pray for those who are in Hell, because he would pray in vain, since there is no redemption in Hell.[9] Therefore we have proved that he only prays for those who are in Purgatory. And this ancient custom of the Church is of such great weight for proving Purgatory, that even if the testimony of Scripture were lacking for proving it, this

---

[1] Cf. Mal. 3, 3.

[2] Cf. Ex. 15, 10. *Homilies on Exodus*, hom. 6, n. 4 (PG 12, 334C-335A).

[3] This work is also titled, *On Faith, Hope and Charity*.

[4] C. 69 (PL 40, 265).

[5] The citation here is to "the fourth sermon on the Commemoration of [All] Souls, which is found among the sermons on the Saints." St. John Fisher (*Assertionis lutheranae confutatio*, fol. 340 r) gives the same when also dealing with Purgatory. But those words are taken from [Pseudo-] St. Augustine's Sermon 104, n. 1 (PL 39, 1946)).

[6] Cf. Ps. 13, 1; 52, 1.

[7] On Is. 65, 24 (PL 24, 678B).

[8] "For although these words may be understood of the fire of tribulation, which men suffer in this world: yet if any will interpret them of the fire of Purgatory, which shall be in the next life: then must he carefully consider, that the Apostle said not that he may be saved by fire, that buildeth upon this foundation iron, brass, or lead, that is, the greater sort of sins, and therefore more hard, and consequently not remissible in that place: but wood, hay, stubble, that is, little and very light sins, which the fire doth easily consume. Yet we have here further to consider, that none can be there purged, no, not for the least sins that be, unless in his lifetime he deserved by virtuous works to find such favor in that place" (C. 39 (PL 77, 369C-D)).

[9] The phrase comes from a responsory of the Office of the Dead, in the third Nocturn of Matins.

alone would suffice according to Augustine's opinion. For in the book, *On Care to be Had For the Dead*, after he had shown from Sacred Scriptures that the suffrages benefit the dead which are performed after their death, speaks thus: "Howbeit even if it were nowhere at all read in the Old Scriptures, not small is the authority, which in this usage is clear, of the whole Church, namely, that in the prayers of the priest which are offered to the Lord God at His altar, the commendation of the dead has also its place."[1] Thus all those testimonies which prove that the suffrages, which are done for the dead after their death, can benefit them, also prove and very clearly show [the existence of] Purgatory, because only those who are in Purgatory can be helped by our prayers or other suffrages. Wherefore we send the reader to that place, namely to the section on "Suffrages," so that in that place they may obtain those testimonies which are lacking here. For in that place we will cite the decree of the Synod of Carthage, which very clearly serviceable for this matter,

Finally, the Council of Florence celebrated under Eugene IV, to which the Greeks with their Constantinopolitan emperor and the Constantinopolitan patriarch were invited, decreed a suitable judgment about this matter, to which the Greeks also consented, containing these words: "It has likewise defined, that, if those truly penitent have departed in the love of God, before they have made satisfaction by the worthy fruits of penance for sins of commission and omission, the souls of these are cleansed after death by purgatorial punishments."[2] There was also published by the Greeks themselves present at the same Council a certain book for proving the place of Purgatory, in which the souls are purged which did not fully satisfy for their sins in this life, which book was produced in Basel in Greek and Latin type.[3] John Eck wrote about this matter a lengthy book divided into four books.[4]

There is a **second heresy** whereby it is taught that the souls present in Purgatory are not outside the state of meriting or demeriting. The author of this heresy is Luther, teaching that souls in Purgatory can still merit or demerit.[5]

The Wise Man clearly condemns this insane heresy of Luther, who in Ecclesiastes says: "Whatsoever thy hand is able to do, do it earnestly: for neither work, nor reason, nor wisdom, nor knowledge shall be in hell, whither thou art hastening" (9, 10). For he does not say that those things are completely not in Hell, because the holy Patriarchs were in Hell [i.e. Limbo]

---

[1] C. 1, n 3 (PL 40, 593).

[2] Dz. 693.

[3] The author here seems to be referring here to a book published by the Protestant Martin Crusius entitled, *Responsio Graecorurn ad positionem Latinorum, opinionem ignis purgatorii fundantium et probantium, quae lecta et data fuit reverendissimis et reverendis Patribus et dominis deputatis die sabbati 13 mensis iunii 1438, in sacristia Fratrum Minorum, Basileae, praesentata Nicolao Cusano*. This book was published in Basel in 1555 under the title: *Orthodoxographa theologiae sacrosanctae ac syncerioris fidei doctores numero LXXVI* [a Is. Heroldo collecta], in-folio. In it is contained a work that was put on the Index of Forbidden Books in 1835 entitled, *Apologia Graecorum de purgatorio igne in concilio Basileensi exhibita, nunc quam primum a Joanne Hartungo latinitate donate*. Clearly, this book does not give a reliable account of the Greek's views as presented at the Council of Florence. A reliable source of these views may be found in the two orations of Archbishop Marc of Ephesus at the said council which may be found the article *Documents relatifs au Concile de Florence…, La question du purgatoire à Ferrare : documents I-VI / textes éd. et trad. par… Mgr. Louis Petit* (Paris, 1920), published in *Patrologia Orientalis*, vol. 15, fasc. 1, n. 72, pp. 39 ff. In the introduction of Mgr. Petit's article, he shows that the above-mentioned booklet was artificially created from Latin into Greek, and Lutheran theology was put into mouths of the Greeks well before the Reformation.

[4] *De purgatorio Iohan. Eckii contra Ludderum: libri IV* (Rome, Marcellus Franck, 1523).

[5] "Furthermore, it does not seem proved, either by reason or by Scripture, that souls in purgatory are outside the state of merit, that is, unable to grow in love." (*95 Theses of Martin Luther*, n. 18 (WA 1, 234)).

at that time, in which there was still reason and wisdom: but the reason why he says that these things are not in Hell is because they can no longer be helped by them, so that they could merit. And again, he says more clearly: "If the tree fall to the south, or to the north, in what place soever it shall fall, there shall it be" (11, 3). Jerome, when interpreting these words in his *Commentary on Ecclesiastes*, speaks thus: "A tree, if in this life it falls and is cut in its state of mortality, either must sin before while it stands and is then placed in the north afterwards, or if it brings forth worthy fruit by the south wind, it will fall down by a southern stroke... And they are not able to advance if they remain in their former places."[1] From whose words it is evident that it is the opinion of the Wise Man that no one can merit or demerit after this life.

Furthermore, our Savior in John's Gospel says: "I must work the works of him that sent me, whilst it is day: the night cometh, when no man can work" (9, 4). In which words one ought to note that He did not say: "The night cometh, when I cannot work"; but He says, so that it may be perceived that He speaks universally: "The night cometh, when no man can work," calling death "night," after which work may not be done. Augustine when treating this passage says the following: "Let man, then, work while he lives, that he may not be overtaken by that night when no man can work. It is now that faith is working by love; and if now we are working, then this is the day—Christ is here. Hear His promise, and think Him not absent. It is Himself who has said, 'Behold, I am with you' (Mt. 28, 20)."[2] And Blessed Chrysostom interprets those words in the same way. For in his fifty-sixth homily on John, he speaks thus: "For He means to say this: 'While it is day,' while men may believe in Me, while this life lasts, 'I must work.' 'The night cometh,' that is, the future time, 'when no man can work.' He said not, 'when I cannot work,' but, 'when no man can work'... Christ calls the future time 'night,' when sinners cannot perform any works."[3] And Blessed Jerome in his commentaries on the Epistle to the Galatians, when expounding the words of the same epistle: "Whilst we have time, let us work good..." (6, 10), interprets those word of Christ in the same way. For he says the following: "As we have said, there is a time for sowing, and that time is now and the life whose course we are running. While we are in this life, we are allowed to sow whatever we want, but when this life passes away, the time for doing work is taken away. Hence the Savior says, 'Work whilst it is day: the night cometh, when no man can work.'"[4] Origen who interprets those words of Christ in the same way, speaks thus: "'The night cometh, when no man can work.' And He says this about that time which will be after this lifetime, in which everyone will receive punishments. Hence, He accordingly calls that future time 'death,' since at that time no one can do any works, but everyone is then treated according to the works which he performed while in this world."[5] Behold four illustrious interpreters of Sacred Scripture who all concordantly think that that night in which, according to the Savior's words, no one can work, is the time after death. Thus, let the prudent reader consider whether it is more correct to assent to Luther alone in the interpretation of Sacred Scripture, than to so many very distinguished men by whose teaching the Church shines like the sun and the moon.

Again, Blessed Paul in the Second Epistle to the Corinthians clearly teaches this same thing, speaking thus: "We must all be manifested before the judgment seat of Christ, that everyone may receive the proper things of the body, according as he hath done (*propria corporis prout gessit*), whether it be good or evil" (5, 10). See that according to Paul no one receives other than according to the proportion of those things which he did when alive in his body: thus after the souls have laid aside their bodies, they cannot merit anything further. Now in

---

[1] On Eccle. 11, 3 (PL 23, 1102C-D).
[2] *Tractates on the Gospel of John*, tract. 44, n. 6 (PL 35, 1716).
[3] N. 2-3 (PG 308-309).
[4] Bk. 3 (PL 26, 432B-C).
[5] Hom. 3 on Ps. 36, 8 (12, 1346A-B).

order that Paul's opinion in this passage may appear more clearly, it will be worthwhile to see how Erasmus of Rotterdam translated this passage. For his translation is as follows: "For we must all appear before the judgment seat of Christ that every man may receive the works of his body according as he hath done (*fiunt per corpus*) whether it be good or evil." This wording is closer to the Greek version, in this wise also it sets forth Paul's meaning, and the Catholic faith, more plainly and clearly, whereby it is believed that after death there is not the time for meriting and demeriting.

And in the Epistle to the Galatians the Apostle likewise says: "And in doing good, let us not fail. For in due time we shall reap, not failing. Therefore, whilst we have time, let us work good to all men" (6, 9-10). Theophylactus, when expounding this passage, says: "Just as it is not always the time for sowing, so neither for reaping: the [wise and foolish] virgins[1] and [poor] Lazarus[2] indicate this. Thus, as long as time remains unto us in the life, let us do good, that is to say, works of beneficence and almsgiving, not merely to rulers and teachers, but also to pagans and Jews." From whose words it is plain that the time which we have for performing good deeds is the time of this life, and not the time after death, because "Praise perisheth from the dead as nothing" (Eccli. 17, 26).

Bishop John [Fisher] of Rochester wrote against this error, in the thirty-eighth article in that work which he made for the assertion of the condemnation of certain articles of Luther, made by Leo X.[3] Jacques Masson, also wrote [against this heresy] in that work which he published for the assertion of the censure of Louvain against Luther.[4] But I have not seen others if they exist.

The **third heresy** was also invented by Luther, and is deduced from the preceding heresy. For from that error whereby he teaches that souls in Purgatory can merit and demerit, he concludes that they are not sure of their salvation: and in this way he draws corrupt and putrid water from a vitiated source.

Wherefore having overthrown the preceding heresy, which is the foundation of this one, this one can nowise stand, without it immediately falling. For if the souls which are purged can neither merit nor demerit, and this cannot be unknown to them, it is proved that they are sure of their own salvation. There is no soul which is purged unless it is founded on Christ. And because upon this foundation it built wood, hay and stubble, that is, certain light and venial sins, hence it suffers loss, so that according to Paul's opinion, he "shall be saved, yet so as by fire" (I Cor. 3, 15). If the soul which is purged has charity, and it cannot now lose it (as we showed in the preceding heresy); therefore it is sure of its salvation. For charity is a certain assurance of the Spirit, and a sort of pledge of eternal happiness, by which the Spirit "giveth testimony to our spirit, that we are the sons of God. And if sons, heirs also; heirs indeed of God, and joint heirs with Christ" (Rom. 8, 16-17). From which things it manifestly appears that every soul which is purged, since it then knows that it is in charity, is certain and secure of its salvation.

Furthermore, it ought to be believed that all souls before they are cast into Purgatory, are firstly examined regarding their deeds and words, and after the examination of those things has been made, they are sent to Purgatory. Otherwise, it would be preposterous if they would first undergo punishments, and afterwards be brought forth for examination, so that a judgment may be made about them. Therefore, it is necessary that after having firstly been examined they render an account, and fully acknowledge both their merits and demerits, and

---

[1] Cf. Mt. 25, 1-13.

[2] Cf. Lk. 16, 19-31.

[3] *Assertionis Lutheranae confutatio* (Paris, Apud Petrum Drouart, 1545), fol. 421v-428v.

[4] *Articulorum doctrinae fratris M. Lutheri per theologos Lovanienses damnatorum ratio ex sacris literis et veteribus tractatoribus* (Antwerp, 1521).

afterwards the sentence be pronounced to them. From which order of judgment, it is proved that all souls which are sent to Purgatory are certain and sure about their salvation, because they know from the sentence pronounced upon them, that as soon as they shall be purged, they will be admitted into heavenly glory. Again, one ought to ask Luther whether he certainly believes that the souls which are purged are then out of danger or not. If he does not believe that they are out of danger, then Purgatory, according to him, will be like the present life a kind of trial, warfare, and contest in which he who runs or does combat is uncertain about victory. But from Job's opinion it is established that the life of man upon (*super*) earth is a warfare or trial.[1] But if man's life beneath (*subtus*) the earth is a warfare, he added without reason "upon earth", when he spoke about man's life. On the other hand, if Luther certainly believes that the souls which are purged are out of danger, how is the soul itself which is purged unaware of this? Has it forgotten by its death those things which it knew before? If we ourselves are sure that the souls that are in Purgatory are now in safety: much more will the souls themselves be sure about their salvation, since in them there is the same faith, hope and charity, and in them also the corruptible body does not weigh down the soul, nor do their minds go a-begging for knowledge of invisible things from visible things, but rather they clearly behold themselves laid bare.

But here perhaps someone could object to us those words which the Church sings in the prayers which it pours out before God for the deceased: "From the gate of hell deliver their souls, O Lord"[2]: and these words: "O Lord Jesus Christ, King of glory, deliver the souls of all the faithful departed from the pains of hell and from the bottomless pit; deliver them out of the lion's mouth, lest hell should swallow them up…"[3] If the souls are sure of their salvation it would be superfluous to pray for them to be delivered from hell, for whom, even if the Church would not pray for them, they could not now descend [into hell].

Let us reply following Bede's opinion, that the place of Purgatory is very close to Hell, and on account of this closeness, and on account of the very great likeness and similarity of punishments of both places, the place of Purgatory is sometimes called by the name of Hell. Now this can also be inferred from the fact that the place in which the Patriarchs were before Christ's death, which place in the Gospel is called Abraham's bosom,[4] is repeatedly called by the name of Hell, and by the name of the pit: while nevertheless in that place the souls were treated more gently than in Purgatory. The Royal Prophet says: "God will redeem my soul from the hand of hell" (Ps. 48, 16). And again: "Thou hast delivered my soul out of the lower hell" (Ps. 85, 13). And it is certain that the [Royal] Prophet did not descend to that place of punishments in which were the damned. And the prophet Zacharias says: "Thou by the blood of thy testament hast sent forth thy prisoners out of the pit, wherein is no water" (9, 11). By which words denoting the deliverance of souls made by Christ, he called the place in which the souls of holy men were, "the pit, wherein is no water." Hence all the more could the place of Purgatory, in which the souls endure very bitter punishments, be called hell and the pit. And the Church prays that the souls be freed from this place and its punishments.

We can reply otherwise, and perhaps better, saying that it is not always doubted about the things which are asked for, whether they shall so happen as is asked. For very often those things are asked for which are certainly known will take place as they are asked to occur: and there are very many testimonies of this thing. For Ecclesiasticus when praying to God says the following: "Reward them that patiently wait for thee, that thy prophets may be found faithful" (36, 18). Yet no one in his right mind will say that Ecclesiasticus doubted about

---

[1] Cf. Job 7, 1.

[2] Versicle and response taken from Office of the Dead.

[3] Offertory of the Requiem Mass.

[4] Cf. Lk. 16, 22.

the fidelity of the prophets of God, or doubted that God would give a reward to those who patiently wait for Him, which nevertheless He asked for. Paul was certain that he would not be separated from the charity of God: he was also certain that a crown of justice was prepared by God the just Judge for him: yet he prayed to God that he would merit to attain it.[1] And if his predestination was known to him, nonetheless he should have prayed to God for the fulfilment of his predestination: "that by good works (according the Apostle Peter's opinion) he may make sure his calling" (II Pet. 1, 10). In this way also the Church, although she certainly knows that the souls that are in Purgatory would not be condemned to Hell, nevertheless ceases not to pray for their deliverance.

Bishop John [Fisher] of Rochester writes against this heresy in the same place in which he writes against the aforesaid heresy.[2]

Luther also devised the **fourth heresy**, whereby he teaches that souls sin without intermission in Purgatory, as long as they seek rest, and dread the punishments, because they seek (as he says) things which are contrary to God's will.

And certainly if the matter were as Luther teaches, purging the souls would be nothing other than to wash a brick[3] and to plow the sea-shore.[4] For if the souls which are cleansed, sin without intermission as long as they dread the punishments; since they dread the punishments at all times, because the dread of punishments is implanted by nature in all men; it follows that they sin at all times, and consequently on account of those sins they will need to be cleansed again. And since they will also dread the purgation of those sins, it follows that they will then sin again, and that it will be necessary from them to be purged again from those sins. And so it would be the same immeasurably without end.

Furthermore, above in the assault on the second heresy about Purgatory, we showed from Holy Writ that no one after death can either merit or sin, by a sin in fact which ought to be imputed to him: thus the souls which are purged, although they dread the punishments, still they do not sin. Again, even if the souls in Purgatory could sin, nevertheless by the fact that they seek rest, and dread punishments, they do not sin. For David did not sin when he said: "My soul hath thirsted after the strong living God; when shall I come and appear before the face of God?" (Ps. 41, 3). Paul also, the vessel of election, says: "I desire to be dissolved and to be with Christ" (Phil. 1, 23). If these men did not sin in desiring rest, why will the souls in Purgatory sin when desiring rest?

And regarding the dread of punishments it is evident that it is not a sin, since this does not come by choice, but from nature, since it is implanted by nature to dread punishments. For Christ soon before His Passion (as Mark says) "began to fear and to be heavy. And he saith to them: My soul is sorrowful even unto death" (14, 33-34). But Christ both never sinned and could not think a sinful thought: therefore, it is not a sin to dread punishments and vexations, especially when it is not by choice, but from a certain natural horror.

---

[1] Cf. II Tim. 4, 8.

[2] *Assertionis Lutheranae confutatio*, art. 38, fol. 421v-428v.

[3] *Laterem lavare*, i.e. πλίνθον πλύνειν, i.e. to wash the color out of a brick, to labor in vain. Cf. Terence, *Phormio*, Act 1, scene 4, ln. 8.

[4] *Litus arare*, i.e. to labor in vain and take useless pains. Cf. Ovid, *Tristia*, bk. 5, poem 4, ln.48.

REGNUM DEI

Kingdom of God

There was a certain error of Cerinthus concerning this matter, saying that Christ's kingdom would be an earthly kingdom after the Resurrection, and in that kingdom there would be the pleasures of the flesh: because he was saying that the kingdom would last a thousand years in this life. But we have already disputed about this error above in the third book in the section on "Beatitude," in the second heresy. And if there are other heresies which pertain to this matter, they have been put by us in that section.

RELIQUIAE SANCTORUM

Relics of the Saints

The Wycliffites, who seem to have been born for removing every Ecclesiastical rite, for eliminating all ceremonies from the Church, among their other blasphemies teach this one, namely, "that the relics of the saints, that is the flesh and bones of dead men, ought neither to be venerated by the people, nor taken from a stinking tomb, nor reposited in a golden or silver case: because those so doing (as they say) do not honor God and His saints, but commit idolatry."[1] The wicked Lollards followed these Wycliffites, one of whom was an Englishman named William White, who was not ashamed to confess all these things publicly and in a judicial tribunal in England. But these men are not the first inventors of this heresy. For nearly [nine hundred[2]] years before them was Vigilantius, a certain Gaul, a priest of the church of Barcelona,[3] who (as we will say below) said that one may not pray to the saints. And so that he might detract the saints more, in whose lot he was not to be reckoned,[4] he taught that the bodies of the saints ought not to be venerated. But neither was this Vigilantius the first author of this heresy, because before him was Eunomius: yet he did not precede him by a long time. Now Jerome testifies concerning Eunomius that he was infected with this pestilence. For in the tract which he wrote against Vigilantius, he says these words: "Do you laugh at the relics of the martyrs, and in company with Eunomius, the father of this heresy, slander the Churches of Christ?"[5] But there is this difference between Vigilantius and the Wycliffites, namely that Vigilantius hated solely the veneration of the saints, but the Wycliffites, being more pestilential than this Vigilantius, just as they do not suffer the relics of the saints to be venerated, so neither do they deem the relics of Christ our Savior to be worthy of any adoration.

Concerning the point that Christ's relics ought to be adored I say nothing now, because above in the section on "Adoration," in the first heresy I fought against the same Wycliffites

---

[1] These words are found in the list of errors abjured by some of William White's disciples (*Heresy trials in the diocese of Norwich, 1428-31* (London, Offices of the Royal Historical Society, 1977), p. 95). Cf. Thomas Netter, *De sacramentalibus* (Venice, typis Antonii Bassanesii ad S. Cantiacum, 1759), c. 128, col. 789B. White was a priest from Kent, who attempted marriage and was executed for heresy in 1428.
[2] The text mistakenly here has "ninety."
[3] Cf. Gennadius, *De Scriptoribus Ecclesiasticis*, c. 35 (PL 58, 1078B).
[4] Cf. Wis. 5, 5.
[5] *Against Vigilantius*, n. 8 (PL 23, 347A).

in favor of the adoration of the Lord's Cross: in which place we said not a little in passing concerning Christ's garments and other things associated with Christ. For what we said in that same place concerning the Lord's Cross, can also likewise be said concerning everything associated to Christ, for example His garments, the sword, if someone were to have it, the table on which He ate, the towel with which He dried His hands, and whatever similar things sanctified by contact with His vivifying Flesh. Because (as Blessed [John] Damascene says) "If of those things which we love, house and couch and garment, are to be longed after, how much the rather should we long after that which belonged to God, our Savior, by means of which we are in truth saved?"[1] For Blessed Jerome reckons that it ought to be so done, who testifies that he did this, saying the following: "I made my way to Egypt. I saw the monasteries of Nitria, and perceived the snakes which lurked among the choirs of the monks. Then making haste I at once returned to Bethlehem, which is now my home, and there poured my perfume upon the manger and cradle of the Savior."[2] And in his epitaph to Paula, he praises that holy Paula, because she adored the crib in which Christ laid when just born, and the sepulcher in which He laid when dead.[3] And it is enough about this.

Let us go on the relics of the saints, and let us show that they are worthy of some veneration, although of not as much as the relics of Christ: because their souls, on account of which we venerate their other things, are not also worthy of such great veneration, as Christ, on account of Whom also, and not on account of themselves, are those things which are associated with Christ adored. Therefore let us go through each thing which is shown veneration in the saints. The first testimony, therefore, of the veneration of the saints is that churches are built in their honor by the institution of the Church: and the Church anathematizes those who teach that this ought not to be done. For the Synod of Gangra speaks thus: "If anyone shall, from a presumptuous disposition, condemn and abhor the assemblies [in honor] of the martyrs, or the services performed there, and the commemoration of them, let him be anathema."[4]

Concerning that the bodies of the saints ought to be honorably buried, it is an ancient rite of the Church practiced from the times of the Apostles until the present time. For Blessed Dionysius the [Pseudo-] Areopagite, the disciple of Paul the Apostle, writes in this manner about this matter: "When the high priest has finished these things, he places the body in a splendid house, with other holy bodies of the same rank. For if, in soul and body, the man fallen asleep passed a life dear to God, there will be honored, with the devout soul, the body also, which contended with it throughout the devout struggles. Hence the Divine justice gives to it, together with its own body, the retributive inheritances, as companion and participator in the devout, or the contrary, life. Wherefore, the Divine institution of sacred rites bequeaths the supremely Divine participations to them both—to the soul, indeed, in pure contemplation and in science of the things being done, and to the body, by sanctifying the whole man, as in a figure with the most Divine ointment, and the most holy symbols of the supremely Divine communion, sanctifying the whole man, and intimating, by purifications of the whole man, that his resurrection will be most complete."[5]

In which words Blessed Dionysius clearly enough indicated that the bodies of the saints are placed in a splendid house: and he says the reason on account of which it ought to so done, namely, because those bodies of the saints cooperated with their souls to do good, and were certain instruments of the souls whereby they performed many things for God's honor and their salvation. Yet these things were said about those whose merits shone brightly in life, or

---

[1] *De fide orthodoxa*, bk. 4, chap. 11 (PG 94, 1131A).

[2] *Apology Against Rufinus*, bk. 3, n. 22 (PL 23, 473C).

[3] Letter 108, n. 9-10 (PL 22, 884).

[4] Canon 20 (PL 67, 60A).

[5] *Ecclesiastical Hierarchy*, c. 7, sect. 9 (PG 3, 582C-D).

who ended their life by martyrdom. For the bodies of these men merited veneration immediately after death, and hence he says that they are put in an honorable house by the high priest. But regarding the others whose life was not manifest by the working of miracles, and for this reason their bodies are not then put in an honorable place, if after death, God so willing, their outstanding merits are rather made known to the world, their bodies are transferred to a more honorable place, and deserve greater honor.

As a confirmation of which matter, besides the very old custom of the Church, which is of very great weight, are also the testimonies of very many holy men, which teach that it ought to be done, and praise it when it has been done. And it is befitting to put the examples of the Fathers of the Old Testament before all, so that the wicked Wycliffites may know that this rite of transferring the bodies of the saints was not recently instituted. For the body of the Patriarch Jacob was translated from Egypt into the land of Chanaan over against Mambre, and was buried there with great veneration of his children, and of the ancients of Egypt.[1] And this was not done by chance, but Jacob himself, when he was in Egypt, before he died, commanded this to be so done, saying: "I am now going to be gathered to my people: bury me with my fathers in the double cave, which is in the field of Ephron the Hethite, over against Mambre in the land of Chanaan, which Abraham bought together with the field of Ephron the Hethite for a possession to bury in" (Gen. 49, 29-30). And also the holy Patriarch Joseph himself likewise being in Egypt: when he was near to death, said to his brethren: "God will visit you, carry my bones with you out of this place" (50, 24). Afterwards, mindful of this precept, Moses with the people of God he brought out of Egypt, took Joseph's bones with them. Let Wycliffe now go out, and call both the children of Israel, namely Joseph and his brethren, and Moses and others, idolaters, due to the fact that they bestowed this honor upon the bones of Jacob and Joseph.

I continue on to the saints of the New Testament, of whose bodies so many translations were made that it would be exceedingly burdensome to relate a hundredth part of them. Wherefore I will relate one or two. Regarding Gervasius and Protasius, whose bodies were nearly unknown to all, and hence had been buried in less decent graves, Blessed Ambrose, to whom their bodies were revealed, when writing says these words: "[The clergy] were bidden to clear away the earth from the spot before the chancel screen of Saints Felix and Nabor. I found the fitting signs, and on bringing in some on whom hands were to be laid, the power of the holy martyrs became so manifest, that even while I was still silent, one was seized and thrown prostrate at the holy burial-place. We found two men of marvelous stature, such as those of ancient days. All the bones were perfect, and there was much blood. During the whole of those two days there was an enormous concourse of people. We quickly arranged the whole in order, and as evening was now coming on transferred them to the basilica of Fausta, where watch was kept during the night, and some received the laying on of hands. On the following day we translated the relics to the basilica called the Ambrosian. During the translation a blind man was healed."[2] What do the Wycliffites say to these things? Perhaps also they are not ashamed to condemn Ambrose, since he transferred the bodies of these holy martyrs to a more honorable and splendid place. But how will they be able to blame that translation, which God willed to confirm with such a great miracle, namely that at that moment of time in which those bodies were transferred, a blind man received sight?

But if they deny this to be true, and they distrust Ambrose, even though he is holy, as an only witness, I will produce another witness, not merely an auricular witness, but an eyewitness, Blessed Augustine: so that in the mouth of two this truth may be confirmed.[3] For Blessed

---

[1] Cf. Gen. 50, 13.

[2] Letter 22, n. 2 (PL 16, 1019B-1020A).

[3] Cf. Deut. 19, 15.

Augustine speaks thus: "The miracle which was wrought at Milan when we were there, and by which a blind man was restored to sight, could come to the knowledge of many; for not only is the city a large one, but also the emperor was there at the time, and the occurrence was witnessed by an immense concourse of people that had gathered to the bodies of the martyrs Protasius and Gervasius, which had long lain concealed and unknown, but were now made known to Bishop Ambrose in a dream, and discovered by him. By virtue of these remains the darkness of that blind man was scattered, and he saw the light of day."[1]

I will put forth another example of this matter declared to us by [Pseudo-] Pope and martyr Saint Cornelius, who transferred the bodies of Saints Peter and Paul into various places. For he himself testifies that he did this, who in a certain letter of his speaks thus: "Wherefore I ask you to give thanks with us: because at the request of a certain devout woman and very noble matron Lucina, the bodies of Peter and Paul were brought up out of the catacombs: and firstly in fact the body of Blessed Paul was brought up in silence, and it was placed in the estate of the aforesaid matron on the Ostian Way, close to the spot where he had been beheaded. But afterwards we received the body of Blessed Peter, Prince of the Apostles, and becomingly we put it near the place where he was crucified, among the bodies of the holy bishops, in the shrine of Apollo, on the Mons Aureus, in the Vatican, by the palace of Nero, on the third day before the calends of July [June 29], praying to God and our Lord Jesus Christ that by His interceding holy Apostles, He may cleanse the stains of your sins, and keep you in His will during the days of your life, and as a fruit of your good works render you persevering."[2] Pope and martyr Cornelius' life and works done by him, having undergone martyrdom for Christ, greatly commend these words.

And to put an end to this dispute, I bring forth Augustine in testimony of this matter. For he says these words about honoring the bodies of the saints: "Nevertheless the bodies of the dead are not on this account to be despised and left unburied; least of all the bodies of the just and faithful, which have been used by the Holy Ghost as His organs and instruments for all good works. For if the clothing of a father, or his ring, or anything he wore, be precious to his children, in proportion to the love they bore him, with how much more reason ought we to care for the bodies of those we love, which they wore far more closely and intimately than any clothing! For the body is not an extraneous ornament or aid, but a part of man's very nature. And therefore, the funeral rites of just men of ancient times were carefully attended to, the earthly remains were honored, and sepulchers provided for them, and obsequies celebrated; and burial foreseen; and they themselves, while yet alive, gave commandment to their sons that their bodies were to be buried or transferred."[3] And the saint likewise commends a certain widow mother and her virgin daughter on account of the remains of the martyr Stephen which they brought away with them, saying the following: "These ladies carry with them relics of the most blessed and glorious martyr Stephen: your Holiness knows how to give due honor to these, as we have done."[4] Blessed Augustine bears witness the he had honored the relics of Saint Stephen: and he exhorts others to do it. And in the *City of God*, he recounts very many miracles which it pleased God to do before the body of that saint on account of his merits.[5]

Therefore, what will they bellow against the testimonies of so many saints, and detract to the veneration of the saints? But they say: The bodies are dead, and they do not perceive as do their souls, wherefore it is not allowed to venerate them, or show them any honor. O mighty argument! Perhaps they do not remember that Christ our Savior said to the Sadducees when

---

[1] *City of God*, bk. 22, c. 8, n. 2 (PL 41, 761).
[2] Letter 1 (PL 3, 842A).
[3] *City of God*, bk. 1, c. 13 (PL 41, 27).
[4] Letter 212 (PL 33, 965).
[5] Bk. 22, c. 8, n. 10-22 (PL 41, 766-769).

they were denying the resurrection: "The God of Abraham, and the God of Isaac, and the God of Jacob is not the God of the dead, but of the living" (Mt. 22, 32). Thus, the saints live to God, on account of Whom they bore hunger, thirst, and other hardships and torments of the body. Let it be granted that their bodies do not live to the Wycliffites, nevertheless they live to God: in Whose sight are everything that their bodies bore for God.

Let it also be granted that they nowise are alive: are they then deserving of no honor? The ark of the covenant was not perceiving neither the tablets, nor that manna, nor the pot concealed within; it was not perceiving the rod, nay the rod was not living which blossomed of old. And yet to these things great honor was given long ago, to such an extent that to no one besides the priest was allowed to touch the ark. And when David brought it forth from the house of Obededom, he girded with a linen ephod, and the whole house of Israel brought it with joyful shouting, and with sound of trumpet. "And David danced with all his might before the Lord" (II Kings 6, 14). And again: "And when the ark of the Lord was come into the city of David, Michol the daughter of Saul, looking out through a window, saw king David leaping and dancing before the Lord" (v. 16). And when Michol reprehended him for this reason, David replied: "Before the Lord, who chose me rather than thy father, and than all his house, and commanded me to be ruler over the people of the Lord in Israel, I will both play and make myself meaner than I have done" (v. 21-22). You see how much worship David showed to the ark of the Lord: because it was a kind of sign representing God, when nevertheless it was not living nor perceiving. In this manner we ought to venerate the bodies of the saints, even though they do neither live nor perceive: but because they were closely joined to the souls of the saints, and according to Paul's opinion they were dwellings and temples of the Holy Ghost.[1] But perhaps the Wycliffites are not ashamed to reprehend David on this account. And I would not be surprised if they tried: for those who are not afraid to rebuke all the saints and the whole Church, it will not be surprising if they try also to make David guilty at the same time with the other saints on this account.

But it is necessary that we clear ourselves from the idolatry of which they accuse us. For they deem all those who venerate the bodies of the saints and their relics to be idolaters, because (as they say) they give Divine honors to creatures. I do not wish to respond to the objection of this kind, because Augustine responds better than I. For he refutes this objection saying the following: "But to our martyrs we build, not temples as if they were gods, but monuments as to dead men whose spirits live with God. Neither do we erect altars at these monuments that we may sacrifice to the martyrs, but to the one God of the martyrs and of ourselves; and in this sacrifice they are named in their own place and rank as men of God who conquered the world by confessing Him, but they are not invoked by the sacrificing priest. For it is to God, not to them, he sacrifices, though he sacrifices at their monument; for he is God's priest, not theirs. The sacrifice itself, too, is the body of Christ, which is not offered to them, because they themselves are that body."[2]

In which words besides the main point, I decided to point out in passing that he says that Christ's Body is the sacrifice which is offered by the priest on the altar to God. Which testimony clearly fights against Luther and Oecolampadius. For Oecolampadius (as we indicated in the section on the "Eucharist) denies that in the sacrifice the true Body of Christ is contained, but merely material bread. Luther, however, even though he admits that the true Body of Christ the Savior is there, still denies that it is offered by the priest: wherefore he says that the Mass is not a sacrifice. But against this heresy I think that I have already spoken abundantly above in the section on the "Mass." Yet because what Augustine now said ought not to have been passed by, I decided to point it out in passing. Thus, after having interjected these words,

---

[1] Cf. II Cor. 6, 16.
[2] *City of God*, bk. 22, c. 10 (PL 41, 772).

regarding the point from which we digressed,[1] let us recall the oration, and let us rejoice that Blessed Augustine refuted so easily and brilliantly the calumny of the adversaries.

But because he answered too leniently and very meekly according to his temperament, and these men against whom we are dealing, as "Phrygians (as it is said in the Proverb) are only made better by beating,"[2] I present Blessed Jerome, who is accustomed to fight harder and more sharply: so that he may treat them as they deserve. For that Blessed Father, when writing against Vigilantius, who also was the author of this error, speaks thus: "Madman, who at any time has adored the martyrs? Who ever thought man was God? Did not Paul and Barnabas, when the people of Lycaonia thought them to be Jupiter and Mercury, and would have offered sacrifices to them, rend their clothes and declare they were men?[3] Not that they were not better than Jupiter and Mercury, who were but men long ago dead, but because, under the mistaken ideas of the Gentiles, the honor due to God was being paid to them. And we read the same respecting Peter, who, when Cornelius wished to adore him, raised him by the hand, and said, 'Arise, I myself also am a man' (Acts 10, 26). And have you the audacity to say that you worship, I do not know what, that which you carry about in a little vessel? I want to know what that thing is which I do not know. Tell us more clearly (that there may be no restraint on your blasphemy) what you mean by the phrase a bit of powder wrapped up in a costly cloth in a tiny vessel. It is nothing less than the relics of the martyrs which he is vexed to see covered with a costly veil, and not bound up with rags or haircloth, or thrown in a sewer, so that drunken and sleeping Vigilantius may be worshipped alone. Are we therefore guilty of sacrilege when we enter the basilicas of the Apostles? Was the Emperor Constantius [I] guilty of sacrilege when he transferred the sacred relics of Andrew, Luke, and Timothy to Constantinople? In their presence the demons cry out, and the devils who dwell in Vigilantius confess that they feel the influence of the saints. And at the present day is the Emperor Arcadius guilty of sacrilege, who after so long a time has conveyed the bones of the Blessed Samuel from Judea to Thrace? Are all the bishops to be considered not only sacrilegious, but silly into the bargain, because they carried that most worthless thing, dust and ashes, wrapped in silk in golden vessel? Are the people of all the churches fools, because they went to meet the sacred relics, and welcomed them with as much joy as if they beheld a living prophet in the midst of them, so that there was one great swarm of people from Palestine to Chalcedon with one voice re-echoing the praises of Christ?"[4] Jerome is not content to repel Vigilantius' calumnies, unless he pierces him and treats him as he deserves.

But so that no place for controversy may lie open, I will bring to the fore a definition of a general council. For the Lateran Council celebrated under Innocent III issued the definition which follows: "Since, because certain ones expose the relics of saints for sale and exhibit them at random, the Christian religion has often suffered detraction; so that it may not suffer detraction in the future, we have ordered by the present decree that from now on ancient relics may by no means be exhibited or exposed for sale outside a case. Moreover let no one presume that newly found relics be venerated publicly, unless first they have been approved by the authority of the Roman Pontiff."[5] Which words are found in the book of the *Decretal Letters* in the title, "Concerning Relics and the Veneration of the Saints."[6] In which words,

---

[1] Cicero is paraphrased here. "Let us return to the point we digressed from [*Eo unde huc digressi sumus revertamur*]" (Cicero, *De natura deorum*, bk. 3, sect. 60).

[2] *Phrygem plagis fieri solera meliorem.* (Cicero, *Pro Flacco*, c. 27, sect. 65). The name of "Phrygian" was long a synonym for "slave."

[3] Cf. Acts 14, 11-14.

[4] *Against Vigilantius*, n. 5 (PL 23, 343A-C).

[5] Dz. 440.

[6] Gregory IX, *Decretales*, bk. III, tit. 45, c. 2.

just as it wisely takes care lest new relics be honored, unless they have been firstly approved by authority of the Roman pontiff: so on the contrary it allows those which have already been authenticated to be honored. And I reckon that I have amply spoken about this matter, in view of that brevity which I promised to keep.

Jerome wrote a tract against this heresy, *Against Vigilantius*, in which place it is testified that Tertullian himself wrote a famous treatise which he called, *Scorpiacum*, against this heresy, which long ago broke out against the Church, and he relates that it was formerly called "the heresy of Cain."[1] Hence it is evident that Eunomius also was not the inventor of this heresy, but it had existed long before him, which sleeping for a long time, afterwards by Eunomius, then by Vigilantius, was finally raised up by John Wycliffe. Thomas Netter also wrote against this heresy in that famous work which he made, *De sacramentalibus*.[2]

RESTITUTIO
Restitution

There is a certain heresy asserting that the restitution of a thing taken by theft is not necessary, such that one could attain eternal life. Guy the Carmelites lists this heresy among the others of the other errors of the Greeks, who says that the priests of the Greeks, for thefts, usury, and clear robbery, do not enjoin that they make satisfaction or give back, but instead anoint the robber with simple oil, whom they oblige to give some portion of the money to themselves, so that they may impart absolution to him: when receiving which money from the thief or robber, they absolve that robber.[3]

Erasmus of Rotterdam gave no small reason for suspicion about this matter. For in his *Annotations on the New Testament*, he suggests that restitution for robbery ought not to be done, but it is enough to give alms, so that the sin of theft or robbery may be forgiven. And lest anyone distrust my words, thinking that I falsely accuse Erasmus about this, I will cite his words which are found in the fourth edition of this work. For when this Erasmus in the annotations on the second chapter of Luke discusses that saying of the Savior: "That which remaineth, give alms" (11, 41): after many words he lastly says: "It ought to be observed that just after having mentioned 'rapine' (v. 39), he does not mention of restitution to be done: he merely promises that when alms are given everything becomes clean."[4] The prudent and impartial reader will easily understand what these words teach. But he removed this suspicion in the fifth edition of this same work, because after those words which we have just cited, he added these words which follow: "But he who is entreated to give to those he owes nothing, is much more entreated to give to him he owes something."[5] Which words completely remove all suspicion about restitution not needing to be done. Yet I wanted to warn the reader about this matter, lest if perhaps he come upon the third or fourth edition of that work, when reading Erasmus' words which are found there, relying upon his authority he would fall into this error. For in those words which are found in the fourth edition, he had given a great occasion for

---

[1] "[Tertullian] wrote a famous treatise which he called most correctly *Scorpiacum*, because, as the scorpion bends itself like a bow to inflict its wound, so what was formerly called the heresy of Cain pours poison into the body of the Church" (*Against Vigilantius*, n. 8 (PL 23, 347B)).

[2] *Doctrinale antiquitatum fidei Catholicae Ecclesiae*, v. 2 (*De Sacramentalibus*), tit. 13, c. 117-121.

[3] *Summa de haeresibus et earum confutationibus*, f. 25r-v, c. 17.

[4] *In Novum Testamentum Annotationes* (Basel, Inclyta Rauracorum, 1527), p. 182.

[5] *In Novum Testamentum Annotationes* (Basel, Froben, 1535), p. 191.

error, on account of which he wanted to remedy this evil. If only he had this mind regarding his other errors.

But now let us go out to do battle against the error of the Greeks, and let us show how foreign this opinion is from the Catholic faith. Firstly, this opinion is clearly opposed to the Natural Law, which says: "See thou never do to another what thou wouldst hate to have done to thee by another" (Tob. 4, 16). And again: "Thou shalt love thy neighbour as thyself" (Mt. 19, 19; 22, 39). But it is rare that a man would not hate to be despoiled of his own goods. And anyone can justly wish that what has been taken from him by stealth be restored: thus, that which one has despoiled of someone by force, he will conversely be obliged to give back. Furthermore, Paul the Apostle commanded this, saying the following: "Render therefore to all men their dues. Tribute, to whom tribute is due: custom, to whom custom: fear, to whom fear: honour, to whom honour. Owe no man anything, but to love one another" (Rom. 13, 7-8). In which words after he ordered that debts are to be paid back to all, lest perhaps it might seem they he had said little by a single precept, he added a prohibition which is a stronger and perpetual obligation, saying: "Owe no man anything."

Next, the renowned holy Tobias when he heard bleating of the kid which his wife had brought home, he said: "Take heed, lest perhaps it be stolen: restore ye it to its owners, for it is not lawful for us either to eat or to touch anything that cometh by theft" (Tob. 2, 21). Again, God Himself requires of him who does true penance that he restore what has been stolen, if he wants to ask for the forgiveness of his sins, saying the following: "If I shall say to the wicked: Thou shalt surely die: and he do penance for his sin, and do judgment and justice, and if that wicked man restore the pledge, and render what he had robbed, and walk in the commandments of life, and do no unjust thing: he shall surely live, and shall not die" (Ez. 33, 14-15). Nothing could be said more clearly than this testimony. For by this law and condition God promises that he will forgive sins to the penitent, if he shall give back what he had robbed. Hence it is that when the condition has not been fulfilled, that is to say, when what he had robbed has not been rendered, God does not forgive sins.

Augustine, in a letter to Macedonius, says: "If the property of another on account of which the sin was committed is not returned, though it can be returned, one does not do penance but only pretends to. But if one truly does penance, the sin is not forgiven unless the stolen property is returned."[1] Which words are found in the book of the *Decretals*.[2] Therefore, let the priests of the Greeks be afraid to set free thieves and robbers from what they have robbed, whom God does not want to set free without restitution. For about these priests the prophet Jeremias seems to me to have spoken, when he says: "They healed the breach of the daughter of my people disgracefully, saying: Peace, peace: and there was no peace" (6, 14); with ignominy he heals the breach of the daughter of the people, who easily grants absolution to one sinning and not legitimately repentant. And it is unnecessary to spend more time in front of such a pestiferous error.

---

[1] Letter 153, c. 6, n. 20 (PL 33, 662).

[2] Gratian, *Concordia discordantium canonum*, causa 14, q. 6 (PL 187, 966A).

RESURRECTIO

Resurrection

Many of the old heretics denied that there would be a resurrection of the body. Which heresy firstly arose among the Jews. For the Sadducees (as appears in the Gospel of Matthew[1]) denied the resurrection of the body. Among those, however, who once put on Christ through Baptism, the first who revived this heresy was Simon the Magician, about whom there is mention in the Acts of the Apostles.[2] For Augustine accuses him of this,[3] although [Pseudo-] Tertullian when speaking about this Simon in his book on heresies,[4] does not accuse him of any such thing. Yet he says that Basilides fell into this error,[5] whom Augustine does not accuse of a similar error.[6] Hymeneus and Philetus, the Apostle Paul bearing witness, said "that the resurrection is past already" (II Tim. 2, 18), and would not happen again. Valentinus and Apelles, according to Augustine[7] and [Pseudo-] Tertullian,[8] thought this same thing. [Pseudo-] Tertullian[9] accuses Marcion and Ophites of this same thing, but Augustine does not.[10] Augustine accuses Marcus,[11] Cerdo,[12] the Cainites,[13] the Severians,[14] the Archontics,[15] and the Hieracites[16] of the same error, but Tertullian does not. Bishop Philastrius of Brescia reproaches the Seleucians[17] and the Proclinianites[18] for this error, whom Augustine also follows regarding this.[19] Brother Bernard of Luxemburg in his *Catalogus haereticorum* relates that Amaury [of Bène or of Chartres],[20] the Albigensians,[21] and the Albanenses[22] upheld this error. Concerning Origen, Augustine relates from the opinion of Epiphanius that he denied the resurrection of the body.[23] But Bishop Theophilus of Alexandria (as we will soon say below) accuses Origen of another error, which is as it were diametrically opposed to this one, because from it is proved that Origen had assented to the resurrection of the body. Now

---

[1] Cf. Mt. 22, 23.
[2] Cf. Acts 8, 9.
[3] *De Haeresibus ad Quodvultdeum*, c. 1 (PL 42, 25).
[4] *Against All Heresies*, c. 1 (PL 2, 61B-62C).
[5] *Ibid.* (PL 2, 63A).
[6] *De Haeresibus ad Quodvultdeum*, c. 4 (PL 42, 26).
[7] *Ibid.*, c. 11 & 23 (PL 42, 28 & 29).
[8] *Against All Heresies*, c. 4 & 5 (PL 2, 69B & 70C).
[9] *Ibid.*, c. 2 & 6 (PL 2, 65A & 70C).
[10] *De Haeresibus ad Quodvultdeum*, c. 17 & 22 (PL 42, 28 & 29).
[11] *Ibid.*, c. 14 (PL 42, 28).
[12] *Ibid.*, c. 21 (PL 42, 29).
[13] *Ibid.*, c. 18 (PL 42, 29).
[14] *Ibid.*, c. 24 (PL 42, 30).
[15] *Ibid.*, c. 20 (PL 42, 29).
[16] *Ibid.*, c. 47 (PL 42, 39).
[17] *Liber de haeresibus*, c. 55 (PL 12, 1170A).
[18] *Liber de haeresibus*, c. 56 (PL 12, 1171A).
[19] *De Haeresibus ad Quodvultdeum*, c. 59-60 (PL 42, 42).
[20] Fol. 21v.
[21] Fol. 22v.
[22] Fol. 23r.
[23] *De Haeresibus ad Quodvultdeum*, c. 43 (PL 42, 33).

which of these two ought to be believed, namely Ephiphanius or Theophilus, I do not see. Actually, in my opinion, neither of them is to be believed, because either both or neither ought to be believed. Now it is impossible that both be believed, since their testimonies against Origen do not agree, but instead contradict each other: thus it is necessary that neither be believed, especially since it is evident from book ten of the *Historia Tripartita* of Cassiodorus, that both, namely Epiphanius and Theophilus, were hostile to the name of Origen.[1]

It is not difficult to dispute against this heresy, since there are very evident and very clear testimonies of Sacred Scripture whereby it can be refuted, especially because we are now armed not against heathen philosophers, but against those who boast that they are Christians, who ought to believe the testimonies of Sacred Scripture. For when the Sadducees were denying the resurrection, our Savior proved it with the testimony of Sacred Scripture, saying: "You err, not knowing the Scriptures, nor the power of God. For in the resurrection, they shall neither marry nor be married; but shall be as the angels of God in heaven. And concerning the resurrection of the dead, have you not read that which was spoken by God, saying to you: I am the God of Abraham, and the God of Isaac, and the God of Jacob?[2] He is not the God of the dead, but of the living" (Mt. 22, 29-32). And Paul the Apostle, in the First Epistle to the Corinthians, when rebuking those who deny the resurrection of the body, speaks thus: "Now if Christ be preached, that he arose again from the dead, how do some among you say that there is no resurrection of the dead? But if there be no resurrection of the dead, then Christ is not risen again. And if Christ be not risen again, then is our preaching vain, and your faith is also vain. Yea, and we are found false witnesses of God: because we have given testimony against God, that he hath raised up Christ; whom he hath not raised up, if the dead rise not again. For if the dead rise not again, neither is Christ risen again. And if Christ be not risen again, your faith is vain" (15, 12-17). And in the Second Epistle to Timothy, he says that Hymeneus and Philetus "have erred from the truth, saying, that the resurrection is past already, and have subverted the faith of some" (2, 18). The symbol of faith [i.e. Creed] published at the Council of Constantinople teaches the same thing.[3] One is loath to cite testimonies for such a clear matter. If someone, however, wishes to know more things about this matter, he may read a certain tract of Blessed Ambrose in the form of an address which is entitled, *On the Belief of the Resurrection*.[4] In which book he not only proves the resurrection by testimonies of Scripture, but also persuades by other arguments.

The **second heresy** is that which teaches that our body in that glory of the resurrection will be impalpable and invisible. The author of this heresy was a certain Eutychius, Bishop of Constantinople,[5] saying that the body after the glory of the resurrection would be air and more subtle than the wind, such that it could neither be touched nor seen. Now by reason of this heresy Blessed Gregory, afterwards the supreme pontiff, was sent by the Apostolic See as legate to Constantinople: when he reached there, he proved before Tiberius [II] Constantine, the then emperor, that this same Eutychius had erred regarding the faith in our resurrection. Which having been done, the emperor himself ordered that the book which Eutychius had published concerning the resurrection be burned.

Against this heresy is that which Job says: "For I know that my Redeemer liveth, and in the last day I shall rise out of the earth. And I shall be clothed again with my skin, and in my flesh I will see my God. Whom I myself shall see, and my eyes shall behold, and not another" (19, 25-27). If the body which is now palpable and visible afterwards will be neither palpable nor

---

[1] C. 10 (PL 69, 1173A-B).

[2] Cf. Ex. 3, 6.

[3] "We look for the resurrection of the dead" (Dz. 86).

[4] *De fide resurrectionis* which is second book of *On the Death of Satyrus* (PL 16, 1315B-1354C).

[5] Eutychius (c. 512-582) was the patriarch of Constantinople from 552 to 565, and from 577 to 582.

visible, but air and more subtle than every wind: then it will be another man who afterwards will rise, and other than he who now lives. And the gloss upon this passage of Job seems to point this out, which says the following: "He expressly indicates the truth of the resurrection. For it is not one person who dies, and another who rises (as those who say that the body will be invisible and impalpable, as Eutychius said) but the very same man."[1] These are the words of the gloss, which is called the "Ordinary Gloss."

Hence it is apparent how miserably deceived was Brother Bernard of Luxemburg, who in his *Catalogus haereticorum* wrote that there were two heretics, one Eutycius, and another Eutychius with an aspirated "c." And so that you may know that he thinks that he was not the same man, notice that after he had printed "Eutycium" in the first edition, in the later edition when adding at the end of the same *Catalogus* other heretics who seemed to be missing in the first edition, he put "Eutychius" with an aspirated "c," as though he were different from him [whose name] he had first written. And since he thought that they were two men he also wants to show us their heresies. A certain Eutycius says that he thought that one man dies, and another rises. But concerning Eutychius he relates that he taught that our bodies rise impalpable and invisible. But if he had carefully examined the matter as he ought, he would have recognized that the man who taught those things is the same, although in different books we may find [his name] written with different letters, in some with a simple "c," but in others with an aspirated "c." Which discrepancy could easily have arisen from a mistake of the copyists, who often copy otherwise than they ought, and change the spelling according to their judgment. Otherwise, that the heresy is the same is very clearly proved from the words of the Ordinary Gloss which we have just cited. For the same gloss points out that Eutychius thought that one man died, and another rises, and that the body dies palpable and visible, and rises impalpable and invisible.

But if the gloss does not show it clearly enough, at least one could learn it from Blessed Gregory, who in his book of *Morals* [*on the Book of Job*], when expounding those words of Job which we have recently cited, tells about his dealings with the same Eutychius, Bishop of Constantinople, and relates that he thought that there is one man who dies, and another who rises: wherefore he believed that the body of a dead man is palpable and visible, and the body of him who rises is impalpable and invisible, because he was saying that it would be air, and more subtle than every wind. And so Blessed Gregory cites that passage of Job which we just cited against the error of this Eutychius, Bishop of Constantinople.[2] I have said these things so that all may see how easily they err who easily make a pronouncement before the matter has been properly examined (as it ought).

But laying aside these things, let us return to our objective. The words of Christ which He said to Martha about Lazarus her then dead brother proves that the same man rises who also died: "Thy brother shall rise again" (Jn. 11, 23). For if the body of the one rising were air and impalpable, Lazarus who rose would not have then been Martha's brother, after the time he did not have that body whereby there was joint consanguinity. Furthermore, our Redeemer, when showing His hands and side to the disciples doubting about His resurrection, offered His flesh and bones to be touched, saying: "Handle, and see: for a spirit hath not flesh and bones, as you see me to have" (Lk. 24, 39). He who desires to know more about this heresy may read Blessed Gregory in his book of *Morals* [*on the Book of Job*], [when he expounds] on the nineteenth chapter of Job, near the end.[3]

The **third heresy** asserts that the bodies after the resurrection will again be mortal, and after that resurrection, when many centuries have passed, it says that the bodies are annihilated.

---

[1] Anselm of Laon, *Glossa Ordinaria* (PL 113, 811A).

[2] Bk. 14, c. 56, n. 72 (PL 75, 1077D).

[3] Bk. 14, c. 56, n. 72-77 (PL 75, 1077C-1080C).

The author of this heresy was Origen. For Theophilus, Bishop of Alexander, accuses him of this in the second book of his Pascal letter, which work Blessed Jerome translated from Greek into Latin.[1] And if it be true that Origen thought this, it is necessary that what Epiphanius relates about him would be false, namely that he denied the resurrection. For he who says that the bodies after the resurrection will be mortal, acknowledges the resurrection clearly enough. But because after this resurrection Origen teaches, according to Theophilus, that the bodies will be annihilated, and will not rise any more, it can happen that Epiphanius understood about this second death when he said that Origen taught that after death there will not be a resurrection. Now whether Origen so thought, or otherwise, I do not know. I certainly know this, that Theophilus relates that he had thought so. Wherefore since he has now been branded for this matter of Origen, it is necessary that we cite some testimonies of Sacred Scripture for refuting his error.

Paul the Apostle, in the Epistle to the Romans, says: "Christ rising again from the dead, dieth now no more, death shall no more have dominion over him" (6, 9). If Christ after the Resurrection dies no more, our bodies after the resurrection will not be mortal: because Christ's resurrection was the exemplar or a certain sign of the resurrection to come in us. And in the First Epistle to the Corinthians, he teaches us this more explicitly, wherein after he made a comparison of a grain of mustard that had died, which at length comes to life, to the resurrection of our body, having come back to the theme he says the following: "It is sown in corruption, it shall rise in incorruption. It is sown in dishonour, it shall rise in glory. It is sown in weakness, it shall rise in power... Behold, I tell you a mystery. We shall all indeed rise again: but we shall not all be changed. In a moment, in the twinkling of an eye, at the last trumpet: for the trumpet shall sound, and the dead shall rise again incorruptible: and we shall be changed. For this corruptible must put on incorruption; and this mortal must put on immortality." (15, 42-43 & 51-53). Nothing clearer could be said for repelling this error. But listen to what the Apostle adds: And when, he says, "This mortal hath put on immortality, then shall come to pass the saying that is written: Death is swallowed up in victory" (v. 54). But death is not perfectly conquered, if fierce death would again overcome the rising bodies. Nor would Christ have perfectly conquered him who had the power of death, that is the devil, if death would be able to possess our bodies. Furthermore, Blessed John in the Apocalypse, when speaking about the just after the resurrection, says: "And God shall wipe away all tears from their eyes: and death shall be no more, nor mourning, nor crying, nor sorrow shall be any more, for the former things are passed away" (21, 4). Since these testimonies are very clear, it is unnecessary to dispute longer on this point.

The **fourth heresy** teaches that Christ rose from the dead on the Saturday after the day of preparation at the sixth hour. Guy [the Carmelite] attributes this error to the Armenians,[2] whom I have always followed in listing the errors of the Armenians: because (as I frankly admit) I could not find any other author whom I might consult on this matter. And in regard this error, I am certainly surprised that a man who has read the Gospel could have fallen into such a plain error. For since it is clear that Christ died on Friday, on the day of preparation, if he rose on Saturday, the next day, how will it be true that he rose on the third day? But the Savior Himself, when foretelling to His disciples the things that were going to happen to Him, says to them: "Behold, we go up to Jerusalem, and all things shall be accomplished which were written by the prophets concerning the Son of man. For he shall be delivered to the Gentiles,

---

[1] "[Origin] says that the bodies which rise, after many centuries will be annihilated, and will not exist except when the souls separated from the lower bodies need new bodies, which other bodies are made again, after the previous ones have been annihilated" (Pascal Letter of the year 401 A. D. to the bishops of all of Egypt, translated by St. Jerome (Letter 96, n. 15 (PL 22, 785)).

[2] C. 14, fol. 34v.

and shall be mocked, and scourged, and spit upon: And after they have scourged him, they will put him to death; and the third day he shall rise again" (Lk. 18, 31-33). Furthermore, our Savior Himself likewise said to the Jews asking for a sign from heaven from Him: "An evil and adulterous generation seeketh a sign: and a sign shall not be given it, but the sign of Jonas the prophet. For as Jonas was in the whale's belly three days and three nights: so shall the Son of man be in the heart of the earth three days and three nights" (Mt. 12, 39-40). If Christ dies on Friday and remains in the heart of the earth three days and three nights, it could not happen that he rose on the next day of Saturday. But it is enough about this.

There is a **fifth heresy** about this matter, which teaches that all men will rise in the male sex, and there will be no female sex after the resurrection. Guy [the Carmelite] accuses the Armenians of this error, and lists in in the twenty[-ninth] place among the errors of the Armenians.[1] Blessed Augustine mentions this error in the *City of God*, saying that there were some who so thought: yet he does not mention who were the promotors of this error.[2]

It can be established that there will be women after the resurrection, for instance from the fact that the Lord made the female just as He made the male. For Scripture says: "Male and female he created them" (Gen. 1, 27). From which words it is evident that the female sex is not a vice, or from a vice, but from nature. For because before sin there was the female, it did not happen from a vice that the female was made. And the sex itself is not a defect: because [if it were,] it would not have been made by God. Hence since the female sex is neither a defect and nor from a defect, but was made by God from the very beginning, it follows that He who made both, would also remake both, and He who instituted both, would likewise restore both.

Besides, Paul, when writing to the Galatians, says: "For as many of you as have been baptized in Christ, have put on Christ. There is neither Jew nor Greek: there is neither bond nor free: there is neither male nor female. For you are all one in Christ Jesus" (3, 27-28). If the female is in Christ Jesus as is the male, why will she not be in glory as is the male? Add to these things what the Lord, when asked by the Sadducees, who were denying the resurrection, about the woman who had married seven brothers so that one of them would raise up seed of the dead brother, whose wife of them would she be after the resurrection, replies: "And Jesus answering, said to them: You err, not knowing the Scriptures, nor the power of God. For in the resurrection they shall neither marry nor be married; but shall be as the angels of God in heaven" (Mt. 22, 29-30). But if there would not be any woman after the resurrection, He would have destroyed their error more easily, saying that there would not be the feminine sex after the resurrection. And since there was very ample room, He would have taught them about this matter: such that He would say that that woman about whom was the question, would be in the future a man, not a woman. But He did not say that, but this: "In the resurrection they shall neither marry nor be married." He denied that there would be marriage after the resurrection: He did not deny the variety of sexes. Nay, He insinuated that there would be this variety there, when He said: "They shall not marry," which befits the [males]; "nor be married [or 'given in marriage']," which applies to [females].[3] Therefore, there will be females who in this world are accustomed to marry, and males who here below have married wives because although He denied that marriage [would be in the next life], He subtly insinuated that there would be a variety of sexes, which is required for marriage. Those members [of females] will indeed be

---

[1] C. 29, fol. 42r.

[2] Bk. 22, c. 17 (PL 41, 778).

[3] "He even affirmed that the sex should exist by saying, 'They shall not be given in marriage,' which can only apply to females; 'Neither shall they marry,' which applies to males" (*Ibid.*). The text here has the sexes reversed, but this has been corrected according to these words of St. Augustine whom the author is following here.

there, but not deputed for their old usage, but for a new beauty, and for setting off to advantage God's wisdom and goodness.[1]

But those who maintain this error object to us those words of Paul from his Epistle to the Ephesians: "Until we all meet into the unity of faith, and of the knowledge of the Son of God, unto a perfect man, unto the measure of the age of the fulness of Christ" (4, 13).

From which passage they argue that all will be resurrected in the male sex: because the Apostle says that "we will all meet... unto a perfect man." Blessed Augustine responds to this objection, saying that in that passage "man" can mean either a male or female human.[2] For just as elsewhere Scripture very often has adopted this usage of the word. For that is clear (so that I may pass over other examples for the present time) which is said in the Psalm: "Blessed is the man to whom the Lord hath not imputed sin" (31, 2). In which place it is evident that by the word "man" the female is also understood: because the female is also blessed, to whom the Lord has not imputed sin.

And Blessed Gregory, in a homily on the passage of the Gospel, "Let your loins be girt" (Lk. 12, 35), suggests the same thing, saying the following: "That the lust of man is in his loins, and that of the woman in her belly, the Lord testifies when he speaks of the devil to Blessed Job, saying: 'His strength,' he says, 'is in his loins, and his force in the navel of his belly' (Job 40, 11). Thus, when the Lord says, 'Let your loins be girt,' it is the lust of the principal sex that is designated by 'loins.'"[3] In which words it is puts forth clearly enough that by speaking of the masculine sex as the more principal sex, the feminine sex is [indirectly] designated.

It can also be otherwise replied, and perhaps more closely to the literal meaning, that we may say in that passage Paul did not refer to the resurrection, but to the perfection of doctrine and the knowledge of truth. For after he had said that some men were given by Christ to be Apostles, some to be prophets, other some Evangelists, other some doctors "for the perfecting of the saints, for the work of the ministry, for the edifying of the body of Christ" (Eph. 4, 12), he immediately added: "Until we all meet into the unity of faith, and of the knowledge of the Son of God, unto a perfect man, unto the measure of the age of the fulness of Christ." [Ambrosiaster], when discussing these words in his commentaries on Paul's Epistles, says these words: "[Paul] says that this order will continue until all those who are predestined to life are of one faith. He exhorts [them] to so labor unto the knowledge of Christ, such that the fulness of faith may be understood, which is this: Christ is full and perfect God, and is not to be measured in human terms, but recognized in the fullness of His Divinity as perfect God. When he speaks about mature manhood, he is not thinking in terms of age and physical stature, but by what he says here, that he wants us to be perfect in the full understanding of the Divinity of the Son of God."[4] And Theophylactus interprets this passage of Paul in the same way.[5]

---

[1] "And the sex of woman is not a vice, but nature. It shall then indeed be superior to carnal intercourse and child-bearing; nevertheless, the female members shall remain adapted not to the old uses, but to a new beauty, which, so far from provoking lust, now extinct, shall excite praise to the wisdom and clemency of God, who both made what was not and delivered from corruption what He made" (*Ibid.*).

[2] "But even if this should be referred to the form in which each one shall rise, what should hinder us from applying to the woman what is expressly said of the man, understanding both sexes to be included under the general term 'man'? For certainly in the saying, 'Blessed is he who fears the Lord,' women also who fear the Lord are included" (*Ibid.*, c. 18 (PL 41, 779).

[3] *Homilies on the Gospels*, hom. 13, n. 1 (PL 76, 1123D).

[4] *Commentaria in Epistolam ad Ephesios*, c. 4, v. 13 (PL 17, 389A-B).

[5] "'Until we all meet into the unity of faith, and of the knowledge of the Son of God.' He says that all we who have received gifts ought to labor and build until we have reached the unity of faith: that is, until we show that we all have one and the same faith, and do not differ in dogmatic teachings, and in our

Finally, it is necessary that we hear the definition of the Church about this matter. For among the Ecclesiastical Dogmas, one is found about this matter in the [seventy-seventh] place, which is the following: "In the resurrection from the dead the kind of sex will not be changed, but the dead man will rise in the form of a man, and the woman in the form of a woman."[1] And it is enough about this subject.

I do not know of anyone who wrote against this heresy besides Blessed Augustine, who in the twenty-second book of the *City of God*, in the seventeenth chapter, discusses some few things.

SACERDOTIUM

Priesthood

It is one of the more pernicious and execrable errors of Luther whereby he teaches that all Christians are priests, and all Christians have equal power, without any distinction made of rank or sex. But even though all Christians may be called priests, still he teaches that no one may use that power except with the consent of the community: because (as he says) "what is common to all, no one can individually usurp unless he be called."[2] Thus this power according to Luther's view was firstly derived from the community, then from that community to him who exercises the priesthood. Luther's words in the book, *The Babylonian Captivity of the Church*, are these: "Let everyone, therefore, who knows himself to be a Christian, be assured of this, that we are all equally priests, that is to say, we have the same power in respect to the Word and the Sacraments."[3] And afterwards he says that the priesthood is nothing other than the power of preaching, and the office of the priest consists in teaching alone.[4]

But here it is necessary to ask Luther whether he believes that the Evangelical priesthood is more abject and of less value than the priesthood of the Old Law? I do not think that he is so insane that he would deny that the Evangelical priesthood is much superior to the Levitical priesthood. But the priesthood of the Old Law was not so abject and of less value such that it was entrusted to all men without distinction. For in Exodus we read that the Lord God said these words to Moses: "Take unto thee also Aaron thy brother with his sons, from among the children of Israel, that they may minister to me in the priest's office: Aaron, Nadab, and Abiu, Eleazar, and Ithamar. And thou shalt make a holy vesture for Aaron thy brother for glory and

---

lives not to be divided among ourselves into particular sects. For when there is both true unity of faith and we both acknowledge the Son of God, and when we both shall have the correct belief in doctrine, then shall we have kept the bond of charity. For Christ is charity.

"'Unto a perfect man, unto the measure of the age of the fulness of Christ.' He calls the more perfect knowledge of the teachings 'a perfect man,' and 'the measure of the age': just as he also calls the whole and entire knowledge and faith regarding Him 'the fulness of Christ': namely, although He was one of the Trinity and equal to the Father, He is made man, one Person and two natures, wills and operations: and He sits beside the Father with His body, and He will come with that same body, and whatever other things are correctly understood and said about Him. Thus, how else does he call our knowledge imperfect? It is in that it is opposed to the future knowledge: but here in respect to its immutability, he calls the knowledge perfect. For when we do not fail, then we are perfect, as appears from the words which follow" (*Commentarius in Epistolam ad Ephesios*, c. 4, v. 13 (PG 124, 1086D-1087B)).

[1] Gennadius, *De ecclesiasticis dogmatibus*, c. 77 (PL 58, 998B).

[2] *On the Babylonian Captivity of the Church* (WA 6, 566, lns. 29-30).

[3] *Ibid.*, lns. 26-28.

[4] "The priesthood is properly nothing but the ministry of the Word—the Word, I say; not the law, but the Gospel" (*Ibid.*, lns. 32-34).

for beauty" (28, 1-2). Notice that you see Aaron and his sons segregated by the Lord's precept from the whole people so that they might perform the priesthood before Him. And to this law is consonant that which Paul, the wonderful interpreter of the Law, says when discoursing about Christ our Savior in the Epistle to the Hebrews: "For he, of whom these things are spoken, is of another tribe, of which no one attended on the altar. For it is evident that our Lord sprung out of Juda: in which tribe Moses spoke nothing concerning priests" (7, 13-14). See Paul testifying that no one of the tribe of Juda, according to the precept of the Mosaic Law, could be a priest.

And the prophet Samuel gave the same testimony before King Saul, who was of the tribe of Benjamin. For he gravely rebuked him on account of the holocaust and peace offering he had offered to God, having performed the office of the priest: and he made known the punishment decreed by God due to this sin, speaking thus: "Thou hast done foolishly, and hast not kept the commandments of the Lord thy God, which he commanded thee. And if thou hadst not done thus, the Lord would now have established thy kingdom over Israel forever. But thy kingdom shall not continue. The Lord hath sought him a man according to his own heart: and him hath the Lord commanded to be prince over his people, because thou hast not observed that which the Lord commanded" (I Kings 13, 13-14).

And now we certainly see the Duke of Saxony, John Fredrick, punished by God with a similar punishment on account of a similar sin. For this man in an astonishing manner supported Luther, the profaner of the Evangelical priesthood: and for this sin, he was vanquished in war by Emperor Charles V, [also titled] King Charles I of the Spains, and captured in war, and despoiled of most of his riches, and also deprived forever of the dignity of imperial elector. All which things, by God so willing, happened, contrary to the expectation of the people, the reason being that since the majority of Germany was infected with the Lutheran heresy, nearly all Germany had rebelled at the same time with this duke against Charles solely on account of the heresy, and had wanted to overthrow the same Charles with a great army from all of Germany. Yet God, in Whose hand are all the victories of war, gave victory to Emperor Charles, and dispersed all the powers which had adhered to the duke of Saxony, as sheep without a shepherd, and handed him over into Charles' hands, who at length deprived him both of his patrimony and dignity, whom if he had also deprived of life, truly Christian men could not have rightly wanted anything from the same emperor.

But let us put these things aside,[1] because they were said only in passing: and let us return to the topic of our disputation. In the book of Numbers, we read that the tribe of Levi was specifically chosen by the Lord for the ministry of the tabernacle, and the sons of Caath were appointed for carrying the vessels of the sanctuary wrapped by Aaron and his sons, so that they would not touch them, lest perchance they would die.[2] What will Luther say here? If God commanded that so much reverence be shown to the vessels of the sanctuary, that they could not be touched by anyone except the priest, one ought to believe that we ought to show much greater reverence to the Most Holy Eucharist, so that the vessels in which It is stored, I do not speak of very Eucharist Itself, we may not allow to be touched by anyone other than a priest? For if such honor is bestowed upon the shadow, is it not right that we give much greater honor to the Body? Dathan, Core, and Abiron were swallowed by the earth, and went down alive as far as hell,[3] because they attempted to usurp the priestly office, and the two hundred and fifty men consenting to them were consumed by fire.[4]

---

[1] The Latin phrase used here, *Missa faciamus* ("let us dismiss from the mind"), is taken from Cicero's *Epistulae ad Familiares*, bk. 9, letter 7 (To M. Terentius Varro), sect. 2.
[2] Cf. Num. 4, 2-20.
[3] Cf. Num. 16, 33.
[4] Cf. Num 16, 35.

And Oza because he "put forth his hand to the ark of God, and took hold of it" (II Kings 6, 6) contrary to the condition of his rank, was suddenly struck by the Lord "for his rashness: and he died there before the ark of God" (v. 7). And Ozias, king of Juda, was struck by the Lord with leprosy on his forehead, because he presumed to usurp the office of the sacerdotal order, by offering incense upon the altar of incense.[1] King Baltasar, who being drunk drank from "the vessels of gold and silver which Nabuchodonosor his father had brought away out of the temple that was in Jerusalem," (Dan. 5, 2), saw a hand writing on the wall, "Mane, Thecel, Phares," (v. 25) and having been slain the same night, "Darius the Mede succeeded to the kingdom" (v. 31). If the Lord was so zealous for the figure, how much more will He be zealous for the reality? He did not permit the shadow to be touched by anyone except a priest, and will he permit His Body to be indiscriminately handled by anyone? Thus let the Lutheran laity beware, and be converted to the Lord, lest perhaps they be cast alive into Hell as Dathan, Core and Abiron.

Furthermore, if the institution of the sacerdotal order, and the time of its institution are considered well, the truth of this matter will easily appear. For priests were ordained by the Lord at the Last Supper, when our Savior having supper with His disciples, said to them: "Do this for a commemoration of me" (Lk. 22, 19). Now they were completed in the priesthood when after the Resurrection, He said to these same disciples: "Whose sins you shall forgive, they are forgiven them; and whose sins you shall retain, they are retained" (Jn. 20, 23). But long before these times the disciples themselves were Christians, because they had already put on Christ through Baptism, although they were not then priests. Therefore, everyone is not (as Luther says) made a priest at Baptism[2]: and it is unnecessary that by the mere fact that someone is a Christian, he would also be a priest, who has power over the real and mystical Body of Christ, that is, the power of consecrating and of absolving.

Again, Blessed Paul, when writing to Timothy, says: "Neglect not the grace that is in thee, which was given thee by prophesy, with imposition of the hands of the priesthood" (I Tim. 4, 14). Or (as Erasmus more clearly translated) "with the authority of the priesthood."[3] And again to the same Timothy, he says: "That thou stir up the grace of God which is in thee, by the imposition of my hands" (II Tim. 1, 6). From which words we gather two things against Luther. One is that Timothy was ordained a priest by Paul. The other is that such ordination was done by the authority of the priests and not (as Luther says) by the consent of the people. And when writing to Titus, Paul says: "For this cause I left thee in Crete, that thou shouldest set in order the things that are wanting, and shouldest ordain priests in every city, as I also appointed thee" (1, 5). If all Christians are priests, it was not necessary to leave Titus in Crete for ordaining priests in the cities. Notice also how Titus was ordained by Paul, and that he exercised the sacerdotal office in Crete by Paul's command alone, and not by the consent or permission of the people. "As I also," Paul says, "appointed thee."

Next, in the Epistle to the Hebrews the Apostle says the same thing: "Neither doth any man take the honour to himself, but he that is called by God, as Aaron was" (5, 4). But Aaron was not called or made a priest by the people, but by God; and his priesthood was derived from God, and not from the people. Thus, much less will the Evangelical priesthood be derived from the people: since the latter is much more worthy of honor than the former. And in the First Epistle to the Corinthians the same Apostle, when enumerating the offices distributed by Christ in the Church, says: "And God indeed hath set some in the church; first apostles, secondly prophets, thirdly doctors; after that miracles; then the graces of healing, helps, gov-

---

[1] II Par. 26, 19.
[2] "How if they were compelled to admit that we all, so many as have been baptized, are equally priests?" (WA 6, 564, lns. 6-7).
[3] *Novum Testamentum omne*, p. 455.

ernments, kinds of tongues, interpretations of speeches" (12, 28). But if everyone can do all things (as Luther says) in vain did He distribute so many offices. Hence Paul deservedly added in that place: "Are all apostles? Are all prophets? Are all doctors? Are all workers of miracles? Have all the grace of healing? Do all speak with tongues? Do all interpret?" (v. 29-30). See that according to Paul's opinion not all are Doctors [i.e. teachers], not all are prophets, not all interpret: hence it is also concluded that not all are priests: especially since according to Luther, the priesthood is nothing other than the power of preaching.

Next the very nature of the most excellent sacrifice which is in the Catholic Church, obliges that for its offering to be done, someone must be appointed a priest who is different from the rest of the people. For pagans also understood this, who for the offering of their sacrifices which they were sacrificing and offering to their gods, always has particular priests distinct from the rest of the people. And they did not want that this office of priesthood be indiscriminately entrusted to all. Hence, since the Church has the most excellent sacrifice of all, it is established that it also has the best priesthood distinct from the people. Yet Luther denies that the Mass is a sacrifice, but we have disputed about this above in the section on the "Mass."

Nevertheless, I caution the reader not to think that I approve of the priesthood of the pagans, from this argument which I now formed from the pagans' priesthood: and hence I proposed it as an example. Far be such a thought from me! For I am not so crazy or so ignorant that I will not understand very well that all their sacrifices were sacrileges, and their whole rite of priesthood was a sacrilege and superstitious. But this evil was coming forth from the fact that they were ignorant of the true God, and those sacrifices which they offered were not to the true God, but to demons whom they thought were gods. Thus, I nevertheless praise the pagans, not in that they were sacrificing to gods, but in that they were not sacrificing indiscriminately and without any distinction of persons by whomever of the people they permitted this to be done. For enlightened by a certain light of natural reason they all understood that the highest honors ought to be bestowed upon God, and the sacrifices offered to God, which they were accustomed to offer not by just anyone, but by some particular men of proven virtue, very specifically appointed for carrying out this office. Now that such is the case is evident both from the pagan's books and also from Sacred Scripture, which when saying that the whole land of Egypt, on account of the great shortage of corn, was made tributary to King Pharaoh, since forced by the famine all were selling their possession to the king: he exempted the priestly land, saying: "Except the land of the priests, which had been given them by the king" (Gen. 47, 22). And afterwards, when Sacred Scripture is relating that a fifth part of the corn was given as tribute, he also exempted the land of the priests, saying: "Except the land of the priests, which was free from this covenant" (v. 26).

Wherefore only for this purpose do we cite this example of the pagans, namely from the fact that all men from every race, at all times, and by all laws always acted in this way, we may prove that this is something known by the light of natural reason, that not any men without distinction ought to be God's priests: but that there be some men set apart from the rest of the people, who take care of this office. And hence we reprehend those who, profaning the Evangelical priesthood, contend that it is common to all without any distinction. For in ancient times God in the same way cited the pagans as an example so that He might reprehend the Jews for their inconstancy, speaking thus through Jeremias: "Pass over to the isles of Cethim, and see: and send into Cedar, and consider diligently: and see if there hath been done anything like this. If a nation hath changed their gods, and indeed they are not gods: but my people have changed their glory into an idol" (2, 10-11). By these words, as it is clear, God did not approve of the idols of the Gentiles, nor of their veneration of idols, which He clearly stated are not gods: but He objected to the Jews the constancy of the Gentiles, whereby they continuously worshipped those whom they at one time believed to be gods, so that He could duly reprehend from it the fickle changeableness of the Jews, who acknowledging the true God with titles, fell away from Him, and went over to strange gods, who were not gods. Having imitated this example of God from the religion of the pagans, which was everywhere and at all times practiced by them, so that they did not make the priesthood common to all without any distinction, I thought that it could be duly proved that the Lutherans who affirm that the Evangelical priesthood, which is more excellent than all others, is common to all man of every condition and age: and not only to men, but also to women, is unheard of until now.

Furthermore, if all Christians are priests, it follows that there is no specific priesthood of the Evangelical Law: because whatever it may be called, all of it will be found in the Mosaic Law. When Luther concedes this, he is forced to also admit that there is no specific law for the time of grace: because the priesthood and the law are so interconnected that when one is taken away it is necessary to take away the other: and when the one is put in place it is necessary that the other follows. For Paul, motivated by this reason, said: "The priesthood being translated, it is necessary that a translation also be made of the law" (Heb. 7, 12). Thus, if there is no specific priesthood in the time of grace, there will also be no specific law for this time of grace. Yet Luther is so foolish that he is not ashamed to assert this, when saying that there is no special Law in the Gospel: but against this error we have already disputed in the section on "Precepts," in the first heresy: and hence it is unnecessary to fight against it a second time.

Again, from the words which Christ said after the Resurrection to the Apostle gathered together at the same time, it can be proved that the sacerdotal power is not common to all. For He said these words to them: "Receive ye the Holy Ghost. Whose sins you shall forgive, they are forgiven them; and whose sins you shall retain, they are retained" (Jn. 20, 22-23). In which words, one ought to observe some things which are worthy of consideration. The first thing is that He says: "Receive ye the Holy Ghost." Now He did not then give the Holy Ghost for working miracles: because that gift of the Holy Ghost He had already given them, when He had sent them to preach. For then, as Luke testifies, "He gave them power and authority over all devils, and to cure diseases" (9, 1). He did not give the Holy Ghost for their sanctification, and the illumination of the Church: because He was given to them in this way on the day of Pentecost. Thus, He gave them the Holy Ghost on the day of the Resurrection because then He gave them the power of forgiving sins. For the remission of sins, even though it is given to the men by the whole Trinity, still it is given in a special manner by the Holy Ghost, just as books [of Scripture] is particularly attributed to Him, which is common to the three Persons. Now the power of forgiving sins, is a kind of judiciary power, for the execution of which it is necessary that there be at least two persons, one who is the party guilty of sin: the other who is judge absolving him from sin. And hence it is gathered that not all men are priests, but one is the priest, and the other is the guilty party.

Perhaps Luther will say that both forgive the other's sins. But if this were the case, Christ would have said, forgive each other, just as James when commending prayer said: "Pray one for another" (5, 16). And there is still something else to be considered in these words, namely that when Christ said these words, there was no woman present, nay no other man present besides the Apostles: and hence it is concluded that it may be understood this power of forgiving sins was granted not to all men, but only to the Apostles, and to those to whom it was afterwards derived through the Apostles: for as often as some gift is Divinely bestowed through some sensible sign, to those only it is believed to have been granted, in whom that sign befell, and not to others who were absent. For the grace of Baptism was only granted to those who were washed with water. The Sacrament of the Eucharist is confected only from the bread and wine upon which the words of consecration were pronounced. Therefore, it simply ought to be believed that the power of forgiving sins was given only to those upon whom the sensible sign of its conferral befell. But the sensible sign of its conferral, which was Christ's breath, befell the Apostles alone when He breathed upon them, saying: "Receive ye the Holy Ghost. Whose sins you shall forgive, they are forgiven them; and whose sins you shall retain, they are retained." Wherefore, the Apostles alone then received that power, and thence others, to whom they, or the bishops, their successors, granted it.

But perhaps someone will object to me here that if this argument were valid, it would also prove that Thomas, one of the twelve Apostles, would not have had the power of forgiving sins, and consequently would not have had the full power of the priesthood, and was not a perfected priest: because, as John bears witness, Thomas was not with the other Apostles when Christ appeared to them, and said to them the aforesaid words, whereby He conferred upon them the power of forgiving sins. Formerly Cyril raised this difficulty and replied to it, saying: All twelve Apostles were chosen by God, that they would be chiefs over the whole world, and would have power as His ministers, of forgiving and retaining sins.[1] Therefore, Christ, Whose power is not limited by space, did not need Thomas' presence so that He might confer this power to him along with the others. Thus, what He deigned to give to all, He gave to Thomas, although absent, when He gave it to the others.

And this ought not to seem to anyone to be difficult, since it is certainly evident that something similar previously occurred in the time of the Old Law. For the Lord commanded Moses to gather seventy men from the elders of Israel, so that God would give them of the spirit of the same Moses, for bearing along with him the burden of the people, which Moses alone was unable to bear. "Moses therefore came, and told the people the words of the Lord, and assembled seventy men of the ancients of Israel, and made them to stand about the tabernacle. And the Lord came down in a cloud, and spoke to him, taking away of the spirit that was in Moses, and giving to the seventy men. And when the spirit had rested on them they prophesied, nor did they cease afterwards. Now there remained in the camp two of the men, of whom one was called Eldad, and the other Medad, upon whom the spirit rested; for they also had been enrolled, but were not gone forth to the tabernacle. And when they prophesied in the camp, there ran a young man, and told Moses, saying: Eldad and Medad prophesy in the camp. Forthwith Josue the son of Nun, the minister of Moses, and chosen out of many, said: My lord Moses forbid them. But he said: Why hast thou emulation for me? O that all the people might prophesy, and that the Lord would give them his spirit!" (Num. 11, 24-29). If sacred history relates that all these things formerly occurred, there is no good reason for anyone to doubt that Christ our Savior gave to Thomas, when absent, but chosen by Him, His Spirit, just as of old He had given His Spirit to Eldad and Medad, because they were chosen for this. For those whom God chooses for the performance of some office, even if they were away from the presence and assembly of those to whom He gives His office, nonetheless they still receive it just like the others: because even if they be absent from the other companions, nevertheless to God, Who calls those things which do not exist just as those things which exist, and to Whom no creature is invisible, they cannot be absent.

Add to these things that, according to Luther's teaching, it is necessary to acknowledge that is a sort of very wretched government, in which would be the worst politics of all of such kind that never existed before, even among the uneducated and barbarian nations. For if the

---

[1] "Thomas, called Didymus, was not with the disciples when Jesus came. How, then, someone may not unreasonably inquire, if he were away, was he in fact made partaker in the Holy Spirit when the Saviour appeared unto the disciples and breathed on them, saying: Receive ye the Holy Ghost? We reply that the power of the Spirit pervaded every man who received grace, and fulfilled the aim of the Lord Who gave Him unto them; and Christ gave the Spirit not to some only but to all the disciples. Therefore, if any were absent, they also received Him, the munificence of the Giver not being confined to those only who were present, but extending to the entire company of the holy Apostles" (Cyril of Alexandria, *On the Gospel According to John*, bk. 12 (PG 74, 718D-719A)).

Church were well arranged and ordered, as Luther contends, there would be no hierarchy in it, and no rank: but everything would be confused, and the Church would be another Babylon. Because no one in it would be subject to another in those things which pertain to the spirit, and which properly belong to the Church: but everyone would be equal to themselves. For Luther denies that the Roman pontiff is the supreme pontiff of the Church: and he says that all bishops are equal, and he denies that anyone is superior to anyone else. He says moreover that the bishops are not superior to the other priests, but all priests are equal to the bishops. Finally, he now says that all Christians are priests. From all which things it is evidently inferred that all Christians are bishops, and no Christian is superior to another in those things which are spiritual and which pertain to the Church. Thus, the Church in this way will be like a flock without a shepherd, or a kingdom without a king, and any nation without one who governs. Therefore, it would necessarily happen in the Church what Solomon says: "Where there is no governor, the people shall fall" (Prov. 11, 14).

In the heavenly Church of the Blessed Angels, they are not all equal: but there are in it many ranks differing in dignity and power, the first and lowest of which is the Angels, the second superior to this rank are called the Archangels, and so on until the last and supreme rank, which is called the Seraphim. Dionysius the [Pseudo-] Areopagite discusses about these ranks in his book, *The Celestial Hierarchy*.[1] This Church militant was formed after the example of that heavenly Church, as the same Dionysius teaches in his book, *The Ecclesiastical Hierarchy*,[2] such that the ranks are also divided in this former Church, just as in the latter. And hence in that same book, when explaining the different states of the Church, he says that the bishop has the highest authority: under him he puts the priests: to these priests he subjects the other ministers, whom they call "deacons"[3]: finally, he says that the people hold the lowest place subject to these ministers.

For on account of this likeness of this lower Church to that higher Church, Bernard says in his book, *On Consideration* [written] to [Pope] Eugenius [III], that John in the Apocalypse said that he saw the city of the new Jerusalem descending from heaven.[4] Bernard's words are these: "Do not despise this appearance on earth because it has its exemplar in heaven. For 'The Son cannot do anything of himself, but what he seeth the Father doing' (Jn. 5, 19), especially since it was said to Him under the name of Moses: 'Look and make it according to the pattern, that was shewn thee in the mount' (Ex. 25, 40). He had seen this who said, 'I saw the holy city, the new Jerusalem, coming down out of heaven prepared by God' (Apoc. 21, 2). For I reckon that it was said on account of its likeness, because just as the Seraphim and Cherubim there, and the other five [choirs] down to the Angels and Archangels are ordered under one Head, God: so also on earth under one supreme pontiff, primate or patriarchs, archbishops, bishops, priests or abbots, and the rest [are ordered] in this manner."[5] Bernard states clearly enough that by God's institution not all Christians are priests, nor are all bishops, but there is a distinction and order among them: just as there is distinction and order among the higher spirits, such that not all are Cherubim, nor are all Seraphim, or Thrones, or Dominations.

I could cite here as a confirmation of this matter many testimonies of the holy Doctors, but being prudent I omit them, due to the fact that the testimonies of Sacred Scripture which we cited are very clear. Yet I will cite one of Tertullian and another of Cyprian, so that from them it may appear how old is this heresy of Luther. For in the book, *Prescription against Heretics*, when describing their conduct, and reprehending it, [Tertullian] speaks thus: "Their

---

[1] PG 3, 119 ff.
[2] PG 3, 369 ff.
[3] The name deacon (*diakonos*) means only minister or servant.
[4] Cf. Apoc. 21, 2.
[5] Bk. 3, c. 4 (PL 182, 768D-769A).

ordinations, are carelessly administered, capricious, changeable. At one time they put novices in office; at another time, men who are bound to some secular employment; at another, persons who have apostatized from us, to bind them by vainglory, since they cannot by the truth. Nowhere is promotion easier than in the camp of rebels, where the mere fact of being there is a foremost service. And so it comes to pass that today one man is their bishop, tomorrow another; today he is a deacon who tomorrow is a reader; today he is a presbyter who tomorrow is a layman. For even on laymen do they impose the functions of priesthood."[1] From whose words these last words ought to be noticed, because when reprehending he says that the heretics impose the functions of priesthood on laymen. If then this is the custom of heretics, Luther also ought also to do this, so that he would not be inconsistent with the customs of his heretical parents.

Cyprian says nearly the same in his letter to Bishop Rogatianus, to whom he writes about a certain deacon, who had been rebellious to the same Rogatianus, his bishop. In which letter after he shows with numerous quotations how much honor priests deserve, he says these words: "But deacons ought to remember that the Lord chose Apostles, that is, bishops and overseers; while Apostles appointed for themselves deacons after the ascent of the Lord into heaven, as ministers of their episcopacy and of the Church. But if we may dare anything against God who makes bishops, deacons may also dare against us by whom they are made; and therefore, it behooves the deacon of whom you write to repent of his audacity, and to acknowledge the honor of the priest, and to satisfy the bishop set over him with full humility. For these things are the beginnings of heretics, and the origins and endeavors of evil-minded schismatics—to please themselves, and with swelling haughtiness to despise him who is set over them. Thus, they depart from the Church—thus a profane altar is set up outside—thus they rebel against the peace of Christ, and the appointment and the unity of God."[2] In which words, besides that which he says, that priests are superior to deacons by God's institution, one especially ought to note this which he says, that such rebellions are "the beginnings of heretics": the beginning, advancement and ending of the heresy of Luther himself taught how true this opinion is. Those things which we disseminated above in the sections of the Sacrament of "Orders," and in the section on "Women," combat this heresy.

There are also the decrees of many councils against it. The IV Synod of Carthage prescribes the manner whereby someone is to be ordained a priest.[3] But if all Christians (as Luther says) are priests, such ordination would be superfluous. The [IV] Lateran Council celebrated under Innocent III, when speaking about the Sacrament of the Eucharist, defines thus: "And surely no one can accomplish this sacrament except a priest who has been rightly ordained according to the keys of the Church which Jesus Christ Himself conceded to the Apostles and to their successors."[4] Now this decree is found in the book of the *Decretal Letters* in the title, *De summa Trinitate et fide Catholica*, in chapter one.[5] The Synod of Rheims, in the second chapter of its decrees defines by these words: "It has come to our knowledge that some priests little esteem the Divine Mysteries to such an extent that they deliver the Lord's Body to a layman or to a woman to carry it to the sick: and to those whom are forbidden to enter the sanctuary, to approach the altar, they entrust to them the Holy of Holies. The [prudence[6]] of all

---

[1] C. 41 (PL 2, 57A).

[2] Letter 65, n. 3 (PL 4, 396B-C).

[3] "When a priest is ordained, the bishop blesses him and places his hand on his head. All the priests who are present do likewise, and they place their hands on his head, next to the hand of the bishop" (Canon 3 (PL 84, 200B)).

[4] Dz. 430.

[5] Gregory IX, *Decretales*, bk. 1, tit. 1 (*De summa Trinitate et fide catholica*), c. 1.

[6] The text mistakenly has "excellence (*praecellentia*)" instead of "prudence (*prudentia*)" as found in

religious men perceives how horrendous and detestable this is. The synod therefore forbids in all places such temerarious presumption to continue; and let the priest himself communicate the sick. But if he shall do otherwise, he will undergo danger to his rank."[1] And these words are found in the book of the *Decretal Letters*,[2] which I have pointed out, because the decrees of that council are not found in the book in which are the decrees of the other councils compiled by [Pseudo-] Isidore.[3] From the words of this council it is evident that not merely is the consecration of the Lord's Body forbidden, but also the touching of the same Body: and it says that it is horrendous and detestable that women and laymen would touch the Lord's Body. What therefore would the council have said if it heard that laymen are attempting to confect the same Lord's Body by consecrating? There is no doubt that it would have executed a more atrocious punishment upon them.

But now it is necessary that we see with what argument Luther supports his proposition. For he says the following: "We are all priests according to that saying of St. Peter: 'You are a chosen generation, a kingly priesthood' (I Pet. 2, 9), but as one cannot be more a man than another; so one can be no more a priest than another. Those, therefore, who are called priests, are no other than laymen, chosen by the consent of the people, or appointed by the bishop, not without the people. For to preach and ordain, are nothing but mere ministry, without anything of Sacrament."[4] O mighty arguer! O another Aristotle! If the office of the priest is nothing, because all are called priests: it will be necessary that you admit for the same reason that Christ is nothing any more than those of whom it was said: "Touch ye not my anointed (*christos*)" (Ps. 104, 15). Furthermore, if according to Peter all are priests, are not all also kings for the same reason? "You are," he says, "a chosen generation, a kingly priesthood." [He does] not [say] any priesthood, but a royal one: so that he might show that they are kings, as well as priests! And in John's Apocalypse the twenty-four ancients who represent the just were crying out, saying: "Thou hast made us to our God a kingdom and priests, and we shall reign on the earth" (5, 10). Thus, if a duly ordained priest is nothing more than any Christian, because all are called priests: it would also be necessary that a king have nothing more than any other Christian, in that all are also called kings. Wherefore it will happen that no one is a king for Luther, just as no one is a priest for him. Again, if on account of those words of Peter it were necessary to acknowledge that all Christians are true priests, it would also be necessary to say that all Jews were priests, since in Exodus it was said by the Lord: "If you will hear my voice, and keep my covenant, you shall be my peculiar possession above all people: for all the earth is mine. And you shall be to me a priestly kingdom, and a holy nation" (19, 5-6). Therefore, since it is very clearly evident that not all Jews were priests, although they were called by God "a priestly kingdom," it is proved that it is also not necessary that all Christians are priests, although Peter called them "a kingly priesthood."

But it remains that we show the true meaning of that text. According to Bede's opinion all Christians are called priests by Peter, because they were united to Christ Who is King and Priest.[5] Didymus [the Blind], of Alexandria, in the exposition which is commonly called, *Su-*

---

the *Decretals* cited here by the author.

[1] PL 187, 1743B.

[2] *Concordia discordantium canonum*, p. 3 (*De consecratione*), dist. 2, c. 29 (*Pervenit*).

[3] The decrees of this council have not been edited. (Cf. F.G.A. Wasserschleben, *Reginonis abbatis Prumiensis libri duo De synodalibus causis et Disciplinis ecclesiasticis... recensuit* (Leipzig, Engelmann, 1840), p. 77, n. 120).

[4] *Defense of the Seven Sacraments*, p. 420.

[5] "'You are a chosen generation, a kingly priesthood...' This, as it were, testimony of praise was given by Moses to the old people of God, which now Peter the Apostle rightly gives to the Gentiles, namely because they have believed in Christ, Who as the cornerstone made the Gentiles one in that salvation

per septem epistolas canonicas, says that Christians are called "a kingly priesthood" because their father, namely Christ, is King and Priest. For after he shows that Christ is King and Priest, he adds these words: "Therefore these things [i.e., kingship and priesthood] having been conferred [upon Christ from His Father], it was necessary, when these things have been handed down by Him, Who is king and priest at the same time, the chosen race would be both royal and at the same time priestly. Their father, in fact, having both dominions, it is necessary that they would be as it were a 'royal' generation from the King, and would be as it were a 'priestly' generation from the Priest. Wherefore they are called 'a holy nation,' having been called by Him Who is Holy, so that they may be 'holy.'"[1] Other interpretations could be given to this text, but I omit them, because Didymus' exposition in my opinion excels all the others, in that it is more germane to the text.

Luther also objects to us, in his book, *De abroganda missa privata*, speaking thus: To the ecclesiastical priests and to the New Law chiefly pertains the ministry of teaching God's word, as the prophet Malachias testifies, saying these words: "The lips of the priest shall keep knowledge, and they shall seek the law at his mouth: because he is the angel of the Lord of hosts" (Mal. 2, 7). But the office of teaching the word of God pertains indiscriminately to all, even to laymen and women. For the Apostle, when speaking about all Christians, writes to the Corinthians: "Such confidence we have, through Christ, towards God. Not that we are sufficient to think anything of ourselves, as of ourselves: but our sufficiency is from God. Who also hath made us fit ministers of the new testament, not in the letter, but in the spirit" (II Cor. 3, 4-6). And Blessed Peter when speaking to all believing in Christ, to whom he directs his first epistle, says: "That you may declare his virtues, who hath called you out of darkness into his marvelous light" (2, 9). Again, Paul directing words to the Corinthian faithful, says: "For you may all prophesy one by one; that all may learn, and all may be exhorted" (I Cor. 14, 31).[2]

But in this argumentation "he lost the labor and the oil,"[3] because both parts of his assumption are false. Firstly, what he says is indeed false, namely that the chief office of a priest is

---

which Israel had in Him" (*Super epistolas Catholicas, In Primam Epistolam Petri*, c. 2 (PL 93, 50D)).

[1] *Enarratio in Epistolas catholicas* (PG 39, 1763C-D).

[2] Luther's actual words are: "Thirdly, let us overthrow the pope's priesthood by means of the office which Christ gave and entrusted to the Apostles. For it belongs to the priest to teach, as is written in Zacharias [sic] in the second chapter: 'The lips of the priest shall keep knowledge, and they shall seek the law at his mouth: because he is the angel of the Lord of hosts' (Mal. 2, 7). For in this way he ought to mediate between God and men, such that he offers to God on behalf of men, and teaches men about God, bringing each one to each other. And here below papist priests seem to themselves to reign, they think that it belongs to them to teach, just as that inflated horn blower, Pope Pelagius, bellows out [*sicut turget immanis illa bucca*] in the *Decretals*: 'Whoever is the authority has the right to command; the rest should and must obey.' [N.B. Gregory of Valencia S.J. calls this fictitious citation "a blasphemous lie" (*Explicatio Verarum Causarum...* (Ingolstadt, Sartorius, 1580) p. 56).] At this point they distort Christ's words: 'He that heareth you, heareth me; and he that despiseth you, despiseth me' (Lk. 10, 16). "Notice here that just as they have fashioned their own priesthood and sacrifice, unknown and foreign to the true Christian, so they have also introduced a new and sacrilegious ministry of the word. In order that this may be clear, we will establish with incontrovertible Scripture that the sole and legitimate ministry of the word, like the priesthood and sacrifice, is common to all Christians. Paul says in II Cor. 4 [sic]: 'Who also hath made us fit ministers of the new testament, not in the letter, but in the spirit' (3, 6). He said these words about all Christians, that he might make all of them ministers of the spirit. Now he who is a minister of the spirit is he who transmits the words of grace, just as the minister of the letter is he who transmits the words of the law. The latter function belonged to Moses, the former to Christ. Peter says to all Christians: 'That you may declare his virtues, who hath called you out of darkness into his marvellous light' (I Pet. 2, 9)." (WA 8, 422, lns. 17-36).

[3] *Oleum et operam perdidi* was a proverbial Roman saying for a waste of time and trouble, "oil" referring to "midnight oil." "Losing both oil and labor," which those were said to do, who had employed

to preach God's word. For this does not pertain to all priests, but only to those who have the care of souls, as their pastors, and hence are bound to feed them with the doctrine of God's word, and concerning these alone Malachias spoke. And concerning these priests alone did Paul say: "Let the priests that rule well, be esteemed worthy of double honour: especially they who labour in the word and doctrine" (I Tim. 5, 17). Thus, there are some priests who do not labor in doctrine. Otherwise, it would not have been necessary to praise more those who labor in the word and doctrine. But those to whom it pertains to labor in the word and doctrine, he sufficiently intimates are they who govern. But to the others who are not pastors of souls, such as are many priests, it does not pertain to preach God's word. And hence it is proved that it is not the chief function of a priest to preach God's word, nor does the sacerdotal ministry consist in that work. "For every high priest taken from among men, is ordained for men in the things that appertain to God, that he may offer up gifts and sacrifices for sins" (Heb. 5, 1). From which words it is evident that the sacerdotal office is to offer, and not to teach. For by this reason alone Paul in that passage proves that Christ is a priest, because He offered, not because He taught. Then, not all teachers of the Old Law were priests; therefore, neither in the Evangelical Law. For the Apostles were ordained priests by Christ at the Last Supper, when He gave them the power of confecting from bread and wine His Body and Blood, and afterwards at the Resurrection He completed [their priesthood], when He gave them the power of forgiving sins. Yet before this time they were sent to preach, as is evident from the Gospels of Matthew and Luke. Philip also was preaching in Samaria, as Luke relates in the Acts of the Apostles, and this man was neither a bishop nor a priest, as is established from the same history: because otherwise it would not have been necessary to send Peter and John to the Samaritans, if Philip could have exercised all the functions of a priest.

The other point which Luther assumes in his argumentation when saying that the office of teaching God's word belongs indiscriminately to all, both laymen and women, is also false. For above in the section of "Preaching," we clearly proved that this opinion is heretical, and that it is not allowed for anyone without permission to preach God's word, as Paul teaches, saying the following: "How shall they preach unless they be sent?" (Rom. 10, 15). Now that he gives women the power of teaching is plain adulation whereby he wants to please them, or so that he might allure by this reason those whom he ardently loved into the love of him. For Paul forbids this to women, speaking thus: "Let the woman learn in silence, with all subjection. But I suffer not a woman to teach" (I Tim. 2, 11-12). Yet Luther, knowing this opinion is opposed to him, distorts it from Paul's mind into another meaning, as for example in the aforementioned tract, saying: Although according to Paul's opinion, where men are performing the function of speaking, women ought not to speak: nevertheless, when no men are speaking, it is necessary that women would speak.[1]

One can easily establish that this is a false interpretation, and very far from Paul's mind if we consider the reason on account of which Paul did not permit women to speak. For the absence of men is not the reason, but the fear of subduction, namely because a woman can easily be seduced: and this can happen more easily when a man is absent, than if a man were present from whom she could be admonished. For this happened to Eve, who was not seduced when her husband was present, but when her husband was absent. Hence Paul after he said that he does not permit a woman to teach, immediately added: "For Adam was first formed; then

---

much time, labor, study, and expense, in endeavoring to attain an object, without being able to effect their purpose. The original Latin phrase *et oleum et operam perdidi* is from act 1, scene 2, of Titus Maccius Plautus' comedy, *Poenulus* (c. 195-189 BC).

[1] "Paul so forbids women to speak, not simply, but in the church, namely where there are men able to speak, so that respectability and order would not be confounded, since a man in many ways is more capable of speaking and it befits him more" (WA 8, 424, lns. 30-33).

Eve. And Adam was not seduced; but the woman being seduced, was in the transgression" (v. 13-14). When Theophylactus interprets these words, he says: "A woman taught once, and the whole world was overthrown: for this reason, this sex may not teach. For it is inconstant, [it easily submits,] and can easily be seduced. For notice that he did not say, 'Eve being seduced,' but 'the woman,' that is to say, as though he were discussing the feminine gender itself. For in the same manner that the whole race perished in Adam, so through Eve inconstancy spread unto all woman; by that inconstancy to be sure that same transgression took place firstly in Eve."[1] Thus, Luther rightly ought to be deemed more fickle, and very fickle, who gives the power of teaching to women, very fickle by nature, and very prone to deception.

But let us see by what very false arguments Luther tries to prove that the power of preaching God's word was committed to all Christians. For the passage which he cites from the Second Epistle to the Corinthians, "He hath made us fit ministers of the new testament" (3, 6), ought to be understood not of all Christians, but alone of Paul himself, and the other fellow Apostles of the Gospel preaching. For these alone were made ministers of the New Testament by Christ, but the others who afterwards were ministers of the same preaching, received that ministry, not from Christ Himself, but from men. And [Ambrosiaster] supports this interpretation who, in his *Commentaria in Epistolas Beati Pauli*, when interpreting the abovementioned words of Paul, says: "Although he indicates his Apostolic dignity, he nevertheless breaks forth into the praise of God, not ascribing it to human merits, but to His grace, Who deigned to ordain salutary preaching for mankind, which would save those whom the Old Law held guilty, after having given the remission of sins through our Lord Jesus Christ."[2] In which words one ought to note especially that by those words Paul indicates his Apostolic dignity, and not that all Christians [have Apostolic dignity]. [Hervé de Bourg-Dieu], agrees with [Ambrosiaster], who when interpreting the same words, says: "He now begins to commend himself in a different way than before, so that he may delineate the false prophets, suggesting that they are ministers of the Old Testament, while he shows that he is a minister of the New."[3]

And although these two illustrious men did not prove this with certitude, still Paul himself was clear enough from those things which he had said at the beginning of the chapter, which it is evident that they were not said to all Christians, but for his commendation alone. "Do we begin again," he says, "to commend ourselves? Or do we need (as some do) epistles of commendation to you, or from you?" (II Cor. 3, 1). And shortly afterwards he added those words, about which we now dispute: "He hath made us fit ministers of the new testament (v. 6)."

Luther also distorts another quotation which he cites from Blessed Peter, from the mind of the same author. For Peter was not speaking about the preaching of God's word in that passage, but about the praise and thanksgiving which all Christians are bound to render to God on account of the immense benefits received from Him. For the prophets and Apostles often use this word "to declare (*annunciare*)," for "to praise" or "to give thanks." Now so that we may show clearly that this is the mind of Blessed Peter, it is necessary to repeat his words just before. "But you are a chosen generation, a kingly priesthood, a holy nation, a purchased people: that you may declare his virtues, who hath called you out of darkness into his marvelous light" (I Pet. 2, 9). In which words he alludes to those things which God gave to the children of Israel, and shows that all those things are figures of those benefits which He gave to the whole Christian people through His Son. The people of Israel were specially chosen by God: as God Himself says through the prophet Osee: "Israel was a child, and I loved him" (11, 1). So the Christian people is now chosen by God, and for this reason Peter calls them

---

[1] *Expositio in Epistolam ad Timotheum* (PG 125, 39A-B).

[2] *Commentaria in Epistolam ad Corinthios Secundam*, c. 3 (PL 17, 286A).

[3] *Commentaria in Epistolas Pauli*: *In Epistolam II ad Corinthios*, c. 3 (PL 181, 1024A).

"a purchased people (*populus acquisitionis*)." God called the people of Israel out of Egypt: and concerning the Christian people Peter says that God called them out of the darkness of ignorance or sin into the marvelous light of the Evangelical Law, to which agrees the passage of Isaias: "The people that walked in darkness, have seen a great light" (9, 2). Thus, just as the people of Israel after they were led out of Egypt gave thanks to God and sang praises to God for the benefits received from Him: so now Peter admonishes the Christian people to give thanks to God for the benefits given to them, because they are "a purchased people," or as Erasmus translates, "a people whom He called into the light"[1]: and because they were called from darkness into His marvelous light. And this is what long before God had foretold through the prophet Isaias: "This people," he says, "have I formed for myself, they shall shew forth my praise" (43, 21).

Next, even if those words of Peter should be understood not only of praise and thanksgiving, but also of the preaching of God's word, still those words ought not to be understood of public and solemn preaching, but of private preaching. And we acknowledge about the latter, which is permitted for every Christian; because anyone can individually exhort his neighbor in this way regarding the faith, according to that which the Wise Man says: "He gave to every one of them commandment concerning his neighbour" (Eccli. 17, 12). But from this power of preaching, Luther foolishly concludes that all men are priests: because, as we already said, the chief office of a priest does not consist in it. Bede supports the previous interpretation, and it also pleases me more, because it is more germane to the text.

Something similar happens regarding another testimony which Luther cites from the First Epistle to the Corinthians, wherein Paul says: "You may all prophesy one by one; that all may learn" (14, 31). For this word, "to prophesy," does not mean for Paul the same thing as "to preach," but "to interpret": because as [Ambrosiaster] points out, "a prophet" in the Evangelical Law is the same thing which "an interpreter" who explains obscure things.[2] For just of old he was called "a prophet," who was seeing those things which could not be seen by others: so now he is called "a prophet," who understands, and thus explains those things which are obscure: and then one is said "to prophesy," when one interprets obscure things. Now it was not granted to all Christians to interpret in this way, as is evident from the very text of Paul, but to those alone who received from God the gift of this kind of prophecy, or interpretation of words. It is also evident that not all Christians can prophesy, from that which Paul says in the Epistle to the Ephesians: "And he gave some apostles, and some prophets, and other some evangelists, and other some pastors and doctors: For the perfecting of the saints, for the work of the ministry, for the edifying of the body of Christ" (4, 11-12). And hence although we may freely grant to Luther that the chief office of a priest consists in preaching God's word, Luther wrongly concludes from this quotation from the First Epistle to the Corinthians that all Christians are priests: because, according to Paul, not all are prophets, nor are all doctors [i.e., teachers].

It remains [to say] that what Luther says, that priests are made priest by the choice and calling of the people, was clearly condemned in the Synod of Laodicea, in the thirteenth chapter of its decrees, where these words are found: "The election of those who are to be appointed to the priesthood is not to be committed to the multitude."[3] In which words it not merely forbids that priests be made by the choice of the people, but also other ministers of the altar. Against the first assertion of this heresy was pronounced canon ten, in session seven of

---

[1] *Novum Testamentum omne*, p. 504.
[2] "Paul is saying that 'prophets' are 'interpreters' of the Scriptures. Just as a prophet speaks of unknown things to come, so a person who clarifies the meaning of the Scriptures, which are obscure to many, is also said to 'prophesy'" (*Commentaria in Epistolam ad Corinthios Primam*, c. 14, v. 4 (PL 17, 254B)).
[3] PL 84, 131A.

the Council of Trent celebrated under Paul III, the words of which are those that follow: "If anyone shall say that all Christians have power to administer the word and all the sacraments: let him be anathema."[1] John Eck in chapter seven, [*On Holy Orders*[2]], in his *Enchiridion locorum communium adversus Lutheranos*,[3] and Josse van Clichtove in his book, *Antilutherus*,[4] wrote against this error of Luther. Johannes Mensign[5] wrote *De sacerdotio ecclesiae Christi catholicae libros duos*.[6] Johann Horst von Romberg[7] composed the *Panegyricus de dignitate et officio sacerdotii evangelici*.[8]

The **second heresy** about this matter teaches that all priests are equal, and there is no distinction among them. The author of this heresy was Aerius. The Waldensians, Marsilius of Padua, and John Wycliffe afterwards revived the same heresy. But we have already disputed about this error above in the section on "Bishops." For in that place we proved against the same heretics that a bishop is superior to a simple priest both in dignity and authority.

The **third heresy** asserts that a priest loses the power of consecrating if he commits a mortal sin. The authors of this heresy (Guy [the Carmelite] bearing witness) were the Waldensians, saying that every just man of their sect can consecrate the Lord's Body, even if he were a layman. If, however, he had committed a mortal sin, they were saying that he lost that power. The first part of this heresy we now conquered in the beginning of this section on the "Priesthood." For we showed there that no layman can exercise the sacerdotal functions. We overthrew the other part of this particular heresy above in the section on "Power." For in that place we proved that no power, lay or ecclesiastical, is lost through a lethal crime, such that if one be a king, or emperor, or bishop, or pope, or priest, he remains in the same state not withstanding whatever sin, unless perhaps the crime of heresy, on account of which according to the opinion of some Catholics, that dignity or authority is lost in the conferral of which a character is not imprinted, of such kind is a kingdom, or empire, or papacy. Yet by such a crime of heresy priestly power is not lost, because the character, which is imprinted in the conferral of the priesthood, is indelible: wherefore a priest once rightly ordained, no matter what crime he afterwards commits, will always be a priest.

The **fourth heresy** reprehends the celibacy of priests, saying that priests ought not to be celibate. The first author of this heresy (as far as I know) is Luther, who mocks the Church in that it forces priests to abstain from wives. Now so that what he taught by word, he could confirm by deed, he seduced a certain nun, and joined himself to her in marriage, and from her begot some children, who are now young. John Oecolampadius, did the same thing, who was a monk of the Order of Saint Bridget. Wolfgang Capito of Strasbourg[9] adhered to the same error in word and deed: when he died, Martin Bucer, a monk also himself of the Order of Saint Dominic, married the wife of this man. And all who are known by the Lutheran name have done this same thing. And hence I consider Luther the first author of this heresy. For those who confound this error with the error of Jovinian, do not seem to me to correctly do so, because even though Jovinian equated marriage with virginity, still he did not reprehend those who wished to remain celibate, nor did he reprehend priests who were without wives,

---

[1] Dz. 853.
[2] An incorrect reference is given here to another work of John Eck, *De sacrificio Missae*,
[3] *Enchiridion locorum communium... adversus Lutheranos*, c. 7, fol. 49r-54r.
[4] Bk. 2, c. 4-7, fol. 70r-78r.
[5] Johannes Mensing (1477–1547) was a German Dominican theologian and controversialist.
[6] *De ecclesiae Christi sacerdotio* (Cologne, Soter, 1532).
[7] Johann Host (1480-1532) was a German Dominican who taught at the University of Cologne.
[8] This book adjoined to *De ecclesiae Christi sacerdotio* (Cologne, Soter, 1532).
[9] Wolfgang Fabricius Capito (c. 1478–1541) was a German Protestant reformer.

because Jovinian himself (as Augustine bears witness in *De Haeresibus* [*ad Quodvultdeum*][1]) wanted not to have a wife, not for the sake of having greater merit in the life to come, but so that he might not have the trials of marriage. Hence it is evident that although there is agreement between Luther and Jovinian about the merit of virginity, they nowise agree about the celibacy of priests. Thus, we need to take up arms against Luther alone.

And firstly, so that Luther's temerity might appear more clearly, who esteems as worthless the decrees and regulations of his mother the Church, in which he was begotten through Baptism, let us show the very old custom of this matter in the Church, and that it is not without weight, but strengthened by a perpetual decree. For the understanding of which it is necessary to point out that a priest can be married in two ways. In one way, such that he who had been previously bound by marriage is afterwards ordained a priest, remaining in the same marriage. In another way, such that he firstly [is ordained] a priest, and after having received the priesthood he marries a wife. And there is certainly a wide difference between these two ways: because in the primitive Church it was observed that he who had married a wife, might be promoted to the priesthood, yet it was not required of him who had been promoted, that he would have firstly married. For John the Evangelist was a virgin, and Blessed Paul according to the opinion of all the Doctors was also a virgin: nevertheless, it is evident that they were priests and bishops. Hence it was not necessary that he who was going to be ordained a priest would have married a wife, even though it was permitted.

Thus, this custom, according to which that one bound by matrimony was promoted to the priesthood, was in use until the time of the Council of Nicea, in which (as it is related) it was established by a general decree that no one having a wife may be ordained a priest. Which statute, since it was nowise observed (as it should have been) by some, Pope Siricius, who ruled the universal Church shortly after the aforesaid Council of Nicea, severely reprehended them about this matter. Since the decree of the Council of Nicea may not be found, it is not inserted here. For many decrees of that council (as [Pseudo-] Isidore testifies) have been lost through negligence, or perhaps the malice of the Arians. I subjoin the words of Pope Siricius, because by them the very pestilential lust of the Lutherans is clearly enough confuted. For that supreme pontiff, in a certain letter to Bishop Himerius of Tarragona, says the following: "Let us come now to the most sacred Orders of clerics, which we learn from your report, beloved, are thus so scorned and disordered throughout your provinces, to the injury of religion which should be venerated, that we should be speaking with the voice of Jeremias, 'Who will give water to my head, or a fountain of tears to my eyes? and I will weep day and night for the slain of the daughter of my people' (9, 1)." And afterwards when relating their crime, he says: "For we learned that many priests and deacons of Christ, long after their ordination, have produced offspring both from their own wives and even through filthy liaisons, and defend their sin with this excuse, that it is read in the Old Testament that the opportunity to procreate was given to priests and ministers. Let him tell me now, whoever is an addict of lusts and a teacher of vices: if he thinks that here and there in the Law of Moses the restraints of indulgence are relaxed by the Lord for Sacred Orders, why does He admonish those to whom the Holy of Holies was committed saying: 'Sanctify yourselves, and be ye holy because I am the Lord your God' (Lev. 20, 7)? Why also were priests ordered to live in the Temple, far from their homes, in the year of their service? Just for this reason: so that they could not engage in carnal intercourse even with wives, and that shining in integrity of conscience they might offer acceptable service to God. The period of service having been completed, use of wives was permitted to them for reason of succession alone, because no one from a tribe other than of Levi was ordered to be admitted to the ministry of God. Whence the Lord Jesus, when He enlightened us by His coming, testified in the Gospel that He had come to fulfill the Law not

---

[1] C. 82 (PL 42, 46).

to destroy it.[1] And hence He willed that the Church, whose spouse He is, handsome in appearance, radiate with the splendor of chastity, so that on the Day of Judgment when He comes again He can find her without stain and blemish, just as He taught through His Apostle.[2] All we priests and deacons are bound by the unbreakable law of those sanctions, so that from the day of our ordination we subject our hearts and bodies to moderation and modesty in order that in every respect we might please our God in these sacrifices which daily we offer."[3] Pope Siricius says many other things about this matter in the same letter. And nevertheless, he does not seem to make a new decree by those words, so that by a new law he obliges priests to celibacy, but rather he makes plain that they have been obliged elsewhere.

After these times it is not found that someone bound by matrimony was made a priest while making use of marriage without punishment. Otherwise, the Church never permitted that an ordained priest after his ordination would marry a wife, nor will it be found that it was done at any time without punishment. Hence it is very clearly proved that the boldfaced audacity of the Lutherans, and the wanton lust of those who fear not after having received the priesthood to enter upon new contacts of marriage, when this was never customary in the Church, nor could they find any vestige of this thing, nay it was ordered by many decrees of councils that anything of the sort may not happen. For the twenty-[sixth] of the speaks thus: "Of those who have been admitted to the clergy unmarried, we ordain, that the readers and singers only may, if they will, marry."[4] From which words it is very clearly proved from the first ages of the Church that it was not lawful for deacons or priests after having received Holy Orders to marry a wife. The Synod of Neocaesaria, in the first chapter of its decrees defines by these words: "If a presbyter marry, let him be removed from his order; but if he commit fornication or adultery, let him be altogether cast out [i.e., of communion] and put to penance."[5]

And what especially confirms this opinion is that the Greeks, for whom the custom is to promote married men to the priesthood, never permitted someone who after having received the priesthood to marry a wife. For the proving of which thing, I will cite two witnesses. Pope Innocent III, in the chapter *Cum olim*, in the title *De clericis conjugatis*, relates these words: "The Eastern Church did not admit the vow of continence, because the Easterners contract marriage in Minor Orders, and in the higher Orders use marriage already contracted."[6] In which words one ought to notice that he says that Easterners "in the higher Orders use marriage already contracted." Hence we proved that they do not contract marriage after having received Sacred Orders, because according to the common rule of the jurists, "The exception affirms the rule in contrary cases."[7] And Gratian in his book of the *Decretals* relates the same thing more expressly, saying: "The Eastern Church did not take vows of chastity. Yet it keeps this incessant observance, that after the priesthood has been acquired, when the first wife has

---

[1] Cf. Mt. 5, 17.

[2] Cf. Eph. 5, 27.

[3] C. 8-10 (PL 13, 1138A-1139A).

[4] PG 137, 87C. The *Apostolic Canons* are apocryphal as mentioned above in the fifth chapter of the Introduction.

[5] Gratian, *Concordia discordantium canonum*, dist. 29, c. 9 (PL 187, 159A). "…penance *among the laity*" is found here and in the text, but not in the translation of Dioysius Exiguus, and so has been omitted here accordingly. Cf. *Corpus iuris canonici* (Graz, Akademische Druck- und Verlagsanstalt, 1959), p. 103.

[6] *Decretals of Pope Gregory IX*, bk. 3, tit. 3 (*De clericis coniugatis*), c. 6. Cf. Innocent III, *Regesta sive epistolae* 2, Liber sextus pontificatus anno VI, Christi 1203, c. 139 (PL 215, 152C).

[7] *Casus exceptus firmat regulam in contrarium*. This is one of the legal axioms of ancient Rome. Cf. Frommelt, *Regulae iuris* (Lipsig, Weiss & Neumeister, 1878), p. 50.

died, with whom the priest had been made, if he shall have married another, he is deposed."[1] From which words it is proved that the Lutherans are worse than the Greek schismatics, and are rebellious to the Church, because the Lutherans even though when they were initiated to Holy [Orders], they professed the vow of continence, nevertheless they do not fear to marry wives after having received the priesthood. But for the Greeks this fulfillment of a religious duty was perpetual, so that they never dared to attempt anything similar.

From all these things, therefore, one ought to conclude two things. One is that from the very beginning of the Church it was never permitted for anyone, after having received the priesthood, to marry a wife. The other is that even though it was sometimes permitted for a married man to be promoted to the priesthood, it is not now permitted, because it has been decreed that no one may receive Holy Orders unless he first vows continence. For Gratian, in distinction twenty-eight, chapter *Ecce ostensum est*, cites the decree of Blessed Gregory, saying the following: "Bishops should not presume to make any one a subdeacon who does not promise to live chastely... since no one ought to approach the ministry of the altar but one who has been of approved chastity before undertaking the ministry."[2] And this decree was not instituted lightly and without reason, nay it decreed that for many urgent reasons it ought to be so kept. For in the Old Law no one was permitted to eat the flesh of the lamb, which was immolated as a figure of Christ's Body and Blood, unless he had his reins girt. Now by that cincture of the loins the bridling of lust was designated: because the Lord in the Gospel when commending chastity used this expression: "Let your loins be girt" (Lk. 12, 35). And in the First Book of Kings we read that when David came to Achimelech the priest, he did not receive the hallowed bread, even when pressed by hunger, until he attested that he and his men were clean from women, and this not only from other women or concubines, but also from their own wives.[3] For so thinks Blessed Jerome in his commentaries on Titus.[4] From which deed of the priest Achimelech, the same Blessed Father concludes that it is all the more necessary that he who is going to receive the Lord's Sacred Body is chaste and pure: because (as he says) "it is the difference between shadow and bodies, between image and truth, between patterns of things to come and the realities themselves which were prefigured through the patterns."

Furthermore, Blessed Paul in the First Epistle to the Corinthians advises those bound by the bond of marriage that they would "not defraud one another, except, perhaps, by consent, for a time, that you may give yourselves to prayer" (7, 5). By which words he suggests clearly enough that it befits them who give themselves to prayer, to abstain from the obligation of marriage. Thus since it pertains to priests of the New Law to pray to God daily for themselves and the people, it is clearly proved that according to Paul's opinion, that they would daily abstain from the obligation of marriage. And certainly [Ambrosiaster] and Jerome conclude from this passage of Paul that it behooves priests to be so chaste, that they would abstain from all intercourse. For [Ambrosiaster] in his exposition on Paul's First Epistle to Timothy says the following: "If Paul commands the common people [or laity] to abstain themselves for a time for the sake of prayer, so that they might give themselves to prayer: how much more the priests and Levites [or deacons] who ought to pray day and night for the people committed to them! Therefore, they ought to be cleaner than others, because they are the stewards of God."[5] And Blessed Jerome in his *Commentaries on the Epistle to Titus*, makes the same conclusion, speaking thus: "But if laymen are commanded to abstain from intercourse with their wives for

---

[1] *Concordia discordantium canonum*, dist. 28, c. 13 (*De Syracusanae*) (PL 187, 162A).

[2] *Concordia discordantium canonum*, dist. 28 (*Ecce ostensum est*), c. 1 (PL 187, 155C). Cf. *Epistles of St. Gregory*, bk. 1, letter 44 (PL 77, 506A-B).

[3] Cf. I Kings 21, 4-5.

[4] On c. 1, v. 8 (PL 26, 569A).

[5] *Commentaria in Epistolam ad Timotheum Primam*, c. 3, v. 13 (PL 17, 471C).

the sake of prayer, what is one to think of him who will daily offer unspotted victims for his own sins and the people's?"[1] Behold you now see how many pressing reasons for establishing the decree about the celibacy of priests. Great, therefore, is the Lutherans' temerity, who against so many statements of the Fathers, against so many decrees of the councils, do not fear, after the vow of continence which they professed in the reception of Orders, to contract marriage, and to persuade others to do likewise.

But it is necessary that we reply to those things which the Lutherans object to us. For they say that chastity, like every other good work, ought to be free and not forced: because forced services do not please God. But the Church (as they say) forces priests to chastity, thus it does not do well by forcing them. I respond that the Church does not force anyone to chastity, but he himself who is ordained a priest obliges himself to the observance of chastity. The Church, on the other hand, forces no one into receiving the priesthood. If the Church would force absolutely and without any condition someone to the priesthood, one would have a just occasion of complaining. Now since it forces no one to receive the priesthood, it is not for this reason that someone may accuse the Church of tyranny. If the celibate priesthood displeases you, abstain from the priesthood, and do not become a priest, because you know that the priesthood has an annexed condition of this kind. But I want (say some Lutheran) to be a priest and to marry a wife. I reply that this does not belong to your choice, or to your judgment, but to the Church alone which can promote whom it wishes to the priesthood if it finds them worthy, and it can repel those whom it knows to be unworthy. A man does not make himself a priest, but the Church makes him a priest through the prelate bishops. Now the Church does not want someone to receive someone for the priesthood, unless he wants to perpetually lead a celibate life, and have the other things which are required for a good priesthood. If the condition is agreeable, it is necessary that you keep your promise. But if before the Holy Order has been received this condition is not agreeable, choose another state of life pleasing to you, and do not receive Holy Orders, to which chastity is annexed.

They secondly object that passage of Paul: "It is better to marry than to be burnt" (I Cor. 7, 9). Thus, since all men (as they say) burn from concupiscence, it will be good to marry so that by marriage such burning of the flesh may be taken away. I reply: Not everyone who is tempted by the flesh burns, but only he who is overcome by the flesh; otherwise Paul himself since he was suffering from a sting of the flesh,[2] would be said to have been burnt. He who is conquered by the flesh, is burnt at that time. And Paul, when speaking about those who are not bound by vow, but have free power over themselves, says that it is better to marry than to be so burnt, that is, to be conquered by the flesh.

They thirdly object that it is very difficult and impossible to perpetually keep chastity, especially by those who are greatly impelled by the flesh, and suffer very ardent burnings of the flesh. Wherefore the Savior when speaking about those who castrated themselves for the kingdom of heaven said: "All men take not this word...He that can take, let him take it" (Mt. 19, 11-12). I answer that chastity is certainly a difficult thing, but it is difficult for the man left to himself and to his own strength: it is not difficult, however, to him who is helped by God's grace. "I can do all things," he says, "in him who strengtheneth me" (Phil. 4, 13). Now God does not deny this grace to anyone doing what lies in himself: but rather gives it to everyone asking. "God is faithful," Paul says, "who will not suffer you to be tempted above that which you are able: but will make also with temptation issue" (I Cor. 10, 13). And the Savior Himself says: "Whatsoever you ask when ye pray... you shall receive" (Mk. 11, 24). Therefore, if the Lutheran thinks that he is so stimulated by the flesh that he cannot resist, let him ask for help from God Who Himself never denies to him doing what he can. "If any of you want

---
[1] On c. 1, v. 8 (PL 26, 568C-D).
[2] Cf. II Cor. 12, 7.

wisdom," James says, "let him ask of God, who giveth to all men abundantly" (1, 5). Hence let the Lutheran do what the Wise Man says about himself: "And as I knew," he says, "that I could not otherwise be continent, except God gave it, and this also was a point of wisdom, to know whose gift it was: I went to the Lord, and besought him" (Wis. 8, 21).

But John Calvin, although he acknowledges that it is a good thing that we ask for help from God for being continent, still says that this calling down of the Divine help is not a sufficient remedy for keeping continence: and then he says that it is necessary to be married. For in that work of his, *The Institutes of Christian Religion*, when reprehending monks on account of the vow of chastity, says these words: "They offer God a promise of perpetual virginity, as if they had previously made a compact with Him to free them from the necessity of marriage. They cannot allege that they make this vow trusting entirely to the grace of God; for, seeing He declares this to be a special gift not given to all,[1] no man has a right to assume that the gift will be his. Let those who have it use it; and if at any time they feel the infirmity of the flesh, let them have recourse to the aid of Him by Whose power they alone can resist. If this avails not, let them not despise the remedy which is offered to them."[2] In which words there are many things which one may not pass over without reprehension and reproof, and hence it is necessary to examine and correct all those words individually. Firstly, in fact, he mocks those who vow chastity, because for this reason they show that they made a compact with God, so that He would free them from the necessity of marriage. He unjustly ridicules them on this account. For the householder who represents God, "having agreed with the labourers for a penny a day, he sent them into his vineyard" (Mt. 20, 2). If God, for eternal life, as all the Holy Doctors interpret that parable of the vineyard, made an agreement with us: undeservedly Calvin ridicules on the grounds that those who promised chastity to God would say that they made an agreement with God, so that He would keep them in chastity. For just as God promised eternal life to one keeping the Commandments: so He promised His assistance and help to everyone calling upon Him, and He comes to their aid.

But lest Calvin say that it is a figment of our imagination and a new teaching whereby we say that God makes agreements with us in this matter, let him hear what Clement of Alexandria says in his *Stromata* [or *Miscellanies*]: "Therefore, continence is the despising of the body, in accordance with the confession of faith in God."[3] Calvin cannot reject Clement of Alexandria for being recent or tricentenary, because he died a thousand three hundred years ago. If perhaps Calvin objects that God does not always keep this agreement, because there are many who do not keep the vow of chastity, I admit that there are many such men. Yet here God does not fail in the keeping of the agreement, but those men fail who do not do what they can, and do not implore God's help and support as they should do.

Next, Calvin said that we ought not entertain confidence in God for doing some work of virtue, namely to believe, to hope, to love God and neighbor, to keep God's Commandments, to recover from sins, to do any other good work. For every such work is a gift from God, and we cannot do it except with God's cooperation. And Calvin acknowledges this in many places, especially in his tract against the acts of the Council of Trent[4]: because "It is God who

---

[1] Cf. Mt. 19, 11.

[2] *Christiani Religionis Institutio* (1539-1554 editions), c. 4, §18 (CR 29, 449).

[3] Bk. 3, c. 1 (PG 8, 1103B). The author here uses a different translation of the Greek into Latin: *Est ergo continentia corporis despicientia, convenienter pactis cum Deo initis*, meaning, "Therefore continence is a despising of the body, after having fittingly entered upon agreements with God."

[4] "God promises not to act so that we may be able to will well, but to make us will well. Nay, he goes farther when he says, 'I will make you to walk;' as was carefully observed by Augustine. The same thing is affirmed by Paul when he teaches, that, 'It is God who worketh in you, both to will and to accomplish, according to his good will' (Phil. 2, 13)" (*Acts of the Council of Trent with the Antidote*, On the sixth

worketh in you, both to will and to accomplish" (Phil. 2, 13). Therefore, since it is certain that not all men have those works of virtue, and consequently those works are not given by God to all: one never ought to have confidence, according to Calvin's teaching, of having some gift from God, because He declares that He does not give [His gifts] to all. For not all married men abstain from adultery, nor do all men abstain from theft, nor all abstain from drunkenness: and yet for any of these God's help is not less needed than for continence; nay, sometimes more: because they are more prone and inclined to drunkenness, or to theft, than to lust, yet one ought always to trust in God, and one ought never to despair about the performance of any virtue: because even though He states that He does not give to all, still we do not know whether we may be those to whom God decreed to give that virtue.

And hence we ought to labor, according to Blessed Peter's teaching, so that by good works we may make sure our calling.[1] And Paul teaches in the First Epistle to Timothy that one ought to have this confidence in God, saying these words: "For they that have ministered well, shall purchase to themselves a good degree, and much confidence in the faith which is in Christ Jesus" (3, 13). [Ambrosiaster], when interpreting these words in his commentaries on Paul, says: "Those who, if they govern well their children and their houses, that is, the servants or domestics, could become worthy of the priesthood, and have confidence before God, that they may know that they can obtain what they ask, now restraining henceforth from the use of women."[2] But much stronger and clearer is the testimony which John gives for this confidence in his First Epistle, saying the following: "And this is the confidence which we have towards him: That, whatsoever we shall ask according to his will, he heareth us" (5, 14).

Moreover, Calvin said in those words recently cited that those who feel themselves troubled by their flesh ought to flee to God's help: and if they do not obtain what they ask, they ought to receive the remedy of marriage, because he says that they are called to marriage by God's determined voice, to whom the ability of being continent is denied.[3] This opinion is worse than the others, because it is more wicked, and exceedingly injurious to God. Now so that I may make this clear to all, I want to ask Calvin whether those to whom God has denied the ability of being continent, did whatever they could of themselves for keeping continence, and so they prayed to God, as was befitting, with fervor and confidence, or perhaps did none of these things. If they did what belongs to them [to do] for keeping continence, and afterwards implored God's favor and help with fervor and confidence, it is most certain and to be held with the Catholic faith, that God would not abandon a supplicant of this kind. Now anyone who would say that God sometimes will deny a person asking in this way for the ability of being continent inflicts a very great injury to God: because he says that He is unfaithful, and nowise keeping His promises. For God denies His favor and help to no one wanting to be continent, or to do any other good thing. In fact, it is a common saying of Augustine, "God welcomes whoever flies to Him, otherwise there would be injustice with Him."[4] For He promises this through the Royal Prophet, saying: "Because he hoped in me I will deliver him: I will protect him because he hath known my name. He shall cry to me, and I will hear him: I am with him in tribulation, I will deliver him, and I will glorify him" (Ps. 90, 14-15). And He

---

session (CR 35, 445)).

[1] Cf. II Pet. 1, 10.

[2] *Commentaria in Epistolam ad Timotheum Primam*, c. 3, v. 12 (PL 17, 471A).

[3] "If the faculty of continence is denied, the voice of God distinctly calls upon them to marry" (*Christiani Religionis Institutio* (1539-1554 editions), c. 4, §18 (CR 29, 449)).

[4] These words are also cited by St. Thomas as being St. Augustine's, but are not found at least as quoted here in his writing. Cf. I-II, q. 112, a. 3 obj. 1. The editions refer to the *Glossa Ordinaria* on Romans 3, 22 and the *Glossa Lombardi* on Romans 3, 21 (PL 191, 1360); also to Rabanus Maurus, *Enarr. In Rom.* 3, 21 (PL 111, 1341). None of these references correspond at all closely to the text cited by St. Thomas.

Himself promised assistance to all without any exception, when He said: "Come to me, all you that labour, and are burdened, and I will refresh you" (Mt. 11, 28).

It cannot be denied that the temptation of the flesh is a heavy burden to the soul, according to the saying of the Wise Man: "The corruptible body is a load upon the soul" (Wis. 9, 15). He who carries this burden, is fatigued with great labor. Hence God calls all these men, just as also any other laboring and burdened men, to Himself, and promises refreshment, that is the granting of those things for which they rightly hunger and thirst. And again, elsewhere the Savior likewise promises the liberality and favor of the Father, saying: "If you ask the Father anything in my name, he will give it you" (Jn. 16, 23). And He also spoke here universally without any exception, not particularly promising this or that, but whatever has been asked. God always fulfills these and other promises of this kind, doing according to that which He promised. For this reason, Paul says that we "hold fast the confession of our hope without wavering (for he is faithful that hath promised)" (Heb. 10, 23).

If Calvin says that those to whom God denies the faculty of being continent did not do what they could for keeping continence, and did not pray to God for it ardently and confidently, then it will be their fault, because they did not do what they could. "You ask, and receive not," James says, "because you ask amiss" (4, 3). Thus, it is the fault of the priests who say that they cannot be continent: because if they had prayed well to God, they would have obtained His favor and help. For, as the [Royal] Prophet says, "The Lord is nigh unto all them that call upon him: to all that call upon him in truth. He will do the will of them that fear him: and he will hear their prayer, and save them" (Ps. 144, 18-19). When [Pseudo-] Jerome interprets these words, he says: "When he delivers them either from the urging of the devil, or from the ardent desire of sin."[1]

But note that the prophet added, "that call upon him in truth." For there are some who ask, not in truth, but in a lie: such are they who ask tepidly: because they do not want what they ask to be given to them, and they lament afterwards if the things requested are granted. To these men God is not nigh when they call upon Him, neither does He hear their prayers, nor does He save them from the urging of the devil, nor from the ardent desire of sin. I think that Calvin and the rest of the Lutheran priests are such, who after having received the priesthood married wives, saying that they could not be continent. I acknowledge that they could not be continent: because they do nothing necessary for keeping continence. Or they dread fasting, they have no abstinence of food, they are gluttons and devourers of meats: they inebriate themselves with wine, and embrace everything inimical to continence. "Be not drunk with wine, wherein is luxury" (Eph. 5, 18). And Jerome says: "A man heated with wine will quickly give the rein to lust."[2] And Isidore [of Seville] says: "By the kindling wood of food, the fires of lust increase: temptation however does not burn the body which abstinence wears down."[3] Calvin, however, and the other Lutheran priests, because they are desirous of lust, and do not want continence, hence they also do not want to abstain from those things which provoke lust: and afterwards say that they are unable to be continent. Similar to this matter seems to me to be a servant, who put the stirrup leather entrusted to his care by his master close to the fire, and afterwards says that he could not keep it unharmed from the fire, and the master rightly punishes this man, because he put it close to the fire.

Now so that Calvin and the other Lutherans might come to know their guilt, because they are not continent: and that the excuse, whereby they say that God denied them this gift of continence, is false, I wish to bring forth four very noble witnesses, and great men without exception. Jerome in his commentaries on Matthew, when interpreting the words of the Savior:

---

[1] *Breviarium in Psalmos* (PL 26, 1248A).

[2] Letter 69 (To Oceanus), n. 9 (PL 22, 663).

[3] *Sententiae*, bk. 2, c. 42, n. 7 (PL 83, 648B).

"All men take not this word, but they to whom it is given" (19, 11), says these words: "But let none think, that wherein He adds, 'but they to whom it is given,' that either fate or fortune is implied, as though they were virgins only whom chance has led to such a fortune. For that is given to those who have sought it of God, who have longed for it, who have striven that they might obtain it. 'For everyone that asketh, receiveth: and he that seeketh, findeth: and to him that knocketh, it shall be opened' (Mt. 7, 8 & Lk. 11, 10)."[1] And afterwards on the words, "He that can take, let him take it" (v. 12), he says these words: "The Lord's word is as it were an exhortation, stirring on His soldiers to the prize of purity. 'He that can take it, let him take it': let him who can, fight, conquer and receive his reward."[2]

Chrysostom, when interpreting the words of the Savior, whereby concerning those "who have made themselves eunuchs for the kingdom of heaven" (Matt. 19, 12), He said, "He that can take it, let him take it," says these words: "[He proceeds again to say, 'He that can take it, let him take it,'] at once making them more earnest by showing that the matter is remarkable and great, and not to include the matter within the necessity of law, on account of His unspeakable gentleness. And this He said, when He showed it to be most possible, in order that the desire of the will might be greater. And if the matter belongs to the will, you will say, why does He say, at the beginning, 'All men take not this word, but they to whom it is given'? It was so that you might learn that the conflict is great; not that you should imagine a sort of casting of lots is necessary. For it is given to those who are willing. But He spoke thus to show that great help of supernal grace is needed by him who enters into this combat, whereof whoever wills to do so shall surely enjoy [the reward]."[3] Nothing clearer against Calvin could be said than these words.

And Theophylactus, when interpreting the same words of the Savior, says: "After the Apostles had said that it would be better not to enter into marriage, the Lord says that virginity is a great possession: but it cannot be rightly kept by everyone, but only those with whom God is their cooperator. For in this passage 'it is given' means 'those with whom God cooperates.' Now to them who ask it is given. For He says, 'Ask, and it shall be given you' (Lk. 11, 9). 'For everyone that asketh,' He says, 'receiveth'" (Mt. 7, 8 & Lk. 11, 10). Theophylactus is here teaching the same thing as Chrysostom.

And before these three men, Origen, when interpreting those words of the Savior in the same way, says these words: "Now because some were finding fault with what Christ said, 'They to whom it is given' (Mt. 19, 11), as though some men, who wished to be in celibacy, but were but were not prevailing, would have an excuse. To whom it ought to be replied that if we only simply accept what was said, 'They to whom it is given,' but we do not pay attention to that which He says elsewhere, 'Ask, and it shall be given you' (Lk. 11, 9), and 'For everyone that asketh, receiveth' (Mt. 7, 8 & Lk. 11, 10); either we are not believers, or those who know the Scriptures. For he who wishes to be able to fulfill what is said about chastity, let him ask believing the One speaking, and he will receive: not doubting about that which was said, 'For everyone that asketh, receiveth' (Mt. 7, 8 & Lk. 11, 10). Thus, who is it who asks? He who believes in Christ speaking. If you stand praying, believe, and you will receive. For he who asks ought to do everything in regard to himself, so that he prays with the spirit, he prays also with the mind,[4] mindful of the Apostolic word which says, 'Pray without ceasing' (I Thess. 5, 17)."[5] From which words it is established that there was long ago those who

---

[1] *Commentary on Matthew*, bk. 3 (PL 26, 135C-D).

[2] *Ibid.* (PL 26, 136B).

[3] Hom. 62, n. (PG 600).

[4] Cf. I Cor. 14, 15.

[5] PG 13, 1249D-1252D. The author here uses an old translation of Origen which is included in Migne's *Patrologia Graeca* at the bottom of the pages cited here.

were giving the same excuse for having violated continence, which the Lutheran priests now give: but Origen says that those men were either unbelievers or those who were not knowing Scripture. Hence let the Lutherans see and choose to which censure they wish to subject themselves: whether they prefer that they are called unbelievers, or those are ignorant of the Scriptures: because it is necessary that they fall into one or the other of these [categories], according to Origen's censure.

To these very reliable witnesses I wish to join a fifth one, more ancient than them all, namely Tertullian, who in his book, *On Monogamy*, says these words: Evangelical "eunuchs not only have lost ignominy, but have even deserved grace, being invited into the kingdoms of the heavens: the law of succeeding to the wife of a brother being buried..., and He says, 'He that can take, let him take it' (Mt. 19, 12); that is, let him who is not able go his way... Choose that which is good: if you cannot, because you will not—for that you can if you will He has shown, because He has proposed each to your free-will—you ought to depart from Him whose will you do not."[1] From these five trustworthy witnesses it is proved that man can be continent if he wills and does those things which are necessary for continence: because to the one doing what he can, God is always ready to help.

But leaving aside these testimonies, so that I may more clearly refute Calvin and the rest of the Lutherans, I ask those of them who have now married wives, what would they do if their wives were to suffer from perpetual sickness, so that they could in no wise have intercourse with them: or if any other impediment were to come in the way, on account of which they would be perpetually deprived of intercourse with them? Would they marry another wife, so that they would comply with the appetite of the flesh? But it is very clearly evident that this is not permitted, because to have two wives at the same time is forbidden by Divine law, as we proved above in the section on "Marriage," in the fourth heresy. And it will not be allowed to have intercourse with another woman, because it would clearly be adultery: because the first wife did not cease to be the wife, neither on account of perpetual sickness nor on account of perpetual absence. Thus, while she is alive her husband cannot be joined to another woman without committing the crime of adultery. What then would Calvin or any other Lutheran priest do in this case? Certainly, it is necessary for him to be continent, unless they prefer to offend God. Therefore, what he would then do for keeping continence, this he may do now before he marries a wife, and he may not say that he cannot keep continence.

Fourthly, they object to us those words of Paul from the First Epistle to the Corinthians: "For fear of fornication, let every man have his own wife" (7, 2). Which words the Lutherans interpret in this sense, that Paul thought that anyone was free to marry a wife when very attracted by his flesh towards venery. But in reality, the Lutherans are mistaken regarding the meaning of these words, or they pretend to be mistaken, so that might at least conceal their lust by the camouflage of their words. For it is not likely that Paul would command marriage, who after a few words in the same epistle and in the same chapter, often gave the counsel of not marrying, and often exhorted to this. "Now concerning virgins," he says, "I have no commandment of the Lord; but I give counsel" (v. 25). And again, "He that is without a wife, is solicitous for the things that belong to the Lord, how he may please God" (v. 32). And after he adds a few words he concludes as follows: "Therefore, both he that giveth his virgin in marriage, doth well; and he that giveth her not, doth better" (v. 38). Now all these words contradict the words cited by the Lutherans, if as they say, Paul by these words either commands or counsels those who are not joined by marriage, that they would contract marriage. Thus, Paul is speaking in these words about those who already had wives, regarding whom, because they were pagans, there was doubt among them, whether when having converted to Christianity, they would necessarily be obliged to leave their wives, or to abstain from intercourse with

---

[1] C. 7 & 14 (PL 2, 938A & 950B-C).

them: and the Corinthians had asked Paul about this matter. Hence when answering them Paul says: "Now concerning the thing whereof you wrote to me: It is good for a man not to touch a woman. But for fear of fornication, let every man have his own wife, and let every woman have her own husband" (v. 1-2). And he consequently explains the obligation which spouses have of rendering the marriage debt to each other. And thereafter from the occasion having been offered, he discusses about virgins, whose state he prefers to matrimony, even though he reckons both to be good. Finally, returning to the married persons about whom he had begun to speak, he repeats again that their union is indissoluble, speaking thus: "A woman is bound by the law as long as her husband liveth" (v. 39).

Therefore, from the whole context of this passage it is clearly gathered that Paul, in those words which the Lutherans cite in favor of themselves, says completely nothing in their favor: because he speaks here about the married, and not about those who are not bound by any bond of marriage. Thus, concerning them he says: "It is good not to touch a woman," that is, it is fitting and useful for a husband to abstain from relations with his wife, and the joining with her flesh, if it is done with her consent. For if she wills to use her husband, he would be obliged, as Paul immediately teaches, to render the debt to his wife. But lest from this abstinence from the wife recommended by the Apostle, they would take an occasion for adultery, he immediately removes the occasion, saying the following: "But for fear of fornication, let every man have his own wife." He did not say, "marry," but "have," that is to say, retain and use her. Also, when saying "his own," he manifestly shows that he speaks of the retention and use of her, which was already his right: and not of her who he was going to marry, and was still not his.

Now in order that I may clearly prove that this is the true and germane meaning of Paul's words, I will cite a number of illustrious men renown for holiness as well as learning in testimony of this matter, any of whom ought to be trusted more than all the Lutherans at the same time. [Ambrosiaster], in his commentaries on Paul, when interpreting the above-mentioned words, says: "Stirred up by the depraved minds of the false Apostles, who in their hypocrisy were teaching that marriage ought to be rejected so that they might appear to be purer than others, the Corinthians wrote to Paul to ask him about these things. Because they were unhappy about this teaching, they ignored everything else and concentrated exclusively on this. Paul replied to them that it was a good thing not to touch a woman, although he did not assert that simply. 'But for fear of fornication,' that is, lest what is against the law be permitted, when what the Law does not forbid is avoided, since 'every man may have his own wife, and every woman may have her own husband' For those who look for a short way, often stray from the right path. For how could it happen that those who abstain from their wives, he finds involved in such serious vices? Therefore he does not permit that those who are abstaining from lawful things to venture to do forbidden things, as the Manichaeans do."[1]

Jerome entirely agrees with this, who in his book, *Against Jovinian*, says these words: Paul said, "'For fear of fornication, let every man have his own wife' (7, 2). He did not say, 'because of fornication let each man marry a wife': otherwise by this excuse he would have thrown the reins to lust, and whenever a man's wife died, he would have to marry another to prevent fornication, but 'have his own wife.' 'Let him,' he says, 'have (and use) his own wife,' whom he had before he became a believer, and whom it would have been good not to touch, and, when once he became a follower of Christ, to know only as a sister, not as a wife unless fornication should make it excusable to touch her. 'The wife hath not power over her own body, but the husband: and likewise also the husband hath not power over his own body, but the wife.' The whole question here concerns those who are married men. Is it lawful for them to do what our Lord forbade in the Gospel, and to put away their wives? Whence it is that the

---

[1] *Commentary on First Corinthians*, c. 7, v. 1 (PL 17, 216B-C).

Apostle says, 'It is good for a man not to touch a woman.' But inasmuch as he who is once married has no power to abstain except by mutual consent, and may not reject an unoffending partner, let the husband render unto the wife her due. He bound himself voluntarily that he might be under compulsion to render it."[1] Jerome could not have spoken more clearly against the Lutherans.

Chrysostom also supports this opinion, who in his nineteenth homily on the First Epistle to the Corinthians, says these words: "Wherefore he says, 'Now concerning the thing whereof you wrote unto me.' For they had written to him, whether it was right to abstain from one's wife, or not: and writing back in answer to this and giving rules about marriage, he introduces also the discourse concerning virginity: 'It is good for a man not to touch a woman.' For if, says he, you enquire what is the excellent and greatly superior course, it is better not to have any usage whatever with a woman: but if you ask what is safe and helpful to your own infirmity, make use of marriage. But since it was likely, as also happens now, that the husband might be willing but the wife not, or perhaps the reverse, mark how he discusses each case... 'Let the husband render the debt to his wife, and the wife also in like manner to the husband.'"[2]

Oecumenius[3] subscribes to this, who when interpreting the above-mentioned words of Paul, says these words: "They had written to Paul, whether one ought to abstain from a wife, or not. 'It is good for a man not to touch a woman'; what however is free from danger, and was given as a help to our weakness, that every man would use his lawful wife, and let every woman would use her lawful husband."[4]

I do not want to cite more witnesses for this opinion, lest I be too prolonged: especially since these four can be enough for a man not completely obstinate. Nevertheless, if anyone would like to see more, I will give their references. Augustine in his letter to Ecdicia.[5] Fulgentius in his second letter, in which he treats the conjugal state;[6] and his third letter, where he treats of the conjugal debt.[7] Theophylactus in his commentaries on Paul.[8] Haymo [of Aux-

---

[1] Bk. 1 (PL 23, 219C-220A).

[2] PG 61, 151-152.

[3] Oecumenius was the Bishop of Trikka (now Trikkala) in Thessaly about 990 A.D.

[4] PG 118, 723B.

[5] "'But for fear of fornication, let every man have his own wife, and let every woman have her own husband...' According to these words of the Apostle, if he had wished to practice continence and you had not, he would have been obliged to render you the debt, and God would have given him credit for continence if he had not refused you marital intercourse, out of consideration for your weakness, not his own, in order to prevent you from falling into the damnable sin of adultery. How much more fitting would it have been for you, to whom subjection was more appropriate, to yield to his will in rendering him the debt in this way, since God would have taken account of your intention to observe continence which you gave up to save your husband from destruction!" (Letter 262, n. 2 (PL 33, 1078)).

[6] "Concerning spouses, it is said: 'But for fear of fornication, let every man have his own wife, and let every woman have her own husband'" (C. 6 (PL 65, 314D)).

[7] "And in order that he might show that he is also writing to married people, he immediately added, 'Now concerning the thing whereof you wrote to me: It is good for a man not to touch a woman. But for fear of fornication, let every man have his own wife, and let every woman have her own husband'" (C. 8 (PL 65, 329B)).

[8] "'But for fear of fornication, let every man have his own wife, and let every woman have her own husband.' He discourses about both spouses. For it is likely that the man loves continence, but not the woman; or vice versa. When saying, 'But for fear of fornication,' he urges us to continence. For if marriage is permitted for fear of fornication, those joined by marriage ought not afterwards to be joined intemperately, but come together chastely" (*Commentariius in Epistolam I ad Corinthios* (PG 124, 639A)).

erre[1]] when interpreting the aforesaid words in *Expositio in Divi Pauli epistolas*.[2] [Hervé de Bourg-Dieu] on the same passage says nearly the same words which [Ambrosiaster] says.[3] Therefore, it will be more reasonable to believe these illustrious men, with whose teaching the Church shines, than two thousand Lutherans, the disciples of Epicurus and Venus.

Fifthly they object to us these words of Paul: "It behoveth therefore a bishop to be… of one wife" (I Tim. 3, 2). From which words the Lutherans infer that it is not merely permitted but also necessary that a bishop and priest have one wife, lest perhaps he takes wives belonging to others, while he lacks his own. If these things were said by uneducated Lutherans, I would not be surprised: but since they are said by those who boast of being very learned, and desire to considered as being learned, I cannot but be surprised that they are so deranged that they are not ashamed to say these things. Hence, either their malice has blinded them, or they so pretend to understand Paul that they may persuade the people, whom they chiefly wish to please, that they married wives not without reason and authority. For Paul in those words does not require marriage in him who to be raised to the episcopacy, as though he who wished to live free of the bond of a wife would be held to be an unworthy priest: but by those words he excludes bigamy from the priesthood, such that he who was bigamous could not perform the priesthood. For otherwise, how could it happen that Paul would require marriage of the priest as something necessary, who elsewhere commends virginity, preferring it to marriage, and exhorting all to it? For it is not likely that he would want the people to be endowed with greater virtue than the bishop.

And consequently, all the holy Doctors received by the Church, who have discoursed about this matter, have so interpreted those words of Paul, as we have just stated. I will cite, therefore, a number of them in testimony, so that I may prove by their testimonies that the Lutherans are very far away from Paul's opinion. Jerome, in the first book of *Against Jovinian*, says these words: "For he does not say: Let a bishop be chosen who marries one wife and begets children; but who marries one wife, and has his children in subjection and well disciplined… To take the other view, if the Apostle's meaning be that marriage is necessary in a bishop, the Apostle himself ought not to have been a bishop, for he said, 'For I would that all men were even as myself' (I Cor. 7, 7). And John [the Evangelist] will be thought unworthy of this rank… [Therefore he ought to be] 'the husband of one wife,' that is, in the past, not in the present."[4] And in a letter to Oceanus he says: "In both epistles [of Paul] commandment is given that only monogamists should be chosen for the clerical office whether as bishops or as presbyters."[5]

Tertullian supports this opinion, who in his book, *On Exhortation to Chastity*, says: "Among us the prescript is more fully and more carefully laid down, that they who are chosen into

---

[1] In Migne's *Patrologia Latina*, this passage is attributed to Haymo of Halberstadt, but as mentioned above (see the section, "Gospel," heresy 2, it has more recently been shown to have been written by Haymo of Auxerre.

[2] "When false Apostles were saying to the Corinthians: 'You who are clean to God ought not to be joined to women, but rather you who believe in Christ ought to leave your wives,' the Corinthians wrote to the Apostle about this matter, whether they ought to be joined to their wives in intercourse or not. To whom the Apostle replies: 'It is indeed good to abstain from a wife, but better to marry than to commit adultery with the wife of another or fornication in some way.'" (*In Epistolam I ad Corinthios* (PL 117, 543C-D)).

[3] "'Let every man have his own wife,' namely his wife, whom he had before he believed." (*In Epistolam I ad Corinthios* (PL 181, 875A)).

[4] N. 34-35 (PL 23, 257A & 258B-C).

[5] Letter 69, n. 3 (PL 22, 656).

the sacerdotal order must be men of one marriage;[1] which rule is so rigidly observed, that I remember some removed from their office for digamy."[2] These are the words of Tertullian who preceded the Council of Nicea by nearly two centuries. I do not want to cite many [Doctors] of the Latins: because they all are suspect of heresy regarding the celibate priesthood, because they [the Lutherans] say that they were overly strict in this matter. If someone wishes to see more, however, he may see [Ambrosiaster] in his commentaries on the [First] Epistle to Timothy;[3] Augustine in his book, *Of the Good of Marriage*;[4] Primasius [of Hadrumetum], a disciple of Augustine, on the first chapter of the Epistle to Titus;[5] Haymo [of Auxerre][6] and [Hervé de Bourg-Dieu][7] on Paul's Epistles.

Wherefore I pass on to the Greeks, who ought to have greater authority with these heretics, because it was commonly boasted that they broke the law in the Council of Nicea regarding the celibacy of priests. Oecumenius, on the first chapter to the Epistle to Titus, says: "'The husband of one wife,' that is, he knew only one wife, who was his lawful wife. This saying imposes silence upon heretics detesting marriage, since some men could anticipate the episcopacy with marriage: but he rejects bigamy, as liable to insult and contempt."[8]

Chrysostom teaches this much more clearly, who on the [First] Epistle to Timothy, says: "'It behoveth therefore a bishop to be... the husband of one wife.' This he does not lay down as a rule, as if he must not be without one, but as prohibiting his having more than one."[9] Chrysostom says many other things in that place in favor of this opinion: and he [i.e. Pseudo-Chrysostom] likewise again confirms it in the second homily of *The Patience of Job*.[10] Theophylactus, as he always does elsewhere, so now also agrees with Chrysostom, speaking thus: "Then, he says this not to make a law, because it would be absolutely necessary for a bishop to be married: for why would he have stated this, who says elsewhere, 'For I would that all men were even as myself' (I Cor. 7, 7)? But it was because those times so required. It is as though he said, 'It may happen that he is the husband of one wife.' But he said this because of the Jews, for to them polygamy was permitted, [that is, to be married to many wives]."[11]

Epiphanius in the second book of his *Against the Heresies*, when he battles against the Cathars, says these words: "Since Christ's Coming, in fact, because the honor and dignity of the priesthood is incredible, God's holy Gospel does not accept men for the priesthood after a first marriage, if they have remarried because their first wife died. And God's holy Church

---

[1] Cf. Tit. 1, 6.

[2] C. 7 (PL 2, 921 C). Digamy is second marriage (as after the death or divorce of a spouse).

[3] "'The husband of one wife.' Although it is not forbidden to have a second wife after the [decease of the] first: however, let him who is worthy of the episcopate even spurn the licit one because of the loftiness of that order, because he who wants this chair ought to be better than others." (C. 3 (PL 17, 468D)).

[4] "It is not lawful to ordain any as a steward of the Church, save the husband of one wife. And this they have understood more acutely who have been of opinion, that neither is he to be ordained, who as a catechumen or as a heathen had a second wife" (*De bono coniugali*, c. 18, n. 21 (PL 40, 387)).

[5] "'If any be without crime, the husband of one wife' (Titus 1, 6). It ought to be noted that for a priest, even licit things are forbidden" (PL 68, 680C).

[6] "'The husband of one wife' (I Tim. 3, 2), that is, before he may be ordained he ought to have one wife, such that he is not bigamous or trigamous; but afterwards he ought to completely abstain" (PL 117, 791D).

[7] "It behoveth him to be 'the husband of one wife,' that is, he who had one wife, not he who had a second" (PL 181, 1421D).

[8] PG 119, 246D-247A.

[9] Hom. 10, n. 1 (PG 62, 547).

[10] PG 56, 569.

[11] PG 125, 42C-D.

observes this with unfailing strictness. She does not even accept the husband of one wife if he is still co-habiting with her and fathering children. She does accept the abstinent husband of one wife, or a widower, as a deacon, presbyter, bishop and subdeacon, [but no other married men], particularly where the Canons of the Church are strictly enforced."[1] Epiphanius lived near to the time of the Council of Nicea: and although he is Greek, he says that at that time they keep the same law about the celibacy of priests among themselves, which is now kept in the Latin Church.

Even though Calvin admits that those words of Paul are so understood by the ancient Doctors of the Church, still he does not hesitate to contradict them all, and he does not shrink from provoking them all, like another Goliath, to battle. For in that work, *The Institutes of Christian Religion*, when disputing against Catholics about the celibacy of priests, after he had objected those words of Paul, "It behoveth a bishop to be... of one wife" (I Tim. 3, 2), he says these words: "I am aware of how they expound this, namely that no one was to be appointed a bishop who had a second wife. And I admit that this interpretation is not new; but it is plainly false from the very context: because it immediately prescribes the kind of wives whom bishops and deacons ought to have. Paul enumerates marriage among the virtues of a bishop; these men declare that, in the ecclesiastical order, marriage is an intolerable vice."[2] Now how can we endure a man so arrogant, and lying so many times so clearly? He admits that this interpretation is not new, but he contends that it is false. Therefore, the Church was always in error: because it always accepted that interpretation, and always acted according to it. How then will it be, as Paul calls it, "the pillar and ground of the truth" (I Tim. 3, 15), if it remained so long in error? The Church should be deemed wretched, which was deceived for so many centuries until Calvin teaching it, freed it from error.

But let us see the arms whereby he thinks that he conquers them all. He firstly says that Paul prescribes what kind of wives the bishops and deacons ought to have. Where in the world does Paul prescribe this? I am undone if this shall ever have been found in Paul. Perhaps Calvin says this on account of those words which Paul immediately adds: "The women in like manner chaste, not slanderers, but sober, faithful in all things" (I Tim. 3, 11). But in these words, as all have interpreted until now, completely nothing about wives of bishops and deacons, nay of any particular wife does Paul treat. And no Catholic interpreter of Paul said that Paul in that passage discoursed about wives. For Primasius,[3] Theophylactus,[4] and [Hervé de Bourg-Dieu][5] say that Paul is speaking in that place about deaconesses, who long ago were had in the Church, and they had some ministry. [Ambrosiaster] however says that Paul is treating about all women in general there, saying the following: "Because he commanded that a holy man would be made bishop, and a deacon likewise: he assuredly did not want the people to be ill-matched, indeed since the Lord says, 'Be ye holy, because I am holy' (Lev. 19, 2). And so also women who are seen to be inferior, he wants to be without crime, so that God's Church may be free from sin."[6] [Ambrosiaster] is very far away from Calvin's meaning. Haymo [of Auxerre] does not approve of the opinion of those who say that Paul in that place treats about

---

[1] *Panarion*, heresy 39 (but 49 of the series), c. 4 (PG 41, 1023A-B).
[2] *Christiani Religionis Institutio* (1539-1554 editions), c. 3, §68 (CR 29, 413)
[3] "Hence it is clear that he speaks about those whom in the east they call deaconesses" (PL 68, 665C).
[4] "'The women in like manner chaste.' He says these things not about any women, but deaconesses" (PG 125, 47C).
[5] "'Women,' that is deaconesses, just like deacons, ought to be 'chaste,' so that the cleanliness of chastity may have rule in them, 'not slanderers,' that is, not seeking by speaking to lessen the good reputation of anyone, 'but sober,' that is, devoid of all drunkenness, and 'faithful in all things,' by their words and deeds, so that they preserve fidelity to God and men" (PL 181, 1424C).
[6] PL 17, 470C.

deaconesses, yet not does not state about whom he speaks. He says moreover that that opinion about deaconesses was rejected by Augustine, but I could not find this in Augustine.[1] I know that others in this age of ours interpret this passage of the wives of bishops and deacons, but they all, although they may not be considered as heretics, nevertheless all of those whom I have known, are suspect of heresy.

Calvin additionally says that Paul enumerates marriage among the bishop's virtues. Perhaps he says this on account of the words, "It behoveth therefore a bishop to be... of one wife" (I Tim. 3, 2). Yet these words, as we have already shown by many testimonies, do not command marriage: but do away with bigamy. If Calvin, therefore, when arguing against this interpretation, once again objects Paul's same words, he commits a fault in disputing, which by the logicians is called begging the question.[2] But let it be granted [for the sake of the argument] that Paul is speaking in those words about the wives of bishops and deacons, still Calvin cannot infer from this that Paul commands bishops to have wives: but only that he permits for that time, in which it was allowed for them, to use those wives which they had before the priesthood, not nevertheless to marry new wives, or to have had more than one.

Sixthly Calvin objects speaking thus: "What could be said more strongly than where Paul denounces from the Holy Ghost that there would be in the last times wicked men, who would forbid marriage,[3] and he does not now call them imposters, but devils."[4] Calvin accuses us from the words of Paul in the First Epistle to Timothy, because we forbid marriages to priests, as though they were illicit in themselves, and intrinsically evil. But I think that Calvin understands very well that that we do not think that marriages are evil in themselves: because we very clearly teach the contrary, and hence we fight against the Encratites and Manichaeans. And so I am persuaded that Calvin, because he shows himself to be learned in other things, deliberately prepared this calumny for us, so that he might object to us that which Paul said against the enemies of marriage.

This quotation was also objected to Jerome long ago, because he preferred virginity to marriage, and was encouraging it. The same Jerome, when replying to this objection in his apology to Pammachius, says these words: "Have I not, I would ask, in the very forefront of my work set the following preface: We are no disciples of Marcion or of Manichaeus, to detract from marriage. Nor are we deceived by the error of Tatian, the chief of the Encratites, into supposing all intercourse unclean. For he condemns and reprobates not marriage only, but foods also which God has created for us to enjoy...[5] We are not ignorant that 'marriage is honorable...and the bed undefiled' (Heb. 13, 4). We have read the first decree of God: 'Increase and multiply, and fill the earth' (Gen. 1, 28). But while we allow marriage, we prefer the virginity which springs from it. Gold is more precious than silver, but is silver on that account the less silver?"[6] Thus, although in these words Paul does battle against the Manichaeans, the Marcionites, and the Encratites, who condemn marriage, he says nothing against us, we who are very far from these men.

Calvin mocks this interpretation of ours and of all Catholics, who in chapter three of his *Institutes of Christian Religion*, after he quotes to us those words of Paul to give the interpretation just mentioned, he says these words: "As though, even granting that this prophecy was

---

[1] "Likewise women ought to be chaste. Certain men wanted this to mean deaconesses, but it should not, as Blessed Augustine says." (PL 117, 792B).

[2] *Petitio principii*, or assuming the conclusion. Cf. Aristotle, *Sophistical Refutations* Part 5 (167b, 1-15).

[3] Cf. I Tim. 4, 1-3.

[4] *Christiani Religionis Institutio* (1539-1554 editions), c. 3, §67 (CR 29, 412).

[5] Cf. I Tim. 4, 3.

[6] Letter 48, n. 2 (PL 22, 494-495).

primarily fulfilled in those heretics, it were not applicable also to themselves; or, as if one could listen to the childish quibble that they do not forbid marriage, because they do not forbid it to all. This is just as if a tyrant were to contend that a law is not unjust because its injustice presses only on a part of the state."[1] In which words as well as in others, he shows both his arrogance and a manifest calumny. For we do not deny that we forbid marriage, because we do not forbid all men: but that we do not forbid by condemning marriage, as the Manichaeans and Encratites forbade it. For in one way does a doctor forbid, who without a command, but only by teaching, asserts that something is bad, and thus exhorts others to abstain from it. But in another way he forbids, who even though he acknowledges something to be good in its nature, yet because what is good for others, for some particular person is not suitable, using a command he orders the person of this kind to abstain from it. In the first way the Encratites and Manichaeans forbid, and hence are condemned by Paul. In the second way the Church forbids matrimony to priests: because a priest ought to be intent upon God, and thinking of those things which are God's. "But he that is with a wife," as Paul says, "is solicitous for the things of the world, how he may please his wife" (I Cor. 7, 33). Now Paul does not condemn this prohibition, nor did he speak about it, as all his interpreters on that passage declare.

Nevertheless, so that we may speak more truthfully and accurately, if we may say so, as we said in the response to the first objection, the Church does not forbid marriage to priests: but God, to whom they promised celibacy, when they were promoted to the priesthood. For God Who through the mouth of the prophet said: "Vow ye, and pay to the Lord your God" (Ps. 75, 12), asks that what was promised to Him, would be given to Him. He also who has received the priesthood from the Church, forbade matrimony to himself, because he received with this condition, that he would lead a perpetually celibate life. He, therefore, who has received the priesthood under this condition, is bound to keep the condition of receipt and expenditure (*accepti datique*[2]), from which one cannot withdraw, just as one cannot withdraw from the priesthood once received. Now Theophylactus testifies in his commentary on Paul that the Church does not forbid marriage of this kind, who when interpreting the aforesaid words from the First Epistle to Timothy, says these words: "They even calumniate marriage... Do we ourselves also forbid marriage? By no means! But rather we exhort a man to virginity who does not wish to marry: for this is more honorable: yet marriage is meanwhile not dishonorable, just as silver is not worthless because gold is more precious."[3] These are the words of Theophylactus, who has followed Chrysostom.[4] Oecumenius teaches the same things on this passage[5]: [Ambrosiaster][6] and all the rest of the holy Doctors agree with them all.

---

[1] *Christiani Religionis Institutio* (1539-1554 editions), c. 3, §67 (CR 29, 412).

[2] "Put all in writing that thou givest out (*datum*) or receivest in (*acceptum*)" (Eccli. 42, 7). This wording in Latin seems to be derived from the Roman use of accounting in which a banking account (*ratio*) had expenditures (*data*) and receipts (*accepta*). Hence the condition attached to the priesthood seems to imply that one ought to balance what one has given to God, with what one has received from God.

[3] *Expositio in Epistolam I ad Timotheum*, c. 4, v. 2 (PG 125, 54A-B).

[4] "And do not we forbid to marry? God forbid. We do not forbid those who wish to marry, but those who do not wish to marry, we exhort to virginity. It is one thing to forbid, and another to leave one to his own free choice. He that forbids, does it once for all, but he who recommends virginity as a higher state, does not forbid marriage, because he prefers virginity" (*Homilies on First Timothy*, hom. 12, n. 2 (PG 62, 560-561)).

[5] "'Forbidding to marry.' What then? Can it be that Christians also forbid one to contract marriage? By no means! 'Marriage honourable in all, and the bed undefiled' (Heb. 13, 4); but they who do not wish to contract marriage are exhorted to virginity: those however who forbid marriage, forbid as though they ward off from something impure" (PG 119, 166D).

[6] *Commentaria in Epistolam ad Timotheum Primam* (PL 17, 473A-B).

Seventhly, Calvin objects to us the decree of the Council of Nicea, in which, as he says, it was decreed that priests would be free to marry wives if they wish. For in that work of his, *The Institutes of Christian Religion*, he says these words: "In the Council of Nicea, indeed, there was a discussion about obliging celibacy: as there are never wanting little men of superstitious minds, who are always devising some novelty as a means of gaining admiration for themselves. What was decided? The opinion of Paphnutius[1] was adopted, who pronounced conjugal intercourse with one's wife to be chastity.[2] The marriage of priests, therefore, continued sacred, and was neither regarded as a disgrace, nor thought to cast any stain on their ministry."[3] When I was reading these words I could not but abominate such shameless audacity of the man, such that he is not afraid to write this very clear lie in order to deceive. In the Council of Nicea, in fact, it was never disputed whether priests could marry a wife, nor did Paphnutius say something about this matter: because this was never customary for Catholic men. Only this was investigated in that council, whether priests or deacons, who before they were promoted to the ministry of this kind, had wives, could use their wives after the reception of the Holy Order. Thus, when someone suggested that a law be made which would forbid priests from using their wives which they had previously married, Paphnutius resisted, and they all consented.

Now so that I may make certain these things which I said, and I may convict Calvin of a lie, I cite Sozomen, the faithful witness who was cited by Cassiodorus in the second book of the *Tripartite History*, who, when speaking about the Council of Nicea, says these words: "Zealous of reforming the life of those who were engaged about the churches, the council enacted laws which were called canons. While they were deliberating about this, some thought that a law ought to be passed enacting that bishops and presbyters, deacons and subdeacons, should hold no intercourse with the wife they had espoused before they entered the priesthood; but Paphnutius, the confessor, stood up and testified against this proposition; he said that marriage was honorable and chaste, and that cohabitation with their own wives was chastity, and advised the council not to frame such a law, for it would be difficult to bear, and might serve as an occasion of incontinence to them and their wives; and he reminded them, that according to the ancient tradition of the church, those who were unmarried when they took part in the communion of sacred orders, were required to remain so, but that those who were married, were not to put away their wives. Such was the advice of Paphnutius, although he was himself unmarried, and in accordance with it, the council concurred with his recommendation, enacted no law about it, but left the matter to the decision of individual judgment, and not to compulsion."[4]

In which words it ought to be especially noticed that he said that in the Council of Nicea it was discussed about whether priests would not have intercourse with the wives they had previously married. From which it is very clearly established that Calvin falsely cited the history of the Nicene Council for proving his opinion. Rightly, therefore, Calvin and others of the same ilk could say that which others said in Isaias: "We have placed our hope in lies, and by falsehood we are protected" (28, 15). Perhaps Calvin, skipping over the rest of the history, only wanted to use Paphnutius' words against us, whereby he said that cohabitation with one's own wife was chastity, and from this he tries to deduce that priests are chaste, who marry wives after having received the priesthood, and have intercourse with them. But Calvin is deceived making such a conclusion, because even though intercourse with one's own wife is chaste, still a priest who before having received the priesthood did not have a wife, when he

---

[1] Paphnutius was the Bishop of a city in the Upper Thebaid in the early fourth century.
[2] *Historia Tripartita*, bk. 2, c. 14 (PL 69, 933C-D).
[3] *Christiani Religionis Institutio* (1539-1554 editions), c. 3, §70 (CR 29, 414).
[4] C. 23 (PG 926B-C).

has intercourse with some woman, although he may say that he is at that time married to her, does not have intercourse with his own wife: because he cannot marry her as his wife, because when receiving the priesthood, he made himself unable to contract marriage.

But Calvin, wishing to excuse the fault of his intercourse, does what Virgil relates in the fourth book of the Aeneid, that Dido after having been known by Aeneas said to excuse her fornication, "She called it marriage, and with this word concealed her guilt."[1] Calvin does the same, and all the rest of his consorts, who in order to excuse their unchaste concubinages, call them marriage, when they are nothing of the sort.

Eighthly and finally, Calvin objects to us the example of the Apostles and of the other holy bishops who had wives. For in that often cited work of his, *The Institutes of Christian Religion*, in chapter three, after he reprehends those who teach that priests ought to be celibate, he says these words: "But if my opponents plead antiquity, my first answer is, that both under the Apostles, and for several ages after, bishops were at liberty to have wives: that the Apostles themselves, and other pastors of primitive authority who succeeded them, had no difficulty in using this liberty, and that the example of the primitive Church ought justly to have more weight than allow us to think that what was then received and practiced with commendation was either illicit or unbecoming."[2]

In which argument he errs no less, and relies upon the lie, which is in the immediately preceding argument. For even though it is true that some Apostles had wives, when they were chosen by Christ for the office of Apostleship, still it is very false that any of them after he was chosen for the Apostleship, married a new wife. And it was never practiced among Catholics that a priest not having a wife, after having received the priesthood, would marry a wife, as Luther, Oecolampadius, Martin Bucer, Calvin and all the other priests of the Lutheran faction did. And for this reason we reproach them, because after having received the priesthood they married wives, or, so that I may speak more truthfully, concubines, which the Catholic Church never approved: yet Calvin, lying very shamelessly, says that this was received with great praise, and was practiced in the Church. Hence, I ask Calvin to name for us from a reliable historical account at least one or two Catholic priests from the primitive Church, who after having received the priesthood married a wife, with commendation, as he says, and I will immediately concede the point. Yet I am sure that he cannot cite any such priest for us, and hence I am astonished that he dared to say with such great impudence, that in the primitive Church that this was received and practiced with commendation. Therefore, I ask the benevolent reader to carefully consider by what kind and by how many lies these heretics deceive the people, and contrive to draw them into their errors.

But here it is necessary to point out that the reader ought not to think that we brand Luther and his followers with the note of heresy because we believe that by Divine institution celibacy is necessary for the reception of Holy Orders, because (as I have just recently taught) in the beginnings of the Church we read that there were married priests. For marriage is not prejudicial to the priesthood by Divine institution. For the Synod of Gangra in fact decrees as follows: "If any one shall maintain, concerning a married presbyter, that is not lawful to partake of the oblation when he offers it, let him be anathema."[3] From its decree is most clearly evident that celibacy is not necessary by Divine law for the reception of Holy Orders. And we have not branded Luther and his followers for this reason, but we accuse them of heresy because they teach contrary to the statute of the Church about the continency of priests, that priests may contract marriage, and they allure priests to do so, and they ridicule the Church for having made such a statute, and they say that it erred in so decreeing. For which reason

---

[1] Line 172.

[2] *Christiani Religionis Institutio* (1539-1554 editions), c. 3, §71 (CR 29, 414).

[3] Canon 4 (PL 67, 58A).

everyone who correctly thinks (as they ought) about the Church's stability and certitude, will deem they have been rightly branded for heresy. We still will say something about this matter below, because some of the things about which we will discuss in the section on "Virginity," and in the section on "Vows," seem to pertain to this topic. For those things are closely related to this subject.

The **fifth heresy** teaches that any lowly priest can exercise the episcopal office in the absence of the bishop. The author of this heresy is the Irishman, [Archbishop] Richard Fitz-Ralph,[1] who in the [eleventh] book of *De questionibus Armenorum*, in the [seventh] chapter, says that lower priests in the absence of a bishop can exercise the sacramental functions, such as the consecration of altars, the blessing of oil or chrism, the conferral of Orders etc. This FitzRalph flourished [i.e., died] in the year of the Lord 1360 under Emperor Charles IV, and the Supreme Pontiff Innocent VI. John Wycliff maintained the same error.

We have already often disputed against this error. For in the section on "Confirmation," we proved that that Sacrament can be only conferred by bishops, and not by any lesser priest. In the section on "Bishops," we proved both from Holy Writ, and from the definition of the Councils, that bishops are both by dignity and power superior to other priests. But if lesser priests could do everything which bishops do, and they themselves do, doubtlessly the former would be equal to bishops, and there would not be any difference between them. But because in those places we did not dispute at all about the conferring of Orders, I will only cite for the settling of this matter the decree of the II Synod of Seville. For in the fifth chapter of the aforesaid council, these words which follow are found: "In the fifth session, we were told by Amano, deacon of Cabra, that in his church, a clergyman was ordained as a priest and two as Levites, the bishop, who suffered from an infirmity of the eyes, was content to put the hands on them, and at this same time, a certain priest gave them the blessing, which is against the ecclesiastical order. Which priest, although he could be condemned for such great audacity by a judgment in the present life, if he lived; nevertheless, since he has already been judged by God, he cannot be accused by a human judgment; but regarding those who are still alive, and they received from him, not the title of consecration, but rather that of ignominy, lest such a usurpation give license to anyone, we have decreed that they be deposed from the rank of the priestly or Levitical Order that they perversely acquired. And they have been rightly judged to be removed, because they were constituted in wickedness."[2] See the judgment of the council on the conferral of Orders, whereby was decided that they were not ordained upon whom the bishop placed his hands, because they received the blessing not from the bishop, but from the priest. Thus, after the judgment of such a great council it would be unjust for us to dispute more about this matter. But if perhaps a curious reader desires to know more things about this matter, he may read Thomas Netter, in his book, *De sacramentalibus*,[3] in the seventh

---

[1] Richard FitzRalph (c. 1300–1360) was an Irish Archbishop of Armagh. He certainly was not a heretic, since at the end of the cited chapter wherein he discusses the powers of simple priests, he finishes by saying that this is just his opinion and that he submits to the correction of the Church and higher authority. Although it normally belongs to a bishop to consecrate altars and to confer minor orders (Cf. 1917 CIC c. 294 §2) as well as holy oils, priests can be delegated to perform these functions. The permission for consecrating holy oils was granted by the Sacred Congregation of Rites on February 23, 1916, because of World War I. See. AAS vol. 8, pg. 73. But Archbishop FitzRaph was incorrect when he wrote in the cited chapter that "If all the bishops were dead, lesser priests could appoint and even consecrate bishops."

[2] PL 130, 597C-D.

[3] *Doctrinale antiquitatum fidei catholicae ecclesiae*, v. 3 (*De sacramentalibus in quo doctrinae antiquitatum fidei Ecclesiae catholicae*), tit. 7, c. 60-63, pp. 382-400.

title. Because in that place the aforesaid author copiously disputes about this matter against FitzRalph and John Wycliffe.

SACRAMENTA

Sacraments

The old enemy of the human race never laid aside his envy towards the human race once it was conceived, and so he is always occupied with doing whatever he can to harm mankind, and strives to impede him from obtaining eternal beatitude. Wherefore the devil, perceiving how much help the Sacraments which God left them give to men for attaining eternal life, by every way that he could tried to lead men away from their reception and use. Now in order to do this better, he deceived certain heretics, making them as it were commanders of his army, so that he might subvert by their hands any Catholic faithful whom he could. For there were many heretics who denied all the Sacraments, such as the Catharists; I do not speak about the Cathari, who by another name are called the Novatians, but those other men much more recent than they, about whom we have already spoken elsewhere. There were other heretics, who even though they admit there to be some Sacraments, yet they deny many others, as we have already shown when we discussed each Sacrament in their own sections. Others again, while accepting some Sacraments, deny that any of them confer grace to the receiver, no matter how much he may prepare his soul for its reception. The originators of this error are the Armenians. The error of these men, after having been driven out of the Church for a long time, Martin Luther took up to be defended, who utters suchlike words about the Sacraments: "It is a heretical opinion, but a common one, that the Sacraments of the New Law give pardoning grace to those who do not set up an obstacle."[1]

Wherefore it seems to me that Luther, like another Nabuzardan, commander of the army of Nabuchodonosor king of Babylon, who destroyed the walls round about Jerusalem and burned the house of the Lord, and took all the gold, silver, and brass vessels in which the priests were ministering to the Lord in the Temple.[2] What else are the Sacraments, and the other ceremonies of the Church, besides a kind of vessels in which one ministers to God in this life? The gold and silver vessels, I say, are the Sacraments: all the other ceremonies of the Church, however, are the brass vessels. The fact that Luther attempts to take away all these things from the Church, clearly demonstrates that he is another Nabuzardan, that is to say, one of the commanders of the diabolic army.

Even though it has been individually disputed against this pestiferous heresy in regard to each Sacrament individually, still at the present time one thing ought to be done, namely that we show very briefly regarding all the Sacraments in general, those ought to be held to be Sacraments which holy Mother Church accepts and maintains as such. For that the Church cannot err due to God's help assisting it, especially in those things in which it ought not err, as we have already often shown elsewhere. And from this we infer that the Church has the capability of distinguishing Divine writings from human ones, and the true from the false meaning, by God daily enlightening it, lest, to wit, it err in those things there would be a dangerous error. But nowhere would there be a more dangerous loss than if it were to accept false Sacraments for true ones, and the traditions of men, nay contrivances of the devil, for the traditions of God's Church, because then the Church would have placed its hope in fictitious and empty signs of bodily things, as sorcerers do, as being Christ's Sacraments. Thus, if

---

[1] *Exsurge Domine*, error n. 1 (Dz. 741).
[2] Cf. IV Kings 25, 1-15.

the Church has this power conferred by God to distinguish God's words from men's words, it is also necessary to acknowledge that it also has this power likewise conferred upon it, to distinguish God's traditions from men's traditions. For otherwise an error to be avoided could with equal reason arise in regard to one or the other. For Christ assisting His Church until the consummation of the world, does not merely do this so that the Church may not err in this or that way, but so that it may not err in any way. And nowhere could it err with greater injury to Christ than if the confidence to be put in Him alone, one puts in completely useless signs completely unsupported by any grace, but empty and void of all trustworthiness, because that would be very evident idolatry, which God abominates above all other vices. Therefore, the Church cannot err in accepting the Sacraments of the faith, no more, I say, than in accepting the Divine Scriptures, in distinguishing which things it cannot err, as we have already shown elsewhere.

Wherefore it was rightly decreed that if anyone were to judge regarding the Sacraments of the Church otherwise than the Roman Church judges, he is reputed a heretic. And because we have already disputed against the individual heresies which have arisen against the individual Sacraments in their own places, it is not needed that we add something: but it will be enough to cite the canons which the Council of Trent celebrated under Paul III in the seventh session issued for the assertion of the Sacraments, and they are those which follow:

"If anyone shall say that the Sacraments of the New Law were not all instituted by Jesus Christ our Lord, or that there are more or less than seven, namely Baptism, Confirmation, Eucharist, Penance, Extreme Unction, Order, and Matrimony, or even that any one of these seven is not truly and strictly speaking a Sacrament: let him be anathema."[1] "If anyone shall say that these same Sacraments of the New Law do not differ from the sacraments of the Old Law, except that the ceremonies are different and the outward rites are different: let him be anathema."[2] "If anyone shall say that these seven Sacraments are equal to each other in such a way that one is not for any reason more worthy than the other: let him be anathema."[3] "If anyone shall say that the Sacraments of the New Law are not necessary for salvation, but are superfluous, and that, although all are not necessary for every individual, without them or without the desire of them through faith alone men obtain from God the grace of justification; let him be anathema."[4] "If anyone shall say that these Sacraments have been instituted for the nourishing of faith alone: let him be anathema."[5] "If anyone shall say that the Sacraments of the New Law do not contain the grace which they signify, or that they do not confer that grace on those who do not place an obstacle in the way, as though they were only outward signs of grace or justice, received through faith, and certain marks of the Christian profession by which the faithful among men are distinguished from the unbelievers: let him be anathema."[6] "If anyone shall say that grace, as far as concerns God's part, is not given through the Sacraments always and to all men, even though they receive them rightly, but only sometimes and to some persons: let him be anathema."[7] "If anyone shall say that by the said Sacraments of the New Law, grace is not conferred from the work which has been worked [*ex opere operato*], but that faith alone in the Divine promise suffices to obtain grace: let him be anathema."[8]

---

[1] Can. 1 (Dz. 844).
[2] Can. 2 (Dz. 845).
[3] Can. 3 (Dz. 846).
[4] Can. 4, (Dz. 847).
[5] Can. 5 (Dz. 848).
[6] Can. 6 (Dz. 849).
[7] Can. 7 (Dz. 850).
[8] Can. 8 (Dz. 851).

After these canons, which pertain to all the Sacraments at the same time, other canons follow, namely the ninth and tenth, which pertain to particular Sacraments: and hence we omit them now, because in those sections to which they pertain, we have already cited them. Then the eleventh canon follows pertaining to this place, which contains the following words: "If anyone shall say that in ministers, when they effect and confer the Sacraments, the intention at least of doing what the Church does is not required: let him be anathema."[1]

The Most Illustrious King of England [Henry VIII] fights vigorously against this heresy in a whole book which he published, *The Defense of the Seven Sacraments*.

There is a **second heresy** about this matter which denies that a character is imprinted in any Sacrament. The author of this heresy is also Luther. But about this error we have already disputed enough (as I think) in the section on "Character." Thus, it is not right that we would repeat again this error for disputation.

SANCTI

Saints

Our adversary the devil has left nothing untried for impeding us from attaining eternal life. For whatever could help us to lay hold of that blessed life, he tries to take away from us. For he who was striving to withdraw men from the reception of the Sacraments, also endeavored to draw them away from the veneration of the saints, namely because he knows that we are very much helped by their prayers, wherefore he sent certain men who, speaking a lie in the spirit of error,[2] would say that the saints ought not to be honored by men, nor ought they pray to them, so that at least in this way men living here below might be defrauded of the helps of the saints who are in heaven. The first author of this pestiferous heresy was (as far as I know) a certain Eustachius,[3] who was condemned on account of this error and many others in the Synod of Gangra.[4] After this man the Gaul Vigilantius, a priest of the church of Barcelona, against whom Blessed Jerome wrote twice about this matter.[5] The Waldensians upheld the same error many years later, who tried to take away all the feast days of the saints from the Church. John Wycliffe, since he always fought for the sect of the Waldensians, did not want to fail them in this matter, such that he would always be like them. Regarding John Hus, there is no need to speak, since he seems to swear by Wycliffe's words more than by Christ's words. But the Bohemians, captivating their understanding unto the obedience of John Hus, maintain this among their other errors. Martin Luther today persists

---

[1] Dz. 854.

[2] Cf. I Jn. 4, 6.

[3] Eustathius of Sebaste (c. 300-c. 377) was one of the chief founders of monasticism in Asia Minor, and for a long time was an intimate friend of St. Basil. He was censured because of the exaggerated asceticism of his followers.

[4] "If anyone shall, through pride, thinking himself to be perfect, reproach the assemblies, which take place in burial places and churches of the holy martyrs, or also thinks that the Masses which are celebrated there are to be despised, and the tombs of the saints ought to be condemned, let him be anathema." (Synod of Gangra, can. 20 in Mansi, vol. 2, col. 1112D-E).

[5] "All at once Vigilantius, or, more correctly, Dormitantius, has arisen, animated by an unclean spirit, to fight against the Spirit of Christ, and to deny that religious reverence is to be paid to the tombs of the martyrs" (PL 23, 339). "You tell me that Vigilantius (whose very name 'Wakeful' is a contradiction: he ought rather to be described as 'Sleepy') has again opened his fetid lips and is pouring forth a torrent of filthy venom upon the relics of the holy martyrs; and that he calls us who cherish them ashmongers and idolaters who pay homage to dead men's bones" (Letter 109 (to Riparius), n. 1 (PL 22, 907)).

in the same condemnation. John Oecolampadius, in his exposition which he published on the prophet Isaias, very often inculcates this error.[1]

The Royal Prophet clearly teaches that the saints ought to be honored, when saying: "But to me thy friends, O God, are made exceedingly honourable" (Ps. 138, 17). He calls the Apostles and the rest of the saints God's friends, who love God with a sincere love. For Christ Himself promises them that after this life has been brought to an end, He would receive them into His friendship, saying: "I will not now call you servants, but friends" (Jn. 15, 15). Thus, it is not right that those whom are held up by David to be honored would be left by us without honor. Furthermore, Truth Himself says in John's Gospel: "If any man minister to me... him will my Father (who is in heaven) honour" (12, 26). What then will the foolish heretics prattle? Is it just that those whom the Father honors in heaven, we would disdain to honor on earth? Especially since the honor shown to the saints, is shown to God Who is glorified in the honor of the saints. "God is wonderful in his saints" (Ps. 67, 36), says the Royal Prophet. Again, Ecclesiasticus exhorts us to honor the saints, saying: "Let us now praise men of renown, and our fathers in their generation" (44, 1). And after he had brought forth some praises of the Patriarchs of the Old Testament, he immediately adds: "All these have gained glory in their generations, and were praised in their days. They that were born of them have left a name behind them, that their praises might be related" (v. 7-8). If then it is permissible to praise them, it will also be permissible to honor them, because praise is a type of honor. For by laudatory words, we bear witness to the esteem which we have for him whom we praise, just as by genuflections and baring the head that we testify to that veneration which we have for another.

Add to these things the authority of the Church itself, which daily celebrates, and commands to be celebrated by the people, feast days in veneration of the saints. And besides this precept which perhaps is recent regarding many feast days that are celebrated, there is the very old and immemorial custom that has always been observed, namely that some days were always celebrated in veneration of the saints. For the sermons of the ancient Doctors of the Church testify to this very thing, in the celebrations of the saints, and in praise of them, which they were making before people. There exist sermons of Ambrose, many more of Augustine, which they preached on the festivals of the saints before the people, so that they might draw the same people to both the imitation and veneration of the saints. But if the saints ought not to be venerated, the Church would never have commanded their feasts to be celebrated, and God would not have allowed His Church, which He assists until the consummation of the world, to err for so long.

I have shown then how the veneration of the saints is in accord with Holy Writ; it remains that we show it to be lawful, lest I say meritorious, to pray to the saints. For the heretics also deny this, as though it would derogate from the Divine clemency that he who ministered to Christ, would be held worthy of this honor, such that he may intercede for others. Abraham prays for Abimelech who had taken Sara for his wife, and Abraham's prayer was heard.[2] And we read in the book of Job: "Call if there be any that will answer thee, and turn to some of the saints" (5, 1). Which words although Eliphaz the Themanite indeed said them to Job, still Job did not reprehend them, but willingly accepted his counsel as sound, although he reprehended him of speaking wrongly about him elsewhere. In the same way Eliu said: "If there shall be an angel speaking for him, one among thousands, to declare man's uprightness, He shall have mercy on him, and shall say: Deliver him, that he may not go down to corruption: I have found wherein I may be merciful to him" (33, 23-24). And in the same book, immediately

---

[1] "It is superstition therefore, that we believe saints wish us to be occupied with worship dedicated to them" (*In Iesaiam Prophetam Hypomnematōn, hoc est, Commentariorum, Ioannis Oecolampadii libri VI* (Basel, Cratander, 1525), fol. 57v).

[2] Cf. Gen. 20, 2 & 17.

after the whole disputation was related which Job had with his friends, in which those friends had offended God, is put God's command whereby He commanded them to go to Job himself, to ask him to pray to God for them. Which when they had done (as God had commanded), Job when praying for them was heard. And the centurion who had a [sick servant], sent the ancients of the Jews to Christ so that they might entreat for the health of the [servant], in that he considered himself unworthy of asking this from Christ.[1] Why may not also we, when diffident about our merits, have recourse to the saints, so that they may pray to God for us, so that we might obtain our petitions more easily?

But because there are these and many other testimonies of Sacred Scripture, whereby we prove that just men when praying to God for other are heard by Him, the heretics take refuge in saying that it is licit to have recourse to holy men while they are alive on earth, and they are heard when they pray for us in this life, not however once they have departed from this life. For so teaches Oecolampadius in his commentaries on Isaias.[2] Long ago, Jerome bears witness that Vigilantius also said this. Wherefore let us hear what Jerome relates about him. For in a certain book, *Against Vigilantius*, he speaks thus: "You say, in your pamphlet, that so long as we are alive we can pray for one another; but once we die, the prayer of no person for another can be heard, and all the more because the martyrs, though they cry for the avenging of their blood, have never been able to obtain their request.[3] If Apostles and martyrs while still in the body can pray for others, when they ought still to be anxious for themselves, how much more must they do so when once they have won their crowns, overcome, and triumphed? A single man, Moses, oft wins pardon from God for six hundred thousand armed men; and Stephen, the follower of his Lord and the first Christian martyr, entreats pardon for his persecutors;[4] and when once they have entered on their life with Christ, shall they have less power than before? The Apostle Paul says that two hundred and seventy-six souls were given to him in the ship;[5] and when, after his dissolution, he has begun to be with Christ, must he shut his mouth, and be unable to say a word for those who throughout the whole world have believed in his Gospel? Shall Vigilantius the live dog be better than Paul the dead lion?[6] You would correctly propound this from Ecclesiastes, if I admitted that Paul were dead in [his] spirit."[7]

But besides these [testimonies] which Jerome objects, there are other much clearer testimonies of Sacred Scripture for proving that the saints who have already died, when praying for us are heard. For Jacob near to death, when he blessed his son Joseph, says: "God, in whose sight my fathers Abraham and Isaac walked, God that feedeth me from my youth until this day; the angel that delivereth me from all evils, bless these boys: and let my name be called upon them, and the names of my fathers Abraham, and Isaac, and may they grow into a multitude upon the earth" (Gen. 48, 15-16). In which words it ought to be noticed that Jacob orders that the names of already deceased Patriarchs be invoked upon the sons of Joseph: because even though they may be dead as to the body, and the world, nevertheless they live before God. For the Truth in the Gospel also says: "He is not the God of the dead, but of the living:

---

[1] Cf. Lk. 7, 2-3 & 6.

[2] "'And he sent Eliacim.' It did not seem enough to the pious king [Ezechias] to pray for himself, he also sends to Isaias to intercede, or because the prayers of many are more easily heard, or because the prophet would pray with more confidence. You have here an example of asking intercessions of the living holy men in this life: but we do not likewise have examples in Scripture, that we may fly to the saints who have passed from this life" (*In Iesaiam Prophetam*, on Is. 37, 2, fol. 198v).

[3] Cf. Apoc. 6, 10.

[4] Cf. Acts 7, 59.

[5] Cf. Acts 27, 24.

[6] Cf. Eccle. 9, 4.

[7] N. 6 (PL 23, 334B-C).

for all live to him" (Lk. 20, 38). Furthermore, Moses, when praying to God for the people, says the following: "Be appeased upon the wickedness of thy people. Remember Abraham, Isaac, and Israel, thy servants… And the Lord was appeased from doing the evil which he had spoken against his people" (Ex. 32, 12-14). Behold you see Moses praying to God through the merits of the Patriarchs, namely Abraham, Isaac, and Jacob. Hence if it were licit for Moses to offer the merits of the Patriarchs, why could not the Patriarchs themselves not better offer their own merits? If you say that they already received a reward for the good deeds which they did here on earth, and cannot merit more, I agree. But we do not say that the saints when praying are heard for the full measure of their merits, but we say that when wayfarers (*in via*) they merited that when praying for us in heaven they would be heard. Wherefore when they are heard, it falls rather to them as a reward of their preceding merits, rather than as new merit. And if they being outside the time of meriting is sufficient reason so that they could not benefit us when praying for us, there will also be sufficient reason that their merits could not benefit us, when Moses praying, offered them to God for the people. And if their merits could benefit when Moses offered them to God, much more could their merits benefit if they [themselves] offer the same [merits] to God.

In the same way Azarias was also praying when put in the fiery furnace: "Deliver us not up for ever, we beseech thee, for thy name's sake, and abolish not thy covenant. And take not away thy mercy from us for the sake of Abraham thy beloved, and Isaac thy servant, and Israel thy holy one: to whom thou hast spoken, promising that thou wouldst multiply their seed as the stars of heaven, and as the sand that is on the sea shore" (Dan. 3, 34-36). Now when praying in this way he was heard, because he was freed with his companions from the fiery furnace. If the merits of the saints already dead could do nothing after their death, in vain Azarias when praying to God offered the merits of those Patriarchs to God. But since he did not pray in vain, but was heard, it is proved that the merits of deceased saints can benefit us after their death, because when living they merited that after their death they could benefit us.

Again, in the book of Zacharias the prophet, the Angel of God prays to God for the Jewish people placed in captivity, saying: "O Lord of hosts, how long wilt thou not have mercy on Jerusalem, and on the cities of Juda, with which thou hast been angry? this is now the seventieth year" (1, 12). By which words the Angel prays to God for the redemption of the Jewish people, recalling the prophecy of the prophet Jeremias whereby he had predicted by the Lord's command that after seventy years He would bring back the Jewish people to their country and freedom. From which passage of Zacharias the prophet the shamelessness of these heretics is proved, who say that the saints who are in heaven ought not to be called upon by us, because they cannot now pray to God for us. And so they say that such invocation of the saints is useless, which will be of no avail. Yet the prophet Zacharias condemns this opinion, since he says that the Angel of the Lord, already beatified, prayed to God for the Jewish people detained in captivity, so that God would deliver them from their captivity.

Next, Onias, the high priest of the Jews, appeared after his death to Judas Machabeus, holding up his hands and praying for all the people of the Jews. In which vision another man similarly appeared, a companion of the same Onias, concerning whom Onias says to Judas Machabeus: "This is a lover of his brethren, and of the people of Israel: this is he that prayeth much for the people, and for all the holy city, Jeremias the prophet of God" (II Mach. 15, 14). If then the saints in Limbo outside the condition of merit (*status meriti*), and not yet enjoying God were praying for their own [people], how much more willingly will they do it once they enjoy God, especially because to pray to God for another is a work of charity? Thus since charity, according to the opinion of Blessed Paul, does not fall away,[1] but rather is perfected in heaven, it is proved that in that same place they pray much more fervently for us, than

---

[1] Cf. I Cor. 13, 8.

they did while they were alive here on earth, or when they were in Limbo. But this testimony from the book of Machabees the Lutherans contemn, because they say that this book does not belong to the canon of the books of Sacred Scripture, but is mere dreams of man having no authority. Yet we showed above that this is very false in the first book, where we proved that the books of the Machabees are truly canonical and sacred.

Next, Blessed John, in the Apocalypse, saw "four living creatures and twenty-four ancients who fell down before the Lamb, having every one of them harps, and golden vials full of odours, which are the prayers of the saints" (5, 8). And in the same Apocalypse again he saw an Angel standing "before the altar, having a golden censer; and there was given to him much incense, that he should offer of the prayers of all saints upon the golden altar, which is before the throne of God. And the smoke of the incense of the prayers of the saints ascended up before God from the hand of the angel" (8, 3-4). Now since according to the Savior's teaching holy men in glory are equal to the Angels of God: it is proved that if the Angels pray for us in heaven, holy men also can pray for us, and be heard.

Finally, since the feasting rich man placed in torments, prayed for his brethren living in this life,[1] much more then it ought to be believed that the souls of the saints put in heaven, who burn with more ardent charity toward their neighbors, pray to God for the salvation of their brethren remaining in this world. For if that rich man, who while he lived, had no care for the salvation of his brethren, when dead intercedes for their salvation, it is much more right to believe that the saints who while they lived prayed for men, would more fervently do this same thing after death, once they enjoy the vision of God.

Therefore, let the heretics be afraid, in the face of so many testimonies of Sacred Scripture, to detract from the glory and honor of the saints, and to defraud living men of their suffrages. I could also cite many more testimonies of the holy Doctors for confirming this matter, which I prudently omit, lest I exceed the limits of the promised brevity. But if the curious reader desires to see them, I will give the references to the places where he can find them: Bernard in his sixty-sixth sermon on the Canticles reprehends some heretics of his time, who were denying that one should pray to the saints;[2] Bede in his homily on the Gospel of Matthew concerning the Canaanite woman;[3] [John] Damascene in the fourth book of *On the Orthodox Faith*;[4]

---

[1] Cf. Lk. 16, 27.

[2] "But look at these slanderers, behold these dogs. They ridicule us because we administer baptism to infants, because we pray for the dead, because we solicit the intercession of the saints... and the living, finally, shall never lack the assistance and consolation of the saints in bliss, who, out of an affection of tender charity, remain always near them, through and in God, everywhere present" (n. 9-10 (PL 183, 1098B & 1099D)).

[3] "But even if the Lord does not respond to the first tears of the beseeching Church, that is, He delays to give requested health of mind to the erring, under these circumstances one ought neither to desist from asking, seeking, knocking, nor give into despair in petitioning: but rather one ought to persevere with so much constancy, the Savior ought to be frequented with such obstinate clamor, also suffrages of His saints ought to be desired during the litanies, until also they from heaven supplicate the Lord for the Church to be heard" (Hom. 19 (PL 92, 104B)).

[4] "To the saints honor must be paid as friends of Christ, as sons and heirs of God" (C. 15 (PG 94, 1163A)).

Augustine in his *Tractates on the Gospel of John*[1] and *Expositions on the Psalms*;[2] Cyril in the sixth book of his *Against Julian the Apostate*;[3] Jerome in his book, *Against Vigilantius*;[4] Cyprian when writing to Pope Cornelius asks whether any of those who had passed away, prays to God for our brothers and sisters, and this is the first of all the letters;[5] and Dionysius the [Pseudo-] Areopagite in [book] seven of the *Ecclesiastical History*.[6]

After so many very clear and very efficacious testimonies there are many decrees of the councils defined about this matter. The Synod of Gangra in the twentieth canon of its decrees speaks in this manner: "If anyone shall, from a presumptuous disposition, condemn and abhor the assemblies [in honor] of the martyrs, or the services performed there, and the commemoration of them, let him be anathema."[7] There are also many other councils which command litanies, that is rogations of the saints solemnly occurring yearly in the Church, in which to all the saints prayers and petitions are uttered, so that they would pray to God for the people. For the [I] Synod of Orléans says the following: "It is resolved that rogations, that is, the litanies, shall be celebrated by all churches before the Ascension of the Lord, such that the preceding three-day fast will have ended on the feast of the Lord's Ascension; and during those three days, servants and handmaidens shall be released from all work, so that as much as possible the entire people may gather. During these three days let all fast and partake

---

[1] "This it was that the blessed martyrs did in their burning love; and if we celebrate their memories in no mere empty form, and, in the banquet whereat they themselves were filled to the full, approach the table of the Lord, we must, as they did, be also ourselves making similar preparations. For on these very grounds we do not commemorate them at that table in the same way, as we do others who now rest in peace, as that we should also pray for them, but rather that they should do so for us, that we may cleave to their footsteps; because they have actually attained that fullness of love, than which, our Lord has told us, there cannot be a greater." (Tract. 84, n. 1 (PL 35, 1847)).

[2] "The persecutors raged against Crispina, whose birthday we are today celebrating… The Lord has prevented us from going with greater joy to the shrine of the martyrs, as we promised yesterday. Beyond suffering and toil, the martyrs are here with us" (On Ps. 120, n. 13 & 15 (PL 37, 1616 & 1618)).

[3] "But we do not say that the holy martyrs are gods, and we certainly are not wont to adore them with Divine worship, but with affection and honor: nay rather we adorn them with the highest honors, for instance because they fought strenuously for the truth, they kept the purity of the faith even to the point that they despised their life, and having disdained the terrors of death, they conquered all danger, and presented themselves as very admirable examples of virtue for men's lives. Wherefore it is not anything absurd, but rather it was necessary that they who excelled with shining deed, are adorned with perpetual honors" (Bk. 6 (PG 76, 810D-811A)).

[4] "If Apostles and martyrs while still in the body can pray for others, when they ought still to be anxious for themselves, how much more must they do so when once they have won their crowns, overcome, and triumphed?" (N. 6 (PL 23, 344B)).

[5] "Let us on both sides always pray for one another. Let us relieve burdens and afflictions by mutual love, that if any one of us, by the swiftness of Divine condescension, shall go hence the first, our love may continue in the presence of the Lord, and our prayers for our brethren and sisters not cease in the presence of the Father's mercy" (Letter 56 (Paris), N. 5 (PL 3, 836A-838A)). In Migne's *Patrologia* this is letter thirteen among the collection the letters of Pope Cornelius. It is the first letter in the order of Erasmus in his first book.

[6] "First, they drove us out; and when alone, and persecuted, and put to death by all, even then we kept the feast. And every place of affliction was to us a place of festival: field, desert, ship, inn, prison; but the perfected martyrs kept the most joyous festival of all, feasting in heaven" (C. 22 (PG 20, 687A)).

[7] PL 67, 60A.

of Lenten foods."[1] The Synod of Girona[2] also commanded that the litanies be made.[3] The V Synod of Toledo, in the first chapter;[4] the VI Synod of Toledo, in the second chapter;[5] and the II Synod of Braga.[6] But these rogations which were commanded by these last three councils are different from those which the [I] Synod of Orléans commanded to be celebrated: because those ones were commanded to be made just before the Ascension, but these are commanded to be celebrated in the month of December.[7] Nevertheless, all those councils agree among themselves about this, because all those councils decided and commanded that solemn rogations would be celebrated at some time.

But if one ought not to pray to the saints, the councils would never have commanded such litanies to be celebrated. For if they do not hear our prayers, or when praying for us they are never heard, we are commanded in vain to pray to them. Therefore, we venerate the saints whom the Heavenly Father so honored, such that He judged them worthy of His friendship. We have recourse to them in our necessities, praying to them, so that they may will to be our intercessors for us to God. Still, we ought not to pray to them with such a confidence that we would place all our hope in them, as though they were able to grant those things which we desire, because we ought to pray in this way to God alone, and to put the prow and the stern in Him alone (as it is said[8]). But the only thing that we ought to ask and hope for from the

---

[1] PL 84, 277B-C. Cf. Gratian, *Concordia discordantium canonum*, c. 3 (PL 187, 1782C). This council was held in 511 A.D.

[2] The Synod of Gerona (Spain) was held in 517 A.D.

[3] "Likewise, the second litanies are to be made on the Calends [i.e., the first day] of November, yet on condition that if a Sunday falls on those days, they are begun in another week according to the prior observance of abstinence on Thursday, and end when Mass is completed on Saturday evening: nevertheless, we have decreed that on those days one must abstain from meat and wine" (PL 84,313C-D).

[4] "Namely that in the whole kingdom granted by God to him [i.e., the Gothic King Chintillan, (606-639 A.D)] a special and particular religious observance be held for all time, namely that from the thirteenth day of [September] a triduum of litanies be everywhere executed and the forgiveness of sins be implored with tears; but if a Sunday occurs, they are celebrated in the week following, so that as iniquity abounds and charity fails to such an extent that malice having spread new crimes are committed, so also may this new said custom arise which can be our purgation before the eyes of the Almighty" (PL 84, 389C). N. B. "the September fast is evidently mentioned by the V Synod of Toledo (can. 1), though obviously by a mistake it calls it *dies Iduum Decembrium* ("Mozarabic Rite," *The Catholic Encyclopedia* (New York: Robert Appleton Company, 1911), vol. 10, p. 616).

[5] "Accepting with great reverence and veneration the devotion of our most religious prince and the constitution of our brother bishops [issued] in the first year of his reign, we are pleased to confirm with our assent [this custom] which is already celebrated each year in his entire realm. Accordingly, with the universal authority of this council, we decree that these days of the litanies, which were instituted in the earlier synod, be celebrated with full observance each year at the same time during which they were ordered to be held, so that they be our expiation before the eyes of Almighty God for those sins which we have committed even to this day" (PL 84, 395D-396A). N.B. The VI Synod of Toledo confirmed the previously cited decree about two years afterwards and made it a general rule for all the churches in Spain, Gallicia, and Gallia Narbonensis, which was at this time under the government of King Chintillan.

[6] "… coming together in the beginning [of Lent] in one of the nearby churches for three days let them celebrate the litanies while walking with psalms through the major churches" (C. 9 (PL 84, 573A)).

[7] December is the month stated in the canon, but as mentioned in the above footnote on the V Synod of Toledo, the September fast should be understood here.

[8] "Cicero, writing to Tiro in the final book of his *Epistulae Familiares*, recalls the saying with these words: 'It was my prow and stern, as the saying of the Greeks goes, to send you away from me so that you could explain my reasoning'. We mean by 'prow and stern' the entirety of our plan, on account of

saints, is that they would want to ask from God that which we wish to obtain. For the divine psalmist clearly suggests this, when saying: "I have lifted up my eyes to the mountains, from whence help shall come to me" (Ps. 120, 1). And lest anyone be deceived, supposing that the mountains themselves, that is the saints, were to give help, he immediately added: "My help is from the Lord, who made heaven and earth" (v. 2). When Blessed Augustine expounds these words, he says: "Think not that the mountains themselves will give you help: for they receive what they may give, give not of their own."[1] And for this reason the Church taught by the Holy Ghost, in the litanies or rogations which it celebrates, prays to God in one way, and in another way prays to the saints. For when praying to God it speaks as follows: "God the Father of Heaven, Have mercy on us. God the Son, Redeemer of the world, Have mercy on us." When, however, it prays to one of the saints, it does not say to him, "Have mercy on us," but it says: "Pray for us." Thus, the when the Church prays, it asks for mercy from God, but for intercession from the saints.

The arguments by which the heretics defend themselves, because they are ridiculous and powerless, I have omitted striving to be brief, especially because from those things which I have said, they can be very easily refuted. Josse Van Clichtove disputes against this heresy in a whole book which he titled, *De veneratione sanctorum*.[2] Cardinal Thomas de Vio Cajetan published a certain tract about this matter.[3] Albert Pighius thoroughly treats this matter, in his book of controversies held in Ratisbon.[4]

SATISFACTIO
Satisfaction

It is one of the most pestilential errors of Luther, whereby he teaches that no satisfaction is needed by the sinner for sins committed because, as he says, when guilt has been forgiven, all punishment which was due to the guilt also stays forgiven.[5] But we have already disputed against this error in the section on "Penance." For in that place, we showed from Holy Writ that after the guilt has been forgiven by God it is necessary that the sinner suffer some punishment for it, either in this world, or in Purgatory. And so it is not necessary that we again dispute about this matter.

---

the fact that the whole ship hangs between stern and prow as if from head to heel" (Erasmus, *Adagia* 1.1.8).

[1] *Expositions on the Psalms*, on Ps. 35, v. 7, n. 9 (PL 36, 347).

[2] *De veneratione sanctorum, opusculum: duos libros complectens* (Paris, ex officina Simonis Colinaei, 1523).

[3] "De adoratione Christi et cultu sactorum," *Theologia universa speculativa dogmatica et moralis, disputatio* (Munich, Jaecklin, 1700), vol. 7, disputatio 20, pp. 533-572.

[4] *Controversiarum præcipuarum in Comitiis Ratisponensibus tractatarum... explicatio* (Paris, Joannes Ruellius, 1549), controversia 13 (*De cultu et invocatione sanctorum*), fol. 190r-195v.

[5] "Nay, when God remits sin, he remits the guilt and the punishment at the same time" (Martin Luther, *Asterisci Lutheri adversus Obeliscos Eckii* (i.e., *The Asterisks of Luther against the Obelisks of Eck*), WA 1, 284, lns. 15-16). Eck published his book, *Obelisks*, against Luther's theses 1518; Luther answered with his *Asterisks*. These titles are taken from the names of the symbols (†*) customarily put in margins to highlight a notable passage. "[The Lutherans] first teach that when the guilt of sin is forgiven all punishment is remitted as well. One who has attained mercy from God upon his sin is no longer bound to any punishment" (Thomas de Vio Cajetan, *De fide et operibus* in *Opuscula omnia* (Antwerp, Johan Keerberg, 1612), bk. 3, tract 10, c. 11, p. 169).

SCRIPTURA SACRA

Sacred Scripture

Nearly all heretics have this one thing in common, namely that they take [books] away from the Scriptures. For they very often at will interpret them otherwise than is correct. And if perhaps some passage is cited against their assertion, which is so clear that its clarity can nowise be obfuscated by their interpretations, immediately they try to remove that book from the canon of Sacred Scripture, saying that that book is unworthy to be included in list of sacred books. For since Sacred Scripture is a kind of mystical tower of David, upon which the armor of strong and Catholic men hang, and for this reason heretics endeavor to reduce the Sacred Scriptures, lest we have the weapons with which we have the force to overthrow their insane teachings. Hence one book is discarded by some, another by others, as it seems expedient to each one, and the teaching of the book conflicts with their assertion. Nevertheless, it is not necessary to dispute in this place against each of them. For since we already demonstrated above in the second chapter of the first book the list of sacred books, it will now be necessary only to relate those heresies which reject some books from the canon of books received by the Church as being apocryphal, and of no authority.

The **first heresy**, therefore, is that which rejects the whole Old Testament. The originator of this heresy is Carpocrates, from whom the Carpocratian, or Carpocratite, heretics were called. After this Carpocrates, Cerdo succeeded in the same error, in the time of Pope and martyr Hyginus, who was the ninth beginning with Blessed Peter supreme pontiff of the whole Church. For Augustine ascribes this to Cerdo in his book, *De Haeresibus*.[1] After Cerdo, Severus, from whom the Severians are named, maintained this heresy. For Augustine relates this in the same book.[2] After the course of a number of years Manichaeus revived the same heresy, under whom it became more well-known: for which reason it happened that Manichaeus is credited by many as the originator of this heresy. Yet it is evident that Manichaeus lived nearly two hundred years after Cerdo. After Manichaeus the Albanenses embraced the same error. For Guy the Carmelite in his *Summa de haeresibus*, when listing the errors of the Albanenses, puts this one among the others in the sixth place.[3] All these heretics united against the Old Testament in reproaching that it was made by an evil origin: wherefore they were also saying that it is evil.

We have already disputed above against this heresy in the section on "Law," in the second heresy. For in that place we proved from testimonies taken from the New Testament that the Law is good, and proceeding from a good origin. And in the section on "God," in the first heresy, we proved from Holy Writ that there is only one God, Who is the origin of all things. Therefore it is unnecessary that we dispute more against this heresy.

The **second heresy** does not accept the books of the Machabees. The author of this heresy is Luther, saying that those books are not canonical, and are unworthy of being listed among the sacred books. Now the reason why Luther does this is because the teaching contained in those books very clearly opposes his teaching. Now in the Second Book of the Machabees the type of suffrages that are made for the dead are praised. Hence Luther, pertinaciously defending his error, rejects these books of Machabees, because they are opposed to his teaching.

---

[1] *De Haeresibus ad Quodvultdeum*, c. 21 (PL 42, 29).
[2] *Ibid.*, c. 24 (PL 42, 30).
[3] *Summa de haeresibus et earum confutationibus*, c. 6, fol. 77v.

SCRIPTURA SACRA

Now Blessed Augustine,[1] [Pope Damasus I],[2] and Pope Innocent I[3] testify that these books ought to be enumerated among the sacred books: lastly the III Synod of Carthage deigned to put these books of Machabees among the canonical scriptures.[4] We cited all which things in the second chapter of the first book.

But Luther and his imitators object to us Jerome saying that such books are not canonical.[5] But in reality, Jerome thinks otherwise than they suppose. For in the preface to the book of Machabees, [Isidore of Seville's[6]] words are these: "Although the books of the Machabees are not contained in the canon of the Hebrews, nevertheless they are counted among the histories of the Divine books."[7] From whose words it is evident that those books were included in the number of sacred books by the Church. But if the Church judged that those books ought to be accepted as Divine, although they are not contained in the Hebrew canon, no one will be able to oppose them without incurring the [theological] note of heresy.

There is a **third heresy** which rejects the sacred Gospels. For Cerdo, about whom we spoke above, was accepting only the Gospel of Luke, while rejecting the other three. For [Pseudo-]Tertullian relates this about him in his book on heresies.[8] Afterwards Marcion, a disciple of Cerdo, as Irenaeus testifies in the first book of his *Against the Heresies*, accepted the error of Cerdo.[9]

There is a **fourth heresy** which, of all four Gospels, only accepts the Gospel of Matthew, contemning the remaining three. Philastrius in his book, *De haeresibus*, assigns this heresy to

---

[1] "[The books of the Maccabees] are held as canonical, not by the Jews, but by the Church, on account of the extreme and wonderful sufferings of certain martyrs, who, before Christ had come in the flesh, contended for the law of God even unto death, and endured most grievous and horrible evils" (*City of God*, bk. 18, c. 36 (PL 41, 596).

[2] "Decree of Damasus" in the Synod of Rome, in the year 382 A.D. (Dz. 84), which is the first ecclesiastical decree on the Church's canonical books of the Sacred Scriptures. The text, however, here cites St. John Damascene, but he merely quotes from these books, thereby indicating that they are canonical: "The second name of God is ὁ Θεός, derived from θέειν, to run, because He courses through all things, or from αἴθειν, to burn: For "God is a consuming fire" (Deut. 4, 24): or from θεᾶσθαι, because He "seeth all things" (II Mach. 9, 5): for nothing can escape Him, and over all He keeps watch" (*An Exposition of the Orthodox Faith*, bk. 1, c. 10 (PG 94, 838A)). Hence, it seems likely that there is a copyist error here, so that "Damascene" in the text should be replaced by "Damasus."

[3] Epistle to Exuperius, in which the complete canon of Sacred Scripture is found (Dz. 97).

[4] Dz. 92.

[5] "As, then, the Church reads Judith, Tobias, and the books of Maccabees, but does not admit them among the canonical Scriptures, so one may read these two volumes for the edification of the people, not for confirming the authority of ecclesiastical dogmas (*Prologue of Jerome to the Books of Solomon*, to Bishops Cromatius and Heliodorus (PL 28, 1243A)).

[6] St. Jerome is incorrectly cited here instead of St. Isidore of Seville. This work had been mistakenly included in an incunabula edition of the works of St. Jerome edited by Bernardinus Gadolus entitled *Opera Diui Hieronymi in hoc volu[mine] co[n] tenta* (Venice, Giovanni and Gregorio de' Gregori, 1497-25 August 1498).

[7] *Prooemia in libros Veteris ac Novi Testamenti* (PL 83, 174D).

[8] "The Gospel of Luke alone, and that not entire, does he receive" (*Against All Heresies*, c. 6 (PL 2, 70C)).

[9] "Besides this, [Marcion] mutilates the Gospel which is according to Luke, removing all that is written respecting the generation of the Lord, and setting aside a great deal of the teaching of the Lord, in which the Lord is recorded as most dearly confessing that the Maker of this universe is His Father. He likewise persuaded his disciples that he himself was more worthy of credit than are those Apostles who have handed down the Gospel to us, furnishing them not with the Gospel, but merely a fragment of it" (C. 27, n. 2 (PG 7, 688B)).

Cerinthus.[1] But Augustine in his tract, *De Haeresibus* [*ad Quodvultdeum*], when discussing about this Cerinthus, makes no mention of this heresy.[2] Irenaeus assigns this error to Ebion, from whom the Ebionite heretics are named.[3]

There is a **fifth heresy** which does not accept the Acts of the Apostles, but tries to remove that book from the list of sacred books. Philastrius also assigns this heresy to Cerinthus along with the preceding,[4] of which Augustine makes no mention, just as he does not mention the preceding one. Eusebius of Caesarea relates that Severus, from whom the Severian heretics are named, did not accept the book of the Acts of the Apostles.[5]

There is a **sixth heresy** which teaches that all the epistles of Paul the Apostle are of no moment. The first author of this pestiferous heresy was Ebion. For Irenaeus assigns this to him.[6] And it is evident that Ebion did this because he taught that the Old Law ought to be observed along with the New. Since Paul very clearly opposes this doctrine in many of his epistles, wherefore Ebion, in order to uphold his error, takes refuge in this asylum, namely that he rejects all of Paul's epistles. After Ebion, Severus succeeded in the same error: although Augustine when speaking about Severus in his book, *De Haeresibus* [*ad Quodvultdeum*], never mentions this error.[7] But Eusebius of Caesarea relates that Severus attacked Paul the Apostle with insults and rejected his epistles.[8] And he clearly intimates that Tatian, the chief of the Encratites, did this same thing,[9] although Augustine when discoursing about Tatian, never accuses him of this.[10] Eusebius also testifies that the Elcesaites[11] accepted this same error.[12]

The **seventh heresy** does not accept the Epistle of James. The author of this heresy is Martin Luther. For although in times past it was doubted by some about it whether belonged to James, still there was nothing yet decided by the Church about it. But since it has now been accepted by the Church in many councils, it is now not permitted to doubt about it. Wherefore Luther, who rejects it contrary to the decision of the Church, is deservedly deemed a heretic for this reason. Now it is clear why Luther would reject this epistle of James the Apostle. For Luther, as it was related in the section on "Faith," feels that faith alone justifies, and it alone is enough for attaining eternal life, even if works be lacking: James, however, in his canonical epistle teaches that "faith without works is dead" (2, 26). Thus, because Luther sees that the Epistle of James opposes his opinion, wherefore he denies this epistle, saying that it is not James' and is unworthy of his Apostolic spirit.[13]

---

[1] C. 36 (PL 12, 1153A).

[2] C. 8 (PL 42, 27).

[3] *Against the Heresies*, bk. 1, c. 26, n. 2 (PG 7, 686B-687A).

[4] C. 36 (PL 12, 1153A).

[5] *Church History*, bk. 4, c. 29, n. 5 (PG 20, 402A).

[6] *Against the Heresies*, bk. 1, c. 26, n. 2 (PG 7, 687A).

[7] C. 24 (PL 42, 30).

[8] *Church History*, bk. 4, c. 29, n. 5 (PG 20, 402A).

[9] "Severus put new strength into the aforesaid heresy [of Tatian]" (PG 20, 299C).

[10] *De Haeresibus ad Quodvultdeum*, c. 25 (PL 42, 30).

[11] The Elcesaites (or Helkesaites) were a sect of Gnostic Ebionites, whose religion was a wild medley of heathen superstitions and Christian doctrines with Judaism.

[12] *Church History*, bk. 6, c. 38 (PG 20, 599A).

[13] Luther's Preface to the New Testament: "In a word, St. John's Gospel and his first Epistle, St. Paul's Epistles, especially Romans, Galatians, and Ephesians, and St. Peter's first Epistle are the books that show you Christ and teach you all that is necessary and good for you to know, even though you were never to see or hear any other book or doctrine. Therefore St. James' Epistle is really an epistle of straw, compared to them; for it has nothing of the nature of the Gospel about it." (*Luthers Werke*, Weimarer Ausgabe Deutsche Bible, vol. 6 (Weimar 1929), p. 10).

And I certainly marvel that he denies this epistle, saying that it is not the Apostle James', since so many illustrious men, and very ancient, bear witness that it belongs to James. Augustine cites a passage from this epistle under the name of James.[1] Jerome, when disputing against the Pelagians, uses a passage from this letter.[2] [Pseudo-] Pope Urban I, a man celebrated for martyrdom, in a letter concerning the common life and offerings of the faithful, cites a passage from this Epistle under the name of James the Apostle.[3] And [Pseudo-] Pope and Martyr Anacletus, who (as he testifies in a certain letter) was ordained a priest by Blessed Peter the Apostle, in a letter concerning the oppression of bishops, in about the middle also cites a passage from this epistle under the name of James.[4] It is more reasonable, therefore, that we believe these very holy and very ancient witnesses, than one foolish and insane Luther, especially since there exists a judgment of the whole Church about this matter, which placed the epistle under the name of James among the canonical scriptures.

The **eighth heresy** does not accept the Gospel of John, nor his Apocalypse. The authors of this heresy were called the Alogians, due to the fact that they were denying that the Son of God is the Word. For *logos* in Greek is *verbum* [meaning "word" in English] in Latin: and hence they were called Alogians, as it were, "without the Word." Since therefore the Gospel of John very clearly testifies that the Son of God is the Word, wherefore they deny that John wrote the Gospel, and they also deny that he wrote the Apocalypse. Eusebius of Caesarea relates that there were some men who rejected the Apocalypse of John, saying that there was nothing in it worthy of the Apostolic dignity, but rather the book was a fiction of the heretic Cerinthus. But that this is not so, besides the definition of the Church, which is the greatest testimony, many sacred and very ancient writers interpreted the Apocalypse as Sacred Scripture, and composed by Blessed John. I omit the more recent writers, to whom not as much trust on this point is due. Augustine, when interpreting the Apocalypse, which he says is by John the Apostle;[5] Dionysius, Bishop of Alexandria, as Eusebius testifies, interpreted the same Apocalypse under the name of Blessed John, although he says that he doubted whether he was John the Apostle, or another John, a holy man in fact, yet not the Apostle. Whosoever's it

---

Luther's preface to the Epistle of James: "Though this Epistle of St. James was rejected by the ancients, I praise it and hold it a good book, because it sets up no doctrine of men and lays great stress upon God's law. But to state my own opinion about it... I consider that it is not the writing of any Apostle. My reasons are as follows. First: Flatly against St. Paul and all the rest of Scripture, it ascribes righteousness to works... James does nothing more than drive to the Law and its works; and he mixes the two up in such disorderly fashion that it seems to me he must have been some good, pious man, who took some sayings of the Apostles' disciples and threw them thus on paper; or perhaps they were written down by someone else from his preaching... In a word, he wants to guard against those who relied on faith without works, and is unequal to the task... and would accomplish by insisting on the Law what the Apostles accomplish by inciting men to love. Therefore, I cannot put him among the true chief books, though I would not thereby prevent anyone from putting him where he pleases and estimating him as he pleases; for there are many good sayings in him" (*Ibid.*, vol. 7, p. 384).

[1] "According to the Epistle of James, however, 'in many things we all offend' (James 3:2)" (*On Merit and the Forgiveness of Sins, and the Baptism of Infants*, bk. 3, c. 7, n. 13 (PL 44, 194)).

[2] "Hear also the words of James: go to now, you that say, 'Behold, now you that say: Today or tomorrow we will go into such a city, and there we will spend a year... All such rejoicing is wicked' (James 4, 13-16)" (Letter 133 (to Ctesiphon), n. 7 (PL 22, 1155)).

[3] This letter is found among the *False Decretals of the Pseudo-Isidore* (PL 130, 137B). It is found among Remigius' canons for his diocese (n. 47 (PL 102, 1097D)) which are described in Migne's *Patrologia Latina* as "spurious" and "very doubtful" (PL 102, 1095B).

[4] *False Decretals of the Pseudo-Isidore* (PL 130, 61B-C).

[5] "A like incident occurred with St. John the Evangelist, who wrote the Apocalypse" (*Sermones de Sanctis*, serm. 273 (On the martyrdom of Bishop Fructuosos), c. 8, n. 8 (PL 38, 1251)).

was, nevertheless, he says that he acknowledges that that writing is sacred, and was accepted by him as such.[1] Melito of Asia, Bishop of Sardis,[2] Hippolytus,[3] and Irenaeus,[4] all these men, Jerome bearing witness in his book, *On Illustrious Men*, interpreted John's Apocalypse.

But even though the testimonies of these men has great force for settling this matter, nevertheless of greater authority is the testimony of the Church itself. For the IV Synod of Toledo, in the sixteenth chapter of its decrees so defines about this matter: "The authority of many councils and the synodical decrees of the Roman prelates prescribe that the book of the Apocalypse is by John the Evangelist, and they determined that it ought to be accepted among the Divine books. And because there are very many who do not accept its authority, and disdain to preach it in the Church of God, if anyone henceforth either does not accept it, or preach it in the Church from Easter until Pentecost, he will have the sentence of excommunication."[5]

François Titelmans, of the Friars Minor, wrote a small book in support of this book against Erasmus of Rotterdam, who in his *Annotations on the New Testament* attempted to detract from the authority of the Apocalypse.[6] Titelmans, however, in that small book by much evidence and many reasons proves that this book ought to be numbered among the canonical books of Sacred Scripture, and was written by John the Evangelist.[7] Then he replies to the

---

[1] "Therefore that he was called John, and that this book is the work of one John, I do not deny. And I agree also that it is the work of a holy and inspired man. But I cannot readily admit that he was the Apostle, the son of Zebedee, the brother of James, by whom the Gospel of John and the Catholic Epistle were written" (*Church History*, bk. 7, c. 25, n. 7 (PG 20, 609C-D)).

[2] *On Illustrious Men*, c. 24 (PL 23, 643B).

[3] *Ibid.*, c. 61 (PL 23, 671B).

[4] *Ibid.*, c. 9 (PL 23, 625A).

[5] C. 17, *Mansi, Sacrorum Conciliorum Nova Amplissima Collectio*, vol. 10, col. 624A-B. C. 16, *False Decretals of the Pseudo-Isidore* (PL 130, 469D).

[6] Erasmus argues firstly that Jerome in his letter to Dardanus (ep. 129) said that the Apocalypse was rejected by the Greeks, and secondly that many learned men thought, that the book's content lacked Apostolic dignity and is no more than a history expressed in figurative or allegorical terms. For example, the author repeats, "I, John," as though he were writing a promissory note (*syngrapham*), whereas he refers to himself only indirectly (if at all) in his Gospel, e.g. as the "disciple whom Jesus loved." Paul, who also had visions, describes them as if they were someone else's. Thirdly, the Greek manuscripts of the Apocalypse that he consulted do not contain the name *Joannes Evangelista* but *Joannes Theologus* in the title. But in practice, he submitted to the "consent of the world and the Church (*consensus orbis et ecclesiae*)." He then suggests based upon Eusebius' *Church History* that Cerinthus is the author. But he refrains from concluding this based upon the testimonies of Justin Martyr and Irenaeus, and shows his willingness to accept the book is a historical account that is merely allegorical. Cf. *Desiderii Erasmi Roterodami Opera omnia emendatiora et...*: vol. 6 (*complectens Novum Testamentum, cui in hac editione sujectae sunt singulis paginis Adnotationes* (Leiden: Petrus vander Aa, 1705) on cols. 1123-1126.

[7] Titelmans cites St. Jerome's letter to Dardanus: "If the custom of the Latins does not receive it among the canonical scriptures, neither, by the same liberty, do the churches of the Greeks accept John's Apocalypse. Yet we accept them both, not following the custom of the present time but the precedent of early writers, who generally make free use of testimonies from both works" (n. 3 (PL 22, 1103)). He then cites Dionysius the Areopagite, Origen, and Dionysius of Alexandria to show that the Greek Church before St. Jerome's time accepted the book of the Apocalypse. He argues that the reason St. John used a different style from the Gospel in the Apocalypse was because of a different subject matter. Lastly, he cites testimonies of Ephraim of Edessa, Suidas, and Theophylactus to prove that John the Evangelists is the same person as John the Theologian. Cf. *Libri duo de authoritate libri Apocalypsis beati Joannis apostoli, in quibus ex antiquissimorum authorum assertionibus, scripturae hujus dignitas et authoritas comprobatur, adversus eos qui nostra hac tempestate, sive falsis assertionibus, sive non bonis dubitationibus, canonicae et divinae hujus scripturae authoritati derogarunt* (Antwerp, Michiel Hillen van Hoochstraten, 1530).

objections which Erasmus had brought forth against this book, and clearly shows that they are of no weight.

Against all these heresies which try to remove some book from the list of sacred books, it is not necessary to dispute now, because those things which we said above in the first book, chapter two, suffice for refuting all these heresies. For there we cited some councils, namely Laodicea, III Carthage, Florence, and Trent, from which it is established that all these books, which we have now related were rejected by various heretics, belong to the canon of Sacred Scripture. It is not necessary to show now how great the Church's authority is in this matter, since there is no other matter in which the Church's authority shows more. The saying of Augustine is very widely known: I would not believe the Gospel, unless I believed the Church.[1] For from nowhere else is one able to know (outside of God's revelation) that such or such a writing is the Gospel, unless from the Church saying to us that this writing is the Gospel. Therefore, since the Church has already taught us that all those books we have now numbered are canonical and sacred, there is no reason to think that someone could oppose them in whatsoever way without heresy.

SCIENTIA
Science

There is nothing which Luther would not treat temerariously: who was not content to condemn all human works, and to brand them as sinful, unless he had also vilified all the sciences. For he says that all speculative sciences ought to be called errors.[2] Now who is able to endure a man so temerarious and brazen, who not only denies the things which faith teaches, but also condemns those things which are manifest by their evident truth? I firmly believe that he does not know what error is: because if he had known, he never would have said that all speculative sciences are errors. For science [or knowledge (*scientia*)] and error are opposed to each other: wherefore it is that they can never be combined into one thing. If there is science, there cannot be error: if there is error, it cannot rightly be called science. And so that these things might be clearer, let us listen to Augustine saying what error is: "[To err is] to receive what is false as if it were true, and to reject what is true as if it were false, or to hold what is uncertain as certain, and what is certain as uncertain."[3] Therefore since many speculative sciences teach many very evident truths, how will they be called errors? There are true things, certain and very evidently manifest, which they teach, such as are those things which are taught in Arithmetic and Geometry: thus they ought not to be branded as errors.

But so that he might camouflage his lie with some color, he says that the reason why all sciences are deemed by him to be errors, is because they necessarily proceed from a heart wicked and not yet healed by grace. For according to him (as we taught above in the section on "Works," and in the section on "Sin") all works, howsoever good, are sins: and the just man sins in every good work. And for this same reason he teaches that all speculative sciences

---

[1] "I should not believe the Gospel, unless the authority of the Catholic Church moved me" (*Against the Epistle of Manichaeus Called Fundamental*, c. 5, n. 6 (PL 42, 176)).

[2] "For all those moral virtues and speculative sciences impair man with a twofold evil: firstly, that they are not true virtues and sciences, but sins and errors, because they necessarily are formed from an evil heart and a heart not yet healed by grace, which cannot but seek itself in all things, and so they make man void and empty; secondly, they deceive and inflate, so that man seems to himself not to be wicked or foolish" (*Decem praecepta Wittenbergensi praedicatii populo*, 1518 (WA 1, 427, lns. 19-24)).

[3] *Enchiridion*, c. 19 (PL 40, 242).

ought to be deemed errors, because they proceed from a wicked heart not yet fully healed in this life by grace. Which argument, if it were valid, would prove that all the mechanical arts, nay also all the liberal arts, namely grammar, logic, and Rhetoric, are errors, and the mathematical disciplines which are the most certain of them all; but Paul refutes this, who in the Epistle to the Romans says: "Is the law sin? God forbid. But I do not know sin, but by the law" (7, 7): the Law (I call) vocal, or written, or mental. But since the Law teaches us to know sin, it will deservedly be called science. And Paul denies that this is a sin. Therefore, not all science ought to be called an error, even though it proceeds from a sinner.

Furthermore, even if we were to grant to Luther that every man is depraved by sin, not on that account are we obliged to concede that everything which proceeds from a sinful man is a sin and error. Because it does not necessarily proceed from man according to that whereby he is wicked: but they can arise from him according to that whereby he is good. For example, according to the gifts of nature, according to which by that nature he is rational, and capable of discipline, by which natural virtue nothing prevents that a wicked man could invent a good art, and understand and teach a both true and certain science. For (according to Blessed Dionysius [the Pseudo-Areopagite]) the natural good in the demons remained unimpaired even after they were hardened in sin.[1] Thus it is not surprising if in men who are still wayfarers, no matter how much depraved by sin, nature is capable of truth, especially since there are so many very useful arts and sciences discovered by the human race: which cannot be denied except very shamelessly, since there are so many serious authors who testify about this matter. Finally, the theological faculty of Paris condemned this perverse teaching of Luther along with many others of his[2]: The Academy of Louvain did this same thing.[3] And I have not deemed it worthy to cross swords any longer about this matter.

SEPULTURA

Burial

Aeneas Sylvius in his book, *De origine Bohemorum*, when enumerating the errors of the Waldensians, intermingles this one among the others, whereby he says they assert that it makes no difference in what ground human bodies are buried, whether it be sacred or not.

And I surely do not know whether this assertion deserves to be called heresy: because if one only says this, that the place does nothing either to increase or lessen the misery of the soul, it is true what he says. For Augustine teaches this same thing in his book, *On Care to be had for the Dead*.[4] And in *The City of God* he affirms the same opinion, saying the following: "The Truth would nowise have said, 'Fear not them which kill the body, but are not able to kill the soul' (Mt. 10, 28), if anything whatever that an enemy could do to the body of the slain

---

[1] *The Divine Names*, c. 4, sect. 23 (PG 3, 725).

[2] *Determinatio theologicae facultatis parisiensis super doctrina Lutheriana hactenus per eam visa* (Paris, Josse Bade, 1521), proposition 98 ("All moral virtues and speculative sciences are not truly virtues and sciences: but sins and errors.") These condemned propositions were selected from various books of Luther.

[3] *Facultatis theologiae Lovanienssi doctrinalis condemnation doctrinae Martini Lutheri* (WA 6, 177, lns. 31-33).

[4] "But as for the burying of the body, whatever is bestowed on that, is no aid of salvation, but an office of humanity, according to that affection by which 'no man ever hates his own flesh' (Eph. 5, 29)" (C. 18, n. 22 (PL 40, 609)).

could be detrimental to the future life. Or will someone perhaps take so absurd a position as to contend that those who kill the body are not to be feared before death, lest they kill the body, but after death, lest they deprive it of burial? If this be so, then that is false which Christ says, 'Be not afraid of them that kill the body, and after that have no more that they can do' (Lk. 12, 4); for it seems they can do great injury to the dead body. Far be it from us to suppose that the Truth can be thus false... Wherefore all these last offices and ceremonies that concern the dead, the careful funeral arrangements, and the equipment of the tomb, and the pomp of obsequies, are rather the solace of the living than the comfort of the dead. If a costly burial does any good to a wicked man, a squalid burial, or none at all, may harm the godly."[1]

And this same thing which he just said, that the funeral burials "are rather the solace of the living than the comfort of the dead," he confirms again in *On Care to be had for the Dead*, speaking thus: "And yet, by reason of that affection of the human heart, whereby 'no man ever hates his own flesh' (Eph. 5, 29), if men have reason to know that after their death their bodies will lack anything which in each man's nation or country the wonted order of sepulture demands, it makes them sorrowful as men; and that which after death reaches not unto them, they do before death fear for their bodies: so that we find in the Books of Kings, God by one prophet threatening another prophet who had transgressed His word, that his carcass should not be brought into the sepulcher of his fathers[2]... Now if in considering what account is to be made of this punishment, we go by the Gospel, where we have learned that after the slaying of the body there is no cause to fear lest the lifeless members should suffer anything, it is not even to be called a punishment. But if we consider a man's human affection towards his own flesh, it was possible for him to be frightened or saddened, while living, by that of which he would have no sense when dead: and this was a punishment, because the mind was pained by that thing about to happen to its body, howsoever when it did happen it would feel no pain."[3] From whose words it appears clearly enough that the place of burial gives no benefit to the soul for either increasing or decreasing glory or misery. And Pope Innocent III teaches the same thing, saying the following: "Although no burial, or a squalid one, does not harm the godly, nevertheless, a splendid, or costly, burial does not do good to the wicked."[4]

Hence if the Waldensians only said this, namely that the burial of bodies profits nothing for increasing the glory of the soul, or lessening the misery of hell, they would have thought rightly, and their opinion ought not to be branded as heresy. But because they absolutely said that completely nothing benefits the soul because the body is buried in a holy place, wherefore rightly their opinion is condemned: because even though it does not benefit for increasing the glory of the soul, still it has another utility not to be contemned. For the living who enter the holy place, in which the body was buried, as often as they recall where the body of the friend or relative was buried, and it comes to mind the holy man or holy woman in whose honor that place was sanctified, they commend the beloved soul of the holy man or holy woman, so that [the soul] is deigned worthy for interceding to God for it. And there is no doubt that such prayer benefits those who died in the state of grace, because when they lived here below, they merited that such things could benefit them after this life: although the living could also do this for those who were not buried in holy places: but they would not be so remembered, unless the grave were to remind them to do so. For when the graves are seen in holy places, the deceased who were buried there are recalled to mind: and if they had not been buried there in the holy place, perhaps there would not have been any remembrance of these dead.

---

[1] Bk. 1, c. 12, n. 1 (PL 41, 26).
[2] "Because thou hast not been obedient to the Lord... thy dead body shall not be brought into the sepulchre of thy fathers" (III Kings 13, 21 & 22).
[3] C. 7, n. 9 (PL 40,598).
[4] *Decretals of Gregory IX*, bk. 3, tit. 28, c. 12.

If, however, it happens that they are remembered outside the holy place, still the soul is not accustomed to be so disposed there to pray to God for them. For on account of this graves are called in Latin *monumenta* [i.e., "memorials"], because they recall [the dead] to mind in the living, so that those buried there may be remembered. But if such great forgetfulness of kindred and friends is had, such that even when the graves of the dead are seen, they do not remember to pray to God for them, there is still something else which manifestly can benefit the cadavers buried in those places: namely suffrages which in every sacred place are accustomed to be made by the ministers of that place for those who were buried within the walls of their cemeteries. For this reason, just as it was a religious obligation to bury the dead: so also, it was a religious duty to consider in what place they would be buried, so that the faithful deceased as well as the living would be separated from the wicked.

And this was observed not only by Christians, but also by the Jews. For the Patriarchs anxiously cared while they were alive about the burial of their bodies. Abraham in fact bought a field from Ephron the Hethite for four hundred sicles of silver for the burial of Sara his wife[1]: Jacob, his grandson, ordered that he would be buried in which place,[2] and Tobias became acceptable to God by burying the dead.[3] The rest of the Patriarchs and prophets cared about the burial of their bodies. But also it was reckoned to be a very good thing to be buried near the bodies of holy men: just as the history of the Kings relates about the prophet of Samaria, who ordered his sons: "Bury me," he said, "in the sepulchre wherein the man of God is buried: lay my bones beside his bones" (III Kings 13, 31). Which deed benefitted him: because King Josias when he destroyed the temples of the idols many years later, so that he might render honor to the holy prophet, ordered that the bones of the other prophet, who was buried next to him, to be left untouched. And from the thirty pieces of silver brought back by Judas the traitor, the chief priests bought the potter's field for the burial of strangers, lest either they would remain unburied, or be buried in a profane place. And about this it is enough.

SILENTIUM

Silence

There were certain heretics devoting themselves so much to silence that putting a finger upon their nose and lips, as though they always practiced silence, applying themselves to nothing else besides keeping silent. In which matter they were saying that they were imitating the prophets, because the prophet David says: "Set a watch, O Lord, before my mouth: and a door round about my lips" (Ps. 140, 3). These heretics were called by the Greek word, Passalorynchitae. πάσσαλος in Greek means "stake," ῥύγχος means "nose." Thus it is evident that they were called Passalorynchitae, as though those putting a stake or finger in the manner of a stake upon the nose. From which it is evident that this word was distorted in Philastrius on account of ignorance of the copyists: because in the writings of Philastrius they are called Passalorinchitae,[4] while nevertheless Augustine calls them Pattalorinchitae[5]: giving this etymology of the word which we just related. Neither Philastrius nor Augustine, however, state at what time this heresy began, or who was its originator.

---

[1] Cf. Gen. 23, 16.

[2] Cf. Gen. 50, 5.

[3] Cf. Tob. 12, 12.

[4] C. 76 (PL 12, 1187B).

[5] Actually, although Pattalorinchitae is found in some old editions of St. Augustine's works, Philastrius' spelling, Passalorynchitae, is now found in Migne's *Patrologia Latina* (C. 63 (PL 42, 42)).

Now so that I may speak about their assertion, these Passalorinchitae seem to me rather to follow the Pythagorean vanity,[1] than the wisdom and piety of the prophets. For the passage of the [Royal] prophet which we cited from the Psalms, nowise supports them. For the prophet does not ask for a wall as a watch for his lips, but a door. "Set a watch, O Lord," says the Psalmist, "before my mouth: and a door round about my lips." He did not say a wall, because if he had asked for a wall, he would seem to have cast away the power of speaking. But he said a door, and not any kind, but around [his lips], namely because it could be opened in a place and time. By which words he asked merely for moderate and temperate speech, and not perpetual silence: namely so that when he ought to be silent, he would be silent: when it would be fitting to speak, he would speak. For (as the son of the same prophet taught after him) there is a time for speaking, just as there is a time for keeping silence.[2] And if keeping silence were always deserving of commendation, Isaias would never have deplored the silence kept by himself, saying: "Woe is me, because I have held my peace" (6, 5). Certainly, against such vain superstition it is irksome to dispute more. Guy the Carmelite never mentions this heresy in his *Summa de haeresibus*, even though Augustine, whom he imitates when enumerating heresies, placed it in the sixty-third place among the other heresies.

SIMONIA

Simony

There was a certain execrable heresy whereby it was believed that spiritual gifts could be bought with money. The author of this heresy was Simon the Magician, about whom in the Acts of the Apostles it is said that after he had been baptized in Samaria by Philip the deacon, "seeing that by the imposition of the hands of the apostles, the Holy Ghost was given, he offered them money, saying: Give me also this power, that on whomsoever I shall lay my hands, he may receive the Holy Ghost" (Acts 8, 18-19). Hence because he firstly, after having received Baptism, believed that spiritual things are salable, wherefore that sin and heresy receives its name from him, such that it is called "simony" from "Simon." The Greeks fall into the same error, who, Guy the Carmelite bearing witness, say that it is permitted to buy ecclesiastical prelatures, and he asserts that it is done by their patriarch.[3] The Armenians are noted for the same error. And this is the first heresy which arose after Christ's Ascension into heaven, which Blessed Peter reproached, saying: "Keep thy money to thyself, to perish with thee, because thou hast thought that the gift of God may be purchased with money" (Acts 8, 20). And immediately he declared him excommunicated, and cast out from the community of the faithful, saying: "Thou hast no part nor lot in this matter. For thy heart is not right in the sight of God. Do penance therefore for this thy wickedness; and pray to God, that perhaps this thought of thy heart may be forgiven thee. For I see thou art in the gall of bitterness, and in the bonds of iniquity" (v. 21-23).

---

[1] "Pythagoras held that the souls of men, after a certain time spent in hell, returned to life again, and passed into a new set of bodies. As a proof of this, he affirmed that he himself had been Euphorbus, at the siege of Troy; and, to prove it, said he knew the shield of that warrior, which he saw hung up in one of the Grecian temples. He was such a handsome person, that his scholars used to call him the Hyperborean Apollo. (*Diog. Laet.*, bk. 8, segm. 2) Lucian calls him by these names, in derision of his vanity, in having endeavored to pass for these persons. But it was not so much vanity, as a sort of fraud in him; because he thereby proposed the reform of men" (*The Select Dialogues of Lucian*, (Philadephia, William Poynell & co., 1804), p. 54).

[2] Eccle. 3, 7.

[3] *Summa de haeresibus*, c. 12, fol. 24v.

Furthermore, Giezi, the servant of the prophet Eliseus, was struck with perpetual leprosy by God, because he accepted money for the benefit of healing which Eliseus had conferred upon Naaman the leper.[1] Again, the Teacher of truth Himself, when sending his disciples to preach, after He had given them the power of healing the sick, of curing leprosy, and of casting out devils, immediately added: "Freely have you received, freely give" (Mt. 10, 8). Next, since in every buying and selling of things, equivalence ought to be kept in the price of things, it is proved that he who believes that the spiritual gifts of God can be equated with a price, also believes that money is equally good and equally precious as God's spiritual gifts. But the Wise Man in the Proverbs thinks the opposite, when saying: "Receive my instruction, and not money: choose knowledge rather than gold. For wisdom is better than all the most precious things: and whatsoever may be desired cannot be compared to it" (8, 10-11). Hence Tharasius, Bishop of Constantinople, in a letter to Pope Hadrian, says the following: "The impious heresy of Macedonius and of those who with him impugned the Holy Ghost, is more endurable [than that of those who are guilty of simony]: since the former in their ravings maintained that the Holy Ghost of Father and Son is a creature and the slave of God, whereas the latter make the same Holy Ghost to be their own slave. For every master sells what he has just as he wills, whether it be his slave or any other of his possessions. Similarly, he who buys, wanting to be the master of what he buys, acquires it by the price of money."[2]

Therefore, since simony is such a serious sin, whereby a very perverse opinion is had of God, wherefore very justly by many decrees of councils it was ordered that no price may be accepted for the conferral of any spiritual thing. For the Synod of Elvira speaks thus: "Those being baptized are not to place money in the baptismal shell since it seems to indicate that the priest is selling what is a free gift."[3] The XI Synod of Toledo defines as follows: "It is absolutely forbidden to make a charge for what is acquired by the consolation of invisible grace, whether by demanding a price or by seeking any kind of return whatever, as the Lord says, 'What you have freely received, freely give' (Mt. 10, 8). And hence whoever henceforth constituted in an ecclesiastical order, either for baptizing or signing[4] the faithful, or the conferring of chrism,[5] or the promotion of Orders, accepts any wage or payments, (unless voluntarily offered) for a favor of this kind, certainly if any such thing be perpetrated with the knowledge of the bishop of the place by his subordinates, the same bishop is subject to an excommunication for two months for having knowingly concealed the wicked deeds, and did not apply the necessary correction. But if the same bishop was unaware any of his subordinates is believed to have accepted for himself anything from the previously specified things, if he is a priest, he is to be punished with an excommunication for three months: if a deacon, four months. But a subdeacon or cleric serving these cupidities, he should be punished with an appropriate punishment and due excommunication."[6] And the II [or III] Synod of Braga[7] decreed that the same thing ought to be done.[8]

---

[1] Cf. IV Kings 5, 27.
[2] Gratian, *Concordia discordantium canonum*, causa 1, q. 1, c. 21 (*Eos*) (PL 187, 489A).
[3] C. 48 (PL 84, 307B). Mansi, vol. 2, col. 304E.
[4] This may refer to the anointing with holy chrism performed after Baptism.
[5] I.e., Confirmation.
[6] *Concordia discordantium canonum*, cause 1, q. 1, c. 101 (*Quicquid invisibilis*) (PL 187, 530B-C); Mansi vol. 11, col. 142, can. 8.
[7] The synod was held in 572 A.D.
[8] "It has been resolved that every bishop ought to command this in his churches, that those who offer their infants for Baptism, if they voluntarily by their own choice offer something, it may be accepted from them; but if through the necessity of poverty they do not have anything to offer, no pledge may be violently taken by the clerics. For many poor people, fearing this, withhold their children from Baptism,

Peter Damascene, who from being a Benedictine monk was the Cardinal Bishop of Ostia, wrote one book against the Simoniacs.[1] Yet I admit that I have not seen this book, but I spoke relying on the testimony of Johannes Trithemius, stating this in his book, *De Ecclesiasticis scriptoribus*.[2]

SPES

Hope

There are so many perverse doctrines of Luther, such that there is scarcely anything pertaining to faith or morals about which Luther did not teach some wicked thing. He thinks wrongly about the virtue of faith, he teaches wrongly about charity: he also teaches very wrongly about hope. For he says that hope does not proceed from merits. And it is not surprising that he would teach these things: because it cannot happen that from a dirty and polluted spring someone may draw clean water, or from a rotten root one can produce good fruit. Now Luther had said that all our works are worth completely nothing: for he says that all our works are sins[3]: and hence it follows that no one then (according to him) may trust in works, or on account of them hope that he will obtain something from God. For Luther places all his hope in faith: and in this way (as we said elsewhere) he extolls faith, such that he completely denigrates works: and for this reason he teaches that by no means ought hope to be based upon our works. Wherefore it is that while he attributes too much to faith, he completely overthrows hope: because in place of hope he teaches presumption, since he teaches men without works to hope for glory. For even though works by their own nature are unworthy that so great a reward, as heavenly glory is, be given: still on account of the agreement which God made with men, whereby He promises that He will give glory to those acting well, our works are then deemed worthy of glory.

For that good householder made an agreement with the laborers for a penny a day. And when the workers who had come early in the morning, hoping that they would receive something more, the householder said to one of them: "Friend, I do thee no wrong: didst thou not agree with me for a penny?" (Mt. 20, 13). For this reason, he said that a penny was owed to the laborer, speaking thus: "Take what is thine, and go thy way" (v. 14). What is "thine"? certainly the penny, for he had agreed to that. For this same reason the Savior says the same thing elsewhere: "The workman is worthy of his meat" (Mt. 10, 10). From which words it is evident that glory is owed to the just man, as a reward to the laborer. It is indeed owed, because it was promised: because unless it had been promised, it would not have been owed.

---

who if perhaps, while they are delayed, were to depart from this life without the grace of Baptism, it is necessary that their perdition would be required of them, when greatly fearing their spoils they withdrew themselves from the grace of Baptism" (*Concordia discordantium canonum*, cause 1, q. 1, c. 103 (*Placuit ut*) (PL 187, 531B); Mansi vol. 9, col. 840B-C, can. 7).

[1] *Contra episcopos Simoniacos* is listed by Trithemius, but this title seems not to be a title of a specific book, but rather a reference to two short works that St. Peter Damian wrote, namely opusc. 30: *De Sacramentis per improbos administratis* & opusc. 31: *Contra Pilargyriam, & munerum cupiditatem* found in *Opera omnia nunc primum in unum collecta ac argumentis, & notationibus illustrata studio ac labore domni Constantini Cajetani* (Paris, Giuseppe Corona, 1743), vol. 3, pp.267-277. He also wrote *Gratissimus* ("Most-Favored Book," *ibid.*, vol. 3, opusc. 6, pp. 42-72) in about 1051 A.D., which treats the problem of simony and the validity of the Sacraments bestowed by a simoniac cleric.

[2] *De scriptoribus ecclesiasticis* (Cologne, Quentel, 1546), p. 141.

[3] "The just man," Luther says, "sins in every good work" (Bull *Exsurge Domine*, condemned proposition 31 (Dz. 771). Cf. WA 1, 356, lns. 23-24).

Thus, this foundation having been laid, I wish to ask Luther what does a laborer hope for, who fatigues himself in another's field? It is certain that he hopes to receive a reward for his labor: for he works for this. But why does he hope? Is it solely on account of the goodness and mercy of the Lord in Whose field he labors? Certainly not, but also on account of his own labor. He indeed hopes based on the Lord's goodness: because had he not believed in Him and had trusted in His promises, he never would have labored in His field: and on account of this relying upon the words said by the Lord, he hopes that he will receive a reward on account of his labors. All just men act in this manner, who rely upon the Lord's goodness and clemency that He will give them eternal glory.

But because they know that He will not give such a great reward to the lazy and idle, they do all they can to labor, so that by their labors they may merit to attain glory. Hence it is said in Job: "The life of man upon earth is a warfare, and his days are like the days of a hireling" (7, 1). Blessed Gregory, when discussing these words in his *Morals on the Book of Job*, says: "Moreover it is to be known, that a hireling anxiously and heedfully sees to it, that never a day pass clear of work, and that the expected end of the time should not come empty for his rewarding. For in his earnestness of labor he sees what he may get in the season of recompense. Thus when his work advances, his assurance in the reward is increased, but when the work is at a stand-still, his hope totters in respect of the recompense. And hence each of the elect reckoning his life as the days of a 'hireling,' stretches forward to the reward so much the more confident in hope, in proportion as he holds on more stoutly against the increase of labor. He considers what the transitory nature of the present life is. He counts the days with works. He dreads lest the moments of life should pass void of labor. He rejoices in adversity, he is refreshed by suffering, he is comforted by mourning, in that he sees himself to be more abundantly recompensed with the rewards of the life to come, the more thoroughly he devotes himself for the love thereof by daily deaths. For it is hence that the citizens of the Land above say to the Creator of it in the words of the Psalmist, 'For thy sake we are killed all the day long' (Ps. 43, 22). Hence Paul says, 'I die daily, I protest by your glory, brethren' (I Cor. 15, 31). Hence he says again, 'For which cause I also suffer these things: but I am not ashamed. For I know whom I have believed, and I am certain that he is able to keep that which I have committed unto him, against that day' (II Tim. 1, 12). Therefore, because holy men now perform labors, commending themselves to the Truth, they already hold so many pledges of their recompense, enclosed within the chamber of hope."[1] From which words it is very clearly established that the hope of the just has its origin from merits, due to the fact that their life is like that of a laborer, who does not hope that he will receive a reward, unless labors precede. Besides, the Apostle Paul teaches this same thing in the Epistle to the Romans, saying the following: "And not only so; but we glory also in tribulations, knowing that tribulation worketh patience; And patience trial; and trial hope" (5, 3-4). [Ambrosiaster] when interpreting this passage, says: "That there should be hope in someone who has been tried and tested is perfectly reasonable, for he will know that he is worthy to receive a reward in the kingdom of God."[2] In which words he clearly teaches that it alone is rightly called hope, which relies upon good and tried works.

But [Hervé of Bourg-Dieu] teaches this much more clearly, who in his comments on the Epistles of Paul, when interpreting the aforesaid passage, speaks thus: "'Trial worketh hope,' because everyone from the fact that he has proved himself to be steadfast, he begins to have hope, that is, the certitude of future glory, which seems to be naught to human reason, but he is strengthened by the testimony of virtue. For if someone who has not yet proved himself hopes, he does not yet hope, but rather presumes. For trials whereby the patience of the faith-

---

[1] Bk. 8, c. 7, n. 12 (PL 75, 808C-809A).

[2] *Commentaries on the Epistle to the Romans*, c. 5, v. 4 (PL 17, 89C).

ful are tried, we ought to take to mean not merely those which occur outwardly, for example [trials] regarding injuries or sicknesses, or from whatever torment of the body, but also those they do or betake to themselves, while they take their rest they afflict and wear down themselves, resisting their passions, refraining [from] lust: and by doing other things which pertain to the good of continence, from which things without a doubt patience is born, which having been made commendable generates hope. Now hope is the expectation of good things to come."[1] What will Luther say now against such distinguished testimonies? If he is not afraid to condemn [Ambrosiaster] and [Hervé of Bourg-Dieu], still it is fitting that he would at least respect Paul, who says: "Trial worketh hope." Therefore, hope is born from good works, tried and tested.

Next, Paul himself, on account of the many good works which he had done, hopes without any doubt that he will receive glory. For so he says: "For I am even now ready to be sacrificed: and the time of my dissolution is at hand. I have fought a good fight, I have finished my course, I have kept the faith. As to the rest, there is laid up for me a crown of justice, which the Lord the just judge will render to me in that day: and not only to me, but to them also that love his coming" (II Tim. 4, 6-8). If someone were to ask Paul, whence did he conceive such certain hope, so that he would say with great confidence that there is laid up for him a crown of justice, [he would answer] because he fought the good fight, he finished the course, he kept the faith. And he not only hopes in this, but also in the justice of the judge, that is, God, Who never denied a merited crown to anyone fighting well. Add to these things that Sacred Scripture itself teaches us to hope partly in good works. For the Royal Prophet speaks thus: "Offer up the sacrifice of justice, and trust in the Lord" (Ps. 4, 6). When [Pseudo-] Jerome expounds these words in his exposition of the Psalms, he speaks thus: "Immolate justice as the sacrifice to God, and consequently you will hope in the Lord."[2] By which words the [Royal] Prophet clearly teaches that hope is not true which the sacrifice of justice does not precede. Paul teaches the same thing in the Epistle to Titus, saying the following: "We should live soberly, and justly, and godly in this world, looking for the blessed hope" (2, 12-13), that is, so that we can securely hope for future beatitude. For Paul understood this [beatitude] by the name of hope there, [because] he firstly admonished to live soberly, and justly, and godly."

From which [testimonies] it is evident that true hope is to a certain extent born from works. But Luther, because he does not want to live soberly, or justly, or godly, would like to have true hope without all these works. Again, the hope of all those who hope without merits, Holy Writ proclaims to be vain. For in the book of Job we read that "The hope of the hypocrite shall perish: his folly shall not please him, and his trust shall be like the spider's web. He shall lean upon his house, and it shall not stand: he shall prop it up, and it shall not rise" (8, 13-15). And again, in the same book: "The eyes of the wicked shall decay, and the way to escape shall fail them, and their hope the abomination of the soul" (11, 20). And the Wise Man in the Proverbs says: "The hope of the wicked shall perish" (10, 28). And in the book of Wisdom: "The hope of the wicked is as dust, which is blown away with the wind, and as a thin froth which is dispersed by the storm: and a smoke that is scattered abroad by the wind: and as the remembrance of a guest of one day that passeth by" (5, 15). And in Ecclesiasticus: "The hopes of a man that is void of understanding are vain and deceitful" (34, 1). Therefore, Luther's hope is vain, who without works trusts that he shall attain to eternal glory.

Finally, this wicked and insane opinion of Luther was rejected by the University of Paris among the many others of his which the faculty condemned.[3] All those things which we said above in the section on "Confidence" fight against this heresy.

---

[1] *Commentaria in epistolas Pauli* (PL 181, 655D).

[2] *Breviarium in Psalmos* (PL 26, 828C).

[3] *Determinatio theologicae facultatis parisiensis*, condemned proposition 87 ("Faith does not come

STUDIA GENERALIA

Colleges[1]

Just as any tyrant who dominates a people by force and violence, takes away from them all weapons with which the people could resist his tyrannical domination, so that he may more easily exercise his tyranny as he pleases, so John Wycliffe seems to me: who when he had scattered many heresies among the people, lest through the knowledge of books his wicked doctrine could be resisted by the people, he attempted to take away from it all colleges, saying that colleges were introduced into the Church by vain paganism, and are of as much value to the Church as the devil. From which opinion it is clearly proved that this man wanted to enervate the power of the Christian religion, by taking away the knowledge of Christians. For "the weapons of our warfare," as Paul says, "are not carnal but spiritual" (II Cor. 10, 4).[2] For our faith ought not to be defended by carnal weapons, but by words, reasons, and arguments, especially by those which can be drawn from Holy Writ. For Paul, when preparing the Ephesians for spiritual combat, says: "In all things taking the shield of faith, wherewith you may be able to extinguish all the fiery darts of the most wicked one. And take unto you the helmet of salvation, and the sword of the Spirit (which is the word of God)" (Eph. 6, 16-17). These are the weapons with which a Catholic fights against a heretic. All the holy and Catholic Doctors have this sword in their hands, and with it they "executed vengeance upon the nations, chastisements among the people" (Ps. 149, 7). Vengeance, I say, because the Jews and the Gentiles, from whom they suffered persecution, by the power of the spiritual sword, namely the word of God, killed the world, and converted it to the faith: they separated them from vices, and turned them toward the virtues, rebuking their evil acts. "For the word of God is living and effectual, and more piercing than any two edged sword" (Heb. 4, 12).

But if these are the weapons with which one ought to do battle, it is necessary that one be exercised in them, lest perhaps when the time of war comes, the soldier never having been trained, would succumb in battle. For a trained soldier in an army fights more dexterously than he who never took up arms. Hence soldiers rightly practice hastiludes[3] among themselves, so that thereby they may learn how to attack enemies, and by what means one ought to withstand them. Along these lines there ought to be a practicing with spiritual weapons, teachers of exercises who teach, contests among the students, debates, questions, so that in this way they may more precisely grasp the right understanding of those things which they discuss, or so that in this way they may become better prepared and more ready for resisting the enemies, that is, the heretics. Now since these things may be better done in the universities than elsewhere, whence it is proved to be right, nay necessary, that universities and colleges be established for having practice of the literary arts.

Moreover, if there were no studies, nor teachers who would teach others, by whom would the uneducated by taught? Would everyone suffice for himself, so that he would not need any teacher? If Wycliffe agrees to this, let him hear Solomon contradicting him: "Lean not upon

---

forth from merits.")

[1] The original name for the university, or the education given at the university, was "general studies." Unlike the seven liberal arts, there was no defined curriculum for the Studia, which necessitated universities to offer the diploma as recognition that a student had successfully studied a branch of studies.

[2] In place of "but spiritual," the Vulgate has "but mighty to God."

[3] "Hastilude is a generic term used in the Middle Ages to refer to many kinds of martial games. The word comes from the Latin *hastiludium*, literally "lance game."

thy own prudence" (Prov. 3, 5). And again: "Be not wise (*sapiens*) in thy own conceit" (v. 7). And Blessed Paul says: "Be not wise (*prudentes*) in your own conceits" (Rom. 12, 16). Theophylactus, when expounding these words, says: "This is to say, do not think that you suffice for yourself, and that it is unnecessary for you to consult someone else, or someone suggesting that which is suitable [to be done]. For even though Moses spoke familiarly with God, still he had need of his father-in-law's advice."[1] Tell me then, Wycliffe, do you wish to act contrary to the command of the Wise Man and of Paul, so that everyone would rely upon his own prudence? If we ought not to be wise in our own conceit [*sapientes apud nosmetipsos*, i.e., wise according to the opinion we have of ourselves], one ought to learn from others: wherefore it is necessary that there be teachers, from whom those who do not know, may learn. But since these teachers are not found everywhere, it is right that there be some public places, such as some cities or towns, in which some men are prepared to teach every man wishing to learn: as in any well governed nation there are places in it assigned for much merchandise, so that someone willing to buy need not roam around the town, uncertain about where those things are sold. Thus, to learn is good and necessary, especially for the ignorant. Therefore, by the same principle, to teach is good and necessary. For just as God put in His Church some Apostles, some prophets, so also He put some teachers.[2] If it is good both to teach and to learn, why will colleges, in which some learn, others teach, be bad? And if those who teach are useful, how will it be true what Wycliffe says, that colleges in which Doctors teach, are of no more value to the Church than the devil?

Otherwise, that he says that colleges were introduced into the Church by a vain paganism, is false just as the rest. For among the Jews of old before Christ's coming there were teachers, who were called Scribes, and who had the charge of teaching the people, and these men were called Rabbi. Hence Augustine, when expounding the passage in John, "And his disciples asked him: Rabbi, who hath sinned" etc. (9, 2), says the following: "You know that 'Rabbi' is Master. They called Him Master, because they desired to learn. The question, at all events, they proposed to the Lord as a master."[3] From whose words it is plain that among the Jews one learned from Rabbis as from teachers, whose office was to teach. Again, the Jews, astonished by Christ's teaching, were saying: "How doth this man know letters, having never learned?" (Jn. 7, 15) And Blessed Paul in the Second Epistle to Timothy says: "But continue thou in those things which thou hast learned, and which have been committed to thee: knowing of whom thou hast learned them. And because from thy infancy thou hast known the holy scriptures" (3, 14-15). From both of these passages it is proved clearly enough that among the Jews one was accustomed to learn the meaning of Holy Writ from some men, and to be taught by others.

Since, therefore, there are such clear testimonies approving teaching and instruction, let us see what motivated John Wycliffe to condemning colleges. Because in them (he says) envies are produced, comparisons of persons and nationality, and many other seedbeds of the father of lies. I admit that these things are there, just as these vices also exist outside the universities and colleges: nevertheless, these vices do not arise from studies, but from the malice of those studying. For otherwise no one could study lest he be stained with these vices. But since there are also many students in the colleges not having part in vices of this kind, it is proved that those vices do not come forth from study, but from the persons themselves who were also infected with the same vices elsewhere. There is not (as I believe) a city or town, no matter how small, in which vices of this kind, such as envies, quarrels, contentions, suspicions, lies, do not often occur. Should perhaps all life which is had in a community or society with others

---

[1] Cf. Ex. 18, 19-24. *Commentarius in Epistolam ad Romanos* (PG 124, 510D).
[2] Cf. Eph. 4, 11.
[3] *Tractates on the Gospel of John*, tract. 44, n. 3 (PL 35, 1714).

be condemned, because they are always produced in any multitude? Far be it, because such a community can be found without these vices. Now that such things exist, comes forth from the malice of some: still not of all, because many live in a community without these vices. Hence colleges ought not to be condemned on this account, otherwise by the same principle every community of people ought to have been condemned.

Add to these things that this use of schools and studies is not as recent as Wycliffe thinks, but began from the very beginnings of the Church. For in Antioch there had been a school for teaching founded by the Apostles, in which there were distinguished teachers engaged in that office. Now this can be inferred from the book of the Acts of the Apostles, where it is so said: "Now there were in the church which was at Antioch, prophets and doctors, among whom was Barnabas, and Simon who was called Niger, and Lucius of Cyrene, and Manahen, who was the foster brother of Herod the tetrarch, and Saul. And as they were ministering to the Lord, and fasting, the Holy Ghost said to them: Separate me Saul and Barnabas, for the work whereunto I have taken them" (13, 1-2). Notice the work and the office for which out of all Christ's disciples only five were chosen, who would teach in Antioch: and from among these five two were promoted to the Apostolate, namely Paul and Barnabas. From which it is evident that at that time one was the office of a teacher, another was that of an Apostle. After this school there was another school erected in Alexandria, about which Eusebius of Caesarea, when speaking about the times of Emperor Antoninus, bears witness by these words: "About that time, Pantaenus, a man highly distinguished for his learning, had charge of the school of the faithful in Alexandria. A school of sacred learning, which continues to our day, was established there in ancient times, and as we have been informed, was managed by men of great ability and zeal for Divine things. Among these it is reported that Pantaenus was at that time especially conspicuous, as he had been educated in the philosophical system of those called Stoics."[1] After this Pantaenus, the same author says Clement succeeded in the same school,[2] and after Clement, Origen,[3] and so successively he relates other teachers who were in charge of that school.[4] Therefore the institution of schools and studies is not as recent as John Wycliffe thinks.

But so that we put an end to this dispute, let us see what the Council of Constance decreed about this matter. For the Council of Constance, in the eighth session, condemned forty-five articles of this John Wycliffe, the twenty-ninth of which is put in that same place in these words: "Universities, studies, colleges, graduations, and offices instruction in the same have been introduced by a vain paganism; they are of as much value to the Church as the devil."[5] Which article along with the others, was therein condemned by a *latae sententiae* excommunication upon them all.

---

[1] *Church History*, bk. 5, c. 10, n. 1-2 (PG 20, 454C-455A).

[2] *Ibid.*, bk. 5, c. 11 (PG 20, 455-458B).

[3] "[Origen] was in his eighteenth year when he took charge of the catechetical school [in Alexandria]" (*Ibid.*, bk. 6, c. 3 (PG 20, 527A).

[4] "It was in the tenth year of the above-mentioned reign that Origen removed from Alexandria to Cæsarea, leaving the charge of the catechetical school in that city to Heraclas" (*Ibid.*, bk. 6, c.26 (PG 20, 586B).

[5] Dz. 609.

SUBDITUS
Submission

There is no state of the Church which John Wycliffe will not have nipped at; there is no authority which he did not denigrate. And he was not content to refuse obedience and submission to his superiors, unless he would also persuade those subject [to authority] to do the same thing. And he thought that it would not be enough unless he would make subjects superior to their rulers, and vassals superior to their lords. For he says that common men can correct their transgressing rulers and lords, and so he asserts that people justly withhold tithes from priests when they know that they are sinners, and to withhold taxes from other authorities on account of their sins. In which matter we perceive that it has happened what Paul says about heretics: "Evil men and seducers shall grow worse and worse: erring, and driving into error" (II Tim. 3, 13). Such is Wycliffe, who in order to gain favor with the people, fell into this mad and pestiferous error, than which no other could be more pestilential. For there is nothing else which could harm the peace and tranquility of a nation more than if you would give to any common man the power of correcting his ruler or lord. Any nation will then be a sort of shadow or image of hell, in which, Job bearing witness, "No order, but everlasting horror dwelleth (10, 22). What kind of order can there be, I ask, where he who ought to be the one corrected, wants to correct? And he who has the duty to correct, undergoes correction? There is certainly no order, nay it is most certainly the opposite of order, that he who rules would be corrected by him whom he rules. For then no one would be superior to another if when any one of them sinned, they could correct each other. Oh, that sort of nation ought to be pitied, which would be governed according to Wycliffe's view. For in it every uncivilized man, the uneducated, the wicked, robbers, adulterers, liars, could correct their rulers and lords, and the worse he was, the more violently he would attack his lord and superior, such that he would be punished by no one, but would remain unpunished in his villainy. For then everything would be confounded. A child would make an uproar against an aged man, a low born man would rise up against a nobleman, fools against a wise man, students against their teacher, children against their parents. And so the nation would be a kind of pit, or (so that I may speak more truly) an abyss of scandals. What would the people not do when given such license? For it is, as it were, a wild people and a very savage beast, than which there is not another more wild or more ferocious.

Besides, if it were permitted for any man from among the people to correct a transgressing ruler: why did David, when in the cave which Saul entered to ease nature, not kill that same Saul, since he could have done it then very easily?[1] Was not Saul at that time a bad king, and deprived of his kingdom by the Lord God? Had he not hitherto killed the priest Achimelech, and eighty-five other men who wore the linen ephod, because he had given hungry David the loaves of proposition?[2] Had he not very often tried to unjustly kill David himself, and would have done so had not the Lord kept His servant from his hand? And yet when all these things were very well known to David himself and to all the people, David did not want to punish him when he could, but merely "secretly cut off the hem of Saul's robe" (I Kings 24, 5), and perhaps still not without some sort of slight fault: which is proved by the fact that afterwards it caused David himself to repent, in that he had cut off the hem of Saul's robe. Wherefore it is that he would have repented much more if he had struck the person of Saul. Hence, he said

---
[1] Cf. I Kings 24, 4.
[2] Cf. I Kings 22, 18.

to his men advising him to kill Saul: "The Lord be merciful unto me, that I may do no such thing to my master the Lord's anointed, as to lay my hand upon him, because he is the Lord's anointed" (v. 7).

Again, Blessed Gregory, when expounding the passage in Job: "Who maketh a man that is a hypocrite [to reign for the sins of the people]" (34, 30), speaks thus: "But because rulers have their own Judge, subjects must be very careful not to judge rashly the conduct of their rulers. For the Lord Himself did not without a reason scatter the money of the changers, and overthrow the seats of them that sold doves,[1] signifying doubtless that He judges the conduct of people through their rulers, but that He examines into the doings of rulers in His own person... As rulers then must take care that their higher position does not puff up their minds with a notion of their singular wisdom, so must subjects be careful not to be offended at the conduct of their rulers. But even if the conduct of rulers is justly blamed, yet it is the duty of subjects to pay them respect, even when they displease them."[2] From whose words it is established that it is not permitted for subjects to judge the life of the shepherd: thus, it will be still less permitted for them to punish the bad life of the shepherd.

Next, since we already proved in the section on "Power" that no power and no authority is lost through mortal sin, it is thence proved that it is not permitted for subjects to punish their transgressing rulers. Otherwise, when they sinned, they would have already lost their power, because as soon as they sin, they are subject to those for correction whom before the sin they had governed. Finally, among the forty-five articles of John Wycliffe condemned in the eighth session of the Council of Constance, the seventeenth says the following: "People can at their will correct masters who offend."[3] Which article was condemned with the others of the same man in the same place.

SUFFRAGIA DEFUNCTORUM

Suffrages for the Deceased

It did not seem enough for Luther to harm the living, unless he had also harmed the dead. For he calls the living away from the veneration of the saints, namely lest they be helped by their prayers, who can do very much before God. But he also defrauds the dead of the suffrages of the living. Therefore he shows himself to be the enemy of the living and the dead. Now we have already disputed about the veneration of the saints; there remains that we fight against Luther in favor of the suffrages of the deceased. For Luther says that prayers, sacrifices, and alms for the deceased, which are done by the living for them, are of no benefit.[4]

---

[1] Cf. Mt. 21, 12.
[2] *Morals on the Book of Job*, bk. 25, c. 16, n. 36-37 (PL 76, 344C-345C).
[3] Dz. 597.
[4] "Now, since this is uncertain, and we do not know whether the soul has been sentenced, it is not a sin to pray for them. However, you should pray in such a way that you let it remain uncertain and say, 'Dear God, if the soul is still in the state that it can be helped, then I pray that Thou would be gracious to it.' When you have done that once or twice, then cease and commend the soul to God. God has promised that He will hear what we pray. Therefore, when you have prayed once or three times, you should believe that He has granted your prayer and never again pray it, so that you do not tempt or mistrust God. But when people institute eternal Masses, vigils, and prayers, and howl all year long, as if God had not granted them the year before—that is the devil and death, in which God is mocked with unbelief; such prayer is nothing but blasphemy of God. Therefore, guard yourself against this and avoid it. God does not care about such annual endowments, but about sincere, devout, believing prayer; that will help the soul, if anything will help it. Vigils and Masses certainly help the bellies of priests, monks, and nuns,

Yet Luther is not the originator of this error, because before him were the Waldensians and Albigensians, who upheld this error. And before these men the Greeks and the Armenians taught the same error, who (as we said elsewhere) completely denied Purgatory, wherefore according to their opinion it would necessarily follow that prayers for the deceased are useless. The first author of this error, as far as I know, was a certain priest, Aerius. For Augustine charges him with this error.[1]

And certainly if the deceased are such men as are these heretics, I admit that sacrifices or prayers ought not to be offered to God for them because such things are offered in vain for those who are in Hell. But for those who are in the place of Purgatory, it is pious and useful to pray to God, or to offer other sacrifices to God. For those who are in Purgatory have charity whereby they are conjoined to Christ the Head, wherefore they are members of the body of the Church, and of which the other living are members. But this is implanted by nature, that upon one suffering member the other members have compassion, and the members help each other when they need one another. Therefore, since those in Purgatory suffer, it is necessary that the living would help them with prayers and sacrifices. For if the living are heard when praying for the living, why not also when they pray for the dead, if they are in need, and are such as those who can be helped? Certainly, another member remaining in the body can give no help to a member that has been cut off. Yet any feeble member as long as it adheres to the body, can be helped by the other members. And hence the prayers of the living do not benefit those who are in Hell: because they are amputated members: but those in Purgatory are members connected to the body, and so can be helped by the other members.

When Jesus saw the faith of some men presenting one sick of the palsy, He said to the one sick of the palsy: "Son, thy sins are forgiven thee" (Mk. 2, 5). If the faith of those presenting benefited the living man sick of the palsy so much, why could not the faith of those presenting sacrifices benefit the deceased, since the latter are before God living members of the same body? Furthermore, the elder Tobias, when instructing his son with good counsels, said: "Lay out thy bread, and thy wine upon the burial of a just man" (4, 18). For unless the offerings made for the dead brought some benefit to them, Tobias would have counseled his son in vain to lay bread and wine upon the burial of a just man. For those things are not laid out for feeding the bodies of the deceased, but of the living, namely of the poor and of the priests, so that these alms offered to the poor, may come to benefit the deceased man himself.

Again, in the Second Book of Machabees, a very clear testimony is contained for the suffrages of the deceased, where it is said thus: "Making a gathering, Judas sent twelve thousand drachms of silver to Jerusalem for sacrifice to be offered for the sins of the dead, thinking well and religiously concerning the resurrection, (For if he had not hoped that they that were slain should rise again, it would have seemed superfluous and vain to pray for the dead), and because he considered that they who had fallen asleep with godliness, had great grace laid up for them. It is therefore a holy and wholesome thought to pray for the dead, that they may be loosed from sins" (12, 43-46). Nothing more explicit could be said than these words for overthrowing this error. Wherefore, the heretics seeing themselves very hard pressed by this testimony, flee to the usual refuge, by saying that the Books of Machabees are not canonical, nor are of so great authority, that its testimony would suffice for disproving some teaching. But it is not necessary to dispute about this now, because, lest we haphazardly undertake this labor, we have shown above in the second chapter of the first book, the list of those books which are called canonical, whose testimony ought to be used in disputing those things which pertain to the faith. In which list the two Books of Machabees are included, even though they

---

but the soul is not at all helped by it, and God is only profaned by it" (*Sermon for the First Sunday after Trinity*, 1522 (WA 10/3, 195-196)).

[1] *De Haeresibus ad Quodvultdeum*, c. 53 (PL 42, 40).

were not reckoned by the Hebrews in the canon, as Blessed Jerome says: Nevertheless, the Church receives those books as canonical.[1]

Otherwise, even if these books were not canonical, and there were no clear testimony of Sacred Scripture, there would be a very powerful testimony for confirming this matter, the very old custom of the whole Catholic Church. Hence Blessed Augustine in his book, *On Care to be had for the Dead*, says: "In the books of the Maccabees we read of sacrifice offered for the dead. Howbeit, even if it were nowhere at all read in the Old Scriptures, not small is the authority, which in this usage is clear, of the whole Church, namely, that in the prayers of the priest which are offered to the Lord God at His altar, the Commendation of the dead has also its place."[2]

There are also many other holy Doctors, illustrious for holiness as well as doctrine, who give testimony in favor of the matter. And (so that I may omit more recent Doctors) I begin with Blessed Gregory, who in the fourth book of the *Dialogues*, says the following: "If the sins after death are not irremissible, then the sacred Oblation of the Holy Host is accustomed to help men's souls, such that the souls of the dead themselves sometimes are seen to ask for that [Oblation, or the Mass]."[3] Now he said, "If the sins after death are not irremissible," on account of those who are in Hell, whose sins are not remissible, and can no longer be redeemed by any satisfaction.

Theophylactus, when expounding the passage of Luke: "Fear ye him, who after he hath killed, hath power to cast into hell" (12, 5), speaks thus: "For here observe, that He did not say, 'Fear ye him who after he hath killed, casts into hell,' but 'hath power to cast into hell.' For sinners who die are not always thrust down into Hell, but they are in God's power, so that they could also be forgiven. Now I say this for the sake of the offerings and prayers which are made for the dead, which serve not a little even for those who have died in serious sins. Hence, after He has killed, He does not universally send to Hell, but has power of casting into Hell. Therefore, let us not cease through alms and intercessions to render Him propitious, Who has power of casting, Who is not always using this power, but is also able to forgive anything."[4] Theophylactus commends clearly enough the suffrages which are made for the dead, and encourages them to be done.

---

[1] These words are not found among St. Jerome's extant writings but can be inferred from the two following quotations: "Therefore, just as the Church also reads the books of Judith, Tobias, and the Maccabees, but does not receive them among the canonical Scriptures, so also one may read these two scrolls for the strengthening of the people, (but) not for confirming the authority of ecclesiastical dogmas" (*Prologue to the Books of Solomon* (PL 28, 1243A)). "Among the Hebrews the Book of Judith is found among the Hagiographa, the authority of which toward confirming those which have come into contention is judged less appropriate. Yet having been written in Chaldean words, it is counted among the histories. But because this book is found by the Nicene Council to have been counted among the number of the Sacred Scriptures, I have acquiesced to your request, indeed a demand, and works having been set aside from which I was forcibly curtailed, I have given to this (book) one short night's work translating more sense from sense than word from word" (*Prologue to the Book of Judith* (PL 29, 37D)). St. Jerome's doubts about the canonicity of the book of Judith seems to have been resolved by the decision of the Council of Nicea, though there are no extant records of this, which can be applied also to the Books of Machabees. Although there indeed exist spurious decrees of the Council of Nicea determining the Scriptural canon, nevertheless, Cassiodorus also makes reference to two conciliar decrees regarding the canon of Sacred Scripture, made by the Council of Nicea and also by the Council of Chalcedon in *De institutione divinarum litterarum*, c. 14 (PL 70, 1126A). Cf. Note "c" in PL 29, 37D-38D.

[2] C. 1, n. 3 (PL 40, 593).

[3] C. 55 (PL 77, 417A).

[4] *Ennaratio in Evangelium Sancti Lucae* (PG 123, 879A-B). St. Thomas Aquinas included this quotation in his *Catena Aurea*.

SUFFRAGIA DEFUNCTORUM

Blessed Chrysostom assigns a very old origin of this thing, saying: "Not in vain did the Apostles order that remembrance should be made of the dead in the dreadful Mysteries. They know that great gain results to them, great benefit."[1] From whose testimony it is evident that this custom has continued since the Apostles, such that in the Sacrifice of the Mass a commemoration for the dead is made, so that the deceased may obtain some benefit from it.

[Pseudo-] Athanasius in the book, *De variis quaestionibus ad Antiochum ducem*, asks in this way: "What then? Do the souls of sinners obtain no benefit, when religious ceremonies, the performance of good deeds and offerings are made for them?" To which question he replies by the following words: "Unless they were partakers of some benefit therefrom, there would be no mention of them in the offering. But in the same way as a grapevine blooming outside in a field, its bottled wine perceives the smell, and at the same time blooms: so we understand that the souls of sinners are partakers of some benefit, from the unbloody Sacrifice and good deeds performed for it, as our God alone, the Ruler of the living and the dead, knows and commands."[2]

And Dionysius the [Pseudo-] Areopagite, a disciple of Paul the Apostle, in his book, *Ecclesiastical Hierarchy*, when describing the ceremonies which were done in the funeral rites done at that time, says: "Then the venerable bishop, advancing, offers a holy prayer over the deceased. After the prayer, both the bishop himself salutes him, and next all who are present. Now the prayer beseeches the supremely Divine Goodness to remit to the deceased all the failings committed by reason of human infirmity, and to set him in light and the land of the living, in the bosom of Abraham, and Isaac, and Jacob: in a place where grief and sorrow and sighing are no more."[3] From whose words it is established clearly enough that at the time of the Apostles this manner of praying for the deceased was kept.

After these testimonies of illustrious men, so that I may put an end to this contention, I will bring to the fore many decrees of various councils. The [Pseudo-] IV Synod of Carthage decreed as follows: "Those who either refuse to the churches the offerings of the deceased, or bestow them with difficulty, are excommunicated as murderers of the poor."[4] The Synod of Vaison-la-Romaine, in the fourth chapter of its decrees, defines thus: "Those who retain the offerings of the deceased, and delay to hand them over to the Church, are to be cast out of the Church as infidels, because it is certain that this exasperation of the Divine justice reaches even a voiding of fidelity, because they defraud both the faithful when departing from their bodies with an abundance of promised offerings, and the poor of the consolation of alms and needed support. For such men as these are as it were murderers of the poor, and not believing God's Judgment is to be undergone. And wherefore a certain one of the Fathers here inserted in his writings a fittingly sentence, which says: 'It is indeed theft to steal from a friend, to

---

[1] *Homilies on Philippians*, hom. 3, n. 4 (PG 62, 204).

[2] *Questiones ad Antiochum ducem*, q. 34 (PG 28, 618A-B). This spurious text takes this analogy from the [Pseudo-] St. Ephraim the Syrian's *Testamentum* (*Sancti Ephraem Syri Omnia Opera* (Rome, Giovani Maria Enrico Salvioni, 1743), p. 239A-C), wherein he says that when grapes ripen in a field, the bottled wine becomes agitated at the same time that the grapes ripen, and likewise onions sown in a field germinate at the same time as onions stored in a house, so it should not be surprising if the souls of the dead are sensibly affected by the commemorations made of them in the offerings (or Masses).

[3] Bk. 7, p. 3, § 5 (PG 3, 559).

[4] C. 4 (Mansi, vol. 8, col. 623B-C). The IV Synod of Carthage, can. 95, is incorrectly cited here, following Gratian's *Concordia discordantium canonum*, causa 13, q. 2, p. 6, c. 10 (PL 187, 943A). The error originates in the *Statuta ecclesiae antiqua*, a late fifth-century collection of canons perhaps compiled by Gennadius of Massilia between 476 and 485. Cf. *Les Statuta ecclesiae antiqua*, ed. C. Munier (Paris, Presses universitaires de France, 1960), pp. 94-95.

defraud the Church is sacrilege.'"[1] And the Synod of Agde, in the fourth chapter, decrees the same thing in nearly the same words.[2] The III Synod of Toledo sets forth this definition: "Those who by the Divine call depart from this life, ought to be brought to the grave with Psalms only, with the voices of those chanting. For we completely forbid the funeral song which is commonly accustomed to be sung for the dead, [or the beating of the breast by oneself, one's neighbors, or one's servants].[3] For it suffices for Christians, whose bodies were buried in hopes of a resurrection, to have the service of Divine song or psalmody bestowed upon them."[4] Finally, the Council of Florence, which was celebrated under Eugene IV for the reunion of the Greeks, defines about this matter thus: "It has likewise defined, that, if those truly penitent have departed in the love of God, before they have made satisfaction by the worthy fruits of penance for sins of commission and omission, the souls of these are cleansed after death by purgatorial punishments; and so that they may be released from punishments of this kind, the suffrages of the living faithful are of advantage to them, namely, the sacrifices of Masses, prayers, and almsgiving, and other works of piety, which are customarily performed by the faithful for other faithful according to the institutions of the Church."[5] I could cite still more decrees of councils, these are enough for refuting the heretics.

TEMPLUM

Church Buildings

King Nabuchodonosor of Babylon, who represents the devil, when he invaded Jerusalem, was not content to despoil the Lord's Temple, and plunder all its precious vessels, but also defiled, polluted, nay in great part destroyed the same Temple, because the Temple's columns, bases, chapter, and many other things were taken away by him from there.[6] King Antiochus acted in the same way, who with a violent hand when invading the Lord's Temple, after he took away "the golden altar, and the candlestick of light, and all the vessels thereof, and the table of proposition, and the pouring vessels, and the vials, and the little mortars of gold, and the veil, and the crowns, and the golden ornament that was before the temple: and he broke them all in pieces" (I Mach. 1, 23): was not content to have taken away all these things, but so that he might show himself to be the most nociferous enemy of the synagogue, he forbade the "holocausts and sacrifices, and atonements to be made in the temple of God" (v. 47). In the same way that ancient enemy of the human race, tried to act in every way that he could. For (as we related above) he put his ministers in place, namely the heretics, who might take away the Sacraments and all the sacramentals, and all the ceremonies and rites from the Church, saying that all those things are completely useless, and mere nonsense. Notice that there are now present other minsters of his, who throw down the temple, and forbid, if they could, sacrifices and prayers to be made in the temple, saying that God's temples are of no utility, and do not benefit in any way in God's Church.

---

[1] *Concordia discordantium canonum*, causa 13, q. 2, p. 6, c. 10 (PL 187, 943B). The Synod of Vaison-la-Romaine was held in 442 A.D. near Avignon.

[2] Mansi, vol. 8, col. 324D.

[3] Such were the ancient pagan customs.

[4] C. 22 (Mansi, vol. 9, col. 998E-999A). The quotation found here in the text has been modified according to the text found in Mansi as cited.

[5] Dz. 693.

[6] IV Kings 25, 13-15.

TEMPLUM

The first author of this heresy was a certain Eustachius of whom mention is made in the Synod of Gangra.[1] This man despised the cathedrals of the martyrs, and the churches dedicated to God under the name of the saints, and he reprehended all who assembled in those same places either to sacrifice or to pray therein. Now this error now long buried, the Waldensians raised up after many centuries, which heretics so that they might appear more illustrious to the world, extended Eustachius' error much further, because he only mocked the churches of God which were consecrated in the name of the saints: these men, on the other hand, detracted every church, saying that the church of the wide open God is the world itself, and those who build churches, monasteries and oratories constrict His majesty, as though the Divine Majesty is found to be more propitious in those places. For Aeneas Sylvius accuses them of this in his book, *De origine Bohemorum*,[2] although Guy [the Carmelite] does not attribute any such thing to them when he recounts the errors of the Waldensians. After the Waldensians were other heretics called the Apostolics, who spoke with still greater injury regarding God's house, saying that a consecrated church avails no more for praying that a pigsty. Certain Bohemian heretics called the Taborites supported the same error more by force and arms than by testimonies of Scripture. The leader and chief was Ziska,[3] a certain nobleman infected with the errors of John Hus, who when gathering a troop of lost men, invaded and ruined the churches. Now so that he might be safe in his crime, and could securely carry out other crimes when he wishes, he chose a naturally fortified place: he surrounded this place with defensive walls, and just as each of his soldiers had erected tents, so he commanded that they build houses for themselves. He named this place Thabor, and he called his followers Thaborite brothers, as though they had seen they had seen the Transfiguration of Christ the Savior with the three Apostles, and then had changed their opinions, which they called the truths of the faith. Thus all these aforesaid heretics thinking in unison, contemn God's house, although one being more insane than another may scorn it more.

Now in order to refute this error it is enough that King Solomon built the Temple by God's command. For although David had first thought to build it, he was rejected by the Lord as unworthy for performing this function, in that he had been a man of war and had shed blood[4]: and this burden of building the Temple passed on to Solomon. If God's Temple were of no utility, Solomon would not have labored so much in its construction; neither would he have expended so much gold and silver in its construction, nor would the Lord God have adorned that Temple with so many and such great privileges, such as are described in the Second Book of Paralipomenon.[5] Furthermore, if God's Temple avails no more (as the wicked Apostolics assert) than a pigsty, the Lord never would have cast out those who sold and bought from it.[6] For since it is permitted to sell and buy in the marketplace, not however in the Temple, it is proved clearly enough that God's Temple is worthy of greater veneration than the marketplace, lest I say than a stable. Again, when Our Lord Jesus Christ was casting out those buying and selling from the Temple, He cited for Himself as a confirmation of the deed the testimony of Isaias saying: "My house shall be called the house of prayer" (Is. 56, 7). From which words it is established clearly enough that God's Temple is a place more destined for prayer than any other place.

Add to these things that the use of temples [i.e. places set apart for worship] is not recent in the Church, but was introduced by the Apostles. For Eusebius of Caesarea in the second

---

[1] Mansi, vol. 2, col. 1122A.
[2] Chapter 35, p. 60.
[3] John Ziska (c. 1360–1424) was a Czech general was a contemporary and follower of John Hus.
[4] I Par. 28, 3.
[5] II Par. 7, 12-16.
[6] Cf. Mt. 21, 12.

book of his *History of the Church*, when relating those things which Philo the Jew had written about the customs of the Christians, speaks thus: "And then a little further on, (he says) after describing the kind of houses which they had, he speaks as follows concerning their churches, which were scattered about here and there: 'In each house there is a sacred chamber which is called a sanctuary (σεμνεῖον) or sacred inner room (μοναστήριον). Σεμνεῖον (a sanctuary) in our language can mean a place of assembly of virtuous men, where, quite alone, they perform the mysteries of the religious life.'"[1] Eusebius relates that Philo wrote these words. Now this Philo (the same Eusebius bearing witness) lived in the time of Emperor Claudius, who was sent as a legate of his people [to the Emperor Caligula[2]], and for this reason came to Rome, where he saw Blessed Peter. Thus it is evident that at the time of the Apostles some places were consecrated for prayer, which we call churches. Finally, the Synod of Gangra in the fifth chapter of its decreed defines thus: "If any one shall teach that the house of God and the assemblies held therein are to be despised, let him be anathema."[3]

TENTATIO

Temptation

Among the many errors which Blessed Bernard attributes to Peter Abelard, there is one whereby he says that he thinks that "The suggestions of devils come to us, as their sagacious wickedness knows how, by the contact of stones and herbs; and that they are able to discern in such natural objects strength suited to excite various passions."[4] And certainly if Peter Abelard would not speak in general about every temptation of the devil, but of a particular one, such that not all but some temptations of the devils are made in us by virtue of stones and herbs, I would not consider it heresy, but true doctrine. For it is certain that many temptations of the soul arise from one's own flesh, because Paul says: "The flesh lusteth against the spirit" (Gal. 5, 17). And such concupiscence of the flesh, is a sort of temptation, whereby the soul is impelled to sin, as James the Apostle says: "Every man is tempted by his own concupiscence, being drawn away and allured" (1, 14). Because there is no one who is not disturbed by the impulses of the flesh, there are various temptations of men by their own bodies. And the devil having come to know the qualities and character of every single body, applies a suitable incitements, whereby the flesh according to its quality can be more enkindled. Hence Blessed Gregory when expounding the passage in Job: "Heat divided upon the earth" (38, 24), says these words: "For the ancient enemy first beholds the character of each person, and then applies the snares of temptations. For one person is of a cheerful, another of a morose, another of a timid, another of a proud disposition.

Our secret adversary, in order then to catch us easily, prepares deceptions closely connected with our various characters. For because pleasure borders on mirth, he holds out lust as a bait to cheerful dispositions. And because moroseness easily slides into anger, he offers the cup of discord for the morose. Because the timid dread punishments, he threatens terrors to the fearful. And because he beholds the proud elated with praises, he draws them on to whatever he pleases, by flattering applause. He lays snares therefore against men one by one, by vices

---

[1] C. 17, n. 9 (PG 20, 178C).

[2] Josephus, *Jewish Antiquities*, bk. 18, c. 8, n. 1. This text mistakenly states that he was sent to Emperor Claudius.

[3] Mansi, vol. 2, col. 1102D.

[4] Letter 190, c. 4, n. 10 (PL 182, 1062B).

TENTATIO

adapted to them."[1] Hence since the devil tempts man according to his different character (which he knows very well): we are certainly obliged to admit that he can tempt man by means of contact with stones or herbs. For there are many powers of stones and herbs which agree with men's characters. Concerning the emerald and topaz it is said that they mitigate the flames of lust.[2] Why will there not also be another stone of contrary power, which increases men's flames? They say that bronze completely expels sadness of heart: on account of which I reckon that it is also possible that there is another stone, which fights against this by its power, such that man's heart may be absorbed by sadness. Now no one doubts that the devil knows these things very well: and wherefore I also do not doubt that the devil by the application and contact of these things can sometimes tempt men, if it be permitted by God.

Furthermore, many theologians of an authority not to be contemned assert that the afflictions and vexations of devils can be mitigated by the application of sensible things, as we read about Saul, who when he was troubled by the devil, was relieved when David played the harp.[3] Nicholas of Lyra agrees to this when interpreting that passage in the First Book of Kings.[4] Richard of Middleton also acknowledges the same thing, who says that the devil's affliction can take hold so little, and the power of the stone or herb be so great, that it not merely mitigates, but completely removes the devil's affliction.[5] If stones and herbs can impede the devil's affliction, what prevents that there be other stones or herbs having the opposite power, which could help the devil in afflicting men? Therefore, it is not against the Catholic faith, to think that the devil can through the contact of stones and herbs impel men to sin.

And if Peter Abelard only thought this, he would not have been censured for heresy on this account. But because I think Blessed Bernard, a learned as well as a holy man, who not unreasonably or undeservedly censured Peter Abelard of heresy in this place: wherefore I think that he spoke about every temptation of the devil: such that there would be no temptation of the devil in us, which does not happen in this way by contact of stones and herbs. And if Peter Abelard so thought, he very clearly erred. For the first temptation of the devil was not by means of stones and herbs, but by means of a serpent, whose appearance he assumed, so that he might form words through its mouth, whereby when speaking to Eve, the first mother of all men, he might persuade the eating of the forbidden fruit. Now so that he might tempt Adam, he made use of Eve, not stones, and not herbs. He indeed had known that his wife was more powerful for this work than all stones and herbs.

And when Satan desires to tempt Job, and seeks permission for this from God, he does not ask for permission to apply stones or herbs: but to remove the fence whereby God had surrounded all his possessions: so that he could tempt him by the destruction of all his possessions.[6] When however he sees that he accomplished too little in this way, he again asks permission for touching his person. And he struck him with a very grievous ulcer, hoping he could break him by adversities.[7] Next when he tempted our Savior in the desert, he did not tempt by the application of herbs and rocks, but by speech, as the Evangelical history relates.

---

[1] *Moralia*, bk. 29, c. 22, n. 45 (PL 76, 501C-D).

[2] Cf. *Ortus sanitatis* (Strassburg, Johann Prüss, 1499), de lapidibus, c. 113 &132.

[3] I Kings 16, 23.

[4] "Melodies draw the attention of the mind towards themselves and consequently withdraws from something else, and in this way can alleviate afflictions caused by the devil in man, insofar as it draws attention to itself and withdraws it from the perception of affliction, but it cannot expel the afflicting devil" (*Bibliorum Sacrorum cum Glossa Ordinaria*, (Venice, 1603), vol. 2, 419B).

[5] *Quodlibeta doctoris eximii Ricardi de Mediavilla ordinis minorum* (Brescia, Tommaso Bozzola, 1591), quodlib. 2, q. 8, pp. 97-97.

[6] Cf. Job. 1, 10-11.

[7] Cf. *Ibid.*, 2, 7.

Firstly he said to Him: "If thou be the Son of God, command that these stones be made bread" etc. (Mt. 4, 3). Furthermore, Sacred Scripture teaches that there are many kinds of temptations, whereby we are tempted by the devil. For sometimes (as Paul the Apostles says) "he transformeth himself into an angel of light" (I Cor. 11, 14), because Satan frequently tempts many showing himself to them as though he were an Angel of light, so that he could deceive them more easily. Hence the Apostles when terrified in the boat, thought that there was an apparition.[1] And Peter the Apostle, when saying to the Lord, "It is I, fear ye not" (Mt. 14, 27): not easily believing, says: "If it be thou, bid me come to thee upon the waters" (v. 28). It was so that if he could firmly have put his foot upon the waters, he would know that it is true that it was not an apparition which appeared. But no one in his right mind would say that such a transformation of the devil whereby he transforms himself into an Angel of light, happens by contact with herbs or stones.

Again, there are some spiritual sins, which have no nearness with the flesh, and hence can nowise arise from that which Paul calls "the spirits of wickedness in the high places" (Eph. 6, 12). Now no one is so insane that he would say that the temptation which solicits to sins of this kind, happens by the contact of stones or herbs: because although these things are corporeal, they have no power of moving the spirit, unless insofar as they are known and loved. The devils could also move the imaginations of men, such that which pleases them more, they present to the imagination, and so tempt men in this way: because what moves the imagination more, that urges more that it be known by the intellect, and that solicits the will more vehemently to love: especially if it is accompanied by delectation of the flesh. And may these things said about this matter suffice. And I have not seen anyone else who has disputed against this heresy: because Blessed Bernard was content with his account alone.

TERRA

Earth

There was one heresy about this matter, which taught that the earth was coeternal with God. A certain Felix, a Manichaean, is called the author of this heresy, with whom Blessed Augustine publicly disputed. And concerning the acts with this Felix two books were published which are included in the works of Blessed Augustine: and in the first of those books there is mention of this heresy.[2]

Against this heresy it is not hard to dispute: since there are very explicit testimonies of Sacred Scripture. For in the book of Genesis it is said: "In the beginning God created heaven and earth" (1, 1). If God created heaven and earth in the beginning, then the earth is not eternal: because what is created, had a beginning at some time. And in the book of Psalms the [Royal] Prophet says: "In the beginning, O Lord, thou foundedst the earth" (101, 26). And Blessed Paul the Apostle in the Epistle to the Hebrews repeats the same words of the Prophet.[3] Furthermore, in the writings of the Prophet Isaias God says: "I made the earth: and I created man upon it" (54, 12). And again: "Thus saith the Lord that created the heavens, God himself that formed the earth, and made it, the very maker thereof: he did not create it in vain: he formed it to be inhabited" (v. 18). If God made the earth, and formed it, it could not happen that it could be coeternal with God: because what has been made, had a beginning at some time.

---

[1] Cf. Mt. 14, 26.

[2] *De actis cum Felice Manichaeo*, bk. 1, c. 18 (PL 42, 532-533).

[3] Cf. Heb. 1, 10.

TIMOR DEI

Lastly there is a definition of a general council against this heresy. For the [IV] Lateran Council celebrated under Innocent III, when speaking about the three persons in God, says these words: "One beginning of all, Creator of all visible and invisible things, of the spiritual and of the corporal; Who by His own omnipotent power at once from the beginning of time created each creature from nothing, spiritual, and corporal, namely, Angelic and mundane, and finally the human, constituted as it were, alike of the spirit and the body."[1] Which words are found in the book of the Decretals in the first chapter *Fidei catholicae, de summa trinitate, et fide catholica*.[2] In which words it ought to be noted that it says: "from the beginning of time created each creature from nothing, spiritual, and corporal." If all creatures are from the beginning of time, then the earth also. If the earth is from the beginning of time, it is not possible that it be eternal at the same time. These few things suffice against such a clear heresy.

TIMOR DEI
Fear of God

One of the pestiferous errors of Luther is that which teaches that the servile fear of God is completely useless, nay even harmful: because he says that it is deserving of punishment. We disputed enough about this error above in the section on "Contrition." Because Luther condemns that contrition for sins, which arises from the hatred of hell: hence it was then necessary to dispute about servile fear. In which place we showed from testimonies of Sacred Scripture that the servile fear of God is good, and is numbered among the Gifts of the Holy Ghost: although no one merits by it, unless it exist along with charity: because there is no work which is worthy of a reward, unless that work arise from the root of charity. But even though what was said in that place suffices for refuting this error, still it will not be useless in this place to add something whereby the truth may shine forth more: especially since this is a more suitable section, in which this disputation ought to be done. And firstly, let us show whence this servile fear originates and from what causes it is generated, so that having shown the goodness of the tree more clearly, the goodness of the fruit may appear more clearly: because according to the saying of our Savior, a good tree brings forth good fruit.[3]

And certainly, as far as I can reckon: the servile fear of God, namely when someone on account of the punishment which he fears, abstains from offending God, has two origins in the sinner himself. One is the love of himself, and of his own wellbeing: hence it happens that he flees adverse things. For the sinner hates and fears punishments, because they take away the rest, peace, pleasure and soundness of the one suffering them. The other origin is the consideration of the Divine omnipotence, and His wisdom and justice. For he considers God to be so powerful, that no one can resist Him, or escape His hand: so wise, that nothing can hide from Him: so just, that He cannot be deflected from justice by either any petitions or gifts, such that He would not punish the evildoer. Therefore, since the sinner hates the punishment, for the inflicting of which he certainly believes that God is powerful, wise and just, he abstains from the sinful deed, lest he suffer such punishment, in such a way however, that the will of sinning is also removed. Such fleeing from sin, I say, for avoiding punishment, is servile fear, which we say is good and useful, unless the will of sinning (as we explained in the section on "Contrition") is mixed with it.

---

[1] Dz. 428.
[2] X, lib. 1, t. 1, c. 1.
[3] Cf. Mt. 7, 17.

For that parable of the king wanting to take an account of his servants shows this clearly enough,[1] which when he began to do, one servant owing ten thousand talents was brought to him: who since he was not paying, was ordered to be sold, that is, (as Augustine interprets[2]) subjected to torments: with his wife and children, that is, with his greed and misdeeds. Which sentence when debtor servant had heard, with horror and hatred of the punishment to which he was now given, pours out prayers to the master, humbly begging him to grant a delay of the payment. And he was not refused; however, when asking for a delay, he received the remission of the debt: which would have remained fixed, had he not afterwards deserved to have this remission revoked, on account of the inhumanity which he had shown towards his fellow servant. Notice that this servant was not converted to his master only out of hatred for the punishment to which he saw he had been sentenced: and having been so converted he was heard. But if servile fear is a sin (as Luther says) the conversion devolving from it would also be evil: and if were evil, it never would have been heard.

Furthermore, our Savior when exhorting us to peace and concord, persuades us to it by this fear. For He speaks thus: "Be at agreement with thy adversary betimes, whilst thou art in the way with him: lest perhaps the adversary deliver thee to the judge, and the judge deliver thee to the officer, and thou be cast into prison. Amen I say to thee, thou shalt not go out from thence till thou repay the last farthing" (Mt. 5, 25-26). Again, the Wise man exhorts parents not to cease to correct and scourge their sons, so that at least in this way they may learn to abstain from evil. "He that spareth the rod," he says, "hateth his son" (Prov. 13, 24): "Thou shalt beat him with the rod, and deliver his soul from hell" (*ibid.*, 23, 14). And again: "Folly is bound up in the heart of a child, and the rod of correction shall drive it away" (*ibid.*, 22, 15). What therefore will you think about the charity of our Father, Who is in heaven, towards His sons? Does He not also punish and scourge His sons, so that at least in this way they may learn to depart from evil? Does He not chastise those whom He loves?[3] Now He loves His sons. Hence every son whom He loves, He corrects.

But why does He correct? Certainly for no other reason than on account of discipline, namely so that they may learn to "decline from evil, and do good" (Ps. 36, 27). This is very clearly gathered from Paul's words themselves. For after he had said that God "scourgeth every son whom he receiveth" (Heb. 12, 6), he immediately added, saying: "Persevere under discipline. God dealeth with you as with his sons; for what son is there, whom the father doth not correct? But if you be without chastisement, whereof all are made partakers, then are you bastards, and not sons" (v. 7-8). You now see for what reason God corrects and scourges his sons, that it is on account of discipline. For some sons are so undisciplined that they are not softened by goodness and mercy, nay they become harder and worse. It is necessary to scourge these sons, so that having been scourged they may learn: because, as a certain prophet says, "Vexation shall make you understand" (Is. 28, 28). And if servile fear were evil, or the operation proceeding from that fear were evil: God would never surround someone with scourges for this purpose, that out of hatred of the scourge he might be converted to acting rightly.

Next the Royal Prophet says: "It is good for me that thou hast humbled me, that I may learn thy justifications" (Ps. 118, 71). David bears witness that he had learned God's justifications because he had been humbled by God: and so he gives thanks to God, because He humbled him: in that from such humiliation a very good thing happened to him, namely that he had learned God's justifications. Hence an action ought not be reckoned to be evil simply because it proceeds from servile fear. And if the action proceeding from it ought not to be called evil

---

[1] Cf. Mt. 18, 23-27.

[2] *Questions on the Gospels*, q. 25 (PL 35, 1328).

[3] Cf. Heb. 12, 6.

TIMOR DEI

for this reason, neither should the fear itself be censured as wicked: because according to the Savior's saying, an evil tree cannot bring forth good fruit.[1]

There are many testimonies of holy men regarding this matter: to present some of them will not be useless. Blessed Bernard in his book, "It is truly a good degree of obedience, if according to the opinion of our master[2] on account of the fear of hell, on account of the holy profession he has professed, someone will obey, yet it is better when one obeys out of love of God."[3] Richard of Saint Victor in his book on the preparation of the soul for contemplation, in chapter eight says that the fear of hell is the beginning of wisdom,[4] and in the following chapter, namely chapter nine when speaking about the same thing, says the following: "The more vehemently a person fears the punishment he deserves, the more sharply he laments the fault he has committed. But it should be known that at whatever hour a sinner shall have been converted and shall have mourned, he will be saved, according to this: 'A contrite and humbled heart, O God, thou wilt not despise' (Ps. 50, 19). How does it seem to you? Is it not right for such a son to be called Simeon, that is 'granting'? For he who truly repents and truly grieves will receive indulgence without doubt and without delay. A prayer that is offered from a contrite and humbled heart is more quickly heard with favor. A heart is humbled through fear, contrite through grief."[5] By which words he teaches clearly enough that servile fear is good: because he asserts that it is the first step to wisdom, and he says that its first offspring is sorrow for sin committed, or contrition, which he affirms merits being heard, which is very far from him wishing to condemn it.

Blessed Augustine although he asserts this in many places, nevertheless does so more explicitly when commenting upon the First Epistle of John the Apostle, wherein when expounding that passage of John, "Fear is not in charity" (4, 18), speaks thus: "Then what say we of him that has begun to fear the day of judgment? If charity in him were perfect, he would not fear. For perfect charity would make perfect righteousness, and he would have nothing to fear: nay rather he would have something to desire; that iniquity may pass away, and God's kingdom come. So then, there is no fear in charity. But in what charity? Not in charity begun: in what then? But perfect charity, says he, casts out fear. Then let fear make the beginning, because the fear of the Lord is the beginning of wisdom. Fear, so to say, prepares a place for charity. But when once charity has begun to inhabit, the fear which prepared the place for it is cast out. For in proportion as this increases, that decreases: and the more this comes to be within, is the fear cast out. Greater charity, less fear; less charity, greater fear. But if no fear, there is no way for charity to come in. As we see in sewing, the thread is introduced by means of the needle; the needle first enters, but except it come out the thread does not come into its place: so fear first occupies the mind, but the fear does not remain there, because it enters only in order to introduce charity."[6] From whose words it is evident that even though servile fear does not remain with perfect charity, still it remains with initial charity, and is the way to perfect charity. If servile fear (as Luther says) were a sin, it would never prepare a place for charity.

Blessed Basil in his exposition of Psalm thirty-three speak thus: "The fear, however, which is salutary and the fear which is productive of holiness, fear which springs up in the soul through devotion and not through passion, what kind would you have me say it is? Whenever you are about to rush head-long into sin, consider that fearful and intolerable tribunal of

---

[1] Cf. Mt. 7, 18.

[2] Cf. *Rule of St. Benedict*, c. 5.

[3] *On Precept and Dispensation*, c. 7, n. 16 (PL 182, 870A).

[4] *Benjamin minor* (*The Twelve Patriarchs*) (PL 196, 6D).

[5] C. 9 (PL 196, 7B).

[6] *Homilies on First John*, hom. 9, n. 4 (PL 35, 2047-2048).

Christ, in which the Judge is seated upon a certain high and sublime throne, and every creature stands trembling beside His glorious presence, and we are about to be led forth, one by one, for the examination of the actions of our life. And beside him who has done many wicked deeds throughout his life certain horrible and dark angels stand, flashing fire from their eyes and breathing fire because of the bitterness of their wills, and with a countenance like the night because of their dejection and their hatred of man. Then, there is the deep pit and the darkness that has no outlet and the light without brightness, which has the power of burning in the darkness but is deprived of its splendor. Next is the poisonous and flesh-devouring class of worms, which eat greedily and are never satiated and cause unbearable pains by their voracity; and lastly, the severest punishment of all, that eternal reproach and shame. Fear these things, and being taught by this fear, check your soul, as with a bit, from its desire for wickedness. The Father promised to teach us this fear of the Lord, and not to teach indiscriminately, but to teach those who wish to heed Him; not those who have long fallen away, but those who run to Him through a desire of being saved; not 'strangers to the testament'[1] but those who are reconciled through Baptism by the word of the adoption of sons. Therefore, He says, 'Come,' that is, 'because of your good deeds approach me, children' since you are considered worthy because of your regeneration to become sons of light.[2] You, who have the ears of your heart open, hear; I shall teach you fear of the Lord, that fear which a little while ago our sermon described."[3] Nothing could be said more explicitly against Luther than these words. For when he speaks about servile fear clearly enough, he says that it leads us to holiness, and is Divinely inspired, and is what the heavenly Father teaches us. Therefore, since we have brought forth so many and such clear testimonies against this error, it is unnecessary that we dispute more about it, especially since many other things were said in the section on "Contrition."

There is a **second heresy** about the fear of God, which Peter Abelard taught, saying that there is fear of the Lord in the life to come. For this is among the errors which Blessed Bernard in his letter one hundred ninety accuses him.[4] And certainly I am surprised that a man in other respect learned would have fallen into so great and very clear error: since for refuting him there is a manifest testimony of the [Royal] Prophet saying: "The fear of the Lord is holy, enduring for ever and ever" (Ps. 18, 10). Augustine, when expounding these words, speaks thus: "Fear of the Lord is not servile but chaste, loving freely, not fearing to be punished by Him Whom it shudders at, but to be separated from Him Whom it loves. This is the chaste fear, not that which consummate charity casts out, but which remains forever."[5] And [Julian of Toledo[6]], in his *Antikeimena* near the end speaks thus: "How does perfect love cast out fear, if the fear of the Lord, which is chaste, endures forever? Hence there is a servile fear, and there is a chaste fear. Servile fear is lest you suffer punishment: chaste fear lest you lose righteousness. Therefore [it ought to be thought that] what the Apostle said pertains to servile fear. It ought to be thought that what the Psalmist says, however, is concerning that chaste fear whereby we will be joined to the Lord forever."[7]

---

[1] Cf. Eph. 2, 12.

[2] Cf. I Thess. 5, 5.

[3] *Homilies on the Psalms* (PG 370D-371C).

[4] "I pass over his saying that the spirit of the fear of the Lord was not in the Lord; that there will be no holy fear of the Lord in the world to come" (C. 4, n. 10 (PL 182, 1062B)).

[5] *Enarrationes in Psalmos*, enarratio II (*sermo ad plebem*), n. 10 (PL 36, 161).

[6] The text incorrectly here cites Salvanius of Marseilles as the author. St. Julian (642-690 A.D.) was archbishop of Toledo.

[7] *Atikeimenon*, bk. 2, *interogatio* 78 (96, 704A). Cf. St. Augustine, *Tractates on the Gospel of John*, tract. 43, n. 5 & 7 (PL 35, 1707-1708).

Furthermore, Blessed Job when speaking about the Angels in remaining heaven says: "The pillars of heaven tremble, and dread at his beck" (26, 11). Now [Pseudo-] Blessed Jerome testifies that he calls the Angels by the name of columns, who in his commentaries on the book of Job when interpreting this passage says: "Thus we understand by the name of columns nothing else but the enduring stability in the nature of the Angels, because they are persevering not merely immovably in holiness, but also in the beautiful glory of eternal beatitude. For concerning the future immobility of men the Son of God speaks thus: 'He that shall overcome, I will make him a pillar in the temple of my God' (Apoc. 3, 12)."[1] These are the words of Jerome, or of whoever is the author of those commentaries. For it evident that it is not Jerome's from the fact that the same Jerome is cited in them. And Blessed Gregory in his *Morals on the Book of Job* after having interpreted those words of Job concerning just men, having turned to the Angels, says: "Which, as we said above, there is nothing hinders being interpreted of the Holy Angels as well; because the very Powers of the heavenly world themselves, which behold Him without ceasing, in that very contemplation of theirs are made to tremble. But that that should not be a trembling of woe to them, it is one not of fear, but of admiration."[2]

And certainly as far as I can reckon, from this source proceeded Peter Abelard's error whereby he supposed that there is not any fear which is not penal. For he ought to have noticed that there is some fear without punishment, which is called reverential fear, or so that I may speak more correctly, it is nothing other than reverence itself. For reverence itself is also very often called by the name of fear in Holy Writ. In the Gospel of Luke we read that after the Lord rose the young son of the widow, "There came a fear on them all: and they glorified God" (Lk. 7, 16). In which place he designates reverence. For all who were standing nearby, having seen such a great miracle reverenced God, because He had sent such a prophet into the world, who could do such miraculous works. Now this can be easily inferred from those things which follow. For after he said that that fear took hold of them all, he added, "they glorified God." Now to glorify God is more the effect of reverence than of penal fear. Likewise, Paul the Apostle in the Epistle to the Romans says: "Render therefore to all men their dues. Tribute, to whom tribute is due: custom, to whom custom: fear, to whom fear: honour, to whom honour" (13, 7). Theophylactus when interpreting which words says the following: "And do not merely give money, but fear also, that is to say reverence and conscientiousness and piety and great honor. Hence he concludes: 'honour, to whom honour.' For fear is twofold: one, whereby those perpetrating crimes are terrified, coming from a bad conscience, which the Apostle already rejected before: but the other, whereby those loving are affected towards the ones loved, that is, an excellent and outstanding honor, as it was said: 'There is no want to them that fear him' (Ps. 33, 10), and 'The fear of the Lord is holy, enduring for ever and ever' (*ibid.* 18, 10). For he suggests piety or reverence here."[3] Therefore there is some fear lacking all torment, and we say that this is in the Blessed. Which if Peter Abelard had understood well, he never would have denied that fear of the Lord is in the world to come.

---

[1] *Commentaria in Iob* (26, 689D).
[2] Bk. 17, c. 19, n. 44 (PL 76, 31C).
[3] *Commentarius in Epistolam ad Romanos* (PG 124, 518A-B).

TYRANNUS

Tyrants

Concerning this matter there was a certain heresy teaching that any tyrant could be licitly and meritoriously killed by any subordinate of his even by hiddenly lying in wait, notwithstanding any compact made between them, even confirmed by oath, and this without sentence or mandate of any judge. The author of this heresy was (as Jean Gerson testifies[1]) a certain Jean Petit.

Against this error many ways lie open by which we are able to conquer it, and firstly from the definition of a tyrant. He is in fact is called a tyrant, according to the meaning of the word which all now use, who rules in a nation not by law, or exercises his authority beyond any just laws of his domain. Wherefore the word "tyrant" belongs not only to a king or another ruler, but to anyone else exercising some authority, if that particular authority does not belong to him: or if it does belong, it is extended to many more things than the law of his domain permits. And so a bishop is a tyrant if he holds the episcopate through forced and violence: or if he possesses it lawfully, yet he does not rule and govern according to justice, but rather extorts taxes beyond what is due, or does other similar things which are not permitted for a bishop. In the same way a pope can be a tyrant. In the same manner a husband could be called a tyrant towards his wife, if he treats her not as his flesh, but as a kind of property. Therefore if any tyrant can be killed by his subject, from this would follow the confusion of all justice: because then the wife could also kill her husband since he rules tyrannically over her: the sheep could also kill their shepherd, whether he be as simple pastor, or bishop, or pope, if any of these would rule tyrannically: children also could kill their parent, if the father would exceed the law of paternal governance in any way. And so this assertion opens the way to any subject not merely to disobedience, but also to inflicting murder to his superior, because it could be alleged that he is a tyrant. How pernicious this is, however, it is not now necessary to teach, since it is clearer than light itself. Furthermore, heresy is a crime much worse than tyranny. But it is not allowed for anyone to kill a heretic; neither therefore will it likewise be permitted for anyone to kill a tyrant.

We can attach this pestiferous heresy in a second way from the notion of deception: because even if it were licit to kill a tyrant, still not by deception and frauds and deceptions. For although we are not bound to reveal to an enemy every truth, we are still bound never to say a lie to him: because "The mouth that belieth, killeth the soul" (Wis. 1, 11). Thus God gave a place of refuge to which he may safely flee, who by chance had killed without deception. But concerning him who killed by deception, falls under the opposite law, saying: "If a man kill his neighbour on set purpose and by lying in wait for him: thou shalt take him away from my altar, that he may die" (Ex. 21, 14).

---

[1] Jean Petit (Lat. *Joannes Parvus*) (c. 1360-1411) was a French theologian. His addresses on the various aspects of the western schism c. 1403 made him a well-known member of the theological faculty of the University of Paris, but his teaching on tyrannicide won him even greater notoriety. On November 23, 1407, Louis, Duke of Orléans, brother of King Charles VI of France, was assassinated in Paris. His cousin, John the Fearless, Duke of Burgundy, who was responsible for the crime, retired to his domains in Flanders and summoned Jean Petit to Amiens to prepare his vindication. Before the king and a carefully selected assemblage in Paris, Petit delivered on March 8, 1408, an ostentatiously learned apologia in defense of his patron's role in the assassination. Cf. *Justificatio ducis Burgundiae* (J. Gerson, *Opera omnia*, ed. L. E. Dupin (Amsterdam 1706) vol. 5, pp. 15–42).

A third way is open whereby the same heresy may be conquered from the notion of a covenant confirmed by oath, because not withstanding such an oath, it asserts that it is permitted for a subordinate to kill a tyrant. The holy Psalmist says: "Thou wilt destroy all that speak a lie. The bloody and the deceitful man the Lord will abhor" (Ps. 5, 7). If God will destroy all who speak a lie, what do you think that He will do to those who commit perjury? When destroying all liars, will He spare perjurers? Far be it. For perjury is also a lie, and not any whatsoever, but one confirmed by oath. But if someone were to say that that oath made with the tyrant does not oblige the subordinate to its observance, many testimonies of Sacred Scripture thwart this response whereby it is proved that any pact or agreement even made with enemies ought to be kept. For due to this reason alone Jacob was troubled and angry with his sons, Simeon and Levi, because they violated the pact made with the Sichemites.[1] And for this reason when he blessed his other sons when dying, he cursed these sons, saying: "Simeon and Levi brethren: vessels of iniquity, waging war. Let not my soul go into their counsel, nor my glory be in their assembly: because in their fury they slew a man, and in their self-will they undermined a wall. Cursed be their fury, because it was stubborn: and their wrath because it was cruel: I will divide them in Jacob, and will scatter them in Israel" (Gen. 49, 5-7). On account of the same reason Sedecias, King of Juda, is reprehended, namely because he rebelled against Nabuchodonosor, King of Babylon, even though he firstly had made an oath to him of keeping fidelity.[2] Blessed Augustine praises Marcus Attilius Regulus, a Roman general, because lest he violate the fidelity which he had confirmed by oath to his Carthaginian enemies, he chose death, and preferred to suffer it rather than violate the fidelity granted to the enemy.[3] Add to these things that if it were licit to break agreements confirmed even by an oath, a door would then be open very wide to complete distrust and to every quarrel. For no one would then trust another promising something, because even if he confirms the promises with an oath, anyone could rightly fear that afterwards he would act contrary to the oath, since he could do it licitly. There will also be no end of controversy, if there is not obligation from an oath, because (as the Apostles says) an oath is the end of every controversy.[4]

There is still another way open, and a very open one, whereby this pestiferous heresy can be overthrown, namely the lack of authority in the killer so that he could justly kill. For no matter how wicked and criminal someone may be, who deserves a thousand deaths, still he cannot justly be killed by anyone except by one having authority and jurisdiction. Cain was a very wicked man, who first shed human blood, and killed his brother: who when he feared that on account of his wicked deeds would he be killed by anyone who found him, God said to him: "No, it shall not be so: but whosoever shall kill Cain, shall be punished sevenfold" (Gen. 4, 15). Furthermore, the rule of law teaches a judgment not made by its judge, is no judgment.[5] And Paul the Apostle clearly reprehends this and similar tyrannies, saying: "Who art thou that judgest another man's servant?" (Rom. 14, 4). For it could very justly be asked of that subject, who killed the tyrant without having waited for the sentence of the superior judge: "By what authority do you do this?" Who constituted you a judge over him? If you have the power of killing, it is necessary that you have it from God: because no one has any power, unless it be

---

[1] Cf. Gen. 34, 30.

[2] "Therefore thus saith the Lord God: As I live, I will lay upon his head the oath he hath despised, and the covenant he hath broken. And I will spread my net over him, and he shall be taken in my net: and I will bring him into Babylon, and will judge him there for the transgression by which he hath despised me" (Ez. 17, 19-20).

[3] *City of God*, bk. 1, c. 15, n. 1 (PL 41, 28-29).

[4] Cf. Heb. 6, 16.

[5] *Sententia non a suo judice lata, nulla est*. Cf. Gratian, *Concordia discordantium canonum*, causa 2, q. 1 (PL 187, 586C). D. *Justiniani Sacratissimi Principis Codicis Repetitae*, bk. 7, tit. 48, n. 3.

given from above. For all power is from God.[1] Therefore show where God gave to subjects this power, so that without the sentence of a judge they can kill tyrants."

We will more easily show that this is forbidden by God. For by the precept: "Thou shalt not kill," according to the interpretation of all the holy Doctors, that killing of man which is by one's authority and without the sentence of the judge. He who without the ruler knowing (the law says[2]) wages war, is guilty of high treason. Again: a king who has supreme authority, cannot without going beyond the order of law, kill someone not warned, not summoned, not convicted: therefore much less could a subject do this. But he who by deception kills someone, does this contrary to the order of law: thus it is not lawful for a subject to kill a tyrant by fraud. Finally, it is contrary to the Natural law that in the settlement or deciding of some dispute the judge and the witness would be the same party, because this belongs to God alone on account of His highest wisdom and goodness. Now when a subject kills a tyrant without the sentence of a higher judge, then he himself is the judge, the party standing against the accused, and the witness. Therefore, there are many things on account of which this pestiferous assertion deserves to be rejected.

Wherefore the Council of Constance condemned this doctrine as being opposed to the Catholic faith, speaking thus: "This most holy synod, being solicitous, as it is duty bound, (having been assembled for that especial purpose), to provide for the extirpation of error and heresies in various parts of the world, has of late heard, that certain propositions erroneous in faith and adverse to good morals, highly scandalous and tending to subvert the established order of government, have been publicly taught, and amongst others this especial one has been reported to it: Any tyrant, can licitly and meritoriously be slain by any of his subjects or vassals, without awaiting the sentence, or order of any judicial authority, though his death be effected by secret fraud, insidious flattery and blandishments, and notwithstanding any pledged oath or engagement entered into with him. This holy synod, anxious to oppose itself to this error, and effectually to eradicate the same, after having maturely considered it, decrees, determines, and declares, this doctrine to be erroneous in faith and in morals: and reprobates and condemns it as heretical, scandalous, and leading to frauds, deceit, lies, and treachery. It moreover determines, decrees, and declares, that all persons pertinaciously holding this most dangerous opinion are heretics, and ought to be punished as such according to canonical regulations."[3] Jean Gerson testifies that a certain book was published in the Council of Constance against this error. But I confess that I have not seen it. Nevertheless, I wished to inform the reader, so that if perhaps he believes that he can find it, let him endeavor to do so.

VERECUNDIA

Shame

There was a certain heresy teaching that one ought not to be ashamed of anything given to us by nature. The authors of this heresy were the Turlupins,[4] who on account of this opinion after the manner of the Cynic philosophers were appearing nude in public, and were having intercourse like beasts in public.

---

[1] Cf. Rom. 13, 1.
[2] Cf. *Justiniani Digestorum seu Pandectarum libri*, bk. 48, tit. 3 (*Ad Legem Juliam Majestatis*), n. 1 (Ulpian).
[3] Mansi, vol. 27, pp. 765-766.
[4] I.e. "The Rascals," from the French word *Turlupin*. The sect was active mainly in the second half of the 14th century around Paris.

VERECUNDIA

And certainly nature itself disproves this heresy, from which we have a certain shame of things. Wherefore the lower parts of the human body by which males and females are united in intercourses (the private parts), are called *verenda* and *pudenda*, from the words *verecundia* (shame) and *pudore* (blush). Even though those lower parts of the human body of themselves are not more depraved than the other parts of the body, still they bear witness to the sin which the first man committed through disobedience. For when Adam ate the apple after having been forbidden by the Divine command, he was punished with reciprocal disobedience, such that he would suffer disobedience of his members in his own body, which he immediately experienced in his genital members. Now this disobedience of the members, remained in all of us as a sort of perpetual punishment in memory of Original sin. For although all the other parts of the body move and rest at the behest and command of our will, only the genital members oppose the behest of the will, and refuse to obey. If you want to raise your hand, it is raised. If you wish it to lower it, the same hand is lowered: and in the same way all the other parts of the body obey the will. Yet it often happens that the genital members are aroused against the will, and the same members sometimes resist when subdued. Therefore we suffer disobedience and rebellion in those parts as a testimony of that disobedience which our first parents exercised against God. If therefore we are justly ashamed of any defect, it is befitting that we be ashamed of those parts of the body, in which both the punishment and testimony of Original sin remains until the present time.

Again, after Adam sinned, when knowing his sin, and wanting to flee from the face of the Lord walking in Paradise, he said to God: "I heard thy voice in paradise; and I was afraid, because I was naked" (Gen. 3, 10). In which passage it is evident that "fear" is used for "shame," which can easily be shown from the cause of the fear which produced that shame. "I was afraid," he said, "because I was naked." For whence was fear, that is shame, because in his naked body he then experienced the disobedience of his body, which was a testimony of his sin. The aprons which they made, so that they might cover the lower parts of the body once they knew that they were naked, bear witness to this shame of Adam and Eve.

Next, if one ought not to be ashamed of anything naturally given, Cham, the son of Noe, is unjustly rebuked because when seeing his inebriated father having his private parts uncovered, he told his brothers: the other brothers, namely Sem and Japheth, are also undeservedly praised because they covered the private parts of their father. But since Cham was cursed by his father on account of that misdeed, and the other sons, on account of the fact that they covered their father, were blessed by their father, it is rightly proved that there are some things about which we ought to be ashamed, even if they were given to us by nature. For on account of this cause of shame alone Sem and Japheth when seeing their father naked turned their faces away, so the they would not see the private parts of their father. Add to this that one of the priestly vestments, with which according the Lord's precept the priest ought to be vested when he entered the Holies, were breeches for covering those parts from which when exposed very great shame arises.[1] Therefore, let the brazen Turlupins be gone, and those things which God covers, may they themselves also be ashamed to uncover.

---

[1] Cf. Ex. 39, 27.

VINUM

Wine

Severus, from whom the Severians originated, taught that it was not allowed at all to drink wine, because by "a lying folly," as Augustine say, they were saying that "wine has sprung from the union of Satan and the earth."[1] None of those who wrote about the heresies (yet those which could be seen) attributed it to anyone else besides Severus. Nevertheless, Blessed Jerome says that this was the error of Tatian. For in his commentaries on the Prophet Amos, when interpreting the passage, "You will present wine to the Nazarites" (2, 12) etc., says the following: "From this passage Tatian, the leader of the Encratites, attempts to base his heresy, asserting that wine ought not to be drunk, since both the Nazarites were commanded by law not to drink wine and now they who present wine to the Nazarites are accused by the prophet. Who if they follow literally in everything, and force the Jewish fables upon Christ's Church, then they also ought to grow their hair and not eat raisins or fresh grapes, and not to go in to for one's dead mother and father: and if perhaps they did these things, and were overcome by either human frailty or necessity, let them shave heads, and all the days of their consecration and labor be void. But if they do not do these things, neither can they adulterate wine with water according to the custom of the Jewish tavern-keepers, shadows of the truth; let them understand the necessity of the grace of the Evangelical law from that drunkenness, whereby one is inebriated by worldly cares and his strength of soul overwhelmed, and whereby they command the prophets, saying, 'Do not prophesy' (*ibid.*), who, conquered by envy, prohibit learned men from bringing forth the message of doctrine."[2] From whose words it is evident that Tatian also taught this heresy. Yet Augustine, or Philastrius, even when they enumerate Tatian's errors, never mention this heresy.

And certainly (so that I may speak candidly) this heresy not only harms the soul, just like any other, but also harms the body: because even if wine taken immoderately harms very much, still when drank moderately provides many benefits to the body. Wherefore the Wise Man Ecclesiasticus says: "Wine drunken with moderation is the joy of the soul and the heart. Sober drinking is health to soul and body" (31, 36-37). Besides, if wine were evil from its nature, our Savior would not have turned water into wine: nor would the wine made from water have been the first of His signs. And if it were not permitted to drink wine, the Savior likewise would not have commanded the waiters at the wedding to bring the wine to the chief steward.[3] Again, the Savior Himself when eating supper with His disciples drank wine, and gave it to His disciples to be drank[4]: and He changed wine into His Blood, and taught them to do likewise, saying: "Do this for a commemoration of me" (Lk. 22, 19). Next, Paul the Apostle when writing to Timothy advised that he not drink water, but that he use a little wine for his stomach's sake, and his frequent infirmities.[5] And it is unnecessary to cite more testimonies, since the heresy is so manifest.

For the rest, that Severus taught that wine ought not to be drunk, because it is evil, and that it is evil because he said that "wine has sprung from the union of Satan and the earth," there is no need now to fight against this: because we have already shown above in the section on

---

[1] *De haeresibus ad Quodvultdeus*, c. 24 (PL 42, 30).
[2] *Commentary on Amos* (PL 25, 1010C-1011A).
[3] Cf. Jn. 2, 8.
[4] Cf. Mt. 26, 27.
[5] Cf. I Tim. 5, 23.

"Creatures" that all creatures are good of themselves, and that they are all from God, and not from any other principle.

VIRGINITAS
Virginity

Jovinian the monk taught that before God virginity is not of greater merit than marriage, but he said that marriage is equal to virginity. On the account of whose teaching many holy virgins advanced in age, after having made a vow, married. Yet Jovinian himself, although he laid aside monastic life did not want to marry a wife: not because he hoped that he would have more merit before God, but he said that he was continent lest he suffer the troubles of marriage. Jerome also accuses Helvidius of this error. Now which of these men first taught this error, is not certain to me: yet it is evident that both of them were contemporaries of Jerome, and Jerome firstly wrote against Helvidius than against Jovinian: because in the first book of *Against Jovinian* he mentions the book which he had written against Helvidius. But which of these men had taught this error before the other is evident from Jerome's words that neither of them was the first author of this heresy, because he attributed the origin to Basilides. For in the second book of *Against Jovinian* near the end he speaks thus: "About four hundred years have passed since the preaching of Christ flashed upon the world, and during that time in which His robe has been torn by countless heresies, almost the whole body of error has been derived from the Chaldean, Syriac, and Greek languages. Basilides, the master of licentiousness and the grossest sensuality, after the lapse of so many years, and like a second Euphorbus,[1] was changed by transmigration into Jovinian, so that the Latin tongue might have a heresy of its own."[2] From whose words it is established that this heresy took its beginning from Basilides. Yet Augustine in his book *De haeresibus [ad Quodvultdeus]* when discussing about this Basilides, does not accuse him of any such thing.[3] Philastrius also when enumerating the errors of Basilides, never mentions this error.[4] Therefore we may believe Jerome as a very diligent investigator of things, especially since the others do not contradict, but are silent. Epiphanius nevertheless when discussing about Basilides in his book on heresies, and enumerating all his heresies, does not say that he equated marriage with virginity, but he says that he taught promiscuous and free intercourse, and other unmentionable types of lust, just as Saturninus his teacher had done.[5] And perhaps for this reason Jerome said that Basilides was changed by transmigration into Jovinian although he had said nothing about virginity.

After these men in our era rose up Martin Luther, who rebuilt Jericho long after it had been destroyed with God's curse, making it much worse than it had been under Jovinian. For

---

[1] Euphorbus is said to have been born again in the person of Pythagoras. See footnote above in the section on "Silence."

[2] N. 37 (PL 23, 335B).

[3] C. 4 (PL 42, 26).

[4] *Liber de Haeresibus*, c. 32 (PL 12, 1144A-1148A).

[5] "Basilides gives his disciples permission to perform the whole of every badness and licentiousness, and gives his converts full instruction in the promiscuous intercourse of an evil kind between men and women. Of them and their kind the Apostle says, 'the wrath of God is revealed from heaven against all ungodliness and injustice of those men that detain the truth of God in injustice' (Rom. 1, 18). For many fall into heresy for this reason of self-indulgence, since through these unnatural acts they find a way of doing their pleasure with impunity." (*Adversus Haereses*, bk. 1, sect. 2, heresy 24, c. 3 (PG 41, 314A)).

he was not content to equate marriage with virginity, as Jovinian had done: but he strove to denigrate virginity to such an extent that he was not afraid to say that it is evil, and contrary to God's command. Now so that the madness of this man may be known to all, I will cite his words, which he wrote in his book, *On Monastic Vows*. Celibacy, he says, virginity, aureoles are nonsense, and mere lies of Satan.[1] And in the book *On Married Life*, when wishing to show that it is impossible to keep virginity, he says these words: "As it is not within my power not to be a man, so it is not my prerogative to be without a woman… 'Increase and multiply, is not a command. It is more than a command, namely, a Divine ordinance [*werck*] which it is not our prerogative to hinder or ignore. Rather, it is just as necessary as the fact that I am a man, and more necessary than sleeping and waking, eating and drinking, and emptying the bowels and bladder."[2] Now so that he might persuade all the people of his teaching, he was not content to teach it by word and writing: but he confirmed it by deed, doing that which he preached to others. For although he was a monk of the family of the Hermits of Saint Augustine, as a shameless dog returning to its vomit, he rejected all monastic life, and married a wife, whom he wanted to be no one but a nun, so that "they might have lettuce like their lips."[3]

This doctrine, since it is very pleasing to the flesh, pleased all those who obey the flesh instead of God, and for this reason the majority of monks and nuns of Germany rejected monastic life, and accepted matrimony. And this was one of the main reasons why the Lutheran heresy gained strength, namely because it always taught those things which please the people, and hence a large part of the people venerated Luther as a prophet of God, and accepted his teaching as God's oracle. For there is always a greater number of fools than wise men in every people. "The number of fools," says the Wise Man, "is infinite" (Eccles. 1, 15). For on account of this reason, as it is known to all who understand correctly, such a great part of the world is subjected to the law of Mohammed: because a very great part of men are attached to the pleasures of the flesh, which he by his law permits to all. And hence it is evident that Luther how wrongly gloried in the great number of his disciples: because for the same reason Mohammed also could glory against Christ: since he also has more disciples and followers than Christ. John Calvin even though he is not particularly well disposed towards virginity, still speaks against it more mildly than Luther. I will prove all these things to everyone afterwards, when I have first cited his words here.

The most effective testimony for the commendation of virginity is that which Christ our Savior says: "There are eunuchs, who have made themselves eunuchs for the kingdom of heaven. He that can take, let him take it" (Mt. 19, 12). For when He had said that it is not permitted for one to put away his wife except on account of fornication: when the disciples heard this thinking that the burden of matrimony on account of its indissoluble bond is very burdensome, said: "If the case of a man with his wife be so, it is not expedient to marry" (v. 10). To whom Christ responded: "All men take not this word, but they to whom it is given" (v. 11). But what is this word which men do not take but they to whom it is given? Certainly it is what He immediately adds: "For there are eunuchs, who were born so from their mother's womb: and there are eunuchs, who were made so by men: and there are eunuchs, who

---

[1] "Therefore what are those magnificent Bulls, whereby virginity, celibacy, the vow are vaunted, then the prerogatives, the aureoles and that kind of foolishness, which are preached, whereby Christians are allured to virginity, but lies of Satan, by which they are incited to pride and to corrupting the virginity of conscience?" (*De votis monasticis Martini Lutheri judicum* (WA 8, 610, ln. 37-611, ln. 2).

[2] *The Estate of Marriage* (*Vom ehelichen Leben*) in *Luther's Works* (Philadelphia, Fortress Press, 1962), vol. 45, p. 18. WA 10/II, 276.

[3] Autarchia quotes a Latin proverb *labia* (or *labra*) *lactucas similes habent*. Cf. Erasmus, Adagia I.x.71. It means that bad things suit each other—coarse meat suits coarse mouths, as an ass eats the thistles for his salad, or a scabbed horse is good enough for a scabbed Squire.

have made themselves eunuchs for the kingdom of heaven. He that can take, let him take it" (v. 12). From these words of Christ it is very clearly established that virginity is preferred to matrimony. For who does not see that that for acquiring which, the strength of all men does not suffice, is much more excellent than that which is so easy, that all can take it? There is no one whose nature is entire, who cannot have intercourse. But it is rare that one could abstain from every kind of intercourse. For not all take this.

Furthermore, Paul the Apostle in the First Epistle to the Corinthians, prefers widowhood to marriage, and he prefers virginity to both, saying: "He that giveth his virgin in marriage, doth well; and he that giveth her not, doth better" (7, 38). What more do we now desire against Jovinian? Could he have said anything more explicit for the vindication of virginity? "He that giveth his virgin in marriage," He says, "doth better." And afterwards when preferring a widow to a married woman He says: "A woman is bound by the law as long as her husband liveth; but if her husband die, she is at liberty: let her marry to whom she will; only in the Lord. But more blessed shall she be, if she so remain, according to my counsel; and I think that I also have the spirit of God" (v. 39-40). Yet before Paul says this statement, he discussed many things whereby he showed that there is wide difference between marriage and virginity. "He that is without a wife," he says, "is solicitous for the things that belong to the Lord, how he may please God. But he that is with a wife, is solicitous for the things of the world, how he may please his wife: and he is divided. And the unmarried woman and the virgin thinketh on the things of the Lord, that she may be holy both in body and in spirit. But she that is married thinketh on the things of the world, how she may please her husband" (v. 32-34).

Let us consider well and faithfully weigh the difference between virginity and marriage. A virgin desires to please the Lord, a married man his wife, and to please his wife, he is solicitous about the things that are in the world, and pertain to the world: and so he is divided, because he who is joined to God, is made one spirit with Him.[1] But where there is unity, there is no division. A virgin therefore is not divided, because desiring to please God alone, he has only one spirit, and this is a Divine spirit. But a married man who also desires to please his wife, as well as God, this man is divided into two parts, one whereby he chooses to please God, if he now chooses: and another whereby he desires to please his wife. Thus let Jovinian now say: Is it not superior to please God, than to please a wife? Is it not better to be joined to God, and to be made one spirit with Him, than to be divided into many parts of solicitudes and miseries? If to please God is better, it follows that virginity is superior to matrimony.

Again, when the Sadducees asked our Savior about the woman who had successively married seven brothers, which of them she would have after the resurrection, the same Savior answers: "In the resurrection they shall neither marry nor be married; but shall be as the angels of God in heaven" (Mt. 22, 30). From which words it is evident that marriage belongs to men: continence however is the proper role of the Angels. Hence as much as Angels are superior to men, so virginity is superior to matrimony.

Next, the great number of virtues which virginity requires for sustaining it also proves this, so that just like another Esther it is supported by them as by its handmaids. For a virgin ought to be abstemious: because wine is a luxurious thing. Abstinence from food is required: because the fires of lust increase by the nourishment of food. Highly necessary is that a covenant be made with the eyes, as Job testifies that he had made, so that one would not so much as think upon a virgin[2]: because as Ecclesiasticus says, many by admiring the beauty of a woman have become reprobate.[3] It is no less necessary to close one's ears to immodest speech: be-

---

[1] Cf. I Cor. 6, 17.

[2] Cf. Job 31, 1.

[3] Cf. Eccli. 9, 11.

VIRGINITAS

cause (as Menander says in Paul[1]) "Evil communications corrupt good manners" (I Cor. 15, 33). Keeping a guard on one's mouth and lips is also necessary, so that one does not incline his heart to evil words, lest perhaps by your light-minded words some woman be wounded in some degree, and she reply like for like, so that she pierces your heart, and draws you away by the flattery of her lips, and you immediately follow her as an ox led to be a victim.[2] One will certainly undergo many troubles, who desires to keep his virginity undefiled. For which reason virginity is deservedly accustomed to be likened to ivory, which due to its great age turns red in color, although it is naturally white, because virginity kept for a long time is equivalent to martyrdom, and is as it were a sort of shedding of blood. In short, virginity can never be alone, but it ought to be like a queen surrounded by vast retinue of handmaids. But how can it happen that virginity is not nobler, which many more virtues serve than matrimony?

Finally, this assertion of Jovinian, as reason and the rule of faith required, was twice condemned by the judgment of the whole Catholic Church. For Pope Syricius,[3] having held a council of priests in Rome, firstly condemned it, so that from his letter concerning the condemnation of Jovinian to the African bishops it can be evident, in which is contained the following words: "We truly do not accept the vows of marriage contemptuously, at which we were present by the veil, but we honor virgins consecrated to God with greater honor. Thus the synod having convened, it is agreed [that all these things] are contrary to our teaching, that is to say, to the Christian law. Hence having followed the precept of the Apostle,[4] that they were teaching otherwise than we have received, it is evident that one judgment has been made by all our priests, deacons, as well as the whole clergy, whereby that Jovinian, Auxentius, Genialis, Germinator, Felix, Prontinus, Martianus, Januarius and Ingeniosus,[5] who were found to be inciters of a new heresy and blasphemy, and have been condemned in perpetuity by Divine sentence, and our judgment, should remain outside the Church."[6] And the [Milanese[7]] bishops having received this letter of Syricius, convened a synod, in which having fully examined the matter (as it ought), approved the condemnation of Jovinian made by Siricius, and wrote back to the same Pope Siricius about this affair. In whose letter these words are had: "It is a savage barking to show no reverence to virginity, observe no rule of chastity, to seek to place everything on a level, to abolish the different degrees of merit, and to introduce a certain meagerness in heavenly rewards, as if Christ had only one palm to bestow, and there was no copious diversity in His rewards. They pretend that they are giving honor to marriage. But what praise is there of marriage, if there is no glory of virginity? We do not deny that marriage was sanctified by Christ, by the Divine Voice saying, 'They two shall be in one flesh' (Gen. 2, 24; Mt. 19, 5), and in one spirit, but our birth precedes our calling, and the mystery of the Divine operation is much more excellent than the remedy of human frailty. A good wife is deservedly praised, but a pious virgin is more properly preferred, for the Apostle says, 'He that giveth his virgin in marriage, doth well; and he that giveth her not, doth better' (I Cor. 7, 38). For 'The one thinketh on the things of the Lord, the other on the things of the world' (v. 34). The one is bound by the chains of marriage, the other is free from chains; the one is under the

---

[1] Menander (in *Thais*) probably derived this saying from Euripides (Socrates, *Ecclesiastical History*, bk. 3, c. 16 (PG 67, 423A)).

[2] Cf. Prov. 7, 21-22.

[3] Pope Syricius reigned from 384-399 A. D.

[4] Cf. Gal. 1, 9: "If anyone preach to you a gospel, besides that which you have received, let him be anathema."

[5] Auxentius, Genialis, Germinator, Felix, Prontinus, Martianus, Januarius and Ingeniosus were the disciples of Jovinian (cf. "Jovinianus," *The Catholic Encyclopedia*, vol. 8, p. 530).

[6] Letter 7, (PL 13, 117).

[7] The text here incorrectly cites the African the Synod of Theleptis (418 A. D.).

Law, the other under grace. Marriage is good, for thereby the means of continuing the human race has been devised, but virginity is better, for thereby the heritage of the heavenly kingdom is regained, and the mode of attaining to heavenly rewards discovered. By a woman care entered the world; by a virgin salvation was brought to pass. Lastly, Christ chose virginity as His own special gift, and displayed the grace of chastity, thus making an exhibition of that in His own Person which in His Mother He had made the object of His choice... Wherefore you are to know that Jovinian, Auxentius, Germinator, Felix, Plotinus, Genialis, Martianus, Januarius and Ingeniosus, whom Your Holiness has condemned, have also, in accordance with your judgment, been condemned by ourselves."[1]

But because we have determined to defend the honor and excellence of virginity against its enemies, it is necessary that we respond to the objections of the adversaries. Now we will do this the more readily, the more we perceive that their objections present little difficulty for us. Firstly in fact they object to us that which God said to the first parents, immediately after God created them. "Increase," He said to them, "and multiply" (Gen. 1, 22). In which words, it is evident from Luther's words cited above, the enemies of virginity say, God gave to every man the command of contracting matrimony. John Calvin, whom I said is not such a bitter enemy of virginity as Luther, asserts this same thing. For in that work, in chapter three of his *Institutes of the Christian Religion*, where he treats of the law, when interpreting the precept: "Thou shalt not commit adultery," he says these words: "As the law under which man was created was not to lead a life of solitude, but enjoy a help meet for him, and ever since he fell under the curse the necessity for this mode of life is increased."[2]

But because these words could be taken in a good sense, such that they are understood to have been said for that time alone: lest they could be so understood by us, he wished to open his mind to us more. For in the same chapter after he had said that it is better to marry than to copulate with a harlot, against priests and monks who promise perpetual chastity to God, says these words: "But Priests, monks, and nuns, forgetful of our sacrifice of this kind, are confident of their fitness for celibacy. But by what oracle have they been instructed, that the chastity which they vow to the end of life, they will be able through life to maintain? They hear the voice of God concerning the universal condition of mankind, 'It is not good for man to be alone' (Gen. 2, 18). They understand, and I wish they did not feel that the sin remaining in us is armed with the sharpest stings. How can they presume to disregard this universal invitation of their nature for a whole lifetime, seeing the gift of continence is more often granted for a certain time as occasion requires?"[3] In which words there are many things, by which he shows that he thinks that even in this time of grace, a universal command is still in effect, which obliges all to contract marriage. For he says that even now it is said to all: 'It is not good for man to be alone," without a wife. He also says that it is not permitted to disregard this universal invitation for a whole lifetime. Now he calls it is a universal invitation whereby we are all called by God to marriage, which calling even if it can be delayed, still it cannot be rejected, as he says, perpetually. Hence he recommends virginity for a certain time: but he condemns perpetual virginity, but it is, so that I may speak with his words, against God's "universal invitation," that is, against the universal command.

Nevertheless, if God granted the gift of virginity to someone in particular, he admits that it is a virtue, but he says that this has not been granted to anyone except for a time. His words in that third chapter are these: "Virginity, I admit, is a virtue not to be despised; but since it is denied to some, and to others granted only for a season, those who are assailed by incontinence, and unable successfully to war against it, should retake themselves to the remedy

---

[1] PG 56, 566B-567B & 570B.

[2] C. 3 (*De lege*), n. 63 (ed. 1554, CR 29, 410).

[3] *Ibid.*, n. 66 (CR 29, 411).

of marriage, and thus cultivate chastity in the way of their calling."[1] From Calvin's words, he differs from Luther by this alone, that Luther completely condemns all virginity; Calvin on the other hand not all virginity, but only that which is through the whole course of life, because he says that this was never granted by God. For after he said that virginity is a virtue, he immediately dividing it, said that it was denied to some, having been granted to others but for a time. Calvin indeed, as I am of the opinion, very clearly saw that testimonies of Sacred Scripture commended virginity which he could not contradict: and so with great care he found the sought way, by which he would commend the least virginity, namely for a certain limited time: but he condemns perpetual virginity, which is the greater and truer virginity. Thus, there is agreement between Luther and Calvin about this, because both say that marriage is commanded to all, and perpetual virginity has been forbidden by Divine precept. Which opinion is so heretical, that it would not be necessary to dispute against, unless we were acting against brazen men, to whom it were necessary to prove the most obvious things. If temporary and limited virginity is a virtue, as Calvin says, perpetual virginity will be a much greater virtue: because the very notion of virginity is much more found in the latter, than in the former. For the difficult good is truly the object of virtue: because it cannot be a virtue unless it pertains to difficult things. Which thing is so well known, that it was manifest not only to Christians, but even to the pagans themselves. For [Pseudo-] Virgil so that I may omit Aristotle and the rest of the philosophers, or that man who interpreted the text of Pythagoras in a mystical sense, said these words:

The Letter [Y] of Pythagoras, cleft by a two-pronged division,
May be seen to display the very image of human life.
For the steep path of virtue takes the righthand way,
And presents difficult access at first to onlookers,
But grants rest to the weary on its lofty summit.[2]

And Ovid in the second book *De Ponto* says:
Tis hard, I admit, yet virtue aims at what is hard.[3]

If the matter of virtue is the difficult good, the consequence is necessarily thence deduced, that virtue is greater in that good, in attainment of which there is greater difficulty. And a certain other noble poet also taught this, namely Lucan in the ninth book of *Pharsalia*, saying the following:

Serpents, thirst, burning-sand
All are welcomed by the brave; endurance finds pleasure in hardship;
virtue rejoices when it pays dear for its existence.[4]

---

[1] *Ibid*, n. 63 (CR 29, 410).

[2] *Litera Pythagorae (discrimine secta bicorni)*
Humanae vitae speciem praeferre videtur:
Nam via virtutis dextrum petit ardua collem,
Difficilem{que} aditum primum spectantibus offert;
Sed requiem praestat fessis in vertice summo.
"The Pythagorean letter, divided into two horns, seems to present an image of human life. For the steep way of virtue, to the right, offers the viewer a difficult approach up a mountainside, but at the top it provides the weary with rest." The twenty-fifth letter of the English alphabet derived from the Greek T. One of the symbols of Pythagoras was the Greek letter Upsilon, T. for which, on account of the similarity of shape, the Romans adopted the letter Y of their own alphabet. Pythagoras said that the two horns of the letter symbolized the two different paths of virtue and vice, the right branch leading to the former and the left to the latter. (*Two Ways of Pythagoras* epigram in *Appendix Vergiliana*).

[3] *Epistulae ex Ponto*, bk. 2, poem, 2, ln. 111.

[4] Alias *De Bello Civili*. "Serpens, sitis, ardor harenae dulcia virtuti; gaudet patientia duris; laetius est, quotiens magno sibi constat, honestum." (Ln. 402).

VIRGINITAS

Therefore, since there is much greater difficulty in the conservation of perpetual virginity, than of temporary virginity limited to a certain time, it is clearly proved that perpetual virginity is a much more excellent virtue than that which is kept for a limited time.

Perhaps Calvin will say here that perpetual virginity, although it has a great difficulty, is not a virtue but a sin, due to the fact that God forbade it, when he commanded matrimony, saying: "Increase and multiply." If Calvin replies in this way, he would be forced to admit that God forbade what is a virtue to men: because perpetual virginity, unless God would have forbade it, as Calvin says, was a virtue by its nature. Next, it is surprising that what is today a virtue, tomorrow is made a vice without any change of things.

But let us pass these matters by, and let us discuss whether it is true what they object to us, that to all men was given a general precept of marriage by those words, "Increase and multiply." This is quite false, and a very clear lie: because I cannot persuade myself that they do not think otherwise than they say, unless perhaps the affection of lust has blinded their minds. For it is unlikely that they did not read Paul, where he says: "Now concerning virgins, I have no commandment of the Lord; but I give counsel... Art thou loosed from a wife? seek not a wife" (I Cor. 7, 25 & 27). If God gave a general precept of marriage to all, as the Lutherans say, then Paul contradicts God, since he counseled virginity against God's precept. Yet far be it that we would say that Paul is opposed to God. Perhaps Calvin will say that Paul merely counseled that virginity, which is restricted to a certain time, which God did not forbid. But Paul's words are so clear and so plain, that they nowise allow that they be distorted into such a sense. For Paul says to the one loosed from a wife, "Seek not a wife": he did not say, "Do not seek a wife for this or that time." But absolutely and without any limitation of time he said, "Seek not a wife." Furthermore, if there were a general precept given to all without any exception, they all would sin who kept perpetual virginity, because they transgressed God's precept. Thus John the Evangelist sinned, and John the Baptist sinned: nay, what is much more horrible than all these things, the Mother of God would have sinned keeping perpetual virginity. Yet there are no pious ears which even allow this to be heard.

Next, if this is a precept, then the sterile would sin even though they are joined in matrimony: because they do not multiply the human race. Now what prudent man would say that they sin on account of the omission of the thing which they cannot perform? Therefore, let us acknowledge that those words of God contain a precept, which of old before Christ's coming and on account of the condition of human nature, He obliged men to those marriages alone so that by them the human race would be propagated. But afterwards when the human race was sufficiently propagated, that precept no longer obliges, and everyone is free to be either a virgin or bound by marriage.

And in testimony of this is that which Jerome long ago responds to Helvidius likewise objecting to that precept against virginity, saying the following: "In accordance with the difference in time and circumstance one rule applied to the (saints of the Old Testament), another to us (in the New Testament) upon whom the ends of the world have come. So long as that Law remained, 'Increase and multiply' (Gen. 1, 28); and 'Cursed is the barren woman that bears not seed in Israel,'[1] they all married and were given in marriage, left father and mother, and became one flesh. But once in tones of thunder the words were heard, 'The time is short... that they who have wives, be as if they had none' (I Cor. 7, 29) ... The world is already full, and the population is too large for the soil. Every day we are being cut down by war, snatched away by disease, swallowed up by shipwreck, although we go to law with one another about the fences of our property."[2] In the first book of *Against Joviniani* he again says: "It was necessary first to plant the wood and to let it grow, so that there might be an after-growth for

---

[1] Cf. Septuagint version of Is. 31, 9 or 66, 9.
[2] *The Perpetual Virginity of Blessed Mary*, n. 20-21 (PL 23, 203C-205B).

cutting down. And at the same time we must bear in mind the meaning of the phrase, replenish the earth. Marriage replenishes the earth, virginity fills Paradise... Our predecessors under the Law served their generation according to their circumstances, and fulfilled the Lord's command: 'Increase and multiply, and fill the earth' (Gen. 1, 23)... To us it is said, 'the time is short; it remaineth, that they also who have wives, be as if they had none' (I Cor. 7, 29)."[1]

But before Jerome Cyprian also taught this in his book, *On the Dress of Virgins*, saying these words: "The first decree commanded to increase and to multiply; the second enjoined continency. While the world is still rough and void, we are propagated by the fruitful begetting of numbers, and we increase to the enlargement of the human race. Now, when the world is filled and the earth supplied, they who can receive continency, living after the manner of eunuchs, are made eunuchs unto the kingdom (of heaven)."[2] But because in Jerome's words it was said that this precept lasted for the time of the Old Testament, I remind the reader, so that he may understand that at that time it was commanded, yet not given to every individual person, but to the body of mankind as a whole. For there are some precepts, which so oblige all men, so that they also oblige the individuals, of which kind are all the precepts of the Decalogue. Again, there are other precepts, which oblige a whole nation, yet not every single individual of that nation. Such are the precepts of the officials in a civil government: and the precepts of the various pastors in the ecclesiastical government. It is indeed a Divine precept that there be various bishops in the Church, and one supreme pastor of the whole Church: yet not all Christians are obliged to be bishops, nor that all would be supreme pontiffs: but only those who were chosen for undertaking this office.

The precept of marriage had the first circumstances, in the beginning when man was created: because at that time each and every man was obliged, due to the fact that then at that time the reason for the precept, namely that multiplication of the human race, remained intact. But afterwards when the human race was sufficiently multiplied before Christ's coming, it was no longer obliging individual men: but the whole of humanity, in which it was necessary that some be joined in marriage but not all. For it was then enough for the multiplication of the human race that there be some who attend to begetting. For if all were then obliged to contracting marriage, it would follow that we could say that Jeremias, Elias, Eliseus, the three young men cast into the furnace in Babylon: as well as Daniel and John the Baptist had sinned because they kept virginity. Nevertheless, far be it that we would turn this into a sin for them, for which Ignatius, Epiphanius, Jerome, Ambrose Damascene and many other holy and learned men praised them, as for a very great virtue, although they lived under the Mosaic Law. Afterwards however the Lord under the Evangelical Law said, "He that can take, let him take it" (Mt. 19, 12): then the liberty was given to all, that they could be virgins if they wished. And hence that precept of marriage was abolished, which was in effect of old, such that neither individuals nor all men are obliged to contracting matrimony.

And Augustine teaches this clearly in the book, *Of the Good of Marriage*, where he firstly says that the holy Fathers of the Old Law were obliged not to abstain from intercourse, because the Son of God was to assume human flesh from them: then at the end of chapter nine he says these words which follow: "But now, whereas, in order to enter upon holy and pure fellowship, there is on all sides from out of all nations an overflowing fullness of spiritual kindred, even they who wish to contract marriage only for the sake of children, are to be admonished, that they use rather the larger good of continence... But I am aware of some that murmur: What, say they, if all men should abstain from all sexual intercourse, whence will the human race exist? Would that all would this, only in 'charity, from a pure heart, and a good conscience, and an unfeigned faith' (I Tim. 1, 5); much more speedily would the City of God

---

[1] N. 16 & 24 (PL 23, 235B & 234D).

[2] N. 23 (PL 4, 463A).

be filled, and the end of the world hastened. For what else does the Apostle, as is manifest, exhort to, when he says, speaking on this head, 'I would that all men were even as myself' (I Cor. 7, 7)?"[1] Although elsewhere Augustine is a promoter of good marriage, still preferring virginity to matrimony prefers that all would be virgins. Luther and Calvin, on the other hand, and all the others of the same ilk, want no one to be virgin and continent, lest they alone seem to be incontinent. But there is something else, which in these words of Augustine, one ought to note in passing, namely that he thinks that Paul is a virgin: which he infers from the words of Paul himself, where he says: "I would that all men were even as myself," and he asserts the same opinion at much greater length in the book, *On the Work of Monks*, wherein he argues explicitly in favor of Paul's virginity.[2]

And [Ambrosiaster] teaches the same thing when interpreting the aforesaid words of Paul.[3] Jerome asserts the same thing in his letter to [Ageruchia],[4] and in another letter to Marcella concerning the praises of Asella,[5] and in another to Eustochium about holy virginity.[6] It was necessary to point out these things in passing on account of those Lutheran heretics, who strive to defend their error by the testimony and example of Paul, saying that Paul was bound by matrimony, and hence they contend that in order to exhort all to matrimony he said, "I would that all men were even as myself." Now it is evident that all these things are false from the testimonies of the holy men which I have cited.

Yet they object to us that Ignatius, who when in his fifth epistle when enumerating holy married men, numbers Paul among them. Nevertheless, what they say is not true: because Ignatius never asserted that about Paul, but the heretics, for whom it is the custom to distort Scripture, either by increasing or lessening them, inserted Paul's name, which Ignatius had not put down, into his epistle. And there is a very convincing proof of this, that in the epistles written by Ignatius' hand, which are found in the old libraries, Paul's name is not found in that place. In Oxford, which is an English university, there is a college of Magdalen, in which

---

[1] C. 9-10, n. 9-10 (PL 40, 380-381).

[2] "The Apostle Paul himself, who assuredly professing highest chastity says, 'I would that all men were even as myself'" (C. 32, n. 40 (PL 40, 579)).

[3] "Paul would not say these things if he were not pure in his own body. If he had had a wife and had told them to be like him, he would hardly be encouraging them to remain virgins. How absurd!" (*Commentary on I Corinthians* (PL 17, 217C).

[4] "[Paul] wishes us — after one marriage — to abide even as he, that is, unmarried, and sets before us in his own apostolic example an instance of the blessedness of which he speaks" (Letter 123, n. 7 (PL 22, 1050). The text here cites St. Jerome's letter to Gerontia, but this addressee is found on some manuscripts while Ageruchia is the addressee in PL 22, 1050, where both names are so mentioned in the footnote.

[5] "And I say nothing of her consecration to the blessed life of virginity, a ceremony which took place when [Ansella] was hardly more than ten years old, a mere babe still wrapped in swaddling clothes. For all that comes before works should be counted of grace; although, doubtless, God foreknew the future when He sanctified Jeremias as yet unborn, when He made John to leap in his mother's womb, and when, before the foundation of the world, He set apart Paul to preach the Gospel of His Son" (Letter 24, n. 2 (PL 22, 427)).

[6] "'Concerning virgins,' says the Apostle, 'I have no commandment of the Lord' (I Cor. 7, 25). Why was this? Because his own virginity was due, not to a command, but to his free choice. For they are not to be heard who feign him to have had a wife; for, when he is discussing continence and commending perpetual chastity, he uses the words, 'I would that all men were even as I myself.' And further on, 'I say, therefore, to the unmarried and widows, it is good for them if they abide even as I' (v. 7-8). And in another place, 'Have we not power to lead about wives even as the rest of the apostles?' (I Cor. 9, 5)." (Letter 22, n. 20 (PL 22, 407)).

these epistles of Ignatius are found written in old and beautiful letters: and in that cited epistle, Paul's name is not there, nay nor any trace of it.

Secondly Luther objects that it is impossible to keep virginity, and hence it is not good: because it exceeds all human powers: and it not only exceeds, as he says, but he says that it is very harmful to one's own life: because for the conservation of one's own life the use of a wife is as necessary as food and drink. And Jovinian was saying this in defense of his error before Luther. For, as Jerome relates about him, he was saying that no one can change which is implanted in him by nature, nor can withstand the instilled inclination of having intercourse. But in fact, these men want to measure the feet of all other men by their own foot. For because those serving the belly and not God cannot live continently,[1] they judge that it is impossible for everyone. Hence it can very appropriately be applied to these men, what a certain Christian poet[2] elegantly said in a similar situation:

The owl does not ever see the sun,
Therefore does the eagle also not see it?
In this way the weakly sort says that something is beyond its strength.
It judges that it has dared to overstep Hercules.[3]

Therefore all these men say that continence is impossible, because they, because they want to obey the flesh, cannot be continent. Yet this which they object, if it were considered carefully, will be reckoned an excuse for their own sin, rather than an argument. But this excuse of theirs is false, and a mere lie, whence it is clearly proved that although it is true that we by our own strength cannot keep virginity, and completely abstain from all intercourse, still with the Divine aid, which God Himself is always prepared to give to all those asking, we can keep virginity unharmed, and especially if He can do other things which are much greater. For Paul when asking God to take away from him the sting of the flesh by which he was greatly afflicted, God replies to him: "My grace is sufficient for thee" (II Cor. 12, 9). And afterwards he said that he had experienced this Divine help in many things. "I can do all these things in him who strengtheneth me" (Phil. 4, 13). If [he can do] all things, then also [he can] keep virginity during the whole course of his life.

But Calvin responds to this argument, saying these words: "And let no man tell me (as many in the present day do) that one can do all things aided by God's help. The help of God is present with those only who walk in his ways,[4] that is, in His calling, from which all withdraw themselves who, omitting the remedies provided by God, vainly and presumptuously strive to struggle with and surmount their needs."[5] All these things are so false and impious, that they seem much worse to me, than the very subject of this disputation, on account of the defense of which these words were said by him. Calvin truly thinks that there is no other remedy for him who is tempted by the flesh, except to marry a wife, and have intercourse with her. For he says that he omits God's remedies, who when tempted by the flesh, does not fly to matrimony: as though there were no other remedy of God besides that one. He does not think that abstinence from food and drink is a remedy. "Without Ceres and Liber," a certain man said, "Venus freezes."[6] And Calvin does not think that a remedy against the burnings of the flesh

---

[1] Cf. Rom. 16, 18.

[2] I.e. Giovanni Battista Spagnuoli (1447-1516), the Mantuan, was an Italian Carmelite reformer, humanist, and poet.

[3] Giovanni Battista Spagnoli, *Carmen panegyricum in Robertum Sanseverinatem* in *Baptistæ Mantuani carmelitae,... Opera omnia* (Antwerp, apud Ioannem Bellerum, 1576), vol. 3, fol. 194r, lns. 6-9.

[4] Cf. Ps. 91, 14.

[5] *Institutes of the Christian Religion*, c. 3, n. 64 (ed. 1554, CR 29, 410).

[6] Terence, Eunuchus, scene 5, act 4, l. 732. In ancient Roman mythology, Ceres was a goddess of agriculture and grain crops. Liber was a god of viticulture and wine.

is scourging, or other similar castigations of the flesh: yet Ecclesiasticus gives the opposite opinion. "The affliction of an hour maketh one forget great delights" (11, 29). Lastly, Calvin does not think that prayer is a remedy in every trial and affliction, not to speak only of the temptation of the flesh. In which matter he does an injury to God Who said: "Whatsoever you shall ask in prayer, you shall receive" (Mt. 21, 22). Moreover, Calvin says that there is vain temerity of him who relying on God's help tries to overcome every temptation of the flesh, especially vehement temptation. Hence with he believes that God in incapable, or unwilling to help. I do not think that he doubts about His omnipotence: if he doubts about God's will, or believes that it is not ready to help all, let him hear what the [Royal] Prophet says: "The Lord is nigh unto all them that call upon him" (Ps. 144, 18). When he says that He "is nigh unto all them that call upon him," it is proved that the Lord does not deny His help to anyone rightly asking for it.

Because I recall that I spoke enough about this matter in the section on "The Priesthood," in the fourth heresy, in which place I fought for the celibacy of the priest, I do not wish to now dispute more: but I only wish to add some testimonies of holy men, which were not cited in that place, for proving that we can conquer temptations of the flesh, when we wish. Augustine in *On Merit and the Forgiveness of Sins, [and the Baptism of Infants]* says: We are not chaste, not because we cannot, but because we do not want.[1] And on Psalm fifty-five he again says: "In yourself is what you may vow and render."[2] And again on Psalm one hundred thirty-one he says these words: "Let no one presume to think he fulfilled by his own strength what he has vowed."[3]

Chrysostom likewise teaches the same thing, saying these words: "And what is more difficult than to play at ball with swords? And tell me what is harder than thoroughly to search out the bottom of the sea? And one might mention innumerable other arts. But easier than all these, if we have the will, is virtue, and the going up into Heaven. For here it is only necessary to have the will, and all [the rest] follows. For we may not say, I am unable, neither accuse the Creator. For if He made us unable, and then commands, it is an accusation against Himself. How is it then (someone says) that many are not able? How is it then that many are not willing? For, if they be willing, all will be able. Therefore also Paul says, 'I would that all men were even as myself' (I Cor. 7, 7), since he knew that all were able to be as himself. For he would not have said this, if it had been impossible. Do you wish to become [such]? Only lay hold on the beginning. Tell me now, in the case of any arts, when we wish to attain them, are we content with wishing, or do we also engage with the things themselves? As for instance, one wishes to become a pilot; he does not say, I wish, and content himself with that, but he also puts his hand to the work. He wishes to become a merchant; he does not merely say, I wish, but he also puts his hand to the work. Again he wishes to travel abroad, and he does not say, I wish, but he puts his hand to the work. In everything then, wishing alone is not sufficient, but work must also be added; and when you wish to mount up to heaven, do you merely say, I wish? How then (he says) did you say that willing is sufficient? [I meant] willing joined with deeds, the laying hold on the thing itself, the laboring. For we have God working with us, and acting with us. Only let us make our choice, only let us apply ourselves to the matter as to work, only let us think earnestly about it, only let us lay it to heart, and all follows."[4]

But before him Origen more clearly taught the same opinion, saying the following: "Have you not heard from Divine Scriptures, that there is a struggle within men of the flesh against

---

[1] "Men are unwilling to do what is right, either because what is right is unknown to them, or because it is unpleasant to them" (Bk. 2, n. 17, n. 26 (PL 44, 167)).

[2] *Enarrationes in Psalmos*, on Ps. 55, 12, n. 19 (PL 36, 659).

[3] *Enarrationes in Psalmos* [2], on Ps. 131, n. 3 (PL 37, 1717).

[4] *Homilies on Hebrews*, hom. 16, n. 4 (PG 63, 126-128).

the spirit, and of the spirit against the flesh?[1] Do you not know that if you only nourish the flesh and you supply it with frequent luxury and an endless flow of delicacies, it will by necessity grow insolent against the spirit and will be made stronger than [the spirit]? But if that happens, without a doubt, it will force the spirit, having been brought into its power, to obey its laws and vices. But if you frequently come to church, if you lend your ear to Divine Writ, if you grasp the explanation of the heavenly precepts, just as the flesh with foods and pleasures, so the spirit will grow strong by the Divine words and thoughts and, having become stronger than the flesh, it will force the flesh to obey itself and to submit to its laws. Therefore, the nourishments of the spirit are the Divine reading, constant prayers, the word of doctrine. With these foods it feeds itself, with them it grows stronger, with them it is made a victor. Because you do not do that, do not lament the infirmity of the flesh, do not say that we want to but we cannot; we want to live temperately but we are deceived by the weakness of the flesh and we are besieged by its stimuli. You give the stimuli to your flesh, you arm it and make it powerful against your spirit when you fill it with flesh, when you flood it with excessive wine, when you stroke it with all luxury and feed it with a view to enticements."[2] From whose and the others' words it is evident that the reason why the Lutherans cannot keep virginity is because they do not want to. They indeed want to conquer, but they do not wish to fight: they want to find rest, but they do not wish to go the way which is necessary for getting there. Furthermore, the opinion of these men is shown to be temerarious by the testimony of Elias, John the Baptist, and John the Evangelist, who it is evident were virgins, and yet not on account of this did they cease to be men. Therefore, let Luther be ashamed saying: "As it is not within my power not to be a man, so it is not my prerogative to be without a woman." Due to his malice Luther wants to conclude the inability of all men.

Thirdly they object to us the examples of the Patriarchs and the Apostles, who although they were very holy, nevertheless had wives. Now who is so arrogant and insolent, that he would dare to say that because he is a virgin, he is better than Blessed Peter the Apostle, or very holy Abraham? I cannot better reply to this objection than Blessed Augustine, and so I will firstly cite him, so that he may reply for us, who in the book, *Of the Good of Marriage*, says these words: "From the period that the fullness of time has come,[3] that it should be said, 'He that can take, let him take it' (Mt. 19, 12), from that period even unto this present, and from henceforth even unto the end, whoever has, works: whoever shall be unwilling to work, let him not falsely say, that he has. And through this means, they, who corrupt good manners by evil communications,[4] with empty and vain craft, say to a Christian man exercising continence, and refusing marriage, 'What then, are you better than Abraham?' But let him not, upon hearing this, be troubled; neither let him dare to say, 'Better,' nor let him fall away from his purpose: for the one he says not truly, the other he does not rightly. But let him say, 'I indeed am not better than Abraham, but the chastity of the unmarried is better than the chastity of marriage'; whereof Abraham had one in use, both in habit. For he lived chastely in the marriage state: but it was in his power to be chaste without marriage, but at that time it behooved not."[5] In which words two things especially ought to be noted. The first is that he calls corrupters of good manners, those who try to detract virginity, and lessen its merit and dignity by the aforesaid objection. The other thing is that he clearly asserts that the chastity of the celibate is better than the chastity of the married.

---

[1] Cf. Gal. 5, 17.
[2] *Homilies on Leviticus*, hom. 9, n. 7 (PG 12, 518C-519A).
[3] Cf. Gal. 4, 4.
[4] Cf. I Cor. 15, 33.
[5] C. 22, n. 27 (PL 40, 391-392).

VIRGINITAS

Calvin fourthly objects to us not actually an irrefutable argument, but a very shameless and very mendacious insult, having imitated on this point him who is the father of lies, as a son imitates a father. For he in that book of his, *Institutes of the Christian Religion*, inveighing against priests, monks and nuns, who defend celibacy, says these words: "As if in their own life they did not furnish a clear proof that celibacy is one thing and chastity another. This life, however, they most impudently style angelical, thereby offering no slight insult to the Angels of God, to whom they compare whoremongers and adulterers, and something much worse and fouler still."[1] From which words, as from the claws of the lion, any prudent and honest man can easily assess Calvin. For all these words are full of lies, contumelies, and impostures. We indeed admit that many priests are whoremongers, adulterers, and ravishers: and also some monks and nuns are similar: but we do not say that the life of anyone of them is angelic: nor do we compare them to Angels, as Calvin mendaciously calumniates, but rather we call all of them wicked, perfidious, and the offspring of Venus: because they degenerated from the parents of their monastic life, and obey their parent Venus rather than the God of all.

Now although the wickedness of these men is so great, even if it were still much greater, still nothing derogates from the state of all these men. Calvin praises marriage with many trumpets, which we ourselves also praise, yet many married men are adulterers, and what is much worse, liers with mankind: but the unbridled and perverse lust of these men derogates nothing from marriage. It is very good that there are government officials in a nation for its right governance: yet many men have the type of government officials who treat them very badly, exercising great tyrannies in them; but the wickedness of these men does not necessitate that government posts are evil in itself, since they are exercised properly by many men. The office of the Apostles was indeed very good, although Judas was very wicked in it. When we dispute about the dignity or merit of any state or of anything else, one ought not to look at those things which come to pass or happen: but what it has of itself, and what belongs to it from its nature. But this or that person is accidental to the state, because other very different and dissimilar persons can be in this state. Therefore when we say that the state of virginity or monasticism is an Angelic life, for the investigation of this the foolish virgins ought not to be put forth as proof, to whom the heavenly gate is closed, and whom the spouse testifies that he knows them not: but the prudent virgins, who hold the correct manner of virginity.[2] And wicked, whoremonger and adulterous monks,, "whose God is their belly; and whose glory is in their shame" (Phil. 3, 19), ought not to be put forth as proof: but those who live chastely and very continently according to the manner of the state, any of those who flee all occasions of lust, and pray very frequently to God, and set all in order, as it is said, "from stern to prow."[3]

But Calvin, in order to support his calumny with a lie, said that we compare whoremonger, adulterous monks, or ones infected with some other filthier unchastity to Angels: which is very great lie. For we compare to Angels only those who when living in the flesh, do not experience the pleasures of the flesh. But Calvin neither concedes this, as I reckon, nay nor can he hear this: because neither he, nor any other teacher of the Lutherans, can endure those things due to their pride and ambition, such that someone would be preferred to them. And hence it happens, that they cannot listen to some excellence of virginity, lest they hear that some men are preferred to themselves: nor can they endure even a little praise of virginity, lest they seem to lack something which is worthy of praise. But lest Calvin accuse us alone because we say that those who are truly virgins or are truly continent are similar to Angels: and that saying this we do no injury to the Angels, I bring forth the testimonies of the holy

---

[1] C. 3, n. 66 (CR 29, 412).

[2] Cf. Mt. 25, 1-12.

[3] I.e. *puppim et proram*.

Fathers as a confirmation of this opinion, any of whom one more rightly ought to believe than a thousand Calvins.

Bernard in his sermon on the Nativity of the Virgin Mary when speaking about that most Blessed Virgin, says these words: "Do not fear the Angel of the Lord, the Lord of the Angel is with you.[1] Then why should you not see the Angels when you live like an Angel? Why should the Angel not visit one who has the same way of life? Why should he not greet one of the saints and a close friend of God. The life of an Angel is clearly that of a virgin, and those who neither marry nor are given in marriage will be like the Angels of God."[2]

But much clearer is that which [Pseudo-[3]] Jerome says in his discourse on the Assumption of the Virgin Mary to Paula and Eustochias, where he says these words: "It is well that an angel be sent to the Virgin; because virginity is ever akin to the Angelic nature. Surely to live in the flesh and not according to the flesh is not an earthly but a heavenly life. Hence to acquire Angelic glory in the flesh is of greater merit, than to have [Angelic glory]."[4] [Pseudo-] Jerome not merely says that virgins are equal to Angels, but he makes them greater.

Ambrose in that book which is called an exhortation to virgins, says these words: "Listen, my children, how great is the reward of virginity. A kingdom is gained, the heavenly kingdom procures the life of the Angels. I recommend this to you, than which nothing is more beautiful, so that you may be Angels among men, who are not bound by any nuptial bond: because women who do not marry, and men who do not take wives, are like Angels upon earth; so that they do not feel the tribulation of the flesh, they do not know servitude, they are relieved from the contagion of worldly thoughts, they turn their minds to Divine things; so that as though they have put off the infirmity of the flesh, they do not think upon the things of man, but those of God."[5] Ambrose clearly enough makes virgins equal to Angels: [the Gloss on I Corinthians 7, 26[6]] makes them higher than Angels, saying these words: "Virginity, by which men are assimilated to Angels, surpasses the condition of human nature. Yet the victory of virgins is greater than that of the Angels. For the Angels live without flesh, but virgins triumph in the flesh."[7]

Cyprian agrees with all these men, who in the book, *On the Dress of Virgins*, near the end of the book when addressing virgins, says these words: "It is the word of the Lord which says, The children of this world beget and are begotten; but they who are counted worthy of that world, and of the resurrection from the dead, neither marry nor are given in marriage: neither shall they die any more: for they are equal to the Angels of God, being the children of the resurrection.[8] That which we shall be, you have already begun to be. You possess already in this world the glory of the resurrection. You pass through the world without the contagion of the world; in that you continue chaste and virgins, you are equal to the Angels of God. Only let your virginity remain and endure substantial and uninjured; and as it began bravely, let it persevere continuously."[9]

Behold the testimonies of holy and very learned men, who say that the state of virginity is an Angelic life, and they make the virgins equal to the Angels, nay in some respect greater.

---

[1] Cf. Lk. 1, 28.

[2] N. 8 (PL 183, 442B).

[3] St. Pashasius Radbert is the author of this work which was formerly attributed to St. Jerome

[4] Letter 9 (*Ad Paulam et Eustochium*), c. 5 (PL 30, 126D-127A).

[5] *Exhortatio virginitatis*, c. 4, n. 19 (PL 16, 342B).

[6] St. Ambrose in his *On Widows* is cited here, very probably because that work is cited in the gloss on the preceding verse.

[7] *Glossa Ordinaria* (PL 114, 531A).

[8] Cf. Lk. 20, 35-36.

[9] N. 22 (PL 4, 462A).

Therefore let Calvin cease to be enraged against us, and to calumniate us, because we place virgins before the married, and we compare them to Angels. He who shall have desired more things against this heresy may read the first book of Blessed Jerome of the two which he wrote against Jovinian. For there he employed all the powers of his eloquence for the vindication of virginity: and he extolled it to such an extent that to some (although undeservedly) it seems not equal enough to matrimony. Blessed Augustine also wrote a book for the vindication of the same virginity, which is entitled, *On Holy Virginity*.

UNCTIONIS EXTREMAE SACRAMENTUM
Sacrament of Extreme Unction

The Sacrament of Extreme Unction was trampled upon by the heretics no less than the others. For the Greeks, Guy the Carmelite bearing witness, assert that this Sacrament does not benefit the sick as to the health of the body.[1] The Waldensians, however, (as Aeneas Sylvius bears witness in his book, *De origine Bohemorum*[2]) do not admit Extreme Unction among the Sacraments of the Church. Yet Guy does not mention this error when he enumerates the errors of the Waldensians. Brother Bernard of Luxemburg in his *Catalogus haereticorum* pins this error upon the Heracleonites, but I do not know his source: because Augustine when speaking about the Heracleonites, does not attribute any such thing to them. Philastrius when discussing these same heretics, makes no mention of this error. Guy who imitates Augustine and Isidore [of Seville] when listing the heresies, never mentions this such that he would pin it upon the Heracleonites.[3]

I omit that good man [Bernard of Luxemburg] who in his *Catalogo haereticorum*, confuses Heracleonites with Hierarchite heretics, thinking that they are the same, only differing in name. It is evident, however, from Augustine and Isidore that they are different sects, waging war under one and another leaders. For when Augustine discusses the Heracleonites in chapter sixteen of his book, *De haeresibus ad Quodvultdeus*,[4] he says that they are so-called from Heracleon, their leader. But the leader of the Hierarchites he calls Hieracha, and he discusses them in chapter forty-seven. And those things which the *Catalogo* relates about the Heracleonites, whom he thinks are also called Hierarchites, are taken from this chapter forty-seven of Augustine, and they are described by the very same words of Augustine, unless because the good man inserted from his own imagination some things, such as regarding this Sacrament of Extreme Unction, about which he says that they assert that it was not instituted by God: even though Augustine, does not accuse either Heracleonites or the Hierarchites of anything of the sort.

Wherefore I do not cease to be amazed that Josse Clichtove, a man other very learned, was deceived in the same way, attributing this error to the Heracleonites, as the *Catalogo* had done. For in that book which he made in support of the assertion of the truths defined at the Council of Sens, in the chapter of the Sacraments of the Church, when discussing the Sacrament of Extreme Unction, he says that to deny that Extreme Unction is a Sacrament was the error of the Heracleonites.[5] And yet Josse when disputing in the same chapter about the Sacrament of Baptism, testifies that in censuring the heretics he imitates that description of

---

[1] *Summa de haeresibus*, fol. 25r, c. 16.
[2] Chapter 35.
[3] Etymologies, b. 8, c. 5, n. 68 (PL 82, 304B).
[4] PL 42, 28.
[5] *Compendium veritatum ad fidem pertinentium...*, c. 15, fol. 81r.

heretics which Guy the Carmelite made, about that Guy we have already said that he does not accuse the Heracleonites of any such thing. Josse Clichtove accuses this same error to John Wycliffe, although in the Council of Constance, in which his errors are condemned, he was not censured for this error: but in the writings of Thomas Netter which very carefully investigated the errors of this Wycliffe, I find a certain trace of this error.

Yet concerning Luther it is certainly evident that he rejected the Sacrament of Extreme Unction: because he denies that it ought to be counted among the Sacraments. For in that book, *The Babylonian Captivity*, he says these words: "I, however, say that if folly has ever been uttered, it has been uttered [about Extreme Unction]."[1] And again in the same place: It is a figment, from this sentence of the Apostle, "Is any man sick among you?" etc. (James 5, 14) that a man ought to be anointed by us, since it is not a Sacrament, but a figment.[2] All the others who gave their names to Luther, agreed with this man: Martin Bucer, Philip Melanchthon, and many others whom it would take a long time to list.

John Calvin in his work which he called *The Institutes of Christian Religion*, in chapter nineteen after he denied that that anointing, about which James the Apostle speaks, is a Sacrament, and said that it does not pertain to the present time, but only to the time of the Apostles, and was merely the grace of healing, says these words: "Even were it granted that this precept of unction, which has nothing to do with the present age, were perfectly adapted to it, they will not even thus have advanced much in support of their unction, with which they have hitherto besmeared us. James would have all the sick to be anointed: these men besmear, with their oil, not the sick, but half-dead carcasses, when life is quivering on the lips, or, as they say, *in extremis*.[3] If they have a present cure in their Sacrament, with which they can either alleviate the bitterness of disease, or at least give some solace to the soul, they are cruel in never curing in time. James would have the sick man to be anointed by the elders of the Church. They admit no anointer but a priestling."[4]

Nevertheless, although Calvin may bark, and resist with all his strength, we ourselves will prove, with God as the guide, that that unction, whereby the sick are anointed according to the rite indicated by Blessed James, is a true Sacrament instituted by Jesus Christ, and has everything which is required for the full nature of a Sacrament. For this is clear because Mark the Evangelist when describing the execution of the that commandment, when Christ sent the twelve Apostles two by two, giving them a certain rule of legation which they ought to follow, says: "And going forth they preached that men should do penance: and they cast out many devils, and anointed with oil many that were sick, and healed them" (6, 12-13).

Now the Apostles made this anointing with oil not on their own authority or out of presumption, but by Christ's command; hence it is proved, piously and in a Christian manner, because one ought not to believe that the Apostles in such and so great a legation would exceed the form of the commandment given to them by Christ. For if they had done something in that legation which was not commanded them, afterwards when they returned to Christ, they would have been rightly reprehended by Him, because since they were disciples, they did not want to be above their teacher, trying to do that about which they had not been instructed by Him. For about this matter, lest they would do something similar, He then admonished them, as Matthew relates, speaking thus: "The disciple is not above the master, nor the servant above his lord" (10, 24). But the Apostles when returning to Christ from this legation,

---

[1] WA 6, 568, lns. 8-9.
[2] WA 5, 570, lns. 29-31. Luther's actual words are: "Nevertheless we boast that this Sacrament, or rather figment, of ours, is founded on and proved by the teaching of the Apostle, from which it is as widely separated as pole from pole."
[3] This Latin phrase, *in extremis*, means "at the point of death."
[4] N. 21 (CR 29, 1080).

as Mark testifies, "related to him all things that they had done and taught" (6, 30): and yet they were not reprehended by Christ about this anointing with oil for the healing of the sick. Now when Christ sent them to preach, as Matthew says, commanded them to "heal the sick" (10, 8), and since the Apostles themselves executing this command healed the sick with oil, and returning to Christ, and relating this to Him, were not reprehended by Him, it is thence proved that this anointing with oil was commanded them by Christ. If they anointed the sick with oil, and healed with this anointing, not on their own authority, but by Christ's command, they were doing it not by the natural power of the oil: because even though oil is medicinal in some sicknesses, still not in all: because there are many sicknesses, in which oil can be harmful rather than beneficial.

Next, if oil could have given the healing from its natural power, no confirmation or preparation of the Gospel teaching could have been taken from that healing, as it was taken from other works of theirs miraculously done, the power for which Christ gave them for confirming the word [of the Gospel], when He sent them to preach the Gospel. Even if this were a natural power of the oil such that it could aid all sicknesses, still it could not give in the same way the health of the soul. Now Christ when He sent the Apostles to preach, did not make them surgeons or doctors, such that they could heal only bodies: but rather the souls. For Christ Himself, their teacher, as all the holy Doctors concordantly teach, did not heal anyone in the body, to whom He did not give the health of the soul, so that He could truly say, that He "healed the whole man on the sabbath day" (Jn. 7, 23).

From all these things it is established that that anointing of oil commanded by Christ to the Apostles and done by them, had the nature of this Sacrament, because it was instituted more for the health of the soul, and of the body. And not only Scholastic theologians give testimony for this our and the Catholic assertion, whom these heretics disdain, and call tricentenary, but also the ancient, holy as well as learned Doctors, a number of whom I will presently cite. Bede in his commentaries on Mark, when interpreting those words, by which he says that the Apostles anointed many sick with oil, says these words: "James the Apostle says: 'Is any man sick among you? Let him bring in the priests of the church, and let them pray over him, anointing him with oil in the name of the Lord...and if he be in sins, they shall be forgiven him' (5, 14-15). Wherefore it is evident from the Apostles themselves, that it is an ancient custom of the holy Church that persons possessed or afflicted with any disease whatever, should be anointed with oil consecrated by priestly blessing."[1] In which words there are many things which one ought to notice. The first is that he says that the oil with which the Apostles, while Christ was alive, anointed the sick, is the same as that about which James the Apostle speaks. The second is that that oil ought to be consecrated by pontifical blessing, and this not from a recent ordinance of the Church, but from the tradition of the Apostles. From which opinion Calvin and all the other Lutherans, who mock and ridicule this pontifical blessing of oil are refuted.

Theophylactus when interpreting the aforesaid words of Mark, says: "Only Mark relates that the Apostles anointed with oil, but James, the brother of the Lord, says this in his Catholic epistle: 'Is any man sick among you? Let him bring in the priests of the church, and let them pray over him, anointing him with oil.' Therefore, in addition to being a help in labors, the fuel of light, and the cause of gladness, oil also signifies the grace of the Holy Ghost, by which we are eased from our labors, and receive light and spiritual joy."[2] In which words one particularly ought to note that he says that that oil is a sign of spiritual grace. Which sentence is enough for proving that that anointing is a Sacrament, according to the definition of a Sacrament which has been accepted by all, and is the following: A Sacrament is a sensible sign

---

[1] *In Evangelium S. Marci*, bk. 2, c. 6 (PL 92, 188B).
[2] PG 123, 550B-C.

UNCTIONIS EXTREMAE SACRAMENTUM

signifying by Divine institution grace, which God promises to give to all receiving it. Calvin, nevertheless, and the rest of the Lutherans deny that grace is given in such an anointing, and that any promise of this grace was given by God.

But besides Theophylactus, let those who contradict on this point listen to [Pseudo-] Jerome, who in his commentaries on Mark, when interpreting those aforesaid words, says these words: "Then the twelve Apostles are sent, and power is given them of teaching the precepts, so that words may accompany deeds at the same time: and visible powers mix with invisible promises: and when they anointed the sick, they strengthen the sick by the power of faith."[1] [Pseudo-] Jerome says that the power of that anointing is to strengthen the sick by the power of faith: he also says that invisible promises are mixed with visible powers. I will cite below still many testimonies of other holy men in the other section, which could also be of service on this matter, if the diligent reader considers them well. From all these things it is very clearly proved that what Calvin and the rest of those of the same ilk say, that that anointing belonged to the time of the Apostles, in which the grace of healing was confined, and not to this age of ours, in which such grace does not abound. For Bede says that that from the Apostles until his time that anointing with oil consecrated by episcopal blessed perdured in the Church. And James the Apostle who moved by the Divine Spirit explained this anointing, did not prescribe any time for its exercise and power: but he spoke without any limitation of time. Therefore you Lutherans, who are accustomed to so persistently demand God's word from us in everything, give to us God's word which says that that anointing was given for only that time. Now since you could not show this word, it follows that according to your teaching, one ought not to believe you on this point: because in support of your opinion you bring forth no word of God.

Next, that that anointing ought not to be called merely the grace of healing, is proved from the fact that it was not given merely for the cure of the body, but for increasing the soul's grace, so that the soul may be stronger at the time in which the devil is accustomed to more diligently and strongly tempt to sin. For it is evident that at the time of the Apostles not all priests had this grace of healing: because diverse are, as Paul says, the gifts of graces.[2] For to some are given, says Paul, the grace of healing, but not to all. But James speaks of all priests, exhorting them to anoint the sick: therefore that anointing of which James speaks, has something more than the grace of healing, namely the grace whereby venial sins are forgiven, but because the testimonies of whatsoever men, even of holy and very learned men, move these heretics but little, even though elsewhere they try with all their might to be helped by their approbations, hence I now wish to bring forth a very clear testimony of Sacred Scripture against them.

Blessed James pronounces a very clear testimony against this heresy, who in his canonical epistle speaks thus: "Is any man sick among you? Let him bring in the priests of the church, and let them pray over him, anointing him with oil in the name of the Lord. And the prayer of faith shall save the sick man: and the Lord shall raise him up: and if he be in sins, they shall be forgiven him" (5, 14-15). Notice the proclamation made by James the Apostle. For from the Apostle's words it is established that in the conferral of Extreme Unction everything which is required for a complete Sacrament is present. For there is there the matter, namely the holy oil with which the sick man is anointed. The form is also expressed, namely the prayer of the priest. Now he stated the effect of this Sacrament, when saying: "And if he be in sins, they shall be forgiven him."

But Luther seeing that he is refuted by this testimony, attempts to reject it, such that he denies that this epistle is of James the Apostle. And if it were of James, he says that it is not

---

[1] *Commentarius in Marcum*, c. 6 (PL 30, 608A).
[2] Cf. I Cor. 12, 4.

UNCTIONIS EXTREMAE SACRAMENTUM

allowed for the Apostle to institute a Sacrament on his own authority, meaning to give a Divine promise with the adjoined sign, since this is the proper function of Christ alone. He therefore tries to weaken this testimony of the Apostle in two ways: firstly, that this epistle is does not belong to James the Apostle; then, and if it were the Apostle's, he says that he did not have the power for instituting a Sacrament. We have confuted (as I think) the first of these above in chapter two of book one, when we disputed about the canonical books of Scripture. For in that place we showed from many decrees of the councils that this Epistle of James the Apostle was put in the list of canonical books. Hence let us come to that in which he openly opposes the Apostles, saying: and if it were James the Apostle's, still it was not allowed for the Apostle to institute a Sacrament.

It is now not surprising that Luther reviles the [Roman] pontiff and the emperor with insults, since he accuses an Apostle of such an atrocious crime, namely that he dared to institute a Sacrament without authority and contrary to Divine law. Certainly no one was ever so demented, and a wicked reviler, who would say that an Apostle was so audacious, that that he would give for a Sacrament what was not a Sacrament. Otherwise, that he says that an Apostle does not have the power of instituting a Sacrament, we also acknowledge: although it is the opinion of others, which does not please me at all, that the Church could institute a Sacrament. Thus we say that the Apostle did not institute the Sacrament, but handed it down by those words to the people that which he had received from Christ, Who wanted to make known some things to the world through Matthew, other things through Mark, other things through Luke, other things again through John. For there are certain things which particular to each Evangelist, of which none of the others mention: about which matter there are the canons published by Eusebius of Caesarea.[1] Therefore, what prevents that Christ also willed to make known to us certain things the His Apostle James, about which neither the Evangelists spoke not a word about? Especially since it is evident that he made known many things to us though the Apostle Paul, which are completely omitted by the Evangelists.

Now we so induce by this testimony of [Pseudo-] Augustine, who in the second book of *De visitatione infirmorum*, when teaching that the sick man ought to confess, receive the Eucharist, and be anointed with holy oil, speaks thus: "That precept of James the Apostle ought not to passed over: 'Is any man sick among you? Let him bring in the priests of the church, and let them pray over him, anointing him with oil in the name of the Lord. And the prayer of faith shall save the sick man: and the Lord shall raise him up: and if he be in sins, they shall be forgiven him.' Therefore, desire that of you, and for you, so it may be done as James the Apostle, yea rather Our Lord by His Apostle did say, for surely the anointing with holy oil is understood to be a figurative anointing of the Holy Ghost."[2] In which words one ought to notice that he says, "yea rather Our Lord by His Apostle did say." By which words he indicates clearly enough that James the Apostle was merely the herald of the Sacrament, not however the institutor.

Furthermore, Pope Innocent I, in a letter to Decentius, Bishop of Gubbio, in the last chapter, speaks thus: "Moreover, because you sought advice about this, as about other things, my own son Celestine the deacon has also written a letter about what you raised concerning the passage in the letter of the Blessed Apostle James: 'Is any man sick among you? Let him bring in the priests of the church, and let them pray over him, anointing him with oil in the name of the Lord. And the prayer of faith shall save the sick man: and the Lord shall raise him up: and if he be in sins, they shall be forgiven him.' There is no doubt but that this ought to be received and understood as referring to the faithful who are ailing, who can be anointed with

---

[1] Eusebius drew up ten tables (*kanones*) dividing the Gospels into ten sections, to show at a glance where each Gospel agreed with or differed from the others.

[2] PL 40, 1154

the holy oil of chrism, which has been made by the bishop, to be used not only by priests, but by all Christians by anointing in their own or others' necessity. Otherwise we see that it is superfluous to add that doubtlessly a bishop is able to do what is it permitted for a priest to do. The passage here mentions priests because the bishops, because the bishops impeded by other duties, are unable to go to all the sick. Still, if the bishop either can visit or have the person brought who is worthy to be visited by him, let him whose very job it is to make chrism visit and bless and touch the sick with chrism without delay."[1] Pope Innocent was in fact a man illustrious for holiness as well as for learning. From whose words it is evident that the institution of this Sacrament is not recent (as Luther imagines). For Innocent governed the universal Church than a thousand and one hundred years before, who based upon the Apostle James' testimony teaches that the sick ought to be anointed with holy oil.

But for a fuller clarification of this matter, let the reader attend to what Bede says when interpreting the previously quoted words of James in his commentaries on the Canonical Epistles. For upon those words, "And let them pray over him, anointing him with oil in the name of the Lord," he says these words: "We read in the Gospel that the Apostles also did this.[2] And now the custom of the Church holds that those who are sick be anointed with consecrated oil by the presbyters, with the prayer that goes with this, so that they may be cured. Not only for the presbyters, but, as Pope Innocent writes, even for all Christians it is lawful to use the same oil for anointing at their own necessity or that of others, but the oil may be consecrated only by bishops. For what he says, 'with oil in the name of the Lord,' means with oil consecrated in the name of the Lord or at least that when they anoint the sick person they ought also to invoke the name of the Lord over him at the same time."[3]

In which words one also ought to note those two things, which we noted above on the other words of his from his commentaries on Mark. But that saying of Innocent where he grants to all Christians, that they could use this blessed oil, "anointing at their own necessity or that of others," ought to be understood that it is permitted for any Christian, that when a necessity occurs he can anoint himself or others with that oil, if the devout affection for that oil motivates him to do this, and hence he hopes that he can attain health from it. Nevertheless, it ought not to be so understood, that any Christian so anointing with the sick with that oil, confects the Sacrament of [Extreme] Unction; because the pope cannot grant this to any Christian, that he can be the minister of this Sacrament, because by Divine institution it can only be administered by a priest. Now that he granted only this can easily be gathered from the words of Innocent himself. For he merely granted that they be anointed with oil, not however that they would say the words by which this Sacrament is confected.

About which thing it was necessary to point out to the reader on account of Calvin's calumnies. For he in the place cited above when speaking about Extreme Unction, and wanting to prove that it is not a Sacrament, and that only priests are its ministers, he says these words: "For they relate that Pope Innocent, who presided over the Church of Rome in the age of Augustine, ordained, that not priests only, but all Christians, should use oil in anointing, in their own necessity, or in that of others. Our authority for this is Sigebert [of Gembloux], in his *Chronicles*."[4] Calvin clearly states that he did not read Innocent, but learned it from Sigebert's *Chronicles*: but if he had read Innocent directly, and he would not have wanted to agree with his opinion; he obviously had understood that the anointing with oil described by Blessed James, which also includes words, can only be administered by priests or bishops: but this notwithstanding that he granted the mere simple use of oil to any Christian, who did not grant

---

[1] C. 8 (PL 56, 517B-518B).

[2] Cf. Mk. 6, 13.

[3] *Commentary on the Seven Catholic Epistles* (PL 93, 39C-D).

[4] C. 19, n. 21 (CR 29, 1081).

[this] so that they might do the rest of the things of which, when done by a valid minister, the Sacrament stands together whole.

Finally, the definition of the Catholic Church confirms this very thing, which until this very day always and everywhere has judged that Extreme Unction is one of the seven Sacraments received by it. For the Council of Florence celebrated under Eugene IV, speaks thus:

The fifth Sacrament is Extreme Unction, whose matter is the olive oil blessed by the bishop. This Sacrament should be given only to the sick of whose death there is fear; and he should be anointed in the following places: on the eyes because of sight, on the ears because of hearing, on the nostrils because of smell, on the mouth because of taste and speech, on the hands because of touch, on the feet because of gait, on the loins because of the delight that flourishes there. The form of this sacrament is the following: *Per istam sanctam unctionem et suam piissimam misericordiam indulgeat tibi Dominus, quidquid per visum*, etc. (Through this holy anointing and his most kind mercy may the Lord forgive you whatever through it, etc.). And similarly on the other members. The minister of this Sacrament is the priest. Now the effect is the healing of the soul and, moreover, in so far as it is expedient for the soul, of the body itself also.[1]

But much more copiously and clearly the Council of Trent discusses about this Sacrament, which in the fourth session celebrated under Julian III, for there were many more other sessions in the same Council under Paul III his predecessor, gave this teaching about this Sacrament:

It has seemed fit to the holy Synod to add to the preceding doctrine on Penance the following matters concerning the Sacrament of Extreme Unction, which was considered by the Fathers the consummation not only of penance, but also of the whole Christian life which should be a perpetual penance. In the first place, therefore, as regards its institution it declares and teaches that our most clement Redeemer, who wished that a provision be made for salutary remedies at all times for His servants against all the weapons of all enemies, just as He made provision for the greatest aids in other Sacraments by which Christians, as long as they live, can preserve themselves free from every very grave spiritual injury, so He fortified the end of life with, as it were, the most powerful defense, by the Sacrament of Extreme Unction. For, although 'our adversary seeks' and seizes throughout our entire life occasions 'to devour'[2] our souls in every manner, yet there is no time when he directs more earnestly all the strength of his cunning to ruin us completely, and if possible to drive us also from trust in the divine mercy, than when he sees that the end of life is upon us.

This sacred unction for the sick, however, was instituted by Christ our Lord as truly and properly a Sacrament of the New Testament, alluded to in Mark,[3] indeed, but recommended to the faithful and promulgated by James the Apostle and brother of the Lord. 'Is any man,' he says, 'sick among you? Let him bring in the priests of the Church, and let them pray over him, anointing him with oil in the name of the Lord and the prayer of faith shall save the sick man, and the Lord shall raise him up; and if he be in sins, they shall be forgiven him' (James 5, 14-15). In these words, as the Church has learned from Apostolic tradition transmitted from hand to hand, he teaches the matter, form, proper ministration, and effect of this salutary Sacrament. For the Church has understood that the matter is the oil blessed by the bishop, since the unction very appropriately represents the grace of the Holy Ghost, with which the soul of the sick person is visibly anointed; and that these words are the form: 'By this holy anointing...'

Furthermore, the significance and effect of this sacrament are explained in these words: 'And the prayer of faith shall save the sick man, and the Lord shall raise him up, and if he

---

[1] Dz. 700.

[2] Cf. I Pet. 5, 8.

[3] Cf. Mk. 6, 13.

UNCTIONIS EXTREMAE SACRAMENTUM

be in sins they shall be forgiven him' (James 5, 15). For the thing signified is the grace of the Holy Ghost, Whose anointing wipes away sins, if there be any still to be expiated, and the remains of sin, and relieves, and strengthens the soul of the sick person by exciting in him great confidence in the Divine mercy, supported by which the sick person bears more lightly the miseries and pains of his illness, and resists more easily the temptations of the evil spirit who lies in wait for His heel,[1] and sometimes attains bodily health, when it is expedient for the salvation of the soul.

And now, as regards the prescribing of those who can receive and administer this Sacrament, this, too, was clearly expressed in the words above. For it is also indicated there that the proper ministers of this Sacrament are the presbyters of the Church, under which name in that place are to be understood not the elders by age or the foremost in rank among the people, but either bishops or priests duly ordained by them with the 'imposition of the hands of the priesthood' (I Tim. 4, 14). It is also declared that this unction is to be applied to the infirm, but especially to those who are so dangerously ill that they seem to be facing the end of life, for which reason it is also called the Sacrament of the dying. But if the sick should recover after the reception of this Sacrament of Extreme Unction, they can with the aid of this Sacrament be strengthened again, when they fall into another similar crisis of life. Therefore, under no condition are they to be listened to, who contrary to so open and clear a statement of the Apostle James[2] teach that this unction is either a figment of the imagination or a rite received from the Fathers, having neither a command of God nor a promise of grace; and likewise those who assert that this has now ceased, as though it were to be referred to the grace of healing only in the primitive Church; and those who maintain that the rite and practice which the holy Roman Church observes in the administration of this Sacrament are opposed to the thought of James the Apostle, and therefore ought to be changed to another; and finally, those who affirm that this Extreme Unction may be contemned by the faithful for all these things very manifestly disagree with the clear words of this great Apostle. Nor, indeed, does the Roman Church, the mother and teacher of all others, observe anything else in the administration of this unction with reference to those matters which constitute the substance of this Sacrament than what the blessed James has prescribed. Nor, indeed, could there be contempt for so great a Sacrament without grievous sin and offense to the Holy Ghost.[3]

But lest anyone teach or temerariously dare to speak in any way against this, it issued four canons containing an automatic sentence of anathema against the temerarious assertors, and they are those which follow:

If anyone says that Extreme Unction is not truly and properly a Sacrament instituted by our Lord Jesus Christ, and promulgated by Blessed James the Apostle, but is only a rite accepted by the Fathers, or a human fiction: let him be anathema.

If anyone says that the sacred anointing of the sick does not confer grace nor remit sins, nor alleviate the sick, but that it has already ceased, as if it had at one time only been a healing grace: let him be anathema.

If anyone says that the rite of Extreme Unction and its practice, which the holy Roman Church observes, is opposed to the statement of the Blessed Apostle James, and that it is therefore to be changed, and can be contemned without sin by Christians: let him be anathema.

If anyone says that the priests of the Church, whom Blessed James exhorts to be brought to anoint the sick, are not the priests ordained by a bishop, but the elders by age in each com-

---

[1] Cf. Gen. 3, 15.
[2] Cf. James 5, 14.
[3] Dz. 907-910.

UNCTIONIS EXTREMAE SACRAMENTUM

munity, and that for this reason a priest alone is not the proper minister of Extreme Unction let him be anathema.[1]

These are the canons of the Council of Trent about the Sacrament of Extreme Unction. Among which the first thing that ought to be noted by Catholics is, as they may understand from it, that the opinion was rejected of certain Scholastic theologians saying that the Sacrament of Extreme Unction was instituted by Blessed James. Which opinion, as I said in the beginning of this section, never pleased me: and although before the definition of this Council it could be upheld in any way whatsoever without the crime of heresy, yet now it is not permitted to be upheld without heresy.

But it is necessary that we respond to the heretics' objections, even though they are so ridiculous that they could be rightly reckoned to be undeserving of a response. Calvin in the place cited above objects these words to us: "Why do they not dedicate some pool of Siloe,[2] into which, at certain seasons the sick may plunge themselves? [That, they say, would be done in vain. Certainly not more in vain than unction.] Why do they not lay themselves on the dead, seeing that Paul, in raising up the dead youth, lay upon him? Why is not clay made of dust and spittle a Sacrament?"[3] And the Wittenbergers support themselves with the same argument in the confession of faith which they presented at the Council of Trent.[4] This argument of all the Lutherans very clearly shows the ignorance of them all: because it is so argued, as if we say that Extreme Unction is a Sacrament merely because the Apostles when anointing with it were conferring to the sick the healing of the body. Yet we do not say that it is a Sacrament because the Apostles by that anointing were conferring health of the body to the sick: but because when they were healing bodies in this way, they were strengthening the soul unto good, which God was then giving to the sick through the ministry of the Apostles, and now confers through the ministry of other priests. The clay, with which the blind man was anointed, had no power of healing, or if it did have any, then it merely contained it, when Christ spread it on the eyes of the blind man: and afterwards it would not have given sight to any blind man, even if anyone else was smeared and afterwards would have washed in the pool of Siloe. Let it be conceded that it gave sight of the body to the blind man, yet it does not follow therefrom that it conferred grace: because God had given no promise about these things, and hence it could not be called a Sacrament, since there would be lacking a Divine promise about the giving of grace. And we say completely the same thing about the pool of Siloe. But that anointing whereby the Apostles were anointing the sick, perdures until the end of the world, will always have equal power in regard to the soul, to which it pertains rather than to the body, from God's promise, which God Himself manifested through James His minister and herald. "And if he be in sins," James says, "they shall be forgiven him." Behold God's promise: because such a remission of sins cannot be given except by God, and is never given without the conferral of grace. Now such a great Apostle would never have dared to give that promise of the forgiveness of sins, unless he were inspired by God, Who alone can give the forgiveness of sins. And hence the lie of the Wittenbergers is very clearly proved,

---

[1] Dz. 926-929.

[2] Cf. Jn. 9, 7.

[3] C. 19, n. 19 (CR 29, 178).

[4] "We confess that the Apostles anointed the sick with oil, and that the sick recovered their bodily health… But these things were then practiced profitably, when as yet the ministers of the Church were endowed with the gift of healing the sick corporally, and wonderfully. But after this gift ceased, the Gospel being confirmed in the Church, the thing itself does witness, this ceremony of anointing is now idly and unfruitfully used. For those who now are anointed, are not accustomed from the anointing to obtain bodily health: yea, this anointing is not used but on them, of whose bodily health men do despair" (The Wittenberg Confession, *Monumentorum ad historiam Concilii Tridentini*, vol. 4, p. 442).

who when discussing in their confession of faith about Extreme Unction say that there does not exist any word of God which will promise, when Christ's Gospel has been spread abroad, that Extreme Unction avails for forgiving sins.

Secondly Calvin objects as follows: "They affirm, indeed, that there is still the same virtue in their unction, but we experience differently."[1] The Wittenbergers say the same thing in their confession of faith. And all these men also show miserable ignorance in this argument of theirs, as well as in the preceding. For they so argue as if we would say that the indubitable effect of this Sacrament, and its true sign, is the healing of the body: and hence they say that they know by certain experience, that there is not such a power of conferring bodily health in this Sacrament, because they see many who after having received the anointing are more weighed down by their sickness, far from being healed. But we say that the indubitable effect of this Sacrament is the consolation of the soul and strength through the grace which God always, unless bad will impedes, confers to the soul of the sick man, so that he can strongly resist the demons then strongly tempting. Now whether or not God confers this grace to the sick after the anointing has been received, neither Calvin nor the Wittenbergers can experience: because God's grace is concealed from human experience, the health of the body however even though it is often conferred by the Sacrament of anointing, still there is not a certain and indubitable effect: because [bodily health] does not have God's promise, except [the health] which God best foresees is more conducive for the health of the soul, which latter [health] the Sacrament rather regards.

Thirdly Calvin objects to us, saying these words: "James would have all the sick to be anointed: these men besmear, with their oil, not the sick, but half-dead carcasses, when life is quivering on the lips, or, as they say, *in extremis*. If they have a present cure in their Sacrament, with which they can either alleviate the bitterness of disease, or at least give some solace to the soul, they are cruel in never curing in time."[2] The Wittenbergers make exactly the same argument against us, yet in fewer words they contrive a greater calumny, saying that we are not accustomed to administer this anointing, "but on them, of whose bodily health men do despair."[3] But this argument proceeds from the same ignorance from which the two other preceding ones also proceeded, and moreover they add a false calumny. For they always argue as if we said that a certain and indubitable effect of this Sacrament is bodily health, and as though they teach us, that this Sacrament was instituted for this, so that it would only be medicine for bodies, and not for souls.

Now that they say that we administer this anointing only to those who are imperiled *in extremis*, or "on them, of whose bodily health men do despair," is clearly a calumny, and a very open lie. For the rule or custom of the Church does not hold this, but teaches and exhorts that all who have a likely danger of death on account of sickness may receive this anointing of holy oil: and then they receive the strength of grace through this Sacrament, when they are tempted more strongly by the devil. And for this same reason this Sacrament is not administered in petty or light sicknesses: because since the devil does not always use such strong temptation, as when death is near, hence a man does not need very powerful help of God's grace, so that one can resist the devil: but the Divine grace which he acquired through the other Sacraments is enough for him, or one can then acquire, through repentance.

Perhaps these heretics looking at the name of Extreme Unction, thought that it is given only to those who are imperiled *in extremis*: because it is called Extreme Unction. But if they so conclude from the name, they are greatly deceived: because not for that reason is it called "extreme" [or "last" anointing]: but because it is the last among the four anointings which the

---

[1] C. 19, n. 19 (CR 29, 178).

[2] *Ibid.*, n. 21 (CR 29, 1080).

[3] The Wittenberg Confession, *Monumentorum ad historiam Concilii Tridentini*, vol. 4, p. 442.

UNCTIONIS EXTREMAE SACRAMENTUM

Church is accustomed to administer to all Christians. For even though the Church has more than four anointings, nevertheless it decided which ones priests and bishops administer not to all Christians, but to some particular ones. Now there are only four which the Church is ready to administer at the appropriate times to all Christians: and the last of these is that whereby the sick are anointed by the hands of the priests. The first is that whereby catechumens are anointed: the second whereby those after having been baptized are anointed: the third is whereby those who receive the Sacrament of Confirmation are anointed: the fourth and last, whereby the ill are anointed by the hands of the priests, when they have some danger of death: and because this is the last, wherefore it is called Extreme Unction by more recent theologians, which by the old Fathers was called the anointing of the ill or the sick.

Fourthly Calvin objects to us, saying the following: "James would have the sick man to be anointed by the elders of the Church. They admit no anointer but a priestling."[1] In which words he openly accuses us about the minister of this Sacrament, whom we say is only the priest: but he, although he concedes that this anointing is a Sacrament, he says that not only a priest is the minister of the Sacrament: because James says, "Let him bring in the priests [or presbyters]," which word since it is Greek, and it means those we call elders [*seniores*] in Latin: but Sacred Scripture judges these men not by age, but by wisdom, and often calls not those who have many years of age, but those who are rich with much wisdom "presbyters" or elders: and because it behooves him who has been adorned with the priestly dignity to be wise, hence it calls priests presbyters rather than others in Sacred Scripture.

Wherefore [Pseudo-] Pope Anacletus a presbyter ordained by Blessed Peter the Apostle, when discussing in the second epistle those who should be chosen to be priests, says these words: "And then it was commanded to Moses that he choose presbyters.[2] Hence it is also said in Proverbs: 'The dignity of old men, their grey hairs' (Prov. 20, 29). But these gray hairs designate wisdom, about which it was written: "The understanding of a man is grey hairs" (Wis. 4, 8). And although we read that men had lived nine hundred and more years from Adam to Abraham, no other was called a presbyter, that is an elder, except Abraham, who is shown to have lived many fewer years. Therefore, not on account of decrepit old age, but on account of wisdom were they named presbyters."[3] From whose words it is evident that all priests were called presbyters because those who were chosen for the priesthood ought to be wise. For Anacletus speaks about the choosing of priests when he said those words.

Besides, that Paul only calls priests presbyters is proved from those words with which he speaks to Titus, saying the following: "For this cause I left thee in Crete, that thou shouldest set in order the things that are wanting, and shouldest ordain priests in every city, as I also appointed thee" (1, 5). In which words he called bishops, who are also called priests, presbyters, as all the sacred Doctors teach. For Titus was left in Crete so that he would make priests through the imposition of his hands, and distribute them through the cities, so that each would be in charge of a city, and not one [bishop] for all [the cities]. But if "presbyters" is interpreted to mean elders, Paul's command will be absurd: because those who were not elders, he could not make elders [or elderly]. Thus because the word "presbyter" ought to be attributed to priests alone, in whom wisdom is especially necessary, James the Apostle called priests alone presbyters, when he said, "Let him bring in the priests of the church" etc. And Chrysostom

---

[1] C. 19, n. 21 (CR 29, 1080).

[2] Cf. Ex. 29, & Num. 11, 16: "Gather unto me seventy men of the ancients of Israel, whom thou knowest to be ancients and masters of the people."

[3] *False Decretals of the Pseudo-Isidore* (PL 130, 71C-D). "Two cardinals, John of Torquemada (1468) and Nicholas of Cusa (1464), declared the earlier documents to be forgeries, especially those purporting to be by Clement and Anacletus" ("False Decretals," *Catholic Encyclopedia* (New York, Robert Appleton Company, 1909), vol. 5, p. 773).

testifies that he spoke about them alone, who in the third book of *On the Priesthood*, when praising the priestly dignity, among many other things says these few words: "For not only at the time of regeneration, but afterwards also, they have authority to forgive sins. 'Is any man sick among you?' it is said, 'Let him bring in the priests of the church, and let them pray over him, anointing him with oil in the name of the Lord. And the prayer of faith shall save the sick man: and the Lord shall raise him up: and if he be in sins, they shall be forgiven him' (James 5, 14-15)."[1] In which words two things especially ought to be noticed. The first is that James in the aforesaid words only calls priests presbyters, for otherwise Chrysostom would have wrongly used the testimony of those words for proving the dignity of priests. The other thing is that he says that priests by that anointing forgive our sins. Therefore Calvin and the Wittenbergers, and all the other recent heretics, ought not to refer the anointing of the sick only to the time of the Apostles, or refer it only to the grace of healing, since sin are forgiven by it.

VOTUM

Vows

It was the opinion of certain heretics that nothing ought to be done out of necessity, but everything ought to be done freely, because the [Royal] Prophet said: "I will freely sacrifice to thee" (Ps. 53, 8). The authors of this heresy are the Lampetians,[2] who having been deceived by this idea, condemned all vows, saying that those things are of no utility, in that they seem to bring in a certain necessity and compulsion upon men. This heresy having been now buried for a long time, after many centuries was revived by the Apostolics, saying that those works which are done without a vow, are destined to a greater reward than those which are done out of necessity. John Wycliffe maintained the same heresy. The last defender of this heresy is now Martin Luther, whose words in the book, *On Monastic Vows*, are these: "Monastic vows, when they cannot be taught as being not more than and not other than faith, are ungodly, heathen, Jewish, sacrilegious, lying, erroneous, satanic, hypocritical, apostate, and even contrary to the examples of the saints. On these grounds they ought to be revoked and given up in complete confidence, even if they were taken with godly and serious intent."[3] But not being content with these things, so that he may show that he has conceived hatred towards monastic vows, and towards monks who profess such vows, he says these words in the same book: "I wish that all monasteries were rooted out, extinguished, and abolished… And would to God that through fire from heaven, through brimstone and pitch, like Sodom and Gomorrha, they would sink into the deepest abyss, so that their memory should die away. The whole world's curses and maledictions are here insufficient."[4] Luther, who had been a monk, and had returned from the monastery to the world, wanted that there would be no trace

---

[1] N. 6 (PG 48, 644).

[2] "The Lampetians taught that monasteries ought to be free, that is, without perpetual vows, as relates Damascene in the book of a hundred heresies, near the end (*De Haeresibus*, n. 98 (PG 94, 759B)). In our time Luther teaches the same thing about monastic vows; they cannot be vowed piously in monasteries, unless by this form: 'I vow chastity, poverty and obedience even to death, that is that I am able to change my mind when I wish'" (St. Robert Bellarmine, *Disputationes de controversiis christianae fidei*, bk. 4 (*On the Marks of the Church*), c. 9 (On the Sixth Mark), n. 19, p. 309).

[3] WA 8, 602-603.

[4] WA 8, 624, lns. 11-15. "In this and in many other places the Latin edition of Luther's words is milder than the original" (J. Verres, *Luther: An Historical Portrait* (New York, Burns & Oates, 1884), p. 156, footnote n. 45).

of any monastery, lest there would remain some testimony of his own apostacy. All the recent heretics have followed Luther on this point, nay on account of this heresy alone many monks from every Order have embraced the other heresies of this man.

When disputing against this heresy, we ought to prove two things from Holy Writ. The first is that vows once pronounced ought to be fulfilled in deed, and they ought not to be taken away by the choice of anyone. The other thing is that it is needful that a work performed from a vow yields a greater reward of the one performing, than if it had been done freely, and without the obligation from the vow. For the proof of the first point a sufficiently convincing testimony is that which the Lord says in the book of Numbers: "If any man make a vow to the Lord, or bind himself by an oath: he shall not make his word void but shall fulfill all that he promised" (Num. 30, 3). Furthermore, the same precept is found again more explicitly in the book of Deuteronomy, where it is thus said: "When thou hast made a vow to the Lord thy God, thou shalt not delay to pay it: because the Lord thy God will require it. And if thou delay, it shall be imputed to thee for a sin. If thou wilt not promise, thou shalt be without sin. But that which is once gone out of thy lips, thou shalt observe, and shalt do as thou hast promised to the Lord thy God, and hast spoken with thy own will and with thy own mouth" (Deut. 23, 21-23). And the Wise Man in Ecclesiastes says: "If thou hast vowed anything to God, defer not to pay it: for an unfaithful and foolish promise displeaseth him: but whatsoever thou hast vowed, pay it. And it is much better not to vow, than after a vow not to perform the things promised" (5, 3-4). Next the Lord, when speaking through the Prophet Baruch about the gods of the heathens, says: "And whether it be evil that one doth unto them, or good, they are not able to recompense it: neither can they set up a king nor put him down: in like manner they can neither give riches, nor requite evil. If a man make a vow to them, and perform it not, they cannot require it" (6, 33-34). From which words it is evident that God will require from him who has vowed a vow, if he does not perform it. And the Royal Prophet very often in his Psalms which he was singing to God, mentions vows, not that they ought to be taken away, but that they be fulfilled in deed and those things which were once promised to God be performed. "Offer to God the sacrifice of praise: and pay thy vows to the most High" (Ps. 49, 14). And again: "I will pay thee my vows, Which my lips have uttered" (Ps. 65, 13-14). And again: "Vow ye, and pay to the Lord your God: all you that are round about him bring presents" (Ps. 75, 12). Here you see how many testimonies there are from the Old Testament, which approve of vows.

But some of these heretics, namely the Lutherans, seeing such clear testimonies for the vindication of vows, flee to this refuge, namely that they say that vows binding for a certain time can be pronounced: because (as they say) through such vows men become slaves, whom God gave freedom. But these miserable men do not attend to the fact that to serve God is to reign, and that Christ did not free us from this servitude, but from the servitude of sin: which liberty no one has better, than he who serves God. For the Apostle says: "Being then freed from sin, we have been made servants of justice" (Rom. 6, 18). Furthermore, he who has married a wife, has entangled himself with an indissolvable bond, such that while the wife is alive he could not be separated from her, nor have an additional wife. Therefore, what prevents that something similar would happen in a perpetual vow? If that servitude, in which man enjoins upon himself, does not oppose the liberty given by Christ, nor also will that servitude which is undertaken by a vow oppose Christian liberty, especially because by marriage both spouses are subjected to each other; but by a vow one is subjected to God.

But now let us examine by way of Sacred Scriptures that perpetuity of vows which they detest. For which matter let us listen to what is said in the First Book of Kings about Anna, the mother of Samuel, before she conceived him: "And Heli the priest sitting upon a stool, before the door of the temple of the Lord: as Anna had her heart full of grief, she prayed to the Lord, shedding many tears, and she made a vow, saying: O Lord, of hosts, if thou wilt look down on the affliction of thy servant, and wilt be mindful of me, and not forget thy handmaid, and wilt give to thy servant a man child: I will give him to the Lord all the days of his life" (1, 9-11). Notice that you see the vow of the mother of the son consecrating to God unto the ministry of the Temple for all the days of his life: afterwards that vow merited to be heard, so far is the vow of that mother from having been condemned by God. And if Anna could pronounce such a perpetual vow about the son, whom she had not yet conceived, why could not anyone vow something similar about himself? Especially because anyone has more of a right over himself, and his will, than any mother over her son.

Furthermore, the Blessed Virgin Mother of pronounced a vow of perpetual virginity to be perpetually observed, which those words clearly testify which she replied to the Angel announcing the conception of the Son of God, saying: "How shall this be done, because I know not man?" (Lk. 1, 34). For that negation, adjoined by the word in the present tense, ought not to be so taken as though it merely denies the act of the present time, but so that she would say the vow in regard to the negation of the act thereafter. For otherwise there would not have been at hand any reason for doubting, and she would seem to have asked without an occasion: because that a woman who never knew man before, afterwards would conceive, is not something difficult, nor do those two things even apparently oppose each other. But a vow of perpetual virginity, and to conceive, seem as though they are diametrically opposed to each other. Hence with reason she asks: "How shall this be done, because I know not man?" that is, I have promised that I would not know a man.

Now some holy Doctors testify that this is the true and genuine meaning of the text. Blessed Bernard in the fourth homily on the Gospel, *Missus est*,[1] speaks thus: "She doubts not the fact, but only inquires about the manner of its accomplishment. She says not 'Will it be done?' but 'How will this be done?' As if she would say: 'Since my Lord knows, and my conscience bears me witness, that His handmaid has made a vow to know no man, by what law shall it please Him to work this wonder? If I must break my vow that I may bring forth such a Son, I rejoice on account of the Son, but I grieve because of my vow. Nevertheless, His will be done.'"[2]

And Venerable Bede, in his homily on the same Gospel, speaks thus: "How (Mary says) can it happen that I would conceive and give birth to a son, who have determined to finish my life in the chasteness of virginity? Now she does not ask, 'How can these things be accomplished,' as though incredulous of the words of the Angel, but certainly because it was necessary that what she then was hearing from the Angel, and what she read had previously been said by the prophet be fulfilled: but she inquires, in what way was it to be fulfilled: namely because the prophet who had predicted that this would come to be, did not say how it could happen, but reserved it to be said by the Angel."[3]

And Blessed Augustine in his book, *On Holy Virginity*, when speaking about the holy Mother of God, speaks thus: "Her virginity also itself was on this account more pleasing and accepted, in that it was not that Christ being conceived in her, rescued it beforehand from a husband who would violate it, Himself to preserve it; but, before He was conceived, chose it, already dedicated to God, as that from which to be born. This is shown by the words which Mary spoke in answer to the Angel announcing to her conception; 'How,' says she, 'shall this be, seeing I know not a man?' Which assuredly she would not say, unless she had before vowed herself unto God as a virgin. But, because the habits of the Israelites as yet refused this, she was espoused to a just man, who would not take from her by violence, but rather

---

[1] "The angel Gabriel was sent (*missus est*) from God into a city of Galilee, called Nazareth" (Lk. 1, 26).
[2] Hom. 4, (On Lk. 1, 32-38), n. 3 (PL 183, 80C-D).
[3] Hom. 1, On the feast of the Annunciation, (PL 94, 12B-C).

guard against violent persons, what she had already vowed."[1] Notice that we have brought forth testimonies of three holy Doctors, from which it is clearly evident that the Virgin Mother of God pronounced a keeping vow of perpetual virginity.

It is also believed that the Apostles pronounced this vow of keeping perpetual virginity, when having left all things they followed Christ. For so thinks Augustine who speaks thus: "For these mighty ones had said, 'Behold we have left all things, and have followed thee' (Mt. 19, 27). They had most mightily vowed this vow. But whence do they receive this, except from Him of whom it is here immediately said, 'Giving the vow to him that vows?'"[2] Again, this is very clearly proved from the testimony of Blessed Paul, who in the First Epistle to Timothy speaks thus: "But the younger widows avoid. For when they have grown wanton in Christ, they will marry: having damnation, because they have made void their first faith" (5, 11-12). What is it to say, "they have made void their first faith"? The meaning is that they violated the vow which they had pronounced in widowhood of keeping continence, since they married after they had pronounced such a vow. And if Paul says that younger widows have damnation, because they made void their first faith: what would he have said about Luther, Oecolampadius, Konrad Pellikan,[3] Francis Lambert,[4] Martin Bucer, and other men of the same ilk, who having cast off the cowl which they were once clothed, after having despised the vow which they had once vowed, like the wife of Lot they looked back, marrying wives?

But these words of Paul, although they are very clear, the heretics attempt to distort into another meaning very far from the text and mind of Paul. For Calvin in his work, *Institutes of the Christian Religion*, in the fourth chapter where he discusses vows, objecting against the aforesaid words of Paul against his own opinion, when responding to them, he says these words which follow: "I by no means deny that widows who dedicated themselves and their labors to the Church, at the same time came under an obligation of perpetual celibacy, not because they regarded it in the light of a religious duty, as afterwards began to be the case, but because they could not perform their functions unless they had their time at their own command, and were free from the nuptial tie. But if, after giving their pledge, they began to look to a new marriage, what else was this but to shake off the calling of God? It is not strange, therefore, when Paul says that by such desires they grow wanton against Christ. In further explanation he afterwards adds, that by not performing their promises to the Church, they violate and nullify their first faith given in Baptism; one of the things contained in this first faith being, that everyone should correspond to his calling... But, first, I deny that they had any other reason for professing celibacy than just because marriage was altogether inconsistent with the function which they undertook. Hence they bound themselves to celibacy only in so far as the nature of their function required. Secondly, I do not admit that they were bound to celibacy in such a sense that it was not better for them to marry than to suffer by the incitements of the flesh, and fall into uncleanness."[5]

---

[1] C. 4, n. 4 (PL 40, 398).

[2] *City of God*, bk. 17, c. 4, n. 6-7 (PL 41, 530). Note that it is the Septuagint version of I Kings 2, 9 that St. Augustine cites here which has the words: *dans votum voventi et benedixit annos justi*, meaming ("Giving the vow to him that vows and He blessed the years of the just"). But in the Vulgate the words the quite different words are: "He will keep the feet of his saints, and the wicked shall be silent in darkness." (Cf. *Vetus Testamentum Graecum Juxta Septuaginta Interpretes* (Paris, A.F. Didot, 1855), vol. 1, p. 397).

[3] Konrad Pellikan (1478-1556) was a German Protestant theologian, humanist, and Protestant reformer who worked chiefly in Switzerland.

[4] Francis Lambert (c. 1486-1530) was a Protestant reformer who abandoned the Franciscan Order at Avignon and died of the plague at Marburg.

[5] N. 19 (CR 29, 450).

By which words, so that he might defend the first opinion which he had rashly uttered against the obligation of vows, he adds a lie to a lie. Thus he says that pledge (*fidem*), which Paul says that widows first gave, is the faith (*fidem*) of the Christian religion promised at Baptism, and not the vow of chastity to be perpetually kept, although he admits that they, when they had been chosen for the ministry of the Church, had accepted the condition of keeping chastity, yet had not obliged themselves to its perpetual observance. But this interpretation of Calvin is very far from Paul's text. For Paul in that passage discussed about the choosing of widows, and teaches, as it is very well known, the kind of widows which ought to be understood: and among other things he prescribes the age of sixty years: because that age, as is very frequently the case, is without the evil solicitations of the flesh, and hence is more disposed to keeping chastity. For the same reason he commands young widows not to be chosen: because that age is inflamed towards lust, especially in those who have at one time experienced the pleasures of the flesh. And hence it happens that when the flesh is stimulated too much they would be luxuriant: which when it happens, they want to marry to please the flesh. Now concerning these marrying in such a way Paul says that they have damnation: now he says that the cause of this damnation is that they made void their first faith. But the pledge given at Baptism was not a promise of not marrying, but of the observation of God's Commandments, among which none is about perpetually keeping vidual chastity: therefore those widows did not make void the pledge given at Baptism, because they married. And hence it is very clearly proved, that the faith which marrying widows violated, is not anything other than the vow of keeping vidual chastity. And all the holy Doctors, who make any mention of these words of Paul, favor this interpretation, any of whom much more rightly ought one to believe than a thousand Calvins or Luthers, or any other men of the like ilk.

Augustine in many and various places renders this interpretation to the aforesaid words of Paul, but more clearly in his exposition on Psalm seventy-five when interpreting the words: "Vow ye, and pay to the Lord your God" (75, 12), where he says these words: "Let each one vow what he shall have willed to vow; let him give heed to this, that he pay what he has vowed. If any man does look back with regard to what he has vowed to God, it is an evil. Some woman or other devoted to continence has willed to marry: what has she willed? The same as any virgin. What has she willed? The same as her own mother. Hath she willed any evil thing? Evil certainly. Why? Because she had already vowed to the Lord her God. For what has the Apostle Paul said concerning such? Though he says that young widows may marry if they will[1]: nevertheless he says in a certain passage, 'But more blessed shall she be, if she so remain, according to my counsel' (I Cor. 7, 40). He shows that she is more blessed, if she shall have so remained; but nevertheless that she is not to be condemned, if she shall have willed to marry. But what does he say concerning certain ones who have vowed and have not paid? 'Having,' he says, 'damnation, because they have made void their first faith' (I Tim. 5, 12). What is, the first faith they have made void? They have vowed, and have not paid... A widow who had vowed to so remain has willed to marry, she has willed the thing which was lawful to her who has married, but to herself was not lawful, because from her place she has looked back."[2]

In the book, *On Holy Virginity*, he again says: "Paul the Apostle censures evil unmarried women, curious and prating, and says that this fault comes of idleness. But at the same time, says he, being idle they learn to go about to houses: but not only idle, but curious also and prating, speaking what they ought not. Of these he had said above, 'But the younger widows avoid. For when they have grown wanton in Christ, they will marry: Having damnation, because they have made void their first faith' (I Tim. 5, 11-12): that is, have not continued in

---

[1] I Tim. 5, 14.
[2] N. 16 (PL 36, 967-968).

that, which they had vowed at the first. And yet he says not, they marry, but they wish to marry. For many of them are recalled from marrying, not by love of a noble purpose, but by fear of open shame, which also itself comes of pride, whereby persons fear to displease men more than God. These, therefore, who wish to marry, and do not marry on this account, because they cannot with impunity, who would do better to marry than to be burned, that is, than to be laid waste in their very conscience by the hidden flame of lust, who repent of their profession, and who feel their confession irksome; unless they correct and set right their heart, and by the fear of God again overcome their lust, must be accounted among the dead."[1] From whose words it is evident that the first faith about which Paul spoke in the aforesaid words, is not the promise made in Baptism, but the vow of continence, against which not only widows who after such a vow marry, but also those who wish to marry, and he says that they ought to be accounted among the dead.

Primasius, Augustine's disciple, agrees with him on this point, who when interpreting those words of Paul, "Having damnation" etc., says these words: "Because they did what was licit but not permitted for themselves, by vowing chastity. But this rule ought to be kept not only by widows, but also by continent virgins."[2]

Isidore [of Seville] in *Ecclesiasticis officiis* interprets the aforesaid words in the same way, saying the following: "The Apostle predicts that widows who desire marriage after a resolution of continence will have damnation: 'For when they have grown wanton in Christ, they will marry: Having damnation, because they have made void their first faith' (I Tim. 5, 11-12), that is, because they did not stand firm in that which they firstly vowed."[3]

The more ancient Jerome agrees with all these men, who when interpreting the words of Paul, "If a virgin marry, she hath not sinned" (I Cor. 7, 28), says these words: "Not that virgin who has once for all dedicated herself to the service of God: for, should one of these marry, she will have damnation, because she has made of no account her first faith. But, if [Jovinian] objects that this saying relates to widows, we reply that it applies with still greater force to virgins, since marriage is forbidden even to widows whose previous marriage had been lawful. For virgins who marry after consecration are rather incestuous than adulterous."[4] And in his commentaries on Ezechiel on chapter forty-four he again says: "Whoever has vowed something and did not fulfill is guilty of the vow. Hence also it is said of widows, 'When they have grown wanton in Christ, they will marry: having damnation, because they have made void their first faith.' For it is better not to promise, than to promise and not to do."[5]

And [Ambrosiaster] does not depart a hair's breadth, as it is said,[6] from these men, who in his commentaries on Paul when interpreting those words, "When they have grown wanton in Christ, they will marry," says these words: "He forbids young widows to be received in this profession. For fidelity tends not to be easily had at the dangerous age: indeed since the examples of certain young widows precedes, who after the profession of life, by the allurement of pleasures, have the name not the actions of widows, and having turned back are incited into

---

[1] C. 33-34, n. 34 (PL 40, 415).

[2] *Commentaria in epistolas S. Pauli* (PL 68, 668B). An unknown author is actually cited here saying, "Which women had promised to remain widows. But this rule not only in widows, but it also ought to be understood of continent virgins, who made void their first faith" (*Commentarii in epistolas Pauli* (PL 30, 883D-884A). But the very similar words written by Primasius have been substituted in the text here.

[3] Bk. 2, c. 19, n. 5 (PL 83, 809A).

[4] Bk. 1, n. 13 (PL 23, 229C).

[5] Bk. 13 (PL 25, 439C-D).

[6] *Latum pilum*. This saying is derived from Cicero. *A recta conscientia transversum unguem non discedere*, "not to depart a finger's breadth in the least" (*Letters to Atticus*, bk. 13, letter 20, section 4).

marriage."[1] And afterwards when interpreting those words, "Having damnation, because they have made void their first faith," he says these words: "He shows why such things remain, lest they impetuously dare what is difficult to accomplish: or if the mind is given to this devotion, she would keep it to herself for a time: because he says that it is temerarious to profess because one ought not be trusted when still at a young age."[2] [Ambrosiaster] states clearly enough that that faith which the young widows made void is the profession of continence: and because they violated it, he says that they have damnation.

Basil the Great, a very holy as well as a very learned man says these words: "Let us see what Paul writes to Timothy. 'But younger widows avoid: For when they have grown wanton in Christ, they will marry: having damnation, because they have made void their first faith.' If, therefore, a widow lies under a very heavy charge, as setting at naught her faith in Christ, what must we think of the virgin, who is the bride of Christ, and a chosen vessel dedicated to the Lord? It is a grave fault even on the part of a slave to give herself away in secret wedlock and fill the house with impurity, and, by her wicked life, to wrong her owner; but it is forsooth far more shocking for the bride to become an adulteress, and, dishonoring her union with the bridegroom, to yield herself to unchaste indulgence. The widow, as being a corrupted slave, is indeed condemned; but the virgin comes under the charge of adultery…One point, however, must be determined beforehand, that the name virgin is given to a woman who voluntarily devotes herself to the Lord, renounces marriage, and embraces a life of holiness."[3]

Chrysostom interprets these words in the same way, in his nineteenth homily on the First Epistle to the Corinthians, the words of which will be cited below for another purpose in this same chapter. I could also cite many other holy and very old Doctors of the Church in testimony for this point, who all interpret the aforesaid words of Paul given about the vow of continence, and not about the pledge in Baptism: but lest I annoy the reader with excessive prolixity, I decided to omit them all, especially because these are enough for convicting Calvin and the rest of the Lutherans of their distorted interpretation of Paul's words. For it is just that in matters of faith and in the interpretation of Sacred Scripture that we would rather believe those holy men renown for holiness as well as their teaching, than Calvin and Luther, and all the rest of the same ilk.

And the holy Doctors were not alone in interpreting these words of Paul: but a number of councils at which many very learned men were gathered together, taught that these words ought to be interpreted in this way. For the IV Synod of Carthage in the last chapter of its decrees speaks thus: "Just as there is a good reward of chastity, so also it ought to be kept with greater observance and prudence, so that if those widows, having been widowed although when still at a young and immature age, who have vowed to God and put off lay clothing according to the testimony of the bishop and the Church, and have appeared in the religious habit, but afterwards passed on to secular marriage, have damnation according to the Apostle Paul, because they dared to make void the pledge of chastity which they vowed to the Lord. Therefore such persons ought to be excluded from the communion of Christians, who also ought not to communicate in the [Eucharistic] banquet with the Christians: for if adulterous spouses are liable to punishment by their husbands for their guilt, how much more will widows who have vowed religiosity to God be censured with the crime of adultery, if they corrupted the consecration which they spontaneously offered to God with libidinous pleasure and made passage to second marriages? Which women, even if have been carried off by force

---

[1] *Commentaria in Epistolam ad Timotheum Primam* (PL 17, 477C).

[2] *Ibid.* (PL 17, 478A).

[3] Letter 199, c. 18 (PG 718B-719B). The author here cites a spurious work, *Liber de viginitate*, c. 40-41 (PG 30, 750C) which he incorrectly attributes to St. Basil; but since St. Basil spoke about this point in one of his letters, the pertinent passage from that letter has been substituted here by the translator.

of violence by someone, and afterwards have consented by libidinous pleasure to remain in the marriage to the abductor or violent man, are held guilty of the damnation related above: for about such woman the Apostle speaks thus: 'For when they have grown wanton in Christ, they will marry' (I Tim. 5, 11)."[1]

The IV Synod of Toledo speaks thus: "There are two kinds of widows: lay and religious (*sanctimoniales*). Lay widows are those who are still disposed to marry; they have not put off their lay clothes. The religious are those who having already put off their secular clothes, have appeared in religious dress in the sight of the priest and the Church. The latter, if they have passed over to marriage, will not be without damnation according to the Apostle, because when firstly vowing [chastity] to God, afterwards they cast off their resolution of chastity."[2] From the words of these two synods it is established that this is the opinion of Paul the Apostle, namely that widows who have vowed perpetual chastity to the Lord, will be damned if they have passed on to a second marriage.

And certainly many councils testify that the marriages of those who once vowed themselves to the Lord ought to be condemned. For the [I] Synod of Valence in the second canon of its decrees, speaks thus: "Concerning young women who have vowed themselves to God, if they have of their own will passed on to earthly marriages, we have decreed that this ought to be observed, that those repenting ought not to be immediately received for forgiveness, and when it has been given nevertheless unless they have full satisfied to God as much as is reasonable, communion is differed unto them."[3]

And in the Synod of Orange in the twenty-seventh chapter decrees thus: "A vow of perpetual widowhood shall be made in the presence of the bishop in the church sacristy, and it shall be indicated by the widow's habit, which is to be bestowed upon her by the bishop. Moreover, the abductor of such women, and the widow herself if she abandons her vow, are justly condemned."[4] The synod again says: "Deserters of the professed chastity of both sexes are to be held as prevaricators, and ought to be put to the penance prescribed by law."[5] There are many other decrees of councils supporting this proposition, which I omit to cite, lest I burden the reader by excessive prolixity. But because someone perhaps will desire to read them, I will indicate merely the places where he can find them. The [II] Synod of Arles in the [forty-sixth[6]] chapter;[7] the Synod of Elvira;[8] the IV Synod of Toledo, in chapter fifty-[five].[9]

---

[1] C. 104 (PL 84, 208A-B; Mansi, vol. 3, col. 958B-E). The IV Synod of Carthage was held in 398 A.D.

[2] C. 56 (PL 84, 378C-D; Mansi, vol. 10, col. 632D-633A). The IV Synod of Toledo was held in 633 A. D.

[3] PL 84, 246A-247A; Mansi, vol. 3, col. 493B. The IV Synod of Valence (in Drôme, France) was held in 374 A. D.

[4] C. 27 (PL 84, 258A; Mansi, vol. 6, col. 440A). The I Synod of Orange was held in 441 A. D.

[5] C. 28 (PL 84, 258A; Mansi, vol. 6, col. 440B).

[6] The text here reads the "seventeenth" chapter, but this is clearly incorrect.

[7] "Professed widows, if they give consent to their seducers, are to be condemned" (Mansi, vol. 7, col. 884B). The II Council of Arles was held in 443 or 452 A. D.

[8] "Virgins who have been consecrated to God Communion, if they have broken the vow of virginity, and served the same lust, not understanding what they have lost, and do not repent, ought not to be given to them even at the end of their life. If, however, they repent that they have fallen by the weakness of the flesh, and they do penance for the rest of their life, and do not engage in intercourse again, they may receive Communion when death approaches" (Mansi, vol. 2, col. 171A-B). The Council of Elvira (Granada, Spain) was held in approximately 305 A. D.

[9] "Whoever among the laity doing penance tonsure themselves, and again prevaricate are made laymen; having been apprehended by their bishop, they may be recalled to the penance to which they abandoned. But if some cannot be recalled to penance, nor convert when admonished, they are truly

From all these decrees it is evident how unjustly some men try to inflict a calumny upon monastic vows: because if it is lawful to pronounce a perpetual vow about something, those vows are much more just about those three things by which the triple concupiscence of this world are overthrown, namely obedience, chastity, and poverty. For by obedience the pride of life is subdued. By the vow of chastity, the concupiscence of the flesh is controlled. And by the vow of poverty, the insatiable concupiscence of the eyes is restrained. Hence it is proved that if there are the three concupiscences of the world, that there would be salutary vows against the three professed in monastic life, because these vows are as it were certain antidotes against those three poisons which the world gives to drink: especially because these three things, about which the vows of monks pertain, are highly commended by Christ. For He commended obedience, saying "If any man will come after me, let him deny himself, and take up his cross, and follow me" (Mt. 16, 24). For one cannot more truly deny himself than when he commits everything to the choice of the superior, so that he would no longer want to do his own will, but that of his superior. He extolled perpetual chastity, saying: "There are eunuchs, who have made themselves eunuchs for the kingdom of heaven. He that can take, let him take it" (Mt. 19, 12). And he commended poverty, when He said: "If thou wilt be perfect, go sell what thou hast, and give to the poor, and thou shalt have treasure in heaven: and come follow me" (v. 21).

Thus since there are such clear testimonies approving monastic vows, let the Lutheran monks be afraid to look back at the world, since they already once put their hand to the plough:[1] and let them take care lest it happen to them just as to Lot's wife, who when fleeing from Sodom, was turned into a statue of salt, because she turned back to Sodom whence she had come out.[2] For when one of Christ's disciples said to Him: "Suffer me first to go and bury my father" (Mt. 8, 21): Christ replied to him: "Let the dead bury their dead" (v. 22). Theophylactus when interpreting which words, says: "If this man was not even permitted to bury his father, woe to those who after they have begun the monastic life turn back to worldly things!"[3] Woe therefore to the lascivious Luther, and his accomplices, who having professed monasticism, heedless of their profession returning to the world, married wives.

Of the two things which we undertook to prove against these heretics, one of which (as I think) we have finished. There now remains that we prove the other, namely that a deed done under a vow is of a better nature, and of greater worth before God, than if it were done without a vow. The holy Psalmist encourages us to vow something to the Lord God, saying: "Vow ye, and pay to the Lord your God: all you that are round about him bring presents" (Ps. 75, 12). But if no merit were to accrue from a vow, the [Royal] Prophet would badly advise us to vow: especially since those not fulfilling, become guilty of them, of which they would not be guilty if they had not vowed: and so according to the heretics' opinion, one vowing exposes himself by a vow to the danger of sin if he does not fulfil, and he is under no hope of a reward

---

condemned as apostates before the Church by the sentence of anathema. Not otherwise they also who having lost their parents, devoted themselves to religion, and afterwards took lay clothes, and having been apprehended by the priest for the service of religion, ought to be recalled to the previous works of penance. But if they cannot be truly converted, they are subject as apostates to the sentence of anathema. Which form will also be kept in the case of widows and holy virgins, and penitent women, who put on the religious habit, and afterwards either put off their habit, or passed on to marriage" (C. 55 (Mansi, vol. 10, col. 632C-D)). Canons forty-eight and fifty-one are cited here, but as they do not pertain to this subject, number fifty-five has been substituted in their place.

[1] Cf. Lk. 9, 62.
[2] Cf. Gen. 19, 26.
[3] PG 123, 223A.

VOTUM -1053-

if he fulfills. Thus if this were the condition of a vow, it is clearly proved that the Prophet did badly when he advised a vow.

Furthermore, the more some deed arises from the root of a better virtue, the better it is. For whence it is that a work done out of charity is better than any work proceeding from another virtue: namely because charity from which it proceeds, is better than any other virtue. For God does not look at how much someone offers, but from how much. And hence that widow was praised, who although she had offered only two mites, was said to have offered more than all the others.[1] From which it is clearly proved that before God not so much is the quantity of the thing offered is esteemed, as the affection of the one offering. Therefore, since a work done from a vow proceeds from the root of obedience, which is better than a victim,[2] but a work done by his own choice and not from a vow, does not arise from that virtue; it follows that the latter is not as good as the former. For he who does something from a vow, being obedient does the thing, and does the thing so that he may obey: thus, since he acts in this way, in addition to the merit which he has corresponding to the work, he now has the merit from obedience; which merit the other does not have who does something by his own choice.

Again, there are many testimonies of holy men in favor of this position. [Pseudo-] Blessed Jerome[3] when discussing the passage of Jeremias in Lamentations: "It is good for a man, when he hath borne the yoke from his youth" (3, 27), says these words: "Thus the perfection of Christ's soldiers is to have a mind divested from all secular businesses, and disturbances of the world, according to that saying of the Apostle: 'No man, being a soldier to God, entangleth himself with secular businesses' etc. (II Tim. 2, 4): and as far as human weakness permits, he hastens to come with Christ: what beauty indeed of the good way of life hermits and monks who are obligated by the vow of monastic discipline, strive to imitate: but [as Cassian says:] 'Perfection is very rare and granted by God's gift to but a very few. For he is truly and not partially perfect who with equal imperturbability can put up with the squalor of the wilderness in the desert, as well as the weaknesses of the brethren in the monastery. And so it is hard to find one who is perfect in both lives, because the anchorite cannot thoroughly acquire a disregard for and stripping oneself of material things, nor the monk purity in contemplation,'[4] but still how much the serenity of a tranquil life surpasses the turbulence of worldly intercourse, he has come to know who has experienced this."[5] In which words there are many things which deserve notice. The first is that at the time of [Pseudo-] Jerome monks bound themselves by a vow, which nevertheless Erasmus pertinaciously denies in many of his works, especially in the life of Jerome which the same Erasmus wrote.[6] But that this is not

---

[1] Cf. Mk. 12, 43.

[2] Cf. Eccle. 4, 17.

[3] This quotation is found in the writings of Rabanus.

[4] *Conferences of the Desert Fathers*, Conference 19, c. 9 (PL 49, 1138B-1140A).

[5] Rabanus, *Commentaria in Jeremiam*, bk. 19, c. 3 (PL 111, 1227B-C).

[6] "Therefore, having weighed and considered everything, the institution of monasticism pleases me: but lest anyone err about this, monasticism was far different at that time from what we see today, hampered as it is by ceremonial formality: yea these monks were making their profession for whom there was liberty of heart in a high degree. For firstly the way of life remained untouched, if someone expressed his choice for very sweet and very free leisure time, the power of coming and going wither one wished remained. They were spurred on to study, fasting, Psalms, vigils by their own choice or they were attracted by the examples [of others], they were not forced by the little constitutions of men. The clothing was simple, and yet it was not prescribed, but taken by the choice of each one, who did not make himself conspicuous or standing out by a shocking novelty, but who displayed Christian simplicity. No fetters of vows, except those which are simply of any Christian. Finally, if repentance had perhaps brought him to his institute, the whole punishment was simply the disgrace of his inconstancy... Indeed that way of life procured these and other benefits: by the pretext of this more honorable way of life it was

as Erasmus says, the words which we have just now cited from Jerome, clearly prove. The second thing is that such a life of monks under the obligation of a vow is good, and is good for the following of Christian perfection. The third is that this life of monks ought to be preferred to the life of others who are involved with secular business. And this is what supports our view, which Erasmus is also not ashamed to deny. And yet I am not surprised: because we have known this having learned from experience, that no one is more a bitter and hostile enemy of some men, that a deserter who runs away and abandons them: now Erasmus was not ashamed to lay aside the monastic life which he had at one time vowed,[1] and hence it happens that he always detracts monks, and very atrociously persecutes them as much as he can: so that he even persuades others by this argument that he acted rightly when he cast off the yoke of monastic life which he had at one time undertook. And yet Jerome judges that to carry this this yoke of monastic life is good.

But, so that I may prove that Erasmus of Rotterdam and other enemies of the monastic profession of a very shameless lie, I wish to cite another witness much more ancient than Jerome, namely the holy Dionysius the [Pseudo-] Areopagite, Paul's disciple, who in his book, *Ecclesiastical Hierarchy*, in the sixth chapter, when describing the rite of monastic consecration and profession, how having been instituted by the Apostles it was then observed in the Church, speaks thus: "But of all the initiates the most exalted order is the sacred rank of the monks which has been purified of all stain and possesses full power and complete holiness in its own activities. To the extent that is permissible, it has entered upon sacred contemplative activity and has achieved intellectual contemplation and communion. This order is entrusted to the perfecting power of those men, the bishops, whose enlightening activities and hierarchical traditions have introduced it, according to capacity, to the holy operations of the sacred mysteries it has beheld. Thanks to their sacred understanding it has been uplifted into the most complete perfection proportionate to this order. This why our blessed leaders considered such men to be worthy of several sacred designations; some gave them the name of *Therapeutae*, or worshippers, and sometimes 'monks,' because of the purity of their duty and service to God and because their lives, far from being dissipated, are focused by their unifying and sacred recollection which excludes all distraction and enables them to achieve a singular mode of life conforming to God and open to the perfection of God's love. Hence the sacred ordinance has bestowed a perfecting grace on them and has deemed them worthy of a sanctifying invocation which is the business of the bishop (he alone confers clerical ordination) but of the devout priests who sacredly perform this secondary rite of the hierarchy. The priest stands before the sacred altar and chants the invocation for the monk. The person being initiated stands behind the priest and does not kneel on either one or both knees. The Scriptures handed down from God are not put on his head. He simply stands while the priest chants the secret invocation over him. First he asks him if he will not only renounce not only

---

permitted to excuse yourself from the ties of friends and relatives, for one to whom, [having been freed from] this very weighty burden, nothing is more sweet than the leisure of studies. And indeed those who had professed the monastic life were held to be wholly excused from public activities and from service and duties at the imperial court. Lastly, they were free from the tyranny of some bishops, who even then became overbearing. At that time, this title [of being a monk] was not held back at all from the functions of the clerical office, and from no rank were bishops more often selected. The profession of a monk was then nothing other than the contemplation belonging to the olden and free, as well as purely Christian, life. I reckoned that these things ought to be pointed out in passing lest, as it is very commonly done, they make Jerome the founder of his institute, to which things he appertains not at all" (Desiderius Erasmus, *Eximii doctoris Hieronymi stridonensis vita* (Basel, Froben, 1519), pp. 16-18.

[1] In 1487 Erasmus entered into the consecrated life as a canon regular of St. Augustine at the canonry of Stein, in South Holland. He took vows there in late 1488 and was ordained to the Catholic priesthood on April 25, 1492. He was dismissed from his monastery and dispensed of his vows by Pope Leo X.

vices, but even imaginations which could be a distraction to his way of life. He reminds him of the rules governing a fully perfect life and openly asserts that he must surpass the median way of life. After the initiate has devoutly promised to do all this the priest makes the sign of the cross on him. He cuts his hair and invokes the three Persons of the Divine beatitude. He takes away all his clothes and gives him others. Then, together with all the other sacred men present at the ceremony he gives him the kiss [of peace] and makes him a partaker of the Divine mysteries."[1] In which words there are many things which ought to be noted. The first is that at that time monks made their profession through the promise of a vow. Which he clearly shows when he said: "After the initiate has devoutly promised to do all this." Thus not only at the time of Jerome, but at a much earlier time, namely from the very beginnings of the Church, monks obliged themselves by a vow to the Lord, promising the renunciation of distracting things [*divisibilia*], that is, of earthly things which are removed and separated from us at death. The other thing which is established from Dionysius is that monastic life, in which one is called to God alone and one renounces secular cares, is more excellent and sublime than all the others.

Blessed Augustine in his letter to Armentarius, who having despised and left the world vowed a vow at the same time with his wife, speaks thus: "Before you were bound by the vow, you were free to live on a lower level, although one should not rejoice over a freedom because of which one does not have a debt whose payment is a gain. But now that God has your vow, I am not inviting you to a great act of justice; rather, I am deterring you from a great injustice. For, if you do not put into practice what you have vowed, you will not be the same sort of person you would have remained if you had not made any such vow. For in that case you would have been less good, but not worse. But now if you break your promise to God, you will be more wretched—God forbid!—to the extent that you would be happier if you kept it. Do not, therefore, regret that you made the vow; rather rejoice that you now may not do what you might have done to your own loss. And so, begin without fear, and put your words into action. He will help you who seeks the fulfillment of your vows. Happy is the necessity that forces one to what is better."[2] In which words there are many things, if the reader observes well, which commend vows.

Blessed Gregory speaks thus: "The difference between a sacrifice and a holocaust is, that, whereas every holocaust is a sacrifice, every sacrifice is not a holocaust. In a sacrifice a part of the victim was immolated; but in a holocaust the entire offering was consumed. And hence the word 'holocaust' means 'all burnt.' Let us then consider what is a sacrifice and what is a holocaust. For when someone vows something of his own to God, and does not vow something [that he has], it is a sacrifice. But when one vows to Almighty God everything that he has, his entire life, all that he takes pleasure in, he is offering a holocaust. For there are some who as yet are retained in mind in this world, and who afford help to the poor from their possessions, and hasten to defend the oppressed. These in the good which they do, offer sacrifices, because of their actions they offer something to God, and keep something for themselves. And there are some who keep nothing for themselves, but sacrifice to Almighty God their tongue, their senses, their life, and the property they possess. What do these do but offer a holocaust, yea rather are made a holocaust? The Israelite people firstly offered sacrifice in Egypt, but secondly in the desert.[3] Therefore he who retains his mind in the world, but now does something good, offers sacrifice to God in Egypt. But he who abandons the present world, and does the good things which he can, as though having forsaken his possessions in Egypt offers sacrifice in the desert: because having driven away the clamor of carnal desires in the quiet of his mind

---

[1] PG 3, 531C-534B.

[2] Letter 127, n. 8 (PL 33, 487).

[3] Cf. Ex. 12 & 13.

and in solitude immolates to God whatever he does. Thus therefore, as it was said, a holocaust is also a sacrifice: yet a holocaust is greater than sacrifice: because with his mind which is not weighed down by the enjoyment of this world, everything which he has is burned as a sacrifice to God."[1] In which words it ought to be noticed that he says, "a holocaust is greater than a sacrifice": and the sacrifice in the desert was greater than the sacrifice in Egypt. From which words it is evident that monks, who have entirely denied their will, and immolate everything in their profession to God through the vow of obedience, have made a holocaust. And in this way it is proved by the same rule that their vow is a sacrifice in the desert, and consequently better than a work done spontaneously by the laity, because it is a sacrifice in Egypt.

Blessed Chrysostom gives testimony in favor of the vow of perpetual poverty, who in his eleventh homily on the Epistle to the Hebrews speaks thus: "And there are also other sacrifices, which are indeed holocausts, the bodies of the martyrs: there both soul and body [are offered]. These have a great savor of a sweet smell. You also art able, if you wish, to bring such a sacrifice. What namely, if you dost not burn your body in the fire? Yet in a different fire you can, for instance, in that of voluntary poverty, in that of affliction. For to have it in one's power to spend one's days in luxury and expense, and yet to take up a life of toil and bitterness, and to mortify the body, is not this a holocaust? Mortify your body, and crucify it, and you shall yourself also receive the crown of this martyrdom. For what in the other case the sword accomplishes, that in this case let a willing mind effect. Let not the love of wealth burn, or possess you, but let this unreasonable appetite itself be consumed and quenched by the fire of the Spirit; let it be cut in pieces by the sword of the Spirit."[2] Chrysostom says clearly enough that one does in the profession of voluntary poverty what the material sword works in the flesh, by the choice of the same poverty, that is the vow [of poverty]: for the latter man becomes Christ's martyr bodily in public, but the former man is a martyr in secret. And just as without a sword or some other equivalent thing a man cannot be Christ's public martyr, so apart from the vow and the desire of poverty, although one may be oppressed by want, one still will not be a martyr in private life.

Add to these things, that omitting that which one had vowed that he would do for God, one sins more gravely then if one had not vowed. For the Wise Man says: "It is much better not to vow, than after a vow not to perform the things promised" (Eccle. 5, 4). In this passage "better" certainly means that which is less bad, as it is said elsewhere: "It were better for him, if that man had not been born" (Mt. 26, 24). Not because one of those things would be good, but because it would have been less evil not to be born, than to have betrayed Christ. So also it ought to be understood in this passage, that it is less evil (as evil is every lack of goodness) not to vow, than after a vow not to render the things promised. For so [Pseudo-] Pope Urban I in his letter on the common life and offerings of the faithful says: "And whoever has received your common life, and vow that he will have nothing of his own, let him take care not to make void his promise, but let him faithfully observe that which he has promised to the Lord, lest he acquire damnation instead of a reward for himself: because it is better not to vow, than not to fulfill a vow, according as it can be better. For those are punished more severely who made a vow and did not perform it, or accepted the faith, and ended their life in bad works, than those who ended their life without a vow, or died without faith, and yet did good works."[3] From whose words it is evident that at that time there were then men who vowing poverty lived in community, just as monks do now. It is also established that those who made a vow and did not fulfill it are to be punished more severely than those who ended their life badly without a vow. If they are punished more severely who do not fulfill [a vow], it must also be that they

---

[1] *Homiliae in Ezechielem*, hom. 8, n. 16 (PL 76, 1037C-1038A).

[2] N. 3 (PG 63, 93).

[3] *False Decretals of the Pseudo-Isidore* (PL 130, 140A).

are rewarded more amply when they do fulfill [a vow]. For otherwise God would not be more inclined to mercy than to punishment.

Finally, so that we may not dispute more about this matter, let us hear the decision of the Church. The IV Synod of Toledo in the [fiftieth] chapter of its decrees speaks thus: "Clerics who desire the monks' way of life, because they desire to follow a better life, free access ought to be granted to them by the bishops, and the wish of those who seek to pass over to the life of contemplation ought not to be forbidden."[1] From its decree it is evident that the life of monks is more perfect than the life of other, secular men: which does not come forth from anywhere but from the vow which they profess, which gives their greater perfection and greater merit.

Now it remains that we would reply to the objections of the heretics, by which they oppose us, and that we show them all to be completely worthless. Firstly they object to us the passage of Paul from the First Epistle to the Corinthians: "If a virgin marry, she hath not sinned" (7, 28). From which words the heretics try to conclude that the religious who have vowed chastity do not sin when they marry men and have intercourse with them. But this is not so, because Paul in the cited words is speaking about virgins who are of their own right, to who it is permitted to marry or not to marry, and not about those who by the vow of chastity which they have vowed, completely cast away from themselves the power of marrying. And Jerome interprets those words according to this opinion in the first book of his *Against Jovinian*, as it easy to see in those words which we cited above for another purpose.

Blessed Chrysostom supports the same interpretation, who in his nineteenth homily on the First Epistle to the Corinthians, when interpreting the aforesaid words, says: "He is not speaking about her who has made choice of virginity, for if it comes to that, she has sinned. Since if the widows are condemned for having to do with second marriages after they have once chosen widowhood, much more the virgins."[2] Chrysostom, who in passing also teaches that those words of Paul from the First Epistle to Timothy, about which we disputed above, ought to be understood of the vow of continence and not of the vow professed in Baptism.

Theophylactus, the perpetual imitator of Chrysostom, gives the same interpretation to the above quoted words of Paul, saying the following: "He calls a virgin here, not her who has been consecrated to God: for she if she marry, she certainly sins, or her who marries an adulterer in place of Christ her spouse: but a still unmarried young woman. For she if she marries, has not sinned: for neither is the marriage something impure."[3]

Isidore interprets in the same way, who in his book, *Ecclesiasticis officiis*, says these words: "They who cannot tolerate the temptation of the flesh, it is necessary that they seek the haven of marriage. Hence also the same Apostle who himself says that he who cannot contain himself, let him marry: For it is better to marry than to be burnt.[4] And again "If thou take a wife, thou hast not sinned. And if a virgin marry, she hath not sinned" (I Cor. 7, 28): and if you do not wish to be greater, take your choice to be less: because to you belongs free will. For marriage is not a sin, but through the care of the world, those who marry, scarcely keep God's law. But on the other hand he says that those do not sin if they marry who have not yet vowed chastity to God. [It is otherwise for him who even has just promised in his heart, if he do otherwise, he has damnation, because he made void, the Apostle says, his first faith.[5]] For what was by its nature licit, by the vow he made illicit."[6]

---

[1] Mansi, vol. 10, col. 631C.
[2] N. 6 (PG 61, 159).
[3] PG 124, 650D.
[4] Cf. I Cor. 7, 9.
[5] Cf. I Tim. 5, 12.
[6] Bk. 2, c. 19, n. 5 (PL 83, 809A).

Photius[1] consents on this point to all these things, who having been cited by Oecumenus says these words: "Paul here understands a virgin to be not her who has been consecrated to God, but an unmarried young woman. For she who has been consecrated to God, makes him who she marries an adulterer to Christ."[2] From the words of all the holy Doctors it is clearly established that those words of Paul do not fight against us, but rather for us.

Secondly, Luther objects in that book of his, *On Monastic Vows*, speaking thus: Monastic vows are opposed to right reason: and especially the vow of chastity, since right reason indeed discerns, that if anything shall have become impossible to us, we are no longer bound to it. Hence any vow, no matter how upright and pious it might be, if it cannot be fulfilled by us, it ceases to be a vow. But in a religious, who has bound himself by the vow of chastity, the weakness of the flesh can be so great, that it cannot be conquered neither by fasting, nor prayers, nor exercises. Thus he can be released with impunity from the vow of chastity, which he was unable to fulfill: and enter the marriage state. Furthermore when he pronounced such a vow before God, it ought to be interpreted conditionally, namely that he would keep celibacy, if in the measure he feels that it is possible for him, and as long as he could keep it entirely.[3] From which words anyone, if he observes carefully, will easily perceive Luther's character, and will know how little consistent he is with himself, and how he changes himself into every shape, like another Proteus. Now so that he might oppose vows, he says that man is not obliged to the impossible, who when he elsewhere disputes about the understanding of two precepts, namely of the love of God and of avoiding concupiscence, said that man was obliged by God to the impossible.

But we replying to his objection acknowledge that no one can be obliged to the impossible: and hence if anyone vows something, which then or afterwards is impossible to him, he is not obliged to the fulfillment of that vow. Now whether that vow is impossible to him or not, he alone ought not to judge: because no one is a good judge in his own cause, especially where the matter itself has some reason for doubting: but one ought to consult a superior, who having well considered the matter from all sides will judge about its possibility or impossibility, and if he shall deem it impossible, by that very fact he will be free from the obligation of his vow. Yet we deny that there can be such weakness of the flesh, that a man is sometimes necessarily forced to yield to it, because there never can be such a vehement temptation of the flesh, such that we cannot resist when supported by the Divine assistance, which God is always prepared to give to everyone asking rightly. Concerning which matter I recall that I said enough above in the section on "Virginity," and in the section on "The Priesthood," in the fourth heresy. Otherwise, that he says that the vow of chastity ought to be vowed conditionally, is something ridiculous: because that condition often gives an occasion for violating the vow. For as often as one would wish to experience the pleasure of the flesh, he would say that he cannot keep continence, because he has been troubled so much by the temptation of the flesh, that he is now unable to resist it.

The third objection of Luther is whereby he says these words: It is completely opposed to right reason, and equally absurd, that someone would vow to God what was nowise put in his power, but entirely placed in another's choice. So that he would be held to be foolish, who would vow to God that he will be a bishop, an Apostle, a ruler or a king, when he knows that none of these things is in the power of the one vowing: but in the power of another, namely of

---

[1] Photius (c. 815-897), Patriarch of Constantinople, was chief author of the great schism between East and West, was born at Constantinople c. 815-897.

[2] Oecumenius, *Commentarius in Epistolam I ad Corinthios* (PG 118, 739A). Oecumenius was the Bishop of Trikka (now Trikala) in Thessaly and wrote in about 990 A. D. He included excerpts of the writings of Photius, among others, in his commentaries.

[3] Cf. WA 8, 629-630.

the one appointing. But he who vows chastity to God, vows something which is completely not, nor could be, in his own hands, since it is the gift of God alone, which man can receive, not offer.[1]

If this argument has some strength, it would also prove that we vow nothing to God, nay the Christian promise itself, which we make in Baptism, is of completely no value: because none of those things which we promise in Baptism, was placed in our power alone. For we cannot execute firmness of faith, full obedience to God's Commandments, the renunciation of Satan without God's special help. "Without me," the Savior says, "you can do nothing" (Jn. 15, 5). And Paul the Apostle says: "Not that we are sufficient to think anything of ourselves, as of ourselves: but our sufficiency is from God" (II Cor. 3, 5). Hence we admit that no one can vow that which is not placed in his own power: yet we deny that the observance of chastity is not placed in our power: because even if man relying upon his own strength alone is unable, still he is able with God's help, which He is prepared to give to all who call upon him in truth. "I can do all these things," Paul says, "in him who strengtheneth me" (Phil. 4, 13). If he can do all things, then he can also keep complete chastity. But that God Himself never denies His help to those asking for it, He Himself bears witness, Who in Mark's Gospel says: "Whatsoever you ask when ye pray, believe that you shall receive; and they shall come unto you" (Mk. 11, 24). If [He will give] all things, then [He will also give] chastity of the flesh. Now we never say that something is in our power, because we can do it without God's help: but because we can do it with God's help, which He is always prepared to give. And for this reason we do not say that it is situated in our power to be a bishop or Apostle, king or ruler: because even though we can attain to any of these offices with God's help, still God is not prepared to confer such help to every man. Thus it is a foolish and ridiculous comparison which Luther has proposed: because the power in us for obtaining the episcopacy is very different from that of keeping chastity. For God is always prepared to help us as to the latter, but not as to the former.

Luther's fourth objection is contained in the following words of his: Some holy men are read to have been taken from monasteries into the episcopacy, into the cardinalate, and the papacy, wherein they certainly passed over from the vow of poverty to using their own possessions. For someone cannot say here that the pope, bishops and cardinals, and similar ecclesiastical rulers, do not possess their own property, since they use them at will. Accordingly, let it be granted that the rulers of monks do not take care of their own possessions: but certainly those ecclesiastical rulers take care of their own possessions, although received from the Church, so that there is nothing which someone could say is not his but that they belong to the Church, which they administer. But if in the prelates on account of obedience and the state of perfection which they assume, the vow of poverty is released, for then they are rich men and owners of their own possessions: on account of the same reason why is not the vow of chastity released in them?[2] From which words it is clearly evident with what irreconcilable hatred Luther hounds the vow of chastity which he had vowed in his profession of monasticism. For so that he can excuse himself there is no stone that he does not move, and hence he fights against it more vehemently and more frequently than against the other vows.

But in this argument he accomplishes absolutely nothing: because he approves of something false, whence he assumes another false thing. For it is false that those who are taken from monastic life are free from the vow of poverty: because even though they are assumed to the episcopacy, they still remain obliged to poverty, just as they were obliged before. And Pope Innocent [I] clearly declared this in the chapter, *De monachis*, whose words are these: "With regard to those monks who after long residence in a monastery attain to the order of

---

[1] Cf. WA 8, 658-659.
[2] Cf. WA 8, 643 ff.

clerics, we bid them not to lay aside their former purpose."[1] Certainly this opinion ought to be understood about those things alone, which are necessary for the substance of the monastic life, and which at the same time can be kept with the episcopal dignity, such as chastity and poverty: for we admit that they are free from other things which conflict with the episcopal office itself, as do obedience, fasting, and silence: because those things cannot be united at the same time with the function of the episcopal office. Now what Luther objects, that they are the owners of those things which by reason of the episcopal office come to them, is false: because they are not the owner of those things, but only the dispensers and administrators. About which matter let he who wishes see Saint Thomas Aquinas,[2] where he discusses this matter very well.

Fifthly Luther objects against the vow of obedience, saying these words: About the vow of obedience religious sin in two ways, both because they represent it as being under a counsel, when it falls under a precept: namely because the inferior obeys the superior, as a son to his father, a wife to her husband, and a servant to his master: and because by it to someone, namely to his own superior, they oblige themselves, and they withdraw themselves from all other superiors and those equal to themselves, saying that they owe it to their superior alone. Therefore, that vow of obedience is irrational and to be condemned.[3] In which words he lied twice. Firstly in fact when he says that the obedience which monks vow falls under a precept. For it is under a precept after the vow of obedience has been professed: yet it is not under a precept before that vow, but only under a counsel. For even though by Divine law every inferior is bound to render obedience to his superior, still it is not sanctioned by Divine law, that a superior of some monastery is the superior to him, who has not professed the monastic life, and hence he is not bound from Divine law to obey him, as long as he was not subject to him. Thus it is under a counsel that a man, who is otherwise free, would spontaneously subject himself to another on account of the love of God, so that he may be ruled and governed by him: it is however under precept that he would obey him, after he promises to God to render obedience to him. Secondly Luther has lied, when he said that monks by the vow of obedience bind themselves by the vow of obedience to only one superior, and to withdraw themselves from all other superiors. For by the same reason whereby a monk is subject to his proximate superior, by that same reason he is also subject to all others, to whom that superior is subject, and he is bound to show to all of them not less, but much greater obedience. And this has always been observed by monks, and no law of theirs ever stated the contrary, nor the practice kept. From all which things it is very clearly proved that this fifth objection of Luther is rather a false calumny, than even an apparent argument.

Luther's sixth objection does not oppose any particular vow, but all vows at the same time in general: The vows of the monastic order is opposed to Evangelical or Christian liberty, which is not only that liberty "reigning...in spirit," says Luther, whereby the conscience is freed from works: but also "whereby all human commandments are removed, and whatever can be observed in external ceremonies, such as all food, all clothing, all person, all gestures, all places, all holy vessels, all days: so that it is permissible to observe or not observe them: as long as, where and how, when and as many times as one pleases, or it lies in the matter itself. And in all, whatsoever is not a Divine Commandment is abolished and surrendered to freedom... But is not the institution of vowing merely something human? Does it not consist in the tonsure, the habit, the food, the drink, the days, the places, the gestures and other ceremonies?" And a few words afterwards, he finally concludes, speaking thus: Therefore

---

[1] Letter to Victricius of Rouen (dated 404), epist. 2 (Gratian, *Concordia discordantium canonum*, causa 16, q. 1 (PL 187, 991B)).

[2] Cf. II-II, q. 185, art. 8.

[3] Cf. WA 8, 645-646.

the monastic vows "are against Evangelical freedom and are completely forbidden by the Divine Commandments": and the institution of vows is a servile teaching of men nowise to be tolerated.[1]

In which words Luther lays bare the basis and foundation of his whole doctrine, by which he drew such a multitude of men to himself. For under the guise and name of Christian liberty he preached to men the brazen license of all vices, allowing them whatever they please, as long as they believe that they will be saved through God's mercy. This license of vices, which Luther call Christian liberty, is the worst slavery: because, as our Savior says, "Whosoever committeth sin, is the servant of sin" (Jn. 8, 34). For the rest, what he says is false, that Christian liberty consists in this, that we are bound to obey no commandments of men. For by this reason it would be necessary to assert that there is no magistrate in the Christian religion, no king, no ruler, no leader: every nation would perish for this reason, and every country, if men are not held to obey any commandments of men. But I recall that I have already spoken enough about this matter above in the section on the "Church," in the third heresy: for in that place we showed from Holy Writ, that there is in the Church the power of making laws, to which all Christians are held to obey.

Next, it is also false what Luther says: that the obligation of vows is of human institution. I indeed acknowledge that the vow itself depends on the human will, and not on a Divine precept: because God does not command, but only counsels us, that we vow something to Him. But after someone has vowed something by his own choice to God, precisely then he is obliged by the Divine precept to rendering to God that which he vowed. In support of which opinion we have cited above in this chapter many and very clear testimonies of Sacred Scriptures, so that save only with very great impudence, can they be contradicted. Thus the institution of vows is not, as Luther very impudently says, a servile human teaching, but the teaching of God saying: "Vow ye, and pay to the Lord your God" (Ps. 75, 12). What Luther says is also false, that monastic vows are "forbidden by the Divine Commandments," because they all, as we have already proved, are certain counsels of Christ, which monks not merely willed do, but willed to oblige themselves to them through the profession of the vow. Therefore, everything which Luther composed in this objection is false, and full of lies, and proceeding from the father of lies.

Seventhly Calvin fights against the vow of chastity in that work of his, *Institutes of the Christian Religion*,[2] wherein he objects to us certain words of Cyprian, and omits the place from which he took them: hence I suspect that he held his peace, lest the reader recurring to Cyprian himself, could easily catch the mendacious calumny: but in order expose Calvin's craftiness, I will cite Cyprian's words more copiously than Calvin, and I will indicate the place, so that one can go to it, and in that place know the true meaning. "Virgins who, after having once determined to continue in their condition, and firmly to maintain their continency,... [according to] the traditions of the Gospel and of the Apostles,... we ought not to allow to dwell with men,—I do not say to sleep together, but to live together—since both their weak sex and their age, still critical, ought to be bridled in all things and ruled by us, lest an occasion should be given to the devil who ensnares us, and desires to rage over us, to hurt them, since the Apostle also says, 'Give not place to the devil' (Eph. 4, 27). The ship is watchfully to be delivered from perilous places, that it may not be broken among the rocks and cliffs; a bundle must swiftly be taken out of the fire, before it is burnt up by the flames

---

[1] Cf. WA 8, 613.

[2] "If virgins have dedicated themselves to Christian faith, let them live modestly and chastely, without pretense. Thus strong and stable, let them wait for the reward of virginity. But if they will not, or cannot persevere, it is better to marry, than by their faults to fall into the fire" (Chap. 4, n. 18 (ed. 1554, CR 29, 450)).

reaching it. No one who is near to danger is long safe, nor will the servant of God be able to escape the devil if he has entangled himself in the devil's nets... But if they have faithfully dedicated themselves to Christ, let them persevere in modesty and chastity, without incurring any evil report, and so in courage and steadiness await the reward of virginity. But if they are unwilling or unable to persevere, it is better that they should marry, than that by their crimes they should fall into the fire."[1] After these words of Cyprian, Calvin says these words: "In the present day, with what invectives would they not lacerate anyone who should seek to temper the vow of continence by such an equitable course? Those, therefore, have wandered far from the ancient custom who not only use no moderation, and grant no pardon when anyone proves unequal to the performance of his vow, but shamelessly declare that it is a more heinous sin to cure the intemperance of the flesh by marriage, than to defile body and soul by whoredom."[2]

Let it be granted that those words of Cyprian ought to have been understood in the way that Calvin thinks, yet one ought not to believe him alone more than so many of all the others whose testimonies we have cited above against Luther and Calvin. But fortunately Cyprian in that same letter very clearly supports us, far from it being the case that he would give the opinion supporting the Lutherans. For in those words Cyprian is not speaking about virgins who have vowed their virginity to God: but about those who have the liberty to marry or not to marry, just as there are those whom nuns are accustomed to call novices, because they are in the year which is given to them for trying, so that in it they can test their strength, and see whether they feel that they are capable of keeping the vow of chastity. And since these virgins, even though they had the firm intention of virginity, and by such an intention dedicated themselves to God: yet because they still have not vowed virginity, if they do not wish to or cannot persevere, it is better that they marry, as Cyprian says, "than that by their crimes they should fall into the fire." For these are those virgins of whom Paul says: "And if a virgin marry, she hath not sinned" (I Cor. 7, 28).

Now that this is the true and genuine meaning of Cyprian's words, it is clearly gathered from the other words which towards the end of the same letter he speaks about virgins who vowed virginity, saying thus: "If a husband come upon his wife, and see her lying with another man, is he not angry and raging, and by the passion of his rage does he not perhaps take his sword into his hand? And what shall Christ and our Lord and Judge think, when He sees His virgin, dedicated to Him, and destined for His holiness, lying with another? How indignant and angry is He, and what penalties does He threaten against such unchaste connections!"[3] And a few words afterwards he adds about the same virgins dedicated to God: "But if any one of them be found to be corrupted, let her abundantly repent, because she who has been guilty of this crime is an adulteress, not (indeed) against a husband, but against Christ."[4]

From which words it is very clearly proved that Cyprian in the other words previously cited was not speaking about virgins who had already vowed their virginity to God, but of the others. For if he were then speaking about the former, how could it be true that which he said, "It is better that they should marry, than that by their crimes they should fall into the fire," if that woman who has intercourse with any man, such that in the words lastly cited he says, she commits adultery and unchastity [*incestum*]? For of her who lies with another man, whosoever he may be, he calls her polluted with unchaste connections. If her connection with any other man is unchaste and adultery, it follows that she also falls into the fire by her sins: and hence it is not possible that it be better for her to marry: because whether she marries or fornicates without marriage, she always commits adultery against Christ, to whom she was

---

[1] Letter 62 (To Pomponius), c. 1-2 (PL 4, 364B-367A).

[2] Chap. 4, n. 18 (ed. 1554, CR 29, 450).

[3] C. 3 (PL 4, 368B-369A).

[4] C. 4 (PL 4, 370A).

espoused. Therefore, lest we say that Cyprian opposes himself, one ought necessarily to acknowledge that his previous words about virgins ought to be understood of virgins who have not yet vowed virginity: but the later words ought to be understood of other virgins who have bound themselves to God by a vow. Hence the craftiness of heretics can be easily understood, who nearly always cite the saints' testimonies which they bring forth at various times in support of their view, maimed and truncated, so that their fallacy may not be detected.

Josse van Clichtove in the third book of his *Antilutherus* wrote against this heresy.[1] The Englishman Richard Smyth[2] also wrote a small booklet for the defense of celibacy and the vows of monks.

There is a **second heresy**, which even though it admits that vows are good and holy, still it denies that something can be vowed to God which is has not been commanded by Him. And on this account it condemns all monastic vows, although it approves of many other vows: because monastic vows are about those things which God did not command, namely about chastity, poverty and obedience. The authors of this heresy are the later Lutherans, who openly admitting to being against Sacred Scripture, condemn all vows and obstinately wishing to persecute monastic vows, coined this saying which they said, that the only vows that please God are those about which He commanded, but all the rest displease Him very much, and ought to be completely condemned. The Wittenbergers teach this in their confession of faith, where in the section on vows, say these words: "There is no doubt that pious, just and legitimate vows ought to be kept and performed, but wicked vows ought to be rescinded. But not without reason is it disputed, in which sort of vows ought monastic vows, of virginity or celibacy, poverty, and obedience, to be placed. For it is manifest that celibacy was not commanded in God's word…Hence he who vows virginity or celibacy, or vows in it as a singular worship of God, consequently, because the state of the celibate was not commanded by God's word, this vow pertains to the commandments of men, about which Christ says: 'In vain do they worship me, teaching doctrines and precepts of men' (Mk. 7, 7). Or they vow it, as something deserving the remission of sins and live everlasting, then it is a manifestly wicked vow, to which no one is obliged."[3] These Wittenbergers afterwards say the same thing about poverty and obedience. Calvin in his work, *Institutes of the Christian Religion*, in the fourth chapter, in which he discusses the monastic life and the vows, says these words: "If we would avoid error in deciding what vows are legitimate, and what preposterous, three things must be attended to—viz. who he is to whom the vow is made; who we are that make it; and, lastly, with what intention we make it. In regard in the first, we should consider that we have to do with God, whom our obedience so delights, that he abominates all will-worship, how specious and splendid soever it be in the eyes of men.[4] If all will-worship, which we devise without authority, is abomination to God, it follows that no worship can be acceptable to him save that which is approved by his word. Therefore, we must not arrogate such license to ourselves as to presume to vow anything to God without evidence of the estimation in which

---

[1] C. 14, fol. 162r-164r.

[2] Richard Smyth, also Smith, (c. 1500-1563) was an English professor and first Regius Professor of Divinity at Oxford and first Chancellor of the University of Douai. He wrote the *Defensio sacri episcoporum et sacerdotum coelibatus... eiusdem de votis monasticis... breuis libellus* (Paris, ex off. Reginaldi Calderii & Claudii ejus filii, 1550).

[3] The Wittenberg Confession, art. 19 (*Monumentorum ad historiam Concilii Tridentini*, vol. 4, p. 447-488). The confession's full title is *Confessio piae doctrinae, quae nomine illustrissimi principis ac domini D. Christophori ducis Wirtembergensis & Teccensis, ac comitis Montisbeligardi, per legatos eius die XXIIII mensis Ianuarii, Anno M.D.LII. congregationi Tridentini concilii proposita est*.

[4] Here Calvin cites Col. 2, 23: "Which things have indeed a shew of wisdom in superstition and humility, and not sparing the body; not in any honour to the filling of the flesh."

he holds it."[1] From which words it is evident that he thinks that nothing can be vowed to God, except that which was commanded by Him: because this alone, as he teaches, has a clear testimony, which pleases God. For these heretics make no distinction, as we related in the section on "Precepts," in the second heresy, between a precept and a counsel, and hence they say that nothing pleases God except that which was commanded by Him. Thus, from this very false opinion they deduce that nothing can be vowed to God except that which was commanded by Him: because it is evident to us that nothing else, they say, pleases God.

For refuting this heresy those things we said in the section on "Precepts, in the second and third heresy, could be enough. For in those places we proved that there is a wide distinction between a precept and a counsel, and that something which is not commanded by God pleases Him. From all which things it is easily inferred that men can vow something to God which He did not command; but besides all those things I wish to bring forth some arguments in particular against this heresy, so that its falsity may be much more clearly made known to all. Firstly, in fact, I offer the testimony from the book of Numbers, where the Lord says through Moses: "If [a wife] vow and bind herself by oath, to afflict her soul by fasting, or abstinence from other things, it shall depend on the will of her husband, whether she shall do it, or not do it. But if the husband hearing it hold his peace, and defer the declaring his mind till another day: whatsoever she had vowed and promised, she shall fulfill: because immediately as he heard it, he held his peace" (Num. 30, 14-15). From which law of God it is very clearly established that something can be vowed to God, which was not commanded by Him. For the wife could vow fasting, and such was not commanded by God, because if it had been commanded by God, her husband could not gainsay such a vow, and make it void. The husband could, however, as it is evident from the law itself, as soon as he had heard, make void the vow: thus that fasting which the wife had vowed, was not commanded by God.

Again, it is clear what sacred history relates about Anna, the wife of Elcana, who when she did not have a child, and had anxiously desired one, "arose after she had eaten and drunk in Silo: and Heli the priest sitting upon a stool, before the door of the temple of the Lord, as Anna had her heart full of grief, she prayed to the Lord, shedding many tears, and she made a vow, saying: O Lord, of hosts, if thou wilt look down on the affliction of thy servant, and wilt be mindful of me, and not forget thy handmaid, and wilt give to thy servant a man child: I will give him to the Lord all the days of his life, and no razor shall come upon his head" (I Kings 1, 9-11). This vow which Anna pronounced, as it is clearly evident, was not about a thing which God had ever commanded her, and yet that vow so pleased God, that on account of its merit God gave Anna her petition. For "When the time was come about, Anna conceived and bore a son, and called his name Samuel: because she had asked him of the Lord" (v. 20). Thus, a vow about something good pleases God, although it was not commanded by Him.

Furthermore, God did not command virginity, Paul bearing witness who says: "Now concerning virgins, I have no commandment of the Lord" (I Cor. 7, 25). But the glorious Mother of God vowed a vow of keeping that same perpetual virginity, which pleased god to such an extent, that He chose her as His mother. Thus every vow which is not about a thing commanded by Him does not displease God. Next, the Apostles pronounced a vow of poverty, as it is evident from the testimony of Augustine, which we cited in the immediately preceding heresy. Now no precept was given by God, but only a counsel about keeping poverty, by which all temporal goods are actually abandoned. Now how much this vow of poverty pleased God, that magnificent promise clearly showed, whereby He promised a very large reward to them on account of that vow. For Peter has asked Christ our Redeemer, what would be given to him and to his fellow disciples, due to the fact that they had left all things in order to follow Him. To which question our Savior responds, speaking thus: "Amen, I say to you, that you,

---

[1] N. 2 (CR (ed. 1554, CR 29, 438)).

who have followed me, in the regeneration, when the Son of man shall sit on the seat of his majesty, you also shall sit on twelve seats judging the twelve tribes of Israel" (Mt. 19, 28). Wherefore, who is so insane that he would say that that on account of which God deigned to give such a great reward, displeased Him? Therefore, a man can justly and holily vow to God what He did not command.

Add to all these things the concordant opinion of holy men, who all teach that man can holily vow to God, what nowise was commanded by Him. Augustine in the first book of his *Adulterous Marriages*, in the twenty-fourth chapter, says these words: "Something it was not wrong for someone to do before making a vow becomes wrong once the person has made a vow never to do it. It is assumed that the vow was one it was right to make, such as a vow of perpetual virginity, or a vow of celibacy made by someone who has become free from the marriage bond after the experience of marriage, or a vow made with mutual consent by a faithful and chaste husband and wife who release each other from their sexual obligations, a vow it is wrong for either of them to make without the other. Once people make these and other similar vows which are properly made, on no condition must they be broken, since they have been made unconditionally. This too is commanded by the Lord, as we should understand from the text, 'Vow ye, and pay to the Lord your God' (Ps. 75, 12). This is why, referring to women who make the vow of virginity and afterwards want to marry, which was certainly not wrong for them to do before they took the vow, the Apostle says: 'Having damnation, because they have made void their first faith' (I Tim. 5, 12)."[1] In which words we can note many things against these heretics: but especially that among the just vows and nowise to be broken he numbers the vow of virginity, which it is evident, was not commanded by God. And he did not say that a vow of temporary but of perpetual virginity is just, and to be kept by all. From which words Calvin is also refuted, who even though he admits and approves of vows, still he condemns all perpetual vows.

And in his commentaries on the Psalms, explaining the verse from Psalm seventy-five: "Vow ye, and pay to the Lord your God" (v. 12), Augustine again says: "Other men also vow, even though they have used such a marriage, that beyond this they will have no such thing, that they will neither desire nor admit the like: and these men have vowed a greater vow than the former. Others vow even virginity from the beginning of life, that they will even know no such thing as those who having experienced have relinquished: and these men have vowed the greatest vow. Others vow that their house shall be a place of entertainment for all the holy men who may come: a great vow they vow. Another vows to relinquish all his goods to be distributed to the poor, and go into a community, into a community of holy men: a great vow he does vow. 'Vow ye, and pay to the Lord our God.' Let each one vow what he shall have willed to vow; let him give heed to this, that he pay what he has vowed."[2] In which words he not merely praises the vows of those things which God did not command, but he says that they are much better than the vows of those things, which God ordered. Jerome, Chrysostom, Photius cited by Oecumenius, Theophylactus, and Isidore support this opinion. For they all when interpreting those words of Paul, "If a virgin marry, she hath not sinned" (I Cor. 7, 28), say that the vow of virginity ought to be kept, which it is evident was not commanded by God. It is not necessary to cite the words of these men now at present because they were cited by me in the immediately preceding heresy.

---

[1] N. 30 (PL 40, 468).
[2] *Exposition on the Book of Psalms*, n. 16 (PL 36, 967).

USURA

USURA

Usury

Guy the Carmelite in his *Summa de haeresibus*, says that the Greeks think that it is not a sin to give something upon usury.[1] And I am certainly surprised that men versed in Holy Writ, and who put some faith in them, have fallen into such a clear heresy, against which there are so many and such manifest testimonies of Sacred Scripture. For in Exodus the Lord's Law says: "If thou lend money to any of my people that is poor, that dwelleth with thee, thou shalt not be hard upon them as an extortioner, nor oppress them with usuries" (22, 25). And in Leviticus: "If thy brother be impoverished... take not usury of him" (25, 35-36). And in Deuteronomy: "Thou shalt not lend to thy brother money to usury, nor corn, nor any other thing: but to the stranger" (23, 19-20). The holy Psalmist when he firstly had asked God who would dwell in His tabernacle, afterwards he himself replying to the same question says: "He that hath not put out his money to usury, nor taken bribes against the innocent" (Ps. 14, 5). There are also many other testimonies in the Old Testament in favor of this matter, which because they are very clear, I prudently omit. From the New Testament there is also that which our Savior says in Luke's Gospel: "Lend, hoping for nothing thereby" (6, 35).

But lest any shameless man pertinaciously also even after having heard these testimonies still attempt to oppose the Catholic faith, it will be worthwhile to bring to the fore the definition of the Church about this matter. The Council of Vienne celebrated upon Pope Clement V, gave this definition about usury: "If anyone shall fall into that error, so that he obstinately presumes to declare that it is not a sin to exercise usury, we decree that he must be punished as a heretic, and we strictly enjoin on local Ordinaries and inquisitors of heresy to proceed against those they find suspect of such error as they would against those suspected of heresy."[2] Which words are had in the book of the Clementine Decretals in the title, *De usuris*, in the chapter, *Ex gravi*.[3] And it is unnecessary that we would cite many testimonies against this heresy, or that we dispute more about this matter. For to discuss what is usury, and how it is committed, requires a very drawn out treatment, and is too unrelated to our purpose: because we took up a disputation not about anything other than heresies. Therefore since we have proved sufficiently (as I believe) that to assert that usury is permitted is a heresy, there is nothing more according to our promise which can be required of us.

TO THE KING

These are, O most Serene KING, the heresies which have troubled the Church from the times of the Apostles until the present day. Now whether I have collected all, is hidden from me, because there were many heresies so hidden that they came to the knowledge of a few or perhaps of no one. There may be others again which even though they were known to many, still they were not those of which they made any mention in their books: wherefore it is necessary that they have passed on to oblivion in the long passage of time. Nevertheless I own this, that I have not omitted in this work any of those assertions which the Church has

---

[1] *Summa de haeresibus et earum confutationibus*, fol. 23r-24r, c. 9.
[2] Cf. Dz. 479 (wherein only the first half of the quotation is cited).
[3] *Clementis Papae V. constitutiones* (Venice, apud Socios Aquilae Renouantis, 1605), p. 197-199.

prescribed, the mention of which is found in the writings of some writer among those which one is permitted to see.

THE END

Index

A

Abelard, Peter xlviii, l, 44, 57, 222, 302–305, 348, 354, 366, 369–370, 481–483, 527–529, 631, 639, 801, 1006–1007, 1012–1013
Adamites 78, 312–313, 726–727, 736
Adelbert Gallus li
Adimantus 166
Aerians 267, 396, 410, 727
Aerius 78, 266–267, 271, 387, 390, 587–588, 591, 952, 1001
Albanenses 157, 159, 342, 602, 609–610, 631, 724, 830, 833, 913–914, 933, 982
Albigensians 157, 342, 601, 933, 1001
Aldebert, or Adalbert li
Alogians 360, 985
Amaury of Bena or of Chartres l, 126–127, 409, 601–602, 933
Anthropomorphites 345–347, 356, 383, 450, 825
Antidicomarianites 651
Apelles 56, 74, 281, 283, 294, 306, 341, 914, 933
Apocaritae 147
Apollinaris 125, 149, 151, 178, 225–226, 282–285, 298, 682
Apostolics 164–165, 167, 338–340, 379, 381, 611, 615, 744, 769, 823, 826–827, 873–874, 918, 1005, 1044
Archontics 724, 933
Arians li, 22, 25, 65, 69, 78, 147, 255, 257, 275–276, 298, 353–359, 363, 410, 822, 953
Arius xlviii, li, 21, 25, 39, 57, 64, 69, 91, 123, 298, 307–308, 352–356, 358–359, 363, 393, 431, 682, 852, 866
Armenians l, 126–128, 178, 182, 184, 193, 197–198, 201, 207, 222–223, 235, 325, 331, 347, 366, 403, 408, 432, 434–435, 437, 450, 454, 602, 730, 744, 763–764, 810, 830, 832–835, 860, 916, 936–937, 972, 991, 1001
Auxentius 255, 650, 1022–1023

B

Bagnolenses 610
Bardesanes 348, 478–479, 631
Basilides 301, 654, 933, 1019
Beghards l, 90–91, 232, 235, 316, 379, 381, 383, 591–592, 769, 780–781, 824, 839–840
Beguines li, 232, 235, 316, 379, 381, 383, 591–592, 769, 780–781, 839–840
Berengarius of Tours 59, 106, 408–409, 412–413, 421–422, 426, 671, 680
Blastus 646, 825
Bohemians 87, 96, 407, 452–453, 464, 809, 916, 974
Borborians 608
Brachitae 147
Bucer, Martin xliv, 26, 215, 266, 449, 520, 541–542, 544, 550, 708, 781, 840, 889–891, 952, 970, 1034, 1047
Bugarius of Montefalcone 778

C

Caelestius 531, 537, 818
Cainites 582, 607, 627, 933
Cajetan (Cardinal Thomas de Vio) xxiv, 16, 131–133, 136, 138–139, 201–209, 439–440, 445–446, 511, 736–737, 739, 741–743, 745–746, 748, 752–754, 757, 763, 768, 981
Calvin, John xliv, 57, 159, 249, 266, 359, 510–511, 518–519, 543, 675, 677, 701–703, 706, 714, 731, 734, 781–782, 788–790, 792, 794, 840–843, 846–852, 882–883, 888, 957–961, 966–967, 969–970, 1020, 1023–1025, 1027–1029, 1031, 1033–1036, 1038, 1041–1044, 1047–1048, 1050, 1061–1063, 1065
Capito, Wolfgang Fabricius xliv, 952
Carlstadt 92, 440, 541, 594, 671
Carpocrates 146, 275, 982
Carpocratians 724
Cassian, John 293, 345, 598, 620, 638, 659–663, 1053
Cataphrygians li, 149, 174–175, 178–180, 728–729, 744
Cathari 267–268, 403, 610, 728, 828, 870, 872, 972
Catharists 267, 403, 611, 972
Cerdo 174, 179, 281–283, 286, 342–343, 410, 627, 647, 933, 982–983
Cerinthus 24–25, 78, 225, 227–229, 275, 280, 305, 336, 625, 724, 925, 984–986
Claudius of Turin xxiv, 78, 101–102, 106, 165, 178, 199, 819
Clement Scotus li
Concorrezenses 610
Cornelius of Antwerp, William 827

D

Desiderius [Sigerius] of Lombardy 828
Dicartitae 147
Diotrephes 854–855
Dolcino of Novara, Fra 164, 873
Donatus xlviii, 8, 17, 193, 373–374

E

Ebion 275, 280, 625, 984
Ebionites 275, 625–626, 984
Elcesaites 625–626, 654–655, 984
Encratites 118–119, 147, 266, 727, 967–968, 984, 1018
Erasmus xxiv, xxv, xxvi, 56–57, 93–94, 107, 159, 173, 270, 273–274, 292, 347, 354, 356–357, 367, 386, 481–482, 494–495, 537, 587–588, 590–591, 657, 669, 674, 695, 744–746, 751–754, 757, 759, 761, 763–765, 767, 769, 784, 792, 811, 819–820, 830, 832, 889–890, 922, 931, 941, 951, 979, 981, 986–987, 1020, 1053–1054
Eunomius 39, 64, 354, 363, 365, 484, 553, 925, 931
Eutyches 39, 126, 292–297, 300, 307, 809
Eutychius of Constantinople 934–935
Evagrius Ponticus li

F

Felix xxiv, 65, 147, 364, 593, 927, 1008, 1022–1023

FitzRalph, Richard 971–972
Flagellants l, 169, 172, 221–222, 396–397, 615
Florinians 312, 315, 608, 646
Florinus 312, 646
Fratricelli 78

G

Galecus, Nicolaus 770
Genialis 1022–1023
Gerard Segarelli 164, 338, 873–874
Germinator 1022–1023
Gnostics li, 146–147, 253–254, 336, 341–342, 582, 608, 647
Grabow, Matthaeus 59
Greeks xliii, 23, 38, 80–81, 176–177, 188, 235, 267–268, 288, 292, 314, 326–327, 358–359, 366–367, 369, 403, 405–407, 432, 435, 438–439, 452–453, 457, 460, 464, 527, 594, 599, 604, 670, 677, 729–730, 732, 744, 763, 808–810, 823, 916, 920, 931–932, 954–955, 965, 980, 986, 991, 1001, 1004, 1033, 1066
Guilliaud, Claude 543–544

H

Helvidius 650–654, 660, 1019, 1025
Heracleon 727, 1033
Heracleonites 727, 1033–1034
Hieracas 657
Hieracha 1033
Hierarchites 1033
Hus, John xlviii, 32, 36, 84, 87, 96, 307, 374–375, 377, 383, 452, 467, 507, 731, 801, 810, 823–824, 874–875, 899–900, 908, 912, 916, 974, 1005
Hussites 33, 65, 78, 87, 381, 407, 467, 635, 769, 912

I

Ingeniosus 1022–1023

J

Jacob of Mies 453
Januarius 30, 330, 458, 1022–1023
Joachim, Abbot 142, 161–162, 398
Joachim of Flora, Abbot 161
John of Jerusalem 145, 159
Jovinian 78, 245–248, 269, 272, 517, 537–540, 552, 583, 586–588, 616, 636, 643, 651, 727, 740, 821, 838–839, 870, 883–884, 886, 905, 952–953, 962, 964, 1019–1023, 1028, 1033, 1049, 1057

L

Lambert, Francis xliv, 1047
Lollards 169–172, 925
Lutherans xiv, xvii, xxiii, xxvii, 21, 33, 44, 53–54, 78, 92, 220, 269, 272, 274, 317, 329,

398, 449–452, 464, 467, 487–488, 491, 494–495, 497, 499, 502–505, 511–512, 516–517, 522–526, 541–544, 548–556, 558–559, 562, 565, 569, 574–575, 577, 583, 594, 620, 633, 635, 641, 675, 692, 694, 701, 706, 769, 777, 788, 801, 854, 863, 881–882, 885, 887–889, 943, 953–956, 959, 961–965, 978, 981, 1025, 1030–1031, 1035–1036, 1041, 1045, 1050, 1062–1063
Luther, Martin xvi, xxi, xxiii, xxiv, xxvi, xliv, xlv, xlviii, 16–17, 21, 24–26, 32–33, 45, 47–49, 52–53, 65, 75, 84, 91–94, 97–99, 106–107, 110–118, 159, 182, 215–221, 249–250, 252–253, 261–262, 264, 266, 272, 307–308, 311, 317–319, 321–322, 325–328, 332–336, 359, 374–375, 378, 380–384, 386–387, 398, 401, 423–427, 431, 439–440, 442–446, 449, 453, 455, 457, 465, 468–469, 471, 473–474, 484, 489–490, 494, 497–498, 511, 513, 517, 520, 526–527, 537, 540–542, 549–553, 565, 586, 594, 599–601, 603, 605, 614, 616, 620, 631–633, 635, 639–640, 642–643, 663, 666–667, 674–676, 691, 693, 700–701, 707–710, 712–715, 718–720, 722–723, 730–732, 734–736, 745, 771–773, 775–776, 778, 780–782, 785–786, 801, 803–805, 809–810, 814–815, 820, 822–823, 834, 840–841, 845–848, 851, 856–857, 859–860, 863, 865–866, 868–869, 875–877, 879–882, 889, 892–896, 898–899, 901, 916, 920–924, 929, 939–953, 970, 972, 974–975, 981–985, 987–988, 993–995, 1000–1001, 1009–1012, 1019–1020, 1023–1024, 1027–1028, 1030, 1034, 1036–1038, 1044–1045, 1047, 1050, 1052, 1058–1062

M

Macedonius 39, 64, 91, 363–365, 932, 992
Magus, Simon xlvii, 3, 78, 145, 393, 562, 839
Mani xlvii, 25, 146, 268, 410
Manichaeans li, 21, 63, 146–149, 182, 249–251, 253–254, 264, 266–268, 274, 282, 286–287, 336–338, 342, 370, 372, 403, 410, 463, 605–606, 608, 648, 743, 962, 967–968
Manichaeism xlvii, 25
Manichaeus xlvii, 146, 266, 268, 283, 287, 294, 336–338, 342–344, 372, 627, 631–632, 636, 646–648, 727, 833, 967, 982, 987
Marcion 25, 73, 80, 118–119, 174, 179, 181, 286, 342, 478, 627, 636, 727, 785, 877, 933, 967, 983
Martianus 1022–1023
Massalians 181–182, 616, 619, 799
Melanchthon, Philip xliv, 26, 215, 218–221, 249, 266, 398, 492–493, 495, 497, 500, 511, 517, 520, 522, 542–543, 549–550, 565, 574, 603, 631, 781, 788–790, 794, 840, 875, 882, 888, 1034
Menander xlvii, 336–337, 724, 1022
Messalians 65, 147, 149, 152–153, 181–182, 184, 386, 435, 798–799
Monothelitism li
Montanus 149, 178, 722, 728–729, 744, 870, 915

N

Nazarenes 271, 625
Nestorians li, 21–22, 70, 296, 461
Nestorius xlviii, li, 39, 46, 64, 91, 285–293, 295–299, 303, 307–308, 354, 369, 381, 408, 420–421, 612, 654, 670, 700, 809
Nicolaites 312, 538, 582, 724
Nicolaus Galecus 770

Nicostratus li
Novatian xlviii, 84, 331, 418, 870, 872–873
Novatians 21, 84, 112, 147, 267, 321, 403, 610, 728–729, 870–872, 972
Novatus xlviii, 728, 870

O

Oecolampadius xliv, 26, 57, 92, 106–107, 249, 253, 337, 409–415, 418, 420–423, 426, 440, 631, 664, 671, 680, 929, 952, 970, 975–976, 1047
Olerii, Petrus li
Olivi 142, 161–162, 182, 184, 305, 398
Olivi, Pierre Jean 142
Ophites 147, 582, 933
Origen 31, 59, 81, 90, 122–126, 132, 154, 159, 230–232, 295, 322, 353, 358, 362, 372, 418, 466–467, 472–473, 527, 602–603, 651, 760–762, 812, 820, 855, 918, 921, 933–934, 936, 960–961, 986, 998, 1029
Osiander, Andreas xliv, 680, 708

P

Passalorynchitae 990
Pelagians 21, 145, 201, 219–220, 534, 537, 776, 795, 801, 821, 846, 895, 897, 916, 985
Pelagius xlviii, 21, 50, 52, 128–130, 200, 207, 354, 442, 531–535, 537–539, 552, 616, 635–636, 643, 667, 801–802, 818, 821, 829–832, 839, 894, 905, 948
Pellikan, Konrad xliv, 1047
Pepuzians 722
Peter of Constantinople li
Peter of Dresden 453
Petilian 198, 377, 655
Petit, Jean 126, 1014
Petrus Olerii li
Petrus Olerius li
Photinus 61, 64, 275, 280, 288
Plotinus 1023
Ponticus, Evagrius li
Priscillian xlviii, 159–160, 266, 268, 337–338, 349, 372, 479–480, 615, 631, 744, 915
Priscillianists 146, 148–149, 264, 266–268, 282, 286, 352, 370–371, 479–480, 615, 727
Proclinianites 281, 608, 933
Psallians 616, 798–799

R

Rhetorians 21, 506, 576, 630
Riswick, Herman 140, 155, 601, 724

S

Sabellians li, 349
Sabellius li, 21, 57, 349–350, 352–353, 358, 364
Sampsaeans 625–626
Saturnians 336, 724
Saturninus 118–119, 312, 336, 724, 1019

Scotus, Clement li
Segarelli, Gerard 873
Seleucians 646, 723, 933
Seleucus 149–150, 172–173, 646, 723
Sethiani 582
Severians 122, 933, 982, 1018
Severus 122, 275, 430, 707, 982, 984, 1018
Sigerius of Lombardy, Desiderius 828
Simon the Magician 1, 312, 336, 724, 933, 991
Spangenberg, Johann 491, 511, 543, 550, 781, 889

T

Tascodrugites 147
Tatian 118–122, 266, 268, 727, 852, 967, 984, 1018
Tertullian xlvii, xlviii, xlix, li, 73, 80, 149–154, 179, 342, 344–345, 607, 636, 717, 728, 784, 811–813, 825, 868, 877, 931, 933, 945, 961, 964–965, 983
Thebuthis 78

V

Valentinus xlvii, 73, 80, 119, 282–283, 286, 294, 337, 342–343, 478–479, 537, 727, 833, 933
Valesians 465, 467
Vigilantius xlviii, 93, 828, 925, 930–931, 974, 976, 979

W

Waldemarius li
Waldensians 65, 90, 97, 199–200, 253, 255, 269, 272, 312–313, 316–317, 319, 327, 378–379, 381, 383–384, 387, 396, 407, 438, 475, 578, 580, 583, 594, 599, 609–610, 617, 619, 668–669, 720, 769–770, 808, 810, 824, 836–837, 873–874, 908, 916, 952, 974, 988–989, 1001, 1005, 1033
Waldo 90, 199
White, William 925
William [Cornelius] of Antwerp 827
William Cornelius of Antwerp 827
William of Saint-Amour 620, 720–721, 828–829
William White 925
Wittenbergers 675–676, 794, 1041–1042, 1044, 1063
Wycliffe, John xix, xlviii, 14, 32, 36, 47–48, 87, 101–104, 169, 199, 201, 255–256, 258–260, 307, 317, 325, 327, 329–330, 339–340, 378–379, 383–390, 392, 396, 409, 421, 423, 426, 467, 471, 507, 527–528, 530, 578, 580, 599–600, 612, 620, 631, 639, 663, 665, 669–670, 674, 720–721, 801–803, 810, 824, 852–854, 874–875, 885, 908, 912, 916, 927, 931, 952, 972, 974, 996–1000, 1034, 1044
Wycliffites 33, 44, 65, 78, 97, 101–103, 169, 253, 258, 467, 475–478, 583, 594, 635, 769, 824, 912, 925, 927, 929

Z

Zwingli xliv, 26, 249, 671, 680